DEMONSTRATION PROBLEM

The Demonstration Problem provides a model for how to solve end-of-chapter material.

DEMONSTRATION PROBLEM

Sky Co., organized in 2014, provided you with the following information.

1. Purchased a license for $20,000 on July 1, 2014. The license gives Sky exclusive rights to sell its services in the tri-state region and will expire on July 1, 2022.
2. Purchased a patent on January 2, 2015, for $40,000. It is estimated to have a 5-year life.
3. Costs incurred to develop an exclusive Internet connection process as of June 1, 2015, were $45,000. The process has an indefinite life.
4. On April 1, 2015, Sky Co. purchased a small circuit board manufacturer for $350,000. Goodwill recorded in the transaction was $90,000.
5. On July 1, 2015, legal fees for successful defense of the patent purchased on January 2, 2015, were $11,400.
6. Research and development costs incurred as of September 1, 2015, were $75,000.

Instructions

(a) Prepare the journal entries to record all the entries related to the patent during 2015.
(b) At December 31, 2015, an impairment test is performed on the license purchased in 2014. It is estimated that the net cash flows to be received from the license will be $13,000, and its fair value is $7,000. Compute the amount of impairment, if any, to be recorded on December 31, 2015.
(c) What is the amount to be reported for intangible assets on the balance sheet at December 31, 2014? At December 31, 2015?

FASB CODIFICATION

The FASB Codification refers students to the relevant FASB literature for the key concepts presented in each chapter.

FASB CODIFICATION

FASB Codification References

[1] FASB ASC 350-10-05. [Predecessor literature: "Goodwill and Other Intangible Assets," *Statement of Financial Accounting Standards No. 142* (Norwalk, Conn.: FASB, 2001).]

[2] FASB ASC 350-30-35. [Predecessor literature: "Goodwill and Other Intangible Assets," *Statement of Financial Accounting Standards No. 142* (Norwalk, Conn.: FASB, 2001), par. 11.]

[3] FASB ASC 805-10. [Predecessor literature: "Business Combinations," *Statement of Financial Accounting Standards No. 141R* (Norwalk, Conn.: FASB, 2007).]

[4] FASB ASC 350-30-35. [Predecessor literature: "Goodwill and Other Intangible Assets," *Statement of Financial Accounting Standards No. 142* (Norwalk, Conn.: FASB, 2001), par. B55.]

[5] FASB ASC 805-10-20. [Predecessor literature: "Business Combinations," *Statement of Financial Accounting Standards No. 141R* (Norwalk, Conn.: FASB, 2007).]

USING YOUR JUDGMENT

The Using Your Judgment section provides students with real-world homework problems covering topics such as financial reporting, financial statement analysis, and professional research.

USING YOUR JUDGMENT

FINANCIAL REPORTING

Financial Reporting Problem

P&G **The Procter & Gamble Company (P&G)**

The financial statements of P&G are presented in Appendix 5B. The company's complete annual report, including the notes to the financial statements, can be accessed at the book's companion website, **www.wiley.com/college/kieso**.

Instructions

Refer to P&G's financial statements and the accompanying notes to answer the following questions.

(a) Does P&G report any intangible assets, especially goodwill, in its 2011 financial statements and accompanying notes?
(b) How much research and development (R&D) cost was expensed by P&G in 2010 and 2011? What percentage of sales revenue and net income did P&G spend on R&D in 2010 and 2011?

PROBLEMS SET B

In addition to the B Set of Exercises, we now provide an additional set of problems for each chapter, based on the problems in the textbook. The B Set of Problems are available in *WileyPLUS* and on the book's companion website, at **www.wiley.com/college/kieso**.

PROBLEMS SET B

See the book's companion website, at **www.wiley.com/college/kieso**, for an additional set of problems.

IFRS INSIGHTS

IFRS Insights offer students a detailed discussion as well as assessment material of international accounting standards at the end of each chapter.

IFRS INSIGHTS

There are some significant differences between IFRS and GAAP in the accounting for both intangible assets and impairments. IFRS related to intangible assets is presented in *IAS 38* ("Intangible Assets"). IFRS related to impairments is found in *IAS 36* ("Impairment of Assets").

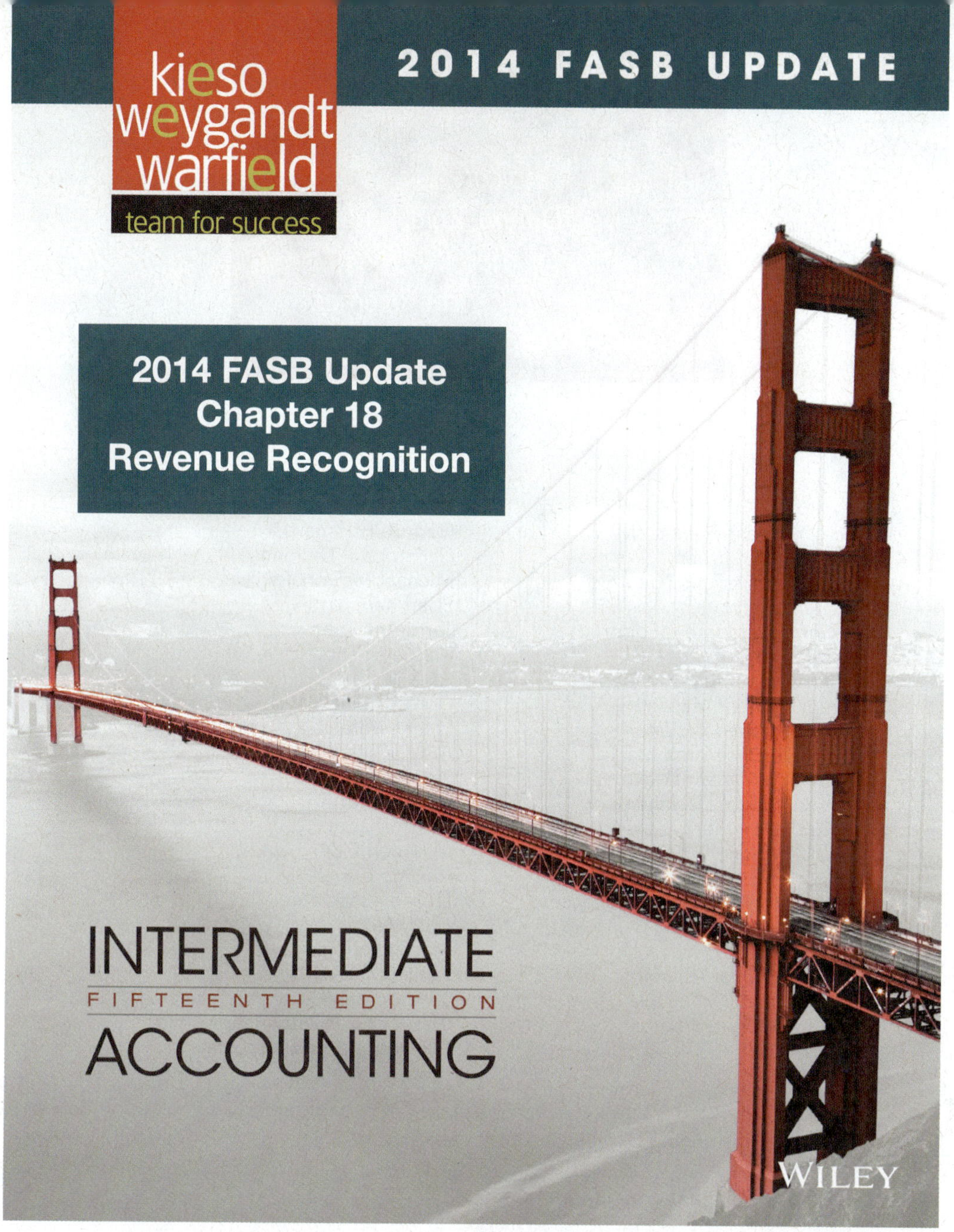

Donald E. Kieso PhD, CPA
Northern Illinois University
DeKalb, Illinois

Jerry J. Weygandt PhD, CPA
University of Wisconsin—Madison
Madison, Wisconsin

Terry D. Warfield, PhD
University of Wisconsin—Madison
Madison, Wisconsin

WILEY

Dedicated to
our wives, ***Donna, Enid, and Mary,***
for their love,
support, and encouragement

Vice President & Executive Publisher	George Hoffman
Associate Publisher	Christopher DeJohn
Senior Acquisitions Editor	Michael McDonald
Content Editor	Brian Kamins
Senior Development Editor	Terry Ann Tatro
Development Editor	Margaret Thompson
Editorial Operations Manager	Yana Mermel
Senior Content Manager	Dorothy Sinclair
Senior Production Editor	Valerie Vargas
Associate Director of Marketing	Amy Scholz
Marketing Manager	Jesse Cruz
Senior Product Designer	Allie K. Morris
Product Designer	Greg Chaput
Senior Designer	Maureen Eide
Designer	Kristine Carney
Production Management Services	Ingrao Associates
Creative Director	Harry Nolan
Senior Photo Editor	Mary Ann Price
Senior Editorial Assistant	Jackie MacKenzie
Cover Photo	JB Broccard/Getty Images, Inc.
Chapter Opener Photo	JB Broccard/Getty Images, Inc.
Cover Credit	JB Broccard/Getty Images, Inc.

This book was set in Palatino LT Std by Aptara®, Inc. and printed and bound by Courier Kendallville. The cover was printed by Courier Kendallville.

This book is printed on acid-free paper. ∞

To order books or for customer service, please call 1-800-CALL WILEY (225-5945).

ISBN-13 978-1-118-98531-1

BRV ISBN-13 978-1-118-93878-2

Printed in the United States of America

10 9 8 7 6 5 4 3 2 1

Brief Contents

Author Commitment

Don Kieso

Donald E. Kieso, PhD, CPA, received his bachelor's degree from Aurora University and his doctorate in accounting from the University of Illinois. He has served as chairman of the Department of Accountancy and is currently the KPMG Emeritus Professor of Accountancy at Northern Illinois University. He has public accounting experience with Price Waterhouse & Co. (San Francisco and Chicago) and Arthur Andersen & Co. (Chicago) and research experience with the Research Division of the American Institute of Certified Public Accountants (New York). He has done post-doctorate work as a Visiting Scholar at the University of California at Berkeley and is a recipient of NIU's Teaching Excellence Award and four Golden Apple Teaching Awards. Professor Kieso is the author of other accounting and business books and is a member of the American Accounting Association, the American Institute of Certified Public Accountants, and the Illinois CPA Society. He has served as a member of the Board of Directors of the Illinois CPA Society, then AACSB's Accounting Accreditation Committees, the State of Illinois Comptroller's Commission, as Secretary-Treasurer of the Federation of Schools of Accountancy, and as Secretary-Treasurer of the American Accounting Association. Professor Kieso is currently serving on the Board of Trustees and Executive Committee of Aurora University, as a member of the Board of Directors of Kishwaukee Community Hospital, and as Treasurer and Director of Valley West Community Hospital. From 1989 to 1993, he served as a charter member of the National Accounting Education Change Commission. He is the recipient of the Outstanding Accounting Educator Award from the Illinois CPA Society, the FSA's Joseph A. Silvoso Award of Merit, the NIU Foundation's Humanitarian Award for Service to Higher Education, a Distinguished Service Award from the Illinois CPA Society, and in 2003 an honorary doctorate from Aurora University.

Jerry Weygandt

Jerry J. Weygandt, PhD, CPA, is Arthur Andersen Alumni Emeritus Professor of Accounting at the University of Wisconsin—Madison. He holds a Ph.D. in accounting from the University of Illinois. Articles by Professor Weygandt have appeared in the *Accounting Review, Journal of Accounting Research, Accounting Horizons, Journal of Accountancy,* and other academic and professional journals. These articles have examined such financial reporting issues as accounting for price-level adjustments, pensions, convertible securities, stock option contracts, and interim reports. Professor Weygandt is author of other accounting and financial reporting books and is a member of the American Accounting Association, the American Institute of Certified Public Accountants, and the Wisconsin Society of Certified Public Accountants. He has served on numerous committees of the American Accounting Association and as a member of the editorial board of the Accounting Review; he also has served as President and Secretary-Treasurer of the American Accounting Association. In addition, he has been actively involved with the American Institute of Certified Public Accountants and has been a member of the Accounting Standards Executive Committee (AcSEC) of that organization. He has served on the FASB task force that examined the reporting issues related to accounting for income taxes and served as a trustee of the Financial Accounting Foundation. Professor Weygandt has received the Chancellor's Award for Excellence in Teaching and the Beta Gamma Sigma Dean's Teaching Award. He is on the board of directors of M & I Bank of Southern Wisconsin. He is the recipient of the Wisconsin Institute of CPA's Outstanding Educator's Award and the Lifetime Achievement Award. In 2001, he received the American Accounting Association's Outstanding Educator Award.

Terry Warfield

Terry D. Warfield, PhD, is the PricewaterhouseCoopers Professor in Accounting at the University of Wisconsin—Madison. He received a B.S. and M.B.A. from Indiana University and a Ph.D. in accounting from the University of Iowa. Professor Warfield's area of expertise is financial reporting, and prior to his academic career, he worked for five years in the banking industry. He served as the Academic Accounting Fellow in the Office of the Chief Accountant at the U.S. Securities and Exchange Commission in Washington, D.C. from 1995–1996. Professor Warfield's primary research interests concern financial accounting standards and disclosure policies. He has published scholarly articles in *The Accounting Review, Journal of Accounting and Economics, Research in Accounting Regulation,* and *Accounting Horizons,* and he has served on the editorial boards of *The Accounting Review, Accounting Horizons,* and *Issues in Accounting Education*. He has served as president of the Financial Accounting and Reporting Section, the Financial Accounting Standards Committee of the American Accounting Association (Chair 1995–1996), and on the AAA-FASB Research Conference Committee. He also served on the Financial Accounting Standards Advisory Council of the Financial Accounting Standards Board. Professor Warfield has received teaching awards at both the University of Iowa and the University of Wisconsin, and he was named to the Teaching Academy at the University of Wisconsin in 1995. Professor Warfield has developed and published several case studies based on his research for use in accounting classes. These cases have been selected for the AICPA Professor-Practitioner Case Development Program and have been published in *Issues in Accounting Education*.

From the Authors

Accounting continues to be one of the most employable, sought-after majors, according to entry-level job site **CollegeGrad.com**. One reason for this interest is found in the statement by former Secretary of the Treasury and Economic Advisor to the President, Lawrence Summers. He noted that the single-most important innovation shaping our capital markets was the idea of generally accepted accounting principles (GAAP). We agree with Mr. Summers. Relevant and reliable financial information is a necessity for viable capital markets. Without it, our markets would be chaotic, and our standard of living would decrease.

This textbook is the market leader in providing the tools needed to understand what GAAP is and how it is applied in practice. Mastery of this material will be invaluable to you in whatever field you select.

Through many editions, this textbook has continued to reflect the constant changes taking place in the GAAP environment. This edition continues this tradition, which has become even more significant as the financial reporting environment is exploding with major change. Here are three areas of major importance that are now incorporated extensively into this edition of the textbook.

Convergence of U.S. GAAP and IFRS

As mentioned above, the most important innovation shaping our capital markets was the idea of U.S. GAAP. It might be said that it would be even better if we had one common set of accounting rules for the whole world, which will make it easier for international investors to compare the financial results of companies from different countries. That is happening quickly as U.S. GAAP and international accounting standards are converging. The convergence process has resulted in a number of common standards between U.S. GAAP and **International Financial Reporting Standards (IFRS)**. And you have the chance to be on the ground floor as we develop for you the similarities and differences in the two systems that ultimately will be one.

> "If this textbook helps you appreciate the challenges, worth, and limitations of financial reporting, if it encourages you to evaluate critically and understand financial accounting concepts and practice, and if it prepares you for advanced study, professional examinations, and the successful and ethical pursuit of your career in accounting or business in a global economy, then we will have attained our objectives."

A Fair Value Movement

The FASB believes that fair value information is more relevant to users than historical cost. As a result, there is more information that is being reported on this basis, and even more will occur in the future. The financial press is full of articles discussing how financial institutions must fair value their assets, which has led to massive losses during the recent credit crisis. In addition, additional insight into the reliability related to fair values is being addressed and disclosed to help investors make important capital allocation decisions. We devote a considerable amount of material that discusses and illustrates fair value concepts in this edition.

A New Way of Looking at Generally Accepted Accounting Principles (GAAP)

Learning GAAP used to be a daunting task, as it is comprised of many standards that vary in form, completeness, and structure. Fortunately, the profession has developed the Financial Accounting Standards Board Codification (often referred to as the Codification). This Codification provides in one place all the GAAP related to a given topic. This textbook is the first to incorporate this Codification—it will make learning GAAP easier and more interesting!

Intermediate Accounting is the market-leading textbook in providing the tools needed to understand what GAAP is and how it is applied in practice. With this Fifteenth Edition, we strive to continue to provide the material needed to understand this subject area. The textbook is comprehensive and up-to-date. We also include proven pedagogical tools, designed to help you learn more effectively and to answer the changing needs of this course. Look inside the front cover for a detailed description of all of the learning tools of the textbook.

We are excited about *Intermediate Accounting*, Fifteenth Edition. We believe it meets an important objective of providing useful information to educators and students interested in learning about both GAAP and IFRS. Suggestions and comments from users of this textbook will be appreciated. Please feel free to e-mail any one of us at *AccountingAuthors@yahoo.com*.

Donald E. Kieso
DeKalb, Illinois

Jerry J. Weygandt
Madison, Wisconsin

Terry D. Warfield
Madison, Wisconsin

What's New?

The Fifteenth Edition expands our emphasis on student learning and improves upon a teaching and learning package that instructors and students have rated the highest in customer satisfaction. Based on extensive reviews, focus groups, and interactions with other intermediate accounting instructors and students, we have developed a number of new pedagogical features and content changes, designed both to help students learn more effectively and to answer the changing needs of the course.

Evolving Issues

As we continue to strive to reflect the constant changes in the accounting environment, we have added a new feature to the Fifteenth Edition, **Evolving Issues**, which highlight and discuss areas in which the profession may be encountering controversy or nearing resolution. Our hope is that these high-interest boxes will increase student engagement, as well as serve as classroom discussion points. For another source of high-interest material, see the **What Do the Numbers Mean?** boxes, most of which are new to this edition.

Demonstration Problems

We understand that students often struggle to apply accounting concepts to realistic business situations. As a result, we include a new **Demonstration Problem** before the end-of-chapter problem material, to serve as a model to help students with their homework assignments.

Updated IFRS Insights Content

We have updated the end-of-chapter section, **IFRS Insights**, throughout the textbook. In addition, in the *Relevant Facts* section, we now present *Similarities* as well as *Differences* between GAAP and IFRS to increase student understanding.

Major Content Revisions

In response to the changing environment, we have significantly revised several chapters.

Chapter 2 Conceptual Framework for Financial Reporting

- New footnote material on the FASB's additional guidance related to the use of fair value in financial statements.
- Updated discussion plus added an illustration on the five steps of revenue recognition.
- Revised Constraints section, as now only cost constraint is included in the conceptual framework.

Chapter 4 Income Statement and Related Information

- Revised Format of the Income Statement section, adding discussion on the intermediate components of the income statement and presenting the multiple-step before the single-step format to reflect current practice.
- Revised Reporting Irregular Items section, to broaden focus on irregular and unusual items. Updated discussion throughout as well as added new material on noncontrolling interest.
- Updated Comprehensive Income discussion, to reflect the most recent accounting standards.
- New illustration showing and explaining the revised income statement sections.

Chapter 18 Revenue Recognition

- We anticipate a new FASB ruling on the revenue recognition principle. As a result, please see the book's companion website, at **www.wiley.com/college/kieso**, for the latest information as well as the availability of an updated, replacement chapter.

Chapter 23 Statement of Cash Flows

- Reorganized chapter, to present the indirect method through preparation of the statement of cash flows first, followed by the discussion of the direct method as well as the advantages and disadvantages of both methods.
- New Evolving Issue, "Direct versus Indirect Controversy," on the arguments in favor of each method.

See the next two pages for a complete list of content revisions by chapter.

Content Changes by Chapter

Chapter 1 Financial Accounting and Accounting Standards

- New opening story, about how the U.S. can improve its financial reporting system to provide reliable accounting information.
- Updated Types of Pronouncements section and increased coverage of the EITF.
- New WDNM box on how different countries' cultures impede international convergence efforts.
- Updated International Accounting Convergence discussion in *IFRS Insights* section.
- New **Evolving Issue**, on the use of fair value accounting.

Chapter 2 Conceptual Framework for Financial Reporting

- Updated WDNM box on earnings with recent information about **Facebook**'s reporting of its first earnings after going public.
- New footnote on the liquidation basis of accounting.
- New footnote material on the FASB's additional guidance related to use of fair value in financial statements.
- Updated discussion plus added an illustration on the five steps of revenue recognition.
- Revised Constraints section, as now only cost constraint is included in the conceptual framework.

Chapter 3 The Accounting Information System

- Revised discussion/terminology used to reflect anticipated new wording of revenue recognition principle.
- Updated material on economic crime in opening story.
- Updated graphics to increase student engagement.
- New WDNM box on companies' need to update their accounting information systems yet unwillingness to interrupt their operations to do so.

Chapter 4 Income Statement and Related Information

- Revised opening story, to discuss **Groupon**'s recent pro forma reporting.
- Revised Format of the Income Statement section, adding discussion on the intermediate components of the income statement and presenting the multiple-step before single-step format to reflect current practice.
- Revised Reporting Irregular Items section, to broaden focus on irregular and unusual items. Updated discussion throughout as well as added discussion on noncontrolling interest.
- Updated Comprehensive Income discussion, to reflect most recent accounting standards.
- New Underlying Concepts marginal note, about how the income statement provides information that is central to the objective of financial reporting.
- Revised the WDNM box on managing earnings to discuss a recent study that reinforces concerns about earnings management.
- New illustration showing and explaining the revised income statement sections.
- New WDNM box on the importance of the top line, in addition to the bottom line, in the income statement when analyzing companies.
- New **Evolving Issue**, on income reporting.

Chapter 5 Balance Sheet and Statement of Cash Flows

- Updated WDNM box on the airline industry, to include recent merger activity.
- Replaced several examples of real-company financial statements.
- Added noncontrolling interest line item to the balance sheet, to reflect recent FASB pronouncement.
- Moved most of **P&G**'s annual report from Appendix 5B to book's companion website.
- New **Evolving Issue**, on balance sheet reporting.

Chapter 6 Accounting and the Time Value of Money

- New opening story, about developing fair value estimates and applying fair value guidance to specific examples.
- New WDNM box on how starting a savings account earlier can significantly affect the value of a retirement fund.
- Revised WDNM box on Fed's ability to adjust interest rates by adding discussion on Fed's more recent use of quantitative easing.

Chapter 7 Cash and Receivables

- New opening story, about banks' boosting earnings by releasing loan loss reserves.
- New WDNM boxes, on tax incentives for companies to move their cash overseas, and recent trends of companies to delay payment of bills.
- New discussion on repurchase agreements (see footnote 14).
- New **Evolving Issue**, on how existing GAAP results in allowances for loan loss that tend to be at their lowest level when they are needed most, the beginning of a downward-trending economic cycle.

Chapter 8 Valuation of Inventories: A Cost-Basis Approach

- New opening story, about why some companies are switching from LIFO to FIFO.

Chapter 9 Inventories: Additional Valuation Issues

- New opening story, about why investors need comparable information about inventory when evaluating retailers' financial statements.

Chapter 10 Acquisition and Disposition of Property, Plant, and Equipment

- New opening story, about importance of capital expenditures and how they can affect a company's income.

Chapter 11 Depreciation, Impairments, and Depletion

- New **Evolving Issue**, on whether to account for exploration costs in the oil and gas industry using full-cost or successful-efforts.

Chapter 12 Intangible Assets

- New opening story, on increasing amount of sustainability information provided by companies.
- New Underlying Concepts marginal note about surrounding controversy for R&D accounting.
- Added more real-world examples to Contract-Related Intangible Assets section.
- Completely rewritten WDNM box, discussing the patent battles between e-tailers and cell phone companies.
- New discussion (footnotes) on qualitative assessment to determine impairment of indefinite-life intangibles.
- Revised WDNM box on impairment risk, to discuss more recent case of **Bank of America**.
- New **Evolving Issue**, on the recognition of R&D and internally generated intangibles.
- Moved Appendix 12A, Accounting for Computer Software Costs, to book's companion website.

Chapter 13 Current Liabilities and Contingencies

- New **Evolving Issue**, on how to account for greenhouse gases.

Chapter 14 Long-Term Liabilities

- New opening story, about the impact of long-term debt on governments and companies.
- New **Evolving Issue**, on how the FASB believes that using the fair value option for liabilities makes sense, as the valuation of a liability is related to a company's credit standing.

Chapter 15 Stockholders' Equity

- Updated opening story, on the global IPO market.
- New WDNM boxes, on Delaware as a tax haven for companies, whether buybacks signal good or bad news about companies, and an analysis of recent company dividend payouts.
- Revised WDNM box to include more recent information about companies going public with two or more classes of stock.
- New information and illustration on recent company buybacks.

Chapter 16 Dilutive Securities and Earnings per Share

- Revised opening story, updating information about companies' use of options and restricted stock.
- Updated material to include recent convergence material on accounting for financial instruments with characteristics of both debt and equity.
- New **Evolving Issue**, on accounting for convertible debt.
- New illustration on company equity grants.
- New footnote on rationale for why companies are moving away from options to restricted stock, and revised footnote about how EPS effects of noncontrolling interest should be presented.
- Completely revised WDNM box, about the effect of companies that expense stock options on their stock prices.

Chapter 17 Investments

- Revised opening story, to include recent FASB position on how banking industry values loans.
- New footnotes on FASB's current exploration for a new impairment model for financial instruments as well as additional disclosures required for items reclassified out of accumulated other comprehensive income.
- New **Evolving Issues**, on fair value controversy as well as proposed new classification and measurement model for financial assets.
- New material on FASB required disclosures for financial instruments, with special emphasis on Level 3 measurements.

Chapter 18 Revenue Recognition

- Updated WDNM boxes, to reflect new disclosure requirements for gift-card issuers and to stress importance of companies reporting sales on a net basis.

Chapter 19 Accounting for Income Taxes

- Updated footnotes on determining the true cost of taxes and deferred tax assets (**Sony**'s experience in post-quake Japan).
- New **Evolving Issue**, on uncertain tax positions.
- New WDNM box, about creative tax accounting at **Apple**, **Google**, and **GE**.

Chapter 20 Accounting for Pensions and Postretirement Benefits

- Updated opening story on pension plan choices.
- Updated statistics on size of pension plan assets globally.
- Updated chart on defined benefit/defined contribution plan mix.
- New **Evolving Issue**, on companies' voluntary choice to abandon corridor amortization.
- Updated WDNM box on funded status of pension plans.
- New WDNM box on guarantees for the PBGC.
- New IFRS Insight section reflecting major amendments to IFRS for pensions (*IAS 19*).

Chapter 21 Accounting for Leases

- Updated opening story on aircraft leasing data and added information about **Rite-Aid**'s off-balance-sheet obligations.
- New **Evolving Issue**, on proposal to address off-balance-sheet reporting of leases.

Chapter 22 Accounting Changes and Error Analysis

- Updated opening story, of recent accounting changes mandated by the FASB and subsequent company restatements.
- Revised WDNM box, on need to protect company statements from negative effects of fraud.

Chapter 23 Statement of Cash Flows

- Reorganized chapter, to present the indirect method through preparation of the statement of cash flows first, followed by the discussion of the direct method as well as advantages and disadvantages of both methods.
- New WDNM box, on how cash flow management can affect the quality of accounting information.
- Reformatted "Direct versus Indirect Controversy" as new **Evolving Issue**, to highlight the arguments in favor of each method.
- Updated WDNM box to show how banks' use of investment classifications can affect operating cash flows.

Chapter 24 Full Disclosure in Financial Reporting

- New discussion in Differential Disclosure section about costs and benefits of a "one size fits all" reporting package.
- New **Evolving Issues**, on ensuring the quantity and quality of financial disclosure, and interim reporting rules.
- New footnote on FASB going concern project.
- New WDNM box, on the difference between British and U.S. forecasting.

Teaching and Learning Supplementary Material

For Instructors

Active-Teaching Aids

Instructors can take advantage of the resources and support available in *WileyPLUS* and the Wiley Faculty Network, as well as a number of helpful assets (such as the Instructor's Manual, Test Bank, PowerPoint presentations, and Solutions Manual) at our book's companion site, **www.wiley.com/college/kieso**.

In addition, instructors will find that we have made a number of additions and enhancements to the Fifteenth Edition instructor and student resources.

Test Bank/Computerized Test Bank. We have made several key enhancements to the Test Bank, both in print and in *WileyPLUS*. These include:

- Newly authored Test Bank questions to cover recent topical additions/expansions (e.g., IFRS, revenue recognition, and fair value).
- New Critical Thinking Questions added to Exercises.
- Removal of outdated questions.

WileyPLUS now includes numerous questions from the Test Bank, offering simple multiple-choice and more complex exercises and problems. Many of these exercises/problems will be algorithmic.

Instructor's Manual, Vols. 1 and 2. Included in each chapter are lecture outlines with teaching tips, chapter reviews, illustrations, and review quizzes.

Solutions Manual, Vols. 1 and 2. Each volume contains detailed solutions to all Brief Exercises, Exercises, and Problems in the textbook, as well as suggested answers to the Concepts for Analysis and *Using Your Judgment* questions and cases.

Narrated PowerPoints. Brief chapter-based videos walk the students through the core concepts in each chapter, as outlined in the PowerPoint Slides.

For Students

Active-Learning Aids

The book's companion site for students, **www.wiley.com/college/kieso**, is home to a number of helpful learning aids, including a B Set of Exercises, B Set of Problems, Self-Study Tests and Additional Self-Tests, Excel templates, annual reports, and a complete glossary of key terms.

B Set of Problems. In addition to the **B Set of Exercises**, we now provide an additional set of problems for each chapter, based on the problems in the textbook. The B Sets of Exercises and Problems are available in *WileyPLUS* and at the book's companion site.

Student Videos. Three new types of videos will be available in *WileyPLUS*:

- Mini lecture videos from Terry Warfield on select difficult topics in intermediate accounting.
- Exercise solution walkthrough videos where a student can see how an exercise similar to one in the textbook is solved.
- Accounting skills videos that demonstrate the basic concepts and skills needed for students to understand how to solve a multitude of intermediate accounting problems.

Student Study Guide, Vols. 1 and 2. Each chapter of the Study Guide contains a chapter review, chapter outline, and a glossary of key terms. Demonstration problems, multiple-choice, true/false, matching, and other exercises are included. Available for purchase at the book's companion site.

Problem-Solving Survival Guide, Vols. 1 and 2. This study guide contains exercises and problems that help students develop their intermediate accounting problem-solving skills. Explanations assist in the approach, set-up, and completion of accounting problems. Tips alert students to common pitfalls and misconceptions. Available for purchase at the book's companion site.

Rockford Corporation: An Accounting Practice Set. This practice set helps students review the accounting cycle and the preparation of financial statements. Available for purchase at the book's companion site. The **computerized Rockford practice set** is a general ledger software version of the printed practice set, also available in *WileyPLUS*.

Gateway to the Profession (accessed at www.wiley.com/college/kieso)

Expanding beyond technical accounting knowledge, the **Gateway to the Profession** materials emphasize certain skills necessary to become a successful accountant or financial manager. The following materials will help students develop needed professional skills:

- Financial Statement Analysis Primer
- Database of Real Companies
- Writing Handbook
- Working in Teams
- Ethics in Accounting

We also include chapter-level resources that help students process and understand key course concepts:

- Interactive Tutorials
- Expanded Discussions
- Spreadsheet Tools
- Additional Internet Links

WileyPLUS

WileyPLUS is a research-based, online environment for effective teaching and learning.

The market-leading homework experience in *WileyPLUS* offers:

A Blank Sheet of Paper Effect

The *WileyPLUS* homework experience, which includes type-ahead for account title entry, imitates a blank sheet of paper format so that students use recall memory when doing homework and will do better in class, on exams, and in their professions.

A Professional Worksheet Style

The professional, worksheet-style problem layouts help students master accounting skills while doing homework that directly applies to the classroom and the real world.

The Opportunity to Catch Mistakes Earlier

Multi-part problems further help students focus by providing feedback at the part-level. Students can catch their mistakes earlier and access content-specific resources at the point of learning.

More Assessment Options

All brief exercises, exercises, and problems from the textbook are now available for assignment in *WileyPLUS* in static or algorithmic format.

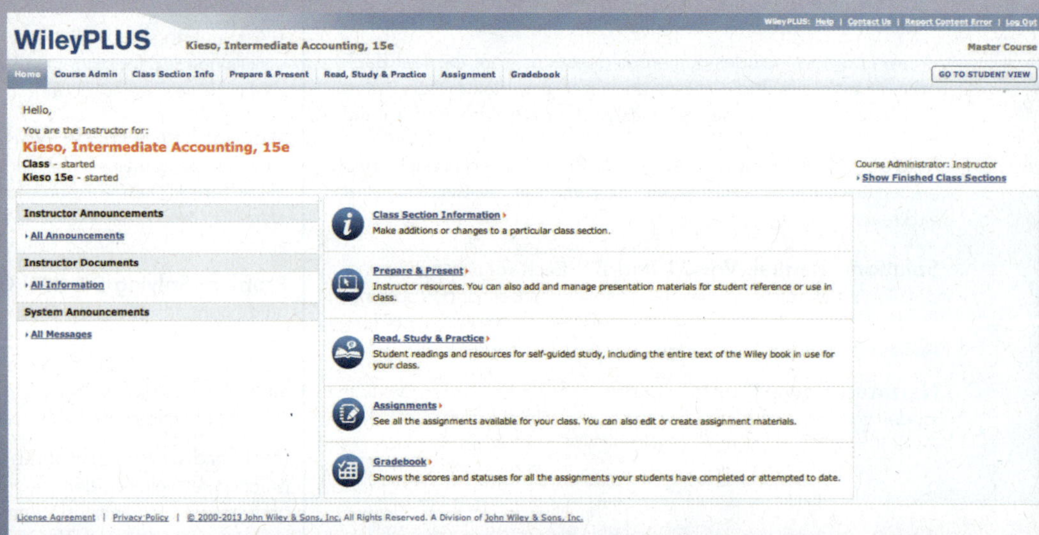

***WileyPLUS* includes a full ebook, interactive tutorials, assessment capabilities, and Blackboard integration.**

www.wileyplus.com

Contents

Chapter 17

Investments 950

What to Do?

Chapter 18

Revenue Recognition 1040

It's Back

Chapter 19

Chapter 20

Chapter 21

Accounting for Leases 1268

Chapter 22

Accounting Changes and Error Analysis 1342

Chapter 23

Statement of Cash Flows 1410

Show Me the Money!

Chapter 24

Full Disclosure in Financial Reporting 1486

High-Quality Financial Reporting—Always in Fashion

Acknowledgments

Intermediate Accounting has benefited greatly from the input of focus group participants, manuscript reviewers, those who have sent comments by letter or e-mail, ancillary authors, and proofers. We greatly appreciate the constructive suggestions and innovative ideas of reviewers and the creativity and accuracy of the ancillary authors and checkers.

Prior Edition Reviewers

We greatly appreciate the over 250 reviewers who have assisted with the prior editions of Intermediate Accounting. *Please visit the book's companion website, at* ***www.wiley.com/college/kieso****, for a full listing of these instructors who have been invaluable in the development and continued improvement of our textbook.*

Fifteenth Edition

Wendy Bailey, *Northeastern University;* Samuel Bass, *Missouri State University;* Susan Bennett, *Wake Technical Community College;* Elise A. Boyas, *University of Pittsburgh;* Jeff Brothers, *Regis University;* John Brozovsky, *Virginia Polytechnic Institute and State University;* Helen Brubeck, *San Jose State University;* Janie Casello Bouges, *University of Massachusetts—Lowell;* Tim Cangeleri, *St. Joseph's College;* Kimberly D. Charland, *Kansas State University;* Elizabeth Conner, *University of Colorado—Denver;* Ming Lu Chun, *Santa Monica College;* Natalie Churyk, *Northern Illinois University;* Eugene Comiskey, *Georgia Institute of Technology;* Tim Coville, *St. John's University;* Illia Dichev, *Emory University;* Bob Eskew, *Purdue University;* Tony Greig, *University of Wisconsin—Madison;* Lynne Hendrix, *Hope College;* Travis Holt, *University of Tennessee;* Allen Hunt, *Southern Illinois University;* John Jiang, *Michigan State University;* Mary Jo Jones, *Eastern University;* Lisa Koonce, *University of Texas—Austin;* Barbara Kren, *Marquette University;* Gaurav Kumar, *University of Arkansas—Little Rock;* Zining Li, *Southern Methodist University;* Ellen Lippman, *University of Portland;* Daphne Main, *Loyola University—New Orleans.*

S.A. Marino, *Westchester Community College;* Ariel Markelevich, *Suffolk University;* Linda McDaniel, *University of Kentucky;* K. Bryan Menk, *Virginia State University;* Gerald Miller, *The College of New Jersey;* Kathleen Moffitt, *Texas State University—San Marcos;* Kanalis Ockree, *Washburn University;* Felicia Olagbemi, *Colorado State University;* Mitch Oler, *Virginia Polytechnic Institute and State University;* Keith Patterson, *Brigham Young University—Idaho;* Charles Pendola, *St. Joseph's College;* Pete Poznanski, *Cleveland State University;* Jay Price, *Utah State University;* Terence Reilly, *Albright University;* Ken Reichelt, *Louisiana State University;* Ada Rodriguez, *Lehman College, CUNY;* Jack Rude, *Bloomsburg University;* Michael Ruff, *Bentley University;* August Saibeni, *Cosumnes River College;* Alexander J. Sannella, *Rutgers University;* Richard Schneible, *University of Albany SUNY;* Stephen Stubben, *University of North Carolina—Chapel Hill;* Stefanie Tate, *University of Massachusetts—Lowell;* Dan Teed, *Troy University;* Robin Thomas, *North Carolina State University;* Thomas Tyson, *St. John Fisher College;* Dan Wangerin, *Michigan State University;* Donna Whitten, *Purdue University North Central;* Kenneth Winter, *University of Wisconsin—Madison;* David Wright, *University of Michigan;* Jim Zapapas, *Regis University;* Lin Zheng, *Mercer University.*

Special thanks to Kurt Pany, Arizona State University, for his input on auditor disclosure issues, and to Stephen A. Zeff, Rice University, for his comments on international accounting.

In addition, we thank the following colleagues who contributed to several of the unique features of this edition.

Gateway to the Profession and Codification Cases

Katie Adler, *Deloitte LLP, Chicago;* Jack Cathey, *University of North Carolina—Charlotte;* Michelle Ephraim, *Worcester Polytechnic Institute;* Erik Frederickson, *Madison, Wisconsin;* Danielle Griffin, *KPMG, Chicago;* Jason Hart, *Deloitte LLP, Milwaukee;* Frank Heflin, *Florida State University;* Mike Katte, *SC Johnson, Racine, WI;* Kelly Krieg, *E & Y, Milwaukee;* Jeremy Kunicki, *Walgreens;* Courtney Meier, *Deloitte LLP, Milwaukee;* Andrew Prewitt, *KPMG, Chicago;* Jeff Seymour, *KPMG, Minneapolis;* Matt Sullivan, *Deloitte LLP, Milwaukee;* Matt Tutaj, *Deloitte LLP, Chicago;* Jen Vaughn, *PricewaterhouseCoopers, Chicago;* Erin Viel, *PricewaterhouseCoopers, Milwaukee.*

Ancillary Authors, Contributors, Proofers, and Accuracy Checkers

LuAnn Bean, *Florida Institute of Technology;* Mary Ann Benson; John C. Borke, *University of Wisconsin—Platteville;* Jack Cathey, *University of North Carolina—Charlotte;* Jim Emig, *Villanova University;* Larry Falcetto, *Emporia State University;* Coby Harmon, *University of California, Santa Barbara;* Marilyn F. Hunt, Douglas W. Kieso, *Aurora University;* Mark Kohlbeck, *Florida Atlantic University;* Steven Lifland, *High Point University;* Ming Lu, *Santa Monica College;* Maureen Mascha, *Marquette University;* Barbara Muller, *Arizona State University;* Jill Misuraca, *University of Tampa;* Yvonne Phang, *Borough of Manhattan Community College;* John Plouffe, *California State Polytechnic University—Pomona;* Mark Riley, *Northern Illinois University;* Lynn Stallworth, *Appalachian State University;* Diane Tanner, *University of North Florida;* Sheila Viel, *University of Wisconsin—Milwaukee;* Dick D. Wasson, *Southwestern College;* Melanie Yon, *San Diego University.*

Advisory Board

We gratefully acknowledge the following members of the Intermediate Accounting Advisory Board for their advice and assistance with this edition.

Steve Balsam, *Temple University;* Jack Cathey, *University of North Carolina—Charlotte;* Uday Chandra, *State University of New York at Albany;* Ruben Davila, *University of Southern California;* Doug deVidal, *University of Texas—Austin;* Sunita Goel, *Siena College;* Jeffrey Hales, *Georgia Institute of Technology;* Celina Jozsi,

University of South Florida; Jocelyn Kauffunger, *University of Pittsburgh;* Adam Koch, *University of Virginia;* Roger Martin, *University of Virginia;* Mark Riley, *Northern Illinois University;* Karen Turner, *University of Northern Colorado.*

Practicing Accountants and Business Executives

From the fields of corporate and public accounting, we owe thanks to the following practitioners for their technical advice and for consenting to interviews.

Mike Crooch, *FASB (retired);* Tracy Golden, *Deloitte LLP;* John Gribble, *PricewaterhouseCoopers (retired);* Darien Griffin, *S.C. Johnson & Son;* Michael Lehman, *Sun Microsystems, Inc.;* Tom Linsmeier, *FASB;* Michele Lippert, *Evoke.com;* Sue McGrath, *Vision Capital Management;* David Miniken, *Sweeney Conrad;* Robert Sack, *University of Virginia;* Clare Schulte, *Deloitte LLP;* Willie Sutton, *Mutual Community Savings Bank, Durham, NC;* Lynn Turner, *former SEC Chief Accountant;* Rachel Woods, *PricewaterhouseCoopers;* Arthur Wyatt, *Arthur Andersen & Co., and the University of Illinois—Urbana.*

Finally, we appreciate the exemplary support and professional commitment given us by the development, marketing, production, and editorial staffs of John Wiley & Sons, including the following: George Hoffman, Susan Elbe, Chris DeJohn, Michael McDonald, Amy Scholz, Jesse Cruz, Valerie Vargas, Brian Kamins, Jackie MacKenzie, Allie Morris, Greg Chaput, Harry Nolan, Maureen Eide, and Kristine Carney. Thanks, too, to Suzanne Ingrao for her production work, to Denise Showers and the staff at Aptara®, Inc. for their work on the textbook, Cyndy Taylor, and to Matt Gauthier and the staff at Integra Publishing Services for their work on the solutions manual.

We also appreciate the cooperation of the American Institute of Certified Public Accountants and the Financial Accounting Standards Board in permitting us to quote from their pronouncements. We thank The Procter & Gamble Company for permitting us to use its 2011 annual report for our specimen financial statements. We also acknowledge permission from the American Institute of Certified Public Accountants, the Institute of Management Accountants, and the Institute of Internal Auditors to adapt and use material from the Uniform CPA Examinations, the CMA Examinations, and the CIA Examinations, respectively.

Suggestions and comments from users of this book will be appreciated. Please feel free to e-mail any one of us at *AccountingAuthors@yahoo.com.*

Donald E. Kieso
Somonauk, Illinois

Jerry J. Weygandt
Madison, Wisconsin

Terry D. Warfield
Madison, Wisconsin

CHAPTER 1

Financial Accounting and Accounting Standards

LEARNING OBJECTIVES

After studying this chapter, you should be able to:

1. Identify the major financial statements and other means of financial reporting.
2. Explain how accounting assists in the efficient use of scarce resources.
3. Identify the objective of financial reporting.
4. Explain the need for accounting standards.
5. Identify the major policy-setting bodies and their role in the standard-setting process.
6. Explain the meaning of generally accepted accounting principles (GAAP) and the role of the Codification for GAAP.
7. Describe the impact of user groups on the rule-making process.
8. Describe some of the challenges facing financial reporting.
9. Understand issues related to ethics and financial accounting.

We Can Do Better

A recent report says it best: "Accounting information is central to the functioning of international capital markets and to managing small businesses, conducting effective government, understanding business processes, and . . . how economic decisions are made. . . . Across the globe, a common characteristic of economies that flourish is the presence of reliable accounting information."

Many in the United States take pride in our system of financial reporting as being the most robust and transparent in the world. But most would also comment that we can do better, particularly in light of the many accounting scandals that have occurred at companies like **AIG**, **WorldCom**, and **Lehman Brothers**, and the financial crisis of 2008.

To better understand where we are today, the Center for Audit Quality conducts a yearly survey that measures investor confidence in such categories as U.S. capital markets, audited financial information, and U.S. publicly traded companies. Here are the results:

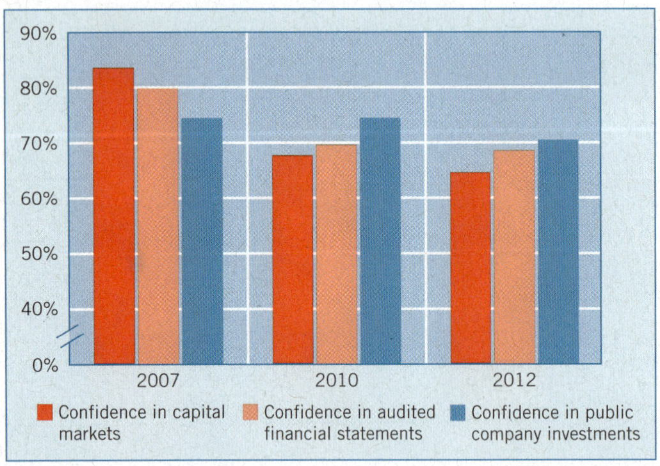

The results indicate that the 2008 financial crisis took a bite out of investor confidence. While investor confidence in U.S. markets, auditors, and public companies has stabilized, the question is how can we improve? Here are some possibilities on how we can enhance the existing system of financial reporting.

1. Today, equity securities are broadly held, with approximately half of American households investing in stocks. This presents a challenge—investors have expressed concerns that **one-size-fits-all financial reports do not meet the needs of the spectrum of investors** who rely on those reports. While many individual investors are more interested in summarized, plain-English reports, market analysts and other investment professionals may desire information at a far more detailed level than is currently provided. Technology may help customize the information that the different types of investors desire.
2. Companies also express concerns with the complexity of the financial reporting system. Companies assert that **when preparing financial reports, it is difficult to ensure compliance with the voluminous and complex requirements contained in U.S. GAAP and SEC reporting rules**. This is a particularly heavy burden on smaller, non-public companies, which may have fewer resources to comply with the wide range of rules.
3. We also need to consider the broader array of information that investors need to make informed decisions. As some have noted, the percentage of a company's market value that can be attributed to accounting book value has declined significantly from the days of a bricks-and-mortar economy. **Thus, we may want to consider a more comprehensive business reporting model, including both financial and nonfinancial key performance indicators.**

4. Finally, we must also consider **how to deliver all of this information in a timelier manner**. In a world where messages can be sent across the world in a blink of an eye, it is ironic that the analysis of financial information is still subject to many manual processes, resulting in delays, increased costs, and errors.

Thus, improving financial reporting involves more than simply trimming or reworking the existing accounting literature. In some cases, major change is already underway. For example:

- The FASB and IASB are working on a convergence project, which will contribute to less-complex, more-understandable standards in the important areas of revenue recognition, leasing, and financial instruments.
- Standard-setters are exploring expanded reporting of key performance indicators, including reports on sustainability and a disclosure framework project to improve the effectiveness of disclosures to clearly communicate the information that is most important to users of financial statements. This project, combined with the introduction of a private-company reporting framework, could go a long way to address one-size-fits-all challenges.
- The SEC now requires the delivery of financial reports using eXtensible Business Reporting Language (XBRL). Reporting through XBRL allows timelier reporting via the Internet and allows statement users to transform accounting reports to meet their specific needs.

Each of these projects will hopefully support improvements in the quality of financial reporting and increase confidence in U.S. capital markets.

Sources: Adapted from The Pathways Commission, "Charting a National Strategy for the Next Generation of Accountants" (AAA, AICPA, July 2012); Conrad W. Hewitt, "Opening Remarks Before the Initial Meeting of the SEC Advisory Committee on Improvements to Financial Reporting," U.S. Securities and Exchange Commission, Washington, D.C. (August 2, 2007); and Center for Audit Quality, *Main Street Investor Survey* (September 2012). See *www.fasb.org* for updates on FASB/IASB convergence, disclosure, and private company decision-making projects.

CONCEPTUAL FOCUS

> See the **Underlying Concepts** on pages 6 and 7.

> Read the **Evolving Issue** on page 17 for a discussion of the use of fair value accounting.

INTERNATIONAL FOCUS

> See the **International Perspectives** on pages 8, 9, 10, 17, and 20.

> Read the **IFRS Insights** on pages 31–39 for a discussion of:

—International standard-setting organizations
—Hierarchy of IFRS
—International accounting convergence

PREVIEW OF CHAPTER 1

As our opening story indicates, the U.S. system of financial reporting has long been the most robust and transparent in the world. However, to ensure that it continues to provide the most relevant and reliable financial information to users, a number of financial reporting issues must be resolved. These issues include such matters as adopting global standards, increasing fair value reporting, and meeting multiple user needs. This chapter explains the environment of financial reporting and the many factors affecting it, as follows.

Financial Accounting and Accounting Standards

Financial Statements and Financial Reporting	Parties Involved in Standard-Setting	Generally Accepted Accounting Principles	Issues in Financial Reporting
• Accounting and capital allocation • Objective • Need to develop standards	• Securities and Exchange Commission • American Institute of CPAs • Financial Accounting Standards Board	• FASB Codification	• Political environment • Expectations gap • Financial reporting challenges • International accounting standards • Ethics

FINANCIAL STATEMENTS AND FINANCIAL REPORTING

LEARNING OBJECTIVE 1
Identify the major financial statements and other means of financial reporting.

The essential characteristics of accounting are (1) the identification, measurement, and communication of financial information about (2) economic entities to (3) interested parties. **Financial accounting** is the process that culminates in the preparation of financial reports on the enterprise for use by both internal and external parties. Users of these financial reports include investors, creditors, managers, unions, and government agencies. In contrast, **managerial accounting** is the process of identifying, measuring, analyzing, and communicating financial information needed by management to plan, control, and evaluate a company's operations.

Financial statements are the principal means through which a company communicates its financial information to those outside it. These statements provide a company's history quantified in money terms. The **financial statements** most frequently provided are (1) the balance sheet, (2) the income statement, (3) the statement of cash flows, and (4) the statement of owners' or stockholders' equity. Note disclosures are an integral part of each financial statement.

Some financial information is better provided, or can be provided only, by means of **financial reporting** other than formal financial statements. Examples include the president's letter or supplementary schedules in the corporate annual report, prospectuses, reports filed with government agencies, news releases, management's forecasts, and social or environmental impact statements. Companies may need to provide such information because of authoritative pronouncement, regulatory rule, or custom. Or they may supply it because management wishes to disclose it voluntarily.

In this textbook, we focus on the development of two types of financial information: (1) the basic financial statements and (2) related disclosures.

Accounting and Capital Allocation

LEARNING OBJECTIVE 2
Explain how accounting assists in the efficient use of scarce resources.

Resources are limited. As a result, people try to conserve them and ensure that they are used effectively. Efficient use of resources often determines whether a business thrives. This fact places a substantial burden on the accounting profession.

Accountants must measure performance accurately and fairly on a timely basis, so that the right managers and companies are able to attract investment capital. For example, relevant and reliable financial information allows investors and creditors to compare the income and assets employed by such companies as **IBM**, **McDonald's**, **Microsoft**, and **Ford**. Because these users can assess the relative return and risks associated with investment opportunities, they channel resources more effectively. Illustration 1-1 shows how this process of capital allocation works.

ILLUSTRATION 1-1
Capital Allocation Process

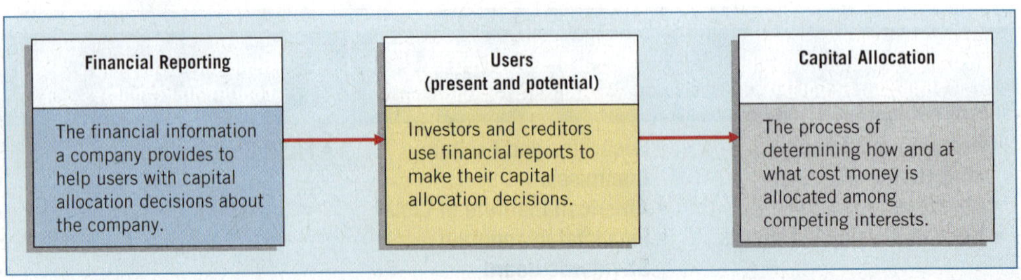

An effective process of capital allocation is critical to a healthy economy. It promotes productivity, encourages innovation, and provides an efficient and liquid market for buying and selling securities and obtaining and granting credit. Unreliable and irrelevant information leads to poor capital allocation, which adversely affects the securities markets.

What do the numbers mean? IT'S THE ACCOUNTING

"It's the accounting." That's what many investors seem to be saying these days. Even the slightest hint of any accounting irregularity at a company leads to a subsequent pounding of the company's stock price. For example, the *Wall Street Journal* has run the following headlines related to accounting and its effects on the economy.

- Stocks take a beating as accounting woes spread beyond Enron.
- Quarterly reports from IBM and Goldman Sachs sent stocks tumbling.
- VeriFone finds accounting issues; stock price cut in half.
- Bank of America admits hiding debt.
- Facebook, Zynga, Groupon: IPO drops due to accounting, not valuation.

It now has become clear that investors must trust the accounting numbers, or they will abandon the market and put their resources elsewhere. With investor uncertainty, the cost of capital increases for companies who need additional resources. In short, relevant and reliable financial information is necessary for markets to be efficient.

Objective of Financial Reporting

3 LEARNING OBJECTIVE
Identify the objective of financial reporting.

What is the objective **(or purpose)** of financial reporting? The objective of general-purpose financial reporting is to **provide financial information about the reporting entity that is useful to present and potential equity investors, lenders, and other creditors in** decisions about providing resources to the entity. Those decisions involve buying, selling, or holding equity and debt instruments, and providing or settling loans and other forms of credit. Information that is decision-useful to capital providers (investors) may also be helpful to other users of financial reporting who are not investors. Let's examine each of the elements of this objective.[1]

General-Purpose Financial Statements

General-purpose financial statements provide financial reporting information to a wide variety of users. For example, when The Hershey Company issues its financial statements, these statements help shareholders, creditors, suppliers, employees, and regulators to better understand its financial position and related performance. Hershey's users need this type of information to make effective decisions. To be cost-effective in providing this information, general-purpose financial statements are most appropriate. In other words, general-purpose financial statements provide at the **least cost the most useful information possible**.

Equity Investors and Creditors

The objective of financial reporting **identifies investors and creditors as the primary users for general-purpose financial statements**. Identifying investors and creditors as the primary users provides an important focus of general-purpose financial reporting. For example, when Hershey issues its financial statements, its primary focus is on investors and creditors because they have the most critical and immediate need for information in financial reports. Investors and creditors need this financial information to assess

[1]Chapter 1, "The Objective of General Purpose Financial Reporting," and Chapter 3, "Qualitative Characteristics of Useful Financial Information," *Statement of Financial Accounting Concepts No. 8* (Norwalk, Conn.: FASB, September 2010), par. OB2.

Underlying Concepts

While the objective of financial reporting is focused on investors and creditors, financial statements may still meet the needs of others.

Hershey's ability to generate net cash inflow and to understand management's ability to protect and enhance the assets of the company, which will be used to generate future net cash inflows. As a result, the primary user groups are not management, regulators, or some other non-investor group.

Entity Perspective

As part of the objective of general-purpose financial reporting, an **entity perspective** is adopted. Companies are viewed as separate and distinct from their owners (present shareholders) using this perspective. The assets of Hershey are viewed as assets of the company and not of a specific creditor or shareholder. Rather, these investors have claims on Hershey's assets in the form of liability or equity claims. The entity perspective is consistent with the present business environment where most companies engaged in financial reporting have substance distinct from their investors (both shareholders and creditors). Thus, a perspective that financial reporting should be focused only on the needs of shareholders—often referred to as the **proprietary perspective**—is not considered appropriate.

What do the numbers mean? DON'T FORGET STEWARDSHIP

In addition to providing decision-useful information about future cash flows, management also is accountable to investors for the custody and safekeeping of the company's economic resources and for their efficient and profitable use. For example, the management of The Hershey Company has the responsibility for protecting its economic resources from unfavorable effects of economic factors, such as price changes, and technological and social changes. Because Hershey's performance in discharging its responsibilities (referred to as its **stewardship** responsibilities) usually affects its ability to generate net cash inflows, financial reporting may also provide decision-useful information to assess management performance in this role.

Source: Chapter 1, "The Objective of General Purpose Financial Reporting," and Chapter 3, "Qualitative Characteristics of Useful Financial Information," *Statement of Financial Accounting Concepts No. 8* (Norwalk, Conn.: FASB, September 2010), paras. OB4–OB10.

Decision-Usefulness

Investors are interested in financial reporting because it provides information that is useful for making decisions (referred to as the **decision-usefulness** approach). As indicated earlier, when making these decisions, investors are interested in assessing (1) the company's ability to generate net cash inflows and (2) management's ability to protect and enhance the capital providers' investments. Financial reporting should therefore help investors assess the amounts, timing, and uncertainty of prospective cash inflows from dividends or interest, and the proceeds from the sale, redemption, or maturity of securities or loans. In order for investors to make these assessments, the economic resources of an enterprise, the claims to those resources, and the changes in them must be understood. Financial statements and related explanations should be a primary source for determining this information.

The emphasis on "assessing cash flow prospects" does not mean that the cash basis is preferred over the accrual basis of accounting. Information based on accrual accounting better indicates a company's present and continuing ability to generate favorable cash flows than does information limited to the financial effects of cash receipts and payments.

Recall from your first accounting course the objective of **accrual-basis accounting**: It ensures that a company records events that change its financial statements in the periods in which the events occur, rather than only in the periods in which it receives or pays cash. Using the accrual basis to determine net income means that a company recognizes revenues when it provides the goods or services rather than when it receives cash. Similarly, it recognizes expenses when it incurs them rather than when it pays them. Under accrual accounting, a company generally recognizes revenues when it makes sales. The company can then relate the revenues to the economic environment of the period in which they occurred. Over the long run, trends in revenues and expenses are generally more meaningful than trends in cash receipts and disbursements.[2]

The Need to Develop Standards

4 LEARNING OBJECTIVE

Explain the need for accounting standards.

The main controversy in setting accounting standards is, "Whose rules should we play by, and what should they be?" The answer is not immediately clear. Users of financial accounting statements have both coinciding and conflicting needs for information of various types. To meet these needs, and to satisfy the stewardship reporting responsibility of management, companies prepare a single set of **general-purpose financial statements**. Users expect these statements to present fairly, clearly, and completely the company's financial operations.

The accounting profession has attempted to develop a set of standards that are generally accepted and universally practiced. Otherwise, each company would have to develop its own standards. Further, readers of financial statements would have to familiarize themselves with every company's peculiar accounting and reporting practices. It would be almost impossible to prepare statements that could be compared.

Underlying Concepts

Preparing financial statements prepared according to accepted accounting standards contributes to the comparability of accounting information.

This common set of standards and procedures is called **generally accepted accounting principles (GAAP)**. The term "generally accepted" means either that an authoritative accounting rule-making body has established a principle of reporting in a given area or that over time a given practice has been accepted as appropriate because of its universal application.[3] Although principles and practices continue to provoke both debate and criticism, most members of the financial community recognize them as the standards that over time have proven to be most useful. We present a more extensive discussion of what constitutes GAAP later in this chapter.

PARTIES INVOLVED IN STANDARD-SETTING

5 LEARNING OBJECTIVE

Identify the major policy-setting bodies and their role in the standard-setting process.

Three organizations are instrumental in the development of financial accounting standards (GAAP) in the United States:

1. Securities and Exchange Commission (SEC)
2. American Institute of Certified Public Accountants (AICPA)
3. Financial Accounting Standards Board (FASB)

Securities and Exchange Commission (SEC)

External financial reporting and auditing developed in tandem with the growth of the industrial economy and its capital markets. However, when the stock market crashed in

[2]As used here, cash flow means "cash generated and used in operations." The term *cash flows* also frequently means cash obtained by borrowing and used to repay borrowing, cash used for investments in resources and obtained from the disposal of investments, and cash contributed by or distributed to owners.

[3]The terms *principles* and *standards* are used interchangeably in practice and throughout this textbook.

International Perspective

The International Organization of Securities Commissions (IOSCO), established in 1987, consists of more than 100 securities regulatory agencies or securities exchanges from all over the world. Collectively, its members represent a substantial proportion of the world's capital markets. The SEC is a member of IOSCO.

1929 and the nation's economy plunged into the Great Depression, there were calls for increased government regulation of business, especially financial institutions and the stock market.

As a result of these events, the federal government established the **Securities and Exchange Commission (SEC)** to help develop and standardize financial information presented to stockholders. The SEC is a federal agency. It administers the Securities Exchange Act of 1934 and several other acts. Most companies that issue securities to the public or are listed on a stock exchange are required to file audited financial statements with the SEC. In addition, the SEC has broad powers to prescribe, in whatever detail it desires, the accounting practices and standards to be employed by companies that fall within its jurisdiction. The SEC currently exercises oversight over 12,000 companies that are listed on the major exchanges (e.g., the New York Stock Exchange and the Nasdaq).

Public/Private Partnership

At the time the SEC was created, no group—public or private—issued accounting standards. The SEC encouraged the creation of a private standard-setting body because it believed that the private sector had the appropriate resources and talent to achieve this daunting task. As a result, accounting standards have developed in the private sector either through the American Institute of Certified Public Accountants (AICPA) or the Financial Accounting Standards Board (FASB).

The SEC has affirmed its support for the FASB by indicating that financial statements conforming to standards set by the FASB are presumed to have substantial authoritative support. In short, the **SEC requires registrants to adhere to GAAP**. In addition, the SEC indicated in its reports to Congress that "it continues to believe that the initiative for establishing and improving accounting standards should remain in the private sector, subject to Commission oversight."

SEC Oversight

The SEC's partnership with the private sector works well. The SEC acts with remarkable restraint in the area of developing accounting standards. Generally, **the SEC relies on the FASB to develop accounting standards**.

The SEC's involvement in the development of accounting standards varies. In some cases, the SEC rejects a standard proposed by the private sector. In other cases, the SEC prods the private sector into taking quicker action on certain reporting problems, such as accounting for investments in debt and equity securities and the reporting of derivative instruments. In still other situations, the SEC communicates problems to the FASB, responds to FASB exposure drafts, and provides the FASB with counsel and advice upon request.

The SEC's mandate is to establish accounting principles. The private sector, therefore, must listen carefully to the views of the SEC. In some sense, the private sector is the formulator and the implementor of the standards.[4] However, when the private sector fails to address accounting problems as quickly as the SEC would like, the partnership between the SEC and the private sector can be strained. This occurred in the deliberations on the

[4]One writer described the relationship of the FASB and SEC and the development of financial reporting standards using the analogy of a pearl. The pearl (a financial reporting standard) "is formed by the reaction of certain oysters (FASB) to an irritant (the SEC)—usually a grain of sand—that becomes embedded inside the shell. The oyster coats this grain with layers of nacre, and ultimately a pearl is formed. The pearl is a joint result of the irritant (SEC) and oyster (FASB); without both, it cannot be created." John C. Burton, "Government Regulation of Accounting and Information," *Journal of Accountancy* (June 1982).

accounting for business combinations and intangible assets. It is also highlighted by concerns over the accounting for off-balance-sheet special-purpose entities, highlighted in the failure of **Enron** and, more recently, the subprime crises that led to the failure of **IndyMac Bank**.

International Perspective

The U.S. legal system is based on English common law, whereby the government generally allows professionals to make the rules. The private sector, therefore, develops these rules (standards). Conversely, some countries have followed codified law, which leads to government-run accounting systems.

Enforcement

As we indicated earlier, companies listed on a stock exchange must submit their financial statements to the SEC. If the SEC believes that an accounting or disclosure irregularity exists regarding the form or content of the financial statements, it sends a deficiency letter to the company. Companies usually resolve these deficiency letters quickly. If disagreement continues, the SEC may issue a "stop order," which prevents the registrant from issuing or trading securities on the exchanges. The Department of Justice may also file criminal charges for violations of certain laws. The SEC process, private sector initiatives, and civil and criminal litigation help to ensure the integrity of financial reporting for public companies.

American Institute of Certified Public Accountants (AICPA)

The **American Institute of Certified Public Accountants (AICPA)**, which is the national professional organization of practicing Certified Public Accountants (CPAs), has been an important contributor to the development of GAAP. Various committees and boards established since the founding of the AICPA have contributed to this effort.

Committee on Accounting Procedure

At the urging of the SEC, the AICPA appointed the Committee on Accounting Procedure in 1939. The **Committee on Accounting Procedure (CAP)** composed of practicing CPAs, issued 51 **Accounting Research Bulletins** during the years 1939 to 1959. These bulletins dealt with a variety of accounting problems. But this problem-by-problem approach failed to provide the needed structured body of accounting principles. In response, in 1959 the AICPA created the Accounting Principles Board.

Accounting Principles Board

The major purposes of the **Accounting Principles Board (APB)** were to (1) advance the written expression of accounting principles, (2) determine appropriate practices, and (3) narrow the areas of difference and inconsistency in practice. To achieve these objectives, the APB's mission was twofold: to develop an overall conceptual framework to assist in the resolution of problems as they become evident and to substantively research individual issues before the AICPA issued pronouncements. The Board's 18 to 21 members, selected primarily from public accounting, also included representatives from industry and academia. The Board's official pronouncements, called **APB Opinions**, were intended to be based mainly on research studies and be supported by reason and analysis. Between its inception in 1959 and its dissolution in 1973, the APB issued 31 opinions.

Unfortunately, the APB came under fire early, charged with lack of productivity and failing to act promptly to correct alleged accounting abuses. Later, the APB tackled numerous thorny accounting issues, only to meet a buzz saw of opposition from industry and CPA firms. It also ran into occasional governmental interference. In 1971, the accounting profession's leaders, anxious to avoid governmental rule-making, appointed a Study Group on Establishment of Accounting Principles. Commonly known as the **Wheat Committee** for its chair Francis Wheat, this group examined the organization and operation of the APB and determined the necessary changes to attain better results. The Study Group submitted its recommendations to the AICPA Council in the spring of 1972, which led to the replacement of the APB with the Financial Accounting Standards Board (FASB) in 1973.

Changing Role of the AICPA

When the FASB replaced the Accounting Principles Board, the AICPA established the **Accounting Standards Executive Committee (AcSEC)** as the committee authorized to speak for the AICPA in the area of financial accounting and reporting. It does so through various written communications:

Audit and Accounting Guides summarize the accounting practices of specific industries and provide specific guidance on matters not addressed by the FASB. Examples are accounting for casinos, airlines, colleges and universities, banks, insurance companies, and many others.

Statements of Position (SOPs) provide guidance on financial reporting topics until the FASB sets standards on the issue in question. SOPs may update, revise, and clarify audit and accounting guides or provide free-standing guidance.

Practice Bulletins indicate the AcSEC's views on narrow financial reporting issues not considered by the FASB.

The role of the AICPA in standard-setting has diminished. The FASB and the AICPA agree that the AICPA and AcSEC no longer will issue authoritative accounting guidance for public companies. Furthermore, while the AICPA has been the leader in developing auditing standards through its **Auditing Standards Board**, the Sarbanes-Oxley Act of 2002 requires the Public Company Accounting Oversight Board to oversee the development of auditing standards. The AICPA continues to develop and grade the CPA examination, which is administered in all 50 states.

International Perspective

The CPA exam is administered internationally at testing sites in Bahrain, Kuwait, Japan, Lebanon, United Arab Emirates (UAE), and Brazil. The CPA exam now has some coverage of IFRS knowledge as part of the financial reporting section of the exam (see *www.aicpa.org/cpa-exam*).

Financial Accounting Standards Board (FASB)

The Wheat Committee's recommendations resulted in the creation of a new standard-setting structure composed of three organizations—the Financial Accounting Foundation (FAF), the Financial Accounting Standards Board (FASB), and the Financial Accounting Standards Advisory Council (FASAC). The **Financial Accounting Foundation** selects the members of the FASB and the Advisory Council, funds their activities, and generally oversees the FASB's activities.

The major operating organization in this three-part structure is the **Financial Accounting Standards Board (FASB)**. Its mission is to establish and improve standards of financial accounting and reporting for the guidance and education of the public, which includes issuers, auditors, and users of financial information. The expectations of success and support for the new FASB relied on several significant differences between it and its predecessor, the APB:

1. ***Smaller membership.*** The FASB consists of seven members, replacing the relatively large 18-member APB.
2. ***Full-time, remunerated membership.*** FASB members are well-paid, full-time members appointed for renewable 5-year terms. The APB members volunteered their part-time work.
3. ***Greater autonomy.*** The APB was a senior committee of the AICPA. The FASB is not part of any single professional organization. It is appointed by and answerable only to the Financial Accounting Foundation.
4. ***Increased independence.*** APB members retained their private positions with firms, companies, or institutions. FASB members must sever all such ties.
5. ***Broader representation.*** All APB members were required to be CPAs and members of the AICPA. Currently, it is not necessary to be a CPA to be a member of the FASB.

In addition to research help from its own staff, the FASB relies on the expertise of various task force groups formed for various projects and on the **Financial Accounting Standards Advisory Council (FASAC)**. The FASAC consults with the FASB on major policy and technical issues and also helps select task force members. Illustration 1-2 shows the current organizational structure for the development of financial reporting standards.[5]

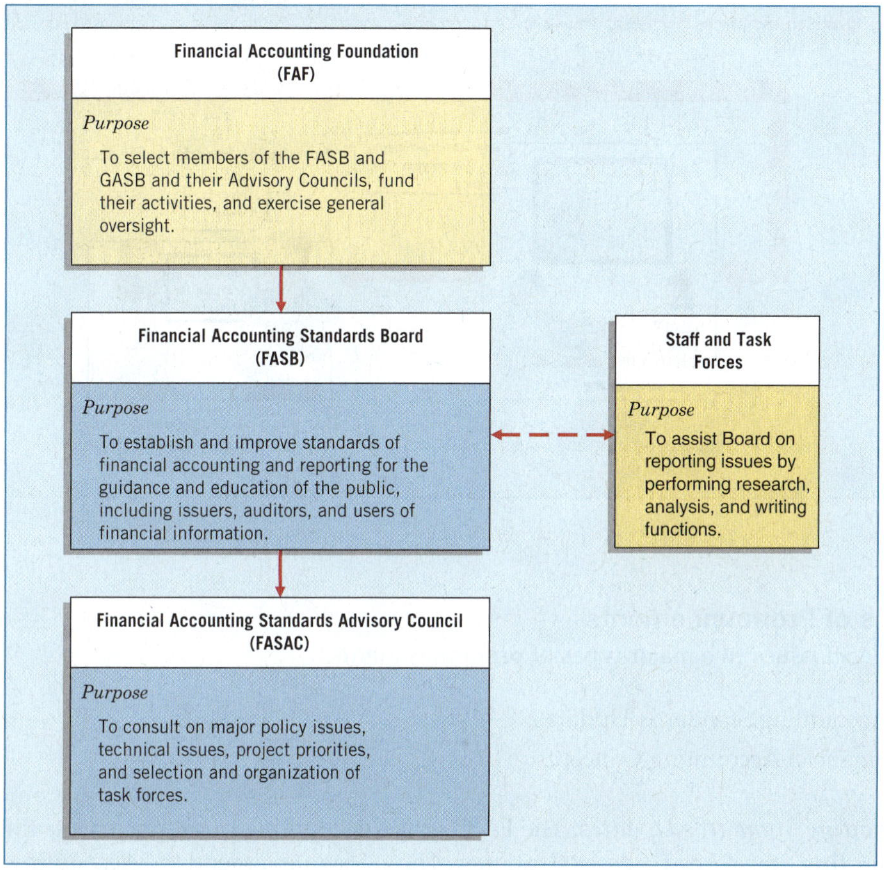

ILLUSTRATION 1-2
Organizational Structure for Setting Accounting Standards

Due Process

In establishing financial accounting standards, the FASB relies on two basic premises. (1) The FASB should be responsive to the needs and viewpoints of the entire economic community, not just the public accounting profession. (2) It should operate in full view of the public through a "due process" system that gives interested persons ample opportunity to make their views known. To ensure the achievement of these goals, the FASB follows specific steps to develop a typical FASB pronouncement, as Illustration 1-3 (page 12) shows.

The passage of new FASB guidance in the form of an Accounting Standards Update requires the support of four of the seven Board members. FASB pronouncements are considered GAAP and thereby binding in practice. All ARBs and APB Opinions implemented by 1973 (when the FASB formed) continue to be effective until amended or superseded by FASB pronouncements. In recognition of possible misconceptions of the term "principles," the FASB uses the term **financial accounting standards** in its pronouncements.

[5]Other advisory groups, such as the Investors Technical Advisory Committee (ITAC), the Not-for-Profit Advisor Committee (NAC), the Valuation Resource Group (VRG), and the recently established Private Company Financial Reporting Committee (PCFRC), share their views and experience with the Board on matters related to projects on the Board's agenda, from the perspective of various constituencies and/or in areas of specific expertise.

ILLUSTRATION 1-3
The Due Process System of the FASB

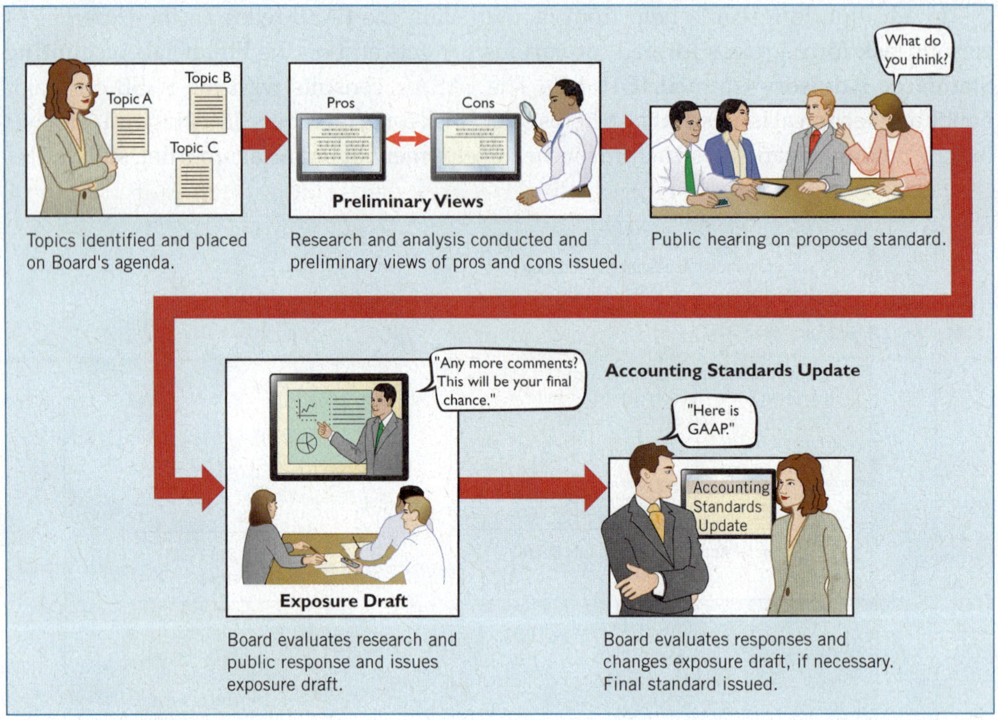

Types of Pronouncements

The FASB issues two major types of pronouncements:

1. Accounting Standards Updates.
2. Financial Accounting Concepts.

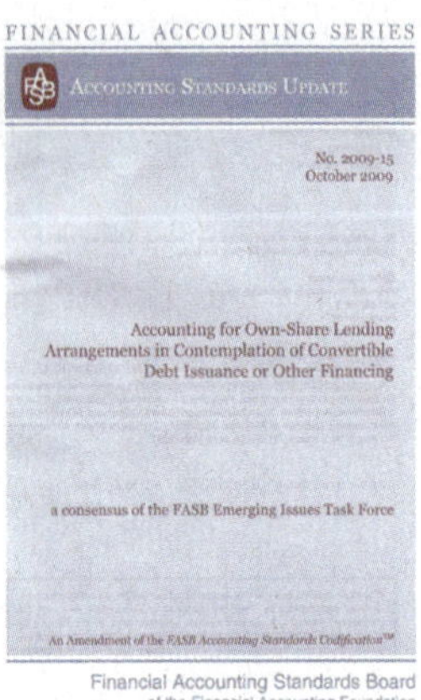
FINANCIAL ACCOUNTING SERIES
ACCOUNTING STANDARDS UPDATE
No. 2009-15
October 2009
Accounting for Own-Share Lending Arrangements in Contemplation of Convertible Debt Issuance or Other Financing
a consensus of the FASB Emerging Issues Task Force
An Amendment of the FASB Accounting Standards Codification™
Financial Accounting Standards Board
of the Financial Accounting Foundation

Accounting Standards Updates. The FASB issues accounting pronouncements through **Accounting Standards Updates** (Updates). These Updates amend the Accounting Standards Codification, which represents the source of authoritative accounting standards, other than standards issued by the SEC. Each Update explains how the Codification has been amended and also includes information to help the reader understand the changes and when those changes will be effective. Common forms of amendments are accounting standards issued that address a broad area of accounting practice (such as the accounting for leases) or interpretations that modify or extend existing standards. Prior standard-setters such as the APB also issued interpretations of APB Opinions.

A second type of Update is a consensus of the **Emerging Issues Task Force (EITF)**, created in 1984 by the FASB. The EITF is comprised of representatives from CPA firms and financial statement preparers. Observers from the SEC and AICPA also attend EITF meetings. The purpose of the task force is to reach a consensus on how to account for new and unusual financial transactions that may potentially create differing financial reporting practices. Examples include accounting for pension plan terminations, revenue from barter transactions by Internet companies, and excessive amounts paid to takeover specialists. The EITF also provided timely guidance for the accounting for loans and investments in the wake of the credit crisis.

The EITF helps the FASB in many ways. The EITF identifies controversial accounting problems as they arise. The EITF determines whether it can quickly resolve them or whether to involve the FASB in solving them. In essence, it becomes a "problem filter" for the FASB. Thus, the FASB will hopefully work on more pervasive long-term problems, while the EITF deals with short-term emerging issues.

We cannot overestimate the importance of the EITF. In one year, for example, the task force examined 61 emerging financial reporting issues and arrived at a consensus on approximately 75 percent of them. The FASB reviews and approves all EITF consensuses. And the SEC indicated that it will view consensus solutions as preferred accounting. Further, it requires persuasive justification for departing from them.

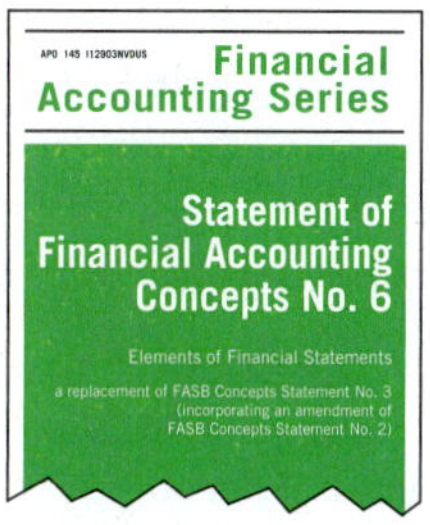

Financial Accounting Concepts. As part of a long-range effort to move away from the problem-by-problem approach, the FASB in November 1978 issued the first in a series of **Statements of Financial Accounting Concepts** as part of its conceptual framework project. (The Concepts Statement can be accessed at *http://www.fasb.org/*.) The series sets forth fundamental objectives and concepts that the Board uses in developing future standards of financial accounting and reporting. The Board intends to form a cohesive set of interrelated concepts—a conceptual framework—that will serve as tools for solving existing and emerging problems in a consistent manner. Unlike a Statement of Financial Accounting Standards, **a Statement of Financial Accounting Concepts does not establish GAAP**. Concepts statements, however, pass through the same due process system (preliminary views, public hearing, exposure draft, etc.) as do standards statements.

GENERALLY ACCEPTED ACCOUNTING PRINCIPLES

6 LEARNING OBJECTIVE
Explain the meaning of generally accepted accounting principles (GAAP) and the role of the Codification for GAAP.

Generally accepted accounting principles (GAAP) have substantial authoritative support. The AICPA's Code of Professional Conduct requires that members prepare financial statements in accordance with GAAP. Specifically, Rule 203 of this Code prohibits a member from expressing an unqualified opinion on financial statements that contain a material departure from generally accepted accounting principles.

What is GAAP? The major sources of GAAP come from the organizations discussed earlier in this chapter. It is composed of a mixture of over 2,000 documents that have been developed over the last 70 years or so. It includes APB Opinions, FASB Standards, and AICPA Research Bulletins. In addition, the FASB has issued **interpretations** and **FASB Staff Positions** that modified or extended existing standards. The APB also issued interpretations of APB Opinions. Both types of interpretations are considered authoritative for purposes of determining GAAP. Since replacing the APB, the FASB has issued over 160 standards, 48 interpretations, and nearly 100 staff positions. Illustration 1-4 highlights the many different types of documents that comprise GAAP.

- AICPA Accounting Interpretations
- FASB Implementation Guides (Q and A)
- Widely recognized and prevalent industry practices
- FASB Emerging Issues Task Force
- AICPA AcSEC Practice Bulletins
- FASB Technical Bulletins
- AICPA Industry Audit and Accounting Guides
- AICPA Statements of Position
- FASB Standards, Interpretations, and Staff Positions
- APB Opinions
- AICPA Accounting Research Bulletins

ILLUSTRATION 1-4
GAAP Documents

What do the numbers mean? YOU HAVE TO STEP BACK

Should the accounting profession have principles-based standards or rules-based standards? Critics of the profession today say that over the past three decades, standard-setters have moved away from broad accounting principles aimed at ensuring that companies' financial statements are fairly presented.

Instead, these critics say, standard-setters have moved toward drafting voluminous rules that, if technically followed in "check-box" fashion, may shield auditors and companies from legal liability. That has resulted in companies creating complex capital structures that comply with GAAP but hide billions of dollars of debt and other obligations. To add fuel to the fire, the chief accountant of the enforcement division of the SEC noted, "One can violate SEC laws and still comply with GAAP."

In short, what he is saying is that it is not enough just to check the boxes. This point was reinforced by the Chief Accountant of the SEC, who remarked that judgments should result in "accounting that reflects the substance of the transaction, as well as being in accordance with the literature." That is, you have to exercise judgment in applying GAAP to achieve high-quality reporting.

Sources: Adapted from S. Liesman, "SEC Accounting Cop's Warning: Playing by the Rules May Not Head Off Fraud Issues," *Wall Street Journal* (February 12, 2002), p. C7. See also "Study Pursuant to Section 108(d) of the Sarbanes-Oxley Act of 2002 on the Adoption by the United States Financial Reporting System of a Principles-Based Accounting System," *SEC* (July 25, 2003); and E. Orenstein, "Accounting as Art vs. Science, and the Role of Professional Judgment," *Accounting Matters,* FEI Financial Reporting Blog (November, 2009).

FASB Codification

Historically, the documents that comprised GAAP varied in format, completeness, and structure. In some cases, these documents were inconsistent and difficult to interpret. As a result, financial statement preparers sometimes were not sure whether they had the right GAAP. Determining what was authoritative and what was not became difficult.

In response to these concerns, the FASB developed the **Financial Accounting Standards Board Accounting Standards Codification** (or more simply, "the Codification"). The FASB's primary goal in developing the Codification is to provide in one place all the authoritative literature related to a particular topic. This will simplify user access to all authoritative U.S. generally accepted accounting principles. The Codification changes the way GAAP is documented, presented, and updated. It explains what GAAP is and eliminates nonessential information such as redundant document summaries, basis for conclusions sections, and historical content. In short, the Codification integrates and synthesizes existing GAAP; it does not create new GAAP. It creates one level of GAAP, which is considered authoritative. All other accounting literature is considered non-authoritative.[6]

To provide easy access to this Codification, the FASB also developed the **Financial Accounting Standards Board Codification Research System (CRS)**. CRS is an online, real-time database that provides easy access to the Codification. The Codification and the related CRS provide a topically organized structure, subdivided into topic, subtopics, sections, and paragraphs, using a numerical index system.

For purposes of referencing authoritative GAAP material in this textbook, we will use the Codification framework. Here is an example of how the Codification framework

[6]The FASB Codification can be accessed at *http://asc.fasb.org/home*. Access to the full functionality of the Codification Research System requires a subscription. Reduced-price academic access is available through the American Accounting Association (see *aaahq.org/FASB/Access.cfm*). Prior to the Codification, the profession relied on *FASB 162*, "The Hierarchy of Generally Accepted Accounting Principles," which defined the meaning of generally accepted accounting principles. In that document, certain documents were deemed more authoritative than others, which led to various levels of GAAP. Fortunately, the Codification does not have different levels of GAAP.

is cited, using Receivables as the example. The purpose of the search shown below is to determine GAAP for accounting for loans and trade receivables not held for sale subsequent to initial measurement.

Topic	Go to FASB ASC 310 to access the Receivables topic.
Subtopics	Go to FASB ASC 310-10 to access the Overall Subtopic of the Topic 310.
Sections	Go to FASB ASC 310-10-35 to access the Subsequent Measurement Section of the Subtopic 310-10.
Paragraph	Go to FASB ASC 310-10-35-47 to access the Loans and Trade Receivables not Held for Sale paragraph of Section 310-10-35.

Illustration 1-5 shows the Codification framework graphically.

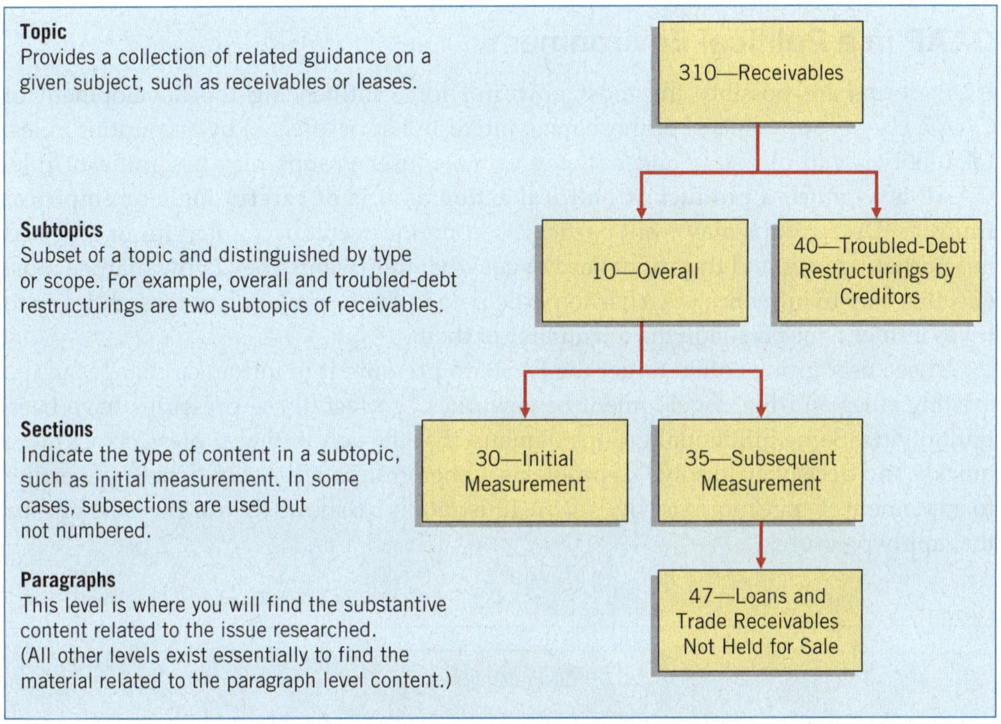

ILLUSTRATION 1-5
FASB Codification Framework

What happens if the Codification does not cover a certain type of transaction or event? In that case, other accounting literature should be considered, such as FASB Concept Statements, international financial reporting standards, and other professional literature. This will happen only rarely.

The expectations for the Codification are high. It is hoped that the Codification will enable users to better understand what GAAP is. As a result, the time to research accounting issues and the risk of noncompliance with GAAP will be reduced, sometimes substantially. In addition, the Web-based format will make updating easier, which will help users stay current with GAAP.[7]

[7]To increase the usefulness of the Codification for public companies, relevant authoritative content issued by the SEC is included in the Codification. In the case of SEC content, an "S" precedes the section number.

For individuals (like you) attempting to learn GAAP, the Codification will be invaluable. It streamlines and simplifies how to determine what GAAP is, which will lead to better financial accounting and reporting. We provide references to the Codification throughout this textbook, using a numbering system. For example, a bracket with a number, such as **[1]**, indicates that the citation to the FASB Codification can be found in the FASB Codification section at the end of the chapter (immediately before the assignment materials).

See the FASB Codification section at the end of each chapter for Codification references and exercises.

ISSUES IN FINANCIAL REPORTING

LEARNING OBJECTIVE 7
Describe the impact of user groups on the rule-making process.

Since the implementation of GAAP may affect many interests, much discussion occurs about who should develop GAAP and to whom it should apply. We discuss some of the major issues below.

GAAP in a Political Environment

User groups are possibly the most powerful force influencing the development of GAAP. User groups consist of those most interested in or affected by accounting rules. Like lobbyists in our state and national capitals, user groups play a significant role. **GAAP is as much a product of political action as it is of careful logic or empirical findings.** User groups may want particular economic events accounted for or reported in a particular way, and they fight hard to get what they want. They know that the most effective way to influence GAAP is to participate in the formulation of these rules or to try to influence or persuade the formulator of them.

These user groups often target the FASB, to pressure it to influence changes in the existing rules and the development of new ones.[8] In fact, these pressures have been multiplying. Some influential groups demand that the accounting profession act more quickly and decisively to solve its problems. Other groups resist such action, preferring to implement change more slowly, if at all. Illustration 1-6 shows the various user groups that apply pressure.

ILLUSTRATION 1-6
User Groups that Influence the Formulation of Accounting Standards

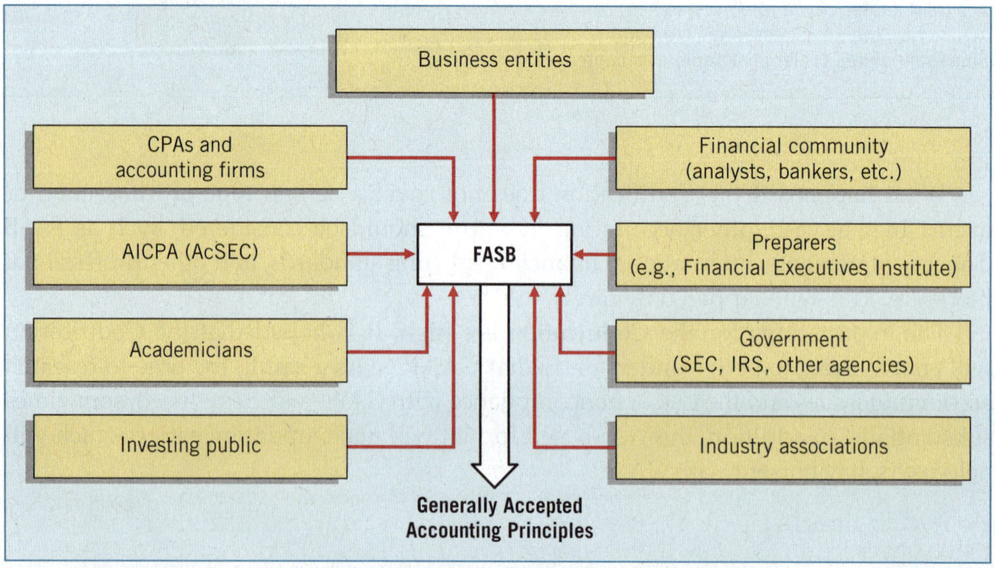

[8]FASB board members acknowledged that they undertook many of the Board's projects, such as "Accounting for Contingencies," "Accounting for Pensions," "Statement of Cash Flows," and "Accounting for Derivatives," due to political pressure.

Should there be politics in establishing GAAP for financial accounting and reporting? Why not? We have politics at home; at school; at the fraternity, sorority, and dormitory; at the office; and at church, temple, and mosque. Politics is everywhere. GAAP is part of the real world, and it cannot escape politics and political pressures.

That is not to say that politics in establishing GAAP is a negative force. Considering the **economic consequences**[9] of many accounting rules, special interest groups should vocalize their reactions to proposed rules. What the Board should *not* do is issue pronouncements that are primarily politically motivated. While paying attention to its constituencies, the Board should base GAAP on sound research and a conceptual framework that has its foundation in economic reality.

Evolving Issue FAIR VALUE, FAIR CONSEQUENCES?

No recent accounting issue better illustrates the economic consequences of accounting than the current debate over the use of fair value accounting for financial assets. Both the FASB and the International Accounting Standards Board (IASB) have standards requiring the use of fair value accounting for financial assets, such as investments and other financial instruments. Fair value provides the most relevant and reliable information for investors about these assets and liabilities. However, in the wake of the recent credit crisis, some countries, their central banks, and bank regulators want to suspend fair value accounting, based on concerns that use of fair value accounting, which calls for recording significant losses on poorly performing loans and investments, could scare investors and depositors and lead to a "run on the bank."

For example, in 2009, Congress ordered the FASB to change its accounting rules so as to reduce the losses banks reported, as the values of their securities had crumbled. These changes were generally supported by banks. But these changes produced a strong reaction from some investors, with one investor group complaining that the changes would "effectively gut the transparent application of fair value measurement." The group also says suspending fair value accounting would delay the recovery of the banking system.

Such political pressure on accounting standard-setters is not confined to the United States. For example, French President Nicolas Sarkozy urged his European Union counterparts to back changes to accounting rules and give banks and insurers some breathing space amid the market turmoil. And more recently, international finance ministers are urging the FASB and IASB to accelerate their work on accounting standards, including the fair value guidance for financial instruments. It is unclear whether these political pressures will have an effect on fair value accounting, but there is no question that the issue has stirred significant worldwide political debate. In short, the numbers have consequences.

Sources: Adapted from Ben Hall and Nikki Tait, "Sarkozy Seeks EU Accounting Change," *The Financial Times Limited* (September 30, 2008); Floyd Norris, "Banks Are Set to Receive More Leeway on Asset Values," *The New York Times* (March 31, 2009); and E. Orenstein, "G20 Finance Ministers Urge FASB, IASB Converge Key Standards by Mid-2013 at the Latest," FEI Financial Reporting Blog (April 2012).

The Expectations Gap

International Perspective

Foreign accounting firms that provide an audit report for a U.S.-listed company are subject to the authority of the accounting oversight board (mandated by the Sarbanes-Oxley Act).

The **Sarbanes-Oxley Act** was passed in response to a string of accounting scandals at companies like **Enron**, **Cendant**, **Sunbeam**, **Rite-Aid**, **Xerox**, and **WorldCom**. This law increased the resources for the SEC to combat fraud and curb poor reporting practices.[10] And the SEC has increased its policing efforts, approving new auditor independence rules and materiality guidelines

[9]*Economic consequences* means the impact of accounting reports on the wealth positions of issuers and users of financial information, and the decision-making behavior resulting from that impact. The resulting behavior of these individuals and groups could have detrimental financial effects on the providers of the financial information. See Stephen A. Zeff, "The Rise of 'Economic Consequences'," *Journal of Accountancy* (December 1978), pp. 56–63. We extend appreciation to Professor Zeff for his insights on this chapter.

[10]*Sarbanes-Oxley Act of 2002,* H. R. Rep. No. 107-610 (2002).

for financial reporting. In addition, the Sarbanes-Oxley Act introduces sweeping changes to the institutional structure of the accounting profession. The following are some of the key provisions of the legislation.

- Establishes an oversight board, the **Public Company Accounting Oversight Board (PCAOB)**, for accounting practices. The PCAOB has oversight and enforcement authority and establishes auditing, quality control, and independence standards and rules.
- Implements stronger independence rules for auditors. Audit partners, for example, are required to rotate every five years, and auditors are prohibited from offering certain types of consulting services to corporate clients.
- Requires CEOs and CFOs to personally certify that financial statements and disclosures are accurate and complete, and requires CEOs and CFOs to forfeit bonuses and profits when there is an accounting restatement.
- Requires audit committees to be comprised of independent members and members with financial expertise.
- Requires codes of ethics for senior financial officers.

In addition, Section 404 of the Sarbanes-Oxley Act requires public companies to attest to the effectiveness of their internal controls over financial reporting. **Internal controls** are a system of checks and balances designed to prevent and detect fraud and errors. Most companies have these systems in place, but many have never completely documented them. Companies are finding that it is a costly process but perhaps badly needed.

While there continues to be debate about the benefits and costs of Sarbanes-Oxley (especially for smaller companies), studies at the time of the act's implementation provide compelling evidence that there was much room for improvement. For example, one study documented 424 companies with deficiencies in internal control.[11] Many problems involved closing the books, revenue recognition deficiencies, reconciling accounts, or dealing with inventory. **SunTrust Bank**, for example, fired three officers after discovering errors in how the company calculates its allowance for bad debts. And **Visteon**, a car parts supplier, said it found problems recording and managing receivables from its largest customer, **Ford Motor**.

Will these changes be enough? The **expectations gap**—what the public thinks accountants *should* do and what accountants think they *can* do—is difficult to close. Due to the number of fraudulent reporting cases, some question whether the profession is doing enough. Although the profession can argue rightfully that accounting cannot be responsible for every financial catastrophe, it must continue to strive to meet the needs of society. However, efforts to meet these needs will become more costly to society. The development of a highly transparent, clear, and reliable system will require considerable resources.

Financial Reporting Challenges

LEARNING OBJECTIVE 8
Describe some of the challenges facing financial reporting.

While our reporting model has worked well in capturing and organizing financial information in a useful and reliable fashion, much still needs to be done. For example, if we move to the year 2025 and look back at financial reporting today, we might read the following.

- ***Nonfinancial measurements.*** Financial reports failed to provide some key performance measures widely used by management, such as customer satisfaction indexes,

[11]Leah Townsend, "Internal Control Deficiency Disclosures—Interim Alert," *Yellow Card—Interim Trend Alert* (April 12, 2005), Glass, Lewis & Co., LLC.

backlog information, reject rates on goods purchased, as well as the results of companies' sustainability efforts.

- ***Forward-looking information.*** Financial reports failed to provide forward-looking information needed by present and potential investors and creditors. One individual noted that financial statements in 2014 should have started with the phrase, "Once upon a time," to signify their use of historical cost and accumulation of past events.
- ***Soft assets.*** Financial reports focused on hard assets (inventory, plant assets) but failed to provide much information about a company's soft assets (intangibles). The best assets are often intangible. Consider **Microsoft**'s know-how and market dominance, **Wal-Mart**'s expertise in supply chain management, and **Procter & Gamble**'s brand image.
- ***Timeliness.*** Companies only prepared financial statements quarterly and provided audited financials annually. Little to no real-time financial statement information was available.
- ***Understandability.*** Investors and market regulators were raising concerns about the complexity and lack of understandability of financial reports.

We believe each of these challenges must be met for the accounting profession to provide the type of information needed for an efficient capital allocation process. We are confident that changes will occur, based on these positive signs:

- Already, some companies voluntarily disclose information deemed relevant to investors. Often such information is nonfinancial. For example, banking companies now disclose data on loan growth, credit quality, fee income, operating efficiency, capital management, and management strategy. Increasingly, companies are preparing reports on their sustainability efforts by reporting such information as water use and conservation, carbon impacts, and labor practices. In some cases, "integrated reports" are provided, which incorporate sustainability reports into the traditional annual report, leading some to call for standards for sustainability reporting.
- Initially, companies used the Internet to provide limited financial data. Now, most companies publish their annual reports in several formats on the Web. The most innovative companies offer sections of their annual reports in a format that the user can readily manipulate, such as in an electronic spreadsheet format. Companies also format their financial reports using eXtensible Business Reporting Language (XBRL), which permits quicker and lower-cost access to companies' financial information.
- More accounting standards now require the recording or disclosing of fair value information. For example, companies either record investments in stocks and bonds, debt obligations, and derivatives at fair value, or companies show information related to fair values in the notes to the financial statements. The FASB and the IASB have a converged standard on fair value measures, which should enhance the usefulness of fair value measures in financial statements.
- The FASB is now working on projects that address disclosure effectiveness and a reporting framework for non-public companies. The projects could go a long way toward addressing complexity and understandability of the information in financial statements, allowing for more-effective, less-complex, and flexible reporting to meet the needs of investors.

Changes in these directions will enhance the relevance of financial reporting and provide useful information to financial statement readers.

International Accounting Standards

Former Secretary of the Treasury, Lawrence Summers, has indicated that the single most important innovation shaping the capital markets was the idea of generally accepted accounting principles. He went on to say that we need something similar internationally.

We believe that the Secretary is right. Relevant and reliable financial information is a necessity for viable capital markets. Unfortunately, companies outside the United States often prepare financial statements using standards different from U.S. GAAP (or simply GAAP). As a result, international companies such as **Coca-Cola**, **Microsoft**, and **IBM** have to develop financial information in different ways. Beyond the additional costs these companies incur, users of the financial statements often must understand at least two sets of accounting standards. (Understanding one set is hard enough!) It is not surprising, therefore, that there is a growing demand for one set of high-quality international standards.

International Perspective

IFRS includes the standards, referred to as International Financial Reporting Standards (IFRS), developed by the IASB. The predecessor to the IASB issued International Accounting Standards (IAS).

Presently, there are two sets of rules accepted for international use—GAAP and **International Financial Reporting Standards (IFRS)**, issued by the London-based **International Accounting Standards Board (IASB)**. U.S. companies that list overseas are still permitted to use GAAP, and foreign companies listed on U.S. exchanges are permitted to use IFRS. As you will learn, there are many similarities between GAAP and IFRS.

Already over 115 countries use IFRS, and the European Union now requires all listed companies in Europe (over 7,000 companies) to use it. The SEC laid out a roadmap by which all U.S. companies might be required to use IFRS by 2015.

Most parties recognize that global markets will best be served if only one set of accounting standards is used. For example, the FASB and the IASB formalized their commitment to the convergence of GAAP and IFRS by issuing a memorandum of understanding (often referred to as the Norwalk agreement). The two Boards agreed to use their best efforts to:

- Make their existing financial reporting standards fully compatible as soon as practicable, and
- Coordinate their future work programs to ensure that once achieved, compatibility is maintained.

International Perspective

The adoption of IFRS by U.S. companies would make it easier to compare U.S. and foreign companies, as well as for U.S. companies to raise capital in foreign markets.

As a result of this agreement, the two Boards identified a number of short-term and long-term projects that would lead to convergence. For example, one short-term project was for the FASB to issue a rule that permits a fair value option for financial instruments. This rule was issued in 2007, and now the FASB and the IASB follow the same accounting in this area. Conversely, the IASB completed a project related to borrowing costs, which makes IFRS consistent with GAAP. Long-term convergence projects relate to such issues as revenue recognition, the conceptual framework, and leases.

Because convergence is such an important issue, we provide a discussion of international accounting standards at the end of each chapter called **IFRS Insights**. This feature will help you understand the changes that are taking place in the financial reporting area as we move to one set of international standards. In addition, throughout the textbook, we provide *International Perspectives* in the margins to help you understand the international reporting environment.

What do the numbers mean? CAN YOU DO THAT?

One of the more difficult issues related to convergence and international accounting standards is that countries have different cultures and customs. For example, the former chair of the IASB explained it this way regarding Europe:

> "In the U.K. everything is permitted unless it is prohibited. In Germany, it is the other way around; everything is prohibited unless it is permitted. In the Netherlands, everything is prohibited even if it is permitted. And in France, everything is permitted even if it is prohibited. Add in countries like Japan, the United States and China, it becomes very difficult to meet the needs of each of these countries."

With this diversity of thinking around the world, it understandable why accounting convergence has been so elusive.

Source: Sir D. Tweedie, "Remarks at the Robert P. Maxon Lectureship," George Washington University (April 7, 2010).

Ethics in the Environment of Financial Accounting

9 LEARNING OBJECTIVE
Understand issues related to ethics and financial accounting.

Robert Sack, a noted commentator on the subject of accounting ethics, observed, "Based on my experience, new graduates tend to be idealistic . . . thank goodness for that! Still it is very dangerous to think that your armor is all in place and say to yourself, 'I would have never given in to that.' The pressures don't explode on us; they build, and we often don't recognize them until they have us."

These observations are particularly appropriate for anyone entering the business world. In accounting, as in other areas of business, we frequently encounter ethical dilemmas. Some of these dilemmas are simple and easy to resolve. However, many are not, requiring difficult choices among allowable alternatives.

Companies that concentrate on "maximizing the bottom line," "facing the challenges of competition," and "stressing short-term results" place accountants in an environment of conflict and pressure. Basic questions such as, "Is this way of communicating financial information good or bad?" "Is it right or wrong?" and "What should I do in the circumstance?" cannot always be answered by simply adhering to GAAP or following the rules of the profession. Technical competence is not enough when encountering ethical decisions.

Gateway to the Profession
Expanded Discussion of Ethical Issues in Financial Reporting

Doing the right thing is not always easy or obvious. The pressures "to bend the rules," "to play the game," or "to just ignore it" can be considerable. For example, "Will my decision affect my job performance negatively?" "Will my superiors be upset?" and "Will my colleagues be unhappy with me?" are often questions business people face in making a tough ethical decision. The decision is more difficult because there is no comprehensive ethical system to provide guidelines.

Time, job, client, personal, and peer pressures can complicate the process of ethical sensitivity and selection among alternatives. Throughout this textbook, **we present ethical considerations to help sensitize you** to the type of situations you may encounter in the performance of your professional responsibility.

Conclusion

Bob Herz, former FASB chairman, believes that there are three fundamental considerations the FASB must keep in mind in its rule-making activities: (1) improvement in financial reporting, (2) simplification of the accounting literature and the rule-making process, and (3) international convergence. These are notable objectives, and the Board is making good progress on all three dimensions. Issues such as off-balance-sheet financing, measurement of fair values, enhanced criteria for revenue recognition, and stock option accounting are examples of where the Board has exerted leadership. Improvements in financial reporting should follow.

Also, the Board is making it easier to understand what GAAP is. GAAP has been contained in a number of different documents. The lack of a single source makes it difficult to access and understand generally accepted principles. As discussed earlier, the Codification now organizes existing GAAP by accounting topic regardless of its source (FASB Statements, APB Opinions, and so on). The codified standards are then considered to be GAAP and to be authoritative. All other literature will be considered nonauthoritative.

Finally, international convergence is underway. Some projects already are completed and differences eliminated. Many more are on the drawing board. It appears to be only a matter of time until we will have one set of global accounting standards that will be established by the IASB. The profession has many challenges, but it has responded in a timely, comprehensive, and effective manner.

You will want to read the **IFRS INSIGHTS** on pages 31–39 for discussion of IFRS and the international reporting environment.

KEY TERMS

Accounting Principles Board (APB), *9*
Accounting Research Bulletins, *9*
Accounting Standards Updates, *12*
accrual-basis accounting, *6*
American Institute of Certified Public Accountants (AICPA), *9*
APB Opinions, *9*
Auditing Standards Board, *10*
Committee on Accounting Procedure (CAP), *9*
decision-usefulness, *6*
Emerging Issues Task Force (EITF), *12*
entity perspective, *6*
expectations gap, *18*
FASB Staff Positions, *13*
financial accounting, *4*
Financial Accounting Standards Board (FASB), *10*
Financial Accounting Standards Board Accounting Standards Codification (Codification), *14*
Financial Accounting Standards Board Codification Research System (CRS), *14*
financial reporting, *4*
financial statements, *4*

SUMMARY OF LEARNING OBJECTIVES

1 Identify the major financial statements and other means of financial reporting. Companies most frequently provide (1) the balance sheet, (2) the income statement, (3) the statement of cash flows, and (4) the statement of owners' or stockholders' equity. Financial reporting other than financial statements may take various forms. Examples include the president's letter and supplementary schedules in the corporate annual report, prospectuses, reports filed with government agencies, news releases, management's forecasts, and descriptions of a company's social or environmental impact.

2 Explain how accounting assists in the efficient use of scarce resources. Accounting provides reliable, relevant, and timely information to managers, investors, and creditors to allow resource allocation to the most efficient enterprises. Accounting also provides measurements of efficiency (profitability) and financial soundness.

3 Identify the objective of financial reporting. The objective of general-purpose financial reporting is to provide financial information about the reporting entity that is useful to present and potential equity investors, lenders, and other creditors in decisions about providing resources to the entity through equity investments and loans or other forms of credit. Information that is decision-useful to investors may also be helpful to other users of financial reporting who are not investors.

4 Explain the need for accounting standards. The accounting profession has attempted to develop a set of standards that is generally accepted and universally practiced. Without this set of standards, each company would have to develop its own standards. Readers of financial statements would have to familiarize themselves with every company's peculiar accounting and reporting practices. As a result, it would be almost impossible to prepare statements that could be compared.

5 Identify the major policy-setting bodies and their role in the standard-setting process. The *Securities and Exchange Commission (SEC)* is a federal agency that has the broad powers to prescribe, in whatever detail it desires, the accounting standards to be employed by companies that fall within its jurisdiction. The *American Institute of Certified Public Accountants (AICPA)* issued standards through its Committee on Accounting Procedure and Accounting Principles Board. The *Financial Accounting Standards Board (FASB)* establishes and improves standards of financial accounting and reporting for the guidance and education of the public.

6 Explain the meaning of generally accepted accounting principles (GAAP) and the role of the Codification for GAAP. Generally accepted accounting principles (GAAP) are those principles that have substantial authoritative support, such as FASB standards, interpretations, and Staff Positions, APB Opinions and interpretations, AICPA Accounting Research Bulletins, and other authoritative pronouncements. All these documents and others are now classified in one document referred to as the Codification. The purpose of the Codification is to simplify user access to all authoritative U.S. GAAP. The Codification changes the way GAAP is documented, presented, and updated.

7 Describe the impact of user groups on the rule-making process. User groups may want particular economic events accounted for or reported in a particular way, and they fight hard to get what they want. They especially target the FASB to influence changes in existing GAAP and in the development of new rules. Because of the accelerated rate of change and the increased complexity of our economy, these pressures have been multiplying. GAAP is as much a product of political action as it is of careful logic or empirical findings. The IASB is working with the FASB toward international convergence of GAAP.

8 Describe some of the challenges facing financial reporting. Financial reports fail to provide (1) some key performance measures widely used by management, (2) forward-looking information needed by investors and creditors, (3) sufficient information on a company's soft assets (intangibles), (4) real-time financial information, and (5) easy-to-comprehend information.

9 Understand issues related to ethics and financial accounting. Financial accountants are called on for moral discernment and ethical decision-making. Decisions sometimes are difficult because a public consensus has not emerged to formulate a comprehensive ethical system that provides guidelines in making ethical judgments.

FASB CODIFICATION

Exercises

Academic access to the FASB Codification is available through university subscriptions, obtained from the American Accounting Association (at *http://aaahq.org/FASB/Access.cfm*), for an annual fee of $150. This subscription covers an unlimited number of students within a single institution. Once this access has been obtained by your school, you should log in (at *http://aaahq.org/ascLogin.cfm*) to prepare responses to the following exercises.

CE1-1 Describe the main elements of the link labeled "Help, FAQ, Learning Guide, and About the Codification."

CE1-2 Describe the procedures for providing feedback.

CE1-3 Briefly describe the purpose and content of the "What's New" link.

An additional accounting research case can be found in the Using Your Judgment section, on page 30.

Be sure to check the book's companion website for a Review and Analysis Exercise, with solution.

WileyPLUS **Brief Exercises, Exercises, Problems, and many more learning and assessment tools and resources are available for practice in WileyPLUS.**

QUESTIONS

1. Differentiate broadly between financial accounting and managerial accounting.
2. Differentiate between "financial statements" and "financial reporting."
3. How does accounting help the capital allocation process?
4. What is the objective of financial reporting?
5. Briefly explain the meaning of decision-usefulness in the context of financial reporting.
6. Of what value is a common set of standards in financial accounting and reporting?
7. What is the likely limitation of "general-purpose financial statements"?
8. In what way is the Securities and Exchange Commission concerned about and supportive of accounting principles and standards?
9. What was the Committee on Accounting Procedure, and what were its accomplishments and failings?
10. For what purposes did the AICPA in 1959 create the Accounting Principles Board?
11. Distinguish among Accounting Research Bulletins, Opinions of the Accounting Principles Board, and Statements of the Financial Accounting Standards Board.
12. If you had to explain or define "generally accepted accounting principles or standards," what essential characteristics would you include in your explanation?
13. In what ways was it felt that the pronouncements issued by the Financial Accounting Standards Board would carry greater weight than the opinions issued by the Accounting Principles Board?
14. How are FASB preliminary views and FASB exposure drafts related to FASB "statements"?
15. Distinguish between FASB Accounting Standards Updates and FASB Statements of Financial Accounting Concepts.
16. What is Rule 203 of the Code of Professional Conduct?
17. The chairman of the FASB at one time noted that "the flow of standards can only be slowed if (1) producers focus less on quarterly earnings per share and tax benefits and more on quality products, and (2) accountants and lawyers rely less on rules and law and more on professional judgment and conduct." Explain his comment.
18. What is the purpose of FASB Staff Positions?
19. Explain the role of the Emerging Issues Task Force in establishing generally accepted accounting principles.
20. What is the difference between the Codification and the Codification Research System?
21. What are the primary advantages of having a Codification of generally accepted accounting principles?
22. What are the sources of pressure that change and influence the development of GAAP?
23. Some individuals have indicated that the FASB must be cognizant of the economic consequences of its pronouncements. What is meant by "economic consequences"? What dangers exist if politics play too much of a role in the development of GAAP?
24. If you were given complete authority in the matter, how would you propose that GAAP should be developed and enforced?
25. One writer recently noted that 99.4 percent of all companies prepare statements that are in accordance with GAAP. Why then is there such concern about fraudulent financial reporting?
26. What is the "expectations gap"? What is the profession doing to try to close this gap?
27. The Sarbanes-Oxley Act was enacted to combat fraud and curb poor reporting practices. What are some key provisions of this legislation?
28. What are some of the major challenges facing the accounting profession?
29. How are financial accountants challenged in their work to make ethical decisions? Is technical mastery of GAAP not sufficient to the practice of financial accounting?

CONCEPTS FOR ANALYSIS

CA1-1 (FASB and Standard-Setting) Presented below are four statements which you are to identify as true or false. If false, explain why the statement is false.

1. GAAP is the term used to indicate the whole body of FASB authoritative literature.
2. Any company claiming compliance with GAAP must comply with most standards and interpretations but does not have to follow the disclosure requirements.
3. The primary governmental body that has influence over the FASB is the SEC.
4. The FASB has a government mandate and therefore does not have to follow due process in issuing a standard.

CA1-2 (GAAP and Standard-Setting) Presented below are four statements which you are to identify as true or false. If false, explain why the statement is false.

1. The objective of financial statements emphasizes a stewardship approach for reporting financial information.
2. The purpose of the objective of financial reporting is to prepare a balance sheet, an income statement, a statement of cash flows, and a statement of owners' or stockholders' equity.
3. Because they are generally shorter, FASB interpretations are subject to less due process, compared to FASB standards.
4. The objective of financial reporting uses an entity rather than a proprietary approach in determining what information to report.

CA1-3 (Financial Reporting and Accounting Standards) Answer the following multiple-choice questions.

1. GAAP stands for:
   (a) governmental auditing and accounting practices.
   (b) generally accepted attest principles.
   (c) government audit and attest policies.
   (d) generally accepted accounting principles.
2. Accounting standard-setters use the following process in establishing accounting standards:
   (a) Research, exposure draft, discussion paper, standard.
   (b) Discussion paper, research, exposure draft, standard.
   (c) Research, preliminary views, discussion paper, standard.
   (d) Research, discussion paper, exposure draft, standard.
3. GAAP is comprised of:
   (a) FASB standards, interpretations, and concepts statements.
   (b) FASB financial standards.
   (c) FASB standards, interpretations, EITF consensuses, and accounting rules issued by FASB predecessor organizations.
   (d) any accounting guidance included in the FASB Codification.
4. The authoritative status of the conceptual framework is as follows.
   (a) It is used when there is no standard or interpretation related to the reporting issues under consideration.
   (b) It is not as authoritative as a standard but takes precedence over any interpretation related to the reporting issue.
   (c) It takes precedence over all other authoritative literature.
   (d) It has no authoritative status.
5. The objective of financial reporting places most emphasis on:
   (a) reporting to capital providers.
   (b) reporting on stewardship.
   (c) providing specific guidance related to specific needs.
   (d) providing information to individuals who are experts in the field.
6. General-purpose financial statements are prepared primarily for:
   (a) internal users.
   (b) external users.
   (c) auditors.
   (d) government regulators.
7. Economic consequences of accounting standard-setting means:
   (a) standard-setters must give first priority to ensuring that companies do not suffer any adverse effect as a result of a new standard.
   (b) standard-setters must ensure that no new costs are incurred when a new standard is issued.
   (c) the objective of financial reporting should be politically motivated to ensure acceptance by the general public.
   (d) accounting standards can have detrimental impacts on the wealth levels of the providers of financial information.
8. The expectations gap is:
   (a) what financial information management provides and what users want.
   (b) what the public thinks accountants should do and what accountants think they can do.
   (c) what the governmental agencies want from standard-setting and what the standard-setters provide.
   (d) what the users of financial statements want from the government and what is provided.

CA1-4 (Financial Accounting) Omar Morena has recently completed his first year of studying accounting. His instructor for next semester has indicated that the primary focus will be the area of financial accounting.

Instructions

(a) Differentiate between financial accounting and managerial accounting.
(b) One part of financial accounting involves the preparation of financial statements. What are the financial statements most frequently provided?
(c) What is the difference between financial statements and financial reporting?

CA1-5 (Objective of Financial Reporting) Karen Sepan, a recent graduate of the local state university, is presently employed by a large manufacturing company. She has been asked by Jose Martinez, controller, to prepare the company's response to a current Preliminary Views published by the Financial Accounting Standards Board (FASB). Sepan knows that the FASB has a conceptual framework, and she believes that these concept statements could be used to support the company's response to the Preliminary Views. She has prepared a rough draft of the response citing the objective of financial reporting.

Instructions

(a) Identify the objective of financial reporting.
(b) Describe the level of sophistication expected of the users of financial information by the objective of financial reporting.

CA1-6 (Accounting Numbers and the Environment) Hardly a day goes by without an article appearing on the crises affecting many of our financial institutions in the United States. It is estimated that the savings and loan (S&L) debacle of the 1980s, for example, ended up costing $500 billion ($2,000 for every man, woman, and child in the United States). Some argue that if the S&Ls had been required to report their investments at fair value instead of cost, large losses would have been reported earlier, which would have signaled regulators to close those S&Ls and, therefore, minimize the losses to U.S. taxpayers.

Instructions

Explain how reported accounting numbers might affect an individual's perceptions and actions. Cite two examples.

CA1-7 (Need for GAAP) Some argue that having various organizations establish accounting principles is wasteful and inefficient. Rather than mandating accounting rules, each company could voluntarily disclose the type of information it considered important. In addition, if an investor wants additional information, the investor could contact the company and pay to receive the additional information desired.

Instructions

Comment on the appropriateness of this viewpoint.

CA1-8 (AICPA's Role in Rule-Making) One of the major groups that has been involved in the standard-setting process is the American Institute of Certified Public Accountants. Initially, it was the primary organization that established accounting principles in the United States. Subsequently, it relinquished its power to the FASB.

Instructions

(a) Identify the two committees of the AICPA that established accounting principles prior to the establishment of the FASB.
(b) Speculate as to why these two organizations failed. In your answer, identify steps the FASB has taken to avoid failure.
(c) What is the present role of the AICPA in the rule-making environment?

CA1-9 (FASB Role in Rule-Making) A press release announcing the appointment of the trustees of the new Financial Accounting Foundation stated that the Financial Accounting Standards Board (to be appointed by the trustees) ". . . will become the established authority for setting accounting principles under which corporations report to the shareholders and others" (AICPA news release July 20, 1972).

Instructions

(a) Identify the sponsoring organization of the FASB and the process by which the FASB arrives at a decision and issues an accounting standard.
(b) Indicate the major types of pronouncements issued by the FASB and the purposes of each of these pronouncements.

CA1-10 (Politicization of GAAP) Some accountants have said that politicization in the development and acceptance of generally accepted accounting principles (i.e., rule-making) is taking place. Some use the term "politicization" in a narrow sense to mean the influence by governmental agencies, particularly the Securities and Exchange Commission, on the development of generally accepted accounting principles. Others use it more broadly to mean the compromise that results when the bodies responsible for developing generally accepted accounting principles are pressured by interest groups (SEC, American Accounting Association, businesses through their various organizations, Institute of Management Accountants, financial analysts, bankers, lawyers, and so on).

Instructions

(a) The Committee on Accounting Procedure of the AICPA was established in the mid- to late 1930s and functioned until 1959, at which time the Accounting Principles Board came into existence. In 1973, the Financial Accounting Standards Board was formed and the APB went out of existence. Do the reasons these groups were formed, their methods of operation while in existence, and the reasons for the demise of the first two indicate an increasing politicization (as the term is used in the broad sense) of accounting standard-setting? Explain your answer by indicating how the CAP, the APB, and the FASB operated or operate. Cite specific developments that tend to support your answer.

(b) What arguments can be raised to support the "politicization" of accounting rule-making?

(c) What arguments can be raised against the "politicization" of accounting rule-making?

(CMA adapted)

CA1-11 (Models for Setting GAAP) Presented below are three models for setting GAAP.

1. The purely political approach, where national legislative action decrees GAAP.
2. The private, professional approach, where GAAP is set and enforced by private professional actions only.
3. The public/private mixed approach, where GAAP is basically set by private-sector bodies that behave as though they were public agencies and whose standards to a great extent are enforced through governmental agencies.

Instructions

(a) Which of these three models best describes standard-setting in the United States? Comment on your answer.

(b) Why do companies, financial analysts, labor unions, industry trade associations, and others take such an active interest in standard-setting?

(c) Cite an example of a group other than the FASB that attempts to establish accounting standards. Speculate as to why another group might wish to set its own standards.

CA1-12 (GAAP Terminology) Wayne Rogers, an administrator at a major university, recently said, "I've got some CDs in my IRA, which I set up to beat the IRS." As elsewhere, in the world of accounting and finance, it often helps to be fluent in abbreviations and acronyms.

Instructions

Presented below is a list of common accounting acronyms. Identify the term for which each acronym stands, and provide a brief definition of each term.

(a) AICPA
(b) CAP
(c) ARB
(d) APB
(e) FAF
(f) FASAC
(g) SOP
(h) GAAP
(i) CPA
(j) FASB
(k) SEC
(l) IASB

CA1-13 (Rule-Making Issues) When the FASB issues new pronouncements, the implementation date is usually 12 months from date of issuance, with early implementation encouraged. Karen Weller, controller, discusses with her financial vice president the need for early implementation of a rule that would result in a fairer presentation of the company's financial condition and earnings. When the financial vice president determines that early implementation of the rule will adversely affect the reported net income for the year, he discourages Weller from implementing the rule until it is required.

Instructions

Answer the following questions.

(a) What, if any, is the ethical issue involved in this case?

(b) Is the financial vice president acting improperly or immorally?

(c) What does Weller have to gain by advocacy of early implementation?

(d) Which stakeholders might be affected by the decision against early implementation?

(CMA adapted)

CA1-14 (Securities and Exchange Commission) The U.S. Securities and Exchange Commission (SEC) was created in 1934 and consists of five commissioners and a large professional staff. The SEC professional staff is organized into five divisions and several principal offices. The primary objective of the SEC is to support fair securities markets. The SEC also strives to foster enlightened stockholder participation in corporate decisions of publicly traded companies. The SEC has a significant presence in financial markets, the development of accounting practices, and corporation-shareholder relations, and has the power to exert influence on entities whose actions lie within the scope of its authority.

Instructions

(a) Explain from where the Securities and Exchange Commission receives its authority.

(b) Describe the official role of the Securities and Exchange Commission in the development of financial accounting theory and practices.

(c) Discuss the interrelationship between the Securities and Exchange Commission and the Financial Accounting Standards Board with respect to the development and establishment of financial accounting theory and practices.

(CMA adapted)

CA1-15 (Financial Reporting Pressures) Presented below is abbreviated testimony from Troy Normand in the WorldCom case. He was a manager in the corporate reporting department and is one of five individuals who pleaded guilty. He is testifying in hopes of receiving no prison time when he is ultimately sentenced.

Q. Mr. Normand, if you could just describe for the jury how the meeting started and what was said during the meeting?

A. I can't recall exactly who initiated the discussion, but right away Scott Sullivan acknowledged that he was aware we had problems with the entries, David Myers had informed him, and we were considering resigning.

He said that he respected our concerns but that we weren't being asked to do anything that he believed was wrong. He mentioned that he acknowledged that the company had lost focus quite a bit due to the preparations for the Sprint merger, and that he was putting plans in place and projects in place to try to determine where the problems were, why the costs were so high.

He did say he believed that the initial statements that we produced, that the line costs in those statements could not have been as high as they were, that he believed something was wrong and there was no way that the costs were that high.

I informed him that I didn't believe the entry we were being asked to do was right, that I was scared, and I didn't want to put myself in a position of going to jail for him or the company. He responded that he didn't believe anything was wrong, nobody was going to be going to jail, but that if it later was found to be wrong, that he would be the person going to jail, not me.

He asked that I stay, don't jump off the plane, let him land it softly, that's basically how he put it. And he mentioned that he had a discussion with Bernie Ebbers, asking Bernie to reduce projections going forward and that Bernie had refused.

Q. Mr. Normand, you said that Mr. Sullivan said something about don't jump out of the plane. What did you understand him to mean when he said that?

A. Not to quit.

Q. During this meeting, did Mr. Sullivan say anything about whether you would be asked to make entries like this in the future?

A. Yes, he made a comment that from that point going forward we wouldn't be asked to record any entries, high-level late adjustments, that the numbers would be the numbers.

Q. What did you understand that to be mean, the numbers would be the numbers?

A. That after the preliminary statements were issued, with the exception of any normal transaction, valid transaction, we wouldn't be asked to be recording any more late entries.

Q. I believe you testified that Mr. Sullivan said something about the line cost numbers not being accurate. Did he ask you to conduct any analysis to determine whether the line cost numbers were accurate?

A. No, he did not.

Q. Did anyone ever ask you to do that?

A. No.

Q. Did you ever conduct any such analysis?

A. No, I didn't.

Q. During this meeting, did Mr. Sullivan ever provide any accounting justification for the entry you were asked to make?

A. No, he did not.

Q. Did anything else happen during the meeting?

A. I don't recall anything else.

Q. How did you feel after this meeting?

A. Not much better actually. I left his office not convinced in any way that what we were asked to do was right. However, I did question myself to some degree after talking with him wondering whether I was making something more out of what was really there.

Instructions

Answer the following questions.

(a) What appears to be the ethical issue involved in this case?

(b) Is Troy Normand acting improperly or immorally?

(c) What would you do if you were Troy Normand?
(d) Who are the major stakeholders in this case?

CA1-16 (Economic Consequences) Presented below are comments made in the financial press.

Instructions

Prepare responses to the requirements in each item.

(a) Rep. John Dingell, at one time the ranking Democrat on the House Commerce Committee, threw his support behind the FASB's controversial derivatives accounting standard and encouraged the FASB to adopt the rule promptly. Indicate why a member of Congress might feel obligated to comment on this proposed FASB standard.

(b) In a strongly worded letter to Senator Lauch Faircloth (R-NC) and House Banking Committee Chairman Jim Leach (R-IA), the American Institute of Certified Public Accountants (AICPA) cautioned against government intervention in the accounting standard-setting process, warning that it had the potential of jeopardizing U.S. capital markets. Explain how government intervention could possibly affect capital markets adversely.

CA1-17 (GAAP and Economic Consequences) The following letter was sent to the SEC and the FASB by leaders of the business community.

> Dear Sirs:
>
> The FASB has been struggling with accounting for derivatives and hedging for many years. The FASB has now developed, over the last few weeks, a new approach that it proposes to adopt as a final standard. We understand that the Board intends to adopt this new approach as a final standard without exposing it for public comment and debate, despite the evident complexity of the new approach, the speed with which it has been developed and the significant changes to the exposure draft since it was released more than one year ago. Instead, the Board plans to allow only a brief review by selected parties, limited to issues of operationality and clarity, and would exclude questions as to the merits of the proposed approach.
>
> As the FASB itself has said throughout this process, its mission does not permit it to consider matters that go beyond accounting and reporting considerations. Accordingly, the FASB may not have adequately considered the wide range of concerns that have been expressed about the derivatives and hedging proposal, including concerns related to the potential impact on the capital markets, the weakening of companies' ability to manage risk, and the adverse control implications of implementing costly and complex new rules imposed at the same time as other major initiatives, including the Year 2000 issues and a single European currency. We believe that these crucial issues must be considered, if not by the FASB, then by the Securities and Exchange Commission, other regulatory agencies, or Congress.
>
> We believe it is essential that the FASB solicit all comments in order to identify and address all material issues that may exist before issuing a final standard. We understand the desire to bring this process to a prompt conclusion, but the underlying issues are so important to this nation's businesses, the customers they serve and the economy as a whole that expediency cannot be the dominant consideration. As a result, we urge the FASB to expose its new proposal for public comment, following the established due process procedures that are essential to acceptance of its standards, and providing sufficient time to affected parties to understand and assess the new approach.
>
> We also urge the SEC to study the comments received in order to assess the impact that these proposed rules may have on the capital markets, on companies' risk management practices, and on management and financial controls. These vital public policy matters deserve consideration as part of the Commission's oversight responsibilities.
>
> We believe that these steps are essential if the FASB is to produce the best possible accounting standard while minimizing adverse economic effects and maintaining the competitiveness of U.S. businesses in the international marketplace.
>
> Very truly yours,
>
> (This letter was signed by the chairs of 22 of the largest U.S. companies.)

Instructions

Answer the following questions.

(a) Explain the "due process" procedures followed by the FASB in developing a financial reporting standard.

(b) What is meant by the term "economic consequences" in accounting standard-setting?

(c) What economic consequences arguments are used in this letter?

(d) What do you believe is the main point of the letter?

(e) Why do you believe a copy of this letter was sent by the business community to influential members of the U.S. Congress?

USING YOUR JUDGMENT

FINANCIAL REPORTING

Financial Reporting Problem

Beverly Crusher, a new staff accountant, is confused because of the complexities involving accounting standard-setting. Specifically, she is confused by the number of bodies issuing financial reporting standards of one kind or another and the level of authoritative support that can be attached to these reporting standards. Beverly decides that she must review the environment in which accounting standards are set, if she is to increase her understanding of the accounting profession.

Beverly recalls that during her accounting education there was a chapter or two regarding the environment of financial accounting and the development of GAAP. However, she remembers that her instructor placed little emphasis on these chapters.

Instructions

(a) Help Beverly by identifying key organizations involved in accounting rule-making.

(b) Beverly asks for guidance regarding authoritative support. Please assist her by explaining what is meant by authoritative support.

(c) Give Beverly a historical overview of how rule-making has evolved so that she will not feel that she is the only one to be confused.

(d) What authority for compliance with GAAP has existed throughout the history of rule-making?

BRIDGE TO THE PROFESSION

Professional Research

As a newly enrolled accounting major, you are anxious to better understand accounting institutions and sources of accounting literature. As a first step, you decide to explore the FASB Conceptual Framework.

Instructions

Go to the FASB website, *http://www.fasb.org,* to access the FASB Concepts Statements. When you have accessed the documents, you can use the search tool in your Internet browser to respond to the following items. (Provide paragraph citations.)

(a) What is the objective of financial reporting?

(b) What other means are there of communicating information, besides financial statements?

(c) Indicate some of the users and the information they are most directly concerned with in economic decision-making.

Additional Professional Resources

See the book's companion website, at **www.wiley.com/college/kieso**, for professional simulations as well as other study resources.

IFRS INSIGHTS

Most agree that there is a need for one set of international accounting standards. Here is why:

10 LEARNING OBJECTIVE
Compare the procedures related to financial accounting and accounting standards under GAAP and IFRS.

- ***Multinational corporations.*** Today's companies view the entire world as their market. For example, **Coca-Cola**, **Intel**, and **McDonald's** generate more than 50 percent of their sales outside the United States, and many foreign companies, such as **Toyota**, **Nestlé**, and **Sony**, find their largest market to be the United States.
- ***Mergers and acquisitions.*** The mergers between **Fiat/Chrysler** and **Vodafone/Mannesmann** suggest that we will see even more such business combinations in the future.
- ***Information technology.*** As communication barriers continue to topple through advances in technology, companies and individuals in different countries and markets are becoming more comfortable buying and selling goods and services from one another.
- ***Financial markets.*** Financial markets are of international significance today. Whether it is currency, equity securities (stocks), bonds, or derivatives, there are active markets throughout the world trading these types of instruments.

RELEVANT FACTS

- International standards are referred to as *International Financial Reporting Standards (IFRS)*, developed by the International Accounting Standards Board (IASB). Recent events in the global capital markets have underscored the importance of financial disclosure and transparency not only in the United States but in markets around the world. As a result, many are examining which accounting and financial disclosure rules should be followed.
- U.S standards, referred to as generally accepted accounting principles (GAAP), are developed by the Financial Accounting Standards Board (FASB). The fact that there are differences between what is in this textbook (which is based on U.S. standards) and IFRS should not be surprising because the FASB and IASB have responded to different user needs. In some countries, the primary users of financial statements are private investors; in others, the primary users are tax authorities or central government planners. It appears that the United States and the international standard-setting environment are primarily driven by meeting the needs of investors and creditors.
- The internal control standards applicable to Sarbanes-Oxley (SOX) apply only to large public companies listed on U.S. exchanges. There is a continuing debate as to whether non-U.S. companies should have to comply with this extra layer of regulation. Debate about international companies (non-U.S.) adopting SOX-type standards centers on whether the benefits exceed the costs. The concern is that the higher costs of SOX compliance are making the U.S. securities markets less competitive.
- The textbook mentions a number of ethics violations, such as at **WorldCom**, **AIG**, and **Lehman Brothers**. These problems have also occurred internationally, for example, at **Satyam Computer Services** (India), **Parmalat** (Italy), and **Royal Ahold** (the Netherlands).
- IFRS tends to be simpler in its accounting and disclosure requirements; some people say more "principles-based." GAAP is more detailed; some people say more "rules-based." This difference in approach has resulted in a debate about the merits of "principles-based" versus "rules-based" standards.

- The SEC allows foreign companies that trade shares in U.S. markets to file their IFRS financial statements without reconciliation to GAAP.

ABOUT THE NUMBERS

World markets are becoming increasingly intertwined. International consumers drive Japanese cars, wear Italian shoes and Scottish woolens, drink Brazilian coffee and Indian tea, eat Swiss chocolate bars, sit on Danish furniture, watch U.S. movies, and use Arabian oil. The tremendous variety and volume of both exported and imported goods indicates the extensive involvement in international trade—for many companies, the world is their market. To provide some indication of the extent of globalization of economic activity, Illustration IFRS1-1 provides a listing of the top 20 global companies in terms of sales.

ILLUSTRATION IFRS1-1
Global Companies

Rank ($ millions)	Company	Country	Revenues	Rank ($ millions)	Company	Country	Revenues
1	**Wal-Mart Stores**	U.S.	421,849	11	**Total**	France	186,055
2	**Royal Dutch Shell**	Netherlands	378,152	12	**ConocoPhillips**	U.S.	184,966
3	**ExxonMobil**	U.S.	354,674	13	**Volkswagen**	Germany	168,041
4	**BP**	U.K.	308,928	14	**AXA**	France	162,236
5	**Sinopec Group**	China	273,422	15	**Fannie Mae**	U.S.	153,825
6	**China National Petroleum**	China	240,192	16	**General Electric**	U.S.	151,628
				17	**ING Group**	Netherlands	147,052
7	**State Grid**	China	226,294	18	**Glencore International**	Switzerland	144,978
8	**Toyota Motor**	Japan	221,760				
9	**Japan Post Holdings**	Japan	203,958	19	**Berkshire Hathaway**	U.S.	136,185
10	**Chevron**	U.S.	196,337	20	**General Motors**	U.S.	135,592

Source: http://money.cnn.com/magazines/fortune/global500/2011/.

As capital markets are increasingly integrated, companies have greater flexibility in deciding where to raise capital. In the absence of market integration, there can be company-specific factors that make it cheaper to raise capital and list/trade securities in one location versus another. With the integration of capital markets, the automatic linkage between the location of the company and location of the capital market is loosening. As a result, companies have expanded choices of where to raise capital, either equity or debt. The move toward adoption of International Financial Reporting Standards has and will continue to facilitate this movement.

International Standard-Setting Organizations

For many years, many nations have relied on their own standard-setting organizations. For example, Canada has the Accounting Standards Board, Japan has the Accounting Standards Board of Japan, Germany has the German Accounting Standards Committee, and the United States has the Financial Accounting Standards Board (FASB). The standards issued by these organizations are sometimes principles-based, rules-based, tax-oriented, or business-based. In other words, they often differ in concept and objective. Starting in 2000, two major standard-setting bodies have emerged as the primary standard-setting bodies in the world. One organization is based in London, United Kingdom, and is called the **International Accounting Standards Board (IASB)**. The IASB issues **International Financial Reporting Standards (IFRS)**, which are used on most foreign exchanges. These standards may also be used by foreign companies listing on U.S. securities exchanges. As indicated earlier, IFRS is presently used in over 115 countries and is rapidly gaining acceptance in other countries as well.

It is generally believed that IFRS has the best potential to provide a common platform on which companies can report and investors can compare financial information. As a result, our discussion focuses on IFRS and the organization involved in developing these standards—the International Accounting Standards Board (IASB). (A detailed discussion of the U.S. system is provided in the chapter.) The two organizations that have a role in international standard-setting are the **International Organization of Securities Commissions (IOSCO)** and the IASB.

International Organization of Securities Commissions (IOSCO)

The International Organization of Securities Commissions (IOSCO) does not set accounting standards. Instead, this organization is dedicated to ensuring that the global markets can operate in an efficient and effective basis. The member agencies (such as from France, Germany, New Zealand, and the U.S. SEC) have resolved to:

- Cooperate to promote high standards of regulation in order to maintain just, efficient, and sound markets.
- Exchange information on their respective experiences in order to promote the development of domestic markets.
- Unite their efforts to establish standards and an effective surveillance of international securities transactions.
- Provide mutual assistance to promote the integrity of the markets by a rigorous application of the standards and by effective enforcement against offenses.

A landmark year for IOSCO was 2005 when it endorsed the IOSCO Memorandum of Understanding (MOU) to facilitate cross-border cooperation, reduce global systemic risk, protect investors, and ensure fair and efficient securities markets. (For more information, go to *http://www.iosco.org/*.)

International Accounting Standards Board (IASB)

The standard-setting structure internationally is composed of four organizations—the International Accounting Standards Committee Foundation, the International Accounting Standards Board (IASB), a Standards Advisory Council, and an International Financial Reporting Interpretations Committee (IFRIC). The trustees of the **International Accounting Standards Committee Foundation (IASCF)** select the members of the IASB and the Standards Advisory Council, fund their activities, and generally oversee the IASB's activities. The IASB is the major operating unit in this four-part structure. Its mission is to develop, in the public interest, a single set of high-quality and understandable IFRS for general-purpose financial statements.

In addition to research help from its own staff, the IASB relies on the expertise of various task force groups formed for various projects and on the **Standards Advisory Council (SAC)**. The SAC consults with the IASB on major policy and technical issues and also helps select task force members. IFRIC develops implementation guidance for consideration by the IASB. Illustration IFRS1-2 (page 34) shows the current organizational structure for the setting of international standards.

As indicated, the standard-setting structure internationally is very similar to the standard-setting structure in the United States (see Illustration 1-2 on page 11). One notable difference is the size of the Board—the IASB has 14 members, while the FASB has just seven members. The larger IASB reflects the need for broader geographic representation in the international setting.

ILLUSTRATION IFRS1-2
International Standard-Setting Structure

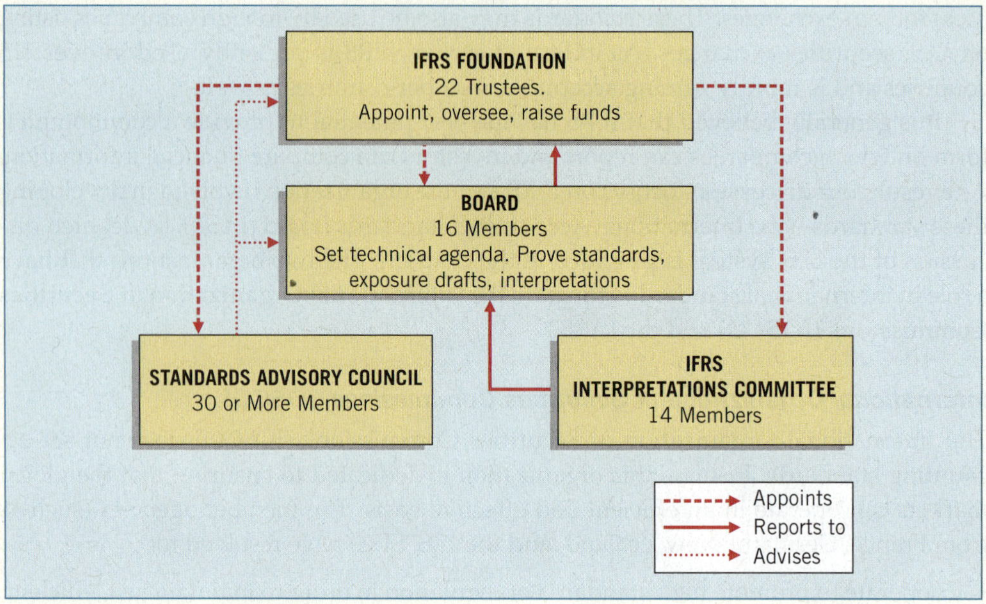

Types of Pronouncements

The IASB issues three major types of pronouncements:

1. International Financial Reporting Standards.
2. Framework for Financial Reporting.
3. International Financial Reporting Interpretations.

International Financial Reporting Standards. Financial accounting standards issued by the IASB are referred to as International Financial Reporting Standards (IFRS). The IASB has issued 13 of these standards to date, covering such subjects as business combinations and share-based payments. Prior to the IASB (formed in 2001), standard-setting on the international level was done by the International Accounting Standards Committee, which issued International Accounting Standards (IAS). The committee issued 41 IASs, many of which have been amended or superseded by the IASB. Those still remaining are considered under the umbrella of IFRS.

Framework for Financial Reporting. As part of a long-range effort to move away from the problem-by-problem approach, the International Accounting Standards Committee (predecessor to the IASB) issued a document entitled "Framework for the Preparation and Presentation of Financial Statements" (also referred to simply as the Framework). This Framework sets forth fundamental objectives and concepts that the Board uses in developing future standards of financial reporting. The intent of the document is to form a cohesive set of interrelated concepts—a conceptual framework—that will serve as tools for solving existing and emerging problems in a consistent manner. For example, the objective of general-purpose financial reporting discussed earlier is part of this Framework. The Framework and any changes to it pass through the same due process (discussion paper, public hearing, exposure draft, etc.) as an IFRS. However, this Framework is not an IFRS and hence does not define standards for any particular measurement or disclosure issue. Nothing in this Framework overrides any specific international accounting standard.

International Financial Reporting Interpretations. Interpretations issued by the **International Financial Reporting Interpretations Committee (IFRIC)** are also considered authoritative and must be followed. These interpretations cover (1) newly identified financial reporting issues not specifically dealt with in IFRS, and (2) issues where unsatisfactory or conflicting interpretations have developed, or seem likely to develop, in the absence of authoritative guidance. The IFRIC has issued over 15 of these interpretations to date. In keeping with the IASB's own approach to setting standards, the IFRIC applies a principles-based approach in providing interpretative guidance. To this end, the IFRIC looks first to the Framework for the Preparation and Presentation of Financial Statements as the foundation for formulating a consensus. It then looks to the principles articulated in the applicable standard, if any, to develop its interpretative guidance and to determine that the proposed guidance does not conflict with provisions in IFRS.

IFRIC helps the IASB in many ways. For example, emerging issues often attract public attention. If not resolved quickly, they can lead to financial crises and scandal. They can also undercut public confidence in current reporting practices. Similar to the EITF in the United States, IFRIC can address controversial accounting problems as they arise. It determines whether it can resolve them or whether to involve the IASB in solving them. In essence, it becomes a "problem filter" for the IASB. Thus, the IASB will hopefully work on more pervasive long-term problems, while the IFRIC deals with short-term emerging issues.

Hierarchy of IFRS

Because it is a private organization, the IASB has no regulatory mandate and therefore no enforcement mechanism. Similar to the U.S. setting, in which the Securities and Exchange Commission enforces the use of FASB standards for public companies, the IASB relies on other regulators to enforce the use of its standards. For example, effective January 1, 2005, the European Union required publicly traded member country companies to use IFRS.

Certain changes have been implemented with respect to use of IFRS in the United States. For example, under American Institute of Certified Public Accountants (AICPA) rules, a member of the AICPA can only report on financial statements prepared in accordance with standards promulgated by standard-setting bodies designated by the AICPA Council. In May 2008, the AICPA Council voted to designate the IASB in London as an international accounting standard-setter for purposes of establishing international financial accounting and reporting principles, and to make related amendments to its rules to provide AICPA members with the option to use IFRS.

Any company indicating that it is preparing its financial statements in conformity with IFRS must use all of the standards and interpretations. The following **hierarchy** is used to determine what recognition, valuation, and disclosure requirements should be used. Companies first look to:

1. International Financial Reporting Standards;
2. International Accounting Standards; and
3. Interpretations originated by the International Financial Reporting Interpretations Committee (IFRIC) or the former Standing Interpretations Committee (SIC).

In the absence of a standard or an interpretation, the following sources in descending order are used: (1) the requirements and guidance in standards and interpretations dealing with similar and related issues; (2) the Framework for financial reporting; and (3) most recent pronouncements of other standard-setting bodies that use a similar conceptual framework to develop accounting standards, other accounting literature, and accepted industry practices, to the extent they do not conflict with the above. The overriding requirement of IFRS is that the financial statements provide a fair presentation (often referred to as a "true and fair view"). Fair representation is assumed to occur if a company follows the guidelines established in IFRS.

International Accounting Convergence

The SEC recognizes that the establishment of a single, widely accepted set of high-quality accounting standards benefits both global capital markets and U.S. investors. U.S. investors will make better-informed investment decisions if they obtain high-quality financial information from U.S. companies that are more comparable to the presently available information from non-U.S. companies operating in the same industry or line of business. Thus, the SEC appears committed to move to IFRS, assuming that certain conditions are met. These conditions are spelled out in a document, referred to as the "**Roadmap**" and in a policy statement issued by the SEC in early 2010.[12]

The FASB and the IASB have been working diligently to (1) make their existing financial reporting standards fully compatible as soon as is practicable, and (2) coordinate their future work programs to ensure that once achieved, compatibility is maintained. This process is referred to as *convergence*, and the Boards have made significant progress in developing high-quality converged standards. However, much work needs to be done. The Boards have identified the issuance of converged standards on financial instruments (investments), revenue, and leases as a key milestone in the convergence process.

SEC Staff Paper on Incorporation of IFRS. The SEC has monitored the convergence process through a staff Work Plan, which considers specific areas and factors relevant to a commission determination as to whether, when, and how the current financial reporting system for U.S. companies should be transitioned to a system incorporating IFRS. Execution of the Work Plan (which addresses such areas as independence of standard- setting, investor understanding of IFRS, and auditor readiness), combined with the completion of the convergence projects of the FASB and the IASB according to their current work plan, will position the SEC to make a decision on required use of IFRS by U.S. issuers.

In July 2012, the SEC staff issued its final report related to the Work Plan elements.[13] The main thrust of the report is that we will have to wait and see for a commission decision on required use of IFRS in the United States. Although the Staff Report did not set out to answer the fundamental question of whether transitioning to IFRS is in the best interests of the U.S. securities markets generally and U.S. investors specifically, it appears that it is unlikely companies would be required to change to IFRS in the near future. Rather, there would be a transition period in which this would be accomplished. With respect to this transition, the SEC staff has suggested gradual incorporation of IFRS into the U.S. financial reporting system.[14]

The approach to incorporation is an "endorsement approach." Rather than adopting IFRS at a point in time (sometimes referred to as a "big bang"), the endorsement approach specifies that the FASB and IASB continue their convergence efforts (over a 5–7-year transition period) to align GAAP and IFRS. As a result, these converged standards (which are also IFRS) will be incorporated into GAAP.

At the end of this period, a U.S. company that is compliant with GAAP would also be compliant with IFRS. Following the transition period, there would be an ongoing endorsement period of IFRS by the FASB to determine if newly issued IFRS will become part of GAAP. Illustration IFRS1-3 shows the timeline for the international accounting convergence process.

[12] "Roadmap for the Potential Use of Financial Statements Prepared in Accordance with International Financial Reporting Standards by U.S. Issuers," *SEC Release No. 33-8982* (November 14, 2008), and "Statement in Support of Convergence and Global Accounting Standards," *SEC Release Nos. 33-9109; 34-61578* (February 24, 2010).

[13] "Work Plan for the Consideration of Incorporating International Financial Reporting Standards into the Financial Reporting System for U.S. Issuers: Final Staff Report SEC" (July 13, 2012), *http://www.sec.gov/spotlight/globalaccountingstandards/ifrs-work-plan-final-report.pdf.*

[14] SEC Staff Paper, "Work Plan for the Consideration of Incorporating International Financial Reporting Standards into the Financial Reporting System for U.S. Issuers: Exploring a Possible Method of Incorporation" (May 26, 2011), available at *www.sec.gov.*

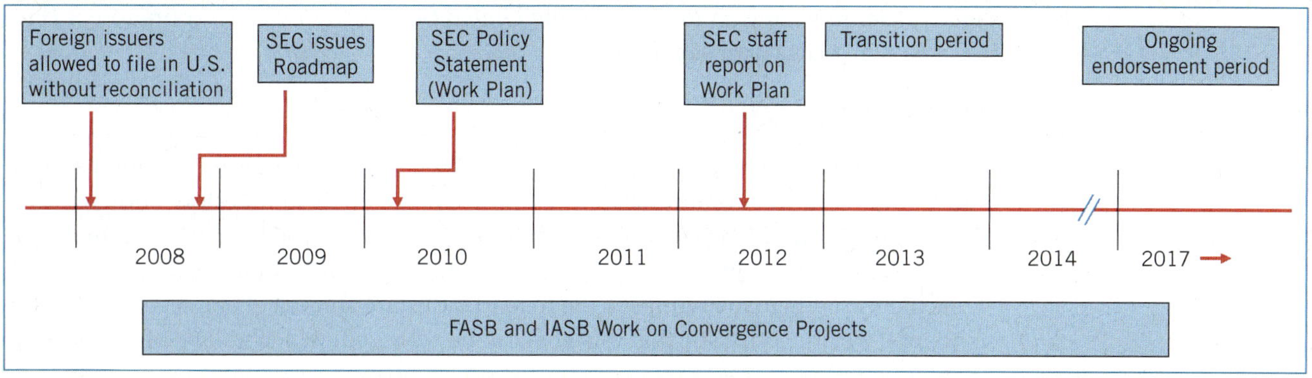

ILLUSTRATION IFRS1-3
International Accounting Convergence Timeline

Transition Period. In the transition period, the FASB and SEC will execute a transition plan for evaluating IFRS for incorporation into GAAP. The transition plan groups IFRS into one of three categories, as summarized in Illustration IFRS1-4.

Category	Transition Plan
1. IFRS subject to current active convergence projects.	The FASB and IASB target completion of active projects (e.g., financial instruments, revenue recognition, and leases) in 2013.
2. IFRS included on the IASB's current standard-setting agenda.	The FASB evaluates other standards that the IASB is likely to issue in the near term to determine potential differences from GAAP. The FASB will review the individual standards to determine how best to incorporate the standards into GAAP.
3. All other existing IFRS not subject to current standard-setting and areas not addressed by IFRS.	The FASB assesses the IFRS not subject to current standard-setting plans for potential incorporation into GAAP. Prospective application of new requirements will be permitted whenever possible after giving consideration to comparability, reliability, cost and benefit, and other relevant factors.

ILLUSTRATION IFRS1-4
Transition Period Elements

As indicated, in the transition period, the FASB will continue to work with the IASB in a convergence process to develop converged standards and to evaluate other existing IFRS for incorporation in GAAP.

Ongoing Endorsement Period. After the transition period, the FASB will continue to have an active role in international standard-setting. This role would differ considerably from the FASB's current standard-setting role and responsibilities. Most significantly, the FASB would participate along with other constituents in the IASB's process for developing IFRS rather than serving as the principal body responsible for developing new accounting standards or modifying existing standards in GAAP.

However, in the ongoing endorsement process, the FASB retains the authority to modify or add to the requirements of newly issued IFRS. Under the endorsement approach, the SEC maintains its oversight of the FASB as the designated U.S. standard-setter. As a result, the SEC staff could issue guidance similar to its process for issuing staff accounting bulletins, although the staff expects that these occurrences would be rare.

Summary. Incorporation of IFRS through the endorsement approach works toward the goal of a single set of high-quality, globally accepted accounting standards, while doing so in a practical manner and in a way that minimizes both the cost and effort needed to incorporate IFRS into the U.S. financial reporting system. The gradual implementation of IFRS reduces adoption costs. Importantly, this IFRS incorporation approach retains GAAP as the basis of financial reporting for U.S. issuers. This avoids the complexities and costs associated with changing the many references to GAAP in U.S. laws and contracts. Based on the endorsement approach, which has been generally well-received by the financial reporting community in the United States, any U.S. incorporation of IFRS in GAAP will occur over several years.

ON THE HORIZON

Financial statements prepared according to IFRS have become an important standard around the world for communicating financial information to investors and creditors. The SEC and the FASB are working with their international counterparts to achieve the goal of a single set of high-quality financial reporting standards for use around the world. While there are still many bumps in the road to the establishment of one set of worldwide standards, we are optimistic that this goal can be achieved, which will be of value to all.

IFRS SELF-TEST QUESTIONS

1. IFRS stands for:
   (a) International Federation of Reporting Services.
   (b) Independent Financial Reporting Standards.
   (c) International Financial Reporting Standards.
   (d) Integrated Financial Reporting Services.
2. The major key players on the international side are the:
   (a) IASB and FASB.
   (b) IOSCO and the SEC.
   (c) SEC and FASB.
   (d) IASB and IOSCO.
3. IFRS is comprised of:
   (a) International Financial Reporting Standards and FASB Financial Reporting Standards.
   (b) International Financial Reporting Standards, International Accounting Standards, and International Accounting Interpretations.
   (c) International Accounting Standards and International Accounting Interpretations.
   (d) FASB Financial Reporting Standards and International Accounting Standards.
4. The authoritative status of the Framework for the Preparation and Presentation of Financial Statements is as follows:
   (a) It is used when there is no standard or interpretation related to the reporting issues under consideration.
   (b) It is not as authoritative as a standard but takes precedence over any interpretation related to the reporting issue.
   (c) It takes precedence over all other authoritative literature.
   (d) It has no authoritative status.
5. Which of the following statements is **true**?
   (a) The IASB has the same number of members as the FASB.
   (b) The IASB structure has both advisory and interpretation functions, but no trustees.
   (c) The IASB has been in existence longer than the FASB.
   (d) The IASB structure is quite similar to the FASB's, except the IASB has a larger number of board members.

IFRS CONCEPTS AND APPLICATION

IFRS1-1 Who are the two key international players in the development of international accounting standards? Explain their role.

IFRS1-2 What might explain the fact that different accounting standard-setters have developed accounting standards that are sometimes quite different in nature?

IFRS1-3 What is the benefit of a single set of high-quality accounting standards?

IFRS1-4 Briefly describe FASB/IASB convergence process and the principles that guide their convergence efforts.

Financial Reporting Case

IFRS1-5 The following comments were made at an Annual Conference of the Financial Executives Institute (FEI).

There is an irreversible movement toward the harmonization of financial reporting throughout the world. The international capital markets require an end to:

1. The confusion caused by international companies announcing different results depending on the set of accounting standards applied.
2. Companies in some countries obtaining unfair commercial advantages from the use of particular national accounting standards.
3. The complications in negotiating commercial arrangements for international joint ventures caused by different accounting requirements.
4. The inefficiency of international companies having to understand and use a myriad of different accounting standards depending on the countries in which they operate and the countries in which they raise capital and debt. Executive talent is wasted on keeping up to date with numerous sets of accounting standards and the never-ending changes to them.
5. The inefficiency of investment managers, bankers, and financial analysts as they seek to compare financial reporting drawn up in accordance with different sets of accounting standards.

Instructions

(a) What is the International Accounting Standards Board?
(b) What stakeholders might benefit from the use of International Accounting Standards?
(c) What do you believe are some of the major obstacles to convergence?

Professional Research

IFRS1-6 As a newly enrolled accounting major, you are anxious to better understand accounting institutions and sources of accounting literature. As a first step, you decide to explore the IASB's Framework for the Preparation and Presentation of Financial Statements.

Instructions

Access the IASB Framework at the IASB website (*http://eifrs.iasb.org/*). (Click on the IFRS tab and then register for free eIFRS access if necessary.) When you have accessed the documents, you can use the search tool in your Internet browser to respond to the following items. (Provide paragraph citations.)

(a) What is the objective of financial reporting?
(b) What other means are there of communicating information, besides financial statements?
(c) Indicate some of the users and the information they are most directly concerned with in economic decision-making.

International Financial Reporting Problem

Marks and Spencer plc

IFRS1-7 The financial statements of Marks and Spencer plc (M&S) are available at the book's companion website or can be accessed at *http://annualreport.marksandspencer.com/_assets/downloads/Marks-and-Spencer-Annual-report-and-financial-statements-2012.pdf.*

Instructions

Refer to M&S's financial statements and the accompanying notes to answer the following questions.

(a) What is the company's main line of business?
(b) In what countries does the company operate?
(c) What is the address of the company's corporate headquarters?
(d) What is the company's reporting currency?

ANSWERS TO IFRS SELF-TEST QUESTIONS

1. c **2.** d **3.** b **4.** a **5.** d

Remember to check the book's companion website to find additional resources for this chapter.

CHAPTER

2 Conceptual Framework for Financial Reporting

LEARNING OBJECTIVES

After studying this chapter, you should be able to:

1 Describe the usefulness of a conceptual framework.

2 Describe the FASB's efforts to construct a conceptual framework.

3 Understand the objective of financial reporting.

4 Identify the qualitative characteristics of accounting information.

5 Define the basic elements of financial statements.

6 Describe the basic assumptions of accounting.

7 Explain the application of the basic principles of accounting.

8 Describe the impact that the cost constraint has on reporting accounting information.

What Is It?

Everyone agrees that accounting needs a framework—a conceptual framework, so to speak—that will help guide the development of standards. To understand the importance of developing this framework, let's see how you would respond in the following two situations.

Situation 1: "Taking a Long Shot . . ."

To supplement donations collected from its general community solicitation, Tri-Cities United Charities holds an annual lottery sweepstakes. In this year's sweepstakes, United Charities is offering a grand prize of $1,000,000 to a single winning ticket holder. A total of 10,000 tickets have been printed, and United Charities plans to sell all the tickets at a price of $150 each.

Since its inception, the sweepstakes has attracted area-wide interest, and United Charities has always been able to meet its sales target. However, in the unlikely event that it might fail to sell a sufficient number of tickets to cover the grand prize, United Charities has reserved the right to cancel the sweepstakes and to refund the price of the tickets to holders.

In recent years, a fairly active secondary market for tickets has developed. This year, buying–selling prices have varied between $75 and $95 before stabilizing at about $90.

When the tickets first went on sale this year, multimillionaire Phil N. Tropic, well-known in Tri-Cities civic circles as a generous but sometimes eccentric donor, bought one of the tickets from United Charities, paying $150 cash.

How would you answer the following questions?

1. Should Phil N. Tropic recognize his lottery ticket as an asset in his financial statements?
2. Assuming that Phil N. Tropic recognizes the lottery ticket as an asset, at what amount should it be reported? Some possible answers are $150, $100, and $90.

CONCEPTUAL FOCUS

This chapter summarizes conceptual elements that will be referred to throughout subsequent chapters.

INTERNATIONAL FOCUS

> See the **International Perspectives** on pages 43, 44, 54, and 55.

> Read the **IFRS Insights** on pages 78–81 for a discussion of:

—Financial statement elements

—Conceptual framework Work Plan

Situation 2: The $20 Million Question

The Hard Rock Mining Company has just completed the first year of operations at its new strip mine, the Lonesome Doe. Hard Rock spent $10 million for the land and $20 million in preparing the site for mining operations. The mine is expected to operate for 20 years. Hard Rock is subject to environmental statutes requiring it to restore the Lonesome Doe mine site on completion of mining operations.

Based on its experience and industry data, as well as current technology, Hard Rock forecasts that restoration will cost about $10 million when it is undertaken. Of those costs, about $4 million is for restoring the topsoil that was removed in preparing the site for mining operations (prior to opening the mine). The rest is directly proportional to the depth of the mine, which in turn is directly proportional to the amount of ore extracted.

How would you answer the following questions?

1. Should Hard Rock recognize a liability for site restoration in conjunction with the opening of the Lonesome Doe Mine? If so, what is the amount of that liability?
2. After Hard Rock has operated the Lonesome Doe Mine for 5 years, new technology is introduced that reduces Hard Rock's estimated future restoration costs to $7 million, $3 million of which relates to restoring the topsoil. How should Hard Rock account for this change in its estimated future liability?

The answer to the questions on the two situations depends on how assets and liabilities are defined and how they should be valued. Hopefully, this chapter will provide you with a framework to resolve questions like these.

Sources: Adapted from Todd Johnson and Kim Petrone, *The FASB Cases on Recognition and Measurement*, Second Edition (New York: John Wiley and Sons, Inc., 1996).

PREVIEW OF CHAPTER 2

As our opening story indicates, users of financial statements can face difficult questions about the recognition and measurement of financial items. To help develop the type of financial information that can be used to answer these questions, financial accounting and reporting relies on a conceptual framework. In this chapter, we discuss the basic concepts underlying the conceptual framework as follows.

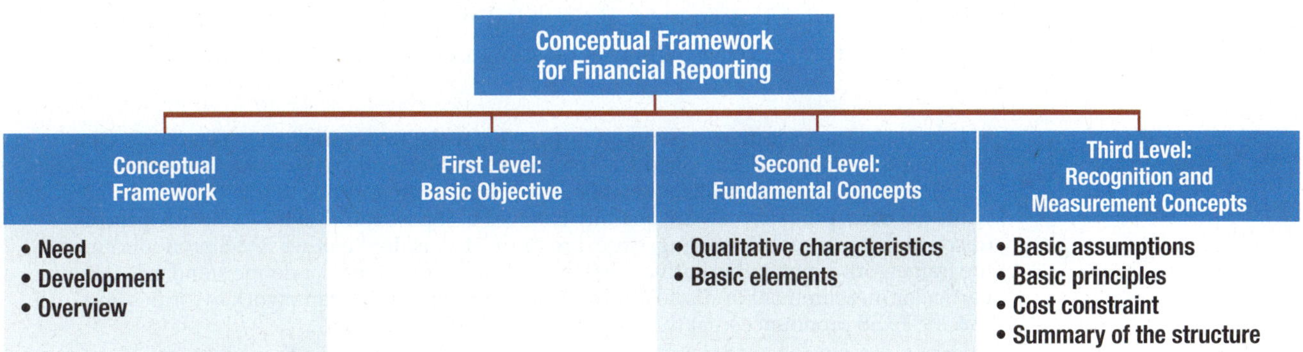

CONCEPTUAL FRAMEWORK

LEARNING OBJECTIVE 1
Describe the usefulness of a conceptual framework.

A **conceptual framework** establishes the concepts that underlie financial reporting. A conceptual framework is a coherent system of concepts that flow from an objective. The objective identifies the purpose of financial reporting. The other concepts provide guidance on (1) identifying the boundaries of financial reporting; (2) selecting the transactions, other events, and circumstances to be represented; (3) how they should be recognized and measured; and (4) how they should be summarized and reported.[1]

Need for a Conceptual Framework

Why do we need a conceptual framework? First, to be useful, rule-making should build on and relate to an established body of concepts. A soundly developed conceptual framework thus enables the FASB to issue **more useful and consistent pronouncements over time; a coherent set of standards should result**. Indeed, without the guidance provided by a soundly developed framework, standard-setting ends up being based on individual concepts developed by each member of the standard-setting body. The following observation by a former standard-setter highlights the problem.

> "As our professional careers unfold, each of us develops a technical conceptual framework. Some individual frameworks are sharply defined and firmly held; others are vague and weakly held; still others are vague and firmly held. . . . At one time or another, most of us have felt the discomfort of listening to somebody buttress a preconceived conclusion by building a convoluted chain of shaky reasoning. Indeed, perhaps on occasion we have voiced such thinking ourselves. . . . My experience . . . taught me many lessons. A major one was that most of us have a natural tendency and an incredible talent for processing new facts in such a way that our prior conclusions remain intact.[2]

In other words, standard-setting that is based on personal conceptual frameworks will lead to different conclusions about identical or similar issues than it did previously. As a result, standards will not be consistent with one another, and past decisions may not be indicative of future ones. Furthermore, the framework should increase financial statement users' understanding of and confidence in financial reporting. It should enhance comparability among companies' financial statements.

Second, as a result of a soundly developed conceptual framework, the profession should be able to more quickly solve new and emerging **practical problems by referring to an existing framework of basic theory**. For example, Sunshine Mining sold two issues of bonds. It can redeem them either with $1,000 in cash or with 50 ounces of silver, whichever is worth more at maturity. Both bond issues have a stated interest rate of 8.5 percent. At what amounts should Sunshine or the buyers of the bonds record them? What is the amount of the premium or discount on the bonds? And how should Sunshine amortize this amount, if the bond redemption payments are to be made in silver (the future value of which is unknown at the date of issuance)? Consider that

[1] "Chapter 1, The Objective of General Purpose Financial Reporting" and "Chapter 3, Qualitative Characteristics of Useful Financial Information," *Statement of Financial Accounting Concepts No. 8* (Norwalk, Conn.: FASB, September 2010). Recall from our discussion in Chapter 1 that while the conceptual framework and any changes to it pass through the same due process (discussion paper, public hearing, exposure draft, etc.) as do the other FASB pronouncements, the framework is not authoritative. That is, the framework does not define standards for any particular measurement or disclosure issue, and nothing in the framework overrides any specific FASB pronouncement that is included in the Codification.

[2] C. Horngren, "Uses and Limitations of a Conceptual Framework," *Journal of Accountancy* (April 1981), p. 90.

Sunshine cannot know, at the date of issuance, the value of future silver bond redemption payments.

It is difficult, if not impossible, for the FASB to prescribe the proper accounting treatment quickly for situations like this or like those represented in our opening story. Practicing accountants, however, must resolve such problems on a daily basis. How? Through good judgment and with the help of a universally accepted conceptual framework, practitioners can quickly focus on an acceptable treatment.

What do the numbers mean? WHAT'S YOUR PRINCIPLE?

The need for a conceptual framework is highlighted by accounting scandals such as those at **Enron** and **Lehman Brothers**. To restore public confidence in the financial reporting process, many have argued that regulators should move toward principles-based rules. They believe that companies exploited the detailed provisions in rules-based pronouncements to manage accounting reports, rather than report the economic substance of transactions. For example, many of the off–balance-sheet arrangements of Enron avoided transparent reporting by barely achieving 3 percent outside equity ownership, a requirement in an obscure accounting rule interpretation. Enron's financial engineers were able to structure transactions to achieve a desired accounting treatment, even if that accounting treatment did not reflect the transaction's true nature. Under principles-based rules, hopefully top management's financial reporting focus will shift from demonstrating compliance with rules to demonstrating that a company has attained the objective of financial reporting.

Development of a Conceptual Framework

2 LEARNING OBJECTIVE
Describe the FASB's efforts to construct a conceptual framework.

Over the years, numerous organizations developed and published their own conceptual frameworks, but no single framework was universally accepted and relied on in practice. In 1976, the FASB began to develop a conceptual framework that would be a basis for setting accounting rules and for resolving financial reporting controversies. The FASB has since issued seven Statements of Financial Accounting Concepts that relate to financial reporting for business enterprises.[3] They are as follows.

1. *SFAC No. 1*, "Objectives of Financial Reporting by Business Enterprises," presents the goals and purposes of accounting (superseded by *SFAC No. 8*, Chapter 1).
2. *SFAC No. 2*, "Qualitative Characteristics of Accounting Information," examines the characteristics that make accounting information useful (superseded by *SFAC No. 8*, Chapter 3).
3. *SFAC No. 3*, "Elements of Financial Statements of Business Enterprises," provides definitions of items in financial statements, such as assets, liabilities, revenues, and expenses (superseded by *SFAC No. 6*).
4. *SFAC No. 5*, "Recognition and Measurement in Financial Statements of Business Enterprises," sets forth fundamental recognition and measurement criteria and guidance on what information should be formally incorporated into financial statements and when.
5. *SFAC No. 6*, "Elements of Financial Statements," replaces *SFAC No. 3* and expands its scope to include not-for-profit organizations.

International Perspective

The IASB has also issued a conceptual framework. The FASB and the IASB have agreed on a joint project to develop a common and improved conceptual framework. The project is being conducted in phases. Phase A on objectives and qualitative characteristics was issued in 2010.

[3]The FASB also issued a Statement of Financial Accounting Concepts that relates to nonbusiness organizations: "Objectives of Financial Reporting by Nonbusiness Organizations," *Statement of Financial Accounting Concepts No. 4* (December 1980).

International Perspective

SFAC No. 8 is the product of a joint conceptual framework project of the FASB and IASB.

6. *SFAC No. 7*, "Using Cash Flow Information and Present Value in Accounting Measurements," provides a framework for using expected future cash flows and present values as a basis for measurement.
7. *SFAC No. 8*, Chapter 1, "The Objective of General Purpose Financial Reporting," and Chapter 3, "Qualitative Characteristics of Useful Financial Information," replaces *SFAC No. 1* and *No. 2*.

Overview of the Conceptual Framework

Illustration 2-1 provides an overview of the FASB's conceptual framework.[4]

ILLUSTRATION 2-1
Framework for Financial Reporting

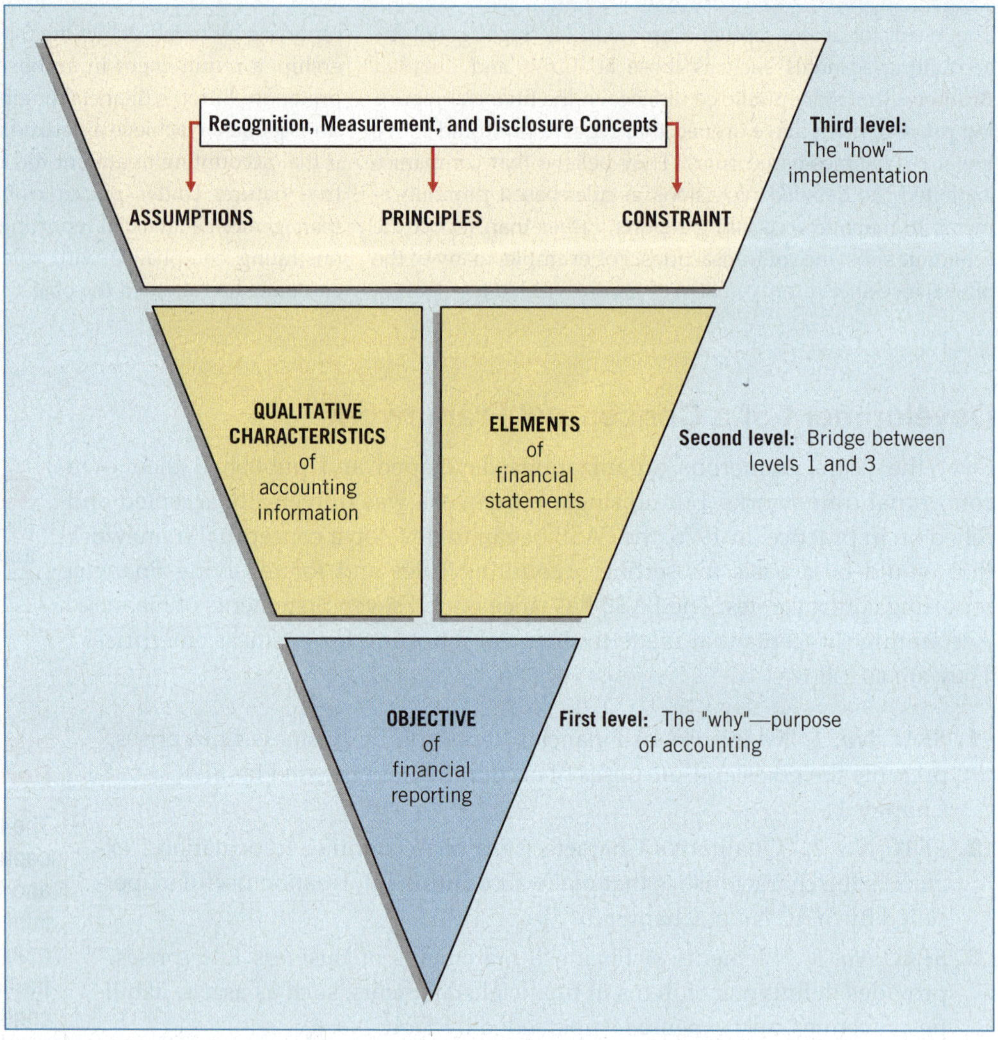

The first level identifies the **objective of financial reporting**—that is, the purpose of financial reporting. The second level provides the **qualitative characteristics** that make accounting information useful and the **elements of financial statements** (assets, liabilities, and so on). The third level identifies the **recognition, measurement, and disclosure concepts** used in establishing and applying accounting standards and the specific concepts to implement the objective. These concepts include assumptions, principles, and a cost constraint that describe the present reporting environment. We examine these three levels of the conceptual framework next.

[4]Adapted from William C. Norby, *The Financial Analysts Journal* (March–April 1982), p. 22.

FIRST LEVEL: BASIC OBJECTIVE

3 LEARNING OBJECTIVE
Understand the objective of financial reporting.

The **objective of financial reporting** is the foundation of the conceptual framework. Other aspects of the framework—qualitative characteristics, elements of financial statements, recognition, measurement, and disclosure—flow logically from the objective. Those aspects of the framework help to ensure that financial reporting achieves its objective.

The objective of general-purpose financial reporting is to provide financial information about the reporting entity that is **useful to present and potential equity investors, lenders, and other creditors in making decisions about providing resources to the entity**. Those decisions involve buying, selling, or holding equity and debt instruments, and providing or settling loans and other forms of credit. Information that is **decision-useful** to capital providers may also be useful to other users of financial reporting, who are not capital providers.[5]

As indicated in Chapter 1, to provide information to decision-makers, companies prepare general-purpose financial statements. **General-purpose financial reporting** helps users who lack the ability to demand all the financial information they need from an entity and therefore must rely, at least partly, on the information provided in financial reports. However, an implicit assumption is that users need reasonable knowledge of business and financial accounting matters to understand the information contained in financial statements. This point is important. It means that financial statement preparers assume a level of competence on the part of users. This assumption impacts the way and the extent to which companies report information.

SECOND LEVEL: FUNDAMENTAL CONCEPTS

4 LEARNING OBJECTIVE
Identify the qualitative characteristics of accounting information.

The objective (first level) focuses on the purpose of financial reporting. Later, we will discuss the ways in which this purpose is implemented (third level). What, then, is the purpose of the second level? The second level provides conceptual building blocks that explain the qualitative characteristics of accounting information and define the elements of financial statements.[6] That is, the second level forms a bridge between the **why** of accounting (the objective) and the **how** of accounting (recognition, measurement, and financial statement presentation).

Qualitative Characteristics of Accounting Information

Should companies like **Walt Disney** or **Kellogg's** provide information in their financial statements on how much it costs them to acquire their assets (historical cost basis) or how much the assets are currently worth (fair value basis)? Should **PepsiCo** combine and show as one company the four main segments of its business, or should it report PepsiCo Beverages, Frito Lay, Quaker Foods, and PepsiCo International as four separate segments?

How does a company choose an acceptable accounting method, the amount and types of information to disclose, and the format in which to present it? The answer: By determining **which alternative provides the most useful information for decision-making purposes (decision-usefulness)**. The FASB identified the **qualitative characteristics** of accounting information that distinguish better (more useful) information from

[5] "Chapter 1, The Objective of General Purpose Financial Reporting," *Statement of Financial Accounting Concepts No. 8* (Norwalk, Conn.: FASB, September 2010), par. OB2.

[6] "Chapter 3, Qualitative Characteristics of Useful Financial Information," *Statement of Financial Accounting Concepts No. 8* (Norwalk, Conn.: FASB, September 2010).

inferior (less useful) information for decision-making purposes. In addition, the FASB identified a cost constraint as part of the conceptual framework (discussed later in the chapter). As Illustration 2-2 shows, the characteristics may be viewed as a hierarchy.

ILLUSTRATION 2-2
Hierarchy of Accounting Qualities

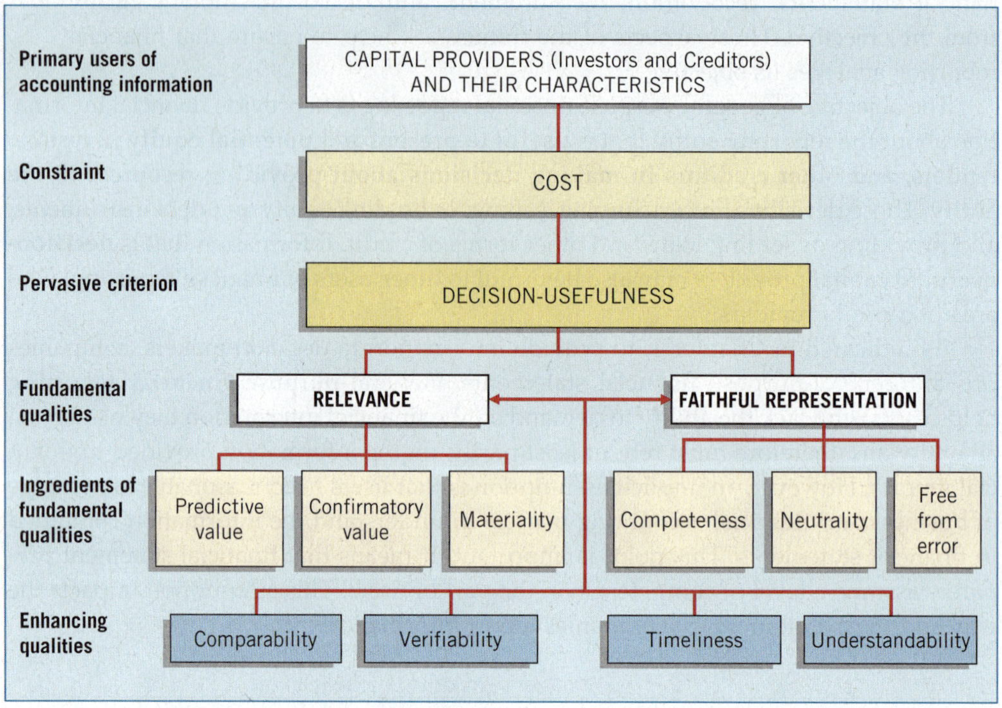

As indicated by Illustration 2-2, qualitative characteristics are either fundamental or enhancing characteristics, depending on how they affect the decision-usefulness of information. Regardless of classification, each qualitative characteristic contributes to the decision-usefulness of financial reporting information. However, providing useful financial information is limited by a pervasive constraint on financial reporting—cost should not exceed the benefits of a reporting practice.

Fundamental Quality—Relevance

Relevance is one of the two fundamental qualities that make accounting information useful for decision-making. Relevance and related ingredients of this fundamental quality are shown below.

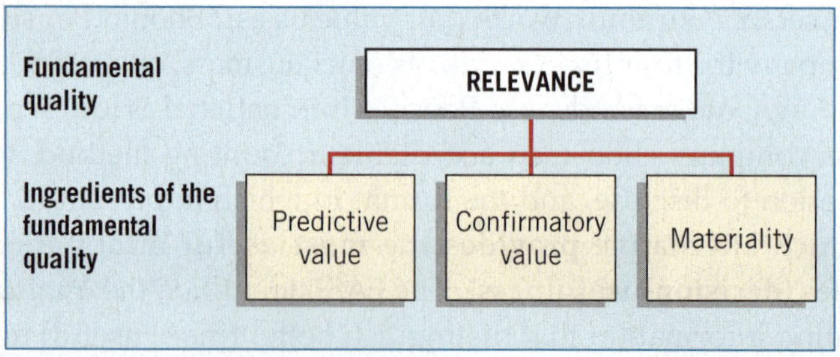

To have **relevance**, accounting information must be capable of making a difference in a decision. Information with no bearing on a decision is irrelevant. Financial information is capable of making a difference when it has predictive value, confirmatory value, or both.

Financial information has **predictive value** if it has value as an input to predictive processes used by investors to form their own expectations about the future. For example, if potential investors are interested in purchasing common shares in **UPS (United Parcel Service)**, they may analyze its current resources and claims to those resources, its dividend payments, and its past income performance to predict the amount, timing, and uncertainty of UPS's future cash flows.

Relevant information also helps users confirm or correct prior expectations; it has **confirmatory value**. For example, when UPS issues its year-end financial statements, it confirms or changes past (or present) expectations based on previous evaluations. It follows that predictive value and confirmatory value are interrelated. For example, information about the current level and structure of UPS's assets and liabilities helps users predict its ability to take advantage of opportunities and to react to adverse situations. The same information helps to confirm or correct users' past predictions about that ability.

Materiality is a company-specific aspect of relevance. Information is material if omitting it or misstating it could influence decisions that users make on the basis of the reported financial information. An individual company determines whether information is material because both the nature and/or magnitude of the item(s) to which the information relates must be considered in the context of an individual company's financial report. Information is *immaterial*, and therefore irrelevant, if it would have no impact on a decision-maker. In short, **it must make a difference** or a company need not disclose it.

Assessing materiality is one of the more challenging aspects of accounting because it requires evaluating both the **relative size and importance** of an item. However, it is difficult to provide firm guidelines in judging when a given item is or is not material. Materiality varies both with relative amount and with relative importance. For example, the two sets of numbers in Illustration 2-3 indicate relative size.

ILLUSTRATION 2-3
Materiality Comparison

	Company A	Company B
Sales	$10,000,000	$100,000
Costs and expenses	9,000,000	90,000
Income from operations	$ 1,000,000	$ 10,000
Unusual gain	$ 20,000	$ 5,000

During the period in question, the revenues and expenses, and therefore the net incomes of Company A and Company B, are proportional. Each reported an unusual gain. In looking at the abbreviated income figures for Company A, it appears insignificant whether the amount of the unusual gain is set out separately or merged with the regular operating income. The gain is only 2 percent of the operating income. If merged, it would not seriously distort the income figure. Company B has had an unusual gain of only $5,000. However, it is relatively much more significant than the larger gain realized by Company A. For Company B, an item of $5,000 amounts to 50 percent of its income from operations. Obviously, the inclusion of such an item in operating income would affect the amount of that income materially. Thus, we see the importance of the **relative size** of an item in determining its materiality.

Companies and their auditors generally adopt the rule of thumb that anything under 5 percent of net income is considered immaterial. However, much can depend on specific rules. For example, one market regulator indicates that a company may use this percentage for an initial assessment of materiality, but it must also consider other factors.[7] For example, companies can no longer fail to record items in order to meet

[7] "Materiality," *SEC Staff Accounting Bulletin No. 99* (Washington, D.C.: SEC, 1999). The auditing profession also adopted this same concept of materiality. See "Audit Risk and Materiality in Conducting an Audit," *Statement on Auditing Standards No. 47* (New York: AICPA, 1983), par. 6.

consensus analysts' earnings numbers, preserve a positive earnings trend, convert a loss to a profit or vice versa, increase management compensation, or hide an illegal transaction like a bribe. In other words, **companies must consider both quantitative and qualitative factors in determining whether an item is material.**

Thus, it is generally not feasible to specify uniform quantitative thresholds at which an item becomes material. Rather, materiality judgments should be made in the context of the nature and the amount of an item. Materiality factors into a great many internal accounting decisions, too. Examples of such judgments that companies must make include the amount of classification required in a subsidiary expense ledger, the degree of accuracy required in allocating expenses among the departments of a company, and the extent to which adjustments should be made for accrued and deferred items. Only by **the exercise of good judgment and professional expertise** can reasonable and appropriate answers be found with respect to materiality issues.

What do the numbers mean? LIVING IN A MATERIAL WORLD

The first line of defense for many companies caught "cooking the books" had been to argue that a questionable accounting item is immaterial. That defense did not work so well in the wake of accounting meltdowns at **Enron** and **Global Crossing** and the tougher rules on materiality issued by the SEC (*SAB 99*).

For example, the SEC alleged in a case against **Sunbeam** that the company's many immaterial adjustments added up to a material misstatement that misled investors about the company's financial position. More recently, the SEC called for a number of companies, such as **Jack in the Box**, **McDonald's**, and **AIG**, to restate prior financial statements for the effects of incorrect accounting. In some cases, the restatements did not meet traditional materiality thresholds. Don Nicholaisen, then SEC chief accountant, observed that whether the amount is material or not, some transactions appear to be "flat out intended to mislead investors." In essence he is saying that any wrong accounting for a transaction can represent important information to the users of financial statements.

Responding to new concerns about materiality, blue-chip companies such as **IBM** and **General Electric** are providing expanded disclosures of transactions that used to fall below the materiality radar. As a result, some good may yet come from the recent accounting failures.

Sources: Adapted from K. Brown and J. Weil, "A Lot More Information Is 'Material' After Enron," *Wall Street Journal Online* (February 22, 2002); S. D. Jones and R. Gibson, "Restaurants Serve Up Restatements," *Wall Street Journal* (January 26, 2005), p. C3; and R. McTauge, "Nicholaisen Says Restatement Needed When Deal Lacks Business Purpose," *Securities Regulation & Law Reporter* (May 9, 2005).

Fundamental Quality—Faithful Representation

Faithful representation is the second fundamental quality that makes accounting information useful for decision-making. Faithful representation and related ingredients of this fundamental quality are shown below.

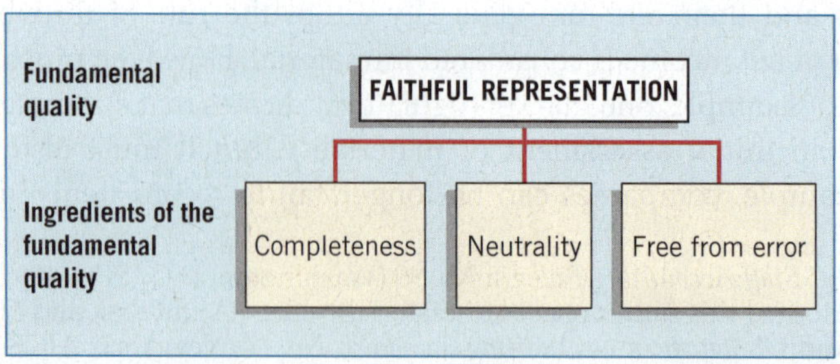

Faithful representation means that the numbers and descriptions match what really existed or happened. Faithful representation is a necessity because most users have neither the time nor the expertise to evaluate the factual content of the information. For example, if **General Motors**' income statement reports sales of $60,510 million when it had sales of $40,510 million, then the statement fails to faithfully represent the proper sales amount. To be a faithful representation, information must be complete, neutral, and free of material error.

Completeness. **Completeness** means that all the information that is necessary for faithful representation is provided. An omission can cause information to be false or misleading and thus not be helpful to the users of financial reports. For example, when **Citigroup** fails to provide information needed to assess the value of its subprime loan receivables (toxic assets), the information is not complete and therefore not a faithful representation of their values.

Neutrality. **Neutrality** means that a company cannot select information to favor one set of interested parties over another. Unbiased information must be the overriding consideration. For example, in the notes to financial statements, tobacco companies such as **R.J. Reynolds** should not suppress information about the numerous lawsuits that have been filed because of tobacco-related health concerns—even though such disclosure is damaging to the company.

Neutrality in rule-making has come under increasing attack. Some argue that the FASB should not issue pronouncements that cause undesirable economic effects on an industry or company. We disagree. Accounting rules (and the standard-setting process) must be free from bias, or we will no longer have credible financial statements. Without credible financial statements, individuals will no longer use this information. An analogy demonstrates the point: Many individuals bet on boxing matches because such contests are assumed not to be fixed. But nobody bets on wrestling matches. Why? Because the public assumes that wrestling matches are rigged. If financial information is biased (rigged), the public will lose confidence and no longer use it.[8]

Free from Error. An information item that is **free from error** will be a more accurate (faithful) representation of a financial item. For example, if **JPMorgan Chase** misstates its loan losses, its financial statements are misleading and not a faithful representation of its financial results. However, faithful representation does not imply total freedom from error. This is because most financial reporting measures involve estimates of various types that incorporate management's judgment. For example, management

[8]Sometimes, in practice, it has been acceptable to invoke prudence or conservatism as a justification for an accounting treatment under conditions of uncertainty. **Prudence** or **conservatism** means when in doubt, choose the solution that will be least likely to overstate assets or income and/or understate liabilities or expenses. The framework indicates that prudence or conservatism generally is in conflict with the quality of neutrality. This is because being prudent or conservative likely leads to a bias in the reported financial position and financial performance. In fact, introducing biased understatement of assets (or overstatement of liabilities) in one period frequently leads to overstating financial performance in later periods—a result that cannot be described as prudent. This is inconsistent with neutrality, which encompasses freedom from bias. Accordingly, the framework does not include prudence or conservatism as desirable qualities of financial reporting information. See "Chapter 3, Qualitative Characteristics of Useful Financial Information," *Statement of Financial Accounting Concepts No. 8* (Norwalk, Conn.: FASB, September 2010), paras. BC3.27–BC3.29.

must estimate the amount of uncollectible accounts to determine bad debt expense. And determination of depreciation expense requires estimation of useful lives of plant and equipment, as well as the salvage value of the assets.

What do the numbers mean? SHOW ME THE EARNINGS!

The emergence of new-economy businesses on the Internet has led to the development of new measures of performance. When Priceline.com splashed on the dot-com scene, it touted steady growth in a measure called "unique offers by users" to explain its heady stock price. To draw investors to its stock, Drugstore.com focused on the number of "unique customers" at its website. After all, new businesses call for new performance measures, right?

Not necessarily. In fact, these indicators failed to show any consistent relationship between profits and website visits. Eventually, as the graphs below show, the profits never materialized, stock prices fell, and the dot-com bubble burst.

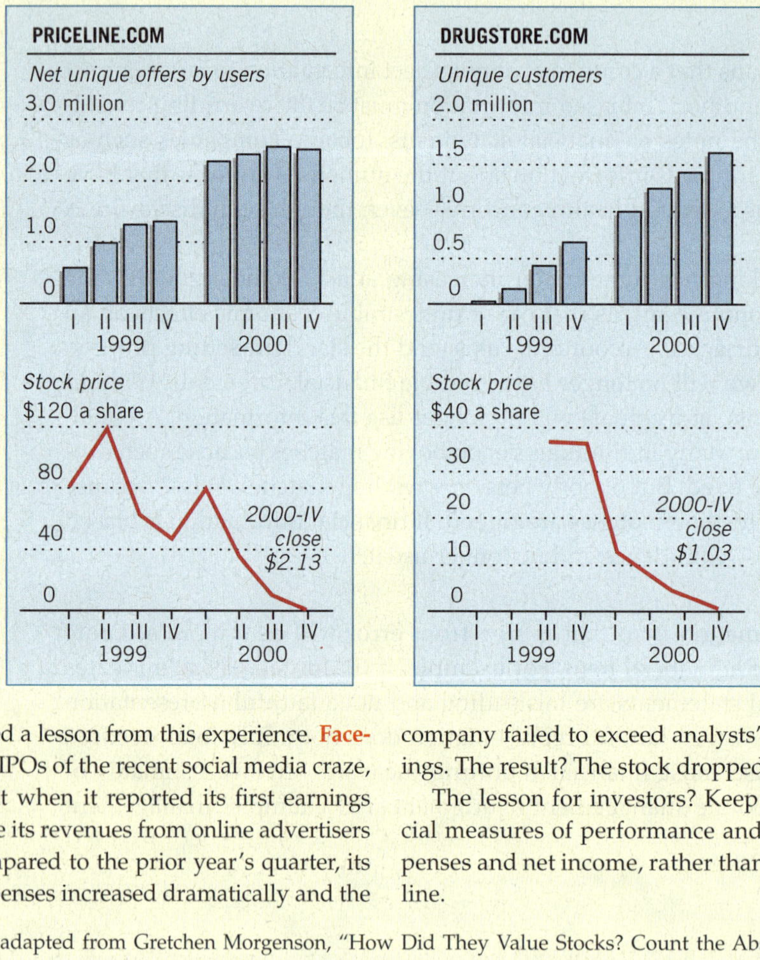

Some have not learned a lesson from this experience. Facebook, one of the hottest IPOs of the recent social media craze, gave investors a big jolt when it reported its first earnings after going public. While its revenues from online advertisers were up 32 percent compared to the prior year's quarter, its marketing and sales expenses increased dramatically and the company failed to exceed analysts' expectations for its earnings. The result? The stock dropped to an all-time low.

The lesson for investors? Keep an eye on reliable financial measures of performance and be sure to count the expenses and net income, rather than focusing on only the top line.

Sources: Story and graphs adapted from Gretchen Morgenson, "How Did They Value Stocks? Count the Absurd Ways," *New York Times* (March 18, 2001), section 3, p. 1; and B. Stone, "Facebook Bellyflops Into Its First Earnings Report," *www.businessweek.com* (July 26, 2012).

Enhancing Qualities

Enhancing qualitative characteristics are complementary to the fundamental qualitative characteristics. These characteristics distinguish more-useful information from less-useful information. Enhancing characteristics, shown below, are comparability, verifiability, timeliness, and understandability.

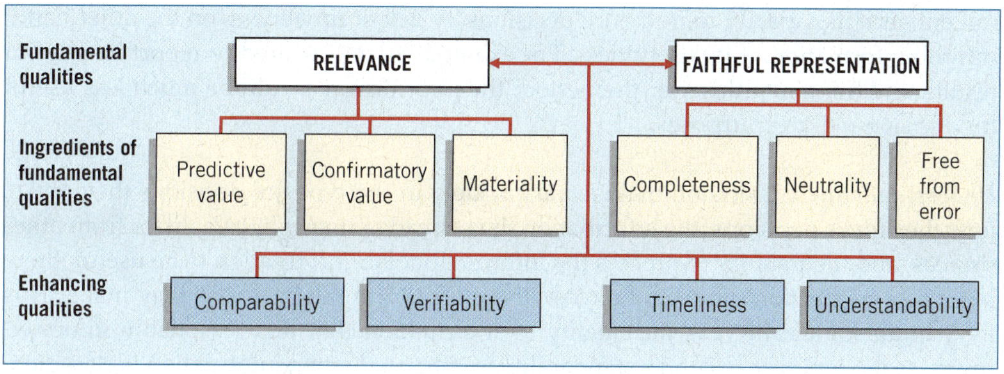

Comparability. Information that is measured and reported in a similar manner for different companies is considered comparable. **Comparability** enables users to identify the real similarities and differences in economic events between companies. For example, historically the accounting for pensions in Japan differed from that in the United States. In Japan, companies generally recorded little or no charge to income for these costs. U.S. companies recorded pension cost as incurred. As a result, it is difficult to compare and evaluate the financial results of **Toyota** or **Honda** to **General Motors** or **Ford**. Investors can only make valid evaluations if comparable information is available.

Another type of comparability, **consistency**, is present when a company applies the same accounting treatment to similar events, from period to period. Through such application, the company shows consistent use of accounting standards. The idea of consistency does not mean, however, that companies cannot switch from one accounting method to another. A company can change methods, but it must first demonstrate that the newly adopted method is preferable to the old. If approved, the company must then disclose the nature and effect of the accounting change, as well as the justification for it, in the financial statements for the period in which it made the change.[9] When a change in accounting principles occurs, the auditor generally refers to it in an explanatory paragraph of the audit report. This paragraph identifies the nature of the change and refers the reader to the note in the financial statements that discusses the change in detail.[10]

Verifiability. **Verifiability** occurs when independent measurers, using the same methods, obtain similar results. Verifiability occurs in the following situations.

1. Two independent auditors count **PepsiCo**'s inventory and arrive at the same physical quantity amount for inventory. Verification of an amount for an asset therefore can occur by simply counting the inventory (referred to as *direct verification*).
2. Two independent auditors compute PepsiCo's inventory value at the end of the year using the FIFO method of inventory valuation. Verification may occur by checking the inputs (quantity and costs) and recalculating the outputs (ending inventory value) using the same accounting convention or methodology (referred to as *indirect verification*).

Timeliness. **Timeliness** means having information available to decision-makers before it loses its capacity to influence decisions. Having relevant information available sooner

[9]Surveys indicate that users highly value consistency. They note that a change tends to destroy the comparability of data before and after the change. Some companies assist users to understand the pre- and post-change data. Generally, however, users say they lose the ability to analyze over time. GAAP guidelines (discussed in Chapter 22) on accounting changes are designed to improve the comparability of the data before and after the change.

[10]These provisions are specified in "Reports on Audited Financial Statements," *Statement on Auditing Standards No. 58* (New York: AICPA, April 1988), par. 34.

can enhance its capacity to influence decisions. A lack of timeliness, on the other hand, can rob information of its usefulness. For example, if **Dell** waited to report its interim results until nine months after the period, the information would be much less useful for decision-making purposes.

Understandability. Decision-makers vary widely in the types of decisions they make, how they make decisions, the information they already possess or can obtain from other sources, and their ability to process the information. For information to be useful, there must be a connection (linkage) between these users and the decisions they make. This link, **understandability**, is the quality of information that lets reasonably informed users see its significance. Understandability is enhanced when information is classified, characterized, and presented clearly and concisely.

For example, assume that **Google** issues a three-months' report that shows interim earnings have declined significantly. This interim report provides relevant and faithfully represented information for decision-making purposes. Some users, upon reading the report, decide to sell their shares. Other users, however, do not understand the report's content and significance. They are surprised when Google declares a smaller year-end dividend and the share price declines. Thus, although Google presented highly relevant information that was a faithful representation, it was useless to those who did not understand it.

Thus, users of financial reports are assumed to have a reasonable knowledge of business and economic activities. In making decisions, users also should review and analyze the information with reasonable diligence. Information that is relevant and faithfully represented should not be excluded from financial reports solely because it is too complex or difficult for some users to understand without assistance.[11]

Basic Elements

LEARNING OBJECTIVE 5

Define the basic elements of financial statements.

An important aspect of developing any theoretical structure is the body of **basic elements** or definitions to be included in it. Accounting uses many terms with distinctive and specific meanings. These terms constitute the language of business or the jargon of accounting.

One such term is **asset**. Is it merely something we own? Or is an asset something we have the right to use, as in the case of leased equipment? Or is it anything of value used by a company to generate revenues—in which case, should we also consider the managers of a company as an asset?

As this example and the lottery ticket example in the opening story illustrate, it therefore seems necessary to develop basic definitions for the elements of financial statements. *SFAC No. 6* defines the 10 interrelated elements that most directly relate to measuring the performance and financial status of a business enterprise. We list them on the next page for review and information purposes; you need not memorize these definitions at this point. We will explain and examine each of these elements in more detail in subsequent chapters.

The FASB classifies the elements into two distinct groups. The first group of three elements—assets, liabilities, and equity—describes amounts of resources and claims to resources at a **moment in time**. The other seven elements describe transactions, events, and circumstances that affect a company during a **period of time**. The first class, affected by elements of the second class, provides at any time the cumulative result of all changes. This interaction is referred to as "articulation." That is, key figures in one financial statement correspond to balances in another.

[11]"Chapter 3, Qualitative Characteristics of Useful Financial Information," *Statement of Financial Accounting Concepts No. 8* (Norwalk, Conn.: FASB, September 2010), paras. QC30–QC31.

ELEMENTS OF FINANCIAL STATEMENTS

ASSETS. Probable future economic benefits obtained or controlled by a particular entity as a result of past transactions or events.

LIABILITIES. Probable future sacrifices of economic benefits arising from present obligations of a particular entity to transfer assets or provide services to other entities in the future as a result of past transactions or events.

EQUITY. Residual interest in the assets of an entity that remains after deducting its liabilities. In a business enterprise, the equity is the ownership interest.

INVESTMENTS BY OWNERS. Increases in net assets of a particular enterprise resulting from transfers to it from other entities of something of value to obtain or increase ownership interests (or equity) in it. Assets are most commonly received as investments by owners, but that which is received may also include services or satisfaction or conversion of liabilities of the enterprise.

DISTRIBUTIONS TO OWNERS. Decreases in net assets of a particular enterprise resulting from transferring assets, rendering services, or incurring liabilities by the enterprise to owners. Distributions to owners decrease ownership interests (or equity) in an enterprise.

COMPREHENSIVE INCOME. Change in equity (net assets) of an entity during a period from transactions and other events and circumstances from nonowner sources. It includes all changes in equity during a period except those resulting from investments by owners and distributions to owners.

REVENUES. Inflows or other enhancements of assets of an entity or settlement of its liabilities (or a combination of both) during a period from delivering or producing goods, rendering services, or other activities that constitute the entity's ongoing major or central operations.

EXPENSES. Outflows or other using up of assets or incurrences of liabilities (or a combination of both) during a period from delivering or producing goods, rendering services, or carrying out other activities that constitute the entity's ongoing major or central operations.

GAINS. Increases in equity (net assets) from peripheral or incidental transactions of an entity and from all other transactions and other events and circumstances affecting the entity during a period except those that result from revenues or investments by owners.

LOSSES. Decreases in equity (net assets) from peripheral or incidental transactions of an entity and from all other transactions and other events and circumstances affecting the entity during a period except those that result from expenses or distributions to owners.[12]

THIRD LEVEL: RECOGNITION AND MEASUREMENT CONCEPTS

6 LEARNING OBJECTIVE
Describe the basic assumptions of accounting.

The third level of the framework consists of concepts that implement the basic objective of level one. These concepts explain how companies should recognize, measure, and report financial elements and events. The FASB sets forth most of these in its *Statement of Financial Accounting Concepts No. 5,* "Recognition and Measurement in Financial Statements of Business Enterprises." According to *SFAC No. 5,* to be recognized, an item (event or transaction) must meet the definition of an "element of

[12]"Elements of Financial Statements," *Statement of Financial Accounting Concepts No. 6* (Stamford, Conn.: FASB, December 1985), pp. ix and x.

financial statements" as defined in *SFAC No. 6* and must be measurable. Most aspects of current practice follow these recognition and measurement concepts.

The accounting profession continues to use the concepts in *SFAC No. 5* as operational guidelines. Here, we identify the concepts as basic assumptions, principles, and a cost constraint. Not everyone uses this classification system, so focus your attention more on **understanding the concepts** than on how we classify and organize them. These concepts serve as guidelines in responding to controversial financial reporting issues.

Basic Assumptions

Four basic **assumptions** underlie the financial accounting structure: (1) **economic entity**, (2) **going concern**, (3) **monetary unit**, and (4) **periodicity**. We'll look at each in turn.

International Perspective

Phase D of the conceptual framework convergence project addresses the reporting entity.

Economic Entity Assumption

The **economic entity assumption** **means that economic activity can be identified with a particular unit of accountability**. In other words, a company keeps its activity separate and distinct from its owners and any other business unit.[13] At the most basic level, the economic entity assumption dictates that **Panera Bread Company** record the company's financial activities separate from those of its owners and managers. Equally important, financial statement users need to be able to distinguish the activities and elements of different companies, such as **General Motors**, **Ford**, and **Chrysler**. If users could not distinguish the activities of different companies, how would they know which company financially outperformed the other?

The entity concept does not apply solely to the segregation of activities among competing companies, such as **Home Depot** and **Lowe's**. An individual, department, division, or an entire industry could be considered a separate entity if we choose to define it in this manner. Thus, **the entity concept does not necessarily refer to a legal entity**. A parent and its subsidiaries are separate **legal** entities, but merging their activities for accounting and reporting purposes does not violate the **economic entity** assumption.[14]

What do the numbers mean? WHOSE COMPANY IS IT?

The importance of the entity assumption is illustrated by scandals involving **W. R. Grace** and, more recently, **Adelphia**. In both cases, senior company employees entered into transactions that blurred the line between the employee's financial interests and those of the company. At Adelphia, among many other self-dealings, the company guaranteed over $2 billion of loans to the founding family. W. R. Grace used company funds to pay for an apartment and chef for the company chairman. As a result of these transactions, these insiders benefitted at the expense of shareholders. Additionally, the financial statements failed to disclose the transactions. Such disclosure would have allowed shareholders to sort out the impact of the employee transactions on company results.

[13]Recently, the FASB has proposed to link the definition of an entity to its financial reporting objective. That is, a reporting entity is described as a circumscribed area of business activity of interest to present and potential equity investors, lenders, and other capital providers. See IASB/FASB, "The Reporting Entity," *Exposure Draft ED/2010/2: Conceptual Framework for Financial Reporting* (March 2010).

[14]The concept of the entity is changing. For example, defining the "outer edges" of companies is now harder. Public companies often consist of multiple public subsidiaries, each with joint ventures, licensing arrangements, and other affiliations. Increasingly, companies form and dissolve joint ventures or customer-supplier relationships in a matter of months or weeks. These "virtual companies" raise accounting issues about how to account for the entity. As discussed in footnote 13, the FASB (and IASB) is addressing these issues in the entity phase of its conceptual framework project.

Going Concern Assumption

Most accounting methods rely on the going concern assumption—**that the company will have a long life**. Despite numerous business failures, most companies have a fairly high continuance rate. As a rule, we expect companies to last long enough to fulfill their objectives and commitments.

This assumption has significant implications. The historical cost principle would be of limited usefulness if we assume eventual liquidation. Under a liquidation approach, for example, a company would better state asset values at net realizable value (sales price less costs of disposal) than at acquisition cost. **Depreciation and amortization policies are justifiable and appropriate only if we assume some permanence to the company.** If a company adopts the liquidation approach, the current/noncurrent classification of assets and liabilities loses much of its significance. Labeling anything a fixed or long-term asset would be difficult to justify. Indeed, listing liabilities on the basis of priority in liquidation would be more reasonable.

The going concern assumption applies in most business situations. **Only where liquidation appears imminent is the assumption inapplicable.** In these cases, a total revaluation of assets and liabilities can provide information that closely approximates the company's net realizable value. You will learn more about accounting problems related to a company in liquidation in advanced accounting courses.[15]

Monetary Unit Assumption

The monetary unit assumption means that money is the common denominator of economic activity and provides an appropriate basis for accounting measurement and analysis. That is, the monetary unit is the most effective means of expressing to interested parties changes in capital and exchanges of goods and services. **The monetary unit is relevant, simple, universally available, understandable, and useful.** Application of this assumption depends on the even more basic assumption that quantitative data are useful in communicating economic information and in making rational economic decisions.

In the United States, accounting ignores price-level changes (inflation and deflation) and assumes that the unit of measure—the dollar—remains reasonably stable. We therefore use the monetary unit assumption to justify adding 1984 dollars to 2014 dollars without any adjustment. The FASB in *SFAC No. 5* indicated that it expects the dollar, unadjusted for inflation or deflation, to continue to be used to measure items recognized in financial statements. Only if circumstances change dramatically (such as if the United States experiences high inflation similar to that in many South American countries) will the FASB again consider "inflation accounting."

International Perspective

Due to their experiences with persistent inflation, several South American countries produce "constant-currency" financial reports. Typically, companies in these countries use a general price-level index to adjust for the effects of inflation.

Periodicity Assumption

To measure the results of a company's activity accurately, we would need to wait until it liquidates. Decision-makers, however, cannot wait that long for such information. Users need to know a company's performance and economic status on a timely basis so that

[15] In response to minimal guidance addressing when it is appropriate to apply, or how to apply, the liquidation basis of accounting, the FASB recently issued a *Proposed Accounting Standards Update*, "Presentation of Financial Statements (Topic 205)—The Liquidation Basis of Accounting" (July 2, 2012). In brief, companies would prepare financial statements using the liquidation basis of accounting when liquidation is imminent (when either a plan for liquidation has been approved or a plan for liquidation is being imposed by other forces, such as involuntary bankruptcy). If liquidation accounting is used, financial statements should reflect relevant information about a company's resources and obligations in liquidation by measuring and presenting assets and liabilities at the amount of cash or other consideration that the company expects to collect or pay in liquidation, along with disclosures about the plan for liquidation, the methods and significant assumptions used to measure assets and liabilities, the type and amount of costs and income accrued, and the expected duration of liquidation.

they can evaluate and compare firms, and take appropriate actions. Therefore, companies must report information periodically.

The **periodicity** (or **time period**) **assumption** implies that a company can divide its economic activities into artificial time periods. These time periods vary, but the most common are monthly, quarterly, and yearly.

The shorter the time period, the more difficult it is to determine the proper net income for the period. A month's results usually prove less verifiable than a quarter's results, and a quarter's results are likely to be less verifiable than a year's results. Investors desire and demand that a company quickly process and disseminate information. Yet the quicker a company releases the information, the more likely the information will include errors. **This phenomenon provides an interesting example of the trade-off between timeliness and accuracy (free from error) in preparing financial data.**

The problem of defining the time period becomes more serious as product cycles shorten and products become obsolete more quickly. Many believe that, given technology advances, companies need to provide more online, real-time financial information to ensure the availability of relevant information.

Basic Principles of Accounting

LEARNING OBJECTIVE 7
Explain the application of the basic principles of accounting.

We generally use four basic **principles of accounting** to record and report transactions: (1) measurement, (2) revenue recognition, (3) expense recognition, and (4) full disclosure. We look at each in turn.

Measurement Principle

We presently have a "mixed-attribute" system that permits the use of various measurement bases. The most commonly used measurements are based on historical cost and fair value. Here, we discuss each.

Historical Cost. GAAP requires that companies account for and report many assets and liabilities on the basis of acquisition price. This is often referred to as the **historical cost principle**. Historical cost has an important advantage over other valuations: **It is generally thought to be verifiable.**

Gateway to the Profession
Expanded Discussion of Accounting and Changing Prices

To illustrate this advantage, consider the problems if companies select current selling price instead. Companies might have difficulty establishing a value for unsold items. Every member of the accounting department might value the assets differently. Further, how often would it be necessary to establish sales value? All companies close their accounts at least annually. But some compute their net income every month. Those companies would have to place a sales value on every asset each time they wished to determine income. Critics raise similar objections against current cost (replacement cost, present value of future cash flows) and any other basis of valuation **except historical cost**.

What about liabilities? Do companies account for them on a cost basis? Yes, they do. Companies issue liabilities, such as bonds, notes, and accounts payable, in exchange for assets (or services), for an agreed-upon price. **This price, established by the exchange transaction, is the "cost" of the liability.** A company uses this amount to record the liability in the accounts and report it in financial statements. Thus, many users prefer historical cost because it provides them with a **verifiable benchmark** for measuring historical trends.

See the FASB Codification section (page 65).

Fair Value. **Fair value** is defined as "the price that would be received to sell an asset or paid to transfer a liability in an orderly transaction between market participants at the measurement date." Fair value is therefore a market-based measure. **[1]** Recently, GAAP has increasingly called for use of fair value measurements in the financial statements. This is often referred to as the **fair value principle**. Fair value information may be more useful than historical cost for certain types of assets and liabilities and in certain industries. For example, companies report many financial instruments, including derivatives, at fair value. Certain industries, such as brokerage houses and mutual funds, prepare their basic financial statements on a fair value basis.

At initial acquisition, historical cost equals fair value. In subsequent periods, as market and economic conditions change, historical cost and fair value often diverge. Thus, fair value measures or estimates often provide more relevant information about the expected future cash flows related to the asset or liability. For example, when long-lived assets decline in value, a fair value measure determines any impairment loss. The FASB believes that fair value information is more relevant to users than historical cost. Fair value measurement, it is argued, provides better insight into the value of a company's assets and liabilities (its financial position) and a better basis for assessing future cash flow prospects.

Recently the Board has taken the additional step of giving companies the option to use fair value (referred to as the **fair value option**) as the basis for measurement of financial assets and financial liabilities. **[2]** The Board considers fair value more relevant than historical cost because it reflects the current cash equivalent value of financial instruments. As a result companies now have the option to record fair value in their accounts for most financial instruments, including such items as receivables, investments, and debt securities.

Use of fair value in financial reporting is increasing. However, measurement based on fair value introduces increased subjectivity into accounting reports when fair value information is not readily available. To increase consistency and comparability in fair value measures, the FASB established a fair value hierarchy that provides insight into the priority of valuation techniques to use to determine fair value. As shown in Illustration 2-4, the fair value hierarchy is divided into three broad levels.

ILLUSTRATION 2-4
Fair Value Hierarchy

Level 1: Observable inputs that reflect quoted prices for identical assets or liabilities in active markets.	Least Subjective
Level 2: Inputs other than quoted prices included in Level 1 that are observable for the asset or liability either directly or through corroboration with observable data.	↓
Level 3: Unobservable inputs (for example, a company's own data or assumptions).	Most Subjective

As Illustration 2-4 indicates, Level 1 is the least subjective because it is based on quoted prices, like a closing stock price in the *Wall Street Journal*. Level 2 is more subjective and would rely on evaluating similar assets or liabilities in active markets. At the most subjective level, Level 3, much judgment is needed, based on the best information available, to arrive at a relevant and representationally faithful fair value measurement.[16]

[16]For major groups of assets and liabilities, companies must disclose (1) the fair value measurement and (2) the fair value hierarchy level of the measurements as a whole, classified by Level 1, 2, or 3. Given the judgment involved, it follows that the more a company depends on Level 3 to determine fair values, the more information about the valuation process the company will need to disclose. Thus, additional disclosures are required for Level 3 measurements; we discuss these disclosures in more detail in subsequent chapters.

Recently, the FASB issued additional guidance related to issues surrounding the use of fair value in financial statements (Accounting Standards Update 2011–04, *Amendments to Achieve Common Fair Value Measurement and Disclosure Requirements in U.S. GAAP and IFRS*). A major benefit of the guidance is to provide a better definitional structure of what is meant by fair value and an improved understanding of how fair value should be measured.

It is easy to arrive at fair values when markets are liquid with many traders, but fair value answers are not readily available in other situations. For example, how do you value the mortgage assets of a subprime lender such as **New Century** given that the market for these securities has essentially disappeared? A great deal of expertise and sound judgment will be needed to arrive at appropriate answers. GAAP also provides guidance on estimating fair values when market-related data is not available. In general, these valuation issues relate to Level 3 fair value measurements. These measurements may be developed using expected cash flow and present value techniques, as described in *Statement of Financial Accounting Concepts No. 7*, "Using Cash Flow Information and Present Value in Accounting," discussed in Chapter 6.

As indicated above, we presently have a "mixed-attribute" system that permits the use of historical cost and fair value. Although the historical cost principle continues to be an important basis for valuation, recording and reporting of fair value information is increasing. The recent measurement and disclosure guidance should increase consistency and comparability when fair value measurements are used in the financial statements and related notes.

Revenue Recognition Principle

When a company agrees to perform a service or sell a product to a customer, it has a **performance obligation**. When the company satisfies this performance obligation, it recognizes revenue. The **revenue recognition principle** therefore requires that companies recognize revenue in the accounting period in which the performance obligation is satisfied. To illustrate, assume that **Klinke Cleaners** cleans clothing on June 30 but customers do not claim and pay for their clothes until the first week of July. Klinke should record revenue in June when it performed the service (satisfied the performance obligation) rather than in July when it received the cash. At June 30, Klinke would report a receivable on its balance sheet and revenue in its income statement for the service performed.

To illustrate the revenue recognition principle in more detail, assume that **Boeing Corporation** signs a contract to sell airplanes to **Delta Air Lines** for $100 million. To determine when to recognize revenue, Boeing uses the five steps shown in Illustration 2-5.

Many revenue transactions pose few problems because the transaction is initiated and completed at the same time. However, when to recognize revenue in other certain situations is often more difficult. The risk of errors and misstatements is significant. Chapter 18 discusses revenue recognition issues in more detail.[17]

Expense Recognition Principle

As indicated in the discussion of financial statement elements, expenses are defined as outflows or other "using up" of assets or incurring of liabilities (or a combination of both) during a period as a result of delivering or producing goods and/or performing services. It follows then that recognition of expenses is related to net changes in assets and earning revenues. In practice, the approach for recognizing expenses is, "Let the expense follow the revenues." This approach is the **expense recognition principle**.

To illustrate, companies recognize expenses not when they pay wages or make a product, but when the work (service) or the product actually contributes to revenue. Thus, companies tie expense recognition to revenue recognition. That is, by matching **efforts (expenses) with accomplishment (revenues), the expense recognition principle**

[17]The framework illustrated here is based on that proposed by the FASB and IASB in their joint project on revenue. See "Revenue from Contracts with Customers," *Proposed Accounting Standards Update (Revised)* (Norwalk, Conn.: FASB, November 14, 2011, and January 4, 2012). The Boards hope to issue a converged standard in early 2013. Application of this new framework to many revenue arrangements results in similar revenue recognition outcomes compared to the current framework (based on earned and realized criteria). However, a new, more general model was needed to respond to the growth of revenue arrangements for which the prior model did not address.

is implemented in accordance with the definition of expense (outflows or other using up of assets or incurring of liabilities).[18]

ILLUSTRATION 2-5
The Five Steps of Revenue Recognition

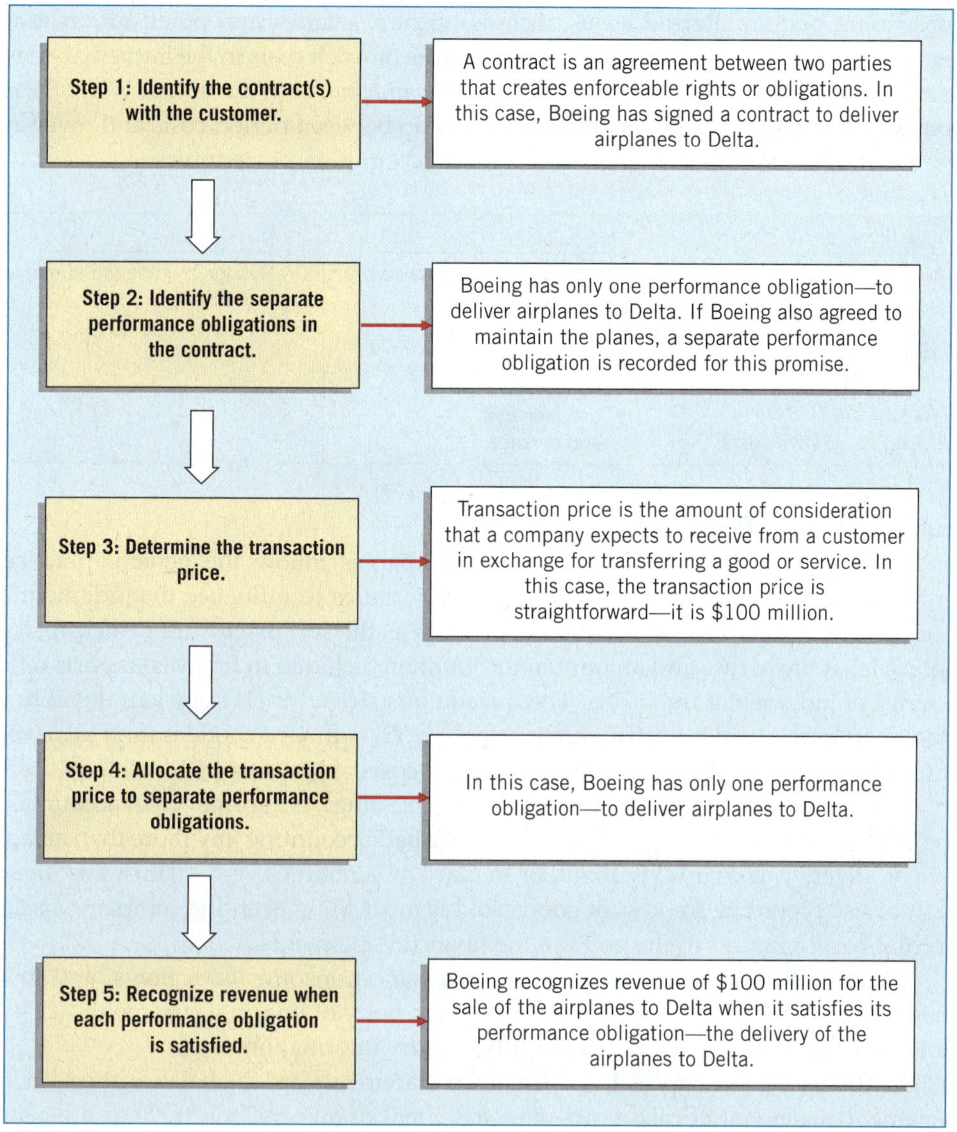

Some costs, however, are difficult to associate with revenue. As a result, some other approach must be developed. Often, companies use a "rational and systematic" allocation policy that will approximate the expense recognition principle. This type of expense recognition involves assumptions about the benefits that a company receives as well as the cost associated with those benefits. For example, a company like **Intel** or **Motorola** allocates the cost of a long-lived asset over all of the accounting periods during which it uses the asset because the asset contributes to the generation of revenue throughout its useful life.

Companies charge some costs to the current period as expenses (or losses) simply because they cannot determine a connection with revenue. Examples of these types of costs are officers' salaries and other administrative expenses.

[18]This approach is commonly referred to as the **matching principle**. However, there is much debate about the conceptual validity of the matching principle. A major concern is that matching permits companies to defer certain costs and treat them as assets on the balance sheet. In fact, these costs may not have future benefits. If abused, this principle permits the balance sheet to become a "dumping ground" for unmatched costs.

Costs are generally classified into two groups: **product costs** and **period costs**. **Product costs**, such as material, labor, and overhead, attach to the product. Companies carry these costs into future periods if they recognize the revenue from the product in subsequent periods. **Period costs**, such as officers' salaries and other administrative expenses, attach to the period. Companies charge off such costs in the immediate period even though benefits associated with these costs may occur in the future. Why? Because companies cannot determine a direct relationship between period costs and revenue.

Illustration 2-6 summarizes these expense recognition procedures.

ILLUSTRATION 2-6
Expense Recognition

Type of Cost	Relationship	Recognition
Product costs: • Material • Labor • Overhead	Direct relationship between cost and revenue.	Recognize in period of revenue (matching).
Period costs: • Salaries • Administrative costs	No direct relationship between cost and revenue.	Expense as incurred.

Full Disclosure Principle

In deciding what information to report, companies follow the general practice of providing information that is of sufficient importance to influence the judgment and decisions of an informed user. Often referred to as the **full disclosure principle**, it recognizes that the nature and amount of information included in financial reports reflects a series of judgmental trade-offs. These trade-offs strive for (1) sufficient detail to disclose matters that **make a difference** to users, yet (2) sufficient condensation to make the **information understandable**, keeping in mind costs of preparing and using it.

Disclosure is not a substitute for proper accounting. As a former chief accountant of the SEC noted, "Good disclosure does not cure bad accounting any more than an adjective or adverb can be used without, or in place of, a noun or verb." Thus, for example, cash-basis accounting for cost of goods sold is misleading even if a company discloses accrual-basis amounts in the notes to the financial statements.

Users find information about financial position, income, cash flows, and investments in one of three places: (1) within the main body of financial statements, (2) in the notes to those statements, or (3) as supplementary information.

As discussed in Chapter 1, the **financial statements** are the balance sheet, income statement, statement of cash flows, and statement of owners' equity. They are a structured means of communicating financial information. To be recognized in the main body of financial statements, **an item should meet the definition of a basic element, be measurable with sufficient certainty, and be relevant and reliable.**[19]

The **notes to financial statements** generally amplify or explain the items presented in the main body of the statements. If the main body of the financial statements gives an incomplete picture of the performance and position of the company, the notes should provide the additional information needed. Information in the notes does not have to be quantifiable, nor does it need to qualify as an element. Notes can be partially or totally narrative. Examples of notes include descriptions of the accounting policies and methods used in measuring the elements reported in the statements, explanations of uncertainties and contingencies, and statistics and details too voluminous for inclusion in the statements. The notes can be essential to understanding the company's performance and position.

Supplementary information may include details or amounts that present a different perspective from that adopted in the financial statements. It may be quantifiable information that is high in relevance but low in faithful representation. For example, oil

[19]*SFAC No. 5*, par. 63.

and gas companies typically provide information on proven reserves as well as the related discounted cash flows.

Supplementary information may also include management's explanation of the financial information and its discussion of the significance of that information. For example, many business combinations have produced financing arrangements that demand new accounting and reporting practices and principles. In each of these situations, the same problem must be faced: making sure the company presents enough information to ensure that the **reasonably prudent investor** will not be misled.

We discuss the content, arrangement, and display of financial statements, along with other facets of full disclosure, in Chapters 4, 5, and 24.[20]

What do the numbers mean? YOU MAY NEED A MAP

Beyond touting nonfinancial measures to investors (see the "What Do the Numbers Mean?" box on page 50), many companies increasingly promote the performance of their companies through the reporting of various "pro forma" earnings measures. A recent survey of newswire reports found 36 instances of the reporting of pro forma measures in just a three-day period.

Pro forma measures are standard measures (such as earnings) that companies adjust, usually for one-time or nonrecurring items. For example, companies usually adjust earnings for the effects of an extraordinary item. Such adjustments make the numbers more comparable to numbers reported in periods without the unusual item.

However, rather than increasing comparability, it appears that some companies use pro forma reporting to accentuate the positive in their results. Examples include **Yahoo!** and **Cisco**, which define pro forma income after adding back payroll tax expense. **Level 8 Systems** transformed an operating loss into a pro forma profit by adding back expenses for depreciation and amortization of intangible assets.

Lynn Turner, former chief accountant at the SEC, calls such earnings measures EBS—"Everything but Bad Stuff." To provide investors a more complete picture of company profitability, not the story preferred by management, the SEC issued Regulation G (REG G). REG G requires companies to reconcile non-GAAP financial measures to GAAP, thereby giving investors a roadmap to analyze adjustments companies make to their GAAP numbers to arrive at pro forma results.

Sources: Adapted from Gretchen Morgenson, "How Did They Value Stocks? Count the Absurd Ways," *New York Times* (March 18, 2001), section 3, p. 1; and Gretchen Morgenson, "Expert Advice: Focus on Profit," *New York Times* (March 18, 2001), section 3, p. 14. See also SEC Regulation G, "Conditions for Use of Non-GAAP Financial Measures," Release No. 33–8176 (March 28, 2003).

Cost Constraint

8 LEARNING OBJECTIVE
Describe the impact that the cost constraint has on reporting accounting information.

In providing information with the qualitative characteristics that make it useful, companies must consider an overriding factor that limits (constrains) the reporting. This is referred to as the **cost constraint** (the **cost-benefit relationship**). That is, companies must weigh the costs of providing the information against the benefits that can be derived from using it. Rule-making bodies and governmental agencies use cost-benefit analysis before making final their informational requirements. In order to justify requiring a particular measurement or disclosure, the benefits perceived to be derived from it must exceed the costs perceived to be associated with it.

A corporate executive made the following remark to the FASB about a proposed rule: "In all my years in the financial arena, I have never seen such an absolutely ridiculous proposal. . . . To dignify these 'actuarial' estimates by recording them as assets and liabilities would be virtually unthinkable except for the fact that the FASB has done equally stupid things in the past. . . . For God's sake, use common sense just this once."[21] Although extreme, this remark indicates the frustration expressed by members of the business community about rule-making, and whether the benefits of a given pronouncement exceed the costs.

[20]Recently, the FASB started a project on disclosure effectiveness to better communicate the information that is most important to users of financial statements. The Board hopes that a sharper focus on important information will result in a reduced volume of notes to the financial statements.

[21]"Decision-Usefulness: The Overriding Objective," *FASB Viewpoints* (October 19, 1983), p. 4.

The difficulty in cost-benefit analysis is that the costs and especially the benefits are not always evident or measurable. The costs are of several kinds: costs of collecting and processing, of disseminating, of auditing, of potential litigation, of disclosure to competitors, and of analysis and interpretation. Benefits to preparers may include greater management control and access to capital at a lower cost. Users may receive better information for allocation of resources, tax assessment, and rate regulation. As noted earlier, benefits are generally more difficult to quantify than are costs.

The implementation of the provisions of the Sarbanes-Oxley Act illustrates the challenges in assessing costs and benefits of standards. One study estimated the increased costs of complying with the new internal-control standards related to the financial reporting process to be an average of $7.8 million per company. However, the study concluded that "quantifying the benefits of improved more reliable financial reporting is not fully possible."[22]

Despite the difficulty in assessing the costs and benefits of its rules, the FASB attempts to determine that each proposed pronouncement will fill a significant need and that the costs imposed to meet the rule are justified in relation to overall benefits of

ILLUSTRATION 2-7
Conceptual Framework for Financial Reporting

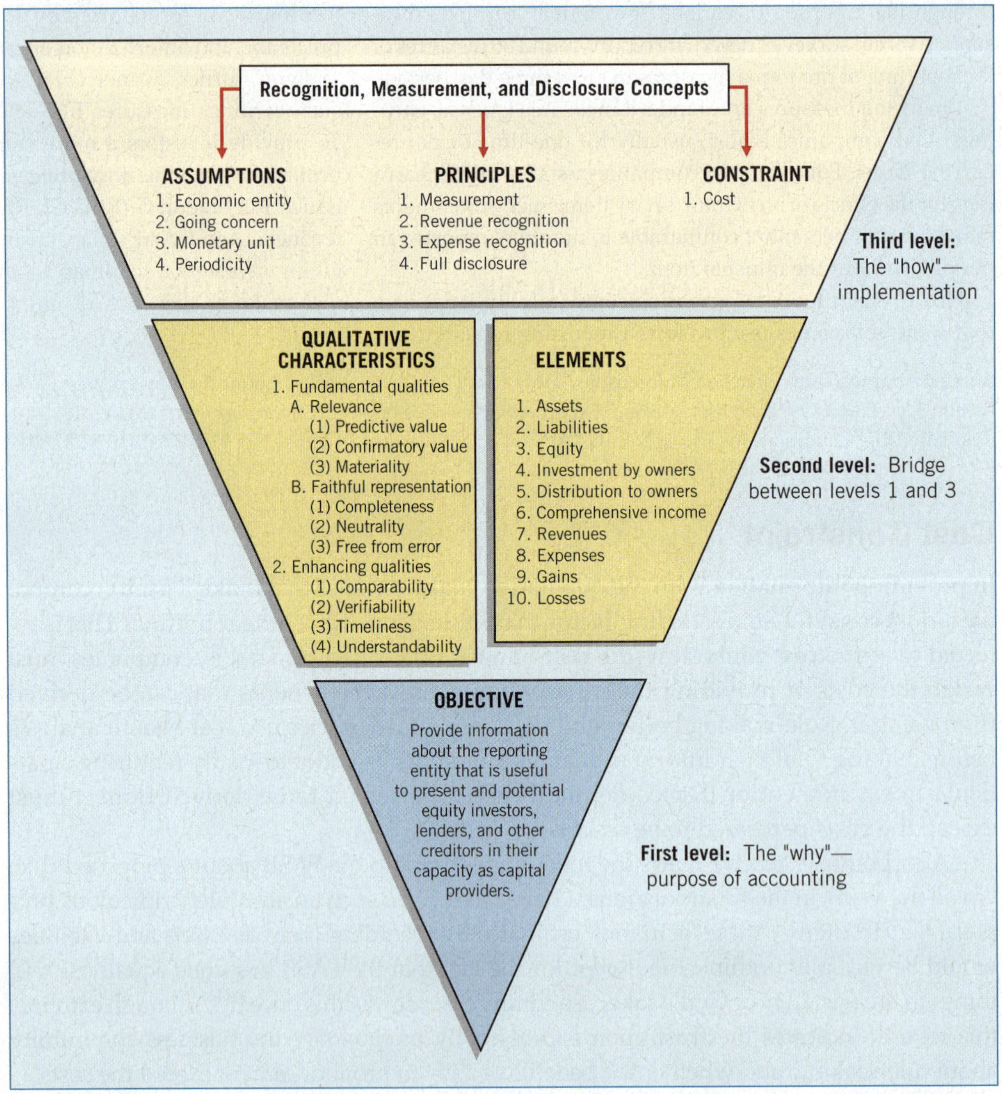

[22]Charles Rivers and Associates, "Sarbanes-Oxley Section 404: Costs and Remediation of Deficiencies," letter from Deloitte and Touche, Ernst and Young, KPMG, and Pricewaterhouse-Coopers to the SEC (April 11, 2005).

the resulting information. In addition, the Board seeks input on costs and benefits as part of its due process.[23]

Summary of the Structure

Illustration 2-7 (page 62) presents the conceptual framework discussed in this chapter. It is similar to Illustration 2-1 except that it provides additional information for each level. We cannot overemphasize the usefulness of this conceptual framework in helping to understand many of the problem areas that we examine in later chapters.

SUMMARY OF LEARNING OBJECTIVES

1 Describe the usefulness of a conceptual framework. The accounting profession needs a conceptual framework to (1) build on and relate to an established body of concepts and objectives, (2) provide a framework for solving new and emerging practical problems, (3) increase financial statement users' understanding of and confidence in financial reporting, and (4) enhance comparability among companies' financial statements.

2 Describe the FASB's efforts to construct a conceptual framework. The FASB issued seven Statements of Financial Accounting Concepts that relate to financial reporting for business enterprises. These concept statements provide the basis for the conceptual framework. They include objectives, qualitative characteristics, and elements. In addition, measurement and recognition concepts are developed. The FASB and the IASB are now working on a joint project to develop an improved common conceptual framework that provides a sound foundation for developing future accounting standards.

3 Understand the objective of financial reporting. The objective of general-purpose financial reporting is to provide financial information about the reporting entity that is **useful to present and potential equity investors, lenders, and other creditors** in making decisions about providing resources to the entity. Those decisions involve buying, selling, or holding equity and debt instruments, and providing or settling loans and other forms of credit. Information that is decision-useful to capital providers may also be helpful to other users of financial reporting who are not capital providers.

4 Identify the qualitative characteristics of accounting information. The overriding criterion by which accounting choices can be judged is decision-usefulness—that is, providing information that is most useful for decision-making. Relevance and faithful representation are the two fundamental qualities that make information decision-useful. Relevant information makes a difference in a decision by having predictive or confirmatory value and is material. Faithful representation is characterized by completeness, neutrality, and being free from error. Enhancing qualities of useful information are (1) comparability, (2) verifiability, (3) timeliness, and (4) understandability.

5 Define the basic elements of financial statements. The basic elements of financial statements are (1) assets, (2) liabilities, (3) equity, (4) investments by owners, (5) distributions to owners, (6) comprehensive income, (7) revenues, (8) expenses, (9) gains, and (10) losses. We define these 10 elements on page 53.

6 Describe the basic assumptions of accounting. Four basic assumptions underlying financial accounting are as follows. (1) *Economic entity:* The activity of a company can be kept separate and distinct from its owners and any other business unit.

[23]For example, as part of its project on "Share-Based Payment" **[3]**, the Board conducted a field study and surveyed commercial software providers to collect information on the costs of measuring the fair values of share-based compensation arrangements.

You will want to read the **IFRS INSIGHTS** on pages 78–81 for discussion of how IFRS relates to the conceptual framework.

KEY TERMS

assumption, *54*
comparability, *51*
completeness, *49*
conceptual framework, *42*
confirmatory value, *47*
conservatism, *49(n)*
consistency, *51*
cost constraint (cost-benefit relationship), *61*
economic entity assumption, *54*
elements, basic, *52*
expense recognition principle, *58*
fair value, *56*
fair value option, *57*
fair value principle, *57*
faithful representation, *49*
financial statements, *60*
free from error, *49*
full disclosure principle, *60*
general-purpose financial reporting, *45*
going concern assumption, *55*
historical cost principle, *56*
matching principle, *59(n)*
materiality, *47*
monetary unit assumption, *55*
neutrality, *49*
notes to financial statements, *60*
objective of financial reporting, *45*
period costs, *59*

(2) *Going concern:* The company will have a long life. (3) *Monetary unit:* Money is the common denominator by which economic activity is conducted, and the monetary unit provides an appropriate basis for measurement and analysis. (4) *Periodicity:* The economic activities of a company can be divided into artificial time periods.

7 Explain the application of the basic principles of accounting. (1) *Measurement principle:* GAAP permits the use of historical cost, fair value, and other valuation bases. Although the historical cost principle (measurement based on acquisition price) continues to be an important basis for valuation, recording and reporting of fair value information is increasing. (2) *Revenue recognition principle:* A company recognizes revenue when it satisfies a performance obligation. (3) *Expense recognition principle:* As a general rule, companies recognize expenses when the service or the product actually makes its contribution to revenue (commonly referred to as *matching*). (4) *Full disclosure principle:* Companies generally provide information that is of sufficient importance to influence the judgment and decisions of an informed user.

8 Describe the impact that the cost constraint has on reporting accounting information. The cost of providing the information must be weighed against the benefits that can be derived from using the information.

DEMONSTRATION PROBLEM

Jeremy Meadow Corporation has hired you to review its accounting records prior to the closing of the revenue and expense accounts as of December 31, the end of the current fiscal year. The following information comes to your attention.

1. During the current year, Jeremy Meadow Corporation changed its policy in regard to expensing purchases of small tools. In the past, it had expensed these purchases because they amounted to less than 2% of net income. Now, the president has decided that the company should follow a policy of capitalization and subsequent depreciation. It is expected that purchases of small tools will not fluctuate greatly from year to year.
2. The company constructed a warehouse at a cost of $1,000,000. It had been depreciating the asset on a straight-line basis over 10 years. In the current year, the controller doubled depreciation expense because the replacement cost of the warehouse had increased significantly.
3. When the balance sheet was prepared, the preparer omitted detailed information as to the amount of cash on deposit in each of several banks. Only the total amount of cash under a caption "Cash in banks" was presented.
4. On July 15 of the current year, Jeremy Meadow Corporation purchased an undeveloped tract of land at a cost of $320,000. The company spent $80,000 in subdividing the land and getting it ready for sale. An appraisal of the property at the end of the year indicated that the land was now worth $500,000. Although none of the lots were sold, the company recognized revenue of $180,000, less related expenses of $80,000, for a net income on the project of $100,000.
5. For a number of years, the company used the FIFO method for inventory valuation purposes. During the current year, the president noted that all the other companies in the industry had switched to the LIFO method. The company decided not to switch to LIFO because net income would decrease $830,000.

Instructions

State whether or not you agree with the decisions made by Jeremy Meadow Corporation. Support your answers with reference, whenever possible, to the generally accepted principles, assumptions, and cost constraint applicable in the circumstances.

Solution

1. From the facts, it is difficult to determine whether to agree or disagree. Consistency, of course, is violated in this situation although its violation may not be material. Furthermore, the change of accounting policies regarding the treatment of small tools cannot be judged good or bad but would depend on the circumstances. In this case, it seems that the result will be approximately the same

whether the corporation capitalizes and expenses, or simply expenses each period, since the purchases are fairly uniform. Perhaps from a cost standpoint (expediency), it might be best to continue the present policy rather than become involved in detailed depreciation schedules, assuming that purchases remain fairly uniform. On the other hand, the president may believe there is a significant unrecorded asset that should be shown on the balance sheet. If such is the case, capitalization and subsequent depreciation would be more appropriate.

2. Disagree. At the present time, accountants do not recognize price level or current value adjustments in the accounts. Hence, it is misleading to deviate from the historical cost principle because conjecture or opinion can take place. Also, depreciation is not so much a matter of valuation as it is a means of cost allocation. Assets are not depreciated on the basis of a decline in their fair value. Rather, they are depreciated on the basis of a systematic charge of expired cost against revenues.
3. Agree. The full disclosure principle recognizes that reasonable condensation and summarization of the details of a corporation's operations and financial position are essential to readability and comprehension. Thus, in determining what is full disclosure, the accountant must decide whether omission will mislead readers of the financial statements. Generally, companies present only the total amount of cash on a balance sheet unless some special circumstance is involved (such as a possible restriction on the use of the cash). In most cases, however, the company's presentation would be considered appropriate and in accordance with the full disclosure principle.
4. Disagree. The historical cost principle indicates that companies account for assets and liabilities on the basis of cost. If sales value were selected, for example, it would be extremely difficult to establish an appraisal value for the given item without selling it. Note, too, that the revenue recognition principle provides guidance on when revenue should be recognized. Revenue should be recognized when the performance obligation is satisfied. In this case, the revenue was not recognized because the critical event, "sale of the land," had not occurred.
5. From the facts, it is difficult to determine whether to agree or disagree with the president. The president's approach is not a violation of any principle. Consistency requires that accounting entities give accountable events the same accounting treatment from period to period for a given business enterprise. It says nothing concerning consistency of accounting principles among business enterprises. From a comparability viewpoint, it might be useful to report the information on a LIFO basis. But, as indicated above, there is no requirement to do so.

FASB CODIFICATION

FASB Codification References

[1] FASB ASC 820-10. [Predecessor literature: "Fair Value Measurement," *Statement of Financial Accounting Standards No. 157* (Norwalk, Conn.: FASB, September 2006).]

[2] FASB ASC 825-10-25. [Predecessor literature: "The Fair Value Option for Financial Assets and Liabilities," *Statement of Financial Accounting Standards No. 159* (Norwalk, Conn.: FASB, 2007).]

[3] FASB ASC 718-10. [Predecessor literature: "Share-Based Payment," *Financial Accounting Standards No. 123(R)* (Norwalk, Conn.: FASB, 2004).]

Exercises

If your school has a subscription to the FASB Codification, go to *http://aaahq.org/ascLogin.cfm* to log in and prepare responses to the following. Provide Codification references for your responses.

CE2-1 Access the glossary ("Master Glossary") at the FASB Codification website to answer the following.

(a) What is the definition of fair value?
(b) What is the definition of revenue?
(c) What is the definition of comprehensive income?

CE2-2 Briefly describe how the organization of the FASB Codification corresponds to the elements of financial statements.

An additional accounting research case can be found in the Using Your Judgment section, on page 77.

Be sure to check the book's companion website for a Review and Analysis Exercise, with solution.

WileyPLUS Brief Exercises, Exercises, Problems, and many more learning and assessment tools and resources are available for practice in WileyPLUS.

QUESTIONS

1. What is a conceptual framework? Why is a conceptual framework necessary in financial accounting?

2. What is the primary objective of financial reporting?

3. What is meant by the term "qualitative characteristics of accounting information"?

4. Briefly describe the two fundamental qualities of useful accounting information.

5. How is materiality (or immateriality) related to the proper presentation of financial statements? What factors and mea-sures should be considered in assessing the materiality of a misstatement in the presentation of a financial statement?

6. What are the enhancing qualities of the qualitative characteristics? What is the role of enhancing qualities in the conceptual framework?

7. According to the FASB conceptual framework, the objective of financial reporting for business enterprises is based on the needs of the users of financial statements. Explain the level of sophistication that the Board assumes about the users of financial statements.

8. What is the distinction between comparability and consistency?

9. Why is it necessary to develop a definitional framework for the basic elements of accounting?

10. Expenses, losses, and distributions to owners are all decreases in net assets. What are the distinctions among them?

11. Revenues, gains, and investments by owners are all increases in net assets. What are the distinctions among them?

12. What are the four basic assumptions that underlie the financial accounting structure?

13. The life of a business is divided into specific time periods, usually a year, to measure results of operations for each such time period and to portray financial conditions at the end of each period.

(a) This practice is based on the accounting assumption that the life of the business consists of a series of time periods and that it is possible to measure accurately the results of operations for each period. Comment on the validity and necessity of this assumption.

(b) What has been the effect of this practice on accounting? What is its relation to the accrual system? What influence has it had on accounting entries and methodology?

14. What is the basic accounting problem created by the monetary unit assumption when there is significant inflation? What appears to be the FASB position on a stable monetary unit?

15. The chairman of the board of directors of the company for which you are chief accountant has told you that he has little use for accounting figures based on historical cost. He believes that replacement values are of far more significance to the board of directors than "out-of-date costs." Present some arguments to convince him that accounting data should still be based on historical cost.

16. What is the definition of fair value?

17. What is the fair value option? Explain how use of the fair value option reflects application of the fair value principle.

18. Briefly describe the fair value hierarchy.

19. Explain the revenue recognition principle.

20. What is a performance obligation, and how is it used to determine when revenue should be recognized?

21. What are the five steps used to determine the proper time to recognize revenue?

22. Selane Eatery operates a catering service specializing in business luncheons for large corporations. Selane requires customers to place their orders 2 weeks in advance of the scheduled events. Selane bills its customers on the tenth day of the month following the date of service and requires that payment be made within 30 days of the billing date. Conceptually, when should Selane recognize revenue related to its catering service?

23. Mogilny Company paid $135,000 for a machine. The Accumulated Depreciation—Equipment account has a balance of $46,500 at the present time. The company could sell the machine today for $150,000. The company president believes that the company has a "right to this gain." What does the president mean by this statement? Do you agree?

24. Three expense recognition methods (associating cause and effect, systematic and rational allocation, and immediate recognition) were discussed in the text under the expense recognition principle. Indicate the basic nature of each of these expense recognition methods and give two examples of each.

25. *Statement of Financial Accounting Concepts No. 5* identifies four characteristics that an item must have before it is recognized in the financial statements. What are these four characteristics?

26. Briefly describe the types of information concerning financial position, income, and cash flows that might be provided (a) within the main body of the financial statements, (b) in the notes to the financial statements, or (c) as supplementary information.

27. In January 2015, Janeway Inc. doubled the amount of its outstanding stock by selling on the market an additional 10,000 shares to finance an expansion of the business. You propose that this information be shown by a footnote on the balance sheet as of December 31, 2014. The president objects, claiming that this sale took place after December 31, 2014, and therefore should not be shown. Explain your position.

28. Describe the major constraint inherent in the presentation of accounting information.

29. What are some of the costs of providing accounting information? What are some of the benefits of accounting information? Describe the cost-benefit factors that should be considered when new accounting standards are being proposed.

30. The treasurer of Landowska Co. has heard that conservatism is a doctrine that is followed in accounting and, therefore, proposes that several policies be followed that are conservative in nature. State your opinion with respect to each of the policies listed.

(a) The company gives a 2-year warranty to its customers on all products sold. The estimated warranty costs incurred from this year's sales should be entered as an expense this year instead of an expense in the period in the future when the warranty is made good.

(b) When sales are made on account, there is always uncertainty about whether the accounts are collectible. Therefore, the treasurer recommends recording the sale when the cash is received from the customers.

(c) A personal liability lawsuit is pending against the company. The treasurer believes there is an even chance that the company will lose the suit and have to pay damages of $200,000 to $300,000. The treasurer recommends that a loss be recorded and a liability created in the amount of $300,000.

BRIEF EXERCISES

4 **BE2-1** Match the qualitative characteristics below with the following statements.

1. Relevance
2. Faithful representation
3. Predictive value
4. Confirmatory value
5. Comparability
6. Completeness
7. Neutrality
8. Timeliness

(a) Quality of information that permits users to identify similarities in and differences between two sets of economic phenomena.
(b) Having information available to users before it loses its capacity to influence decisions.
(c) Information about an economic phenomenon that has value as an input to the processes used by capital providers to form their own expectations about the future.
(d) Information that is capable of making a difference in the decisions of users in their capacity as capital providers.
(e) Absence of bias intended to attain a predetermined result or to induce a particular behavior.

4 **BE2-2** Match the qualitative characteristics below with the following statements.

1. Timeliness
2. Completeness
3. Free from error
4. Understandability
5. Faithful representation
6. Relevance
7. Neutrality
8. Confirmatory value

(a) Quality of information that assures users that information represents the economic phenomena that it purports to represent.
(b) Information about an economic phenomenon that corrects past or present expectations based on previous evaluations.
(c) The extent to which information is accurate in representing the economic substance of a transaction.
(d) Includes all the information that is necessary for a faithful representation of the economic phenomena that it purports to represent.
(e) Quality of information that allows users to comprehend its meaning.

4 **BE2-3** Discuss whether the changes described in each of the cases below require recognition in the CPA's audit report as to consistency. (Assume that the amounts are material.)

(a) The company changed its inventory method to FIFO from weighted-average, which had been used in prior years.
(b) The company disposed of one of the two subsidiaries that had been included in its consolidated statements for prior years.
(c) The estimated remaining useful life of plant property was reduced because of obsolescence.

4 **BE2-4** Identify which qualitative characteristic of accounting information is best described in each item below. (Do not use relevance and faithful representation.)

(a) The annual reports of **Best Buy Co.** are audited by certified public accountants.
(b) **Black & Decker** and **Cannondale Corporation** both use the FIFO cost flow assumption.
(c) **Starbucks Corporation** has used straight-line depreciation since it began operations.
(d) **Motorola** issues its quarterly reports immediately after each quarter ends.

4 **BE2-5** Presented below are three different transactions related to materiality. Explain whether you would classify these transactions as material.

(a) Blair Co. has reported a positive trend in earnings over the last 3 years. In the current year, it reduces its bad debt allowance to ensure another positive earnings year. The impact of this adjustment is equal to 3% of net income.
(b) Hindi Co. has an extraordinary gain of $3.1 million on the sale of plant assets and a $3.3 million loss on the sale of investments. It decides to net the gain and loss because the net effect is considered immaterial. Hindi Co.'s income for the current year was $10 million.
(c) Damon Co. expenses all capital equipment under $25,000 on the basis that it is immaterial. The company has followed this practice for a number of years.

5 **BE2-6** For each item below, indicate to which category of elements of financial statements it belongs.

(a) Retained earnings
(b) Sales
(c) Additional paid-in capital
(d) Inventory
(e) Depreciation
(f) Loss on sale of equipment
(g) Interest payable
(h) Dividends
(i) Gain on sale of investment
(j) Issuance of common stock

6 **BE2-7** Identify which basic assumption of accounting is best described in each item below.

(a) The economic activities of **FedEx Corporation** are divided into 12-month periods for the purpose of issuing annual reports.
(b) **Solectron Corporation, Inc.** does not adjust amounts in its financial statements for the effects of inflation.
(c) **Walgreen Co.** reports current and noncurrent classifications in its balance sheet.
(d) The economic activities of **General Electric** and its subsidiaries are merged for accounting and reporting purposes.

7 **BE2-8** Identify which basic principle of accounting is best described in each item below.

(a) **Norfolk Southern Corporation** reports revenue in its income statement when the performance obligation is satisfied instead of when the cash is collected.
(b) **Yahoo!** recognizes depreciation expense for a machine over the 2-year period during which that machine helps the company earn revenue.
(c) **Oracle Corporation** reports information about pending lawsuits in the notes to its financial statements.
(d) **Eastman Kodak Company** reports land on its balance sheet at the amount paid to acquire it, even though the estimated fair value is greater.

7 **BE2-9** Vande Velde Company made three investments during 2014. (1) It purchased 1,000 shares of Sastre Company, a start-up company. Vande Velde made the investment based on valuation estimates from an internally developed model. (2) It purchased 2,000 shares of **GE** stock, which trades on the NYSE. (3) It invested $10,000 in local development authority bonds. Although these bonds do not trade on an active market, their value closely tracks movements in U.S. Treasury bonds. Where will Vande Velde report these investments in the fair value hierarchy?

6 **BE2-10** If the going concern assumption is not made in accounting, discuss the differences in the amounts shown in the financial statements for the following items.

(a) Land.
(b) Unamortized bond premium.
(c) Depreciation expense on equipment.
(d) Inventory.
(e) Prepaid insurance.

6 7 **BE2-11** What accounting assumption, principle, or constraint would Target Corporation use in each of the
8 situations below?

- **(a)** Target was involved in litigation over the last year. This litigation is disclosed in the financial statements.
- **(b)** Target allocates the cost of its depreciable assets over the life it expects to receive revenue from these assets.
- **(c)** Target records the purchase of a new Dell PC at its cash equivalent price.

5 **BE2-12** Explain how you would decide whether to record each of the following expenditures as an asset or an expense. Assume all items are material.

- **(a)** Legal fees paid in connection with the purchase of land are $1,500.
- **(b)** Eduardo, Inc. paves the driveway leading to the office building at a cost of $21,000.
- **(c)** A meat market purchases a meat-grinding machine at a cost of $3,500.
- **(d)** On June 30, Monroe and Meno, medical doctors, pay 6 months' office rent to cover the month of July and the next 5 months.
- **(e)** Smith's Hardware Company pays $9,000 in wages to laborers for construction on a building to be used in the business.
- **(f)** Alvarez's Florists pays wages of $2,100 for the month an employee who serves as driver of their delivery truck.

EXERCISES

1 3 **E2-1 (Usefulness, Objective of Financial Reporting)** Indicate whether the following statements about the conceptual framework are true or false. If false, provide a brief explanation supporting your position.

- **(a)** Accounting rule-making that relies on a body of concepts will result in useful and consistent pronouncements.
- **(b)** General-purpose financial reports are most useful to company insiders in making strategic business decisions.
- **(c)** Accounting standards based on individual conceptual frameworks generally will result in consistent and comparable accounting reports.
- **(d)** Capital providers are the only users who benefit from general-purpose financial reporting.
- **(e)** Accounting reports should be developed so that users without knowledge of economics and business can become informed about the financial results of a company.
- **(f)** The objective of financial reporting is the foundation from which the other aspects of the framework logically result.

1 3 **E2-2 (Usefulness, Objective of Financial Reporting, Qualitative Characteristics)** Indicate whether the
4 following statements about the conceptual framework are true or false. If false, provide a brief explanation supporting your position.

- **(a)** The fundamental qualitative characteristics that make accounting information useful are relevance and verifiability.
- **(b)** Relevant information only has predictive value, confirmatory value, or both.
- **(c)** Information that is a faithful representation is characterized as having predictive or confirmatory value.
- **(d)** Comparability pertains only to the reporting of information in a similar manner for different companies.
- **(e)** Verifiability is solely an enhancing characteristic for faithful representation.
- **(f)** In preparing financial reports, it is assumed that users of the reports have reasonable knowledge of business and economic activities.

4 8 **E2-3 (Qualitative Characteristics)** *SFAC No. 8* identifies the qualitative characteristics that make accounting information useful. Presented below are a number of questions related to these qualitative characteristics and underlying constraint.

- **(a)** What is the quality of information that enables users to confirm or correct prior expectations?
- **(b)** Identify the pervasive constraint developed in the conceptual framework.
- **(c)** The chairman of the SEC at one time noted, "If it becomes accepted or expected that accounting principles are determined or modified in order to secure purposes other than economic measurement, we assume a grave risk that confidence in the credibility of our financial information system

will be undermined." Which qualitative characteristic of accounting information should ensure that such a situation will not occur? (Do not use faithful representation.)

(d) Muruyama Corp. switches from FIFO to average-cost to FIFO over a 2-year period. Which qualitative characteristic of accounting information is not followed?

(e) Assume that the profession permits the savings and loan industry to defer losses on investments it sells because immediate recognition of the loss may have adverse economic consequences on the industry. Which qualitative characteristic of accounting information is not followed? (Do not use relevance or faithful representation.)

(f) What are the two fundamental qualities that make accounting information useful for decision-making?

(g) Watteau Inc. does not issue its first-quarter report until after the second quarter's results are reported. Which qualitative characteristic of accounting is not followed? (Do not use relevance.)

(h) Predictive value is an ingredient of which of the two fundamental qualities that make accounting information useful for decision-making purposes?

(i) Duggan, Inc. is the only company in its industry to depreciate its plant assets on a straight-line basis. Which qualitative characteristic of accounting information may not be followed?

(j) Roddick Company has attempted to determine the replacement cost of its inventory. Three different appraisers arrive at substantially different amounts for this value. The president, nevertheless, decides to report the middle value for external reporting purposes. Which qualitative characteristic of information is lacking in these data? (Do not use relevance or faithful representation.)

4 **E2-4 (Qualitative Characteristics)** The qualitative characteristics that make accounting information useful for decision-making purposes are as follows.

Relevance	Neutrality	Verifiability
Faithful representation	Completeness	Understandability
Predictive value	Timeliness	Comparability
Confirmatory value	Materiality	Free from error

Instructions

Identify the appropriate qualitative characteristic(s) to be used given the information provided below.

(a) Qualitative characteristic being employed when companies in the same industry are using the same accounting principles.
(b) Quality of information that confirms users' earlier expectations.
(c) Imperative for providing comparisons of a company from period to period.
(d) Ignores the economic consequences of a standard or rule.
(e) Requires a high degree of consensus among individuals on a given measurement.
(f) Predictive value is an ingredient of this fundamental quality of information.
(g) Four qualitative characteristics that are related to both relevance and faithful representation.
(h) An item is not recorded because its effect on income would not change a decision.
(i) Neutrality is an ingredient of this fundamental quality of accounting information.
(j) Two fundamental qualities that make accounting information useful for decision-making purposes.
(k) Issuance of interim reports is an example of what enhancing quality of relevance?

5 **E2-5 (Elements of Financial Statements)** Ten interrelated elements that are most directly related to measuring the performance and financial status of an enterprise are provided below.

Assets	Distributions to owners	Expenses
Liabilities	Comprehensive income	Gains
Equity	Revenues	Losses
Investments by owners		

Instructions

Identify the element or elements associated with the 12 items below.

(a) Arises from peripheral or incidental transactions.
(b) Obligation to transfer resources arising from a past transaction.
(c) Increases ownership interest.
(d) Declares and pays cash dividends to owners.
(e) Increases in net assets in a period from nonowner sources.
(f) Items characterized by service potential or future economic benefit.
(g) Equals increase in assets less liabilities during the year, after adding distributions to owners and subtracting investments by owners.
(h) Arises from income statement activities that constitute the entity's ongoing major or central operations.
(i) Residual interest in the assets of the enterprise after deducting its liabilities.

(j) Increases assets during a period through sale of product.
(k) Decreases assets during the period by purchasing the company's own stock.
(l) Includes all changes in equity during the period, except those resulting from investments by owners and distributions to owners.

6 7 8 **E2-6 (Assumptions, Principles, and Constraint)** Presented below are the assumptions, principles, and constraint used in this chapter.

1. Economic entity assumption	**5.** Measurement principle (historical cost)	**7.** Expense recognition principle
2. Going concern assumption		**8.** Full disclosure principle
3. Monetary unit assumption	**6.** Measurement principle (fair value)	**9.** Cost constraint
4. Periodicity assumption		**10.** Revenue recognition principle

Instructions

Identify by number the accounting assumption, principle, or constraint that describes each situation below. Do not use a number more than once.

(a) Allocates expenses to revenues in the proper period.
(b) Indicates that fair value changes subsequent to purchase are not recorded in the accounts. (Do not use revenue recognition principle.)
(c) Ensures that all relevant financial information is reported.
(d) Rationale why plant assets are not reported at liquidation value. (Do not use historical cost principle.)
(e) Indicates that personal and business record keeping should be separately maintained.
(f) Separates financial information into time periods for reporting purposes.
(g) Assumes that the dollar is the "measuring stick" used to report on financial performance.

6 7 8 **E2-7 (Assumptions, Principles, and Constraint)** Presented below are a number of operational guidelines and practices that have developed over time.

Instructions

Select the assumption, principle, or constraint that most appropriately justifies these procedures and practices. (Do not use qualitative characteristics.)

(a) Fair value changes are not recognized in the accounting records.
(b) Financial information is presented so that investors will not be misled.
(c) Intangible assets are capitalized and amortized over periods benefited.
(d) Repair tools are expensed when purchased.
(e) Agricultural companies use fair value for purposes of valuing crops.
(f) Each enterprise is kept as a unit distinct from its owner or owners.
(g) All significant post-balance-sheet events are reported.
(h) Revenue is recorded at point of sale.
(i) All important aspects of bond indentures are presented in financial statements.
(j) Rationale for accrual accounting.
(k) The use of consolidated statements is justified.
(l) Reporting must be done at defined time intervals.
(m) An allowance for doubtful accounts is established.
(n) Goodwill is recorded only at time of purchase.
(o) A company charges its sales commission costs to expense.

7 **E2-8 (Full Disclosure Principle)** Presented below are a number of facts related to Weller, Inc. Assume that no mention of these facts was made in the financial statements and the related notes.

Instructions

Assume that you are the auditor of Weller, Inc. and that you have been asked to explain the appropriate accounting and related disclosure necessary for each of these items.

(a) The company decided that, for the sake of conciseness, only net income should be reported on the income statement. Details as to revenues, cost of goods sold, and expenses were omitted.
(b) Equipment purchases of $170,000 were partly financed during the year through the issuance of a $110,000 notes payable. The company offset the equipment against the notes payable and reported plant assets at $60,000.
(c) Weller has reported its ending inventory at $2,100,000 in the financial statements. No other information related to inventories is presented in the financial statements and related notes.
(d) The company changed its method of valuing inventories from weighted-average to FIFO. No mention of this change was made in the financial statements.

7 **E2-9 (Accounting Principles—Comprehensive)** Presented below are a number of business transactions that occurred during the current year for Gonzales, Inc.

Instructions

In each of the situations, discuss the appropriateness of the journal entries in terms of generally accepted accounting principles.

(a) The president of Gonzales, Inc. used his expense account to purchase a new Suburban solely for personal use. The following journal entry was made.

Miscellaneous Expense	29,000	
Cash		29,000

(b) Merchandise inventory that cost $620,000 is reported on the balance sheet at $690,000, the expected selling price less estimated selling costs. The following entry was made to record this increase in value.

Inventory	70,000	
Sales Revenue		70,000

(c) The company is being sued for $500,000 by a customer who claims damages for personal injury apparently caused by a defective product. Company attorneys feel extremely confident that the company will have no liability for damages resulting from the situation. Nevertheless, the company decides to make the following entry.

Loss from Lawsuit	500,000	
Liability for Lawsuit		500,000

(d) Because the general level of prices increased during the current year, Gonzales, Inc. determined that there was a $16,000 understatement of depreciation expense on its equipment and decided to record it in its accounts. The following entry was made.

Depreciation Expense	16,000	
Accumulated Depreciation—Equipment		16,000

(e) Gonzales, Inc. has been concerned about whether intangible assets could generate cash in case of liquidation. As a consequence, goodwill arising from a purchase transaction during the current year and recorded at $800,000 was written off as follows.

Retained Earnings	800,000	
Goodwill		800,000

(f) Because of a "fire sale," equipment obviously worth $200,000 was acquired at a cost of $155,000. The following entry was made.

Equipment	200,000	
Cash		155,000
Sales Revenue		45,000

7 **E2-10 (Accounting Principles—Comprehensive)** Presented below is information related to Cramer, Inc.

Instructions

Comment on the appropriateness of the accounting procedures followed by Cramer, Inc.

(a) Depreciation expense on the building for the year was $60,000. Because the building was increasing in value during the year, the controller decided to charge the depreciation expense to retained earnings instead of to net income. The following entry is recorded.

Retained Earnings	60,000	
Accumulated Depreciation—Buildings		60,000

(b) Materials were purchased on January 1, 2014, for $120,000 and this amount was entered in the Materials account. On December 31, 2014, the materials would have cost $141,000, so the following entry is made.

Inventory	21,000	
Gain on Inventories		21,000

(c) During the year, the company purchased equipment through the issuance of common stock. The stock had a par value of $135,000 and a fair value of $450,000. The fair value of the equipment was not easily determinable. The company recorded this transaction as follows.

Equipment	135,000	
Common Stock		135,000

(d) During the year, the company sold certain equipment for $285,000, recognizing a gain of $69,000. Because the controller believed that new equipment would be needed in the near future, she decided to defer the gain and amortize it over the life of any new equipment purchased.

(e) An order for $61,500 has been received from a customer for products on hand. This order was shipped on January 9, 2015. The company made the following entry in 2014.

Accounts Receivable	61,500	
Sales Revenue		61,500

EXERCISES SET B

See the book's companion website, at **www.wiley.com/college/kieso**, for an additional set of exercises.

CONCEPTS FOR ANALYSIS

CA2-1 (Conceptual Framework—General) Wayne Cooper has some questions regarding the theoretical framework in which GAAP is set. He knows that the FASB and other predecessor organizations have attempted to develop a conceptual framework for accounting theory formulation. Yet, Wayne's supervisors have indicated that these theoretical frameworks have little value in the practical sense (i.e., in the real world). Wayne did notice that accounting rules seem to be established after the fact rather than before. He thought this indicated a lack of theory structure but never really questioned the process at school because he was too busy doing the homework.

Wayne feels that some of his anxiety about accounting theory and accounting semantics could be alleviated by identifying the basic concepts and definitions accepted by the profession and considering them in light of his current work. By doing this, he hopes to develop an appropriate connection between theory and practice.

Instructions

(a) Help Wayne recognize the purpose of and benefit of a conceptual framework.

(b) Identify any Statements of Financial Accounting Concepts issued by the FASB that may be helpful to Wayne in developing his theoretical background.

CA2-2 (Conceptual Framework—General) The Financial Accounting Standards Board (FASB) has developed a conceptual framework for financial accounting and reporting. The FASB has issued eight Statements of Financial Accounting Concepts. These statements are intended to set forth the objective and fundamentals that will be the basis for developing financial accounting and reporting standards. The objective identifies the goals and purposes of financial reporting. The fundamentals are the underlying concepts of financial accounting that guide the selection of transactions, events, and circumstances to be accounted for; their recognition and measurement; and the means of summarizing and communicating them to interested parties.

The purpose of the statement on qualitative characteristics is to examine the characteristics that make accounting information useful. These characteristics or qualities of information are the ingredients that make information useful and the qualities to be sought when accounting choices are made.

Instructions

(a) Identify and discuss the benefits that can be expected to be derived from the FASB's conceptual framework study.

(b) What is the most important quality for accounting information as identified in the conceptual framework? Explain why it is the most important.

(c) *Statement of Financial Accounting Concepts No. 8* describes a number of key characteristics or qualities for accounting information. Briefly discuss the importance of any three of these qualities for financial reporting purposes.

(CMA adapted)

CA2-3 (Objective of Financial Reporting) Homer Winslow and Jane Alexander are discussing various aspects of the FASB's concepts statement on the objective of financial reporting. Homer indicates that this pronouncement provides little, if any, guidance to the practicing professional in resolving accounting controversies. He believes that the statement provides such broad guidelines that it would be impossible to apply the objective to present-day reporting problems. Jane concedes this point but indicates that the objective is still needed to provide a starting point for the FASB in helping to improve financial reporting.

Instructions

(a) Indicate the basic objective established in the conceptual framework.

(b) What do you think is the meaning of Jane's statement that the FASB needs a starting point to resolve accounting controversies?

CA2-4 (Qualitative Characteristics) Accounting information provides useful information about business transactions and events. Those who provide and use financial reports must often select and evaluate accounting alternatives. The FASB statement on qualitative characteristics of accounting information examines the characteristics of accounting information that make it useful for decision-making. It also points out that various limitations inherent in the measurement and reporting process may necessitate trade-offs or sacrifices among the characteristics of useful information.

Instructions

(a) Describe briefly the following characteristics of useful accounting information.

(1) Relevance.
(2) Faithful representation.
(3) Understandability.
(4) Comparability.
(5) Consistency.

(b) For each of the following pairs of information characteristics, give an example of a situation in which one of the characteristics may be sacrificed in return for a gain in the other.

(1) Relevance and faithful representation.
(2) Relevance and consistency.
(3) Comparability and consistency.
(4) Relevance and understandability.

(c) What criterion should be used to evaluate trade-offs between information characteristics?

CA2-5 (Revenue Recognition Principle) After the presentation of your report on the examination of the financial statements to the board of directors of Piper Publishing Company, one of the new directors expresses surprise that the income statement assumes that an equal proportion of the revenue is recognized with the publication of every issue of the company's magazine. She feels that the "crucial event" in the process of earning revenue in the magazine business is the cash sale of the subscription. She says that she does not understand why most of the revenue cannot be "recognized" in the period of the cash sale.

Instructions

Discuss the propriety of timing the recognition of revenue in Piper Publishing Company's accounts with:

(a) The cash sale of the magazine subscription.

(b) The publication of the magazine every month.

(c) Both events, by recognizing a portion of the revenue with the cash sale of the magazine subscription and a portion of the revenue with the publication of the magazine every month.

CA2-6 (Expense Recognition Principle) An accountant must be familiar with the concepts involved in determining earnings of a business entity. The amount of earnings reported for a business entity is dependent on the proper recognition, in general, of revenues and expenses for a given time period. In some situations, costs are recognized as expenses at the time of product sale. In other situations, guidelines have been developed for recognizing costs as expenses or losses by other criteria.

Instructions

(a) Explain the rationale for recognizing costs as expenses at the time of product sale.

(b) What is the rationale underlying the appropriateness of treating costs as expenses of a period instead of assigning the costs to an asset? Explain.

(c) In what general circumstances would it be appropriate to treat a cost as an asset instead of as an expense? Explain.

(d) Some expenses are assigned to specific accounting periods on the basis of systematic and rational allocation of asset cost. Explain the underlying rationale for recognizing expenses on the basis of systematic and rational allocation of asset cost.

(e) Identify the conditions under which it would be appropriate to treat a cost as a loss.

(AICPA adapted)

CA2-7 (Expense Recognition Principle) Accountants try to prepare income statements that are as accurate as possible. A basic requirement in preparing accurate income statements is to record costs and revenues properly. Proper recognition of costs and revenues requires that costs resulting from typical business operations be recognized in the period in which they expired.

Instructions

(a) List three criteria that can be used to determine whether such costs should appear as charges in the income statement for the current period.

(b) As generally presented in financial statements, the following items or procedures have been criticized as improperly recognizing costs. Briefly discuss each item from the viewpoint of matching costs with revenues and suggest corrective or alternative means of presenting the financial information.
  (1) Receiving and handling costs.
  (2) Cash discounts on purchases.

CA2-8 (Expense Recognition Principle) Daniel Barenboim sells and erects shell houses, that is, frame structures that are completely finished on the outside but are unfinished on the inside except for flooring, partition studding, and ceiling joists. Shell houses are sold chiefly to customers who are handy with tools and who have time to do the interior wiring, plumbing, wall completion and finishing, and other work necessary to make the shell houses livable dwellings.

Barenboim buys shell houses from a manufacturer in unassembled packages consisting of all lumber, roofing, doors, windows, and similar materials necessary to complete a shell house. Upon commencing operations in a new area, Barenboim buys or leases land as a site for its local warehouse, field office, and display houses. Sample display houses are erected at a total cost of $30,000 to $44,000 including the cost of the unassembled packages. The chief element of cost of the display houses is the unassembled packages, inasmuch as erection is a short, low-cost operation. Old sample models are torn down or altered into new models every 3 to 7 years. Sample display houses have little salvage value because dismantling and moving costs amount to nearly as much as the cost of an unassembled package.

Instructions

(a) A choice must be made between (1) expensing the costs of sample display houses in the periods in which the expenditure is made and (2) spreading the costs over more than one period. Discuss the advantages of each method.

(b) Would it be preferable to amortize the cost of display houses on the basis of (1) the passage of time or (2) the number of shell houses sold? Explain.

(AICPA adapted)

CA2-9 (Qualitative Characteristics) Recently, your uncle, Carlos Beltran, who knows that you always have your eye out for a profitable investment, has discussed the possibility of your purchasing some corporate bonds. He suggests that you may wish to get in on the "ground floor" of this deal. The bonds being issued by Neville Corp. are 10-year debentures which promise a 40% rate of return. Neville manufactures novelty/party items.

You have told Neville that, unless you can take a look at its financial statements, you would not feel comfortable about such an investment. Believing that this is the chance of a lifetime, Uncle Carlos has procured a copy of Neville's most recent, unaudited financial statements which are a year old. These statements were prepared by Mrs. Andy Neville. You peruse these statements, and they are quite impressive. The balance sheet showed a debt-to-equity ratio of 0.10 and, for the year shown, the company reported net income of $2,424,240.

The financial statements are not shown in comparison with amounts from other years. In addition, no significant note disclosures about inventory valuation, depreciation methods, loan agreements, etc. are available.

Instructions

Write a letter to Uncle Carlos explaining why it would be unwise to base an investment decision on the financial statements that he has provided to you. Be sure to explain why these financial statements are neither relevant nor representationally faithful.

CA2-10 (Expense Recognition Principle) Anderson Nuclear Power Plant will be "mothballed" at the end of its useful life (approximately 20 years) at great expense. The expense recognition principle requires that expenses be matched to revenue. Accountants Ana Alicia and Ed Bradley argue whether it is better to allocate the expense of mothballing over the next 20 years or ignore it until mothballing occurs.

Instructions

Answer the following questions.

(a) What stakeholders should be considered?
(b) What ethical issue, if any, underlies the dispute?
(c) What alternatives should be considered?
(d) Assess the consequences of the alternatives.
(e) What decision would you recommend?

CA2-11 (Cost Constraint) The AICPA Special Committee on Financial Reporting proposed the following constraints related to financial reporting.

1. Business reporting should exclude information outside of management's expertise or for which management is not the best source, such as information about competitors.

2. Management should not be required to report information that would significantly harm the company's competitive position.
3. Management should not be required to provide forecasted financial statements. Rather, management should provide information that helps users forecast for themselves the company's financial future.
4. Other than for financial statements, management need report only the information it knows. That is, management should be under no obligation to gather information it does not have, or does not need, to manage the business.
5. Companies should present certain elements of business reporting only if users and management agree they should be reported—a concept of flexible reporting.
6. Companies should not have to report forward-looking information unless there are effective deterrents to unwarranted litigation that discourages companies from doing so.

Instructions

For each item, briefly discuss how the proposed constraint addresses concerns about the costs and benefits of financial reporting.

USING YOUR JUDGMENT

FINANCIAL REPORTING

Financial Reporting Problem

P&G

The Procter & Gamble Company (P&G)

The financial statements of P&G are presented in Appendix 5B. The company's complete annual report, including the notes to the financial statements, can be accessed at the book's companion website, **www.wiley.com/college/kieso**.

Instructions

Refer to P&G's financial statements and the accompanying notes to answer the following questions.

(a) Using the notes to the consolidated financial statements, determine P&G's revenue recognition policies. Discuss the impact of trade promotions on P&G's financial statements.

(b) Give two examples of where historical cost information is reported in P&G's financial statements and related notes. Give two examples of the use of fair value information reported in either the financial statements or related notes.

(c) How can we determine that the accounting principles used by P&G are prepared on a basis consistent with those of last year?

(d) What is P&G's accounting policy related to advertising? What accounting principle does P&G follow regarding accounting for advertising? Where are advertising expenses reported in the financial statements?

Comparative Analysis Case

The Coca-Cola Company and PepsiCo, Inc.

Instructions

Go to the book's companion website, and use information found there to answer the following questions related to The Coca-Cola Company and PepsiCo, Inc.

(a) What are the primary lines of business of these two companies as shown in their notes to the financial statements?

(b) Which company has the dominant position in beverage sales?

(c) How are inventories for these two companies valued? What cost allocation method is used to report inventory? How does their accounting for inventories affect comparability between the two companies?

(d) Which company changed its accounting policies, which then affected the consistency of the financial results from the previous year? What were these changes?

Financial Statement Analysis Case

Wal-Mart Stores, Inc.

Wal-Mart Stores, Inc. provided the following disclosure in a recent annual report.

> *New accounting pronouncement (partial)* . . . the Securities and Exchange Commission issued Staff Accounting Bulletin No. 101—"Revenue Recognition in Financial Statements" (*SAB 101*). This SAB deals with various revenue recognition issues, several of which are common within the retail industry. As a result of the issuance of this SAB . . . the Company is currently evaluating the effects of the SAB on its method of recognizing revenues related to layaway sales and will make any accounting method changes necessary during the first quarter of [next year].

In response to *SAB 101*, Wal-Mart changed its revenue recognition policy for layaway transactions, in which Wal-Mart sets aside merchandise for customers who make partial payment. Before the change, Wal-Mart recognized all revenue on the sale at the time of the layaway. After the change, Wal-Mart does not recognize revenue until customers satisfy all payment obligations and take possession of the merchandise.

Instructions

(a) Discuss the expected effect on income (1) in the year that Wal-Mart makes the changes in its revenue recognition policy, and (2) in the years following the change.

(b) Evaluate the extent to which Wal-Mart's previous revenue policy was consistent with the revenue recognition principle.

(c) If all retailers had used a revenue recognition policy similar to Wal-Mart's before the change, are there any concerns with respect to the qualitative characteristic of comparability? Explain.

Accounting, Analysis, and Principles

William Murray achieved one of his life-long dreams by opening his own business, The Caddie Shack Driving Range, on May 1, 2014. He invested $20,000 of his own savings in the business. He paid $6,000 cash to have a small building constructed to house the operations and spent $800 on golf clubs, golf balls, and yardage signs. Murray leased 4 acres of land at a cost of $1,000 per month. (He paid the first month's rent in cash.) During the first month, advertising costs totaled $750, of which $150 was unpaid at the end of the month. Murray paid his three nephews $400 for retrieving golf balls. He deposited in the company's bank account all revenues from customers ($4,700). On May 15, Murray withdrew $800 in cash for personal use. On May 31, the company received a utility bill for $100 but did not immediately pay it. On May 31, the balance in the company bank account was $15,100.

Murray is feeling pretty good about results for the first month, but his estimate of profitability ranges from a loss of $4,900 to a profit of $1,650.

Accounting

Prepare a balance sheet at May 31, 2014. Murray appropriately records any depreciation expense on a quarterly basis. How could Murray have determined that the business operated at a profit of $1,650? How could Murray conclude that the business operated at a loss of $4,900?

Analysis

Assume Murray has asked you to become a partner in his business. Under the partnership agreement, after paying him $10,000, you would share equally in all future profits. Which of the two income measures above would be more useful in deciding whether to become a partner? Explain.

Principles

What is income according to GAAP? What concepts do the differences in the three income measures for The Caddie Shack Driving Range illustrate?

BRIDGE TO THE PROFESSION

Professional Research

Your aunt recently received the annual report for a company in which she has invested. The report notes that the statements have been prepared in accordance with "generally accepted accounting principles." She has also heard that certain terms have special meanings in accounting relative to everyday use. She would like you to explain the meaning of terms she has come across related to accounting.

Instructions

Go to *http://www.fasb.org* and access the FASB Concepts Statements and respond to the following items. (Provide paragraph citations.) When you have accessed the documents, you can use the search tool in your Internet browser.

(a) How is "materiality" defined in the conceptual framework?

(b) The concepts statements provide several examples in which specific quantitative materiality guidelines are provided to firms. Identity at least two of these examples. Do you think the materiality guidelines should be quantified? Why or why not?

(c) The concepts statements discuss the concept of "articulation" between financial statement elements. Briefly summarize the meaning of this term and how it relates to an entity's financial statements.

Additional Professional Resources

See the book's companion website, at **www.wiley.com/college/kieso**, for professional simulations as well as other study resources.

IFRS INSIGHTS

LEARNING OBJECTIVE 9
Compare the conceptual frameworks underlying GAAP and IFRS.

The IASB and the FASB are working on a joint project to develop a common conceptual framework. This framework is based on the existing conceptual frameworks underlying GAAP and IFRS. The objective of this joint project is to develop a conceptual framework that leads to standards that are principles-based and internally consistent and that leads to the most useful financial reporting.

RELEVANT FACTS

Following are the key similarities and differences between GAAP and IFRS related to the conceptual framework.

Similarities

- In 2010, the IASB and FASB completed the first phase of a jointly created conceptual framework. In this first phase, they agreed on the objective of financial reporting and a common set of desired qualitative characteristics. These were presented in the Chapter 2 discussion. Note that prior to this converged phase, the IASB Framework gave more emphasis to the objective of providing information on management's performance (stewardship).
- The existing conceptual frameworks underlying GAAP and IFRS are very similar. That is, they are organized in a similar manner (objective, elements, qualitative characteristics, etc.). There is no real need to change many aspects of the existing frameworks other than to converge different ways of discussing essentially the same concepts.
- The converged framework should be a single document, unlike the two conceptual frameworks that presently exist. It is unlikely that the basic structure related to the concepts will change.
- Both the IASB and FASB have similar measurement principles, based on historical cost and fair value. In 2011, the Boards issued a converged standard fair value measurement so that the definition of fair value, measurement techniques, and disclosures are the same between GAAP and IFRS when fair value is used in financial statements.

Differences

- Although both GAAP and IFRS are increasing the use of fair value to report assets, at this point IFRS has adopted it more broadly. As examples, under IFRS, companies can apply fair value to property, plant, and equipment; natural resources; and in some cases, intangible assets.
- GAAP has a concept statement to guide estimation of fair values when market-related data is not available (*Statement of Financial Accounting Concepts No. 7*, "Using Cash Flow Information and Present Value in Accounting"). The IASB has not issued a similar concept statement; it has issued a fair value standard *(IFRS 13)* that is converged with GAAP.
- The monetary unit assumption is part of each framework. However, the unit of measure will vary depending on the currency used in the country in which the company is incorporated (e.g., Chinese yuan, Japanese yen, and British pound). IFRS makes an explicit assumption that financial statements are prepared on an accrual basis.
- The economic entity assumption is also part of each framework, although some cultural differences result in differences in its application. For example, in Japan many companies have formed alliances that are so strong that they act similar to related corporate divisions although they are not actually part of the same company.

ABOUT THE NUMBERS

Financial Statement Elements

While the conceptual framework that underlies IFRS is very similar to that used to develop GAAP, the elements identified and their definitions under IFRS are different. The IASB elements and their definitions are as follows.

> ***Assets.*** A resource controlled by the entity as a result of past events and from which future economic benefits are expected to flow to the entity.
>
> ***Liabilities.*** A present obligation of the entity arising from past events, the settlement of which is expected to result in an outflow from the entity of resources embodying economic benefits. Liabilities may be legally enforceable via a contract or law, but need not be, i.e., they can arise due to normal business practice or customs.
>
> ***Equity.*** A residual interest in the assets of the entity after deducting all its liabilities.
>
> ***Income.*** Increases in economic benefits that result in increases in equity (other than those related to contributions from shareholders). Income includes both revenues (resulting from ordinary activities) and gains.
>
> ***Expenses.*** Decreases in economic benefits that result in decreases in equity (other than those related to distributions to shareholders). Expenses includes losses that are not the result of ordinary activities.

Conceptual Framework Work Plan

The work on the conceptual framework is being done in phases. As discussed, Phase A related to objectives and qualitative characteristics has been issued in 2010. Work on the remaining core phases—(1) a chapter on the reporting entity (Phase D), (2) a chapter related to measurement (Phase C), and (3) elements and recognition (Phase B)—are currently on hold as the focus is on completing key convergence projects on revenue, financial instruments, and leases.

ON THE HORIZON

The IASB and the FASB face a difficult task in attempting to update, modify, and complete a converged conceptual framework. There are many difficult issues. For example: How do we trade off characteristics such as highly relevant information that is difficult to verify? How do we define control when we are developing a definition of an asset? Is a liability the future sacrifice itself or the obligation to make the sacrifice? Should a single measurement method, such as historical cost or fair value, be used, or does it depend on whether it is an asset or liability that is being measured? We are optimistic that the new document will be a significant improvement over its predecessors and will lead to principles-based standards that help users of the financial statements make better decisions.

IFRS SELF-TEST QUESTIONS

1. Which of the following statements about the IASB and FASB conceptual frameworks is **not** correct?
   (a) The IASB conceptual framework does not identify the element *comprehensive income*.
   (b) The existing IASB and FASB conceptual frameworks are organized in similar ways.
   (c) The FASB and IASB agree that the objective of financial reporting is to provide useful information to investors and creditors.
   (d) IFRS does not allow use of fair value as a measurement basis.
2. Which of the following statements is **false**?
   (a) The monetary unit assumption is used under IFRS.
   (b) Under IFRS, companies may use fair value for property, plant, and equipment.
   (c) The FASB and IASB are working on a joint conceptual framework project.
   (d) Under IFRS, there are the same number of financial statement elements as in GAAP.
3. Companies that use IFRS:
   (a) must report all their assets on the statement of financial position (balance sheet) at fair value.
   (b) may report property, plant, and equipment and natural resources at fair value.
   (c) may refer to a concept statement on estimating fair values when market data are not available.
   (d) may only use historical cost as the measurement basis in financial reporting.
4. The issues that the FASB and IASB must address in developing a common conceptual framework include all of the following **except**:
   (a) should the characteristic of relevance be traded-off in favor of information that is verifiable?
   (b) should a single measurement method such as historical cost be used?
   (c) should the common framework lead to standards that are principles-based or rules-based?
   (d) should the role of financial reporting focus on internal decision-making as well as providing information to assist users in decision-making?
5. With respect to the converged FASB/IASB conceptual framework:
   (a) work is being conducted on the framework as a whole, and it will not be issued until all parts are completed.
   (b) work on the framework has a higher priority than projects on revenue and leases.
   (c) work is being conducted on the framework in phases, and completed parts will be issued as completed.
   (d) the framework will not address measurement issues.

IFRS CONCEPTS AND APPLICATION

IFRS2-1 What two assumptions are central to the IASB conceptual framework?

IFRS2-2 Do the IASB and FASB conceptual frameworks differ in terms of the role of financial reporting? Explain.

IFRS2-3 What are some of the differences in elements in the IASB and FASB conceptual frameworks?

IFRS2-4 What are some of the challenges to the FASB and IASB in developing a converged conceptual framework?

Financial Reporting Case

IFRS2-5 As discussed in Chapter 1, the **International Accounting Standards Board (IASB)** develops accounting standards for many international companies. The IASB also has developed a conceptual framework to help guide the setting of accounting standards. While the FASB and IASB have issued converged concepts statements on the objective and qualitative characteristics, other parts of their frameworks differ.

Instructions

Briefly discuss the similarities and differences between the FASB and IASB conceptual frameworks as related to elements and their definitions.

Professional Research

IFRS2-6 Your aunt recently received the annual report for a company in which she has invested. The report notes that the statements have been prepared in accordance with IFRS. She has also heard that certain terms have special meanings in accounting relative to everyday use. She would like you to explain the meaning of terms she has come across related to accounting.

Instructions

Access the IASB Framework at the IASB website (*http://eifrs.iasb.org/*). (Click on the IFRS tab and then register for free eIFRS access if necessary.) When you have accessed the documents, you can use the search tool in your Internet browser to prepare responses to the following items. (Provide paragraph citations.)

(a) How is "materiality" defined in the framework?
(b) Briefly discuss how materiality relates to (1) the relevance of financial information, and (2) completeness.
(c) Your aunt observes that under IFRS, the financial statements are prepared on the accrual basis. According to the framework, what does "accrual basis" mean?

International Financial Reporting Problem
Marks and Spencer plc

IFRS2-7 The financial statements of **Marks and Spencer plc (M&S)** are available at the book's companion website or can be accessed at *http://annualreport.marksandspencer.com/_assets/downloads/Marks-and-Spencer-Annual-report-and-financial-statements-2012.pdf.*

Instructions

Refer to M&S's financial statements and the accompanying notes to answer the following questions.

(a) Using the notes to the consolidated financial statements, determine M&S's revenue recognition policies.
(b) Give two examples of where historical cost information is reported in M&S's financial statements and related notes. Give two examples of the use of fair value information reported in either the financial statements or related notes.
(c) How can we determine that the accounting principles used by M&S are prepared on a basis consistent with those of last year?
(d) What is M&S's accounting policy related to refunds and loyalty schemes? Why does M&S include the accounting for refunds and loyalty schemes in its critical accounting estimates and judgments?

ANSWERS TO IFRS SELF-TEST QUESTIONS

1. d **2.** d **3.** b **4.** d **5.** c

Remember to check the book's companion website to find additional resources for this chapter.

CHAPTER

3 The Accounting Information System

LEARNING OBJECTIVES

After studying this chapter, you should be able to:

1 Understand basic accounting terminology.

2 Explain double-entry rules.

3 Identify steps in the accounting cycle.

4 Record transactions in journals, post to ledger accounts, and prepare a trial balance.

5 Explain the reasons for preparing adjusting entries and identify major types of adjusting entries.

6 Prepare financial statements from the adjusted trial balance.

7 Prepare closing entries.

8 Prepare financial statements for a merchandising company.

Needed: A Reliable Information System

Maintaining a set of accounting records is not optional. Regulators require that businesses prepare and retain a set of records and documents that can be audited. The U.S. Foreign Corrupt Practices Act, for example, requires public companies to "make and keep books, records, and accounts, which, in reasonable detail, accurately and fairly reflect the transactions and dispositions of the assets." But beyond these two reasons, a company that fails to keep an accurate record of its business transactions may lose revenue and is more likely to operate inefficiently.

One reason accurate records are not provided is because of economic crime or corruption. It is clear that economic crime remains a persistent and difficult problem for many companies. For example, it was recently estimated that 53 percent of U.S. companies experienced significant economic crime. And its global counterparts are not far behind, with a reported rate of 43 percent. While global rates appear lower, U.S. companies often have more stringent internal controls and are more likely to find and report crime. Presented to the right is a chart that indicates the types of economic crime experienced in a recent period.

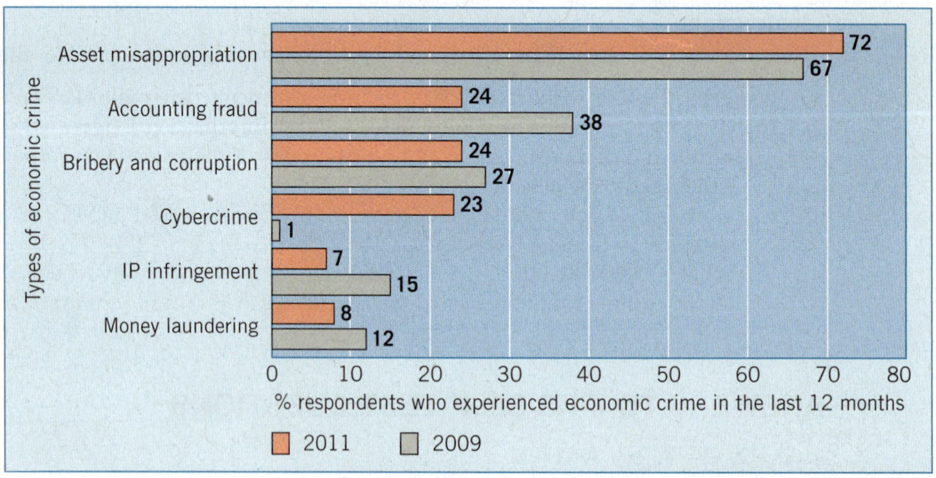

The top four economic crimes are asset misappropriation, accounting fraud, bribery and corruption, and cybercrime. Cybercrime is a new phenomenon as new types of fraud are emerging in this area. Smartphones and tablet devices, social media, and cloud computing all offer companies interesting business opportunities but can also lead to risks related to the disclosure of sensitive and confidential data.

In some of these cases, such as money laundering or infringement of intellectual property, a sound system of internal controls focused on financial accounting and reporting may not work. Nonetheless, many believe that effective internal control sends a message that a company is serious about finding not only economic crime but also errors or misstatements. As a result, many companies are taking a proactive look as to how they can better prevent both economic crime as well as basic errors in their systems. The chart on the next page indicates the percentage of companies that identified certain factors influencing their decision to implement controls to deter economic crime.

CONCEPTUAL FOCUS

> See the **Underlying Concepts** on page 90.

INTERNATIONAL FOCUS

> Read the **IFRS Insights** on pages 153–157 for a discussion of:
> —Accounting system internal controls
> —First-time adoption of IFRS

Reasons for Internal Controls

	U.S.	Global
Sarbanes-Oxley Act	99%	84%
U.S. Patriot Act	85	29
Advice from external consultants	63	50
FCPA/OECD Anti-Bribery Convention	38	23
Public discussion/media	38	33
Federal sentencing guidelines	38	29
Incidents of economic crime	31	34
Local legislation	24	51
Bad experience and/or advice from law enforcement	17	36

What happens when companies fail to keep an accurate record of their business transactions? Consider **Adecco**, the largest international employment services company, which confirmed existence of weakness in its internal controls systems and Adecco staffing operations in certain countries. Manipulation involved such matters as reconciliation of payroll bank accounts, accounts receivable, and documentation in revenue recognition. These irregularities forced an indefinite delay in reporting the company's income figures, which led to significant decline in share price. Or consider **Nortel Networks Corp.**, which overstated and understated its reserve accounts to manage its earnings. This eventually led to the liquidation of the company.

Even the use of computers is no assurance of accuracy and efficiency. "The conversion to a new system called MasterNet fouled up data processing records to the extent that **Bank of America** was frequently unable to produce or deliver customer statements on a timely basis," said an executive at one of the country's largest banks.

Although these situations may occur only rarely in large organizations, they illustrate the point: Companies must properly maintain accounts and detailed records or face unnecessary costs.

Sources: Adapted from "Economic Crime: People, Culture, and Controls," *The Fourth Biennial Global Economic Crime Survey* (PricewaterhouseCoopers, 2007); and "Cybercrime: Protecting Against the Growing Threat," *Global Economic Crime Survey* (PricewaterhouseCoopers, 2012).

PREVIEW OF CHAPTER 3

As the opening story indicates, a reliable information system is a necessity for all companies. The purpose of this chapter is to explain and illustrate the features of an accounting information system. The content and organization of this chapter are as follows.

The Accounting Information System

Accounting Information System	The Accounting Cycle	Financial Statements for Merchandisers
• Basic terminology • Debits and credits • Accounting equation • Financial statements and ownership structure	• Identifying and recording • Journalizing • Posting • Trial balance • Adjusting entries • Adjusted trial balance • Preparing financial statements • Closing • Post-closing trial balance • Reversing entries	• Income statement • Statement of retained earnings • Balance sheet • Closing entries

ACCOUNTING INFORMATION SYSTEM

LEARNING OBJECTIVE 1
Understand basic accounting terminology.

An **accounting information system** collects and processes transaction data and then disseminates the financial information to interested parties. Accounting information systems vary widely from one business to another. Various factors shape these systems: the nature of the business and the transactions in which it engages, the size of the firm, the volume of data to be handled, and the informational demands that management and others require.

As we discussed in Chapters 1 and 2, in response to the requirements of the Sarbanes-Oxley Act, companies are placing a renewed focus on their accounting systems to ensure relevant and reliable information is reported in financial statements.[1] A good accounting information system helps management answer such questions as:

- How much and what kind of debt is outstanding?
- Were our sales higher this period than last?
- What assets do we have?
- What were our cash inflows and outflows?
- Did we make a profit last period?
- Are any of our product lines or divisions operating at a loss?
- Can we safely increase our dividends to stockholders?
- Is our rate of return on net assets increasing?

Management can answer many other questions with the data provided by an efficient accounting system. A well-devised accounting information system benefits every type of company.

Basic Terminology

Financial accounting rests on a set of concepts (discussed in Chapters 1 and 2) for identifying, recording, classifying, and interpreting transactions and other events relating to enterprises. You therefore need to understand the **basic terminology employed in collecting accounting data**.

BASIC TERMINOLOGY

EVENT. A happening of consequence. An event generally is the source or cause of changes in assets, liabilities, and equity. Events may be external or internal.

TRANSACTION. An **external event** involving a transfer or exchange between two or more entities.

ACCOUNT. A systematic arrangement that shows the effect of transactions and other events on a specific element (asset, liability, and so on). Companies keep a separate account

[1]A recent survey indicated nearly one in three companies view the benefits of Sarbanes-Oxley (SOX) to outweigh its costs. Approximately half of the companies believe the costs exceed the benefits of SOX to some degree. Management view their companies generally as benefiting from SOX but overall have a slightly negative view toward the legislation. In a large percentage of companies, the internal control over financial reporting has improved since SOX became a requirement. See "Where U.S.-Listed Companies Stand: Reviewing Cost, Time, Effort and Processes," *2012 Sarbanes-Oxley Compliance Survey* (Protiviti Company, May 2012).

for each asset, liability, revenue, and expense, and for capital (owners' equity). Because the format of an account often resembles the letter T, it is sometimes referred to as a **T-account**. (See Illustration 3-3, page 87.)

REAL AND NOMINAL ACCOUNTS. Real (permanent) **accounts** are asset, liability, and equity accounts; they appear on the balance sheet. **Nominal** (temporary) **accounts** are revenue, expense, and dividend accounts; except for dividends, they appear on the income statement. Companies periodically close nominal accounts; they do not close real accounts.

LEDGER. The book (or computer printouts) containing the accounts. A **general ledger** is a collection of all the asset, liability, owners' equity, revenue, and expense accounts. A **subsidiary ledger** contains the details related to a given general ledger account.

JOURNAL. The "book of original entry" where the company initially records transactions and selected other events. Various amounts are transferred from the book of original entry, the journal, to the ledger. Entering transaction data in the journal is known as **journalizing**.

POSTING. The process of transferring the essential facts and figures from the book of original entry to the ledger accounts.

TRIAL BALANCE. The list of all open accounts in the ledger and their balances. The trial balance taken immediately after all adjustments have been posted is called an **adjusted trial balance**. A trial balance taken immediately after closing entries have been posted is called a **post-closing** (or **after-closing**) **trial balance**. Companies may prepare a trial balance at any time.

ADJUSTING ENTRIES. Entries made at the end of an accounting period to bring all accounts up to date on an accrual basis, so that the company can prepare correct financial statements.

FINANCIAL STATEMENTS. Statements that reflect the collection, tabulation, and final summarization of the accounting data. Four statements are involved. (1) The **balance sheet** shows the financial condition of the enterprise at the end of a period. (2) The **income statement** measures the results of operations during the period. (3) The **statement of cash flows** reports the cash provided and used by operating, investing, and financing activities during the period. (4) The **statement of retained earnings** reconciles the balance of the retained earnings account from the beginning to the end of the period.

CLOSING ENTRIES. The formal process by which the enterprise reduces all nominal accounts to zero and determines and transfers the net income or net loss to an owners' equity account. Also known as "closing the ledger," "closing the books," or merely "closing."

Debits and Credits

2 LEARNING OBJECTIVE
Explain double-entry rules.

The terms **debit** (Dr.) and **credit** (Cr.) mean left and right, respectively. These terms do not mean increase or decrease, but instead describe *where* a company makes entries in the recording process. That is, when a company enters an amount on the left side of an account, it **debits** the account. When it makes an entry on the right side, it **credits** the account. When comparing the totals of the two sides, an account shows a **debit balance** if the total of the debit amounts exceeds the credits. An account shows a **credit balance** if the credit amounts exceed the debits.

The positioning of debits on the left and credits on the right is simply an accounting custom. We could function just as well if we reversed the sides. However, the United

States adopted the custom, now the rule, of having debits on the left side of an account and credits on the right side, similar to the custom of driving on the right-hand side of the road. This rule applies to all accounts.

The equality of debits and credits provides the basis for the double-entry system of recording transactions (sometimes referred to as double-entry bookkeeping). Under the universally used **double-entry accounting** system, a company records the dual (two-sided) effect of each transaction in appropriate accounts. This system provides a logical method for recording transactions. It also offers a means of proving the accuracy of the recorded amounts. If a company records every transaction with equal debits and credits, then the sum of all the debits to the accounts must equal the sum of all the credits.

Illustration 3-1 presents the basic guidelines for an accounting system. Increases to all asset and expense accounts occur on the left (or debit side) and decreases on the right (or credit side). Conversely, increases to all liability and revenue accounts occur on the right (or credit side) and decreases on the left (or debit side). A company increases stockholders' equity accounts, such as Common Stock and Retained Earnings, on the credit side, but increases Dividends on the debit side.

ILLUSTRATION 3-1
Double-Entry (Debit and Credit) Accounting System

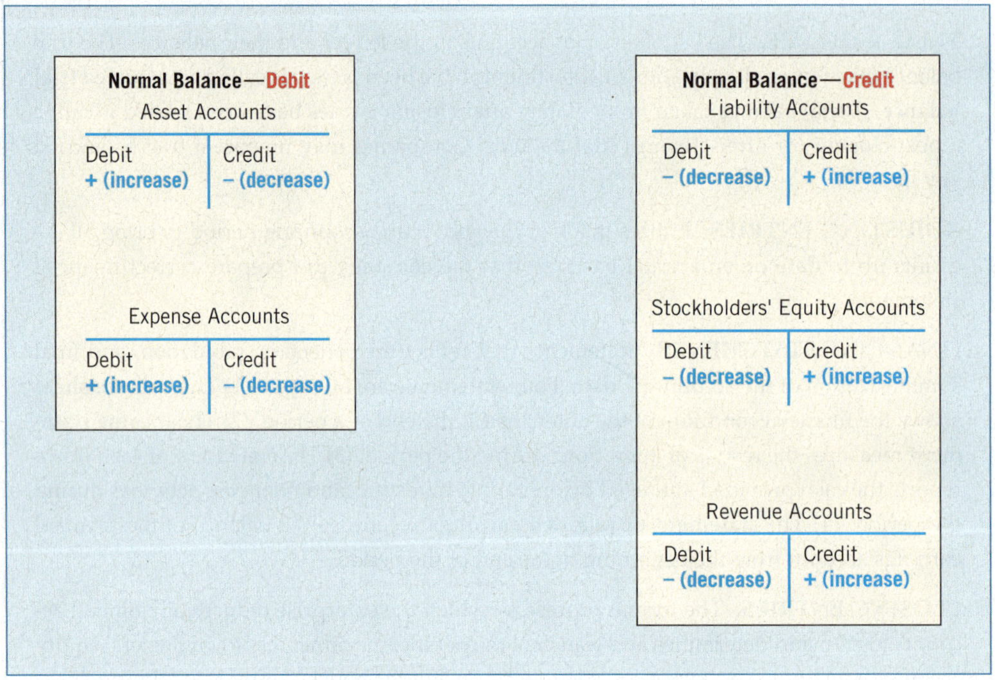

The Accounting Equation

In a double-entry system, for every debit there must be a credit, and vice versa. This leads us, then, to the basic equation in accounting (Illustration 3-2).

ILLUSTRATION 3-2
The Basic Accounting Equation

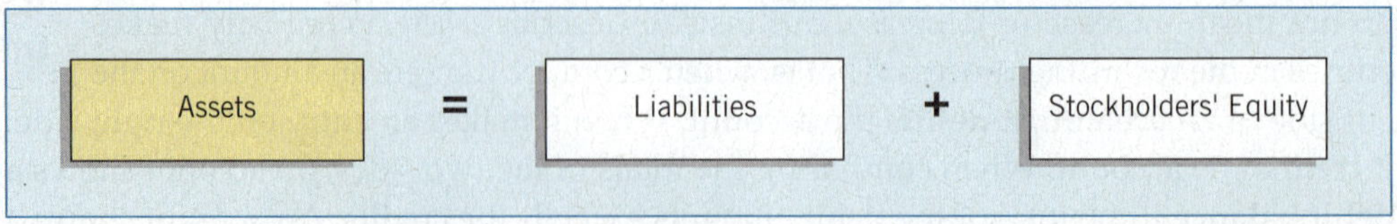

Illustration 3-3 expands this equation to show the accounts that make up stockholders' equity. The figure also shows the debit/credit rules and effects on each type of account. Study this diagram carefully. It will help you understand the fundamentals of the double-entry system. Like the basic equation, the expanded equation must also balance (total debits equal total credits).

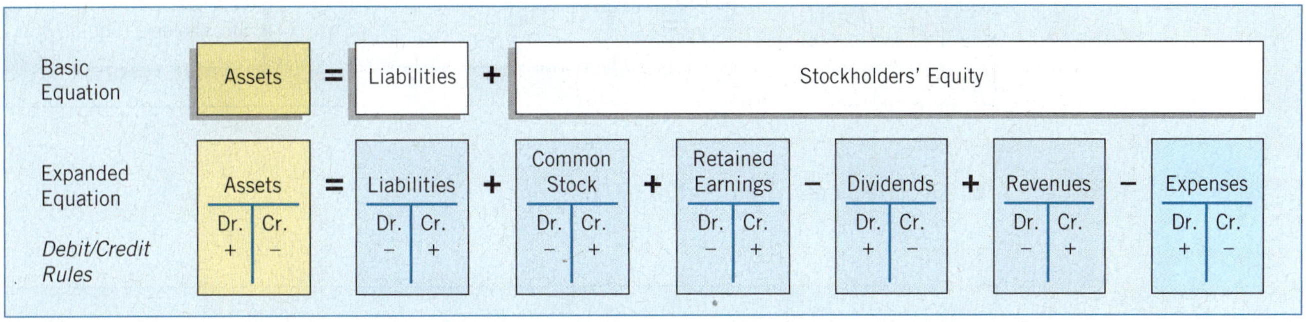

ILLUSTRATION 3-3
Expanded Equation and Debit/Credit Rules and Effects

Every time a transaction occurs, the elements of the accounting equation change. However, the basic equality remains. To illustrate, consider the following eight different transactions for Perez Inc.

1. Owners invest $40,000 in exchange for common stock.

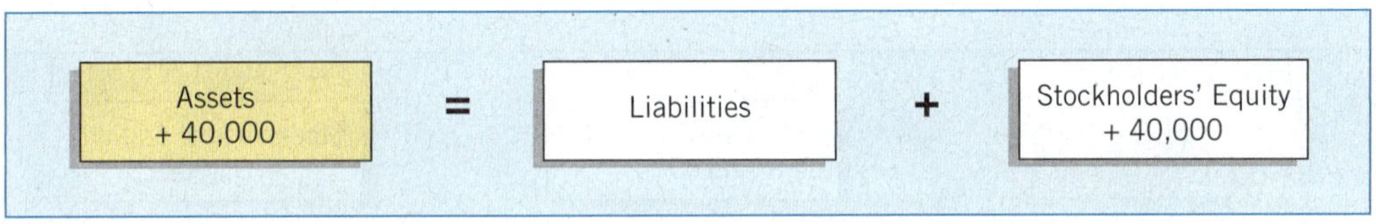

2. Disburse $600 cash for secretarial wages.

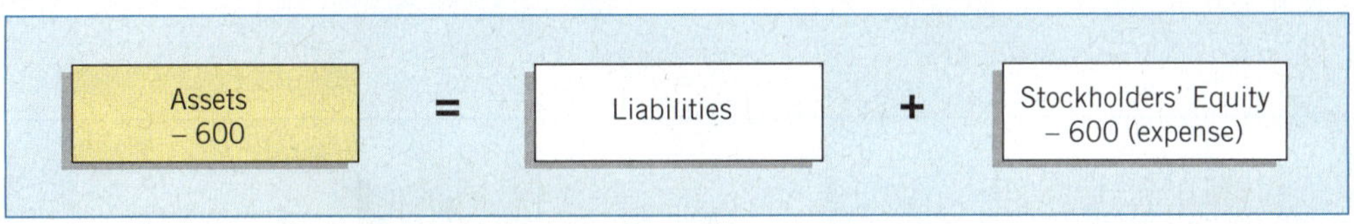

3. Purchase office equipment priced at $5,200, giving a 10 percent promissory note in exchange.

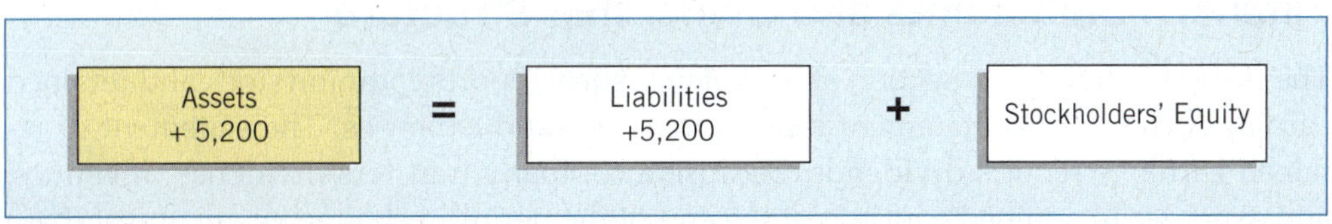

4. Receive $4,000 cash for services performed.

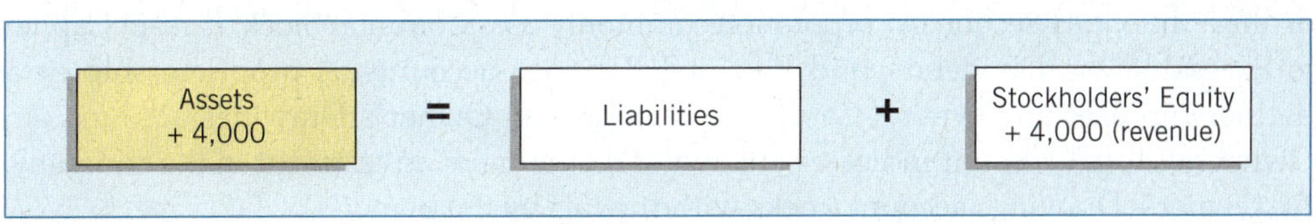

5. Pay off a short-term liability of $7,000.

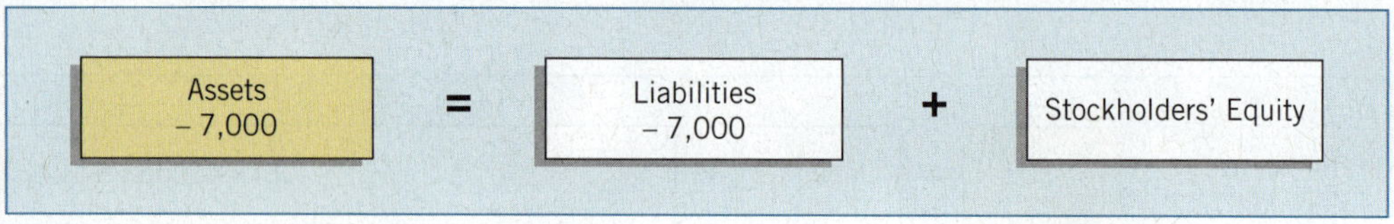

6. Declare a cash dividend of $5,000.

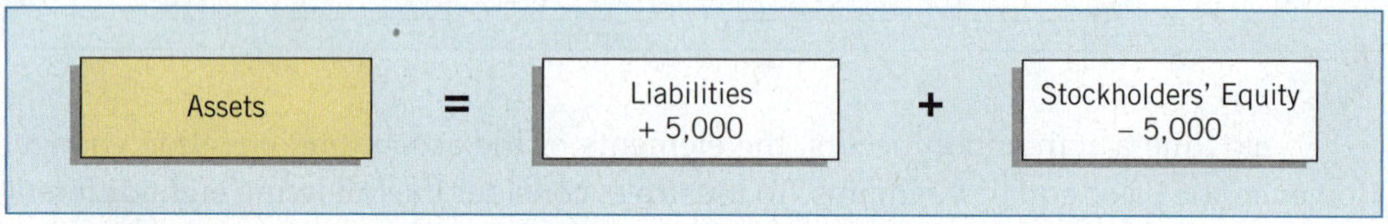

7. Convert a long-term liability of $80,000 into common stock.

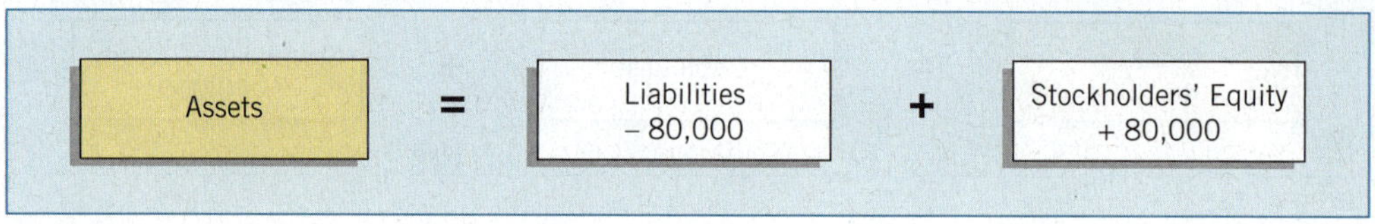

8. Pay cash of $16,000 for a delivery van.

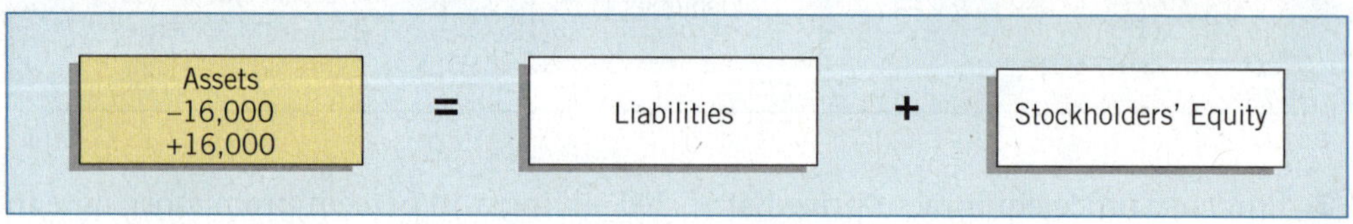

Financial Statements and Ownership Structure

The stockholders' equity section of the balance sheet reports common stock and retained earnings. The income statement reports revenues and expenses. The statement of retained earnings reports dividends. Because a company transfers dividends, revenues, and expenses to retained earnings at the end of the period, a change in any one of these three items affects stockholders' equity. Illustration 3-4 shows the stockholders' equity relationships.

The company's ownership structure dictates the types of accounts that are part of or affect the equity section. A corporation commonly uses Common Stock, Paid-in Capital in Excess of Par, Dividends, and Retained Earnings accounts. A proprietorship or a partnership uses an Owner's Capital account and an Owner's Drawings account. An Owner's Capital account indicates the owner's or owners' investment in the company. An Owner's Drawings account tracks withdrawals by the owner(s).

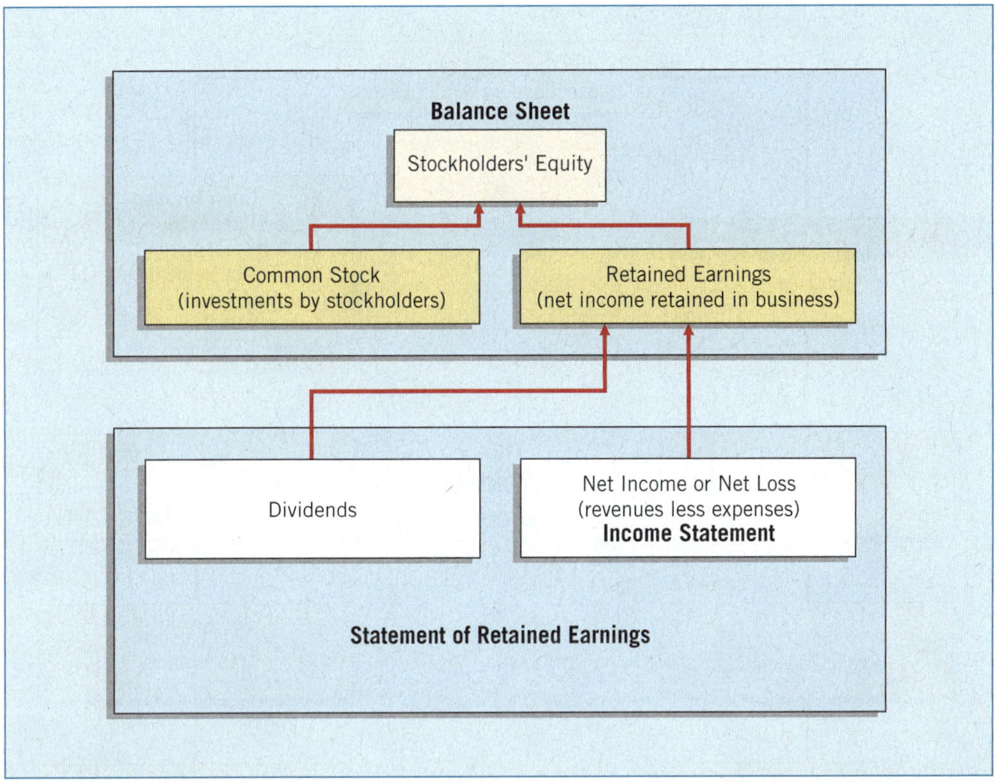

ILLUSTRATION 3-4
Financial Statements and Ownership Structure

Illustration 3-5 summarizes and relates the transactions affecting owners' equity to the nominal (temporary) and real (permanent) classifications and to the types of business ownership.

ILLUSTRATION 3-5
Effects of Transactions on Owners' Equity Accounts

		Ownership Structure			
		Proprietorships and Partnerships		Corporations	
Transactions Affecting Owners' Equity	Impact on Owners' Equity	Nominal (Temporary) Accounts	Real (Permanent) Accounts	Nominal (Temporary) Accounts	Real (Permanent) Accounts
Investment by owner(s)	Increase		Capital		Common Stock and related accounts
Revenues recognized	Increase	Revenue		Revenue	
Expenses incurred	Decrease	Expense	Capital	Expense	Retained Earnings
Withdrawal by owner(s)	Decrease	Drawing		Dividends	

THE ACCOUNTING CYCLE

Illustration 3-6 (on page 90) shows the steps in the **accounting cycle**. A company normally uses these accounting procedures to record transactions and prepare financial statements.

3 LEARNING OBJECTIVE
Identify steps in the accounting cycle.

Identifying and Recording Transactions and Other Events

The first step in the accounting cycle is analysis of transactions and selected other events. The first problem is to determine what to record. Although GAAP provides guidelines, no simple rules exist that state which events a company should record. Although

ILLUSTRATION 3-6
The Accounting Cycle

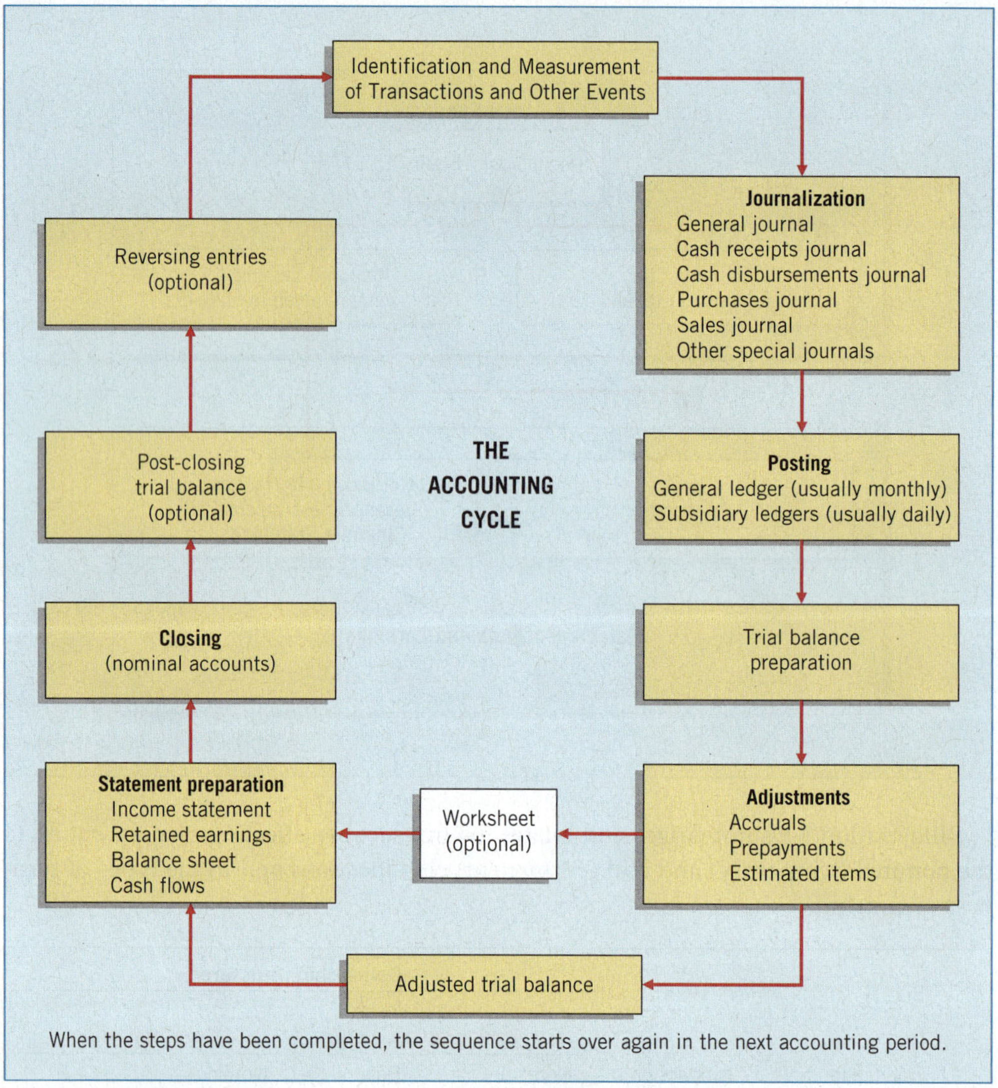

changes in a company's personnel or managerial policies may be important, the company should not record these items in the accounts. On the other hand, a company should record all cash sales or purchases—no matter how small.

The concepts we presented in Chapter 2 determine what to recognize in the accounts. An item should be recognized in the financial statements if it is an element, is measurable, and is relevant and representationally faithful. Consider human resources. **R. G. Barry & Co.** at one time reported as supplemental data total assets of $14,055,926, including $986,094 for "Net investments in human resources." **AT&T** and **ExxonMobil** also experimented with human resource accounting. Should we value employees for balance sheet and income statement purposes? Certainly skilled employees are an important asset (highly relevant), but the problems of determining their value and measuring it reliably have not yet been solved. Consequently, human resources are not recorded. Perhaps when measurement techniques become more sophisticated and accepted, such information will be presented, if only in supplemental form.

Underlying Concepts

Assets are probable economic benefits controlled by a particular entity as a result of a past transaction or event. Do human resources of a company meet this definition?

The FASB uses the phrase "transactions and other events and circumstances that affect a business enterprise" to describe the sources or causes of changes in an entity's assets, liabilities, and equity.[2] Events are of two types. (1) **External**

[2]"Elements of Financial Statements of Business Enterprises," *Statement of Financial Accounting Concepts No. 6* (Stamford, Conn.: FASB, 1985), pp. 259–260.

events involve interaction between an entity and its environment, such as a transaction with another entity, a change in the price of a good or service that an entity buys or sells, a flood or earthquake, or an improvement in technology by a competitor. (2) **Internal events** occur within an entity, such as using buildings and machinery in operations, or transferring or consuming raw materials in production processes.

Many events have both external and internal elements. For example, hiring an employee, which involves an exchange of salary for labor, is an external event. Using the services of labor is part of production, an internal event. Further, an entity may initiate and control events, such as the purchase of merchandise or use of a machine. Or, events may be beyond its control, such as an interest rate change, theft, or a tax hike.

Transactions are types of external events. They may be an exchange between two entities where each receives and sacrifices value, such as purchases and sales of goods or services. Or, transactions may be transfers in one direction only. For example, an entity may incur a liability without directly receiving value in exchange, such as charitable contributions. Other examples include investments by owners, distributions to owners, payment of taxes, gifts, casualty losses, and thefts.

In short, a company records as many events as possible that affect its financial position. As discussed earlier in the case of human resources, it omits some events because of tradition and others because of complicated measurement problems. Recently, however, the accounting profession shows more receptiveness to accepting the challenge of measuring and reporting events previously viewed as too complex and immeasurable.

Journalizing

4 LEARNING OBJECTIVE
Record transactions in journals, post to ledger accounts, and prepare a trial balance.

A company records in **accounts** those transactions and events that affect its assets, liabilities, and equities. The **general ledger** contains all the asset, liability, and stockholders' equity accounts. An account (see Illustration 3-3, on page 87) shows the effect of transactions on particular asset, liability, equity, revenue, and expense accounts.

In practice, companies do not record transactions and selected other events originally in the ledger. A transaction affects two or more accounts, each of which is on a different page in the ledger. Therefore, in order to have a complete record of each transaction or other event in one place, a company uses a **journal** (also called "the book of original entry"). In its simplest form, a **general journal** chronologically lists transactions and other events, expressed in terms of debits and credits to accounts.

Illustration 3-7 shows the technique of journalizing, using the first two transactions for Softbyte, Inc. These transactions were:

September 1 Stockholders invested $15,000 cash in the corporation in exchange for shares of stock.
Purchased computer equipment for $7,000 cash.

The J1 indicates these two entries are on the first page of the general journal.

ILLUSTRATION 3-7
Technique of Journalizing

GENERAL JOURNAL				J1
Date	Account Titles and Explanation	Ref.	Debit	Credit
2014				
Sept. 1	Cash		15,000	
	Common Stock			15,000
	(Issued shares of stock for cash)			
1	Equipment		7,000	
	Cash			7,000
	(Purchased equipment for cash)			

Each **general journal entry** consists of four parts: (1) the accounts and amounts to be debited (Dr.), (2) the accounts and amounts to be credited (Cr.), (3) a date, and (4) an explanation. A company enters debits first, followed by the credits (slightly indented). The explanation begins below the name of the last account to be credited and may take one or more lines. A company completes the "Ref." column at the time it posts the accounts.

Gateway to the Profession

Expanded Discussion of Special Journals

In some cases, a company uses **special journals** in addition to the general journal. Special journals summarize transactions possessing a common characteristic (e.g., cash receipts, sales, purchases, cash payments). As a result, using them reduces bookkeeping time.

Posting

Transferring journal entries to the ledger accounts is called **posting**. Posting involves the following steps.

1. In the **ledger**, in the appropriate columns of the account(s) debited, enter the date, journal page, and debit amount shown in the journal.
2. In the reference column of the **journal**, write the account number to which the debit amount was posted.
3. In the **ledger**, in the appropriate columns of the account(s) credited, enter the date, journal page, and credit amount shown in the journal.
4. In the reference column of the **journal**, write the account number to which the credit amount was posted.

Illustration 3-8 diagrams these four steps, using the first journal entry of Softbyte, Inc. The illustration shows the general ledger accounts in **standard account form**. Some companies call this form the **three-column form of account** because it has three money

ILLUSTRATION 3-8
Posting a Journal Entry

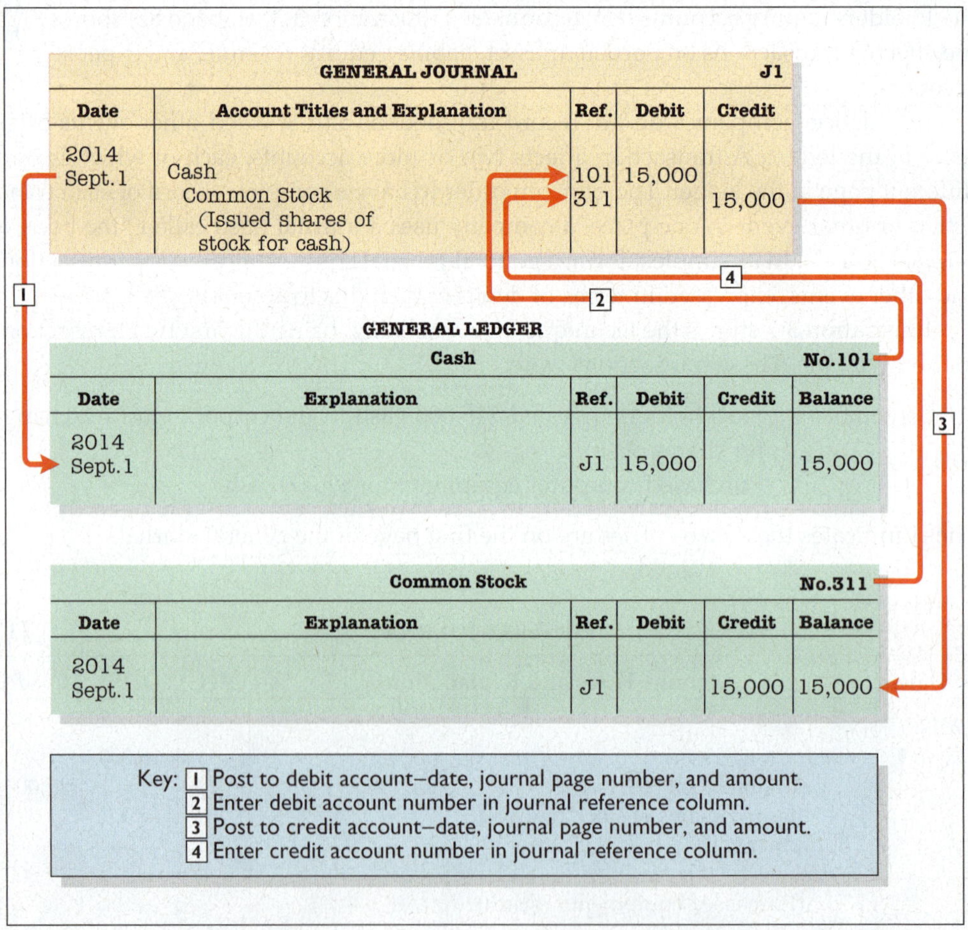

columns—debit, credit, and balance. The balance in the account is determined after each transaction. The explanation space and reference columns provide special information about the transaction. The boxed numbers indicate the sequence of the steps.

The numbers in the "Ref." column of the general journal refer to the ledger accounts to which a company posts the respective items. For example, the "101" placed in the column to the right of "Cash" indicates that the company posted this $15,000 item to Account No. 101 in the ledger.

The posting of the general journal is completed when a company records all of the posting reference numbers opposite the account titles in the journal. Thus, the number in the posting reference column serves two purposes. (1) It indicates the ledger account number of the account involved. (2) It indicates the completion of posting for the particular item. Each company selects its own numbering system for its ledger accounts. Many begin numbering with asset accounts and then follow with liabilities, owners' equity, revenue, and expense accounts, in that order.

The ledger accounts in Illustration 3-8 show the accounts after completion of the posting process. The reference J1 (General Journal, page 1) indicates the source of the data transferred to the ledger account.

An Expanded Example

To show an expanded example of the basic steps in the recording process, we use the October transactions of Pioneer Advertising Agency Inc. Pioneer's accounting period is a month. Illustrations 3-9 through 3-18 show the journal entry and posting of each transaction. For simplicity, we use a T-account form instead of the standard account form. Study the transaction analyses carefully.

The purpose of transaction analysis is (1) to identify the type of account involved, and (2) to determine whether a debit or a credit is required. You should always perform this type of analysis before preparing a journal entry. Doing so will help you understand the journal entries discussed in this chapter as well as more complex journal entries in later chapters. Keep in mind that every journal entry affects one or more of the following items: assets, liabilities, stockholders' equity, revenues, or expenses.

1. October 1: Stockholders invest $100,000 cash in an advertising venture to be known as Pioneer Advertising Agency Inc.

ILLUSTRATION 3-9
Investment of Cash by Stockholders

Journal Entry

Date	Account	Ref.	Debit	Credit
Oct. 1	Cash	101	100,000	
	Common Stock	311		100,000
	(Issued shares of stock for cash)			

Posting

Cash 101	
Oct. 1 100,000	

Common Stock 311	
	Oct. 1 100,000

2. October 1: Pioneer Advertising purchases office equipment costing $50,000 by signing a 3-month, 12%, $50,000 note payable.

ILLUSTRATION 3-10
Purchase of Office Equipment

Journal Entry

Date	Account	Ref.	Debit	Credit
Oct. 1	Equipment	157	50,000	
	Notes Payable	200		50,000
	(Issued 3-month, 12% note for office equipment)			

Posting

Equipment 157	
Oct. 1 50,000	

Notes Payable 200	
	Oct. 1 50,000

3. October 2: Pioneer Advertising receives a $12,000 cash advance from R. Knox, a client, for advertising services that are expected to be completed by December 31.

ILLUSTRATION 3-11
Receipt of Cash for Future Service

Journal Entry

Oct. 2	Cash	101	12,000	
	Unearned Service Revenue	209		12,000
	(Received cash from R. Knox for future service)			

Posting

Cash 101	
Oct. 1 100,000	
2 12,000	

Unearned Service Revenue 209	
	Oct. 2 12,000

4. October 3: Pioneer Advertising pays $9,000 office rent, in cash, for October.

ILLUSTRATION 3-12
Payment of Monthly Rent

Journal Entry

Oct. 3	Rent Expense	729	9,000	
	Cash	101		9,000
	(Paid October rent)			

Posting

Cash 101	
Oct. 1 100,000	Oct. 3 9,000
2 12,000	

Rent Expense 729	
Oct. 3 9,000	

5. October 4: Pioneer Advertising pays $6,000 for a one-year insurance policy that will expire next year on September 30.

ILLUSTRATION 3-13
Payment for Insurance

Journal Entry

Oct. 4	Prepaid Insurance	130	6,000	
	Cash	101		6,000
	(Paid one-year policy; effective date October 1)			

Posting

Cash 101	
Oct. 1 100,000	Oct. 3 9,000
2 12,000	4 6,000

Prepaid Insurance 130	
Oct. 4 6,000	

6. October 5: Pioneer Advertising purchases, for $25,000 on account, an estimated 3-month supply of advertising materials from Aero Supply.

ILLUSTRATION 3-14
Purchase of Supplies on Account

Journal Entry

Oct. 5	Supplies	126	25,000	
	Accounts Payable	201		25,000
	(Purchased supplies on account from Aero Supply)			

Posting

Supplies 126	
Oct. 5 25,000	

Accounts Payable 201	
	Oct. 5 25,000

7. October 9: Pioneer Advertising signs a contract with a local newspaper for advertising inserts (flyers) to be distributed starting the last Sunday in November. Pioneer will start work on the content of the flyers in November. Payment of $7,000 is due following delivery of the Sunday papers containing the flyers.

ILLUSTRATION 3-15
Signing a Contract

A business transaction has not occurred. There is only an agreement between Pioneer Advertising and the newspaper for the services to be performed in November. Therefore, no journal entry is necessary in October.

8. October 20: Pioneer Advertising's board of directors declares and pays a $5,000 cash dividend to stockholders.

ILLUSTRATION 3-16
Declaration and Payment of Dividend by Corporation

Journal Entry

Oct. 20	Dividends	332	5,000	
	Cash	101		5,000
	(Declared and paid a cash dividend)			

Posting

Cash	101		
Oct. 1	100,000	Oct. 3	9,000
2	12,000	4	6,000
		20	5,000

Dividends	332
Oct. 20 5,000	

9. October 26: Pioneer Advertising pays employee salaries and wages in cash. Employees are paid once a month, every four weeks. The total payroll is $10,000 per week, or $2,000 per day. In October, the pay period began on Monday, October 1. As a result, the pay period ended on Friday, October 26, with salaries and wages of $40,000 being paid.

ILLUSTRATION 3-17
Payment of Salaries and Wages

Journal Entry

Oct. 26	Salaries and Wages Expense	726	40,000	
	Cash	101		40,000
	(Paid salaries to date)			

Posting

Cash	101		
Oct. 1	100,000	Oct. 3	9,000
2	12,000	4	6,000
		20	5,000
		26	40,000

Salaries and Wages Expense	726
Oct. 26 40,000	

10. October 31: Pioneer Advertising receives $28,000 in cash and bills Copa Company $72,000 for advertising services of $100,000 performed in October.

ILLUSTRATION 3-18
Recognize Revenue for Services Performed

Journal Entry

Oct. 31	Cash	101	28,000	
	Accounts Receivable	112	72,000	
	Service Revenue	400		100,000
	(Recognize revenue for services performed)			

Posting

Cash	101		
Oct. 1	100,000	Oct. 3	9,000
2	12,000	4	6,000
31	28,000	20	5,000
		26	40,000

Accounts Receivable	112
Oct. 31 72,000	

Service Revenue	400
	Oct. 31 100,000

Trial Balance

A **trial balance** is a list of accounts and their balances at a given time. A company usually prepares a trial balance at the end of an accounting period. The trial balance lists the accounts in the order in which they appear in the ledger, with debit balances listed in the left column and credit balances in the right column. The totals of the two columns must agree.

The trial balance proves the mathematical equality of debits and credits after posting. Under the double-entry system, this equality occurs when the sum of the debit account balances equals the sum of the credit account balances. A trial balance also uncovers errors in journalizing and posting. In addition, it is useful in the preparation of financial statements. The procedures for preparing a trial balance consist of:

1. List the account titles and their balances in the appropriate debit or credit column.
2. Total the debit and credit columns.
3. Prove the equality of the two columns.

Illustration 3-19 presents the trial balance prepared from the ledger of Pioneer Advertising Agency Inc. Note that the total debits ($287,000) equal the total credits ($287,000). A trial balance also often shows account numbers to the left of the account titles.

ILLUSTRATION 3-19
Trial Balance (Unadjusted)

PIONEER ADVERTISING AGENCY INC.
TRIAL BALANCE
OCTOBER 31, 2014

	Debit	Credit
Cash	$ 80,000	
Accounts Receivable	72,000	
Supplies	25,000	
Prepaid Insurance	6,000	
Equipment	50,000	
Notes Payable		$ 50,000
Accounts Payable		25,000
Unearned Service Revenue		12,000
Common Stock		100,000
Dividends	5,000	
Service Revenue		100,000
Salaries and Wages Expense	40,000	
Rent Expense	9,000	
	$287,000	$287,000

A trial balance does not prove that a company recorded all transactions or that the ledger is correct. Numerous errors may exist even though the trial balance columns agree. For example, the trial balance may balance even when a company (1) fails to journalize a transaction, (2) omits posting a correct journal entry, (3) posts a journal entry twice, (4) uses incorrect accounts in journalizing or posting, or (5) makes offsetting errors in recording the amount of a transaction. In other words, as long as a company posts equal debits and credits, even to the wrong account or in the wrong amount, the total debits will equal the total credits.

LEARNING OBJECTIVE 5
Explain the reasons for preparing adjusting entries and identify major types of adjusting entries.

Adjusting Entries

In order for revenues to be recorded in the period in which services are performed and for expenses to be recognized in the period in which they are incurred, companies make **adjusting entries**. In short, adjustments ensure that a company like McDonald's follows the revenue recognition and expense recognition principles.

The use of adjusting entries makes it possible to report on the balance sheet the appropriate assets, liabilities, and owners' equity at the statement date. Adjusting entries also make it possible to report on the income statement the proper revenues and expenses for the period. However, the trial balance—the first pulling together of the transaction data—may not contain up-to-date and complete data. This occurs for the following reasons.

1. Some events are not recorded daily because it is not efficient to do so. Examples are the use of supplies and the earning of wages by employees.
2. Some costs are not recorded during the accounting period because these costs expire with the passage of time rather than as a result of recurring daily transactions. Examples of such costs are building and equipment depreciation and rent and insurance.
3. Some items may be unrecorded. An example is a utility service bill that will not be received until the next accounting period.

Adjusting entries are required every time a company, such as **Coca-Cola**, prepares financial statements. At that time, Coca-Cola must analyze each account in the trial balance to determine whether it is complete and up-to-date for financial statement purposes. The analysis requires a thorough understanding of Coca-Cola's operations and the interrelationship of accounts. Because of this involved process, usually a skilled accountant prepares the adjusting entries. In gathering the adjustment data, Coca-Cola may need to make inventory counts of supplies and repair parts. Further, it may prepare supporting schedules of insurance policies, rental agreements, and other contractual commitments. Companies often prepare adjustments after the balance sheet date. However, they date the entries as of the balance sheet date.

Types of Adjusting Entries

Adjusting entries are classified as either deferrals or accruals. Each of these classes has two subcategories, as Illustration 3-20 shows.

ILLUSTRATION 3-20
Categories of Adjusting Entries

Deferrals:
1. **Prepaid expenses:** Expenses paid in cash before they are used or consumed.
2. **Unearned revenues:** Cash received before services are performed.

Accruals:
1. **Accrued revenues:** Revenues for services performed but not yet received in cash or recorded.
2. **Accrued expenses:** Expenses incurred but not yet paid in cash or recorded.

We review specific examples and explanations of each type of adjustment in subsequent sections. We base each example on the October 31 trial balance of Pioneer Advertising Agency Inc. (Illustration 3-19). We assume that Pioneer uses an accounting period of one month. Thus, Pioneer will make monthly adjusting entries, dated October 31.

Adjusting Entries for Deferrals

To defer means to postpone or delay. **Deferrals** are expenses or revenues that are recognized at a date later than the point when cash was originally exchanged. The two types of deferrals are prepaid expenses and unearned revenues.

If a company does not make an adjustment for these deferrals, the asset and liability are overstated, and the related expense and revenue are understated. For example, in Pioneer's trial balance (Illustration 3-19), the balance in the asset Supplies shows only supplies purchased. This balance is overstated; the related expense account, Supplies Expense, is understated because the cost of supplies used has not been recognized. Thus, the adjusting entry for deferrals will decrease a balance sheet account and increase an income statement account. Illustration 3-21 shows the effects of adjusting entries for deferrals.

ILLUSTRATION 3-21
Adjusting Entries for Deferrals

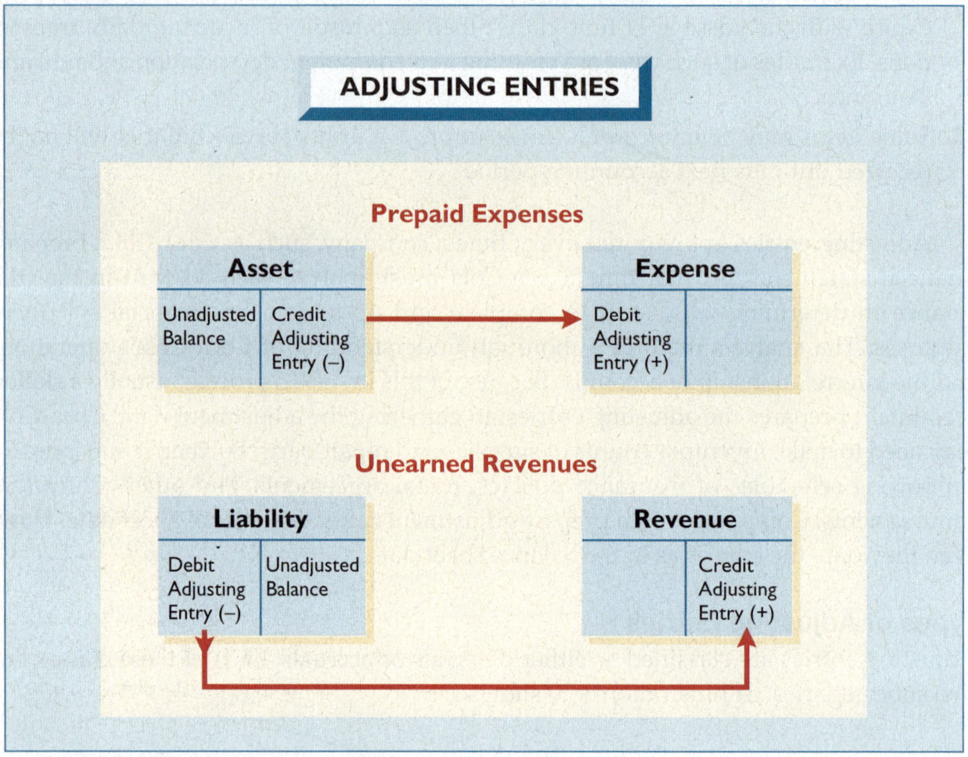

Prepaid Expenses. Assets paid for and recorded before a company uses them are called **prepaid expenses**. When expenses are prepaid, a company debits an asset account to show the service or benefit it will receive in the future. Examples of common prepayments are insurance, supplies, advertising, and rent. In addition, companies make prepayments when they purchase buildings and equipment.

Prepaid expenses are costs that expire either with the passage of time (e.g., rent and insurance) or through use and consumption (e.g., supplies). The expiration of these costs does not require daily entries, an unnecessary and impractical task. Accordingly, a company like **Walgreens** usually postpones the recognition of such cost expirations until it prepares financial statements. At each statement date, Walgreens makes adjusting entries to record the expenses that apply to the current accounting period and to show the remaining amounts in the asset accounts.

As shown above, prior to adjustment, assets are overstated and expenses are understated. **Thus, an adjusting entry for prepaid expenses results in a debit to an expense account and a credit to an asset account.**

Supplies. A business may use several different types of supplies. For example, a CPA firm will use office supplies such as stationery, envelopes, and accounting paper. An advertising firm will stock advertising supplies such as graph paper, video film, and poster paper. Supplies are generally debited to an asset account when they are acquired. Recognition of supplies used is generally deferred until the adjustment process. At that time, a physical inventory (count) of supplies is taken. The difference between the balance in the Supplies (asset) account and the cost of supplies on hand represents the supplies used (an expense) for the period.

For example, Pioneer Advertising purchased advertising supplies costing $25,000 on October 5. Pioneer therefore debited the asset Supplies. This account shows a balance of $25,000 in the October 31 trial balance (see Illustration 3-19 on page 96). An inventory count at the close of business on October 31 reveals that $10,000 of supplies are still on hand. Thus, the cost of supplies used is $15,000 ($25,000 − $10,000). The analysis and adjustment for advertising supplies is summarized in Illustration 3-22.

Supplies

Oct. 5

Supplies purchased; record asset

Oct. 31

Supplies used; record supplies expense

Basic Analysis: The expense Supplies Expense is increased $15,000, and the asset Supplies is decreased $15,000.

Equation Analysis:

(1)	Assets	=	Liabilities	+	Stockholders' Equity
	Supplies	=			Supplies Expense
	−$15,000				−$15,000

Debit–Credit Analysis: Debits increase expenses: debit Supplies Expense $15,000. Credits decrease assets: credit Supplies $15,000.

Journal Entry:

		Debit	Credit
Oct. 31	Supplies Expense	15,000	
	Supplies		15,000
	(To record supplies used)		

Posting:

Supplies			
Oct. 5	25,000	Oct. 31	Adj. 15,000
Oct. 31	Bal. 10,000		

Supplies Expense		
Oct. 31	Adj. 15,000	
Oct. 31	Bal. 15,000	

A	=	L	+	SE
				−15,000
−15,000				

Cash Flows
no effect

ILLUSTRATION 3-22
Adjustment for Supplies

After adjustment, the asset account Supplies shows a balance of $10,000, which equals the cost of supplies on hand at the statement date. In addition, Supplies Expense shows a balance of $15,000, which equals the cost of supplies used in October. **Without an adjusting entry, October expenses are understated and net income overstated by $15,000. Moreover, both assets and stockholders' equity are overstated by $15,000 on the October 31 balance sheet.**

Insurance. Most companies maintain fire and theft insurance on merchandise and equipment, personal liability insurance for accidents suffered by customers, and automobile insurance on company cars and trucks. The extent of protection against loss determines the cost of the insurance (the amount of the premium to be paid). The insurance policy specifies the term and coverage. The minimum term usually covers one year, but three- to five-year terms are available and may offer lower annual premiums. A company usually debits insurance premiums to the asset account Prepaid Insurance when paid. At the financial statement date, it then debits Insurance Expense and credits Prepaid Insurance for the cost that expired during the period.

For example, on October 4, Pioneer Advertising paid $6,000 for a one-year fire insurance policy. Coverage began on October 1. Pioneer debited the cost of the premium to Prepaid Insurance at that time. This account still shows a balance of $6,000 in the October 31 trial balance. The analysis and adjustment for insurance is summarized in Illustration 3-23 (page 100).

Insurance

Oct. 1

Insurance purchased; record asset

Insurance Policy			
Oct $500	Nov $500	Dec $500	Jan $500
Feb $500	March $500	April $500	May $500
June $500	July $500	Aug $500	Sept $500
1 YEAR $6,000			

Oct. 31
Insurance expired; record insurance expense.

ILLUSTRATION 3-23
Adjustment for Insurance

Basic Analysis	The expense Insurance Expense is increased $500, and the asset Prepaid Insurance is decreased $500.
Equation Analysis	(2) **Assets** = **Liabilities** + **Stockholders' Equity** Prepaid Insurance = Insurance Expense −$500 = −$500
Debit–Credit Analysis	Debits increase expenses: debit Insurance Expense $500. Credits decrease assets: credit Prepaid Insurance $500.
Journal Entry	Oct. 31 Insurance Expense 500 Prepaid Insurance 500 (To record insurance expired)

Posting

Prepaid Insurance			
Oct. 4	6,000	Oct. 31	**Adj. 500**
Oct. 31	Bal. 5,500		

Insurance Expense	
Oct. 31	**Adj. 500**
Oct. 31	Bal. 500

A	=	L	+	SE
				−500
−500				

Cash Flows
no effect

The asset Prepaid Insurance shows a balance of $5,500, which represents the unexpired cost for the remaining 11 months of coverage. At the same time, the balance in Insurance Expense equals the insurance cost that expired in October. **Without an adjusting entry, October expenses are understated by $500 and net income overstated by $500. Moreover, both assets and stockholders' equity also are overstated by $500 on the October 31 balance sheet.**

Depreciation. Companies like **Caterpillar** or **Boeing** typically own various productive facilities, such as buildings, equipment, and motor vehicles. These assets provide a service for a number of years. The term of service is commonly referred to as the **useful life** of the asset. Because Caterpillar, for example, expects an asset such as a building to provide service for many years, Caterpillar records the building as an asset, rather than an expense, in the year the building is acquired. Caterpillar records such assets at cost, as required by the historical cost principle.

To follow the expense recognition principle, Caterpillar reports a portion of the cost of a long-lived asset as an expense during each period of the asset's useful life. **Depreciation** is the process of allocating the cost of an asset to expense over its useful life in a rational and systematic manner.

Depreciation

Oct. 2

Equipment purchased; record asset

Equipment			
Oct $400	Nov $400	Dec $400	Jan $400
Feb $400	March $400	April $400	May $400
June $400	July $400	Aug $400	Sept $400
Depreciation = $4,800/year			

Oct. 31
Depreciation recognized; record depreciation expense

Need for depreciation adjustment. Generally accepted accounting principles (GAAP) view the acquisition of productive facilities as a long-term prepayment for services. The need for making periodic adjusting entries for depreciation is, therefore, the same as we described for other prepaid expenses. That is, a company recognizes the expired cost (expense) during the period and reports the unexpired cost (asset) at the end of the period. The primary causes of depreciation of a productive facility are actual use, deterioration due to the elements, and obsolescence. For example, at the time Caterpillar acquires an asset, the effects of these factors cannot be known with certainty. Therefore, Caterpillar must estimate them. **Thus, depreciation is an estimate rather than a factual measurement of the expired cost.**

To estimate depreciation expense, Caterpillar often divides the cost of the asset by its useful life. For example, if Caterpillar purchases equipment for $10,000 and expects its useful life to be 10 years, Caterpillar records annual depreciation of $1,000.

In the case of Pioneer Advertising, it estimates depreciation on its office equipment to be $4,800 a year (cost $50,000 less salvage value $2,000 divided by useful life of 10 years), or $400 per month. The analysis and adjustment for depreciation is summarized in Illustration 3-24.

ILLUSTRATION 3-24
Adjustment for Depreciation

Basic Analysis	The expense Depreciation Expense is increased $400, and the contra asset Accumulated Depreciation—Equipment is increased $400.
Equation Analysis	**Assets** = **Liabilities** + **Stockholders' Equity** Accumulated Depreciation—Equipment −$400 = Depreciation Expense −$400
Debit–Credit Analysis	Debits increase expenses: debit Depreciation Expense $400. Credits increase contra assets: credit Accumulated Depreciation—Equipment $400.

Journal Entry

Oct. 31	Depreciation Expense	400	
	Accumulated Depreciation—Equipment		400
	(To record monthly depreciation)		

Posting

Equipment			
Oct. 2	50,000		
Oct. 31	Bal. 50,000		

Accumulated Depreciation—Equipment			
		Oct. 31	Adj. 400
		Oct. 31	Bal. 400

Depreciation Expense			
Oct. 31	Adj. 400		
Oct. 31	Bal. 400		

A	=	L	+	SE
				−400
−400				

Cash Flows
no effect

The balance in the Accumulated Depreciation—Equipment account will increase $400 each month. Therefore, after recording and posting the adjusting entry at November 30, the balance will be $800.

Statement presentation. Accumulated Depreciation—Equipment is a contra asset account. A **contra asset account** offsets an asset account on the balance sheet. This means that the Accumulated Depreciation—Equipment account offsets the Equipment account on the balance sheet. Its normal balance is a credit. Pioneer uses this account instead of crediting Equipment in order to disclose both the original cost of the equipment and the total expired cost to date. In the balance sheet, Pioneer deducts Accumulated Depreciation—Equipment from the related asset account as follows.

ILLUSTRATION 3-25
Balance Sheet Presentation of Accumulated Depreciation

Equipment	$50,000	
Less: Accumulated depreciation—equipment	400	$49,600

The **book value** of any depreciable asset is the difference between its cost and its related accumulated depreciation. In Illustration 3-25, the book value of the equipment at the balance sheet date is $49,600. Note that the asset's book value generally differs from its fair value. The reason: **Depreciation is an allocation concept, not a valuation concept.** That is, depreciation **allocates an asset's cost to the periods in which it is used. Depreciation does not attempt to report the actual change in the value of the asset.**

Depreciation expense identifies that portion of the asset's cost that expired during the period (in this case, October). **Without this adjusting entry, total assets, total stockholders' equity, and net income are overstated, and depreciation expense is understated.**

A company records depreciation expense for each piece of equipment, such as trucks or machinery, and for all buildings. A company also establishes related accumulated depreciation accounts for the above, such as Accumulated Depreciation—Trucks, Accumulated Depreciation—Machinery, and Accumulated Depreciation—Buildings.

Unearned Revenues

Oct. 2

Cash is received in advance; liability is recorded

Oct. 31

Some service has been performed; some revenue is recorded

Unearned Revenues. When companies receive cash before services are performed, they record a liability by increasing (crediting) a liability account called **unearned revenues**. In other words, a company now has a performance obligation (liability) to provide service to one its customers. Items like rent, magazine subscriptions, and customer deposits for future service may result in unearned revenues. Airlines, such as **Delta**, **American**, and **Southwest**, treat receipts from the sale of tickets as unearned revenue until they provide the flight service. Tuition received prior to the start of a semester is another example of unearned revenue.

Unearned revenues are the opposite of prepaid expenses. Indeed, unearned revenue on the books of one company is likely to be a prepayment on the books of the company that made the advance payment. For example, if we assume identical accounting periods, a landlord will have unearned rent revenue when a tenant has prepaid rent.

When a company such as **Intel** receives payment for services to be performed in a future accounting period, it credits an unearned revenue (a liability) account to recognize the liability that exists. Intel subsequently recognizes revenue when it performs the service. However, making daily entries to record this revenue is impractical. Instead, Intel delays recognition of revenue until the adjustment process. Then, Intel makes an adjusting entry to record the revenue for services performed during the period and to show the liability that remains at the end of the accounting period. In the typical case, liabilities are overstated and revenues are understated prior to adjustment. **Thus, the adjusting entry for unearned revenues results in a debit (decrease) to a liability account and a credit (increase) to a revenue account.**

For example, Pioneer Advertising received $12,000 on October 2 from R. Knox for advertising services expected to be completed by December 31. Pioneer credited the payment to Unearned Service Revenue. This liability account shows a balance of $12,000 in the October 31 trial balance. Based on an evaluation of the service Pioneer performed for Knox during October, the company determines that it should recognize $4,000 of revenue in October. The liability (Unearned Service Revenue) is therefore decreased and stockholders' equity (Service Revenue) is increased, as shown in Illustration 3-26.

The liability Unearned Service Revenue now shows a balance of $8,000. This amount represents the remaining advertising services expected to be performed in the future. At the same time, Service Revenue shows total revenue recognized in October of $104,000. **Without this adjustment, revenues and net income are understated by $4,000 in the income statement. Moreover, liabilities will be overstated and stockholders' equity will be understated by $4,000 on the October 31 balance sheet.**

Adjusting Entries for Accruals

The second category of adjusting entries is accruals. Companies make adjusting entries for accruals to record revenues for services performed and expenses incurred in the current accounting period. Without an accrual adjustment, the revenue account (and the

ILLUSTRATION 3-26
Adjustment for Unearned Service Revenue

Basic Analysis: The liability Unearned Service Revenue is decreased $4,000, and the revenue Service Revenue is increased $4,000.

Equation Analysis:

Assets	=	Liabilities	+	Stockholders' Equity
		Unearned Service Revenue		Service Revenue
		−$4,000		+$4,000

Debit–Credit Analysis: Debits decrease liabilities: debit Unearned Service Revenue $4,000. Credits increase revenues: credit Service Revenue $4,000.

Journal Entry:

Oct. 31	Unearned Service Revenue	4,000	
	Service Revenue		4,000
	(To record revenue for services performed)		

Posting:

Unearned Service Revenue			
Oct. 31	**Adj. 4,000**	Oct. 2	12,000
		Oct. 31	Bal. 8,000

Service Revenue			
		Oct. 3	100,000
		31	**Adj. 4,000**
		Oct. 31	Bal. 104,000

A	=	L	+	SE
		−4,000		
				+4,000

Cash Flows
no effect

related asset account) or the expense account (and the related liability account) are understated. Thus, the adjusting entry for accruals **will increase both a balance sheet and an income statement account**. Illustration 3-27 shows adjusting entries for accruals.

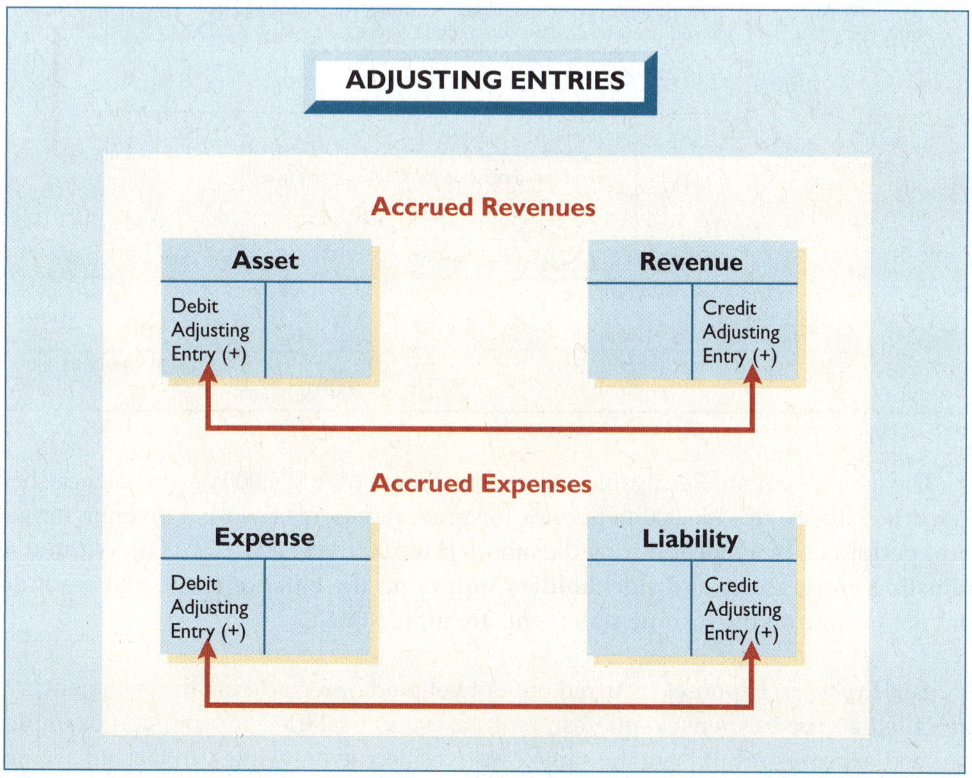

ILLUSTRATION 3-27
Adjusting Entries for Accruals

Accrued Revenues. Revenues for services performed but not yet recorded at the statement date are **accrued revenues**. Accrued revenues may accumulate (accrue) with the passing of time, as in the case of interest revenue. These are unrecorded because the earning of interest does not involve daily transactions. Companies do not record interest revenue on a daily basis because it is often impractical to do so. Accrued revenues also may result from services that have been performed but not yet billed nor collected, as in the case of commissions and fees. These may be unrecorded because only a portion of the total service has been performed and the clients will not be billed until the service has been completed.

Accrued Revenues

Revenue and receivable are recorded for unbilled services

An adjusting entry records the receivable that exists at the balance sheet date and the revenue for the services performed during the period. Prior to adjustment, both assets and revenues are understated. Accordingly, **an adjusting entry** for accrued revenues results in a debit (increase) to an asset account and a credit (increase) to a revenue account.

In October, Pioneer Advertising performed services worth $2,000 that were not billed to clients on or before October 31. Because these services are not billed, they are not recorded. The accrual of unrecorded service revenue increases an asset account, Accounts Receivable. It also increases stockholders' equity by increasing a revenue account, Service Revenue, as shown in Illustration 3-28.

ILLUSTRATION 3-28
Accrual Adjustment for Receivable and Revenue Accounts

Basic Analysis: The asset Accounts Receivable is increased $2,000, and the revenue Service Revenue is increased $2,000.

Equation Analysis:

Assets	=	Liabilities	+	Stockholders' Equity
Accounts Receivable				Service Revenue
+$2,000	=			+$2,000

Debit–Credit Analysis: Debits increase assets: debit Accounts Receivable $2,000.
Credits increase revenues: credit Service Revenue $2,000.

Journal Entry:

Date	Account	Debit	Credit
Oct. 31	Accounts Receivable	2,000	
	Service Revenue		2,000
	(To record revenue for services performed)		

Posting:

Accounts Receivable			
Oct. 1	72,000		
31 Adj.	2,000		
Oct. 31 Bal.	74,000		

Service Revenue			
		Oct. 3	100,000
		31	4,000
		31 Adj.	2,000
		Oct. 31 Bal.	106,000

A	=	L	+	SE
+2,000				
				+2,000

Cash Flows
no effect

The asset Accounts Receivable shows that clients owe $74,000 at the balance sheet date. The balance of $106,000 in Service Revenue represents the total revenue for services performed by Pioneer during the month ($100,000 + $4,000 + $2,000). **Without an adjusting entry, assets and stockholders' equity on the balance sheet, and revenues and net income on the income statement, are understated.**

Accrued Expenses. Expenses incurred but not yet paid or recorded at the statement date are called **accrued expenses**. Interest, rent, taxes, and salaries are common examples. Accrued expenses result from the same causes as accrued revenues. In fact, an accrued expense on the books of one company is an accrued revenue to another company. For example, the $2,000 accrual of service revenue by Pioneer is an accrued expense to the client that received the service.

Adjustments for accrued expenses record the obligations that exist at the balance sheet date and recognize the expenses that apply to the current accounting period. Prior to adjustment, both liabilities and expenses are understated. Therefore, the adjusting entry for accrued expenses results in a debit (increase) to an expense account and a credit (increase) to a liability account.

Accrued interest. Pioneer Advertising signed a three-month note payable in the amount of $50,000 on October 1. The note requires interest at an annual rate of 12 percent. Three factors determine the amount of the interest accumulation: (1) the face value of the note; (2) the interest rate, which is always expressed as an annual rate; and (3) the length of time the note is outstanding. For Pioneer, the total interest due on the $50,000 note at its maturity date three months' in the future is $1,500 ($50,000 × 12% × 3/12), or $500 for one month. Illustration 3-29 shows the formula for computing interest and its application to Pioneer. Note that the formula expresses the time period as a fraction of a year.

ILLUSTRATION 3-29
Formula for Computing Interest

Face Value of Note	×	Annual Interest Rate	×	Time in Terms of One Year	=	Interest
$50,000	×	12%	×	1/12	=	**$500**

As Illustration 3-30 shows, the accrual of interest at October 31 increases a liability account, Interest Payable. It also decreases stockholders' equity by increasing an expense account, Interest Expense.

ILLUSTRATION 3-30
Adjustment for Interest

Basic Analysis
The expense Interest Expense is increased $500, and the liability Interest Payable is increased $500.

Equation Analysis

Assets	=	Liabilities	+	Stockholders' Equity
		Interest Payable		Interest Expense
		+$500		−$500

Debit–Credit Analysis
Debits increase expenses: debit Interest Expense $500.
Credits increase liabilities: credit Interest Payable $500.

Journal Entry

Oct. 31	Interest Expense	500	
	Interest Payable		500
	(To record interest on notes payable)		

Posting

Interest Expense			
Oct. 31	**Adj. 500**		
Oct. 31	Bal. 500		

Interest Payable			
		Oct. 31	**Adj. 500**
		Oct. 31	Bal. 500

A	=	L	+	SE
				−500
		+500		

Cash Flows
no effect

Interest Expense shows the interest charges for the month of October. Interest Payable shows the amount of interest owed at the statement date. Pioneer will not pay this amount until the note comes due at the end of three months. Why does Pioneer use the

Interest Payable account instead of crediting Notes Payable? By recording interest payable separately, Pioneer discloses the two different types of obligations—interest and principal—in the accounts and statements. **Without this adjusting entry, liabilities and interest expense are understated, and both net income and stockholders' equity are overstated.**

Accrued salaries and wages. Companies pay for some types of expenses, such as employee salaries and wages, after the services have been performed. For example, Pioneer Advertising last paid salaries and wages on October 26. It will not pay salaries and wages again until November 23. However, as shown in the calendar below, three working days remain in October (October 29–31).

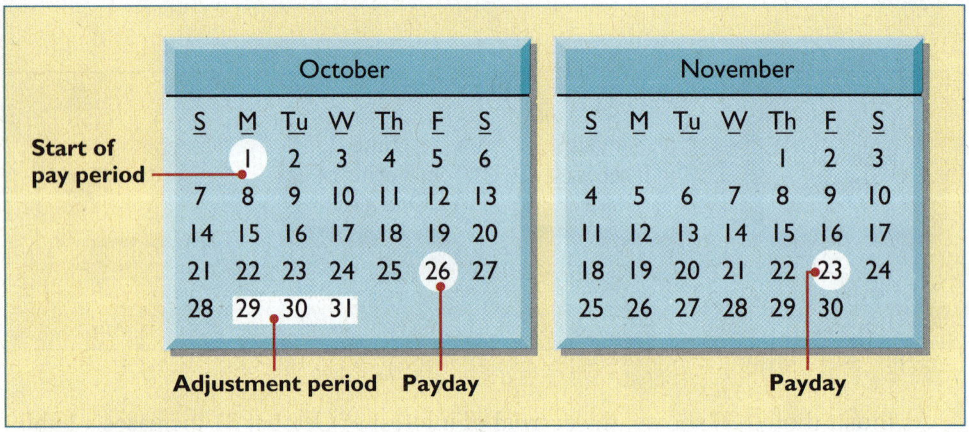

At October 31, the salaries and wages for these days represent an accrued expense and a related liability to Pioneer. The employees receive total salaries and wages of $10,000 for a five-day work week, or $2,000 per day. Thus, accrued salaries and wages at October 31 are $6,000 ($2,000 × 3). The analysis and adjustment process is summarized in Illustration 3-31.

ILLUSTRATION 3-31
Adjustment for Salaries and Wages Expense

Basic Analysis	The expense Salaries and Wages Expense is increased $6,000, and the liability account Salaries and Wages Payable is increased $6,000.
Equation Analysis	**Assets** = **Liabilities** (Salaries and Wages Payable +$6,000) + **Stockholders' Equity** (Salaries and Wages Expense −$6,000)
Debit–Credit Analysis	Debits increase expenses: debit Salaries and Wages Expense $6,000. Credits increase liabilities: credit Salaries and Wages Payable $6,000.
Journal Entry	Oct. 31 Salaries and Wages Expense 6,000 Salaries and Wages Payable 6,000 (To record accrued salaries)
Posting	see T-accounts below

Date	Account	Debit	Credit
Oct. 31	Salaries and Wages Expense	6,000	
	Salaries and Wages Payable		6,000
	(To record accrued salaries)		

Salaries and Wages Expense

Debit	Credit
Oct. 26 40,000	
31 **Adj. 6,000**	
Oct. 31 Bal. 46,000	

Salaries and Wages Payable

Debit	Credit
	Oct. 31 **Adj. 6,000**
	Oct. 31 Bal. 6,000

A	=	L	+	SE
				−6,000
		+6,000		

Cash Flows
no effect

After this adjustment, the balance in Salaries and Wages Expense of $46,000 (23 days × $2,000) is the actual salaries and wages expense for October. The balance in Salaries and Wages Payable of $6,000 is the amount of the liability for salaries and wages owed as of October 31. **Without the $6,000 adjustment for salaries, both Pioneer's expenses and liabilities are understated by $6,000.**

Pioneer pays salaries and wages every four weeks. Consequently, the next payday is November 23, when it will again pay total salaries and wages of $40,000. The payment consists of $6,000 of salaries and wages payable at October 31 plus $34,000 of salaries and wages expense for November (17 working days as shown in the November calendar × $2,000). Therefore, Pioneer makes the following entry on November 23.

Nov. 23		
Salaries and Wages Payable	6,000	
Salaries and Wages Expense	34,000	
Cash		40,000
(To record November 23 payroll)		

A	=	L	+	SE
		−6,000		
				−34,000
−40,000				

Cash Flows
−40,000

This entry eliminates the liability for Salaries and Wages Payable that Pioneer recorded in the October 31 adjusting entry. This entry also records the proper amount of Salaries and Wages Expense for the period between November 1 and November 23.

What do the numbers mean? AM I COVERED?

Rather than purchasing insurance to cover casualty losses and other obligations, some companies "self-insure." That is, a company decides to pay for any possible claims, as they arise, out of its own resources. The company also purchases an insurance policy to cover losses that exceed certain amounts.

For example, **Almost Family, Inc.**, a healthcare services company, has a self-insured employee health-benefit program. However, Almost Family ran into accounting problems when it failed to record an accrual of the liability for benefits not covered by its back-up insurance policy. This led to restatement of Almost Family's fiscal results for the accrual of the benefit expense.

Bad debts. Proper recognition of revenues and expenses dictates recording bad debts as an expense of the period in which a company recognizes revenue for services performed instead of the period in which the company writes off the accounts or notes. The proper valuation of the receivable balance also requires recognition of uncollectible receivables. Proper recognition and valuation require an adjusting entry.

Bad Debts

Oct. 31
Uncollectible accounts; record bad debt expense

At the end of each period, a company such as **General Mills** estimates the amount of receivables that will later prove to be uncollectible. General Mills bases the estimate on various factors: the amount of bad debts it experienced in past years, general economic conditions, how long the receivables are past due, and other factors that indicate the extent of uncollectibility. To illustrate, assume that, based on past experience, Pioneer Advertising reasonably estimates a bad debt expense for the month of $1,600. The analysis and adjustment process for bad debts is summarized in Illustration 3-32 (page 108).

ILLUSTRATION 3-32
Adjustment for Bad Debt Expense

Basic Analysis

The expense Bad Debt Expense is increased $1,600, and the contra asset Allowance for Doubtful Accounts is increased $1,600.

Equation Analysis

Assets	=	Liabilities	+	Stockholders' Equity
Allowance for Doubtful Accounts	=			Bad Debt Expense
−$1,600				−$1,600

Debit–Credit Analysis

Debits increase expenses: debit Bad Debt Expense $1,600.
Credits increase contra assets: credit Allowance for Doubtful Accounts $1,600.

Journal Entry

Date	Account	Debit	Credit
Oct. 31	Bad Debt Expense	1,600	
	Allowance for Doubtful Accounts		1,600
	(To record monthly bad debt expense)		

Posting

Accounts Receivable

	Debit		Credit
Oct. 2	72,000		
31	2,000		
Oct. 31	Bal. 74,000		

Allowance for Doubtful Accounts

	Debit		Credit
		Oct. 31	**Adj. 1,600**
		Oct. 31	Bal. 1,600

Bad Debt Expense

	Debit		Credit
Oct. 31	**Adj. 1,600**		
Oct. 31	Bal. 1,600		

A = L + SE
−1,600 (SE)
−1,600 (A)
Cash Flows
no effect

A company often expresses bad debts as a percentage of the revenue on account for the period. Or, a company may compute bad debts by adjusting Allowance for Doubtful Accounts to a certain percentage of the trade accounts receivable and trade notes receivable at the end of the period.

Adjusted Trial Balance

After journalizing and posting all adjusting entries, Pioneer Advertising prepares another trial balance from its ledger accounts (shown in Illustration 3-33 on page 109). This trial balance is called an **adjusted trial balance**. The purpose of an adjusted trial balance is to **prove the equality** of the total debit balances and the total credit balances in the ledger after all adjustments. Because the accounts contain all data needed for financial statements, the adjusted trial balance is the **primary basis for the preparation of financial statements**.

Preparing Financial Statements

LEARNING OBJECTIVE 6
Prepare financial statements from the adjusted trial balance.

As indicated above, **Pioneer Advertising can prepare financial statements directly from the adjusted trial balance.** Illustrations 3-34 (page 109) and 3-35 (page 110) show the interrelationships of data in the adjusted trial balance and the financial statements.

As Illustration 3-34 shows, Pioneer prepares the income statement from the revenue and expense accounts. Next, it derives the retained earnings statement from the retained earnings and dividends accounts and the net income (or net loss) shown in the income statement.

ILLUSTRATION 3-33
Adjusted Trial Balance

PIONEER ADVERTISING AGENCY INC.
Adjusted Trial Balance
October 31, 2014

	Debit	Credit
Cash	$ 80,000	
Accounts Receivable	74,000	
Allowance for Doubtful Accounts		$ 1,600
Supplies	10,000	
Prepaid Insurance	5,500	
Equipment	50,000	
Accumulated Depreciation—Equipment		400
Notes Payable		50,000
Accounts Payable		25,000
Interest Payable		500
Unearned Service Revenue		8,000
Salaries and Wages Payable		6,000
Common Stock		100,000
Dividends	5,000	
Service Revenue		106,000
Salaries and Wages Expense	46,000	
Supplies Expense	15,000	
Rent Expense	9,000	
Insurance Expense	500	
Interest Expense	500	
Depreciation Expense	400	
Bad Debt Expense	1,600	
	$297,500	$297,500

ILLUSTRATION 3-34
Preparation of the Income Statement and Retained Earnings Statement from the Adjusted Trial Balance

PIONEER ADVERTISING AGENCY INC.
Adjusted Trial Balance
October 31, 2014

Account	Debit	Credit
Cash	$80,000	
Accounts Receivable	74,000	
Allowance for Doubtful Accounts		$ 1,600
Supplies	10,000	
Prepaid Insurance	5,500	
Equipment	50,000	
Accumulated Depreciation—Equipment		400
Notes Payable		50,000
Accounts Payable		25,000
Unearned Service Revenue		8,000
Salaries and Wages Payable		6,000
Interest Payable		500
Common Stock		100,000
Retained Earnings		–0–
Dividends	5,000	
Service Revenue		106,000
Salaries and Wages Expense	46,000	
Supplies Expense	15,000	
Rent Expense	9,000	
Insurance Expense	500	
Interest Expense	500	
Depreciation Expense	400	
Bad Debt Expense	1,600	
	$297,500	$297,500

PIONEER ADVERTISING AGENCY INC.
Income Statement
For the Month Ended October 31, 2014

Revenues		
Service revenue		$106,000
Expenses		
Salaries and wages expense	$46,000	
Supplies expense	15,000	
Rent expense	9,000	
Insurance expense	500	
Interest expense	500	
Depreciation expense	400	
Bad debt expense	1,600	
Total expenses		73,000
Net income		$ 33,000

PIONEER ADVERTISING AGENCY INC.
Retained Earnings Statement
For the Month Ended October 31, 2014

Retained earnings, October 1	$ –0–
Add: Net income	33,000
	33,000
Less: Dividends	5,000
Retained earnings, October 31	$28,000

To balance sheet

As Illustration 3-35 shows, Pioneer then prepares the balance sheet from the asset and liability accounts, the common stock account, and the ending retained earnings balance as reported in the retained earnings statement.

PIONEER ADVERTISING AGENCY INC.
Adjusted Trial Balance
October 31, 2014

Account	Debit	Credit
Cash	$80,000	
Accounts Receivable	74,000	
Allowance for Doubtful Accounts		$ 1,600
Supplies	10,000	
Prepaid Insurance	5,500	
Equipment	50,000	
Accumulated Depreciation—Equipment		400
Notes Payable		50,000
Accounts Payable		25,000
Unearned Service Revenue		8,000
Salaries and Wages Payable		6,000
Interest Payable		500
Common Stock		100,000
Retained Earnings		–0–
Dividends	5,000	
Service Revenue		106,000
Salaries and Wages Expense	46,000	
Supplies Expense	15,000	
Rent Expense	9,000	
Insurance Expense	500	
Interest Expense	500	
Depreciation Expense	400	
Bad Debt Expense	1,600	
	$297,500	$297,500

PIONEER ADVERTISING AGENCY INC.
Balance Sheet
October 31, 2014

Assets		
Cash		$ 80,000
Accounts receivable	$74,000	
Less: Allowance for doubtful accounts	1,600	72,400
Supplies		10,000
Prepaid insurance		5,500
Equipment	50,000	
Less: Accumulated depreciation—equipment	400	49,600
Total assets		$217,500
Liabilities and Stockholders' Equity		
Liabilities		
Notes payable		$ 50,000
Accounts payable		25,000
Unearned service revenue		8,000
Salaries and wages payable		6,000
Interest payable		500
Total liabilities		89,500
Stockholders' equity		
Common stock		100,000
Retained earnings		28,000
Total liabilities and stockholders' equity		$217,500

Balance at Oct. 31 from Retained Earnings Statement in Illustration 3-34

ILLUSTRATION 3-35
Preparation of the Balance Sheet from the Adjusted Trial Balance

What do the numbers mean? 24/7 ACCOUNTING

To achieve the vision of "24/7 accounting," a company must be able to update revenue, income, and balance sheet numbers every day within the quarter and publish them on the Internet. Such real-time reporting responds to the demand for more timely financial information made available to all investors—not just to analysts with access to company management.

Two obstacles typically stand in the way of 24/7 accounting: having the necessary accounting systems to close the books on a daily basis, and reliability concerns associated with unaudited real-time data. Only a few companies have the necessary accounting capabilities. Cisco Systems, which pioneered the concept of the 24-hour close, is one such company.

Closing

Basic Process

LEARNING OBJECTIVE 7
Prepare closing entries.

The **closing process** reduces the balance of nominal (temporary) accounts to zero in order to prepare the accounts for the next period's transactions. In the closing process, Pioneer Advertising transfers all of the revenue and expense account balances (income statement items) to a clearing or suspense account called Income Summary. The Income Summary account matches revenues and expenses.

Pioneer uses this clearing account only at the end of each accounting period. The account represents the net income or net loss for the period. It then transfers this amount (the net income or net loss) to an owners' equity account. (For a corporation, the owners' equity account is retained earnings; for proprietorships and partnerships, it is a capital account.) Companies post all such **closing entries** to the appropriate general ledger accounts.

Closing Entries

In practice, companies generally prepare closing entries only at the end of a company's annual accounting period. However, to illustrate the journalizing and posting of closing entries, we will assume that Pioneer Advertising closes its books monthly. Illustration 3-36 shows the closing entries at October 31.

ILLUSTRATION 3-36
Closing Entries Journalized

GENERAL JOURNAL			J3
Date	**Account Titles and Explanation**	**Debit**	**Credit**
	Closing Entries		
	(1)		
Oct. 31	Service Revenue	106,000	
	Income Summary		106,000
	(To close revenue account)		
	(2)		
31	Income Summary	73,000	
	Supplies Expense		15,000
	Depreciation Expense		400
	Insurance Expense		500
	Salaries and Wages Expense		46,000
	Rent Expense		9,000
	Interest Expense		500
	Bad Debt Expense		1,600
	(To close expense accounts)		
	(3)		
31	Income Summary	33,000	
	Retained Earnings		33,000
	(To close net income to retained earnings)		
	(4)		
31	Retained Earnings	5,000	
	Dividends		5,000
	(To close dividends to retained earnings)		

A couple of cautions about preparing closing entries. (1) Avoid unintentionally doubling the revenue and expense balances rather than zeroing them. (2) Do not close Dividends through the Income Summary account. **Dividends are not expenses, and they are not a factor in determining net income.**

Posting Closing Entries

Illustration 3-37 (page 112) shows the posting of closing entries and the underlining (ruling) of accounts. All temporary accounts have zero balances after posting the closing entries. In addition, note that the balance in Retained Earnings represents the accumulated undistributed earnings of Pioneer at the end of the accounting period. Pioneer reports this

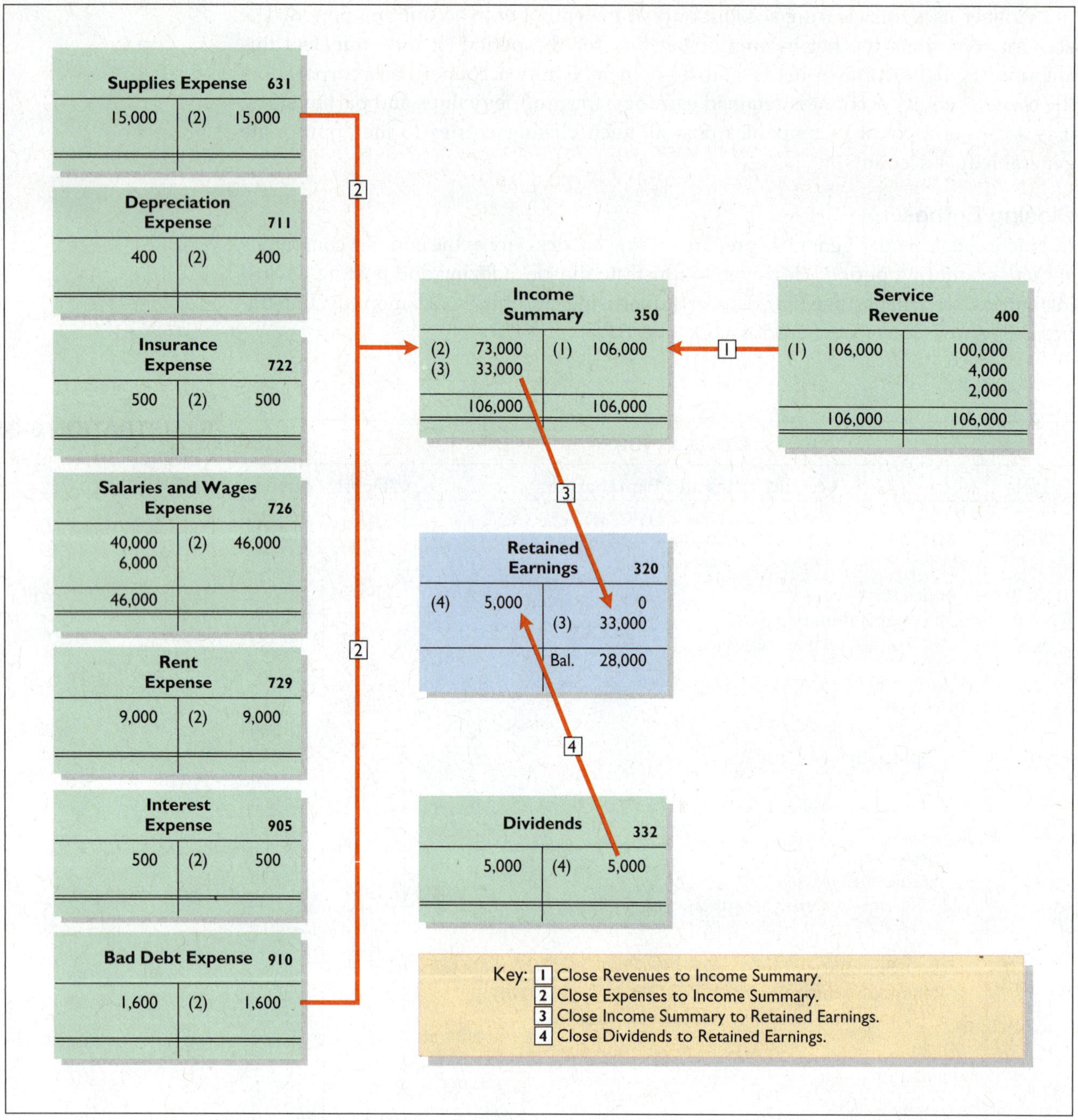

ILLUSTRATION 3-37
Posting of Closing Entries

amount in the balance sheet as the ending amount reported on the retained earnings statement. As noted above, **Pioneer uses the Income Summary account only in closing**. It does not journalize and post entries to this account during the year.

As part of the closing process, Pioneer totals, balances, and double-underlines the **temporary accounts**—revenues, expenses, and dividends—as shown in T-account form in Illustration 3-37. It does not close the **permanent accounts**—assets, liabilities, and stockholders' equity (Common Stock and Retained Earnings). Instead, Pioneer draws a single underline beneath the current period entries for the permanent accounts. The account balance is then entered below the single underline and is carried forward to the next period (see, for example, Retained Earnings).

After the closing process, each income statement account and the dividend account are balanced out to zero and are ready for use in the next accounting period.

Post-Closing Trial Balance

Recall that a trial balance is prepared after entering the regular transactions of the period, and that a second trial balance (the adjusted trial balance) occurs after posting the adjusting entries. A company may take a third trial balance after posting the closing entries. The trial balance after closing is called the **post-closing trial balance**. The purpose of the post-closing trial balance is **to prove the equality of the permanent account balances that the company carries forward into the next accounting period**. Since all temporary accounts will have zero balances, **the post-closing trial balance will contain only permanent (real)—balance sheet—accounts.**

Illustration 3-38 shows the post-closing trial balance of Pioneer Advertising Agency Inc.

ILLUSTRATION 3-38
Post-Closing Trial Balance

PIONEER ADVERTISING AGENCY INC.
POST-CLOSING TRIAL BALANCE
OCTOBER 31, 2014

Account	Debit	Credit
Cash	$ 80,000	
Accounts Receivable	74,000	
Allowance for Doubtful Accounts		$ 1,600
Supplies	10,000	
Prepaid Insurance	5,500	
Equipment	50,000	
Accumulated Depreciation—Equipment		400
Notes Payable		50,000
Accounts Payable		25,000
Unearned Service Revenue		8,000
Salaries and Wages Payable		6,000
Interest Payable		500
Common Stock		100,000
Retained Earnings		28,000
	$219,500	$219,500

A post-closing trial balance provides evidence that the company has properly journalized and posted the closing entries. It also shows that the accounting equation is in balance at the end of the accounting period. However, like the other trial balances, it does not prove that Pioneer has recorded all transactions or that the ledger is correct. For example, the post-closing trial balance will balance if a transaction is not journalized and posted, or if a transaction is journalized and posted twice.

Reversing Entries—An Optional Step

Some accountants prefer to reverse the effects of certain adjusting entries by making a **reversing entry** at the beginning of the next accounting period. A reversing entry is the exact opposite of the adjusting entry made in the previous period. **Use of reversing entries is an optional bookkeeping procedure; it is not a required step in the accounting cycle.** Accordingly, we have chosen to cover this topic in Appendix 3B at the end of the chapter.

The Accounting Cycle Summarized

A summary of the steps in the accounting cycle shows a logical sequence of the accounting procedures used during a fiscal period:

1. Enter the transactions of the period in appropriate journals.
2. Post from the journals to the ledger (or ledgers).
3. Take an unadjusted trial balance (trial balance).
4. Prepare adjusting journal entries and post to the ledger(s).
5. Take a trial balance after adjusting (adjusted trial balance).
6. Prepare the financial statements from the second trial balance.
7. Prepare closing journal entries and post to the ledger(s).
8. Take a post-closing trial balance (**optional**).
9. Prepare reversing entries (**optional**) and post to the ledger(s).

A company normally completes all of these steps in every fiscal period.

What do the numbers mean? HEY, IT'S COMPLICATED

The economic volatility of the past few years has left companies hungering for more timely and uniform financial information to help them react quickly to fast-changing conditions. As one expert noted, companies were extremely focused on trying to reduce costs and plan for the future better, but a lot of them discovered that they didn't have the information they needed and they didn't have the ability to get that information. The unsteady recession environment also made it risky for companies to interrupt their operations to get new systems up to speed.

So what to do? Try to piecemeal upgrades each year or start a major overhaul of their internal systems? **Best Buy**, for example, has standardized as many of its systems as possible and has been steadily upgrading them over the past decade. Acquisitions can wreak havoc on reporting systems. Best Buy is choosy about when to standardize for companies it acquires, but it sometimes has to implement new systems after international deals.

In other situations, a major overhaul is needed. For example, it is common for companies with a steady stream of acquisitions to have 50 to 70 general ledger systems. In those cases, a company cannot react well unless its systems are made compatible. So is it the big bang (major overhaul) or the piecemeal approach? It seems to depend. One thing is certain—good accounting systems are a necessity. Without one, the risk of failure is high.

Source: Emily Chasan, "The Financial-Data Dilemma," *Wall Street Journal* (July 24, 2012), p. B4.

FINANCIAL STATEMENTS FOR A MERCHANDISING COMPANY

LEARNING OBJECTIVE 8
Prepare financial statements for a merchandising company.

Pioneer Advertising Agency Inc. is a service company. In this section, we show a detailed set of financial statements for a merchandising company, Uptown Cabinet Corp. The financial statements (see pages 115–116) are prepared from the adjusted trial balance.

Income Statement

The income statement for Uptown, shown in Illustration 3-39, is self-explanatory. The income statement classifies amounts into such categories as gross profit on sales, income from operations, income before taxes, and net income. Although earnings per share information is required to be shown on the face of the income statement for a corporation, we omit this item here as it will be discussed more fully later in the textbook. *For homework problems, do not present earnings per share information unless required to do so.*

ILLUSTRATION 3-39
Income Statement for a Merchandising Company

UPTOWN CABINET CORP. INCOME STATEMENT FOR THE YEAR ENDED DECEMBER 31, 2014			
Net sales			$400,000
Cost of goods sold			316,000
Gross profit on sales			84,000
Selling expenses			
Salaries and wages expense (sales)		$20,000	
Advertising expense		10,200	
Total selling expenses		30,200	
Administrative expenses			
Salaries and wages expense (general)	$19,000		
Depreciation expense—equipment	6,700		
Property tax expense	5,300		
Rent expense	4,300		
Bad debt expense	1,000		
Telephone and Internet expense	600		
Insurance expense	360		
Total administrative expenses		37,260	
Total selling and administrative expenses			67,460
Income from operations			16,540
Other revenues and gains			
Interest revenue			800
			17,340
Other expenses and losses			
Interest expense			1,700
Income before income taxes			15,640
Income tax			3,440
Net income			$ 12,200

Statement of Retained Earnings

A corporation may retain the net income earned in the business, or it may distribute it to stockholders by payment of dividends. In Illustration 3-40, Uptown added the net income earned during the year to the balance of retained earnings on January 1, thereby increasing the balance of retained earnings. Deducting dividends of $2,000 results in the ending retained earnings balance of $26,400 on December 31.

ILLUSTRATION 3-40
Statement of Retained Earnings for a Merchandising Company

UPTOWN CABINET CORP. STATEMENT OF RETAINED EARNINGS FOR THE YEAR ENDED DECEMBER 31, 2014	
Retained earnings, January 1	$16,200
Add: Net income	12,200
	28,400
Less: Dividends	2,000
Retained earnings, December 31	$26,400

Balance Sheet

The balance sheet for Uptown, shown in Illustration 3-41 (page 116), is a classified balance sheet. Interest receivable, inventory, prepaid insurance, and prepaid rent are included as current assets. Uptown considers these assets current because they will be converted into cash or used by the business within a relatively short period of time. Uptown deducts the amount of Allowance for Doubtful Accounts from the total of accounts, notes, and interest receivable because it estimates that only $54,800 of $57,800 will be collected in cash.

ILLUSTRATION 3-41
Balance Sheet for a Merchandising Company

UPTOWN CABINET CORP.
BALANCE SHEET
AS OF DECEMBER 31, 2014

Assets			
Current assets			
Cash			$ 1,200
Notes receivable	$16,000		
Accounts receivable	41,000		
Interest receivable	800	$57,800	
Less: Allowance for doubtful accounts		3,000	54,800
Inventory			40,000
Prepaid insurance			540
Prepaid rent			500
Total current assets			97,040
Property, plant, and equipment			
Equipment		67,000	
Less: Accumulated depreciation—equipment		18,700	
Total property, plant, and equipment			48,300
Total assets			$145,340
Liabilities and Stockholders' Equity			
Current liabilities			
Notes payable			$ 20,000
Accounts payable			13,500
Property taxes payable			2,000
Income taxes payable			3,440
Total current liabilities			38,940
Long-term liabilities			
Bonds payable, due June 30, 2022			30,000
Total liabilities			68,940
Stockholders' equity			
Common stock, $5.00 par value, issued and outstanding, 10,000 shares		$50,000	
Retained earnings		26,400	
Total stockholders' equity			76,400
Total liabilities and stockholders' equity			$145,340

In the property, plant, and equipment section, Uptown deducts the Accumulated Depreciation—Equipment from the cost of the equipment. The difference represents the book or carrying value of the equipment.

The balance sheet shows property taxes payable as a current liability because it is an obligation that is payable within a year. The balance sheet also shows other short-term liabilities such as accounts payable.

The bonds payable, due in 2022, are long-term liabilities. As a result, the balance sheet shows the account in a separate section. (The company paid interest on the bonds on December 31.)

Because Uptown is a corporation, the capital section of the balance sheet, called the stockholders' equity section in the illustration, differs somewhat from the capital section for a proprietorship. Total stockholders' equity consists of the common stock, which is the original investment by stockholders, and the earnings retained in the business. *For homework purposes, unless instructed otherwise, prepare an unclassified balance sheet.*

What do the numbers mean? STATEMENTS, PLEASE

The use of a worksheet at the end of each month or quarter enables a company to prepare interim financial statements even though it closes the books only at the end of each year. For example, assume that **Google** closes its books on December 31, but it wants monthly financial statements. To do this, at the end of January, Google prepares an adjusted trial balance (using a worksheet as illustrated in Appendix 3C) to supply the information needed for statements for January.

At the end of February, it uses a worksheet again. Note that because Google did not close the accounts at the end of January, the income statement taken from the adjusted trial balance on February 28 will present the net income for two months. If Google wants an income statement for only the month of February, the company obtains it by subtracting the items in the January income statement from the corresponding items in the income statement for the two months of January and February.

If Google executes such a process daily, it can realize "24/7 accounting" (see the "What Do the Numbers Mean?" box on page 110).

Closing Entries

Uptown makes closing entries in its general journal as shown below.

December 31, 2014		
Interest Revenue	800	
Sales Revenue	400,000	
Income Summary		400,800
(To close revenues to Income Summary)		
Income Summary	388,600	
Cost of Goods Sold		316,000
Salaries and Wages Expense (sales)		20,000
Advertising Expense		10,200
Salaries and Wages Expense (general)		19,000
Depreciation Expense		6,700
Rent Expense		4,300
Property Tax Expense		5,300
Bad Debt Expense		1,000
Telephone and Internet Expense		600
Insurance Expense		360
Interest Expense		1,700
Income Tax Expense		3,440
(To close expenses to Income Summary)		
Income Summary	12,200	
Retained Earnings		12,200
(To close Income Summary to Retained Earnings)		
Retained Earnings	2,000	
Dividends		2,000
(To close Dividends to Retained Earnings)		

You will want to read the **IFRS INSIGHTS** on pages 153–157 for discussion of IFRS related to information systems.

SUMMARY OF LEARNING OBJECTIVES

1 Understand basic accounting terminology. Understanding the following eleven terms helps in understanding key accounting concepts: (1) Event. (2) Transaction. (3) Account. (4) Real and nominal accounts. (5) Ledger. (6) Journal. (7) Posting. (8) Trial balance. (9) Adjusting entries. (10) Financial statements. (11) Closing entries.

2 Explain double-entry rules. The left side of any account is the debit side; the right side is the credit side. All asset and expense accounts are increased on the left or

KEY TERMS

account, *84*
accounting cycle, *89*
accounting information system, *84*
accrued expenses, *104*
accrued revenues, *103*
adjusted trial balance, *85, 108*
adjusting entry, *85, 96*

balance sheet, 85
book value, 101
closing entries, 85, 111
closing process, 110
contra asset account, 101
credit, 85
debit, 85
depreciation, 100
double-entry accounting, 86
event, 84
financial statements, 85
general journal, 91
general ledger, 85, 91
income statement, 85
journal, 85
journalizing, 85
ledger, 85
nominal accounts, 85
post-closing trial balance, 85, 113
posting, 85, 92
prepaid expenses, 98
real accounts, 85
reversing entries, 113
special journals, 92
statement of cash flows, 85
statement of retained earnings, 85
subsidiary ledger, 85
T-account, 85
transaction, 84
trial balance, 85, 96
unearned revenues, 102

debit side and decreased on the right or credit side. Conversely, all liability and revenue accounts are increased on the right or credit side and decreased on the left or debit side. Stockholders' equity accounts, Common Stock and Retained Earnings, are increased on the credit side. Dividends is increased on the debit side.

3 Identify steps in the accounting cycle. The basic steps in the accounting cycle are (1) identifying and measuring transactions and other events; (2) journalizing; (3) posting; (4) preparing an unadjusted trial balance; (5) making adjusting entries; (6) preparing an adjusted trial balance; (7) preparing financial statements; and (8) closing.

4 Record transactions in journals, post to ledger accounts, and prepare a trial balance. The simplest journal form chronologically lists transactions and events expressed in terms of debits and credits to particular accounts. The items entered in a general journal must be transferred (posted) to the general ledger. Companies should prepare an unadjusted trial balance at the end of a given period after they have recorded the entries in the journal and posted them to the ledger.

5 Explain the reasons for preparing adjusting entries and identify major types of adjusting entries. Adjustments achieve a proper recognition of revenues and expenses, so as to determine net income for the current period and to achieve an accurate statement of end-of-the-period balances in assets, liabilities, and owners' equity accounts. The major types of adjusting entries are deferrals (prepaid expenses and unearned revenues) and accruals (accrued revenues and accrued expenses).

6 Prepare financial statements from the adjusted trial balance. Companies can prepare financial statements directly from the adjusted trial balance. The income statement is prepared from the revenue and expense accounts. The statement of retained earnings is prepared from the retained earnings account, dividends, and net income (or net loss). The balance sheet is prepared from the asset, liability, and equity accounts.

7 Prepare closing entries. In the closing process, the company transfers all of the revenue and expense account balances (income statement items) to a clearing account called Income Summary, which is used only at the end of the fiscal year. Revenues and expenses are matched in the Income Summary account. The net result of this matching represents the net income or net loss for the period. That amount is then transferred to an owners' equity account (Retained Earnings for a corporation and capital accounts for proprietorships and partnerships).

8 Prepare financial statements for a merchandising company. The financial statements for a merchandiser differ from those for a service company, as a merchandiser must account for gross profit on sales. The accounting cycle, however, is performed the same.

APPENDIX 3A CASH-BASIS ACCOUNTING VERSUS ACCRUAL-BASIS ACCOUNTING

LEARNING OBJECTIVE 9
Differentiate the cash basis of accounting from the accrual basis of accounting.

Most companies use **accrual-basis accounting**: They recognize revenue when the performance obligation is satisfied and expenses in the period incurred, without regard to the time of receipt or payment of cash.

Some small companies and the average individual taxpayer, however, use a strict or modified cash-basis approach. Under the **strict cash basis**, companies record revenue only when they receive cash. They record expenses only when they disperse cash. Determining income on the cash basis rests upon collecting revenue and paying expenses. The cash basis ignores two principles: the revenue recognition principle and the expense recognition principle. Consequently, cash-basis financial statements are not in conformity with GAAP.

An illustration will help clarify the differences between accrual-basis and cash-basis accounting. Assume that Quality Contractor signs an agreement to construct a garage for $22,000. In January, Quality begins construction, incurs costs of $18,000 on credit, and by the end of January delivers a finished garage to the buyer. In February, Quality collects $22,000 cash from the customer. In March, Quality pays the $18,000 due the creditors. Illustrations 3A-1 and 3A-2 show the net incomes for each month under cash-basis accounting and accrual-basis accounting.

ILLUSTRATION 3A-1
Income Statement—Cash Basis

QUALITY CONTRACTOR
INCOME STATEMENT—CASH BASIS
FOR THE MONTH OF

	January	February	March	Total
Cash receipts	$-0-	$22,000	$ -0-	$22,000
Cash payments	-0-	-0-	18,000	18,000
Net income (loss)	$-0-	$22,000	$(18,000)	$ 4,000

ILLUSTRATION 3A-2
Income Statement—Accrual Basis

QUALITY CONTRACTOR
INCOME STATEMENT—ACCRUAL BASIS
FOR THE MONTH OF

	January	February	March	Total
Revenues	$22,000	$-0-	$-0-	$22,000
Expenses	18,000	-0-	-0-	18,000
Net income (loss)	$ 4,000	$-0-	$-0-	$ 4,000

For the three months combined, total net income is the same under both cash-basis accounting and accrual-basis accounting. The difference is in the **timing** of revenues and expenses. The basis of accounting also affects the balance sheet. Illustrations 3A-3 and 3A-4 (page 120) show Quality Contractor's balance sheets at each month-end under the cash basis and the accrual basis.

ILLUSTRATION 3A-3
Balance Sheets—Cash Basis

QUALITY CONTRACTOR
BALANCE SHEET—CASH BASIS
AS OF

	January 31	February 28	March 31
Assets			
Cash	$-0-	$22,000	$4,000
Total assets	$-0-	$22,000	$4,000
Liabilities and Owners' Equity			
Owners' equity	$-0-	$22,000	$4,000
Total liabilities and owners' equity	$-0-	$22,000	$4,000

ILLUSTRATION 3A-4
Balance Sheets—Accrual Basis

QUALITY CONTRACTOR
BALANCE SHEET—ACCRUAL BASIS
AS OF

	January 31	February 28	March 31
Assets			
Cash	$ -0-	$22,000	$4,000
Accounts receivable	22,000	-0-	-0-
Total assets	$22,000	$22,000	$4,000
Liabilities and Owners' Equity			
Accounts payable	$18,000	$18,000	$-0-
Owners' equity	4,000	4,000	4,000
Total liabilities and owners' equity	$22,000	$22,000	$4,000

Analysis of Quality's income statements and balance sheets shows the ways in which cash-basis accounting is inconsistent with basic accounting theory:

1. The cash basis understates revenues and assets from the construction and delivery of the garage in January. It ignores the $22,000 of accounts receivable, representing a near-term future cash inflow.
2. The cash basis understates expenses incurred with the construction of the garage and the liability outstanding at the end of January. It ignores the $18,000 of accounts payable, representing a near-term future cash outflow.
3. The cash basis understates owners' equity in January by not recognizing the revenues and the asset until February. It also overstates owners' equity in February by not recognizing the expenses and the liability until March.

In short, cash-basis accounting violates the accrual concept underlying financial reporting.

The **modified cash basis** is a mixture of the cash basis and the accrual basis. It is based on the strict cash basis but with modifications that have substantial support, such as capitalizing and depreciating plant assets or recording inventory. This method is often followed by professional services firms (doctors, lawyers, accountants, and consultants) and by retail, real estate, and agricultural operations.[3]

CONVERSION FROM CASH BASIS TO ACCRUAL BASIS

Not infrequently, companies want to convert a cash basis or a modified cash basis set of financial statements to the accrual basis for presentation to investors and creditors. To illustrate this conversion, assume that Dr. Diane Windsor, like many small business owners, keeps her accounting records on a cash basis. In the year 2014, Dr. Windsor

[3]Companies in the following situations might use a cash or modified cash basis.

(1) A company that is primarily interested in cash flows (for example, a group of physicians that distributes cash-basis earnings for salaries and bonuses).

(2) A company that has a limited number of financial statement users (small, closely held company with little or no debt).

(3) A company that has operations that are relatively straightforward (small amounts of inventory, long-term assets, or long-term debt).

received $300,000 from her patients and paid $170,000 for operating expenses, resulting in an excess of cash receipts over disbursements of $130,000 ($300,000 − $170,000). At January 1 and December 31, 2014, she has accounts receivable, unearned service revenue, accrued liabilities, and prepaid expenses as shown in Illustration 3A-5.

	January 1, 2014	December 31, 2014
Accounts receivable	$12,000	$9,000
Unearned service revenue	-0-	4,000
Accrued liabilities	2,000	5,500
Prepaid expenses	1,800	2,700

ILLUSTRATION 3A-5
Financial Information Related to Dr. Diane Windsor

Service Revenue Computation

To convert the amount of cash received from patients to service revenue on an accrual basis, we must consider changes in accounts receivable and unearned service revenue during the year. Accounts receivable at the beginning of the year represents revenues recognized last year that are collected this year. Ending accounts receivable indicates revenues recognized this year that are not yet collected. Therefore, to compute revenue on an accrual basis, we subtract beginning accounts receivable and add ending accounts receivable, as the formula in Illustration 3A-6 shows.

Cash receipts from customers { **− Beginning accounts receivable** / **+ Ending accounts receivable** } = **Revenue on an accrual basis**

ILLUSTRATION 3A-6
Conversion of Cash Receipts to Revenue—Accounts Receivable

Similarly, beginning unearned service revenue represents cash received last year for revenues recognized this year. Ending unearned service revenue results from collections this year that will be recognized as revenue next year. Therefore, to compute revenue on an accrual basis, we add beginning unearned service revenue and subtract ending unearned service revenue, as the formula in Illustration 3A-7 shows.

Cash receipts from customers { **+ Beginning unearned service revenue** / **− Ending unearned service revenue** } = **Revenue on an accrual basis**

ILLUSTRATION 3A-7
Conversion of Cash Receipts to Revenue—Unearned Service Revenue

Therefore, for Dr. Windsor's dental practice, to convert cash collected from customers to service revenue on an accrual basis, we would make the computations shown in Illustration 3A-8.

Cash receipts from customers		$300,000
− Beginning accounts receivable	$(12,000)	
+ Ending accounts receivable	9,000	
+ Beginning unearned service revenue	-0-	
− Ending unearned service revenue	(4,000)	(7,000)
Service revenue (accrual)		$293,000

ILLUSTRATION 3A-8
Conversion of Cash Receipts to Service Revenue

Operating Expense Computation

To convert cash paid for operating expenses during the year to operating expenses on an accrual basis, we must consider changes in prepaid expenses and accrued liabilities. First, we need to recognize as this year's expenses the amount of beginning prepaid expenses. (The cash payment for these occurred last year.) Therefore, to arrive at operating expense on an accrual basis, we add the beginning prepaid expenses balance to cash paid for operating expenses.

Conversely, ending prepaid expenses result from cash payments made this year for expenses to be reported next year. (Under the accrual basis, Dr. Windsor would have deferred recognizing these payments as expenses until a future period.) To convert these cash payments to operating expenses on an accrual basis, we deduct ending prepaid expenses from cash paid for expenses, as the formula in Illustration 3A-9 shows.

ILLUSTRATION 3A-9
Conversion of Cash Payments to Expenses—Prepaid Expenses

$$\text{Cash paid for operating expenses} \begin{cases} + \text{Beginning prepaid expenses} \\ - \text{Ending prepaid expenses} \end{cases} = \text{Expenses on an accrual basis}$$

Similarly, beginning accrued liabilities result from expenses recognized last year that require cash payments this year. Ending accrued liabilities relate to expenses recognized this year that have not been paid. To arrive at expenses on an accrual basis, we deduct beginning accrued liabilities and add ending accrued liabilities to cash paid for expenses, as the formula in Illustration 3A-10 shows.

ILLUSTRATION 3A-10
Conversion of Cash Payments to Expenses—Accrued Liabilities

$$\text{Cash paid for operating expenses} \begin{cases} - \text{Beginning accrued liabilities} \\ + \text{Ending accrued liabilities} \end{cases} = \text{Expenses on an accrual basis}$$

Therefore, for Dr. Windsor's dental practice, to convert cash paid for operating expenses to operating expenses on an accrual basis, we would make the computations shown in Illustration 3A-11.

ILLUSTRATION 3A-11
Conversion of Cash Paid to Operating Expenses

Cash paid for operating expenses		$170,000
+ Beginning prepaid expense	$ 1,800	
− Ending prepaid expense	(2,700)	
− Beginning accrued liabilities	(2,000)	
+ Ending accrued liabilities	5,500	2,600
Operating expenses (accrual)		$172,600

This entire conversion can be completed in worksheet form, as shown in Illustration 3A-12.

ILLUSTRATION 3A-12
Conversion of Statement of Cash Receipts and Disbursements to Income Statement

Diane Windsor.xls

DIANE WINDSOR, D.D.S.
Conversion of Income Statement Data from Cash Basis to Accrual Basis
For the Year 2014

Account Titles	Cash Basis	Adjustments: Add	Adjustments: Deduct	Accrual Basis
Collections from customers	$300,000			
– Accounts receivable, Jan. 1			$12,000	
+ Accounts receivable, Dec. 31		$9,000		
+ Unearned service revenue, Jan. 1		—	—	
– Unearned service revenue, Dec. 31			4,000	
Service revenue				$293,000
Disbursement for expenses	170,000			
+ Prepaid expenses, Jan. 1		1,800		
– Prepaid expenses, Dec. 31			2,700	
– Accrued liabilities, Jan. 1			2,000	
+ Accrued liabilities, Dec. 31		5,500		
Operating expenses				172,600
Excess of cash collections over disbursements—cash basis	$130,000			
Net income—accrual basis				$120,400

Using this approach, we adjust collections and disbursements on a cash basis to revenue and expense on an accrual basis, to arrive at accrual net income. In any conversion from the cash basis to the accrual basis, depreciation or amortization is an additional expense in arriving at net income on an accrual basis.

THEORETICAL WEAKNESSES OF THE CASH BASIS

The cash basis reports exactly when cash is received and when cash is disbursed. To many people, that information represents something concrete. Isn't cash what it is all about? Does it make sense to invent something, design it, produce it, market and sell it, if you aren't going to get cash for it in the end? Many frequently say, "Cash is the real bottom line," and also, "Cash is the oil that lubricates the economy." If so, then what is the merit of accrual accounting?

Today's economy is considerably more lubricated by credit than by cash. The accrual basis, not the cash basis, recognizes all aspects of the credit phenomenon. Investors, creditors, and other decision-makers seek timely information about a company's *future* cash flows. Accrual-basis accounting provides this information by reporting the cash inflows and outflows associated with earnings activities as soon as these companies can estimate these cash flows with an acceptable degree of certainty. Receivables and payables are forecasters of future cash inflows and outflows. In other words, accrual-basis accounting aids in predicting future cash flows by reporting transactions and other events with cash consequences at the time the transactions and events occur, rather than when the cash is received and paid.

KEY TERMS

accrual-basis accounting, *118*
modified cash basis, *120*
strict cash basis, *118*

SUMMARY OF LEARNING OBJECTIVE FOR APPENDIX 3A

9 Differentiate the cash basis of accounting from the accrual basis of accounting. The cash basis of accounting records revenues when cash is received and expenses when cash is paid. The accrual basis recognizes revenue when the performance obligation is satisfied and expenses in the period incurred, without regard to the time of the receipt or payment of cash. Accrual-basis accounting is theoretically preferable because it provides information about future cash inflows and outflows associated with earnings activities as soon as companies can estimate these cash flows with an acceptable degree of certainty. Cash-basis accounting is not in conformity with GAAP.

APPENDIX 3B USING REVERSING ENTRIES

LEARNING OBJECTIVE 10
Identify adjusting entries that may be reversed.

Use of reversing entries simplifies the recording of transactions in the next accounting period. The use of reversing entries, however, does not change the amounts reported in the financial statements for the previous period.

ILLUSTRATION OF REVERSING ENTRIES—ACCRUALS

A company most often uses reversing entries to reverse two types of adjusting entries: accrued revenues and accrued expenses. To illustrate the optional use of reversing entries for accrued expenses, we use the following transaction and adjustment data.

1. October 24 (initial salaries and wages entry): Paid $4,000 of salaries and wages incurred between October 10 and October 24.
2. October 31 (adjusting entry): Incurred salaries and wages between October 25 and October 31 of $1,200, to be paid in the November 8 payroll.
3. November 8 (subsequent salaries and wages entry): Paid salaries and wages of $2,500. Of this amount, $1,200 applied to accrued salaries and wages payable at October 31 and $1,300 to salaries and wages payable for November 1 through November 8.

Illustration 3B-1 shows the comparative entries.

The comparative entries show that the first three entries are the same whether or not the company uses reversing entries. The last two entries differ. The November 1 reversing entry eliminates the $1,200 balance in Salaries and Wages Payable, created by the October 31 adjusting entry. The reversing entry also creates a $1,200 credit balance in the Salaries and Wages Expense account. As you know, it is unusual for an expense account to have a credit balance. However, the balance is correct in this instance. Why? Because the company will debit the entire amount of the first salaries and wages payment in the new accounting period to Salaries and Wages Expense. This debit eliminates the credit balance. The resulting debit balance in the expense account will equal the salaries and wages expense incurred in the new accounting period ($1,300 in this example).

Reversing Entries Not Used				Reversing Entries Used			
Initial Salary Entry							
Oct. 24	Salaries and Wages Expense	4,000		Oct. 24	Salaries and Wages Expense	4,000	
	Cash		4,000		Cash		4,000
Adjusting Entry							
Oct. 31	Salaries and Wages Expense	1,200		Oct. 31	Salaries and Wages Expense	1,200	
	Salaries and Wages Payable		1,200		Salaries and Wages Payable		1,200
Closing Entry							
Oct. 31	Income Summary	5,200		Oct. 31	Income Summary	5,200	
	Salaries and Wages Expense		5,200		Salaries and Wages Expense		5,200
Reversing Entry							
Nov. 1	No entry is made.			Nov. 1	Salaries and Wages Payable	1,200	
					Salaries and Wages Expense		1,200
Subsequent Salary Entry							
Nov. 8	Salaries and Wages Payable	1,200		Nov. 8	Salaries and Wages Expense	2,500	
	Salaries and Wages Expense	1,300			Cash		2,500
	Cash		2,500				

ILLUSTRATION 3B-1
Comparison of Entries for Accruals, with and without Reversing Entries

When a company makes reversing entries, it debits all cash payments of expenses to the related expense account. This means that on November 8 (and every payday), the company debits Salaries and Wages Expense for the amount paid without regard to the existence of any accrued salaries and wages payable. Repeating the same entry simplifies the recording process in an accounting system.

ILLUSTRATION OF REVERSING ENTRIES—DEFERRALS

Up to this point, we assumed the recording of all deferrals as prepaid expense or unearned revenue. In some cases, though, a company records deferrals directly in expense or revenue accounts. When this occurs, a company may also reverse deferrals.

To illustrate the use of reversing entries for prepaid expenses, we use the following transaction and adjustment data.

1. December 10 (initial entry): Purchased $20,000 of office supplies with cash.
2. December 31 (adjusting entry): Determined that $5,000 of office supplies are on hand.

Illustration 3B-2 (page 126) shows the comparative entries.

After the adjusting entry on December 31 (regardless of whether using reversing entries), the asset account Supplies shows a balance of $5,000, and Supplies Expense shows a balance of $15,000. If the company initially debits Supplies Expense when it purchases the supplies, it then makes a reversing entry to return to the expense account the cost of unconsumed supplies. The company then continues to debit Supplies Expense for additional purchases of supplies during the next period.

Deferrals are generally entered in real accounts (assets and liabilities), thus making reversing entries unnecessary. This approach is used because it is advantageous for items that a company needs to apportion over several periods (e.g., supplies and parts inventories). However, for other items that do not follow this regular pattern and that may or may not involve two or more periods, a company ordinarily enters them initially

Reversing Entries Not Used				Reversing Entries Used			
Initial Purchase of Supplies Entry							
Dec. 10	Supplies	20,000		Dec. 10	Supplies Expense	20,000	
	Cash		20,000		Cash		20,000
Adjusting Entry							
Dec. 31	Supplies Expense	15,000		Dec. 31	Supplies	5,000	
	Supplies		15,000		Supplies Expense		5,000
Closing Entry							
Dec. 31	Income Summary	15,000		Dec. 31	Income Summary	15,000	
	Supplies Expense		15,000		Supplies Expense		15,000
Reversing Entry							
Jan. 1	No entry			Jan. 1	Supplies Expense	5,000	
					Supplies		5,000

ILLUSTRATION 3B-2
Comparison of Entries for Deferrals, with and without Reversing Entries

in revenue or expense accounts. The revenue and expense accounts may not require adjusting, and the company thus systematically closes them to Income Summary.

Using the nominal accounts adds consistency to the accounting system. It also makes the recording more efficient, particularly when a large number of such transactions occur during the year. For example, the bookkeeper knows to expense invoice items (except for capital asset acquisitions). He or she need not worry whether an item will result in a prepaid expense at the end of the period because the company will make adjustments at the end of the period.

SUMMARY OF REVERSING ENTRIES

We summarize guidelines for reversing entries as follows.

1. All accruals should be reversed.
2. All deferrals for which a company debited or credited the original cash transaction to an expense or revenue account should be reversed.
3. Adjusting entries for depreciation and bad debts are not reversed.

Recognize that reversing entries do not have to be used. Therefore, some accountants avoid them entirely.

SUMMARY OF LEARNING OBJECTIVE FOR APPENDIX 3B

10 Identify adjusting entries that may be reversed. Reversing entries are most often used to reverse two types of adjusting entries: accrued revenues and accrued expenses. Deferrals may also be reversed if the initial entry to record the transaction is made to an expense or revenue account.

APPENDIX 3C USING A WORKSHEET: THE ACCOUNTING CYCLE REVISITED

11 LEARNING OBJECTIVE
Prepare a 10-column worksheet.

In this appendix, we provide an additional illustration of the end-of-period steps in the accounting cycle and illustrate the use of a worksheet in this process. Using a **worksheet** often facilitates the end-of-period (monthly, quarterly, or annually) accounting and reporting process. Use of a worksheet helps a company prepare the financial statements on a more timely basis. How? With a worksheet, a company need not wait until it journalizes and posts the adjusting and closing entries.

A company prepares a worksheet either on columnar paper or within a computer spreadsheet. In either form, a company uses the worksheet to adjust account balances and to prepare financial statements.

The worksheet does not replace the financial statements. Instead, it is an informal device for accumulating and sorting information needed for the financial statements. Completing the worksheet provides considerable assurance that a company properly handled all of the details related to the end-of-period accounting and statement preparation. The 10-column worksheet in Illustration 3C-1 (on page 128) provides columns for the first trial balance, adjustments, adjusted trial balance, income statement, and balance sheet.

WORKSHEET COLUMNS

Trial Balance Columns

Uptown Cabinet Corp., shown in Illustration 3C-1 (page 128), obtains data for the trial balance from its ledger balances at December 31. The amount for Inventory, $40,000, is the year-end inventory amount, which results from the application of a perpetual inventory system.

Adjustments Columns

After Uptown enters all adjustment data on the worksheet, it establishes the equality of the adjustment columns. It then extends the balances in all accounts to the adjusted trial balance columns.

ADJUSTMENTS ENTERED ON THE WORKSHEET

Items (a) through (g) below serve as the basis for the adjusting entries made in the worksheet for Uptown shown in Illustration 3C-1.

(a) Depreciation of equipment at the rate of 10 percent per year based on original cost of $67,000.

(b) Estimated bad debts of one-quarter of 1 percent of sales ($400,000).

(c) Insurance expired during the year $360.

(d) Interest accrued on notes receivable as of December 31, $800.

(e) The Rent Expense account contains $500 rent paid in advance, which is applicable to next year.

(f) Property taxes accrued December 31, $2,000.

(g) Income taxes payable estimated $3,440.

Uptown Cabinet Corp.xls

Home Insert Page Layout Formulas Data Review View

P18 fx

UPTOWN CABINET CORP.
Ten-Column Worksheet
For the Year Ended December 31, 2014

	A	B	C	D	E	F	G	H	I	J	K
5–6		Trial Balance		Adjustments		Adjusted Trial Balance		Income Statement		Balance Sheet	
7	Account Titles	Dr.	Cr.	Dr.	Cr.	Dr.	Cr.	Dr.	Cr.	Dr.	Cr.
8	Cash	1,200				1,200				1,200	
9	Notes receivable	16,000				16,000				16,000	
10	Accounts receivable	41,000				41,000				41,000	
11	Allowance for doubtful accounts		2,000		(b) 1,000		3,000				3,000
12	Inventory	40,000				40,000				40,000	
13	Prepaid insurance	900			(c) 360	540				540	
14	Equipment	67,000				67,000				67,000	
15	Accumulated depreciation—equipment		12,000		(a) 6,700		18,700				18,700
16	Notes payable		20,000				20,000				20,000
17	Accounts payable		13,500				13,500				13,500
18	Bonds payable		30,000				30,000				30,000
19	Common stock		50,000				50,000				50,000
20	Retained earnings, Jan. 1, 2014		16,200				16,200				16,200
21	Dividends	2,000				2,000				2,000	
22	Sales revenue		400,000				400,000		400,000		
23	Cost of goods sold	316,000				316,000		316,000			
24	Salaries and wages expense (sales)	20,000				20,000		20,000			
25	Advertising expense	10,200				10,200		10,200			
26	Salaries and wages expense (general)	19,000				19,000		19,000			
27	Telephone and Internet expense	600				600		600			
28	Rent expense	4,800			(e) 500	4,300		4,300			
29	Property tax expense	3,300		(f) 2,000		5,300		5,300			
30	Interest expense	1,700				1,700		1,700			
31	Totals	543,700	543,700								
32	Depreciation expense			(a) 6,700		6,700		6,700			
33	Bad debt expense			(b) 1,000		1,000		1,000			
34	Insurance expense			(c) 360		360		360			
35	Interest receivable			(d) 800		800				800	
36	Interest revenue				(d) 800		800		800		
37	Prepaid rent			(e) 500		500				500	
38	Property taxes payable				(f) 2,000		2,000				2,000
39	Income tax expense			(g) 3,440		3,440		3,440			
40	Income tax payable				(g) 3,440		3,440				3,440
41	Totals			14,800	14,800	557,640	557,640	388,600	400,800		
42	Net income							12,200			12,200
43	Totals							400,800	400,800	169,040	169,040

ILLUSTRATION 3C-1
Use of a Worksheet

The adjusting entries shown on the December 31, 2014, worksheet are as follows.

	(a)		
Depreciation Expense		6,700	
Accumulated Depreciation—Equipment			6,700
	(b)		
Bad Debt Expense		1,000	
Allowance for Doubtful Accounts			1,000
	(c)		
Insurance Expense		360	
Prepaid Insurance			360
	(d)		
Interest Receivable		800	
Interest Revenue			800
	(e)		
Prepaid Rent		500	
Rent Expense			500
	(f)		
Property Tax Expense		2,000	
Property Taxes Payable			2,000
	(g)		
Income Tax Expense		3,440	
Income Taxes Payable			3,440

Uptown Cabinet transfers the adjusting entries to the Adjustments columns of the worksheet, often designating each by letter. The trial balance lists any new accounts resulting from the adjusting entries, as illustrated on the worksheet. (For example, see the accounts listed in rows 32 through 40 in Illustration 3C-1.) Uptown then totals and balances the Adjustments columns.

Adjusted Trial Balance

The adjusted trial balance shows the balance of all accounts after adjustment at the end of the accounting period. For example, Uptown adds the $2,000 shown opposite the Allowance for Doubtful Accounts in the Trial Balance Cr. column to the $1,000 in the Adjustments Cr. column. The company then extends the $3,000 total to the Adjusted Trial Balance Cr. column. Similarly, Uptown reduces the $900 debit opposite Prepaid Insurance by the $360 credit in the Adjustments column. The result, $540, is shown in the Adjusted Trial Balance Dr. column.

Income Statement and Balance Sheet Columns

Uptown extends all the debit items in the Adjusted Trial Balance columns into the Income Statement or Balance Sheet columns to the right. It similarly extends all the credit items.

The next step is to total the Income Statement columns. Uptown needs the amount of net income or loss for the period to balance the debit and credit columns. The net income of $12,200 is shown in the Income Statement Dr. column because revenues exceeded expenses by that amount.

Uptown then balances the Income Statement columns. The company also enters the net income of $12,200 in the Balance Sheet Cr. column as an increase in retained earnings.

PREPARING FINANCIAL STATEMENTS FROM A WORKSHEET

The worksheet provides the information needed for preparation of the financial statements without reference to the ledger or other records. In addition, the worksheet sorts that data into appropriate columns, which facilitates the preparation of the statements. The financial statements of Uptown Cabinet are shown in Chapter 3 (pages 115–116).

KEY TERMS

worksheet, *127*

SUMMARY OF LEARNING OBJECTIVE FOR APPENDIX 3C

11 **Prepare a 10-column worksheet.** The 10-column worksheet provides columns for the first trial balance, adjustments, adjusted trial balance, income statement, and balance sheet. The worksheet does not replace the financial statements. Instead, it is an informal device for accumulating and sorting information needed for the financial statements.

DEMONSTRATION PROBLEM

Nalezny Advertising Agency was founded by Casey Hayward in January 2005. Presented below are both the adjusted and unadjusted trial balances as of December 31, 2014.

NALEZNY ADVERTISING AGENCY
TRIAL BALANCE
DECEMBER 31, 2014

	Unadjusted		Adjusted	
	Dr.	Cr.	Dr.	Cr.
Cash	$ 11,000		$ 11,000	
Accounts Receivable	20,000		21,500	
Supplies	8,400		5,000	
Equipment	60,000		60,000	
Accumulated Depreciation—Equipment		$ 28,000		$ 35,000
Accounts Payable		5,000		5,000
Unearned Advertising Revenue		7,000		5,600
Salaries and Wages Payable		-0-		1,300
Common Stock		10,000		10,000
Retained Earnings		4,800		4,800
Advertising Revenue		58,600		61,500
Salaries and Wages Expense	10,000		11,300	
Depreciation Expense			7,000	
Supplies Expense			3,400	
Rent Expense	4,000		4,000	
	$113,400	$113,400	$123,200	$123,200

Instructions

(a) Journalize the annual adjusting entries that were made.

(b) Prepare an income statement for the year ending December 31, 2014, and a balance sheet at December 31.

(c) Describe the remaining steps in the accounting cycle to be completed by Nalezny for 2014.

Solution

(a)

Date	Account	Debit	Credit
Dec. 31	Accounts Receivable	1,500	
	Advertising Revenue		1,500
31	Unearned Advertising Revenue	1,400	
	Advertising Revenue		1,400
31	Supplies Expense	3,400	
	Supplies		3,400
31	Depreciation Expense	7,000	
	Accumulated Depreciation—Equipment		7,000
31	Salaries and Wages Expense	1,300	
	Salaries and Wages Payable		1,300

(b)

NALEZNY ADVERTISING AGENCY
INCOME STATEMENT
FOR THE YEAR ENDED DECEMBER 31, 2014

Revenues		
Advertising revenue		$61,500
Expenses		
Salaries and wages expense	$11,300	
Depreciation expense	7,000	
Rent expense	4,000	
Supplies expense	3,400	
Total expenses		25,700
Net income		$35,800

NALEZNY ADVERTISING AGENCY
BALANCE SHEET
DECEMBER 31, 2014

Assets

Cash		$11,000
Accounts receivable		21,500
Supplies		5,000
Equipment	$60,000	
Less: Accumulated depreciation—equipment	35,000	25,000
Total assets		$62,500

Liabilities and Stockholders' Equity

Liabilities		
Accounts payable		$ 5,000
Unearned advertising revenue		5,600
Salaries and wage payable		1,300
Total liabilities		11,900
Stockholders' equity		
Common stock	$10,000	
Retained earnings	40,600*	50,600
Total liabilities and stockholders' equity		$62,500

*Retained earnings, Jan. 1, 2014	$ 4,800
Add: Net income	35,800
Retained earnings, Dec. 31, 2014	$40,600

(c) Following preparation of financial statements (part (b)), Nalezny would prepare closing entries to reduce the temporary accounts to zero. Some companies prepare a post-closing trial balance and reversing entries.

Be sure to check the book's companion website for a Review and Analysis Exercise, with solution.

Note: All asterisked Questions, Exercises, and Problems relate to material in the appendices to the chapter.

QUESTIONS

1. Give an example of a transaction that results in:

(a) A decrease in an asset and a decrease in a liability.

(b) A decrease in one asset and an increase in another asset.

(c) A decrease in one liability and an increase in another liability.

2. Do the following events represent business transactions? Explain your answer in each case.

(a) A computer is purchased on account.

(b) A customer returns merchandise and is given credit on account.

(c) A prospective employee is interviewed.

(d) The owner of the business withdraws cash from the business for personal use.

(e) Merchandise is ordered for delivery next month.

3. Name the accounts debited and credited for each of the following transactions.

(a) Billing a customer for work done.

(b) Receipt of cash from customer on account.

(c) Purchase of office supplies on account.

(d) Purchase of 15 gallons of gasoline for the delivery truck.

4. Why are revenue and expense accounts called temporary or nominal accounts?

5. Andrea Pafko, a fellow student, contends that the double-entry system means that each transaction must be recorded twice. Is Andrea correct? Explain.

6. Is it necessary that a trial balance be taken periodically? What purpose does it serve?

7. Indicate whether each of the following items is a real or nominal account and whether it appears in the balance sheet or the income statement.

(a) Prepaid Rent.

(b) Salaries and Wages Payable.

(c) Inventory.

(d) Accumulated Depreciation—Equipment.

(e) Equipment.

(f) Service Revenue.

(g) Salaries and Wages Expense.

(h) Supplies.

8. Employees are paid every Saturday for the preceding work week. If a balance sheet is prepared on Wednesday, December 31, what does the amount of wages earned during the first three days of the week (12/29, 12/30, 12/31) represent? Explain.

9. (a) How are the components of revenues and expenses different for a merchandising company? (b) Explain the income measurement process of a merchandising company.

10. What differences are there between the trial balance before closing and the trial balance after closing with respect to the following accounts?

(a) Accounts Payable.

(b) Expense accounts.

(c) Revenue accounts.

(d) Retained Earnings account.

(e) Cash.

11. What are adjusting entries and why are they necessary?

12. What are closing entries and why are they necessary?

13. Jay Hawk, maintenance supervisor for Boston Insurance Co., has purchased a riding lawnmower and accessories to be used in maintaining the grounds around corporate headquarters. He has sent the following information to the accounting department.

Cost of mower and accessories	$4,000	Date purchased	7/1/14
Estimated useful life	5 yrs	Monthly salary of groundskeeper	$1,100
Salvage value	$0	Estimated annual fuel cost	$150

Compute the amount of depreciation expense (related to the mower and accessories) that should be reported on Boston's December 31, 2014, income statement. Assume straight-line depreciation.

14. Midwest Enterprises made the following entry on December 31, 2014.

Interest Expense	10,000	
Interest Payable		10,000
(To record interest expense due on loan from Anaheim National Bank)		

What entry would Anaheim National Bank make regarding its outstanding loan to Midwest Enterprises? Explain why this must be the case.

***15.** Distinguish between cash-basis accounting and accrual-basis accounting. Why is accrual-basis accounting acceptable for most businesses and the cash-basis unacceptable in the preparation of an income statement and a balance sheet?

***16.** When salaries and wages expense for the year is computed, why are beginning accrued salaries and wages subtracted from, and ending accrued salaries and wages added to, salaries and wages paid during the year?

***17.** List two types of transactions that would receive different accounting treatment using (a) strict cash-basis accounting, and (b) a modified cash basis.

***18.** What are reversing entries, and why are they used?

***19.** "A worksheet is a permanent accounting record, and its use is required in the accounting cycle." Do you agree? Explain.

BRIEF EXERCISES

4 **BE3-1** Transactions for Mehta Company for the month of May are presented below. Prepare journal entries for each of these transactions. (You may omit explanations.)

May	1	B.D. Mehta invests $4,000 cash in exchange for common stock in a small welding corporation.
	3	Buys equipment on account for $1,100.
	13	Pays $400 to landlord for May rent.
	21	Bills Noble Corp. $500 for welding work done.

4 **BE3-2** Agazzi Repair Shop had the following transactions during the first month of business as a proprietorship. Journalize the transactions. (Omit explanations.)

Aug.	2	Invested $12,000 cash and $2,500 of equipment in the business.
	7	Purchased supplies on account for $500. (Debit asset account.)
	12	Performed services for clients, for which $1,300 was collected in cash and $670 was billed to the clients.
	15	Paid August rent $600.
	19	Counted supplies and determined that only $270 of the supplies purchased on August 7 are still on hand.

4 5 **BE3-3** On July 1, 2014, Crowe Co. pays $15,000 to Zubin Insurance Co. for a 3-year insurance policy. Both companies have fiscal years ending December 31. For Crowe Co., journalize the entry on July 1 and the adjusting entry on December 31.

4 5 **BE3-4** Using the data in BE3-3, journalize the entry on July 1 and the adjusting entry on December 31 for Zubin Insurance Co. Zubin uses the accounts Unearned Service Revenue and Service Revenue.

4 5 **BE3-5** Assume that on February 1, **Procter & Gamble (P&G)** paid $720,000 in advance for 2 years' insurance coverage. Prepare P&G's February 1 journal entry and the annual adjusting entry on June 30.

4 5 **BE3-6** LaBouche Corporation owns a warehouse. On November 1, it rented storage space to a lessee (tenant) for 3 months for a total cash payment of $2,400 received in advance. Prepare LaBouche's November 1 journal entry and the December 31 annual adjusting entry.

4 5 **BE3-7** Dresser Company's weekly payroll, paid on Fridays, totals $8,000. Employees work a 5-day week. Prepare Dresser's adjusting entry on Wednesday, December 31, and the journal entry to record the $8,000 cash payment on Friday, January 2.

5 **BE3-8** Included in Gonzalez Company's December 31 trial balance is a note receivable of $12,000. The note is a 4-month, 10% note dated October 1. Prepare Gonzalez's December 31 adjusting entry to record $300 of accrued interest, and the February 1 journal entry to record receipt of $12,400 from the borrower.

5 **BE3-9** Prepare the following adjusting entries at August 31 for **Walgreens**.

(a) Interest on notes payable of $300 is accrued.
(b) Services performed but unbilled total $1,400.
(c) Salaries and wages earned by employees of $700 have not been recorded.
(d) Bad debt expense for year is $900.

Use the following account titles: Service Revenue, Accounts Receivable, Interest Expense, Interest Payable, Salaries and Wages Expense, Salaries and Wages Payable, Allowance for Doubtful Accounts, and Bad Debt Expense.

5 **BE3-10** At the end of its first year of operations, the trial balance of Alonzo Company shows Equipment $30,000 and zero balances in Accumulated Depreciation—Equipment and Depreciation Expense. Depreciation for the year is estimated to be $2,000. Prepare the adjusting entry for depreciation at December 31, and indicate the balance sheet presentation for the equipment at December 31.

7 **BE3-11** Side Kicks has year-end account balances of Sales Revenue $808,900; Interest Revenue $13,500; Cost of Goods Sold $556,200; Administrative Expenses $189,000; Income Tax Expense $35,100; and Dividends $18,900. Prepare the year-end closing entries.

9 ***BE3-12** Kelly Company had cash receipts from customers in 2014 of $142,000. Cash payments for operating expenses were $97,000. Kelly has determined that at January 1, accounts receivable was $13,000, and prepaid expenses were $17,500. At December 31, accounts receivable was $18,600, and prepaid expenses were $23,200. Compute (a) service revenue and (b) operating expenses.

10 ***BE3-13** Assume that **Best Buy** made a December 31 adjusting entry to debit Salaries and Wages Expense and credit Salaries and Wages Payable for $4,200 for one of its departments. On January 2, Best Buy paid the weekly payroll of $7,000. Prepare Best Buy's (a) January 1 reversing entry; (b) January 2 entry (assuming the reversing entry was prepared); and (c) January 2 entry (assuming the reversing entry was not prepared).

EXERCISES

4 **E3-1 (Transaction Analysis—Service Company)** Beverly Crusher is a licensed CPA. During the first month of operations of her business (a sole proprietorship), the following events and transactions occurred.

April	2	Invested $32,000 cash and equipment valued at $14,000 in the business.
	2	Hired a secretary-receptionist at a salary of $290 per week payable monthly.
	3	Purchased supplies on account $700. (Debit an asset account.)
	7	Paid office rent of $600 for the month.
	11	Completed a tax assignment and billed client $1,100 for services rendered. (Use Service Revenue account.)
	12	Received $3,200 advance on a management consulting engagement.
	17	Received cash of $2,300 for services completed for Ferengi Co.
	21	Paid insurance expense $110.
	30	Paid secretary-receptionist $1,160 for the month.
	30	A count of supplies indicated that $120 of supplies had been used.
	30	Purchased a new computer for $6,100 with personal funds. (The computer will be used exclusively for business purposes.)

Instructions

Journalize the transactions in the general journal. (Omit explanations.)

4 **E3-2 (Corrected Trial Balance)** The trial balance of Wanda Landowska Company (shown on the next page) does not balance. Your review of the ledger reveals the following. (a) Each account had a normal balance. (b) The debit footings in Prepaid Insurance, Accounts Payable, and Property Tax Expense were each understated $100. (c) A transposition error was made in Accounts Receivable and Service Revenue; the correct balances for Accounts Receivable and Service Revenue are $2,750 and $6,690, respectively. (d) A debit posting to Advertising Expense of $300 was omitted. (e) A $1,500 cash drawing by the owner was debited to Owner's Capital and credited to Cash.

WANDA LANDOWSKA COMPANY
TRIAL BALANCE
APRIL 30, 2014

	Debit	Credit
Cash	$ 4,800	
Accounts Receivable	2,570	
Prepaid Insurance	700	
Equipment		$ 8,000
Accounts Payable		4,500
Property Taxes Payable	560	
Owner's Capital		11,200
Service Revenue	6,960	
Salaries and Wages Expense	4,200	
Advertising Expense	1,100	
Property Tax Expense		800
	$20,890	$24,500

Instructions

Prepare a correct trial balance.

4 **E3-3 (Corrected Trial Balance)** The trial balance of Blues Traveler Corporation does not balance.

BLUES TRAVELER CORPORATION
TRIAL BALANCE
APRIL 30, 2014

	Debit	Credit
Cash	$ 5,912	
Accounts Receivable	5,240	
Supplies	2,967	
Equipment	6,100	
Accounts Payable		$ 7,044
Common Stock		8,000
Retained Earnings		2,000
Service Revenue		5,200
Office Expense	4,320	
	$24,539	$22,244

An examination of the ledger shows these errors.

1. Cash received from a customer on account was recorded (both debit and credit) as $1,380 instead of $1,830.
2. The purchase on account of a computer costing $3,200 was recorded as a debit to Office Expense and a credit to Accounts Payable.
3. Services were performed on account for a client, $2,250, for which Accounts Receivable was debited $2,250 and Service Revenue was credited $225.
4. A payment of $95 for telephone charges was entered as a debit to Office Expense and a debit to Cash.
5. The Service Revenue account was totaled at $5,200 instead of $5,280.

Instructions

From this information prepare a corrected trial balance.

4 **E3-4 (Corrected Trial Balance)** The trial balance of Watteau Co. (shown on the next page) does not balance.

WATTEAU CO.
TRIAL BALANCE
JUNE 30, 2014

	Debit	Credit
Cash		$ 2,870
Accounts Receivable	$ 3,231	
Supplies	800	
Equipment	3,800	
Accounts Payable		2,666
Unearned Service Revenue	1,200	
Common Stock		6,000
Retained Earnings		3,000
Service Revenue		2,380
Salaries and Wages Expense	3,400	
Office Expense	940	
	$13,371	$16,916

Each of the listed accounts should have a normal balance per the general ledger. An examination of the ledger and journal reveals the following errors.

1. Cash received from a customer on account was debited for $570, and Accounts Receivable was credited for the same amount. The actual collection was for $750.
2. The purchase of a computer printer on account for $500 was recorded as a debit to Supplies for $500 and a credit to Accounts Payable for $500.
3. Services were performed on account for a client for $890. Accounts Receivable was debited for $890 and Service Revenue was credited for $89.
4. A payment of $65 for telephone charges was recorded as a debit to Office Expense for $65 and a debit to Cash for $65.
5. When the Unearned Service Revenue account was reviewed, it was found that service revenue amounting to $325 was performed prior to June 30 (related to Unearned Service Revenue).
6. A debit posting to Salaries and Wages Expense of $670 was omitted.
7. A payment on account for $206 was credited to Cash for $206 and credited to Accounts Payable for $260.
8. A dividend of $575 was debited to Salaries and Wages Expense for $575 and credited to Cash for $575.

Instructions

Prepare a correct trial balance. (*Note:* It may be necessary to add one or more accounts to the trial balance.)

5 **E3-5 (Adjusting Entries)** The ledger of Duggan Rental Agency on March 31 of the current year includes the following selected accounts before adjusting entries have been prepared.

XLS

	Debit	Credit
Prepaid Insurance	$ 3,600	
Supplies	2,800	
Equipment	25,000	
Accumulated Depreciation—Equipment		$ 8,400
Notes Payable		20,000
Unearned Rent Revenue		9,300
Rent Revenue		60,000
Interest Expense	–0–	
Salaries and Wages Expense	14,000	

An analysis of the accounts shows the following.

1. The equipment depreciates $250 per month.
2. One-third of the unearned rent was recognized as revenue during the quarter.
3. Interest of $500 is accrued on the notes payable.
4. Supplies on hand total $850.
5. Insurance expires at the rate of $300 per month.

Instructions

Prepare the adjusting entries at March 31, assuming that adjusting entries are made quarterly. Additional accounts are Depreciation Expense, Insurance Expense, Interest Payable, and Supplies Expense. (Omit explanations.)

5 **E3-6 (Adjusting Entries)** Karen Weller, D.D.S., opened a dental practice on January 1, 2014. During the first month of operations, the following transactions occurred.

1. Performed services for patients who had dental plan insurance. At January 31, $750 of such services was performed but not yet billed to the insurance companies.
2. Utility expenses incurred but not paid prior to January 31 totaled $520.
3. Purchased dental equipment on January 1 for $80,000, paying $20,000 in cash and signing a $60,000, 3-year note payable. The equipment depreciates $400 per month. Interest is $500 per month.
4. Purchased a one-year malpractice insurance policy on January 1 for $12,000.
5. Purchased $1,600 of dental supplies. On January 31, determined that $500 of supplies were on hand.

Instructions

Prepare the adjusting entries on January 31. (Omit explanations.) Account titles are Accumulated Depreciation—Equipment, Depreciation Expense, Service Revenue, Accounts Receivable, Insurance Expense, Interest Expense, Interest Payable, Prepaid Insurance, Supplies, Supplies Expense, Utilities Expense, and Accounts Payable.

5 **E3-7 (Analyze Adjusted Data)** A partial adjusted trial balance of Piper Company at January 31, 2014, shows the following.

PIPER COMPANY
ADJUSTED TRIAL BALANCE
JANUARY 31, 2014

	Debit	Credit
Supplies	$ 700	
Prepaid Insurance	2,400	
Salaries and Wages Payable		$ 800
Unearned Service Revenue		750
Supplies Expense	950	
Insurance Expense	400	
Salaries and Wages Expense	1,800	
Service Revenue		2,000

Instructions

Answer the following questions, assuming the year begins January 1.

(a) If the amount in Supplies Expense is the January 31 adjusting entry, and $850 of supplies was purchased in January, what was the balance in Supplies on January 1?
(b) If the amount in Insurance Expense is the January 31 adjusting entry, and the original insurance premium was for one year, what was the total premium and when was the policy purchased?
(c) If $2,500 of salaries was paid in January, what was the balance in Salaries and Wages Payable at December 31, 2013?
(d) If $1,600 was received in January for services performed in January, what was the balance in Unearned Service Revenue at December 31, 2013?

5 **E3-8 (Adjusting Entries)** Andy Roddick is the new owner of Ace Computer Services. At the end of August 2014, his first month of ownership, Roddick is trying to prepare monthly financial statements. Below is some information related to unrecorded expenses that the business incurred during August.

1. At August 31, Roddick owed his employees $1,900 in wages that will be paid on September 1.
2. At the end of the month, he had not yet received the month's utility bill. Based on past experience, he estimated the bill would be approximately $600.
3. On August 1, Roddick borrowed $30,000 from a local bank on a 15-year mortgage. The annual interest rate is 8%.
4. A telephone bill in the amount of $117 covering August charges is unpaid at August 31.

Instructions

Prepare the adjusting journal entries as of August 31, 2014, suggested by the information above.

g Entries) Selected accounts of Urdu Company are shown below.

Supplies			
l.	800	10/31	470

Accounts Receivable			
10/17	2,400		
10/31	1,650		

Salaries and Wages Expense			
10/15	800		
10/31	600		

Salaries and Wages Payable			
		10/31	600

Unearned Service Revenue			
10/31	400	10/20	650

Supplies Expense			
10/31	470		

Service Revenue			
		10/17	2,400
		10/31	1,650
		10/31	400

Instructions

From an analysis of the T-accounts, reconstruct (a) the October transaction entries, and (b) the adjusting journal entries that were made on October 31, 2014. Prepare explanations for each journal entry.

5 **E3-10 (Adjusting Entries)** Greco Resort opened for business on June 1 with eight air-conditioned units. Its trial balance on August 31 is as follows.

GRECO RESORT
TRIAL BALANCE
AUGUST 31, 2014

	Debit	Credit
Cash	$ 19,600	
Prepaid Insurance	4,500	
Supplies	2,600	
Land	20,000	
Buildings	120,000	
Equipment	16,000	
Accounts Payable		$ 4,500
Unearned Rent Revenue		4,600
Mortgage Payable		60,000
Common Stock		91,000
Retained Earnings		9,000
Dividends	5,000	
Rent Revenue		76,200
Salaries and Wages Expense	44,800	
Utilities Expenses	9,200	
Maintenance and Repairs Expense	3,600	
	$245,300	$245,300

Other data:

1. The balance in prepaid insurance is a one-year premium paid on June 1, 2014.
2. An inventory count on August 31 shows $450 of supplies on hand.
3. Annual depreciation rates are buildings (4%) and equipment (10%). Salvage value is estimated to be 10% of cost.
4. Unearned Rent Revenue of $3,800 was earned prior to August 31.
5. Salaries of $375 were unpaid at August 31.
6. Rentals of $800 were due from tenants at August 31.
7. The mortgage interest rate is 8% per year.

Instructions

(a) Journalize the adjusting entries on August 31 for the 3-month period June 1–August 31. (Omit explanations.)

(b) Prepare an adjusted trial balance on August 31.

6 **E3-11 (Prepare Financial Statements)** The adjusted trial balance of Anderson Cooper Co. as of December 31, 2014, contains the following.

ANDERSON COOPER CO.
ADJUSTED TRIAL BALANCE
DECEMBER 31, 2014

Account Titles	Dr.	Cr.
Cash	$19,472	
Accounts Receivable	6,920	
Prepaid Rent	2,280	
Equipment	18,050	
Accumulated Depreciation—Equipment		$ 4,895
Notes Payable		5,700
Accounts Payable		5,472
Common Stock		20,000
Retained Earnings		11,310
Dividends	3,000	
Service Revenue		11,590
Salaries and Wages Expense	6,840	
Rent Expense	2,260	
Depreciation Expense	145	
Interest Expense	83	
Interest Payable		83
	$59,050	$59,050

Instructions

(a) Prepare an income statement.

(b) Prepare a statement of retained earnings.

(c) Prepare a classified balance sheet.

6 **E3-12 (Prepare Financial Statements)** Santo Design Agency was founded by Thomas Grant in January 2008. Presented below is the adjusted trial balance as of December 31, 2014.

SANTO DESIGN AGENCY
ADJUSTED TRIAL BALANCE
DECEMBER 31, 2014

	Dr.	Cr.
Cash	$ 11,000	
Accounts Receivable	21,500	
Supplies	5,000	
Prepaid Insurance	2,500	
Equipment	60,000	
Accumulated Depreciation—Equipment		$ 35,000
Accounts Payable		5,000
Interest Payable		150
Notes Payable		5,000
Unearned Service Revenue		5,600
Salaries and Wages Payable		1,300
Common Stock		10,000
Retained Earnings		3,500
Service Revenue		61,500
Salaries and Wages Expense	11,300	
Insurance Expense	850	
Interest Expense	500	
Depreciation Expense	7,000	
Supplies Expense	3,400	
Rent Expense	4,000	
	$127,050	$127,050

Instructions

(a) Prepare an income statement and a statement of retained earnings for the year ending December 31, 2014, and an unclassified balance sheet at December 31.

(b) Answer the following questions.

(1) If the note has been outstanding 6 months, what is the annual interest rate on that note?

(2) If the company paid $17,500 in salaries in 2014, what was the balance in Salaries and Wages Payable on December 31, 2013?

7 8 **E3-13 (Closing Entries)** The adjusted trial balance of Lopez Company shows the following data pertaining to sales at the end of its fiscal year, October 31, 2014: Sales Revenue $800,000, Delivery Expense $12,000, Sales Returns and Allowances $24,000, and Sales Discounts $15,000.

Instructions

(a) Prepare the revenues section of the income statement.

(b) Prepare separate closing entries for (1) sales and (2) the contra accounts to sales.

7 8 **E3-14 (Closing Entries)** Presented below is information related to Gonzales Corporation for the month of January 2014.

Cost of goods sold	$208,000	Salaries and wages expense	$ 61,000
Delivery expense	7,000	Sales discounts	8,000
Insurance expense	12,000	Sales returns and allowances	13,000
Rent expense	20,000	Sales revenue	350,000

Instructions

Prepare the necessary closing entries.

8 **E3-15 (Missing Amounts)** Presented below is financial information for two different companies.

	Alatorre Company	Eduardo Company
Sales revenue	$90,000	(d)
Sales returns and allowances	(a)	$ 5,000
Net sales	81,000	95,000
Cost of goods sold	56,000	(e)
Gross profit	(b)	38,000
Operating expenses	15,000	23,000
Net income	(c)	15,000

Instructions

Compute the missing amounts.

7 **E3-16 (Closing Entries for a Corporation)** Presented below are selected account balances for Homer Winslow Co. as of December 31, 2014.

Inventory 12/31/14	$ 60,000	Cost of Goods Sold	$225,700
Common Stock	75,000	Selling Expenses	16,000
Retained Earnings	45,000	Administrative Expenses	38,000
Dividends	18,000	Income Tax Expense	30,000
Sales Returns and Allowances	12,000		
Sales Discounts	15,000		
Sales Revenue	410,000		

Instructions

Prepare closing entries for Homer Winslow Co. on December 31, 2014. (Omit explanations.)

4 **E3-17 (Transactions of a Corporation, Including Investment and Dividend)** Scratch Miniature Golf and Driving Range Inc. was opened on March 1 by Scott Verplank. The following selected events and transactions occurred during March.

Mar. 1 Invested $50,000 cash in the business in exchange for common stock.

3 Purchased Michelle Wie's Golf Land for $38,000 cash. The price consists of land $10,000, building $22,000, and equipment $6,000. (Make one compound entry.)

5 Advertised the opening of the driving range and miniature golf course, paying advertising expenses of $1,600.

6 Paid cash $1,480 for a one-year insurance policy.

10 Purchased golf equipment for $2,500 from Singh Company, payable in 30 days.

Mar. 18	Received golf fees of $1,200 in cash.
25	Declared and paid a $500 cash dividend.
30	Paid wages of $900.
30	Paid Singh Company in full.
31	Received $750 of fees in cash.

Scratch uses the following accounts: Cash, Prepaid Insurance, Land, Buildings, Equipment, Accounts Payable, Common Stock, Dividends, Service Revenue, Advertising Expense, and Salaries and Wages Expense.

Instructions

Journalize the March transactions. (Provide explanations for the journal entries.)

9 ***E3-18 (Cash to Accrual Basis)** Jill Accardo, M.D., maintains the accounting records of Accardo Clinic on a cash basis. During 2014, Dr. Accardo collected $142,600 from her patients and paid $55,470 in expenses. At January 1, 2014, and December 31, 2014, she had accounts receivable, unearned service revenue, accrued expenses, and prepaid expenses as follows. (All long-lived assets are rented.)

	January 1, 2014	December 31, 2014
Accounts receivable	$9,250	$15,927
Unearned service revenue	2,840	4,111
Accrued expenses	3,435	2,108
Prepaid expenses	1,917	3,232

Instructions

Prepare a schedule that converts Dr. Accardo's "excess of cash collected over cash disbursed" for the year 2014 to net income on an accrual basis for the year 2014.

9 ***E3-19 (Cash and Accrual Basis)** Wayne Rogers Corp. maintains its financial records on the cash basis of accounting. Interested in securing a long-term loan from its regular bank, Wayne Rogers Corp. requests you as its independent CPA to convert its cash-basis income statement data to the accrual basis. You are provided with the following summarized data covering 2013, 2014, and 2015.

	2013	2014	2015
Cash receipts from sales:			
On 2013 sales	$295,000	$160,000	$ 30,000
On 2014 sales	–0–	355,000	90,000
On 2015 sales			408,000
Cash payments for expenses:			
On 2013 expenses	185,000	67,000	25,000
On 2014 expenses	40,000[a]	160,000	55,000
On 2015 expenses		45,000[b]	218,000

[a]Prepayments of 2014 expenses.
[b]Prepayments of 2015 expenses.

Instructions

(a) Using the data above, prepare abbreviated income statements for the years 2013 and 2014 on the cash basis.

(b) Using the data above, prepare abbreviated income statements for the years 2013 and 2014 on the accrual basis.

5 10 ***E3-20 (Adjusting and Reversing Entries)** When the accounts of Daniel Barenboim Inc. are examined, the adjusting data listed below are uncovered on December 31, the end of an annual fiscal period.

1. The prepaid insurance account shows a debit of $5,280, representing the cost of a 2-year fire insurance policy dated August 1 of the current year.
2. On November 1, Rent Revenue was credited for $1,800, representing revenue from a subrental for a 3-month period beginning on that date.
3. Purchase of advertising materials for $800 during the year was recorded in the Advertising Expense account. On December 31, advertising materials of $290 are on hand.
4. Interest of $770 has accrued on notes payable.

Instructions

Prepare the following in general journal form.

(a) The adjusting entry for each item.

(b) The reversing entry for each item where appropriate.

11 *E3-21 (Worksheet) Presented below are selected accounts for Alvarez Company as reported in the worksheet at the end of May 2014.

Alvarez Company.xls

ALVAREZ CO.
Worksheet
For The Month Ended May 31, 2014

Account Titles	Adjusted Trial Balance Dr.	Adjusted Trial Balance Cr.	Income Statement Dr.	Income Statement Cr.	Balance Sheet Dr.	Balance Sheet Cr.
Cash	9,000					
Inventory	80,000					
Sales Revenue		450,000				
Sales Returns and Allowances	10,000					
Sales Discounts	5,000					
Cost of Goods Sold	250,000					

Instructions
Complete the worksheet by extending amounts reported in the adjusted trial balance to the appropriate columns in the worksheet. Do not total individual columns.

11 *E3-22 (Worksheet and Balance Sheet Presentation) The adjusted trial balance for Ed Bradley Co. is presented in the following worksheet for the month ended April 30, 2014.

Ed Bradley Co.xls

ED BRADLEY CO.
Worksheet (PARTIAL)
For The Month Ended April 30, 2014

Account Titles	Adjusted Trial Balance Dr.	Adjusted Trial Balance Cr.	Income Statement Dr.	Income Statement Cr.	Balance Sheet Dr.	Balance Sheet Cr.
Cash	$18,972					
Accounts Receivable	6,920					
Prepaid Rent	2,280					
Equipment	18,050					
Accumulated Depreciation—Equipment		$4,895				
Notes Payable		5,700				
Accounts Payable		4,472				
Common Stock		34,960				
Retained Earnings—April 1, 2014		1,000				
Dividends	6,650					
Service Revenue		12,590				
Salaries and Wages Expense	6,840					
Rent Expense	3,760					
Depreciation Expense	145					
Interest Expense	83					
Interest Payable		83				

Instructions
Complete the worksheet and prepare a classified balance sheet.

11 *__E3-23 (Partial Worksheet Preparation)__ Jurassic Park Co. prepares monthly financial statements from a worksheet. Selected portions of the January worksheet showed the following data.

Jurassic Park Co.xls

Home Insert Page Layout Formulas Data Review View

P18 *fx*

	A	B	C	D	E	F	G
1							
2	**JURASSIC PARK CO.**						
3	**Worksheet (PARTIAL)**						
4	**For The Month Ended Jan. 31, 2014**						
5						Adjusted	
6		Trial Balance		Adjustments		Trial Balance	
7	Account Titles	Dr.	Cr.	Dr.	Cr.	Dr.	Cr.
8	Supplies	3,256			(a) 1,500	1,756	
9	Accumulated Depreciation—Equipment		6,682		(b) 257		6,939
10	Interest Payable		100		(c) 50		150
11	Supplies Expense			(a) 1,500		1,500	
12	Depreciation Expense			(b) 257		257	
13	Interest Expense			(c) 50		50	

During February, no events occurred that affected these accounts. But at the end of February, the following information was available.

(a) Supplies on hand	$715
(b) Monthly depreciation	$257
(c) Accrued interest	$ 50

Instructions

Reproduce the data that would appear in the February worksheet, and indicate the amounts that would be shown in the January income statement.

EXERCISES SET B

See the book's companion website, at **www.wiley.com/college/kieso**, for an additional set of exercises.

PROBLEMS

4 6 7 **P3-1 (Transactions, Financial Statements—Service Company)** Listed below are the transactions of Yasunari Kawabata, D.D.S., for the month of September.

Sept.	1	Kawabata begins practice as a dentist and invests $20,000 cash.
	2	Purchases dental equipment on account from Green Jacket Co. for $17,280.
	4	Pays rent for office space, $680 for the month.
	4	Employs a receptionist, Michael Bradley.
	5	Purchases dental supplies for cash, $942.
	8	Receives cash of $1,690 from patients for services performed.
	10	Pays miscellaneous office expenses, $430.
	14	Bills patients $5,820 for services performed.
	18	Pays Green Jacket Co. on account, $3,600.
	19	Withdraws $3,000 cash from the business for personal use.
	20	Receives $980 from patients on account.
	25	Bills patients $2,110 for services performed.
	30	Pays the following expenses in cash: Salaries and wages $1,800; miscellaneous office expenses $85.
	30	Dental supplies used during September, $330.

Instructions

(a) Enter the transactions shown above in appropriate general ledger accounts (use T-accounts). Use the following ledger accounts: Cash, Accounts Receivable, Supplies, Equipment, Accumulated Depreciation—Equipment, Accounts Payable, Owner's Capital, Service Revenue, Rent Expense, Office Expense, Salaries and Wages Expense, Supplies Expense, Depreciation Expense, and Income Summary. Allow 10 lines for the Cash and Income Summary accounts, and 5 lines for each of the other accounts needed. Record depreciation using a 5-year life on the equipment, the straight-line method, and no salvage value. Do not use a drawing account.

(b) Prepare a trial balance.

(c) Prepare an income statement, a statement of owner's equity, and an unclassified balance sheet.

(d) Close the ledger.

(e) Prepare a post-closing trial balance.

5 6 **P3-2 (Adjusting Entries and Financial Statements)** Mason Advertising Agency was founded in January 2010. Presented below are adjusted and unadjusted trial balances as of December 31, 2014.

XLS

MASON ADVERTISING AGENCY
TRIAL BALANCE
DECEMBER 31, 2014

	Unadjusted		Adjusted	
	Dr.	Cr.	Dr.	Cr.
Cash	$ 11,000		$ 11,000	
Accounts Receivable	20,000		23,500	
Supplies	8,400		3,000	
Prepaid Insurance	3,350		2,500	
Equipment	60,000		60,000	
Accumulated Depreciation—Equipment		$ 28,000		$ 33,000
Accounts Payable		5,000		5,000
Interest Payable		-0-		150
Notes Payable		5,000		5,000
Unearned Service Revenue		7,000		5,600
Salaries and Wages Payable		-0-		1,300
Common Stock		10,000		10,000
Retained Earnings		3,500		3,500
Service Revenue		58,600		63,500
Salaries and Wages Expense	10,000		11,300	
Insurance Expense			850	
Interest Expense	350		500	
Depreciation Expense			5,000	
Supplies Expense			5,400	
Rent Expense	4,000		4,000	
	$117,100	$117,100	$127,050	$127,050

Instructions

(a) Journalize the annual adjusting entries that were made. (Omit explanations.)

(b) Prepare an income statement and a statement of retained earnings for the year ending December 31, 2014, and an unclassified balance sheet at December 31.

(c) Answer the following questions.

 (1) If the note has been outstanding 3 months, what is the annual interest rate on that note?

 (2) If the company paid $12,500 in salaries and wages in 2014, what was the balance in Salaries and Wages Payable on December 31, 2013?

5 **P3-3 (Adjusting Entries)** A review of the ledger of Baylor Company at December 31, 2014, produces the following data pertaining to the preparation of annual adjusting entries.

1. Salaries and Wages Payable $0. There are eight employees. Salaries and wages are paid every Friday for the current week. Five employees receive $700 each per week, and three employees earn $600 each per week. December 31 is a Tuesday. Employees do not work weekends. All employees worked the last 2 days of December.

2. Unearned Rent Revenue $429,000. The company began subleasing office space in its new building on November 1. Each tenant is required to make a $5,000 security deposit that is not refundable until occupancy is terminated. At December 31, the company had the following rental contracts that are paid in full for the entire term of the lease.

Date	Term (in months)	Monthly Rent	Number of Leases
Nov. 1	6	$6,000	5
Dec. 1	6	$8,500	4

3. Prepaid Advertising $13,200. This balance consists of payments on two advertising contracts. The contracts provide for monthly advertising in two trade magazines. The terms of the contracts are as shown below.

Contract	Date	Amount	Number of Magazine Issues
A650	May 1	$6,000	12
B974	Oct. 1	7,200	24

The first advertisement runs in the month in which the contract is signed.

4. Notes Payable $60,000. This balance consists of a note for one year at an annual interest rate of 12%, dated June 1.

Instructions

Prepare the adjusting entries at December 31, 2014. (Show all computations).

4 5 6 7 8 **P3-4 (Financial Statements, Adjusting and Closing Entries)** The trial balance of Bellemy Fashion Center contained the following accounts at November 30, the end of the company's fiscal year.

BELLEMY FASHION CENTER
TRIAL BALANCE
NOVEMBER 30, 2014

	Debit	Credit
Cash	$ 28,700	
Accounts Receivable	33,700	
Inventory	45,000	
Supplies	5,500	
Equipment	133,000	
Accumulated Depreciation—Equipment		$ 24,000
Notes Payable		51,000
Accounts Payable		48,500
Common Stock		90,000
Retained Earnings		8,000
Sales Revenue		757,200
Sales Returns and Allowances	4,200	
Cost of Goods Sold	495,400	
Salaries and Wages Expense	140,000	
Advertising Expense	26,400	
Utilities Expenses	14,000	
Maintenance and Repairs Expense	12,100	
Delivery Expense	16,700	
Rent Expense	24,000	
	$978,700	$978,700

Adjustment data:

1. Supplies on hand totaled $1,500.
2. Depreciation is $15,000 on the equipment.
3. Interest of $11,000 is accrued on notes payable at November 30.

Other data:

1. Salaries expense is 70% selling and 30% administrative.
2. Rent expense and utilities expenses are 80% selling and 20% administrative.
3. $30,000 of notes payable are due for payment next year.
4. Maintenance and repairs expense is 100% administrative.

Instructions

(a) Journalize the adjusting entries.
(b) Prepare an adjusted trial balance.
(c) Prepare a multiple-step income statement and retained earnings statement for the year and a classified balance sheet as of November 30, 2014.
(d) Journalize the closing entries.
(e) Prepare a post-closing trial balance.

5 **P3-5 (Adjusting Entries)** The accounts listed below appeared in the December 31 trial balance of the Savard Theater.

	Debit	Credit
Equipment	$192,000	
Accumulated Depreciation—Equipment		$ 60,000
Notes Payable		90,000
Admissions Revenue		380,000
Advertising Expense	13,680	
Salaries and Wages Expense	57,600	
Interest Expense	1,400	

Instructions

(a) From the account balances listed above and the information given below, prepare the annual adjusting entries necessary on December 31. (Omit explanations.)
  (1) The equipment has an estimated life of 16 years and a salvage value of $24,000 at the end of that time. (Use straight-line method.)
  (2) The note payable is a 90-day note given to the bank October 20 and bearing interest at 8%. (Use 360 days for denominator.)
  (3) In December, 2,000 coupon admission books were sold at $30 each. They could be used for admission any time after January 1.
  (4) Advertising expense paid in advance and included in Advertising Expense $1,100.
  (5) Salaries and wages accrued but unpaid $4,700.
(b) What amounts should be shown for each of the following on the income statement for the year?
  (1) Interest expense.
  (2) Admissions revenue.
  (3) Advertising expense.
  (4) Salaries and wages expense.

5 6 **P3-6 (Adjusting Entries and Financial Statements)** The following are the trial balance and the other information related to Yorkis Perez, a consulting engineer.

YORKIS PEREZ, CONSULTING ENGINEER
TRIAL BALANCE
DECEMBER 31, 2014

	Debit	Credit
Cash	$ 29,500	
Accounts Receivable	49,600	
Allowance for Doubtful Accounts		$ 750
Inventory	1,960	
Prepaid Insurance	1,100	
Equipment	25,000	
Accumulated Depreciation—Equipment		6,250
Notes Payable		7,200
Owner's Capital		35,010
Service Revenue		100,000
Rent Expense	9,750	
Salaries and Wages Expense	30,500	
Utilities Expenses	1,080	
Office Expense	720	
	$149,210	$149,210

1. Fees received in advance from clients $6,000.
2. Services performed for clients that were not recorded by December 31, $4,900.
3. Bad debt expense for the year is $1,430.
4. Insurance expired during the year $480.
5. Equipment is being depreciated at 10% per year.
6. Yorkis Perez gave the bank a 90-day, 10% note for $7,200 on December 1, 2014.
7. Rent of the building is $750 per month. The rent for 2014 has been paid, as has that for January 2015.
8. Office salaries and wages earned but unpaid December 31, 2014, $2,510.

Instructions

(a) From the trial balance and other information given, prepare annual adjusting entries as of December 31, 2014. (Omit explanations.)

(b) Prepare an income statement for 2014, a statement of owner's equity, and a classified balance sheet. Yorkis Perez withdrew $17,000 cash for personal use during the year.

5 6 **P3-7 (Adjusting Entries and Financial Statements)** Rolling Hills Golf Inc. was organized on July 1, 2014. Quarterly financial statements are prepared. The unadjusted trial balance and adjusted trial balance on September 30 are shown here.

ROLLING HILLS GOLF INC.
TRIAL BALANCE
SEPTEMBER 30, 2014

	Unadjusted		Adjusted	
	Dr.	Cr.	Dr.	Cr.
Cash	$ 6,700		$ 6,700	
Accounts Receivable	400		1,000	
Prepaid Rent	1,800		900	
Supplies	1,200		180	
Equipment	15,000		15,000	
Accumulated Depreciation—Equipment				$ 350
Notes Payable		$ 5,000		5,000
Accounts Payable		1,070		1,070
Salaries and Wages Payable				600
Interest Payable				50
Unearned Rent Revenue		1,000		800
Common Stock		14,000		14,000
Retained Earnings		0		0
Dividends	600		600	
Service Revenue		14,100		14,700
Rent Revenue		700		900
Salaries and Wages Expense	8,800		9,400	
Rent Expense	900		1,800	
Depreciation Expense			350	
Supplies Expense			1,020	
Utilities Expenses	470		470	
Interest Expense			50	
	$35,870	$35,870	$37,470	$37,470

Instructions

(a) Journalize the adjusting entries that were made.

(b) Prepare an income statement and a retained earnings statement for the 3 months ending September 30 and a classified balance sheet at September 30.

(c) Identify which accounts should be closed on September 30.

(d) If the note bears interest at 12%, how many months has it been outstanding?

5 6 **P3-8 (Adjusting Entries and Financial Statements)** Vedula Advertising Agency was founded by Murali Vedula in January 2009. Presented on the next page are both the adjusted and unadjusted trial balances as of December 31, 2014.

VEDULA ADVERTISING AGENCY
TRIAL BALANCE
DECEMBER 31, 2014

	Unadjusted		Adjusted	
	Dr.	Cr.	Dr.	Cr.
Cash	$ 11,000		$ 11,000	
Accounts Receivable	16,000		19,500	
Supplies	9,400		6,500	
Prepaid Insurance	3,350		1,790	
Equipment	60,000		60,000	
Accumulated Depreciation—Equipment		$ 25,000		$ 30,000
Notes Payable		8,000		8,000
Accounts Payable		2,000		2,000
Interest Payable		0		560
Unearned Service Revenue		5,000		3,100
Salaries and Wages Payable		0		820
Common Stock		20,000		20,000
Retained Earnings		5,500		5,500
Dividends	10,000		10,000	
Service Revenue		57,600		63,000
Salaries and Wages Expense	9,000		9,820	
Insurance Expense			1,560	
Interest Expense			560	
Depreciation Expense			5,000	
Supplies Expense			2,900	
Rent Expense	4,350		4,350	
	$123,100	$123,100	$132,980	$132,980

Instructions

(a) Journalize the annual adjusting entries that were made.
(b) Prepare an income statement and a retained earnings statement for the year ended December 31, and a classified balance sheet at December 31.
(c) Identify which accounts should be closed on December 31.
(d) If the note has been outstanding 10 months, what is the annual interest rate on that note?
(e) If the company paid $10,500 in salaries and wages in 2014, what was the balance in Salaries and Wages Payable on December 31, 2013?

4 5 6 7 **P3-9 (Adjusting and Closing)** Presented below is the trial balance of the Crestwood Golf Club, Inc. as of December 31. The books are closed annually on December 31.

CRESTWOOD GOLF CLUB, INC.
TRIAL BALANCE
DECEMBER 31

	Debit	Credit
Cash	$ 15,000	
Accounts Receivable	13,000	
Allowance for Doubtful Accounts		$ 1,100
Prepaid Insurance	9,000	
Land	350,000	
Buildings	120,000	
Accumulated Depreciation—Buildings		38,400
Equipment	150,000	
Accumulated Depreciation—Equipment		70,000
Common Stock		400,000
Retained Earnings		82,000
Dues Revenue		200,000
Green Fees Revenue		5,900
Rent Revenue		17,600
Utilities Expenses	54,000	
Salaries and Wages Expense	80,000	
Maintenance and Repairs Expense	24,000	
	$815,000	$815,000

Instructions

(a) Enter the balances in ledger accounts. Allow five lines for each account.

(b) From the trial balance and the information given below, prepare annual adjusting entries and post to the ledger accounts. (Omit explanations.)

  (1) The buildings have an estimated life of 30 years with no salvage value (straight-line method).

  (2) The equipment is depreciated at 10% per year.

  (3) Insurance expired during the year $3,500.

  (4) The rent revenue represents the amount received for 11 months for dining facilities. The December rent has not yet been received.

  (5) It is estimated that 12% of the accounts receivable will be uncollectible.

  (6) Salaries and wages earned but not paid by December 31, $3,600.

  (7) Dues received in advance from members $8,900.

(c) Prepare an adjusted trial balance.

(d) Prepare closing entries and post.

4 5 6 7 8 **P3-10 (Adjusting and Closing)** Presented below is the December 31 trial balance of New York Boutique.

NEW YORK BOUTIQUE
TRIAL BALANCE
DECEMBER 31

	Debit	Credit
Cash	$ 18,500	
Accounts Receivable	32,000	
Allowance for Doubtful Accounts		$ 700
Inventory, December 31	80,000	
Prepaid Insurance	5,100	
Equipment	84,000	
Accumulated Depreciation—Equipment		35,000
Notes Payable		28,000
Common Stock		80,600
Retained Earnings		10,000
Sales Revenue		600,000
Cost of Goods Sold	408,000	
Salaries and Wages Expense (sales)	50,000	
Advertising Expense	6,700	
Salaries and Wages Expense (administrative)	65,000	
Supplies Expense	5,000	
	$754,300	$754,300

Instructions

(a) Construct T-accounts and enter the balances shown.

(b) Prepare adjusting journal entries for the following and post to the T-accounts. (Omit explanations.) Open additional T-accounts as necessary. (The books are closed yearly on December 31.)

  (1) Bad debt expense is estimated to be $1,400.

  (2) Equipment is depreciated based on a 7-year life (no salvage value).

  (3) Insurance expired during the year $2,550.

  (4) Interest accrued on notes payable $3,360.

  (5) Sales salaries and wages earned but not paid $2,400.

  (6) Advertising paid in advance $700.

  (7) Office supplies on hand $1,500, charged to Supplies Expense when purchased.

(c) Prepare closing entries and post to the accounts.

9 ***P3-11 (Cash and Accrual Basis)** On January 1, 2014, Norma Smith and Grant Wood formed a computer sales and service company in Soapsville, Arkansas, by investing $90,000 cash. The new company, Arkansas Sales and Service, has the following transactions during January.

1. Pays $6,000 in advance for 3 months' rent of office, showroom, and repair space.
2. Purchases 40 personal computers at a cost of $1,500 each, 6 graphics computers at a cost of $2,500 each, and 25 printers at a cost of $300 each, paying cash upon delivery.

3. Sales, repair, and office employees earn $12,600 in salaries and wages during January, of which $3,000 was still payable at the end of January.
4. Sells 30 personal computers at $2,550 each, 4 graphics computers for $3,600 each, and 15 printers for $500 each; $75,000 is received in cash in January, and $23,400 is sold on a deferred payment basis.
5. Other operating expenses of $8,400 are incurred and paid for during January; $2,000 of incurred expenses are payable at January 31.

Instructions

(a) Using the transaction data above, prepare (1) a cash-basis income statement and (2) an accrual-basis income statement for the month of January.

(b) Using the transaction data above, prepare (1) a cash-basis balance sheet and (2) an accrual-basis balance sheet as of January 31, 2014.

(c) Identify the items in the cash-basis financial statements that make cash-basis accounting inconsistent with the theory underlying the elements of financial statements.

5 6 7 11 ***P3-12 (Worksheet, Balance Sheet, Adjusting and Closing Entries)** Cooke Company has a fiscal year ending on September 30. Selected data from the September 30 worksheet are presented below.

Cooke Co.xls

COOKE COMPANY
Worksheet
For The Month Ended September 30, 2014

	Trial Balance		Adjusted Trial Balance	
Account Titles	Dr.	Cr.	Dr.	Cr.
Cash	37,400		37,400	
Supplies	18,600		4,200	
Prepaid Insurance	31,900		3,900	
Land	80,000		80,000	
Equipment	120,000		120,000	
Accumulated Depreciation—Equipment		36,200		42,000
Accounts Payable		14,600		14,600
Unearned Service Revenue		2,700		700
Mortgage Payable		50,000		50,000
Common Stock		107,700		107,700
Retained Earnings, Sept. 1, 2014		2,000		2,000
Dividends	14,000		14,000	
Service Revenue		278,500		280,500
Salaries and Wages Expense	109,000		109,000	
Maintenance and Repairs Expense	30,500		30,500	
Advertising Expense	9,400		9,400	
Utilities Expenses	16,900		16,900	
Property Tax Expense	18,000		21,000	
Interest Expense	6,000		12,000	
Totals	491,700	491,700		
Insurance Expense			28,000	
Supplies Expense			14,400	
Interest Payable				6,000
Depreciation Expense			5,800	
Property Taxes Payable				3,000
Totals			506,500	506,500

Instructions

(a) Prepare a complete worksheet.
(b) Prepare a classified balance sheet. (*Note:* $10,000 of the mortgage payable is due for payment in the next fiscal year.)
(c) Journalize the adjusting entries using the worksheet as a basis..
(d) Journalize the closing entries using the worksheet as a basis.
(e) Prepare a post-closing trial balance.

PROBLEMS SET B

See the book's companion website, at **www.wiley.com/college/kieso**, for an additional set of problems.

USING YOUR JUDGMENT

FINANCIAL REPORTING

Financial Reporting Problem

P&G

The Procter & Gamble Company (P&G)

The financial statements of P&G are presented in Appendix 5B. The company's complete annual report, including the notes to the financial statements, can be accessed at the book's companion website, **www.wiley.com/college/kieso**.

Instructions

Refer to these financial statements and the accompanying notes to answer the following questions.

(a) What were P&G's total assets at June 30, 2011? At June 30, 2010?
(b) How much cash (and cash equivalents) did P&G have on June 30, 2011?
(c) What were P&G's research and development costs in 2010? In 2011?
(d) What were P&G's revenues in 2010? In 2011?
(e) Using P&G's financial statements and related notes, identify items that may result in adjusting entries for deferrals and accruals.
(f) What were the amounts of P&G's depreciation and amortization expense in 2009, 2010, and 2011?

Comparative Analysis Case

The Coca-Cola Company and PepsiCo, Inc.

Instructions

Go to the book's companion website and use information found there to answer the following questions related to The Coca-Cola Company and PepsiCo, Inc.

(a) Which company had the greater percentage increase in total assets from 2010 to 2011?
(b) Using the Selected Financial Data section of these two companies, determine their 5-year average growth rates related to net sales and income from continuing operations.
(c) Which company had more depreciation and amortization expense for 2011? Provide a rationale as to why there is a difference in these amounts between the two companies.

Financial Statement Analysis Case

Kellogg Company

Kellogg Company has its headquarters in Battle Creek, Michigan. The company manufactures and sells ready-to-eat breakfast cereals and convenience foods including cookies, toaster pastries, and cereal bars.

Selected data from Kellogg Company's 2011 annual report follows (dollar amounts in millions).

	2011	2010	2009
Sales	$13,198.00	$12,397.00	$12,575.00
Gross profit %	41.28	42.66	42.87
Operating profit	1,976.00	1,990.00	2,001.00
Net cash flow less capital expenditures	1,001.00	534.00	1,266.00
Net earnings	1,231.00	1,247.00	1,212.00

In its annual reports, Kellogg Company has indicated that it plans to achieve sustainability of its operating results with operating principles that emphasize profit-rich, sustainable sales growth, as well as cash flow and return on invested capital. Kellogg believes its steady earnings growth, strong cash flow, and continued investment during a multi-year period demonstrates the strength and flexibility of its business model.

Instructions

(a) Compute the percentage change in sales, operating profit, net cash flow less capital expenditures, and net earnings from year to year for the years presented.

(b) Evaluate Kellogg's performance. Which trend seems most favorable? Which trend seems least favorable? What are the implications of these trends for Kellogg's sustainable performance objectives? Explain.

Accounting, Analysis, and Principles

The Amato Theater is nearing the end of the year and is preparing for a meeting with its bankers to discuss the renewal of a loan. The accounts listed below appeared in the December 31, 2014, trial balance.

	Debit	Credit
Prepaid Advertising	$ 6,000	
Equipment	192,000	
Accumulated Depreciation—Equipment		$ 60,000
Notes Payable		90,000
Unearned Service Revenue		17,500
Ticket Revenue		360,000
Advertising Expense	18,680	
Salaries and Wages Expense	67,600	
Interest Expense	1,400	

Additional information is available as follows.

1. The equipment has an estimated useful life of 16 years and a salvage value of $40,000 at the end of that time. Amato uses the straight-line method for depreciation.
2. The note payable is a one-year note given to the bank January 31 and bearing interest at 10%. Interest is calculated on a monthly basis.
3. Late in December 2014, the theater sold 350 coupon ticket books at $50 each. One hundred fifty of these ticket books can be used only for admission any time after January 1, 2015. The cash received was recorded as Unearned Service Revenue.
4. Advertising paid in advance was $6,000 and was debited to Prepaid Advertising. The company has used $2,500 of the advertising as of December 31, 2014.
5. Salaries and wages accrued but unpaid at December 31, 2014, were $3,500.

Accounting

Prepare any adjusting journal entries necessary for the year ended December 31, 2014.

Analysis

Determine Amato's income before and after recording the adjusting entries. Use your analysis to explain why Amato's bankers should be willing to wait for Amato to complete its year-end adjustment process before making a decision on the loan renewal.

Principles

Although Amato's bankers are willing to wait for the adjustment process to be completed before they receive financial information, they would like to receive financial reports more frequently than annually or even quarterly. What trade-offs, in terms of relevance and faithful representation, are inherent in preparing financial statements for shorter accounting time periods?

BRIDGE TO THE PROFESSION

Professional Research

Recording transactions in the accounting system requires knowledge of the important characteristics of the elements of financial statements, such as assets and liabilities. In addition, accountants must understand the inherent uncertainty in accounting measures and distinctions between related accounting concepts that are important in evaluating the effects of transactions on the financial statements.

Instructions

Go to *http://aaahq.org/asclogin.cfm* to log in and provide explanations for the following items. (Provide paragraph citations.) When you have accessed the documents, you can use the search tool in your Internet browser.

(a) The three essential characteristics of assets.

(b) The three essential characteristics of liabilities.

(c) Uncertainty and its effect on financial statements.

(d) The difference between realization and recognition.

Additional Professional Resources

See the book's companion website, at **www.wiley.com/college/kieso**, for professional simulations as well as other study resources.

IFRS INSIGHTS

12 LEARNING OBJECTIVE
Compare the accounting information systems under GAAP and IFRS.

As indicated in this chapter, companies must have an effective accounting system. In the wake of accounting scandals at U.S. companies like **Sunbeam**, **Rite-Aid**, **Xerox**, and **WorldCom**, U.S. lawmakers demanded higher assurance on the quality of accounting reports. Since the passage of the Sarbanes-Oxley Act of 2002 (SOX), companies that trade on U.S. exchanges are required to place renewed focus on their accounting systems to ensure accurate reporting.

RELEVANT FACTS

Following are the key similarities and differences between GAAP and IFRS related to accounting information systems.

Similarities

- International companies use the same set of procedures and records to keep track of transaction data. Thus, the material in Chapter 3 dealing with the account, general rules of debit and credit, and steps in the recording process—the journal, ledger, and chart of accounts—is the same under both GAAP and IFRS.
- Transaction analysis is the same under GAAP and IFRS but, as you will see in later chapters, different standards sometimes impact how transactions are recorded.
- Both the FASB and IASB go beyond the basic definitions provided in this textbook for the key elements of financial statements, that is, assets, liabilities, equity, revenues, and expenses.
- A trial balance under IFRS follows the same format as shown in the textbook. As shown in the textbook, dollar signs are typically used only in the trial balance and the financial statements. The same practice is followed under IFRS, using the currency of the country in which the reporting company is headquartered.

Differences

- Rules for accounting for specific events sometimes differ across countries. For example, European companies rely less on historical cost and more on fair value than U.S. companies. Despite the differences, the double-entry accounting system is the basis of accounting systems worldwide.
- Internal controls are a system of checks and balances designed to prevent and detect fraud and errors. While most public U.S. companies have these systems in place, many non-U.S. companies have never completely documented them nor had an independent auditor attest to their effectiveness. Both of these actions are required under SOX. These enhanced internal control standards apply only to large public companies listed on U.S. exchanges.

ABOUT THE NUMBERS

Accounting System Internal Controls

There is continuing debate over whether foreign issuers should have to comply with the extra layer of regulation related to internal controls attestation.[4] Companies find that internal control review is a costly process but needed. One study estimates the cost of compliance for U.S. companies at over $35 billion, with audit fees doubling in the first year of compliance. At the same time, examination of internal controls indicates lingering problems in the way companies operate. One study of first compliance with the internal control testing provisions documented material weaknesses for about 13 percent of companies reporting in 2004 and 2005.

Debate about requiring foreign companies to comply with SOX centers on whether the higher costs of a good information system are making the U.S. securities markets less competitive. Presented below are statistics for initial public offerings (IPOs) in the years since the passage of SOX.

Share of IPO Proceeds: U.S., Europe, and China (U.S. $, billions)

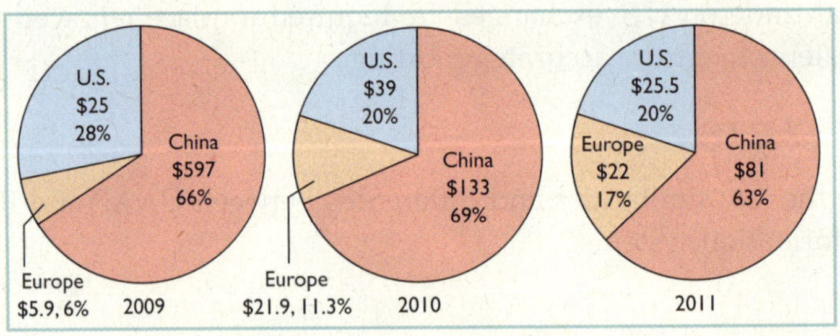

	2009 IPOs	2010 IPOs	2011 IPOs
U.S.	69	168	134
Europe	126	380	430
China	208	502	432

Source: PricewaterhouseCoopers, U.S. IPO Watch: 2011 Analysis and Trends.

Note the U.S. share of IPOs has steadily declined. Some critics of the SOX provisions attribute the decline to the increased cost of complying with the internal control rules. Others, looking at these same trends, are not so sure about SOX being the cause of the relative decline of U.S. IPOs. These commentators argue that growth in non-U.S. markets is a natural consequence of general globalization of capital flows.

[4]See Greg Ip, Kara Scannel, and Deborah Solomon, "Trade Winds in Call to Deregulate Business, A Global Twist," *Wall Street Journal* (January 25, 2007), p. A1.

First-Time Adoption of IFRS

As discussed in Chapter 1, IFRS is growing in acceptance around the world. For example, recent statistics indicate 40 percent of the Global Fortune 500 companies use IFRS. And the chair of the IASB predicts that IFRS adoption will grow from its current level of over 115 countries to nearly 150 countries in the near future.

When countries accept IFRS for use as accepted accounting policies, companies need guidance to ensure that their first IFRS financial statements contain high-quality information. Specifically, *IFRS 1* requires that information in a company's first IFRS statements (1) be transparent, (2) provide a suitable starting point, and (3) have a cost that does not exceed the benefits. As a result, many companies will be going through a substantial conversion process to switch from their reporting standards to IFRS.

The overriding principle in converting to IFRS is full retrospective application of IFRS. Retrospective application—recasting prior financial statements on the basis of IFRS—provides financial statement users with comparable information. As indicated, the objective of the conversion process is to present a set of IFRS statements as if the company always reported using IFRS. To achieve this objective, a company follows these steps:

1. Identify the timing of its first IFRS statements.
2. Prepare an opening balance sheet at the date of transition to IFRS.
3. Select accounting principles that comply with IFRS, and apply these principles retrospectively.
4. Make extensive disclosures to explain the transition to IFRS.

Once a company decides to convert to IFRS, it must decide on the transition date and the reporting date. The transition date is the beginning of the earliest period for which full comparative IFRS information is presented. The reporting date is the closing balance sheet date for the first IFRS financial statements.

To illustrate, assume that FirstChoice Company plans to provide its first IFRS statements for the year ended December 31, 2016. FirstChoice decides to present comparative information for one year only. Therefore, its date of transition to IFRS is January 1, 2015, and its reporting date is December 31, 2016. The timeline for first-time adoption is presented in the following graphic.

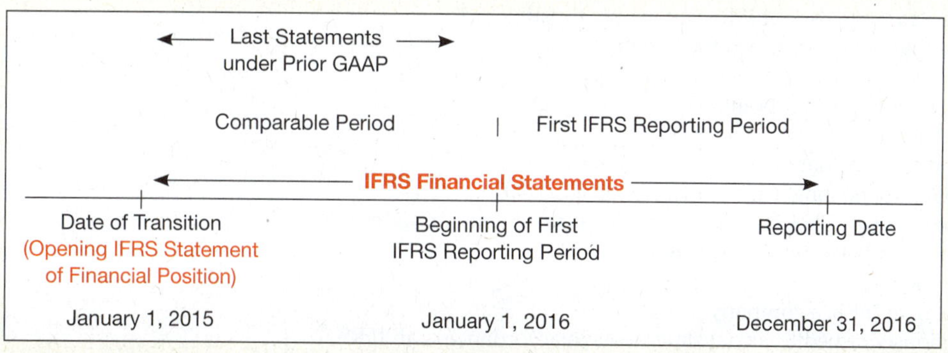

The graphic shows the following.

1. The opening IFRS statement of financial position for FirstChoice on January 1, 2015, serves as the starting point (date of transition) for the company's accounting under IFRS.
2. The first full IFRS statements are shown for FirstChoice for December 31, 2016. In other words, a minimum of two years of IFRS statements must be presented before

a conversion to IFRS occurs. As a result, FirstChoice must prepare at least one year of comparative financial statements for 2016 using IFRS.

3. FirstChoice presents financial statements in accordance with GAAP annually to December 31, 2015.

Following this conversion process, FirstChoice provides users of the financial statements with comparable IFRS statements for 2015 and 2016. Upon first-time adoption of IFRS, a company must present at least one year of comparative information under IFRS.

ON THE HORIZON

The basic recording process shown in this textbook is followed by companies around the globe. It is unlikely to change in the future. The definitional structure of assets, liabilities, equity, revenues, and expenses may change over time as the IASB and FASB evaluate their overall conceptual framework for establishing accounting standards. In addition, high-quality international accounting requires both high-quality accounting standards and high-quality auditing. Similar to the convergence of GAAP and IFRS, there is a movement to improve international auditing standards. The International Auditing and Assurance Standards Board (IAASB) functions as an independent standard-setting body. It works to establish high-quality auditing and assurance and quality-control standards throughout the world. Whether the IAASB adopts internal control provisions similar to those in SOX remains to be seen. You can follow developments in the international audit arena at *http://www.ifac.org/iaasb/*.

IFRS SELF-TEST QUESTIONS

1. Which statement is **correct** regarding IFRS?
   - **(a)** IFRS reverses the rules of debits and credits, that is, debits are on the right and credits are on the left.
   - **(b)** IFRS uses the same process for recording transactions as GAAP.
   - **(c)** The chart of accounts under IFRS is different because revenues follow assets.
   - **(d)** None of the above statements are correct.
2. Information in a company's first IFRS statements must:
   - **(a)** have a cost that does not exceed the benefits.
   - **(b)** be transparent.
   - **(c)** provide a suitable starting point.
   - **(d)** All the above.
3. The transition date is the date:
   - **(a)** when a company no longer reports under its national standards.
   - **(b)** when the company issues its most recent financial statement under IFRS.
   - **(c)** three years prior to the reporting date.
   - **(d)** None of the above.
4. When converting to IFRS, a company must:
   - **(a)** recast previously issued financial statements in accordance with IFRS.
   - **(b)** use GAAP in the reporting period but subsequently use IFRS.
   - **(c)** prepare at least three years of comparative statements.
   - **(d)** use GAAP in the transition year but IFRS in the reporting year.
5. The purpose of presenting comparative information in the transition to IFRS is:
   - **(a)** to ensure that the information is a faithful representation.
   - **(b)** in accordance with the Sarbanes-Oxley Act.
   - **(c)** to provide users of the financial statements with information on GAAP in one period and IFRS in the other period.
   - **(d)** to provide users of the financial statements with information on IFRS for at least two periods.

IFRS CONCEPTS AND APPLICATION

IFRS3-1 How is the date of transition and the date of reporting determined in first-time adoption of IFRS?

IFRS3-2 What are the characteristics of high-quality information in a company's first IFRS financial statements?

IFRS3-3 What are the steps to be completed in preparing the opening IFRS statement of financial position?

IFRS3-4 Becker Ltd. is planning to adopt IFRS and prepare its first IFRS financial statements at December 31, 2015. What is the date of Becker's opening balance sheet, assuming one year of comparative information? What periods will be covered in Becker's first IFRS financial statements?

Professional Research

IFRS3-5 Recording transactions in the accounting system requires knowledge of the important characteristics of the elements of financial statements, such as assets and liabilities. In addition, accountants must understand the inherent uncertainty in accounting measures and distinctions between related accounting concepts that are important in evaluating the effects of transactions on the financial statements.

Instructions

Access the IASB Framework at the IASB website (*http://eifrs.iasb.org/*). (Click on the IFRS tab and then register for free eIFRS access if necessary.) When you have accessed the documents, you can use the search tool in your Internet browser to respond to the following items. (Provide paragraph citations.)

(a) Provide the definition of an asset and discuss how the economic benefits embodied in an asset might flow to a company.

(b) Provide the definition of a liability and discuss how a company might satisfy a liability.

(c) What is "accrual basis"? How do adjusting entries illustrate application of the accrual basis?

International Financial Reporting Problem
Marks and Spencer plc

IFRS3-6 The financial statements of **Marks and Spencer plc (M&S)** are available at the book's companion website or can be accessed at *http://annualreport.marksandspencer.com/_assets/downloads/Marks-and-Spencer-Annual-report-and-financial-statements-2012.pdf.*

Instructions

Refer to M&S's financial statements and the accompanying notes to answer the following questions.

(a) What were M&S's total assets at 31 March 2012? At 2 April 2011?

(b) How much cash (and cash equivalents) did M&S have on 31 March 2012?

(c) What were M&S's selling and marketing expenses in 2012? In 2011?

(d) What were M&S's revenues in 2012? In 2011?

(e) Using M&S's financial statements and related notes, identify items that may result in adjusting entries for prepayments and accruals.

(f) What were the amounts of M&S's depreciation and amortization expense in 2011 and 2012?

ANSWERS TO IFRS SELF-TEST QUESTIONS

1. b **2.** d **3.** d **4.** a **5.** d

Remember to check the book's companion website to find additional resources for this chapter.

CHAPTER 4

Income Statement and Related Information

LEARNING OBJECTIVES

After studying this chapter, you should be able to:

1. Understand the uses and limitations of an income statement.
2. Describe the content and format of the income statement.
3. Prepare an income statement.
4. Explain how to report various income items.
5. Identify where to report earnings per share information.
6. Understand the reporting of accounting changes and errors.
7. Prepare a retained earnings statement.
8. Explain how to report other comprehensive income.

Financial Statements Are Changing

The 2011 annual report of **Groupon** presents the following additional information in its financial statements regarding a calculation of its consolidated segment operating (loss) income (CSOI).

The following is a reconciliation of CSOI to the most comparable U.S. GAAP measure, "Loss from operations," for the years ended December 31, 2010 and 2011.

	Year Ended December 31,	
	2010	2011
(in thousands)		
Loss from operations	$(420,344)	$(233,386)
Adjustments:		
Stock-based compensation	36,168	93,590
Acquisition-related costs	203,183	(4,537)
Total adjustments	239,351	89,053
CSOI	$(180,993)	$(144,333)

Management of Groupon explained that CSOI is the consolidated operating (loss) income, after adjustment for acquisition-related costs and stock-based compensation expense. They explained, "We consider CSOI to be an important measure for management to evaluate the performance of our business as it excludes certain non-cash expenses. We believe it is important to view CSOI as a complement to our entire consolidated statements of operations. When evaluating our performance, you should consider CSOI as a complement to other financial performance measures, including various cash flow metrics, net loss and our other U.S. GAAP results."

Why do companies report these adjusted income numbers (sometimes referred to as pro forma measures)? One major reason is that companies believe some items on the income statement are not representative of operating results. Here is another example, using **Amazon.com**. At one time, Amazon reported in a separate schedule adjustments to net income for items such as share-based compensation, amortization of goodwill and intangibles, impairment charges, and equity in losses of its subsidiaries. All these adjustments make the adjusted income measure higher than reported income. Amazon defends its pro forma reporting, saying it gives better insight into the fundamental operations of the business. However, while management asserts pro forma is useful to investors, others raise concerns.

Skeptics of pro forma reporting often note that these adjustments generally lead to higher adjusted net income and, as a result, often report *earnings before bad stuff (EBS)*. In Groupon's case, the add-backs more than halved its operating loss in 2010 and resulted in an improving trend in operating performance over the two-year period. And pro forma puffery is not an isolated phenomenon. In a recent four-quarter earnings cycle, nearly 50 percent of S&P 500 companies also reported an income measure that they adjusted for certain items. Analysis of pro forma to GAAP numbers indicate that about 30 percent of the S&P 500 companies report pro forma income in excess of operating income. In general, pro forma profits were 18 percent higher than operating earnings. Another concern with pro forma is that it is difficult to compare these adjusted numbers

because companies have different views as to what is fundamental to their business.

In many ways, the pro forma reporting practices by companies like Groupon and Amazon represent implied criticisms of certain financial reporting standards, including how the information is presented on the income statement. In response, the SEC issued Regulation G, which requires companies to reconcile non-GAAP financial measures to GAAP. This regulation provides investors with a roadmap to analyze adjustments that companies make to their GAAP numbers to arrive at pro forma results. Regulation G helps investors compare one company's pro forma measures with results reported by another company.

The FASB (and IASB) are working on a joint project on financial statement presentation to address users' concerns about these practices. Users believe too many alternatives exist for classifying and reporting income statement information. They note that information is often highly aggregated and inconsistently presented. As a result, it is difficult to assess the financial performance of the company and compare its results with other companies. This trend toward more transparent income reporting is encouraging, but managers still like pro forma reporting, as indicated by a recent survey in response to the FASB financial statement presentation project. Over 55 percent polled indicated they would continue to practice pro forma reporting, even with a revised income statement format.

Sources: A. Stuart, "A New Vision for Accounting: Robert Herz and FASB Are Preparing a Radical New Format for Financial Statements," *CFO Magazine* (February 2008), pp. 49–53; SEC Regulation G, *"Conditions for Use of Non-GAAP Financial Measures,"* Release No. 33-8176 (March 28, 2003) and *Compliance & Disclosure Interpretations: Non-GAAP Financial Measures* (January 15, 2010), available at *www.sec.gov/divisions/corpfin/guidance/nongaapinterp.htm*; and R. Cyran, A. Currie, and R. Cox, "Fuzzy Accounting Enriches Groupon," *The New York Times* (June 12, 2011).

CONCEPTUAL FOCUS

> See the **Underlying Concepts** on pages 161 and 179.

> Read the **Evolving Issue** on page 185 for a discussion of income reporting.

INTERNATIONAL FOCUS

> See the **International Perspectives** on pages 169, 174, and 183.

> Read the **IFRS Insights** on pages 205–211 for a discussion of:
—Income reporting
—Expense classifications

PREVIEW OF CHAPTER 4

As indicated in the opening story, companies are attempting to provide income statement information they believe is useful for decision-making. Investors need complete and comparable information on income and its components to assess company profitability correctly. In this chapter, we examine the many different types of revenues, expenses, gains, and losses that affect the income statement and related information, as follows.

Income Statement and Related Information

Income Statement	Format of the Income Statement	Reporting Various Income Items	Other Reporting Issues
• Usefulness • Limitations • Quality of earnings	• Elements • Intermediate components • Condensed income statements • Single-step income statements	• Unusual gains and losses • Discontinued operations • Extraordinary items • Noncontrolling interest • Earnings per share	• Accounting changes and errors • Retained earnings statement • Comprehensive income

INCOME STATEMENT

LEARNING OBJECTIVE 1
Understand the uses and limitations of an income statement.

The **income statement** is the report that measures the success of company operations for a given period of time. (It is also often called the statement of income or statement of earnings.[1]) The business and investment community uses the income statement to determine profitability, investment value, and creditworthiness. It provides investors and creditors with information that helps them predict the **amounts, timing, and uncertainty of future cash flows**.

Usefulness of the Income Statement

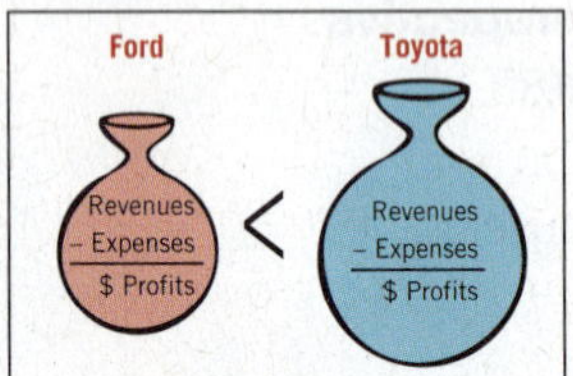

Which company did better last year?

The income statement helps users of financial statements predict future cash flows in a number of ways. For example, investors and creditors use the income statement information to:

1. *Evaluate the past performance of the company.* Examining revenues and expenses indicates how the company performed and allows comparison of its performance to its competitors. For example, analysts use the income data provided by **Ford** to compare its performance to that of **Toyota**.

Hmmm... Where am I headed?

2. *Provide a basis for predicting future performance.* Information about past performance helps to determine important trends that, if continued, provide information about future performance. For example, **General Electric** at one time reported consistent increases in revenues. Obviously, past success does not necessarily translate into future success. However, analysts can better predict future revenues, and hence earnings and cash flows, if a reasonable correlation exists between past and future performance.

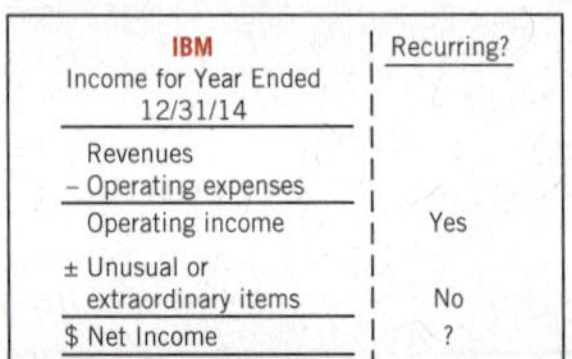

Recurring items are more certain in the future.

3. *Help assess the risk or uncertainty of achieving future cash flows.* Information on the various components of income—revenues, expenses, gains, and losses—highlights the relationships among them. It also helps to assess the risk of not achieving a particular level of cash flows in the future. For example, investors and creditors often segregate **IBM**'s operating performance from other nonrecurring sources of income because IBM primarily generates revenues and cash through its operations. Thus, results from continuing operations usually have greater significance for predicting future performance than do results from nonrecurring activities and events.

In summary, information in the income statement—revenues, expenses, gains, and losses—helps users evaluate past performance. It also provides insights into the likelihood of achieving a particular level of cash flows in the future.

Limitations of the Income Statement

You left something out!

Because net income is an estimate and reflects a number of assumptions, income statement users need to be aware of certain limitations associated with its information. Some of these limitations include:

1. *Companies omit items from the income statement that they cannot measure reliably.* Current practice prohibits recognition of certain items from the determination of income even though the effects of these items can arguably affect the company's

[1]We will use the term *income statement* except in situations where a company reports other comprehensive income (discussed later in the chapter). In that case, we will use the term **statement of comprehensive income**.

performance. For example, a company may not record unrealized gains and losses on certain investment securities in income when there is uncertainty that it will ever realize the changes in value. In addition, more and more companies, like **Cisco Systems** and **Microsoft**, experience increases in value due to brand recognition, customer service, and product quality. A common framework for identifying and reporting these types of values is still lacking.

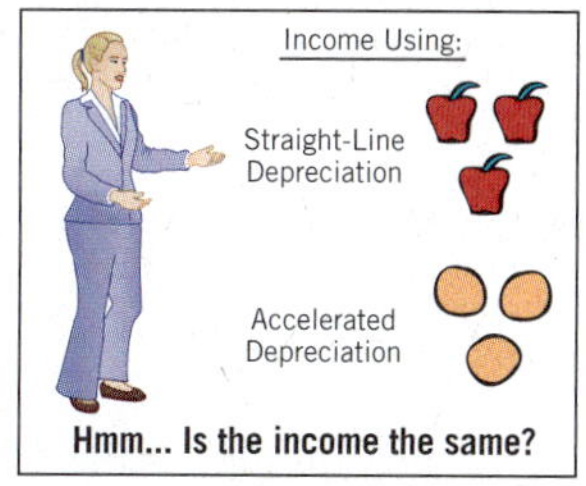

2. ***Income numbers are affected by the accounting methods employed.*** One company may depreciate its plant assets on an accelerated basis; another chooses straight-line depreciation. Assuming all other factors are equal, the first company will report lower income. In effect, we are comparing apples to oranges.

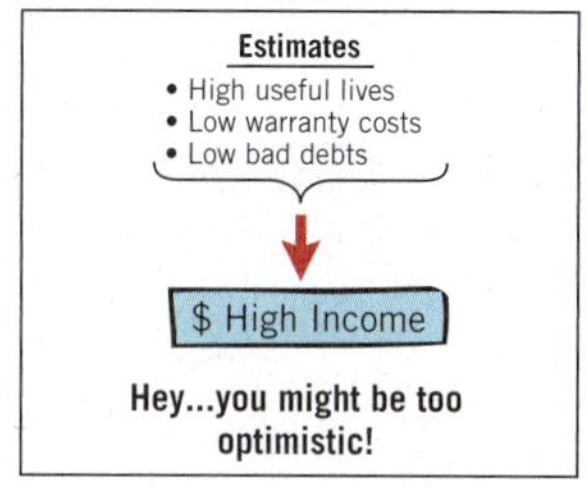

3. ***Income measurement involves judgment.*** For example, one company in good faith may estimate the useful life of an asset to be 20 years while another company uses a 15-year estimate for the same type of asset. Similarly, some companies may make optimistic estimates of future warranty costs and bad debt write-offs, which result in lower expense and higher income.

In summary, several limitations of the income statement reduce the usefulness of its information for predicting the amounts, timing, and uncertainty of future cash flows.

Quality of Earnings

Underlying Concepts

The income statement provides important information to help assess the amounts, timing, and uncertainty of future cash flows—the central element of the objective of financial reporting.

So far, our discussion has highlighted the importance of information in the income statement for investment and credit decisions, including the evaluation of the company and its managers.[2] Companies try to meet or beat Wall Street expectations so that the market price of their stock and the value of management's stock options increase. As a result, companies have incentives to manage income to meet earnings targets or to make earnings look less risky.

The SEC has expressed concern that the motivations to meet earnings targets may override good business practices. This erodes the quality of earnings and the quality of financial reporting. As indicated by one SEC chairperson, "Managing may be giving way to manipulation; integrity may be losing out to illusion."[3] As a result, the SEC has taken decisive action to prevent the practice of earnings management.

What is **earnings management**? It is often defined as the planned timing of revenues, expenses, gains, and losses to smooth out bumps in earnings. In most cases, companies use earnings management to increase income in the current year at the expense of income in future years. For example, they prematurely recognize sales in order to boost earnings. As one commentator noted, "it's like popping a cork in [opening] a bottle of wine before it is ready."

Companies also use earnings management to decrease current earnings in order to increase income in the future. The classic case is the use of "cookie jar" reserves. Companies establish these reserves by using unrealistic assumptions to estimate liabilities for such items as loan losses, restructuring charges, and warranty returns. The companies then reduce these reserves in the future to increase reported income in the future.

[2]In support of the usefulness of income information, accounting researchers have documented an association between companies' market prices and reported incomes. See W. H. Beaver, "Perspectives on Recent Capital Markets Research," *The Accounting Review* (April 2002), pp. 453–474.

[3]A. Levitt, "The Numbers Game," Remarks to NYU Center for Law and Business, September 28, 1998 (Securities and Exchange Commission, 1998).

Such earnings management negatively affects the **quality of earnings** if it distorts the information in a way that is less useful for predicting future earnings and cash flows. Markets rely on trust. The bond between shareholders and the company must remain strong. Investors or others losing faith in the numbers reported in the financial statements will damage U.S. capital markets. As we mentioned in the opening story, we need heightened scrutiny of income measurement and reporting to ensure the quality of earnings and investors' confidence in the income statement.

What do the numbers mean? *FOUR: THE LONELIEST NUMBER*

Managing earnings up or down adversely affects the quality of earnings. Why do companies engage in such practices? Some recent research concludes that many companies tweak quarterly earnings to meet investor expectations. How do they do it? Research findings indicate that companies tend to nudge their earnings numbers up by a 10th of a cent or two. That lets them round results up to the highest cent, as illustrated in the following chart.

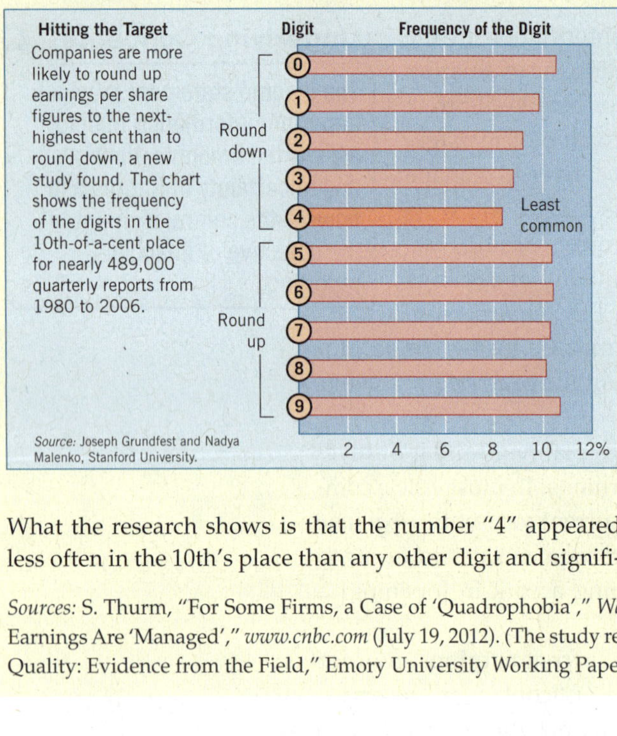

What the research shows is that the number "4" appeared less often in the 10th's place than any other digit and significantly less often than would be expected by chance. This effect is called "quadrophobia." For the typical company in the study, an increase of $31,000 in quarterly net income would boost earnings per share by a 10th of a cent. A more recent analysis of quarterly results for more than 2,600 companies found that rounding up remains more common than rounding down.

Another recent study reinforces the concerns about earnings management. Based on a survey of 169 public-company chief financial officers (and with in-depth interviews of 12), the study concludes that high-quality earnings are sustainable when backed by actual cash flows and "avoiding unreliable long-term estimates." However, about 20 percent of firms manage earnings to misrepresent their economic performance. And when they do manage earnings, it could move EPS by an average of 10 percent.

Is such earnings management a problem for investors? It is if they cannot determine the impact on earnings quality. Indeed, the surveyed CFOs "believe that it is difficult for outside observers to unravel earnings management, especially when such earnings are managed using subtle unobservable choices or real actions." What's an investor to do? The survey authors say the CFOs "advocate paying close attention to the key managers running the firm, the lack of correlation between earnings and cash flows, significant deviations between firm and peer experience, and unusual behavior in accruals."

Sources: S. Thurm, "For Some Firms, a Case of 'Quadrophobia'," *Wall Street Journal* (February 14, 2010); and H. Greenberg, "CFOs Concede Earnings Are 'Managed'," *www.cnbc.com* (July 19, 2012). (The study referred to is by I. Dichev, J. Graham, C. Harvey, and S. Rajgopal, "Earnings Quality: Evidence from the Field," Emory University Working Paper (July 2012).

FORMAT OF THE INCOME STATEMENT

LEARNING OBJECTIVE 2
Describe the content and format of the income statement.

Elements of the Income Statement

Net income results from revenue, expense, gain, and loss transactions. The income statement summarizes these transactions. This method of income measurement, the **transaction approach**, focuses on the income-related activities that have occurred during the period.[4] The statement can further classify income by customer, product line, or function, or by operating and nonoperating, continuing and discontinued, and regular and irregular categories.[5] The following lists more formal definitions of income-related items, referred to as the major elements of the income statement.

ELEMENTS OF FINANCIAL STATEMENTS

REVENUES. Inflows or other enhancements of assets of an entity or settlements of its liabilities during a period from delivering or producing goods, rendering services, or other activities that constitute the entity's ongoing major or central operations.

EXPENSES. Outflows or other using-up of assets or incurrences of liabilities during a period from delivering or producing goods, rendering services, or carrying out other activities that constitute the entity's ongoing major or central operations.

GAINS. Increases in equity (net assets) from peripheral or incidental transactions of an entity except those that result from revenues or investments by owners.

LOSSES. Decreases in equity (net assets) from peripheral or incidental transactions of an entity except those that result from expenses or distributions to owners.[6]

Revenues take many forms, such as sales, fees, interest, dividends, and rents. Expenses also take many forms, such as cost of goods sold, depreciation, interest, rent, salaries and wages, and taxes. Gains and losses also are of many types, resulting from the sale of investments or plant assets, settlement of liabilities, and write-offs of assets due to impairments or casualty.

The distinction between revenues and gains, and between expenses and losses, depend to a great extent on the typical activities of the company. For example, when **McDonald's** sells a hamburger, it records the selling price as revenue. However, when McDonald's sells land, it records any excess of the selling price over the book value as a gain. This difference in treatment results because the sale of the hamburger is part of McDonald's regular operations. The sale of land is not.

We cannot overemphasize the importance of reporting these elements. Most decision-makers find the *parts* of a financial statement to be more useful than the whole. As we indicated earlier, investors and creditors are interested in predicting the amounts, timing, and uncertainty of future income and cash flows. Having income statement elements shown in some detail and in comparison with prior years' data allows decision-makers to better assess future income and cash flows.

[4]The most common alternative to the transaction approach is the **capital maintenance approach** to income measurement. Under this approach, a company determines income for the period based on the change in equity, after adjusting for capital contributions (e.g., investments by owners) or distributions (e.g., dividends). The main drawback associated with the capital maintenance approach is that the components of income are not evident in its measurement. The Internal Revenue Service uses the capital maintenance approach to identify unreported income and refers to this approach as the "net worth check."

[5]The term "irregular" encompasses transactions and other events that are derived from developments outside the normal operations of the business.

[6]"Elements of Financial Statements," *Statement of Financial Accounting Concepts No. 6* (Stamford, Conn.: FASB, 1985), paras. 78–89.

Intermediate Components of the Income Statement

LEARNING OBJECTIVE 3
Prepare an income statement.

It is common for companies to present some or all of the following sections and totals within the income statement as shown in Illustration 4-1. This format is often referred to as the **multiple-step income statement**.

ILLUSTRATION 4-1
Income Statement Sections

1. OPERATING SECTION. A report of the revenues and expenses of the company's principal operations.
   (a) **Sales or Revenue Section.** A subsection presenting sales, discounts, allowances, returns, and other related information. Its purpose is to arrive at the net amount of sales revenue.
   (b) **Cost of Goods Sold Section.** A subsection that shows the cost of goods that were sold to produce the sales.
   (c) **Selling Expenses.** A subsection that lists expenses resulting from the company's efforts to make sales.
   (d) **Administrative or General Expenses.** A subsection reporting expenses of general administration.[7]
2. NONOPERATING SECTION. A report of revenues and expenses resulting from secondary or auxiliary activities of the company. In addition, special gains and losses that are infrequent or unusual, but not both, are normally reported in this section. Generally these items break down into two main subsections:
   (a) **Other Revenues and Gains.** A list of the revenues recognized or gains incurred, generally net of related expenses, from nonoperating transactions.
   (b) **Other Expenses and Losses.** A list of the expenses or losses incurred, generally net of any related incomes, from nonoperating transactions.
3. INCOME TAX. A section reporting federal and state taxes levied on income from continuing operations.
4. DISCONTINUED OPERATIONS. Material gains or losses resulting from the disposition of a component of the business.
5. EXTRAORDINARY ITEMS. Unusual and infrequent material gains and losses.
6. NONCONTROLLING INTEREST. Allocation of income to noncontrolling shareholders.
7. EARNINGS PER SHARE.

As indicated, companies report all revenues, gains, expenses, and losses on the income statement. This statement separates operating transactions from nonoperating transactions, and matches costs and expenses with related revenues. It highlights certain intermediate components of income that analysts use to compute ratios for assessing the performance of the company. Companies present nonoperating revenues, gains, expenses, and losses in a separate section, before income taxes and income from operations. Companies report irregular items, such as discontinued operations of a component of a business and extraordinary items, as separate elements in the income statement. Segregating income with different characteristics and providing intermediate income figures helps readers evaluate earnings information in assessing the amounts, timing, and uncertainty of future cash flows.

[7]Although the content of the operating section is always the same, the organization of the material can differ. The breakdown above uses a **natural expense classification**. Manufacturing concerns and merchandising companies in the wholesale trade commonly use this. Another classification of operating expenses, recommended for retail stores, uses a **functional expense classification** of administrative, occupancy, publicity, buying, and selling expenses.

Illustration 4-2 presents an income statement for Cabrera Company. Cabrera's income statement includes all of the major items shown in Illustration 4-1, except for discontinued operations, extraordinary items, and noncontrolling interest. In arriving at net income, the statement presents the following subtotals and totals: gross profit, income from operations, income before income tax, and net income.[8]

ILLUSTRATION 4-2
Multiple-Step Income Statement

CABRERA COMPANY
INCOME STATEMENT
FOR THE YEAR ENDED DECEMBER 31, 2014

Sales			
Sales revenue			$3,053,081
Less: Sales discounts		$ 24,241	
Sales returns and allowances		56,427	80,668
Net sales			2,972,413
Cost of goods sold			1,982,541
Gross profit			989,872
Operating Expenses			
Selling expenses			
Sales salaries and commissions	$202,644		
Sales office salaries	59,200		
Travel and entertainment	48,940		
Advertising expense	38,315		
Delivery expense	41,209		
Shipping supplies and expense	24,712		
Postage and stationery	16,788		
Telephone and Internet expense	12,215		
Depreciation of sales equipment	9,005	453,028	
Administrative expenses			
Officers' salaries	186,000		
Office salaries	61,200		
Legal and professional services	23,721		
Utilities expense	23,275		
Insurance expense	17,029		
Depreciation of building	18,059		
Depreciation of office equipment	16,000		
Stationery, supplies, and postage	2,875		
Miscellaneous office expenses	2,612	350,771	803,799
Income from operations			186,073
Other Revenues and Gains			
Dividend revenue		98,500	
Rent revenue		72,910	171,410
			357,483
Other Expenses and Losses			
Interest on bonds and notes			126,060
Income before income tax			231,423
Income tax			66,934
Net income for the year			$ 164,489
Earnings per common share			$1.74

The disclosure of net sales is useful because Cabrera reports regular revenues as a separate item. It discloses irregular or incidental revenues elsewhere in the income statement. As a result, analysts can more easily understand and assess trends in revenue from continuing operations.

Similarly, the reporting of gross profit provides a useful number for evaluating performance and predicting future earnings. Statement readers may study the trend in gross

[8]Companies must include *earnings per share* or *net loss per share* on the face of the income statement.

profits to determine how successfully a company uses its resources. They also may use that information to understand how competitive pressure affected profit margins.

Finally, disclosing income from operations highlights the difference between regular and irregular or incidental activities. This disclosure helps users recognize that incidental or irregular activities are unlikely to continue at the same level. Furthermore, disclosure of operating earnings may assist in comparing different companies and assessing operating efficiencies.

What do the numbers mean? TOP LINE OR BOTTOM LINE?

The importance of the components of income, as well as the bottom line, is illustrated in the recent case of **Chipotle**. Its stock had climbed fourfold in five years and for good reason. The company had been reporting surprisingly high bottom-line income and investors were clamoring to buy. However, in a recent month, that pattern was broken—that is, Chipotle posted solid earnings, but investors sold. The reason? Analysts attribute the sell-off to Chipotle missing its target for *revenues*. The stock fell 21 percent, from $404 to $317, in a day. And Chipotle was not alone. Six in 10 large companies reported results in that same quarter that missed revenue targets. In response to the bad revenue news, **Priceline.com** fell $117 to $562 after reporting revenue that was lower than analysts had expected. The story has been the same for dozens of companies across industries, from **Coach**, a luxury goods retailer, to **Boston Scientific**, which sells medical devices, to glass-container maker **Owens-Illinois**.

The recent focus on the top line, revenue, arises because market expectations for revenues do not seem to jive with the companies' optimistic profit picture. For example, revenues are expected to drop by about 2 percent in 2013 for companies in the S&P 500. And while companies might report a surprise in earnings, analysts will be focusing on revenues. Companies have been able to cut costs to compensate—laying off workers, squeezing remaining staff, and using technology to run more efficiently—but there's a limit to how much you can squeeze your workers and use technology to produce more. U.S. companies are just about as lean as any time in history.

As one analyst noted (in this economic environment), "you won't be able to grow earnings much faster than revenue. . . . Analysts will have to revise down their earnings." So watch the top line, as well as the bottom line.

Source: Associated Press, "Why Some Stocks Are Sinking Despite Big Profits," *The New York Times* (August 12, 2012).

Condensed Income Statements

In some cases, a single income statement cannot possibly present all the desired expense detail. To solve this problem, a company includes only the totals of expense groups in the statement of income. It then also prepares supplementary schedules to support the totals. This format may thus reduce the income statement itself to a few lines on a single sheet. For this reason, readers who wish to study all the reported data on operations must give their attention to the supporting schedules. For example, consider the income statement shown in Illustration 4-3 for Cabrera Company. This statement is a condensed version of the more detailed multiple-step statement presented in Illustration 4-2 (page 165). It is more representative of the type found in practice. Illustration 4-4 then shows an example of a supporting schedule, cross-referenced as Note D and detailing the selling expenses.

How much detail should a company include in the income statement? On the one hand, a company wants to present a simple, summarized statement so that readers can readily discover important factors. On the other hand, it wants to disclose the results of all activities and to provide more than just a skeleton report. As we showed in Illustrations 4-3 and 4-4, the income statement always includes certain basic elements, but companies can present them in various formats.

ILLUSTRATION 4-3
Condensed Income Statement

CABRERA COMPANY INCOME STATEMENT FOR THE YEAR ENDED DECEMBER 31, 2014		
Net sales		$2,972,413
Cost of goods sold		1,982,541
Gross profit		989,872
Selling expenses (see Note D)	$453,028	
Administrative expenses	350,771	803,799
Income from operations		186,073
Other revenues and gains		171,410
		357,483
Other expenses and losses		126,060
Income before income tax		231,423
Income tax		66,934
Net income for the year		$ 164,489
Earnings per share		$1.74

ILLUSTRATION 4-4
Sample Supporting Schedule

Note D: Selling expenses	
Sales salaries and commissions	$202,644
Sales office salaries	59,200
Travel and entertainment	48,940
Advertising expense	38,315
Delivery expense	41,209
Shipping supplies and expense	24,712
Postage and stationery	16,788
Telephone and Internet expense	12,215
Depreciation of sales equipment	9,005
Total selling expenses	$453,028

Single-Step Income Statements

In reporting revenues, gains, expenses, and losses, some companies often use a format known as the **single-step income statement** instead of a multiple-step income statement. The single-step statement consists of just two groupings: revenues and expenses. Expenses are deducted from revenues to arrive at net income or loss, hence the expression "single-step." Frequently, companies report income tax separately as the last item before net income to indicate its relationship to income before income tax. Illustration 4-5 (page 168) shows the single-step income statement of Cabrera Company.

Companies that use the single-step income statement in financial reporting typically do so because of its simplicity. That is, **the primary advantage of the single-step format lies in its simple presentation and the absence of any implication that one type of revenue or expense item has priority over another.** This format thus eliminates potential classification problems.[9]

[9] *Accounting Trends and Techniques* (New York: AICPA) recently reported that of the 500 companies surveyed, 411 employed the multiple-step form, and 89 employed the single-step income statement format. This is a reversal from 1983, when 314 used the single-step form and 286 used the multiple-step form.

ILLUSTRATION 4-5
Single-Step Income Statement

CABRERA COMPANY INCOME STATEMENT FOR THE YEAR ENDED DECEMBER 31, 2014	
Revenues	
Net sales	$2,972,413
Dividend revenue	98,500
Rent revenue	72,910
Total revenues	3,143,823
Expenses	
Cost of goods sold	1,982,541
Selling expenses	453,028
Administrative expenses	350,771
Interest expense	126,060
Income tax expense	66,934
Total expenses	2,979,334
Net income	$ 164,489
Earnings per common share	$1.74

REPORTING VARIOUS INCOME ITEMS

LEARNING OBJECTIVE 4
Explain how to report various income items.

GAAP allows flexibility in the presentation of the components of income. However, the FASB developed specific guidelines in two important areas: what to include in income and how to report certain unusual or irregular items.

What should be reported in net income and where it should be reported is controversial. For example, should companies report a gain or loss on sale of an investment as part of net income or report it directly in retained earnings? Should a company report a loss on discontinued operations differently than interest expense? What we therefore need is consistent and comparable income reporting practices. Developing a framework for reporting income components is important to ensure useful information.

Furthermore, as our opening story discusses, we need consistent and comparable income reporting practices to avoid "promotional" information reported by companies.[10] Some users advocate a **current operating performance approach** to income reporting. These analysts argue that the most useful income measure reflects only regular and recurring revenue and expense elements. Some irregular items do not reflect a company's future earning power.

In contrast, others warn that a focus on operating income potentially misses important information about a company's performance. Any gain or loss experienced by the company, whether directly or indirectly related to operations, contributes to its long-run profitability. As one analyst notes, "write-offs matter. . . . They speak to the volatility of (past) earnings."[11] As a result, analysts can use some nonoperating items to assess the riskiness of future earnings. Furthermore, determining which items are operating and which are irregular or unusual requires judgment. This might lead to differences in the treatment of irregular items and to possible manipulation of income measures.

[10]The FASB and the IASB are working on a joint project on financial statement presentation, which is studying how to best report income as well as information presented in the balance sheet and the statement of cash flows. See *http://www.fasb.org/project/financial_statement_presentation.shtml*.

[11]D. McDermott, "Latest Profit Data Stir Old Debate Between Net and Operating Income," *Wall Street Journal* (May 3, 1999). A recent survey of 500 large public companies (*Accounting Trends and Techniques—2012* (New York: AICPA)) documented that 106 of the 500 survey companies reported a write-down of assets (see also Illustration 4-6 on page 169). This highlights the importance of good reporting for these irregular items.

So, what to do? The accounting profession has **adopted a modified all-inclusive concept**. In this approach, companies record most items, including unusual or irregular ones, as part of net income.[12] In addition, companies are required to highlight these items in the financial statements so that users can better determine the long-run earning power of the company. These income items fall into four general categories, which we discuss in the following sections:

International Perspective

In many countries, the "modified all-inclusive" income statement approach does not parallel that of the United States. For example, companies in these countries take some gains and losses directly to owners' equity accounts instead of reporting them on the income statement.

1. Unusual gains and losses.
2. Discontinued operations.
3. Extraordinary items.
4. Noncontrolling interest.

Unusual Gains and Losses

The following items may need separate disclosure in the income statement to help users predict the amounts, timing, and uncertainty of future cash flows.

- Losses on the write-down or write-off of receivables; inventories; property, plant, and equipment; deferred research and development costs; or other intangible assets.
- Gains or losses from exchange or translation of foreign currencies, including those relating to major devaluations and revaluations.
- Restructuring charges.
- Other gains or losses from sale or abandonment of property, plant, or equipment used in the business.
- Effects of a strike, including those against competitors and major suppliers.
- Adjustment of accruals on long-term contracts. [1]

See the FASB Codification section (page 188).

Illustration 4-6 identifies the most common types of unusual gains and losses reported in a survey of 500 large companies. Note that more than 40 percent of the surveyed firms reported restructuring charges, and nearly 60 percent of the companies reported write-downs or gains or losses on asset sales.

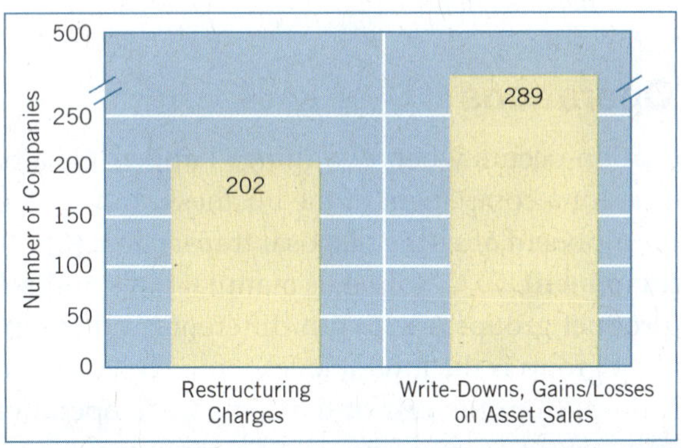

ILLUSTRATION 4-6
Number of Unusual Items Reported in a Recent Year by 500 Large Companies

Companies sometimes show these unusual gains and losses with their normal recurring revenues and expenses. For example, **PepsiCo, Inc.** presented an unusual charge in its income statement, as Illustration 4-7 (page 170) shows.

[12]The FASB issued a statement of concepts that offers some guidance on this topic: "Recognition and Measurement in Financial Statements of Business Enterprises," *Statement of Financial Accounting Concepts No. 5* (Stamford, Conn.: FASB, 1984).

ILLUSTRATION 4-7
Income Statement Presentation of Unusual Charges

PepsiCo, Inc.
(in millions)

Net sales	$20,917
Costs and expenses, net	
Cost of sales	8,525
Selling, general, and administrative expenses	9,241
Amortization of intangible assets	199
Unusual items (Note 2)	290
Operating income	$ 2,662

Note 2 (Restructuring Charge)

Dispose and write down assets	$183
Improve productivity	94
Strengthen the international bottler structure	13
Net loss	$290

The net charge to strengthen the international bottler structure includes proceeds of $87 million associated with a settlement related to a previous Venezuelan bottler agreement, which were partially offset by related costs.

Restructuring charges, like the one PepsiCo reported in Note 2 above, are common in recent years (see also Illustration 4-6 on page 169). A **restructuring charge** relates to a major reorganization of company affairs, such as costs associated with employee layoffs, plant closing costs, write-offs of assets, and so on. A company should not report a restructuring charge as an extraordinary item because these write-offs are part of a company's ordinary and typical activities.

Companies tend to **report unusual items in a separate section just above "Income from operations before income taxes,"** especially when there are multiple unusual items. For example, when General Electric experienced multiple unusual items in one year, it reported them in a separate "Unusual items" section of the income statement below "Income before unusual items and income taxes." *When preparing a multiple-step income statement for homework purposes, you should report unusual gains and losses in the "Other revenues and gains" or "Other expenses and losses" section unless you are instructed to prepare a separate unusual items section.*[13]

Discontinued Operations

A **discontinued operation** occurs when two things happen: (1) a company eliminates the results of operations of a component of the business, and (2) there is no significant involvement in that component after the disposal transaction. **[2]**

To illustrate a **component**, S. C. Johnson manufactures and sells consumer products. It has several product groups, each with different product lines and brands. For S. C. Johnson, a product group is the lowest level at which it can clearly distinguish the operations and cash flows from the rest of the company's operations. Therefore, each product group is a component of the company. If a component were disposed of, S. C. Johnson would classify it as a discontinued operation.

[13]Many companies report "one-time items." However, some companies take restructuring charges practically every year. Citicorp (now Citigroup) took restructuring charges six years in a row; Eastman Kodak Co. did so five out of six years. Research indicates that the market discounts the earnings of companies that report a series of "nonrecurring" items. Such evidence supports the contention that these elements reduce the quality of earnings. See J. Elliott and D. Hanna, "Repeated Accounting Write-Offs and the Information Content of Earnings," *Journal of Accounting Research* (Supplement, 1996).

Here is another example. Assume that Softso Inc. has experienced losses with certain brands in its beauty-care products group. As a result, Softso decides to sell that part of its business. It will discontinue any continuing involvement in the product group after the sale. In this case, Softso eliminates the operations and the cash flows of the product group from its ongoing operations and reports it as a discontinued operation.

On the other hand, assume Softso decides to remain in the beauty-care business but will discontinue the brands that experienced losses. Because Softso cannot differentiate the cash flows from the brands from the cash flows of the product group as a whole, it cannot consider the brands a component. Softso does not classify any gain or loss on the sale of the brands as a discontinued operation.

Companies report as discontinued operations (in a separate income statement category) the gain or loss from **disposal of a component of a business**. In addition, companies report the **results of operations of a component that has been or will be disposed of** separately from continuing operations. Companies show the effects of discontinued operations net of tax as a separate category, after continuing operations. **[3]**

To illustrate, Multiplex Products, Inc., a highly diversified company, decides to discontinue its electronics division. During the current year, the electronics division lost $300,000 (net of tax). Multiplex sold the division at the end of the year at a loss of $500,000 (net of tax). Illustration 4-8 shows the reporting of discontinued operations for Multiplex.

ILLUSTRATION 4-8
Income Statement Presentation of Discontinued Operations

Income from continuing operations		$20,000,000
Discontinued operations		
Loss from operation of discontinued electronics division (net of tax)	$300,000	
Loss from disposal of electronics division (net of tax)	500,000	(800,000)
Net income		$19,200,000

Companies use the phrase **"Income from continuing operations"** only when gains or losses on discontinued operations occur.[14]

A company that reports a discontinued operation must report per share amounts for discontinued operations either on the face of the income statement or in the notes to the financial statements. To illustrate, consider the income statement for Poquito Industries Inc., shown in Illustration 4-9 (page 172). Poquito had 100,000 shares outstanding for the entire year. Notice the order in which Poquito shows the data, with per share information at the bottom. The Poquito income statement, as Illustration 4-9 shows, is highly condensed. Poquito would need to describe items such as "Other expenses and losses" and "Discontinued operations" fully and appropriately in the statement or related notes.

Intraperiod Tax Allocation

As indicated in Illustration 4-8, companies report discontinued operations on the income statement net of tax. The allocation of tax to this item is called **intraperiod tax allocation**, that is, allocation within a period. It relates the income tax expense (sometimes referred to as the income tax provision) of the fiscal period to the specific items that give rise to the amount of the income tax provision.

Intraperiod tax allocation helps financial statement users better understand the impact of income taxes on the various components of net income. For example, readers

[14]In practice, a company will generally report only one line on the income statement, such as "Loss on discontinued operations," and then in the notes explain the two components of the loss that total $800,000. *For homework purposes, report both amounts on the face of the income statement, net of tax, if both amounts are provided.*

ILLUSTRATION 4-9
Income Statement

POQUITO INDUSTRIES INC. INCOME STATEMENT FOR THE YEAR ENDED DECEMBER 31, 2014		
Sales revenue		$1,420,000
Cost of goods sold		600,000
Gross profit		820,000
Selling and administrative expenses		320,000
Other revenues and gains		
Interest revenue	$ 10,000	
Other expenses and losses		
Loss on disposal of part of Textile Division	(5,000)	
Loss on sale of investments	(30,000)	(25,000)
Income from operations		475,000
Interest expense		15,000
Income before income tax		460,000
Income tax		184,000
Income from continuing operations		276,000
Discontinued operations		
Income from operations of Pizza Division, less applicable income tax of $24,800	54,000	
Loss on disposal of Pizza Division, less applicable income tax of $41,000	(90,000)	(36,000)
Net income		$240,000
Per share		
Income from continuing operations		$2.76
Income from operations of discontinued division, net of tax		0.54
Loss on disposal of discontinued operation, net of tax		(0.90)
Net income		$2.40

of financial statements will understand how much income tax expense relates to "Income from continuing operations" and how much to discontinued operations. This approach helps users to better predict the amount, timing, and uncertainty of future cash flows. In addition, intraperiod tax allocation discourages statement readers from using pretax measures of performance when evaluating financial results, and thereby recognizes that income tax expense is a real cost.

Companies use intraperiod tax allocation on the income statement for the following items: (1) income from continuing operations, (2) discontinued operations, and (3) extraordinary items (discussed below). The general concept is **"let the tax follow the income."**

To compute the income tax expense attributable to "Income from continuing operations," a company computes the income tax expense related to both the revenue and expense transactions as well as other income and expense used in determining this income subtotal. (In this computation, the company does not consider the tax consequences of items excluded from the determination of "Income from continuing operations.") Companies then associate a separate tax effect (e.g., for discontinued operations). Here, we look in more detail at the calculation of intraperiod tax allocation for a discontinued gain or discontinued loss.

Discontinued Operations (Gain)

In applying the concept of intraperiod tax allocation, assume that Schindler Co. has income before income tax of $250,000. It has a gain of $100,000 from a discontinued operation. Assuming a 30 percent income tax rate, Schindler presents the following information on the income statement.

Income before income tax		$250,000
Income tax		75,000
Income from continuing operations		175,000
Gain on discontinued operations	$100,000	
Less: Applicable income tax	30,000	70,000
Net income		$245,000

ILLUSTRATION 4-10
Intraperiod Tax Allocation, Discontinued Operations Gain

Schindler determines the income tax of $75,000 ($250,000 × 30%) attributable to "Income before income tax" from revenue and expense transactions related to this income. Schindler omits the tax consequences of items excluded from the determination of "Income before income tax." The company shows a separate tax effect of $30,000 related to the "Gain on discontinued operations."

Discontinued Operations (Loss)

To illustrate the reporting of a loss from discontinued operations, assume that Schindler Co. has income before income tax of $250,000. It also has a loss from discontinued operations of $100,000. Assuming a 30 percent tax rate, Schindler presents the income tax on the income statement as shown in Illustration 4-11. In this case, the loss provides a positive tax benefit of $30,000. Schindler, therefore, subtracts it from the $100,000 loss.

Income before income tax		$250,000
Income tax		75,000
Income from continuing operations		175,000
Loss from discontinued operations	$100,000	
Less: Applicable income tax reduction	30,000	70,000
Net income		$105,000

ILLUSTRATION 4-11
Intraperiod Tax Allocation, Discontinued Operations Loss

Companies may also report the tax effect of a discontinued item by means of a note disclosure, as illustrated below.

Income before income tax	$250,000
Income tax	75,000
Income from continuing operations	175,000
Loss on discontinued operations, less applicable income tax reduction (Note 1)	70,000
Net income	$105,000

Note 1: During the year, the Company suffered a loss on discontinuing operations of $70,000, net of applicable income tax reduction of $30,000.

ILLUSTRATION 4-12
Note Disclosure of Intraperiod Tax Allocation

Extraordinary Items

Extraordinary items are nonrecurring **material** items that differ significantly from a company's typical business activities. The criteria for extraordinary items are as follows.

> Extraordinary items are events and transactions that are distinguished by their unusual nature **and** by the infrequency of their occurrence. Classifying an event or transaction as an extraordinary item requires meeting **both** of the following criteria:
>
> **(a)** ***Unusual nature.*** The underlying event or transaction should possess a high degree of abnormality and be of a type clearly unrelated to, or only incidentally

related to, the ordinary and typical activities of the company, taking into account the environment in which it operates.

(b) ***Infrequency of occurrence.*** The underlying event or transaction should be of a type that the company does not reasonably expect to recur in the foreseeable future, taking into account the environment in which the company operates. **[4]**

International Perspective

Special reporting for extraordinary items is prohibited under IFRS.

Only rarely does an event or transaction clearly meet the criteria for an extraordinary item.[15] For example, a company classifies gains or losses as extraordinary if they **resulted directly from a major casualty** (such as an earthquake), an **expropriation**, or a **prohibition under a newly enacted law or regulation**. Such circumstances clearly meet the criteria of unusual and infrequent. For example, **Weyerhaeuser Company** (forest and lumber) incurred an extraordinary item (an approximate $36 million loss) as a result of volcanic activity at Mount St. Helens. The eruption destroyed standing timber, logs, buildings, equipment, and transportation systems covering 68,000 acres.

In determining whether an item is extraordinary, **a company must consider the environment in which it operates**. The environment includes such factors as industry characteristics, geographic location, and the nature and extent of governmental regulations. Thus, the FASB accords extraordinary item treatment to the loss from hail damages to a tobacco grower's crops if hailstorm damage in its locality is rare. On the other hand, frost damage to a citrus grower's crop in Florida does not qualify as extraordinary because frost damage normally occurs there every three or four years.

Similarly, when a company sells the only significant security investment it has ever owned, the gain or loss meets the criteria of an extraordinary item. Another company, however, that has a portfolio of securities acquired for investment purposes would not report such a sale as an extraordinary item. Sale of such securities is part of its ordinary and typical activities.

In addition, considerable judgment must be exercised in determining whether to report an item as extraordinary. For example, the government condemned the forestlands of some paper companies to preserve state or national parks or forests. Is such an event extraordinary, or is it part of a paper company's normal operations? Such determination is not easy. Much depends on the frequency of previous condemnations, the expectation of future condemnations, materiality, and the like.[16]

Extraordinary Gains

To illustrate the reporting of an extraordinary gain, assume that Logan Co. has income before income tax and extraordinary item of $250,000. It has an extraordinary gain of $100,000 from a condemnation settlement received on one its properties. Assuming a 30 percent income tax rate, Logan presents the following information on the income statement.

ILLUSTRATION 4-13
Extraordinary Gain

Income before income tax and extraordinary item		$250,000
Income tax		75,000
Income before extraordinary item		175,000
Extraordinary gain—condemnation settlement	$100,000	
Less: Applicable income tax	30,000	70,000
Net income		$245,000

[15] *Accounting Trends and Techniques—2012* (New York: AICPA) indicates that just 1 of the 500 companies surveyed reported an extraordinary item.

[16] Because assessing the materiality of individual items requires judgment, determining what is extraordinary is difficult. However, in making materiality judgments, companies should consider extraordinary items individually and not in the aggregate. **[5]**

Logan determines the income tax of $75,000 ($250,000 × 30%) attributable to "Income before income tax and extraordinary item" from revenue and expense transactions related to this income. Logan omits the tax consequences of items excluded from the determination of "Income before income tax and extraordinary item." The company shows a separate tax effect of $30,000 related to the "Extraordinary gain—condemnation settlement."

Extraordinary Losses

To illustrate the reporting of an extraordinary loss, assume that Logan Co. has income before income tax and extraordinary item of $250,000. It suffers an extraordinary loss from a major casualty of $100,000. Assuming a 30 percent tax rate, Logan presents the income tax on the income statement as shown in Illustration 4-14. In this case, the loss provides a positive tax benefit of $30,000. Logan, therefore, subtracts it from the $100,000 loss.

ILLUSTRATION 4-14
Intraperiod Tax Allocation, Extraordinary Loss

Income before income tax and extraordinary item		$250,000
Income tax		75,000
Income before extraordinary item		175,000
Extraordinary item—casualty loss	$100,000	
Less: Applicable income tax reduction	30,000	70,000
Net income		$105,000

Companies may also report the tax effect of an extraordinary item by means of a note disclosure, as illustrated below.

ILLUSTRATION 4-15
Note Disclosure of Intraperiod Tax Allocation

Income before income tax and extraordinary item	$250,000
Income tax	75,000
Income before extraordinary item	175,000
Extraordinary item—casualty loss, less applicable income tax reduction (Note 1)	70,000
Net income	$105,000

Note 1: During the year, the Company suffered a major casualty loss of $70,000, net of applicable income tax reduction of $30,000.

A presentation showing both discontinued operations and extraordinary items is shown in Illustration 4-19 (page 178).[17]

What do the numbers mean? EXTRAORDINARY TIMES

No event better illustrates the difficulties of determining whether a transaction meets the definition of extraordinary than the financial impacts of the terrorist attack on the World Trade Center on September 11, 2001.

To many, this event, which resulted in the tragic loss of lives, jobs, and in some cases entire businesses, clearly meets the criteria for unusual and infrequent. For example, in the wake of the terrorist attack that destroyed the World Trade Center and turned much of lower Manhattan including Wall Street into a war zone, airlines, insurance companies, and other businesses recorded major losses due to property damage, business disruption, and suspension of airline travel and of securities trading.

But, to the surprise of many, the FASB did not permit extraordinary item reporting for losses arising from the terrorist attacks. The reason? After much deliberation, the

[17]As indicated earlier, discontinued operations and extraordinary items are shown net of tax, while unusual gains and losses are not reported net of tax. The Board specifically **prohibited a net-of-tax treatment for these latter items**, to ensure that users of financial statements can easily differentiate extraordinary items—reported net of tax—from material items that are unusual or infrequent, but not both.

Emerging Issues Task Force (EITF) of the FASB decided that measurement of the possible loss was too difficult.

Take the airline industry as an example. What portion of the airlines' losses after September 11 was related to the terrorist attack, and what portion was due to the ongoing recession? Also, the FASB did not want companies to use the attack as a reason for reporting as extraordinary some losses that had little direct relationship to the attack. Indeed, energy company **AES** and shoe retailer **Footstar**, which both were experiencing profit pressure before 9/11, put some of the blame for their poor performance on the attack. The FASB came to a similar conclusion—no extraordinary treatment—for the effects of the recent huricanes Katrina and Sandy.

Sources: Julie Creswell, "Bad News Bearers Shift the Blame," *Fortune* (October 15, 2001), p. 44; and CFO Journal, "Companies Must Walk Fine Line in Accounting for Sandy," *Wall Street Journal* (November 13, 2012).

Noncontrolling Interest

A company like **The Coca-Cola Company** owns substantial interests in other companies. Coca-Cola generally consolidates the financial results of these companies into its own financial statements. In these cases, Coca-Cola is referred to as the parent, and the other companies are referred to as subsidiaries. **Noncontrolling interest** is then the portion of equity (net assets) interest in a subsidiary not attributable to the parent company.

To illustrate, assume that Coca-Cola acquires 70 percent of the outstanding stock of Koch Company. Because Coca-Cola owns more than 50 percent of Koch, it consolidates Koch's financial results with its own. Consolidated net income is then allocated to the controlling (Coca-Cola) and noncontrolling shareholders' percentage of ownership in Koch. In other words, under this arrangement, the ownership of Koch is divided into two classes: (1) the majority interest represented by stockholders who own the controlling interest and (2) the noncontrolling interest (sometimes referred to as the minority interest) represented by stockholders who are not part of the controlling group. When Coca-Cola prepares a consolidated income statement, GAAP requires that net income be allocated to the controlling and noncontrolling interest. This allocation is reported at the bottom of the income statement, after net income.

An example of how Coca-Cola reports its noncontrolling interest is shown in Illustration 4-16.

ILLUSTRATION 4-16
Presentation of Noncontrolling Interest

The Coca-Cola Company

Consolidated net income	$8,634
Less: Net income attributable to noncontrolling interests	62
Net income attributable to shareowners of The Coca-Cola Company	$8,572

The noncontrolling interest amounts are not an expense or dividend, but are allocations of net income (loss) to the noncontrolling interest. **[6]**

Summary of Various Income Items

Because of the numerous intermediate income figures created by the reporting of irregular items, readers must carefully evaluate earnings information reported by the financial press. Illustration 4-17 summarizes the basic concepts that we previously discussed. Although simplified, the chart provides a useful framework for determining the treatment of special items affecting the income statement.

Type of Situation	Criteria	Examples	Placement on Income Statement
Unusual gains or losses, not considered extraordinary	Material; character typical of the customary business activities; unusual or infrequent but not both.	Write-downs of receivables, inventories; adjustments of accrued contract prices; gains or losses from fluctuations of foreign exchange; gains or losses from sales of assets used in business.	Show in separate section above income before extraordinary items. Often reported in "Other revenues and gains" or "Other expenses and losses" section. **(Not shown net of tax.)**
Discontinued operations	Disposal of a component of a business for which the company can clearly distinguish operations and cash flows from the rest of the company's operations.	Sale by diversified company of major division that represents only activities in electronics industry. Food distributor that sells wholesale to supermarket chains and through fast-food restaurants decides to discontinue the division that sells to one of two classes of customers.	Show in separate section after continuing operations but before extraordinary items. **(Shown net of tax.)**
Extraordinary items	Material, and both unusual and infrequent (nonrecurring).	Gains or losses resulting from casualties, an expropriation, or a prohibition under a new law.	Show in separate section entitled "Extraordinary items." **(Shown net of tax.)**
Noncontrolling interest	Allocation of net income or loss divided between two classes: (1) the majority interest represented by the shareholders who own the controlling interest, and (2) the noncontrolling interest (often referred to as the *minority interest*).	Net profit (loss) attributable to noncontrolling shareholders.	Report as a separate item below net income or loss as an allocation of the net income or loss **(not as an item of income or expense).**

ILLUSTRATION 4-17
Summary of Various Items in the Income Statement

Earnings per Share

5 LEARNING OBJECTIVE
Identify where to report earnings per share information.

A company customarily sums up the results of its operations in one important figure: net income. However, the financial world has widely accepted an even more distilled and compact figure as the most significant business indicator—**earnings per share (EPS)**.

The computation of earnings per share is usually straightforward. **Earnings per share is net income minus preferred dividends (income available to common stockholders), divided by the weighted average of common shares outstanding.**[18]

To illustrate, assume that Lancer, Inc. reports net income of $350,000. It declares and pays preferred dividends of $50,000 for the year. The weighted-average number of common shares outstanding during the year is 100,000 shares. Lancer computes earnings per share of $3, as shown in Illustration 4-18.

$$\frac{\text{Net Income} - \text{Preferred Dividends}}{\text{Weighted Average of Common Shares Outstanding}} = \text{Earnings per Share}$$

$$\frac{\$350{,}000 - \$50{,}000}{100{,}000} = \$3$$

ILLUSTRATION 4-18
Equation Illustrating Computation of Earnings per Share

Note that EPS measures the number of dollars earned by each share of common stock. It does not represent the dollar amount paid to stockholders in the form of dividends.

Prospectuses, proxy material, and annual reports to stockholders commonly use the "net income per share" or "earnings per share" ratio. The financial press, statistical

[18]In calculating earnings per share, companies deduct preferred dividends from net income if the dividends are declared or if they are cumulative though not declared. Only the net income attributable to the controlling interest should be used in computing earnings per share.

services like Standard & Poor's, and Wall Street securities analysts also highlight EPS. Because of its importance, **companies must disclose earnings per share on the face of the income statement**. A company that reports a discontinued operation or an extraordinary item must report per share amounts for these line items either on the face of the income statement or in the notes to the financial statements. [7]

To illustrate, consider the income statement for Poquito Industries Inc. shown in Illustration 4-19. Notice the order in which Poquito shows the data, with per share information at the bottom. Assume that the company had 100,000 shares outstanding for the entire year. The Poquito income statement, as Illustration 4-19 shows, is highly condensed. Poquito would need to describe items such as "Loss on disposal of part of Textile Division," "Discontinued operations," and "Extraordinary item" fully and appropriately in the statement or related notes.

ILLUSTRATION 4-19
Income Statement

POQUITO INDUSTRIES INC.
INCOME STATEMENT
FOR THE YEAR ENDED DECEMBER 31, 2014

Sales revenue		$1,420,000
Cost of goods sold		600,000
Gross profit		820,000
Selling and administrative expenses		320,000
Income from operations		500,000
Other revenues and gains		
Interest revenue		10,000
Other expenses and losses		
Loss on disposal of part of Textile Division	$ 5,000	
Loss on sale of investments	45,000	50,000
Income from continuing operations before income tax		460,000
Income tax		184,000
Income from continuing operations		276,000
Discontinued operations		
Income from operations of Pizza Division, less applicable income tax of $24,800	54,000	
Loss on disposal of Pizza Division, less applicable income tax of $41,000	90,000	36,000
Income before extraordinary item		240,000
Extraordinary item—loss from earthquake, less applicable income tax of $23,000		45,000
Net income		$ 195,000
Per share of common stock		
Income from continuing operations		$2.76
Income from operations of discontinued division, net of tax		0.54
Loss on disposal of discontinued operation, net of tax		0.90
Income before extraordinary item		2.40
Extraordinary loss, net of tax		0.45
Net income		$1.95

Many corporations have simple capital structures that include only common stock. For these companies, a presentation such as "Earnings per common share" is appropriate on the income statement. In many instances, however, companies' earnings per share are subject to dilution (reduction) in the future because existing contingencies permit the issuance of additional common shares. [8][19]

[19]The earnings per share effects of noncontrolling interest should also be presented. In addition, the amounts of income from continuing operations and discontinued operations (if present) attributable to the controlling interest should be disclosed. We discuss the computational problems involved in accounting for these dilutive securities in earnings per share computations in Chapter 16.

What do the numbers mean? DIFFERENT INCOME CONCEPTS

As mentioned in the opening story, the FASB and the IASB are collaborating on a joint project related to presentation of financial statements. In 2008, these two groups issued an exposure draft that presented examples of what these new financial statements might look like. The Boards also conducted field tests on two groups: preparers and users. Preparers were asked to recast their financial statements and then comment on the results. Users examined the recast statements and commented on their usefulness.

One part of the field test asked analysts to indicate which primary performance metric they use or create from a company's income statement. They were provided with the following options: (a) Net income; (b) Pretax income; (c) Income before interest and taxes (EBIT); (d) Income before interest, taxes, depreciation, and amortization (EBITDA); (e) Operating income; (f) Comprehensive income; and (g) Other. The adjacent chart highlights their responses.

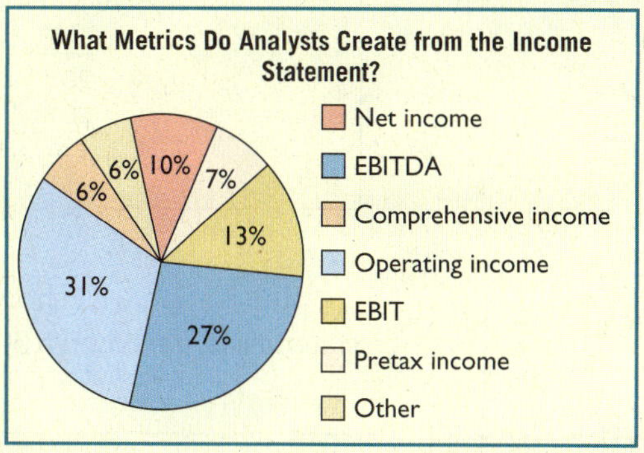

As indicated, Operating income (31%) and EBITDA (27%) were identified as the two primary performance metrics that respondents use or create from a company's income statement. A majority of the respondents identified a primary performance metric that uses net income as its foundation (pretax income would be in this group). Clearly, users and preparers look at more than just the bottom-line income number, which supports the common practice of providing subtotals within the income statement.

Source: "FASB-IASB Report on Analyst Field Test Results," Financial Statement Presentation Informational Board Meeting (September 21, 2009).

OTHER REPORTING ISSUES

In this section, we discuss reporting issues related to (1) accounting changes and errors, (2) retained earnings statement, and (3) comprehensive income.

6 LEARNING OBJECTIVE
Understand the reporting of accounting changes and errors.

Accounting Changes and Errors

Changes in accounting principle, change in estimates, and corrections of errors require unique reporting provisions.

Changes in Accounting Principle

Changes in accounting occur frequently in practice because important events or conditions may be in dispute or uncertain at the statement date. One type of accounting change results when a company adopts a different accounting principle. **Changes in accounting principle** include a change in the method of inventory pricing from FIFO to average-cost, or a change in accounting for construction contracts from the percentage-of-completion to the completed-contract method. **[9]**[20]

Underlying Concepts

Companies can change principles, but they must demonstrate that the newly adopted principle is preferable to the old one. Such changes result in lost consistency from period to period.

A company recognizes a change in accounting principle by making a **retrospective adjustment** to the financial statements. Such an adjustment recasts the prior years' statements on a basis consistent with the newly adopted principle. The company records the cumulative effect of the change for prior periods as an adjustment to beginning retained earnings of the earliest year presented.

To illustrate, Gaubert Inc. decided in March 2014 to change from FIFO to weighted-average inventory pricing. Gaubert's income before income tax, using the new weighted-average method in 2014, is $30,000. Illustration 4-20 (page 180) presents the pretax income data for 2012 and 2013 for this example.

[20]In Chapter 22, we examine in greater detail the problems related to accounting changes, and changes in estimates and errors.

ILLUSTRATION 4-20
Calculation of a Change in Accounting Principle

Year	FIFO	Weighted-Average Method	Excess of FIFO over Weighted-Average Method
2012	$40,000	$35,000	$5,000
2013	30,000	27,000	3,000
Total			$8,000

Illustration 4-21 shows the information Gaubert presented in its comparative income statements, based on a 30 percent tax rate.

ILLUSTRATION 4-21
Income Statement Presentation of a Change in Accounting Principle

	2014	2013	2012
Income before income tax	$30,000	$27,000	$35,000
Income tax	9,000	8,100	10,500
Net income	$21,000	$18,900	$24,500

Thus, under the retrospective approach, the company recasts the prior years' income numbers under the newly adopted method. This approach therefore preserves comparability across years.

Changes in Accounting Estimates

Changes in accounting estimates are inherent in the accounting process. For example, companies estimate useful lives and salvage values of depreciable assets, uncollectible receivables, inventory obsolescence, and the number of periods expected to benefit from a particular expenditure. Not infrequently, due to time, circumstances, or new information, even estimates originally made in good faith must be changed. A company accounts for such changes in estimates in the period of change if they affect only that period, or in the period of change and future periods if the change affects both.

To illustrate a change in estimate that affects only the period of change, assume that DuPage Materials Corp. consistently estimated its bad debt expense at 1 percent of credit sales. In 2014, however, DuPage determines that it must revise upward the estimate of bad debts for the current year's credit sales to 2 percent, or double the prior years' percentage. The 2 percent rate is necessary to reduce accounts receivable to net realizable value. Using 2 percent results in a bad debt charge of $240,000, or double the amount using the 1 percent estimate for prior years. DuPage records the bad debt expense and related allowance at December 31, 2014, as follows.

Bad Debt Expense	240,000	
Allowance for Doubtful Accounts		240,000

DuPage includes the entire change in estimate in 2014 income because the change does not affect future periods. **Companies do not handle changes in estimate retrospectively.** That is, such changes are not carried back to adjust prior years. **Changes in estimate are not considered errors.**

Corrections of Errors

Errors occur as a result of mathematical mistakes, mistakes in the application of accounting principles, or oversight or misuse of facts that existed at the time financial statements were prepared. In recent years, many companies have corrected for errors in their financial statements. The errors involved such items as improper reporting of revenue, accounting for stock options, allowances for receivables, inventories, and other provisions.

Companies correct errors by making proper entries in the accounts and reporting the corrections in the financial statements. Corrections of errors are treated as **prior period adjustments**, similar to changes in accounting principles. Companies record a correction of an error in the year in which it is discovered. They report the error in the financial statements as an adjustment to the beginning balance of retained earnings. If a company prepares comparative financial statements, it should restate the prior statements for the effects of the error.

To illustrate, in 2015, Hillsboro Co. determined that it incorrectly overstated its accounts receivable and sales revenue by $100,000 in 2014. In 2015, Hillsboro makes the following entry to correct for this error (ignore income taxes).

Retained Earnings	100,000	
Accounts Receivable		100,000

Beginning retained earnings is debited in 2015 because sales revenue, and therefore net income, was overstated in 2014 (hence, Retained Earnings was overstated). Accounts Receivable is credited to reduce this overstated balance to the correct amount.

Summary

The impact of changes in accounting principle and error corrections are debited or credited directly to retained earnings for the amounts related to prior periods. Illustration 4-22 summarizes the basic concepts related to these two items, as well as the accounting and reporting for changes in estimates. Although simplified, the chart provides a useful framework for determining the treatment of special items affecting the income statement.

ILLUSTRATION 4-22
Summary of Accounting Changes and Errors

Type of Situation	Criteria	Examples	Placement on Income Statement
Changes in accounting principle	Change from one generally accepted accounting principle to another.	Change in the basis of inventory pricing from FIFO to average-cost.	Recast prior years' income statement on the same basis as the newly adopted principle. **(Shown net of tax.)**
Changes in estimates	Normal, recurring corrections and adjustments.	Changes in the realizability of receivables and inventories; changes in estimated lives of equipment, intangible assets; changes in estimated liability for warranty costs, income taxes, and salary payments.	Show change only in the affected accounts in current and future periods. **(Not shown net of tax.)**
Corrections of errors	Mistake, misuse of facts.	Error in reporting income and expenses.	Treat as prior period adjustment; restate prior years' income statements to correct for error. **(Shown net of tax.)**

Retained Earnings Statement

7 LEARNING OBJECTIVE
Prepare a retained earnings statement.

Net income increases retained earnings. A net loss decreases retained earnings. Both cash and stock dividends decrease retained earnings. Changes in accounting principles (generally) and prior period adjustments may increase or decrease retained earnings. Companies charge or credit these adjustments (net of tax) to the opening balance of retained earnings. This excludes the adjustments from the determination of net income for the current period.

Companies may show retained earnings information in different ways. For example, some companies prepare a separate retained earnings statement, as Illustration 4-23 (page 182) shows.

ILLUSTRATION 4-23
Retained Earnings Statement

STRICKER INC. RETAINED EARNINGS STATEMENT FOR THE YEAR ENDED DECEMBER 31, 2014		
Retained earnings, January 1, as reported		$1,050,000
Correction for understatement of net income in prior period (inventory error)		50,000
Retained earnings, January 1, as adjusted		1,100,000
Add: Net income		360,000
		1,460,000
Less: Cash dividends	$100,000	
Stock dividends	200,000	300,000
Retained earnings, December 31		$1,160,000

The reconciliation of the beginning to the ending balance in retained earnings provides information about why net assets increased or decreased during the year.[21] The association of dividend distributions with net income for the period indicates what management is doing with earnings: It may be "plowing back" into the business part or all of the earnings, distributing all current income, or distributing current income plus the accumulated earnings of prior years.

Restrictions of Retained Earnings

Companies often restrict retained earnings to comply with contractual requirements, board of directors' policy, or current necessity. Generally, companies disclose in the notes to the financial statements the amounts of restricted retained earnings. In some cases, companies transfer the amount of retained earnings restricted to an account titled **Appropriated Retained Earnings**. The retained earnings section may therefore report two separate amounts—(1) retained earnings free (unrestricted) and (2) retained earnings appropriated (restricted). The total of these two amounts equals the total retained earnings.

Comprehensive Income

LEARNING OBJECTIVE 8
Explain how to report other comprehensive income.

Companies generally include in income all revenues, expenses, gains, and losses recognized during the period. These items are classified within the income statement so that financial statement readers can better understand the significance of various components of net income. Changes in accounting principles and corrections of errors are excluded from the calculation of net income because their effects relate to prior periods.

In recent years, there is increased use of fair values for measuring assets and liabilities. Furthermore, possible reporting of gains and losses related to changes in fair value have placed a strain on income reporting. Because fair values are continually changing, some argue that recognizing these gains and losses in net income is misleading. The FASB agrees and has identified a limited number of transactions that should be recorded in other comprehensive income, which affects accumulated other comprehensive income reported in stockholders' equity. One example is unrealized gains and losses on available-for-sale securities.[22] These gains and losses are excluded from net income, thereby

[21] *Accounting Trends and Techniques—2012* (New York: AICPA) indicates that most companies (490 of 500 surveyed) present changes in retained earnings either within the statement of stockholders' equity (486 firms) or in a separate statement of retained earnings (4 firms). Only 1 of the 500 companies prepares a combined statement of income and retained earnings.

[22] We further discuss available-for-sale securities in Chapter 17. Additional examples of other comprehensive items are translation gains and losses on foreign currency, unrealized gains and losses on certain hedging transactions, and adjustments related to pensions. Corrections of errors and changes in accounting principles are not considered other comprehensive income items.

reducing volatility in net income due to fluctuations in fair value. At the same time, disclosure of the potential gain or loss is provided.

Companies include these items that bypass the income statement in a measure called comprehensive income. **Comprehensive income** includes all changes in equity during a period *except* those resulting from investments by owners and distributions to owners. Comprehensive income, therefore, includes the following: all revenues and gains, expenses and losses reported in net income, and all gains and losses that bypass net income but affect stockholders' equity. These items—non-owner changes in equity that bypass the income statement—are referred to as **other comprehensive income**.

International Perspective

GAAP and IFRS are now converged with respect to comprehensive income reporting.

Companies must display the components of other comprehensive income in one of two ways: (1) a single continuous statement (**one statement approach**) or (2) two separate, but consecutive statements of net income and other comprehensive income (**two statement approach**). The one statement approach is often referred to as the statement of comprehensive income. The two statement approach uses the traditional term income statement for the first statement and the comprehensive income statement for the second statement. **[10]**

Under either approach, companies display each component of net income and each component of other comprehensive income. In addition, net income and comprehensive income are reported. Companies are not required to report earnings per share information related to comprehensive income.[23]

We illustrate these two alternatives in the next two sections. In each case, assume that V. Gill Inc. reports the following information for 2014: sales revenue $800,000; cost of goods sold $600,000; operating expenses $90,000; and an unrealized holding gain on available-for-sale securities of $30,000, net of tax.

One Statement Approach

In this approach, the traditional net income is a subtotal, with total comprehensive income shown as a final total. The combined statement has the advantage of not requiring the creation of a new financial statement. However, burying net income as a subtotal on the statement is a disadvantage. Illustration 4-24 shows the one statement format for V. Gill.

ILLUSTRATION 4-24
One Statement Format: Comprehensive Income

V. GILL INC.
STATEMENT OF COMPREHENSIVE INCOME
FOR THE YEAR ENDED DECEMBER 31, 2014

Sales revenue	$800,000
Cost of goods sold	600,000
Gross profit	200,000
Operating expenses	90,000
Net income	110,000
Other comprehensive income	
Unrealized holding gain, net of tax	30,000
Comprehensive income	$140,000

[23]A company must display the components of other comprehensive income either (1) net of related tax effects, or (2) before related tax effects, with one amount shown for the aggregate amount of tax related to the total amount of other comprehensive income. Both alternatives must show each component of other comprehensive income, net of related taxes either in the face of the statement or in the notes. *Accounting Trends and Techniques—2012* indicates that 89 of 490 surveyed companies reporting tax effects provided it in the notes.

Two Statement Approach

Illustration 4-25 shows the two statement format for V. Gill. Reporting comprehensive income in a separate statement indicates that the gains and losses identified as other comprehensive income have the same status as traditional gains and losses.

ILLUSTRATION 4-25
Two Statement Format: Comprehensive Income

V. GILL INC.
INCOME STATEMENT
FOR THE YEAR ENDED DECEMBER 31, 2014

Sales revenue	$800,000
Cost of goods sold	600,000
Gross profit	200,000
Operating expenses	90,000
Net income	$110,000

V. GILL INC.
COMPREHENSIVE INCOME STATEMENT
FOR THE YEAR ENDED DECEMBER 31, 2014

Net income	$110,000
Other comprehensive income	
Unrealized holding gain, net of tax	30,000
Comprehensive income	$140,000

Statement of Stockholders' Equity

In addition to a comprehensive income statement, companies also present a **statement of stockholders' equity** (often referred to as statement of changes in stockholders' equity). This statement reports the changes in each stockholders' equity account and in total stockholders' equity during the year. Companies often prepare **in columnar form** the statement of stockholders' equity. In this format, they use columns for each account and for total stockholders' equity. Stockholders' equity is generally comprised of contributed capital (common and preferred stock and additional paid-in capital), retained earnings, and the accumulated balances in other comprehensive income. The statement reports the change in each stockholders' equity account and in total stockholders' equity for the period. The following items are disclosed in this statement.

1. Contributions (issuances of shares) and distributions (dividends) to owners.
2. Reconciliation of the carrying amount of each component of stockholders' equity from the beginning to the end of the period.

To illustrate, assume the same information for V. Gill (on page 183). The company has the following stockholders' equity account balances at the beginning of 2014: Common Stock $300,000, Retained Earnings $50,000, and Accumulated Other Comprehensive Income $60,000. No changes in the Common Stock account occurred during the year. Illustration 4-26 shows a statement of stockholders' equity for V. Gill.

ILLUSTRATION 4-26
Presentation of Comprehensive Income in Stockholders' Equity Statement

V. GILL INC.
STATEMENT OF STOCKHOLDERS' EQUITY
FOR THE YEAR ENDED DECEMBER 31, 2014

	Total	Retained Earnings	Accumulated Other Comprehensive Income	Common Stock
Beginning balance	$410,000	$ 50,000	$60,000	$300,000
Net income	110,000	110,000		
Other comprehensive income				
Unrealized holding gain, net of tax	30,000		30,000	
Ending balance	$550,000	$160,000	$90,000	$300,000

Balance Sheet Presentation

Regardless of the display format used, V. Gill reports **accumulated other comprehensive income** of $90,000 in the stockholders' equity section of the balance sheet as follows.

ILLUSTRATION 4-27
Presentation of Accumulated Other Comprehensive Income in the Balance Sheet

V. GILL INC.
BALANCE SHEET
AS OF DECEMBER 31, 2014
(STOCKHOLDERS' EQUITY SECTION)

Stockholders' equity	
Common stock	$300,000
Retained earnings	160,000
Accumulated other comprehensive income	90,000
Total stockholders' equity	$550,000

You will want to read the **IFRS INSIGHTS** on pages 205–211 for discussion of IFRS related to the income statement.

By providing information on the components of comprehensive income, as well as accumulated other comprehensive income, the company communicates information about all changes in net assets. With this information, users will better understand the quality of the company's earnings.

Evolving Issue INCOME REPORTING

As indicated in the chapter, information reported in the income statement is important to meeting the objective of financial reporting. However, there is debate over income reporting practices, be it the controversy over pro forma reporting or whether to report comprehensive income in a one statement or a two statement format. In response to these debates and to differences between income reporting under U.S. GAAP and IFRS, standard-setters are working on a project to improve the usefulness of the income statement.

Work to date has resulted in two core principles for financial statement presentation (for the income statement, balance sheet, and the statement of cash flows) based on the objective of financial reporting:

1. **Disaggregate information so that it is useful in predicting an entity's future cash flows.** Disaggregation means separating resources by the activity in which they are used and by their economic characteristics.
2. **Portray a cohesive financial picture of a company's activities.** A cohesive financial picture means that the relationship between items across financial statements is clear and that a company's financial statements complement each other as much as possible.

Cohesiveness will be addressed by using the same classifications across the balance sheet, income statement, and statement of cash flows. The proposed model classifies activities as business or financing, although some have suggested that each statement be segregated into operating, investing, and financing activities.

The statement presentation project is currently inactive on the Boards' joint agenda (see *www.fasb.org* and click on Inactive Joint FASB/IASB Projects under the Projects tab), but it is expected to restart once the projects on financial instruments, revenue recognition, and leases are completed.

KEY TERMS

SUMMARY OF LEARNING OBJECTIVES

1 Understand the uses and limitations of an income statement. The income statement provides investors and creditors with information that helps them predict the amounts, timing, and uncertainty of future cash flows. Also, the income statement helps users determine the risk (level of uncertainty) of not achieving particular cash flows. The limitations of an income statement are as follows. (1) The statement does not include many items that contribute to general growth and well-being of a company. (2) Income numbers are often affected by the accounting methods used. (3) Income measures are subject to estimates.

The transaction approach focuses on the activities that occurred during a given period. Instead of presenting only a net change in net assets, it discloses the components of the change. The transaction approach to income measurement requires the use of revenue, expense, loss, and gain accounts.

2 Describe the content and format of the income statement. The major elements of the income statement are as follows. (1) *Revenues:* Inflows or other enhancements of assets of an entity or settlements of its liabilities during a period from delivering or producing goods, rendering services, or other activities that constitute the entity's ongoing major or central operations. (2) *Expenses:* Outflows or other using-up of assets or incurrences of liabilities during a period from delivering or producing goods, rendering services, or carrying out other activities that constitute the entity's ongoing major or central operations. (3) *Gains:* Increases in equity (net assets) from peripheral or incidental transactions of an entity except those that result from revenues or investments by owners. (4) *Losses:* Decreases in equity (net assets) from peripheral or incidental transactions of an entity except those that result from expenses or distributions to owners.

3 Prepare an income statement. In a single-step income statement, just two groupings exist: revenues and expenses. Expenses are deducted from revenues to arrive at net income or loss—a single subtraction. Frequently, companies report income tax separately as the last item before net income.

A multiple-step income statement shows two further classifications: (1) a separation of operating results from those obtained through the subordinate or nonoperating activities of the company, and (2) a classification of expenses by functions, such as merchandising or manufacturing, selling, and administration.

4 Explain how to report various income items. Companies generally include irregular gains or losses or nonrecurring items in the income statement as follows. (1) Other items of a material amount that are of an unusual or nonrecurring nature and are not considered extraordinary are separately disclosed as a component of continuing operations. (2) Discontinued operations of a component of a business are classified as a separate item, after continuing operations. (3) The unusual, material, nonrecurring items that are significantly different from the customary business activities are shown in a separate section for extraordinary items, below discontinued operations. If a company holds a noncontrolling interest in a subsidiary company, it must present an allocation of net income or loss that is attributable to the noncontrolling interest.

5 Identify where to report earnings per share information. Because of the inherent dangers of focusing attention solely on earnings per share, the profession concluded that companies must disclose earnings per share on the face of the income statement. A company that reports a discontinued operation or an extraordinary item must report per share amounts for these line items either on the face of the income statement or in the notes to the financial statements.

6 Understand the reporting of accounting changes and errors. Changes in accounting principle and corrections of errors are adjusted through retained earnings. Changes in estimates are a normal part of the accounting process. The effects of these changes are handled prospectively, with the effects recorded in income in the period of change and in future periods without adjustment to retained earnings.

7 Prepare a retained earnings statement. The retained earnings statement should disclose net income (loss), dividends, adjustments due to changes in accounting principles, error corrections, and restrictions of retained earnings.

8 Explain how to report other comprehensive income. Companies report the components of other comprehensive income in one of two ways: (1) a single statement of comprehensive income (one statement format) or (2) in a second statement (two statement format).

DEMONSTRATION PROBLEM

Presented below are 11 income statement items from Braun Company for the year ended December 31, 2014.

Sales revenue	$2,700,000
Cost of goods sold	1,150,000
Interest revenue	15,000
Loss from abandonment of plant assets	45,000
Gain from extinguishment of debt	28,000
Unrealized holding loss on an available-for-sale investment, net of tax	12,000
Selling expenses	290,000
Administrative expenses	190,000
Effect of change in estimated useful lives of fixed assets	35,000
Loss from earthquake (unusual and infrequent)	30,000
Gain on disposal of a component of Braun's business	50,000

Instructions

(a) Using the information above, prepare a condensed multiple-step income statement. Assume a tax rate of 30% and 100,000 shares of common stock outstanding during 2014.

(b) Compute comprehensive income for Braun in 2014.

Solution

(a)

BRAUN COMPANY
INCOME STATEMENT
FOR THE YEAR ENDED DECEMBER 31, 2014

Sales revenue		$2,700,000
Cost of goods sold		1,150,000
Gross profit		1,550,000
Selling expenses	$290,000	
Administrative expenses	190,000	480,000
Income from operations		1,070,000
Other revenues and gains		
Interest revenue	15,000	
Gain on debt extinguishment	28,000	43,000

Other expenses and losses		
Loss from plant abandonment		(45,000)
Income before income taxes		1,068,000
Income taxes (30%)		320,400
Income from continuing operations		747,600
Discontinued operations		
Gain from disposal of component of business	50,000	
Less: Applicable income tax	15,000	35,000
Income before extraordinary items		782,600
Extraordinary items		
Loss from earthquake	30,000	
Less: Applicable income tax	9,000	(21,000)
Net income		$ 761,600
Per share of common stock		
Income from continuing operations		$ 7.48
Discontinued operations		0.35
Income before extraordinary item		7.83
Extraordinary item, net of tax		(0.21)
Net income		$ 7.61

(b)

Net income	$761,600
Unrealized holding loss on available-for-sale investment, net of tax	12,000
Comprehensive income	$749,600

FASB CODIFICATION

FASB Codification References

[1] FASB ASC 225-20-45-4. [Predecessor literature: "Reporting the Results of Operations," *Opinions of the Accounting Principles Board No. 30* (New York: AICPA, 1973), par. 23, as amended by "Accounting for the Impairment or Disposal of Long-lived Assets," *Statement of Financial Accounting Standards No. 144* (Norwalk, Conn.: FASB, 2001).]

[2] FASB ASC 224-20-45-2. [Predecessor literature: "Reporting the Results of Operations," *Opinions of the Accounting Principles Board No. 30* (New York: AICPA, 1973), par. 20.]

[3] FASB ASC 205-20-45. [Predecessor literature: "Accounting for the Impairment or Disposal of Long-lived Assets," *Statement of Financial Accounting Standards No. 144* (Norwalk, Conn.: FASB, 2001), par. 4.]

[4] FASB ASC 225-20-45-2. [Predecessor literature: "Reporting the Results of Operations," *Opinions of the Accounting Principles Board No. 30* (New York: AICPA, 1973), par. 20.]

[5] FASB ASC 225-20-45-3. [Predecessor literature: "Reporting the Results of Operations," *Opinions of the Accounting Principles Board No. 30* (New York: AICPA, 1973), par. 24, as amended by "Accounting for the Impairment or Disposal of Long-lived Assets," *Statement of Financial Accounting Standards No. 144* (Norwalk, Conn.: FASB, 2001).]

[6] FASB ASC 810-10-45. [Predecessor literature: "Consolidated Financial Statements," *Accounting Research Bulletin No. 51* (August 1959).]

[7] FASB ASC 260. [Predecessor literature: "Earnings Per Share," *Statement of Financial Accounting Standards No. 128* (Norwalk, Conn.: FASB, 1996).]

[8] FASB ASC 260-10-10-2. [Predecessor literature: "Earnings Per Share," *Statement of Financial Accounting Standards No. 128* (Norwalk, Conn.: FASB, 1996), par. 11.]

[9] FASB ASC 250. [Predecessor literature: "Accounting Changes and Error Corrections," *Statement of Financial Accounting Standards No. 154* (Norwalk, Conn.: FASB, 2005).]

[10] FASB ASC 220. [Predecessor literature: "Reporting Comprehensive Income," *Statement of Financial Accounting Standards No. 130* (Norwalk, Conn.: FASB, 1997).]

Exercises

If your school has a subscription to the FASB Codification, go to *http://aahq.org/asclogin.cfm* to log in and prepare responses to the following. Provide Codification references for your responses.

CE4-1 Access the glossary ("Master Glossary") to answer the following.

(a) What is a change in accounting estimate?

(b) How is a change in accounting principle distinguished from a "change in accounting estimate effected by a change in accounting principle"?

(c) What is the formal definition of comprehensive income?

CE4-2 What distinguishes an item that is "unusual in nature" from an item that is considered "extraordinary"?

CE4-3 Enyart Company experienced a catastrophic loss in the second quarter of the year. The loss meets the criteria for extraordinary item reporting, but Enyart's controller is unsure whether this item should be reported as extraordinary in the second quarter interim report. Advise the controller.

CE4-4 What guidance does the SEC provide for public companies with respect to the reporting of the "effect of preferred stock dividends and accretion of carrying amount of preferred stock on earnings per share"?

An additional Codification case can be found in the Using Your Judgment section, on page 205.

Be sure to check the book's companion website for a Review and Analysis Exercise, with solution.

WileyPLUS **Brief Exercises, Exercises, Problems, and many more learning and assessment tools and resources are available for practice in WileyPLUS.**

QUESTIONS

1. What kinds of questions about future cash flows do investors and creditors attempt to answer with information in the income statement?

2. How can information based on past transactions be used to predict future cash flows?

3. Identify at least two situations in which important changes in value are not reported in the income statement.

4. Identify at least two situations in which application of different accounting methods or accounting estimates results in difficulties in comparing companies.

5. Explain the transaction approach to measuring income. Why is the transaction approach to income measurement preferable to other ways of measuring income?

6. What is earnings management?

7. How can earnings management affect the quality of earnings?

8. Why should caution be exercised in the use of the net income figure derived in an income statement? What are the objectives of generally accepted accounting principles in their application to the income statement?

9. A *Wall Street Journal* article noted that **Apple** reported higher income than its competitors by using a more aggressive policy for recognizing revenue on future upgrades to its products. Some contend that Apple's quality of earnings is low. What does the term "quality of earnings" mean?

10. What is the major distinction (a) between revenues and gains and (b) between expenses and losses?

11. What are the advantages and disadvantages of the single-step income statement?

12. What is the basis for distinguishing between operating and nonoperating items?

13. Distinguish between the modified all-inclusive income statement and the current operating performance income statement. According to present generally accepted accounting principles, which is recommended? Explain.

14. How should correction of errors be reported in the financial statements?

15. Discuss the appropriate treatment in the financial statements of each of the following.

(a) An amount of $113,000 realized in excess of the cash surrender value of an insurance policy on the life of one of the founders of the company who died during the year.

(b) A profit-sharing bonus to employees computed as a percentage of net income.

(c) Additional depreciation on factory machinery because of an error in computing depreciation for the previous year.

(d) Rent received from subletting a portion of the office space.

(e) A patent infringement suit, brought 2 years ago against the company by another company, was settled this year by a cash payment of $725,000.

(f) A reduction in the Allowance for Doubtful Accounts balance because the account appears to be considerably in excess of the probable loss from uncollectible receivables.

16. Indicate where the following items would ordinarily appear on the financial statements of Boleyn, Inc. for the year 2014.

(a) The service life of certain equipment was changed from 8 to 5 years. If a 5-year life had been used previously, additional depreciation of $425,000 would have been charged.

(b) In 2014, a flood destroyed a warehouse that had a book value of $1,600,000. Floods are rare in this locality.

(c) In 2014, the company wrote off $1,000,000 of inventory that was considered obsolete.

(d) An income tax refund related to the 2011 tax year was received.

(e) In 2011, a supply warehouse with an expected useful life of 7 years was erroneously expensed.

(f) Boleyn, Inc. changed from weighted-average to FIFO inventory pricing.

17. Indicate the section of a multiple-step income statement in which each of the following is shown.

(a) Loss on inventory write-down.

(b) Loss from strike.

(c) Bad debt expense.

(d) Loss on disposal of a component of the business.

(e) Gain on sale of machinery.

(f) Interest revenue.

(g) Depreciation expense.

(h) Material write-offs of notes receivable.

18. Perlman Land Development, Inc. purchased land for $70,000 and spent $30,000 developing it. It then sold the land for $160,000. Sheehan Manufacturing purchased land for a future plant site for $100,000. Due to a change in plans, Sheehan later sold the land for $160,000. Should these two companies report the land sales, both at gains of $60,000, in a similar manner?

19. You run into Greg Norman at a party and begin discussing financial statements. Greg says, "I prefer the single-step income statement because the multiple-step format generally overstates income." How should you respond to Greg?

20. Santo Corporation has eight expense accounts in its general ledger which could be classified as selling expenses. Should Santo report these eight expenses separately in its income statement or simply report one total amount for selling expenses?

21. Cooper Investments reported an unusual gain from the sale of certain assets in its 2014 income statement. How does intraperiod tax allocation affect the reporting of this unusual gain?

22. Discuss the appropriate treatment in the income statement for the following items:

(a) Loss on discontinued operations.

(b) Noncontrolling interest allocation.

(c) Earnings per share.

(d) Gain on sale of equipment.

23. Lebron Co. owns most but not all of the shares of its subsidiary Bryant Inc. Lebron reported net income of $124,700. The amount to be attributed to the noncontrolling interest in Bryant is $30,000. Indicate how Lebron will report the noncontrolling interest in its income statement.

24. What effect does intraperiod tax allocation have on reported net income?

25. Neumann Company computed earnings per share as follows.

$$\frac{\text{Net income}}{\text{Common shares outstanding at year-end}}$$

Neumann has a simple capital structure. What possible errors might the company have made in the computation? Explain.

26. Qualls Corporation reported 2014 earnings per share of $7.21. In 2015, Qualls reported earnings per share as follows.

On income before extraordinary item	$6.40
On extraordinary item	1.88
On net income	$8.28

Is the increase in earnings per share from $7.21 to $8.28 a favorable trend?

27. What is meant by "tax allocation within a period"? What is the justification for such practice?

28. When does tax allocation within a period become necessary? How should this allocation be handled?

29. During 2014, Liselotte Company earned income of $1,500,000 before income taxes and realized a gain of $450,000 on a government-forced condemnation sale of a division plant facility. The income is subject to income taxation at the rate of 34%. The gain on the sale of the plant is taxed at 30%. Proper accounting suggests that the unusual gain be reported as an extraordinary item. Illustrate an appropriate presentation of these items in the income statement.

30. On January 30, 2013, a suit was filed against Frazier Corporation under the Environmental Protection Act. On August 6, 2014, Frazier Corporation agreed to settle the action and pay $920,000 in damages to certain current and former employees. How should this settlement be reported in the 2014 financial statements? Discuss.

31. Linus Paper Company decided to close two small pulp mills in Conway, New Hampshire, and Corvallis, Oregon. Would these closings be reported in a separate section entitled "Discontinued operations after income from continuing operations"? Discuss.

32. What major types of items are reported in the retained earnings statement?

33. Generally accepted accounting principles usually require the use of accrual accounting to "fairly present" income. If the cash receipts and disbursements method of accounting will "clearly reflect" taxable income, why does this method not usually also "fairly present" income?

34. State some of the more serious problems encountered in seeking to achieve the ideal measurement of periodic net income. Explain what accountants do as a practical alternative.

35. What is meant by the terms *elements* and *items* as they relate to the income statement? Why might items have to be disclosed in the income statement?

36. What are the two ways that other comprehensive income may be displayed (reported)?

37. How should the disposal of a component of a business be disclosed in the income statement?

BRIEF EXERCISES

3 **BE4-1** Starr Co. had sales revenue of $540,000 in 2014. Other items recorded during the year were:

Cost of goods sold	$330,000
Salaries and wages expense	120,000
Income tax expense	25,000
Increase in value of company reputation	15,000
Other operating expenses	10,000
Unrealized gain on value of patents	20,000

Prepare a single-step income statement for Starr for 2014. Starr has 100,000 shares of stock outstanding.

3 **BE4-2** Brisky Corporation had net sales of $2,400,000 and interest revenue of $31,000 during 2014. Expenses for 2014 were cost of goods sold $1,450,000; administrative expenses $212,000; selling expenses $280,000; and interest expense $45,000. Brisky's tax rate is 30%. The corporation had 100,000 shares of common stock authorized and 70,000 shares issued and outstanding during 2014. Prepare a single-step income statement for the year ended December 31, 2014.

3 **BE4-3** Using the information provided in BE4-2, prepare a condensed multiple-step income statement for Brisky Corporation.

2 3 4 **BE4-4** Finley Corporation had income from continuing operations of $10,600,000 in 2014. During 2014, it disposed of its restaurant division at an after-tax loss of $189,000. Prior to disposal, the division operated at a loss of $315,000 (net of tax) in 2014. Finley had 10,000,000 shares of common stock outstanding during 2014. Prepare a partial income statement for Finley beginning with income from continuing operations.

2 3 4 **BE4-5** Stacy Corporation had income before income taxes for 2014 of $6,300,000. In addition, it suffered an unusual and infrequent pretax loss of $770,000 from a volcano eruption. The corporation's tax rate is 30%. Prepare a partial income statement for Stacy beginning with income before income taxes. The corporation had 5,000,000 shares of common stock outstanding during 2014.

6 **BE4-6** During 2014, Williamson Company changed from FIFO to weighted-average inventory pricing. Pretax income in 2013 and 2012 (Williamson's first year of operations) under FIFO was $160,000 and $180,000, respectively. Pretax income using weighted-average pricing in the prior years would have been $145,000 in 2013 and $170,000 in 2012. In 2014, Williamson Company reported pretax income (using weighted-average pricing) of $180,000. Show comparative income statements for Williamson Company, beginning with "Income before income tax," as presented on the 2014 income statement. (The tax rate in all years is 30%.)

6 **BE4-7** Vandross Company has recorded bad debt expense in the past at a rate of 1½% of net sales. In 2014, Vandross decides to increase its estimate to 2%. If the new rate had been used in prior years, cumulative bad debt expense would have been $380,000 instead of $285,000. In 2014, bad debt expense will be $120,000 instead of $90,000. If Vandross's tax rate is 30%, what amount should it report as the cumulative effect of changing the estimated bad debt rate?

5 **BE4-8** In 2014, Hollis Corporation reported net income of $1,000,000. It declared and paid preferred stock dividends of $250,000. During 2014, Hollis had a weighted average of 190,000 common shares outstanding. Compute Hollis's 2014 earnings per share.

7 **BE4-9** Portman Corporation has retained earnings of $675,000 at January 1, 2014. Net income during 2014 was $1,400,000, and cash dividends declared and paid during 2014 totaled $75,000. Prepare a retained earnings statement for the year ended December 31, 2014.

6 7 **BE4-10** Using the information from BE4-9, prepare a retained earnings statement for the year ended December 31, 2014. Assume an error was discovered: land costing $80,000 (net of tax) was charged to maintenance and repairs expense in 2011.

8 **BE4-11** On January 1, 2014, Richards Inc. had cash and common stock of $60,000. At that date, the company had no other asset, liability, or equity balances. On January 2, 2014, it purchased for cash $20,000 of equity securities that it classified as available-for-sale. It received cash dividends of $3,000 during the year on these securities. In addition, it has an unrealized holding gain on these securities of $4,000 net of tax. Determine the following amounts for 2014: (a) net income, (b) comprehensive income, (c) other comprehensive income, and (d) accumulated other comprehensive income (end of 2014).

EXERCISES

2 **E4-1 (Computation of Net Income)** Presented below are changes in all the account balances of Fritz Reiner Furniture Co. during the current year, except for retained earnings.

	Increase (Decrease)		Increase (Decrease)
Cash	$ 79,000	Accounts Payable	$ (51,000)
Accounts Receivable (net)	45,000	Bonds Payable	82,000
Inventory	127,000	Common Stock	125,000
Investments	(47,000)	Paid-In Capital in Excess of Par—Common Stock	13,000

Instructions

Compute the net income for the current year, assuming that there were no entries in the Retained Earnings account except for net income and a dividend declaration of $19,000 which was paid in the current year.

2 4 **E4-2 (Compute Income Measures)** Presented below is information related to Viel Company at December 31, 2014, the end of its first year of operations.

Sales revenue	$310,000
Cost of goods sold	140,000
Selling and administrative expenses	50,000
Gain on sale of plant assets	30,000
Unrealized gain on available-for-sale investments	10,000
Interest expense	6,000
Loss on discontinued operations	12,000
Allocation to noncontrolling interest	40,000
Dividends declared and paid	5,000

Instructions

Compute the following: (a) income from operations, (b) net income, (c) net income attributable to Viel Company's controlling shareholders, (d) comprehensive income, and (e) retained earnings balance at December 31, 2014.

2 4 **E4-3 (Income Statement Items)** Presented below are certain account balances of Paczki Products Co.

Rent revenue	$ 6,500	Sales discounts	$ 7,800
Interest expense	12,700	Selling expenses	99,400
Beginning retained earnings	114,400	Sales revenue	390,000
Ending retained earnings	134,000	Income tax expense	31,000
Dividend revenue	71,000	Cost of goods sold	184,400
Sales returns and allowances	12,400	Administrative expenses	82,500
Allocation to noncontrolling interest	17,000		

Instructions

From the foregoing, compute the following: (a) total net revenue, (b) net income, (c) dividends declared, and (d) income attributable to controlling stockholders.

2 3 **E4-4 (Single-Step Income Statement)** The financial records of LeRoi Jones Inc. were destroyed by fire at the end of 2014. Fortunately, the controller had kept certain statistical data related to the income statement as follows.

1. The beginning merchandise inventory was $92,000 and decreased 20% during the current year.
2. Sales discounts amount to $17,000.
3. 20,000 shares of common stock were outstanding for the entire year.
4. Interest expense was $20,000.
5. The income tax rate is 30%.
6. Cost of goods sold amounts to $500,000.
7. Administrative expenses are 20% of cost of goods sold but only 8% of gross sales.
8. Four-fifths of the operating expenses relate to sales activities.

Instructions

From the foregoing information prepare an income statement for the year 2014 in single-step form.

2 3 **E4-5 (Multiple-Step and Single-Step)** Two accountants for the firm of Elwes and Wright are arguing about the merits of presenting an income statement in a multiple-step versus a single-step format. The discussion involves the following 2014 information related to P. Bride Company ($000 omitted).

XLS

Administrative expense	
Officers' salaries	$ 4,900
Depreciation of office furniture and equipment	3,960
Cost of goods sold	60,570
Rent revenue	17,230
Selling expense	
Delivery expense	2,690
Sales commissions	7,980
Depreciation of sales equipment	6,480
Sales revenue	96,500
Income tax	9,070
Interest expense	1,860

Instructions

(a) Prepare an income statement for the year 2014 using the multiple-step form. Common shares outstanding for 2014 total 40,550 (000 omitted).

(b) Prepare an income statement for the year 2014 using the single-step form.

(c) Which one do you prefer? Discuss.

2 3 5 **E4-6 (Multiple-Step and Extraordinary Items)** The following balances were taken from the books of Maria Conchita Alonzo Corp. on December 31, 2014.

Interest revenue	$ 86,000	Accumulated depreciation—equipment	$ 40,000
Cash	51,000	Accumulated depreciation—buildings	28,000
Sales revenue	1,380,000	Notes receivable	155,000
Accounts receivable	150,000	Selling expenses	194,000
Prepaid insurance	20,000	Accounts payable	170,000
Sales returns and allowances	150,000	Bonds payable	100,000
Allowance for doubtful accounts	7,000	Administrative and general expenses	97,000
Sales discounts	45,000	Accrued liabilities	32,000
Land	100,000	Interest expense	60,000
Equipment	200,000	Notes payable	100,000
Buildings	140,000	Loss from earthquake damage	
Cost of goods sold	621,000	(extraordinary item)	150,000
		Common stock	500,000
		Retained earnings	21,000

Assume the total effective tax rate on all items is 34%.

Instructions

Prepare a multiple-step income statement; 100,000 shares of common stock were outstanding during the year.

2 3 5 **E4-7 (Multiple-Step and Single-Step)** The accountant of Latifa Shoe Co. has compiled the following information from the company's records as a basis for an income statement for the year ended December 31, 2014.

Rent revenue	$ 29,000
Interest expense	18,000
Market appreciation on land above cost	31,000
Salaries and wages expense (selling)	114,800
Supplies (selling)	17,600
Income tax	37,400
Salaries and wages expense (administrative)	135,900

Other administrative expenses	$ 51,700
Cost of goods sold	496,000
Net sales	980,000
Depreciation on plant assets (70% selling, 30% administrative)	65,000
Cash dividends declared	16,000

There were 20,000 shares of common stock outstanding during the year.

Instructions

(a) Prepare a multiple-step income statement.
(b) Prepare a single-step income statement.
(c) Which format do you prefer? Discuss.

3 4 5 **E4-8 (Income Statement, EPS)** Presented below are selected ledger accounts of Tucker Corporation as of December 31, 2014.

Cash	$ 50,000
Administrative expenses	100,000
Selling expenses	80,000
Net sales	540,000
Cost of goods sold	210,000
Cash dividends declared (2014)	20,000
Cash dividends paid (2014)	15,000
Discontinued operations (loss before income taxes)	40,000
Depreciation expense, not recorded in 2013	30,000
Retained earnings, December 31, 2013	90,000
Effective tax rate 30%	

Instructions

(a) Compute net income for 2014.
(b) Prepare a partial income statement beginning with income from continuing operations before income tax, and including appropriate earnings per share information. Assume 10,000 shares of common stock were outstanding during 2014.

3 4 5 7 **E4-9 (Multiple-Step Statement with Retained Earnings)** Presented below is information related to Ivan Calderon Corp. for the year 2014.

Net sales	$1,300,000	Write-off of inventory due to obsolescence	$ 80,000
Cost of goods sold	780,000	Depreciation expense omitted by accident in 2013	55,000
Selling expenses	65,000	Casualty loss (extraordinary item) before taxes	50,000
Administrative expenses	48,000	Cash dividends declared	45,000
Dividend revenue	20,000	Retained earnings at December 31, 2013	980,000
Interest revenue	7,000	Effective tax rate of 34% on all items	

Instructions

(a) Prepare a multiple-step income statement for 2014. Assume that 60,000 shares of common stock are outstanding.
(b) Prepare a separate retained earnings statement for 2014.

5 **E4-10 (Earnings per Share)** The stockholders' equity section of Tkachuk Corporation appears below as of December 31, 2014.

8% preferred stock, $50 par value, authorized 100,000 shares, outstanding 90,000 shares		$ 4,500,000
Common stock, $1.00 par, authorized and issued 10 million shares		10,000,000
Additional paid-in capital		20,500,000
Retained earnings	$134,000,000	
Net income	33,000,000	167,000,000
		$202,000,000

Net income for 2014 reflects a total effective tax rate of 34%. Included in the net income figure is a loss of $18,000,000 (before tax) as a result of a major casualty, which should be classified as an extraordinary item. Preferred stock dividends of $360,000 were declared and paid in 2014. Dividends of $1,000,000 were declared and paid to common stockholders in 2014.

Instructions

Compute earnings per share data as it should appear on the income statement of Tkachuk Corporation.

3 4 5 7 **E4-11 (Condensed Income Statement—Periodic Inventory Method)** The following are selected ledger accounts of Spock Corporation at December 31, 2014.

Cash	$ 185,000	Salaries and wages expense (sales)	$284,000
Inventory	535,000	Salaries and wages expense (office)	346,000
Sales revenue	4,275,000	Purchase returns	15,000
Unearned sales revenue	117,000	Sales returns and allowances	79,000
Purchases	2,786,000	Freight-in	72,000
Sales discounts	34,000	Accounts receivable	142,500
Purchase discounts	27,000	Sales commissions	83,000
Selling expenses	69,000	Telephone and Internet expense (sales)	17,000
Accounting and legal services	33,000	Utilities expense (office)	32,000
Insurance expense (office)	24,000	Miscellaneous office expenses	8,000
Advertising expense	54,000	Rent revenue	240,000
Delivery expense	93,000	Extraordinary loss (before tax)	70,000
Depreciation expense (office equipment)	48,000	Interest expense	176,000
Depreciation expense (sales equipment)	36,000	Common stock ($10 par)	900,000

Spock's effective tax rate on all items is 34%. A physical inventory indicates that the ending inventory is $686,000.

Instructions

Prepare a condensed 2014 income statement for Spock Corporation.

7 **E4-12 (Retained Earnings Statement)** Eddie Zambrano Corporation began operations on January 1, 2011. During its first 3 years of operations, Zambrano reported net income and declared dividends as follows.

	Net Income	Dividends Declared
2011	$ 40,000	$ –0–
2012	125,000	50,000
2013	160,000	50,000

The following information relates to 2014.

Income before income tax	$240,000
Prior period adjustment: understatement of 2012 depreciation expense (before taxes)	$ 25,000
Cumulative decrease in income from change in inventory methods (before taxes)	$ 35,000
Dividends declared (of this amount, $25,000 will be paid on Jan. 15, 2015)	$100,000
Effective tax rate	40%

Instructions

(a) Prepare a 2014 retained earnings statement for Eddie Zambrano Corporation.

(b) Assume Eddie Zambrano Corp. restricted retained earnings in the amount of $70,000 on December 31, 2014. After this action, what would Zambrano report as total retained earnings in its December 31, 2014, balance sheet?

5 **E4-13 (Earnings per Share)** At December 31, 2013, Shiga Naoya Corporation had the following stock outstanding.

10% cumulative preferred stock, $100 par, 107,500 shares	$10,750,000
Common stock, $5 par, 4,000,000 shares	20,000,000

During 2014, Shiga Naoya did not issue any additional common stock. The following also occurred during 2014.

Income from continuing operations before taxes	$23,650,000
Discontinued operations (loss before taxes)	$ 3,225,000
Preferred dividends declared	$ 1,075,000
Common dividends declared	$ 2,200,000
Effective tax rate	35%

Instructions

Compute earnings per share data as it should appear in the 2014 income statement of Shiga Naoya Corporation. (Round to two decimal places.)

4 **E4-14 (Change in Accounting Principle)** Tim Mattke Company began operations in 2012 and for simplicity reasons, adopted weighted-average pricing for inventory. In 2014, in accordance with other companies in its industry, Mattke changed its inventory pricing to FIFO. The pretax income data is reported below.

Year	Weighted-Average	FIFO
2012	$370,000	$395,000
2013	390,000	430,000
2014	410,000	450,000

Instructions

(a) What is Mattke's net income in 2014? Assume a 35% tax rate in all years.

(b) Compute the cumulative effect of the change in accounting principle from weighted-average to FIFO inventory pricing.

(c) Show comparative income statements for Tim Mattke Company, beginning with income before income tax, as presented on the 2014 income statement.

3 8 **E4-15 (Comprehensive Income)** Roxanne Carter Corporation reported the following for 2014: net sales $1,200,000; cost of goods sold $750,000; selling and administrative expenses $320,000; and an unrealized holding gain on available-for-sale securities $18,000.

Instructions

Prepare a statement of comprehensive income, using (a) the one statement format, and (b) the two statement format. (Ignore income taxes and earnings per share.)

7 8 **E4-16 (Comprehensive Income)** C. Reither Co. reports the following information for 2014: sales revenue $700,000; cost of goods sold $500,000; operating expenses $80,000; and an unrealized holding loss on available-for-sale securities for 2014 of $60,000. It declared and paid a cash dividend of $10,000 in 2014.

C. Reither Co. has January 1, 2014, balances in common stock $350,000; accumulated other comprehensive income $80,000; and retained earnings $90,000. It issued no stock during 2014.

Instructions

Prepare a statement of stockholders' equity.

3 4 5 7 8 **E4-17 (Various Reporting Formats)** The following information was taken from the records of Roland Carlson Inc. for the year 2014. Income tax applicable to income from continuing operations $187,000; income tax applicable to loss on discontinued operations $25,500; income tax applicable to extraordinary gain $32,300; income tax applicable to extraordinary loss $20,400; and unrealized holding gain on available-for-sale securities $15,000.

Extraordinary gain	$ 95,000	Cash dividends declared	$ 150,000
Loss on discontinued operations	75,000	Retained earnings January 1, 2014	600,000
Administrative expenses	240,000	Cost of goods sold	850,000
Rent revenue	40,000	Selling expenses	300,000
Extraordinary loss	60,000	Sales revenue	1,900,000

Shares outstanding during 2014 were 100,000.

Instructions

(a) Prepare a single-step income statement.

(b) Prepare a comprehensive income statement for 2014, using the two statement format.

(c) Prepare a retained earnings statement for 2014.

EXERCISES SET B

See the book's companion website, at **www.wiley.com/college/kieso**, for an additional set of exercises.

PROBLEMS

3 4 5 7 **P4-1 (Multiple-Step Income, Retained Earnings)** The following information is related to Dickinson Company for 2014.

Retained earnings balance, January 1, 2014	$ 980,000
Sales revenue	25,000,000
Cost of goods sold	16,000,000
Interest revenue	70,000
Selling and administrative expenses	4,700,000
Write-off of goodwill	820,000
Income taxes for 2014	1,244,000
Gain on the sale of investments (normal recurring)	110,000
Loss due to flood damage—extraordinary item (net of tax)	390,000
Loss on the disposition of the wholesale division (net of tax)	440,000
Loss on operations of the wholesale division (net of tax)	90,000

Dividends declared on common stock	$250,000
Dividends declared on preferred stock	80,000

Dickinson Company decided to discontinue its entire wholesale operations and to retain its manufacturing operations. On September 15, Dickinson sold the wholesale operations to Rogers Company. During 2014, there were 500,000 shares of common stock outstanding all year.

Instructions

Prepare a multiple-step income statement and a retained earnings statement.

3 5 **P4-2 (Single-Step Income, Retained Earnings, Periodic Inventory)** Presented below is the trial balance
7 of Thompson Corporation at December 31, 2014.

THOMPSON CORPORATION
TRIAL BALANCE
DECEMBER 31, 2014

	Debit	Credit
Purchase Discounts		$ 10,000
Cash	$ 189,700	
Accounts Receivable	105,000	
Rent Revenue		18,000
Retained Earnings		160,000
Salaries and Wages Payable		18,000
Sales Revenue		1,100,000
Notes Receivable	110,000	
Accounts Payable		49,000
Accumulated Depreciation—Equipment		28,000
Sales Discounts	14,500	
Sales Returns and Allowances	17,500	
Notes Payable		70,000
Selling Expenses	232,000	
Administrative Expenses	99,000	
Common Stock		300,000
Income Tax Expense	53,900	
Cash Dividends	45,000	
Allowance for Doubtful Accounts		5,000
Supplies	14,000	
Freight-In	20,000	
Land	70,000	
Equipment	140,000	
Bonds Payable		100,000
Gain on Sale of Land		30,000
Accumulated Depreciation—Buildings		19,600
Inventory	89,000	
Buildings	98,000	
Purchases	610,000	
Totals	$1,907,600	$1,907,600

A physical count of inventory on December 31 resulted in an inventory amount of $64,000; thus, cost of goods sold for 2014 is $645,000.

Instructions

Prepare a single-step income statement and a retained earnings statement. Assume that the only changes in retained earnings during the current year were from net income and dividends. Thirty thousand shares of common stock were outstanding the entire year.

3 4 **P4-3 (Irregular Items)** Maher Inc. reported income from continuing operations before taxes during 2014
5 of $790,000. Additional transactions occurring in 2014 but not considered in the $790,000 are as follows.

1. The corporation experienced an uninsured flood loss (extraordinary) in the amount of $90,000 during the year. The tax rate on this item is 46%.
2. At the beginning of 2012, the corporation purchased a machine for $54,000 (salvage value of $9,000) that had a useful life of 6 years. The bookkeeper used straight-line depreciation for 2012, 2013, and 2014 but failed to deduct the salvage value in computing the depreciation base.
3. Sale of securities held as a part of its portfolio resulted in a loss of $57,000 (pretax).

4. When its president died, the corporation realized $150,000 from an insurance policy. The cash surrender value of this policy had been carried on the books as an investment in the amount of $46,000 (the gain is nontaxable).
5. The corporation disposed of its recreational division at a loss of $115,000 before taxes. Assume that this transaction meets the criteria for discontinued operations.
6. The corporation decided to change its method of inventory pricing from average-cost to the FIFO method. The effect of this change on prior years is to increase 2012 income by $60,000 and decrease 2013 income by $20,000 before taxes. The FIFO method has been used for 2014. The tax rate on these items is 40%.

Instructions

Prepare an income statement for the year 2014 starting with income from continuing operations before taxes. Compute earnings per share as it should be shown on the face of the income statement. Common shares outstanding for the year are 120,000 shares. (Assume a tax rate of 30% on all items, unless indicated otherwise.)

3 4 **P4-4 (Multiple- and Single-Step Income, Retained Earnings)** The following account balances were in-
5 6 cluded in the trial balance of Twain Corporation at June 30, 2014.

7

Sales revenue	$1,578,500	Depreciation expense (office furniture and equipment)	$ 7,250
Sales discounts	31,150	Property tax expense	7,320
Cost of goods sold	896,770	Bad debt expense (selling)	4,850
Salaries and wages expense (sales)	56,260	Maintenance and repairs expense (administration)	9,130
Sales commissions	97,600	Office expense	6,000
Travel expense (salespersons)	28,930	Sales returns and allowances	62,300
Delivery expense	21,400	Dividends received	38,000
Entertainment expense	14,820	Interest expense	18,000
Telephone and Internet expense (sales)	9,030	Income tax expense	102,000
Depreciation expense (sales equipment)	4,980	Depreciation understatement due to error—2011 (net of tax)	17,700
Maintenance and repairs expense (sales)	6,200	Dividends declared on preferred stock	9,000
Miscellaneous selling expenses	4,715	Dividends declared on common stock	37,000
Office supplies used	3,450		
Telephone and Internet expense (administration)	2,820		

The Retained Earnings account had a balance of $337,000 at July 1, 2013. There are 80,000 shares of common stock outstanding.

Instructions

(a) Using the multiple-step form, prepare an income statement and a retained earnings statement for the year ended June 30, 2014.

(b) Using the single-step form, prepare an income statement and a retained earnings statement for the year ended June 30, 2014.

3 4 **P4-5 (Irregular Items)** Presented below is a combined single-step income and retained earnings statement
5 6 for Nerwin Company for 2014.

7

		(000 omitted)
Net sales revenue		$640,000
Costs and expenses		
Cost of goods sold	$500,000	
Selling, general, and administrative expenses	66,000	
Other, net	17,000	583,000
Income before income tax		57,000
Income tax		19,400
Net income		37,600
Retained earnings at beginning of period, as previously reported	141,000	
Adjustment required for correction of error	(7,000)	
Retained earnings at beginning of period, as restated		134,000
Dividends on common stock		(12,200)
Retained earnings at end of period		$159,400

Additional facts are as follows.

1. "Selling, general, and administrative expenses" for 2014 included a charge of $8,500,000 that was usual but infrequently occurring.

2. "Other, net" for 2014 included an extraordinary item (charge) of $6,000,000. If the extraordinary item (charge) had not occurred, income taxes for 2014 would have been $21,400,000 instead of $19,400,000.
3. "Adjustment required for correction of an error" was a result of a change in estimate (useful life of certain assets reduced to 8 years and a catch-up adjustment made).
4. Nerwin Company disclosed earnings per common share for net income in the notes to the financial statements.

Instructions

Determine from these additional facts whether the presentation of the facts in the Nerwin Company income and retained earnings statement is appropriate. If the presentation is not appropriate, describe the appropriate presentation and discuss its theoretical rationale. (Do not prepare a revised statement.)

4 6 **P4-6 (Retained Earnings Statement, Prior Period Adjustment)** Below is the Retained Earnings account
7 for the year 2014 for Acadian Corp.

Retained earnings, January 1, 2014		$257,600
Add:		
Gain on sale of investments (net of tax)	$41,200	
Net income	84,500	
Refund on litigation with government, related to the year 2011 (net of tax)	21,600	
Recognition of income earned in 2013, but omitted from income statement in that year (net of tax)	25,400	172,700
		430,300
Deduct:		
Loss on discontinued operations (net of tax)	35,000	
Write-off of goodwill (net of tax)	60,000	
Cumulative effect on income of prior years in changing from LIFO to FIFO inventory valuation in 2014 (net of tax)	23,200	
Cash dividends declared	32,000	150,200
Retained earnings, December 31, 2014		$280,100

Instructions

(a) Prepare a corrected retained earnings statement. Acadian Corp. normally sells investments of the type mentioned above. FIFO inventory was used in 2014 to compute net income.

(b) State where the items that do not appear in the corrected retained earnings statement should be shown.

3 4 **P4-7 (Income Statement, Irregular Items)** Wade Corp. has 150,000 shares of common stock outstanding.
5 6 In 2014, the company reports income from continuing operations before income tax of $1,210,000. Additional transactions not considered in the $1,210,000 are as follows.

1. In 2014, Wade Corp. sold equipment for $40,000. The machine had originally cost $80,000 and had accumulated depreciation of $30,000. The gain or loss is considered ordinary.
2. The company discontinued operations of one of its subsidiaries during the current year at a loss of $190,000 before taxes. Assume that this transaction meets the criteria for discontinued operations. The loss from operations of the discontinued subsidiary was $90,000 before taxes; the loss from disposal of the subsidiary was $100,000 before taxes.
3. An internal audit discovered that amortization of intangible assets was understated by $35,000 (net of tax) in a prior period. The amount was charged against retained earnings.
4. The company had a gain of $125,000 on the condemnation of much of its property. The gain is taxed at a total effective rate of 40%. Assume that the transaction meets the requirements of an extraordinary item.

Instructions

Analyze the above information and prepare an income statement for the year 2014, starting with income from continuing operations before income tax. Compute earnings per share as it should be shown on the face of the income statement. (Assume a total effective tax rate of 38% on all items, unless otherwise indicated.)

PROBLEMS SET B

See the book's companion website, at **www.wiley.com/college/kieso**, for an additional set of problems.

CONCEPTS FOR ANALYSIS

CA4-1 (Identification of Income Statement Deficiencies) O'Malley Corporation was incorporated and began business on January 1, 2014. It has been successful and now requires a bank loan for additional working capital to finance expansion. The bank has requested an audited income statement for the year 2014. The accountant for O'Malley Corporation provides you with the following income statement which O'Malley plans to submit to the bank.

O'MALLEY CORPORATION
INCOME STATEMENT

Sales revenue		$850,000
Dividends		32,300
Gain on recovery of insurance proceeds from earthquake loss (extraordinary)		38,500
		920,800
Less:		
Selling expenses	$101,100	
Cost of goods sold	510,000	
Advertising expense	13,700	
Loss on obsolescence of inventories	34,000	
Loss on discontinued operations	48,600	
Administrative expense	73,400	780,800
Income before income tax		140,000
Income tax		56,000
Net income		$ 84,000

Instructions

Indicate the deficiencies in the income statement presented above. Assume that the corporation desires a single-step income statement.

CA4-2 (Earnings Management) Bobek Inc. has recently reported steadily increasing income. The company reported income of $20,000 in 2011, $25,000 in 2012, and $30,000 in 2013. A number of market analysts have recommended that investors buy the stock because they expect the steady growth in income to continue. Bobek is approaching the end of its fiscal year in 2014, and it again appears to be a good year. However, it has not yet recorded warranty expense.

Based on prior experience, this year's warranty expense should be around $5,000, but some managers have approached the controller to suggest a larger, more conservative warranty expense should be recorded this year. Income before warranty expense is $43,000. Specifically, by recording a $7,000 warranty accrual this year, Bobek could report an increase in income for this year and still be in a position to cover its warranty costs in future years.

Instructions

(a) What is earnings management?

(b) Assume income before warranty expense is $43,000 for both 2014 and 2015 and that total warranty expense over the 2-year period is $10,000. What is the effect of the proposed accounting in 2014? In 2015?

(c) What is the appropriate accounting in this situation?

CA4-3 (Earnings Management) Charlie Brown, controller for Kelly Corporation, is preparing the company's income statement at year-end. He notes that the company lost a considerable sum on the sale of some equipment it had decided to replace. Since the company has sold equipment routinely in the past, Brown knows the losses cannot be reported as extraordinary. He also does not want to highlight it as a material loss since he feels that will reflect poorly on him and the company. He reasons that if the company had recorded more depreciation during the assets' lives, the losses would not be so great. Since depreciation is included among the company's operating expenses, he wants to report the losses along with the company's expenses, where he hopes it will not be noticed.

Instructions

(a) What are the ethical issues involved?

(b) What should Brown do?

CA4-4 (Income Reporting Items) Simpson Corp. is an entertainment firm that derives approximately 30% of its income from the Casino Knights Division, which manages gambling facilities. As auditor for Simpson Corp., you have recently overheard the following discussion between the controller and financial vice president.

VICE PRESIDENT: If we sell the Casino Knights Division, it seems ridiculous to segregate the results of the sale in the income statement. Separate categories tend to be absurd and confusing to the stockholders. I believe that we should simply report the gain on the sale as other income or expense without detail.

CONTROLLER: Professional pronouncements would require that we report this information separately in the income statement. If a sale of this type is considered unusual and infrequent, it must be reported as an extraordinary item.

VICE PRESIDENT: What about the walkout we had last month when employees were upset about their commission income? Would this situation not also be an extraordinary item?

CONTROLLER: I am not sure whether this item would be reported as extraordinary or not.

VICE PRESIDENT: Oh well, it doesn't make any difference because the net effect of all these items is immaterial, so no disclosure is necessary.

Instructions

(a) On the basis of the foregoing discussion, answer the following questions. Who is correct about handling the sale? What would be the correct income statement presentation for the sale of the Casino Knights Division?

(b) How should the walkout by the employees be reported?

(c) What do you think about the vice president's observation on materiality?

(d) What are the earnings per share implications of these topics?

CA4-5 (Identification of Income Statement Weaknesses) The following financial statement was prepared by employees of Walters Corporation.

WALTERS CORPORATION
INCOME STATEMENT
YEAR ENDED DECEMBER 31, 2014

Revenues	
Gross sales, including sales taxes	$1,044,300
Less: Returns, allowances, and cash discounts	56,200
Net sales	988,100
Dividends, interest, and purchase discounts	30,250
Recoveries of accounts written off in prior years	13,850
Total revenues	1,032,200
Costs and expenses	
Cost of goods sold, including sales taxes	465,900
Salaries and related payroll expenses	60,500
Rent	19,100
Delivery expense and freight-in	3,400
Bad debt expense	27,800
Total costs and expenses	576,700
Income before extraordinary items	455,500
Extraordinary items	
Loss on discontinued styles (Note 1)	71,500
Loss on sale of marketable securities (Note 2)	39,050
Loss on sale of warehouse (Note 3)	86,350
Total extraordinary items	196,900
Net income	$ 258,600
Net income per share of common stock	$2.30

Note 1: New styles and rapidly changing consumer preferences resulted in a $71,500 loss on the disposal of discontinued styles and related accessories.

Note 2: The corporation sold an investment in marketable securities at a loss of $39,050. The corporation normally sells securities of this nature.

Note 3: The corporation sold one of its warehouses at an $86,350 loss.

Instructions

Identify and discuss the weaknesses in classification and disclosure in the single-step income statement above. You should explain why these treatments are weaknesses and what the proper presentation of the items would be in accordance with GAAP.

CA4-6 (Classification of Income Statement Items) As audit partner for Grupo and Rijo, you are in charge of reviewing the classification of unusual items that have occurred during the current year. The following material items have come to your attention.

1. A merchandising company incorrectly overstated its ending inventory 2 years ago. Inventory for all other periods is correctly computed.
2. An automobile dealer sells for $137,000 an extremely rare 1930 S type Invicta which it purchased for $21,000 10 years ago. The Invicta is the only such display item the dealer owns.
3. A drilling company during the current year extended the estimated useful life of certain drilling equipment from 9 to 15 years. As a result, depreciation for the current year was materially lowered.
4. A retail outlet changed its computation for bad debt expense from 1% to ½ of 1% of sales because of changes in its customer clientele.
5. A mining concern sells a foreign subsidiary engaged in uranium mining, although it (the seller) continues to engage in uranium mining in other countries.
6. A steel company changes from the average-cost method to the FIFO method for inventory costing purposes.
7. A construction company, at great expense, prepared a major proposal for a government loan. The loan is not approved.
8. A water pump manufacturer has had large losses resulting from a strike by its employees early in the year.
9. Depreciation for a prior period was incorrectly understated by $950,000. The error was discovered in the current year.
10. A large sheep rancher suffered a major loss because the state required that all sheep in the state be killed to halt the spread of a rare disease. Such a situation has not occurred in the state for 20 years.
11. A food distributor that sells wholesale to supermarket chains and to fast-food restaurants (two distinguishable classes of customers) decides to discontinue the division that sells to one of the two classes of customers.

Instructions

From the foregoing information, indicate in what section of the income statement or retained earnings statement these items should be classified. Provide a brief rationale for your position.

CA4-7 (Comprehensive Income) Willie Nelson, Jr., controller for Jenkins Corporation, is preparing the company's financial statements at year-end. Currently, he is focusing on the income statement and determining the format for reporting comprehensive income. During the year, the company earned net income of $400,000 and had unrealized gains on available-for-sale securities of $15,000. In the previous year, net income was $410,000, and the company had no unrealized gains or losses.

Instructions

(a) Show how income and comprehensive income will be reported on a comparative basis for the current and prior years, using the two statement format.

(b) Show how income and comprehensive income will be reported on a comparative basis for the current and prior years, using the one statement format.

(c) Which format should Nelson recommend?

USING YOUR JUDGMENT

FINANCIAL REPORTING

Financial Reporting Problem

The Procter & Gamble Company (P&G)

The financial statements of P&G are presented in Appendix 5B. The company's complete annual report, including the notes to the financial statements, can be accessed at the book's companion website, **www.wiley.com/college/kieso**.

Instructions

Refer to P&G's financial statements and the accompanying notes to answer the following questions.

(a) What type of income statement format does P&G use? Indicate why this format might be used to present income statement information.

(b) What are P&G's primary revenue sources?

(c) Compute P&G's gross profit for each of the years 2009–2011. Explain why gross profit decreased in 2011.

(d) Why does P&G make a distinction between operating and nonoperating revenue?

(e) What financial ratios did P&G choose to report in its "Financial Summary" section covering the years 2001–2011?

Comparative Analysis Case

The Coca-Cola Company and PepsiCo, Inc.

Instructions

Go to the book's companion website and use information found there to answer the following questions related to **The Coca-Cola Company** and **PepsiCo, Inc.**

(a) What type of income format(s) is used by these two companies? Identify any differences in income statement format between these two companies.

(b) What are the gross profits, operating profits, and net incomes for these two companies over the 3-year period 2009–2011? Which company has had better financial results over this period of time?

(c) Identify the irregular items reported by these two companies in their income statements over the 3-year period 2009–2011. Do these irregular items appear to be significant?

Financial Statement Analysis Cases

Case 1 Bankruptcy Prediction

The Z-score bankruptcy prediction model uses balance sheet and income information to arrive at a Z-Score, which can be used to predict financial distress:

$$Z = \frac{\text{Working capital}}{\text{Total assets}} \times 1.2 + \frac{\text{Retained earnings}}{\text{Total assets}} \times 1.4 + \frac{\text{EBIT}}{\text{Total assets}} \times 3.3 + \frac{\text{Sales}}{\text{Total assets}} \times .99 + \frac{\text{MV equity}}{\text{Total liabilities}} \times 0.6$$

EBIT is earnings before interest and taxes. MV equity is the market value of common equity, which can be determined by multiplying stock price by shares outstanding.

Following extensive testing, it has been shown that companies with Z-scores above 3.0 are unlikely to fail; those with Z-scores below 1.81 are very likely to fail. While the original model was developed for publicly held manufacturing companies, the model has been modified to apply to companies in various industries, emerging companies, and companies not traded in public markets.

Instructions

(a) Use information in the financial statements of a company like **Walgreens** or **Deere & Co.** to compute the Z-score for the past 2 years.

(b) Interpret your result. Where does the company fall in the financial distress range?

(c) The Z-score uses EBIT as one of its elements. Why do you think this income measure is used?

Case 2 Dresser Industries

Dresser Industries provides products and services to oil and natural gas exploration, production, transmission, and processing companies. The following is taken from a recent income statement. (Dollar amounts are in millions.)

Sales revenue	$2,697.0
Service revenue	1,933.9
Share of earnings of unconsolidated affiliates	92.4
Total revenues	4,723.3
Cost of sales	1,722.7
Cost of services	1,799.9
Total costs of sales and services	3,522.6

Gross earnings	$1,200.7
Selling, engineering, administrative and general expenses	(919.8)
Special charges	(70.0)
Other income (deductions)	
Interest expense	(47.4)
Interest earned	19.1
Other, net	4.8
Earnings before income taxes and other items below	187.4
Income taxes	(79.4)
Noncontrolling interest	(10.3)
Earnings from continuing operations	97.7
Discontinued operations	(35.3)
Earnings before extraordinary items	62.4
Extraordinary items	(6.3)
Net earnings	$ 56.1

Instructions

Assume that 177,636,000 shares of stock were issued and outstanding. Prepare the per share portion of the income statement. Remember to begin with "Earnings from continuing operations."

Case 3 P/E Ratios

One of the more closely watched ratios by investors is the price/earnings (P/E) ratio. By dividing price per share by earnings per share, analysts get insight into the value the market attaches to a company's earnings. More specifically, a high P/E ratio (in comparison to companies in the same industry) may suggest the stock is overpriced. Also, there is some evidence that companies with low P/E ratios are underpriced and tend to outperform the market. However, the ratio can be misleading.

P/E ratios are sometimes misleading because the E (earnings) is subject to a number of assumptions and estimates that could result in overstated earnings and a lower P/E. Some analysts conduct "revenue analysis" to evaluate the quality of an earnings number. Revenues are less subject to management estimates and all earnings must begin with revenues. These analysts also compute the price-to-sales ratio (PSR = price per share ÷ sales per share) to assess whether a company is performing well compared to similar companies. If a company has a price-to-sales ratio significantly higher than its competitors, investors may be betting on a stock that has yet to prove itself. [*Source:* Janice Revell, "Beyond P/E," *Fortune* (May 28, 2001), p. 174.]

Instructions

(a) Identify some of the estimates or assumptions that could result in overstated earnings.

(b) Compute the P/E ratio and the PSR for Tootsie Roll and Hershey for 2011.

(c) Use these data to compare the quality of each company's earnings.

Accounting, Analysis, and Principles

Counting Crows Inc. provided the following information for the year 2014.

Retained earnings, January 1, 2014	$ 600,000
Administrative expenses	240,000
Selling expenses	300,000
Sales revenue	1,900,000
Cash dividends declared	80,000
Cost of goods sold	850,000
Extraordinary gain	95,000
Loss on discontinued operations	75,000
Rent revenue	40,000
Unrealized holding gain on available-for-sale securities	17,000
Income tax applicable to continuing operations	187,000
Income tax benefit applicable to loss on discontinued operations	25,500
Income tax applicable to extraordinary gain	32,300
Income tax applicable to unrealized holding gain on available-for-sale securities	2,000

Accounting

Prepare (a) a single-step income statement for 2014, (b) a retained earnings statement for 2014, and (c) a statement of comprehensive income using the two statement format. Shares outstanding during 2014 were 100,000.

Analysis

Explain how a multiple-step income statement format can provide useful information to a financial statement user.

Principles

In a recent meeting with its auditor, Counting Crows' management argued that the company should be able to prepare a pro forma income statement with some one-time administrative expenses reported similar to extraordinary items and discontinued operations. Is such reporting consistent with the qualitative characteristics of accounting information as discussed in the conceptual framework? Explain.

BRIDGE TO THE PROFESSION

Professional Research: FASB Codification

Your client took accounting a number of years ago and was unaware of comprehensive income reporting. He is not convinced that any accounting standards exist for comprehensive income.

Instructions

Go to *http://aahq.org/asclogin.cfm* to log in and prepare responses to the following. Provide Codification references for your responses.

(a) What authoritative literature addresses comprehensive income? When was it issued?

(b) Provide the definition of comprehensive income.

(c) Define classifications within net income and give examples.

(d) Define classifications within other comprehensive income and give examples.

(e) What are reclassification adjustments?

Additional Professional Resources

See the book's companion website, at **www.wiley.com/college/kieso**, for professional simulations as well as other study resources.

IFRS INSIGHTS

9 LEARNING OBJECTIVE
Compare the accounting procedures for income reporting under GAAP and IFRS.

As in GAAP, the income statement is a required statement for IFRS. In addition, the content and presentation of an IFRS income statement is similar to the one used for GAAP. *IAS 1*, "Presentation of Financial Statements," provides general guidelines for the reporting of income statement information. Subsequently, a number of international standards have been issued that provide additional guidance to issues related to income statement presentation.

RELEVANT FACTS

Following are the key similarities and differences between GAAP and IFRS related to the income statement.

Similarities

- Both GAAP and IFRS require companies to indicate the amount of net income attributable to noncontrolling interest.

- Both GAAP and IFRS follow the same presentation guidelines for discontinued operations, but IFRS defines a discontinued operation more narrowly. Both standard-setters have indicated a willingness to develop a similar definition to be used in the joint project on financial statement presentation.
- Both GAAP and IFRS have items that are recognized in equity as part of comprehensive income but do not affect net income. Both GAAP and IFRS allow a one statement or two statement approach to preparing the statement of comprehensive income.

Differences

- Presentation of the income statement under GAAP follows either a single-step or multiple-step format. IFRS does not mention a single-step or multiple-step approach. In addition, under GAAP, companies must report an item as extraordinary if it is unusual in nature and infrequent in occurrence. Extraordinary items are prohibited under IFRS.
- Under IFRS, companies must classify expenses by either nature or function. GAAP does not have that requirement, but the SEC requires a functional presentation.
- IFRS identifies certain minimum items that should be presented on the income statement. GAAP has no minimum information requirements. However, the SEC rules have more rigorous presentation requirements.
- IFRS does not define key measures like income from operations. SEC regulations define many key measures and provide requirements and limitations on companies reporting non-GAAP/IFRS information.
- Under IFRS, revaluation of property, plant, and equipment, and intangible assets is permitted and is reported as other comprehensive income. The effect of this difference is that application of IFRS results in more transactions affecting equity but not net income.

ABOUT THE NUMBERS

Income Reporting

Illustration IFRS4-1 provides a summary of the primary income items under IFRS. As indicated in the table, similar to GAAP, companies report all revenues, gains, expenses, and losses on the income statement and, at the end of the period, close them to Income Summary. They provide useful subtotals on the income statement, such as gross profit, income from operations, income before income tax, and net income. Companies classify discontinued operations of a component of a business as a separate item in the income statement, after "Income from continuing operations." Companies present other income and expense in a separate section, before income from operations. Providing intermediate income figures helps readers evaluate earnings information in assessing the amounts, timing, and uncertainty of future cash flows.

Expense Classifications

Companies are required to present an analysis of expenses classified either by their nature (such as cost of materials used, direct labor incurred, delivery expense, advertising expense, employee benefits, depreciation expense, and amortization expense) or their function (such as cost of goods sold, selling expenses, and administrative expenses).

Type of Situation	Criteria	Examples	Placement on Income Statement
Sales or service revenues	Revenue arising from the ordinary activities of the company	Sales revenue, service revenue	Sales or revenue section
Cost of goods sold	Expense arising from the cost of inventory sold or services provided	In a merchandising company, cost of goods sold; in a service company, cost of services	Deduct from sales (to arrive at gross profit) or service revenue
Selling and administrative expenses	Expenses arising from the ordinary activities of the company	Sales salaries, delivery expense, rent, depreciation, utilities	Deduct from gross profit; if the function-of-expense approach is used, depreciation and amortization expense and labor costs must be disclosed
Other income and expense	Gains and losses and other ancillary revenues and expenses	Gain on sale of long-lived assets, impairment loss on intangible assets, investment revenue, dividend and interest revenue, casualty losses	Report as part of income from operations
Financing costs	Separates cost of financing from operating costs	Interest expense	Report in separate section between income from operations and income before income tax
Income tax	Levies imposed by governmental bodies on the basis of income	Taxes computed on income before income tax	Report in separate section between income before income tax and net income
Discontinued operations	A component of a company that has either been disposed of or is classified as held-for-sale	A sale by diversified company of a major division representing its only activities in the electronics industry Food distributor that sells wholesale to supermarkets decides to discontinue the division in a major geographic area	Report gains or losses on discontinued operations net of tax in a separate section between income from continuing operations and net income
Non-controlling interest	Allocation of net income of loss divided between two classes: (1) the majority interest represented by the shareholders who own the controlling interest, and (2) the non-controlling interest (often referred to as the minority interest)	Net profit (loss) attributable to non-controlling shareholders	Report as a separate item below net income or loss as an allocation of the net income or loss (not as an item of income or expense)

ILLUSTRATION IFRS4-1
Summary of Income Items under IFRS

An advantage of the **nature-of-expense method** is that it is simple to apply because allocations of expense to different functions are not necessary. For manufacturing companies that must allocate costs to the product produced, using a nature-of-expense approach permits companies to report expenses without making arbitrary allocations.

The **function-of-expense method**, however, is often viewed as more relevant because this method identifies the major cost drivers of the company and therefore helps users assess whether these amounts are appropriate for the revenue generated. As indicated, a disadvantage of this method is that the allocation of costs to the varying functions may be arbitrary and therefore the expense classification becomes misleading.

To illustrate these two methods, assume that the accounting firm of Telaris Co. performs audit, tax, and consulting services. It has the following revenues and expenses.

Service revenues	$400,000
Cost of services	
Staff salaries (related to various services performed)	145,000
Supplies expense (related to various services performed)	10,000
Selling expenses	
Advertising costs	20,000
Entertainment expense	3,000
Administrative expenses	
Utilities expense	5,000
Depreciation on building	12,000

If Telaris Co. uses the nature-of-expense approach, its income statement presents each expense item but does not classify the expenses into various subtotals, as follows.

TELARIS CO.
INCOME STATEMENT
FOR THE MONTH OF JANUARY 2014

Service revenues	$400,000
Staff salaries	145,000
Supplies expense	10,000
Advertising costs	20,000
Utilities expense	5,000
Depreciation on building	12,000
Entertainment expense	3,000
Net income	$205,000

If Telaris uses the function-of-expense approach, its income statement is as follows.

TELARIS CO.
INCOME STATEMENT
FOR THE MONTH OF JANUARY 2014

Service revenues	$400,000
Cost of services	155,000
Selling expenses	23,000
Administrative expenses	17,000
Net income	$205,000

The function-of-expense method is generally used in practice although many companies believe both approaches have merit. These companies use the function-of-expense approach on the income statement but provide detail of the expenses (as in the nature-of-expense approach) in the notes to the financial statements. The IASB-FASB discussion paper on financial statement presentation also recommends the dual approach.

ON THE HORIZON

The IASB and FASB are working on a project that would rework the structure of financial statements. One stage of this project will address the issue of how to classify various items in the income statement. A main goal of this new approach is to provide information that better represents how businesses are run. The FASB and IASB have issued a proposal to require comprehensive income be reported in a combined statement of comprehensive income. This approach draws attention away from just one number—net income.

IFRS SELF-TEST QUESTIONS

1. Which of the following is **not** reported in an income statement under IFRS?
   (a) Discontinued operations.
   (b) Extraordinary items.
   (c) Cost of goods sold.
   (d) Income tax.
2. Which of the following statements is **correct** regarding income reporting under IFRS?
   (a) IFRS does not permit revaluation of property, plant, and equipment, and intangible assets.
   (b) IFRS provides the same options for reporting comprehensive income as GAAP.
   (c) Companies must classify expenses by nature.
   (d) IFRS provides a definition for all items presented in the income statement.
3. Which statement is **correct** regarding IFRS?
   (a) An advantage of the nature-of-expense method is that it is simple to apply because allocations of expense to different functions are not necessary.
   (b) The function-of-expense approach never requires arbitrary allocations.
   (c) An advantage of the function-of-expense method is that allocation of costs to the varying functions is rarely arbitrary.
   (d) IFRS requires use of the nature-of-expense approach.
4. The non-controlling interest section of the income statement is:
   (a) required under GAAP but not under IFRS.
   (b) required under IFRS but not under GAAP.
   (c) required under IFRS and GAAP.
   (d) not reported under GAAP or IFRS.
5. Which of the following is **not** an acceptable way of displaying the components of other comprehensive income under IFRS?
   (a) Within the statement of retained earnings.
   (b) Second income statement.
   (c) Combined statement of comprehensive income.
   (d) All of these choices are acceptable.

IFRS CONCEPTS AND APPLICATION

IFRS4-1 Explain the difference between the "nature-of-expense" and "function-of-expense" classifications.

IFRS4-2 Discuss the appropriate treatment in the income statement for the following items:

(a) Loss on discontinued operations.
(b) Non-controlling interest allocation.

IFRS4-3 Bradshaw Company experienced a loss that was deemed to be both unusual in nature and infrequent in occurrence. How should Bradshaw report this item in accordance with IFRS?

IFRS4-4 Presented below is information related to Viel Company at December 31, 2014, the end of its first year of operations.

Sales revenue	$310,000
Cost of goods sold	140,000
Selling and administrative expenses	50,000
Gain on sale of plant assets	30,000
Unrealized gain on non-trading equity securities	10,000
Interest expense	6,000
Loss on discontinued operations	12,000
Allocation to non-controlling interest	40,000
Dividends declared and paid	5,000

Instructions

Compute the following: (a) income from operations, (b) net income, (c) net income attributable to Viel Company controlling shareholders, (d) comprehensive income, and (e) retained earnings balance at December 31, 2014. (Ignore income taxes.)

IFRS4-5 Below is the income statement for a British company, **Avon Rubber plc**. Avon prepares its financial statements in accordance with IFRS.

Avon Rubber plc

Consolidated Income Statement for the Year Ended 30 September

	2011	2010
Continuing operations		
Revenue	107,600	117,574
Cost of sales	(77,892)	(89,256)
Gross profit	29,708	28,318
Distribution costs	(4,832)	(4,527)
Administrative expenses	(13,740)	(14,536)
Other operating income	–	–
Operating profit/(loss) from continuing operations	11,136	9,255
Operating profit/(loss) is analysed as:		
Before depreciation, amortization and exceptional items	15,723	13,577
Depreciation and amortization	(4,587)	(4,322)
Operating profit/(loss) before exceptional items	11,136	9,255
Exceptional operating items		
Finance income	5	16
Finance costs	(486)	(985)
Other finance income	(443)	(1,152)
Profit/(loss) before taxation	991	(12,391)
Taxation	(3,094)	(2,808)
Profit/(loss) for the year from continuing operations	(2,103)	(15,199)
Discontinued operations		
Profit/(loss) for the year from discontinued operations	–	–
Loss for the year	–	–
Earnings/(loss) per share		
Basic	25.2p	15.2p
Diluted	23.3p	14.4p
Earnings/(loss) per share from continuing operations		
Basic	25.2p	15.2p
Diluted	23.3p	14.4p

Instructions

(a) Review the Avon Rubber income statement and identify at least three differences between the IFRS income statement and an income statement of a U.S. company as presented in the chapter.

(b) Identify any irregular items reported by Avon Rubber. Is the reporting of these irregular items in Avon's income statement similar to reporting of these items in U.S. companies' income statements? Explain.

Professional Research

IFRS4-6 Your client took accounting a number of years ago and was unaware of comprehensive income reporting. He is not convinced that any accounting standards exist for comprehensive income.

Instructions

Access the IFRS authoritative literature at the IASB website (*http://www.iasb.org/*). (Click on the IFRS tab and then register for free eIFRS access if necessary.) When you have accessed the documents, you can use the search tool in your Internet browser to respond to the following questions. (Provide paragraph citations.)

(a) What IFRS addresses reporting in the statement of comprehensive income? When was it issued?
(b) Provide the definition of total comprehensive income.
(c) Explain the rationale for presenting additional line items, headings, and subtotals in the statement of comprehensive income.
(d) What items of income or expense may be presented either in the statement of comprehensive income or in the notes?

International Financial Reporting Problem
Marks and Spencer plc

IFRS4-7 The financial statements of **Marks and Spencer plc (M&S)** are available at the book's companion website or can be accessed at *http://annualreport.marksandspencer.com/_assets/downloads/Marks-and-Spencer-Annual-report-and-financial-statements-2012.pdf.*

Instructions

Refer to M&S's financial statements and the accompanying notes to answer the following questions.

(a) What type of income statement format does M&S use? Indicate why this format might be used to present income statement information.
(b) What are M&S's primary revenue sources?
(c) Compute M&S's gross profit for each of the years 2011 and 2012. Explain why gross profit increased in 2012.
(d) Why does M&S make a distinction between operating and non-operating profit?
(e) Does M&S report any non-GAAP measures? Explain.

ANSWERS TO IFRS SELF-TEST QUESTIONS

1. b **2.** b **3.** a **4.** c **5.** a

Remember to check the book's companion website to find additional resources for this chapter.

CHAPTER 5

Balance Sheet and Statement of Cash Flows

LEARNING OBJECTIVES

After studying this chapter, you should be able to:

1 Explain the uses and limitations of a balance sheet.

2 Identify the major classifications of the balance sheet.

3 Prepare a classified balance sheet using the report and account formats.

4 Indicate the purpose of the statement of cash flows.

5 Identify the content of the statement of cash flows.

6 Prepare a basic statement of cash flows.

7 Understand the usefulness of the statement of cash flows.

8 Determine which balance sheet information requires supplemental disclosure.

9 Describe the major disclosure techniques for the balance sheet.

Hey, It Doesn't Balance!

A good accounting student knows by now that Total Assets = Total Liabilities + Total Equity. From this equation, we can also determine net assets, which are determined as follows: Total Assets − Total Liabilities = Net Assets. O.K., this is simple so far. But let's look at the recent discussion paper by the FASB/IASB on how the statement of financial position (the balance sheet) should be structured.

The statement of financial position is divided into five major parts, with many assets and liabilities netted against one another. Here is the general framework for the new statement of financial position:

BUSINESS
- Operating assets and liabilities
- Investing assets and liabilities

FINANCING
- Financing assets
- Financing liabilities

INCOME TAXES

DISCONTINUED OPERATIONS

EQUITY

The statement does look a bit different than the traditional balance sheet. Let's put some numbers to the statement and see how it works. (See the example on the facing page.)

Well, it does balance—in that net assets equal equity—but isn't it important to know total assets and total liabilities? As some have observed, the statement of financial position will not balance the way we expect it to. That is, assets won't equal liabilities and equity. This is because the assets and liabilities are grouped into the business, financing, discontinued operations, and income taxes categories. This new model raises a number of questions, such as:

- Does separating "business activities from financing activities" provide information that is more decision-useful?
- Does information on income taxes and discontinued operations merit separate categories?

The FASB and IASB are working to get answers to these and other questions about this proposed model. One thing is for sure—adoption of the new financial statements will be a dramatic change but hopefully one for the better.

> **CONCEPTUAL FOCUS**
>
> > See the **Underlying Concepts** on pages 227, 228, 237, 240, and 241.
>
> > Read the **Evolving Issue** on page 243 for a discussion of balance sheet reporting.

> **INTERNATIONAL FOCUS**
>
> > See the **International Perspectives** on pages 231 and 242.
>
> > Read the **IFRS Insights** on pages 277–284 for a discussion of:
>
> —Classification in the statement of financial position
>
> —Equity
>
> —Revaluation equity
>
> —Fair presentation

STATEMENT OF FINANCIAL POSITION

BUSINESS		
Operating		
Inventories	$ 400,000	
Receivables	200,000	
Total short-term assets		$ 600,000
Property (net)	500,000	
Intangible assets	50,000	
Total long-term assets		550,000
Accounts payable	30,000	
Wages payable	40,000	
Total short-term liabilities		(70,000)
Lease liability	10,000	
Other long-term debt	35,000	
Total long-term liabilities		(45,000)
Net operating assets		**1,035,000**
Investing		
Trading securities	45,000	
Other securities	5,000	
Total investing assets		50,000
TOTAL NET BUSINESS ASSETS		**1,085,000**
FINANCING		
Financing assets		
Cash	30,000	
Total financing assets		30,000
Financing liabilities		
Short- and long-term borrowing	130,000	
Total financing liabilities		(130,000)
NET FINANCING LIABILITIES		**(100,000)**
DISCONTINUED OPERATIONS		
Assets held for sale		420,000
INCOME TAXES		
Deferred income taxes		70,000
NET ASSETS		**$1,475,000**
EQUITY		
Share capital—ordinary	$1,000,000	
Retained earnings	475,000	
TOTAL EQUITY		**$1,475,000**

Sources: Marie Leone and Tim Reason, "How Extreme Is the Makeover?" *CFO Magazine* (March 1, 2009); and *Preliminary Views on Financial Statement Presentation*, FASB/IASB Discussion Paper (October 2008).

PREVIEW OF CHAPTER 5

As the opening story indicates, the FASB and IASB are working to improve the presentation of financial information on the balance sheet, as well as other financial statements. In this chapter, we examine the many different types of assets, liabilities, and equity items that affect the balance sheet and the statement of cash flows. The content and organization of the chapter are as follows.

Balance Sheet and Statement of Cash Flows

Balance Sheet	Statement of Cash Flows	Additional Information
• Usefulness • Limitations • Classification • Format	• Purpose • Content and format • Preparation overview • Usefulness	• Supplemental disclosures • Techniques of disclosure

BALANCE SHEET

LEARNING OBJECTIVE 1
Explain the uses and limitations of a balance sheet.

The **balance sheet**, sometimes referred to as the **statement of financial position**, reports the assets, liabilities, and stockholders' equity of a business enterprise at a specific date. This financial statement provides information about the nature and amounts of investments in enterprise resources, obligations to creditors, and the owners' equity in net resources. It therefore helps in predicting the amounts, timing, and uncertainty of future cash flows.

Usefulness of the Balance Sheet

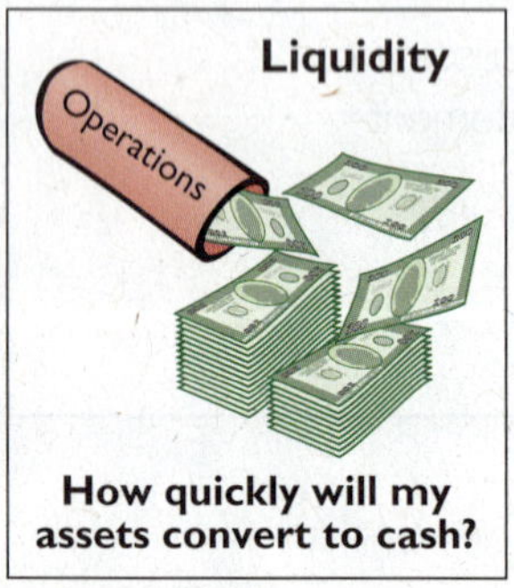

By providing information on assets, liabilities, and stockholders' equity, the balance sheet provides a basis for computing rates of return and evaluating the capital structure of the enterprise. Analysts also use information in the balance sheet to assess a company's risk[1] and future cash flows. In this regard, analysts use the balance sheet to assess a company's liquidity, solvency, and financial flexibility.

Liquidity describes "the amount of time that is expected to elapse until an asset is realized or otherwise converted into cash or until a liability has to be paid."[2] Creditors are interested in short-term liquidity ratios, such as the ratio of cash (or near cash) to short-term liabilities. These ratios indicate whether a company, like **Amazon.com**, will have the resources to pay its current and maturing obligations. Similarly, stockholders assess liquidity to evaluate the possibility of future cash dividends or the buyback of shares. In general, the greater Amazon's liquidity, the lower its risk of failure.

Solvency refers to the ability of a company to pay its debts as they mature. For example, when a company carries a high level of long-term debt relative to assets, it has lower solvency than a similar company with a low level of long-term debt. Companies with higher debt are relatively more risky because they will need more of their assets to meet their fixed obligations (interest and principal payments).

Liquidity and solvency affect a company's **financial flexibility**, which measures the "ability of an enterprise to take effective actions to alter the amounts and timing of cash flows so it can respond to unexpected needs and opportunities."[3] For example, a company may become so loaded with debt—so financially inflexible—that it has little or no sources of cash to finance expansion or to pay off maturing debt. A company with a high degree of financial flexibility is better able to survive bad times, to recover from unexpected setbacks, and to take advantage of profitable and unexpected investment opportunities. Generally, the greater an enterprise's financial flexibility, the lower its risk of failure.

Limitations of the Balance Sheet

Some of the major limitations of the balance sheet are:

1. Most assets and liabilities are reported at **historical cost**. As a result, the information provided in the balance sheet is often criticized for not reporting a more relevant fair value. For example, **Georgia-Pacific** owns timber and other assets that may appreciate in value after purchase. Yet, Georgia-Pacific reports any increase only if and when it sells the assets.

[1]Risk conveys the unpredictability of future events, transactions, circumstances, and results of the company.

[2]"Reporting Income, Cash Flows, and Financial Position of Business Enterprises," *Proposed Statement of Financial Accounting Concepts* (Stamford, Conn.: FASB, 1981), par. 29.

[3]"Reporting Income, Cash Flows, and Financial Position of Business Enterprises," *Proposed Statement of Financial Accounting Concepts* (Stamford, Conn.: FASB, 1981), par. 25.

2. Companies use **judgments and estimates** to determine many of the items reported in the balance sheet. For example, in its balance sheet, **Dell** estimates the amount of receivables that it will collect, the useful life of its warehouses, and the number of computers that will be returned under warranty.
3. The balance sheet necessarily **omits many items that are of financial value** but that a company cannot record objectively. For example, the knowledge and skill of **Intel** employees in developing new computer chips are arguably the company's most significant assets. However, because Intel cannot reliably measure the value of its employees and other intangible assets (such as customer base, research superiority, and reputation), it does not recognize these items in the balance sheet. Similarly, many liabilities are reported in an "off-balance-sheet" manner, if at all.

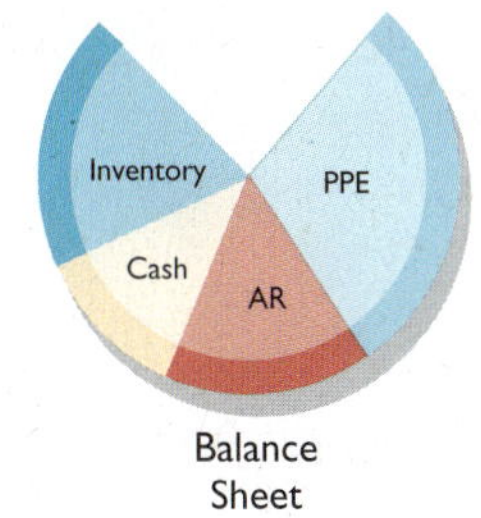

Hey....we left out the value of the employees!

The bankruptcy of **Enron**, the seventh-largest U.S. company at the time, highlights the omission of important items in the balance sheet. In Enron's case, it failed to disclose certain off-balance-sheet financing obligations in its main financial statements.[4]

What do the numbers mean? GROUNDED

The terrorist attacks of September 11, 2001, showed how vulnerable the major airlines are to falling demand for their services. Since that infamous date, major airlines have reduced capacity and slashed jobs to avoid bankruptcy. **United Airlines**, **Northwest Airlines**, **US Airways**, and several smaller competitors filed for bankruptcy in the wake of 9/11.

Delta Airlines made the following statements in its annual report issued shortly after 9/11:

> "If we are unsuccessful in further reducing our operating costs . . . we will need to restructure our costs under Chapter 11 of the U.S. Bankruptcy Code. . . . We have substantial liquidity needs and there is no assurance that we will be able to obtain the necessary financing to meet those needs on acceptable terms, if at all."

These financial flexibility challenges have continued, exacerbated by ever-increasing fuel prices, labor costs, and the economic downturn in response to the financial crisis. Not surprisingly, several of the major airlines (Delta and Northwest, **Continental** and United, and **Airtran** and **Southwest**) merged recently as a way to build some competitive synergies and to bolster their financial flexibility. Others (**American Airlines** and US Airways) are exploring mergers.

Source: R. Seaney, "Airline Mergers: Good for Travelers?" *http://abcnews.go.com/Travel/airline-merger-mania-cost/story?id=16227892* (April 27, 2012).

Classification in the Balance Sheet

2 LEARNING OBJECTIVE
Identify the major classifications of the balance sheet.

Balance sheet accounts are **classified**. That is, balance sheets group together similar items to arrive at significant subtotals. Furthermore, the material is arranged so that important relationships are shown.

The FASB has often noted that the parts and subsections of financial statements can be more informative than the whole. Therefore, the FASB discourages the reporting of summary accounts alone (total assets, net assets, total liabilities, etc.). Instead, companies should report and classify individual items in sufficient detail to permit users to assess the amounts, timing, and uncertainty of future cash flows. Such

[4]We discuss several of these omitted items (such as leases and other off-balance-sheet arrangements) in later chapters. See Wayne Upton, Jr., *Special Report: Business and Financial Reporting, Challenges from the New Economy* (Norwalk, Conn.: FASB, 2001); and U.S. Securities and Exchange Commission, "Disclosure in Management's Discussion and Analysis about Off-Balance Sheet Arrangements and Aggregate Contractual Obligations," *http://www.sec.gov/rules/final/33-8182.htm* (May 2003).

classification also makes it easier for users to evaluate the company's liquidity, financial flexibility, profitability, and risk.

To classify items in financial statements, companies group those items with similar characteristics and separate items with different characteristics.[5] For example, companies should report separately:

1. Assets that differ in their **type or expected function** in the company's central operations or other activities. For example, IBM reports merchandise inventories separately from property, plant, and equipment.
2. Assets and liabilities with **different implications for the company's financial flexibility**. For example, a company that uses assets in its operations, like Walgreens, should report those assets separately from assets held for investment and assets subject to restrictions, such as leased equipment.
3. Assets and liabilities with **different general liquidity characteristics**. For example, Boeing Company reports cash separately from inventories.

The three general classes of items included in the balance sheet are assets, liabilities, and equity. We defined them in Chapter 2 as follows.

ELEMENTS OF THE BALANCE SHEET

1. **ASSETS.** Probable future economic benefits obtained or controlled by a particular entity as a result of past transactions or events.
2. **LIABILITIES.** Probable future sacrifices of economic benefits arising from present obligations of a particular entity to transfer assets or provide services to other entities in the future as a result of past transactions or events.
3. **EQUITY.** Residual interest in the assets of an entity that remains after deducting its liabilities. In a business enterprise, the equity is the ownership interest.[6]

Companies then further divide these items into several subclassifications. Illustration 5-1 indicates the general format of balance sheet presentation.

ILLUSTRATION 5-1
Balance Sheet Classifications

Assets	Liabilities and Owners' Equity
Current assets	Current liabilities
Long-term investments	Long-term debt
Property, plant, and equipment	Owners' (stockholders') equity
Intangible assets	
Other assets	

A company may classify the balance sheet in some other manner, but in practice you usually see little departure from these major subdivisions. A proprietorship or partnership does present the classifications within the owners' equity section a little differently, as we will show later in the chapter.

[5]"Reporting Income, Cash Flows, and Financial Positions of Business Enterprises," *Proposed Statement of Financial Accounting Concepts* (Stamford, Conn.: FASB, 1981), par. 51.

[6]"Elements of Financial Statements of Business Enterprises," *Statement of Financial Accounting Concepts No. 6* (Stamford, Conn.: FASB, 1985), paras. 25, 35, and 49.

Current Assets

Current assets are cash and other assets a company expects to convert into cash, sell, or consume either in one year or in the operating cycle, whichever is longer. The operating cycle is the average time between when a company acquires materials and supplies and when it receives cash for sales of the product (for which it acquired the materials and supplies). The cycle operates from cash through inventory, production, receivables, and back to cash. When several operating cycles occur within one year (which is generally the case for service companies), a company uses the one-year period. If the operating cycle is more than one year, a company uses the longer period.

Current assets are presented in the balance sheet in order of liquidity. The five major items found in the current assets section, and their bases of valuation, are shown in Illustration 5-2.

ILLUSTRATION 5-2
Current Assets and Basis of Valuation

Item	Basis of Valuation
Cash and cash equivalents	Fair value
Short-term investments	Generally, fair value
Receivables	Estimated amount collectible
Inventories	Lower-of-cost-or-market
Prepaid expenses	Cost

A company does not report these five items as current assets if it does not expect to realize them in one year or in the operating cycle, whichever is longer. For example, a company excludes from the current assets section cash restricted for purposes other than payment of current obligations or for use in current operations. **Generally, if a company expects to convert an asset into cash or to use it to pay a current liability within a year or the operating cycle, whichever is longer, it classifies the asset as current.**

This rule, however, is subject to interpretation. A company classifies an investment in common stock as either a current asset or a noncurrent asset depending on management's intent. When it has small holdings of common stocks or bonds that it will hold long-term, it should not classify them as current.

Although a current asset is well defined, certain theoretical problems also develop. For example, how is including prepaid expenses in the current assets section justified? The rationale is that if a company did not pay these items in advance, it would instead need to use other current assets during the operating cycle. If we follow this logic to its ultimate conclusion, however, any asset previously purchased saves the use of current assets during the operating cycle and would be considered current.

Another problem occurs in the current-asset definition when a company consumes plant assets during the operating cycle. Conceptually, it seems that a company should place in the current assets section an amount equal to the current depreciation charge on the plant assets, because it will consume them in the next operating cycle. However, this conceptual problem is ignored. This example illustrates that the formal distinction made between some current and noncurrent assets is somewhat arbitrary.

Cash. Cash is generally considered to consist of currency and demand deposits (monies available on demand at a financial institution). **Cash equivalents** are short-term highly liquid investments that will mature within three months or less. Most companies use the caption "Cash and cash equivalents," and they indicate that this amount approximates fair value.

A company must disclose any restrictions or commitments related to the availability of cash. As an example, see the excerpt from the annual report of **Alterra Healthcare Corp.** in Illustration 5-3 (page 218).

ILLUSTRATION 5-3
Balance Sheet Presentation of Restricted Cash

Alterra Healthcare Corp.

Current assets	
Cash	$18,728,000
Restricted cash and investments (Note 7)	7,191,000

Note 7: Restricted Cash and Investments. Restricted cash and investments consist of certificates of deposit restricted as collateral for lease arrangements and debt service with interest rates ranging from 4.0% to 5.5%.

Alterra Healthcare restricted cash to meet an obligation due currently. Therefore, Alterra included this restricted cash under current assets.

If a company restricts cash for purposes other than current obligations, it excludes the cash from current assets. Illustration 5-4 shows an example of this, from the annual report of **Owens Corning, Inc.**

ILLUSTRATION 5-4
Balance Sheet Presentation of Current and Noncurrent Restricted Cash

Owens Corning, Inc.
(in millions)

Current assets	
Cash and cash equivalents	$ 70
Restricted securities—Fibreboard—current portion (Note 23)	900
Other assets	
Restricted securities—Fibreboard (Note 23)	938

Note 23 (in part). The Insurance Settlement funds are held in and invested by the Fibreboard Settlement Trust (the "Trust") and are available to satisfy Fibreboard's pending and future asbestos related liabilities. . . . The assets of the Trust are comprised of cash and marketable securities (collectively, the "Trust Assets") and are reflected on Owens Corning's consolidated balance sheet as restricted assets. These assets are reflected as current assets or other assets, with each category denoted "Restricted securities—Fibreboard."

Short-Term Investments. Companies group investments in debt and equity securities into three separate portfolios for valuation and reporting purposes:

Held-to-maturity: Debt securities that a company has the positive intent and ability to hold to maturity.

Trading: Debt and equity securities bought and held primarily for sale in the near term to generate income on short-term price differences.

Available-for-sale: Debt and equity securities not classified as held-to-maturity or trading securities.

A company should report trading securities (whether debt or equity) as current assets. It classifies individual held-to-maturity and available-for-sale securities as current or noncurrent depending on the circumstances. It should report held-to-maturity securities at amortized cost. All trading and available-for-sale securities are reported at fair value. **[1]**[7]

See the FASB Codification section (page 255).

[7]Under the fair value option, companies may elect to use fair value as the measurement basis for selected financial assets and liabilities. For these companies, some of their financial assets (and liabilities) may be recorded at historical cost, while others are recorded at fair value. **[2]**

For example, Illustration 5-5 is an excerpt from the annual report of **Intuit Inc.** with respect to its available-for-sale investments.

ILLUSTRATION 5-5
Balance Sheet Presentation of Investments in Securities

Intuit Inc.
(in thousands)

Assets	
Cash and cash equivalents	$ 170,043
Short-term investments (Note 2)	1,036,758

Note 2 (in part). The following schedule summarizes the estimated fair value of our short-term investments (all available-for-sale):

Corporate notes	$ 50,471
Municipal bonds	931,374
U.S. government securities	54,913

Receivables. A company should clearly identify any anticipated loss due to uncollectibles, the amount and nature of any nontrade receivables, and any receivables used as collateral. Major categories of receivables should be shown in the balance sheet or the related notes. For receivables arising from unusual transactions (such as sale of property, or a loan to affiliates or employees), companies should separately classify these as long-term, unless collection is expected within one year. **Stanley Black & Decker** reported its receivables as shown in Illustration 5-6.

ILLUSTRATION 5-6
Balance Sheet Presentation of Receivables

Stanley Black & Decker
(in millions)

Current assets	
Cash and cash equivalents	$ 906.9
Accounts and notes receivable, net	1,553.2
Inventories, net	1,438.6
Prepaid expenses	209.0
Other current assets	215.0
Total current assets	4,322.7

Note B (in part): Accounts and Notes Receivable

Trade accounts receivable	$1,484.0
Trade notes receivable	100.3
Other accounts receivables	32.8
Gross accounts and notes receivable	1,617.1
Allowance for doubtful accounts	(63.9)
Accounts and notes receivable, net	$1,553.2

Inventories. To present inventories properly, a company discloses the basis of valuation (e.g., lower-of-cost-or-market) and the cost flow assumption used (e.g., FIFO or LIFO). A manufacturing concern (like **Abbott Laboratories**, shown in Illustration 5-7 on page 220) also indicates the stage of completion of the inventories.

ILLUSTRATION 5-7
Balance Sheet Presentation of Inventories, Showing Stage of Completion

Abbott Laboratories
(in thousands)

Current assets	
Inventories	
Finished products	$ 772,478
Work in process	338,818
Materials	384,148
Total inventories	1,495,444

Note 1 (in part): Inventories. Inventories are stated at the lower-of-cost- (first-in, first-out basis) or-market.

Weyerhaeuser Company, a forestry company and lumber manufacturer with several finished-goods product lines, reported its inventory as shown in Illustration 5-8.

ILLUSTRATION 5-8
Balance Sheet Presentation of Inventories, Showing Product Lines

Weyerhaeuser Company

Current assets	
Inventories—at FIFO lower of cost or market	
Logs and chips	$ 68,471,000
Lumber, plywood and panels	86,741,000
Pulp, newsprint and paper	47,377,000
Containerboard, paperboard, containers and cartons	59,682,000
Other products	161,717,000
Total product inventories	423,988,000
Materials and supplies	175,540,000

Prepaid Expenses. A company includes prepaid expenses in current assets if it will receive benefits (usually services) within one year or the operating cycle, whichever is longer. As we discussed earlier, these items are current assets because if they had not already been paid, they would require the use of cash during the next year or the operating cycle. A company reports prepaid expenses at the amount of the unexpired or unconsumed cost.

A common example is the prepayment for an insurance policy. A company classifies it as a prepaid expense because the payment precedes the receipt of the benefit of coverage. Other common prepaid expenses include prepaid rent, advertising, taxes, and office or operating supplies. **Hasbro, Inc.**, for example, listed its prepaid expenses in current assets as shown in Illustration 5-9.

ILLUSTRATION 5-9
Balance Sheet Presentation of Prepaid Expenses

Hasbro, Inc.
(in thousands)

Current assets	
Cash and cash equivalents	$ 715,400
Accounts receivable, less allowances of $27,700	556,287
Inventories	203,337
Prepaid expenses and other current assets	243,291
Total current assets	$1,718,315

Noncurrent Assets

Noncurrent assets are those not meeting the definition of current assets. They include a variety of items, as we discuss in the following sections.

Long-Term Investments. **Long-term investments**, often referred to simply as investments, normally consist of one of four types:

1. Investments in securities, such as bonds, common stock, or long-term notes.
2. Investments in tangible fixed assets not currently used in operations, such as land held for speculation.
3. Investments set aside in special funds, such as a sinking fund, pension fund, or plant expansion fund. This includes the cash surrender value of life insurance.
4. Investments in nonconsolidated subsidiaries or affiliated companies.

Companies expect to hold long-term investments for many years. They usually present them on the balance sheet just below "Current assets," in a separate section called "Investments." Realize that many securities classified as long-term investments are, in fact, readily marketable. But a company does not include them as current assets unless it **intends to convert them to cash in the short-term**—that is, within a year or in the operating cycle, whichever is longer. As indicated earlier, securities classified as available-for-sale are reported at fair value, and held-to-maturity securities are reported at amortized cost.

Motorola, Inc. reported its investments section, located between "Property, plant, and equipment" and "Other assets," as shown in Illustration 5-10.

ILLUSTRATION 5-10
Balance Sheet Presentation of Long-Term Investments

Motorola, Inc.
(in millions)

Investments	
Equity investments	$ 872
Other investments	2,567
Fair value adjustment to available-for-sale securities	2,487
Total	$5,926

Property, Plant, and Equipment. **Property, plant, and equipment** are tangible long-lived assets used in the regular operations of the business. These assets consist of physical property such as land, buildings, machinery, furniture, tools, and wasting resources (timberland, minerals). With the exception of land, a company either depreciates (e.g., buildings) or depletes (e.g., timberlands or oil reserves) these assets.

Mattel, Inc. presented its property, plant, and equipment in its balance sheet as shown in Illustration 5-11 (page 222).

A company discloses the basis it uses to value property, plant, and equipment; any liens against the properties; and accumulated depreciation—usually in the notes to the financial statements.

ILLUSTRATION 5-11
Balance Sheet Presentation of Property, Plant, and Equipment

Mattel, Inc.

Property, plant, and equipment	
Land	$ 32,793,000
Buildings	257,430,000
Machinery and equipment	564,244,000
Capitalized leases	23,271,000
Leasehold improvements	74,988,000
	952,726,000
Less: Accumulated depreciation	472,986,000
	479,740,000
Tools, dies and molds, net	168,092,000
Property, plant, and equipment, net	647,832,000

Intangible Assets. **Intangible assets** lack physical substance and are not financial instruments (see page 238 for the definition of a financial instrument). They include patents, copyrights, franchises, goodwill, trademarks, trade names, and customer lists. A company writes off (amortizes) limited-life intangible assets over their useful lives. It periodically assesses indefinite-life intangibles (such as goodwill) for impairment. Intangibles can represent significant economic resources, yet financial analysts often ignore them, because valuation is difficult.

PepsiCo, Inc. reported intangible assets in its balance sheet as shown in Illustration 5-12.

ILLUSTRATION 5-12
Balance Sheet Presentation of Intangible Assets

PepsiCo, Inc.
(in millions)

Intangible assets	
Goodwill	$3,374
Trademarks	1,320
Other identifiable intangibles	147
Total intangibles	$4,841

Other Assets. The items included in the section "Other assets" vary widely in practice. Some include items such as long-term prepaid expenses, prepaid pension cost, and noncurrent receivables. Other items that might be included are assets in special funds, deferred income taxes, property held for sale, and restricted cash or securities. A company should limit this section to include only unusual items sufficiently different from assets included in specific categories.

Liabilities

Similar to assets, companies classify liabilities as current or long-term.

Current Liabilities. **Current liabilities** are the obligations that a company reasonably expects to liquidate either through the use of current assets or the creation of other current liabilities. This concept includes:

1. Payables resulting from the acquisition of goods and services: accounts payable, wages payable, taxes payable, and so on.

2. Collections received in advance for the delivery of goods or performance of services, such as unearned rent revenue or unearned subscriptions revenue.

3. Other liabilities whose liquidation will take place within the operating cycle, such as the portion of long-term bonds to be paid in the current period or short-term obligations arising from the purchase of equipment.

At times, a liability that is payable within the next year is not included in the current liabilities section. This occurs either when the company expects to refinance the debt through another long-term issue **[3]** or to retire the debt out of noncurrent assets. This approach is used because liquidation does not result from the use of current assets or the creation of other current liabilities.

Companies do not report current liabilities in any consistent order. In general, though, companies most commonly list notes payable, accounts payable, or short-term debt as the first item. Income taxes payable, current maturities of long-term debt, or other current liabilities are commonly listed last. For example, see **Halliburton Company**'s current liabilities section in Illustration 5-13.

ILLUSTRATION 5-13
Balance Sheet Presentation of Current Liabilities

Halliburton Company
(in millions)

Current liabilities	
Short-term notes payable	$1,570
Accounts payable	782
Accrued employee compensation and benefits	267
Unearned revenues	386
Income taxes payable	113
Accrued special charges	6
Current maturities of long-term debt	8
Other current liabilities	694
Total current liabilities	3,826

Current liabilities include such items as trade and nontrade notes and accounts payable, advances received from customers, and current maturities of long-term debt. If the amounts are material, companies classify income taxes and other accrued items separately. A company should fully describe in the notes any information about a secured liability—for example, stock held as collateral on notes payable—to identify the assets providing the security.

The excess of total current assets over total current liabilities is referred to as **working capital** (or sometimes **net working capital**). Working capital represents the net amount of a company's relatively liquid resources. That is, it is the liquidity buffer available to meet the financial demands of the operating cycle.

Companies seldom disclose on the balance sheet an amount for working capital. But bankers and other creditors compute it as an indicator of the short-run liquidity of a company. To determine the actual liquidity and availability of working capital to meet current obligations, however, requires analysis of the composition of the current assets and their nearness to cash.

What do the numbers mean? "SHOW ME THE ASSETS!"

Before the dot-com bubble burst, concerns about liquidity and solvency led creditors of many dot-com companies to demand more assurances that these companies could pay their bills when due. A key indicator for creditors is the amount of working capital. For example, when a report predicted that **Amazon.com**'s working capital would turn negative, the company's vendors began to explore steps that would ensure that Amazon would pay them.

Some vendors demanded that their dot-com customers sign notes stating that the goods shipped to them would serve as collateral for the transaction. Other vendors began shipping goods on consignment—an arrangement whereby the vendor retains ownership of the goods until a third party buys and pays for them.

Another recent bubble in the real estate market created a working capital and liquidity crisis for no less a revered financial institution than **Bear Stearns**. What happened? Bear Stearns was one of the biggest investors in mortgage-backed securities. But when the housing market cooled off and the value of the collateral backing Bear Stearns's mortgage securities dropped dramatically, the market began to question Bear Stearns's ability to meet its obligations. The result: The Federal Reserve stepped in to avert a collapse of the company, backing a bailout plan that guaranteed *$30 billion* of Bear Stearns's investments. This paved the way for a buy-out by **JPMorgan Chase** at $2 per share (later amended to $10 a share)—quite a bargain since Bear Stearns had been trading above $80 a share just a month earlier.

Source: Robin Sidel, Greg Ip, Michael M. Phillips, and Kate Kelly, "The Week That Shook Wall Street: Inside the Demise of Bear Stearns," *Wall Street Journal* (March 18, 2008), p. A1.

Long-Term Liabilities. **Long-term liabilities** are obligations that a company does not reasonably expect to liquidate within the normal operating cycle. Instead, it expects to pay them at some date beyond that time. The most common examples are bonds payable, notes payable, some deferred income tax amounts, lease obligations, and pension obligations. **Companies classify long-term liabilities that mature within the current operating cycle as current liabilities if payment of the obligation requires the use of current assets.**

Generally, long-term liabilities are of three types:

1. Obligations arising from specific financing situations, such as the issuance of bonds, long-term lease obligations, and long-term notes payable.
2. Obligations arising from the ordinary operations of the company, such as pension obligations and deferred income tax liabilities.
3. Obligations that depend on the occurrence or non-occurrence of one or more future events to confirm the amount payable, the payee, or the date payable, such as service or product warranties and other contingencies.

Companies generally provide a great deal of supplementary disclosure for long-term liabilities because most long-term debt is subject to various covenants and restrictions for the protection of lenders.[8]

It is desirable to report any premium or discount separately as an addition to or subtraction from the bonds payable. Companies frequently describe the terms of all long-term liability agreements (including maturity date or dates, rates of interest, nature of obligation, and any security pledged to support the debt) in notes to the financial statements. Illustration 5-14 provides an example of this, taken from an excerpt from **The Great Atlantic & Pacific Tea Company**'s financials.

[8]Companies usually explain the pertinent rights and privileges of the various securities (both debt and equity) outstanding in the notes to the financial statements. Examples of information that companies should disclose are dividend and liquidation preferences, participation rights, call prices and dates, conversion or exercise prices or rates and pertinent dates, sinking fund requirements, unusual voting rights, and significant terms of contracts to issue additional shares. [4]

ILLUSTRATION 5-14
Balance Sheet Presentation of Long-Term Debt

The Great Atlantic & Pacific Tea Company, Inc.

Total current liabilities	$978,109,000
Long-term debt (See note)	254,312,000
Obligations under capital leases	252,618,000
Deferred income taxes	57,167,000
Other non-current liabilities	127,321,000

Note: Indebtedness. Debt consists of:	
9.5% senior notes, due in annual installments of $10,000,000	$ 40,000,000
Mortgages and other notes due through 2011 (average interest rate of 9.9%)	107,604,000
Bank borrowings at 9.7%	67,225,000
Commercial paper at 9.4%	100,102,000
	314,931,000
Less: Current portion	(60,619,000)
Total long-term debt	$254,312,000

Owners' Equity

The **owners' equity** (**stockholders' equity**) section is one of the most difficult sections to prepare and understand. This is due to the complexity of capital stock agreements and the various restrictions on stockholders' equity imposed by state corporation laws, liability agreements, and boards of directors. Companies usually divide the section into six parts:

STOCKHOLDERS' EQUITY SECTION

1. **CAPITAL STOCK.** The par or stated value of the shares issued.
2. **ADDITIONAL PAID-IN CAPITAL.** The excess of amounts paid in over the par or stated value.
3. **RETAINED EARNINGS.** The corporation's undistributed earnings.
4. **ACCUMULATED OTHER COMPREHENSIVE INCOME.** The aggregate amount of the other comprehensive income items.
5. **TREASURY STOCK.** Generally, the amount of ordinary shares repurchased.
6. **NONCONTROLLING INTEREST (MINORITY INTEREST).** A portion of the equity of subsidiaries not wholly owned by the reporting company.

For capital stock, companies must disclose the par value and the authorized, issued, and outstanding share amounts. A company usually presents the additional paid-in capital in one amount although subtotals are informative if the sources of additional capital are varied and material. The retained earnings amount may be divided between the **unappropriated** (the amount that is usually available for dividend distribution) and **restricted** (e.g., by bond indentures or other loan agreements) amounts. In addition, companies show any capital stock reacquired (treasury stock) as a reduction of stockholders' equity. Accumulated other comprehensive income includes such items as unrealized gains and losses on available-for-sale investments and unrealized gains and losses on certain derivative transactions. Noncontrolling interest (discussed in Chapter 4 and sometimes referred to as *minority interest*) is also shown as a separate item (where applicable) as a part of equity.

Illustration 5-15 (page 226) presents an example of the stockholders' equity section from **Las Vegas Sands Corporation**.

The ownership or stockholders' equity accounts in a corporation differ considerably from those in a partnership or proprietorship. Partners show separately their permanent

ILLUSTRATION 5-15
Balance Sheet Presentation of Stockholders' Equity

Las Vegas Sands Corporation

Equity	
Preferred stock, \$0.001 par value, 50,000,000 shares authorized, 3,614,923 shares issued and outstanding	\$ 207,356
Common stock, \$0.001 par value, 1,000,000,000 shares authorized, 707,507,982 shares issued and outstanding	708
Capital in excess of par value	5,444,705
Accumulated other comprehensive income	129,519
Retained earnings	880,703
Total Las Vegas Sands Corp. stockholders' equity	6,662,991
Noncontrolling interests	1,268,197
Total equity	\$7,931,188

capital accounts and the balance in their temporary accounts (drawing accounts). Proprietorships ordinarily use a single capital account that handles all of the owner's equity transactions.

What do the numbers mean? WARNING SIGNALS

Analysts use balance sheet information in models designed to predict financial distress. Researcher E. I. Altman pioneered a bankruptcy-prediction model that derives a "Z-score" by combining balance sheet and income measures in the following equation.

$$Z = \frac{\text{Working capital}}{\text{Total assets}} \times 1.2 + \frac{\text{Retained earnings}}{\text{Total assets}} \times 1.4 + \frac{\text{EBIT}}{\text{Total assets}} \times 3.3 + \frac{\text{Sales}}{\text{Total assets}} \times 0.99 + \frac{\text{MV equity}}{\text{Total liabilities}} \times 0.6$$

Following extensive testing, Altman found that companies with Z-scores above 3.0 are unlikely to fail. Those with Z-scores below 1.81 are very likely to fail.

Altman developed the original model for publicly held manufacturing companies. He and others have modified the model to apply to companies in various industries, emerging companies, and companies not traded in public markets.

At one time, the use of Z-scores was virtually unheard of among practicing accountants. Today, auditors, management consultants, and courts of law use this measure to help evaluate the overall financial position and trends of a firm. In addition, banks use Z-scores for loan evaluation. While a low score does not guarantee bankruptcy, the model has been proven accurate in many situations.

Source: Adapted from E. I. Altman and E. Hotchkiss, *Corporate Financial Distress and Bankruptcy*, Third Edition (New York: John Wiley and Sons, 2005).

Balance Sheet Format

LEARNING OBJECTIVE 3
Prepare a classified balance sheet using the report and account formats.

One common arrangement that companies use in presenting a classified balance sheet is the **account form**. It lists assets, by sections, on the left side, and liabilities and stockholders' equity, by sections, on the right side. The main disadvantage is the need for a sufficiently wide space in which to present the items side by side. Often, the account form requires two facing pages.

To avoid this disadvantage, the **report form** lists the sections one above the other, on the same page. See, for example, Illustration 5-16, which lists assets, followed by liabilities and stockholders' equity directly below, on the same page.[9]

[9] *Accounting Trends and Techniques* (New York: AICPA) recently indicates that all of the 500 companies surveyed use either the "report form" (484) or the "account form" (16), sometimes collectively referred to as the "customary form."

ILLUSTRATION 5-16
Classified Report Form Balance Sheet

SCIENTIFIC PRODUCTS, INC.
BALANCE SHEET
DECEMBER 31, 2014

Assets			
Current assets			
Cash		$ 42,485	
Investments (available-for-sale)		28,250	
Accounts receivable	$165,824		
Less: Allowance for doubtful accounts	1,850	163,974	
Notes receivable		23,000	
Inventories—at average-cost		489,713	
Supplies on hand		9,780	
Prepaid expenses		16,252	
Total current assets			$ 773,454
Long-term investments			
Equity investments			87,500
Property, plant, and equipment			
Land—at cost		125,000	
Buildings—at cost	975,800		
Less: Accumulated depreciation	341,200	634,600	
Total property, plant, and equipment			759,600
Intangible assets			
Goodwill			100,000
Total assets			$1,720,554
Liabilities and Stockholders' Equity			
Current liabilities			
Notes payable to banks		$ 50,000	
Accounts payable		197,532	
Accrued interest on notes payable		500	
Income taxes payable		62,520	
Accrued salaries, wages, and other liabilities		9,500	
Deposits received from customers		420	
Total current liabilities			$ 320,472
Long-term debt			
Twenty-year 12% debentures, due January 1, 2022			500,000
Total liabilities			820,472
Stockholders' equity			
Paid in on capital stock			
Preferred, 7%, cumulative			
Authorized, issued, and outstanding, 30,000 shares of $10 par value	$300,000		
Common—			
Authorized, 500,000 shares of $1 par value; issued and outstanding, 400,000 shares	400,000		
Additional paid-in capital	37,500	$737,500	
Retained earnings		153,182	
Accumulated other comprehensive income		8,650	
Less: Treasury stock		12,750	
Equity attributable to Scientific Products, Inc.			886,582
Equity attributable to noncontrolling interest			13,500
Total stockholders' equity			900,082
Total liabilities and stockholders' equity			$1,720,554

Underlying Concepts

The presentation of balance sheet information meets the objective of financial reporting—to provide information about entity resources, claims to resources, and changes in them.

Infrequently, companies use other balance sheet formats. For example, companies sometimes deduct current liabilities from current assets to arrive at working capital. Or, they deduct all liabilities from all assets.

STATEMENT OF CASH FLOWS

LEARNING OBJECTIVE 4
Indicate the purpose of the statement of cash flows.

Chapter 2 indicated that an important element of the objective of financial reporting is "assessing the amounts, timing, and uncertainty of cash flows." The three financial statements we have looked at so far—the income statement, the statement of stockholders' equity, and the balance sheet—each present some information about the cash flows of an enterprise during a period. But they do so to a limited extent. For instance, the income statement provides information about resources provided by operations but not exactly cash. The statement of stockholders' equity shows the amount of cash used to pay dividends or purchase treasury stock. Comparative balance sheets might show what assets the company has acquired or disposed of, and what liabilities it has incurred or liquidated.

Underlying Concepts
The statement of cash flows meets the objective of financial reporting—to help assess the amounts, timing, and uncertainty of future cash flows.

Useful as they are, none of these statements presents a detailed summary of all the cash inflows and outflows, or the sources and uses of cash during the period. To fill this need, the FASB requires the **statement of cash flows** (also called the **cash flow statement**). **[5]**

What do the numbers mean? WATCH THAT CASH FLOW

Investors usually focus on net income measured on an accrual basis. However, information on cash flows can be important for assessing a company's liquidity, financial flexibility, and overall financial performance. The graph below shows **W. T. Grant**'s financial performance over 7 years.

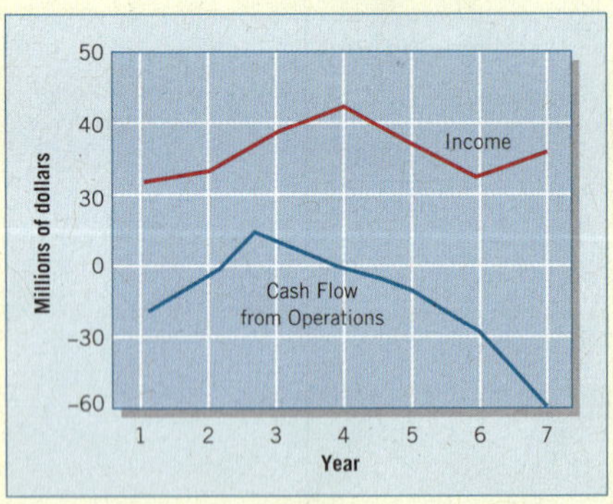

Although W. T. Grant showed consistent profits and even some periods of earnings growth, its cash flow began to "go south" starting in about year 3. The company filed for bankruptcy shortly after year 7. Financial statement readers who studied the company's cash flows would have found early warnings of its problems. The Grant experience is a classic case, illustrating the importance of cash flows as an early-warning signal of financial problems.

A more recent retailer case is **Target**. Although Target has shown good profits, some are concerned that a bit too much of its sales have been made on credit rather than cash. Why is this a problem? Like W. T. Grant, the earnings of profitable lenders can get battered in future periods if they have to start adding large amounts to their bad-loan reserve to catch up with credit losses. And if losses ramp up on Target-branded credit cards, Target may get hit in this way.

Source: Peter Eavis, "Is Target Corp.'s Credit Too Generous?" *Wall Street Journal* (March 11, 2008), p. C1.

Purpose of the Statement of Cash Flows

The primary purpose of a statement of cash flows is to provide relevant information about the cash receipts and cash payments of an enterprise during a period. To achieve this purpose, the statement of cash flows reports the following: (1) the cash effects of operations during a period, (2) investing transactions, (3) financing transactions, and (4) the net increase or decrease in cash during the period.[10]

[10]The FASB recommends the basis as "cash and cash equivalents." **Cash equivalents** are liquid investments that mature within three months or less.

Reporting the sources, uses, and net increase or decrease in cash helps investors, creditors, and others know what is happening to a company's most liquid resource. Because most individuals maintain a checkbook and prepare a tax return on a cash basis, they can comprehend the information reported in the statement of cash flows.

The statement of cash flows provides answers to the following simple but important questions:

1. Where did the cash come from during the period?
2. What was the cash used for during the period?
3. What was the change in the cash balance during the period?

Content and Format of the Statement of Cash Flows

5 LEARNING OBJECTIVE
Identify the content of the statement of cash flows.

Companies classify cash receipts and cash payments during a period into three different activities in the statement of cash flows—operating, investing, and financing activities, defined as follows.

1. **Operating activities** involve the cash effects of transactions that enter into the determination of net income.
2. **Investing activities** include making and collecting loans and acquiring and disposing of investments (both debt and equity) and property, plant, and equipment.
3. **Financing activities** involve liability and owners' equity items. They include (a) obtaining resources from owners and providing them with a return on their investment, and (b) borrowing money from creditors and repaying the amounts borrowed.

Illustration 5-17 shows the basic format of the statement of cash flows.

ILLUSTRATION 5-17
Basic Format of Cash Flow Statement

STATEMENT OF CASH FLOWS	
Cash flows from operating activities	$XXX
Cash flows from investing activities	XXX
Cash flows from financing activities	XXX
Net increase (decrease) in cash	XXX
Cash at beginning of year	XXX
Cash at end of year	$XXX

Illustration 5-18 (page 230) graphs the inflows and outflows of cash classified by activity.

The statement's value is that it helps users evaluate liquidity, solvency, and financial flexibility. As stated earlier, **liquidity** refers to the "nearness to cash" of assets and liabilities. **Solvency** is the firm's ability to pay its debts as they mature. **Financial flexibility** is a company's ability to respond and adapt to financial adversity and unexpected needs and opportunities.

We have devoted Chapter 23 entirely to the detailed preparation and content of the statement of cash flows. The intervening chapters will cover several elements and complex topics that affect the content of a typical statement of cash flows. The presentation in this chapter is introductory—a reminder of the existence of the statement of cash flows and its usefulness.

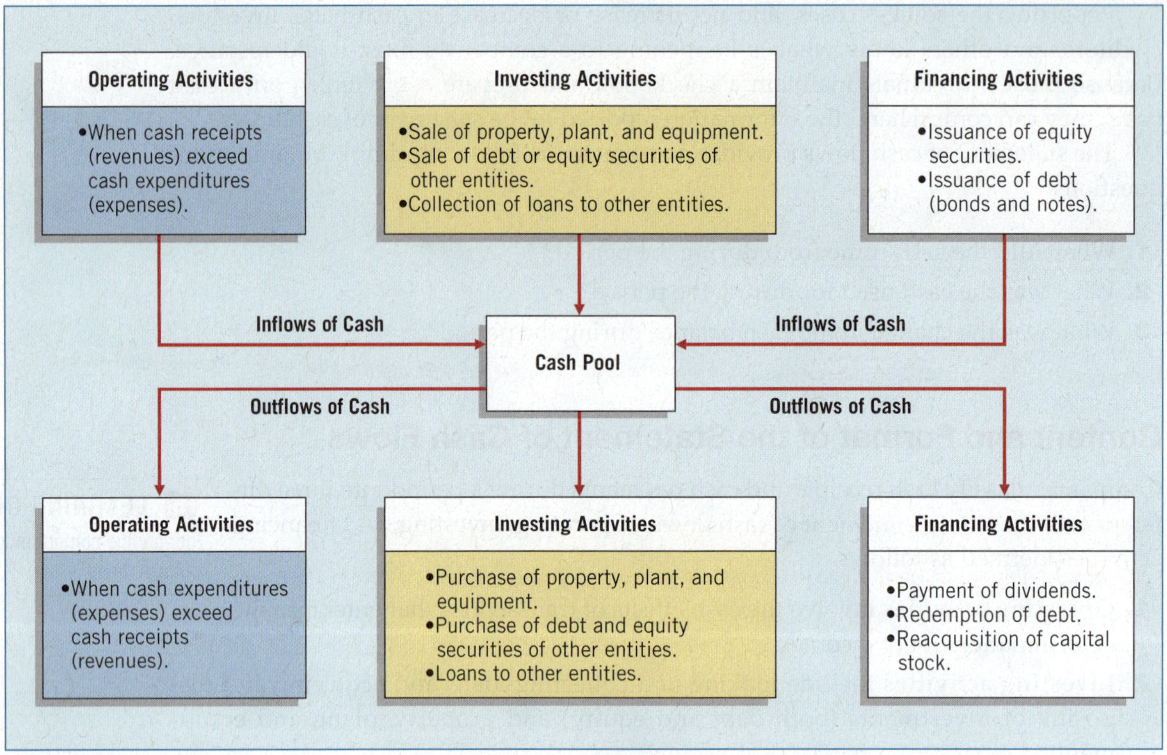

ILLUSTRATION 5-18
Cash Inflows and Outflows

Overview of the Preparation of the Statement of Cash Flows

Sources of Information

LEARNING OBJECTIVE 6
Prepare a basic statement of cash flows.

Companies obtain the information to prepare the statement of cash flows from several sources: (1) comparative balance sheets, (2) the current income statement, and (3) selected transaction data.

The following simple example demonstrates how companies use these sources in preparing a statement of cash flows.

On January 1, 2014, in its first year of operations, Telemarketing Inc. issued 50,000 shares of $1 par value common stock for $50,000 cash. The company rented its office space, furniture, and telecommunications equipment and performed marketing services throughout the first year. In June 2014, the company purchased land for $15,000. Illustration 5-19 shows the company's comparative balance sheets at the beginning and end of 2014.

ILLUSTRATION 5-19
Comparative Balance Sheets

TELEMARKETING INC.
BALANCE SHEETS

	Dec. 31, 2014	Jan. 1, 2014	Increase/Decrease
Assets			
Cash	$31,000	$-0-	$31,000 Increase
Accounts receivable	41,000	-0-	41,000 Increase
Land	15,000	-0-	15,000 Increase
Total	$87,000	$-0-	
Liabilities and Stockholders' Equity			
Accounts payable	$12,000	$-0-	12,000 Increase
Common stock	50,000	-0-	50,000 Increase
Retained earnings	25,000	-0-	25,000 Increase
Total	$87,000	$-0-	

Illustration 5-20 presents the income statement and additional information.

ILLUSTRATION 5-20
Income Statement Data

TELEMARKETING INC.
INCOME STATEMENT
FOR THE YEAR ENDED DECEMBER 31, 2014

Revenues	$172,000
Operating expenses	120,000
Income before income tax	52,000
Income tax	13,000
Net income	$ 39,000

Additional information:
Dividends of $14,000 were paid during the year.

Preparing the Statement of Cash Flows

Preparing the statement of cash flows from these sources involves four steps:

1. Determine the net cash provided by (or used in) operating activities.
2. Determine the net cash provided by (or used in) investing and financing activities.
3. Determine the change (increase or decrease) in cash during the period.
4. Reconcile the change in cash with the beginning and the ending cash balances.

Net cash provided by operating activities is the excess of cash receipts over cash payments from operating activities. Companies determine this amount by converting net income on an accrual basis to a cash basis. To do so, they add to or deduct from net income those items in the income statement that do not affect cash. This procedure requires that a company analyze not only the current year's income statement but also the comparative balance sheets and selected transaction data.

Analysis of Telemarketing's comparative balance sheets reveals two items that will affect the computation of net cash provided by operating activities:

1. The increase in accounts receivable reflects a noncash increase of $41,000 in revenues.
2. The increase in accounts payable reflects a noncash increase of $12,000 in expenses.

Therefore, to arrive at net cash provided by operating activities, Telemarketing Inc. deducts from net income the increase in accounts receivable ($41,000), and it adds back to net income the increase in accounts payable ($12,000). As a result of these adjustments, the company determines net cash provided by operating activities to be $10,000, computed as shown in Illustration 5-21.

ILLUSTRATION 5-21
Computation of Net Cash Provided by Operating Activities

Net income		$39,000
Adjustments to reconcile net income to net cash provided by operating activities:		
Increase in accounts receivable	$(41,000)	
Increase in accounts payable	12,000	(29,000)
Net cash provided by operating activities		$10,000

International Perspective

IFRS requires a statement of cash flows. Both IFRS and GAAP specify that the cash flows must be classified as operating, investing, or financing.

Next, the company determines its investing and financing activities. Telemarketing Inc.'s only **investing activity** was the land purchase. It had two **financing activities**. (1) Common stock increased $50,000 from the issuance of 50,000 shares for cash. (2) The company paid $14,000 cash in dividends. Knowing the amounts provided/used by operating, investing, and financing activities, the company determines the **net increase in cash**. Illustration 5-22 (page 232) presents Telemarketing Inc.'s statement of cash flows for 2014.

ILLUSTRATION 5-22
Statement of Cash Flows

TELEMARKETING INC. STATEMENT OF CASH FLOWS FOR THE YEAR ENDED DECEMBER 31, 2014		
Cash flows from operating activities		
Net income		$39,000
Adjustments to reconcile net income to net cash provided by operating activities:		
Increase in accounts receivable	$(41,000)	
Increase in accounts payable	12,000	(29,000)
Net cash provided by operating activities		10,000
Cash flows from investing activities		
Purchase of land	(15,000)	
Net cash used by investing activities		(15,000)
Cash flows from financing activities		
Issuance of common stock	50,000	
Payment of cash dividends	(14,000)	
Net cash provided by financing activities		36,000
Net increase in cash		31,000
Cash at beginning of year		–0–
Cash at end of year		$31,000

The increase in cash of $31,000 reported in the statement of cash flows **agrees with** the increase of $31,000 in cash calculated from the comparative balance sheets.

Significant Noncash Activities

Not all of a company's significant activities involve cash. Examples of significant noncash activities are:

1. Issuance of common stock to purchase assets.
2. Conversion of bonds into common stock.
3. Issuance of debt to purchase assets.
4. Exchanges of long-lived assets.

Significant financing and investing activities that do not affect cash are not reported in the body of the statement of cash flows. Rather, these activities are reported in either a separate schedule at the bottom of the statement of cash flows or in separate notes to the financial statements. Such reporting of these noncash activities satisfies the full disclosure principle.

Illustration 5-23 shows an example of a comprehensive statement of cash flows. Note that the company purchased equipment through the issuance of $50,000 of bonds, which is a significant noncash transaction. *In solving homework assignments, you should present significant noncash activities in a separate schedule at the bottom of the statement of cash flows.*

Usefulness of the Statement of Cash Flows

LEARNING OBJECTIVE 7
Understand the usefulness of the statement of cash flows.

"Happiness is a positive cash flow" is certainly true. Although net income provides a long-term measure of a company's success or failure, cash is its lifeblood. Without cash, a company will not survive. For small and newly developing companies, cash flow is the single most important element for survival. Even medium and large companies must control cash flow.

Creditors examine the cash flow statement carefully because they are concerned about being paid. They begin their examination by finding net cash provided by operating activities. A high amount indicates that a company is able to generate sufficient cash from

ILLUSTRATION 5-23
Comprehensive Statement of Cash Flows

NESTOR COMPANY
STATEMENT OF CASH FLOWS
FOR THE YEAR ENDED DECEMBER 31, 2014

Cash flows from operating activities		
Net income		$320,750
Adjustments to reconcile net income to net cash provided by operating activities:		
Depreciation expense	$ 88,400	
Amortization of intangibles	16,300	
Gain on sale of plant assets	(8,700)	
Increase in accounts receivable (net)	(11,000)	
Decrease in inventory	15,500	
Decrease in accounts payable	(9,500)	91,000
Net cash provided by operating activities		411,750
Cash flows from investing activities		
Sale of plant assets	90,500	
Purchase of equipment	(182,500)	
Purchase of land	(70,000)	
Net cash used by investing activities		(162,000)
Cash flows from financing activities		
Payment of cash dividend	(19,800)	
Issuance of common stock	100,000	
Redemption of bonds	(50,000)	
Net cash provided by financing activities		30,200
Net increase in cash		279,950
Cash at beginning of year		135,000
Cash at end of year		$414,950
Noncash investing and financing activities		
Purchase of equipment through issuance of $50,000 of bonds		

operations to pay its bills without further borrowing. Conversely, a low or negative amount of net cash provided by operating activities indicates that a company may have to borrow or issue equity securities to acquire sufficient cash to pay its bills. Consequently, creditors look for answers to the following questions in the company's cash flow statements.

1. How successful is the company in generating net cash provided by operating activities?
2. What are the trends in net cash flow provided by operating activities over time?
3. What are the major reasons for the positive or negative net cash provided by operating activities?

You should recognize that companies can fail even though they report net income. The difference between net income and net cash provided by operating activities can be substantial. Companies such as **W. T. Grant Company** and **Prime Motor Inn**, for example, reported high net income numbers but negative net cash provided by operating activities. Eventually, both companies filed for bankruptcy.

In addition, substantial increases in receivables and/or inventory can explain the difference between positive net income and negative net cash provided by operating activities. For example, in its first year of operations, Hu Inc. reported a net income of $80,000. Its net cash provided by operating activities, however, was a negative $95,000, as shown in Illustration 5-24 (page 234).

Hu could easily experience a "cash crunch" because it has its cash tied up in receivables and inventory. If Hu encounters problems in collecting receivables, or if inventory moves slowly or becomes obsolete, its creditors may have difficulty collecting on their loans.

ILLUSTRATION 5-24
Negative Net Cash Provided by Operating Activities

HU INC.
NET CASH FLOW FROM OPERATING ACTIVITIES

Cash flows from operating activities		
Net income		$ 80,000
Adjustments to reconcile net income to net cash provided by operating activities:		
Increase in receivables	$ (75,000)	
Increase in inventories	(100,000)	(175,000)
Net cash provided by operating activities		$(95,000)

Financial Liquidity

Readers of financial statements often assess liquidity by using the **current cash debt coverage**. It indicates whether the company can pay off its current liabilities from its operations in a given year. Illustration 5-25 shows the formula for this ratio.

ILLUSTRATION 5-25
Formula for Current Cash Debt Coverage

$$\frac{\text{Net Cash Provided by Operating Activities}}{\text{Average Current Liabilities}} = \text{Current Cash Debt Coverage}$$

The higher the current cash debt coverage, the less likely a company will have liquidity problems. For example, a ratio near 1:1 is good. It indicates that the company can meet all of its current obligations from internally generated cash flow.

Financial Flexibility

The **cash debt coverage** provides information on financial flexibility. It indicates a company's ability to repay its liabilities from net cash provided by operating activities, without having to liquidate the assets employed in its operations. Illustration 5-26 shows the formula for this ratio. Notice its similarity to the current cash debt coverage. However, because it uses average total liabilities in place of average current liabilities, it takes a somewhat longer-range view.

ILLUSTRATION 5-26
Formula for Cash Debt Coverage

$$\frac{\text{Net Cash Provided by Operating Activities}}{\text{Average Total Liabilities}} = \text{Cash Debt Coverage}$$

The higher this ratio, the less likely the company will experience difficulty in meeting its obligations as they come due. It signals whether the company can pay its debts and survive if external sources of funds become limited or too expensive.

Free Cash Flow

A more sophisticated way to examine a company's financial flexibility is to develop a free cash flow analysis. **Free cash flow** is the amount of discretionary cash flow a company has. It can use this cash flow to purchase additional investments, retire its debt, purchase treasury stock, or simply add to its liquidity. Financial statement users calculate free cash flow as shown in Illustration 5-27.

ILLUSTRATION 5-27
Formula for Free Cash Flow

$$\text{Net Cash Provided by Operating Activities} - \text{Capital Expenditures} - \text{Dividends} = \text{Free Cash Flow}$$

In a free cash flow analysis, we first deduct capital spending, to indicate it is the least discretionary expenditure a company generally makes. (Without continued efforts to maintain and expand facilities, it is unlikely that a company can continue to maintain its competitive position.) We then deduct dividends. Although a company *can* cut its dividend, it usually will do so only in **a financial emergency**. The amount resulting after these deductions is the company's free cash flow. Obviously, the greater the amount of free cash flow, the greater the company's financial flexibility.

Questions that a free cash flow analysis answers are:

1. Is the company able to pay its dividends without resorting to external financing?
2. If business operations decline, will the company be able to maintain its needed capital investment?
3. What is the amount of discretionary cash flow that can be used for additional investment, retirement of debt, purchase of treasury stock, or addition to liquidity?

Illustration 5-28 is a free cash flow analysis using the cash flow statement for Nestor Company (shown in Illustration 5-23 on page 233).

ILLUSTRATION 5-28
Free Cash Flow Computation

NESTOR COMPANY
FREE CASH FLOW ANALYSIS

Net cash provided by operating activities	$411,750
Less: Capital expenditures	252,500
Dividends	19,800
Free cash flow	$139,450

This computation shows that Nestor has a positive, and substantial, net cash provided by operating activities of $411,750. Nestor's statement of cash flows reports that the company purchased equipment of $182,500 and land of $70,000 for total capital spending of $252,500. Nestor has more than sufficient cash flow to meet its dividend payment and therefore has satisfactory financial flexibility.

As you can see from looking back at Illustration 5-23 (page 233), Nestor used its free cash flow to redeem bonds and add to its liquidity. If it finds additional investments that are profitable, it can increase its spending without putting its dividend or basic capital spending in jeopardy. Companies that have strong financial flexibility can take advantage of profitable investments even in tough times. In addition, strong financial flexibility frees companies from worry about survival in poor economic times. In fact, those with strong financial flexibility often fare better in a poor economy because they can take advantage of opportunities that other companies cannot.

What do the numbers mean? "THERE OUGHT TO BE A LAW"

As one manager noted, "There ought to be a law that before you can buy a stock, you must be able to read a balance sheet." We agree, and the same can be said for a statement of cash flows.

Krispy Kreme Doughnuts provides an example of how stunning earnings growth can hide real problems. Not long ago, the doughnut maker was a glamour stock with a 60 percent earnings per share growth rate and a price-earnings ratio around 70. Seven months later, its stock price had dropped 72 percent. What happened? Stockholders alleged that Krispy Kreme may have been inflating its revenues and not taking enough bad debt expense (which inflated both assets and income). In addition, Krispy Kreme's operating cash flow was negative. Most financially sound companies generate positive cash flow.

On the next page are additional examples of how one rating agency rated the earnings quality of some companies, using some key balance sheet and statement of cash flow measurements.

Earnings-Quality Winners Company	Earnings-Quality Indicators	Earnings-Quality Losers Company	Earnings-Quality Indicators
Avon Products	Strong cash flow	Ford Motor	High debt and underfunded pension plan
Capital One Financial	Conservatively capitalized		
Ecolab	Good management of working capital	Kroger	High goodwill and debt
Timberland	Minimal off-balance-sheet commitments	Ryder System	Negative free cash flow
		Teco Energy	Selling assets to meet liquidity needs

Another rating organization uses a metric to adjust for shortcomings in amounts reported in the balance sheet. Just as improving balance sheet and cash flow information is a leading indicator of improved earnings, a deteriorating balance sheet and statement of cash flows warn of earnings declines (and falling stock prices). This was the case at Avon; its strong cash flow rating subsequently declined, such that its free cash flow was just 76 percent of net income. This raised red flags about the results on foreign investments by Avon.

Sources: Adapted from Gretchen Morgenson, "How Did They Value Stocks? Count the Absurd Ways," *New York Times on the Web* (March 18, 2001); K. Badanhausen, J. Gage, C. Hall, and M. Ozanian, "Beyond Balance Sheet: Earnings Quality," *Forbes.com* (January 28, 2005); and H. Karp, "Avon's Investments Fall Short," *Wall Street Journal* (December 8, 2011).

ADDITIONAL INFORMATION

LEARNING OBJECTIVE 8

Determine which balance sheet information requires supplemental disclosure.

In both Chapter 4 and this chapter, we have discussed the primary financial statements that all companies prepare in accordance with GAAP. However, the primary financial statements cannot provide the complete picture related to the financial position and financial performance of the company. Additional descriptive information in supplemental disclosures and certain techniques of disclosure expand on and amplify the items presented in the main body of the statements.

Supplemental Disclosures

The balance sheet is not complete if a company simply lists the assets, liabilities, and owners' equity accounts. It still needs to provide important supplemental information. This may be information not presented elsewhere in the statement, or it may elaborate on items in the balance sheet. The four types of information that are usually supplemental to account titles and amounts presented in the balance sheet are as follows.

SUPPLEMENTAL BALANCE SHEET INFORMATION

1. **CONTINGENCIES.** Material events that have an uncertain outcome.
2. **ACCOUNTING POLICIES.** Explanations of the valuation methods used or the basic assumptions made concerning inventory valuations, depreciation methods, investments in subsidiaries, etc.
3. **CONTRACTUAL SITUATIONS.** Explanations of certain restrictions or covenants attached to specific assets or, more likely, to liabilities.
4. **FAIR VALUES.** Disclosures of fair values, particularly for financial instruments.

Contingencies

A **contingency** is an existing situation involving uncertainty as to possible gain (gain contingency) or loss (loss contingency) that will ultimately be resolved when one or more future events occur or fail to occur. In short, contingencies are material events with an uncertain future. Examples of gain contingencies are tax operating-loss carryforwards or company litigation against another party. Typical loss contingencies relate to litigation, environmental issues, possible tax assessments, or government investigations. We examine the accounting and reporting requirements involving contingencies more fully in Chapter 13.

Underlying Concepts

The basis for including additional information should meet the *full disclosure principle.* That is, the information should be of sufficient importance to influence the judgment of an informed user.

Accounting Policies

GAAP recommends disclosure for all significant accounting principles and methods that involve selection from among alternatives or those that are peculiar to a given industry. **[6]** For instance, companies can compute inventories under several cost flow assumptions (e.g., LIFO and FIFO), depreciate plant and equipment under several accepted methods (e.g., double-declining-balance and straight-line), and carry investments at different valuations (e.g., cost, equity, and fair value). Sophisticated users of financial statements know of these possibilities and examine the statements closely to determine the methods used.

Companies must also disclose information about the nature of their operations, the use of estimates in preparing financial statements, certain significant estimates, and vulnerabilities due to certain concentrations. **[7]** Illustration 5-29 shows an example of such a disclosure.

ILLUSTRATION 5-29
Balance Sheet Disclosure of Significant Risks and Uncertainties

Chesapeake Corporation

Risks and Uncertainties. Chesapeake operates in three business segments which offer a diversity of products over a broad geographic base. The Company is not dependent on any single customer, group of customers, market, geographic area or supplier of materials, labor or services. Financial statements include, where necessary, amounts based on the judgments and estimates of management. These estimates include allowances for bad debts, accruals for landfill closing costs, environmental remediation costs, loss contingencies for litigation, self-insured medical and workers' compensation insurance and determinations of discount and other rate assumptions for pensions and postretirement benefit expenses.

Disclosure of significant accounting principles and methods and of risks and uncertainties is particularly useful if given in a separate **Summary of Significant Accounting Policies** preceding the notes to the financial statements or as the initial note.

Contractual Situations

Companies should disclose contractual situations, if significant, in the notes to the financial statements. For example, they must clearly state the essential provisions of lease contracts, pension obligations, and stock option plans in the notes. Analysts want to know not only the amount of the liabilities but also how the different contractual provisions affect the company at present and in the future.

Companies must disclose the following commitments if the amounts are material: commitments related to obligations to maintain working capital, to limit the payment of dividends, to restrict the use of assets, and to require the maintenance of certain financial ratios. Management must exercise considerable judgment to determine whether omission of such information is misleading. The rule in this situation is, "When in doubt, disclose." It is better to disclose a little too much information than not enough.

What do the numbers mean? WHAT ABOUT YOUR COMMITMENTS?

Many of the recent accounting scandals related to the nondisclosure of significant contractual obligations. In response, the SEC has mandated that companies disclose contractual obligations in a tabular summary in the management discussion and analysis section of the company's annual report.

Presented below, as an example, is a disclosure from The Procter & Gamble Company.

Contractual Commitments, as of June 30, 2011 (in millions of dollars)

	Total	Less Than 1 Year	1–3 Years	3–5 Years	After 5 Years
Recorded Liabilities					
Total debt	$31,494	$ 9,933	$ 5,959	$5,095	$10,507
Capital leases	407	46	89	75	197
Uncertain tax positions (1)	77	77	—	—	—
Other					
Interest payments relating to long-term debt	9,897	1,002	1,744	1,313	5,838
Operating leases (2)	1,499	264	416	314	505
Minimum pension funding (3)	1,070	391	679	—	—
Purchase obligations (4)	3,012	1,351	1,130	258	273
Total contractual commitments	$47,456	$13,064	$10,017	$7,055	$17,320

(1) As of June 30, 2011, the Company's Consolidated Balance Sheet reflects a liability for uncertain tax positions of $2.4 billion, including $555 million of interest and penalties. Due to the high degree of uncertainty regarding the timing of future cash outflows of liabilities for uncertain tax positions beyond one year, a reasonable estimate of the period of cash settlement beyond twelve months from the balance sheet date of June 30, 2011 cannot be made.
(2) Operating lease obligations are shown net of guaranteed sublease income.
(3) Represents future pension payments to comply with local funding requirements. The projected payments beyond fiscal year 2014 are not currently determinable.
(4) Primarily reflects future contractual payments under various take-or-pay arrangements entered into as part of the normal course of business.

Fair Values

As we have discussed, fair value information may be more useful than historical cost for certain types of assets and liabilities. This is particularly so in the case of financial instruments. **Financial instruments** are defined as cash, an ownership interest, or a contractual right to receive or obligation to deliver cash or another financial instrument. Such contractual rights to receive cash or other financial instruments are assets. Contractual obligations to pay are liabilities. Cash, investments, accounts receivable, and payables are examples of financial instruments.

Given the expanded use of fair value measurements, as discussed in Chapter 2, GAAP also has expanded disclosures about fair value measurements. **[8]** To increase consistency and comparability in the use of fair value measures, companies follow a fair value hierarchy that provides insight into how to determine fair value. The hierarchy has three levels. **Level 1** measures (the least subjective) are based on observable inputs, such as market prices for identical assets or liabilities. **Level 2** measures (more subjective) are based on market-based inputs other than those included in Level 1, such as those based on market prices for similar assets or liabilities. **Level 3** measures (most subjective) are based on unobservable inputs, such as a company's own data or assumptions.[11]

For major groups of assets and liabilities, companies must make the following fair value disclosures: (1) the fair value measurement and (2) the fair value hierarchy level of the measurements as a whole, classified by Level 1, 2, or 3. Illustration 5-30 provides a disclosure for Devon Energy for its assets and liabilities measured at fair value.

[11] Level 3 fair value measurements may be developed using expected cash flow and present value techniques, as described in "Using Cash Flow Information and Present Value in Accounting," *Statement of Financial Accounting Concepts No. 7*, as discussed in Chapter 6.

ILLUSTRATION 5-30
Disclosure of Fair Values

Devon Energy Corporation

Note 7: Fair Value Measurements (in part). Certain of Devon's assets and liabilities are reported at fair value in the accompanying balance sheets. The following table provides fair value measurement information for such assets and liabilities.

		Fair Value Measurements Using:		
	Total Fair Value	Quoted Prices in Active Markets (Level 1)	Significant Other Observable Inputs (Level 2)	Significant Unobservable Inputs (Level 3)
		(In millions)		
Assets:				
Short-term investments	$ 341	$ 341	$ —	$ —
Investment in Chevron common stock	1,327	1,327	—	—
Financial instruments	8	—	8	—
Liabilities:				
Financial instruments	497	—	497	—
Asset retirement obligation (ARO)	1,300	—	—	1,300

GAAP establishes a fair value hierarchy that prioritizes the inputs to valuation techniques used to measure fair value. As presented in the table above, this hierarchy consists of three broad levels. Level 1 inputs on the hierarchy consist of unadjusted quoted prices in active markets for identical assets and liabilities and have the highest priority. Level 3 inputs have the lowest priority. Devon uses appropriate valuation techniques based on the available inputs to measure the fair values of its assets and liabilities. When available, Devon measures fair value using Level 1 inputs because they generally provide the most reliable evidence of fair value.

In addition, companies must provide significant additional disclosure related to Level 3 measurements. The disclosures related to Level 3 are substantial and must identify what assumptions the company used to generate the fair value numbers and any related income effects. Companies will want to use Level 1 and 2 measurements as much as possible. In most cases, these valuations should be very reliable, as the fair value measurements are based on market information. In contrast, a company that uses Level 3 measurements extensively must be carefully evaluated to understand the impact these valuations have on the financial statements.

Techniques of Disclosure

9 LEARNING OBJECTIVE
Describe the major disclosure techniques for the balance sheet.

Companies should disclose as completely as possible the effect of various contingencies on financial condition, the methods of valuing assets and liabilities, and the company's contracts and agreements. To disclose this pertinent information, companies may use parenthetical explanations, notes, cross-reference and contra items, and supporting schedules.

Parenthetical Explanations

Companies often provide additional information by parenthetical explanations following the item. For example, Illustration 5-31 shows a parenthetical explanation of the

ILLUSTRATION 5-31
Parenthetical Disclosure of Shares Issued—Ford Motor Company

Ford Motor Company

Stockholders' Equity (in millions)	
Common stock, par value $0.01 per share (1,837 million shares issued)	$18

Underlying Concepts

The user-specific quality of *understandability* requires accountants to be careful in describing transactions and events.

number of shares issued by **Ford Motor Company** on the balance sheet under "Stockholders' equity."

This additional pertinent balance sheet information adds clarity and completeness. It has an advantage over a note because it brings the additional information into the **body of the statement** where readers will less likely overlook it. Companies, however, should avoid lengthy parenthetical explanations, which might be distracting.

Notes

Companies use notes if they cannot conveniently show additional explanations as parenthetical explanations. Illustration 5-32 shows how **International Paper Company** reported its inventory costing methods in its accompanying notes.

ILLUSTRATION 5-32
Note Disclosure

International Paper Company

Note 11

Inventories by major category were (millions):

Raw materials	$ 371
Finished pulp, paper and packaging products	1,796
Finished lumber and panel products	184
Operating supplies	351
Other	16
Total inventories	$2,718

The last-in, first-out inventory method is used to value most of International Paper's U.S. inventories. Approximately 70% of total raw materials and finished products inventories were valued using this method. If the first-in, first-out method had been used, it would have increased total inventories balances by approximately $170 million.

Companies commonly use notes to disclose the following: the existence and amount of any preferred stock dividends in arrears, the terms of or obligations imposed by purchase commitments, special financial arrangements and instruments, depreciation policies, any changes in the application of accounting principles, and the existence of contingencies.

Notes therefore must present all essential facts as completely and succinctly as possible. Careless wording may mislead rather than aid readers. Notes should add to the total information made available in the financial statements, not raise unanswered questions or contradict other portions of the statements. The note disclosures in Illustration 5-33 show the presentation of such information.

ILLUSTRATION 5-33
More Note Disclosures

Alberto-Culver Company

Note 3: Long-Term Debt. Various borrowing arrangements impose restrictions on such items as total debt, working capital, dividend payments, treasury stock purchases and interest expense. The company was in compliance with these arrangements and $68 million of consolidated retained earnings was not restricted as to the payment of dividends and purchases of treasury stock.

ILLUSTRATION 5-33
(Continued)

Apple Inc.

Note 7: Commitments and Contingencies.

Other Commitments

As of September 24, 2011, the Company had outstanding off-balance sheet commitments for outsourced manufacturing and component purchases of $13.9 billion. Additionally, other outstanding obligations were $2.4 billion as of September 24, 2011, and were comprised mainly of commitments under long term supply agreements to make additional inventory component prepayments and to acquire capital equipment, commitments to acquire product tooling and manufacturing process equipment, and commitments related to advertising, research and development, Internet and telecommunications services and other obligations.

Underlying Concepts

The FASB recently issued an invitation to comment on disclosure effectiveness, in order to get input on how disclosures in the footnotes can be made more useful.

Willamette Industries, Inc.

Note 4: Property, Plant, and Equipment (partial): The company changed its accounting estimates relating to depreciation. The estimated service lives for most machinery and equipment were extended five years. The change was based upon a study performed by the company's engineering department, comparisons to typical industry practices, and the effect of the company's extensive capital investments which have resulted in a mix of assets with longer productive lives due to technological advances. As a result of the change, net income was increased $51,900, or $0.46 per diluted share.

Cross-Reference and Contra Items

Companies "cross-reference" a direct relationship between an asset and a liability on the balance sheet. For example, as shown in Illustration 5-34, on December 31, 2014, a company might show the following entries—one listed among the current assets, and the other listed among the current liabilities.

ILLUSTRATION 5-34
Cross-Referencing and Contra Items

Current Assets (in part)	
Cash on deposit with sinking fund trustee for redemption of bonds payable—see Current liabilities	$800,000

Current Liabilities (in part)	
Bonds payable to be redeemed in 2015—see Current assets	$2,300,000

This cross-reference points out that the company will redeem $2,300,000 of bonds payable currently, for which it has only set aside $800,000. Therefore, it needs additional cash from unrestricted cash, from sales of investments, from profits, or from some other source. Alternatively, the company can show the same information parenthetically.

Another common procedure is to establish contra or adjunct accounts. A **contra account** on a balance sheet reduces either an asset, liability, or owners' equity account. Examples include Accumulated Depreciation and Discount on Bonds Payable. Contra accounts provide some flexibility in presenting the financial information. With the use of the Accumulated Depreciation account, for example, a reader of the statement can see the original cost of the asset as well as the depreciation to date.

An **adjunct account**, on the other hand, increases either an asset, liability, or owners' equity account. An example is Premium on Bonds Payable, which, when added to the Bonds Payable account, describes the total bond liability of the company.

Supporting Schedules

Often a company needs a separate schedule to present more detailed information about certain assets or liabilities, as shown in Illustration 5-35.

ILLUSTRATION 5-35
Disclosure through Use of Supporting Schedules

Property, plant, and equipment	
Land, buildings, equipment, and other fixed assets—net (see Schedule 3)	$643,300

SCHEDULE 3
LAND, BUILDINGS, EQUIPMENT, AND OTHER FIXED ASSETS

	Total	Land	Buildings	Equip.	Other Fixed Assets
Balance January 1, 2014	$740,000	$46,000	$358,000	$260,000	$76,000
Additions in 2014	161,200		120,000	38,000	3,200
	901,200	46,000	478,000	298,000	79,200
Assets retired or sold in 2014	31,700			27,000	4,700
Balance December 31, 2014	869,500	46,000	478,000	271,000	74,500
Depreciation taken to January 1, 2014	196,000		102,000	78,000	16,000
Depreciation taken in 2014	56,000		28,000	24,000	4,000
	252,000		130,000	102,000	20,000
Depreciation on assets retired in 2014	25,800			22,000	3,800
Depreciation accumulated December 31, 2014	226,200		130,000	80,000	16,200
Book value of assets	$643,300	$46,000	$348,000	$191,000	$58,300

International Perspective

Internationally, accounting terminology is a problem. Confusion arises even between nations that share a language. For example, U.S. investors normally think of "stock" as "equity" or "ownership." To the British, "stocks" means inventory. In the United States, "fixed assets" generally refers to "property, plant, and equipment." In Britain, the category includes more items.

Terminology

The account titles in the general ledger do not necessarily represent the best terminology for balance sheet purposes. Companies often use brief account titles and include technical terms that only accountants understand. But many persons unacquainted with accounting terminology examine balance sheets. Thus, balance sheets should contain descriptions that readers will generally understand and clearly interpret.

For example, companies have used the term "reserve" in differing ways: to describe amounts deducted from assets (contra accounts such as accumulated depreciation and allowance for doubtful accounts), as a part of the title of contingent or estimated liabilities, and to describe an appropriation of retained earnings. Because of the different meanings attached to this term, misinterpretation often resulted from its use. Therefore, the profession has recommended that companies use the word **reserve** only to describe an appropriation of retained earnings. The use of the term in this narrower sense—to describe appropriated retained earnings—has resulted in a better understanding of its significance when it appears in a balance sheet. However, the term "appropriated" appears more logical, and we encourage its use.

For years, the profession has recommended that the use of the word **surplus** be discontinued in balance sheet presentations of stockholders' equity. The use of the terms *capital surplus, paid-in surplus,* and *earned surplus* is confusing. Although condemned by the profession, these terms appear all too frequently in current financial statements.

You will want to read the **IFRS INSIGHTS** on pages 277–284 for discussion of IFRS related to the balance sheet and statement of cash flows.

Evolving Issue BALANCE SHEET REPORTING: GROSS OR NET?

In addition to the issue of financial statement presentation discussed in the opening story, a second area of controversy for balance sheet reporting is the issue of offsetting (or netting) of assets and liabilities. It is generally accepted that offsetting of recognized assets and recognized liabilities detracts from the ability of users both to understand the transactions and conditions that have occurred and to assess the company's future cash flows. In other words, providing information on assets, liabilities, and stockholders' equity helps users to compute rates of return and evaluate capital structure. However, netting assets and liabilities limits a user's ability to assess the future economic benefits and obligations. That is, offsetting hides the existence of assets and liabilities, making it difficult to evaluate liquidity, solvency, and financial flexibility. As a result, GAAP does not permit the reporting of summary accounts alone (e.g., total assets, net assets, and total liabilities).

Recently, the IASB and FASB have worked to develop common criteria for offsetting on the balance sheet. Current offsetting rules under IFRS are more restrictive than GAAP. The rules proposed would allow offsetting only in rare circumstances (e.g., when right of offset is legally enforceable). Implementation of these new rules in the United States would result in a dramatic "grossing up" of balance sheets (particularly for financial institutions). For example, one study estimated that the new rules would gross up U.S. banks' balance sheets by $900 billion (or an average of 68%, ranging from a 31.4% increase for **Citigroup** to 104.7% for **Morgan Stanley**).* Not surprisingly, the FASB received significant push-back from some of its constituents (particularly financial institutions) to the proposed rules.

As a result, to date the Boards have not been able to agree on a converged standard, thereby stalling this project. However, the Boards have issued converged disclosure requirements. The disclosure rules require companies to disclose both gross information and net information about instruments and transactions that are eligible for offset in the balance sheet. While the Boards have not been able to develop a converged set of criteria for offsetting, the information provided under the new converged disclosure rules should enable users of a company's financial statements to evaluate the effects of netting arrangements on its financial position. In doing so, the new rules support the full disclosure principle.

*See Y. N'Diaye, "S&P: Accounting Rule Could Boost Bank Balance Sheets by Average 68%," *https://mninews.deutsche-boerse.com* (September 22, 2011).

SUMMARY OF LEARNING OBJECTIVES

1 Explain the uses and limitations of a balance sheet. The balance sheet provides information about the nature and amounts of investments in a company's resources, obligations to creditors, and owners' equity. The balance sheet contributes to financial reporting by providing a basis for (1) computing rates of return, (2) evaluating the capital structure of the enterprise, and (3) assessing the liquidity, solvency, and financial flexibility of the enterprise.

KEY TERMS

account form, *226*
adjunct account, *242*
available-for-sale investments, *218*
balance sheet, *214*
cash debt coverage, *234*
contingency, *237*
contra account, *241*

current assets, *217*
current cash debt coverage, *234*
current liabilities, *222*
financial flexibility, *214*
financial instruments, *238*
financing activities, *229*
free cash flow, *234*
held-to-maturity investments, *218*
intangible assets, *222*
investing activities, *229*
liquidity, *214*
long-term investments, *221*
long-term liabilities, *224*
operating activities, *229*
owners' (stockholders') equity, *225*
property, plant, and equipment, *221*
report form, *226*
reserve, *242*
solvency, *214*
statement of cash flows, *228*
trading investments, *218*
working capital, *223*

Three limitations of a balance sheet are as follows. (1) The balance sheet does not reflect fair value because accountants use a historical cost basis in valuing and reporting most assets and liabilities. (2) Companies must use judgments and estimates to determine certain amounts, such as the collectibility of receivables and the useful life of long-term tangible and intangible assets. (3) The balance sheet omits many items that are of financial value to the business but cannot be recorded objectively, such as human resources, customer base, and reputation.

2 **Identify the major classifications of the balance sheet.** The general elements of the balance sheet are assets, liabilities, and equity. The major classifications of assets are current assets; long-term investments; property, plant, and equipment; intangible assets; and other assets. The major classifications of liabilities are current and long-term liabilities. The balance sheet of a corporation generally classifies owners' equity as capital stock, additional paid-in capital, and retained earnings.

3 **Prepare a classified balance sheet using the report and account formats.** The report form lists liabilities and stockholders' equity directly below assets on the same page. The account form lists assets, by sections, on the left side, and liabilities and stockholders' equity, by sections, on the right side.

4 **Indicate the purpose of the statement of cash flows.** The primary purpose of a statement of cash flows is to provide relevant information about a company's cash receipts and cash payments during a period. Reporting the sources, uses, and net change in cash enables financial statement readers to know what is happening to a company's most liquid resource.

5 **Identify the content of the statement of cash flows.** In the statement of cash flows, companies classify the period's cash receipts and cash payments into three different activities. (1) *Operating activities*: Involve the cash effects of transactions that enter into the determination of net income. (2) *Investing activities*: Include making and collecting loans, and acquiring and disposing of investments (both debt and equity) and of property, plant, and equipment. (3) *Financing activities*: Involve liability and owners' equity items. Financing activities include (a) obtaining capital from owners and providing them with a return on their investment, and (b) borrowing money from creditors and repaying the amounts borrowed.

6 **Prepare a basic statement of cash flows.** The information to prepare the statement of cash flows usually comes from comparative balance sheets, the current income statement, and selected transaction data. Companies follow four steps to prepare the statement of cash flows from these sources. (1) Determine the net cash provided by (or used in) operating activities. (2) Determine the net cash provided by (or used in) investing and financing activities. (3) Determine the change (increase or decrease) in cash during the period. (4) Reconcile the change in cash with the beginning and ending cash balances.

7 **Understand the usefulness of the statement of cash flows.** Creditors examine the statement of cash flows carefully because they are concerned about being paid. The net cash flow provided by operating activities in relation to the company's liabilities is helpful in making this assessment. Two ratios used in this regard are the current cash debt ratio and the cash debt ratio. In addition, the amount of free cash flow provides creditors and stockholders with a picture of the company's financial flexibility.

8 **Determine which balance sheet information requires supplemental disclosure.** Four types of information normally are supplemental to account titles and amounts presented in the balance sheet. (1) *Contingencies:* Material events that have an uncertain outcome. (2) *Accounting policies:* Explanations of the valuation methods used or the basic assumptions made concerning inventory valuation, depreciation methods, investments in subsidiaries, etc. (3) *Contractual situations:* Explanations of certain restrictions or covenants attached to specific assets or, more likely, to liabilities. (4) *Fair values:* Disclosures related to fair values, particularly related to financial instruments.

9 Describe the major disclosure techniques for the balance sheet. Companies use four methods to disclose pertinent information in the balance sheet. (1) *Parenthetical explanations:* Parenthetical information provides additional information or description following the item. (2) *Notes:* A company uses notes if it cannot conveniently show additional explanations or descriptions as parenthetical explanations. (3) *Cross-reference and contra items:* Companies "cross-reference" a direct relationship between an asset and a liability on the balance sheet. (4) *Supporting schedules:* Often a company uses a separate schedule to present more detailed information than just the single summary item shown in the balance sheet.

APPENDIX 5A RATIO ANALYSIS—A REFERENCE

USING RATIOS TO ANALYZE PERFORMANCE

10 LEARNING OBJECTIVE
Identify the major types of financial ratios and what they measure.

Analysts and other interested parties can gather qualitative information from financial statements by examining relationships between items on the statements and identifying trends in these relationships. A useful starting point in developing this information is ratio analysis.

A **ratio** expresses the mathematical relationship between one quantity and another. **Ratio analysis** expresses the relationship among pieces of selected financial statement data, in a **percentage**, a **rate**, or a simple **proportion**.

To illustrate, **IBM Corporation** recently had current assets of $46,970 million and current liabilities of $39,798 million. We find the ratio between these two amounts by dividing current assets by current liabilities. The alternative means of expression are:

Percentage:	Current assets are 118% of current liabilities.
Rate:	Current assets are 1.18 times as great as current liabilities.
Proportion:	The relationship of current assets to current liabilities is 1.18:1.

To analyze financial statements, we classify ratios into four types, as follows.

MAJOR TYPES OF RATIOS

LIQUIDITY RATIOS. Measures of the company's short-term ability to pay its maturing obligations.

ACTIVITY RATIOS. Measures of how effectively the company uses its assets.

PROFITABILITY RATIOS. Measures of the degree of success or failure of a given company or division for a given period of time.

COVERAGE RATIOS. Measures of the degree of protection for long-term creditors and investors.

Gateway to the Profession

Expanded Discussion of Financial Statement Analysis

In Chapter 5, we discussed three measures related to the statement of cash flows (current cash debt coverage, cash debt coverage, and free cash flow). Throughout the remainder of the textbook, we provide ratios to help you understand and interpret the information presented in financial statements. Illustration 5A-1 presents the ratios that we will use throughout the textbook. You should find this chart helpful as you examine these ratios in more detail in the following chapters. An appendix to Chapter 24 further discusses financial statement analysis.

ILLUSTRATION 5A-1
A Summary of Financial Ratios

Ratio	Formula	Purpose or Use
I. Liquidity		
1. Current ratio	$\frac{\text{Current assets}}{\text{Current liabilities}}$	Measures short-term debt-paying ability
2. Quick or acid-test ratio	$\frac{\text{Cash, short-term investments, and net receivables}}{\text{Current liabilities}}$	Measures immediate short-term liquidity
3. Current cash debt coverage	$\frac{\text{Net cash provided by operating activities}}{\text{Average current liabilities}}$	Measures a company's ability to pay off its current liabilities in a given year from its operations
II. Activity		
4. Accounts receivable turnover	$\frac{\text{Net sales}}{\text{Average trade receivables (net)}}$	Measures liquidity of receivables
5. Inventory turnover	$\frac{\text{Cost of goods sold}}{\text{Average inventory}}$	Measures liquidity of inventory
6. Asset turnover	$\frac{\text{Net sales}}{\text{Average total assets}}$	Measures how efficiently assets are used to generate sales
III. Profitability		
7. Profit margin on sales	$\frac{\text{Net income}}{\text{Net sales}}$	Measures net income generated by each dollar of sales
8. Return on assets	$\frac{\text{Net income}}{\text{Average total assets}}$	Measures overall profitability of assets
9. Return on common stock equity	$\frac{\text{Net income minus preferred dividends}}{\text{Average common stockholders' equity}}$	Measures profitability of owners' investment
10. Earnings per share	$\frac{\text{Net income minus preferred dividends}}{\text{Weighted-average number of shares outstanding}}$	Measures net income earned on each share of common stock
11. Price-earnings ratio	$\frac{\text{Market price of stock}}{\text{Earnings per share}}$	Measures the ratio of the market price per share to earnings per share
12. Payout ratio	$\frac{\text{Cash dividends}}{\text{Net income}}$	Measures percentage of earnings distributed in the form of cash dividends
IV. Coverage		
13. Debt to assets	$\frac{\text{Total liabilities}}{\text{Total assets}}$	Measures the percentage of total assets provided by creditors
14. Times interest earned	$\frac{\text{Income before income taxes and interest expense}}{\text{Interest expense}}$	Measures ability to meet interest payments as they come due
15. Cash debt coverage	$\frac{\text{Net cash provided by operating activities}}{\text{Average total liabilities}}$	Measures a company's ability to repay its total liabilities in a given year from its operations
16. Book value per share	$\frac{\text{Common stockholders' equity}}{\text{Outstanding shares}}$	Measures the amount each share would receive if the company were liquidated at the amounts reported on the balance sheet
17. Free cash flow	Net cash provided by operating activities − Capital expenditures − Dividends	Measures the amount of discretionary cash flow

SUMMARY OF LEARNING OBJECTIVE FOR APPENDIX 5A

10 Identify the major types of financial ratios and what they measure. Ratios express the mathematical relationship between one quantity and another, expressed as a percentage, a rate, or a proportion. *Liquidity* ratios measure the short-term ability to pay maturing obligations. *Activity* ratios measure the effectiveness of asset usage. *Profitability* ratios measure the success or failure of an enterprise. *Coverage* ratios measure the degree of protection for long-term creditors and investors.

KEY TERMS

activity ratios, *245*
coverage ratios, *245*
liquidity ratios, *245*
profitability ratios, *245*
ratio analysis, *245*

APPENDIX 5B SPECIMEN FINANCIAL STATEMENTS: THE PROCTER & GAMBLE COMPANY

The Procter & Gamble Company (P&G) manufactures and markets a range of consumer products in various countries throughout the world. The company markets over 300 branded products in more than 160 countries. It manages its business in six product segments: Fabric and Home Care, Baby and Family Care, Beauty Care, Health Care, Snacks, and Pet Care and Grooming.

P&G

The content and organization of corporate annual reports have become fairly standardized. Excluding the public relations part of the report (pictures, products, etc.), the following are the traditional financial portions of the annual report:

- Letter to the Stockholders
- Financial Highlights
- Management's Discussion and Analysis
- Management Certification of Financial Statements
- Management's Report on Internal Control
- Auditor's Reports
- Financial Statements
- Notes to the Financial Statements
- Supplementary Financial Information (e.g., 10-year financial summary)

The following pages contain excerpts from the president's letter and the financial statements from P&G's 2011 annual report. **The complete P&G annual report can be accessed at the book's companion website, www.wiley.com/college/kieso.** You will see examples of the standard annual report elements by examining the P&G annual report.

We do not expect that you will comprehend P&G's financial statements and the accompanying notes in their entirety at your first reading. But we expect that by the time you complete the material in this textbook, your level of understanding and interpretive ability will have grown enormously.

At this point, we recommend that you go online and take 20 to 30 minutes to scan the annual report, especially the financial statements and notes. Your goal should be to familiarize yourself with the contents and accounting elements. Throughout the following 19 chapters, when you are asked to refer to specific parts of P&G's financial statements, do so! Then, when you have completed reading this textbook, we challenge you to reread P&G's financials to see how much greater and more sophisticated your understanding of them has become.

Letter to Shareholders

Dear Shareholders,

Last year, I described P&G's Purpose-inspired Growth Strategy, which is to touch and improve more consumers' lives in more parts of the world more completely. I told you that we intend to deliver total shareholder return that consistently ranks P&G among the top third of our peers—the best performing consumer products companies in the world. To do this, we must deliver the Company's long-term annual growth goals, which are to:

- **Grow organic sales 1% to 2% faster than market growth in the categories and countries where we compete.**
- **Deliver core earnings per share (core EPS) growth of high single to low double digits.**
- **Generate free cash flow productivity of 90% or greater.**

We made meaningful progress toward these long-term goals for fiscal 2011, despite significant external challenges.

- **Organic sales grew 4%. Organic volume grew 5%.**
- **Core earnings per share grew 8%.**
- **Free cash flow productivity was 84% of net earnings.**

We increased our quarterly dividend by 9%, making this the 121st consecutive year that P&G has paid a dividend and the 55th consecutive year that the dividend has increased.

Over the past 55 years, P&G's dividend has increased at an annual compound average rate of approximately 9.5%. In total, we paid approximately $5.8 billion in dividends in fiscal 2011. We also returned $7.0 billion to shareholders through the repurchase of P&G stock. Based on our current market capitalization, dividends and share repurchase, we provided shareholders with an effective cash yield of nearly 7%, with additional potential for capital appreciation.

This is good performance in a very demanding business and economic environment. It is not yet great performance. I am confident, however, that we will continue to grow our business on the strength of our Purpose-inspired Growth Strategy:

- **We are executing the strategy as planned, with unrelenting focus on innovation.**
- **We are increasing productivity, which frees up resources to invest in innovation.**
- **We continue to strengthen our portfolio of businesses.**
- **We are tackling growth challenges head on.**
- **We have solid, executable plans in place to capture the enormous growth potential that our strategy creates.**

Further, P&G people are inspired and are performing heroically to improve lives, to grow our business, and to create value for our shareholders.

Robert A. McDonald
Chairman of the Board, President and
Chief Executive Officer

Financials

Net Sales ($ billions)

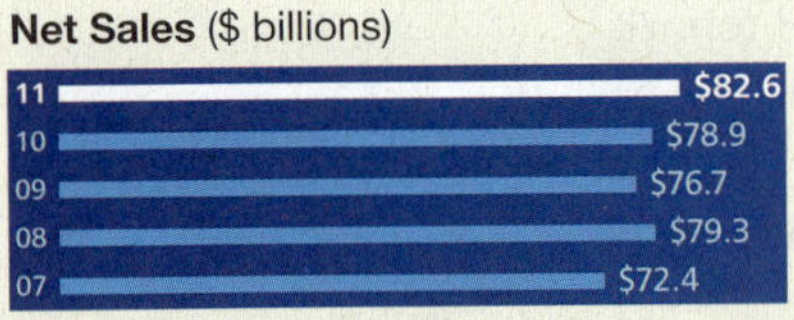

Operating Cash Flow ($ billions)

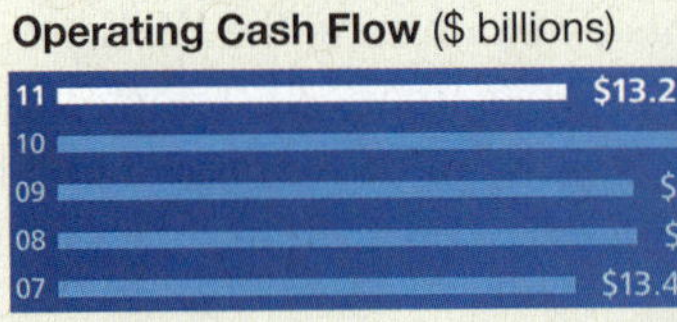

Diluted Net Earnings (per common share)

Financial Highlights (Unaudited)

Amounts in millions, except per share amounts	2011	2010	2009	2008	2007
Net Sales	$82,559	$78,938	$76,694	$79,257	$72,441
Operating Income	15,818	16,021	15,374	15,979	14,485
Net Earnings	11,797	12,736	13,436	12,075	10,340
Net Earnings Margin from Continuing Operations	14.3%	13.9%	13.9%	14.2%	13.3%
Diluted Net Earnings per Common Share from Continuing Operations	$ 3.93	$ 3.53	$ 3.39	$ 3.40	$ 2.84
Diluted Net Earnings per Common Share	3.93	4.11	4.26	3.64	3.04
Dividends per Common Share	1.97	1.80	1.64	1.45	1.28

Consolidated Statements of Earnings

Amounts in millions except per share amounts; Years ended June 30	2011	2010	2009
NET SALES	**$82,559**	$78,938	$76,694
Cost of products sold	**40,768**	37,919	38,690
Selling, general and administrative expense	**25,973**	24,998	22,630
OPERATING INCOME	**15,818**	16,021	15,374
Interest expense	**831**	946	1,358
Other non-operating income/(expense), net	**202**	(28)	397
EARNINGS FROM CONTINUING OPERATIONS BEFORE INCOME TAXES	**15,189**	15,047	14,413
Income taxes on continuing operations	**3,392**	4,101	3,733
NET EARNINGS FROM CONTINUING OPERATIONS	**11,797**	10,946	10,680
NET EARNINGS FROM DISCONTINUED OPERATIONS	**—**	1,790	2,756
NET EARNINGS	**$11,797**	$12,736	$13,436
BASIC NET EARNINGS PER COMMON SHARE:			
Earnings from continuing operations	**$ 4.12**	$ 3.70	$ 3.55
Earnings from discontinued operations	**—**	0.62	0.94
BASIC NET EARNINGS PER COMMON SHARE	**4.12**	4.32	4.49
DILUTED NET EARNINGS PER COMMON SHARE:			
Earnings from continuing operations	**3.93**	3.53	3.39
Earnings from discontinued operations	**—**	0.58	0.87
DILUTED NET EARNINGS PER COMMON SHARE	**3.93**	4.11	4.26
DIVIDENDS PER COMMON SHARE	**$ 1.97**	$ 1.80	$ 1.64

Consolidated Balance Sheets

Amounts in millions; June 30

Assets	2011	2010
CURRENT ASSETS		
Cash and cash equivalents	$ 2,768	$ 2,879
Accounts receivable	6,275	5,335
INVENTORIES		
Materials and supplies	2,153	1,692
Work in process	717	604
Finished goods	4,509	4,088
Total inventories	7,379	6,384
Deferred income taxes	1,140	990
Prepaid expenses and other current assets	4,408	3,194
TOTAL CURRENT ASSETS	21,970	18,782
PROPERTY, PLANT AND EQUIPMENT		
Buildings	7,753	6,868
Machinery and equipment	32,820	29,294
Land	934	850
Total property, plant and equipment	41,507	37,012
Accumulated depreciation	(20,214)	(17,768)
NET PROPERTY, PLANT AND EQUIPMENT	21,293	19,244
GOODWILL AND OTHER INTANGIBLE ASSETS		
Goodwill	57,562	54,012
Trademarks and other intangible assets, net	32,620	31,636
NET GOODWILL AND OTHER INTANGIBLE ASSETS	90,182	85,648
OTHER NONCURRENT ASSETS	4,909	4,498
TOTAL ASSETS	$138,354	$128,172

Liabilities and Shareholders' Equity	2011	2010
CURRENT LIABILITIES		
Accounts payable	$ 8,022	$ 7,251
Accrued and other liabilities	9,290	8,559
Debt due within one year	9,981	8,472
TOTAL CURRENT LIABILITIES	27,293	24,282
LONG-TERM DEBT	22,033	21,360
DEFERRED INCOME TAXES	11,070	10,902
OTHER NONCURRENT LIABILITIES	9,957	10,189
TOTAL LIABILITIES	70,353	66,733
SHAREHOLDERS' EQUITY		
Convertible Class A preferred stock, stated value $1 per share (600 shares authorized)	1,234	1,277
Non-Voting Class B preferred stock, stated value $1 per share (200 shares authorized)	—	—
Common stock, stated value $1 per share (10,000 shares authorized; shares issued: 2011—4,007.9, 2010—4,007.6)	4,008	4,008
Additional paid-in capital	62,405	61,697
Reserve for ESOP debt retirement	(1,357)	(1,350)
Accumulated other comprehensive income/(loss)	(2,054)	(7,822)
Treasury stock, at cost (shares held: 2011—1,242.2, 2010—1,164.1)	(67,278)	(61,309)
Retained earnings	70,682	64,614
Noncontrolling interest	361	324
TOTAL SHAREHOLDERS' EQUITY	68,001	61,439
TOTAL LIABILITIES AND SHAREHOLDERS' EQUITY	$138,354	$128,172

Consolidated Statements of Shareholders' Equity

Dollars in millions/Shares in thousands	Common Shares Outstanding	Common Stock	Preferred Stock	Additional Paid-In Capital	Reserve for ESOP Debt Retirement	Accumulated Other Comprehensive Income/(loss)	Non-controlling Interest	Treasury Stock	Retained Earnings	Total
BALANCE JUNE 30, 2008	3,032,717	$4,002	$1,366	$60,307	$(1,325)	$ 3,746	$290	$(47,588)	$48,986	$69,784
Net earnings									13,436	13,436
Other comprehensive income:										
Financial statement translation						(6,151)				(6,151)
Hedges and investment securities, net of $452 tax						748				748
Defined benefit retirement plans, net of $879 tax						(1,701)				(1,701)
Total comprehensive income										$ 6,332
Cumulative impact for adoption of new accounting guidance[(1)]									(84)	(84)
Dividends to shareholders:										
Common									(4,852)	(4,852)
Preferred, net of tax benefits									(192)	(192)
Treasury purchases	(98,862)							(6,370)		(6,370)
Employee plan issuances	16,841	5		804				428		1,237
Preferred stock conversions	4,992		(42)	7				35		—
Shares tendered for Folgers coffee subsidiary	(38,653)							(2,466)		(2,466)
ESOP debt impacts					(15)				15	—
Noncontrolling interest							(7)			(7)
BALANCE JUNE 30, 2009	2,917,035	4,007	1,324	61,118	(1,340)	(3,358)	283	(55,961)	57,309	63,382
Net earnings									12,736	12,736
Other comprehensive income:										
Financial statement translation						(4,194)				(4,194)
Hedges and investment securities, net of $520 tax						867				867
Defined benefit retirement plans, net of $465 tax						(1,137)				(1,137)
Total comprehensive income										$ 8,272
Dividends to shareholders:										
Common									(5,239)	(5,239)
Preferred, net of tax benefits									(219)	(219)
Treasury purchases	(96,759)							(6,004)		(6,004)
Employee plan issuances	17,616	1		574				616		1,191
Preferred stock conversions	5,579		(47)	7				40		—
ESOP debt impacts					(10)				27	17
Noncontrolling interest				(2)			41			39
BALANCE JUNE 30, 2010	2,843,471	4,008	1,277	61,697	(1,350)	(7,822)	324	(61,309)	64,614	61,439
Net earnings									**11,797**	**11,797**
Other comprehensive income:										
Financial statement translation						**6,493**				**6,493**
Hedges and investment securities, net of $711 tax						**(1,178)**				**(1,178)**
Defined benefit retirement plans, net of $302 tax						**453**				**453**
Total comprehensive income										**$17,565**
Dividends to shareholders:										
Common									**(5,534)**	**(5,534)**
Preferred, net of tax benefits									**(233)**	**(233)**
Treasury purchases	**(112,729)**							**(7,039)**		**(7,039)**
Employee plan issuances	**29,729**	**—**		**702**				**1,033**		**1,735**
Preferred stock conversions	**5,266**		**(43)**	**6**				**37**		**—**
ESOP debt impacts					**(7)**				**38**	**31**
Noncontrolling interest				**—**			**37**			**37**
BALANCE JUNE 30, 2011	**2,765,737**	**$4,008**	**$1,234**	**$62,405**	**$(1,357)**	**$(2,054)**	**$361**	**$(67,278)**	**$70,682**	**$68,001**

(1) Cumulative impact of adopting new accounting guidance relates to split-dollar life insurance arrangements.

Consolidated Statements of Cash Flows

Amounts in millions; Years ended June 30	2011	2010	2009
CASH AND CASH EQUIVALENTS, BEGINNING OF YEAR	$ 2,879	$ 4,781	$ 3,313
OPERATING ACTIVITIES			
Net earnings	11,797	12,736	13,436
Depreciation and amortization	2,838	3,108	3,082
Share-based compensation expense	414	453	516
Deferred income taxes	128	36	596
Gain on sale of businesses	(203)	(2,670)	(2,377)
Change in accounts receivable	(426)	(14)	415
Change in inventories	(501)	86	721
Change in accounts payable, accrued and other liabilities	358	2,446	(742)
Change in other operating assets and liabilities	(1,190)	(305)	(758)
Other	16	196	30
TOTAL OPERATING ACTIVITIES	13,231	16,072	14,919
INVESTING ACTIVITIES			
Capital expenditures	(3,306)	(3,067)	(3,238)
Proceeds from asset sales	225	3,068	1,087
Acquisitions, net of cash acquired	(474)	(425)	(368)
Change in investments	73	(173)	166
TOTAL INVESTING ACTIVITIES	(3,482)	(597)	(2,353)
FINANCING ACTIVITIES			
Dividends to shareholders	(5,767)	(5,458)	(5,044)
Change in short-term debt	151	(1,798)	(2,420)
Additions to long-term debt	1,536	3,830	4,926
Reductions of long-term debt	(206)	(8,546)	(2,587)
Treasury stock purchases	(7,039)	(6,004)	(6,370)
Impact of stock options and other	1,302	721	681
TOTAL FINANCING ACTIVITIES	(10,023)	(17,255)	(10,814)
EFFECT OF EXCHANGE RATE CHANGES ON CASH AND CASH EQUIVALENTS	163	(122)	(284)
CHANGE IN CASH AND CASH EQUIVALENTS	(111)	(1,902)	1,468
CASH AND CASH EQUIVALENTS, END OF YEAR	$ 2,768	$ 2,879	$ 4,781

SUPPLEMENTAL DISCLOSURE			
Cash payments for:			
Interest	$ 806	$ 1,184	$ 1,226
Income taxes	2,992	4,175	3,248
Assets acquired through non-cash capital leases	13	20	8
Divestiture of coffee business in exchange for shares of P&G stock	—	—	2,466

DEMONSTRATION PROBLEMS

Demonstration Problem 1: Assume that Sanchez Company has the following accounts at the end of the current year.

1. Common Stock.
2. Discount on Bonds Payable.
3. Treasury Stock (at cost).
4. Notes Payable (short-term).
5. Raw Materials.
6. Preferred Stock Investments (long-term).
7. Unearned Rent Revenue.
8. Work in Process.
9. Copyrights.
10. Buildings.
11. Notes Receivable (short-term).
12. Cash.
13. Salaries and Wages Payable.
14. Accumulated Depreciation—Buildings.
15. Accumulated Other Comprehensive Income.
16. Cash Restricted for Plant Expansion.
16. Land Held for Future Plant Site.
17. Noncontrolling Interest.
18. Allowance for Doubtful Accounts—Accounts Receivable.
19. Retained Earnings.
20. Paid-in Capital in Excess of Par—Common Stock.
21. Unearned Subscriptions Revenue.
22. Receivables—Officers (due in one year).
23. Finished Goods.
24. Accounts Receivable.
25. Bonds Payable (due in 4 years).

Instructions

Prepare a classified balance sheet in good form. (No monetary amounts are necessary.)

Solution to Demonstration Problem 1

SANCHEZ COMPANY
BALANCE SHEET
DECEMBER 31, 20XX

Assets			
Current assets			
Cash (less cash restricted for plant expansion)		$XXX	
Accounts receivable	$XXX		
Less: Allowance for doubtful accounts	XXX	XXX	
Notes receivable		XXX	
Receivables—officers		XXX	
Inventory			
Finished goods	XXX		
Work in process	XXX		
Raw materials	XXX	XXX	
Total current assets			$XXX
Long-term investments			
Preferred stock investments		XXX	
Land held for future plant site		XXX	
Cash restricted for plant expansion		XXX	
Total long-term investments			XXX
Property, plant, and equipment			
Buildings		XXX	
Less: Accumulated depreciation—buildings		XXX	XXX
Intangible assets			
Copyrights			XXX
Total assets			$XXX

Liabilities and Stockholders' Equity			
Current liabilities			
Salaries and wages payable		$XXX	
Notes payable (short-term)		XXX	
Unearned subscriptions revenue		XXX	
Unearned rent revenue		XXX	
Total current liabilities			$XXX
Long-term debt			
Bonds payable (due in four years)		XXX	
Discount on bonds payable		(XXX)	XXX
Total liabilities			XXX
Stockholders' equity			
Capital stock:			
Common stock	$XXX		
Additional paid-in capital:			
Paid in capital in excess of par—common stock	XXX		
Total paid-in capital		XXX	
Retained earnings		XXX	
Accumulated other comprehensive income		XXX	
Treasury stock (at cost)		(XXX)	
Total equity attributable to Sanchez shareholders			XXX
Equity attributable to noncontrolling interest			XXX
Total liabilities and stockholders' equity			$XXX

Demonstration Problem 2: Cassy Corporation's balance sheet at the end of 2013 included the following items.

Current assets	$282,000	Current liabilities	$180,000
Land	36,000	Bonds payable	120,000
Buildings	144,000	Common stock	216,000
Equipment	108,000	Retained earnings	52,800
Accumulated depreciation—buildings	(36,000)	Total	$568,800
Accumulated depreciation—equipment	(13,200)		
Patents	48,000		
Total	$568,800		

The following information is available for 2014.

1. Treasury stock was purchased at a cost of $13,200.
2. Cash dividends of $36,000 were declared and paid.
3. A long-term investment in stock was purchased for $19,200.
4. Current assets other than cash increased by $34,800. Current liabilities increased by $15,600.
5. Depreciation expense was $4,800 on the building and $10,800 on equipment.
6. Net income was $66,000.
7. Bonds payable of $60,000 were issued.
8. An addition to the building was completed at a cost of $32,400.
9. Patent amortization was $3,000.
10. Equipment (cost $24,000 and accumulated depreciation $9,600) was sold for $12,000.

Instructions

(a) Prepare a balance sheet at December 31, 2014.
(b) Prepare a statement of cash flows for 2014.

Solution to Demonstration Problem 2

(a)

CASSY CORPORATION
BALANCE SHEET
DECEMBER 31, 2014

Assets			
Current assets ($282,000 + $34,800 + $39,000)			$355,800
Long-term investments			19,200
Property, plant, and equipment			
Land		$ 36,000	
Buildings ($144,000 + $32,400)	$176,400		
Less: Accumulated depreciation—buildings ($36,000 + $4,800)	40,800	135,600	
Equipment ($108,000 − $24,000)	84,000		
Less: Accumulated depreciation—equipment ($13,200 − $9,600 + $10,800)	14,400	69,600	
Total			241,200
Intangible assets—patents ($48,000 − $3,000)			45,000
Total assets			$661,200

Liabilities and Stockholders' Equity	
Current liabilities ($180,000 + $15,600)	$195,600
Long-term liabilities	
Bonds payable ($120,000 + $60,000)	180,000
Total liabilities	375,600

Stockholders' equity		
Common stock	$216,000	
Retained earnings ($52,800 + $66,000 − $36,000)	82,800	
Total	298,800	
Less: Cost of treasury stock	(13,200)	
Total stockholders' equity		285,600
Total liabilities and stockholders' equity		$661,200

Notes: The amount determined for current assets is computed last and is a "plug" figure. That is, total liabilities and stockholders' equity is computed because information is available to determine this amount. Because the total assets amount is the same as the total liabilities and stockholders' equity amount, the amount of total assets is determined. Information is available to compute all the asset amounts except current assets. Therefore, current assets can be determined by deducting the total of all the other asset balances from the total asset balance (i.e., $661,200 − $45,000 − $241,200 − $19,200).

(b)

CASSY CORPORATION
STATEMENT OF CASH FLOWS
FOR THE YEAR ENDED DECEMBER 31, 2014

Cash flows from operating activities		
Net income		$66,000
Adjustments to reconcile net income to net cash provided by operating activities:		
Loss on sale of equipment	$ 2,400	
Depreciation expense	15,600	
Patent amortization	3,000	
Increase in current liabilities	15,600	
Increase in current assets (other than cash)	(34,800)	1,800
Net cash provided by operating activities		67,800
Cash flows from investing activities		
Sale of equipment	12,000	
Addition to building	(32,400)	
Investment in stock	(19,200)	
Net cash used by investing activities		(39,600)
Cash flows from financing activities		
Issuance of bonds	60,000	
Payment of dividends	(36,000)	
Purchase of treasury stock	(13,200)	
Net cash provided by financing activities		10,800
Net increase in cash		$39,000

FASB CODIFICATION

FASB Codification References

[1] FASB ASC 320-10-35-1. [Predecessor literature: "Accounting for Certain Investments in Debt and Equity Securities," *Statement of Financial Accounting Standards No. 115* (Norwalk, Conn.: FASB, 1993).]

[2] FASB ASC 825-10-25-1. [Predecessor literature: "The Fair Value Option for Financial Assets and Liabilities, Including an Amendment of FASB Statement No. 115," *Statement of Financial Accounting Standards No. 159* (Norwalk, Conn.: FASB, February 2007).]

[3] FASB ASC 470-10-05-6. [Predecessor literature: "Classification of Short-term Obligations Expected to Be Refinanced," *Statement of Financial Accounting Standards No. 6* (Stamford, Conn.: FASB, 1975).]

[4] FASB ASC 505-10-50. [Predecessor literature: "Disclosure of Information about Capital Structure," *Statement of Financial Accounting Standards No. 129* (Norwalk: FASB, 1997), par. 4).]

[5] FASB ASC 230-10-05. [Predecessor literature: "Statement of Cash Flows," *Statement of Financial Accounting Standards No. 95* (Stamford, Conn.: FASB, 1987).]

[6] FASB ASC 235-10-05. [Predecessor literature: "Disclosure of Accounting Policies," *Opinions of the Accounting Principles Board No. 22* (New York: AICPA, 1972).]

[7] FASB ASC 275-10-05. [Predecessor literature: "Disclosure of Certain Significant Risks and Uncertainties," *Statement of Position 94-6* (New York: AICPA, 1994).]

[8] FASB ASC 820-10-15. [Predecessor literature: "Fair Value Measurement," *Statement of Financial Accounting Standards No. 157* (Norwalk, Conn.: FASB, September 2006).]

Exercises

If your school has a subscription to the FASB Codification, go to *http://aaahq.org/asclogin.cfm* to log in and prepare responses to the following. Provide Codification references for your responses.

CE5-1 Access the Codification glossary ("Master Glossary") to answer the following.

(a) What is the definition provided for current assets?
(b) What is the definition of an intangible asset? In what section of the Codification are intangible assets addressed?
(c) What are cash equivalents?
(d) What are financing activities?

CE5-2 What guidance does the Codification provide on the classification of current liabilities?

CE5-3 What guidance does the Codification provide concerning the format of accounting disclosures?

CE5-4 What are the objectives related to the statement of cash flows?

An additional Codification case can be found in the Using Your Judgment section, on page 277.

Be sure to check the book's companion website for a Review and Analysis Exercise, with solution.

WileyPLUS **Brief Exercises, Exercises, Problems, and many more learning and assessment tools and resources are available for practice in WileyPLUS.**

QUESTIONS

1. How does information from the balance sheet help users of the financial statements?

2. What is meant by solvency? What information in the balance sheet can be used to assess a company's solvency?

3. A recent financial magazine indicated that the airline industry has poor financial flexibility. What is meant by financial flexibility, and why is it important?

4. Discuss at least two situations in which estimates could affect the usefulness of information in the balance sheet.

5. Perez Company reported an increase in inventories in the past year. Discuss the effect of this change on the current ratio (current assets ÷ current liabilities). What does this tell a statement user about Perez Company's liquidity?

6. What is meant by liquidity? Rank the following assets from one to five in order of liquidity.

(a) Goodwill.

(b) Inventory.

(c) Buildings.

(d) Short-term investments.

(e) Accounts receivable.

7. What are the major limitations of the balance sheet as a source of information?

8. Discuss at least two items that are important to the value of companies like **Intel** or **IBM** but that are not recorded in their balance sheets. What are some reasons why these items are not recorded in the balance sheet?

9. How does separating current assets from property, plant, and equipment in the balance sheet help analysts?

10. In its December 31, 2014, balance sheet Oakley Corporation reported as an asset, "Net notes and accounts receivable, $7,100,000." What other disclosures are necessary?

11. Should available-for-sale securities always be reported as a current asset? Explain.

12. What is the relationship between current assets and current liabilities?

13. The New York Knicks, Inc. sold 10,000 season tickets at $2,000 each. By December 31, 2014, 16 of the 40 home games had been played. What amount should be reported as a current liability at December 31, 2014?

14. What is working capital? How does working capital relate to the operating cycle?

15. In what section of the balance sheet should the following items appear, and what balance sheet terminology would you use?

(a) Treasury stock (recorded at cost).

(b) Checking account at bank.

(c) Land (held as an investment).

(d) Sinking fund.

(e) Unamortized premium on bonds payable.

(f) Copyrights.

(g) Pension fund assets.

(h) Premium on capital stock.

(i) Long-term investments (pledged against bank loans payable).

16. Where should the following items be shown on the balance sheet, if shown at all?

(a) Allowance for doubtful accounts.

(b) Merchandise held on consignment.

(c) Advances received on sales contract.

(d) Cash surrender value of life insurance.

(e) Land.

(f) Merchandise out on consignment.

(g) Franchises.

(h) Accumulated depreciation of equipment.

(i) Materials in transit—purchased f.o.b. destination.

17. State the generally accepted accounting principle applicable to balance sheet valuation of each of the following assets.

(a) Trade accounts receivable.

(b) Land.

(c) Inventories.

(d) Trading securities (common stock of other companies).

(e) Prepaid expenses.

18. Refer to the definition of assets on page 216. Discuss how a leased building might qualify as an asset of the lessee (tenant) under this definition.

19. Kathleen Battle says, "Retained earnings should be reported as an asset, since it is earnings which are reinvested in the business." How would you respond to Battle?

20. The creditors of Chester Company agree to accept promissory notes for the amount of its indebtedness with a proviso that two-thirds of the annual profits must be applied to their liquidation. How should these notes be reported on the balance sheet of the issuing company? Give a reason for your answer.

21. What is the purpose of a statement of cash flows? How does it differ from a balance sheet and an income statement?

22. The net income for the year for Genesis, Inc. is $750,000, but the statement of cash flows reports that the net cash provided by operating activities is $640,000. What might account for the difference?

23. Net income for the year for Carrie, Inc. was $750,000, but the statement of cash flows reports that net cash provided by operating activities was $860,000. What might account for the difference?

24. Differentiate between operating activities, investing activities, and financing activities.

25. Each of the following items must be considered in preparing a statement of cash flows. Indicate where each item is to be reported in the statement, if at all. Assume that net income is reported as $90,000.

(a) Accounts receivable increased from $34,000 to $39,000 from the beginning to the end of the year.

(b) During the year, 10,000 shares of preferred stock with a par value of $100 per share were issued at $115 per share.

(c) Depreciation expense amounted to $14,000, and bond premium amortization amounted to $5,000.

(d) Land increased from $10,000 to $30,000.

26. Sergey Co. has net cash provided by operating activities of $1,200,000. Its average current liabilities for the period are $1,000,000, and its average total liabilities are $1,500,000. Comment on the company's liquidity and financial flexibility, given this information.

27. Net income for the year for Tanizaki, Inc. was $750,000, but the statement of cash flows reports that net cash provided by operating activities was $860,000. Tanizaki also reported capital expenditures of $75,000 and paid dividends in the amount of $30,000. Compute Tanizaki's free cash flow.

28. What is the purpose of a free cash flow analysis?

29. What are some of the techniques of disclosure for the balance sheet?

30. What is a "Summary of Significant Accounting Policies"?

31. What types of contractual obligations must be disclosed in great detail in the notes to the balance sheet? Why do you think these detailed provisions should be disclosed?

32. What is the profession's recommendation in regard to the use of the term "surplus"? Explain.

BRIEF EXERCISES

3 **BE5-1** Harding Corporation has the following accounts included in its December 31, 2014, trial balance: Accounts Receivable $110,000; Inventory $290,000; Allowance for Doubtful Accounts $8,000; Patents $72,000; Prepaid Insurance $9,500; Accounts Payable $77,000; Cash $30,000. Prepare the current assets section of the balance sheet, listing the accounts in proper sequence.

3 **BE5-2** Koch Corporation's adjusted trial balance contained the following asset accounts at December 31, 2014: Cash $7,000; Land $40,000; Patents $12,500; Accounts Receivable $90,000; Prepaid Insurance $5,200; Inventory $30,000; Allowance for Doubtful Accounts $4,000; Equity Investments (trading) $11,000. Prepare the current assets section of the balance sheet, listing the accounts in proper sequence.

3 **BE5-3** Included in Outkast Company's December 31, 2014, trial balance are the following accounts: Prepaid Rent $5,200; Debt Investments (trading) $56,000; Unearned Fees $17,000; Land (held for investment) $39,000; Notes Receivable (long-term) $42,000. Prepare the long-term investments section of the balance sheet.

3 **BE5-4** Lowell Company's December 31, 2014, trial balance includes the following accounts: Inventory $120,000; Buildings $207,000; Accumulated Depreciation—Equipment $19,000; Equipment $190,000; Land (held for investment) $46,000; Accumulated Depreciation—Buildings $45,000; Land $71,000; Timberland $70,000. Prepare the property, plant, and equipment section of the balance sheet.

3 **BE5-5** Crane Corporation has the following accounts included in its December 31, 2014, trial balance: Equity Investments (trading) $21,000; Goodwill $150,000; Prepaid Insurance $12,000; Patents $220,000; Franchises $130,000. Prepare the intangible assets section of the balance sheet.

3 **BE5-6** Patrick Corporation's adjusted trial balance contained the following asset accounts at December 31, 2014: Prepaid Rent $12,000; Goodwill $50,000; Franchise Fees Receivable $2,000; Franchises $47,000; Patents $33,000; Trademarks $10,000. Prepare the intangible assets section of the balance sheet.

3 **BE5-7** Thomas Corporation's adjusted trial balance contained the following liability accounts at December 31, 2014: Bonds Payable (due in 3 years) $100,000; Accounts Payable $72,000; Notes Payable (due in 90 days) $22,500; Salaries and Wages Payable $4,000; Income Taxes Payable $7,000. Prepare the current liabilities section of the balance sheet.

3 **BE5-8** Included in Adams Company's December 31, 2014, trial balance are the following accounts: Accounts Payable $220,000; Pension Liability $375,000; Discount on Bonds Payable $29,000; Unearned Rent Revenue $41,000; Bonds Payable $400,000; Salaries and Wages Payable $27,000; Interest Payable $12,000; Income Taxes Payable $29,000. Prepare the current liabilities section of the balance sheet.

3 **BE5-9** Use the information presented in BE5-8 for Adams Company to prepare the long-term liabilities section of the balance sheet.

3 **BE5-10** Hawthorn Corporation's adjusted trial balance contained the following accounts at December 31, 2014: Retained Earnings $120,000; Common Stock $750,000; Bonds Payable $100,000; Paid-in Capital in Excess of Par—Common Stock $200,000; Goodwill $55,000; Accumulated Other Comprehensive Loss $150,000; Noncontrolling Interest $35,000. Prepare the stockholders' equity section of the balance sheet.

3 **BE5-11** Stowe Company's December 31, 2014, trial balance includes the following accounts: Investment in Common Stock $70,000; Retained Earnings $114,000; Trademarks $31,000; Preferred Stock $152,000; Common Stock $55,000; Deferred Income Taxes $88,000; Paid-in Capital in Excess of Par—Common Stock $174,000; Noncontrolling Interest $63,000. Prepare the stockholders' equity section of the balance sheet.

6 **BE5-12** Keyser Beverage Company reported the following items in the most recent year.

Net income	$40,000
Dividends paid	5,000
Increase in accounts receivable	10,000
Increase in accounts payable	7,000
Purchase of equipment (capital expenditure)	8,000
Depreciation expense	4,000
Issue of notes payable	20,000

Compute net cash provided by operating activities, the net change in cash during the year, and free cash flow.

6 **BE5-13** Ames Company reported 2014 net income of $151,000. During 2014, accounts receivable increased by $13,000 and accounts payable increased by $9,500. Depreciation expense was $44,000. Prepare the cash flows from operating activities section of the statement of cash flows.

6 **BE5-14** Martinez Corporation engaged in the following cash transactions during 2014.

Sale of land and building	$191,000
Purchase of treasury stock	40,000
Purchase of land	37,000
Payment of cash dividend	95,000
Purchase of equipment	53,000
Issuance of common stock	147,000
Retirement of bonds	100,000

Compute the net cash provided (used) by investing activities.

6 **BE5-15** Use the information presented in BE5-14 for Martinez Corporation to compute the net cash used (provided) by financing activities.

7 **BE5-16** Using the information in BE5-14, determine Martinez's free cash flow, assuming that it reported net cash provided by operating activities of $400,000.

EXERCISES

2 3 **E5-1 (Balance Sheet Classifications)** Presented below are a number of balance sheet accounts of Deep Blue Something, Inc.

(a) Investment in Preferred Stock.
(b) Treasury Stock.
(c) Common Stock.
(d) Dividends Payable.
(e) Accumulated Depreciation—Equipment.
(f) Construction in Process.
(g) Petty Cash.
(h) Interest Payable.
(i) Deficit.
(j) Equity Investments (trading).
(k) Income Taxes Payable.
(l) Unearned Subscriptions Revenue.
(m) Work in Process.
(n) Salaries and Wages Payable.

Instructions

For each of the accounts above, indicate the proper balance sheet classification. In the case of borderline items, indicate the additional information that would be required to determine the proper classification.

2 3 **E5-2 (Classification of Balance Sheet Accounts)** Presented below are the captions of Faulk Company's balance sheet.

(a) Current assets.
(b) Investments.
(c) Property, plant, and equipment.
(d) Intangible assets.
(e) Other assets.
(f) Current liabilities.
(g) Noncurrent liabilities.
(h) Capital stock.
(i) Additional paid-in capital.
(j) Retained earnings.

Instructions

Indicate by letter where each of the following items would be classified.

1. Preferred stock.
2. Goodwill.
3. Salaries and wages payable.
4. Accounts payable.
5. Buildings.
6. Equity investments (trading).
7. Current maturity of long-term debt.
8. Premium on bonds payable.
9. Allowance for doubtful accounts.
10. Accounts receivable.
11. Cash surrender value of life insurance.
12. Notes payable (due next year).
13. Supplies.
14. Common stock.
15. Land.
16. Bond sinking fund.
17. Inventory.
18. Prepaid insurance.
19. Bonds payable.
20. Income taxes payable.

2 3 **E5-3 (Classification of Balance Sheet Accounts)** Assume that Fielder Enterprises uses the following headings on its balance sheet.

(a) Current assets.
(b) Investments.
(c) Property, plant, and equipment.
(d) Intangible assets.
(e) Other assets.
(f) Current liabilities.
(g) Long-term liabilities.
(h) Capital stock.
(i) Paid-in capital in excess of par.
(j) Retained earnings.

Instructions

Indicate by letter how each of the following usually should be classified. If an item should appear in a note to the financial statements, use the letter "N" to indicate this fact. If an item need not be reported at all on the balance sheet, use the letter "X."

1. Prepaid insurance.
2. Stock owned in affiliated companies.
3. Unearned service revenue.
4. Advances to suppliers.
5. Unearned rent revenue.
6. Preferred stock.
7. Additional paid-in capital on preferred stock.
8. Copyrights.
9. Petty cash fund.
10. Sales taxes payable.
11. Accrued interest on notes receivable.
12. Twenty-year issue of bonds payable that will mature within the next year. (No sinking fund exists, and refunding is not planned.)
13. Machinery retired from use and held for sale.
14. Fully depreciated machine still in use.
15. Accrued interest on bonds payable.
16. Salaries that company budget shows will be paid to employees within the next year.
17. Discount on bonds payable. (Assume related to bonds payable in item 12.)
18. Accumulated depreciation—buildings.
19. Noncontrolling interest.

2 3 **E5-4 (Preparation of a Classified Balance Sheet)** Assume that Denis Savard Inc. has the following accounts at the end of the current year.

1. Common Stock.
2. Discount on Bonds Payable.
3. Treasury Stock (at cost).
4. Notes Payable (short-term).
5. Raw Materials.
6. Preferred Stock Investments (long-term).
7. Unearned Rent Revenue.
8. Work in Process.
9. Copyrights.
10. Buildings.
11. Notes Receivable (short-term).
12. Cash.
13. Salaries and Wages Payable.
14. Accumulated Depreciation—Buildings.
15. Restricted Cash for Plant Expansion.
16. Land Held for Future Plant Site.
17. Allowance for Doubtful Accounts.
18. Retained Earnings.
19. Paid-in Capital in Excess of Par—Common Stock.
20. Unearned Subscriptions Revenue.
21. Receivables—Officers (due in one year).
22. Inventory (finished goods).
23. Accounts Receivable.
24. Bonds Payable (due in 4 years).
25. Noncontrolling Interest.

Instructions

Prepare a classified balance sheet in good form. (No monetary amounts are necessary.)

3 **E5-5 (Preparation of a Corrected Balance Sheet)** Uhura Company has decided to expand its operations. The bookkeeper recently completed the balance sheet presented below in order to obtain additional funds for expansion.

UHURA COMPANY
BALANCE SHEET
FOR THE YEAR ENDED 2014

Current assets	
Cash	$230,000
Accounts receivable (net)	340,000
Inventory (lower-of-average-cost-or-market)	401,000
Equity investments (trading)—at cost (fair value $120,000)	140,000
Property, plant, and equipment	
Buildings (net)	570,000
Equipment (net)	160,000
Land held for future use	175,000

Intangible assets	
Goodwill	80,000
Cash surrender value of life insurance	90,000
Prepaid expenses	12,000
Current liabilities	
Accounts payable	135,000
Notes payable (due next year)	125,000
Pension obligation	82,000
Rent payable	49,000
Premium on bonds payable	53,000
Long-term liabilities	
Bonds payable	500,000
Stockholders' equity	
Common stock, \$1.00 par, authorized 400,000 shares, issued 290,000	290,000
Additional paid-in capital	160,000
Retained earnings	?

Instructions

Prepare a revised balance sheet given the available information. Assume that the accumulated depreciation balance for the buildings is \$160,000 and for the equipment, \$105,000. The allowance for doubtful accounts has a balance of \$17,000. The pension obligation is considered a long-term liability.

2 3 **E5-6 (Corrections of a Balance Sheet)** The bookkeeper for Geronimo Company has prepared the following balance sheet as of July 31, 2014.

GERONIMO COMPANY
BALANCE SHEET
AS OF JULY 31, 2014

Cash	\$ 69,000	Notes and accounts payable	\$ 44,000
Accounts receivable (net)	40,500	Long-term liabilities	75,000
Inventory	60,000	Stockholders' equity	155,500
Equipment (net)	84,000		\$274,500
Patents	21,000		
	\$274,500		

The following additional information is provided.

1. Cash includes \$1,200 in a petty cash fund and \$15,000 in a bond sinking fund.
2. The net accounts receivable balance is comprised of the following two items: (a) accounts receivable \$44,000 and (b) allowance for doubtful accounts \$3,500.
3. Inventory costing \$5,300 was shipped out on consignment on July 31, 2014. The ending inventory balance does not include the consigned goods. Receivables in the amount of \$5,300 were recognized on these consigned goods.
4. Equipment had a cost of \$112,000 and an accumulated depreciation balance of \$28,000.
5. Income taxes payable of \$6,000 were accrued on July 31. Geronimo Company, however, had set up a cash fund to meet this obligation. This cash fund was not included in the cash balance but was offset against the income taxes payable amount.

Instructions

Prepare a corrected classified balance sheet as of July 31, 2014, from the available information, adjusting the account balances using the additional information.

3 **E5-7 (Current Assets Section of the Balance Sheet)** Presented below are selected accounts of Yasunari Kawabata Company at December 31, 2014.

Inventory (finished goods)	\$ 52,000	Cost of Goods Sold	\$2,100,000
Unearned Service Revenue	90,000	Notes Receivable	40,000
Equipment	253,000	Accounts Receivable	161,000
Inventory (work in process)	34,000	Inventory (raw materials)	207,000
Cash	37,000	Supplies Expense	60,000
Equity Investments (short-term)	31,000	Allowance for Doubtful Accounts	12,000
Customer Advances	36,000	Licenses	18,000
Restricted Cash for Plant Expansion	50,000	Additional Paid-in Capital	88,000
		Treasury Stock	22,000

The following additional information is available.

1. Inventories are valued at lower-of-cost-or-market using LIFO.
2. Equipment is recorded at cost. Accumulated depreciation, computed on a straight-line basis, is $50,600.
3. The short-term investments have a fair value of $29,000. (Assume they are trading securities.)
4. The notes receivable are due April 30, 2016, with interest receivable every April 30. The notes bear interest at 6%. (*Hint:* Accrued interest due on December 31, 2014.)
5. The allowance for doubtful accounts applies to the accounts receivable. Accounts receivable of $50,000 are pledged as collateral on a bank loan.
6. Licenses are recorded net of accumulated amortization of $14,000.
7. Treasury stock is recorded at cost.

Instructions

Prepare the current assets section of Yasunari Kawabata Company's December 31, 2014, balance sheet, with appropriate disclosures.

2 **E5-8 (Current vs. Long-term Liabilities)** Frederic Chopin Corporation is preparing its December 31, 2014, balance sheet. The following items may be reported as either a current or long-term liability.

1. On December 15, 2014, Chopin declared a cash dividend of $2.50 per share to stockholders of record on December 31. The dividend is payable on January 15, 2015. Chopin has issued 1,000,000 shares of common stock, of which 50,000 shares are held in treasury.
2. At December 31, bonds payable of $100,000,000 are outstanding. The bonds pay 12% interest every September 30 and mature in installments of $25,000,000 every September 30, beginning September 30, 2015.
3. At December 31, 2013, customer advances were $12,000,000. During 2014, Chopin collected $30,000,000 of customer advances; advances of $25,000,000 should be recognized in income.

Instructions

For each item above, indicate the dollar amounts to be reported as a current liability and as a long-term liability, if any.

2 3 **E5-9 (Current Assets and Current Liabilities)** The current assets and current liabilities sections of the balance sheet of Allessandro Scarlatti Company appear as follows.

ALLESSANDRO SCARLATTI COMPANY
BALANCE SHEET (PARTIAL)
DECEMBER 31, 2014

Cash		$ 40,000	Accounts payable	$ 61,000
Accounts receivable	$89,000		Notes payable	67,000
Less: Allowance for doubtful accounts	7,000	82,000		$128,000
Inventory		171,000		
Prepaid expenses		9,000		
		$302,000		

The following errors in the corporation's accounting have been discovered:

1. January 2015 cash disbursements entered as of December 2014 included payments of accounts payable in the amount of $39,000, on which a cash discount of 2% was taken.
2. The inventory included $27,000 of merchandise that had been received at December 31 but for which no purchase invoices had been received or entered. Of this amount, $12,000 had been received on consignment; the remainder was purchased f.o.b. destination, terms 2/10, n/30.
3. Sales for the first four days in January 2015 in the amount of $30,000 were entered in the sales journal as of December 31, 2014. Of these, $21,500 were sales on account and the remainder were cash sales.

4. Cash, not including cash sales, collected in January 2015 and entered as of December 31, 2014, totaled $35,324. Of this amount, $23,324 was received on account after cash discounts of 2% had been deducted; the remainder represented the proceeds of a bank loan.

Instructions

(a) Restate the current assets and current liabilities sections of the balance sheet in accordance with good accounting practice. (Assume that both accounts receivable and accounts payable are recorded gross.)

(b) State the net effect of your adjustments on Allessandro Scarlatti Company's retained earnings balance.

2 3 **E5-10 (Current Liabilities)** Norma Smith is the controller of Baylor Corporation and is responsible for the preparation of the year-end financial statements. The following transactions occurred during the year.

(a) On December 20, 2014, a former employee filed a legal action against Baylor for $100,000 for wrongful dismissal. Management believes the action to be frivolous and without merit. The likelihood of payment to the employee is remote.

(b) Bonuses to key employees based on net income for 2014 are estimated to be $150,000.

(c) On December 1, 2014, the company borrowed $600,000 at 8% per year. Interest is paid quarterly.

(d) Credit sales for the year amounted to $10,000,000. Baylor's expense provision for doubtful accounts is estimated to be 3% of credit sales.

(e) On December 15, 2014, the company declared a $2.00 per share dividend on the 40,000 shares of common stock outstanding, to be paid on January 5, 2015.

(f) During the year, customer advances of $160,000 were received; $50,000 of this amount was earned by December 31, 2014.

Instructions

For each item above, indicate the dollar amount to be reported as a current liability. If a liability is not reported, explain why.

3 **E5-11 (Balance Sheet Preparation)** Presented below is the adjusted trial balance of Kelly Corporation at December 31, 2014.

XLS

	Debit	Credit
Cash	$?	
Supplies	1,200	
Prepaid Insurance	1,000	
Equipment	48,000	
Accumulated Depreciation—Equipment		$ 4,000
Trademarks	950	
Accounts Payable		10,000
Salaries and Wages Payable		500
Unearned Service Revenue		2,000
Bonds Payable (due 2021)		9,000
Common Stock		10,000
Retained Earnings		25,000
Service Revenue		10,000
Salaries and Wages Expense	9,000	
Insurance Expense	1,400	
Rent Expense	1,200	
Interest Expense	900	
Total	$?	$?

Additional information:

1. Net loss for the year was $2,500.
2. No dividends were declared during 2014.

Instructions

Prepare a classified balance sheet as of December 31, 2014.

3 **E5-12 (Preparation of a Balance Sheet)** Presented below is the trial balance of Scott Butler Corporation at December 31, 2014.

	Debit	Credit
Cash	$ 197,000	
Sales Revenue		$ 8,100,000
Debt Investments (trading) (at cost, $145,000)	153,000	
Cost of Goods Sold	4,800,000	
Debt Investments (long-term)	299,000	
Equity Investments (long-term)	277,000	
Notes Payable (short-term)		90,000
Accounts Payable		455,000
Selling Expenses	2,000,000	
Investment Revenue		63,000
Land	260,000	
Buildings	1,040,000	
Dividends Payable		136,000
Accrued Liabilities		96,000
Accounts Receivable	435,000	
Accumulated Depreciation—Buildings		152,000
Allowance for Doubtful Accounts		25,000
Administrative Expenses	900,000	
Interest Expense	211,000	
Inventory	597,000	
Gain (extraordinary)		80,000
Notes Payable (long-term)		900,000
Equipment	600,000	
Bonds Payable		1,000,000
Accumulated Depreciation—Equipment		60,000
Franchises	160,000	
Common Stock ($5 par)		1,000,000
Treasury Stock	191,000	
Patents	195,000	
Retained Earnings		78,000
Paid-in Capital in Excess of Par		80,000
Totals	$12,315,000	$12,315,000

Instructions

Prepare a balance sheet at December 31, 2014, for Scott Butler Corporation. (Ignore income taxes.)

5 **E5-13 (Statement of Cash Flows—Classifications)** The major classifications of activities reported in the statement of cash flows are operating, investing, and financing. Classify each of the transactions listed below as:

1. Operating activity—add to net income.
2. Operating activity—deduct from net income.
3. Investing activity.
4. Financing activity.
5. Reported as significant noncash activity.

The transactions are as follows.

(a) Issuance of common stock.
(b) Purchase of land and building.
(c) Redemption of bonds.
(d) Sale of equipment.
(e) Depreciation of machinery.
(f) Amortization of patent.
(g) Issuance of bonds for plant assets.
(h) Payment of cash dividends.
(i) Exchange of furniture for office equipment.
(j) Purchase of treasury stock.
(k) Loss on sale of equipment.
(l) Increase in accounts receivable during the year.
(m) Decrease in accounts payable during the year.

6 **E5-14 (Preparation of a Statement of Cash Flows)** The comparative balance sheets of Constantine Cavamanlis Inc. at the beginning and the end of the year 2014 are as follows.

CONSTANTINE CAVAMANLIS INC.
BALANCE SHEETS

Assets	Dec. 31, 2014	Jan. 1, 2014	Inc./Dec.
Cash	$ 45,000	$ 13,000	$32,000 Inc.
Accounts receivable	91,000	88,000	3,000 Inc.
Equipment	39,000	22,000	17,000 Inc.
Less: Accumulated depreciation—equipment	17,000	11,000	6,000 Inc.
Total	$158,000	$112,000	
Liabilities and Stockholders' Equity			
Accounts payable	$ 20,000	$ 15,000	5,000 Inc.
Common stock	100,000	80,000	20,000 Inc.
Retained earnings	38,000	17,000	21,000 Inc.
Total	$158,000	$112,000	

Net income of $44,000 was reported, and dividends of $23,000 were paid in 2014. New equipment was purchased and none was sold.

Instructions

Prepare a statement of cash flows for the year 2014.

6 7 **E5-15 (Preparation of a Statement of Cash Flows)** Presented below is a condensed version of the comparative balance sheets for Zubin Mehta Corporation for the last two years at December 31.

	2014	2013
Cash	$177,000	$ 78,000
Accounts receivable	180,000	185,000
Investments	52,000	74,000
Equipment	298,000	240,000
Accumulated depreciation—equipment	(106,000)	(89,000)
Current liabilities	134,000	151,000
Common stock	160,000	160,000
Retained earnings	307,000	177,000

Additional information:

Investments were sold at a loss (not extraordinary) of $10,000; no equipment was sold; cash dividends paid were $30,000; and net income was $160,000.

Instructions

(a) Prepare a statement of cash flows for 2014 for Zubin Mehta Corporation.
(b) Determine Zubin Mehta Corporation's free cash flow.

6 7 **E5-16 (Preparation of a Statement of Cash Flows)** A comparative balance sheet for Shabbona Corporation is presented below.

	December 31	
Assets	2014	2013
Cash	$ 73,000	$ 22,000
Accounts receivable	82,000	66,000
Inventory	180,000	189,000
Land	71,000	110,000
Equipment	260,000	200,000
Accumulated depreciation—equipment	(69,000)	(42,000)
Total	$597,000	$545,000
Liabilities and Stockholders' Equity		
Accounts payable	$ 34,000	$ 47,000
Bonds payable	150,000	200,000
Common stock ($1 par)	214,000	164,000
Retained earnings	199,000	134,000
Total	$597,000	$545,000

Additional information:

1. Net income for 2014 was $125,000. No gains or losses were recorded in 2014.
2. Cash dividends of $60,000 were declared and paid.
3. Bonds payable amounting to $50,000 were retired through issuance of common stock.

Instructions

(a) Prepare a statement of cash flows for 2014 for Shabbona Corporation.

(b) Determine Shabbona Corporation's current cash debt coverage, cash debt coverage, and free cash flow. Comment on its liquidity and financial flexibility.

3 6 **E5-17 (Preparation of a Statement of Cash Flows and a Balance Sheet)** Grant Wood Corporation's balance sheet at the end of 2013 included the following items.

Current assets	$235,000	Current liabilities	$150,000
Land	30,000	Bonds payable	100,000
Buildings	120,000	Common stock	180,000
Equipment	90,000	Retained earnings	44,000
Accum. depr.—buildings	(30,000)	Total	$474,000
Accum. depr.—equipment	(11,000)		
Patents	40,000		
Total	$474,000		

The following information is available for 2014.

1. Net income was $55,000.
2. Equipment (cost $20,000 and accumulated depreciation $8,000) was sold for $10,000.
3. Depreciation expense was $4,000 on the building and $9,000 on equipment.
4. Patent amortization was $2,500.
5. Current assets other than cash increased by $29,000. Current liabilities increased by $13,000.
6. An addition to the building was completed at a cost of $27,000.
7. A long-term investment in stock was purchased for $16,000.
8. Bonds payable of $50,000 were issued.
9. Cash dividends of $30,000 were declared and paid.
10. Treasury stock was purchased at a cost of $11,000.

Instructions

(Show only totals for current assets and current liabilities.)

(a) Prepare a statement of cash flows for 2014.

(b) Prepare a balance sheet at December 31, 2014.

6 7 **E5-18 (Preparation of a Statement of Cash Flows, Analysis)** The comparative balance sheets of Madrasah Corporation at the beginning and end of the year 2014 appear below.

MADRASAH CORPORATION
BALANCE SHEETS

Assets	Dec. 31, 2014	Jan. 1, 2014	Inc./Dec.
Cash	$ 20,000	$ 13,000	$ 7,000 Inc.
Accounts receivable	106,000	88,000	18,000 Inc.
Equipment	39,000	22,000	17,000 Inc.
Less: Accumulated depreciation—equipment	17,000	11,000	6,000 Inc.
Total	$148,000	$112,000	
Liabilities and Stockholders' Equity			
Accounts payable	$ 20,000	$ 15,000	5,000 Inc.
Common stock	100,000	80,000	20,000 Inc.
Retained earnings	28,000	17,000	11,000 Inc.
Total	$148,000	$112,000	

Net income of $44,000 was reported, and dividends of $33,000 were paid in 2014. New equipment was purchased and none was sold.

Instructions

(a) Prepare a statement of cash flows for the year 2014.

(b) Compute the current ratio (current assets ÷ current liabilities) as of January 1, 2014, and December 31, 2014, and compute free cash flow for the year 2014.

(c) In light of the analysis in (b), comment on Madrasah's liquidity and financial flexibility.

EXERCISES SET B

See the book's companion website, at **www.wiley.com/college/kieso**, for an additional set of exercises.

PROBLEMS

3 **P5-1 (Preparation of a Classified Balance Sheet, Periodic Inventory)** Presented below is a list of accounts in alphabetical order.

Accounts Receivable
Accumulated Depreciation—Buildings
Accumulated Depreciation—Equipment
Accumulated Other Comprehensive Income
Advances to Employees
Advertising Expense
Allowance for Doubtful Accounts
Bond Sinking Fund
Bonds Payable
Buildings
Cash (in bank)
Cash (on hand)
Cash Surrender Value of Life Insurance
Commission Expense
Common Stock
Copyrights
Debt Investments (trading)
Dividends Payable
Equipment
Freight-In
Gain on Disposal of Equipment
Interest Receivable
Inventory—Beginning
Inventory—Ending
Land
Land for Future Plant Site
Loss from Flood
Noncontrolling Interest
Notes Payable (due next year)
Paid-in Capital in Excess of Par—Preferred Stock
Patents
Payroll Taxes Payable
Pension Liability
Petty Cash
Preferred Stock
Premium on Bonds Payable
Prepaid Rent
Purchase Returns and Allowances
Purchases
Retained Earnings
Salaries and Wages Expense (sales)
Salaries and Wages Payable
Sales Discounts
Sales Revenue
Treasury Stock (at cost)
Unearned Subscriptions Revenue

Instructions

Prepare a classified balance sheet in good form. (No monetary amounts are to be shown.)

3 **P5-2 (Balance Sheet Preparation)** Presented below are a number of balance sheet items for Montoya, Inc., for the current year, 2014.

XLS

Goodwill	$ 125,000	Accumulated depreciation—equipment	$ 292,000
Payroll taxes payable	177,591	Inventory	239,800
Bonds payable	300,000	Rent payable (short-term)	45,000
Discount on bonds payable	15,000	Income taxes payable	98,362
Cash	360,000	Rent payable (long-term)	480,000
Land	480,000	Common stock, $1 par value	200,000
Notes receivable	445,700	Preferred stock, $10 par value	150,000
Notes payable (to banks)	265,000	Prepaid expenses	87,920
Accounts payable	490,000	Equipment	1,470,000
Retained earnings	?	Equity investments (trading)	121,000
Income taxes receivable	97,630	Accumulated depreciation—buildings	270,200
Notes payable (long-term)	1,600,000	Buildings	1,640,000

Instructions

Prepare a classified balance sheet in good form. Common stock authorized was 400,000 shares, and preferred stock authorized was 20,000 shares. Assume that notes receivable and notes payable are short-term, unless stated otherwise. Cost and fair value of equity investments (trading) are the same.

3 **P5-3 (Balance Sheet Adjustment and Preparation)** The adjusted trial balance of Eastwood Company and other related information for the year 2014 are presented as follows.

EASTWOOD COMPANY
ADJUSTED TRIAL BALANCE
DECEMBER 31, 2014

	Debit	Credit
Cash	$ 41,000	
Accounts Receivable	163,500	
Allowance for Doubtful Accounts		$ 8,700
Prepaid Insurance	5,900	
Inventory	208,500	
Equity Investments (long-term)	339,000	
Land	85,000	
Construction in Process (building)	124,000	
Patents	36,000	
Equipment	400,000	
Accumulated Depreciation—Equipment		240,000
Discount on Bonds Payable	20,000	
Accounts Payable		148,000
Accrued Liabilities		49,200
Notes Payable		94,000
Bonds Payable		200,000
Common Stock		500,000
Paid-in Capital in Excess of Par—Common Stock		45,000
Retained Earnings		138,000
	$1,422,900	$1,422,900

Additional information:

1. The LIFO method of inventory value is used.
2. The cost and fair value of the long-term investments that consist of stocks and bonds is the same.
3. The amount of the Construction in Progress account represents the costs expended to date on a building in the process of construction. (The company rents factory space at the present time.) The land on which the building is being constructed cost $85,000, as shown in the trial balance.
4. The patents were purchased by the company at a cost of $40,000 and are being amortized on a straight-line basis.
5. Of the discount on bonds payable, $2,000 will be amortized in 2015.
6. The notes payable represent bank loans that are secured by long-term investments carried at $120,000. These bank loans are due in 2015.
7. The bonds payable bear interest at 8% payable every December 31, and are due January 1, 2025.
8. 600,000 shares of common stock of a par value of $1 were authorized, of which 500,000 shares were issued and outstanding.

Instructions

Prepare a balance sheet as of December 31, 2014, so that all important information is fully disclosed.

3 **P5-4 (Preparation of a Corrected Balance Sheet)** The balance sheet of Kishwaukee Corporation as of December 31, 2014, is as follows.

KISHWAUKEE CORPORATION
BALANCE SHEET
DECEMBER 31, 2014

Assets	
Goodwill (Note 2)	$ 120,000
Buildings (Note 1)	1,640,000
Inventory	312,100
Land	950,000
Accounts receivable	170,000
Treasury stock (50,000 shares)	87,000
Cash on hand	175,900
Assets allocated to trustee for plant expansion	
Cash in bank	70,000
Debt investments (held-to-maturity)	138,000
	$3,663,000

Equities	
Notes payable (Note 3)	$ 600,000
Common stock, authorized and issued, 1,000,000 shares, no par	1,150,000
Retained earnings	803,000
Noncontrolling interest	55,000
Appreciation capital (Note 1)	570,000
Income tax payable	75,000
Reserve for depreciation recorded to date on the building	410,000
	$3,663,000

Note 1: Buildings are stated at cost, except for one building that was recorded at appraised value. The excess of appraisal value over cost was $570,000. Depreciation has been recorded based on cost.

Note 2: Goodwill in the amount of $120,000 was recognized because the company believed that book value was not an accurate representation of the fair value of the company. The gain of $120,000 was credited to Retained Earnings.

Note 3: Notes payable are long-term except for the current installment due of $100,000.

Instructions

Prepare a corrected classified balance sheet in good form. The notes above are for information only.

3 **P5-5 (Balance Sheet Adjustment and Preparation)** Presented below is the balance sheet of Sargent Corporation for the current year, 2014.

SARGENT CORPORATION
BALANCE SHEET
DECEMBER 31, 2014

Current assets	$ 485,000	Current liabilities	$ 380,000
Investments	640,000	Long-term liabilities	1,000,000
Property, plant, and equipment	1,720,000	Stockholders' equity	1,770,000
Intangible assets	305,000		$3,150,000
	$3,150,000		

The following information is presented.

1. The current assets section includes cash $150,000, accounts receivable $170,000 less $10,000 for allowance for doubtful accounts, inventories $180,000, and unearned rent revenue $5,000. Inventoy is stated on the lower-of-FIFO-cost-or-market.
2. The investments section includes the cash surrender value of a life insurance contract $40,000; investments in common stock, short-term (trading) $80,000 and long-term (available-for-sale) $270,000; and bond sinking fund $250,000. The cost and fair value of investments in common stock are the same.
3. Property, plant, and equipment includes buildings $1,040,000 less accumulated depreciation $360,000; equipment $450,000 less accumulated depreciation $180,000; land $500,000; and land held for future use $270,000.
4. Intangible assets include a franchise $165,000; goodwill $100,000; and discount on bonds payable $40,000.
5. Current liabilities include accounts payable $140,000; notes payable—short-term $80,000 and long-term $120,000; and income taxes payable $40,000.
6. Long-term liabilities are composed solely of 7% bonds payable due 2022.
7. Stockholders' equity has preferred stock, no par value, authorized 200,000 shares, issued 70,000 shares for $450,000; and common stock, $1.00 par value, authorized 400,000 shares, issued 100,000 shares at an average price of $10. In addition, the corporation has retained earnings of $320,000.

Instructions

Prepare a balance sheet in good form, adjusting the amounts in each balance sheet classification as affected by the information given above.

3 6 7 **P5-6 (Preparation of a Statement of Cash Flows and a Balance Sheet)** Lansbury Inc. had the following balance sheet at December 31, 2013.

XLS

LANSBURY INC.
BALANCE SHEET
DECEMBER 31, 2013

Cash	$ 20,000	Accounts payable	$ 30,000
Accounts receivable	21,200	Notes payable (long-term)	41,000
Investments	32,000	Common stock	100,000
Plant assets (net)	81,000	Retained earnings	23,200
Land	40,000		$194,200
	$194,200		

During 2014, the following occurred.

1. Lansbury Inc. sold part of its investment portfolio for $15,000. This transaction resulted in a gain of $3,400 for the firm. The company classifies its investments as available-for-sale.
2. A tract of land was purchased for $18,000 cash.
3. Long-term notes payable in the amount of $16,000 were retired before maturity by paying $16,000 cash.
4. An additional $20,000 in common stock was issued at par.
5. Dividends of $8,200 were declared and paid to stockholders.
6. Net income for 2014 was $32,000 after allowing for depreciation of $11,000.
7. Land was purchased through the issuance of $30,000 in bonds.
8. At December 31, 2014, Cash was $32,000, Accounts Receivable was $41,600, and Accounts Payable remained at $30,000.

Instructions

(a) Prepare a statement of cash flows for 2014.
(b) Prepare an unclassified balance sheet as it would appear at December 31, 2014.
(c) How might the statement of cash flows help the user of the financial statements? Compute two cash flow ratios.

1 3 6 7 **P5-7 (Preparation of a Statement of Cash Flows and Balance Sheet)** Aero Inc. had the following balance sheet at December 31, 2013.

AERO INC.
BALANCE SHEET
DECEMBER 31, 2013

Cash	$ 20,000	Accounts payable	$ 30,000
Accounts receivable	21,200	Bonds payable	41,000
Investments	32,000	Common stock	100,000
Plant assets (net)	81,000	Retained earnings	23,200
Land	40,000		$194,200
	$194,200		

During 2014, the following occurred.

1. Aero liquidated its available-for-sale investment portfolio at a loss of $5,000.
2. A tract of land was purchased for $38,000.
3. An additional $30,000 in common stock was issued at par.
4. Dividends totaling $10,000 were declared and paid to stockholders.
5. Net income for 2014 was $35,000, including $12,000 in depreciation expense.
6. Land was purchased through the issuance of $30,000 in additional bonds.
7. At December 31, 2014, Cash was $70,200, Accounts Receivable was $42,000, and Accounts Payable was $40,000.

Instructions

(a) Prepare a statement of cash flows for the year 2014 for Aero.
(b) Prepare the unclassified balance sheet as it would appear at December 31, 2014.
(c) Compute Aero's free cash flow and current cash debt coverage for 2014.
(d) Use the analysis of Aero to illustrate how information in the balance sheet and statement of cash flows helps the user of the financial statements.

PROBLEMS SET B

See the book's companion website, at **www.wiley.com/college/kieso**, for an additional set of problems.

CONCEPTS FOR ANALYSIS

CA5-1 (Reporting the Financial Effects of Varied Transactions) In an examination of Arenes Corporation as of December 31, 2014, you have learned that the following situations exist. No entries have been made in the accounting records for these items.

1. The corporation erected its present factory building in 1999. Depreciation was calculated by the straight-line method, using an estimated life of 35 years. Early in 2014, the board of directors conducted a careful survey and estimated that the factory building had a remaining useful life of 25 years as of January 1, 2014.
2. An additional assessment of 2013 income taxes was levied and paid in 2014.
3. When calculating the accrual for officers' salaries at December 31, 2014, it was discovered that the accrual for officers' salaries for December 31, 2013, had been overstated.
4. On December 15, 2014, Arenes Corporation declared a cash dividend on its common stock outstanding, payable February 1, 2015, to the common stockholders of record December 31, 2014.

Instructions

Describe fully how each of the items above should be reported in the financial statements of Arenes Corporation for the year 2014.

CA5-2 (Identifying Balance Sheet Deficiencies) The assets of Fonzarelli Corporation are presented below (000s omitted).

FONZARELLI CORPORATION
BALANCE SHEET (PARTIAL)
DECEMBER 31, 2014

Assets		
Current assets		
Cash		$ 100,000
Unclaimed payroll checks		27,500
Debt investments (trading) (fair value $30,000) at cost		37,000
Accounts receivable (less bad debt reserve)		75,000
Inventory—at lower-of-cost- (determined by the next-in, first-out method) or-market		240,000
Total current assets		479,500
Tangible assets		
Land (less accumulated depreciation)		80,000
Buildings and equipment	$800,000	
Less: Accumulated depreciation	250,000	550,000
Net tangible assets		630,000
Long-term investments		
Stocks and bonds		100,000
Treasury stock		70,000
Total long-term investments		170,000
Other assets		
Discount on bonds payable		19,400
Sinking fund		975,000
Total other assets		994,400
Total assets		$2,273,900

Instructions

Indicate the deficiencies, if any, in the foregoing presentation of Fonzarelli Corporation's assets.

CA5-3 (Critique of Balance Sheet Format and Content) Presented below is the balance sheet of Sameed Brothers Corporation (000s omitted).

SAMEED BROTHERS CORPORATION
BALANCE SHEET
DECEMBER 31, 2014

Assets		
Current assets		
Cash	$26,000	
Marketable securities	18,000	
Accounts receivable	25,000	
Inventory	20,000	
Supplies	4,000	
Stock investment in subsidiary company	20,000	$113,000
Investments		
Treasury stock		25,000
Property, plant, and equipment		
Buildings and land	91,000	
Less: Reserve for depreciation	31,000	60,000
Other assets		
Cash surrender value of life insurance		19,000
Total assets		$217,000
Liabilities and Stockholders' Equity		
Current liabilities		
Accounts payable	$22,000	
Reserve for income taxes	15,000	
Customers' accounts with credit balances	1	$ 37,001
Deferred credits		
Unamortized premium on bonds payable		2,000
Long-term liabilities		
Bonds payable		60,000
Total liabilities		99,001
Common stock		
Common stock, par $5	85,000	
Earned surplus	24,999	
Cash dividends declared	8,000	117,999
Total liabilities and stockholders' equity		$217,000

Instructions

Evaluate the balance sheet presented. State briefly the proper treatment of any item criticized.

CA5-4 (Presentation of Property, Plant, and Equipment) Carol Keene, corporate comptroller for Dumaine Industries, is trying to decide how to present "Property, plant, and equipment" in the balance sheet. She realizes that the statement of cash flows will show that the company made a significant investment in purchasing new equipment this year, but overall she knows the company's plant assets are rather old. She feels that she can disclose one figure titled "Property, plant, and equipment, net of depreciation," and the result will be a low figure. However, it will not disclose the age of the assets. If she chooses to show the cost less accumulated depreciation, the age of the assets will be apparent. She proposes the following.

Property, plant, and equipment, net of depreciation	$10,000,000
rather than	
Property, plant, and equipment	$50,000,000
Less: Accumulated depreciation	40,000,000
Net book value	$10,000,000

Instructions

Answer the following questions.

(a) What are the ethical issues involved?
(b) What should Keene do?

CA5-5 (Cash Flow Analysis) The partner in charge of the Kappeler Corporation audit comes by your desk and leaves a letter he has started to the CEO and a copy of the cash flow statement for the year ended December 31, 2014. Because he must leave on an emergency, he asks you to finish the letter by explaining: (1) the disparity between net income and cash flow, (2) the importance of operating cash flow, (3) the renewable source(s) of cash flow, and (4) possible suggestions to improve the cash position.

KAPPELER CORPORATION
STATEMENT OF CASH FLOWS
FOR THE YEAR ENDED DECEMBER 31, 2014

Cash flows from operating activities		
Net income		$ 100,000
Adjustments to reconcile net income to net cash provided by operating activities:		
Depreciation expense	$ 10,000	
Amortization expense	1,000	
Loss on sale of fixed assets	5,000	
Increase in accounts receivable (net)	(40,000)	
Increase in inventory	(35,000)	
Decrease in accounts payable	(41,000)	(100,000)
Net cash provided by operating activities		-0-
Cash flows from investing activities		
Sale of plant assets	25,000	
Purchase of equipment	(100,000)	
Purchase of land	(200,000)	
Net cash used by investing activities		(275,000)
Cash flows from financing activities		
Payment of dividends	(10,000)	
Redemption of bonds	(100,000)	
Net cash used by financing activities		(110,000)
Net decrease in cash		(385,000)
Cash balance, January 1, 2014		400,000
Cash balance, December 31, 2014		$ 15,000

Date

President Kappeler, CEO
Kappeler Corporation
125 Wall Street
Middleton, Kansas 67458

Dear Mr. Kappeler:

I have good news and bad news about the financial statements for the year ended December 31, 2014. The good news is that net income of $100,000 is close to what we predicted in the strategic plan last year, indicating strong performance this year. The bad news is that the cash balance is seriously low. Enclosed is the Statement of Cash Flows, which best illustrates how both of these situations occurred simultaneously . . .

Instructions

Complete the letter to the CEO, including the four components requested by your boss.

USING YOUR JUDGMENT

FINANCIAL REPORTING

Financial Reporting Problem

P&G

The Procter & Gamble Company (P&G)

The financial statements of P&G are presented in Appendix 5B. The company's complete annual report, including the notes to the financial statments, can be accessed at the book's companion website, **www.wiley.com/college/kieso**.

Instructions

Refer to P&G's financial statements and the related information in the annual report to answer the following questions.

(a) What alternative formats could P&G have adopted for its balance sheet? Which format did it adopt?

(b) Identify the various techniques of disclosure P&G might have used to disclose additional pertinent financial information. Which technique does it use in its financials?

(c) In what classifications are P&G's investments reported? What valuation basis does P&G use to report its investments? How much working capital did P&G have on June 30, 2011? On June 30, 2010?

(d) What were P&G's cash flows from its operating, investing, and financing activities for 2011? What were its trends in net cash provided by operating activities over the period 2009 to 2011? Explain why the change in accounts payable and in accrued and other liabilities is added to net income to arrive at net cash provided by operating activities.

(e) Compute P&G's (1) current cash debt coverage, (2) cash debt coverage, and (3) free cash flow for 2011. What do these ratios indicate about P&G's financial condition?

Comparative Analysis Case

The Coca-Cola Company and PepsiCo, Inc.

Instructions

Go to the book's companion website and use information found there to answer the following questions related to The Coca-Cola Company and PepsiCo, Inc.

(a) What format(s) did these companies use to present their balance sheets?

(b) How much working capital did each of these companies have at the end of 2011? Speculate as to their rationale for the amount of working capital they maintain.

(c) What is the most significant difference in the asset structure of the two companies? What causes this difference?

(d) What are the companies' annual and 5-year (2007–2011) growth rates in total assets and long-term debt?

(e) What were these two companies' trends in net cash provided by operating activities over the period 2007–2011?

(f) Compute both companies' (1) current cash debt coverage, (2) cash debt coverage, and (3) free cash flow. What do these ratios indicate about the financial condition of the two companies?

Financial Statement Analysis Cases

Case 1: Uniroyal Technology Corporation

Uniroyal Technology Corporation (UTC), with corporate offices in Sarasota, Florida, is organized into three operating segments. The high-performance plastics segment is responsible for research, development, and manufacture of a wide variety of products, including orthopedic braces, graffiti-resistant seats for buses and airplanes, and a static-resistant plastic used in the central processing units of microcomputers. The coated fabrics segment manufactures products such as automobile seating, door and instrument panels, and specialty items such as waterproof seats for personal watercraft and stain-resistant, easy-cleaning upholstery fabrics. The foams and adhesives segment develops and manufactures products used in commercial roofing applications.

The following items relate to operations in a recent year.

1. Serious pressure was placed on profitability by sharply increasing raw material prices. Some raw materials increased in price 50% during the past year. Cost containment programs were instituted and

product prices were increased whenever possible, which resulted in profit margins actually improving over the course of the year.

2. The company entered into a revolving credit agreement, under which UTC may borrow the lesser of $15,000,000 or 80% of eligible accounts receivable. At the end of the year, approximately $4,000,000 was outstanding under this agreement. The company plans to use this line of credit in the upcoming year to finance operations and expansion.

Instructions

(a) Should investors be informed of raw materials price increases, such as described in item 1? Does the fact that the company successfully met the challenge of higher prices affect the answer? Explain.

(b) How should the information in item 2 be presented in the financial statements of UTC?

Case 2: Sherwin-Williams Company

Sherwin-Williams, based in Cleveland, Ohio, manufactures a wide variety of paint and other coatings, which are marketed through its specialty stores and in other retail outlets. The company also manufactures paint for automobiles. The Automotive Division has had financial difficulty. During a recent year, five branch locations of the Automotive Division were closed, and new management was put in place for the branches remaining.

The following titles were shown on Sherwin-Williams's balance sheet for that year.

Accounts payable
Accounts receivable, less allowance
Accrued taxes
Buildings
Cash and cash equivalents
Common stock
Employee compensation payable
Finished goods inventories
Intangibles and other assets
Land
Long-term debt
Machinery and equipment
Other accruals
Other capital
Other current assets
Other long-term liabilities
Postretirement obligations other than pensions
Retained earnings
Short-term investments
Taxes payable
Work in process and raw materials inventories

Instructions

(a) Organize the accounts in the general order in which they would have been presented in a classified balance sheet.

(b) When several of the branch locations of the Automotive Division were closed, what balance sheet accounts were most likely affected? Did the balance in those accounts decrease or increase?

Case 3: Deere & Company

Presented below is the SEC-mandated disclosure of contractual obligations provided by Deere & Company in a recent annual report. Deere & Company reported current assets of $27,208 and total current liabilities of $15,922 at year-end. All dollars are in millions.

Aggregate Contractual Obligations

The payment schedule for the company's contractual obligations at year-end in millions of dollars is as follows:

	Total	Less than 1 year	2&3 years	4&5 years	More than 5 years
Debt					
Equipment operations	$ 2,061	$ 130	$ 321		$1,610
Financial services	19,598	8,515	7,025	$3,003	1,055
Total	21,659	8,645	7,346	3,003	2,665
Interest on debt	3,857	941	1,102	557	1,257
Purchase obligations	3,212	3,172	26	9	5
Operating leases	358	100	120	58	80
Capital leases	29	3	6	4	16
Total	$29,115	$12,861	$8,600	$3,631	$4,023

Instructions

(a) Compute Deere & Company's working capital and current ratio (current assets ÷ current liabilities) with and without the contractual obligations reported in the schedule.

(b) Briefly discuss how the information provided in the contractual obligation disclosure would be useful in evaluating Deere & Company for loans (1) due in one year and (2) due in five years.

Case 4: Amazon.com

The incredible growth of Amazon.com has put fear into the hearts of traditional retailers. Amazon's stock price has soared to amazing levels. However, it is often pointed out in the financial press that it took the company several years to report its first profit. The following financial information is taken from a recent annual report.

($ in millions)	Current Year	Prior Year
Current assets	$ 3,373	$2,929
Total assets	4,363	3,696
Current liabilities	2,532	1,899
Total liabilities	3,932	3,450
Cash provided by operations	702	733
Capital expenditures	216	204
Dividends paid	0	0
Net income(loss)	190	359
Sales	10,711	8,490

Instructions

(a) Calculate free cash flow for Amazon for the current and prior years, and discuss its ability to finance expansion from internally generated cash. Thus far Amazon has avoided purchasing large warehouses. Instead, it has used those of others. It is possible, however, that in order to increase customer satisfaction the company may have to build its own warehouses. If this happens, how might your impression of its ability to finance expansion change?

(b) Discuss any potential implications of the change in Amazon's cash provided by operations from the prior year to the current year.

Accounting, Analysis, and Principles

Early in January 2015, Hopkins Company is preparing for a meeting with its bankers to discuss a loan request. Its bookkeeper provided the following accounts and balances at December 31, 2014.

	Debit	Credit
Cash	$ 75,000	
Accounts Receivable (net)	38,500	
Inventory	65,300	
Equipment (net)	84,000	
Patents	15,000	
Notes and Accounts Payable		$ 52,000
Notes Payable (due 2016)		75,000
Common Stock		100,000
Retained Earnings		50,800
	$277,800	$277,800

Except for the following items, Hopkins has recorded all adjustments in its accounts.

1. Cash includes $500 petty cash and $15,000 in a bond sinking fund.
2. Net accounts receivable is comprised of $52,000 in accounts receivable and $13,500 in allowance for doubtful accounts.
3. Equipment had a cost of $112,000 and accumulated depreciation of $28,000.
4. On January 8, 2015, one of Hopkins' customers declared bankruptcy. At December 31, 2014, this customer owed Hopkins $9,000.

Accounting

Prepare a corrected December 31, 2014, balance sheet for Hopkins Company.

Analysis

Hopkins' bank is considering granting an additional loan in the amount of $45,000, which will be due December 31, 2015. How can the information in the balance sheet provide useful information to the bank about Hopkins' ability to repay the loan?

Principles

In the upcoming meeting with the bank, Hopkins plans to provide additional information about the fair value of its equipment and some internally generated intangible assets related to its customer lists. This information indicates that Hopkins has significant unrealized gains on these assets, which are not reflected on the balance sheet. What objections is the bank likely to raise about the usefulness of this information in evaluating Hopkins for the loan renewal?

BRIDGE TO THE PROFESSION

Professional Research: FASB Codification

In light of the full disclosure principle, investors and creditors need to know the balances for assets, liabilities, and equity as well as the accounting policies adopted by management to measure the items reported in the balance sheet.

Instructions

If your school has a subscription to the FASB Codification, go to *http://aaahq.org/asclogin.cfm* to log in and prepare responses to the following. Provide Codification references for your responses.

(a) Identify the literature that addresses the disclosure of accounting policies.

(b) How are accounting policies defined in the literature?

(c) What are the three scenarios that would result in detailed disclosure of the accounting methods used?

(d) What are some examples of common disclosures that are required under this statement?

Additional Professional Resources

See the book's companion website, at **www.wiley.com/college/kieso**, for professional simulations as well as other study resources.

IFRS INSIGHTS

11 LEARNING OBJECTIVE

Compare the accounting procedures related to the balance sheet under GAAP and IFRS.

As in GAAP, the balance sheet and the statement of cash flows are required statements for IFRS. In addition, the content and presentation of an IFRS statement of financial position (balance sheet) and cash flow statement are similar to those used for GAAP. In general, the disclosure requirements related to the balance sheet and the statement of cash flows are much more extensive and detailed in the United States. *IAS 1*, "Presentation of Financial Statements," provides the overall IFRS requirements for balance sheet information. *IAS 7*, "Cash Flow Statements," provides the overall IFRS requirements for cash flow information. IFRS insights on the statement of cash flows are presented in Chapter 23.

RELEVANT FACTS

Following are the key similarities and differences between GAAP and IFRS related to the balance sheet.

Similarities

- Both IFRS and GAAP allow the use of title "balance sheet" or "statement of financial position." IFRS recommends but does not require the use of the title "statement of financial position" rather than balance sheet.
- Both IFRS and GAAP require disclosures about (1) accounting policies followed, (2) judgments that management has made in the process of applying the entity's accounting policies, and (3) the key assumptions and estimation uncertainty that could result in a material adjustment to the carrying amounts of assets and liabilities within the next financial year. Comparative prior period information must be presented and financial statements must be prepared annually.
- IFRS and GAAP require presentation of non-controlling interests in the equity section of the balance sheet.

Differences

- IFRS requires a classified statement of financial position except in very limited situations. IFRS follows the same guidelines as this textbook for distinguishing between current and non-current assets and liabilities. However, under GAAP, public companies must follow SEC regulations, which require specific line items. In addition, specific GAAP mandates certain forms of reporting for this information.
- Under IFRS, current assets are usually listed in the reverse order of liquidity. For example, under GAAP cash is listed first, but under IFRS it is listed last.
- IFRS has many differences in terminology that you will notice in this textbook. For example, in the sample statement of financial position illustrated on page 279, notice in the equity section common stock is called share capital—ordinary.
- Use of the term "reserve" is discouraged in GAAP, but there is no such prohibition in IFRS.

ABOUT THE NUMBERS

Classification in the Statement of Financial Position

Statement of financial position accounts are **classified**. That is, a statement of financial position groups together similar items to arrive at significant subtotals. Furthermore, the material is arranged so that important relationships are shown. The IASB indicates that the parts and subsections of financial statements are more informative than the whole. Therefore, the IASB discourages the reporting of summary accounts alone (total assets, net assets, total liabilities, etc.).

Instead, companies should report and classify individual items in sufficient detail to permit users to assess the amounts, timing, and uncertainty of future cash flows. Such classification also makes it easier for users to evaluate the company's liquidity and financial flexibility, profitability, and risk. Companies then further divide these items into several subclassifications. A representative statement of financial position presentation is shown on the next page.

SCIENTIFIC PRODUCTS, INC.
STATEMENT OF FINANCIAL POSITION
DECEMBER 31, 2014

Assets			
Non-current assets			
Long-term investments			
Investments in held-for-collection securities		$ 82,000	
Land held for future development		5,500	$ 87,500
Property, plant, and equipment			
Land		125,000	
Buildings	$975,800		
Less: Accumulated depreciation	341,200	634,600	
Total property, plant, and equipment			759,600
Intangible assets			
Capitalized development costs		6,000	
Goodwill		66,000	
Other identifiable intangible assets		28,000	100,000
Total non-current assets			**947,100**
Current assets			
Inventories		489,713	
Prepaid expenses		16,252	
Accounts receivable	165,824		
Less: Allowance for doubtful accounts	1,850	163,974	
Short-term investments		51,030	
Cash and cash equivalents		52,485	
Total current assets			**773,454**
Total assets			**$1,720,554**
Equity and Liabilities			
Equity			
Share capital—preference	$300,000		
Share capital—ordinary	400,000		
Share premium—preference	10,000		
Share premium—ordinary	27,500		
Retained earnings	153,182		
Accumulated other comprehensive income	8,650		
Less: Treasury shares	12,750		
Equity attributable to Scientific Products, Inc.		$886,582	
Equity attributable to non-controlling interest		13,500	
Total equity			**$ 900,082**
Non-current liabilities			
Bond liabilities due January 31, 2022	425,000		
Provisions related to pensions	75,000		
Total non-current liabilities		**500,000**	
Current liabilities			
Notes payable	80,000		
Accounts payable	197,532		
Interest payable	20,500		
Salary and wages payable	5,560		
Provisions related to warranties	12,500		
Deposits received from customers	4,380		
Total current liabilities		**320,472**	
Total liabilities			**820,472**
Total equity and liabilities			**$1,720,554**

The statement presented is in "report form" format. Some companies use other statement of financial position formats. For example, companies sometimes deduct current liabilities from current assets to arrive at working capital. Or, they deduct all liabilities from all assets. Some companies report the subtotal *net assets*, which equals total assets minus total liabilities.

Equity

The **equity** (also referred to as **shareholders' equity**) section is one of the most difficult sections to prepare and understand. This is due to the complexity of ordinary and preference share agreements and the various restrictions on equity imposed by corporation laws, liability agreements, and boards of directors. Companies usually divide the section into six parts:

EQUITY SECTION

1. **SHARE CAPITAL.** The par or stated value of shares issued. It includes ordinary shares (sometimes referred to as *common shares*) and preference shares (sometimes referred to as *preferred shares*).
2. **SHARE PREMIUM.** The excess of amounts paid-in over the par or stated value.
3. **RETAINED EARNINGS.** The corporation's undistributed earnings.
4. **ACCUMULATED OTHER COMPREHENSIVE INCOME.** The aggregate amount of the other comprehensive income items.
5. **TREASURY SHARES.** Generally, the amount of ordinary shares repurchased.
6. **NON-CONTROLLING INTEREST (MINORITY INTEREST).** A portion of the equity of subsidiaries not owned by the reporting company.

For ordinary shares, companies must disclose the par value and the authorized, issued, and outstanding share amounts. The same holds true for preference shares. A company usually presents the share premium (for both ordinary and preference shares) in one amount, although subtotals are informative if the sources of additional capital are varied and material. The retained earnings amount may be divided between the **unappropriated** (the amount that is usually available for dividend distribution) and **restricted** (e.g., by bond indentures or other loan agreements) amounts. In addition, companies show any shares reacquired (treasury shares) as a reduction of equity.

Accumulated other comprehensive income (sometimes referred to as *reserves* or *other reserves*) includes such items as unrealized gains and losses on non-trading equity investments and unrealized gains and losses on certain derivative transactions. Non-controlling interest, sometimes referred to as minority interest, is also shown as a separate item (where applicable) as a part of equity.

Delhaize Group presented its equity section as follows.

Delhaize Group
(000,000)

Share capital	€ 50
Share premium	2,725
Treasury shares	(56)
Retained earnings	2,678
Other reserves	(1,254)
Shareholders' equity	4,143
Minority interests	52
Total equity	€4,195

Many companies reporting under IFRS often use the term "reserve" as an all-inclusive catch-all for items such as retained earnings, share premium, and accumulated other comprehensive income.

Revaluation Equity

GAAP and IFRS differ in the IFRS provision for balance sheet revaluations of property, plant, and equipment. Under the *revaluation model*, revaluations are recorded and reported as part of equity. To illustrate, Richardson Company uses IFRS and has property and equipment on an historical cost basis of $2,000,000. At the end of the year, Richardson appraises its property and equipment and determines it had a revaluation increase of $243,000.

Richardson records this revaluation under IFRS with an increase to property and equipment as well as a valuation reserve in equity. A note to the financial statements explains the change in the revaluation equity account from one period to the next, as shown below for Richardson Company, assuming a beginning balance of $11,345,000.

Note 30. Reserves (in part)

(,000)	2014
Properties Revaluation Reserve	
Balance at beginning of year	$11,345
Increase (decrease) on revaluation of plant and equipment	243
Impairment losses	—
Reversals of impairment losses	—
Balance at end of year	$11,588

Fair Presentation

Companies must present fairly the financial position, financial performance, and cash flows of the company. Fair presentation means the faithful representation of transactions and events using the definitions and recognition criteria in the IASB conceptual framework. It is presumed that the use of IFRS with appropriate disclosure results in financial statements that are fairly presented. In other words, inappropriate use of accounting policies cannot be overcome by explanatory notes to the financial statements. In some rare cases, as indicated in Chapter 2, companies can use a "true and fair" override. This situation develops, for example, when the IFRS for a given company appears to conflict with the objective of financial reporting. This situation might occur when a regulatory body indicates that a specific IFRS may be misleading. As indicated earlier, a true and fair override is highly unlikely in today's reporting environment.

One recent and highly publicized exception is the case of **Société Générale** (SocGen), a French bank. The bank used the true and fair rule to justify reporting losses that occurred in 2008 in the prior year. Although allowed under the true and fair rule, such reporting was questioned because it permitted the bank to "take a bath," that is, record as many losses as possible in 2007, which was already a bad year for the bank. As a result, SocGen's 2008 reports looked better. [See F. Norris, "SocGen Changes Its Numbers," *The New York Times* (May 13, 2008).]

ON THE HORIZON

The FASB and the IASB are working on a project to converge their standards related to financial statement presentation. A key feature of the proposed framework is that each of the statements will be organized, in the same format, to separate an entity's financing activities from its operating and investing activities and, further, to separate financing activities into transactions with owners and creditors. Thus, the same classifications used in the statement of financial position would also be used in the statement of comprehensive income and the statement of cash flows. The project has three phases. You can follow the joint financial presentation project at the following link: *http://www.fasb.org/project/financial_statement_presentation.shtml.*

IFRS SELF-TEST QUESTIONS

1. Which of the following statements about IFRS and GAAP accounting and reporting requirements for the balance sheet is **not** correct?
   (a) Both IFRS and GAAP distinguish between current and non-current assets and liabilities.
   (b) The presentation formats required by IFRS and GAAP for the balance sheet are similar.
   (c) Both IFRS and GAAP require that comparative information be reported.
   (d) One difference between the reporting requirements under IFRS and those of the GAAP balance sheet is that an IFRS balance sheet may list long-term assets first.
2. Current assets under IFRS are listed generally:
   (a) by importance.
   (b) in the reverse order of their expected conversion to cash.
   (c) by longevity.
   (d) alphabetically.
3. Companies that use IFRS:
   (a) may report all their assets on the statement of financial position at fair value.
   (b) are not allowed to net assets (assets − liabilities) on their statement of financial positions.
   (c) may report non-current assets before current assets on the statement of financial position.
   (d) do not have any guidelines as to what should be reported on the statement of financial position.
4. Franco Company uses IFRS and owns property, plant, and equipment with a historical cost of $5,000,000. At December 31, 2013, the company reported a valuation reserve of $690,000. At December 31, 2014, the property, plant, and equipment was appraised at $5,325,000. The valuation reserve will show what balance at December 31, 2014?
   (a) $365,000.
   (b) $325,000.
   (c) $690,000.
   (d) $0.
5. A company has purchased a tract of land and expects to build a production plant on the land in approximately 5 years. During the 5 years before construction, the land will be idle. Under IFRS, the land should be reported as:
   (a) land expense.
   (b) property, plant, and equipment.
   (c) an intangible asset.
   (d) a long-term investment.

IFRS CONCEPTS AND APPLICATION

IFRS5-1 Where can authoritative IFRS guidance be found related to the statement of financial position (balance sheet) and the statement of cash flows?

IFRS5-2 Briefly describe some of the similarities and differences between GAAP and IFRS with respect to statement of financial position (balance sheet) reporting.

IFRS5-3 Briefly describe the convergence efforts related to financial statement presentation.

IFRS5-4 Rainmaker Company prepares its financial statements in accordance with IFRS. In 2014, Rainmaker recorded the following revaluation adjustments related to its buildings and land: The company's building increased in value by $200,000; its land declined by $35,000. How will these revaluation adjustments affect Rainmaker's balance sheet? Will the reporting differ under GAAP? Explain.

International Reporting Case

IFRS5-5 Presented below is the balance sheet for **Tomkins plc**, a British company.

Tomkins plc
Consolidated Balance Sheet
(amounts in £ millions)

Non-current assets	
Goodwill	436.0
Other intangible assets	78.0
Property, plant and equipment	1,122.8
Investments in associates	20.6
Trade and other receivables	81.1
Deferred tax assets	82.9
Post-employment benefit surpluses	1.3
	1,822.7
Current assets	
Inventories	590.8
Trade and other receivables	753.0
Income tax recoverable	49.0
Available-for-sale investments	1.2
Cash and cash equivalents	445.0
	1,839.0
Assets held for sale	11.9
Total assets	3,673.6
Current liabilities	
Bank overdrafts	4.8
Bank and other loans	11.2
Obligations under finance leases	1.0
Trade and other payables	677.6
Income tax liabilities	15.2
Provisions	100.3
	810.1
Non-current liabilities	
Bank and other loans	687.3
Obligations under finance leases	3.6
Trade and other payables	27.1
Post-employment benefit obligations	343.5
Deferred tax liabilities	25.3
Income tax liabilities	79.5
Provisions	19.2
	1,185.5
Total liabilities	1,995.6
Net assets	1,678.0
Capital and reserves	
Ordinary share capital	79.6
Share premium account	799.2
Own shares	(8.2)
Capital redemption reserve	921.8
Currency translation reserve	(93.0)
Available-for-sale reserve	(0.9)
Accumulated deficit	(161.9)
Shareholders' equity	1,536.6
Minority interests	141.4
Total equity	1,678.0

Instructions

(a) Identify at least three differences in balance sheet reporting between British and U.S. firms, as shown in Tomkins' balance sheet.

(b) Review Tomkins' balance sheet and identify how the format of this financial statement provides useful information, as illustrated in the chapter.

Professional Research

IFRS5-6 In light of the full disclosure principle, investors and creditors need to know the balances for assets, liabilities, and equity, as well as the accounting policies adopted by management to measure the items reported in the statement of financial position.

Instructions

Access the IFRS authoritative literature at the IASB website (*http://eifrs.iasb.org/*). (If necessary, click on the IFRS tab and then register for eIFRS free access.) When you have accessed the documents, you can use the search tool in your Internet browser to respond to the following questions. (Provide paragraph citations.)

(a) Identify the literature that addresses the disclosure of accounting policies.

(b) How are accounting policies defined in the literature?

(c) What are the guidelines concerning consistency in applying accounting policies?

(d) What are some examples of common disclosures that are required under this statement?

International Financial Reporting Problem

Marks and Spencer plc

IFRS5-7 The financial statements of **Marks and Spencer plc (M&S)** are available at the book's companion website or can be accessed at *http://annualreport.marksandspencer.com/_assets/downloads/Marks-and-Spencer-Annual-report-and-financial-statements-2012.pdf*.

Instructions

Refer to M&S's financial statements and the accompanying notes to answer the following questions.

(a) What alternative formats could M&S have adopted for its statement of financial position? Which format did it adopt?

(b) Identify the various techniques of disclosure M&S might have used to disclose additional pertinent financial information. Which technique does it use in its financials?

(c) In what classifications are M&S's investments reported? What valuation basis does M&S use to report its investments? How much working capital did M&S have on 31 March 2012? On 2 April 2011?

(d) What were M&S's cash flows from its operating, investing, and financing activities for 2012? What were its trends in net cash provided by operating activities over the period 2011 to 2012? Explain why the change in accounts payable and in accrued and other liabilities is added to net income to arrive at net cash provided by operating activities.

(e) Compute M&S's (1) current cash debt coverage, (2) cash debt coverage, and (3) free cash flow for 2012. What do these ratios indicate about M&S's financial conditions?

ANSWERS TO IFRS SELF-TEST QUESTIONS

1. b **2.** b **3.** c **4.** b **5.** d

Remember to check the book's companion website to find additional resources for this chapter.

CHAPTER 6 Accounting and the Time Value of Money

LEARNING OBJECTIVES

After studying this chapter, you should be able to:

1. Identify accounting topics where the time value of money is relevant.
2. Distinguish between simple and compound interest.
3. Use appropriate compound interest tables.
4. Identify variables fundamental to solving interest problems.
5. Solve future and present value of 1 problems.
6. Solve future value of ordinary and annuity due problems.
7. Solve present value of ordinary and annuity due problems.
8. Solve present value problems related to deferred annuities and bonds.
9. Apply expected cash flows to present value measurement.

How Do I Measure That?

A significant part of accounting is measurement. And as we discussed in Chapter 2, we have a mixed-attribute measurement model. That is, many items are measured based on historical cost (e.g., property, plant, and equipment, inventory), but increasingly accounting measurements are based on fair value (e.g., financial instruments, impairments). Determining fair value of an item is fairly straightforward when market prices are available (Level 1 in the fair value hierarchy). However, when a market price is not available, accountants must rely on valuation models to develop a fair value estimate (Level 3 of the fair value hierarchy).

Developing fair value estimates based on a valuation model generally involves discounted cash flow techniques, which has three primary elements: (1) estimating the amounts and timing of future cash flows, (2) developing probability estimates for those cash flows, and (3) determining the appropriate discount rate to apply to the expected cash flows to arrive at a fair value estimate. Seems pretty straightforward, right? Actually, this can be a challenging process when applied to a variety of complex assets and liabilities for which GAAP requires a fair value estimate.

Many companies, particularly financial institutions, faced this challenge during the financial crisis when securities markets seized up to the point that valid market prices for investments and loans were not readily available. Major banks, such as **HSBC Holdings**, **Wells Fargo**, and **Bank of America**, confronted this issue with respect to their mortgage-backed securities and interest rate swaps used to hedge interest rate risk. **Kohl's Department Stores** dealt with a similar situation for its investment in auction rates securities (ARS). The fair value of ARS is generally determined at quarterly auctions. However, these auctions failed during the financial crisis, and Kohl's and other ARS investors were forced to use a valuation model rather than market prices to determine fair value.

The FASB provides fair value estimation guidance (FASB ASC 820), but the Board also performs ongoing assessment of whether and to what extent additional valuation guidance is needed. In this regard, the Board established the **Valuation Resource Group (VRG)**. The VRG is comprised of accounting and valuation professionals, preparers and users of financial statements, regulators, and other industry representatives. The VRG provides the Board and the FASB staff with multiple viewpoints on application issues relating to fair value for financial reporting purposes. Here is a sampling of the issues discussed by the VRG:

- Measurement of contingent consideration in a business combination.
- Incorporating multi-period excess earnings in valuing intangible assets.
- Effects of premiums and discounts in fair value measurements.

CONCEPTUAL FOCUS

> The time value of money is fundamental to the measurement concept in GAAP.

INTERNATIONAL FOCUS

> The time value of money concept is universal and applied the same, regardless of whether a company follows GAAP or IFRS.

- Determining the carrying amount of a reporting unit when performing the goodwill impairment test.
- Measurement uncertainty analysis disclosures.

As indicated, the list of topics is revealing as to the variety and complexity of the issues that must be addressed in implementing the fair value measurement principle. Discussion of these items by the VRG helped the FASB develop appropriate approaches for applying fair value guidance to specific examples. For example, with respect to the contingent consideration topic, the VRG noted that taxes must be considered when developing future cash flow estimates and that, in some cases, these tax effects are different for assets and liabilities.

The VRG has and will provide good counsel to the FASB with respect to applying the fair value measurement principle. After studying this chapter, you should have a better understanding of time value of money principles and discounted cash flow techniques as they are applied in accounting measurements.

Sources: Ernst and Young, "Valuation Resource Group: Highlights of November 2010 Meeting," *Hot Topic—Update on Major Accounting and Auditing Activities, No: 2010-59* (5 November 2010).

PREVIEW OF CHAPTER 6

As we indicated in the opening story, as a financial expert in today's accounting environment, you will be expected to make present and future value measurements and to understand their implications. The purpose of this chapter is to present the tools and techniques that will help you measure the present value of future cash inflows and outflows. The content and organization of the chapter are as follows.

Accounting and the Time Value of Money

Basic Time Value Concepts	Single-Sum Problems	Annuities	More Complex Situations	Present Value Measurement
• Applications • The nature of interest • Simple interest • Compound interest • Fundamental variables	• Future value of a single sum • Present value of a single sum • Solving for other unknowns	• Future value of ordinary annuity • Future value of annuity due • Examples of FV of annuity • Present value of ordinary annuity • Present value of annuity due • Examples of PV of annuity	• Deferred annuities • Valuation of long-term bonds • Effective-interest method of bond discount/premium amortization	• Choosing an appropriate interest rate • Example of expected cash flow

BASIC TIME VALUE CONCEPTS

LEARNING OBJECTIVE 1
Identify accounting topics where the time value of money is relevant.

In accounting (and finance), the phrase **time value of money** indicates a relationship between time and money—that a dollar received today is worth more than a dollar promised at some time in the future. Why? Because of the opportunity to invest today's dollar and receive interest on the investment. Yet, when deciding among investment or borrowing alternatives, it is essential to be able to compare today's dollar and tomorrow's dollar on the same footing—to compare "apples to apples." Investors do that by using the concept of **present value**, which has many applications in accounting.

Applications of Time Value Concepts

Financial reporting uses different measurements in different situations—historical cost for equipment, net realizable value for inventories, fair value for investments. As we discussed in Chapters 2 and 5, the FASB increasingly is requiring the use of fair values in the measurement of assets and liabilities. According to the FASB's recent guidance on fair value measurements, the most useful fair value measures are based on market prices in active markets. Within the fair value hierarchy these are referred to as Level 1. Recall that Level 1 fair value measures are the least subjective because they are based on quoted prices, such as a closing stock price in the *Wall Street Journal*.

However, for many assets and liabilities, market-based fair value information is not readily available. In these cases, fair value can be estimated based on the expected future cash flows related to the asset or liability. Such fair value estimates are generally considered Level 3 (most subjective) in the fair value hierarchy because they are based on unobservable inputs, such as a company's own data or assumptions related to the expected future cash flows associated with the asset or liability. As discussed in the fair value guidance, present value techniques are used to convert expected cash flows into present values, which represent an estimate of fair value. **[1]**

See the FASB Codification section (page 320).

Because of the increased use of present values in this and other contexts, it is important to understand present value techniques.[1] We list some of the applications of present value-based measurements to accounting topics below; we discuss many of these in the following chapters.

PRESENT VALUE-BASED ACCOUNTING MEASUREMENTS

1. **NOTES.** Valuing noncurrent receivables and payables that carry no stated interest rate or a lower than market interest rate.
2. **LEASES.** Valuing assets and obligations to be capitalized under long-term leases and measuring the amount of the lease payments and annual leasehold amortization.
3. **PENSIONS AND OTHER POSTRETIREMENT BENEFITS.** Measuring service cost components of employers' postretirement benefits expense and postretirement benefits obligation.
4. **LONG-TERM ASSETS.** Evaluating alternative long-term investments by discounting future cash flows. Determining the value of assets acquired under deferred payment contracts. Measuring impairments of assets.

[1]GAAP addresses present value as a measurements basis for a broad array of transactions, such as accounts and loans receivable **[2]**, leases **[3]**, postretirement benefits **[4]**, asset impairments **[5]**, and stock-based compensation **[6]**.

5. **STOCK-BASED COMPENSATION.** Determining the fair value of employee services in compensatory stock-option plans.
6. **BUSINESS COMBINATIONS.** Determining the value of receivables, payables, liabilities, accruals, and commitments acquired or assumed in a "purchase."
7. **DISCLOSURES.** Measuring the value of future cash flows from oil and gas reserves for disclosure in supplementary information.
8. **ENVIRONMENTAL LIABILITIES.** Determining the fair value of future obligations for asset retirements.

In addition to accounting and business applications, compound interest, annuity, and present value concepts apply to personal finance and investment decisions. In purchasing a home or car, planning for retirement, and evaluating alternative investments, you will need to understand time value of money concepts.

The Nature of Interest

Interest is payment for the use of money. It is the excess cash received or repaid over and above the amount lent or borrowed (**principal**). For example, Corner Bank lends Hillfarm Company $10,000 with the understanding that it will repay $11,500. The excess over $10,000, or $1,500, represents interest expense for Hillfarm and interest revenue for Corner Bank.

The lender generally states the amount of interest as a rate over a specific period of time. For example, if Hillfarm borrowed $10,000 for one year before repaying $11,500, the rate of interest is 15 percent per year ($1,500 ÷ $10,000). The custom of expressing interest as a percentage rate is an established business practice.[2] In fact, business managers make investing and borrowing decisions on the basis of the rate of interest involved, rather than on the actual dollar amount of interest to be received or paid.

How is the interest rate determined? One important factor is the level of credit risk (risk of nonpayment) involved. Other factors being equal, the higher the credit risk, the higher the interest rate. Low-risk borrowers like **Microsoft** or **Intel** can probably obtain a loan at or slightly below the going market rate of interest. However, a bank would probably charge the neighborhood delicatessen several percentage points above the market rate, if granting the loan at all.

The amount of interest involved in any financing transaction is a function of three variables:

VARIABLES IN INTEREST COMPUTATION

1. **PRINCIPAL.** The amount borrowed or invested.
2. **INTEREST RATE.** A percentage of the outstanding principal.
3. **TIME.** The number of years or fractional portion of a year that the principal is outstanding.

Thus, the following three relationships apply:

- The larger the principal amount, the larger the dollar amount of interest.
- The higher the interest rate, the larger the dollar amount of interest.
- The longer the time period, the larger the dollar amount of interest.

[2]Federal law requires the disclosure of interest rates on an annual basis in all contracts. That is, instead of stating the rate as "1% per month," contracts must state the rate as "12% per year" if it is simple interest or "12.68% per year" if it is compounded monthly.

Simple Interest

LEARNING OBJECTIVE 2
Distinguish between simple and compound interest.

Companies compute **simple interest** on the amount of the principal only. It is the return on (or growth of) the principal for one time period. The following equation expresses simple interest.[3]

$$\textbf{Interest} = p \times i \times n$$

where

$$p = \text{principal}$$
$$i = \text{rate of interest for a single period}$$
$$n = \text{number of periods}$$

To illustrate, Barstow Electric Inc. borrows \$10,000 for 3 years with a simple interest rate of 8% per year. It computes the total interest it will pay as follows.

$$\begin{aligned}\textbf{Interest} &= p \times i \times n \\ &= \$10{,}000 \times .08 \times 3 \\ &= \$2{,}400\end{aligned}$$

If Barstow borrows \$10,000 for 3 months at 8%, the interest is \$200, computed as follows.

$$\begin{aligned}\text{Interest} &= \$10{,}000 \times .08 \times 3/12 \\ &= \$200\end{aligned}$$

Compound Interest

LEARNING OBJECTIVE 3
Use appropriate compound interest tables.

John Maynard Keynes, the legendary English economist, supposedly called it magic. Mayer Rothschild, the founder of the famous European banking firm, proclaimed it the eighth wonder of the world. Today, people continue to extol its wonder and its power. The object of their affection? Compound interest.

We compute **compound interest** on principal **and** on any interest earned that has not been paid or withdrawn. It is the return on (or growth of) the principal for two or more time periods. Compounding computes interest not only on the principal but also on the interest earned to date on that principal, assuming the interest is left on deposit.

To illustrate the difference between simple and compound interest, assume that Vasquez Company deposits \$10,000 in the Last National Bank, where it will earn simple interest of 9% per year. It deposits another \$10,000 in the First State Bank, where it will earn compound interest of 9% per year compounded annually. In both cases, Vasquez will not withdraw any interest until 3 years from the date of deposit. Illustration 6-1 shows the computation of interest Vasquez will receive, as well as its accumulated year-end balance.

ILLUSTRATION 6-1
Simple vs. Compound Interest

Last National Bank

	Simple Interest Calculation	Simple Interest	Accumulated Year-End Balance
Year 1	\$10,000.00 × 9%	\$ 900.00	\$10,900.00
Year 2	\$10,000.00 × 9%	900.00	\$11,800.00
Year 3	\$10,000.00 × 9%	900.00	\$12,700.00
		\$2,700.00	

First State Bank

	Compound Interest Calculation	Compound Interest	Accumulated Year-End Balance
Year 1	\$10,000.00 × 9%	\$ 900.00	\$10,900.00
Year 2	\$10,900.00 × 9%	981.00	\$11,881.00
Year 3	\$11,881.00 × 9%	1,069.29	\$12,950.29
		\$2,950.29	

\$250.29 Difference

[3]Business mathematics and business finance textbooks traditionally state simple interest as *I* (interest) = *P* (principal) × *R* (rate) × *T* (time).

Note in Illustration 6-1 that simple interest uses the initial principal of $10,000 to compute the interest in all 3 years. **Compound interest uses the accumulated balance (principal plus interest to date) at each year-end to compute interest in the succeeding year.** This explains the larger balance in the compound interest account.

Obviously, any rational investor would choose compound interest, if available, over simple interest. In the example above, compounding provides $250.29 of additional interest revenue. For practical purposes, compounding assumes that unpaid interest earned becomes a part of the principal. Furthermore, the accumulated balance at the end of each year becomes the new principal sum on which interest is earned during the next year.

Compound interest is the typical interest computation applied in business situations. This occurs particularly in our economy, where companies use and finance large amounts of long-lived assets over long periods of time. Financial managers view and evaluate their investment opportunities in terms of a series of periodic returns, each of which they can reinvest to yield additional returns. Simple interest usually applies only to short-term investments and debts that involve a time span of one year or less.

What do the numbers mean? A PRETTY GOOD START

The continuing debate on Social Security reform provides a great context to illustrate the power of compounding. One proposed idea is for the government to give $1,000 to every citizen at birth. This gift would be deposited in an account that would earn interest tax-free until the citizen retires. Assuming the account earns a modest 5% annual return until retirement at age 65, the $1,000 would grow to $23,839. With monthly compounding, the $1,000 deposited at birth would grow to $25,617.

Why start so early? If the government waited until age 18 to deposit the money, it would grow to only $9,906 with annual compounding. That is, reducing the time invested by a third results in more than a 50% reduction in retirement money. This example illustrates the importance of starting early when the power of compounding is involved.

Compound Interest Tables (see pages 334–343)

We present five different types of compound interest tables at the end of this chapter. These tables should help you study this chapter as well as solve other problems involving interest.

INTEREST TABLES AND THEIR CONTENTS

1. **FUTURE VALUE OF 1 *TABLE*.** Contains the amounts to which 1 will accumulate if deposited now at a specified rate and left for a specified number of periods (Table 6-1).
2. **PRESENT VALUE OF 1 *TABLE*.** Contains the amounts that must be deposited now at a specified rate of interest to equal 1 at the end of a specified number of periods (Table 6-2).
3. **FUTURE VALUE OF AN ORDINARY ANNUITY OF 1 *TABLE*.** Contains the amounts to which periodic rents of 1 will accumulate if the payments (rents) are invested at the **end** of each period at a specified rate of interest for a specified number of periods (Table 6-3).
4. **PRESENT VALUE OF AN ORDINARY ANNUITY OF 1 *TABLE*.** Contains the amounts that must be deposited now at a specified rate of interest to permit withdrawals of 1 at the **end** of regular periodic intervals for the specified number of periods (Table 6-4).
5. **PRESENT VALUE OF AN ANNUITY DUE OF 1 *TABLE*.** Contains the amounts that must be deposited now at a specified rate of interest to permit withdrawals of 1 at the **beginning** of regular periodic intervals for the specified number of periods (Table 6-5).

Illustration 6-2 lists the general format and content of these tables. It shows how much principal plus interest a dollar accumulates to at the end of each of five periods, at three different rates of compound interest.

ILLUSTRATION 6-2
Excerpt from Table 6-1

FUTURE VALUE OF 1 AT COMPOUND INTEREST
(EXCERPT FROM TABLE 6-1, PAGE 334)

Period	9%	10%	11%
1	1.09000	1.10000	1.11000
2	1.18810	1.21000	1.23210
3	1.29503	1.33100	1.36763
4	1.41158	1.46410	1.51807
5	1.53862	1.61051	1.68506

The compound tables rely on basic formulas. For example, the formula to determine the future value factor (*FVF*) for 1 is:

$$FVF_{n,i} = (1 + i)^n$$

where

$FVF_{n,i}$ = future value factor for n periods at i interest
n = number of periods
i = rate of interest for a single period

Gateway to the Profession
Financial Calculator and Spreadsheet Tools

Financial calculators include preprogrammed $FVF_{n,i}$ and other time value of money formulas.

To illustrate the use of interest tables to calculate compound amounts, assume an interest rate of 9%. Illustration 6-3 shows the future value to which 1 accumulates (the future value factor).

ILLUSTRATION 6-3
Accumulation of Compound Amounts

Period	Beginning-of-Period Amount	×	Multiplier $(1 + i)$	=	End-of-Period Amount*	Formula $(1 + i)^n$
1	1.00000		1.09		1.09000	$(1.09)^1$
2	1.09000		1.09		1.18810	$(1.09)^2$
3	1.18810		1.09		1.29503	$(1.09)^3$

*Note that these amounts appear in Table 6-1 in the 9% column.

Throughout our discussion of compound interest tables, note the intentional use of the term **periods** instead of **years**. Interest is generally expressed in terms of an annual rate. However, many business circumstances dictate a compounding period of less than one year. In such circumstances, a company must convert the annual interest rate to correspond to the length of the period. To convert the "annual interest rate" into the "compounding period interest rate," a company **divides the annual rate by the number of compounding periods per year.**

In addition, companies determine the number of periods by **multiplying the number of years involved by the number of compounding periods per year.** To illustrate, assume an investment of $1 for 6 years at 8% annual interest compounded **quarterly**. Using Table 6-1, page 334, read the factor that appears in the 2% column on the 24th row—6 years × 4 compounding periods per year, namely 1.60844, or approximately $1.61. Thus, all compound interest tables use the term **periods**, not **years**, to express the quantity of n. Illustration 6-4 shows how to determine (1) the interest rate per compounding period and (2) the number of compounding periods in four situations of differing compounding frequency.[4]

ILLUSTRATION 6-4
Frequency of Compounding

12% Annual Interest Rate over 5 Years Compounded	Interest Rate per Compounding Period	Number of Compounding Periods
Annually (1)	.12 ÷ 1 = .12	5 years × 1 compounding per year = 5 periods
Semiannually (2)	.12 ÷ 2 = .06	5 years × 2 compoundings per year = 10 periods
Quarterly (4)	.12 ÷ 4 = .03	5 years × 4 compoundings per year = 20 periods
Monthly (12)	.12 ÷ 12 = .01	5 years × 12 compoundings per year = 60 periods

How often interest is compounded can substantially affect the rate of return. For example, a 9% annual interest compounded **daily** provides a 9.42% yield, or a difference of 0.42%. The 9.42% is the **effective yield.**[5] The annual interest rate (9%) is the **stated, nominal,** or **face rate.** When the compounding frequency is greater than once a year, the effective-interest rate will always exceed the stated rate.

Illustration 6-5 shows how compounding for five different time periods affects the effective yield and the amount earned by an investment of $10,000 for one year.

ILLUSTRATION 6-5
Comparison of Different Compounding Periods

	Compounding Periods				
Interest Rate	Annually	Semiannually	Quarterly	Monthly	Daily
8%	8.00% $800	8.16% $816	8.24% $824	8.30% $830	8.33% $833
9%	9.00% $900	9.20% $920	9.31% $931	9.38% $938	9.42% $942
10%	10.00% $1,000	10.25% $1,025	10.38% $1,038	10.47% $1,047	10.52% $1,052

[4]Because interest is theoretically earned (accruing) every second of every day, it is possible to calculate interest that is **compounded continuously**. Using the natural, or Napierian, system of logarithms facilitates computations involving continuous compounding. As a practical matter, however, most business transactions assume interest to be compounded no more frequently than daily.

[5]The formula for calculating the **effective rate**, in situations where the compounding frequency (n) is greater than once a year, is as follows.

$$\text{Effective rate} = (1 + i)^n - 1$$

To illustrate, if the stated annual rate is 8% compounded quarterly (or 2% per quarter), the effective annual rate is:

$$\begin{aligned}\text{Effective rate} &= (1 + .02)^4 - 1\\ &= (1.02)^4 - 1\\ &= 1.0824 - 1\\ &= .0824\\ &= 8.24\%\end{aligned}$$

LEARNING OBJECTIVE 4
Identify variables fundamental to solving interest problems.

Fundamental Variables

The following four variables are fundamental to all compound interest problems.

FUNDAMENTAL VARIABLES

1. **RATE OF INTEREST.** This rate, unless otherwise stated, is an annual rate that must be adjusted to reflect the length of the compounding period if less than a year.
2. **NUMBER OF TIME PERIODS.** This is the number of compounding periods. (A period may be equal to or less than a year.)
3. **FUTURE VALUE.** The value at a future date of a given sum or sums invested assuming compound interest.
4. **PRESENT VALUE.** The value now (present time) of a future sum or sums discounted assuming compound interest.

Illustration 6-6 depicts the relationship of these four fundamental variables in a **time diagram**.

ILLUSTRATION 6-6
Basic Time Diagram

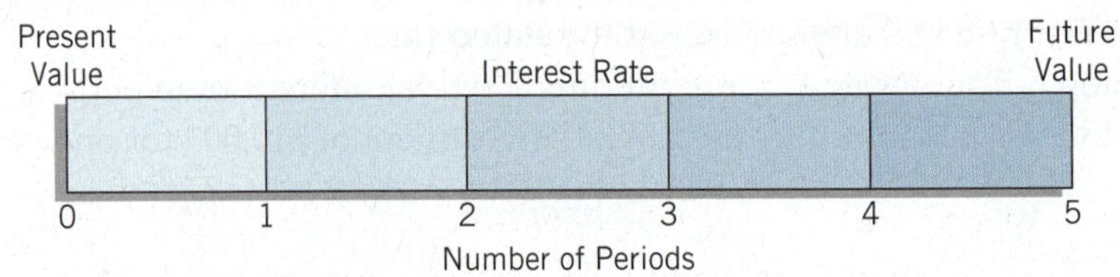

In some cases, all four of these variables are known. However, at least one variable is unknown in many business situations. To better understand and solve the problems in this chapter, we encourage you to sketch compound interest problems in the form of the preceding time diagram.

SINGLE-SUM PROBLEMS

LEARNING OBJECTIVE 5
Solve future and present value of 1 problems.

Many business and investment decisions involve a single amount of money that either exists now or will in the future. Single-sum problems are generally classified into one of the following two categories.

1. Computing the **unknown future value** of a known single sum of money that is invested now for a certain number of periods at a certain interest rate.
2. Computing the **unknown present value** of a known single sum of money in the future that is discounted for a certain number of periods at a certain interest rate.

When analyzing the information provided, determine first whether the problem involves a future value or a present value. Then apply the following general rules, depending on the situation:

- **If solving for a future value,** *accumulate* all cash flows to a future point. In this instance, interest increases the amounts or values over time so that the future value exceeds the present value.

- **If solving for a present value,** *discount* all cash flows from the future to the present. In this case, **discounting** reduces the amounts or values, so that the present value is less than the future amount.

Preparation of time diagrams aids in identifying the unknown as an item in the future or the present. Sometimes the problem involves neither a future value nor a present value. Instead, the unknown is the interest or discount rate, or the number of compounding or discounting periods.

Future Value of a Single Sum

To determine the **future value** of a single sum, multiply the future value factor by its present value (principal), as follows.

$$FV = PV\,(FVF_{n,i})$$

where

FV = future value

PV = present value (principal or single sum)

$FVF_{n,i}$ = future value factor for n periods at i interest

To illustrate, Bruegger Co. wants to determine the future value of $50,000 invested for 5 years compounded annually at an interest rate of 11%. Illustration 6-7 shows this investment situation in time-diagram form.

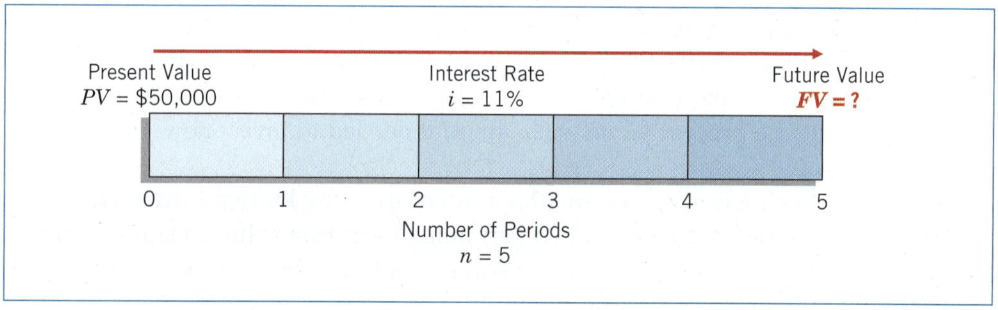

ILLUSTRATION 6-7
Future Value Time Diagram ($n = 5$, $i = 11\%$)

Using the future value formula, Bruegger solves this investment problem as follows.

$$\begin{aligned} \textbf{Future value} &= PV\,(FVF_{n,i}) \\ &= \$50{,}000\,(FVF_{5,11\%}) \\ &= \$50{,}000\,(1 + .11)^5 \\ &= \$50{,}000\,(1.68506) \\ &= \$84{,}253 \end{aligned}$$

To determine the future value factor of 1.68506 in the formula above, Bruegger uses a financial calculator or reads the appropriate table, in this case Table 6-1 (11% column and the 5-period row).

Companies can apply this time diagram and formula approach to routine business situations. To illustrate, assume that **Commonwealth Edison Company** deposited $250 million in an escrow account with **Northern Trust Company** at the beginning of 2014 as a commitment toward a power plant to be completed December 31, 2017. How much will the company have on deposit at the end of 4 years if interest is 10%, compounded semiannually?

With a known present value of $250 million, a total of 8 compounding periods (4×2), and an interest rate of 5% per compounding period ($.10 \div 2$), the company can time-diagram this problem and determine the future value as shown in Illustration 6-8.

ILLUSTRATION 6-8
Future Value Time Diagram ($n = 8, i = 5\%$)

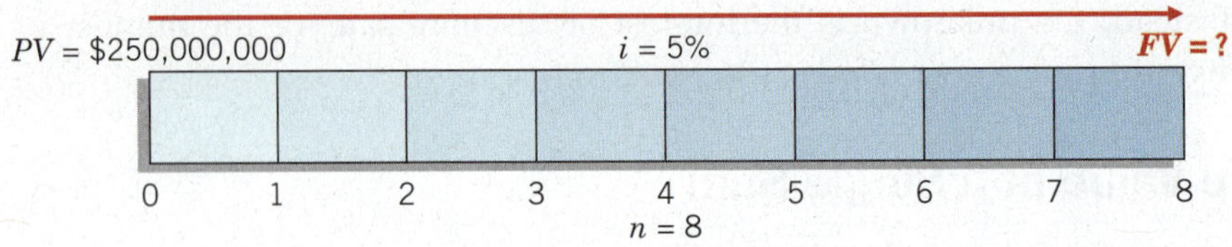

$$\text{Future value} = \$250,000,000\ (FVF_{8,5\%})$$
$$= \$250,000,000\ (1 + .05)^8$$
$$= \$250,000,000\ (1.47746)$$
$$= \$369,365,000$$

Using a future value factor found in Table 6-1 (5% column, 8-period row), we find that the deposit of $250 million will accumulate to $369,365,000 by December 31, 2017.

Present Value of a Single Sum

The Bruegger example on page 295 showed that $50,000 invested at an annually compounded interest rate of 11% will equal $84,253 at the end of 5 years. It follows, then, that $84,253, 5 years in the future, is worth $50,000 now. That is, $50,000 is the present value of $84,253. The **present value** is the amount needed to invest now, to produce a known future value.

The present value is always a smaller amount than the known future value, due to earned and accumulated interest. In determining the future value, a company moves forward in time using a process of **accumulation**. In determining present value, it moves backward in time using a process of **discounting**.

As indicated earlier, a "present value of 1 table" appears at the end of this chapter as Table 6-2. Illustration 6-9 demonstrates the nature of such a table. It shows the present value of 1 for five different periods at three different rates of interest.

ILLUSTRATION 6-9
Excerpt from Table 6-2

PRESENT VALUE OF 1 AT COMPOUND INTEREST
(EXCERPT FROM TABLE 6-2, PAGE 337)

Period	9%	10%	11%
1	0.91743	0.90909	0.90090
2	0.84168	0.82645	0.81162
3	0.77218	0.75132	0.73119
4	0.70843	0.68301	0.65873
5	0.64993	0.62092	0.59345

The following formula is used to determine the present value of 1 (present value factor):

$$PVF_{n,i} = \frac{1}{(1+i)^n}$$

where

$PVF_{n,i}$ = present value factor for n periods at i interest

To illustrate, assuming an interest rate of 9%, the present value of 1 discounted for three different periods is as shown in Illustration 6-10.

ILLUSTRATION 6-10
Present Value of $1 Discounted at 9% for Three Periods

Discount Periods	1	÷	$(1+i)^n$	=	Present Value*	Formula $1/(1+i)^n$
1	1.00000		1.09		.91743	$1/(1.09)^1$
2	1.00000		$(1.09)^2$		.84168	$1/(1.09)^2$
3	1.00000		$(1.09)^3$		.77218	$1/(1.09)^3$

*Note that these amounts appear in Table 6-2 in the 9% column.

The present value of any single sum (future value), then, is as follows.

$$PV = FV\,(PVF_{n,i})$$

where

PV = present value
FV = future value
$PVF_{n,i}$ = present value factor for n periods at i interest

To illustrate, what is the present value of $84,253 to be received or paid in 5 years discounted at 11% compounded annually? Illustration 6-11 shows this problem as a time diagram.

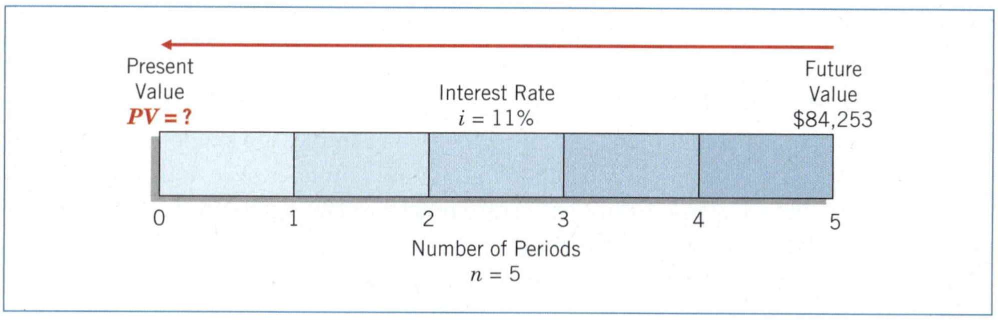

ILLUSTRATION 6-11
Present Value Time Diagram ($n = 5$, $i = 11\%$)

Using the formula, we solve this problem as follows.

$$\begin{aligned}\textbf{Present value} &= FV\,(PVF_{n,i})\\ &= \$84{,}253\,(PVF_{5,11\%})\\ &= \$84{,}253\left(\frac{1}{(1+.11)^5}\right)\\ &= \$84{,}253\,(.59345)\\ &= \$50{,}000 \text{ (rounded by \$.06)}\end{aligned}$$

To determine the present value factor of 0.59345, use a financial calculator or read the present value of a single sum in Table 6-2 (11% column, 5-period row).

The time diagram and formula approach can be applied in a variety of situations. For example, assume that your rich uncle decides to give you $2,000 for a trip to Europe when you graduate from college 3 years from now. He proposes to finance the trip by investing a sum of money now at 8% compound interest that will provide you with $2,000 upon your graduation. The only conditions are that you graduate and that you tell him how much to invest now.

To impress your uncle, you set up the time diagram in Illustration 6-12 and solve this problem as follows.

ILLUSTRATION 6-12
Present Value Time Diagram ($n = 3, i = 8\%$)

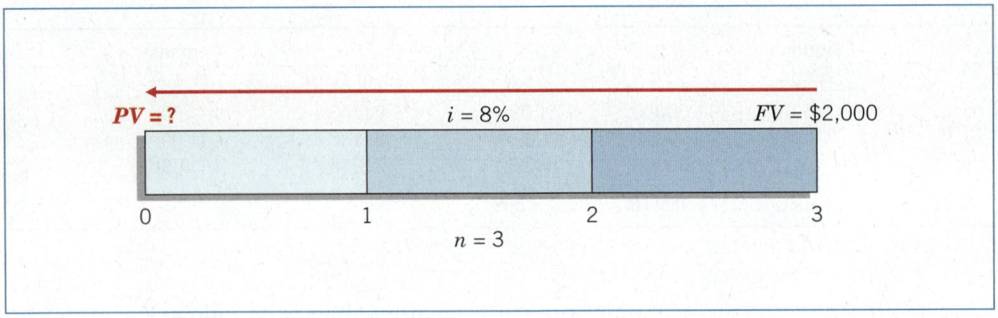

$$\text{Present value} = 2{,}000\,(PVF_{3,8\%})$$
$$= \$2{,}000\left(\frac{1}{(1+.08)^3}\right)$$
$$= \$2{,}000\,(.79383)$$
$$= \$1{,}587.66$$

Advise your uncle to invest $1,587.66 now to provide you with $2,000 upon graduation. To satisfy your uncle's other condition, you must pass this course (and many more).

Solving for Other Unknowns in Single-Sum Problems

In computing either the future value or the present value in the previous single-sum illustrations, both the number of periods and the interest rate were known. In many business situations, both the future value and the present value are known, but the number of periods or the interest rate is unknown. The following two examples are single-sum problems (future value and present value) with either an unknown number of periods (n) or an unknown interest rate (i). These examples, and the accompanying solutions, demonstrate that knowing any three of the four values (future value, *FV*; present value, *PV*; number of periods, n; interest rate, i) allows you to derive the remaining unknown variable.

Example—Computation of the Number of Periods

The Village of Somonauk wants to accumulate $70,000 for the construction of a veterans monument in the town square. At the beginning of the current year, the Village deposited $47,811 in a memorial fund that earns 10% interest compounded annually. How many years will it take to accumulate $70,000 in the memorial fund?

In this illustration, the Village knows both the present value ($47,811) and the future value ($70,000), along with the interest rate of 10%. Illustration 6-13 depicts this investment problem as a time diagram.

ILLUSTRATION 6-13
Time Diagram to Solve for Unknown Number of Periods

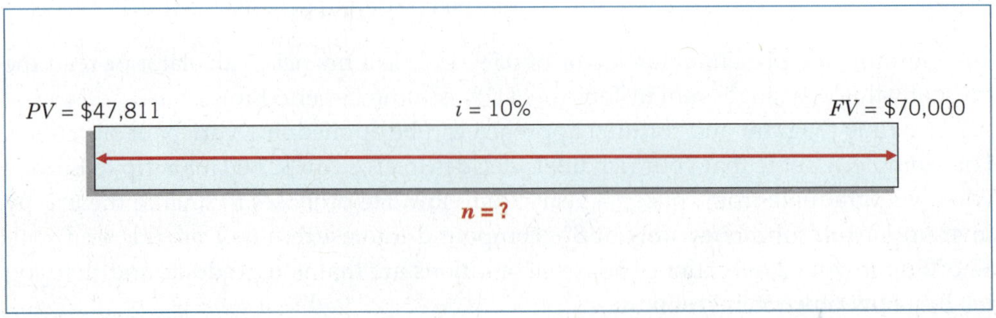

Knowing both the present value and the future value allows the Village to solve for the unknown number of periods. It may use either the future value or the present value formulas, as shown in Illustration 6-14.

ILLUSTRATION 6-14
Solving for Unknown Number of Periods

Future Value Approach	Present Value Approach
$FV = PV\,(FVF_{n,10\%})$	$PV = FV\,(PVF_{n,10\%})$
$\$70{,}000 = \$47{,}811\,(FVF_{n,10\%})$	$\$47{,}811 = \$70{,}000\,(PVF_{n,10\%})$
$FVF_{n,10\%} = \dfrac{\$70{,}000}{\$47{,}811} = 1.46410$	$PVF_{n,10\%} = \dfrac{\$47{,}811}{\$70{,}000} = .68301$

Using the future value factor of 1.46410, refer to Table 6-1 and read down the 10% column to find that factor in the 4-period row. Thus, it will take 4 years for the $47,811 to accumulate to $70,000 if invested at 10% interest compounded annually. Or, using the present value factor of 0.68301, refer to Table 6-2 and read down the 10% column to find that factor in the 4-period row.

Example—Computation of the Interest Rate

Advanced Design, Inc. needs $1,409,870 for basic research 5 years from now. The company currently has $800,000 to invest for that purpose. At what rate of interest must it invest the $800,000 to fund basic research projects of $1,409,870, 5 years from now?

The time diagram in Illustration 6-15 depicts this investment situation.

ILLUSTRATION 6-15
Time Diagram to Solve for Unknown Interest Rate

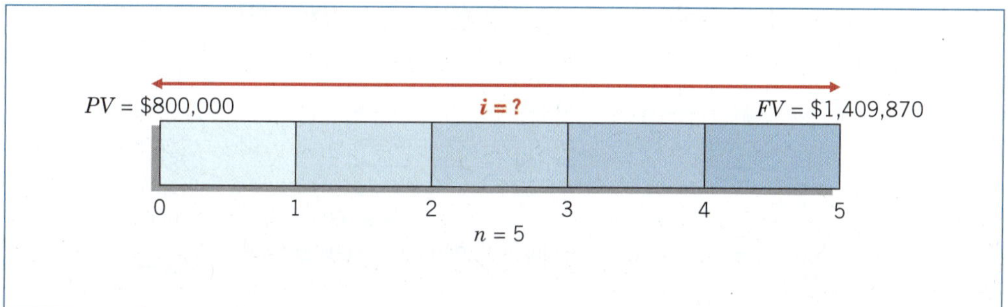

Advanced Design may determine the unknown interest rate from either the future value approach or the present value approach, as Illustration 6-16 shows.

ILLUSTRATION 6-16
Solving for Unknown Interest Rate

Future Value Approach	Present Value Approach
$FV = PV\,(FVF_{5,i})$	$PV = FV\,(PVF_{5,i})$
$\$1{,}409{,}870 = \$800{,}000\,(FVF_{5,i})$	$\$800{,}000 = \$1{,}409{,}870\,(PVF_{5,i})$
$FVF_{5,i} = \dfrac{\$1{,}409{,}870}{\$800{,}000} = 1.76234$	$PVF_{5,i} = \dfrac{\$800{,}000}{\$1{,}409{,}870} = .56743$

Using the future value factor of 1.76234, refer to Table 6-1 and read across the 5-period row to find that factor in the 12% column. Thus, the company must invest the $800,000 at 12% to accumulate to $1,409,870 in 5 years. Or, using the present value factor of .56743 and Table 6-2, again find that factor at the juncture of the 5-period row and the 12% column.

ANNUITIES

6 LEARNING OBJECTIVE
Solve future value of ordinary and annuity due problems.

The preceding discussion involved only the accumulation or discounting of a single principal sum. However, many situations arise in which a series of dollar amounts are paid or received periodically, such as installment loans or sales; regular, partially recovered invested funds; or a series of realized cost savings.

For example, a life insurance contract involves a series of equal payments made at equal intervals of time. Such a process of periodic payment represents the accumulation of a sum of money through an annuity. An **annuity**, by definition, requires the following: (1) periodic payments or receipts (called **rents**) of the same amount, (2) the same-length interval between such rents, and (3) compounding of **interest** once each interval. The **future value of an annuity** is the sum of all the rents plus the accumulated compound interest on them.

Note that the rents may occur at either the beginning or the end of the periods. If the rents occur at the end of each period, an annuity is classified as an **ordinary annuity**. If the rents occur at the beginning of each period, an annuity is classified as an **annuity due**.

Future Value of an Ordinary Annuity

One approach to determining the future value of an annuity computes the value to which **each** of the rents in the series will accumulate, and then totals their individual future values.

For example, assume that $1 is deposited at the **end** of each of 5 years (an ordinary annuity) and earns 12% interest compounded annually. Illustration 6-17 shows the computation of the future value, using the "future value of 1" table (Table 6-1) for each of the five $1 rents.

ILLUSTRATION 6-17
Solving for the Future Value of an Ordinary Annuity

END OF PERIOD IN WHICH $1.00 IS TO BE INVESTED

Present	1	2	3	4	5	Value at End of Year 5
	$1.00					$1.57352
		$1.00				1.40493
			$1.00			1.25440
				$1.00		1.12000
					$1.00	1.00000
Total (future value of an ordinary annuity of $1.00 for 5 periods at 12%)						$6.35285

Because an ordinary annuity consists of rents deposited at the end of the period, those rents earn no interest during the period. For example, the third rent earns interest for only two periods (periods four and five). It earns no interest for the third period since it is not deposited until the end of the third period. When computing the future value of an ordinary annuity, the number of compounding periods will always be **one less than the number of rents**.

The foregoing procedure for computing the future value of an ordinary annuity always produces the correct answer. However, it can become cumbersome if the number of rents is large. A formula provides a more efficient way of expressing the future value of an ordinary annuity of 1. This formula sums the individual rents plus the compound interest, as follows.

$$FVF\text{-}OA_{n,i} = \frac{(1+i)^n - 1}{i}$$

where

$FVF\text{-}OA_{n,i}$ = future value factor of an ordinary annuity
i = rate of interest per period
n = number of compounding periods

For example, $FVF\text{-}OA_{5,12\%}$ refers to the value to which an ordinary annuity of 1 will accumulate in 5 periods at 12% interest.

Using the formula above has resulted in the development of tables, similar to those used for the "future value of 1" and the "present value of 1" for both an ordinary annuity and an annuity due. Illustration 6-18 provides an excerpt from the "future value of an ordinary annuity of 1" table.

FUTURE VALUE OF AN ORDINARY ANNUITY OF 1
(EXCERPT FROM TABLE 6-3, PAGE 339)

Period	10%	11%	12%
1	1.00000	1.00000	1.00000
2	2.10000	2.11000	2.12000
3	3.31000	3.34210	3.37440
4	4.64100	4.70973	4.77933
5	6.10510	6.22780	6.35285*

*Note that this annuity table factor is the same as the sum of the future values of 1 factors shown in Illustration 6-17.

ILLUSTRATION 6-18
Excerpt from Table 6-3

Interpreting the table, if $1 is invested at the end of each year for 4 years at 11% interest compounded annually, the value of the annuity at the end of the fourth year is $4.71 (4.70973 × $1.00). Now, multiply the factor from the appropriate line and column of the table by the dollar amount of **one rent** involved in an ordinary annuity. The result: the accumulated sum of the rents and the compound interest to the date of the last rent.

The following formula computes the future value of an ordinary annuity.

$$\text{Future value of an ordinary annuity} = R\,(FVF\text{-}OA_{n,i})$$

where

$$R = \text{periodic rent}$$
$$FVF\text{-}OA_{n,i} = \text{future value of an ordinary annuity factor for } n \text{ periods at } i \text{ interest}$$

To illustrate, what is the future value of five $5,000 deposits made at the end of each of the next 5 years, earning interest of 12%? Illustration 6-19 depicts this problem as a time diagram.

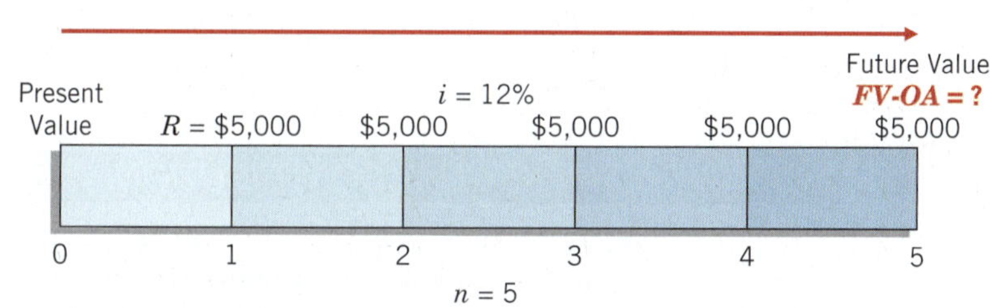

ILLUSTRATION 6-19
Time Diagram for Future Value of Ordinary Annuity ($n = 5, i = 12\%$)

Use of the formula solves this investment problem as follows.

$$\begin{aligned}\text{Future value of an ordinary annuity} &= R\,(FVF\text{-}OA_{n,i})\\ &= 5{,}000\,(FVF\text{-}OA_{5,12\%})\\ &= \$5{,}000\left(\frac{(1+.12)^5-1}{.12}\right)\\ &= \$5{,}000\,(6.35285)\\ &= \$31{,}764.25\end{aligned}$$

To determine the future value of an ordinary annuity factor of 6.35285 in the formula on page 301, use a financial calculator or read the appropriate table, in this case, Table 6-3 (12% column and the 5-period row).

To illustrate these computations in a business situation, assume that Hightown Electronics deposits $75,000 at the end of each 6-month period for the next 3 years, to accumulate enough money to meet debts that mature in 3 years. What is the future value that the company will have on deposit at the end of 3 years if the annual interest rate is 10%? The time diagram in Illustration 6-20 depicts this situation.

ILLUSTRATION 6-20
Time Diagram for Future Value of Ordinary Annuity ($n = 6, i = 5\%$)

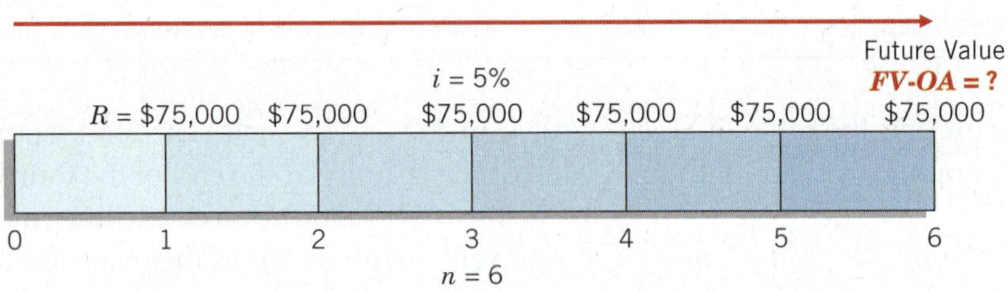

The formula solution for the Hightown Electronics situation is as follows.

$$\textbf{Future value of an ordinary annuity} = R\,(FVF\text{-}OA_{n,i})$$
$$= \$75{,}000\,(FVF\text{-}OA_{6,5\%})$$
$$= \$75{,}000\left(\frac{(1 + .05)^6 - 1}{.05}\right)$$
$$= \$75{,}000\,(6.80191)$$
$$= \$510{,}143.25$$

Thus, six 6-month deposits of $75,000 earning 5% per period will grow to $510,143.25.

What do the numbers mean? DON'T WAIT TO MAKE THAT CONTRIBUTION!

There is great power in compounding of interest, and there is no better illustration of this maxim than the case of retirement savings, especially for young people. Under current tax rules for individual retirement accounts (IRAs), you can contribute up to $5,000 in an investment fund, which will grow tax-free until you reach retirement age. What's more, you get a tax deduction for the amount contributed in the current year. Financial planners encourage young people to take advantage of the tax benefits of IRAs. By starting early, you can use the power of compounding to grow a pretty good nest egg. As shown in the adjacent chart, starting earlier can have a big impact on the value of your retirement fund.

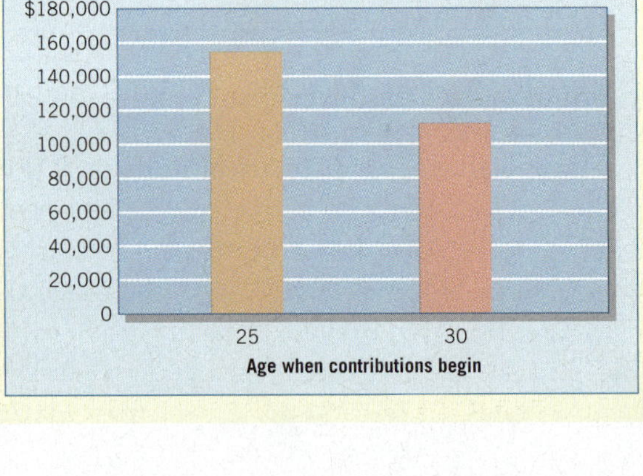

As shown, by setting aside \$1,000 each year, beginning when you are 25 and assuming a rate of return of 6%, your retirement account at age 65 will have a tidy balance of \$154,762 (\$1,000 × 154.76197 ($FVF\text{-}OA_{40,6\%}$)). That's the power of compounding. Not too bad you say, but hey, there are a lot of things you might want to spend that \$1,000 on (clothes, a trip to Vegas or Europe, new golf clubs). However, if you delay starting those contributions until age 30, your retirement fund will grow only to a value of \$111,435 (\$1,000 × 111.43478 ($FVF\text{-}OA_{35,6\%}$)). That is quite a haircut—about 28%. That is, by delaying or missing contributions, you miss out on the power of compounding and put a dent in your projected nest egg.

Source: Adapted from T. Rowe Price, "A Roadmap to Financial Security for Young Adults," *Invest with Confidence* (*troweprice.com*).

Future Value of an Annuity Due

The preceding analysis of an ordinary annuity assumed that the periodic rents occur at the **end** of each period. Recall that an **annuity due** assumes periodic rents occur at the **beginning** of each period. This means an annuity due will accumulate interest during the first period (in contrast to an ordinary annuity rent, which will not). In other words, the two types of annuities differ in the number of interest accumulation periods involved even though the same number of rents occur.

If rents occur at the end of a period (ordinary annuity), in determining the **future value of an annuity** there will be one less interest period than if the rents occur at the beginning of the period (annuity due). Illustration 6-21 shows this distinction.

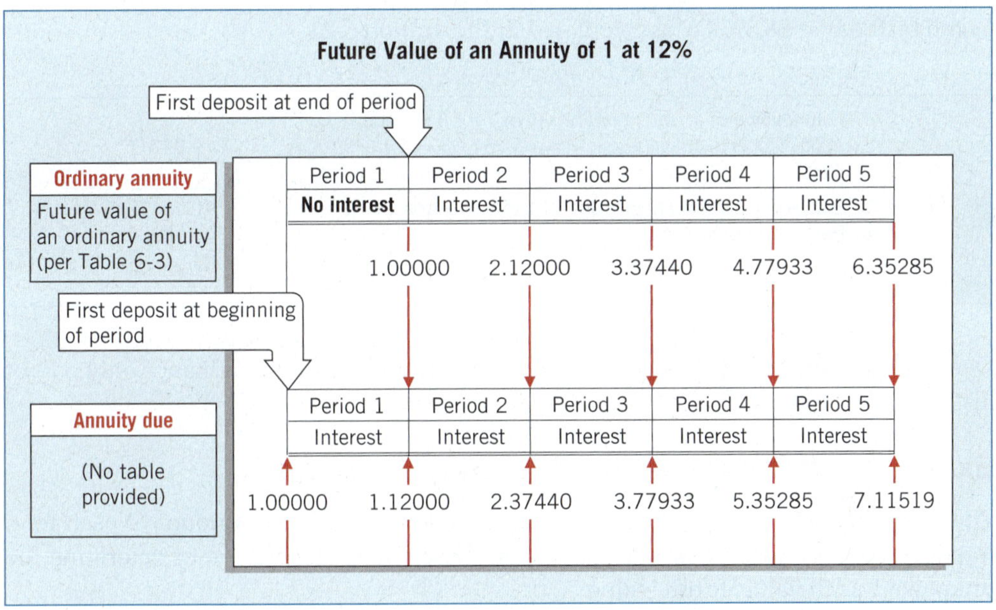

ILLUSTRATION 6-21
Comparison of the Future Value of an Ordinary Annuity with an Annuity Due

In this example, the cash flows from the annuity due come exactly one period earlier than for an ordinary annuity. As a result, the future value of the annuity due factor is exactly 12% higher than the ordinary annuity factor. For example, the value of an ordinary annuity factor at the end of period one at 12% is 1.00000, whereas for an annuity due it is 1.12000.

To find the future value of an annuity due factor, multiply the future value of an ordinary annuity factor by 1 plus the interest rate. For example, to determine the future value of an annuity due interest factor for 5 periods at 12% compound interest, simply multiply the future value of an ordinary annuity interest factor for 5 periods (6.35285), by one plus the interest rate (1 + .12), to arrive at 7.11519 (6.35285 × 1.12).

To illustrate the use of the ordinary annuity tables in converting to an annuity due, assume that Sue Lotadough plans to deposit $800 a year on each birthday of her son Howard. She makes the first deposit on his tenth birthday, at 6% interest compounded annually. Sue wants to know the amount she will have accumulated for college expenses by her son's eighteenth birthday.

If the first deposit occurs on Howard's tenth birthday, Sue will make a total of 8 deposits over the life of the annuity (assume no deposit on the eighteenth birthday), as shown in Illustration 6-22. Because all the deposits are made at the beginning of the periods, they represent an annuity due.

ILLUSTRATION 6-22
Annuity Due Time Diagram

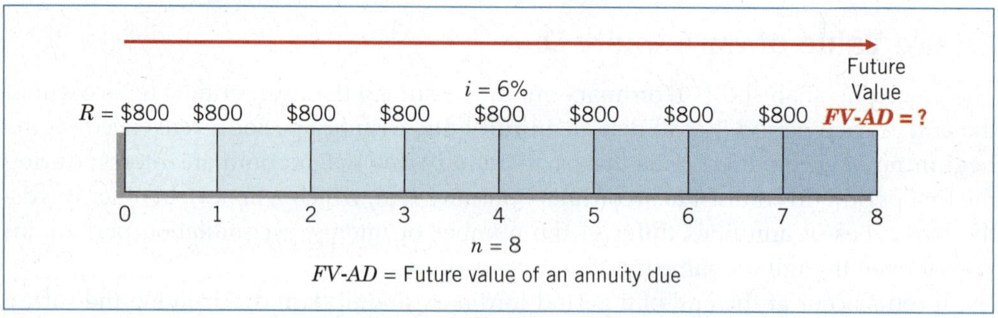

Referring to the "future value of an ordinary annuity of 1" table for 8 periods at 6%, Sue finds a factor of 9.89747. She then multiplies this factor by (1 + .06) to arrive at the future value of an annuity due factor. As a result, the accumulated value on Howard's eighteenth birthday is $8,393.06, as calculated in Illustration 6-23.

ILLUSTRATION 6-23
Computation of Accumulated Value of Annuity Due

1. Future value of an ordinary annuity of 1 for 8 periods at 6% (Table 6-3)	9.89747
2. Factor (1 + .06)	× 1.06
3. Future value of an annuity due of 1 for 8 periods at 6%	10.49132
4. Periodic deposit (rent)	× $800
5. Accumulated value on son's 18th birthday	$8,393.06

Depending on the college he chooses, Howard may have enough to finance only part of his first year of school.

Examples of Future Value of Annuity Problems

The foregoing annuity examples relied on three known values—amount of each rent, interest rate, and number of periods. Using these values enables us to determine the unknown fourth value, future value.

The first two future value problems we present illustrate the computations of (1) the amount of the rents and (2) the number of rents. The third problem illustrates the computation of the future value of an annuity due.

Computation of Rent

Assume that you plan to accumulate $14,000 for a down payment on a condominium apartment 5 years from now. For the next 5 years, you earn an annual return of 8% compounded semiannually. How much should you deposit at the end of each 6-month period?

The $14,000 is the future value of 10 (5 × 2) semiannual end-of-period payments of an unknown amount, at an interest rate of 4% (8% ÷ 2). Illustration 6-24 depicts this problem as a time diagram.

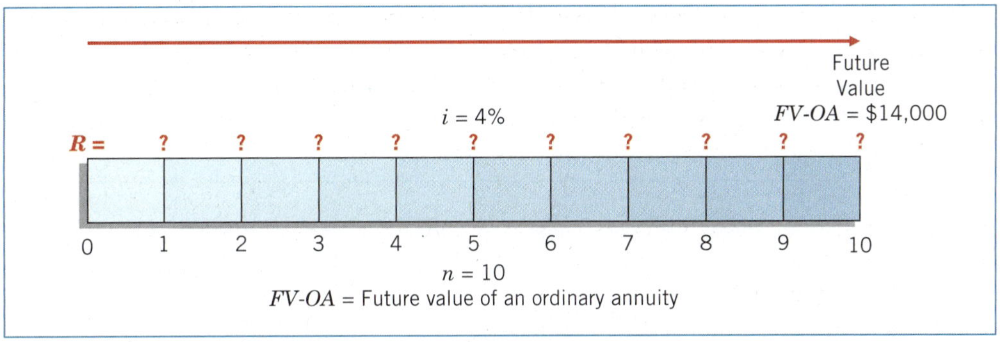

ILLUSTRATION 6-24
Future Value of Ordinary Annuity Time Diagram (n = 10, i = 4%)

Using the formula for the future value of an ordinary annuity, you determine the amount of each rent as follows.

$$\text{Future value of an ordinary annuity} = R\,(FVF\text{-}OA_{n,i})$$
$$\$14{,}000 = R\,(FVF\text{-}OA_{10,4\%})$$
$$\$14{,}000 = R\,(12.00611)$$
$$R = \$1{,}166.07$$

Thus, you must make 10 semiannual deposits of $1,166.07 each in order to accumulate $14,000 for your down payment.

Computation of the Number of Periodic Rents

Suppose that a company's goal is to accumulate $117,332 by making periodic deposits of $20,000 at the end of each year, which will earn 8% compounded annually while accumulating. How many deposits must it make?

The $117,332 represents the future value of n(?) $20,000 deposits, at an 8% annual rate of interest. Illustration 6-25 depicts this problem in a time diagram.

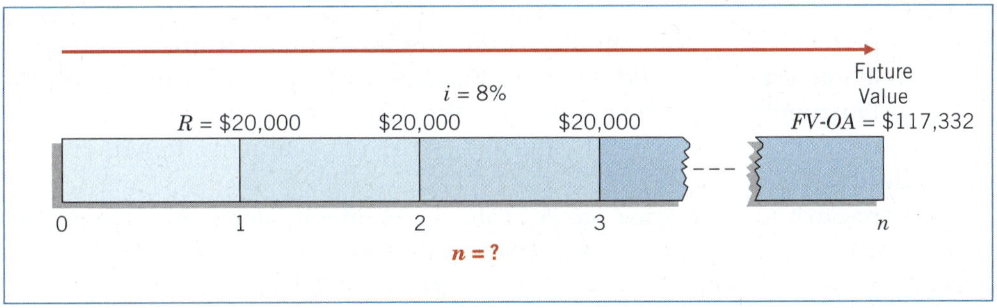

ILLUSTRATION 6-25
Future Value of Ordinary Annuity Time Diagram, to Solve for Unknown Number of Periods

Using the future value of an ordinary annuity formula, the company obtains the following factor.

$$\text{Future value of an ordinary annuity} = R\,(FVF\text{-}OA_{n,i})$$
$$\$117{,}332 = \$20{,}000\,(FVF\text{-}OA_{n,8\%})$$
$$FVF\text{-}OA_{n,8\%} = \frac{\$117{,}332}{\$20{,}000} = 5.86660$$

Use Table 6-3 and read down the 8% column to find 5.86660 in the 5-period row. Thus, the company must make five deposits of $20,000 each.

Computation of the Future Value

To create his retirement fund, Walter Goodwrench, a mechanic, now works weekends. Mr. Goodwrench deposits $2,500 today in a savings account that earns 9% interest.

He plans to deposit $2,500 every year for a total of 30 years. How much cash will Mr. Goodwrench accumulate in his retirement savings account, when he retires in 30 years? Illustration 6-26 depicts this problem in a time diagram.

ILLUSTRATION 6-26
Future Value Annuity Due Time Diagram ($n = 30, i = 9\%$)

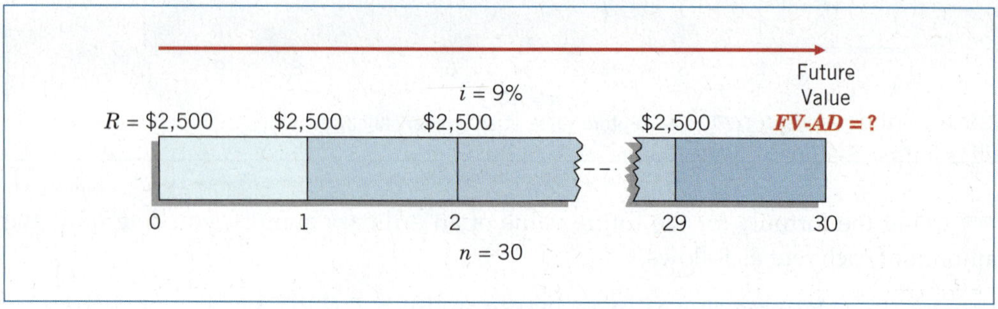

Using the "future value of an ordinary annuity of 1" table, Mr. Goodwrench computes the solution as shown in Illustration 6-27.

ILLUSTRATION 6-27
Computation of Accumulated Value of an Annuity Due

1. Future value of an ordinary annuity of 1 for 30 periods at 9%	136.30754
2. Factor (1 + .09)	× 1.09
3. Future value of an annuity due of 1 for 30 periods at 9%	148.57522
4. Periodic rent	× $2,500
5. Accumulated value at end of 30 years	$371,438

Present Value of an Ordinary Annuity

LEARNING OBJECTIVE 7
Solve present value of ordinary and annuity due problems.

The present value of an annuity is **the single sum** that, if invested at compound interest now, would provide for an annuity (a series of withdrawals) for a certain number of future periods. In other words, the present value of an ordinary annuity is the present value of a series of equal rents, to withdraw at equal intervals.

One approach to finding the present value of an annuity determines the present value of each of the rents in the series and then totals their individual present values. For example, we may view an annuity of $1, to be received at the **end** of each of 5 periods, as separate amounts. We then compute each present value using the table of present values (see Table 6-2 on pages 336–337), assuming an interest rate of 12%. Illustration 6-28 shows this approach.

ILLUSTRATION 6-28
Solving for the Present Value of an Ordinary Annuity

END OF PERIOD IN WHICH $1.00 IS TO BE RECEIVED

Present Value at Beg. of Year 1	1	2	3	4	5
$0.89286 ←	$1.00				
.79719 ←		$1.00			
.71178 ←			$1.00		
.63552 ←				$1.00	
.56743 ←					$1.00
$3.60478 Total (present value of an ordinary annuity of $1.00 for five periods at 12%)					

This computation tells us that if we invest the single sum of \$3.61 today at 12% interest for 5 periods, we will be able to withdraw \$1 at the end of each period for 5 periods. We can summarize this cumbersome procedure by the following formula.

$$PVF\text{-}OA_{n,i} = \frac{1 - \dfrac{1}{(1+i)^n}}{i}$$

The expression $PVF\text{-}OA_{n,i}$ refers to the present value of an ordinary annuity of 1 factor for n periods at i interest. Ordinary annuity tables base present values on this formula. Illustration 6-29 shows an excerpt from such a table.

ILLUSTRATION 6-29
Excerpt from Table 6-4

PRESENT VALUE OF AN ORDINARY ANNUITY OF 1
(EXCERPT FROM TABLE 6-4, PAGE 341)

Period	10%	11%	12%
1	0.90909	0.90090	0.89286
2	1.73554	1.71252	1.69005
3	2.48685	2.44371	2.40183
4	3.16986	3.10245	3.03735
5	3.79079	3.69590	3.60478*

*Note that this annuity table factor is equal to the sum of the present value of 1 factors shown in Illustration 6-28.

The general formula for the present value of any ordinary annuity is as follows.

$$\text{Present value of an ordinary annuity} = R\,(PVF\text{-}OA_{n,i})$$

where

$$R = \text{periodic rent (ordinary annuity)}$$
$$PVF\text{-}OA_{n,i} = \text{present value of an ordinary annuity of 1 for } n \text{ periods at } i \text{ interest}$$

To illustrate with an example, what is the present value of rental receipts of \$6,000 each, to be received at the end of each of the next 5 years when discounted at 12%? This problem may be time-diagrammed and solved as shown in Illustration 6-30.

ILLUSTRATION 6-30
Present Value of Ordinary Annuity Time Diagram

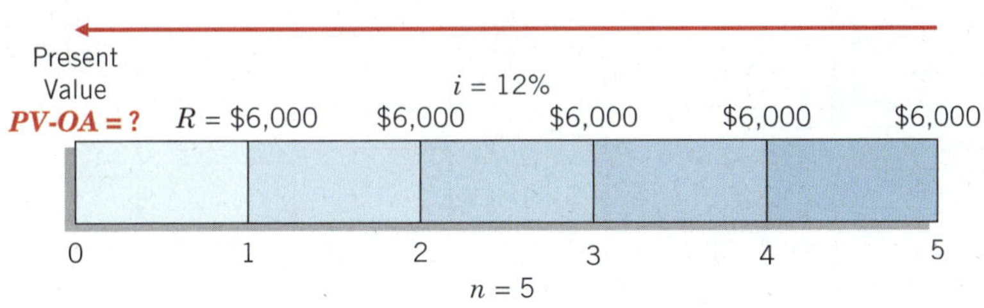

The formula for this calculation is as shown below.

$$\begin{aligned}\text{Present value of an ordinary annuity} &= R\,(PVF\text{-}OA_{n,i})\\ &= \$6{,}000\,(PVF\text{-}OA_{5,12\%})\\ &= \$6{,}000\,(3.60478)\\ &= \$21{,}628.68\end{aligned}$$

The present value of the 5 ordinary annuity rental receipts of \$6,000 each is \$21,628.68. To determine the present value of the ordinary annuity factor 3.60478, use a financial calculator or read the appropriate table, in this case Table 6-4 (12% column and 5-period row).

What do the numbers mean? UP IN SMOKE

Time value of money concepts also can be relevant to public policy debates. For example, several states had to determine how to receive the payments from tobacco companies as settlement for a national lawsuit against the companies for the healthcare costs of smoking.

The **State of Wisconsin** was due to collect 25 years of payments totaling \$5.6 billion. The state could wait to collect the payments, or it could sell the payments to an investment bank (a process called *securitization*). If it were to sell the payments, it would receive a lump-sum payment today of \$1.26 billion. Is this a good deal for the state? Assuming a discount rate of 8% and that the payments will be received in equal amounts (e.g., an annuity), the present value of the tobacco payment is:

$$\$5.6 \text{ billion} \div 25 = \$224 \text{ million}$$

$$\$224 \text{ million} \times 10.67478^{*} = \$2.39 \text{ billion}$$

$^{*}PV\text{-}OA\ (i = 8\%, n = 25)$

Why would some in the state be willing to take just \$1.26 billion today for an annuity whose present value is almost twice that amount? One reason is that Wisconsin was facing a hole in its budget that could be plugged in part by the lump-sum payment. Also, some believed that the risk of not getting paid by the tobacco companies in the future makes it prudent to get the money earlier.

If this latter reason has merit, then the present value computation above should have been based on a higher interest rate. Assuming a discount rate of 15%, the present value of the annuity is \$1.448 billion (\$5.6 billion ÷ 25 = \$224 million; \$224 million × 6.46415), which is much closer to the lump-sum payment offered to the State of Wisconsin.

Present Value of an Annuity Due

In our discussion of the present value of an ordinary annuity, we discounted the final rent based on the number of rent periods. In determining the present value of an annuity due, there is always one fewer discount period. Illustration 6-31 shows this distinction.

ILLUSTRATION 6-31
Comparison of Present Value of an Ordinary Annuity with an Annuity Due

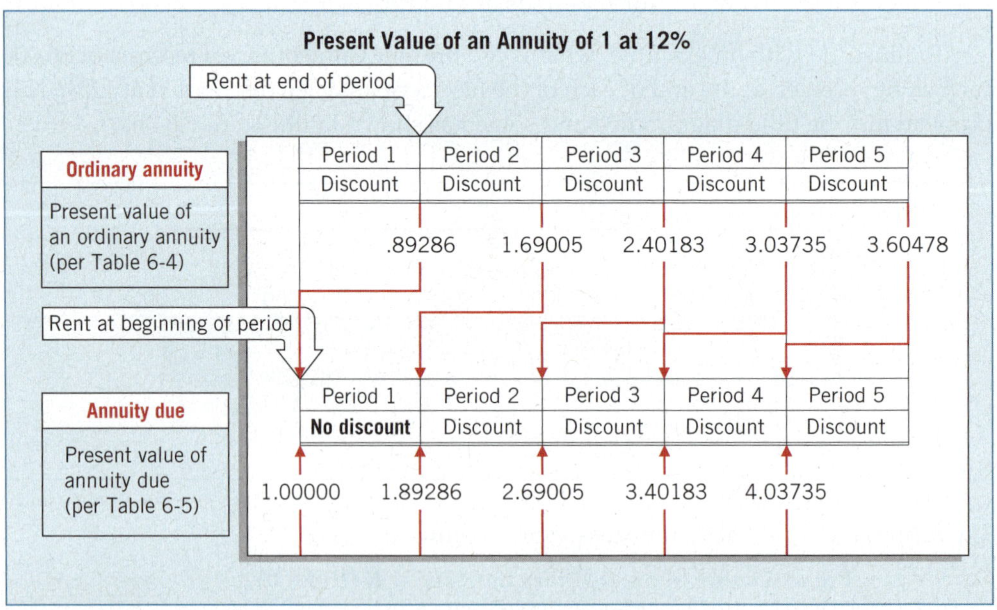

Because each cash flow comes exactly one period sooner in the present value of the annuity due, the present value of the cash flows is exactly 12% higher than the present value of an ordinary annuity. Thus, **to find the present value of an annuity due factor, multiply the present value of an ordinary annuity factor by 1 plus the interest rate** (that is, $1 + i$).

To determine the present value of an annuity due interest factor for 5 periods at 12% interest, take the present value of an ordinary annuity for 5 periods at 12% interest (3.60478) and multiply it by 1.12 to arrive at the present value of an annuity due, 4.03735 (3.60478 × 1.12). We provide present value of annuity due factors in Table 6-5.

To illustrate, Space Odyssey, Inc., rents a communications satellite for 4 years with annual rental payments of $4.8 million to be made at the beginning of each year. If the relevant annual interest rate is 11%, what is the present value of the rental obligations? Illustration 6-32 shows the company's time diagram for this problem.

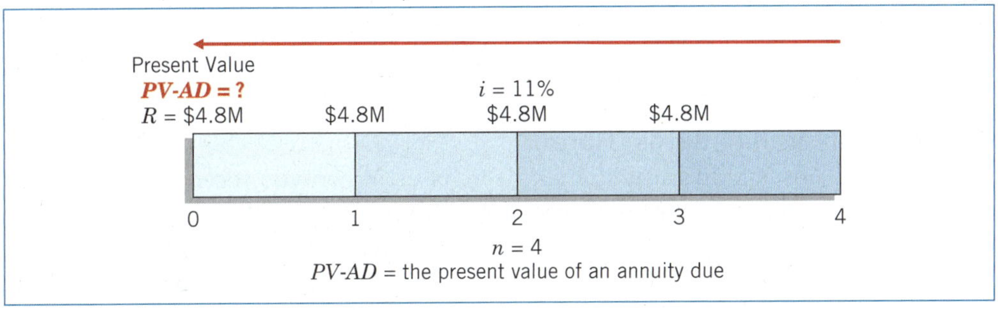

ILLUSTRATION 6-32
Present Value of Annuity Due Time Diagram ($n = 4, i = 11\%$)

Illustration 6-33 shows the computations to solve this problem.

ILLUSTRATION 6-33
Computation of Present Value of an Annuity Due

1. Present value of an ordinary annuity of 1 for 4 periods at 11% (Table 6-4)	3.10245
2. Factor (1 + .11)	× 1.11
3. Present value of an annuity due of 1 for 4 periods at 11%	3.44372
4. Periodic deposit (rent)	× $4,800,000
5. Present value of payments	$16,529,856

Using Table 6-5 also locates the desired factor 3.44371 and computes the present value of the lease payments to be $16,529,808. (The difference in computations is due to rounding.)

Examples of Present Value of Annuity Problems

In the following three examples, we demonstrate the computation of (1) the present value, (2) the interest rate, and (3) the amount of each rent.

Computation of the Present Value of an Ordinary Annuity

You have just won a lottery totaling $4,000,000. You learn that you will receive a check in the amount of $200,000 at the end of each of the next 20 years. What amount have you really won? That is, what is the present value of the $200,000 checks you will receive over the next 20 years? Illustration 6-34 (page 310) shows a time diagram of this enviable situation (assuming an appropriate interest rate of 10%).

You calculate the present value as follows.

$$\text{Present value of an ordinary annuity} = R\,(PVF\text{-}OA_{n,i})$$
$$= \$200{,}000\,(PVF\text{-}OA_{20,10\%})$$
$$= \$200{,}000\,(8.51356)$$
$$= \$1{,}702{,}712$$

ILLUSTRATION 6-34
Time Diagram to Solve for Present Value of Lottery Payments

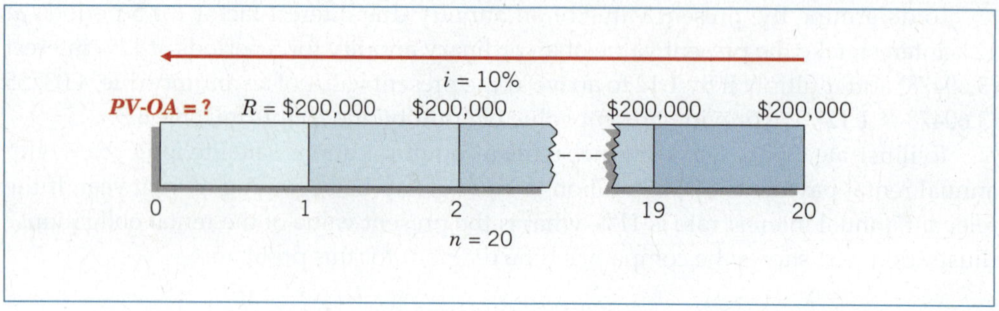

As a result, if the state deposits $1,702,712 now and earns 10% interest, it can withdraw $200,000 a year for 20 years to pay you the $4,000,000.

Computation of the Interest Rate

Many shoppers use credit cards to make purchases. When you receive the statement for payment, you may pay the total amount due or you may pay the balance in a certain number of payments. For example, assume you receive a statement from **MasterCard** with a balance due of $528.77. You may pay it off in 12 equal monthly payments of $50 each, with the first payment due one month from now. What rate of interest would you be paying?

The $528.77 represents the present value of the 12 payments of $50 each at an unknown rate of interest. The time diagram in Illustration 6-35 depicts this situation.

ILLUSTRATION 6-35
Time Diagram to Solve for Effective-Interest Rate on Loan

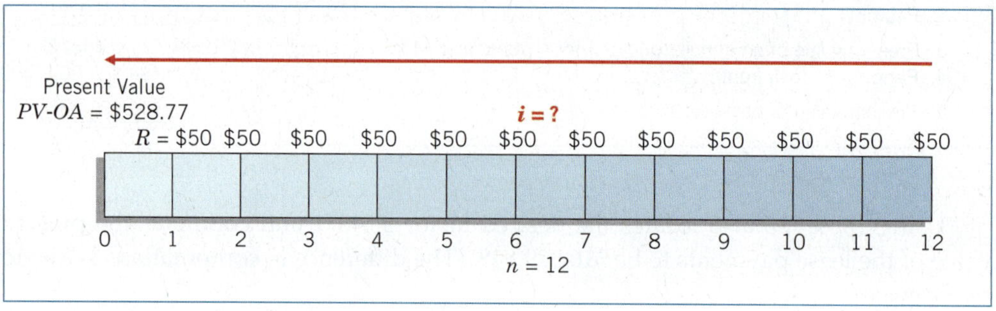

You calculate the rate as follows.

$$\text{Present value of an ordinary annuity} = R\,(PVF\text{-}OA_{n,i})$$

$$\$528.77 = \$50\,(PVF\text{-}OA_{12,i})$$

$$(PVFOA_{12,i}) = \frac{\$528.77}{\$50} = 10.57540$$

Referring to Table 6-4 and reading across the 12-period row, you find 10.57534 in the 2% column. Since 2% is a monthly rate, the nominal annual rate of interest is 24% (12 × 2%). The effective annual rate is 26.82423% $[(1 + .02)^{12} - 1]$. Obviously, you are better off paying the entire bill now if possible.

Computation of a Periodic Rent

Norm and Jackie Remmers have saved $36,000 to finance their daughter Dawna's college education. They deposited the money in the Bloomington Savings and Loan Association, where it earns 4% interest compounded semiannually. What equal amounts can their daughter withdraw at the end of every 6 months during her 4 college years, without exhausting the fund? Illustration 6-36 shows a time diagram of this situation.

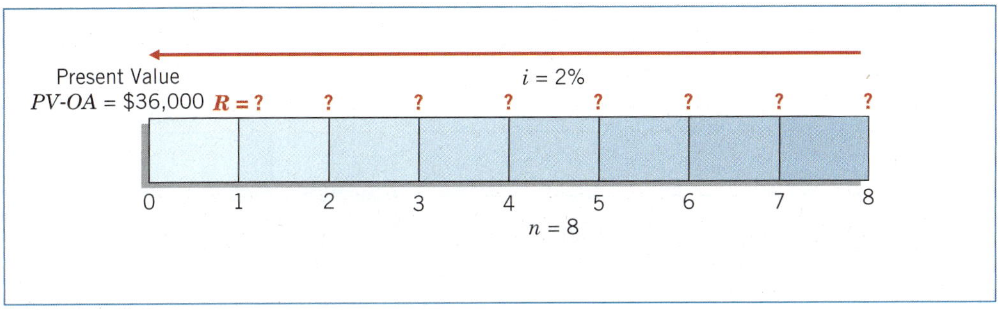

ILLUSTRATION 6-36
Time Diagram for Ordinary Annuity for a College Fund

Determining the answer by simply dividing $36,000 by 8 withdrawals is wrong. Why? Because that ignores the interest earned on the money remaining on deposit. Dawna must consider that interest is compounded semiannually at 2% (4% ÷ 2) for 8 periods (4 years × 2). Thus, using the same present value of an ordinary annuity formula, she determines the amount of each withdrawal that she can make as follows.

$$\text{Present value of an ordinary annuity} = R\ (PVF\text{-}OA_{n,i})$$
$$\$36{,}000 = R\ (PVF\text{-}OA_{8,2\%})$$
$$\$36{,}000 = R\ (7.32548)$$
$$R = \$4{,}914.35$$

MORE COMPLEX SITUATIONS

8 LEARNING OBJECTIVE
Solve present value problems related to deferred annuities and bonds.

Solving time value problems often requires using more than one table. For example, a business problem may need computations of both present value of a single sum and present value of an annuity. Two such common situations are:

1. Deferred annuities.
2. Bond problems.

Deferred Annuities

A **deferred annuity** is an annuity in which the rents begin after a specified number of periods. A deferred annuity does not begin to produce rents until two or more periods have expired. For example, "an **ordinary annuity** of six annual rents deferred 4 years" means that no rents will occur during the first 4 years and that the first of the six rents will occur at the end of the fifth year. "An **annuity due** of six annual rents deferred 4 years" means that no rents will occur during the first 4 years and that the first of six rents will occur at the beginning of the fifth year.

Future Value of a Deferred Annuity

Computing the future value of a deferred annuity is relatively straightforward. Because there is no accumulation or investment on which interest may accrue, the future value of a deferred annuity is the same as the future value of an annuity not deferred. That is, computing the future value simply ignores the deferred period.

To illustrate, assume that Sutton Corporation plans to purchase a land site in 6 years for the construction of its new corporate headquarters. Because of cash flow problems, Sutton budgets deposits of $80,000 on which it expects to earn 5% annually, only at the end of the fourth, fifth, and sixth periods. What future value will Sutton have accumulated at the end of the sixth year? Illustration 6-37 (page 312) shows a time diagram of this situation.

ILLUSTRATION 6-37
Time Diagram for Future Value of Deferred Annuity

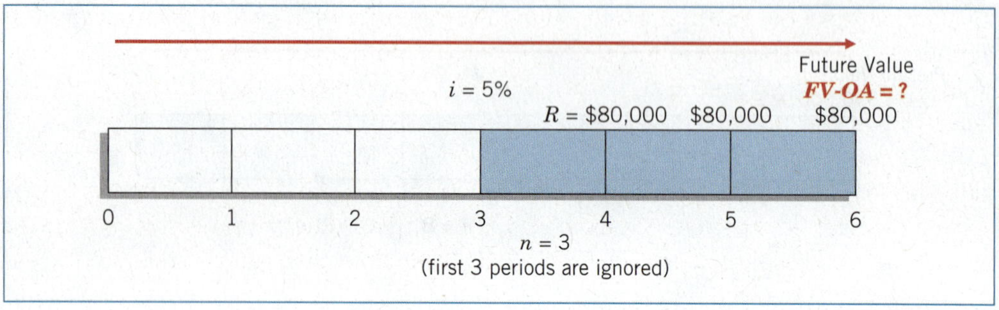

Sutton determines the value accumulated by using the standard formula for the future value of an ordinary annuity:

$$\text{Future value of an ordinary annuity} = R\,(FVF\text{-}OA_{n,i})$$
$$= \$80{,}000\,(FVF\text{-}OA_{3,5\%})$$
$$= \$80{,}000\,(3.15250)$$
$$= \$252{,}200$$

Present Value of a Deferred Annuity

Computing the present value of a deferred annuity must recognize the interest that accrues on the original investment during the deferral period.

To compute the present value of a deferred annuity, we compute the present value of an ordinary annuity of 1 as if the rents had occurred for the entire period. We then subtract the present value of rents that were not received during the deferral period. We are left with the present value of the rents actually received subsequent to the deferral period.

To illustrate, Bob Bender has developed and copyrighted tutorial software for students in advanced accounting. He agrees to sell the copyright to Campus Micro Systems for 6 annual payments of $5,000 each. The payments will begin 5 years from today. Given an annual interest rate of 8%, what is the present value of the 6 payments?

This situation is an ordinary annuity of 6 payments deferred 4 periods. The time diagram in Illustration 6-38 depicts this sales agreement.

ILLUSTRATION 6-38
Time Diagram for Present Value of Deferred Annuity

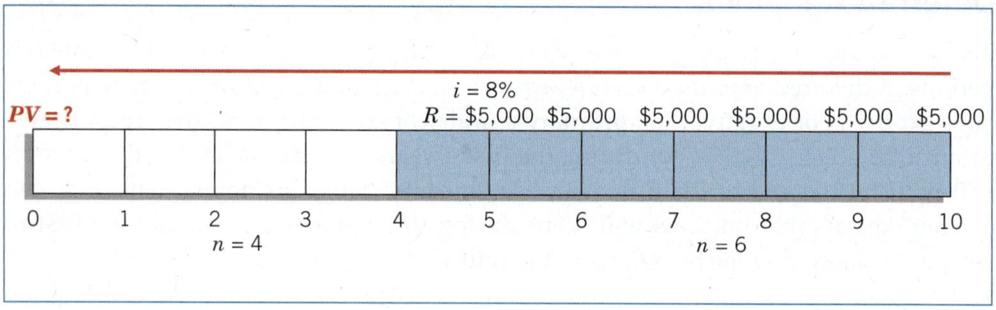

Two options are available to solve this problem. The first is to use only Table 6-4, as shown in Illustration 6-39.

ILLUSTRATION 6-39
Computation of the Present Value of a Deferred Annuity

1. Each periodic rent		$5,000
2. Present value of an ordinary annuity of 1 for total periods (10) [number of rents (6) plus number of deferred periods (4)] at 8%	6.71008	
3. Less: Present value of an ordinary annuity of 1 for the number of deferred periods (4) at 8%	3.31213	
4. Difference		× 3.39795
5. Present value of 6 rents of $5,000 deferred 4 periods		$16,989.75

The subtraction of the present value of an annuity of 1 for the deferred periods eliminates the nonexistent rents during the deferral period. It converts the present value of an ordinary annuity of $1.00 for 10 periods to the present value of 6 rents of $1.00, deferred 4 periods.

Alternatively, Bender can use both Table 6-2 and Table 6-4 to compute the present value of the 6 rents. He can first discount the annuity 6 periods. However, because the annuity is deferred 4 periods, he must treat the present value of the annuity as a future amount to be discounted another 4 periods. The time diagram in Illustration 6-40 depicts this two-step process.

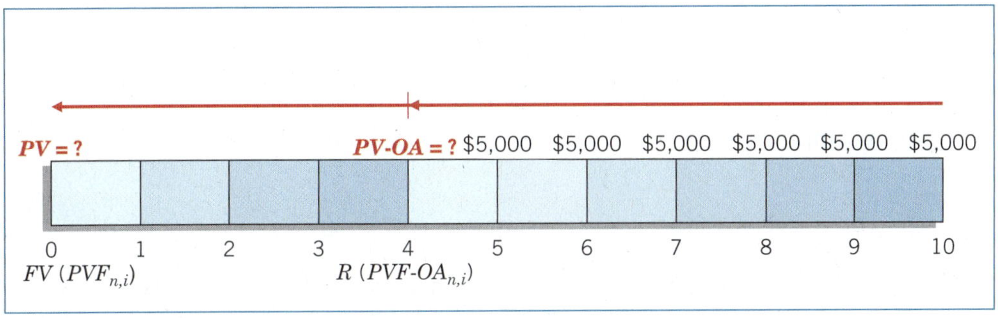

ILLUSTRATION 6-40
Time Diagram for Present Value of Deferred Annuity (2-Step Process)

Calculation using formulas would be done in two steps, as follows.

Step 1: Present value of an ordinary annuity $= R\ (PVF\text{-}OA_{n,i})$
$= \$5{,}000\ (PVF\text{-}OA_{6,8\%})$
$= \$5{,}000\ (4.62288)$
(Table 6-4, Present value of an ordinary annuity)
$= \$23{,}114.40$

Step 2: Present value of a single sum $= FV\ (PVF_{n,i})$
$= \$23{,}114.40\ (PVF_{4,8\%})$
$= \$23{,}114.40\ (.73503)$
(Table 6-2, Present value of a single sum)
$= \$16{,}989.78$

The present value of $16,989.78 computed above is the same as in Illustration 6-39 although computed differently. (The $0.03 difference is due to rounding.)

Valuation of Long-Term Bonds

A long-term bond produces two cash flows: (1) periodic interest payments during the life of the bond, and (2) the principal (face value) paid at maturity. At the date of issue, bond buyers determine the present value of these two cash flows using the market rate of interest.

The periodic interest payments represent an annuity. The principal represents a single-sum problem. The current market value of the bonds is the combined present values of the interest annuity and the principal amount.

To illustrate, Alltech Corporation on January 1, 2014, issues $100,000 of 9% bonds due in 5 years with interest payable annually at year-end. The current market rate of interest for bonds of similar risk is 11%. What will the buyers pay for this bond issue?

The time diagram in Illustration 6-41 depicts both cash flows.

ILLUSTRATION 6-41
Time Diagram to Solve for Bond Valuation

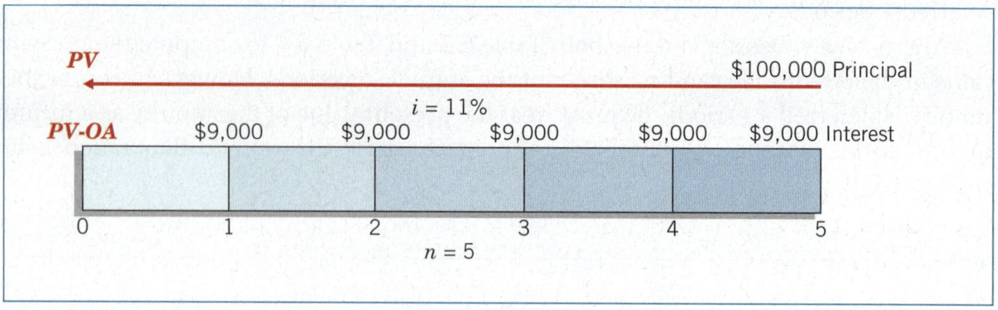

Alltech computes the present value of the two cash flows by discounting at 11% as follows.

ILLUSTRATION 6-42
Computation of the Present Value of an Interest-Bearing Bond

1. Present value of the principal: $FV\ (PVF_{5,11\%}) = \$100{,}000\ (.59345)$	$59,345.00
2. Present value of the interest payments: $R\ (PVF\text{-}OA_{5,11\%}) = \$9{,}000\ (3.69590)$	33,263.10
3. Combined present value (market price)—carrying value of bonds	$92,608.10

By paying $92,608.10 at date of issue, the buyers of the bonds will realize an effective yield of 11% over the 5-year term of the bonds. This is true because Alltech discounted the cash flows at 11%.

Effective-Interest Method of Amortization of Bond Discount or Premium

In the previous example (Illustration 6-42), Alltech Corporation issued bonds at a discount, computed as follows.

ILLUSTRATION 6-43
Computation of Bond Discount

Maturity value (face amount) of bonds		$100,000.00
Present value of the principal	$59,345.00	
Present value of the interest	33,263.10	
Proceeds (present value and cash received)		(92,608.10)
Discount on bonds issued		$ 7,391.90

Alltech amortizes (writes off to interest expense) the amount of this discount over the life of the bond issue.

The preferred procedure for amortization of a discount or premium is the **effective-interest method**. Under the effective-interest method:

Gateway to the Profession
Use of Spreadsheets to Calculate Bond Amortization

1. The company issuing the bond first computes bond interest expense by multiplying the carrying value of the bonds at the beginning of the period by the effective-interest rate.
2. The company then determines the bond discount or premium amortization by comparing the bond interest expense with the interest to be paid.

Illustration 6-44 depicts the computation of bond amortization.

ILLUSTRATION 6-44
Amortization Computation

Bond Interest Expense				Bond Interest Paid				
(Carrying Value of Bonds at Beginning of Period	×	Effective-Interest Rate)	−	(Face Amount of Bonds	×	Stated Interest Rate)	=	**Amortization Amount**

The effective-interest method produces a periodic interest expense equal to a **constant percentage of the carrying value of the bonds**. Since the percentage used is the effective rate of interest incurred by the borrower at the time of issuance, the effective-interest method results in matching expenses with revenues.

We can use the data from the Alltech Corporation example to illustrate the effective-interest method of amortization. Alltech issued $100,000 face value of bonds at a discount of $7,391.90, resulting in a carrying value of $92,608.10. Illustration 6-45 shows the effective-interest amortization schedule for Alltech's bonds.

ILLUSTRATION 6-45
Effective-Interest Amortization Schedule

SCHEDULE OF BOND DISCOUNT AMORTIZATION
5-YEAR, 9% BONDS SOLD TO YIELD 11%

Date	Cash Interest Paid	Interest Expense	Bond Discount Amortization	Carrying Value of Bonds
1/1/12				$ 92,608.10
12/31/12	$ 9,000[a]	$10,186.89[b]	$1,186.89[c]	93,794.99[d]
12/31/13	9,000	10,317.45	1,317.45	95,112.44
12/31/14	9,000	10,462.37	1,462.37	96,574.81
12/31/15	9,000	10,623.23	1,623.23	98,198.04
12/31/16	9,000	10,801.96[e]	1,801.96	100,000.00
	$45,000	$52,391.90	$7,391.90	

[a]$100,000 × .09 = $9,000
[b]$92,608.10 × .11 = $10,186.89
[c]$10,186.89 − $9,000 = $1,186.89
[d]$92,608.10 + $1,186.89 = $93,794.99
[e]$0.18 difference due to rounding.

We use the amortization schedule illustrated above for note and bond transactions in Chapters 7 and 14.

PRESENT VALUE MEASUREMENT

9 LEARNING OBJECTIVE
Apply expected cash flows to present value measurement.

In the past, most accounting calculations of present value relied on the most likely cash flow amount. *Concepts Statement No. 7* introduces an **expected cash flow approach**.[6] It uses a range of cash flows and incorporates the probabilities of those cash flows to provide a more relevant measurement of present value.

To illustrate the expected cash flow model, assume that there is a 30% probability that future cash flows will be $100, a 50% probability that they will be $200, and a 20% probability that they will be $300. In this case, the expected cash flow would be $190 [($100 × 0.3) + ($200 × 0.5) + ($300 × 0.2)]. Traditional present value approaches would use the most likely estimate ($200). However, that estimate fails to consider the different probabilities of the possible cash flows.

[6]"Using Cash Flow Information and Present Value in Accounting Measurements," *Statement of Financial Accounting Concepts No. 7* (Norwalk, Conn.: FASB, 2000).

Choosing an Appropriate Interest Rate

After determining expected cash flows, a company must then use the proper interest rate to discount the cash flows. The interest rate used for this purpose has three components:

THREE COMPONENTS OF INTEREST

1. **PURE RATE OF INTEREST (2%–4%).** This would be the amount a lender would charge if there were no possibilities of default and no expectation of inflation.
2. **EXPECTED INFLATION RATE OF INTEREST (0%–?).** Lenders recognize that in an inflationary economy, they are being paid back with less valuable dollars. As a result, they increase their interest rate to compensate for this loss in purchasing power. When inflationary expectations are high, interest rates are high.
3. **CREDIT RISK RATE OF INTEREST (0%–5%).** The government has little or no credit risk (i.e., risk of nonpayment) when it issues bonds. A business enterprise, however, depending upon its financial stability, profitability, etc., can have a low or a high credit risk.

The FASB takes the position that after computing the expected cash flows, a company should discount those cash flows by the **risk-free rate of return**. That rate is defined as **the pure rate of return plus the expected inflation rate**. The Board notes that the expected cash flow framework adjusts for credit risk because it incorporates the probability of receipt or payment into the computation of expected cash flows. Therefore, the rate used to discount the expected cash flows should consider only the pure rate of interest and the inflation rate.

What do the numbers mean? HOW LOW CAN THEY GO?

Management of the level of interest rates is an important policy tool of the Federal Reserve Bank and its chair, Ben Bernanke. Through a number of policy options, the Fed has the ability to move interest rates up or down, and these rate changes can affect the wealth of all market participants. For example, if the Fed wants to raise rates (because the overall economy is getting overheated), it can raise the *discount rate*, which is the rate banks pay to borrow money from the Fed. This rate increase will factor into the rates banks and other creditors use to lend money. As a result, companies will think twice about borrowing money to expand their businesses. The result will be a slowing economy. A rate cut does just the opposite. It makes borrowing cheaper, and it can help the economy expand as more companies borrow to expand their operations.

Keeping rates low had been the Fed's policy in the early 2000s. The low rates did help keep the economy humming. But these same low rates may have also resulted in too much real estate lending and the growth of a real estate bubble, as the price of housing was fueled by cheaper low-interest mortgage loans. But, as the old saying goes, "What goes up, must come down." That is what real estate prices did, triggering massive loan write-offs, a seizing up of credit markets, and a slowing economy.

So just when a rate cut might help the economy, the Fed's rate-cutting toolbox is empty. As a result, the Fed began to explore other options, such as repurchasing long-term government bonds—referred to as "quantitative easing." These repurchases put money into the market, increase the demand for long-term bonds, and reduce long-term interest rates. The Fed has conducted three rounds of quantitative easing in an attempt to spur the economy out of its persistent funk.

Source: Adam Shell, "Five Investments to Consider if the Fed Uncorks QE3," *USA TODAY* (September 1, 2012).

Example of Expected Cash Flow

To illustrate, assume that Al's Appliance Outlet offers a 2-year warranty on all products sold. In 2014, Al's Appliance sold $250,000 of a particular type of clothes dryer. Al's Appliance entered into an agreement with Ralph's Repair to provide all warranty service on the dryers sold in 2014. To determine the warranty expense to record in 2014 and the amount of warranty liability to record on the December 31, 2014, balance sheet, Al's Appliance must measure the fair value of the agreement. Since there is not a ready market for these warranty contracts, Al's Appliance uses expected cash flow techniques to value the warranty obligation.

Based on prior warranty experience, Al's Appliance estimates the expected cash outflows associated with the dryers sold in 2014, as shown in Illustration 6-46.

ILLUSTRATION 6-46
Expected Cash Outflows—Warranties

	Cash Flow Estimate	×	Probability Assessment	=	Expected Cash Flow
2014	$3,800		20%		$ 760
	6,300		50%		3,150
	7,500		30%		2,250
			Total		$6,160
2015	$5,400		30%		$1,620
	7,200		50%		3,600
	8,400		20%		1,680
			Total		$6,900

Applying expected cash flow concepts to these data, Al's Appliance estimates warranty cash outflows of $6,160 in 2014 and $6,900 in 2015.

Illustration 6-47 shows the present value of these cash flows, assuming a risk-free rate of 5% and cash flows occurring at the end of the year.

ILLUSTRATION 6-47
Present Value of Cash Flows

Year	Expected Cash Flow	×	PV Factor, $i = 5\%$	=	Present Value
2014	$6,160		0.95238		$ 5,866.66
2015	6,900		0.90703		6,258.51
			Total		$12,125.17

SUMMARY OF LEARNING OBJECTIVES

1 Identify accounting topics where the time value of money is relevant. Some of the applications of present value–based measurements to accounting topics are (1) notes, (2) leases, (3) pensions and other postretirement benefits, (4) long-term assets, (5) sinking funds, (6) business combinations, (7) disclosures, and (8) installment contracts.

2 Distinguish between simple and compound interest. See items 1 and 2 in the Fundamental Concepts on page 318.

3 Use appropriate compound interest tables. In order to identify which of the five compound interest tables to use, determine whether you are solving for (1) the future value of a single sum, (2) the present value of a single sum, (3) the future value of a series of sums (an annuity), or (4) the present value of a series of sums (an annuity). In addition, when a series of sums (an annuity) is involved, identify whether these sums are received or paid (1) at the beginning of each period (annuity due) or (2) at the end of each period (ordinary annuity).

4 Identify variables fundamental to solving interest problems. The following four variables are fundamental to all compound interest problems. (1) *Rate of interest:*

KEY TERMS

annuity, *300*
annuity due, *300*
compound interest, *290*
deferred annuity, *311*
discounting, *295*
effective yield, *293*
effective-interest method, *314*
expected cash flow approach, *315*
face rate, *293*
future value, *294*
future value of an annuity, *300*
interest, *289*
nominal rate, *293*
ordinary annuity, *300*
present value, *294*

unless otherwise stated, an annual rate, adjusted to reflect the length of the compounding period if less than a year. (2) *Number of time periods:* the number of compounding periods (a period may be equal to or less than a year). (3) *Future value:* the value at a future date of a given sum or sums invested assuming compound interest. (4) *Present value:* the value now (present time) of a future sum or sums discounted assuming compound interest.

5 **Solve future and present value of 1 problems.** See items 5(a) and 6(a) in the Fundamental Concepts below.

6 **Solve future value of ordinary and annuity due problems**. See item 5(b) in the Fundamental Concepts below.

7 **Solve present value of ordinary and annuity due problems.** See item 6(b) in the Fundamental Concepts on page 319.

8 **Solve present value problems related to deferred annuities and bonds.** Deferred annuities are annuities in which rents begin after a specified number of periods. The future value of a deferred annuity is computed the same as the future value of an annuity not deferred. To find the present value of a deferred annuity, compute the present value of an ordinary annuity of 1 as if the rents had occurred for the entire period, and then subtract the present value of rents not received during the deferral period. The current market price of bonds combines the present values of the interest annuity and the principal amount.

9 **Apply expected cash flows to present value measurement.** The expected cash flow approach uses a range of cash flows and the probabilities of those cash flows to provide the most likely estimate of expected cash flows. The proper interest rate used to discount the cash flows is the risk-free rate of return.

FUNDAMENTAL CONCEPTS

1. SIMPLE INTEREST. Interest on principal only, regardless of interest that may have accrued in the past.

2. COMPOUND INTEREST. Interest accrues on the unpaid interest of past periods as well as on the principal.

3. RATE OF INTEREST. Interest is usually expressed as an annual rate, but when the compounding period is shorter than one year, the interest rate for the shorter period must be determined.

4. ANNUITY. A series of payments or receipts (called rents) that occur at equal intervals of time. Types of annuities:

(a) Ordinary Annuity. Each rent is payable (receivable) at the end of the period.

(b) Annuity Due. Each rent is payable (receivable) at the beginning of the period.

5. FUTURE VALUE. Value at a later date of a single sum that is invested at compound interest.

(a) Future Value of 1 (or value of a single sum). The future value of $1 (or a single given sum), *FV*, at the end of *n* periods at *i* compound interest rate (Table 6-1).

(b) Future Value of an Annuity. The future value of a series of rents invested at compound interest. In other words, the accumulated total that results from a series of equal deposits at regular intervals invested at compound interest. Both deposits and interest increase the accumulation.

(1) **Future Value of an Ordinary Annuity.** The future value on the date of the last rent (Table 6-3).

(2) **Future Value of an Annuity Due.** The future value one period after the date of the last rent. When an annuity due table is not available, use Table 6-3 with the following formula.

Value of annuity due of 1 for n rents	=	(Value of ordinary annuity for n rents) × (1 + interest rate)

6. PRESENT VALUE. The value at an earlier date (usually now) of a given future sum discounted at compound interest.

(a) Present Value of 1 (or present value of a single sum). The present value (worth) of $1 (or a given sum), due n periods hence, discounted at i compound interest (Table 6-2).

(b) Present Value of an Annuity. The present value (worth) of a series of rents discounted at compound interest. In other words, it is the sum when invested at compound interest that will permit a series of equal withdrawals at regular intervals.

(1) **Present Value of an Ordinary Annuity.** The value now of $1 to be received or paid at the end of each period (rents) for n periods, discounted at i compound interest (Table 6-4).

(2) **Present Value of an Annuity Due.** The value now of $1 to be received or paid at the beginning of each period (rents) for n periods, discounted at i compound interest (Table 6-5). To use Table 6-4 for an annuity due, apply this formula.

Present value of annuity due of 1 for n rents	=	(Present value of an ordinary annuity of n rents) × (1 + interest rate)

DEMONSTRATION PROBLEM

Messier Company is a manufacturer of cycling equipment. It is facing several decisions involving time value of money considerations.

Instructions

Provide the requested information for (a)–(d) below. (Round all answers to the nearest dollar.)

(a) Messier recently signed a lease for a new office building for a lease period of 10 years. Under the lease agreement, a security deposit of $12,000 is made, with the deposit to be returned at the expiration of the lease, with interest compounded at 10% per year. What amount will the company receive at the time the lease expires?

(b) Recently, the vice president of operations of the company has requested construction of a new plant to meet the increasing demand for the company's bikes. After a careful evaluation of the request, the board of directors has decided to raise funds for the new plant by issuing $3,000,000 of 11% term corporate bonds on March 1, 2014, due on March 1, 2029, with interest payable each March 1 and September 1. At the time of issuance, the market interest rate for similar financial instruments is 10%. Determine the selling price of the bonds.

(c) The company, having issued the bonds in part (b), is committed to make annual sinking fund deposits of $90,000. The deposits are made on the last day of each year and yield a return of 10%. Will the fund at the end of 15 years be sufficient to retire the bonds? If not, what will the deficiency be?

(d) Messier has 50 employees. Recently, after a long negotiation with the local labor union, the company decided to initiate a pension plan as a part of its employee compensation plan. The plan will start on January 1, 2014. Each employee covered by the plan is entitled to a pension payment each year after retirement. As required by accounting standards, the controller of the company needs to report the pension obligation (liability). The following estimates have been collected.

Average length of time to retirement	15 years
Expected life duration after retirement	10 years
Total pension payment expected each year after retirement for all employees	$800,000 per year

On the basis of the information above, determine the present value of the pension liability. Assume payment made at the end of the year and the interest rate to be used is 8%.

Solution

(a) Future value of $12,000 at 10% for 10 years

($12,000 × 2.59374) = $ 31,125

(b) Formula for the interest payments:

$PV\text{-}OA = R\,(PVF\text{-}OA_{n,i})$
$PV\text{-}OA = \$165{,}000\,(PVF\text{-}OA_{30,5\%})$
$PV\text{-}OA = \$165{,}000\,(15.37245)$
$PV\text{-}OA = \$2{,}536{,}454$

Formula for the principal:

$PV = FV\,(PVF_{n,i})$
$PV = \$3{,}000{,}000\,(PVF_{30,5\%})$
$PV = \$3{,}000{,}000\,(0.23138)$
$PV = \$694{,}140$

The selling price of the bonds = $2,536,454 + $694,140 = $3,230,594.

(c) Future value of an ordinary annuity of $90,000 at 10% for 15 years ($90,000 × 31.77248) $2,859,523

Deficiency ($3,000,000 − $2,859,523) $ 140,477

(d) Compute the value of the deferred annuity and then discount that amount to the present.

(i) Present value of the expected annual pension payments at the end of the tenth year:

$PV\text{-}OA = R\,(PVF\text{-}OA_{n,i})$
$PV\text{-}OA = \$800{,}000\,(PVF\text{-}OA_{10,8\%})$
$PV\text{-}OA = \$800{,}000\,(6.71008)$
$PV\text{-}OA = \$5{,}368{,}064$

(ii) Present value of the expected annual pension payments at the beginning of the current year:

$PV = FV\,(PVF_{n,i})$
$PV = \$5{,}368{,}064\,(PVF_{15,8\%})$
$PV = \$5{,}368{,}064\,(0.31524)$
$PV = \$1{,}692{,}228$

The company's pension obligation (liability) is $1,692,228.

FASB CODIFICATION

FASB Codification References

[1] FASB ASC 820-10. [Predecessor literature: "Fair Value Measurement," *Statement of Financial Accounting Standards No. 157* (Norwalk, Conn.: FASB, September 2006).]

[2] FASB ASC 310-10. [Predecessor literature: "Accounting by Creditors for Impairment of a Loan," *FASB Statement No. 114* (Norwalk, Conn.: FASB, May 1993).]

[3] FASB ASC 840-30-30. [Predecessor literature: "Accounting for Leases," *FASB Statement No. 13* as amended and interpreted through May 1980 (Stamford, Conn.: FASB, 1980).]

[4] FASB ASC 715-30-35. [Predecessor literature: "Employers' Accounting for Pension Plans," *Statement of Financial Accounting Standards No. 87* (Stamford, Conn.: FASB, 1985).]

[5] FASB ASC 360-10-35. [Predecessor literature: "Accounting for the Impairment or Disposal of Long-Lived Assets," *Statement of Financial Accounting Standards No. 144* (Norwalk, Conn.: FASB, 2001).]

[6] FASB ASC 718-10-10. [Predecessor literature: "Accounting for Stock-Based Compensation," *Statement of Financial Accounting Standards No. 123* (Norwalk, Conn: FASB, 1995); and "Share-Based Payment," *Statement of Financial Accounting Standard No. 123(R)* (Norwalk, Conn: FASB, 2004).]

Exercises

If your school has a subscription to the FASB Codification, go to *http://aaahq.org/asclogin.cfm* to log in and prepare responses to the following. Provide Codification references for your responses.

CE6-1 Access the glossary ("Master Glossary") to answer the following.
- **(a)** What is the definition of present value?
- **(b)** Briefly describe the term "discount rate adjustment technique."
- **(c)** Identify the other codification references to present value.

CE6-2 In addition to the list of topics identified in footnote 1 on page 288, identify three areas in which present value is used as a measurement basis. Briefly describe one topic related to:
(a) Assets. **(b)** Liabilities. **(c)** Revenues or expenses.

CE6-3 What is interest cost? Briefly describe imputation of interest.

An additional Codification case can be found in the Using Your Judgment section, on page 333.

Be sure to check the book's companion website for a Review and Analysis Exercise, with solution.

WileyPLUS **Brief Exercises, Exercises, Problems, and many more learning and assessment tools and resources are available for practice in WileyPLUS.**

QUESTIONS

1. What is the time value of money? Why should accountants have an understanding of compound interest, annuities, and present value concepts?

2. Identify three situations in which accounting measures are based on present values. Do these present value applications involve single sums or annuities, or both single sums and annuities? Explain.

3. What is the nature of interest? Distinguish between "simple interest" and "compound interest."

4. What are the components of an interest rate? Why is it important for accountants to understand these components?

5. The following are a number of values taken from compound interest tables involving the same number of periods and the same rate of interest. Indicate what each of these four values represents.

(a) 6.71008. **(c)** .46319.
(b) 2.15892. **(d)** 14.48656.

6. Jose Oliva is considering two investment options for a $1,500 gift he received for graduation. Both investments have 8% annual interest rates. One offers quarterly compounding; the other compounds on a semiannual basis. Which investment should he choose? Why?

7. Regina Henry deposited $20,000 in a money market certificate that provides interest of 10% compounded quarterly if the amount is maintained for 3 years. How much will Regina Henry have at the end of 3 years?

8. Will Smith will receive $80,000 on December 31, 2019 (5 years from now), from a trust fund established by his father. Assuming the appropriate interest rate for discounting is 12% (compounded semiannually), what is the present value of this amount today?

9. What are the primary characteristics of an annuity? Differentiate between an "ordinary annuity" and an "annuity due."

10. Kehoe, Inc. owes $40,000 to Ritter Company. How much would Kehoe have to pay each year if the debt is retired through four equal payments (made at the end of the year), given an interest rate on the debt of 12%? (Round to two decimal places.)

11. The Kellys are planning for a retirement home. They estimate they will need $200,000 4 years from now to purchase this home. Assuming an interest rate of 10%, what amount must be deposited at the end of each of the 4 years to fund the home price? (Round to two decimal places.)

12. Assume the same situation as in Question 11, except that the four equal amounts are deposited at the beginning of the period rather than at the end. In this case, what amount must be deposited at the beginning of each period? (Round to two decimals.)

13. Explain how the future value of an ordinary annuity interest table is converted to the future value of an annuity due interest table.

14. Explain how the present value of an ordinary annuity interest table is converted to the present value of an annuity due interest table.

15. In a book named *Treasure*, the reader has to figure out where a 2.2 pound, 24 kt gold horse has been buried. If the horse is found, a prize of $25,000 a year for 20 years is provided. The actual cost to the publisher to purchase an annuity to pay for the prize is $245,000. What interest rate (to the nearest percent) was used to determine the amount of the annuity? (Assume end-of-year payments.)

16. Alexander Enterprises leases property to Hamilton, Inc. Because Hamilton, Inc. is experiencing financial difficulty, Alexander agrees to receive five rents of $20,000 at the end of each year, with the rents deferred 3 years. What is the present value of the five rents discounted at 12%?

17. Answer the following questions.

(a) On May 1, 2014, Goldberg Company sold some machinery to Newlin Company on an installment contract basis. The contract required five equal annual payments, with the first payment due on May 1, 2014. What present value concept is appropriate for this situation?

(b) On June 1, 2014, Seymour Inc. purchased a new machine that it does not have to pay for until May 1, 2016. The total payment on May 1, 2016, will include both principal and interest. Assuming interest at a 12% rate, the cost of the machine would be the total payment multiplied by what time value of money concept?

(c) Costner Inc. wishes to know how much money it will have available in 5 years if five equal amounts of $35,000 are invested, with the first amount invested immediately. What interest table is appropriate for this situation?

(d) Megan Hoffman invests in a "jumbo" $200,000, 3-year certificate of deposit at First Wisconsin Bank. What table would be used to determine the amount accumulated at the end of 3 years?

18. Recently, Glenda Estes was interested in purchasing a Honda Acura. The salesperson indicated that the price of the car was either $27,600 cash or $6,900 at the end of each of 5 years. Compute the effective-interest rate to the nearest percent that Glenda would pay if she chooses to make the five annual payments.

19. Recently, property/casualty insurance companies have been criticized because they reserve for the total loss as much as 5 years before it may happen. The IRS has joined the debate because it says the full reserve is unfair from a taxation viewpoint. What do you believe is the IRS position?

BRIEF EXERCISES

(Unless instructed otherwise, round answers to the nearest dollar.)

5 **BE6-1** Chris Spear invested $15,000 today in a fund that earns 8% compounded annually. To what amount will the investment grow in 3 years? To what amount would the investment grow in 3 years if the fund earns 8% annual interest compounded semiannually?

5 **BE6-2** Tony Bautista needs $25,000 in 4 years. What amount must he invest today if his investment earns 12% compounded annually? What amount must he invest if his investment earns 12% annual interest compounded quarterly?

5 **BE6-3** Candice Willis will invest $30,000 today. She needs $150,000 in 21 years. What annual interest rate must she earn?

5 **BE6-4** Bo Newman will invest $10,000 today in a fund that earns 5% annual interest. How many years will it take for the fund to grow to $17,100?

6 **BE6-5** Sally Medavoy will invest $8,000 a year for 20 years in a fund that will earn 12% annual interest. If the first payment into the fund occurs today, what amount will be in the fund in 20 years? If the first payment occurs at year-end, what amount will be in the fund in 20 years?

6 **BE6-6** Steve Madison needs $250,000 in 10 years. How much must he invest at the end of each year, at 11% interest, to meet his needs?

5 **BE6-7** John Fillmore's lifelong dream is to own his own fishing boat to use in his retirement. John has recently come into an inheritance of $400,000. He estimates that the boat he wants will cost $300,000 when he retires in 5 years. How much of his inheritance must he invest at an annual rate of 12% (compounded annually) to buy the boat at retirement?

5 **BE6-8** Refer to the data in BE6-7. Assuming quarterly compounding of amounts invested at 12%, how much of John Fillmore's inheritance must be invested to have enough at retirement to buy the boat?

6 **BE6-9** Morgan Freeman is investing $16,380 at the end of each year in a fund that earns 10% interest. In how many years will the fund be at $100,000?

7 **BE6-10** Henry Quincy wants to withdraw $30,000 each year for 10 years from a fund that earns 8% interest. How much must he invest today if the first withdrawal is at year-end? How much must he invest today if the first withdrawal takes place immediately?

7 **BE6-11** Leon Tyler's VISA balance is $793.15. He may pay it off in 12 equal end-of-month payments of $75 each. What interest rate is Leon paying?

7 **BE6-12** Maria Alvarez is investing $300,000 in a fund that earns 8% interest compounded annually. What equal amounts can Maria withdraw at the end of each of the next 20 years?

6 **BE6-13** Adams Inc. will deposit $30,000 in a 12% fund at the end of each year for 8 years beginning December 31, 2014. What amount will be in the fund immediately after the last deposit?

7 **BE6-14** Amy Monroe wants to create a fund today that will enable her to withdraw $25,000 per year for 8 years, with the first withdrawal to take place 5 years from today. If the fund earns 8% interest, how much must Amy invest today?

8 **BE6-15** Clancey Inc. issues $2,000,000 of 7% bonds due in 10 years with interest payable at year-end. The current market rate of interest for bonds of similar risk is 8%. What amount will Clancey receive when it issues the bonds?

7 **BE6-16** Zach Taylor is settling a $20,000 loan due today by making 6 equal annual payments of $4,727.53. Determine the interest rate on this loan, if the payments begin one year after the loan is signed.

7 **BE6-17** Consider the loan in BE6-16. What payments must Zach Taylor make to settle the loan at the same interest rate but with the 6 payments beginning on the day the loan is signed?

EXERCISES

(Unless instructed otherwise, round answers to the nearest dollar. Interest rates are per annum unless otherwise indicated.)

3 **E6-1 (Using Interest Tables)** For each of the following cases, indicate (a) to what rate columns, and (b) to what number of periods you would refer in looking up the interest factor.

1. In a future value of 1 table

Annual Rate	Number of Years Invested	Compounded
a. 9%	9	Annually
b. 12%	5	Quarterly
c. 10%	15	Semiannually

2. In a present value of an annuity of 1 table

Annual Rate	Number of Years Involved	Number of Rents Involved	Frequency of Rents
a. 9%	25	25	Annually
b. 10%	15	30	Semiannually
c. 12%	7	28	Quarterly

2 5 **E6-2 (Simple and Compound Interest Computations)** Alan Jackson invests $20,000 at 8% annual interest, leaving the money invested without withdrawing any of the interest for 8 years. At the end of the 8 years, Alan withdraws the accumulated amount of money.

Instructions

(a) Compute the amount Alan would withdraw assuming the investment earns simple interest.

(b) Compute the amount Alan would withdraw assuming the investment earns interest compounded annually.

(c) Compute the amount Alan would withdraw assuming the investment earns interest compounded semiannually.

5 6 7 **E6-3 (Computation of Future Values and Present Values)** Using the appropriate interest table, answer each of the following questions. (Each case is independent of the others.)

(a) What is the future value of $7,000 at the end of 5 periods at 8% compounded interest?

(b) What is the present value of $7,000 due 8 periods hence, discounted at 11%?

(c) What is the future value of 15 periodic payments of $7,000 each made at the end of each period and compounded at 10%?

(d) What is the present value of $7,000 to be received at the end of each of 20 periods, discounted at 5% compound interest?

6 7 **E6-4 (Computation of Future Values and Present Values)** Using the appropriate interest table, answer the following questions. (Each case is independent of the others).

(a) What is the future value of 20 periodic payments of $4,000 each made at the beginning of each period and compounded at 8%?

(b) What is the present value of $2,500 to be received at the beginning of each of 30 periods, discounted at 10% compound interest?

(c) What is the future value of 15 deposits of $2,000 each made at the beginning of each period and compounded at 10%? (Future value as of the end of the fifteenth period.)

(d) What is the present value of six receipts of $1,000 each received at the beginning of each period, discounted at 9% compounded interest?

7 **E6-5 (Computation of Present Value)** Using the appropriate interest table, compute the present values of the following periodic amounts due at the end of the designated periods.

(a) $30,000 receivable at the end of each period for 8 periods compounded at 12%.

(b) $30,000 payments to be made at the end of each period for 16 periods at 9%.

(c) $30,000 payable at the end of the seventh, eighth, ninth, and tenth periods at 12%.

5 6 7 **E6-6 (Future Value and Present Value Problems)** Presented below are three unrelated situations.

(a) Dwayne Wade Company recently signed a lease for a new office building, for a lease period of 10 years. Under the lease agreement, a security deposit of $12,000 is made, with the deposit to be returned at the expiration of the lease, with interest compounded at 10% per year. What amount will the company receive at the time the lease expires?

(b) Serena Williams Corporation, having recently issued a $20 million, 15-year bond issue, is committed to make annual sinking fund deposits of $600,000. The deposits are made on the last day of each year and yield a return of 10%. Will the fund at the end of 15 years be sufficient to retire the bonds? If not, what will the deficiency be?

(c) Under the terms of his salary agreement, president Rex Walters has an option of receiving either an immediate bonus of $40,000, or a deferred bonus of $70,000 payable in 10 years. Ignoring tax considerations and assuming a relevant interest rate of 8%, which form of settlement should Walters accept?

8 **E6-7 (Computation of Bond Prices)** What would you pay for a $50,000 debenture bond that matures in 15 years and pays $5,000 a year in interest if you wanted to earn a yield of:

(a) 8%? **(b)** 10%? **(c)** 12%?

8 **E6-8 (Computations for a Retirement Fund)** Clarence Weatherspoon, a super salesman contemplating retirement on his fifty-fifth birthday, decides to create a fund on an 8% basis that will enable him to withdraw $20,000 per year on June 30, beginning in 2018 and continuing through 2021. To develop this fund, Clarence intends to make equal contributions on June 30 of each of the years 2014–2017.

Instructions

(a) How much must the balance of the fund equal on June 30, 2017, in order for Clarence Weatherspoon to satisfy his objective?

(b) What are each of Clarence's contributions to the fund?

5 **E6-9 (Unknown Rate)** LEW Company purchased a machine at a price of $100,000 by signing a note payable, which requires a single payment of $123,210 in 2 years. Assuming annual compounding of interest, what rate of interest is being paid on the loan?

5 **E6-10 (Unknown Periods and Unknown Interest Rate)** Consider the following independent situations.

(a) Mike Finley wishes to become a millionaire. His money market fund has a balance of $92,296 and has a guaranteed interest rate of 10%. How many years must Mike leave that balance in the fund in order to get his desired $1,000,000?

(b) Assume that Sally Williams desires to accumulate $1 million in 15 years using her money market fund balance of $182,696. At what interest rate must Sally's investment compound annually?

7 **E6-11 (Evaluation of Purchase Options)** Sosa Excavating Inc. is purchasing a bulldozer. The equipment has a price of $100,000. The manufacturer has offered a payment plan that would allow Sosa to make 10 equal annual payments of $16,274.53, with the first payment due one year after the purchase.

Instructions

(a) How much total interest will Sosa pay on this payment plan?

(b) Sosa could borrow $100,000 from its bank to finance the purchase at an annual rate of 9%. Should Sosa borrow from the bank or use the manufacturer's payment plan to pay for the equipment?

7 **E6-12 (Analysis of Alternatives)** The Black Knights Inc., a manufacturer of low-sugar, low-sodium, low-cholesterol TV dinners, would like to increase its market share in the Sunbelt. In order to do so, Black Knights has decided to locate a new factory in the Panama City area. Black Knights will either buy or lease a site depending upon which is more advantageous. The site location committee has narrowed down the available sites to the following three buildings.

Building A: Purchase for a cash price of $600,000, useful life 25 years.

Building B: Lease for 25 years with annual lease payments of $69,000 being made at the beginning of the year.

Building C: Purchase for $650,000 cash. This building is larger than needed; however, the excess space can be sublet for 25 years at a net annual rental of $7,000. Rental payments will be received at the end of each year. The Black Knights Inc. has no aversion to being a landlord.

Instructions

In which building would you recommend that The Black Knights Inc. locate, assuming a 12% cost of funds?

8 **E6-13 (Computation of Bond Liability)** George Hincapie Inc. manufactures cycling equipment. Recently, the vice president of operations of the company has requested construction of a new plant to meet the increasing demand for the company's bikes. After a careful evaluation of the request, the board of directors has decided to raise funds for the new plant by issuing $2,000,000 of 11% term corporate bonds on March 1, 2014, due on March 1, 2029, with interest payable each March 1 and September 1. At the time of issuance, the market interest rate for similar financial instruments is 10%.

Instructions

As the controller of the company, determine the selling price of the bonds.

8 **E6-14 (Computation of Pension Liability)** Nerwin, Inc. is a furniture manufacturing company with 50 employees. Recently, after a long negotiation with the local labor union, the company decided to initiate a pension plan as a part of its compensation plan. The plan will start on January 1, 2014. Each employee covered by the plan is entitled to a pension payment each year after retirement. As required by accounting standards, the controller of the company needs to report the pension obligation (liability). On the basis of a discussion with the supervisor of the Personnel Department and an actuary from an insurance company, the controller develops the following information related to the pension plan.

Average length of time to retirement	15 years
Expected life duration after retirement	10 years
Total pension payment expected each year after retirement for all employees. Payment made at the end of the year.	$700,000 per year

The interest rate to be used is 8%.

Instructions

On the basis of the information above, determine the present value of the pension obligation (liability).

5 6 **E6-15 (Investment Decision)** Andrew Bogut just received a signing bonus of $1,000,000. His plan is to invest this payment in a fund that will earn 8%, compounded annually.

Instructions

(a) If Bogut plans to establish the AB Foundation once the fund grows to $1,999,000, how many years until he can establish the foundation?

(b) Instead of investing the entire $1,000,000, Bogut invests $300,000 today and plans to make 9 equal annual investments into the fund beginning one year from today. What amount should the payments be if Bogut plans to establish the $1,999,000 foundation at the end of 9 years?

6 **E6-16 (Retirement of Debt)** Jesper Parnevik borrowed $70,000 on March 1, 2012. This amount plus accrued interest at 12% compounded semiannually is to be repaid March 1, 2022. To retire this debt, Jesper plans to contribute to a debt retirement fund five equal amounts starting on March 1, 2017, and for the next 4 years. The fund is expected to earn 10% per annum.

Instructions

How much must be contributed each year by Jesper Parnevik to provide a fund sufficient to retire the debt on March 1, 2022?

7 **E6-17 (Computation of Amount of Rentals)** Your client, Keith Moreland Leasing Company, is preparing a contract to lease a machine to Souvenirs Corporation for a period of 25 years. Moreland has an investment cost of $365,755 in the machine, which has a useful life of 25 years and no salvage value at the end of that time. Your client is interested in earning an 11% return on its investment and has agreed to accept 25 equal rental payments at the end of each of the next 25 years.

Instructions

You are requested to provide Moreland with the amount of each of the 25 rental payments that will yield an 11% return on investment.

7 **E6-18 (Least Costly Payoff)** Assume that Sonic Foundry Corporation has a contractual debt outstanding. Sonic has available two means of settlement. It can either make immediate payment of $2,600,000, or it can make annual payments of $300,000 for 15 years, each payment due on the last day of the year.

Instructions

Which method of payment do you recommend, assuming an expected effective interest rate of 8% during the future period?

7 **E6-19 (Least Costly Payoff)** Assuming the same facts as those in E6-18 except that the payments must begin now and be made on the first day of each of the 15 years, what payment method would you recommend?

9 **E6-20 (Expected Cash Flows)** For each of the following, determine the expected cash flows.

	Cash Flow Estimate	Probability Assessment
(a)	$ 4,800	20%
	6,300	50%
	7,500	30%
(b)	$ 5,400	30%
	7,200	50%
	8,400	20%
(c)	$(1,000)	10%
	3,000	80%
	5,000	10%

9 **E6-21 (Expected Cash Flows and Present Value)** Keith Bowie is trying to determine the amount to set aside so that he will have enough money on hand in 2 years to overhaul the engine on his vintage used car. While there is some uncertainty about the cost of engine overhauls in 2 years, by conducting some research online, Keith has developed the following estimates.

Engine Overhaul Estimated Cash Outflow	Probability Assessment
$200	10%
450	30%
600	50%
750	10%

Instructions

How much should Keith Bowie deposit today in an account earning 6%, compounded annually, so that he will have enough money on hand in 2 years to pay for the overhaul?

9 **E6-22 (Fair Value Estimate)** Killroy Company owns a trade name that was purchased in an acquisition of McClellan Company. The trade name has a book value of $3,500,000, but according to GAAP, it is assessed for impairment on an annual basis. To perform this impairment test, Killroy must estimate the fair value of the trade name. (You will learn more about intangible asset impairments in Chapter 12.) It has developed the following cash flow estimates related to the trade name based on internal information. Each cash flow estimate reflects Killroy's estimate of annual cash flows over the next 8 years. The trade name is assumed to have no salvage value after the 8 years. (Assume the cash flows occur at the end of each year.)

Cash Flow Estimate	Probability Assessment
$380,000	20%
630,000	50%
750,000	30%

Instructions

(a) What is the estimated fair value of the trade name? Killroy determines that the appropriate discount rate for this estimation is 8%.

(b) Is the estimate developed for part (a) a Level 1 or Level 3 fair value estimate? Explain.

EXERCISES SET B

See the book's companion website, at **www.wiley.com/college/kieso**, for an additional set of exercises.

PROBLEMS

(Unless instructed otherwise, round answers to the nearest dollar. Interest rates are per annum unless otherwise indicated.)

5 7 **P6-1 (Various Time Value Situations)** Answer each of these unrelated questions.

(a) On January 1, 2014, Fishbone Corporation sold a building that cost $250,000 and that had accumulated depreciation of $100,000 on the date of sale. Fishbone received as consideration a $240,000 non-interest-bearing note due on January 1, 2017. There was no established exchange price for the building, and the note had no ready market. The prevailing rate of interest for a note of this type on January 1, 2014, was 9%. At what amount should the gain from the sale of the building be reported?

(b) On January 1, 2014, Fishbone Corporation purchased 300 of the $1,000 face value, 9%, 10-year bonds of Walters Inc. The bonds mature on January 1, 2024, and pay interest annually beginning January 1, 2015. Fishbone purchased the bonds to yield 11%. How much did Fishbone pay for the bonds?

(c) Fishbone Corporation bought a new machine and agreed to pay for it in equal annual installments of $4,000 at the end of each of the next 10 years. Assuming that a prevailing interest rate of 8% applies to this contract, how much should Fishbone record as the cost of the machine?

(d) Fishbone Corporation purchased a special tractor on December 31, 2014. The purchase agreement stipulated that Fishbone should pay $20,000 at the time of purchase and $5,000 at the end of each of the next 8 years. The tractor should be recorded on December 31, 2014, at what amount, assuming an appropriate interest rate of 12%?

(e) Fishbone Corporation wants to withdraw $120,000 (including principal) from an investment fund at the end of each year for 9 years. What should be the required initial investment at the beginning of the first year if the fund earns 11%?

5 6 **P6-2 (Various Time Value Situations)** Using the appropriate interest table, provide the solution to each of
7 the following four questions by computing the unknowns.

(a) What is the amount of the payments that Ned Winslow must make at the end of each of 8 years to accumulate a fund of $90,000 by the end of the eighth year, if the fund earns 8% interest, compounded annually?

(b) Robert Hitchcock is 40 years old today and he wishes to accumulate $500,000 by his sixty-fifth birthday so he can retire to his summer place on Lake Hopatcong. He wishes to accumulate this amount by making equal deposits on his fortieth through his sixty-fourth birthdays. What annual deposit must Robert make if the fund will earn 12% interest compounded annually?

(c) Diane Ross has $20,000 to invest today at 9% to pay a debt of $47,347. How many years will it take her to accumulate enough to liquidate the debt?

(d) Cindy Houston has a $27,600 debt that she wishes to repay 4 years from today; she has $19,553 that she intends to invest for the 4 years. What rate of interest will she need to earn annually in order to accumulate enough to pay the debt?

5 7 **P6-3 (Analysis of Alternatives)** Assume that **Wal-Mart Stores, Inc.** has decided to surface and maintain for 10 years a vacant lot next to one of its stores to serve as a parking lot for customers. Management is considering the following bids involving two different qualities of surfacing for a parking area of 12,000 square yards.

Bid A: A surface that costs $5.75 per square yard to install. This surface will have to be replaced at the end of 5 years. The annual maintenance cost on this surface is estimated at 25 cents per square yard for each year except the last year of its service. The replacement surface will be similar to the initial surface.

Bid B: A surface that costs $10.50 per square yard to install. This surface has a probable useful life of 10 years and will require annual maintenance in each year except the last year, at an estimated cost of 9 cents per square yard.

Instructions

Prepare computations showing which bid should be accepted by Wal-Mart. You may assume that the cost of capital is 9%, that the annual maintenance expenditures are incurred at the end of each year, and that prices are not expected to change during the next 10 years.

7 **P6-4 (Evaluating Payment Alternatives)** Howie Long has just learned he has won a $500,000 prize in the lottery. The lottery has given him two options for receiving the payments. (1) If Howie takes all the money today, the state and federal governments will deduct taxes at a rate of 46% immediately. (2) Alternatively, the lottery offers Howie a payout of 20 equal payments of $36,000 with the first payment occurring when Howie turns in the winning ticket. Howie will be taxed on each of these payments at a rate of 25%.

Instructions

Assuming Howie can earn an 8% rate of return (compounded annually) on any money invested during this period, which pay-out option should he choose?

5 7 **P6-5 (Analysis of Alternatives)** Julia Baker died, leaving to her husband Brent an insurance policy contract that provides that the beneficiary (Brent) can choose any one of the following four options.

(a) $55,000 immediate cash.

(b) $4,000 every 3 months payable at the end of each quarter for 5 years.

(c) $18,000 immediate cash and $1,800 every 3 months for 10 years, payable at the beginning of each 3-month period.

(d) $4,000 every 3 months for 3 years and $1,500 each quarter for the following 25 quarters, all payments payable at the end of each quarter.

Instructions

If money is worth 2½% per quarter, compounded quarterly, which option would you recommend that Brent exercise?

8 **P6-6 (Purchase Price of a Business)** During the past year, Stacy McGill planted a new vineyard on 150 acres of land that she leases for $30,000 a year. She has asked you, as her accountant, to assist her in determining the value of her vineyard operation.

The vineyard will bear no grapes for the first 5 years (1–5). In the next 5 years (6–10), Stacy estimates that the vines will bear grapes that can be sold for $60,000 each year. For the next 20 years (11–30), she expects the harvest will provide annual revenues of $110,000. But during the last 10 years (31–40) of the vineyard's life, she estimates that revenues will decline to $80,000 per year.

During the first 5 years, the annual cost of pruning, fertilizing, and caring for the vineyard is estimated at $9,000; during the years of production, 6–40, these costs will rise to $12,000 per year. The relevant market rate of interest for the entire period is 12%. Assume that all receipts and payments are made at the end of each year.

Instructions

Dick Button has offered to buy Stacy's vineyard business by assuming the 40-year lease. On the basis of the current value of the business, what is the minimum price Stacy should accept?

5 6 7 **P6-7 (Time Value Concepts Applied to Solve Business Problems)** Answer the following questions related to Dubois Inc.

(a) Dubois Inc. has $600,000 to invest. The company is trying to decide between two alternative uses of the funds. One alternative provides $80,000 at the end of each year for 12 years, and the other is to receive a single lump-sum payment of $1,900,000 at the end of the 12 years. Which alternative should Dubois select? Assume the interest rate is constant over the entire investment.

(b) Dubois Inc. has completed the purchase of new Dell computers. The fair value of the equipment is $824,150. The purchase agreement specifies an immediate down payment of $200,000 and semiannual payments of $76,952 beginning at the end of 6 months for 5 years. What is the interest rate, to the nearest percent, used in discounting this purchase transaction?

(c) Dubois Inc. loans money to John Kruk Corporation in the amount of $800,000. Dubois accepts an 8% note due in 7 years with interest payable semiannually. After 2 years (and receipt of interest for 2 years), Dubois needs money and therefore sells the note to Chicago National Bank, which demands interest on the note of 10% compounded semiannually. What is the amount Dubois will receive on the sale of the note?

(d) Dubois Inc. wishes to accumulate $1,300,000 by December 31, 2024, to retire bonds outstanding. The company deposits $200,000 on December 31, 2014, which will earn interest at 10% compounded quarterly, to help in the retirement of this debt. In addition, the company wants to know how much should be deposited at the end of each quarter for 10 years to ensure that $1,300,000 is available at the end of 2024. (The quarterly deposits will also earn at a rate of 10%, compounded quarterly.) (Round to even dollars.)

7 **P6-8 (Analysis of Alternatives)** Ellison Inc., a manufacturer of steel school lockers, plans to purchase a new punch press for use in its manufacturing process. After contacting the appropriate vendors, the purchasing department received differing terms and options from each vendor. The Engineering Department has determined that each vendor's punch press is substantially identical and each has a useful life of 20 years. In addition, Engineering has estimated that required year-end maintenance costs will be $1,000 per year for the first 5 years, $2,000 per year for the next 10 years, and $3,000 per year for the last 5 years. Following is each vendor's sale package.

Vendor A: $55,000 cash at time of delivery and 10 year-end payments of $18,000 each. Vendor A offers all its customers the right to purchase at the time of sale a separate 20-year maintenance service contract, under which Vendor A will perform all year-end maintenance at a one-time initial cost of $10,000.

Vendor B: Forty semiannual payments of $9,500 each, with the first installment due upon delivery. Vendor B will perform all year-end maintenance for the next 20 years at no extra charge.

Vendor C: Full cash price of $150,000 will be due upon delivery.

Instructions

Assuming that both Vendors A and B will be able to perform the required year-end maintenance, that Ellison's cost of funds is 10%, and the machine will be purchased on January 1, from which vendor should the press be purchased?

5 7 **P6-9 (Analysis of Business Problems)** James Kirk is a financial executive with McDowell Enterprises. Although James Kirk has not had any formal training in finance or accounting, he has a "good sense" for numbers and has helped the company grow from a very small company ($500,000 sales) to a large operation ($45 million in sales). With the business growing steadily, however, the company needs to make a number of difficult financial decisions in which James Kirk feels a little "over his head." He therefore has decided to hire a new employee with "numbers" expertise to help him. As a basis for determining whom to employ, he has decided to ask each prospective employee to prepare answers to questions relating to the following situations he has encountered recently. Here are the questions.

(a) In 2013, McDowell Enterprises negotiated and closed a long-term lease contract for newly constructed truck terminals and freight storage facilities. The buildings were constructed on land owned by the company. On January 1, 2014, McDowell took possession of the leased property. The 20-year lease is effective for the period January 1, 2014, through December 31, 2033. Advance rental payments of $800,000 are payable to the lessor (owner of facilities) on January 1 of each of the first 10 years of the lease term. Advance payments of $400,000 are due on January 1 for each of the last 10 years of the lease term. McDowell has an option to purchase all the leased facilities for $1 on December 31, 2033. At the time the lease was negotiated, the fair value of the truck terminals and freight storage facilities was approximately $7,200,000. If the company had borrowed the money to purchase the facilities, it would have had to pay 10% interest. Should the company have purchased rather than leased the facilities?

(b) Last year the company exchanged a piece of land for a non-interest-bearing note. The note is to be paid at the rate of $15,000 per year for 9 years, beginning one year from the date of disposal of the land. An appropriate rate of interest for the note was 11%. At the time the land was originally purchased, it cost $90,000. What is the fair value of the note?

(c) The company has always followed the policy to take any cash discounts on goods purchased. Recently, the company purchased a large amount of raw materials at a price of $800,000 with terms 1/10, n/30 on which it took the discount. McDowell has recently estimated its cost of funds at 10%. Should McDowell continue this policy of always taking the cash discount?

5 7 **P6-10 (Analysis of Lease vs. Purchase)** Dunn Inc. owns and operates a number of hardware stores in the New England region. Recently, the company has decided to locate another store in a rapidly growing area of Maryland. The company is trying to decide whether to purchase or lease the building and related facilities.

Purchase: The company can purchase the site, construct the building, and purchase all store fixtures. The cost would be $1,850,000. An immediate down payment of $400,000 is required, and the remaining $1,450,000 would be paid off over 5 years at $350,000 per year (including interest payments made at end of year). The property is expected to have a useful life of 12 years, and then it will be sold for $500,000. As the owner of the property, the company will have the following out-of-pocket expenses each period.

Property taxes (to be paid at the end of each year)	$40,000
Insurance (to be paid at the beginning of each year)	27,000
Other (primarily maintenance which occurs at the end of each year)	16,000
	$83,000

Lease: First National Bank has agreed to purchase the site, construct the building, and install the appropriate fixtures for Dunn Inc. if Dunn will lease the completed facility for 12 years. The annual costs for the lease would be $270,000. Dunn would have no responsibility related to the facility over the 12 years. The terms of the lease are that Dunn would be required to make 12 annual payments (the first payment to be made at the time the store opens and then each following year). In addition, a deposit of $100,000 is required when the store is opened. This deposit will be returned at the end of the twelfth year, assuming no unusual damage to the building structure or fixtures.

Instructions

Which of the two approaches should Dunn Inc. follow? (Currently, the cost of funds for Dunn Inc. is 10%.)

8 **P6-11 (Pension Funding)** You have been hired as a benefit consultant by Jean Honore, the owner of Attic Angels. She wants to establish a retirement plan for herself and her three employees. Jean has provided the following information. The retirement plan is to be based upon annual salary for the last year before retirement and is to provide 50% of Jean's last-year annual salary and 40% of the last-year annual salary for each employee. The plan will make annual payments at the beginning of each year for 20 years from the date of retirement. Jean wishes to fund the plan by making 15 annual deposits beginning January 1, 2014. Invested funds will earn 12% compounded annually. Information about plan participants as of January 1, 2014, is as follows.

Jean Honore, owner: Current annual salary of $48,000; estimated retirement date January 1, 2039.

Colin Davis, flower arranger: Current annual salary of $36,000; estimated retirement date January 1, 2044.

Anita Baker, sales clerk: Current annual salary of $18,000; estimated retirement date January 1, 2034.

Gavin Bryars, part-time bookkeeper: Current annual salary of $15,000; estimated retirement date January 1, 2029.

In the past, Jean has given herself and each employee a year-end salary increase of 4%. Jean plans to continue this policy in the future.

Instructions

(a) Based upon the above information, what will be the annual retirement benefit for each plan participant? (Round to the nearest dollar.) (*Hint:* Jean will receive raises for 24 years.)

(b) What amount must be on deposit at the end of 15 years to ensure that all benefits will be paid? (Round to the nearest dollar.)

(c) What is the amount of each annual deposit Jean must make to the retirement plan?

8 **P6-12 (Pension Funding)** Craig Brokaw, newly appointed controller of STL, is considering ways to reduce his company's expenditures on annual pension costs. One way to do this is to switch STL's pension fund assets from First Security to NET Life. STL is a very well-respected computer manufacturer that recently has experienced a sharp decline in its financial performance for the first time in its 25-year history. Despite financial problems, STL still is committed to providing its employees with good pension and postretirement health benefits.

Under its present plan with First Security, STL is obligated to pay $43 million to meet the expected value of future pension benefits that are payable to employees as an annuity upon their retirement from the company. On the other hand, NET Life requires STL to pay only $35 million for identical future pension benefits. First Security is one of the oldest and most reputable insurance companies in North America. NET Life has a much weaker reputation in the insurance industry. In pondering the significant difference in annual pension costs, Brokaw asks himself, "Is this too good to be true?"

Instructions

Answer the following questions.

(a) Why might NET Life's pension cost requirement be $8 million less than First Security's requirement for the same future value?

(b) What ethical issues should Craig Brokaw consider before switching STL's pension fund assets?

(c) Who are the stakeholders that could be affected by Brokaw's decision?

7 9 **P6-13 (Expected Cash Flows and Present Value)** Danny's Lawn Equipment sells high-quality lawn mowers and offers a 3-year warranty on all new lawn mowers sold. In 2014, Danny sold $300,000 of new specialty mowers for golf greens for which Danny's service department does not have the equipment to do the service. Danny has entered into an agreement with Mower Mavens to provide all warranty service on the special mowers sold in 2014. Danny wishes to measure the fair value of the agreement to determine the warranty liability for sales made in 2014. The controller for Danny's Lawn Equipment estimates the following expected warranty cash outflows associated with the mowers sold in 2014.

Year	Cash Flow Estimate	Probability Assessment
2015	$2,500	20%
	4,000	60%
	5,000	20%
2016	$3,000	30%
	5,000	50%
	6,000	20%
2017	$4,000	30%
	6,000	40%
	7,000	30%

Instructions

Using expected cash flow and present value techniques, determine the value of the warranty liability for the 2014 sales. Use an annual discount rate of 5%. Assume all cash flows occur at the end of the year.

7 9 **P6-14 (Expected Cash Flows and Present Value)** At the end of 2014, Sawyer Company is conducting an impairment test and needs to develop a fair value estimate for machinery used in its manufacturing operations. Given the nature of Sawyer's production process, the equipment is for special use. (No secondhand market values are available.) The equipment will be obsolete in 2 years, and Sawyer's accountants have developed the following cash flow information for the equipment.

Year	Net Cash Flow Estimate	Probability Assessment
2015	$6,000	40%
	9,000	60%
2016	$ (500)	20%
	2,000	60%
	4,000	20%
	Scrap value	
2016	$ 500	50%
	900	50%

Instructions

Using expected cash flow and present value techniques, determine the fair value of the machinery at the end of 2014. Use a 6% discount rate. Assume all cash flows occur at the end of the year.

8 9 **P6-15 (Fair Value Estimate)** Murphy Mining Company recently purchased a quartz mine that it intends to work for the next 10 years. According to state environmental laws, Murphy must restore the mine site to its original natural prairie state after it ceases mining operations at the site. To properly account for the mine, Murphy must estimate the fair value of this asset retirement obligation. This amount will be recorded as a liability and added to the value of the mine on Murphy's books. (You will learn more about these asset retirement obligations in Chapters 10 and 13.)

There is no active market for retirement obligations such as these, but Murphy has developed the following cash flow estimates based on its prior experience in mining-site restoration. It will take 3 years to restore the mine site when mining operations cease in 10 years. Each estimated cash outflow reflects an annual payment at the end of each year of the 3-year restoration period.

Restoration Estimated Cash Outflow	Probability Assessment
$15,000	10%
22,000	30%
25,000	50%
30,000	10%

Instructions

(a) What is the estimated fair value of Murphy's asset retirement obligation? Murphy determines that the appropriate discount rate for this estimation is 5%. Round calculations to the nearest dollar.

(b) Is the estimate developed for part (a) a Level 1 or Level 3 fair value estimate? Explain.

PROBLEMS SET B

See the book's companion website, at **www.wiley.com/college/kieso**, for an additional set of problems.

USING YOUR JUDGMENT

FINANCIAL REPORTING

P&G

Financial Reporting Problem

The Procter & Gamble Company (P&G)

The financial statements of P&G are presented in Appendix 5B. The company's complete annual report, including the notes to the financial statements, can be accessed at the book's companion website, **www.wiley.com/college/kieso**.

Instructions

(a) Examining each item in P&G's balance sheet, identify those items that require present value, discounting, or interest computations in establishing the amount reported. (The accompanying notes are an additional source for this information.)

(b) (1) What interest rates are disclosed by P&G as being used to compute interest and present values? (2) Why are there so many different interest rates applied to P&G's financial statement elements (assets, liabilities, revenues, and expenses)?

Financial Statement Analysis Case

Consolidated Natural Gas Company

Consolidated Natural Gas Company (CNG), with corporate headquarters in Pittsburgh, Pennsylvania, is one of the largest producers, transporters, distributors, and marketers of natural gas in North America.

Periodically, the company experiences a decrease in the value of its gas- and oil-producing properties, and a special charge to income was recorded in order to reduce the carrying value of those assets.

Assume the following information. In 2013, CNG estimated the cash inflows from its oil- and gas-producing properties to be $375,000 per year. During 2014, the write-downs described above caused the estimate to be decreased to $275,000 per year. Production costs (cash outflows) associated with all these properties were estimated to be $125,000 per year in 2013, but this amount was revised to $155,000 per year in 2014.

Instructions

(Assume that all cash flows occur at the end of the year.)

(a) Calculate the present value of net cash flows for 2013–2015 (three years), using the 2013 estimates and a 10% discount factor.

(b) Calculate the present value of net cash flows for 2014–2016 (three years), using the 2014 estimates and a 10% discount factor.

(c) Compare the results using the two estimates. Is information on future cash flows from oil- and gas-producing properties useful, considering that the estimates must be revised each year? Explain.

Accounting, Analysis, and Principles

Johnson Co. accepts a note receivable from a customer in exchange for some damaged inventory. The note requires the customer make semiannual installments of $50,000 each for 10 years. The first installment begins six months from the date the customer took delivery of the damaged inventory. Johnson's management estimates that the fair value of the damaged inventory is $679,517.

Accounting

(a) What interest rate is Johnson implicitly charging the customer? Express the rate as an annual rate but assume semiannual compounding.

(b) At what dollar amount do you think Johnson should record the note receivable on the day the customer takes delivery of the damaged inventory?

Analysis

Assume the note receivable for damaged inventory makes up a significant portion of Johnson's assets. If interest rates increase, what happens to the fair value of the receivable? Briefly explain why.

Principles

The Financial Accounting Standards Board recently issued an accounting standard that allows companies to report assets such as notes receivable at fair value. Discuss how fair value versus historical cost potentially involves a trade-off of one desired quality of accounting information against another.

BRIDGE TO THE PROFESSION

Professional Research

At a recent meeting of the accounting staff in your company, the controller raised the issue of using present value techniques to conduct impairment tests for some of the company's fixed assets. Some of the more senior members of the staff admitted having little knowledge of present value concepts in this context, but they had heard about a FASB Concepts Statement that may be relevant. As the junior staff in the department, you have been asked to conduct some research of the authoritative literature on this topic and report back at the staff meeting next week.

Instructions

If your school has a subscription to the FASB Codification, go to *http://aaahq.org/asclogin.cfm* to log in and access the FASB Statements of Financial Accounting Concepts. When you have accessed the documents, you can use the search tool in your Internet browser to respond to the following items. (Provide paragraph citations.)

(a) Identify the recent concept statement that addresses present value measurement in accounting.

(b) What are some of the contexts in which present value concepts are applied in accounting measurement?

(c) Provide definitions for the following terms:

- **(1)** Best estimate.
- **(2)** Estimated cash flow (contrasted to expected cash flow).
- **(3)** Fresh-start measurement.
- **(4)** Interest methods of allocation.

Additional Professional Resources

See the book's companion website, at **www.wiley.com/college/kieso**, for professional simulations as well as other study resources.

Remember to check the book's companion website to find additional resources for this chapter.

TABLE 6-1 FUTURE VALUE OF 1 (FUTURE VALUE OF A SINGLE SUM)

$FVF_{n,i} = (1 + i)^n$

(n) Periods	2%	2½%	3%	4%	5%	6%
1	1.02000	1.02500	1.03000	1.04000	1.05000	1.06000
2	1.04040	1.05063	1.06090	1.08160	1.10250	1.12360
3	1.06121	1.07689	1.09273	1.12486	1.15763	1.19102
4	1.08243	1.10381	1.12551	1.16986	1.21551	1.26248
5	1.10408	1.13141	1.15927	1.21665	1.27628	1.33823
6	1.12616	1.15969	1.19405	1.26532	1.34010	1.41852
7	1.14869	1.18869	1.22987	1.31593	1.40710	1.50363
8	1.17166	1.21840	1.26677	1.36857	1.47746	1.59385
9	1.19509	1.24886	1.30477	1.42331	1.55133	1.68948
10	1.21899	1.28008	1.34392	1.48024	1.62889	1.79085
11	1.24337	1.31209	1.38423	1.53945	1.71034	1.89830
12	1.26824	1.34489	1.42576	1.60103	1.79586	2.01220
13	1.29361	1.37851	1.46853	1.66507	1.88565	2.13293
14	1.31948	1.41297	1.51259	1.73168	1.97993	2.26090
15	1.34587	1.44830	1.55797	1.80094	2.07893	2.39656
16	1.37279	1.48451	1.60471	1.87298	2.18287	2.54035
17	1.40024	1.52162	1.65285	1.94790	2.29202	2.69277
18	1.42825	1.55966	1.70243	2.02582	2.40662	2.85434
19	1.45681	1.59865	1.75351	2.10685	2.52695	3.02560
20	1.48595	1.63862	1.80611	2.19112	2.65330	3.20714
21	1.51567	1.67958	1.86029	2.27877	2.78596	3.39956
22	1.54598	1.72157	1.91610	2.36992	2.92526	3.60354
23	1.57690	1.76461	1.97359	2.46472	3.07152	3.81975
24	1.60844	1.80873	2.03279	2.56330	3.22510	4.04893
25	1.64061	1.85394	2.09378	2.66584	3.38635	4.29187
26	1.67342	1.90029	2.15659	2.77247	3.55567	4.54938
27	1.70689	1.94780	2.22129	2.88337	3.73346	4.82235
28	1.74102	1.99650	2.28793	2.99870	3.92013	5.11169
29	1.77584	2.04641	2.35657	3.11865	4.11614	5.41839
30	1.81136	2.09757	2.42726	3.24340	4.32194	5.74349
31	1.84759	2.15001	2.50008	3.37313	4.53804	6.08810
32	1.88454	2.20376	2.57508	3.50806	4.76494	6.45339
33	1.92223	2.25885	2.65234	3.64838	5.00319	6.84059
34	1.96068	2.31532	2.73191	3.79432	5.25335	7.25103
35	1.99989	2.37321	2.81386	3.94609	5.51602	7.68609
36	2.03989	2.43254	2.89828	4.10393	5.79182	8.14725
37	2.08069	2.49335	2.98523	4.26809	6.08141	8.63609
38	2.12230	2.55568	3.07478	4.43881	6.38548	9.15425
39	2.16474	2.61957	3.16703	4.61637	6.70475	9.70351
40	2.20804	2.68506	3.26204	4.80102	7.03999	10.28572

TABLE 6-1 FUTURE VALUE OF 1

8%	9%	10%	11%	12%	15%	(*n*) Periods
1.08000	1.09000	1.10000	1.11000	1.12000	1.15000	1
1.16640	1.18810	1.21000	1.23210	1.25440	1.32250	2
1.25971	1.29503	1.33100	1.36763	1.40493	1.52088	3
1.36049	1.41158	1.46410	1.51807	1.57352	1.74901	4
1.46933	1.53862	1.61051	1.68506	1.76234	2.01136	5
1.58687	1.67710	1.77156	1.87041	1.97382	2.31306	6
1.71382	1.82804	1.94872	2.07616	2.21068	2.66002	7
1.85093	1.99256	2.14359	2.30454	2.47596	3.05902	8
1.99900	2.17189	2.35795	2.55803	2.77308	3.51788	9
2.15892	2.36736	2.59374	2.83942	3.10585	4.04556	10
2.33164	2.58043	2.85312	3.15176	3.47855	4.65239	11
2.51817	2.81267	3.13843	3.49845	3.89598	5.35025	12
2.71962	3.06581	3.45227	3.88328	4.36349	6.15279	13
2.93719	3.34173	3.79750	4.31044	4.88711	7.07571	14
3.17217	3.64248	4.17725	4.78459	5.47357	8.13706	15
3.42594	3.97031	4.59497	5.31089	6.13039	9.35762	16
3.70002	4.32763	5.05447	5.89509	6.86604	10.76126	17
3.99602	4.71712	5.55992	6.54355	7.68997	12.37545	18
4.31570	5.14166	6.11591	7.26334	8.61276	14.23177	19
4.66096	5.60441	6.72750	8.06231	9.64629	16.36654	20
5.03383	6.10881	7.40025	8.94917	10.80385	18.82152	21
5.43654	6.65860	8.14028	9.93357	12.10031	21.64475	22
5.87146	7.25787	8.95430	11.02627	13.55235	24.89146	23
6.34118	7.91108	9.84973	12.23916	15.17863	28.62518	24
6.84847	8.62308	10.83471	13.58546	17.00000	32.91895	25
7.39635	9.39916	11.91818	15.07986	19.04007	37.85680	26
7.98806	10.24508	13.10999	16.73865	21.32488	43.53532	27
8.62711	11.16714	14.42099	18.57990	23.88387	50.06561	28
9.31727	12.17218	15.86309	20.62369	26.74993	57.57545	29
10.06266	13.26768	17.44940	22.89230	29.95992	66.21177	30
10.86767	14.46177	19.19434	25.41045	33.55511	76.14354	31
11.73708	15.76333	21.11378	28.20560	37.58173	87.56507	32
12.67605	17.18203	23.22515	31.30821	42.09153	100.69983	33
13.69013	18.72841	25.54767	34.75212	47.14252	115.80480	34
14.78534	20.41397	28.10244	38.57485	52.79962	133.17552	35
15.96817	22.25123	30.91268	42.81808	59.13557	153.15185	36
17.24563	24.25384	34.00395	47.52807	66.23184	176.12463	37
18.62528	26.43668	37.40434	52.75616	74.17966	202.54332	38
20.11530	28.81598	41.14479	58.55934	83.08122	232.92482	39
21.72452	31.40942	45.25926	65.00087	93.05097	267.86355	40

TABLE 6-2 PRESENT VALUE OF 1 (PRESENT VALUE OF A SINGLE SUM)

$$PVF_{n,i} = \frac{1}{(1+i)^n} = (1+i)^{-n}$$

(n) Periods	2%	2½%	3%	4%	5%	6%
1	.98039	.97561	.97087	.96154	.95238	.94340
2	.96117	.95181	.94260	.92456	.90703	.89000
3	.94232	.92860	.91514	.88900	.86384	.83962
4	.92385	.90595	.88849	.85480	.82270	.79209
5	.90573	.88385	.86261	.82193	.78353	.74726
6	.88797	.86230	.83748	.79031	.74622	.70496
7	.87056	.84127	.81309	.75992	.71068	.66506
8	.85349	.82075	.78941	.73069	.67684	.62741
9	.83676	.80073	.76642	.70259	.64461	.59190
10	.82035	.78120	.74409	.67556	.61391	.55839
11	.80426	.76214	.72242	.64958	.58468	.52679
12	.78849	.74356	.70138	.62460	.55684	.49697
13	.77303	.72542	.68095	.60057	.53032	.46884
14	.75788	.70773	.66112	.57748	.50507	.44230
15	.74301	.69047	.64186	.55526	.48102	.41727
16	.72845	.67362	.62317	.53391	.45811	.39365
17	.71416	.65720	.60502	.51337	.43630	.37136
18	.70016	.64117	.58739	.49363	.41552	.35034
19	.68643	.62553	.57029	.47464	.39573	.33051
20	.67297	.61027	.55368	.45639	.37689	.31180
21	.65978	.59539	.53755	.43883	.35894	.29416
22	.64684	.58086	.52189	.42196	.34185	.27751
23	.63416	.56670	.50669	.40573	.32557	.26180
24	.62172	.55288	.49193	.39012	.31007	.24698
25	.60953	.53939	.47761	.37512	.29530	.23300
26	.59758	.52623	.46369	.36069	.28124	.21981
27	.58586	.51340	.45019	.34682	.26785	.20737
28	.57437	.50088	.43708	.33348	.25509	.19563
29	.56311	.48866	.42435	.32065	.24295	.18456
30	.55207	.47674	.41199	.30832	.23138	.17411
31	.54125	.46511	.39999	.29646	.22036	.16425
32	.53063	.45377	.38834	.28506	.20987	.15496
33	.52023	.44270	.37703	.27409	.19987	.14619
34	.51003	.43191	.36604	.26355	.19035	.13791
35	.50003	.42137	.35538	.25342	.18129	.13011
36	.49022	.41109	.34503	.24367	.17266	.12274
37	.48061	.40107	.33498	.23430	.16444	.11579
38	.47119	.39128	.32523	.22529	.15661	.10924
39	.46195	.38174	.31575	.21662	.14915	.10306
40	.45289	.37243	.30656	.20829	.14205	.09722

TABLE 6-2 PRESENT VALUE OF 1

8%	9%	10%	11%	12%	15%	(*n*) Periods
.92593	.91743	.90909	.90090	.89286	.86957	1
.85734	.84168	.82645	.81162	.79719	.75614	2
.79383	.77218	.75132	.73119	.71178	.65752	3
.73503	.70843	.68301	.65873	.63552	.57175	4
.68058	.64993	.62092	.59345	.56743	.49718	5
.63017	.59627	.56447	.53464	.50663	.43233	6
.58349	.54703	.51316	.48166	.45235	.37594	7
.54027	.50187	.46651	.43393	.40388	.32690	8
.50025	.46043	.42410	.39092	.36061	.28426	9
.46319	.42241	.38554	.35218	.32197	.24719	10
.42888	.38753	.35049	.31728	.28748	.21494	11
.39711	.35554	.31863	.28584	.25668	.18691	12
.36770	.32618	.28966	.25751	.22917	.16253	13
.34046	.29925	.26333	.23199	.20462	.14133	14
.31524	.27454	.23939	.20900	.18270	.12289	15
.29189	.25187	.21763	.18829	.16312	.10687	16
.27027	.23107	.19785	.16963	.14564	.09293	17
.25025	.21199	.17986	.15282	.13004	.08081	18
.23171	.19449	.16351	.13768	.11611	.07027	19
.21455	.17843	.14864	.12403	.10367	.06110	20
.19866	.16370	.13513	.11174	.09256	.05313	21
.18394	.15018	.12285	.10067	.08264	.04620	22
.17032	.13778	.11168	.09069	.07379	.04017	23
.15770	.12641	.10153	.08170	.06588	.03493	24
.14602	.11597	.09230	.07361	.05882	.03038	25
.13520	.10639	.08391	.06631	.05252	.02642	26
.12519	.09761	.07628	.05974	.04689	.02297	27
.11591	.08955	.06934	.05382	.04187	.01997	28
.10733	.08216	.06304	.04849	.03738	.01737	29
.09938	.07537	.05731	.04368	.03338	.01510	30
.09202	.06915	.05210	.03935	.02980	.01313	31
.08520	.06344	.04736	.03545	.02661	.01142	32
.07889	.05820	.04306	.03194	.02376	.00993	33
.07305	.05340	.03914	.02878	.02121	.00864	34
.06763	.04899	.03558	.02592	.01894	.00751	35
.06262	.04494	.03235	.02335	.01691	.00653	36
.05799	.04123	.02941	.02104	.01510	.00568	37
.05369	.03783	.02674	.01896	.01348	.00494	38
.04971	.03470	.02430	.01708	.01204	.00429	39
.04603	.03184	.02210	.01538	.01075	.00373	40

TABLE 6-3 FUTURE VALUE OF AN ORDINARY ANNUITY OF 1

$$FVF\text{-}OA_{n,i} = \frac{(1 + i)^n - 1}{i}$$

(n) Periods	2%	2½%	3%	4%	5%	6%
1	1.00000	1.00000	1.00000	1.00000	1.00000	1.00000
2	2.02000	2.02500	2.03000	2.04000	2.05000	2.06000
3	3.06040	3.07563	3.09090	3.12160	3.15250	3.18360
4	4.12161	4.15252	4.18363	4.24646	4.31013	4.37462
5	5.20404	5.25633	5.30914	5.41632	5.52563	5.63709
6	6.30812	6.38774	6.46841	6.63298	6.80191	6.97532
7	7.43428	7.54743	7.66246	7.89829	8.14201	8.39384
8	8.58297	8.73612	8.89234	9.21423	9.54911	9.89747
9	9.75463	9.95452	10.15911	10.58280	11.02656	11.49132
10	10.94972	11.20338	11.46338	12.00611	12.57789	13.18079
11	12.16872	12.48347	12.80780	13.48635	14.20679	14.97164
12	13.41209	13.79555	14.19203	15.02581	15.91713	16.86994
13	14.68033	15.14044	15.61779	16.62684	17.71298	18.88214
14	15.97394	16.51895	17.08632	18.29191	19.59863	21.01507
15	17.29342	17.93193	18.59891	20.02359	21.57856	23.27597
16	18.63929	19.38022	20.15688	21.82453	23.65749	25.67253
17	20.01207	20.86473	21.76159	23.69751	25.84037	28.21288
18	21.41231	22.38635	23.41444	25.64541	28.13238	30.90565
19	22.84056	23.94601	25.11687	27.67123	30.53900	33.75999
20	24.29737	25.54466	26.87037	29.77808	33.06595	36.78559
21	25.78332	27.18327	28.67649	31.96920	35.71925	39.99273
22	27.29898	28.86286	30.53678	34.24797	38.50521	43.39229
23	28.84496	30.58443	32.45288	36.61789	41.43048	46.99583
24	30.42186	32.34904	34.42647	39.08260	44.50200	50.81558
25	32.03030	34.15776	36.45926	41.64591	47.72710	54.86451
26	33.67091	36.01171	38.55304	44.31174	51.11345	59.15638
27	35.34432	37.91200	40.70963	47.08421	54.66913	63.70577
28	37.05121	39.85980	42.93092	49.96758	58.40258	68.52811
29	38.79223	41.85630	45.21885	52.96629	62.32271	73.63980
30	40.56808	43.90270	47.57542	56.08494	66.43885	79.05819
31	42.37944	46.00027	50.00268	59.32834	70.76079	84.80168
32	44.22703	48.15028	52.50276	62.70147	75.29883	90.88978
33	46.11157	50.35403	55.07784	66.20953	80.06377	97.34316
34	48.03380	52.61289	57.73018	69.85791	85.06696	104.18376
35	49.99448	54.92821	60.46208	73.65222	90.32031	111.43478
36	51.99437	57.30141	63.27594	77.59831	95.83632	119.12087
37	54.03425	59.73395	66.17422	81.70225	101.62814	127.26812
38	56.11494	62.22730	69.15945	85.97034	107.70955	135.90421
39	58.23724	64.78298	72.23423	90.40915	114.09502	145.05846
40	60.40198	67.40255	75.40126	95.02552	120.79977	154.76197

TABLE 6-3 FUTURE VALUE OF AN ORDINARY ANNUITY OF 1

8%	9%	10%	11%	12%	15%	(*n*) Periods
1.00000	1.00000	1.00000	1.00000	1.00000	1.00000	1
2.08000	2.09000	2.10000	2.11000	2.12000	2.15000	2
3.24640	3.27810	3.31000	3.34210	3.37440	3.47250	3
4.50611	4.57313	4.64100	4.70973	4.77933	4.99338	4
5.86660	5.98471	6.10510	6.22780	6.35285	6.74238	5
7.33592	7.52334	7.71561	7.91286	8.11519	8.75374	6
8.92280	9.20044	9.48717	9.78327	10.08901	11.06680	7
10.63663	11.02847	11.43589	11.85943	12.29969	13.72682	8
12.48756	13.02104	13.57948	14.16397	14.77566	16.78584	9
14.48656	15.19293	15.93743	16.72201	17.54874	20.30372	10
16.64549	17.56029	18.53117	19.56143	20.65458	24.34928	11
18.97713	20.14072	21.38428	22.71319	24.13313	29.00167	12
21.49530	22.95339	24.52271	26.21164	28.02911	34.35192	13
24.21492	26.01919	27.97498	30.09492	32.39260	40.50471	14
27.15211	29.36092	31.77248	34.40536	37.27972	47.58041	15
30.32428	33.00340	35.94973	39.18995	42.75328	55.71747	16
33.75023	36.97371	40.54470	44.50084	48.88367	65.07509	17
37.45024	41.30134	45.59917	50.39593	55.74972	75.83636	18
41.44626	46.01846	51.15909	56.93949	63.43968	88.21181	19
45.76196	51.16012	57.27500	64.20283	72.05244	102.44358	20
50.42292	56.76453	64.00250	72.26514	81.69874	118.81012	21
55.45676	62.87334	71.40275	81.21431	92.50258	137.63164	22
60.89330	69.53194	79.54302	91.14788	104.60289	159.27638	23
66.76476	76.78981	88.49733	102.17415	118.15524	184.16784	24
73.10594	84.70090	98.34706	114.41331	133.33387	212.79302	25
79.95442	93.32398	109.18177	127.99877	150.33393	245.71197	26
87.35077	102.72314	121.09994	143.07864	169.37401	283.56877	27
95.33883	112.96822	134.20994	159.81729	190.69889	327.10408	28
103.96594	124.13536	148.63093	178.39719	214.58275	377.16969	29
113.28321	136.30754	164.49402	199.02088	241.33268	434.74515	30
123.34587	149.57522	181.94343	221.91317	271.29261	500.95692	31
134.21354	164.03699	201.13777	247.32362	304.84772	577.10046	32
145.95062	179.80032	222.25154	275.52922	342.42945	644.66553	33
158.62667	196.98234	245.47670	306.83744	384.52098	765.36535	34
172.31680	215.71076	271.02437	341.58955	431.66350	881.17016	35
187.10215	236.12472	299.12681	380.16441	484.46312	1014.34568	36
203.07032	258.37595	330.03949	422.98249	543.59869	1167.49753	37
220.31595	282.62978	364.04343	470.51056	609.83053	1343.62216	38
238.94122	309.06646	401.44778	523.26673	684.01020	1546.16549	39
259.05652	337.88245	442.59256	581.82607	767.09142	1779.09031	40

TABLE 6-4 PRESENT VALUE OF AN ORDINARY ANNUITY OF 1

$$PVF\text{-}OA_{n,i} = \frac{1 - \dfrac{1}{(1+i)^n}}{i}$$

(n) Periods	2%	2½%	3%	4%	5%	6%
1	.98039	.97561	.97087	.96154	.95238	.94340
2	1.94156	1.92742	1.91347	1.88609	1.85941	1.83339
3	2.88388	2.85602	2.82861	2.77509	2.72325	2.67301
4	3.80773	3.76197	3.71710	3.62990	3.54595	3.46511
5	4.71346	4.64583	4.57971	4.45182	4.32948	4.21236
6	5.60143	5.50813	5.41719	5.24214	5.07569	4.91732
7	6.47199	6.34939	6.23028	6.00205	5.78637	5.58238
8	7.32548	7.17014	7.01969	6.73274	6.46321	6.20979
9	8.16224	7.97087	7.78611	7.43533	7.10782	6.80169
10	8.98259	8.75206	8.53020	8.11090	7.72173	7.36009
11	9.78685	9.51421	9.25262	8.76048	8.30641	7.88687
12	10.57534	10.25776	9.95400	9.38507	8.86325	8.38384
13	11.34837	10.98319	10.63496	9.98565	9.39357	8.85268
14	12.10625	11.69091	11.29607	10.56312	9.89864	9.29498
15	12.84926	12.38138	11.93794	11.11839	10.37966	9.71225
16	13.57771	13.05500	12.56110	11.65230	10.83777	10.10590
17	14.29187	13.71220	13.16612	12.16567	11.27407	10.47726
18	14.99203	14.35336	13.75351	12.65930	11.68959	10.82760
19	15.67846	14.97889	14.32380	13.13394	12.08532	11.15812
20	16.35143	15.58916	14.87747	13.59033	12.46221	11.46992
21	17.01121	16.18455	15.41502	14.02916	12.82115	11.76408
22	17.65805	16.76541	15.93692	14.45112	13.16300	12.04158
23	18.29220	17.33211	16.44361	14.85684	13.48857	12.30338
24	18.91393	17.88499	16.93554	15.24696	13.79864	12.55036
25	19.52346	18.42438	17.41315	15.62208	14.09394	12.78336
26	20.12104	18.95061	17.87684	15.98277	14.37519	13.00317
27	20.70690	19.46401	18.32703	16.32959	14.64303	13.21053
28	21.28127	19.96489	18.76411	16.66306	14.89813	13.40616
29	21.84438	20.45355	19.18845	16.98371	15.14107	13.59072
30	22.39646	20.93029	19.60044	17.29203	15.37245	13.76483
31	22.93770	21.39541	20.00043	17.58849	15.59281	13.92909
32	23.46833	21.84918	20.38877	17.87355	15.80268	14.08404
33	23.98856	22.29188	20.76579	18.14765	16.00255	14.23023
34	24.49859	22.72379	21.13184	18.41120	16.19290	14.36814
35	24.99862	23.14516	21.48722	18.66461	16.37419	14.49825
36	25.48884	23.55625	21.83225	18.90828	16.54685	14.62099
37	25.96945	23.95732	22.16724	19.14258	16.71129	14.73678
38	26.44064	24.34860	22.49246	19.36786	16.86789	14.84602
39	26.90259	24.73034	22.80822	19.58448	17.01704	14.94907
40	27.35548	25.10278	23.11477	19.79277	17.15909	15.04630

TABLE 6-4 PRESENT VALUE OF AN ORDINARY ANNUITY OF 1

8%	9%	10%	11%	12%	15%	(n) Periods
.92593	.91743	.90909	.90090	.89286	.86957	1
1.78326	1.75911	1.73554	1.71252	1.69005	1.62571	2
2.57710	2.53130	2.48685	2.44371	2.40183	2.28323	3
3.31213	3.23972	3.16986	3.10245	3.03735	2.85498	4
3.99271	3.88965	3.79079	3.69590	3.60478	3.35216	5
4.62288	4.48592	4.35526	4.23054	4.11141	3.78448	6
5.20637	5.03295	4.86842	4.71220	4.56376	4.16042	7
5.74664	5.53482	5.33493	5.14612	4.96764	4.48732	8
6.24689	5.99525	5.75902	5.53705	5.32825	4.77158	9
6.71008	6.41766	6.14457	5.88923	5.65022	5.01877	10
7.13896	6.80519	6.49506	6.20652	5.93770	5.23371	11
7.53608	7.16073	6.81369	6.49236	6.19437	5.42062	12
7.90378	7.48690	7.10336	6.74987	6.42355	5.58315	13
8.24424	7.78615	7.36669	6.98187	6.62817	5.72448	14
8.55948	8.06069	7.60608	7.19087	6.81086	5.84737	15
8.85137	8.31256	7.82371	7.37916	6.97399	5.95424	16
9.12164	8.54363	8.02155	7.54879	7.11963	6.04716	17
9.37189	8.75563	8.20141	7.70162	7.24967	6.12797	18
9.60360	8.95012	8.36492	7.83929	7.36578	6.19823	19
9.81815	9.12855	8.51356	7.96333	7.46944	6.25933	20
10.01680	9.29224	8.64869	8.07507	7.56200	6.31246	21
10.20074	9.44243	8.77154	8.17574	7.64465	6.35866	22
10.37106	9.58021	8.88322	8.26643	7.71843	6.39884	23
10.52876	9.70661	8.98474	8.34814	7.78432	6.43377	24
10.67478	9.82258	9.07704	8.42174	7.84314	6.46415	25
10.80998	9.92897	9.16095	8.48806	7.89566	6.49056	26
10.93516	10.02658	9.23722	8.54780	7.94255	6.51353	27
11.05108	10.11613	9.30657	8.60162	7.98442	6.53351	28
11.15841	10.19828	9.36961	8.65011	8.02181	6.55088	29
11.25778	10.27365	9.42691	8.69379	8.05518	6.56598	30
11.34980	10.34280	9.47901	8.73315	8.08499	6.57911	31
11.43500	10.40624	9.52638	8.76860	8.11159	6.59053	32
11.51389	10.46444	9.56943	8.80054	8.13535	6.60046	33
11.58693	10.51784	9.60858	8.82932	8.15656	6.60910	34
11.65457	10.56682	9.64416	8.85524	8.17550	6.61661	35
11.71719	10.61176	9.67651	8.87859	8.19241	6.62314	36
11.77518	10.65299	9.70592	8.89963	8.20751	6.62882	37
11.82887	10.69082	9.73265	8.91859	8.22099	6.63375	38
11.87858	10.72552	9.75697	8.93567	8.23303	6.63805	39
11.92461	10.75736	9.77905	8.95105	8.24378	6.64178	40

TABLE 6-5 PRESENT VALUE OF AN ANNUITY DUE OF 1

$$PVF\text{-}AD_{n,i} = 1 + \frac{1 - \dfrac{1}{(1+i)^{n-1}}}{i}$$

(n) Periods	2%	2½%	3%	4%	5%	6%
1	1.00000	1.00000	1.00000	1.00000	1.00000	1.00000
2	1.98039	1.97561	1.97087	1.96154	1.95238	1.94340
3	2.94156	2.92742	2.91347	2.88609	2.85941	2.83339
4	3.88388	3.85602	3.82861	3.77509	3.72325	3.67301
5	4.80773	4.76197	4.71710	4.62990	4.54595	4.46511
6	5.71346	5.64583	5.57971	5.45182	5.32948	5.21236
7	6.60143	6.50813	6.41719	6.24214	6.07569	5.91732
8	7.47199	7.34939	7.23028	7.00205	6.78637	6.58238
9	8.32548	8.17014	8.01969	7.73274	7.46321	7.20979
10	9.16224	8.97087	8.78611	8.43533	8.10782	7.80169
11	9.98259	9.75206	9.53020	9.11090	8.72173	8.36009
12	10.78685	10.51421	10.25262	9.76048	9.30641	8.88687
13	11.57534	11.25776	10.95400	10.38507	9.86325	9.38384
14	12.34837	11.98319	11.63496	10.98565	10.39357	9.85268
15	13.10625	12.69091	12.29607	11.56312	10.89864	10.29498
16	13.84926	13.38138	12.93794	12.11839	11.37966	10.71225
17	14.57771	14.05500	13.56110	12.65230	11.83777	11.10590
18	15.29187	14.71220	14.16612	13.16567	12.27407	11.47726
19	15.99203	15.35336	14.75351	13.65930	12.68959	11.82760
20	16.67846	15.97889	15.32380	14.13394	13.08532	12.15812
21	17.35143	16.58916	15.87747	14.59033	13.46221	12.46992
22	18.01121	17.18455	16.41502	15.02916	13.82115	12.76408
23	18.65805	17.76541	16.93692	15.45112	14.16300	13.04158
24	19.29220	18.33211	17.44361	15.85684	14.48857	13.30338
25	19.91393	18.88499	17.93554	16.24696	14.79864	13.55036
26	20.52346	19.42438	18.41315	16.62208	15.09394	13.78336
27	21.12104	19.95061	18.87684	16.98277	15.37519	14.00317
28	21.70690	20.46401	19.32703	17.32959	15.64303	14.21053
29	22.28127	20.96489	19.76411	17.66306	15.89813	14.40616
30	22.84438	21.45355	20.18845	17.98371	16.14107	14.59072
31	23.39646	21.93029	20.60044	18.29203	16.37245	14.76483
32	23.93770	22.39541	21.00043	18.58849	16.59281	14.92909
33	24.46833	22.84918	21.38877	18.87355	16.80268	15.08404
34	24.98856	23.29188	21.76579	19.14765	17.00255	15.23023
35	25.49859	23.72379	22.13184	19.41120	17.19290	15.36814
36	25.99862	24.14516	22.48722	19.66461	17.37419	15.49825
37	26.48884	24.55625	22.83225	19.90828	17.54685	15.62099
38	26.96945	24.95732	23.16724	20.14258	17.71129	15.73678
39	27.44064	25.34860	23.49246	20.36786	17.86789	15.84602
40	27.90259	25.73034	23.80822	20.58448	18.01704	15.94907

TABLE 6-5 PRESENT VALUE OF AN ANNUITY DUE OF 1

8%	9%	10%	11%	12%	15%	(*n*) Periods
1.00000	1.00000	1.00000	1.00000	1.00000	1.00000	1
1.92593	1.91743	1.90909	1.90090	1.89286	1.86957	2
2.78326	2.75911	2.73554	2.71252	2.69005	2.62571	3
3.57710	3.53130	3.48685	3.44371	3.40183	3.28323	4
4.31213	4.23972	4.16986	4.10245	4.03735	3.85498	5
4.99271	4.88965	4.79079	4.69590	4.60478	4.35216	6
5.62288	5.48592	5.35526	5.23054	5.11141	4.78448	7
6.20637	6.03295	5.86842	5.71220	5.56376	5.16042	8
6.74664	6.53482	6.33493	6.14612	5.96764	5.48732	9
7.24689	6.99525	6.75902	6.53705	6.32825	5.77158	10
7.71008	7.41766	7.14457	6.88923	6.65022	6.01877	11
8.13896	7.80519	7.49506	7.20652	6.93770	6.23371	12
8.53608	8.16073	7.81369	7.49236	7.19437	6.42062	13
8.90378	8.48690	8.10336	7.74987	7.42355	6.58315	14
9.24424	8.78615	8.36669	7.98187	7.62817	6.72448	15
9.55948	9.06069	8.60608	8.19087	7.81086	6.84737	16
9.85137	9.31256	8.82371	8.37916	7.97399	6.95424	17
10.12164	9.54363	9.02155	8.54879	8.11963	7.04716	18
10.37189	9.75563	9.20141	8.70162	8.24967	7.12797	19
10.60360	9.95012	9.36492	8.83929	8.36578	7.19823	20
10.81815	10.12855	9.51356	8.96333	8.46944	7.25933	21
11.01680	10.29224	9.64869	9.07507	8.56200	7.31246	22
11.20074	10.44243	9.77154	9.17574	8.64465	7.35866	23
11.37106.	10.58021	9.88322	9.26643	8.71843	7.39884	24
11.52876	10.70661	9.98474	9.34814	8.78432	7.43377	25
11.67478	10.82258	10.07704	9.42174	8.84314	7.46415	26
11.80998	10.92897	10.16095	9.48806	8.89566	7.49056	27
11.93518	11.02658	10.23722	9.54780	8.94255	7.51353	28
12.05108	11.11613	10.30657	9.60162	8.98442	7.53351	29
12.15841	11.19828	10.36961	9.65011	9.02181	7.55088	30
12.25778	11.27365	10.42691	9.69379	9.05518	7.56598	31
12.34980	11.34280	10.47901	9.73315	9.08499	7.57911	32
12.43500	11.40624	10.52638	9.76860	9.11159	7.59053	33
12.51389	11.46444	10.56943	9.80054	9.13535	7.60046	34
12.58693	11.51784	10.60858	9.82932	9.15656	7.60910	35
12.65457	11.56682	10.64416	9.85524	9.17550	7.61661	36
12.71719	11.61176	10.67651	9.87859	9.19241	7.62314	37
12.77518	11.65299	10.70592	9.89963	9.20751	7.62882	38
12.82887	11.69082	10.73265	9.91859	9.22099	7.63375	39
12.87858	11.72552	10.75697	9.93567	9.23303	7.63805	40

CHAPTER

7 Cash and Receivables

LEARNING OBJECTIVES

After studying this chapter, you should be able to:

1. Identify items considered cash.
2. Indicate how to report cash and related items.
3. Define receivables and identify the different types of receivables.
4. Explain accounting issues related to recognition of accounts receivable.
5. Explain accounting issues related to valuation of accounts receivable.
6. Explain accounting issues related to recognition and valuation of notes receivable.
7. Explain the fair value option.
8. Explain accounting issues related to disposition of accounts and notes receivable.
9. Describe how to report and analyze receivables.

Please Release Me?

In recent quarters, several U.S. banks have reported increases in net income compared to the same quarter in the previous year. How did the market greet this news? With a resounding "blah." For example, **Wells Fargo**'s report led to a share price decline of 8.4 percent, and **Citigroup** saw a 1.7 percent drop in its share price when it announced earnings. What gives?

It seems that the source of earnings increase matters to the market. And in the case of banks, a significant portion of recent earnings increases are the result of decreases in the banks' bad debt expense, not increased revenues on loans and investments. These decreases happen when the banks' reserves that have accumulated in the allowance for loan losses are judged to be too high. How big is the effect? As shown in the chart below, in a recent quarter, of the $14.3 billion in earnings reported by the top 10 U.S. banks, $3.5 billion came from releasing loan loss reserves. For Citi, without the reserve release, it would have reported a loss.

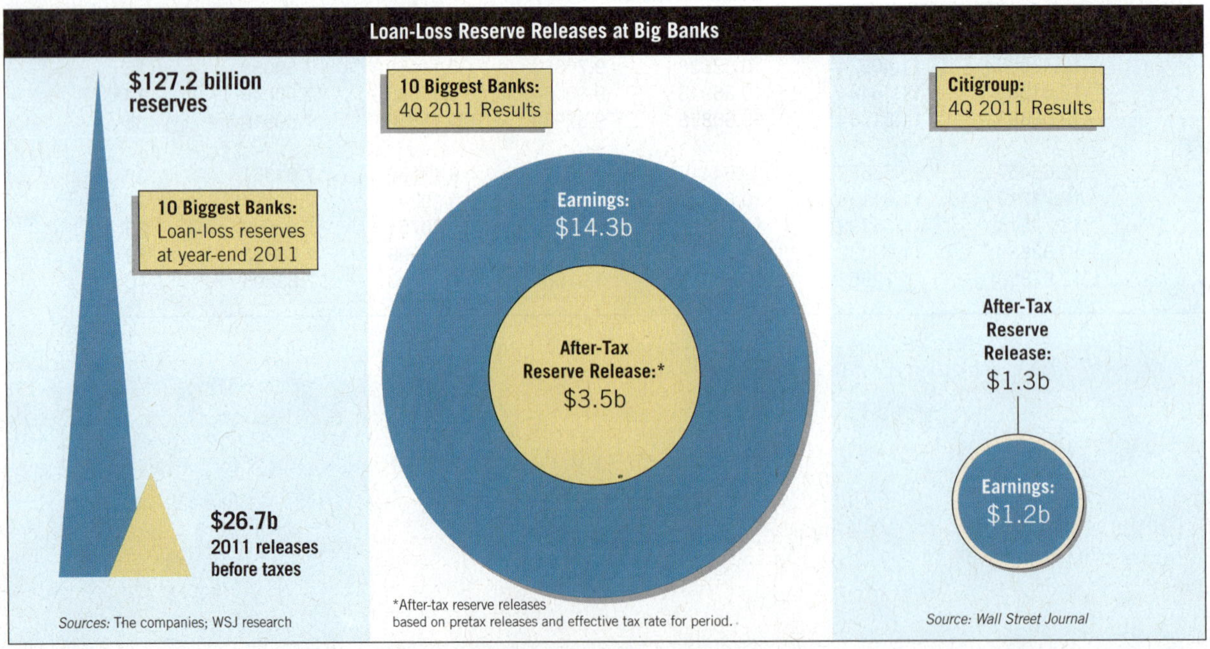

CONCEPTUAL FOCUS

- See the **Underlying Concepts** on pages 352, 356, and 373.
- Read the **Evolving Issue** on page 374 for a discussion of accounting for loan losses.

INTERNATIONAL FOCUS

- See the **International Perspectives** on pages 365, 370, and 372.
- Read the **IFRS Insights** on pages 408–412 for a discussion of:
  - —Impairment evaluation
  - —Recovery of impairment losses

As shown in the left side of the chart, the 10 largest banks had $127.2 billion in the allowance for loan losses at the end of 2011, and $26.7 billion was drawn down (released) in that same year.

So is this a problem? Supposedly, reserves should be released when there is a decline in the likelihood that loans will not be paid. However, some market-watchers doubt that banks can afford to keep up the pace of reserve releases. Lowering reserves could increase pressure on profits that are being hit by slow economic growth, low interest rates, and tighter rules. According to one analyst, "The releases are masking some horrible operating performance. . . . The bottom line is your earnings power is decreasing."

To be fair, analysts often criticize banks when they increase the allowance for loan losses during profitable periods. In some cases, the banks are accused of managing earnings. That is, in good times they increase loan loss reserves, which reduces (or smoothes) earnings. Then in bad times, the reserves can be released, thereby increasing earnings. The SEC has reprimanded some banks for this alleged earnings management—in not only the tough times, but the good times as well.

Sources: S. Kapner, "Citi Shines, but Investors Shrug," *Wall Street Journal* (October 18, 2011), p. C1; and M. Rapoport, "Banks Depleting Earnings Backstop: Days Numbered for Using Reserves to Increase Profit," *Wall Street Journal* (February 8, 2012), p. C1.

PREVIEW OF CHAPTER 7

As our opening story indicates, measurement and remeasurement of the allowance for doubtful accounts has important implications for accurate reporting of net accounts receivable, operating profits, net income, and assets. In this chapter, we discuss cash and receivables—two assets that are important to banks such as **Citigroup** and nonbank companies such as **Wal-Mart Stores, Inc.** The content and organization of the chapter are as follows.

Cash and Receivables

- **Cash**
  - What is cash?
  - Reporting cash
  - Summary of cash-related items
- **Accounts Receivable**
  - Recognition of accounts receivable
  - Valuation of accounts receivable
- **Notes Receivable**
  - Recognition of notes receivable
  - Valuation of notes receivable
- **Special Issues**
  - Fair value option
  - Disposition of accounts and notes receivable
  - Presentation and analysis

CASH

What Is Cash?

LEARNING OBJECTIVE 1
Identify items considered cash.

Cash, the most liquid of assets, is the standard medium of exchange and the basis for measuring and accounting for all other items. Companies generally classify cash as a current asset. Cash consists of coin, currency, and available funds on deposit at the bank. Negotiable instruments such as money orders, certified checks, cashier's checks, personal checks, and bank drafts are also viewed as cash. What about savings accounts? Banks do have the legal right to demand notice before withdrawal. But, because banks rarely demand prior notice, savings accounts nevertheless are considered cash.

Some negotiable instruments provide small investors with an opportunity to earn interest. These items, more appropriately classified as temporary investments than as cash, include money market funds, money market savings certificates, certificates of deposit (CDs), and similar types of deposits and "short-term paper."[1] These securities usually contain restrictions or penalties on their conversion to cash. Money market funds that provide checking account privileges, however, are usually classified as cash.

Certain items present classification problems: Companies treat **postdated checks and I.O.U.s** as receivables. They also treat **travel advances** as receivables if collected from employees or deducted from their salaries. Otherwise, companies classify the travel advance as a prepaid expense. **Postage stamps on hand** are classified as part of office supplies inventory or as a prepaid expense. Because **petty cash funds and change funds are used** to meet current operating expenses and liquidate current liabilities, companies include these funds in current assets as cash.

Reporting Cash

LEARNING OBJECTIVE 2
Indicate how to report cash and related items.

Although the reporting of cash is relatively straightforward, a number of issues merit special attention. These issues relate to the reporting of:

1. Cash equivalents.
2. Restricted cash.
3. Bank overdrafts.

Cash Equivalents

A current classification that has become popular is "Cash and cash equivalents."[2] **Cash equivalents** are short-term, highly liquid investments that are both (a) readily convertible to known amounts of cash, and (b) so near their maturity that they present insignificant risk of changes in value because of changes in interest rates. Generally, only investments with original maturities of three months or less qualify under these definitions. Examples of cash

[1]A variety of "short-term paper" is available for investment. For example, **certificates of deposit** (CDs) represent formal evidence of indebtedness, issued by a bank, subject to withdrawal under the specific terms of the instrument. Issued in various denominations, they have maturities anywhere from 7 days to 10 years and generally pay interest at the short-term interest rate in effect at the date of issuance.

In **money-market funds**, a variation of the mutual fund, the mix of Treasury bills and commercial paper making up the fund's portfolio determines the yield. Most money-market funds require an initial minimum investment of $1,000; many allow withdrawal by check or wire transfer.

Treasury bills are U.S. government obligations generally issued with 4-, 13-, and 26-week maturities; they are sold at weekly government auctions in denominations of $1,000 up to a maximum purchase of $5 million.

Commercial paper is a short-term note issued by corporations with good credit ratings. Often issued in $5,000 and $10,000 denominations, these notes generally yield a higher rate than Treasury bills.

[2]*Accounting Trends and Techniques* recently indicated that approximately 2 percent of the companies surveyed use the caption "Cash," 89 percent use "Cash and cash equivalents," and 2 percent use a caption such as "Cash and marketable securities" or similar terminology.

equivalents are Treasury bills, commercial paper, and money market funds. Some companies combine cash with temporary investments on the balance sheet. In these cases, they describe the amount of the temporary investments either parenthetically or in the notes.

Most individuals think of cash equivalents as cash. Unfortunately, that is not always the case. Companies like **Kohl's** and **ADC Telecommunications** have found out the hard way and are taking sizable write-downs on cash equivalents. Their losses resulted because they purchased auction-rate notes that declined in value. These notes carry interest rates that usually reset weekly and often have long-maturity dates (as long as 30 years). Companies argued that such notes should be classified as cash equivalents because they can be routinely traded at auction on a daily basis. (In short, they are liquid and risk-free.) Auditors agreed and permitted cash-equivalent treatment even though maturities extended well beyond three months. But when the credit crunch hit, the auctions stopped, and the value of these securities dropped because no market existed. In retrospect, the cash-equivalent classification was misleading.

It now appears likely that the FASB will eliminate the cash-equivalent classification from financial statement presentations altogether. Companies will now report only cash. If an asset is not cash and is short-term in nature, it should be reported as a temporary investment. An interesting moral to this story is that when times are good, some careless accounting may work. But in bad times, it quickly becomes apparent that sloppy accounting can lead to misleading and harmful effects for users of the financial statements.

Restricted Cash

Petty cash, payroll, and dividend funds are examples of cash set aside for a particular purpose. In most situations, these fund balances are not material. Therefore, companies do not segregate them from cash in the financial statements. When material in amount, companies segregate **restricted cash** from "regular" cash for reporting purposes. Companies classify restricted cash either in the current assets or in the long-term assets section, depending on the date of availability or disbursement. Classification in the current section is appropriate if using the cash for payment of existing or maturing obligations (within a year or the operating cycle, whichever is longer). On the other hand, companies show the restricted cash in the long-term section of the balance sheet if holding the cash for a longer period of time. Among other potential restrictions, companies need to determine whether any of the cash in accounts outside the United States is restricted by regulations against exportation of currency.

Cash classified in the long-term section is frequently set aside for plant expansion, retirement of long-term debt, or, in the case of **International Thoroughbred Breeders**, for entry fee deposits.

ILLUSTRATION 7-1
Disclosure of Restricted Cash

International Thoroughbred Breeders

Restricted cash and investments (See Note)	$3,730,000

Note: Restricted Cash. At year-end, the Company had approximately $3,730,000, which was classified as restricted cash and investments. These funds are primarily cash received from horsemen for nomination and entry fees to be applied to upcoming racing meets, purse winnings held in trust for horsemen, and amounts held for unclaimed ticketholder winnings.

Banks and other lending institutions often require customers to maintain minimum cash balances in checking or savings accounts. The SEC defines these minimum balances, called **compensating balances**, as "that portion of any demand deposit (or any time deposit or certificate of deposit) maintained by a corporation which constitutes support for existing borrowing arrangements of the corporation with a lending institution. Such arrangements would include both outstanding borrowings and the assurance of future credit availability." **[1]**

See the FASB Codification section (page 385).

To avoid misleading investors about the amount of cash available to meet recurring obligations, the SEC recommends that companies state separately **legally restricted deposits** held as compensating balances against **short-term** borrowing arrangements among the "Cash and cash equivalent items" in current assets. Companies should classify separately restricted deposits held as compensating balances against **long-term** borrowing arrangements as noncurrent assets in either the investments or other assets sections, using a caption such as "Cash on deposit maintained as compensating balance." In cases where compensating balance arrangements exist without agreements that restrict the use of cash amounts shown on the balance sheet, companies should describe the arrangements and the amounts involved in the notes.

Bank Overdrafts

Bank overdrafts occur when a company writes a check for more than the amount in its cash account. Companies should report bank overdrafts in the current liabilities section, adding them to the amount reported as accounts payable. If material, companies should disclose these items separately, either on the face of the balance sheet or in the related notes.[3]

Bank overdrafts are generally not offset against the cash account. A major exception is when available cash is present in another account in the same bank on which the overdraft occurred. Offsetting in this case is required.

Summary of Cash-Related Items

Cash and cash equivalents include the medium of exchange and most negotiable instruments. If the item cannot be quickly converted to coin or currency, a company separately classifies it as an investment, receivable, or prepaid expense. Companies segregate and classify cash that is unavailable for payment of currently maturing liabilities in the long-term assets section. Illustration 7-2 summarizes the classification of cash-related items.

ILLUSTRATION 7-2
Classification of Cash-Related Items

Classification of Cash, Cash Equivalents, and Noncash Items

Item	Classification	Comment
Cash	Cash	If unrestricted, report as cash. If restricted, identify and classify as current and noncurrent assets.
Petty cash and change funds	Cash	Report as cash.
Short-term paper	Cash equivalents	Investments with maturity of less than 3 months, often combined with cash.
Short-term paper	Temporary investments	Investments with maturity of 3 to 12 months.
Postdated checks and I.O.U.s	Receivables	Assumed to be collectible.
Travel advances	Receivables	Assumed to be collected from employees or deducted from their salaries.
Postage on hand (as stamps or in postage meters)	Prepaid expenses	May also be classified as office supplies inventory.
Bank overdrafts	Current liability	If right of offset exists, reduce cash.
Compensating balances	Cash separately classified as a deposit maintained as compensating balance	Classify as current or noncurrent in the balance sheet. Disclose separately in notes details of the arrangement.

[3]Bank overdrafts usually occur because of a simple oversight by the company writing the check. Banks often expect companies to have overdrafts from time to time and therefore negotiate a fee as payment for this possible occurrence. However, at one time, E. F. Hutton (a large brokerage firm) began intentionally overdrawing its accounts by astronomical amounts—on some days exceeding $1 billion—thus obtaining interest-free loans that it could invest. Because the amounts were so large and fees were not negotiated in advance, E. F. Hutton came under criminal investigation for its actions.

What do the numbers mean? LUCK OF THE IRISH

Recently, **Apple** executives explained what they are planning to do with their $98 billion in cash (pay a $2.65 dividend and buy back some of their shares). However, what they were really talking about was not the full $98 billion but the $34 billion the company has here in the United States. The other $64 billion is sitting in overseas subsidiaries and may never find its way back to the United States. The reason: U.S. tax laws allow companies to defer taxes on their profits from international operations until they bring the cash back into the country.

So what do many companies do? Either the cash just sits there in foreign bank accounts or is reinvested in factories and acquisitions overseas. After all, why should a company send its cash back to the United States when it can reinvest this cash overseas without any tax payments? As a result, companies now have the incentive to move as much of their earnings overseas to low-tax jurisdictions such as a country like Ireland. As one expert noted, it cannot be the luck of the Irish that explains the extraordinary and systematic profitability of Irish subsidiaries of U.S. companies.

So when investors analyze an annual report and find a company reporting a large cash balance, they may believe that this cash is available for increased dividends or for acquisitions in the United States. But that is not necessarily so—much of the cash may be overseas and may never return.

Unfortunately, the problem is getting bigger, not smaller. Untaxed foreign earnings are now growing at a much faster rate than earnings generated in the United States. For example, in a recent five-year period, the accumulated untaxed foreign earnings have reached over $1 trillion and are growing at a rate of 22 percent as compared to 5 percent for domestic earnings. A majority of these earnings are concentrated in three sectors—health care, technology, and industrials. Presented below is a chart that shows total accumulated untaxed foreign earnings, untaxed foreign earnings for the current year and its relationship to net income, and cash flow provided by operations for the top five companies in the S&P 500. Note that the top 40 companies in the S&P 500 have 73 percent of the total untaxed foreign earnings in the index.

Company	Accumulated Untaxed Foreign Earnings (UFE)*	Untaxed Foreign Earnings in Current Year*	Untaxed Foreign Earnings as a % of Net Income	Untaxed Foreign Earnings as a % of Operating Cash Flow
Microsoft	$ 44,800	$15,300	66%	57%
Pfizer	63,000	14,800	169	73
ExxonMobil	47,000	12,000	28	22
Apple	23,400	11,100	43	30
General Electric	102,000	8,000	56	24

*In $ millions.

What this all tells us is that the U.S. taxpayer is presently holding the bag because many of these companies may never be taxed as the cash from these earnings will not be invested in the Unites States. At a minimum, investors need more information about foreign earnings, the amount of cash in foreign deposits, and cash generated from foreign operations where untaxed foreign earnings were reported. Capital markets are well served when good information is provided. You would think that cash is cash and the amount is certain, but unfortunately some cash is better than other cash.

Source: J. Ciesielski, "Growing, Glowing Earnings: S&P 500's 2011 Untaxed Income," *The Analyst's Accounting Observer* (March 26, 2012).

ACCOUNTS RECEIVABLE

3 LEARNING OBJECTIVE
Define receivables and identify the different types of receivables.

Receivables are claims held against customers and others for money, goods, or services. For financial statement purposes, companies classify receivables as either **current** (short-term) or **noncurrent** (long-term). Companies expect to collect **current receivables** within a year or during the current operating cycle, whichever is longer. They classify all other receivables as **noncurrent**. Receivables are further classified in the balance sheet as either trade or nontrade receivables.

Customers often owe a company amounts for goods bought or services rendered. A company may subclassify these **trade receivables**, usually the most significant item it possesses, into accounts receivable and notes receivable. **Accounts receivable** are oral promises of the purchaser to pay for goods and services sold. They represent "open accounts" resulting from short-term extensions of credit. A company normally collects them within 30 to 60 days. **Notes receivable** are written promises to pay a certain sum of money on a specified future date. They may arise from sales, financing, or other transactions. Notes may be short-term or long-term.

Nontrade receivables arise from a variety of transactions. Some examples of nontrade receivables are:

1. Advances to officers and employees.
2. Advances to subsidiaries.
3. Deposits paid to cover potential damages or losses.
4. Deposits paid as a guarantee of performance or payment.
5. Dividends and interest receivable.
6. Claims against:
   (a) Insurance companies for casualties sustained.
   (b) Defendants under suit.
   (c) Governmental bodies for tax refunds.
   (d) Common carriers for damaged or lost goods.
   (e) Creditors for returned, damaged, or lost goods.
   (f) Customers for returnable items (crates, containers, etc.).

Because of the peculiar nature of nontrade receivables, companies generally report them as separate items in the balance sheet. Illustration 7-3 shows the reporting of trade and nontrade receivables in the balance sheets of **Molson Coors Brewing Company** and **Seaboard Corporation**.

Molson Coors Brewing Company
(in thousands)

Current assets	
Cash and cash equivalents	$ 377,023
Accounts and notes receivable	
Trade, less allowance for doubtful accounts of $8,827	758,526
Current notes receivable and other receivables, less allowance for doubtful accounts of $3,181	112,626
Inventories	369,521
Maintenance and operating supplies, less allowance for obsolete supplies of $10,556	34,782
Other current assets, less allowance for advertising supplies of $948	124,336
Total current assets	$1,776,814

Seaboard Corporation
(in thousands)

Current assets		
Cash and cash equivalents		$ 47,346
Short-term investments		286,660
Receivables		
Trade	$251,005	
Due from foreign affiliates	90,019	
Other	26,349	
		367,373
Allowance for doubtful accounts		(8,060)
Net receivables		359,313
Inventories		392,946
Deferred income taxes		19,558
Other current assets		77,710
Total current assets		$1,183,533

ILLUSTRATION 7-3
Receivables Balance Sheet Presentations

The basic issues in accounting for accounts and notes receivable are the same: **recognition, valuation,** and **disposition**. We discuss these basic issues for accounts and notes receivable next.

Recognition of Accounts Receivable

> **4 LEARNING OBJECTIVE**
> Explain accounting issues related to recognition of accounts receivable.

In most receivables transactions, the amount to be recognized is the exchange price between the two parties. **The exchange price is the amount due from the debtor** (a customer or a borrower). Some type of business document, often an invoice, serves as evidence of the exchange price. Two factors may complicate the measurement of the exchange price: (1) the availability of discounts (trade and cash discounts), and (2) the length of time between the sale and the due date of payments (the interest element).

Trade Discounts

Prices may be subject to a trade or quantity discount. Companies use such **trade discounts** to avoid frequent changes in catalogs, to alter prices for different quantities purchased, or to hide the true invoice price from competitors.

Trade discounts are commonly quoted in percentages. For example, say your cell phone has a list price of $90, and the manufacturer sells it to **Best Buy** for list less a 30 percent trade discount. The manufacturer then records the receivable at $63 per phone. The manufacturer, per normal practice, simply deducts the trade discount from the list price and bills the customer net.

As another example, **Maxwell House** at one time sold a 10-ounce jar of its instant coffee listing at $5.85 to supermarkets for $5.05, a trade discount of approximately 14 percent. The supermarkets in turn sold the instant coffee for $5.20 per jar. Maxwell House records the receivable and related sales revenue at $5.05 per jar, not $5.85.

Cash Discounts (Sales Discounts)

Companies offer **cash discounts (sales discounts)** to induce prompt payment. Cash discounts generally presented in terms such as 2/10, n/30 (2 percent if paid within 10 days, gross amount due in 30 days), or 2/10, E.O.M., net 30, E.O.M. (2 percent if paid any time before the tenth day of the following month, with full payment due by the thirtieth of the following month).

Companies usually take sales discounts unless their cash is severely limited. Why? A company that receives a 1 percent reduction in the sales price for payment within 10 days, total payment due within 30 days, effectively earns 18.25 percent [.01 ÷ (20/365)], or at least avoids that rate of interest cost.

Companies usually record sales and related sales discount transactions by entering the receivable and sale at the gross amount. Under this method, companies recognize sales discounts only when they receive payment within the discount period. The income statement shows sales discounts as a deduction from sales to arrive at net sales.

Some contend that sales discounts not taken reflect penalties added to an established price to encourage prompt payment. That is, the seller offers sales on account at a slightly higher price than if selling for cash. The cash discount offered offsets the increase. Thus, customers who pay within the discount period actually purchase at the cash price. Those who pay after expiration of the discount period pay a penalty for the delay—an amount in excess of the cash price. Per this reasoning, some companies record sales and receivables net. They subsequently debit any discounts not taken to Accounts Receivable and credit to Sales Discounts Forfeited. The entries in Illustration 7-4 (page 352) show the difference between the gross and net methods.

If using the gross method, a company reports sales discounts as a deduction from sales in the income statement. Proper expense recognition dictates that the company also reasonably estimates the expected discounts to be taken and charges that amount

ILLUSTRATION 7-4
Entries under Gross and Net Methods of Recording Cash (Sales) Discounts

Gross Method			Net Method		
Sales of $10,000, terms 2/10, n/30					
Accounts Receivable	10,000		Accounts Receivable	9,800	
Sales Revenue		10,000	Sales Revenue		9,800
Payment on $4,000 of sales received within discount period					
Cash	3,920		Cash	3,920	
Sales Discounts	80		Accounts Receivable		3,920
Accounts Receivable		4,000			
Payment on $6,000 of sales received after discount period					
Cash	6,000		Accounts Receivable	120	
Accounts Receivable		6,000	Sales Discounts Forfeited		120
			Cash	6,000	
			Accounts Receivable		6,000

against sales. If using the net method, a company considers Sales Discounts Forfeited as an "Other revenue" item.[4]

Theoretically, the recognition of Sales Discounts Forfeited is correct. The receivable is stated closer to its realizable value, and the net sales figure measures the revenue recognized from the sale. As a practical matter, however, companies seldom use the net method because it requires additional analysis and bookkeeping. For example, the net method requires adjusting entries to record sales discounts forfeited on accounts receivable that have passed the discount period.

Nonrecognition of Interest Element

Ideally, a company should measure receivables in terms of their present value, that is, the discounted value of the cash to be received in the future. When expected cash receipts require a waiting period, the receivable face amount is not worth the amount that the company ultimately receives.

To illustrate, assume that **Best Buy** makes a sale on account for $1,000 with payment due in four months. The applicable annual rate of interest is 12 percent, and payment is made at the end of four months. The present value of that receivable is not $1,000 but $961.54 ($1,000 × .96154). In other words, the $1,000 Best Buy receives four months from now is not the same as the $1,000 received today.

Underlying Concepts

Materiality means it must make a difference to a decision-maker. The FASB believes that present value concepts can be ignored for short-term receivables.

Theoretically, any revenue after the period of sale is interest revenue. In practice, companies ignore interest revenue related to accounts receivable because the amount of the discount is not usually material in relation to the net income for the period. The profession specifically excludes from present value considerations "receivables arising from transactions with customers in the normal course of business which are due in customary trade terms not exceeding approximately one year." [2]

Valuation of Accounts Receivable

LEARNING OBJECTIVE 5
Explain accounting issues related to valuation of accounts receivable.

Reporting of receivables involves (1) classification and (2) valuation on the balance sheet. Classification involves determining the length of time each receivable will be outstanding. Companies classify receivables intended to be collected within a

[4]To the extent that discounts not taken reflect a short-term financing, some argue that companies could use an interest revenue account to record these amounts.

year or the operating cycle, whichever is longer, as current. All other receivables are classified as long-term.

Companies value and report short-term receivables at net realizable value—the net amount they expect to receive in cash. Determining net realizable value requires estimating both uncollectible receivables and any returns or allowances to be granted.

Uncollectible Accounts Receivable

As one revered accountant aptly noted, the credit manager's idea of heaven probably would be a place where everyone (eventually) paid his or her debts.[5] Unfortunately, this situation often does not occur. For example, a customer may not be able to pay because of a decline in its sales revenue due to a downturn in the economy. Similarly, individuals may be laid off from their jobs or faced with unexpected hospital bills. Companies record credit losses as debits to Bad Debt Expense (or Uncollectible Accounts Expense). Such losses are a normal and necessary risk of doing business on a credit basis.

Two methods are used in accounting for uncollectible accounts: (1) the direct write-off method and (2) the allowance method. The following sections explain these methods.

Direct Write-Off Method for Uncollectible Accounts

Under the direct write-off method, when a company determines a particular account to be uncollectible, it charges the loss to Bad Debt Expense. Assume, for example, that on December 10 Cruz Co. writes off as uncollectible Yusado's $8,000 balance. The entry is:

December 10		
Bad Debt Expense	8,000	
Accounts Receivable (Yusado)		8,000
(To record write-off of Yusado account)		

Under this method, Bad Debt Expense will show only **actual losses** from uncollectibles. The company will report accounts receivable at its gross amount.

Supporters of the **direct write-off-method** (which is often used for tax purposes) contend that it records facts, not estimates. It assumes that a good account receivable resulted from each sale, and that later events revealed certain accounts to be uncollectible and worthless. From a practical standpoint, this method is simple and convenient to apply. But the direct write-off method is theoretically deficient. It usually fails to record expenses in the same period as associated revenues. Nor does it result in receivables being stated at net realizable value on the balance sheet. **As a result, using the direct write-off method is not considered appropriate, except when the amount uncollectible is immaterial.**

Allowance Method for Uncollectible Accounts

The allowance method of accounting for bad debts involves estimating uncollectible accounts at the end of each period. This ensures that companies state receivables on the balance sheet at their net realizable value. Net realizable value is the net amount the company expects to receive in cash. The FASB considers the collectibility of receivables a loss contingency. Thus, the allowance method is appropriate in situations where it is probable that an asset has been impaired and that the amount of the loss can be reasonably estimated. **[3]**

Although estimates are involved, companies can predict the percentage of uncollectible receivables from past experiences, present market conditions, and an analysis of the outstanding balances. Many companies set their credit policies to provide for a certain percentage of uncollectible accounts. (In fact, many feel that failure to reach that

[5]William J. Vatter, *Managerial Accounting* (Englewood Cliffs, N.J.: Prentice-Hall, 1950), p. 60.

percentage means that they are losing sales due to overly restrictive credit policies.) Thus, the FASB requires the allowance method for financial reporting purposes when bad debts are material in amount. This method has three essential features:

1. Companies **estimate** uncollectible accounts receivable. They match this estimated expense **against revenues** in the same accounting period in which they record the revenues.
2. Companies debit estimated uncollectibles to Bad Debt Expense and credit them to Allowance for Doubtful Accounts (a contra asset account) through an adjusting entry at the end of each period.
3. When companies write off a specific account, they debit actual uncollectibles to Allowance for Doubtful Accounts and credit that amount to Accounts Receivable.

Recording Estimated Uncollectibles. To illustrate the allowance method, assume that Brown Furniture has credit sales of $1,800,000 in 2014. Of this amount, $150,000 remains uncollected at December 31. The credit manager estimates that $10,000 of these sales will be uncollectible. The adjusting entry to record the estimated uncollectibles is:

December 31, 2014		
Bad Debt Expense	10,000	
Allowance for Doubtful Accounts		10,000
(To record estimate of uncollectible accounts)		

Brown reports Bad Debt Expense in the income statement as an operating expense. Thus, the estimated uncollectibles are matched with sales in 2014. Brown records the expense in the same year it made the sales.

As Illustration 7-5 shows, the company deducts the allowance account from accounts receivable in the current assets section of the balance sheet.

ILLUSTRATION 7-5
Presentation of Allowance for Doubtful Accounts

BROWN FURNITURE
BALANCE SHEET (PARTIAL)

Current assets		
Cash		$ 15,000
Accounts receivable	$150,000	
Less: Allowance for doubtful accounts	10,000	140,000
Inventory		300,000
Prepaid insurance		25,000
Total current assets		$480,000

Allowance for Doubtful Accounts shows the estimated amount of claims on customers that the company expects will become uncollectible in the future.[6] Companies use a contra account instead of a direct credit to Accounts Receivable because they do not know which customers will not pay. The credit balance in the allowance account will absorb the specific write-offs when they occur. The amount of $140,000 in Illustration 7-5 represents the **net realizable value** of the accounts receivable at the statement date. **Companies do not close Allowance for Doubtful Accounts at the end of the fiscal year.**

[6]The account description employed for the allowance account is usually Allowance for Doubtful Accounts or simply Allowance. *Accounting Trends and Techniques* recently indicated that approximately 83 percent of the companies surveyed used "allowance" in their description.

Recording the Write-Off of an Uncollectible Account. When companies have exhausted all means of collecting a past-due account and collection appears impossible, the company should write off the account. In the credit card industry, for example, it is standard practice to write off accounts that are 210 days past due.

To illustrate a receivables write-off, assume that the financial vice president of Brown Furniture authorizes a write-off of the $1,000 balance owed by Randall Co. on March 1, 2015. The entry to record the write-off is:

March 1, 2015		
Allowance for Doubtful Accounts	1,000	
Accounts Receivable (Randall Co.)		1,000
(Write-off of Randall Co. account)		

Bad Debt Expense does not increase when the write-off occurs. **Under the allowance method, companies debit every bad debt write-off to the allowance account rather than to Bad Debt Expense.** A debit to Bad Debt Expense would be incorrect because the company has already recognized the expense when it made the adjusting entry for estimated bad debts. Instead, the entry to record the write-off of an uncollectible account reduces both Accounts Receivable and Allowance for Doubtful Accounts.

Recovery of an Uncollectible Account. Occasionally, a company collects from a customer after it has written off the account as uncollectible. The company makes two entries to record the recovery of a bad debt: (1) It reverses the entry made in writing off the account. This reinstates the customer's account. (2) It journalizes the collection in the usual manner.

To illustrate, assume that on July 1, 2015, Randall Co. pays the $1,000 amount that Brown had written off on March 1. These are the entries:

July 1, 2015		
Accounts Receivable (Randall Co.)	1,000	
Allowance for Doubtful Accounts		1,000
(To reverse write-off of account)		
Cash	1,000	
Accounts Receivable (Randall Co.)		1,000
(Collection of account)		

Note that the recovery of a bad debt, like the write-off of a bad debt, affects **only balance sheet accounts**. The net effect of the two entries above is a debit to Cash and a credit to Allowance for Doubtful Accounts for $1,000.[7]

Bases Used for Allowance Method. To simplify the preceding explanation, we assumed we knew the amount of the expected uncollectibles. In "real life," companies must estimate that amount when they use the allowance method. Two bases are used to determine this amount: **(1) percentage of sales** and **(2) percentage of receivables**. Both bases are generally accepted. The choice is a management decision. It depends on the relative emphasis that management wishes to give to expenses and revenues on the one hand or to net realizable value of the accounts receivable on the other. The choice is whether to emphasize income statement or balance sheet relationships. Illustration 7-6 (page 356) compares the two bases.

[7]If using the direct write-off approach, the company debits the amount collected to Cash and credits a revenue account entitled Uncollectible Amounts Recovered, with proper notation in the customer's account.

ILLUSTRATION 7-6
Comparison of Bases for Estimating Uncollectibles

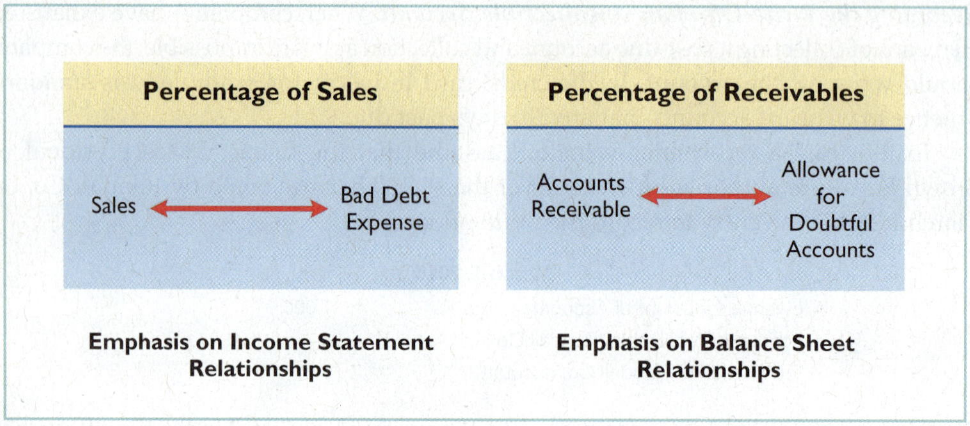

Underlying Concepts

The percentage-of-sales method illustrates the expense recognition principle, which relates expenses to revenues recognized.

The percentage-of-sales basis results in a better matching of expenses with revenues—an income statement viewpoint. The percentage-of-receivables basis produces the better estimate of net realizable value—a balance sheet viewpoint. Under both bases, the company must determine its past experience with bad debt losses.

Percentage-of-sales (income statement) approach. In the **percentage-of-sales approach**, management estimates what percentage of credit sales will be uncollectible. This percentage is based on past experience and anticipated credit policy.

The company applies this percentage to either total credit sales or net credit sales of the current year. To illustrate, assume that Gonzalez Company elects to use the percentage-of-sales basis. It concludes that 1 percent of net credit sales will become uncollectible. If net credit sales for 2014 are $800,000, the estimated bad debts expense is $8,000 (1% × $800,000). The adjusting entry is:

December 31, 2014		
Bad Debt Expense	8,000	
Allowance for Doubtful Accounts		8,000

After the adjusting entry is posted, assuming the allowance account already has a credit balance of $1,723, the accounts of Gonzalez Company will show the following:

ILLUSTRATION 7-7
Bad Debt Accounts after Posting

Bad Debt Expense				Allowance for Doubtful Accounts	
Dec. 31 Adj.	8,000			Jan. 1 Bal.	1,723
				Dec. 31 Adj.	8,000
				Dec. 31 Bal.	9,723

The amount of bad debt expense and the related credit to the allowance account are unaffected by any balance currently existing in the allowance account. Because the bad debt expense estimate is related to a nominal account (Sales Revenue), any balance in the allowance is ignored. Therefore, the percentage-of-sales method achieves a proper matching of cost and revenues. This method is frequently referred to as the **income statement approach**.

Percentage-of-receivables (balance sheet) approach. Using past experience, a company can estimate the percentage of its outstanding receivables that will become uncollectible, without identifying specific accounts. This procedure provides a reasonably accurate estimate of the receivables' realizable value. But, it does not fit the concept of matching cost and revenues. Rather, it simply reports receivables in the balance sheet at net realizable value. Hence, it is referred to as the **percentage-of-receivables** (or balance sheet) **approach**.

Companies may apply this method using one **composite rate** that reflects an estimate of the uncollectible receivables. Or, companies may set up an **aging schedule** of accounts receivable, which applies a different percentage based on past experience to the various age categories. An aging schedule also identifies which accounts require special attention by indicating the extent to which certain accounts are past due. The schedule of Wilson & Co. in Illustration 7-8 is an example.

ILLUSTRATION 7-8
Accounts Receivable Aging Schedule

WILSON & CO.
AGING SCHEDULE

Name of Customer	Balance Dec. 31	Under 60 days	60–90 days	91–120 days	Over 120 days
Western Stainless Steel Corp.	$ 98,000	$ 80,000	$18,000		
Brockway Steel Company	320,000	320,000			
Freeport Sheet & Tube Co.	55,000				$55,000
Allegheny Iron Works	74,000	60,000		$14,000	
	$547,000	$460,000	$18,000	$14,000	$55,000

Summary

Age	Amount	Percentage Estimated to Be Uncollectible	Required Balance in Allowance
Under 60 days old	$460,000	4%	$18,400
60–90 days old	18,000	15%	2,700
91–120 days old	14,000	20%	2,800
Over 120 days	55,000	25%	13,750
Year-end balance of allowance for doubtful accounts			$37,650

Wilson reports bad debt expense of $37,650 for this year, assuming that no balance existed in the allowance account.

To change the illustration slightly, **assume that the allowance account had a credit balance of $800 before adjustment**. In this case, Wilson adds $36,850 ($37,650 − $800) to the allowance account and makes the following entry.

Bad Debt Expense	36,850	
Allowance for Doubtful Accounts		36,850

Wilson therefore states the balance in the allowance account at $37,650. **If the Allowance for Doubtful Accounts balance before adjustment had a debit balance of $200**, then Wilson records bad debt expense of $37,850 ($37,650 desired balance + $200 debit balance). In the percentage-of-receivables method, Wilson cannot ignore the balance in the allowance account because the percentage is related to a real account (Accounts Receivable).

Companies usually do not prepare an aging schedule to determine bad debt expense. Rather, they prepare it as a control device to determine the composition of receivables and to identify delinquent accounts. Companies base the estimated loss percentage developed for each category on previous loss experience and the advice of credit department personnel.

Whether using a composite rate or an aging schedule, the primary objective of the percentage of outstanding receivables method for financial statement purposes is to report receivables in the balance sheet at net realizable value. However, it is deficient in that it may not match the bad debt expense to the period in which the sale takes place.

Gateway to the Profession

Tutorial on Recording Uncollectible Accounts

The allowance for doubtful accounts as a percentage of receivables will vary, depending on the industry and the economic climate. Companies such as **Eastman Kodak**, **General Electric**, and **Monsanto** have recorded allowances ranging from $3 to $6 per $100 of accounts receivable. Other large companies, such as **CPC International** ($1.48), **Texaco** ($1.23), and **USX Corp.** ($0.78), have had bad debt allowances of less than $1.50 per $100. At the other extreme are hospitals that allow for $15 to $20 per $100 of accounts receivable.

Regardless of the method chosen—percentage-of-sales or -receivables—determining the expense associated with uncollectible accounts requires a large degree of judgment. Recent concern exists that, similar to **Citigroup** in our opening story, some banks use this judgment to manage earnings. By overestimating the amounts of uncollectible loans in a good earnings year, the bank can "save for a rainy day" in a future period. In future (less-profitable) periods, banks can reduce the overly conservative allowance for loan loss account to increase earnings.[8]

What do the numbers mean? I'M STILL WAITING

Small companies are in a bind. Many of their suppliers are demanding payment earlier, and their customers (represented by their accounts receivable) are taking longer to pay. That means companies with the least clout get squeezed the hardest. As one company executive noted, "The slowdown of currency, of money, the exchange, puts us in a very precarious position."

The average time small companies took to collect accounts receivable increased to 27 days in 2010 from about 23 days in the previous four-year period. Many small companies are seeing their payments from larger customers stretch from 30 days to 60 and even 90 days after an invoice is issued. **Wal-Mart Stores, Inc.**, for example, took 29.5 days to pay its bills in the first quarter of 2010, up from 27 days a year earlier. **Apple** took 52 days, up from 43 days a year earlier. As one individual stated, "If you are working with one of these large companies, as your only customer, they have the power. They can go to somebody else, but you can't go anywhere."

The chart on the right indicates that, overall, companies are increasing their payment times past the due date regardless of their size. For example, in the first quarter of 2012, companies paid their bills an average of 7.6 days past due, a 14.1 percent increase from the same period the previous period. The very small companies and the large companies generally have delayed payment the most.

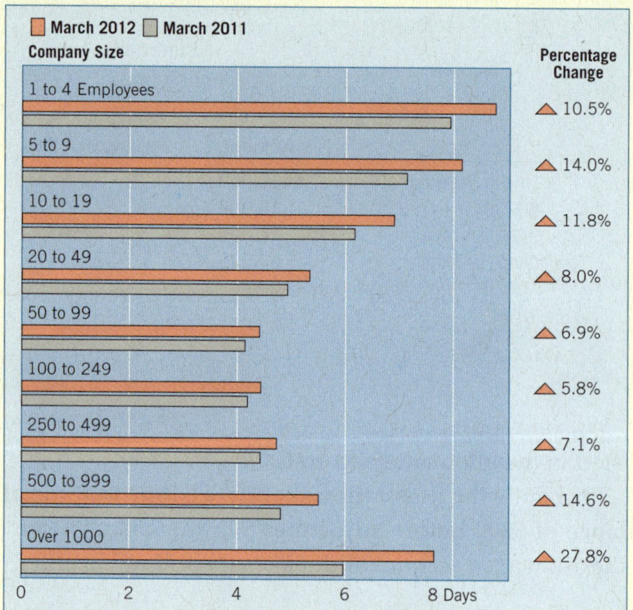

Source: Experian-Moody's Q1 2012 benchmark report.

The recession is taking its toll. As companies get squeezed between late payments and tighter credit terms, nonpayments often result. As a result, much judgment must be exercised in determining the proper percentage to record for bad debts.

Sources: Anonymous, "A Cash-Flow Crisis Is the Recession's Legacy," *Bloomberg Businessweek* (March 28–April 3, 2011), pp. 59–60; and A. Loten, "Small Firms' Big Customers Are Slow to Pay," *Wall Street Journal* (June 7, 2012), p. B7.

[8] The SEC brought action against **Suntrust Banks**, requiring a reversal of $100 million of bad debt expense. This reversal increased after-tax profit by $61 million. Recall from our earnings management discussion in Chapter 4 that increasing or decreasing income through management manipulation can reduce the quality of financial reports.

NOTES RECEIVABLE

6 LEARNING OBJECTIVE
Explain accounting issues related to recognition and valuation of notes receivable.

A note receivable is supported by a formal **promissory note**, a written promise to pay a certain sum of money at a specific future date. Such a note is a negotiable instrument that a **maker** signs in favor of a designated **payee** who may legally and readily sell or otherwise transfer the note to others. Although all notes contain an interest element because of the time value of money, companies classify them as interest-bearing or non-interest-bearing. **Interest-bearing notes** have a stated rate of interest. **Zero-interest-bearing notes** (non-interest-bearing) include interest as part of their face amount. Notes receivable are considered fairly liquid, even if long-term, because companies may easily convert them to cash (although they might pay a fee to do so).

Companies frequently accept notes receivable from customers who need to extend the payment period of an outstanding receivable. Or they require notes from high-risk or new customers. In addition, companies often use notes in loans to employees and subsidiaries, and in the sales of property, plant, and equipment. In some industries (e.g., the pleasure and sport boat industry), notes support all credit sales. The majority of notes, however, originate from lending transactions. The basic issues in accounting for notes receivable are the same as those for accounts receivable: **recognition, valuation, and disposition**.

Recognition of Notes Receivable

Companies generally record short-term notes at face value (less allowances) because the interest implicit in the maturity value is immaterial. A general rule is that notes treated as cash equivalents (maturities of three months or less and easily converted to cash) are not subject to premium or discount amortization.

However, companies should record and report long-term notes receivable at the **present value of the cash they expect to collect**. When the interest stated on an interest-bearing note equals the effective (market) rate of interest, the note sells at face value.[9] When the stated rate differs from the market rate, the cash exchanged (present value) differs from the face value of the note. Companies then record this difference, either a discount or a premium, and amortize it over the life of a note to approximate the effective (market) interest rate. This illustrates one of the many situations in which time value of money concepts are applied to accounting measurement.

Note Issued at Face Value

To illustrate the discounting of a note issued at face value, assume that Bigelow Corp. lends Scandinavian Imports $10,000 in exchange for a $10,000, three-year note bearing interest at 10 percent annually. The market rate of interest for a note of similar risk is also 10 percent. We show the time diagram depicting both cash flows in Illustration 7-9 (page 360).

[9]The **stated interest rate**, also referred to as the face rate or the coupon rate, is the rate contracted as part of the note. The **effective-interest rate**, also referred to as the market rate or the effective yield, is the rate used in the market to determine the value of the note—that is, the discount rate used to determine present value.

ILLUSTRATION 7-9
Time Diagram for Note Issued at Face Value

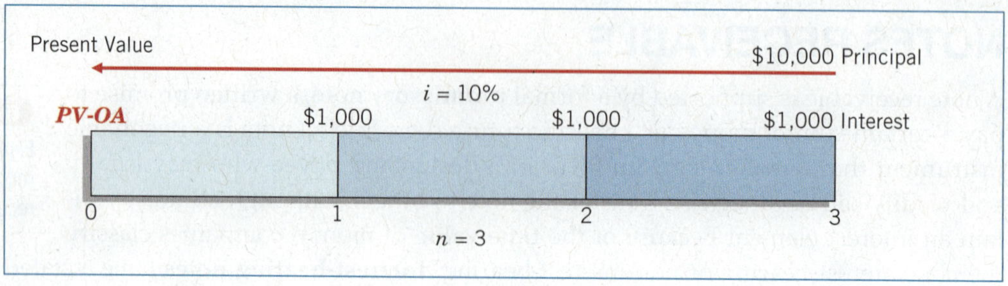

Bigelow computes the present value or exchange price of the note as follows.

ILLUSTRATION 7-10
Present Value of Note—Stated and Market Rates the Same

Face value of the note		$10,000
Present value of the principal:		
$10,000 ($PVF_{3,10\%}$) = $10,000 × .75132	$7,513	
Present value of the interest:		
$1,000 ($PVF\text{-}OA_{3,10\%}$) = $1,000 × 2.48685	2,487	
Present value of the note		10,000
Difference		$ -0-

You can use a financial calculator to solve this problem.

Calculator Solution for Present Value of Note Receivable

	Inputs	Answer
N	3	
I	10	
PV	?	-10,000
PMT	1,000	
FV	10,000	

In this case, the present value of the note equals its face value because the effective and stated rates of interest are also the same. Bigelow records the receipt of the note as follows.

Notes Receivable	10,000	
Cash		10,000

Bigelow recognizes the interest earned each year as follows.

Cash	1,000	
Interest Revenue		1,000

Note Not Issued at Face Value

Zero-Interest-Bearing Notes. If a company receives a zero-interest-bearing note, its present value is the cash paid to the issuer. Because the company knows both the future amount and the present value of the note, it can compute the interest rate. This rate is often referred to as the **implicit interest rate**. Companies record the difference between the future (face) amount and the present value (cash paid) as a discount and amortize it to interest revenue over the life of the note.

To illustrate, Jeremiah Company receives a three-year, $10,000 zero-interest-bearing note, the present value of which is $7,721.80. The implicit rate that equates the total cash to be received ($10,000 at maturity) to the present value of the future cash flows ($7,721.80) is 9 percent (the present value of 1 for three periods at 9 percent is .77218). We show the time diagram depicting the one cash flow in Illustration 7-11.

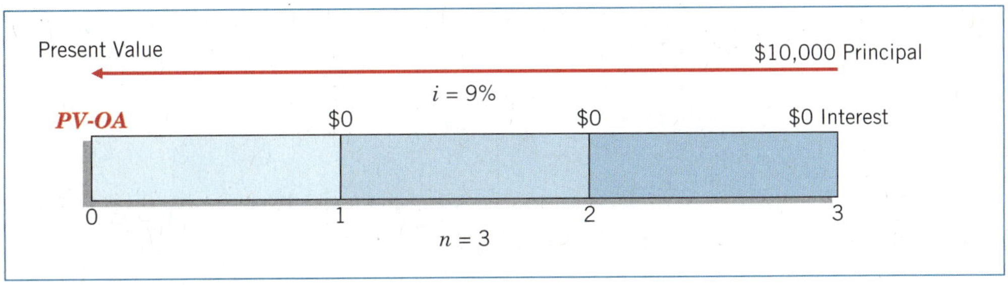

ILLUSTRATION 7-11
Time Diagram for Zero-Interest-Bearing Note

Calculator Solution for Effective-Interest Rate on Note

	Inputs	Answer
N	3	
I	?	9
PV		−7,721.80
PMT	0	
FV	10,000	

Jeremiah records the transaction as follows.

Notes Receivable	10,000.00	
Discount on Notes Receivable ($10,000 − $7,721.80)		2,278.20
Cash		7,721.80

Discount on Notes Receivable is a valuation account. Companies report it on the balance sheet as a contra asset account to notes receivable. They then amortize the discount, and recognize interest revenue annually using the **effective-interest method**. Illustration 7-12 shows the three-year discount amortization and interest revenue schedule.

ILLUSTRATION 7-12
Discount Amortization Schedule—Effective-Interest Method

SCHEDULE OF NOTE DISCOUNT AMORTIZATION
EFFECTIVE-INTEREST METHOD
0% NOTE DISCOUNTED AT 9%

	Cash Received	Interest Revenue	Discount Amortized	Carrying Amount of Note
Date of issue				$ 7,721.80
End of year 1	$ -0-	$ 694.96[a]	$ 694.96[b]	8,416.76[c]
End of year 2	-0-	757.51	757.51	9,174.27
End of year 3	-0-	825.73[d]	825.73	10,000.00
	$ -0-	$2,278.20	$2,278.20	

[a]$7,721.80 × .09 = $694.96
[b]$694.96 − 0 = $694.96
[c]$7,721.80 + $694.96 = $8,416.76
[d]5¢ adjustment to compensate for rounding

Jeremiah records interest revenue at the end of the first year using the effective-interest method as follows.

Discount on Notes Receivable	694.96	
Interest Revenue ($7,721.80 × 9%)		694.96

The amount of the discount, $2,278.20 in this case, represents the interest revenue Jeremiah will receive from the note over the three years.

Interest-Bearing Notes. Often the stated rate and the effective rate differ. The zero-interest-bearing note is one example.

To illustrate a more common situation, assume that Morgan Corp. makes a loan to Marie Co. and receives in exchange a three-year, $10,000 note bearing interest at 10 percent annually. The market rate of interest for a note of similar risk is 12 percent. We show the time diagram depicting both cash flows in Illustration 7-13 (page 362).

ILLUSTRATION 7-13
Time Diagram for Interest-Bearing Note

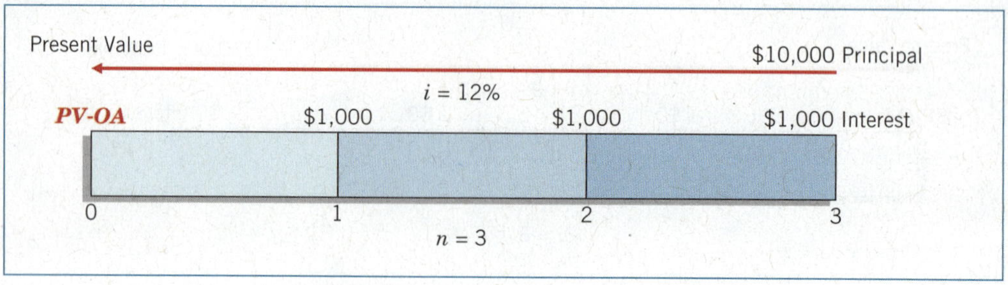

Morgan computes the present value of the two cash flows as follows.

ILLUSTRATION 7-14
Computation of Present Value—Effective Rate Different from Stated Rate

Face value of the note		$10,000
Present value of the principal:		
$10,000 ($PVF_{3,12\%}$) = $10,000 × .71178	$7,118	
Present value of the interest:		
$1,000 ($PVF\text{-}OA_{3,12\%}$) = $1,000 × 2.40183	2,402	
Present value of the note		9,520
Difference (Discount)		$ 480

In this case, because the effective rate of interest (12 percent) exceeds the stated rate (10 percent), the present value of the note is less than the face value. That is, Morgan exchanged the note at a **discount**. Morgan records the receipt of the note at a discount as follows.

Notes Receivable	10,000	
Discount on Notes Receivable		480
Cash		9,520

Morgan then amortizes the discount and recognizes interest revenue annually using the **effective-interest method**. Illustration 7-15 shows the three-year discount amortization and interest revenue schedule.

ILLUSTRATION 7-15
Discount Amortization Schedule—Effective-Interest Method

SCHEDULE OF NOTE DISCOUNT AMORTIZATION
EFFECTIVE-INTEREST METHOD
10% NOTE DISCOUNTED AT 12%

	Cash Received	Interest Revenue	Discount Amortized	Carrying Amount of Note
Date of issue				$ 9,520
End of year 1	$1,000[a]	$1,142[b]	$142[c]	9,662[d]
End of year 2	1,000	1,159	159	9,821
End of year 3	1,000	1,179	179	10,000
	$3,000	$3,480	$480	

[a]$10,000 × 10% = $1,000
[b]$9,520 × 12% = $1,142
[c]$1,142 − $1,000 = $142
[d]$9,520 + $142 = $9,662

On the date of issue, the note has a present value of $9,520. Its unamortized discount—additional interest revenue spread over the three-year life of the note—is $480.

At the end of year 1, Morgan receives $1,000 in cash. But its interest revenue is $1,142 ($9,520 × 12%). The difference between $1,000 and $1,142 is the amortized discount, $142. Morgan records receipt of the annual interest and amortization of the discount for the first year as follows (amounts per amortization schedule).

Cash	1,000	
Discount on Notes Receivable	142	
Interest Revenue		1,142

The carrying amount of the note is now $9,662 ($9,520 + $142). Morgan repeats this process until the end of year 3.

When the present value exceeds the face value, the note is exchanged at a premium. Companies record the premium on a note receivable as a debit and amortize it using the effective-interest method over the life of the note as annual reductions in the amount of interest revenue recognized.

Notes Received for Property, Goods, or Services. When a **note is received in exchange for property, goods, or services** in a bargained transaction entered into at arm's length, the stated interest rate is presumed to be fair unless:

1. No interest rate is stated, or
2. The stated interest rate is unreasonable, or
3. The face amount of the note is materially different from the current cash sales price for the same or similar items or from the current fair value of the debt instrument. **[4]**

In these circumstances, the company measures the present value of the note by the fair value of the property, goods, or services or by an amount that reasonably approximates the fair value of the note.

To illustrate, Oasis Development Co. sold a corner lot to Rusty Pelican as a restaurant site. Oasis accepted in exchange a five-year note having a maturity value of $35,247 and no stated interest rate. The land originally cost Oasis $14,000. At the date of sale, the land had a fair value of $20,000. Given the criterion above, Oasis uses the fair value of the land, $20,000, as the present value of the note. Oasis therefore records the sale as:

Notes Receivable	35,247	
Discount on Notes Receivable ($35,247 – $20,000)		15,247
Land		14,000
Gain on Disposal of Land ($20,000 – $14,000)		6,000

Calculator Solution for Effective-Interest Rate on Note

	Inputs	Answer
N	5	
I	?	12
PV	–20,000	
PMT	0	
FV	35,247	

Oasis amortizes the discount to interest revenue over the five-year life of the note using the effective-interest method.

Choice of Interest Rate

In note transactions, other factors involved in the exchange, such as the fair value of the property, goods, or services, determine the effective or real interest rate. But, if a company cannot determine that fair value and if the note has no ready market, determining the present value of the note is more difficult. To estimate the present value of a note under such circumstances, the company must approximate an applicable interest rate that may differ from the stated interest rate. This process of interest-rate approximation is called **imputation**. The resulting interest rate is called an **imputed interest rate**.

The prevailing rates for similar instruments, from issuers with similar credit ratings, affect the choice of a rate. Restrictive covenants, collateral, payment schedule, and the existing prime interest rate also impact the choice. A company determines the imputed interest rate when it receives the note. It ignores any subsequent changes in prevailing interest rates.

Valuation of Notes Receivable

Like accounts receivable, companies record and report short-term notes receivable at their net realizable value—that is, at their face amount less all necessary allowances. The primary notes receivable allowance account is Allowance for Doubtful Accounts. The computations and estimations involved in valuing short-term notes receivable and in recording bad debt expense and the related allowance **exactly parallel that for trade accounts receivable**. Companies estimate the amount of uncollectibles by using either a percentage-of-sales revenue or an analysis of the receivables.

Long-term notes receivable involve additional estimation problems. For example, the value of a note receivable can change significantly over time from its original cost. That is, with the passage of time, historical numbers become less and less relevant. As discussed earlier (in Chapters 2, 5, and 6), the FASB requires that for financial instruments such as receivables, companies disclose not only their cost but also their fair value in the notes to the financial statements.

Impairments. A note receivable may become impaired. A note receivable is considered **impaired** when it is probable that the creditor will be unable to collect all amounts due (both principal and interest) according to the contractual terms of the receivable. In this case, a loss is recorded for the amount of the impairment. Appendix 7B further discusses impairments of receivables.

What do the numbers mean? *ECONOMIC CONSEQUENCES AND WRITE-OFFS*

The massive write-downs that financial firms are posting have begun to spur a backlash among some investors and executives, who are blaming accounting rules for exaggerating the losses and are seeking new, more forgiving ways to value investments.

The rules—which last made headlines back in the **Enron** era—require companies to value many of the securities they hold at whatever price prevails in the market, no matter how sharply those prices swing.

Some analysts and executives argue this triggers a domino effect. The market falls, forcing banks to take write-offs, pushing the market lower, causing more write-offs. Companies like **AIG** and **Citicorp** argue that their write-downs may never actually result in a true charge to the company. It's a sore point because companies feel they are being forced to take big financial hits on holdings that they have no intention of actually selling at current prices.

Companies believe they are strong enough to simply keep the holdings in their portfolios until the crisis passes. Forcing companies to value securities based on what they would fetch if sold today "is an attempt to apply liquidation accounting to a going concern," says one analyst. Bob Herz, former FASB chairperson, acknowledges the difficulty but notes, "you tell me what a better answer is. . . . Is just pretending that things aren't decreasing in value a better answer? Should you just let everybody say they think it's going to recover?"

Others who favor the use of market values say that for all its imperfections, market value also imposes discipline on companies. "It forces you to realistically confront what's happening to you much quicker, so it plays a useful purpose," said Sen. Jack Reed (D., R.I.), a member of the Senate banking committee.

Japan stands out as an example of how ignoring problems can lead to years-long stagnation. "Look at Japan, where they ignored write-downs at all their financial institutions when loans went bad," said Jeff Mahoney, general counsel at the Council for Institutional Investors.

In addition, companies don't always have the luxury of waiting out a storm until assets recover the long-term value that executives believe exists. A classic example relates to many European banks that hold loans to countries like Greece, Spain, Ireland, and Portugal. Although these loans are clearly toxic (values overstated), some banks still contend that they should not be written down (partly because they can be held to maturity). However, this contention is suspect, and impairment losses are rising. For example, **Bankia Group**, Spain's third largest bank, recently restated its 2011 results to show a €3.3 billion ($4.2 billion) loss rather than the previously reported €40.9 billion profit.

Sources: Adapted from David Reilly, "Wave of Write-Offs Rattles Market: Accounting Rules Blasted as Dow Falls; A $600 Billion Toll?" *Wall Street Journal* (March 1, 2008), p. Al; and J. Weil, "The E4 Smiled While Spain's Banks Cooked the Books," *Bloomberg* (June 14, 2012).

SPECIAL ISSUES

Three additional special issues for accounting and reporting of receivables relate to the following.

1. Fair value option.
2. Disposition of receivables.
3. Presentation and disclosure.

Fair Value Option

7 LEARNING OBJECTIVE
Explain the fair value option.

Recently, the FASB has given companies the option to use fair value as the basis of measurement in the financial statements. **[5]** The Board believes that fair value measurement for financial instruments provides more relevant and understandable information than historical cost. It considers fair value to be more relevant because it reflects the current cash equivalent value of financial instruments. As a result, companies now have the option to record fair value in their accounts for most financial instruments, including receivables.

International Perspective

IFRS also has the fair value option.

If companies choose the **fair value option**, the receivables are recorded at fair value, with unrealized holding gains or losses reported as part of net income. An **unrealized holding gain or loss** is the net change in the fair value of the receivable from one period to another, exclusive of interest revenue. As a result, the company reports the receivable at fair value each reporting date. In addition, it reports the change in value as part of net income.

Companies may elect to use the fair value option at the time the financial instrument is originally recognized or when some event triggers a new basis of accounting (such as when a business acquisition occurs). If a company elects the fair value option for a financial instrument, it must continue to use fair value measurement for that instrument until the company no longer owns this instrument. If the company does not elect the fair value option for a given financial instrument at the date of recognition, it may not use this option on that specific instrument in subsequent periods.

Recording Fair Value Option

Assume that Escobar Company has notes receivable that have a fair value of $810,000 and a carrying amount of $620,000. Escobar decides on December 31, 2014, to use the fair value option for these receivables. This is the first valuation of these recently acquired receivables. Having elected to use the fair value option, Escobar must value these receivables **at fair value in all subsequent periods in which it holds these receivables**. Similarly, if Escobar elects *not* to use the fair value option, it must use its carrying amount for all future periods.

When using the fair value option, Escobar reports the receivables at fair value, with any unrealized holding gains and losses reported as part of net income. The **unrealized holding gain** is the difference between the fair value and the carrying amount at December 31, 2014, which for Escobar is $190,000 ($810,000 − $620,000). At December 31, 2014, Escobar makes an adjusting entry to record the increase in value of notes receivable and to record the unrealized holding gain, as follows.

December 31, 2014		
Notes Receivable	190,000	
Unrealized Holding Gain or Loss—Income		190,000

Escobar adds the difference between fair value and the cost of the notes receivable to arrive at the fair value reported on the balance sheet. In subsequent periods, the company will report **any change in fair value** as an unrealized holding gain or loss. For example, if at December 31, 2015, the fair value of the notes receivable is $800,000, Escobar would recognize an unrealized holding loss of $10,000 ($810,000 − $800,000) and reduce the Notes Receivable account.

Disposition of Accounts and Notes Receivable

8 LEARNING OBJECTIVE
Explain accounting issues related to disposition of accounts and notes receivable.

In the normal course of events, companies collect accounts and notes receivable when due and then remove them from the books. However, the growing size and significance of credit sales and receivables has led to changes in this "normal course of events." **In order to accelerate the receipt of cash from receivables, the owner may transfer accounts or notes receivables to another company for cash.**

There are various reasons for this early transfer. First, for competitive reasons, providing sales financing for customers is virtually mandatory in many industries. In the sale of durable goods, such as automobiles, trucks, industrial and farm equipment, computers, and appliances, most sales are on an installment contract basis. Many major companies in these industries have created wholly owned subsidiaries specializing in receivables financing. For example, **Ford** has **Ford Motor Credit**, and **John Deere** has **John Deere Credit**.

Second, the **holder** may sell receivables because money is tight and access to normal credit is unavailable or too expensive. Also, a firm may sell its receivables, instead of borrowing, to avoid violating existing lending agreements.

Finally, billing and collection of receivables are often time-consuming and costly. Credit card companies such as **MasterCard**, **Visa**, **American Express**, **Diners Club**, **Discover**, and others take over the collection process and provide merchants with immediate cash.

Conversely, some **purchasers** of receivables buy them to obtain the legal protection of ownership rights afforded a purchaser of assets versus the lesser rights afforded a secured creditor. In addition, banks and other lending institutions may need to purchase receivables because of legal lending limits. That is, they cannot make any additional loans but they can buy receivables and charge a fee for this service.

The transfer of receivables to a third party for cash happens in one of two ways:

1. Secured borrowing.
2. Sales of receivables.

Secured Borrowing

A company often uses receivables as collateral in a borrowing transaction. In fact, a creditor often requires that the debtor designate (assign) or pledge[10] receivables as security for the loan. If the loan is not paid when due, the creditor can convert the collateral to cash—that is, collect the receivables.

To illustrate, on March 1, 2014, Howat Mills, Inc. provides (assigns) $700,000 of its accounts receivable to Citizens Bank as collateral for a $500,000 note. Howat Mills continues to collect the accounts receivable; the account debtors are not notified of the arrangement. Citizens Bank assesses a finance charge of 1 percent of the accounts receivable and interest on the note of 12 percent. Howat Mills makes monthly payments to the bank for all cash it collects on the receivables. Illustration 7-16 shows the entries for the secured borrowing for Howat Mills and Citizens Bank.

In addition to recording the collection of receivables, Howat Mills must recognize all discounts, returns and allowances, and bad debts. Each month Howat Mills uses the proceeds from the collection of the accounts receivable to retire the note obligation. In addition, it pays interest on the note.[11]

Sales of Receivables

Sales of receivables have increased substantially in recent years. A common type is a sale to a factor. **Factors** are finance companies or banks that buy receivables from businesses

[10] If a company transfers the receivables for custodial purposes, the custodial arrangement is often referred to as a **pledge**.

[11] What happens if Citizens Bank collected the transferred accounts receivable rather than Howat Mills? Citizens Bank would simply remit the cash proceeds to Howat Mills, and Howat Mills would make the same entries shown in Illustration 7-16. As a result, Howat Mills reports these "collaterized" receivables as an asset on the balance sheet.

Howat Mills, Inc.			Citizens Bank		
Transfer of accounts receivable and issuance of note on March 1, 2014					
Cash	493,000		Notes Receivable	500,000	
Interest Expense	7,000*		Interest Revenue		7,000*
Notes Payable		500,000	Cash		493,000
*(1% × $700,000)					
Collection in March of $440,000 of accounts less cash discounts of $6,000 plus receipt of $14,000 sales returns					
Cash	434,000				
Sales Discounts	6,000				
Sales Returns and Allowances	14,000		(No entry)		
Accounts Receivable					
($440,000 + $14,000 = $454,000)		454,000			
Remitted March collections plus accrued interest to the bank on April 1, 2014					
Interest Expense	5,000*		Cash	439,000	
Notes Payable	434,000		Interest Revenue		5,000*
Cash		439,000	Notes Receivable		434,000
*($500,000 × .12 × 1/12)					
Collection in April of the balance of accounts less $2,000 written off as uncollectible					
Cash	244,000				
Allowance for Doubtful Accounts	2,000		(No entry)		
Accounts Receivable		246,000*			
*($700,000 − $454,000)					
Remitted the balance due of $66,000 ($500,000 − $434,000) on the note plus interest on May 1, 2014					
Interest Expense	660*		Cash	66,660	
Notes Payable	66,000		Interest Revenue		660*
Cash		66,660	Notes Receivable		66,000
*($66,000 × .12 × 1/12)					

ILLUSTRATION 7-16
Entries for Transfer of Receivables—Secured Borrowing

for a fee and then collect the remittances directly from the customers. **Factoring receivables** is traditionally associated with the textile, apparel, footwear, furniture, and home furnishing industries.[12] Illustration 7-17 shows a typical factoring arrangement.

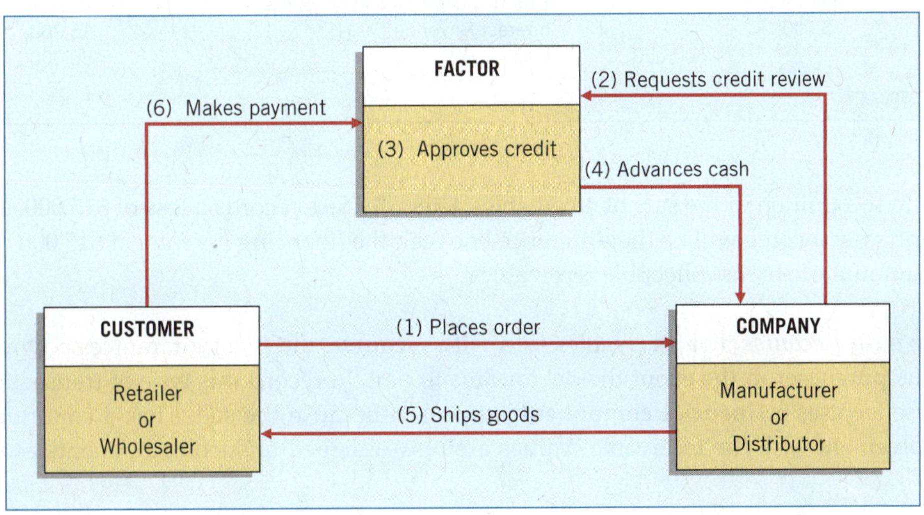

ILLUSTRATION 7-17
Basic Procedures in Factoring

[12]Credit cards like **MasterCard** and **Visa** are a type of factoring arrangement. Typically, the purchaser of the receivable charges a ¾–1½ percent commission of the receivables purchased (the commission is 4–5 percent for credit card factoring).

A recent phenomenon in the sale (transfer) of receivables is securitization. **Securitization** takes a pool of assets, such as credit card receivables, mortgage receivables, or car loan receivables, and sells shares in these pools of interest and principal payments. This, in effect, creates securities backed by these pools of assets. Virtually every asset with a payment stream and a long-term payment history is a candidate for securitization.

What are the differences between factoring and securitization? Factoring usually involves sale to only one company, fees are high, the quality of the receivables is low, and the seller afterward does not service the receivables. In a securitization, many investors are involved, margins are tight, the receivables are of generally higher quality, and the seller usually continues to service the receivables.

In either a factoring or a securitization transaction, a company sells receivables on either a **without recourse** or a **with recourse** basis.[13]

Sale without Recourse. When buying receivables **without recourse**, the purchaser assumes the risk of collectibility and absorbs any credit losses. The transfer of accounts receivable in a nonrecourse transaction is an outright sale of the receivables both in form (transfer of title) and substance (transfer of control). In nonrecourse transactions, as in any sale of assets, the seller debits Cash for the proceeds and credits Accounts Receivable for the face value of the receivables. The seller recognizes the difference, reduced by any provision for probable adjustments (discounts, returns, allowances, etc.), as a Loss on Sale of Receivables. The seller uses a Due from Factor account (reported as a receivable) to account for the proceeds retained by the factor to cover probable sales discounts, sales returns, and sales allowances.

Gateway to the Profession

Comprehensive Illustration of Sale without Recourse

To illustrate, Crest Textiles, Inc. factors $500,000 of accounts receivable with Commercial Factors, Inc., on a **without recourse** basis. Crest Textiles transfers the receivable records to Commercial Factors, which will receive the collections. Commercial Factors assesses a finance charge of 3 percent of the amount of accounts receivable and retains an amount equal to 5 percent of the accounts receivable (for probable adjustments). Crest Textiles and Commercial Factors make the following journal entries for the receivables transferred without recourse.

ILLUSTRATION 7-18
Entries for Sale of Receivables without Recourse

Crest Textiles, Inc.		
Cash	460,000	
Due from Factor	25,000*	
Loss on Sale of Receivables	15,000**	
Accounts (Notes) Receivable		500,000

*(5% × $500,000) **(3% × $500,000)

Commercial Factors, Inc.		
Accounts (Notes) Receivable	500,000	
Due to Customer (Crest Textiles)		25,000
Interest Revenue		15,000
Cash		460,000

In recognition of the sale of receivables, Crest Textiles records a loss of $15,000. The factor's net income will be the difference between the financing revenue of $15,000 and the amount of any uncollectible receivables.

Sale with Recourse. For receivables sold **with recourse**, the seller guarantees payment to the purchaser in the event the debtor fails to pay. To record this type of transaction, the seller uses a **financial components approach** because the seller has a continuing involvement with the receivable. Values are now assigned to such components as the

[13]**Recourse** is the right of a transferee of receivables to receive payment from the transferor of those receivables for (1) failure of the debtors to pay when due, (2) the effects of prepayments, or (3) adjustments resulting from defects in the eligibility of the transferred receivables. [6]

recourse provision, servicing rights, and agreement to reacquire. In this approach, each party to the sale only recognizes the assets and liabilities that it controls after the sale.

To illustrate, assume the same information as in Illustration 7-18 for Crest Textiles and for Commercial Factors, except that Crest Textiles sold the receivables on a with recourse basis. Crest Textiles determines that this recourse liability has a fair value of $6,000. To determine the loss on the sale of the receivables, Crest Textiles computes the net proceeds from the sale as follows.

Cash received	$460,000	
Due from factor	25,000	$485,000
Less: Recourse liability		6,000
Net proceeds		$479,000

ILLUSTRATION 7-19
Net Proceeds Computation

Net proceeds are cash or other assets received in a sale less any liabilities incurred. Crest Textiles then computes the loss as follows.

Carrying (book) value	$500,000
Net proceeds	479,000
Loss on sale of receivables	$ 21,000

ILLUSTRATION 7-20
Loss on Sale Computation

Illustration 7-21 shows the journal entries for both Crest Textiles and Commercial Factors for the receivables sold with recourse.

Crest Textiles, Inc.			Commercial Factors, Inc.		
Cash	460,000		Accounts Receivable	500,000	
Due from Factor	25,000		Due to Customer		
Loss on Sale of			(Crest Textiles)		25,000
Receivables	21,000		Interest Revenue		15,000
Accounts (Notes)			Cash		460,000
Receivable		500,000			
Recourse Liability		6,000			

ILLUSTRATION 7-21
Entries for Sale of Receivables with Recourse

In this case, Crest Textiles recognizes a loss of $21,000. In addition, it records a liability of $6,000 to indicate the probable payment to Commercial Factors for uncollectible receivables. If Commercial Factors collects all the receivables, Crest Textiles eliminates its recourse liability and increases income. Commercial Factors' net income is the interest revenue of $15,000. It will have no bad debts related to these receivables.

Gateway to the Profession

Tutorial on the Disposition of Receivables

Secured Borrowing versus Sale

The FASB concluded that a sale occurs only if the seller surrenders control of the receivables to the buyer. The following three conditions must be met before a company can record a sale:

1. The transferred asset has been isolated from the transferor (put beyond reach of the transferor and its creditors).

2. The transferees have obtained the right to pledge or exchange either the transferred assets or beneficial interests in the transferred assets.
3. The transferor does not maintain effective control over the transferred assets through an agreement to repurchase or redeem them before their maturity.

If the three conditions are met, a sale occurs. Otherwise, the transferor should record the transfer as a secured borrowing. If sale accounting is appropriate, a company must still consider assets obtained and liabilities incurred in the transaction. Illustration 7-22 shows the rules of accounting for transfers of receivables.

ILLUSTRATION 7-22
Accounting for Transfers of Receivables

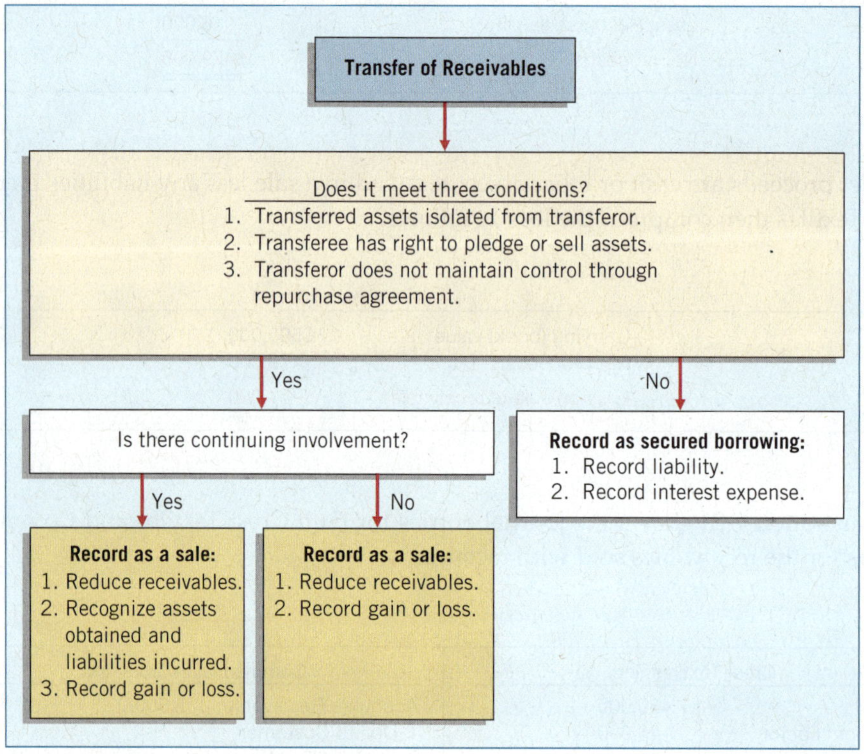

International Perspective

With recent changes in U.S. GAAP, the accounting guidance for transfers is substantially converged.

As indicated, if there is continuing involvement in a sale transaction, a company must record the assets obtained and liabilities incurred.[14]

[14]In response to the financial crisis, which was partly caused by securitizations gone bad (see the "What Do the Numbers Mean?" box on page 371), the FASB issued new rules to tighten up the conditions when a transfer of receivables is recorded as a sale. The changes in the rules apply primarily to transfers that involve participating interests (which is the case for many securitizations). In order for a transfer with participating interests to be accounted for as a sale, all participating investors must have a pro rata share ownership interest in the transferred assets. That is, all parties to the transfer must receive benefits or be exposed to risks of the transferred assets in proportion to their ownership share. If these criteria are not met (e.g., some investors get paid first or others absorb more losses than others on the transferred receivables), then the transfer is accounted for as a secured borrowing. [7] As a result of these new rules, sale treatment for transfers of receivables will be significantly reduced.

In response to the use of **repurchase agreements** by some financial institutions during the financial crisis (e.g., Lehman Brothers' Repo 105) to "window-dress" their balance sheets and show lower leverage, the FASB also recently issued new guidance on transfers of assets in repurchase agreements. [8] The new rules tighten the requirements for meeting the control criterion, which raises the bar for companies to be able to assert sale accounting in a repurchase agreement.

What do the numbers mean? RETURN TO LENDER

It used to be that lenders of mortgages and other types of debt securities carried them on their books as a loan receivable. But thanks to Wall Street, many lenders learned how to package these loans together and sell (securitize) them, and record a gain on the sale. In fact, virtually every asset with a payment stream and a long-term payment history is a candidate for securitization. And, for a while, everyone was happy to be part of the mortgage securitization game. The graphic below illustrates the way the process worked.

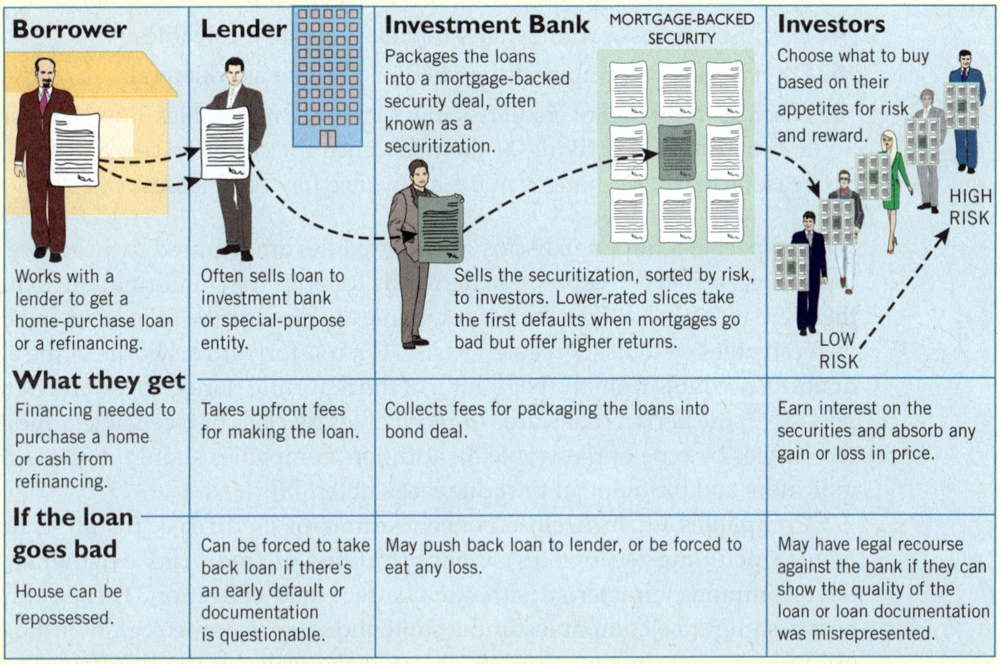

As indicated, once the mortgage loan is signed by the borrower, the lender sells the loans to an investment bank or a trust (special-purpose entity), reports a gain, and generally earns fees for servicing the debt. The trust, with the help of the investment bank, raises the money to buy these loans by selling some type of interest-bearing security to the investing public. These investors are happy because they earn a return that they believe is excellent, given the risk they take.

There were two big problems with these arrangements. First, as indicated in our discussion in the text, the lender has to make sure it does not keep control. Otherwise, it cannot sell the receivable *and* receive gain-on-sale treatment. Unfortunately, the accounting rules were loose enough that lenders were able to argue that they do not have control in most cases. Second, lenders realized that lending to subprime borrowers could be very profitable. They focused on these customers because the bank earns a fee for origination of the loan, sells the loans for a gain, and earns servicing revenue—a triple bump to the bottom line. However, when the housing market collapsed, the subprime borrowers could not repay their loans, and the credit markets collapsed. The result was a credit crisis.

So, who loses? Investors, primarily. But many investors are not ready to let lenders off the hook. They argue that in many of these sales, the lender must take back loans that defaulted or contained mistakes or fraud (bogus appraisals, inflated borrower incomes, and other misrepresentations). For example, **Countrywide Financial Corp.**, the largest mortgage lender in the United States, indicated that its liability for such claims increased by nearly $600 million from March 31, 2007, to March 31, 2008.

The moral of the story is that accounting matters. Lenders have strong incentives to want to report upfront gains on sales of loans. But, in most cases, these gains should never have been booked. In response, the FASB has issued new rules to tighten up "gain-on-sale" accounting for securitizations with participating interests (see footnote 14 on page 370). With these new rules, lenders will have to keep the loan on its balance sheet. Under these conditions, lenders would be much less likely to lend so much money to individuals with poor credit ratings.

Source: M. Hudson, "How Wall Street Stoked the Mortgage Meltdown," *Wall Street Journal* (June 27, 2007), p. A10.

LEARNING OBJECTIVE 9

Describe how to report and analyze receivables.

Presentation and Analysis

Presentation of Receivables

The general rules in classifying receivables are:

1. Segregate the different types of receivables that a company possesses, if material.
2. Appropriately offset the valuation accounts against the proper receivable accounts.
3. Determine that receivables classified in the current assets section will be converted into cash within the year or the operating cycle, whichever is longer.
4. Disclose any loss contingencies that exist on the receivables.
5. Disclose any receivables designated or pledged as collateral.
6. Disclose the nature of credit risk inherent in the receivables, how that risk is analyzed and assessed in arriving at the allowance for credit losses, and the changes and reasons for those changes in the allowance for credit losses.

With respect to additional disclosures, companies are required to disaggregate based on type of receivable. In response to demands for additional information about credit risk, the FASB recently issued rules for companies to provide the following disclosures about its receivables on a disaggregated basis: (1) a roll-forward schedule of the allowance for doubtful accounts from the beginning of the reporting period to the end of the reporting period, (2) the nonaccrual status of receivables by class of receivables, and (3) impaired receivables by type of receivable. In addition, companies should disclose credit quality indicators and the aging of past due receivables. **[9]**

Companies must disclose concentrations of credit risk for all financial instruments (including receivables). Concentrations of credit risk exist when receivables have common characteristics that may affect their collection. These common characteristics might be companies in the same industry or same region of the country. For example, **Quantum Corporation** reported that sales of its disk drives to its top five customers (including **Hewlett-Packard**) represented nearly 40 percent of its revenues in a recent year. Financial statements users want to know if a substantial amount of receivables from such sales are to customers facing uncertain economic conditions. No numerical guidelines are provided as to what is meant by a "concentration of credit risk."[15]

The assets sections of Colton Corporation's balance sheet in Illustration 7-23 show many of the disclosures required for receivables.

International Perspective

Holding receivables that it will receive in a foreign currency represents risk that the exchange rate may move against the company. This results in a decrease in the amount collected in terms of U.S. dollars. Companies engaged in cross-border transactions often "hedge" these receivables by buying contracts to exchange currencies at specified amounts at future dates.

Analysis of Receivables

Accounts Receivable Turnover. Analysts frequently compute financial ratios to evaluate the liquidity of a company's accounts receivable. To assess the liquidity of the receivables, they use the **accounts receivable turnover** ratio. This ratio measures the number of times, on average, a company collects receivables during the period. The ratio is computed by dividing net sales by average (net) receivables outstanding during the year. Theoretically, the numerator should include only net credit sales, but this information is frequently unavailable. However, if the relative amounts of credit and cash sales remain fairly constant, the trend indicated by the ratio will still be valid. Barring significant seasonal

[15]Three items should be disclosed with an identified concentration: (1) information on the characteristic that determines the concentration, (2) the amount of loss that could occur upon nonperformance, and (3) information on any collateral related to the receivable. **[10]**

ILLUSTRATION 7-23
Disclosure of Receivables

COLTON CORPORATION
BALANCE SHEET (PARTIAL)
AS OF DECEMBER 31, 2014

Current assets		
Cash and cash equivalents		$ 1,870,250
Accounts and notes receivable (Note 2)	$10,509,673	
Less: Allowance for doubtful accounts	500,226	
	10,009,447	
Advances to subsidiaries due 9/30/14	2,090,000	
Federal income taxes refundable	146,704	
Dividends and interest receivable	75,500	
Other receivables and claims (including debit balances in accounts payable)	174,620	12,496,271
Total current assets		$14,366,521
Noncurrent receivables		
Notes receivable from officers and key employees		376,090
Claims receivable (litigation settlement to be collected over four years)		585,000

Segregate different types of receivables

Note 2: Accounts and Notes Receivable. All noncurrent receivables are due within five years from the balance sheet date. Trade receivables that are less than three months past due are not considered impaired. At December 31, the aging analysis of receivables is as follows.

Amounts ($000)	Total	Neither Past Due or Impaired	Past Due but Not Impaired <30 days	30–60 days	60–90 days	90–120 days	>120 days
2014	10,510	5,115	2,791	1,582	570	360	92

Disclose aging of receivables

As at December 31, 2014, trade receivables at initial value of $109 were impaired and fully provided for. The following table summarises movements in the provision for impairment of receivables.

	Total $000
At January 1, 2014	98
Expense for the year	26
Written off	(9)
Recoveries	(6)
At December 31, 2014	109

Presentation of impaired receivables

Certain subsidiaries transferred receivable balances amounting to $1,014 to a bank in exchange for cash during the year ended December 31, 2014. The transaction has been accounted for as a secured borrowing. In case of default under the loan agreement, the borrower has the right to receive the cash flows from the receivables transferred. Without default, the subsidiaries will collect the receivables and assign new receivables as collateral.

Disclose collateral arrangements

factors, average receivables outstanding can be computed from the beginning and ending balances of net trade receivables.

To illustrate, **Best Buy** reported 2011 net sales of $50,705 million, its beginning and ending accounts receivable balances were $2,288 million and $2,348 million, respectively. Illustration 7-24 shows the computation of its accounts receivable turnover.

Underlying Concepts

Providing information that will help users assess a company's current liquidity and prospective cash flows is a primary objective of accounting.

ILLUSTRATION 7-24
Computation of Accounts Receivable Turnover

$$\frac{\textbf{Net Sales}}{\textbf{Average Trade Receivables (net)}} = \textbf{Accounts Receivable Turnover}$$

$$\frac{\$50{,}705}{(\$2{,}288 + \$2{,}348)/2} = 21.9 \text{ times, or every 16.7 days } (365 \div 21.9)$$

This information[16] shows how successful the company is in collecting its outstanding receivables. If possible, an aging schedule should also be prepared to help determine how long receivables have been outstanding. A satisfactory accounts receivable turnover may have resulted because certain receivables were collected quickly though others have been outstanding for a relatively long period. An aging schedule would reveal such patterns.

You will want to read the **IFRS INSIGHTS** on pages 408–412 for discussion of IFRS related to cash and receivables.

Often the accounts receivable turnover is transformed to **days to collect accounts receivable or days outstanding**—an average collection period. In this case, 21.9 is divided into 365 days, resulting in 16.7 days. Companies frequently use the average collection period to assess the effectiveness of a company's credit and collection policies. The general rule is that the average collection period should not greatly exceed the credit term period. That is, if customers are given a 60-day period for payment, then the average collection period should not be too much in excess of 60 days.

Evolving Issue — A CURE FOR "TOO LITTLE, TOO LATE"?

A significant accounting weakness revealed during the financial crisis relates to the accounting for loan losses (or allowance for doubtful accounts). The concern is that the existing GAAP (and IFRS) results in allowances for loan loss that tend to be at their lowest level when they are needed the most—at the beginning of a downward-trending economic cycle (the "too little, too late" concern). Therefore, the FASB and IASB have been working to develop a standard that ensures that the allowance for loan loss balance better reflects all estimated credit losses.

The Boards agree that a company should recognize an impairment in net income when it does not expect to collect all contractual amounts due on a loan. Furthermore, the Boards indicate that it is inappropriate to defer an impairment loss over the life of a loan. In other words, if a company does not expect to collect all amounts due, a loss exists and should be recognized immediately. The Boards are exploring two different approaches to an improved impairment model.

The first approach, referred to as the three-bucket approach, would classify loans and other financial assets into three buckets, which reflect assets of increasing severity of impairment. In this model, financial assets start out in Bucket 1 with reserves equal to 12 months of expected losses. Then, assets move to Bucket 2 or 3, and reserves increase to reflect expected losses over the life of those assets if the credit quality deteriorates and if there is an expectation that substantially all of the contractual cash flows will not be recovered.

In response to criticisms that the three-bucket model is overly complex, the FASB is exploring a second model—referred to as the "Current Expected Credit Loss" (CECL) model. Unlike the three-bucket approach, the CECL model uses a single-measurement objective—current estimate of lifetime expected credit losses—in contrast to the three-bucket model's requirement to distinguish between "12 months of expected credit losses" (Bucket 1) and "lifetime expected credit losses" (Buckets 2 and 3).

Under the CECL model, the impairment estimate reflects management's estimate of the contractual cash flows that the company does not expect to collect. Thus, the balance sheet will reflect the current estimate of expected credit losses at the reporting date, while the income statement will indicate the effects of credit deterioration or improvement that has taken place during the period.

While these proposed models represent a significant change from current practice, they have gained support because the loan loss allowance captures expected losses in response to deterioration in credit quality. In addition, in contrast to current GAAP, which is based on an "incurred loss" model, estimated loan losses are recognized earlier.

Source: K. Tysiac, "FASB Takes New Path in Contentious Financial Instruments Project," *Journal of Accountancy* (August 31, 2012).

[16]Several figures other than 365 could be used. A common alternative is 360 days because it is divisible by 30 (days) and 12 (months). *Use 365 days in any homework computations.*

SUMMARY OF LEARNING OBJECTIVES

1 Identify items considered cash. To be reported as "cash," an asset must be readily available for the payment of current obligations and free from contractual restrictions that limit its use in satisfying debts. Cash consists of coin, currency, and available funds on deposit at the bank. Negotiable instruments such as money orders, certified checks, cashier's checks, personal checks, and bank drafts are also viewed as cash. Savings accounts are usually classified as cash.

2 Indicate how to report cash and related items. Companies report cash as a current asset in the balance sheet. The reporting of other related items are as follows. (1) *Restricted cash:* The SEC recommends that companies state separately legally restricted deposits held as compensating balances against short-term borrowing among the "Cash and cash equivalent items" in current assets. Restricted deposits held against long-term borrowing arrangements should be separately classified as noncurrent assets in either the investments or other assets sections. (2) *Bank overdrafts:* Companies should report overdrafts in the current liabilities section and usually add them to the amount reported as accounts payable. If material, these items should be separately disclosed either on the face of the balance sheet or in the related notes. (3) *Cash equivalents:* Companies often report this item together with cash as "Cash and cash equivalents."

3 Define receivables and identify the different types of receivables. Receivables are claims held against customers and others for money, goods, or services. The receivables are classified into three types: (1) current or noncurrent, (2) trade or nontrade, and (3) accounts receivable or notes receivable.

4 Explain accounting issues related to recognition of accounts receivable. Two issues that may complicate the measurement of accounts receivable are (1) the availability of discounts (trade and cash discounts), and (2) the length of time between the sale and the payment due dates (the interest element).

Ideally, companies should measure receivables in terms of their present value—that is, the discounted value of the cash to be received in the future. The profession specifically excludes from the present value considerations receivables arising from normal business transactions that are due in customary trade terms within approximately one year.

5 Explain accounting issues related to valuation of accounts receivable. Companies value and report short-term receivables at net realizable value—the net amount expected to be received in cash, which is not necessarily the amount legally receivable. Determining net realizable value requires estimating uncollectible receivables.

6 Explain accounting issues related to recognition and valuation of notes receivable. Companies record short-term notes at face value and long-term notes receivable at the present value of the cash they expect to collect. When the interest stated on an interest-bearing note equals the effective (market) rate of interest, the note sells at face value. When the stated rate differs from the effective rate, a company records either a discount or premium. Like accounts receivable, companies record and report short-term notes receivable at their net realizable value. The same is also true of long-term receivables.

7 Explain the fair value option. Companies have the option to record receivables at fair value. Once the fair value option is chosen, the receivable is reported on the balance sheet at fair value, with the change in fair value recorded in income.

8 Explain accounting issues related to disposition of accounts and notes receivable. To accelerate the receipt of cash from receivables, the owner may transfer the receivables to another company for cash in one of two ways. (1) *Secured borrowing:*

KEY TERMS

accounts receivable, *350*
accounts receivable turnover, *372*
aging schedule, *357*
allowance method, *353*
bank overdrafts, *348*
cash, *346*
cash discounts, *351*
cash equivalents, *346*
compensating balances, *347*
direct write-off method, *353*
factoring receivables, *367*
fair value option, *365*
financial components approach, *368*
imputed interest rate, *363*
net realizable value, *353*
nontrade receivables, *350*
notes receivable, *350*
percentage-of-receivables approach, *357*
percentage-of-sales approach, *356*
promissory note, *359*
receivables, *349*
restricted cash, *347*
sales discounts, *351*
securitization, *368*
trade discounts, *351*
trade receivables, *349*
unrealized holding gain or loss, *365*
without recourse, *368*
with recourse, *368*
zero-interest-bearing notes, *359*

A creditor often requires that the debtor designate or pledge receivables as security for the loan. (2) *Sales (factoring) of receivables:* Factors are finance companies or banks that buy receivables from businesses and then collect the remittances directly from the customers. In many cases, transferors may have some continuing involvement with the receivable sold. Companies use a financial components approach to record this type of transaction.

9 **Describe how to report and analyze receivables.** Companies should report receivables with appropriate offset of valuation accounts against receivables, classify receivables as current or noncurrent, identify pledged or designated receivables, and disclose the credit risk inherent in the receivables. Analysts assess receivables based on turnover and the days outstanding.

APPENDIX 7A CASH CONTROLS

LEARNING OBJECTIVE 10

Explain common techniques employed to control cash.

Cash is the asset most susceptible to improper diversion and use. Management faces two problems in accounting for cash transactions: (1) to establish proper controls to prevent any unauthorized transactions by officers or employees, and (2) to provide information necessary to properly manage cash on hand and cash transactions. Yet even with sophisticated control devices, errors can and do happen. For example, the *Wall Street Journal* ran a story entitled "A $7.8 Million Error Has a Happy Ending for a Horrified Bank." The story described how Manufacturers Hanover Trust Co. mistakenly overpaid about $7.8 million in cash dividends to its stockholders. (As implied in the headline, most stockholders returned the monies.)

To safeguard cash and to ensure the accuracy of the accounting records for cash, companies need effective **internal control** over cash. Provisions of the Sarbanes-Oxley Act call for enhanced efforts to increase the quality of internal control (for cash and other assets). Such efforts are expected to result in improved financial reporting. In this appendix, we discuss some of the basic control issues related to cash.

USING BANK ACCOUNTS

To obtain desired control objectives, a company can vary the number and location of banks and the types of bank accounts. For large companies operating in multiple locations, the location of bank accounts can be important. Establishing collection accounts in strategic locations can accelerate the flow of cash into the company by shortening the time between a customer's mailing of a payment and the company's use of the cash. Multiple collection centers generally reduce the size of a company's **collection float**. This is the difference between the amount on deposit according to the company's records and the amount of collected cash according to the bank record.

International Perspective

Multinational corporations often have cash accounts in more than one currency. For financial statement purposes, these corporations typically translate these currencies into U.S. dollars, using the exchange rate in effect at the balance sheet date.

Large, multilocation companies frequently use **lockbox accounts** to collect in cities with heavy customer billing. The company rents a local post office box and authorizes a local bank to pick up the remittances mailed to that box number. The bank empties the box at least once a day and immediately credits the company's account for collections. The greatest advantage of a lockbox is that it accelerates the availability of collected cash. Generally, in a lockbox arrangement the bank microfilms the checks for record purposes and provides the company with a deposit slip, a list of collections, and any customer correspondence. Thus, a lockbox system improves the control over cash and accelerates collection of cash. If the income generated from accelerating the receipt of funds exceeds the cost of the lockbox system, then it is a worthwhile undertaking.

The **general checking account** is the principal bank account in most companies and frequently the only bank account in small businesses. A company deposits in and disburses cash from this account. A company cycles all transactions through it. For example, a company deposits from and disburses to all other bank accounts through the general checking account.

Companies use **imprest bank accounts** to make a specific amount of cash available for a limited purpose. The account acts as a clearing account for a large volume of checks or for a specific type of check. To clear a specific and intended amount through the imprest account, a company transfers that amount from the general checking account or other source. Companies often use imprest bank accounts for disbursing payroll checks, dividends, commissions, bonuses, confidential expenses (e.g., officers' salaries), and travel expenses.

THE IMPREST PETTY CASH SYSTEM

Almost every company finds it necessary to pay small amounts for miscellaneous expenses such as taxi fares, minor office supplies, and employees' lunches. Disbursements by check for such items is often impractical, yet some control over them is important. A simple method of obtaining reasonable control, while adhering to the rule of disbursement by check, is the **imprest system for petty cash** disbursements. This is how the system works:

1. The company designates a petty cash custodian, and gives the custodian a small amount of currency from which to make payments. It records transfer of funds to petty cash as:

Petty Cash	300	
Cash		300

2. The petty cash custodian obtains signed receipts from each individual to whom he or she pays cash, attaching evidence of the disbursement to the petty cash receipt. Petty cash transactions are not recorded until the fund is reimbursed; someone other than the petty cash custodian records those entries.
3. When the supply of cash runs low, the custodian presents to the controller or accounts payable cashier a request for reimbursement supported by the petty cash receipts and other disbursement evidence. The custodian receives a company check to replenish the fund. At this point, the company records transactions based on petty cash receipts.

Supplies Expense	42	
Postage Expense	53	
Miscellaneous Expense	76	
Cash Over and Short	2	
Cash		173

4. If the company decides that the amount of cash in the petty cash fund is excessive, it lowers the fund balance as follows.

Cash	50	
Petty Cash		50

Subsequent to establishment, a company makes entries to the Petty Cash account only to increase or decrease the size of the fund.

A company uses a **Cash Over and Short** account when the petty cash fund fails to prove out. That is, an error occurs such as incorrect change, overpayment of expense, or lost receipt. If cash proves out **short** (i.e., the sum of the receipts and cash in the fund is less than the imprest amount), the company debits the shortage to the Cash Over and

Short account. If cash proves out **over**, it credits the overage to Cash Over and Short. The company closes Cash Over and Short only at the end of the year. It generally shows Cash Over and Short on the income statement as an "Other expense or revenue."

There are usually expense items in the fund except immediately after reimbursement. Therefore, to maintain accurate financial statements, a company must reimburse the funds at the end of each accounting period and also when nearly depleted.

Under the imprest system, the petty cash custodian is responsible at all times for the amount of the fund on hand either as cash or in the form of signed receipts. These receipts provide the evidence required by the disbursing officer to issue a reimbursement check. Further, a company follows two additional procedures to obtain more complete control over the petty cash fund:

1. A superior of the petty cash custodian makes surprise counts of the fund from time to time to determine that a satisfactory accounting of the fund has occurred.
2. The company cancels or mutilates petty cash receipts after they have been submitted for reimbursement, so that they cannot be used to secure a second reimbursement.

PHYSICAL PROTECTION OF CASH BALANCES

Not only must a company safeguard cash receipts and cash disbursements through internal control measures, but it must also protect the cash on hand and in banks. Because receipts become cash on hand and disbursements are made from cash in banks, adequate control of receipts and disbursements is part of the protection of cash balances, along with certain other procedures.

Physical protection of cash is so elementary a necessity that it requires little discussion. A company should make every effort to minimize the cash on hand in the office. It should only have on hand a petty cash fund, the current day's receipts, and perhaps funds for making change. Insofar as possible, it should keep these funds in a vault, safe, or locked cash drawer. The company should transmit intact each day's receipts to the bank as soon as practicable. Accurately stating the amount of available cash both in internal management reports and in external financial statements is also extremely important.

Every company has a record of cash received, disbursed, and the balance. Because of the many cash transactions, however, errors or omissions may occur in keeping this record. Therefore, a company must periodically prove the balance shown in the general ledger. It can count cash actually present in the office—petty cash, change funds, and undeposited receipts—for comparison with the company records. For cash on deposit, a company prepares a bank reconciliation—a reconciliation of the company's record and the bank's record of the company's cash.

RECONCILIATION OF BANK BALANCES

At the end of each calendar month the bank supplies each customer with a **bank statement** (a copy of the bank's account with the customer) together with the customer's checks that the bank paid during the month.[17] If neither the bank nor the customer made any errors, if all deposits made and all checks drawn by the customer reached the bank

[17]As we mentioned in Chapter 7, paper checks continue to be used as a means of payment. However, ready availability of desktop publishing software and hardware has created new opportunities for check fraud in the form of duplicate, altered, and forged checks. At the same time, new fraud-fighting technologies, such as ultraviolet imaging, high-capacity barcodes, and biometrics, are being developed. These technologies convert paper documents into electronically processed document files, thereby reducing the risk of fraud.

within the same month, and if no unusual transactions occurred that affected either the company's or the bank's record of cash, the balance of cash reported by the bank to the customer equals that shown in the customer's own records. This condition seldom occurs due to one or more of the reconciling items presented below. Hence, a company expects differences between its record of cash and the bank's record. Therefore, it must reconcile the two to determine the nature of the differences between the two amounts.

RECONCILING ITEMS

1. **DEPOSITS IN TRANSIT.** End-of-month deposits of cash recorded on the depositor's books in one month are received and recorded by the bank in the following month.
2. **OUTSTANDING CHECKS.** Checks written by the depositor are recorded when written but may not be recorded by (may not "clear") the bank until the next month.
3. **BANK CHARGES.** Charges recorded by the bank against the depositor's balance for such items as bank services, printing checks, **not-sufficient-funds (NSF) checks**, and safe-deposit box rentals. The depositor may not be aware of these charges until the receipt of the bank statement.
4. **BANK CREDITS.** Collections or deposits by the bank for the benefit of the depositor that may be unknown to the depositor until receipt of the bank statement. Examples are note collection for the depositor and interest earned on interest-bearing checking accounts.
5. **BANK OR DEPOSITOR ERRORS.** Errors on either the part of the bank or the part of the depositor cause the bank balance to disagree with the depositor's book balance.

A **bank reconciliation** is a schedule explaining any differences between the bank's and the company's records of cash. If the difference results only from transactions not yet recorded by the bank, the company's record of cash is considered correct. But, if some part of the difference arises from other items, either the bank or the company must adjust its records.

A company may prepare two forms of a bank reconciliation. One form reconciles from the bank statement balance to the book balance or vice versa. The other form reconciles both the bank balance and the book balance to a correct cash balance. Most companies use this latter form. Illustration 7A-1 shows a sample of that form and its common reconciling items.

ILLUSTRATION 7A-1
Bank Reconciliation Form and Content

Balance per bank statement (end of period)		$$$
Add: Deposits in transit	$$	
Undeposited receipts (cash on hand)	$$	
Bank errors that understate the bank statement balance	$$	$$
		$$$
Deduct: Outstanding checks	$$	
Bank errors that overstate the bank statement balance	$$	$$
Correct cash balance		$$$
Balance per depositor's books		$$$
Add: Bank credits and collections not yet recorded in the books	$$	
Book errors that understate the book balance	$$	$$
		$$$
Deduct: Bank charges not yet recorded in the books	$$	
Book errors that overstate the book balance	$$	$$
Correct cash balance		$$$

This form of reconciliation consists of two sections: (1) "Balance per bank statement" and (2) "Balance per depositor's books." Both sections end with the same "Correct cash balance." The correct cash balance is the amount to which the books must be adjusted and is the amount reported on the balance sheet. **Companies prepare adjusting journal entries for all the addition and deduction items appearing in the "Balance per depositor's books" section.** Companies should immediately call to the bank's attention any errors attributable to it.

To illustrate, Nugget Mining Company's books show a cash balance at the Denver National Bank on November 30, 2014, of $20,502. The bank statement covering the month of November shows an ending balance of $22,190. An examination of Nugget's accounting records and November bank statement identified the following reconciling items.

1. A deposit of $3,680 that Nugget mailed November 30 does not appear on the bank statement.
2. Checks written in November but not charged to the November bank statement are:

Check #7327	$ 150
#7348	4,820
#7349	31

3. Nugget has not yet recorded the $600 of interest collected by the bank November 20 on Sequoia Co. bonds held by the bank for Nugget.
4. Bank service charges of $18 are not yet recorded on Nugget's books.
5. The bank returned one of Nugget's customer's checks for $220 with the bank statement, marked "NSF." The bank treated this bad check as a disbursement.
6. Nugget discovered that it incorrectly recorded check #7322, written in November for $131 in payment of an account payable, as $311.
7. A check for Nugent Oil Co. in the amount of $175 that the bank incorrectly charged to Nugget accompanied the statement.

Nugget reconciled the bank and book balances to the correct cash balance of $21,044 as shown in Illustration 7A-2.

ILLUSTRATION 7A-2
Sample Bank Reconciliation

NUGGET MINING COMPANY
BANK RECONCILIATION
DENVER NATIONAL BANK, NOVEMBER 30, 2014

Balance per bank statement (end of period)			$22,190
Add: Deposit in transit	(1)	$3,680	
Bank error—incorrect check charged to account by bank	(7)	175	3,855
			26,045
Deduct: Outstanding checks	(2)		5,001
Correct cash balance			$21,044
Balance per books			$20,502
Add: Interest collected by the bank	(3)	$ 600	
Error in recording check #7322	(6)	180	780
			21,282
Deduct: Bank service charges	(4)	18	
NSF check returned	(5)	220	238
Correct cash balance			$21,044

The journal entries required to adjust and correct Nugget's books in early December 2014 are taken from the items in the "Balance per books" section and are as follows.

Cash	600	
Interest Revenue		600
(To record interest on Sequoia Co. bonds, collected by bank)		
Cash	180	
Accounts Payable		180
(To correct error in recording amount of check #7322)		
Office Expense (bank charges)	18	
Cash		18
(To record bank service charges for November)		
Accounts Receivable	220	
Cash		220
(To record customer's check returned NSF)		

Gateway to the Profession

Expanded Discussion of a Four-Column Bank Reconciliation

After posting the entries, Nugget's cash account will have a balance of $21,044. Nugget should return the Nugent Oil Co. check to Denver National Bank, informing the bank of the error.

SUMMARY OF LEARNING OBJECTIVE FOR APPENDIX 7A

KEY TERMS

bank reconciliation, *379*

imprest system for petty cash, *377*

not-sufficient-funds (NSF) checks, *379*

10 **Explain common techniques employed to control cash.** The common techniques employed to control cash are as follows. (1) *Using bank accounts:* A company can vary the number and location of banks and the types of accounts to obtain desired control objectives. (2) *The imprest petty cash system:* It may be impractical to require small amounts of various expenses be paid by check, yet some control over them is important. (3) *Physical protection of cash balances:* Adequate control of receipts and disbursements is a part of the protection of cash balances. Every effort should be made to minimize the cash on hand in the office. (4) *Reconciliation of bank balances:* Cash on deposit is not available for count and is proved by preparing a bank reconciliation.

APPENDIX 7B IMPAIRMENTS OF RECEIVABLES

11 LEARNING OBJECTIVE

Describe the accounting for a loan impairment.

Companies continually evaluate their receivables to determine their ultimate collectibility. As discussed in the chapter, the FASB considers the collectibility of receivables a *loss contingency*. Thus, the allowance method is appropriate in situations where it is probable that an asset has been impaired and the amount of the loss can be reasonably estimated. Generally, companies start with historical loss rates and modify these rates for changes in economic conditions that could affect a borrower's ability to repay the loan. The discussion in the chapter assumed use of this approach to determine the amount of bad debts to be recorded for a period.

However, for long-term receivables such as loans that are identified as impaired, companies perform an additional impairment evaluation.[18] GAAP has specific rules for

[18] A loan is defined as "a contractual right to receive money on demand or on fixed and determinable dates that is recognized as an asset in the creditor's statement of financial position." For example, accounts receivable with terms exceeding one year are considered loans. **[11]**

measurement and reporting of these impairments. These rules relate to determining the value of these loans and how much loss to recognize if the holder of the loans plans to keep them in hope that the market will recover. More complex rules arise when these loans are sold as part of the securitization process, especially when the original terms of the notes are modified.[19]

IMPAIRMENT MEASUREMENT AND REPORTING

A company considers a loan receivable impaired when it is probable, based on current information and events, that it will not collect all amounts due (both principal and interest). If a loan is determined to be individually impaired, the company should measure the loss due to the **impairment**. This impairment loss is calculated as the difference between the investment in the loan (generally the principal plus accrued interest) and the expected future cash flows discounted at the loan's historical effective-interest rate.[20] When using the historical effective loan rate, the value of the investment will change only if some of the legally contracted cash flows are reduced. A company recognizes a loss in this case because the expected future cash flows are now lower. The company ignores interest rate changes caused by current economic events that affect the fair value of the loan. In estimating future cash flows, the creditor should use reasonable and supportable assumptions and projections. **[13]**

Impairment Loss Example

At December 31, 2013, Ogden Bank recorded an investment of $100,000 in a loan to Carl King. The loan has an historical effective-interest rate of 10 percent, the principal is due in full at maturity in three years, and interest is due annually. Unfortunately, King is experiencing financial difficulty and thinks he will have a difficult time making full payment. The loan officer performs a review of the loan's expected future cash flows and utilizes the present value method for measuring the required impairment loss. Illustration 7B-1 shows the cash flow schedule prepared by the loan officer.

ILLUSTRATION 7B-1
Impaired Loan Cash Flows

Dec. 31	Contractual Cash Flow	Expected Cash Flow	Loss of Cash Flow
2014	$ 10,000	$ 5,000	$ 5,000
2015	10,000	5,000	5,000
2016	$110,000	105,000	5,000
Total cash flows	$130,000	$115,000	$15,000

As indicated, this loan is impaired. The expected cash flows of $115,000 are less than the contractual cash flows, including principal and interest, of $130,000. The amount of the impairment to be recorded equals the difference between the recorded investment of $100,000 and the present value of the expected cash flows, as shown in Illustration 7B-2.

[19]Note that the impairment test shown in this appendix only applies to specific loans. However, if the loans are bundled into a security (e.g., the mortgage-backed securities), the impairment test is different. Impairments of securities are measured based on fair value. We discuss this accounting in Chapter 17.

[20]The creditor may also, for the sake of expediency, use the market price of the loan (if such a price is available) or the fair value of the collateral if it is a collateralized loan. **[12]** Recognize that if the value of the investment is based on the historical rate, generally the resultant value will not be equal to the fair value of the loan in subsequent periods. We consider this accounting inconsistent with fair value principles as applied to other financial instruments.

ILLUSTRATION 7B-2
Computation of Impairment Loss

Recorded investment		$100,000
Less: Present value of $100,000 due in 3 years at 10% (Table 6-2); *FV* (*PVF*$_{3,10\%}$); ($100,000 × .75132)	$75,132	
Present value of $5,000 interest payable annually for 3 years at 10% R (*PVF-OA*$_{3,10\%}$); ($5,000 × 2.48685)	12,434	87,566
Loss on impairment		$ 12,434

The loss due to the impairment is $12,434. Why isn't it $15,000 ($130,000 – $115,000)? Because Ogden Bank must measure the loss at a present-value amount, not at an undiscounted amount, when it records the loss.

Recording Impairment Losses

Ogden Bank (the creditor) recognizes an impairment loss of $12,434 by debiting Bad Debt Expense for the expected loss. At the same time, it reduces the overall value of the receivable by crediting Allowance for Doubtful Accounts. The journal entry to record the loss is therefore as follows.[21]

Bad Debt Expense	12,434	
Allowance for Doubtful Accounts		12,434

What entry does Carl King (the debtor) make? The debtor makes no entry because he still legally owes $100,000.

In some cases, debtors like King negotiate a modification in the terms of the loan agreement. In such cases, the accounting entries from Ogden Bank are the same as the situation in which the loan officer must estimate the future cash flows—except that the calculation for the amount of the loss becomes more reliable (because the revised expected cash flow amounts are contractually specified in the loan agreement).[22] The entries related to the debtor in this case often change; they are discussed in Appendix 14A.

What do the numbers mean? LOST IN TRANSLATION

Floyd Norris, noted financial writer for the *New York Times*, recently wrote in his blog that he attended a conference to discuss the financial crisis in subprime lending. He highlighted, and provided "translations" of, some of the statements he heard at that conference:

- "There is a problem of misaligned incentives."

  Translation: Many parties in the lending process were complicit in not performing due diligence on loans because there were lots of fees to be had if the loans were made, good loans or bad.

- "It is pretty clear that there was a failure in some key assumptions that were supporting our analytics and our models."

  Translation: The rating agencies that evaluated the risk level of these securities made many miscalculations. Some structured finance products that were given superior ratings are no longer worth much.

- "The plumbing of the U.S. economy has been deeply damaged. It is a long window of vulnerability."

  Translation: The U.S. has caused a financial crisis as a result of poor lending practices, and many financial institutions are fighting to survive.

- "I'm glad that this time we did not cause it."

  Translation: Other countries realized they had caused financial crises in the past but were not to blame for the current U.S. financial situation.

[21]In the event of a loan write-off, the company charges the loss against the allowance. In subsequent periods, if revising estimated expected cash flows based on new information, the company adjusts the allowance account and bad debt expense account (either increased or decreased depending on whether conditions improved or worsened) in the same fashion as the original impairment. We use the terms "loss" and "bad debt expense" interchangeably throughout this discussion. Companies should charge losses related to receivables transactions to Bad Debt Expense or the related Allowance for Doubtful Accounts because they use these accounts to recognize changes in values affecting receivables.

[22]Many alternatives are permitted to recognize income by Ogden Bank in subsequent periods. **[14]**

- "What you see is what you get. If you don't see it, it will get you."

Translation: A large number of financial institutions have to take losses on assets that are not reported on their balance sheets. Their continuing interest in some of the loans that they supposedly sold is now coming back to them and they will have to report losses.

Source: Floyd Norris blog, *http://www.norris.blogs.nytimes.com/* (accessed June 2008).

KEY TERM

impairment, 382

SUMMARY OF LEARNING OBJECTIVE FOR APPENDIX 7B

11 Describe the accounting for a loan impairment. A creditor bases an impairment loan loss on the difference between the present value of the future cash flows (using the historical effective-interest rate) and the carrying amount of the note.

DEMONSTRATION PROBLEM

The trial balance before adjustment for Slamar Company shows the following balances.

	Debit	Credit
Net sales	$860,000	
Accounts receivable	338,000	
Allowance for doubtful accounts		$4,240

Consider the following independent situations:

1. To obtain additional cash, Slamar factors without recourse $50,000 of accounts receivable with Pierce Finance. The finance charge is 11% of the amount factored.
2. To obtain a 1-year loan of $75,000, Slamar assigns $80,000 of specific receivable accounts to Milo Financial. The finance charge is 9% of the loan; the cash is received and the accounts turned over to Milo Financial.
3. The company wants to maintain Allowance for Doubtful Accounts at 6% of gross accounts receivable.
4. The company wishes to increase the allowance account by 2% of net sales.

Instructions

(a) Using the data above, give the journal entries required to record situations 1–4.

(b) Discuss how analysis based on the current ratio and the accounts receivable turnover would be affected if Slamar had transferred the receivables in situation 1 using a secured borrowing.

Solution

(a)

		Debit	Credit
1.	Cash	44,500	
	Loss on Sale of Receivables ($50,000 × 11%)	5,500	
	Accounts Receivable		50,000
2.	Cash	68,250	
	Interest Expense ($75,000 × 9%)	6,750	
	Notes Payable		75,000

3. Bad Debt Expense	24,520	
Allowance for Doubtful Accounts [(\$338,000 × 6%) + \$4,240]		24,520
4. Bad Debt Expense	17,200	
Allowance for Doubtful Accounts (\$860,000 × 2%)		17,200

(b) With a secured borrowing, the receivables would stay on Slamar's books, and Slamar would record a note payable. This would reduce the current ratio and accounts receivable turnover.

FASB CODIFICATION

FASB Codification References

[1] FASB ASC 210-10-S99-1. [Predecessor literature: "Amendments to Regulations S-X and Related Interpretations and Guidelines Regarding the Disclosure of Compensating Balances and Short-Term Borrowing Arrangements," *Accounting Series Release No. 148*, Securities and Exchange Commission (November 13, 1973).]

[2] FASB ASC 835-30-15-3. [Predecessor literature: "Interest on Receivables and Payables," *Opinions of the Accounting Principles Board No. 21* (New York: AICPA, 1971), par. 3(a).]

[3] FASB ASC 310-10-35-8. [Predecessor literature: "Accounting for Contingencies," *Statement of Financial Accounting Standards No. 5* (Stamford, Conn.: FASB, 1975), par. 8.]

[4] FASB ASC 835-30-05. [Predecessor literature: "Interest on Receivables and Payables," *Opinions of the Accounting Principles Board No. 21* (New York: AICPA, 1971), par. 3(a).]

[5] FASB ASC 825-10-25. [Predecessor literature: "The Fair Value Option for Financial Assets and Liabilities—Including an Amendment to FASB No. 115," *Statement of Financial Accounting Standards No. 159* (Norwalk, Conn.: FASB, 2007).]

[6] FASB ASC 860-40 and FASB ASC 860-10-5-15. [Predecessor literature: "Accounting for Transfers and Servicing of Financial Assets and Extinguishments of Liabilities," *Statement of Financial Accounting Standards No. 140* (Stamford, Conn.: FASB, 2000), p. 155.]

[7] FASB ASC 860-10-40. [Predecessor literature: None.]

[8] FASB ASC 860. [Predecessor literature: "Transfers and Servicing," *Accounting Standards Update 2011–03* (April 2011).]

[9] FASB ASC 310-10-50. [Predecessor literature: None.]

[10] FASB ASC 825-10-50-20 through 22. [Predecessor literature: "Disclosures about Fair Value of Financial Instruments," *Statement of Financial Accounting Standards No. 107* (Norwalk, Conn.: FASB, 1991), par. 15.]

[11] FASB ASC 310-10-35-22. [Predecessor literature: "Accounting by Creditors for Impairment of a Loan," *FASB Statement No. 114* (Norwalk, Conn.: FASB, May 1993).]

[12] FASB ASC 310-10-35-22. [Predecessor literature: "Accounting by Creditors for Impairment of a Loan," *FASB Statement No. 114* (Norwalk, Conn.: FASB, May 1993), par. 13.]

[13] FASB ASC 310-10-35-26. [Predecessor literature: "Accounting by Creditors for Impairment of a Loan," *FASB Statement No. 114* (Norwalk, Conn.: FASB, May 1993), par. 15.]

[14] FASB ASC 310-10-35-40. [Predecessor literature: "Accounting by Creditors for Impairment of a Loan—Income Recognition and Disclosures," *FASB Statement No. 118* (Norwalk, Conn.: FASB, October 1994).]

Exercises

If your school has a subscription to the FASB Codification, go to *http://aaahq.org/asclogin.cfm* to log in and prepare responses to the following. Provide Codification references for your responses.

CE7-1 Access the glossary ("Master Glossary") to answer the following.

(a) What is the definition of cash?
(b) What is the definition of securitization?
(c) What are the three contexts that give rise to recourse?

CE7-2 Carrie Underwood believes that by establishing a loss contingency for uncollectible receivables, a company provides financial protection against the loss. What does the authoritative literature say about this belief?

CE7-3 In addition to securitizations, what are the other types of transfers of financial assets identified in the Codification?

CE7-4 The controller for Nesheim Construction Company believes that it is appropriate to offset a note payable to Oregon Bank against an account receivable from Oregon Bank related to remodeling services provided to the bank. What is the authoritative guidance concerning the criteria to be met to allow such offsetting?

An additional Codification case can be found in the Using Your Judgment section, on page 407.

Be sure to check the book's companion website for a Review and Analysis Exercise, with solution.

WileyPLUS Brief Exercises, Exercises, Problems, and many more learning and assessment tools and resources are available for practice in WileyPLUS.

Note: All asterisked Questions, Exercises, and Problems relate to material in the appendices to the chapter.

QUESTIONS

1. What may be included under the heading of "cash"?

2. In what accounts should the following items be classified?

- **(a)** Coins and currency.
- **(b)** U.S. Treasury (government) bonds.
- **(c)** Certificate of deposit.
- **(d)** Cash in a bank that is in receivership.
- **(e)** NSF check (returned with bank statement).
- **(f)** Deposit in foreign bank (exchangeability limited).
- **(g)** Postdated checks.
- **(h)** Cash to be used for retirement of long-term bonds.
- **(i)** Deposits in transit.
- **(j)** 100 shares of Dell stock (intention is to sell in one year or less).
- **(k)** Savings and checking accounts.
- **(l)** Petty cash.
- **(m)** Stamps.
- **(n)** Travel advances.

3. Define a "compensating balance." How should a compensating balance be reported?

4. Springsteen Inc. reported in a recent annual report "Restricted cash for debt redemption." What section of the balance sheet would report this item?

5. What are the reasons that a company gives trade discounts? Why are trade discounts not recorded in the accounts like cash discounts?

6. What are two methods of recording accounts receivable transactions when a cash discount situation is involved? Which is more theoretically correct? Which is used in practice more of the time? Why?

7. What are the basic problems that occur in the valuation of accounts receivable?

8. What is the theoretical justification of the allowance method as contrasted with the direct write-off method of accounting for bad debts?

9. Indicate how well the percentage-of-sales method and the aging method accomplish the objectives of the allowance method of accounting for bad debts.

10. Of what merit is the contention that the allowance method lacks the objectivity of the direct write-off method? Discuss in terms of accounting's measurement function.

11. Explain how the accounting for bad debts can be used for earnings management.

12. Because of calamitous earthquake losses, Bernstein Company, one of your client's oldest and largest customers, suddenly and unexpectedly became bankrupt. Approximately 30% of your client's total sales have been made to Bernstein Company during each of the past several years. The amount due from Bernstein Company—none of which is collectible—equals 22% of total accounts receivable, an amount that is considerably in excess of what was determined to be an adequate provision for doubtful accounts at the close of the preceding year. How would your client record the write-off of the Bernstein Company receivable if it is using the allowance method of accounting for bad debts? Justify your suggested treatment.

13. What is the normal procedure for handling the collection of accounts receivable previously written off using the direct write-off method? The allowance method?

14. On January 1, 2014, Lombard Co. sells property for which it had paid $690,000 to Sargent Company, receiving in return Sargent's zero-interest-bearing note for $1,000,000 payable in 5 years. What entry would Lombard make to record the sale, assuming that Lombard frequently sells similar items of property for a cash sales price of $640,000?

15. What is "imputed interest"? In what situations is it necessary to impute an interest rate for notes receivable? What are the considerations in imputing an appropriate interest rate?

16. What is the fair value option? Where do companies that elect the fair value option report unrealized holding gains and losses?

17. Indicate three reasons why a company might sell its receivables to another company.

18. When is the financial components approach to recording the transfers of receivables used? When should a transfer of receivables be recorded as a sale?

19. Moon Hardware is planning to factor some of its receivables. The cash received will be used to pay for inventory purchases. The factor has indicated that it will require "recourse" on the sold receivables. Explain to the controller of Moon Hardware what "recourse" is and how the recourse will be reflected in Moon's financial statements after the sale of the receivables.

20. Horizon Outfitters Company includes in its trial balance for December 31 an item for Accounts Receivable $789,000. This balance consists of the following items:

Due from regular customers	$523,000
Refund receivable on prior year's income taxes (an established claim)	15,500
Travel advance to employees	22,000
Loan to wholly owned subsidiary	45,500
Advances to creditors for goods ordered	61,000
Accounts receivable assigned as security for loans payable	75,000
Notes receivable past due plus interest on these notes	47,000
Total	$789,000

Illustrate how these items should be shown in the balance sheet as of December 31.

21. What is the accounts receivable turnover, and what type of information does it provide?

22. You are evaluating Woodlawn Racetrack for a potential loan. An examination of the notes to the financial statements indicates restricted cash at year-end amounts to $100,000. Explain how you would use this information in evaluating Woodlawn's liquidity.

***23.** Distinguish among the following: (1) a general checking account, (2) an impress bank account, and (3) a lockbox account.

***24.** What are the general rules for measuring and recognizing gain or loss by both the debtor and the creditor in an impairment?

***25.** What is meant by impairment of a loan? Under what circumstances should a creditor recognize an impaired loan?

BRIEF EXERCISES

1 **BE7-1** Kraft Enterprises owns the following assets at December 31, 2014.

Cash in bank—savings account	68,000	Checking account balance	17,000
Cash on hand	9,300	Postdated checks	750
Cash refund due from IRS	31,400	Certificates of deposit (180-day)	90,000

What amount should be reported as cash?

4 **BE7-2** Restin Co. uses the gross method to record sales made on credit. On June 1, 2014, it made sales of $50,000 with terms 3/15, n/45. On June 12, 2014, Restin received full payment for the June 1 sale. Prepare the required journal entries for Restin Co.

4 **BE7-3** Use the information from BE7-2, assuming Restin Co. uses the net method to account for cash discounts. Prepare the required journal entries for Restin Co.

5 **BE7-4** Wilton, Inc. had net sales in 2014 of $1,400,000. At December 31, 2014, before adjusting entries, the balances in selected accounts were: Accounts Receivable $250,000 debit, and Allowance for Doubtful Accounts $2,400 credit. If Wilton estimates that 2% of its net sales will prove to be uncollectible, prepare the December 31, 2014, journal entry to record bad debt expense.

5 **BE7-5** Use the information presented in BE7-4 for Wilton, Inc.

(a) Instead of estimating the uncollectibles at 2% of net sales, assume that 10% of accounts receivable will prove to be uncollectible. Prepare the entry to record bad debt expense.

(b) Instead of estimating uncollectibles at 2% of net sales, assume Wilton prepares an aging schedule that estimates total uncollectible accounts at $24,600. Prepare the entry to record bad debt expense.

6 **BE7-6** Milner Family Importers sold goods to Tung Decorators for $30,000 on November 1, 2014, accepting Tung's $30,000, 6-month, 6% note. Prepare Milner's November 1 entry, December 31 annual adjusting entry, and May 1 entry for the collection of the note and interest.

6 **BE7-7** Dold Acrobats lent $16,529 to Donaldson, Inc., accepting Donaldson's 2-year, $20,000, zero-interest-bearing note. The implied interest rate is 10%. Prepare Dold's journal entries for the initial transaction, recognition of interest each year, and the collection of $20,000 at maturity.

8 **BE7-8** On October 1, 2014, Chung, Inc. assigns $1,000,000 of its accounts receivable to Seneca National Bank as collateral for a $750,000 note. The bank assesses a finance charge of 2% of the receivables assigned and interest on the note of 9%. Prepare the October 1 journal entries for both Chung and Seneca.

8 **BE7-9** Wood Incorporated factored $150,000 of accounts receivable with Engram Factors Inc. on a without-recourse basis. Engram assesses a 2% finance charge of the amount of accounts receivable and retains an amount equal to 6% of accounts receivable for possible adjustments. Prepare the journal entry for Wood Incorporated and Engram Factors to record the factoring of the accounts receivable to Engram.

8 **BE7-10** Use the information in BE7-9 for Wood. Assume that the receivables are sold with recourse. Prepare the journal entry for Wood to record the sale, assuming that the recourse liability has a fair value of $7,500.

8 **BE7-11** Arness Woodcrafters sells $250,000 of receivables to Commercial Factors, Inc. on a with recourse basis. Commercial assesses a finance charge of 5% and retains an amount equal to 4% of accounts receivable. Arness estimates the fair value of the recourse liability to be $8,000. Prepare the journal entry for Arness to record the sale.

8 **BE7-12** Use the information presented in BE7-11 for Arness Woodcrafters but assume that the recourse liability has a fair value of $4,000, instead of $8,000. Prepare the journal entry and discuss the effects of this change in the value of the recourse liability on Arness's financial statements.

9 **BE7-13** Recent financial statements of **General Mills, Inc.** report net sales of $12,442,000,000. Accounts receivable are $912,000,000 at the beginning of the year and $953,000,000 at the end of the year. Compute General Mills' accounts receivable turnover. Compute General Mills' average collection period for accounts receivable in days.

10 ***BE7-14** Finman Company designated Jill Holland as petty cash custodian and established a petty cash fund of $200. The fund is reimbursed when the cash in the fund is at $15. Petty cash receipts indicate funds were disbursed for office supplies $94 and miscellaneous expense $87. Prepare journal entries for the establishment of the fund and the reimbursement.

10 ***BE7-15** Horton Corporation is preparing a bank reconciliation and has identified the following potential reconciling items. For each item, indicate if it is (1) added to balance per bank statement, (2) deducted from balance per bank statement, (3) added to balance per books, or (4) deducted from balance per books.

(a) Deposit in transit $5,500.
(b) Bank service charges $25.
(c) Interest credited to Horton's account $31.
(d) Outstanding checks $7,422.
(e) NSF check returned $377.

10 ***BE7-16** Use the information presented in BE7-15 for Horton Corporation. Prepare any entries necessary to make Horton's accounting records correct and complete.

11 ***BE7-17** Assume that Toni Braxton Company has recently fallen into financial difficulties. By reviewing all available evidence on December 31, 2014, one of Toni Braxton's creditors, the National American Bank, determined that Toni Braxton would pay back only 65% of the principal at maturity. As a result, the bank decided that the loan was impaired. If the loss is estimated to be $225,000, what entry(ies) should National American Bank make to record this loss?

EXERCISES

1 **E7-1 (Determining Cash Balance)** The controller for Clint Eastwood Co. is attempting to determine the amount of cash to be reported on its December 31, 2014, balance sheet. The following information is provided.

1. Commercial savings account of $600,000 and a commercial checking account balance of $900,000 are held at First National Bank of Yojimbo.

2. Money market fund account held at Volonte Co. (a mutual fund organization) permits Eastwood to write checks on this balance, $5,000,000.
3. Travel advances of $180,000 for executive travel for the first quarter of next year (employee to reimburse through salary reduction).
4. A separate cash fund in the amount of $1,500,000 is restricted for the retirement of long-term debt.
5. Petty cash fund of $1,000.
6. An I.O.U. from Marianne Koch, a company customer, in the amount of $190,000.
7. A bank overdraft of $110,000 has occurred at one of the banks the company uses to deposit its cash receipts. At the present time, the company has no deposits at this bank.
8. The company has two certificates of deposit, each totaling $500,000. These CDs have a maturity of 120 days.
9. Eastwood has received a check that is dated January 12, 2015, in the amount of $125,000.
10. Eastwood has agreed to maintain a cash balance of $500,000 at all times at First National Bank of Yojimbo to ensure future credit availability.
11. Eastwood has purchased $2,100,000 of commercial paper of Sergio Leone Co. which is due in 60 days.
12. Currency and coin on hand amounted to $7,700.

Instructions

(a) Compute the amount of cash to be reported on Eastwood Co.'s balance sheet at December 31, 2014.

(b) Indicate the proper reporting for items that are not reported as cash on the December 31, 2014, balance sheet.

1 **E7-2 (Determining Cash Balance)** Presented below are a number of independent situations.

Instructions

For each individual situation, determine the amount that should be reported as cash. If the item(s) is not reported as cash, explain the rationale.

1. Checking account balance $925,000; certificate of deposit $1,400,000; cash advance to subsidiary of $980,000; utility deposit paid to gas company $180.
2. Checking account balance $600,000; an overdraft in special checking account at same bank as normal checking account of $17,000; cash held in a bond sinking fund $200,000; petty cash fund $300; coins and currency on hand $1,350.
3. Checking account balance $590,000; postdated check from customer $11,000; cash restricted due to maintaining compensating balance requirement of $100,000; certified check from customer $9,800; postage stamps on hand $620.
4. Checking account balance at bank $37,000; money market balance at mutual fund (has checking privileges) $48,000; NSF check received from customer $800.
5. Checking account balance $700,000; cash restricted for future plant expansion $500,000; short-term Treasury bills $180,000; cash advance received from customer $900 (not included in checking account balance); cash advance of $7,000 to company executive, payable on demand; refundable deposit of $26,000 paid to federal government to guarantee performance on construction contract.

3 4 **E7-3 (Financial Statement Presentation of Receivables)** Jim Carrie Company shows a balance of $181,140 in the Accounts Receivable account on December 31, 2013. The balance consists of the following.

Installment accounts due in 2014	$23,000
Installment accounts due after 2014	34,000
Overpayments to vendors	2,640
Due from regular customers, of which $40,000 represents accounts pledged as security for a bank loan	79,000
Advances to employees	1,500
Advance to subsidiary company (due in 2015)	81,000

Instructions

Illustrate how the information above should be shown on the balance sheet of Jim Carrie Company on December 31, 2013.

3 4 **E7-4 (Determining Ending Accounts Receivable)** Your accounts receivable clerk, Mitra Adams, to whom you pay a salary of $1,500 per month, has just purchased a new Acura. You decided to test the accuracy of the accounts receivable balance of $82,000 as shown in the ledger.

The following information is available for your *first year* in business.

(1) Collections from customers	$198,000
(2) Merchandise purchased	320,000
(3) Ending merchandise inventory	90,000
(4) Goods are marked to sell at 40% above cost	

Instructions

Compute an estimate of the ending balance of accounts receivable from customers that should appear in the ledger and any apparent shortages. Assume that all sales are made on account.

4 **E7-5 (Recording Sales Gross and Net)** On June 3, Arnold Company sold to Chester Company merchandise having a sale price of $3,000 with terms of 2/10, n/60, f.o.b. shipping point. An invoice totaling $90, terms n/30, was received by Chester on June 8 from John Booth Transport Service for the freight cost. On June 12, the company received a check for the balance due from Chester Company.

Instructions

(a) Prepare journal entries on the Arnold Company books to record all the events noted above under each of the following bases.

(1) Sales and receivables are entered at gross selling price.

(2) Sales and receivables are entered at net of cash discounts.

(b) Prepare the journal entry under basis 2, assuming that Chester Company did not remit payment until July 29.

4 **E7-6 (Recording Sales Transactions)** Presented below is information from Perez Computers Incorporated.

July 1	Sold $20,000 of computers to Robertson Company with terms 3/15, n/60. Perez uses the gross method to record cash discounts.
10	Perez received payment from Robertson for the full amount owed from the July transactions.
17	Sold $200,000 in computers and peripherals to The Clark Store with terms of 2/10, n/30.
30	The Clark Store paid Perez for its purchase of July 17.

Instructions

Prepare the necessary journal entries for Perez Computers.

5 **E7-7 (Recording Bad Debts)** Duncan Company reports the following financial information before adjustments.

	Dr.	Cr.
Accounts Receivable	$100,000	
Allowance for Doubtful Accounts		$ 2,000
Sales Revenue (all on credit)		900,000
Sales Returns and Allowances	50,000	

Instructions

Prepare the journal entry to record Bad Debt Expense assuming Duncan Company estimates bad debts at (a) 1% of net sales and (b) 5% of accounts receivable.

5 **E7-8 (Recording Bad Debts)** At the end of 2014, Aramis Company has accounts receivable of $800,000 and an allowance for doubtful accounts of $40,000. On January 16, 2015, Aramis Company determined that its receivable from Ramirez Company of $6,000 will not be collected, and management authorized its write-off.

Instructions

(a) Prepare the journal entry for Aramis Company to write off the Ramirez receivable.

(b) What is the net realizable value of Aramis Company's accounts receivable before the write-off of the Ramirez receivable?

(c) What is the net realizable value of Aramis Company's accounts receivable after the write-off of the Ramirez receivable?

5 **E7-9 (Computing Bad Debts and Preparing Journal Entries)** The trial balance before adjustment of Reba McIntyre Inc. shows the following balances.

	Dr.	Cr.
Accounts Receivable	$90,000	
Allowance for Doubtful Accounts	1,750	
Sales Revenue (all on credit)		$680,000

Instructions

Give the entry for estimated bad debts assuming that the allowance is to provide for doubtful accounts on the basis of (a) 4% of gross accounts receivable and (b) 1% of net sales.

5 **E7-10 (Bad-Debt Reporting)** The chief accountant for Dickinson Corporation provides you with the following list of accounts receivable written off in the current year.

Date	Customer	Amount
March 31	E. L. Masters Company	$7,800
June 30	Stephen Crane Associates	6,700
September 30	Amy Lowell's Dress Shop	7,000
December 31	R. Frost, Inc.	9,830

Dickinson Corporation follows the policy of debiting Bad Debt Expense as accounts are written off. The chief accountant maintains that this procedure is appropriate for financial statement purposes because the Internal Revenue Service will not accept other methods for recognizing bad debts.

All of Dickinson Corporation's sales are on a 30-day credit basis. Sales for the current year total $2,200,000, and research has determined that bad debt losses approximate 2% of sales.

Instructions

(a) Do you agree or disagree with Dickinson's policy concerning recognition of bad debt expense? Why or why not?

(b) By what amount would net income differ if bad debt expense was computed using the percentage-of-sales approach?

5 **E7-11 (Bad Debts—Aging)** Danica Patrick, Inc. includes the following account among its trade receivables.

Hopkins Co.					
1/1	Balance forward	700	1/28	Cash (#1710)	1,100
1/20	Invoice #1710	1,100	4/2	Cash (#2116)	1,350
3/14	Invoice #2116	1,350	4/10	Cash (1/1 Balance)	155
4/12	Invoice #2412	1,710	4/30	Cash (#2412)	1,000
9/5	Invoice #3614	490	9/20	Cash (#3614 and part of #2412)	790
10/17	Invoice #4912	860			
11/18	Invoice #5681	2,000	10/31	Cash (#4912)	860
12/20	Invoice #6347	800	12/1	Cash (#5681)	1,250
			12/29	Cash (#6347)	800

Instructions

Age the balance and specify any items that apparently require particular attention at year-end.

4 5 8 **E7-12 (Journalizing Various Receivable Transactions)** Presented below is information related to James Garfield Corp.

July 1 James Garfield Corp. sold to Warren Harding Co. merchandise having a sales price of $8,000 with terms 2/10, net/60. Garfield records its sales and receivables net.

5 Accounts receivable of $9,000 (gross) are factored with Andrew Jackson Credit Corp. without recourse at a financing charge of 9%. Cash is received for the proceeds; collections are handled by the finance company. (These accounts were all past the discount period.)

9 Specific accounts receivable of $9,000 (gross) are pledged to Alf Landon Credit Corp. as security for a loan of $6,000 at a finance charge of 6% of the amount of the loan. The finance company will make the collections. (All the accounts receivable are past the discount period.)

Dec. 29 Warren Harding Co. notifies Garfield that it is bankrupt and will pay only 10% of its account. Give the entry to write off the uncollectible balance using the allowance method. (*Note*: First record the increase in the receivable on July 11 when the discount period passed.)

Instructions

Prepare all necessary entries in general journal form for Garfield Corp.

8 **E7-13 (Assigning Accounts Receivable)** On April 1, 2014, Rasheed Company assigns $400,000 of its accounts receivable to the Third National Bank as collateral for a $200,000 loan due July 1, 2014. The assignment agreement calls for Rasheed Company to continue to collect the receivables. Third National Bank assesses a finance charge of 2% of the accounts receivable, and interest on the loan is 10% (a realistic rate of interest for a note of this type).

Instructions

(a) Prepare the April 1, 2014, journal entry for Rasheed Company.

(b) Prepare the journal entry for Rasheed's collection of $350,000 of the accounts receivable during the period from April 1, 2014, through June 30, 2014.

(c) On July 1, 2014, Rasheed paid Third National all that was due from the loan it secured on April 1, 2014. Prepare the journal entry to record this payment.

5 8 **E7-14 (Journalizing Various Receivable Transactions)** The trial balance before adjustment for Phil Collins Company shows the following balances.

	Dr.	Cr.
Accounts Receivable	$82,000	
Allowance for Doubtful Accounts	2,120	
Sales Revenue		$430,000

Instructions

Using the data above, give the journal entries required to record each of the following cases. (Each situation is independent.)

1. To obtain additional cash, Collins factors without recourse $25,000 of accounts receivable with Stills Finance. The finance charge is 10% of the amount factored.
2. To obtain a 1-year loan of $55,000, Collins assigns $65,000 of specific receivable accounts to Crosby Financial. The finance charge is 8% of the loan; the cash is received and the accounts turned over to Crosby Financial.
3. The company wants to maintain the Allowance for Doubtful Accounts at 5% of gross accounts receivable.
4. The company wishes to increase the allowance account by 1½% of net sales.

8 **E7-15 (Transfer of Receivables with Recourse)** Ames Quartet Inc. factors receivables with a carrying amount of $200,000 to Joffrey Company for $160,000 on a with recourse basis.

Instructions

The recourse provision has a fair value of $1,000. This transaction should be recorded as a sale. Prepare the appropriate journal entry to record this transaction on the books of Ames Quartet Inc.

8 **E7-16 (Transfer of Receivables with Recourse)** Beyoncé Corporation factors $175,000 of accounts receivable with Kathleen Battle Financing, Inc. on a with recourse basis. Kathleen Battle Financing will collect the receivables. The receivables records are transferred to Kathleen Battle Financing on August 15, 2014. Kathleen Battle Financing assesses a finance charge of 2% of the amount of accounts receivable and also reserves an amount equal to 4% of accounts receivable to cover probable adjustments.

Instructions

(a) What conditions must be met for a transfer of receivables with recourse to be accounted for as a sale?

(b) Assume the conditions from part (a) are met. Prepare the journal entry on August 15, 2014, for Beyoncé to record the sale of receivables, assuming the recourse obligation has a fair value of $2,000.

8 **E7-17 (Transfer of Receivables without Recourse)** JFK Corp. factors $300,000 of accounts receivable with LBJ Finance Corporation on a without recourse basis on July 1, 2014. The receivables records are transferred to LBJ Finance, which will receive the collections. LBJ Finance assesses a finance charge of 1½% of the amount of accounts receivable and retains an amount equal to 4% of accounts receivable to cover sales discounts, returns, and allowances. The transaction is to be recorded as a sale.

Instructions

(a) Prepare the journal entry on July 1, 2014, for JFK Corp. to record the sale of receivables without recourse.

(b) Prepare the journal entry on July 1, 2014, for LBJ Finance Corporation to record the purchase of receivables without recourse.

6 **E7-18 (Note Transactions at Unrealistic Interest Rates)** On July 1, 2014, Agincourt Inc. made two sales.

1. It sold land having a fair value of $700,000 in exchange for a 4-year zero-interest-bearing promissory note in the face amount of $1,101,460. The land is carried on Agincourt's books at a cost of $590,000.
2. It rendered services in exchange for a 3%, 8-year promissory note having a face value of $400,000 (interest payable annually).

Agincourt Inc. recently had to pay 8% interest for money that it borrowed from British National Bank. The customers in these two transactions have credit ratings that require them to borrow money at 12% interest.

Instructions

Record the two journal entries that should be recorded by Agincourt Inc. for the sales transactions above that took place on July 1, 2014.

6 7 **E7-19 (Notes Receivable with Unrealistic Interest Rate)** On December 31, 2012, Ed Abbey Co. performed environmental consulting services for Hayduke Co. Hayduke was short of cash, and Abbey Co. agreed to

accept a $200,000 zero-interest-bearing note due December 31, 2014, as payment in full. Hayduke is somewhat of a credit risk and typically borrows funds at a rate of 10%. Abbey is much more creditworthy and has various lines of credit at 6%.

Instructions

(a) Prepare the journal entry to record the transaction of December 31, 2012, for the Ed Abbey Co.
(b) Assuming Ed Abbey Co.'s fiscal year-end is December 31, prepare the journal entry for December 31, 2013.
(c) Assuming Ed Abbey Co.'s fiscal year-end is December 31, prepare the journal entry for December 31, 2014.

9 **E7-20 (Analysis of Receivables)** Presented below is information for Jones Company.

1. Beginning-of-the-year Accounts Receivable balance was $15,000.
2. Net sales (all on account) for the year were $100,000. Jones does not offer cash discounts.
3. Collections on accounts receivable during the year were $70,000.

Instructions

(a) Prepare (summary) journal entries to record the items noted above.
(b) Compute Jones's accounts receivable turnover for the year. The company does not believe it will have any bad debts.
(c) Use the turnover ratio computed in (b) to analyze Jones's liquidity. The turnover ratio last year was 6.0.

8 **E7-21 (Transfer of Receivables)** Use the information for Jones Company as presented in E7-20. Jones is planning to factor some accounts receivable at the end of the year. Accounts totaling $25,000 will be transferred to Credit Factors, Inc. with recourse. Credit Factors will retain 5% of the balances for probable adjustments and assesses a finance charge of 4%. The fair value of the recourse obligation is $1,200.

Instructions

(a) Prepare the journal entry to record the sale of the receivables.
(b) Compute Jones's accounts receivable turnover for the year, assuming the receivables are sold, and discuss how factoring of receivables affects the turnover ratio.

10 ***E7-22 (Petty Cash)** Carolyn Keene, Inc. decided to establish a petty cash fund to help ensure internal control over its small cash expenditures. The following information is available for the month of April.

1. On April 1, it established a petty cash fund in the amount of $200.
2. A summary of the petty cash expenditures made by the petty cash custodian as of April 10 is as follows.

Delivery charges paid on merchandise purchased	$60.00
Supplies purchased and used	25.00
Postage expense	33.00
I.O.U. from employees	17.00
Miscellaneous expense	36.00

The petty cash fund was replenished on April 10. The balance in the fund was $27.

3. The petty cash fund balance was increased $100 to $300 on April 20.

Instructions

Prepare the journal entries to record transactions related to petty cash for the month of April.

10 ***E7-23 (Petty Cash)** The petty cash fund of Fonzarelli's Auto Repair Service, a sole proprietorship, contains the following.

1. Coins and currency		$ 15.20
2. Postage stamps		2.90
3. An I.O.U. from Richie Cunningham, an employee, for cash advance		40.00
4. Check payable to Fonzarelli's Auto Repair from Pottsie Weber, an employee, marked NSF		34.00
5. Vouchers for the following:		
Stamps	$ 20.00	
Two Rose Bowl tickets for Nick Fonzarelli	170.00	
Printer cartridge	14.35	204.35
		$296.45

The general ledger account Petty Cash has a balance of $300.

Instructions

Prepare the journal entry to record the reimbursement of the petty cash fund.

10 *E7-24 **(Bank Reconciliation and Adjusting Entries)** Angela Lansbury Company deposits all receipts and makes all payments by check. The following information is available from the cash records.

June 30 Bank Reconciliation

Balance per bank	$ 7,000
Add: Deposits in transit	1,540
Deduct: Outstanding checks	(2,000)
Balance per books	$ 6,540

Month of July Results

	Per Bank	Per Books
Balance July 31	$8,650	$9,250
July deposits	5,000	5,810
July checks	4,000	3,100
July note collected (not included in July deposits)	1,000	—
July bank service charge	15	—
July NSF check from a customer, returned by the bank (recorded by bank as a charge)	335	—

Instructions

(a) Prepare a bank reconciliation going from balance per bank and balance per book to correct cash balance.

(b) Prepare the general journal entry or entries to correct the Cash account.

10 *E7-25 **(Bank Reconciliation and Adjusting Entries)** Logan Bruno Company has just received the August 31, 2014, bank statement, which is summarized below.

County National Bank	Disbursements	Receipts	Balance
Balance, August 1			$ 9,369
Deposits during August		$32,200	41,569
Note collected for depositor, including $40 interest		1,040	42,609
Checks cleared during August	$34,500		8,109
Bank service charges	20		8,089
Balance, August 31			8,089

The general ledger Cash account contained the following entries for the month of August.

Cash

Balance, August 1	10,050	Disbursements in August	34,903
Receipts during August	35,000		

Deposits in transit at August 31 are $3,800, and checks outstanding at August 31 total $1,050. Cash on hand at August 31 is $310. The bookkeeper improperly entered one check in the books at $146.50 which was written for $164.50 for supplies (expense); it cleared the bank during the month of August.

Instructions

(a) Prepare a bank reconciliation dated August 31, 2014, proceeding to a correct balance.

(b) Prepare any entries necessary to make the books correct and complete.

(c) What amount of cash should be reported in the August 31 balance sheet?

11 *E7-26 **(Impairments)** On December 31, 2014, Iva Majoli Company borrowed $62,092 from Paris Bank, signing a 5-year, $100,000 zero-interest-bearing note. The note was issued to yield 10% interest. Unfortunately, during 2016, Majoli began to experience financial difficulty. As a result, at December 31, 2016, Paris Bank determined that it was probable that it would receive back only $75,000 at maturity. The market rate of interest on loans of this nature is now 11%.

Instructions

(a) Prepare the entry to record the issuance of the loan by Paris Bank on December 31, 2014.

(b) Prepare the entry, if any, to record the impairment of the loan on December 31, 2016, by Paris Bank.

11 ***E7-27 (Impairments)** On December 31, 2014, Conchita Martinez Company signed a $1,000,000 note to Sauk City Bank. The market interest rate at that time was 12%. The stated interest rate on the note was 10%, payable annually. The note matures in 5 years. Unfortunately, because of lower sales, Conchita Martinez's financial situation worsened. On December 31, 2016, Sauk City Bank determined that it was probable that the company would pay back only $600,000 of the principal at maturity. However, it was considered likely that interest would continue to be paid, based on the $1,000,000 loan.

Instructions

(a) Determine the amount of cash Conchita Martinez received from the loan on December 31, 2014.
(b) Prepare a note amortization schedule for Sauk City Bank up to December 31, 2016.
(c) Determine the loss on impairment that Sauk City Bank should recognize on December 31, 2016.

EXERCISES SET B

See the book's companion website, at **www.wiley.com/college/kieso**, for an additional set of exercises.

PROBLEMS

2 **P7-1 (Determine Proper Cash Balance)** Francis Equipment Co. closes its books regularly on December 31, but at the end of 2014 it held its cash book open so that a more favorable balance sheet could be prepared for credit purposes. Cash receipts and disbursements for the first 10 days of January were recorded as December transactions. The information is given below.

1. January cash receipts recorded in the December cash book totaled $45,640, of which $28,000 represents cash sales, and $17,640 represents collections on account for which cash discounts of $360 were given.
2. January cash disbursements recorded in the December check register liquidated accounts payable of $22,450 on which discounts of $250 were taken.
3. The ledger has not been closed for 2014.
4. The amount shown as inventory was determined by physical count on December 31, 2014.

The company uses the periodic method of inventory.

Instructions

(a) Prepare any entries you consider necessary to correct Francis's accounts at December 31.
(b) To what extent was Francis Equipment Co. able to show a more favorable balance sheet at December 31 by holding its cash book open? (Compute working capital and the current ratio.) Assume that the balance sheet that was prepared by the company showed the following amounts:

	Dr.	Cr.
Cash	$39,000	
Accounts receivable	42,000	
Inventory	67,000	
Accounts payable		$45,000
Other current liabilities		14,200

5 **P7-2 (Bad-Debt Reporting)** The following are a series of unrelated situations.

1. Halen Company's unadjusted trial balance at December 31, 2014, included the following accounts.

	Debit	Credit
Allowance for doubtful accounts	$4,000	
Net sales		$1,200,000

Halen Company estimates its bad debt expense to be 1½% of net sales. Determine its bad debt expense for 2014.

2. An analysis and aging of Stuart Corp. accounts receivable at December 31, 2014, disclosed the following.

Amounts estimated to be uncollectible	$ 180,000
Accounts receivable	1,750,000
Allowance for doubtful accounts (per books)	125,000

What is the net realizable value of Stuart's receivables at December 31, 2014?

3. Shore Co. provides for doubtful accounts based on 3% of credit sales. The following data are available for 2014.

Credit sales during 2014	$2,400,000
Allowance for doubtful accounts 1/1/14	17,000
Collection of accounts written off in prior years (customer credit was reestablished)	8,000
Customer accounts written off as uncollectible during 2014	30,000

What is the balance in Allowance for Doubtful Accounts at December 31, 2014?

4. At the end of its first year of operations, December 31, 2014, Darden Inc. reported the following information.

Accounts receivable, net of allowance for doubtful accounts	$950,000
Customer accounts written off as uncollectible during 2014	24,000
Bad debt expense for 2014	84,000

What should be the balance in accounts receivable at December 31, 2014, before subtracting the allowance for doubtful accounts?

5. The following accounts were taken from Bullock Inc.'s trial balance at December 31, 2014.

	Debit	Credit
Net credit sales		$750,000
Allowance for doubtful accounts	$ 14,000	
Accounts receivable	310,000	

If doubtful accounts are 3% of accounts receivable, determine the bad debt expense to be reported for 2014.

Instructions

Answer the questions relating to each of the five independent situations as requested.

5 **P7-3 (Bad-Debt Reporting—Aging)** Manilow Corporation operates in an industry that has a high rate of bad debts. Before any year-end adjustments, the balance in Manilow's Accounts Receivable account was $555,000 and Allowance for Doubtful Accounts had a credit balance of $40,000. The year-end balance reported in the balance sheet for Allowance for Doubtful Accounts will be based on the aging schedule shown below.

XLS

Days Account Outstanding	Amount	Probability of Collection
Less than 16 days	$300,000	.98
Between 16 and 30 days	100,000	.90
Between 31 and 45 days	80,000	.85
Between 46 and 60 days	40,000	.80
Between 61 and 75 days	20,000	.55
Over 75 days	15,000	.00

Instructions

(a) What is the appropriate balance for Allowance for Doubtful Accounts at year-end?

(b) Show how accounts receivable would be presented on the balance sheet.

(c) What is the dollar effect of the year-end bad debt adjustment on the before-tax income?

(CMA adapted)

5 **P7-4 (Bad-Debt Reporting)** From inception of operations to December 31, 2014, Fortner Corporation provided for uncollectible accounts receivable under the allowance method. Provisions were made monthly at 2% of credit sales, bad debts written off were charged to the allowance account; recoveries of bad debts previously written off were credited to the allowance account, and no year-end adjustments to the allowance account were made. Fortner's usual credit terms are net 30 days.

The balance in Allowance for Doubtful Accounts was $130,000 at January 1, 2014. During 2014, credit sales totaled $9,000,000, interim provisions for doubtful accounts were made at 2% of credit sales, $90,000 of bad debts were written off, and recoveries of accounts previously written off amounted to $15,000. Fortner installed a computer system in November 2014, and an aging of accounts receivable was prepared for the first time as of December 31, 2014. A summary of the aging is as follows.

Classification by Month of Sale	Balance in Each Category	Estimated % Uncollectible
November–December 2014	$1,080,000	2%
July–October	650,000	10%
January–June	420,000	25%
Prior to 1/1/14	150,000	80%
	$2,300,000	

Based on the review of collectibility of the account balances in the "prior to 1/1/14" aging category, additional receivables totaling $60,000 were written off as of December 31, 2014. The 80% uncollectible estimate applies to the remaining $90,000 in the category. Effective with the year ended December 31, 2014, Fortner adopted a different method for estimating the allowance for doubtful accounts at the amount indicated by the year-end aging analysis of accounts receivable.

Instructions

(a) Prepare a schedule analyzing the changes in Allowance for Doubtful Accounts for the year ended December 31, 2014. Show supporting computations in good form. (*Hint:* In computing the 12/31/14 allowance, subtract the $60,000 write-off.)

(b) Prepare the journal entry for the year-end adjustment to Allowance for Doubtful Accounts balance as of December 31, 2014.

(AICPA adapted)

5 **P7-5 (Bad-Debt Reporting)** Presented below is information related to the Accounts Receivable accounts of Gulistan Inc. during the current year 2014.

1. An aging schedule of the accounts receivable as of December 31, 2014, is as follows.

Age	Net Debit Balance	% to Be Applied after Correction Is Made
Under 60 days	$172,342	1%
60–90 days	136,490	3%
91–120 days	39,924*	6%
Over 120 days	23,644	$3,700 definitely uncollectible; estimated remainder uncollectible is 25%
	$372,400	

*The $3,240 write-off of receivables is related to the 91-to-120 day category.

2. The Accounts Receivable control account has a debit balance of $372,400 on December 31, 2014.
3. Two entries were made in the Bad Debt Expense account during the year: (1) a debit on December 31 for the amount credited to Allowance for Doubtful Accounts, and (2) a credit for $3,240 on November 3, 2014, and a debit to Allowance for Doubtful Accounts because of a bankruptcy.
4. Allowance for Doubtful Accounts is as follows for 2014.

Allowance for Doubtful Accounts

Nov. 3	Uncollectible accounts written off	3,240	Jan. 1	Beginning balance	8,750
			Dec. 31	5% of $372,400	18,620

5. A credit balance exists in Accounts Receivable (60–90 days) of $4,840, which represents an advance on a sales contract.

Instructions

Assuming that the books have not been closed for 2014, make the necessary correcting entries.

3 4 5 **P7-6 (Journalize Various Accounts Receivable Transactions)** The balance sheet of Starsky Company at December 31, 2013, includes the following.

Notes receivable	$ 36,000	
Accounts receivable	182,100	
Less: Allowance for doubtful accounts	17,300	$200,800

Transactions in 2014 include the following.

1. Accounts receivable of $138,000 were collected including accounts of $60,000 on which 2% sales discounts were allowed.
2. $5,300 was received in payment of an account which was written off the books as worthless in 2013.
3. Customer accounts of $17,500 were written off during the year.
4. At year-end, Allowance for Doubtful Accounts was estimated to need a balance of $20,000. This estimate is based on an analysis of aged accounts receivable.

Instructions
Prepare all journal entries necessary to reflect the transactions above.

8 **P7-7 (Assigned Accounts Receivable—Journal Entries)** Salen Company finances some of its current operations by assigning accounts receivable to a finance company. On July 1, 2014, it assigned, under guarantee, specific accounts amounting to $150,000. The finance company advanced to Salen 80% of the accounts assigned (20% of the total to be withheld until the finance company has made its full recovery), less a finance charge of ½% of the total accounts assigned.

On July 31, Salen Company received a statement that the finance company had collected $80,000 of these accounts and had made an additional charge of ½% of the total accounts outstanding as of July 31. This charge is to be deducted at the time of the first remittance due Salen Company from the finance company. (*Hint:* Make entries at this time.) On August 31, 2014, Salen Company received a second statement from the finance company, together with a check for the amount due. The statement indicated that the finance company had collected an additional $50,000 and had made a further charge of ½% of the balance outstanding as of August 31.

Instructions
Make all entries on the books of Salen Company that are involved in the transactions above.

(AICPA adapted)

6 **P7-8 (Notes Receivable with Realistic Interest Rate)** On October 1, 2014, Arden Farm Equipment Company sold a pecan-harvesting machine to Valco Brothers Farm, Inc. In lieu of a cash payment Valco Brothers Farm gave Arden a 2-year, $120,000, 8% note (a realistic rate of interest for a note of this type). The note required interest to be paid annually on October 1. Arden's financial statements are prepared on a calendar-year basis.

Instructions
Assuming Valco Brothers Farm fulfills all the terms of the note, prepare the necessary journal entries for Arden Farm Equipment Company for the entire term of the note.

6 **P7-9 (Notes Receivable Journal Entries)** On December 31, 2014, Oakbrook Inc. rendered services to Beghun Corporation at an agreed price of $102,049, accepting $40,000 down and agreeing to accept the balance in four equal installments of $20,000 receivable each December 31. An assumed interest rate of 11% is imputed.

Instructions
Prepare the entries that would be recorded by Oakbrook Inc. for the sale and for the receipts and interest on the following dates. (Assume that the effective-interest method is used for amortization purposes.)

(a) December 31, 2014.
(b) December 31, 2015.
(c) December 31, 2016.
(d) December 31, 2017.
(e) December 31, 2018.

6 **P7-10 (Comprehensive Receivables Problem)** Braddock Inc. had the following long-term receivable account balances at December 31, 2013.

Note receivable from sale of division	$1,500,000
Note receivable from officer	400,000

Transactions during 2014 and other information relating to Braddock's long-term receivables were as follows.

1. The $1,500,000 note receivable is dated May 1, 2013, bears interest at 9%, and represents the balance of the consideration received from the sale of Braddock's electronics division to New York Company. Principal payments of $500,000 plus appropriate interest are due on May 1, 2014, 2015, and 2016. The first principal and interest payment was made on May 1, 2014. Collection of the note installments is reasonably assured.
2. The $400,000 note receivable is dated December 31, 2013, bears interest at 8%, and is due on December 31, 2016. The note is due from Sean May, president of Braddock Inc. and is collateralized by 10,000 shares of Braddock's common stock. Interest is payable annually on December 31, and all interest payments were paid on their due dates through December 31, 2014. The quoted market price of Braddock's common stock was $45 per share on December 31, 2014.

3. On April 1, 2014, Braddock sold a patent to Pennsylvania Company in exchange for a $100,000 zero-interest-bearing note due on April 1, 2016. There was no established exchange price for the patent, and the note had no ready market. The prevailing rate of interest for a note of this type at April 1, 2014, was 12%. The present value of $1 for two periods at 12% is 0.797 (use this factor). The patent had a carrying value of $40,000 at January 1, 2014, and the amortization for the year ended December 31, 2014, would have been $8,000. The collection of the note receivable from Pennsylvania is reasonably assured.
4. On July 1, 2014, Braddock sold a parcel of land to Splinter Company for $200,000 under an installment sale contract. Splinter made a $60,000 cash down payment on July 1, 2014, and signed a 4-year 11% note for the $140,000 balance. The equal annual payments of principal and interest on the note will be $45,125 payable on July 1, 2015, through July 1, 2018. The land could have been sold at an established cash price of $200,000. The cost of the land to Braddock was $150,000. Circumstances are such that the collection of the installments on the note is reasonably assured.

Instructions

(a) Prepare the long-term receivables section of Braddock's balance sheet at December 31, 2014.

(b) Prepare a schedule showing the current portion of the long-term receivables and accrued interest receivable that would appear in Braddock's balance sheet at December 31, 2014.

(c) Prepare a schedule showing interest revenue from the long-term receivables that would appear on Braddock's income statement for the year ended December 31, 2014.

8 9 **P7-11 (Income Effects of Receivables Transactions)** Sandburg Company requires additional cash for its business. Sandburg has decided to use its accounts receivable to raise the additional cash and has asked you to determine the income statement effects of the following contemplated transactions.

1. On July 1, 2014, Sandburg assigned $400,000 of accounts receivable to Keller Finance Company. Sandburg received an advance from Keller of 80% of the assigned accounts receivable less a commission of 3% on the advance. Prior to December 31, 2014, Sandburg collected $220,000 on the assigned accounts receivable, and remitted $232,720 to Keller, $12,720 of which represented interest on the advance from Keller.
2. On December 1, 2014, Sandburg sold $300,000 of net accounts receivable to Wunsch Company for $270,000. The receivables were sold outright on a without recourse basis.
3. On December 31, 2014, an advance of $120,000 was received from First Bank by pledging $160,000 of Sandburg's accounts receivable. Sandburg's first payment to First Bank is due on January 30, 2015.

Instructions

Prepare a schedule showing the income statement effects for the year ended December 31, 2014, as a result of the above facts.

10 ***P7-12 (Petty Cash, Bank Reconciliation)** Bill Jovi is reviewing the cash accounting for Nottleman, Inc., a local mailing service. Jovi's review will focus on the petty cash account and the bank reconciliation for the month ended May 31, 2014. He has collected the following information from Nottleman's bookkeeper for this task.

Petty Cash

1. The petty cash fund was established on May 10, 2014, in the amount of $250.
2. Expenditures from the fund by the custodian as of May 31, 2014, were evidenced by approved receipts for the following.

Postage expense	$33.00
Mailing labels and other supplies	65.00
I.O.U. from employees	30.00
Shipping charges (to customer)	57.45
Newspaper advertising	22.80
Miscellaneous expense	15.35

On May 31, 2014, the petty cash fund was replenished and increased to $300; currency and coin in the fund at that time totaled $26.40.

Bank Reconciliation

THIRD NATIONAL BANK
BANK STATEMENT

	Disbursements	Receipts	Balance
Balance, May 1, 2014			$8,769
Deposits		$28,000	
Note payment direct from customer (interest of $30)		930	
Checks cleared during May	$31,150		
Bank service charges	27		
Balance, May 31, 2014			6,522

Nottleman's Cash Account	
Balance, May 1, 2014	$ 8,850
Deposits during May 2014	31,000
Checks written during May 2014	(31,835)

Deposits in transit are determined to be $3,000, and checks outstanding at May 31 total $850. Cash on hand (besides petty cash) at May 31, 2014, is $246.

Instructions

(a) Prepare the journal entries to record the transactions related to the petty cash fund for May.

(b) Prepare a bank reconciliation dated May 31, 2014, proceeding to a correct cash balance, and prepare the journal entries necessary to make the books correct and complete.

(c) What amount of cash should be reported in the May 31, 2014, balance sheet?

10 ***P7-13 (Bank Reconciliation and Adjusting Entries)** The cash account of Aguilar Co. showed a ledger balance of $3,969.85 on June 30, 2014. The bank statement as of that date showed a balance of $4,150. Upon comparing the statement with the cash records, the following facts were determined.

1. There were bank service charges for June of $25.
2. A bank memo stated that Bao Dai's note for $1,200 and interest of $36 had been collected on June 29, and the bank had made a charge of $5.50 on the collection. (No entry had been made on Aguilar's books when Bao Dai's note was sent to the bank for collection.)
3. Receipts for June 30 for $3,390 were not deposited until July 2.
4. Checks outstanding on June 30 totaled $2,136.05.
5. The bank had charged the Aguilar Co.'s account for a customer's uncollectible check amounting to $253.20 on June 29.
6. A customer's check for $90 had been entered as $60 in the cash receipts journal by Aguilar on June 15.
7. Check no. 742 in the amount of $491 had been entered in the cash journal as $419, and check no. 747 in the amount of $58.20 had been entered as $582. Both checks had been issued to pay for purchases of equipment.

Instructions

(a) Prepare a bank reconciliation dated June 30, 2014, proceeding to a correct cash balance.

(b) Prepare any entries necessary to make the books correct and complete.

10 ***P7-14 (Bank Reconciliation and Adjusting Entries)** Presented below is information related to Haselhof Inc.

Balance per books at October 31, $41,847.85; receipts $173,523.91; disbursements $164,893.54. Balance per bank statement November 30, $56,274.20.

The following checks were outstanding at November 30.

1224	$1,635.29
1230	2,468.30
1232	2,125.15
1233	482.17

Included with the November bank statement and not recorded by the company were a bank debit memo for $27.40 covering bank charges for the month, a debit memo for $372.13 for a customer's check returned and marked NSF, and a credit memo for $1,400 representing bond interest collected by the bank in the name of Haselhof Inc. Cash on hand at November 30 recorded and awaiting deposit amounted to $1,915.40.

Instructions

(a) Prepare a bank reconciliation (to the correct balance) at November 30, for Haselhof Inc. from the information above.

(b) Prepare any journal entries required to adjust the cash account at November 30.

11 ***P7-15 (Loan Impairment Entries)** On January 1, 2014, Botosan Company issued a $1,200,000, 5-year, zero-interest-bearing note to National Organization Bank. The note was issued to yield 8% annual interest. Unfortunately, during 2015 Botosan fell into financial trouble due to increased competition. After reviewing all available evidence on December 31, 2015, National Organization Bank decided that the loan was impaired. Botosan will probably pay back only $800,000 of the principal at maturity.

Instructions

(a) Prepare journal entries for both Botosan Company and National Organization Bank to record the issuance of the note on January 1, 2014. (Round to the nearest $10.)

(b) Assuming that both Botosan Company and National Organization Bank use the effective-interest method to amortize the discount, prepare the amortization schedule for the note.

(c) Under what circumstances can National Organization Bank consider Botosan's note to be impaired?

(d) Compute the loss National Organization Bank will suffer from Botosan's financial distress on December 31, 2015. What journal entries should be made to record this loss?

PROBLEMS SET B

See the book's companion website, at **www.wiley.com/college/kieso**, for an additional set of problems.

CONCEPTS FOR ANALYSIS

CA7-1 (Bad-Debt Accounting) Simms Company has significant amounts of trade accounts receivable. Simms uses the allowance method to estimate bad debts instead of the direct write-off method. During the year, some specific accounts were written off as uncollectible, and some that were previously written off as uncollectible were collected.

Instructions

(a) What are the deficiencies of the direct write-off method?

(b) What are the two basic allowance methods used to estimate bad debts, and what is the theoretical justification for each?

(c) How should Simms account for the collection of the specific accounts previously written off as uncollectible?

CA7-2 (Various Receivable Accounting Issues) Kimmel Company uses the net method of accounting for sales discounts. Kimmel also offers trade discounts to various groups of buyers.

On August 1, 2014, Kimmel sold some accounts receivable on a without recourse basis. Kimmel incurred a finance charge.

Kimmel also has some notes receivable bearing an appropriate rate of interest. The principal and total interest are due at maturity. The notes were received on October 1, 2014, and mature on September 30, 2016. Kimmel's operating cycle is less than one year.

Instructions

(a) **(1)** Using the net method, how should Kimmel account for the sales discounts at the date of sale? What is the rationale for the amount recorded as sales under the net method?

(2) Using the net method, what is the effect on Kimmel's sales revenues and net income when customers do not take the sales discounts?

(b) What is the effect of trade discounts on sales revenues and accounts receivable? Why?

(c) How should Kimmel account for the accounts receivable factored on August 1, 2014? Why?

(d) How should Kimmel account for the note receivable and the related interest on December 31, 2014? Why?

CA7-3 (Bad-Debt Reporting Issues) Clark Pierce conducts a wholesale merchandising business that sells approximately 5,000 items per month with a total monthly average sales value of $250,000. Its annual bad debt rate has been approximately 1½% of sales. In recent discussions with his bookkeeper, Mr. Pierce has become confused by all the alternatives apparently available in handling the Allowance for Doubtful Accounts balance. The following information has been presented to Pierce.

1. An allowance can be set up (a) on the basis of a percentage of sales or (b) on the basis of a valuation of all past due or otherwise questionable accounts receivable. Those considered uncollectible can be charged to such allowance at the close of the accounting period, or specific items can be charged off directly against (1) Gross Sales or to (2) Bad Debt Expense in the year in which they are determined to be uncollectible.
2. Collection agency and legal fees, and so on, incurred in connection with the attempted recovery of bad debts can be charged to (a) Bad Debt Expense, (b) Allowance for Doubtful Accounts, (c) Legal Expense, or (d) Administrative Expense.
3. Debts previously written off in whole or in part but currently recovered can be credited to (a) Other Revenue, (b) Bad Debt Expense, or (c) Allowance for Doubtful Accounts.

Instructions

Which of the foregoing methods would you recommend to Mr. Pierce in regard to (1) allowances and charge-offs, (2) collection expenses, and (3) recoveries? State briefly and clearly the reasons supporting your recommendations.

CA7-4 (Basic Note and Accounts Receivable Transactions)

Part 1: On July 1, 2014, Wallace Company, a calendar-year company, sold special-order merchandise on credit and received in return an interest-bearing note receivable from the customer. Wallace Company will receive interest at the prevailing rate for a note of this type. Both the principal and interest are due in one lump sum on June 30, 2015.

Instructions

When should Wallace Company report interest revenue from the note receivable? Discuss the rationale for your answer.

Part 2: On December 31, 2014, Wallace Company had significant amounts of accounts receivable as a result of credit sales to its customers. Wallace uses the allowance method based on credit sales to estimate bad debts. Past experience indicates that 2% of credit sales normally will not be collected. This pattern is expected to continue.

Instructions

(a) Discuss the rationale for using the allowance method based on credit sales to estimate bad debts. Contrast this method with the allowance method based on the balance in the trade receivables accounts.

(b) How should Wallace Company report the allowance for doubtful accounts on its balance sheet at December 31, 2014? Also, describe the alternatives, if any, for presentation of bad debt expense in Wallace Company's 2014 income statement.

(AICPA adapted)

CA7-5 (Sale of Notes Receivable) Corrs Wholesalers Co. sells industrial equipment for a standard 3-year note receivable. Revenue is recognized at time of sale. Each note is secured by a lien on the equipment and has a face amount equal to the equipment's list price. Each note's stated interest rate is below the customer's market rate at date of sale. All notes are to be collected in three equal annual installments beginning one year after sale. Some of the notes are subsequently sold to a bank with recourse, some are subsequently sold without recourse, and some are retained by Corrs. At year end, Corrs evaluates all outstanding notes receivable and provides for estimated losses arising from defaults.

Instructions

(a) What is the appropriate valuation basis for Corrs's notes receivable at the date it sells equipment?

(b) How should Corrs account for the sale, without recourse, of a February 1, 2014, note receivable sold on May 1, 2014? Why is it appropriate to account for it in this way?

(c) At December 31, 2014, how should Corrs measure and account for the impact of estimated losses resulting from notes receivable that it

(1) Retained and did **not** sell?

(2) Sold to bank with recourse?

(AICPA adapted)

CA7-6 (Zero-Interest-Bearing Note Receivable) On September 30, 2013, Rolen Machinery Co. sold a machine and accepted the customer's zero-interest-bearing note. Rolen normally makes sales on a cash basis. Since the machine was unique, its sales price was not determinable using Rolen's normal pricing practices.

After receiving the first of two equal annual installments on September 30, 2014, Rolen immediately sold the note with recourse. On October 9, 2015, Rolen received notice that the note was dishonored, and it paid all amounts due. At all times prior to default, the note was reasonably expected to be paid in full.

Instructions

(a) **(1)** How should Rolen determine the sales price of the machine?

(2) How should Rolen report the effects of the zero-interest-bearing note on its income statement for the year ended December 31, 2013? Why is this accounting presentation appropriate?

(b) What are the effects of the sale of the note receivable with recourse on Rolen's income statement for the year ended December 31, 2014, and its balance sheet at December 31, 2014?

(c) How should Rolen account for the effects of the note being dishonored?

CA7-7 (Reporting of Notes Receivable, Interest, and Sale of Receivables) On July 1, 2014, Moresan Company sold special-order merchandise on credit and received in return an interest-bearing note receivable from the customer. Moresan will receive interest at the prevailing rate for a note of this type. Both the principal and interest are due in one lump sum on June 30, 2015.

On September 1, 2014, Moresan sold special-order merchandise on credit and received in return a zero-interest-bearing note receivable from the customer. The prevailing rate of interest for a note of this type is determinable. The note receivable is due in one lump sum on August 31, 2016.

Moresan also has significant amounts of trade accounts receivable as a result of credit sales to its customers. On October 1, 2014, some trade accounts receivable were assigned to Indigo Finance Company on a non-notification (Moresan handles collections) basis for an advance of 75% of their amount at an interest charge of 8% on the balance outstanding.

On November 1, 2014, other trade accounts receivable were sold on a without recourse basis. The factor withheld 5% of the trade accounts receivable factored as protection against sales returns and allowances and charged a finance charge of 3%.

Instructions

(a) How should Moresan determine the interest revenue for 2014 on the:
- **(1)** Interest-bearing note receivable? Why?
- **(2)** Zero-interest-bearing note receivable? Why?

(b) How should Moresan report the interest-bearing note receivable and the zero-interest-bearing note receivable on its balance sheet at December 31, 2014?

(c) How should Moresan account for subsequent collections on the trade accounts receivable assigned on October 1, 2014, and the payments to Indigo Finance? Why?

(d) How should Moresan account for the trade accounts receivable factored on November 1, 2014? Why?

(AICPA adapted)

CA7-8 (Accounting for Zero-Interest-Bearing Note) Soon after beginning the year-end audit work on March 10 at Engone Company, the auditor has the following conversation with the controller.

CONTROLLER: The year ended March 31st should be our most profitable in history and, as a consequence, the board of directors has just awarded the officers generous bonuses.

AUDITOR: I thought profits were down this year in the industry, according to your latest interim report.

CONTROLLER: Well, they were down, but 10 days ago we closed a deal that will give us a substantial increase for the year.

AUDITOR: Oh, what was it?

CONTROLLER: Well, you remember a few years ago our former president bought stock in Henderson Enterprises because he had those grandiose ideas about becoming a conglomerate. For 6 years we have not been able to sell this stock, which cost us $3,000,000 and has not paid a nickel in dividends. Thursday we sold this stock to Bimini Inc. for $4,000,000. So, we will have a gain of $700,000 ($1,000,000 pretax) which will increase our net income for the year to $4,000,000, compared with last year's $3,800,000. As far as I know, we'll be the only company in the industry to register an increase in net income this year. That should help the market value of the stock!

AUDITOR: Do you expect to receive the $4,000,000 in cash by March 31st, your fiscal year-end?

CONTROLLER: No. Although Bimini Inc. is an excellent company, they are a little tight for cash because of their rapid growth. Consequently, they are going to give us a $4,000,000 zero-interest-bearing note with payments of $400,000 per year for the next 10 years. The first payment is due on March 31 of next year.

AUDITOR: Why is the note zero-interest-bearing?

CONTROLLER: Because that's what everybody agreed to. Since we don't have any interest-bearing debt, the funds invested in the note do not cost us anything and besides, we were not getting any dividends on the Henderson Enterprises stock.

Instructions

Do you agree with the way the controller has accounted for the transaction? If not, how should the transaction be accounted for?

CA7-9 (Receivables Management) As the manager of the accounts receivable department for Beavis Leather Goods, Ltd., you recently noticed that Kelly Collins, your accounts receivable clerk who is paid $1,200 per month, has been wearing unusually tasteful and expensive clothing. (This is Beavis's first year in business.) This morning, Collins drove up to work in a brand new Lexus.

Naturally suspicious by nature, you decide to test the accuracy of the accounts receivable balance of $192,000 as shown in the ledger. The following information is available for your first year (precisely 9 months ended September 30, 2014) in business.

(1) Collections from customers	$188,000
(2) Merchandise purchased	360,000
(3) Ending merchandise inventory	90,000
(4) Goods are marked to sell at 40% above cost.	

Instructions

Assuming all sales were made on account, compute the ending accounts receivable balance that should appear in the ledger, noting any apparent shortage. Then, draft a memo dated October 3, 2014, to Mark Price, the branch manager, explaining the facts in this situation. Remember that this problem is serious, and you do not want to make hasty accusations.

CA7-10 (Bad-Debt Reporting) Marvin Company is a subsidiary of Hughes Corp. The controller believes that the yearly allowance for doubtful accounts for Marvin should be 2% of net credit sales. Given the recession and the high interest rate environment, the president, nervous that the parent company might expect the subsidiary to sustain its 10% growth rate, suggests that the controller increase the allowance for doubtful accounts to 3% yearly. The president thinks that the lower net income, which reflects a 6% growth rate, will be a more sustainable rate for Marvin Company.

Instructions

(a) In a recessionary environment with tight credit and high interest rates:
   (1) Identify steps Marvin Company might consider to improve the accounts receivable situation.
   (2) Then evaluate each step identified in terms of the risks and costs involved.

(b) Should the controller be concerned with Marvin Company's growth rate in estimating the allowance? Explain your answer.

(c) Does the president's request pose an ethical dilemma for the controller? Give your reasons.

USING YOUR JUDGMENT

FINANCIAL REPORTING

Financial Reporting Problem

P&G

The Procter & Gamble Company (P&G)

The financial statements of P&G are presented in Appendix 5B. The company's complete annual report, including the notes to the financial statements, can be accessed at the book's companion website, **www.wiley.com/college/kieso**.

Instructions

Refer to P&G's financial statements and the accompanying notes to answer the following questions.

(a) What criteria does P&G use to classify "Cash and cash equivalents" as reported in its balance sheet?

(b) As of June 30, 2011, what balances did P&G have in cash and cash equivalents? What were the major uses of cash during the year?

(c) P&G reports no allowance for doubtful accounts, suggesting that bad debt expense is not material for this company. Is it reasonable that a company like P&G would not have material bad debt expense? Explain.

Comparative Analysis Case

The Coca-Cola Company and PepsiCo, Inc.

Instructions

Go to the book's companion website and use the information found there to answer the following questions related to The Coca-Cola Company and PepsiCo, Inc.

(a) What were the cash and cash equivalents reported by Coca-Cola and PepsiCo at the end of 2011? What does each company classify as cash equivalents?

(b) What were the accounts receivable (net) for Coca-Cola and PepsiCo at the end of 2011? Which company reports the greater allowance for doubtful accounts (amount and percentage of gross receivable) at the end of 2011?

(c) Assuming that all "net operating revenues" (Coca-Cola) and all "net sales" (PepsiCo) were net *credit* sales, compute the accounts receivable turnover for 2011 for Coca-Cola and PepsiCo; also compute the days outstanding for receivables. What is your evaluation of the difference?

Financial Statement Analysis Cases

Case 1 Occidental Petroleum Corporation

Occidental Petroleum Corporation reported the following information in a recent annual report.

Occidental Petroleum Corporation
Consolidated Balance Sheets
(in millions)

Assets at December 31,	Current year	Prior year
Current assets		
Cash and cash equivalents	$ 683	$ 146
Trade receivables, net of allowances	804	608
Receivables from joint ventures, partnerships, and other	330	321
Inventories	510	491
Prepaid expenses and other	147	307
Total current assets	2,474	1,873
Long-term receivables, net	264	275

Notes to Consolidated Financial Statements

Cash and Cash Equivalents. Cash equivalents consist of highly liquid investments. Cash equivalents totaled approximately $661 million and $116 million at current and prior year-ends, respectively.

Trade Receivables. Occidental has agreement to sell, under a revolving sale program, an undivided percentage ownership interest in a designated pool of non-interest-bearing receivables. Under this program, Occidental serves as the collection agent with respect to the receivables sold. An interest in new receivables is sold as collections are made from customers. The balance sold at current year-end was $360 million.

Instructions

(a) What items other than coin and currency may be included in "cash"?

(b) What items may be included in "cash equivalents"?

(c) What are compensating balance arrangements, and how should they be reported in financial statements?

(d) What are the possible differences between cash equivalents and short-term (temporary) investments?

(e) Assuming that the sale agreement meets the criteria for sale accounting, cash proceeds were $345 million, the carrying value of the receivables sold was $360 million, and the fair value of the recourse liability was $15 million, what was the effect on income from the sale of receivables?

(f) Briefly discuss the impact of the transaction in (e) on Occidental's liquidity.

Case 2 Microsoft Corporation

Microsoft is the leading developer of software in the world. To continue to be successful Microsoft must generate new products, which requires significant amounts of cash. The following is the current asset and current liability information from Microsoft's current balance sheets (in millions). Following the Microsoft data is the current asset and current liability information from **Oracle**'s current balance sheets (in millions). Oracle is another major software developer.

Microsoft Corporation
Balance Sheets (partial)
As of June 30
(in millions)

Current assets	2011	2010
Cash and equivalents	$ 9,610	$ 5,505
Short-term investments	43,162	31,283
Accounts receivable	14,987	13,014
Other	7,159	5,874
Total current assets	$74,918	$55,676
Total current liabilities	$28,774	$26,147

Oracle
Balance Sheets (partial)
As of May 31
(in millions)

Current assets	2011	2010
Cash and equivalents	$16,163	$ 9,914
Short-term investments	12,685	8,555
Receivables	6,628	5,585
Other current assets	3,698	2,950
Total current assets	$39,174	$27,004
Current liabilities	$14,192	$14,691

Part 1 (Cash and Cash Equivalents)

Instructions

(a) What is the definition of a cash equivalent? Give some examples of cash equivalents. How do cash equivalents differ from other types of short-term investments?

(b) Calculate (1) the current ratio and (2) working capital for each company for 2011 and discuss your results.

(c) Is it possible to have too many liquid assets?

Part 2 (Accounts Receivable)

Microsoft provided the following disclosure related to its accounts receivable.

Allowance for Doubtful Accounts. The allowance for doubtful accounts reflects our best estimate of probable losses inherent in the accounts receivable balance. We determine the allowance based on known troubled accounts, historical experience, and other currently available evidence. Activity in the allowance for doubtful accounts is as follows:

(in millions)

Year Ended June 30	Balance at beginning of period	Charged to costs and expenses	Write-offs	Balance at end of period
2009	$153	$360	$(62)	$451
2010	451	45	(121)	375
2011	375	14	(56)	333

Instructions

(a) Compute Microsoft's accounts receivable turnover for 2011 and discuss your results. Microsoft had sales revenue of $69,943 million in 2011.

(b) Reconstruct the summary journal entries for 2011 based on the information in the disclosure.

(c) Briefly discuss how the accounting for bad debts affects the analysis in Part 2 (a).

Accounting, Analysis, and Principles

The Flatiron Pub provides catering services to local businesses. The following information was available for The Flatiron Pub for the years ended December 31, 2013 and 2014.

	December 31, 2013	December 31, 2014
Cash	$ 2,000	$ 1,685
Accounts receivable	46,000	?
Allowance for doubtful accounts	550	?
Other current assets	8,500	7,925
Current liabilities	37,000	44,600
Total credit sales	205,000	255,000
Collections on accounts receivable	190,000	228,000

Flatiron management is preparing for a meeting with its bank concerning renewal of a loan and has collected the following information related to the above balances.

1. The cash reported at December 31, 2014, reflects the following items: petty cash $1,575 and postage stamps $110. The other current assets balance at December 31, 2014, includes the checking account balance of $4,000.
2. On November 30, 2014, Flatiron agreed to accept a 6-month, $5,000 note bearing 12% interest, payable at maturity, from a major client in settlement of a $5,000 bill. The above balances do not reflect this transaction.
3. Flatiron factored some accounts receivable at the end of 2014. It transferred accounts totaling $10,000 to Final Factor, Inc. with recourse. Final Factor will receive the collections from Flatiron's customers and will retain 2% of the balances. Final Factor assesses Flatiron a finance charge of 3% on this transfer. The fair value of the recourse liability is $400. However, management has determined that the amount due from the factor and the fair value of the resource obligation have not been recorded, and neither are included in the balances above.
4. Flatiron charged off uncollectible accounts with balances of $1,600. On the basis of the latest available information, the 2014 provision for bad debts is estimated to be 2.5% of accounts receivable.

Accounting

(a) Based on the above transactions, determine the balance for (1) Accounts Receivable and (2) Allowance for Doubtful Accounts at December 31, 2014.

(b) Prepare the current assets section of The Flatiron Pub's balance sheet at December 31, 2014.

Analysis

(a) Compute Flatiron's current ratio and accounts receivable turnover for December 31, 2014. Use these measures to analyze Flatiron's liquidity. The accounts receivable turnover in 2013 was 4.37.

(b) Discuss how the analysis you did above of Flatiron's liquidity would be affected if Flatiron had transferred the receivables in a secured borrowing transaction.

Principles

What is the conceptual basis for recording bad debt expense based on the percentage-of-receivables approach at December 31, 2014?

BRIDGE TO THE PROFESSION

C Professional Research: FASB Codification

As the new staff person in your company's treasury department, you have been asked to conduct research related to a proposed transfer of receivables. Your supervisor wants the authoritative sources for the following items that are discussed in the securitization agreement.

Instructions

If your school has a subscription to the FASB Codification, go to *http://aaahq.org/asclogin.cfm* to log in and prepare responses to the following. Provide Codification references for your responses.

(a) Identify relevant Codification section that addresses transfers of receivables.
(b) What are the objectives for reporting transfers of receivables?
(c) Provide definitions for the following:
  (1) Transfer.
  (2) Recourse.
  (3) Collateral.
(d) Provide other examples (besides recourse and collateral) that qualify as continuing involvement.

Additional Professional Resources

See the book's companion website, at **www.wiley.com/college/kieso**, for professional simulations as well as other study resources.

IFRS INSIGHTS

LEARNING OBJECTIVE 12
Compare the accounting procedures for cash and receivables under GAAP and IFRS.

The basic accounting and reporting issues related to recognition and measurement of receivables, such as the use of allowance accounts, how to record discounts, use of the allowance method to account for bad debts, and factoring, are similar for both IFRS and GAAP. *IAS 1* ("Presentation of Financial Statements") is the only standard that discusses issues specifically related to cash. *IFRS 7* ("Financial Instruments: Disclosure") and *IAS 39* ("Financial Instruments: Recognition and Measurement") are the two international standards that address issues related to financial instruments and more specifically receivables.

RELEVANT FACTS

Following are the key similarities and differences between GAAP and IFRS related to cash and receivables.

Similarities

- The accounting and reporting related to cash is essentially the same under both IFRS and GAAP. In addition, the definition used for cash equivalents is the same.
- Like GAAP, cash and receivables are generally reported in the current assets section of the statement of financial position under IFRS.
- Similar to GAAP, IFRS requires that loans and receivables be accounted for at amortized cost, adjusted for allowances for doubtful accounts. IFRS sometimes refers to these allowances as *provisions*. The entry to record the allowance would be as follows.

Bad Debt Expense	xxxxxx	
Provision for Doubtful Accounts		xxxxxx

Differences

- Under IFRS, companies may report cash and receivables as the last items in current assets under IFRS. Under GAAP, these items are reported in order of liquidity.
- While IFRS implies that receivables with different characteristics should be reported separately, there is no standard that mandates this segregation. GAAP has explicit guidance in the area.

- The fair value option is similar under GAAP and IFRS but not identical. The international standard related to the fair value option is subject to certain qualifying criteria not in the U.S. standard. In addition, there is some difference in the financial instruments covered.
- Under IFRS, bank overdrafts are generally reported as cash. Under GAAP, such balances are reported as liabilities.
- IFRS and GAAP differ in the criteria used to account for transfers of receivables. IFRS is a combination of an approach focused on risks and rewards and loss of control. GAAP uses loss of control as the primary criterion. In addition, IFRS generally permits partial transfers; GAAP does not.

ABOUT THE NUMBERS

Impairment Evaluation Process

IFRS provides detailed guidelines to assess whether receivables should be considered uncollectible (often referred to as *impaired*). GAAP does not identify a specific approach. Under IFRS, companies assess their receivables for impairment each reporting period and start the impairment assessment by considering whether objective evidence indicates that one or more loss events have occurred. Examples of possible loss events are:

- Significant financial problems of the customer.
- Payment defaults.
- Renegotiation of terms of the receivable due to financial difficulty of the customer.
- Measurable decrease in estimated future cash flows from a group of receivables since initial recognition, although the decrease cannot yet be identified with individual assets in the group.

A receivable is considered impaired when a loss event indicates a negative impact on the estimated future cash flows to be received from the customer (*IAS 39*, paragraphs 58–70). The IASB requires that the impairment assessment should be performed as follows.

1. Receivables that are individually significant are considered for impairment separately; if impaired, the company recognizes it. Receivables that are not individually significant may also be assessed individually, but it is not necessary to do so.
2. Any receivable individually assessed that is not considered impaired is included with a group of assets with similar credit-risk characteristics and collectively assessed for impairment.
3. Any receivables **not individually assessed are collectively assessed** for impairment.

To illustrate, assume that Hector Company has the following receivables classified into individually significant and all other receivables.

Individually significant receivables		
Yaan Company	$ 40,000	
Randon Inc.	100,000	
Fernando Co.	60,000	
Blanchard Ltd.	50,000	$250,000
All other receivables		500,000
Total		$750,000

Hector determines that Yaan's receivable is impaired by $15,000, and Blanchard's receivable is totally impaired. Both Randon's and Fernando's receivables are not considered impaired. Hector also determines a composite rate of 2% is appropriate to measure impairment on all other receivables. The total impairment is computed as follows.

Accounts Receivable Impairments		
Individually assessed receivables		
Yaan Company		$15,000
Blanchard Ltd.		50,000
Collectively assessed receivables	$500,000	
Add: Randon Inc.	100,000	
Fernando Co.	60,000	
Total collectively assessed receivables	$660,000	
Collectively assessed impairments ($660,000 × 2%)		13,200
Total impairment		$78,200

Hector therefore has an impairment related to its receivables of $78,200. The most controversial part of this computation is that Hector must include in the collective assessment the receivables from Randon and Fernando that were individually assessed and not considered impaired. The rationale for including Randon and Fernando in the collective assessment is that companies often do not have all the information at hand to make an informed decision for individual assessment.

Recovery of Impairment Loss

The accounting for loan impairments is similar between GAAP and IFRS. Subsequent to recording an impairment, events or economic conditions may change such that the extent of the impairment loss decreases (e.g., due to an impairment in the debtor's credit rating). Under IFRS, some or all of the previously recognized impairment loss shall be reversed either directly, with a debit to Accounts Receivable, or by debiting the allowance account and crediting Bad Debt Expense. Such reversals of impairment losses are not allowed under GAAP.

To illustrate, recall the Ogden Bank impairment example of page 382. In that situation, Ogden Bank (the creditor) recognized an impairment loss of $12,434 by debiting Bad Debt Expense for the expected loss. At the same time, it reduced the overall value of the receivable by crediting Allowance for Doubtful Accounts. Ogden made the following entry to record the loss.

Bad Debt Expense	12,434	
Allowance for Doubtful Accounts		12,434

Now, assume that in the year following the impairment recorded by Ogden, Carl King (the borrower) has worked his way out of financial difficulty. Ogden now expects to receive all payments on the loan according to the original loan terms. Based on this new information, the present value of the expected payments is $100,000. Thus, Ogden makes the following entry to reverse the previously recorded impairment.

Allowance for Doubtful Accounts	12,434	
Bad Debt Expense		12,434

Note that the reversal of impairment losses shall not result in carrying amount of the receivable that exceeds the amortized cost that would have been reported had the impairment not been recognized. Under GAAP, reversal of an impairment is not permitted. Rather, the balance of the loan after the impairment becomes the new basis for the loan.

ON THE HORIZON

The question of recording fair values for financial instruments will continue to be an important issue to resolve as the Boards work toward convergence. Both the IASB and the FASB have indicated that they believe that financial statements would be more transparent and understandable if companies recorded and reported all financial instruments at fair value. That said, in *IFRS 9,* which was issued in 2009, the IASB created a split model, where some financial instruments are recorded at fair value but other financial assets, such as loans and receivables, can be accounted for at amortized cost if certain criteria are met. Critics say that this can result in two companies with identical securities accounting for those securities in different ways. A proposal by the FASB would require that nearly all financial instruments, including loans and receivables, be accounted for at fair value. It has been suggested that *IFRS 9* will likely be changed or replaced as the FASB and IASB continue to deliberate the best treatment for financial instruments. In fact, one member of the IASB said that companies should ignore *IFRS 9* and continue to report under the old standard, because in his opinion, it is extremely likely that it would be changed before the mandatory adoption date of this standard in 2015.

IFRS SELF-TEST QUESTIONS

1. Under IFRS, cash and cash equivalents are reported:
   (a) the same as GAAP.
   (b) as separate items.
   (c) similar to GAAP, except for the reporting of bank overdrafts.
   (d) always as the first items in the current assets section.
2. Under IFRS, receivables are to be reported on the balance sheet at:
   (a) amortized cost.
   (b) amortized cost adjusted for estimated loss provisions.
   (c) historical cost.
   (d) replacement cost.
3. Which of the following statements is **false**?
   (a) Receivables include equity securities purchased by the company.
   (b) Receivables include credit card receivables.
   (c) Receivables include amounts owed by employees as result of company loans to employees.
   (d) Receivables include amounts resulting from transactions with customers.
4. Under IFRS:
   (a) the entry to record estimated uncollected accounts is the same as GAAP.
   (b) loans and receivables should only be tested for impairment as a group.
   (c) it is always acceptable to use the direct write-off method.
   (d) all financial instruments are recorded at fair value.
5. Which of the following statements is **true**?
   (a) The fair value option requires that some types of financial instruments be recorded at fair value.
   (b) The fair value option requires that all noncurrent financial instruments be recorded at amortized cost.
   (c) The fair value option allows, but does not require, that some types of financial instruments be recorded at fair value.
   (d) The FASB and IASB would like to reduce the reliance on fair value accounting for financial instruments in the future.

IFRS CONCEPTS AND APPLICATION

IFRS7-1 Briefly describe the impairment evaluation process and assessment of receivables on an individual or collective basis.

IFRS7-2 What are some steps taken by both the FASB and IASB to move to fair value measurement for financial instruments? In what ways have some of the approaches differed?

IFRS7-3 On December 31, 2014, Firth Company borrowed $62,092 from Paris Bank, signing a 5-year, $100,000 zero-interest-rate note. The note was issued to yield 10% interest. Unfortunately, during 2016, Firth began to experience financial difficulty. As a result, at December 31, 2016, Paris Bank determined that it was probable that it would collect only $75,000 at maturity. The market rate of interest on loans of this nature is now 11%.

Instructions

(a) Prepare the entry (if any) to record the impairment of the loan on December 31, 2016, by Paris Bank.

(b) Prepare the entry on March 31, 2017, if Paris learns that Firth will be able to repay the loan under the original terms.

Professional Research

IFRS7-4 As the new staff person in your company's treasury department, you have been asked to conduct research related to a proposed transfer of receivables. Your supervisor wants the authoritative sources for the following items that are discussed in the receivables transfer agreement.

Instructions

Access the IFRS authoritative literature at the IASB website (*http://eifrs.iasb.org/*). (Click on the IFRS tab and then register for free eIFRS access if necessary.) When you have accessed the documents, you can use the search tool in your Internet browser to prepare responses to the following items. **(a)** Identify relevant IFRSs that address transfers of receivables. **(b)** What are the objectives for reporting transfers of receivables? **(c)** Provide the definition for "Amortized cost."

International Financial Reporting Problem

Marks and Spencer plc

IFRS7-5 The financial statements of **Marks and Spencer plc (M&S)** are available at the book's companion website or can be accessed at *http://annualreport.marksandspencer.com/_assets/downloads/Marks-and-Spencer-Annual-report-and-financial-statements-2012.pdf.*

Instructions

Refer to M&S's financial statements and the accompanying notes to answer the following questions.

(a) What criteria does M&S use to classify "Cash and cash equivalents" as reported in its statement of financial position?

(b) As of 31 March 2012, what balances did M&S have in cash and cash equivalents? What were the major uses of cash during the year?

(c) What amounts related to trade receivables does M&S report? Does M&S have any past due but not impaired receivables?

ANSWERS TO IFRS SELF-TEST QUESTIONS

1. c **2.** b **3.** a **4.** a **5.** c

Remember to check the book's companion website to find additional resources for this chapter.

CHAPTER 8 Valuation of Inventories: A Cost-Basis Approach

LEARNING OBJECTIVES

After studying this chapter, you should be able to:

1 Identify major classifications of inventory.

2 Distinguish between perpetual and periodic inventory systems.

3 Determine the goods included in inventory and the effects of inventory errors on the financial statements.

4 Understand the items to include as inventory cost.

5 Describe and compare the cost flow assumptions used to account for inventories.

6 Explain the significance and use of a LIFO reserve.

7 Understand the effect of LIFO liquidations.

8 Explain the dollar-value LIFO method.

9 Identify the major advantages and disadvantages of LIFO.

10 Understand why companies select given inventory methods.

To Switch or Not to Switch

Many companies use the last-in, first-out (LIFO) cost flow assumption in the accounting for inventories. LIFO has a lot going for it in terms of tax savings and providing an income number that better reflects the gross profit associated with inventories with different historical costs. However, in the wake of international convergence discussions (LIFO is not permitted under IFRS) and tax policy debates (LIFO is one of a number of "tax loopholes" that if closed could help address our budget and deficit challenges), more companies are seriously considering the switch from LIFO to first-in, first-out (FIFO) or average-cost inventory methods. For example, of the 449 large public companies surveyed by the AICPA in 2012, just 163 indicated LIFO use (a 25% decline relative to 2001). Here are some of the reasons to support the switch from LIFO.

- While many believe that LIFO provides a more useful income measure, other methods, such as FIFO and average-cost, better reflect the current value of inventory on the balance sheet.
- Many companies discontinued LIFO use to support uniformity of inventory valuation across operations. That is, companies were using LIFO in their U.S. operations but FIFO and/or average-cost in international units. The switch from LIFO simplifies the external reporting for these multinational companies.
- There is also a "bandwagon" effect—when some companies make the switch, their peers likely follow suit to enhance comparability for financial statement users.
- The recent periods of low inflation have resulted in less significant tax benefits associated with LIFO use. That is, in times of rising costs, by expensing the most recently purchased items, cost of goods sold is higher (compared to FIFO or average-cost) and taxable income is lower. A number of companies do not believe the smaller tax benefits of LIFO offset the costs. For example, **Kraft Foods** switched from LIFO to average-cost in 2009, noting that in the recent stable price environment, its cost of goods sold was $95 million *higher* under average-cost.

CONCEPTUAL FOCUS

> See the **Underlying Concepts** on pages 422, 425, and 427.

> Read the **Evolving Issue** on page 445 for a discussion of LIFO.

INTERNATIONAL FOCUS

> See the **International Perspectives** on pages 421, 426, 429, 431, and 444.

> **IFRS Insights** related to inventory are presented in Chapter 9 on pages 525–534.

- Finally, the companies most resistant to make the switch from LIFO are those with large inventory balances. That is, the higher the inventory balance, the higher the additional tax payment will be upon the switch to FIFO. However, a growing number of companies have implemented just-in-time (JIT) or other lean manufacturing techniques, under which much lower inventories are kept on hand. In the extreme, JIT leads to zero inventory and no LIFO effect relative to other methods. For example, **JCPenney** recently switched from LIFO to FIFO in the same period that it rolled out its "Door-to-Floor" lean inventory strategy. As a result, the accounting effect of the change to FIFO was immaterial.

The merits of LIFO use (about which you will learn more in this chapter) are many. However, these benefits appear to be waning. We expect more companies to weigh a voluntary switch away from LIFO in the future.

Source: Adapted from L. Hughes, J. Livingstone, and D. Upton, "Switching from LIFO: Strategies for Change," *The CPA Journal* (April 2011), pp. 26–29.

PREVIEW OF CHAPTER 8

As our opening story indicates, the accounting choice related to inventory is affected by operating strategies, tax consequences, and is important for providing information that is useful for predicting financial performance. In this chapter, we discuss the basic issues related to accounting and reporting for inventory. The content and organization of the chapter are as follows.

Valuation of Inventories: A Cost-Basis Approach

Inventory Issues	Physical Goods Included in Inventory	Costs Included in Inventory	Cost Flow Assumptions	LIFO: Special Issues	Basis for Selection
• Classification • Cost flow • Control • Basic inventory valuation	• Goods in transit • Consigned goods • Special sales agreements • Effect of inventory errors	• Product costs • Period costs • Purchase discounts	• Specific identification • Average-cost • FIFO • LIFO	• LIFO reserve • LIFO liquidation • Dollar-value LIFO • Comparison of LIFO approaches • Advantages of LIFO • Disadvantages of LIFO	• Summary of inventory valuation methods

INVENTORY ISSUES

Classification

LEARNING OBJECTIVE 1
Identify major classifications of inventory.

Inventories are asset items that a company holds for sale in the ordinary course of business, or goods that it will use or consume in the production of goods to be sold. The description and measurement of inventory require careful attention. The investment in inventories is frequently the largest current asset of merchandising (retail) and manufacturing businesses.

A **merchandising concern**, such as **Wal-Mart Stores, Inc.**, usually purchases its merchandise in a form ready for sale. It reports the cost assigned to unsold units left on hand as **merchandise inventory**. Only one inventory account, Inventory, appears in the financial statements.

Manufacturing concerns, on the other hand, produce goods to sell to merchandising firms. Many of the largest U.S. businesses are manufacturers, such as **Boeing**, **IBM**, **ExxonMobil**, **Procter & Gamble**, **Ford**, and **Motorola**. Although the products they produce may differ, manufacturers normally have three inventory accounts—Raw Materials, Work in Process, and Finished Goods.

A company reports the cost assigned to goods and materials on hand but not yet placed into production as **raw materials inventory**. Raw materials include the wood to make a baseball bat or the steel to make a car. These materials can be traced directly to the end product.

At any point in a continuous production process, some units are only partially processed. The cost of the raw material for these unfinished units, plus the direct labor cost applied specifically to this material and a ratable share of manufacturing overhead costs, constitute the **work in process inventory**.

Companies report the costs identified with the completed but unsold units on hand at the end of the fiscal period as **finished goods inventory**. Illustration 8-1 contrasts the financial statement presentation of inventories of **Wal-Mart Stores, Inc.** (a merchandising company) with those of **Sherwin-Williams Company** (a manufacturing company.) The remainder of the balance sheet is essentially similar for the two types of companies.

ILLUSTRATION 8-1
Comparison of Presentation of Current Assets for Merchandising and Manufacturing Companies

Merchandising Company
Wal-Mart Stores, Inc.

Balance Sheet
January 31, 2012

Current assets (in millions)	
Cash and cash equivalents	$ 6,550
Receivables, net	5,937
Inventories	40,714
Prepaid expenses and other	1,774
Total current assets	$54,975

Manufacturing Company
Sherwin-Williams Company

Balance Sheet
December 31, 2011

Current assets (in thousands)		
Cash and cash equivalents		$ 32,696
Accounts receivable, less allowance		989,873
Inventories:		
Finished goods	$730,727	
Work in process and raw materials	196,082	926,809
Deferred income taxes		149,207
Other current assets		163,008
Total current assets		$ 2,261,593

A manufacturing company like **Sherwin-Williams** also might include a Manufacturing or Factory **Supplies Inventory** account. In it, Sherwin-Williams would include such items as machine oils, nails, cleaning material, and the like—supplies that are used in production but are not the primary materials being processed.

Illustration 8-2 shows the differences in the flow of costs through a merchandising company and a manufacturing company.

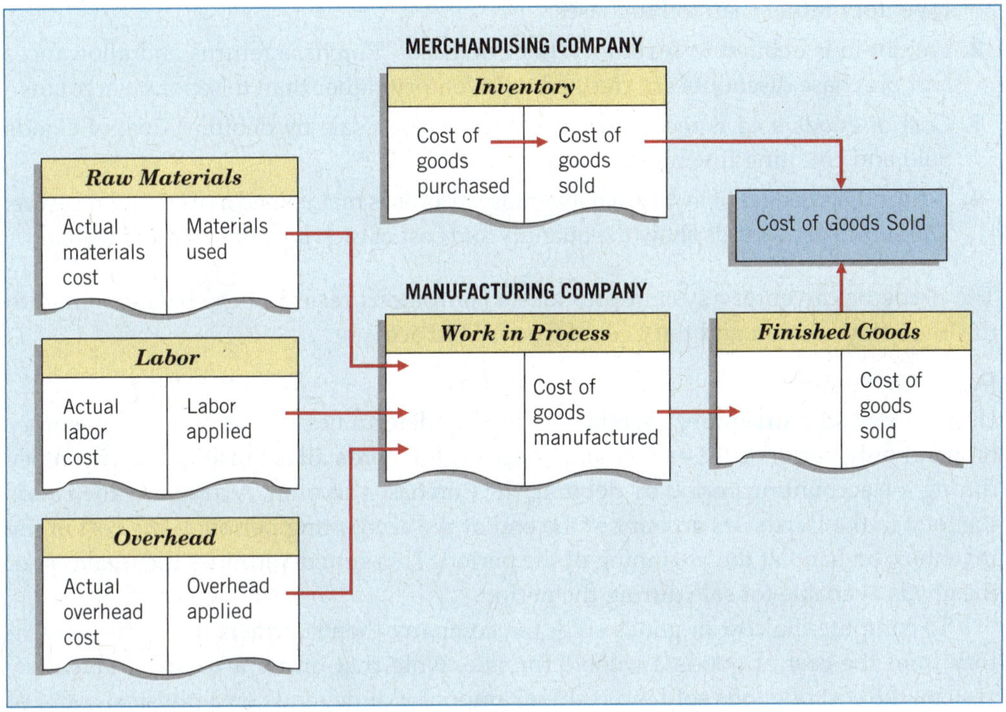

ILLUSTRATION 8-2
Flow of Costs through Manufacturing and Merchandising Companies

Inventory Cost Flow

2 LEARNING OBJECTIVE
Distinguish between perpetual and periodic inventory systems.

Companies that sell or produce goods report inventory and cost of goods sold at the end of each accounting period. The flow of costs for a company is as follows. Beginning inventory plus the cost of goods purchased is the cost of goods available for sale. As goods are sold, they are assigned to cost of goods sold. Those goods that are not sold by the end of the accounting period represent ending inventory. Illustration 8-3 describes these relationships.

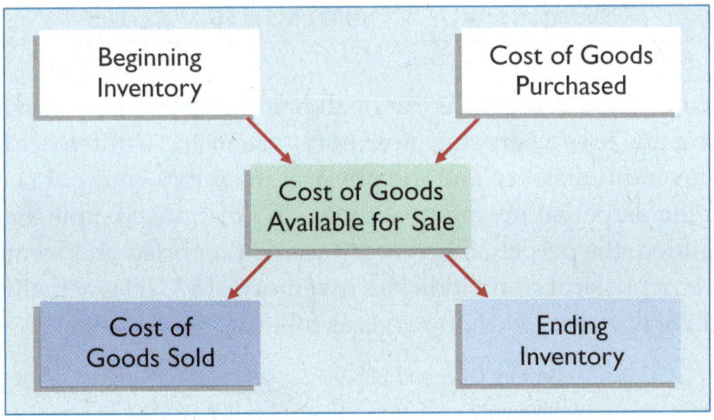

ILLUSTRATION 8-3
Inventory Cost Flow

Companies use one of two types of systems for maintaining accurate inventory records for these costs—the perpetual system or the periodic system.

Perpetual System

A **perpetual inventory system** continuously tracks changes in the Inventory account. That is, a company records all purchases and sales (issues) of goods directly in the Inventory account **as they occur**. The accounting features of a perpetual inventory system are as follows.

1. Purchases of merchandise for resale or raw materials for production are debited to Inventory rather than to Purchases.
2. Freight-in is debited to Inventory, not Purchases. Purchase returns and allowances and purchase discounts are credited to Inventory rather than to separate accounts.
3. Cost of goods sold is recorded at the time of each sale by debiting Cost of Goods Sold and crediting Inventory.
4. A subsidiary ledger of individual inventory records is maintained as a control measure. The subsidiary records show the quantity and cost of each type of inventory on hand.

The perpetual inventory system provides a continuous record of the balances in both the Inventory account and the Cost of Goods Sold account.

Periodic System

Under a **periodic inventory system**, a company determines the quantity of inventory on hand only periodically, as the name implies. It records all acquisitions of inventory during the accounting period by debiting the Purchases account. A company then adds the total in the Purchases account at the end of the accounting period to the cost of the inventory on hand at the beginning of the period. This sum determines the total cost of the goods available for sale during the period.

To compute the cost of goods sold, the company then subtracts the ending inventory from the cost of goods available for sale. Note that under a periodic inventory system, the cost of goods sold is a residual amount that depends on a physical count of ending inventory. This process is referred to as "taking a physical inventory." Companies that use the periodic system take a physical inventory at least once a year.

Comparing Perpetual and Periodic Systems

To illustrate the difference between a perpetual and a periodic system, assume that Fesmire Company had the following transactions during the current year.

Beginning inventory	100 units at $6	= $ 600
Purchases	900 units at $6	= $5,400
Sales	600 units at $12	= $7,200
Ending inventory	400 units at $6	= $2,400

Fesmire records these transactions during the current year as shown in Illustration 8-4.

When a company uses a perpetual inventory system and a difference exists between the perpetual inventory balance and the physical inventory count, it needs a separate entry to adjust the perpetual inventory account. To illustrate, assume that at the end of the reporting period, the perpetual inventory account reported an inventory balance of $4,000. However, a physical count indicates inventory of $3,800 is actually on hand. The entry to record the necessary write-down is as follows.

Inventory Over and Short	200	
Inventory		200

Perpetual inventory overages and shortages generally represent a misstatement of cost of goods sold. The difference results from normal and expected shrinkage, breakage,

ILLUSTRATION 8-4
Comparative Entries—Perpetual vs. Periodic

Perpetual Inventory System			Periodic Inventory System		
Beginning inventory, 100 units at $6					
The Inventory account shows the inventory on hand at $600.			The Inventory account shows the inventory on hand at $600.		
Purchase 900 units at $6					
Inventory	5,400		Purchases	5,400	
Accounts Payable		5,400	Accounts Payable		5,400
Sale of 600 units at $12					
Accounts Receivable	7,200		Accounts Receivable	7,200	
Sales Revenue		7,200	Sales Revenue		7,200
Cost of Goods Sold (600 at $6)	3,600		(No entry)		
Inventory		3,600			
End-of-period entries for inventory accounts, 400 units at $6					
No entry necessary.			Inventory (ending, by count)	2,400	
The Inventory account shows the ending balance of $2,400 ($600 + $5,400 – $3,600).			Cost of Goods Sold	3,600	
			Purchases		5,400
			Inventory (beginning)		600

shoplifting, incorrect recordkeeping, and the like. Inventory Over and Short therefore adjusts Cost of Goods Sold. In practice, companies sometimes report Inventory Over and Short in the "Other revenues and gains" or "Other expenses and losses" section of the income statement.

Note that a company using the periodic inventory system does not report the account Inventory Over and Short. The reason: The periodic method does not have accounting records against which to compare the physical count. As a result, a company buries inventory overages and shortages in cost of goods sold.

Inventory Control

For various reasons, management is vitally interested in inventory planning and control. Whether a company manufactures or merchandises goods, it needs an accurate accounting system with up-to-date records. It may lose sales and customers if it does not stock products in the desired style, quality, and quantity. Further, companies must monitor inventory levels carefully to limit the financing costs of carrying large amounts of inventory.

In a perfect world, companies would like a continuous record of both their inventory levels and their cost of goods sold. The popularity and affordability of accounting software makes the perpetual system cost-effective for many kinds of businesses. Companies like **Target**, **Best Buy**, and **Sears Holdings** now incorporate the recording of sales with optical scanners at the cash register into perpetual inventory systems.

However, many companies cannot afford a complete perpetual system. But, most of these companies need current information regarding their inventory levels, to protect against stock-outs or overpurchasing, and to aid in preparation of monthly or quarterly financial data. As a result, these companies use a **modified perpetual inventory system**. This system provides detailed inventory records of increases and decreases in quantities only—not dollar amounts. It is merely a memorandum device outside the double-entry system, which helps in determining the level of inventory at any point in time.

Whether a company maintains a complete perpetual inventory in quantities and dollars or a modified perpetual inventory system, it probably takes a physical inventory once a year. No matter what type of inventory records companies use, they all face the danger of loss and error. Waste, breakage, theft, improper entry, failure to prepare or record requisitions, and other similar possibilities may cause the inventory records to differ from the actual inventory on hand. Thus, **all companies** need periodic verification of the inventory records by actual count, weight, or measurement, with the counts compared with the detailed inventory records. As indicated earlier, a company corrects the records to agree with the quantities actually on hand.

Insofar as possible, companies should take the physical inventory near the end of their fiscal year, to properly report inventory quantities in their annual accounting reports. Because this is not always possible, however, physical inventories taken within two or three months of the year's end are satisfactory if a company maintains detailed inventory records with a fair degree of accuracy.[1]

What do the numbers mean? *STAYING LEAN*

Wal-Mart Stores, Inc. uses its buying power in the supply chain to purchase an increasing proportion of its goods directly from manufacturers and on a combined basis across geographic borders. Wal-Mart estimates that it saves 5–15% across its supply chain by implementing direct purchasing on a combined basis for the 15 countries in which it operates. Thus, Wal-Mart has a good handle on what products it needs to stock, and it gets the best prices when it purchases.

Wal-Mart also provides a classic example of the use of tight inventory controls. Department managers use a scanner that when placed over the bar code corresponding to a particular item, will tell them how many of the items the store sold yesterday, last week, and over the same period last year. It will tell them how many of those items are in stock, how many are on the way, and how many the neighboring Walmart stores are carrying (in case one store runs out). Wal-Mart's inventory management practices have helped it become one of the top-ranked companies on the Fortune 500 in terms of sales.

Source: J. Birchall, "Walmart Aims to Cut Supply Chain Cost," *Financial Times* (January 4, 2010).

Basic Issues in Inventory Valuation

Goods sold (or used) during an accounting period seldom correspond exactly to the goods bought (or produced) during that period. As a result, inventories either increase or decrease during the period. Companies must then allocate the cost of all the goods available for sale (or use) between the goods that were sold or used and those that are still on hand. The **cost of goods available for sale or use** is the *sum* of (1) the cost of the goods on hand at the beginning of the period, and (2) the cost of the goods acquired or produced during the period. The **cost of goods sold** is the *difference* between (1) the cost of goods available for sale during the period, and (2) the cost of goods on hand at the end of the period. Illustration 8-5 shows these calculations.

ILLUSTRATION 8-5
Computation of Cost of Goods Sold

Beginning inventory, Jan. 1	$100,000
Cost of goods acquired or produced during the year	800,000
Total cost of goods available for sale	900,000
Ending inventory, Dec. 31	(200,000)
Cost of goods sold during the year	$700,000

[1]Some companies have developed methods of determining inventories, including statistical sampling, that are sufficiently reliable to make unnecessary an annual physical count of each item of inventory.

Valuing inventories can be complex. It requires determining the following.

1. **The physical goods to include in inventory** (who owns the goods?—goods in transit, consigned goods, special sales agreements).
2. **The costs to include in inventory** (product vs. period costs).
3. **The cost flow assumption to adopt** (specific identification, average-cost, FIFO, LIFO, retail, etc.)

We explore these basic issues in the next three sections.

International Perspective

Who owns the goods, as well as the costs to include in inventory, are essentially accounted for the same under IFRS and GAAP.

PHYSICAL GOODS INCLUDED IN INVENTORY

3 LEARNING OBJECTIVE

Determine the goods included in inventory and the effects of inventory errors on the financial statements.

Technically, a company should record purchases when it obtains legal title to the goods. In practice, however, a company records acquisitions when it receives the goods. Why? Because it is difficult to determine the exact time of legal passage of title for every purchase. In addition, no material error likely results from such a practice if consistently applied. Illustration 8-6 indicates the general guidelines companies use in evaluating whether the seller or buyer reports an item as inventory. Exceptions to the general guidelines can arise for goods in transit and consigned goods.

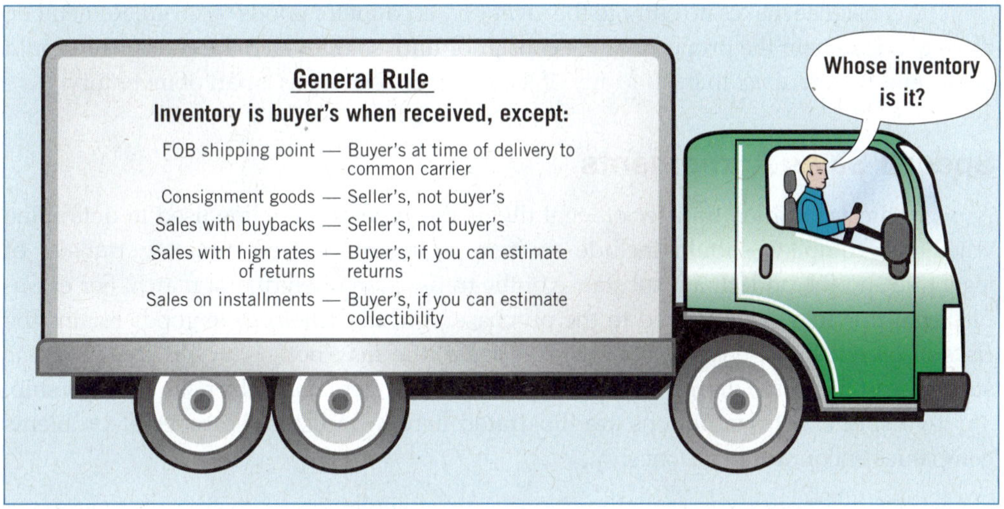

ILLUSTRATION 8-6
Guidelines for Determining Ownership

Goods in Transit

Sometimes purchased merchandise remains in transit—not yet received—at the end of a fiscal period. The accounting for these shipped goods depends on who owns them. For example, a company like **Walgreens** determines ownership by applying the "passage of title" rule. If a supplier ships goods to Walgreens **f.o.b. shipping point**, title passes to Walgreens when the supplier delivers the goods to the common carrier, who acts as an agent for Walgreens. (The abbreviation f.o.b. stands for free on board.) If the supplier ships the goods **f.o.b. destination**, title passes to Walgreens only when it receives the goods from the common carrier. "Shipping point" and "destination" are often designated by a particular location, for example, f.o.b. Denver.

When Walgreens obtains legal title to goods, it must record them as purchases in that fiscal period, assuming a periodic inventory system. Thus, goods shipped to Walgreens f.o.b. shipping point, but in transit at the end of the period, belong to Walgreens. It should show the purchase in its records because legal title to these goods passed to

Walgreens upon shipment of the goods. To disregard such purchases results in understating inventories and accounts payable in the balance sheet, and understating purchases and ending inventories in the income statement.

Consigned Goods

Companies market certain products through a **consignment** shipment. Under this arrangement, a company like Williams' Art Gallery (the consignor) ships various art merchandise to Sotheby's Holdings (the consignee), who acts as Williams' agent in selling the consigned goods. Sotheby's agrees to accept the goods without any liability, except to exercise due care and reasonable protection from loss or damage, until it sells the goods to a third party. When Sotheby's sells the goods, it remits the revenue, less a selling commission and expenses incurred in accomplishing the sale, to Williams.

Goods out on consignment remain the property of the consignor (Williams in the example above). Williams thus includes the goods in its inventory at purchase price or production cost. Occasionally, and only for a significant amount, the consignor shows the inventory out on consignment as a separate item. Sometimes a consignor reports the inventory on consignment in the notes to the financial statements. For example, Eagle Clothes, Inc. reported the following related to consigned goods: "Inventories consist of finished goods shipped on consignment to customers of the Company's subsidiary April-Marcus, Inc."

The consignee makes no entry to the inventory account for goods received. Remember, these goods remain the property of the consignor until sold. In fact, the consignee should be extremely careful *not* to include any of the goods consigned as a part of inventory.

Special Sales Agreements

As we indicated earlier, transfer of legal title is the general guideline used to determine whether a company should include an item in inventory. Unfortunately, transfer of legal title and the underlying substance of the transaction often do not match. For example, legal title may have passed to the purchaser, but the seller of the goods retains the risks of ownership. Conversely, transfer of legal title may not occur, but the economic substance of the transaction is such that the seller no longer retains the risks of ownership.

Two special sales situations are illustrated here to indicate the types of problems companies encounter in practice:

1. Sales with buyback agreement.
2. Sales with high rates of return.

Sales with Buyback Agreement

Sometimes an enterprise finances its inventory without reporting either the liability or the inventory on its balance sheet. This approach, often referred to as a **product financing arrangement**, usually involves a "sale" with either an implicit or explicit "buyback" agreement.

Underlying Concepts

Recognizing revenue at the time the inventory is "parked" violates the revenue recognition principle. That is, a performance obligation is met when the risks and rewards of ownership are transferred to the buyer.

To illustrate, Hill Enterprises transfers ("sells") inventory to Chase, Inc. and simultaneously agrees to repurchase this merchandise at a specified price over a specified period of time. Chase then uses the inventory as collateral and borrows against it. Chase uses the loan proceeds to pay Hill, which repurchases the inventory in the future. Chase employs the proceeds from repayment to meet its loan obligation.

The essence of this transaction is that Hill Enterprises is financing its inventory—and retaining risk of ownership—even though it transferred to Chase technical legal title to the merchandise. By structuring a transaction in this manner, Hill avoids personal property taxes in certain states. Other advantages of this transaction for Hill are the removal of the current liability from its balance sheet and the ability to manipulate income. For Chase, the purchase of the goods may solve a LIFO liquidation problem (discussed later), or Chase may enter into a similar reciprocal agreement at a later date.

These arrangements are often described in practice as "**parking transactions**." In this situation, Hill simply parks the inventory on Chase's balance sheet for a short period of time. Generally, when a repurchase agreement exists, Hill should report the inventory and related liability on its books. **[1]** The reason? Hill has retained the risks and rewards of ownership.

See the FASB Codification section (page 449).

Sales with High Rates of Return

In industries such as publishing, music, toys, and sporting goods, formal or informal agreements often exist that permit purchasers to return inventory for a full or partial refund.

To illustrate, Quality Publishing Company sells textbooks to Campus Bookstores with an agreement that Campus may return for full credit any books not sold. Historically, Campus Bookstores returned approximately 25 percent of the textbooks from Quality Publishing. How should Quality Publishing report its sales transactions?

One alternative is to record the sale at the full amount and establish an estimated sales returns and allowances account until the return period has expired. A second possibility is to not record any sales until circumstances indicate the amount of inventory the buyer will return. The key question is: Under what circumstances should Quality Publishing consider the inventory sold? The answer is that **when Quality Publishing can reasonably estimate the amount of returns**, it should consider the goods sold but establish a return liability for the amount of the estimated returns. Conversely, if returns are unpredictable, Quality Publishing should not consider the goods sold and it should not remove the goods from its inventory. **[2]**

What do the numbers mean? NO PARKING!

In one of the more elaborate accounting frauds, employees at **Kurzweil Applied Intelligence Inc.** booked millions of dollars in phony inventory sales during a two-year period that straddled two audits and an initial public stock offering. They dummied up phony shipping documents and logbooks to support bogus sales transactions. Then they shipped high-tech equipment, not to customers, but to a public warehouse for "temporary" storage, where some of it sat for 17 months. (Kurzweil still had ownership.)

To foil auditors' attempts to verify the existence of the inventory, Kurzweil employees moved the goods from warehouse to warehouse. To cover the fraudulently recorded sales transactions as auditors closed in, the employees brought back the still-hidden goods, under the pretense that the goods were returned by customers. When auditors uncovered the fraud, the bottom dropped out of Kurzweil's stock.

Similar inventory shenanigans occurred at **Delphi**, which used side-deals with third parties to get inventory off its books and to record sales. The overstatement in income eventually led to a bankruptcy filing for Delphi.

More recently and with an international twist, concerns about inventory shenanigans are surfacing in China. Following years of torrid growth, the global economic slowdown has resulted in a huge buildup of unsold goods that is cluttering shop floors, clogging car dealerships, and filling factory warehouses. The large inventory overhang is raising alarms about phantom profits and suspect economic data coming out of China.

Sources: Adapted from "Anatomy of a Fraud," *BusinessWeek* (September 16, 1996), pp. 90–94; J. McCracken, "Delphi Executives Named in Suit over Inventory Practices," *Wall Street Journal* (May 5, 2005), p. A3; and K. Bradsher, "China Confronts Mounting Piles of Unsold Goods," *New York Times* (August 23, 2012).

Effect of Inventory Errors

Items incorrectly included or excluded in determining cost of goods sold through inventory misstatements will result in errors in the financial statements. Let's look at two cases, assuming a periodic inventory system.

Ending Inventory Misstated

What would happen if IBM correctly records its beginning inventory and purchases, but fails to include some items in ending inventory? In this situation, we would have the following effects on the financial statements at the end of the period.

ILLUSTRATION 8-7
Financial Statement Effects of Misstated Ending Inventory

Balance Sheet		Income Statement	
Inventory	Understated	Cost of goods sold	Overstated
Retained earnings	Understated		
Working capital	Understated	Net income	Understated
Current ratio	Understated		

If ending inventory is understated, working capital (current assets less current liabilities) and the current ratio (current assets divided by current liabilities) are understated. If cost of goods sold is overstated, then net income is understated.

To illustrate the effect on net income over a two-year period (2013–2014), assume that Jay Weiseman Corp. understates its ending inventory by $10,000 in 2013; all other items are correctly stated. The effect of this error is to decrease net income in 2013 and to increase net income in 2014. The error is counterbalanced (offset) in 2014 because beginning inventory is understated and net income is overstated. As Illustration 8-8 shows, the income statement misstates the net income figures for both 2013 and 2014 although the *total* for the two years is correct.

ILLUSTRATION 8-8
Effect of Ending Inventory Error on Two Periods

JAY WEISEMAN CORP.
(All Figures Assumed)

	Incorrect Recording		Correct Recording	
	2013	2014	2013	2014
Revenues	$100,000	$100,000	$100,000	$100,000
Cost of goods sold				
Beginning inventory	25,000	→20,000	25,000	→30,000
Purchased or produced	45,000	60,000	45,000	60,000
Goods available for sale	70,000	80,000	70,000	90,000
Less: Ending inventory	20,000*	40,000	30,000	40,000
Cost of goods sold	50,000	40,000	40,000	50,000
Gross profit	50,000	60,000	60,000	50,000
Administrative and selling expenses	40,000	40,000	40,000	40,000
Net income	$ 10,000	$ 20,000	$ 20,000	$ 10,000
	Total income for two years = $30,000		Total income for two years = $30,000	

*Ending inventory understated by $10,000 in 2013.

If Weiseman *overstates* ending inventory in 2013, the reverse effect occurs. Inventory, working capital, current ratio, and net income are overstated, and cost of goods sold is understated. The effect of the error on net income will be counterbalanced in 2014, but the income statement misstates both years' net income figures.

Purchases and Inventory Misstated

Suppose that Bishop Company does not record as a purchase certain goods that it owns and does not count them in ending inventory. The effect on the financial statements (assuming this is a purchase on account) is as follows.

ILLUSTRATION 8-9
Financial Statement Effects of Misstated Purchases and Inventory

Balance Sheet		Income Statement	
Inventory	Understated	Purchases	Understated
Retained earnings	No effect	Cost of goods sold	No effect
Accounts payable	Understated	Net income	No effect
Working capital	No effect	Inventory (ending)	Understated
Current ratio	Overstated		

Omission of goods from purchases and inventory results in an understatement of inventory and accounts payable in the balance sheet. It also results in an understatement of purchases and ending inventory in the income statement. However, the omission of such goods does not affect net income for the period. Why not? Because Bishop understates both purchases and ending inventory by the same amount—the error is thereby offset in cost of goods sold. Total working capital is unchanged, but the current ratio is overstated because of the omission of equal amounts from inventory and accounts payable.

To illustrate the effect on the current ratio, assume that Bishop *understated* accounts payable and ending inventory by $40,000. Illustration 8-10 shows the understated and correct data.

ILLUSTRATION 8-10
Effects of Purchases and Ending Inventory Errors

Purchases and Ending Inventory Understated		Purchases and Ending Inventory Correct	
Current assets	$120,000	Current assets	$160,000
Current liabilities	$ 40,000	Current liabilities	$ 80,000
Current ratio	3 to 1	Current ratio	2 to 1

The understated data indicate a current ratio of 3 to 1, whereas the correct ratio is 2 to 1. Thus, understatement of accounts payable and ending inventory can lead to a "window-dressing" of the current ratio. That is, Bishop can make the current ratio appear better than it is.

If Bishop *overstates* both purchases (on account) and ending inventory, then the effects on the balance sheet are exactly the reverse. The financial statements overstate inventory and accounts payable, and understate the current ratio. The overstatement does not affect cost of goods sold and net income because the errors offset one another. Similarly, working capital is not affected.

Underlying Concepts

When inventory is misstated, its presentation is not representationally faithful.

We cannot overemphasize the importance of proper inventory measurement in presenting accurate financial statements. For example, **Leslie Fay**, a women's apparel maker, had accounting irregularities that wiped out one year's net income and caused a restatement of the prior year's earnings. One reason: It inflated inventory and deflated cost of goods sold. **Anixter Bros. Inc.** had to restate its income by $1.7 million because an accountant in the antenna manufacturing division overstated the ending inventory, thereby reducing its cost of sales. Similarly, **AM International** allegedly recorded as sold products that were only being rented. As a result, inaccurate inventory and sales figures inappropriately added $7.9 million to pretax income.

COSTS INCLUDED IN INVENTORY

4 LEARNING OBJECTIVE
Understand the items to include as inventory cost.

One of the most important problems in dealing with inventories concerns the dollar amount at which to carry the inventory in the accounts. **Companies generally account for the acquisition of inventories, like other assets, on a cost basis.**

Product Costs

Product costs are those costs that "attach" to the inventory. As a result, a company records product costs in the inventory account. These costs are directly connected with bringing the goods to the buyer's place of business and converting such goods to a salable condition. Such charges include freight charges on goods purchased, other direct costs of acquisition, and labor and other production costs incurred in processing the goods up to the time of sale.

It seems proper also to allocate to inventories a share of any buying costs or expenses of a purchasing department, storage costs, and other costs incurred in storing or handling the goods before their sale. However, because of the practical difficulties involved in allocating such costs and expenses, companies usually exclude these items in valuing inventories.

A manufacturing company's costs include direct materials, direct labor, and manufacturing overhead costs. Manufacturing overhead costs include indirect materials, indirect labor, and various costs, such as depreciation, taxes, insurance, and heat and electricity.

Period Costs

Period costs are those costs that are indirectly related to the acquisition or production of goods. Period costs such as selling expenses and, under ordinary circumstances, general and administrative expenses are therefore not included as part of inventory cost.

International Perspective

GAAP has more detailed rules related to the accounting for inventories, compared to IFRS.

Yet, conceptually, these expenses are as much a cost of the product as the initial purchase price and related freight charges attached to the product. Why then do companies exclude these costs from inventoriable items? Because companies generally consider selling expenses as more directly related to the cost of goods sold than to the unsold inventory. In addition, period costs, especially administrative expenses, are so unrelated or indirectly related to the immediate production process that any allocation is purely arbitrary.[2]

Interest is another period cost. Companies usually expense **interest costs** associated with getting inventories ready for sale. Supporters of this approach argue that interest costs are really a **cost of financing**. Others contend that interest costs incurred to finance activities associated with readying inventories for sale are as much a **cost of the asset** as materials, labor, and overhead. Therefore, they reason, companies should capitalize interest costs.

The FASB ruled that companies should capitalize interest costs related to assets constructed for internal use or assets produced as discrete projects (such as ships or real estate projects) for sale or lease [4].[3] The FASB emphasized that these discrete projects should take considerable time, entail substantial expenditures, and be likely to involve significant amounts of interest cost. A company should not capitalize interest costs for inventories that it routinely manufactures or otherwise produces in large quantities on a repetitive basis. In this case, the informational benefit does not justify the cost.

Treatment of Purchase Discounts

The use of a **Purchase Discounts** account in a periodic inventory system indicates that the company is reporting its purchases and accounts payable at the gross amount. If a

[2]Companies should not record abnormal freight, handling costs, and amounts of wasted materials (spoilage) as inventory costs. If the costs associated with the actual level of spoilage or product defects are greater than the costs associated with normal spoilage or defects, the company should charge the excess as an expense in the current period. [3]

[3]The reporting rules related to interest cost capitalization have their greatest impact in accounting for long-term assets. We therefore discuss them in Chapter 10.

company uses this **gross method**, it reports purchase discounts as a deduction from purchases on the income statement.

Another approach is to record the purchases and accounts payable at an amount **net of the cash discounts**. In this approach, the company records failure to take a purchase discount within the discount period in a Purchase Discounts Lost account. If a company uses this **net method**, it considers purchase discounts lost as a financial expense and reports it in the "Other expenses and losses" section of the income statement. This treatment is considered better for two reasons. (1) It provides a correct reporting of the cost of the asset and related liability. (2) It can measure management inefficiency by holding management responsible for discounts not taken.

To illustrate the difference between the gross and net methods, assume the following transactions.

ILLUSTRATION 8-11
Entries under Gross and Net Methods

Gross Method			Net Method		
Purchase cost $10,000, terms 2/10, net 30					
Purchases	10,000		Purchases	9,800	
Accounts Payable		10,000	Accounts Payable		9,800
Invoices of $4,000 are paid within discount period					
Accounts Payable	4,000		Accounts Payable	3,920	
Purchase Discounts		80	Cash		3,920
Cash		3,920			
Invoices of $6,000 are paid after discount period					
Accounts Payable	6,000		Accounts Payable	5,880	
Cash		6,000	Purchase Discounts Lost	120	
			Cash		6,000

Many believe that the somewhat more complicated net method is not justified by the resulting benefits. This could account for the widespread use of the less logical but simpler gross method. In addition, some contend that management is reluctant to report in the financial statements the amount of purchase discounts lost.

Underlying Concepts

Not using the net method because of resultant difficulties is an example of the application of the cost constraint.

What do the numbers mean? YOU MAY NEED A MAP

Does it really matter *where* a company reports certain costs in its income statement as long as it includes them all as expenses in computing income?

For e-tailers, such as **Amazon.com** or **Drugstore.com**, *where* they report certain selling costs does appear to be important. Contrary to well-established retailer practices, these companies insist on reporting some selling costs—fulfillment costs related to inventory shipping and warehousing—as part of administrative expenses, instead of as cost of goods sold. This practice is allowable within GAAP, *if* applied consistently and adequately disclosed. Although the practice doesn't affect the bottom line, it does make the e-tailers' gross margins look better. For example, at one time Amazon reported $265 million of these costs in one quarter. Some experts thought Amazon should include those charges in costs of goods sold, which would substantially lower its gross profit, as shown below (in millions).

	E-tailer Reporting	Traditional Reporting
Sales	$2,795	$2,795
Cost of goods sold	2,132	2,397
Gross profit	$ 663	$ 398
Gross margin %	24%	14%

Similarly, if **Drugstore.com** and **eToys.com** made similar adjustments, their gross margins would go from positive to negative.

Thus, if you want to be able to compare the operating results of e-tailers to other traditional retailers, it might be a good idea to have a good accounting map in order to navigate their income statements and how they report certain selling costs.

Source: Adapted from P. Elstrom, "The End of Fuzzy Math?" *BusinessWeek, e.Biz—Net Worth* (December 11, 2000). According to GAAP **[5]**, companies must disclose the accounting policy for classifying these selling costs in income.

WHICH COST FLOW ASSUMPTION TO ADOPT?

LEARNING OBJECTIVE 5
Describe and compare the cost flow assumptions used to account for inventories.

During any given fiscal period, companies typically purchase merchandise at several different prices. If a company prices inventories at cost and it made numerous purchases at different unit costs, which cost price should it use? Conceptually, a specific identification of the given items sold and unsold seems optimal. But this measure often proves both expensive and impossible to achieve. Consequently, companies use one of several systematic inventory **cost flow assumptions**.

Indeed, the actual physical flow of goods and the cost flow assumption often greatly differ. **There is no requirement that the cost flow assumption adopted be consistent with the physical movement of goods.** A company's major objective in selecting a method should be to choose the one that, under the circumstances, most clearly reflects periodic income. **[6]**

To illustrate, assume that Call-Mart Inc. had the following transactions in its first month of operations.

Date	Purchases	Sold or Issued	Balance
March 2	2,000 @ $4.00		2,000 units
March 15	6,000 @ $4.40		8,000 units
March 19		4,000 units	4,000 units
March 30	2,000 @ $4.75		6,000 units

From this information, Call-Mart computes the ending inventory of 6,000 units and the cost of goods available for sale (beginning inventory + purchases) of $43,900 [(2,000 at $4.00) + (6,000 at $4.40) + (2,000 at $4.75)]. The question is, which price or prices should it assign to the 6,000 units of ending inventory? The answer depends on which cost flow assumption it uses.

Specific Identification

Specific identification calls for identifying each item sold and each item in inventory. A company includes in cost of goods sold the costs of the specific items sold. It includes in inventory the costs of the specific items on hand. This method may be used only in instances where it is practical to separate physically the different purchases made. As a result, most companies only use this method when handling a relatively small number of costly, easily distinguishable items. In the retail trade, this includes some types of jewelry, fur coats, automobiles, and some furniture. In manufacturing, it includes special orders and many products manufactured under a job cost system.

To illustrate, assume that Call-Mart Inc.'s 6,000 units of inventory consists of 1,000 units from the March 2 purchase, 3,000 from the March 15 purchase, and 2,000 from the March 30 purchase. Illustration 8-12 shows how Call-Mart computes the ending inventory and cost of goods sold.

ILLUSTRATION 8-12
Specific Identification Method

Date	No. of Units	Unit Cost	Total Cost
March 2	1,000	$4.00	$ 4,000
March 15	3,000	4.40	13,200
March 30	2,000	4.75	9,500
Ending inventory	6,000		$26,700

Cost of goods available for sale (computed in previous section)	$43,900
Deduct: Ending inventory	26,700
Cost of goods sold	$17,200

This method appears ideal. Specific identification matches actual costs against actual revenue. Thus, a company reports ending inventory at actual cost. In other words, **under specific identification the cost flow matches the physical flow of the goods**. On closer observation, however, this method has certain deficiencies.

Some argue that specific identification allows a company to manipulate net income. For example, assume that a wholesaler purchases identical plywood early in the year at three different prices. When it sells the plywood, the wholesaler can select either the lowest or the highest price to charge to expense. It simply selects the plywood from a specific lot for delivery to the customer. A business manager, therefore, can manipulate net income by delivering to the customer the higher- or lower-priced item, depending on whether the company seeks lower or higher reported earnings for the period.

International Perspective

IFRS indicates specific identification is the preferred inventory method, unless it is impracticable to use.

Another problem relates to the arbitrary allocation of costs that sometimes occurs with specific inventory items. For example, a company often faces difficulty in relating shipping charges, storage costs, and discounts directly to a given inventory item. This results in allocating these costs somewhat arbitrarily, leading to a "breakdown" in the precision of the specific identification method.[4]

Average-Cost

As the name implies, the **average-cost method** prices items in the inventory on the basis of the average cost of all similar goods available during the period. To illustrate use of the periodic inventory method (amount of inventory computed at the end of the period), Call-Mart computes the ending inventory and cost of goods sold using a **weighted-average method** as follows.

ILLUSTRATION 8-13
Weighted-Average Method—Periodic Inventory

Date of Invoice	No. Units	Unit Cost	Total Cost
March 2	2,000	$4.00	$ 8,000
March 15	6,000	4.40	26,400
March 30	2,000	4.75	9,500
Total goods available	10,000		$43,900

Weighted-average cost per unit $\frac{\$43,900}{10,000} = \$4.39$

Inventory in units 6,000 units
Ending inventory $6,000 \times \$4.39 = \$26,340$

Cost of goods available for sale	$43,900
Deduct: Ending inventory	26,340
Cost of goods sold	$17,560

[4]The motion picture industry provides a good illustration of the cost allocation problem. Often actors receive a percentage of net income for a given movie or television program. Some actors, however, have alleged that their programs have been extremely profitable to the motion picture studios but they have received little in the way of profit-sharing. Actors contend that the studios allocate additional costs to successful projects to avoid sharing profits.

In computing the average cost per unit, Call-Mart includes the beginning inventory, if any, both in the total units available and in the total cost of goods available.

Companies use the **moving-average method** with perpetual inventory records. Illustration 8-14 shows the application of the average-cost method for perpetual records.

ILLUSTRATION 8-14
Moving-Average Method—Perpetual Inventory

Date	Purchased		Sold or Issued	Balance	
March 2	(2,000 @ $4.00)	$ 8,000		(2,000 @ $4.00)	$ 8,000
March 15	(6,000 @ 4.40)	26,400		(8,000 @ 4.30)	34,400
March 19			(4,000 @ $4.30) $17,200	(4,000 @ 4.30)	17,200
March 30	(2,000 @ 4.75)	9,500		(6,000 @ 4.45)	26,700

In this method, Call-Mart computes a **new average unit cost** each time it makes a purchase. For example, on March 15, after purchasing 6,000 units for $26,400, Call-Mart has 8,000 units costing $34,400 ($8,000 plus $26,400) on hand. The average unit cost is $34,400 divided by 8,000, or $4.30. Call-Mart uses this unit cost in costing withdrawals until it makes another purchase. At that point, Call-Mart computes a new average unit cost. Accordingly, the company shows the cost of the 4,000 units withdrawn on March 19 at $4.30, for a total cost of goods sold of $17,200. On March 30, following the purchase of 2,000 units for $9,500, Call-Mart determines a new unit cost of $4.45, for an ending inventory of $26,700.

Companies often use average-cost methods for practical rather than conceptual reasons. These methods are both simple to apply and objective. They are not as subject to income manipulation as some of the other inventory pricing methods. In addition, proponents of the average-cost methods reason that measuring a specific physical flow of inventory is often impossible. Therefore, it is better to cost items on an average-price basis. This argument is particularly persuasive when dealing with similar inventory items.

First-In, First-Out (FIFO)

The **FIFO (first-in, first-out) method** assumes that a company uses goods in the order in which it purchases them. In other words, the FIFO method assumes that **the first goods purchased are the first used** (in a manufacturing concern) **or the first sold** (in a merchandising concern). The inventory remaining must therefore represent the most recent purchases.

To illustrate, assume that Call-Mart uses the periodic inventory system. It determines its cost of the ending inventory by taking the cost of the most recent purchase and working back until it accounts for all units in the inventory. Call-Mart determines its ending inventory and cost of goods sold as shown in Illustration 8-15.

ILLUSTRATION 8-15
FIFO Method—Periodic Inventory

Date	No. Units	Unit Cost	Total Cost
March 30	2,000	$4.75	$ 9,500
March 15	4,000	4.40	17,600
Ending inventory	6,000		$27,100

Cost of goods available for sale	$43,900
Deduct: Ending inventory	27,100
Cost of goods sold	$16,800

If Call-Mart instead uses a perpetual inventory system in quantities and dollars, it attaches a cost figure to each withdrawal. Then the cost of the 4,000 units removed on March 19 consists of the cost of the items purchased on March 2 and March 15. Illustration 8-16 shows the inventory on a FIFO basis perpetual system for Call-Mart.

ILLUSTRATION 8-16
FIFO Method—Perpetual Inventory

Date	Purchased		Sold or Issued	Balance	
March 2	(2,000 @ $4.00)	$ 8,000		2,000 @ $4.00	$ 8,000
March 15	(6,000 @ 4.40)	26,400		2,000 @ 4.00 6,000 @ 4.40	34,400
March 19			2,000 @ $4.00 2,000 @ 4.40 ($16,800)	4,000 @ 4.40	17,600
March 30	(2,000 @ 4.75)	9,500		4,000 @ 4.40 2,000 @ 4.75	27,100

Here, the ending inventory is $27,100, and the cost of goods sold is $16,800 [(2,000 @ $4.00) + (2,000 @ $4.40)].

Notice that in these two FIFO examples, the cost of goods sold ($16,800) and ending inventory ($27,100) are the same. **In all cases where FIFO is used, the inventory and cost of goods sold would be the same at the end of the month whether a perpetual or periodic system is used.** Why? Because the same costs will always be first in and, therefore, first out. This is true whether a company computes cost of goods sold as it sells goods throughout the accounting period (the perpetual system) or as a residual at the end of the accounting period (the periodic system).

One objective of FIFO is to approximate the physical flow of goods. When the physical flow of goods is actually first-in, first-out, the FIFO method closely approximates specific identification. At the same time, it prevents manipulation of income. With FIFO, a company cannot pick a certain cost item to charge to expense.

Another advantage of the FIFO method is that the ending inventory is close to current cost. Because the first goods in are the first goods out, the ending inventory amount consists of the most recent purchases. This is particularly true with rapid inventory turnover. This approach generally approximates replacement cost on the balance sheet when price changes have not occurred since the most recent purchases.

However, the FIFO method fails to match current costs against current revenues on the income statement. A company charges the oldest costs against the more current revenue, possibly distorting gross profit and net income.

Last-In, First-Out (LIFO)

International Perspective

IFRS does not permit LIFO.

The **LIFO (last-in, first-out) method** matches the cost of the last goods purchased against revenue. If Call-Mart Inc. uses a periodic inventory system, it assumes that **the cost of the total quantity sold or issued during the month comes from the most recent purchases.** Call-Mart prices the ending inventory by using the total units as a basis of computation and disregards the exact dates of sales or issuances. For example, Call-Mart would assume that the cost of the 4,000 units withdrawn absorbed the 2,000 units purchased on March 30 and 2,000 of the 6,000 units purchased on March 15. Illustration 8-17 (page 432) shows how Call-Mart computes the inventory and related cost of goods sold, using the periodic inventory method.

If Call-Mart keeps a perpetual inventory record in quantities and dollars, use of the LIFO method results in **different ending inventory and cost of goods sold amounts**

ILLUSTRATION 8-17
LIFO Method—Periodic Inventory

Date of Invoice	No. Units	Unit Cost	Total Cost
March 2	2,000	$4.00	$ 8,000
March 15	4,000	4.40	17,600
Ending inventory	6,000		$25,600

Goods available for sale	$43,900
Deduct: Ending inventory	25,600
Cost of goods sold	$18,300

than the amounts calculated under the periodic method. Illustration 8-18 shows these differences under the perpetual method.

ILLUSTRATION 8-18
LIFO Method—Perpetual Inventory

Date	Purchased		Sold or Issued	Balance	
March 2	(2,000 @ $4.00)	$ 8,000		2,000 @ $4.00	$ 8,000
March 15	(6,000 @ 4.40)	26,400		2,000 @ 4.00 6,000 @ 4.40	34,400
March 19			(4,000 @ $4.40) $17,600	2,000 @ 4.00 2,000 @ 4.40	16,800
March 30	(2,000 @ 4.75)	9,500		2,000 @ 4.00 2,000 @ 4.40 2,000 @ 4.75	26,300

Gateway to the Profession
Tutorial on Inventory Methods

The month-end periodic inventory computation presented in Illustration 8-17 (inventory $25,600 and cost of goods sold $18,300) shows a different amount from the perpetual inventory computation (inventory $26,300 and cost of goods sold $17,600). The periodic system matches the total withdrawals for the month with the total purchases for the month in applying the last-in, first-out method. In contrast, the perpetual system matches each withdrawal with the immediately preceding purchases. In effect, the periodic computation assumed that Call-Mart included the cost of the goods that it purchased on March 30 in the sale or issue on March 19.

SPECIAL ISSUES RELATED TO LIFO

LIFO Reserve

LEARNING OBJECTIVE 6
Explain the significance and use of a LIFO reserve.

Many companies use LIFO for tax and external reporting purposes. However, they maintain a FIFO, average-cost, or standard cost system for internal reporting purposes. There are several reasons to do so. (1) Companies often base their pricing decisions on a FIFO, average, or standard cost assumption, rather than on a LIFO basis. (2) Recordkeeping on some other basis is easier because the LIFO assumption usually does not approximate the physical flow of the product. (3) Profit-sharing and other bonus arrangements often depend on a non-LIFO inventory assumption. (4) The use of a pure LIFO system is troublesome for interim periods, which require estimates of year-end quantities and prices.

The difference between the inventory method used for internal reporting purposes and LIFO is the Allowance to Reduce Inventory to LIFO account or the **LIFO reserve**. The change in the allowance balance from one period to the next is the **LIFO effect**. The LIFO effect is the adjustment that companies must make to the accounting records in a given year.

To illustrate, assume that Acme Boot Company uses the FIFO method for internal reporting purposes and LIFO for external reporting purposes. At January 1, 2014, the Allowance to Reduce Inventory to LIFO balance is $20,000. At December 31, 2014, the balance should be $50,000. As a result, Acme Boot realizes a LIFO effect of $30,000 and makes the following entry at year-end.

Cost of Goods Sold	30,000	
Allowance to Reduce Inventory to LIFO		30,000

Acme Boot deducts Allowance to Reduce Inventory to LIFO from inventory to ensure that it states the inventory on a LIFO basis at year-end.

Companies should disclose either the LIFO reserve or the replacement cost of the inventory, as shown in Illustration 8-19. **[7]**

ILLUSTRATION 8-19
Note Disclosures of LIFO Reserve

American Maize-Products Company

Inventories (Note 3)	$80,320,000

Note 3: Inventories. At December 31, $31,516,000 of inventories were valued using the LIFO method. This amount is less than the corresponding replacement value by $3,765,000.

Brown Shoe Company, Inc.
(in thousands)

	Current Year	Previous Year
Inventories, (Note 1)	$365,989	$362,274

Note 1 (partial): Inventories. Inventories are valued at the lower of cost or market determined principally by the last-in, first-out (LIFO) method. If the first-in, first-out (FIFO) cost method had been used, inventories would have been $11,709 higher in the current year and $13,424 higher in the previous year.

What do the numbers mean? COMPARING APPLES TO APPLES

Investors commonly use the current ratio to evaluate a company's liquidity. They compute the current ratio as current assets divided by current liabilities. A higher current ratio indicates that a company is better able to meet its current obligations when they come due. However, it is not meaningful to compare the current ratio for a company using LIFO to one for a company using FIFO. It would be like comparing apples to oranges since the two companies measure inventory (and cost of goods sold) differently.

To make the current ratio comparable on an apples-to-apples basis, analysts use the LIFO reserve. The following adjustments should do the trick:

> Inventory Adjustment: LIFO inventory + LIFO reserve = FIFO inventory

(For cost of goods sold, deduct the *change* in the LIFO reserve from LIFO cost of goods sold to yield the comparable FIFO amount.)

For **Brown Shoe, Inc.** (see Illustration 8-19), with current assets of $487.8 million and current liabilities of $217.8 million, the current ratio using LIFO is $487.8 ÷ $217.8 = 2.2. After adjusting for the LIFO effect, Brown Shoe's current ratio under FIFO would be ($487.8 + $11.7) ÷ $217.8 = 2.3.

Thus, without the LIFO adjustment, the Brown Shoe current ratio is understated.

LIFO Liquidation

LEARNING OBJECTIVE 7

Understand the effect of LIFO liquidations.

Up to this point, we have emphasized a **specific-goods approach** to costing LIFO inventories (also called **traditional LIFO** or **unit LIFO**). This approach is often unrealistic for two reasons:

1. When a company has many different inventory items, the accounting cost of tracking each inventory item is expensive.
2. Erosion of the LIFO inventory can easily occur. Referred to as **LIFO liquidation**, this often distorts net income and leads to substantial tax payments.

To understand the LIFO liquidation problem, assume that Basler Co. has 30,000 pounds of steel in its inventory on December 31, 2014, with cost determined on a specific-goods LIFO approach.

Ending Inventory (2014)

	Pounds	Unit Cost	LIFO Cost
2011	8,000	$ 4	$ 32,000
2012	10,000	6	60,000
2013	7,000	9	63,000
2014	5,000	10	50,000
	30,000		$205,000

As indicated, the ending 2014 inventory for Basler comprises costs from past periods. These costs are called **layers** (increases from period to period). The first layer is identified as the base layer. Illustration 8-20 shows the layers for Basler.

ILLUSTRATION 8-20
Layers of LIFO Inventory

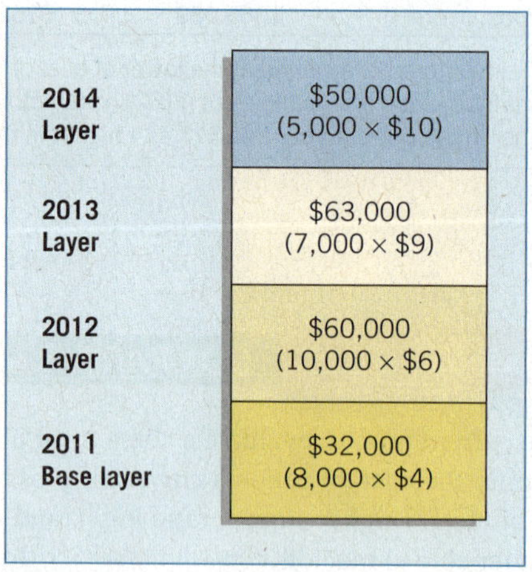

Note the increased price of steel over the four-year period. In 2015, due to metal shortages, Basler had to liquidate much of its inventory (a LIFO liquidation). At the end of 2015, only 6,000 pounds of steel remained in inventory. Because the company uses LIFO, Basler liquidates the most recent layer, 2014, first, followed by the 2013 layer, and so on. The result: Basler matches costs from preceding periods against sales revenues reported in current dollars. As Illustration 8-21 shows, this leads to a distortion in net income and increased taxable income in the current period. Unfortunately, **LIFO liquidations can occur frequently when using a specific-goods LIFO approach.**

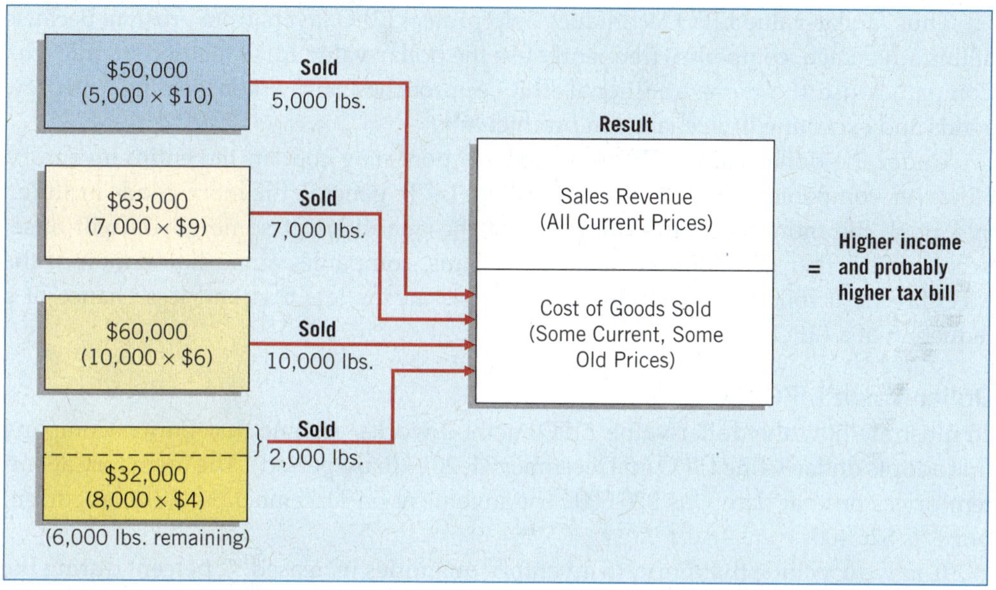

ILLUSTRATION 8-21
LIFO Liquidation

To alleviate the LIFO liquidation problems and to simplify the accounting, companies can combine goods into pools. A **pool** groups items of a similar nature. Thus, instead of only identical units, a company combines, and counts as a group, a number of similar units or products. This method, the **specific-goods pooled LIFO approach**, usually results in fewer LIFO liquidations. Why? Because the reduction of one quantity in the pool may be offset by an increase in another.

The specific-goods pooled LIFO approach eliminates some of the disadvantages of the specific-goods (traditional) accounting for LIFO inventories. This pooled approach, using quantities as its measurement basis, however, creates other problems.

First, most companies continually change the mix of their products, materials, and production methods. As a result, in employing a pooled approach using quantities, companies must continually redefine the pools. This can be time-consuming and costly. Second, even when practical, the approach often results in an erosion ("LIFO liquidation") of the layers, thereby losing much of the LIFO costing benefit. Erosion of the layers occurs when a specific good or material in the pool is replaced with another good or material. The new item may not be similar enough to be treated as part of the old pool. Therefore, a company may need to recognize any inflationary profit deferred on the old goods as it replaces them.

Dollar-Value LIFO

8 LEARNING OBJECTIVE
Explain the dollar-value LIFO method.

The dollar-value LIFO method overcomes the problems of redefining pools and eroding layers. **The dollar-value LIFO method determines and measures any increases and decreases in a pool in terms of total dollar value, not the physical quantity of the goods in the inventory pool.**

Such an approach has two important advantages over the specific-goods pooled approach. First, companies may include a broader range of goods in a dollar-value LIFO pool. Second, a dollar-value LIFO pool permits replacement of goods that are similar items, similar in use, or interchangeable. (In contrast, a specific-goods LIFO pool only allows replacement of items that are substantially identical.)

Thus, dollar-value LIFO techniques help protect LIFO layers from erosion. Because of this advantage, companies frequently use the dollar-value LIFO method in practice.[5] Companies use the more traditional LIFO approaches only when dealing with few goods and expecting little change in product mix.

Under the dollar-value LIFO method, one pool may contain the entire inventory. However, companies generally use several pools.[6] In general, the more goods included in a pool, the more likely that increases in the quantities of some goods will offset decreases in other goods in the same pool. Thus, companies avoid liquidation of the LIFO layers. It follows that having fewer pools means less cost and less chance of a reduction of a LIFO layer.[7]

Gateway to the Profession

Tutorial on Dollar-Value LIFO

Dollar-Value LIFO Example

To illustrate how the dollar-value LIFO method works, assume that Enrico Company first adopts dollar-value LIFO on December 31, 2013 (base period). The inventory at current prices on that date was $20,000. The inventory on December 31, 2014, at current prices is $26,400.

Can we conclude that Enrico's inventory quantities increased 32 percent during the year ($26,400 ÷ $20,000 = 132%)? First, we need to ask: What is the value of the ending inventory in terms of beginning-of-the-year prices? Assuming that prices have increased 20 percent during the year, the ending inventory at beginning-of-the-year prices amounts to $22,000 ($26,400 ÷ 120%). Therefore, the inventory quantity has increased only 10 percent, or from $20,000 to $22,000 in terms of beginning-of-the-year prices.

The next step is to price this real-dollar quantity increase. This real-dollar quantity increase of $2,000 valued at year-end prices is $2,400 (120% × $2,000). This increment (layer) of $2,400, when added to the beginning inventory of $20,000, totals $22,400 for the December 31, 2014, inventory, as shown below.

First layer—(beginning inventory) in terms of 100	$20,000
Second layer—(2014 increase) in terms of 120	2,400
Dollar-value LIFO inventory, December 31, 2014	$22,400

Note that a layer forms only when the ending inventory at base-year prices exceeds the beginning inventory at base-year prices. And only when a new layer forms must Enrico compute a new index.

[5]A study by James M. Reeve and Keith G. Stanga disclosed that the vast majority of respondent companies applying LIFO use the dollar-value method or the dollar-value retail method to apply LIFO. Only a small minority of companies use the specific-goods (unit LIFO) approach or the specific-goods pooling approach. See J.M. Reeve and K.G. Stanga, "The LIFO Pooling Decision," *Accounting Horizons* (June 1987), p. 27.

[6]The Reeve and Stanga study (*ibid.*) reports that most companies have only a few pools—the median is six for retailers and three for nonretailers. But the distributions are highly skewed; some companies have 100 or more pools. Retailers that use LIFO have significantly more pools than nonretailers. About a third of the nonretailers (mostly manufacturers) use a single pool for their entire LIFO inventory.

[7]A later study shows that when quantities are increasing, multiple pools over a period of time may produce (under rather general conditions) significantly higher cost of goods sold deductions than a single-pool approach. When a stock-out occurs, a single-pool approach may lessen the layer liquidation for that year, but it may not erase the cumulative cost of goods sold advantage accruing to the use of multiple pools built up over the preceding years. See William R. Coon and Randall B. Hayes, "The Dollar Value LIFO Pooling Decision: The Conventional Wisdom Is Too General," *Accounting Horizons* (December 1989), pp. 57–70.

Comprehensive Dollar-Value LIFO Example

To illustrate the use of the dollar-value LIFO method in a more complex situation, assume that Bismark Company develops the following information.

December 31		Inventory at End-of-Year Prices	÷	Price Index (percentage)	=	End-of-Year Inventory at Base-Year Prices
(Base year)	2011	$200,000		100		$200,000
	2012	299,000		115		260,000
	2013	300,000		120		250,000
	2014	351,000		130		270,000

At December 31, 2011, Bismark computes the ending inventory under dollar-value LIFO as $200,000, as Illustration 8-22 shows.

ILLUSTRATION 8-22
Computation of 2011 Inventory at LIFO Cost

Ending Inventory at Base-Year Prices	Layer at Base-Year Prices		Price Index (percentage)		Ending Inventory at LIFO Cost
$200,000	$200,000	×	100	=	$200,000

At December 31, 2012, a comparison of the ending inventory at base-year prices ($260,000) with the beginning inventory at base-year prices ($200,000) indicates that the quantity of goods (in base-year prices) increased $60,000 ($260,000 − $200,000). Bismark prices this increment (layer) at the 2012 index of 115 percent to arrive at a new layer of $69,000. Ending inventory for 2012 is $269,000, composed of the beginning inventory of $200,000 and the new layer of $69,000. Illustration 8-23 shows the computations.

ILLUSTRATION 8-23
Computation of 2012 Inventory at LIFO Cost

Ending Inventory at Base-Year Prices	Layers at Base-Year Prices			Price Index (percentage)		Ending Inventory at LIFO Cost
$260,000 →	2011	$200,000	×	100	=	$200,000
→	2012	60,000	×	115	=	69,000
		$260,000				$269,000

At December 31, 2013, a comparison of the ending inventory at base-year prices ($250,000) with the beginning inventory at base-year prices ($260,000) indicates a decrease in the quantity of goods of $10,000 ($250,000 − $260,000). If the ending inventory at base-year prices is less than the beginning inventory at base-year prices, **a company must subtract the decrease from the most recently added layer. When a decrease occurs, the company "peels off" previous layers at the prices in existence when it added the layers.** In Bismark's situation, this means that it removes $10,000 in base-year prices from the 2012 layer of $60,000 at base-year prices. It values the balance of $50,000 ($60,000 − $10,000) at base-year prices at the 2012 price index of 115 percent. As a result, it now values this 2012 layer at $57,500 ($50,000 × 115%). Therefore, Bismark computes the ending inventory at $257,500, consisting of the beginning inventory of $200,000 and the second layer of $57,500. Illustration 8-24 (page 438) shows the computations for 2013.

ILLUSTRATION 8-24
Computation of 2013 Inventory at LIFO Cost

Ending Inventory at Base-Year Prices	Layers at Base-Year Prices			Price Index (percentage)		Ending Inventory at LIFO Cost
$250,000	2011	$200,000	×	100	=	$200,000
	2012	50,000	×	115	=	57,500
		$250,000				$257,500

Note that if Bismark eliminates a layer or base (or portion thereof), it cannot rebuild it in future periods. That is, the layer is gone forever.

At December 31, 2014, a comparison of the ending inventory at base-year prices ($270,000) with the beginning inventory at base-year prices ($250,000) indicates an increase in the quantity of goods (in base-year prices) of $20,000 ($270,000 − $250,000). After converting the $20,000 increase, using the 2014 price index, the ending inventory is $283,500, composed of the beginning layer of $200,000, a 2012 layer of $57,500, and a 2014 layer of $26,000 ($20,000 × 130%). Illustration 8-25 shows this computation.

ILLUSTRATION 8-25
Computation of 2014 Inventory at LIFO Cost

Ending Inventory at Base-Year Prices	Layers at Base-Year Prices			Price Index (percentage)		Ending Inventory at LIFO Cost
$270,000	2011	$200,000	×	100	=	$200,000
	2012	50,000	×	115	=	57,500
	2014	20,000	×	130	=	26,000
		$270,000				$283,500

The ending inventory at base-year prices must always equal the total of the layers at base-year prices. Checking that this situation exists will help to ensure correct dollar-value computations.

Selecting a Price Index

Obviously, price changes are critical in dollar-value LIFO. How do companies determine the price indexes? Many companies use the general price-level index that the federal government prepares and publishes each month. The most popular general external price-level index is the **Consumer Price Index for Urban Consumers** (CPI-U).[8] Companies also use more-specific external price indexes. For instance, various organizations compute and publish daily indexes for most commodities (gold, silver, other metals, corn, wheat, and other farm products). Many trade associations prepare indexes for specific product lines or industries. Any of these indexes may be used for dollar-value LIFO purposes.

When a relevant specific external price index is not readily available, a company may compute its own specific internal price index. The desired approach is to price ending inventory at the most current cost. Therefore, a company that chose to compute its own specific internal price index would ordinarily determine current cost by referring to the actual cost of the goods it most recently had purchased. The price index provides a measure of the change in price or cost levels between the base year and the current year. The company then computes the index for each year after the base year. The general formula for computing the index is as follows.

[8]Indexes may be **general** (composed of several commodities, goods, or services) or **specific** (for one commodity, good, or service). Additionally, they may be **external** (computed by an outside party, such as the government, commodity exchange, or trade association) or **internal** (computed by the enterprise for its own product or service).

$$\frac{\text{Ending Inventory for the Period at Current Cost}}{\text{Ending Inventory for the Period at Base-Year Cost}} = \text{Price Index for Current Year}$$

ILLUSTRATION 8-26
Formula for Computing a Price Index

This approach is generally referred to as the **double-extension method**. As its name implies, the value of the units in inventory is extended at *both* base-year prices and current-year prices.

To illustrate this computation, assume that Toledo Company's base-year inventory (January 1, 2014) consisted of the following.

Items	Quantity	Cost per Unit	Total Cost
A	1,000	$ 6	$ 6,000
B	2,000	20	40,000
January 1, 2014, inventory at base-year costs			$46,000

Examination of the ending inventory indicates that the company holds 3,000 units of Item A and 6,000 units of Item B on December 31, 2014. The most recent actual purchases related to these items were as follows.

Items	Purchase Date	Quantity Purchased	Cost per Unit
A	December 1, 2014	4,000	$ 7
B	December 15, 2014	5,000	25
B	November 16, 2014	1,000	22

Toledo double-extends the inventory as shown in Illustration 8-27.

ILLUSTRATION 8-27
Double-Extension Method of Determining a Price Index

	12/31/14 Inventory at Base-Year Costs			12/31/14 Inventory at Current-Year Costs		
Items	Units	Base-Year Cost per Unit	Total	Units	Current-Year Cost per Unit	Total
A	3,000	$ 6	$ 18,000	3,000	$ 7	$ 21,000
B	6,000	20	120,000	5,000	25	125,000
B				1,000	22	22,000
			$138,000			$168,000

After the inventories are double-extended, Toledo uses the formula in Illustration 8-26 to develop the index for the current year (2014), as follows.

$$\frac{\text{Ending Inventory for the Period at Current Cost}}{\text{Ending Inventory for the Period at Base-Year Cost}} = \frac{\$168{,}000}{\$138{,}000} = 121.74\%$$

ILLUSTRATION 8-28
Computation of 2014 Index

Toledo then applies this index (121.74%) to the layer added in 2014. Note in this illustration that Toledo used the most recent actual purchases to determine current cost. Alternatively, it could have used other approaches such as FIFO and average-cost. Whichever flow assumption is adopted, a company must use it consistently from one period to another.

Use of the double-extension method is time-consuming and difficult where substantial technological change has occurred or where many items are involved. That is, as time passes, the company must determine a new base-year cost for new products, and must keep a base-year cost for each inventory item.[9]

What do the numbers mean? QUITE A DIFFERENCE

As indicated, significant differences can arise in inventory measured according to current cost and dollar-value LIFO. Let's look at an additional summary example.

Truman Company uses the dollar-value LIFO method of computing its inventory. Inventory for the last three years is as shown below.

Year Ended December 31	Inventory at Current-Year Cost	Price Index
2012	$60,000	100
2013	84,000	105
2014	87,000	116

The values of the 2012, 2013, and 2014 inventories using the dollar-value LIFO method are presented in the table below.

Year	Inventory at End-of-Year Prices	Inventory at Base-Year Prices	Layers at Base-Year Prices	×	Price-Index Layers at LIFO Cost	Dollar-Value LIFO Inventory
2012	$60,000	$60,000 ÷ 100 = $60,000	2012 $60,000	×	100 = $60,000	$60,000
2013	84,000	$84,000 ÷ 105 = $80,000	2012 $60,000	×	100 = $60,000	
			2013 20,000	×	105 = $21,000	$81,000
2014	87,000	$87,000 ÷ 116 = $75,000	2012 $60,000	×	100 = $60,000	
			2013 15,000	×	105 = $15,750	$75,750

As indicated, consistent with LIFO costing in times of rising prices, the dollar-value LIFO inventory amount is less than inventory stated at end-of-year prices. The company did not add layers at the 2014 prices. This is because the increase in inventory at end-of-year (current) prices was primarily due to higher prices. Also, establishing the LIFO layers based on price-adjusted dollars relative to base-year layers reduces the likelihood of a LIFO liquidation.

Comparison of LIFO Approaches

We present three different approaches to computing LIFO inventories in this chapter—specific-goods LIFO, specific-goods pooled LIFO, and dollar-value LIFO. As we indicated earlier, the use of the specific-goods LIFO is unrealistic. Most companies have numerous goods in inventory at the end of a period. Costing (pricing) them on a unit basis is extremely expensive and time-consuming.

The specific-goods pooled LIFO approach reduces recordkeeping and clerical costs. In addition, it is more difficult to erode the layers because the reduction of one quantity in the pool may be offset by an increase in another. Nonetheless, the pooled approach using quantities as its measurement basis can lead to untimely LIFO liquidations.

As a result, **most companies using a LIFO system employ dollar-value LIFO**. Although the approach appears complex, the logic and the computations are actually quite simple, after determining an appropriate index.

[9]To simplify the analysis, companies may use another approach, initially sanctioned by the Internal Revenue Service for tax purposes. Under this method, a company obtains an index from an outside source or by double-extending only a sample portion of the inventory. For example, the IRS allows all companies to use as their inflation rate for a LIFO pool 80 percent of the inflation rate reported by the appropriate consumer or producer price indexes prepared by the Bureau of Labor Statistics (BLS). Once the company obtains the index, it divides the ending inventory at current cost by the index to find the base-year cost. Using generally available external indexes greatly simplifies LIFO computations, and frees companies from having to compute internal indexes.

However, problems do exist with the dollar-value LIFO method. The selection of the items to be put in a pool can be subjective.[10] Such a determination, however, is extremely important because manipulation of the items in a pool without conceptual justification can affect reported net income. For example, the SEC noted that some companies have set up pools that are easy to liquidate. As a result, to increase income, a company simply decreases inventory, thereby matching low-cost inventory items to current revenues.

To curb this practice, the SEC has taken a much harder line on the number of pools that companies may establish. In a well-publicized case, **Stauffer Chemical Company** increased the number of LIFO pools from 8 to 280, boosting its net income by $16,515,000 or approximately 13 percent. Stauffer justified the change in its annual report on the basis of "achieving a better matching of cost and revenue." The SEC required Stauffer to reduce the number of its inventory pools, contending that some pools were inappropriate and alleging income manipulation.

Major Advantages of LIFO

9 LEARNING OBJECTIVE
Identify the major advantages and disadvantages of LIFO.

One obvious advantage of LIFO approaches is that the LIFO cost flow often approximates the physical flow of the goods in and out of inventory. For instance, in a coal pile, the last coal in is the first coal out because it is on the top of the pile. The coal remover is not going to take the coal from the bottom of the pile! The coal taken first is the coal placed on the pile last.

However, this is one of only a few situations where the actual physical flow corresponds to LIFO. Therefore, most adherents of LIFO use other arguments for its widespread use, as follows.

Matching

LIFO matches the more recent costs against current revenues to provide a better measure of current earnings. During periods of inflation, many challenge the quality of non-LIFO earnings, noting that failing to match current costs against current revenues **creates transitory or "paper" profits ("inventory profits")**. Inventory profits occur when the inventory costs matched against sales are less than the inventory replacement cost. This results in understating the cost of goods sold and overstating profit. Using LIFO (rather than a method such as FIFO) matches current costs against revenues, thereby reducing inventory profits.

Tax Benefits/Improved Cash Flow

LIFO's popularity mainly stems from its tax benefits. As long as the price level increases and inventory quantities do not decrease, a deferral of income tax occurs. Why? Because a company matches the items it most recently purchased (at the higher price level) against revenues. For example, when **Fuqua Industries** switched to LIFO, it realized a tax savings of about $4 million. Even if the price level decreases later, the company still temporarily deferred its income taxes. Thus, use of LIFO in such situations improves a company's cash flow.[11]

[10]It is suggested that companies analyze how inventory purchases are affected by price changes, how goods are stocked, how goods are used, and if future liquidations are likely. See William R. Cron and Randall Hayes, *ibid.*, p. 57.

[11]In periods of rising prices, the use of fewer pools will translate into greater income tax benefits through the use of LIFO. The use of fewer pools allows companies to offset inventory reductions on some items and inventory increases in others. In contrast, the use of more pools increases the likelihood of liquidating old, low-cost inventory layers and incurring negative tax consequences. See Reeve and Stanga, *ibid.*, pp. 28–29.

The tax law requires that if a company uses LIFO for tax purposes, it must also use LIFO for financial accounting purposes[12] (although neither tax law nor GAAP requires a company to pool its inventories in the same manner for book and tax purposes). This requirement is often referred to as the **LIFO conformity rule**. Other inventory valuation methods do not have this requirement.

Future Earnings Hedge

With LIFO, future price declines will not substantially affect a company's future reported earnings. The reason: Since the company records the most recent inventory as sold first, there is not much ending inventory at high prices vulnerable to a price decline. Thus LIFO eliminates or substantially minimizes write-downs to market as a result of price decreases. In contrast, inventory costed under FIFO is more vulnerable to price declines, which can reduce net income substantially.

Major Disadvantages of LIFO

Despite its advantages, LIFO has the following drawbacks.

Reduced Earnings

Many corporate managers view the lower profits reported under the LIFO method in inflationary times as a distinct disadvantage. They would rather have higher reported profits than lower taxes. Some fear that investors may misunderstand an accounting change to LIFO, and that the lower profits may cause the price of the company's stock to fall.

Inventory Understated

LIFO may have a distorting effect on a company's balance sheet. The inventory valuation is normally outdated because the oldest costs remain in inventory. This understatement makes the working capital position of the company appear worse than it really is. A good example is **Caterpillar**, which uses LIFO costing for most of its inventory, valued at $14.5 billion at year-end 2011. Under FIFO costing, Caterpillar's inventories have a value of $16.7 billion—approximately 5 percent higher than the LIFO amount.

The magnitude and direction of this variation between the carrying amount of inventory and its current price depend on the degree and direction of the price changes and the amount of inventory turnover. The combined effect of rising product prices and avoidance of inventory liquidations increases the difference between the inventory carrying value at LIFO and current prices of that inventory. This magnifies the balance sheet distortion attributed to the use of LIFO.

Physical Flow

LIFO does not approximate the physical flow of the items except in specific situations (such as the coal pile discussed earlier). Originally, companies could use LIFO only in certain circumstances. This situation has changed over the years. Now, physical flow characteristics no longer determine whether a company may employ LIFO.

Involuntary Liquidation/Poor Buying Habits

If a company eliminates the base or layers of old costs, it may match old, irrelevant costs against current revenues. A distortion in reported income for a given period may result, as well as detrimental income tax consequences. For example, **Caterpillar** recently experienced a LIFO liquidation, resulting in an increased tax bill of $60 million.[13]

[12]Management often selects an accounting procedure because a lower tax results from its use, instead of an accounting method that is conceptually more appealing. Throughout this textbook, we identify accounting procedures that provide income tax benefits to the user.

[13]Companies should disclose the effects on income of LIFO inventory liquidations in the notes to the financial statements. [8]

Because of the liquidation problem, LIFO may cause poor buying habits. A company may simply purchase more goods and match these goods against revenue to avoid charging the old costs to expense. Furthermore, recall that with LIFO, a company may attempt to manipulate its net income at the end of the year simply by altering its pattern of purchases.[14]

One survey uncovered the following reasons why companies reject LIFO.[15]

ILLUSTRATION 8-29
Why Do Companies Reject LIFO? Summary of Responses

Reasons to Reject LIFO	Number	% of Total*
No expected tax benefits		
No required tax payment	34	16%
Declining prices	31	15
Rapid inventory turnover	30	14
Immaterial inventory	26	12
Miscellaneous tax related	38	17
	159	74%
Regulatory or other restrictions	26	12%
Excessive cost		
High administrative costs	29	14%
LIFO liquidation–related costs	12	6
	41	20%
Other adverse consequences		
Lower reported earnings	18	8%
Bad accounting	7	3
	25	11%

*Percentage totals more than 100% as some companies offered more than one explanation.

BASIS FOR SELECTION OF INVENTORY METHOD

10 LEARNING OBJECTIVE
Understand why companies select given inventory methods.

How does a company choose among the various inventory methods? Although no absolute rules can be stated, preferability for LIFO usually occurs in either of the following circumstances: (1) if selling prices and revenues have been increasing faster than costs, thereby distorting income, and (2) in situations where LIFO has been traditional, such as department stores and industries where a fairly constant "base stock" is present (such as refining, chemicals, and glass).[16]

Conversely, LIFO is probably inappropriate in the following circumstances: (1) where prices tend to lag behind costs; (2) in situations where specific identification is traditional, such as in the sale of automobiles, farm equipment, art, and antique jewelry; or (3) where unit costs tend to decrease as production increases, thereby nullifying the tax benefit that LIFO might provide.[17]

[14]For example, **General Tire and Rubber** accelerated raw material purchases at the end of the year to minimize the book profit from a liquidation of LIFO inventories and to minimize income taxes for the year.

[15]Michael H. Granof and Daniel Short, "Why Do Companies Reject LIFO?" *Journal of Accounting, Auditing, and Finance* (Summer 1984), pp. 323–333 and Table 1, p. 327.

[16]*Accounting Trends and Techniques—2012* reports that of 669 inventory method disclosures, 163 used LIFO, 312 used FIFO, 133 used average-cost, and 56 used other methods. As discussed in the opening story, because of steady or falling raw materials costs and costs savings from electronic data interchange and just-in-time technologies in recent years, many businesses using LIFO no longer experience substantial tax benefits. Even some companies for which LIFO is creating a benefit are finding that the administrative costs associated with LIFO are higher than the LIFO benefit obtained. As a result, some companies are moving to FIFO or average-cost.

[17]See Barry E. Cushing and Marc J. LeClere, "Evidence on the Determinants of Inventory Accounting Policy Choice," *The Accounting Review* (April 1992), pp. 355–366 and Table 4, p. 363, for a list of factors hypothesized to affect FIFO–LIFO choices.

Tax consequences are another consideration. Switching from FIFO to LIFO usually results in an immediate tax benefit. However, switching from LIFO to FIFO can result in a substantial tax burden. For example, when **Chrysler** changed from LIFO to FIFO, it became responsible for an additional $53 million in taxes that the company had deferred over 14 years of LIFO inventory valuation. Why, then, would Chrysler, and other companies, change to FIFO? The major reason was the profit crunch of that era. Although Chrysler showed a loss of $7.6 million after the switch, the loss would have been $20 million *more* if the company had not changed its inventory valuation from LIFO to FIFO.

It is questionable whether companies should switch from LIFO to FIFO for the sole purpose of increasing reported earnings. Intuitively, we would assume that companies with higher reported earnings would have a higher share valuation (common stock price). However, some studies have indicated that the users of financial data exhibit a much higher sophistication than might be expected. Share prices are the same and, in some cases, even higher under LIFO in spite of lower reported earnings.[18]

The concern about reduced income resulting from adoption of LIFO has even less substance now because the IRS has also relaxed the LIFO conformity rule which requires a company employing LIFO for tax purposes to use it for book purposes as well. The IRS has also relaxed restrictions against providing non-LIFO income numbers as supplementary information. As a result, companies now provide supplemental non-LIFO disclosures. While not intended to override the basic LIFO method adopted for financial reporting, these disclosures may be useful in comparing operating income and working capital with companies not on LIFO.

For example, **Sherwin-Williams Company**, a LIFO user, presented the information in its annual report as shown in Illustration 8-30.

ILLUSTRATION 8-30
Supplemental Non-LIFO Disclosure

Sherwin-Williams Company

Inventories were stated at the lower of cost or market with cost determined principally on the last-in, first-out (LIFO) method. The following presents the effect on inventories, net income and net income per common share had the Company used the first-in, first-out (FIFO) inventory valuation method adjusted for income taxes at the statutory rate and assuming no other adjustments.

	2011	2010
Percentage of total inventories on LIFO	77%	76%
Excess of FIFO over LIFO	$378,986	$277,164
(Decrease) increase in net income due to LIFO	(62,636)	(16,394)
(Decrease) increase in net income per common share due to LIFO	(.59)	(.15)

International Perspective

Many U.S. companies that have international operations use LIFO for U.S. purposes but use FIFO for their foreign subsidiaries.

Relaxation of the LIFO conformity rule has led some companies to select LIFO as their inventory valuation method because they will be able to disclose FIFO income numbers in the financial reports if they so desire.[19]

Companies often combine inventory methods. For example, **John Deere** uses LIFO for most of its inventories, and prices the remainder using FIFO. **The Hershey Company** follows the same practice. One reason for these practices is

[18]See, for example, Shyam Sunder, "Relationship Between Accounting Changes and Stock Prices: Problems of Measurement and Some Empirical Evidence," *Empirical Research in Accounting: Selected Studies, 1973* (Chicago: University of Chicago), pp. 1–40. But see Robert Moren Brown, "Short-Range Market Reaction to Changes to LIFO Accounting Using Preliminary Earnings Announcement Dates," *The Journal of Accounting Research* (Spring 1980), which found that companies that do change to LIFO suffer a short-run decline in the price of their stock.

[19]Note that a company can use one variation of LIFO for financial reporting purposes and another for tax without violating the LIFO conformity rule. Such a relaxation has caused many problems because the general approach to accounting for LIFO has been "whatever is good for tax is good for financial reporting."

that certain product lines can be highly susceptible to deflation instead of inflation. In addition, if the level of inventory is unstable, unwanted involuntary liquidations may result in certain product lines if using LIFO. Finally, for high inventory turnover in certain product lines, a company cannot justify LIFO's additional recordkeeping and expense. In such cases, a company often uses average-cost because it is easy to compute.[20]

Although a company may use a variety of inventory methods to assist in accurate computation of net income, once it selects a pricing method, it must apply it consistently thereafter. If conditions indicate that the inventory pricing method in use is unsuitable, the company must seriously consider all other possibilities before selecting another method. It should clearly explain any change and disclose its effect in the financial statements.

Evolving Issue REPEAL LIFO!

In some situations, use of LIFO can result in significant tax savings for companies. For example, **Sherwin-Williams Company** estimates its tax bill would increase by $16 million if it were to change from LIFO to FIFO. The option to use LIFO to reduce taxes has become a political issue because of the growing federal deficit. Some are proposing elimination of LIFO (and other tax law changes) to help reduce the federal deficit. Why pick on LIFO? Well, one recent budget estimate indicates that repeal of LIFO would help plug the budget deficit with over $61 billion in additional tax collections. In addition, since IFRS does not permit LIFO, its repeal will contribute to international accounting convergence.

Source: R. Bloom and W. Cenker, "The Death of LIFO?" *Journal of Accountancy* (January 2009), pp. 44–49.

Inventory Valuation Methods—Summary Analysis

The preceding sections of this chapter described a number of inventory valuation methods. Here we present a brief summary of the three major inventory methods to show the effects these valuation methods have on the financial statements. This comparison assumes periodic inventory procedures and the following selected data.

Selected Data		
Beginning cash balance		$ 7,000
Beginning retained earnings		$10,000
Beginning inventory:	4,000 units @ $3	$12,000
Purchases:	6,000 units @ $4	$24,000
Sales:	5,000 units @ $12	$60,000
Operating expenses		$10,000
Income tax rate		40%

Illustration 8-31 (page 446) shows the comparative results on net income of the use of average-cost, FIFO, and LIFO. Notice that gross profit and net income are lowest under LIFO, highest under FIFO, and somewhere in the middle under average-cost.

[20]For an interesting discussion of the reasons for and against the use of FIFO and average-cost, see Michael H. Granof and Daniel G. Short, "For Some Companies, FIFO Accounting Makes Sense," *Wall Street Journal* (August 30, 1982); and the subsequent rebuttal by Gary C. Biddle, "Taking Stock of Inventory Accounting Choices," *Wall Street Journal* (September 15, 1982).

ILLUSTRATION 8-31
Comparative Results of Average-Cost, FIFO, and LIFO Methods

	Average-Cost	FIFO	LIFO
Sales	$60,000	$60,000	$60,000
Cost of goods sold	18,000[a]	16,000[b]	20,000[c]
Gross profit	42,000	44,000	40,000
Operating expenses	10,000	10,000	10,000
Income before taxes	32,000	34,000	30,000
Income taxes (40%)	12,800	13,600	12,000
Net income	$19,200	$20,400	$18,000
	[a]4,000 @ $3 = $12,000 6,000 @ $4 = 24,000 $36,000 $36,000 ÷ 10,000 = $3.60 $3.60 × 5,000 = $18,000	[b]4,000 @ $3 = $12,000 1,000 @ $4 = 4,000 $16,000	[c]5,000 @ $4 = $20,000

Illustration 8-32 shows the final balances of selected items at the end of the period.

ILLUSTRATION 8-32
Balances of Selected Items under Alternative Inventory Valuation Methods

	Inventory	Gross Profit	Taxes	Net Income	Retained Earnings	Cash
Average-Cost	$18,000 (5,000 × $3.60)	$42,000	$12,800	$19,200	$29,200 ($10,000 + $19,200)	$20,200[a]
FIFO	$20,000 (5,000 × $4)	$44,000	$13,600	$20,400	$30,400 ($10,000 + $20,400)	$19,400[a]
LIFO	$16,000 (4,000 × $3) (1,000 × $4)	$40,000	$12,000	$18,000	$28,000 ($10,000 + $18,000)	$21,000[a]

[a]Cash at year-end	=	Beg. Balance	+	Sales	−	Purchases	−	Operating expenses	−	Taxes
Average-cost—$20,200	=	$7,000	+	$60,000	−	$24,000	−	$10,000	−	$12,800
FIFO—$19,400	=	$7,000	+	$60,000	−	$24,000	−	$10,000	−	$13,600
LIFO—$21,000	=	$7,000	+	$60,000	−	$24,000	−	$10,000	−	$12,000

LIFO results in the highest cash balance at year-end (because taxes are lower). This example assumes that prices are rising. The opposite result occurs if prices are declining.

KEY TERMS

average-cost method, 429
consigned goods, 422
cost flow assumptions, 428
dollar-value LIFO, 435
double-extension method, 439
finished goods inventory, 416
first-in, first-out (FIFO) method, 430
f.o.b. destination, 421
f.o.b. shipping point, 421
gross method, 427
inventories, 416
last-in, first-out (LIFO) method, 431

SUMMARY OF LEARNING OBJECTIVES

1 Identify major classifications of inventory. Only one inventory account, Inventory, appears in the financial statements of a merchandising concern. A manufacturer normally has three inventory accounts: Raw Materials, Work in Process, and Finished Goods. Companies report the cost assigned to goods and materials on hand but not yet placed into production as raw materials inventory. They report the cost of the raw materials on which production has been started but not completed, plus the direct labor cost applied specifically to this material and a ratable share of manufacturing overhead costs, as work in process inventory. Finally, they report the costs identified with the completed but unsold units on hand at the end of the fiscal period as finished goods inventory.

2 Distinguish between perpetual and periodic inventory systems. A perpetual inventory system maintains a continuous record of inventory changes in the Inventory account. That is, a company records all purchases and sales (issues) of goods directly in the Inventory account as they occur. Under a periodic inventory system, companies determine the quantity of inventory on hand only periodically. A company debits a Purchases account, but the Inventory account remains the same. It determines cost of goods sold at the end of the period by subtracting ending inventory from cost of goods available for sale. A company ascertains ending inventory by physical count.

3 Determine the goods included in inventory and the effects of inventory errors on the financial statements. Companies record purchases of inventory when they obtain legal title to the goods (generally when they receive the goods). Shipping terms must be evaluated to determine when legal title passes, and careful consideration must be made for cost of goods sold on consignment and sales with buy-back agreements and high rates of return. *If the company misstates ending inventory:* (1) In the balance sheet, the inventory and retained earnings will be misstated, which will lead to miscalculation of the working capital and current ratio, and (2) in the income statement, the cost of goods sold and net income will be misstated. *If the company misstates purchases (and related accounts payable) and inventory:* (1) In the balance sheet, the inventory and accounts payable will be misstated, which will lead to miscalculation of the current ratio, and (2) in the income statement, purchases and ending inventory will be misstated.

4 Understand the items to include as inventory cost. Product costs are those costs that attach to the inventory and are recorded in the Inventory account. Such charges include freight charges on goods purchased, other direct costs of acquisition, and labor and other production costs incurred in processing the goods up to the time of sale. Period costs are those costs that are indirectly related to the acquisition or production of goods. These changes, such as selling expense and general and administrative expenses, are therefore not included as part of inventory cost.

5 Describe and compare the cost flow assumptions used to account for inventories. (1) *Average-cost* prices items in the inventory on the basis of the average cost of all similar goods available during the period. (2) *First-in, first-out (FIFO)* assumes that a company uses goods in the order in which it purchases them. The inventory remaining must therefore represent the most recent purchases. (3) *Last-in, first-out (LIFO)* matches the cost of the last goods purchased against revenue.

6 Explain the significance and use of a LIFO reserve. The difference between the inventory method used for internal reporting purposes and LIFO is referred to as Allowance to Reduce Inventory to LIFO, or the LIFO reserve. The change in LIFO reserve is referred to as the LIFO effect. Companies should disclose either the LIFO reserve or the replacement cost of the inventory in the financial statements.

7 Understand the effect of LIFO liquidations. LIFO liquidations match costs from preceding periods against sales revenues reported in current dollars. This distorts net income and results in increased taxable income in the current period. LIFO liquidations can occur frequently when using a specific-goods LIFO approach.

8 Explain the dollar-value LIFO method. For the dollar-value LIFO method, companies determine and measure increases and decreases in a pool in terms of total dollar value, not the physical quantity of the goods in the inventory pool.

9 Identify the major advantages and disadvantages of LIFO. The major advantages of LIFO are the following. (1) It matches recent costs against current revenues to provide a better measure of current earnings. (2) As long as the price level increases and inventory quantities do not decrease, a deferral of income tax occurs in LIFO. (3) Because of the deferral of income tax, cash flow improves. Major disadvantages are (1) reduced earnings, (2) understated inventory, (3) does not approximate physical flow of the items except in peculiar situations, and (4) involuntary liquidation issues.

10 Understand why companies select given inventory methods. Companies ordinarily prefer LIFO in the following circumstances: (1) if selling prices and revenues have been increasing faster than costs and (2) if a company has a fairly constant "base stock." Conversely, LIFO would probably not be appropriate in the following circumstances: (1) if sale prices tend to lag behind costs, (2) if specific identification is traditional, and (3) when unit costs tend to decrease as production increases, thereby nullifying the tax benefit that LIFO might provide.

DEMONSTRATION PROBLEM

Clinton Company makes specialty cases for smart phones and other handheld devices. The company has experienced strong growth, and you are especially interested in how well Clinton is managing its inventory balances. You have collected the following information for the current year.

Inventory at the beginning of year	$ 1,555 million
Inventory at the end of year, before any adjustments	$ 1,267 million
Total cost of goods sold, before any adjustments	$17,844 million

The company values inventory at lower-of-cost (using LIFO cost flow assumption)-or-market.

Instructions

Prepare a schedule (a computer worksheet would serve well) showing the impact of the following items on Clinton's inventory turnover.

(a) Shipping contracts changed 2 months ago from f.o.b. shipping point to f.o.b. destination. At the end of the year, $5 million of products are en route to China (and will not arrive until after financial statements are released). Current inventory balances do not reflect this change in policy.

(b) During the year, Clinton recorded sales and costs of goods sold on $2 million of units shipped to various wholesalers on consignment. At year-end, none of these units have been sold by wholesalers.

(c) To be more consistent with industry inventory valuation practices, Clinton changed from LIFO to FIFO for its inventory of iPad cases. This inventory is currently carried at $724 million. Data for this item of inventory for the year are as follows.

Month	Units Purchased	Inventory Sold	Price per Unit	Units Balance
January 1	100		$3.10	100
April 15	150		3.20	250
October 25		130		120
November 10	250		3.50	370
December 20		150		220

(d) Explain to Clinton management the advantages of adopting the LIFO cost flow assumption. Are there any drawbacks? Explain.

Solution

(a)–(c)

Clinton.xls

	A	B	C	D	E	F
1		Unadjusted				
2		Balance	Adjustment (a)	Adjustment (b)	Adjustment (c)	Adjusted Balance
3	Beginning inventory	$ 1,555.00	–	–	–	$ 1,555.00
4	Ending inventory	1,267.00	$ 5.00	$ 2.00	$ 46.00	1,320.00
5	Average inventory	1,411.00	–	–	–	1,437.50
6	Cost of goods sold	17,844.00	$(5.00)	$(2.00)	$(46.00)	17,791.00
7	Inventory turnover	12.65	–	–	–	12.38
8						
9	Explanation		Goods officially change hands at the point of destination.	Clinton should include the goods on consignment to other sellers.	Ending inventory under FIFO would be $770 (220 @ $3.50), which is $46 ($770 - $724) lower than LIFO.	
10						

(d) The major advantages of the LIFO inventory method include better matching of costs with revenues, deferral of income taxes, improved cash flow, and minimization of the impact of future price declines on future earnings. Better matching arises in the use of LIFO because the most recent costs are matched with current revenues. In times of rising prices, this matching will result in lower taxable income, which in turn will reduce current taxes. The deferral of taxes under LIFO contributes to a higher cash flow. As illustrated in the analysis above, the switch to FIFO resulted in a higher ending inventory, which leads to a lower cost of goods sold and higher income. Thus, Clinton's reported income will be higher but so will its taxes. Note that under LIFO, future taxes may be higher when lower cost items of inventory are sold in future periods and matched with higher sales prices.

FASB CODIFICATION

FASB Codification References

[1] FASB ASC 470-40-05. [Predecessor literature: "Accounting for Product Financing Arrangements," *Statement of Financial Accounting Standards No. 49* (Stamford, Conn.: FASB, 1981).]

[2] FASB ASC 605-15-15. [Predecessor literature: "Revenue Recognition When Right of Return Exists," *Statement of Financial Accounting Standards No. 48* (Stamford, Conn.: FASB, 1981).]

[3] FASB ASC 330-10-30-7. [Predecessor literature: "Inventory Costs: An Amendment of ARB No. 43, Chapter 4," *Statement of Financial Accounting Standards No. 151* (Norwalk, Conn.: FASB 2004).]

[4] FASB ASC 835-20-05. [Predecessor literature: "Capitalization of Interest Cost," *Statement of Financial Accounting Standards No. 34* (Stamford, Conn.: FASB, 1979).]

[5] FASB ASC 645-45-05. [Predecessor literature: "Accounting for Shipping and Handling Fees and Costs," *EITF No. 00–10* (2000).]

[6] FASB ASC 330-10-30. [Predecessor literature: "Restatement and Revision of Accounting Research Bulletins," *Accounting Research Bulletin No. 43* (New York: AICPA, 1953), Ch. 4, Statement 4.]

[7] FASB ASC 330-10-S99-1. [Predecessor literature: "AICPA Task Force on LIFO Inventory Problems, *Issues Paper* (New York: AICPA, November 30, 1984), pp. 2–24.]

[8] FASB ASC 330-10-S99-3. [Predecessor literature: "AICPA Task Force on LIFO Inventory Problems, *Issues Paper* (New York: AICPA, November 30, 1984), pp. 36–37.]

Exercises

If your school has a subscription to the FASB Codification, go to *http://aaahq.org/asclogin.cfm* to log in and prepare responses to the following. Provide Codification references for your responses.

CE8-1 Access the glossary ("Master Glossary") to answer the following.

- **(a)** What is the definition provided for inventory?
- **(b)** What is a customer?
- **(c)** Under what conditions is a distributor considered a customer?
- **(d)** What is a product financing arrangement? What inventory measurement issues are raised through these arrangements?

CE8-2 Due to rising fuel costs, your client, Overstock.com, is considering adding a charge for shipping and handling costs on products sold through its website. What is the authoritative guidance for reporting these costs?

CE8-3 What guidance does the Codification provide concerning reporting inventories above cost?

CE8-4 What is the nature of the SEC guidance concerning the reporting of LIFO liquidations?

An additional Codification case can be found in the Using Your Judgment section, on page 471.

Be sure to check the book's companion website for a Review and Analysis Exercise, with solution.

QUESTIONS

1. In what ways are the inventory accounts of a retailing company different from those of a manufacturing company?

2. Why should inventories be included in (a) a statement of financial position and (b) the computation of net income?

3. What is the difference between a perpetual inventory and a physical inventory? If a company maintains a perpetual inventory, should its physical inventory at any date be equal to the amount indicated by the perpetual inventory records? Why?

4. Mishima, Inc. indicated in a recent annual report that approximately $19 million of merchandise was received on consignment. Should Mishima, Inc. report this amount on its balance sheet? Explain.

5. What is a product financing arrangement? How should product financing arrangements be reported in the financial statements?

6. Where, if at all, should the following items be classified on a balance sheet?

   (a) Goods out on approval to customers.

   (b) Goods in transit that were recently purchased f.o.b. destination.

   (c) Land held by a realty firm for sale.

   (d) Raw materials.

   (e) Goods received on consignment.

   (f) Manufacturing supplies.

7. At the balance sheet date, Clarkson Company held title to goods in transit amounting to $214,000. This amount was omitted from the purchases figure for the year and also from the ending inventory. What is the effect of this omission on the net income for the year as calculated when the books are closed? What is the effect on the company's financial position as shown in its balance sheet? Is materiality a factor in determining whether an adjustment for this item should be made?

8. Define "cost" as applied to the valuation of inventories.

9. Distinguish between product costs and period costs as they relate to inventory.

10. Ford Motor Co. is considering alternate methods of accounting for the cash discounts it takes when paying suppliers promptly. One method suggested was to report these discounts as financial income when payments are made. Comment on the propriety of this approach.

11. Zonker Inc. purchases 500 units of an item at an invoice cost of $30,000. What is the cost per unit? If the goods are shipped f.o.b. shipping point and the freight bill was $1,500, what is the cost per unit if Zonker Inc. pays the freight charges? If these items were bought on 2/10, n/30 terms and the invoice and the freight bill were paid within the 10-day period, what would be the cost per unit?

12. Specific identification is sometimes said to be the ideal method of assigning cost to inventory and to cost of goods sold. Briefly indicate the arguments for and against this method of inventory valuation.

13. FIFO, average-cost, and LIFO methods are often used instead of specific identification for inventory valuation purposes. Compare these methods with the specific identification method, discussing the theoretical propriety of each method in the determination of income and asset valuation.

14. How might a company obtain a price index in order to apply dollar-value LIFO?

15. Describe the LIFO double-extension method. Using the following information, compute the index at December 31, 2014, applying the double-extension method to a LIFO pool consisting of 25,500 units of product A and 10,350 units of product B. The base-year cost of product A is $10.20 and of product B is $37.00. The price at December 31, 2014, for product A is $21.00 and for product B is $45.60. (Round to two decimal places.)

16. As compared with the FIFO method of costing inventories, does the LIFO method result in a larger or smaller net income in a period of rising prices? What is the comparative effect on net income in a period of falling prices?

17. What is the dollar-value method of LIFO inventory valuation? What advantage does the dollar-value method have over the specific goods approach of LIFO inventory valuation? Why will the traditional LIFO inventory costing method and the dollar-value LIFO inventory costing method produce different inventory valuations if the composition of the inventory base changes?

18. Explain the following terms.

   (a) LIFO layer.

   (b) LIFO reserve.

   (c) LIFO effect.

19. On December 31, 2013, the inventory of Powhattan Company amounts to $800,000. During 2014, the company decides to use the dollar-value LIFO method of costing inventories. On December 31, 2014, the inventory is $1,053,000 at December 31, 2014, prices. Using the December 31, 2013, price level of 100 and the December 31, 2014, price level of 108, compute the inventory value at December 31, 2014, under the dollar-value LIFO method.

20. In an article that appeared in the *Wall Street Journal*, the phrases "phantom (paper) profits" and "high LIFO profits" through involuntary liquidation were used. Explain these phrases.

BRIEF EXERCISES

1 **BE8-1** Included in the December 31 trial balance of Rivera Company are the following assets.

Cash	$ 190,000	Work in process	$200,000
Equipment (net)	1,100,000	Accounts receivable (net)	400,000
Prepaid insurance	41,000	Patents	110,000
Raw materials	335,000	Finished goods	170,000

Prepare the current assets section of the December 31 balance sheet.

2 **BE8-2** Matlock Company uses a perpetual inventory system. Its beginning inventory consists of 50 units that cost $34 each. During June, the company purchased 150 units at $34 each, returned 6 units for credit, and sold 125 units at $50 each. Journalize the June transactions.

4 **BE8-3** Stallman Company took a physical inventory on December 31 and determined that goods costing $200,000 were on hand. Not included in the physical count were $25,000 of goods purchased from Pelzer Corporation, f.o.b. shipping point, and $22,000 of goods sold to Alvarez Company for $30,000, f.o.b. destination. Both the Pelzer purchase and the Alvarez sale were in transit at year-end. What amount should Stallman report as its December 31 inventory?

3 **BE8-4** Bienvenu Enterprises reported cost of goods sold for 2014 of $1,400,000 and retained earnings of $5,200,000 at December 31, 2014. Bienvenu later discovered that its ending inventories at December 31, 2013 and 2014, were overstated by $110,000 and $35,000, respectively. Determine the corrected amounts for 2014 cost of goods sold and December 31, 2014, retained earnings.

5 **BE8-5** Amsterdam Company uses a periodic inventory system. For April, when the company sold 600 units, the following information is available.

	Units	Unit Cost	Total Cost
April 1 inventory	250	$10	$ 2,500
April 15 purchase	400	12	4,800
April 23 purchase	350	13	4,550
	1,000		$11,850

Compute the April 30 inventory and the April cost of goods sold using the average-cost method.

5 **BE8-6** Data for Amsterdam Company are presented in BE8-5. Compute the April 30 inventory and the April cost of goods sold using the FIFO method.

5 **BE8-7** Data for Amsterdam Company are presented in BE8-5. Compute the April 30 inventory and the April cost of goods sold using the LIFO method.

8 **BE8-8** Midori Company had ending inventory at end-of-year prices of $100,000 at December 31, 2013; $119,900 at December 31, 2014; and $134,560 at December 31, 2015. The year-end price indexes were 100 at 12/31/13, 110 at 12/31/14, and 116 at 12/31/15. Compute the ending inventory for Midori Company for 2013 through 2015 using the dollar-value LIFO method.

8 **BE8-9** Arna, Inc. uses the dollar-value LIFO method of computing its inventory. Data for the past 3 years follow.

Year Ended December 31	Inventory at Current-Year Cost	Price Index
2013	$19,750	100
2014	22,140	108
2015	25,935	114

Instructions

Compute the value of the 2014 and 2015 inventories using the dollar-value LIFO method.

EXERCISES

4 **E8-1 (Inventoriable Costs)** Presented below is a list of items that may or may not be reported as inventory in a company's December 31 balance sheet.

1. Goods out on consignment at another company's store.
2. Goods sold on an installment basis (bad debts can be reasonably estimated).
3. Goods purchased f.o.b. shipping point that are in transit at December 31.
4. Goods purchased f.o.b. destination that are in transit at December 31.
5. Goods sold to another company, for which our company has signed an agreement to repurchase at a set price that covers all costs related to the inventory.
6. Goods sold where large returns are predictable.
7. Goods sold f.o.b. shipping point that are in transit at December 31.
8. Freight charges on goods purchased.
9. Interest costs incurred for inventories that are routinely manufactured.
10. Costs incurred to advertise goods held for resale.
11. Materials on hand not yet placed into production by a manufacturing firm.
12. Office supplies.
13. Raw materials on which a manufacturing firm has started production but which are not completely processed.
14. Factory supplies.
15. Goods held on consignment from another company.
16. Costs identified with units completed by a manufacturing firm but not yet sold.
17. Goods sold f.o.b. destination that are in transit at December 31.
18. Short-term investments in stocks and bonds that will be resold in the near future.

Instructions

Indicate which of these items would typically be reported as inventory in the financial statements. If an item should **not** be reported as inventory, indicate how it should be reported in the financial statements.

4 **E8-2 (Inventoriable Costs)** In your audit of Jose Oliva Company, you find that a physical inventory on December 31, 2014, showed merchandise with a cost of $441,000 was on hand at that date. You also discover the following items were all excluded from the $441,000.

XLS

1. Merchandise of $61,000 which is held by Oliva on consignment. The consignor is the Max Suzuki Company.
2. Merchandise costing $38,000 which was shipped by Oliva f.o.b. destination to a customer on December 31, 2014. The customer was expected to receive the merchandise on January 6, 2015.
3. Merchandise costing $46,000 which was shipped by Oliva f.o.b. shipping point to a customer on December 29, 2014. The customer was scheduled to receive the merchandise on January 2, 2015.
4. Merchandise costing $83,000 shipped by a vendor f.o.b. destination on December 30, 2014, and received by Oliva on January 4, 2015.
5. Merchandise costing $51,000 shipped by a vendor f.o.b. shipping point on December 31, 2014, and received by Oliva on January 5, 2015.

Instructions

Based on the above information, calculate the amount that should appear on Oliva's balance sheet at December 31, 2014, for inventory.

4 **E8-3 (Inventoriable Costs)** Assume that in an annual audit of Harlowe Inc. at December 31, 2014, you find the following transactions near the closing date.

1. A special machine, fabricated to order for a customer, was finished and specifically segregated in the back part of the shipping room on December 31, 2014. The customer was billed on that date and the machine excluded from inventory although it was shipped on January 4, 2015.
2. Merchandise costing $2,800 was received on January 3, 2015, and the related purchase invoice recorded January 5. The invoice showed the shipment was made on December 29, 2014, f.o.b. destination.
3. A packing case containing a product costing $3,400 was standing in the shipping room when the physical inventory was taken. It was not included in the inventory because it was marked "Hold for shipping instructions." Your investigation revealed that the customer's order was dated December 18, 2014, but that the case was shipped and the customer billed on January 10, 2015. The product was a stock item of your client.

4. Merchandise received on January 6, 2015, costing $680 was entered in the purchase journal on January 7, 2015. The invoice showed shipment was made f.o.b. supplier's warehouse on December 31, 2014. Because it was not on hand at December 31, it was not included in inventory.
5. Merchandise costing $720 was received on December 28, 2014, and the invoice was not recorded. You located it in the hands of the purchasing agent; it was marked "on consignment."

Instructions

Assuming that each of the amounts is material, state whether the merchandise should be included in the client's inventory, and give your reason for your decision on each item.

2 4 **E8-4 (Inventoriable Costs—Perpetual)** Colin Davis Machine Company maintains a general ledger account for each class of inventory, debiting such accounts for increases during the period and crediting them for decreases. The transactions below relate to the Raw Materials inventory account, which is debited for materials purchased and credited for materials requisitioned for use.

1. An invoice for $8,100, terms f.o.b. destination, was received and entered January 2, 2014. The receiving report shows that the materials were received December 28, 2013.
2. Materials costing $28,000, shipped f.o.b. destination, were not entered by December 31, 2013, "because they were in a railroad car on the company's siding on that date and had not been unloaded."
3. Materials costing $7,300 were returned to the supplier on December 29, 2013, and were shipped f.o.b. shipping point. The return was entered on that date, even though the materials are not expected to reach the supplier's place of business until January 6, 2014.
4. An invoice for $7,500, terms f.o.b. shipping point, was received and entered December 30, 2013. The receiving report shows that the materials were received January 4, 2014, and the bill of lading shows that they were shipped January 2, 2014.
5. Materials costing $19,800 were received December 30, 2013, but no entry was made for them because "they were ordered with a specified delivery of no earlier than January 10, 2014."

Instructions

Prepare correcting general journal entries required at December 31, 2013, assuming that the books have not been closed.

3 4 **E8-5 (Inventoriable Costs—Error Adjustments)** Craig Company asks you to review its December 31, 2014, inventory values and prepare the necessary adjustments to the books. The following information is given to you.

1. Craig uses the periodic method of recording inventory. A physical count reveals $234,890 of inventory on hand at December 31, 2014.
2. Not included in the physical count of inventory is $13,420 of merchandise purchased on December 15 from Browser. This merchandise was shipped f.o.b. shipping point on December 29 and arrived in January. The invoice arrived and was recorded on December 31.
3. Included in inventory is merchandise sold to Champy on December 30, f.o.b. destination. This merchandise was shipped after it was counted. The invoice was prepared and recorded as a sale on account for $12,800 on December 31. The merchandise cost $7,350, and Champy received it on January 3.
4. Included in inventory was merchandise received from Dudley on December 31 with an invoice price of $15,630. The merchandise was shipped f.o.b. destination. The invoice, which has not yet arrived, has not been recorded.
5. Not included in inventory is $8,540 of merchandise purchased from Glowser Industries. This merchandise was received on December 31 after the inventory had been counted. The invoice was received and recorded on December 30.
6. Included in inventory was $10,438 of inventory held by Craig on consignment from Jackel Industries.
7. Included in inventory is merchandise sold to Kemp f.o.b. shipping point. This merchandise was shipped after it was counted. The invoice was prepared and recorded as a sale for $18,900 on December 31. The cost of this merchandise was $10,520, and Kemp received the merchandise on January 5.
8. Excluded from inventory was a carton labeled "Please accept for credit." This carton contains merchandise costing $1,500 which had been sold to a customer for $2,600. No entry had been made to the books to reflect the return, but none of the returned merchandise seemed damaged.

Instructions

(a) Determine the proper inventory balance for Craig Company at December 31, 2014.
(b) Prepare any correcting entries to adjust inventory to its proper amount at December 31, 2014. Assume the books have not been closed.

4 **E8-6 (Determining Merchandise Amounts—Periodic)** Two or more items are omitted in each of the following tabulations of income statement data. Fill in the amounts that are missing.

	2013	2014	2015
Sales revenue	$290,000	$?	$410,000
Sales returns and allowances	11,000	13,000	?
Net sales	?	347,000	?
Beginning inventory	20,000	32,000	?
Ending inventory	?	?	?
Purchases	?	260,000	298,000
Purchase returns and allowances	5,000	8,000	10,000
Freight-in	8,000	9,000	12,000
Cost of goods sold	233,000	?	293,000
Gross profit on sales	46,000	91,000	97,000

4 **E8-7 (Purchases Recorded Net)** Presented below are transactions related to Tom Brokaw, Inc.

May 10	Purchased goods billed at $15,000 subject to cash discount terms of 2/10, n/60.
11	Purchased goods billed at $13,200 subject to terms of 1/15, n/30.
19	Paid invoice of May 10.
24	Purchased goods billed at $11,500 subject to cash discount terms of 2/10, n/30.

Instructions

(a) Prepare general journal entries for the transactions above under the assumption that purchases are to be recorded at net amounts after cash discounts and that discounts lost are to be treated as financial expense.

(b) Assuming no purchase or payment transactions other than those given above, prepare the adjusting entry required on May 31 if financial statements are to be prepared as of that date.

4 **E8-8 (Purchases Recorded, Gross Method)** Cruise Industries purchased $10,800 of merchandise on February 1, 2014, subject to a trade discount of 10% and with credit terms of 3/15, n/60. It returned $2,500 (gross price before trade or cash discount) on February 4. The invoice was paid on February 13.

Instructions

(a) Assuming that Cruise uses the perpetual method for recording merchandise transactions, record the purchase, return, and payment using the gross method.

(b) Assuming that Cruise uses the periodic method for recording merchandise transactions, record the purchase, return, and payment using the gross method.

(c) At what amount would the purchase on February 1 be recorded if the net method were used?

2 **E8-9 (Periodic versus Perpetual Entries)** Fong Sai-Yuk Company sells one product. Presented below is information for January for Fong Sai-Yuk Company.

XLS

Jan. 1	Inventory	100 units at $5 each
4	Sale	80 units at $8 each
11	Purchase	150 units at $6 each
13	Sale	120 units at $8.75 each
20	Purchase	160 units at $7 each
27	Sale	100 units at $9 each

Fong Sai-Yuk uses the FIFO cost flow assumption. All purchases and sales are on account.

Instructions

(a) Assume Fong Sai-Yuk uses a periodic system. Prepare all necessary journal entries, including the end-of-month closing entry to record cost of goods sold. A physical count indicates that the ending inventory for January is 110 units.

(b) Compute gross profit using the periodic system.

(c) Assume Fong Sai-Yuk uses a perpetual system. Prepare all necessary journal entries.

(d) Compute gross profit using the perpetual system.

3 **E8-10 (Inventory Errors—Periodic)** Ann M. Martin Company makes the following errors during the current year. (Evaluate each case independently and assume ending inventory in the following year is correctly stated.)

1. Ending inventory is overstated, but purchases and related accounts payable are recorded correctly.
2. Both ending inventory and purchases and related accounts payable are understated. (Assume this purchase was recorded and paid for in the following year.)
3. Ending inventory is correct, but a purchase on account was not recorded. (Assume this purchase was recorded and paid for in the following year.)

Instructions

Indicate the effect of each of these errors on working capital, current ratio (assume that the current ratio is greater than 1), retained earnings, and net income for the current year and the subsequent year.

3 **E8-11 (Inventory Errors)** At December 31, 2013, Stacy McGill Corporation reported current assets of $370,000 and current liabilities of $200,000. The following items may have been recorded incorrectly.

1. Goods purchased costing $22,000 were shipped f.o.b. shipping point by a supplier on December 28. McGill received and recorded the invoice on December 29, 2013, but the goods were not included in McGill's physical count of inventory because they were not received until January 4, 2014.
2. Goods purchased costing $15,000 were shipped f.o.b. destination by a supplier on December 26. McGill received and recorded the invoice on December 31, but the goods were not included in McGill's 2013 physical count of inventory because they were not received until January 2, 2014.
3. Goods held on consignment from Claudia Kishi Company were included in McGill's December 31, 2013, physical count of inventory at $13,000.
4. Freight-in of $3,000 was debited to advertising expense on December 28, 2013.

Instructions

(a) Compute the current ratio based on McGill's balance sheet.
(b) Recompute the current ratio after corrections are made.
(c) By what amount will income (before taxes) be adjusted up or down as a result of the corrections?

3 **E8-12 (Inventory Errors)** The net income per books of Linda Patrick Company was determined without knowledge of the errors indicated.

Year	Net Income per Books	Error in Ending Inventory	
2009	$50,000	Overstated	$ 3,000
2010	52,000	Overstated	9,000
2011	54,000	Understated	11,000
2012	56,000	No error	
2013	58,000	Understated	2,000
2014	60,000	Overstated	8,000

Instructions

Prepare a worksheet to show the adjusted net income figure for each of the 6 years after taking into account the inventory errors.

2 5 **E8-13 (FIFO and LIFO—Periodic and Perpetual)** Inventory information for Part 311 of Monique Aaron Corp. discloses the following information for the month of June.

June 1	Balance	300 units @ $10	June 10	Sold	200 units @ $24
11	Purchased	800 units @ $12	15	Sold	500 units @ $25
20	Purchased	500 units @ $13	27	Sold	300 units @ $27

Instructions

(a) Assuming that the periodic inventory method is used, compute the cost of goods sold and ending inventory under (1) LIFO and (2) FIFO.
(b) Assuming that the perpetual inventory method is used and costs are computed at the time of each withdrawal, what is the value of the ending inventory at LIFO?
(c) Assuming that the perpetual inventory method is used and costs are computed at the time of each withdrawal, what is the gross profit if the inventory is valued at FIFO?
(d) Why is it stated that LIFO usually produces a lower gross profit than FIFO?

5 **E8-14 (FIFO, LIFO and Average-Cost Determination)** John Adams Company's record of transactions for the month of April was as follows.

Purchases			Sales	
April 1	(balance on hand)	600 @ $ 6.00	April 3	500 @ $10.00
4		1,500 @ 6.08	9	1,400 @ 10.00
8		800 @ 6.40	11	600 @ 11.00
13		1,200 @ 6.50	23	1,200 @ 11.00
21		700 @ 6.60	27	900 @ 12.00
29		500 @ 6.79		4,600
		5,300		

Instructions

(a) Assuming that periodic inventory records are kept in units only, compute the inventory at April 30 using (1) LIFO and (2) average-cost.

(b) Assuming that perpetual inventory records are kept in dollars, determine the inventory using (1) FIFO and (2) LIFO.

(c) Compute cost of goods sold assuming periodic inventory procedures and inventory priced at FIFO.

(d) In an inflationary period, which inventory method—FIFO, LIFO, average-cost—will show the highest net income?

5 **E8-15 (FIFO, LIFO, Average-Cost Inventory)** Shania Twain Company was formed on December 1, 2013. The following information is available from Twain's inventory records for Product BAP.

	Units	Unit Cost
January 1, 2014 (beginning inventory)	600	$ 8.00
Purchases:		
January 5, 2014	1,200	9.00
January 25, 2014	1,300	10.00
February 16, 2014	800	11.00
March 26, 2014	600	12.00

A physical inventory on March 31, 2014, shows 1,600 units on hand.

Instructions

Prepare schedules to compute the ending inventory at March 31, 2014, under each of the following inventory methods.

(a) FIFO. **(b)** LIFO. **(c)** Weighted-average (round unit costs to two decimal places).

5 **E8-16 (Compute FIFO, LIFO, Average-Cost—Periodic)** Presented below is information related to Blowfish radios for the Hootie Company for the month of July.

Date	Transaction	Units In	Unit Cost	Total	Units Sold	Selling Price	Total
July 1	Balance	100	$4.10	$ 410			
6	Purchase	800	4.20	3,360			
7	Sale				300	$7.00	$ 2,100
10	Sale				300	7.30	2,190
12	Purchase	400	4.50	1,800			
15	Sale				200	7.40	1,480
18	Purchase	300	4.60	1,380			
22	Sale				400	7.40	2,960
25	Purchase	500	4.58	2,290			
30	Sale				200	7.50	1,500
	Totals	2,100		$9,240	1,400		$10,230

Instructions

(a) Assuming that the periodic inventory method is used, compute the inventory cost at July 31 under each of the following cost flow assumptions.

(1) FIFO.

(2) LIFO.

(3) Weighted-average.

(b) Answer the following questions.

(1) Which of the methods used above will yield the lowest figure for gross profit for the income statement? Explain why.

(2) Which of the methods used above will yield the lowest figure for ending inventory for the balance sheet? Explain why.

2 5 **E8-17 (FIFO and LIFO—Periodic and Perpetual)** The following is a record of Pervis Ellison Company's transactions for Boston Teapots for the month of May 2014.

May 1 Balance 400 units @ $20	May 10 Sale 300 units @ $38
12 Purchase 600 units @ $25	20 Sale 540 units @ $38
28 Purchase 400 units @ $30	

Instructions

(a) Assuming that perpetual inventories are **not** maintained and that a physical count at the end of the month shows 560 units on hand, what is the cost of the ending inventory using (1) FIFO and (2) LIFO?

(b) Assuming that perpetual records are maintained and they tie into the general ledger, calculate the ending inventory using (1) FIFO and (2) LIFO.

5 **E8-18 (FIFO and LIFO; Income Statement Presentation)** The board of directors of Ichiro Corporation is considering whether or not it should instruct the accounting department to shift from a first-in, first-out (FIFO) basis of pricing inventories to a last-in, first-out (LIFO) basis. The following information is available.

Sales	21,000 units @ $50
Inventory, January 1	6,000 units @ 20
Purchases	6,000 units @ 22
	10,000 units @ 25
	7,000 units @ 30
Inventory, December 31	8,000 units @ ?
Operating expenses	$200,000

Instructions

Prepare a condensed income statement for the year on both bases for comparative purposes.

5 **E8-19 (FIFO and LIFO Effects)** You are the vice president of finance of Sandy Alomar Corporation, a retail company that prepared two different schedules of gross margin for the first quarter ended March 31, 2014. These schedules appear below.

	Sales ($5 per unit)	Cost of Goods Sold	Gross Margin
Schedule 1	$150,000	$124,900	$25,100
Schedule 2	150,000	129,400	20,600

The computation of cost of goods sold in each schedule is based on the following data.

	Units	Cost per Unit	Total Cost
Beginning inventory, January 1	10,000	$4.00	$40,000
Purchase, January 10	8,000	4.20	33,600
Purchase, January 30	6,000	4.25	25,500
Purchase, February 11	9,000	4.30	38,700
Purchase, March 17	11,000	4.40	48,400

Jane Torville, the president of the corporation, cannot understand how two different gross margins can be computed from the same set of data. As the vice president of finance, you have explained to Ms. Torville that the two schedules are based on different assumptions concerning the flow of inventory costs, i.e., FIFO and LIFO. Schedules 1 and 2 were not necessarily prepared in this sequence of cost flow assumptions.

Instructions

Prepare two separate schedules computing cost of goods sold and supporting schedules showing the composition of the ending inventory under both cost flow assumptions.

5 **E8-20 (FIFO and LIFO—Periodic)** Johnny Football Shop began operations on January 2, 2014. The following stock record card for footballs was taken from the records at the end of the year.

Date	Voucher	Terms	Units Received	Unit Invoice Cost	Gross Invoice Amount
1/15	10624	Net 30	50	$20	$1,000
3/15	11437	1/5, net 30	65	16	1,040
6/20	21332	1/10, net 30	90	15	1,350
9/12	27644	1/10, net 30	84	12	1,008
11/24	31269	1/10, net 30	76	11	836
	Totals		365		$5,234

A physical inventory on December 31, 2014, reveals that 100 footballs were in stock. The bookkeeper informs you that all the discounts were taken. Assume that Johnny Football Shop uses the invoice price less discount for recording purchases.

Instructions

(a) Compute the December 31, 2014, inventory using the FIFO method.
(b) Compute the 2014 cost of goods sold using the LIFO method.
(c) What method would you recommend to the owner to minimize income taxes in 2014, using the inventory information for footballs as a guide?

6 **E8-21 (LIFO Effect)** The following example was provided to encourage the use of the LIFO method. In a nutshell, LIFO subtracts inflation from inventory costs, deducts it from taxable income, and records it in a LIFO reserve account on the books. The LIFO benefit grows as inflation widens the gap between current-year and past-year (minus inflation) inventory costs. This gap is:

	With LIFO	Without LIFO
Revenues	$3,200,000	$3,200,000
Cost of goods sold	2,800,000	2,800,000
Operating expenses	150,000	150,000
Operating income	250,000	250,000
LIFO adjustment	40,000	0
Taxable income	$ 210,000	$ 250,000
Income taxes @ 36%	$ 75,600	$ 90,000
Cash flow	$ 174,400	$ 160,000
Extra cash	$ 14,400	0
Increased cash flow	9%	0%

Instructions

(a) Explain what is meant by the LIFO reserve account.
(b) How does LIFO subtract inflation from inventory costs?
(c) Explain how the cash flow of $174,400 in this example was computed. Explain why this amount may not be correct.
(d) Why does a company that uses LIFO have extra cash? Explain whether this situation will always exist.

5 8 **E8-22 (Alternative Inventory Methods—Comprehensive)** Tori Amos Corporation began operations on December 1, 2013. The only inventory transaction in 2013 was the purchase of inventory on December 10, 2013, at a cost of $20 per unit. None of this inventory was sold in 2013. Relevant information is as follows.

Ending inventory units		
December 31, 2013		100
December 31, 2014, by purchase date		
December 2, 2014	100	
July 20, 2014	50	150

During the year, the following purchases and sales were made.

Purchases		Sales	
March 15	300 units at $24	April 10	200
July 20	300 units at 25	August 20	300
September 4	200 units at 28	November 18	150
December 2	100 units at 30	December 12	200

The company uses the periodic inventory method.

Instructions

(a) Determine ending inventory under (1) specific identification, (2) FIFO, (3) LIFO, and (4) average-cost.
(b) Determine ending inventory using dollar-value LIFO. Assume that the December 2, 2014, purchase cost is the current cost of inventory. (*Hint:* The beginning inventory is the base layer priced at $20 per unit.)

8 **E8-23 (Dollar-Value LIFO)** Oasis Company has used the dollar-value LIFO method for inventory cost determination for many years. The following data were extracted from Oasis' records.

Date	Price Index	Ending Inventory at Base Prices	Ending Inventory at Dollar-Value LIFO
December 31, 2014	105	$92,000	$92,600
December 31, 2015	?	97,000	98,350

Instructions

Calculate the index used for 2015 that yielded the above results.

8 **E8-24 (Dollar-Value LIFO)** The dollar-value LIFO method was adopted by Enya Corp. on January 1, 2014. Its inventory on that date was $160,000. On December 31, 2014, the inventory at prices existing on that date amounted to $140,000. The price level at January 1, 2014, was 100, and the price level at December 31, 2014, was 112.

Instructions

(a) Compute the amount of the inventory at December 31, 2014, under the dollar-value LIFO method.

(b) On December 31, 2015, the inventory at prices existing on that date was $172,500, and the price level was 115. Compute the inventory on that date under the dollar-value LIFO method.

8 **E8-25 (Dollar-Value LIFO)** Presented below is information related to Dino Radja Company.

Date	Ending Inventory (End-of-Year Prices)	Price Index
December 31, 2011	$ 80,000	100
December 31, 2012	115,500	105
December 31, 2013	108,000	120
December 31, 2014	122,200	130
December 31, 2015	154,000	140
December 31, 2016	176,900	145

Instructions

Compute the ending inventory for Dino Radja Company for 2011 through 2016 using the dollar-value LIFO method.

8 **E8-26 (Dollar-Value LIFO)** The following information relates to the Jimmy Johnson Company.

Date	Ending Inventory (End-of-Year Prices)	Price Index
December 31, 2010	$ 70,000	100
December 31, 2011	90,300	105
December 31, 2012	95,120	116
December 31, 2013	105,600	120
December 31, 2014	100,000	125

Instructions

Use the dollar-value LIFO method to compute the ending inventory for Johnson Company for 2010 through 2014.

EXERCISES SET B

See the book's companion website, at **www.wiley.com/college/kieso**, for an additional set of exercises.

PROBLEMS

4 5 8 **P8-1 (Various Inventory Issues)** The following independent situations relate to inventory accounting.

1. Kim Co. purchased goods with a list price of $175,000, subject to trade discounts of 20% and 10%, with no cash discounts allowable. How much should Kim Co. record as the cost of these goods?
2. Keillor Company's inventory of $1,100,000 at December 31, 2014, was based on a physical count of goods priced at cost and before any year-end adjustments relating to the following items.
   (a) Goods shipped from a vendor f.o.b. shipping point on December 24, 2014, at an invoice cost of $69,000 to Keillor Company were received on January 4, 2015.
   (b) The physical count included $29,000 of goods billed to Sakic Corp. f.o.b. shipping point on December 31, 2014. The carrier picked up these goods on January 3, 2015.
   What amount should Keillor report as inventory on its balance sheet?
3. Zimmerman Corp. had 1,500 units of part M.O. on hand May 1, 2014, costing $21 each. Purchases of part M.O. during May were as follows.

	Units	Unit Cost
May 9	2,000	$22.00
17	3,500	23.00
26	1,000	24.00

A physical count on May 31, 2014, shows 2,000 units of part M.O. on hand. Using the FIFO method, what is the cost of part M.O. inventory at May 31, 2014? Using the LIFO method, what is the inventory cost? Using the average-cost method, what is the inventory cost?

4. Ashbrook Company adopted the dollar-value LIFO method on January 1, 2014 (using internal price indexes and multiple pools). The following data are available for inventory pool A for the 2 years following adoption of LIFO.

Inventory	At Base-Year Cost	At Current-Year Cost
1/1/14	$200,000	$200,000
12/31/14	240,000	264,000
12/31/15	256,000	286,720

Computing an internal price index and using the dollar-value LIFO method, at what amount should the inventory be reported at December 31, 2015?

5. Donovan Inc., a retail store chain, had the following information in its general ledger for the year 2015.

Merchandise purchased for resale	$909,400
Interest on notes payable to vendors	8,700
Purchase returns	16,500
Freight-in	22,000
Freight-out (delivery expense)	17,100
Cash discounts on purchases	6,800

What is Donovan's inventoriable cost for 2015?

Instructions

Answer each of the preceding questions about inventories, and explain your answers.

3 4 **P8-2 (Inventory Adjustments)** Dimitri Company, a manufacturer of small tools, provided the following information from its accounting records for the year ended December 31, 2014.

Inventory at December 31, 2014 (based on physical count of goods in Dimitri's plant, at cost, on December 31, 2014)	$1,520,000
Accounts payable at December 31, 2014	1,200,000
Net sales (sales less sales returns)	8,150,000

Additional information is as follows.

1. Included in the physical count were tools billed to a customer f.o.b. shipping point on December 31, 2014. These tools had a cost of $31,000 and were billed at $40,000. The shipment was on Dimitri's loading dock waiting to be picked up by the common carrier.
2. Goods were in transit from a vendor to Dimitri on December 31, 2014. The invoice cost was $76,000, and the goods were shipped f.o.b. shipping point on December 29, 2014.
3. Work in process inventory costing $30,000 was sent to an outside processor for plating on December 30, 2014.
4. Tools returned by customers and held pending inspection in the returned goods area on December 31, 2014, were not included in the physical count. On January 8, 2015, the tools costing $32,000 were inspected and returned to inventory. Credit memos totaling $47,000 were issued to the customers on the same date.
5. Tools shipped to a customer f.o.b. destination on December 26, 2014, were in transit at December 31, 2014, and had a cost of $26,000. Upon notification of receipt by the customer on January 2, 2015, Dimitri issued a sales invoice for $42,000.
6. Goods, with an invoice cost of $27,000, received from a vendor at 5:00 p.m. on December 31, 2014, were recorded on a receiving report dated January 2, 2015. The goods were not included in the physical count, but the invoice was included in accounts payable at December 31, 2014.
7. Goods received from a vendor on December 26, 2014, were included in the physical count. However, the related $56,000 vendor invoice was not included in accounts payable at December 31, 2014, because the accounts payable copy of the receiving report was lost.
8. On January 3, 2015, a monthly freight bill in the amount of $8,000 was received. The bill specifically related to merchandise purchased in December 2014, one-half of which was still in the inventory at December 31, 2014. The freight charges were not included in either the inventory or in accounts payable at December 31, 2014.

Instructions

Using the format shown below, prepare a schedule of adjustments as of December 31, 2014, to the initial amounts per Dimitri's accounting records. Show separately the effect, if any, of each of the eight transactions on the December 31, 2014, amounts. If the transactions would have no effect on the initial amount shown, enter NONE.

	Inventory	Accounts Payable	Net Sales
Initial amounts	$1,520,000	$1,200,000	$8,150,000
Adjustments—increase (decrease)			
1			
2			
3			
4			
5			
6			
7			
8			
Total adjustments			
Adjusted amounts	$	$	$

(AICPA adapted)

4 **P8-3 (Purchases Recorded Gross and Net)** Some of the transactions of Torres Company during August are listed below. Torres uses the periodic inventory method.

XLS

August 10	Purchased merchandise on account, $12,000, terms 2/10, n/30.
13	Returned part of the purchase of August 10, $1,200, and received credit on account.
15	Purchased merchandise on account, $16,000, terms 1/10, n/60.
25	Purchased merchandise on account, $20,000, terms 2/10, n/30.
28	Paid invoice of August 15 in full.

Instructions

(a) Assuming that purchases are recorded at gross amounts and that discounts are to be recorded when taken:
  (1) Prepare general journal entries to record the transactions.
  (2) Describe how the various items would be shown in the financial statements.

(b) Assuming that purchases are recorded at net amounts and that discounts lost are treated as financial expenses:
  (1) Prepare general journal entries to enter the transactions.
  (2) Prepare the adjusting entry necessary on August 31 if financial statements are to be prepared at that time.
  (3) Describe how the various items would be shown in the financial statements.

(c) Which of the two methods do you prefer and why?

2 5 **P8-4 (Compute FIFO, LIFO, and Average-Cost)** Hull Company's record of transactions concerning part X for the month of April was as follows.

XLS

Purchases		Sales	
April 1 (balance on hand)	100 @ $5.00	April 5	300
4	400 @ 5.10	12	200
11	300 @ 5.30	27	800
18	200 @ 5.35	28	150
26	600 @ 5.60		
30	200 @ 5.80		

Instructions

(a) Compute the inventory at April 30 on each of the following bases. Assume that perpetual inventory records are kept in units only. Carry unit costs to the nearest cent.
  (1) First-in, first-out (FIFO).
  (2) Last-in, first-out (LIFO).
  (3) Average-cost.

(b) If the perpetual inventory record is kept in dollars, and costs are computed at the time of each withdrawal, what amount would be shown as ending inventory in (1), (2), and (3) above? (Carry average unit costs to four decimal places.)

2 5 **P8-5 (Compute FIFO, LIFO, and Average-Cost)** Some of the information found on a detail inventory card for Slatkin Inc. for the first month of operations is as follows.

Date	Received: No. of Units	Received: Unit Cost	Issued, No. of Units	Balance, No. of Units
January 2	1,200	$3.00		1,200
7			700	500
10	600	3.20		1,100
13			500	600
18	1,000	3.30	300	1,300
20			1,100	200
23	1,300	3.40		1,500
26			800	700
28	1,600	3.50		2,300
31			1,300	1,000

Instructions

(a) From these data compute the ending inventory on each of the following bases. Assume that perpetual inventory records are kept in units only. (Carry unit costs to the nearest cent and ending inventory to the nearest dollar.)

(1) First-in, first-out (FIFO).

(2) Last-in, first-out (LIFO).

(3) Average-cost.

(b) If the perpetual inventory record is kept in dollars, and costs are computed at the time of each withdrawal, would the amounts shown as ending inventory in (1), (2), and (3) above be the same? Explain and compute. (Round average unit costs to four decimal places.)

2 5 **P8-6 (Compute FIFO, LIFO, Average-Cost—Periodic and Perpetual)** Ehlo Company is a multiproduct firm. Presented below is information concerning one of its products, the Hawkeye.

Date	Transaction	Quantity	Price/Cost
1/1	Beginning inventory	1,000	$12
2/4	Purchase	2,000	18
2/20	Sale	2,500	30
4/2	Purchase	3,000	23
11/4	Sale	2,200	33

Instructions

Compute cost of goods sold, assuming Ehlo uses:

(a) Periodic system, FIFO cost flow.

(b) Perpetual system, FIFO cost flow.

(c) Periodic system, LIFO cost flow.

(d) Perpetual system, LIFO cost flow.

(e) Periodic system, weighted-average cost flow.

(f) Perpetual system, moving-average cost flow.

5 **P8-7 (Financial Statement Effects of FIFO and LIFO)** The management of Tritt Company has asked its accounting department to describe the effect upon the company's financial position and its income statements of accounting for inventories on the LIFO rather than the FIFO basis during 2014 and 2015. The accounting department is to assume that the change to LIFO would have been effective on January 1, 2014, and that the initial LIFO base would have been the inventory value on December 31, 2013. Presented below are the company's financial statements and other data for the years 2014 and 2015 when the FIFO method was employed.

	Financial Position as of 12/31/13	12/31/14	12/31/15
Cash	$ 90,000	$130,000	$154,000
Accounts receivable	80,000	100,000	120,000
Inventory	120,000	140,000	176,000
Other assets	160,000	170,000	200,000
Total assets	$450,000	$540,000	$650,000
Accounts payable	$ 40,000	$ 60,000	$ 80,000
Other liabilities	70,000	80,000	110,000
Common stock	200,000	200,000	200,000
Retained earnings	140,000	200,000	260,000
Total liabilities and equity	$450,000	$540,000	$650,000

	Income for Years Ended	
	12/31/14	12/31/15
Sales revenue	$900,000	$1,350,000
Less: Cost of goods sold	505,000	756,000
Other expenses	205,000	304,000
	710,000	1,060,000
Income before income taxes	190,000	290,000
Income taxes (40%)	76,000	116,000
Net income	$114,000	$ 174,000

Other data:

1. Inventory on hand at December 31, 2013, consisted of 40,000 units valued at $3.00 each.
2. Sales (all units sold at the same price in a given year):

   2014—150,000 units @ $6.00 each   2015—180,000 units @ $7.50 each

3. Purchases (all units purchased at the same price in given year):

   2014—150,000 units @ $3.50 each   2015—180,000 units @ $4.40 each

4. Income taxes at the effective rate of 40% are paid on December 31 each year.

Instructions

Name the account(s) presented in the financial statements that would have different amounts for 2015 if LIFO rather than FIFO had been used, and state the new amount for each account that is named. Show computations.

(CMA adapted)

8 **P8-8 (Dollar-Value LIFO)** Norman's Televisions produces television sets in three categories: portable, midsize, and flat-screen. On January 1, 2014, Norman adopted dollar-value LIFO and decided to use a single inventory pool. The company's January 1 inventory consists of:

Category	Quantity	Cost per Unit	Total Cost
Portable	6,000	$100	$ 600,000
Midsize	8,000	250	2,000,000
Flat-screen	3,000	400	1,200,000
	17,000		$3,800,000

During 2014, the company had the following purchases and sales.

Category	Quantity Purchased	Cost per Unit	Quantity Sold	Selling Price per Unit
Portable	15,000	$110	14,000	$150
Midsize	20,000	300	24,000	405
Flat-screen	10,000	500	6,000	600
	45,000		44,000	

Instructions

(Round to four decimals.)

(a) Compute ending inventory, cost of goods sold, and gross profit.
(b) Assume the company uses three inventory pools instead of one. Repeat instruction (a).

8 **P8-9 (Internal Indexes—Dollar-Value LIFO)** On January 1, 2014, Bonanza Wholesalers Inc. adopted the dollar-value LIFO inventory method for income tax and external financial reporting purposes. However, Bonanza continued to use the FIFO inventory method for internal accounting and management purposes. In applying the LIFO method, Bonanza uses internal conversion price indexes and the multiple pools approach under which substantially identical inventory items are grouped into LIFO inventory pools. The following data were available for inventory pool no. 1, which comprises products A and B, for the 2 years following the adoption of LIFO.

	FIFO Basis per Records		
	Units	Unit Cost	Total Cost
Inventory, 1/1/14			
Product A	10,000	$30	$300,000
Product B	9,000	25	225,000
			$525,000
Inventory, 12/31/14			
Product A	17,000	36	$612,000
Product B	9,000	26	234,000
			$846,000
Inventory, 12/31/15			
Product A	13,000	40	$520,000
Product B	10,000	32	320,000
			$840,000

Instructions

(a) Prepare a schedule to compute the internal conversion price indexes for 2014 and 2015. Round indexes to two decimal places.

(b) Prepare a schedule to compute the inventory amounts at December 31, 2014 and 2015, using the dollar-value LIFO inventory method.

(AICPA adapted)

8 **P8-10 (Internal Indexes—Dollar-Value LIFO)** Presented below is information related to Kaisson Corporation for the last 3 years.

	Quantities	Base-Year Cost		Current-Year Cost	
Item	in Ending Inventories	Unit Cost	Amount	Unit Cost	Amount
December 31, 2013					
A	9,000	$2.00	$18,000	$2.20	$19,800
B	6,000	3.00	18,000	3.55	21,300
C	4,000	5.00	20,000	5.40	21,600
		Totals	$56,000		$62,700
December 31, 2014					
A	9,000	$2.00	$18,000	$2.60	$23,400
B	6,800	3.00	20,400	3.75	25,500
C	6,000	5.00	30,000	6.40	38,400
		Totals	$68,400		$87,300
December 31, 2015					
A	8,000	$2.00	$16,000	$2.70	$21,600
B	8,000	3.00	24,000	4.00	32,000
C	6,000	5.00	30,000	6.20	37,200
		Totals	$70,000		$90,800

Instructions

Compute the ending inventories under the dollar-value LIFO method for 2013, 2014, and 2015. The base period is January 1, 2013, and the beginning inventory cost at that date was $45,000. Compute indexes to two decimal places.

8 **P8-11 (Dollar-Value LIFO)** Richardson Company cans a variety of vegetable-type soups. Recently, the company decided to value its inventories using dollar-value LIFO pools. The clerk who accounts for inventories does not understand how to value the inventory pools using this new method, so, as a private consultant, you have been asked to teach him how this new method works.

He has provided you with the following information about purchases made over a 6-year period.

Date	Ending Inventory (End-of-Year Prices)	Price Index
Dec. 31, 2010	$ 80,000	100
Dec. 31, 2011	111,300	105
Dec. 31, 2012	108,000	120
Dec. 31, 2013	128,700	130
Dec. 31, 2014	147,000	140
Dec. 31, 2015	174,000	145

You have already explained to him how this inventory method is maintained, but he would feel better about it if you were to leave him detailed instructions explaining how these calculations are done and why he needs to put all inventories at a base-year value.

Instructions

(a) Compute the ending inventory for Richardson Company for 2010 through 2015 using dollar-value LIFO.

(b) Using your computation schedules as your illustration, write a step-by-step set of instructions explaining how the calculations are done. Begin your explanation by briefly explaining the theory behind this inventory method, including the purpose of putting all amounts into base-year price levels.

PROBLEMS SET B

See the book's companion website, at **www.wiley.com/college/kieso**, for an additional set of problems.

CONCEPTS FOR ANALYSIS

CA8-1 (Inventoriable Costs) You are asked to travel to Milwaukee to observe and verify the inventory of the Milwaukee branch of one of your clients. You arrive on Thursday, December 30, and find that the inventory procedures have just been started. You spot a railway car on the sidetrack at the unloading door and ask the warehouse superintendent, Buck Rogers, how he plans to inventory the contents of the car. He responds, "We are not going to include the contents in the inventory."

Later in the day, you ask the bookkeeper for the invoice on the carload and the related freight bill. The invoice lists the various items, prices, and extensions of the goods in the car. You note that the carload was shipped December 24 from Albuquerque, f.o.b. Albuquerque, and that the total invoice price of the goods in the car was $35,300. The freight bill called for a payment of $1,500. Terms were net 30 days. The bookkeeper affirms the fact that this invoice is to be held for recording in January.

Instructions

(a) Does your client have a liability that should be recorded at December 31? Discuss.

(b) Prepare a journal entry(ies), if required, to reflect any accounting adjustment required. Assume a perpetual inventory system is used by your client.

(c) For what possible reason(s) might your client wish to postpone recording the transaction?

CA8-2 (Inventoriable Costs) Brian Erlacher, an inventory control specialist, is interested in better understanding the accounting for inventories. Although Brian understands the more sophisticated computer inventory control systems, he has little knowledge of how inventory cost is determined. In studying the records of Strider Enterprises, which sells normal brand-name goods from its own store and on consignment through Chavez Inc., he asks you to answer the following questions.

Instructions

(a) Should Strider Enterprises include in its inventory normal brand-name goods purchased from its suppliers but not yet received if the terms of purchase are f.o.b. shipping point (manufacturer's plant)? Why?

(b) Should Strider Enterprises include freight-in expenditures as an inventory cost? Why?

(c) If Strider Enterprises purchases its goods on terms 2/10, net 30, should the purchases be recorded gross or net? Why?

(d) What are products on consignment? How should they be reported in the financial statements?

(AICPA adapted)

CA8-3 (Inventoriable Costs) George Solti, the controller for Garrison Lumber Company, has recently hired you as assistant controller. He wishes to determine your expertise in the area of inventory accounting and therefore asks you to answer the following unrelated questions.

(a) A company is involved in the wholesaling and retailing of automobile tires for foreign cars. Most of the inventory is imported, and it is valued on the company's records at the actual inventory cost plus freight-in. At year-end, the warehousing costs are prorated over cost of goods sold and ending inventory. Are warehousing costs considered a product cost or a period cost?

(b) A certain portion of a company's "inventory" is composed of obsolete items. Should obsolete items that are not currently consumed in the production of "goods or services to be available for sale" be classified as part of inventory?

(c) A company purchases airplanes for sale to others. However, until they are sold, the company charters and services the planes. What is the proper way to report these airplanes in the company's financial statements?

(d) A company wants to buy coal deposits but does not want the financing for the purchase to be reported on its financial statements. The company therefore establishes a trust to acquire the coal deposits. The company agrees to buy the coal over a certain period of time at specified prices. The trust is able to finance the coal purchase and pay off the loan as it is paid by the company for the minerals. How should this transaction be reported?

CA8-4 (Accounting Treatment of Purchase Discounts) Shawnee Corp., a household appliances dealer, purchases its inventories from various suppliers. Shawnee has consistently stated its inventories at the lower-of-cost (FIFO)-or-market.

Instructions

Shawnee is considering alternate methods of accounting for the cash discounts it takes when paying its suppliers promptly. From a theoretical standpoint, discuss the acceptability of each of the following methods.

(a) Financial income when payments are made.

(b) Reduction of cost of goods sold for the period when payments are made.

(c) Direct reduction of purchase cost.

(AICPA adapted)

CA8-5 (General Inventory Issues) In January 2014, Susquehanna Inc. requested and secured permission from the commissioner of the Internal Revenue Service to compute inventories under the last-in, first-out (LIFO) method and elected to determine inventory cost under the dollar-value LIFO method. Susquehanna Inc. satisfied the commissioner that cost could be accurately determined by use of an index number computed from a representative sample selected from the company's single inventory pool.

Instructions

(a) Why should inventories be included in (1) a balance sheet and (2) the computation of net income?

(b) The Internal Revenue Code allows some accountable events to be considered differently for income tax reporting purposes and financial accounting purposes, while other accountable events must be reported the same for both purposes. Discuss why it might be desirable to report some accountable events differently for financial accounting purposes than for income tax reporting purposes.

(c) Discuss the ways and conditions under which the FIFO and LIFO inventory costing methods produce different inventory valuations. Do not discuss procedures for computing inventory cost.

(AICPA adapted)

CA8-6 (LIFO Inventory Advantages) Jane Yoakam, president of Estefan Co., recently read an article that claimed that at least 100 of the country's largest 500 companies were either adopting or considering adopting the last-in, first-out (LIFO) method for valuing inventories. The article stated that the firms were switching to LIFO to (1) neutralize the effect of inflation in their financial statements, (2) eliminate inventory profits, and (3) reduce income taxes. Ms. Yoakam wonders if the switch would benefit her company.

Estefan currently uses the first-in, first-out (FIFO) method of inventory valuation in its periodic inventory system. The company has a high inventory turnover rate, and inventories represent a significant proportion of the assets.

Ms. Yoakam has been told that the LIFO system is more costly to operate and will provide little benefit to companies with high turnover. She intends to use the inventory method that is best for the company in the long run rather than selecting a method just because it is the current fad.

Instructions

(a) Explain to Ms. Yoakam what "inventory profits" are and how the LIFO method of inventory valuation could reduce them.

(b) Explain to Ms. Yoakam the conditions that must exist for Estefan Co. to receive tax benefits from a switch to the LIFO method.

CA8-7 (Average-Cost, FIFO, and LIFO) Prepare a memorandum containing responses to the following items.

(a) Describe the cost flow assumptions used in average-cost, FIFO, and LIFO methods of inventory valuation.

(b) Distinguish between weighted-average-cost and moving-average-cost for inventory costing purposes.

(c) Identify the effects on both the balance sheet and the income statement of using the LIFO method instead of the FIFO method for inventory costing purposes over a substantial time period when purchase prices of inventoriable items are rising. State why these effects take place.

CA8-8 (LIFO Application and Advantages) Geddes Corporation is a medium-sized manufacturing company with two divisions and three subsidiaries, all located in the United States. The Metallic Division manufactures metal castings for the automotive industry, and the Plastic Division produces small plastic items for electrical products and other uses. The three subsidiaries manufacture various products for other industrial users.

Geddes Corporation plans to change from the lower of first-in, first-out (FIFO)-cost-or market method of inventory valuation to the last-in, first-out (LIFO) method of inventory valuation to obtain tax benefits. To make the method acceptable for tax purposes, the change also will be made for its annual financial statements.

Instructions

(a) Describe the establishment of and subsequent pricing procedures for each of the following LIFO inventory methods.

(1) LIFO applied to units of product when the periodic inventory system is used.

(2) Application of the dollar-value method to LIFO units of product.

(b) Discuss the specific advantages and disadvantages of using the dollar-value LIFO application as compared to specific goods LIFO (unit LIFO). (Ignore income tax considerations.)

(c) Discuss the general advantages and disadvantages claimed for LIFO methods.

CA8-9 (Dollar-Value LIFO Issues) Arruza Co. is considering switching from the specific-goods LIFO approach to the dollar-value LIFO approach. Because the financial personnel at Arruza know very little about dollar-value LIFO, they ask you to answer the following questions.

(a) What is a LIFO pool?

(b) Is it possible to use a LIFO pool concept and not use dollar-value LIFO? Explain.

(c) What is a LIFO liquidation?

(d) How are price indexes used in the dollar-value LIFO method?

(e) What are the advantages of dollar-value LIFO over specific-goods LIFO?

CA8-10 (FIFO and LIFO) Harrisburg Company is considering changing its inventory valuation method from FIFO to LIFO because of the potential tax savings. However, management wishes to consider all of the effects on the company, including its reported performance, before making the final decision.

The inventory account, currently valued on the FIFO basis, consists of 1,000,000 units at $8 per unit on January 1, 2014. There are 1,000,000 shares of common stock outstanding as of January 1, 2014, and the cash balance is $400,000.

The company has made the following forecasts for the period 2014–2016.

	2014	2015	2016
Unit sales (in millions of units)	1.1	1.0	1.3
Sales price per unit	$10	$12	$12
Unit purchases (in millions of units)	1.0	1.1	1.2
Purchase price per unit	$8	$9	$10
Annual depreciation (in thousands of dollars)	$300	$300	$300
Cash dividends per share	$0.15	$0.15	$0.15
Cash payments for additions to and replacement of plant and equipment (in thousands of dollars)	$350	$350	$350
Income tax rate	40%	40%	40%
Operating expenses (exclusive of depreciation) as a percent of sales	15%	15%	15%
Common shares outstanding (in millions)	1	1	1

Instructions

(a) Prepare a schedule that illustrates and compares the following data for Harrisburg Company under the FIFO and the LIFO inventory method for 2014–2016. Assume the company would begin LIFO at the beginning of 2014.

(1) Year-end inventory balances.
(2) Annual net income after taxes.
(3) Earnings per share.
(4) Cash balance.

Assume all sales are collected in the year of sale and all purchases, operating expenses, and taxes are paid during the year incurred.

(b) Using the data above, your answer to (a), and any additional issues you believe need to be considered, prepare a report that recommends whether or not Harrisburg Company should change to the LIFO inventory method. Support your conclusions with appropriate arguments.

(CMA adapted)

CA8-11 (LIFO Choices) Wilkens Company uses the LIFO method for inventory costing. In an effort to lower net income, company president Mike Wilkens tells the plant accountant to take the unusual step of recommending to the purchasing department a large purchase of inventory at year-end. The price of the item to be purchased has nearly doubled during the year, and the item represents a major portion of inventory value.

Instructions

Answer the following questions.

(a) Identify the major stakeholders. If the plant accountant recommends the purchase, what are the consequences?

(b) If Wilkens Company were using the FIFO method of inventory costing, would Mike Wilkens give the same order? Why or why not?

USING YOUR JUDGMENT

FINANCIAL REPORTING

Financial Statement Analysis Cases

Case 1 T J International

T J International was founded in 1969 as Trus Joist International. The firm, a manufacturer of specialty building products, has its headquarters in Boise, Idaho. The company, through its partnership in the Trus Joist MacMillan joint venture, develops and manufactures engineered lumber. This product is a high-quality substitute for structural lumber and uses lower-grade wood and materials formerly considered waste. The company also is majority owner of the Outlook Window Partnership, which is a consortium of three wood and vinyl window manufacturers.

Following is T J International's adapted income statement and information concerning inventories from its annual report.

T J International

Sales	$618,876,000
Cost of goods sold	475,476,000
Gross profit	143,400,000
Selling and administrative expenses	102,112,000
Income from operations	41,288,000
Other expense	24,712,000
Income before income tax	16,576,000
Income taxes	7,728,000
Net income	$ 8,848,000

Inventories. Inventories are valued at the lower of cost or market and include material, labor, and production overhead costs. Inventories consisted of the following:

	Current Year	Prior Year
Finished goods	$27,512,000	$23,830,000
Raw materials and work-in-progress	34,363,000	33,244,000
	61,875,000	57,074,000
Reduction to LIFO cost	(5,263,000)	(3,993,000)
	$56,612,000	$53,081,000

The last-in, first-out (LIFO) method is used for determining the cost of lumber, veneer, Microllam lumber, TJI joists, and open web joists. Approximately 35 percent of total inventories at the end of the current year were valued using the LIFO method. The first-in, first-out (FIFO) method is used to determine the cost of all other inventories.

Instructions

(a) How much would income before taxes have been if FIFO costing had been used to value all inventories?

(b) If the income tax rate is 46.6%, what would income tax have been if FIFO costing had been used to value all inventories? In your opinion, is this difference in net income between the two methods material? Explain.

(c) Does the use of a different costing system for different types of inventory mean that there is a different physical flow of goods among the different types of inventory? Explain.

Case 2 Noven Pharmaceuticals, Inc.

Noven Pharmaceuticals, Inc., headquartered in Miami, Florida, describes itself in a recent annual report as follows.

Noven Pharmaceuticals, Inc.

Noven is a place of ideas—a company where scientific excellence and state-of-the-art manufacturing combine to create new answers to human needs. Our transdermal delivery systems speed drugs painlessly and effortlessly into the bloodstream by means of a simple skin patch. This technology has proven applications in estrogen replacement, but at Noven we are developing a variety of systems incorporating bestselling drugs that fight everything from asthma, anxiety and dental pain to cancer, heart disease and neurological illness. Our research portfolio also includes new technologies, such as iontophoresis, in which drugs are delivered through the skin by means of electrical currents, as well as products that could satisfy broad consumer needs, such as our anti-microbial mouthrinse.

Noven also reported in its annual report that its activities to date have consisted of product development efforts, some of which have been independent and some of which have been completed in conjunction with **Rhone-Poulenc Rorer (RPR)** and **Ciba-Geigy**. The revenues so far have consisted of money received from licensing fees, "milestone" payments (payments made under licensing agreements when certain stages of the development of a certain product have been completed), and interest on its investments. The company expects that it will have significant revenue in the upcoming fiscal year from the launch of its first product, a transdermal estrogen delivery system.

The current assets portion of Noven's balance sheet follows.

Cash and cash equivalents	$12,070,272
Securities held to maturity	23,445,070
Inventory of supplies	1,264,553
Prepaid and other current assets	825,159
Total current assets	$37,605,054

Inventory of supplies is recorded at the lower-of-cost (first-in, first-out)-or-net realizable value and consists mainly of supplies for research and development.

Instructions

(a) What would you expect the physical flow of goods for a pharmaceutical manufacturer to be most like: FIFO, LIFO, or random (flow of goods does not follow a set pattern)? Explain.

(b) What are some of the factors that Noven should consider as it selects an inventory measurement method?

(c) Suppose that Noven had $49,000 in an inventory of transdermal estrogen delivery patches. These patches are from an initial production run and will be sold during the coming year. Why do you think that this amount is not shown in a separate inventory account? In which of the accounts shown is the inventory likely to be? At what point will the inventory be transferred to a separate inventory account?

Case 3 SUPERVALU

SUPERVALU reported the following data in its annual report.

	Feb. 27, 2010	Feb. 26, 2011	Feb. 25, 2012
Total revenues	$40,597	$37,534	$36,100
Cost of sales (using LIFO)	31,444	29,124	28,010
Year-end inventories using FIFO	2,606	2,552	2,492
Year-end inventories using LIFO	2,342	2,270	2,150

(a) Compute SUPERVALU's inventory turnovers for 2011 and 2012, using:

(1) Cost of sales and LIFO inventory.

(2) Cost of sales and FIFO inventory.

(b) Some firms calculate inventory turnover using sales rather than cost of goods sold in the numerator. Calculate SUPERVALU's 2011 and 2012 turnover, using:

(1) Sales and LIFO inventory.

(2) Sales and FIFO inventory.

(c) Describe the method that SUPERVALU's appears to use.

(d) State which method you would choose to evaluate SUPERVALU's performance. Justify your choice.

Accounting, Analysis, and Principles

Englehart Company sells two types of pumps. One is large and is for commercial use. The other is smaller and is used in residential swimming pools. The following inventory data is available for the month of March.

	Units	Price per Unit	Total
Residential Pumps			
Inventory at Feb. 28:	200	$ 400	$ 80,000
Purchases:			
March 10	500	$ 450	$225,000
March 20	400	$ 475	$190,000
March 30	300	$ 500	$150,000
Sales:			
March 15	500	$ 540	$270,000
March 25	400	$ 570	$228,000
Inventory at March 31:	500		
Commercial Pumps			
Inventory at Feb. 28:	600	$ 800	$480,000
Purchases:			
March 3	600	$ 900	$540,000
March 12	300	$ 950	$285,000
March 21	500	$1,000	$500,000
Sales:			
March 18	900	$1,080	$972,000
March 29	600	$1,140	$684,000
Inventory at March 31:	500		

Accounting

(a) Assuming Englehart uses a periodic inventory system, determine the cost of inventory on hand at March 31 and the cost of goods sold for March under first-in, first-out (FIFO).

(b) Assume Englehart uses dollar-value LIFO and one pool, consisting of the combination of residential and commercial pumps. Determine the cost of inventory on hand at March 31 and the cost of goods sold for March. Assume Englehart's initial adoption of LIFO is on March 1. Use the double-extension method to determine the appropriate price indices. (*Hint:* The price index for February 28/March 1 should be 1.00.) (Round the index to three decimal places.)

Analysis

(a) Assume you need to compute a current ratio for Englehart. Which inventory method (FIFO or dollar-value LIFO) do you think would give you a more meaningful current ratio?

(b) Some of Englehart's competitors use LIFO inventory costing and some use FIFO. How can an analyst compare the results of companies in an industry, when some use LIFO and others use FIFO?

Principles

Can companies change from one inventory accounting method to another? If a company changes to an inventory accounting method used by most of its competitors, what are the trade-offs in terms of the conceptual framework discussed in Chapter 2 of the textbook?

BRIDGE TO THE PROFESSION

Professional Research: FASB Codification

In conducting year-end inventory counts, your audit team is debating the impact of the client's right of return policy both on inventory valuation and revenue recognition. The assistant controller argues that there is no need to worry about the return policies since they have not changed in a while. The audit senior wants a more authoritative answer and has asked you to conduct some research of the authoritative literature before she presses the point with the client.

Instructions

If your school has a subscription to the FASB Codification, go to *http://aaahq.org/asclogin.cfm* to log in and prepare responses to the following. Provide Codification references for your responses.

(a) What is the authoritative guidance for revenue recognition when right of return exists?

(b) When is this guidance important for a company?

(c) Sales with high rates of return can ultimately cause inventory to be misstated. Why are returns allowed? Should different industries be able to make different types of return policies?

(d) In what situations would a reasonable estimate of returns be difficult to make?

Additional Professional Resources

See the book's companion website, at **www.wiley.com/college/kieso**, for professional simulations as well as other study resources.

Remember to check the book's companion website to find additional resources for this chapter.

CHAPTER

9 Inventories: Additional Valuation Issues

LEARNING OBJECTIVES

After studying this chapter, you should be able to:

1 Describe and apply the lower-of-cost-or-market rule.

2 Explain when companies value inventories at net realizable value.

3 Explain when companies use the relative sales value method to value inventories.

4 Discuss accounting issues related to purchase commitments.

5 Determine ending inventory by applying the gross profit method.

6 Determine ending inventory by applying the retail inventory method.

7 Explain how to report and analyze inventory.

Not What It Seems to Be

Investors need comparable information about inventory when evaluating a retailer's financial statements. To do so, investors need to determine what inventory method a retailer is using (FIFO, LIFO, average-cost, or a combination of methods) and then adjust the company to a common method. That is a good start. What investors often then do is compute relevant information about the company such as inventory turnover, number of days sales in inventory, gross profit rate, and liquidity measures such as the acid-test ratio. These calculations are critical. Inventory is a significant component of working capital and the gross profit resulting from sales of inventory is often viewed as the most important income component in measuring a retailer's progress. For example, consider the financial statements of **Best Buy** shown in the following table. Inventory comprises over 50 percent of current assets, and gross profit represents 24 percent of sales revenue.

BEST BUY ($ IN MILLIONS)			
Consolidated Balance Sheets		**Consolidated Statements of Earnings**	
Current Assets		Revenue	$50,705
Cash and cash equivalents	$ 1,199	Cost of goods sold	38,132
Receivables	2,288	Gross profit	$12,573
Merchandise inventories	5,731		
Other current assets	1,101	Net income (loss)	$ (1,231)
Total current assets	$10,319		

Therefore, analysis is based on these numbers. However, there often are still questions about the reliability of the information reported in the financial statements. That is, subjective estimates are involved because of the possible impairment of the inventory. For example, Best Buy provides disclosures related to inventory in its annual report, shown on the next page.

CONCEPTUAL FOCUS

> See the **Underlying Concepts** on pages 479, 480, and 484.

INTERNATIONAL FOCUS

> See the **International Perspectives** on pages 474, 475, and 482.

> Read the **IFRS Insights** on pages 525–534 for a discussion of:
—Lower-of-cost-or-net realizable value (LCNRV)
—Agricultural inventory

As indicated in the table below, subjective estimates concerning the measurement and valuation of inventory (related to markdowns and inventory losses) could have a significant impact on an investor's ability to compare inventory levels (and their impact on gross profit) at Best Buy relative to other retailers. Thus, inventory balances may not be what they seem, not only due to the cost flow assumptions (e.g., LIFO/FIFO) you learned about in Chapter 8 but also due to significant markdowns and losses that you will learn about in this chapter.

Critical Accounting Estimates in Preparation of the Financial Statements: Inventory	Judgments and Uncertainties
We value our inventory at the lower of cost or market through the establishment of markdown and inventory loss adjustments. Our inventory valuation reflects markdowns for the excess of the cost over the amount we expect to realize from the ultimate sale or other disposal of the inventory. Markdowns establish a new cost basis for our inventory. Subsequent changes in facts or circumstances do not result in the reversal of previously recorded markdowns or an increase in that newly established cost basis.	Our markdown adjustment contains uncertainties because the calculation requires management to make assumptions and to apply judgment regarding inventory aging, forecast consumer demand, the promotional environment and technological obsolescence.
Our inventory valuation also reflects adjustments for anticipated physical inventory losses (e.g., theft) that have occurred since the last physical inventory. Physical inventory counts are taken on a regular basis to ensure that the inventory reported in our consolidated financial statements is properly stated.	Our inventory loss adjustment contains uncertainties because the calculation requires management to make assumptions and to apply judgment regarding a number of factors, including historical results and current inventory loss trends.

PREVIEW OF CHAPTER 9

As our opening story indicates, information on inventories is important to investors. In this chapter, we discuss some of the valuation and estimation concepts that companies use to develop relevant inventory information. The content and organization of the chapter are as follows.

Inventories: Additional Valuation Issues

Lower-of-Cost-or-Market
- Ceiling and floor
- How LCM works
- Application of LCM
- "Market"
- Use of allowance
- Multiple periods
- Evaluation of rule

Valuation Bases
- Net realizable value
- Relative sales value
- Purchase commitments

Gross Profit Method
- Gross profit percentage
- Evaluation of method

Retail Inventory Method
- Concepts
- Conventional method
- Special items
- Evaluation of method

Presentation and Analysis
- Presentation
- Analysis

LOWER-OF-COST-OR-MARKET

LEARNING OBJECTIVE 1
Describe and apply the lower-of-cost-or-market rule.

Inventories are recorded at their cost. However, if inventory declines in value below its original cost, a major departure from the historical cost principle occurs. Whatever the reason for a decline—obsolescence, price-level changes, or damaged goods—a company should write down the inventory to market to report this loss. **A company abandons the historical cost principle when the future utility (revenue-producing ability) of the asset drops below its original cost.** Companies therefore **report inventories at the lower-of-cost-or-market** at each reporting period.

Illustration 9-1 shows how Target and Best Buy reported this information.

ILLUSTRATION 9-1
Lower-of-Cost-or-Market Disclosures

Target
(in millions)

	As of January 28, 2012	
Current Assets		
Inventory		$7,918

Notes to Consolidated Financial Statements (in part)

11. Inventory

Substantially all inventory and the related cost of sales are accounted for under the retail inventory accounting method (RIM) using the last-in, first-out (LIFO) method. Inventory is stated at the lower of LIFO cost or market. Cost includes purchase price as reduced by vendor income. Inventory is also reduced for estimated losses related to shrinkage and markdowns. The LIFO provision is calculated based on inventory levels, markup rates and internally measured retail price indices.

Best Buy
(in millions)

	March 3, 2012	
Current Assets		
Merchandise inventories		$5,731

Summary of Significant Accounting Policies (in part)

Merchandise inventories are recorded at the lower of cost using either the average cost or first-in-first-out method, or market.

International Perspective

IFRS defines *market* as net realizable value; GAAP defines *market* as replacement cost subject to certain constraints.

Recall that **cost** is the acquisition price of inventory computed using one of the historical cost-based methods—specific identification, average-cost, FIFO, or LIFO. The term **market** in the phrase "the lower-of-cost-or-market" (LCM) generally means the cost to replace the item by purchase or reproduction. For a retailer like Nordstrom, the term "market" refers to the market in which it purchases goods, not the market in which it sells them. For a manufacturer like William Wrigley Jr., the term "market" refers to the cost to reproduce. Thus the rule really means that **companies value goods at cost or cost to replace, whichever is lower**.

For example, say Target purchased a Timex wristwatch for $30 for resale. Target can sell the wristwatch for $48.95 and replace it for $25. It should therefore value the wristwatch at $25 for inventory purposes under the lower-of-cost-or-market rule. Target can use the lower-of-cost-or-market rule of valuation after applying any of the cost flow methods discussed above to determine the inventory cost.

A departure from cost is justified because **a company should charge a loss of utility against revenues in the period in which the loss occurs**, not in the period of sale. Note also that the lower-of-cost-or-market method is **a conservative approach to inventory valuation**. That is, when doubt exists about the value of an asset, a company should use the lower value for the asset, which also reduces net income.

Ceiling and Floor

Why use replacement cost to represent market value? Because a decline in the replacement cost of an item usually reflects or predicts a decline in selling price. Using replacement cost allows a company to maintain a consistent rate of gross profit on sales (normal profit margin). Sometimes, however, a reduction in the replacement cost of an item fails to indicate a corresponding reduction in its utility. This requires using two additional valuation limitations to value ending inventory—net realizable value and net realizable value less a normal profit margin.

Net realizable value (NRV) is the estimated selling price in the ordinary course of business, less reasonably predictable costs of completion and disposal (often referred to as net selling price). A normal profit margin is subtracted from that amount to arrive at **net realizable value less a normal profit margin**.

To illustrate, assume that Jerry Mander Corp. has unfinished inventory with a sales value of $1,000, estimated cost of completion and disposal of $300, and a normal profit margin of 10 percent of sales. Jerry Mander determines the following net realizable value.

ILLUSTRATION 9-2
Computation of Net Realizable Value

Inventory—sales value	$1,000
Less: Estimated cost of completion and disposal	300
Net realizable value	700
Less: Allowance for normal profit margin (10% of sales)	100
Net realizable value less a normal profit margin	$ 600

The general lower-of-cost-or-market rule is: A company values inventory at the lower-of-cost-or-market, with market limited to an amount that is not more than net realizable value or less than net realizable value less a normal profit margin. [1]

See the FASB Codification section (page 504).

The **upper limit (ceiling)** is the net realizable value of inventory. The **lower limit (floor)** is the net realizable value less a normal profit margin. What is the rationale for these two limitations? Establishing these limits for the value of the inventory prevents companies from over- or understating inventory.

The maximum limitation, **not to exceed the net realizable value (ceiling),** prevents overstatement of the value of obsolete, damaged, or shopworn inventories. That is, if the replacement cost of an item exceeds its net realizable value, a company should not report inventory at replacement cost. The company can receive only the selling price less cost of disposal. To report the inventory at replacement cost would result in an overstatement of inventory and understatement of the loss in the current period.

To illustrate, assume that **Staples** paid $1,000 for a color laser printer that it can now replace for $900. The printer's net realizable value is $700. At what amount should Staples report the laser printer in its financial statements? To report the replacement cost of $900 overstates the ending inventory and understates the loss for the period. Therefore, Staples should report the printer at $700.

The minimum limitation (floor) is **not to be less than net realizable value reduced by an allowance for an approximately normal profit margin**. The floor establishes a value below which a company should not price inventory, regardless of replacement cost. It makes no sense to price inventory below net realizable value less a normal margin. This minimum amount (floor) measures

International Perspective

IFRS does not use a ceiling or floor to determine market.

what the company can receive for the inventory and still earn a normal profit. Use of a floor deters understatement of inventory and overstatement of the loss in the current period.

Illustration 9-3 graphically presents the guidelines for valuing inventory at the lower-of-cost-or-market.

ILLUSTRATION 9-3
Inventory Valuation—Lower-of-Cost-or-Market

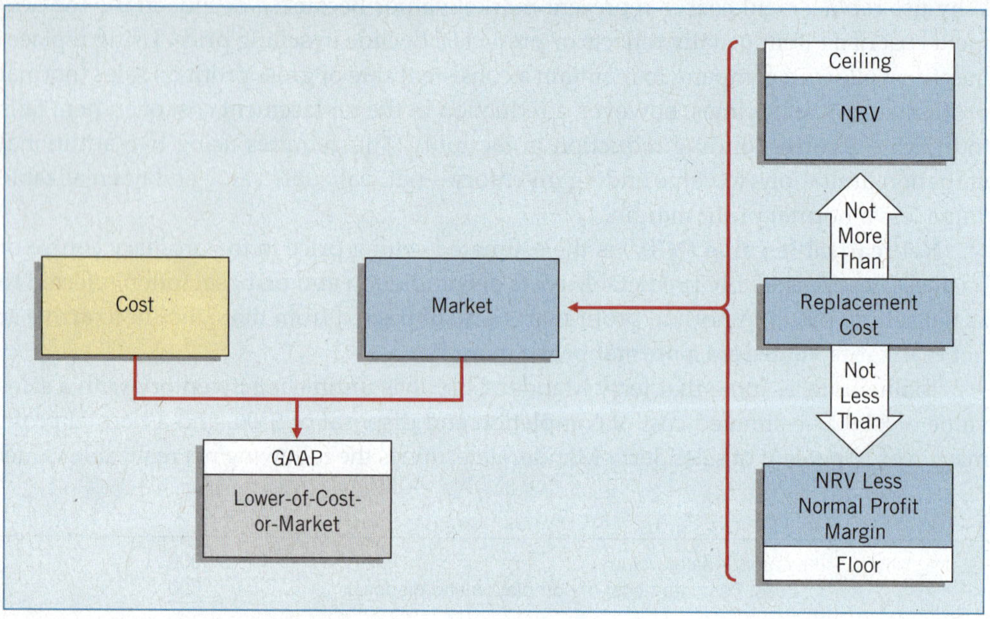

How Lower-of-Cost-or-Market Works

The **designated market value** is the amount that a company compares to cost. It is **always the middle value of three amounts**: replacement cost, net realizable value, and net realizable value less a normal profit margin. To illustrate how to compute designated market value, assume the information relative to the inventory of Regner Foods, Inc., as shown in Illustration 9-4.

ILLUSTRATION 9-4
Computation of Designated Market Value

Food	Replacement Cost	Net Realizable Value (Ceiling)	Net Realizable Value Less a Normal Profit Margin (Floor)	Designated Market Value
Spinach	$ 88,000	$120,000	$104,000	$104,000
Carrots	90,000	100,000	70,000	90,000
Cut beans	45,000	40,000	27,500	40,000
Peas	36,000	72,000	48,000	48,000
Mixed vegetables	105,000	92,000	80,000	92,000

Designated Market Value Decision:

Spinach	Net realizable value less a normal profit margin is selected because it is the middle value.
Carrots	Replacement cost is selected because it is the middle value.
Cut beans	Net realizable value is selected because it is the middle value.
Peas	Net realizable value less a normal profit margin is selected because it is the middle value.
Mixed vegetables	Net realizable value is selected because it is the middle value.

Regner Foods then compares designated market value to cost to determine the lower-of-cost-or-market. It determines the final inventory value as shown in Illustration 9-5.

ILLUSTRATION 9-5
Determining Final Inventory Value

Food	Cost	Replacement Cost	Net Realizable Value (Ceiling)	Net Realizable Value Less a Normal Profit Margin (Floor)	Designated Market Value	Final Inventory Value
Spinach	$ 80,000	$ 88,000	$120,000	$104,000	$104,000	$ 80,000
Carrots	100,000	90,000	100,000	70,000	90,000	90,000
Cut beans	50,000	45,000	40,000	27,500	40,000	40,000
Peas	90,000	36,000	72,000	48,000	48,000	48,000
Mixed vegetables	95,000	105,000	92,000	80,000	92,000	92,000
						$350,000

Final Inventory Value:

Spinach	Cost ($80,000) is selected because it is lower than designated market value (net realizable value less a normal profit margin).
Carrots	Designated market value (replacement cost, $90,000) is selected because it is lower than cost.
Cut beans	Designated market value (net realizable value, $40,000) is selected because it is lower than cost.
Peas	Designated market value (net realizable value less a normal profit margin, $48,000) is selected because it is lower than cost.
Mixed vegetables	Designated market value (net realizable value, $92,000) is selected because it is lower than cost.

The application of the lower-of-cost-or-market rule incorporates only losses in value that occur in the normal course of business from such causes as style changes, shift in demand, or regular shop wear. A company reduces damaged or deteriorated goods to net realizable value. When material, it may carry such goods in separate inventory accounts.

Methods of Applying Lower-of-Cost-or-Market

In the Regner Foods illustration, we assumed that the company applied the lower-of-cost-or-market rule to each individual type of food. However, companies may apply the lower-of-cost-or-market rule either directly to each item, to each category, or to the total of the inventory. If a company follows a major category or total inventory approach in applying the lower-of-cost-or-market rule, increases in market prices tend to offset decreases in market prices. To illustrate, assume that Regner Foods separates its food products into two major categories, frozen and canned, as shown in Illustration 9-6.

ILLUSTRATION 9-6
Alternative Applications of Lower-of-Cost-or-Market

			Lower-of-Cost-or-Market by:		
	Cost	Designated Market	Individual Items	Major Categories	Total Inventory
Frozen					
Spinach	$ 80,000	$104,000	$ 80,000		
Carrots	100,000	90,000	90,000		
Cut beans	50,000	40,000	40,000		
Total frozen	230,000	234,000		$230,000	
Canned					
Peas	90,000	48,000	48,000		
Mixed vegetables	95,000	92,000	92,000		
Total canned	185,000	140,000		140,000	
Total	$415,000	$374,000	$350,000	$370,000	$374,000

If Regner Foods applied the lower-of-cost-or-market rule to individual items, the amount of inventory is $350,000. If applying the rule to major categories, it jumps to

$370,000. If applying LCM to the total inventory, it totals $374,000. Why this difference? When a company uses a major categories or total inventory approach, market values higher than cost offset market values lower than cost. For Regner Foods, using the major categories approach partially offsets the high market value for spinach. Using the total inventory approach totally offsets the high market value for spinach.

Companies usually price inventory on an item-by-item basis. In fact, tax rules require that companies use an individual-item basis barring practical difficulties. In addition, the individual-item approach gives the most conservative valuation for balance sheet purposes.[1] Often, a company prices inventory on a total-inventory basis when it offers only one end product (comprised of many different raw materials). If it produces several end products, a company might use a category approach instead. The method selected should be the one that most clearly reflects income. **Whichever method a company selects, it should apply the method consistently from one period to another.**[2]

Recording "Market" Instead of Cost

One of two methods may be used to record the income effect of valuing inventory at market. One method, referred to as the **cost-of-goods-sold method**, debits cost of goods sold for the write-down of the inventory to market. As a result, the company does not report a loss in the income statement because the cost of goods sold already includes the amount of the loss. The second method, referred to as the **loss method**, debits a loss account for the write-down of the inventory to market. We use the following inventory data for Ricardo Company to illustrate entries under both methods.

Cost of goods sold (before adjustment to market)	$108,000
Ending inventory (cost)	82,000
Ending inventory (at market)	70,000

Illustration 9-7 shows the entries for both the cost-of-goods-sold and loss methods, assuming the use of a perpetual inventory system.

ILLUSTRATION 9-7
Accounting for the Reduction of Inventory to Market—Perpetual Inventory System

Cost-of-Goods-Sold Method			Loss Method		
To reduce inventory from cost to market					
Cost of Goods Sold	12,000		Loss Due to Decline of Inventory to Market	12,000	
Inventory		12,000	Inventory		12,000

The cost-of-goods-sold method buries the loss in the Cost of Goods Sold account. The loss method, by identifying the loss due to the write-down, shows the loss separate from Cost of Goods Sold in the income statement.

Illustration 9-8 contrasts the differing amounts reported in the income statement under the two approaches, using data from the Ricardo example.

[1]If a company uses dollar-value LIFO, determining the LIFO cost of an individual item may be more difficult. The company might decide that it is more appropriate to apply the lower-of-cost-or-market rule to the total amount of each pool. The AICPA Task Force on LIFO Inventory Problems concluded that the most reasonable approach to applying the lower-of-cost-or-market provisions to LIFO inventories is to base the determination on reasonable groupings of items. A pool constitutes a reasonable grouping.

[2]Inventory accounting for financial statement purposes can be different from income tax purposes. For example, companies cannot use the lower-of-cost-or-market rule with LIFO for tax purposes. However, companies may use the lower-of-cost-or-market and LIFO for financial accounting purposes.

Cost-of-Goods-Sold Method	
Sales revenue	$200,000
Cost of goods sold (after adjustment to market*)	120,000
Gross profit on sales	$ 80,000
*Cost of goods sold (before adjustment to market)	$108,000
Difference between inventory at cost and market ($82,000 – $70,000)	12,000
Cost of goods sold (after adjustment to market)	$120,000

Loss Method	
Sales revenue	$200,000
Cost of goods sold	108,000
Gross profit on sales	92,000
Loss due to decline of inventory to market	12,000
	$ 80,000

ILLUSTRATION 9-8
Income Statement Presentation—Cost-of-Goods-Sold and Loss Methods of Reducing Inventory to Market

GAAP does not specify a particular account to debit for the write-down. We believe the loss method presentation is preferable because it clearly discloses the loss resulting from a decline in inventory to market.

Underlying Concepts

The income statement under the cost-of-goods-sold method presentation lacks *representational faithfulness*. The cost-of-goods-sold method does not indicate what it purports to represent. However, allowing this presentation illustrates the concept of materiality.

Use of an Allowance

Instead of crediting the Inventory account for market adjustments, companies generally use an allowance account, often referred to as Allowance to Reduce Inventory to Market. For example, using an allowance account under the loss method, Ricardo Company makes the following entry to record the inventory write-down to market.

Loss Due to Decline of Inventory to Market	12,000	
Allowance to Reduce Inventory to Market		12,000

Use of the allowance account results in reporting both the cost and the market of the inventory. Ricardo reports inventory in the balance sheet as follows.

Inventory (at cost)	$ 82,000
Allowance to reduce inventory to market	(12,000)
Inventory (at market)	$ 70,000

ILLUSTRATION 9-9
Presentation of Inventory Using an Allowance Account

The use of the allowance under the cost-of-goods-sold or loss method permits the balance sheet to reflect inventory measured at $82,000, although the balance sheet shows a net amount of $70,000. It also keeps subsidiary inventory ledgers and records in correspondence with the control account without changing prices. *For homework purposes, use an allowance account to record market adjustments, unless instructed otherwise.*

With respect to accounting for the allowance in the subsequent period, if the company still has on hand the merchandise in question, it should retain the allowance account. If it does not keep that account, the company will overstate beginning inventory and cost of goods. However, **if the company has sold the goods**, then it should close the account. It then establishes a "new allowance account" for any decline in inventory value that takes place in the current year.[3]

[3]The AICPA Task Force on LIFO Inventory Problems concluded that for LIFO inventories, companies should close the allowance from the prior year and should base the allowance at the end of the year on a new lower-of-cost-or-market computation. **[2]**

Use of an Allowance—Multiple Periods

Underlying Concepts

The inconsistency in the presentation of inventory is an example of the trade-off between *relevance and faithful representation.* Market is more relevant than cost, and cost is more representationally faithful than market. Apparently, relevance takes precedence in a down market, and faithful representation is more important in an up market.

In general, accountants leave the allowance account on the books. They merely adjust the balance at the next year-end to agree with the discrepancy between cost and the lower-of-cost-or-market at that balance sheet date. Thus, if prices are falling, the company records an additional write-down. If prices are rising, the company records an increase in income, as shown in Illustration 9-10.

We can think of the net increase in income as the excess of the credit effect of closing the beginning allowance balance over the debit effect of setting up the current year-end allowance account. Recognizing the increases and decreases has the same effect on net income as closing the allowance balance to beginning inventory or to cost of goods sold.

ILLUSTRATION 9-10
Effect on Net Income of Reducing Inventory to Market

Date	Inventory at Cost	Inventory at Market	Amount Required in Valuation Account	Adjustment of Valuation Account Balance	Effect on Net Income
Dec. 31, 2013	$188,000	$176,000	$12,000	$12,000 inc.	Decrease
Dec. 31, 2014	194,000	187,000	7,000	5,000 dec.	Increase
Dec. 31, 2015	173,000	174,000	0	7,000 dec.	Increase
Dec. 31, 2016	182,000	180,000	2,000	2,000 inc.	Decrease

What do the numbers mean? "PUT IT IN REVERSE"

The lower-of-cost-or-market rule is designed to provide timely information about the decline in the value of inventory. When the value of inventory declines, income takes a hit in the period of the write-down.

What happens in the periods after the write-down? For some companies, gross margins and bottom lines get a boost when they sell inventory that had been written down in a previous period. For example, as the table below shows, **Vishay Intertechnology**, **Transwitch**, and **Cisco Systems** reported gains from selling inventory that had previously been written down. The table also evaluates how clearly these companies disclosed the effects of the reversal of inventory write-downs.

For Transwitch, the reversal of fortunes amounted to 23 percent of net income. The problem is that the $600,000 credit had little to do with the company's ongoing operations, and the company did not do a good job disclosing the effect of the reversal on current-year profitability.

Even when companies do disclose a reversal, it is sometimes hard to determine the impact on income. For example, **Intel** disclosed that it had sold inventory that had been written down in prior periods but did not specify how much reserved inventory was sold.

Transparency of financial reporting should be a top priority. With better disclosure of the reversals that boost profits in the current period, financial transparency would also get a boost.

Company	Gain from Reversal	Disclosure
Vishay Intertechnology	Not available	Poor—The semiconductor company did not mention the gain in its earnings announcement. Two weeks later in an SEC filing, Vishay disclosed the gain on the inventory that it had written down.
Transwitch	$600,000	Poor—The company did not mention the gain in its earnings announcement. Three weeks later in an SEC filing, the company disclosed the gain on the inventory that it had written down.
Cisco Systems	$525 million	Good—The networking giant detailed in its earnings release and in SEC filings the gains from selling inventory it had previously written off.

Source: S. E. Ante, "The Secret Behind Those Profit Jumps," *BusinessWeek Online* (December 8, 2003).

Evaluation of the Lower-of-Cost-or-Market Rule

The lower-of-cost-or-market rule suffers some conceptual deficiencies:

1. A company recognizes decreases in the value of the asset and the charge to expense in the period in which the loss in utility occurs—not in the period of sale. On the other hand, it recognizes increases in the value of the asset only at the point of sale. This inconsistent treatment can distort income data.
2. Application of the rule results in inconsistency because a company may value the inventory at cost in one year and at market in the next year.
3. Lower-of-cost-or-market values the inventory in the balance sheet conservatively, but its effect on the income statement may or may not be conservative. Net income for the year in which a company takes the loss is definitely lower. Net income of the subsequent period may be higher than normal if the expected reductions in sales price do not materialize.
4. Application of the lower-of-cost-or-market rule uses a "normal profit" in determining inventory values. Since companies estimate "normal profit" based on past experience (which they may not attain in the future), this subjective measure presents an opportunity for income manipulation.

Many financial statement users appreciate the lower-of-cost-or-market rule because they at least know that it prevents overstatement of inventory. In addition, recognizing all losses but anticipating no gains generally avoids overstating income.

VALUATION BASES

Valuation at Net Realizable Value

2 LEARNING OBJECTIVE

Explain when companies value inventories at net realizable value.

For the most part, companies record inventory at cost or at the lower-of-cost-or-market.[4] However, many believe that for purposes of applying the lower-of-cost-or-market rule, companies should define "market" as **net realizable value** (selling price less estimated costs to complete and sell) rather than as replacement cost. This argument is based on the fact that the amount that companies will collect from this inventory in the future is the net realizable value.[5]

Under limited circumstances, support exists for **recording inventory at net realizable value**, even if that amount is above cost. GAAP permits this exception to the

[4]Manufacturing companies frequently employ a **standardized cost system** that predetermines the unit costs for material, labor, and manufacturing overhead and that values raw materials, work in process, and finished goods inventories at their standard costs. For financial reporting purposes, it is acceptable to price inventories at standard costs if there is no significant difference between the actual costs and standard costs. If there is a significant difference, companies should adjust the inventory amounts to actual cost. In *Accounting Research and Terminology Bulletin, Final Edition,* the profession notes that **"standard costs are acceptable if adjusted at reasonable intervals to reflect current conditions."** Burlington Industries and Hewlett-Packard use standard costs for valuing at least a portion of their inventories.

[5]"The Accounting Basis of Inventories," *Accounting Research Study No. 13* (New York: AICPA, 1973) recommends that companies adopt net realizable value. We also should note that companies frequently fail to apply the rules of lower-of-cost-or-market in practice. For example, companies rarely compute and apply the lower limit—net realizable value less a normal markup—because it is a fairly subjective computation. In addition, companies often do not reduce inventory to market unless its disposition is expected to result in a loss. Furthermore, if the net realizable value of finished goods exceeds cost, companies usually assume that both work in process and raw materials do also. In practice, therefore, authoritative literature [3] is considered a guide, and accountants often exercise professional judgment in lieu of following the pronouncements literally.

International Perspective

Similar to GAAP, certain agricultural products and mineral products can be reported at net realizable value using IFRS.

normal recognition rule under the following conditions: (1) when there is a controlled market with a quoted price applicable to all quantities, and (2) when no significant costs of disposal are involved. For example, mining companies ordinarily report inventories of certain minerals (rare metals, especially) at selling prices because there is often a controlled market without significant costs of disposal. Similar treatment is given agricultural products that are immediately marketable at quoted prices.

A third reason for allowing valuation at net realizable value is that sometimes it is too difficult to obtain the cost figures. Cost figures are not difficult to determine in, say, a manufacturing plant, where the company combines various raw materials and purchased parts to create a finished product. The manufacturer can use the cost basis to account for various items in inventory because it knows the cost of each individual component part. The situation is different in a meat-packing plant, however. The "raw material" consists of, say, cattle, each unit of which the company purchases as a whole and then divides into parts that are the products. Instead of one product out of many raw materials or parts, the meat-packing company makes many products from one "unit" of raw material. To allocate the cost of the animal "on the hoof" into the cost of, say, ribs, chuck, and shoulders, is a practical impossibility. It is much easier and more useful for the company to determine the market price of the various products and value them in the inventory at selling price less the various costs necessary to get them to market (costs such as shipping and handling). Hence, because of a peculiarity of the industry, meat-packing companies sometimes carry **inventories at sales price less distribution costs**.

Valuation Using Relative Sales Value

LEARNING OBJECTIVE 3

Explain when companies use the relative sales value method to value inventories.

A special problem arises when a company buys a group of varying units in a single **lump-sum purchase**, also called a **basket purchase**. To illustrate, assume that Woodland Developers purchases land for $1 million that it will subdivide into 400 lots. These lots are of different sizes and shapes but can be roughly sorted into three groups graded A, B, and C. As Woodland sells the lots, it apportions the purchase cost of $1 million among the lots sold and the lots remaining on hand.

You might wonder why Woodland would not simply divide the total cost of $1 million by 400 lots, to get a cost of $2,500 for each lot. This approach would not recognize that the lots vary in size, shape, and attractiveness. Therefore, to accurately value each unit, the common and most logical practice is to allocate the total among the various units on the basis of their **relative sales value**.

Illustration 9-11 shows the allocation of relative sales value for the Woodland Developers example.

ILLUSTRATION 9-11
Allocation of Costs, Using Relative Sales Value

Lots	Number of Lots	Sales Price per Lot	Total Sales Price	Relative Sales Price	Total Cost	Cost Allocated to Lots	Cost per Lot
A	100	$10,000	$1,000,000	100/250	$1,000,000	$ 400,000	$4,000
B	100	6,000	600,000	60/250	1,000,000	240,000	2,400
C	200	4,500	900,000	90/250	1,000,000	360,000	1,800
			$2,500,000			$1,000,000	

Woodland determines the cost of lots sold and the gross profit, using the amounts given in the "Cost per Lot" column, as follows.

Lots	Number of Lots Sold	Cost per Lot	Cost of Lots Sold	Sales	Gross Profit
A	77	$4,000	$308,000	$ 770,000	$ 462,000
B	80	2,400	192,000	480,000	288,000
C	100	1,800	180,000	450,000	270,000
			$680,000	$1,700,000	$1,020,000

ILLUSTRATION 9-12
Determination of Gross Profit, Using Relative Sales Value

The ending inventory is therefore $320,000 ($1,000,000 − $680,000).

Woodland also can compute this inventory amount another way. The ratio of cost to selling price for all the lots is $1 million divided by $2,500,000, or 40 percent. Accordingly, if the total sales price of lots sold is, say $1,700,000, then the cost of the lots sold is 40 percent of $1,700,000, or $680,000. The inventory of lots on hand is then $1 million less $680,000, or $320,000.

The petroleum industry widely uses the relative sales value method to value (at cost) the many products and by-products obtained from a barrel of crude oil.

Purchase Commitments—A Special Problem

4 LEARNING OBJECTIVE
Discuss accounting issues related to purchase commitments.

In many lines of business, a company's survival and continued profitability depends on its having a sufficient stock of merchandise to meet customer demand. Consequently, it is quite common for a company to make **purchase commitments**, which are agreements to buy inventory weeks, months, or even years in advance. Generally, the seller retains title to the merchandise or materials covered in the purchase commitments. Indeed, the goods may exist only as natural resources as unplanted seed (in the case of agricultural commodities), or as work in process (in the case of a product).[6]

Usually, it is not necessary for the buyer to make any entries to reflect commitments for purchases of goods that the seller has not shipped. Ordinary orders, for which the buyer and seller will determine prices at the time of shipment and **which are subject to cancellation**, do not represent either an asset or a liability to the buyer. Therefore, the buyer need not record such purchase commitments or report them in the financial statements.

What happens, though, if a buyer enters into a formal, noncancelable purchase contract? Even then, the buyer recognizes no asset or liability at the date of inception, **because the contract is "executory" in nature**: Neither party has fulfilled its part of the contract. However, if material, the buyer should disclose such contract details in a note to its financial statements. Illustration 9-13 shows an example of a purchase commitment disclosure.

Note 1: Contracts for the purchase of raw materials in 2014 have been executed in the amount of $600,000. The market price of such raw materials on December 31, 2013, is $640,000.

ILLUSTRATION 9-13
Disclosure of Purchase Commitment

In the disclosure in Illustration 9-13, the contract price was less than the market price at the balance sheet date. **If the contract price is greater than the market price and the buyer expects that losses will occur when the purchase is effected, the buyer**

[6]One study noted that about 30 percent of public companies have purchase commitments outstanding, with an estimated value of $725 billion ("SEC Staff Report on Off-Balance Sheet Arrangements, Special Purpose Entities, and Related Issues," *http://www.sec.gov/news/ studies/ soxoffbalancerpt.pdf,* June 2005). Purchase commitments are popular because the buyer can secure a supply of inventory at a known price. The seller also benefits in these arrangements by knowing how much to produce.

should recognize losses in the period during which such declines in market prices take place. [4][7]

As an example, at one time many Northwest forest-product companies such as **Boise Cascade**, **Georgia-Pacific**, and **Weyerhaeuser** signed long-term timber-cutting contracts with the **U.S. Forest Service**. These contracts required that the companies pay $310 per thousand board feet for timber-cutting rights. Unfortunately, the market price for timber-cutting rights in the latter part of the year dropped to $80 per thousand board feet. As a result, a number of these companies had long-term contracts that, if fulfilled, would result in substantial future losses.

Underlying Concepts

Reporting the loss is *conservative*. However, reporting the decline in market price is debatable because no asset is recorded. This area demonstrates the need for good definitions of assets and liabilities.

To illustrate the accounting problem, assume that St. Regis Paper Co. signed timber-cutting contracts to be executed in 2015 at a price of $10,000,000. Assume further that the market price of the timber cutting rights on December 31, 2014, dropped to $7,000,000. St. Regis would make the following entry on December 31, 2014.

Unrealized Holding Gain or Loss—Income (Purchase Commitments)	3,000,000	
Estimated Liability on Purchase Commitments		3,000,000

St. Regis would report this unrealized holding loss in the income statement under "Other expenses and losses." And because the contract is to be executed within the next fiscal year, St. Regis would report the Estimated Liability on Purchase Commitments in the current liabilities section on the balance sheet. When St. Regis cuts the timber at a cost of $10 million, it would make the following entry.

Purchases (Inventory)	7,000,000	
Estimated Liability on Purchase Commitments	3,000,000	
Cash		10,000,000

The result of the purchase commitment was that St. Regis paid $10 million for a contract worth only $7 million. It recorded the loss in the previous period—when the price actually declined.

If St. Regis can partially or fully recover the contract price before it cuts the timber, it reduces the Estimated Liability on Purchase Commitments. In that case, it then reports in the period of the price increase a resulting gain for the amount of the partial or full recovery. For example, Congress permitted some of the forest-products companies to buy out of their contracts at reduced prices in order to avoid potential bankruptcies. To illustrate, assume that Congress permitted St. Regis to reduce its contract price and therefore its commitment by $1,000,000. The entry to record this transaction is as follows.

Estimated Liability on Purchase Commitments	1,000,000	
Unrealized Holding Gain or Loss—Income (Purchase Commitments)		1,000,000

If the market price at the time St. Regis cuts the timber is more than $2,000,000 below the contract price, St. Regis will have to recognize an additional loss in the period of cutting and record the purchase at the lower-of-cost-or-market.

[7]There is a long-standing controversy on the accounting in this area. See, for example, Yuji Ijiri, *Recognition of Contractual Rights and Obligations, Research Report* (Stamford, Conn.: FASB, 1980), who argues that companies should capitalize firm purchase commitments. "Firm" means that it is unlikely that companies can avoid performance under the contract without a severe penalty.

Also, see Mahendra R. Gujarathi and Stanley F. Biggs, "Accounting for Purchase Commitments: Some Issues and Recommendations," *Accounting Horizons* (September 1988), pp. 75–78. They conclude, "Recording an asset and liability on the date of inception for the noncancelable purchase commitments is suggested as the first significant step towards alleviating the accounting problems associated with the issue. At year-end, the potential gains and losses should be treated as contingencies which provide a coherent structure for the reporting of such gains and losses."

Are purchasers at the mercy of market price declines? Not totally. Purchasers can protect themselves against the possibility of market price declines of goods under contract by hedging. In **hedging**, the purchaser in the purchase commitment simultaneously enters into a contract in which it agrees to sell in the future the same quantity of the same (or similar) goods at a fixed price. Thus the company holds a *buy position* in a purchase commitment and a *sell position* in a futures contract in the same commodity. The purpose of the hedge is to offset the price risk of the buy and sell positions. The company will be better off under one contract by approximately (maybe exactly) the same amount by which it is worse off under the other contract.

For example, St. Regis Paper Co. could have hedged its purchase commitment contract with a futures contract for timber rights of the same amount. In that case, its loss of $3,000,000 on the purchase commitment could have been offset by a $3,000,000 gain on the futures contract.[8]

As easy as this makes it sound, accounting for purchase commitments is still unsettled and controversial. Some argue that companies should report purchase commitments as assets and liabilities at the time they sign the contract. Others believe that the present recognition at the delivery date is more appropriate. *FASB Concepts Statement No. 6* states, "a purchase commitment involves both an item that might be recorded as an asset and an item that might be recorded as a liability. That is, it involves both a right to receive assets and an obligation to pay. . . . If both the right to receive assets and the obligation to pay were recorded at the time of the purchase commitment, the nature of the loss and the valuation account that records it when the price falls would be clearly seen." Although the discussion in *Concepts Statement No. 6* does not exclude the possibility of recording assets and liabilities for purchase commitments, it contains no conclusions or implications about whether companies should record them.[9]

THE GROSS PROFIT METHOD OF ESTIMATING INVENTORY

5 LEARNING OBJECTIVE

Determine ending inventory by applying the gross profit method.

Companies take a physical inventory to verify the accuracy of the perpetual inventory records or, if no records exist, to arrive at an inventory amount. Sometimes, however, taking a physical inventory is impractical. In such cases, companies use substitute measures to approximate inventory on hand.

One substitute method of verifying or determining the inventory amount is the **gross profit method** (also called the **gross margin method**). Auditors widely use this method in situations where they need only an estimate of the company's inventory (e.g., interim reports). Companies also use this method when fire or other catastrophe destroys either inventory or inventory records. The gross profit method relies on three assumptions:

1. The beginning inventory plus purchases equal total goods to be accounted for.
2. Goods not sold must be on hand.
3. The sales, reduced to cost, deducted from the sum of the opening inventory plus purchases, equal ending inventory.

To illustrate, assume that Cetus Corp. has a beginning inventory of $60,000 and purchases of $200,000, both at cost. Sales at selling price amount to $280,000. The gross profit on selling price is 30 percent.

[8]Appendix 17A provides a complete discussion of hedging and the use of derivatives such as futures.

[9]"Elements of Financial Statements," *Statement of Financial Accounting Concepts No. 6* (Stamford, Conn.: FASB, 1985), paras. 251–253.

Cetus applies the gross profit method as follows.

ILLUSTRATION 9-14
Application of Gross Profit Method

Beginning inventory (at cost)		$ 60,000
Purchases (at cost)		200,000
Goods available (at cost)		260,000
Sales (at selling price)	$280,000	
Less: Gross profit (30% of $280,000)	84,000	
Sales (at cost)		196,000
Approximate inventory (at cost)		$ 64,000

The current period's records contain all the information Cetus needs to compute inventory at cost, except for the gross profit percentage. Cetus determines the gross profit percentage by reviewing company policies or prior period records. In some cases, companies must adjust this percentage if they consider prior periods unrepresentative of the current period.[10]

Computation of Gross Profit Percentage

In most situations, the **gross profit percentage** is stated as a percentage of selling price. The previous illustration, for example, used a 30 percent gross profit on sales. Gross profit on selling price is the common method for quoting the profit for several reasons. (1) Most companies state goods on a retail basis, not a cost basis. (2) A profit quoted on selling price is lower than one based on cost. This lower rate gives a favorable impression to the consumer. (3) The gross profit based on selling price can never exceed 100 percent.[11]

In Illustration 9-14, the gross profit was a given. But how did Cetus derive that figure? To see how to compute a gross profit percentage, assume that an article cost $15 and sells for $20, a gross profit of $5. As shown in the computations in Illustration 9-15, this markup is ¼ or 25 percent of retail, and ⅓ or, 33⅓ percent of cost.

ILLUSTRATION 9-15
Computation of Gross Profit Percentage

$$\frac{\text{Markup}}{\text{Retail}} = \frac{\$5}{\$20} = 25\% \text{ at retail} \qquad \frac{\text{Markup}}{\text{Cost}} = \frac{\$5}{\$15} = 33\tfrac{1}{3}\% \text{ on cost}$$

Although companies normally compute the gross profit on the basis of selling price, you should understand the basic relationship between markup on cost and markup on

[10]An alternative method of estimating inventory using the gross profit percentage is considered by some to be less complicated than the traditional method. This alternative method uses the standard income statement format as follows. (Assume the same data as in the Cetus example above.)

Relationships			Solution	
Sales revenue		$280,000		$280,000
Cost of sales				
Beginning inventory	$ 60,000		$ 60,000	
Purchases	200,000		200,000	
Goods available for sale	260,000		260,000	
Ending inventory	(3) ?		(3) 64,000 Est.	
Cost of goods sold		(2) ?		(2)196,000 Est.
Gross profit on sales (30%)		(1) ?		(1) 84,000 Est.

Compute the unknowns as follows: first the gross profit amount, then cost of goods sold, and finally the ending inventory, as shown below.

(1) $280,000 × 30% = $84,000 (gross profit on sales).
(2) $280,000 − $84,000 = $196,000 (cost of goods sold).
(3) $260,000 − $196,000 = $64,000 (ending inventory).

[11]The terms *gross margin percentage, rate of gross profit,* and *percentage markup* are synonymous, although companies more commonly use *markup* in reference to cost and *gross profit* in reference to sales.

selling price. For example, assume that a company marks up a given item by 25 percent. What, then, is the **gross profit on selling price**? To find the answer, assume that the item sells for $1. In this case, the following formula applies.

$$\textbf{Cost} + \textbf{Gross profit} = \textbf{Selling price}$$
$$C + .25C = SP$$
$$(1 + .25)C = SP$$
$$1.25C = \$1.00$$
$$C = \$0.80$$

The gross profit equals $0.20 ($1.00 − $0.80). The rate of gross profit on selling price is therefore 20 percent ($0.20/$1.00).

Conversely, assume that the gross profit on selling price is 20 percent. What is the **markup on cost**? To find the answer, again assume that the item sells for $1. Again, the same formula holds:

$$\textbf{Cost} + \textbf{Gross profit} = \textbf{Selling price}$$
$$C + .20SP = SP$$
$$C = (1 - .20)SP$$
$$C = .80SP$$
$$C = .80(\$1.00)$$
$$C = \$0.80$$

As in the previous example, the markup equals $0.20 ($1.00 − $0.80). The markup on cost is 25 percent ($0.20/$0.80).

Retailers use the following formulas to express these relationships:

$$\text{1. Gross profit on selling price} = \frac{\text{Percentage markup on cost}}{100\% + \text{Percentage markup on cost}}$$

$$\text{2. Percentage markup on cost} = \frac{\text{Gross profit on selling price}}{100\% - \text{Gross profit on selling price}}$$

ILLUSTRATION 9-16
Formulas Relating to Gross Profit

To understand how to use these formulas, consider their application in the following calculations.

Gross Profit on Selling Price		Percentage Markup on Cost
Given: 20%	→	$\frac{.20}{1.00 - .20} = 25\%$
Given: 25%	→	$\frac{.25}{1.00 - .25} = 33\frac{1}{3}\%$
$\frac{.25}{1.00 + .25} = 20\%$	←	Given: 25%
$\frac{.50}{1.00 + .50} = 33\frac{1}{3}\%$	←	Given: 50%

ILLUSTRATION 9-17
Application of Gross Profit Formulas

Because selling price exceeds cost and with the gross profit amount the same for both, **gross profit on selling price will always be less than the related percentage based on cost.** Note that companies do not multiply sales by a cost-based markup percentage. Instead, they must convert the gross profit percentage to a percentage based on selling price.

Evaluation of Gross Profit Method

What are the major disadvantages of the gross profit method? One disadvantage is that **it provides an estimate**. As a result, companies must take a physical inventory once a year to verify the inventory. Second, the gross profit method **uses past percentages** in determining the markup. Although the past often provides answers to the future, a current rate is more appropriate. Note that whenever significant fluctuations occur, companies should adjust the percentage as appropriate. Third, companies must be **careful in applying a blanket gross profit rate**. Frequently, a store or department handles merchandise with widely varying rates of gross profit. In these situations, the company may need to apply the gross profit method by subsections, lines of merchandise, or a similar basis that classifies merchandise according to their respective rates of gross profit. The gross profit method is normally unacceptable for financial reporting purposes because it provides only an estimate. GAAP requires a physical inventory as additional verification of the inventory indicated in the records. Nevertheless, GAAP permits the gross profit method to determine ending inventory for interim (generally quarterly) reporting purposes, provided a company discloses the use of this method. Note that the gross profit method will follow closely the inventory method used (FIFO, LIFO, average-cost) because it relies on historical records.

What do the numbers mean? THE SQUEEZE

Managers and analysts closely follow gross profits. A small change in the gross profit rate can significantly affect the bottom line. At one time, **Apple** suffered a textbook case of shrinking gross profits. In response to pricing wars in the personal computer market, Apple had to quickly reduce the price of its signature Macintosh computers—reducing prices more quickly than it could reduce its costs. As a result, its gross profit rate fell from 44 percent to 40 percent in one year. Though the drop of 4 percent seems small, its impact on the bottom line caused Apple's stock price to drop from $57 per share to $27.50 per share in a two-month period (with a recent share price over $500, it would have been great to get into Apple stock at those lower prices!)

As another, more recent example, **Nike**—the largest global manufacturer of athletic footwear—in a recent quarter reported earnings that indicated falling gross profit, leading market analysts to adjust Nike's stock price downward. The cause—continuing downward pressure on its gross profit. On the positive side, an increase in the gross profit rate provides a positive signal to the market. For example, just a 1 percent boost in **Dr. Pepper**'s gross profit rate cheered the market, indicating the company was able to avoid the squeeze of increased commodity costs by raising its prices.

Sources: Trefis, "Nike's Earnings Reiterate Gross Margin Pressure," *http://seekingalpha.com* (March 23, 2011); and D. Kardous, "Higher Pricing Helps Boost Dr. Pepper Snapple's Net," *Wall Street Journal Online* (June 5, 2008).

RETAIL INVENTORY METHOD

LEARNING OBJECTIVE 6
Determine ending inventory by applying the retail inventory method.

Accounting for inventory in a retail operation presents several challenges. Retailers with certain types of inventory may use the specific identification method to value their inventories. Such an approach makes sense when a retailer holds significant individual inventory units, such as automobiles, pianos, or fur coats. However, imagine attempting to use such an approach at **Target**, **Home Depot**, **Sears Holdings**, or **Bloomingdale's**—high-volume retailers that have many different types of merchandise. It would be extremely difficult to determine the cost of each sale, to enter cost codes on the tickets, to change the codes to reflect declines in value of the merchandise, to allocate costs such as transportation, and so on.

An alternative is to compile the inventories at retail prices. For most retailers, an observable pattern between cost and price exists. The retailer can then use a formula to convert retail prices to cost. This method is called the **retail inventory method**. **It requires**

that the retailer keep a record of (1) the total cost and retail value of goods purchased, (2) the total cost and retail value of the goods available for sale, and (3) the sales for the period. Use of the retail inventory method is very common. For example, **Safeway** supermarkets, **Target**, **Wal-Mart**, and **Best Buy** use the retail inventory method.

Here is how it works at a company like **Best Buy**. Beginning with the retail value of the goods available for sale, Best Buy deducts the sales revenue for the period. This calculation determines an estimated inventory (goods on hand) at retail. It next computes the **cost-to-retail ratio** for all goods. The formula for this computation is to divide the total goods available for sale at cost by the total goods available at retail price. Finally, to obtain ending inventory at cost, Best Buy applies the cost-to-retail ratio to the ending inventory valued at retail. Illustration 9-18 shows the retail inventory method calculations for Best Buy (assumed data).

ILLUSTRATION 9-18
Retail Inventory Method

BEST BUY
(current period)

	Cost	Retail
Beginning inventory	$14,000	$ 20,000
Purchases	63,000	90,000
Goods available for sale	$77,000	110,000
Deduct: Sales revenue		85,000
Ending inventory, at retail		$ 25,000

Cost-to-retail ratio ($77,000 ÷ $110,000) = 70%
Ending inventory at cost (70% of $25,000) = $17,500

There are different versions of the retail inventory method. These include the **conventional** method (based on lower-of-average-cost-or-market), the **cost** method, the **LIFO retail** method, and the **dollar-value LIFO** retail method. Regardless of which version a company uses, the IRS, various retail associations, and the accounting profession all sanction use of the retail inventory method. One of its advantages is that a company like Best Buy can approximate the inventory balance **without a physical count**. However, to avoid a potential overstatement of the inventory, Target makes periodic inventory counts. Such counts are especially important in retail operations where loss due to shoplifting or breakage is common.

The retail inventory method is particularly useful for any type of **interim report** because such reports usually need a fairly quick and reliable measure of the inventory. Also, similar to use of the gross profit method, insurance adjusters often use this method to **estimate losses** from fire, flood, or other type of casualty. This method also acts as a **control device** because a company will have to explain any deviations from a physical count at the end of the year. Finally, the retail method **expedites the physical inventory count** at the end of the year. The crew taking the physical inventory need record only the retail price of each item. The crew does not need to look up each item's invoice cost, thereby saving time and expense.

Retail-Method Concepts

The amounts shown in the "Retail" column of Illustration 9-18 above represent the original retail prices, assuming no price changes. In practice, though, retailers frequently mark up or mark down the prices they charge buyers.

For retailers, the term **markup** means an additional markup of the original retail price. (In another context, such as the gross profit discussion on pages 485–488, we often think of markup on the basis of cost.) **Markup cancellations** are decreases in prices of merchandise that the retailer had marked up above the original retail price.

In a competitive market, retailers often need to use **markdowns**, which are decreases in the original sales prices. Such cuts in sales prices may be necessary because of a decrease in the general level of prices, special sales, soiled or damaged goods, overstocking, and market competition. Markdowns are common in retailing these days. **Markdown cancellations** occur when the markdowns are later offset by increases in the prices of goods that the retailer had marked down—such as after a one-day sale, for example. Neither a markup cancellation nor a markdown cancellation can exceed the original markup or markdown.

To illustrate these concepts, assume that Designer Clothing Store recently purchased 100 dress shirts from Marroway, Inc. The cost for these shirts was $1,500, or $15 a shirt. Designer Clothing established the selling price on these shirts at $30 a shirt. The shirts were selling quickly in anticipation of Father's Day, so the manager added a markup of $5 per shirt. This markup made the price too high for customers, and sales slowed. The manager then reduced the price to $32. At this point we would say that the shirts at Designer Clothing have had a markup of $5 and a markup cancellation of $3.

Right after Father's Day, the manager marked down the remaining shirts to a sale price of $23. At this point, an additional markup cancellation of $2 has taken place, and a $7 markdown has occurred. If the manager later increases the price of the shirts to $24, a markdown cancellation of $1 would occur.

Retail Inventory Method with Markups and Markdowns—Conventional Method

Retailers use markup and markdown concepts in developing the proper inventory valuation at the end of the accounting period. To obtain the appropriate inventory figures, companies must give proper treatment to markups, markup cancellations, markdowns, and markdown cancellations.

To illustrate the different possibilities, consider the data for In-Fusion Inc., shown in Illustration 9-19. In-Fusion can calculate its ending inventory at cost under two assumptions, A and B. (We'll explain the reasons for the two later.)

Assumption A: Computes a cost ratio after markups (and markup cancellations) but before markdowns.

Assumption B: Computes a cost ratio after both markups and markdowns (and cancellations).

The computations for In-Fusion are:

Ending inventory at retail × Cost ratio = Value of ending inventory

Assumption A: $12,500 × 53.9% = $6,737.50

Assumption B: $12,500 × 54.7% = $6,837.50

The question becomes: Which assumption and which percentage should In-Fusion use to compute the ending inventory valuation? The answer depends on which retail inventory method In-Fusion chooses.

One approach uses only assumption A (a cost ratio using markups but not markdowns). It approximates the lower-of-average-cost-or-market. We will refer to this approach as the **conventional retail inventory method** or the **lower-of-cost-or-market approach.**

To understand why this method considers only the markups, not the markdowns, in the cost percentage, you must understand how a retail business operates. A markup normally indicates an increase in the market value of the item. On the other hand, a markdown means a decline in the utility of that item. Therefore, to approximate the lower-of-cost-or-market, we would consider markdowns a current loss and so would not

ILLUSTRATION 9-19
Retail Inventory Method with Markups and Markdowns

	Cost	Retail
Beginning inventory	$ 500	$ 1,000
Purchases (net)	20,000	35,000
Markups		3,000
Markup cancellations		1,000
Markdowns		2,500
Markdown cancellations		2,000
Sales (net)		25,000

IN-FUSION INC.

	Cost		Retail
Beginning inventory	$ 500		$ 1,000
Purchases (net)	20,000		35,000
Merchandise available for sale	20,500		36,000
Add: Markups		$3,000	
Less: Markup cancellations		1,000	
Net markups			2,000
	20,500		38,000

(A) Cost-to-retail ratio $= \frac{\$20,500}{\$38,000} = 53.9\%$

	Cost		Retail
Deduct:			
Markdowns		2,500	
Markdown cancellations		(2,000)	
Net markdowns			500
	$20,500		37,500

(B) Cost-to-retail ratio $= \frac{\$20,500}{\$37,500} = 54.7\%$

	Retail
Deduct: Sales (net)	25,000
Ending inventory at retail	$12,500

include them in calculating the cost-to-retail ratio. Omitting the markdowns would make the cost-to-retail ratio lower, which leads to an approximate lower-of-cost-or-market.

An example will make the distinction between the two methods clear. In-Fusion purchased two items for $5 apiece; the original sales price was $10 each. One item was subsequently written down to $2. Assuming no sales for the period, **if markdowns are considered** in the cost-to-retail ratio (assumption B—the **cost method)**, we compute the ending inventory in the following way.

ILLUSTRATION 9-20
Retail Inventory Method Including Markdowns—Cost Method

Markdowns Included in Cost-to-Retail Ratio

	Cost	Retail
Purchases	$10	$20
Deduct: Markdowns		8
Ending inventory, at retail		$12

Cost-to-retail ratio $= \frac{\$10}{\$12} = 83.3\%$

Ending inventory at cost ($12 × .833) = $10

This approach (the cost method) reflects an **average cost** of the two items of the commodity without considering the loss on the one item. It values ending inventory at $10.

If markdowns are not considered in the cost-to-retail ratio (assumption A—the **conventional retail method**), we compute the ending inventory as follows.

ILLUSTRATION 9-21
Retail Inventory Method Excluding Markdowns—Conventional Method (LCM)

Markdowns Not Included in Cost-to-Retail Ratio

	Cost	Retail
Purchases	$10	$20

$$\text{Cost-to-retail ratio} = \frac{\$10}{\$20} = 50\%$$

Deduct: Markdowns		8
Ending inventory, at retail		$12

Ending inventory at cost ($12 × .50) = $6

Under this approach (the conventional retail method, in which markdowns are **not considered**), ending inventory would be $6. The inventory valuation of $6 reflects two inventory items, one inventoried at $5 and the other at $1. It reflects the fact that In-Fusion reduced the sales price from $10 to $2, and reduced the cost from $5 to $1.[12]

To approximate the lower-of-cost-or-market, In-Fusion must establish the **cost-to-retail ratio**. It does this by dividing the cost of goods available for sale by the sum of the original retail price of these goods plus the net markups. This calculation excludes markdowns and markdown cancellations. Illustration 9-22 shows the basic format for the retail inventory method using the lower-of-cost-or-market approach along with the In-Fusion Inc. information.

ILLUSTRATION 9-22
Comprehensive Conventional Retail Inventory Method Format

IN-FUSION INC.

	Cost		Retail
Beginning inventory	$ 500		$ 1,000
Purchases (net)	20,000		35,000
Totals	20,500		36,000
Add: Net markups			
Markups		$3,000	
Markup cancellations		1,000	2,000
Totals	$20,500	←→	38,000
Deduct: Net markdowns			
Markdowns		2,500	
Markdown cancellations		2,000	500
Sales price of goods available			37,500
Deduct: Sales (net)			25,000
Ending inventory, at retail			$12,500

$$\text{Cost-to-retail ratio} = \frac{\text{Cost of goods available}}{\text{Original retail price of goods available, plus net markups}}$$

$$= \frac{\$20{,}500}{\$38{,}000} = 53.9\%$$

Ending inventory at lower-of-cost-or-market (53.9% × $12,500) = $6,737.50

[12]This figure is not really market (replacement cost), but it is net realizable value less the normal margin that is allowed. In other words, the sale price of the goods written down is $2, but subtracting a normal margin of 50 percent ($5 cost, $10 price), the figure becomes $1.

Because an averaging effect occurs, an exact lower-of-cost-or-market inventory valuation is ordinarily not obtained, but an adequate approximation can be achieved. In contrast, adding net markups **and** deducting net markdowns yields **approximate cost**.

Special Items Relating to Retail Method

The retail inventory method becomes more complicated when we consider such items as freight-in, purchase returns and allowances, and purchase discounts. In the retail method, we treat such items as follows.

- **Freight costs** are part of the purchase cost.
- **Purchase returns** are ordinarily considered as a reduction of the price at both cost and retail.
- **Purchase discounts and allowances** usually are considered as a reduction of the cost of purchases.

In short, the treatment for the items affecting the cost column of the retail inventory approach follows the computation for cost of goods available for sale.[13]

Note also that **sales returns and allowances** are considered as proper adjustments to gross sales. However, when sales are recorded gross, companies do not recognize **sales discounts**. To adjust for the sales discount account in such a situation would provide an ending inventory figure at retail that would be overvalued.

In addition, a number of special items require careful analysis:

- **Transfers-in** from another department are reported in the same way as purchases from an outside company.
- **Normal shortages** (breakage, damage, theft, shrinkage) should reduce the retail column because these goods are no longer available for sale. Such costs are reflected in the selling price because a certain amount of shortage is considered normal in a retail enterprise. As a result, companies do not consider this amount in computing the cost-to-retail percentage. Rather, to arrive at ending inventory at retail, they show normal shortages as a deduction similar to sales.
- **Abnormal shortages**, on the other hand, are deducted from both the cost and retail columns and reported as a special inventory amount or as a loss. To do otherwise distorts the cost-to-retail ratio and overstates ending inventory.
- **Employee discounts** (given to employees to encourage loyalty, better performance, and so on) are deducted from the retail column in the same way as sales. These discounts should not be considered in the cost-to-retail percentage because they do not reflect an overall change in the selling price.[14]

Illustration 9-23 (page 494) shows some of these concepts. The company, Extreme Sport Apparel, determines its inventory using the conventional retail inventory method.

Evaluation of Retail Inventory Method

Companies like **Gap Inc.**, **Home Depot**, or your local department store use the retail inventory method of computing inventory for the following reasons: (1) to permit the computation of net income without a physical count of inventory, (2) as a control measure in determining inventory shortages, (3) in regulating quantities of merchandise on hand, and (4) for insurance information.

[13]When the purchase allowance is not reflected by a reduction in the selling price, no adjustment is made to the retail column.

[14]Note that if employee sales are recorded gross, no adjustment is necessary for employee discounts in the retail column.

ILLUSTRATION 9-23
Conventional Retail Inventory Method—Special Items Included

EXTREME SPORT APPAREL			
	Cost		Retail
Beginning inventory	$ 1,000		$ 1,800
Purchases	30,000		60,000
Freight-in	600		—
Purchase returns	(1,500)		(3,000)
Totals	30,100		58,800
Net markups			9,000
Abnormal shortage	(1,200)		(2,000)
Totals	$28,900	←→	65,800
Deduct:			
Net markdowns			1,400
Sales revenue		$36,000	
Sales returns		(900)	35,100
Employee discounts			800
Normal shortage			1,300
			$27,200

Cost-to-retail ratio $= \frac{\$28,900}{\$65,800} = 43.9\%$

Ending inventory at lower-of-cost-or-market (43.9% × $27,200) = $11,940.80

One characteristic of the retail inventory method is that it **has an averaging effect on varying rates of gross profit**. This can be problematic when companies apply the method to an entire business, where rates of gross profit vary among departments. There is no allowance for possible distortion of results because of such differences. Companies refine the retail method under such conditions by computing inventory separately by departments or by classes of merchandise with similar gross profits. In addition, the reliability of this method assumes that the distribution of items in inventory is similar to the "mix" in the total goods available for sale.

PRESENTATION AND ANALYSIS

Presentation of Inventories

LEARNING OBJECTIVE 7
Explain how to report and analyze inventory.

Accounting standards require financial statement disclosure of the composition of the inventory, inventory financing arrangements, and the inventory costing methods employed. The standards also require the consistent application of costing methods from one period to another.

Manufacturers should report the inventory composition either in the balance sheet or in a separate schedule in the notes. The relative mix of raw materials, work in process, and finished goods helps in assessing liquidity and in computing the stage of inventory completion.

Significant or unusual financing arrangements relating to inventories may require note disclosure. Examples include transactions with related parties, product financing arrangements, firm purchase commitments, involuntary liquidation of LIFO inventories, and pledging of inventories as collateral. Companies should present inventories pledged as collateral for a loan in the current assets section rather than as an offset to the liability.

A company should also report the basis on which it states inventory amounts (lower-of-cost-or-market) and the method used in determining cost (LIFO, FIFO, average-cost, etc.). For example, the annual report of **Mumford of Wyoming** contains the following disclosures.

ILLUSTRATION 9-24
Disclosure of Inventory Methods

Mumford of Wyoming

Note A: Significant Accounting Policies

Live feeder cattle and feed—last-in, first-out (LIFO) cost, which is below approximate market	$854,800
Live range cattle—lower of principally identified cost or market	$1,240,500
Live sheep and supplies—lower of first-in, first-out (FIFO) cost or market	$674,000
Dressed meat and by-products—principally at market less allowances for distribution and selling expenses	$362,630

Illustration 9-24 shows that a company can use different pricing methods for different elements of its inventory. If Mumford changes the method of pricing any of its inventory elements, it must report a change in accounting principle. For example, if Mumford changes its method of accounting for live sheep from FIFO to average-cost, it should separately report this change, along with the effect on income, in the current and prior periods. Changes in accounting principle require an explanatory paragraph in the auditor's report describing the change in method.

Fortune Brands, Inc. reported its inventories in its annual report as follows (note the "trade practice" followed in classifying inventories among the current assets).

ILLUSTRATION 9-25
Disclosure of Trade Practice in Valuing Inventories

Fortune Brands, Inc.

Current assets

(in millions)	December 31
Inventories	
Maturing spirits	$1,243.0
Other raw materials, supplies and work in process	322.7
Finished products	450.9
Total inventories	$2,016.6

Significant Accounting Policies (in part)

Inventories The first-in, first-out (FIFO) inventory method is our principal inventory method across all segments. In accordance with generally recognized trade practice, maturing spirits inventories are classified as current assets, although the majority of these inventories ordinarily will not be sold within one year, due to the duration of aging processes. Inventory provisions are recorded to reduce inventory to the lower of cost or market value for obsolete or slow moving inventory based on assumptions about future demand and marketability of products, the impact of new product introductions, inventory turns, product spoilage and specific identification of items, such as product discontinuance or engineering/material changes.

Analysis of Inventories

As our opening story illustrates, the amount of inventory that a company carries can have significant economic consequences. As a result, companies must manage inventories. But, inventory management is a double-edged sword. It requires constant attention. On the one hand, management wants to stock a great variety and quantity of items. Doing so will provide customers with the greatest selection. However, such an inventory policy may incur excessive carrying costs (e.g., investment, storage, insurance, taxes, obsolescence, and damage). On the other hand, low inventory levels lead to stock-outs, lost sales, and disgruntled customers.

Using financial ratios helps companies to chart a middle course between these two dangers. Common ratios used in the management and evaluation of inventory levels are inventory turnover and a related measure, average days to sell inventory.

Inventory Turnover

The **inventory turnover** measures the number of times on average a company sells the inventory during the period. It measures the liquidity of the inventory. To compute inventory turnover, divide the cost of goods sold by the average inventory on hand during the period.

Barring seasonal factors, analysts compute average inventory from beginning and ending inventory balances. For example, in its 2011 annual report **Kellogg Company** reported a beginning inventory of $1,056 million, an ending inventory of $1,132 million, and cost of goods sold of $7,750 million for the year. Illustration 9-26 shows the inventory turnover formula and Kellogg Company's 2011 ratio computation below.

ILLUSTRATION 9-26
Inventory Turnover

$$\text{Inventory Turnover} = \frac{\text{Cost of Goods Sold}}{\text{Average Inventory}} = \frac{\$7{,}750}{(\$1{,}132 + \$1{,}056)/2} = 7.08 \text{ times}$$

You will want to read the **IFRS INSIGHTS** on pages 525–534 for discussion of IFRS related to inventories.

Average Days to Sell Inventory

A variant of the inventory turnover is the **average days to sell inventory**. This measure represents the average number of days' sales for which a company has inventory on hand. For example, the inventory turnover for **Kellogg Company** of 7.08 times divided into 365 is approximately 51.6 days.

There are typical levels of inventory in every industry. However, companies that keep their inventory at lower levels with higher turnovers than those of their competitors, and that still can satisfy customer needs, are the most successful.

KEY TERMS

SUMMARY OF LEARNING OBJECTIVES

1 Describe and apply the lower-of-cost-or-market rule. If inventory declines in value below its original cost, for whatever reason, a company should write down the inventory to reflect this loss. The general rule is to abandon the historical cost principle when the future utility (revenue-producing ability) of the asset drops below its original cost.

2 Explain when companies value inventories at net realizable value. Companies value inventory at net realizable value when (1) there is a controlled market with a quoted price applicable to all quantities, (2) no significant costs of disposal are involved, and (3) the cost figures are too difficult to obtain.

3 Explain when companies use the relative sales value method to value inventories. When a company purchases a group of varying units at a single lump-sum price—a so-called basket purchase—the company may allocate the total purchase price to the individual items on the basis of relative sales value.

4 Discuss accounting issues related to purchase commitments. Accounting for purchase commitments is controversial. Some argue that companies should report purchase commitment contracts as assets and liabilities at the time the contract is signed. Others believe that recognition at the delivery date is most appropriate. The

FASB neither excludes nor recommends the recording of assets and liabilities for purchase commitments. However, companies record losses when market prices fall relative to the commitment price.

5 Determine ending inventory by applying the gross profit method. Companies follow these steps to determine ending inventory by the gross profit method. (1) Compute the gross profit percentage on selling price. (2) Compute gross profit by multiplying net sales by the gross profit percentage. (3) Compute cost of goods sold by subtracting gross profit from net sales. (4) Compute ending inventory by subtracting cost of goods sold from total goods available for sale.

6 Determine ending inventory by applying the retail inventory method. Companies follow these steps to determine ending inventory by the conventional retail method. (1) To estimate inventory at retail, deduct the sales for the period from the retail value of the goods available for sale. (2) To find the cost-to-retail ratio for all goods passing through a department or firm, divide the total goods available for sale at cost by the total goods available at retail. (3) Convert the inventory valued at retail to approximate cost by applying the cost-to-retail ratio.

7 Explain how to report and analyze inventory. Accounting standards require financial statement disclosure of (1) the composition of the inventory (in the balance sheet or a separate schedule in the notes), (2) significant or unusual inventory financing arrangements, and (3) inventory costing methods employed (which may differ for different elements of inventory). Accounting standards also require the consistent application of costing methods from one period to another. Common ratios used in the management and evaluation of inventory levels are inventory turnover and average days to sell inventory.

APPENDIX 9A LIFO RETAIL METHODS

8 LEARNING OBJECTIVE
Determine ending inventory by applying the LIFO retail methods.

A number of retail establishments have changed from the more conventional treatment to a **LIFO retail method**. For example, the world's largest retailer, **Wal-Mart Stores, Inc.**, uses the LIFO retail method. The primary reason to do so is for the tax advantages associated with valuing inventories on a LIFO basis. In addition, adoption of LIFO results in a better matching of costs and revenues.

The use of LIFO retail is made under two assumptions: (1) stable prices and (2) fluctuating prices.

STABLE PRICES—LIFO RETAIL METHOD

It is much more complex to compute the final inventory balance using a LIFO flow than using the conventional retail method. Under the LIFO retail method, companies like **Wal-Mart** or **Target** consider **both markups and markdowns** in obtaining the proper cost-to-retail percentage. Furthermore, since the LIFO method is concerned only with the additional layer, or the amount that should be subtracted from the previous layer, the beginning inventory is excluded from the cost-to-retail percentage.

A major assumption of the LIFO retail method is that the markups and markdowns apply only to the goods purchased during the current period and not to the beginning inventory. This assumption is debatable and may explain why some companies do not adopt this method.

Illustration 9A-1 presents the major concepts involved in the LIFO retail method applied to the Hernandez Company. Note that, to simplify the accounting, we have assumed that the price level has remained unchanged.

ILLUSTRATION 9A-1
LIFO Retail Method—Stable Prices

	Cost	Retail
Beginning inventory—2014	$ 27,000	$ 45,000
Net purchases during the period	346,500	480,000
Net markups		20,000
Net markdowns		(5,000)
Total (excluding beginning inventory)	346,500	←→ 495,000
Total (including beginning inventory)	$373,500	540,000
Net sales during the period		(484,000)
Ending inventory at retail		$ 56,000

Establishment of cost-to-retail percentage under assumptions of LIFO retail ($346,500 ÷ $495,000) = 70%

Illustration 9A-2 indicates that the inventory is composed of two layers: the beginning inventory and the additional increase that occurred in the inventory this period (2014). When we start the next period (2015), the beginning inventory will be composed of those two layers. If an increase in inventory occurs again, an additional layer will be added.

ILLUSTRATION 9A-2
Ending Inventory at LIFO Cost, 2014—Stable Prices

Ending Inventory at Retail Prices—2014		Layers at Retail Prices		Cost-to-Retail (Percentage)		Ending Inventory at LIFO Cost
$56,000	2013	$45,000	×	60%*	=	$27,000
	2014	11,000	×	70	=	7,700
		$56,000				$34,700

*$27,000 / $45,000 (prior year's cost-to-retail)

However, if the final inventory figure is below the beginning inventory, Hernandez must reduce the beginning inventory starting with the most recent layer. For example, assume that the ending inventory for 2015 at retail is $50,000. Illustration 9A-3 shows the computation of the ending inventory at cost. Notice that the 2014 layer is reduced from $11,000 to $5,000.

ILLUSTRATION 9A-3
Ending Inventory at LIFO Cost, 2015—Stable Prices

Ending Inventory at Retail Prices—2015		Layers at Retail Prices		Cost-to-Retail (Percentage)		Ending Inventory at LIFO Cost
$50,000	2013	$45,000	×	60%	=	$27,000
	2014	5,000	×	70	=	3,500
		$50,000				$30,500

FLUCTUATING PRICES—DOLLAR-VALUE LIFO RETAIL METHOD

The previous example simplified the LIFO retail method by ignoring changes in the selling price of the inventory. Let us now assume that a change in the price level of the inventories occurs (as is usual). If the price level does change, the company must

eliminate the price change so as to measure the real increase in inventory, not the dollar increase. This approach is referred to as the **dollar-value LIFO retail method**.

To illustrate, assume that the beginning inventory had a retail market value of \$10,000 and the ending inventory had a retail market value of \$15,000. Assume further that the price level has risen from 100 to 125. It is inappropriate to suggest that a real increase in inventory of \$5,000 has occurred. Instead, the company must deflate the ending inventory at retail, as the computation in Illustration 9A-4 shows.

ILLUSTRATION 9A-4
Ending Inventory at Retail—Deflated and Restated

Ending inventory at retail (deflated) \$15,000 ÷ 1.25*	\$12,000	
Beginning inventory at retail	10,000	
Real increase in inventory at retail	\$ 2,000	
Ending inventory at retail on LIFO basis:		
First layer	\$10,000	
Second layer (\$2,000 × 1.25)	2,500	\$12,500

*1.25 = 125 ÷ 100

This approach is essentially the dollar-value LIFO method discussed in Chapter 8. In computing the LIFO inventory under a dollar-value LIFO approach, the company finds the dollar increase in inventory and deflates it to beginning-of-the-year prices. This indicates whether actual increases or decreases in quantity have occurred. If an increase in quantities occurs, the company prices this increase at the new index, in order to compute the value of the new layer. If a decrease in quantities happens, the company subtracts the increase from the most recent layers to the extent necessary.

The following computations, based on those in Illustration 9A-1 for Hernandez Company, illustrate the differences between the dollar-value LIFO retail method and the regular LIFO retail approach. Assume that the current 2014 price index is 112 (prior year = 100) and that the inventory (\$56,000) has remained unchanged. In comparing Illustrations 9A-1 and 9A-5 (see below), note that the computations involved in finding the cost-to-retail percentage are exactly the same. However, the dollar-value method determines the increase that has occurred in the inventory in terms of base-year prices.

ILLUSTRATION 9A-5
Dollar-Value LIFO Retail Method—Fluctuating Prices

	Cost	Retail	
Beginning inventory—2014	\$ 27,000	\$ 45,000	
Net purchases during the period	346,500	480,000	
Net markups		20,000	
Net markdowns		(5,000)	
Total (excluding beginning inventory)	346,500 ←	→ 495,000	
Total (including beginning inventory)	\$373,500	540,000	
Net sales during the period at retail		(484,000)	
Ending inventory at retail		\$ 56,000	
Establishment of cost-to-retail percentage under assumptions of LIFO retail (\$346,500 ÷ \$495,000) =			70%
A. Ending inventory at retail prices deflated to base-year prices (\$56,000 ÷ 1.12)			\$50,000
B. Beginning inventory (retail) at base-year prices			45,000
C. Inventory increase (retail) from beginning of period			\$ 5,000

From this information, we compute the inventory amount at cost:

ILLUSTRATION 9A-6
Ending Inventory at LIFO Cost, 2014—Fluctuating Prices

Ending Inventory at Base-Year Retail Prices—2014	Layers at Base-Year Retail Prices			Price Index (percentage)		Cost-to-Retail (percentage)		Ending Inventory at LIFO Cost
$50,000 →	2013	$45,000	×	100%	×	60%	=	$27,000
	2014	5,000	×	112	×	70	=	3,920
		$50,000						$30,920

As Illustration 9A-6 shows, before the conversion to cost takes place, Hernandez must restate layers of a particular year to the prices in effect in the year when the layer was added.

Note the difference between the LIFO approach (stable prices) and the dollar-value LIFO method as indicated below.

ILLUSTRATION 9A-7
Comparison of Effect of Price Assumptions

	LIFO (stable prices)	LIFO (fluctuating prices)
Beginning inventory	$27,000	$27,000
Increment	7,700	3,920
Ending inventory	$34,700	$30,920

The difference of $3,780 ($34,700 − $30,920) results from an increase in the **price** of goods, not from an increase in the **quantity** of goods.

SUBSEQUENT ADJUSTMENTS UNDER DOLLAR-VALUE LIFO RETAIL

The dollar-value LIFO retail method follows the same procedures in subsequent periods as the traditional dollar-value method discussed in Chapter 8. That is, when a real increase in inventory occurs, Hernandez adds a new layer.

To illustrate, using the data from the previous example, assume that the retail value of the 2015 ending inventory at current prices is $64,800, the 2015 price index is 120 percent of base-year, and the cost-to-retail percentage is 75 percent. In base-year dollars, the ending inventory is therefore $54,000 ($64,800/120%). Illustration 9A-8 shows the computation of the ending inventory at LIFO cost.

ILLUSTRATION 9A-8
Ending Inventory at LIFO Cost, 2015—Fluctuating Prices

Ending Inventory at Base-Year Retail Prices—2015	Layers at Base-Year Retail Prices			Price Index (percentage)		Cost-to-Retail (percentage)		Ending Inventory at LIFO Cost
$54,000 →	2013	$45,000	×	100%	×	60%	=	$27,000
	2014	5,000	×	112	×	70	=	3,920
	2015	4,000	×	120	×	75	=	3,600
		$54,000						$34,520

Conversely, when a real decrease in inventory develops, Hernandez "peels off" previous layers at prices in existence when the layers were added. To illustrate, assume that in 2015 the ending inventory in base-year prices is $48,000. The computation of the LIFO inventory is as follows.

ILLUSTRATION 9A-9
Ending Inventory at LIFO Cost, 2015—Fluctuating Prices

Ending Inventory at Base-Year Retail Prices—2015	Layers at Base-Year Retail Prices			Price Index (percentage)		Cost-to-Retail (percentage)		Ending Inventory at LIFO Cost
$48,000	2013	$45,000	×	100%	×	60%	=	$27,000
	2014	3,000	×	112	×	70	=	2,352
		$48,000						$29,352

The advantages and disadvantages of the lower-of-cost-or-market method (conventional retail) versus LIFO retail are the same for retail operations as for non-retail operations. As a practical matter, a company's selection of which retail inventory method to use often involves determining which method provides a lower taxable income. It might appear that retail LIFO will provide the lower taxable income in a period of rising prices. But this is not always the case. LIFO will provide an approximate current cost matching, but it states ending inventory at cost. The conventional retail method may have a large write-off because of the use of the lower-of-cost-or-market approach, which may offset the LIFO current cost matching.

CHANGING FROM CONVENTIONAL RETAIL TO LIFO

Because conventional retail is a lower-of-cost-or-market approach, the company must restate beginning inventory to a cost basis when changing from the conventional retail to the LIFO method.[15] The usual approach is to compute the cost basis from the purchases of the prior year, adjusted for both markups and markdowns.[16]

To illustrate, assume that Hakeman Clothing Store employs the conventional retail method but wishes to change to the LIFO retail method beginning in 2015. The amounts shown on the company's books are as follows.

	At Cost	At Retail
Inventory, January 1, 2014	$ 5,210	$ 15,000
Net purchases in 2014	47,250	100,000
Net markups in 2014		7,000
Net markdowns in 2014		2,000
Sales revenue in 2014		95,000

Illustration 9A-10 (page 502) shows computation of ending inventory under the **conventional retail method** for 2014.

[15]Changing from the conventional retail method to LIFO retail represents a change in accounting principle. We provide an expanded discussion of accounting principle changes in Chapter 22.

[16]A logical question to ask is, "Why are only the purchases from the prior period considered and not also the beginning inventory?" Apparently, the IRS believes that "the purchases-only approach" provides a more reasonable cost basis. The IRS position is debatable. However, for our purposes, it seems appropriate to use the purchases-only approach.

ILLUSTRATION 9A-10
Conventional Retail Inventory Method

	Cost	Retail
Inventory January 1, 2014	$ 5,210	$ 15,000
Net purchases	47,250	100,000
Net additional markups		7,000
	$52,460	122,000
Net markdowns		(2,000)
Sales revenue		(95,000)
Ending inventory at retail		$ 25,000
Establishment of cost-to-retail percentage ($52,460 ÷ $122,000) =		43%
December 31, 2014, inventory at cost		
Inventory at retail		$ 25,000
Cost-to-retail ratio		× 43%
Inventory at cost under conventional retail		$ 10,750

Hakeman Clothing can then quickly approximate the ending inventory for 2014 under the **LIFO retail method,** as shown in Illustration 9A-11.

ILLUSTRATION 9A-11
Conversion to LIFO Retail Inventory Method

December 31, 2014, Inventory at LIFO Cost

$$\text{Ending inventory} = \frac{\text{Retail}}{\$25{,}000} \times \frac{\text{Ratio}}{45\%^*} = \frac{\text{LIFO}}{\$11{,}250}$$

*The cost-to-retail ratio was computed as follows.

$$\frac{\text{Net purchases at cost}}{\text{Net purchases at retail plus markups less markdowns}} = \frac{\$47{,}250}{\$100{,}000 + \$7{,}000 - \$2{,}000} = 45\%$$

The difference of $500 ($11,250 − $10,750) between the LIFO retail method and the conventional retail method in the ending inventory for 2014 is the amount by which the company must adjust beginning inventory for 2015. The entry to adjust the inventory to a cost basis is as follows.

	Debit	Credit
Inventory	500	
Adjustment to Record Inventory at Cost		500

KEY TERMS

dollar-value LIFO retail method, *499*

LIFO retail method, *497*

SUMMARY OF LEARNING OBJECTIVE FOR APPENDIX 9A

8 Determine ending inventory by applying the LIFO retail methods. The application of LIFO retail is made under two assumptions: stable prices and fluctuating prices.

Procedures under stable prices: (a) Because the LIFO method is a cost method, both markups and markdowns must be considered in obtaining the proper cost-to-retail percentage. (b) Since the LIFO method is concerned only with the additional layer, or the amount that should be subtracted from the previous layer, the beginning inventory is excluded from the cost-to-retail percentage. (c) The markups and markdowns apply only to the goods purchased during the current period and not to the beginning inventory.

Procedures under fluctuating prices: The steps are the same as for stable prices except that in computing the LIFO inventory under a dollar-value LIFO approach, the dollar increase in inventory is found and deflated to beginning-of-the-year prices. Doing so will determine whether actual increases or decreases in quantity have occurred. If quantities increase, this increase is priced at the new index to compute the new layer. If quantities decrease, the decrease is subtracted from the most recent layers to the extent necessary.

DEMONSTRATION PROBLEM

Norwood Company makes miniature circuit boards that are components of wireless phones and personal organizers. The company has experienced strong growth, and you are especially interested in how well Norwood is managing its inventory balances. You have collected the following information for the current year.

Inventory at the beginning of year	$ 1,026,000
Inventory at the end of year, before any adjustments	1,007,000
Total cost of goods sold, before any adjustments	11,776,000

The company values inventory at lower-of-cost (using LIFO cost flow assumption)-or-market.

Instructions

(a) Compute Norwood's inventory turnover before any adjustment.

(b) Recompute the inventory turnover after adjusting Norwood's inventory information for the following items.

1. During the year, Norwood recorded sales and costs of goods sold on $22,000 of units shipped to various wholesalers on consignment. At year-end, none of these units have been sold by wholesalers.
2. Shipping contracts changed 2 months ago from f.o.b. shipping point to f.o.b. destination point. At the end of the year, $25,000 of products are en route to China and will not arrive until after financial statements are released. Current inventory balances do not reflect this change in policy.
3. At the end of the year, Norwood determined that a certain section of inventory with an historical cost of $112,000 has a replacement cost of $100,800, net realizable value of $101,000 and net realizable value less a normal profit margin of $90,400. There is no need to make a lower-of-cost-or-market adjustment to other inventory.

Solution

(a) $$\frac{\$11{,}776{,}000}{(\$1{,}026{,}000 \times \$1{,}007{,}000)/2} = 11.6 \text{ times}$$

(b) Adjustments to ending inventory

Item	Adjustment to Ending Inventory	Explanation
1. Consigned goods	$22,000	Norwood should count the goods it has consigned in other stores.
2. Goods in transit	$25,000	Goods officially change hands at the point of destination. Norwood should still show these goods in inventory (not cost of goods sold), until they reach the destination.
3. Lower-of-cost-or-market	$(11,200)	($112,000 – $100,800). The correct valuation is $100,800 since the market designation of $100,800 is less than the original cost.

$$\text{Adjusted inventory turnover} = \frac{\$11{,}740{,}000^{a}}{(\$1{,}026{,}000 \times \$1{,}042{,}800^{b})/2}$$
$$= 11.3 \text{ times}$$

[a]Cost of goods sold: $11,776,000 − $22,000 − $25,000 + $11,200 = $11,740,200
[b]Ending inventory: $1,007,000 + $22,000 + $25,000 − $11,200 = $1,042,800

FASB CODIFICATION

FASB Codification References

[1] FASB ASC 330-10-35. [Predecessor literature: "Restatement and Revision of Accounting Research Bulletins," *Accounting Research Bulletin No. 43* (New York: AICPA, 1953), Ch. 4, par. 8.]

[2] FASB ASC 330-10-S99-3. [Predecessor literature: "AICPA Task Force on LIFO Inventory Problems," *Issues Paper* (New York: AICPA, November 30, 1984), pp. 50–55.]

[3] FASB ASC 330-10-35. [Predecessor literature: "Restatement and Revision of Accounting Research Bulletins," *Accounting Research Bulletin No. 43* (New York: AICPA, 1953), Ch. 4.]

[4] FASB ASC 330-10-35-16 through 18. [Predecessor literature: "Restatement and Revision of Accounting Research Bulletins," *Accounting Research Bulletin No. 43* (New York: AICPA, 1953), Ch. 4, par. 16.]

Exercises

If your school has a subscription to the FASB Codification, go to *http://aaahq.org/asclogin.cfm* to log in and prepare responses to the following. Provide Codification references for your responses.

CE9-1 Access the glossary ("Master Glossary") to answer the following.

(a) What is the definition of inventory?
(b) What is the definition of market as it relates to inventory?
(c) What is the definition of net realizable value?

CE9-2 Based on increased competition for one of its key products, Tutaj Company is concerned that it will not be able to sell its products at a price that would cover its costs. Since the company is already having a bad year, the sales manager proposes writing down the inventory to the lowest level possible, so that all the bad news will be in the current year. Explain to the sales manager the rationale for lower-of-cost-or-market adjustments, according to GAAP.

CE9-3 What are the provisions for subsequent measurement of inventory in the context of a hedging transaction?

CE9-4 What is the nature of the SEC guidance concerning inventory disclosures?

An additional Codification case can be found in the Using Your Judgment section, on page 525.

Be sure to check the book's companion website for a Review and Analysis Exercise, with solution.

WileyPLUS Brief Exercises, Exercises, Problems, and many more learning and assessment tools and resources are available for practice in WileyPLUS.

Note: All asterisked Questions, Exercises, and Problems relate to material in the appendix to the chapter.

QUESTIONS

1. Where there is evidence that the utility of inventory goods, as part of their disposal in the ordinary course of business, will be less than cost, what is the proper accounting treatment?

2. Explain the rationale for the ceiling and floor in the lower-of-cost-or-market method of valuing inventories.

3. Why are inventories valued at the lower-of-cost-or-market? What are the arguments against the use of the LCM method of valuing inventories?

4. What approaches may be employed in applying the lower-of-cost-or-market procedure? Which approach is normally used and why?

5. In some instances, accounting principles require a departure from valuing inventories at cost alone. Determine the proper unit inventory price in the following cases.

	Cases				
	1	2	3	4	5
Cost	$15.90	$16.10	$15.90	$15.90	$15.90
Net realizable value	14.50	19.20	15.20	10.40	16.40
Net realizable value less normal profit	12.80	17.60	13.75	8.80	14.80
Market (replacement cost)	14.80	17.20	12.80	9.70	16.80

6. What method(s) might be used in the accounts to record a loss due to a price decline in the inventories? Discuss.

7. What factors might call for inventory valuation at sales prices (net realizable value or market price)?

8. Under what circumstances is relative sales value an appropriate basis for determining the price assigned to inventory?

9. At December 31, 2014, Ashley Co. has outstanding purchase commitments for 150,000 gallons, at $6.20 per gallon, of a raw material to be used in its manufacturing process. The company prices its raw material inventory at cost or market, whichever is lower. Assuming that the market price as of December 31, 2014, is $5.90, how would you treat this situation in the accounts?

10. What are the major uses of the gross profit method?

11. Distinguish between gross profit as a percentage of cost and gross profit as a percentage of sales price. Convert the following gross profit percentages based on cost to gross profit percentages based on sales price: 25% and 33⅓%. Convert the following gross profit percentages based on sales price to gross profit percentages based on cost: 33⅓% and 60%.

12. Adriana Co., with annual net sales of $5 million, maintains a markup of 25% based on cost. Adriana's expenses average 15% of net sales. What is Adriana's gross profit and net profit in dollars?

13. A fire destroys all of the merchandise of Assante Company on February 10, 2014. Presented below is information compiled up to the date of the fire.

Inventory, January 1, 2014	$ 400,000
Sales revenue to February 10, 2014	1,950,000
Purchases to February 10, 2014	1,140,000
Freight-in to February 10, 2014	60,000
Rate of gross profit on selling price	40%

What is the approximate inventory on February 10, 2014?

14. What conditions must exist for the retail inventory method to provide valid results?

15. The conventional retail inventory method yields results that are essentially the same as those yielded by the lower-of-cost-or-market method. Explain. Prepare an illustration of how the retail inventory method reduces inventory to market.

16. (a) Determine the ending inventory under the conventional retail method for the furniture department of Mayron Department Stores from the following data.

	Cost	Retail
Inventory, Jan. 1	$ 149,000	$ 283,500
Purchases	1,400,000	2,160,000
Freight-in	70,000	
Markups, net		92,000
Markdowns, net		48,000
Sales revenue		2,175,000

(b) If the results of a physical inventory indicated an inventory at retail of $295,000, what inferences would you draw?

17. Deere and Company reported inventory in its balance sheet as follows.

Inventories	$1,999,100,000

What additional disclosures might be necessary to present the inventory fairly?

18. Of what significance is inventory turnover to a retail store?

*19. What modifications to the conventional retail method are necessary to approximate a LIFO retail flow?

BRIEF EXERCISES

1 2 **BE9-1** Presented below is information related to Rembrandt Inc.'s inventory.

(per unit)	Skis	Boots	Parkas
Historical cost	$190.00	$106.00	$53.00
Selling price	212.00	145.00	73.75
Cost to distribute	19.00	8.00	2.50
Current replacement cost	203.00	105.00	51.00
Normal profit margin	32.00	29.00	21.25

Determine the following: (a) the two limits to market value (i.e., the ceiling and the floor) that should be used in the lower-of-cost-or-market computation for skis, (b) the cost amount that should be used in the lower-of-cost-or-market comparison of boots, and (c) the market amount that should be used to value parkas on the basis of the lower-of-cost-or-market.

1 2 **BE9-2** Floyd Corporation has the following four items in its ending inventory.

Item	Cost	Replacement Cost	Net Realizable Value (NRV)	NRV Less Normal Profit Margin
Jokers	$2,000	$2,050	$2,100	$1,600
Penguins	5,000	5,100	4,950	4,100
Riddlers	4,400	4,550	4,625	3,700
Scarecrows	3,200	2,990	3,830	3,070

Determine the final lower-of-cost-or-market inventory value for each item.

1 2 **BE9-3** Kumar Inc. uses a perpetual inventory system. At January 1, 2014, inventory was $214,000 at both cost and market value. At December 31, 2014, the inventory was $286,000 at cost and $265,000 at market value. Prepare the necessary December 31 entry under (a) the cost-of-goods-sold method and (b) the loss method.

3 **BE9-4** Bell, Inc. buys 1,000 computer game CDs from a distributor who is discontinuing those games. The purchase price for the lot is $8,000. Bell will group the CDs into three price categories for resale, as indicated below.

Group	No. of CDs	Price per CD
1	100	$ 5
2	800	10
3	100	15

Determine the cost per CD for each group, using the relative sales value method.

4 **BE9-5** Kemper Company signed a long-term noncancelable purchase commitment with a major supplier to purchase raw materials in 2015 at a cost of $1,000,000. At December 31, 2014, the raw materials to be purchased have a market value of $950,000. Prepare any necessary December 31, 2014, entry.

4 **BE9-6** Use the information for Kemper Company from BE9-5. In 2015, Kemper paid $1,000,000 to obtain the raw materials which were worth $950,000. Prepare the entry to record the purchase.

5 **BE9-7** Fosbre Corporation's April 30 inventory was destroyed by fire. January 1 inventory was $150,000, and purchases for January through April totaled $500,000. Sales revenue for the same period were $700,000. Fosbre's normal gross profit percentage is 35% on sales. Using the gross profit method, estimate Fosbre's April 30 inventory that was destroyed by fire.

6 **BE9-8** Boyne Inc. had beginning inventory of $12,000 at cost and $20,000 at retail. Net purchases were $120,000 at cost and $170,000 at retail. Net markups were $10,000; net markdowns were $7,000; and sales revenue was $147,000. Compute ending inventory at cost using the conventional retail method.

7 **BE9-9** In its 2012 annual report, Gap Inc. reported inventory of $1,615 million on January 25, 2012, and $1,620 million on January 29, 2011, cost of sales of $9,275 million for fiscal year 2012, and net sales of $14,549 million. Compute Gap's inventory turnover and the average days to sell inventory for the fiscal year 2012.

8 ***BE9-10** Use the information for Boyne Inc. from BE9-8. Compute ending inventory at cost using the LIFO retail method.

8 ***BE9-11** Use the information for Boyne Inc. from BE9-8, and assume the price level increased from 100 at the beginning of the year to 115 at year-end. Compute ending inventory at cost using the dollar-value LIFO retail method.

EXERCISES

E9-1 (Lower-of-Cost-or-Market) The inventory of 3T Company on December 31, 2014, consists of the following items.

Part No.	Quantity	Cost per Unit	Cost to Replace per Unit
110	600	$ 90	$100
111	1,000	60	52
112	500	80	76
113	200	170	180
120	400	205	208
121[a]	1,600	16	14
122	300	240	235

[a]Part No. 121 is obsolete and has a realizable value of $0.20 each as scrap.

Instructions

(a) Determine the inventory as of December 31, 2014, by the lower-of-cost-or-market method, applying this method directly to each item.

(b) Determine the inventory by the lower-of-cost-or-market method, applying the method to the total of the inventory.

E9-2 (Lower-of-Cost-or-Market) Smashing Pumpkins Company uses the lower-of-cost-or-market method, on an individual-item basis, in pricing its inventory items. The inventory at December 31, 2014, consists of products D, E, F, G, H, and I. Relevant per-unit data for these products appear below.

	Item D	Item E	Item F	Item G	Item H	Item I
Estimated selling price	$120	$110	$95	$90	$110	$90
Cost	75	80	80	80	50	36
Replacement cost	120	72	70	30	70	30
Estimated selling expense	30	30	30	25	30	30
Normal profit	20	20	20	20	20	20

Instructions

Using the lower-of-cost-or-market rule, determine the proper unit value for balance sheet reporting purposes at December 31, 2014, for each of the inventory items above.

E9-3 (Lower-of-Cost-or-Market) Michael Bolton Company follows the practice of pricing its inventory at the lower-of-cost-or-market, on an individual-item basis.

Item No.	Quantity	Cost per Unit	Cost to Replace	Estimated Selling Price	Cost of Completion and Disposal	Normal Profit
1320	1,200	$3.20	$3.00	$4.50	$0.35	$1.25
1333	900	2.70	2.30	3.50	0.50	0.50
1426	800	4.50	3.70	5.00	0.40	1.00
1437	1,000	3.60	3.10	3.20	0.25	0.90
1510	700	2.25	2.00	3.25	0.80	0.60
1522	500	3.00	2.70	3.80	0.40	0.50
1573	3,000	1.80	1.60	2.50	0.75	0.50
1626	1,000	4.70	5.20	6.00	0.50	1.00

Instructions

From the information above, determine the amount of Bolton Company inventory.

E9-4 (Lower-of-Cost-or-Market—Journal Entries) Corrs Company began operations in 2013 and determined its ending inventory at cost and at lower-of-cost-or-market at December 31, 2013, and December 31, 2014. This information is presented below.

	Cost	Lower-of-Cost-or-Market
12/31/13	$346,000	$327,000
12/31/14	410,000	395,000

Instructions

(a) Prepare the journal entries required at December 31, 2013, and December 31, 2014, assuming that the inventory is recorded at market, and a perpetual inventory system (direct method) is used.

(b) Prepare journal entries required at December 31, 2013, and December 31, 2014, assuming that the inventory is recorded at cost and an allowance account is adjusted at each year-end under a perpetual system.

(c) Which of the two methods above provides the higher net income in each year?

1 2 **E9-5 (Lower-of-Cost-or-Market—Valuation Account)** Presented below is information related to Candlebox Enterprises.

	Jan. 31	Feb. 28	Mar. 31	Apr. 30
Inventory at cost	$15,000	$15,100	$17,000	$13,000
Inventory at the lower-of-cost-or-market	14,500	12,600	15,600	12,300
Purchases for the month		20,000	24,000	26,500
Sales revenue for the month		29,000	35,000	40,000

Instructions

(a) From the information, prepare (as far as the data permit) monthly income statements in columnar form for February, March, and April. The inventory is to be shown in the statement at cost, the gain or loss due to market fluctuations is to be shown separately, and a valuation account is to be set up for the difference between cost and the lower of cost or market.

(b) Prepare the journal entry required to establish the valuation account at January 31 and entries to adjust it monthly thereafter.

1 2 **E9-6 (Lower-of-Cost-or-Market—Error Effect)** Winans Company uses the lower-of-cost-or-market method, on an individual-item basis, in pricing its inventory items. The inventory at December 31, 2013, included product X. Relevant per-unit data for product X appear below.

Estimated selling price	$45
Cost	40
Replacement cost	35
Estimated selling expense	14
Normal profit	9

There were 1,000 units of product X on hand at December 31, 2013. Product X was incorrectly valued at $35 per unit for reporting purposes. All 1,000 units were sold in 2014.

Instructions

Compute the effect of this error on net income for 2013 and the effect on net income for 2014, and indicate the direction of the misstatement for each year.

3 **E9-7 (Relative Sales Value Method)** Phil Collins Realty Corporation purchased a tract of unimproved land for $55,000. This land was improved and subdivided into building lots at an additional cost of $34,460. These building lots were all of the same size but owing to differences in location were offered for sale at different prices as follows.

Group	No. of Lots	Price per Lot
1	9	$3,000
2	15	4,000
3	17	2,400

Operating expenses for the year allocated to this project total $18,200. Lots unsold at the year-end were as follows.

Group 1	5 lots
Group 2	7 lots
Group 3	2 lots

Instructions

At the end of the fiscal year Phil Collins Realty Corporation instructs you to arrive at the net income realized on this operation to date.

3 **E9-8 (Relative Sales Value Method)** During 2014, Pretenders Furniture Company purchases a carload of wicker chairs. The manufacturer sells the chairs to Pretenders for a lump sum of $59,850 because it is discontinuing manufacturing operations and wishes to dispose of its entire stock. Three types of chairs are included in the carload. The three types and the estimated selling price for each are listed below.

Type	No. of Chairs	Estimated Selling Price Each
Lounge chairs	400	$90
Armchairs	300	80
Straight chairs	700	50

During 2014, Pretenders sells 200 lounge chairs, 100 armchairs, and 120 straight chairs.

Instructions

What is the amount of gross profit realized during 2014? What is the amount of inventory of unsold straight chairs on December 31, 2014?

4 **E9-9 (Purchase Commitments)** Marvin Gaye Company has been having difficulty obtaining key raw materials for its manufacturing process. The company therefore signed a long-term noncancelable purchase commitment with its largest supplier of this raw material on November 30, 2014, at an agreed price of $400,000. At December 31, 2014, the raw material had declined in price to $365,000.

Instructions

What entry would you make on December 31, 2014, to recognize these facts?

4 **E9-10 (Purchase Commitments)** At December 31, 2014, Indigo Girls Company has outstanding noncancelable purchase commitments for 36,000 gallons, at $3.00 per gallon, of raw material to be used in its manufacturing process. The company prices its raw material inventory at cost or market, whichever is lower.

Instructions

(a) Assuming that the market price as of December 31, 2014, is $3.30, how would this matter be treated in the accounts and statements? Explain.

(b) Assuming that the market price as of December 31, 2014, is $2.70, instead of $3.30, how would you treat this situation in the accounts and statements?

(c) Give the entry in January 2015, when the 36,000-gallon shipment is received, assuming that the situation given in (b) above existed at December 31, 2014, and that the market price in January 2015 was $2.70 per gallon. Give an explanation of your treatment.

5 **E9-11 (Gross Profit Method)** Each of the following gross profit percentages is expressed in terms of cost.

1. 20%.
2. 25%.
3. 33⅓%.
4. 50%.

Instructions

Indicate the gross profit percentage in terms of sales for each of the above.

5 **E9-12 (Gross Profit Method)** Mark Price Company uses the gross profit method to estimate inventory for monthly reporting purposes. Presented below is information for the month of May.

Inventory, May 1	$ 160,000
Purchases (gross)	640,000
Freight-in	30,000
Sales revenue	1,000,000
Sales returns	70,000
Purchase discounts	12,000

Instructions

(a) Compute the estimated inventory at May 31, assuming that the gross profit is 30% of sales.

(b) Compute the estimated inventory at May 31, assuming that the gross profit is 30% of cost.

5 **E9-13 (Gross Profit Method)** Tim Legler requires an estimate of the cost of goods lost by fire on March 9. Merchandise on hand on January 1 was $38,000. Purchases since January 1 were $72,000; freight-in, $3,400; purchase returns and allowances, $2,400. Sales are made at 33⅓% above cost and totaled $100,000 to March 9. Goods costing $10,900 were left undamaged by the fire; remaining goods were destroyed.

Instructions

(a) Compute the cost of goods destroyed.

(b) Compute the cost of goods destroyed, assuming that the gross profit is 33⅓% of sales.

5 **E9-14 (Gross Profit Method)** Rasheed Wallace Company lost most of its inventory in a fire in December just before the year-end physical inventory was taken. The corporation's books disclosed the following.

Beginning inventory	$170,000	Sales revenue	$650,000
Purchases for the year	390,000	Sales returns	24,000
Purchase returns	30,000	Rate of gross profit on net sales	40%

Merchandise with a selling price of $21,000 remained undamaged after the fire. Damaged merchandise with an original selling price of $15,000 had a net realizable value of $5,300.

Instructions

Compute the amount of the loss as a result of the fire, assuming that the corporation had no insurance coverage.

5 **E9-15 (Gross Profit Method)** You are called by Tim Duncan of Spurs Co. on July 16 and asked to prepare a claim for insurance as a result of a theft that took place the night before. You suggest that an inventory be taken immediately. The following data are available.

Inventory, July 1	$ 38,000
Purchases—goods placed in stock July 1–15	85,000
Sales revenue—goods delivered to customers (gross)	116,000
Sales returns—goods returned to stock	4,000

Your client reports that the goods on hand on July 16 cost $30,500, but you determine that this figure includes goods of $6,000 received on a consignment basis. Your past records show that sales are made at approximately 40% over cost. Duncan's insurance covers only goods owned.

Instructions

Compute the claim against the insurance company.

5 **E9-16 (Gross Profit Method)** Gheorghe Moresan Lumber Company handles three principal lines of merchandise with these varying rates of gross profit on cost.

Lumber	25%
Millwork	30%
Hardware and fittings	40%

On August 18, a fire destroyed the office, lumber shed, and a considerable portion of the lumber stacked in the yard. To file a report of loss for insurance purposes, the company must know what the inventories were immediately preceding the fire. No detail or perpetual inventory records of any kind were maintained. The only pertinent information you are able to obtain are the following facts from the general ledger, which was kept in a fireproof vault and thus escaped destruction.

	Lumber	Millwork	Hardware
Inventory, Jan. 1, 2014	$ 250,000	$ 90,000	$ 45,000
Purchases to Aug. 18, 2014	1,500,000	375,000	160,000
Sales revenue to Aug. 18, 2014	2,080,000	533,000	210,000

Instructions

Submit your estimate of the inventory amounts immediately preceding the fire.

5 **E9-17 (Gross Profit Method)** Presented below is information related to Aaron Rodgers Corporation for the current year.

Beginning inventory	$ 600,000	
Purchases	1,500,000	
Total goods available for sale		$2,100,000
Sales revenue		2,500,000

Instructions

Compute the ending inventory, assuming that **(a)** gross profit is 45% of sales; **(b)** gross profit is 60% of cost; **(c)** gross profit is 35% of sales; and **(d)** gross profit is 25% of cost.

6 **E9-18 (Retail Inventory Method)** Presented below is information related to Bobby Engram Company.

	Cost	Retail
Beginning inventory	$ 58,000	$100,000
Purchases (net)	122,000	200,000
Net markups		10,345
Net markdowns		26,135
Sales revenue		186,000

Instructions

(a) Compute the ending inventory at retail.

(b) Compute a cost-to-retail percentage (round to two decimals) under the following conditions.

(1) Excluding both markups and markdowns.

(2) Excluding markups but including markdowns.

(3) Excluding markdowns but including markups.

(4) Including both markdowns and markups.

(c) Which of the methods in (b) above (1, 2, 3, or 4) does the following?

(1) Provides the most conservative estimate of ending inventory.

(2) Provides an approximation of lower-of-cost-or-market.

(3) Is used in the conventional retail method.

(d) Compute ending inventory at lower-of-cost-or-market (round to nearest dollar).

(e) Compute cost of goods sold based on (d).

(f) Compute gross margin based on (d).

6 **E9-19 (Retail Inventory Method)** Presented below is information related to Ricky Henderson Company.

	Cost	Retail
Beginning inventory	$ 200,000	$ 280,000
Purchases	1,375,000	2,140,000
Markups		95,000
Markup cancellations		15,000
Markdowns		35,000
Markdown cancellations		5,000
Sales revenue		2,200,000

Instructions

Compute the inventory by the conventional retail inventory method.

6 **E9-20 (Retail Inventory Method)** The records of Ellen's Boutique report the following data for the month of April.

Sales revenue	$99,000	Purchases (at cost)	$48,000
Sales returns	2,000	Purchases (at sales price)	88,000
Markups	10,000	Purchase returns (at cost)	2,000
Markup cancellations	1,500	Purchase returns (at sales price)	3,000
Markdowns	9,300	Beginning inventory (at cost)	30,000
Markdown cancellations	2,800	Beginning inventory (at sales price)	46,500
Freight on purchases	2,400		

Instructions

Compute the ending inventory by the conventional retail inventory method.

7 **E9-21 (Analysis of Inventories)** The financial statements of ConAgra Foods, Inc.'s 2012 annual report disclose the following information.

(in millions)	May 27, 2012	May 29, 2011	May 30, 2010
Inventories	$1,870	$1,803	$1,598

	Fiscal Year	
	2012	2011
Net sales	$13,263	$12,303
Cost of goods sold	10,436	9,390
Net income	474	818

Instructions

Compute ConAgra's **(a)** inventory turnover and **(b)** the average days to sell inventory for 2012 and 2011.

8 ***E9-22 (Retail Inventory Method—Conventional and LIFO)** Helen Keller Company began operations on January 1, 2013, adopting the conventional retail inventory system. None of the company's merchandise was marked down in 2013 and, because there was no beginning inventory, its ending inventory for 2013 of $38,100 would have been the same under either the conventional retail system or the LIFO retail system.

On December 31, 2014, the store management considers adopting the LIFO retail system and desires to know how the December 31, 2014, inventory would appear under both systems. All pertinent data regarding purchases, sales, markups, and markdowns are shown below. There has been no change in the price level.

	Cost	Retail
Inventory, Jan. 1, 2014	$ 38,100	$ 60,000
Markdowns (net)		13,000
Markups (net)		22,000
Purchases (net)	130,900	178,000
Sales (net)		167,000

Instructions

Determine the cost of the 2014 ending inventory under both **(a)** the conventional retail method and **(b)** the LIFO retail method.

8 ***E9-23 (Retail Inventory Method—Conventional and LIFO)** Leonard Bernstein Company began operations late in 2013 and adopted the conventional retail inventory method. Because there was no beginning inventory for 2013 and no markdowns during 2013, the ending inventory for 2013 was $14,000 under both the conventional retail method and the LIFO retail method. At the end of 2014, management wants to compare the results of applying the conventional and LIFO retail methods. There was no change in the price level during 2014. The following data are available for computations.

	Cost	Retail
Inventory, January 1, 2014	$14,000	$20,000
Sales revenue		80,000
Net markups		9,000
Net markdowns		1,600
Purchases	58,800	81,000
Freight-in	7,500	
Estimated theft		2,000

Instructions

Compute the cost of the 2014 ending inventory under both **(a)** the conventional retail method and **(b)** the LIFO retail method.

8 ***E9-24 (Dollar-Value LIFO Retail)** You assemble the following information for Seneca Department Store, which computes its inventory under the dollar-value LIFO method.

	Cost	Retail
Inventory on January 1, 2014	$216,000	$300,000
Purchases	364,800	480,000
Increase in price level for year		9%

Instructions

Compute the cost of the inventory on December 31, 2014, assuming that the inventory at retail is **(a)** $294,300 and **(b)** $365,150.

8 ***E9-25 (Dollar-Value LIFO Retail)** Presented below is information related to Langston Hughes Corporation.

	Price Index	LIFO Cost	Retail
Inventory on December 31, 2014, when dollar-value LIFO is adopted	100	$36,000	$ 74,500
Inventory, December 31, 2015	110	?	100,100

Instructions

Compute the ending inventory under the dollar-value LIFO method at December 31, 2015. The cost-to-retail ratio for 2015 was 60%.

8 ***E9-26 (Conventional Retail and Dollar-Value LIFO Retail)** Amiras Corporation began operations on January 1, 2014, with a beginning inventory of $30,100 at cost and $50,000 at retail. The following information relates to 2014.

	Retail
Net purchases ($108,500 at cost)	$150,000
Net markups	10,000
Net markdowns	5,000
Sales revenue	126,900

Instructions

(a) Assume Amiras decided to adopt the conventional retail method. Compute the ending inventory to be reported in the balance sheet.

(b) Assume instead that Amiras decides to adopt the dollar-value LIFO retail method. The appropriate price indexes are 100 at January 1 and 110 at December 31. Compute the ending inventory to be reported in the balance sheet.

(c) On the basis of the information in part (b), compute cost of goods sold.

8 ***E9-27 (Dollar-Value LIFO Retail)** Connie Chung Corporation adopted the dollar-value LIFO retail inventory method on January 1, 2013. At that time the inventory had a cost of $54,000 and a retail price of $100,000. The following information is available.

	Year-End Inventory at Retail	Current Year Cost—Retail %	Year-End Price Index
2013	$118,720	57%	106
2014	138,750	60%	111
2015	125,350	61%	115
2016	162,500	58%	125

The price index at January 1, 2013, is 100.

Instructions

Compute the ending inventory at December 31 of the years 2013–2016. (Round to the nearest dollar.)

8 ***E9-28 (Change to LIFO Retail)** John Olerud Ltd., a local retailing concern in the Bronx, New York, has decided to change from the conventional retail inventory method to the LIFO retail method starting on January 1, 2015. The company recomputed its ending inventory for 2014 in accordance with the procedures necessary to switch to LIFO retail. The inventory computed was $212,600.

Instructions

Assuming that John Olerud Ltd.'s ending inventory for 2014 under the conventional retail inventory method was $205,000, prepare the appropriate journal entry on January 1, 2015.

EXERCISES SET B

See the book's companion website, at **www.wiley.com/college/kieso**, for an additional set of exercises.

PROBLEMS

1 2 **P9-1 (Lower-of-Cost-or-Market)** Remmers Company manufactures desks. Most of the company's desks are standard models and are sold on the basis of catalog prices. At December 31, 2014, the following finished desks appear in the company's inventory.

Finished Desks	A	B	C	D
2014 catalog selling price	$450	$480	$900	$1,050
FIFO cost per inventory list 12/31/14	470	450	830	960
Estimated current cost to manufacture (at December 31, 2014, and early 2015)	460	430	610	1,000
Sales commissions and estimated other costs of disposal	50	60	80	130
2015 catalog selling price	500	540	900	1,200

The 2014 catalog was in effect through November 2014, and the 2015 catalog is effective as of December 1, 2014. All catalog prices are net of the usual discounts. Generally, the company attempts to obtain a 20% gross profit on selling price and has usually been successful in doing so.

Instructions

At what amount should each of the four desks appear in the company's December 31, 2014, inventory, assuming that the company has adopted a lower-of-FIFO-cost-or-market approach for valuation of inventories on an individual-item basis?

1 2 **P9-2 (Lower-of-Cost-or-Market)** Garcia Home Improvement Company installs replacement siding, windows, and louvered glass doors for single-family homes and condominium complexes in northern New Jersey and southern New York. The company is in the process of preparing its annual financial statements for the fiscal year ended May 31, 2014, and Jim Alcide, controller for Garcia, has gathered the following data concerning inventory.

XLS

At May 31, 2014, the balance in Garcia's Raw Materials Inventory account was $408,000, and Allowance to Reduce Inventory to Market had a credit balance of $27,500. Alcide summarized the relevant inventory cost and market data at May 31, 2014, in the schedule below.

Alcide assigned Patricia Devereaux, an intern from a local college, the task of calculating the amount that should appear on Garcia's May 31, 2014, financial statements for inventory under the lower-of-cost-or-market rule as applied to each item in inventory. Devereaux expressed concern over departing from the historical cost principle.

	Cost	Replacement Cost	Sales Price	Net Realizable Value	Normal Profit
Aluminum siding	$ 70,000	$ 62,500	$ 64,000	$ 56,000	$ 5,100
Cedar shake siding	86,000	79,400	94,000	84,800	7,400
Louvered glass doors	112,000	124,000	186,400	168,300	18,500
Thermal windows	140,000	126,000	154,800	140,000	15,400
Total	$408,000	$391,900	$499,200	$449,100	$46,400

Instructions

(a) (1) Determine the proper balance in Allowance to Reduce Inventory to Market at May 31, 2014.

(2) For the fiscal year ended May 31, 2014, determine the amount of the gain or loss that would be recorded due to the change in Allowance to Reduce Inventory to Market.

(b) Explain the rationale for the use of the lower-of-cost-or-market rule as it applies to inventories.

(CMA adapted)

1 2 **P9-3 (Entries for Lower-of-Cost-or-Market—Cost-of-Goods-Sold and Loss)** Malone Company determined its ending inventory at cost and at lower-of-cost-or-market at December 31, 2013, December 31, 2014, and December 31, 2015, as shown below.

	Cost	Lower-of-Cost-or-Market
12/31/13	$650,000	$650,000
12/31/14	780,000	712,000
12/31/15	905,000	830,000

Instructions

(a) Prepare the journal entries required at December 31, 2014, and at December 31, 2015, assuming that the cost-of-goods-sold method of adjusting to lower-of-cost-or-market is used.

(b) Prepare the journal entries required at December 31, 2014, and at December 31, 2015, assuming that the loss method of adjusting to lower-of-cost-or-market is used.

5 **P9-4 (Gross Profit Method)** Eastman Company lost most of its inventory in a fire in December just before the year-end physical inventory was taken. Corporate records disclose the following.

Inventory (beginning)	$ 80,000	Sales revenue	$415,000
Purchases	290,000	Sales returns	21,000
Purchase returns	28,000	Gross profit % based on net selling price	35%

Merchandise with a selling price of $30,000 remained undamaged after the fire, and damaged merchandise has a net realizable value of $8,150. The company does not carry fire insurance on its inventory.

Instructions

Prepare a formal labeled schedule computing the fire loss incurred. (Do not use the retail inventory method.)

5 **P9-5 (Gross Profit Method)** On April 15, 2015, fire damaged the office and warehouse of Stanislaw Corporation. The only accounting record saved was the general ledger, from which the trial balance below was prepared.

STANISLAW CORPORATION
TRIAL BALANCE
MARCH 31, 2015

Cash	$ 20,000	
Accounts receivable	40,000	
Inventory, December 31, 2014	75,000	
Land	35,000	
Buildings	110,000	
Accumulated depreciation		$ 41,300
Equipment	3,600	
Accounts payable		23,700
Other accrued expenses		10,200
Common stock		100,000
Retained earnings		52,000
Sales revenue		135,000
Purchases	52,000	
Miscellaneous expense	26,600	
	$362,200	$362,200

The following data and information have been gathered.

1. The fiscal year of the corporation ends on December 31.
2. An examination of the April bank statement and canceled checks revealed that checks written during the period April 1–15 totaled $13,000: $5,700 paid to accounts payable as of March 31, $3,400 for April merchandise shipments, and $3,900 paid for other expenses. Deposits during the same period amounted to $12,950, which consisted of receipts on account from customers with the exception of a $950 refund from a vendor for merchandise returned in April.
3. Correspondence with suppliers revealed unrecorded obligations at April 15 of $15,600 for April merchandise shipments, including $2,300 for shipments in transit (f.o.b. shipping point) on that date.
4. Customers acknowledged indebtedness of $46,000 at April 15, 2015. It was also estimated that customers owed another $8,000 that will never be acknowledged or recovered. Of the acknowledged indebtedness, $600 will probably be uncollectible.
5. The companies insuring the inventory agreed that the corporation's fire-loss claim should be based on the assumption that the overall gross profit rate for the past 2 years was in effect during the current year. The corporation's audited financial statements disclosed this information:

	Year Ended December 31	
	2014	2013
Net sales	$530,000	$390,000
Net purchases	280,000	235,000
Beginning inventory	50,000	66,000
Ending inventory	75,000	50,000

6. Inventory with a cost of $7,000 was salvaged and sold for $3,500. The balance of the inventory was a total loss.

Instructions

Prepare a schedule computing the amount of inventory fire loss. The supporting schedule of the computation of the gross profit should be in good form.

(AICPA adapted)

6 **P9-6 (Retail Inventory Method)** The records for the Clothing Department of Sharapova's Discount Store are summarized below for the month of January.

XLS

Inventory, January 1: at retail $25,000; at cost $17,000
Purchases in January: at retail $137,000; at cost $82,500
Freight-in: $7,000
Purchase returns: at retail $3,000; at cost $2,300
Transfers in from suburban branch: at retail $13,000; at cost $9,200
Net markups: $8,000
Net markdowns: $4,000
Inventory losses due to normal breakage, etc.: at retail $400
Sales revenue at retail: $95,000
Sales returns: $2,400

Instructions

(a) Compute the inventory for this department as of January 31, at retail prices.
(b) Compute the ending inventory using lower-of-average-cost-or-market.

6 **P9-7 (Retail Inventory Method)** Presented below is information related to Waveland Inc.

	Cost	Retail
Inventory, 12/31/14	$250,000	$ 390,000
Purchases	914,500	1,460,000
Purchase returns	60,000	80,000
Purchase discounts	18,000	—
Gross sales revenue (after employee discounts)	—	1,410,000
Sales returns	—	97,500
Markups	—	120,000
Markup cancellations	—	40,000
Markdowns	—	45,000
Markdown cancellations	—	20,000
Freight-in	42,000	—
Employee discounts granted	—	8,000
Loss from breakage (normal)	—	4,500

Instructions

Assuming that Waveland Inc. uses the conventional retail inventory method, compute the cost of its ending inventory at December 31, 2015.

6 **P9-8 (Retail Inventory Method)** Fuque Inc. uses the retail inventory method to estimate ending inventory for its monthly financial statements. The following data pertain to a single department for the month of October 2015.

Inventory, October 1, 2015	
At cost	$ 52,000
At retail	78,000
Purchases (exclusive of freight and returns)	
At cost	272,000
At retail	423,000
Freight-in	16,600
Purchase returns	
At cost	5,600
At retail	8,000
Markups	9,000
Markup cancellations	2,000
Markdowns (net)	3,600
Normal spoilage and breakage	10,000
Sales revenue	390,000

Instructions

(a) Using the conventional retail method, prepare a schedule computing estimated lower-of-cost-or-market inventory for October 31, 2015.

(b) A department store using the conventional retail inventory method estimates the cost of its ending inventory as $60,000. An accurate physical count reveals only $47,000 of inventory at lower-of-cost-or-market. List the factors that may have caused the difference between the computed inventory and the physical count.

1 2 4 7 **P9-9 (Statement and Note Disclosure, LCM, and Purchase Commitment)** Maddox Specialty Company, a division of Lost World Inc., manufactures three models of gear shift components for bicycles that are sold to bicycle manufacturers, retailers, and catalog outlets. Since beginning operations in 1990, Maddox has used normal absorption costing and has assumed a first-in, first-out cost flow in its perpetual inventory system. The balances of the inventory accounts at the end of Maddox's fiscal year, November 30, 2014, are shown below. The inventories are stated at cost before any year-end adjustments.

Finished goods	$647,000
Work in process	112,500
Raw materials	264,000
Factory supplies	69,000

The following information relates to Maddox's inventory and operations.

1. The finished goods inventory consists of the items analyzed below.

	Cost	Market
Down tube shifter		
Standard model	$ 67,500	$ 67,000
Click adjustment model	94,500	89,000
Deluxe model	108,000	110,000
Total down tube shifters	270,000	266,000
Bar end shifter		
Standard model	83,000	90,050
Click adjustment model	99,000	97,550
Total bar end shifters	182,000	187,600
Head tube shifter		
Standard model	78,000	77,650
Click adjustment model	117,000	119,300
Total head tube shifters	195,000	196,950
Total finished goods	$647,000	$650,550

2. One-half of the head tube shifter finished goods inventory is held by catalog outlets on consignment.
3. Three-quarters of the bar end shifter finished goods inventory has been pledged as collateral for a bank loan.
4. One-half of the raw materials balance represents derailleurs acquired at a contracted price 20% above the current market price. The market value of the rest of the raw materials is $127,400.
5. The total market value of the work in process inventory is $108,700.
6. Included in the cost of factory supplies are obsolete items with an historical cost of $4,200. The market value of the remaining factory supplies is $65,900.
7. Maddox applies the lower-of-cost-or-market method to each of the three types of shifters in finished goods inventory. For each of the other three inventory accounts, Maddox applies the lower-of-cost-or-market method to the total of each inventory account.
8. Consider all amounts presented above to be material in relation to Maddox's financial statements taken as a whole.

Instructions

(a) Prepare the inventory section of Maddox's balance sheet as of November 30, 2014, including any required note(s).

(b) Without prejudice to your answer to (a), assume that the market value of Maddox's inventories is less than cost. Explain how this decline would be presented in Maddox's income statement for the fiscal year ended November 30, 2014.

(c) Assume that Maddox has a firm purchase commitment for the same type of derailleur included in the raw materials inventory as of November 30, 2014, and that the purchase commitment is at a contracted price 15% greater than the current market price. These derailleurs are to be delivered to Maddox after November 30, 2014. Discuss the impact, if any, that this purchase commitment would have on Maddox's financial statements prepared for the fiscal year ended November 30, 2014.

(CMA adapted)

1 2 **P9-10 (Lower-of-Cost-or-Market)** Fiedler Co. follows the practice of valuing its inventory at the lower-of-cost-or-market. The following information is available from the company's inventory records as of December 31, 2014.

Item	Quantity	Unit Cost	Replacement Cost/Unit	Estimated Selling Price/Unit	Completion & Disposal Cost/Unit	Normal Profit Margin/Unit
A	1,100	$7.50	$8.40	$10.50	$1.50	$1.80
B	800	8.20	7.90	9.40	0.90	1.20
C	1,000	5.60	5.40	7.20	1.15	0.60
D	1,000	3.80	4.20	6.30	0.80	1.50
E	1,400	6.40	6.30	6.70	0.70	1.00

Instructions

Greg Forda is an accounting clerk in the accounting department of Fiedler Co., and he cannot understand why the market value keeps changing from replacement cost to net realizable value to something that he cannot even figure out. Greg is very confused, and he is the one who records inventory purchases and calculates ending inventory. You are the manager of the department and an accountant.

(a) Calculate the lower-of-cost-or-market using the "individual item" approach.

(b) Show the journal entry he will need to make in order to write down the ending inventory from cost to market.

(c) Then write a memo to Greg explaining what designated market value is as well as how it is computed. Use your calculations to aid in your explanation.

8 ***P9-11 (Conventional and Dollar-Value LIFO Retail)** As of January 1, 2014, Aristotle Inc. installed the retail method of accounting for its merchandise inventory.

To prepare the store's financial statements at June 30, 2014, you obtain the following data.

	Cost	Selling Price
Inventory, January 1	$ 30,000	$ 43,000
Markdowns		10,500
Markups		9,200
Markdown cancellations		6,500
Markup cancellations		3,200
Purchases	104,800	155,000
Sales revenue		154,000
Purchase returns	2,800	4,000
Sales returns and allowances		8,000

Instructions

(a) Prepare a schedule to compute Aristotle's June 30, 2014, inventory under the conventional retail method of accounting for inventories.

(b) Without prejudice to your solution to part (a), assume that you computed the June 30, 2014, inventory to be $59,400 at retail and the ratio of cost to retail to be 70%. The general price level has increased from 100 at January 1, 2014, to 108 at June 30, 2014. Prepare a schedule to compute the June 30, 2014, inventory at the June 30 price level under the dollar-value LIFO retail method.

(AICPA adapted)

8 ***P9-12 (Retail, LIFO Retail, and Inventory Shortage)** Late in 2011, Joan Seceda and four other investors took the chain of Becker Department Stores private, and the company has just completed its third year of operations under the ownership of the investment group. Andrea Selig, controller of Becker Department Stores, is in the process of preparing the year-end financial statements. Based on the preliminary financial statements, Seceda has expressed concern over inventory shortages, and she has asked Selig to determine whether an abnormal amount of theft and breakage has occurred. The accounting records of Becker Department Stores contain the following amounts on November 30, 2014, the end of the fiscal year.

	Cost	Retail
Beginning inventory	$ 68,000	$100,000
Purchases	255,000	400,000
Net markups		50,000
Net markdowns		110,000
Sales revenue		320,000

According to the November 30, 2014, physical inventory, the actual inventory at retail is $115,000.

Instructions

(a) Describe the circumstances under which the retail inventory method would be applied and the advantages of using the retail inventory method.

(b) Assuming that prices have been stable, calculate the value, at cost, of Becker Department Stores' ending inventory using the last-in, first-out (LIFO) retail method. Be sure to furnish supporting calculations.

(c) Estimate the amount of shortage, at retail, that has occurred at Becker Department Stores during the year ended November 30, 2014.

(d) Complications in the retail method can be caused by such items as (1) freight-in costs, (2) purchase returns and allowances, (3) sales returns and allowances, and (4) employee discounts. Explain how each of these four special items is handled in the retail inventory method.

(CMA adapted)

8 ***P9-13 (Change to LIFO Retail)** Diderot Stores Inc., which uses the conventional retail inventory method, wishes to change to the LIFO retail method beginning with the accounting year ending December 31, 2014.

Amounts as shown below appear on the store's books before adjustment.

	Cost	Retail
Inventory, January 1, 2014	$ 15,800	$ 24,000
Purchases in 2014	116,200	184,000
Markups in 2014		12,000
Markdowns in 2014		5,500
Sales revenue in 2014		175,000

You are to assume that all markups and markdowns apply to 2014 purchases, and that it is appropriate to treat the entire inventory as a single department.

Instructions

Compute the inventory at December 31, 2014, under the following methods.

(a) The conventional retail method.

(b) The last-in, first-out retail method, effecting the change in method as of January 1, 2014. Assume that the cost-to-retail percentage for 2013 was recomputed correctly in accordance with procedures necessary to change to LIFO. This ratio was 59%.

(AICPA adapted)

8 ***P9-14 (Change to LIFO Retail; Dollar-Value LIFO Retail)** Davenport Department Store converted from the conventional retail method to the LIFO retail method on January 1, 2014, and is now considering converting to the dollar-value LIFO inventory method. During your examination of the financial statements for the year ended December 31, 2015, management requested that you furnish a summary showing certain computations of inventory cost for the past 3 years.

Here is the available information.

1. The inventory at January 1, 2013, had a retail value of $56,000 and cost of $29,800 based on the conventional retail method.
2. Transactions during 2013 were as follows.

	Cost	Retail
Purchases	$311,000	$554,000
Purchase returns	5,200	10,000
Purchase discounts	6,000	
Gross sales revenue (after employee discounts)		551,000
Sales returns		9,000
Employee discounts		3,000
Freight-in	17,600	
Net markups		20,000
Net markdowns		12,000

3. The retail value of the December 31, 2014, inventory was $75,600, the cost ratio for 2014 under the LIFO retail method was 61%, and the regional price index was 105% of the January 1, 2014, price level.
4. The retail value of the December 31, 2015, inventory was $62,640, the cost ratio for 2015 under the LIFO retail method was 60%, and the regional price index was 108% of the January 1, 2014, price level.

Instructions

(a) Prepare a schedule showing the computation of the cost of inventory on hand at December 31, 2013, based on the conventional retail method.

(b) Prepare a schedule showing the recomputation of the inventory to be reported on December 31, 2013, in accordance with procedures necessary to convert from the conventional retail method to the LIFO retail method beginning January 1, 2014. Assume that the retail value of the December 31, 2013, inventory was $60,000.

(c) Without prejudice to your solution to part (b), assume that you computed the December 31, 2013, inventory (retail value $60,000) under the LIFO retail method at a cost of $33,300. Prepare a schedule showing the computations of the cost of the store's 2014 and 2015 year-end inventories under the dollar-value LIFO method.

(AICPA adapted)

PROBLEMS SET B

See the book's companion website, at **www.wiley.com/college/kieso**, for an additional set of problems.

CONCEPTS FOR ANALYSIS

CA9-1 (Lower-of-Cost-or-Market) You have been asked by the financial vice president to develop a short presentation on the lower-of-cost-or-market method for inventory purposes. The financial VP needs to explain this method to the president because it appears that a portion of the company's inventory has declined in value.

Instructions

The financial VP asks you to answer the following questions.

(a) What is the purpose of the lower-of-cost-or-market method?

(b) What is meant by "market"? (*Hint:* Discuss the ceiling and floor constraints.)

(c) Do you apply the lower-of-cost-or-market method to each individual item, to a category, or to the total of the inventory? Explain.

(d) What are the potential disadvantages of the lower-of-cost-or-market method?

CA9-2 (Lower-of-Cost-or-Market) The market value of Lake Corporation's inventory has declined below its cost. Sheryl Conan, the controller, wants to use the loss method to write down inventory because it more clearly discloses the decline in market value and does not distort the cost of goods sold. Her supervisor, financial vice president Dick Wright, prefers the cost-of-goods-sold method to write down inventory because it does not call attention to the decline in market value.

Instructions

Answer the following questions.

(a) What, if any, is the ethical issue involved?

(b) Is any stakeholder harmed if Dick Wright's preference is used?

(c) What should Sheryl Conan do?

CA9-3 (Lower-of-Cost-or-Market) Ogala Corporation purchased a significant amount of raw materials inventory for a new product that it is manufacturing.

Ogala uses the lower-of-cost-or-market rule for these raw materials. The replacement cost of the raw materials is above the net realizable value, and both are below the original cost.

Ogala uses the average-cost inventory method for these raw materials. In the last 2 years, each purchase has been at a lower price than the previous purchase, and the ending inventory quantity for each period has been higher than the beginning inventory quantity for that period.

Instructions

(a) (1) At which amount should Ogala's raw materials inventory be reported on the balance sheet? Why?

(2) In general, why is the lower-of-cost-or-market rule used to report inventory?

(b) What would have been the effect on ending inventory and cost of goods sold had Ogala used the LIFO inventory method instead of the average-cost inventory method for the raw materials? Why?

CA9-4 (Retail Inventory Method) Saurez Company, your client, manufactures paint. The company's president, Maria Saurez, has decided to open a retail store to sell Saurez paint as well as wallpaper and other supplies that would be purchased from other suppliers. She has asked you for information about the conventional retail method of pricing inventories at the retail store.

Instructions

Prepare a report to the president explaining the retail method of pricing inventories. Your report should include the following points.

(a) Description and accounting features of the method.

(b) The conditions that may distort the results under the method.

(c) A comparison of the advantages of using the retail method with those of using cost methods of inventory pricing.

(d) The accounting theory underlying the treatment of net markdowns and net markups under the method.

(AICPA adapted)

CA9-5 (Cost Determination, LCM, Retail Method) Olson Corporation, a retailer and wholesaler of national brand-name household lighting fixtures, purchases its inventories from various suppliers.

Instructions

(a) (1) What criteria should be used to determine which of Olson's costs are inventoriable?

(2) Are Olson's administrative costs inventoriable? Defend your answer.

(b) (1) Olson uses the lower-of-cost-or-market rule for its wholesale inventories. What are the theoretical arguments for that rule?

(2) The replacement cost of the inventories is below the net realizable value less a normal profit margin, which, in turn, is below the original cost. What amount should be used to value the inventories? Why?

(c) Olson calculates the estimated cost of its ending inventories held for sale at retail using the conventional retail inventory method. How would Olson treat the beginning inventories and net markdowns in calculating the cost ratio used to determine its ending inventories? Why?

(AICPA adapted)

CA9-6 (Purchase Commitments) Prophet Company signed a long-term purchase contract to buy timber from the U.S. Forest Service at $300 per thousand board feet. Under these terms, Prophet must cut and pay $6,000,000 for this timber during the next year. Currently, the market value is $250 per thousand board feet. At this rate, the market price is $5,000,000. Jerry Herman, the controller, wants to recognize the loss in value on the year-end financial statements, but the financial vice president, Billie Hands, argues that the loss is temporary and should be ignored. Herman notes that market value has remained near $250 for many months, and he sees no sign of significant change.

Instructions

(a) What are the ethical issues, if any?

(b) Is any particular stakeholder harmed by the financial vice president's decision?

(c) What should the controller do?

USING YOUR JUDGMENT

FINANCIAL REPORTING

Financial Reporting Problem

P&G

The Procter & Gamble Company (P&G)

The financial statements of P&G are presented in Appendix 5B. The company's complete annual report, including the notes to the financial statements, can be accessed at the book's companion website, **www.wiley.com/college/kieso**.

Instructions

Refer to P&G's financial statements and the accompanying notes to answer the following questions.

(a) How does P&G value its inventories? Which inventory costing method does P&G use as a basis for reporting its inventories?

(b) How does P&G report its inventories in the balance sheet? In the notes to its financial statements, what three descriptions are used to classify its inventories?

(c) What costs does P&G include in Inventory and Cost of Products Sold?

(d) What was P&G's inventory turnover in 2011? What is its gross profit percentage? Evaluate P&G's inventory turnover and its gross profit percentage.

Comparative Analysis Case

The Coca-Cola Company and PepsiCo, Inc.

Instructions

Go to the book's companion website and use information found there to answer the following questions related to The Coca-Cola Company and PepsiCo, Inc.

(a) What is the amount of inventory reported by Coca-Cola at December 31, 2011, and by PepsiCo at December 31, 2011? What percent of total assets is invested in inventory by each company?

(b) What inventory costing methods are used by Coca-Cola and PepsiCo? How does each company value its inventories?

(c) In the notes, what classifications (description) are used by Coca-Cola and PepsiCo to categorize their inventories?

(d) Compute and compare the inventory turnovers and days to sell inventory for Coca-Cola and PepsiCo for 2011. Indicate why there might be a significant difference between the two companies.

Financial Statement Analysis Cases

Case 1 Robots, Inc.

Robots, Inc. reported the following information regarding 2013–2014 inventory.

Robots, Inc.

	2014	2013
Current assets		
Cash	$ 153,010	$ 538,489
Accounts receivable, net of allowance for doubtful accounts of $46,000 in 2014 and $160,000 in 2013	1,627,980	2,596,291
Inventories (Note 2)	1,340,494	1,734,873
Other current assets	123,388	90,592
Assets of discontinued operations	–	32,815
Total current assets	3,244,872	4,993,060

Notes to Consolidated Financial Statements

Note 1 (in part): Nature of Business and Significant Accounting Policies

Inventories—Inventories are stated at the lower-of-cost-or-market. Cost is determined by the last-in, first-out (LIFO) method by the parent company and by the first-in, first-out (FIFO) method by its subsidiaries.

Note 2: Inventories

Inventories consist of the following.

	2014	2013
Raw materials	$1,264,646	$2,321,178
Work in process	240,988	171,222
Finished goods and display units	129,406	711,252
Total inventories	1,635,040	3,203,652
Less: Amount classified as long-term	294,546	1,468,779
Current portion	$1,340,494	$1,734,873

Inventories are stated at the lower of cost determined by the LIFO method or market for Robots, Inc. Inventories for the two wholly-owned subsidiaries, Robot Command, Inc. (U.S.) and Robot Limited (U.K.), are stated on the FIFO method which amounted to $566,000 at October 31, 2013. No inventory is stated on the FIFO method at October 31, 2014. Included in inventory stated at FIFO cost was $32,815 at October 31, 2013, of Robot Command inventory classified as an asset from discontinued operations (see Note 14). If the FIFO method had been used for the entire consolidated group, inventories after an adjustment to the lower-of-cost-or-market would have been approximately $2,000,000 and $3,800,000 at October 31, 2014 and 2013, respectively.

Inventory has been written down to estimated net realizable value, and results of operations for 2014, 2013, and 2012 include a corresponding charge of approximately $868,000, $960,000, and $273,000, respectively, which represents the excess of LIFO cost over market.

Inventory of $294,546 and $1,468,779 at October 31, 2014 and 2013, respectively, shown on the balance sheet as a noncurrent asset represents that portion of the inventory that is not expected to be sold currently.

Reduction in inventory quantities during the years ended October 31, 2014, 2013, and 2012 resulted in liquidation of LIFO inventory quantities carried at a lower cost prevailing in prior years as compared with the cost of fiscal 2011 purchases. The effect of these reductions was to decrease the net loss by approximately $24,000, $157,000, and $90,000 at October 31, 2014, 2013, and 2012, respectively.

Instructions

(a) Why might Robots, Inc., use two different methods for valuing inventory?

(b) Comment on why Robots, Inc., might disclose how its LIFO inventories would be valued under FIFO.

(c) Why does the LIFO liquidation reduce operating costs?

(d) Comment on whether Robots, Inc. would report more or less income if it had been on a FIFO basis for all its inventory.

Case 2 Barrick Gold Corporation

Barrick Gold Corporation, with headquarters in Toronto, Canada, is the world's most profitable and largest gold mining company outside South Africa. Part of the key to Barrick's success has been due to its ability to maintain cash flow while improving production and increasing its reserves of gold-containing property. In the most recent year, Barrick achieved record growth in cash flow, production, and reserves.

The company maintains an aggressive policy of developing previously identified target areas that have the possibility of a large amount of gold ore, and that have not been previously developed. Barrick limits the riskiness of this development by choosing only properties that are located in politically stable regions, and by the company's use of internally generated funds, rather than debt, to finance growth.

Barrick's inventories are as follows.

Barrick Gold Corporation

Inventories (in millions, US dollars)	
Current	
Gold in process	$133
Mine operating supplies	82
	$215
Non-current (included in Other assets)	
Ore in stockpiles	$65

Instructions

(a) Why do you think that there are no finished goods inventories? Why do you think the raw material, ore in stockpiles, is considered to be a non-current asset?

(b) Consider that Barrick has no finished goods inventories. What journal entries are made to record a sale?

(c) Suppose that gold bullion that cost $1.8 million to produce was sold for $2.4 million. The journal entry was made to record the sale, but no entry was made to remove the gold from the gold in process inventory. How would this error affect the following?

Balance Sheet		Income Statement	
Inventory	?	Cost of goods sold	?
Retained earnings	?	Net income	?
Accounts payable	?		
Working capital	?		
Current ratio	?		

Accounting, Analysis, and Principles

Englehart Company sells two types of pumps. One is large and is for commercial use. The other is smaller and is used in residential swimming pools. The following inventory data is available for the month of March.

	Units	Price per Unit	Total
Residential Pumps			
Inventory at Feb. 28:	200	$ 400	$ 80,000
Purchases:			
March 10	500	$ 450	$225,000
March 20	400	$ 475	$190,000
March 30	300	$ 500	$150,000
Sales:			
March 15	500	$ 540	$270,000
March 25	400	$ 570	$228,000
Inventory at March 31:	500		
Commercial Pumps			
Inventory at Feb. 28:	600	$ 800	$480,000
Purchases:			
March 3	600	$ 900	$540,000
March 12	300	$ 950	$285,000
March 21	500	$1,000	$500,000
Sales:			
March 18	900	$1,080	$972,000
March 29	600	$1,140	$684,000
Inventory at March 31:	500		

In addition to the above information, due to a downturn in the economy that has hit Englehart's commercial customers especially hard, Englehart expects commercial pump prices from March 31 onward to be considerably different (and lower) than at the beginning of and during March. Englehart has developed the following additional information.

	Commercial Pumps	Residential Pumps
Expected selling price (per unit, net of costs to sell)	$1,050	$580
Replacement cost	$ 900	$550

The normal profit margin is 16.67% of cost. Englehart uses the FIFO accounting method.

Accounting

(a) Determine the dollar amount that Englehart should report on its March 31 balance sheet for inventory. Assume Englehart applies lower-of-cost-or-market at the individual product level.

(b) Repeat part (a) but assume Englehart applies lower-of-cost-or-market at the major category level. Englehart places both commercial and residential pumps into the same (and only) category.

Analysis

Which of the two approaches above (individual product level or major categories) for applying LCM do you think gives the financial statement reader better information?

Principles

Assume that during April, the replacement cost of commercial pumps rebounds to $1,050 (assume this will be designated market value).

(a) Briefly describe how Englehart will report in its April financial statements the inventory remaining from March 31.

(b) Briefly describe the conceptual trade-offs inherent in the accounting in part (a).

BRIDGE TO THE PROFESSION

Professional Research: FASB Codification

Jones Co. is in a technology-intensive industry. Recently, one of its competitors introduced a new product with technology that might render obsolete some of Jones's inventory. The accounting staff wants to follow the appropriate authoritative literature in determining the accounting for this significant market event.

Instructions

If your school has a subscription to the FASB Codification, go to *http://aaahg.org/asclogin.cfm* to log in and prepare responses to the following. Provide Codification references for your responses.

(a) Identify the primary authoritative guidance for the accounting for inventories. What is the predecessor literature?

(b) List three types of goods that are classified as inventory. What characteristic will automatically exclude an item from being classified as inventory?

(c) Define "market" as used in the phrase "lower-of-cost-or-market."

(d) Explain when it is acceptable to state inventory above cost and which industries allow this practice.

Additional Professional Resources

See the book's companion website, at **www.wiley.com/college/kieso**, for professional simulations as well as other study resources.

IFRS INSIGHTS

9 LEARNING OBJECTIVE
Compare the accounting procedures related to valuation of inventories under GAAP and IFRS.

The major IFRS requirements related to accounting and reporting for inventories are found in *IAS 2* ("Inventories"), *IAS 18* ("Revenue"), and *IAS 41* ("Agriculture"). In most cases, IFRS and GAAP are the same. The major differences are that IFRS prohibits the use of the LIFO cost flow assumption and records market in the lower-of-cost-or-market differently.

RELEVANT FACTS

Following are the key similarities and differences between GAAP and IFRS related to inventories.

Similarities

- IFRS and GAAP account for inventory acquisitions at historical cost and evaluate inventory for lower-of-cost-or-market subsequent to acquisition.
- Who owns the goods—goods in transit, consigned goods, special sales agreements—as well as the costs to include in inventory are essentially accounted for the same under IFRS and GAAP.

Differences

- The requirements for accounting for and reporting inventories are more principles-based under IFRS. That is, GAAP provides more detailed guidelines in inventory accounting.
- A major difference between IFRS and GAAP relates to the LIFO cost flow assumption. GAAP permits the use of LIFO for inventory valuation. IFRS prohibits its use. FIFO and average-cost are the only two acceptable cost flow assumptions permitted under IFRS. Both sets of standards permit specific identification where appropriate.
- In the lower-of-cost-or-market test for inventory valuation, IFRS defines market as net realizable value. GAAP, on the other hand, defines market as replacement cost subject to the constraints of net realizable value (the ceiling) and net realizable value less a normal markup (the floor). IFRS does not use a ceiling or a floor to determine market.
- Under GAAP, if inventory is written down under the lower-of-cost-or-market valuation, the new basis is now considered its cost. As a result, the inventory may not be written back up to its original cost in a subsequent period. Under IFRS, the write-down may be reversed in a subsequent period up to the amount of the previous write-down. Both the write-down and any subsequent reversal should be reported on the income statement. IFRS accounting for lower-of-cost-or-market is discussed more fully in the *About the Numbers* section below.
- IFRS requires both biological assets and agricultural produce at the point of harvest to be reported at net realizable value. GAAP does not require companies to account for all biological assets in the same way. Furthermore, these assets generally are not reported at net realizable value. Disclosure requirements also differ between the two sets of standards. IFRS accounting for agriculture and biological assets is discussed more fully in the *About the Numbers* section.

ABOUT THE NUMBERS

Lower-of-Cost-or-Net Realizable Value (LCNRV)

Inventories are recorded at their cost. However, if inventory declines in value below its original cost, a major departure from the historical cost principle occurs. Whatever the reason for a decline—obsolescence, price-level changes, or damaged goods—a company should write down the inventory to net realizable value to report this loss. **A company abandons the historical cost principle when the future utility (revenue-producing ability) of the asset drops below its original cost.**

Net Realizable Value

Recall that **cost** is the acquisition price of inventory computed using one of the historical cost-based methods—specific identification, average-cost, or FIFO. The term **net realizable value (NRV)** refers to the net amount that a company expects to realize from the sale of inventory. Specifically, net realizable value is the estimated selling price in the normal course of business less estimated costs to complete and estimated costs to make a sale.

To illustrate, assume that Mander Corp. has unfinished inventory with a cost of $950, a sales value of $1,000, estimated cost of completion of $50, and estimated selling costs of $200. Mander's net realizable value is computed as follows.

Inventory value—unfinished		$1,000
Less: Estimated cost of completion	$ 50	
Estimated cost to sell	200	250
Net realizable value		$ 750

Mander reports inventory on its statement of financial position (balance sheet) at $750. In its income statement, Mander reports a Loss on Inventory Write-Down of $200 ($950−$750).

A departure from cost is justified because inventories should not be reported at amounts higher than their expected realization from sale or use. In addition, a company like Mander should charge the loss of utility against revenues in the period in which the loss occurs, not in the period of sale. Companies therefore report their inventories at the **lower-of-cost-or-net realizable value (LCNRV)** at each reporting date.

Illustration of LCNRV

As indicated, a company values inventory at LCNRV. A company estimates net realizable value based on the most reliable evidence of the inventories' realizable amounts (expected selling price, expected costs to completion, and expected costs to sell). To illustrate, Regner Foods computes its inventory at LCNRV, as shown in Illustration IFRS9-1.

ILLUSTRATION IFRS9-1
LCNRV Data

Food	Cost	Net Realizable Value	Final Inventory Value
Spinach	$ 80,000	$120,000	$ 80,000
Carrots	100,000	110,000	100,000
Cut beans	50,000	40,000	40,000
Peas	90,000	72,000	72,000
Mixed vegetables	95,000	92,000	92,000
			$384,000

Final Inventory Value:

Spinach	Cost ($80,000) is selected because it is lower than net realizable value.
Carrots	Cost ($100,000) is selected because it is lower than net realizable value.
Cut beans	Net realizable value ($40,000) is selected because it is lower than cost.
Peas	Net realizable value ($72,000) is selected because it is lower than cost.
Mixed vegetables	Net realizable value ($92,000) is selected because it is lower than cost.

As indicated, the final inventory value of $384,000 equals the sum of the LCNRV for each of the inventory items. That is, Regner Foods applies the LCNRV rule to each individual type of food. Similar to GAAP, under IFRS, companies may apply the LCNRV rule to a group of similar or related items, or to the total of the inventory. If a company follows a group-of-similar-or-related-items or total-inventory approach in determining LCNRV, increases in market prices tend to offset decreases in market prices. In most situations, companies price inventory on an item-by-item basis. In fact, tax rules in some countries require that companies use an individual-item basis, barring practical difficulties.

In addition, the individual-item approach gives the lowest valuation for statement of financial position purposes. In some cases, a company prices inventory on a total-inventory basis when it offers only one end product (comprised of many different raw materials). If it produces several end products, a company might use a similar-or-related approach instead. **Whichever method a company selects, it should apply the method consistently from one period to another.**

Recording Net Realizable Value Instead of Cost

Similar to GAAP, one of two methods may be used to record the income effect of valuing inventory at net realizable value. One method, referred to as the **cost-of-goods-sold method**, debits cost of goods sold for the write-down of the inventory to net realizable value. As a result, the company does not report a loss in the income statement because the cost of goods sold already includes the amount of the loss. The second method, referred to as the **loss method**, debits a loss account for the write-down of the inventory to net realizable value. We use the following inventory data for Ricardo Company to illustrate entries under both methods.

Cost of goods sold (before adjustment to net realizable value)	$108,000
Ending inventory (cost)	82,000
Ending inventory (at net realizable value)	70,000

Illustration IFRS9-2 shows the entries for both the cost-of-goods-sold and loss methods, assuming the use of a perpetual inventory system.

ILLUSTRATION IFRS9-2
LCNRV Entries

Cost-of-Goods-Sold Method			Loss Method		
To reduce inventory from cost to net realizable value					
Cost of Goods Sold	12,000		Loss Due to Decline of Inventory to Net Realizable Value	12,000	
Inventory		12,000	Inventory		12,000

The cost-of-goods-sold method buries the loss in the Cost of Goods Sold account. The loss method, by identifying the loss due to the write-down, shows the loss separate from Cost of Goods Sold in the income statement. Illustration IFRS9-3 contrasts the differing amounts reported in the income statement under the two approaches, using data from the Ricardo example.

ILLUSTRATION IFRS9-3
Income Statement Reporting—LCNRV

Cost-of-Goods-Sold Method	
Sales revenue	$200,000
Cost of goods sold (after adjustment to net realizable value*)	120,000
Gross profit on sales	$ 80,000
*Cost of goods sold (before adjustment to net realizable value)	$108,000
Difference between inventory at cost and net realizable value ($82,000 − $70,000)	12,000
Cost of goods sold (after adjustment to net realizable value)	$120,000

Loss Method	
Sales revenue	$200,000
Cost of goods sold	108,000
Gross profit on sales	92,000
Loss due to decline of inventory to net realizable value	12,000
	$ 80,000

IFRS does not specify a particular account to debit for the write-down. We believe the loss method presentation is preferable because it clearly discloses the loss resulting from a decline in inventory net realizable values.

Use of an Allowance

Instead of crediting the Inventory account for net realizable value adjustments, companies generally use an allowance account, often referred to as Allowance to Reduce Inventory to Net Realizable Value. For example, using an allowance account under the loss method, Ricardo Company makes the following entry to record the inventory write-down to net realizable value.

Loss Due to Decline of Inventory to Net Realizable Value	12,000	
Allowance to Reduce Inventory to Net Realizable Value		12,000

Use of the allowance account results in reporting both the cost and the net realizable value of the inventory. Ricardo reports inventory in the statement of financial position as follows.

ILLUSTRATION IFRS9-4
Presentation of Inventory Using an Allowance Account

Inventory (at cost)	$82,000
Allowance to reduce inventory to net realizable value	(12,000)
Inventory (at net realizable value)	$70,000

The use of the allowance under the cost-of-goods-sold or loss method permits both the income statement and the statement of financial position to reflect inventory measured at $82,000, although the statement of financial position shows a net amount of $70,000. It also keeps subsidiary inventory ledgers and records in correspondence with the control account without changing prices. *For homework purposes, use an allowance account to record net realizable value adjustments, unless instructed otherwise.*

Recovery of Inventory Loss

In periods following the write-down, economic conditions may change such that the net realizable value of inventories previously written down may be *greater* than cost or there is clear evidence of an increase in the net realizable value. In this situation, the amount of the write-down is reversed, with the reversal limited to the amount of the original write-down.

Continuing the Ricardo example, assume that in the subsequent period, market conditions change, such that the net realizable value increases to $74,000 (an increase of $4,000). As a result, only $8,000 is needed in the allowance. Ricardo makes the following entry, using the loss method.

Allowance to Reduce Inventory to Net Realizable Value	4,000	
Recovery of Inventory Loss ($74,000 − $70,000)		4,000

Valuation Bases

For the most part, companies record inventory at LCNRV. However, there are some situations in which companies depart from the LCNRV rule. Such treatment may be justified in situations when cost is difficult to determine, the items are readily marketable at quoted market prices, and units of product are interchangeable. In this section, we discuss agricultural assets (including biological assets and agricultural produce), for which net realizable value is the general rule for valuing inventory.

Agricultural Inventory

Under IFRS, net realizable value measurement is used for inventory when the inventory is related to agricultural activity. In general, agricultural activity results in two types of agricultural assets: (1) biological assets or (2) agricultural produce at the point of harvest.

A **biological asset** (classified as a non-current asset) is a living animal or plant, such as sheep, cows, fruit trees, or cotton plants. **Agricultural produce** is the harvested product of a biological asset, such as wool from a sheep, milk from a dairy cow, picked fruit from a fruit tree, or cotton from a cotton plant.

Biological assets are measured on initial recognition and at the end of each reporting period at fair value less costs to sell (net realizable value). Companies record a gain or loss due to changes in the net realizable value of biological assets in income when it arises. For example, a gain may arise on initial recognition of a biological asset, such as when a calf is born. A gain or loss may arise on initial recognition of agricultural produce as a result of harvesting. Losses may arise on initial recognition for agricultural assets because costs to sell are deducted in determining fair value less costs to sell.

Agricultural produce (which are harvested from biological assets) are measured at fair value less costs to sell (net realizable value) at the point of harvest. Once harvested, the net realizable value of the agricultural produce becomes its cost, and this asset is accounted for similar to other inventories held for sale in the normal course of business. Measurement at fair value or selling price less point-of-sale costs corresponds to the net realizable value measure in the LCNRV test (selling price less estimated costs to complete and sell) since at harvest, the agricultural product is complete and is ready for sale.

Illustration of Agricultural Accounting at Net Realizable Value

To illustrate the accounting at net realizable value for agricultural assets, assume that Bancroft Dairy produces milk for sale to local cheese-makers. Bancroft began operations on January 1, 2014, by purchasing 420 milking cows for $460,000. Bancroft provides the following information related to the milking cows.

ILLUSTRATION IFRS9-5
Agricultural Assets—Bancroft Dairy

Milking cows		
Carrying value, January 1, 2014*		$460,000
Change in fair value due to growth and price changes	$35,000	
Decrease in fair value due to harvest	(1,200)	
Change in carrying value		33,800
Carrying value, January 31, 2014		$493,800
Milk harvested during January**		$ 36,000

*The carrying value is measured at fair value less costs to sell (net realizable value). The fair value of milking cows is determined based on market prices of livestock of similar age, breed, and genetic merit.
**Milk is initially measured at its fair value less costs to sell (net realizable value) at the time of milking. The fair value of milk is determined based on market prices in the local area.

As indicated, the carrying value of the milking cows increased during the month. Part of the change is due to changes in market prices (less costs to sell) for milking cows. The change in market price may also be affected by growth—the increase in value as the cows mature and develop increased milking capacity. At the same time, as mature cows are milked, their milking capacity declines (fair value decrease due to harvest). For example, changes in fair value arising from growth and harvesting from mature cows can be estimated based on changes in market prices of different age cows in the herd.

Bancroft makes the following entry to record the change in carrying value of the milking cows.

Biological Asset—Milking Cows ($493,800 − $460,000)	33,800	
Unrealized Holding Gain or Loss—Income		33,800

As a result of this entry, Bancroft's statement of financial position reports Biological Asset—Milking Cows as a non-current asset at fair value less costs to sell (net realizable value). In addition, the unrealized gains and losses are reported as other income and expense on the income statement. In subsequent periods at each reporting date, Bancroft continues to report Biological Asset—Milking Cows at net realizable value and records any related unrealized gains or losses in income. Because there is a ready market for the biological assets (milking cows), valuation at net realizable value provides more relevant information about these assets.

In addition to recording the change in the biological asset, Bancroft makes the following summary entry to record the milk harvested for the month of January.

Milk Inventory	36,000	
Unrealized Holding Gain or Loss—Income		36,000

The milk inventory is recorded at net realizable value at the time it is harvested, and Unrealized Holding Gain or Loss—Income is recognized in income. As with the biological assets, net realizable value is considered the most relevant for purposes of valuation at harvest. What happens to the milk inventory that Bancroft recorded upon harvesting the milk from the cows? Assuming the milk harvested in January was sold to a local cheese-maker for $38,500, Bancroft records the sale as follows.

Cash	38,500	
Cost of Goods Sold	36,000	
Milk Inventory		36,000
Sales Revenue		38,500

Thus, once harvested, the net realizable value of the harvested milk becomes its cost, and the milk is accounted for similar to other inventories held for sale in the normal course of business.

A final note: Some animals or plants may not be considered biological assets but would be classified and accounted for as other types of assets (not at net realizable value). For example, a pet shop may hold an inventory of dogs purchased from breeders that it then sells. Because the pet shop is not breeding the dogs, these dogs are not considered biological assets. As a result, the dogs are accounted for as inventory held for sale (at LCNRV).

ON THE HORIZON

One issue that will be difficult to resolve relates to the use of the LIFO cost flow assumption. As indicated, IFRS specifically prohibits its use. Conversely, the LIFO cost flow assumption is widely used in the United States because of its favorable tax advantages. In addition, many argue that LIFO from a financial reporting point of view provides a better matching of current costs against revenue and therefore enables companies to compute a more realistic income.

IFRS SELF-TEST QUESTIONS

1. All of the following are key similarities between GAAP and IFRS with respect to accounting for inventories **except**:
(a) costs to include in inventories are similar.
(b) LIFO cost flow assumption where appropriate is used by both sets of standards.
(c) fair value valuation of inventories is prohibited by both sets of standards.
(d) guidelines on ownership of goods are similar.

2. All of the following are key differences between GAAP and IFRS with respect to accounting for inventories **except** the:
(a) definition of the lower-of-cost-or-market test for inventory valuation differs between GAAP and IFRS.
(b) average-cost method is prohibited under IFRS.
(c) inventory basis determination for write-downs differs between GAAP and IFRS.
(d) guidelines are more principles-based under IFRS than they are under GAAP.

3. Starfish Company (a company using GAAP and the LIFO inventory method) is considering changing to IFRS and the FIFO inventory method. How would a comparison of these methods affect Starfish's financials?
(a) During a period of inflation, working capital would decrease when IFRS and the FIFO inventory method are used as compared to GAAP and LIFO.
(b) During a period of inflation, the taxes will decrease when IFRS and the FIFO inventory method are used as compared to GAAP and LIFO.
(c) During a period of inflation, net income would be greater if IFRS and the FIFO inventory method are used as compared to GAAP and LIFO.
(d) During a period of inflation, the current ratio would decrease when IFRS and the FIFO inventory method are used as compared to GAAP and LIFO.

4. Assume that Darcy Industries had the following inventory values.

Inventory cost (on December 31, 2014)	$1,500
Inventory market (on December 31, 2014)	$1,350
Inventory net realizable value (on December 31, 2014)	$1,320

Under IFRS, what is the inventory carrying value on December 31, 2014?
(a) $1,500.
(b) $1,570.
(c) $1,560.
(d) $1,320.

5. Under IFRS, agricultural activity results in which of the following types of assets?
I. Agricultural produce
II. Biological assets
(a) I only.
(b) II only.
(c) I and II.
(d) Neither I nor II.

IFRS CONCEPTS AND APPLICATION

IFRS9-1 Briefly describe some of the similarities and differences between GAAP and IFRS with respect to the accounting for inventories.

IFRS9-2 LaTour Inc. is based in France and prepares its financial statements in accordance with IFRS. In 2014, it reported cost of goods sold of $578 million and average inventory of $154 million. Briefly discuss how analysis of LaTour's inventory turnover (and comparisons to a company using GAAP) might be affected by differences in inventory accounting between IFRS and GAAP.

IFRS9-3 Reed Pentak, a finance major, has been following globalization and made the following observation concerning accounting convergence: "I do not see many obstacles concerning development of a single accounting standard for inventories." Prepare a response to Reed to explain the main obstacle to achieving convergence in the area of inventory accounting.

IFRS9-4 Briefly describe the valuation of (a) biological assets and (b) agricultural produce.

IFRS9-5 In some instances, accounting principles require a departure from valuing inventories at cost alone. Determine the proper unit inventory price in the following cases.

	Cases				
	1	2	3	4	5
Cost	$15.90	$16.10	$15.90	$15.90	$15.90
Sales price	14.80	19.20	15.20	10.40	17.80
Estimated cost to complete	1.50	1.90	1.65	.80	1.00
Estimated cost to sell	.50	.70	.55	.40	.60

IFRS9-6 Riegel Company uses the LCNRV method, on an individual-item basis, in pricing its inventory items. The inventory at December 31, 2014, consists of products D, E, F, G, H, and I. Relevant per unit data for these products appear below.

	Item D	Item E	Item F	Item G	Item H	Item I
Estimated selling price	$120	$110	$95	$90	$110	$90
Cost	75	80	80	80	50	36
Cost to complete	30	30	25	35	30	30
Selling costs	10	18	10	20	10	20

Using the LCNRV rule, determine the proper unit value for statement of financial position reporting purposes at December 31, 2014, for each of the inventory items above.

IFRS9-7 Dover Company began operations in 2014 and determined its ending inventory at cost and at LCNRV at December 31, 2014, and December 31, 2015. This information is presented below.

	Cost	Net Realizable Value
12/31/14	$346,000	$322,000
12/31/15	410,000	390,000

(a) Prepare the journal entries required at December 31, 2014, and December 31, 2015, assuming that the inventory is recorded at LCNRV and a perpetual inventory system using the cost-of-goods-sold method is used.

(b) Prepare journal entries required at December 31, 2014, and December 31, 2015, assuming that the inventory is recorded at cost and a perpetual system using the loss method is used.

(c) Which of the two methods above provides the higher net income in each year?

IFRS9-8 Keyser's Fleece Inc. holds a drove of sheep. Keyser shears the sheep on a semiannual basis and then sells the harvested wool into the specialty knitting market. Keyser has the following information related to the shearing sheep at January 1, 2014, and during the first six months of 2014.

	Shearing Sheep
Carrying value (equal to net realizable value), January 1, 2014	$74,000
Change in fair value due to growth and price changes	4,700
Change in fair value due to harvest	(575)
Wool harvested during the first 6 months (at NRV)	9,000

Prepare the journal entry(ies) for Keyser's biological asset (shearing sheep) for the first six months of 2014.

IFRS9-9 Refer to the data in IFRS9-8 for Keyser's Fleece Inc. Prepare the journal entries for (a) the wool harvested in the first six months of 2014, and (b) the wool harvested that is sold for $10,500 in July 2014.

Professional Research

IFRS9-10 Jones Co. is in a technology-intensive industry. Recently, one of its competitors introduced a new product with technology that might render obsolete some of Jones's inventory. The accounting staff wants to follow the appropriate authoritative literature in determining the accounting for this significant market event.

Instructions

Access the IFRS authoritative literature at the IASB website (*http://eifrs.iasb.org/*). (Click on the IFRS tab and then register for free eIFRS access if necessary.) When you have accessed the documents, you can use the search tool in your Internet browser to respond to the following questions. (Provide paragraph citations.)

(a) Identify the authoritative literature addressing inventory pricing.
(b) List three types of goods that are classified as inventory. What characteristic will automatically exclude an item from being classified as inventory?
(c) Define "net realizable value" as used in the phrase "lower-of-cost-or-net realizable value."
(d) Explain when it is acceptable to state inventory above cost and which industries allow this practice.

International Financial Reporting Problem

Marks and Spencer plc

IFRS9-11 The financial statements of **Marks and Spencer plc (M&S)** are available at the book's companion website or can be accessed at *http://annualreport.marksandspencer.com/_assets/downloads/Marks-and-Spencer-Annual-report-and-financial-statements-2012.pdf.*

Instructions

Refer to M&S's financial statements and the accompanying notes to answer the following questions.

(a) How does M&S value its inventories? Which inventory costing method does M&S use as a basis for reporting its inventories?
(b) How does M&S report its inventories in the statement of financial position? In the notes to its financial statements, what three descriptions are used to classify its inventories?
(c) What costs does M&S include in Inventory and Cost of Sales?
(d) What was M&S's inventory turnover in 2012? What is its gross profit percentage? Evaluate M&S's inventory turnover and its gross profit percentage.

ANSWERS TO IFRS SELF-TEST QUESTIONS

1. b **2.** b **3.** c **4.** d **5.** c

Remember to check the book's companion website to find additional resources for this chapter.

CHAPTER 10 Acquisition and Disposition of Property, Plant, and Equipment

LEARNING OBJECTIVES

After studying this chapter, you should be able to:

1. Describe property, plant, and equipment.
2. Identify the costs to include in initial valuation of property, plant, and equipment.
3. Describe the accounting problems associated with self-constructed assets.
4. Describe the accounting problems associated with interest capitalization.
5. Understand accounting issues related to acquiring and valuing plant assets.
6. Describe the accounting treatment for costs subsequent to acquisition.
7. Describe the accounting treatment for the disposal of property, plant, and equipment.

Watch Your Spending

Investments in long-lived assets, such as property, plant, and equipment, are important elements in many companies' balance sheets. As Table 1 shows, capital expenditures on structures and equipment (whether new or used) are starting to grow again after the effects of the 2008 financial crisis.

Table 1: Total Capital Expenditures by Type for All U.S. Businesses, 2001 to 2010

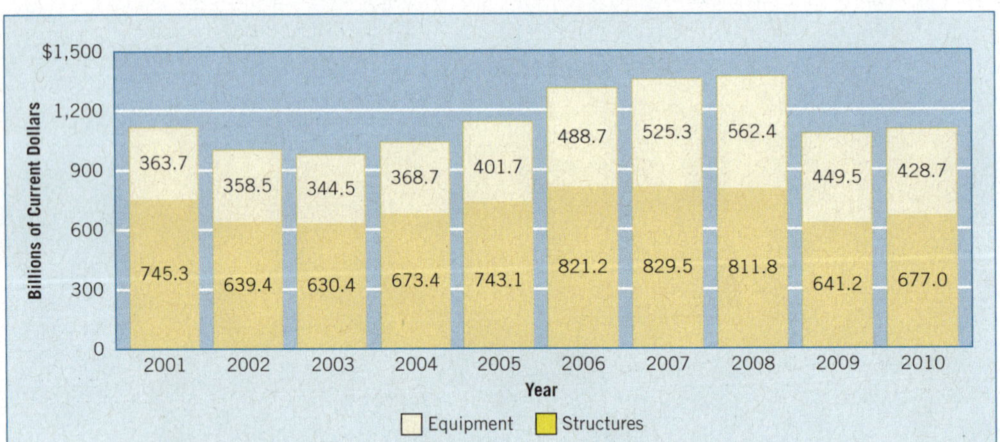

Sources: Annual Capital Expenditures Survey, 2012 Capital Spending Report and, U.S. Census (2012).

Unfortunately, Table 1 also shows that capital expenditures' growth is overall stagnant in the last 10 years. However, better times may be ahead. To illustrate, the food and beverage industry increased its capital expenditures by 20 percent in 2011 and is estimated to increase them again by 4 percent in 2012. Table 2 identifies the five companies in this industry with the largest capital expenditures in 2011 and 2012.

Table 2: Capital Spending ($ in millions)

Company	2012 Budget	% Change from 2011	2011 Actual	2011 Budget	% Change from 2010 Actual	2010 Actual
Anheuser-Busch InBev	$3,200	2%	$3,256	$2,800	31%	$2,350
Coca-Cola	3,100M	6	2,920	3,100	40	2,215
PepsiCo	3,000	9	3,300	3,700	14	3,253
Kraft Foods	2,000	13	1,771	1,800	9	1,661
Tyson	825	28	643	700	27	550

CONCEPTUAL FOCUS

- See the **Underlying Concepts** on pages 538, 542, and 557.

INTERNATIONAL FOCUS

- See the **International Perspectives** on pages 538, 542, 546, 550, and 555.
- **IFRS Insights** related to property, plant, and equipment are presented in Chapter 11.

Capital expenditures are significant for many companies. For example, at **Jet Blue Airways**, plant assets are 69 percent of its total assets. For **Wal-Mart Stores, Inc.**, it's 53 percent. Conversely, **Microsoft**'s percentage is just 3 percent. Amounts for companies' capital expenditures are reported on a company's balance sheet and directly affect such items as total assets, depreciation expense, cash flows, and net income. Companies that overspend in this area find that income is reduced as depreciation increases without corresponding increases in revenues. As a result, these companies often lose financial flexibility. That is, they find themselves in a cash bind as their cash flows from operations can no longer meet their obligations.

A good example is **Baker Hughes, Inc.** (an oilfield-services company), which in the first half of 2012 reported cash flow from operations of $24 million but capital expenditures of $1,442 million. Although the company is presently stable, the unfavorable relationship of cash flow from operations to capital expenditures is a cause for concern.

Companies can also affect income by reducing capital expenditures. For example, **Cintas** (a uniform rental business) cut back on capital expenditures in recent years. In response, depreciation expense declined to $152 million in 2010 relative to $158 million in the prior year. That lifted its earnings per share by seven cents. Similarly, **Norfolk Southern** added eight cents per share to its bottom line through lower depreciation charges.

Thus, not only do companies have to be careful in planning the proper amount of capital expenditures, but users must understand the impact of these expenditures on measures of financial performance. As illustrated by the examples above, the level of capital expenditures, depreciation expense, cash flow from operations, and net income all play a role in assessing a company's ability to generate future cash flows.

Sources: Adapted from L. Strauss, "Depreciation: An Appreciation," *Barrons Online* (April 30, 2011); and D. Phelps, "Top 100 Capital Spending Report: Greek Yogurt Plants Are Stacking Up," *www.FoodProcessing.com* (April 9, 2012).

PREVIEW OF CHAPTER 10

As we indicate in the opening story, a company like **Jet Blue Airways** has a substantial investment in property, plant, and equipment. Conversely, other companies, such as **Microsoft**, have a minor investment in these types of assets. In this chapter, we discuss the proper accounting for the acquisition, use, and disposition of property, plant, and equipment. The content and organization of the chapter are as follows.

Acquisition and Disposition of Property, Plant, and Equipment

Acquisition
- Acquisition costs: land, buildings, equipment
- Self-constructed assets
- Interest costs
- Observations

Valuation
- Cash discounts
- Deferred contracts
- Lump-sum purchases
- Stock issuance
- Nonmonetary exchanges
- Contributions
- Other valuation methods

Costs Subsequent to Acquisition
- Additions
- Improvements and replacements
- Rearrangement and reinstallation
- Repairs
- Summary

Disposition
- Sale
- Involuntary conversion
- Miscellaneous problems

PROPERTY, PLANT, AND EQUIPMENT

LEARNING OBJECTIVE 1

Describe property, plant, and equipment.

Companies like Boeing, Target, and Starbucks use assets of a durable nature. Such assets are called **property, plant, and equipment**. Other terms commonly used are **plant assets** and **fixed assets**. We use these terms interchangeably. Property, plant, and equipment include land, building structures (offices, factories, warehouses), and equipment (machinery, furniture, tools). The major characteristics of property, plant, and equipment are as follows.

1. ***They are acquired for use in operations and not for resale.*** Only assets used in normal business operations are classified as property, plant, and equipment. For example, an idle building is more appropriately classified separately as an investment. Land developers or subdividers classify land as inventory.
2. ***They are long-term in nature and usually depreciated.*** Property, plant, and equipment yield services over a number of years. Companies allocate the cost of the investment in these assets to future periods through periodic depreciation charges. The exception is land, which is depreciated only if a material decrease in value occurs, such as a loss in fertility of agricultural land because of poor crop rotation, drought, or soil erosion.
3. ***They possess physical substance.*** Property, plant, and equipment are tangible assets characterized by physical existence or substance. This differentiates them from intangible assets, such as patents or goodwill. Unlike raw material, however, property, plant, and equipment do not physically become part of a product held for resale.

Underlying Concepts

Fair value is relevant to inventory but less so for property, plant, and equipment which, consistent with the going-concern assumption, are held for use in the business, not for sale like inventory.

Acquisition of Property, Plant, and Equipment

LEARNING OBJECTIVE 2

Identify the costs to include in initial valuation of property, plant, and equipment.

Most companies use historical cost as the basis for valuing property, plant, and equipment. **Historical cost measures the cash or cash equivalent price of obtaining the asset and bringing it to the location and condition necessary for its intended use.** For example, companies like Kellogg Co. consider the purchase price, freight costs, sales taxes, and installation costs of a productive asset as part of the asset's cost. It then allocates these costs to future periods through depreciation. Further, Kellogg **adds to the asset's original cost** any related costs incurred **after the asset's acquisition**, such as additions, improvements, or replacements, **if they provide future service potential**. Otherwise, Kellogg expenses these costs immediately.[1]

Subsequent to acquisition, companies should not write up property, plant, and equipment to reflect fair value when it is above cost. The main reasons for this position are as follows.

1. Historical cost involves actual, not hypothetical, transactions and so is the most reliable.
2. Companies should not anticipate gains and losses but should recognize gains and losses only when the asset is sold.

International Perspective

Under international accounting standards, historical cost is the benchmark (preferred) treatment for property, plant, and equipment. However, companies may also use revalued amounts. When using revaluation, companies must revalue the class of assets regularly.

Even those who favor fair value measurement for inventory and financial instruments often take the position that property, plant, and equipment should not be revalued. The major concern is the difficulty of developing a reliable fair value for these types

[1]Additional costs to be included in the cost of property, plant, and equipment are those related to asset retirement obligations (AROs). These costs, such as those related to decommissioning nuclear facilities or reclamation or restoration of a mining facility, reflect a legal requirement to retire the asset at the end of its useful life. The expected costs are recorded in the asset cost and depreciated over the useful life (see Chapter 13).

of assets. For example, how does one value a **General Motors** automobile manufacturing plant or a nuclear power plant owned by **Consolidated Edison**?

However, if the fair value of the property, plant, and equipment is less than its carrying amount, the asset may be written down. These situations occur when the asset is impaired (discussed in Chapter 11) and in situations where the asset is being held for sale. A long-lived asset classified as held for sale should be measured at the lower of its carrying amount or fair value less costs to sell. In that case, a reasonable valuation for the asset can be obtained, based on the sales price. A long-lived asset is not depreciated if it is classified as held for sale. This is because such assets are not being used to generate revenues. **[1]**

See the FASB Codification section (page 564).

Cost of Land

All expenditures made to acquire land and ready it for use are considered part of the land cost. Thus, when **Wal-Mart Stores, Inc.** or **Home Depot** purchases land on which to build a new store, its land costs typically include (1) the purchase price; (2) closing costs, such as title to the land, attorney's fees, and recording fees; (3) costs incurred in getting the land in condition for its intended use, such as grading, filling, draining, and clearing; (4) assumption of any liens, mortgages, or encumbrances on the property; and (5) any additional land improvements that have an indefinite life.

Gateway to the Profession

Expanded Discussion of Alternative Valuation Methods

For example, when Home Depot purchases land for the purpose of constructing a building, it considers all costs incurred up to the excavation for the new building as land costs. **Removal of old buildings—clearing, grading, and filling—is a land cost because this activity is necessary to get the land in condition for its intended purpose.** Home Depot treats any proceeds from getting the land ready for its intended use, such as salvage receipts on the demolition of an old building or the sale of cleared timber, as **reductions in the price of the land**.

In some cases, when Home Depot purchases land, it may assume certain obligations on the land such as back taxes or liens. In such situations, the cost of the land is the cash paid for it, plus the encumbrances. In other words, if the purchase price of the land is $50,000 cash but Home Depot assumes accrued property taxes of $5,000 and liens of $10,000, its land cost is $65,000.

Home Depot also might incur **special assessments** for local improvements, such as pavements, street lights, sewers, and drainage systems. It should charge these costs to the Land account because they are relatively permanent in nature. That is, after installation, they are maintained by the local government. In addition, Home Depot should charge any permanent improvements it makes, such as landscaping, to the Land account. It records separately any **improvements with limited lives**, such as private driveways, walks, fences, and parking lots, as Land Improvements. These costs are depreciated over their estimated lives.

Generally, land is part of property, plant, and equipment. However, if the major purpose of acquiring and holding land is speculative, a company more appropriately classifies the land as an **investment**. If a real estate concern holds the land for resale, it should classify the land as **inventory**.

In cases where land is held as an investment, what accounting treatment should be given for taxes, insurance, and other direct costs incurred while holding the land? Many believe these costs should be capitalized. The reason: They are not generating revenue from the investment at this time. Companies generally use this approach except when the asset is currently producing revenue (such as rental property).

Cost of Buildings

The cost of buildings should include all expenditures related directly to their acquisition or construction. These costs include (1) materials, labor, and overhead costs incurred during construction, and (2) professional fees and building permits. Generally, companies contract others to construct their buildings. Companies consider all costs incurred, from excavation to completion, as part of the building costs.

But how should companies account for an old building that is on the site of a newly proposed building? Is the cost of removal of the old building a cost of the land or a cost of the new building? Recall that **if a company purchases land with an old building on it, then the cost of demolition less its salvage value is a cost of getting the land ready for its intended use and relates to the land rather than to the new building**. In other words, all costs of getting an asset ready for its intended use are costs of that asset.

Cost of Equipment

The term "equipment" in accounting includes delivery equipment, office equipment, machinery, furniture and fixtures, furnishings, factory equipment, and similar fixed assets. The cost of such assets includes the purchase price, freight and handling charges incurred, insurance on the equipment while in transit, cost of special foundations if required, assembling and installation costs, and costs of conducting trial runs. Costs thus include all expenditures incurred in acquiring the equipment and preparing it for use.

Self-Constructed Assets

LEARNING OBJECTIVE 3
Describe the accounting problems associated with self-constructed assets.

Occasionally, companies construct their own assets. Determining the cost of such machinery and other fixed assets can be a problem. Without a purchase price or contract price, the company must allocate costs and expenses to arrive at the cost of the **self-constructed asset**. Materials and direct labor used in construction pose no problem. A company can trace these costs directly to work and material orders related to the fixed assets constructed.

However, the assignment of indirect costs of manufacturing creates special problems. These indirect costs, called **overhead** or burden, include power, heat, light, insurance, property taxes on factory buildings and equipment, factory supervisory labor, depreciation of fixed assets, and supplies.

Companies can handle indirect costs in one of two ways:

1. *Assign no fixed overhead to the cost of the constructed asset.* The major argument for this treatment is that indirect overhead is generally fixed in nature. It does not increase as a result of a company constructing its own plant or equipment. This approach assumes that the company will have the same costs regardless of whether it constructs the asset or not. Therefore, to charge a portion of the overhead costs to the equipment will normally reduce current expenses and consequently overstate income of the current period. However, the company would assign to the cost of the constructed asset variable overhead costs that increase as a result of the construction.
2. *Assign a portion of all overhead to the construction process.* This approach, called a **full-costing approach**, follows the belief that costs should attach to all products and assets manufactured or constructed. Under this approach, a company assigns a portion of all overhead to the construction process, as it would to normal production. Advocates say that failure to allocate overhead costs understates the initial cost of the asset and results in an inaccurate future allocation.

Companies should assign to the asset **a pro rata portion** of the fixed overhead to determine its cost. Companies use this treatment extensively because many believe that it results in a better recognition of these costs in periods benefited.

If the allocated overhead results in recording construction costs in excess of the costs that an outside independent producer would charge, the company should record the excess overhead as a period loss rather than capitalize it. This avoids capitalizing the asset at more than its probable fair value.[2]

Interest Costs During Construction

4 LEARNING OBJECTIVE
Describe the accounting problems associated with interest capitalization.

The proper accounting for interest costs has been a long-standing controversy. Three approaches have been suggested to account for the interest incurred in financing the construction of property, plant, and equipment:

1. ***Capitalize no interest charges during construction.*** Under this approach, interest is considered a cost of financing and not a cost of construction. Some contend that if a company had used stock (equity) financing rather than debt, it would not incur this cost. The major argument against this approach is that the use of cash, whatever its source, has an associated implicit interest cost, which should not be ignored.
2. ***Charge construction with all costs of funds employed, whether identifiable or not.*** This method maintains that the cost of construction should include the cost of financing, whether by cash, debt, or stock. Its advocates say that all costs necessary to get an asset ready for its intended use, including interest, are part of the asset's cost. Interest, whether actual or imputed, is a cost, just as are labor and materials. A major criticism of this approach is that imputing the cost of equity capital (stock) is subjective and outside the framework of an historical cost system.
3. ***Capitalize only the actual interest costs incurred during construction.*** This approach agrees in part with the logic of the second approach—that interest is just as much a cost as are labor and materials. But this approach capitalizes only interest costs incurred through debt financing. (That is, it does not try to determine the cost of equity financing.) Under this approach, a company that uses debt financing will have an asset of higher cost than a company that uses stock financing. Some consider this approach unsatisfactory because they believe the cost of an asset should be the same whether it is financed with cash, debt, or equity.

Illustration 10-1 shows how a company might add interest costs (if any) to the cost of the asset under the three capitalization approaches.

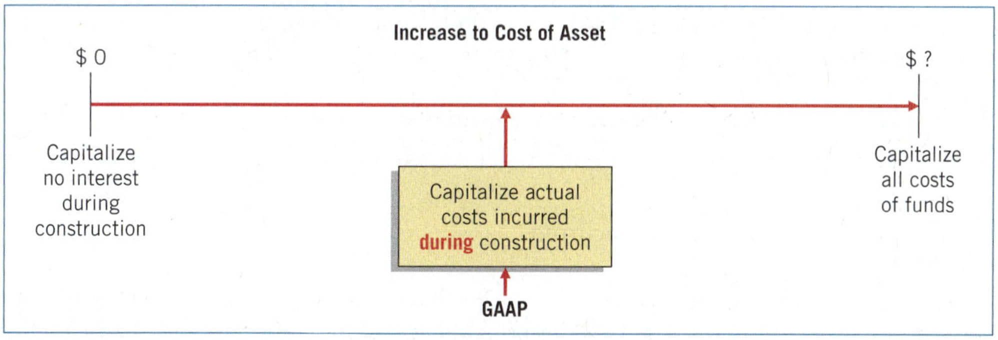

ILLUSTRATION 10-1
Capitalization of Interest Costs

[2]A committee of the AICPA argues against allocation of overhead. Instead, it supports capitalization of only direct costs (costs directly related to the specific activities involved in the construction process). AcSEC was concerned that the allocation of overhead costs may lead to overly aggressive allocations and therefore misstatements of income. In addition, not reporting these costs as period costs during the construction period may affect comparisons of period costs and resulting net income from one period to the next. See Accounting Standards Executive Committee, "Accounting for Certain Costs and Activities Related to Property, Plant, and Equipment," Exposure Draft (New York: AICPA, June 29, 2001).

GAAP requires the third approach—capitalizing actual interest (with modification). This method follows the concept that the **historical cost of acquiring an asset includes all costs (including interest) incurred to bring the asset to the condition and location necessary for its intended use.** The rationale for this approach is that during construction, the asset is not generating revenues. Therefore, a company should defer (capitalize) interest costs. [2] Once construction is complete, the asset is ready for its intended use and a company can earn revenues. At this point, the company should report interest as an expense and match it to these revenues. It follows that the company should expense any interest cost incurred in purchasing an asset that is ready for its intended use.

Underlying Concepts

The objective of capitalizing interest is to obtain a measure of acquisition cost that reflects a company's total investment in the asset and to charge that cost to future periods benefited.

To implement this general approach, companies consider three items:

1. Qualifying assets.
2. Capitalization period.
3. Amount to capitalize.

Qualifying Assets

To qualify for interest capitalization, assets must require a period of time to get them ready for their intended use. A company capitalizes interest costs starting with the first expenditure related to the asset. Capitalization continues until the company substantially readies the asset for its intended use.

Assets that qualify for interest cost capitalization include assets under construction for a company's own use (including buildings, plants, and large machinery) and assets intended for sale or lease that are constructed or otherwise produced as discrete projects (e.g., ships or real estate developments).

Examples of assets that do not qualify for interest capitalization are (1) assets that are in use or ready for their intended use, and (2) assets that the company does not use in its earnings activities and that are not undergoing the activities necessary to get them ready for use. Examples of this second type include land remaining undeveloped and assets not used because of obsolescence, excess capacity, or need for repair.

International Perspective

Recently, IFRS changed to require companies to capitalize borrowing costs related to qualifying assets. These changes were made as part of the IASB's and FASB's convergence project.

Capitalization Period

The **capitalization period** is the period of time during which a company must capitalize interest. It begins with the presence of three conditions:

1. Expenditures for the asset have been made.
2. Activities that are necessary to get the asset ready for its intended use are in progress.
3. Interest cost is being incurred.

Interest capitalization **continues as long as these three conditions are present.** The capitalization period ends when the asset is substantially complete and ready for its intended use.

Amount to Capitalize

The amount of interest to capitalize is limited to the lower of actual interest cost incurred during the period or avoidable interest. **Avoidable interest** is the amount of interest cost during the period that a company could theoretically avoid if it had not made expenditures for the asset. If the actual interest cost for the period is $90,000 and the avoidable interest is $80,000, the company capitalizes only $80,000. Or, if the actual interest cost is $80,000 and the avoidable interest is $90,000, it still capitalizes only $80,000. In no situation should interest cost include a cost of capital charge for stockholders' equity. Furthermore, GAAP requires interest capitalization for a qualifying asset only if its effect, compared with the effect of expensing interest, is material. **[3]**

To apply the avoidable interest concept, a company determines the potential amount of interest that it may capitalize during an accounting period by multiplying the interest rate(s) by the **weighted-average accumulated expenditures** for qualifying assets during the period.

Weighted-Average Accumulated Expenditures. In computing the weighted-average accumulated expenditures, a company weights the construction expenditures by the amount of time (fraction of a year or accounting period) that it can incur interest cost on the expenditure.

To illustrate, assume a 17-month bridge construction project with current-year payments to the contractor of $240,000 on March 1, $480,000 on July 1, and $360,000 on November 1. The company computes the weighted-average accumulated expenditures for the year ended December 31 as follows.

ILLUSTRATION 10-2
Computation of Weighted-Average Accumulated Expenditures

Expenditures					
Date	Amount	×	Capitalization Period*	=	Weighted-Average Accumulated Expenditures
March 1	$ 240,000		10/12		$200,000
July 1	480,000		6/12		240,000
November 1	360,000		2/12		60,000
	$1,080,000				$500,000

*Months between date of expenditure and date interest capitalization stops or end of year, whichever comes first (in this case December 31).

To compute the weighted-average accumulated expenditures, a company weights the expenditures by the amount of time that it can incur interest cost on each one. For the March 1 expenditure, the company associates 10 months' interest cost with the expenditure. For the expenditure on July 1, it incurs only 6 months' interest costs. For the expenditure made on November 1, the company incurs only 2 months of interest cost.

Interest Rates. Companies follow the below principles in selecting the appropriate interest rates to be applied to the weighted-average accumulated expenditures:

1. For the portion of weighted-average accumulated expenditures that is less than or equal to any amounts borrowed specifically to finance construction of the assets, **use the interest rate incurred on the specific borrowings.**
2. For the portion of weighted-average accumulated expenditures that is greater than any debt incurred specifically to finance construction of the assets, **use a weighted average of interest rates incurred on all other outstanding debt during the period.**[3]

[3]The interest rate to be used may rely exclusively on an average rate of all the borrowings, if desired. For our purposes, we use the specific borrowing rate followed by the average interest rate because we believe it to be more conceptually consistent. Either method can be used; GAAP does not provide explicit guidance on this measurement. For a discussion of this issue and others related to interest capitalization, see Kathryn M. Means and Paul M. Kazenski, "SFAS 34: Recipe for Diversity," *Accounting Horizons* (September 1988); and Wendy A. Duffy, "A Graphical Analysis of Interest Capitalization," *Journal of Accounting Education* (Fall 1990).

Illustration 10-3 shows the computation of a weighted-average interest rate for debt greater than the amount incurred specifically to finance construction of the assets.

ILLUSTRATION 10-3
Computation of Weighted-Average Interest Rate

	Principal	Interest
12%, 2-year note	$ 600,000	$ 72,000
9%, 10-year bonds	2,000,000	180,000
7.5%, 20-year bonds	5,000,000	375,000
	$7,600,000	$627,000

$$\text{Weighted-average interest rate} = \frac{\textbf{Total interest}}{\textbf{Total principal}} = \frac{\$627,000}{\$7,600,000} = 8.25\%$$

Comprehensive Example of Interest Capitalization

To illustrate the issues related to interest capitalization, assume that on November 1, 2013, Shalla Company contracted Pfeifer Construction Co. to construct a building for $1,400,000 on land costing $100,000 (purchased from the contractor and included in the first payment). Shalla made the following payments to the construction company during 2014.

January 1	March 1	May 1	December 31	Total
$210,000	$300,000	$540,000	$450,000	$1,500,000

Pfeifer Construction completed the building, ready for occupancy, on December 31, 2014. Shalla had the following debt outstanding at December 31, 2014.

Specific Construction Debt	
1. 15%, 3-year note to finance purchase of land and construction of the building, dated December 31, 2013, with interest payable annually on December 31	$750,000
Other Debt	
2. 10%, 5-year note payable, dated December 31, 2010, with interest payable annually on December 31	$550,000
3. 12%, 10-year bonds issued December 31, 2009, with interest payable annually on December 31	$600,000

Shalla computed the weighted-average accumulated expenditures during 2014 as shown in Illustration 10-4.

ILLUSTRATION 10-4
Computation of Weighted-Average Accumulated Expenditures

Expenditures			Current-Year		
Date	Amount	×	Capitalization Period	=	Weighted-Average Accumulated Expenditures
January 1	$ 210,000		12/12		$210,000
March 1	300,000		10/12		250,000
May 1	540,000		8/12		360,000
December 31	450,000		0		0
	$1,500,000				$820,000

Note that the expenditure made on December 31, the last day of the year, does not have any interest cost.

Shalla computes the avoidable interest as shown in Illustration 10-5.

ILLUSTRATION 10-5
Computation of Avoidable Interest

Weighted-Average Accumulated Expenditures	×	Interest Rate	=	Avoidable Interest
$750,000		.15 (construction note)		$112,500
70,000[a]		.1104 (weighted average of other debt)[b]		7,728
$820,000				$120,228

[a]The amount by which the weighted-average accumulated expenditures exceeds the specific construction loan.

[b]Weighted-average interest rate computation:

	Principal	Interest
10%, 5-year note	$ 550,000	$ 55,000
12%, 10-year bonds	600,000	72,000
	$1,150,000	$127,000

$$\text{Weighted-average interest rate} = \frac{\text{Total interest}}{\text{Total principal}} = \frac{\$127,000}{\$1,150,000} = 11.04\%$$

The company determines the actual interest cost, which represents the maximum amount of interest that it may capitalize during 2014, as shown in Illustration 10-6.

ILLUSTRATION 10-6
Computation of Actual Interest Cost

Construction note	$750,000 × .15 =	$112,500
5-year note	$550,000 × .10 =	55,000
10-year bonds	$600,000 × .12 =	72,000
Actual interest		$239,500

The interest cost that Shalla capitalizes is the lesser of $120,228 (avoidable interest) and $239,500 (actual interest), or $120,228.

Shalla records the following journal entries during 2014:

	Debit	Credit
January 1		
Land	100,000	
Buildings (or Construction in Process)	110,000	
Cash		210,000
March 1		
Buildings	300,000	
Cash		300,000
May 1		
Buildings	540,000	
Cash		540,000
December 31		
Buildings	450,000	
Cash		450,000
Buildings (Capitalized Interest)	120,228	
Interest Expense ($239,500 − $120,228)	119,272	
Cash ($112,500 + $55,000 + $72,000)		239,500

Gateway to the Profession

Tutorial on Interest Capitalization

Shalla should write off capitalized interest cost as part of depreciation over the useful life of the assets involved and not over the term of the debt. It should disclose the total interest cost incurred during the period, with the portion charged to expense and the portion capitalized indicated.

At December 31, 2014, Shalla discloses the amount of interest capitalized either as part of the nonoperating section of the income statement or in the notes accompanying the financial statements. We illustrate both forms of disclosure, in Illustrations 10-7 and 10-8.[4]

ILLUSTRATION 10-7
Capitalized Interest Reported in the Income Statement

Income from operations		XXXX
Other expenses and losses:		
Interest expense	$239,500	
Less: Capitalized interest	120,228	119,272
Income before income taxes		XXXX
Income taxes		XXX
Net income		XXXX

ILLUSTRATION 10-8
Capitalized Interest Disclosed in a Note

Note 1: Accounting Policies. *Capitalized Interest.* During 2014, total interest cost was $239,500, of which $120,228 was capitalized and $119,272 was charged to expense.

What do the numbers mean? WHAT'S IN YOUR INTEREST?

The requirement to capitalize interest can significantly impact financial statements. For example, when earnings of building manufacturer **Jim Walter's Corporation** dropped from $1.51 to $1.17 per share, the company offset 11 cents per share of the decline by capitalizing the interest on coal mining projects and several plants under construction.

How do statement users determine the impact of interest capitalization on a company's bottom line? They examine the notes to the financial statements. Companies with material interest capitalization must disclose the amounts of capitalized interest relative to total interest costs. For example, **Anadarko Petroleum Corporation** capitalized nearly 30 percent of its total interest costs in a recent year and provided the following footnote related to capitalized interest.

Financial Footnotes
Total interest costs incurred during the year were $82,415,000. Of this amount, the Company capitalized $24,716,000. Capitalized interest is included as part of the cost of oil and gas properties. The capitalization rates are based on the Company's weighted-average cost of borrowings used to finance the expenditures.

Special Issues Related to Interest Capitalization

Two issues related to interest capitalization merit special attention:

1. Expenditures for land.
2. Interest revenue.

Expenditures for Land. When a company purchases land with the intention of developing it for a particular use, interest costs associated with those expenditures qualify for interest capitalization. If it purchases land as a site for a structure (such as a plant site), **interest costs capitalized during the period of construction are part of the cost of the plant, not the land.** Conversely, if the company develops land for lot sales, it includes any capitalized interest cost as part of the acquisition cost of the developed land. However, it should **not** capitalize interest costs involved in purchasing land held **for speculation** because the asset is ready for its intended use.

International Perspective

IFRS requires that interest revenue earned on specific borrowings should offset interest costs capitalized. The rationale is that the interest revenue earned is directly related to the interest cost incurred on the specific borrowing.

Interest Revenue. Companies frequently borrow money to finance construction of assets. They temporarily invest the excess borrowed funds in interest-bearing securities until they need the funds to pay for construction. During the early stages of construction, interest revenue earned may exceed the interest cost incurred on the borrowed funds.

[4]In subsequent years of a multi-year project, Shalla would follow the same procedures as presented for year 1. That is, interest to be capitalized each year is determined, based on weighted-average expenditures in that year multiplied by the appropriate interest rate, and then compared to actual interest. Total interest for the year is then allocated to interest expense and capitalized interest.

Should companies offset interest revenue against interest cost when determining the amount of interest to capitalize as part of the construction cost of assets? In general, **companies should not net or offset interest revenue against interest cost**. Temporary or short-term investment decisions are not related to the interest incurred as part of the acquisition cost of assets. Therefore, companies should capitalize the interest incurred on qualifying assets whether or not they temporarily invest excess funds in short-term securities. Some criticize this approach because a company can defer the interest cost but report the interest revenue in the current period.

Observations

The interest capitalization requirement is still debated. From a conceptual viewpoint, many believe that, for the reasons mentioned earlier, companies should either capitalize **no interest cost** or **all interest costs**, actual or imputed.

VALUATION OF PROPERTY, PLANT, AND EQUIPMENT

5 LEARNING OBJECTIVE
Understand accounting issues related to acquiring and valuing plant assets.

Like other assets, **companies should record property, plant, and equipment at the fair value of what they give up or at the fair value of the asset received, whichever is more clearly evident**. However, the process of asset acquisition sometimes obscures fair value. For example, if a company buys land and buildings together for one price, how does it determine separate values for the land and buildings? We examine these types of accounting problems in the following sections.

Cash Discounts

When a company purchases plant assets subject to cash discounts for prompt payment, how should it report the discount? If it takes the discount, the company should consider the discount as a reduction in the purchase price of the asset. But should the company reduce the asset cost even if it does not take the discount?

Two points of view exist on this question. One approach considers the discount—whether taken or not—as a reduction in the cost of the asset. The rationale for this approach is that the real cost of the asset is the cash or cash equivalent price of the asset. In addition, some argue that the terms of cash discounts are so attractive that failure to take them indicates management error or inefficiency.

Proponents of the other approach argue that failure to take the discount should not always be considered a loss. The terms may be unfavorable, or it might not be prudent for the company to take the discount. At present, companies use both methods though most prefer the former method.

Deferred-Payment Contracts

Companies frequently purchase plant assets on long-term credit contracts, using notes, mortgages, bonds, or equipment obligations. **To properly reflect cost, companies account for assets purchased on long-term credit contracts at the present value of the consideration exchanged between the contracting parties at the date of the transaction.**

For example, Greathouse Company purchases an asset today in exchange for a $10,000 zero-interest-bearing note payable four years from now. The company would not record the asset at $10,000. Instead, the present value of the $10,000 note establishes the exchange price of the transaction (the purchase price of the asset). Assuming an appropriate interest rate of 9 percent at which to discount this single payment of $10,000 due four years from now, Greathouse records this asset at $7,084.30 ($10,000 × .70843). [See Table 6-2 (page 337) for the present value of a single sum, $PV = \$10,000\ (PVF_{4,9\%})$.]

When no interest rate is stated or if the specified rate is unreasonable, the company imputes an appropriate interest rate. The objective is to approximate the interest rate that the buyer and seller would negotiate at arm's length in a similar borrowing transaction. In imputing an interest rate, companies consider such factors as the borrower's credit rating, the amount and maturity date of the note, and prevailing interest rates. **The company uses the cash exchange price of the asset acquired (if determinable) as the basis for recording the asset and measuring the interest element.**

To illustrate, Sutter Company purchases a specially built robot spray painter for its production line. The company issues a $100,000, five-year, zero-interest-bearing note to Wrigley Robotics, Inc. for the new equipment. The prevailing market rate of interest for obligations of this nature is 10 percent. Sutter is to pay off the note in five $20,000 installments, made at the end of each year. Sutter cannot readily determine the fair value of this specially built robot. Therefore, Sutter approximates the robot's value by establishing the fair value (present value) of the note. Entries for the date of purchase and dates of payments, plus computation of the present value of the note, are as follows.

Date of Purchase

Equipment	75,816*	
Discount on Notes Payable	24,184	
Notes Payable		100,000

*Present value of note = $20,000 ($PVF\text{-}OA_{5,10\%}$)
= $20,000 (3.79079); Table 6-4
= $75,816

End of First Year

Interest Expense	7,582	
Notes Payable	20,000	
Cash		20,000
Discount on Notes Payable		7,582

Interest expense in the first year under the effective-interest approach is $7,582 [($100,000 − $24,184) × 10%]. The entry at the end of the second year to record interest and principal payment is as follows.

End of Second Year

Interest Expense	6,340	
Notes Payable	20,000	
Cash		20,000
Discount on Notes Payable		6,340

Interest expense in the second year under the effective-interest approach is $6,340 [($100,000 − $24,184) − ($20,000 − $7,582)] × 10%.

If Sutter did not impute an interest rate for deferred-payment contracts, it would record the asset at an amount greater than its fair value and overstate depreciation expense. In addition, Sutter would understate interest expense in the income statement for all periods involved.

Lump-Sum Purchases

A special problem of valuing fixed assets arises when a company purchases a group of plant assets at a single **lump-sum price**. When this common situation occurs, the company allocates the total cost among the various assets on the basis of their relative fair values. The assumption is that costs will vary in direct proportion to fair value. This is the same principle that companies apply to allocate a lump-sum cost among different inventory items.

To determine fair value, a company should use valuation techniques that are appropriate in the circumstances. In some cases, a single valuation technique will be appropriate. In other cases, multiple valuation approaches might have to be used.[5]

To illustrate, Norduct Homes, Inc. decides to purchase several assets of a small heating concern, Comfort Heating, for $80,000. Comfort Heating is in the process of liquidation. Its assets sold are:

	Book Value	Fair Value
Inventory	$30,000	$ 25,000
Land	20,000	25,000
Building	35,000	50,000
	$85,000	$100,000

Norduct Homes allocates the $80,000 purchase price on the basis of the relative fair values (assuming specific identification of costs is impracticable) in the following manner.

ILLUSTRATION 10-9
Allocation of Purchase Price—Relative Fair Value Basis

Inventory	$\frac{\$25,000}{\$100,000} \times \$80,000 = \$20,000$
Land	$\frac{\$25,000}{\$100,000} \times \$80,000 = \$20,000$
Building	$\frac{\$50,000}{\$100,000} \times \$80,000 = \$40,000$

Issuance of Stock

When companies acquire property by issuing securities, such as common stock, the par or stated value of such stock fails to properly measure the property cost. If trading of the stock is active, **the market price of the stock issued is a fair indication of the cost of the property acquired. The stock is a good measure of the current cash equivalent price.**

For example, Upgrade Living Co. decides to purchase some adjacent land for expansion of its carpeting and cabinet operation. In lieu of paying cash for the land, the company issues to Deedland Company 5,000 shares of common stock (par value $10) that have a fair value of $12 per share. Upgrade Living Co. records the following entry.

Land (5,000 × $12)	60,000	
Common Stock		50,000
Paid-In Capital in Excess of Par—Common Stock		10,000

If the company cannot determine the market price of the common stock exchanged, it establishes the fair value of the property. It then uses the value of the property as the basis for recording the asset and issuance of the common stock.

[5]The valuation approaches that should be used are the market, income, or cost approach, or a combination of these approaches. The *market approach* uses observable prices and other relevant information generated by market transactions involving comparable assets. The *income approach* uses valuation techniques to convert future amounts (for example, cash flows or earnings) to a single present value amount (discounted). The *cost approach* is based on the amount that currently would be required to replace the service capacity of an asset (often referred to as current replacement cost). In determining the fair value, the company should assume the highest and best use of the asset. **[4]**

Exchanges of Nonmonetary Assets

The proper accounting for exchanges of nonmonetary assets, such as property, plant, and equipment, is controversial.[6] Some argue that companies should account for these types of exchanges based on the fair value of the asset given up or the fair value of the asset received, with a gain or loss recognized. Others believe that they should account for exchanges based on the recorded amount (book value) of the asset given up, with no gain or loss recognized. Still others favor an approach that recognizes losses in all cases but defers gains in special situations.

Ordinarily, companies account for the exchange of **nonmonetary assets** on the basis of **the fair value of the asset given up or the fair value of the asset received, whichever is clearly more evident**. [5] Thus, companies **should recognize immediately** any gains or losses on the exchange. The rationale for immediate recognition is that most transactions have **commercial substance**, and therefore gains and losses should be recognized.

International Perspective

The FASB changed its accounting for exchanges to converge with IFRS. Previously, the FASB used a "similar in nature" criterion for exchanged assets to determine whether gains should be recognized. With use of the commercial substance test, GAAP and IFRS are now very similar.

Meaning of Commercial Substance

As indicated above, fair value is the basis for measuring an asset acquired in a nonmonetary exchange if the transaction has commercial substance. An exchange has **commercial substance** if the future cash flows change as a result of the transaction. That is, if the two parties' economic positions change, the transaction has commercial substance.

For example, Andrew Co. exchanges some of its equipment for land held by Roddick Inc. It is likely that the timing and amount of the cash flows arising for the land will differ significantly from the cash flows arising from the equipment. As a result, both Andrew Co. and Roddick Inc. are in different economic positions. Therefore, the exchange has commercial substance, and the companies recognize a gain or loss on the exchange.

What if companies exchange similar assets, such as one truck for another truck? Even in an exchange of similar assets, a change in the economic position of the company can result. For example, let's say the useful life of the truck received is significantly longer than that of the truck given up. The cash flows for the trucks can differ significantly. As a result, the transaction has commercial substance, and the company should use fair value as a basis for measuring the asset received in the exchange.

However, it is possible to exchange similar assets but not have a significant difference in cash flows. That is, the company is in the same economic position as before the exchange. In that case, the company recognizes a loss but generally defers a gain.

As we will see in the following examples, use of fair value generally results in recognizing a gain or loss at the time of the exchange. Consequently, companies must determine if the transaction has commercial substance. To make this determination, they must carefully evaluate the cash flow characteristics of the assets exchanged.[7]

Illustration 10-10 summarizes asset exchange situations and the related accounting.

[6]Nonmonetary assets are items whose price in terms of the monetary unit may change over time. Monetary assets—cash and short- or long-term accounts and notes receivable—are fixed in terms of units of currency by contract or otherwise.

[7]The determination of the commercial substance of a transaction requires significant judgment. In determining whether future cash flows change, it is necessary to do one of two things. (1) Determine whether the risk, timing, and amount of cash flows arising for the asset received differ from the cash flows associated with the outbound asset. Or, (2) evaluate whether cash flows are affected with the exchange versus without the exchange. Also note that if companies cannot determine fair values of the assets exchanged, then they should use recorded book values in accounting for the exchange.

ILLUSTRATION 10-10
Accounting for Exchanges

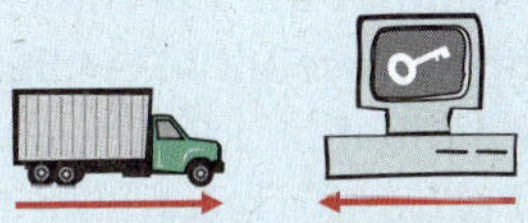

Type of Exchange	Accounting Guidance
Exchange has commercial substance.	Recognize gains and losses immediately.
Exchange lacks commercial substance—no cash received.	Defer gains; recognize losses immediately.
Exchange lacks commercial substance—cash received.	Recognize partial gain; recognize losses immediately.*

*If cash is 25% or more of the fair value of the exchange, recognize entire gain because earnings process is complete.

As Illustration 10-10 indicates, companies immediately recognize losses they incur on all exchanges. The accounting for gains depends on whether the exchange has commercial substance. If the exchange has commercial substance, the company recognizes the gain immediately. However, the profession modifies the rule for immediate recognition of a gain when an exchange lacks commercial substance: **If the company receives no cash in such an exchange, it defers recognition of a gain. If the company receives cash in such an exchange, it recognizes part of the gain immediately.**

To illustrate the accounting for these different types of transactions, we examine various loss and gain exchange situations.

Exchanges—Loss Situation

When a company exchanges nonmonetary assets and a loss results, the company recognizes the loss immediately. The rationale: Companies should not value assets at more than their cash equivalent price. If the loss were deferred, assets would be overstated. Therefore, companies recognize a loss immediately whether the exchange has commercial substance or not.

For example, Information Processing, Inc. trades its used machine for a new model at Jerrod Business Solutions Inc. The exchange has commercial substance. The used machine has a book value of $8,000 (original cost $12,000 less $4,000 accumulated depreciation) and a fair value of $6,000. The new model lists for $16,000. Jerrod gives Information Processing a trade-in allowance of $9,000 for the used machine. Information Processing computes the cost of the new asset as follows.

ILLUSTRATION 10-11
Computation of Cost of New Machine

List price of new machine	$16,000
Less: Trade-in allowance for used machine	9,000
Cash payment due	7,000
Fair value of used machine	6,000
Cost of new machine	$13,000

Information Processing records this transaction as follows.

Equipment	13,000	
Accumulated Depreciation—Equipment	4,000	
Loss on Disposal of Equipment	2,000	
Equipment		12,000
Cash		7,000

We verify the loss on the disposal of the used machine as follows.

ILLUSTRATION 10-12
Computation of Loss on Disposal of Used Machine

Fair value of used machine	$6,000
Less: Book value of used machine	8,000
Loss on disposal of used machine	$2,000

Why did Information Processing not use the trade-in allowance or the book value of the old asset as a basis for the new equipment? The company did not use the trade-in allowance because it included a price concession (similar to a price discount). Few individuals pay list price for a new car. Dealers such as Jerrod often inflate trade-in allowances on the used car so that actual selling prices fall below list prices. To record the car at list price would state it at an amount in excess of its cash equivalent price because of the new car's inflated list price. Similarly, use of book value in this situation would overstate the value of the new machine by $2,000.[8]

Exchanges—Gain Situation

Has Commercial Substance. Now let's consider the situation in which a nonmonetary exchange has commercial substance and a gain is realized. In such a case, a company usually records the cost of a nonmonetary asset acquired in exchange for another nonmonetary asset at the **fair value of the asset given up** and immediately recognizes a gain. The company should use the **fair value of the asset received** only if it is more clearly evident than the fair value of the asset given up.

To illustrate, Interstate Transportation Company exchanged a number of used trucks plus cash for a semi-truck. The used trucks have a combined book value of $42,000 (cost $64,000 less $22,000 accumulated depreciation). Interstate's purchasing agent, experienced in the secondhand market, indicates that the used trucks have a fair value of $49,000. In addition to the trucks, Interstate must pay $11,000 cash for the semi-truck. Interstate computes the cost of the semi-truck as follows.

ILLUSTRATION 10-13
Computation of Semi-Truck Cost

Fair value of trucks exchanged	$49,000
Cash paid	11,000
Cost of semi-truck	$60,000

Interstate records the exchange transaction as follows.

Trucks (semi)	60,000	
Accumulated Depreciation—Trucks	22,000	
Trucks (used)		64,000
Gain on Disposal of Trucks		7,000
Cash		11,000

The gain is the difference between the fair value of the used trucks and their book value. We verify the computation as follows.

ILLUSTRATION 10-14
Computation of Gain on Disposal of Used Trucks

Fair value of used trucks		$49,000
Cost of used trucks	$64,000	
Less: Accumulated depreciation	22,000	
Book value of used trucks		(42,000)
Gain on disposal of used trucks		$ 7,000

In this case, Interstate is in a different economic position, and therefore the transaction has commercial substance. Thus, it **recognizes a gain.**

Lacks Commercial Substance—No Cash Received. We now assume that the Interstate Transportation Company exchange lacks commercial substance. That is, the economic

[8]Recognize that for Jerrod (the dealer), the asset given up in the exchange is considered inventory. As a result, Jerrod records a sale and related cost of goods sold. The used machine received by Jerrod is recorded at fair value.

position of Interstate did not change significantly as a result of this exchange. In this case, Interstate defers the gain of $7,000 and reduces the basis of the semi-truck. Illustration 10-15 shows two different but acceptable computations to illustrate this reduction.

Fair value of semi-truck	$60,000		Book value of used trucks	$42,000
Less: Gain deferred	7,000	OR	Plus: Cash paid	11,000
Basis of semi-truck	$53,000		Basis of semi-truck	$53,000

ILLUSTRATION 10-15
Basis of Semi-Truck—Fair Value vs. Book Value

Interstate records this transaction as follows.

Trucks (semi)	53,000	
Accumulated Depreciation—Trucks	22,000	
Trucks (used)		64,000
Cash		11,000

If the exchange lacks commercial substance, the company recognizes the gain (reflected in the basis of the semi-truck) through lower depreciation expense or when it later sells the semi-truck, not at the time of the exchange.

Lacks Commercial Substance—Some Cash Received. When a company receives cash (sometimes referred to as "boot") in an exchange that lacks commercial substance, it must immediately recognize a portion of the gain.[9] Illustration 10-16 shows the general formula for gain recognition when an exchange includes some cash.

$$\frac{\textbf{Cash Received (Boot)}}{\textbf{Cash Received (Boot) + Fair Value of Other Assets Received}} \times \textbf{Total Gain} = \textbf{Recognized Gain}$$

ILLUSTRATION 10-16
Formula for Gain Recognition, Some Cash Received

To illustrate, assume that Queenan Corporation traded in used machinery with a book value of $60,000 (cost $110,000 less accumulated depreciation $50,000) and a fair value of $100,000. It receives in exchange a machine with a fair value of $90,000 plus cash of $10,000. Illustration 10-17 shows calculation of the total gain on the exchange.

Fair value of machine given up	$100,000
Less: Book value of machine given up	60,000
Total gain	$ 40,000

ILLUSTRATION 10-17
Computation of Total Gain

Generally, when a transaction lacks commercial substance, a company defers any gain. But because Queenan received $10,000 in cash, it recognizes a partial gain. The portion of the gain a company recognizes is the ratio of monetary assets (cash in this case) to the total consideration received. Queenan computes the partial gain as follows.

$$\frac{\$10{,}000}{\$10{,}000 + \$90{,}000} \times \$40{,}000 = \$4{,}000$$

ILLUSTRATION 10-18
Computation of Gain Based on Ratio of Cash Received to Total Consideration Received

[9]When the monetary consideration is significant, i.e., **25 percent or more** of the fair value of the exchange, both parties consider the transaction a **monetary exchange**. Such "monetary" exchanges rely on the fair values to measure the gains or losses that are recognized in their entirety. **[6]**

Because Queenan recognizes only a gain of $4,000 on this transaction, it defers the remaining $36,000 ($40,000 − $4,000) and reduces the basis (recorded cost) of the new machine. Illustration 10-19 shows the computation of the basis.

ILLUSTRATION 10-19
Computation of Basis

Fair value of new machine	$90,000		Book value of old machine	$60,000
Less: Gain deferred	36,000	OR	Less: Portion of book value presumed sold	6,000*
Basis of new machine	$54,000		Basis of new machine	$54,000

$$^*\frac{\$10,000}{\$100,000} \times \$60,000 = \$6,000$$

Queenan records the transaction with the following entry.

Cash	10,000	
Machinery (new)	54,000	
Accumulated Depreciation—Machinery	50,000	
Machinery (old)		110,000
Gain on Disposal of Machinery		4,000

The rationale for the treatment of a partial gain is as follows. Before a nonmonetary exchange that includes some cash, a company has an unrecognized gain, which is the difference between the book value and the fair value of the old asset. When the exchange occurs, a portion of the fair value is converted to a more liquid asset. The ratio of this liquid asset to the total consideration received is the portion of the total gain that the company realizes. Thus, the company recognizes and records that amount.

Illustration 10-20 presents in summary form the accounting requirements for recognizing gains and losses on exchanges of nonmonetary assets.[10]

ILLUSTRATION 10-20
Summary of Gain and Loss Recognition on Exchanges of Nonmonetary Assets

1. Compute the total gain or loss on the transaction. This amount is equal to the difference between the fair value of the asset given up and the book value of the asset given up.
2. If a loss is computed in step 1, always recognize the entire loss.
3. If a gain is computed in step 1,
   (a) and the exchange has commercial substance, recognize the entire gain.
   (b) and the exchange lacks commercial substance,
      (1) and no cash is involved, no gain is recognized.
      (2) and some cash is given, no gain is recognized.
      (3) and some cash is received, the following portion of the gain is recognized:

$$\frac{\text{Cash Received (Boot)}}{\text{Cash Received (Boot)} + \text{Fair Value of Other Assets Received}} \times \text{Total Gain}^*$$

*If the amount of cash exchanged is 25% or more, both parties recognize entire gain or loss.

Companies disclose in their financial statements nonmonetary exchanges during a period. Such disclosure indicates the nature of the transaction(s), the method of accounting for the assets exchanged, and gains or losses recognized on the exchanges. [7]

[10]Adapted from an article by Robert Capettini and Thomas E. King, "Exchanges of Nonmonetary Assets: Some Changes," *The Accounting Review* (January 1976).

What do the numbers mean? *ABOUT THOSE SWAPS*

In a press release, Roy Olofson, former vice president of finance for **Global Crossing**, accused company executives of improperly describing the company's revenue to the public. He said the company had improperly recorded long-term sales immediately rather than over the term of the contract, had improperly booked as cash transactions swaps of capacity with other carriers, and had fired him when he blew the whistle.

The accounting for the swaps involves exchanges of similar network capacity. Companies have said they engage in such deals because swapping is quicker and less costly than building segments of their own networks, or because such pacts provide redundancies to make their own networks more reliable. In one expert's view, an exchange of similar network capacity is the equivalent of trading a blue truck for a red truck—it shouldn't boost a company's revenue.

But Global Crossing and **Qwest**, among others, counted as revenue the money received from the other company in the swap. (In general, in transactions involving leased capacity, the companies booked the revenue over the life of the contract.) Some of these companies then treated their own purchases as capital expenditures, which were not run through the income statement. Instead, the spending led to the addition of assets on the balance sheet (and an inflated bottom line).

The SEC questioned some of these capacity exchanges, because it appeared they were a device to pad revenue. This reaction was not surprising, since revenue growth was a key factor in the valuation of companies such as Global Crossing and Qwest during the craze for tech stocks in the late 1990s and 2000.

Source: Adapted from Henny Sender, "Telecoms Draw Focus for Moves in Accounting," *Wall Street Journal* (March 26, 2002), p. C7.

Accounting for Contributions

Companies sometimes receive or make contributions (donations or gifts). Such contributions, **nonreciprocal transfers**, transfer assets in one direction. A contribution is often some type of asset (such as cash, securities, land, buildings, or use of facilities), but it also could be the forgiveness of a debt.

When companies acquire assets as donations, a strict cost concept dictates that the valuation of the asset should be zero. However, a departure from the historical cost principle seems justified; the only costs incurred (legal fees and other relatively minor expenditures) are not a reasonable basis of accounting for the assets acquired. To record nothing is to ignore the economic realities of an increase in wealth and assets. Therefore, companies use the **fair value of the asset** to establish its value on the books.

International Perspective

IFRS provides detailed guidance on how to account for contributions and government grants.

What then is the proper accounting for the credit in this transaction? Some believe the credit should be made to Donated Capital (an additional paid-in capital account). This approach views the increase in assets from a donation as contributed capital, rather than as earned revenue.

Others argue that companies should report donations as revenues from contributions. Their reasoning is that only the owners of a business contribute capital. At issue in this approach is whether the company should report revenue immediately or over the period that the asset is employed. For example, to attract new industry a city may offer land, but the receiving enterprise may incur additional costs in the future (e.g., transportation or higher state income taxes) because the location is not the most desirable. As a consequence, some argue that the company should defer the revenue and recognize it as the costs are incurred.

The FASB's position is that **in general, companies should recognize contributions received as revenues in the period received.** **[8]**[11] Companies measure contributions at the fair value of the assets received. **[9]** To illustrate, Max Wayer Meat Packing, Inc. has

[11]GAAP is silent on how to account for the transfers of assets from governmental units to business enterprises. However, we believe that the basic requirements should hold also for these types of contributions. Therefore, companies should record all assets at fair value and all credits as revenue.

recently accepted a donation of land with a fair value of $150,000 from the Memphis Industrial Development Corp. In return, Max Wayer Meat Packing promises to build a packing plant in Memphis. Max Wayer's entry is:

Land	150,000	
Contribution Revenue		150,000

When a company contributes a nonmonetary asset, it should record the amount of the donation as an expense at the fair value of the donated asset. If a difference exists between the fair value of the asset and its book value, the company should recognize a gain or loss. To illustrate, Kline Industries donates land to the city of Los Angeles for a city park. The land cost $80,000 and has a fair value of $110,000. Kline Industries records this donation as follows.

Contribution Expense	110,000	
Land		80,000
Gain on Disposal of Land		30,000

In some cases, companies promise to give (pledge) some type of asset in the future. Should companies record this promise immediately or when they give the assets? If the promise is **unconditional** (depends only on the passage of time or on demand by the recipient for performance), the company should report the contribution expense and related payable immediately. If the promise is **conditional**, the company recognizes expense in the period benefited by the contribution, generally when it transfers the asset.

Other Asset Valuation Methods

The exception to the historical cost principle for assets acquired through donation is based on fair value. Another exception is the **prudent cost** concept. This concept states that if for some reason a company ignorantly paid too much for an asset originally, it is theoretically preferable to charge a loss immediately.

For example, assume that a company constructs an asset at a cost much greater than its present economic usefulness. It would be appropriate to charge these excess costs as a loss to the current period, rather than capitalize them as part of the cost of the asset. In practice, the need to use the prudent cost approach seldom develops. Companies typically either use good reasoning in paying a given price or fail to recognize that they have overpaid.

What happens, on the other hand, if a company makes a bargain purchase or internally constructs a piece of equipment at a cost savings? Such savings should not result in immediate recognition of a gain under any circumstances.

COSTS SUBSEQUENT TO ACQUISITION

LEARNING OBJECTIVE 6

Describe the accounting treatment for costs subsequent to acquisition.

After installing plant assets and readying them for use, a company incurs additional costs that range from ordinary repairs to significant additions. The major problem is allocating these costs to the proper time periods. **In general, costs incurred to achieve greater future benefits should be capitalized, whereas expenditures that simply maintain a given level of services should be expensed.** In order to capitalize costs, one of three conditions must be present:

1. The useful life of the asset must be increased.
2. The quantity of units produced from the asset must be increased.
3. The quality of the units produced must be enhanced.

For example, a company like **Boeing** should expense expenditures that do not increase an asset's future benefits. That is, it expenses immediately ordinary repairs that maintain the existing condition of the asset or restore it to normal operating efficiency.

Companies expense most expenditures below an established arbitrary minimum amount, say, $100 or $500. Although conceptually this treatment may be incorrect, expediency demands it. Otherwise, companies would set up depreciation schedules for an item such as a wastepaper basket.

Underlying Concepts

Expensing long-lived wastepaper baskets is an application of the materiality concept.

The distinction between a **capital expenditure (asset)** and a **revenue expenditure (expense)** is not always clear-cut. Yet, in most cases, **consistent application of a capital/expense policy** is more important than attempting to provide general theoretical guidelines for each transaction. Generally, companies incur four major types of expenditures relative to existing assets.

MAJOR TYPES OF EXPENDITURES

ADDITIONS. Increase or extension of existing assets.

IMPROVEMENTS AND REPLACEMENTS. Substitution of an improved asset for an existing one.

REARRANGEMENT AND REINSTALLATION. Movement of assets from one location to another.

REPAIRS. Expenditures that maintain assets in condition for operation.

What do the numbers mean? DISCONNECTED

It all started with a check of the books by an internal auditor for **WorldCom Inc.** The telecom giant's newly installed chief executive had asked for a financial review, and the auditor was spot-checking records of capital expenditures. She found the company was using an unorthodox technique to account for one of its biggest expenses: charges paid to local telephone networks to complete long-distance calls.

Instead of recording these charges as operating expenses, WorldCom recorded a significant portion as capital expenditures. The maneuver was worth hundreds of millions of dollars to WorldCom's bottom line. It effectively turned a loss for all of 2001 and the first quarter of 2002 into a profit. The graph below compares WorldCom's accounting to that under GAAP. Soon after this discovery, WorldCom filed for bankruptcy.

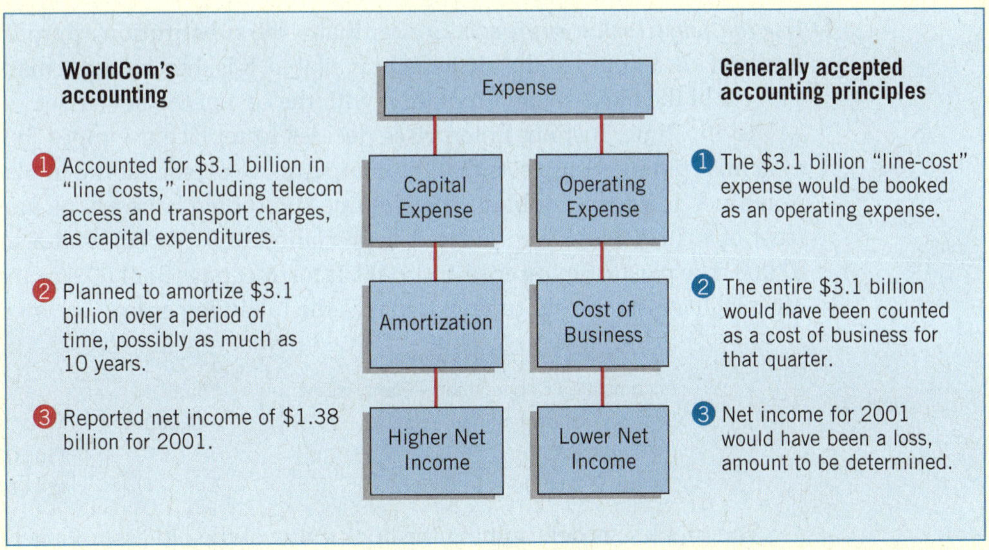

Source: Adapted from Jared Sandberg, Deborah Solomon, and Rebecca Blumenstein, "Inside WorldCom's Unearthing of a Vast Accounting Scandal," *Wall Street Journal* (June 27, 2002), p. A1.

Additions

Additions should present no major accounting problems. By definition, **companies capitalize any addition to plant assets because a new asset is created**. For example, the addition of a wing to a hospital, or of an air conditioning system to an office, increases the service potential of that facility. Companies should capitalize such expenditures and match them against the revenues that will result in future periods.

One problem that arises in this area is the accounting for any changes related to the existing structure as a result of the addition. Is the cost incurred to tear down an old wall, to make room for the addition, a cost of the addition or an expense or loss of the period? The answer is that it depends on the original intent. If the company had anticipated building an addition later, then this cost of removal is a proper cost of the addition. But if the company had not anticipated this development, it should properly report the removal as a loss in the current period on the basis of inefficient planning. Normally, the company retains the carrying amount of the old wall in the accounts, although theoretically the company should remove it.

Improvements and Replacements

Companies substitute one asset for another through **improvements** and **replacements**. What is the difference between an improvement and a replacement? An **improvement** (**betterment**) is the substitution of a **better asset** for the one currently used (say, a concrete floor for a wooden floor). A **replacement**, on the other hand, is the substitution of a **similar asset** (a wooden floor for a wooden floor).

Many times improvements and replacements result from a general policy to modernize or rehabilitate an older building or piece of equipment. The problem is differentiating these types of expenditures from normal repairs. Does the expenditure increase the **future service potential** of the asset? Or does it merely **maintain the existing level** of service? Frequently, the answer is not clear-cut. Good judgment is required to correctly classify these expenditures.

If the expenditure increases the future service potential of the asset, a company should capitalize it. The accounting is therefore handled in one of three ways, depending on the circumstances:

1. ***Use the substitution approach.*** Conceptually, the **substitution approach** is correct if the carrying amount of the old asset is available. It is then a simple matter to remove the cost of the old asset and replace it with the cost of the new asset.

   To illustrate, Instinct Enterprises decides to replace the pipes in its plumbing system. A plumber suggests that the company use plastic tubing in place of the cast iron pipes and copper tubing. The old pipe and tubing have a book value of $15,000 (cost of $150,000 less accumulated depreciation of $135,000), and a scrap value of $1,000. The plastic tubing costs $125,000. If Instinct pays $124,000 for the new tubing after exchanging the old tubing, it makes the following entry:

Plant Assets (plumbing system)	125,000	
Accumulated Depreciation—Plant Assets	135,000	
Loss on Disposal of Plant Assets	14,000	
Plant Assets		150,000
Cash ($125,000 − $1,000)		124,000

   The problem is determining the book value of the old asset. Generally, the components of a given asset depreciate at different rates. However, generally no separate accounting is made. For example, the tires, motor, and body of a truck depreciate at different rates, but most companies use one rate for the entire truck. Companies can set separate depreciation rates, but it is often impractical. If a company cannot determine the carrying amount of the old asset, it adopts one of two other approaches.

2. ***Capitalize the new cost.*** Another approach capitalizes the improvement and keeps the carrying amount of the old asset on the books. The justification for this approach is that the item is sufficiently depreciated to reduce its carrying amount almost to zero. Although this assumption may not always be true, the differences are often insignificant. Companies usually handle improvements in this manner.
3. ***Charge to accumulated depreciation.*** In cases when a company does not improve the quantity or quality of the asset itself but instead extends its useful life, the company debits the expenditure to Accumulated Depreciation rather than to an asset account. The theory behind this approach is that the replacement extends the useful life of the asset and thereby recaptures some or all of the past depreciation. The net carrying amount of the asset is the same whether debiting the asset or accumulated depreciation.

Rearrangement and Reinstallation

Companies incur **rearrangement and reinstallation costs** to benefit future periods. An example is the rearrangement and reinstallation of machines to facilitate future production.

If a company like **The Coca-Cola Company** can determine or estimate the original installation cost and the accumulated depreciation to date, it handles the rearrangement and reinstallation cost as a replacement. If not, which is generally the case, Coca-Cola should capitalize the new costs (if material in amount) as an asset to be amortized over future periods expected to benefit. If these costs are immaterial, if they cannot be separated from other operating expenses, or if their future benefit is questionable, the company should immediately expense them.

Repairs

A company makes **ordinary repairs** to maintain plant assets in operating condition. It charges ordinary repairs to an expense account in the period incurred, on the basis that **it is the primary period benefited.** Maintenance charges that occur regularly include replacing minor parts, lubricating and adjusting equipment, repainting, and cleaning. A company treats these as ordinary operating expenses.

It is often difficult to distinguish a repair from an improvement or replacement. The major consideration is whether the expenditure benefits more than one year or one operating cycle, whichever is longer. If a **major repair** (such as an overhaul) occurs, several periods will benefit. A company should handle the cost as an addition, improvement, or replacement.[12]

An interesting question is whether a company can accrue planned maintenance overhaul costs *before* the actual costs are incurred. For example, assume that **Southwest Airlines** schedules major overhauls of its planes every three years. Should Southwest be permitted to accrue these costs and related liability over the three-year period? Some argue that this accrue-in-advance approach better matches expenses to revenues and reports Southwest's obligation for these costs. However, reporting a liability is inappropriate. To whom does Southwest owe? In other words, Southwest has no obligation to an outside party until it has to pay for the overhaul costs, and therefore it has no liability. As a result, companies are not permitted to accrue in advance for planned major overhaul costs either for interim or annual periods. **[10]**

[12]A committee of the AICPA has proposed (see footnote 2) that companies expense as incurred costs involved for planned major expenditures unless they represent an *additional* component or the *replacement* of an existing component.

Summary of Costs Subsequent to Acquisition

Illustration 10-21 summarizes the accounting treatment for various costs incurred subsequent to the acquisition of capitalized assets.

ILLUSTRATION 10-21
Summary of Costs Subsequent to Acquisition of Property, Plant, and Equipment

Type of Expenditure	Normal Accounting Treatment
Additions	Capitalize cost of addition to asset account.
Improvements and replacements	(a) **Carrying value known:** Remove cost of and accumulated depreciation on old asset, recognizing any gain or loss. Capitalize cost of improvement/replacement. (b) **Carrying value unknown:** 1. If the asset's useful life is extended, debit accumulated depreciation for cost of improvement/replacement. 2. If the quantity or quality of the asset's productivity is increased, capitalize cost of improvement/replacement to asset account.
Rearrangement and reinstallation	(a) If original installation cost is **known**, account for cost of rearrangement/reinstallation as a replacement (carrying value known). (b) If original installation cost is **unknown** and rearrangement/reinstallation cost is **material** in amount and benefits future periods, capitalize as an asset. (c) If original installation cost is **unknown** and rearrangement/reinstallation cost is **not material or future benefit is questionable**, expense the cost when incurred.
Repairs	(a) **Ordinary:** Expense cost of repairs when incurred. (b) **Major:** As appropriate, treat as an addition, improvement, or replacement.

DISPOSITION OF PROPERTY, PLANT, AND EQUIPMENT

LEARNING OBJECTIVE 7
Describe the accounting treatment for the disposal of property, plant, and equipment.

A company, like **Intel**, may retire plant assets voluntarily or dispose of them by sale, exchange, involuntary conversion, or abandonment. Regardless of the type of disposal, depreciation must be taken up to the date of disposition. Then, Intel should remove all accounts related to the retired asset. Generally, the book value of the specific plant asset does not equal its disposal value. As a result, a gain or loss develops. The reason: Depreciation is an estimate of cost allocation and not a process of valuation. **The gain or loss is really a correction of net income** for the years during which Intel used the fixed asset.

Intel should show gains or losses on the disposal of plant assets in the income statement along with other items from customary business activities. However, if it sold, abandoned, spun off, or otherwise disposed of the "operations of a component of a business," then it should report the results separately in the discontinued operations section of the income statement (as discussed in Chapter 4). That is, Intel should report any gain or loss from disposal of a business component with the related results of discontinued operations.

Sale of Plant Assets

Companies record depreciation for the period of time between the date of the last depreciation entry and the date of sale. To illustrate, assume that Barret Company recorded depreciation on a machine costing $18,000 for 9 years at the rate of $1,200 per year. If it sells the machine in the middle of the tenth year for $7,000, Barret records depreciation to the date of sale as:

Depreciation Expense ($1,200 × $\frac{1}{2}$)	600	
Accumulated Depreciation—Machinery		600

The entry for the sale of the asset then is:

Cash	7,000	
Accumulated Depreciation—Machinery	11,400	
[($1,200 × 9) + $600]		
Machinery		18,000
Gain on Disposal of Machinery		400

The book value of the machinery at the time of the sale is $6,600 ($18,000 − $11,400). Because the machinery sold for $7,000, the amount of the gain on the sale is $400.

Involuntary Conversion

Sometimes an asset's service is terminated through some type of **involuntary conversion** such as fire, flood, theft, or condemnation. Companies report the difference between the amount recovered (e.g., from a condemnation award or insurance recovery), if any, and the asset's book value as a gain or loss. They treat these gains or losses like any other type of disposition. In some cases, these gains or losses may be reported as extraordinary items in the income statement **if the conditions of the disposition are unusual and infrequent in nature.**

To illustrate, Camel Transport Corp. had to sell a plant located on company property that stood directly in the path of an interstate highway. For a number of years, the state had sought to purchase the land on which the plant stood, but the company resisted. The state ultimately exercised its right of eminent domain, which the courts upheld. In settlement, Camel received $500,000, which substantially exceeded the $200,000 book value of the plant and land (cost of $400,000 less accumulated depreciation of $200,000). Camel made the following entry.

Cash	500,000	
Accumulated Depreciation—Plant Assets	200,000	
Plant Assets		400,000
Gain on Disposal of Plant Assets		300,000

If the conditions surrounding the condemnation are judged to be unusual and infrequent, Camel's gain of $300,000 is reported as an extraordinary item.

Some object to the recognition of a gain or loss in certain *involuntary* conversions. For example, the federal government often condemns forests for national parks. The paper companies that owned these forests must report a gain or loss on the condemnation. However, companies such as **Georgia-Pacific** contend that no gain or loss should be reported because they must replace the condemned forest land immediately and so are in the same economic position as they were before. The issue is whether condemnation and subsequent purchase should be viewed as one or two transactions. GAAP requires "that a gain or loss be recognized when a nonmonetary asset is involuntarily converted to monetary assets even though an enterprise reinvests or is obligated to reinvest the monetary assets in replacement nonmonetary assets." **[11]**

Miscellaneous Problems

If a company scraps or abandons an asset without any cash recovery, it recognizes a loss equal to the asset's book value. If scrap value exists, the gain or loss that occurs is the difference between the asset's scrap value and its book value. If an asset still can be used even though it is fully depreciated, it may be kept on the books at historical cost less depreciation.

Companies must disclose in notes to the financial statements the amount of fully depreciated assets in service. For example, **Petroleum Equipment Tools Inc.** in its annual report disclosed, "The amount of fully depreciated assets included in property, plant, and equipment at December 31 amounted to approximately $98,900,000."

KEY TERMS

additions, 558
avoidable interest, 542
capital expenditure, 557
capitalization period, 542
commercial substance, 550
fixed assets, 538
historical cost, 538
improvements (betterments), 558
involuntary conversion, 561
lump-sum price, 548
major repairs, 559
nonmonetary assets, 550
nonreciprocal transfers, 555
ordinary repairs, 559
plant assets, 538
property, plant, and equipment, 538
prudent cost, 556
rearrangement and reinstallation costs, 559
replacements, 558
revenue expenditure, 557
self-constructed asset, 540
weighted-average accumulated expenditures, 543

SUMMARY OF LEARNING OBJECTIVES

1 Describe property, plant, and equipment. The major characteristics of property, plant, and equipment are as follows. (1) They are acquired for use in operations and not for resale. (2) They are long-term in nature and usually subject to depreciation. (3) They possess physical substance.

2 Identify the costs to include in initial valuation of property, plant, and equipment. The costs included in initial valuation of property, plant, and equipment are as follows.

Cost of land: Includes all expenditures made to acquire land and to ready it for use. Land costs typically include (1) the purchase price; (2) closing costs, such as title to the land, attorney's fees, and recording fees; (3) costs incurred in getting the land in condition for its intended use, such as grading, filling, draining, and clearing; (4) assumption of any liens, mortgages, or encumbrances on the property; and (5) any additional land improvements that have an indefinite life.

Cost of buildings: Includes all expenditures related directly to their acquisition or construction. These costs include (1) materials, labor, and overhead costs incurred during construction, and (2) professional fees and building permits.

Cost of equipment: Includes the purchase price, freight and handling charges incurred, insurance on the equipment while in transit, cost of special foundations if required, assembling and installation costs, and costs of conducting trial runs.

3 Describe the accounting problems associated with self-constructed assets. Indirect costs of manufacturing create special problems because companies cannot easily trace these costs directly to work and material orders related to the constructed assets. Companies might handle these costs in one of two ways. (1) Assign no fixed overhead to the cost of the constructed asset, or (2) assign a portion of all overhead to the construction process. Companies use the second method extensively.

4 Describe the accounting problems associated with interest capitalization. Only actual interest (with modifications) should be capitalized. The rationale for this approach is that during construction, the asset is not generating revenue and therefore companies should defer (capitalize) interest cost. Once construction is completed, the asset is ready for its intended use and revenues can be recognized. Any interest cost incurred in purchasing an asset that is ready for its intended use should be expensed.

5 Understand accounting issues related to acquiring and valuing plant assets. The following issues relate to acquiring and valuing plant assets. (1) *Cash discounts:* Whether taken or not, they are generally considered a reduction in the cost of the asset; the real cost of the asset is the cash or cash equivalent price of the asset. (2) *Deferred-payment contracts:* Companies account for assets purchased on long-term credit contracts at the present value of the consideration exchanged between the contracting parties. (3) *Lump-sum purchase:* Allocate the total cost among the various assets on the basis of their relative fair values. (4) *Issuance of stock:* If the stock is actively traded, the market price of the stock issued is a fair indication of the cost of the property acquired. If the market price of the common stock exchanged is not determinable, establish the fair value of the property and use it as the basis for recording the asset and issuance of the common stock. (5) *Exchanges of nonmonetary assets*: The accounting for exchanges of nonmonetary assets depends on whether the exchange has commercial substance. See Illustrations 10-10 (page 551) and 10-20 (page 554) for summaries of how to account for exchanges. (6) *Contributions:* Record at the fair value of the asset received, and credit revenue for the same amount.

6 Describe the accounting treatment for costs subsequent to acquisition. Illustration 10-21 (page 560) summarizes how to account for costs subsequent to acquisition.

7 Describe the accounting treatment for the disposal of property, plant, and equipment. Regardless of the time of disposal, companies take depreciation up to the date of disposition and then remove all accounts related to the retired asset. Gains or losses on the retirement of plant assets are shown in the income statement along with other items that arise from customary business activities. Gains or losses on involuntary conversions, if unusual and infrequent, may be reported as extraordinary items.

DEMONSTRATION PROBLEM

Columbia Company, which manufactures machine tools, had the following transactions related to plant assets in 2014.

Asset A: On June 2, 2014, Columbia purchased a stamping machine at a retail price of $12,000. Columbia paid 6% sales tax on this purchase. Columbia paid a contractor $2,800 for a specially wired platform for the machine, to ensure noninterrupted power to the machine. Columbia estimates the machine will have a 4-year useful life, with a salvage value of $2,000 at the end of 4 years. The machine was put into use on July 1, 2014.

Asset B: On January 1, 2014, Columbia, Inc. signed a fixed-price contract for construction of a warehouse facility at a cost of $1,000,000. It was estimated that the project will be completed by December 31, 2014. On March 1, 2014, to finance the construction cost, Columbia borrowed $1,000,000 payable April 1, 2015, plus interest at the rate of 10%. During 2014, Columbia made deposit and progress payments totaling $750,000 under the contract; the weighted-average amount of accumulated expenditures was $400,000 for the year. The excess-borrowed funds were invested in short-term securities, from which Columbia realized investment revenue of $13,000. The warehouse was completed on December 1, 2014, at which time Columbia made the final payment to the contractor. Columbia estimates the warehouse will have a 25-year useful life, with a salvage value of $20,000.

Columbia uses straight-line depreciation and employs the "half-year" convention in accounting for partial-year depreciation. Columbia's fiscal year ends on December 31.

Instructions

(a) At what amount should Columbia record the acquisition cost of the machine?

(b) What amount of capitalized interest should Columbia include in the cost of the warehouse?

(c) On July 1, 2016, Columbia decides to outsource its stamping operation to Medek, Inc. As part of this plan, Columbia sells the machine (and the platform) to Medek, Inc. for $7,000. What is the impact of this disposal on Columbia's 2016 income before taxes?

Solution

(a) Historical cost is measured by the cash or cash equivalent price of obtaining the asset and bringing it to the location and condition for its intended use. For Columbia, this is:

Price	$12,000
Tax ($12,000 × .06)	720
Platform	2,800
Total	$15,520

(b) $40,000 ($400,000 × .10)—Weighted-Average Accumulated Expenditures × Interest Rate = Avoidable Interest

Since Columbia has outstanding debt incurred specifically for the construction project, in an amount greater than the weighted-average accumulated expenditures of $400,000, the interest rate of 10% is used for capitalization purposes. Capitalization stops upon completion of the project at December 31, 2014. Therefore, the avoidable interest is $40,000, which is less than the actual interest. The investment revenue of $13,000 is irrelevant to the question addressed in this problem because such interest earned on the unexpended portion of the loan is not to be offset against the amount eligible for capitalization.

(c) The income effect is a gain or loss, determined by comparing the book value of the asset to the disposal value:

Cost	$15,520
Less: Accumulated depreciation ($1,690 + $3,380 + $1,690)	6,760*
Book value of machine and platform	8,760
Less: Cash received for machine and platform	7,000
Loss before income taxes	$ 1,760

*Depreciable base: $15,520 − $2,000 = $13,520. Depreciation expense: $13,520 ÷ 4 = $3,380 per year.

2014: ½ year ($3,380 × .50)	$1,690
2015: full year	3,380
2016: ½ year	1,690
Total	$6,760

FASB CODIFICATION

FASB Codification References

[1] FASB ASC 360-10-35-43. [Predecessor literature: "Accounting for the Impairment or Disposal of Long-lived Assets," *Statement of Financial Accounting Standards No. 144* (Norwalk, Conn.: FASB, 2001), par. 34.]

[2] FASB ASC 835-20-05. [Predecessor literature: "Capitalization of Interest Cost," *Statement of Financial Accounting Standards No. 34* (Stamford, Conn.: FASB, 1979).]

[3] FASB ASC 835-20-15-4. [Predecessor literature: "Determining Materiality for Capitalization of Interest Cost," *Statement of Financial Accounting Standards No. 42* (Stamford, Conn.: FASB, 1980), par. 10.]

[4] FASB ASC 820-10-35. [Predecessor literature: "(Predecessor literature: "Fair Value Measurement," *Statement of Financial Accounting Standards No. 157* (Norwalk, Conn.: FASB, September 2006), paras. 13–18.]

[5] FASB ASC 845-10-30. [Predecessor literature: "Accounting for Nonmonetary Transactions," *Opinions of the Accounting Principles Board No. 29* (New York: AICPA, 1973), par. 18, and "Exchanges of Nonmonetary Assets, an Amendment of *APB Opinion No. 29*," *Statement of Financial Accounting Standards No. 153* (Norwalk, Conn.: FASB, 2004).]

[6] FASB ASC 845-10-25-6. [Predecessor literature: "Interpretations of *APB Opinion No. 29*," EITF Abstracts No. 01-02 (Norwalk, Conn.: FASB, 2002).]

[7] FASB ASC 845-10-50-1. [Predecessor literature: "Accounting for Nonmonetary Transactions," *Opinions of the Accounting Principles Board No. 29* (New York: AICPA, 1973), par. 28, and "Exchanges of Nonmonetary Assets, an Amendment of *APB Opinion No. 29*," *Statement of Financial Accounting Standards No. 153* (Norwalk, Conn.: FASB, 2004).]

[8] FASB ASC 958-605-25-2. [Predecessor literature: "Accounting for Contributions Received and Contributions Made," *Statement of Financial Accounting Standards No. 116* (Norwalk, Conn.: FASB, 1993).]

[9] FASB ASC 845-10-30. [Predecessor literature: "Accounting for Nonmonetary Transactions," *Opinions of the Accounting Principles Board No. 29* (New York: AICPA, 1973), par. 18, and "Exchanges of Nonmonetary Assets, an Amendment of *APB Opinion No. 29*," *Statement of Financial Accounting Standards No. 153* (Norwalk, Conn.: FASB, 2004).]

[10] FASB ASC 360-10-25-5. [Predecessor literature: "Accounting for Planned Major Maintenance Activities," FASB Staff Position AUG-AIR-1 (Norwalk, Conn.: FASB, September 2006), par. 5.]

[11] FASB ASC 605-40-25-2. [Predecessor literature: "Accounting for Involuntary Conversions of Nonmonetary Assets to Monetary Assets," *FASB Interpretation No. 30* (Stamford, Conn.: FASB, 1979), summary paragraph.]

Exercises

If your school has a subscription to the FASB Codification, go to *http://aaahq.org/asclogin.cfm* to log in and prepare responses to the following. Provide Codification references for your responses.

CE10-1 Access the glossary ("Master Glossary") to answer the following.

(a) What does it mean to "capitalize" an item?
(b) What is the definition of a nonmonetary asset?

(c) What is a nonreciprocal transfer?

(d) What is the definition of "contribution"?

CE10-2 Herb Scholl, the owner of Scholl's Company, wonders whether interest costs associated with developing land can ever be capitalized. What does the Codification say on this matter?

CE10-3 What guidance does the Codification provide on the accrual of costs associated with planned major maintenance activities?

CE10-4 Briefly describe how the purchases and sales of inventory with the same counterparty are similar to the accounting for other nonmonetary exchanges.

An additional Codification case can be found in the Using Your Judgment section, on page 586.

Be sure to check the book's companion website for a Review and Analysis Exercise, with solution.

WileyPLUS **Brief Exercises, Exercises, Problems, and many more learning and assessment tools and resources are available for practice in WileyPLUS.**

QUESTIONS

1. What are the major characteristics of plant assets?

2. Mickelson Inc. owns land that it purchased on January 1, 2000, for $450,000. At December 31, 2014, its current value is $770,000 as determined by appraisal. At what amount should Mickelson report this asset on its December 31, 2014, balance sheet? Explain.

3. Name the items, in addition to the amount paid to the former owner or contractor, that may properly be included as part of the acquisition cost of the following plant assets.

   (a) Land.

   (b) Machinery and equipment.

   (c) Buildings.

4. Indicate where the following items would be shown on a balance sheet.

   (a) A lien that was attached to the land when purchased.

   (b) Landscaping costs.

   (c) Attorney's fees and recording fees related to purchasing land.

   (d) Variable overhead related to construction of machinery.

   (e) A parking lot servicing employees in the building.

   (f) Cost of temporary building for workers during construction of building.

   (g) Interest expense on bonds payable incurred during construction of a building.

   (h) Assessments for sidewalks that are maintained by the city.

   (i) The cost of demolishing an old building that was on the land when purchased.

5. Two positions have normally been taken with respect to the recording of fixed manufacturing overhead as an element of the cost of plant assets constructed by a company for its own use:

   (a) It should be excluded completely.

   (b) It should be included at the same rate as is charged to normal operations.

   What are the circumstances or rationale that support or deny the application of these methods?

6. The Buildings account of Postera Inc. includes the following items that were used in determining the basis for depreciating the cost of a building.

   (a) Organization and promotion expenses.

   (b) Architect's fees.

   (c) Interest and taxes during construction.

   (d) Interest revenue on investments held to fund construction of a building.

   Do you agree with these charges? If not, how would you deal with each of the items above in the corporation's books and in its annual financial statements?

7. Burke Company has purchased two tracts of land. One tract will be the site of its new manufacturing plant, while the other is being purchased with the hope that it will be sold in the next year at a profit. How should these two tracts of land be reported in the balance sheet?

8. One financial accounting issue encountered when a company constructs its own plant is whether the interest cost on funds borrowed to finance construction should be capitalized and then amortized over the life of the assets constructed. What is the justification for capitalizing such interest?

9. Provide examples of assets that do not qualify for interest capitalization.

10. What interest rates should be used in determining the amount of interest to be capitalized? How should the amount of interest to be capitalized be determined?

11. How should the amount of interest capitalized be disclosed in the notes to the financial statements? How should interest revenue from temporarily invested excess funds borrowed to finance the construction of assets be accounted for?

12. Discuss the basic accounting problem that arises in handling each of the following situations.

    (a) Assets purchased by issuance of common stock.

    (b) Acquisition of plant assets by gift or donation.

    (c) Purchase of a plant asset subject to a cash discount.

    (d) Assets purchased on a long-term credit basis.

    (e) A group of assets acquired for a lump sum.

    (f) An asset traded in or exchanged for another asset.

13. Magilke Industries acquired equipment this year to be used in its operations. The equipment was delivered by the suppliers, installed by Magilke, and placed into operation. Some of it was purchased for cash with discounts available for prompt payment. Some of it was purchased under long-term payment plans for which the interest charges approximated prevailing rates. What costs should Magilke capitalize for the new equipment purchased this year? Explain.

14. Schwartzkopf Co. purchased for $2,200,000 property that included both land and a building to be used in operations. The seller's book value was $300,000 for the land and $900,000 for the building. By appraisal, the fair value was estimated to be $500,000 for the land and $2,000,000 for the building. At what amount should Schwartzkopf report the land and the building at the end of the year?

15. Pueblo Co. acquires machinery by paying $10,000 cash and signing a $5,000, 2-year, zero-interest-bearing note payable. The note has a present value of $4,208, and Pueblo purchased a similar machine last month for $13,500. At what cost should the new equipment be recorded?

16. Stan Ott is evaluating two recent transactions involving exchanges of equipment. In one case, the exchange has commercial substance. In the second situation, the exchange lacks commercial substance. Explain to Stan the differences in accounting for these two situations.

17. Crowe Company purchased a heavy-duty truck on July 1, 2011, for $30,000. It was estimated that it would have a useful life of 10 years and then would have a trade-in value of $6,000. The company uses the straight-line method. It was traded on August 1, 2015, for a similar truck costing $42,000; $16,000 was allowed as trade-in value (also fair value) on the old truck and $26,000 was paid in cash. A comparison of expected cash flows for the trucks indicates the exchange lacks commercial substance. What is the entry to record the trade-in?

18. Once equipment has been installed and placed in operation, subsequent expenditures relating to this equipment are frequently thought of as repairs or general maintenance and, hence, chargeable to operations in the period in which the expenditure is made. Actually, determination of whether such an expenditure should be charged to operations or capitalized involves a much more careful analysis of the character of the expenditure. What are the factors that should be considered in making such a decision? Discuss fully.

19. What accounting treatment is normally given to the following items in accounting for plant assets?

    (a) Additions.

    (b) Major repairs.

    (c) Improvements and replacements.

20. New machinery, which replaced a number of employees, was installed and put in operation in the last month of the fiscal year. The employees had been dismissed after payment of an extra month's wages, and this amount was added to the cost of the machinery. Discuss the propriety of the charge. If it was improper, describe the proper treatment.

21. To what extent do you consider the following items to be proper costs of the fixed asset? Give reasons for your opinions.

    (a) Overhead of a business that builds its own equipment.

    (b) Cash discounts on purchases of equipment.

    (c) Interest paid during construction of a building.

    (d) Cost of a safety device installed on a machine.

    (e) Freight on equipment returned before installation, for replacement by other equipment of greater capacity.

    (f) Cost of moving machinery to a new location.

    (g) Cost of plywood partitions erected as part of the remodeling of the office.

    (h) Replastering of a section of the building.

    (i) Cost of a new motor for one of the trucks.

22. Neville Enterprises has a number of fully depreciated assets that are still being used in the main operations of the business. Because the assets are fully depreciated, the president of the company decides not to show them on the balance sheet or disclose this information in the notes. Evaluate this procedure.

23. What are the general rules for how gains or losses on retirement of plant assets should be reported in income?

BRIEF EXERCISES

2 **BE10-1** Previn Brothers Inc. purchased land at a price of $27,000. Closing costs were $1,400. An old building was removed at a cost of $10,200. What amount should be recorded as the cost of the land?

4 **BE10-2** Hanson Company is constructing a building. Construction began on February 1 and was completed on December 31. Expenditures were $1,800,000 on March 1, $1,200,000 on June 1, and $3,000,000 on December 31. Compute Hanson's weighted-average accumulated expenditures for interest capitalization purposes.

4 **BE10-3** Hanson Company (see BE10-2) borrowed $1,000,000 on March 1 on a 5-year, 12% note to help finance construction of the building. In addition, the company had outstanding all year a 10%, 5-year, $2,000,000 note payable and an 11%, 4-year, $3,500,000 note payable. Compute the weighted-average interest rate used for interest capitalization purposes.

4 **BE10-4** Use the information for Hanson Company from BE10-2 and BE10-3. Compute avoidable interest for Hanson Company.

5 **BE10-5** Garcia Corporation purchased a truck by issuing an $80,000, 4-year, zero-interest-bearing note to Equinox Inc. The market rate of interest for obligations of this nature is 10%. Prepare the journal entry to record the purchase of this truck.

5 **BE10-6** Mohave Inc. purchased land, building, and equipment from Laguna Corporation for a cash payment of $315,000. The estimated fair values of the assets are land $60,000, building $220,000, and equipment $80,000. At what amounts should each of the three assets be recorded?

5 **BE10-7** Fielder Company obtained land by issuing 2,000 shares of its $10 par value common stock. The land was recently appraised at $85,000. The common stock is actively traded at $40 per share. Prepare the journal entry to record the acquisition of the land.

5 **BE10-8** Navajo Corporation traded a used truck (cost $20,000, accumulated depreciation $18,000) for a small computer worth $3,300. Navajo also paid $500 in the transaction. Prepare the journal entry to record the exchange. (The exchange has commercial substance.)

5 **BE10-9** Use the information for Navajo Corporation from BE10-8. Prepare the journal entry to record the exchange, assuming the exchange lacks commercial substance.

5 **BE10-10** Mehta Company traded a used welding machine (cost $9,000, accumulated depreciation $3,000) for office equipment with an estimated fair value of $5,000. Mehta also paid $3,000 cash in the transaction. Prepare the journal entry to record the exchange. (The exchange has commercial substance.)

5 **BE10-11** Cheng Company traded a used truck for a new truck. The used truck cost $30,000 and has accumulated depreciation of $27,000. The new truck is worth $37,000. Cheng also made a cash payment of $36,000. Prepare Cheng's entry to record the exchange. (The exchange lacks commercial substance.)

5 **BE10-12** Slaton Corporation traded a used truck for a new truck. The used truck cost $20,000 and has accumulated depreciation of $17,000. The new truck is worth $35,000. Slaton also made a cash payment of $33,000. Prepare Slaton's entry to record the exchange. (The exchange has commercial substance.)

6 **BE10-13** Indicate which of the following costs should be expensed when incurred.

(a) $13,000 paid to rearrange and reinstall machinery.
(b) $200,000 paid for addition to building.
(c) $200 paid for tune-up and oil change on delivery truck.
(d) $7,000 paid to replace a wooden floor with a concrete floor.
(e) $2,000 paid for a major overhaul on a truck, which extends the useful life.

7 **BE10-14** Ottawa Corporation owns machinery that cost $20,000 when purchased on July 1, 2011. Depreciation has been recorded at a rate of $2,400 per year, resulting in a balance in accumulated depreciation of $8,400 at December 31, 2014. The machinery is sold on September 1, 2015, for $10,500. Prepare journal entries to (a) update depreciation for 2015 and (b) record the sale.

7 **BE10-15** Use the information presented for Ottawa Corporation in BE10-14, but assume the machinery is sold for $5,200 instead of $10,500. Prepare journal entries to (a) update depreciation for 2015 and (b) record the sale.

EXERCISES

2 **E10-1 (Acquisition Costs of Realty)** The following expenditures and receipts are related to land, land improvements, and buildings acquired for use in a business enterprise. The receipts are enclosed in parentheses.

(a)	Money borrowed to pay building contractor (signed a note)	$(275,000)
(b)	Payment for construction from note proceeds	275,000
(c)	Cost of land fill and clearing	8,000
(d)	Delinquent real estate taxes on property assumed by purchaser	7,000
(e)	Premium on 6-month insurance policy during construction	6,000
(f)	Refund of 1-month insurance premium because construction completed early	(1,000)
(g)	Architect's fee on building	22,000
(h)	Cost of real estate purchased as a plant site (land $200,000 and building $50,000)	250,000
(i)	Commission fee paid to real estate agency	9,000
(j)	Installation of fences around property	4,000
(k)	Cost of razing and removing building	11,000
(l)	Proceeds from salvage of demolished building	(5,000)
(m)	Interest paid during construction on money borrowed for construction	13,000
(n)	Cost of parking lots and driveways	19,000
(o)	Cost of trees and shrubbery planted (permanent in nature)	14,000
(p)	Excavation costs for new building	3,000

Instructions

Identify each item by letter and list the items in columnar form, using the headings shown below. All receipt amounts should be reported in parentheses. For any amounts entered in the Other Accounts column, also indicate the account title.

Item	Land	Land Improvements	Buildings	Other Accounts

2 **E10-2 (Acquisition Costs of Realty)** Martin Buber Co. purchased land as a factory site for $400,000. The process of tearing down two old buildings on the site and constructing the factory required 6 months.

XLS

The company paid $42,000 to raze the old buildings and sold salvaged lumber and brick for $6,300. Legal fees of $1,850 were paid for title investigation and drawing the purchase contract. Martin Buber paid $2,200 to an engineering firm for a land survey, and $68,000 for drawing the factory plans. The land survey had to be made before definitive plans could be drawn. Title insurance on the property cost $1,500, and a liability insurance premium paid during construction was $900. The contractor's charge for construction was $2,740,000. The company paid the contractor in two installments: $1,200,000 at the end of 3 months and $1,540,000 upon completion. Interest costs of $170,000 were incurred to finance the construction.

Instructions

Determine the cost of the land and the cost of the building as they should be recorded on the books of Martin Buber Co. Assume that the land survey was for the building.

2 **E10-3 (Acquisition Costs of Trucks)** Kelly Clarkson Corporation operates a retail computer store. To improve delivery services to customers, the company purchases four new trucks on April 1, 2014. The terms of acquisition for each truck are described below.

XLS

1. Truck #1 has a list price of $15,000 and is acquired for a cash payment of $13,900.
2. Truck #2 has a list price of $16,000 and is acquired for a down payment of $2,000 cash and a zero-interest-bearing note with a face amount of $14,000. The note is due April 1, 2015. Clarkson would normally have to pay interest at a rate of 10% for such a borrowing, and the dealership has an incremental borrowing rate of 8%.
3. Truck #3 has a list price of $16,000. It is acquired in exchange for a computer system that Clarkson carries in inventory. The computer system cost $12,000 and is normally sold by Clarkson for $15,200. Clarkson uses a perpetual inventory system.
4. Truck #4 has a list price of $14,000. It is acquired in exchange for 1,000 shares of common stock in Clarkson Corporation. The stock has a par value per share of $10 and a market price of $13 per share.

Instructions

Prepare the appropriate journal entries for the above transactions for Clarkson Corporation.

2 3 **E10-4 (Purchase and Self-Constructed Cost of Assets)** Worf Co. both purchases and constructs various equipment it uses in its operations. The following items for two different types of equipment were recorded in random order during the calendar year 2014.

Purchase	
Cash paid for equipment, including sales tax of $5,000	$105,000
Freight and insurance cost while in transit	2,000
Cost of moving equipment into place at factory	3,100
Wage cost for technicians to test equipment	4,000
Insurance premium paid during first year of operation on this equipment	1,500
Special plumbing fixtures required for new equipment	8,000
Repair cost incurred in first year of operations related to this equipment	1,300
Construction	
Material and purchased parts (gross cost $200,000; failed to take 2% cash discount)	$200,000
Imputed interest on funds used during construction (stock financing)	14,000
Labor costs	190,000
Allocated overhead costs (fixed—$20,000; variable—$30,000)	50,000
Profit on self-construction	30,000
Cost of installing equipment	4,400

Instructions

Compute the total cost for each of these two pieces of equipment. If an item is not capitalized as a cost of the equipment, indicate how it should be reported.

2 3 4 **E10-5 (Treatment of Various Costs)** Ben Sisko Supply Company, a newly formed corporation, incurred the following expenditures related to Land, to Buildings, and to Machinery and Equipment.

Abstract company's fee for title search		$ 520
Architect's fees		3,170
Cash paid for land and dilapidated building thereon		87,000
Removal of old building	$20,000	
Less: Salvage	5,500	14,500
Interest on short-term loans during construction		7,400
Excavation before construction for basement		19,000
Machinery purchased (subject to 2% cash discount, which was not taken)		55,000
Freight on machinery purchased		1,340
Storage charges on machinery, necessitated by noncompletion of building when machinery was delivered		2,180
New building constructed (building construction took 6 months from date of purchase of land and old building)		485,000
Assessment by city for drainage project		1,600
Hauling charges for delivery of machinery from storage to new building		620
Installation of machinery		2,000
Trees, shrubs, and other landscaping after completion of building (permanent in nature)		5,400

Instructions

Determine the amounts that should be debited to Land, to Buildings, and to Machinery and Equipment. Assume the benefits of capitalizing interest during construction exceed the cost of implementation. Indicate how any costs not debited to these accounts should be recorded.

3 4 **E10-6 (Correction of Improper Cost Entries)** Plant acquisitions for selected companies are as follows.

1. Belanna Industries Inc. acquired land, buildings, and equipment from a bankrupt company, Torres Co., for a lump-sum price of $700,000. At the time of purchase, Torres's assets had the following book and appraisal values.

	Book Values	Appraisal Values
Land	$200,000	$150,000
Buildings	250,000	350,000
Equipment	300,000	300,000

To be conservative, the company decided to take the lower of the two values for each asset acquired. The following entry was made.

Land	150,000	
Buildings	250,000	
Equipment	300,000	
Cash		700,000

2. Harry Enterprises purchased store equipment by making a $2,000 cash down payment and signing a 1-year, $23,000, 10% note payable. The purchase was recorded as follows.

Equipment	27,300	
Cash		2,000
Notes Payable		23,000
Interest Payable		2,300

3. Kim Company purchased office equipment for $20,000, terms 2/10, n/30. Because the company intended to take the discount, it made no entry until it paid for the acquisition. The entry was:

Equipment	20,000	
Cash		19,600
Purchase Discounts		400

4. Kaisson Inc. recently received at zero cost land from the Village of Cardassia as an inducement to locate its business in the Village. The appraised value of the land is $27,000. The company made no entry to record the land because it had no cost basis.
5. Zimmerman Company built a warehouse for $600,000. It could have purchased the building for $740,000. The controller made the following entry.

Buildings	740,000	
Cash		600,000
Profit on Construction		140,000

Instructions

Prepare the entry that should have been made at the date of each acquisition.

4 **E10-7 (Capitalization of Interest)** Harrisburg Furniture Company started construction of a combination office and warehouse building for its own use at an estimated cost of $5,000,000 on January 1, 2014. Harrisburg expected to complete the building by December 31, 2014. Harrisburg has the following debt obligations outstanding during the construction period.

Construction loan—12% interest, payable semiannually, issued December 31, 2013	$2,000,000
Short-term loan—10% interest, payable monthly, and principal payable at maturity on May 30, 2015	1,400,000
Long-term loan—11% interest, payable on January 1 of each year. Principal payable on January 1, 2018	1,000,000

Instructions

(Carry all computations to two decimal places.)

(a) Assume that Harrisburg completed the office and warehouse building on December 31, 2014, as planned at a total cost of $5,200,000, and the weighted-average amount of accumulated expenditures was $3,600,000. Compute the avoidable interest on this project.

(b) Compute the depreciation expense for the year ended December 31, 2015. Harrisburg elected to depreciate the building on a straight-line basis and determined that the asset has a useful life of 30 years and a salvage value of $300,000.

4 **E10-8 (Capitalization of Interest)** On December 31, 2013, Main Inc. borrowed $3,000,000 at 12% payable annually to finance the construction of a new building. In 2014, the company made the following expenditures related to this building: March 1, $360,000; June 1, $600,000; July 1, $1,500,000; December 1, $1,500,000. The building was completed in February 2015. Additional information is provided as follows.

1. Other debt outstanding	
10-year, 13% bond, December 31, 2007, interest payable annually	$4,000,000
6-year, 10% note, dated December 31, 2011, interest payable annually	$1,600,000
2. March 1, 2014, expenditure included land costs of $150,000	
3. Interest revenue earned in 2014	$49,000

Instructions

(a) Determine the amount of interest to be capitalized in 2014 in relation to the construction of the building.

(b) Prepare the journal entry to record the capitalization of interest and the recognition of interest expense, if any, at December 31, 2014.

4 **E10-9 (Capitalization of Interest)** On July 31, 2014, Amsterdam Company engaged Minsk Tooling Company to construct a special-purpose piece of factory machinery. Construction was begun immediately

and was completed on November 1, 2014. To help finance construction, on July 31 Amsterdam issued a $300,000, 3-year, 12% note payable at Netherlands National Bank, on which interest is payable each July 31. $200,000 of the proceeds of the note was paid to Minsk on July 31. The remainder of the proceeds was temporarily invested in short-term marketable securities (trading securities) at 10% until November 1. On November 1, Amsterdam made a final $100,000 payment to Minsk. Other than the note to Netherlands, Amsterdam's only outstanding liability at December 31, 2014, is a $30,000, 8%, 6-year note payable, dated January 1, 2011, on which interest is payable each December 31.

Instructions

(a) Calculate the interest revenue, weighted-average accumulated expenditures, avoidable interest, and total interest cost to be capitalized during 2014. (Round all computations to the nearest dollar.)

(b) Prepare the journal entries needed on the books of Amsterdam Company at each of the following dates.

(1) July 31, 2014.
(2) November 1, 2014.
(3) December 31, 2014.

4 **E10-10 (Capitalization of Interest)** The following three situations involve the capitalization of interest.

Situation I: On January 1, 2014, Oksana Baiul, Inc. signed a fixed-price contract to have Builder Associates construct a major plant facility at a cost of $4,000,000. It was estimated that it would take 3 years to complete the project. Also on January 1, 2014, to finance the construction cost, Oksana Baiul borrowed $4,000,000 payable in 10 annual installments of $400,000, plus interest at the rate of 10%. During 2014, Oksana Baiul made deposit and progress payments totaling $1,500,000 under the contract; the weighted-average amount of accumulated expenditures was $800,000 for the year. The excess borrowed funds were invested in short-term securities, from which Oksana Baiul realized investment income of $250,000.

Instructions

What amount should Oksana Baiul report as capitalized interest at December 31, 2014?

Situation II: During 2014, Midori Ito Corporation constructed and manufactured certain assets and incurred the following interest costs in connection with those activities.

	Interest Costs Incurred
Warehouse constructed for Ito's own use	$30,000
Special-order machine for sale to unrelated customer, produced according to customer's specifications	9,000
Inventories routinely manufactured, produced on a repetitive basis	8,000

All of these assets required an extended period of time for completion.

Instructions

Assuming the effect of interest capitalization is material, what is the total amount of interest costs to be capitalized?

Situation III: Peggy Fleming, Inc. has a fiscal year ending April 30. On May 1, 2014, Peggy Fleming borrowed $10,000,000 at 11% to finance construction of its own building. Repayments of the loan are to commence the month following completion of the building. During the year ended April 30, 2015, expenditures for the partially completed structure totaled $7,000,000. These expenditures were incurred evenly throughout the year. Interest earned on the unexpended portion of the loan amounted to $650,000 for the year.

Instructions

How much should be shown as capitalized interest on Peggy Fleming's financial statements at April 30, 2015?

(CPA adapted)

2 3 5 **E10-11 (Entries for Equipment Acquisitions)** Jane Geddes Engineering Corporation purchased conveyor equipment with a list price of $10,000. Presented below are three independent cases related to the equipment. (Round to the nearest dollar.)

(a) Geddes paid cash for the equipment 8 days after the purchase. The vendor's credit terms are 2/10, n/30. Assume that equipment purchases are initially recorded gross.

(b) Geddes traded in equipment with a book value of $2,000 (initial cost $8,000), and paid $9,500 in cash one month after the purchase. The old equipment could have been sold for $400 at the date of trade. (The exchange has commercial substance.)

(c) Geddes gave the vendor a $10,800 zero-interest-bearing note for the equipment on the date of purchase. The note was due in one year and was paid on time. Assume that the effective-interest rate in the market was 9%.

Instructions

Prepare the general journal entries required to record the acquisition and payment in each of the independent cases above.

2 3 5 **E10-12 (Entries for Asset Acquisition, Including Self-Construction)** Below are transactions related to Duffner Company.

(a) The City of Pebble Beach gives the company 5 acres of land as a plant site. The fair value of this land is determined to be $81,000.

(b) 13,000 shares of common stock with a par value of $50 per share are issued in exchange for land and buildings. The property has been appraised at a fair value of $810,000, of which $180,000 has been allocated to land and $630,000 to buildings. The stock of Duffner Company is not listed on any exchange, but a block of 100 shares was sold by a stockholder 12 months ago at $65 per share, and a block of 200 shares was sold by another stockholder 18 months ago at $58 per share.

(c) No entry has been made to remove from the accounts for Materials, Direct Labor, and Overhead the amounts properly chargeable to plant asset accounts for machinery constructed during the year. The following information is given relative to costs of the machinery constructed.

Materials used	$12,500
Factory supplies used	900
Direct labor incurred	15,000
Additional overhead (over regular) caused by construction of machinery, excluding factory supplies used	2,700
Fixed overhead rate applied to regular manufacturing operations	60% of direct labor cost
Cost of similar machinery if it had been purchased from outside suppliers	44,000

Instructions

Prepare journal entries on the books of Duffner Company to record these transactions.

2 5 **E10-13 (Entries for Acquisition of Assets)** Presented below is information related to Zonker Company.

1. On July 6, Zonker Company acquired the plant assets of Doonesbury Company, which had discontinued operations. The appraised value of the property is:

Land	$ 400,000
Buildings	1,200,000
Equipment	800,000
Total	$2,400,000

Zonker Company gave 12,500 shares of its $100 par value common stock in exchange. The stock had a market price of $168 per share on the date of the purchase of the property.

2. Zonker Company expended the following amounts in cash between July 6 and December 15, the date when it first occupied the building.

Repairs to building	$105,000
Construction of bases for equipment to be installed later	135,000
Driveways and parking lots	122,000
Remodeling of office space in building, including new partitions and walls	161,000
Special assessment by city on land	18,000

3. On December 20, the company paid cash for equipment, $260,000, subject to a 2% cash discount, and freight on equipment of $10,500.

Instructions

Prepare entries on the books of Zonker Company for these transactions.

5 **E10-14 (Purchase of Equipment with Zero-Interest-Bearing Debt)** Chippewas Inc. has decided to purchase equipment from Central Michigan Industries on January 2, 2014, to expand its production capacity to meet customers' demand for its product. Chippewas issues an $800,000, 5-year, zero-interest-bearing note to Central Michigan for the new equipment when the prevailing market rate of interest for obligations of this nature is 12%. The company will pay off the note in five $160,000 installments due at the end of each year over the life of the note.

Instructions

(Round to nearest dollar in all computations.)

(a) Prepare the journal entry(ies) at the date of purchase.

(b) Prepare the journal entry(ies) at the end of the first year to record the payment and interest, assuming that the company employs the effective-interest method.

(c) Prepare the journal entry(ies) at the end of the second year to record the payment and interest.
(d) Assuming that the equipment had a 10-year life and no salvage value, prepare the journal entry necessary to record depreciation in the first year. (Straight-line depreciation is employed.)

5 **E10-15 (Purchase of Computer with Zero-Interest-Bearing Debt)** Cardinals Corporation purchased a computer on December 31, 2013, for $105,000, paying $30,000 down and agreeing to pay the balance in five equal installments of $15,000 payable each December 31 beginning in 2014. An assumed interest rate of 10% is implicit in the purchase price.

Instructions

(Round to two decimal places.)

(a) Prepare the journal entry(ies) at the date of purchase.
(b) Prepare the journal entry(ies) at December 31, 2014, to record the payment and interest (effective-interest method employed).
(c) Prepare the journal entry(ies) at December 31, 2015, to record the payment and interest (effective-interest method employed).

5 **E10-16 (Asset Acquisition)** Hayes Industries purchased the following assets and constructed a building as well. All this was done during the current year.

Assets 1 and 2: These assets were purchased as a lump sum for $100,000 cash. The following information was gathered.

Description	Initial Cost on Seller's Books	Depreciation to Date on Seller's Books	Book Value on Seller's Books	Appraised Value
Machinery	$100,000	$50,000	$50,000	$90,000
Equipment	60,000	10,000	50,000	30,000

Asset 3: This machine was acquired by making a $10,000 down payment and issuing a $30,000, 2-year, zero-interest-bearing note. The note is to be paid off in two $15,000 installments made at the end of the first and second years. It was estimated that the asset could have been purchased outright for $35,900.

Asset 4: This machinery was acquired by trading in used machinery. (The exchange lacks commercial substance.) Facts concerning the trade-in are as follows.

Cost of machinery traded	$100,000
Accumulated depreciation to date of sale	40,000
Fair value of machinery traded	80,000
Cash received	10,000
Fair value of machinery acquired	70,000

Asset 5: Equipment was acquired by issuing 100 shares of $8 par value common stock. The stock had a market price of $11 per share.

Construction of Building: A building was constructed on land purchased last year at a cost of $150,000. Construction began on February 1 and was completed on November 1. The payments to the contractor were as follows.

Date	Payment
2/1	$120,000
6/1	360,000
9/1	480,000
11/1	100,000

To finance construction of the building, a $600,000, 12% construction loan was taken out on February 1. The loan was repaid on November 1. The firm had $200,000 of other outstanding debt during the year at a borrowing rate of 8%.

Instructions

Record the acquisition of each of these assets.

5 **E10-17 (Nonmonetary Exchange)** Busytown Corporation, which manufactures shoes, hired a recent college graduate to work in its accounting department. On the first day of work, the accountant was assigned to total a batch of invoices with the use of an adding machine. Before long, the accountant, who had never before seen such a machine, managed to break the machine. Busytown Corporation gave the machine plus $340 to Dick Tracy Business Machine Company (dealer) in exchange for a new machine. Assume the following information about the machines.

	Busytown Corp. (Old Machine)	Dick Tracy Co. (New Machine)
Machine cost	$290	$270
Accumulated depreciation	140	–0–
Fair value	85	425

Instructions

For each company, prepare the necessary journal entry to record the exchange. (The exchange has commercial substance.)

5 **E10-18 (Nonmonetary Exchange)** Cannondale Company purchased an electric wax melter on April 30, 2014, by trading in its old gas model and paying the balance in cash. The following data relate to the purchase.

List price of new melter	$15,800
Cash paid	10,000
Cost of old melter (5-year life, $700 salvage value)	11,200
Accumulated depreciation—old melter (straight-line)	6,300
Secondhand fair value of old melter	5,200

Instructions

Prepare the journal entry(ies) necessary to record this exchange, assuming that the exchange **(a)** has commercial substance, and **(b)** lacks commercial substance. Cannondale's fiscal year ends on December 31, and depreciation has been recorded through December 31, 2013.

5 **E10-19 (Nonmonetary Exchange)** Carlos Arruza Company exchanged equipment used in its manufacturing operations plus $3,000 in cash for similar equipment used in the operations of Tony LoBianco Company. The following information pertains to the exchange.

	Carlos Arruza Co.	Tony LoBianco Co.
Equipment (cost)	$28,000	$28,000
Accumulated depreciation	19,000	10,000
Fair value of equipment	12,500	15,500
Cash given up	3,000	

Instructions

(a) Prepare the journal entries to record the exchange on the books of both companies. Assume that the exchange lacks commercial substance.

(b) Prepare the journal entries to record the exchange on the books of both companies. Assume that the exchange has commercial substance.

5 **E10-20 (Nonmonetary Exchange)** Dana Ashbrook Inc. has negotiated the purchase of a new piece of automatic equipment at a price of $8,000 plus trade-in, f.o.b. factory. Dana Ashbrook Inc. paid $8,000 cash and traded in used equipment. The used equipment had originally cost $62,000; it had a book value of $42,000 and a secondhand fair value of $47,800, as indicated by recent transactions involving similar equipment. Freight and installation charges for the new equipment required a cash payment of $1,100.

Instructions

(a) Prepare the general journal entry to record this transaction, assuming that the exchange has commercial substance.

(b) Assuming the same facts as in (a) except that fair value information for the assets exchanged is not determinable, prepare the general journal entry to record this transaction.

6 **E10-21 (Analysis of Subsequent Expenditures)** King Donovan Resources Group has been in its plant facility for 15 years. Although the plant is quite functional, numerous repair costs are incurred to maintain it in sound working order. The company's plant asset book value is currently $800,000, as indicated below.

Original cost	$1,200,000
Accumulated depreciation	400,000
Book value	$ 800,000

During the current year, the following expenditures were made to the plant facility.

(a) Because of increased demands for its product, the company increased its plant capacity by building a new addition at a cost of $270,000.

(b) The entire plant was repainted at a cost of $23,000.

(c) The roof was an asbestos cement slate. For safety purposes, it was removed and replaced with a wood shingle roof at a cost of $61,000. Book value of the old roof was $41,000.

(d) The electrical system was completely updated at a cost of $22,000. The cost of the old electrical system was not known. It is estimated that the useful life of the building will not change as a result of this updating.

(e) A series of major repairs were made at a cost of $47,000, because parts of the wood structure were rotting. The cost of the old wood structure was not known. These extensive repairs are estimated to increase the useful life of the building.

Instructions

Indicate how each of these transactions would be recorded in the accounting records.

6 **E10-22 (Analysis of Subsequent Expenditures)** The following transactions occurred during 2014. Assume that depreciation of 10% per year is charged on all machinery and 5% per year on buildings, on a straight-line basis, with no estimated salvage value. Depreciation is charged for a full year on all fixed assets acquired during the year, and no depreciation is charged on fixed assets disposed of during the year.

Jan. 30	A building that cost $132,000 in 1997 is torn down to make room for a new building. The wrecking contractor was paid $5,100 and was permitted to keep all materials salvaged.
Mar. 10	Machinery that was purchased in 2007 for $16,000 is sold for $2,900 cash, f.o.b. purchaser's plant. Freight of $300 is paid on the sale of this machinery.
Mar. 20	A gear breaks on a machine that cost $9,000 in 2009. The gear is replaced at a cost of $2,000. The replacement does not extend the useful life of the machine but does make the machine more efficient.
May 18	A special base installed for a machine in 2008 when the machine was purchased has to be replaced at a cost of $5,500 because of defective workmanship on the original base. The cost of the machinery was $14,200 in 2008. The cost of the base was $3,500, and this amount was charged to the Machinery account in 2008.
June 23	One of the buildings is repainted at a cost of $6,900. It had not been painted since it was constructed in 2010.

Instructions

(Round to the nearest dollar.)

Prepare general journal entries for the transactions.

6 **E10-23 (Analysis of Subsequent Expenditures)** Plant assets often require expenditures subsequent to acquisition. It is important that they be accounted for properly. Any errors will affect both the balance sheets and income statements for a number of years.

Instructions

For each of the following items, indicate whether the expenditure should be capitalized (C) or expensed (E) in the period incurred.

(a) ________ Improvement.

(b) ________ Replacement of a minor broken part on a machine.

(c) ________ Expenditure that increases the useful life of an existing asset.

(d) ________ Expenditure that increases the efficiency and effectiveness of a productive asset but does not increase its salvage value.

(e) ________ Expenditure that increases the efficiency and effectiveness of a productive asset and increases the asset's salvage value.

(f) ________ Expenditure that increases the quality of the output of the productive asset.

(g) ________ Improvement to a machine that increased its fair market value and its production capacity by 30% without extending the machine's useful life.

(h) ________ Ordinary repairs.

7 **E10-24 (Entries for Disposition of Assets)** On December 31, 2014, Travis Tritt Inc. has a machine with a book value of $940,000. The original cost and related accumulated depreciation at this date are as follows.

Machine	$1,300,000
Less: Accumulated depreciation	360,000
Book value	$ 940,000

Depreciation is computed at $60,000 per year on a straight-line basis.

Instructions

Presented below is a set of independent situations. For each independent situation, indicate the journal entry to be made to record the transaction. Make sure that depreciation entries are made to update the book value of the machine prior to its disposal.

(a) A fire completely destroys the machine on August 31, 2015. An insurance settlement of $430,000 was received for this casualty. Assume the settlement was received immediately.

(b) On April 1, 2015, Tritt sold the machine for $1,040,000 to Dwight Yoakam Company.

(c) On July 31, 2015, the company donated this machine to the Mountain King City Council. The fair value of the machine at the time of the donation was estimated to be $1,100,000.

7 **E10-25 (Disposition of Assets)** On April 1, 2014, Gloria Estefan Company received a condemnation award of $430,000 cash as compensation for the forced sale of the company's land and building, which stood in the path of a new state highway. The land and building cost $60,000 and $280,000, respectively, when they were acquired. At April 1, 2014, the accumulated depreciation relating to the building amounted to $160,000. On August 1, 2014, Estafan purchased a piece of replacement property for cash. The new land cost $90,000, and the new building cost $400,000.

Instructions

Prepare the journal entries to record the transactions on April 1 and August 1, 2014.

EXERCISES SET B

See the book's companion website, at **www.wiley.com/college/kieso**, for an additional set of exercises.

PROBLEMS

2 **P10-1 (Classification of Acquisition and Other Asset Costs)** At December 31, 2013, certain accounts included in the property, plant, and equipment section of Reagan Company's balance sheet had the following balances.

Land	$230,000
Buildings	890,000
Leasehold improvements	660,000
Equipment	875,000

During 2014, the following transactions occurred.

1. Land site number 621 was acquired for $850,000. In addition, to acquire the land Reagan paid a $51,000 commission to a real estate agent. Costs of $35,000 were incurred to clear the land. During the course of clearing the land, timber and gravel were recovered and sold for $13,000.
2. A second tract of land (site number 622) with a building was acquired for $420,000. The closing statement indicated that the land value was $300,000 and the building value was $120,000. Shortly after acquisition, the building was demolished at a cost of $41,000. A new building was constructed for $330,000 plus the following costs.

Excavation fees	$38,000
Architectural design fees	11,000
Building permit fee	2,500
Imputed interest on funds used during construction (stock financing)	8,500

   The building was completed and occupied on September 30, 2014.
3. A third tract of land (site number 623) was acquired for $650,000 and was put on the market for resale.
4. During December 2014, costs of $89,000 were incurred to improve leased office space. The related lease will terminate on December 31, 2016, and is not expected to be renewed. (*Hint:* Leasehold improvements should be handled in the same manner as land improvements.)
5. A group of new machines was purchased under a royalty agreement that provides for payment of royalties based on units of production for the machines. The invoice price of the machines was $87,000, freight costs were $3,300, installation costs were $2,400, and royalty payments for 2014 were $17,500.

Instructions

(a) Prepare a detailed analysis of the changes in each of the following balance sheet accounts for 2014.

Land	Leasehold Improvements
Buildings	Equipment

Disregard the related accumulated depreciation accounts.

(b) List the items in the situation that were not used to determine the answer to (a) above, and indicate where, or if, these items should be included in Reagan's financial statements.

(AICPA adapted)

2 7 **P10-2 (Classification of Acquisition Costs)** Selected accounts included in the property, plant, and equipment section of Lobo Corporation's balance sheet at December 31, 2013, had the following balances.

Land	$ 300,000
Land improvements	140,000
Buildings	1,100,000
Equipment	960,000

During 2014, the following transactions occurred.

1. A tract of land was acquired for $150,000 as a potential future building site.
2. A plant facility consisting of land and building was acquired from Mendota Company in exchange for 20,000 shares of Lobo's common stock. On the acquisition date, Lobo's stock had a closing market price of $37 per share on a national stock exchange. The plant facility was carried on Mendota's books at $110,000 for land and $320,000 for the building at the exchange date. Current appraised values for the land and building, respectively, are $230,000 and $690,000.
3. Items of machinery and equipment were purchased at a total cost of $400,000. Additional costs were incurred as follows.

Freight and unloading	$13,000
Sales taxes	20,000
Installation	26,000

4. Expenditures totaling $95,000 were made for new parking lots, streets, and sidewalks at the corporation's various plant locations. These expenditures had an estimated useful life of 15 years.
5. A machine costing $80,000 on January 1, 2006, was scrapped on June 30, 2014. Double-declining-balance depreciation has been recorded on the basis of a 10-year life.
6. A machine was sold for $20,000 on July 1, 2014. Original cost of the machine was $44,000 on January 1, 2011, and it was depreciated on the straight-line basis over an estimated useful life of 7 years and a salvage value of $2,000.

Instructions

(Round to the nearest dollar.)

(a) Prepare a detailed analysis of the changes in each of the following balance sheet accounts for 2014.

Land	Buildings
Land Improvements	Equipment

(*Hint:* Disregard the related accumulated depreciation accounts.)

(b) List the items in the fact situation that were not used to determine the answer to (a), showing the pertinent amounts and supporting computations in good form for each item. In addition, indicate where, or if, these items should be included in Lobo's financial statements.

(AICPA adapted)

2 3 5 **P10-3 (Classification of Land and Building Costs)** Spitfire Company was incorporated on January 2, 2015, but was unable to begin manufacturing activities until July 1, 2015, because new factory facilities were not completed until that date.

The Land and Buildings account reported the following items during 2015.

January 31	Land and buildings	$160,000
February 28	Cost of removal of building	9,800
May 1	Partial payment of new construction	60,000
May 1	Legal fees paid	3,770
June 1	Second payment on new construction	40,000
June 1	Insurance premium	2,280
June 1	Special tax assessment	4,000
June 30	General expenses	36,300
July 1	Final payment on new construction	30,000
December 31	Asset write-up	53,800
		399,950
December 31	Depreciation—2015 at 1%	(4,000)
December 31, 2015	Account balance	$395,950

The following additional information is to be considered.

1. To acquire land and building, the company paid $80,000 cash and 800 shares of its 8% cumulative preferred stock, par value $100 per share. Fair value of the stock is $117 per share.
2. Cost of removal of old buildings amounted to $9,800, and the demolition company retained all materials of the building.
3. Legal fees covered the following.

Cost of organization	$ 610
Examination of title covering purchase of land	1,300
Legal work in connection with construction contract	1,860
	$3,770

4. Insurance premium covered the building for a 2-year term beginning May 1, 2015.
5. The special tax assessment covered street improvements that are permanent in nature.
6. General expenses covered the following for the period from January 2, 2015, to June 30, 2015.

President's salary	$32,100
Plant superintendent's salary—supervision of new building	4,200
	$36,300

7. Because of a general increase in construction costs after entering into the building contract, the board of directors increased the value of the building $53,800, believing that such an increase was justified to reflect the current market at the time the building was completed. Retained earnings was credited for this amount.
8. Estimated life of building—50 years.
   Depreciation for 2015—1% of asset value (1% of $400,000, or $4,000).

Instructions

(a) Prepare entries to reflect correct land, buildings, and depreciation accounts at December 31, 2015.
(b) Show the proper presentation of land, buildings, and depreciation on the balance sheet at December 31, 2015.

(AICPA adapted)

2 5 **P10-4 (Dispositions, Including Condemnation, Demolition, and Trade-In)** Presented below is a schedule
7 of property dispositions for Hollerith Co.

Schedule of Property Dispositions

	Cost	Accumulated Depreciation	Cash Proceeds	Fair Value	Nature of Disposition
Land	$40,000	—	$31,000	$31,000	Condemnation
Building	15,000	—	3,600	—	Demolition
Warehouse	70,000	$16,000	74,000	74,000	Destruction by fire
Machine	8,000	2,800	900	7,200	Trade-in
Furniture	10,000	7,850	—	3,100	Contribution
Automobile	9,000	3,460	2,960	2,960	Sale

The following additional information is available.

Land: On February 15, a condemnation award was received as consideration for unimproved land held primarily as an investment, and on March 31, another parcel of unimproved land to be held as an investment was purchased at a cost of $35,000.

Building: On April 2, land and building were purchased at a total cost of $75,000, of which 20% was allocated to the building on the corporate books. The real estate was acquired with the intention of demolishing the building, and this was accomplished during the month of November. Cash proceeds received in November represent the net proceeds from demolition of the building.

Warehouse: On June 30, the warehouse was destroyed by fire. The warehouse was purchased January 2, 2011, and had depreciated $16,000. On December 27, the insurance proceeds and other funds were used to purchase a replacement warehouse at a cost of $90,000.

Machine: On December 26, the machine was exchanged for another machine having a fair value of $6,300 and cash of $900 was received. (The exchange lacks commercial substance.)

Furniture: On August 15, furniture was contributed to a qualified charitable organization. No other contributions were made or pledged during the year.

Automobile: On November 3, the automobile was sold to Jared Winger, a stockholder.

Instructions

Indicate how these items would be reported on the income statement of Hollerith Co.

(AICPA adapted)

2 4 **P10-5 (Classification of Costs and Interest Capitalization)** On January 1, 2014, Blair Corporation purchased for $500,000 a tract of land (site number 101) with a building. Blair paid a real estate broker's commission of $36,000, legal fees of $6,000, and title guarantee insurance of $18,000. The closing statement indicated that the land value was $500,000 and the building value was $100,000. Shortly after acquisition, the building was razed at a cost of $54,000.

Blair entered into a $3,000,000 fixed-price contract with Slatkin Builders, Inc. on March 1, 2014, for the construction of an office building on land site number 101. The building was completed and occupied on September 30, 2015. Additional construction costs were incurred as follows.

Plans, specifications, and blueprints	$21,000
Architects' fees for design and supervision	82,000

The building is estimated to have a 40-year life from date of completion and will be depreciated using the 150% declining-balance method.

To finance construction costs, Blair borrowed $3,000,000 on March 1, 2014. The loan is payable in 10 annual installments of $300,000 starting on March 1, 2015, plus interest at the rate of 10%. Blair's weighted-average amounts of accumulated building construction expenditures were as follows.

For the period March 1 to December 31, 2014	$1,300,000
For the period January 1 to September 30, 2015	1,900,000

Instructions

(a) Prepare a schedule that discloses the individual costs making up the balance in the land account in respect of land site number 101 as of September 30, 2015.

(b) Prepare a schedule that discloses the individual costs that should be capitalized in the office building account as of September 30, 2015. Show supporting computations in good form.

(AICPA adapted)

2 4 **P10-6 (Interest During Construction)** Grieg Landscaping began construction of a new plant on December 1, 2014. On this date, the company purchased a parcel of land for $139,000 in cash. In addition, it paid $2,000 in surveying costs and $4,000 for a title insurance policy. An old dwelling on the premises was demolished at a cost of $3,000, with $1,000 being received from the sale of materials.

Architectural plans were also formalized on December 1, 2014, when the architect was paid $30,000. The necessary building permits costing $3,000 were obtained from the city and paid for on December 1 as well. The excavation work began during the first week in December with payments made to the contractor as follows.

Date of Payment	Amount of Payment
March 1	$240,000
May 1	330,000
July 1	60,000

The building was completed on July 1, 2015.

To finance construction of this plant, Grieg borrowed $600,000 from the bank on December 1, 2014. Grieg had no other borrowings. The $600,000 was a 10-year loan bearing interest at 8%.

Instructions

Compute the balance in each of the following accounts at December 31, 2014, and December 31, 2015. (Round amounts to the nearest dollar.)

(a) Land.
(b) Buildings.
(c) Interest Expense.

4 **P10-7 (Capitalization of Interest)** Laserwords Inc. is a book distributor that had been operating in its original facility since 1987. The increase in certification programs and continuing education requirements in several professions has contributed to an annual growth rate of 15% for Laserwords since 2009. Laserwords' original facility became obsolete by early 2014 because of the increased sales volume and the fact that Laserwords now carries CDs in addition to books.

On June 1, 2014, Laserwords contracted with Black Construction to have a new building constructed for $4,000,000 on land owned by Laserwords. The payments made by Laserwords to Black Construction are shown in the schedule below.

Date	Amount
July 30, 2014	$ 900,000
January 30, 2015	1,500,000
May 30, 2015	1,600,000
Total payments	$4,000,000

Construction was completed and the building was ready for occupancy on May 27, 2015. Laserwords had no new borrowings directly associated with the new building but had the following debt outstanding at May 31, 2015, the end of its fiscal year.

10%, 5-year note payable of $2,000,000, dated April 1, 2011, with interest payable annually on April 1.
12%, 10-year bond issue of $3,000,000 sold at par on June 30, 2007, with interest payable annually on June 30.

The new building qualifies for interest capitalization. The effect of capitalizing the interest on the new building, compared with the effect of expensing the interest, is material.

Instructions

(a) Compute the weighted-average accumulated expenditures on Laserwords' new building during the capitalization period.
(b) Compute the avoidable interest on Laserwords' new building. (Round to one decimal place.)
(c) Some interest cost of Laserwords Inc. is capitalized for the year ended May 31, 2015.
  (1) Identify the items relating to interest costs that must be disclosed in Laserwords' financial statements.
  (2) Compute the amount of each of the items that must be disclosed.

(CMA adapted)

5 **P10-8 (Nonmonetary Exchanges)** Holyfield Corporation wishes to exchange a machine used in its operations. Holyfield has received the following offers from other companies in the industry.

1. Dorsett Company offered to exchange a similar machine plus $23,000. (The exchange has commercial substance for both parties.)
2. Winston Company offered to exchange a similar machine. (The exchange lacks commercial substance for both parties.)
3. Liston Company offered to exchange a similar machine, but wanted $3,000 in addition to Holyfield's machine. (The exchange has commercial substance for both parties.)

In addition, Holyfield contacted Greeley Corporation, a dealer in machines. To obtain a new machine, Holyfield must pay $93,000 in addition to trading in its old machine.

	Holyfield	Dorsett	Winston	Liston	Greeley
Machine cost	$160,000	$120,000	$152,000	$160,000	$130,000
Accumulated depreciation	60,000	45,000	71,000	75,000	–0–
Fair value	92,000	69,000	92,000	95,000	185,000

Instructions

For each of the four independent situations, prepare the journal entries to record the exchange on the books of each company.

5 **P10-9 (Nonmonetary Exchanges)** On August 1, Hyde, Inc. exchanged productive assets with Wiggins, Inc. Hyde's asset is referred to below as "Asset A," and Wiggins' is referred to as "Asset B." The following facts pertain to these assets.

	Asset A	Asset B
Original cost	$96,000	$110,000
Accumulated depreciation (to date of exchange)	40,000	47,000
Fair value at date of exchange	60,000	75,000
Cash paid by Hyde, Inc.	15,000	
Cash received by Wiggins, Inc.		15,000

Instructions

(a) Assuming that the exchange of Assets A and B has commercial substance, record the exchange for both Hyde, Inc. and Wiggins, Inc. in accordance with generally accepted accounting principles.

(b) Assuming that the exchange of Assets A and B lacks commercial substance, record the exchange for both Hyde, Inc. and Wiggins, Inc. in accordance with generally accepted accounting principles.

5 **P10-10 (Nonmonetary Exchanges)** During the current year, Marshall Construction trades an old crane that has a book value of $90,000 (original cost $140,000 less accumulated depreciation $50,000) for a new crane from Brigham Manufacturing Co. The new crane cost Brigham $165,000 to manufacture and is classified as inventory. The following information is also available.

	Marshall Const.	Brigham Mfg. Co.
Fair value of old crane	$ 82,000	
Fair value of new crane		$200,000
Cash paid	118,000	
Cash received		118,000

Instructions

(a) Assuming that this exchange is considered to have commercial substance, prepare the journal entries on the books of (1) Marshall Construction and (2) Brigham Manufacturing.

(b) Assuming that this exchange lacks commercial substance for Marshall, prepare the journal entries on the books of Marshall Construction.

(c) Assuming the same facts as those in (a), except that the fair value of the old crane is $98,000 and the cash paid is $102,000, prepare the journal entries on the books of (1) Marshall Construction and (2) Brigham Manufacturing.

(d) Assuming the same facts as those in (b), except that the fair value of the old crane is $97,000 and the cash paid $103,000, prepare the journal entries on the books of (1) Marshall Construction and (2) Brigham Manufacturing.

2 5 **P10-11 (Purchases by Deferred Payment, Lump-Sum, and Nonmonetary Exchanges)** Klamath Company, a manufacturer of ballet shoes, is experiencing a period of sustained growth. In an effort to expand its production capacity to meet the increased demand for its product, the company recently made several acquisitions of plant and equipment. Rob Joffrey, newly hired in the position of fixed-asset accountant, requested that Danny Nolte, Klamath's controller, review the following transactions.

Transaction 1: On June 1, 2014, Klamath Company purchased equipment from Wyandot Corporation. Klamath issued a $28,000, 4-year, zero-interest-bearing note to Wyandot for the new equipment. Klamath will pay off the note in four equal installments due at the end of each of the next 4 years. At the date of the transaction, the prevailing market rate of interest for obligations of this nature was 10%. Freight costs of $425 and installation costs of $500 were incurred in completing this transaction. The appropriate factors for the time value of money at a 10% rate of interest are given below.

Future value of $1 for 4 periods	1.46
Future value of an ordinary annuity for 4 periods	4.64
Present value of $1 for 4 periods	0.68
Present value of an ordinary annuity for 4 periods	3.17

Transaction 2: On December 1, 2014, Klamath Company purchased several assets of Yakima Shoes Inc., a small shoe manufacturer whose owner was retiring. The purchase amounted to $220,000 and included the assets listed below. Klamath Company engaged the services of Tennyson Appraisal Inc., an independent appraiser, to determine the fair values of the assets which are also presented below.

	Yakima Book Value	Fair Value
Inventory	$ 60,000	$ 50,000
Land	40,000	80,000
Buildings	70,000	120,000
	$170,000	$250,000

During its fiscal year ended May 31, 2015, Klamath incurred $8,000 for interest expense in connection with the financing of these assets.

Transaction 3: On March 1, 2015, Klamath Company exchanged a number of used trucks plus cash for vacant land adjacent to its plant site. (The exchange has commercial substance.) Klamath intends to use the land for a parking lot. The trucks had a combined book value of $35,000, as Klamath had recorded $20,000 of accumulated depreciation against these assets. Klamath's purchasing agent, who has had previous dealings in the secondhand market, indicated that the trucks had a fair value of $46,000 at the time of the transaction. In addition to the trucks, Klamath Company paid $19,000 cash for the land.

Instructions

(a) Plant assets such as land, buildings, and equipment receive special accounting treatment. Describe the major characteristics of these assets that differentiate them from other types of assets.

(b) For each of the three transactions described above, determine the value at which Klamath Company should record the acquired assets. Support your calculations with an explanation of the underlying rationale.

(c) The books of Klamath Company show the following additional transactions for the fiscal year ended May 31, 2015.

(1) Acquisition of a building for speculative purposes.

(2) Purchase of a 2-year insurance policy covering plant equipment.

(3) Purchase of the rights for the exclusive use of a process used in the manufacture of ballet shoes.

For each of these transactions, indicate whether the asset should be classified as a plant asset. If it is a plant asset, explain why it is. If it is not a plant asset, explain why not, and identify the proper classification.

(CMA adapted)

PROBLEMS SET B

See the book's companion website, at **www.wiley.com/college/kieso**, for an additional set of problems.

CONCEPTS FOR ANALYSIS

CA10-1 (Acquisition, Improvements, and Sale of Realty) Tonkawa Company purchased land for use as its corporate headquarters. A small factory that was on the land when it was purchased was torn down before construction of the office building began. Furthermore, a substantial amount of rock blasting and removal had to be done to the site before construction of the building foundation began. Because the office building was set back on the land far from the public road, Tonkawa Company had the contractor construct a paved road that led from the public road to the parking lot of the office building.

Three years after the office building was occupied, Tonkawa Company added four stories to the office building. The four stories had an estimated useful life of 5 years more than the remaining estimated useful life of the original office building.

Ten years later, the land and building were sold at an amount more than their net book value, and Tonkawa Company had a new office building constructed in another state for use as its new corporate headquarters.

Instructions

(a) Which of the expenditures above should be capitalized? How should each be depreciated or amortized? Discuss the rationale for your answers.

(b) How would the sale of the land and building be accounted for? Include in your answer an explanation of how to determine the net book value at the date of sale. Discuss the rationale for your answer.

CA10-2 (Accounting for Self-Constructed Assets) Troopers Medical Labs, Inc., began operations 5 years ago producing stetrics, a new type of instrument it hoped to sell to doctors, dentists, and hospitals. The demand for stetrics far exceeded initial expectations, and the company was unable to produce enough stetrics to meet demand.

The company was manufacturing its product on equipment that it built at the start of its operations. To meet demand, more efficient equipment was needed. The company decided to design and build the equipment, because the equipment currently available on the market was unsuitable for producing stetrics.

In 2014, a section of the plant was devoted to development of the new equipment and a special staff was hired. Within 6 months, a machine developed at a cost of $714,000 increased production dramatically and reduced labor costs substantially. Elated by the success of the new machine, the company built three more machines of the same type at a cost of $441,000 each.

Instructions

(a) In general, what costs should be capitalized for self-constructed equipment?

(b) Discuss the propriety of including in the capitalized cost of self-constructed assets:

  (1) The increase in overhead caused by the self-construction of fixed assets.

  (2) A proportionate share of overhead on the same basis as that applied to goods manufactured for sale.

(c) Discuss the proper accounting treatment of the $273,000 ($714,000 − $441,000) by which the cost of the first machine exceeded the cost of the subsequent machines. This additional cost should not be considered research and development costs.

CA10-3 (Capitalization of Interest) Vania Magazine Company started construction of a warehouse building for its own use at an estimated cost of $5,000,000 on January 1, 2013, and completed the building on December 31, 2013. During the construction period, Vania has the following debt obligations outstanding.

Construction loan—12% interest, payable semiannually, issued December 31, 2012	$2,000,000
Short-term loan—10% interest, payable monthly, and principal payable at maturity, on May 30, 2014	1,400,000
Long-term loan—11% interest, payable on January 1 of each year; principal payable on January 1, 2016	1,000,000

Total cost amounted to $5,200,000, and the weighted average of accumulated expenditures was $3,500,000.

Jane Esplanade, the president of the company, has been shown the costs associated with this construction project and capitalized on the balance sheet. She is bothered by the "avoidable interest" included in the cost. She argues that, first, all the interest is unavoidable—no one lends money without expecting to be compensated for it. Second, why can't the company use all the interest on all the loans when computing this avoidable interest? Finally, why can't her company capitalize all the annual interest that accrued over the period of construction?

Instructions

(Round the weighted-average interest rate to two decimal places.)

You are the manager of accounting for the company. In a memo, explain what avoidable interest is, how you computed it (being especially careful to explain why you used the interest rates that you did), and why the company cannot capitalize all its interest for the year. Attach a schedule supporting any computations that you use.

CA10-4 (Nonmonetary Exchanges) You have two clients that are considering trading machinery with each other. Although the machines are different from each other, you believe that an assessment of expected cash flows on the exchanged assets will indicate the exchange lacks commercial substance. Your clients would prefer that the exchange be deemed to have commercial substance, to allow them to record gains. Here are the facts:

	Client A	Client B
Original cost	$100,000	$150,000
Accumulated depreciation	40,000	80,000
Fair value	80,000	100,000
Cash received (paid)	(20,000)	20,000

Instructions

(a) Record the trade-in on Client A's books assuming the exchange has commercial substance.

(b) Record the trade-in on Client A's books assuming the exchange lacks commercial substance.

(c) Write a memo to the controller of Company A indicating and explaining the dollar impact on current and future statements of treating the exchange as having, versus lacking, commercial substance.

(d) Record the entry on Client B's books assuming the exchange has commercial substance.

(e) Record the entry on Client B's books assuming the exchange lacks commercial substance.

(f) Write a memo to the controller of Company B indicating and explaining the dollar impact on current and future statements of treating the exchange as having, versus lacking, commercial substance.

CA10-5 (Costs of Acquisition) The invoice price of a machine is $50,000. Various other costs relating to the acquisition and installation of the machine including transportation, electrical wiring, special base, and so on amount to $7,500. The machine has an estimated life of 10 years, with no salvage value at the end of that period.

The owner of the business suggests that the incidental costs of $7,500 be charged to expense immediately for the following reasons.

1. If the machine should be sold, these costs cannot be recovered in the sales price.
2. The inclusion of the $7,500 in the machinery account on the books will not necessarily result in a closer approximation of the market price of this asset over the years, because of the possibility of changing demand and supply levels.
3. Charging the $7,500 to expense immediately will reduce federal income taxes.

Instructions

Discuss each of the points raised by the owner of the business.

(AICPA adapted)

CA10-6 (Cost of Land vs. Building—Ethics) Tones Company purchased a warehouse in a downtown district where land values are rapidly increasing. Gerald Carter, controller, and Wilma Ankara, financial vice president, are trying to allocate the cost of the purchase between the land and the building. Noting that depreciation can be taken only on the building, Carter favors placing a very high proportion of the cost on the warehouse itself, thus reducing taxable income and income taxes. Ankara, his supervisor, argues that the allocation should recognize the increasing value of the land, regardless of the depreciation potential of the warehouse. Besides, she says, net income is negatively impacted by additional depreciation and will cause the company's stock price to go down.

Instructions

Answer the following questions.

(a) What stakeholder interests are in conflict?
(b) What ethical issues does Carter face?
(c) How should these costs be allocated?

USING YOUR JUDGMENT

FINANCIAL REPORTING

Financial Statement Analysis Case

Johnson & Johnson

Johnson & Johnson, the world's leading and most diversified health-care corporation, serves its customers through specialized worldwide franchises. Each of its franchises consists of a number of companies throughout the world that focus on a particular health-care market, such as surgical sutures, consumer pharmaceuticals, or contact lenses. Information related to its property, plant, and equipment in its 2011 annual report is shown in the notes to the financial statements below.

1. Property, Plant and Equipment and Depreciation

Property, plant and equipment are stated at cost. The Company utilizes the straight-line method of depreciation over the estimated useful lives of the assets:

Building and building equipment	20–40 years
Land and leasehold improvements	10–20 years
Machinery and equipment	2–13 years

4. Property, Plant and Equipment

At the end of 2011 and 2010, property, plant and equipment at cost and accumulated depreciation were:

(dollars in millions)	2011	2010
Land and land improvements	$ 754	$ 738
Buildings and building equipment	9,389	9,079
Machinery and equipment	19,182	18,032
Construction in progress	2,504	2,577
	31,829	30,426
Less accumulated depreciation	17,090	15,873
	$14,739	$14,553

The Company capitalizes interest expense as part of the cost of construction of facilities and equipment. Interest expense capitalized in 2011, 2010 and 2009 was $84 million, $73 million and $101 million, respectively.

Depreciation expense, including the amortization of capitalized interest in 2011, 2010 and 2009 was $2.3 billion, $2.2 billion and $2.1 billion, respectively.

Johnson & Johnson's provided the following selected information in its 2011 cash flow statement.

Johnson & Johnson
2011 Annual Report

Consolidated Financial Statements (excerpts)

Net cash flows from operating activities	$14,298
Cash flows from investing activities	
Additions to property, plant and equipment	(2,893)
Proceeds from the disposal of assets	1,342
Acquisitions, net of cash acquired	(2,797)
Purchases of investments	(29,882)
Sales of investments	30,396
Other (primarily intangibles)	(778)
Net cash used by investing activities	(4,612)
Cash flows from financing activities	
Dividends to shareholders	(6,156)
Repurchase of common stock	(2,525)
Proceeds from short-term debt	9,729
Retirement of short-term debt	(11,200)
Proceeds from long-term debt	4,470
Retirement of long-term debt	(16)
Proceeds from the exercise of stock options/excess tax benefits	1,246
Net cash used by financing activities	(4,452)
Effect of exchange rate changes on cash and cash equivalents	(47)
Increase in cash and cash equivalents	5,187
Cash and cash equivalents, beginning of year (Note 1)	19,355
Cash and cash equivalents, end of year (Note 1)	$24,542
Supplemental cash flow data	
Cash paid during the year for:	
Interest	$ 576
Income taxes	2,970

Instructions

(a) What was the cost of buildings and building equipment at the end of 2011?

(b) Does Johnson & Johnson use a conservative or liberal method to depreciate its property, plant, and equipment?

(c) What was the actual interest expense paid by the company in 2011?

(d) What is Johnson & Johnson's free cash flow? From the information provided, comment on Johnson & Johnson's financial flexibility.

Accounting, Analysis, and Principles

Durler Company purchased equipment on January 2, 2010, for $112,000. The equipment had an estimated useful life of 5 years with an estimated salvage value of $12,000. Durler uses straight-line depreciation on all assets. On January 2, 2014, Durler exchanged this equipment plus $12,000 in cash for newer equipment. The old equipment has a fair value of $50,000.

Accounting

Prepare the journal entry to record the exchange on the books of Durler Company. Assume that the exchange has commercial substance.

Analysis

How will this exchange affect comparisons of the return on asset ratio for Durler in the year of the exchange compared to prior years?

Principles

How does the concept of commercial substance affect the accounting and analysis of this exchange?

BRIDGE TO THE PROFESSION

Professional Research: FASB Codification

Your client is in the planning phase for a major plant expansion, which will involve the construction of a new warehouse. The assistant controller does not believe that interest cost can be included in the cost of the warehouse, because it is a financing expense. Others on the planning team believe that some interest cost can be included in the cost of the warehouse, but no one could identify the specific authoritative guidance for this issue. Your supervisor asks you to research this issue.

Instructions

If your school has a subscription to the FASB Codification, go to *http://aaahq.org/asclogin.cfm* to log in and prepare responses to the following. Provide Codification references for your responses.

(a) Is it permissible to capitalize interest into the cost of assets? Provide authoritative support for your answer.

(b) What are the objectives for capitalizing interest?

(c) Discuss which assets qualify for interest capitalization.

(d) Is there a limit to the amount of interest that may be capitalized in a period?

(e) If interest capitalization is allowed, what disclosures are required?

Additional Professional Resources

See the book's companion website, at **www.wiley.com/college/kieso**, for professional simulations as well as other study resources.

Remember to check the book's companion website to find additional resources for this chapter.

CHAPTER

11 Depreciation, Impairments, and Depletion

LEARNING OBJECTIVES

After studying this chapter, you should be able to:

1. Explain the concept of depreciation.
2. Identify the factors involved in the depreciation process.
3. Compare activity, straight-line, and decreasing-charge methods of depreciation.
4. Explain special depreciation methods.
5. Explain the accounting issues related to asset impairment.
6. Explain the accounting procedures for depletion of natural resources.
7. Explain how to report and analyze property, plant, equipment, and natural resources.

Here Come the Write-Offs

The credit crisis starting in late 2008 affected many financial and nonfinancial institutions. Many of the statistics related to this crisis are sobering, as noted below.

- In October 2008, the FTSE 100 in the United Kingdom suffered its biggest one-day fall since October 1987. The index closed at its lowest level since October 2004.
- The Dow Jones Industrial Average fell below the 8,000 level for the first time since 2003.
- Germany's benchmark DAX tumbled after the collapse of the proposed rescue plan for **Hypo Real Estate**.
- Tightening credit and less disposable income led to Japanese electronic groups losing value. The Nikkei fell to its lowest point since February 2004.
- The Hong Kong Hang Seng dropped in line with the rest of Asia, closing below 17,000 points for the first time in two years in October 2008 and below 11,000 by November of that year.
- Governments spent billions of dollars bailing out financial institutions.

Although some financial rebound has occurred since October 2008, it is clear that most economies of the world are now in a slower growth pattern. This slowdown raises many questions related to the proper accounting for many long-term assets, such as property, plant, and equipment; intangible assets; and many types of financial assets. One of the most difficult issues relates to the possibility of higher impairment charges related to these assets and the related disclosures that may be needed. The following is an example of a recent impairment charge taken by **Fujitsu Limited**.

Impairment Losses (in part)

Due to the worsening of the global business environment, Fujitsu recognized consolidated impairment losses of 58.9 billion yen in relation to property, plant, and equipment of businesses with decreased profitability. The main losses are as follows:

(1) Property, Plant, and Equipment of LSI Business
Impairment losses related to the property, plant, and equipment of the LSI business of Fujitsu Microelectronics Limited totaled 49.9 billion yen. In January, Fujitsu Microelectronics announced business reforms in response to a sharp downturn in customer demand that began last autumn.

(2) Property, Plant, and Equipment of Optical Transmission Systems and Other Businesses
Consolidated impairment losses of 8.9 billion yen were recognized in relation to the property, plant, and equipment of the optical transmission systems business, the electronic components business and other businesses due to their decreased profitability.

(3) Property, Plant, and Equipment of HDD Business (included in business restructuring expenses)
Impairment losses of 16.2 billion yen have been recognized in relation to the property, plant, and equipment of the reorganized HDD business. These losses are included in business restructuring expenses. The impairment loss includes 5.3 billion yen recognized in the third quarter for the discontinuation of the HDD head business.

CONCEPTUAL FOCUS

> See the **Underlying Concepts** on pages 592, 593, 594, and 601.

> Read the **Evolving Issue** on page 609 for a discussion of using the full-cost versus successful-efforts method for accounting for exploration costs.

INTERNATIONAL FOCUS

> See the **International Perspectives** on pages 597, 602, 603, and 609.

> Read the **IFRS Insights** on pages 637–646 for a discussion of:
—Component depreciation
—Impairments
—Revaluations

Impairment losses for property, plant, and equipment for many companies in the next few years will be substantial. Here are some of the questions that will need to be addressed regarding possible impairments.

1. How often should a company test for impairment?
2. What are key impairment indicators?
3. What disclosures are necessary for impairments?
4. How do companies match their cash flows to the asset that is potentially impaired?

Assessing whether a company has impaired assets is difficult. For example, in addition to the technical accounting issues, the environment can change quickly. Reduced spending by consumers, lack of confidence in global economic decisions, and higher volatility in both stock and commodity markets are factors to consider. Nevertheless, for investors and creditors to have assurance that the amounts reported on the balance sheet for property, plant, and equipment are relevant and representationally faithful, appropriate impairment charges must be reported on a timely basis.

Source: A portion of this discussion is taken from "Top 10 Tips for Impairment Testing," PricewaterhouseCoopers (December 2008).

PREVIEW OF CHAPTER 11

As noted in the opening story, both U.S. and foreign companies are affected by impairment rules. These rules recognize that when economic conditions deteriorate, companies may need to write off an asset's cost to indicate the decline in its usefulness. The purpose of this chapter is to examine the depreciation process and the methods of writing off the cost of property, plant, and equipment and natural resources. The content and organization of the chapter are as follows.

Depreciation, Impairments, and Depletion

Depreciation	Impairments	Depletion	Presentation and Analysis
• Factors involved • Methods of depreciation • Special methods • Special issues	• Recognizing impairments • Measuring impairments • Restoration of loss • Assets to be disposed of	• Establishing a base • Write-off of resource cost • Estimating reserves • Liquidating dividends • Continuing controversy	• Presentation • Analysis

DEPRECIATION—A METHOD OF COST ALLOCATION

LEARNING OBJECTIVE 1
Explain the concept of depreciation.

Most individuals at one time or another purchase and trade in an automobile. The automobile dealer and the buyer typically discuss what the trade-in value of the old car is. Also, they may talk about what the trade-in value of the new car will be in several years. In both cases, a decline in value is considered to be an example of depreciation.

To accountants, however, depreciation is not a matter of valuation. Rather, **depreciation is a means of cost allocation. Depreciation is the accounting process of allocating the cost of tangible assets to expense in a systematic and rational manner to those periods expected to benefit from the use of the asset.** For example, a company like Goodyear (one of the world's largest tire manufacturers) does not depreciate assets on the basis of a decline in their fair value. Instead, it depreciates through systematic charges to expense.

This approach is employed because the value of the asset may fluctuate between the time the asset is purchased and the time it is sold or junked. Attempts to measure these interim value changes have not been well received because values are difficult to measure objectively. Therefore, Goodyear charges the asset's cost to depreciation expense over its estimated life. It makes no attempt to value the asset at fair value between acquisition and disposition. Companies use the cost allocation approach because it recognizes the expense in the periods expected to benefit and because fluctuations in fair value are uncertain and difficult to measure.

When companies write off the cost of long-lived assets over a number of periods, they typically use the term **depreciation**. They use the term **depletion** to describe the reduction in the cost of natural resources (such as timber, gravel, oil, and coal) over a period of time. The expiration of intangible assets, such as patents or copyrights, is called **amortization**.

Factors Involved in the Depreciation Process

LEARNING OBJECTIVE 2
Identify the factors involved in the depreciation process.

Before establishing a pattern of charges to revenue, a company must answer three basic questions:

1. What depreciable base is to be used for the asset?
2. What is the asset's useful life?
3. What method of cost apportionment is best for this asset?

The answers to these questions involve combining several estimates into one single figure. Note the calculations assume perfect knowledge of the future, which is never attainable.

Depreciable Base for the Asset

Gateway to the Profession
Tutorial on Depreciation Methods

The base established for depreciation is a function of two factors: the original cost, and salvage or disposal value. We discussed historical cost in Chapter 10. **Salvage value** is the estimated amount that a company will receive when it sells the asset or removes it from service. It is the amount to which a company writes down or depreciates the asset during its useful life. If an asset has a cost of $10,000 and a salvage value of $1,000, its **depreciation base** is $9,000.

ILLUSTRATION 11-1
Computation of Depreciation Base

Original cost	$10,000
Less: Salvage value	1,000
Depreciation base	$ 9,000

From a practical standpoint, companies often assign a zero salvage value. Some long-lived assets, however, have substantial salvage values.

Estimation of Service Lives

The service life of an asset often differs from its physical life. A piece of machinery may be physically capable of producing a given product for many years beyond its service life. But a company may not use the equipment for all that time because the cost of producing the product in later years may be too high. For example, the old Slater cotton mill in Pawtucket, Rhode Island, is preserved in remarkable physical condition as an historic landmark in U.S. industrial development, although its service life was terminated many years ago.[1]

Companies retire assets for two reasons: **physical factors** (such as casualty or expiration of physical life) and **economic factors** (obsolescence). Physical factors are the wear and tear, decay, and casualties that make it difficult for the asset to perform indefinitely. These physical factors set the outside limit for the service life of an asset.

We can classify the economic or functional factors into three categories:

1. **Inadequacy** results when an asset ceases to be useful to a company because the demands of the firm have changed. An example would be the need for a larger building to handle increased production. Although the old building may still be sound, it may have become inadequate for the company's purpose.
2. **Supersession** is the replacement of one asset with another more efficient and economical asset. Examples would be the replacement of the mainframe computer with a PC network, or the replacement of the Boeing 767 with the Boeing 787.
3. **Obsolescence** is the catchall for situations not involving inadequacy and supersession.

Because the distinction between these categories appears artificial, it is probably best to consider economic factors collectively instead of trying to make distinctions that are not clear-cut.

To illustrate the concepts of physical and economic factors, consider a new nuclear power plant. Which is more important in determining the useful life of a nuclear power plant—physical factors or economic factors? The limiting factors seem to be (1) ecological considerations, (2) competition from other power sources, and (3) safety concerns. Physical life does not appear to be the primary factor affecting useful life. Although the plant's physical life may be far from over, the plant may become obsolete in 10 years.

For a house, physical factors undoubtedly are more important than the economic or functional factors relative to useful life. Whenever the physical nature of the asset primarily determines useful life, maintenance plays an extremely vital role. The better the maintenance, the longer the life of the asset.[2]

In most cases, a company estimates the useful life of an asset based on its past experience with the same or similar assets. Others use sophisticated statistical methods to establish a useful life for accounting purposes. And in some cases, companies select arbitrary service lives. In a highly industrial economy such as that of the United States, where research and innovation are so prominent, technological factors have as much effect, if not more, on service lives of tangible plant assets as physical factors do.

[1]Taken from J. D. Coughlan and W. K. Strand, *Depreciation Accounting, Taxes and Business Decisions* (New York: The Ronald Press, 1969), pp. 10–12.

[2]The airline industry also illustrates the type of problem involved in estimation. In the past, aircraft were assumed not to wear out—they just became obsolete. However, some jets have been in service as long as 20 years, and maintenance of these aircraft has become increasingly expensive. As a result, some airlines now replace aircraft not because of obsolescence but because of physical deterioration.

What do the numbers mean? ALPHABET DUPE

Some companies try to imply that depreciation is not a cost. For example, in their press releases they will often make a bigger deal over earnings before interest, taxes, depreciation, and amortization (often referred to as EBITDA) than net income under GAAP. They like it because it "dresses up" their earnings numbers. Some on Wall Street buy this hype because they don't like the allocations that are required to determine net income. Some banks, without batting an eyelash, even let companies base their loan covenants on EBITDA.

For example, look at **Premier Parks**, which operates the Six Flags chain of amusement parks. Premier touts its EBITDA performance. But that number masks a big part of how the company operates—and how it spends its money. Premier argues that analysts should ignore depreciation for big-ticket items like roller coasters because the rides have a long life. Critics, however, say that the amusement industry has to spend as much as 50 percent of its EBITDA just to keep its rides and attractions current. Those expenses are not optional—let the rides get a little rusty, and ticket sales start to tail off. That means analysts really should view depreciation associated with the costs of maintaining the rides (or buying new ones) as an everyday expense. It also means investors in those companies should have strong stomachs.

What's the risk of trusting a fad accounting measure? Just look at one year's bankruptcy numbers. Of the 147 companies tracked by Moody's that defaulted on their debt, most borrowed money based on EBITDA performance. The bankers in those deals probably wish they had looked at a few other factors. On the other hand, nonfinancial companies in the S&P 500 generated a substantial EBITDA margin of 20.9 percent in 2011. Some analysts are concerned that such a high number suggests that companies are reluctant to incur costs and want to stockpile cash. The lesson? Investors will do well to avoid focus on any single accounting measure.

Sources: Adapted from Herb Greenberg, "Alphabet Dupe: Why EBITDA Falls Short," *Fortune* (July 10, 2000), p. 240; and V. Monga, "Operating Efficiency Runs High at U.S. Firms," *Wall Street Journal* (February 28, 2012), p. B7.

Methods of Depreciation

LEARNING OBJECTIVE 3
Compare activity, straight-line, and decreasing-charge methods of depreciation.

The third factor involved in the depreciation process is the **method** of cost apportionment. The profession requires that the depreciation method employed be "systematic and rational." Companies may use a number of depreciation methods, as follows.

Underlying Concepts
Depreciation attempts to recognize the cost of an asset to the periods that benefit from the use of that asset.

1. Activity method (units of use or production).
2. Straight-line method.
3. Decreasing-charge methods (accelerated):
   (a) Sum-of-the-years'-digits.
   (b) Declining-balance method.
4. Special depreciation methods:
   (a) Group and composite methods.
   (b) Hybrid or combination methods.[3]

To illustrate these depreciation methods, assume that Stanley Coal Mines recently purchased an additional crane for digging purposes. Illustration 11-2 contains the pertinent data concerning this purchase.

ILLUSTRATION 11-2
Data Used to Illustrate Depreciation Methods

Cost of crane	$500,000
Estimated useful life	5 years
Estimated salvage value	$ 50,000
Productive life in hours	30,000 hours

[3]*Accounting Trends and Techniques—2012* reports that of its 500 surveyed companies, for reporting purposes, 490 used straight-line, 9 used declining-balance, 2 used sum-of-the-years'-digits, 9 used an accelerated method (not specified), 12 used units-of-production, and 17 used group/composite.

Activity Method

The activity method (also called the **variable-charge** or **units-of-production approach**) assumes that depreciation is **a function of use or productivity, instead of the passage of time**. A company considers the life of the asset in terms of either the **output** it provides (units it produces) or an **input** measure such as the number of hours it works. Conceptually, the proper cost association relies on output instead of hours used, but often the output is not easily measurable. In such cases, an input measure such as machine hours is a more appropriate method of measuring the dollar amount of depreciation charges for a given accounting period.

The crane poses no particular depreciation problem. Stanley can measure the usage (hours) relatively easily. If Stanley uses the crane for 4,000 hours the first year, the depreciation charge is:

$$\frac{(\text{Cost less salvage value}) \times \text{Hours this year}}{\text{Total estimated hours}} = \text{Depreciation charge}$$

$$\frac{(\$500{,}000 - \$50{,}000) \times 4{,}000}{30{,}000} = \$60{,}000$$

ILLUSTRATION 11-3
Depreciation Calculation, Activity Method—Crane Example

The major limitation of this method is that it is inappropriate in situations in which depreciation is a function of time instead of activity. For example, a building steadily deteriorates due to the elements (time) regardless of its use. In addition, where economic or functional factors affect an asset, independent of its use, the activity method loses much of its significance. For example, if a company is expanding rapidly, a particular building may soon become obsolete for its intended purposes. In both cases, activity is irrelevant. Another problem in using an activity method is the difficulty of estimating units of output or service hours received.

In cases where loss of services results from activity or productivity, the activity method does the best to record expenses in the same period as associated revenues. Companies that desire low depreciation during periods of low productivity, and high depreciation during high productivity, either adopt or switch to an activity method. In this way, a plant running at 40 percent of capacity generates 60 percent lower depreciation charges. **Inland Steel**, for example, switched to units-of-production depreciation at one time and reduced its losses by $43 million, or $1.20 per share.

Straight-Line Method

The straight-line method considers depreciation as a **function of time rather than a function of usage**. Companies widely use this method because of its simplicity. The straight-line procedure is often the most conceptually appropriate, too. When creeping obsolescence is the primary reason for a limited service life, the decline in usefulness may be constant from period to period. Stanley computes the depreciation charge for the crane as follows.

Underlying Concepts

If benefits flow on a "straight-line" basis, then justification exists for recording the cost of the asset on a straight-line basis with these benefits.

$$\frac{\text{Cost less salvage value}}{\text{Estimated service life}} = \text{Depreciation charge}$$

$$\frac{\$500{,}000 - \$50{,}000}{5} = \$90{,}000$$

ILLUSTRATION 11-4
Depreciation Calculation, Straight-Line Method—Crane Example

The major objection to the straight-line method is that it rests on two tenuous assumptions. (1) The asset's economic usefulness is the same each year, and (2) the maintenance and repair expense is essentially the same each period.

One additional problem that occurs in using straight-line—as well as some others—is that distortions in the rate of return analysis (income/assets) develop.

Illustration 11-5 indicates how the rate of return increases, given constant revenue flows, because the asset's book value decreases.

ILLUSTRATION 11-5
Depreciation and Rate of Return Analysis—Crane Example

Year	Depreciation Expense	Undepreciated Asset Balance (book value)	Income (after depreciation expense)	Rate of Return (Income ÷ Assets)
0		$500,000		
1	$90,000	410,000	$100,000	24.4%
2	90,000	320,000	100,000	31.2%
3	90,000	230,000	100,000	43.5%
4	90,000	140,000	100,000	71.4%
5	90,000	50,000	100,000	200.0%

Decreasing-Charge Methods

Underlying Concepts

The expense recognition principle does not justify a constant charge to income. If the benefits from the asset decline as the asset ages, then a decreasing charge to income better matches cost to benefits.

The **decreasing-charge methods** provide for a higher depreciation cost in the earlier years and lower charges in later periods. Because these methods allow for higher early-year charges than in the straight-line method, they are often called **accelerated depreciation methods**.

What is the main justification for this approach? The rationale is that companies should charge more depreciation in earlier years because the asset is most productive in its earlier years. Furthermore, the accelerated methods provide a constant cost because the depreciation charge is lower in the later periods, at the time when the repair and maintenance costs are often higher. Generally, companies use one of two decreasing-charge methods: the sum-of-the-years'-digits method or the declining-balance method.

Sum-of-the-Years'-Digits. The **sum-of-the-years'-digits method** results in a decreasing depreciation charge based on a decreasing fraction of depreciable cost (original cost less salvage value). Each fraction uses the sum of the years as a denominator (5 + 4 + 3 + 2 + 1 = 15). The numerator is the number of years of estimated life remaining as of the beginning of the year. In this method, the numerator decreases year by year, and the denominator remains constant (5/15, 4/15, 3/15, 2/15, and 1/15). At the end of the asset's useful life, the balance remaining should equal the salvage value. Illustration 11-6 shows this method of computation.[4]

ILLUSTRATION 11-6
Sum-of-the-Years'-Digits Depreciation Schedule—Crane Example

Year	Depreciation Base	Remaining Life in Years	Depreciation Fraction	Depreciation Expense	Book Value, End of Year
1	$450,000	5	5/15	$150,000	$350,000
2	450,000	4	4/15	120,000	230,000
3	450,000	3	3/15	90,000	140,000
4	450,000	2	2/15	60,000	80,000
5	450,000	1	1/15	30,000	50,000[a]
		15	15/15	$450,000	

[a]Salvage value.

[4]What happens if the estimated service life of the asset is, let us say, 51 years? How would we calculate the sum-of-the-years'-digits? Fortunately mathematicians have developed the following formula that permits easy computation:

$$\frac{n(n+1)}{2} = \frac{51(51+1)}{2} = 1{,}326$$

Declining-Balance Method. The **declining-balance method** utilizes a depreciation rate (expressed as a percentage) that is some multiple of the straight-line method. For example, the double-declining rate for a 10-year asset is 20 percent (double the straight-line rate, which is 1/10 or 10 percent). Companies apply the constant rate to the declining book value each year.

Unlike other methods, the declining-balance method **does not deduct the salvage value** in computing the depreciation base. The declining-balance rate is multiplied by the book value of the asset at the beginning of each period. Since the depreciation charge reduces the book value of the asset each period, applying the constant-declining-balance rate to a successively lower book value results in lower depreciation charges each year. This process continues until the book value of the asset equals its estimated salvage value. At that time, the company discontinues depreciation.

Companies use various multiples in practice. For example, the **double-declining-balance method** depreciates assets at twice (200 percent) the straight-line rate. Illustration 11-7 shows Stanley's depreciation charges if using the double-declining approach.

ILLUSTRATION 11-7
Double-Declining Depreciation Schedule—Crane Example

Year	Book Value of Asset First of Year	Rate on Declining Balance[a]	Depreciation Expense	Balance Accumulated Depreciation	Book Value, End of Year
1	$500,000	40%	$200,000	$200,000	$300,000
2	300,000	40%	120,000	320,000	180,000
3	180,000	40%	72,000	392,000	108,000
4	108,000	40%	43,200	435,200	64,800
5	64,800	40%	14,800[b]	450,000	50,000

[a]Based on twice the straight-line rate of 20% ($90,000/$450,000 = 20%; 20% × 2 = 40%).
[b]Limited to $14,800 because book value should not be less than salvage value.

Companies often switch from the declining-balance method to the straight-line method near the end of the asset's useful life to ensure that they depreciate the asset only to its salvage value.[5]

Special Depreciation Methods

4 LEARNING OBJECTIVE
Explain special depreciation methods.

Sometimes companies adopt special depreciation methods. Reasons for doing so might be that a company's assets have unique characteristics, or the nature of the industry. Two of these special methods are:

1. Group and composite methods.
2. Hybrid or combination methods.

Group and Composite Methods

Companies often depreciate multiple-asset accounts using one rate. For example, AT&T might depreciate telephone poles, microwave systems, or switchboards by groups.

Two methods of depreciating multiple-asset accounts exist: the group method and the composite method. The choice of method depends on the nature of the assets involved. Companies frequently use the **group method** when the assets are similar in nature and

[5]A pure form of the declining-balance method (sometimes appropriately called the "fixed percentage of book value method") has also been suggested as a possibility. This approach finds a rate that depreciates the asset exactly to salvage value at the end of its expected useful life. The formula for determination of this rate is as follows.

$$\text{Depreciation rate} = 1 - \sqrt[n]{\frac{\text{Salvage value}}{\text{Acquisition cost}}}$$

The life in years is n. After computing the depreciation rate, a company applies it on the declining book value of the asset from period to period, which means that depreciation expense will be successively lower. This method is not used extensively in practice due to cumbersome computations. Further, it is not permitted for tax purposes.

have approximately the same useful lives. They use the **composite approach** when the assets are dissimilar and have different lives. The group method more closely approximates a single-unit cost procedure because the dispersion from the average is not as great. The computation for group or composite methods is essentially the same: find an average and depreciate on that basis.

Companies determine the **composite depreciation rate** by dividing the depreciation per year by the total cost of the assets. To illustrate, Mooney Motors establishes the composite depreciation rate for its fleet of cars, trucks, and campers as shown in Illustration 11-8.

ILLUSTRATION 11-8
Depreciation Calculation, Composite Basis

Asset	Original Cost	Salvage Value	Depreciation Cost	Estimated Life (yrs.)	Depreciation per Year (straight-line)
Cars	$145,000	$25,000	$120,000	3	$40,000
Trucks	44,000	4,000	40,000	4	10,000
Campers	35,000	5,000	30,000	5	6,000
	$224,000	$34,000	$190,000		$56,000

$$\text{Composite depreciation rate} = \frac{\$56{,}000}{\$224{,}000} = 25\%$$

Composite life = 3.39 years ($190,000 ÷ $56,000)

If there are no changes in the asset account, Mooney will depreciate the group of assets to the residual or salvage value at the rate of $56,000 ($224,000 × 25%) a year. As a result, it will take Mooney 3.39 years to depreciate these assets. The length of time it takes a company to depreciate its assets on a composite basis is called the **composite life.**

We can highlight the differences between the group or composite method and the single-unit depreciation method by looking at asset retirements. If Mooney retires an asset before or after the average service life of the group is reached, it buries the resulting gain or loss in the Accumulated Depreciation account. This practice is justified because Mooney will retire some assets before the average service life and others after the average life. For this reason, the debit to Accumulated Depreciation is the difference between original cost and cash received. Mooney does not record a gain or loss on disposition.

To illustrate, suppose that Mooney Motors sold one of the campers with a cost of $5,000 for $2,600 at the end of the third year. The entry is:

Accumulated Depreciation—Plant Assets	2,400	
Cash	2,600	
Cars, Trucks, and Campers		5,000

If Mooney purchases a new type of asset (mopeds, for example), it must compute a new depreciation rate and apply this rate in subsequent periods.

Illustration 11-9 presents a typical financial statement disclosure of the group depreciation method for **Ampco-Pittsburgh Corporation**.

ILLUSTRATION 11-9
Disclosure of Group Depreciation Method

Ampco-Pittsburgh Corporation

Depreciation rates are based on estimated useful lives of the asset groups. Gains or losses on normal retirements or replacements of depreciable assets, subject to composite depreciation methods, are not recognized; the difference between the cost of the assets retired or replaced and the related salvage value is charged or credited to the accumulated depreciation.

The group or composite method simplifies the bookkeeping process and tends to average out errors caused by over- or underdepreciation. As a result, gains or losses on disposals of assets do not distort periodic income.

On the other hand, the unit method (depreciation of single assets) has several advantages over the group or composite methods. (1) It simplifies the computation mathematically. (2) It identifies gains and losses on disposal. (3) It isolates depreciation on idle equipment. (4) It represents the best estimate of the depreciation of each asset, not the result of averaging the cost over a longer period of time. As a consequence, companies generally use the unit method.[6] *Unless stated otherwise, you should use the unit method in homework problems.*

Hybrid or Combination Methods

Gateway to the Profession

Expanded Discussion—Special Depreciation Methods

In addition to the depreciation methods already discussed, companies are free to develop their own special or tailor-made depreciation methods. GAAP requires only that the method result in the allocation of an asset's cost over the asset's life in a **systematic and rational manner**.

For example, the steel industry widely uses a hybrid depreciation method, called the **production variable method**, that is a combination straight-line/activity approach. The following note from **WHX Corporation**'s annual report explains one variation of this method.

ILLUSTRATION 11-10
Disclosure of Hybrid Depreciation Method

WHX Corporation

The Company utilizes the modified units of production method of depreciation which recognizes that the depreciation of steelmaking machinery is related to the physical wear of the equipment as well as a time factor. The modified units of production method provides for straight-line depreciation charges modified (adjusted) by the level of raw steel production. In the prior year, depreciation under the modified units of production method was $21.6 million or 40% less than straight-line depreciation, and in the current year it was $1.1 million or 2% more than straight-line depreciation.

What do the numbers mean? DECELERATING DEPRECIATION

Which depreciation method should management select? Many believe that the method that best matches revenues with expenses should be used. For example, if revenues generated by the asset are constant over its useful life, select straight-line depreciation. On the other hand, if revenues are higher (or lower) at the beginning of the asset's life, then use a decreasing (or increasing) method. Thus, if a company can reliably estimate revenues from the asset, selecting a depreciation method that best matches costs with those revenues would seem to provide the most useful information to investors and creditors for assessing the future cash flows from the asset.

Managers in the real estate industry face a different challenge when considering depreciation choices. Real estate managers object to traditional depreciation methods because in their view, real estate often does not decline in value. In addition, because real estate is highly debt-financed, most real estate concerns report losses in earlier years of operations when the sum of depreciation and interest exceeds the revenue from the real estate project. As a result, real estate companies, like **Kimco Realty**, argue for some form of **increasing-charge** method of depreciation (lower depreciation at the beginning and higher depreciation at the end). With such a method, companies would report higher total assets and net income in the earlier years of the project.[7]

International Perspective

IFRS requires use of component depreciation.

[6]A committee of the AICPA has indicated in an exposure draft that companies should use the unit approach whenever feasible. In fact, it indicates that an even better way to depreciate property, plant, and equipment is to use *component depreciation*. Under component depreciation, a company should depreciate over its expected useful life any part or portion of property, plant, and equipment that can be separately identified as an asset. For example, a company could separate the various components of a building (e.g., roof, heating and cooling system, elevator, leasehold improvements) and depreciate each component over its useful life.

[7]In this regard, real estate investment trusts (REITs) often report (in addition to net income) an earnings measure, funds from operations (FFO), that adjusts income for depreciation expense and other noncash expenses. This method is not GAAP. There is mixed empirical evidence about whether FFO or GAAP income is more useful to real estate investment trust investors. See, for example, Richard Gore and David Stott, "Toward a More Informative Measure of Operating Performance in the REIT Industry: Net Income vs. FFO," *Accounting Horizons* (December 1998); and Linda Vincent, "The Information Content of FFO for REITs," *Journal of Accounting and Economics* (January 1999).

Special Depreciation Issues

We still need to discuss several special issues related to depreciation:

1. How should companies compute depreciation for partial periods?
2. Does depreciation provide for the replacement of assets?
3. How should companies handle revisions in depreciation rates?

Depreciation and Partial Periods

Companies seldom purchase plant assets on the first day of a fiscal period or dispose of them on the last day of a fiscal period. A practical question is: How much depreciation should a company charge for the partial periods involved?

In computing depreciation expense for partial periods, companies must determine the depreciation expense for the full year and then prorate this depreciation expense between the two periods involved. This process should continue throughout the useful life of the asset.

Assume, for example, that Steeltex Company purchases an automated drill machine with a five-year life for \$45,000 (no salvage value) on June 10, 2013. The company's fiscal year ends December 31. Steeltex therefore charges depreciation for only 6⅔ months during that year. The total depreciation for a full year (assuming straight-line depreciation) is \$9,000 (\$45,000/5). The depreciation for the first, partial year is therefore:

$$\frac{6^2/_3}{12} \times \$9,000 = \$5,000$$

The partial-period calculation is relatively simple when Steeltex uses straight-line depreciation. But how is partial-period depreciation handled when it uses an accelerated method such as sum-of-the-years'-digits or double-declining-balance? As an illustration, assume that Steeltex purchased another machine for \$10,000 on July 1, 2013, with an estimated useful life of five years and no salvage value. Illustration 11-11 shows the depreciation figures for 2013, 2014, and 2015.

ILLUSTRATION 11-11
Calculation of Partial-Period Depreciation, Two Accelerated Methods

	Sum-of-the-Years'-Digits	Double-Declining-Balance
1st full year	(5/15 × \$10,000) = \$3,333.33	(40% × \$10,000) = \$4,000
2nd full year	(4/15 × 10,000) = 2,666.67	(40% × 6,000) = 2,400
3rd full year	(3/15 × 10,000) = 2,000.00	(40% × 3,600) = 1,440
Depreciation from July 1, 2013, to December 31, 2013		
	6/12 × \$3,333.33 = \$1,666.67	6/12 × \$4,000 = \$2,000
Depreciation for 2014		
	6/12 × \$3,333.33 = \$1,666.67	6/12 × \$4,000 = \$2,000
	6/12 × 2,666.67 = 1,333.33	6/12 × 2,400 = 1,200
	\$3,000.00	\$3,200
		or (\$10,000 − \$2,000) × 40% = \$3,200
Depreciation for 2015		
	6/12 × \$2,666.67 = \$1,333.33	6/12 × \$2,400 = \$1,200
	6/12 × 2,000.00 = 1,000.00	6/12 × 1,440 = 720
	\$2,333.33	\$1,920
		or (\$10,000 − \$5,200) × 40% = \$1,920

Sometimes a company like Steeltex modifies the process of allocating costs to a partial period to handle acquisitions and disposals of plant assets more simply. One variation is to take no depreciation in the year of acquisition and a full year's depreciation in the year of disposal. Other variations charge one-half year's depreciation both in the year of acquisition and in the year of disposal (referred to as the **half-year convention**), or charge a full year in the year of acquisition and none in the year of disposal.

In fact, Steeltex may adopt any one of these fractional-year policies in allocating cost to the first and last years of an asset's life so long as it applies the method consistently. However, **unless otherwise stipulated, companies normally compute depreciation on the basis of the nearest full month.**

Illustration 11-12 shows depreciation allocated under five different fractional-year policies using the straight-line method on the $45,000 automated drill machine purchased by Steeltex Company on June 10, 2013, discussed earlier.

ILLUSTRATION 11-12
Fractional-Year Depreciation Policies

Machine Cost = $45,000	Depreciation Allocated per Period Over 5-Year Life*					
Fractional-Year Policy	2013	2014	2015	2016	2017	2018
1. Nearest fraction of a year.	$5,000[a]	$9,000	$9,000	$9,000	$9,000	$4,000[b]
2. Nearest full month.	5,250[c]	9,000	9,000	9,000	9,000	3,750[d]
3. Half year in period of acquisition and disposal.	4,500	9,000	9,000	9,000	9,000	4,500
4. Full year in period of acquisition, none in period of disposal.	9,000	9,000	9,000	9,000	9,000	–0–
5. None in period of acquisition, full year in period of disposal.	–0–	9,000	9,000	9,000	9,000	9,000

[a]6.667/12 ($9,000) [b]5.333/12 ($9,000) [c]7/12 ($9,000) [d]5/12 ($9,000)
*Rounded to nearest dollar.

Depreciation and Replacement of Property, Plant, and Equipment

A common misconception about depreciation is that it provides funds for the replacement of fixed assets. Depreciation is like other expenses in that it reduces net income. It differs, though, in that **it does not involve a current cash outflow**.

To illustrate why depreciation does not provide funds for replacement of plant assets, assume that a business starts operating with plant assets of $500,000 that have a useful life of five years. The company's balance sheet at the beginning of the period is:

Plant assets	$500,000	Stockholders' equity	$500,000

If we assume that the company earns no revenue over the five years, the income statements are:

	Year 1	Year 2	Year 3	Year 4	Year 5
Revenue	$ –0–	$ –0–	$ –0–	$ –0–	$ –0–
Depreciation	(100,000)	(100,000)	(100,000)	(100,000)	(100,000)
Loss	$(100,000)	$(100,000)	$(100,000)	$(100,000)	$(100,000)

Total depreciation of the plant assets over the five years is $500,000. The balance sheet at the end of the five years therefore is:

Plant assets	–0–	Stockholders' equity	–0–

This extreme example illustrates that depreciation **in no way** provides funds for the replacement of assets. **The funds for the replacement of the assets come from the revenues** (generated through use of the asset). Without the revenues, no income materializes and no cash inflow results.

Revision of Depreciation Rates

When purchasing a plant asset, companies carefully determine depreciation rates based on past experience with similar assets and other pertinent information. The provisions for depreciation are only estimates, however. Companies may need to revise them during the life of the asset. Unexpected physical deterioration or unforeseen obsolescence may decrease the estimated useful life of the asset. Improved maintenance procedures, revision of operating procedures, or similar developments may prolong the life of the asset beyond the expected period.[8]

For example, assume that **International Paper Co.** purchased machinery with an original cost of $90,000. It estimates a 20-year life with no salvage value. However, during year 6, International Paper estimates that it will use the machine for an additional 25 years. Its total life, therefore, will be 30 years instead of 20. Depreciation has been recorded at the rate of 1/20 of $90,000, or $4,500 per year by the straight-line method. On the basis of a 30-year life, International Paper should have recorded depreciation as 1/30 of $90,000, or $3,000 per year. It has therefore overstated depreciation, and understated net income, by $1,500 for each of the past five years, or a total amount of $7,500. Illustration 11-13 shows this computation.

ILLUSTRATION 11-13
Computation of Accumulated Difference Due to Revisions

	Per Year	For 5 Years
Depreciation charged per books (1/20 × $90,000)	$4,500	$22,500
Depreciation based on a 30-year life (1/30 × $90,000)	(3,000)	(15,000)
Excess depreciation charged	$1,500	$ 7,500

International Paper should report this change in estimate in the current and prospective periods (prospectively): It should not make any changes in previously reported results. And it does not adjust opening balances nor attempt to "catch up" for prior periods. The reason? Changes in estimates are a continual and inherent part of any estimation process. Continual restatement of prior periods would occur for revisions of estimates unless handled prospectively. Therefore, no entry is made at the time the change in estimate occurs. Charges for depreciation in subsequent periods (assuming use of the straight-line method) are determined by **dividing the remaining book value less any salvage value by the remaining estimated life.**

ILLUSTRATION 11-14
Computing Depreciation after Revision of Estimated Life

Machinery	$90,000
Less: Accumulated depreciation	22,500
Book value of machinery at end of 5th year	$67,500

Depreciation (future periods) = $67,500 book value ÷ 25 years remaining life = $2,700

The entry to record depreciation for each of the remaining 25 years is:

Depreciation Expense	2,700	
Accumulated Depreciation—Machinery		2,700

[8]As an example of a change in operating procedures, **General Motors (GM)** used to write off its tools—such as dies and equipment used to manufacture car bodies—over the life of the body type. Through this procedure, it expensed tools twice as fast as **Ford** and three times as fast as **Chrysler**. However, it slowed the depreciation process on these tools and lengthened the lives on its plant and equipment. These revisions reduced depreciation and amortization charges by approximately $1.23 billion, or $2.55 per share, in the year of the change. In Chapter 22, we provide a more complete discussion of changes in estimates.

What do the numbers mean? DEPRECIATION CHOICES

The amount of depreciation expense recorded depends on both the depreciation method used and estimates of service lives and salvage values of the assets. Differences in these choices and estimates can significantly impact a company's reported results and can make it difficult to compare the depreciation numbers of different companies.

For example, when **Willamette Industries** extended the estimated service lives of its machinery and equipment by five years, it increased income by nearly $54 million (see Note 4 to the right).

An analyst determines the impact of these management choices and judgments on the amount of depreciation expense by examining the notes to financial statements. For example, Willamette Industries provided the following note to its financial statements.

Note 4: Property, Plant, and Equipment (partial)

	Range of Useful Lives
Land	—
Buildings	15–35
Machinery & equipment	5–25
Furniture & fixtures	3–15

During the year, the estimated service lives for most machinery and equipment were extended five years. The change was based upon a study performed by the company's engineering department, comparisons to typical industry practices, and the effect of the company's extensive capital investments which have resulted in a mix of assets with longer productive lives due to technological advances. As a result of the change, net income was increased by $54,000,000.

IMPAIRMENTS

5 LEARNING OBJECTIVE
Explain the accounting issues related to asset impairment.

The general accounting standard of **lower-of-cost-or-market for inventories does not apply to property, plant, and equipment**. Even when property, plant, and equipment has suffered partial obsolescence, accountants have been reluctant to reduce the asset's carrying amount. Why? Because, unlike inventories, it is difficult to arrive at a fair value for property, plant, and equipment that is not subjective and arbitrary.

For example, **Falconbridge Ltd. Nickel Mines** had to decide whether to write off all or a part of its property, plant, and equipment in a nickel-mining operation in the Dominican Republic. The project had been incurring losses because nickel prices were low and operating costs were high. Only if nickel prices increased by approximately 33 percent would the project be reasonably profitable. Whether a write-off was appropriate depended on the future price of nickel. Even if the company decided to write off the asset, how much should be written off?

Underlying Concepts

The *going concern concept* assumes that the company can recover the investment in its assets. Under GAAP, companies do not report the fair value of long-lived assets because a going concern does not plan to sell such assets. However, if the assumption of being able to recover the cost of the investment is not valid, then a company should report a reduction in value.

Recognizing Impairments

As discussed in the opening story, the credit crisis starting in late 2008 has affected many financial and nonfinancial institutions. As a result of the global slump, many companies are considering write-offs of some of their long-lived assets. These write-offs are referred to as **impairments**.

Various events and changes in circumstances might lead to an impairment. Examples are:

- A significant decrease in the fair value of an asset.
- A significant change in the extent or manner in which an asset is used.
- A significant adverse change in legal factors or in the business climate that affects the value of an asset.

- An accumulation of costs significantly in excess of the amount originally expected to acquire or construct an asset.
- A projection or forecast that demonstrates continuing losses associated with an asset.

See the FASB Codification section (page 618).

These events or changes in circumstances indicate that the company may not be able to recover the carrying amount of the asset. In that case, a **recoverability test** is used to determine whether an impairment has occurred. **[1]**

To apply the first step of the recoverability test, a company like **UPS** estimates the future net cash flows expected from the **use of that asset and its eventual disposition.** If the sum of the expected future net cash flows (undiscounted) is **less than the carrying amount** of the asset, UPS considers the asset impaired. Conversely, if the sum of the expected future net cash flows (undiscounted) is **equal to or greater than the carrying amount** of the asset, no impairment has occurred.

The recoverability test therefore screens for asset impairment. For example, if the expected future net cash flows from an asset are $400,000 and its carrying amount is $350,000, no impairment has occurred. However, if the expected future net cash flows are $300,000, an impairment has occurred. The rationale for the recoverability test relies on a basic presumption: A balance sheet should report long-lived assets at no more than the carrying amounts that are recoverable.

Measuring Impairments

If the recoverability test indicates an impairment, UPS computes a loss. The **impairment loss** is the amount by which the carrying amount of the asset **exceeds its fair value.** How does UPS determine the fair value of an asset? It is measured based on the market price if an active market for the asset exists. If no active market exists, UPS uses the **present value of expected future net cash flows to determine fair value.**

International Perspective

IFRS also uses a fair value test to measure the impairment loss. However, IFRS does not use the first-stage recoverability test used under GAAP—comparing the undiscounted cash flows to the carrying amount. As a result, the IFRS test is more strict than GAAP.

To summarize, the process of determining an impairment loss is as follows.

1. Review events or changes in circumstances for possible impairment.
2. If the review indicates a possible impairment, apply the recoverability test. If the sum of the expected future net cash flows from the long-lived asset is less than the carrying amount of the asset, an impairment has occurred.
3. Assuming an impairment, the impairment loss is the amount by which the carrying amount of the asset exceeds the fair value of the asset. The fair value is the market price of the asset or the present value of expected future net cash flows.

Impairment—Example 1

M. Alou Inc. has equipment that, due to changes in its use, it reviews for possible impairment. The equipment's carrying amount is $600,000 ($800,000 cost less $200,000 accumulated depreciation). Alou determines the expected future net cash flows (undiscounted) from the use of the equipment and its eventual disposal to be $650,000.

The recoverability test indicates that the $650,000 of expected future net cash flows from the equipment's use exceed the carrying amount of $600,000. As a result, no impairment occurred. (Recall that the undiscounted future net cash flows must be less than the carrying amount for Alou to deem an asset to be impaired and to measure the impairment loss.) Therefore, M. Alou Inc. does not recognize an impairment loss in this case.

Impairment—Example 2

Assume the same facts as in Example 1, except that the expected future net cash flows from Alou's equipment are $580,000 (instead of $650,000). The recoverability test indicates that the expected future net cash flows of $580,000 from the use of the asset are less than its carrying amount of $600,000. Therefore, an impairment has occurred.

The difference between the carrying amount of Alou's asset and its fair value is the impairment loss. Assuming this asset has a fair value of $525,000, Illustration 11-15 shows the loss computation.

ILLUSTRATION 11-15
Computation of Impairment Loss

Carrying amount of the equipment	$600,000
Fair value of equipment	(525,000)
Loss on impairment	$ 75,000

M. Alou records the impairment loss as follows.

Loss on Impairment	75,000	
Accumulated Depreciation—Equipment		75,000

M. Alou Inc. reports the impairment loss as part of income from continuing operations, in the "Other expenses and losses" section. Generally, Alou **should not report this loss as an extraordinary item**. Costs associated with an impairment loss are the same costs that would flow through operations and that it would report as part of continuing operations. Alou will continue to use these assets in operations. Therefore, it should not report the loss below "Income from continuing operations."

A company that recognizes an impairment loss should disclose the asset(s) impaired, the events leading to the impairment, the amount of the loss, and how it determined fair value (disclosing the interest rate used, if appropriate).

Restoration of Impairment Loss

After recording an impairment loss, the reduced carrying amount of an asset held for use becomes its new cost basis. A company does not change the new cost basis except for depreciation or amortization in future periods or for additional impairments.

To illustrate, assume that Damon Company at December 31, 2013, has equipment with a carrying amount of $500,000. Damon determines this asset is impaired and writes it down to its fair value of $400,000. At the end of 2014, Damon determines that the fair value of the asset is $480,000. The carrying amount of the equipment should not change in 2014 except for the depreciation taken in 2014. Damon **may not restore an impairment loss for an asset held for use**. The rationale for not writing the asset up in value is that the new cost basis puts the impaired asset on an equal basis with other assets that are unimpaired.

International Perspective

IFRS permits write-ups for subsequent recoveries of impairment, back up to the original amount before the impairment. GAAP prohibits those write-ups, except for assets to be disposed of.

Impairment of Assets to Be Disposed Of

What happens if a company intends to dispose of the impaired asset, instead of holding it for use? At one time, Kroger recorded an impairment loss of $54 million on property, plant, and equipment it no longer needed due to store closures. In this case, Kroger reports the impaired asset at the lower-of-cost-or-net realizable value (fair value less costs to sell). Because Kroger intends to dispose of the assets in a short period of time, it uses net realizable value in order to provide a better measure of the net cash flows that it will receive from these assets.

Kroger does not depreciate or amortize assets held for disposal during the period it holds them. The rationale is that depreciation is inconsistent with the notion of assets to be disposed of and with the use of the lower-of-cost-or-net realizable value. In other words, **assets held for disposal are like inventory; companies should report them at the lower-of-cost-or-net realizable value.**

Because Kroger will recover assets held for disposal through sale rather than through operations, it continually revalues them. Each period, the assets are reported at the lower-of-cost-or-net realizable value. Thus, **Kroger can write up or down an asset held for disposal in future periods, as long as the carrying value after the write-up never exceeds the carrying amount of the asset before the impairment.** Companies should report losses or gains related to these impaired assets as part of **income from continuing operations.**

Illustration 11-16 summarizes the key concepts in accounting for impairments.

ILLUSTRATION 11-16
Graphic of Accounting for Impairments

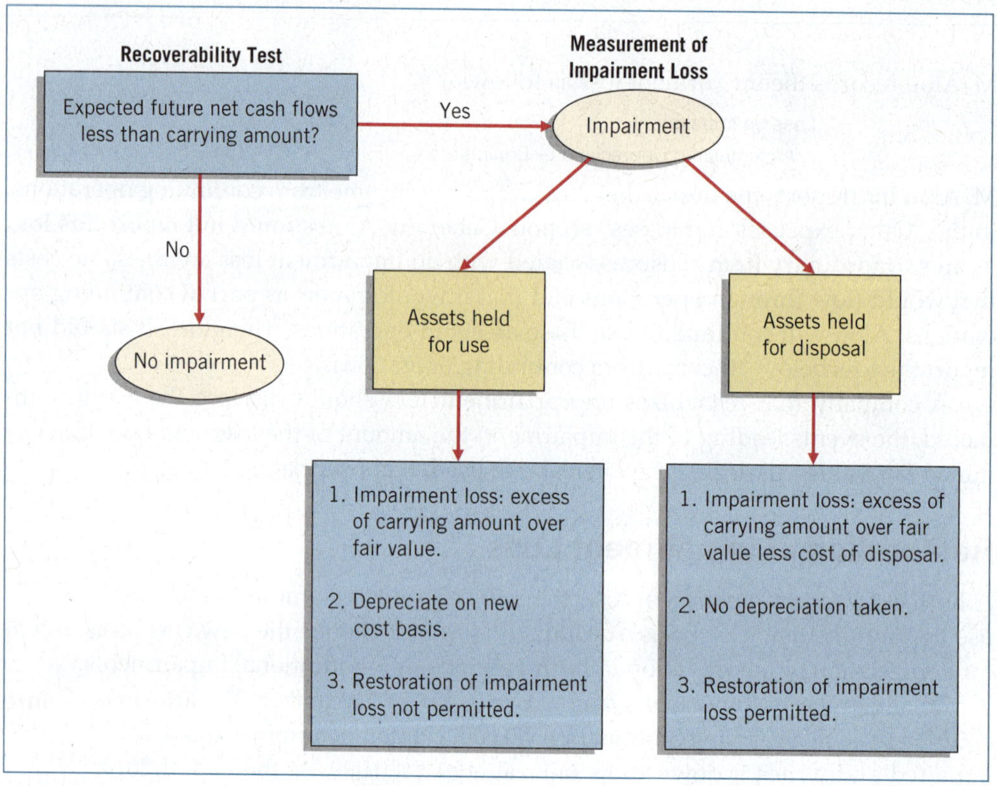

DEPLETION

LEARNING OBJECTIVE 6
Explain the accounting procedures for depletion of natural resources.

Natural resources, often called wasting assets, include petroleum, minerals, and timber. They have two main features: (1) the complete removal (consumption) of the asset, and (2) replacement of the asset only by an act of nature. Unlike plant and equipment, natural resources are consumed physically over the period of use and do not maintain their physical characteristics. Still, the accounting problems associated with natural resources are similar to those encountered with fixed assets. The questions to be answered are:

1. How do companies establish the cost basis for write-off?
2. What pattern of allocation should companies employ?

Recall that the accounting profession uses the term **depletion** for the process of allocating the cost of natural resources.

Establishing a Depletion Base

How do we determine the depletion base for natural resources? For example, a company like **ExxonMobil** makes sizable expenditures to find natural resources. And for every successful discovery, there are many failures. Furthermore, the company encounters long delays between the time it incurs costs and the time it obtains the benefits from the extracted resources. As a result, a company in the extractive industries, like ExxonMobil, frequently adopts a conservative policy in accounting for the expenditures related to finding and extracting natural resources.

Computation of the depletion base involves four factors: (1) acquisition cost of the deposit, (2) exploration costs, (3) development costs, and (4) restoration costs.

Acquisition Costs

Acquisition cost is the price ExxonMobil pays to obtain the property right to search and find an undiscovered natural resource. It also can be the price paid for an already-discovered resource. A third type of acquisition cost can be lease payments for property containing a productive natural resource. Included in these acquisition costs are royalty payments to the owner of the property.

Generally, the acquisition cost of natural resources is recorded in an account titled Undeveloped Property. ExxonMobil later assigns that cost to the natural resource if exploration efforts are successful. If the efforts are unsuccessful, it writes off the acquisition cost as a loss.

Exploration Costs

As soon as a company has the right to use the property, it often incurs **exploration costs** needed to find the resource. When exploration costs are substantial, some companies capitalize them into the depletion base. In the oil and gas industry, where the costs of finding the resource are significant and the risks of finding the resource are very uncertain, most large companies expense these costs. Smaller oil and gas companies often capitalize these exploration costs. We examine the unique issues related to the oil and gas industry on pages 608–609 (see "Continuing Controversy").

Development Costs

Companies divide **development costs** into two parts: (1) tangible equipment costs and (2) intangible development costs. Tangible equipment costs include all of the transportation and other heavy equipment needed to extract the resource and get it ready for market. Because companies can move the heavy equipment from one extracting site to another, companies do not normally include **tangible equipment costs in the depletion base**. Instead, they use separate depreciation charges to allocate the costs of such equipment. However, some tangible assets (e.g., a drilling rig foundation) cannot be moved. Companies depreciate these assets over their useful life or the life of the resource, whichever is shorter.

Intangible development costs, on the other hand, are such items as drilling costs, tunnels, shafts, and wells. These costs have no tangible characteristics but are needed for the production of the natural resource. **Intangible development costs are considered part of the depletion base.**

Restoration Costs

Companies sometimes incur substantial costs to restore property to its natural state after extraction has occurred. These are **restoration costs**. Companies consider **restoration costs part of the depletion base**. The amount included in the depletion base is the fair value of the obligation to restore the property after extraction. A more complete discussion of the accounting for restoration costs and related liabilities (sometimes referred to as asset retirement obligations) is provided in Chapter 13. Similar to other long-lived assets, companies deduct from the depletion base any salvage value to be received on the property.

Write-Off of Resource Cost

Once the company establishes the depletion base, the next problem is determining how to allocate the cost of the natural resource to accounting periods.

Normally, companies compute depletion (often referred to as **cost depletion**) on a **units-of-production method** (an activity approach). Thus, depletion is a function of the number of units extracted during the period. In this approach, the total cost of the natural resource less salvage value is divided by the number of units estimated to be in the resource deposit, to obtain a **cost per unit of product**. To compute depletion, the cost per unit is then multiplied by the number of units extracted.

For example, MaClede Co. acquired the right to use 1,000 acres of land in Alaska to mine for gold. The lease cost is $50,000, and the related exploration costs on the property are $100,000. Intangible development costs incurred in opening the mine are $850,000. Total costs related to the mine before the first ounce of gold is extracted are, therefore, $1,000,000. MaClede estimates that the mine will provide approximately 100,000 ounces of gold. Illustration 11-17 shows computation of the depletion cost per unit (depletion rate).

ILLUSTRATION 11-17
Computation of Depletion Rate

$$\frac{\text{Total cost} - \text{Salvage value}}{\text{Total estimated units available}} = \text{Depletion cost per unit}$$

$$\frac{\$1{,}000{,}000}{100{,}000} = \$10 \text{ per ounce}$$

If MaClede extracts 25,000 ounces in the first year, then the depletion for the year is $250,000 (25,000 ounces × $10). It records the depletion as follows.

Inventory (gold)	250,000	
Gold Mine		250,000

MaClede debits Inventory for the total depletion for the year and credits Gold Mine to reduce the carrying value of the natural resource. MaClede credits Inventory when it sells the inventory and debits Cost of Goods Sold. The amount not sold remains in inventory and is reported in the current assets section of the balance sheet.[9]

Sometimes companies use an Accumulated Depletion account. In that case, MaClede's balance sheet would present the cost of the natural resource and the amount of accumulated depletion entered to date as follows.

ILLUSTRATION 11-18
Balance Sheet Presentation of Natural Resource

Gold mine (at cost)	$1,000,000	
Less: Accumulated depletion	250,000	$750,000

For purposes of homework, credit depletion to the asset account.

[9] The tax law has long provided a deduction against revenue from oil, gas, and most minerals for the greater of cost or **percentage depletion**. The percentage (statutory) depletion allows some companies a write-off ranging from 5 percent to 22 percent (depending on the natural resource) of gross revenue received. As a result of this tax benefit, the amount of depletion may exceed the cost assigned to a given natural resource. An asset's carrying amount may be zero, but the company may take a depletion deduction if it has gross revenue. The significance of the percentage depletion allowance is now greatly reduced since Congress repealed it for most oil and gas companies.

MaClede may also depreciate on a units-of-production basis the tangible equipment used in extracting the gold. This approach is appropriate if it can directly assign the estimated lives of the equipment to one given resource deposit. If MaClede uses the equipment on more than one job, other cost allocation methods such as straight-line or accelerated depreciation methods would be more appropriate.

Estimating Recoverable Reserves

Sometimes companies need to change the estimate of recoverable reserves. They do so either because they have new information or because more sophisticated production processes are available. Natural resources such as oil and gas deposits and some rare metals have recently provided the greatest challenges. Estimates of these reserves are in large measure merely "knowledgeable guesses."

This problem is the **same as accounting for changes in estimates for the useful lives of plant and equipment**. The procedure is to **revise the depletion rate on a prospective basis**: A company divides the remaining cost by the new estimate of the recoverable reserves. This approach has much merit because the required estimates are so uncertain.

What do the numbers mean? RESERVE SURPRISE

Cuts in the estimates of oil and natural gas reserves at **Royal Dutch Shell**, **El Paso Corporation**, and other energy companies at one time highlighted the importance of reserve disclosures. Investors appeared to believe that these disclosures provide useful information for assessing the future cash flows from a company's oil and gas reserves. For example, when Shell's estimates turned out to be overly optimistic (to the tune of 3.9 billion barrels or 20 percent of reserves), Shell's stock price fell.

The experience at Shell and other companies has led the SEC to look at how companies are estimating their "proved" reserves. *Proved reserves* are quantities of oil and gas that can be shown "with reasonable certainty to be recoverable in future years. . . ." The phrase "reasonable certainty" is crucial to this guidance, but differences in interpretation of what is reasonably certain can result in a wide range of estimates.

In one case, for example, **ExxonMobil**'s estimate was 29 percent higher than an estimate the SEC developed. ExxonMobil was more optimistic about the effects of new technology that enables the industry to retrieve more of the oil and gas it finds. Thus, to ensure the continued usefulness of reserve information disclosures, the SEC continues to work on a measurement methodology that keeps up with technology changes in the oil and gas industry.

Sources: S. Labaton and J. Gerth, "At Shell, New Accounting and Rosier Outlook," *New York Times* (*nytimes.com*) (March 12, 2004); and J. Ball, C. Cummins, and B. Bahree, "Big Oil Differs with SEC on Methods to Calculate the Industry's Reserves," *Wall Street Journal* (February 24, 2005), p. C1.

Liquidating Dividends

A company often owns as its only major asset a property from which it intends to extract natural resources. If the company does not expect to purchase additional properties, it may gradually distribute to stockholders their capital investments by paying **liquidating dividends**, which are dividends greater than the amount of accumulated net income.

The major accounting problem is to distinguish between dividends that are a return of capital and those that are not. Because the dividend is a return of the investor's original contribution, the company issuing a liquidating dividend should debit Paid-in Capital in Excess of Par for that portion related to the original investment, instead of debiting Retained Earnings.

To illustrate, at year-end, Callahan Mining had a retained earnings balance of $1,650,000, accumulated depletion on mineral properties of $2,100,000, and paid-in capital in excess of par of $5,435,493. Callahan's board declared a dividend of $3 per share on the 1,000,000 shares outstanding. It records the $3,000,000 cash dividend as follows.

Retained Earnings	1,650,000	
Paid-in Capital in Excess of Par—Common Stock	1,350,000	
Cash		3,000,000

Callahan must inform stockholders that the $3 dividend per share represents a $1.65 ($1,650,000 ÷ 1,000,000 shares) per share return on investment and a $1.35 ($1,350,000 ÷ 1,000,000 shares) per share liquidating dividend.

Continuing Controversy

A major controversy relates to the accounting for exploration costs in the oil and gas industry. Conceptually, the question is whether unsuccessful ventures are a cost of those that are successful. Those who hold the **full-cost concept** argue that the cost of drilling a dry hole is a cost needed to find the commercially profitable wells. Others believe that companies should capitalize only the costs of successful projects. This is the **successful-efforts concept**. Its proponents believe that the only relevant measure for a project is the cost directly related to that project, and that companies should report any remaining costs as period charges. In addition, they argue that an unsuccessful company will end up capitalizing many costs that will make it, over a short period of time, show no less income than does one that is successful.[10]

The FASB has attempted to narrow the available alternatives, with little success. Here is a brief history of the debate.

1. *1977—The FASB required oil and gas companies to follow successful-efforts accounting.* Small oil and gas producers, voicing strong opposition, lobbied extensively in Congress. Governmental agencies assessed the implications of this standard from a public interest perspective and reacted contrary to the FASB's position.[11]
2. ***1978—In response to criticisms of the FASB's actions, the SEC reexamined the issue and found both the successful-efforts and full-cost approaches inadequate. Neither method, said the SEC, reflects the economic substance of oil and gas exploration.*** As a substitute, the SEC argued in favor of a yet-to-be developed method, **reserve recognition accounting (RRA)**, which it believed would provide more useful information. Under RRA, as soon as a company discovers oil, it reports the value of the oil on the balance sheet and in the income statement. Thus, RRA is a fair value approach, in contrast to full-costing and successful-efforts, which are historical cost approaches. The use of RRA would make a substantial difference in the balance sheets and income statements of oil companies. For example, **Atlantic Richfield Co.** at one time reported net producing property of $2.6 billion. Under RRA, the same properties would be valued at $11.8 billion.
3. ***1979–1981—As a result of the SEC's actions, the FASB issued another standard that suspended the requirement that companies follow successful-efforts accounting.***

[10]Large international oil companies such as **ExxonMobil** use the successful-efforts approach. Most of the smaller, exploration-oriented companies use the full-cost approach. The differences in net income figures under the two methods can be staggering. Analysts estimated that the difference between full-cost and successful-efforts for **ChevronTexaco** would be $500 million over a 10-year period (income lower under successful-efforts).

[11]The Department of Energy indicated that companies using the full-cost method at that time would reduce their exploration activities because of the unfavorable earnings impact associated with successful-efforts accounting. The Justice Department asked the SEC to postpone adoption of one uniform method of accounting in the oil and gas industry until the SEC could determine whether the information reported to investors would be enhanced and competition constrained by adoption of the successful-efforts method.

Therefore, full-costing was again permissible. In attempting to implement RRA, however, the SEC encountered practical problems in estimating **(1) the amount of the reserves, (2) the future production costs, (3) the periods of expected disposal, (4) the discount rate, and (5) the selling price**. Companies needed an estimate for each of these to arrive at an accurate valuation of existing reserves. Estimating the future selling price, appropriate discount rate, and future extraction and delivery costs of reserves that are years away from realization can be a formidable task.

4. ***1981—The SEC abandoned RRA in the primary financial statements of oil and gas producers.*** The SEC decided that RRA did not possess the required degree of reliability for use as a primary method of financial reporting. However, it continued to stress the need for some form of fair-value-based disclosure for oil and gas reserves. As a result, the profession now requires fair value disclosures for those natural resources.

Currently, companies can use either the full-cost approach or the successful-efforts approach. It does seem ironic that Congress directed the FASB to develop one method of accounting for the oil and gas industry, and when the FASB did so, the government chose not to accept it. Subsequently, the SEC attempted to develop a new approach, failed, and then urged the FASB to develop the disclosure requirements in this area. After all these changes, the two alternatives still exist.[12]

International Perspective

IFRS also permits companies to use either full-cost or successful-efforts approaches.

Evolving Issue FULL-COST OR SUCCESSFUL-EFFORTS?

The controversy in the oil and gas industry provides a number of lessons. First, it demonstrates the strong influence that the federal government has in financial reporting matters. Second, the concern for economic consequences places pressure on the FASB to weigh the economic effects of any required standard. Third, the experience with RRA highlights the problems that accompany any proposed change from an historical cost to a fair value approach. Fourth, this controversy illustrates the difficulty of establishing standards when affected groups have differing viewpoints.

Indeed, failure to consider the economic consequences of accounting principles is a frequent criticism of the profession. However, the neutrality concept requires that the statements be free from bias. Freedom from bias requires that the statements reflect economic reality, even if undesirable effects occur. Finally, the debate over oil and gas accounting reinforces the need for a conceptual framework with carefully developed guidelines for recognition, measurement, and reporting, so that interested parties can more easily resolve issues of this nature in the future.

PRESENTATION AND ANALYSIS

Presentation of Property, Plant, Equipment, and Natural Resources

7 LEARNING OBJECTIVE

Explain how to report and analyze property, plant, equipment, and natural resources.

A company should disclose the basis of valuation—usually historical cost—for property, plant, equipment, and natural resources along with pledges, liens, and other commitments related to these assets. It should not offset any liability secured by property, plant, equipment, and natural resources against these assets. Instead, this obligation should be reported in the liabilities section. The company should

[12]One requirement of the full-cost approach is that companies can capitalize costs only up to a ceiling, which is the present value of company reserves. Companies must expense costs above that ceiling. When the price of oil fell in the mid-1980s, so did the present value of companies' reserves, which forced expensing of costs beyond the ceiling. Companies lobbied for leniency, but the SEC decided that the write-offs had to be taken. Mesa Limited Partnerships restated its $31 million profit to a $169 million loss, and Pacific Lighting restated its $44.5 million profit to a $70.5 million loss.

segregate property, plant, and equipment not currently employed as producing assets in the business (such as idle facilities or land held as an investment) from assets used in operations.

When depreciating assets, a company credits a valuation account such as Accumulated Depreciation—Equipment. Using an accumulated depreciation account permits the user of the financial statements to see the original cost of the asset and the amount of depreciation that the company charged to expense in past years.

When depleting natural resources, some companies use an accumulated depletion account. Many, however, simply credit the natural resource account directly. The rationale for this approach is that the natural resources are physically consumed, making direct reduction of the cost of the natural resources appropriate.

Because of the significant impact on the financial statements of the depreciation method(s) used, companies should disclose the following.

1. Depreciation expense for the period.
2. Balances of major classes of depreciable assets, by nature and function.
3. Accumulated depreciation, either by major classes of depreciable assets or in total.
4. A general description of the method or methods used in computing depreciation with respect to major classes of depreciable assets. **[2]**[13]

Special disclosure requirements relate to the oil and gas industry. Companies engaged in these activities must disclose the following in their financial statements: (1) the basic method of accounting for those costs incurred in oil and gas producing activities (e.g., full-cost versus successful-efforts), and (2) how the company disposes of costs relating to extractive activities (e.g., dispensing immediately versus depreciation and depletion). **[3]**[14]

The 2011 annual report of **International Paper Company** in Illustration 11-19 shows an acceptable disclosure. It uses condensed balance sheet data supplemented with details and policies in notes to the financial statements.

ILLUSTRATION 11-19
Disclosures for Property, Plant, Equipment, and Natural Resources

International Paper Company

Consolidated Balance Sheet (partial)

In millions at December 31	2011	2010
Assets		
Total current assets	$10,456	$ 8,028
Plants, properties and equipment, net	11,817	12,002
Forestlands	660	747
Investments	632	1,092
Goodwill	2,346	2,308
Deferred charges and other assets	1,082	1,191
Total assets	$26,993	$25,368

[13]Some believe that companies should disclose the average useful life of the assets or the range of years of asset life to help users understand the age and life of property, plant, and equipment.

[14]Public companies, in addition to these two required disclosures, must include as supplementary information numerous schedules reporting reserve quantities; capitalized costs; acquisition, exploration, and development activities; and a standardized measure of discounted future net cash flows related to proved oil and gas reserve quantities. Given the importance of these disclosures, the SEC has issued rules for disclosures to help investors better understand the nature of oil and gas company operations. These rules provide updated guidance on (1) estimates of quantities of proved reserves, (2) estimates of future net revenues, and (3) disclosure of reserve information. See "Modernization of Oil and Gas Reporting," SEC Financial Reporting Release No. 78 (Release No. 33-8995) (December 31, 2008).

ILLUSTRATION 11-19
(continued)

Note 1 (partial)

Plants, Properties and Equipment. Plants, properties and equipment are stated at cost, less accumulated depreciation. Expenditures for betterments are capitalized, whereas normal repairs and maintenance are expensed as incurred. The units-of-production method of depreciation is used for major pulp and paper mills, and the straight-line method is used for other plants and equipment. Annual straight-line depreciation rates are, for buildings—2 1/2% to 8 1/2%, and for machinery and equipment—5% to 33%.

Forestlands. At December 31, 2011, International Paper and its subsidiaries owned or managed approximately 325,000 acres of forestlands in Brazil, and through licenses and forest management agreements, had harvesting rights on government-owned forestlands in Russia. Costs attributable to timber are charged against income as trees are cut. The rate charged is determined annually based on the relationship of incurred costs to estimated current merchantable volume.

Note 7 (partial)

Plants, properties and equipment by major classification were:

In millions at December 31	2011	2010
Pulp, paper and packaging facilities		
Mills	$22,494	$22,935
Packaging plants	6,358	6,534
Other plants, properties and equipment	1,556	1,524
Gross cost	30,408	30,993
Less: Accumulated depreciation	18,591	18,991
Plants, properties and equipment, net	$11,817	$12,002

In millions	2011	2010	2009
Depreciation expense	$1,263	$1,396	$1,416

Analysis of Property, Plant, and Equipment

Analysts evaluate assets relative to activity (turnover) and profitability.

Asset Turnover

How efficiently a company uses its assets to generate sales is measured by the **asset turnover**. This ratio divides net sales by average total assets for the period. The resulting number is the dollars of sales produced by each dollar invested in assets. To illustrate, we use the following data from the **Johnson & Johnson** 2011 annual report. Illustration 11-20 shows computation of the asset turnover.

Johnson & Johnson

	(in millions)
Net sales	$ 65,030
Total assets, 1/2/12	113,644
Total assets, 1/2/11	102,908
Net income	9,672

ILLUSTRATION 11-20
Asset Turnover

$$\text{Asset turnover} = \frac{\textbf{Net sales}}{\textbf{Average total assets}} = \frac{\$65{,}030}{(\$113{,}644 + \$102{,}908)/2} = .60$$

The asset turnover shows that Johnson & Johnson generated sales of $0.60 per dollar of assets in the year ended January 2, 2012.

Asset turnovers vary considerably among industries. For example, a large utility like **Ameren** has a ratio of 0.32 times. A large grocery chain like **Kroger** has a ratio of 2.73 times. Thus, in comparing performance among companies based on the asset turnover ratio, you need to consider the ratio within the context of the industry in which a company operates.

Profit Margin on Sales

Another measure for analyzing the use of property, plant, and equipment is the **profit margin on sales** (return on sales). Calculated as net income divided by net sales, this profitability ratio does not, by itself, answer the question of how profitably a company uses its assets. But by relating the profit margin on sales to the asset turnover during a period of time, we can ascertain how profitably the company used assets during that period of time in a measure of the return on assets. Using the Johnson & Johnson data shown on page 611, we compute the profit margin on sales and the return on assets as follows.

ILLUSTRATION 11-21
Profit Margin on Sales

$$\text{Profit margin on sales} = \frac{\text{Net income}}{\text{Net sales}} = \frac{\$9{,}672}{\$65{,}030} = 14.87\%$$

$$\text{Return on assets} = \text{Profit margin on sales} \times \text{Asset turnover} = 14.87\% \times .6006 = 8.93\%$$

Return on Assets

The **return on assets (ROA)** is computed directly by dividing net income by average total assets. Using Johnson & Johnson's data, we compute the ratio as follows.

ILLUSTRATION 11-22
Return on Assets

$$\text{Return on assets} = \frac{\text{Net income}}{\text{Average total assets}} = \frac{\$9{,}672}{(\$113{,}644 + \$102{,}908)/2} = 8.93\%$$

You will want to read the **IFRS INSIGHTS** on pages 637–646 for discussion of IFRS related to property, plant, and equipment.

The 8.93 percent return on assets computed in this manner equals the 8.93 percent rate computed by multiplying the profit margin on sales by the asset turnover. The rate of return on assets measures profitability well because it combines the effects of profit margin and asset turnover.

KEY TERMS

accelerated depreciation methods, *594*
activity method, *593*
amortization, *590*
asset turnover, *611*
composite approach, *596*
composite depreciation rate, *596*
cost depletion, *606*

SUMMARY OF LEARNING OBJECTIVES

1 Explain the concept of depreciation. Depreciation allocates the cost of tangible assets to expense in a systematic and rational manner to those periods expected to benefit from the use of the asset.

2 Identify the factors involved in the depreciation process. Three factors involved in the depreciation process are (1) determining the depreciation base for the asset, (2) estimating service lives, and (3) selecting a method of cost apportionment (depreciation).

3 Compare activity, straight-line, and decreasing-charge methods of depreciation. (1) *Activity method:* Assumes that depreciation is a function of use or productivity instead of the passage of time. The life of the asset is considered in terms of either the output it provides, or an input measure such as the number of hours it works. (2) *Straight-line method:* Considers depreciation a function of time instead of a function of usage. The straight-line procedure is often the most conceptually appropriate when the decline in usefulness is constant from period to period. (3) *Decreasing-charge methods:* Provide for a higher depreciation cost in the earlier years and lower charges in later periods. The main justification for this approach is that the asset is the most productive in its early years.

4 Explain special depreciation methods. Two special depreciation methods are as follows. (1) *Group and composite methods:* The group method is frequently used when the assets are fairly similar in nature and have approximately the same useful lives. The composite method may be used when the assets are dissimilar and have different lives. (2) *Hybrid or combination methods:* These methods may combine straight-line/activity approaches.

5 Explain the accounting issues related to asset impairment. The process to determine an impairment loss is as follows. (1) Review events and changes in circumstances for possible impairment. (2) If events or changes suggest impairment, determine if the sum of the expected future net cash flows from the long-lived asset is less than the carrying amount of the asset. If less, measure the impairment loss. (3) The impairment loss is the amount by which the carrying amount of the asset exceeds the fair value of the asset.

After a company records an impairment loss, the reduced carrying amount of the long-lived asset is its new cost basis. Impairment losses may not be restored for assets held for use. If the company expects to dispose of the asset, it should report the impaired asset at the lower-of-cost-or-net realizable value. It is not depreciated. It can be continuously revalued, as long as the write-up is never to an amount greater than the carrying amount before impairment.

6 Explain the accounting procedures for depletion of natural resources. To account for depletion of natural resources, companies (1) establish the depletion base and (2) write off resource cost. Four factors are part of establishing the depletion base: (a) acquisition costs, (b) exploration costs, (c) development costs, and (d) restoration costs. To write off resource cost, companies normally compute depletion on the units-of-production method. Thus, depletion is a function of the number of units withdrawn during the period. To obtain a cost per unit of product, the total cost of the natural resource less salvage value is divided by the number of units estimated to be in the resource deposit, to obtain a cost per unit of product. To compute depletion, this cost per unit is multiplied by the number of units withdrawn.

7 Explain how to report and analyze property, plant, equipment, and natural resources. The basis of valuation for property, plant, and equipment and for natural resources should be disclosed along with pledges, liens, and other commitments related to these assets. Companies should not offset any liability secured by property, plant, and equipment or by natural resources against these assets, but should report it in the liabilities section. When depreciating assets, credit a valuation account normally called Accumulated Depreciation. When depleting assets, use an accumulated depletion account, or credit the depletion directly to the natural resource account. Companies engaged in significant oil and gas producing activities must provide additional disclosures about these activities. Analysis may be performed to evaluate the asset turnover, profit margin on sales, and return on assets.

declining-balance method, *595*
decreasing-charge methods, *594*
depletion, *590, 604*
depreciation, *590*
depreciation base, *590*
development costs, *605*
double-declining-balance method, *595*
exploration costs, *605*
full-cost concept, *608*
group method, *595*
impairment, *601*
inadequacy, *591*
liquidating dividends, *607*
natural resources, *604*
obsolescence, *591*
percentage depletion, *606(n)*
profit margin on sales, *612*
recoverability test, *602*
reserve recognition accounting (RRA), *608*
restoration costs, *605*
return on assets (ROA), *612*
salvage value, *590*
straight-line method, *593*
successful-efforts concept, *608*
sum-of-the-years'-digits method, *594*
supersession, *591*

APPENDIX 11A INCOME TAX DEPRECIATION

LEARNING OBJECTIVE 8
Describe income tax methods of depreciation.

For the most part, a financial accounting course does not address issues related to the computation of income taxes. However, because the concepts of tax depreciation are similar to those of book depreciation and because tax depreciation methods are sometimes adopted for book purposes, we present an overview of this subject.

Congress passed the Accelerated Cost Recovery System (ACRS) as part of the Economic Recovery Tax Act of 1981. The goal was to stimulate capital investment through faster write-offs and to bring more uniformity to the write-off period. For assets purchased in the years 1981 through 1986, companies use ACRS and its preestablished "cost recovery periods" for various classes of assets.

In the Tax Reform Act of 1986 Congress enacted a **Modified Accelerated Cost Recovery System**, known as **MACRS**. It applies to depreciable assets placed in service in 1987 and later. The following discussion is based on these MACRS rules. Realize that tax depreciation rules are subject to change annually.[15]

MODIFIED ACCELERATED COST RECOVERY SYSTEM

The computation of depreciation under MACRS differs from the computation under GAAP in three respects: (1) a mandated tax life, which is generally shorter than the economic life; (2) cost recovery on an accelerated basis; and (3) an assigned salvage value of zero.

Tax Lives (Recovery Periods)

Each item of depreciable property belongs to a property class. The recovery period (depreciable tax life) of an asset depends on its property class. Illustration 11A-1 presents the MACRS property classes.

ILLUSTRATION 11A-1
MACRS Property Classes

3-year property	Includes small tools, horses, and assets used in research and development activities
5-year property	Includes automobiles, trucks, computers and peripheral equipment, and office machines
7-year property	Includes office furniture and fixtures, agriculture equipment, oil exploration and development equipment, railroad track, manufacturing equipment, and any property not designated by law as being in any other class
10-year property	Includes railroad tank cars, mobile homes, boilers, and certain public utility property
15-year property	Includes roads, shrubbery, and certain low-income housing
20-year property	Includes waste-water treatment plants and sewer systems
27.5-year property	Includes residential rental property
39-year property	Includes nonresidential real property

[15]For example, in an effort to jump-start the economy following the September 11, 2001, terrorist attacks, Congress passed the Job Creation and Worker Assistance Act of 2002 (the Act). The Act allows a 30 percent first-year bonus depreciation for assets placed into service after September 11, 2001, but before September 11, 2004. A follow-up provision enacted in 2003 extended the tax savings to assets placed in service before January 1, 2005. And in 2010, Congress extended bonus depreciation for smaller companies. These laws encourage companies to invest in fixed assets because they can front-load depreciation expense, which lowers taxable income and amount of taxes companies pay in the early years of an asset's life. Although the Act may be a good thing for the economy, it can distort cash flow measures—making them look artificially strong when the allowances are in place but reversing once the bonus depreciation expires. See D. Zion and B. Carcache, "Bonus Depreciation Boomerang," *Credit Suisse First Boston Equity Research* (February 19, 2004).

Tax Depreciation Methods

Companies compute depreciation expense using the tax basis—usually the cost—of the asset. The depreciation method depends on the MACRS property class, as shown below.

ILLUSTRATION 11A-2
Depreciation Method for Various MACRS Property Classes

MACRS Property Class	Depreciation Method
3-, 5-, 7-, and 10-year property	Double-declining-balance
15- and 20-year property	150% declining-balance
27.5- and 39-year property	Straight-line

Depreciation computations for income tax purposes are based on the **half-year convention**. That is, a half year of depreciation is allowable in the year of acquisition and in the year of disposition.[16] A company depreciates an asset to a zero value so that there is no salvage value at the end of its MACRS life.

Use of IRS-published tables, shown in Illustration 11A-3, simplifies application of these depreciation methods.

ILLUSTRATION 11A-3
IRS Table of MACRS Depreciation Rates, by Property Class

	MACRS Depreciation Rates by Class of Property					
Recovery Year	3-year (200% DB)	5-year (200% DB)	7-year (200% DB)	10-year (200% DB)	15-year (150% DB)	20-year (150% DB)
1	33.33	20.00	14.29	10.00	5.00	3.750
2	44.45	32.00	24.49	18.00	9.50	7.219
3	14.81*	19.20	17.49	14.40	8.55	6.677
4	7.41	11.52*	12.49	11.52	7.70	6.177
5		11.52	8.93*	9.22	6.93	5.713
6		5.76	8.92	7.37	6.23	5.285
7			8.93	6.55*	5.90*	4.888
8			4.46	6.55	5.90	4.522
9				6.56	5.91	4.462*
10				6.55	5.90	4.461
11				3.28	5.91	4.462
12					5.90	4.461
13					5.91	4.462
14					5.90	4.461
15					5.91	4.462
16					2.95	4.461
17						4.462
18						4.461
19						4.462
20						4.461
21						2.231

*Switchover to straight-line depreciation.

Example of MACRS

To illustrate depreciation computations under both MACRS and GAAP straight-line accounting, assume the following facts for a computer and peripheral equipment purchased by Denise Rode Company on January 1, 2013.

[16]The tax law requires mid-quarter and mid-month conventions for MACRS purposes in certain circumstances.

Acquisition Date	January 1, 2013
Cost	$100,000
Estimated useful life	7 years
Estimated salvage value	$16,000
MACRS class life	5 years
MACRS method	200% declining-balance
GAAP method	Straight-line
Disposal proceeds—January 2, 2020	$11,000

Using the rates from the MACRS depreciation rate schedule for a 5-year class of property, Rode computes depreciation as follows for tax purposes.

ILLUSTRATION 11A-4
Computation of MACRS Depreciation

MACRS Depreciation

2013	$100,000 × .20	=	$ 20,000
2014	$100,000 × .32	=	32,000
2015	$100,000 × .192	=	19,200
2016	$100,000 × .1152	=	11,520
2017	$100,000 × .1152	=	11,520
2018	$100,000 × .0576	=	5,760
	Total depreciation		$100,000

Rode computes the depreciation under GAAP straight-line method, with $16,000 of estimated salvage value and an estimated useful life of 7 years, as shown in Illustration 11A-5.

ILLUSTRATION 11A-5
Computation of GAAP Depreciation

GAAP Depreciation

($100,000 − $16,000) ÷ 7 =	$12,000 annual depreciation
	× 7 years
1/1/13–1/2/20	$84,000 total depreciation

The MACRS depreciation recovers the total cost of the asset on an accelerated basis. But, a taxable gain of $11,000 results from the sale of the asset at January 2, 2020. Therefore, the net effect on taxable income for the years 2013 through 2020 is $89,000 ($100,000 depreciation − $11,000 gain).

Under GAAP, the company recognizes a loss on disposal of $5,000 ($16,000 book value − $11,000 disposal proceeds). The net effect on income before income taxes for the years 2013 through 2020 is $89,000 ($84,000 depreciation + $5,000 loss), the same as the net effect of MACRS on taxable income.

Even though the net effects are equal in amount, the deferral of income tax payments under MACRS from early in the life of the asset to later in life is desirable. The different amounts of depreciation for income tax reporting and financial GAAP reporting in each year are a matter of timing and result in temporary differences, which require **interperiod tax allocation**. (See Chapter 19 for an extended treatment of this topic.)

OPTIONAL STRAIGHT-LINE METHOD

An alternate MACRS method exists for determining depreciation deductions. Based on the straight-line method, it is referred to as the **optional** (elective) **straight-line method**. This method applies to the six classes of property described earlier. The alternate

MACRS applies the straight-line method to the MACRS recovery periods. It ignores salvage value.

Under the optional straight-line method, in the first year in which the property is put in service, the company deducts half of the amount of depreciation that would be permitted for a full year (half-year convention). *Use the half-year convention for homework problems.*

TAX VERSUS BOOK DEPRECIATION

GAAP requires that companies allocate the cost of depreciable assets to expense over the expected useful life of the asset in a systematic and rational manner. Some argue that from a cost-benefit perspective it would be better for companies to adopt the MACRS approach in order to eliminate the necessity of maintaining two different sets of records.

However, the tax laws and financial reporting have different objectives. The purpose of taxation is to raise revenue from constituents in an equitable manner. The purpose of financial reporting is to reflect the economic substance of a transaction as closely as possible and to help predict the amounts, timing, and uncertainty of future cash flows. Because these objectives differ, the adoption of one method for both tax and book purposes in all cases is not in accordance with GAAP.

SUMMARY OF LEARNING OBJECTIVE FOR APPENDIX 11A

KEY TERM

Modified Accelerated Cost Recovery System (MACRS), *614*

8 Describe income tax methods of depreciation. Congress enacted a Modified Accelerated Cost Recovery System (MACRS) in the Tax Reform Act of 1986. It applies to depreciable assets placed in service in 1987 and later. The computation of depreciation under MACRS differs from the computation under GAAP in three respects: (1) a mandated tax life, which is generally shorter than the economic life; (2) cost recovery on an accelerated basis; and (3) an assigned salvage value of zero.

DEMONSTRATION PROBLEM

Norwel Company manufactures miniature circuit boards used in smartphones. On June 5, 2014, Norwel purchased a circuit board stamping machine at a retail price of $24,000. Norwel paid 5% sales tax on this purchase and hired a contractor to build a specially wired platform for the machine for $1,800, to meet OSHA safety requirements. Norwel estimates the machine will have a 5-year useful life, with a salvage value of $2,000 at the end of 5 years. Norwel uses straight-line depreciation and employs the "half-year" convention in accounting for partial-year depreciation. Norwel's fiscal year ends on December 31.

Instructions

(a) At what amount should Norwel record the acquisition cost of the machine?

(b) How much depreciation expense should Norwel record in 2014 and in 2015?

(c) At what amount will the machine be reported in Norwel's balance sheet at December 31, 2015?

(d) During 2016, Norwel's circuit board business is experiencing significant competition from companies with more advanced low-heat circuit boards. As a result, at June 30, 2016, Norwel conducts an impairment evaluation of the stamping machine purchased in 2014. Norwel determines that undiscounted future cash flows for the machine are estimated to be $15,200 and the fair value of the machine, based on prices in the re-sale market, to be $13,400. Prepare the journal entry to record an impairment, if any, on the stamping machine.

Solution

(a) Historical cost is measured by the cash or cash equivalent price of obtaining the asset and bringing it to the location and condition for its intended use. For Norwel, this is:

Price	$24,000
Tax ($24,000 × .05)	1,200
Platform	1,800
Total	$27,000

(b) Depreciable base: $27,000 − $2,000 = $25,000

Depreciation expense: $25,000 ÷ 5 = $5,000 per year

2014: 1/2 year = $5,000 × .50 = $2,500
2015: full year = $5,000

(c) The amount reported on the balance sheet is the cost of the asset less accumulated depreciation:

Machinery	$27,000
Less: Accumulated depreciation	7,500
Book value	$19,500

(d) Norwel first conducts the recoverability test, comparing the book value of the machine to the undiscounted future cash flows. This indicates the future cash flows ($15,200) are less than the book value ($17,000*).

*Cost	$27,000
Less: Accumulated depreciation ($2,500 + $5,000 + $2,500)	10,000
Book value of machine and platform	$17,000

Thus, Norwel will record an impairment, based on comparison of the fair value of the machine and platform to the book value. The entry is as follows.

Loss on Impairment ($17,000 − $13,400)	3,600	
Accumulated Depreciation—Machinery		3,600

FASB CODIFICATION

FASB Codification References

[1] FASB ASC 360-10-05. [Predecessor literature: "Accounting for the Impairment or Disposal of Long-lived Assets," *Statement of Financial Accounting Standards No. 144* (Norwalk, Conn.: 2001).]

[2] FASB ASC 360-10-50-1. [Predecessor literature: "Omnibus Opinion—1967," *Opinions of the Accounting Principles Board No. 12* (New York: AICPA, 1967), par. 5.]

[3] FASB ASC 932-235-50-1. [Predecessor literature: "Disclosures about Oil and Gas Producing Activities," *Statement of Financial Accounting Standards Board No. 69* (Stamford, Conn.: FASB, 1982).]

Exercises

If your school has a subscription to the FASB Codification, go to *http://aaahq.org/asclogin.cfm* to log in and prepare responses to the following. Provide Codification references for your responses.

CE11-1 Access the glossary ("Master Glossary") to answer the following.

(a) What is the definition of amortization?
(b) What is the definition of impairment?
(c) What is the definition of recoverable amount?
(d) What are activities, as they relate to the construction of an asset?

CE11-2 Your client, Barriques Inc., is contemplating a restructuring of its operations, including the possibility of spinning off some of its assets to the original owners. However, management is unsure of the accounting for any impairment on the assets. What does the authoritative literature say about these types of impairments?

CE11-3 Your great-uncle, who is a CPA, is impressed that you are majoring in accounting. But, he believes that depreciation is something that companies do based on past practice, not on the basis of any authoritative guidance. Provide the authoritative literature to support the practice of fixed-asset depreciation.

CE11-4 What is the nature of SEC guidance concerning property, plant, and equipment disclosures?

An additional Codification case can be found in the Using Your Judgment section, on page 637.

Be sure to check the book's companion website for a Review and Analysis Exercise, with solution.

WileyPLUS **Brief Exercises, Exercises, Problems, and many more learning and assessment tools and resources are available for practice in WileyPLUS.**

Note: All asterisked Questions, Exercises, and Problems relate to material in the appendix to the chapter.

QUESTIONS

1. Distinguish among depreciation, depletion, and amortization.
2. Identify the factors that are relevant in determining the annual depreciation charge, and explain whether these factors are determined objectively or whether they are based on judgment.
3. Some believe that accounting depreciation measures the decline in the value of fixed assets. Do you agree? Explain.
4. Explain how estimation of service lives can result in unrealistically high carrying values for fixed assets.
5. The plant manager of a manufacturing firm suggested in a conference of the company's executives that accountants should speed up depreciation on the machinery in the finishing department because improvements were rapidly making those machines obsolete, and a depreciation fund big enough to cover their replacement is needed. Discuss the accounting concept of depreciation and the effect on a business concern of the depreciation recorded for plant assets, paying particular attention to the issues raised by the plant manager.
6. For what reasons are plant assets retired? Define inadequacy, supersession, and obsolescence.
7. What basic questions must be answered before the amount of the depreciation charge can be computed?
8. Workman Company purchased a machine on January 2, 2014, for $800,000. The machine has an estimated useful life of 5 years and a salvage value of $100,000. Depreciation was computed by the 150% declining-balance method. What is the amount of accumulated depreciation at the end of December 31, 2015?
9. Silverman Company purchased machinery for $162,000 on January 1, 2014. It is estimated that the machinery will have a useful life of 20 years, salvage value of $15,000, production of 84,000 units, and working hours of 42,000. During 2014, the company uses the machinery for 14,300 hours, and the machinery produces 20,000 units. Compute depreciation under the straight-line, units-of-output, working hours, sum-of-the-years'-digits, and double-declining-balance methods.
10. What are the major factors considered in determining what depreciation method to use?
11. Under what conditions is it appropriate for a business to use the composite method of depreciation for its plant assets? What are the advantages and disadvantages of this method?
12. If Remmers, Inc. uses the composite method and its composite rate is 7.5% per year, what entry should it make when plant assets that originally cost $50,000 and have been used for 10 years are sold for $14,000?

13. A building that was purchased on December 31, 2000, for $2,500,000 was originally estimated to have a life of 50 years with no salvage value at the end of that time. Depreciation has been recorded through 2014. During 2015, an examination of the building by an engineering firm discloses that its estimated useful life is 15 years after 2014. What should be the amount of depreciation for 2015?

14. Charlie Parker, president of Spinners Company, has recently noted that depreciation increases cash provided by operations and therefore depreciation is a good source of funds. Do you agree? Discuss.

15. Andrea Torbert purchased a computer for $8,000 on July 1, 2014. She intends to depreciate it over 4 years using the double-declining-balance method. Salvage value is $1,000. Compute depreciation for 2015.

16. Walkin Inc. is considering the write-down of its long-term plant because of a lack of profitability. Explain to the management of Walkin how to determine whether a write-down is permitted.

17. Last year, Wyeth Company recorded an impairment on an asset held for use. Recent appraisals indicate that the asset has increased in value. Should Wyeth record this recovery in value?

18. Toro Co. has equipment with a carrying amount of $700,000. The expected future net cash flows from the equipment are $705,000, and its fair value is $590,000. The equipment is expected to be used in operations in the future. What amount (if any) should Toro report as an impairment to its equipment?

19. Explain how gains or losses on impaired assets should be reported in income.

20. It has been suggested that plant and equipment could be replaced more quickly if depreciation rates for income tax and accounting purposes were substantially increased. As a result, business operations would receive the benefit of more modern and more efficient plant facilities. Discuss the merits of this proposition.

21. Neither depreciation on replacement cost nor depreciation adjusted for changes in the purchasing power of the dollar has been recognized as generally accepted accounting principles for inclusion in the primary financial statements. Briefly present the accounting treatment that might be used to assist in the maintenance of the ability of a company to replace its productive capacity.

22. List (a) the similarities and (b) the differences in the accounting treatments of depreciation and cost depletion.

23. Describe cost depletion and percentage depletion. Why is the percentage depletion method permitted?

24. In what way may the use of percentage depletion violate sound accounting theory?

25. In the extractive industries, businesses may pay dividends in excess of net income. What is the maximum permissible? How can this practice be justified?

26. The following statement appeared in a financial magazine: "RRA—or Rah-Rah, as it's sometimes dubbed—has kicked up quite a storm. Oil companies, for example, are convinced that the approach is misleading. Major accounting firms agree." What is RRA? Why might oil companies believe that this approach is misleading?

27. Shumway Oil uses successful-efforts accounting and also provides full-cost results as well. Under full-cost, Shumway Oil would have reported retained earnings of $42 million and net income of $4 million. Under successful-efforts, retained earnings were $29 million, and net income was $3 million. Explain the difference between full-costing and successful-efforts accounting.

28. Target in 2012 reported net income of $2.9 billion, net sales of $69.8 billion, and average total assets of $45.2 billion. What is Target's asset turnover? What is Target's return on assets?

*29. What is a modified accelerated cost recovery system (MACRS)? Speculate as to why this system is now required for tax purposes.

BRIEF EXERCISES

2 3 **BE11-1** Fernandez Corporation purchased a truck at the beginning of 2014 for $50,000. The truck is estimated to have a salvage value of $2,000 and a useful life of 160,000 miles. It was driven 23,000 miles in 2014 and 31,000 miles in 2015. Compute depreciation expense for 2014 and 2015.

2 3 **BE11-2** Lockard Company purchased machinery on January 1, 2014, for $80,000. The machinery is estimated to have a salvage value of $8,000 after a useful life of 8 years. (a) Compute 2014 depreciation expense using the straight-line method. (b) Compute 2014 depreciation expense using the straight-line method assuming the machinery was purchased on September 1, 2014.

2 3 **BE11-3** Use the information for Lockard Company given in BE11-2. (a) Compute 2014 depreciation expense using the sum-of-the-years'-digits method. (b) Compute 2014 depreciation expense using the sum-of-the-years'-digits method, assuming the machinery was purchased on April 1, 2014.

2 3 **BE11-4** Use the information for Lockard Company given in BE11-2. (a) Compute 2014 depreciation expense using the double-declining-balance method. (b) Compute 2014 depreciation expense using the double-declining-balance method, assuming the machinery was purchased on October 1, 2014.

2 3 **BE11-5** Cominsky Company purchased a machine on July 1, 2015, for $28,000. Cominsky paid $200 in title fees and county property tax of $125 on the machine. In addition, Cominsky paid $500 shipping charges for delivery, and $475 was paid to a local contractor to build and wire a platform for the machine on the plant floor. The machine has an estimated useful life of 6 years with a salvage value of $3,000. Determine the depreciation base of Cominsky's new machine. Cominsky uses straight-line depreciation.

4 **BE11-6** Dickinson Inc. owns the following assets.

Asset	Cost	Salvage	Estimated Useful Life
A	$70,000	$7,000	10 years
B	50,000	5,000	5 years
C	82,000	4,000	12 years

Compute the composite depreciation rate and the composite life of Dickinson's assets.

4 **BE11-7** Holt Company purchased a computer for $8,000 on January 1, 2013. Straight-line depreciation is used, based on a 5-year life and a $1,000 salvage value. In 2015, the estimates are revised. Holt now feels the computer will be used until December 31, 2016, when it can be sold for $500. Compute the 2015 depreciation.

5 **BE11-8** Jurassic Company owns equipment that cost $900,000 and has accumulated depreciation of $380,000. The expected future net cash flows from the use of the asset are expected to be $500,000. The fair value of the equipment is $400,000. Prepare the journal entry, if any, to record the impairment loss.

6 **BE11-9** Everly Corporation acquires a coal mine at a cost of $400,000. Intangible development costs total $100,000. After extraction has occurred, Everly must restore the property (estimated fair value of the obligation is $80,000), after which it can be sold for $160,000. Everly estimates that 4,000 tons of coal can be extracted. If 700 tons are extracted the first year, prepare the journal entry to record depletion.

7 **BE11-10** In its 2011 annual report, **Campbell Soup Company** reports beginning-of-the-year total assets of $6,276 million, end-of-the-year total assets of $6,862 million, total sales of $7,719 million, and net income of $805 million. (a) Compute Campbell's asset turnover. (b) Compute Campbell's profit margin on sales. (c) Compute Campbell's return on assets using (1) asset turnover and profit margin and (2) net income.

8 *__BE11-11__ Francis Corporation purchased an asset at a cost of $50,000 on March 1, 2014. The asset has a useful life of 8 years and a salvage value of $4,000. For tax purposes, the MACRS class life is 5 years. Compute tax depreciation for each year 2014–2019.

EXERCISES

2 3 **E11-1 (Depreciation Computations—SL, SYD, DDB)** Deluxe Ezra Company purchases equipment on January 1, Year 1, at a cost of $469,000. The asset is expected to have a service life of 12 years and a salvage value of $40,000.

Instructions

(a) Compute the amount of depreciation for each of Years 1 through 3 using the straight-line depreciation method.

(b) Compute the amount of depreciation for each of Years 1 through 3 using the sum-of-the-years'-digits method.

(c) Compute the amount of depreciation for each of Years 1 through 3 using the double-declining-balance method. (In performing your calculations, round constant percentage to the nearest one-hundredth of a point and round answers to the nearest dollar.)

2 3 **E11-2 (Depreciation—Conceptual Understanding)** Rembrandt Company acquired a plant asset at the beginning of Year 1. The asset has an estimated service life of 5 years. An employee has prepared depreciation schedules for this asset using three different methods to compare the results of using one method with the results of using other methods. You are to assume that the following schedules have been correctly prepared for this asset using (1) the straight-line method, (2) the sum-of-the-years'-digits method, and (3) the double-declining-balance method.

Year	Straight-Line	Sum-of-the-Years'-Digits	Double-Declining-Balance
1	$ 9,000	$15,000	$20,000
2	9,000	12,000	12,000
3	9,000	9,000	7,200
4	9,000	6,000	4,320
5	9,000	3,000	1,480
Total	$45,000	$45,000	$45,000

Instructions

Answer the following questions.

(a) What is the cost of the asset being depreciated?
(b) What amount, if any, was used in the depreciation calculations for the salvage value for this asset?
(c) Which method will produce the highest charge to income in Year 1?
(d) Which method will produce the highest charge to income in Year 4?
(e) Which method will produce the highest book value for the asset at the end of Year 3?
(f) If the asset is sold at the end of Year 3, which method would yield the highest gain (or lowest loss) on disposal of the asset?

2 3 **E11-3 (Depreciation Computations—SYD, DDB—Partial Periods)** Judds Company purchased a new plant asset on April 1, 2014, at a cost of $711,000. It was estimated to have a service life of 20 years and a salvage value of $60,000. Judds' accounting period is the calendar year.

Instructions

(a) Compute the depreciation for this asset for 2014 and 2015 using the sum-of-the-years'-digits method.
(b) Compute the depreciation for this asset for 2014 and 2015 using the double-declining-balance method.

2 3 **E11-4 (Depreciation Computations—Five Methods)** Jon Seceda Furnace Corp. purchased machinery for $315,000 on May 1, 2014. It is estimated that it will have a useful life of 10 years, salvage value of $15,000, production of 240,000 units, and working hours of 25,000. During 2015, Seceda Corp. uses the machinery for 2,650 hours, and the machinery produces 25,500 units.

XLS

Instructions

From the information given, compute the depreciation charge for 2015 under each of the following methods. (Round to the nearest dollar.)

(a) Straight-line.
(b) Units-of-output.
(c) Working hours.
(d) Sum-of-the-years'-digits.
(e) Declining-balance (use 20% as the annual rate).

2 3 **E11-5 (Depreciation Computations—Four Methods)** Robert Parish Corporation purchased a new machine for its assembly process on August 1, 2014. The cost of this machine was $117,900. The company estimated that the machine would have a salvage value of $12,900 at the end of its service life. Its life is estimated at 5 years, and its working hours are estimated at 21,000 hours. Year-end is December 31.

Instructions

Compute the depreciation expense under the following methods. Each of the following should be considered unrelated.

(a) Straight-line depreciation for 2014.
(b) Activity method for 2014, assuming that machine usage was 800 hours.
(c) Sum-of-the-years'-digits for 2015.
(d) Double-declining-balance for 2015.

2 3 **E11-6 (Depreciation Computations—Five Methods, Partial Periods)** Muggsy Bogues Company purchased equipment for $212,000 on October 1, 2014. It is estimated that the equipment will have a useful life of 8 years and a salvage value of $12,000. Estimated production is 40,000 units and estimated working hours are 20,000. During 2014, Bogues uses the equipment for 525 hours and the equipment produces 1,000 units.

Instructions

Compute depreciation expense under each of the following methods. Bogues is on a calendar-year basis ending December 31.

(a) Straight-line method for 2014.
(b) Activity method (units of output) for 2014.

(c) Activity method (working hours) for 2014.
(d) Sum-of-the-years'-digits method for 2016.
(e) Double-declining-balance method for 2015.

2 3 **E11-7 (Different Methods of Depreciation)** Jackel Industries presents you with the following information.

Description	Date Purchased	Cost	Salvage Value	Life in Years	Depreciation Method	Accumulated Depreciation to 12/31/15	Depreciation for 2016
Machine A	2/12/14	$142,500	$16,000	10	**(a)**	$33,350	**(b)**
Machine B	8/15/13	**(c)**	21,000	5	SL	29,000	**(d)**
Machine C	7/21/12	75,400	23,500	8	DDB	**(e)**	**(f)**
Machine D	10/12/**(g)**	219,000	69,000	5	SYD	70,000	**(h)**

Instructions

Complete the table for the year ended December 31, 2016. The company depreciates all assets using the half-year convention.

2 3 **E11-8 (Depreciation Computation—Replacement, Nonmonetary Exchange)** George Zidek Corporation bought a machine on June 1, 2012, for $31,000, f.o.b. the place of manufacture. Freight to the point where it was set up was $200, and $500 was expended to install it. The machine's useful life was estimated at 10 years, with a salvage value of $2,500. On June 1, 2013, an essential part of the machine is replaced, at a cost of $1,980, with one designed to reduce the cost of operating the machine. The cost of the old part and related depreciation cannot be determined with any accuracy.

On June 1, 2016, the company buys a new machine of greater capacity for $35,000, delivered, trading in the old machine which has a fair value and trade-in allowance of $20,000. To prepare the old machine for removal from the plant cost $75, and expenditures to install the new one were $1,500. It is estimated that the new machine has a useful life of 10 years, with a salvage value of $4,000 at the end of that time. (The exchange has commercial substance.)

Instructions

Assuming that depreciation is to be computed on the straight-line basis, compute the annual depreciation on the new equipment that should be provided for the fiscal year beginning June 1, 2016. (Round to the nearest dollar.)

4 **E11-9 (Composite Depreciation)** Presented below is information related to LeBron James Manufacturing Corporation.

Asset	Cost	Estimated Salvage	Estimated Life (in years)
A	$40,500	$5,500	10
B	33,600	4,800	9
C	36,000	3,600	9
D	19,000	1,500	7
E	23,500	2,500	6

Instructions

(a) Compute the rate of depreciation per year to be applied to the plant assets under the composite method.
(b) Prepare the adjusting entry necessary at the end of the year to record depreciation for the year.
(c) Prepare the entry to record the sale of asset D for cash of $4,800. It was used for 6 years, and depreciation was entered under the composite method.

2 3 **E11-10 (Depreciation Computations, SYD)** Five Satins Company purchased a piece of equipment at the beginning of 2011. The equipment cost $430,000. It has an estimated service life of 8 years and an expected salvage value of $70,000. The sum-of-the-years'-digits method of depreciation is being used. Someone has already correctly prepared a depreciation schedule for this asset. This schedule shows that $60,000 will be depreciated for a particular calendar year.

Instructions

Show calculations to determine for what particular year the depreciation amount for this asset will be $60,000.

2 3 4 **E11-11 (Depreciation—Change in Estimate)** Machinery purchased for $60,000 by Tom Brady Co. in 2010 was originally estimated to have a life of 8 years with a salvage value of $4,000 at the end of that time. Depreciation has been entered for 5 years on this basis. In 2015, it is determined that the total estimated life should be 10 years with a salvage value of $4,500 at the end of that time. Assume straight-line depreciation.

Instructions

(a) Prepare the entry to correct the prior years' depreciation, if necessary.
(b) Prepare the entry to record depreciation for 2015.

2 3 4 **E11-12 (Depreciation Computation—Addition, Change in Estimate)** In 1987, Herman Moore Company completed the construction of a building at a cost of $2,000,000 and first occupied it in January 1988. It was estimated that the building will have a useful life of 40 years and a salvage value of $60,000 at the end of that time.

Early in 1998, an addition to the building was constructed at a cost of $500,000. At that time, it was estimated that the remaining life of the building would be, as originally estimated, an additional 30 years, and that the addition would have a life of 30 years and a salvage value of $20,000.

In 2016, it is determined that the probable life of the building and addition will extend to the end of 2047, or 20 years beyond the original estimate.

Instructions

(a) Using the straight-line method, compute the annual depreciation that would have been charged from 1988 through 1997.
(b) Compute the annual depreciation that would have been charged from 1998 through 2015.
(c) Prepare the entry, if necessary, to adjust the account balances because of the revision of the estimated life in 2016.
(d) Compute the annual depreciation to be charged, beginning with 2016.

2 3 4 **E11-13 (Depreciation—Replacement, Change in Estimate)** Greg Maddox Company constructed a building at a cost of $2,200,000 and occupied it beginning in January 1995. It was estimated at that time that its life would be 40 years, with no salvage value.

In January 2015, a new roof was installed at a cost of $300,000, and it was estimated then that the building would have a useful life of 25 years from that date. The cost of the old roof was $160,000.

Instructions

(a) What amount of depreciation should have been charged annually from the years 1995 to 2014? (Assume straight-line depreciation.)
(b) What entry should be made in 2015 to record the replacement of the roof?
(c) Prepare the entry in January 2015 to record the revision in the estimated life of the building, if necessary.
(d) What amount of depreciation should be charged for the year 2015?

2 3 **E11-14 (Error Analysis and Depreciation, SL and SYD)** Mike Devereaux Company shows the following entries in its Equipment account for 2015. All amounts are based on historical cost.

Equipment

2015			2015		
Jan. 1	Balance	134,750	June 30	Cost of equipment sold (purchased prior to 2015)	23,000
Aug. 10	Purchases	32,000			
12	Freight on equipment purchased	700			
25	Installation costs	2,700			
Nov. 10	Repairs	500			

Instructions

(a) Prepare any correcting entries necessary.
(b) Assuming that depreciation is to be charged for a full year on the ending balance in the asset account, compute the proper depreciation charge for 2015 under each of the methods listed below. Assume an estimated life of 10 years, with no salvage value. The machinery included in the January 1, 2015, balance was purchased in 2013.
(1) Straight-line. (2) Sum-of-the-years'-digits.

2 3 **E11-15 (Depreciation for Fractional Periods)** On March 10, 2016, Lost World Company sells equipment that it purchased for $192,000 on August 20, 2009. It was originally estimated that the equipment would have a life of 12 years and a salvage value of $16,800 at the end of that time, and depreciation has been computed on that basis. The company uses the straight-line method of depreciation.

Instructions

(a) Compute the depreciation charge on this equipment for 2009, for 2016, and the total charge for the period from 2010 to 2015, inclusive, under each of the six following assumptions with respect to partial periods.

(1) Depreciation is computed for the exact period of time during which the asset is owned. (Use 365 days for base.)
(2) Depreciation is computed for the full year on the January 1 balance in the asset account.
(3) Depreciation is computed for the full year on the December 31 balance in the asset account.
(4) Depreciation for one-half year is charged on plant assets acquired or disposed of during the year.
(5) Depreciation is computed on additions from the beginning of the month following acquisition and on disposals to the beginning of the month following disposal.
(6) Depreciation is computed for a full period on all assets in use for over one-half year, and no depreciation is charged on assets in use for less than one-half year. (Use 365 days for base.)

(b) Briefly evaluate the methods above, considering them from the point of view of basic accounting theory as well as simplicity of application.

5 **E11-16 (Impairment)** Presented below is information related to equipment owned by Suarez Company at December 31, 2014.

Cost	$9,000,000
Accumulated depreciation to date	1,000,000
Expected future net cash flows	7,000,000
Fair value	4,800,000

Assume that Suarez will continue to use this asset in the future. As of December 31, 2014, the equipment has a remaining useful life of 4 years.

Instructions

(a) Prepare the journal entry (if any) to record the impairment of the asset at December 31, 2014.
(b) Prepare the journal entry to record depreciation expense for 2015.
(c) The fair value of the equipment at December 31, 2015, is $5,100,000. Prepare the journal entry (if any) necessary to record this increase in fair value.

5 **E11-17 (Impairment)** Assume the same information as E11-16, except that Suarez intends to dispose of the equipment in the coming year. It is expected that the cost of disposal will be $20,000.

Instructions

(a) Prepare the journal entry (if any) to record the impairment of the asset at December 31, 2014.
(b) Prepare the journal entry (if any) to record depreciation expense for 2015.
(c) The asset was not sold by December 31, 2015. The fair value of the equipment on that date is $5,300,000. Prepare the journal entry (if any) necessary to record this increase in fair value. It is expected that the cost of disposal is still $20,000.

5 **E11-18 (Impairment)** The management of Petro Garcia Inc. was discussing whether certain equipment should be written off as a charge to current operations because of obsolescence. This equipment has a cost of $900,000 with depreciation to date of $400,000 as of December 31, 2014. On December 31, 2014, management projected its future net cash flows from this equipment to be $300,000 and its fair value to be $230,000. The company intends to use this equipment in the future.

Instructions

(a) Prepare the journal entry (if any) to record the impairment at December 31, 2014.
(b) Where should the gain or loss (if any) on the write-down be reported in the income statement?
(c) At December 31, 2015, the equipment's fair value increased to $260,000. Prepare the journal entry (if any) to record this increase in fair value.
(d) What accounting issues did management face in accounting for this impairment?

6 **E11-19 (Depletion Computations—Timber)** Stanislaw Timber Company owns 9,000 acres of timberland purchased in 2003 at a cost of $1,400 per acre. At the time of purchase, the land without the timber was valued at $400 per acre. In 2004, Stanislaw built fire lanes and roads, with a life of 30 years, at a cost of $84,000. Every year, Stanislaw sprays to prevent disease at a cost of $3,000 per year and spends $7,000 to maintain the fire lanes and roads. During 2005, Stanislaw selectively logged and sold 700,000 board feet of timber, of the estimated 3,500,000 board feet. In 2006, Stanislaw planted new seedlings to replace the trees cut at a cost of $100,000.

Instructions

(a) Determine the depreciation expense and the cost of timber sold related to depletion for 2005.
(b) Stanislaw has not logged since 2005. If Stanislaw logged and sold 900,000 board feet of timber in 2016, when the timber cruise (appraiser) estimated 5,000,000 board feet, determine the cost of timber sold related to depletion for 2016.

6 **E11-20 (Depletion Computations—Oil)** Diderot Drilling Company has leased property on which oil has been discovered. Wells on this property produced 18,000 barrels of oil during the past year that sold at an average sales price of $55 per barrel. Total oil resources of this property are estimated to be 250,000 barrels.

The lease provided for an outright payment of $500,000 to the lessor (owner) before drilling could be commenced and an annual rental of $31,500. A premium of 5% of the sales price of every barrel of oil removed is to be paid annually to the lessor. In addition, Diderot (lessee) is to clean up all the waste and debris from drilling and to bear the costs of reconditioning the land for farming when the wells are abandoned. The estimated fair value, at the time of the lease, of this clean-up and reconditioning is $30,000.

Instructions

From the provisions of the lease agreement, you are to compute the cost per barrel for the past year, exclusive of operating costs, to Diderot Drilling Company.

6 **E11-21 (Depletion Computations—Timber)** Forda Lumber Company owns a 7,000-acre tract of timber purchased in 2000 at a cost of $1,300 per acre. At the time of purchase, the land was estimated to have a value of $300 per acre without the timber. Forda Lumber Company has not logged this tract since it was purchased. In 2014, Forda had the timber cruised. The cruise (appraiser) estimated that each acre contained 8,000 board feet of timber. In 2014, Forda built 10 miles of roads at a cost of $7,840 per mile. After the roads were completed, Forda logged and sold 3,500 trees containing 850,000 board feet.

Instructions

- **(a)** Determine the cost of timber sold related to depletion for 2014.
- **(b)** If Forda depreciates the logging roads on the basis of timber cut, determine the depreciation expense for 2014.
- **(c)** If Forda plants five seedlings at a cost of $4 per seedling for each tree cut, how should Forda treat the reforestation?

6 **E11-22 (Depletion Computations—Mining)** Alcide Mining Company purchased land on February 1, 2014, at a cost of $1,190,000. It estimated that a total of 60,000 tons of mineral was available for mining. After it has removed all the natural resources, the company will be required to restore the property to its previous state because of strict environmental protection laws. It estimates the fair value of this restoration obligation at $90,000. It believes it will be able to sell the property afterwards for $100,000. It incurred developmental costs of $200,000 before it was able to do any mining. In 2014, resources removed totaled 30,000 tons. The company sold 22,000 tons.

Instructions

Compute the following information for 2014.

- **(a)** Per unit material cost.
- **(b)** Total material cost of December 31, 2014, inventory.
- **(c)** Total material cost in cost of goods sold at December 31, 2014.

6 **E11-23 (Depletion Computations—Minerals)** At the beginning of 2014, Aristotle Company acquired a mine for $970,000. Of this amount, $100,000 was ascribed to the land value and the remaining portion to the minerals in the mine. Surveys conducted by geologists have indicated that approximately 12,000,000 units of the ore appear to be in the mine. Aristotle incurred $170,000 of development costs associated with this mine prior to any extraction of minerals. It also determined that the fair value of its obligation to prepare the land for an alternative use when all of the mineral has been removed was $40,000. During 2014, 2,500,000 units of ore were extracted and 2,100,000 of these units were sold.

Instructions

Compute the following.

- **(a)** The total amount of depletion for 2014.
- **(b)** The amount that is charged as an expense for 2014 for the cost of the minerals sold during 2014.

7 **E11-24 (Ratio Analysis)** The 2011 Annual Report of **Tootsie Roll Industries** contains the following information.

(in millions)	December 31, 2011	December 31, 2010
Total assets	$857.9	$858.0
Total liabilities	191.9	190.6
Net sales	528.4	517.1
Net income	43.9	53.0

Instructions

Compute the following ratios for Tootsie Roll for 2011.

(a) Asset turnover.
(b) Return on assets.
(c) Profit margin on sales.
(d) How can the asset turnover be used to compute the return on assets?

8 ***E11-25 (Book vs. Tax (MACRS) Depreciation)** Futabatei Enterprises purchased a delivery truck on January 1, 2014, at a cost of $27,000. The truck has a useful life of 7 years with an estimated salvage value of $6,000. The straight-line method is used for book purposes. For tax purposes, the truck, having an MACRS class life of 7 years, is classified as 5-year property; the optional MACRS tax rate tables are used to compute depreciation. In addition, assume that for 2014 and 2015 the company has revenues of $200,000 and operating expenses (excluding depreciation) of $130,000.

Instructions

(a) Prepare income statements for 2014 and 2015. (The final amount reported on the income statement should be income before income taxes.)
(b) Compute taxable income for 2014 and 2015.
(c) Determine the total depreciation to be taken over the useful life of the delivery truck for both book and tax purposes.
(d) Explain why depreciation for book and tax purposes will generally be different over the useful life of a depreciable asset.

8 ***E11-26 (Book vs. Tax (MACRS) Depreciation)** Shimei Inc. purchased computer equipment on March 1, 2014, for $31,000. The computer equipment has a useful life of 10 years and a salvage value of $1,000. For tax purposes, the MACRS class life is 5 years.

Instructions

(a) Assuming that the company uses the straight-line method for book and tax purposes, what is the depreciation expense reported in (1) the financial statements for 2014 and (2) the tax return for 2014?
(b) Assuming that the company uses the double-declining-balance method for both book and tax purposes, what is the depreciation expense reported in (1) the financial statements for 2014 and (2) the tax return for 2014?
(c) Why is depreciation for tax purposes different from depreciation for book purposes even if the company uses the same depreciation method to compute them both?

EXERCISES SET B

See the book's companion website, at **www.wiley.com/college/kieso**, for an additional set of exercises.

PROBLEMS

2 3 **P11-1 (Depreciation for Partial Period—SL, SYD, and DDB)** Alladin Company purchased Machine #201 on May 1, 2014. The following information relating to Machine #201 was gathered at the end of May.

Price	$85,000
Credit terms	2/10, n/30
Freight-in	$ 800
Preparation and installation costs	$ 3,800
Labor costs during regular production operations	$10,500

It is expected that the machine could be used for 10 years, after which the salvage value would be zero. Alladin intends to use the machine for only 8 years, however, after which it expects to be able to sell it for $1,500. The invoice for Machine #201 was paid May 5, 2014. Alladin uses the calendar year as the basis for the preparation of financial statements.

Instructions

(a) Compute the depreciation expense for the years indicated using the following methods. (Round to the nearest dollar.)

(1) Straight-line method for 2014.
(2) Sum-of-the-years'-digits method for 2015.
(3) Double-declining-balance method for 2014.

(b) Suppose Kate Crow, the president of Alladin, tells you that because the company is a new organization, she expects it will be several years before production and sales reach optimum levels. She asks you to recommend a depreciation method that will allocate less of the company's depreciation expense to the early years and more to later years of the assets' lives. What method would you recommend?

2 3 **P11-2 (Depreciation for Partial Periods—SL, Act., SYD, and Declining-Balance)** The cost of equipment purchased by Charleston, Inc., on June 1, 2014, is $89,000. It is estimated that the machine will have a $5,000 salvage value at the end of its service life. Its service life is estimated at 7 years, its total working hours are estimated at 42,000, and its total production is estimated at 525,000 units. During 2014, the machine was operated 6,000 hours and produced 55,000 units. During 2015, the machine was operated 5,500 hours and produced 48,000 units.

Instructions

Compute depreciation expense on the machine for the year ending December 31, 2014, and the year ending December 31, 2015, using the following methods.

(a) Straight-line.
(b) Units-of-output.
(c) Working hours.
(d) Sum-of-the-years'-digits.
(e) Declining-balance (twice the straight-line rate).

2 3 **P11-3 (Depreciation—SYD, Act., SL, and DDB)** The following data relate to the Machinery account of Eshkol, Inc. at December 31, 2014.

	Machinery			
	A	B	C	D
Original cost	$46,000	$51,000	$80,000	$80,000
Year purchased	2009	2010	2011	2013
Useful life	10 years	15,000 hours	15 years	10 years
Salvage value	$ 3,100	$ 3,000	$ 5,000	$ 5,000
Depreciation method	Sum-of-the-years'-digits	Activity	Straight-line	Double-declining-balance
Accum. depr. through 2014*	$31,200	$35,200	$15,000	$16,000

*In the year an asset is purchased, Eshkol, Inc. does not record any depreciation expense on the asset. In the year an asset is retired or traded in, Eshkol, Inc. takes a full year's depreciation on the asset.

The following transactions occurred during 2015.

(a) On May 5, Machine A was sold for $13,000 cash. The company's bookkeeper recorded this retirement in the following manner in the cash receipts journal.

Cash	13,000	
Machinery (Machine A)		13,000

(b) On December 31, it was determined that Machine B had been used 2,100 hours during 2015.

(c) On December 31, before computing depreciation expense on Machine C, the management of Eshkol, Inc. decided the useful life remaining from January 1, 2015, was 10 years.

(d) On December 31, it was discovered that a machine purchased in 2014 had been expensed completely in that year. This machine cost $28,000 and has a useful life of 10 years and no salvage value. Management has decided to use the double-declining-balance method for this machine, which can be referred to as "Machine E."

Instructions

Prepare the necessary correcting entries for the year 2015. Record the appropriate depreciation expense on the above-mentioned machines.

2 3 **P11-4 (Depreciation and Error Analysis)** A depreciation schedule for semi-trucks of Ichiro Manufacturing Company was requested by your auditor soon after December 31, 2015, showing the additions, retirements,

depreciation, and other data affecting the income of the company in the 4-year period 2012 to 2015, inclusive. The following data were ascertained.

Balance of Trucks account, Jan. 1, 2012	
Truck No. 1 purchased Jan. 1, 2009, cost	$18,000
Truck No. 2 purchased July 1, 2009, cost	22,000
Truck No. 3 purchased Jan. 1, 2011, cost	30,000
Truck No. 4 purchased July 1, 2011, cost	24,000
Balance, Jan. 1, 2012	$94,000

The Accumulated Depreciation—Trucks account previously adjusted to January 1, 2012, and entered in the ledger, had a balance on that date of $30,200 (depreciation on the four trucks from the respective dates of purchase, based on a 5-year life, no salvage value). No charges had been made against the account before January 1, 2012.

Transactions between January 1, 2012, and December 31, 2015, which were recorded in the ledger, are as follows.

July 1, 2012	Truck No. 3 was traded for a larger one (No. 5), the agreed purchase price of which was $40,000. Ichiro Mfg. Co. paid the automobile dealer $22,000 cash on the transaction. The entry was a debit to Trucks and a credit to Cash, $22,000. The transaction has commercial substance.
Jan. 1, 2013	Truck No. 1 was sold for $3,500 cash; entry debited Cash and credited Trucks, $3,500.
July 1, 2014	A new truck (No. 6) was acquired for $42,000 cash and was charged at that amount to the Trucks account. (Assume truck No. 2 was not retired.)
July 1, 2014	Truck No. 4 was damaged in a wreck to such an extent that it was sold as junk for $700 cash. Ichiro Mfg. Co. received $2,500 from the insurance company. The entry made by the bookkeeper was a debit to Cash, $3,200, and credits to Miscellaneous Income, $700, and Trucks, $2,500.

Entries for depreciation had been made at the close of each year as follows: 2012, $21,000; 2013, $22,500; 2014, $25,050; and 2015, $30,400.

Instructions

(a) For each of the 4 years, compute separately the increase or decrease in net income arising from the company's errors in determining or entering depreciation or in recording transactions affecting trucks, ignoring income tax considerations.

(b) Prepare one compound journal entry as of December 31, 2015, for adjustment of the Trucks account to reflect the correct balances as revealed by your schedule, assuming that the books have not been closed for 2015.

3 6 **P11-5 (Depletion and Depreciation—Mining)** Khamsah Mining Company has purchased a tract of mineral land for $900,000. It is estimated that this tract will yield 120,000 tons of ore with sufficient mineral content to make mining and processing profitable. It is further estimated that 6,000 tons of ore will be mined the first and last year and 12,000 tons every year in between. (Assume 11 years of mining operations.) The land will have a salvage value of $30,000.

The company builds necessary structures and sheds on the site at a cost of $36,000. It is estimated that these structures can serve 15 years but, because they must be dismantled if they are to be moved, they have no salvage value. The company does not intend to use the buildings elsewhere. Mining machinery installed at the mine was purchased secondhand at a cost of $60,000. This machinery cost the former owner $150,000 and was 50% depreciated when purchased. Khamsah Mining estimates that about half of this machinery will still be useful when the present mineral resources have been exhausted, but that dismantling and removal costs will just about offset its value at that time. The company does not intend to use the machinery elsewhere. The remaining machinery will last until about one-half the present estimated mineral ore has been removed and will then be worthless. Cost is to be allocated equally between these two classes of machinery.

Instructions

(a) As chief accountant for the company, you are to prepare a schedule showing estimated depletion and depreciation costs for each year of the expected life of the mine.

(b) Also compute the depreciation and depletion for the first year assuming actual production of 5,000 tons. Nothing occurred during the year to cause the company engineers to change their estimates of either the mineral resources or the life of the structures and equipment.

6 **P11-6 (Depletion, Timber, and Extraordinary Loss)** Conan O'Brien Logging and Lumber Company owns 3,000 acres of timberland on the north side of Mount Leno, which was purchased in 2002 at a cost of $550 per acre. In 2014, O'Brien began selectively logging this timber tract. In May 2014, Mount Leno erupted, burying the timberland of O'Brien under a foot of ash. All of the timber on the O'Brien tract was downed. In addition, the logging roads, built at a cost of $150,000, were destroyed, as well as the logging equipment, with a net book value of $300,000.

At the time of the eruption, O'Brien had logged 20% of the estimated 500,000 board feet of timber. Prior to the eruption, O'Brien estimated the land to have a value of $200 per acre after the timber was harvested. O'Brien includes the logging roads in the depletion base.

O'Brien estimates it will take 3 years to salvage the downed timber at a cost of $700,000. The timber can be sold for pulp wood at an estimated price of $3 per board foot. The value of the land is unknown, but must be considered nominal due to future uncertainties.

Instructions

(a) Determine the depletion cost per board foot for the timber harvested prior to the eruption of Mount Leno.
(b) Prepare the journal entry to record the depletion prior to the eruption.
(c) If this tract represents approximately half of the timber holdings of O'Brien, determine the amount of the extraordinary loss due to the eruption of Mount Leno for the year ended December 31, 2014.

6 **P11-7 (Natural Resources—Timber)** Bronson Paper Products purchased 10,000 acres of forested timberland in March 2014. The company paid $1,700 per acre for this land, which was above the $800 per acre most farmers were paying for cleared land. During April, May, June, and July 2014, Bronson cut enough timber to build roads using moveable equipment purchased on April 1, 2014. The cost of the roads was $250,000, and the cost of the equipment was $225,000; this equipment was expected to have a $9,000 salvage value and would be used for the next 15 years. Bronson selected the straight-line method of depreciation for the moveable equipment. Bronson began actively harvesting timber in August and by December had harvested and sold 540,000 board feet of timber of the estimated 6,750,000 board feet available for cutting.

In March 2015, Bronson planted new seedlings in the area harvested during the winter. Cost of planting these seedlings was $120,000. In addition, Bronson spent $8,000 in road maintenance and $6,000 for pest spraying during calendar-year 2015. The road maintenance and spraying are annual costs. During 2015, Bronson harvested and sold 774,000 board feet of timber of the estimated 6,450,000 board feet available for cutting.

In March 2016, Bronson again planted new seedlings at a cost of $150,000, and also spent $15,000 on road maintenance and pest spraying. During 2016, the company harvested and sold 650,000 board feet of timber of the estimated 6,500,000 board feet available for cutting.

Instructions

Compute the amount of depreciation and depletion expense for each of the 3 years (2014, 2015, and 2016). Assume that the roads are usable only for logging and therefore are included in the depletion base.

2 3 **P11-8 (Comprehensive Fixed-Asset Problem)** Darby Sporting Goods Inc. has been experiencing growth in the demand for its products over the last several years. The last two Olympic Games greatly increased the popularity of basketball around the world. As a result, a European sports retailing consortium entered into an agreement with Darby's Roundball Division to purchase basketballs and other accessories on an increasing basis over the next 5 years.

To be able to meet the quantity commitments of this agreement, Darby had to obtain additional manufacturing capacity. A real estate firm located an available factory in close proximity to Darby's Roundball manufacturing facility, and Darby agreed to purchase the factory and used machinery from Encino Athletic Equipment Company on October 1, 2013. Renovations were necessary to convert the factory for Darby's manufacturing use.

The terms of the agreement required Darby to pay Encino $50,000 when renovations started on January 1, 2014, with the balance to be paid as renovations were completed. The overall purchase price for the factory and machinery was $400,000. The building renovations were contracted to Malone Construction at $100,000. The payments made, as renovations progressed during 2014, are shown below. The factory was placed in service on January 1, 2015.

	1/1	4/1	10/1	12/31
Encino	$50,000	$90,000	$110,000	$150,000
Malone		30,000	30,000	40,000

On January 1, 2014, Darby secured a $500,000 line-of-credit with a 12% interest rate to finance the purchase cost of the factory and machinery, and the renovation costs. Darby drew down on the line-of-credit to meet the payment schedule shown above; this was Darby's only outstanding loan during 2014.

Bob Sprague, Darby's controller, will capitalize the maximum allowable interest costs for this project. Darby's policy regarding purchases of this nature is to use the appraisal value of the land for book purposes and prorate the balance of the purchase price over the remaining items. The building had originally cost Encino $300,000 and had a net book value of $50,000, while the machinery originally cost $125,000 and had a net book value of $40,000 on the date of sale. The land was recorded on Encino's books at $40,000. An appraisal, conducted by independent appraisers at the time of acquisition, valued the land at $290,000, the building at $105,000, and the machinery at $45,000.

Angie Justice, chief engineer, estimated that the renovated plant would be used for 15 years, with an estimated salvage value of $30,000. Justice estimated that the productive machinery would have a remaining useful life of 5 years and a salvage value of $3,000. Darby's depreciation policy specifies the 200% declining-balance method for machinery and the 150% declining-balance method for the plant. One-half year's depreciation is taken in the year the plant is placed in service, and one-half year is allowed when the property is disposed of or retired. Darby uses a 360-day year for calculating interest costs.

Instructions

(a) Determine the amounts to be recorded on the books of Darby Sporting Goods Inc. as of December 31, 2014, for each of the following properties acquired from Encino Athletic Equipment Company.
(1) Land. **(2)** Buildings. **(3)** Machinery.

(b) Calculate Darby Sporting Goods Inc.'s 2015 depreciation expense, for book purposes, for each of the properties acquired from Encino Athletic Equipment Company.

(c) Discuss the arguments for and against the capitalization of interest costs.

(CMA adapted)

5 **P11-9 (Impairment)** Roland Company uses special strapping equipment in its packaging business. The equipment was purchased in January 2013 for $10,000,000 and had an estimated useful life of 8 years with no salvage value. At December 31, 2014, new technology was introduced that would accelerate the obsolescence of Roland's equipment. Roland's controller estimates that expected future net cash flows on the equipment will be $6,300,000 and that the fair value of the equipment is $5,600,000. Roland intends to continue using the equipment, but it is estimated that the remaining useful life is 4 years. Roland uses straight-line depreciation.

Instructions

(a) Prepare the journal entry (if any) to record the impairment at December 31, 2014.

(b) Prepare any journal entries for the equipment at December 31, 2015. The fair value of the equipment at December 31, 2015, is estimated to be $5,900,000.

(c) Repeat the requirements for (a) and (b), assuming that Roland intends to dispose of the equipment and that it has not been disposed of as of December 31, 2015.

2 3 **P11-10 (Comprehensive Depreciation Computations)** Kohlbeck Corporation, a manufacturer of steel products, began operations on October 1, 2013. The accounting department of Kohlbeck has started the fixed-asset and depreciation schedule presented on page 632. You have been asked to assist in completing this schedule. In addition to ascertaining that the data already on the schedule are correct, you have obtained the following information from the company's records and personnel.

1. Depreciation is computed from the first of the month of acquisition to the first of the month of disposition.
2. Land A and Building A were acquired from a predecessor corporation. Kohlbeck paid $800,000 for the land and building together. At the time of acquisition, the land had an appraised value of $90,000, and the building had an appraised value of $810,000.
3. Land B was acquired on October 2, 2013, in exchange for 2,500 newly issued shares of Kohlbeck's common stock. At the date of acquisition, the stock had a par value of $5 per share and a fair value of $30 per share. During October 2013, Kohlbeck paid $16,000 to demolish an existing building on this land so it could construct a new building.
4. Construction of Building B on the newly acquired land began on October 1, 2014. By September 30, 2015, Kohlbeck had paid $320,000 of the estimated total construction costs of $450,000. It is estimated that the building will be completed and occupied by July 2016.
5. Certain equipment was donated to the corporation by a local university. An independent appraisal of the equipment when donated placed the fair value at $40,000 and the salvage value at $3,000.
6. Machinery A's total cost of $182,900 includes installation expense of $600 and normal repairs and maintenance of $14,900. Salvage value is estimated at $6,000. Machinery A was sold on February 1, 2015.
7. On October 1, 2014, Machinery B was acquired with a down payment of $5,740 and the remaining payments to be made in 11 annual installments of $6,000 each beginning October 1, 2014. The prevailing interest rate was 8%. The following data were abstracted from present value tables (rounded).

Present value of $1.00 at 8%	
10 years	.463
11 years	.429
15 years	.315

Present value of an ordinary annuity of $1.00 at 8%	
10 years	6.710
11 years	7.139
15 years	8.559

KOHLBECK CORPORATION
Fixed-Asset and Depreciation Schedule
For Fiscal Years Ended September 30, 2014, and September 30, 2015

Assets	Acquisition Date	Cost	Salvage	Depreciation Method	Estimated Life in Years	Depreciation Expense Year Ended September 30 2014	2015
Land A	October 1, 2013	$ (1)	N/A*	N/A	N/A	N/A	N/A
Building A	October 1, 2013	(2)	$40,000	Straight-line	(3)	$13,600	(4)
Land B	October 2, 2013	(5)	N/A	N/A	N/A	N/A	N/A
Building B	Under Construction	$320,000 to date	—	Straight-line	30	—	(6)
Donated Equipment	October 2, 2013	(7)	3,000	150% declining-balance	10	(8)	(9)
Machinery A	October 2, 2013	(10)	6,000	Sum-of-the-years'-digits	8	(11)	(12)
Machinery B	October 1, 2014	(13)	—	Straight-line	20	—	(14)

*N/A—Not applicable

Instructions

For each numbered item on the schedule above, supply the correct amount. (Round each answer to the nearest dollar.)

2 3 **P11-11 (Depreciation for Partial Periods—SL, Act., SYD, and DDB)** On January 1, 2012, a machine was purchased for $90,000. The machine has an estimated salvage value of $6,000 and an estimated useful life of 5 years. The machine can operate for 100,000 hours before it needs to be replaced. The company closed its books on December 31 and operates the machine as follows: 2012, 20,000 hours; 2013, 25,000 hours; 2014, 15,000 hours; 2015, 30,000 hours; and 2016, 10,000 hours.

Instructions

(a) Compute the annual depreciation charges over the machine's life assuming a December 31 year-end for each of the following depreciation methods.

(1) Straight-line method.
(2) Activity method.
(3) Sum-of-the-years'-digits method.
(4) Double-declining-balance method.

(b) Assume a fiscal year-end of September 30. Compute the annual depreciation charges over the asset's life applying each of the following methods.

(1) Straight-line method.
(2) Sum-of-the-years'-digits method.
(3) Double-declining-balance method.

2 3 8 ***P11-12 (Depreciation—SL, DDB, SYD, Act., and MACRS)** On January 1, 2013, Locke Company, a small machine-tool manufacturer, acquired for $1,260,000 a piece of new industrial equipment. The new equipment had a useful life of 5 years, and the salvage value was estimated to be $60,000. Locke estimates that the new equipment can produce 12,000 machine tools in its first year. It estimates that production will decline by 1,000 units per year over the remaining useful life of the equipment.

The following depreciation methods may be used: (1) straight-line, (2) double-declining-balance, (3) sum-of-the-years'-digits, and (4) units-of-output. For tax purposes, the class life is 7 years. Use the MACRS tables for computing depreciation.

Instructions

(a) Which depreciation method would maximize net income for financial statement reporting for the 3-year period ending December 31, 2015? Prepare a schedule showing the amount of accumulated depreciation at December 31, 2015, under the method selected. Ignore present value, income tax, and deferred income tax considerations.

(b) Which depreciation method (MACRS or optional straight-line) would minimize net income for income tax reporting for the 3-year period ending December 31, 2015? Determine the amount of accumulated depreciation at December 31, 2015. Ignore present value considerations.

(AICPA adapted)

PROBLEMS SET B

See the book's companion website, at **www.wiley.com/college/kieso**, for an additional set of problems.

CONCEPTS FOR ANALYSIS

CA11-1 (Depreciation Basic Concepts) Burnitz Manufacturing Company was organized on January 1, 2014. During 2014, it has used in its reports to management the straight-line method of depreciating its plant assets.

On November 8, you are having a conference with Burnitz's officers to discuss the depreciation method to be used for income tax and stockholder reporting. James Bryant, president of Burnitz, has suggested the use of a new method, which he feels is more suitable than the straight-line method for the needs of the company during the period of rapid expansion of production and capacity that he foresees. Following is an example in which the proposed method is applied to a fixed asset with an original cost of $248,000, an estimated useful life of 5 years, and a salvage value of approximately $8,000.

Year	Years of Life Used	Fraction Rate	Depreciation Expense	Accumulated Depreciation at End of Year	Book Value at End of Year
1	1	1/15	$16,000	$ 16,000	$232,000
2	2	2/15	32,000	48,000	200,000
3	3	3/15	48,000	96,000	152,000
4	4	4/15	64,000	160,000	88,000
5	5	5/15	80,000	240,000	8,000

The president favors the new method because he has heard that:

1. It will increase the funds recovered during the years near the end of the assets' useful lives when maintenance and replacement disbursements are high.
2. It will result in increased write-offs in later years and thereby will reduce taxes.

Instructions

(a) What is the purpose of accounting for depreciation?

(b) Is the president's proposal within the scope of generally accepted accounting principles? In making your decision, discuss the circumstances, if any, under which use of the method would be reasonable and those, if any, under which it would not be reasonable.

(c) The president wants your advice on the following issues.

(1) Do depreciation charges recover or create funds? Explain.

(2) Assume that the Internal Revenue Service accepts the proposed depreciation method in this case. If the proposed method were used for stockholder and tax reporting purposes, how would it affect the availability of cash flows generated by operations?

CA11-2 (Unit, Group, and Composite Depreciation) The certified public accountant is frequently called upon by management for advice regarding methods of computing depreciation. Of comparable importance, although it arises less frequently, is the question of whether the depreciation method should be based on consideration of the assets as units, as a group, or as having a composite life.

Instructions

(a) Briefly describe the depreciation methods based on treating assets as (1) units and (2) a group or as having a composite life.

(b) Present the arguments for and against the use of each of the two methods.

(c) Describe how retirements are recorded under each of the two methods.

(AICPA adapted)

CA11-3 (Depreciation—Strike, Units-of-Production, Obsolescence) Presented on page 634 are three different and unrelated situations involving depreciation accounting. Answer the question(s) at the end of each situation.

Situation I: Recently, Broderick Company experienced a strike that affected a number of its operating plants. The controller of this company indicated that it was not appropriate to report depreciation expense during this period because the equipment did not depreciate and an improper matching of costs and revenues would result. She based her position on the following points.

1. It is inappropriate to charge the period with costs for which there are no related revenues arising from production.
2. The basic factor of depreciation in this instance is wear and tear. Because equipment was idle, no wear and tear occurred.

Instructions

Comment on the appropriateness of the controller's comments.

Situation II: Etheridge Company manufactures electrical appliances, most of which are used in homes. Company engineers have designed a new type of blender which, through the use of a few attachments, will perform more functions than any blender currently on the market. Demand for the new blender can be projected with reasonable probability. In order to make the blenders, Etheridge needs a specialized machine that is not available from outside sources. It has been decided to make such a machine in Etheridge's own plant.

Instructions

(a) Discuss the effect of projected demand in units for the new blenders (which may be steady, decreasing, or increasing) on the determination of a depreciation method for the machine.

(b) What other matters should be considered in determining the depreciation method? (Ignore income tax considerations.)

Situation III: Haley Paper Company operates a 300-ton-per-day kraft pulp mill and four sawmills in Wisconsin. The company is in the process of expanding its pulp mill facilities to a capacity of 1,000 tons per day and plans to replace three of its older, less efficient sawmills with an expanded facility. One of the mills to be replaced did not operate for most of 2014 (current year), and there are no plans to reopen it before the new sawmill facility becomes operational.

In reviewing the depreciation rates and in discussing the salvage values of the sawmills that were to be replaced, it was noted that if present depreciation rates were not adjusted, substantial amounts of plant costs on these three mills would not be depreciated by the time the new mill came on stream.

Instructions

What is the proper accounting for the four sawmills at the end of 2014?

CA11-4 (Depreciation Concepts) As a cost accountant for San Francisco Cannery, you have been approached by Phil Perriman, canning room supervisor, about the 2014 costs charged to his department. In particular, he is concerned about the line item "depreciation." Perriman is very proud of the excellent condition of his canning room equipment. He has always been vigilant about keeping all equipment serviced and well oiled. He is sure that the huge charge to depreciation is a mistake; it does not at all reflect the cost of minimal wear and tear that the machines have experienced over the last year. He believes that the charge should be considerably lower.

The machines being depreciated are six automatic canning machines. All were put into use on January 1, 2014. Each cost $625,000, having a salvage value of $55,000 and a useful life of 12 years. San Francisco depreciates this and similar assets using double-declining-balance depreciation. Perriman has also pointed out that if you used straight-line depreciation, the charge to his department would not be so great.

Instructions

Write a memo to Phil Perriman to clear up his misunderstanding of the term "depreciation." Also, calculate year-1 depreciation on all machines using both methods. Explain the theoretical justification for double-declining-balance and why, in the long run, the aggregate charge to depreciation will be the same under both methods.

CA11-5 (Depreciation Choice—Ethics) Jerry Prior, Beeler Corporation's controller, is concerned that net income may be lower this year. He is afraid upper-level management might recommend cost reductions by laying off accounting staff, including him.

Prior knows that depreciation is a major expense for Beeler. The company currently uses the double-declining-balance method for both financial reporting and tax purposes, and he's thinking of selling equipment that, given its age, is primarily used when there are periodic spikes in demand. The equipment has a carrying value of $2,000,000 and a fair value of $2,180,000. The gain on the sale would be reported in the income statement. He doesn't want to highlight this method of increasing income. He thinks, "Why don't I increase the estimated useful lives and the salvage values? That will decrease depreciation expense and require less extensive disclosure, since the changes are accounted for prospectively. I may be able to save my job and those of my staff."

Instructions

Answer the following questions.

(a) Who are the stakeholders in this situation?

(b) What are the ethical issues involved?

(c) What should Prior do?

USING YOUR JUDGMENT

FINANCIAL REPORTING

Financial Reporting Problem

P&G

The Procter & Gamble Company (P&G)

The financial statements of P&G are presented in Appendix 5B. The company's complete annual report, including the notes to the financial statements, can be accessed at the book's companion website, **www.wiley.com/college/kieso**.

Instructions

Refer to P&G's financial statements and the accompanying notes to answer the following questions.

(a) What descriptions are used by P&G in its balance sheet to classify its property, plant, and equipment?

(b) What method or methods of depreciation does P&G use to depreciate its property, plant, and equipment?

(c) Over what estimated useful lives does P&G depreciate its property, plant, and equipment?

(d) What amounts for depreciation and amortization expense did P&G charge to its income statement in 2011, 2010, and 2009?

(e) What were the capital expenditures for property, plant, and equipment made by P&G in 2011, 2010, and 2009?

Comparative Analysis Case

The Coca-Cola Company and PepsiCo., Inc.

Instructions

Go to the book's companion website and use information found there to answer the following questions related to The Coca-Cola Company and PepsiCo, Inc.

(a) What amount is reported in the balance sheets as property, plant, and equipment (net) of Coca-Cola at December 31, 2011, and of PepsiCo at December 31, 2011? What percentage of total assets is invested in property, plant, and equipment by each company?

(b) What depreciation methods are used by Coca-Cola and PepsiCo for property, plant, and equipment? How much depreciation was reported by Coca-Cola and PepsiCo in 2011? In 2010?

(c) Compute and compare the following ratios for Coca-Cola and PepsiCo for 2011.

(1) Asset turnover.

(2) Profit margin on sales.

(3) Return on assets.

(d) What amount was spent in 2011 for capital expenditures by Coca-Cola and PepsiCo? What amount of interest was capitalized in 2011?

Financial Statement Analysis Case

McDonald's Corporation

McDonald's is the largest and best-known global food-service retailer, with more than 32,000 restaurants in 118 countries. On any day, McDonald's serves approximately 1 percent of the world's population. Presented on the next page is information related to McDonald's property and equipment.

McDonald's Corporation
Summary of Significant Accounting Policies Section

Property and Equipment. Property and equipment are stated at cost, with depreciation and amortization provided using the straight-line method over the following estimated useful lives: buildings—up to 40 years; leasehold improvements—the lesser of useful lives of assets or lease terms, which generally include option periods; and equipment—three to 12 years.

[In the notes to the financial statements:]

Property and Equipment
Net property and equipment consisted of:

(In millions)	December 31 2011	2010
Land	$ 5,328.3	$ 5,200.5
Buildings and improvements on owned land	13,079.9	12,399.4
Buildings and improvements on leased land	12,021.8	11,732.0
Equipment, signs and seating	4,757.2	4,608.5
Other	550.4	542.0
	35,737.6	34,482.4
Accumulated depreciation and amortization	(12,903.1)	(12,421.8)
Net property and equipment	$22,834.5	$22,060.6

Depreciation and amortization expense was (in millions): 2011—$1,329.6; 2010—$1,200.4; 2009—$1,160.8.

[In its 6-year summary, McDonald's provides the following information.]

Cash Provided by Operations

(dollars in millions)	2011	2010	2009
Cash provided by operations	$7,150	$6,342	$5,751
Capital expenditures	$2,730	$2,135	$1,952

Instructions

(a) What method of depreciation does McDonald's use?

(b) Does depreciation and amortization expense cause cash flow from operations to increase? Explain.

(c) What does the schedule of cash flow measures indicate?

Accounting, Analysis, and Principles

Electroboy Enterprises, Inc. operates several stores throughout the western United States. As part of an operational and financial reporting review in a response to a downturn in its markets, the company's management has decided to perform an impairment test on five stores (combined). The five stores' sales have declined due to aging facilities and competition from a rival that opened new stores in the same markets. Management has developed the following information concerning the five stores as of the end of fiscal 2013.

Original cost	$36 million
Accumulated depreciation	$10 million
Estimated remaining useful life	4 years
Estimated expected future annual cash flows (not discounted)	$4.0 million per year
Appropriate discount rate	5 percent

Accounting

(a) Determine the amount of impairment loss, if any, that Electroboy should report for fiscal 2013 and the book value at which Electroboy should report the five stores on its fiscal year-end 2013 balance sheet. Assume that the cash flows occur at the end of each year.

(b) Repeat part (a), but instead assume that (1) the estimated remaining useful life is 10 years, (2) the estimated annual cash flows are $2,720,000 per year, and (3) the appropriate discount rate is 6 percent.

Analysis

Assume that you are a financial analyst and you participate in a conference call with Electroboy management in early 2014 (before Electroboy closes the books on fiscal 2013). During the conference call, you learn that management is considering selling the five stores, but the sale won't likely be completed until the second quarter of fiscal 2014. Briefly discuss what implications this would have for Electroboy's 2013 financial statements. Assume the same facts as in part (b) above.

Principles

Electroboy management would like to know the accounting for the impaired asset in periods subsequent to the impairment. Can the assets be written back up? Briefly discuss the conceptual arguments for this accounting.

BRIDGE TO THE PROFESSION

Professional Research: FASB Codification

Matt Holmes recently joined Klax Company as a staff accountant in the controller's office. Klax Company provides warehousing services for companies in several midwestern cities.

The location in Dubuque, Iowa, has not been performing well due to increased competition and the loss of several customers that have recently gone out of business. Matt's department manager suspects that the plant and equipment may be impaired and wonders whether those assets should be written down. Given the company's prior success, this issue has never arisen in the past, and Matt has been asked to conduct some research on this issue.

Instructions

If your school has a subscription to the FASB Codification, go to *http://aaahq.org/asclogin.cfm* to log in and prepare responses to the following. Provide Codification references for your responses.

(a) What is the authoritative guidance for asset impairments? Briefly discuss the scope of the standard (i.e., explain the types of transactions to which the standard applies).

(b) Give several examples of events that would cause an asset to be tested for impairment. Does it appear that Klax should perform an impairment test? Explain.

(c) What is the best evidence of fair value? Describe alternate methods of estimating fair value.

Additional Professional Resources

See the book's companion website, at **www.wiley.com/college/kieso**, for professional simulations as well as other study resources.

IFRS INSIGHTS

9 LEARNING OBJECTIVE
Compare the accounting for property, plant, and equipment under GAAP and IFRS.

GAAP adheres to many of the same principles of IFRS in the accounting for property, plant, and equipment. Major differences relate to use of component depreciation, impairments, and revaluations.

RELEVANT FACTS

Following are the key similarities and differences between GAAP and IFRS related to property, plant, and equipment.

Similarities

- The definition of property, plant, and equipment is essentially the same under GAAP and IFRS.

- Under both GAAP and IFRS, changes in depreciation method and changes in useful life are treated in the current and future periods. Prior periods are not affected.
- The accounting for plant asset disposals is the same under GAAP and IFRS.
- The accounting for the initial costs to acquire natural resources is similar under GAAP and IFRS.
- Under both GAAP and IFRS, interest costs incurred during construction must be capitalized. Recently, IFRS converged to GAAP.
- The accounting for exchanges of non-monetary assets is essentially the same between IFRS and GAAP. GAAP requires that gains on exchanges of non-monetary assets be recognized if the exchange has commercial substance. This is the same framework used in IFRS.
- GAAP and IFRS both view depreciation as allocation of cost over an asset's life. GAAP permits the same depreciation methods (straight-line, diminishing-balance, units-of-production) as IFRS.

Differences

- IFRS requires component depreciation. Under GAAP, component depreciation is permitted but is rarely used.
- Under IFRS, companies can use either the historical cost model or the revaluation model. GAAP does not permit revaluations of property, plant, and equipment or mineral resources.
- In testing for impairments of long-lived assets, GAAP uses a different model than IFRS to test for impairments (details of the IFRS impairment test is presented in the *About the Numbers* discussion). As long as future undiscounted cash flows exceed the carrying amount of the asset, no impairment is recorded. The IFRS impairment test is stricter. However, unlike GAAP, reversals of impairment losses are permitted.

ABOUT THE NUMBERS

Component Depreciation

Under IFRS, companies are required to use **component depreciation**. IFRS requires that each part of an item of property, plant, and equipment that is significant to the total cost of the asset must be depreciated separately. Companies therefore have to exercise judgment to determine the proper allocations to the components. As an example, when a company like **Nokia** purchases a building, it must determine how the various building components (e.g., the foundation, structure, roof, heating and cooling system, and elevators) should be segregated and depreciated.

To illustrate the accounting for component depreciation, assume that EuroAsia Airlines purchases an airplane for $100,000,000 on January 1, 2014. The airplane has a useful life of 20 years and a residual value of $0. EuroAsia uses the straight-line method of depreciation for all its airplanes. EuroAsia identifies the following components, amounts, and useful lives, as shown in Illustration IFRS11-1.

ILLUSTRATION IFRS11-1
Airplane Components

Components	Component Amount	Component Useful Life
Airframe	$60,000,000	20 years
Engine components	32,000,000	8 years
Other components	8,000,000	5 years

Illustration IFRS11-2 shows the computation of depreciation expense for EuroAsia for 2014.

Components	Component Amount	÷	Useful Life	=	Component Depreciation
Airframe	$ 60,000,000		20		$3,000,000
Engine components	32,000,000		8		4,000,000
Other components	8,000,000		5		1,600,000
Total	$100,000,000				$8,600,000

ILLUSTRATION IFRS11-2
Computation of Component Depreciation

As indicated, EuroAsia records depreciation expense of $8,600,000 in 2014 as follows.

Depreciation Expense	8,600,000	
Accumulated Depreciation—Airplane		8,600,000

On the statement of financial position at the end of 2014, EuroAsia reports the airplane as a single amount. The presentation is shown in Illustration IFRS11-3.

Non-current assets	
Airplane	$100,000,000
Less: Accumulated depreciation—airplane	8,600,000
	$ 91,400,000

ILLUSTRATION IFRS11-3
Presentation of Carrying Amount of Airplane

In many situations, a company may not have a good understanding of the cost of the individual components purchased. In that case, the cost of individual components should be estimated based on reference to current market prices (if available), discussion with experts in valuation, or use of other reasonable approaches.

Recognizing Impairments

As discussed in the textbook, the credit crisis starting in late 2008 has affected many financial and non-financial institutions. As a result of this global slump, many companies are considering write-offs of some of their long-lived assets. These write-offs are referred to as **impairments**. The accounting for impairments is different under GAAP and IFRS.

A long-lived tangible asset is impaired when a company is not able to recover the asset's carrying amount either through using it or by selling it. To determine whether an asset is impaired, **on an annual basis, companies review the asset for indicators of impairments**—that is, a decline in the asset's cash-generating ability through use or sale. This review should consider internal sources (e.g., adverse changes in performance) and external sources (e.g., adverse changes in the business or regulatory environment) of information. **If impairment indicators are present, then an impairment test must be conducted.** This test compares the asset's recoverable amount with its carrying amount. If the carrying amount is higher than the recoverable amount, the difference is an impairment loss. If the recoverable amount is greater than the carrying amount, no impairment is recorded.

Recoverable amount is defined as the higher of fair value less costs to sell or value-in-use. **Fair value less costs to sell** means what the asset could be sold for after deducting costs of disposal. **Value-in-use** is the present value of cash flows expected from the future use and eventual sale of the asset at the end of its useful life. Illustration IFRS11-4 (page 640) highlights the nature of the impairment test.

ILLUSTRATION IFRS11-4
Impairment Test

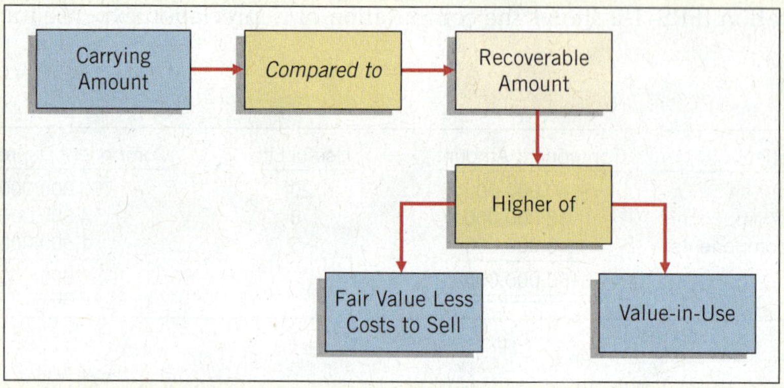

If either the fair value less costs to sell or value-in-use is higher than the carrying amount, there is no impairment. If both the fair value less costs to sell and value-in-use are lower than the carrying amount, a loss on impairment occurs.

Example: No Impairment

Assume that Cruz Company performs an impairment test for its equipment. The carrying amount of Cruz's equipment is $200,000, its fair value less costs to sell is $180,000, and its value-in-use is $205,000. In this case, the value-in-use of Cruz's equipment is higher than its carrying amount of $200,000. As a result, there is no impairment. (If a company can more readily determine value-in-use (or fair value less costs to sell) and it determines that no impairment is needed, it is not required to compute the other measure.)

Example: Impairment

Assume the same information for Cruz Company above except that the value-in-use of Cruz's equipment is $175,000 rather than $205,000. Cruz measures the impairment loss as the difference between the carrying amount of $200,000 and the higher of fair value less costs to sell ($180,000) or value-in-use ($175,000). Cruz therefore uses the fair value less cost of disposal to record an impairment loss of $20,000 ($200,000 − $180,000). Cruz makes the following entry to record the impairment loss.

Loss on Impairment	20,000	
Accumulated Depreciation—Equipment		20,000

Loss on Impairment is reported in the income statement in the "Other income and expense" section. The company then either credits Equipment or Accumulated Depreciation—Equipment to reduce the carrying amount of the equipment for the impairment. *For purposes of homework, credit accumulated depreciation when recording an impairment for a depreciable asset.*

Reversal of Impairment Loss

After recording the impairment loss, the recoverable amount becomes the basis of the impaired asset. What happens if a review in a future year indicates that the asset is no longer impaired because the recoverable amount of the asset is higher than the carrying amount? In that case, the impairment loss may be reversed.

To illustrate, assume that Tan Company purchases equipment on January 1, 2014, for $300,000, with a useful life of three years, and no residual value. Its depreciation and related carrying amount over the three years is as follows.

Year	Depreciation Expense	Carrying Amount
2014	$100,000 ($300,000/3)	$200,000
2015	$100,000 ($300,000/3)	$100,000
2016	$100,000 ($300,000/3)	0

At December 31, 2014, Tan determines it has an impairment loss of $20,000 and therefore makes the following entry.

Loss on Impairment	20,000	
Accumulated Depreciation—Equipment		20,000

Tan's depreciation expense and related carrying amount after the impairment is as indicated in Illustration IFRS11-5.

ILLUSTRATION IFRS11-5
Carrying Value of Impaired Asset

Year	Depreciation Expense	Carrying Amount
2015	$90,000 ($180,000/2)	$90,000
2016	$90,000 ($180,000/2)	0

At the end of 2015, Tan determines that the recoverable amount of the equipment is $96,000, which is greater than its carrying amount of $90,000. In this case, Tan reverses the previously recognized impairment loss with the following entry.

Accumulated Depreciation—Equipment	6,000	
Recovery of Loss from Impairment		6,000

The recovery of the impairment loss is reported in the "Other income and expense" section of the income statement. The carrying amount of Tan's equipment is now $96,000 ($90,000 + $6,000) at December 31, 2015. The general rule related to reversals of impairments is as follows. The amount of the recovery of the loss is limited to the carrying amount that would result if the impairment had not occurred. For example, the carrying amount of Tan's equipment at the end of 2015 would be $100,000, assuming no impairment. The $6,000 recovery is therefore permitted because Tan's carrying amount on the equipment is now only $96,000.

However, any recovery above $10,000 is not permitted. The reason is that any recovery above $10,000 results in Tan carrying the asset at a value above its historical cost.

Revaluations

Up to this point, we have assumed that companies use the historical cost principle to value long-lived tangible assets after acquisition. However, under IFRS companies have a choice. They may value these assets at cost or at fair value.

Recognizing Revaluations

Network Rail (a company in Great Britain) is an example of a company that elected to use fair values to account for its railroad network. Its use of fair value led to an increase of £4,289 million to its long-lived tangible assets. When companies choose to fair value their long-lived tangible assets subsequent to acquisition, they account for the change in the fair value by adjusting the appropriate asset account and establishing an unrealized gain on the revalued long-lived tangible asset. This unrealized gain is often referred to as **revaluation surplus**.

Revaluation—Land. To illustrate revaluation of land, assume that Siemens Group purchased land for $1,000,000 on January 5, 2014. The company elects to use revaluation accounting for the land in subsequent periods. At December 31, 2014, the land's fair value is $1,200,000. The entry to record the land at fair value is as follows.

Land	200,000	
Unrealized Gain on Revaluation (land)		200,000

The land is reported on the statement of financial position at $1,200,000, and Unrealized Gain on Revaluation (land) increases other comprehensive income in the statement of comprehensive income. In addition, if this is the only revaluation adjustment to date, the statement of financial position reports accumulated other comprehensive income of $200,000.

Revaluation—Depreciable Assets. To illustrate the accounting for revaluations of depreciable assets, assume that Lenovo Group purchases equipment for $500,000 on January 2, 2014. The equipment has a useful life of five years, is depreciated using the straight-line method of depreciation, and its residual value is zero. Lenovo chooses to revalue its equipment to fair value over the life of the equipment. Lenovo records depreciation expense of $100,000 ($500,000 ÷ 5) at December 31, 2014, as follows.

December 31, 2014		
Depreciation Expense	100,000	
Accumulated Depreciation—Equipment		100,000
(To record depreciation expense in 2014)		

After this entry, Lenovo's equipment has a carrying amount of $400,000 ($500,000 – $100,000). Lenovo receives an independent appraisal for the fair value of equipment at December 31, 2014, which is $460,000. To report the equipment at fair value, Lenovo does the following.

1. Reduces the Accumulated Depreciation—Equipment account to zero.
2. Reduces the Equipment account by $40,000—it then is reported at its fair value of $460,000.
3. Records Unrealized Gain on Revaluation (equipment) for the difference between the fair value and carrying amount of the equipment, or $60,000 ($460,000 – $400,000).

The entry to record this revaluation at December 31, 2014, is as follows.

December 31, 2014		
Accumulated Depreciation—Equipment	100,000	
Equipment		40,000
Unrealized Gain on Revaluation (equipment)		60,000
(To adjust the equipment to fair value and record revaluation increase)		

The equipment is now reported at its fair value of $460,000 ($500,000 – $40,000). As an alternative to the one shown here, companies restate on a proportionate basis the cost and accumulated depreciation of the asset, such that the carrying amount of the asset after revaluation equals its revalued amount.

The increase in the fair value of $60,000 is reported on the statement of comprehensive income as other comprehensive income. In addition, the ending balance is reported in accumulated other comprehensive income on the statement of financial position in the equity section. Illustration IFRS11-6 shows the presentation of revaluation elements.

ILLUSTRATION IFRS11-6
Financial Statement Presentation—Revaluations

On the statement of comprehensive income:	
Depreciation expense	$100,000
Other comprehensive income	
Unrealized gain on revaluation (equipment)	$ 60,000
On the statement of financial position:	
Non-current assets	
Equipment ($500,000 – $40,000)	$460,000
Accumulated depreciation—equipment ($100,000 – $100,000)	–0–
Carrying amount	$460,000
Equity	
Accumulated other comprehensive income	$ 60,000

As indicated, at December 31, 2014, the carrying amount of the equipment is now \$460,000. Lenovo reports depreciation expense of \$100,000 in the income statement and Unrealized Gain on Revaluation (equipment) of \$60,000 in "Other comprehensive income." Assuming no change in the useful life of the equipment, depreciation in 2015 is \$115,000 (\$460,000 ÷ 4).

In summary, a revaluation increase generally goes to equity. A revaluation decrease is reported as an expense (as an impairment loss), unless it offsets previously recorded revaluation increases. If the revaluation increase offsets a revaluation decrease that went to expense, then the increase is reported in income. **Under no circumstances can the Accumulated Other Comprehensive Income account related to revaluations have a negative balance.**

ON THE HORIZON

With respect to revaluations, as part of the conceptual framework project, the Boards will examine the measurement bases used in accounting. It is too early to say whether a converged conceptual framework will recommend fair value measurement (and revaluation accounting) for property, plant, and equipment. However, this is likely to be one of the more contentious issues, given the long-standing use of historical cost as a measurement basis in GAAP.

IFRS SELF-TEST QUESTIONS

1. Mandall Company constructed a warehouse for \$280,000 on January 2, 2014. Mandall estimates that the warehouse has a useful life of 20 years and no residual value. Construction records indicate that \$40,000 of the cost of the warehouse relates to its heating, ventilation, and air conditioning (HVAC) system, which has an estimated useful life of only 10 years. What is the first year of depreciation expense using straight-line component depreciation under IFRS?
   (a) \$28,000. **(c)** \$16,000.
   (b) \$14,000. **(d)** \$4,000.
2. Francisco Corporation is constructing a new building at a total initial cost of \$10,000,000. The building is expected to have a useful life of 50 years with no residual value. The building's finished surfaces (e.g., roof cover and floor cover) are 5% of this cost and have a useful life of 20 years. Building services systems (e.g., electric, heating, and plumbing) are 20% of the cost and have a useful life of 25 years. The depreciation in the first year using component depreciation, assuming straight-line depreciation with no residual value, is:
   (a) \$200,000. **(c)** \$255,000.
   (b) \$215,000. **(d)** None of the above.
3. Which of the following statements is **correct**?
   (a) Both IFRS and GAAP permit revaluation of property, plant, and equipment.
   (b) IFRS permits revaluation of property, plant, and equipment but not GAAP.
   (c) Both IFRS and GAAP do not permit revaluation of property, plant, and equipment.
   (d) GAAP permits revaluation of property, plant, and equipment but not IFRS.
4. Hilo Company has land that cost \$350,000 but now has a fair value of \$500,000. Hilo Company decides to use the revaluation method specified in IFRS to account for the land. Which of the following statements is **correct**?
   (a) Hilo Company must continue to report the land at \$350,000.
   (b) Hilo Company would report a net income increase of \$150,000 due to an increase in the value of the land.
   (c) Hilo Company would debit Revaluation Surplus for \$150,000.
   (d) Hilo Company would credit Revaluation Surplus by \$150,000.
5. Under IFRS, value-in-use is defined as:
   (a) net realizable value.
   (b) fair value.
   (c) future cash flows discounted to present value.
   (d) total future undiscounted cash flows.

IFRS CONCEPTS AND APPLICATION

IFRS11-1 Walkin Inc. is considering the write-down of its long-term plant because of a lack of profitability. Explain to the management of Walkin how to determine whether a write-down is permitted.

IFRS11-2 Last year, Wyeth Company recorded an impairment on an asset held for use. Recent appraisals indicate that the asset has increased in value. Should Wyeth record this recovery in value?

IFRS11-3 Toro Co. has equipment with a carrying amount of $700,000. The value-in-use of the equipment is $705,000, and its fair value less costs of disposal is $590,000. The equipment is expected to be used in operations in the future. What amount (if any) should Toro report as an impairment to its equipment?

IFRS11-4 Explain how gains or losses on impaired assets should be reported in income.

IFRS11-5 Tanaka Company has land that cost $15,000,000. Its fair value on December 31, 2014, is $20,000,000. Tanaka chooses the revaluation model to report its land. Explain how the land and its related valuation should be reported.

IFRS11-6 Why might a company choose not to use revaluation accounting?

IFRS11-7 Ortiz purchased a piece of equipment that cost $202,000 on January 1, 2014. The equipment has the following components.

Component	Cost	Residual Value	Estimated Useful Life
A	$70,000	$7,000	10 years
B	50,000	5,000	5 years
C	82,000	4,000	12 years

Compute the depreciation expense for this equipment at December 31, 2014.

IFRS11-8 Tan Chin Company purchases a building for $11,300,000 on January 2, 2014. An engineer's report shows that of the total purchase price, $11,000,000 should be allocated to the building (with a 40-year life), $150,000 to 15-year property, and $150,000 to 5-year property. No residual (salvage) value should be considered. Compute depreciation expense for 2014 using component depreciation.

IFRS11-9 Brazil Group purchases a vehicle at.a cost of $50,000 on January 2, 2014. Individual components of the vehicle and useful lives are as follows.

	Cost	Useful Lives
Tires	$ 6,000	2 years
Transmission	10,000	5 years
Trucks	34,000	10 years

Instructions

(Assume no residual (salvage) value.)

(a) Compute depreciation expense for 2014, assuming Brazil depreciates the vehicle as a single unit.
(b) Compute depreciation expense for 2014, assuming Brazil uses component depreciation.
(c) Why might a company want to use component depreciation to depreciate its assets?

IFRS11-10 Jurassic Company owns machinery that cost $900,000 and has accumulated depreciation of $380,000. The present value of expected future net cash flows from the use of the asset are expected to be $500,000. The fair value less cost of disposal of the equipment is $400,000. Prepare the journal entry, if any, to record the impairment loss.

IFRS11-11 Presented below is information related to equipment owned by Pujols Company at December 31, 2014.

Cost (residual value $0)	$9,000,000
Accumulated depreciation to date	1,000,000
Value-in-use	5,500,000
Fair value less cost of disposal	4,400,000

Assume that Pujols will continue to use this asset in the future. As of December 31, 2014, the equipment has a remaining useful life of 8 years. Pujols uses straight-line depreciation.

Instructions

(a) Prepare the journal entry (if any) to record the impairment of the asset at December 31, 2014.
(b) Prepare the journal entry to record depreciation expense for 2015.
(c) The recoverable amount of the equipment at December 31, 2015, is $6,050,000. Prepare the journal entry (if any) necessary to record this increase.

IFRS11-12 Assume the same information as in IFRS11-11, except that Pujols intends to dispose of the equipment in the coming year.

Instructions

(a) Prepare the journal entry (if any) to record the impairment of the asset at December 31, 2014.
(b) Prepare the journal entry (if any) to record depreciation expense for 2015.
(c) The asset was not sold by December 31, 2015. The fair value of the equipment on that date is $5,100,000. Prepare the journal entry (if any) necessary to record this increase. It is expected that the cost of disposal is $20,000.

IFRS11-13 Falcetto Company acquired equipment on January 1, 2013, for $12,000. Falcetto elects to value this class of equipment using revaluation accounting. This equipment is being depreciated on a straight-line basis over its 6-year useful life. There is no residual value at the end of the 6-year period. The appraised value of the equipment approximates the carrying amount at December 31, 2013 and 2015. On December 31, 2014, the fair value of the equipment is determined to be $7,000.

Instructions

(a) Prepare the journal entries for 2013 related to the equipment.
(b) Prepare the journal entries for 2014 related to the equipment.
(c) Determine the amount of depreciation expense that Falcetto will record on the equipment in 2015.

International Reporting Case

IFRS11-14 Companies following international accounting standards are permitted to revalue fixed assets above the assets' historical costs. Such revaluations are allowed under various countries' standards and the standards issued by the IASB. **Liberty International**, a real estate company headquartered in the United Kingdom (U.K.), follows U.K. standards. In a recent year, Liberty disclosed the following information on revaluations of its tangible fixed assets. The revaluation reserve measures the amount by which tangible fixed assets are recorded above historical cost and is reported in Liberty's stockholders' equity.

Liberty International

Completed Investment Properties

Completed investment properties are professionally valued on a market value basis by external valuers at the balance sheet date. Surpluses and deficits arising during the year are reflected in the revalution reserve.

Liberty reported the following additional data. Amounts for **Kimco Realty** (which follows GAAP) in the same year are provided for comparison.

	Liberty (pounds sterling, in thousands)	Kimco (dollars, in millions)
Total revenues	£ 741	$ 517
Average total assets	5,577	4,696
Net income	125	297

Instructions

(a) Compute the following ratios for Liberty and Kimco.
(1) Return on assets.
(2) Profit margin on sales.
(3) Asset turnover.
How do these companies compare on these performance measures?
(b) Liberty reports a revaluation surplus of £1,952. Assume that £1,550 of this amount arose from an increase in the net replacement value of investment properties during the year. Prepare the journal entry to record this increase.

(c) Under U.K. (and IASB) standards, are Liberty's assets and equity overstated? If so, why? When comparing Liberty to U.S. companies, like Kimco, what adjustments would you need to make in order to have valid comparisons of ratios such as those computed in (a) above?

Professional Research

IFRS11-15 Matt Holmes recently joined Klax Company as a staff accountant in the controller's office. Klax Company provides warehousing services for companies in several European cities. The location in Koblenz, Germany, has not been performing well due to increased competition and the loss of several customers that have recently gone out of business. Matt's department manager suspects that the plant and equipment may be impaired and wonders whether those assets should be written down. Given the company's prior success, this issue has never arisen in the past, and Matt has been asked to conduct some research on this issue.

Instructions

Access the IFRS authoritative literature at the IASB website (*http://eifrs.iasb.org/*). (Click on the IFRS tab and then register for free eIFRS access if necessary.) When you have accessed the documents, you can use the search tool in your Internet browser to respond to the following questions. (Provide paragraph citations.)

(a) What is the authoritative guidance for asset impairments? Briefly discuss the scope of the standard (i.e., explain the types of transactions to which the standard applies).

(b) Give several examples of events that would cause an asset to be tested for impairment. Does it appear that Klax should perform an impairment test? Explain.

(c) What is the best evidence of fair value? Describe alternate methods of estimating fair value.

International Financial Reporting Problem

Marks and Spencer plc

IFRS11-16 The financial statements of **Marks and Spencer plc (M&S)** are available at the book's companion website or can be accessed at *http://annualreport.marksandspencer.com/_assets/downloads/Marks-and-Spencer-Annual-report-and-financial-statements-2012.pdf.*

Instructions

Refer to M&S's financial statements and the accompanying notes to answer the following questions.

(a) What descriptions are used by M&S in its statement of financial position to classify its property, plant, and equipment?

(b) What method or methods of depreciation does M&S use to depreciate its property, plant, and equipment?

(c) Over what estimated useful lives does M&S depreciate its property, plant, and equipment?

(d) What amounts for depreciation and amortization expense did M&S charge to its income statement in 2012 and 2011?

(e) What were the capital expenditures for property, plant, and equipment made by M&S in 2012 and 2011?

ANSWERS TO IFRS SELF-TEST QUESTIONS

1. c **2.** c **3.** b **4.** d **5.** c

Remember to check the book's companion website to find additional resources for this chapter.

CHAPTER 12 Intangible Assets

LEARNING OBJECTIVES

After studying this chapter, you should be able to:

1. Describe the characteristics of intangible assets.
2. Identify the costs to include in the initial valuation of intangible assets.
3. Explain the procedure for amortizing intangible assets.
4. Describe the types of intangible assets.
5. Explain the accounting issues for recording goodwill.
6. Explain the accounting issues related to intangible-asset impairments.
7. Identify the conceptual issues related to research and development costs.
8. Describe the accounting for research and development and similar costs.
9. Indicate the presentation of intangible assets and related items.

Is This Sustainable?

Companies are increasing their focus on sustainability issues. Companies like **Southwest Airlines**, **Clorox**, and **Northrop Grumman** are executing strategic initiatives including fuel-spill control, use of recycled materials, and water conservation. Why the growing importance of responsible management of resource use? One reason is that market participants are now more interested in investing in companies that are pursuing sustainability strategies.

For example, as indicated in the following graph, sustainable investing by professional portfolio managers in the United States has increased from below $500 billion in the mid-1990s to over $2.5 trillion (or 12.5% of the total under management) in 2010.

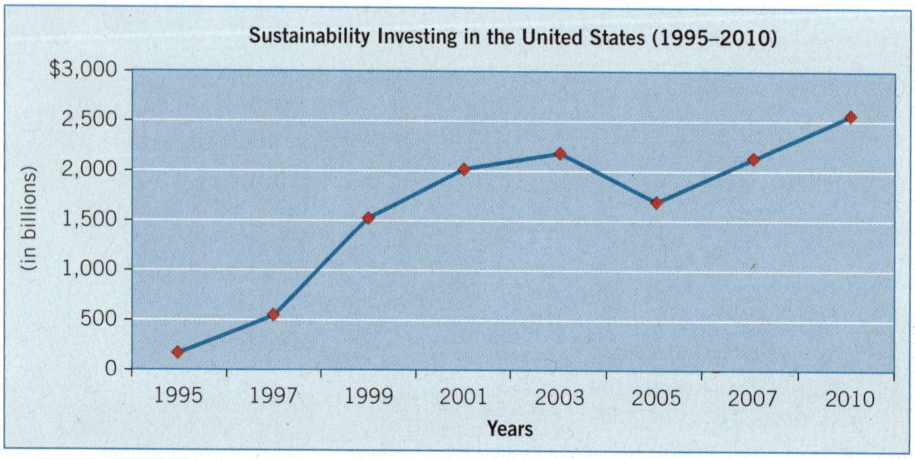

Source: Social Investment Forum.

In light of investor focus on sustainability, it is not surprising that companies are increasing the amount of information reported to the market about their sustainability efforts. However, rather than adding a line item in the income statement or balance sheet, companies instead provide more useful information about the future cash flow consequences of sustainability strategies, which are intangible and usually "nonfinancial" in nature.

CONCEPTUAL FOCUS

> See the **Underlying Concepts** on pages 651, 659, and 662.

> Read the **Evolving Issue** on page 673 for a discussion of recognition of R&D and internally generated intangibles.

INTERNATIONAL FOCUS

> See the **International Perspectives** on pages 652 and 666.

> Read the **IFRS Insights** on pages 693–699 for a discussion of:
—Development costs
—Impairments of intangibles

Consider, for example, the disclosure of information about greenhouse gases. In 2010, the Securities and Exchange Commission clarified the circumstances in which public companies should disclose information related to climate change, as well as the impact on financial performance of their efforts to manage the consequences of greenhouse gas emissions. So here's the paradox: If nonfinancial data, such as greenhouse gas emissions per dollar of revenue, is included in a financial report for investors, how can it still be called nonfinancial?

As with the reporting of research and development expenditures and other intangible assets—many of which do not show up on a balance sheet or income statement—companies are now exploring ways to combine the nonfinancial information with mandated disclosures in what is called an **integrated report**. In such a report, a company might disclose data on any of dozens of metrics beyond conventional balance sheet accounting, whether they are "integrated" or released separately. Practitioners collectively refer sustainability reporting as **ESG** for the three major categories of data—environmental, social, and corporate governance.

While 228 U.S. companies issued a sustainability report in 2011, there was significant variation in the content and format. Only a handful, like those prepared by **Clorox**, **Northrop Grumman**, **SAS**, **Genentech**, and **Polymer Group Inc.**, integrated a sustainability report with the financial statements. As with accounting reports prepared under GAAP, perhaps sustainability reporting is in need of standards?

Sources: S. Lopresti and P. Lilak, "Do Investors Care About Sustainability?" *PwC* (March 2012); and E. Rostin, "Non-Financial Data Are Material: The Sustainability Paradox," *www.bloombergnews.com* (April 13, 2012).

PREVIEW OF CHAPTER 12

As our opening story indicates, sustainability strategies are taking on increased importance for companies like **Southwest Airlines** and **Clorox**. Reporting challenges for effective sustainability investments are similar to those for intangible assets. In this chapter, we explain the basic conceptual and reporting issues related to intangible assets. The content and organization of the chapter are as follows.

Intangible Assets

Intangible Asset Issues	Types of Intangibles	Impairment of Intangibles	Research and Development Costs	Presentation of Intangibles and Related Items
• Characteristics • Valuation • Amortization	• Marketing-related • Customer-related • Artistic-related • Contract-related • Technology-related • Goodwill	• Limited-life intangibles • Indefinite-life intangibles other than goodwill • Goodwill • Summary	• Identifying R&D • Accounting for R&D • Similar costs	• Intangible assets • R&D costs

INTANGIBLE ASSET ISSUES

Characteristics

LEARNING OBJECTIVE 1
Describe the characteristics of intangible assets.

Gap Inc.'s most important asset is its brand image, not its store fixtures. The Coca-Cola Company's success comes from its secret formula for making Coca-Cola, not its plant facilities. America Online's subscriber base, not its Internet connection equipment, provides its most important asset. The U.S. economy is dominated by information and service providers. For these companies, their major assets are often intangible in nature.

See the FASB Codification section (page 676).

What exactly are intangible assets? **Intangible assets** have two main characteristics. [1]

1. ***They lack physical existence.*** Tangible assets such as property, plant, and equipment have physical form. Intangible assets, in contrast, derive their value from the rights and privileges granted to the company using them.
2. ***They are not financial instruments.*** Assets such as bank deposits, accounts receivable, and long-term investments in bonds and stocks also lack physical substance. However, financial instruments derive their value from the right (claim) to receive cash or cash equivalents in the future. Financial instruments are not classified as intangibles.

In most cases, intangible assets provide benefits over a period of years. Therefore, companies normally classify them as long-term assets.

Following a discussion of the general valuation and accounting provisions for intangible assets, we present a more extensive discussion of the types of intangible assets and their accounting.

Valuation

Purchased Intangibles

LEARNING OBJECTIVE 2
Identify the costs to include in the initial valuation of intangible assets.

Companies **record at cost** intangibles purchased from another party. Cost includes all acquisition costs plus expenditures to make the intangible asset ready for its intended use. Typical costs include purchase price, legal fees, and other incidental expenses.

Sometimes companies acquire intangibles in exchange for stock or other assets. In such cases, **the cost of the intangible is the fair value of the consideration given or the fair value of the intangible received, whichever is more clearly evident**. What if a company buys several intangibles, or a combination of intangibles and tangibles? In such a "basket purchase," the company should allocate the cost on the basis of fair values. Essentially, the accounting treatment for purchased intangibles closely parallels that for purchased tangible assets.[1]

Internally Created Intangibles

Sometimes a company may incur substantial research and development (R&D) costs to create an intangible. For example, Google expensed the R&D costs incurred to develop its valuable search engine. Costs incurred internally to create intangibles are generally expensed.

[1]The accounting in this section relates to the acquisition of a single asset or group of assets. The accounting for intangible assets acquired in a **business combination** (transaction in which the purchaser obtains control of one or more businesses) is discussed later in this chapter.

How do companies justify this approach? Some argue that the costs incurred internally to create intangibles bear no relationship to their real value. Therefore, they reason, expensing these costs is appropriate. Others note that it is difficult to associate internal costs with a specific intangible. Still others contend that due to the underlying subjectivity related to intangibles, companies should follow a conservative approach—that is, expense as incurred. As a result, **companies capitalize only direct costs** incurred in developing the intangible, such as legal costs, and expense the rest.

Underlying Concepts

The controversy surrounding the accounting for R&D expenditures reflects a debate about whether such expenditures meet the definition of an asset. If so, then an "expense all R&D costs" policy results in overstated expenses and understated assets.

Amortization of Intangibles

3 LEARNING OBJECTIVE

Explain the procedure for amortizing intangible assets.

The allocation of the cost of intangible assets in a systematic way is called **amortization**. Intangibles have either a **limited (finite) useful life** or an **indefinite useful life**. For example, a company like **Walt Disney Company** has both types of intangibles. Disney **amortizes** its **limited-life** intangible assets (e.g., copyrights on its movies and licenses related to its branded products). It **does not amortize indefinite-life** intangible assets (e.g., the Disney trade name or its Internet domain name).

Limited-Life Intangibles

Companies amortize their limited-life intangibles by systematic charges to expense over their useful life. The useful life should reflect the periods over which these assets will contribute to cash flows. Disney, for example, considers these factors in determining useful life:

1. The expected use of the asset by the company.
2. The expected useful life of another asset or a group of assets to which the useful life of the intangible asset may relate (such as lease rights to a studio lot).
3. Any legal, regulatory, or contractual provisions that may limit the useful life.
4. Any provisions (legal, regulatory, or contractual) that enable renewal or extension of the asset's legal or contractual life without substantial cost. This factor assumes that there is evidence to support renewal or extension. Disney also must be able to accomplish renewal or extension without material modifications of the existing terms and conditions.
5. The effects of obsolescence, demand, competition, and other economic factors. Examples include the stability of the industry, known technological advances, legislative action that results in an uncertain or changing regulatory environment, and expected changes in distribution channels.
6. The level of maintenance expenditure required to obtain the expected future cash flows from the asset. For example, a material level of required maintenance in relation to the carrying amount of the asset may suggest a very limited useful life. [2]

The amount of amortization expense for a limited-life intangible asset should reflect the pattern in which the company consumes or uses up the asset, if the company can reliably determine that pattern. For example, assume that Second Wave, Inc. purchases a license to provide a specified quantity of a gene product called Mega. Second Wave should amortize the cost of the license following the pattern of use of Mega. If Second Wave's license calls for it to provide 30 percent of the total the first year, 20 percent the second year, and 10 percent per year until the license expires, it would amortize the license cost using that pattern. If it cannot determine the pattern of production or consumption, Second Wave should use the straight-line method of amortization. (*For homework problems, assume the use of the straight-line method unless stated otherwise.*) **When Second Wave amortizes these licenses, it should show the charges as expenses. It should credit either the appropriate asset accounts or separate accumulated amortization accounts.**

The amount of an intangible asset to be amortized should be its cost less residual value. The residual value is assumed to be zero unless at the end of its useful life the intangible asset has value to another company. For example, if Hardy Co. commits to purchasing an intangible asset from U2D Co. at the end of the asset's useful life, U2D Co. should reduce the cost of its intangible asset by the residual value. Similarly, U2D Co. should consider fair values, if reliably determined, for residual values.

What happens if the life of a limited-life intangible asset changes? In that case, the remaining carrying amount should be amortized over the revised remaining useful life. Companies should, on a regular basis, evaluate the limited-life intangibles for **impairment**. Similar to the accounting for property, plant, and equipment, an impairment loss should be recognized if the carrying amount of the intangible is not recoverable and its carrying amount exceeds its fair value. (We will cover impairment of intangibles in more detail later in the chapter.)

Indefinite-Life Intangibles

If no factors (legal, regulatory, contractual, competitive, or other) limit the useful life of an intangible asset, a company considers its useful life indefinite. An **indefinite life** means that there is no foreseeable limit on the period of time over which the intangible asset is expected to provide cash flows. A company **does not amortize** an intangible asset with an indefinite life. To illustrate, assume that Double Clik Inc. acquired a trademark that it uses to distinguish a leading consumer product. It renews the trademark every 10 years. All evidence indicates that this trademarked product will generate cash flows for an indefinite period of time. In this case, the trademark has an indefinite life; Double Clik does not record any amortization.

International Perspective

IFRS requires capitalization of some development costs.

Companies should test indefinite-life intangibles for **impairment** at least annually. As we will discuss in more detail later in the chapter, the **impairment test** for indefinite-life intangibles differs from the one for limited-life intangibles. Only the fair value test is performed for indefinite-life intangibles; there is no recoverability test for these intangibles. The reason? Indefinite-life intangible assets might never fail the undiscounted cash flows recoverability test because cash flows could extend indefinitely into the future.

Illustration 12-1 summarizes the accounting treatment for intangible assets.

ILLUSTRATION 12-1
Accounting Treatment for Intangibles

Type of Intangible	Manner Acquired: Purchased	Manner Acquired: Internally Created	Amortization	Impairment Test
Limited-life intangibles	Capitalize	Expense*	Over useful life	Recoverability test and then fair value test
Indefinite-life intangibles	Capitalize	Expense*	Do not amortize	Fair value test only

*Except for direct costs, such as legal costs.

What do the numbers mean? *DEFINITELY INDEFINITE*

The importance of intangible asset classification as either limited-life or indefinite-life is illustrated in the experience of **Outdoor Channel Holdings**. Here's what happened. Outdoor Channel recorded an intangible asset related to the value of an important distributor relationship, purchased from another company. At that time, it classified the relationship as indefinite-life. Thus, in the first two years of the asset's life, Outdoor Channel recorded no amortization expense on this asset. In the third year, investors were surprised to find that Outdoor Channel changed the classification of the distributor relationship to limited-life, with an expected life of 21.33 years (a fairly definite useful life) and, shortly thereafter, wrote off this intangible completely.

Apparently, the company was overly optimistic about the expected future cash flows arising from the distributor relationship. As a result of that optimism, income in the second year was overstated by $9.5 million, or 14 percent, and the impairment recorded in the third year amounted to 7 percent of assets. From indefinite-life to limited-life to worthless in two short years—investors were surely hurt by Outdoor's aggressive intangible asset classification.

Source: Jack Ciesielski, *The AAO Weblog, www.accountingobserver.com/blog/* (January 12, 2007).

TYPES OF INTANGIBLE ASSETS

4 LEARNING OBJECTIVE
Describe the types of intangible assets.

As indicated, the accounting for intangible assets depends on whether the intangible has a limited or an indefinite life. There are many different types of intangibles, often classified into the following six major categories. **[3]**

1. Marketing-related intangible assets.
2. Customer-related intangible assets.
3. Artistic-related intangible assets.
4. Contract-related intangible assets.
5. Technology-related intangible assets.
6. Goodwill.

Marketing-Related Intangible Assets

Companies primarily use **marketing-related intangible assets** in the marketing or promotion of products or services. Examples are trademarks or trade names, newspaper mastheads, Internet domain names, and noncompetition agreements.

A **trademark** or **trade name** is a word, phrase, or symbol that distinguishes or identifies a particular company or product. Trade names like Kleenex, Pepsi-Cola, Buick, Excedrin, Wheaties, and Sunkist create immediate product identification in our minds, thereby enhancing marketability. Under common law, the right to use a trademark or trade name, whether registered or not, rests exclusively with the original user as long as the original user continues to use it. Registration with the U.S. Patent and Trademark Office provides legal protection for an **indefinite number of renewals for periods of 10 years each**. Therefore, a company that uses an established trademark or trade name may properly consider it to have an indefinite life and does not amortize its cost.

If a company buys a trademark or trade name, it capitalizes the cost at the purchase price. If a company develops a trademark or trade name, it capitalizes costs related to securing it, such as attorney fees, registration fees, design costs, consulting fees, and successful legal defense costs. However, it excludes research and development costs. When the total cost of a trademark or trade name is insignificant, a company simply expenses it.

The value of a marketing-related intangible can be substantial. Consider Internet **domain names**. The name **Drugs.com** at one time sold for $800,000. The bidding for the name **Loans.com** approached $500,000. An expansion of domain names will allow industries to use terms like .cars or even Internet slang like lol. This expansion has led to a new wave of domain name activity. For a fee of $185,000, companies can register their own domain names. Applications received include company names (such as **Microsoft**, which would have the name .microsoft) and for city-based domains (such as .nyc and .berlin).

Company names also identify qualities and characteristics that companies work hard and spend much to develop. In a recent year, an estimated 1,230 companies took on new names in an attempt to forge new identities and paid over $250 million to corporate-identity consultants. Among these were **Primerica** (formerly American Can), **Navistar** (formerly International Harvester), and **Nissan** (formerly Datsun).

What do the numbers mean? KEEP YOUR HANDS OFF MY INTANGIBLE!

Companies go to great extremes to protect their valuable intangible assets. Consider how the creators of the highly successful game *Trivial Pursuit* protected their creation. First, they copyrighted the 6,000 questions that are at the heart of the game. Then they shielded the *Trivial Pursuit* name by applying for a registered trademark. As a third mode of protection, they obtained a design patent on the playing board's design as a unique graphic creation.

Another example is the iPhone trade name. **Cisco Systems** sued **Apple** for using the iPhone trade name when Apple introduced its hot new phone in 2007. Not so fast, said Cisco, which had held the iPhone trade name since 2000 and was using it on its own Voice over Internet Protocol (VoIP) products. The two companies came to an agreement for joint use of the name. It was not disclosed what Apple paid for this arrangement, but it is not surprising why Apple would want to settle—to avoid a costly delay to the launch of its highly anticipated iPhone.

Source: Nick Wingfield, "Apple, Cisco Reach Accord Over iPhone," *Wall Street Journal Online* (February 22, 2007).

Customer-Related Intangible Assets

Customer-related intangible assets result from interactions with outside parties. Examples include customer lists, order or production backlogs, and both contractual and noncontractual customer relationships.

To illustrate, assume that Green Market Inc. acquires the customer list of a large newspaper for $6,000,000 on January 1, 2014. This customer database includes names, contact information, order history, and demographic information. Green Market expects to benefit from the information evenly over a three-year period. In this case, the customer list is a limited-life intangible that Green Market should amortize on a straight-line basis.

Green Market records the purchase of the customer list and the amortization of the customer list at the end of each year as follows.

January 1, 2014		
Customer List	6,000,000	
Cash		6,000,000
(To record purchase of customer list)		
December 31, 2014, 2015, 2016		
Amortization Expense	2,000,000	
Customer List (or Accumulated Customer List Amortization)		2,000,000
(To record amortization expense)		

The preceding example assumed no residual value for the customer list. But what if Green Market determines that it can sell the list for $60,000 to another company at the end of three years? In that case, Green Market should subtract this residual value from the cost in order to determine the amortization expense for each year. Amortization expense would be $1,980,000, as shown in Illustration 12-2.

Cost	$6,000,000
Less: Residual value	60,000
Amortization base	$5,940,000
Amortization expense per period: $1,980,000 ($5,940,000 ÷ 3)	

ILLUSTRATION 12-2
Calculation of Amortization Expense with Residual Value

Companies should assume a zero residual value unless the asset's useful life is less than the economic life and reliable evidence is available concerning the residual value. **[4]**

Artistic-Related Intangible Assets

Artistic-related intangible assets involve ownership rights to plays, literary works, musical works, pictures, photographs, and video and audiovisual material. Copyrights protect these ownership rights.

A **copyright** is a federally granted right that all authors, painters, musicians, sculptors, and other artists have in their creations and expressions. A copyright is granted for the **life of the creator plus 70 years**. It gives the owner or heirs the exclusive right to reproduce and sell an artistic or published work. Copyrights are not renewable.

Copyrights can be valuable. In the late 1990s, **Walt Disney Company** faced the loss of its copyright on Mickey Mouse, which could have affected sales of billions of dollars of Mickey-related goods and services (including theme parks). This copyright was so important that Disney and many other big entertainment companies fought all the way to the Supreme Court—and won an extension of copyright lives from 50 to 70 years.

As another example, **Really Useful Group** owns copyrights on the musicals of Andrew Lloyd Webber—*Cats, Phantom of the Opera, Jesus Christ Superstar*, and others. The company has little in the way of tangible assets, yet analysts value it at over $300 million.

Companies capitalize the costs of acquiring and defending a copyright. They amortize any capitalized costs over the useful life of the copyright if less than its legal life (life of the creator plus 70 years). For example, Really Useful Group should allocate the costs of its copyrights to the years in which it expects to receive the benefits. The difficulty of determining the number of years over which it will receive benefits typically encourages a company like Really Useful Group to write off these costs over a fairly short period of time. Companies must expense the research and development costs that lead to a copyright as those costs are incurred.

Contract-Related Intangible Assets

Contract-related intangible assets represent the value of rights that arise from contractual arrangements. Examples are franchise and licensing agreements, construction permits, broadcast rights, and service or supply contracts.

A **franchise** is a contractual arrangement under which the franchisor grants the franchisee the right to sell certain products or services, to use certain trademarks or trade names, or to perform certain functions, usually within a designated geographical area. When you purchase a Prius from a **Toyota** dealer, fill up your tank at the corner **Shell** station, eat lunch at **Subway**, or make reservations at a **Marriott** hotel, you are dealing with franchises.

The franchisor, having developed a unique concept or product, protects its concept or product through a patent, copyright, or trademark or trade name. The franchisee acquires the right to exploit the franchisor's idea or product by signing a franchise agreement.

Another type of franchise, granted by a governmental body, permits the business to use public property in performing its services. Examples are the use of city streets for a bus line or taxi service; the use of public land for telephone, electric, and cable television lines; and the use of airwaves for radio or TV broadcasting. Such operating rights are referred to as **licenses** or **permits**. For example, **Fox**, **CBS**, and **NBC** recently agreed to pay $27.9 billion for the right to broadcast **NFL** football games over an eight-year period.

Franchises and licenses may be for a definite period of time, for an indefinite period of time, or perpetual. The company securing the franchise or license carries an intangible asset account (entitled Franchises or Licenses) on its books, only when it can identify costs with the acquisition of the operating right. (Such costs might be legal fees or an advance lump-sum payment, for example.) **A company should amortize the cost of a franchise (or license) with a limited life as an operating expense over the life of the franchise.** It should not amortize a franchise with an indefinite life nor a perpetual franchise; the company should instead carry such franchises at cost.

Annual payments made under a franchise agreement should be entered as operating expenses in the period in which they are incurred. These payments do not represent an asset since they do not relate to *future rights* to use the property.

Technology-Related Intangible Assets

Technology-related intangible assets relate to innovations or technological advances. Examples are patented technology and trade secrets granted by the U.S. Patent and Trademark Office.

A **patent** gives the holder exclusive right to use, manufacture, and sell a product or process **for a period of 20 years** without interference or infringement by others. Companies such as **Merck**, **Polaroid**, and **Xerox** were founded on patents and built on the exclusive rights thus granted.[2] The two principal kinds of patents are **product patents**, which cover actual physical products, and **process patents**, which govern the process of making products.

If a company like **Qualcomm** purchases a patent from an inventor, the purchase price represents its cost. Qualcomm can capitalize other costs incurred in connection with securing a patent, as well as attorneys' fees and other unrecovered costs of a successful legal suit to protect the patent, as part of the patent cost. However, it **must expense as incurred** any research and development costs related to the **development** of the product, process, or idea that it subsequently patents. (We discuss accounting for research and development costs in more detail on pages 665–667.)

Companies should amortize the cost of a patent over its legal life or its useful life (the period in which benefits are received), **whichever is shorter**. If Qualcomm owns a patent from the date it is granted and expects the patent to be useful during its entire legal life, the company should amortize it over 20 years. If it appears that the patent will be useful for a shorter period of time, say for five years, it should amortize its cost over five years.

[2]Consider the opposite result. Sir Alexander Fleming, who discovered penicillin, decided not to use a patent to protect his discovery. He hoped that foregoing a patent would help companies produce the medication more quickly. Companies, however, refused to develop it because they did not have the patent shield and, therefore, were afraid to make the investment.

Changing demand, new inventions superseding old ones, inadequacy, and other factors often limit the useful life of a patent to less than the legal life. For example, the useful life of pharmaceutical patents is frequently less than the legal life because of the testing and approval period that follows their issuance. A typical drug patent has several years knocked off its 20-year legal life. Why? Because a drug-maker spends one to four years on animal tests, four to six years on human tests, and two to three years for the Food and Drug Administration to review the tests. All this time occurs *after* issuing the patent but *before* the product goes on pharmacists' shelves.

What do the numbers mean? PATENT BATTLES

From online retailing to cell phone features, global competition is bringing to the boiling point battles over patents. For example, to protect its patented "one-click" shopping technology that saves your shipping and credit card information when you shop online, **Amazon.com** filed a complaint against **Barnesandnoble.com**, its rival in the e-tailing wars.

The smartphone industry is another patent battleground. For example, **Nokia** filed patent lawsuits against **Apple** (and Apple countersued) over cell phone features such as swiping gestures on touch screens and the "app store" for downloading software. Apple also targeted **HTC** for infringing on Apple's patented feature that allows screens to detect more than one finger touch at a time. This facilitates the popular zoom-in and zoom-out capability. HTC, in turn, sued Apple for infringing on patented technology that helps extend battery life.

Sources: Adapted from L. Rohde, "Amazon, Barnes and Noble Settle Patent Dispute," *CNN.com* (March 8, 2002); and J. Mintz, "Smart Phone Makers in Legal Fights over Patents," *Wisconsin State Journal* (December 19, 2010), p. F4.

As mentioned earlier, companies capitalize the costs of defending copyrights. The accounting treatment for a patent defense is similar. **A company charges all unrecovered legal fees and other costs incurred in successfully defending a patent suit to Patents,** an asset account. Such costs should be amortized along with acquisition cost over the remaining useful life of the patent.

Amortization expense should reflect the pattern, if reliably determined, in which a company uses up the patent.[3] A company may credit amortization of patents directly to the Patents account or to an Accumulated Patent Amortization account. To illustrate, assume that Harcott Co. incurs $180,000 in legal costs on January 1, 2014, to successfully defend a patent. The patent's useful life after defense is 12 years, amortized on a straight-line basis. Harcott records the legal fees and the amortization at the end of 2014 as follows.

January 1, 2014		
Patents	180,000	
Cash		180,000
(To record legal fees related to patent)		
December 31, 2014		
Amortization Expense ($180,000 ÷ 12)	15,000	
Patents (or Accumulated Patent Amortization)		15,000
(To record amortization of patent)		

We've indicated that a patent's useful life should not extend beyond its legal life of 20 years. However, companies often make small modifications or additions that lead to a new patent. For example, **Astra Zeneca plc** filed for additional patents on minor modifications to its heartburn drug Prilosec. The effect may be to extend the life of the old

[3]Companies may compute amortization on a units-of-production basis in a manner similar to that described for depreciation on property, plant, and equipment.

patent. If the new patent provides essentially the same benefits, Astra Zeneca can apply the unamortized costs of the old patent to the new patent.[4]

Alternatively, if a patent becomes impaired because demand drops for the product, the asset should be written down or written off immediately to expense.

What do the numbers mean? THE VALUE OF A SECRET FORMULA

After several espionage cases were uncovered, the secrets contained within the Los Alamos nuclear lab seemed easier to check out than a library book. But **The Coca-Cola Company** has managed to keep the recipe for the world's best-selling soft drink under wraps for more than 100 years. The company offers almost no information about its lifeblood, and the only written copy of the formula resides in a bank vault in Atlanta. This handwritten sheet is available to no one except by vote of Coca-Cola's board of directors.

Can't science offer some clues? Coke purportedly contains 17 to 18 ingredients. That includes the usual caramel color and corn syrup, as well as a blend of oils known as 7X (rumored to be a mix of orange, lemon, cinnamon, and others). Distilling natural products like these is complicated since they are made of thousands of compounds. One ingredient you will not find, by the way, is cocaine. Although the original formula did contain trace amounts, today's Coke doesn't. When was it removed? That too is a secret.

Some experts indicate that the power of the Coca-Cola formula and related brand image account for almost $72 billion, or roughly 6 percent, of Coke's $1,128 billion stock value.

Sources: Adapted from Reed Tucker, "How Has Coke's Formula Stayed a Secret?" *Fortune* (July 24, 2000), p. 42; and "Best Global Brands 2011," *www.interbrand.com* (accessed July 5, 2012).

Goodwill

LEARNING OBJECTIVE 5
Explain the accounting issues for recording goodwill.

Although companies may capitalize certain costs incurred in developing specifically identifiable assets such as patents and copyrights, the amounts capitalized are generally insignificant. But companies do record material amounts of intangible assets when purchasing them, particularly in situations involving a business combination (the purchase of another business).

To illustrate, assume that Portofino Company decides to purchase Aquinas Company. In this situation, Portofino measures the assets acquired and the liabilities assumed at fair value. In measuring these assets and liabilities, Portofino must identify all the assets and liabilities of Aquinas. As a result, Portofino may recognize some assets or liabilities not previously recognized by Aquinas. For example, Portofino may recognize intangible assets such as a brand name, patent, or customer list that were not recorded by Aquinas. In this case, Aquinas may not have recognized these assets because they were developed internally and charged to expense.

In many business combinations, the purchasing company records goodwill. **Goodwill** is measured as the excess of the cost of the purchase over the fair value of the identifiable net assets (assets less liabilities) purchased. For example, if Portofino paid $2,000,000 to purchase Aquinas's identifiable net assets (with a fair value of $1,500,000), Portofino records goodwill of $500,000. Goodwill is therefore measured as a residual rather than measured directly. That is why goodwill is sometimes referred to as a **plug**, a **gap filler**, or a **master valuation account**.[5]

[4]Another classic example is **Eli Lilly's** drug Prozac (prescribed to treat depression). In 1998, this product accounted for 43 percent of Eli Lilly's sales. The patent on Prozac expired in 2001, and the company was unable to extend its protection with a second-use patent for the use of Prozac to treat appetite disorders. Sales of the product slipped substantially as generic equivalents entered the market.

[5]GAAP **[5]** provides detailed guidance regarding the recognition of identifiable intangible assets in a business combination. With this guidance, companies should recognize more identifiable intangible assets, and less goodwill, in the financial statements as a result of business combinations.

Conceptually, goodwill represents the future economic benefits arising from the other assets acquired in a business combination that are not individually identified and separately recognized. It is often called "the most intangible of the intangible assets" because it is identified only with the business as a whole. The only way to sell goodwill is to sell the business.

Recording Goodwill

Internally Created Goodwill. **Goodwill generated internally should not be capitalized in the accounts.** The reason? Measuring the components of goodwill is simply too complex, and associating any costs with future benefits is too difficult. The future benefits of goodwill may have no relationship to the costs incurred in the development of that goodwill. To add to the mystery, goodwill may even exist in the absence of specific costs to develop it. Finally, because no objective transaction with outside parties takes place, a great deal of subjectivity—even misrepresentation—may occur.

Purchased Goodwill. As indicated earlier, **goodwill is recorded only when an entire business is purchased**. To record goodwill, a company compares the fair value of the net tangible and identifiable intangible assets with the purchase price of the acquired business. The difference is considered goodwill. **Goodwill is the residual—the excess of cost over fair value of the identifiable net assets acquired.**

Underlying Concepts

Capitalizing goodwill only when it is purchased in an arm's-length transaction, and not capitalizing any goodwill generated internally, is another example of faithful representation winning out over relevance.

To illustrate, Multi-Diversified, Inc. decides that it needs a parts division to supplement its existing tractor distributorship. The president of Multi-Diversified is interested in buying Tractorling Company, a small concern in Chicago. Illustration 12-3 presents the balance sheet of Tractorling Company.

ILLUSTRATION 12-3
Tractorling Co. Balance Sheet

TRACTORLING CO.
BALANCE SHEET
AS OF DECEMBER 31, 2014

Assets		Liabilities and Equity	
Cash	$ 25,000	Current liabilities	$ 55,000
Accounts receivable	35,000	Capital stock	100,000
Inventory	42,000	Retained earnings	100,000
Property, plant, and equipment, net	153,000		
Total assets	$255,000	Total liabilities and equity	$255,000

After considerable negotiation, Tractorling Company decides to accept Multi-Diversified's offer of $400,000. What, then, is the value of the goodwill, if any?

Gateway to the Profession

Expanded Discussion—Valuing Goodwill

The answer is not obvious. Tractorling's historical cost-based balance sheet does not disclose the fair values of its identifiable assets. Suppose, though, that as the negotiations progress, Multi-Diversified investigates Tractorling's underlying assets to determine their fair values. Such an investigation may be accomplished either through a purchase audit undertaken by Multi-Diversified or by an independent appraisal from some other source. The investigation determines the valuations shown in Illustration 12-4 (page 660).

Normally, differences between current fair value and book value are more common among long-term assets than among current assets. Cash obviously poses no problems as to value. Receivables normally are fairly close to current valuation although they may at times need certain adjustments due to inadequate bad debt provisions. Liabilities usually are stated at book value. However, if interest rates have changed since the company incurred the liabilities, a different valuation (such as present value based on

ILLUSTRATION 12-4
Fair Value of Tractorling's Net Assets

Fair Values	
Cash	$ 25,000
Accounts receivable	35,000
Inventory	122,000
Property, plant, and equipment, net	205,000
Patents	18,000
Liabilities	(55,000)
Fair value of net assets	$350,000

expected cash flows) is appropriate. Careful analysis must be made to determine that no unrecorded liabilities are present.

The $80,000 difference in Tractorling's inventories ($122,000 − $42,000) could result from a number of factors. The most likely is that the company uses LIFO. Recall that during periods of inflation, LIFO better matches expenses against revenues. However, it also creates a balance sheet distortion. Ending inventory consists of older layers costed at lower valuations.

In many cases, the values of long-term assets such as property, plant, and equipment, and intangibles may have increased substantially over the years. This difference could be due to inaccurate estimates of useful lives, continual expensing of small expenditures (say, less than $300), inaccurate estimates of residual values, and the discovery of some unrecorded assets. (For example, in Tractorling's case, analysis determines Patents have a fair value of $18,000.) Or, fair values may have substantially increased.

Since the investigation now determines the fair value of net assets to be $350,000, why would Multi-Diversified pay $400,000? Undoubtedly, Tractorling points to its established reputation, good credit rating, top management team, well-trained employees, and so on. These factors make the value of the business greater than $350,000. Multi-Diversified places a premium on the future earning power of these attributes as well as on the basic asset structure of the company today.

Multi-Diversified labels the difference between the purchase price of $400,000 and the fair value of net assets of $350,000 as goodwill. Goodwill is viewed as one or a group of unidentifiable values (intangible assets), the cost of which "is measured by the difference between the cost of the group of assets or enterprise acquired and the sum of the assigned costs of individual tangible and identifiable intangible assets acquired less liabilities assumed."[6] This procedure for valuation is called a **master valuation approach**. It assumes goodwill covers all the values that cannot be specifically identified with any identifiable tangible or intangible asset. Illustration 12-5 shows this approach.

ILLUSTRATION 12-5
Determination of Goodwill—Master Valuation Approach

Assigned to purchase price of $400,000

Cash	$ 25,000
Accounts receivable	35,000
Inventory	122,000
Property, plant, and equipment, net	205,000
Patents	18,000
Liabilities	(55,000)
Fair value of net identifiable assets	$350,000
Purchase price	400,000
Value assigned to goodwill	$ 50,000

[6]The FASB expressed concern about measuring goodwill as a residual but noted that there is no real measurement alternative since goodwill is not separable from the company as a whole. **[6]**

Multi-Diversified records this transaction as follows.

Cash	25,000	
Accounts Receivable	35,000	
Inventory	122,000	
Property, Plant, and Equipment	205,000	
Patents	18,000	
Goodwill	50,000	
Liabilities		55,000
Cash		400,000

Companies often identify goodwill on the balance sheet as the **excess of cost over the fair value** of the net assets acquired.

Goodwill Write-Off

Companies that recognize goodwill in a business combination **consider it to have an indefinite life and therefore should not amortize it**. Although goodwill may decrease in value over time, predicting the actual life of goodwill and an appropriate pattern of amortization is extremely difficult. In addition, investors find the amortization charge of little use in evaluating financial performance.

Furthermore, the investment community wants to know the amount invested in goodwill, which often is the largest intangible asset on a company's balance sheet. Therefore, **companies adjust its carrying value only when goodwill is impaired**. This approach significantly impacts the income statements of some companies.

Some believe that goodwill's value eventually disappears. Therefore, they argue, companies should charge goodwill to expense over the periods affected, to better match expense with revenues. Others note that the accounting treatment for purchased goodwill and goodwill created internally should be consistent. They point out that companies immediately expense goodwill created internally and should follow the same treatment for purchased goodwill. Though these arguments may have some merit, nonamortization of goodwill combined with an adequate impairment test should provide the most useful financial information to the investment community. We discuss the accounting for goodwill impairments later in the chapter.

Bargain Purchase

In a few cases, the purchaser in a business combination pays *less than* the fair value of the identifiable net assets. Such a situation is referred to as a **bargain purchase**. A bargain purchase results from a market imperfection. That is, the seller would have been better off to sell the assets individually than in total. However, situations do occur (e.g., a forced liquidation or distressed sale due to the death of a company founder) in which the purchase price is less than the value of the net identifiable assets. **This excess amount is recorded as a gain by the purchaser.**

The FASB notes that an economic gain is inherent in a bargain purchase. The purchaser is better off by the amount by which the fair value of what is acquired exceeds the amount paid. Some expressed concern that some companies may attempt inappropriate gain recognition by making an intentional error in measurement of the assets or liabilities. As a result, the FASB requires companies to disclose the nature of this gain transaction. Such disclosure will help users to better evaluate the quality of the earnings reported.[7]

[7]This gain is not reported as an extraordinary item, **[7]** which is consistent with convergence in international accounting standards. IFRS does not permit extraordinary item reporting.

IMPAIRMENT OF INTANGIBLE ASSETS

LEARNING OBJECTIVE 6
Explain the accounting issues related to intangible-asset impairments.

In some cases, the carrying amount of a long-lived asset (property, plant, and equipment, or intangible assets) is not recoverable. Therefore, a company needs to record a write-off. As discussed in Chapter 11, this write-off is referred to as an **impairment**.

Impairment of Limited-Life Intangibles

The rules that apply to **impairments of property, plant, and equipment also apply to limited-life intangibles**. As discussed in Chapter 11, a company should review property, plant, and equipment for impairment at certain points—whenever events or changes in circumstances indicate that the carrying amount of the asset may not be recoverable. In performing this **recoverability test**, the company estimates the future cash flows expected from use of the asset and its eventual disposal. If the sum of the expected future net cash flows (undiscounted) is less than the carrying amount of the asset, the company would measure and recognize an impairment loss. [8]

The company then uses the **fair value test**. This test measures the impairment loss by comparing the asset's fair value with its carrying amount. The impairment loss is the carrying amount of the asset less the fair value of the impaired asset. As with other impairments, the loss on the limited-life intangible is reported as part of income from continuing operations. The entry generally appears in the "Other expenses and losses" section.

To illustrate, assume that Lerch, Inc. has a patent on how to extract oil from shale rock. Unfortunately, several recent non-shale oil discoveries adversely affected the demand for shale-oil technology. Thus, the patent has provided little income to date. As a result, Lerch performs a recoverability test. It finds that the expected future net cash flows from this patent are $35 million. Lerch's patent has a carrying amount of $60 million. Because the expected future net cash flows of $35 million are less than the carrying amount of $60 million, Lerch must determine an impairment loss.

Discounting the expected future net cash flows at its market rate of interest, Lerch determines the fair value of its patent to be $20 million. Illustration 12-6 shows the impairment loss computation (based on fair value).

ILLUSTRATION 12-6
Computation of Loss on Impairment of Patent

Carrying amount of patent	$60,000,000
Less: Fair value (based on present value computation)	20,000,000
Loss on impairment	$40,000,000

Lerch records this loss as follows.

Loss on Impairment	40,000,000	
Patents		40,000,000

Underlying Concepts

The basic attributes of intangibles, their uncertainty as to future benefits, and their uniqueness have discouraged valuation in excess of cost.

After recognizing the impairment, the reduced carrying amount of the patents is its new cost basis. Lerch should amortize the patent's new cost over its remaining useful life or legal life, whichever is shorter. Even if shale-oil prices increase in subsequent periods and the value of the patent increases, Lerch **may not recognize restoration of the previously recognized impairment loss**.

Impairment of Indefinite-Life Intangibles Other Than Goodwill

Companies should test indefinite-life intangibles other than goodwill for impairment at least annually. The impairment test for an indefinite-life asset other than goodwill is a **fair value test**. This test compares the fair value of the intangible asset with the asset's carrying amount. If the fair value is less than the carrying amount, the company recognizes an impairment. Companies use this one-step test because many indefinite-life assets easily meet the recoverability test (because cash flows may extend many years into the future). **Thus, companies do not use the recoverability test.**

To illustrate, assume that Arcon Radio purchased a broadcast license for $2,000,000. The license is renewable every 10 years if the company provides appropriate service and does not violate Federal Communications Commission (FCC) rules. Arcon Radio has renewed the license with the FCC twice, at a minimal cost. Because it expects cash flows to last indefinitely, Arcon reports the license as an indefinite-life intangible asset. Recently, the FCC decided to auction significantly more of these licenses. As a result, Arcon Radio expects reduced cash flows for the remaining two years of its existing license. It performs an impairment test and determines that the fair value of the intangible asset is $1,500,000. Arcon therefore reports an impairment loss of $500,000, computed as follows.

ILLUSTRATION 12-7
Computation of Loss on Impairment of Broadcast License

Carrying amount of broadcast license	$2,000,000
Less: Fair value of broadcast license	1,500,000
Loss on impairment	$ 500,000

Arcon Radio now reports the license at $1,500,000, its fair value. Even if the value of the license increases in the remaining two years, Arcon may not restore the previously recognized impairment loss.

Companies have the option to perform a qualitative assessment to determine whether it is more likely than not (i.e., a likelihood of more than 50 percent) that an indefinite-life intangible asset is impaired. **[9]** If the qualitative assessment indicates that the fair value of the reporting unit is more likely than not to be greater than the carrying value (i.e., the asset is not impaired), **the company need not continue with the fair value test**. As a result, use of the qualitative assessment option should reduce both the cost and complexity of performing the impairment test.[8]

Impairment of Goodwill

Goodwill must be tested for impairment at least annually. **The impairment rule for goodwill is a two-step process.** First, a company compares the fair value of the reporting unit to its carrying amount, including goodwill. If the fair value of the reporting unit exceeds the carrying amount, goodwill is not impaired. The company does not have to do anything else. Similar to other indefinite-life intangibles, companies may instead perform an optional qualitative assessment to determine whether it is more likely than not that goodwill is impaired. If the qualitative assessment indicates that the fair value of the reporting unit is more likely than not to be greater than the carrying value, the company need not continue with the two-step impairment test.[9]

To illustrate, assume that Kohlbuy Corporation has three divisions. It purchased one division, Pritt Products, four years ago for $2 million. Unfortunately, Pritt experienced operating losses over the last three quarters. Kohlbuy management is now reviewing the

[8] Examples of events and circumstances to be evaluated include but are not limited to (1) deterioration in general economic conditions; (2) an increased competitive environment, a decline in market-dependent multiples or metrics, a change in the market for a company's products or services, or a regulatory or political development; (3) cost factors such as increases in raw materials, labor, or other costs that have a negative effect on earnings; and (4) overall financial performance such as negative or declining cash flows or a decline in actual or planned revenue or earnings.

[9] The qualitative assessment examines similar factors as those used in the optional qualitative test for other indefinite-life intangibles but are based on events and circumstances related to the reporting unit. **[10]**

division for purposes of recognizing an impairment. Illustration 12-8 lists the Pritt Division's net assets, including the associated goodwill of $900,000 from the purchase.

ILLUSTRATION 12-8
Net Assets of Pritt Division, Including Goodwill

Cash	$ 200,000
Accounts receivable	300,000
Inventory	700,000
Property, plant, and equipment (net)	800,000
Goodwill	900,000
Accounts and notes payable	(500,000)
Net assets	$2,400,000

Kohlbuy determines that the fair value of Pritt Division is $2,800,000. **Because the fair value of the division exceeds the carrying amount of the net assets, Kohlbuy does not recognize any impairment.**

However, if the fair value of Pritt Division were less than the carrying amount of the net assets, then Kohlbuy would perform a second step to determine possible impairment. In the second step, Kohlbuy determines the fair value of the goodwill (implied value of goodwill) and compares it to its carrying amount. To illustrate, assume that the fair value of the Pritt Division is $1,900,000 instead of $2,800,000. Illustration 12-9 computes the implied value of the goodwill in this case.[10]

ILLUSTRATION 12-9
Determination of Implied Value of Goodwill

Fair value of Pritt Division	$1,900,000
Less: Net identifiable assets (excluding goodwill) ($2,400,000 − $900,000)	1,500,000
Implied value of goodwill	$ 400,000

Kohlbuy then compares the implied value of the goodwill to the recorded goodwill to measure the impairment, as shown in Illustration 12-10.

ILLUSTRATION 12-10
Measurement of Goodwill Impairment

Carrying amount of goodwill	$900,000
Less: Implied value of goodwill	400,000
Loss on impairment	$500,000

Impairment Summary

Illustration 12-11 summarizes the impairment tests for various intangible assets.

ILLUSTRATION 12-11
Summary of Intangible Asset Impairment Tests

Type of Intangible Asset	Impairment Test
Limited life	Recoverability test, then fair value test
Indefinite life other than goodwill	Fair value test*
Goodwill	Fair value test on reporting unit, then fair value test on implied goodwill*

*An optional qualitative assessment may be performed to determine whether the fair value test needs to be performed.

[10] Illustration 12-9 assumes that the carrying amount equals the fair value of net identifiable assets (excluding goodwill). If different, companies use the fair value of the net identifiable assets (excluding goodwill) to determine the implied goodwill.

What do the numbers mean? IMPAIRMENT RISK

As shown in the chart below, goodwill impairments spiked in 2008 and 2009, coinciding with the stock market downturn in the wake of the financial crisis.

A spike in impairments when the market declines is understandable because declines in stock price are indicators that the fair values of acquired assets have declined below the carrying value. And while there is a declining trend in impairments in 2009 and 2010, notable goodwill impairments are being reported. For example, **Microsoft** posted a goodwill impairment charge of $6.3 billion in 2012. Some are expecting more goodwill impairments for other companies with book values well above market value of equity ($1.8 trillion for about 10 percent of companies in the S&P 500 at the end of 2001). As one analyst noted, "Anybody looking at a decline in market price could see the company was placing a much higher value on its assets than the market thought they were worth."

Investors need to keep watch. Such asset write-downs—for brand names, franchise rights, and other intangible assets (including goodwill)—are important because they tell investors that management have concluded their companies' future cash flows will not achieve previous estimates.

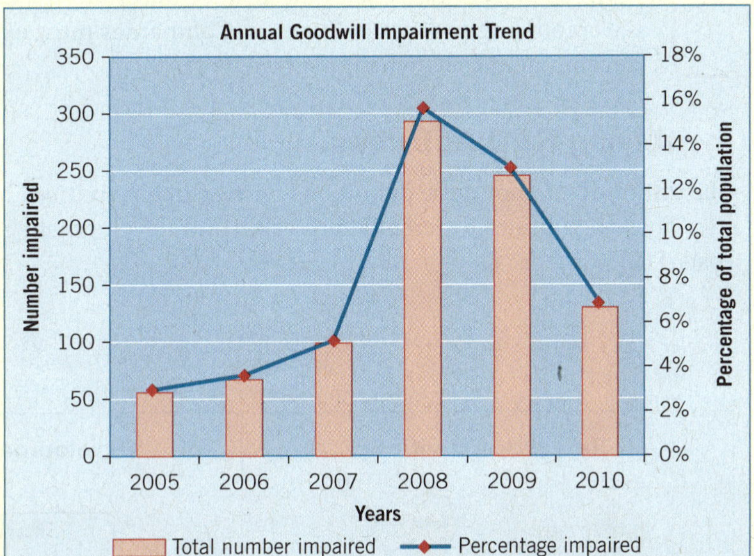

Source: "Evaluating Impairment Risk: Goodwill Impairment Continues Downward Trend in 2010" (KPMG LLP), 2010.

Sources: M. Murphy, "The Big Number," *Wall Street Journal* (November 16, 2011), p. B5; and S. Thurm, "Buyers Beware: The Goodwill Games," *Wall Street Journal* (August 13, 2012).

RESEARCH AND DEVELOPMENT COSTS

7 LEARNING OBJECTIVE
Identify the conceptual issues related to research and development costs.

Research and development (R&D) costs are not in themselves intangible assets. However, we present the accounting for R&D costs here because R&D activities frequently result in the development of patents or copyrights (such as a new product, process, idea, formula, composition, or literary work) that may provide future value.

Many companies spend considerable sums on research and development. Illustration 12-12 (page 666) shows the outlays for R&D made by selected global companies.

Two difficulties arise in accounting for R&D expenditures: (1) identifying the costs associated with particular activities, projects, or achievements, and (2) determining the

ILLUSTRATION 12-12
R&D Outlays, as a Percentage of Sales

Company	Sales (millions)	R&D/Sales
Canon	$3,557,433	8.65%
Daimler	€106,540	3.92%
GlaxoSmithKline	£27,387	14.64%
Johnson & Johnson	$65,030	11.61%
Nokia	€38,659	14.52%
Roche	CHF42,531	19.58%
Procter & Gamble	$82,559	2.42%
Samsung	₩ 165,002	6.05%

International Perspective

IFRS requires the capitalization of appropriate development expenditures. This conflicts with GAAP.

magnitude of the future benefits and length of time over which such benefits may be realized. Because of these latter uncertainties, the FASB has simplified the accounting practice in this area. **Companies must expense all research and development costs when incurred. [11]**

Identifying R&D Activities

Illustration 12-13 shows the definitions for **research activities** and **development activities**. These definitions differentiate research and development costs from other similar costs. **[12]**

ILLUSTRATION 12-13
Research Activities versus Development Activities

Research Activities	Development Activities

Planned search or critical investigation aimed at discovery of new knowledge.	Translation of research findings or other knowledge into a plan or design for a new product or process or for a significant improvement to an existing product or process whether intended for sale or use.
Examples	**Examples**
Laboratory research aimed at discovery of new knowledge; searching for applications of new research findings.	Conceptual formulation and design of possible product or process alternatives; construction of prototypes and operation of pilot plants.

R&D activities do not include routine or periodic alterations to existing products, production lines, manufacturing processes, and other ongoing operations, even though these alterations may represent improvements. For example, routine ongoing efforts to refine, enrich, or improve the qualities of an existing product are not considered R&D activities.

Accounting for R&D Activities

8 LEARNING OBJECTIVE
Describe the accounting for research and development and similar costs.

The costs associated with R&D activities and the accounting treatments accorded them are as follows.

1. ***Materials, equipment, and facilities.*** Expense the entire costs, **unless the items have alternative future uses** (in other R&D projects or otherwise). If there are alternative future uses, carry the items as inventory and allocate as consumed, or capitalize and depreciate as used.
2. ***Personnel.*** Expense as incurred salaries, wages, and other related costs of personnel engaged in R&D.
3. ***Purchased intangibles.*** Recognize and measure at fair value. After initial recognition, account for in accordance with their nature (as either limited-life or indefinite-life intangibles).[11]
4. ***Contract services.*** Expense the costs of services performed by others in connection with the R&D as incurred.
5. ***Indirect costs.*** Include a reasonable allocation of indirect costs in R&D costs, except for general and administrative cost, which must be clearly related in order to be included in R&D. **[14]**

Consistent with item 1 above, if a company owns a research facility that conducts R&D activities and that has alternative future uses (in other R&D projects or otherwise), it should capitalize the facility as an operational asset. The company accounts for depreciation and other costs related to such research facilities as R&D expenses.[12]

To illustrate, assume that Next Century Incorporated develops, produces, and markets laser machines for medical, industrial, and defense uses.[13] Illustration 12-14 (on the next page) lists the types of expenditures related to its laser-machine activities, along with the recommended accounting treatment.

Costs Similar to R&D Costs

Many costs have characteristics similar to research and development costs. Examples are:

1. Start-up costs for a new operation.
2. Initial operating losses.
3. Advertising costs.
4. Computer software costs.

[11]If R&D-related intangibles (often referred to as **in-process R&D**) are also acquired in a business combination, they are also recognized and measured at fair value. After initial recognition, these intangible assets are accounted for in accordance with their nature (as either limited-life or indefinite-life intangibles). **[13]**

[12]Companies in **the extractive industries** can use the following accounting treatment for the unique costs of research, exploration, and development activities and for those costs that are similar to but not classified as R&D costs: (1) expense as incurred, (2) capitalize and either depreciate or amortize over an appropriate period of time, or (3) accumulate as part of inventoriable costs. Choice of the appropriate accounting treatment for such costs is based on the degree of certainty of future benefits and the principle of matching revenues and expenses.

[13]Sometimes companies conduct R&D activities for other companies under a contractual arrangement. In this case, the contract usually specifies that the company performing the R&D work be reimbursed for all direct costs and certain specific indirect costs, plus a profit element. Because reimbursement is expected, the company doing the R&D work records the R&D costs as a receivable. The company for whom the work has been performed reports these costs as R&D and expenses them as incurred. For a more complete discussion of how an enterprise should account for funding of its R&D by others, see **[15]**.

NEXT CENTURY INCORPORATED		
Type of Expenditure	Accounting Treatment	Rationale
1. Construction of long-range research facility for use in current and future projects (three-story, 400,000-square-foot building).	Capitalize and depreciate as R&D expense.	Has alternative future use.
2. Acquisition of R&D equipment for use on current project only.	Expense immediately as R&D.	Research cost.
3. Acquisition of machinery for use on current and future R&D projects.	Capitalize and depreciate as R&D expense.	Has alternative future use.
4. Purchase of materials for use on current and future R&D projects.	Inventory and allocate to R&D projects; expense as consumed.	Has alternative future use.
5. Salaries of research staff designing new laser bone scanner.	Expense immediately as R&D.	Research cost.
6. Research costs incurred under contract with New Horizon, Inc., and billable monthly.	Record as a receivable.	Not R&D cost (reimbursable expense).
7. Material, labor, and overhead costs of prototype laser scanner.	Expense immediately as R&D.	Development cost.
8. Costs of testing prototype and design modifications.	Expense immediately as R&D.	Development cost.
9. Legal fees to obtain patent on new laser scanner.	Capitalize as patent and amortize to overhead as part of cost of goods manufactured.	Direct cost of patent.
10. Executive salaries.	Expense as operating expense.	Not R&D cost (general and administrative expense).
11. Cost of marketing research to promote new laser scanner.	Expense as operating expense.	Not R&D cost (selling expense).
12. Engineering costs incurred to advance the laser scanner to full production stage.	Expense immediately as R&D.	Development cost.
13. Costs of successfully defending patent on laser scanner.	Capitalize as patent and amortize to overhead as part of cost of goods manufactured.	Direct cost of patent.
14. Commissions to sales staff marketing new laser scanner.	Expense as operating expense.	Not R&D cost (selling expense).

ILLUSTRATION 12-14
Sample R&D Expenditures and Their Accounting Treatment

For the most part, these costs are expensed as incurred, similar to the accounting for R&D costs. We briefly explain these costs in the following sections.

Start-Up Costs

Start-up costs are incurred for one-time activities to start a new operation. Examples include opening a new plant, introducing a new product or service, or conducting business in a new territory. Start-up costs include **organizational costs**, such as legal and state fees incurred to organize a new business entity.

The accounting for start-up costs is straightforward: **Expense start-up costs as incurred.** The profession recognizes that companies incur start-up costs with the expectation of future revenues or increased efficiencies. However, to determine the amount and timing of future benefits is so difficult that a conservative approach—expensing these costs as incurred—is required. [16]

To illustrate examples of start-up costs, assume that U.S.-based Hilo Beverage Company decides to construct a new plant in Brazil. This represents Hilo's first entry into the Brazilian market. Hilo plans to introduce the company's major U.S. brands into Brazil on a locally produced basis. The following costs might be involved:

1. Travel-related costs; costs related to employee salaries; and costs related to feasibility studies, accounting, tax, and government affairs.

2. Training of local employees related to product, maintenance, computer systems, finance, and operations.
3. Recruiting, organizing, and training related to establishing a distribution network.

Hilo Beverage should expense all these start-up costs as incurred.

Start-up activities commonly occur at the same time as activities involving the acquisition of assets. For example, as it is incurring start-up costs for the new plant, Hilo probably is also buying or building property, plant, equipment, and inventory. Hilo should not immediately expense the costs of these tangible assets. Instead, it should report them on the balance sheet using appropriate GAAP reporting guidelines.

Initial Operating Losses

Some contend that companies should be allowed to capitalize initial operating losses incurred in the start-up of a business. They argue that such operating losses are an unavoidable cost of starting a business.

For example, assume that Hilo lost money in its first year of operations and wishes to capitalize this loss. Hilo's CEO argues that as the company becomes profitable, it will offset these losses in future periods. What do you think? We believe that this approach is unsound since losses have no future service potential and therefore cannot be considered an asset.

GAAP requires that operating losses during the early years **should not be capitalized**. In short, **the accounting and reporting standards should be no different for an enterprise trying to establish a new business than they are for other enterprises.** [17][14]

Advertising Costs

Over the years, PepsiCo has hired various pop stars, such as Elton John and Beyoncé, to advertise its products. How should it report such advertising costs related to its star spokespeople? Pepsi could expense the costs in various ways:

1. When the pop stars have completed their singing assignments.
2. The first time the advertising runs.
3. Over the estimated useful life of the advertising.
4. In an appropriate fashion to each of the three periods identified above.
5. Over the period revenues are expected to result.

For the most part, Pepsi must expense advertising costs as incurred or the first time the advertising takes place. Whichever of these two approaches is followed, the results are essentially the same. On the other hand, companies record as assets any tangible assets used in advertising, such as billboards or blimps. The rationale is that such assets do have alternative future uses. Again the profession has taken a conservative approach to recording advertising costs because defining and measuring the future benefits can be so difficult. [18][15]

Computer Software Costs

A special problem arises in distinguishing R&D costs from selling and administrative activities. The FASB's intent was that companies exclude from the definition of R&D activities the acquisition, development, or improvement of a product or process **for use in their selling or administrative activities.** For example, the costs of software incurred by an airline

Gateway to the Profession

Expanded Discussion—Software Development Costs

[14]A company is considered to be in the developing stages when it is directing its efforts toward establishing a new business and either the company has not started the principal operations or it has earned no significant revenue.

[15]There are some exceptions for immediate expensing of advertising costs when they relate to direct-response advertising, but that subject is beyond the scope of this book.

in improving its computerized reservation system or the costs incurred in developing a company's management information system **are not** research and development costs.

What do the numbers mean? BRANDED

For many companies, developing a strong brand image is as important as developing the products they sell. Now more than ever, companies see the power of a strong brand, enhanced by significant and effective advertising investments.

As the following chart indicates, the value of brand investments is substantial. **Coca-Cola** heads the list with an estimated brand value of about $72 billion.

The World's 10 Most Valuable Brands
(in billions)

1	Coca-Cola	$71.9
2	IBM	69.9
3	Microsoft	59.0
4	Google	55.3
5	GE	42.8
6	McDonald's	35.6
7	Intel	35.2
8	Apple	33.5
9	Disney	29.0
10	HP	28.9

Source: 2011 data, from Interbrand Corp.

Occasionally you may find the value of a brand included in a company's financial statements under goodwill. But generally you will not find the estimated values of brands recorded in companies' balance sheets. The reason? The subjectivity that goes into estimating a brand's value. In some cases, analysts base an estimate of brand value on opinion polls or on some multiple of ad spending. For example, in estimating the brand values shown to the left, **Interbrand Corp.** estimates the percentage of the overall future revenues the brand will generate and then discounts the net cash flows, to arrive at a present value.

Some analysts believe that information on brand values is relevant. Others voice valid concerns about the reliability of brand value estimates due to subjectivity in the estimates for revenues, costs, and the risk component of the discount rate. For example, another brand valuation firm, **Millward Brown**, ranks **Apple** as number one with an estimated brand value of $183 billion (or about one-third of Apple's market value). These data support the highly subjective nature of brand valuation estimates.

Sources: "Best Global Brands 2011," *www.interbrand.com* (accessed July 5, 2012); and S. Vranica and J. Hansegard, "Ikea Discloses an $11 Billion Secret," *Wall Street Journal* (August 9, 2012).

PRESENTATION OF INTANGIBLES AND RELATED ITEMS

Presentation of Intangible Assets

LEARNING OBJECTIVE 9
Indicate the presentation of intangible assets and related items.

The reporting of intangible assets is similar to the reporting of property, plant, and equipment. However, contra accounts are not normally shown for intangibles on the balance sheet. As Illustration 12-15 shows, on the balance sheet companies should report as a separate item all intangible assets other than goodwill. If goodwill is present, companies should report it separately. The FASB concluded that since goodwill and other intangible assets differ significantly from other types of assets, such disclosure benefits users of the balance sheet.

On the income statement, companies should present amortization expense and impairment losses for intangible assets other than goodwill separately and as part of continuing operations. Again, see Illustration 12-15. Goodwill impairment losses should also be presented as a separate line item in the continuing operations section, unless the goodwill impairment is associated with a discontinued operation.

The notes to the financial statements should include information about acquired intangible assets, including the aggregate amortization expense for each of the succeeding five years. If separate accumulated amortization accounts are not used, accumulated amortization should be disclosed in the notes. The notes should include information about changes in the carrying amount of goodwill during the period.

ILLUSTRATION 12-15
Intangible Asset Disclosures

HARBAUGH COMPANY

Balance Sheet (partial)
(in thousands)

Intangible assets (Note C)	$3,840
Goodwill (Note D)	2,575

Income Statement (partial)
(in thousands)

as part of Continuing operations	
Amortization expense	$380
Impairment losses (goodwill)	46

Notes to the Financial Statements

Note C: Acquired Intangible Assets

	As of December 31, 2014	
	Gross Carrying Amount	Accumulated Amortization
Amortized intangible assets		
Trademark	$2,000	$(100)
Customer list	500	(310)
Other	60	(10)
Total	$2,560	$(420)
Unamortized intangible assets		
Licenses	$1,300	
Trademark	400	
Total	$1,700	

Types of intangibles and carrying values

Aggregate Amortization Expense

For year ended 12/31/14	$380

Estimated Amortization Expense

For year ended 12/31/15	$200
For year ended 12/31/16	90
For year ended 12/31/17	70
For year ended 12/31/18	60
For year ended 12/31/19	50

Current and future expense

Note D: Goodwill
The changes in the carrying amount of goodwill for the year ended December 31, 2014, are as follows.

($000s)	Technology Segment	Communications Segment	Total
Balance as of January 1, 2014	$1,413	$904	$2,317
Goodwill acquired during year	189	115	304
Impairment losses	—	(46)	(46)
Balance as of December 31, 2014	$1,602	$973	$2,575

Goodwill by segment and carrying values

The Communications segment is tested for impairment in the third quarter, after the annual forecasting process. Due to an increase in competition in the Texas and Louisiana cable industry, operating profits and cash flows were lower than expected in the fourth quarter of 2013 and the first and second quarters of 2014. Based on that trend, the earnings forecast for the next 5 years was revised. In September 2014, a goodwill impairment loss of $46 was recognized in the Communications reporting unit. The fair value of that reporting unit was estimated using the expected present value of future cash flows.

Impairment methodology

Presentation of Research and Development Costs

Companies should disclose in the financial statements (generally in the notes) the total R&D costs charged to expense each period for which they present an income statement. **Merck & Co., Inc.**, a global research pharmaceutical company, reported both internal and acquired research and development in its recent income statement, as shown in Illustration 12-16.

ILLUSTRATION 12-16
Income Statement Disclosure of R&D Costs

Merck & Co., Inc.
(in millions)

	Years Ended December 31		
	2011	2010	2009
Sales	$48,047	$45,987	$27,428.3
Costs, expenses and other			
Materials and production	16,871	18,396	9,018.9
Marketing and administrative	13,733	13,125	8,543.2
Research and development	8,467	11,111	5,845.0
Restructuring costs	1,306	985	1,633.9
Equity income from affiliates	(610)	(587)	(2,235.0)
Other (income) expense, net	946	1,304	(10,669.5)
	$40,713	$44,334	$12,136.5

In addition, Merck provides a discussion about R&D expenditures in its annual report, as shown in Illustration 12-17.

ILLUSTRATION 12-17
Merck's R&D Disclosure

Merck & Co., Inc.

Research and development in the pharmaceutical industry is inherently a long-term process. The following data show the trend of the Company's research and development spending. For the period 1998 to 2011, the compounded annual growth rate in research and development was approximately 21%.

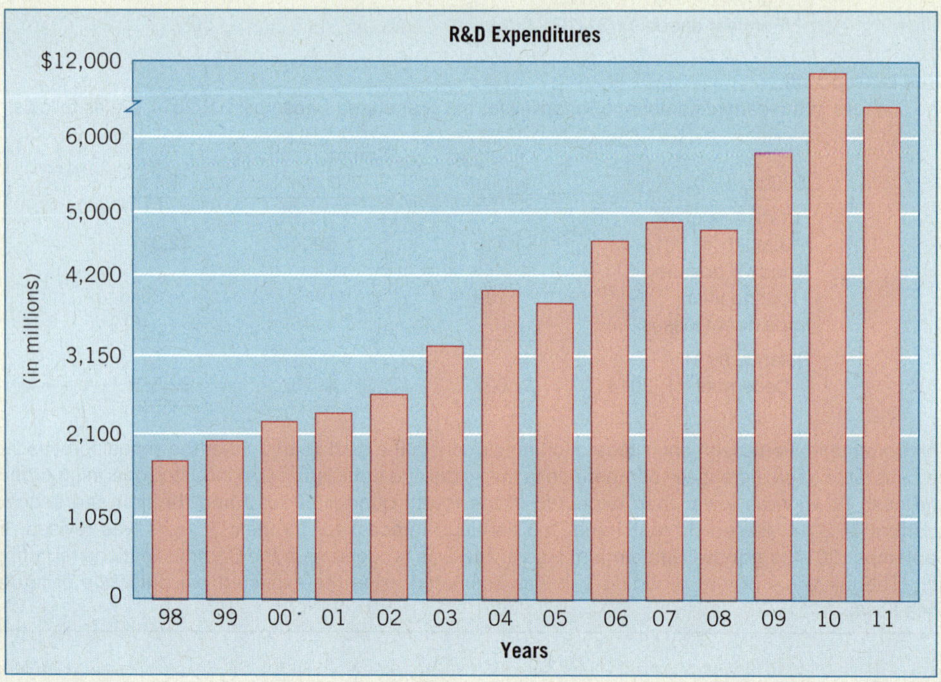

You will want to read the **IFRS INSIGHTS** on pages 693–699 for discussion of IFRS related to intangible assets.

Evolving Issue RECOGNITION OF R&D AND INTERNALLY GENERATED INTANGIBLES

The requirement that companies expense immediately all R&D costs (as well as start-up costs) incurred internally is a practical solution. It ensures consistency in practice and uniformity among companies. But the practice of immediately writing off expenditures made in the expectation of benefiting future periods is conceptually incorrect.

Proponents of immediate expensing contend that from an income statement standpoint, long-run application of this standard frequently makes little difference. They argue that because of the ongoing nature of most companies' R&D activities, the amount of R&D cost charged to expense each accounting period is about the same, whether there is immediate expensing or capitalization and subsequent amortization.

Others criticize this practice. They believe that the balance sheet should report an intangible asset related to expenditures that have future benefit. To preclude capitalization of all R&D expenditures removes from the balance sheet what may be a company's most valuable asset.

Indeed, research findings indicate that capitalizing R&D costs may be helpful to investors. For example, one study showed a significant relationship between R&D outlays and subsequent benefits in the form of increased productivity, earnings, and shareholder value for R&D-intensive companies. Another study found that there was a significant decline in earnings usefulness for companies that were forced to switch from capitalizing to expensing R&D costs, and that the decline appears to persist over time.

The current accounting for R&D and other internally generated intangible assets represents one of the many trade-offs made among relevance, faithful representation, and cost-benefit considerations. The FASB and IASB have completed some limited-scope projects on the accounting for intangible assets, and the Boards have contemplated a joint project on the accounting for identifiable intangible assets (i.e., excluding goodwill). Such a project would address concerns that the current accounting requirements lead to inconsistent treatments for some types of intangible assets depending on how they arise. (See *http://www.ifrs.org/Current+Projects/IASB+Projects/Intangible+Assets/Intangible+Assets.htm.*)

Sources for research studies: Baruch Lev and Theodore Sougiannis, "The Capitalization, Amortization, and Value-Relevance of R&D," *Journal of Accounting and Economics* (February 1996); and Martha L. Loudder and Bruce K. Behn, "Alternative Income Determination Rules and Earnings Usefulness: The Case of R&D Costs," *Contemporary Accounting Research* (Fall 1995).

SUMMARY OF LEARNING OBJECTIVES

1 Describe the characteristics of intangible assets. Intangible assets have two main characteristics: (1) They lack physical existence, and (2) they are not financial instruments. In most cases, intangible assets provide services over a period of years and so are normally classified as long-term assets.

2 Identify the costs to include in the initial valuation of intangible assets. Intangibles are recorded at cost. Cost includes all acquisition costs and expenditures needed to make the intangible asset ready for its intended use. If intangibles are acquired in exchange for stock or other assets, the cost of the intangible is the fair value of the consideration given or the fair value of the intangible received, whichever is more clearly evident. When a company makes a "basket purchase" of several intangibles or a combination of intangibles and tangibles, it should allocate the cost on the basis of fair values.

3 Explain the procedure for amortizing intangible assets. Intangibles have either a limited useful life or an indefinite useful life. Companies amortize limited-life intangibles. They do not amortize indefinite-life intangibles. Limited-life intangibles should be amortized by systematic charges to expense over their useful life. The useful life should reflect the period over which these assets will contribute to cash flows. The

KEY TERMS

amortization, *651*
bargain purchase, *661*
business combination, *650(n)*
copyright, *655*
development activities, *666*
fair value test, *662*
franchise, *655*
goodwill, *658*
impairment, *662*
indefinite-life intangibles, *651*
intangible assets, *650*
license (permit), *656*
limited-life intangibles, *651*
master valuation approach, *660*
organizational costs, *668*

amount to report for amortization expense should reflect the pattern in which a company consumes or uses up the asset, if it can reliably determine that pattern. Otherwise, use a straight-line approach.

4 Describe the types of intangible assets. Major types of intangibles are (1) *marketing-related intangibles,* used in the marketing or promotion of products or services; (2) *customer-related intangibles,* resulting from interactions with outside parties; (3) *artistic-related intangibles,* giving ownership rights to such items as plays and literary works; (4) *contract-related intangibles,* representing the value of rights that arise from contractual arrangements; (5) *technology-related intangibles,* relating to innovations or technological advances; and (6) *goodwill,* arising from business combinations.

5 Explain the accounting issues for recording goodwill. Unlike receivables, inventories, and patents that a company can sell or exchange individually in the marketplace, goodwill can be identified only with the company as a whole. Goodwill is a "going concern" valuation and is recorded only when an entire business is purchased. A company should not capitalize goodwill generated internally. The future benefits of goodwill may have no relationship to the costs incurred in the development of that goodwill. Goodwill may exist even in the absence of specific costs to develop it.

To record goodwill, a company compares the fair value of the net tangible and identifiable intangible assets with the purchase price of the acquired business. The difference is considered goodwill. Goodwill is the residual. Goodwill is often identified on the balance sheet as the excess of cost over the fair value of the net assets acquired.

6 Explain the accounting issues related to intangible-asset impairments. Impairment occurs when the carrying amount of the intangible asset is not recoverable. Companies use a recoverability test and a fair value test to determine impairments for limited-life intangibles. They use only a fair value test for indefinite-life intangibles. Goodwill impairments require a two-step process. First, test the fair value of the reporting unit, then do the fair value test on implied goodwill.

7 Identify the conceptual issues related to research and development costs. R&D costs are not in themselves intangible assets, but R&D activities frequently result in the development of something a company patents or copyrights. The difficulties in accounting for R&D expenditures are (1) identifying the costs associated with particular activities, projects, or achievements, and (2) determining the magnitude of the future benefits and length of time over which a company may realize such benefits. Because of these latter uncertainties, companies are required to expense all research and development costs when incurred.

8 Describe the accounting for research and development and similar costs. Illustration 12-14 (page 668) shows typical costs associated with R&D activities and the accounting treatment accorded them. Many costs have characteristics similar to R&D costs. Examples are start-up costs, initial operating losses, and advertising costs. For the most part, these costs are expensed as incurred, similar to the accounting for R&D costs.

9 Indicate the presentation of intangible assets and related items. On the balance sheet, companies should report all intangible assets other than goodwill as a separate item. Contra accounts are not normally shown. If goodwill is present, it too should be reported as a separate item. On the income statement, companies should report amortization expense and impairment losses in continuing operations. The notes to the financial statements have additional detailed information. Financial statements must disclose the total R&D costs charged to expense each period for which an income statement is presented.

DEMONSTRATION PROBLEM

Sky Co., organized in 2014, provided you with the following information.

1. Purchased a license for $20,000 on July 1, 2014. The license gives Sky exclusive rights to sell its services in the tri-state region and will expire on July 1, 2022.
2. Purchased a patent on January 2, 2015, for $40,000. It is estimated to have a 5-year life.
3. Costs incurred to develop an exclusive Internet connection process as of June 1, 2015, were $45,000. The process has an indefinite life.
4. On April 1, 2015, Sky Co. purchased a small circuit board manufacturer for $350,000. Goodwill recorded in the transaction was $90,000.
5. On July 1, 2015, legal fees for successful defense of the patent purchased on January 2, 2015, were $11,400.
6. Research and development costs incurred as of September 1, 2015, were $75,000.

Instructions

(a) Prepare the journal entries to record all the entries related to the patent during 2015.

(b) At December 31, 2015, an impairment test is performed on the license purchased in 2014. It is estimated that the net cash flows to be received from the license will be $13,000, and its fair value is $7,000. Compute the amount of impairment, if any, to be recorded on December 31, 2015.

(c) What is the amount to be reported for intangible assets on the balance sheet at December 31, 2014? At December 31, 2015?

Solution

(a)

	Debit	Credit
January 2, 2015		
Patents	40,000	
Cash		40,000
July 1, 2015		
Patents	11,400	
Cash		11,400
December 31, 2015		
Patent Amortization Expense	9,267	
Patents		9,267

Computation of patent expense:

$40,000 × 12/60 =	$8,000
$11,400 × 6/54 =	1,267
Total	$9,267

(b) Computation of impairment loss:

Cost	$20,000
Less: Accumulated amortization ($20,000 × 18/96)	3,750
Book value	$16,250

Book value of $16,250 is greater than net cash flows of $13,000. Therefore, the license is impaired. The impairment loss is computed as follows.

Book value	$16,250
Fair value	7,000
Loss on impairment	$ 9,250

(c) Intangible assets as of December 31, 2014:

License	$18,750*
*Cost	$20,000
Less: Accumulated amortization ($20,000 × 6/96)	1,250
Total	$18,750

Intangible assets as of December 31, 2015:

License	$ 7,000
Patents ($40,000 + $11,400 − $9,267)	$42,133
Goodwill	$90,000

All the costs to develop the Internet connection process and the research and development costs are expensed as incurred.

FASB CODIFICATION

FASB Codification References

[1] FASB ASC 350-10-05. [Predecessor literature: "Goodwill and Other Intangible Assets," *Statement of Financial Accounting Standards No. 142* (Norwalk, Conn.: FASB, 2001).]

[2] FASB ASC 350-30-35. [Predecessor literature: "Goodwill and Other Intangible Assets," *Statement of Financial Accounting Standards No. 142* (Norwalk, Conn.: FASB, 2001), par. 11.]

[3] FASB ASC 805-10. [Predecessor literature: "Business Combinations," *Statement of Financial Accounting Standards No. 141R* (Norwalk, Conn.: FASB, 2007).]

[4] FASB ASC 350-30-35. [Predecessor literature: "Goodwill and Other Intangible Assets," *Statement of Financial Accounting Standards No. 142* (Norwalk, Conn.: FASB, 2001), par. B55.]

[5] FASB ASC 805-10-20. [Predecessor literature: "Business Combinations," *Statement of Financial Accounting Standards No. 141R* (Norwalk, Conn.: FASB, 2007).]

[6] FASB ASC 805-10-30. [Predecessor literature: "Business Combinations," *Statement of Financial Accounting Standards No. 141R* (Norwalk, Conn.: FASB, 2007).]

[7] FASB ASC 805-10-30. [Predecessor literature: "Business Combinations," *Statement of Financial Accounting Standards No. 141R* (Norwalk, Conn.: FASB, 2007).]

[8] FASB ASC 360-10-05. [Predecessor literature: "Accounting for the Impairment or Disposal of Long-lived Assets," *Statement of Financial Accounting Standards No. 144* (Norwalk, Conn.: 2001).]

[9] FASB ASC 350-30-35-17A-19. [Predecessor literature: "Goodwill and Other Intangible Assets," *Statement of Financial Accounting Standards No. 142* (Norwalk, Conn.: FASB, 2001).]

[10] FASB ASC 350-20-35. [Predecessor literature: "Goodwill and Other Intangible Assets," *Statement of Financial Accounting Standards No. 142* (Norwalk, Conn.: FASB, 2001).]

[11] FASB ASC 735-10-25-1. [Predecessor literature: "Accounting for Research and Development Costs," *Statement of Financial Accounting Standards No. 2* (Stamford, Conn.: FASB, 1974), par. 12.]

[12] FASB ASC Master Glossary. [Predecessor literature: "Accounting for Research and Development Costs," *Statement of Financial Accounting Standards No. 2* (Stamford, Conn.: FASB, 1974), par. 8.]

[13] FASB ASC 805-10. [Predecessor literature: "Business Combinations," *Statement of Financial Accounting Standards No. 141–Revised* (Norwalk, Conn.: FASB, 2007), par. E11.]

[14] FASB ASC 730-10-25-2. [Predecessor literature: "Accounting for Research and Development Costs," *Statement of Financial Accounting Standards No. 2* (Stamford, Conn.: FASB, 1974), par. 11.]

[15] FASB ASC 730-20-05. [Predecessor literature: "Research and Development Arrangements," *Statement of Financial Accounting Standards No. 68* (Stamford, Conn.: FASB, 1982).]

[16] FASB ASC 720-15-25. [Predecessor literature: "Reporting on the Costs of Start-up Activities," *Statement of Position 98-5* (New York: AICPA, 1998).]

[17] FASB ASC 915-205-45-1. [Predecessor literature: "Accounting and Reporting by Development Stage Enterprises," *Statement of Financial Accounting Standards No. 7* (Stamford, Conn.: FASB, 1975), par. 10.]

[18] FASB ASC 720-35-05-3. [Predecessor literature: "Reporting on Advertising Costs," *Statement of Position 93-7* (New York: AICPA, 1993).]

Exercises

If your school has a subscription to the FASB Codification, go to *http://aaahq.org/asclogin.cfm* to log in and prepare responses to the following. Provide Codification references for your responses.

CE12-1 Access the Codification glossary ("Master Glossary") to answer the following.

- **(a)** What is the definition provided for an intangible asset?
- **(b)** What is the definition of goodwill?
- **(c)** What is the definition of research and development (R&D)?
- **(d)** What is a development stage entity?

CE12-2 Your friend Harry does not understand the concept of an indefinite-life intangible asset. He wonders, "Does this mean the life is infinite?" What does the authoritative literature say about indefinite-life intangible assets?

CE12-3 What guidance does the Codification provide concerning the disclosure of research and development (R&D) costs?

CE12-4 What is the nature of the authoritative guidance for advertising costs for entertainment companies?

An additional Codification case can be found in the Using Your Judgment section, on page 692.

Be sure to check the book's companion website for a Review and Analysis Exercise, with solution.

WileyPLUS **Brief Exercises, Exercises, Problems, and many more learning and assessment tools and resources are available for practice in WileyPLUS.**

QUESTIONS

1. What are the two main characteristics of intangible assets?

2. If intangibles are acquired for stock, how is the cost of the intangible determined?

3. Intangibles have either a limited useful life or an indefinite useful life. How should these two different types of intangibles be amortized?

4. Why does the accounting profession make a distinction between internally created intangibles and purchased intangibles?

5. In 2014, Ghostbusters Corp. spent $420,000 for "goodwill" visits by sales personnel to key customers. The purpose of these visits was to build a solid, friendly relationship for the future and to gain insight into the problems and needs of the companies served. How should this expenditure be reported?

6. What are factors to be considered in estimating the useful life of an intangible asset?

7. What should be the pattern of amortization for a limited-life intangible?

8. Columbia Sportswear Company acquired a trademark that is helpful in distinguishing one of its new products. The trademark is renewable every 10 years at minimal cost. All evidence indicates that this trademarked product will generate cash flows for an indefinite period of time. How should this trademark be amortized?

9. McNabb Company spent $190,000 developing a new process, $45,000 in legal fees to obtain a patent, and $91,000 to market the process that was patented, all in the year 2014. How should these costs be accounted for in 2014?

10. Izzy Inc. purchased a patent for $350,000 which has an estimated useful life of 10 years. Its pattern of use or consumption cannot be reliably determined. Prepare the entry to record the amortization of the patent in its first year of use.

11. Explain the difference between artistic-related intangible assets and contract-related intangible assets.

12. What is goodwill? What is a bargain purchase?

13. Under what circumstances is it appropriate to record goodwill in the accounts? How should goodwill, properly recorded on the books, be written off in order to conform with generally accepted accounting principles?

14. In examining financial statements, financial analysts often write off goodwill immediately. Comment on this procedure.

15. Braxton Inc. is considering the write-off of a limited-life intangible because of its lack of profitability. Explain to the management of Braxton how to determine whether a write-off is permitted.

16. Last year, Zeno Company recorded an impairment on an intangible asset held for use. Recent appraisals indicate that the asset has increased in value. Should Zeno record this recovery in value?

17. Explain how losses on impaired intangible assets should be reported in income.

18. Simon Company determines that its goodwill is impaired. It finds that its implied goodwill is $360,000 and its recorded goodwill is $400,000. The fair value of its identifiable assets is $1,450,000. What is the amount of goodwill impaired?

19. What is the nature of research and development costs?

20. Research and development activities may include (a) personnel costs, (b) materials and equipment costs, and (c) indirect costs. What is the recommended accounting treatment for these three types of R&D costs?

21. Which of the following activities should be expensed currently as R&D costs?

    (a) Testing in search for or evaluation of product or process alternatives.

    (b) Engineering follow-through in an early phase of commercial production.

    (c) Legal work in connection with patent applications or litigation, and the sale or licensing of patents.

22. Indicate the proper accounting for the following items.

    (a) Organization costs.

    (b) Advertising costs.

    (c) Operating losses.

23. In 2013, Austin Powers Corporation developed a new product that will be marketed in 2014. In connection with the development of this product, the following costs were incurred in 2013: research and development costs $400,000; materials and supplies consumed $60,000; and compensation paid to research consultants $125,000. It is anticipated that these costs will be recovered in 2016. What is the amount of research and development costs that Austin Powers should record in 2013 as a charge to expense?

24. Recently, a group of university students decided to incorporate for the purposes of selling a process to recycle the waste product from manufacturing cheese. Some of the initial costs involved were legal fees and office expenses incurred in starting the business, state incorporation fees, and stamp taxes. One student wishes to charge these costs against revenue in the current period. Another wishes to defer these costs and amortize them in the future. Which student is correct?

25. An intangible asset with an estimated useful life of 30 years was acquired on January 1, 2004, for $540,000. On January 1, 2014, a review was made of intangible assets and their expected service lives, and it was determined that this asset had an estimated useful life of 30 more years from the date of the review. What is the amount of amortization for this intangible in 2014?

BRIEF EXERCISES

2 3 **BE12-1** Celine Dion Corporation purchases a patent from Salmon Company on January 1, 2014, for $54,000. The patent has a remaining legal life of 16 years. Celine Dion feels the patent will be useful for 10 years. Prepare Celine Dion's journal entries to record the purchase of the patent and 2014 amortization.

2 3 **BE12-2** Use the information provided in BE12-1. Assume that at January 1, 2016, the carrying amount of the patent on Celine Dion's books is $43,200. In January, Celine Dion spends $24,000 successfully defending a patent suit. Celine Dion still feels the patent will be useful until the end of 2023. Prepare the journal entries to record the $24,000 expenditure and 2016 amortization.

2 3 **BE12-3** Larry Byrd, Inc., spent $68,000 in attorney fees while developing the trade name of its new product, the Mean Bean Machine. Prepare the journal entries to record the $68,000 expenditure and the first year's amortization, using an 8-year life.

2 3 **BE12-4** Gershwin Corporation obtained a franchise from Sonic Hedgehog Inc. for a cash payment of $120,000 on April 1, 2014. The franchise grants Gershwin the right to sell certain products and services for a period of 8 years. Prepare Gershwin's April 1 journal entry and December 31 adjusting entry.

5 **BE12-5** On September 1, 2014, Winans Corporation acquired Aumont Enterprises for a cash payment of $700,000. At the time of purchase, Aumont's balance sheet showed assets of $620,000, liabilities of $200,000, and owners' equity of $420,000. The fair value of Aumont's assets is estimated to be $800,000. Compute the amount of goodwill acquired by Winans.

6 **BE12-6** Kenoly Corporation owns a patent that has a carrying amount of $300,000. Kenoly expects future net cash flows from this patent to total $210,000. The fair value of the patent is $110,000. Prepare Kenoly's journal entry, if necessary, to record the loss on impairment.

6 **BE12-7** Waters Corporation purchased Johnson Company 3 years ago and at that time recorded goodwill of $400,000. The Johnson Division's net assets, including the goodwill, have a carrying amount of $800,000. The fair value of the division is estimated to be $1,000,000. Prepare Waters' journal entry, if necessary, to record impairment of the goodwill.

6 **BE12-8** Use the information provided in BE12-7. Assume that the fair value of the division is estimated to be $750,000 and the implied goodwill is $350,000. Prepare Waters' journal entry, if necessary, to record impairment of the goodwill.

8 **BE12-9** Capriati Corporation commenced operations in early 2014. The corporation incurred $60,000 of costs such as fees to underwriters, legal fees, state fees, and promotional expenditures during its formation. Prepare journal entries to record the $60,000 expenditure and 2014 amortization, if any.

8 **BE12-10** Treasure Land Corporation incurred the following costs in 2014.

Cost of laboratory research aimed at discovery of new knowledge	$120,000
Cost of testing in search for product alternatives	100,000
Cost of engineering activity required to advance the design of a product to the manufacturing stage	210,000
	$430,000

Prepare the necessary 2014 journal entry or entries for Treasure Land.

8 **BE12-11** Indicate whether the following items are capitalized or expensed in the current year.

(a) Purchase cost of a patent from a competitor.
(b) Research and development costs.
(c) Organizational costs.
(d) Costs incurred internally to create goodwill.

3 9 **BE12-12** Nieland Industries had one patent recorded on its books as of January 1, 2014. This patent had a book value of $288,000 and a remaining useful life of 8 years. During 2014, Nieland incurred research and development costs of $96,000 and brought a patent infringement suit against a competitor. On December 1, 2014, Nieland received the good news that its patent was valid and that its competitor could not use the process Nieland had patented. The company incurred $85,000 to defend this patent. At what amount should patent(s) be reported on the December 31, 2014, balance sheet, assuming monthly amortization of patents?

3 9 **BE12-13** Sinise Industries acquired two copyrights during 2014. One copyright related to a textbook that was developed internally at a cost of $9,900. This textbook is estimated to have a useful life of 3 years from September 1, 2014, the date it was published. The second copyright (a history research textbook) was purchased from University Press on December 1, 2014, for $24,000. This textbook has an indefinite useful life. How should these two copyrights be reported on Sinise's balance sheet as of December 31, 2014?

EXERCISES

1 4 **E12-1 (Classification Issues—Intangibles)** Presented below is a list of items that could be included in the intangible assets section of the balance sheet.

1. Investment in a subsidiary company.
2. Timberland.
3. Cost of engineering activity required to advance the design of a product to the manufacturing stage.

4. Lease prepayment (6 months' rent paid in advance).
5. Cost of equipment obtained.
6. Cost of searching for applications of new research findings.
7. Costs incurred in the formation of a corporation.
8. Operating losses incurred in the start-up of a business.
9. Training costs incurred in start-up of new operation.
10. Purchase cost of a franchise.
11. Goodwill generated internally.
12. Cost of testing in search for product alternatives.
13. Goodwill acquired in the purchase of a business.
14. Cost of developing a patent.
15. Cost of purchasing a patent from an inventor.
16. Legal costs incurred in securing a patent.
17. Unrecovered costs of a successful legal suit to protect the patent.
18. Cost of conceptual formulation of possible product alternatives.
19. Cost of purchasing a copyright.
20. Research and development costs.
21. Long-term receivables.
22. Cost of developing a trademark.
23. Cost of purchasing a trademark.

Instructions

(a) Indicate which items on the list above would generally be reported as intangible assets in the balance sheet.

(b) Indicate how, if at all, the items not reportable as intangible assets would be reported in the financial statements.

1 4 **E12-2 (Classification Issues—Intangibles)** Presented below is selected information related to Martin Burke Inc. at year-end. All these accounts have debit balances.

Cable television franchises	Film contract rights
Music copyrights	Customer lists
Research and development costs	Prepaid expenses
Goodwill	Covenants not to compete
Cash	Brand names
Discount on notes payable	Notes receivable
Accounts receivable	Investments in affiliated companies
Property, plant, and equipment	Organization costs
Internet domain name	Land

Instructions

Identify which items should be classified as an intangible asset. For those items not classified as an intangible asset, indicate where they would be reported in the financial statements.

1 4 **E12-3 (Classification Issues—Intangible Assets)** Joni Hyde Inc. has the following amounts reported in its general ledger at the end of the current year.

XLS

Organization costs	$24,000
Trademarks	15,000
Discount on bonds payable	35,000
Deposits with advertising agency for ads to promote goodwill of company	10,000
Excess of cost over fair value of net identifiable assets of acquired subsidiary	75,000
Cost of equipment acquired for research and development projects; the equipment has an alternative future use	90,000
Costs of developing a secret formula for a product that is expected to be marketed for at least 20 years	80,000

Instructions

(a) On the basis of the information above, compute the total amount to be reported by Hyde for intangible assets on its balance sheet at year-end.

(b) If an item is not to be included in intangible assets, explain its proper treatment for reporting purposes.

3 8 **E12-4 (Intangible Amortization)** Presented below is selected information for Alatorre Company.

1. Alatorre purchased a patent from Vania Co. for $1,000,000 on January 1, 2012. The patent is being amortized over its remaining legal life of 10 years, expiring on January 1, 2022. During 2014, Alatorre determined that the economic benefits of the patent would not last longer than 6 years from the date of acquisition. What amount should be reported in the balance sheet for the patent, net of accumulated amortization, at December 31, 2014?
2. Alatorre bought a franchise from Alexander Co. on January 1, 2013, for $400,000. The carrying amount of the franchise on Alexander's books on January 1, 2013, was $500,000. The franchise agreement had an estimated useful life of 30 years. Because Alatorre must enter a competitive bidding at the end of 2015, it is unlikely that the franchise will be retained beyond 2022. What amount should be amortized for the year ended December 31, 2014?
3. On January 1, 2014, Alatorre incurred organization costs of $275,000. What amount of organization expense should be reported in 2014?
4. Alatorre purchased the license for distribution of a popular consumer product on January 1, 2014, for $150,000. It is expected that this product will generate cash flows for an indefinite period of time. The license has an initial term of 5 years but by paying a nominal fee, Alatorre can renew the license indefinitely for successive 5-year terms. What amount should be amortized for the year ended December 31, 2014?

Instructions

Answer the questions asked about each of the factual situations.

2 3 **E12-5 (Correct Intangible Assets Account)** As the recently appointed auditor for William J. Bryan Corpo-
7 ration, you have been asked to examine selected accounts before the 6-month financial statements of June 30, 2014, are prepared. The controller for William J. Bryan Corporation mentions that only one account is kept for intangible assets. The account is shown below.

Intangible Assets

		Debit	Credit	Balance
Jan. 4	Research and development costs	940,000		940,000
Jan. 5	Legal costs to obtain patent	75,000		1,015,000
Jan. 31	Payment of 7 months' rent on property leased by Bryan	91,000		1,106,000
Feb. 11	Premium on common stock		250,000	856,000
March 31	Unamortized bond discount on bonds due March 31, 2034	84,000		940,000
April 30	Promotional expenses related to start-up of business	207,000		1,147,000
June 30	Operating losses for first 6 months	241,000		1,388,000

Instructions

Prepare the entry or entries necessary to correct this account. Assume that the patent has a useful life of 10 years.

3 8 **E12-6 (Recording and Amortization of Intangibles)** Rolanda Marshall Company, organized in 2013, has set up a single account for all intangible assets. The following summary discloses the debit entries that have been recorded during 2014.

1/2/14	Purchased patent (8-year life)	$ 350,000
4/1/14	Purchase goodwill (indefinite life)	360,000
7/1/14	Purchased franchise with 10-year life; expiration date 7/1/24	450,000
8/1/14	Payment of copyright (5-year life)	156,000
9/1/14	Research and development costs	215,000
		$1,531,000

Instructions

Prepare the necessary entries to clear the Intangible Assets account and to set up separate accounts for distinct types of intangibles. Make the entries as of December 31, 2014, recording any necessary amortization and reflecting all balances accurately as of that date. (Use straight-line amortization.)

2 3 **E12-7 (Accounting for Trade Name)** In early January 2013, Outkast Corporation applied for a trade name, incurring legal costs of $16,000. In January 2014, Outkast incurred $7,800 of legal fees in a successful defense of its trade name.

Instructions

(a) Compute 2013 amortization, 12/31/13 book value, 2014 amortization, and 12/31/14 book value if the company amortizes the trade name over 10 years.

(b) Compute the 2014 amortization and the 12/31/14 book value, assuming that at the beginning of 2014, Outkast determines that the trade name will provide no future benefits beyond December 31, 2017.

(c) Ignoring the response for part (b), compute the 2015 amortization and the 12/31/15 book value, assuming that at the beginning of 2015, based on new market research, Outkast determines that the fair value of the trade name is $15,000. Estimated total future cash flows from the trade name is $16,000 on January 3, 2015.

8 **E12-8 (Accounting for Organization Costs)** Horace Greeley Corporation was organized in 2013 and began operations at the beginning of 2014. The company is involved in interior design consulting services. The following costs were incurred prior to the start of operations.

Attorney's fees in connection with organization of the company	$15,000
Purchase of drafting and design equipment	10,000
Costs of meetings of incorporators to discuss organizational activities	7,000
State filing fees to incorporate	1,000
	$33,000

Instructions

(a) Compute the total amount of organization costs incurred by Greeley.

(b) Prepare the journal entry to record organization costs for 2014.

2 3 7 **E12-9 (Accounting for Patents, Franchises, and R&D)** Jimmy Carter Company has provided information on intangible assets as follows.

A patent was purchased from Gerald Ford Company for $2,000,000 on January 1, 2013. Carter estimated the remaining useful life of the patent to be 10 years. The patent was carried in Ford's accounting records at a net book value of $2,000,000 when Ford sold it to Carter.

During 2014, a franchise was purchased from Ronald Reagan Company for $480,000. In addition, 5% of revenue from the franchise must be paid to Reagan. Revenue from the franchise for 2014 was $2,500,000. Carter estimates the useful life of the franchise to be 10 years and takes a full year's amortization in the year of purchase.

Carter incurred research and development costs in 2014 as follows.

Materials and equipment	$142,000
Personnel	189,000
Indirect costs	102,000
	$433,000

Carter estimates that these costs will be recouped by December 31, 2017. The materials and equipment purchased have no alternative uses.

On January 1, 2014, because of recent events in the field, Carter estimates that the remaining life of the patent purchased on January 1, 2013, is only 5 years from January 1, 2014.

Instructions

(a) Prepare a schedule showing the intangibles section of Carter's balance sheet at December 31, 2014. Show supporting computations in good form.

(b) Prepare a schedule showing the income statement effect (related to expenses) for the year ended December 31, 2014, as a result of the facts above. Show supporting computations in good form.

(AICPA adapted)

2 3 **E12-10 (Accounting for Patents)** During 2010, George Winston Corporation spent $170,000 in research and development costs. As a result, a new product called the New Age Piano was patented. The patent was obtained on October 1, 2010, and had a legal life of 20 years and a useful life of 10 years. Legal costs of $18,000 related to the patent were incurred as of October 1, 2010.

Instructions

(a) Prepare all journal entries required in 2010 and 2011 as a result of the transactions above.

(b) On June 1, 2012, Winston spent $9,480 to successfully prosecute a patent infringement suit. As a result, the estimate of useful life was extended to 12 years from June 1, 2012. Prepare all journal entries required in 2012 and 2013.

(c) In 2014, Winston determined that a competitor's product would make the New Age Piano obsolete and the patent worthless by December 31, 2015. Prepare all journal entries required in 2014 and 2015.

2 3 **E12-11 (Accounting for Patents)** Tones Industries has the following patents on its December 31, 2013, balance sheet.

Patent Item	Initial Cost	Date Acquired	Useful Life at Date Acquired
Patent A	$30,600	3/1/10	17 years
Patent B	$15,000	7/1/11	10 years
Patent C	$14,400	9/1/12	4 years

The following events occurred during the year ended December 31, 2014.

1. Research and development costs of $245,700 were incurred during the year.
2. Patent D was purchased on July 1 for $36,480. This patent has a useful life of 9½ years.
3. As a result of reduced demands for certain products protected by Patent B, a possible impairment of Patent B's value may have occurred at December 31, 2014. The controller for Tones estimates the expected future cash flows from Patent B will be as follows.

Year	Expected Future Cash Flows
2015	$2,000
2016	2,000
2017	2,000

The proper discount rate to be used for these flows is 8%. (Assume that the cash flows occur at the end of the year.)

Instructions

(a) Compute the total carrying amount of Tones' patents on its December 31, 2013, balance sheet.

(b) Compute the total carrying amount of Tones' patents on its December 31, 2014, balance sheet.

5 **E12-12 (Accounting for Goodwill)** Fred Moss, owner of Moss Interiors, is negotiating for the purchase of Zweifel Galleries. The balance sheet of Zweifel is given in an abbreviated form below.

ZWEIFEL GALLERIES
BALANCE SHEET
AS OF DECEMBER 31, 2014

Assets		Liabilities and Stockholders' Equity		
Cash	$100,000	Accounts payable		$ 50,000
Land	70,000	Notes payable (long-term)		300,000
Buildings (net)	200,000	Total liabilities		350,000
Equipment (net)	175,000	Common stock	$200,000	
Copyrights (net)	30,000	Retained earnings	25,000	225,000
Total assets	$575,000	Total liabilities and stockholders' equity		$575,000

Moss and Zweifel agree that:

1. Land is undervalued by $30,000.
2. Equipment is overvalued by $5,000.

Zweifel agrees to sell the gallery to Moss for $350,000.

Instructions

Prepare the entry to record the purchase of Zweifel Galleries on Moss's books.

3 5 **E12-13 (Accounting for Goodwill)** On July 1, 2014, Brigham Corporation purchased Young Company by paying $250,000 cash and issuing a $100,000 note payable to Steve Young. At July 1, 2014, the balance sheet of Young Company was as follows.

Cash	$ 50,000	Accounts payable	$200,000
Accounts receivable	90,000	Stockholders' equity	235,000
Inventory	100,000		$435,000
Land	40,000		
Buildings (net)	75,000		
Equipment (net)	70,000		
Trademarks	10,000		
	$435,000		

The recorded amounts all approximate current values except for land (fair value of $60,000), inventory (fair value of $125,000), and trademarks (fair value of $15,000).

Instructions

(a) Prepare the July 1 entry for Brigham Corporation to record the purchase.
(b) Prepare the December 31 entry for Brigham Corporation to record amortization of intangibles. The trademark has an estimated useful life of 4 years with a residual value of $3,000.

6 **E12-14 (Copyright Impairment)** Presented below is information related to copyrights owned by Walter de la Mare Company at December 31, 2014.

Cost	$8,600,000
Carrying amount	4,300,000
Expected future net cash flows	4,000,000
Fair value	3,200,000

Assume that Walter de la Mare Company will continue to use this copyright in the future. As of December 31, 2014, the copyright is estimated to have a remaining useful life of 10 years.

Instructions

(a) Prepare the journal entry (if any) to record the impairment of the asset at December 31, 2014. The company does not use accumulated amortization accounts.
(b) Prepare the journal entry to record amortization expense for 2015 related to the copyrights.
(c) The fair value of the copyright at December 31, 2015, is $3,400,000. Prepare the journal entry (if any) necessary to record the increase in fair value.

5 6 **E12-15 (Goodwill Impairment)** Presented below is net asset information related to the Carlos Division of Santana, Inc.

CARLOS DIVISION
NET ASSETS
AS OF DECEMBER 31, 2014
(IN MILLIONS)

Cash	$ 50
Accounts receivable	200
Property, plant, and equipment (net)	2,600
Goodwill	200
Less: Notes payable	(2,700)
Net assets	$ 350

The purpose of the Carlos Division is to develop a nuclear-powered aircraft. If successful, traveling delays associated with refueling could be substantially reduced. Many other benefits would also occur. To date, management has not had much success and is deciding whether a write-down at this time is appropriate. Management estimated its future net cash flows from the project to be $400 million. Management has also received an offer to purchase the division for $335 million. All identifiable assets' and liabilities' book and fair value amounts are the same.

Instructions

(a) Prepare the journal entry (if any) to record the impairment at December 31, 2014.
(b) At December 31, 2015, it is estimated that the division's fair value increased to $345 million. Prepare the journal entry (if any) to record this increase in fair value.

8 **E12-16 (Accounting for R&D Costs)** Leontyne Price Company from time to time embarks on a research program when a special project seems to offer possibilities. In 2013, the company expends $325,000 on a research project, but by the end of 2013 it is impossible to determine whether any benefit will be derived from it.

Instructions

(a) What account should be charged for the $325,000, and how should it be shown in the financial statements?

(b) The project is completed in 2014, and a successful patent is obtained. The R&D costs to complete the project are $110,000. The administrative and legal expenses incurred in obtaining patent number 472-1001-84 in 2014 total $16,000. The patent has an expected useful life of 5 years. Record these costs in journal entry form. Also, record patent amortization (full year) in 2014.

(c) In 2015, the company successfully defends the patent in extended litigation at a cost of $47,200, thereby extending the patent life to December 31, 2022. What is the proper way to account for this cost? Also, record patent amortization (full year) in 2015.

(d) Additional engineering and consulting costs incurred in 2015 required to advance the design of a product to the manufacturing stage total $60,000. These costs enhance the design of the product considerably. Discuss the proper accounting treatment for this cost.

8 **E12-17 (Accounting for R&D Costs)** Thomas More Company incurred the following costs during the current year in connection with its research and development activities.

Cost of equipment acquired that will have alternative uses in future R&D projects over the next 5 years (uses straight-line depreciation)	$280,000
Materials consumed in R&D projects	59,000
Consulting fees paid to outsiders for R&D projects	100,000
Personnel costs of persons involved in R&D projects	128,000
Indirect costs reasonably allocable to R&D projects	50,000
Materials purchased for future R&D projects	34,000

Instructions

Compute the amount to be reported as research and development expense by More on its current year income statement. Assume equipment is purchased at the beginning of the year.

EXERCISES SET B

See the book's companion website, at **www.wiley.com/college/kieso**, for an additional set of exercises.

PROBLEMS

2 3 **P12-1 (Correct Intangible Assets Account)** Reichenbach Co., organized in 2013, has set up a single account for all intangible assets. The following summary discloses the debit entries that have been recorded during 2014 and 2015.

Intangible Assets

7/1/14	8-year franchise; expiration date 6/30/22	$ 48,000
10/1/14	Advance payment on laboratory space (2-year lease)	24,000
12/31/14	Net loss for 2013 including state incorporation fee, $1,000, and related legal fees of organizing, $5,000 (all fees incurred in 2013)	16,000
1/2/15	Patent purchased (10-year life)	84,000
3/1/15	Cost of developing a secret formula (indefinite life)	75,000
4/1/15	Goodwill purchased (indefinite life)	278,400
6/1/15	Legal fee for successful defense of patent purchased above	12,650
9/1/15	Research and development costs	160,000

Instructions

Prepare the necessary entries to clear the Intangible Assets account and to set up separate accounts for distinct types of intangibles. Make the entries as of December 31, 2015, recording any necessary amortization and reflecting all balances accurately as of that date. (Ignore income tax effects.)

2 3 **P12-2 (Accounting for Patents)** Fields Laboratories holds a valuable patent (No. 758-6002-1A) on a precipitator that prevents certain types of air pollution. Fields does not manufacture or sell the products and processes it develops. Instead, it conducts research and develops products and processes which it patents, and then assigns the patents to manufacturers on a royalty basis. Occasionally it sells a patent. The history of Fields patent number 758-6002-1A is as follows.

Date	Activity	Cost
2005–2006	Research conducted to develop precipitator	$384,000
Jan. 2007	Design and construction of a prototype	87,600
March 2007	Testing of models	42,000
Jan. 2008	Fees paid engineers and lawyers to prepare patent application; patent granted June 30, 2008	59,500
Nov. 2009	Engineering activity necessary to advance the design of the precipitator to the manufacturing stage	81,500
Dec. 2010	Legal fees paid to successfully defend precipitator patent	42,000
April 2011	Research aimed at modifying the design of the patented precipitator	43,000
July 2015	Legal fees paid in unsuccessful patent infringement suit against a competitor	34,000

Fields assumed a useful life of 17 years when it received the initial precipitator patent. On January 1, 2013, it revised its useful life estimate downward to 5 remaining years. Amortization is computed for a full year if the cost is incurred prior to July 1, and no amortization for the year if the cost is incurred after June 30. The company's year ends December 31.

Instructions

Compute the carrying value of patent No. 758-6002-1A on each of the following dates:

(a) December 31, 2008.
(b) December 31, 2012.
(c) December 31, 2015.

2 3 **P12-3 (Accounting for Franchise, Patents, and Trademark)** Information concerning Sandro Corporation's intangible assets is as follows.

1. On January 1, 2014, Sandro signed an agreement to operate as a franchisee of Hsian Copy Service, Inc. for an initial franchise fee of $75,000. Of this amount, $15,000 was paid when the agreement was signed, and the balance is payable in 4 annual payments of $15,000 each, beginning January 1, 2015. The agreement provides that the down payment is not refundable and no future services are required of the franchisor. The present value at January 1, 2014, of the 4 annual payments discounted at 14% (the implicit rate for a loan of this type) is $43,700. The agreement also provides that 5% of the revenue from the franchise must be paid to the franchisor annually. Sandro's revenue from the franchise for 2014 was $900,000. Sandro estimates the useful life of the franchise to be 10 years. (*Hint:* You may want to refer to Chapter 18 to determine the proper accounting treatment for the franchise fee and payments.)
2. Sandro incurred $65,000 of experimental and development costs in its laboratory to develop a patent that was granted on January 2, 2014. Legal fees and other costs associated with registration of the patent totaled $17,600. Sandro estimates that the useful life of the patent will be 8 years.
3. A trademark was purchased from Shanghai Company for $36,000 on July 1, 2011. Expenditures for successful litigation in defense of the trademark totaling $10,200 were paid on July 1, 2014. Sandro estimates that the useful life of the trademark will be 20 years from the date of acquisition.

Instructions

(a) Prepare a schedule showing the intangible assets section of Sandro's balance sheet at December 31, 2014. Show supporting computations in good form.
(b) Prepare a schedule showing all expenses resulting from the transactions that would appear on Sandro's income statement for the year ended December 31, 2014. Show supporting computations in good form.

(AICPA adapted)

8 9 **P12-4 (Accounting for R&D Costs)** During 2012, Robin Wright Tool Company purchased a building site for its proposed research and development laboratory at a cost of $60,000. Construction of the building was started in 2012. The building was completed on December 31, 2013, at a cost of $320,000 and was placed in service on January 2, 2014. The estimated useful life of the building for depreciation

purposes was 20 years. The straight-line method of depreciation was to be employed, and there was no estimated residual value.

Management estimates that about 50% of the projects of the research and development group will result in long-term benefits (i.e., at least 10 years) to the corporation. The remaining projects either benefit the current period or are abandoned before completion. A summary of the number of projects and the direct costs incurred in conjunction with the research and development activities for 2014 appears below.

	Number of Projects	Salaries and Employee Benefits	Other Expenses (excluding Building Depreciation Charges)
Completed projects with long-term benefits	15	$ 90,000	$50,000
Abandoned projects or projects that benefit the current period	10	65,000	15,000
Projects in process—results indeterminate	5	40,000	12,000
Total	30	$195,000	$77,000

Upon recommendation of the research and development group, Robin Wright Tool Company acquired a patent for manufacturing rights at a cost of $88,000. The patent was acquired on April 1, 2013, and has an economic life of 10 years.

Instructions

If generally accepted accounting principles were followed, how would the items above relating to research and development activities be reported on the following financial statements?

(a) The company's income statement for 2014.
(b) The company's balance sheet as of December 31, 2014.

Be sure to give account titles and amounts, and briefly justify your presentation.

(CMA adapted)

5 6 **P12-5 (Goodwill, Impairment)** On July 31, 2014, Mexico Company paid $3,000,000 to acquire all of the common stock of Conchita Incorporated, which became a division of Mexico. Conchita reported the following balance sheet at the time of the acquisition.

XLS

Current assets	$ 800,000	Current liabilities	$ 600,000
Noncurrent assets	2,700,000	Long-term liabilities	500,000
Total assets	$3,500,000	Stockholders' equity	2,400,000
		Total liabilities and stockholders' equity	$3,500,000

It was determined at the date of the purchase that the fair value of the identifiable net assets of Conchita was $2,750,000. Over the next 6 months of operations, the newly purchased division experienced operating losses. In addition, it now appears that it will generate substantial losses for the foreseeable future. At December 31, 2014, Conchita reports the following balance sheet information.

Current assets	$ 450,000
Noncurrent assets (including goodwill recognized in purchase)	2,400,000
Current liabilities	(700,000)
Long-term liabilities	(500,000)
Net assets	$1,650,000

It is determined that the fair value of the Conchita Division is $1,850,000. The recorded amount for Conchita's net assets (excluding goodwill) is the same as fair value, except for property, plant, and equipment, which has a fair value $150,000 above the carrying value.

Instructions

(a) Compute the amount of goodwill recognized, if any, on July 31, 2014.
(b) Determine the impairment loss, if any, to be recorded on December 31, 2014.
(c) Assume that fair value of the Conchita Division is $1,600,000 instead of $1,850,000. Determine the impairment loss, if any, to be recorded on December 31, 2014.
(d) Prepare the journal entry to record the impairment loss, if any, and indicate where the loss would be reported in the income statement.

2 3 5 6 9 **P12-6 (Comprehensive Intangible Assets)** Montana Matt's Golf Inc. was formed on July 1, 2013, when Matt Magilke purchased the Old Master Golf Company. Old Master provides video golf instruction at kiosks in shopping malls. Magilke plans to integrate the instructional business into his golf equipment and accessory stores. Magilke paid $770,000 cash for Old Master. At the time, Old Master's balance sheet reported assets of $650,000 and liabilities of $200,000 (thus owners' equity was $450,000). The fair value of Old Master's assets is estimated to be $800,000. Included in the assets is the Old Master trade name with a fair value of $10,000 and a copyright on some instructional books with a fair value of $24,000. The trade name has a remaining life of 5 years and can be renewed at nominal cost indefinitely. The copyright has a remaining life of 40 years.

Instructions

(a) Prepare the intangible assets section of Montana Matt's Golf Inc. at December 31, 2013. How much amortization expense is included in Montana Matt's income for the year ended December 31, 2013? Show all supporting computations.

(b) Prepare the journal entry to record amortization expense for 2014. Prepare the intangible assets section of Montana Matt's Golf Inc. at December 31, 2014. (No impairments are required to be recorded in 2014.)

(c) At the end of 2015, Magilke is evaluating the results of the instructional business. Due to fierce competition from online and television (e.g., the Golf Channel), the Old Master reporting unit has been losing money. Its book value is now $500,000. The fair value of the Old Master reporting unit is $420,000. The implied value of goodwill is $90,000. Magilke has collected the following information related to the company's intangible assets.

Intangible Asset	Expected Cash Flows (undiscounted)	Fair Values
Trade names	$ 9,000	$ 3,000
Copyrights	30,000	25,000

Prepare the journal entries required, if any, to record impairments on Montana Matt's intangible assets. (Assume that any amortization for 2015 has been recorded.) Show supporting computations.

PROBLEMS SET B

See the book's companion website, at **www.wiley.com/college/kieso**, for an additional set of problems.

CONCEPTS FOR ANALYSIS

CA12-1 (Accounting for Pre-Opening Costs) After securing lease commitments from several major stores, Auer Shopping Center, Inc. was organized and built a shopping center in a growing suburb.

The shopping center would have opened on schedule on January 1, 2014, if it had not been struck by a severe tornado in December. Instead, it opened for business on October 1, 2014. All of the additional construction costs that were incurred as a result of the tornado were covered by insurance.

In July 2013, in anticipation of the scheduled January opening, a permanent staff had been hired to promote the shopping center, obtain tenants for the uncommitted space, and manage the property.

A summary of some of the costs incurred in 2013 and the first nine months of 2014 follows.

	2013	January 1, 2014 through September 30, 2014
Interest on mortgage bonds	$720,000	$540,000
Cost of obtaining tenants	300,000	360,000
Promotional advertising	540,000	557,000

The promotional advertising campaign was designed to familiarize shoppers with the center. Had it been known in time that the center would not open until October 2014, the 2013 expenditure for promotional advertising would not have been made. The advertising had to be repeated in 2014.

All of the tenants who had leased space in the shopping center at the time of the tornado accepted the October occupancy date on condition that the monthly rental charges for the first 9 months of 2014 be canceled.

Instructions

Explain how each of the costs for 2013 and the first 9 months of 2014 should be treated in the accounts of the shopping center corporation. Give the reasons for each treatment.

(AICPA adapted)

CA12-2 (Accounting for Patents) On June 30, 2014, your client, Ferry Company, was granted two patents covering plastic cartons that it had been producing and marketing profitably for the past 3 years. One patent covers the manufacturing process, and the other covers the related products.

Ferry executives tell you that these patents represent the most significant breakthrough in the industry in the past 30 years. The products have been marketed under the registered trademarks Evertight, Duratainer, and Sealrite. Licenses under the patents have already been granted by your client to other manufacturers in the United States and abroad, and are producing substantial royalties.

On July 1, Ferry commenced patent infringement actions against several companies whose names you recognize as those of substantial and prominent competitors. Ferry's management is optimistic that these suits will result in a permanent injunction against the manufacture and sale of the infringing products as well as collection of damages for loss of profits caused by the alleged infringement.

The financial vice president has suggested that the patents be recorded at the discounted value of expected net royalty receipts.

Instructions

(a) What is the meaning of "discounted value of expected net receipts"? Explain.
(b) How would such a value be calculated for net royalty receipts?
(c) What basis of valuation for Ferry's patents would be generally accepted in accounting? Give supporting reasons for this basis.
(d) Assuming no practical problems of implementation, and ignoring generally accepted accounting principles, what is the preferable basis of valuation for patents? Explain.
(e) What would be the preferable theoretical basis of amortization? Explain.
(f) What recognition, if any, should be made of the infringement litigation in the financial statements for the year ending September 30, 2014? Discuss.

(AICPA adapted)

CA12-3 (Accounting for Research and Development Costs) Cuevas Co. is in the process of developing a revolutionary new product. A new division of the company was formed to develop, manufacture, and market this new product. As of year-end (December 31, 2014), the new product has not been manufactured for resale. However, a prototype unit was built and is in operation.

Throughout 2014, the new division incurred certain costs. These costs include design and engineering studies, prototype manufacturing costs, administrative expenses (including salaries of administrative personnel), and market research costs. In addition, approximately $900,000 in equipment (with an estimated useful life of 10 years) was purchased for use in developing and manufacturing the new product. Approximately $315,000 of this equipment was built specifically for the design development of the new product. The remaining $585,000 of equipment was used to manufacture the pre-production prototype and will be used to manufacture the new product once it is in commercial production.

Instructions

(a) How are "research" and "development" defined in the authoritative literature (GAAP)?
(b) Briefly indicate the practical and conceptual reasons for the conclusion reached by the Financial Accounting Standards Board on accounting and reporting practices for research and development costs.
(c) In accordance with GAAP, how should the various costs of Cuevas described above be recorded on the financial statements for the year ended December 31, 2014?

(AICPA adapted)

CA12-4 (Accounting for Research and Development Costs) Czeslaw Corporation's research and development department has an idea for a project it believes will culminate in a new product that would be very profitable for the company. Because the project will be very expensive, the department requests approval from the company's controller, Jeff Reid.

Reid recognizes that corporate profits have been down lately and is hesitant to approve a project that will incur significant expenses that cannot be capitalized due to the requirements of the authoritative literature. He knows that if they hire an outside firm that does the work and obtains a patent for the process, Czeslaw Corporation can purchase the patent from the outside firm and record the expenditure as an asset. Reid knows that the company's own R&D department is first-rate, and he is confident they can do the work well.

Instructions

Answer the following questions.

(a) Who are the stakeholders in this situation?
(b) What are the ethical issues involved?
(c) What should Reid do?

USING YOUR JUDGMENT

FINANCIAL REPORTING

Financial Reporting Problem

P&G

The Procter & Gamble Company (P&G)

The financial statements of P&G are presented in Appendix 5B. The company's complete annual report, including the notes to the financial statements, can be accessed at the book's companion website, **www.wiley.com/college/kieso**.

Instructions

Refer to P&G's financial statements and the accompanying notes to answer the following questions.

(a) Does P&G report any intangible assets, especially goodwill, in its 2011 financial statements and accompanying notes?

(b) How much research and development (R&D) cost was expensed by P&G in 2010 and 2011? What percentage of sales revenue and net income did P&G spend on R&D in 2010 and 2011?

Comparative Analysis Case

The Coca-Cola Company and PepsiCo, Inc.

Instructions

Go to the book's companion website and use information found there to answer the following questions related to **The Coca-Cola Company** and **PepsiCo, Inc.**

(a) **(1)** What amounts for intangible assets were reported in their respective balance sheets by Coca-Cola and PepsiCo?

(2) What percentage of total assets is each of these reported amounts?

(3) What was the change in the amount of intangibles from 2010 to 2011 for Coca-Cola and PepsiCo?

(b) **(1)** On what basis and over what periods of time did Coca-Cola and PepsiCo amortize their intangible assets?

(2) What were the amounts of accumulated amortization reported by Coca-Cola and PepsiCo at the end of 2011 and 2010?

(3) What was the composition of the identifiable and unidentifiable intangible assets reported by Coca-Cola and PepsiCo at the end of 2011?

Financial Statement Analysis Cases

Case 1: Merck and Johnson & Johnson

Merck & Co., Inc. and Johnson & Johnson are two leading producers of health-care products. Each has considerable assets, and each expends considerable funds each year toward the development of new products. The development of a new health-care product is often very expensive, and risky. New products frequently must undergo considerable testing before approval for distribution to the public. For example, it took Johnson & Johnson 4 years and $200 million to develop its 1-DAY ACUVUE contact lenses. Below are some basic data compiled from the financial statements of these two companies.

(all dollars in millions)	Johnson & Johnson	Merck
Total assets	$53,317	$42,573
Total revenue	47,348	22,939
Net income	8,509	5,813
Research and development expense	5,203	4,010
Intangible assets	11,842	2,765

Instructions

(a) What kinds of intangible assets might a health-care products company have? Does the composition of these intangibles matter to investors—that is, would it be perceived differently if all of Merck's intangibles were goodwill than if all of its intangibles were patents?

(b) Suppose the president of Merck has come to you for advice. He has noted that by eliminating research and development expenditures the company could have reported $4 billion more in net income. He is frustrated because much of the research never results in a product, or the products take years to develop. He says shareholders are eager for higher returns, so he is considering eliminating research and development expenditures for at least a couple of years. What would you advise?

(c) The notes to Merck's financial statements note that Merck has goodwill of $1.1 billion. Where does recorded goodwill come from? Is it necessarily a good thing to have a lot of goodwill on a company's books?

Case 2: Analysis of Goodwill

As a new intern for the local branch office of a national brokerage firm, you are excited to get an assignment that allows you to use your accounting expertise. Your supervisor provides you the spreadsheet below, which contains data for the most recent quarter for three companies that the firm has been recommending to its clients as "buys." Each of the companies' returns on assets has outperformed their industry cohorts in the past. But, given recent challenges in their markets, there is concern that the companies may experience operating challenges and lower earnings. (All numbers in millions, except return on assets.)

	A	B	C	D	E
1	Company	Fair Value of Company	Book Value (Net Assets)	Carrying Value of Goodwill	Return on Assets
2	Sprint Nextel	$36,361	$51,271	$30,718	3.5%
3	Washington Mutual	11,742	23,941	9,062	2.4%
4	E* Trade Financial	1,639	4,104	2,035	5.6%
5					

Instructions

(a) The fair value for each of these companies is lower than the corresponding book value. What implications does this have for each company's future prospects?

(b) To date, none of these companies has recorded goodwill impairments. Your supervisor suspects that they will need to record impairments in the near future, but he is unsure about the goodwill impairment rules. Is it likely that these companies will recognize impairments? Explain.

(c) Estimate the amount of goodwill impairment for each company and prepare the journal entry to record the impairment. For each company, you may assume that the book value less the carrying value of the goodwill approximates the fair value of the companies' net assets.

(d) Discuss the effects of your entries in part (c) on your evaluation of these companies based on the return on assets ratio.

Accounting, Analysis, and Principles

On January 2, 2014, Raconteur Corp. reported the following intangible assets: (1) copyright with a carrying value of $15,000, and (2) a trade name with a carrying value of $8,500. The trade name has a remaining life of 5 years and can be renewed at nominal cost indefinitely. The copyright has a remaining life of 10 years.

At December 31, 2014, Raconteur assessed the intangible assets for possible impairment and developed the following information.

	Estimated Undiscounted Expected Future Cash Flows	Estimated Fair Value
Copyright	$20,000	$16,000
Trade name	10,000	5,000

Accounting

Prepare any journal entries required for Raconteur's intangible assets at December 31, 2014.

Analysis

Many stock analysts indicate a preference for less-volatile operating income measures. Such measures make it easier to predict future income and cash flows, using reported income measures. How does the accounting for impairments of intangible assets affect the volatility of operating income?

Principles

Many accounting issues involve a trade-off between the primary characteristics of relevant and representationally faithful information. How does the accounting for intangible asset impairments reflect this trade-off?

BRIDGE TO THE PROFESSION

Professional Research: FASB Codification

King Company is contemplating the purchase of a smaller company, which is a distributor of King's products. Top management of King is convinced that the acquisition will result in significant synergies in its selling and distribution functions. The financial management group (of which you are a part) has been asked to prepare some analysis of the effects of the acquisition on the combined company's financial statements. This is the first acquisition for King, and some of the senior staff insist that based on their recollection of goodwill accounting, any goodwill recorded on the acquisition will result in a "drag" on future earnings for goodwill amortization. Other younger members on the staff argue that goodwill accounting has changed. Your supervisor asks you to research this issue.

Instructions

If your school has a subscription to the FASB Codification, go to *http://aaahq.org/asclogin.cfm* to log in and prepare responses to the following. Provide Codification references for your responses.

(a) Identify the accounting literature that addresses goodwill and other intangible assets.

(b) Define goodwill.

(c) Is goodwill subject to amortization? Explain.

(d) When goodwill is recognized by a subsidiary, should it be tested for impairment at the consolidated level or the subsidiary level? Discuss.

Additional Professional Resources

See the book's companion website, at **www.wiley.com/college/kieso**, for professional simulations as well as other study resources.

IFRS INSIGHTS

There are some significant differences between IFRS and GAAP in the accounting for both intangible assets and impairments. IFRS related to intangible assets is presented in *IAS 38* ("Intangible Assets"). IFRS related to impairments is found in *IAS 36* ("Impairment of Assets").

10 LEARNING OBJECTIVE
Compare the accounting for intangible assets under GAAP and IFRS.

RELEVANT FACTS

Following are the key similarities and differences between GAAP and IFRS related to intangible assets.

Similarities

- Like GAAP, under IFRS intangible assets (1) lack physical substance and (2) are not financial instruments. In addition, under IFRS an intangible asset is identifiable. To be identifiable, an intangible asset must either be separable from the company (can be sold or transferred) or it arises from a contractual or legal right from which economic benefits will flow to the company. Fair value is used as the measurement basis for intangible assets under IFRS, if it is more clearly evident.
- With issuance of a recent converged statement on business combinations (*IFRS 3* and *SFAS No. 141—Revised*), IFRS and GAAP are very similar for intangibles acquired in a business combination. That is, companies recognize an intangible asset separately from goodwill if the intangible represents contractual or legal rights or is capable of being separated or divided and sold, transferred, licensed, rented, or exchanged. In addition, under both GAAP and IFRS, companies recognize acquired in-process research and development (IPR&D) as a separate intangible asset if it meets the definition of an intangible asset and its fair value can be measured reliably.
- As in GAAP, under IFRS the costs associated with research and development are segregated into the two components. Costs in the research phase are always expensed under both IFRS and GAAP.

Differences

- IFRS permits revaluation on limited-life intangible assets. Revaluations are not permitted for goodwill and other indefinite-life intangible assets.
- IFRS permits some capitalization of internally generated intangible assets (e.g., brand value) if it is probable there will be a future benefit and the amount can be reliably measured. GAAP requires expensing of all costs associated with internally generated intangibles.
- IFRS requires an impairment test at each reporting date for long-lived assets and intangibles, and records an impairment if the asset's carrying amount exceeds its recoverable amount. The recoverable amount is the higher of the asset's fair value less costs to sell and its value-in-use. **Value-in-use** is the future cash flows to be derived from the particular assets, discounted to present value. Under GAAP, impairment loss is measured as the excess of the carrying amount over the asset's fair value.
- IFRS allows reversal of impairment losses when there has been a change in economic conditions or in the expected use of limited-life intangibles. Under GAAP, impairment losses cannot be reversed for assets to be held and used; the impairment loss

results in a new cost basis for the asset. IFRS and GAAP are similar in the accounting for impairments of assets held for disposal.

- Under IFRS, costs in the development phase of a research and development project are capitalized once technological feasibility (referred to as **economic viability**) is achieved.

ABOUT THE NUMBERS

Development Costs

Businesses frequently incur costs on a variety of intangible resources, such as scientific or technological knowledge, market research, intellectual property, and brand names. These costs are commonly referred to as research and development (R&D) costs. Intangible assets that might arise from these expenditures include patents, computer software, copyrights, and trademarks. For example, Nokia incurred R&D costs to develop its cell phones, resulting in patents related to its technology. In determining the accounting for these costs, Nokia must determine whether its R&D project is at a sufficiently advanced stage to be considered economically viable. To perform this assessment, Nokia evaluates costs incurred during the research phase and the development phase. Illustration IFRS12-1 indicates the two stages of research and development activities, along with the accounting treatment for costs incurred during these phases.

ILLUSTRATION IFRS12-1
Research and Development Stages

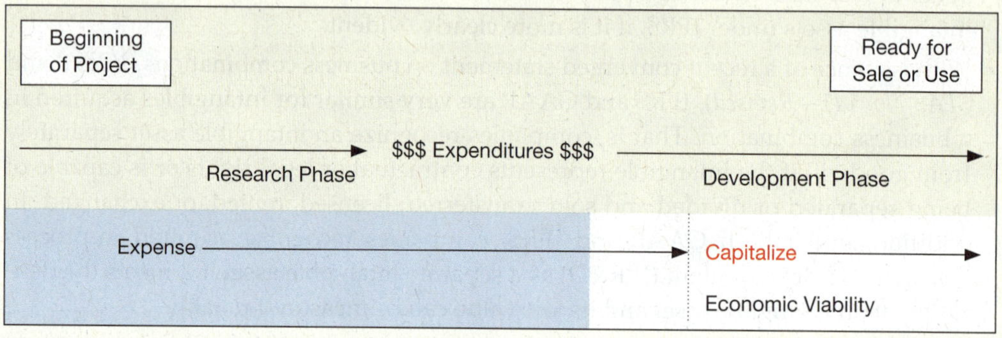

As indicated, all costs incurred in the research phase are expensed as incurred. Once a project moves to the development phase, certain development costs are capitalized. Specifically, development costs are capitalized when certain criteria are met, indicating that an economically viable intangible asset will result from the R&D project. In essence, economic viability indicates that the project is far enough along in the process such that the economic benefits of the R&D project will flow to the company. Therefore, development costs incurred from that point forward meet the recognition criteria and should be recorded as an intangible asset.

In summary, companies expense all research phase costs and some development phase costs. Certain development costs are capitalized once economic viability criteria are met.

Impairment of Intangible Assets

An intangible asset is **impaired** when a company is not able to recover the asset's carrying amount either through using it or by selling it. As discussed in Chapter 11, to determine whether a long-lived asset (property, plant, and equipment, or intangible asset) is impaired, a review is made of the asset's cash-generating ability through use or sale. If the carrying amount is higher than the recoverable amount, the difference is an impairment loss. If the recoverable amount is greater than the carrying amount, no impairment is recorded. The specific procedures for recording impairments depend on the type of intangible asset—limited-life or indefinite-life (including goodwill).

Impairment of Limited-Life Intangibles

The rules that apply to **impairments of property, plant, and equipment also apply to limited-life intangibles.** At each statement of financial position date, a company should review limited-life intangibles for impairment. Information indicating that an impairment test should be performed might be internal (e.g., physical damage or adverse changes in performance) or external (e.g., adverse changes in the business or regulatory environment, or technological or competitive developments). If there is an indication that an intangible asset is impaired, the company performs an impairment test: compare the carrying value of the intangible asset to the recoverable amount.

Recall that **recoverable amount** is defined as the higher of fair value less costs to sell or value-in-use. Fair value less costs to sell means what the asset could be sold for after deducting costs of disposal. Value-in-use is the present value of cash flows expected from the future use and eventual sale of the asset at the end of its useful life. The **impairment loss** is the carrying amount of the asset less the recoverable amount of the impaired asset. As with other impairments, the loss is reported in profit or loss.

Companies generally report the loss in the "Other income and expense" section. To illustrate, assume that Lerch, Inc. has a patent on how to extract oil from shale rock, with a carrying value of $5,000,000 at the end of 2014. Unfortunately, several recent non-shale-oil discoveries adversely affected the demand for shale-oil technology, indicating that the patent is impaired. Lerch determines the recoverable amount for the patent, based on value-in-use (because there is no active market for the patent). Lerch estimates the patent's value-in-use at $2,000,000, based on the discounted expected future net cash flows at its market rate of interest. Illustration IFRS12-2 shows the impairment loss computation (based on value-in-use).

Carrying value of patent	$5,000,000
Recoverable amount (based on value-in-use)	(2,000,000)
Loss on impairment	$3,000,000

ILLUSTRATION IFRS12-2
Computation of Loss on Impairment of Patent

Lerch records this loss as follows.

Loss on Impairment	3,000,000	
Patents		3,000,000

After recognizing the impairment, the recoverable amount of $2,000,000 is the new cost basis of the patent. Lerch should amortize the patent's recoverable amount (new carrying amount) over its remaining useful life or legal life, whichever is shorter.

Reversal of Impairment Loss

What happens if a review in a future year indicates that an intangible asset is no longer impaired because the recoverable amount of the asset is higher than the carrying amount? In that case, the impairment loss may be reversed. To illustrate, continuing the Lerch patent example, assume that the remaining life of the patent is five years with zero residual value. Recall the carrying value of the patent after impairment is $2,000,000 ($5,000,000 − $3,000,000). Thus, Lerch's amortization is $400,000 ($2,000,000 ÷ 5) over the remaining five years of the patent's life. The amortization expense and related carrying amount after the impairment is shown in Illustration IFRS12-3.

Early in 2016, based on improving conditions in the market for shale-oil technology, Lerch remeasures the recoverable amount of the patent to be $1,750,000. In this case, Lerch reverses a portion of the recognized impairment loss with the following entry.

Patents ($1,750,000 − $1,600,000)	150,000	
Recovery of Loss on Impairment		150,000

ILLUSTRATION IFRS12-3
Post-Impairment Carrying Value of Patent

Year	Amortization Expense	Carrying Amount	
2015	$400,000	$1,600,000	($2,000,000 − $400,000)
2016	400,000	1,200,000	($1,600,000 − $400,000)
2017	400,000	800,000	($1,200,000 − $400,000)
2018	400,000	400,000	($800,000 − $400,000)
2019	400,000	0	($400,000 − $400,000)

The recovery of the impairment loss is reported in the "Other income and expense" section of the income statement. The carrying amount of the patent is now $1,750,000 ($1,600,000 + $150,000). Assuming the remaining life of the patent is four years, Lerch records $437,500 ($1,750,000 ÷ 4) amortization expense in 2016.

Impairment of Indefinite-Life Intangibles Other Than Goodwill

Companies test indefinite-life intangibles (including goodwill) for impairment annually. To illustrate, assume that Arcon Radio purchased a broadcast license for $2,000,000. The license is renewable every 10 years if the company provides appropriate service and does not violate Government Communications Commission (GCC) rules. Arcon Radio has renewed the license with the GCC twice, at a minimal cost. Because it expects cash flows to last indefinitely, Arcon reports the license as an indefinite-life intangible asset. Recently, the GCC decided to issue significantly more of these licenses, which will reduce the value of Arcon's license. Based on recent auctions of similar licenses, Arcon Radio estimates the fair value less costs to sell (the recoverable amount) of its license to be $1,500,000. Arcon therefore reports an impairment loss of $500,000, computed as follows.

ILLUSTRATION IFRS12-4
Computation of Loss on Impairment of Broadcast License

Carrying value of broadcast license	$ 2,000,000
Recoverable amount (based on fair value less costs to sell)	(1,500,000)
Loss on impairment	$ 500,000

Impairment of Goodwill

The timing of the impairment test for goodwill is the same as that for other indefinite-life intangibles. That is, companies must test goodwill at least annually. However, because goodwill generates cash flows only in combination with other assets, the impairment test is conducted based on the cash-generating unit to which the goodwill is assigned. Recall from our discussion in Chapter 11 that companies identify a **cash-generating unit** based on the smallest identifiable group of assets that generate cash flows independently of the cash flows from other assets. Under IFRS, when a company records goodwill in a business combination, it must assign the goodwill to the cash-generating unit that is expected to benefit from the synergies and other benefits arising from the business combination.

To illustrate, assume that Kohlbuy Corporation has three divisions. It purchased one division, Pritt Products, four years ago for $2 million. Unfortunately, Pritt experienced operating losses over the last three quarters. Kohlbuy management is now reviewing the division (the cash-generating unit), for purposes of its annual impairment testing. Illustration IFRS12-5 lists the Pritt Division's net assets, including the associated goodwill of $900,000 from the purchase.

ILLUSTRATION IFRS12-5
Net Assets of Pritt Division, Including Goodwill

Property, plant, and equipment (net)	$ 800,000
Goodwill	900,000
Inventory	700,000
Receivables	300,000
Cash	200,000
Accounts and notes payable	(500,000)
Net assets	$2,400,000

Kohlbuy determines the recoverable amount for the Pritt Division to be $2,800,000, based on a value-in-use estimate. **Because the recoverable amount of the division exceeds the carrying amount of the net assets, Kohlbuy does not recognize any impairment.** However, if the recoverable amount for the Pritt Division were less than the carrying amount of the net assets, then Kohlbuy must record an impairment. To illustrate, assume that the recoverable amount for the Pritt Division is $1,900,000 instead of $2,800,000. Illustration IFRS12-6 computes the amount of the impairment loss to be recorded.

Recoverable amount of Pritt Division	$ 1,900,000
Net identifiable assets	(2,400,000)
Loss on impairment	$ 500,000

ILLUSTRATION IFRS12-6
Determination of Impairment for the Pritt Division

Kohlbuy makes the following entry to record the impairment.

Loss on Impairment	500,000	
Goodwill		500,000

Following this entry, the carrying value of the goodwill is $400,000 ($900,000 − $500,000). If conditions change in subsequent periods, such that the recoverable amount of the Pritt Division's assets other than goodwill exceeds their carrying value, Kohlbuy may reverse an impairment loss on the Pritt Division assets other than goodwill. **Goodwill impairment loss reversals are not permitted.**

ON THE HORIZON

The IASB and FASB have identified a project, in a very preliminary stage, which would consider expanded recognition of internally generated intangible assets. As indicated, IFRS permits more recognition of intangibles compared to GAAP. Thus, it will be challenging to develop converged standards for intangible assets, given the long-standing prohibition on capitalizing internally generated intangible assets and research and development in GAAP. Learn more about the timeline for the intangible asset project at the IASB website *http://www.iasb.org/current_Projects/IASB_Projects/IASB_Work_Plan.htm.*

IFRS SELF-TEST QUESTIONS

1. All of the following are key similarities between GAAP and IFRS with respect to accounting for intangible assets **except**:
   (a) for accounting purposes, costs associated with research and development activities are segregated into the two components.
   (b) the accounting for intangibles acquired in a business combination.
   (c) recovery of impairments on intangibles other than goodwill.
   (d) the accounting for impairments of assets held for disposal.
2. Research and development costs are:
   (a) expensed under GAAP.
   (b) expensed under IFRS.
   (c) expensed under both GAAP and IFRS.
   (d) None of the above.
3. Which of the following statements is **correct**?
   (a) Both IFRS and GAAP permit revaluation of property, plant, and equipment, and intangible assets (except for goodwill).
   (b) GAAP permits capitalization of development costs.
   (c) IFRS requires capitalization of research and development costs once economic viability is met.
   (d) IFRS requires capitalization of development costs once economic viability is met.

4. A loss on impairment of an intangible asset under IFRS is the asset's:
   (a) carrying amount less the expected future net cash flows.
   (b) carrying amount less its recoverable amount.
   (c) recoverable amount less the expected future net cash flows.
   (d) book value less its fair value.
5. Recovery of impairment is recognized under IFRS for all the following **except**:
   (a) patent held for sale. (c) trademark.
   (b) patent held for use. (d) goodwill.

IFRS CONCEPTS AND APPLICATION

IFRS12-1 Where can authoritative IFRS guidance related to intangible assets be found?

IFRS12-2 Briefly describe some of the similarities and differences between GAAP and IFRS with respect to the accounting for intangible assets.

IFRS12-3 Briefly discuss the convergence efforts that are underway in the area of intangible assets.

IFRS12-4 Treasure Land Corporation incurred the following costs in 2014.

Cost of laboratory research aimed at discovery of new knowledge	$120,000
Cost of testing in search for product alternatives	100,000
Cost of engineering activity required to advance the design of a product to the manufacturing stage	210,000
Prototype testing subsequent to meeting economic viability	75,000
	$505,000

Prepare the necessary 2014 journal entry(ies) for Treasure Land.

IFRS12-5 Indicate whether the following items are capitalized or expensed in the current year.

(a) Purchase cost of a patent from a competitor.
(b) Research costs.
(c) Development costs (after achieving economic viability).
(d) Organizational costs.
(e) Costs incurred internally to create goodwill.

IFRS12-6 Kenoly Corporation owns a patent that has a carrying amount of $300,000. Kenoly expects future net cash flows from this patent to total $210,000 over its remaining life of 10 years. The recoverable amount of the patent is $110,000. Prepare Kenoly's journal entry, if necessary, to record the loss on impairment.

IFRS12-7 Use the information in IFRS12-6. Assume that at the end of the year following the impairment (after recording amortization expense), the estimated recoverable amount for the patent is $130,000. Prepare Kenoly's journal entry, if needed.

IFRS12-8 Waters Corporation purchased Johnson Company 3 years ago and at that time recorded goodwill of $400,000. The Johnson Division's net assets, including the goodwill, have a carrying amount of $800,000. The recoverable amount of the division is estimated to be $1,000,000. Prepare Waters' journal entry, if necessary, to record impairment of the goodwill.

IFRS12-9 Use the information provided in IFRS12-8. Assume that the recoverable amount of the division is estimated to be $750,000. Prepare Waters' journal entry, if necessary, to record impairment of the goodwill.

IFRS12-10 Margaret Avery Company from time to time embarks on a research program when a special project seems to offer possibilities. In 2012, the company expends $325,000 on a research project, but by the end of 2012, it is impossible to determine whether any benefit will be derived from it.

(a) What account should be charged for the $325,000, and how should it be shown in the financial statements?
(b) The project is completed in 2013, and a successful patent is obtained. The R&D costs to complete the project are $130,000 ($36,000 of these costs were incurred after achieving economic viability). The

administrative and legal expenses incurred in obtaining patent number 472-1001-84 in 2013 total $24,000. The patent has an expected useful life of 5 years. Record these costs in journal entry form. Also, record patent amortization (full year) in 2013.

(c) In 2014, the company successfully defends the patent in extended litigation at a cost of $47,200, thereby extending the patent life to December 31, 2021. What is the proper way to account for this cost? Also, record patent amortization (full year) in 2014.

(d) Additional engineering and consulting costs incurred in 2014 required to advance the design of a new version of the product to the manufacturing stage total $60,000. These costs enhance the design of the product considerably, but it is highly uncertain if there will be a market for the new version of the product. Discuss the proper accounting treatment for this cost.

Professional Research

IFRS12-11 King Company is contemplating the purchase of a smaller company, which is a distributor of King's products. Top management of King is convinced that the acquisition will result in significant synergies in its selling and distribution functions. The financial management group (of which you are a part) has been asked to analyze the effects of the acquisition on the combined company's financial statements. This is the first acquisition for King, and some of the senior staff insist that based on their recollection of goodwill accounting, any goodwill recorded on the acquisition will result in a "drag" on future earnings for goodwill amortization. Other younger members on the staff argue that goodwill accounting has changed. Your supervisor asks you to research this issue.

Instructions

Access the IFRS authoritative literature at the IASB website (*http://eifrs.iasb.org/*). (Click on the IFRS tab and then register for free eIFRS access if necessary.) When you have accessed the documents, you can use the search tool in your Internet browser to respond to the following questions. (Provide paragraph citations.)

(a) Identify the accounting literature that addresses goodwill and other intangible assets.
(b) Define goodwill.
(c) Is goodwill subject to amortization? Explain.
(d) When goodwill is recognized by a subsidiary, should it be tested for impairment at the consolidated level or the subsidiary level? Discuss.

International Financial Reporting Problem
Marks and Spencer plc

IFRS12-12 The financial statements of **Marks and Spencer plc (M&S)** are available at the book's companion website or can be accessed at *http://corporate.marksandspencer.com/documents/publications/2012/Annual_Report_2012.*

Instructions

Refer to M&S's financial statements and the accompanying notes to answer the following questions.

(a) Does M&S report any intangible assets and goodwill in its financial statements and accompanying notes? Briefly explain.
(b) How much selling and marketing expenses does M&S report in 2011 and 2012? Briefly discuss the significance of these expenses to M&S's operating results.

ANSWERS TO IFRS SELF-TEST QUESTIONS

1. c **2.** a **3.** d **4.** b **5.** d

Remember to check the book's companion website to find additional resources for this chapter.

CHAPTER 13 Current Liabilities and Contingencies

LEARNING OBJECTIVES

After studying this chapter, you should be able to:

1. Describe the nature, type, and valuation of current liabilities.
2. Explain the classification issues of short-term debt expected to be refinanced.
3. Identify types of employee-related liabilities.
4. Identify the criteria used to account for and disclose gain and loss contingencies.
5. Explain the accounting for different types of loss contingencies.
6. Indicate how to present and analyze liabilities and contingencies.

Now You See It, Now You Don't

A look at the liabilities side of the balance sheet of the company **Beru AG Corporation**, dated March 31, 2003, shows how international standards have changed regarding the reporting of financial information. Here is how one liability was shown on this date:

Anticipated losses arising from pending transactions	3,285,000 euros

Do you believe a liability should be reported for such transactions? *Anticipated losses* means the losses have not yet occurred. *Pending transactions* means that the condition that might cause the loss has also not occurred. So where is the liability? To whom does the company owe something? Where is the obligation?

German accounting rules in 2003 were permissive. They allowed companies to report liabilities for possible future events. In essence, the establishment of this general-purpose "liability" provides a buffer for Beru if losses do materialize. If you take a more skeptical view, you might say the accounting rules let Beru smooth its income by charging expenses in good years and reducing expenses in bad years.

The story has a happy ending: European companies switched to International Financial Reporting Standards (IFRS) in 2005. Under IFRS, liabilities like "Anticipated losses arising from pending transactions" disappear. So when we look at Beru's 2005 financial statements, we find a note stating that the company has reported as liabilities only obligations arising from past transactions that can be reasonably estimated.

Standard-setters continue to work on the financial reporting of certain "contingent" liabilities, such as those related to pending lawsuits and other possible losses for which a company might be liable. As you will learn in this chapter, standard-setters have provided much more transparency in reporting liability-type transactions. However, much still needs to be done. For example, the IASB is considering major changes in how to recognize and measure contingent liabilities. The task will not be easy. Consider a simple illustration involving a company that sells hamburgers:

- The hamburgers are sold in a jurisdiction where the law states that the seller must pay $100,000 to each customer that purchases a contaminated hamburger;
- At the end of the reporting period, the company has sold one hamburger; and
- Past experience indicates there is a one in a million chance that a hamburger sold by the entity is contaminated. No other information is available.

Does the company have a liability? What is the conceptual justification, if any, to record a liability or for that matter, not to record a liability? And if you conclude that the sale of the hamburger results in a liability, how do you measure it? Another way to ask the question is whether the hamburger issue is a recognition issue or a measurement issue. This example illustrates some of the difficult questions that the IASB faces in this area.

The FASB recently proposed expanded disclosure about the nature of contingencies, more quantitative and qualitative background on contingencies, and, maybe most welcome of all, required tabular presentation of the changes in contingencies, including explanation of the changes. Note that these disclosures are similar to those required in IFRS. What's not to like about these enhanced disclosures? Well quite a bit, according to early responses by some companies and the legal profession. These parties are concerned that the information in these enhanced disclosures could be used against them in a lawsuit, and they are voicing strong opposition to the proposed rules. We do not know the end of this liability story. However, the controversy over the proposed rules illustrates the challenges of developing accounting rules for liabilities that meet the needs of investors while avoiding harm to the companies reporting the information.

CONCEPTUAL FOCUS

> See the **Underlying Concepts** on pages 702, 707, 712, 721, and 725.

> Read the **Evolving Issue** on page 730 for a discussion of how to account for greenhouse gases.

INTERNATIONAL FOCUS

> See the **International Perspectives** on pages 706, 727, and 729.

> Read the **IFRS Insights** on pages 753–761 for a discussion of:
—Refinancing criteria
—Provisions
—Contingencies

PREVIEW OF CHAPTER 13

As our opening story indicates, the convergence of GAAP and IFRS should lead to improved reporting of liabilities. In this chapter, we explain the basic issues related to accounting and reporting for current and contingent liabilities. The content and organization of the chapter are as follows.

Current Liabilities and Contingencies

Current Liabilities	Contingencies	Presentation and Analysis
• Accounts payable • Notes payable • Current maturities of long-term debt • Short-term obligations • Dividends payable • Customer advances and deposits, unearned revenues • Taxes payable • Employee-related liabilities	• Gain contingencies • Loss contingencies	• Presentation of current liabilities • Presentation of contingencies • Analysis of current liabilities

CURRENT LIABILITIES

LEARNING OBJECTIVE 1
Describe the nature, type, and valuation of current liabilities.

The question, "What is a liability?" is not easy to answer. For example, is preferred stock a liability or an ownership claim? The first reaction is to say that preferred stock is in fact an ownership claim, and companies should report it as part of stockholders' equity. In fact, preferred stock has many elements of debt as well.[1] The issuer (and in some cases the holder) often has the right to call the stock within a specific period of time—making it similar to a repayment of principal. The dividend on the preferred stock is in many cases almost guaranteed (the cumulative provision)—making it look like interest. As a result, preferred stock is but one of many financial instruments that are difficult to classify.[2]

Underlying Concepts

To determine the appropriate classification of specific financial instruments, companies need proper definitions of assets, liabilities, and equities. They often use the conceptual framework definitions as the basis for resolving controversial classification issues.

To help resolve some of these controversies, the FASB, as part of its conceptual framework, defined **liabilities** as **"probable future sacrifices of economic benefits arising from present obligations of a particular entity to transfer assets or provide services to other entities in the future as a result of past transactions or events."**[3] In other words, a liability has three essential characteristics:

1. It is a present obligation that entails settlement by probable future transfer or use of cash, goods, or services.
2. It is an unavoidable obligation.
3. The transaction or other event creating the obligation has already occurred.

Because liabilities involve future disbursements of assets or services, one of their most important features is the date on which they are payable. A company must satisfy currently maturing obligations in the ordinary course of business to continue operating. Liabilities with a more distant due date do not, as a rule, represent a claim on the company's current resources. They are therefore in a slightly different category. This feature gives rise to the basic division of liabilities into (1) current liabilities and (2) long-term debt.

Recall that current assets are cash or other assets that companies reasonably expect to convert into cash, sell, or consume in operations within a single operating cycle or within a year (if completing more than one cycle each year). **Current liabilities** are **"obligations whose liquidation is reasonably expected to require use of existing resources properly classified as current assets, or the creation of other current liabilities."** **[2]** This definition has gained wide acceptance because it recognizes operating cycles of varying lengths in different industries. This definition also considers the important relationship between current assets and current liabilities. **[3]**

The **operating cycle** is the period of time elapsing between the acquisition of goods and services involved in the manufacturing process and the final cash realization resulting from sales and subsequent collections. Industries that manufacture products requiring an aging process, and certain capital-intensive industries, have an operating cycle of considerably more than one year. On the other hand, most retail and service establishments have several operating cycles within a year.

See the FASB Codification section (page 733).

[1]This illustration is not just a theoretical exercise. In practice, a number of preferred stock issues have all the characteristics of a debt instrument, except that they are called and legally classified as preferred stock. In some cases, the IRS has even permitted companies to treat the dividend payments as interest expense for tax purposes.

[2]The FASB has issued a standard to address the accounting for some of these securities **[1]** and is working with the IASB on a broader project to address the accounting for securities with debt and equity features.

[3]"Elements of Financial Statements of Business Enterprises," *Statement of Financial Accounting Concepts No. 6* (Stamford, Conn.: FASB, 1980).

Here are some typical current liabilities:

1. Accounts payable.
2. Notes payable.
3. Current maturities of long-term debt.
4. Short-term obligations expected to be refinanced.
5. Dividends payable.
6. Customer advances and deposits.
7. Unearned revenues.
8. Sales taxes payable.
9. Income taxes payable.
10. Employee-related liabilities.

Accounts Payable

Accounts payable, or **trade accounts payable**, are balances owed to others for goods, supplies, or services purchased on open account. Accounts payable arise because of the time lag between the receipt of services or acquisition of title to assets and the payment for them. The terms of the sale (e.g., 2/10, n/30 or 1/10, E.O.M.) usually state this period of extended credit, commonly 30 to 60 days.

Most companies record liabilities for purchases of goods upon receipt of the goods. If title has passed to the purchaser before receipt of the goods, the company should record the transaction at the time of title passage. A company must pay special attention to transactions occurring near the end of one accounting period and at the beginning of the next. It needs to ascertain that the record of goods received (the inventory) agrees with the liability (accounts payable), and that it records both in the proper period.

Measuring the amount of an account payable poses no particular difficulty. The invoice received from the creditor specifies the due date and the exact outlay in money that is necessary to settle the account. The only calculation that may be necessary concerns the amount of cash discount. See Chapter 8 for illustrations of entries related to accounts payable and purchase discounts.

Notes Payable

Notes payable are written promises to pay a certain sum of money on a specified future date. They may arise from purchases, financing, or other transactions. Some industries require notes (often referred to as **trade notes payable**) as part of the sales/purchases transaction in lieu of the normal extension of open account credit. Notes payable to banks or loan companies generally arise from cash loans. Companies classify notes as short-term or long-term, depending on the payment due date. Notes may also be interest-bearing or zero-interest-bearing.

Interest-Bearing Note Issued

Assume that Castle National Bank agrees to lend $100,000 on March 1, 2014, to Landscape Co. if Landscape signs a $100,000, 6 percent, four-month note. Landscape records the cash received on March 1 as follows.

March 1		
Cash	100,000	
Notes Payable		100,000
(To record issuance of 6%, 4-month note to Castle National Bank)		

If Landscape prepares financial statements semiannually, it makes the adjusting entry (shown at the top of page 704) to recognize interest expense and interest payable of $2,000 ($100,000 × 6% × 4/12) at June 30.

June 30		
Interest Expense	2,000	
Interest Payable		2,000
(To accrue interest for 4 months on Castle National Bank note)		

If Landscape prepares financial statements monthly, its adjusting entry at the end of each month is $500 ($100,000 × 6% × 1/12).

At maturity (July 1), Landscape must pay the face value of the note ($100,000) plus $2,000 interest ($100,000 × 6% × 4/12). Landscape records payment of the note and accrued interest as follows.

July 1		
Notes Payable	100,000	
Interest Payable	2,000	
Cash		102,000
(To record payment of Castle National Bank interest-bearing note and accrued interest at maturity)		

Zero-Interest-Bearing Note Issued

A company may issue a zero-interest-bearing note instead of an interest-bearing note. A zero-interest-bearing note does not explicitly state an interest rate on the face of the note. **Interest is still charged**, however. At maturity, the borrower must pay back an amount greater than the cash received at the issuance date. In other words, the borrower receives in cash the present value of the note. The present value equals the face value of the note at maturity minus the interest or discount charged by the lender for the term of the note. In essence, the bank takes its fee "up front" rather than on the date the note matures.

To illustrate, assume that Landscape issues a $102,000, four-month, zero-interest-bearing note to Castle National Bank. The present value of the note is $100,000.[4] Landscape records this transaction as follows.

March 1		
Cash	100,000	
Discount on Notes Payable	2,000	
Notes Payable		102,000
(To record issuance of 4-month, zero-interest-bearing note to Castle National Bank)		

Landscape credits the Notes Payable account for the face value of the note, which is $2,000 more than the actual cash received. It debits the difference between the cash received and the face value of the note to Discount on Notes Payable. **Discount on Notes Payable is a contra account to Notes Payable, and therefore is subtracted from Notes Payable on the balance sheet.** Illustration 13-1 shows the balance sheet presentation on March 1.

ILLUSTRATION 13-1
Balance Sheet Presentation of Discount

Current liabilities		
Notes payable	$102,000	
Less: Discount on notes payable	2,000	$100,000

The amount of the discount, $2,000 in this case, represents the cost of borrowing $100,000 for 4 months. Accordingly, Landscape charges the discount to interest expense over the life of the note. That is, the Discount on Notes Payable balance **represents interest expense chargeable to future periods**. Thus, Landscape should not debit

[4]The bank discount rate used in this example to find the present value is 5.96 percent.

Interest Expense for $2,000 at the time of obtaining the loan. We discuss additional accounting issues related to notes payable in Chapter 14.

Current Maturities of Long-Term Debt

PepsiCo reports as part of its current liabilities the portion of bonds, mortgage notes, and other long-term indebtedness that matures within the next fiscal year. It categorizes this amount as **current maturities of long-term debt**. Companies, like PepsiCo, exclude long-term debts maturing currently as current liabilities if they are to be:

1. Retired by assets accumulated for this purpose that properly have not been shown as current assets,
2. Refinanced, or retired from the proceeds of a new debt issue, or
3. Converted into capital stock.

In these situations, the use of current assets or the creation of other current liabilities does not occur. Therefore, classification as a current liability is inappropriate. A company should disclose the plan for liquidation of such a debt either parenthetically or by a note to the financial statements. When only a part of a long-term debt is to be paid within the next 12 months, as in the case of serial bonds that it retires through a series of annual installments, **the company reports the maturing portion of long-term debt as a current liability**, and the remaining portion as a long-term debt.

However, a company should classify as current any liability that is **due on demand** (callable by the creditor) or will be due on demand within a year (or operating cycle, if longer). Liabilities often become callable by the creditor when there is a violation of the debt agreement. For example, most debt agreements specify a given level of equity to debt be maintained, or specify that working capital be of a minimum amount. If the company violates an agreement, it must classify the debt as current because it is a reasonable expectation that existing working capital will be used to satisfy the debt. Only if a company can show that it is **probable** that it will cure (satisfy) the violation within the grace period specified in the agreements can it classify the debt as noncurrent. [4]

Short-Term Obligations Expected to Be Refinanced

2 LEARNING OBJECTIVE

Explain the classification issues of short-term debt expected to be refinanced.

Short-term obligations are debts scheduled to mature within one year after the date of a company's balance sheet or within its operating cycle, whichever is longer. Some **short-term obligations** are **expected to be refinanced** on a long-term basis. These short-term obligations will not require the use of working capital during the next year (or operating cycle).[5]

At one time, the accounting profession generally supported the exclusion of short-term obligations from current liabilities if they were "expected to be refinanced." But the profession provided no specific guidelines, so companies determined whether a short-term obligation was "expected to be refinanced" based solely on management's **intent** to refinance on a long-term basis. Classification was not clear-cut. For example, a company might obtain a five-year bank loan but handle the actual financing with 90-day notes, which it must keep turning over (renewing). In this case, is the loan a long-term debt or a current liability? Another example was the Penn Central Railroad before it went bankrupt. The railroad was deep into short-term debt but classified it as long-term debt. Why? Because the railroad believed it had commitments from lenders to keep

[5]*Refinancing a short-term obligation on a long-term basis* means either replacing it with a long-term obligation or equity securities, or renewing, extending, or replacing it with short-term obligations for an uninterrupted period extending beyond one year (or the operating cycle, if longer) from the date of the enterprise's balance sheet.

refinancing the short-term debt. When those commitments suddenly disappeared, it was "good-bye Pennsy." As the Greek philosopher Epictetus once said, "Some things in this world are not and yet appear to be."

Refinancing Criteria

To resolve these classification problems, the accounting profession has developed criteria for determining the circumstances under which short-term obligations may be properly excluded from current liabilities. A company is required to exclude a short-term obligation from current liabilities if **both** of the following conditions are met:

1. It must **intend to refinance** the obligation on a long-term basis.
2. It must **demonstrate an ability** to consummate the refinancing. [5]

Intention to refinance on a long-term basis means that the company intends to refinance the short-term obligation so that it will not require the use of working capital during the ensuing fiscal year (or operating cycle, if longer).

The company demonstrates the **ability** to consummate the refinancing by:

(a) **Actually refinancing** the short-term obligation by issuing a long-term obligation or equity securities after the date of the balance sheet but before it is issued; or

(b) Entering into a **financing agreement** that clearly permits the company to refinance the debt on a long-term basis on terms that are readily determinable.

If an actual refinancing occurs, the portion of the short-term obligation to be excluded from current liabilities may not exceed the proceeds from the new obligation or equity securities used to retire the short-term obligation. For example, Montavon Winery had $3,000,000 of short-term debt. Subsequent to the balance sheet date, but before issuing the balance sheet, the company issued 100,000 shares of common stock, intending to use the proceeds to liquidate the short-term debt at its maturity. If Montavon's net proceeds from the sale of the 100,000 shares total $2,000,000, it can exclude from current liabilities only $2,000,000 of the short-term debt.

International Perspective

IFRS requires that the current portion of long-term debt be classified as current unless an agreement to refinance on a long-term basis is completed before the date of the financial statements.

An additional question is whether a company should exclude from current liabilities a short-term obligation if it is paid off after the balance sheet date and replaced by long-term debt before the balance sheet is issued. To illustrate, Marquardt Company pays off short-term debt of $40,000 on January 17, 2015, and issues long-term debt of $100,000 on February 3, 2015. Marquardt's financial statements, dated December 31, 2014, are to be issued March 1, 2015. Should Marquardt exclude the $40,000 short-term debt from current liabilities? No—here's why: Repayment of the short-term obligation required the use of **existing** current assets **before** the company obtained funds through long-term financing. Therefore, Marquardt must include the short-term obligations in current liabilities at the balance sheet date (as shown in Illustration 13-2).

ILLUSTRATION 13-2
Short-Term Debt Paid Off after Balance Sheet Date and Later Replaced by Long-Term Debt

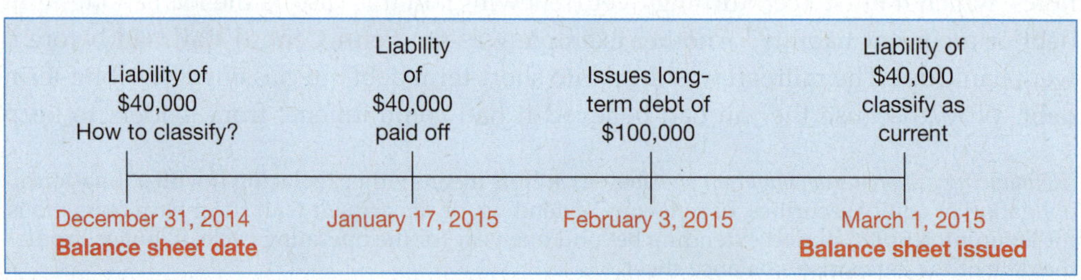

What do the numbers mean? WHAT ABOUT THAT SHORT-TERM DEBT?

The evaluation of credit quality involves more than simply assessing a company's ability to repay loans. Credit analysts also evaluate debt management strategies. Analysts and investors will reward what they view as prudent management decisions with lower debt service costs and a higher stock price. The wrong decisions can bring higher debt costs and lower stock prices.

General Electric Capital Corp., a subsidiary of **General Electric**, experienced the negative effects of market scrutiny of its debt management policies. Analysts complained that GE had been slow to refinance its mountains of short-term debt. GE had issued these current obligations, with maturities of 270 days or less, when interest rates were low. However, in light of expectations that the Fed would raise interest rates, analysts began to worry about the higher interest costs GE would pay when it refinanced these loans. Some analysts recommended that it was time to reduce dependence on short-term credit. The reasoning goes that a shift to more dependable long-term debt, thereby locking in slightly higher rates for the long-term, is the better way to go.

Thus, scrutiny of GE debt strategies led to analysts' concerns about GE's earnings prospects. Investors took the analysis to heart, and GE experienced a two-day 6 percent drop in its stock price. Recently, GE and other companies, such as **UPS**, have responded to these criticisms and have been increasing issuance of long-term debt to lock-in continuing low interest rates.

Sources: Adapted from Steven Vames, "Credit Quality, Stock Investing Seem to Go Hand in Hand," *Wall Street Journal* (April 1, 2002), p. R4; and V. Monga, "Companies Feast on Cheap Money Market for 30-Year Bonds, Priced at Stark Lows, Brings Out GE, UPS and Other Once-Shy Issuers," *Wall Street Journal* (October 8, 2012).

Dividends Payable

A **cash dividend payable** is an amount owed by a corporation to its stockholders as a result of board of directors' authorization. At the date of declaration, the corporation assumes a liability that places the stockholders in the position of creditors in the amount of dividends declared. Because companies always pay cash dividends within one year of declaration (generally within three months), they classify them as current liabilities.

On the other hand, companies do not recognize accumulated but undeclared dividends on cumulative preferred stock as a liability. Why? Because **preferred dividends in arrears** are not an obligation until the board of directors authorizes the payment. Nevertheless, companies should disclose the amount of cumulative dividends unpaid in a note, or show it parenthetically in the capital stock section.

Underlying Concepts

Preferred dividends in arrears do represent a probable future economic sacrifice, but the expected sacrifice does not result from a past transaction or past event. The sacrifice will result from a future event (declaration by the board of directors). Note disclosure improves the predictive value of the financial statements.

Dividends payable in the form of additional shares of stock are not recognized as a liability. Such **stock dividends** (as we discuss in Chapter 15) do not require future outlays of assets or services. Companies generally report such undistributed stock dividends in the stockholders' equity section because they represent retained earnings in the process of transfer to paid-in capital.

Customer Advances and Deposits

Current liabilities may include **returnable cash deposits** received from customers and employees. Companies may receive deposits from customers to guarantee performance of a contract or service or as guarantees to cover payment of expected future obligations. For example, a company like **Alltel Corp.** often requires a deposit on equipment that customers use to connect to the Internet or to access its other services. Alltel also may receive deposits from customers as guarantees for possible damage to property. Additionally, some companies require their employees to make deposits for the return of keys or other company property.

The classification of these items as current or noncurrent liabilities depends on the time between the date of the deposit and the termination of the relationship that required the deposit.

Unearned Revenues

A magazine publisher, such as **Golf Digest**, receives payment when a customer subscribes to its magazines. An airline company, such as **American Airlines**, sells tickets for future flights. And software companies, like **Microsoft**, issue coupons that allow customers to upgrade to the next version of their software. How do these companies account for **unearned revenues** that they receive before delivering goods or rendering services?

1. When a company receives an advance payment, it debits Cash, and credits a current liability account identifying the source of the unearned revenue.
2. When a company recognizes revenue, it debits the unearned revenue account, and credits a revenue account.

To illustrate, assume that Allstate University sells 10,000 season football tickets at $50 each for its five-game home schedule. Allstate University records the sales of season tickets as follows.

August 6

Cash	500,000	
Unearned Sales Revenue		500,000
(To record sale of 10,000 season tickets)		

As each game is completed, Allstate University makes the following entry.

September 7

Unearned Sales Revenue	100,000	
Sales Revenue		100,000
(To record football ticket revenue)		

The account Unearned Sales Revenue represents unearned revenue. Allstate University reports it as a current liability in the balance sheet as the school has a performance obligation. As the school recognizes revenue, it reclassifies the amount from Unearned Sales Revenue to Sales Revenue. Unearned revenue is material for some companies. In the airline industry, for example, tickets sold for future flights represent almost 50 percent of total current liabilities.

Illustration 13-3 shows specific unearned revenue and revenue accounts used in elected types of businesses.

ILLUSTRATION 13-3
Unearned Revenue and Revenue Accounts

Type of Business	Account Title: Unearned Revenue	Account Title: Revenue
Airline	Unearned Ticket Revenue	Passenger Revenue
Magazine publisher	Unearned Subscription Revenue	Subscription Revenue
Hotel	Unearned Rent Revenue	Rent Revenue
Auto dealer	Unearned Warranty Revenue	Warranty Revenue
Retailers	Unearned Gift Card Revenue	Sales Revenue

The balance sheet reports obligations for any commitments that are redeemable in goods and services. The income statement reports revenues related to performance obligations satisfied during the period.

What do the numbers mean? *MICROSOFT'S LIABILITIES—GOOD OR BAD?*

Users of financial statements generally examine current liabilities to assess a company's liquidity and overall financial flexibility. Companies must pay many current liabilities, such as accounts payable, wages payable, and taxes payable, sooner rather than later. A substantial increase in these liabilities should raise a red flag about a company's financial position.

This is not the case for all current liabilities. For example, **Microsoft** has a current liability entitled "Short-term unearned revenue" of $18,653 million in 2012 that has increased year after year. Unearned revenue is a liability that arises from sales of Microsoft products such as *Internet Explorer* and *Windows*. Microsoft also has provided coupons for upgrades to its programs to bolster sales of its XBox consoles. At the time of a sale, customers pay not only for the current version of the software but also for future upgrades. Microsoft recognizes sales revenue from the current version of the software and records as a liability (unearned revenue) the value of future upgrades to the software that it "owes" to customers.

Market analysts read such an increase in unearned revenue as a positive signal about Microsoft's sales and profitability. When Microsoft's sales are growing, its unearned revenue account increases. Thus, an *increase* in a liability is good news about Microsoft sales. At the same time, a decline in unearned revenue is bad news. As one analyst noted, a slowdown or reversal of the growth in Microsoft's unearned revenues indicates slowing sales, which is bad news for investors. Thus, increases in current liabilities can sometimes be viewed as good signs instead of bad.

Sources: Adapted from David Bank, "Some Fans Cool to Microsoft, Citing Drop in Old Indicator," *Wall Street Journal* (October 28, 1999); and Bloomberg News, "Microsoft Profit Hit by Deferred Sales; Forecast Raised," *The Globe and Mail* (January 26, 2007), p. B8.

Sales Taxes Payable

Retailers like **Wal-Mart**, **Best Buy**, and **Gap Inc.** must collect sales taxes from customers on transfers of tangible personal property and on certain services and then must remit these taxes to the proper governmental authority. Gap, for example, sets up a liability to provide for taxes collected from customers but not yet remitted to the tax authority. The Sales Taxes Payable account should reflect the liability for sales taxes due various governments.

The entry below illustrates use of the Sales Taxes Payable account on a sale of $3,000 when a 4 percent sales tax is in effect.

Cash	3,120	
Sales Revenue		3,000
Sales Taxes Payable		120

Sometimes the sales tax collections credited to the liability account are not equal to the liability as computed by the governmental formula. In such a case, Gap makes an adjustment of the liability account by recognizing a gain or a loss on sales tax collections.

Many companies do not segregate the sales tax and the amount of the sale at the time of sale. Instead, the company credits both amounts in total in the Sales Revenue account. Then, to reflect correctly the actual amount of sales and the liability for sales taxes, the company would debit the Sales Revenue account for the amount of the sales taxes due the government on these sales, and would credit the Sales Taxes Payable account for the same amount.

To illustrate, assume that the Sales Revenue account balance of $150,000 includes sales taxes of 4 percent. Thus, the amount recorded in the Sales Revenue account is comprised of the sales amount plus sales tax of 4 percent of the sales amount. Sales therefore are $144,230.77 ($150,000 ÷ 1.04) and the sales tax liability is $5,769.23 ($144,230.77 × 0.04; or $150,000 − $144,230.77). The following entry would record the amount due the taxing unit.

Sales Revenue	5,769.23	
Sales Taxes Payable		5,769.23

Income Taxes Payable

Any federal or state income tax varies in proportion to the amount of annual income. Using the best information and advice available, a business must prepare an income tax return and compute the income taxes payable resulting from the operations of the

Gateway to the Profession

Expanded Discussion of Property Taxes Payable

current period. Corporations should classify as a current liability the taxes payable on net income, as computed per the tax return.[6] Unlike a corporation, proprietorships and partnerships are not taxable entities. Because the individual proprietor and the members of a partnership are subject to personal income taxes on their share of the business's taxable income, income tax liabilities do not appear on the financial statements of proprietorships and partnerships.

Most corporations must make periodic tax payments throughout the year in an authorized bank depository or a Federal Reserve Bank. These payments are based upon estimates of the total annual tax liability. As the estimated total tax liability changes, the periodic contributions also change. If in a later year the taxing authority assesses an additional tax on the income of an earlier year, the company should credit Income Taxes Payable and charge the related debit to current operations.

Differences between taxable income under the tax laws and accounting income under generally accepted accounting principles sometimes occur. Because of these differences, the amount of income taxes payable to the government in any given year may differ substantially from income tax expense as reported on the financial statements. Chapter 19 is devoted solely to income tax matters and presents an extensive discussion of this complex topic.

Employee-Related Liabilities

LEARNING OBJECTIVE 3
Identify types of employee-related liabilities.

Companies also report as a current liability amounts owed to employees for salaries or wages at the end of an accounting period. In addition, they often also report as current liabilities the following items related to employee compensation.

1. Payroll deductions.
2. Compensated absences.
3. Bonuses.

Payroll Deductions

The most common types of payroll deductions are taxes, insurance premiums, employee savings, and union dues. **To the extent that a company has not remitted the amounts deducted to the proper authority at the end of the accounting period, it should recognize them as current liabilities.**

Social Security Taxes. Since January 1, 1937, Social Security legislation has provided federal **Old Age, Survivor, and Disability Insurance (OASDI)** benefits for certain individuals and their families. Funds for these payments come from taxes levied on both the employer and the employee. Employers collect the employee's share of this tax by deducting it from the employee's gross pay, and remit it to the government along with their share. The government taxes both the employer and the employee at the same rate, currently 6.2 percent based on the employee's gross pay up to a $113,700 annual limit. The OASDI tax is usually referred to as **FICA** (the Federal Insurance Contribution Act).

In 1965, Congress passed the first federal health insurance program for the aged—popularly known as **Medicare**. This two-part program alleviates the high cost of medical care for those over age 65. A separate Hospital Insurance tax, paid by both the employee and the employer at the rate of 1.45 percent on the employee's total compensation,

[6]Corporate taxes are based on a progressive tax rate structure. Companies with taxable income of $50,000 or less are taxed at a 15 percent rate. Higher levels of income are taxed at much higher rates.

finances the Basic Plan, which provides hospital and other institutional services.[7] The Voluntary Plan covers the major part of doctors' bills and other medical and health services. Monthly payments from all who enroll, plus matching funds from the federal government, finance this plan.

The combination of the OASDI tax (FICA) and the federal Hospital Insurance Tax is commonly referred to as the **Social Security tax**. The combined rate for these taxes, 7.65 percent on an employee's wages to $113,700 and 1.45 percent in excess of $113,700, changes intermittently by acts of Congress. **Companies should report the amount of unremitted employee and employer Social Security tax on gross wages paid as a current liability.**

Unemployment Taxes. Another payroll tax levied by the federal government in co-operation with state governments provides a system of unemployment insurance. All employers who meet the following criteria are subject to the **Federal Unemployment Tax Act (FUTA)**: (1) those who paid wages of $1,500 or more during any calendar quarter in the year or preceding year, or (2) those who employed at least one individual on at least one day in each of 20 weeks during the current or preceding calendar year.

Only employers pay the unemployment tax. The rate of this tax is 6.2 percent on the first $7,000 of compensation paid to each employee during the calendar year. The employer receives a tax credit not to exceed 5.4 percent for contributions paid to a state plan for unemployment compensation. Thus, if an employer is subject to a state unemployment tax of 5.4 percent or more, it pays only 0.8 percent tax to the federal government.

State unemployment compensation laws differ both from the federal law and among various states. Therefore, employers must refer to the unemployment tax laws in each state in which they pay wages and salaries. The normal state tax may range from 3 percent to 7 percent or higher. However, all states provide for some form of **merit rating**, which reduces the state contribution rate. Employers who display by their benefit and contribution experience that they provide steady employment may receive this reduction—if the size of the state fund is adequate. In order not to penalize an employer who has earned a reduction in the state contribution rate, federal law allows a credit of 5.4 percent, even when the effective state contribution rate is less than 5.4 percent.

To illustrate, Appliance Repair Co. has a taxable payroll of $100,000. It is subject to a federal rate of 6.2 percent and a state contribution rate of 5.7 percent. However, its stable employment experience reduces the company's state rate to 1 percent. Appliance Repair computes its federal and state unemployment taxes as shown in Illustration 13-4.

ILLUSTRATION 13-4
Computation of Unemployment Taxes

State unemployment tax payment (1% × $100,000)	$1,000
Federal unemployment tax [(6.2% − 5.4%) × $100,000]	800
Total federal and state unemployment tax	$1,800

Companies pay federal unemployment tax quarterly, and file a tax form annually. Companies also generally pay state contributions quarterly as well. Because both the federal and the state unemployment taxes accrue on earned compensation, companies should record the amount of accrued but unpaid employer contributions **as an operating expense and as a current liability when preparing financial statements at year-end**.

Income Tax Withholding. Federal and some state income tax laws require employers to withhold from each employee's pay the applicable income tax due on those wages. The

[7]As a result of the new health-care law, the Affordable Care Act, the actual rate for Medicare is higher for married couples, generally with incomes in excess of $250,000.

employer computes the amount of income tax to withhold according to a government-prescribed formula or withholding tax table. That amount depends on the length of the pay period and each employee's taxable wages, marital status, and claimed dependents. If the income tax withheld plus the employee and the employer Social Security taxes exceeds specified amounts per month, the employer must make remittances to the government during the month. Illustration 13-5 summarizes payroll deductions and liabilities.

ILLUSTRATION 13-5
Summary of Payroll Liabilities

Item	Who Pays	
Income tax withholding FICA taxes—employee share Union dues	Employee	Employer reports these amounts as liabilities until remitted.
FICA taxes—employer share Federal unemployment State unemployment	Employer	

Payroll Deductions Example. Assume a weekly payroll of $10,000 entirely subject to FICA and Medicare (7.65%), federal (0.8%) and state (4%) unemployment taxes, with income tax withholding of $1,320 and union dues of $88 deducted. The company records the salaries and wages paid and the **employee payroll deductions** as follows.

Salaries and Wages Expense	10,000	
Withholding Taxes Payable		1,320
FICA Taxes Payable		765
Union Dues Payable		88
Cash		7,827

It records the **employer payroll taxes** as follows.

Payroll Tax Expense	1,245	
FICA Taxes Payable		765
FUTA Taxes Payable		80
SUTA Taxes Payable		400

The employer must remit to the government its share of FICA tax along with the amount of FICA tax deducted from each employee's gross compensation. It records all unremitted employer FICA taxes as payroll tax expense and payroll tax payable.[8]

Compensated Absences

Underlying Concepts

When these four conditions exist, all elements in the definition of a liability exist. In addition, the expense recognition principle requires that the company report the expense for the services in the period consumed.

Compensated absences are paid absences from employment—such as vacation, illness, and holidays.[9] Companies should accrue a liability for the cost of compensation for future absences if **all of the following conditions** exist. [6]

(a) The employer's obligation relating to employees' rights to receive compensation for future absences is attributable to employees' services **already rendered**.

(b) The obligation relates to the rights that **vest or accumulate**.

(c) Payment of the compensation is **probable**.

(d) The amount can be **reasonably estimated**. [7]

[8]A manufacturing company allocates all of the payroll costs (wages, payroll taxes, and fringe benefits) to appropriate cost accounts such as Direct Labor, Indirect Labor, Sales Salaries, Administrative Salaries, and the like. This abbreviated and somewhat simplified discussion of payroll costs and deductions is not indicative of the volume of records and clerical work that may be involved in maintaining a sound and accurate payroll system.

[9]In addition, companies provide **postemployment benefits** to past or inactive employees **after employment but prior to retirement**. Examples include salary continuation, supplemental unemployment benefits, severance pay, job training, and continuation of health and life insurance coverage.

Illustration 13-6 shows an example of an accrual for compensated absences, in an excerpt from the balance sheet of **Clarcor Inc.**

ILLUSTRATION 13-6
Balance Sheet Presentation of Accrual for Compensated Absences

Clarcor Inc.

Current liabilities	
Accounts payable	$ 6,308
Accrued salaries, wages and commissions	2,278
Compensated absences	2,271
Accrued pension liabilities	1,023
Other accrued liabilities	4,572
	$16,452

If an employer meets conditions (a), (b), and (c) but does not accrue a liability because of a failure to meet condition (d), it should disclose that fact. Illustration 13-7 shows an example of such a disclosure, in a note from the financial statements of **Gotham Utility Company**.

ILLUSTRATION 13-7
Disclosure of Policy for Compensated Absences

Gotham Utility Company

Employees of the Company are entitled to paid vacation, personal, and sick days off, depending on job status, length of service, and other factors. Due to numerous differing union contracts and other agreements with nonunion employees, it is impractical to estimate the amount of compensation for future absences, and, accordingly, no liability has been reported in the accompanying financial statements. The Company's policy is to recognize the cost of compensated absences when actually paid to employees; compensated absence payments to employees totaled $2,786,000.

The following considerations are relevant to the accounting for compensated absences.

Vested rights exist when an employer has an obligation to make payment to an employee even after terminating his or her employment. Thus, vested rights are not contingent on an employee's future service. **Accumulated rights** are those that employees can carry forward to future periods if not used in the period in which earned. For example, assume that you earn four days of vacation pay as of December 31, the end of your employer's fiscal year. Company policy is that you will be paid for this vacation time even if you terminate employment. In this situation, your four days of vacation pay are vested, and your employer must accrue the amount.

Now assume that your vacation days are not vested but that you can carry the four days over into later periods. Although the rights are not vested, they are accumulated rights for which the employer must make an accrual. However, the amount of the accrual is adjusted to allow for estimated forfeitures due to turnover.

A modification of the general rules relates to the issue of **sick pay**. If sick pay benefits vest, a company must accrue them. If sick pay benefits accumulate but do not vest, a company may choose whether to accrue them. Why this distinction? Companies may administer compensation designated as sick pay in one of two ways. In some companies, employees receive sick pay only if illness causes their absence. Therefore, these companies may or may not accrue a liability because its payment depends on future employee illness. Other companies allow employees to accumulate unused sick pay and take compensated time off from work even when not ill. For this type of sick pay, a company must accrue a liability because the company will pay it, regardless of whether employees become ill.

Companies should recognize the expense and related liability for compensated absences in the year earned by employees. For example, if new employees receive rights to two weeks' paid vacation at the beginning of their second year of employment, a company considers the vacation pay to be earned during the first year of employment.

What rate should a company use to accrue the compensated absence cost—the current rate or an estimated future rate? GAAP is silent on this subject. Therefore, companies will likely use the current rather than future rate. The future rate is less certain and raises time value of money issues. To illustrate, assume that Amutron Inc. began operations on January 1, 2014. The company employs 10 individuals and pays each $480 per week. Employees earned 20 unused vacation weeks in 2014. In 2015, the employees used the vacation weeks, but now they each earn $540 per week. Amutron accrues the accumulated vacation pay on December 31, 2014, as follows.

Salaries and Wages Expense	9,600	
Salaries and Wages Payable ($480 × 20)		9,600

At December 31, 2014, the company reports on its balance sheet a liability of $9,600. In 2015, it records the payment of vacation pay as follows.

Salaries and Wages Payable	9,600	
Salaries and Wages Expense	1,200	
Cash ($540 × 20)		10,800

In 2015, the use of the vacation weeks extinguishes the liability. Note that Amutron records the difference between the amount of cash paid and the reduction in the liability account as an adjustment to Salaries and Wages Expense in the period when paid. This difference arises because it accrues the liability account at the rates of pay in effect during the period when employees **earned** the compensated time. The cash paid, however, depends on the rates in effect during the period when employees **used** the compensated time. If Amutron used the future rates of pay to compute the accrual in 2014, then the cash paid in 2015 would equal the liability.[10]

Gateway to the Profession

Expanded Discussion of Bonus Computations

Bonus Agreements

Many companies give a **bonus** to certain or all employees in addition to their regular salaries or wages. Frequently the bonus amount depends on the company's yearly profit. For example, employees at **Ford Motor Company** share in the success of the company's operations on the basis of a complicated formula using net income as its primary basis for computation. A company may consider **bonus payments to employees** as additional wages and should include them as a deduction in determining the net income for the year.

To illustrate the entries for an employee bonus, assume that Palmer Inc. shows income for the year 2014 of $100,000. It will pay out bonuses of $10,700 in January 2015. Palmer makes an adjusting entry dated December 31, 2014, to record the bonuses as follows.

Salaries and Wages Expense	10,700	
Salaries and Wages Payable		10,700

In January 2015, when Palmer pays the bonus, it makes this journal entry:

Salaries and Wages Payable	10,700	
Cash		10,700

[10]Some companies also have obligations for benefits paid to employees after they retire. The accounting and reporting standards for postretirement benefit payments are complex. These standards relate to two different types of **postretirement benefits**: (1) pensions, and (2) postretirement health-care and life insurance benefits. We discuss these issues extensively in Chapter 20.

Palmer should show the expense account in the income statement as an operating expense. **The liability, Salaries and Wages Payable, is usually payable within a short period of time. Companies should include it as a current liability in the balance sheet.** Similar to bonus agreements are contractual agreements for **conditional expenses**. Examples would be agreements covering rents or royalty payments conditional on the amount of revenues recognized or the quantity of product produced or extracted. Conditional expenses based on revenues or units produced are usually less difficult to compute than bonus arrangements.

For example, assume that a lease calls for a fixed rent payment of $500 per month and 1 percent of all sales over $300,000 per year. The company's annual rent obligation would amount to $6,000 plus $0.01 of each dollar of revenue over $300,000. Or, a royalty agreement may give to a patent owner $1 for every ton of product resulting from the patented process, or give to a mineral rights owner $0.50 on every barrel of oil extracted. As the company produces or extracts each additional unit of product, it creates an additional obligation, usually a current liability.

CONTINGENCIES

4 LEARNING OBJECTIVE

Identify the criteria used to account for and disclose gain and loss contingencies.

Companies often are involved in situations where uncertainty exists about whether an obligation to transfer cash or other assets has arisen and/or the amount that will be required to settle the obligation. For example:

- **Merck** may be a defendant in a lawsuit, and any payment is contingent upon the outcome of a settlement or an administrative or court proceeding.
- **Ford Motor Company** provides a warranty for a car it sells, and any payments are contingent on the number of cars that qualify for benefits under the warranty.
- **Briggs & Stratton** acts as a guarantor on a loan for another entity, and any payment is contingent on whether the other entity defaults.

Broadly, these situations are called contingencies. A **contingency** is "an existing condition, situation, or set of circumstances involving uncertainty as to possible gain **(gain contingency)** or loss **(loss contingency)** to an enterprise that will ultimately be resolved when one or more future events occur or fail to occur." **[8]**[11]

Gain Contingencies

Gain contingencies are claims or rights to receive assets (or have a liability reduced) whose existence is uncertain but which may become valid eventually. The typical gain contingencies are:

1. Possible receipts of monies from gifts, donations, asset sales, and so on.
2. Possible refunds from the government in tax disputes.
3. Pending court cases with a probable favorable outcome.
4. Tax loss carryforwards (discussed in Chapter 19).

Companies follow a conservative policy in this area; they do not record gain contingencies. A company discloses gain contingencies in the notes only when a high probability exists for realizing them. As a result, it is unusual to find information about

[11]According to *Accounting Trends and Techniques—2012,* the most common gain contingencies are related to operating loss carryforwards and other tax credits and to tax credit carryforwards.

contingent gains in the financial statements and the accompanying notes. Illustration 13-8 presents an example of a gain contingency disclosure.

ILLUSTRATION 13-8
Disclosure of Gain Contingency

BMC Industries, Inc.

Note 13: Legal Matters. In the first quarter, a U.S. District Court in Miami, Florida, awarded the Company a $5.1 million judgment against Barth Industries (Barth) of Cleveland, Ohio and its parent, Nesco Holdings, Inc. (Nesco). The judgment relates to an agreement under which Barth and Nesco were to help automate the plastic lens production plant in Fort Lauderdale, Florida. The Company has not recorded any income relating to this judgment because Barth and Nesco have filed an appeal.

Loss Contingencies

LEARNING OBJECTIVE 5
Explain the accounting for different types of loss contingencies.

Loss contingencies involve possible losses. A liability incurred as a result of a loss contingency is by definition a contingent liability. **Contingent liabilities** depend on the occurrence of one or more future events to confirm either the amount payable, the payee, the date payable, or its existence. That is, these factors depend on a contingency.

International Perspective
IFRS uses the term *provisions* to refer to estimated liabilities.

Likelihood of Loss

When a loss contingency exists, the likelihood that the future event or events will confirm the incurrence of a liability can range from probable to remote. The FASB uses the terms **probable**, **reasonably possible**, and **remote** to identify three areas within that range and assigns the following meanings.

Probable. The future event or events are likely to occur.

Reasonably possible. The chance of the future event or events occurring is more than remote but less than likely.

Remote. The chance of the future event or events occurring is slight.

Companies should accrue an estimated loss from a loss contingency by a charge to expense and a liability recorded only if **both** of the following conditions are met.[12]

1. Information available prior to the issuance of the financial statements indicates that it is **probable that a liability has been incurred** at the date of the financial statements.
2. The amount of the loss can be **reasonably estimated.**

To record a liability, a company does not need to know the exact payee nor the exact date payable. **What a company must know is whether it is probable that it incurred a liability.**

To meet the second criterion, a company needs to be able to reasonably determine an amount for the liability. To determine a reasonable estimate of the liability, a company may use its own experience, experience of other companies in the industry, engineering or research studies, legal advice, or educated guesses by qualified personnel. Illustration 13-9 shows disclosure of an accrual recorded for a loss contingency, from the annual report of Quaker State Oil Refining Company.

[12]We discuss loss contingencies that result in the incurrence of a liability in this chapter. We discuss loss contingencies that result in the impairment of an asset (e.g., collectibility of receivables or threat of expropriation of assets) in other sections of this textbook.

ILLUSTRATION 13-9
Disclosure of Accrual for Loss Contingency

Quaker State Oil Refining Company

Note 5: Contingencies. During the period from November 13 to December 23, a change in an additive component purchased from one of its suppliers caused certain oil refined and shipped to fail to meet the Company's low-temperature performance requirements. The Company has recalled this product and has arranged for reimbursement to its customers and the ultimate consumers of all costs associated with the product. Estimated cost of the recall program, net of estimated third party reimbursement, in the amount of $3,500,000 has been charged to current operations.

Use of the terms probable, reasonably possible, and remote to classify contingencies involves judgment and subjectivity. Illustration 13-10 lists examples of loss contingencies and the general accounting treatment accorded them.

ILLUSTRATION 13-10
Accounting Treatment of Loss Contingencies

Usually Accrued

Loss Related to:

1. Collectibility of receivables
2. Obligations related to product warranties and product defects
3. Premiums offered to customers

Not Accrued

Loss Related to:

4. Risk of loss or damage of enterprise property by fire, explosion, or other hazards
5. General or unspecified business risks
6. Risk of loss from catastrophes assumed by property and casualty insurance companies, including reinsurance companies

May Be Accrued*

Loss Related to:

7. Threat of expropriation of assets
8. Pending or threatened litigation
9. Actual or possible claims and assessments**
10. Guarantees of indebtedness of others
11. Obligations of commercial banks under "standby letters of credit"
12. Agreements to repurchase receivables (or the related property) that have been sold

*Should be accrued when both criteria—probable and reasonably estimable—are met.
**Estimated amounts of losses incurred prior to the balance sheet date but settled subsequently should be accrued as of the balance sheet date.

Practicing accountants express concern over the diversity that now exists in the interpretation of "probable," "reasonably possible," and "remote." Current practice relies heavily on the exact language used in responses received from lawyers (such language is necessarily biased and protective rather than predictive). As a result, accruals and disclosures of contingencies vary considerably in practice. Some of the more common loss contingencies are:[13]

1. Litigation, claims, and assessments.
2. Guarantee and warranty costs.
3. Premiums and coupons.
4. Environmental liabilities.

[13] *Accounting Trends and Techniques—2012* indicates that 500 companies report loss contingencies for the following: litigation, 355; environmental, 195; possible tax assessments, 124; insurance, 154; governmental investigation, 101; and others, 71.

As discussed in the opening story, companies do not record or report in the notes to the financial statements general risk contingencies inherent in business operations (e.g., the possibility of war, strike, uninsurable catastrophes, or a business recession).

Litigation, Claims, and Assessments

Companies must consider the following factors, among others, in determining whether to record a liability with respect to **pending or threatened** litigation and actual or possible claims and assessments.

1. The **time period** in which the underlying cause of action occurred.
2. The **probability** of an unfavorable outcome.
3. The ability to make a **reasonable estimate** of the amount of loss.

To report a loss and a liability in the financial statements, **the cause for litigation must have occurred on or before the date of the financial statements**. It does not matter that the company became aware of the existence or possibility of the lawsuit or claims after the date of the financial statements but before issuing them. To evaluate the probability of an unfavorable outcome, a company considers the following: the nature of the litigation, the progress of the case, the opinion of legal counsel, its own and others' experience in similar cases, and any management response to the lawsuit.

Companies can seldom predict the outcome of pending litigation, however, with any assurance. And, even if evidence available at the balance sheet date does not favor the company, it is hardly reasonable to expect the company to publish in its financial statements a dollar estimate of the probable negative outcome. Such specific disclosures might weaken the company's position in the dispute and encourage the plaintiff to intensify its efforts. A typical example of the wording of such a disclosure is the note to the financial statements of **Apple Inc.**, relating to its litigation concerning repetitive stress injuries, as shown in Illustration 13-11.

ILLUSTRATION 13-11
Disclosure of Litigation

Apple Inc.

"Repetitive Stress Injury" Litigation. The Company is named in numerous lawsuits (fewer than 100) alleging that the plaintiff incurred so-called "repetitive stress injury" to the upper extremities as a result of using keyboards and/or mouse input devices sold by the Company. In a trial of one of these cases (*Dorsey v. Apple*) in the United States District Court for the Eastern District of New York, the jury rendered a verdict in favor of the Company, and final judgment in favor of the Company has been entered. The other cases are in various stages of pretrial activity. These suits are similar to those filed against other major suppliers of personal computers. Ultimate resolution of the litigation against the Company may depend on progress in resolving this type of litigation in the industry overall.

With respect to **unfiled suits** and **unasserted claims and assessments**, a company must determine (1) the degree of **probability** that a suit may be filed or a claim or assessment may be asserted, and (2) the **probability** of an unfavorable outcome. For example, assume that the Federal Trade Commission investigates the Nawtee Company for restraint of trade, and institutes enforcement proceedings. Private claims of triple damages for redress often follow such proceedings. In this case, Nawtee must determine the probability of the claims being asserted **and** the probability of triple damages being awarded. If both are probable, if the loss is reasonably estimable, and if the cause for action is dated on or before the date of the financial statements, then Nawtee should accrue the liability.[14]

Guarantee and Warranty Costs

A **warranty** **(product guarantee)** is a promise made by a seller to a buyer to make good on a deficiency of quantity, quality, or performance in a product. Manufacturers commonly use it as a sales promotion technique. Automakers, for instance, "hyped" their sales by extending their new-car warranty to seven years or 100,000 miles. For a specified period of time following the date of sale to the consumer, the manufacturer may promise to bear all or part of the cost of replacing defective parts, to perform any necessary repairs or servicing without charge, to refund the purchase price, or even to "double your money back."

Warranties and guarantees entail future costs. These additional costs, sometimes called "after costs" or "post-sale costs," frequently are significant. Although the future cost is indefinite as to amount, due date, and even customer, a liability is probable in most cases. Companies should recognize this liability in the accounts if they can reasonably estimate it. The estimated amount of the liability includes all the costs that the company will incur after sale and delivery and that are incident to the correction of defects or deficiencies required under the warranty provisions. Warranty costs are a classic example of a loss contingency.

Companies use two basic methods of accounting for warranty costs: (1) the cash-basis method and (2) the accrual method.

Cash Basis. Under the **cash-basis method**, companies expense warranty costs as incurred. In other words, a **seller or manufacturer charges warranty costs to the period in which it complies with the warranty**. The company does not record a liability for future costs arising from warranties, nor does it charge the period of sale. Companies frequently justify use of this method, the only one recognized for income tax purposes, on the basis of expediency when warranty costs are immaterial or when the warranty period is relatively short. A company uses the cash-basis method when it does not accrue a warranty liability in the year of sale either because:

1. It is not probable that a liability has been incurred, or
2. It cannot reasonably estimate the amount of the liability.

Accrual Basis. If it is probable that customers will make warranty claims and a company can reasonably estimate the costs involved, the company must use the accrual method. Under the **accrual method**, companies charge warranty costs to operating expense **in the year of sale**. The accrual method is the generally accepted method. Companies should use it whenever the warranty is an integral and inseparable part of the sale and is viewed as a loss contingency. We refer to this approach as the **expense warranty approach**.

Example of expense warranty approach. To illustrate the expense warranty method, assume that Denson Machinery Company begins production on a new machine in July 2014,

[14]Companies need not disclose contingencies involving an unasserted claim or assessment when no claimant has come forward unless (1) it is considered probable that a claim will be asserted, and (2) there is a reasonable possibility that the outcome will be unfavorable. The FASB recently had a project to develop disclosures that are sufficient to enable users of financial statements to assess the likelihood, timing, and amount of future cash flows associated with loss contingencies. As indicated in the opening story, this project and its proposed recommendations were extremely controversial. Although the SEC continues to focus on these disclosures, the FASB has now removed the project from its active agenda (see *http://www.cooley.com/66716*).

and sells 100 units at $5,000 each by its year-end, December 31, 2014. Each machine is under warranty for one year. Denson estimates, based on past experience with a similar machine, that the warranty cost will average $200 per unit. Further, as a result of parts replacements and services rendered in compliance with machinery warranties, it incurs $4,000 in warranty costs in 2014 and $16,000 in 2015.

1. Sale of 100 machines at $5,000 each, July through December 2014:

Cash or Accounts Receivable	500,000	
Sales Revenue		500,000
(To record sales revenue)		

2. Recognition of warranty expense, July through December 2014:

Warranty Expense	4,000	
Cash, Inventory, Accrued Payroll		4,000
(Warranty costs incurred)		
Warranty Expense	16,000	
Warranty Liability		16,000
(To accrue estimated warranty costs)		

The December 31, 2014, balance sheet reports "Warranty liability" as a current liability of $16,000, and the income statement for 2014 reports "Warranty expense" of $20,000.

3. Recognition of warranty costs incurred in 2015 (on 2014 machinery sales):

Warranty Liability	16,000	
Cash, Inventory, Accrued Payroll		16,000
(Warranty costs incurred)		

If Denson Machinery applies the cash-basis method, it reports $4,000 as warranty expense in 2014 and $16,000 as warranty expense in 2015. It records all of the sale price as revenue in 2014. In many instances, application of the cash-basis method fails to record the warranty costs relating to the products sold during a given period with the revenues derived from such products. As such, **it violates the expense recognition principle**. However, where ongoing warranty policies exist year after year, the differences between the cash and the expense warranty bases probably would not be so great.

Sales warranty approach. A warranty is sometimes **sold separately from the product**. For example, when you purchase a television set or Blu-ray player, you are entitled to the manufacturer's warranty. You also will undoubtedly be offered an extended warranty on the product at an additional cost.[15]

In this case, the seller should recognize separately the sale of the television or Blu-ray player, with the manufacturer's warranty and the sale of the extended warranty. **[9]** This approach is referred to as the **sales warranty approach**. **Companies defer revenue on the sale of the extended warranty** and generally recognize it on a straight-line basis over the life of the contract. The seller of the warranty defers revenue because it has an obligation to perform services over the life of the contract. The seller should only defer and amortize costs that vary with, and are directly related to, the sale of the contracts (mainly commissions). It expenses those costs, such as employees' salaries, advertising, and general and administrative expenses, that it would have incurred even if it did not sell a contract.

To illustrate, assume you purchase a new automobile from Hanlin Auto for $20,000. In addition to the regular warranty on the auto (the manufacturer will pay for all repairs

[15] A company separately prices a contract if the customer has the option to purchase the services provided under the contract for an expressly stated amount separate from the price of the product. An extended warranty or product maintenance contract usually meets these conditions.

for the first 36,000 miles or three years, whichever comes first), you purchase at a cost of $600 an extended warranty that protects you for an additional three years or 36,000 miles. Hanlin Auto records the sale of the automobile (with the regular warranty) and the sale of the extended warranty on January 2, 2014, as follows.

Cash	20,600	
Sales Revenue		20,000
Unearned Warranty Revenue		600

It recognizes revenue at the end of the fourth year (using straight-line amortization) as follows.

Unearned Warranty Revenue	200	
Warranty Revenue		200

Because the extended warranty contract only starts after the regular warranty expires, Hanlin Auto defers revenue recognition until the fourth year. If it incurs the costs of performing services under the extended warranty contract on other than a straight-line basis (as historical evidence might indicate), Hanlin Auto should recognize revenue over the contract period as it performs services under the contract. **[10]**[16]

Premiums and Coupons

Numerous companies offer premiums (either on a limited or continuing basis) to customers in return for boxtops, certificates, coupons, labels, or wrappers. The **premium** may be silverware, dishes, a small appliance, a toy, or free transportation. Also, **printed coupons** that can be redeemed for a cash discount on items purchased are extremely popular. A more recent marketing innovation is the **cash rebate**, which the buyer can obtain by returning the store receipt, a rebate coupon, and Universal Product Code (UPC label) or "bar code" to the manufacturer.[17]

Companies offer premiums, coupon offers, and rebates to stimulate sales. Thus companies should charge the **costs of premiums and coupons to expense in the period of the sale** that benefits from the plan. The period that benefits is not necessarily the period in which the company offered the premium. At the end of the accounting period, many premium offers may be outstanding and must be redeemed when presented in subsequent periods. In order to reflect the existing current liability and to match costs with revenues, the company estimates the number of outstanding premium offers that customers will present for redemption. The company then charges the cost of premium offers to Premium Expense. It credits the outstanding performance obligation to an account titled Premium Liability.

Underlying Concepts

Warranties and coupons are loss contingencies that satisfy the conditions necessary for a liability. Regarding the income statement, the *expense recognition principle* requires that companies report the related expense in the period in which the sale occurs.

The following example illustrates the accounting treatment for a premium offer. Fluffy Cakemix Company offered its customers a large, nonbreakable mixing bowl in exchange for 25 cents and 10 boxtops. The mixing bowl costs Fluffy Cakemix Company 75 cents, and the company estimates that customers will redeem 60 percent of the boxtops. The premium offer began in June 2014 and resulted in the transactions journalized

[16]The FASB requires additional disclosure requirements for warranties. A company must disclose its accounting policy and the method used to determine its warranty liability, and must present a tabular reconciliation of the changes in the product warranty liability. **[11]**

[17]Nearly 40 percent of cash rebates never get redeemed, and some customers complain about how difficult the rebate process is. See B. Grow, "The Great Rebate Runaround," *BusinessWeek* (December 5, 2005), pp. 34–37. Approximately 4 percent of coupons are redeemed. Redeemed coupons eventually make their way to the corporate headquarters of the stores that accept them. From there they are shipped to clearinghouses operated by A. C. Nielsen Company (of TV-rating fame) that count them and report back to the manufacturers who, in turn, reimburse the stores.

below. Fluffy Cakemix Company records purchase of 20,000 mixing bowls at 75 cents as follows.

Inventory of Premiums	15,000	
Cash		15,000

The entry to record sales of 300,000 boxes of cake mix at 80 cents would be:

Cash	240,000	
Sales Revenue		240,000

Fluffy records the actual redemption of 60,000 boxtops, the receipt of 25 cents per 10 boxtops, and the delivery of the mixing bowls as follows.

Cash [(60,000 ÷ 10) × $0.25]	1,500	
Premium Expense	3,000	
Inventory of Premiums		4,500
Computation: (60,000 ÷ 10) × $0.75 = $4,500		

Finally, Fluffy makes an end-of-period adjusting entry for estimated liability for outstanding premium offers (boxtops) as follows.

Premium Expense	6,000	
Premium Liability		6,000

Computation:

Total boxtops sold in 2014	300,000
Total estimated redemptions (60%)	180,000
Boxtops redeemed in 2014	60,000
Estimated future redemptions	120,000
Cost of estimated claims outstanding (120,000 ÷ 10) × ($0.75 − $0.25) = $6,000	

The December 31, 2014, balance sheet of Fluffy Cakemix Company reports an "Inventory of premiums" of $10,500 for the premium mixing bowls as a current asset and "Premium liability" of $6,000 as a current liability. The 2014 income statement reports a $9,000 "Premium expense" among the selling expenses.

What do the numbers mean? *FREQUENT FLYERS*

Numerous companies offer premiums to customers in the form of a promise of future goods or services as an incentive for purchases today. Premium plans that have widespread adoption are the frequent-flyer programs used by all major airlines. On the basis of mileage accumulated, frequent-flyer members receive discounted or free airline tickets. Airline customers can earn miles toward free travel by making long-distance phone calls, staying in hotels, and charging gasoline and groceries on a credit card. Those free tickets represent an enormous potential liability because people using them may displace paying passengers.

When airlines first started offering frequent-flyer bonuses, everyone assumed that they could accommodate the free-ticket holders with otherwise-empty seats. That made the additional cost of the program so minimal that airlines didn't accrue it or report the small liability. But, as more and more paying passengers have been crowded off flights by frequent-flyer awardees, the loss of revenues has grown enormously. For example, **Delta Air Lines** reported liabilities of over $4.5 billion for frequent-flyer tickets.

Environmental Liabilities

Estimates to clean up existing toxic waste sites total upward of $752 billion over a 30-year period. In addition, cost estimates of cleaning up our air and preventing future deterioration of the environment run even higher. These costs are likely to only grow, considering "Superfund legislation." This federal legislation provides the Environmental

Protection Agency (EPA) with the power to clean up waste sites and charge the clean-up costs to parties the EPA deems responsible for contaminating the site. These potentially responsible parties can have a significant liability.

In many industries, the construction and operation of long-lived assets involves obligations for the retirement of those assets. When a mining company opens up a strip mine, it may also commit to restore the land once it completes mining. Similarly, when an oil company erects an offshore drilling platform, it may be legally obligated to dismantle and remove the platform at the end of its useful life.

Accounting Recognition of Asset Retirement Obligations. A company must recognize an **asset retirement obligation (ARO)** when it has an existing legal obligation associated with the retirement of a long-lived asset and when it can reasonably estimate the amount of the liability. Companies should record the ARO at fair value. **[12]**

Obligating events. Examples of existing legal obligations, which require recognition of a liability include, but are not limited to:

- Decommissioning nuclear facilities;
- Dismantling, restoring, and reclamation of oil and gas properties;
- Certain closure, reclamation, and removal costs of mining facilities; and
- Closure and post-closure costs of landfills.

In order to capture the benefits of these long-lived assets, **the company is generally legally obligated for the costs associated with retirement of the asset, whether the company hires another party to perform the retirement activities or performs the activities with its own workforce and equipment**. AROs give rise to various recognition patterns. For example, the obligation may arise at the outset of the asset's use (e.g., erection of an oil-rig), or it may build over time (e.g., a landfill that expands over time).

Measurement. A company initially measures an ARO at fair value, which is defined as the amount that the company would pay in an active market to settle the ARO. While active markets do not exist for many AROs, companies should estimate fair value based on the best information available. Such information could include market prices of similar liabilities, if available. Alternatively, companies may use present value techniques to estimate fair value.

Recognition and allocation. To record an ARO in the financial statements, a company includes the cost associated with the ARO in the carrying amount of the related long-lived asset, and records a liability for the same amount. It records an asset retirement cost as part of the related asset because these costs are directly related to operating the asset and are necessary to prepare the asset for its intended use. Therefore, the specific asset (e.g., mine, drilling platform, nuclear power plant) should be increased because the future economic benefit comes from the use of this productive asset. **Companies should not record the capitalized asset retirement costs in a separate account because there is no future economic benefit that can be associated with these costs alone.**

In subsequent periods, companies allocate the cost of the ARO to expense over the period of the related asset's useful life. Companies may use the straight-line method for this allocation, as well as other systematic and rational allocations.

Example of ARO accounting provisions. To illustrate the accounting for AROs, assume that on January 1, 2014, Wildcat Oil Company erected an oil platform in the Gulf of

Mexico. Wildcat is legally required to dismantle and remove the platform at the end of its useful life, estimated to be five years. Wildcat estimates that dismantling and removal will cost $1,000,000. Based on a 10 percent discount rate, the fair value of the asset retirement obligation is estimated to be $620,920 ($1,000,000 × .62092). Wildcat records this ARO as follows.

January 1, 2014		
Drilling Platform	620,920	
Asset Retirement Obligation		620,920

During the life of the asset, Wildcat allocates the asset retirement cost to expense. Using the straight-line method, Wildcat makes the following entries to record this expense.

December 31, 2014, 2015, 2016, 2017, 2018		
Depreciation Expense ($620,920 ÷ 5)	124,184	
Accumulated Depreciation—Plant Assets		124,184

In addition, Wildcat must accrue interest expense each period. Wildcat records interest expense and the related increase in the asset retirement obligation on December 31, 2014, as follows.

December 31, 2014		
Interest Expense ($620,920 × 10%)	62,092	
Asset Retirement Obligation		62,092

On January 10, 2019, Wildcat contracts with Rig Reclaimers, Inc. to dismantle the platform at a contract price of $995,000. Wildcat makes the following journal entry to record settlement of the ARO.

January 10, 2019		
Asset Retirement Obligation	1,000,000	
Gain on Settlement of ARO		5,000
Cash		995,000

Companies provide extensive disclosure regarding environmental liabilities. In addition, some believe that companies should record more of these liabilities. The SEC recommends that companies not delay recognition of a liability due to significant uncertainty. The SEC argues that if the liability is within a range, and no amount within the range is the best estimate, then management should recognize the minimum amount of the range. That treatment is in accordance with GAAP. The SEC also believes that companies should report environmental liabilities in the balance sheet independent of recoveries from third parties. Thus, companies may not net possible insurance recoveries against liabilities but must show them separately. Because there is much litigation regarding recovery of insurance proceeds, these "assets" appear to be gain contingencies. Therefore, companies should not report these on the balance sheet.[18]

[18]As we indicated earlier, the FASB requires that, when some amount within the range appears at the time to be a better estimate than any other amount within the range, a company accrues that amount. When no amount within the range is a better estimate than any other amount, the company accrues the dollar amount at the low end of the range and discloses the dollar amount at the high end of the range. Unfortunately, in many cases, zero may arguably be the low point of the range, resulting in no liability being recognized. **[13], [14]**

Self-Insurance

As discussed earlier, contingencies are not recorded for general risks (e.g., losses that might arise due to poor expected economic conditions). Similarly, companies do not record contingencies for more specific future risks such as allowances for repairs. The reason: These items do meet the definition of a liability because they do not arise from a past transaction but instead relate to future events.

Underlying Concepts

Even if companies can estimate the amount of losses with a high degree of certainty, the losses are not liabilities because they result from a future event and not from a past event.

Some companies take out insurance policies against the potential losses from fire, flood, storm, and accident. Other companies do not. The reasons: Some risks are not insurable, the insurance rates are prohibitive (e.g., earthquakes and riots), or they make a business decision to self-insure. Self-insurance is another item that is not recognized as a contingency.

Despite its name, **self-insurance** is **not insurance but risk assumption**. Any company that assumes its own risks puts itself in the position of incurring expenses or losses as they happen. There is little theoretical justification for the establishment of a liability based on a hypothetical charge to insurance expense. This is "as if" accounting. The conditions for accrual stated in GAAP are not satisfied prior to the occurrence of the event. Until that time there is no diminution in the value of the property. And unlike an insurance company, which has contractual obligations to reimburse policyholders for losses, a company can have no such obligation to itself and, hence, no liability either before or after the occurrence of damage. **[15]**[19]

The note shown in Illustration 13-12 from the annual report of **Molson Coors Brewing Company** is typical of the self-insurance disclosure.

Molson Coors Brewing Company

Notes to Financial Statements (in part)

Note 21: Insurance. We are self-insured for certain insurable risks consisting primarily of employee health insurance programs, as well as workers' compensation, general liability, automobile liability, and property insurance deductibles or retentions . . . we fully insured future risks for long-term disability, and, in most states, workers' compensation, but maintained a self-insured position for workers' compensation for certain self-insured states and for claims incurred prior to the inception of the insurance coverage in Colorado in 1997.

ILLUSTRATION 13-12
Disclosure of Self-Insurance

Exposure to **risks of loss resulting from uninsured past injury to others**, however, is an existing condition involving uncertainty about the amount and timing of losses that may develop. In such a case, a contingency exists. A company with a fleet of vehicles for example, would have to accrue uninsured losses resulting from injury to others or damage to the property of others that took place prior to the date of the financial statements (if the experience of the company or other information enables it to make a reasonable estimate of the liability). However, it should not establish a liability for **expected future injury** to others or damage to the property of others, even if it can reasonably estimate the amount of losses.

[19]A commentary in *Forbes* (June 15, 1974, p. 42) stated its position on this matter quite succinctly: "The simple and unquestionable fact of life is this: Business is cyclical and full of unexpected surprises. Is it the role of accounting to disguise this unpleasant fact and create a fairyland of smoothly rising earnings? Or, should accounting reflect reality, warts and all—floods, expropriations and all manner of rude shocks?"

What do the numbers mean? MORE DISCLOSURE, PLEASE

On November 19, 2001, **Enron** filed its third-quarter financial statements and reported on its balance sheet debt of approximately $13 billion. Yet on the same day, at a meeting to discuss its liquidity crisis, Enron informed its bankers that its debt was approximately $38 billion. Company officers described the difference of *$25 billion* as being either off-balance-sheet or on the balance sheet other than debt.

As a result of the Enron bankruptcy and other financial reporting scandals, Congress passed the Sarbanes-Oxley Act of 2002. One of its provisions mandates that the Securities and Exchange Commission conduct a study to determine the extent of off-balance-sheet transactions occurring in U.S. businesses.

Table 1 below indicates the extent of disclosure and recognition of contingent liabilities. The study classified contingent liabilities into three categories: (1) litigation contingent liabilities, (2) environmental liabilities, and (3) guarantees. The statistics provided relate to reports filed by 10,100 companies listed on the U.S. stock exchanges in 2005.

Table 1

Type of Contingency	Companies Disclosing	Companies Recording
Litigation contingent liabilities	46.3%	5.1%
Environmental contingent liabilities	10.2%	5.1%
Guarantees	35.4%	10.2%

As Table 1 indicates, approximately 46 percent of companies disclosed litigation contingent liabilities, but only 5.1 percent recorded any liability related to these contingencies. On the other hand, 35 percent of the companies disclosed guarantees but a third of these companies (10.2 percent) recorded a liability for these contingencies.

Table 2 below shows the dollar amounts of the contingent liabilities companies disclosed and recorded.

Table 2

Type of Contingency	Companies Disclosing ($ millions)	Companies Recording ($ millions)
Litigation contingent liabilities	$52,354	$11,814
Environmental contingent liabilities	$23,414	$18,723
Guarantees	$46,535,399	$123,949

Table 2 indicates that companies disclosed litigation contingent liabilities of approximately $52 billion, but recorded only $11.8 billion as liabilities. Incredibly, companies disclosed more than *$46 trillion* of guarantees, a small fraction of which (just $124 billion) they recorded as liabilities.

The results of this study suggest that the FASB must continue to address the issue of contingencies to ensure that companies provide relevant and representationally faithful information for these types of financial events.

Source: "Report and Recommendations Pursuant to Section 401(c) of the Sarbanes-Oxley Act of 2002 on Arrangements with Off-Balance Sheet Implications, Special Purpose Entities, and Transparency of Filings by Issuers," United States Securities and Exchange Commission, Office of Chief Accountant, Office of Economic Analyses, Division of Corporation Finance (June 2005).

PRESENTATION AND ANALYSIS

Presentation of Current Liabilities

LEARNING OBJECTIVE 6
Indicate how to present and analyze liabilities and contingencies.

In practice, current liabilities are usually recorded and reported in financial statements at their full maturity value. Because of the short time periods involved, frequently less than one year, the difference between the present value of a current liability and the maturity value is usually not large. The profession accepts as immaterial any slight overstatement of liabilities that results from carrying current liabilities at maturity value. **[16]**[20]

[20]GAAP specifically exempts from present value measurements those payables arising from transactions with suppliers in the normal course of business that do not exceed approximately one year.

The current liabilities accounts are commonly presented as the first classification in the liabilities and stockholders' equity section of the balance sheet. Within the current liabilities section, companies may list the accounts in order of maturity, in descending order of amount, or in order of liquidation preference. Illustration 13-13 presents an excerpt of **Best Buy Co.**'s financial statements that is representative of the reports of large corporations.

ILLUSTRATION 13-13
Balance Sheet Presentation of Current Liabilities

Best Buy Co.
(dollars in thousands)

	March 3, 2012	February 26, 2011
Current assets		
Cash and cash equivalents	$ 1,199	$ 1,103
Short-term investments	—	22
Receivables	2,288	2,348
Merchandise inventories	5,731	5,897
Other current assets	1,079	1,103
Total current assets	$10,297	$10,473
Current liabilities		
Accounts payable	$ 5,364	$ 4,894
Unredeemed gift card liabilities	456	474
Accrued compensation and related expenses	539	570
Accrued liabilities	1,685	1,471
Accrued income taxes	288	256
Short-term debt	480	557
Current portion of long-term debt	43	441
Total current liabilities	$ 8,855	$ 8,663

Detail and supplemental information concerning current liabilities should be sufficient to meet the requirement of full disclosure. Companies should clearly identify secured liabilities, as well as indicate the related assets pledged as collateral. If the due date of any liability can be extended, a company should disclose the details. Companies should not offset current liabilities against assets that it will apply to their liquidation. Finally, current maturities of long-term debt are classified as current liabilities.

International Perspective

Companies reporting under IFRS often report noncurrent liabilities before current liabilities.

A major exception exists when a company will pay a currently maturing obligation from assets classified as long-term. For example, if a company will retire a bond payable using a bond sinking fund that is classified as a long-term asset, it should report the bonds payable in the long-term liabilities section. Presentation of this debt in the current liabilities section would distort the working capital position of the company.

If a company excludes a short-term obligation from current liabilities because of refinancing, it should include the following in the note to the financial statements:

1. A general description of the financing agreement.
2. The terms of any new obligation incurred or to be incurred.
3. The terms of any equity security issued or to be issued.

When a company expects to refinance on a long-term basis by issuing equity securities, it is not appropriate to include the short-term obligation in stockholders' equity. At the date of the balance sheet, the obligation is a liability and not stockholders' equity. Illustration 13-14 (on page 728) shows the disclosure requirements for an actual refinancing situation.

ILLUSTRATION 13-14
Actual Refinancing of Short-Term Debt

	December 31, 2014
Current liabilities	
Accounts payable	$ 3,600,000
Accrued payables	2,500,000
Income taxes payable	1,100,000
Current portion of long-term debt	1,000,000
Total current liabilities	$ 8,200,000
Long-term debt	
Notes payable refinanced in January 2015 (Note 1)	$ 2,000,000
11% bonds due serially through 2025	15,000,000
Total long-term debt	$17,000,000

Note 1: On January 19, 2015, the Company issued 50,000 shares of common stock and received proceeds totaling $2,385,000, of which $2,000,000 was used to liquidate notes payable that matured on February 1, 2015. Accordingly, such notes payable have been classified as long-term debt at December 31, 2014.

Presentation of Contingencies

A company records a loss contingency and a liability if the loss is both probable and estimable. But, if the loss is **either probable or estimable but not both**, and if there is at least a **reasonable possibility** that a company may have incurred a liability, it must disclose the following in the notes.

1. The nature of the contingency.
2. An estimate of the possible loss or range of loss or a statement that an estimate cannot be made.

Illustration 13-15 presents an extensive litigation disclosure note from the financial statements of **Raymark Corporation**. The note indicates that Raymark charged actual losses to operations and that a further liability may exist, but that the company cannot currently estimate this liability.

ILLUSTRATION 13-15
Disclosure of Loss Contingency through Litigation

Raymark Corporation

Note I: Litigation. Raymark is a defendant or co-defendant in a substantial number of lawsuits alleging wrongful injury and/or death from exposure to asbestos fibers in the air. The following table summarizes the activity in these lawsuits:

Claims	
Pending at beginning of year	8,719
Received during year	4,494
Settled or otherwise disposed of	(1,445)
Pending at end of year	11,768
Average indemnification cost	$3,364
Average cost per case, including defense costs	$6,499
Trial activity	
Verdicts for the Company	23
Total trials	36

The following table presents the cost of defending asbestos litigation, together with related insurance and workers' compensation expenses.

Included in operating profit	$ 1,872,000
Nonoperating expense	9,077,000
Total	$10,949,000

The Company is seeking to reasonably determine its liability. However, it is not possible to predict which theory of insurance will apply, the number of lawsuits still to be filed, the cost of settling and defending the existing and unfiled cases, or the ultimate impact of these lawsuits on the Company's consolidated financial statements.

Companies should disclose certain other contingent liabilities, even though the possibility of loss may be remote, as follows.

International Perspective

GAAP provides more guidance on the content of disclosures about contingencies than does IFRS.

1. Guarantees of indebtedness of others.
2. Obligations of commercial banks under "stand-by letters of credit."
3. Guarantees to repurchase receivables (or any related property) that have been sold or assigned.

Disclosure should include the nature and amount of the guarantee and, if estimable, the amount that the company can recover from outside parties.[21] Cities Service Company disclosed its guarantees of others' indebtedness in the following note.

Cities Service Company

Note 10: Contingent Liabilities. The Company and certain subsidiaries have guaranteed debt obligations of approximately $62 million of companies in which substantial stock investments are held. Also, under long-term agreements with certain pipeline companies in which stock interests are held, the Company and its subsidiaries have agreed to provide minimum revenue for product shipments. The Company has guaranteed mortgage debt ($80 million) incurred by a 50 percent owned tanker affiliate for construction of tankers which are under long-term charter contracts to the Company and others. It is not anticipated that any loss will result from any of the above described agreements.

ILLUSTRATION 13-16
Disclosure of Guarantees of Indebtedness

Analysis of Current Liabilities

The distinction between current liabilities and long-term debt is important. It provides information about the liquidity of the company. Liquidity regarding a liability is the expected time to elapse before its payment. In other words, a liability soon to be paid is a current liability. A liquid company is better able to withstand a financial downturn. Also, it has a better chance of taking advantage of investment opportunities that develop.

Analysts use certain basic ratios such as net cash flow provided by operating activities to current liabilities, and the turnover ratios for receivables and inventory, to assess liquidity. Two other ratios used to examine liquidity are the current ratio and the acid-test ratio.

Current Ratio

The **current ratio** is the ratio of total current assets to total current liabilities. Illustration 13-17 shows its formula.

$$\text{Current ratio} = \frac{\text{Current assets}}{\text{Current liabilities}}$$

ILLUSTRATION 13-17
Formula for Current Ratio

The ratio is frequently expressed as a coverage of so many times. Sometimes it is called the **working capital ratio** because working capital is the excess of current assets over current liabilities.

[21]As discussed earlier (footnote 16), the FASB has issued additional disclosure and recognition requirements for guarantees. The interpretation responds to confusion about the reporting of guarantees used in certain transactions. The new rules expand existing disclosure requirements for most guarantees, including loan guarantees such as standby letters of credit. It also will result in companies recognizing more liabilities at fair value for the obligations assumed under a guarantee. [17]

A satisfactory current ratio does not disclose that a portion of the current assets may be tied up in slow-moving inventories. With inventories, especially raw materials and work in process, there is a question of how long it will take to transform them into the finished product and what ultimately will be realized in the sale of the merchandise. Eliminating the inventories, along with any prepaid expenses, from the amount of current assets might provide better information for short-term creditors. Therefore, some analysts use the acid-test ratio in place of the current ratio.

Acid-Test Ratio

Many analysts favor an **acid-test** or **quick ratio** that relates total current liabilities to cash, marketable securities, and receivables. Illustration 13-18 shows the formula for this ratio. As you can see, the acid-test ratio does not include inventories.

ILLUSTRATION 13-18
Formula for Acid-Test Ratio

$$\text{Acid-test ratio} = \frac{\text{Cash} + \text{Short-term investments} + \text{Net receivables}}{\text{Current liabilities}}$$

To illustrate the computation of these two ratios, we use the information for **Best Buy Co.** in Illustration 13-13 (on page 727). Illustration 13-19 shows the computation of the current and acid-test ratios for Best Buy.

ILLUSTRATION 13-19
Computation of Current and Acid-Test Ratios for Best Buy Co.

$$\text{Current ratio} = \frac{\text{Current assets}}{\text{Current liabilities}} = \frac{\$10{,}297}{\$8{,}855} = 1.16 \text{ times}$$

$$\text{Acid-test ratio} = \frac{\text{Cash} + \text{Short-term investments} + \text{Net receivables}}{\text{Current liabilities}} = \frac{\$3{,}487}{\$8{,}855} = 0.39 \text{ times}$$

You will want to read the **IFRS INSIGHTS** on pages 753–761 for discussion of IFRS related to current liabilities and contingencies.

From this information, it appears that Best Buy's current position is adequate. However, the acid-test ratio is well below 1. A comparison to another retailer, **RadioShack**, whose current ratio is 2.73 and whose acid-test ratio is 1.44, indicates that Best Buy is less liquid and carrying more inventory than its industry counterparts.

Evolving Issue GREENHOUSE GASES: LET'S BE STANDARD-SETTERS

Ok, here is your chance to determine what to do about a very fundamental issue—how to account for greenhouse gases (GHG), often referred to as carbon emissions. Many governments are trying a market-based system, in which companies pay for an excessive amount of carbon emissions put into the atmosphere. In this market-based system, companies are granted carbon allowance permits. Each permit allows them to discharge, as an example, one metric ton of carbon dioxide (CO_2). In some cases, companies may receive a number of these permits free—in other situations, they must pay for them. Other approaches require companies only to pay when they exceed a certain amount. The question is, how to account for these permits and related liabilities? For example, what happens when the permits issued by the government are free? Should an asset and revenue be reported? And if an asset is recorded, should the debit be to an intangible asset or inventory? Also, should the company recognize a liability related to its pollution? And how do we account for companies that have to purchase permits because they have exceeded their allowance?

Two views seem to have emerged. The first is referred to as the **net liability approach**. In this approach, a company does not recognize an asset or liability. A company only recognizes a liability once GHG exceed the permits granted. To illustrate, Holton Refinery receives permits on January 1, 2014, representing the right to emit 10,000 tons of GHG for the year 2014. Other data:

- The market price of each permit at date of issuance is $10 per ton.

- During the year, Holton emits 12,000 tons.
- The market price for a permit is now \$16 per ton at December 31, 2014.

Under the net liability approach, Holton records only a liability of \$32,000 for the additional amount that it must pay for the 2,000 permits it must purchase at \$16 per ton.

Another approach is referred to as the **government grant approach.** In this approach, permits granted by the government are recorded at their fair value based on the initial price of \$10 per ton. The asset recorded is an intangible asset. At the same time, an Unearned Revenue account is credited, which is subsequently recognized in income over the 2014 year. During 2014, a liability and a related emission expense of \$132,000 is recognized (10,000 tons × \$10 + 2,000 tons × \$16). The chart below compares the results of each approach on the financial statements.

	Net Liability Approach	Government Grant Approach
Income Statement		
Revenues	\$ 0	\$100,000
Emission expenses	32,000	132,000
Net loss	\$32,000	\$ 32,000
Balance Sheet		
Assets	\$ 0	\$100,000
Liabilities	32,000	132,000

So what do you think—net liability or government grant approach? As indicated, companies presently can report this information either way, plus some other variants which were not mentioned here. Please feel free to contact the FASB regarding your views.

SUMMARY OF LEARNING OBJECTIVES

1 Describe the nature, type, and valuation of current liabilities. Current liabilities are obligations whose liquidation a company reasonably expects to require the use of current assets or the creation of other current liabilities. Theoretically, liabilities should be measured by the present value of the future outlay of cash required to liquidate them. In practice, companies usually record and report current liabilities at their full maturity value.

There are several types of current liabilities, such as (1) accounts payable, (2) notes payable, (3) current maturities of long-term debt, (4) dividends payable, (5) customer advances and deposits, (6) unearned revenues, (7) taxes payable, and (8) employee-related liabilities.

2 Explain the classification issues of short-term debt expected to be refinanced. A short-term obligation is excluded from current liabilities if both of the following conditions are met. (1) The company must intend to refinance the obligation on a long-term basis, *and* (2) it must demonstrate an ability to consummate the refinancing.

3 Identify types of employee-related liabilities. The employee-related liabilities are (1) payroll deductions, (2) compensated absences, and (3) bonus agreements.

4 Identify the criteria used to account for and disclose gain and loss contingencies. Gain contingencies are not recorded. Instead, they are disclosed in the notes only when the probabilities are high that a gain contingency will occur. A company should accrue an estimated loss from a loss contingency by charging expense and recording a liability only if *both* of the following conditions are met. (1) Information available prior to the issuance of the financial statements indicates that it is probable

KEY TERMS

accumulated rights, *713*
acid-test (quick) ratio, *730*
asset retirement obligation, *723*
bonus, *714*
cash dividend payable, *707*
compensated absences, *712*
contingency, *715*
contingent liabilities, *716*
current liabilities, *702*
current maturities of long-term debt, *705*
current ratio, *729*
expense warranty approach, *719*
FICA, *710*
FUTA, *711*
gain contingencies, *715*
liabilities, *702*
litigation, claims, and assessments, *718*
loss contingencies, *716*

that a liability has been incurred at the date of the financial statements, and (2) the amount of the loss can be reasonably estimated.

5 Explain the accounting for different types of loss contingencies. The following factors must be considered in determining whether to record a liability with respect to pending or threatened litigation and actual or possible claims and assessments: (1) the time period in which the underlying cause for action occurred, (2) the probability of an unfavorable outcome, and (3) the ability to reasonably estimate the amount of loss.

If it is probable that customers will make claims under warranties relating to goods or services that have been sold and it can reasonably estimate the costs involved, the company uses the accrual method. It charges warranty costs under the accrual basis to operating expense in the year of sale.

Premiums, coupon offers, and rebates are made to stimulate sales. Companies should charge their costs to expense in the period of the sale that benefits from the premium plan.

A company must recognize asset retirement obligations when it has an existing legal obligation related to the retirement of a long-lived asset and it can reasonably estimate the amount.

6 Indicate how to present and analyze liabilities and contingencies. The current liability accounts are usually presented as the first classification in the liabilities and stockholders' equity section of the balance sheet. Within the current liabilities section, companies may list the accounts in order of maturity, in descending order of amount, or in order of liquidation preference. Detail and supplemental information concerning current liabilities should be sufficient to meet the requirement of full disclosure. If the loss is either probable or estimable but not both, and if there is at least a reasonable possibility that a company may have incurred a liability, it should disclose in the notes both the nature of the contingency and an estimate of the possible loss. Two ratios used to analyze liquidity are the current and acid-test ratios.

DEMONSTRATION PROBLEM

Listed below are selected transactions of Baileys' Department Store for the current year ending December 31.

1. On December 5, the store received $500 from the Jackson Players as a deposit to be returned after certain furniture to be used in stage production was returned on January 15.
2. During December, cash sales totaled $798,000, which includes the 5% sales tax that must be remitted to the state by the fifteenth day of the following month.
3. On December 10, the store purchased for cash three delivery trucks for $120,000. The trucks were purchased in a state that applies a 5% sales tax.
4. The store determined it will cost $100,000 to restore the area (considered a land improvement) surrounding one of its store parking lots, when the store is closed in 2 years. Baileys' estimates the fair value of the obligation at December 31 is $84,000.
5. As a result of uninsured accidents during the year, personal injury suits for $350,000 and $60,000 have been filed against the company. It is the judgment of Baileys' legal counsel that an unfavorable outcome is unlikely in the $60,000 case but that an unfavorable verdict approximating $250,000 (reliably estimated) will probably result in the $350,000 case.
6. Baileys' Midwest store division consisting of 12 stores in "Tornado Alley" is uninsurable because of the special risk of injury to customers, employees, and losses due to severe weather and subpar construction standards in older malls. The year 2014 is considered one of the safest (luckiest) in the division's history because no loss due to injury or casualty was suffered. Having suffered an average of three casualties a year during the rest of the past decade (ranging from $60,000 to $700,000), management is certain that next year the company will probably not be so fortunate.

Instructions

(a) Prepare all the journal entries necessary to record the transactions noted above as they occurred and any adjusting journal entries relative to the transactions that would be required to present fair financial statements at December 31. Date each entry. For simplicity, assume that adjusting entries are recorded only once a year on December 31.

(b) For items 5 and 6, indicate what should be reported relative to each situation in the financial statements and accompanying notes. Explain why.

Solution

			Debit	Credit
(a)	1. Dec. 5	Cash	500	
		Due to Customer		500
	2. Dec. 1–31	Cash	798,000	
		Sales Revenue ($798,000 ÷ 1.05)		760,000
		Sales Taxes Payable ($760,000 × .05)		38,000
	3. Dec. 10	Trucks ($120,000 × 1.05)	126,000	
		Cash		126,000
	4. Dec. 31	Land Improvements	84,000	
		Asset Retirement Obligation		84,000
	5.	Lawsuit Loss	250,000	
		Lawsuit Liability		250,000

6. No entry required.

(b) 5. A loss and a liability have been recorded in the first case because (i) information is available prior to the issuance of the financial statements that indicates it is probable that a liability had been incurred at the date of the financial statements and (ii) the amount is reasonably estimable. That is, the occurrence of the uninsured accidents during the year plus the outstanding injury suits and the attorney's estimate of probable loss required recognition of a loss contingency.

6. Even though Baileys' Midwest store division is uninsurable due to high risk and has sustained repeated losses in the past, as of the balance sheet date no assets have been impaired or liabilities incurred, nor is an amount reasonably estimable. Therefore, this situation does not satisfy the criteria for recognition of a loss contingency. Also, unless a casualty has occurred or there is some other evidence to indicate impairment of an asset prior to the issuance of the financial statements, there is no disclosure required relative to a loss contingency. Disclosure is required when one or both of the criteria for a loss contingency are not satisfied and there is a reasonable possibility that a liability may have been incurred or an asset impaired, or it is probable that a claim will be asserted and there is a reasonable possibility of an unfavorable outcome.

FASB CODIFICATION

FASB Codification References

[1] FASB ASC 480-10-05. [Predecessor literature: "Accounting for Certain Financial Instruments with Characteristics of Both Liabilities and Equity," *Statement of Financial Accounting Standards No. 150* (Norwalk, Conn.: FASB, 2003).]

[2] FASB ASC 210-10-45-6. [Predecessor literature: Committee on Accounting Procedure, American Institute of Certified Public Accountants, "Accounting Research and Terminology Bulletins," Final Edition (New York: AICPA, 1961), p. 21.]

[3] FASB ASC 470-10-05-7. [Predecessor literature: "Classification of Short-term Obligations Expected to Be Refinanced," *Statement of Financial Accounting Standards No. 6* (Stamford, Conn.: FASB, 1975), par. 2.]

[4] FASB ASC 470-10-45-11. [Predecessor literature: "Classification of Obligations That Are Callable by the Creditor," *Statement of Financial Accounting Standards No. 78* (Stamford, Conn.: FASB, 1983).]

[5] FASB ASC 470-10-45-14. [Predecessor literature: "Classification of Short-term Obligations Expected to Be Refinanced," *Statement of Financial Accounting Standards No. 6* (Stamford, Conn.: FASB, 1975), paras. 10 and 11.]

[6] FASB ASC 710-10-25-1. [Predecessor literature: "Accounting for Compensated Absences," *Statement of Financial Accounting Standards No. 43* (Stamford, Conn.: FASB, 1980), par. 6.]

[7] FASB ASC 712-10-05. [Predecessor literature: "Employers' Accounting for Postemployment Benefits," *Statement of Financial Accounting Standards No. 112* (Norwalk, Conn.: FASB, November 1992), par. 18.]

[8] FASB ASC 450-10-05-4. [Predecessor literature: "Accounting for Contingencies," *Statement of Financial Accounting Standards No. 5* (Stamford, Conn.: FASB, 1975), par. 1.]

[9] FASB ASC 605-20-25. [Predecessor literature: "Accounting for Separately Extended Warranty and Product Maintenance Contracts," *FASB Technical Bulletin No. 90-1* (Stamford, Conn.: FASB, 1990).]

[10] FASB ASC 605-20-25-3. [Predecessor literature: "Accounting for Separately Extended Warranty and Product Maintenance Contracts," *FASB Technical Bulletin No. 90-1* (Stamford, Conn.: FASB, 1990).]

[11] FASB ASC 460-10-50-8. [Predecessor literature: "Guarantor's Accounting and Disclosure Requirements for Guarantees, Including Indirect Guarantees of Indebtedness of Others," *FASB Interpretation No. 45* (Norwalk, Conn.: FASB, 2002).]

[12] FASB ASC 410-20-05. [Predecessor literature: "Accounting for Asset Retirement Obligations," *Statement of Financial Accounting Standards No. 143* (Norwalk, Conn.: FASB, 2001).]

[13] FASB ASC 450-20-30-1. [Predecessor literature: "Reasonable Estimation of the Amount of a Loss," *FASB Interpretation No. 14* (Stamford, Conn.: FASB, 1976), par. 3.]

[14] FASB ASC 450-10-05. [Predecessor literature: "Accounting for Contingencies," *FASB Statement No. 5* (Stamford, Conn.: FASB, 1975).]

[15] FASB ASC 450-20-55-5. [Predecessor literature: "Accounting for Contingencies," *FASB Statement No. 5* (Stamford, Conn.: FASB, 1975), par. 28.]

[16] FASB ASC 835-30-15-3. [Predecessor literature: "Interest on Receivables and Payables," *Opinions of the Accounting Principles Board No. 21* (New York: AICPA, 1971), par. 3.]

[17] FASB ASC 460-10-50-8. [Predecessor literature: "Guarantor's Accounting and Disclosure Requirements for Guarantees, Including Indirect Guarantees of Indebtedness of Others," *FASB Interpretation No. 45* (Norwalk, Conn.: FASB, 2002).]

Exercises

If your school has a subscription to the FASB Codification, go to *http://aaahq.org/asclogin.cfm* to log in and prepare responses to the following. Provide Codification references for your responses.

CE13-1 Access the glossary ("Master Glossary") to answer the following.

(a) What is an asset retirement obligation?
(b) What is the definition of "current liabilities"?
(c) What does it mean if something is "reasonably possible"?
(d) What is a warranty?

CE13-2 What must an entity disclose about its asset retirement obligations?

CE13-3 What are three examples of estimates that are used in accounting that are not contingencies? Can you explain why they are not considered contingencies?

CE13-4 Under what conditions must an employer accrue a liability for employees' compensation for future absences?

An additional Codification case can be found in the Using Your Judgment section, on page 753.

Be sure to check the book's companion website for a Review and Analysis Exercise, with solution.

WileyPLUS **Brief Exercises, Exercises, Problems, and many more learning and assessment tools and resources are available for practice in WileyPLUS.**

QUESTIONS

1. Distinguish between a current liability and a long-term debt.

2. Assume that your friend Will Morris, who is a music major, asks you to define and discuss the nature of a liability. Assist him by preparing a definition of a liability and by explaining to him what you believe are the elements or factors inherent in the concept of a liability.

3. Why is the liabilities section of the balance sheet of primary significance to bankers?

4. How are current liabilities related by definition to current assets? How are current liabilities related to a company's operating cycle?

5. Leon Wight, a newly hired loan analyst, is examining the current liabilities of a corporate loan applicant. He observes that unearned revenues have declined in the current year compared to the prior year. Is this a positive indicator about the client's liquidity? Explain.

6. How is present value related to the concept of a liability?

7. What is the nature of a "discount" on notes payable?

8. How should a debt callable by the creditor be reported in the debtor's financial statements?

9. Under what conditions should a short-term obligation be excluded from current liabilities?

10. What evidence is necessary to demonstrate the ability to consummate the refinancing of short-term debt?

11. Discuss the accounting treatment or disclosure that should be accorded a declared but unpaid cash dividend, an accumulated but undeclared dividend on cumulative preferred stock, and a stock dividend distributable.

12. How does unearned revenue arise? Why can it be classified properly as a current liability? Give several examples of business activities that result in unearned revenues.

13. What are compensated absences?

14. Under what conditions must an employer accrue a liability for the cost of compensated absences?

15. Under what conditions is an employer required to accrue a liability for sick pay? Under what conditions is an employer permitted but not required to accrue a liability for sick pay?

16. Faith Battle operates a health food store, and she has been the only employee. Her business is growing, and she is considering hiring some additional staff to help her in the store. Explain to her the various payroll deductions that she will have to account for, including their potential impact on her financial statements, if she hires additional staff.

17. Define (a) a contingency and (b) a contingent liability.

18. Under what conditions should a contingent liability be recorded?

19. Distinguish between a determinable current liability and a contingent liability. Give two examples of each type.

20. How are the terms "probable," "reasonably possible," and "remote" related to contingent liabilities?

21. Contrast the cash-basis method and the accrual method of accounting for warranty costs.

22. Grant Company has had a record-breaking year in terms of growth in sales and profitability. However, market research indicates that it will experience operating losses in two of its major businesses next year. The controller has proposed that the company record a provision for these future losses this year, since it can afford to take the charge and still show good results. Advise the controller on the appropriateness of this charge.

23. How does the expense warranty approach differ from the sales warranty approach?

24. Southeast Airlines Inc. awards members of its Flightline program a second ticket at half price, valid for 2 years anywhere on its flight system, when a full-price ticket is purchased. How would you account for the full-fare and half-fare tickets?

25. Pacific Airlines Co. awards members of its Frequent Fliers Club one free round-trip ticket, anywhere on its flight system, for every 50,000 miles flown on its planes. How would you account for the free ticket award?

26. When must a company recognize an asset retirement obligation?

27. Should a liability be recorded for risk of loss due to lack of insurance coverage? Discuss.

28. What factors must be considered in determining whether or not to record a liability for pending litigation? For threatened litigation?

29. Within the current liabilities section, how do you believe the accounts should be listed? Defend your position.

30. How does the acid-test ratio differ from the current ratio? How are they similar?

31. When should liabilities for each of the following items be recorded on the books of an ordinary business corporation?

(a) Acquisition of goods by purchase on credit.

(b) Officers' salaries.

(c) Special bonus to employees.

(d) Dividends.

(e) Purchase commitments.

BRIEF EXERCISES

1 **BE13-1** Roley Corporation uses a periodic inventory system and the gross method of accounting for purchase discounts. On July 1, Roley purchased $60,000 of inventory, terms 2/10, n/30, FOB shipping point. Roley paid freight costs of $1,200. On July 3, Roley returned damaged goods and received credit of $6,000. On July 10, Roley paid for the goods. Prepare all necessary journal entries for Roley.

1 **BE13-2** Upland Company borrowed $40,000 on November 1, 2014, by signing a $40,000, 9%, 3-month note. Prepare Upland's November 1, 2014, entry; the December 31, 2014, annual adjusting entry; and the February 1, 2015, entry.

1 **BE13-3** Takemoto Corporation borrowed $60,000 on November 1, 2014, by signing a $61,350, 3-month, zero-interest-bearing note. Prepare Takemoto's November 1, 2014, entry; the December 31, 2014, annual adjusting entry; and the February 1, 2015, entry.

1 2 **BE13-4** At December 31, 2014, Burr Corporation owes $500,000 on a note payable due February 15, 2015. (a) If Burr refinances the obligation by issuing a long-term note on February 14 and using the proceeds to pay off the note due February 15, how much of the $500,000 should be reported as a current liability at December 31, 2014? (b) If Burr pays off the note on February 15, 2015, and then borrows $1,000,000 on a long-term basis on March 1, how much of the $500,000 should be reported as a current liability at December 31, 2014, the end of the fiscal year?

1 **BE13-5** Sport Pro Magazine sold 12,000 annual subscriptions on August 1, 2014, for $18 each. Prepare Sport Pro's August 1, 2014, journal entry and the December 31, 2014, annual adjusting entry, assuming the magazines are published and delivered monthly.

1 **BE13-6** Dillons Corporation made credit sales of $30,000 which are subject to 6% sales tax. The corporation also made cash sales which totaled $20,670 including the 6% sales tax. (a) Prepare the entry to record Dillons' credit sales. (b) Prepare the entry to record Dillons' cash sales.

3 **BE13-7** Lexington Corporation's weekly payroll of $24,000 included FICA taxes withheld of $1,836, federal taxes withheld of $2,990, state taxes withheld of $920, and insurance premiums withheld of $250. Prepare the journal entry to record Lexington's payroll.

3 **BE13-8** Kasten Inc. provides paid vacations to its employees. At December 31, 2014, 30 employees have each earned 2 weeks of vacation time. The employees' average salary is $500 per week. Prepare Kasten's December 31, 2014, adjusting entry.

3 **BE13-9** Mayaguez Corporation provides its officers with bonuses based on net income. For 2014, the bonuses total $350,000 and are paid on February 15, 2015. Prepare Mayaguez's December 31, 2014, adjusting entry and the February 15, 2015, entry.

4 5 **BE13-10** Scorcese Inc. is involved in a lawsuit at December 31, 2014. (a) Prepare the December 31 entry assuming it is probable that Scorcese will be liable for $900,000 as a result of this suit. (b) Prepare the December 31 entry, if any, assuming it is *not* probable that Scorcese will be liable for any payment as a result of this suit.

4 5 **BE13-11** Buchanan Company recently was sued by a competitor for patent infringement. Attorneys have determined that it is probable that Buchanan will lose the case and that a reasonable estimate of damages to be paid by Buchanan is $300,000. In light of this case, Buchanan is considering establishing a $100,000 self-insurance allowance. What entry(ies), if any, should Buchanan record to recognize this loss contingency?

4 5 **BE13-12** Calaf's Drillers erects and places into service an off-shore oil platform on January 1, 2015, at a cost of $10,000,000. Calaf is legally required to dismantle and remove the platform at the end of its useful life in 10 years. Calaf estimates it will cost $1,000,000 to dismantle and remove the platform at the end of its useful life in 10 years. (The fair value at January 1, 2015, of the dismantle and removal costs is $450,000.) Prepare the entry to record the asset retirement obligation.

4 5 **BE13-13** Streep Factory provides a 2-year warranty with one of its products which was first sold in 2014. In that year, Streep spent $70,000 servicing warranty claims. At year-end, Streep estimates that an additional $400,000 will be spent in the future to service warranty claims related to 2014 sales. Prepare Streep's journal entry to record the $70,000 expenditure and the December 31 adjusting entry, assuming the expenditures are inventory costs.

4 5 **BE13-14** Leppard Corporation sells DVD players. The corporation also offers its customers a 2-year warranty contract. During 2014, Leppard sold 20,000 warranty contracts at $99 each. The corporation spent $180,000 servicing warranties during 2014, and it estimates that an additional $900,000 will be spent in the future to service the warranties. Prepare Leppard's journal entries for (a) the sale of contracts, (b) the cost of servicing the warranties, and (c) the recognition of warranty revenue. Assume the service costs are inventory costs.

4 5 **BE13-15** Wynn Company offers a set of building blocks to customers who send in 3 UPC codes from Wynn cereal, along with 50¢. The block sets cost Wynn $1.10 each to purchase and 60¢ each to mail to customers. During 2014, Wynn sold 1,200,000 boxes of cereal. The company expects 30% of the UPC codes to be sent in. During 2014, 120,000 UPC codes were redeemed. Prepare Wynn's December 31, 2014, adjusting entry.

EXERCISES

1 **E13-1 (Balance Sheet Classification of Various Liabilities)** How would each of the following items be reported on the balance sheet?

(a) Accrued vacation pay.
(b) Estimated taxes payable.
(c) Service warranties on appliance sales.
(d) Bank overdraft.
(e) Employee payroll deductions unremitted.
(f) Unpaid bonus to officers.
(g) Deposit received from customer to guarantee performance of a contract.
(h) Sales taxes payable.
(i) Gift certificates sold to customers but not yet redeemed.
(j) Premium offers outstanding.
(k) Discount on notes payable.
(l) Personal injury claim pending.
(m) Current maturities of long-term debts to be paid from current assets.
(n) Cash dividends declared but unpaid.
(o) Dividends in arrears on preferred stock.
(p) Loans from officers.

1 **E13-2 (Accounts and Notes Payable)** The following are selected 2014 transactions of Sean Astin Corporation.

XLS

Sept. 1	Purchased inventory from Encino Company on account for $50,000. Astin records purchases gross and uses a periodic inventory system.
Oct. 1	Issued a $50,000, 12-month, 8% note to Encino in payment of account.
Oct. 1	Borrowed $50,000 from the Shore Bank by signing a 12-month, zero-interest-bearing $54,000 note.

Instructions

(a) Prepare journal entries for the selected transactions above.
(b) Prepare adjusting entries at December 31.
(c) Compute the total net liability to be reported on the December 31 balance sheet for:
  (1) The interest-bearing note.
  (2) The zero-interest-bearing note.

2 **E13-3 (Refinancing of Short-Term Debt)** On December 31, 2014, Hattie McDaniel Company had $1,200,000 of short-term debt in the form of notes payable due February 2, 2015. On January 21, 2015, the company issued 25,000 shares of its common stock for $38 per share, receiving $950,000 proceeds after brokerage fees and other costs of issuance. On February 2, 2015, the proceeds from the stock sale, supplemented by an additional $250,000 cash, are used to liquidate the $1,200,000 debt. The December 31, 2014, balance sheet is issued on February 23, 2015.

Instructions

Show how the $1,200,000 of short-term debt should be presented on the December 31, 2014, balance sheet, including note disclosure.

2 **E13-4 (Refinancing of Short-Term Debt)** On December 31, 2014, Kate Holmes Company has $7,000,000 of short-term debt in the form of notes payable to Gotham State Bank due in 2015. On January 28, 2015, Holmes enters into a refinancing agreement with Gotham that will permit it to borrow up to 60% of the gross amount of its accounts receivable. Receivables are expected to range between a low of $6,000,000 in May to a high of $8,000,000 in October during the year 2015. The interest cost of the maturing short-term debt is 15%, and the new agreement calls for a fluctuating interest at 1% above the prime rate on notes due in 2019. Holmes's December 31, 2014, balance sheet is issued on February 15, 2015.

Instructions

Prepare a partial balance sheet for Holmes at December 31, 2014, showing how its $7,000,000 of short-term debt should be presented, including footnote disclosure.

3 **E13-5 (Compensated Absences)** Matt Broderick Company began operations on January 2, 2013. It employs 9 individuals who work 8-hour days and are paid hourly. Each employee earns 10 paid vacation days and 6 paid sick days annually. Vacation days may be taken after January 15 of the year following the year in which they are earned. Sick days may be taken as soon as they are earned; unused sick days accumulate. Additional information is as follows.

Actual Hourly Wage Rate		Vacation Days Used by Each Employee		Sick Days Used by Each Employee	
2013	2014	2013	2014	2013	2014
$10	$11	0	9	4	5

Matt Broderick Company has chosen to accrue the cost of compensated absences at rates of pay in effect during the period when earned and to accrue sick pay when earned.

Instructions

(a) Prepare journal entries to record transactions related to compensated absences during 2013 and 2014.

(b) Compute the amounts of any liability for compensated absences that should be reported on the balance sheet at December 31, 2013 and 2014.

3 **E13-6 (Compensated Absences)** Assume the facts in E13-5 except that Matt Broderick Company has chosen not to accrue paid sick leave until used, and has chosen to accrue vacation time at expected future rates of pay without discounting. The company used the following projected rates to accrue vacation time.

Year in Which Vacation Time Was Earned	Projected Future Pay Rates Used to Accrue Vacation Pay
2013	$10.75
2014	11.60

Instructions

(a) Prepare journal entries to record transactions related to compensated absences during 2013 and 2014.

(b) Compute the amounts of any liability for compensated absences that should be reported on the balance sheet at December 31, 2013, and 2014.

1 **E13-7 (Adjusting Entry for Sales Tax)** During the month of June, Rowling Boutique had cash sales of $233,200 and credit sales of $153,700, both of which include the 6% sales tax that must be remitted to the state by July 15.

Instructions

Prepare the adjusting entry that should be recorded to fairly present the June 30 financial statements.

3 **E13-8 (Payroll Tax Entries)** The payroll of YellowCard Company for September 2013 is as follows.

Total payroll was $480,000, of which $110,000 is exempt from Social Security tax because it represented amounts paid in excess of $113,700 to certain employees. The amount paid to employees in excess of $7,000 was $400,000. Income taxes in the amount of $80,000 were withheld, as was $9,000 in union dues. The state unemployment tax is 3.5%, but YellowCard Company is allowed a credit of 2.3% by the state for its unemployment experience. Also, assume that the current FICA tax is 7.65% on an employee's wages to $113,700 and 1.45% in excess of $113,700. No employee for YellowCard makes more than $125,000. The federal unemployment tax rate is 0.8% after state credit.

Instructions

Prepare the necessary journal entries if the wages and salaries paid and the employer payroll taxes are recorded separately.

3 **E13-9 (Payroll Tax Entries)** Green Day Hardware Company's payroll for November 2014 is summarized below.

		Amount Subject to Payroll Taxes		
			Unemployment Tax	
Payroll	Wages Due	FICA	Federal	State
Factory	$120,000	$120,000	$40,000	$40,000
Sales	32,000	32,000	4,000	4,000
Administrative	36,000	36,000	—	—
Total	$188,000	$188,000	$44,000	$44,000

At this point in the year, some employees have already received wages in excess of those to which payroll taxes apply. Assume that the state unemployment tax is 2.5%. The FICA rate is 7.65% on an employee's wages to $113,700 and 1.45% in excess of $113,700. Of the $188,000 wages subject to FICA tax, $20,000 of the sales wages is in excess of $113,700. Federal unemployment tax rate is 0.8% after credits. Income tax withheld amounts to $16,000 for factory, $7,000 for sales, and $6,000 for administrative.

Instructions

(a) Prepare a schedule showing the employer's total cost of wages for November by function. (Round all computations to nearest dollar.)

(b) Prepare the journal entries to record the factory, sales, and administrative payrolls including the employer's payroll taxes.

5 **E13-10 (Warranties)** Soundgarden Company sold 200 color laser copiers in 2014 for $4,000 apiece, together with a one-year warranty. Maintenance on each copier during the warranty period averages $330.

Instructions

(a) Prepare entries to record the sale of the copiers and the related warranty costs, assuming that the accrual method is used. Actual warranty costs incurred in 2014 were $17,000.

(b) On the basis of the data above, prepare the appropriate entries, assuming that the cash-basis method is used.

5 **E13-11 (Warranties)** Sheryl Crow Equipment Company sold 500 Rollomatics during 2014 at $6,000 each. During 2014, Crow spent $20,000 servicing the 2-year warranties that accompany the Rollomatic. All applicable transactions are on a cash basis.

Instructions

(a) Prepare 2014 entries for Crow using the expense warranty approach. Assume that Crow estimates the total cost of servicing the warranties will be $120,000 for 2 years.

(b) Prepare 2014 entries for Crow assuming that the warranties are not an integral part of the sale. Assume that of the sales total, $150,000 relates to sales of warranty contracts. Crow estimates the total cost of servicing the warranties will be $120,000 for 2 years. Estimate revenues to be recognized on the basis of costs incurred and estimated costs.

5 **E13-12 (Premium Entries)** No Doubt Company includes 1 coupon in each box of soap powder that it packs, and 10 coupons are redeemable for a premium (a kitchen utensil). In 2014, No Doubt Company purchased 8,800 premiums at 80 cents each and sold 110,000 boxes of soap powder at $3.30 per box; 44,000 coupons were presented for redemption in 2014. It is estimated that 60% of the coupons will eventually be presented for redemption.

Instructions

Prepare all the entries that would be made relative to sales of soap powder and to the premium plan in 2014.

4 5 **E13-13 (Contingencies)** Presented below are three independent situations. Answer the question at the end of each situation.

1. During 2014, Salt-n-Pepa Inc. became involved in a tax dispute with the IRS. Salt-n-Pepa's attorneys have indicated that they believe it is probable that Salt-n-Pepa will lose this dispute. They also believe that Salt-n-Pepa will have to pay the IRS between $900,000 and $1,400,000. After the 2014 financial statements were issued, the case was settled with the IRS for $1,200,000. What amount, if any, should be reported as a liability for this contingency as of December 31, 2014?
2. On October 1, 2014, Alan Jackson Chemical was identified as a potentially responsible party by the Environmental Protection Agency. Jackson's management along with its counsel have concluded that it is probable that Jackson will be responsible for damages, and a reasonable estimate of these damages is $5,000,000. Jackson's insurance policy of $9,000,000 has a deductible clause of $500,000. How should Alan Jackson Chemical report this information in its financial statements at December 31, 2014?
3. Melissa Etheridge Inc. had a manufacturing plant in Sudan, which was destroyed in the civil war. It is not certain who will compensate Etheridge for this destruction, but Etheridge has been assured by governmental officials that it will receive a definite amount for this plant. The amount of the compensation will be less than the fair value of the plant, but more than its book value. How should the contingency be reported in the financial statements of Etheridge Inc.?

5 **E13-14 (Asset Retirement Obligation)** Oil Products Company purchases an oil tanker depot on January 1, 2014, at a cost of $600,000. Oil Products expects to operate the depot for 10 years, at which time it is legally required to dismantle the depot and remove the underground storage tanks. It is estimated that it will cost $75,000 to dismantle the depot and remove the tanks at the end of the depot's useful life.

Instructions

(a) Prepare the journal entries to record the depot and the asset retirement obligation for the depot on January 1, 2014. Based on an effective-interest rate of 6%, the present value of the asset retirement obligation on January 1, 2014, is $41,879.

(b) Prepare any journal entries required for the depot and the asset retirement obligation at December 31, 2014. Oil Products uses straight-line depreciation; the estimated salvage value for the depot is zero.

(c) On December 31, 2023, Oil Products pays a demolition firm to dismantle the depot and remove the tanks at a price of $80,000. Prepare the journal entry for the settlement of the asset retirement obligation.

5 **E13-15 (Premiums)** Presented below and on page 740 are three independent situations.

1. Hairston Stamp Company records stamp service revenue and provides for the cost of redemptions in the year stamps are sold to licensees. Hairston's past experience indicates that only 80% of the

stamps sold to licensees will be redeemed. Hairston's liability for stamp redemptions was $13,000,000 at December 31, 2013. Additional information for 2014 is as follows.

Stamp service revenue from stamps sold to licensees	$9,500,000
Cost of redemptions (stamps sold prior to 1/1/14)	6,000,000

If all the stamps sold in 2014 were presented for redemption in 2015, the redemption cost would be $5,200,000. What amount should Hairston report as a liability for stamp redemptions at December 31, 2014?

2. In packages of its products, Burnitz Inc. includes coupons that may be presented at retail stores to obtain discounts on other Burnitz products. Retailers are reimbursed for the face amount of coupons redeemed plus 10% of that amount for handling costs. Burnitz honors requests for coupon redemption by retailers up to 3 months after the consumer expiration date. Burnitz estimates that 60% of all coupons issued will ultimately be redeemed. Information relating to coupons issued by Burnitz during 2014 is as follows.

Consumer expiration date	12/31/14
Total face amount of coupons issued	$800,000
Total payments to retailers as of 12/31/14	330,000

What amount should Burnitz report as a liability for unredeemed coupons at December 31, 2014?

3. Roland Company sold 700,000 boxes of pie mix under a new sales promotional program. Each box contains one coupon, which submitted with $4.00, entitles the customer to a baking pan. Roland pays $6.00 per pan and $0.50 for handling and shipping. Roland estimates that 70% of the coupons will be redeemed, even though only 250,000 coupons had been processed during 2014. What amount should Roland report as a liability for unredeemed coupons at December 31, 2014?

(AICPA adapted)

6 **E13-16 (Financial Statement Impact of Liability Transactions)** Presented below is a list of possible transactions.

1. Purchased inventory for $80,000 on account (assume perpetual system is used).
2. Issued an $80,000 note payable in payment on account (see item 1 above).
3. Recorded accrued interest on the note from item 2 above.
4. Borrowed $100,000 from the bank by signing a 6-month, $112,000, zero-interest-bearing note.
5. Recognized 4 months' interest expense on the note from item 4 above.
6. Recorded cash sales of $75,260, which includes 6% sales tax.
7. Recorded wage expense of $35,000. The cash paid was $25,000; the difference was due to various amounts withheld.
8. Recorded employer's payroll taxes.
9. Accrued accumulated vacation pay.
10. Recorded an asset retirement obligation.
11. Recorded bonuses due to employees.
12. Recorded a contingent loss on a lawsuit that the company will probably lose.
13. Accrued warranty expense (assume expense warranty approach).
14. Paid warranty costs that were accrued in item 13 above.
15. Recorded sales of product and related warranties (assume sales warranty approach).
16. Paid warranty costs under contracts from item 15 above.
17. Recognized warranty revenue (see item 15 above).
18. Recorded estimated liability for premium claims outstanding.

Instructions

Set up a table using the format shown below and analyze the effect of the 18 transactions on the financial statement categories indicated.

#	Assets	Liabilities	Owners' Equity	Net Income
1				

Use the following code:

I: Increase D: Decrease NE: No net effect

6 **E13-17 (Ratio Computations and Discussion)** Sprague Company has been operating for several years, and on December 31, 2014, presented the following balance sheet.

SPRAGUE COMPANY
BALANCE SHEET
DECEMBER 31, 2014

Cash	$ 40,000	Accounts payable	$ 80,000
Receivables	75,000	Mortgage payable	140,000
Inventory	95,000	Common stock ($1 par)	150,000
Plant assets (net)	220,000	Retained earnings	60,000
	$430,000		$430,000

The net income for 2014 was $25,000. Assume that total assets are the same in 2013 and 2014.

Instructions

Compute each of the following ratios. For each of the four, indicate the manner in which it is computed and its significance as a tool in the analysis of the financial soundness of the company.

(a) Current ratio.
(b) Acid-test ratio.
(c) Debt to assets.
(d) Return on assets.

6 **E13-18 (Ratio Computations and Analysis)** Prior Company's condensed financial statements provide the following information.

PRIOR COMPANY
BALANCE SHEET

	Dec. 31, 2014	Dec. 31, 2013
Cash	$ 52,000	$ 60,000
Accounts receivable (net)	198,000	80,000
Short-term investments	80,000	40,000
Inventory	440,000	360,000
Prepaid expenses	3,000	7,000
Total current assets	$ 773,000	$ 547,000
Property, plant, and equipment (net)	857,000	853,000
Total assets	$1,630,000	$1,400,000
Current liabilities	240,000	160,000
Bonds payable	400,000	400,000
Common stockholders' equity	990,000	840,000
Total liabilities and stockholders' equity	$1,630,000	$1,400,000

INCOME STATEMENT
FOR THE YEAR ENDED 2014

Sales revenue	$1,640,000
Cost of goods sold	(800,000)
Gross profit	840,000
Selling and administrative expenses	(440,000)
Interest expense	(40,000)
Net income	$ 360,000

Instructions

(a) Determine the following for 2014.
   (1) Current ratio at December 31.
   (2) Acid-test ratio at December 31.
   (3) Accounts receivable turnover.
   (4) Inventory turnover.
   (5) Return on assets.
   (6) Profit margin on sales.

(b) Prepare a brief evaluation of the financial condition of Prior Company and of the adequacy of its profits.

6 **E13-19 (Ratio Computations and Effect of Transactions)** Presented below is information related to Carver Inc.

CARVER INC.
BALANCE SHEET
DECEMBER 31, 2014

Cash		$ 45,000	Notes payable (short-term)	$ 50,000
Receivables	$110,000		Accounts payable	32,000
Less: Allowance	15,000	95,000	Accrued liabilities	5,000
Inventory		170,000	Common stock (par $5)	260,000
Prepaid insurance		8,000	Retained earnings	141,000
Land		20,000		
Equipment (net)		150,000		
		$488,000		$488,000

CARVER INC.
INCOME STATEMENT
FOR THE YEAR ENDED DECEMBER 31, 2014

Sales revenue		$1,400,000
Cost of goods sold		
Inventory, Jan. 1, 2014	$200,000	
Purchases	790,000	
Cost of goods available for sale	990,000	
Inventory, Dec. 31, 2014	(170,000)	
Cost of goods sold		820,000
Gross profit on sales		580,000
Operating expenses		170,000
Net income		$ 410,000

Instructions

(a) Compute the following ratios or relationships of Carver Inc. Assume that the ending account balances are representative unless the information provided indicates differently.
(1) Current ratio.
(2) Inventory turnover.
(3) Accounts receivable turnover.
(4) Earnings per share.
(5) Profit margin on sales.
(6) Return on assets on December 31, 2014.

(b) Indicate for each of the following transactions whether the transaction would improve, weaken, or have no effect on the current ratio of Carver Inc. at December 31, 2014.
(1) Write off an uncollectible account receivable, $2,200.
(2) Purchase additional capital stock for cash.
(3) Pay $40,000 on notes payable (short-term).
(4) Collect $23,000 on accounts receivable.
(5) Buy equipment on account.
(6) Give an existing creditor a short-term note in settlement of account.

EXERCISES SET B

See the book's companion website, at **www.wiley.com/college/kieso**, for an additional set of exercises.

PROBLEMS

1 **P13-1 (Current Liability Entries and Adjustments)** Described below are certain transactions of Edwardson Corporation. The company uses the periodic inventory system.

1. On February 2, the corporation purchased goods from Martin Company for $70,000 subject to cash discount terms of 2/10, n/30. Purchases and accounts payable are recorded by the corporation at net amounts after cash discounts. The invoice was paid on February 26.
2. On April 1, the corporation bought a truck for $50,000 from General Motors Company, paying $4,000 in cash and signing a one-year, 12% note for the balance of the purchase price.
3. On May 1, the corporation borrowed $83,000 from Chicago National Bank by signing a $92,000 zero-interest-bearing note due one year from May 1.
4. On August 1, the board of directors declared a $300,000 cash dividend that was payable on September 10 to stockholders of record on August 31.

Instructions

(a) Make all the journal entries necessary to record the transactions above using appropriate dates.

(b) Edwardson Corporation's year-end is December 31. Assuming that no adjusting entries relative to the transactions above have been recorded, prepare any adjusting journal entries concerning interest that are necessary to present fair financial statements at December 31. Assume straight-line amortization of discounts.

1 5 **P13-2 (Liability Entries and Adjustments)** Listed below are selected transactions of Schultz Department Store for the current year ending December 31.

1. On December 5, the store received $500 from the Selig Players as a deposit to be returned after certain furniture to be used in stage production was returned on January 15.
2. During December, cash sales totaled $798,000, which includes the 5% sales tax that must be remitted to the state by the fifteenth day of the following month.
3. On December 10, the store purchased for cash three delivery trucks for $120,000. The trucks were purchased in a state that applies a 5% sales tax.
4. The store determined it will cost $100,000 to restore the area (considered a land improvement) surrounding one of its store parking lots, when the store is closed in 2 years. Schultz estimates the fair value of the obligation at December 31 is $84,000.

Instructions

Prepare all the journal entries necessary to record the transactions noted above as they occurred and any adjusting journal entries relative to the transactions that would be required to present fair financial statements at December 31. Date each entry. For simplicity, assume that adjusting entries are recorded only once a year on December 31.

3 **P13-3 (Payroll Tax Entries)** Cedarville Company pays its office employee payroll weekly. Below is a partial list of employees and their payroll data for August. Because August is their vacation period, vacation pay is also listed.

Employee	Earnings to July 31	Weekly Pay	Vacation Pay to Be Received in August
Mark Hamill	$4,200	$200	—
Karen Robbins	3,500	150	$300
Brent Kirk	2,700	110	220
Alec Guinness	7,400	250	—
Ken Sprouse	8,000	330	660

Assume that the federal income tax withheld is 10% of wages. Union dues withheld are 2% of wages. Vacations are taken the second and third weeks of August by Robbins, Kirk, and Sprouse. The state unemployment tax rate is 2.5% and the federal is 0.8%, both on a $7,000 maximum. The FICA rate is 7.65% on employee and employer on a maximum of $113,700 per employee. In addition, a 1.45% rate is charged both employer and employee for an employee's wages in excess of $113,700.

Instructions

Make the journal entries necessary for each of the four August payrolls. The entries for the payroll and for the company's liability are made separately. Also make the entry to record the monthly payment of accrued payroll liabilities.

3 **P13-4 (Payroll Tax Entries)** Below is a payroll sheet for Otis Import Company for the month of September 2014. The company is allowed a 1% unemployment compensation rate by the state; the federal unemployment tax rate is 0.8% and the maximum for both is $7,000. Assume a 10% federal income tax rate for all employees and a 7.65% FICA tax on employee and employer on a maximum of $113,700. In addition, 1.45% is charged both employer and employee for an employee's wages in excess of $113,700 per employee.

Name	Earnings to Aug. 31	September Earnings	Income Tax Withholding	FICA	Unemployment Tax State	Unemployment Tax Federal
B.D. Williams	$ 6,800	$ 800				
D. Raye	6,500	700				
K. Baker	7,600	1,100				
F. Lopez	13,600	1,900				
A. Daniels	107,000	13,000				
B. Kingston	112,000	16,000				

Instructions

(a) Complete the payroll sheet and make the necessary entry to record the payment of the payroll.
(b) Make the entry to record the payroll tax expenses of Otis Import Company.
(c) Make the entry to record the payment of the payroll liabilities created. Assume that the company pays all payroll liabilities at the end of each month.

5 **P13-5 (Warranties, Accrual, and Cash Basis)** Brooks Corporation sells computers under a 2-year warranty contract that requires the corporation to replace defective parts and to provide the necessary repair labor. During 2014, the corporation sells for cash 400 computers at a unit price of $2,500. On the basis of past experience, the 2-year warranty costs are estimated to be $155 for parts and $185 for labor per unit. (For simplicity, assume that all sales occurred on December 31, 2014.) The warranty is not sold separately from the computer.

Instructions

(a) Record any necessary journal entries in 2014, applying the cash-basis method.
(b) Record any necessary journal entries in 2014, applying the expense warranty accrual method.
(c) What liability relative to these transactions would appear on the December 31, 2014, balance sheet and how would it be classified if the cash-basis method is applied?
(d) What liability relative to these transactions would appear on the December 31, 2014, balance sheet and how would it be classified if the expense warranty accrual method is applied?

In 2015, the actual warranty costs to Brooks Corporation were $21,400 for parts and $39,900 for labor.

(e) Record any necessary journal entries in 2015, applying the cash-basis method.
(f) Record any necessary journal entries in 2015, applying the expense warranty accrual method.

5 **P13-6 (Extended Warranties)** Dos Passos Company sells televisions at an average price of $900 and also offers to each customer a separate 3-year warranty contract for $90 that requires the company to perform periodic services and to replace defective parts. During 2014, the company sold 300 televisions and 270 warranty contracts for cash. It estimates the 3-year warranty costs as $20 for parts and $40 for labor, and accounts for warranties separately. Assume sales occurred on December 31, 2014, and straight-line recognition of warranty revenues occurs.

Instructions

(a) Record any necessary journal entries in 2014.
(b) What liability relative to these transactions would appear on the December 31, 2014, balance sheet and how would it be classified?

In 2015, Dos Passos Company incurred actual costs relative to 2014 television warranty sales of $2,000 for parts and $4,000 for labor.

(c) Record any necessary journal entries in 2015 relative to 2014 television warranties.
(d) What amounts relative to the 2014 television warranties would appear on the December 31, 2015, balance sheet and how would they be classified?

4 5 **P13-7 (Warranties, Accrual, and Cash Basis)** Alvarado Company sells a machine for $7,400 with a 12-month warranty agreement that requires the company to replace all defective parts and to provide the repair labor at no cost to the customers. With sales being made evenly throughout the year, the company sells 600 machines in 2014 (warranty expense is incurred half in 2014 and half in 2015). As a result of product testing, the company estimates that the warranty cost is $390 per machine ($170 parts and $220 labor).

Instructions

Assuming that actual warranty costs are incurred exactly as estimated, what journal entries would be made relative to the following facts?

(a) Under application of the expense warranty accrual method for:
- **(1)** Sale of machinery in 2014.
- **(2)** Warranty costs incurred in 2014.
- **(3)** Warranty expense charged against 2014 revenues.
- **(4)** Warranty costs incurred in 2015.

(b) Under application of the cash-basis method for:
- **(1)** Sale of machinery in 2014.
- **(2)** Warranty costs incurred in 2014.
- **(3)** Warranty expense charged against 2014 revenues.
- **(4)** Warranty costs incurred in 2015.

(c) What amount, if any, is disclosed in the balance sheet as a liability for future warranty costs as of December 31, 2014, under each method?

(d) Which method best reflects the income in 2014 and 2015 of Alvarado Company? Why?

5 **P13-8 (Premium Entries)** To stimulate the sales of its Alladin breakfast cereal, Loptien Company places 1 coupon in each box. Five coupons are redeemable for a premium consisting of a children's hand puppet. In 2015, the company purchases 40,000 puppets at $1.50 each and sells 480,000 boxes of Alladin at $3.75 a box. From its experience with other similar premium offers, the company estimates that 40% of the coupons issued will be mailed back for redemption. During 2015, 115,000 coupons are presented for redemption.

Instructions

Prepare the journal entries that should be recorded in 2015 relative to the premium plan.

5 6 **P13-9 (Premium Entries and Financial Statement Presentation)** Sycamore Candy Company offers an MP3 download (seven-single medley) as a premium for every five candy bar wrappers presented by customers together with $2.50. The candy bars are sold by the company to distributors for 30 cents each. The purchase price of each download code to the company is $2.25. In addition, it costs 50 cents to distribute each code. The results of the premium plan for the years 2014 and 2015 are as follows. (All purchases and sales are for cash.)

	2014	2015
MP3 codes purchased	250,000	330,000
Candy bars sold	2,895,400	2,743,600
Wrappers redeemed	1,200,000	1,500,000
2014 wrappers expected to be redeemed in 2015	290,000	
2015 wrappers expected to be redeemed in 2016		350,000

Instructions

(a) Prepare the journal entries that should be made in 2014 and 2015 to record the transactions related to the premium plan of the Sycamore Candy Company.

(b) Indicate the account names, amounts, and classifications of the items related to the premium plan that would appear on the balance sheet and the income statement at the end of 2014 and 2015.

4 5 **P13-10 (Loss Contingencies: Entries and Essay)** On November 24, 2014, 26 passengers on Windsor Airlines Flight No. 901 were injured upon landing when the plane skidded off the runway. Personal injury suits for damages totaling $9,000,000 were filed on January 11, 2015, against the airline by 18 injured passengers. The airline carries no insurance. Legal counsel has studied each suit and advised Windsor that it can reasonably expect to pay 60% of the damages claimed. The financial statements for the year ended December 31, 2014, were issued February 27, 2015.

Instructions

(a) Prepare any disclosures and journal entries required by the airline in preparation of the December 31, 2014, financial statements.

(b) Ignoring the November 24, 2014, accident, what liability due to the risk of loss from lack of insurance coverage should Windsor Airlines record or disclose? During the past decade, the company has experienced at least one accident per year and incurred average damages of $3,200,000. Discuss fully.

4 5 **P13-11 (Loss Contingencies: Entries and Essays)** Polska Corporation, in preparation of its December 31, 2014, financial statements, is attempting to determine the proper accounting treatment for each of the following situations.

1. As a result of uninsured accidents during the year, personal injury suits for $350,000 and $60,000 have been filed against the company. It is the judgment of Polska's legal counsel that an unfavorable outcome is unlikely in the $60,000 case but that an unfavorable verdict approximating $250,000 will probably result in the $350,000 case.
2. Polska Corporation owns a subsidiary in a foreign country that has a book value of $5,725,000 and an estimated fair value of $9,500,000. The foreign government has communicated to Polska its intention to expropriate the assets and business of all foreign investors. On the basis of settlements other firms have received from this same country, Polska expects to receive 40% of the fair value of its properties as final settlement.
3. Polska's chemical product division consisting of five plants is uninsurable because of the special risk of injury to employees and losses due to fire and explosion. The year 2014 is considered one of the safest (luckiest) in the division's history because no loss due to injury or casualty was suffered. Having suffered an average of three casualties a year during the rest of the past decade (ranging from $60,000 to $700,000), management is certain that next year the company will probably not be so fortunate.

Instructions

(a) Prepare the journal entries that should be recorded as of December 31, 2014, to recognize each of the situations above.

(b) Indicate what should be reported relative to each situation in the financial statements and accompanying notes. Explain why.

5 **P13-12 (Warranties and Premiums)** Garison Music Emporium carries a wide variety of musical instruments, sound reproduction equipment, recorded music, and sheet music. Garison uses two sales promotion techniques—warranties and premiums—to attract customers.

Musical instruments and sound equipment are sold with a one-year warranty for replacement of parts and labor. The estimated warranty cost, based on past experience, is 2% of sales.

The premium is offered on the recorded and sheet music. Customers receive a coupon for each dollar spent on recorded music or sheet music. Customers may exchange 200 coupons and $20 for a digital MP3 player. Garison pays $32 for each player and estimates that 60% of the coupons given to customers will be redeemed.

Garison's total sales for 2014 were $7,200,000—$5,700,000 from musical instruments and sound reproduction equipment and $1,500,000 from recorded music and sheet music. Replacement parts and labor for warranty work totaled $164,000 during 2014. A total of 6,500 players used in the premium program were purchased during the year and there were 1,200,000 coupons redeemed in 2014.

The accrual method is used by Garison to account for the warranty and premium costs for financial reporting purposes. The balances in the accounts related to warranties and premiums on January 1, 2014, were as shown below.

Inventory of Premiums	$ 37,600
Premium Liability	44,800
Warranty Liability	136,000

Instructions

Garison Music Emporium is preparing its financial statements for the year ended December 31, 2014. Determine the amounts that will be shown on the 2014 financial statements for the following.

(a) Warranty Expense.
(b) Warranty Liability.
(c) Premium Expense.
(d) Inventory of Premiums.
(e) Premium Liability.

(CMA adapted)

4 5 **P13-13 (Liability Errors)** You are the independent auditor engaged to audit Millay Corporation's December 31, 2014, financial statements. Millay manufactures household appliances. During the course of your audit, you discovered the following contingent liabilities.

1. Millay began production of a new dishwasher in June 2014 and, by December 31, 2014, sold 120,000 to various retailers for $500 each. Each dishwasher is under a one-year warranty. The company estimates that its warranty expense per dishwasher will amount to $25. At year-end, the company had already paid out $1,000,000 in warranty expenses. Millay's income statement shows warranty expenses of $1,000,000 for 2014. Millay accounts for warranty costs on the accrual basis.
2. In response to your attorney's letter, Morgan Sondgeroth, Esq., has informed you that Millay has been cited for dumping toxic waste into the Kishwaukee River. Clean-up costs and fines amount to $2,750,000. Although the case is still being contested, Sondgeroth is certain that Millay will most probably have to pay the fine and clean-up costs. No disclosure of this situation was found in the financial statements.

3. Millay is the defendant in a patent infringement lawsuit by Megan Drabek over Millay's use of a hydraulic compressor in several of its products. Sondgeroth claims that, if the suit goes against Millay, the loss may be as much as $5,000,000. However, Sondgeroth believes the loss of this suit to be only reasonably possible. Again, no mention of this suit is made in the financial statements.

As presented, these contingencies are not reported in accordance with GAAP, which may create problems in issuing a favorable audit report. You feel the need to note these problems in the work papers.

Instructions

Heading each page with the name of the company, balance sheet date, and a brief description of the problem, write a brief narrative for each of the above issues in the form of **a memorandum** to be incorporated in the audit work papers. Explain what led to the discovery of each problem, what the problem really is, and what you advised your client to do (along with any appropriate journal entries) in order to bring these contingencies in accordance with GAAP.

5 **P13-14 (Warranty and Coupon Computation)** Schmitt Company must make computations and adjusting entries for the following independent situations at December 31, 2015.

1. Its line of amplifiers carries a 3-year warranty against defects. On the basis of past experience the estimated warranty costs related to dollar sales are first year after sale—2% of sales revenue; second year after sale—3% of sales revenue; and third year after sale—5% of sales revenue. Sales and actual warranty expenditures for the first 3 years of business were:

	Sales Revenue	Warranty Expenditures
2013	$ 800,000	$ 6,500
2014	1,100,000	17,200
2015	1,200,000	62,000

Instructions

Compute the amount that Schmitt Company should report as a liability in its December 31, 2015, balance sheet. Assume that all sales are made evenly throughout each year with warranty expenses also evenly spaced relative to the rates above.

2. With some of its products, Schmitt Company includes coupons that are redeemable in merchandise. The coupons have no expiration date and, in the company's experience, 40% of them are redeemed. The liability for unredeemed coupons at December 31, 2014, was $9,000. During 2015, coupons worth $30,000 were issued, and merchandise worth $8,000 was distributed in exchange for coupons redeemed.

Instructions

Compute the amount of the liability that should appear on the December 31, 2015, balance sheet.

(AICPA adapted)

PROBLEMS SET B

See the book's companion website, at **www.wiley.com/college/kieso**, for an additional set of problems.

CONCEPTS FOR ANALYSIS

CA13-1 (Nature of Liabilities) Presented below is the current liabilities section of Micro Corporation.

	($000) 2015	2014
Current liabilities		
Notes payable	$ 68,713	$ 7,700
Accounts payable	179,496	101,379
Compensation to employees	60,312	31,649
Accrued liabilities	158,198	77,621
Income taxes payable	10,486	26,491
Current maturities of long-term debt	16,592	6,649
Total current liabilities	$493,797	$251,489

Instructions

Answer the following questions.

(a) What are the essential characteristics that make an item a liability?
(b) How does one distinguish between a current liability and a long-term liability?
(c) What are accrued liabilities? Give three examples of accrued liabilities that Micro might have.
(d) What is the theoretically correct way to value liabilities? How are current liabilities usually valued?
(e) Why are notes payable reported first in the current liabilities section?
(f) What might be the items that comprise Micro's liability for "Compensation to employees"?

CA13-2 (Current versus Noncurrent Classification) Rodriguez Corporation includes the following items in its liabilities at December 31, 2014.

1. Notes payable, $25,000,000, due June 30, 2015.
2. Deposits from customers on equipment ordered by them from Rodriguez, $6,250,000.
3. Salaries and wages payable, $3,750,000, due January 14, 2015.

Instructions

Indicate in what circumstances, if any, each of the three liabilities above would be excluded from current liabilities.

CA13-3 (Refinancing of Short-Term Debt) Dumars Corporation reports in the current liability section of its balance sheet at December 31, 2014 (its year-end), short-term obligations of $15,000,000, which includes the current portion of 12% long-term debt in the amount of $10,000,000 (matures in March 2015). Management has stated its intention to refinance the 12% debt whereby no portion of it will mature during 2015. The date of issuance of the financial statements is March 25, 2015.

Instructions

(a) Is management's intent enough to support long-term classification of the obligation in this situation?
(b) Assume that Dumars Corporation issues $13,000,000 of 10-year debentures to the public in January 2015 and that management intends to use the proceeds to liquidate the $10,000,000 debt maturing in March 2015. Furthermore, assume that the debt maturing in March 2015 is paid from these proceeds prior to the issuance of the financial statements. Will this have any impact on the balance sheet classification at December 31, 2014? Explain your answer.
(c) Assume that Dumars Corporation issues common stock to the public in January and that management intends to entirely liquidate the $10,000,000 debt maturing in March 2015 with the proceeds of this equity securities issue. In light of these events, should the $10,000,000 debt maturing in March 2015 be included in current liabilities at December 31, 2014?
(d) Assume that Dumars Corporation, on February 15, 2015, entered into a financing agreement with a commercial bank that permits Dumars Corporation to borrow at any time through 2016 up to $15,000,000 at the bank's prime rate of interest. Borrowings under the financing agreement mature three years after the date of the loan. The agreement is not cancelable except for violation of a provision with which compliance is objectively determinable. No violation of any provision exists at the date of issuance of the financial statements. Assume further that the current portion of long-term debt does not mature until August 2015. In addition, management intends to refinance the $10,000,000 obligation under the terms of the financial agreement with the bank, which is expected to be financially capable of honoring the agreement.
    (1) Given these facts, should the $10,000,000 be classified as current on the balance sheet at December 31, 2014?
    (2) Is disclosure of the refinancing method required?

CA13-4 (Loss Contingencies) On February 1, 2015, one of the huge storage tanks of Viking Manufacturing Company exploded. Windows in houses and other buildings within a one-mile radius of the explosion were severely damaged, and a number of people were injured. As of February 15, 2015 (when the December 31, 2014, financial statements were completed and sent to the publisher for printing and public distribution), no suits had been filed or claims asserted against the company as a consequence of the explosion. The company fully anticipates that suits will be filed and claims asserted for injuries and damages. Because the casualty was uninsured and the company considered at fault, Viking Manufacturing will have to cover the damages from its own resources.

Instructions

Discuss fully the accounting treatment and disclosures that should be accorded the casualty and related contingent losses in the financial statements dated December 31, 2014.

CA13-5 (Loss Contingency) Presented below is a note disclosure for Matsui Corporation.

> **Litigation and Environmental:** The Company has been notified, or is a named or a potentially responsible party in a number of governmental (federal, state and local) and private actions associated with environmental matters, such as those relating to hazardous wastes, including certain sites which are on the United States EPA National Priorities List ("Superfund"). These actions seek clean-up costs, penalties and/or damages for personal injury or to property or natural resources.
>
> In 2014, the Company recorded a pre-tax charge of $56,229,000, included in the "Other expense (income)—net" caption of the Company's consolidated income statements, as an additional provision for environmental matters. These expenditures are expected to take place over the next several years and are indicative of the Company's commitment to improve and maintain the environment in which it operates. At December 31, 2014, environmental accruals amounted to $69,931,000, of which $61,535,000 are considered noncurrent and are included in the "Deferred credits and other liabilities" caption of the Company's consolidated balance sheets.
>
> While it is impossible at this time to determine with certainty the ultimate outcome of environmental matters, it is management's opinion, based in part on the advice of independent counsel (after taking into account accruals and insurance coverage applicable to such actions) that when the costs are finally determined they will not have a material adverse effect on the financial position of the Company.

Instructions

Answer the following questions.

(a) What conditions must exist before a loss contingency can be recorded in the accounts?

(b) Suppose that Matsui Corporation could not reasonably estimate the amount of the loss, although it could establish with a high degree of probability the minimum and maximum loss possible. How should this information be reported in the financial statements?

(c) If the amount of the loss is uncertain, how would the loss contingency be reported in the financial statements?

CA13-6 (Warranties and Loss Contingencies) The following two independent situations involve loss contingencies.

Part 1: Benson Company sells two products, Grey and Yellow. Each carries a one-year warranty.

1. Product Grey—Product warranty costs, based on past experience, will normally be 1% of sales.
2. Product Yellow—Product warranty costs cannot be reasonably estimated because this is a new product line. However, the chief engineer believes that product warranty costs are likely to be incurred.

Instructions

How should Benson report the estimated product warranty costs for each of the two types of merchandise above? Discuss the rationale for your answer. Do not discuss disclosures that should be made in Benson's financial statements or notes.

Part 2: Constantine Company is being sued for $4,000,000 for an injury caused to a child as a result of alleged negligence while the child was visiting the Constantine Company plant in March 2014. The suit was filed in July 2014. Constantine's lawyer states that it is probable that Constantine will lose the suit and be found liable for a judgment costing anywhere from $400,000 to $2,000,000. However, the lawyer states that the most probable judgment is $1,000,000.

Instructions

How should Constantine report the suit in its 2014 financial statements? Discuss the rationale for your answer. Include in your answer disclosures, if any, that should be made in Constantine's financial statements or notes.

(AICPA adapted)

CA13-7 (Warranties) The Dotson Company, owner of Bleacher Mall, charges Rich Clothing Store a rental fee of $600 per month plus 5% of yearly profits over $500,000. Matt Rich, the owner of the store, directs his accountant, Ron Hamilton, to increase the estimate of bad debt expense and warranty costs in order to keep profits at $475,000.

Instructions

Answer the following questions.

(a) Should Hamilton follow his boss's directive?

(b) Who is harmed if the estimates are increased?

(c) Is Matt Rich's directive ethical?

USING YOUR JUDGMENT

FINANCIAL REPORTING

Financial Reporting Problem

P&G

The Procter & Gamble Company (P&G)

The financial statements of P&G are presented in Appendix 5B. The company's complete annual report, including the notes to the financial statements, can be accessed at the book's companion website, **www.wiley.com/college/kieso**.

Instructions

Refer to these financial statements and the accompanying notes to answer the following questions.

(a) What was P&G's 2011 short-term debt and related weighted-average interest rate on this debt?

(b) What was P&G's 2011 working capital, acid-test ratio, and current ratio? Comment on P&G's liquidity.

(c) What types of commitments and contingencies has P&G's reported in its financial statements? What is management's reaction to these contingencies?

Comparative Analysis Case

The Coca-Cola Company and PepsiCo, Inc.

Instructions

Go to the book's companion website and use information found there to answer the following questions related to The Coca-Cola Company and PepsiCo, Inc.

(a) How much working capital do each of these companies have at the end of 2011?

(b) Compute each company's (a) current cash debt coverage, (b) cash debt coverage, (c) current ratio, (d) acid-test ratio, (e) accounts receivable turnover, and (f) inventory turnover for 2011. Comment on each company's overall liquidity.

(c) In PepsiCo's financial statements, it reports in the long-term debt section "short-term borrowings, reclassified." How can short-term borrowings be classified as long-term debt?

(d) What types of loss or gain contingencies do these two companies have at the end of 2011?

Financial Statement Analysis Cases

Case 1 Northland Cranberries

Despite being a publicly traded company only since 1987, Northland Cranberries of Wisconsin Rapids, Wisconsin, is one of the world's largest cranberry growers. During its short life as a publicly traded corporation, it has engaged in an aggressive growth strategy. As a consequence, the company has taken on significant amounts of both short-term and long-term debt. The following information is taken from recent annual reports of the company.

Northland Cranberries

	Current Year	Prior Year
Current assets	$ 6,745,759	$ 5,598,054
Total assets	107,744,751	83,074,339
Current liabilities	10,168,685	4,484,687
Total liabilities	73,118,204	49,948,787
Shareholders' equity	34,626,547	33,125,552
Net sales	21,783,966	18,051,355
Cost of goods sold	13,057,275	8,751,220
Interest expense	3,654,006	2,393,792
Income tax expense	1,051,000	1,917,000
Net income	1,581,707	2,942,954

Instructions

(a) Evaluate the company's liquidity by calculating and analyzing working capital and the current ratio.

(b) The discussion of the company's liquidity, shown below, was provided by the company in the Management Discussion and Analysis section of the company's annual report. Comment on whether you agree with management's statements, and what might be done to remedy the situation.

> The lower comparative current ratio in the current year was due to $3 million of short-term borrowing then outstanding which was incurred to fund the Yellow River Marsh acquisitions last year. As a result of the extreme seasonality of its business, the company does not believe that its current ratio or its underlying stated working capital at the current, fiscal year-end is a meaningful indication of the Company's liquidity. As of March 31 of each fiscal year, the Company has historically carried no significant amounts of inventories and by such date all of the Company's accounts receivable from its crop sold for processing under the supply agreements have been paid in cash, with the resulting cash received from such payments used to reduce indebtedness. The Company utilizes its revolving bank credit facility, together with cash generated from operations, to fund its working capital requirements throughout its growing season.

Case 2 Mohican Company

Presented below is the current liabilities section and related note of Mohican Company.

	(dollars in thousands)	
	Current Year	Prior Year
Current liabilities		
Current portion of long-term debt	$ 15,000	$ 10,000
Short-term debt	2,668	405
Accounts payable	29,495	42,427
Accrued warranty	16,843	16,741
Accrued marketing programs	17,512	16,585
Other accrued liabilities	35,653	33,290
Accrued and deferred income taxes	16,206	17,348
Total current liabilities	$133,377	$136,796

Notes to Consolidated Financial Statements

Note 1 (in part): Summary of Significant Accounting Policies and Related Data

Accrued Warranty The company provides an accrual for future warranty costs based upon the relationship of prior years' sales to actual warranty costs.

Instructions

Answer the following questions.

(a) What is the difference between the cash basis and the accrual basis of accounting for warranty costs?

(b) Under what circumstance, if any, would it be appropriate for Mohican Company to recognize deferred revenue on warranty contracts?

(c) If Mohican Company recognized deferred revenue on warranty contracts, how would it recognize this revenue in subsequent periods?

Case 3 BOP Clothing Co.

As discussed in the chapter, an important consideration in evaluating current liabilities is a company's operating cycle. The operating cycle is the average time required to go from cash to cash in generating revenue. To determine the length of the operating cycle, analysts use two measures: the average days to sell inventory (*inventory days*) and the average days to collect receivables (*receivable days*). The inventory-days computation measures the average number of days it takes to move an item from raw materials or purchase to final sale (from the day it comes in the company's door to the point it is converted to cash or an account receivable). The receivable-days computation measures the average number of days it takes to collect an account.

Most businesses must then determine how to finance the period of time when the liquid assets are tied up in inventory and accounts receivable. To determine how much to finance, companies first determine accounts payable days—how long it takes to pay creditors. Accounts payable days measures the number of days it takes to pay a supplier invoice. Consider the following operating cycle worksheet for BOP Clothing Co.

	2013	2014
Cash	$ 45,000	$ 30,000
Accounts receivable	250,000	325,000
Inventory	830,000	800,000
Accounts payable	720,000	775,000
Purchases	1,100,000	1,425,000
Cost of goods sold	1,145,000	1,455,000
Sales	1,750,000	1,950,000
Operating Cycle		
Inventory days[1]	264.6	200.7
Receivable days[2]	52.1	60.8
Operating cycle	316.7	261.5
Less: Accounts payable days[3]	238.9	198.5
Days to be financed	77.8	63.0
Working capital	$ 405,000	$ 380,000
Current ratio	1.56	1.49
Acid-test ratio	0.41	0.46

[1]Inventory days = (Inventory × 365) ÷ Cost of goods sold
[2]Receivable days = (Accounts receivable × 365) ÷ Sales
[3]Accounts payable days = (Accounts payable × 365) ÷ Purchases

Purchases = Cost of goods sold + Ending inventory − Beginning inventory.
The ratios above assume that other current assets and liabilities are negligible.

These data indicate that BOP has reduced its overall operating cycle (to 261.5 days) as well as the number of days to be financed with sources of funds other than accounts payable (from 78 to 63 days). Most businesses cannot finance the operating cycle with accounts payable financing alone, so working capital financing, usually short-term interest-bearing loans, is needed to cover the shortfall. In this case, BOP would need to borrow less money to finance its operating cycle in 2014 than in 2013.

Instructions

(a) Use the BOP analysis to briefly discuss how the operating cycle data relate to the amount of working capital and the current and acid-test ratios.

(b) Select two other real companies that are in the same industry and complete the operating cycle worksheet, along with the working capital and ratio analysis. Briefly summarize and interpret the results. To simplify the analysis, you may use ending balances to compute turnover ratios.

[Adapted from Operating Cycle Worksheet at *www.entrepreneur.com*]

Accounting, Analysis, and Principles

(*Note:* For any part of this problem requiring an interest or discount rate, use 10%.)

YellowCard Company manufactures accessories for iPods. It had the following selected transactions during 2014.

1. YellowCard provides a 2-year warranty on its docking stations, which it began selling in 2014. During 2014, YellowCard spent $6,000 servicing warranty claims. At year-end, YellowCard estimates that an additional $45,000 will be spent in the future to service warranties related to 2014 sales.
2. YellowCard has a $200,000 loan outstanding from First Trust Corp. The loan is set to mature on February 28, 2015. For several years, First Trust has agreed to extend the loan, as long as YellowCard makes all its quarterly interest payments (interest is due on the last days of each February, May, August, and November) and maintains an acid-test ratio (also called "quick ratio") of at least 1.25. First Trust has provided YellowCard a "commitment letter" indicating that First Trust will extend the loan another 12 months, providing YellowCard makes the interest payment due on March 31.
3. During 2013, YellowCard constructed a small manufacturing facility specifically to manufacture one particular accessory. YellowCard paid the construction contractor $5,000,000 cash (which was the total contract price) and placed the facility into service on January 1, 2014. Because of technological change, YellowCard anticipates that the manufacturing facility will be useful for no more than 10 years. The local government where the facility is located required that, at the end of the 10-year period, YellowCard remediate the facility so that it can be used as a community center. YellowCard estimates the cost of remediation to be $500,000.

Accounting

Prepare all 2014 journal entries relating to (a) YellowCard's warranties, (b) YellowCard's loan from First Trust Corp., and (c) the new manufacturing facility YellowCard opened on January 1, 2014.

Analysis

Describe how the transactions above affect ratios that might be used to assess YellowCard's liquidity. How important is the commitment letter that YellowCard has from First Trust Corp. to these ratios?

Principles

YellowCard is contemplating offering an extended warranty. If customers pay an additional $50 at the time of product purchase, YellowCard would extend the warranty an additional two years. Would the extended warranty meet the definition of a liability under current generally accepted accounting principles? Briefly explain.

BRIDGE TO THE PROFESSION

Professional Research: FASB Codification

Pleasant Co. manufactures specialty bike accessories. The company is known for product quality, and it has offered one of the best warranties in the industry on its higher-priced products—a lifetime guarantee, performing all the warranty work in its own shops. The warranty on these products is included in the sales price.

Due to the recent introduction and growth in sales of some products targeted to the low-price market, Pleasant is considering partnering with another company to do the warranty work on this line of products, if customers purchase a service contract at the time of original product purchase. Pleasant has called you to advise the company on the accounting for this new warranty arrangement.

Instructions

If your school has a subscription to the FASB Codification, go to *http://aaahq.org/asclogin.cfm* to log in and prepare responses to the following. Provide Codification references for your responses.

(a) Identify the accounting literature that addresses the accounting for the type of separately priced warranty that Pleasant is considering.

(b) When are warranty contracts considered separately priced?

(c) What are incremental direct acquisition costs and how should they be treated?

Additional Professional Resources

See the book's companion website, at **www.wiley.com/college/kieso**, for professional simulations as well as other study resources.

IFRS INSIGHTS

7 LEARNING OBJECTIVE
Compare the accounting procedures for current liabilities and contingencies under GAAP and IFRS.

IFRS and GAAP have similar definitions for liabilities. IFRS related to reporting and recognition of liabilities is found in *IAS 1* ("Presentation of Financial Statements") and *IAS 37* ("Provisions, Contingent Liabilities, and Contingent Assets").

RELEVANT FACTS

Following are the key similarities and differences between GAAP and IFRS related to current liabilities and contingencies.

Similarities

- Similar to U.S. practice, IFRS requires that companies present current and non-current liabilities on the face of the statement of financial position (balance sheet), with current liabilities generally presented in order of liquidity. However, many companies using IFRS present non-current liabilities before current liabilities on the statement of financial position.
- The basic definition of a liability under GAAP and IFRS is very similar. In a more technical way, liabilities are defined by the IASB as a present obligation of the entity arising from past events, the settlement of which is expected to result in an outflow from the entity of resources embodying economic benefits. Liabilities may be legally enforceable via a contract or law but need not be. That is, they can arise due to normal business practices or customs.
- IFRS requires that companies classify liabilities as current or non-current on the face of the statement of financial position (balance sheet), except in industries where a presentation based on liquidity would be considered to provide more useful information (such as financial institutions).

Differences

- Under IFRS, the measurement of a provision related to a contingency is based on the best estimate of the expenditure required to settle the obligation. If a range of estimates is predicted and no amount in the range is more likely than any other amount in the range, the "midpoint" of the range is used to measure the liability. In GAAP, the minimum amount in a range is used.
- Both IFRS and GAAP prohibit the recognition of liabilities for future losses. However, IFRS permits recognition of a restructuring liability, once a company has committed to a restructuring plan. GAAP has additional criteria (i.e., related to communicating the plan to employees) before a restructuring liability can be established.
- IFRS and GAAP are similar in the treatment of asset retirement obligations (AROs). However, the recognition criteria for an ARO are more stringent under GAAP: The ARO is not recognized unless there is a present legal obligation and the fair value of the obligation can be reasonably estimated.
- Under IFRS, short-term obligations expected to be refinanced can be classified as non-current if the refinancing is completed by the financial statement date. GAAP uses the date the financial statements are issued.
- IFRS uses the term *provisions* to refer to estimated liabilities. Under IFRS, contingencies are not recorded but are often disclosed. The accounting for provisions under IFRS and estimated liabilities under GAAP are very similar.
- GAAP uses the term *contingency* in a different way than IFRS. Contingent liabilities are not recognized in the financial statements under IFRS, whereas under GAAP, a contingent liability is sometimes recognized.

ABOUT THE NUMBERS

Refinancing Criteria

The IASB has developed criteria for determining the circumstances under which short-term obligations may be properly excluded from current liabilities. Specifically, a company can exclude a short-term obligation from current liabilities if both of the following conditions are met:

1. It must intend to refinance the obligation on a long-term basis; and
2. It must have an unconditional right to defer settlement of the liability for at least 12 months after the reporting date.

Intention to refinance on a long-term basis means that the company intends to refinance the short-term obligation so that it will not require the use of working capital during the ensuing fiscal year (or operating cycle, if longer). Entering into a financing arrangement that clearly permits the company to refinance the debt on a long-term basis on terms that are readily determinable before the next reporting date is one way to satisfy the second condition. In addition, the fact that a company has the right to refinance at any time and intends to do so permits the company to classify the liability as non-current.

To illustrate, assume that Haddad Company provides the following information related to its note payable.

- Issued note payable of $3,000,000 on November 30, 2013, due on February 28, 2014. Haddad's reporting date is December 31, 2013.
- Haddad intends to extend the maturity date of the loan (refinance the loan) to June 30, 2015.
- Its December 31, 2013, financial statements are authorized for issue on March 15, 2014.
- The necessary paperwork to refinance the loan is completed on January 15, 2014. Haddad did not have an unconditional right to defer settlement of the obligation at December 31, 2013.

A graphical representation of the refinancing events is provided in Illustration IFRS13-1.

ILLUSTRATION IFRS13-1
Refinancing Events

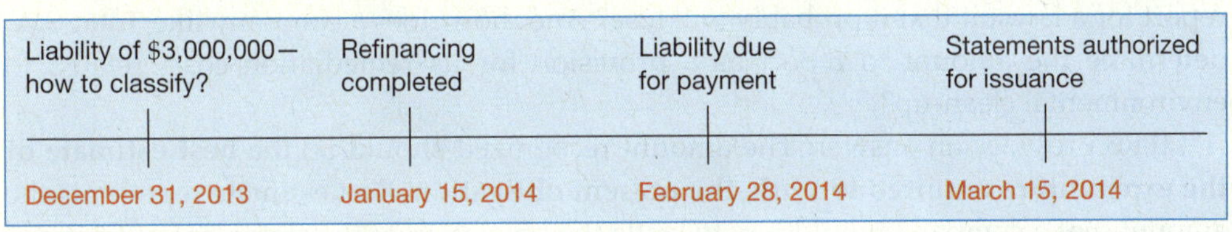

In this case, Haddad must classify its note payable as a current liability because the refinancing was not completed by December 31, 2013, the financial reporting date. Only if the refinancing was completed before December 31, 2013, can Haddad classify the note obligation as non-current. The rationale: Refinancing a liability after the statement of financial position date does not affect the liquidity or solvency at the date of the statement of financial position, the reporting of which should reflect contractual agreements in force on that date.

What happens if Haddad has both the intention and the discretion (within the loan agreement) to refinance or roll over its $3,000,000 note payable to June 30, 2015? In this case, Haddad should classify the note payable as non-current because it has the ability to defer the payment to June 30, 2015.

Provisions

As indicated in the *Relevant Facts* section, a **provision** is a liability of uncertain timing or amount (sometimes referred to as an *estimated liability*). Provisions are very common and may be reported either as current or non-current depending on the date of expected payment. Common types of provisions are obligations related to litigation, warrantees or product guarantees, business restructurings, and environmental damage.

The difference between a provision and other liabilities (such as accounts or notes payable, salaries payable, and dividends payable) is that **a provision has greater uncertainty about the timing or amount of the future expenditure required to settle the obligation**. For example, when **Siemens AG** reports an accounts payable, there is an invoice or formal agreement as to the existence and the amount of the liability. Similarly, when Siemens accrues interest payable, the timing and the amount are known.[22]

[22]The distinction is important because provisions are subject to disclosure requirements that do not apply to other types of payables.

Recognition of a Provision

Companies accrue an expense and related liability for a provision only if the following three conditions are met:

1. A company has a present obligation (legal or constructive) as a result of a past event;
2. It is probable that an outflow of resources embodying economic benefits will be required to settle the obligation; and.
3. A reliable estimate can be made of the amount of the obligation.

If any of these three conditions are not met, no provision is recognized.

In applying the first condition, the past event (often referred to as the *past obligatory event*) must have occurred. In applying the second condition, the term **probable** is defined as "more likely than not to occur." This phrase is interpreted to mean the probability of occurrence is greater than 50 percent. If the probability is 50 percent or less, the provision is not recognized.

Measurement of Provisions

How does a company like **Toyota**, for example, determine the amount to report for its warranty cost on its automobiles? How does a company like **Carrefour** determine its liability for customer refunds? Or, how does **Novartis** determine the amount to report for a lawsuit that it probably will lose? And, how does a company like **Total S.A.** determine the amount to report as a provision for its remediation costs related to environmental clean-up?

IFRS provides an answer: The amount recognized should be the **best estimate of the expenditure required to settle the present obligation.** Best estimate represents the amount that a company would pay to settle the obligation at the statement of financial position date.

Measurement Examples. In determining the best estimate, the management of a company must use judgment, based on past or similar transactions, discussions with experts, and any other pertinent information. Here is how this judgment might be used in three different types of situations to arrive at best estimate:

- ***Toyota warranties.*** Toyota sells many cars and must make an estimate of the number of warranty repairs and related costs it will incur. Because it is dealing with a large population of automobiles, it is often best to weight all possible outcomes by associated probabilities. For example, it might determine that 80 percent of its cars will not have any warranty cost, 12 percent will have substantial costs, and 8 percent will have a much smaller cost. In this case, by weighting all the possible outcomes by their associated probabilities, Toyota **arrives at an expected value** for its warranty liability.
- ***Carrefour refunds.*** Carrefour sells many items at varying selling prices. Refunds to customers for products sold may be viewed as a continuous range of refunds, with each point in the range having the same probability of occurrence. In this case, the **midpoint in the range** can be used as the basis for measuring the amount of the refunds.
- ***Novartis lawsuit.*** Large companies like Novartis are involved in numerous litigation issues related to their products. Where a single obligation such as a lawsuit is being measured, **the most likely outcome** of the lawsuit may be the best estimate of the liability.

Common Types of Provisions

Here are some common areas for which provisions may be recognized in the financial statements:

1. Lawsuits	**4.** Environmental
2. Warranties	**5.** Onerous contracts
3. Premiums	**6.** Restructuring

IFRS accounting guidance is similar to GAAP for these items. Although companies generally report only one current and one non-current amount for provisions in the statement of financial position, IFRS also requires extensive disclosure related to provisions in the notes to the financial statements. Companies do not record or report in the notes to the financial statements general risk contingencies inherent in business operations (e.g., the possibility of war, strike, uninsurable catastrophes, or a business recession).

Onerous Contract Provisions

Sometimes, companies have what are referred to as **onerous contracts**. These contracts are ones in which "the unavoidable costs of meeting the obligations exceed the economic benefits expected to be received." An example of an onerous contract is a loss recognized on unfavorable non-cancelable purchase commitments related to inventory items.

To illustrate another situation, assume that Sumart Sports operates profitably in a factory that it has leased and on which it pays monthly rentals. Sumart decides to relocate its operations to another facility. However, the lease on the old facility continues for the next three years. Unfortunately, Sumart cannot cancel the lease nor will it be able to sublet the factory to another party. The expected costs to satisfy this onerous contract are $200,000. In this case, Sumart makes the following entry.

Loss on Lease Contract	200,000	
Lease Contract Liability		200,000

The expected costs should reflect the least net cost of exiting from the contract, which is the lower of (1) the cost of fulfilling the contract, or (2) the compensation or penalties arising from failure to fulfill the contract.

Contingencies

In a general sense, all provisions are contingent because they are uncertain in timing or amount. However, IFRS uses the term "contingent" for liabilities and assets that are not recognized in the financial statements.

Contingent Liabilities

Contingent liabilities are not recognized in the financial statements because they are (1) a possible obligation (not yet confirmed as a present obligation), (2) a present obligation for which it is not probable that payment will be made, or (3) a present obligation for which a reliable estimate of the obligation cannot be made. Examples of contingent liabilities are:

- A lawsuit in which it is only possible that the company might lose.
- A guarantee related to collectability of a receivable.

Illustration IFRS13-2 presents the general guidelines for the accounting and reporting of contingent liabilities.

ILLUSTRATION IFRS13-2
Contingent Liability Guidelines

Outcome	Probability*	Accounting Treatment
Virtually certain	At least 90%	Report as liability (provision).
Probable (more likely than not)	51–89% probable	Report as liability (provision).
Possible but not probable	5–50%	Disclosure required.
Remote	Less than 5%	No disclosure required.

*In practice, the percentages for virtually certain and remote may deviate from those presented here.

Unless the possibility of any outflow in settlement is remote, companies should disclose the contingent liability at the end of the reporting period, providing a brief description of the nature of the contingent liability and, where practicable:

1. An estimate of its financial effect;
2. An indication of the uncertainties relating to the amount or timing of any outflow; and
3. The possibility of any reimbursement.

Contingent Assets

A **contingent asset** is a possible asset that arises from past events and whose existence will be confirmed by the occurrence or non-occurrence of uncertain future events not wholly within the control of the company. Typical contingent assets are:

1. Possible receipts of monies from gifts, donations, bonuses.
2. Possible refunds from the government in tax disputes.
3. Pending court cases with a probable favorable outcome.

Contingent assets are not recognized on the statement of financial position. If realization of the contingent asset is virtually certain, it is no longer considered a contingent asset and is recognized as an asset. **Virtually certain** is generally interpreted to be at least a probability of 90 percent or more.

The general rules related to contingent assets are presented in Illustration IFRS13-3.

ILLUSTRATION IFRS13-3
Contingent Asset Guidelines

Outcome	Probability*	Accounting Treatment
Virtually certain	At least 90% probable	Report as asset (no longer contingent).
Probable (more likely than not)	51–90% probable	Disclose.
Possible but not probable	5–50%	No disclosure required.
Remote	Less than 5%	No disclosure required.

*In practice, the percentages for virtually certain and remote may deviate from those presented here.

Contingent assets are disclosed when an inflow of economic benefits is considered more likely than not to occur (greater than 50 percent). However, it is important that disclosures for contingent assets avoid giving misleading indications of the likelihood of income arising. As a result, it is not surprising that the thresholds for allowing recognition of contingent assets are more stringent relative to those for liabilities.

What might be an example of a contingent asset that becomes an asset to be recorded? To illustrate, assume that Marcus Realty leases a property to **Marks and Spencer plc (M&S)**. The contract is non-cancelable for five years. On December 1, 2013, before the end of the contract, M&S withdraws from the contract and is required to pay £245,000 as a penalty. At the time M&S cancels the contract, a receivable and related income should be reported by Marcus. The disclosure includes the nature and, where practicable, the estimated financial effects of the asset.

IFRS SELF-TEST QUESTIONS

1. The presentation of current and non-current liabilities in the statement of financial position (balance sheet):
   (a) is shown only on GAAP financial statements.
   (b) is shown on both a GAAP and an IFRS statement of financial position.

(c) is always shown with current liabilities reported first in an IFRS statement of financial position.
(d) includes contingent liabilities under IFRS.

2. In accounting for short-term debt expected to be refinanced to long-term debt:
   (a) GAAP uses the authorization date to determine classification of short-term debt to be refinanced.
   (b) IFRS uses the authorization date to determine classification of short-term debt to be refinanced.
   (c) IFRS uses the financial statement date to determine classification of short-term debt to be refinanced.
   (d) GAAP uses the date of issue, but only for secured debt, to determine classification of short-term debt to be refinanced.
3. Under IFRS, a provision is the same as:
   (a) a contingent liability.
   (b) an estimated liability.
   (c) a contingent gain.
   (d) None of the above.
4. A typical provision is:
   (a) bonds payable.
   (b) cash.
   (c) a warranty liability.
   (d) accounts payable.
5. In determining the amount of a provision, a company using IFRS should generally measure:
   (a) using the midpoint of the range between the lowest possible loss and the highest possible loss.
   (b) using the minimum amount of the loss in the range.
   (c) using the best estimate of the amount of the loss expected to occur.
   (d) using the maximum amount of the loss in the range.

IFRS CONCEPTS AND APPLICATION

IFRS13-1 Under what conditions should a short-term obligation be excluded from current liabilities?

IFRS13-2 What evidence is necessary to demonstrate the ability to defer settlement of short-term debt?

IFRS13-3 Define a provision, and give three examples of a provision.

IFRS13-4 Under what conditions should a provision be recorded?

IFRS13-5 Distinguish between a current liability, such as accounts payable, and a provision.

IFRS13-6 What is an onerous contract? Give two examples of an onerous contract.

IFRS13-7 On December 31, 2014, Alexander Company had $1,200,000 of short-term debt in the form of notes payable due February 2, 2015. On January 21, 2015, the company issued 25,000 ordinary shares for $36 per share, receiving $900,000 proceeds after brokerage fees and other costs of issuance. On February 2, 2015, the proceeds from the share sale, supplemented by an additional $300,000 cash, are used to liquidate the $1,200,000 debt. The December 31, 2014, statement of financial position is authorized for issue on February 23, 2015.

Instructions

Show how the $1,200,000 of short-term debt should be presented on the December 31, 2014, statement of financial position.

IFRS13-8 Presented below are two different situations related to Mckee Corporation's debt obligations. Mckee's next financial reporting date is December 31, 2014. The financial statements are authorized for issuance on March 1, 2015.

1. Mckee has a long-term obligation of $400,000, which is maturing over 4 years in the amount of $100,000 per year. The obligation is dated November 1, 2014, and the first maturity date is November 1, 2015.
2. Mckee has a short-term obligation due February 15, 2015. Its lender agrees to extend the maturity date of this loan to February 15, 2017. The agreement for extension is signed on January 15, 2015.

Instructions

Indicate how each of these debt obligations is reported on Mckee's statement of financial position on December 31, 2014.

IFRS13-9 The following situations relate to Bolivia Company.

1. Bolivia provides a warranty with all its products it sells. It estimates that it will sell 1,000,000 units of its product for the year ended December 31, 2014, and that its total revenue for the

product will be $100,000,000. It also estimates that 60% of the product will have no defects, 30% will have major defects, and 10% will have minor defects. The cost of a minor defect is estimated to be $5 for each product sold, and the cost for a major defect cost is $15. The company also estimates that the minimum amount of warranty expense will be $2,000,000 and the maximum will be $10,000,000.

2. Bolivia is involved in a tax dispute with the tax authorities. The most likely outcome of this dispute is that Bolivia will lose and have to pay $400,000. The minimum it will lose is $20,000 and the maximum is $2,500,000.

Instructions

Prepare the journal entry to record provisions, if any, for Bolivia at December 31, 2014.

IFRS13-10 Kobayashi Corporation reports in the current liability section of its statement of financial position at December 31, 2014 (its year-end), short-term obligations of $15,000,000, which includes the current portion of 12% long-term debt in the amount of $10,000,000 (matures in March 2015). Management has stated its intention to refinance the 12% debt whereby no portion of it will mature during 2015. The date of issuance of the financial statements is March 25, 2015.

Instructions

(a) Is management's intent enough to support long-term classification of the obligation in this situation?

(b) Assume that Kobayashi Corporation issues $13,000,000 of 10-year debentures to the public in January 2015 and that management intends to use the proceeds to liquidate the $10,000,000 debt maturing in March 2015. Furthermore, assume that the debt maturing in March 2015 is paid from these proceeds prior to the authorization to issue the financial statements. Will this have any impact on the statement of financial position classification at December 31, 2014? Explain your answer.

(c) Assume that Kobayashi Corporation issues ordinary shares to the public in January and that management intends to entirely liquidate the $10,000,000 debt maturing in March 2015 with the proceeds of this equity securities issue. In light of these events, should the $10,000,000 debt maturing in March 2015 be included in current liabilities at December 31, 2014?

Professional Research

IFRS13-11 Hincapie Co. manufactures specialty bike accessories. The company is most well known for its product quality, and it has offered one of the best warranties in the industry on its higher-priced products—a lifetime guarantee. The warranty on these products is included in the sales price. Hincapie has a contract with a service company, which performs all warranty work on Hincapie products. Under the contract, Hincapie guarantees the service company at least $200,000 of warranty work for each year of the 3-year contract.

The recent economic recession has been hard on Hincapie's business, and sales for its higher-end products have been especially adversely impacted. As a result, Hincapie is planning to restructure its high-quality lines by moving manufacturing for those products into one of its other factories, shutting down assembly lines, and terminating workers. In order to keep some workers on-board, Hincapie plans to bring all warranty work in-house. It can terminate the current warranty contract by making a one-time termination payment of $75,000.

The restructuring plans have been discussed by management during November 2013; they plan to get approval from the board of directors at the December board meeting and execute the restructuring in early 2014. Given the company's past success, the accounting for restructuring activities has never come up. Hincapie would like you to do some research on how it should account for this restructuring according to IFRS.

Instructions

Access the IFRS authoritative literature at the IASB website (*http://eifrs.iasb.org/*). (Click on the IFRS tab and then register for free eIFRS access if necessary.) When you have accessed the documents, you can use the search tool in your Internet browser to respond to the following questions. (Provide paragraph citations.)

(a) Identify the accounting literature that addresses the accounting for the various costs that will be incurred in the restructuring.

(b) Advise Hincapie on the restructuring costs. When should Hincapie recognize liabilities arising from the restructuring? What costs can be included? What costs are excluded?

(c) Does Hincapie have a liability related to the service contract? Explain. If Hincapie has a liability, at what amount should it be recorded?

International Financial Reporting Problem

Marks and Spencer plc

IFRS13-12 The financial statements of **Marks and Spencer plc (M&S)** are available at the book's companion website or can be accessed at *http://annualreport.marksandspencer.com/_assets/downloads/Marks-and-Spencer-Annual-report-and-financial-statements-2012.pdf.*

Instructions

Refer to M&S's financial statements and the accompanying notes to answer the following questions.

(a) What was M&S's 2012 short-term debt and related weighted-average interest rate on this debt?

(b) What was M&S's 2012 working capital, acid-test ratio, and current ratio? Comment on M&S's liquidity.

(c) What types of commitments and contingencies has M&S reported in its financial statements?

ANSWERS TO IFRS SELF-TEST QUESTIONS

1. b **2.** c **3.** b **4.** c **5.** c

Remember to check the book's companion website to find additional resources for this chapter.

CHAPTER 14 Long-Term Liabilities

LEARNING OBJECTIVES

After studying this chapter, you should be able to:

1. Describe the formal procedures associated with issuing long-term debt.
2. Identify various types of bond issues.
3. Describe the accounting valuation for bonds at date of issuance.
4. Apply the methods of bond discount and premium amortization.
5. Describe the accounting for the extinguishment of debt.
6. Explain the accounting for long-term notes payable.
7. Describe the accounting for the fair value option.
8. Explain the reporting of off-balance-sheet financing arrangements.
9. Indicate how to present and analyze long-term debt.

Going Long

The clock is ticking. Every second, it seems, someone in the world takes on more debt. The idea of a debt clock for an individual nation is familiar to anyone who has been to Times Square in New York, where the American public shortfall is revealed. The global debt clock shown below (accessed in October 2012) indicates the global figure for almost all government debts in dollar terms.

Current Global Public Debt

$ 049, 041, 235, 945, 311

Does it matter? After all, world governments owe the money to their own citizens, not to the Martians. But the rising total is important for two reasons. First, when government debt rises faster than economic output (as it has been doing in recent years), this implies more state interference in the economy and higher taxes in the future. Second, debt must be rolled over at regular intervals. This creates a recurring popularity test for individual governments, much like reality-TV contestants facing a public phone vote every week. Fail that vote, as various euro-zone governments have done, and the country (and its neighbors) can be plunged into crisis.

In addition to government debt, companies are issuing corporate debt at a record pace. Why this trend? For one thing, low interest rates and rising inflows into fixed-income funds have triggered record bond issuances as banks cut back lending. In addition, for some high-rated companies, it can be riskier to borrow from a bank than the bond markets. The reason: High-rated companies tend to rely on short-term commercial paper, backed up by undrawn loans, to fund working capital but are left stranded when these markets freeze up. Some are now financing themselves with longer-term bonds instead.

In fact, nonfinancial companies are issuing 30-year bonds at a record pace, as they look to increase long-term borrowings, lock in low interest rates, and take advantage of investor demand. The charts on the next page show the substantial increase in bonds issues as interest rates have fallen.

Companies, like **Phillip Morris**, **Medtronic**, **Plains All American Pipeline**, and **Simon Property Group**, have all sold 30-year bonds recently. Increases in the issuance of these bonds suggest confidence in the economy as investors appear comfortable holding such long-term investments. In addition, companies have a strong appetite for issuing these bonds

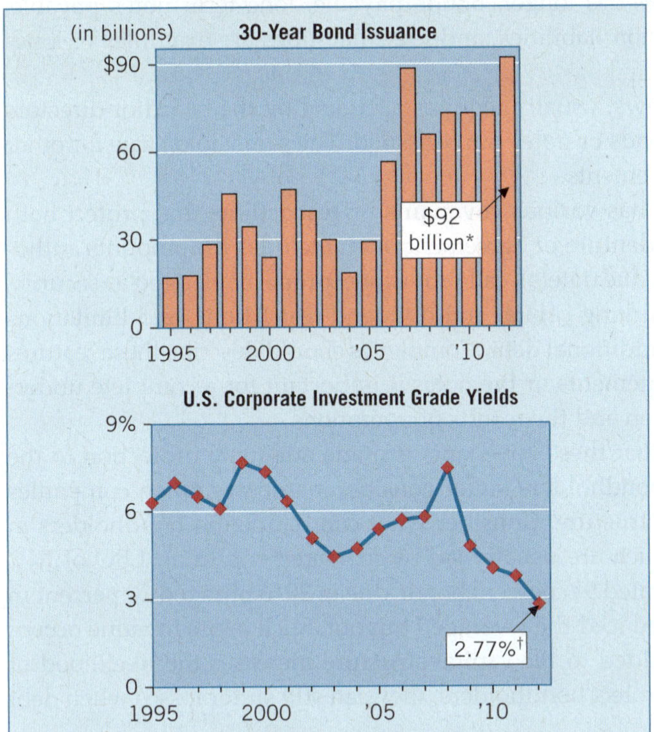

*Year to date. †As of Oct. 5. Other yield data are recorded on the last day of each year.

Sources: Dealogic (bond issuance); Barclays (yields); and *Wall Street Journal*.

CONCEPTUAL FOCUS

> See the **Underlying Concepts** on page 774.

> Read the **Evolving Issue** on page 788 for a discussion of recognizing debt using the fair value option.

INTERNATIONAL FOCUS

> See the **International Perspectives** on pages 770, 775, and 785.

> Read the **IFRS Insights** on pages 815–819 for a discussion of:

—Effective-interest method
—Extinguishments with modifications of terms

because they provide a substantial cash infusion at a relatively low interest rate. Hopefully, it will work out for both the investor and the company in the long run.

Sources: A. Sakoui and N. Bullock, "Companies Choose Bonds for Cheap Funds," *Financial Times* (October 12, 2009); *http://www.economist.com/content/global_debt_clock*; and V. Monga, "Companies Feast on Cheap Money Market for 30-Year Bonds, Priced at Stark Lows, Brings Out GE, UPS and Other Once-Shy Issuers," *Wall Street Journal* (October 8, 2012).

PREVIEW OF CHAPTER 14

As our opening story indicates, companies may rely on different forms of long-term borrowing, depending on market conditions and the features of various noncurrent liabilities. In this chapter, we explain the accounting issues related to long-term liabilities. The content and organization of the chapter are as follows.

Long-Term Liabilities

Bonds Payable
- Issuing bonds
- Types of bonds

Valuation of Bonds Payable
- Issued at par
- Issued at discount or premium
- Issued between interest dates
- Effective-interest method
- Costs of issuing
- Extinguishment

Long-Term Notes Payable
- Notes issued at face value
- Notes not issued at face value
- Special situations
- Mortgage notes payable
- Fair value option

Reporting and Analyzing Liabilities
- Off-balance-sheet financing
- Presentation and analysis

BONDS PAYABLE

LEARNING OBJECTIVE 1
Describe the formal procedures associated with issuing long-term debt.

Long-term debt consists of probable future sacrifices of economic benefits arising from present obligations that are not payable within a year or the operating cycle of the company, whichever is longer. Bonds payable, long-term notes payable, mortgages payable, pension liabilities, and lease liabilities are examples of long-term liabilities.

A corporation, per its bylaws, usually requires approval by the board of directors and the stockholders before bonds or notes can be issued. The same holds true for other types of long-term debt arrangements.

Generally, long-term debt has various **covenants** or **restrictions** that protect both lenders and borrowers. The indenture or agreement often includes the amounts authorized to be issued, interest rate, due date(s), call provisions, property pledged as security, sinking fund requirements, working capital and dividend restrictions, and limitations concerning the assumption of additional debt. Companies should describe these features in the body of the financial statements or the notes if important for a complete understanding of the financial position and the results of operations.

Although it would seem that these covenants provide adequate protection to the long-term debtholder, many bondholders suffer considerable losses when companies add more debt to the capital structure. Consider what can happen to bondholders in leveraged buyouts (LBOs), which are usually led by management. In an LBO of RJR Nabisco, for example, solidly rated 9⅜ percent bonds due in 2016 plunged 20 percent in value when management announced the leveraged buyout. Such a loss in value occurs because the additional debt added to the capital structure increases the likelihood of default. Although covenants protect bondholders, they can still suffer losses when debt levels get too high.

Issuing Bonds

A bond arises from a contract known as a **bond indenture**. A bond represents a promise to pay (1) a sum of money at a designated maturity date, plus (2) periodic interest at a specified rate on the maturity amount (face value). Individual bonds are evidenced by a paper certificate and typically have a $1,000 face value. Companies usually make bond interest payments semiannually, although the interest rate is generally expressed as an annual rate. The main purpose of bonds is to borrow for the long term when the amount of capital needed is too large for one lender to supply. By issuing bonds in $100, $1,000, or $10,000 denominations, a company can divide a large amount of long-term indebtedness into many small investing units, thus enabling more than one lender to participate in the loan.

A company may sell an entire bond issue to an investment bank, which acts as a selling agent in the process of marketing the bonds. In such arrangements, investment banks may either underwrite the entire issue by guaranteeing a certain sum to the company, thus taking the risk of selling the bonds for whatever price they can get (firm underwriting). Or they may sell the bond issue for a commission on the proceeds of the sale (best-efforts underwriting). Alternatively, the issuing company may sell the bonds directly to a large institution, financial or otherwise, without the aid of an underwriter (private placement).

Types of Bonds

LEARNING OBJECTIVE 2
Identify various types of bond issues.

Presented on the next page, we define some of the more common types of bonds found in practice.

TYPES OF BONDS

SECURED AND UNSECURED BONDS. **Secured bonds** are backed by a pledge of some sort of collateral. Mortgage bonds are secured by a claim on real estate. Collateral trust bonds are secured by stocks and bonds of other corporations. Bonds not backed by collateral are **unsecured.** A **debenture bond** is unsecured. A "junk bond" is unsecured and also very risky, and therefore pays a high interest rate. Companies often use these bonds to finance leveraged buyouts.

TERM, SERIAL BONDS, AND CALLABLE BONDS. Bond issues that mature on a single date are called **term bonds.** Issues that mature in installments are called **serial bonds.** Serially maturing bonds are frequently used by school or sanitary districts, municipalities, or other local taxing bodies that receive money through a special levy. **Callable bonds** give the issuer the right to call and redeem the bonds prior to maturity.

CONVERTIBLE, COMMODITY-BACKED, AND DEEP-DISCOUNT BONDS. If bonds are convertible into other securities of the corporation for a specified time after issuance, they are **convertible bonds.**

Two types of bonds have been developed in an attempt to attract capital in a tight money market—commodity-backed bonds and deep-discount bonds. **Commodity-backed bonds** (also called **asset-linked bonds**) are redeemable in measures of a commodity, such as barrels of oil, tons of coal, or ounces of rare metal. To illustrate, **Sunshine Mining**, a silver-mining company, sold two issues of bonds redeemable with either $1,000 in cash or 50 ounces of silver, whichever is greater at maturity, and that have a stated interest rate of 8½ percent. The accounting problem is one of projecting the maturity value, especially since silver has fluctuated between $4 and $40 an ounce since issuance.

JCPenney Company sold the first publicly marketed long-term debt securities in the United States that do not bear interest. These **deep-discount bonds**, also referred to as **zero-interest debenture bonds**, are sold at a discount that provides the buyer's total interest payoff at maturity.

REGISTERED AND BEARER (COUPON) BONDS. Bonds issued in the name of the owner are **registered bonds** and require surrender of the certificate and issuance of a new certificate to complete a sale. A **bearer** or **coupon bond**, however, is not recorded in the name of the owner and may be transferred from one owner to another by mere delivery.

INCOME AND REVENUE BONDS. **Income bonds** pay no interest unless the issuing company is profitable. **Revenue bonds**, so called because the interest on them is paid from specified revenue sources, are most frequently issued by airports, school districts, counties, toll-road authorities, and governmental bodies.

What do the numbers mean? ALL ABOUT BONDS

How do investors monitor their bond investments? One way is to review the bond listings found in the newspaper or online. Corporate bond listings show the coupon (interest) rate, maturity date, and last price. However, because corporate bonds are more actively held by large institutional investors, the listings also indicate the current yield and the volume traded. Corporate bond listings would look like those below.

Issuer	Maturity	Amount ($ millions)	Price	Coupon	Yield
Wal-Mart Stores, Inc.	08/15/2037	3,000	145.4	6.50	3.69
General Electric	12/06/2017	4,000	118.2	5.25	1.58

The companies issuing the bonds are listed in the first column, in this case, Wal-Mart Stores, Inc. and General Electric. Immediately after the names is a column with the maturity date, followed by the amount and price of the bonds. As indicated, Wal-Mart pays a coupon rate of 6.5 percent and yields 3.69 percent. General Electric pays a coupon rate of 5.25 percent and yields 1.58 percent. The lower yield for General Electric arises because the time to maturity is much shorter than Wal-Mart's.

Also, interest rates and the bond's term to maturity have a real effect on bond prices. For example, an increase in interest rates will lead to a decline in bond values. Similarly, a decrease in interest rates will lead to a rise in bond values. The data reported in the table to the right, based on three different bond funds, demonstrate these relationships between interest rate changes and bond values.

Bond Price Changes in Response to Interest Rate Changes	1% Interest Rate Increase	1% Interest Rate Decrease
Short-term fund (2–5 years)	−2.5%	+2.5%
Intermediate-term fund (5 years)	−5%	+5%
Long-term fund (10 years)	−10%	+10%

Data source: The Vanguard Group.

Another factor that affects bond prices is the call feature, which decreases the value of the bond. Investors must be rewarded for the risk that the issuer will call the bond if interest rates decline, which would force the investor to reinvest at lower rates.

VALUATION OF BONDS PAYABLE—DISCOUNT AND PREMIUM

LEARNING OBJECTIVE 3
Describe the accounting valuation for bonds at date of issuance.

The issuance and marketing of bonds to the public does not happen overnight. It usually takes weeks or even months. First, the issuing company must arrange for underwriters that will help market and sell the bonds. Then, it must obtain the Securities and Exchange Commission's approval of the bond issue, undergo audits, and issue a prospectus (a document which describes the features of the bond and related financial information). Finally, the company must generally have the bond certificates printed. Frequently, the issuing company establishes the terms of a bond indenture well in advance of the sale of the bonds. Between the time the company sets these terms and the time it issues the bonds, the market conditions and the financial position of the issuing corporation may change significantly. Such changes affect the marketability of the bonds and thus their selling price.

The selling price of a bond issue is set by the supply and demand of buyers and sellers, relative risk, market conditions, and the state of the economy. The investment community values a bond at the **present value of its expected future cash flows**, which consist of (1) interest and (2) principal. The rate used to compute the present value of these cash flows is the interest rate that provides an acceptable return on an investment commensurate with the issuer's risk characteristics.

The interest rate written in the terms of the bond indenture (and often printed on the bond certificate) is known as the **stated**, **coupon**, or **nominal rate**. The issuer of the bonds sets this rate. The stated rate is expressed as a percentage of the **face value** of the bonds (also called the **par value**, **principal amount**, or **maturity value**).

If the rate employed by the investment community (buyers) differs from the stated rate, the present value of the bonds computed by the buyers (and the current purchase price) will differ from the face value of the bonds. The difference between the face value and the present value of the bonds determines the actual price that buyers pay for the bonds. This difference is either a discount or premium.[1]

[1]It is generally the case that the stated rate of interest on bonds is set in rather precise decimals (such as 6.875%). Companies usually attempt to align the stated rate as closely as possible with the market or effective rate at the time of issue.

- If the bonds sell for less than face value, they sell at a **discount**.
- If the bonds sell for more than face value, they sell at a **premium**.

The rate of interest actually earned by the bondholders is called the **effective yield** or **market rate**. If bonds sell at a discount, the effective yield exceeds the stated rate. Conversely, if bonds sell at a premium, the effective yield is lower than the stated rate. Several variables affect the bond's price while it is outstanding, most notably the market rate of interest. There is an inverse relationship between the market interest rate and the price of the bond.

Here we consider an example to illustrate the computation of the **present value of a bond issue**. Assume that ServiceMaster issues $100,000 in bonds, due in five years with 9 percent interest payable annually at year-end. At the time of issue, the market rate for such bonds is 11 percent. The time diagram in Illustration 14-1 depicts both the interest and the principal cash flows.

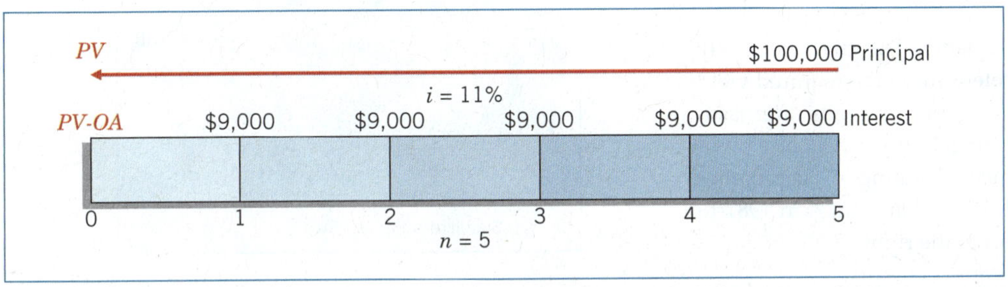

ILLUSTRATION 14-1
Time Diagram for Bond Cash Flows

The actual principal and interest cash flows are discounted at an 11 percent rate for five periods, as shown in Illustration 14-2.

Present value of the principal:	
$100,000 × .59345 (Table 6-2)	$59,345.00
Present value of the interest payments:	
$9,000 × 3.69590 (Table 6-4)	33,263.10
Present value (selling price) of the bonds	$92,608.10

ILLUSTRATION 14-2
Present Value Computation of Bond Selling at a Discount

By paying $92,608.10 at the date of issue, investors earn an effective rate or yield of 11 percent over the five-year term of the bonds. These bonds would sell at a discount of $7,391.90 ($100,000 − $92,608.10). The price at which the bonds sell is typically stated as a **percentage** of the face or par value of the bonds. For example, the ServiceMaster bonds sold for 92.6 (92.6% of par). If ServiceMaster had received $102,000, then the bonds sold for 102 (102% of par).

When bonds sell at less than face value, it means that investors demand a rate of interest **higher** than the stated rate. Usually this occurs because the investors can earn a greater rate on alternative investments of equal risk. They cannot change the stated rate, so they refuse to pay face value for the bonds. Thus, by changing the amount invested, they alter the effective rate of return. The investors receive interest at the stated rate computed on the face value, but they actually earn at **an effective rate that exceeds the stated rate because they paid less than face value for the bonds**. (Later in the chapter, in Illustrations 14-6 and 14-7 (pages 772–773), we show an illustration for a bond that sells at a premium.)

What do the numbers mean? HOW'S MY RATING?

Two major publication companies, **Moody's Investors Service** and **Standard & Poor's Corporation**, issue quality ratings on every public debt issue. The following table summarizes the ratings issued by Standard & Poor's, along with historical default rates on bonds with different ratings.

Original rating	AAA	AA	A	BBB	BB	B	CCC
Default rate	0.52%	1.31	2.32	6.64	19.52	35.76	54.38

Data source: Standard & Poor's Corp.

As expected, bonds receiving the highest quality rating of AAA have the lowest historical default rates. Bonds rated below BBB, which are considered below investment grade ("junk bonds"), experience default rates ranging from 20 to 50 percent.

Debt ratings reflect credit quality. The market closely monitors these ratings when determining the required yield and pricing of bonds at issuance and in periods after issuance, especially if a bond's rating is upgraded or downgraded. Unfortunately, the median rating of companies assessed by Standard & Poor's has fallen from A in 1981 to BBB today, as shown in the chart to the right.

The BBB rating is the lowest possible "investment grade" or, to put it another way, is just one notch above "junk" bond status. It should be noted that investors who seek triple-A debt are running out of options. Standard & Poor's recently gave its top rating to just four U.S. industrial companies: **Automatic Data Processing**, **ExxonMobil**, **Johnson & Johnson**, and **Microsoft**.

Standard & Poor's Median Corporate-Credit Rating

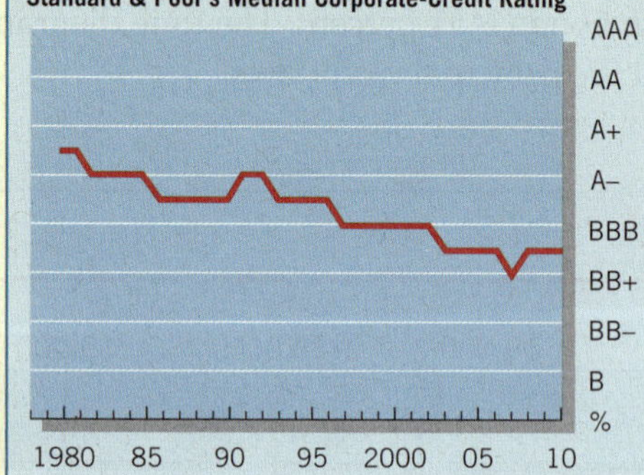

Source: Standard & Poor's.

Sources: A. Borrus, M. McNamee, and H. Timmons, "The Credit Raters: How They Work and How They Might Work Better," *BusinessWeek* (April 8, 2002), pp. 38–40; Standard and Poor's, *Global Fixed Income Research*, "Fallen Angel Activity" (February 6, 2007); and "Betting the Balance Sheet," *The Economist* (June 24, 2010).

Bonds Issued at Par on Interest Date

When a company issues bonds on an interest payment date at par (face value), it accrues no interest. No premium or discount exists. The company simply records the cash proceeds and the face value of the bonds. To illustrate, if Buchanan Company issues at par 10-year term bonds with a par value of $800,000, dated January 1, 2014, and bearing interest at an annual rate of 10 percent payable semiannually on January 1 and July 1, it records the following entry.

Cash	800,000	
Bonds Payable		800,000

Buchanan records the first semiannual interest payment of $40,000 ($800,000 × .10 × 1/2) on July 1, 2014, as follows.

Interest Expense	40,000	
Cash		40,000

It records accrued interest expense at December 31, 2014 (year-end), as follows.

Interest Expense	40,000	
Interest Payable		40,000

LEARNING OBJECTIVE 4
Apply the methods of bond discount and premium amortization.

Bonds Issued at Discount or Premium on Interest Date

If Buchanan Company issues the $800,000 of bonds on January 1, 2014, at 97 (meaning 97% of par), it records the issuance as shown on the top of the next page.

Cash ($800,000 × .97)	776,000	
Discount on Bonds Payable	24,000	
Bonds Payable		800,000

Recall from our earlier discussion that because of its relation to interest, **companies amortize the discount and charge it to interest expense over the period of time that the bonds are outstanding.**

The **straight-line method** amortizes a constant amount each interest period (in this case 20 interest periods).[2] For example, using the bond discount of $24,000, Buchanan amortizes $1,200 to interest expense each period for 20 periods ($24,000 ÷ 20).

Buchanan records the first semiannual interest payment of $40,000 ($800,000 × 10% × ½) and the bond discount on July 1, 2014, as follows.

Interest Expense	41,200	
Discount on Bonds Payable		1,200
Cash		40,000

At December 31, 2014, Buchanan makes the following adjusting entry.

Interest Expense	41,200	
Discount on Bonds Payable		1,200
Interest Payable		40,000

At the end of the first year, 2014, the balance in the Discount on Bonds Payable account is $21,600 ($24,000 − $1,200 − $1,200). Over the term of the bonds, the balance in Discount on Bonds Payable will decrease by the same amount until it has zero balance at the maturity date of the bonds.

If instead of issuing the bonds on January 1, 2014, Buchanan dates and sells the bonds on October 1, 2014, and if the fiscal year of the corporation ends on December 31, the discount amortized during 2014 would be only 3/12 of 1/10 of $24,000, or $600. Buchanan must also record three months of accrued interest on December 31.

Premium on Bonds Payable is accounted for in a manner similar to that for Discount on Bonds Payable. If Buchanan dates and sells 10-year bonds with a par value of $800,000 on January 1, 2014, at 103, it records the issuance as follows.

Cash ($800,000 × 1.03)	824,000	
Premium on Bonds Payable		24,000
Bonds Payable		800,000

With the bond premium of $24,000, Buchanan amortizes $1,200 to interest expense each period for 20 periods ($24,000 ÷ 20).

Buchanan records the first semiannual interest payment of $40,000 ($800,000 × 10% × ½) and the bond premium on July 1, 2014, as follows.

Interest Expense	38,800	
Premium on Bonds Payable	1,200	
Cash		40,000

At December 31, 2014, Buchanan makes the following adjusting entry.

Interest Expense	38,800	
Premium on Bonds Payable	1,200	
Interest Payable		40,000

Amortization of a discount increases interest expense. Amortization of a premium decreases interest expense. Later in the chapter, we discuss amortization of a discount or premium under the effective-interest method.

[2]The effective-interest method is preferred for amortization of discount or premium. To keep these initial illustrations simple, we have chosen to use the straight-line method.

The issuer may call some bonds at a stated price after a certain date. This call feature gives the issuing corporation the opportunity to reduce its bonded indebtedness or take advantage of lower interest rates. **Whether callable or not, a company must amortize any premium or discount over the bond's life to maturity because early redemption (call of the bond) is not a certainty.**

Bonds Issued Between Interest Dates

Companies usually make bond interest payments semiannually, on dates specified in the bond indenture. When companies issue bonds on other than the interest payment dates, **buyers of the bonds will pay the seller the interest accrued from the last interest payment date to the date of issue.** The purchasers of the bonds, in effect, pay the bond issuer in advance for that portion of the full six-months' interest payment to which they are not entitled because they have not held the bonds for that period. **Then, on the next semiannual interest payment date, purchasers will receive the full six-months' interest payment.**

To illustrate, assume that on March 1, 2014, Taft Corporation issues 10-year bonds, dated January 1, 2014, with a par value of $800,000. These bonds have an annual interest rate of 6 percent, payable semiannually on January 1 and July 1. Because Taft issues the bonds between interest dates, it records the bond issuance at **par plus accrued interest** as follows.

Cash	808,000	
Bonds Payable		800,000
Interest Expense ($800,000 × .06 × 2/12)		8,000
(Interest Payable might be credited instead)		

The purchaser advances two months' interest. On July 1, 2014, four months after the date of purchase, Taft pays the purchaser six months' interest. Taft makes the following entry on July 1, 2014.

Interest Expense	24,000	
Cash		24,000

The Interest Expense account now contains a debit balance of $16,000, which represents the proper amount of interest expense—four months at 6 percent on $800,000.

The illustration above was simplified by having the January 1, 2014, bonds issued on March 1, 2014, **at par**. If, however, Taft issued the 6 percent bonds at 102, its March 1 entry would be:

Cash [($800,000 × 1.02) + ($800,000 × .06 × 2/12)]	824,000	
Bonds Payable		800,000
Premium on Bonds Payable ($800,000 × .02)		16,000
Interest Expense		8,000

Taft would amortize the premium **from the date of sale** (March 1, 2014), not from the date of the bonds (January 1, 2014).

International Perspective

IFRS requires the use of the effective-interest method. GAAP permits the use of the straight-line method if not materially different than the effective-interest method.

Effective-Interest Method

The preferred procedure for amortization of a discount or premium is the **effective-interest method** (also called **present value amortization**). Under the effective-interest method, companies:

1. Compute bond interest expense first by multiplying the **carrying value** (book value) of the bonds at the beginning of the period by the effective-interest rate.[3]

[3]The carrying value is the face amount minus any unamortized discount or plus any unamortized premium. The term *carrying value* is synonymous with *book value*.

2. Determine the bond discount or premium amortization next by comparing the bond interest expense with the interest (cash) to be paid.

Illustration 14-3 depicts graphically the computation of the amortization.

Bond Interest Expense				Bond Interest Paid				
Carrying Value of Bonds at Beginning of Period	×	Effective-Interest Rate	−	Face Amount of Bonds	×	Stated Interest Rate	=	Amortization Amount

ILLUSTRATION 14-3
Bond Discount and Premium Amortization Computation

The effective-interest method produces a periodic interest expense equal to **a constant percentage of the carrying value of the bonds**. Since the percentage is the effective rate of interest incurred by the borrower at the time of issuance, the effective-interest method matches expenses with revenues better than the straight-line method.

Both the effective-interest and straight-line methods result in the **same total amount of interest expense over the term of the bonds**. However, when the annual amounts are materially different, generally accepted accounting principles require use of the effective-interest method. [1]

See the FASB Codification section (page 798).

Bonds Issued at a Discount

To illustrate amortization of a discount under the effective-interest method, Evermaster Corporation issued $100,000 of 8 percent term bonds on January 1, 2014, due on January 1, 2019, with interest payable each July 1 and January 1. Because the investors required an effective-interest rate of 10 percent, they paid $92,278 for the $100,000 of bonds, creating a $7,722 discount. Evermaster computes the $7,722 discount as follows.[4]

Maturity value of bonds payable		$100,000
Present value of $100,000 due in 5 years at 10%, interest payable semiannually (Table 6-2); $FV(PVF_{10,5\%})$; ($100,000 × .61391)	$61,391	
Present value of $4,000 interest payable semiannually for 5 years at 10% annually (Table 6-4); $R(PVF\text{-}OA_{10,5\%})$; ($4,000 × 7.72173)	30,887	
Less: Proceeds from sale of bonds		92,278
Discount on bonds payable		$ 7,722

ILLUSTRATION 14-4
Computation of Discount on Bonds Payable

The five-year amortization schedule appears in Illustration 14-5 (page 772).

Evermaster records the issuance of its bonds at a discount on January 1, 2014, as follows.

Cash	92,278	
Discount on Bonds Payable	7,722	
Bonds Payable		100,000

It records the first interest payment on July 1, 2014, and amortization of the discount as follows.

Interest Expense	4,614	
Discount on Bonds Payable		614
Cash		4,000

[4]Because companies pay interest semiannually, the interest rate used is 5% (10% × $^6/_{12}$). The number of periods is 10 (5 years × 2).

ILLUSTRATION 14-5
Bond Discount Amortization Schedule

Calculator Solution for Present Value of Bonds:

	Inputs	Answer
N	10	
I/YR	5	
PV	?	92,278
PMT	-4,000	
FV	-100,000	

SCHEDULE OF BOND DISCOUNT AMORTIZATION
EFFECTIVE-INTEREST METHOD—SEMIANNUAL INTEREST PAYMENTS
5-YEAR, 8% BONDS SOLD TO YIELD 10%

Date	Cash Paid	Interest Expense	Discount Amortized	Carrying Amount of Bonds
1/1/14				$ 92,278
7/1/14	$ 4,000[a]	$ 4,614[b]	$ 614[c]	92,892[d]
1/1/15	4,000	4,645	645	93,537
7/1/15	4,000	4,677	677	94,214
1/1/16	4,000	4,711	711	94,925
7/1/16	4,000	4,746	746	95,671
1/1/17	4,000	4,783	783	96,454
7/1/17	4,000	4,823	823	97,277
1/1/18	4,000	4,864	864	98,141
7/1/18	4,000	4,907	907	99,048
1/1/19	4,000	4,952	952	100,000
	$40,000	$47,722	$7,722	

[a]$4,000 = $100,000 × .08 × 6/12
[b]$4,614 = $92,278 × .10 × 6/12
[c]$614 = $4,614 − $4,000
[d]$92,892 = $92,278 + $614

Evermaster records the interest expense accrued at December 31, 2014 (year-end), and amortization of the discount as follows.

Interest Expense	4,645	
Interest Payable		4,000
Discount on Bonds Payable		645

Bonds Issued at a Premium

Now assume that for the bond issue by Evermaster Corporation (page 771), investors are willing to accept an effective-interest rate of 6 percent. In that case, they would pay $108,530 or a premium of $8,530, computed as follows.

ILLUSTRATION 14-6
Computation of Premium on Bonds Payable

Maturity value of bonds payable		$100,000
Present value of $100,000 due in 5 years at 6%, interest payable semiannually (Table 6-2); $FV(PVF_{10,3\%})$; ($100,000 × .74409)	$74,409	
Present value of $4,000 interest payable semiannually for 5 years at 6% annually (Table 6-4); $R(PVF\text{-}OA_{10,3\%})$; ($4,000 × 8.53020)	34,121	
Less: Proceeds from sale of bonds		108,530
Premium on bonds payable		$ 8,530

The five-year amortization schedule appears in Illustration 14-7.

Evermaster records the issuance of its bonds at a premium on January 1, 2014, as follows.

Cash	108,530	
Premium on Bonds Payable		8,530
Bonds Payable		100,000

Evermaster records the first interest payment on July 1, 2014, and amortization of the premium as follows.

Interest Expense	3,256	
Premium on Bonds Payable	744	
Cash		4,000

SCHEDULE OF BOND PREMIUM AMORTIZATION
EFFECTIVE-INTEREST METHOD—SEMIANNUAL INTEREST PAYMENTS
5-YEAR, 8% BONDS SOLD TO YIELD 6%

Date	Cash Paid	Interest Expense	Premium Amortized	Carrying Amount of Bonds
1/1/14				$108,530
7/1/14	$ 4,000[a]	$ 3,256[b]	$ 744[c]	107,786[d]
1/1/15	4,000	3,234	766	107,020
7/1/15	4,000	3,211	789	106,231
1/1/16	4,000	3,187	813	105,418
7/1/16	4,000	3,162	838	104,580
1/1/17	4,000	3,137	863	103,717
7/1/17	4,000	3,112	888	102,829
1/1/18	4,000	3,085	915	101,914
7/1/18	4,000	3,057	943	100,971
1/1/19	4,000	3,029	971	100,000
	$40,000	$31,470	$8,530	

[a]$4,000 = $100,000 × .08 × 6/12
[b]$3,256 = $108,530 × .06 × 6/12
[c]$744 = $4,000 − $3,256
[d]$107,786 = $108,530 − $744

ILLUSTRATION 14-7
Bond Premium Amortization Schedule

Calculator Solution for Present Value of Bonds:

	Inputs	Answer
N	10	
I/YR	3	
PV	?	108,530
PMT	−4,000	
FV	−100,000	

Evermaster should amortize the discount or premium as an adjustment to interest expense over the life of the bond in such a way as to result in a **constant rate of interest** when applied to the carrying amount of debt outstanding at the beginning of any given period.

Accruing Interest

In our previous examples, the interest payment dates and the date the financial statements were issued were essentially the same. For example, when Evermaster sold bonds at a premium, the two interest payment dates coincided with the financial reporting dates. However, what happens if Evermaster wishes to report financial statements at the end of February 2014? In this case, the company **prorates** the premium by the appropriate number of months, to arrive at the proper interest expense, as follows.

Interest accrual ($4,000 × 2/6)	$1,333.33
Premium amortized ($744 × 2/6)	(248.00)
Interest expense (Jan.–Feb.)	$1,085.33

ILLUSTRATION 14-8
Computation of Interest Expense

Evermaster records this accrual as follows.

Interest Expense	1,085.33	
Premium on Bonds Payable	248.00	
Interest Payable		1,333.33

If the company prepares financial statements six months later, it follows the same procedure. That is, the premium amortized would be as follows.

Premium amortized (March–June) ($744 × 4/6)	$496.00
Premium amortized (July–August) ($766 × 2/6)	255.33
Premium amortized (March–August)	$751.33

ILLUSTRATION 14-9
Computation of Premium Amortization

The interest-accrual computation is much simpler if the company uses the straight-line method. For example, the total premium is $8,530, which Evermaster allocates evenly over the five-year period. Thus, premium amortization per month is $142.17 ($8,530 ÷ 60 months).

Classification of Discount and Premium

Discount on bonds payable is **not an asset**. It does not provide any future economic benefit. In return for the use of borrowed funds, a company must pay interest. A bond discount means that the company borrowed less than the face or maturity value of the bond. It therefore faces an actual (effective) interest rate higher than the stated (nominal) rate. Conceptually, discount on bonds payable is a liability valuation account. That is, it reduces the face or maturity amount of the related liability.[5] This account is referred to as a **contra account**.

Similarly, premium on bonds payable has no existence apart from the related debt. The lower interest cost results because the proceeds of borrowing exceed the face or maturity amount of the debt. Conceptually, premium on bonds payable is a *liability* valuation account. It adds to the face or maturity amount of the related liability.[6] This account is referred to as an **adjunct account**. As a result, **companies report bond discounts and bond premiums as a direct deduction from or addition to the face amount of the bond.**

Costs of Issuing Bonds

Underlying Concepts

Because bond issue costs do not meet the definition of an asset, some argue they should be expensed at issuance.

The issuance of bonds involves engraving and printing costs, legal and accounting fees, commissions, promotion costs, and other similar charges. Companies are required to charge these costs to an asset account (usually long-term), often referred to as Unamortized Bond Issue Costs. Companies then allocate Unamortized Bond Issue Costs to expense over the life of the debt, in a manner similar to that used for discount on bonds. **[2]**

We disagree with this approach. Unamortized bond issue cost in our view is an expense (or a reduction of the related liability).

Apparently the FASB also disagrees with the current GAAP treatment and notes in *Concepts Statement No. 6* that debt issue cost is not considered an asset because it provides no future economic benefit. The cost of issuing bonds, in effect, reduces the proceeds of the bonds issued and increases the effective-interest rate. Companies may thus account for it the same as the unamortized discount.

There is an obvious difference between GAAP and *Concepts Statement No. 6*'s view of debt issue costs. However, until an issued standard supersedes existing GAAP, **unamortized bond issue costs are treated as a deferred charge and amortized over the life of the debt.**

To illustrate the accounting for costs of issuing bonds, assume that Microchip Corporation sold $20,000,000 of 10-year debenture bonds for $20,795,000 on January 1, 2014 (also the date of the bonds). Costs of issuing the bonds were $245,000. Microchip records the issuance of the bonds and amortization of the bond issue costs as follows.

January 1, 2014		
Cash	20,550,000	
Unamortized Bond Issue Costs	245,000	
Premium on Bonds Payable		795,000
Bonds Payable		20,000,000
(To record issuance of bonds)		

December 31, 2014		
Bond Issue Expense	24,500	
Unamortized Bond Issue Costs		24,500
(To amortize one year of bond issue costs—straight-line method)		

[5]"Elements of Financial Statements of Business Enterprises," *Statement of Financial Accounting Concepts No. 6* (Stamford, Conn.: FASB, 1980).

[6]*Ibid.*, par. 238.

Microchip continues to amortize the bond issue costs in the same way over the life of the bonds. Although the effective-interest method is preferred, in practice companies may use the straight-line method to amortize bond issue costs because it is easier and the results are not materially different.

International Perspective

IFRS requires that issue costs reduce the carrying amount of the bond, which increases the effective-interest rate.

Extinguishment of Debt

5 LEARNING OBJECTIVE

Describe the accounting for the extinguishment of debt.

How do companies record the payment of debt—often referred to as **extinguishment of debt**? If a company holds the bonds (or any other form of debt security) to maturity, the answer is straightforward: The company does not compute any gains or losses. It will have fully amortized any premium or discount and any issue costs at the date the bonds mature. As a result, the carrying amount will equal the maturity (face) value of the bond. As the maturity or face value will also equal the bond's fair value at that time, no gain or loss exists.

In some cases, a company extinguishes debt before its maturity date.[7] The amount paid on extinguishment or redemption before maturity, including any call premium and expense of reacquisition, is called the **reacquisition price**. On any specified date, the **net carrying amount** of the bonds is the amount payable at maturity, adjusted for unamortized premium or discount, and cost of issuance. Any excess of the net carrying amount over the reacquisition price is a **gain from extinguishment**. The excess of the reacquisition price over the net carrying amount is a **loss from extinguishment**. At the time of reacquisition, **the unamortized premium or discount, and any costs of issue applicable to the bonds, must be amortized up to the reacquisition date**.

To illustrate, assume that on January 1, 2007, General Bell Corp. issued at 97 bonds with a par value of $800,000, due in 20 years. It incurred bond issue costs totaling $16,000. Eight years after the issue date, General Bell calls the entire issue at 101 and cancels it.[8] At that time, the unamortized discount balance is $14,400, and the unamortized issue cost balance is $9,600. Illustration 14-10 indicates how General Bell computes the loss on redemption (extinguishment).

ILLUSTRATION 14-10
Computation of Loss on Redemption of Bonds

Reacquisition price ($800,000 × 1.01)		$808,000
Net carrying amount of bonds redeemed:		
Face value	$800,000	
Unamortized discount ($24,000* × 12/20)	(14,400)	
Unamortized issue costs ($16,000 × 12/20)		
(both amortized using straight-line basis)	(9,600)	(776,000)
Loss on redemption		$ 32,000

*[$800,000 × (1 − .97)]

[7]Some companies have attempted to extinguish debt through an in-substance defeasance. **In-substance defeasance** is an arrangement whereby a company provides for the future repayment of a long-term debt issue by placing purchased securities in an irrevocable trust. The company pledges the principal and interest of the securities in the trust to pay off the principal and interest of its own debt securities as they mature. However, it is not legally released from its primary obligation for the debt that is still outstanding. In some cases, debtholders are not even aware of the transaction and continue to look to the company for repayment. This practice is not considered an extinguishment of debt, and therefore the company does not record a gain or loss.

[8]The issuer of callable bonds must generally exercise the call on an interest date. Therefore, the amortization of any discount or premium will be up to date, and there will be no accrued interest. However, early extinguishments through purchases of bonds in the open market are more likely to be on other than an interest date. If the purchase is not made on an interest date, the discount or premium must be amortized, and the interest payable must be accrued from the last interest date to the date of purchase.

General Bell records the reacquisition and cancellation of the bonds as follows.

Bonds Payable	800,000	
Loss on Redemption of Bonds	32,000	
Discount on Bonds Payable		14,400
Unamortized Bond Issue Costs		9,600
Cash		808,000

Note that it is often advantageous for the issuer to acquire the **entire** outstanding bond issue and replace it with a new bond issue bearing a lower rate of interest. The replacement of an existing issuance with a new one is called **refunding**. Whether the early redemption or other extinguishment of outstanding bonds is a nonrefunding or a refunding situation, a company should recognize the difference (gain or loss) between the reacquisition price and the net carrying amount of the redeemed bonds in income of the period of redemption.[9]

What do the numbers mean? YOUR DEBT IS KILLING MY EQUITY

Traditionally, investors in the equity and bond markets operate in their own separate worlds. However, in recent volatile markets, even quiet murmurs in the bond market have been amplified into movements (usually negative) in share prices. At one extreme, these gyrations heralded the demise of a company well before the investors could sniff out the problem.

The swift decline of **Enron** in late 2001 provided the ultimate lesson: A company with no credit is no company at all. As one analyst remarked, "You can no longer have an opinion on a company's shares without having an appreciation for its credit rating." Indeed, other energy companies also felt the effect of Enron's troubles as lenders tightened or closed down the credit supply and raised interest rates on already-high levels of debt. The result? Stock prices took a hit.

Other industries are not immune from the negative shareholder effects of credit problems. For example, analysts at **TheStreet.com** compiled a list of companies with a focus on debt levels. Companies like **Copel CIA** (an energy distribution company) were rewarded with improved stock ratings, based on their manageable debt levels. In contrast, other companies with high debt levels and low ability to cover interest costs were not viewed very favorably. Among them is **Goodyear Tire and Rubber**, which reported debt six times greater than its equity.

Goodyear is a classic example of how swift and crippling a heavy debt-load can be. Not too long ago, Goodyear had a good credit rating and was paying a good dividend. But, with mounting operating losses, Goodyear's debt became a huge burden, its debt rating fell to junk status, the company cut its dividend, and its stock price dropped 80 percent. Only recently has Goodyear been able to dig out of its debt ditch. This was yet another example of stock prices taking a hit due to concerns about credit quality. Thus, even if your investment tastes are in equity, keep an eye on the liabilities.

Sources: Adapted from Steven Vames, "Credit Quality, Stock Investing Seem to Go Hand in Hand," *Wall Street Journal* (April 1, 2002), p. R4; Herb Greenberg, "The Hidden Dangers of Debt," *Fortune* (July 21, 2003), p. 153; and Christine Richard, "Holders of Corporate Bonds Seek Protection from Risk," *Wall Street Journal* (December 17–18, 2005), p. B4.

LONG-TERM NOTES PAYABLE

LEARNING OBJECTIVE 6
Explain the accounting for long-term notes payable.

The difference between current notes payable and **long-term notes payable** is the maturity date. As discussed in Chapter 13, short-term notes payable are those that companies expect to pay within a year or the operating cycle, whichever is longer. Long-term notes are similar in substance to bonds in that both have fixed maturity dates and carry either a stated or implicit interest rate. However, notes do not trade as readily as bonds in the organized public securities markets. Noncorporate and small corporate enterprises issue notes as their long-term instruments. Larger corporations issue both long-term notes and bonds.

[9] At one time, companies were required to report gains and losses on extinguishment of debt as extraordinary items. In response to increasing debt extinguishments as part of normal risk management, the FASB concluded that such gains or losses are neither unusual nor infrequent. As a result, the FASB eliminated the requirement for extraordinary item treatment for extinguishment of debt. [3]

Accounting for notes and bonds is quite similar. **Like a bond, a note is valued at the present value of its future interest and principal cash flows. The company amortizes any discount or premium over the life of the note**, just as it would the discount or premium on a bond.[10] Companies compute the present value of an **interest-bearing note**, record its issuance, and amortize any discount or premium and accrual of interest in the same way that they do for bonds (as shown on pages 768–773 of this chapter).

As you might expect, accounting for long-term notes payable parallels accounting for long-term notes receivable as was presented in Chapter 7.

Notes Issued at Face Value

In Chapter 7, we discussed the recognition of a $10,000, three-year note Scandinavian Imports issued at face value to Bigelow Corp. In this transaction, the stated rate and the effective rate were both 10 percent. The time diagram and present value computation on page 360 of Chapter 7 (see Illustration 7-9) for Bigelow Corp. are the same for the issuer of the note, Scandinavian Imports, in recognizing a note payable. Because the present value of the note and its face value are the same, $10,000, Scandinavian recognizes no premium or discount. It records the issuance of the note as follows.

Cash	10,000	
Notes Payable		10,000

Scandinavian Imports recognizes the interest incurred each year as follows.

Interest Expense	1,000	
Cash		1,000

Notes Not Issued at Face Value

Zero-Interest-Bearing Notes

If a company issues a zero-interest-bearing (non-interest-bearing) note[11] solely for cash, it measures the note's present value by the cash received. The implicit interest rate is the **rate that equates the cash received with the amounts to be paid in the future.** The issuing company records the difference between the face amount and the present value (cash received) as **a discount and amortizes that amount to interest expense over the life of the note.**

An example of such a transaction is Beneficial Corporation's offering of $150 million of zero-coupon notes (deep-discount bonds) having an eight-year life. With a face value of $1,000 each, these notes sold for $327—a deep discount of $673 each. The present value of each note is the cash proceeds of $327. We can calculate the interest rate by determining the rate that equates the amount the investor currently pays with the amount to be received in the future. Thus, Beneficial amortizes the discount over the eight-year life of the notes using an effective-interest rate of 15 percent.[12]

Calculator Solution for Effective Interest on Note:

	Inputs	Answer
N	8	
I/YR	?	15
PV	−327	
PMT	0	
FV	1,000	

[10] All payables that represent commitments to pay money at a determinable future date are subject to present value measurement techniques, except for the following specifically excluded types:

1. Normal accounts payable due within one year.
2. Security deposits, retainages, advances, or progress payments.
3. Transactions between parent and subsidiary.
4. Obligations payable at some indeterminable future date. [4]

[11] Although we use the term "note" throughout this discussion, the basic principles and methodology apply equally to other long-term debt instruments.

[12] $\$327 = \$1{,}000(PVF_{8,i})$

$$PVF_{8,i} = \frac{\$327}{\$1{,}000} = .327$$

.327 = 15% (in Table 6-2 locate .32690).

To illustrate the entries and the amortization schedule for a long-term note payable, assume that Turtle Cove Company issued the three-year, $10,000, zero-interest-bearing note to Jeremiah Company illustrated on page 361 of Chapter 7 (notes receivable). The implicit rate that equated the total cash to be paid ($10,000 at maturity) to the present value of the future cash flows ($7,721.80 cash proceeds at date of issuance) was 9 percent. (The present value of $1 for 3 periods at 9% is $0.77218.) Illustration 14-11 shows the time diagram for the single cash flow.

ILLUSTRATION 14-11
Time Diagram for Zero-Interest-Bearing Note

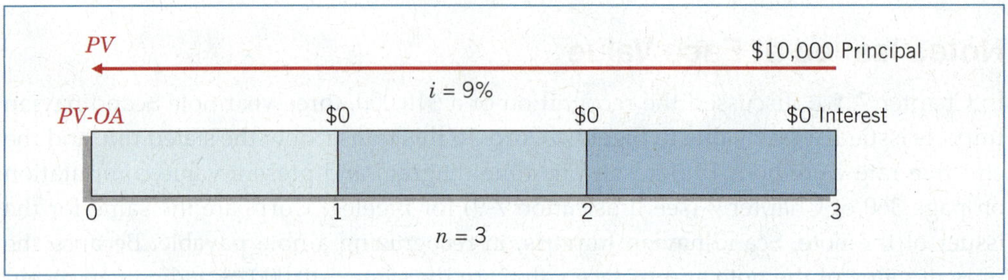

Turtle Cove records issuance of the note as follows.

Cash	7,721.80	
Discount on Notes Payable	2,278.20	
Notes Payable		10,000.00

Turtle Cove amortizes the discount and recognizes interest expense annually using the **effective-interest method**. Illustration 14-12 shows the three-year discount amortization and interest expense schedule. (This schedule is similar to the note receivable schedule of Jeremiah Company in Illustration 7-12.)

ILLUSTRATION 14-12
Schedule of Note Discount Amortization

SCHEDULE OF NOTE DISCOUNT AMORTIZATION
EFFECTIVE-INTEREST METHOD
0% NOTE DISCOUNTED AT 9%

	Cash Paid	Interest Expense	Discount Amortized	Carrying Amount of Note
Date of issue				$ 7,721.80
End of year 1	$-0-	$ 694.96[a]	$ 694.96[b]	8,416.76[c]
End of year 2	-0-	757.51	757.51	9,174.27
End of year 3	-0-	825.73[d]	825.73	10,000.00
	$-0-	$2,278.20	$2,278.20	

[a]$7,721.80 × .09 = $694.96
[b]$694.96 − 0 = $694.96
[c]$7,721.80 + $694.96 = $8,416.76
[d]5¢ adjustment to compensate for rounding.

Turtle Cove records interest expense at the end of the first year using the effective-interest method as follows.

Interest Expense ($7,721.80 × 9%)	694.96	
Discount on Notes Payable		694.96

The total amount of the discount, $2,278.20 in this case, represents the expense that Turtle Cove Company will incur on the note over the three years.

Interest-Bearing Notes

The zero-interest-bearing note above is an example of the extreme difference between the stated rate and the effective rate. In many cases, the difference between these rates is not so great.

Consider the example from Chapter 7 where Marie Co. issued for cash a $10,000, three-year note bearing interest at 10 percent to Morgan Corp. The market rate of interest for a note of similar risk is 12 percent. Illustration 7-13 (page 362) shows the time diagram depicting the cash flows and the computation of the present value of this note. In this case, because the effective rate of interest (12%) is greater than the stated rate (10%), the present value of the note is less than the face value. That is, the note is exchanged at a **discount**. Marie Co. records the issuance of the note as follows.

Cash	9,520	
Discount on Notes Payable	480	
Notes Payable		10,000

Marie Co. then amortizes the discount and recognizes interest expense annually using the **effective-interest method**. Illustration 14-13 shows the three-year discount amortization and interest expense schedule.

ILLUSTRATION 14-13
Schedule of Note Discount Amortization

SCHEDULE OF NOTE DISCOUNT AMORTIZATION
EFFECTIVE-INTEREST METHOD
10% NOTE DISCOUNTED AT 12%

	Cash Paid	Interest Expense	Discount Amortized	Carrying Amount of Note
Date of issue				$ 9,520
End of year 1	$1,000[a]	$1,142[b]	$142[c]	9,662[d]
End of year 2	1,000	1,159	159	9,821
End of year 3	1,000	1,179	179	10,000
	$3,000	$3,480	$480	

[a]$10,000 × 10% = $1,000
[b]$9,520 × 12% = $1,142
[c]$1,142 − $1,000 = $142
[d]$9,520 + $142 = $9,662

Marie Co. records payment of the annual interest and amortization of the discount for the first year as follows (amounts per amortization schedule).

Interest Expense	1,142	
Discount on Notes Payable		142
Cash		1,000

When the present value exceeds the face value, Marie Co. exchanges the note at a premium. It does so by recording the premium as a credit and amortizing it using the effective-interest method over the life of the note as annual reductions in the amount of interest expense recognized.

Special Notes Payable Situations

Notes Issued for Property, Goods, or Services

Sometimes, companies may receive property, goods, or services in exchange for a note payable. When exchanging the debt instrument for property, goods, or services in a bargained transaction entered into at arm's length, the stated interest rate is presumed to be fair unless:

1. No interest rate is stated, or
2. The stated interest rate is unreasonable, or
3. The stated face amount of the debt instrument is materially different from the current cash sales price for the same or similar items or from the current fair value of the debt instrument.

In these circumstances, the company measures the present value of the debt instrument by the fair value of the property, goods, or services or by an amount that reasonably approximates the fair value of the note. **[5]** If there is **no stated rate of interest, the amount of interest is the difference between the face amount of the note and the fair value of the property**.

For example, assume that Scenic Development Company sells land having a cash sale price of $200,000 to Health Spa, Inc. In exchange for the land, Health Spa gives a five-year, $293,866, zero-interest-bearing note. The $200,000 cash sale price represents the present value of the $293,866 note discounted at 8 percent for five years. Should both parties record the transaction on the sale date at the face amount of the note, which is $293,866? No—if they did, Health Spa's Land account and Scenic's sales would be overstated by $93,866 (the interest for five years at an effective rate of 8%). Similarly, interest revenue to Scenic and interest expense to Health Spa for the five-year period would be understated by $93,866.

Because the difference between the cash sale price of $200,000 and the $293,866 face amount of the note represents interest at an effective rate of 8 percent, the companies' transaction is recorded at the exchange date as shown in Illustration 14-14.

ILLUSTRATION 14-14
Entries for Noncash Note Transactions

Health Spa, Inc. (Buyer)			Scenic Development Company (Seller)		
Land	200,000		Notes Receivable	293,866	
Discount on Notes Payable	93,866		Discount on Notes Rec.		93,866
Notes Payable		293,866	Sales Revenue		200,000

During the five-year life of the note, Health Spa amortizes annually a portion of the discount of $93,866 as a charge to interest expense. Scenic Development records interest revenue totaling $93,866 over the five-year period by also amortizing the discount. The effective-interest method is required, unless the results obtained from using another method are not materially different from those that result from the effective-interest method.

Choice of Interest Rate

In note transactions, the effective or market interest rate is either evident or determinable by other factors involved in the exchange, such as the fair value of what is given or received. But, if a company cannot determine the fair value of the property, goods, services, or other rights, and if the note has no ready market, the problem of determining the present value of the note is more difficult. To estimate the present value of a note under such circumstances, a company must approximate an applicable interest rate that may differ from the stated interest rate. This process of interest-rate approximation is called **imputation**, and the resulting interest rate is called an **imputed interest rate**.

The prevailing rates for similar instruments of issuers with similar credit ratings affect the choice of a rate. Other factors such as restrictive covenants, collateral, payment schedule, and the existing prime interest rate also play a part. Companies determine the imputed interest rate when they issue a note; any subsequent changes in prevailing interest rates are ignored.

To illustrate, assume that on December 31, 2014, Wunderlich Company issued a promissory note to Brown Interiors Company for architectural services. The note has a face value of $550,000, a due date of December 31, 2019, and bears a stated interest rate of 2 percent, payable at the end of each year. Interest paid each period is therefore $11,000 ($550,000 × 2%). Wunderlich cannot readily determine the fair value of the architectural services, nor is the note readily marketable. On the basis of Wunderlich's credit rating, the absence of collateral, the prime interest rate at that date, and the prevailing interest on Wunderlich's other outstanding debt, the company imputes an 8 percent interest rate as appropriate in this circumstance. Illustration 14-15 shows the time diagram depicting both cash flows.

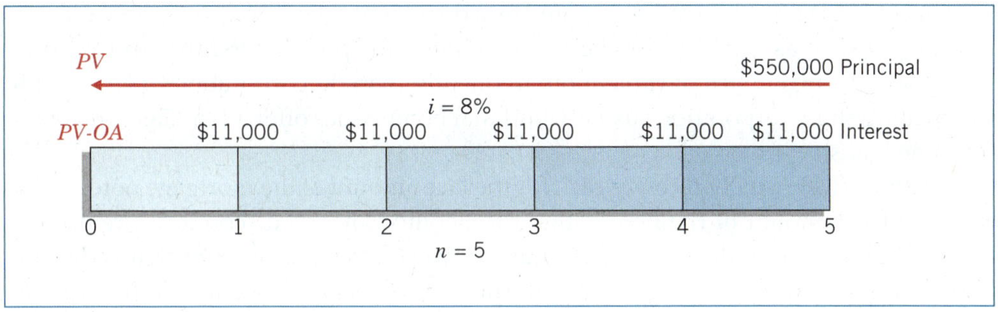

ILLUSTRATION 14-15
Time Diagram for Interest-Bearing Note

The present value of the note and the imputed fair value of the architectural services are determined as follows.

Face value of the note		$550,000
Present value of $550,000 due in 5 years at 8% interest payable annually (Table 6-2); $FV(PVF_{5,8\%})$; ($550,000 × .68058)	$374,319	
Present value of $11,000 interest payable annually for 5 years at 8%; $R(PVF\text{-}OA_{5,8\%})$; ($11,000 × 3.99271)	43,920	
Present value of the note		(418,239)
Discount on notes payable		$131,761

ILLUSTRATION 14-16
Computation of Imputed Fair Value and Note Discount

Wunderlich records issuance of the note in payment for the architectural services as follows.

December 31, 2014		
Buildings (or Construction in Process)	418,239	
Discount on Notes Payable	131,761	
Notes Payable		550,000

The five-year amortization schedule appears below.

SCHEDULE OF NOTE DISCOUNT AMORTIZATION
EFFECTIVE-INTEREST METHOD
2% NOTE DISCOUNTED AT 8% (IMPUTED)

Date	Cash Paid (2%)	Interest Expense (8%)	Discount Amortized	Carrying Amount of Note
12/31/14				$418,239
12/31/15	$11,000[a]	$ 33,459[b]	$ 22,459[c]	440,698[d]
12/31/16	11,000	35,256	24,256	464,954
12/31/17	11,000	37,196	26,196	491,150
12/31/18	11,000	39,292	28,292	519,442
12/31/19	11,000	41,558[e]	30,558	550,000
	$55,000	$186,761	$131,761	

[a]$550,000 × 2% = $11,000
[b]$418,239 × 8% = $33,459
[c]$33,459 − $11,000 = $22,459
[d]$418,239 + $22,459 = $440,698
[e]$3 adjustment to compensate for rounding.

ILLUSTRATION 14-17
Schedule of Discount Amortization Using Imputed Interest Rate

Calculator Solution for the Fair Value of Services:

	Inputs	Answer
N	5	
I/YR	8	
PV	?	418,241*
PMT	−11,000	
FV	−550,000	

*Difference due to rounding.

Wunderlich records payment of the first year's interest and amortization of the discount as follows.

December 31, 2015		
Interest Expense	33,459	
Discount on Notes Payable		22,459
Cash		11,000

Mortgage Notes Payable

The most common form of long-term notes payable is a mortgage note payable. A **mortgage note payable** is a promissory note secured by a document called a mortgage that pledges title to property as security for the loan. Individuals, proprietorships, and partnerships use mortgage notes payable more frequently than do corporations. (As noted in the opening story, corporations usually find that bond issues offer advantages in obtaining large loans.)

The borrower usually receives cash for the face amount of the mortgage note. In that case, the face amount of the note is the true liability, and no discount or premium is involved. When the lender assesses "points," however, the total amount received by the borrower is less than the face amount of the note.[13] Points raise the effective-interest rate above the rate specified in the note. A **point** is 1 percent of the face of the note.

For example, assume that Harrick Co. borrows $1,000,000, signing a 20-year mortgage note with a stated interest rate of 10.75 percent as part of the financing for a new plant. If Associated Savings demands 4 points to close the financing, Harrick will receive 4 percent less than $1,000,000—or $960,000—but it will be obligated to repay the entire $1,000,000 at the rate of $10,150 per month. Because Harrick received only $960,000, and must repay $1,000,000, its effective-interest rate is increased to approximately 11.3 percent on the money actually borrowed.

On the balance sheet, Harrick should report the mortgage note payable as a liability using a title such as "Mortgage Payable" or "Notes Payable—Secured," with a brief disclosure of the property pledged in notes to the financial statements.

Mortgages may be payable in full at maturity or in installments over the life of the loan. If payable at maturity, Harrick classifies its mortgage payable as a long-term liability on the balance sheet until such time as the approaching maturity date warrants showing it as a current liability. If it is payable in installments, Harrick shows the current installments due as current liabilities, with the remainder as a long-term liability.

Lenders have partially replaced the traditional **fixed-rate mortgage** with alternative mortgage arrangements. Most lenders offer **variable-rate mortgages** (also called *floating-rate* or *adjustable-rate* mortgages) featuring interest rates tied to changes in the fluctuating market rate. Generally, the variable-rate lenders adjust the interest rate at either one- or three-year intervals, pegging the adjustments to changes in the prime rate or the U.S. Treasury bond rate.

Fair Value Option

LEARNING OBJECTIVE 7
Describe the accounting for the fair value option.

As indicated earlier, noncurrent liabilities, such as bonds and notes payable, are generally measured at amortized cost (face value of the payable, adjusted for any payments and amortization of any premium or discount). However, companies have the option to record fair value in their accounts for most financial assets and liabilities, including bonds and notes payable. [6] As discussed in Chapter 7 (page 365), the FASB believes that fair value measurement for financial instruments, including financial liabilities, provides more relevant and understandable information than amortized cost. It considers fair value to be more relevant because it reflects the current cash equivalent value of financial instruments.

Fair Value Measurement

If companies choose the **fair value option**, noncurrent liabilities, such as bonds and notes payable, are recorded at fair value, with unrealized holding gains or losses reported as part of net income. An **unrealized holding gain or loss** is the net change in the

[13] Points, in mortgage financing, are analogous to the original issue discount of bonds.

fair value of the liability from one period to another, exclusive of interest expense recognized but not recorded. As a result, the company reports the liability at fair value each reporting date. In addition, it reports the change in value as part of net income.

To illustrate, Edmonds Company has issued $500,000 of 6 percent bonds at face value on May 1, 2014. Edmonds chooses the fair value option for these bonds. At December 31, 2014, the value of the bonds is now $480,000 because interest rates in the market have increased to 8 percent. The value of the debt securities falls because the bond is paying less than market rate for similar securities. Under the fair value option, Edmonds makes the following entry.

Bonds Payable	20,000	
Unrealized Holding Gain or Loss—Income		20,000

As the journal entry indicates, the value of the bonds declined. This decline leads to a reduction in the bond liability and a resulting unrealized holding gain, which is reported as part of net income. The value of Edmonds' debt declined because interest rates increased. It should be emphasized that Edmonds must continue to value the bonds payable at fair value in all subsequent periods.

Fair Value Controversy

With the Edmonds bonds, we assumed that the decline in value of the bonds was due to an interest rate increase. In other situations, the decline may occur because the bonds become more likely to default. That is, **if the creditworthiness of Edmonds Company declines, the value of its debt also declines**. If its creditworthiness declines, its bond investors are receiving a lower rate relative to investors with similar-risk investments. If Edmonds is using the fair value option, changes in the fair value of the bonds payable for a decline in creditworthiness are included as part of income. Some question how Edmonds can record a gain when its creditworthiness is becoming worse. As one writer noted, "It seems counterintuitive." However, the FASB notes that the debtholders' loss is the shareholders' gain. That is, the shareholders' claims on the assets of the company increase when the value of the debtholders' claims declines. In addition, the worsening credit position may indicate that the assets of the company are declining in value as well. Thus, the company may be reporting losses on the asset side, which will be offsetting gains on the liability side.[14]

REPORTING AND ANALYZING LIABILITIES

8 LEARNING OBJECTIVE
Explain the reporting of off-balance-sheet financing arrangements.

Reporting liabilities and long-term debt is one of the most controversial areas in financial reporting. Because long-term debt has a significant impact on the cash flows of the company, reporting requirements must be substantive and informative. One problem is that the definition of a liability established in *Concepts Statement No. 6* and the recognition criteria established in *Concepts Statement No. 5* are sufficiently imprecise that some continue to argue that certain obligations need not be reported as debt.

Off-Balance-Sheet Financing

What do **Krispy Kreme**, **Cisco**, **Enron**, and **Adelphia Communications** have in common? They all have been accused of using off-balance-sheet financing to minimize the reporting of debt on their balance sheets. **Off-balance-sheet financing** is an attempt to borrow monies in such a way to prevent recording the obligations. It has become an issue of

[14]This issue is discussed further in the "Evolving Issue" box on page 788.

extreme importance. Many allege that Enron, in one of the largest corporate failures on record, hid a considerable amount of its debt off the balance sheet. As a result, any company that uses off-balance-sheet financing today risks investors dumping the company's stock. Consequently, the company's share price will suffer. Nevertheless, a considerable amount of off-balance-sheet financing continues to exist. As one writer noted, "The basic drives of humans are few: to get enough food, to find shelter, and to keep debt off the balance sheet."

Different Forms

Off-balance-sheet financing can take many different forms:

1. ***Non-consolidated subsidiary.*** Under GAAP, a parent company does not have to consolidate a subsidiary company that is less than 50 percent owned. In such cases, the parent therefore does not report the assets and liabilities of the subsidiary. All the parent reports on its balance sheet is the investment in the subsidiary. As a result, users of the financial statements may not understand that the subsidiary has considerable debt for which the parent may ultimately be liable if the subsidiary runs into financial difficulty.
2. ***Special-purpose entity (SPE).*** A company creates a **special-purpose entity (SPE)** to perform a special project. To illustrate, assume that Clarke Company decides to build a new factory. However, management does not want to report the plant or the borrowing used to fund the construction on its balance sheet. It therefore creates an SPE, the purpose of which is to build the plant. (This arrangement is called a **project financing arrangement**.) The SPE finances and builds the plant. In return, Clarke guarantees that it or some outside party will purchase all the products produced by the plant. (Some refer to this as a **take-or-pay contract**.) As a result, Clarke might not report the asset or liability on its books. The accounting rules in this area are complex. We discuss the accounting for SPEs in Appendix 17B.
3. ***Operating leases.*** Another way that companies keep debt off the balance sheet is by leasing. Instead of owning the assets, companies lease them. Again, by meeting certain conditions, the company has to report only rent expense each period and to provide note disclosure of the transaction. Note that SPEs often use leases to accomplish off-balance-sheet treatment. We discuss accounting for lease transactions extensively in Chapter 21.

Rationale

Why do companies engage in off-balance-sheet financing? A major reason is that many believe that **removing debt enhances the quality of the balance sheet** and permits credit to be obtained more readily and at less cost.

Second, loan covenants often limit the amount of debt a company may have. As a result, the company uses off-balance-sheet financing because **these types of commitments might not be considered in computing the debt limitation**.

Third, some argue that the asset side of the balance sheet is severely understated. For example, companies that use LIFO costing for inventories and depreciate assets on an accelerated basis will often have carrying amounts for inventories and property, plant, and equipment that are much lower than their fair values. As an offset to these lower values, some believe that part of the debt does not have to be reported. In other words, **if companies report assets at fair values**, less pressure would undoubtedly exist for off-balance-sheet financing arrangements.

Whether the arguments above have merit is debatable. The general idea of "out of sight, out of mind" may not be true in accounting. Many users of financial statements indicate that they factor these off-balance-sheet financing arrangements into their computations when assessing debt-to-equity relationships. Similarly, many loan covenants also attempt to account for these complex arrangements. Nevertheless, many companies still believe that benefits will accrue if they omit certain obligations from the balance sheet.

As a response to off-balance-sheet financing arrangements, the FASB has increased disclosure (note) requirements. This response is consistent with an "efficient markets" philosophy: The important question is not whether the presentation is off-balance-sheet or not, but whether the items are disclosed at all. In addition, the SEC, in response to the Sarbanes-Oxley Act of 2002, now requires companies to provide related information in their management discussion and analysis sections. Specifically, companies must disclose (1) all contractual obligations in a tabular format and (2) contingent liabilities and commitments in either a textual or tabular format.[15]

We believe that recording more obligations on the balance sheet will enhance financial reporting. Given the problems with companies such as **Enron**, **Dynegy**, **Williams Company**, **Chesapeake Energy**, and **Calpine**, and the Sarbanes-Oxley requirements, we expect that less off-balance-sheet financing will occur in the future.

International Perspective

There is no comparable institution to the SEC in international securities markets. As a result, many international companies (those not registered with the SEC) are not required to provide disclosures such as those related to contractual obligations.

What do the numbers mean? OBLIGATED

The off-balance-sheet world is slowly but surely becoming more on-balance-sheet. New interpretations on guarantees (discussed in Chapter 13) and variable-interest entities (discussed in Appendix 17B) are doing their part to increase the amount of debt reported on corporate balance sheets.

In addition, the SEC has rules that require companies to disclose off-balance-sheet arrangements and contractual obligations that currently have, or are reasonably likely to have, a material future effect on the companies' financial condition. Companies now must include a tabular disclosure (following a prescribed format) in the management discussion and analysis section of the annual report. Presented below is **Best Buy Co.**'s tabular disclosure of its contractual obligations.

Best Buy Co.
Contractual Obligations

The following table presents information regarding our contractual obligations by fiscal year ($ in millions):

		Payments due by period			
Contractual Obligations	**Total**	**Less than 1 year**	**1–3 years**	**3–5 years**	**More than 5 years**
Short-term debt obligations	$ 480	$ 480	—	—	—
Long-term debt obligations	1,498	—	$ 500	$ 349	$ 649
Capital lease obligations	81	18	35	11	17
Financing lease obligations	149	22	47	40	40
Interest payments	500	101	142	105	152
Operating lease obligations	7,517	1,216	2,217	1,732	2,352
Purchase obligations	3,548	1,771	1,499	278	—
	$13,773	$3,608	$4,440	$2,515	$3,210
Other					
Unrecognized tax benefits	$ 387	—	—	—	—
Deferred compensation	62	—	—	—	—

Note: For additional information refer to Note 8, Debt; Note 11, Leases; Note 13, Income Taxes and Note 15, Contingencies and Commitments, in the Notes to Consolidated Financial Statements, included in Item 8, Financial Statements and Supplementary Data, of this Annual Report on Form 10-K.

Enron's abuse of off-balance-sheet financing to hide debt was shocking and inappropriate. One silver lining in the Enron debacle, however, is that the standard-setting bodies in the accounting profession are now providing increased guidance on companies' reporting of contractual obligations. We believe the new SEC rule, which requires companies to report their obligations over a period of time, will be extremely useful to the investment community.

[15]It is unlikely that the FASB will be able to stop all types of off-balance-sheet transactions. Financial engineering is the "Holy Grail" of Wall Street. Developing new financial instruments and arrangements to sell and market to customers is not only profitable but also adds to the prestige of the investment firms that create them. Thus, new financial products will continue to appear that will test the ability of the FASB to develop appropriate accounting standards for them.

Presentation and Analysis of Long-Term Debt

Presentation of Long-Term Debt

LEARNING OBJECTIVE 9
Indicate how to present and analyze long-term debt.

Companies that have large amounts and numerous issues of long-term debt frequently report only one amount in the balance sheet, supported with comments and schedules in the accompanying notes. Long-term debt that **matures within one year** should be reported as a current liability, unless using noncurrent assets to accomplish redemption. If the company plans to refinance debt, convert it into stock, or retire it from a bond retirement fund, it should continue to report the debt as noncurrent. However, the company should disclose the method it will use in its liquidation. [7], [8]

Note disclosures generally indicate the nature of the liabilities, maturity dates, interest rates, call provisions, conversion privileges, restrictions imposed by the creditors, and assets designated or pledged as security. Companies should show any assets pledged as security for the debt in the assets section of the balance sheet. The fair value of the long-term debt should also be disclosed if it is practical to estimate fair value. Finally, companies must disclose future payments for sinking fund requirements and maturity amounts of long-term debt during each of the next five years. These disclosures aid financial statement users in evaluating the amounts and timing of future cash flows. Illustration 14-18 shows an example of the type of information provided for Target Corporation. Note that if the company has any off-balance-sheet financing, it must provide extensive note disclosure. [9]

ILLUSTRATION 14-18
Long-Term Debt Disclosure

Target Corporation
(dollars in millions)

	January 28, 2012	January 29, 2011
Total current assets	$16,449	$17,213
Current liabilities		
Accounts payable	$ 6,857	$ 6,625
Accrued and other current liabilities	3,644	3,326
Unsecured debt and other borrowings	3,036	119
Nonrecourse debt collateralized by credit card receivables	750	—
Total current liabilities	14,287	10,070
Total noncurrent liabilities	16,522	18,148

19. Notes Payable and Long-Term Debt (in part)

At January 28, 2012, the carrying value and maturities of our debt portfolio were as follows:

Debt Maturities (millions)	January 28, 2012 Rate *(a)*	Balance
Due fiscal 2012–2016	2.8%	$ 6,281
Due fiscal 2017–2021	4.8	4,604
Due fiscal 2022–2026	8.7	64
Due fiscal 2027–2031	6.8	680
Due fiscal 2032–2036	6.3	551
Due fiscal 2037	6.8	3,500
Total notes and debentures	4.6	15,680
Swap valuation adjustments		114
Capital lease obligations		1,689
Less:		
Amounts due within one year		(3,786)
Long-term debt		$13,697

(a) Reflects the weighted-average stated interest rate as of year-end.

Required principal payments on notes and debentures over the next five years are as follows:

Required Principal Payments (millions)	2012	2013	2014	2015	2016
Unsecured	$3,001	$501	$1,001	$27	$751
Nonrecourse	750	250	—	—	—
Total required principal payments	$3,751	$751	$1,001	$27	$751

ILLUSTRATION 14-18
(continued)

Analysis of Long-Term Debt

Long-term creditors and stockholders are interested in a company's long-run solvency, particularly its ability to pay interest as it comes due and to repay the face value of the debt at maturity. Debt to assets and times interest earned are two ratios that provide information about debt-paying ability and long-run solvency.

Debt to Assets. The **debt to assets ratio** measures the percentage of the total assets provided by creditors. To compute it, divide total debt (both current and long-term liabilities) by total assets, as Illustration 14-19 shows.

$$\text{Debt to assets} = \frac{\text{Total liabilities}}{\text{Total assets}}$$

ILLUSTRATION 14-19
Computation of Debt to Assets Ratio

The higher the percentage of total liabilities to total assets, the greater the risk that the company may be unable to meet its maturing obligations.

Times Interest Earned. The **times interest earned** ratio indicates the company's ability to meet interest payments as they come due. As shown in Illustration 14-20, it is computed by dividing income before interest expense and income taxes by interest expense.

$$\text{Times interest earned} = \frac{\text{Income before income taxes and interest expense}}{\text{Interest expense}}$$

ILLUSTRATION 14-20
Computation of Times Interest Earned

To illustrate these ratios, we use data from **Target**'s 2011 annual report. Target has total liabilities of $30,809 million, total assets of $46,630 million, interest expense of $869 million, income taxes of $1,527 million, and net income of $2,929 million. We compute Target's debt to assets and times interest earned ratios as shown in Illustration 14-21.

Even though Target has a relatively high debt to assets percentage of 66.1 percent, its interest coverage of 6.12 times indicates it can easily meet its interest payments as they come due.

You will want to read the **IFRS INSIGHTS** on pages 815–819 for discussion of IFRS related to long-term liabilities.

$$\text{Debt to assets} = \frac{\$30{,}809}{\$46{,}630} = 66.1\%$$

$$\text{Times interest earned} = \frac{(\$2{,}929 + \$869 + \$1{,}527)}{\$869} = 6.12 \text{ times}$$

ILLUSTRATION 14-21
Computation of Long-Term Debt Ratios for Target

Evolving Issue: FAIR VALUE OF LIABILITIES: PICK A NUMBER, ANY NUMBER

In 2011, Citigroup's third-quarter earnings rose 68 percent from a year earlier, partly due to an accounting adjustment. The accounting adjustment was a $1.9 billion gain related to a change in the valuation of its debt obligations. A similar situation resulted in the third quarter of 2011 for JPMorgan. Its results were enhanced by decreasing the value of its debt, also by $1.9 billion. How does a company recognize a gain on its debt when it has not sold it?

Here is how it works. Say a company records a $100 million liability for bonds it issues. Subsequently, the bond's credit rating drops from AA to BB. As a result, the price of the bond trading in the market drops to $90 million. As we discussed earlier, if the fair value option is used to value debt, the company makes the following entry.

Bonds Payable	10,000,000	
Unrealized Holding Gain or Loss—Income		10,000,000

Presto! The company's net income increases even though its credit rating drops. This result seems counterintuitive—how does a company that is actually doing worse have its income increase?

The FASB has struggled with this issue for years. It defends the present position by indicating that the valuation of a liability is related to its credit standing. Therefore, if a company's credit standing drops, the liability value drops as well. And if the value of a company's liability is less, the company is better off and should record a gain. It should be noted that it can work the other way as well. That is, if a company's credit standing increases, the value of the liability increases and therefore the company records a loss.

Another major argument in favor of the present approach is that by forcing companies to highlight their credit weakness, it raises a question about the asset side of the balance sheet. In other words, if you see a credit weakness, you should ask, "Where is the impaired asset?" If a company's credit is bad, it may mean there are losses on the asset side that are not being recognized or disclosed.

The FASB (and IASB) are debating this issue in the financial instruments project. Some have suggested that the gain or loss be part of other comprehensive income. Others disagree and believe it should be part of net income. Still others believe that changes in the value of the liability should not be reported in income until the liability is extinguished. As one expert noted, "At its worse, bank accounting can seem like the mirrors in a fun house. Reality is reflected, but the distortions can be very large."

Sources: Floyd Norris, "Distortions in Baffling Financial Statements," *The New York Times* (November 10, 2011); and Marie Leone, "The Fair Value Deadbeat Debate Returns," *CFO.com* (June 25, 2009).

KEY TERMS

bearer (coupon) bonds, *765*
bond discount, *767*
bond indenture, *764*
bond premium, *767*
callable bonds, *765*
carrying value, *770*
commodity-backed bonds, *765*
convertible bonds, *765*
debenture bonds, *765*
debt to assets ratio, *787*
deep-discount (zero-interest debenture) bonds, *765*
discount, *767*
effective-interest method, *770*
effective yield, or market rate, *767*
extinguishment of debt, *775*
face, par, principal, or maturity value, *766*

SUMMARY OF LEARNING OBJECTIVES

1 Describe the formal procedures associated with issuing long-term debt. Incurring long-term debt is often a formal procedure. The bylaws of corporations usually require approval by the board of directors and the stockholders before corporations can issue bonds or can make other long-term debt arrangements. Generally, long-term debt has various covenants or restrictions. The covenants and other terms of the agreement between the borrower and the lender are stated in the bond indenture or note agreement.

2 Identify various types of bond issues. Various types of bond issues are (1) secured and unsecured bonds; (2) term, serial, and callable bonds; (3) convertible, commodity-backed, and deep-discount bonds; (4) registered and bearer (coupon) bonds; and (5) income and revenue bonds. The variety in the types of bonds results from attempts to attract capital from different investors and risk-takers and to satisfy the cash flow needs of the issuers.

3 Describe the accounting valuation for bonds at date of issuance. The investment community values a bond at the present value of its future cash flows, which consist of interest and principal. The rate used to compute the present value of these cash flows is the interest rate that provides an acceptable return on an investment commensurate with the issuer's risk characteristics. The interest rate written in the terms of the bond indenture and ordinarily appearing on the bond certificate is the stated, coupon, or nominal rate. The issuer of the bonds sets the rate and expresses it as a percentage of the face value (also called the par value, principal amount, or maturity value) of the bonds. If the rate employed by the buyers differs from the stated rate, the present value of the bonds computed by the buyers will differ from the face value of the bonds. The difference between the face value and the present value of the bonds is either a discount or premium.

4 **Apply the methods of bond discount and premium amortization.** The discount (premium) is amortized and charged (credited) to interest expense over the life of the bonds. Amortization of a discount increases bond interest expense, and amortization of a premium decreases bond interest expense. The profession's preferred procedure for amortization of a discount or premium is the effective-interest method. Under the effective-interest method, (1) bond interest expense is computed by multiplying the carrying value of the bonds at the beginning of the period by the effective-interest rate; then, (2) the bond discount or premium amortization is determined by comparing the bond interest expense with the interest to be paid.

5 **Describe the accounting for the extinguishment of debt.** At the time of extinguishment (reacquisition, redemption, or refunding) of long-term debt, the unamortized premium or discount and any costs of issue applicable to the debt must be amortized up to the reacquisition date. The reacquisition price is the amount paid on extinguishment or redemption before maturity, including any call premium and expense of reacquisition. On any specified date, the net carrying amount of the debt is the amount payable at maturity, adjusted for unamortized premium or discount and issue costs. Any excess of the net carrying amount over the reacquisition price is a gain from extinguishment. The excess of the reacquisition price over the net carrying amount is a loss from extinguishment. Gains and losses on extinguishments are recognized currently in income.

6 **Explain the accounting for long-term notes payable.** Accounting procedures for notes and bonds are similar. Like a bond, a note is valued at the present value of its expected future interest and principal cash flows, with any discount or premium being similarly amortized over the life of the note. Whenever the face amount of the note does not reasonably represent the present value of the consideration in the exchange, a company must evaluate the entire arrangement in order to properly record the exchange and the subsequent interest.

7 **Describe the accounting for the fair value option.** Companies have the option to record fair value in their accounts for most financial assets and liabilities, including noncurrent liabilities. Fair value measurement for financial instruments, including financial liabilities, provides more relevant and understandable information than amortized cost. If companies choose the fair value option, noncurrent liabilities, such as bonds and notes payable, are recorded at fair value, with unrealized holding gains or losses reported as part of net income. An unrealized holding gain or loss is the net change in the fair value of the liability from one period to another, exclusive of interest expense recognized but not recorded.

8 **Explain the reporting of off-balance-sheet financing arrangements.** Off-balance-sheet financing is an attempt to borrow funds in such a way to prevent recording obligations. Examples of off-balance-sheet arrangements are (1) non-consolidated subsidiaries, (2) special-purpose entities, and (3) operating leases.

9 **Indicate how to present and analyze long-term debt.** Companies that have large amounts and numerous issues of long-term debt frequently report only one amount in the balance sheet and support this with comments and schedules in the accompanying notes. Any assets pledged as security for the debt should be shown in the assets section of the balance sheet. Long-term debt that matures within one year should be reported as a current liability, unless redemption is to be accomplished with other than current assets. If a company plans to refinance the debt, convert it into stock, or retire it from a bond retirement fund, it should continue to report it as noncurrent, accompanied

fair value option, *782*
imputation, *780*
imputed interest rate, *780*
income bonds, *765*
long-term debt, *764*
long-term notes payable, *776*
mortgage notes payable, *782*
off-balance-sheet financing, *783*
premium, *767*
refunding, *776*
registered bonds, *765*
revenue bonds, *765*
secured bonds, *765*
serial bonds, *765*
special-purpose entity (SPE), *784*
stated, coupon, or nominal rate, *766*
straight-line method, *769*
term bonds, *765*
times interest earned, *787*
zero-interest debenture bonds, *765*

with a note explaining the method it will use in the debt's liquidation. Disclosure is required of future payments for sinking fund requirements and maturity amounts of long-term debt during each of the next five years. Debt to assets and times interest earned are two ratios that provide information about debt-paying ability and long-run solvency.

APPENDIX 14A TROUBLED-DEBT RESTRUCTURINGS

LEARNING OBJECTIVE 10
Describe the accounting for a debt restructuring.

Practically every day, the *Wall Street Journal* runs a story about some company in financial difficulty. In most troubled-debt situations, the creditor usually first recognizes a loss on impairment. Subsequently, the creditor either modifies the terms of the loan or the debtor settles the loan on terms unfavorable to the creditor. In unusual cases, the creditor forces the debtor into bankruptcy in order to ensure the highest possible collection on the loan. Illustration 14A-1 shows this continuum.

ILLUSTRATION 14A-1
Usual Progression in Troubled-Debt Situations

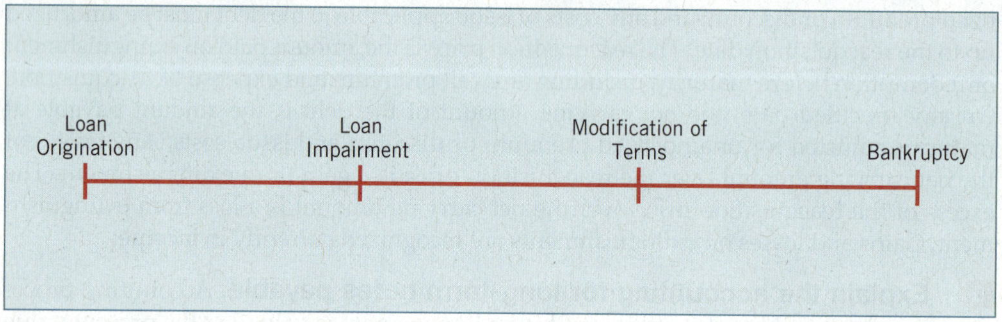

To illustrate, consider the case of **Huffy Corp.**, a name that adorned the first bicycle of many American children. Before its bankruptcy, Huffy's creditors likely recognized a loss on impairment. Subsequently, the creditors either modified the terms of the loan or settled it on terms unfavorable to the creditor. Finally, the creditors forced Huffy into bankruptcy, and the suppliers received a 30 percent equity stake in Huffy. These terms helped ensure the highest possible collection on the Huffy loan.

We discussed the accounting for loan impairments in Appendix 7B. The purpose of this appendix is to explain how creditors and debtors report information in financial statements related to troubled-debt restructurings.

International Perspective
IFRS generally assumes that all restructurings be accounted for as extinguishments of debt.

A **troubled-debt restructuring** occurs when a creditor "for economic or legal reasons related to the debtor's financial difficulties grants a concession to the debtor that it would not otherwise consider." **[10]** Thus, a troubled-debt restructuring does not apply to modifications of a debt obligation that reflect general economic conditions leading to a reduced interest rate. Nor does it apply to the refunding of an old debt with new debt having an effective-interest rate approximately equal to that of similar debt issued by nontroubled debtors.

A troubled-debt restructuring involves one of two basic types of transactions:[16]

1. Settlement of debt at less than its carrying amount.
2. Continuation of debt with a modification of terms.

[16] Recently, the FASB issued Accounting Standards Update 2011-02, Receivables (Topic 310): *A Creditor's Determination of Whether a Restructuring Is a Troubled Debt Restructuring*, to help determine when a troubled-debt restructuring (TDR) occurs. The new rule provides additional guidance for determining whether a TDR has occurred by clarifying when the creditor has granted a concession and whether the debtor is experiencing financial difficulty. As a result of this rule, creditors will likely determine that more restructurings are troubled-debt restructurings, which will lead to more losses on receivables being reported.

SETTLEMENT OF DEBT

In addition to using cash, settling a debt obligation can involve either a transfer of noncash assets (real estate, receivables, or other assets) or the issuance of the debtor's stock. In these situations, **the creditor should account for the noncash assets or equity interest received at their fair value.**

The debtor must determine the excess of the carrying amount of the payable over the fair value of the assets or equity transferred (gain). Likewise, the creditor must determine the excess of the receivable over the fair value of those same assets or equity interests transferred (loss). The debtor recognizes a gain equal to the amount of the excess. The creditor normally charges the excess (loss) against Allowance for Doubtful Accounts. In addition, the debtor recognizes a gain or loss on disposition of assets to the extent that the fair value of those assets differs from their carrying amount (book value).

Transfer of Assets

Assume that American City Bank loaned $20,000,000 to Union Mortgage Company. Union Mortgage, in turn, invested these monies in residential apartment buildings. However, because of low occupancy rates, it cannot meet its loan obligations. American City Bank agrees to accept from Union Mortgage real estate with a fair value of $16,000,000 in full settlement of the $20,000,000 loan obligation. The real estate has a carrying value of $21,000,000 on the books of Union Mortgage. American City Bank (creditor) records this transaction as follows.

Land	16,000,000	
Allowance for Doubtful Accounts	4,000,000	
Notes Receivable (from Union Mortgage)		20,000,000

The bank records the real estate at fair value. Further, it makes a charge to Allowance for Doubtful Accounts to reflect the bad debt write-off.

Union Mortgage (debtor) records this transaction as follows.

Notes Payable (to American City Bank)	20,000,000	
Loss on Disposal of Land	5,000,000	
Land		21,000,000
Gain on Restructuring of Debt		4,000,000

Union Mortgage has a loss on the disposition of real estate in the amount of $5,000,000 (the difference between the $21,000,000 book value and the $16,000,000 fair value). It should show this as an ordinary loss on the income statement. In addition, it has a gain on restructuring of debt of $4,000,000 (the difference between the $20,000,000 carrying amount of the note payable and the $16,000,000 fair value of the real estate).

Granting of Equity Interest

Assume that American City Bank agrees to accept from Union Mortgage 320,000 shares of common stock ($10 par) that has a fair value of $16,000,000, in full settlement of the $20,000,000 loan obligation. American City Bank (creditor) records this transaction as follows.

Equity Investments	16,000,000	
Allowance for Doubtful Accounts	4,000,000	
Notes Receivable (from Union Mortgage)		20,000,000

It records the stock as an investment at the fair value at the date of restructure.

Union Mortgage (debtor) records this transaction as follows.

Notes Payable (to American City Bank)	20,000,000	
Common Stock		3,200,000
Paid-in Capital in Excess of Par—Common Stock		12,800,000
Gain on Restructuring of Debt		4,000,000

It records the stock issued in the normal manner. It records the difference between the par value and the fair value of the stock as additional paid-in capital.

MODIFICATION OF TERMS

In some cases, a debtor's serious short-run cash flow problems will lead it to request one or a combination of the following modifications:

1. Reduction of the stated interest rate.
2. Extension of the maturity date of the face amount of the debt.
3. Reduction of the face amount of the debt.
4. Reduction or deferral of any accrued interest.

The creditor's loss is based on expected cash flows discounted at the historical effective rate of the loan. [11] The debtor calculates its gain based on **undiscounted amounts.** As a consequence, **the gain recorded by the debtor will not equal the loss recorded by the creditor under many circumstances.**[17]

Two examples demonstrate the accounting for a troubled-debt restructuring by debtors and creditors:

1. The debtor does not record a gain.
2. The debtor does record a gain.

In both instances the creditor has a loss.

Example 1—No Gain for Debtor

This example demonstrates a restructuring in which the debtor records no gain.[18] On December 31, 2013, Morgan National Bank enters into a debt restructuring agreement with Resorts Development Company, which is experiencing financial difficulties. The bank restructures a $10,500,000 loan receivable issued at par (interest paid to date) by:

1. Reducing the principal obligation from $10,500,000 to $9,000,000;
2. Extending the maturity date from December 31, 2013, to December 31, 2017; and
3. Reducing the interest rate from 12% to 8%.

[17]In response to concerns expressed about this nonsymmetric treatment, the FASB stated that it did not address debtor accounting because expansion of the scope of the statement would delay its issuance. By basing the debtor calculation on undiscounted amounts, the amount of gain (if any) recognized by the debtor is reduced at the time the modification of terms occurs. If fair value were used, the gain recognized would be greater. The result of this approach is to spread the unrecognized gain over the life of the new agreement. We believe that this accounting is inappropriate and hopefully will change as more fair value measurements are introduced into the financial statements.

[18]Note that the examples given for restructuring assume the creditor made no previous entries for impairment. In actuality, it is likely that the creditor would have already made an entry when the loan initially became impaired. Restructuring would, therefore, simply require an adjustment of the initial estimated bad debt by the creditor. Recall, however, that the debtor makes no entry upon impairment.

Debtor Calculations

The total future cash flow, after restructuring of $11,880,000 ($9,000,000 of principal plus $2,880,000 of interest payments[19]), exceeds the total pre-restructuring carrying amount of the debt of $10,500,000. Consequently, **the debtor records no gain nor makes any adjustment** to the carrying amount of the payable. As a result, Resorts Development (debtor) makes no entry at the date of restructuring.

The debtor must compute a new effective-interest rate in order to record interest expense in future periods. The new effective-interest rate equates the present value of the future cash flows specified by the new terms with the pre-restructuring carrying amount of the debt. In this case, Resorts Development computes the new rate by relating the pre-restructure carrying amount ($10,500,000) to the total future cash flow ($11,880,000). The rate necessary to discount the total future cash flow ($11,880,000), to a present value equal to the remaining balance ($10,500,000), is 3.46613 percent.[20]

On the basis of the effective rate of 3.46613 percent, the debtor prepares the schedule shown in Illustration 14A-2.

ILLUSTRATION 14A-2
Schedule Showing Reduction of Carrying Amount of Note

RESORTS DEVELOPMENT CO. (DEBTOR)

Date	Cash Paid (8%)	Interest Expense (3.46613%)	Reduction of Carrying Amount	Carrying Amount of Note
12/31/13				$10,500,000
12/31/14	$ 720,000[a]	$ 363,944[b]	$ 356,056[c]	10,143,944
12/31/15	720,000	351,602	368,398	9,775,546
12/31/16	720,000	338,833	381,167	9,394,379
12/31/17	720,000	325,621	394,379	9,000,000
	$2,880,000	$1,380,000	$1,500,000	

[a]$720,000 = $9,000,000 × .08
[b]$363,944 = $10,500,000 × 3.46613%
[c]$356,056 = $720,000 − $363,944

Calculator Solution for Interest Rate

	Inputs	Answer
N	4	
I/YR	?	3.466
PV	10,500,000	
PMT	-720,000	
FV	-9,000,000	

Thus, on December 31, 2014 (date of first interest payment after restructure), the debtor makes the following entry.

December 31, 2014

Notes Payable	356,056	
Interest Expense	363,944	
Cash		720,000

The debtor makes a similar entry (except for different amounts for debits to Notes Payable and Interest Expense) each year until maturity. At maturity, Resorts Development makes the following entry.

December 31, 2017

Notes Payable	9,000,000	
Cash		9,000,000

[19]Total interest payments are $9,000,000 × .08 × 4 years = $2,880,000.

[20]An accurate interest rate i can be found by using the formulas given at the tops of Tables 6-2 and 6-4 to set up the following equation.

$$\$10{,}500{,}000 = \underset{\text{(from Table 6-2)}}{\frac{1}{(1+i)^4}} \times \$9{,}000{,}000 + \underset{\text{(from Table 6-4)}}{\frac{1 - \frac{1}{(1+i)^4}}{i}} \times \$720{,}000$$

Solving algebraically for i, we find that $i = 3.46613\%$.

Creditor Calculations

Morgan National Bank (creditor) must calculate its loss based on the expected future cash flows discounted at the historical effective rate of the loan. It calculates this loss as shown in Illustration 14A-3.

ILLUSTRATION 14A-3
Computation of Loss to Creditor on Restructuring

Pre-restructure carrying amount		$10,500,000
Present value of restructured cash flows:		
Present value of $9,000,000 due in 4 years at 12%, interest payable annually (Table 6-2); $FV(PVF_{4,12\%})$; ($9,000,000 × .63552)	$5,719,680	
Present value of $720,000 interest payable annually for 4 years at 12% (Table 6-4); $R(PVF\text{-}OA_{4,12\%})$; ($720,000 × 3.03735)	2,186,892	
Present value of restructured cash flows		(7,906,572)
Loss on restructuring		$ 2,593,428

As a result, Morgan National Bank records bad debt expense as follows (assuming no establishment of an allowance balance from recognition of an impairment).

Bad Debt Expense	2,593,428	
Allowance for Doubtful Accounts		2,593,428

In subsequent periods, Morgan National Bank reports interest revenue based on the historical effective rate. Illustration 14A-4 provides the following interest and amortization information.

ILLUSTRATION 14A-4
Schedule of Interest and Amortization after Debt Restructuring

MORGAN NATIONAL BANK (CREDITOR)

Date	Cash Received (8%)	Interest Revenue (12%)	Increase of Carrying Amount	Carrying Amount of Note
12/31/13				$7,906,572
12/31/14	$ 720,000[a]	$ 948,789[b]	$ 228,789[c]	8,135,361
12/31/15	720,000	976,243	256,243	8,391,604
12/31/16	720,000	1,006,992	286,992	8,678,596
12/31/17	720,000	1,041,404[d]	321,404[d]	9,000,000
Total	$2,880,000	$3,973,428	$1,093,428	

[a]$720,000 = $9,000,000 × .08
[b]$948,789 = $7,906,572 × .12
[c]$228,789 = $948,789 − $720,000
[d]$28 adjustment to compensate for rounding.

On December 31, 2014, Morgan National Bank makes the following entry.

December 31, 2014

Cash	720,000	
Allowance for Doubtful Accounts	228,789	
Interest Revenue		948,789

Morgan National Bank makes a similar entry (except for different amounts debited to Allowance for Doubtful Accounts and credited to Interest Revenue) each year until maturity. At maturity, the company makes the following entry.

December 31, 2017

Cash	9,000,000	
Allowance for Doubtful Accounts	1,500,000	
Notes Receivable		10,500,000

Example 2—Gain for Debtor

If the pre-restructure carrying amount exceeds the total future cash flows as a result of a modification of the terms, the debtor records a gain. To illustrate, assume the facts in the previous example except that Morgan National Bank reduces the principal to $7,000,000 (and extends the maturity date to December 31, 2017, and reduces the interest from 12% to 8%). The total future cash flow is now $9,240,000 ($7,000,000 of principal plus $2,240,000 of interest[21]), which is $1,260,000 ($10,500,000 − $9,240,000) less than the pre-restructure carrying amount of $10,500,000.

Under these circumstances, Resorts Development (debtor) reduces the carrying amount of its payable $1,260,000 and records a gain of $1,260,000. On the other hand, Morgan National Bank (creditor) debits its Bad Debt Expense for $4,350,444. Illustration 14A-5 shows this computation.

ILLUSTRATION 14A-5
Computation of Loss to Creditor on Restructuring

Pre-restructure carrying amount		$10,500,000
Present value of restructured cash flows:		
Present value of $7,000,000 due in 4 years at 12%, interest payable annually (Table 6-2); $FV(PVF_{4,12\%})$; ($7,000,000 × .63552)	$4,448,640	
Present value of $560,000 interest payable annually for 4 years at 12% (Table 6-4); $R(PVF\text{-}OA_{4,12\%})$; ($560,000 × 3.03735)	1,700,916	(6,149,556)
Creditor's loss on restructuring		$ 4,350,444

Illustration 14A-6 shows the entries to record the gain and loss on the debtor's and creditor's books at the date of restructure, December 31, 2013.

December 31, 2013 (date of restructure)					
Resorts Development Co. (Debtor)			**Morgan National Bank (Creditor)**		
Notes Payable	1,260,000		Bad Debt Expense	4,350,444	
Gain on Restructuring of Debt		1,260,000	Allowance for Doubtful Accounts		4,350,444

ILLUSTRATION 14A-6
Debtor and Creditor Entries to Record Gain and Loss on Note

For Resorts Development (debtor), because the new carrying value of the note ($10,500,000 − $1,260,000 = $9,240,000) equals the sum of the undiscounted cash flows ($9,240,000), the imputed interest rate is 0 percent. Consequently, all of the future cash flows reduce the principal balance, and the company recognizes no interest expense.

Morgan National reports the interest revenue in the same fashion as the previous example—that is, using the historical effective-interest rate applied toward the newly discounted value of the note. Illustration 14A-7 (on page 796) shows interest computations.

[21]Total interest payments are $7,000,000 × .08 × 4 years = $2,240,000.

ILLUSTRATION 14A-7
Schedule of Interest and Amortization after Debt Restructuring

MORGAN NATIONAL BANK (CREDITOR)

Date	Cash Received (8%)	Interest Revenue (12%)	Increase in Carrying Amount	Carrying Amount of Note
12/31/13				$6,149,556
12/31/14	$ 560,000[a]	$ 737,947[b]	$177,947[c]	6,327,503
12/31/15	560,000	759,300	199,300	6,526,803
12/31/16	560,000	783,216	223,216	6,750,019
12/31/17	560,000	809,981[d]	249,981[d]	7,000,000
Total	$2,240,000	$3,090,444	$850,444	

[a]$560,000 = $7,000,000 × .08
[b]$737,947 = $6,149,556 × .12
[c]$177,947 = $737,947 − $560,000
[d]$21 adjustment to compensate for rounding.

The journal entries in Illustration 14A-8 demonstrate the accounting by debtor and creditor for periodic interest payments and final principal payment.

Resorts Development Co. (Debtor)			Morgan National Bank (Creditor)		
December 31, 2014 (date of first interest payment following restructure)					
Notes Payable	560,000		Cash	560,000	
Cash		560,000	Allowance for Doubtful Accounts	177,947	
			Interest Revenue		737,947
December 31, 2015, 2016, and 2017 (dates of 2nd, 3rd, and last interest payments)					
(Debit and credit same accounts as 12/31/14 using applicable amounts from appropriate amortization schedules.)					
December 31, 2017 (date of principal payment)					
Notes Payable	7,000,000		Cash	7,000,000	
Cash		7,000,000	Allowance for Doubtful Accounts	3,500,000	
			Notes Receivable		10,500,000

ILLUSTRATION 14A-8
Debtor and Creditor Entries to Record Periodic Interest and Final Principal Payments

CONCLUDING REMARKS

The accounting for troubled debt is complex because the accounting standards allow for use of different measurement standards to determine the loss or gain reported. In addition, the assets and liabilities reported are sometimes not stated at historical cost or fair value, but at amounts adjusted for certain events but not others. This cumbersome accounting demonstrates the need for adoption of a comprehensive fair-value model for financial instruments that is consistent with finance concepts for pricing these financial instruments.

KEY TERM

troubled-debt restructuring, 790

SUMMARY OF LEARNING OBJECTIVE FOR APPENDIX 14A

10 Describe the accounting for a debt restructuring. There are two types of debt settlements: (1) transfer of noncash assets, and (2) granting of equity interest. Creditors and debtors record losses and gains on settlements based on fair values. For accounting purposes, there are also two types of restructurings with continuation of debt with modified terms: (1) the carrying amount of debt is less than the future cash flows, and (2) the carrying amount of debt exceeds the total future cash flows. Creditors record losses on these restructurings based on the expected future cash flows discounted at the historical effective-interest rate. The debtor determines its gain based on undiscounted cash flows.

DEMONSTRATION PROBLEM

Consider the following independent situations:

(a) On March 1, 2014, Heide Co. issued at 103 plus accrued interest $3,000,000, 9% bonds. The bonds are dated January 1, 2010, and pay interest semiannually on July 1 and January 1. In addition, Heide Co. incurred $27,000 of bond issuance costs. Compute the net amount of cash received by Heide Co. as a result of the issuance of these bonds.

(b) On January 1, 2014, Reymont Co. issued 9% bonds with a face value of $500,000 for $469,280 to yield 10%. The bonds are dated January 1, 2014, and pay interest annually. What amount is reported as bond discount on the issue date? Prepare the journal entry to record interest expense on December 31, 2014.

(c) Czeslaw Building Co. has a number of long-term bonds outstanding at December 31, 2014. These long-term bonds have the following sinking fund requirements and maturities for the next 6 years.

	Sinking Fund	Maturities
2015	$300,000	$100,000
2016	100,000	250,000
2017	100,000	100,000
2018	200,000	—
2019	200,000	150,000
2020	200,000	100,000

Indicate how this information should be reported in the financial statements at December 31, 2014.

Instructions

Prepare responses for each item above.

Solution

(a) Heide Co.

Selling price of the bonds ($3,000,000 × 103%)	$3,090,000
Accrued interest from January 1 to February 28, 2014 ($3,000,000 × 9% × 2/12)	45,000
Total cash received from issuance of the bonds	3,135,000
Less: Bond issuance costs	27,000
Net amount of cash received	$3,108,000

(b) Reymont Co.

Face value of bonds	$500,000
Issue price	(469,280)
Bond discount on issue late	$ 30,720

December 31, 2014

Interest Expense ($469,280 × 10%)	46,928	
Discount on Bonds Payable ($46,928 − $45,000)		1,928
Interest Payable ($500,000 × 9%)		45,000

(c) Czeslaw Building Co.

Maturities and sinking fund requirements on long-term debt for the next five year are as follows.

2015	$400,000	2018	$200,000
2016	350,000	2019	350,000
2017	200,000		

FASB CODIFICATION

FASB Codification References

[1] FASB ASC 835-30-55-2. [Predecessor literature: "Interest on Receivables and Payables," *Opinions of the Accounting Principles Board No. 21* (New York: AICPA, 1971), par. 16.]

[2] FASB ASC 835-30-35-2. [Predecessor literature: "Interest on Receivables and Payables," *Opinions of the Accounting Principles Board No. 21* (New York: AICPA, 1971), par. 15.]

[3] FASB ASC 470-50-45. [Predecessor literature: "Rescission of *FASB Statements No. 4, 44,* and *64* and Technical Corrections," *Statement of Accounting Standards No. 145* (Norwalk, Conn.: FASB, 2002).]

[4] FASB ASC 835-30-15-3. [Predecessor literature: "Interest on Receivables and Payables," *Opinions of the Accounting Principles Board No. 21* (New York: AICPA, 1971).]

[5] FASB ASC 835-30-05-2. [Predecessor literature: "Interest on Receivables and Payables," *Opinions of the Accounting Principles Board No. 21* (New York: AICPA, 1971), par. 12.]

[6] FASB ASC 825-10-25. [Predecessor literature: "The Fair Value Option for Financial Assets and Liabilities—Including an Amendment to FASB No. 115," *Statement of Financial Accounting Standards No. 159* (Norwalk, Conn.: FASB, 2007).]

[7] FASB ASC 470-10-50-4. [Predecessor literature: "Balance Sheet Classification of Short-Term Obligations Expected to Be Refinanced," *FASB Statement of Financial Accounting Standards No. 6* (Stamford, Conn.: FASB, 1975), par. 15.]

[8] FASB ASC 505-10-50-3. [Predecessor literature: "Disclosure of Information about Capital Structure," *FASB Statement of Financial Accounting Standards No. 129* (Norwalk, Conn.: 1997), par. 4.]

[9] FASB ASC 470-10-50-1. [Predecessor literature: "Disclosure of Long-Term Obligations," *FASB Statement of Financial Accounting Standards No. 47* (Stamford, Conn.: 1981), par. 10.]

[10] FASB ASC 310-40-15-2. [Predecessor literature: "Accounting by Debtors and Creditors for Troubled Debt Restructurings," *FASB Statement No. 15* (Norwalk, Conn.: FASB, June, 1977), par. 1.]

[11] FASB ASC 310-10-35. [Predecessor literature: "Accounting by Creditors for Impairment of a Loan," *FASB Statement No. 114* (Norwalk, Conn.: FASB, May 1993), par. 42.]

Exercises

If your school has a subscription to the FASB Codification, go to *http://aaahq.org/ascLogin.cfm* to log in and prepare responses to the following. Provide Codification references for your responses.

CE14-1 Access the glossary (Master Glossary) to answer the following.

(a) What does the term "callable obligation" mean?
(b) What is an imputed interest rate?
(c) What is a long-term obligation?
(d) What is the definition of "effective-interest rate"?

CE14-2 What guidance does the Codification provide on the disclosure of long-term obligations?

CE14-3 Describe how a company would classify debt that includes covenants. What conditions must exist in order to depart from the normal rule?

CE14-4 A company proposes to include in its SEC registration statement a balance sheet showing its subordinate debt as a portion of stockholders' equity. Will the SEC allow this? Why or why not?

An additional Codification case can be found in the Using Your Judgment section, on page 814.

Be sure to check the book's companion website for a Review and Analysis Exercise, with solution.

Note: All asterisked Questions, Exercises, and Problems relate to material in the appendix to the chapter.

(Unless instructed otherwise, round all answers to the nearest dollar.)

QUESTIONS

1. (a) From what sources might a corporation obtain funds through long-term debt? (b) What is a bond indenture? What does it contain? (c) What is a mortgage?

2. Potlatch Corporation has issued various types of bonds such as term bonds, income bonds, and debentures. Differentiate between term bonds, mortgage bonds, debenture bonds, income bonds, callable bonds, registered bonds, bearer or coupon bonds, convertible bonds, commodity-backed bonds, and deep discount bonds.

3. Distinguish between the following interest rates for bonds payable:
   (a) Yield rate.
   (b) Nominal rate.
   (c) Stated rate.
   (d) Market rate.
   (e) Effective rate.

4. Distinguish between the following values relative to bonds payable:
   (a) Maturity value.
   (b) Face value.
   (c) Market (fair) value.
   (d) Par value.

5. Under what conditions of bond issuance does a discount on bonds payable arise? Under what conditions of bond issuance does a premium on bonds payable arise?

6. How should discount on bonds payable be reported on the financial statements? Premium on bonds payable?

7. What are the two methods of amortizing discount and premium on bonds payable? Explain each.

8. Zopf Company sells its bonds at a premium and applies the effective-interest method in amortizing the premium. Will the annual interest expense increase or decrease over the life of the bonds? Explain.

9. Briggs and Stratton reported unamortized debt issue costs of $5.1 million. How should the costs of issuing these bonds be accounted for and classified in the financial statements?

10. Will the amortization of Discount on Bonds Payable increase or decrease Bond Interest Expense? Explain.

11. What is the "call" feature of a bond issue? How does the call feature affect the amortization of bond premium or discount?

12. Why would a company wish to reduce its bond indebtedness before its bonds reach maturity? Indicate how this can be done and the correct accounting treatment for such a transaction.

13. How are gains and losses from extinguishment of a debt classified in the income statement? What disclosures are required of such transactions?

14. What is done to record properly a transaction involving the issuance of a non-interest-bearing long-term note in exchange for property?

15. How is the present value of a non-interest-bearing note computed?

16. When is the stated interest rate of a debt instrument presumed to be fair?

17. What are the considerations in imputing an appropriate interest rate?

18. Differentiate between a fixed-rate mortgage and a variable-rate mortgage.

19. What is the fair value option? Briefly describe the controversy of applying the fair value option to financial liabilities.

20. Pierre Company has a 12% note payable with a carrying value of $20,000. Pierre applies the fair value option to this note. Given an increase in market interest rates, the fair value of the note is $22,600. Prepare the entry to record the fair value option for this note.

21. What disclosures are required relative to long-term debt and sinking fund requirements?

22. What is off-balance-sheet financing? Why might a company be interested in using off-balance-sheet financing?

23. What are some forms of off-balance-sheet financing?

24. Explain how a non-consolidated subsidiary can be a form of off-balance-sheet financing.

*25. What are the types of situations that result in troubled debt?

*26. What are the general rules for measuring gain or loss by both creditor and debtor in a troubled-debt restructuring involving a settlement?

*27. (a) In a troubled-debt situation, why might the creditor grant concessions to the debtor?
   (b) What type of concessions might a creditor grant the debtor in a troubled-debt situation?

*28. What are the general rules for measuring and recognizing gain or loss by both the debtor and the creditor in a troubled-debt restructuring involving a modification of terms?

*29. What is meant by "accounting symmetry" between the entries recorded by the debtor and creditor in a troubled-debt restructuring involving a modification of terms? In what ways is the accounting for troubled-debt restructurings non-symmetrical?

*30. Under what circumstances would a transaction be recorded as a troubled-debt restructuring by only one of the two parties to the transaction?

BRIEF EXERCISES

3 **BE14-1** Whiteside Corporation issues $500,000 of 9% bonds, due in 10 years, with interest payable semiannually. At the time of issue, the market rate for such bonds is 10%. Compute the issue price of the bonds.

3 4 **BE14-2** The Colson Company issued $300,000 of 10% bonds on January 1, 2014. The bonds are due January 1, 2020, with interest payable each July 1 and January 1. The bonds are issued at face value. Prepare Colson's journal entries for (a) the January issuance, (b) the July 1 interest payment, and (c) the December 31 adjusting entry.

3 4 **BE14-3** Assume the bonds in BE14-2 were issued at 98. Prepare the journal entries for (a) January 1, (b) July 1, and (c) December 31. Assume The Colson Company records straight-line amortization semiannually.

3 4 **BE14-4** Assume the bonds in BE14-2 were issued at 103. Prepare the journal entries for (a) January 1, (b) July 1, and (c) December 31. Assume The Colson Company records straight-line amortization semiannually.

3 4 **BE14-5** Devers Corporation issued $400,000 of 6% bonds on May 1, 2014. The bonds were dated January 1, 2014, and mature January 1, 2017, with interest payable July 1 and January 1. The bonds were issued at face value plus accrued interest. Prepare Devers's journal entries for (a) the May 1 issuance, (b) the July 1 interest payment, and (c) the December 31 adjusting entry.

3 4 **BE14-6** On January 1, 2014, JWS Corporation issued $600,000 of 7% bonds, due in 10 years. The bonds were issued for $559,224, and pay interest each July 1 and January 1. JWS uses the effective-interest method. Prepare the company's journal entries for (a) the January 1 issuance, (b) the July 1 interest payment, and (c) the December 31 adjusting entry. Assume an effective-interest rate of 8%.

3 4 **BE14-7** Assume the bonds in BE14-6 were issued for $644,636 and the effective-interest rate is 6%. Prepare the company's journal entries for (a) the January 1 issuance, (b) the July 1 interest payment, and (c) the December 31 adjusting entry.

3 4 **BE14-8** Teton Corporation issued $600,000 of 7% bonds on November 1, 2014, for $644,636. The bonds were dated November 1, 2014, and mature in 10 years, with interest payable each May 1 and November 1. Teton uses the effective-interest method with an effective rate of 6%. Prepare Teton's December 31, 2014, adjusting entry.

9 **BE14-9** At December 31, 2014, Hyasaki Corporation has the following account balances:

Bonds payable, due January 1, 2023	$2,000,000
Discount on bonds payable	88,000
Interest payable	80,000

Show how the above accounts should be presented on the December 31, 2014, balance sheet, including the proper classifications.

4 **BE14-10** Wasserman Corporation issued 10-year bonds on January 1, 2014. Costs associated with the bond issuance were $160,000. Wasserman uses the straight-line method to amortize bond issue costs. Prepare the December 31, 2014, entry to record 2014 bond issue cost amortization.

5 **BE14-11** On January 1, 2014, Henderson Corporation redeemed $500,000 of bonds at 99. At the time of redemption, the unamortized premium was $15,000 and unamortized bond issue costs were $5,250. Prepare the corporation's journal entry to record the reacquisition of the bonds.

6 **BE14-12** Coldwell, Inc. issued a $100,000, 4-year, 10% note at face value to Flint Hills Bank on January 1, 2014, and received $100,000 cash. The note requires annual interest payments each December 31. Prepare Coldwell's journal entries to record (a) the issuance of the note and (b) the December 31 interest payment.

6 **BE14-13** Samson Corporation issued a 4-year, $75,000, zero-interest-bearing note to Brown Company on January 1, 2014, and received cash of $47,664. The implicit interest rate is 12%. Prepare Samson's journal entries for (a) the January 1 issuance and (b) the December 31 recognition of interest.

6 **BE14-14** McCormick Corporation issued a 4-year, $40,000, 5% note to Greenbush Company on January 1, 2014, and received a computer that normally sells for $31,495. The note requires annual interest payments each December 31. The market rate of interest for a note of similar risk is 12%. Prepare McCormick's journal entries for (a) the January 1 issuance and (b) the December 31 interest.

6 **BE14-15** Shlee Corporation issued a 4-year, $60,000, zero-interest-bearing note to Garcia Company on January 1, 2014, and received cash of $60,000. In addition, Shlee agreed to sell merchandise to Garcia at an amount less than regular selling price over the 4-year period. The market rate of interest for similar notes is 12%. Prepare Shlee Corporation's January 1 journal entry.

7 **BE14-16** Shonen Knife Corporation has elected to use the fair value option for one of its notes payable. The note was issued at an effective rate of 11% and has a carrying value of $16,000. At year-end, Shonen Knife's borrowing rate has declined; the fair value of the note payable is now $17,500. (a) Determine the unrealized holding gain or loss on the note. (b) Prepare the entry to record any unrealized holding gain or loss.

EXERCISES

2 **E14-1 (Classification of Liabilities)** Presented below are various account balances of K.D. Lang Inc.

(a) Unamortized premium on bonds payable, of which $3,000 will be amortized during the next year.
(b) Bank loans payable of a winery, due March 10, 2018. (The product requires aging for 5 years before sale.)
(c) Serial bonds payable, $1,000,000, of which $200,000 are due each July 31.
(d) Amounts withheld from employees' wages for income taxes.
(e) Notes payable due January 15, 2017.
(f) Credit balances in customers' accounts arising from returns and allowances after collection in full of account.
(g) Bonds payable of $2,000,000 maturing June 30, 2016.
(h) Overdraft of $1,000 in a bank account. (No other balances are carried at this bank.)
(i) Deposits made by customers who have ordered goods.

Instructions

Indicate whether each of the items above should be classified on December 31, 2014, as a current liability, a long-term liability, or under some other classification. Consider each one independently from all others; that is, do not assume that all of them relate to one particular business. If the classification of some of the items is doubtful, explain why in each case.

2 **E14-2 (Classification)** The following items are found in the financial statements.

(a) Discount on bonds payable.
(b) Interest expense (credit balance).
(c) Unamortized bond issue costs.
(d) Gain on repurchase of debt.
(e) Mortgage payable (payable in equal amounts over next 3 years).
(f) Debenture bonds payable (maturing in 5 years).
(g) Notes payable (due in 4 years).
(h) Premium on bonds payable.
(i) Treasury bonds.
(j) Bonds payable (due in 3 years).

Instructions

Indicate how each of these items should be classified in the financial statements.

3 4 **E14-3 (Entries for Bond Transactions)** Presented below are two independent situations.

1. On January 1, 2014, Simon Company issued $200,000 of 9%, 10-year bonds at par. Interest is payable quarterly on April 1, July 1, October 1, and January 1.
2. On June 1, 2014, Garfunkel Company issued $100,000 of 12%, 10-year bonds dated January 1 at par plus accrued interest. Interest is payable semiannually on July 1 and January 1.

Instructions

For each of these two independent situations, prepare journal entries to record the following.

(a) The issuance of the bonds.
(b) The payment of interest on July 1.
(c) The accrual of interest on December 31.

3 4 **E14-4 (Entries for Bond Transactions—Straight-Line)** Celine Dion Company issued $600,000 of 10%, 20-year bonds on January 1, 2014, at 102. Interest is payable semiannually on July 1 and January 1. Dion Company uses the straight-line method of amortization for bond premium or discount.

XLS

Instructions

Prepare the journal entries to record the following.

(a) The issuance of the bonds.

(b) The payment of interest and the related amortization on July 1, 2014.
(c) The accrual of interest and the related amortization on December 31, 2014.

3 4 **E14-5 (Entries for Bond Transactions—Effective-Interest)** Assume the same information as in E14-4, except that Celine Dion Company uses the effective-interest method of amortization for bond premium or discount. Assume an effective yield of 9.7705%.

Instructions

Prepare the journal entries to record the following. (Round to the nearest dollar.)

(a) The issuance of the bonds.
(b) The payment of interest and related amortization on July 1, 2014.
(c) The accrual of interest and the related amortization on December 31, 2014.

3 4 **E14-6 (Amortization Schedule—Straight-Line)** Devon Harris Company sells 10% bonds having a maturity value of $2,000,000 for $1,855,816. The bonds are dated January 1, 2014, and mature January 1, 2019. Interest is payable annually on January 1.

Instructions

Set up a schedule of interest expense and discount amortization under the straight-line method. (Round answers to the nearest cent.)

3 4 **E14-7 (Amortization Schedule—Effective-Interest)** Assume the same information as E14-6.

Instructions

Set up a schedule of interest expense and discount amortization under the effective-interest method. (*Hint:* The effective-interest rate must be computed.)

3 4 **E14-8 (Determine Proper Amounts in Account Balances)** Presented below are three independent situations.

(a) CeCe Winans Corporation incurred the following costs in connection with the issuance of bonds: (1) printing and engraving costs, $12,000; (2) legal fees, $49,000; and (3) commissions paid to underwriter, $60,000. What amount should be reported as Unamortized Bond Issue Costs, and where should this amount be reported on the balance sheet?
(b) George Gershwin Co. sold $2,000,000 of 10%, 10-year bonds at 104 on January 1, 2014. The bonds were dated January 1, 2014, and pay interest on July 1 and January 1. If Gershwin uses the straight-line method to amortize bond premium or discount, determine the amount of interest expense to be reported on July 1, 2014, and December 31, 2014.
(c) Ron Kenoly Inc. issued $600,000 of 9%, 10-year bonds on June 30, 2014, for $562,500. This price provided a yield of 10% on the bonds. Interest is payable semiannually on December 31 and June 30. If Kenoly uses the effective-interest method, determine the amount of interest expense to record if financial statements are issued on October 31, 2014.

3 4 **E14-9 (Entries and Questions for Bond Transactions)** On June 30, 2014, Mischa Auer Company issued $4,000,000 face value of 13%, 20-year bonds at $4,300,920, a yield of 12%. Auer uses the effective-interest method to amortize bond premium or discount. The bonds pay semiannual interest on June 30 and December 31.

Instructions

(Round answers to the nearest cent.)

(a) Prepare the journal entries to record the following transactions.
   (1) The issuance of the bonds on June 30, 2014.
   (2) The payment of interest and the amortization of the premium on December 31, 2014.
   (3) The payment of interest and the amortization of the premium on June 30, 2015.
   (4) The payment of interest and the amortization of the premium on December 31, 2015.
(b) Show the proper balance sheet presentation for the liability for bonds payable on the December 31, 2015, balance sheet.
(c) Provide the answers to the following questions.
   (1) What amount of interest expense is reported for 2015?
   (2) Will the bond interest expense reported in 2015 be the same as, greater than, or less than the amount that would be reported if the straight-line method of amortization were used?
   (3) Determine the total cost of borrowing over the life of the bond.
   (4) Will the total bond interest expense for the life of the bond be greater than, the same as, or less than the total interest expense if the straight-line method of amortization were used?

3 4 **E14-10 (Entries for Bond Transactions)** On January 1, 2014, Aumont Company sold 12% bonds having a maturity value of $500,000 for $537,907.37, which provides the bondholders with a 10% yield. The bonds

are dated January 1, 2014; and mature January 1, 2019, with interest payable December 31 of each year. Aumont Company allocates interest and unamortized discount or premium on the effective-interest basis.

Instructions

(Round answers to the nearest cent.)

(a) Prepare the journal entry at the date of the bond issuance.
(b) Prepare a schedule of interest expense and bond amortization for 2014–2016.
(c) Prepare the journal entry to record the interest payment and the amortization for 2014.
(d) Prepare the journal entry to record the interest payment and the amortization for 2016.

3 **E14-11 (Information Related to Various Bond Issues)** Karen Austin Inc. has issued three types of debt on January 1, 2014, the start of the company's fiscal year.

(a) $10 million, 10-year, 15% unsecured bonds, interest payable quarterly. Bonds were priced to yield 12%.
(b) $25 million par of 10-year, zero-coupon bonds at a price to yield 12% per year.
(c) $20 million, 10-year, 10% mortgage bonds, interest payable annually to yield 12%.

Instructions

Prepare a schedule that identifies the following items for each bond: (1) maturity value, (2) number of interest periods over life of bond, (3) stated rate per each interest period, (4) effective-interest rate per each interest period, (5) payment amount per period, and (6) present value of bonds at date of issue.

3 4 5 **E14-12 (Entry for Redemption of Bond; Bond Issue Costs)** On January 2, 2009, Banno Corporation issued $1,500,000 of 10% bonds at 97 due December 31, 2018. Legal and other costs of $24,000 were incurred in connection with the issue. Interest on the bonds is payable annually each December 31. The $24,000 issue costs are being deferred and amortized on a straight-line basis over the 10-year term of the bonds. The discount on the bonds is also being amortized on a straight-line basis over the 10 years. (Straight-line is not materially different in effect from the preferable "interest method.")

The bonds are callable at 101 (i.e., at 101% of face amount), and on January 2, 2014, Banno called $900,000 face amount of the bonds and redeemed them.

Instructions

Ignoring income taxes, compute the amount of loss, if any, to be recognized by Banno as a result of retiring the $900,000 of bonds in 2014 and prepare the journal entry to record the redemption.

(AICPA adapted)

3 4 5 **E14-13 (Entries for Redemption and Issuance of Bonds)** Matt Perry, Inc. had outstanding $6,000,000 of 11% bonds (interest payable July 31 and January 31) due in 10 years. On July 1, it issued $9,000,000 of 10%, 15-year bonds (interest payable July 1 and January 1) at 98. A portion of the proceeds was used to call the 11% bonds at 102 on August 1. Unamortized bond discount and issue cost applicable to the 11% bonds were $120,000 and $30,000, respectively.

Instructions

Prepare the journal entries necessary to record issue of the new bonds and the refunding of the bonds.

3 4 5 **E14-14 (Entries for Redemption and Issuance of Bonds)** On June 30, 2006, County Company issued 12% bonds with a par value of $800,000 due in 20 years. They were issued at 98 and were callable at 104 at any date after June 30, 2014. Because of lower interest rates and a significant change in the company's credit rating, it was decided to call the entire issue on June 30, 2015, and to issue new bonds. New 10% bonds were sold in the amount of $1,000,000 at 102; they mature in 20 years. County Company uses straight-line amortization. Interest payment dates are December 31 and June 30.

Instructions

(a) Prepare journal entries to record the redemption of the old issue and the sale of the new issue on June 30, 2015.
(b) Prepare the entry required on December 31, 2015, to record the payment of the first 6 months' interest and the amortization of premium on the bonds.

3 4 5 **E14-15 (Entries for Redemption and Issuance of Bonds)** Linda Day George Company had bonds outstanding with a maturity value of $300,000. On April 30, 2014, when these bonds had an unamortized discount of $10,000, they were called in at 104. To pay for these bonds, George had issued other bonds a month earlier bearing a lower interest rate. The newly issued bonds had a life of 10 years. The new bonds were issued at 103 (face value $300,000). Issue costs related to the new bonds were $3,000.

Instructions

Ignoring interest, compute the gain or loss and record this refunding transaction.

(AICPA adapted)

6 **E14-16 (Entries for Zero-Interest-Bearing Notes)** On January 1, 2014, Ellen Greene Company makes the two following acquisitions.

1. Purchases land having a fair value of $200,000 by issuing a 5-year, zero-interest-bearing promissory note in the face amount of $337,012.
2. Purchases equipment by issuing a 6%, 8-year promissory note having a maturity value of $250,000 (interest payable annually).

The company has to pay 11% interest for funds from its bank.

Instructions

(Round answers to the nearest cent.)

(a) Record the two journal entries that should be recorded by Ellen Greene Company for the two purchases on January 1, 2014.

(b) Record the interest at the end of the first year on both notes using the effective-interest method.

6 **E14-17 (Imputation of Interest)** Presented below are two independent situations.

(a) On January 1, 2014, Robin Wright Inc. purchased land that had an assessed value of $350,000 at the time of purchase. A $550,000, zero-interest-bearing note due January 1, 2017, was given in exchange. There was no established exchange price for the land, nor a ready fair value for the note. The interest rate charged on a note of this type is 12%. Determine at what amount the land should be recorded at January 1, 2014, and the interest expense to be reported in 2014 related to this transaction.

(b) On January 1, 2014, Field Furniture Co. borrowed $5,000,000 (face value) from Gary Sinise Co., a major customer, through a zero-interest-bearing note due in 4 years. Because the note was zero-interest-bearing, Field Furniture agreed to sell furniture to this customer at lower than market price. A 10% rate of interest is normally charged on this type of loan. Prepare the journal entry to record this transaction and determine the amount of interest expense to report for 2014.

6 **E14-18 (Imputation of Interest with Right)** On January 1, 2014, Margaret Avery Co. borrowed and received $400,000 from a major customer evidenced by a zero-interest-bearing note due in 3 years. As consideration for the zero-interest-bearing feature, Avery agrees to supply the customer's inventory needs for the loan period at lower than the market price. The appropriate rate at which to impute interest is 8%.

Instructions

(a) Prepare the journal entry to record the initial transaction on January 1, 2014. (Round all computations to the nearest dollar.)

(b) Prepare the journal entry to record any adjusting entries needed at December 31, 2014. Assume that the sales of Avery's product to this customer occur evenly over the 3-year period.

7 **E14-19 (Fair Value Option)** Fallen Company commonly issues long-term notes payable to its various lenders. Fallen has had a pretty good credit rating such that its effective borrowing rate is quite low (less than 8% on an annual basis). Fallen has elected to use the fair value option for the long-term notes issued to Barclay's Bank and has the following data related to the carrying and fair value for these notes.

	Carrying Value	Fair Value
December 31, 2014	$54,000	$54,000
December 31, 2015	44,000	42,500
December 31, 2016	36,000	38,000

Instructions

(a) Prepare the journal entry at December 31 (Fallen's year-end) for 2014, 2015, and 2016, to record the fair value option for these notes.

(b) At what amount will the note be reported on Fallen's 2015 balance sheet?

(c) What is the effect of recording the fair value option on these notes on Fallen's 2016 income?

(d) Assuming that general market interest rates have been stable over the period, does the fair value data for the notes indicate that Fallen's creditworthiness has improved or declined in 2016? Explain.

9 **E14-20 (Long-Term Debt Disclosure)** At December 31, 2014, Redmond Company has outstanding three long-term debt issues. The first is a $2,000,000 note payable which matures June 30, 2017. The second is a $6,000,000 bond issue which matures September 30, 2018. The third is a $12,500,000 sinking fund debenture with annual sinking fund payments of $2,500,000 in each of the years 2016 through 2020.

Instructions

Prepare the required note disclosure for the long-term debt at December 31, 2014.

10 ***E14-21 (Settlement of Debt)** Strickland Company owes $200,000 plus $18,000 of accrued interest to Moran State Bank. The debt is a 10-year, 10% note. During 2014, Strickland's business deteriorated due to a faltering regional economy. On December 31, 2014, Moran State Bank agrees to accept an old machine and cancel the entire debt. The machine has a cost of $390,000, accumulated depreciation of $221,000, and a fair value of $180,000.

Instructions

(a) Prepare journal entries for Strickland Company and Moran State Bank to record this debt settlement.
(b) How should Strickland report the gain or loss on the disposition of machine and on restructuring of debt in its 2014 income statement?
(c) Assume that, instead of transferring the machine, Strickland decides to grant 15,000 shares of its common stock ($10 par) which has a fair value of $180,000 in full settlement of the loan obligation. If Moran State Bank treats Strickland's stock as a trading investment, prepare the entries to record the transaction for both parties.

10 ***E14-22 (Term Modification without Gain—Debtor's Entries)** On December 31, 2014, the American Bank enters into a debt restructuring agreement with Barkley Company, which is now experiencing financial trouble. The bank agrees to restructure a 12%, issued at par, $3,000,000 note receivable by the following modifications:

1. Reducing the principal obligation from $3,000,000 to $2,400,000.
2. Extending the maturity date from December 31, 2014, to January 1, 2018.
3. Reducing the interest rate from 12% to 10%.

Barkley pays interest at the end of each year. On January 1, 2018, Barkley Company pays $2,400,000 in cash to Firstar Bank.

Instructions

(a) Will the gain recorded by Barkley be equal to the loss recorded by American Bank under the debt restructuring?
(b) Can Barkley Company record a gain under the term modification mentioned above? Explain.
(c) Assuming that the interest rate Barkley should use to compute interest expense in future periods is 1.4276%, prepare the interest payment schedule of the note for Barkley Company after the debt restructuring.
(d) Prepare the interest payment entry for Barkley Company on December 31, 2016.
(e) What entry should Barkley make on January 1, 2018?

10 ***E14-23 (Term Modification without Gain—Creditor's Entries)** Using the same information as in E14-22, answer the following questions related to American Bank (creditor).

Instructions

(a) What interest rate should American Bank use to calculate the loss on the debt restructuring?
(b) Compute the loss that American Bank will suffer from the debt restructuring. Prepare the journal entry to record the loss.
(c) Prepare the interest receipt schedule for American Bank after the debt restructuring.
(d) Prepare the interest receipt entry for American Bank on December 31, 2016.
(e) What entry should American Bank make on January 1, 2018?

10 ***E14-24 (Term Modification with Gain—Debtor's Entries)** Use the same information as in E14-22 above except that American Bank reduced the principal to $1,900,000 rather than $2,400,000. On January 1, 2018, Barkley pays $1,900,000 in cash to American Bank for the principal.

Instructions

(a) Can Barkley Company record a gain under this term modification? If yes, compute the gain for Barkley Company.
(b) Prepare the journal entries to record the gain on Barkley's books.
(c) What interest rate should Barkley use to compute its interest expense in future periods? Will your answer be the same as in E14-22 above? Why or why not?
(d) Prepare the interest payment schedule of the note for Barkley Company after the debt restructuring.
(e) Prepare the interest payment entries for Barkley Company on December 31, of 2015, 2016, and 2017.
(f) What entry should Barkley make on January 1, 2018?

10 ***E14-25 (Term Modification with Gain—Creditor's Entries)** Using the same information as in E14-22 and E14-24, answer the following questions related to American Bank (creditor).

Instructions

(a) Compute the loss American Bank will suffer under this new term modification. Prepare the journal entry to record the loss on American's books.

(b) Prepare the interest receipt schedule for American Bank after the debt restructuring.

(c) Prepare the interest receipt entry for American Bank on December 31, 2015, 2016, and 2017.

(d) What entry should American Bank make on January 1, 2018?

10 ***E14-26 (Debtor/Creditor Entries for Settlement of Troubled Debt)** Gottlieb Co. owes $199,800 to Ceballos Inc. The debt is a 10-year, 11% note. Because Gottlieb Co. is in financial trouble, Ceballos Inc. agrees to accept some property and cancel the entire debt. The property has a book value of $90,000 and a fair value of $140,000.

Instructions

(a) Prepare the journal entry on Gottlieb's books for debt restructure.

(b) Prepare the journal entry on Ceballos's books for debt restructure.

10 ***E14-27 (Debtor/Creditor Entries for Modification of Troubled Debt)** Vargo Corp. owes $270,000 to First Trust. The debt is a 10-year, 12% note due December 31, 2014. Because Vargo Corp. is in financial trouble, First Trust agrees to extend the maturity date to December 31, 2016, reduce the principal to $220,000, and reduce the interest rate to 5%, payable annually on December 31.

Instructions

(a) Prepare the journal entries on Vargo's books on December 31, 2014, 2015, 2016.

(b) Prepare the journal entries on First Trust's books on December 31, 2014, 2015, 2016.

EXERCISES SET B

See the book's companion website, at **www.wiley.com/college/kieso**, for an additional set of exercises.

PROBLEMS

3 4 **P14-1 (Analysis of Amortization Schedule and Interest Entries)** The following amortization and interest schedule reflects the issuance of 10-year bonds by Capulet Corporation on January 1, 2008, and the subsequent interest payments and charges. The company's year-end is December 31, and financial statements are prepared once yearly.

Amortization Schedule

Year	Cash	Interest	Amount Unamortized	Carrying Value
1/1/2008			$5,651	$ 94,349
2008	$11,000	$11,322	5,329	94,671
2009	11,000	11,361	4,968	95,032
2010	11,000	11,404	4,564	95,436
2011	11,000	11,452	4,112	95,888
2012	11,000	11,507	3,605	96,395
2013	11,000	11,567	3,038	96,962
2014	11,000	11,635	2,403	97,597
2015	11,000	11,712	1,691	98,309
2016	11,000	11,797	894	99,106
2017	11,000	11,894		100,000

Instructions

(a) Indicate whether the bonds were issued at a premium or a discount and how you can determine this fact from the schedule.

(b) Indicate whether the amortization schedule is based on the straight-line method or the effective-interest method, and how you can determine which method is used.

(c) Determine the stated interest rate and the effective-interest rate.

(d) On the basis of the schedule above, prepare the journal entry to record the issuance of the bonds on January 1, 2008.
(e) On the basis of the schedule above, prepare the journal entry or entries to reflect the bond transactions and accruals for 2008. (Interest is paid January 1.)
(f) On the basis of the schedule above, prepare the journal entry or entries to reflect the bond transactions and accruals for 2015. Capulet Corporation does not use reversing entries.

3 4 5 **P14-2 (Issuance and Redemption of Bonds)** Venezuela Co. is building a new hockey arena at a cost of $2,500,000. It received a downpayment of $500,000 from local businesses to support the project, and now needs to borrow $2,000,000 to complete the project. It therefore decides to issue $2,000,000 of 10.5%, 10-year bonds. These bonds were issued on January 1, 2013, and pay interest annually on each January 1. The bonds yield 10%. Venezuela paid $50,000 in bond issue costs related to the bond sale.

XLS

Instructions

(a) Prepare the journal entry to record the issuance of the bonds and the related bond issue costs incurred on January 1, 2013.
(b) Prepare a bond amortization schedule up to and including January 1, 2017, using the effective-interest method.
(c) Assume that on July 1, 2016, Venezuela Co. redeems half of the bonds at a cost of $1,065,000 plus accrued interest. Prepare the journal entry to record this redemption.

3 4 6 **P14-3 (Negative Amortization)** Good-Deal Inc. developed a new sales gimmick to help sell its inventory of new automobiles. Because many new car buyers need financing, Good-Deal offered a low downpayment and low car payments for the first year after purchase. It believes that this promotion will bring in some new buyers.

On January 1, 2014, a customer purchased a new $33,000 automobile, making a downpayment of $1,000. The customer signed a note indicating that the annual rate of interest would be 8% and that quarterly payments would be made over 3 years. For the first year, Good-Deal required a $400 quarterly payment to be made on April 1, July 1, October 1, and January 1, 2015. After this one-year period, the customer was required to make regular quarterly payments that would pay off the loan as of January 1, 2017.

Instructions

(a) Prepare a note amortization schedule for the first year.
(b) Indicate the amount the customer owes on the contract at the end of the first year.
(c) Compute the amount of the new quarterly payments.
(d) Prepare a note amortization schedule for these new payments for the next 2 years.
(e) What do you think of the new sales promotion used by Good-Deal?

3 4 5 9 **P14-4 (Issuance and Redemption of Bonds; Income Statement Presentation)** Holiday Company issued its 9%, 25-year mortgage bonds in the principal amount of $3,000,000 on January 2, 2000, at a discount of $150,000, which it proceeded to amortize by charges to expense over the life of the issue on a straight-line basis. The indenture securing the issue provided that the bonds could be called for redemption in total but not in part at any time before maturity at 104% of the principal amount, but it did not provide for any sinking fund.

On December 18, 2014, the company issued its 11%, 20-year debenture bonds in the principal amount of $4,000,000 at 102, and the proceeds were used to redeem the 9%, 25-year mortgage bonds on January 2, 2015. The indenture securing the new issue did not provide for any sinking fund or for redemption before maturity.

Instructions

(a) Prepare journal entries to record the issuance of the 11% bonds and the redemption of the 9% bonds.
(b) Indicate the income statement treatment of the gain or loss from redemption and the note disclosure required.

3 4 5 **P14-5 (Comprehensive Bond Problem)** In each of the following independent cases the company closes its books on December 31.

XLS

1. Sanford Co. sells $500,000 of 10% bonds on March 1, 2014. The bonds pay interest on September 1 and March 1. The due date of the bonds is September 1, 2017. The bonds yield 12%. Give entries through December 31, 2015.
2. Titania Co. sells $400,000 of 12% bonds on June 1, 2014. The bonds pay interest on December 1 and June 1. The due date of the bonds is June 1, 2018. The bonds yield 10%. On October 1, 2015, Titania buys back $120,000 worth of bonds for $126,000 (includes accrued interest). Give entries through December 1, 2016.

Instructions

For the two cases prepare all of the relevant journal entries from the time of sale until the date indicated. Use the effective-interest method for discount and premium amortization (construct amortization tables where applicable). Amortize premium or discount on interest dates and at year-end. (Assume that no reversing entries were made.)

3 4 5 **P14-6 (Issuance of Bonds between Interest Dates, Straight-Line, Redemption)** Presented below are selected transactions on the books of Simonson Corporation.

May 1, 2014 Bonds payable with a par value of $900,000, which are dated January 1, 2014, are sold at 106 plus accrued interest. They are coupon bonds, bear interest at 12% (payable annually at January 1), and mature January 1, 2024. (Use interest expense account for accrued interest.)

Dec. 31 Adjusting entries are made to record the accrued interest on the bonds, and the amortization of the proper amount of premium. (Use straight-line amortization.)

Jan. 1, 2015 Interest on the bonds is paid.

April 1 Bonds with par value of $360,000 are called at 102 plus accrued interest, and redeemed. (Bond premium is to be amortized only at the end of each year.)

Dec. 31 Adjusting entries are made to record the accrued interest on the bonds, and the proper amount of premium amortized.

Instructions

(Round to two decimal places.)

Prepare journal entries for the transactions above.

3 4 5 **P14-7 (Entries for Life Cycle of Bonds)** On April 1, 2014, Seminole Company sold 15,000 of its 11%, 15-year, $1,000 face value bonds at 97. Interest payment dates are April 1 and October 1, and the company uses the straight-line method of bond discount amortization. On March 1, 2015, Seminole took advantage of favorable prices of its stock to extinguish 6,000 of the bonds by issuing 200,000 shares of its $10 par value common stock. At this time, the accrued interest was paid in cash. The company's stock was selling for $31 per share on March 1, 2015.

Instructions

Prepare the journal entries needed on the books of Seminole Company to record the following.

(a) April 1, 2014: issuance of the bonds.
(b) October 1, 2014: payment of semiannual interest.
(c) December 31, 2014: accrual of interest expense.
(d) March 1, 2015: extinguishment of 6,000 bonds. (No reversing entries made.)

6 **P14-8 (Entries for Zero-Interest-Bearing Note)** On December 31, 2014, Faital Company acquired a computer from Plato Corporation by issuing a $600,000 zero-interest-bearing note, payable in full on December 31, 2018. Faital Company's credit rating permits it to borrow funds from its several lines of credit at 10%. The computer is expected to have a 5-year life and a $70,000 salvage value.

Instructions

(Round answers to the nearest cent.)

(a) Prepare the journal entry for the purchase on December 31, 2014.
(b) Prepare any necessary adjusting entries relative to depreciation (use straight-line) and amortization (use effective-interest method) on December 31, 2015.
(c) Prepare any necessary adjusting entries relative to depreciation and amortization on December 31, 2016.

6 **P14-9 (Entries for Zero-Interest-Bearing Note; Payable in Installments)** Sabonis Cosmetics Co. purchased machinery on December 31, 2013, paying $50,000 down and agreeing to pay the balance in four equal installments of $40,000 payable each December 31. An assumed interest of 8% is implicit in the purchase price.

Instructions

Prepare the journal entries that would be recorded for the purchase and for the payments and interest on the following dates. (Round answers to the nearest cent.)

(a) December 31, 2013.
(b) December 31, 2014.
(c) December 31, 2015.
(d) December 31, 2016.
(e) December 31, 2017.

3 4 5 9 **P14-10 (Comprehensive Problem: Issuance, Classification, Reporting)** Presented on the next page are four independent situations.

(a) On March 1, 2015, Wilke Co. issued at 103 plus accrued interest $4,000,000, 9% bonds. The bonds are dated January 1, 2015, and pay interest semiannually on July 1 and January 1. In addition, Wilke Co. incurred $27,000 of bond issuance costs. Compute the net amount of cash received by Wilke Co. as a result of the issuance of these bonds.

(b) On January 1, 2014, Langley Co. issued 9% bonds with a face value of $700,000 for $656,992 to yield 10%. The bonds are dated January 1, 2014, and pay interest annually. What amount is reported for interest expense in 2014 related to these bonds, assuming that Langley used the effective-interest method for amortizing bond premium and discount?

(c) Tweedie Building Co. has a number of long-term bonds outstanding at December 31, 2014. These long-term bonds have the following sinking fund requirements and maturities for the next 6 years.

	Sinking Fund	Maturities
2015	$300,000	$100,000
2016	100,000	250,000
2017	100,000	100,000
2018	200,000	—
2019	200,000	150,000
2020	200,000	100,000

Indicate how this information should be reported in the financial statements at December 31, 2014.

(d) In the long-term debt structure of Beckford Inc., the following three bonds were reported: mortgage bonds payable $10,000,000; collateral trust bonds $5,000,000; bonds maturing in installments, secured by plant equipment $4,000,000. Determine the total amount, if any, of debenture bonds outstanding.

4 **P14-11 (Effective-Interest Method)** Samantha Cordelia, an intermediate accounting student, is having difficulty amortizing bond premiums and discounts using the effective-interest method. Furthermore, she cannot understand why GAAP requires that this method be used instead of the straight-line method. She has come to you with the following problem, looking for help.

On June 30, 2014, Hobart Company issued $2,000,000 face value of 11%, 20-year bonds at $2,171,600, a yield of 10%. Hobart Company uses the effective-interest method to amortize bond premiums or discounts. The bonds pay semiannual interest on June 30 and December 31. Prepare an amortization schedule for four periods.

Instructions

Using the data above for illustrative purposes, write a short memo (1–1.5 pages double-spaced) to Samantha, explaining what the effective-interest method is, why it is preferable, and how it is computed. (Do not forget to include an amortization schedule, referring to it whenever necessary.)

10 ***P14-12 (Debtor/Creditor Entries for Continuation of Troubled Debt)** Daniel Perkins is the sole shareholder of Perkins Inc., which is currently under protection of the U.S. bankruptcy court. As a "debtor in possession," he has negotiated the following revised loan agreement with United Bank. Perkins Inc.'s $600,000, 12%, 10-year note was refinanced with a $600,000, 5%, 10-year note.

Instructions

(a) What is the accounting nature of this transaction?

(b) Prepare the journal entry to record this refinancing:

(1) On the books of Perkins Inc.

(2) On the books of United Bank.

(c) Discuss whether generally accepted accounting principles provide the proper information useful to managers and investors in this situation.

10 ***P14-13 (Restructure of Note under Different Circumstances)** Halvor Corporation is having financial difficulty and therefore has asked Frontenac National Bank to restructure its $5 million note outstanding. The present note has 3 years remaining and pays a current rate of interest of 10%. The present market rate for a loan of this nature is 12%. The note was issued at its face value.

Instructions

Presented below and on the next page are four independent situations. Prepare the journal entry that Halvor and Frontenac National Bank would make for each of these restructurings.

(a) Frontenac National Bank agrees to take an equity interest in Halvor by accepting common stock valued at $3,700,000 in exchange for relinquishing its claim on this note. The common stock has a par value of $1,700,000.

(b) Frontenac National Bank agrees to accept land in exchange for relinquishing its claim on this note. The land has a book value of $3,250,000 and a fair value of $4,000,000.

(c) Frontenac National Bank agrees to modify the terms of the note, indicating that Halvor does not have to pay any interest on the note over the 3-year period.

(d) Frontenac National Bank agrees to reduce the principal balance due to $4,166,667 and require interest only in the second and third year at a rate of 10%.

10 *__P14-14 (Debtor/Creditor Entries for Continuation of Troubled Debt with New Effective Interest)__ Crocker Corp. owes D. Yaeger Corp. a 10-year, 10% note in the amount of $330,000 plus $33,000 of accrued interest. The note is due today, December 31, 2014. Because Crocker Corp. is in financial trouble, D. Yaeger Corp. agrees to forgive the accrued interest, $30,000 of the principal, and to extend the maturity date to December 31, 2017. Interest at 10% of revised principal will continue to be due on 12/31 each year.

Assume the following present value factors for 3 periods.

	2¼%	2⅜%	2½%	2⅝%	2¾%	3%
Single sum	.93543	.93201	.92859	.92521	.92184	.91514
Ordinary annuity of 1	2.86989	2.86295	2.85602	2.84913	2.84226	2.82861

Instructions

(a) Compute the new effective-interest rate for Crocker Corp. following restructure. (*Hint:* Find the interest rate that establishes approximately $363,000 as the present value of the total future cash flows.)

(b) Prepare a schedule of debt reduction and interest expense for the years 2014 through 2017.

(c) Compute the gain or loss for D. Yaeger Corp. and prepare a schedule of receivable reduction and interest revenue for the years 2014 through 2017.

(d) Prepare all the necessary journal entries on the books of Crocker Corp. for the years 2014, 2015, and 2016.

(e) Prepare all the necessary journal entries on the books of D. Yaeger Corp. for the years 2014, 2015, and 2016.

PROBLEMS SET B

See the book's companion website, at **www.wiley.com/college/kieso**, for an additional set of problems.

CONCEPTS FOR ANALYSIS

CA14-1 (Bond Theory: Balance Sheet Presentations, Interest Rate, Premium) On January 1, 2014, Nichols Company issued for $1,085,800 its 20-year, 11% bonds that have a maturity value of $1,000,000 and pay interest semiannually on January 1 and July 1. Bond issue costs were not material in amount. Below are three presentations of the long-term liability section of the balance sheet that might be used for these bonds at the issue date.

1. Bonds payable (maturing January 1, 2034)	$1,000,000
Unamortized premium on bonds payable	85,800
Total bond liability	$1,085,800
2. Bonds payable—principal (face value $1,000,000 maturing January 1, 2034)	$ 142,050[a]
Bonds payable—interest (semiannual payment $55,000)	943,750[b]
Total bond liability	$1,085,800
3. Bonds payable—principal (maturing January 1, 2034)	$1,000,000
Bonds payable—interest ($55,000 per period for 40 periods)	2,200,000
Total bond liability	$3,200,000

[a]The present value of $1,000,000 due at the end of 40 (6-month) periods at the yield rate of 5% per period.
[b]The present value of $55,000 per period for 40 (6-month) periods at the yield rate of 5% per period.

Instructions

(a) Discuss the conceptual merit(s) of each of the date-of-issue balance sheet presentations shown above for these bonds.

(b) Explain why investors would pay $1,085,800 for bonds that have a maturity value of only $1,000,000.

(c) Assuming that a discount rate is needed to compute the carrying value of the obligations arising from a bond issue at any date during the life of the bonds, discuss the conceptual merit(s) of using for this purpose:
(1) The coupon or nominal rate.
(2) The effective or yield rate at date of issue.

(d) If the obligations arising from these bonds are to be carried at their present value computed by means of the current market rate of interest, how would the bond valuation at dates subsequent to the date of issue be affected by an increase or a decrease in the market rate of interest?

(AICPA adapted)

CA14-2 (Bond Theory: Price, Presentation, and Redemption) On March 1, 2014, Sealy Company sold its 5-year, $1,000 face value, 9% bonds dated March 1, 2014, at an effective annual interest rate (yield) of 11%. Interest is payable semiannually, and the first interest payment date is September 1, 2014. Sealy uses the effective-interest method of amortization. Bond issue costs were incurred in preparing and selling the bond issue. The bonds can be called by Sealy at 101 at any time on or after March 1, 2015.

Instructions

(a) (1) How would the selling price of the bond be determined?
(2) Specify how all items related to the bonds would be presented in a balance sheet prepared immediately after the bond issue was sold.

(b) What items related to the bond issue would be included in Sealy's 2014 income statement, and how would each be determined?

(c) Would the amount of bond discount amortization using the effective-interest method of amortization be lower in the second or third year of the life of the bond issue? Why?

(d) Assuming that the bonds were called in and redeemed on March 1, 2015, how should Sealy report the redemption of the bonds on the 2015 income statement?

(AICPA adapted)

CA14-3 (Bond Theory: Amortization and Gain or Loss Recognition)

Part I: The appropriate method of amortizing a premium or discount on issuance of bonds is the effective-interest method.

Instructions

(a) What is the effective-interest method of amortization and how is it different from and similar to the straight-line method of amortization?

(b) How is amortization computed using the effective-interest method, and why and how do amounts obtained using the effective-interest method differ from amounts computed under the straight-line method?

Part II: Gains or losses from the early extinguishment of debt that is refunded can theoretically be accounted for in three ways:

1. Amortized over remaining life of old debt.
2. Amortized over the life of the new debt issue.
3. Recognized in the period of extinguishment.

Instructions

(a) Develop supporting arguments for each of the three theoretical methods of accounting for gains and losses from the early extinguishment of debt.

(b) Which of the methods above is generally accepted and how should the appropriate amount of gain or loss be shown in a company's financial statements?

(AICPA adapted)

CA14-4 (Off-Balance-Sheet Financing) Matt Ryan Corporation is interested in building its own soda can manufacturing plant adjacent to its existing plant in Partyville, Kansas. The objective would be to ensure a steady supply of cans at a stable price and to minimize transportation costs. However, the company has been experiencing some financial problems and has been reluctant to borrow any additional cash to fund the project. The company is not concerned with the cash flow problems of making payments, but rather with the impact of adding additional long-term debt to its balance sheet.

The president of Ryan, Andy Newlin, approached the president of the Aluminum Can Company (ACC), its major supplier, to see if some agreement could be reached. ACC was anxious to work out an arrangement, since it seemed inevitable that Ryan would begin its own can production. The Aluminum Can Company could not afford to lose the account.

After some discussion, a two-part plan was worked out. First, ACC was to construct the plant on Ryan's land adjacent to the existing plant. Second, Ryan would sign a 20-year purchase agreement. Under the purchase agreement, Ryan would express its intention to buy all of its cans from ACC, paying a unit price which at normal capacity would cover labor and material, an operating management fee, and the debt service requirements on the plant. The expected unit price, if transportation costs are taken into consideration, is lower than current market. If Ryan did not take enough production in any one year and if the excess cans could not be sold at a high enough price on the open market, Ryan agrees to make up any cash shortfall so that ACC could make the payments on its debt. The bank will be willing to make a 20-year loan for the plant, taking the plant and the purchase agreement as collateral. At the end of 20 years, the plant is to become the property of Ryan.

Instructions

(a) What are project financing arrangements using special-purpose entities?
(b) What are take-or-pay contracts?
(c) Should Ryan record the plant as an asset together with the related obligation?
(d) If not, should Ryan record an asset relating to the future commitment?
(e) What is meant by off-balance-sheet financing?

CA14-5 (Bond Issue) Donald Lennon is the president, founder, and majority owner of Wichita Medical Corporation, an emerging medical technology products company. Wichita is in dire need of additional capital to keep operating and to bring several promising products to final development, testing, and production. Donald, as owner of 51% of the outstanding stock, manages the company's operations. He places heavy emphasis on research and development and long-term growth. The other principal stockholder is Nina Friendly who, as a nonemployee investor, owns 40% of the stock. Nina would like to deemphasize the R & D functions and emphasize the marketing function to maximize short-run sales and profits from existing products. She believes this strategy would raise the market price of Wichita's stock.

All of Donald's personal capital and borrowing power is tied up in his 51% stock ownership. He knows that any offering of additional shares of stock will dilute his controlling interest because he won't be able to participate in such an issuance. But, Nina has money and would likely buy enough shares to gain control of Wichita. She then would dictate the company's future direction, even if it meant replacing Donald as president and CEO.

The company already has considerable debt. Raising additional debt will be costly, will adversely affect Wichita's credit rating, and will increase the company's reported losses due to the growth in interest expense. Nina and the other minority stockholders express opposition to the assumption of additional debt, fearing the company will be pushed to the brink of bankruptcy. Wanting to maintain his control and to preserve the direction of "his" company, Donald is doing everything to avoid a stock issuance and is contemplating a large issuance of bonds, even if it means the bonds are issued with a high effective-interest rate.

Instructions

(a) Who are the stakeholders in this situation?
(b) What are the ethical issues in this case?
(c) What would you do if you were Donald?

USING YOUR JUDGMENT

FINANCIAL REPORTING

Financial Reporting Problem

P&G

The Procter & Gamble Company (P&G)

The financial statements of P&G are presented in Appendix 5B. The company's complete annual report, including the notes to the financial statements, can be accessed at the book's companion website, **www.wiley.com/college/kieso**.

Instructions

Refer to P&G's 2011 financial statements and the accompanying notes to answer the following questions.

(a) What cash outflow obligations related to the repayment of long-term debt does P&G have over the next 5 years?

(b) P&G indicates that it believes that it has the ability to meet business requirements in the foreseeable future. Prepare an assessment of its liquidity, solvency, and financial flexibility using ratio analysis.

Comparative Analysis Case

The Coca-Cola Company and PepsiCo, Inc.

Instructions

Go to the book's companion website and use information found there to answer the following questions related to The Coca-Cola Company and PepsiCo, Inc.

(a) Compute the debt to assets and the times interest earned ratios for these two companies. Comment on the quality of these two ratios for both Coca-Cola and PepsiCo.

(b) What is the difference between the fair value and the historical cost (carrying amount) of each company's debt at year-end 2011? Why might a difference exist in these two amounts?

(c) Both companies have debt issued in foreign countries. Speculate as to why these companies may use foreign debt to finance their operations. What risks are involved in this strategy, and how might they adjust for this risk?

Financial Statement Analysis Case

Commonwealth Edison Co.

The following article appeared in the *Wall Street Journal.*

Bond Markets

Giant Commonwealth Edison Issue Hits Resale Market With $70 Million Left Over

NEW YORK—Commonwealth Edison Co.'s slow-selling new 9¼% bonds were tossed onto the resale market at a reduced price with about $70 million still available from the $200 million offered Thursday, dealers said.

The Chicago utility's bonds, rated double-A by Moody's and double-A-minus by Standard & Poor's, originally had been priced at 99.803, to yield 9.3% in 5 years. They were marked down yesterday the equivalent of about $5.50 for each $1,000 face amount, to about 99.25, where their yield jumped to 9.45%.

Instructions

(a) How will the development above affect the accounting for Commonwealth Edison's bond issue?

(b) Provide several possible explanations for the markdown and the slow sale of Commonwealth Edison's bonds.

Accounting, Analysis, and Principles

The following information is taken from the 2014 annual report of Bugant, Inc. Bugant's fiscal year ends December 31 of each year. Bugant's December 31, 2014, balance sheet is as follows.

Bugant, Inc.
Balance Sheet
December 31, 2014

Assets	
Cash	$ 450
Inventory	1,800
Total current assets	2,250
Plant and equipment	2,000
Accumulated depreciation	(160)
Total assets	$4,090
Liabilities	
Bonds payable (net of discount)	$1,426
Stockholders' equity	
Common stock	1,500
Retained earnings	1,164
Total liabilities and stockholders' equity	$4,090

Note X: Long Term Debt:
On January 1, 2015, Bugant issued bonds with face value of $1,500 and a coupon rate equal to 10%. The bonds were issued to yield 12% and mature on January 1, 2020.

Additional information concerning 2015 is as follows.

1. Sales were $3,500, all for cash.
2. Purchases were $2,000, all paid in cash.
3. Salaries were $700, all paid in cash.
4. Property, plant, and equipment was originally purchased for $2,000 and is depreciated straight-line over a 25-year life with no salvage value.
5. Ending inventory was $1,900.
6. Cash dividends of $100 were declared and paid by Bugant.
7. Ignore taxes.
8. The market rate of interest on bonds of similar risk was 12% during all of 2015.
9. Interest on the bonds is paid semiannually each June 30 and December 31.

Accounting

Prepare a balance sheet for Bugant, Inc. at December 31, 2015, and an income statement for the year ending December 31, 2015. Assume semiannual compounding of the bond interest.

Analysis

Use common ratios for analysis of long-term debt to assess Bugant's long-run solvency. Has Bugant's solvency changed much from 2014 to 2015? Bugant's net income in 2014 was $550 and interest expense was $169.

Principles

Recently, the FASB and the IASB allowed companies the option of recognizing in their financial statements the fair values of their long-term debt. That is, companies have the option to change the balance sheet value of their long-term debt to the debt's fair value and report the change in balance sheet value as a gain or loss in income. In terms of the qualitative characteristics of accounting information (Chapter 2), briefly describe the potential trade-off(s) involved in reporting long-term debt at its fair value.

BRIDGE TO THE PROFESSION

Professional Research: FASB Codification

Wie Company has been operating for just 2 years, producing specialty golf equipment for women golfers. To date, the company has been able to finance its successful operations with investments from its principal owner, Michelle Wie, and cash flows from operations. However, current expansion plans will require some borrowing to expand the company's production line.

As part of the expansion plan, Wie will acquire some used equipment by signing a zero-interest-bearing note. The note has a maturity value of $50,000 and matures in 5 years. A reliable fair value measure for the equipment is not available, given the age and specialty nature of the equipment. As a result, Wie's accounting staff is unable to determine an established exchange price for recording the equipment (nor the interest rate to be used to record interest expense on the long-term note). They have asked you to conduct some accounting research on this topic.

Instructions

If your school has a subscription to the FASB Codification, go to *http://aaahq.org/ascLogin.cfm* to log in and prepare responses to the following. Provide Codification references for your responses.

(a) Identify the authoritative literature that provides guidance on the zero-interest-bearing note. Use some of the examples to explain how the standard applies in this setting.

(b) How is present value determined when an established exchange price is not determinable and a note has no ready market? What is the resulting interest rate often called?

(c) Where should a discount or premium appear in the financial statements? What about issue costs?

Additional Professional Resources

See the book's companion website, at **www.wiley.com/college/kieso**, for professional simulations as well as other study resources.

IFRS INSIGHTS

As indicated in Chapter 13, IFRS and GAAP have similar definitions of liabilities.

11 LEARNING OBJECTIVE
Compare the accounting procedures for long-term liabilities under GAAP and IFRS.

RELEVANT FACTS

Following are the key similarities and differences between GAAP and IFRS related to long-term liabilities.

Similarities

- As indicated in our earlier discussions, GAAP and IFRS have similar liability definitions, and liabilities are classified as current and non-current.
- Much of the accounting for bonds and long-term notes is the same for GAAP and IFRS.

Differences

- Under GAAP, companies are permitted to use the straight-line method of amortization for bond discount or premium, provided that the amount recorded is not materially different than that resulting from effective-interest amortization. However, the effective-interest method is preferred and is generally used. Under IFRS, companies must use the effective-interest method.
- Under IFRS, companies do not use premium or discount accounts but instead show the bond at its net amount. For example, if a $100,000 bond was issued at 97, under IFRS a company would record:

Cash	97,000	
Bonds Payable		97,000

- Under GAAP, bond issue costs are recorded as an asset. Under IFRS, bond issue costs are netted against the carrying amount of the bonds.
- GAAP uses the term *troubled-debt restructurings* and has developed specific guidelines related to that category of loans. IFRS generally assumes that all restructurings will be accounted for as extinguishments of debt.
- IFRS requires a liability and related expense or cost be recognized when a contract is onerous. Under GAAP, losses on onerous contracts are generally not recognized under GAAP unless addressed by industry or transaction-specific requirements.

ABOUT THE NUMBERS

Effective-Interest Method

As discussed earlier, by paying more or less at issuance, investors earn a rate different than the coupon rate on the bond. Recall that the issuing company pays the contractual interest rate over the term of the bonds but also must pay the face value at maturity. If the bond is issued at a discount, the amount paid at maturity is more than the issue amount. If issued at a premium, the company pays less at maturity relative to the issue price.

The company records this adjustment to the cost as **bond interest expense** over the life of the bonds through a process called **amortization. Amortization of a discount increases bond interest expense. Amortization of a premium decreases bond interest expense.**

Under IFRS, the required procedure for amortization of a discount or premium is the **effective-interest method** (also called **present value amortization**). Under the effective-interest method, companies:

1. Compute bond interest expense first by multiplying the **carrying value** (book value) of the bonds at the beginning of the period by the effective-interest rate.
2. Determine the bond discount or premium amortization next by comparing the bond interest expense with the interest (cash) to be paid.

Illustration IFRS14-1 depicts graphically the computation of the amortization.

ILLUSTRATION IFRS14-1
Bond Discount and Premium Amortization Computation

Bond Interest Expense		Bond Interest Paid		
Carrying Value of Bonds at Beginning of Period × Effective-Interest Rate	−	Face Amount of Bonds × Stated Interest Rate	=	Amortization Amount

The effective-interest method produces a periodic interest expense equal to **a constant percentage of the carrying value of the bonds**. The issuance of bonds involves engraving and printing costs, legal and accounting fees, commissions, promotion costs, and other similar charges. These costs should be recorded as a reduction to the issue amount of the bond payable and then amortized into expense over the life of the bond, through an adjustment to the effective-interest rate. For example, if the face value of the bond is $100,000 and issue costs are $1,000, then the bond payable (net of the bond issue costs) is recorded at $99,000. Thus, the effective-interest rate will be higher, based on the reduced carrying value.

Bonds Issued at a Discount

To illustrate amortization of a discount under the effective-interest method, Evermaster Corporation issued $100,000 of 8 percent term bonds on January 1, 2014, due on January 1, 2019, with interest payable each July 1 and January 1. Because the investors required an effective-interest rate of 10 percent, they paid $92,278 for the $100,000 of bonds, creating a $7,722 discount. Evermaster computes the $7,722 discount as follows.

ILLUSTRATION IFRS14-2
Computation of Discount on Bonds Payable

Maturity value of bonds payable		$100,000
Present value of $100,000 due in 5 years at 10%, interest payable semiannually (Table 6-2); $FV(PVF_{10,5\%})$; ($100,000 × .61391)	$61,391	
Present value of $4,000 interest payable semiannually for 5 years at 10% annually (Table 6-4); $R(PVF\text{-}OA_{10,5\%})$; ($4,000 × 7.72173)	30,887	
Proceeds from sale of bonds		(92,278)
Discount on bonds payable		$ 7,722

The five-year amortization schedule appears in Illustration IFRS14-3.

Evermaster records the issuance of its bonds at a discount on January 1, 2014, as follows.

Cash	92,278	
Bonds Payable		92,278

It records the first interest payment on July 1, 2014, and amortization of the discount as follows.

Interest Expense	4,614	
Bonds Payable		614
Cash		4,000

ILLUSTRATION IFRS14-3
Bond Discount Amortization Schedule

SCHEDULE OF BOND DISCOUNT AMORTIZATION
EFFECTIVE-INTEREST METHOD—SEMIANNUAL INTEREST PAYMENTS
5-YEAR, 8% BONDS SOLD TO YIELD 10%

Date	Cash Paid	Interest Expense	Discount Amortized	Carrying Amount of Bonds
1/1/14				$ 92,278
7/1/14	$ 4,000[a]	$ 4,614[b]	$ 614[c]	92,892[d]
1/1/15	4,000	4,645	645	93,537
7/1/15	4,000	4,677	677	94,214
1/1/16	4,000	4,711	711	94,925
7/1/16	4,000	4,746	746	95,671
1/1/17	4,000	4,783	783	96,454
7/1/17	4,000	4,823	823	97,277
1/1/18	4,000	4,864	864	98,141
7/1/18	4,000	4,907	907	99,048
1/1/19	4,000	4,952	952	100,000
	$40,000	$47,722	$7,722	

[a]$4,000 = $100,000 × .08 × 6/12
[b]$4,614 = $92,278 × .10 × 6/12
[c]$614 = $4,614 − $4,000
[d]$92,892 = $92,278 + $614

Evermaster records the interest expense accrued at December 31, 2014 (year-end), and amortization of the discount as follows.

Interest Expense	4,645	
Interest Payable		4,000
Bonds Payable		645

Extinguishment with Modification of Terms

Practically every day, the *Wall Street Journal* or the *Financial Times* runs a story about some company in financial difficulty. Notable recent examples are **Nakheel**, **Parmalat**, and **General Motors**. In many of these situations, the creditor may grant a borrower concessions with respect to settlement. The creditor offers these concessions to ensure the highest possible collection on the loan. For example, a creditor may offer one or a combination of the following modifications:

1. Reduction of the stated interest rate.
2. Extension of the maturity date of the face amount of the debt.
3. Reduction of the face amount of the debt.
4. Reduction or deferral of any accrued interest.

As with other extinguishments, when a creditor grants favorable concessions on the terms of a loan, the debtor has an economic gain. Thus, the accounting for debt modifications is similar to that for other extinguishments. That is, the original obligation is extinguished, the new payable is recorded at fair value, and a gain is recognized for the difference in the fair value of the new obligation and the carrying value of the old obligation. Thus, under IFRS, debt modifications are similar to troubled-debt restructurings in GAAP. In general, IFRS treats debt modifications as debt extinguishments.

An exception to the general rule is when the modification of terms is not substantial. A substantial modification is defined as one in which the discounted cash flows under the terms of the new debt (using the historical effective-interest rate) differ by at least 10 percent of the carrying value of the original debt. If a modification is not substantial, the difference (gain) is deferred and amortized over the remaining life of the debt at the historical effective-interest rate. In the case of a non-substantial modification, in essence, the new loan is a continuation of the old loan. Therefore, the debtor should record interest at the historical effective-interest rate.

ON THE HORIZON

The FASB and IASB are currently involved in two projects, each of which has implications for the accounting for liabilities. One project is investigating approaches to differentiate between debt and equity instruments. The other project, the elements phase of the conceptual framework project, will evaluate the definitions of the fundamental building blocks of accounting. The results of these projects could change the classification of many debt and equity securities.

IFRS SELF-TEST QUESTIONS

1. Under IFRS, bond issuance costs, including the printing costs and legal fees associated with the issuance, should be:
   - **(a)** expensed in the period when the debt is issued.
   - **(b)** recorded as a reduction in the carrying value of bonds payable.
   - **(c)** accumulated in a deferred charge account and amortized over the life of the bonds.
   - **(d)** reported as an expense in the period the bonds mature or are redeemed.
2. Which of the following is stated correctly?
   - **(a)** Current liabilities follow non-current liabilities on the statement of financial position under GAAP but non-current liabilities follow current liabilities under IFRS.
   - **(b)** IFRS does not treat debt modifications as extinguishments of debt.
   - **(c)** Bond issuance costs are recorded as a reduction of the carrying value of the debt under GAAP but are recorded as an asset and amortized to expense over the term of the debt under IFRS.
   - **(d)** Under GAAP, bonds payable is recorded at the face amount and any premium or discount is recorded in a separate account. Under IFRS, bonds payable is recorded at the carrying value so no separate premium or discount accounts are used.
3. All of the following are differences between IFRS and GAAP in accounting for liabilities **except:**
   - **(a)** When a bond is issued at a discount, GAAP records the discount in a separate contra liability account. IFRS records the bond net of the discount.
   - **(b)** Under IFRS, bond issuance costs reduce the carrying value of the debt. Under GAAP, these costs are recorded as an asset and amortized to expense over the terms of the bond.
   - **(c)** GAAP, but not IFRS, uses the term "troubled-debt restructurings."
   - **(d)** GAAP, but not IFRS, uses the term "provisions" for contingent liabilities which are accrued.
4. On January 1, Patterson Inc. issued $5,000,000, 9% bonds for $4,695,000. The market rate of interest for these bonds is 10%. Interest is payable annually on December 31. Patterson uses the effective-interest method of amortizing bond discount. At the end of the first year, Patterson should report bonds payable of:
   - **(a)** $4,725,500.
   - **(b)** $4,714,500.
   - **(c)** $258,050.
   - **(d)** $4,745,000.
5. On January 1, Martinez Inc. issued $3,000,000, 11% bonds for $3,195,000. The market rate of interest for these bonds is 10%. Interest is payable annually on December 31. Martinez uses the effective-interest method of amortizing bond premium. At the end of the first year, Martinez should report bonds payable of:
   - **(a)** $3,185,130.
   - **(b)** $3,184,500.
   - **(c)** $3,173,550.
   - **(d)** $3,165,000.

IFRS CONCEPTS AND APPLICATION

IFRS14-1 What is the required method of amortizing discount and premium on bonds payable? Explain the procedures.

IFRS14-2 What are the general rules for measuring and recognizing gain or loss by a debt extinguishment with modification?

IFRS14-3 On January 1, 2014, JWS Corporation issued $600,000 of 7% bonds, due in 10 years. The bonds were issued for $559,224, and pay interest each July 1 and January 1. Prepare the company's journal entries for (a) the January 1 issuance, (b) the July 1 interest payment, and (c) the December 31 adjusting entry. Assume an effective-interest rate of 8%.

IFRS14-4 Assume the bonds in IFRS14-3 were issued for $644,636 and the effective-interest rate is 6%. Prepare the company's journal entries for (a) the January 1 issuance, (b) the July 1 interest payment, and (c) the December 31 adjusting entry. (Round to the nearest dollar.)

IFRS14-5 Foreman Company issued $800,000 of 10%, 20-year bonds on January 1, 2014, at 119.792 to yield 8%. Interest is payable semiannually on July 1 and January 1. Prepare the journal entries to record (a) the issuance of the bonds, (b) the payment of interest and the related amortization on July 1, 2014, and (c) the accrual of interest and the related amortization on December 31, 2014. (Round to the nearest dollar.)

IFRS14-6 Assume the same information as in IFRS14-5, except that the bonds were issued at 84.95 to yield 12%. Prepare the journal entries to record (a) the issuance of the bonds, (b) the payment of interest and related amortization on July 1, 2014, and (c) the accrual of interest and the related amortization on December 31, 2014. (Round to the nearest dollar.)

Professional Research

IFRS14-7 Wie Company has been operating for just 2 years, producing specialty golf equipment for women golfers. To date, the company has been able to finance its successful operations with investments from its principal owner, Michelle Wie, and cash flows from operations. However, current expansion plans will require some borrowing to expand the company's production line.

As part of the expansion plan, Wie is contemplating a borrowing on a note payable or issuance of bonds. In the past, the company has had little need for external borrowing so the management team has a number of questions concerning the accounting for these new non-current liabilities. They have asked you to conduct some research on this topic.

Instructions

Access the IFRS authoritative literature at the IASB website (*http://eifrs.iasb.org/*). (Click on the IFRS tab and then register for free eIFRS access if necessary.) When you have accessed the documents, you can use the search tool in your Internet browser to respond to the following questions. (Provide paragraph citations.)

(a) With respect to a decision of issuing notes or bonds, management is aware of certain costs (e.g., printing, marketing, selling) associated with a bond issue. How will these costs affect Wie's reported earnings in the year of issue and while the bonds are outstanding?

(b) If all goes well with the plant expansion, the financial performance of Wie Company could dramatically improve. As a result, Wie's market rate of interest (which is currently around 12%) could decline. This raises the possibility of retiring or exchanging the debt, in order to get a lower borrowing rate. How would such a debt extinguishment be accounted for?

International Financial Reporting Problem
Marks and Spencer plc

IFRS14-8 The financial statements of **Marks and Spencer plc (M&S)** are available at the book's companion website or can be accessed at *http://annualreport.marksandspencer.com/_assets/downloads/Marks-and-Spencer-Annual-report-and-financial-statements-2012.pdf.*

Instructions

Refer to M&S's financial statements and the accompanying notes to answer the following questions.

(a) What cash outflow obligations related to the repayment of long-term debt does M&S have over the next 5 years?

(b) M&S indicates that it believes that it has the ability to meet business requirements in the foreseeable future. Prepare an assessment of its liquidity, solvency, and financial flexibility using ratio analysis.

ANSWERS TO IFRS SELF-TEST QUESTIONS

1. b **2.** d **3.** d **4.** b **5.** b

Remember to check the book's companion website to find additional resources for this chapter.

CHAPTER

15 Stockholders' Equity

LEARNING OBJECTIVES

After studying this chapter, you should be able to:

1. Discuss the characteristics of the corporate form of organization.
2. Identify the key components of stockholders' equity.
3. Explain the accounting procedures for issuing shares of stock.
4. Describe the accounting for treasury stock.
5. Explain the accounting for and reporting of preferred stock.
6. Describe the policies used in distributing dividends.
7. Identify the various forms of dividend distributions.
8. Explain the accounting for small and large stock dividends, and for stock splits.
9. Indicate how to present and analyze stockholders' equity.

It's a Global Market

As mentioned in prior chapters, we are moving rapidly toward one set of global financial reporting standards and one "common language" for financial information. This change will probably lead to more consolidation of our capital markets. To understand how quickly the global financial world is changing, let's examine a few trends occurring on stock exchanges around the world.

In 2007, the New York Stock Exchange (NYSE) merged with Paris-based Euronext, creating the world's first transatlantic stock exchange. **NYSE Euronext** is the world's largest exchange group, now with 8,000 listed issuers representing over 40 percent of global equity trading in 2010. Similarly, NASDAQ, the world's largest electronic stock market, merged with OMX, the Nordic stock market operator. This electronic exchange operates in 29 countries, on six continents, and has over 4,000 listed issuers, with a market value of approximately $5.5 trillion. (Further exchange consolidation may be in the offing, with **IntercontinentalExchange** and international exchanges in Asia exploring mergers with NYSE Euronext.)

Another reason behind the movement to international financial reporting standards can be found in recent initial public offerings (IPOs). The emerging markets are driving the global IPO market. As shown in the following table, Greater China is at the top in IPO volume, with Poland, Korea, and India also in the top 10.

2011 Global IPOs by Domicile Country—Top 10 by Number of Deals

Country	Number of Deals	% of Global Total
Greater China*	388	31.70%
Poland	137	11.20
United States	108	8.80
Australia	98	8.00
South Korea	69	5.60
Canada	64	5.20
India	40	3.30
Japan	37	3.00
United Kingdom	28	2.30
Indonesia	26	2.10
Rest of world** (52 countries)	230	18.80
Total	1,225	100.00%

Source: Based on the listed company domicile.
*Includes Mainland China, Hong Kong, and Taiwan.
**Includes countries with 1% or less of IPO activity by number of deals or capital raised.

CONCEPTUAL FOCUS

> See the **Underlying Concepts** on pages 830 and 842.

INTERNATIONAL FOCUS

> See the **International Perspectives** on pages 823 and 824.

> Read the **IFRS Insights** on pages 874–880 for a discussion of:
—Equity
—Accounting for preference shares
—Presentation of equity

Finally, globalization has also been an enormous boon for some of the biggest names in corporate America, along with investors who own the stocks in those companies. As shown in the following table, these 10 large U.S. companies—often called "multinationals" for good reason—have increasingly followed globalization of markets.

Company	Total Revenues	% of Revenues Overseas
Intel	$ 44	85
Dow	54	67
McDonald's	24	66
IBM	100	64
General Electric	149	54
Ford	129	51
Nike	21	50
Wal-Mart	420	45
ExxonMobil	342	45
Amazon.com	34	45

As indicated, **Intel** has 85 percent of its sales overseas, **McDonald's** in a recent year sold more hamburgers overseas than in the United States, and **Ford Motor Company**'s sales would be much less except for success in the European market. Overall, about 40 percent of profit for firms listed in the S&P 500 stock index are now coming in from overseas sales. Foreign exposure allows U.S.-based companies to capitalize on rapid growth in emerging markets like China, India, and Latin America, and earn much stronger profits than if they were totally dependent on the struggling U.S. economy. As one analyst noted, "[Returns for companies] . . . in the S&P 500 continue to outgrow the U.S. economy. Earnings power is decoupled from U.S. GDP."

Sources: Ernst and Young, *Growth During Economic Uncertainty: Global IPO Trends Report* (2012); *www. euronext.com;* and R. Newman, "Why U.S. Companies Aren't So American Anymore," *http://money.usnews.com* (June 30, 2011).

PREVIEW OF CHAPTER 15

As our opening story indicates, the growth of global equity capital markets indicates that investors around the world need useful information. In this chapter, we explain the accounting issues related to the stockholders' equity of a corporation. The content and organization of the chapter are as follows.

Stockholders' Equity

The Corporate Form
- State corporate law
- Capital stock or share system
- Variety of ownership interests

Corporate Capital
- Issuance of stock
- Reacquisition of shares

Preferred Stock
- Features
- Accounting for and reporting preferred stock

Dividend Policy
- Financial condition and dividend distributions
- Types of dividends
- Stock dividends and stock splits
- Disclosure of restrictions

Presentation and Analysis
- Presentation
- Analysis

THE CORPORATE FORM OF ORGANIZATION

LEARNING OBJECTIVE 1
Discuss the characteristics of the corporate form of organization.

Of the three **primary forms of business organization**—the proprietorship, the partnership, and the corporation—the corporate form dominates. The corporation is by far the leader in terms of the aggregate amount of resources controlled, goods and services produced, and people employed. All of the "Fortune 500" largest industrial firms are corporations. Although the corporate form has a number of advantages (as well as disadvantages) over the other two forms, its principal advantage is its facility for attracting and accumulating large amounts of capital.

The special characteristics of the corporate form that affect accounting include:

1. Influence of state corporate law.
2. Use of the capital stock or share system.
3. Development of a variety of ownership interests.

State Corporate Law

Anyone who wishes to establish a corporation must submit **articles of incorporation** to the state in which incorporation is desired. After fulfilling requirements, the state issues a corporation charter, thereby recognizing the company as a legal entity subject to state law. Regardless of the number of states in which a corporation has operating divisions, it is incorporated in only one state.

It is to the company's advantage to incorporate in a state whose laws favor the corporate form of business organization. For example, consider that nearly half of all public corporations in the United States are incorporated in Delaware. Why Delaware? The state has a favorable tax and regulatory environment, resulting in Delaware being home to more corporations—public and private—than people.[1]

Each state has its own business incorporation act. The accounting for stockholders' equity follows the provisions of these acts. In many cases, states have adopted the principles contained in the Model Business Corporate Act prepared by the American Bar Association. State laws are complex and vary both in their provisions and in their definitions of certain terms. Some laws fail to define technical terms. As a result, terms often mean one thing in one state and another thing in a different state. These problems may be further compounded because legal authorities often interpret the effects and restrictions of the laws differently.

What do the numbers mean? 1209 NORTH ORANGE STREET

Nothing about 1209 North Orange Street hints at the secrets inside. It's a humdrum office building, a low-slung affair with a faded awning and a view of a parking garage. Hardly worth a second glance, if even a first one. But behind its doors is one of the most remarkable corporate collections in the world: 1209 North Orange, you see, is the legal address of no fewer than 285,000 separate businesses.

Its occupants, on paper, include giants like **American Airlines**, **Apple**, **Bank of America**, **Berkshire Hathaway**, **Cargill**, **Coca-Cola**, **Ford**, **General Electric**, **Google**, **JPMorgan Chase**, and **Wal-Mart**. These companies do business across the nation and around the world. Here at 1209 North Orange, they simply have a dropbox.

What brings these marquee names to 1209 North Orange, and to other Delaware addresses, also attracts less-upstanding corporate citizens. For instance, 1209 North Orange was, until recently, a business address of Timothy S. Durham, known as "the Midwest Madoff." On June 20, Durham was found guilty of bilking 5,000 mostly middle-class and elderly investors out of $207 million. It was also an address of Stanko Subotic, a Serbian businessman and convicted smuggler—just one of many Eastern Europeans drawn to the state.

Big corporations, small-time businesses, rogues, scoundrels, and worse—all have turned up at Delaware addresses in hopes of minimizing taxes, skirting regulations, plying friendly courts, or, when needed, covering their tracks.

[1]L. Wayne, "How Delaware Thrives as a Corporate Tax Haven," *The New York Times* (June 30, 2012).

Federal authorities worry that, in addition to the legitimate businesses flocking here, drug-traffickers, embezzlers, and money-launderers are increasingly heading to Delaware, too. It's easy to set up shell companies here, no questions asked.

Of course, business—the legal kind—has been the mainstay of Delaware since 1792, when the state established its Court of Chancery to handle business affairs. By the early 20th century, the state was writing friendly corporate and tax laws to lure companies from New York, New Jersey, and elsewhere. Today, Delaware regularly tops lists of domestic and foreign tax havens because it allows companies to lower their taxes in another state—for instance, the state in which they actually do business or have their headquarters—by shifting royalties and similar revenues to holding companies in Delaware, where they are not taxed. In tax circles, the arrangement is known as "the Delaware loophole." Over the last decade, the Delaware loophole has enabled corporations to reduce the taxes paid to other states by an estimated $9.5 billion.

Source: L. Wayne, "How Delaware Thrives as a Corporate Tax Haven," *The New York Times* (June 30, 2012).

Capital Stock or Share System

Stockholders' equity in a corporation generally consists of a large number of units or shares. Within a given class of stock, each share exactly equals every other share. The number of shares possessed determines each owner's interest. If a company has one class of stock divided into 1,000 shares, a person who owns 500 shares controls one-half of the ownership interest. One holding 10 shares has a one-hundredth interest.

Each share of stock has certain rights and privileges. Only by special contract can a company restrict these rights and privileges at the time it issues the shares. Owners must examine the articles of incorporation, stock certificates, and the provisions of the state law to ascertain such restrictions on or variations from the standard rights and privileges. In the absence of restrictive provisions, each share carries the following rights:

International Perspective

In the United States, stockholders are treated equally as far as access to financial information. That is not always the case in other countries. For example, in Mexico, foreign investors as well as minority investors often have difficulty obtaining financial data. These restrictions are rooted in the habits of companies that, for many years, were tightly controlled by a few stockholders and managers.

1. To share proportionately in profits and losses.
2. To share proportionately in management (the right to vote for directors).
3. To share proportionately in corporate assets upon liquidation.
4. To share proportionately in any new issues of stock of the same class—called the **preemptive right**.[2]

The first three rights are self-explanatory. The last right is used to protect each stockholder's proportional interest in the company. **The preemptive right protects an existing stockholder from involuntary dilution of ownership interest.** Without this right, stockholders might find their interest reduced by the issuance of additional stock without their knowledge and at prices unfavorable to them. However, many corporations have eliminated the preemptive right. Why? Because this right makes it inconvenient for corporations to issue large amounts of additional stock, as they frequently do in acquiring other companies.

The share system easily allows one individual to transfer an interest in a company to another investor. For example, individuals owning shares in Google **may sell them to others at any time and at any price without obtaining the consent of the company or other stockholders.** Each share is personal property of the owner, who may dispose of it at will. Google simply maintains a list or subsidiary ledger of stockholders as a guide to dividend payments, issuance of stock rights, voting proxies, and the like. Because owners freely and frequently transfer shares, Google must revise the subsidiary

[2]This privilege is referred to as a **stock right** or **warrant**. The warrants issued in these situations are of short duration, unlike the warrants issued with other securities.

ledger of stockholders periodically, generally in advance of every dividend payment or stockholders' meeting.

In addition, the major stock exchanges require ownership controls that the typical corporation finds uneconomic to provide. Thus, corporations often use **registrars and transfer agents** who specialize in providing services for recording and transferring stock. The Uniform Stock Transfer Act and the Uniform Commercial Code govern the negotiability of stock certificates.

Variety of Ownership Interests

In every corporation, one class of stock must represent the basic ownership interest. That class is called common stock. **Common stock** is the residual corporate interest that bears the ultimate risks of loss and receives the benefits of success. Common stockholders are not guaranteed dividends or assets upon dissolution. But common stockholders generally control the management of the corporation and tend to profit most if the company is successful. In the event that a corporation has only one authorized issue of capital stock, that issue is by definition common stock, whether so designated in the charter or not.

International Perspective

The U.S. and British systems of corporate governance and finance depend to a large extent on equity financing and the widely dispersed ownership of shares traded in highly liquid markets. The German and Japanese systems have relied more on debt financing, interlocking stock ownership, and banker/director and worker/shareholder rights.

In an effort to broaden investor appeal, corporations may offer two or more classes of stock, each with different rights or privileges. As indicated in the preceding section, each share of stock of a given issue has the same four inherent rights as other shares of the same issue. By special stock contracts between the corporation and its stockholders, however, the stockholder may sacrifice certain of these rights in return for other special rights or privileges. Thus, special classes of stock, usually called **preferred stock**, are created. In return for any special preference, the preferred stockholder always sacrifices some of the inherent rights of common stock ownership.

A common type of preference is to give the preferred stockholders a prior claim on earnings. The corporation thus assures them a dividend, usually at a stated rate, before it distributes any amount to the common stockholders. In return for this preference, the preferred stockholders may sacrifice their right to a voice in management or their right to share in profits beyond the stated rate.

CORPORATE CAPITAL

LEARNING OBJECTIVE 2
Identify the key components of stockholders' equity.

Owners' equity in a corporation is defined as stockholders' equity, shareholders' equity, or corporate capital. The following three categories normally appear as part of stockholders' equity:

1. Capital stock.
2. Additional paid-in capital.
3. Retained earnings.

The first two categories, capital stock and additional paid-in capital, constitute contributed (paid-in) capital. **Retained earnings** represents the earned capital of the company. **Contributed (paid-in) capital** is the total amount paid in on capital stock—the amount provided by stockholders to the corporation for use in the business. Contributed capital includes items such as the par value of all outstanding stock and premiums less discounts on issuance. **Earned capital** is the capital that develops from profitable operations. It consists of all undistributed income that remains invested in the company.

Stockholders' equity is the difference between the assets and the liabilities of the company. That is, the owners' or stockholders' interest in a company like **The Walt Disney Company** is a **residual interest**.[3] **Stockholders' (owners') equity** represents the cumulative net contributions by stockholders plus retained earnings. As a residual interest, stockholders' equity has no existence apart from the assets and liabilities of Disney—stockholders' equity equals net assets. Stockholders' equity is not a claim to specific assets but a claim against a portion of the total assets. Its amount is not specified or fixed; it depends on Disney's profitability. Stockholders' equity grows if the company is profitable. It shrinks, or may disappear entirely, if Disney loses money.

Issuance of Stock

3 LEARNING OBJECTIVE
Explain the accounting procedures for issuing shares of stock.

In issuing stock, companies follow these procedures. First, the state must authorize the stock, generally in a certificate of incorporation or charter. Next, the corporation offers shares for sale, entering into contracts to sell stock. Then, after receiving amounts for the stock, the corporation issues shares. The corporation generally makes no entry in the general ledger accounts when it receives its stock authorization from the state of incorporation.

We discuss the accounting problems involved in the issuance of stock under the following topics.

1. Accounting for par value stock.
2. Accounting for no-par stock.
3. Accounting for stock issued in combination with other securities (lump-sum sales).
4. Accounting for stock issued in noncash transactions.
5. Accounting for costs of issuing stock.

Par Value Stock

The par value of a stock has no relationship to its fair value. At present, the par value associated with most capital stock issuances is very low. For example, **PepsiCo**'s par value is 1⅔¢, **Kellogg**'s is \$0.25, and **Hershey**'s is \$1. Such values contrast dramatically with the situation in the early 1900s, when practically all stock issued had a par value of \$100. Low par values help companies avoid the contingent liability associated with stock sold below par.[4]

To show the required information for issuance of par value stock, corporations maintain accounts for each class of stock as follows.

1. ***Preferred Stock or Common Stock.*** Together, these two stock accounts reflect the par value of the corporation's issued shares. The company credits these accounts when it originally issues the shares. It makes no additional entries in these accounts unless it issues additional shares or retires them.
2. ***Paid-in Capital in Excess of Par (also called Additional Paid-in Capital).*** The **Paid-in Capital in Excess of Par** account indicates any excess over par value paid in by stockholders in return for the shares issued to them. Once paid in, the excess over par becomes a part of the corporation's additional paid-in capital. The individual stockholder has no greater claim on the excess paid in than all other holders of the same class of shares.

[3]"Elements of Financial Statements," *Statement of Financial Accounting Concepts No. 6* (Stamford, Conn.: FASB, 1985), par. 60.

[4]Companies rarely, if ever, issue stock at a value below par value. If issuing stock below par, the company records the discount as a debit to Additional Paid-in Capital. In addition, the corporation may call on the original purchaser or the current holder of the shares issued below par to pay in the amount of the discount to prevent creditors from sustaining a loss upon liquidation of the corporation.

No-Par Stock

Many states permit the issuance of capital stock without par value, called **no-par stock**. The reasons for issuance of no-par stock are twofold. First, issuance of no-par stock **avoids the contingent liability** (see footnote 4) that might occur if the corporation issued par value stock at a discount. Second, some confusion exists over the relationship (or rather the absence of a relationship) between the par value and fair value. If shares have no-par value, **the questionable treatment of using par value as a basis for fair value never arises.** This is particularly advantageous whenever issuing stock for property items such as intangible or tangible fixed assets.

A major disadvantage of no-par stock is that some states levy a high tax on these issues. In addition, in some states the total issue price for no-par stock may be considered legal capital, which could reduce the flexibility in paying dividends.

Corporations sell no-par shares, like par value shares, for whatever price they will bring. However, unlike par value shares, corporations issue them without a premium or a discount. The exact amount received represents the credit to common or preferred stock. For example, Video Electronics Corporation is organized with authorized common stock of 10,000 shares without par value. Video Electronics makes only a memorandum entry for the authorization, inasmuch as no amount is involved. If Video Electronics then issues 500 shares for cash at $10 per share, it makes the following entry.

Cash	5,000	
Common Stock (no-par value)		5,000

If it issues another 500 shares for $11 per share, Video Electronics makes this entry:

Cash	5,500	
Common Stock (no-par value)		5,500

True no-par stock should be carried in the accounts at issue price without any additional paid-in capital or discount reported. But some states require that no-par stock have a **stated value**. The stated value is a minimum value below which a company cannot issue it. Thus, instead of being no-par stock, such stated-value stock becomes, in effect, stock with a very low par value. It thus is open to all the criticism and abuses that first encouraged the development of no-par stock.[5]

If no-par stock has a stated value of $5 per share but sells for $11, all such amounts in excess of $5 are recorded as additional paid-in capital, which in many states is fully or partially available for dividends. Thus, no-par value stock with a low stated value permits a new corporation to commence its operations with additional paid-in capital that may exceed its stated capital. For example, if a company issued 1,000 of the shares with a $5 stated value at $15 per share for cash, it makes the following entry.

Cash	15,000	
Common Stock		5,000
Paid-in Capital in Excess of Stated Value—Common Stock		10,000

Most corporations account for no-par stock with a stated value as if it were par value stock with par equal to the stated value.

Stock Issued with Other Securities (Lump-Sum Sales)

Generally, corporations sell classes of stock separately from one another. The reason to do so is to track the proceeds relative to each class, as well as relative to each lot. Occasionally, a corporation issues two or more classes of securities for a single payment

[5] *Accounting Trends and Techniques—2012* indicates that its 500 surveyed companies reported 461 issues of outstanding common stock, 453 par value issues, and 40 no-par issues; 3 of the no-par issues were shown at their stated (assigned) values.

or lump sum (e.g., in the acquisition of another company). The accounting problem in such lump-sum sales is how to allocate the proceeds among the several classes of securities. Companies use one of two methods of allocation: (1) the proportional method and (2) the incremental method.

Proportional Method. If the fair value or other sound basis for determining relative value is available for each class of security, **the company allocates the lump sum received among the classes of securities on a proportional basis**. For instance, assume a company issues 1,000 shares of $10 stated value common stock having a market price of $20 a share, and 1,000 shares of $10 par value preferred stock having a market price of $12 a share, for a lump sum of $30,000. Illustration 15-1 shows how the company allocates the $30,000 to the two classes of stock.

ILLUSTRATION 15-1
Allocation in Lump-Sum Securities Issuance—Proportional Method

Fair value of common (1,000 × $20) =	$20,000		
Fair value of preferred (1,000 × $12) =	12,000		
Aggregate fair value	$32,000		
Allocated to common:	$20,000 / $32,000	× $30,000 =	$18,750
Allocated to preferred:	$12,000 / $32,000	× $30,000 =	$11,250
Total allocation			$30,000

Incremental Method. In instances where a company cannot determine the fair value of all classes of securities, it may use the incremental method. It uses the fair value of the securities as a basis for those classes that it knows, and allocates the remainder of the lump sum to the class for which it does not know the fair value. For instance, if a company issues 1,000 shares of $10 stated value common stock having a fair value of $20, and 1,000 shares of $10 par value preferred stock having no established fair value, for a lump sum of $30,000, it allocates the $30,000 to the two classes as shown in Illustration 15-2.

ILLUSTRATION 15-2
Allocation in Lump-Sum Securities Issuance—Incremental Method

Lump-sum receipt	$30,000
Allocated to common (1,000 × $20)	(20,000)
Balance allocated to preferred	$10,000

If a company cannot determine fair value for any of the classes of stock involved in a lump-sum exchange, it may need to use other approaches. It may rely on an expert's appraisal. Or, if the company knows that one or more of the classes of securities issued will have a determinable fair value in the near future, it may use a best estimate basis with the intent to adjust later, upon establishment of the future fair value.

Stock Issued in Noncash Transactions

Accounting for the issuance of shares of stock for property or services involves an issue of valuation. **The general rule is: Companies should record stock issued for services or property other than cash at either the fair value of the stock issued or the fair value of the noncash consideration received, whichever is more clearly determinable.**

If a company can readily determine both, and the transaction results from an arm's-length exchange, there will probably be little difference in their fair values. In such cases, the basis for valuing the exchange should not matter.

If a company cannot readily determine either the fair value of the stock it issues or the property or services it receives, it should employ an appropriate valuation technique.

Depending on available data, the valuation may be based on market transactions involving comparable assets or the use of discounted expected future cash flows. Companies should avoid the use of the book, par, or stated values as a basis of valuation for these transactions.

A company may exchange unissued stock or treasury stock (issued shares that it has reacquired but not retired) for property or services. If it uses treasury shares, the cost of the treasury shares **should not** be considered the decisive factor in establishing the fair value of the property or services. Instead, it should use the fair value of the treasury stock, if known, to value the property or services. Otherwise, if it does not know the fair value of the treasury stock, it should use the fair value of the property or services received, if determinable.

The following series of transactions illustrates the procedure for recording the issuance of 10,000 shares of $10 par value common stock for a patent for Marlowe Company, in various circumstances.

1. Marlowe cannot readily determine the fair value of the patent, but it knows the fair value of the stock is $140,000.

Patents	140,000	
Common Stock (10,000 shares × $10 per share)		100,000
Paid-in Capital in Excess of Par—Common Stock		40,000

2. Marlowe cannot readily determine the fair value of the stock, but it determines the fair value of the patent is $150,000.

Patents	150,000	
Common Stock (10,000 shares × $10 per share)		100,000
Paid-in Capital in Excess of Par—Common Stock		50,000

3. Marlowe cannot readily determine the fair value of the stock nor the fair value of the patent. An independent consultant values the patent at $125,000 based on discounted expected cash flows.

Patents	125,000	
Common Stock (10,000 shares × $10 share)		100,000
Paid-in Capital in Excess of Par—Common Stock		25,000

In corporate law, the board of directors has the power to set the value of noncash transactions. However, boards sometimes abuse this power. The issuance of stock for property or services has resulted in cases of overstated corporate capital through intentional overvaluation of the property or services received. The overvaluation of the stockholders' equity resulting from inflated asset values creates **watered stock**. The corporation should eliminate the "water" by simply writing down the overvalued assets.

If, as a result of the issuance of stock for property or services, a corporation undervalues the recorded assets, it creates **secret reserves**. An understated corporate structure (secret reserve) may also result from other methods: excessive depreciation or amortization charges, expensing capital expenditures, excessive write-downs of inventories or receivables, or any other understatement of assets or overstatement of liabilities. An example of a liability overstatement is an excessive provision for estimated product warranties that ultimately results in an understatement of owners' equity, thereby creating a secret reserve.

Costs of Issuing Stock

When a company like **Walgreens** issues common stock, it should report direct costs incurred to sell stock, such as underwriting costs, accounting and legal fees, printing costs, and taxes, as a reduction of the amounts paid in. Walgreens therefore debits issue costs to Paid-in Capital in Excess of Par—Common Stock because they are unrelated to corporate operations. In effect, **issue costs are a cost of financing**. As such, issue costs should reduce the proceeds received from the sale of the stock.

Walgreens should expense management salaries and other indirect costs related to the stock issue because it is difficult to establish a relationship between these costs and the sale proceeds. In addition, Walgreens expenses recurring costs, primarily registrar and transfer agents' fees, as incurred.

What do the numbers mean? THE CASE OF THE DISAPPEARING RECEIVABLE

Sometimes companies issue stock but may not receive cash in return. As a result, a company records a receivable.

Controversy existed regarding the presentation of this receivable on the balance sheet. Some argued that the company should report the receivable as an asset similar to other receivables. Others argued that the company should report the receivable as a deduction from stockholders' equity (similar to the treatment of treasury stock). The SEC settled this issue: It requires companies to use the contra equity approach because the risk of collection in this type of transaction is often very high.

This accounting issue surfaced in **Enron**'s accounting. Starting in early 2000, Enron issued shares of its common stock to four "special-purpose entities" in exchange for which it received a note receivable. Enron then increased its assets (by recording a receivable) and stockholders' equity, a move the company now calls an accounting error. As a result of this accounting treatment, Enron overstated assets and stockholders' equity by $172 million in its 2000 audited financial statements and by $828 million in its unaudited 2001 statements. This $1 billion overstatement was 8.5 percent of Enron's previously reported stockholders' equity at that time.

As Lynn Turner, former chief accountant of the SEC, noted, "It is a basic accounting principle that you don't record equity until you get cash, and a note doesn't count as cash." Situations like this led investors, creditors, and suppliers to lose faith in the credibility of Enron, which eventually caused its bankruptcy.

Source: Adapted from Jonathan Weil, "Basic Accounting Tripped Up Enron—Financial Statements Didn't Add Up—Auditors Overlook a Simple Rule," *Wall Street Journal* (November 11, 2001), p. C1.

Reacquisition of Shares

4 LEARNING OBJECTIVE
Describe the accounting for treasury stock.

Companies often buy back their own shares. In fact, share buybacks now exceed dividends as a form of distribution to stockholders. For example, oil producer **ConocoPhillips**, healthcare–products giant **Johnson & Johnson**, and discount retailer **Wal-Mart Stores** have ambitious buyback plans. As shown in Illustration 15-3, companies in the S&P 500 are on track to buy back more than $429 billion of their own shares in 2012.[6]

ILLUSTRATION 15-3
Share Buybacks in 2012

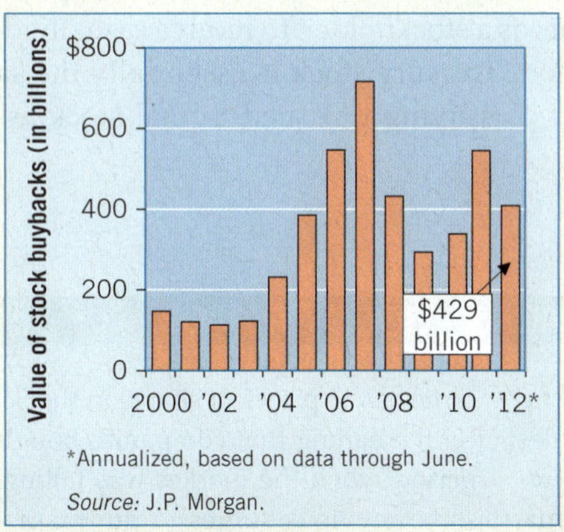

Corporations purchase their outstanding stock for several reasons:

1. *To provide tax-efficient distributions of excess cash to shareholders.* Capital gain rates on sales of stock to the company by the stockholders have been approximately half the ordinary tax rate for many investors. This advantage has been somewhat diminished by recent changes in the tax law related to dividends.

[6] T. Lauricella, "Post-Rally Risks in U.S. Stocks," *Wall Street Journal* (October 1, 2012), p. C11.

2. *To increase earnings per share and return on equity.* Reducing both shares outstanding and stockholders' equity often enhances certain performance ratios. However, strategies to hype performance measures might increase performance in the short-run, but these tactics add no real long-term value.
3. *To provide stock for employee stock compensation contracts or to meet potential merger needs.* Honeywell Inc. reported that it would use part of its purchase of one million common shares for employee stock option contracts. Other companies acquire shares to have them available for business acquisitions.
4. *To thwart takeover attempts or to reduce the number of stockholders.* By reducing the number of shares held by the public, existing owners and managements bar "outsiders" from gaining control or significant influence. When Ted Turner attempted to acquire CBS, CBS started a substantial buyback of its stock. Companies may also use stock purchases to eliminate dissident stockholders.
5. *To make a market in the stock.* As one company executive noted, "Our company is trying to establish a floor for the stock." Purchasing stock in the marketplace creates a demand. This may stabilize the stock price or, in fact, increase it.

Some publicly held corporations have chosen to "go private," that is, to eliminate public (outside) ownership entirely by purchasing all of their outstanding stock. Companies often accomplish such a procedure through a **leveraged buyout (LBO)**, in which the company borrows money to finance the stock repurchases.

Underlying Concepts

As we indicated in Chapter 2, an asset should have probable future economic benefits. Treasury stock simply reduces common stock outstanding.

After reacquiring shares, a company may either retire them or hold them in the treasury for reissue. If not retired, such shares are referred to as **treasury stock** (**treasury shares**). Technically, treasury stock is a corporation's own stock, reacquired after having been issued and fully paid.

Treasury stock is not an asset. When a company purchases treasury stock, a reduction occurs in both assets and stockholders' equity. It is inappropriate to imply that a corporation can own a part of itself. A corporation may sell treasury stock to obtain funds, but that does not make treasury stock a balance sheet asset. When a corporation buys back some of its own outstanding stock, it has not acquired an asset; it reduces net assets.

The possession of treasury stock does not give the corporation the right to vote, to exercise preemptive rights as a stockholder, to receive cash dividends, or to receive assets upon corporate liquidation. **Treasury stock is essentially the same as unissued capital stock.** No one advocates classifying unissued capital stock as an asset in the balance sheet.[7]

What do the numbers mean? BUYBACKS—GOOD OR BAD?

As indicated in Illustration 15-3, companies have ramped up repurchases of their own stock. Notable buyback companies are ExxonMobil, which recently bought back $5 billion of its stock during that period, and ConocoPhillips, which repurchased $3.1 billion of its shares. The surge in repurchases came as the prices of shares in the S&P 500 dropped 3.3 percent, meaning that companies bought more shares during a period when the market was falling. That is a far cry from some previous surges in buybacks, such as the one in the fourth quarter of 2007, when companies repurchased a record

[7]The possible justification for classifying these shares as assets is that the company will use them to liquidate a specific liability that appears on the balance sheet. *Accounting Trends and Techniques—2012* reported that out of 500 companies surveyed, 341 disclosed treasury stock, but none classified it as an asset.

dollar amount of shares even as the stock market was peaking.

Is this good or bad news for investors? Maybe neither. While it might appear that companies are getting better at timing their purchases (when prices are falling), they also buy shares for reasons that go beyond giving a boost to shareholders—everything from mergers and acquisitions to eliminating the impact of equity compensation. And unlike dividend payments, buybacks haven't been shown to make investors better off in the long run. For example, from 2004, when companies first were required to disclose monthly share repurchases, through the end of 2011, 31 percent of S&P 500 companies have seen the value of those shares fall and just 36 percent have returned more than 7 percent. As one analyst notes, "It's important to look at what a company is paying relative to what its shares are worth. If they overpay, wealth is being transferred to the sellers."

The conventional wisdom is that companies which buy back shares believe their shares are undervalued. Thus, analysts view the buyback announcement as an important piece of inside information about future company prospects. On the other hand, buybacks can actually hurt businesses and their shareholders over the long run. For example, drug-makers **Merck**, **Pfizer**, and **Amgen** spent heavily on stock repurchases, possibly at the expense of research and development. And whether the buyback is a good thing appears to depend a lot on why the company did the buyback and what the repurchased shares were used for.

One study found that companies often increased their buybacks when earnings growth slowed. This allowed the companies to prop up earnings per share (based on fewer shares outstanding). Furthermore, many buybacks do not actually result in a net reduction in shares outstanding. For example, companies such as **Microsoft** and **Broadcom** bought back shares to meet share demands for stock option exercises, resulting in higher net shares outstanding when they reissued the repurchased shares to the option holders upon exercise. In this case, the buyback actually indicated a further dilution in the share ownership in the buyback company.

This does not mean you should never trust a buyback signal. But if the buyback is intended to manage the company's earnings or if the buyback results in dilution, take a closer look.

Sources: Adapted from W. Lazonick, "The Buyback Boondoggle," *BusinessWeek* (August 24, 2009); and B. Levisohn, "Beware All Those Buybacks," *Wall Street Journal* (September 29–30, 2012), p. B9.

Purchase of Treasury Stock

Gateway to the Profession

Discussion of Using Par or Stated Value for Treasury Stock Transactions

Companies use two general methods of handling treasury stock in the accounts: the cost method and the par value method. Both methods are generally acceptable. The cost method enjoys more widespread use.[8]

- The **cost method** results in debiting the Treasury Stock account for the reacquisition cost and in reporting this account as a deduction from the total paid-in capital **and** retained earnings on the balance sheet.
- The **par (stated) value method** records all transactions in treasury shares at their par value and reports the treasury stock as a deduction from capital stock only.

No matter which method a company uses, most states consider the cost of the treasury shares acquired as a restriction on retained earnings.

Companies generally use the cost method to account for treasury stock. This method derives its name from the fact that a company maintains the Treasury Stock account at the cost of the shares purchased.[9] Under the cost method, the company debits the Treasury Stock account for the cost of the shares acquired. Upon reissuance of the shares, it credits the account for this same cost. The original price received for the stock does not affect the entries to record the acquisition and reissuance of the treasury stock.

To illustrate, assume that Pacific Company issued 100,000 shares of $1 par value common stock at a price of $10 per share. In addition, it has retained earnings of $300,000.

[8]*Accounting Trends and Techniques—2012* indicates that of its selected list of 500 companies, of the 341 companies with treasury stock, all carried common stock in treasury at cost. Only one company carried preferred stock in treasury.

[9]If making numerous acquisitions of blocks of treasury shares at different prices, a company may use inventory costing methods—such as specific identification, average-cost, or FIFO—to identify the cost at date of reissuance.

Illustration 15-4 shows the stockholders' equity section on December 31, 2013, before purchase of treasury stock.

ILLUSTRATION 15-4
Stockholders' Equity with No Treasury Stock

Stockholders' equity	
Paid-in capital	
Common stock, $1 par value, 100,000 shares issued and outstanding	$ 100,000
Additional paid-in capital	900,000
Total paid-in capital	1,000,000
Retained earnings	300,000
Total stockholders' equity	$1,300,000

On January 20, 2014, Pacific acquires 10,000 shares of its stock at $11 per share. Pacific records the reacquisition as follows.

January 20, 2014		
Treasury Stock	110,000	
Cash		110,000

Note that Pacific debited Treasury Stock for the cost of the shares purchased. The original paid-in capital account, Common Stock, is not affected because the number of issued shares does not change. The same is true for the Paid-in Capital in Excess of Par—Common Stock account. Pacific deducts treasury stock from total paid-in capital and retained earnings in the stockholders' equity section.

Illustration 15-5 shows the stockholders' equity section for Pacific after purchase of the treasury stock.

ILLUSTRATION 15-5
Stockholders' Equity with Treasury Stock

Stockholders' equity	
Paid-in capital	
Common stock, $1 par value, 100,000 shares issued and 90,000 outstanding	$ 100,000
Additional paid-in capital	900,000
Total paid-in capital	1,000,000
Retained earnings	300,000
Total paid-in capital and retained earnings	1,300,000
Less: Cost of treasury stock (10,000 shares)	110,000
Total stockholders' equity	$1,190,000

Pacific subtracts the cost of the treasury stock from the total of common stock, additional paid-in capital, and retained earnings. It therefore reduces stockholders' equity. Many states require a corporation to restrict retained earnings for the cost of treasury stock purchased. The restriction keeps intact the corporation's legal capital that it temporarily holds as treasury stock. When the corporation sells the treasury stock, it lifts the restriction.

Pacific discloses both the number of shares issued (100,000) and the number in the treasury (10,000). The difference is the number of shares of stock outstanding (90,000). The term **outstanding stock** means the number of shares of issued stock that stockholders own.

Sale of Treasury Stock

Companies usually reissue or retire treasury stock. When selling treasury shares, the accounting for the sale depends on the price. If the selling price of the treasury stock equals its cost, the company records the sale of the shares by debiting Cash and crediting

Treasury Stock. In cases where the selling price of the treasury stock is not equal to cost, then accounting for treasury stock sold **above cost** differs from the accounting for treasury stock sold **below cost**. However, the sale of treasury stock either above or below cost increases both total assets and stockholders' equity.

Sale of Treasury Stock above Cost. When the selling price of shares of treasury stock exceeds its cost, a company credits the difference to Paid-in Capital from Treasury Stock. To illustrate, assume that Pacific acquired 10,000 shares of its treasury stock at $11 per share. It now sells 1,000 shares at $15 per share on March 10. Pacific records the entry as follows.

March 10, 2014		
Cash	15,000	
Treasury Stock		11,000
Paid-in Capital from Treasury Stock		4,000

There are two reasons why Pacific does not credit $4,000 to Gain on Sale of Treasury Stock. (1) Gains on sales occur when selling **assets**; treasury stock is not an asset. (2) A gain or loss should not be recognized from stock transactions with its own stockholders. Thus, Pacific should not include paid-in capital arising from the sale of treasury stock in the measurement of net income. Instead, it lists paid-in capital from treasury stock separately on the balance sheet, as a part of paid-in capital.

Sale of Treasury Stock below Cost. When a corporation sells treasury stock below its cost, it usually debits the excess of the cost over selling price to Paid-in Capital from Treasury Stock. Thus, if Pacific sells an additional 1,000 shares of treasury stock on March 21 at $8 per share, it records the sale as follows.

March 21, 2014		
Cash	8,000	
Paid-in Capital from Treasury Stock	3,000	
Treasury Stock		11,000

We can make several observations based on the two sale entries (sale above cost and sale below cost). (1) Pacific credits Treasury Stock at cost in each entry. (2) Pacific uses Paid-in Capital from Treasury Stock for the difference between the cost and the resale price of the shares. (3) Neither entry affects the original paid-in capital account, Common Stock.

After eliminating the credit balance in Paid-in Capital from Treasury Stock, the corporation debits any additional excess of cost over selling price to Retained Earnings. To illustrate, assume that Pacific sells an additional 1,000 shares at $8 per share on April 10. Illustration 15-6 shows the balance in the Paid-in Capital from Treasury Stock account (before the April 10 purchase).

ILLUSTRATION 15-6
Treasury Stock Transactions in Paid-in Capital Account

Paid-in Capital from Treasury Stock			
Mar. 21	3,000	Mar. 10	4,000
		Balance	1,000

In this case, Pacific debits $1,000 of the excess to Paid-in Capital from Treasury Stock. It debits the remainder to Retained Earnings. The entry is:

April 10, 2014		
Cash	8,000	
Paid-in Capital from Treasury Stock	1,000	
Retained Earnings	2,000	
Treasury Stock		11,000

Retiring Treasury Stock

The board of directors may approve the retirement of treasury shares. This decision results in cancellation of the treasury stock and a reduction in the number of shares of issued stock. Retired treasury shares have the status of authorized and unissued shares. The accounting effects are similar to the sale of treasury stock except that corporations debit the **paid-in capital accounts applicable to the retired shares** instead of cash. For example, if a corporation originally sells the shares at par, it debits Common Stock for the par value per share. If it originally sells the shares at $3 above par value, it also debits Paid-in Capital in Excess of Par—Common Stock for $3 per share at retirement.

PREFERRED STOCK

LEARNING OBJECTIVE 5
Explain the accounting for and reporting of preferred stock.

As noted earlier, preferred stock is a special class of shares that possesses certain preferences or features not possessed by the common stock.[10] The following features are those most often associated with preferred stock issues.

1. Preference as to dividends.
2. Preference as to assets in the event of liquidation.
3. Convertible into common stock.
4. Callable at the option of the corporation.
5. Nonvoting.

The features that distinguish preferred from common stock may be of a more restrictive and negative nature than preferences. For example, the preferred stock may be nonvoting, noncumulative, and nonparticipating.

Companies usually issue preferred stock with a par value, expressing the dividend preference as a **percentage of the par value**. Thus, holders of 8 percent preferred stock with a $100 par value are entitled to an annual dividend of $8 per share. This stock is commonly referred to as 8 percent preferred stock. In the case of no-par preferred stock, a corporation expresses a dividend preference as a **specific dollar amount** per share, for example, $7 per share. This stock is commonly referred to as $7 preferred stock.

A preference as to dividends does not assure the payment of dividends. It merely assures that **the corporation must pay the stated dividend rate or amount applicable to the preferred stock before paying any dividends on the common stock**.

A company often issues preferred stock (instead of debt) because of a high debt-to-equity ratio. In other instances, it issues preferred stock through private placements with other corporations at a lower-than-market dividend rate because the acquiring corporation receives largely tax-free dividends (owing to the IRS's 70 percent or 80 percent dividends received deduction).

Features of Preferred Stock

A corporation may attach whatever preferences or restrictions, in whatever combination it desires, to a preferred stock issue, as long as it does not specifically violate its state incorporation law. Also, it may issue more than one class of preferred stock. We discuss the most common features attributed to preferred stock on the next page.

[10] *Accounting Trends and Techniques—2012* reports that of its 500 surveyed companies, 35 had preferred stock outstanding.

Cumulative Preferred Stock

Cumulative preferred stock requires that if a corporation fails to pay a dividend in any year, it must make it up in a later year before paying any dividends to common stockholders. If the directors fail to declare a dividend at the normal date for dividend action, the dividend is said to have been "passed." Any passed dividend on cumulative preferred stock constitutes a **dividend in arrears**. Because no liability exists until the board of directors declares a dividend, a corporation does not record a dividend in arrears as a liability but discloses it in a note to the financial statements. A corporation seldom issues noncumulative preferred stock because a passed dividend is lost forever to the preferred stockholder. As a result, this stock issue would be less marketable.

Participating Preferred Stock

Holders of **participating preferred stock** share ratably with the common stockholders in any profit distributions beyond the prescribed rate. That is, 5 percent preferred stock, if fully participating, will receive not only its 5 percent return, but also dividends at the same rates as those paid to common stockholders if paying amounts in excess of 5 percent of par or stated value to common stockholders. Note that participating preferred stock may be only partially participating. Although seldom used, examples of companies that have issued participating preferred stock are **LTV Corporation**, **Southern California Edison**, and **Allied Products Corporation**.

Convertible Preferred Stock

Convertible preferred stock allows stockholders, at their option, to exchange preferred shares for common stock at a predetermined ratio. The convertible preferred stockholder not only enjoys a preferred claim on dividends but also has the option of converting into a common stockholder with unlimited participation in earnings.

Callable Preferred Stock

Callable preferred stock permits the corporation at its option to call or redeem the outstanding preferred shares at specified future dates and at stipulated prices. Many preferred issues are callable. The corporation usually sets the call or redemption price slightly above the original issuance price and commonly states it in terms related to the par value. The callable feature permits the corporation to use the capital obtained through the issuance of such stock until the need has passed or it is no longer advantageous.

The existence of a call price or prices tends to set a ceiling on the market price of the preferred shares unless they are convertible into common stock. When a corporation redeems preferred stock, it must pay any dividends in arrears.

Redeemable Preferred Stock

Recently, more and more issuances of preferred stock have features that make the security more like debt (legal obligation to pay) than an equity instrument. For example, **redeemable preferred stock** has a mandatory redemption period or a redemption feature that the issuer cannot control.

Previously, public companies were not permitted to report these debt-like preferred stock issues in equity, but they were not required to report them as a liability either. There were concerns about classification of these debt-like securities, which may have been reported as equity or in the "mezzanine" section of balance sheets between debt and equity. There also was diversity in practice as to how dividends on these securities were reported. The FASB now requires debt-like securities, such as redeemable preferred stock, to be classified as liabilities and be measured and accounted for similar to liabilities. **[1]**

See the FASB Codification section (page 856).

What do the numbers mean? A CLASS (B) ACT

Some companies grant preferences to different shareholders by issuing different classes of common stock. Recent stock bids put the spotlight on dual-class stock structures. For example, ownership of **Dow Jones & Co.** was controlled by family members who owned Class B shares, which carry super voting powers. The same is true for the Ford family's control of **Ford Motor Co.** Class B shares are often criticized for protecting owners' interest at the expense of shareholder return. These shares often can determine if a takeover deal gets done, or not. Here are some notable companies with two-tiered shares.

Company	Votes Controlled by Class B Shareholders	Company	Votes Controlled by Class B Shareholders
Ford	40%	**Estée Lauder**	88%
New York Times	70%	**Polo Ralph Lauren**	88%
Meredith	71%	**Martha Stewart Living**	91%
Cablevision Systems	73%	**1-800-Flowers**	93%
Google	78%		

Data: Bloomberg Financial Markets, *BusinessWeek*, company documents.

For most retail investors, voting rights are not that important. Indeed, in 2011, 20 companies (including **Zynga**, **Groupon**, and **LinkedIn**) went public in the United States with two or more classes of stock. For family-controlled companies, issuing newer classes of lower or nonvoting stock effectively creates currency for acquisitions, increases liquidity, or puts a public value on the company without diluting the family's voting control. This was one of the main reasons **Facebook** gave when it created a dual-class share structure in 2009. In that IPO, Facebook founder Mark Zuckerberg owns only a quarter of the stock but still holds 57 percent of Facebook's voting rights. Thus, investors must carefully compare the apparent bargain prices for some classes of stock—they may end up as second-class citizens with no voting rights.

Sources: Adapted from Andy Serwer, "Dual-Listed Companies Aren't Fair or Balanced," *Fortune* (September 20, 2004), p. 83; Alex Halperin, "A Class (B) Act," *BusinessWeek* (May 28, 2007), p. 12; The Big Number, "20 Companies That Went Public in 2011 with Two or More Classes of Stock," *Wall Street Journal* (February 8, 2012), p. B5; and MoneyWatch, "Facebook's IPO by the Important Numbers," *www.cbsnews.com* (May 17, 2012).

Accounting for and Reporting Preferred Stock

The accounting for preferred stock at issuance is similar to that for common stock. A corporation allocates proceeds between the par value of the preferred stock and additional paid-in capital. To illustrate, assume that Bishop Co. issues 10,000 shares of $10 par value preferred stock for $12 cash per share. Bishop records the issuance as follows.

	Debit	Credit
Cash	120,000	
Preferred Stock		100,000
Paid-in Capital in Excess of Par—Preferred Stock		20,000

Thus, Bishop maintains separate accounts for these different classes of shares.

In contrast to convertible bonds (recorded as a liability on the date of issue), corporations consider convertible preferred stock as a part of stockholders' equity. In addition, when exercising convertible preferred stock, there is no theoretical justification for recognition of a gain or loss. A company recognizes no gain or loss when dealing with stockholders in their capacity as business owners. Instead, the company **employs the book value method**: debit Preferred Stock, along with any related Paid-in Capital in Excess of Par—Preferred Stock, and credit Common Stock and Paid-in Capital in Excess of Par—Common Stock (if an excess exists).

Preferred stock generally has no maturity date. Therefore, no legal obligation exists to pay the preferred stockholder. As a result, companies classify preferred stock as part of stockholders' equity. Companies generally report preferred stock at par value as the first item in the stockholders' equity section. They report any excess over par value as part of additional paid-in capital. They also consider dividends on preferred stock as a distribution of income and not an expense. Companies must disclose the pertinent rights of the preferred stock outstanding. [2]

DIVIDEND POLICY

6 LEARNING OBJECTIVE
Describe the policies used in distributing dividends.

Dividend payouts can be important signals to the market. The practice of paying dividends declined sharply in the 1980s and 1990s as companies focused on growth and plowed profits back into the business. A resurgence in dividend payouts is due in large part to the dividend tax cut of 2003, which reduced the rate of tax on dividends to 15 percent (quite a bit lower than the ordinary income rate charged in the past). In addition, investors who were burned by accounting scandals in recent years began demanding higher payouts in the form of dividends. Why? A dividend check provides proof that at least some portion of a company's profits is genuine.[11] As one analyst noted, "Companies with the ability to grow dividends over time tend to be durable businesses with strong cash flow and relatively predictable earnings. . . . So you're more likely to get a return on your investment year in and year out."

Determining the proper amount of dividends to pay is a difficult financial management decision. Companies paying dividends are extremely reluctant to reduce or eliminate their dividend. They fear that the securities market might negatively view this action. As a consequence, dividend-paying companies will make every effort to continue to do so. In addition, the type of shareholder the company has (taxable or nontaxable, retail investor or institutional investor) plays a large role in determining dividend policy.

Very few companies pay dividends in amounts equal to their legally available retained earnings. The major reasons are as follows.

1. To maintain agreements (bond covenants) with specific creditors, to retain all or a portion of the earnings, in the form of assets, to build up additional protection against possible loss.
2. To meet state corporation requirements, that earnings equivalent to the cost of treasury shares purchased be restricted against dividend declarations.
3. To retain assets that would otherwise be paid out as dividends, to finance growth or expansion. This is sometimes called internal financing, reinvesting earnings, or "plowing" the profits back into the business.
4. To smooth out dividend payments from year to year by accumulating earnings in good years and using such accumulated earnings as a basis for dividends in bad years.
5. To build up a cushion or buffer against possible losses or errors in the calculation of profits.

The reasons above are self-explanatory except for the second. The laws of some states require that the corporation restrict its legal capital from distribution to stockholders, to protect against loss for creditors.[12] The applicable state law determines the legality of a dividend.

Financial Condition and Dividend Distributions

Effective management of a company requires attention to more than the legality of dividend distributions. Management must also consider economic conditions, most importantly, liquidity. Assume an extreme situation as shown in Illustration 15-7 (page 838).

[11]"Dividend Stocks: Yield, Growth, and Possible Tax Hikes," *T. Rowe Price Report* (Fall 2011). From 1926 to 2011, dividends have contributed 42% of the total return of the S&P 500 Index. See "Dividend Growth Stocks May Be Timely as the Economy Sputters," *T. Rowe Price Report* (Fall 2011).

[12]If the corporation buys its own outstanding stock, it reduces its legal capital and distributes assets to stockholders. If permitted, the corporation could, by purchasing treasury stock at any price desired, return to the stockholders their investments and leave creditors with little or no protection against loss.

ILLUSTRATION 15-7
Balance Sheet, Showing a Lack of Liquidity

BALANCE SHEET			
Plant assets	$500,000	Capital stock	$400,000
		Retained earnings	100,000
	$500,000		$500,000

The depicted company has a retained earnings credit balance. Unless restricted, it can declare a dividend of $100,000. But because all its assets are plant assets used in operations, payment of a cash dividend of $100,000 would require the sale of plant assets or borrowing.

Even if a balance sheet shows current assets, as in Illustration 15-8, the question remains as to whether the company needs its cash for other purposes.

ILLUSTRATION 15-8
Balance Sheet, Showing Cash but Minimal Working Capital

BALANCE SHEET				
Cash	$100,000	Current liabilities		$ 60,000
Plant assets	460,000	Capital stock	$400,000	
		Retained earnings	100,000	500,000
	$560,000			$560,000

The existence of current liabilities strongly implies that the company needs some of the cash to meet current debts as they mature. In addition, day-to-day cash requirements for payrolls and other expenditures not included in current liabilities also require cash.

Thus, before declaring a dividend, management must consider **availability of funds to pay the dividend.** A company should not pay a dividend unless both the present and future financial position warrant the distribution.

The SEC encourages companies to disclose their dividend policy in their annual report, especially those that (1) have earnings but fail to pay dividends, or (2) do not expect to pay dividends in the foreseeable future. In addition, the SEC encourages companies that consistently pay dividends to indicate whether they intend to continue this practice in the future.

Types of Dividends

LEARNING OBJECTIVE 7
Identify the various forms of dividend distributions.

Companies generally base dividend distributions either on accumulated profits (that is, retained earnings) or on some other capital item such as additional paid-in capital. Dividends are of the following types.

1. Cash dividends.
2. Property dividends.
3. Liquidating dividends.

Although commonly paid in cash, companies occasionally pay dividends in stock or some other asset.[13] **All dividends, except for stock dividends, reduce the total stockholders' equity in the corporation.** When declaring a stock dividend, the corporation does not pay out assets or incur a liability. It issues additional shares of stock to each stockholder and nothing more.

[13] *Accounting Trends and Techniques—2012* reported that of its 500 surveyed companies, 343 paid a cash dividend on common stock, 33 paid a cash dividend on preferred stock, 2 issued stock dividends, and 1 issued or paid dividends in kind. Some companies declare more than one type of dividend in a given year.

The natural expectation of any stockholder who receives a dividend is that the corporation has operated successfully. As a result, he or she is receiving a share of its profits. A company should disclose a **liquidating dividend**—that is, a dividend not based on retained earnings—to the stockholders so that they will not misunderstand its source.

Cash Dividends

The board of directors votes on the declaration of **cash dividends**. Upon approval of the resolution, the board declares a dividend. Before paying it, however, the company must prepare a current list of stockholders. For this reason, there is usually a time lag between declaration and payment. For example, the board of directors might approve a resolution at the January 10 (**date of declaration**) meeting and declare it payable February 5 (**date of payment**) to all stockholders of record January 25 (**date of record**).[14] In this example, the period from January 10 to January 25 gives time for the company to complete and register any transfers in process. The time from January 25 to February 5 provides an opportunity for the transfer agent or accounting department, depending on who does this work, to prepare a list of stockholders as of January 25 and to prepare and mail dividend checks.

A declared cash dividend is a liability. Because payment is generally required very soon, it is usually a current liability. Companies record the following entries to record the declaration and payment of a cash dividend. To illustrate, Roadway Freight Corp. on June 10 declared a cash dividend of 50 cents a share on 1.8 million shares payable July 16 to all stockholders of record June 24.

At date of declaration (June 10)		
Retained Earnings (Cash Dividends Declared)	900,000	
Dividends Payable		900,000
At date of record (June 24)		
No entry		
At date of payment (July 16)		
Dividends Payable	900,000	
Cash		900,000

To set up a ledger account that shows the amount of dividends declared during the year, Roadway Freight might debit Cash Dividends Declared instead of Retained Earnings at the time of declaration. It then closes this account to Retained Earnings at year-end.

A company may declare dividends either as a certain percent of par, such as a 6 percent dividend on preferred stock, or as an amount per share, such as 60 cents per share on no-par common stock. In the first case, the rate multiplied by the par value of outstanding shares equals the total dividend. In the second, the dividend equals the amount per share multiplied by the number of shares outstanding. **Companies do not declare or pay cash dividends on treasury stock.**

Dividend policies vary among corporations. Some companies, such as **JP Morgan Chase**, **Clorox Co.**, and **Tootsie Roll Industries**, take pride in a long, unbroken string of quarterly dividend payments. They would lower or pass the dividend only if forced to do so by a sustained decline in earnings or a critical shortage of cash.

[14]Theoretically, the ex-dividend date is the day after the date of record. However, to allow time for transfer of the shares, the stock exchanges generally advance the ex-dividend date two to four days. Therefore, the party who owns the stock on the day prior to the expressed ex-dividend date receives the dividends. The party who buys the stock on and after the ex-dividend date does not receive the dividend. Between the declaration date and the ex-dividend date, the market price of the stock includes the dividend.

"Growth" companies, on the other hand, pay little or no cash dividends because their policy is to expand as rapidly as internal and external financing permit. For example, **Questcor Pharmaceuticals Inc.** has never paid cash dividends to its common stockholders. These investors hope that the price of their shares will appreciate in value. The investors will then realize a profit when they sell their shares. Many companies focus more on increasing share price, stock repurchase programs, and corporate earnings than on dividend payout.

Property Dividends

Dividends payable in assets of the corporation other than cash are called **property dividends** or **dividends in kind**. Property dividends may be merchandise, real estate, or investments, or whatever form the board of directors designates. **Ranchers Exploration and Development Corp.** reported one year that it would pay a fourth-quarter dividend in gold bars instead of cash. Because of the obvious difficulties of divisibility of units and delivery to stockholders, the usual property dividend is in the form of securities of other companies that the distributing corporation holds as an investment.

For example, after ruling that **DuPont**'s 23 percent stock interest in **General Motors** (GM) violated antitrust laws, the Supreme Court ordered DuPont to divest itself of the GM stock within 10 years. The stock represented 63 million shares of GM's 281 million shares then outstanding. DuPont could not sell the shares in one block of 63 million. Further, it could not sell 6 million shares annually for the next 10 years without severely depressing the value of the GM stock. DuPont solved its problem by declaring a property dividend and distributing the GM shares as a dividend to its own stockholders.

When declaring a property dividend, the corporation should **restate at fair value the property it will distribute, recognizing any gain or loss** as the difference between the property's fair value and carrying value at date of declaration. The corporation may then record the declared dividend as a debit to Retained Earnings (or Property Dividends Declared) and a credit to Property Dividends Payable, at an amount equal to the fair value of the distributed property. Upon distribution of the dividend, the corporation debits Property Dividends Payable and credits the account containing the distributed asset (restated at fair value).

For example, Trendler, Inc. transferred to stockholders some of its equity investments costing $1,250,000 by declaring a property dividend on December 28, 2013, to be distributed on January 30, 2014, to stockholders of record on January 15, 2014. At the date of declaration, the securities have a fair value of $2,000,000. Trendler makes the following entries.

At date of declaration (December 28, 2013)		
Equity Investments	750,000	
Unrealized Holding Gain or Loss—Income		750,000
Retained Earnings (Property Dividends Declared)	2,000,000	
Property Dividends Payable		2,000,000

At date of distribution (January 30, 2014)		
Property Dividends Payable	2,000,000	
Equity Investments		2,000,000

Liquidating Dividends

Some corporations use paid-in capital as a basis for dividends. Without proper disclosure of this fact, stockholders may erroneously believe the corporation has been operating at a profit. To avoid this type of deception, intentional or unintentional, a clear statement of the source of every dividend should accompany the dividend check.

Dividends based on other than retained earnings are sometimes described as **liquidating dividends**. This term implies that such dividends are a return of the stockholder's investment rather than of profits. In other words, **any dividend not based on earnings reduces corporate paid-in capital and to that extent, it is a liquidating dividend**. Companies in the extractive industries may pay dividends equal to the total of accumulated income and depletion. The portion of these dividends in excess of accumulated income represents a return of part of the stockholder's investment.

For example, McChesney Mines Inc. issued a "dividend" to its common stockholders of $1,200,000. The cash dividend announcement noted that stockholders should consider $900,000 as income and the remainder a return of capital. McChesney Mines records the dividend as follows.

At date of declaration		
Retained Earnings	900,000	
Paid-in Capital in Excess of Par—Common Stock	300,000	
Dividends Payable		1,200,000
At date of payment		
Dividends Payable	1,200,000	
Cash		1,200,000

In some cases, management simply decides to cease business and declares a liquidating dividend. In these cases, liquidation may take place over a number of years to ensure an orderly and fair sale of assets. For example, when **Overseas National Airways** dissolved, it agreed to pay a liquidating dividend to its stockholders over a period of years equivalent to $8.60 per share. Each liquidating dividend payment in such cases reduces paid-in capital.

Stock Dividends and Stock Splits

Stock Dividends

8 LEARNING OBJECTIVE
Explain the accounting for small and large stock dividends, and for stock splits.

If management wishes to "capitalize" part of the earnings (i.e., reclassify amounts from earned to contributed capital) and thus retain earnings in the business on a permanent basis, it may issue a stock dividend. In this case, **the company distributes no assets**. Each stockholder maintains exactly the same proportionate interest in the corporation and the same total book value after the company issues the stock dividend. Of course, the book value per share is lower because each stockholder holds more shares.

A **stock dividend** therefore is the issuance by a corporation of its own stock to its stockholders on a pro rata basis, without receiving any consideration. In recording a stock dividend, some believe that the company should transfer the **par value of the stock issued** as a dividend from retained earnings to capital stock. Others believe that it should transfer the **fair value of the stock issued**—its market value at the declaration date—from retained earnings to capital stock and additional paid-in capital.

The fair value position was adopted, at least in part, in order to influence the stock dividend policies of corporations. Evidently in 1941, both the New York Stock Exchange and many in the accounting profession regarded periodic stock dividends as objectionable. They believed that the term dividend when used with a distribution of additional stock was misleading because investors' net assets did not increase as a result of this "dividend." As a result, these groups decided to make it more difficult for corporations to sustain a series of such stock dividends out of their accumulated

Underlying Concepts

By requiring fair value, the intent was to punish companies that used stock dividends. This approach violates the neutrality concept (that is, that standards-setting should be even-handed).

earnings, by requiring the use of fair value when it substantially exceeded book value.[15]

When the stock dividend is less than 20–25 percent of the common shares outstanding at the time of the dividend declaration, the company is therefore required to transfer the **fair value** of the stock issued from retained earnings. Stock dividends of less than 20–25 percent are often referred to as **small (ordinary) stock dividends**. This method of handling stock dividends is justified on the grounds that "many recipients of stock dividends look upon them as distributions of corporate earnings and usually in an amount equivalent to the fair value of the additional shares received." **[3]** We consider this argument unconvincing. It is generally agreed that stock dividends are not income to the recipients. Therefore, sound accounting should not recommend procedures simply because some recipients think they are income.[16]

To illustrate a small stock dividend, assume that Vine Corporation has outstanding 1,000 shares of $100 par value common stock and retained earnings of $50,000. If Vine declares a 10 percent stock dividend, it issues 100 additional shares to current stockholders. If the fair value of the stock at the time of the stock dividend is $130 per share, the entry is:

At date of declaration

Retained Earnings	13,000	
Common Stock Dividend Distributable		10,000
Paid-in Capital in Excess of Par—Common Stock		3,000

Note that the stock dividend does not affect any asset or liability. **The entry merely reflects a reclassification of stockholders' equity.** If Vine prepares a balance sheet between the dates of declaration and distribution, it should show the common stock dividend distributable in the stockholders' equity section as an addition to common stock (whereas it shows cash or property dividends payable as current liabilities).

When issuing the stock, the entry is:

At date of distribution

Common Stock Dividend Distributable	10,000	
Common Stock		10,000

No matter what the fair value is at the time of the stock dividend, each stockholder retains the same proportionate interest in the corporation.

Some state statutes specifically prohibit the issuance of stock dividends on treasury stock. In those states that permit treasury shares to participate in the distribution accompanying a stock dividend or stock split, the planned use of the treasury shares influences corporate practice. For example, if a corporation issues treasury shares in connection with employee stock options, the treasury shares may participate in the distribution because the corporation usually adjusts the number of shares under option for any stock dividends or splits. But no useful purpose is served by issuing additional shares to the treasury stock without a specific purpose, since they are essentially equivalent to authorized but unissued shares.

[15]This was perhaps the earliest instance of "economic consequences" affecting an accounting pronouncement. The Committee on Accounting Procedure described its action as required by "proper accounting and corporate policy." See Stephen A. Zeff, "The Rise of 'Economic Consequences,'" *The Journal of Accountancy* (December 1978), pp. 53–66.

[16]One study concluded that *small* stock dividends do not always produce significant amounts of extra value on the date after issuance (ex date) and that *large* stock dividends almost always fail to generate extra value on the ex-dividend date. Taylor W. Foster III and Don Vickrey, "The Information Content of Stock Dividend Announcements," *The Accounting Review*, Vol. LIII, No. 2 (April 1978), pp. 360–370.

To continue with our example of the effect of the small stock dividend, note in Illustration 15-9 that the stock dividend does not change the total stockholders' equity. Also, it does not change the proportion of the total shares outstanding held by each stockholder.

ILLUSTRATION 15-9
Effects of a Small (10%) Stock Dividend

Before dividend	
Common stock, 1,000 shares at $100 par	$100,000
Retained earnings	50,000
Total stockholders' equity	$150,000
Stockholders' interests:	
A. 400 shares, 40% interest, book value	$ 60,000
B. 500 shares, 50% interest, book value	75,000
C. 100 shares, 10% interest, book value	15,000
	$150,000
After declaration but before distribution of 10% stock dividend	
If fair value ($130) is used as basis for entry:	
Common stock, 1,000 shares at $100 par	$100,000
Common stock distributable, 100 shares at $100 par	10,000
Paid-in capital in excess of par—common stock	3,000
Retained earnings ($50,000 − $13,000)	37,000
Total stockholders' equity	$150,000
After declaration and distribution of 10% stock dividend	
If fair value ($130) is used as basis for entry:	
Common stock, 1,100 shares at $100 par	$110,000
Paid-in capital in excess of par—common stock	3,000
Retained earnings ($50,000 − $13,000)	37,000
Total stockholders' equity	$150,000
Stockholders' interest:	
A. 440 shares, 40% interest, book value	$ 60,000
B. 550 shares, 50% interest, book value	75,000
C. 110 shares, 10% interest, book value	15,000
	$150,000

Stock Splits

If a company has undistributed earnings over several years and accumulates a sizable balance in retained earnings, the market value of its outstanding shares likely increases. Stock issued at prices less than $50 a share can easily attain a market price in excess of $200 a share. The higher the market price of a stock, however, the less readily some investors can purchase it.

The managements of many corporations believe that better public relations depend on wider ownership of the corporation stock. They therefore target a market price sufficiently low to be within range of the majority of potential investors. To reduce the market price of shares, they use the common device of a **stock split**. For example, after its stock price increased by 25-fold, **Qualcomm Inc.** split its stock 4-for-1. Qualcomm's stock had risen above $500 per share, raising concerns that Qualcomm could not meet an analyst target of $1,000 per share. The split reduced the analysts' target to $250, which it could better meet with wider distribution of shares at lower trading prices.[17]

From an accounting standpoint, Qualcomm **records no entry for a stock split.** However, it enters a memorandum note to indicate the changed par value of the shares

[17]Another classic case is **Coca-Cola**. Coca-Cola recently split its stock for the 11th time. If it had not done all of these splits, one of Coke's original shares would be worth $10.3 *million*. See S. Jakab, "Coca-Cola's Currency Is Its Resilience," *Wall Street Journal* (July 16, 2012).

and the increased number of shares. Illustration 15-10 shows the lack of change in stockholders' equity for a 2-for-1 stock split on 1,000 shares of $100 par value stock with the par being halved upon issuance of the additional shares.

ILLUSTRATION 15-10
Effects of a Stock Split

Stockholders' Equity before 2-for-1 Split		Stockholders' Equity after 2-for-1 Split	
Common stock, 1,000 shares at $100 par	$100,000	Common stock, 2,000 shares at $50 par	$100,000
Retained earnings	50,000	Retained earnings	50,000
	$150,000		$150,000

What do the numbers mean? SPLITSVILLE

Stock splits were all the rage in the booming stock market of the 1990s. Of major companies on the New York Stock Exchange, fewer than 80 companies split shares in 1990. By 1998, with stock prices soaring, over 200 companies split shares. Although the split does not increase a stockholder's proportionate ownership of the company, studies show that split shares usually outperform those that don't split, as well as the market as a whole, for several years after the split. In addition, the splits help the company keep the shares in more attractive price ranges.

What about when the market "turns south"? A number of companies who split their shares in the boom markets of the 1990s have since seen their share prices decline to a point considered too low. For example, Lucent traded at less than $5 a share following a 4-for-1 split. For some investors, these low-priced stocks are unattractive because some brokerage commissions rely on the number of shares traded, not the dollar amount. Others are concerned that low-priced shares are easier for would-be scamsters to manipulate. And if a company's per share price falls below $1 for 30 consecutive days, it is a violation of stock exchange listing requirements.

Some companies are considering reverse stock splits in which, say, 5 shares are consolidated into one. Thus, a stock previously trading at $5 per share would be part of an unsplit share trading at $25. Unsplitting might thus avoid some of the negative consequences of a low trading price. The downside to this strategy is that analysts might view reverse splits as additional bad news about the direction of the stock price. For example, Webvan, a failed Internet grocer, did a 1-for-25 reverse split just before it entered bankruptcy. And struggling Tenet Healthcare executed a 1-for-4 reverse split in combination with a debt restructuring, in order to get its stock price into a more favorable trading range.

Sources: Adapted from David Henry, "Stocks: The Case for Unsplitting," *BusinessWeek Online* (April 1, 2002); and M. Murphy, "Tenet CFO Says Reverse Split Could Help Land New Business," *Wall Street Journal* (October 2, 2012).

Stock Split and Stock Dividend Differentiated

From a legal standpoint, a stock split differs from a stock dividend. How? A stock split increases the number of shares outstanding and decreases the par or stated value per share. **A stock dividend, although it increases the number of shares outstanding, does not decrease the par value; thus, it increases the total par value of outstanding shares.**

The reasons for issuing a stock dividend are numerous and varied. Stock dividends can be primarily a publicity gesture **because many consider stock dividends as dividends**. Another reason is that the corporation may simply wish to retain profits in the business by capitalizing a part of retained earnings. In such a situation, it makes a transfer on declaration of a stock dividend from earned capital to contributed capital.

A corporation may also use a stock dividend, like a stock split, to increase the marketability of the stock, although marketability is often a secondary consideration. If the stock dividend is large, it has the same effect on market price as a stock split. **Whenever corporations issue additional shares for the purpose of reducing the unit market price, then the distribution more closely resembles a stock split than a stock dividend. This effect usually results only if the number of shares issued is more than 20–25 percent of the number of shares previously outstanding.** [4] A stock dividend of more than 20–25 percent of the number of shares previously outstanding is called a

large stock dividend.[18] Such a distribution should not be called a stock dividend but instead "a split-up effected in the form of a dividend" or "stock split."

Also, since a split-up effected in the form of a dividend does not alter the par value per share, companies generally are required to transfer the par value amount from retained earnings. In other words, companies transfer from retained earnings to capital stock **the par value of the stock issued**, as opposed to a transfer of the market price of the shares issued as in the case of a small stock dividend.[19] For example, **Brown Group, Inc.** at one time authorized a 2-for-1 split, effected in the form of a stock dividend. As a result of this authorization, it distributed approximately 10.5 million shares, and transferred more than $39 million representing the par value of the shares issued from Retained Earnings to the Common Stock account.

To illustrate a large stock dividend (stock split-up effected in the form of a dividend), Rockland Steel, Inc. declared a 30 percent stock dividend on November 20, payable December 29 to stockholders of record December 12. At the date of declaration, 1,000,000 shares, par value $10, are outstanding and with a fair value of $200 per share. The entries are:

At date of declaration (November 20)

Retained Earnings	3,000,000	
Common Stock Dividend Distributable		3,000,000

Computation: 1,000,000 shares × 30% = 300,000; 300,000 Additional shares × $10 Par value = $3,000,000

At date of distribution (December 29)

Common Stock Dividend Distributable	3,000,000	
Common Stock		3,000,000

Illustration 15-11 summarizes and compares the effects in the balance sheet and related items of various types of dividends and stock splits.

ILLUSTRATION 15-11
Effects of Dividends and Stock Splits on Financial Statement Elements

Effect on:	Declaration of Cash Dividend	Payment of Cash Dividend	Declaration and Distribution of Small Stock Dividend	Declaration and Distribution of Large Stock Dividend	Stock Split
Retained earnings	Decrease	–0–	Decrease[a]	Decrease[b]	–0–
Capital stock	–0–	–0–	Increase[b]	Increase[b]	–0–
Additional paid-in capital	–0–	–0–	Increase[c]	–0–	–0–
Total stockholders' equity	Decrease	–0–	–0–	–0–	–0–
Working capital	Decrease	–0–	–0–	–0–	–0–
Total assets	–0–	Decrease	–0–	–0–	–0–
Number of shares outstanding	–0–	–0–	Increase	Increase	Increase

[a]Market price of shares. [b]Par or stated value of shares. [c]Excess of market price over par.

[18]The SEC has added more precision to the 20–25 percent rule. Specifically, the SEC indicates that companies should consider distributions of 25 percent or more as a "split-up effected in the form of a dividend." Companies should account for distributions of less than 25 percent as a stock dividend. The SEC more precisely defined GAAP here. As a result, public companies follow the SEC rule.

[19]Often, a company records a split-up effected in the form of a dividend as a debit to Paid-in Capital instead of Retained Earnings to indicate that this transaction should affect only paid-in capital accounts. No reduction of retained earnings is required except as indicated by legal requirements. *For homework purposes, assume that the debit is to Retained Earnings.* See, for example, Taylor W. Foster III and Edmund Scribner, "Accounting for Stock Dividends and Stock Splits: Corrections to Textbook Coverage," *Issues in Accounting Education* (February 1998).

What do the numbers mean? DIVIDENDS UP, DIVIDENDS DOWN

As the economy recovered from the financial crisis, a number of U.S. companies increased their dividend payout in a sign of growing confidence and rising cash balances. For example, early in 2011 a number of companies increased dividends, including **CVS/Caremark Corp.**, **Family Dollar Stores Inc.**, and **Schlumberger Ltd.** The number was up from the prior year amid concerns that dividend payouts would level off if the economy slows.

In such a slow growth environment, with interest rates persistently low and the tax treatment of dividends still favorable, an investment strategy focusing on stocks with the potential of *increasing* dividends may be particularly timely. Said one market watcher, "Investors too often overlook the importance of dividends, particularly the contribution to total return from reinvested dividends. . . . Dividends also can provide a good hedge against inflation in the form of a growing stream of income."

A look at the returns for "dividend growers" compared to "dividend cutters" in the following chart supports the advice to keep an eye on dividend growth.

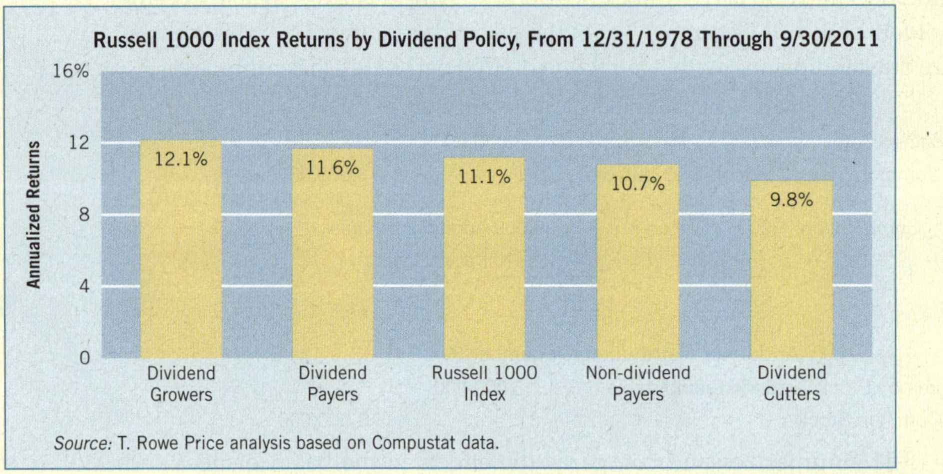

As indicated, from 1979 through the end of 2011, stocks in the Russell 1000 Index that were growing their dividends outperformed dividend-paying stocks, the index itself, non-dividend-paying stocks, and stocks that cut their dividends. During that time, an investment of $100 in dividend growers would have risen to $4,018 compared with $3,134 based on the index return. Dividend payers outperformed non-dividend payers during down and flat markets, and offered lower volatility of returns in all market environments.

Furthermore, the best performers are stocks with the combination of a relatively high yield—though not always the very highest—and a high dividend growth rate. This is because high yields sometimes are a function of beaten-down stock prices due to poor corporate earnings prospects or other issues. Indeed, in such cases, dividend cuts could be in the offing. By contrast, stocks that have performed best historically have been those in which the company's true growth potential has been undervalued by investors. Thus, companies with growing dividends are signaling confidence about their future earnings and most likely to perform well throughout market cycles, which make them good candidates for long-term growth.

Source: "Dividend Growth Stocks May Be Timely as the Economy Sputters," *T. Rowe Price Report* (Fall 2011).

Disclosure of Restrictions on Retained Earnings

Many corporations restrict retained earnings or dividends, without any formal journal entries. Such restrictions are **best disclosed by note**. Parenthetical notations are sometimes used, but restrictions imposed by bond indentures and loan agreements commonly require an extended explanation. Notes provide a medium for more complete explanations and free the financial statements from abbreviated notations. The note disclosure should reveal the source of the restriction, pertinent provisions, and the amount of retained earnings subject to restriction, or the amount not restricted.

Restrictions may be based on the retention of a certain retained earnings balance, the ability to maintain certain working capital requirements, additional borrowing, and other considerations. The example from the annual report of **Alberto-Culver Company** in Illustration 15-12 shows a note disclosing potential restrictions on retained earnings and dividends.

ILLUSTRATION 15-12
Disclosure of Restrictions on Retained Earnings and Dividends

Alberto-Culver Company

Note 3 (in part): The $200 million revolving credit facility, the term note, and the receivables agreement impose restrictions on such items as total debt, working capital, dividend payments, treasury stock purchases, and interest expense. At year-end, the company was in compliance with these arrangements, and $220 million of consolidated retained earnings was not restricted as to the payment of dividends.

PRESENTATION AND ANALYSIS OF STOCKHOLDERS' EQUITY

Presentation

Balance Sheet

9 LEARNING OBJECTIVE
Indicate how to present and analyze stockholders' equity.

Illustration 15-13 shows a comprehensive stockholders' equity section from the balance sheet of Frost Company that includes most of the equity items we discussed in this chapter.

ILLUSTRATION 15-13
Comprehensive Stockholders' Equity Presentation

FROST COMPANY
STOCKHOLDERS' EQUITY
DECEMBER 31, 2014

Capital stock		
Preferred stock, $100 par value, 7% cumulative, 100,000 shares authorized, 30,000 shares issued and outstanding		$ 3,000,000
Common stock, no-par, stated value $10 per share, 500,000 shares authorized, 400,000 shares issued		4,000,000
Common stock dividend distributable, 20,000 shares		200,000
Total capital stock		7,200,000
Additional paid-in capital[20]		
Excess over par—preferred	$150,000	
Excess over stated value—common	840,000	990,000
Total paid-in capital		8,190,000
Retained earnings		4,360,000
Total paid-in capital and retained earnings		12,550,000
Less: Cost of treasury stock (2,000 shares, common)		190,000
Accumulated other comprehensive loss[21]		360,000
Total stockholders' equity		$12,000,000

[20]*Accounting Trends and Techniques—2012* reports that of its 500 surveyed companies, 465 had additional paid-in capital.

[21]Companies may include a number of items in the "Accumulated other comprehensive income (loss)." *Accounting Trends and Techniques—2012* reports that of its 500 surveyed companies, 407 reported cumulative translation adjustments, 386 reported defined benefit postretirement plan adjustments (discussed in Chapter 20), 286 reported changes in the fair value of derivatives (discussed in Appendix 17A), and 218 reported unrealized losses/gains on certain investments (discussed in Chapter 17). A number of companies had more than one item.

Frost should disclose the pertinent rights and privileges of the various securities outstanding. For example, companies must disclose all of the following: dividend and liquidation preferences, participation rights, call prices and dates, conversion or exercise prices and pertinent dates, sinking fund requirements, unusual voting rights, and significant terms of contracts to issue additional shares. Liquidation preferences should be disclosed in the equity section of the balance sheet, rather than in the notes to the financial statements, to emphasize the possible effect of this restriction on future cash flows. [5]

Statement of Stockholders' Equity

The **statement of stockholders' equity** is frequently presented in the following basic format.

1. Balance at the beginning of the period.
2. Additions.
3. Deductions.
4. Balance at the end of the period.

Companies must disclose changes in the separate accounts comprising stockholders' equity, to make the financial statements sufficiently informative. Such changes may be disclosed in separate statements or in the basic financial statements or notes thereto.[22]

A **columnar format** for the presentation of changes in stockholders' equity items in published annual reports is gaining in popularity. An example is ConAgra Foods' statement of common stockholders' equity, shown in Illustration 15-14.

ConAgra Foods, Inc. and Subsidiaries

For the Fiscal Year Ended May 2012

(Dollars in millions except per share amounts)	Common Shares	Common Stock	Additional Paid-in Capital	Retained Earnings	Accumulated Other Comprehensive Income (Loss)	Treasury Stock	Noncontrolling Interests	Total Equity
Balance of May 29, 2011	567.9	$2,839.7	$899.1	$4,690.3	$ (91.2)	$(3,668.2)	$ 7.0	$4,676.7
Stock option and incentive plans			3.9	(1.3)		252.9		255.5
Currency translation adjustment, net of reclassification adjustment					(52.0)		(4.4)	(56.4)
Repurchase of common shares						(352.4)		(352.4)
Unrealized loss on securities					(0.1)			(0.1)
Derivative adjustment, net of reclassification adjustment					(89.1)			(89.1)
Acquisition of majority interest in ATFL							92.6	92.6
Activities of noncontrolling interests			(1.5)				1.3	(0.2)
Pension and postretirement healthcare benefits					(66.7)			(66.7)
Dividends declared on common stock; $0.95 per share				(391.8)				(391.8)
Net income attributable to ConAgra Foods, Inc.				467.9				467.9
Balance at May 27, 2012	567.9	$2,839.7	$901.5	$4,765.1	$(299.1)	$(3,767.7)	$96.5	$4,536.0

ILLUSTRATION 15-14
Columnar Format for Statement of Common Stockholders' Equity

[22]*Accounting Trends and Techniques—2012* reports that of the 500 companies surveyed, 486 presented statements of stockholders' equity, 4 presented separate statements of retained earnings only, 1 presented combined statements of income and retained earnings, and 9 presented changes in equity items in the notes only.

Analysis

Analysts use stockholders' equity ratios to evaluate a company's profitability and long-term solvency. We discuss and illustrate the following three ratios below.

Gateway to the Profession

Financial Analysis Primer

1. Return on common stock equity.
2. Payout ratio.
3. Book value per share.

Return on Common Stock Equity

The **return on common stock equity**, often referred to as **return on equity (ROE)**, measures profitability from the common stockholders' viewpoint. This ratio shows how many dollars of net income the company earned for each dollar invested by the owners. Return on equity also helps investors judge the worthiness of a stock when the overall market is not doing well. For example, **Best Buy** shares dropped nearly 40 percent, along with the broader market in 2001–2002. But a review of its return on equity during this period and since shows a steady return of 20 to 22 percent while the overall market ROE declined from 16 percent to 8 percent. More importantly, Best Buy and other stocks, such as **3M** and **Procter & Gamble**, recovered their lost market value, while other stocks with less robust ROEs stayed in the doldrums.

Return on equity equals net income less preferred dividends, divided by average common stockholders' equity. For example, assume that Gerber's Inc. had net income of \$360,000, declared and paid preferred dividends of \$54,000, and average common stockholders' equity of \$2,550,000. Illustration 15-15 shows how to compute Gerber's ratio.

$$\text{Return on Common Stock Equity} = \frac{\text{Net Income} - \text{Preferred Dividends}}{\text{Average Common Stockholders' Equity}}$$

$$= \frac{\$360{,}000 - \$54{,}000}{\$2{,}550{,}000}$$

$$= 12\%$$

ILLUSTRATION 15-15
Computation of Return on Common Stock Equity

As shown in Illustration 15-15, when preferred stock is present, income available to common stockholders equals net income less preferred dividends. Similarly, the amount of common stock equity used in this ratio equals **total stockholders' equity less the par value of preferred stock.**

A company can improve its return on common stock equity through the prudent use of debt or preferred stock financing. **Trading on the equity** describes the practice of using borrowed money or issuing preferred stock in hopes of obtaining a higher rate of return on the money used. Shareholders win if return on the assets is higher than the cost of financing these assets. When this happens, the return on common stock equity will exceed the return on total assets. In short, the company is "trading on the equity at a gain." In this situation, the money obtained from bondholders or preferred stockholders earns enough to pay the interest or preferred dividends and leaves a profit for the common stockholders. On the other hand, if the cost of the financing is higher that the rate earned on the assets, the company is trading on equity at a loss and stockholders lose.

Payout Ratio

Another ratio of interest to investors, the **payout ratio**, is the ratio of cash dividends to net income. If preferred stock is outstanding, this ratio equals cash dividends paid to common stockholders, divided by net income available to common stockholders.

For example, assume that Troy Co. has cash dividends of $100,000 and net income of $500,000, and no preferred stock outstanding. Illustration 15-16 shows the payout ratio computation.

ILLUSTRATION 15-16
Computation of Payout Ratio

$$\text{Payout Ratio} = \frac{\text{Cash Dividends}}{\text{Net Income}}$$

$$= \frac{\$100,000}{\$500,000}$$

$$= 20\%$$

Recently, the payout ratio has plummeted. In 1982, more than half of earnings were converted to dividends. In the fourth quarter of 2011, just 36 percent of the earnings of the S&P 500 was distributed via dividends.[23]

You will want to read the **IFRS INSIGHTS** on pages 874–880 for discussion of IFRS related to stockholders' equity.

Book Value per Share

A much-used basis for evaluating net worth is found in the book value or equity value per share of stock. **Book value per share** of stock is the amount each share would receive if the company were liquidated **on the basis of amounts reported on the balance sheet.** However, the figure loses much of its relevance if the valuations on the balance sheet fail to approximate fair value of the assets. Book value per share equals common stockholders' equity divided by outstanding common shares. Assume that Chen Corporation's common stockholders' equity is $1,000,000 and it has 100,000 shares of common stock outstanding. Illustration 15-17 shows its book value per share computation.

ILLUSTRATION 15-17
Computation of Book Value per Share

$$\text{Book Value per Share} = \frac{\text{Common Stockholders' Equity}}{\text{Outstanding Shares}}$$

$$= \frac{\$1,000,000}{100,000}$$

$$= \$10 \text{ per share}$$

KEY TERMS

Additional Paid-in Capital, 825
book value per share, 850
callable preferred stock, 835
cash dividends, 839
common stock, 824
contributed (paid-in) capital, 824
convertible preferred stock, 835
cost method, 831
cumulative preferred stock, 835
dividend in arrears, 835
earned capital, 824
large stock dividend, 845
leveraged buyout (LBO), 830

SUMMARY OF LEARNING OBJECTIVES

1 Discuss the characteristics of the corporate form of organization. Among the specific characteristics of the corporate form that affect accounting are the (1) influence of state corporate law, (2) use of the capital stock or share system, and (3) development of a variety of ownership interests. In the absence of restrictive provisions, each share of stock carries the right to share proportionately in (1) profits and losses, (2) management (the right to vote for directors), (3) corporate assets upon liquidation, and (4) any new issues of stock of the same class (called the preemptive right).

2 Identify the key components of stockholders' equity. Stockholders' or owners' equity is classified into two categories: contributed capital and earned capital. Contributed capital (paid-in capital) describes the total amount paid in on capital stock. Put another way, it is the amount that stockholders invested in the corporation for use in the business. Contributed capital includes items such as the par value of all outstanding capital stock and premiums less any discounts on issuance. Earned capital is the

[23]R. Shaw, "S&P 500 Dividend Payout Ratio Still Giving Off Caution Signals," *http://seekingalpha.com* (January 16, 2012).

capital that develops if the business operates profitably; it consists of all undistributed income that remains invested in the company.

3 Explain the accounting procedures for issuing shares of stock. Accounts are kept for the following different types of stock. *Par value stock:* (a) preferred stock or common stock, (b) paid-in capital in excess of par or additional paid-in capital, and (c) discount on stock. *No-par stock:* common stock or common stock and additional paid-in capital, if stated value used. *Stock issued in combination with other securities (lump-sum sales):* The two methods of allocation available are (a) the proportional method and (b) the incremental method. *Stock issued in noncash transactions:* When issuing stock for services or property other than cash, the company should record the property or services at either the fair value of the stock issued, or the fair value of the noncash consideration received, whichever is more clearly determinable.

4 Describe the accounting for treasury stock. The cost method is generally used in accounting for treasury stock. This method derives its name from the fact that a company maintains the Treasury Stock account at the cost of the shares purchased. Under the cost method, a company debits the Treasury Stock account for the cost of the shares acquired and credits it for this same cost upon reissuance. The price received for the stock when originally issued does not affect the entries to record the acquisition and reissuance of the treasury stock.

5 Explain the accounting for and reporting of preferred stock. Preferred stock is a special class of shares that possesses certain preferences or features not possessed by the common stock. The features that are most often associated with preferred stock issues are (1) preference as to dividends, (2) preference as to assets in the event of liquidation, (3) convertible into common stock, (4) callable at the option of the corporation, and (5) nonvoting. At issuance, the accounting for preferred stock is similar to that for common stock. When convertible preferred stock is converted, a company uses the book value method. It debits Preferred Stock, along with any related Paid-in Capital in Excess of Par—Preferred Stock and credits Common Stock and Paid-in Capital in Excess of Par—Common Stock (if an excess exists).

6 Describe the policies used in distributing dividends. The state incorporation laws normally provide information concerning the legal restrictions related to the payment of dividends. Corporations rarely pay dividends in an amount equal to the legal limit. This is due, in part, to the fact that companies use assets represented by undistributed earnings to finance future operations of the business. If a company is considering declaring a dividend, it must ask two preliminary questions. (1) Is the condition of the corporation such that the dividend is **legally permissible**? (2) Is the condition of the corporation such that a dividend is **economically sound**?

7 Identify the various forms of dividend distributions. Dividends are of the following types: (1) cash dividends, (2) property dividends, (3) liquidating dividends (dividends based on other than retained earnings), and (4) stock dividends (the issuance by a corporation of its own stock to its stockholders on a pro rata basis, but without receiving consideration).

8 Explain the accounting for small and large stock dividends, and for stock splits. Generally accepted accounting principles require that the accounting for small stock dividends (less than 20–25 percent) rely on the fair value of the stock issued. When declaring a common stock dividend, a company debits Retained Earnings at the fair value of the stock it distributes. The entry includes a credit to Common Stock Dividend Distributable at par value times the number of shares, with any excess credited to Paid-in Capital in Excess of Par—Common Stock. If the number of shares issued exceeds 20–25 percent of the shares outstanding (large stock dividend), it debits Retained Earnings at par value and credits Common Stock Distributable—there is no additional paid-in capital.

A stock dividend is a capitalization of retained earnings that reduces retained earnings and increases certain contributed capital accounts. The par value per share and total

Gateway to the Profession

Expanded Discussion of Quasi-Reorganization

stockholders' equity remain unchanged with a stock dividend, and all stockholders retain their same proportionate share of ownership. A stock split results in an increase or decrease in the number of shares outstanding, with a corresponding decrease or increase in the par or stated value per share. No accounting entry is required for a stock split.

9 Indicate how to present and analyze stockholders' equity. The stockholders' equity section of a balance sheet includes capital stock, additional paid-in capital, and retained earnings. A company might also present additional items such as treasury stock and accumulated other comprehensive income. Companies often provide a statement of stockholders' equity. Common ratios that use stockholders' equity amounts are return on common stock equity, payout ratio, and book value per share.

APPENDIX 15A DIVIDEND PREFERENCES AND BOOK VALUE PER SHARE

DIVIDEND PREFERENCES

LEARNING OBJECTIVE 10
Explain the different types of preferred stock dividends and their effect on book value per share.

Illustrations 15A-1 to 15A-4 indicate the **effects** of various **dividend preferences** on dividend distributions to common and preferred stockholders. Assume that in 2014, Mason Company is to distribute $50,000 as cash dividends, its outstanding common stock has a par value of $400,000, and its 6 percent preferred stock has a par value of $100,000. Mason would distribute dividends to each class, employing the assumptions given, as follows.

1. If the preferred stock is noncumulative and nonparticipating:

ILLUSTRATION 15A-1
Dividend Distribution, Noncumulative and Nonparticipating Preferred

	Preferred	Common	Total
6% of $100,000	$6,000		$ 6,000
The remainder to common		$44,000	44,000
Totals	$6,000	$44,000	$50,000

2. If the preferred stock is cumulative and nonparticipating, and Mason Company did not pay dividends on the preferred stock in the preceding two years:

ILLUSTRATION 15A-2
Dividend Distribution, Cumulative and Nonparticipating Preferred, with Dividends in Arrears

	Preferred	Common	Total
Dividends in arrears, 6% of $100,000 for 2 years	$12,000		$12,000
Current year's dividend, 6% of $100,000	6,000		6,000
The remainder to common		$32,000	32,000
Totals	$18,000	$32,000	$50,000

3. If the preferred stock is noncumulative and is fully participating:[24]

[24]When preferred stock is participating, there may be different agreements as to how the participation feature is to be executed. However, in the absence of any specific agreement the following procedure is recommended:

a. After the preferred stock is assigned its current year's dividend, the common stock will receive a "like" percentage of par value outstanding. In example (3) in Illustration 15A-3, this amounts to 6 percent of $400,000.

b. In example (3), shown in Illustration 15A-3, the remainder of the declared dividend is $20,000. We divide this amount by total par value ($500,000) to find the rate of participation to be applied to each class of stock. In this case, the rate of participation is 4 percent ($20,000 ÷ $500,000), which we then multiply by the par value of each class of stock to determine the amount of participation.

ILLUSTRATION 15A-3
Dividend Distribution, Noncumulative and Fully Participating Preferred

	Preferred	Common	Total
Current year's dividend, 6%	$ 6,000	$24,000	$30,000
Participating dividend of 4%	4,000	16,000	20,000
Totals	$10,000	$40,000	$50,000

The participating dividend was determined as follows.

Current year's dividend:	
Preferred, 6% of $100,000 = $ 6,000	
Common, 6% of $400,000 = 24,000	$ 30,000
Amount available for participation ($50,000 − $30,000)	$ 20,000
Par value of stock that is to participate ($100,000 + $400,000)	$500,000
Rate of participation ($20,000 ÷ $500,000)	4%
Participating dividend:	
Preferred, 4% of $100,000	$ 4,000
Common, 4% of $400,000	16,000
	$ 20,000

4. If the preferred stock is cumulative and is fully participating, and Mason Company did not pay dividends on the preferred stock in the preceding two years:

ILLUSTRATION 15A-4
Dividend Distribution, Cumulative and Fully Participating Preferred, with Dividends in Arrears

	Preferred	Common	Total
Dividends in arrears, 6% of $100,000 for 2 years	$12,000		$12,000
Current year's dividend, 6%	6,000	$24,000	30,000
Participating dividend, 1.6% ($8,000 ÷ $500,000)	1,600	6,400	8,000
Totals	$19,600	$30,400	$50,000

BOOK VALUE PER SHARE

Book value per share in its simplest form is computed as net assets divided by outstanding common shares at the end of the year. The computation of book value per share becomes more complicated if a company has preferred stock in its capital structure. For example, if preferred dividends are in arrears, if the preferred stock is participating, or if preferred stock has a redemption or liquidating value higher than its carrying amount, the company must allocate retained earnings between the preferred and common stockholders in computing book value.

To illustrate, assume that the following situation exists.

ILLUSTRATION 15A-5
Computation of Book Value per Share—No Dividends in Arrears

Stockholders' equity	Preferred	Common
Preferred stock, 5%	$300,000	
Common stock		$400,000
Excess of issue price over par of common stock		37,500
Retained earnings		162,582
Totals	$300,000	$600,082
Common shares outstanding		4,000
Book value per share		$150.02

The situation in Illustration 15A-5 assumes that no preferred dividends are in arrears and that the preferred is not participating. Now assume that the same facts exist except that the 5 percent preferred is cumulative, participating up to 8 percent, and that dividends for three years before the current year are in arrears. Illustration 15A-6 (page 854) shows how to compute the book value of the common stock, assuming that no action has yet been taken concerning dividends for the current year.

ILLUSTRATION 15A-6
Computation of Book Value per Share—with Dividends in Arrears

Stockholders' equity	Preferred	Common
Preferred stock, 5%	$300,000	
Common stock		$400,000
Excess of issue price over par of common stock		37,500
Retained earnings:		
Dividends in arrears (3 years at 5% a year)	45,000	
Current year requirement at 5%	15,000	20,000
Participating—additional 3%	9,000	12,000
Remainder to common		61,582
Totals	$369,000	$531,082
Shares outstanding		4,000
Book value per share		$132.77

In connection with the book value computation, the analyst must know how to handle the following items: the number of authorized and unissued shares; the number of treasury shares on hand; any commitments with respect to the issuance of unissued shares or the reissuance of treasury shares; and the relative rights and privileges of the various types of stock authorized. As an example, if the liquidating value of the preferred stock is higher than its carrying amount, the liquidating amount should be used in the book value computation.

SUMMARY OF LEARNING OBJECTIVE FOR APPENDIX 15A

10 Explain the different types of preferred stock dividends and their effect on book value per share. The dividend preferences of preferred stock affect the dividends paid to stockholders. Preferred stock can be (1) cumulative or noncumulative, and (2) fully participating, partially participating, or nonparticipating. If preferred dividends are in arrears, if the preferred stock is participating, or if preferred stock has a redemption or liquidation value higher than its carrying amount, allocate retained earnings between preferred and common stockholders in computing book value per share.

DEMONSTRATION PROBLEM

D'Ouville Company was formed on July 1, 2011. It was authorized to issue 500,000 shares of $10 par value common stock and 100,000 shares of 8%, $25 par value, cumulative and nonparticipating preferred stock. D'Ouville Company has a July 1–June 30 fiscal year. The following information relates to the stockholders' equity accounts of D'Ouville Company.

Common Stock: Prior to the 2013–2014 fiscal year, D'Ouville Company had 110,000 shares of outstanding common stock issued as follows.

1. 95,000 shares were issued for cash on July 1, 2011, at $31 per share.
2. On July 24, 2011, 5,000 shares were exchanged for a plot of land which cost the seller $70,000 in 2005 and had an estimated fair value of $220,000 on July 24, 2011.
3. 10,000 shares were issued on March 1, 2013, for $42 per share.

During the 2013–2014 fiscal year, the following transactions regarding common stock took place.

November 30, 2013 — D'Ouville purchased 2,000 shares of its own stock on the open market at $39 per share. D'Ouville uses the cost method for treasury stock.

December 15, 2013	D'Ouville declared a 5% stock dividend for stockholders of record on January 15, 2014, to be issued on January 31, 2014. D'Ouville was having a liquidity problem and could not afford a cash dividend at the time. D'Ouville's common stock was selling at $52 per share on December 15, 2013.
June 20, 2014	D'Ouville sold 500 shares of its own common stock that it had purchased on November 30, 2013, for $21,000.

Preferred Stock: D'Ouville issued 100,000 shares of preferred stock at $44 per share on July 1, 2012.

Cash Dividends: D'Ouville has followed a schedule of declaring cash dividends in December and June, with payment being made to stockholders of record in the following month. The cash dividends which have been declared since inception of the company through June 30, 2014, are shown below.

Declaration Date	Common Stock	Preferred Stock
12/15/12	$0.30 per share	$0.50 per share
6/15/13	$0.30 per share	$0.50 per share
12/15/13	—	$0.50 per share

No cash dividends were declared during June 2014 due to the company's liquidity problems.

Retained Earnings: As of June 30, 2013, D'Ouville retained earnings account had a balance of $550,000. For the fiscal year ending June 30, 2014, D'Ouville reported net income of $120,000.

Instructions

Prepare the stockholders' equity section of the balance sheet, including appropriate notes, for D'Ouville Company as of June 30, 2014, as it should appear in its annual report to the shareholders.

Solution

D'OUVILLE COMPANY
STOCKHOLDERS' EQUITY
JUNE 30, 2014

Capital stock		
4% preferred stock, $25 par value, cumulative and nonparticipating, 100,000 shares authorized, 100,000 shares issued and outstanding—Note A		$2,500,000
Common stock, $10 par value, 500,000 shares authorized, 115,400 shares issued, with 1,500 shares held in the treasury		1,154,000
Additional paid-in capital		
On preferred stock	$1,900,000	
On common stock	2,711,800*	
On treasury stock	1,500	4,613,300
Total paid-in capital		8,267,300
Retained earnings		339,200**
Total paid-in capital and retained earnings		8,606,500
Less: Treasury stock, 1,500 shares at cost		58,500
Total stockholders' equity		$8,548,000

Note A: D'Ouville Company is in arrears on the preferred stock in the amount of $100,000.

*Premium on Common Stock:

Issue of 95,000 shares × ($31 − $10)	$1,995,000
Issue of 5,000 shares for plot of land ($220,000 − $50,000)	170,000
10,000 shares issued (3/1/13) [10,000 × ($42 − $10)]	320,000
5,400 shares as dividend [5,400 × ($52 − $10)]	226,800
	$2,711,800

**Retained Earnings:

Beginning balance	+	Income	−	Stock dividend	−	Preferred dividend	=	Ret. earnings, ending balance
$550,000	+	$120,000	−	$280,800	−	$50,000	=	$339,200

FASB CODIFICATION

FASB Codification References

[1] FASB ASC 480-10-05. [Predecessor literature: "Accounting for Certain Financial Instruments with Characteristics of Both Liabilities and Equity," *Statement of Financial Accounting Standards No. 150* (Norwalk Conn.: FASB, 2003).]

[2] FASB ASC 505-10-50-3. [Predecessor literature: "Disclosure of Information about Capital Structure," *Statement of Financial Accounting Standards No. 129* (Norwalk, Conn.: FASB, 1997).]

[3] FASB ASC 505-20-05-2. [Predecessor literature: American Institute of Certified Public Accountants, *Accounting Research and Terminology Bulletins, No. 43* (New York: AICPA, 1961), Ch. 7, par. 10.]

[4] FASB ASC 505-20-25-3. [Predecessor literature: American Institute of Certified Public Accountants, *Accounting Research and Terminology Bulletins, No. 43* (New York: AICPA, 1961), par. 13.]

[5] FASB ASC 505-10-50-3. [Predecessor literature: "Disclosure of Information about Capital Structure," *Statement of Financial Accounting Standards No. 129* (Norwalk, Conn.: FASB, February 1997), par. 4.]

Exercises

If your school has a subscription to the FASB Codification, go to *http://aaahq.org/ascLogin.cfm* to log in and prepare responses to the following. Provide Codification references for your responses.

CE15-1 Access the glossary ("Master Glossary") to answer the following.

(a) What is a "convertible security"?
(b) What is a "stock dividend"?
(c) What is a "stock split"?
(d) What are "participation rights"?

CE15-2 At what percentage point can the issuance of additional shares still qualify as a stock dividend, as opposed to a stock split?

CE15-3 A company plans to issue shares and wants to know the SEC's stance on the accounting treatment for the costs of issuing stock. Can these costs be deferred, or must they be expensed immediately?

CE15-4 If a company chooses to purchase its own shares and then either (1) retires the repurchased shares and issues additional shares, or (2) resells the repurchased shares, can a gain or loss be recognized by the company? Why or why not?

An additional Codification case can be found in the Using Your Judgment section, on page 873.

Be sure to check the book's companion website for a Review and Analysis Exercise, with solution.

WileyPLUS **Brief Exercises, Exercises, Problems, and many more learning and assessment tools and resources are available for practice in WileyPLUS.**

Note: All asterisked Questions, Exercises, and Problems relate to material in the appendix to the chapter.

QUESTIONS

1. In the absence of restrictive provisions, what are the basic rights of stockholders of a corporation?
2. Why is a preemptive right important?
3. Distinguish between common and preferred stock.
4. Why is the distinction between paid-in capital and retained earnings important?
5. Explain each of the following terms: authorized capital stock, unissued capital stock, issued capital stock, outstanding capital stock, and treasury stock.
6. What is meant by par value, and what is its significance to stockholders?

7. Describe the accounting for the issuance for cash of no-par value common stock at a price in excess of the stated value of the common stock.

8. Explain the difference between the proportional method and the incremental method of allocating the proceeds of lump-sum sales of capital stock.

9. What are the different bases for stock valuation when assets other than cash are received for issued shares of stock?

10. Explain how underwriting costs and accounting and legal fees associated with the issuance of stock should be recorded.

11. For what reasons might a corporation purchase its own stock?

12. Discuss the propriety of showing:

(a) Treasury stock as an asset.

(b) "Gain" or "loss" on sale of treasury stock as additions to or deductions from income.

(c) Dividends received on treasury stock as income.

13. What features or rights may alter the character of preferred stock?

14. Dagwood Inc. recently noted that its 4% preferred stock and 4% participating preferred stock, which are both cumulative, have priority as to dividends up to 4% of their par value. Its participating preferred stock participates equally with the common stock in any dividends in excess of 4%. What is meant by the term participating? Cumulative?

15. Where in the financial statements is preferred stock normally reported?

16. List possible sources of additional paid-in capital.

17. Satchel Inc. purchases 10,000 shares of its own previously issued $10 par common stock for $290,000. Assuming the shares are held in the treasury with intent to reissue, what effect does this transaction have on (a) net income, (b) total assets, (c) total paid-in capital, and (d) total stockholders' equity?

18. Indicate how each of the following accounts should be classified in the stockholders' equity section.

(a) Common Stock.

(b) Retained Earnings.

(c) Paid-in Capital in Excess of Par—Common Stock.

(d) Treasury Stock.

(e) Paid-in Capital from Treasury Stock.

(f) Paid-in Capital in Excess of Stated Value—Common Stock.

(g) Preferred Stock.

19. What factors influence the dividend policy of a company?

20. What are the principal considerations of a board of directors in making decisions involving dividend declarations? Discuss briefly.

21. Dividends are sometimes said to have been paid "out of retained earnings." What is the error, if any, in that statement?

22. Distinguish among: cash dividends, property dividends, liquidating dividends, and stock dividends.

23. Describe the accounting entry for a stock dividend, if any. Describe the accounting entry for a stock split, if any.

24. Stock splits and stock dividends may be used by a corporation to change the number of shares of its stock outstanding.

(a) What is meant by a stock split effected in the form of a dividend?

(b) From an accounting viewpoint, explain how the stock split effected in the form of a dividend differs from an ordinary stock dividend.

(c) How should a stock dividend that has been declared but not yet issued be classified in a balance sheet? Why?

25. The following comment appeared in the notes of Colorado Corporation's annual report: "Such distributions, representing proceeds from the sale of Sarazan, Inc., were paid in the form of partial liquidating dividends and were in lieu of a portion of the Company's ordinary cash dividends." How would a partial liquidating dividend be accounted for in the financial records?

26. This comment appeared in the annual report of MacCloud Inc.: "The Company could pay cash or property dividends on the Class A common stock without paying cash or property dividends on the Class B common stock. But if the Company pays any cash or property dividends on the Class B common stock, it would be required to pay at least the same dividend on the Class A common stock." How is a property dividend accounted for in the financial records?

27. For what reasons might a company restrict a portion of its retained earnings?

28. How are restrictions of retained earnings reported?

***29.** McNabb Corp. had $100,000 of 7%, $20 par value preferred stock and 12,000 shares of $25 par value common stock outstanding throughout 2014.

(a) Assuming that total dividends declared in 2014 were $64,000, and that the preferred stock is not cumulative but is fully participating, common stockholders should receive 2014 dividends of what amount?

(b) Assuming that total dividends declared in 2014 were $64,000, and that the preferred stock is fully participating and cumulative with preferred dividends in arrears for 2013, preferred stockholders should receive 2014 dividends totaling what amount?

(c) Assuming that total dividends declared in 2014 were $30,000, that the preferred stock is cumulative, nonparticipating, and was issued on January 1, 2013, and that $5,000 of preferred dividends were declared and paid in 2013, the common stockholders should receive 2014 dividends totaling what amount?

BRIEF EXERCISES

3 **BE15-1** Buttercup Corporation issued 300 shares of $10 par value common stock for $4,500. Prepare Buttercup's journal entry.

3 **BE15-2** Swarten Corporation issued 600 shares of no-par common stock for $8,200. Prepare Swarten's journal entry if (a) the stock has no stated value, and (b) the stock has a stated value of $2 per share.

4 9 **BE15-3** Wilco Corporation has the following account balances at December 31, 2014.

Common stock, $5 par value	$ 510,000
Treasury stock	90,000
Retained earnings	2,340,000
Paid-in capital in excess of par—common stock	1,320,000

Prepare Wilco's December 31, 2014, stockholders' equity section.

3 **BE15-4** Ravonette Corporation issued 300 shares of $10 par value common stock and 100 shares of $50 par value preferred stock for a lump sum of $13,500. The common stock has a market price of $20 per share, and the preferred stock has a market price of $90 per share. Prepare the journal entry to record the issuance.

3 **BE15-5** On February 1, 2014, Buffalo Corporation issued 3,000 shares of its $5 par value common stock for land worth $31,000. Prepare the February 1, 2014, journal entry.

3 **BE15-6** Moonwalker Corporation issued 2,000 shares of its $10 par value common stock for $60,000. Moonwalker also incurred $1,500 of costs associated with issuing the stock. Prepare Moonwalker's journal entry to record the issuance of the company's stock.

4 **BE15-7** Sprinkle Inc. has outstanding 10,000 shares of $10 par value common stock. On July 1, 2014, Sprinkle reacquired 100 shares at $87 per share. On September 1, Sprinkle reissued 60 shares at $90 per share. On November 1, Sprinkle reissued 40 shares at $83 per share. Prepare Sprinkle's journal entries to record these transactions using the cost method.

4 **BE15-8** Arantxa Corporation has outstanding 20,000 shares of $5 par value common stock. On August 1, 2014, Arantxa reacquired 200 shares at $80 per share. On November 1, Arantxa reissued the 200 shares at $70 per share. Arantxa had no previous treasury stock transactions. Prepare Arantxa's journal entries to record these transactions using the cost method.

5 **BE15-9** Hinges Corporation issued 500 shares of $100 par value preferred stock for $61,500. Prepare Hinges's journal entry.

6 **BE15-10** Woolford Inc. declared a cash dividend of $1.00 per share on its 2 million outstanding shares. The dividend was declared on August 1, payable on September 9 to all stockholders of record on August 15. Prepare all journal entries necessary on those three dates.

6 7 **BE15-11** Cole Inc. owns shares of Marlin Corporation stock classified as an available-for-sale investment. At December 31, 2014, the available-for-sale securities were carried in Cole's accounting records at their cost of $875,000, which equals their fair value. On September 21, 2015, when the fair value of the securities was $1,200,000, Cole declared a property dividend whereby the Marlin securities are to be distributed on October 23, 2015 to stockholders of record on October 8, 2015. Prepare all journal entries necessary on those three dates.

6 7 **BE15-12** Graves Mining Company declared, on April 20, a dividend of $500,000 payable on June 1. Of this amount, $125,000 is a return of capital. Prepare the April 20 and June 1 entries for Graves.

8 **BE15-13** Green Day Corporation has outstanding 400,000 shares of $10 par value common stock. The corporation declares a 5% stock dividend when the fair value of the stock is $65 per share. Prepare the journal entries for Green Day Corporation for both the date of declaration and the date of distribution.

8 **BE15-14** Use the information from BE15-13, but assume Green Day Corporation declared a 100% stock dividend rather than a 5% stock dividend. Prepare the journal entries for both the date of declaration and the date of distribution.

10 ***BE15-15** Nottebart Corporation has outstanding 10,000 shares of $100 par value, 6% preferred stock and 60,000 shares of $10 par value common stock. The preferred stock was issued in January 2014, and no dividends were declared in 2014 or 2015. In 2016, Nottebart declares a cash dividend of $300,000. How will the dividend be shared by common and preferred stockholders if the preferred is (a) noncumulative and (b) cumulative?

EXERCISES

3 **E15-1 (Recording the Issuances of Common Stock)** During its first year of operations, Collin Raye Corporation had the following transactions pertaining to its common stock.

Jan. 10	Issued 80,000 shares for cash at $6 per share.
Mar. 1	Issued 5,000 shares to attorneys in payment of a bill for $35,000 for services rendered in helping the company to incorporate.
July 1	Issued 30,000 shares for cash at $8 per share.
Sept. 1	Issued 60,000 shares for cash at $10 per share.

Instructions

(a) Prepare the journal entries for these transactions, assuming that the common stock has a par value of $5 per share.

(b) Prepare the journal entries for these transactions, assuming that the common stock is no-par with a stated value of $3 per share.

3 **E15-2 (Recording the Issuance of Common and Preferred Stock)** Kathleen Battle Corporation was organized on January 1, 2014. It is authorized to issue 10,000 shares of 8%, $100 par value preferred stock, and 500,000 shares of no-par common stock with a stated value of $1 per share. The following stock transactions were completed during the first year.

Jan. 10	Issued 80,000 shares of common stock for cash at $5 per share.
Mar. 1	Issued 5,000 shares of preferred stock for cash at $108 per share.
Apr. 1	Issued 24,000 shares of common stock for land. The asking price of the land was $90,000; the fair value of the land was $80,000.
May 1	Issued 80,000 shares of common stock for cash at $7 per share.
Aug. 1	Issued 10,000 shares of common stock to attorneys in payment of their bill of $50,000 for services rendered in helping the company organize.
Sept. 1	Issued 10,000 shares of common stock for cash at $9 per share.
Nov. 1	Issued 1,000 shares of preferred stock for cash at $112 per share.

Instructions

Prepare the journal entries to record the above transactions.

3 **E15-3 (Stock Issued for Land)** Twenty-five thousand shares reacquired by Elixir Corporation for $53 per share were exchanged for undeveloped land that has an appraised value of $1,700,000. At the time of the exchange, the common stock was trading at $62 per share on an organized exchange.

Instructions

(a) Prepare the journal entry to record the acquisition of land assuming that the purchase of the stock was originally recorded using the cost method.

(b) Briefly identify the possible alternatives (including those that are totally unacceptable) for quantifying the cost of the land and briefly support your choice.

3 **E15-4 (Lump-Sum Sale of Stock with Bonds)** Faith Evans Corporation is a regional company which is an SEC registrant. The corporation's securities are thinly traded on NASDAQ. Faith Evans Corp. has issued 10,000 units. Each unit consists of a $500 par, 12% subordinated debenture and 10 shares of $5 par common stock. The investment banker has retained 400 units as the underwriting fee. The other 9,600 units were sold to outside investors for cash at $880 per unit. Prior to this sale, the 2-week ask price of common stock was $40 per share. Twelve percent is a reasonable market yield for the debentures, and therefore the par value of the bonds is equal to the fair value.

Instructions

(a) Prepare the journal entry to record Evans' transaction, under the following conditions.

(1) Employing the incremental method.

(2) Employing the proportional method, assuming the recent price quote on the common stock reflects fair value.

(b) Briefly explain which method is, in your opinion, the better method.

3 5 **E15-5 (Lump-Sum Sales of Stock with Preferred Stock)** Dave Matthew Inc. issues 500 shares of $10 par value common stock and 100 shares of $100 par value preferred stock for a lump sum of $100,000.

Instructions

(a) Prepare the journal entry for the issuance when the market price of the common shares is $165 each and market price of the preferred is $230 each. (Round to nearest dollar.)

(b) Prepare the journal entry for the issuance when only the market price of the common stock is known and it is $170 per share.

3 4 **E15-6 (Stock Issuances and Repurchase)** Lindsey Hunter Corporation is authorized to issue 50,000 shares of $5 par value common stock. During 2014, Lindsey Hunter took part in the following selected transactions.

1. Issued 5,000 shares of stock at $45 per share, less costs related to the issuance of the stock totaling $7,000.
2. Issued 1,000 shares of stock for land appraised at $50,000. The stock was actively traded on a national stock exchange at approximately $46 per share on the date of issuance.
3. Purchased 500 shares of treasury stock at $43 per share. The treasury shares purchased were issued in 2010 at $40 per share.

Instructions

(a) Prepare the journal entry to record item 1.
(b) Prepare the journal entry to record item 2.
(c) Prepare the journal entry to record item 3 using the cost method.

4 **E15-7 (Effect of Treasury Stock Transactions on Financials)** Joe Dumars Company has outstanding 40,000 shares of $5 par common stock which had been issued at $30 per share. Joe Dumars then entered into the following transactions.

1. Purchased 5,000 treasury shares at $45 per share.
2. Resold 2,000 of the treasury shares at $49 per share.
3. Resold 500 of the treasury shares at $40 per share.

Instructions

Use the following code to indicate the effect each of the three transactions has on the financial statement categories listed in the table below, assuming Joe Dumars Company uses the cost method (I = Increase; D = Decrease; NE = No effect).

#	Assets	Liabilities	Stockholders' Equity	Paid-in Capital	Retained Earnings	Net Income
1						
2						
3						

3 **E15-8 (Preferred Stock Entries and Dividends)** Otis Thorpe Corporation has 10,000 shares of $100 par value, 8%, preferred stock and 50,000 shares of $10 par value common stock outstanding at December 31, 2014.

Instructions

Answer the questions in each of the following independent situations.

(a) If the preferred stock is cumulative and dividends were last paid on the preferred stock on December 31, 2011, what are the dividends in arrears that should be reported on the December 31, 2014, balance sheet? How should these dividends be reported?
(b) If the preferred stock is convertible into seven shares of $10 par value common stock and 4,000 shares are converted, what entry is required for the conversion assuming the preferred stock was issued at par value?
(c) If the preferred stock was issued at $107 per share, how should the preferred stock be reported in the stockholders' equity section?

3 4 **E15-9 (Correcting Entries for Equity Transactions)** Pistons Inc. recently hired a new accountant with extensive experience in accounting for partnerships. Because of the pressure of the new job, the accountant was unable to review what he had learned earlier about corporation accounting. During the first month, he made the following entries for the corporation's capital stock.

May 2	Cash	192,000	
	Capital Stock		192,000
	(Issued 12,000 shares of $5 par value common stock at $16 per share)		
10	Cash	600,000	
	Capital Stock		600,000
	(Issued 10,000 shares of $30 par value preferred stock at $60 per share)		

May 15	Capital Stock	15,000	
	Cash		15,000
	(Purchased 1,000 shares of common stock for the treasury at $15 per share)		
31	Cash	8,500	
	Capital Stock		5,000
	Gain on Sale of Stock		3,500
	(Sold 500 shares of treasury stock at $17 per share)		

Instructions

On the basis of the explanation for each entry, prepare the entries that should have been made for the capital stock transactions.

3 4 **E15-10 (Analysis of Equity Data and Equity Section Preparation)** For a recent 2-year period, the balance sheet of Santana Dotson Company showed the following stockholders' equity data at December 31 (in millions).

	2014	2013
Additional paid-in capital	$ 931	$ 817
Common stock	545	540
Retained earnings	7,167	5,226
Treasury stock	1,564	918
Total stockholders' equity	$7,079	$5,665
Common stock shares issued	218	216
Common stock shares authorized	500	500
Treasury stock shares	34	27

Instructions

(a) Answer the following questions.

(1) What is the par value of the common stock?

(2) What is the cost per share of treasury stock at December 31, 2014, and at December 31, 2013?

(b) Prepare the stockholders' equity section at December 31, 2014.

7 8 **E15-11 (Equity Items on the Balance Sheet)** The following are selected transactions that may affect stockholders' equity.

1. Recorded accrued interest earned on a note receivable.
2. Declared a cash dividend.
3. Declared and distributed a stock split.
4. Approved a retained earnings restriction.
5. Recorded the expiration of insurance coverage that was previously recorded as prepaid insurance.
6. Paid the cash dividend declared in item 2 above.
7. Recorded accrued interest expense on a note payable.
8. Declared a stock dividend.
9. Distributed the stock dividend declared in item 8.

Instructions

In the following table, indicate the effect each of the nine transactions has on the financial statement elements listed. Use the following code: I = Increase, D = Decrease, NE = No effect.

Item	Assets	Liabilities	Stockholders' Equity	Paid-in Capital	Retained Earnings	Net Income

7 **E15-12 (Cash Dividend and Liquidating Dividend)** Lotoya Davis Corporation has 10 million shares of common stock issued and outstanding. On June 1, the board of directors voted an 80 cents per share cash dividend to stockholders of record as of June 14, payable June 30.

Instructions

(a) Prepare the journal entry for each of the dates above assuming the dividend represents a distribution of earnings.

(b) How would the entry differ if the dividend were a liquidating dividend?

8 **E15-13 (Stock Split and Stock Dividend)** The common stock of Alexander Hamilton Inc. is currently selling at $120 per share. The directors wish to reduce the share price and increase share volume prior to a new issue. The per share par value is $10; book value is $70 per share. Nine million shares are issued and outstanding.

Instructions

Prepare the necessary journal entries assuming the following.

(a) The board votes a 2-for-1 stock split.

(b) The board votes a 100% stock dividend.

(c) Briefly discuss the accounting and securities market differences between these two methods of increasing the number of shares outstanding.

8 **E15-14 (Entries for Stock Dividends and Stock Splits)** The stockholders' equity accounts of G.K. Chesterton Company have the following balances on December 31, 2014.

Common stock, $10 par, 300,000 shares issued and outstanding	$3,000,000
Paid-in capital in excess of par—common stock	1,200,000
Retained earnings	5,600,000

Shares of G.K. Chesterton Company stock are currently selling on the Midwest Stock Exchange at $37.

Instructions

Prepare the appropriate journal entries for each of the following cases.

(a) A stock dividend of 5% is declared and issued.

(b) A stock dividend of 100% is declared and issued.

(c) A 2-for-1 stock split is declared and issued.

7 8 **E15-15 (Dividend Entries)** The following data were taken from the balance sheet accounts of Masefield Corporation on December 31, 2013.

XLS

Current assets	$540,000
Debt investments	624,000
Common stock (par value $10)	500,000
Paid-in capital in excess of par	150,000
Retained earnings	840,000

Instructions

Prepare the required journal entries for the following unrelated items.

(a) A 5% stock dividend is declared and distributed at a time when the market price per share is $39.

(b) The par value of the common stock is reduced to $2 with a 5-for-1 stock split.

(c) A dividend is declared January 5, 2014, and paid January 25, 2014, in bonds held as an investment. The bonds have a book value of $100,000 and a fair value of $135,000.

6 7 8 **E15-16 (Computation of Retained Earnings)** The following information has been taken from the ledger accounts of Isaac Stern Corporation.

Total income since incorporation	$317,000
Total cash dividends paid	60,000
Total value of stock dividends distributed	30,000
Gains on treasury stock transactions	18,000
Unamortized discount on bonds payable	32,000

Instructions

Determine the current balance of retained earnings.

9 **E15-17 (Stockholders' Equity Section)** Bruno Corporation's post-closing trial balance at December 31, 2014, is shown on the next page.

BRUNO CORPORATION
POST-CLOSING TRIAL BALANCE
DECEMBER 31, 2014

	Dr.	Cr.
Accounts payable		$ 310,000
Accounts receivable	$ 480,000	
Accumulated depreciation—buildings		185,000
Additional paid-in capital in excess		
of par—common		1,300,000
From treasury stock		160,000
Allowance for doubtful accounts		30,000
Bonds payable		300,000
Buildings	1,450,000	
Cash	190,000	
Common stock ($1 par)		200,000
Dividends payable (preferred stock—cash)		4,000
Inventory	560,000	
Land	400,000	
Preferred stock ($50 par)		500,000
Prepaid expenses	40,000	
Retained earnings		301,000
Treasury stock (common at cost)	170,000	
Totals	$3,290,000	$3,290,000

At December 31, 2014, Bruno had the following number of common and preferred shares.

	Common	Preferred
Authorized	600,000	60,000
Issued	200,000	10,000
Outstanding	190,000	10,000

The dividends on preferred stock are $4 cumulative. In addition, the preferred stock has a preference in liquidation of $50 per share.

Instructions

Prepare the stockholders' equity section of Bruno's balance sheet at December 31, 2014.

(AICPA adapted)

4 7 8 **E15-18 (Dividends and Stockholders' Equity Section)** Anne Cleves Company reported the following amounts in the stockholders' equity section of its December 31, 2013, balance sheet.

Preferred stock, 10%, $100 par (10,000 shares authorized, 2,000 shares issued)	$200,000
Common stock, $5 par (100,000 shares authorized, 20,000 shares issued)	100,000
Additional paid-in capital	125,000
Retained earnings	450,000
Total	$875,000

During 2014, Cleves took part in the following transactions concerning stockholders' equity.

1. Paid the annual 2013 $10 per share dividend on preferred stock and a $2 per share dividend on common stock. These dividends had been declared on December 31, 2013.
2. Purchased 1,700 shares of its own outstanding common stock for $40 per share. Cleves uses the cost method.
3. Reissued 700 treasury shares for land valued at $30,000.
4. Issued 500 shares of preferred stock at $105 per share.
5. Declared a 10% stock dividend on the outstanding common stock when the stock is selling for $45 per share.
6. Issued the stock dividend.
7. Declared the annual 2014 $10 per share dividend on preferred stock and the $2 per share dividend on common stock. These dividends are payable in 2015.

Instructions

(a) Prepare journal entries to record the transactions described above.
(b) Prepare the December 31, 2014, stockholders' equity section. Assume 2014 net income was $330,000.

9 **E15-19 (Comparison of Alternative Forms of Financing)** Shown below is the liabilities and stockholders' equity section of the balance sheet for Jana Kingston Company and Mary Ann Benson Company. Each has assets totaling $4,200,000.

Jana Kingston Co.		Mary Ann Benson Co.	
Current liabilities	$ 300,000	Current liabilities	$ 600,000
Long-term debt, 10%	1,200,000	Common stock ($20 par)	2,900,000
Common stock ($20 par)	2,000,000	Retained earnings (Cash dividends, $328,000)	700,000
Retained earnings (Cash dividends, $220,000)	700,000		
	$4,200,000		$4,200,000

For the year, each company has earned the same income before interest and taxes.

	Jana Kingston Co.	Mary Ann Benson Co.
Income before interest and taxes	$1,200,000	$1,200,000
Interest expense	120,000	-0-
	1,080,000	1,200,000
Income taxes (45%)	486,000	540,000
Net income	$ 594,000	$ 660,000

At year end, the market price of Kingston's stock was $101 per share, and Benson's was $63.50.

Instructions

(a) Which company is more profitable in terms of return on total assets?
(b) Which company is more profitable in terms of return on common stock equity?
(c) Which company has the greater net income per share of stock? Neither company issued or reacquired shares during the year.
(d) From the point of view of net income, is it advantageous to the stockholders of Jana Kingston Co. to have the long-term debt outstanding? Why?
(e) What is the book value per share for each company?

9 **E15-20 (Trading on the Equity Analysis)** Presented below is information from the annual report of Emporia Plastics, Inc.

Operating income	$ 532,150
Bond interest expense	135,000
	397,150
Income taxes	183,432
Net income	$ 213,718
Bonds payable	$1,000,000
Common stock	875,000
Retained earnings	375,000

Instructions

(a) Compute the return on common stock equity and the rate of interest paid on bonds. (Assume balances for debt and equity accounts approximate averages for the year.)
(b) Is Emporia Plastics Inc. trading on the equity successfully? Explain.

10 ***E15-21 (Preferred Dividends)** The outstanding capital stock of Edna Millay Corporation consists of 2,000 shares of $100 par value, 8% preferred, and 5,000 shares of $50 par value common.

Instructions

Assuming that the company has retained earnings of $90,000, all of which is to be paid out in dividends, and that preferred dividends were not paid during the 2 years preceding the current year, state how much each class of stock should receive under each of the following conditions.

(a) The preferred stock is noncumulative and nonparticipating.
(b) The preferred stock is cumulative and nonparticipating.

(c) The preferred stock is cumulative and participating. (Round dividend rate percentages to four decimal places.)

10 ***E15-22 (Preferred Dividends)** Matt Schmidt Company's ledger shows the following balances on December 31, 2014.

7% Preferred stock—$10 par value, outstanding 20,000 shares	$ 200,000
Common stock—$100 par value, outstanding 30,000 shares	3,000,000
Retained earnings	630,000

Instructions

Assuming that the directors decide to declare total dividends in the amount of $366,000, determine how much each class of stock should receive under each of the conditions stated below. One year's dividends are in arrears on the preferred stock.

(a) The preferred stock is cumulative and fully participating.
(b) The preferred stock is noncumulative and nonparticipating.
(c) The preferred stock is noncumulative and is participating in distributions in excess of a 10% dividend rate on the common stock.

10 ***E15-23 (Preferred Stock Dividends)** Cajun Company has outstanding 2,500 shares of $100 par, 6% preferred stock and 15,000 shares of $10 par value common. The following schedule shows the amount of dividends paid out over the last 4 years.

Instructions

Allocate the dividends to each type of stock under assumptions (a) and (b). Express your answers in per-share amounts using the format shown below.

		Assumptions			
		(a) Preferred, noncumulative, and nonparticipating		(b) Preferred, cumulative, and fully participating	
Year	Paid-out	Preferred	Common	Preferred	Common
2012	$13,000				
2013	$26,000				
2014	$57,000				
2015	$76,000				

10 ***E15-24 (Computation of Book Value per Share)** Morgan Sondgeroth Inc. began operations in January 2012 and reported the following results for each of its 3 years of operations.

2012	$260,000 net loss	2013	$40,000 net loss	2014	$800,000 net income

At December 31, 2014, Morgan Sondgeroth Inc. capital accounts were as follows.

8% cumulative preferred stock, par value $100; authorized, issued, and outstanding 5,000 shares	$500,000
Common stock, par value $1.00; authorized 1,000,000 shares; issued and outstanding 750,000 shares	$750,000

Morgan Sondgeroth Inc. has never paid a cash or stock dividend. There has been no change in the capital accounts since Sondgeroth began operations. The state law permits dividends only from retained earnings.

Instructions

(a) Compute the book value of the common stock at December 31, 2014.
(b) Compute the book value of the common stock at December 31, 2014, assuming that the preferred stock has a liquidating value of $106 per share.

EXERCISES SET B

See the book's companion website, at **www.wiley.com/college/kieso**, for an additional set of exercises.

PROBLEMS

3 4 **P15-1 (Equity Transactions and Statement Preparation)** On January 5, 2014, Phelps Corporation received
9 a charter granting the right to issue 5,000 shares of $100 par value, 8% cumulative and nonparticipating preferred stock, and 50,000 shares of $10 par value common stock. It then completed these transactions.

Jan. 11	Issued 20,000 shares of common stock at $16 per share.
Feb. 1	Issued to Sanchez Corp. 4,000 shares of preferred stock for the following assets: equipment with a fair value of $50,000; a factory building with a fair value of $160,000; and land with an appraised value of $270,000.
July 29	Purchased 1,800 shares of common stock at $17 per share. (Use cost method.)
Aug. 10	Sold the 1,800 treasury shares at $14 per share.
Dec. 31	Declared a $0.25 per share cash dividend on the common stock and declared the preferred dividend.
Dec. 31	Closed the Income Summary account. There was a $175,700 net income.

XLS

Instructions

(a) Record the journal entries for the transactions listed above.

(b) Prepare the stockholders' equity section of Phelps Corporation's balance sheet as of December 31, 2014.

4 9 **P15-2 (Treasury Stock Transactions and Presentation)** Clemson Company had the following stockholders' equity as of January 1, 2014.

Common stock, $5 par value, 20,000 shares issued	$100,000
Paid-in capital in excess of par—common stock	300,000
Retained earnings	320,000
Total stockholders' equity	$720,000

During 2014, the following transactions occurred.

Feb. 1	Clemson repurchased 2,000 shares of treasury stock at a price of $19 per share.
Mar. 1	800 shares of treasury stock repurchased above were reissued at $17 per share.
Mar. 18	500 shares of treasury stock repurchased above were reissued at $14 per share.
Apr. 22	600 shares of treasury stock repurchased above were reissued at $20 per share.

Instructions

(a) Prepare the journal entries to record the treasury stock transactions in 2014, assuming Clemson uses the cost method.

(b) Prepare the stockholders' equity section as of April 30, 2014. Net income for the first 4 months of 2014 was $130,000.

3 4 **P15-3 (Equity Transactions and Statement Preparation)** Hatch Company has two classes of capital stock
7 8 outstanding: 8%, $20 par preferred and $5 par common. At December 31, 2014, the following accounts were included in stockholders' equity.

Preferred Stock, 150,000 shares	$ 3,000,000
Common Stock, 2,000,000 shares	10,000,000
Paid-in Capital in Excess of Par—Preferred Stock	200,000
Paid-in Capital in Excess of Par—Common Stock	27,000,000
Retained Earnings	4,500,000

The following transactions affected stockholders' equity during 2015.

Jan. 1	30,000 shares of preferred stock issued at $22 per share.
Feb. 1	50,000 shares of common stock issued at $20 per share.
June 1	2-for-1 stock split (par value reduced to $2.50).
July 1	30,000 shares of common treasury stock purchased at $10 per share. Hatch uses the cost method.
Sept. 15	10,000 shares of treasury stock reissued at $11 per share.
Dec. 31	The preferred dividend is declared, and a common dividend of 50¢ per share is declared.
Dec. 31	Net income is $2,100,000.

Instructions

Prepare the stockholders' equity section for Hatch Company at December 31, 2015. Show all supporting computations.

3 5 **P15-4 (Stock Transactions—Lump Sum)** Seles Corporation's charter authorized issuance of 100,000 shares of $10 par value common stock and 50,000 shares of $50 preferred stock. The following transactions involving the issuance of shares of stock were completed. Each transaction is independent of the others.

1. Issued a $10,000, 9% bond payable at par and gave as a bonus one share of preferred stock, which at that time was selling for $106 a share.
2. Issued 500 shares of common stock for equipment. The equipment had been appraised at $7,100; the seller's book value was $6,200. The most recent market price of the common stock is $16 a share.
3. Issued 375 shares of common and 100 shares of preferred for a lump sum amounting to $10,800. The common had been selling at $14 and the preferred at $65.
4. Issued 200 shares of common and 50 shares of preferred for equipment. The common had a fair value of $16 per share; the equipment has a fair value of $6,500.

Instructions

Record the transactions listed above in journal entry form.

4 **P15-5 (Treasury Stock—Cost Method)** Before Gordon Corporation engages in the treasury stock transactions listed below, its general ledger reflects, among others, the following account balances (par value of its stock is $30 per share).

XLS

Paid-in Capital in Excess of Par—Common Stock	Common Stock	Retained Earnings
$99,000	$270,000	$80,000

Instructions

Record the treasury stock transactions (given below) under the cost method of handling treasury stock; use the FIFO method for purchase-sale purposes.

(a) Bought 380 shares of treasury stock at $40 per share.
(b) Bought 300 shares of treasury stock at $45 per share.
(c) Sold 350 shares of treasury stock at $42 per share.
(d) Sold 110 shares of treasury stock at $38 per share.

4 7 9 **P15-6 (Treasury Stock—Cost Method—Equity Section Preparation)** Washington Company has the following stockholders' equity accounts at December 31, 2014.

Common Stock ($100 par value, authorized 8,000 shares)	$480,000
Retained Earnings	294,000

Instructions

(a) Prepare entries in journal form to record the following transactions, which took place during 2015.
  (1) 280 shares of outstanding stock were purchased at $97 per share. (These are to be accounted for using the cost method.)
  (2) A $20 per share cash dividend was declared.
  (3) The dividend declared in (2) above was paid.
  (4) The treasury shares purchased in (1) above were resold at $102 per share.
  (5) 500 shares of outstanding stock were purchased at $105 per share.
  (6) 350 of the shares purchased in (5) above were resold at $96 per share.

(b) Prepare the stockholders' equity section of Washington Company's balance sheet after giving effect to these transactions, assuming that the net income for 2015 was $94,000. State law requires restriction of retained earnings for the amount of treasury stock.

4 7 **P15-7 (Cash Dividend Entries)** The books of Conchita Corporation carried the following account balances as of December 31, 2014.

Cash	$ 195,000
Preferred Stock (6% cumulative, nonparticipating, $50 par)	300,000
Common Stock (no-par value, 300,000 shares issued)	1,500,000
Paid-in Capital in Excess of Par—Preferred Stock	150,000
Treasury Stock (common 2,800 shares at cost)	33,600
Retained Earnings	105,000

The company decided not to pay any dividends in 2014.

The board of directors, at their annual meeting on December 21, 2015, declared the following: "The current year dividends shall be 6% on the preferred and $.30 per share on the common. The dividends in arrears shall be paid by issuing 1,500 shares of treasury stock." At the date of declaration, the preferred is selling at $80 per share, and the common at $12 per share. Net income for 2015 is estimated at $77,000.

Instructions

(a) Prepare the journal entries required for the dividend declaration and payment, assuming that they occur simultaneously.

(b) Could Conchita Corporation give the preferred stockholders 2 years' dividends and common stockholders a 30 cents per share dividend, all in cash?

7 8 **P15-8 (Dividends and Splits)** Myers Company provides you with the following condensed balance sheet information.

Assets		Liabilities and Stockholders' Equity		
Current assets	$ 40,000	Current and long-term liabilities		$100,000
Equity investments (trading)	60,000	Stockholders' equity		
Equipment (net)	250,000	Common stock ($5 par)	$ 20,000	
Intangibles	60,000	Paid-in capital in excess of par	110,000	
Total assets	$410,000	Retained earnings	180,000	310,000
		Total liabilities and stockholders' equity		$410,000

Instructions

For each transaction below, indicate the dollar impact (if any) on the following five items: (1) total assets, (2) common stock, (3) paid-in capital in excess of par, (4) retained earnings, and (5) stockholders' equity. (Each situation is independent.)

(a) Myers declares and pays a $0.50 per share cash dividend.

(b) Myers declares and issues a 10% stock dividend when the market price of the stock is $14 per share.

(c) Myers declares and issues a 30% stock dividend when the market price of the stock is $15 per share.

(d) Myers declares and distributes a property dividend. Myers gives one share of its equity investment (ABC stock) for every two shares of Myers Company stock held. Myers owns 10,000 shares of ABC. ABC is selling for $10 per share on the date the property dividend is declared.

(e) Myers declares a 2-for-1 stock split and issues new shares.

3 4 7 9 **P15-9 (Stockholders' Equity Section of Balance Sheet)** The following is a summary of all relevant transactions of Vicario Corporation since it was organized in 2014.

In 2014, 15,000 shares were authorized and 7,000 shares of common stock ($50 par value) were issued at a price of $57. In 2015, 1,000 shares were issued as a stock dividend when the stock was selling for $60. Three hundred shares of common stock were bought in 2016 at a cost of $64 per share. These 300 shares are still in the company treasury.

In 2015, 10,000 preferred shares were authorized and the company issued 5,000 of them ($100 par value) at $113. Some of the preferred stock was reacquired by the company and later reissued for $4,700 more than it cost the company.

The corporation has earned a total of $610,000 in net income after income taxes and paid out a total of $312,600 in cash dividends since incorporation.

Instructions

Prepare the stockholders' equity section of the balance sheet in proper form for Vicario Corporation as of December 31, 2016. Account for treasury stock using the cost method.

8 **P15-10 (Stock Dividends and Stock Split)** Oregon Inc. $10 par common stock is selling for $110 per share. Four million shares are currently issued and outstanding. The board of directors wishes to stimulate interest in Oregon common stock before a forthcoming stock issue but does not wish to distribute capital at this time. The board also believes that too many adjustments to the stockholders' equity section, especially retained earnings, might discourage potential investors.

The board has considered three options for stimulating interest in the stock:

1. A 20% stock dividend.
2. A 100% stock dividend.
3. A 2-for-1 stock split.

Instructions

Acting as financial advisor to the board, you have been asked to report briefly on each option and, considering the board's wishes, make a recommendation. Discuss the effects of each of the foregoing options.

7 8 9 **P15-11 (Stock and Cash Dividends)** Earnhart Corporation has outstanding 3,000,000 shares of common stock of a par value of $10 each. The balance in its Retained Earnings account at January 1, 2014, was $24,000,000, and it then had Paid-in Capital in Excess of Par—Common Stock of $5,000,000. During 2014,

the company's net income was $4,700,000. A cash dividend of $0.60 a share was declared on May 5, 2014, and was paid June 30, 2014, and a 6% stock dividend was declared on November 30, 2014, and distributed to stockholders of record at the close of business on December 31, 2014. You have been asked to advise on the proper accounting treatment of the stock dividend.

The existing stock of the company is quoted on a national stock exchange. The market price of the stock has been as follows.

October 31, 2014	$31
November 30, 2014	$34
December 31, 2014	$38

Instructions

(a) Prepare the journal entry to record the declaration and payment of the cash dividend.

(b) Prepare the journal entry to record the declaration and distribution of the stock dividend.

(c) Prepare the stockholders' equity section (including schedules of retained earnings and additional paid-in capital) of the balance sheet of Earnhart Corporation for the year 2014 on the basis of the foregoing information. Draft a note to the financial statements setting forth the basis of the accounting for the stock dividend, and add separately appropriate comments or explanations regarding the basis chosen.

3 4 7 8 9 **P15-12 (Analysis and Classification of Equity Transactions)** Penn Company was formed on July 1, 2012. It was authorized to issue 300,000 shares of $10 par value common stock and 100,000 shares of 8% $25 par value, cumulative and nonparticipating preferred stock. Penn Company has a July 1–June 30 fiscal year.

The following information relates to the stockholders' equity accounts of Penn Company.

Common Stock

Prior to the 2014–2015 fiscal year, Penn Company had 110,000 shares of outstanding common stock issued as follows.

1. 85,000 shares were issued for cash on July 1, 2012, at $31 per share.
2. On July 24, 2012, 5,000 shares were exchanged for a plot of land which cost the seller $70,000 in 2006 and had an estimated fair value of $220,000 on July 24, 2012.
3. 20,000 shares were issued on March 1, 2013, for $42 per share.

During the 2014–2015 fiscal year, the following transactions regarding common stock took place.

November 30, 2014	Penn purchased 2,000 shares of its own stock on the open market at $39 per share. Penn uses the cost method for treasury stock.
December 15, 2014	Penn declared a 5% stock dividend for stockholders of record on January 15, 2015, to be issued on January 31, 2015. Penn was having a liquidity problem and could not afford a cash dividend at the time. Penn's common stock was selling at $52 per share on December 15, 2014.
June 20, 2015	Penn sold 500 shares of its own common stock that it had purchased on November 30, 2014, for $21,000.

Preferred Stock

Penn issued 40,000 shares of preferred stock at $44 per share on July 1, 2013.

Cash Dividends

Penn has followed a schedule of declaring cash dividends in December and June, with payment being made to stockholders of record in the following month. The cash dividends which have been declared since inception of the company through June 30, 2015, are shown below.

Declaration Date	Common Stock	Preferred Stock
12/15/13	$0.30 per share	$1.00 per share
6/15/14	$0.30 per share	$1.00 per share
12/15/14	—	$1.00 per share

No cash dividends were declared during June 2015 due to the company's liquidity problems.

Retained Earnings

As of June 30, 2014, Penn's retained earnings account had a balance of $690,000. For the fiscal year ending June 30, 2015, Penn reported net income of $40,000.

Instructions

Prepare the stockholders' equity section of the balance sheet, including appropriate notes, for Penn Company as of June 30, 2015, as it should appear in its annual report to the shareholders.

(CMA adapted)

PROBLEMS SET B

See the book's companion website, at **www.wiley.com/college/kieso**, for an additional set of problems.

CONCEPTS FOR ANALYSIS

CA15-1 (Preemptive Rights and Dilution of Ownership) Wallace Computer Company is a small, closely held corporation. Eighty percent of the stock is held by Derek Wallace, president. Of the remainder, 10% is held by members of his family and 10% by Kathy Baker, a former officer who is now retired. The balance sheet of the company at June 30, 2014, was substantially as shown below.

Assets		Liabilities and Stockholders' Equity	
Cash	$ 22,000	Current liabilities	$ 50,000
Other	450,000	Common stock	250,000
	$472,000	Retained earnings	172,000
			$472,000

Additional authorized common stock of $300,000 par value had never been issued. To strengthen the cash position of the company, Wallace issued common stock with a par value of $100,000 to himself at par for cash. At the next stockholders' meeting, Baker objected and claimed that her interests had been injured.

Instructions

(a) Which stockholder's right was ignored in the issue of shares to Derek Wallace?
(b) How may the damage to Baker's interests be repaired most simply?
(c) If Derek Wallace offered Baker a personal cash settlement and they agreed to employ you as an impartial arbitrator to determine the amount, what settlement would you propose? Present your calculations with sufficient explanation to satisfy both parties.

CA15-2 (Issuance of Stock for Land) Martin Corporation is planning to issue 3,000 shares of its own $10 par value common stock for two acres of land to be used as a building site.

Instructions

(a) What general rule should be applied to determine the amount at which the land should be recorded?
(b) Under what circumstances should this transaction be recorded at the fair value of the land?
(c) Under what circumstances should this transaction be recorded at the fair value of the stock issued?
(d) Assume Martin intentionally records this transaction at an amount greater than the fair value of the land and the stock. Discuss this situation.

CA15-3 (Conceptual Issues—Equity) Statements of Financial Accounting Concepts set forth financial accounting and reporting objectives and fundamentals that will be used by the Financial Accounting Standards Board in developing standards. *Concepts Statement No. 6* defines various elements of financial statements.

Instructions

Answer the following questions based on *SFAC No. 6*.

(a) Define and discuss the term "equity."
(b) What transactions or events change owners' equity?
(c) Define "investments by owners" and provide examples of this type of transaction. What financial statement element other than equity is typically affected by owner investments?
(d) Define "distributions to owners" and provide examples of this type of transaction. What financial statement element other than equity is typically affected by distributions?
(e) What are examples of changes within owners' equity that do not change the total amount of owners' equity?

CA15-4 (Stock Dividends and Splits) The directors of Merchant Corporation are considering the issuance of a stock dividend. They have asked you to discuss the proposed action by answering the following questions.

Instructions

(a) What is a stock dividend? How is a stock dividend distinguished from a stock split (1) from a legal standpoint, and (2) from an accounting standpoint?

(b) For what reasons does a corporation usually declare a stock dividend? A stock split?

(c) Discuss the amount, if any, of retained earnings to be capitalized in connection with a stock dividend.

(AICPA adapted)

CA15-5 (Stock Dividends) Kulikowski Inc., a client, is considering the authorization of a 10% common stock dividend to common stockholders. The financial vice president of Kulikowski wishes to discuss the accounting implications of such an authorization with you before the next meeting of the board of directors.

Instructions

(a) The first topic the vice president wishes to discuss is the nature of the stock dividend to the recipient. Discuss the case against considering the stock dividend as income to the recipient.

(b) The other topic for discussion is the propriety of issuing the stock dividend to all "stockholders of record" or to "stockholders of record exclusive of shares held in the name of the corporation as treasury stock." Discuss the case against issuing stock dividends on treasury shares.

(AICPA adapted)

CA15-6 (Stock Dividend, Cash Dividend, and Treasury Stock) Mask Company has 30,000 shares of $10 par value common stock authorized and 20,000 shares issued and outstanding. On August 15, 2014, Mask purchased 1,000 shares of treasury stock for $18 per share. Mask uses the cost method to account for treasury stock. On September 14, 2014, Mask sold 500 shares of the treasury stock for $20 per share.

In October 2014, Mask declared and distributed 1,950 shares as a stock dividend from unissued shares when the market price of the common stock was $21 per share.

On December 20, 2014, Mask declared a $1 per share cash dividend, payable on January 10, 2015, to shareholders of record on December 31, 2014.

Instructions

(a) How should Mask account for the purchase and sale of the treasury stock, and how should the treasury stock be presented in the balance sheet at December 31, 2014?

(b) How should Mask account for the stock dividend, and how would it affect the stockholders' equity at December 31, 2014? Why?

(c) How should Mask account for the cash dividend, and how would it affect the balance sheet at December 31, 2014? Why?

(AICPA adapted)

CA15-7 (Treasury Stock—Ethics) Lois Kenseth, president of Sycamore Corporation, is concerned about several large stockholders who have been very vocal lately in their criticisms of her leadership. She thinks they might mount a campaign to have her removed as the corporation's CEO. She decides that buying them out by purchasing their shares could eliminate them as opponents, and she is confident they would accept a "good" offer. Kenseth knows the corporation's cash position is decent, so it has the cash to complete the transaction. She also knows the purchase of these shares will increase earnings per share, which should make other investors quite happy. (Earnings per share is calculated by dividing net income available for the common shareholders by the weighted-average number of shares outstanding. Therefore, if the number of shares outstanding is decreased by purchasing treasury shares, earnings per share increases.)

Instructions

Answer the following questions.

(a) Who are the stakeholders in this situation?

(b) What are the ethical issues involved?

(c) Should Kenseth authorize the transaction?

USING YOUR JUDGMENT

FINANCIAL REPORTING

Financial Reporting Problem

The Procter & Gamble Company (P&G)

The financial statements of P&G are presented in Appendix 5B. The company's complete annual report, including the notes to the financial statements, can be accessed at the book's companion website, **www.wiley.com/college/kieso**.

Instructions

Refer to P&G's financial statements and the accompanying notes to answer the following questions.

(a) What is the par or stated value of P&G's preferred stock?

(b) What is the par or stated value of P&G's common stock?

(c) What percentage of P&G's authorized common stock was issued at June 30, 2011?

(d) How many shares of common stock were outstanding at June 30, 2011, and June 30, 2010?

(e) What was the dollar amount effect of the cash dividends on P&G's stockholders' equity?

(f) What is P&G's return on common stock equity for 2011 and 2010?

(g) What is P&G's payout ratio for 2011 and 2010?

(h) What was the market price range (high/low) of P&G's common stock during the quarter ended June 30, 2011?

Comparative Analysis Case

The Coca-Cola Company and PepsiCo, Inc.

Instructions

Go to the book's companion website and use information found there to answer the following questions related to The Coca-Cola Company and PepsiCo, Inc.

(a) What is the par or stated value of Coca-Cola's and PepsiCo's common or capital stock?

(b) What percentage of authorized shares was issued by Coca-Cola at December 31, 2011, and by PepsiCo at December 31, 2011?

(c) How many shares are held as treasury stock by Coca-Cola at December 31, 2011, and by PepsiCo at December 31, 2011?

(d) How many Coca-Cola common shares are outstanding at December 31, 2011? How many PepsiCo shares of capital stock are outstanding at December 31, 2011?

(e) What amounts of cash dividends per share were declared by Coca-Cola and PepsiCo in 2011? What were the dollar amount effects of the cash dividends on each company's stockholders' equity?

(f) What are Coca-Cola's and PepsiCo's return on common/capital stock equity for 2011 and 2010? Which company gets the higher return on the equity of its shareholders?

(g) What are Coca-Cola's and PepsiCo's payout ratios for 2011?

(h) What was the market price range (high/low) for Coca-Cola's common stock and PepsiCo's capital stock during the fourth quarter of 2011? Which company's (Coca-Cola's or PepsiCo's) stock price increased more (%) during 2011?

Financial Statement Analysis Cases

Case 1 Kellogg Company

Kellogg Company is the world's leading producer of ready-to-eat cereal products. In recent years, the company has taken numerous steps aimed at improving its profitability and earnings per share. Presented below are some basic facts for Kellogg.

	2011	2010
Net sales	$13,198	$12,397
Net income	1,229	1,240
Total assets	11,901	11,847
Total liabilities	10,139	9,693
Common stock, $0.25 par value	105	105
Capital in excess of par value	522	495
Retained earnings	6,721	6,122
Treasury stock, at cost	3,130	2,650
Number of shares outstanding (in millions)	357	366

Instructions

(a) What are some of the reasons that management purchases its own stock?

(b) Explain how earnings per share might be affected by treasury stock transactions.

(c) Calculate the ratio of debt to assets for 2010 and 2011, and discuss the implications of the change.

Case 2 Wiebold, Incorporated

The following note related to stockholders' equity was reported in Wiebold, Inc.'s annual report.

> On February 1, the Board of Directors declared a 3-for-2 stock split, distributed on February 22 to shareholders of record on February 10. Accordingly, all numbers of common shares, except unissued shares and treasury shares, and all per share data have been restated to reflect this stock split.
>
> On the basis of amounts declared and paid, the annualized quarterly dividends per share were $0.80 in the current year and $0.75 in the prior year.

Instructions

(a) What is the significance of the date of record and the date of distribution?

(b) Why might Wiebold have declared a 3-for-2 for stock split?

(c) What impact does Wiebold's stock split have on (1) total stockholders' equity, (2) total par value, (3) outstanding shares, and (4) book value per share?

Accounting, Analysis, and Principles

On January 1, 2014, Agassi Corporation had the following stockholders' equity accounts.

Common Stock ($10 par value, 60,000 shares issued and outstanding)	$600,000
Paid-in Capital in Excess of Par—Common Stock	500,000
Retained Earnings	620,000

During 2014, the following transactions occurred.

Jan. 15	Declared and paid a $1.05 cash dividend per share to stockholders.
Apr. 15	Declared and paid a 10% stock dividend. The market price of the stock was $14 per share.
May 15	Reacquired 2,000 common shares at a market price of $15 per share.
Nov. 15	Reissued 1,000 shares held in treasury at a price of $18 per share.
Dec. 31	Determined that net income for the year was $370,000.

Accounting

Journalize the above transactions. (Include entries to close net income to Retained Earnings.) Determine the ending balances for Paid-in Capital, Retained Earnings, and Stockholders' Equity.

Analysis

Calculate the payout ratio and the return on common stock equity.

Principles

R. Federer is examining Agassi's financial statements and wonders whether the "gains" or "losses" on Agassi's treasury stock transactions should be included in income for the year. Briefly explain whether, and the conceptual reasons why, gains or losses on treasury stock transactions should be recorded in income.

BRIDGE TO THE PROFESSION

Professional Research: FASB Codification

Recall from Chapter 13 that Hincapie Co. (a specialty bike-accessory manufacturer) is expecting growth in sales of some products targeted to the low-price market. Hincapie is contemplating a preferred stock issue to help finance this expansion in operations. The company is leaning toward participating preferred stock because ownership will not be diluted, but the investors will get an extra dividend if the company does well. The company management wants to be certain that its reporting of this transaction is transparent to its current shareholders and wants you to research the disclosure requirements related to its capital structure.

Instructions

If your school has a subscription to the FASB Codification, go to *http://aaahq.org/ascLogin.cfm* to log in and prepare responses to the following. Provide Codification references for your responses.

(a) Identify the authoritative literature that addresses disclosure of information about capital structure.

(b) Find definitions of the following:

(1) Securities.

(2) Participation rights.

(3) Preferred stock.

(c) What information about securities must companies disclose? Discuss how Hincapie should report the proposed preferred stock issue.

Additional Professional Resources

See the book's companion website, at **www.wiley.com/college/kieso**, for professional simulations as well as other study resources.

IFRS INSIGHTS

LEARNING OBJECTIVE 11

Compare the procedures for accounting for stockholders' equity under GAAP and IFRS.

The primary IFRS related to stockholders' equity are *IAS 1* ("Presentation of Financial Statements"), *IAS 32* ("Financial Instruments: Presentation"), and *IAS 39* ("Financial Instruments: Recognition and Measurement").

RELEVANT FACTS

Following are the key similarities and differences between GAAP and IFRS related to stockholders' equity.

Similarities

- The accounting for the issuance of shares and purchase of treasury stock are similar under both IFRS and GAAP.
- The accounting for declaration and payment of dividends and the accounting for stock splits are similar under both IFRS and GAAP.

Differences

- Major differences relate to terminology used, introduction of concepts such as revaluation surplus, and presentation of stockholders' equity information.
- Many countries have different investor groups than the United States. For example, in Germany, financial institutions like banks are not only the major creditors but often are the largest shareholders as well. In the United States and the United Kingdom, many companies rely on substantial investment from private investors.
- The accounting for treasury share retirements differs between IFRS and GAAP. Under GAAP, a company has three options: (1) charge the excess of the cost of treasury shares over par value to retained earnings, (2) allocate the difference between paid-in capital and retained earnings, or (3) charge the entire amount to paid-in capital. Under IFRS, the excess may have to be charged to paid-in capital, depending on the original transaction related to the issuance of the shares.
- The statement of changes in equity is usually referred to as the statement of stockholders' equity (or shareholders' equity) under GAAP.
- Both IFRS and GAAP use the term retained earnings. However, IFRS relies on the term "reserve" as a dumping ground for other types of equity transactions, such as other comprehensive income items as well as various types of unusual transactions related

to convertible debt and share option contracts. GAAP relies on the account Accumulated Other Comprehensive Income (Loss). We also use this account in the discussion below, as it appears this account is gaining prominence within the IFRS literature.

- Under IFRS, it is common to report "revaluation surplus" related to increases or decreases in items such as property, plant, and equipment; mineral resources; and intangible assets. The term surplus is generally not used in GAAP. In addition, unrealized gains on the above items are not reported in the financial statements under GAAP.

ABOUT THE NUMBERS

Equity

Equity is the residual interest in the assets of the company after deducting all liabilities. Equity is often referred to as shareholders' equity, stockholders' equity, or corporate capital. Equity is often subclassified on the statement of financial position (balance sheet) into the following categories (as discussed in Chapter 5).

1. Share capital.
2. Share premium.
3. Retained earnings.
4. Accumulated other comprehensive income.
5. Treasury shares.
6. Non-controlling interest (minority interest).

Such classifications help financial statement users to better understand the legal or other restrictions related to the ability of the company to pay dividends or otherwise use its equity for certain defined purposes. Companies often make a distinction between contributed capital (paid-in capital) and earned capital. **Contributed capital (paid-in capital)** is the total amount paid in on capital shares—the amount provided by shareholders to the corporation for use in the business. Contributed capital includes items such as the par value of all outstanding shares and premiums less discounts on issuance. **Earned capital** is the capital that develops from profitable operations. It consists of all undistributed income that remains invested in the company. **Retained earnings** represents the earned capital of the company.

As indicated above, equity is a **residual interest** and therefore its value is derived from the amount of the corporations' assets and liabilities. Only in unusual cases will a company's equity equal the total fair value of its shares. For example, BMW recently had total equity of €20,265 million and a market capitalization of €21,160 million. BMW's equity represents the net contributions from shareholders (from both majority and minority shareholders) plus retained earnings and accumulated other comprehensive income. As a residual interest, its equity has no existence apart from the assets and liabilities of BMW—equity equals net assets. Equity is not a claim to specific assets but a claim against a portion of the total assets. Its amount is not specified or fixed; it depends on BMW's profitability. Equity grows if it is profitable. It shrinks, or may disappear entirely, if BMW loses money.

Issuance of Ordinary Shares

Under IFRS, the accounting for share issuances is similar to GAAP. The primary difference is the account titles. GAAP uses an account, Common Stock, for the par value of shares, while IFRS uses an account labeled Share Capital. What about no-par shares? In some countries, as in the United States, the total issue price for no-par shares may be considered legal capital, which could reduce the flexibility in paying dividends. Corporations sell no-par shares, like par value shares, for whatever price they will bring. However, unlike par value shares, corporations issue them without a premium or a discount. The exact amount received represents the credit to ordinary or preference shares.

For example, Video Electronics Corporation is organized with 10,000 ordinary shares authorized without par value. Video Electronics makes only a memorandum entry for the authorization, inasmuch as no amount is involved. If Video Electronics then issues 500 shares for cash at $10 per share, it makes the following entry.

Cash	5,000	
Share Capital—Ordinary		5,000

If it issues another 500 shares for $11 per share, Video Electronics makes this entry.

Cash	5,500	
Share Capital—Ordinary		5,500

True no-par shares should be carried in the accounts at issue price without any share premium reported. But some countries require that no-par shares have a **stated value**. The stated value is a minimum value below which a company cannot issue it. Thus, instead of being no-par shares, such stated-value shares become, in effect, shares with a very low par value. It thus is open to all the criticism and abuses that first encouraged the development of no-par shares.

If no-par shares have a stated value of $5 per share but sell for $11, all such amounts in excess of $5 are recorded as share premium, which in many jurisdictions is fully or partially available for dividends. Thus, no-par value shares, with a low stated value, permit a new corporation to commence its operations with share premium that may exceed its stated capital. For example, if a company issued 1,000 of the shares with a $5 stated value at $15 per share for cash, it makes the following entry.

Cash	15,000	
Share Capital—Ordinary		5,000
Share Premium—Ordinary		10,000

Most corporations account for no-par shares with a stated value as if they were par value shares with par equal to the stated value.

Accounting for and Reporting Preference Shares

The accounting for preference shares at issuance is similar to that for ordinary shares. A corporation allocates proceeds between the par value of the preference shares and share premium. To illustrate, assume that Bishop Co. issues 10,000 shares of $10 par value preference shares for $12 cash per share. Bishop records the issuance as follows.

Cash	120,000	
Share Capital—Preference		100,000
Share Premium—Preference		20,000

Thus, Bishop maintains separate accounts for these different classes of shares. Corporations consider convertible preference shares as a part of equity. In addition, when exercising convertible preference shares, there is no theoretical justification for recognition of a gain or loss. A company recognizes no gain or loss when dealing with shareholders in their capacity as business owners. Instead, the company **employs the book value method**: debit Share Capital—Preference, along with any related Share Premium—Preference; credit Share Capital—Ordinary and Share Premium—Ordinary (if an excess exists).

Preference shares generally have no maturity date. Therefore, no legal obligation exists to pay the preference shareholder. As a result, companies classify preference shares as part of equity. Companies generally report preference shares at par value as the first item in the equity section. They report any excess over par value as part of share premium. They also consider dividends on preference shares as a distribution of income and not an expense. Companies must disclose the pertinent rights of the preference shares outstanding.

Presentation of Equity

Statement of Financial Position

Illustration IFRS15-1 shows a comprehensive equity section from the statement of financial position of Frost Company that includes the equity items we discussed previously.

ILLUSTRATION IFRS15-1
Comprehensive Equity Presentation

FROST COMPANY EQUITY DECEMBER 31, 2014		
Share capital—preference, $100 par value, 7% cumulative, 100,000 shares authorized, 30,000 shares issued and outstanding	$3,000,000	
Share capital—ordinary, no-par, stated value $10 per share, 500,000 shares authorized, 400,000 shares issued	4,000,000	
Ordinary share dividend distributable	200,000	$ 7,200,000
Share premium—preference	150,000	
Share premium—ordinary	840,000	990,000
Retained earnings		4,360,000
Treasury shares (2,000 ordinary shares)		(190,000)
Accumulated other comprehensive loss		(360,000)
Total equity		$12,000,000

Frost should disclose the pertinent rights and privileges of the various securities outstanding. For example, companies must disclose all of the following: dividend and liquidation preferences, participation rights, call prices and dates, conversion or exercise prices and pertinent dates, sinking fund requirements, unusual voting rights, and significant terms of contracts to issue additional shares. Liquidation preferences should be disclosed in the equity section of the statement of financial position, rather than in the notes to the financial statements, to emphasize the possible effect of this restriction on future cash flows.

Presentation of Statement of Changes in Equity

Companies are also required to present a **statement of changes in equity**. The statement of changes in equity includes the following.

1. Total comprehensive income for the period, showing separately the total amounts attributable to owners of the parent and to non-controlling interests.
2. For each component of equity, the effects of retrospective application or retrospective restatement.
3. For each component of equity, a reconciliation between the carrying amount at the beginning and the end of the period, separately disclosing changes resulting from:
   (a) Profit or loss;
   (b) Each item of other comprehensive income; and
   (c) Transactions with owners in their capacity as owners, showing separately contributions by and distributions to owners and changes in ownership interests in subsidiaries that do not result in a loss of control.

A typical statement of changes in equity is shown in Illustration IFRS15-2.

ILLUSTRATION IFRS15-2
Statement of Changes in Equity

	Share Capital	Retained Earnings	Unrealized Holding Gain (Loss) on Non-Trading Equity Investments	Unrealized Holding Gain (Loss) on Property, Plant, and Equipment	Total
Balance—December 31, 2014	$600,000	$120,000	$22,000	$15,000	$ 757,000
Issue of Ordinary Shares	200,000				200,000
Total Comprehensive Income		70,000	11,000	8,000	89,000
Dividends		(20,000)			(20,000)
Balance—December 31, 2015	$800,000	$170,000	$33,000	$23,000	$1,026,000

In addition, companies are required to present, either in the statement of changes in equity or in the notes, the amount of dividends recognized as distributions to owners during the period and the related amount per share.

ON THE HORIZON

As indicated in earlier discussions, the IASB and the FASB are currently working on a project related to financial statement presentation. An important part of this study is to determine whether certain line items, subtotals, and totals should be clearly defined and required to be displayed in the financial statements. For example, it is likely that the statement of changes in equity and its presentation will be examined closely. In addition, the options of how to present other comprehensive income under GAAP will change in any converged standard.

IFRS SELF-TEST QUESTIONS

1. Which of the following does **not** represent a pair of GAAP/IFRS-comparable terms?
   (a) Additional paid-in capital/Share premium.
   (b) Treasury stock/Repurchase reserve.
   (c) Common stock/Share capital—ordinary.
   (d) Preferred stock/Preference shares.
2. Under IFRS, the amount of capital received in excess of par value would be credited to:
   (a) Retained Earnings.
   (b) Contributed Capital.
   (c) Share Premium.
   (d) Par value is not used under IFRS.
3. The term *reserves* is used under IFRS with reference to all of the following **except**:
   (a) gains and losses on revaluation of property, plant, and equipment.
   (b) capital received in excess of the par value of issued shares.
   (c) retained earnings.
   (d) fair value differences.
4. Which of the following is **false**?
   (a) Under GAAP, companies cannot record gains on transactions involving their own shares.
   (b) Under IFRS, companies cannot record gains on transactions involving their own shares.
   (c) Under IFRS, the statement of stockholders' equity is a required statement.
   (d) Under IFRS, a company records a revaluation surplus when it experiences an increase in the price of its common stock.
5. Under IFRS, a purchase by a company of its own shares results in:
   (a) an increase in treasury shares.
   (b) a decrease in assets.
   (c) a decrease in equity.
   (d) All of the above.

IFRS CONCEPTS AND APPLICATION

IFRS15-1 Where can authoritative IFRS guidance related to stockholders' equity be found?

IFRS15-2 Briefly describe some of the similarities and differences between GAAP and IFRS with respect to the accounting for stockholders' equity.

IFRS15-3 Briefly discuss the implications of the financial statement presentation project for the reporting of stockholders' equity.

IFRS15-4 Mary Tokar is comparing a GAAP-based company to a company that uses IFRS. Both companies report equity investments. The IFRS company reports unrealized losses on these investments under the heading "Reserves" in its equity section. However, Mary can find no similar heading in the GAAP-based company financial statements. Can Mary conclude that the GAAP-based company has no unrealized gains or losses on its non-trading equity investments? Explain.

IFRS15-5 Explain each of the following terms: authorized ordinary shares, unissued ordinary shares, issued ordinary shares, outstanding ordinary shares, and treasury shares.

IFRS15-6 Indicate how each of the following accounts should be classified in the equity section.

(a) Share Capital—Ordinary.
(b) Retained Earnings.
(c) Share Premium—Ordinary.
(d) Treasury Shares.
(e) Share Premium—Treasury.
(f) Share Capital—Preference.
(g) Accumulated Other Comprehensive Income.

IFRS15-7 Kaymer Corporation issued 300 shares of $10 par value ordinary shares for $4,500. Prepare Kaymer's journal entry.

IFRS15-8 Wilco Corporation has the following account balances at December 31, 2014.

Share capital—ordinary, $5 par value	$ 510,000
Treasury shares	90,000
Retained earnings	2,340,000
Share premium—ordinary	1,320,000

Instructions

Prepare Wilco's December 31, 2014, equity section.

IFRS15-9 Ravonette Corporation issued 300 shares of $10 par value ordinary shares and 100 shares of $50 par value preference shares for a lump sum of $13,500. The ordinary shares have a market price of $20 per share, and the preference shares have a market price of $90 per share.

Instructions

Prepare the journal entry to record the issuance.

IFRS15-10 Weisberg Corporation has 10,000 shares of $100 par value, 6%, preference shares and 50,000 ordinary shares of $10 par value outstanding at December 31, 2014.

Instructions

Answer the questions in each of the following independent situations.

(a) If the preference shares are cumulative and dividends were last paid on the preference shares on December 31, 2011, what are the dividends in arrears that should be reported on the December 31, 2014, statement of financial position? How should these dividends be reported?

(b) If the preference shares are convertible into seven shares of $10 par value ordinary shares and 3,000 shares are converted, what entry is required for the conversion, assuming the preference shares were issued at par value?

(c) If the preference shares were issued at $107 per share, how should the preference shares be reported in the equity section?

IFRS15-11 Teller Corporation's post-closing trial balance at December 31, 2014, was as follows.

TELLER CORPORATION
POST-CLOSING TRIAL BALANCE
DECEMBER 31, 2014

	Dr.	Cr.
Accounts payable		$ 310,000
Accounts receivable	$ 480,000	
Accumulated depreciation—building and equipment		185,000
Allowance for doubtful accounts		30,000
Bonds payable		700,000
Building and equipment	1,450,000	
Cash	190,000	
Dividends payable on preference shares—cash		4,000
Inventories	560,000	
Land	400,000	
Prepaid expenses	40,000	
Retained earnings		201,000
Share capital—ordinary ($1 par value)		200,000
Share capital—preference ($50 par value)		500,000
Share premium—ordinary		1,000,000
Share premium—treasury		160,000
Treasury shares—ordinary at cost	170,000	
Totals	$3,290,000	$3,290,000

At December 31, 2014, Teller had the following number of ordinary and preference shares.

	Ordinary	Preference
Authorized	600,000	60,000
Issued	200,000	10,000
Outstanding	190,000	10,000

The dividends on preference shares are $4 cumulative. In addition, the preference shares have a preference in liquidation of $50 per share.

Instructions

Prepare the equity section of Teller's statement of financial position at December 31, 2014.

Professional Research

IFRS15-12 Hincapie Co. (a specialty bike-accessory manufacturer) is expecting growth in sales of some products targeted to the low-price market. Hincapie is contemplating a preference share issue to help finance this expansion in operations. The company is leaning toward preference shares because ownership will not be diluted, but the investors will get an extra dividend if the company does well. The company management wants to be certain that its reporting of this transaction is transparent to its current shareholders and wants you to research the disclosure requirements related to its capital structure.

Instructions

Access the IFRS authoritative literature at the IASB website (*http://eifrs.iasb.org/*). (Click on the IFRS tab and then register for free eIFRS access if necessary.) When you have accessed the documents, you can use the search tool in your Internet browser to respond to the following questions. (Provide paragraph citations.)

(a) Identify the authoritative literature that addresses disclosure of information about capital structure.

(b) What information about share capital must companies disclose? Discuss how Hincapie should report the proposed preference share issue.

International Financial Reporting Problem

Marks and Spencer plc

IFRS15-13 The financial statements of **Marks and Spencer plc (M&S)** are available at the book's companion website or can be accessed at *http://annualreport.marksandspencer.com/_assets/downloads/Marks-and-Spencer-Annual-report-and-financial-statements-2012.pdf.*

Instructions

Refer to M&S's financial statements and the accompanying notes to answer the following questions.

(a) What is the par or stated value of M&S's preference shares?

(b) What is the par or stated value of M&S's ordinary shares?

(c) What percentage of M&S's authorized ordinary shares was issued at 31 March 2012?

(d) How many ordinary shares were outstanding at 31 March 2012, and 2 April 2011?

(e) What was the pound amount effect of the cash dividends on M&S's equity?

(f) What is M&S's return on ordinary share equity for 2012 and 2011?

(g) What is M&S's payout ratio for 2012 and 2011?

ANSWERS TO IFRS SELF-TEST QUESTIONS

1. b **2.** c **3.** b **4.** d **5.** d

Remember to check the book's companion website to find additional resources for this chapter.

CHAPTER

16 Dilutive Securities and Earnings per Share

LEARNING OBJECTIVES

After studying this chapter, you should be able to:

1. Describe the accounting for the issuance, conversion, and retirement of convertible securities.
2. Explain the accounting for convertible preferred stock.
3. Contrast the accounting for stock warrants and for stock warrants issued with other securities.
4. Describe the accounting for stock compensation plans.
5. Discuss the controversy involving stock compensation plans.
6. Compute earnings per share in a simple capital structure.
7. Compute earnings per share in a complex capital structure.

Kicking the Habit

Some habits die hard. Take stock options—called by some "the crack cocaine of incentives." Stock options are a form of compensation that gives key employees the choice to purchase shares at a given (usually lower-than-market) price. For many years, companies were hooked on these products. Why? The combination of a hot equity market and favorable accounting treatment made stock options the incentive of choice. They were compensation with no expense to the companies that granted them, and they were popular with key employees, so companies granted them with abandon. However, the accounting rules that took effect in 2005 required *expensing* the fair value of stock options. This new treatment has made it easier for companies to kick this habit.

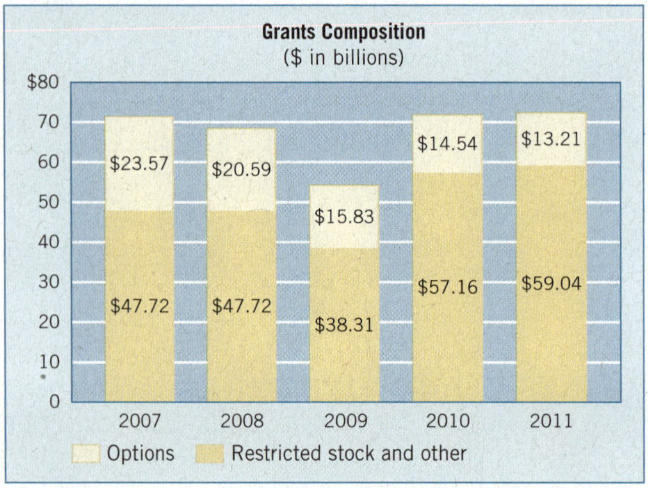

As shown in the chart above, a review of option use for the U.S. companies in the S&P 500 indicates a decline in the use of option-based compensation and an increase in restricted-stock plans. Fewer companies are granting stock options, following implementation of stock-option expensing. As a spokesperson at one company commented, "Once you begin expensing options, the attractiveness significantly drops."

CONCEPTUAL FOCUS

> See the **Underlying Concepts** on pages 890 and 897.

> Read the **Evolving Issue** on page 890 for a discussion of convertible debt.

INTERNATIONAL FOCUS

> See the **International Perspectives** on pages 885, 892, 896, 901, and 904.

> Read the **IFRS Insights** on pages 941–949 for a discussion of:
—Accounting for convertible debt
—Employee share-purchase plans

In the 1990s, executives with huge option stockpiles had an almost irresistible incentive to do whatever it took to increase the stock price and cash in their options. By reining in options, many companies are taking the first steps toward curbing both out-of-control executive pay and the era of corporate corruption that it spawned.

As indicated earlier, some of the ways that companies are curbing option grants include replacing options with restricted shares. Further analysis of these trends indicates that restricted-stock use is more than 10 times the magnitude of options grants in the financial industry. Even after excluding financial companies from the statistics, restricted shares are now the plan of choice. And in the information technology area (where in the past, share options were heavily favored), the fair value of restricted-share plans exceeds that for share options. In this industry, some companies are simply reducing option grants, without offering a replacement, while others, like **Microsoft** and **Yahoo!**, have switched to restricted-stock plans completely. Is this a good trend? Most believe it is; the requirement to expense stock-based compensation similar to other forms of compensation has changed the focus of compensation plans to rewarding talent and performance without breaking the bank. The positive impact on corporate behavior, while hard to measure, should benefit investors in years to come.

Sources: Adapted from: Louis Lavelle, "Kicking the Stock-Options Habit," *BusinessWeek Online* (February 16, 2005). Graph from J. Ciesielski, "S&P 500 Executive Pay: The Bread Keeps Rising," *The Analyst's Accounting Observer* (June 25, 2012).

PREVIEW OF CHAPTER 16

As the opening story indicates, companies are rethinking the use of various forms of stock-based compensation. The purpose of this chapter is to discuss the proper accounting for stock-based compensation. In addition, the chapter examines issues related to other types of financial instruments, such as convertible securities, warrants, and contingent shares, including their effects on reporting earnings per share. The content and organization of the chapter are as follows.

Dilutive Securities and Earnings per Share

Dilutive Securities
- Debt and equity
- Convertible debt
- Convertible preferred stock
- Stock warrants

Accounting for Stock Compensation
- Stock-option plans
- Restricted stock
- Employee stock-purchase plans
- Disclosure of compensation plans
- Debate

Computing Earnings per Share
- Simple capital structure
- Complex capital structure

DILUTIVE SECURITIES

Debt and Equity

LEARNING OBJECTIVE 1
Describe the accounting for the issuance, conversion, and retirement of convertible securities.

Many of the controversies related to the accounting for financial instruments such as stock options, convertible securities, and preferred stock relate to whether companies should report these instruments as a liability or as equity. For example, companies should classify nonredeemable common shares as equity because the issuer has no **obligation** to pay dividends or repurchase the stock. Declaration of dividends is at the issuer's discretion, as is the decision to repurchase the stock. Similarly, preferred stock that is not redeemable does not require the issuer to pay dividends or repurchase the stock. Thus, nonredeemable common or preferred stock lacks an important characteristic of a liability—an obligation to pay the holder of the common or preferred stock at some point in the future.

However the classification is not as clear-cut for other financial instruments. For example, in Chapter 15 we discussed the accounting for mandatorily redeemable preferred stock. Companies originally classified this security as part of equity. The SEC then prohibited equity classification, and most companies classified these securities between debt and equity on the balance sheet in a separate section often referred to as the "mezzanine section." The FASB now requires companies to report these types of securities as a liability.[1] **[1]**

See the FASB Codification section (page 923).

In this chapter, we discuss securities that have characteristics of *both* debt and equity. For example, a convertible bond has both debt and equity characteristics. Should a company classify this security as debt, as equity, or as part debt and part equity? In addition, how should a company compute earnings per share if it has convertible bonds and other convertible securities in its capital structure? Convertible securities as well as options, warrants, and other securities are often called **dilutive securities** because upon exercise they may reduce (dilute) earnings per share.

Accounting for Convertible Debt

Convertible bonds can be changed into other corporate securities during some specified period of time after issuance. A convertible bond combines the benefits of a bond with the privilege of exchanging it for stock at the holder's option. Investors who purchase it desire the security of a bond holding (guaranteed interest and principal) plus the added option of conversion if the value of the stock appreciates significantly.

Corporations issue convertibles for two main reasons. One is to raise equity capital without giving up more ownership control than necessary. To illustrate, assume a company wants to raise $1 million; its common stock is selling at $45 a share. To raise the $1 million, the company would have to sell 22,222 shares (ignoring issue costs). By selling 1,000 bonds at $1,000 par, each convertible into 20 shares of common stock, the company could raise $1 million by committing only 20,000 shares of its common stock.

[1] The FASB (and IASB) have studied the accounting for financial instruments with characteristics of both debt and equity. At one time, the Boards proposed a definition of equity that is far more restrictive than current practice. Under the proposed "basic ownership approach," only common stock is classified as equity. All other instruments (e.g., preferred stock, options, and convertible debt) are classified as liabilities. Instruments classified as liabilities are measured at fair value, and changes are reported in income. Adoption of a narrow definition provides fewer opportunities to structure instruments and arrangements to achieve a desired accounting treatment. See "*Financial Instruments with Characteristics of Equity*" (November 30, 2007) at *http://www.fasb.org*. While the Boards have agreed on some provisions to improve and simplify the financial reporting requirements for financial instruments with characteristics of debt and equity, the project is currently inactive as the Boards have focused on other major convergence projects.

A second reason to issue convertibles is to obtain debt financing at cheaper rates. Many companies could issue debt only at high interest rates unless they attach a convertible covenant. The conversion privilege entices the investor to accept a lower interest rate than would normally be the case on a straight debt issue. For example, Amazon.com at one time issued convertible bonds that pay interest at an effective yield of 4.75 percent. This rate was much lower than Amazon would have had to pay by issuing straight debt. For this lower interest rate, the investor receives the right to buy Amazon's common stock at a fixed price until the bond's maturity.[2]

As indicated earlier, the accounting for convertible debt involves reporting issues at the time of (1) issuance, (2) conversion, and (3) retirement.

At Time of Issuance

The method for recording convertible bonds **at the date of issue follows the method used to record straight debt issues**. None of the proceeds are recorded as equity. Companies amortize to the maturity date any discount or premium that results from the issuance of convertible bonds. Why this treatment? Because it is difficult to predict when, if at all, conversion will occur. However, the accounting for convertible debt as a straight debt issue is controversial; we discuss it more fully later in the chapter.

International Perspective

IFRS requires that the issuer of convertible debt record the liability and equity components separately.

At Time of Conversion

If converting bonds into other securities, a company uses the **book value method** to record the conversion. The book value method records the securities exchanged for the bond at the carrying amount (book value) of the bond.

To illustrate, assume that Hilton, Inc. has a $1,000 bond that is convertible into 10 shares of common stock (par value $10). At the time of conversion, the unamortized premium is $50. Hilton records the conversion of the bonds as follows.

Bonds Payable	1,000	
Premium on Bonds Payable	50	
Common Stock		100
Paid-in Capital in Excess of Par—Common Stock		950

Support for the book value approach is based on the argument that an agreement was established at the date of the issuance either to pay a stated amount of cash at maturity or to issue a stated number of shares of equity securities. Therefore, when the debtholder converts the debt to equity in accordance with the preexisting contract terms, the issuing company recognizes no gain or loss upon conversion.

Induced Conversions

Sometimes the issuer wishes to encourage prompt conversion of its convertible debt to equity securities in order to reduce interest costs or to improve its debt to equity ratio. Thus, the issuer may offer some form of additional consideration (such as cash or common stock), called a "sweetener," to **induce conversion**. The issuing company reports the sweetener as an expense of the current period. Its amount is the fair value of the additional securities or other consideration given.

[2]As with any investment, a buyer has to be careful. For example, Wherehouse Entertainment Inc., which had 6¼ percent convertibles outstanding, was taken private in a leveraged buyout. As a result, the convertible was suddenly as risky as a junk bond of a highly leveraged company with a coupon of only 6¼ percent. As one holder of the convertibles noted, "What's even worse is that the company will be so loaded down with debt that it probably won't have enough cash flow to make its interest payments. And the convertible debt we hold is subordinated to the rest of Wherehouse's debt." These types of situations make convertibles less attractive and lead to the introduction of takeover protection covenants in some convertible bond offerings. Or, sometimes convertibles are permitted to be called at par, and therefore the conversion premium may be lost.

Assume that Helloid, Inc. has outstanding $1,000,000 par value convertible debentures convertible into 100,000 shares of $1 par value common stock. Helloid wishes to reduce its annual interest cost. To do so, Helloid agrees to pay the holders of its convertible debentures an additional $80,000 if they will convert. Assuming conversion occurs, Helloid makes the following entry.

Debt Conversion Expense	80,000	
Bonds Payable	1,000,000	
Common Stock		100,000
Paid-in Capital in Excess of Par—Common Stock		900,000
Cash		80,000

Helloid records the additional $80,000 as **an expense of the current period** and not as a reduction of equity.

Some argue that the cost of a conversion inducement is a cost of obtaining equity capital. As a result, they contend, companies should recognize the cost of conversion as a cost of (a reduction of) the equity capital acquired, and not as an expense. However, the FASB indicated that when an issuer makes an additional payment to encourage conversion, the payment is for a service (bondholders converting at a given time) and should be reported as an expense. The issuing company does not report this expense as an extraordinary item. **[2]**

Retirement of Convertible Debt

As indicated earlier, the method for recording the **issuance** of convertible bonds follows that used in recording straight debt issues. Specifically this means that issuing companies should not attribute any portion of the proceeds to the conversion feature, nor should it credit a paid-in capital account.

Although some raise theoretical objections to this approach, to be consistent, companies need to recognize a gain or loss on **retiring convertible debt in the same way that they recognize a gain or loss on retiring nonconvertible debt**. For this reason, companies should report differences between the cash acquisition price of debt and its carrying amount **in current income as a gain or loss.**

Convertible Preferred Stock

LEARNING OBJECTIVE 2
Explain the accounting for convertible preferred stock.

Convertible preferred stock includes an option for the holder to convert preferred shares into a fixed number of common shares. The major difference between accounting for a convertible bond and convertible preferred stock at the date of issue is their classification. Convertible bonds are considered liabilities, whereas convertible preferreds (unless mandatory redemption exists) are considered part of stockholders' equity.

In addition, when stockholders exercise convertible preferred stock, there is no theoretical justification for recognizing a gain or loss. A company does not recognize a gain or loss when it deals with stockholders in their capacity as business owners. Therefore, companies do not recognize a gain or loss when stockholders exercise convertible preferred stock.

In accounting for the exercise of convertible preferred stock, a company uses the **book value method**. It debits Preferred Stock, along with any related Paid-in Capital in Excess of Par—Preferred Stock, and it credits Common Stock and Paid-in Capital in Excess of Par—Common Stock (if an excess exists). The treatment differs when the par value of the common stock issued **exceeds** the book value of the preferred stock. In that case, the company usually debits Retained Earnings for the difference.

To illustrate, assume Host Enterprises issued 1,000 shares of common stock (par value $2) upon conversion of 1,000 shares of preferred stock (par value $1) that was originally issued for a $200 premium. The entry would be:

Convertible Preferred Stock	1,000	
Paid-in Capital in Excess of Par—Preferred Stock	200	
Retained Earnings	800	
Common Stock		2,000

The rationale for the debit to Retained Earnings is that Host has offered the preferred stockholders an **additional return** to facilitate their conversion to common stock. In this example, Host charges the additional return to retained earnings. Many states, however, require that this charge simply reduce additional paid-in capital from other sources.

What do the numbers mean? HOW LOW CAN YOU GO?

Financial engineers are always looking for the next innovation in security design to meet the needs of both issuers and investors. Consider the convertible bonds issued by **STMicroelectronics (STM)**. STM's 10-year bonds have a zero coupon and are convertible into STM common stock at an exercise price of $33.43. When issued, the bonds sold at an effective yield of −*0.05* percent. That's right—a negative yield.

How could this happen? When STM issued the bonds, investors thought the options to convert were so valuable that they were willing to take zero interest payments and invest an amount *in excess of* the maturity value of the bonds. In essence, the investors are paying interest to STM, and STM records interest revenue. Why would investors do this? If the stock price rises, as many thought it would for STM and many tech companies at this time, these bond investors could convert and get a big gain in the stock.

Investors did get some additional protection in the deal: They can redeem the $1,000 bonds after three years and receive $975 (and after five and seven years, for lower amounts), if it looks like the bonds will never convert. In the end, STM has issued bonds with a significant equity component. And because the entire bond issue is classified as debt, STM records negative interest expense.

Source: STM Financial Reports. See also Floyd Norris, "Legal but Absurd: They Borrow a Billion and Report a Profit," *The New York Times* (August 8, 2003), p. C1.

Stock Warrants

3 LEARNING OBJECTIVE
Contrast the accounting for stock warrants and for stock warrants issued with other securities.

Warrants are certificates entitling the holder to acquire shares of stock at a certain price within a stated period. This option is similar to the conversion privilege in a convertible bond. Warrants, if exercised, become common stock and usually have a dilutive effect (reduce earnings per share) similar to that of the conversion of convertible securities. However, a substantial difference between convertible securities and stock warrants is that upon exercise of the warrants, the holder has to pay a certain amount of money to obtain the shares.

The issuance of warrants or options to buy additional shares normally arises under three situations:

1. When issuing different types of securities, such as bonds or preferred stock, companies often include warrants **to make the security more attractive**—by providing an "equity kicker."
2. Upon the issuance of additional common stock, existing stockholders have a **preemptive right to purchase common stock** first. Companies may issue warrants to evidence that right.
3. Companies give warrants, often referred to as *stock options*, **to executives and employees** as a form of **compensation**.

The problems in accounting for stock warrants are complex and present many difficulties—some of which remain unresolved. The following sections address the accounting for stock warrants in the three situations listed above.

Stock Warrants Issued with Other Securities

Warrants issued with other securities are basically long-term options to buy common stock at a fixed price. Generally the life of warrants is five years, occasionally 10 years; very occasionally, a company may offer perpetual warrants.

A warrant works like this. Tenneco, Inc. offered a unit comprising one share of stock and one detachable warrant. As its name implies, the **detachable stock warrant** can be detached (separated) from the stock and traded as a separate security. The Tenneco warrant in this example is exercisable at $24.25 per share and good for five years. The unit (share of stock plus detachable warrant) sold for 22.75 ($22.75). Since the price of the common stock the day before the sale was 19.88 ($19.88), the difference suggests a price of 2.87 ($2.87) for the warrant.

The investor pays for the warrant in order to receive the right to buy the stock, at a fixed price of $24.25, sometime in the future. It would not be profitable at present for the purchaser to exercise the warrant and buy the stock, because the price of the stock was much below the exercise price.[3] But if, for example, the price of the stock rises to $30, the investor gains $2.88 ($30 − $24.25 − $2.87) on an investment of $2.87, a 100 percent increase! If the price never rises, the investor loses the full $2.87 per warrant.[4]

A company should allocate the proceeds from the sale of debt with detachable stock warrants **between the two securities.**[5] The profession takes the position that two separable instruments are involved, that is, (1) a bond and (2) a warrant giving the holder the right to purchase common stock at a certain price. Companies can trade detachable warrants separately from the debt. This allows the determination of a fair value. The two methods of allocation available are:

1. The proportional method.
2. The incremental method.

Proportional Method. At one time, AT&T issued bonds with detachable five-year warrants to buy one share of common stock (par value $5) at $25. At the time, a share of AT&T stock was selling for approximately $50. These warrants enabled AT&T to price its bond offering at par with an 8¾ percent yield (quite a bit lower than prevailing rates at that time). To account for the proceeds from this offering, AT&T would place a value on the two securities: (1) the value of the bonds without the warrants, and (2) the value of the warrants. The **proportional method** then allocates the proceeds using the proportion of the two amounts, based on fair values.

For example, assume that AT&T's bonds (par $1,000) sold for 99 without the warrants soon after their issue. The market price of the warrants at that time was $30. (Prior to sale the warrants will not have a fair value.) The allocation relies on an estimate of fair value, generally as established by an investment banker, or on the relative fair value of the bonds and the warrants soon after the company issues and trades them. The price paid for 10,000, $1,000 bonds with the warrants attached was par, or $10,000,000. Illustration 16-1 shows the proportional allocation of the bond proceeds between the bonds and warrants.

[3]Later in this discussion, we will show that the value of the warrant is normally determined on the basis of a relative fair value approach because of the difficulty of imputing a warrant value in any other manner.

[4]From the illustration, it is apparent that buying warrants can be an "all or nothing" proposition.

[5]A detachable warrant means that the warrant can sell separately from the bond. GAAP makes a distinction between detachable and nondetachable warrants because companies must sell nondetachable warrants with the security as a complete package. Thus, no allocation is permitted. [3]

Fair value of bonds (without warrants) ($10,000,000 × .99)		$ 9,900,000
Fair value of warrants (10,000 × $30)		300,000
Aggregate fair value		$10,200,000

$$\text{Allocated to bonds: } \frac{\$9,900,000}{\$10,200,000} \times \$10,000,000 = \$\ 9,705,882$$

$$\text{Allocated to warrants: } \frac{\$300,000}{\$10,200,000} \times \$10,000,000 = \$\ \ \ 294,118$$

$$\text{Total allocation} \qquad \$10,000,000$$

ILLUSTRATION 16-1
Proportional Allocation of Proceeds between Bonds and Warrants

In this situation, the bonds sell at a discount. AT&T records the sale as follows.

Cash	9,705,882	
Discount on Bonds Payable	294,118	
Bonds Payable		10,000,000

In addition, AT&T sells warrants that it credits to paid-in capital. It makes the following entry.

Cash	294,118	
Paid-in Capital—Stock Warrants		294,118

AT&T may combine the entries if desired. Here, we show them separately, to indicate that the purchaser of the bond is buying not only a bond but also a possible future claim on common stock in the form of the stock warrant.

Assuming investors exercise all 10,000 warrants (one warrant per one share of stock), AT&T makes the following entry.

Cash (10,000 × $25)	250,000	
Paid-in Capital—Stock Warrants	294,118	
Common Stock (10,000 × $5)		50,000
Paid-in Capital in Excess of Par—Common Stock		494,118

What if investors fail to exercise the warrants? In that case, AT&T debits Paid-in Capital—Stock Warrants for $294,118 and credits Paid-in Capital—Expired Stock Warrants for a like amount. The additional paid-in capital reverts to the former stockholders.

Incremental Method. In instances where a company cannot determine the fair value of either the warrants or the bonds, it applies the **incremental method** used in lump-sum security purchases (as explained in Chapter 15, page 827). That is, the company uses the security for which it *can* determine the fair value. It allocates the remainder of the purchase price to the security for which it does not know the fair value.

For example, assume that the fair value of the AT&T warrants is $300,000, but the company cannot determine the fair value of the bonds without the warrants. Illustration 16-2 shows the amount allocated to the warrants and the stock in this case.

Lump-sum receipt	$10,000,000
Allocated to the warrants	(300,000)
Balance allocated to bonds	$ 9,700,000

ILLUSTRATION 16-2
Incremental Allocation of Proceeds between Bonds and Warrants

Conceptual Questions. The question arises whether the allocation of value to the warrants is consistent with the handling of convertible debt, in which companies allocate no value to the conversion privilege. The FASB stated that the features of a convertible security are **inseparable** in the sense that choices are mutually exclusive. The holder either converts the bonds or redeems them for cash, but cannot do both. No basis, therefore, exists for recognizing the conversion value in the accounts.

Underlying Concepts

Reporting a convertible bond solely as debt is not representationally faithful. However, the cost constraint is used to justify the failure to allocate between debt and equity.

The Board, however, indicated that the issuance of bonds with **detachable warrants** involves *two* securities, one a debt security, which will remain outstanding until maturity, and the other a warrant to purchase common stock. At the time of issuance, separable instruments exist. The existence of two instruments therefore justifies separate treatment. **Nondetachable warrants,** however, **do not require an allocation of the proceeds between the bonds and the warrants.** Similar to the accounting for convertible bonds, companies record the entire proceeds from nondetachable warrants as debt.[6]

Evolving Issue IS THAT ALL DEBT?

Many argue that the conversion feature of a convertible bond is not significantly different in nature from the call represented by a warrant. The question is whether, although the legal forms differ, sufficient similarities of substance exist to support the same accounting treatment. Some contend that inseparability *per se* is an insufficient basis for restricting allocation between identifiable components of a transaction.

Examples of allocation between assets of value in a single transaction *do* exist, such as allocation of values in basket purchases and separation of principal and interest in capitalizing long-term leases. Critics of the current accounting for convertibles say that to deny recognition of value to the conversion feature merely looks to the form of the instrument and does not deal with the substance of the transaction. In an exposure draft on this subject (project now inactive), the FASB indicates that companies should separate the debt and equity components of securities such as convertible debt or bonds issued with nondetachable warrants (see footnotes 1 and 6).

We agree with this position. In both situations (convertible debt and debt issued with warrants), the investor has made a payment to the company for an equity feature—the right to acquire an equity instrument in the future. The only real distinction between them is that the additional payment made when the equity instrument is formally acquired takes different forms. The warrant holder pays additional cash to the issuing company; the convertible debt holder pays for stock by forgoing the receipt of interest from conversion date until maturity date and by forgoing the receipt of the maturity value itself. Thus, the difference is one of method or form of payment only, rather than one of substance. However, until the profession officially reverses its stand with respect to accounting for convertible debt, companies will continue to report convertible debt and bonds issued with nondetachable warrants solely as debt.

Rights to Subscribe to Additional Shares

If the directors of a corporation decide to issue new shares of stock, the old stockholders generally have the right (**preemptive privilege**) to purchase newly issued shares in proportion to their holdings. This privilege, referred to as a **stock right**, saves existing stockholders from suffering a dilution of voting rights without their consent. Also, it may allow them to purchase stock somewhat below its fair value. Unlike the warrants issued with other securities, the warrants issued for stock rights are of short duration.

The certificate representing the stock right states the number of shares the holder of the right may purchase. Each share of stock owned ordinarily gives the owner one stock right. The certificate also states the price at which the new shares may be purchased. The

[6]GAAP requires that for convertible debt that can be settled in cash, companies should account for the liability and equity components separately. In deliberations of the debt/equity project (see footnote 1), the FASB has proposed that all convertible bonds be separated into liability and equity components. As indicated, this project is inactive at this time. **[4]** Academic research indicates that estimates of the debt and equity components of convertible bonds are subject to considerable measurement error. See Mary Barth, Wayne Landsman, and Richard Rendleman, Jr., "Option Pricing–Based Bond Value Estimates and a Fundamental Components Approach to Account for Corporate Debt," *The Accounting Review* (January 1998). This and other challenges explain in part the extended time needed to develop new standards in this area.

price is normally less than the current market price of such shares, which gives the rights a value in themselves. From the time they are issued until they expire, holders of stock rights may purchase and sell them like any other security.

Companies make only a memorandum entry when they issue rights to existing stockholders. This entry indicates the number of rights issued to existing stockholders in order to ensure that the company has additional unissued stock registered for issuance in case the rights are exercised. Companies make no formal entry at this time because they have not yet issued stock nor received cash.

If holders exercise the stock rights, a cash payment of some type usually is involved. If the company receives cash equal to the par value, it makes an entry crediting Common Stock at par value. If the company receives cash in excess of par value, it credits Paid-in Capital in Excess of Par—Common Stock. If it receives cash less than par value, a debit to Paid-in Capital in Excess of Par—Common Stock is appropriate.

Stock Compensation Plans

The third form of warrant arises in stock compensation plans to pay and motivate employees. This warrant is a **stock option**, which gives key employees the option to purchase common stock at a given price over an extended period of time.

A consensus of opinion is that effective compensation programs are ones that do the following: (1) base compensation on employee and company performance, (2) motivate employees to high levels of performance, (3) help retain executives and allow for recruitment of new talent, (4) maximize the employee's after-tax benefit and minimize the employer's after-tax cost, and (5) use performance criteria over which the employee has control. Straight cash-compensation plans (salary and perhaps a bonus), though important, are oriented to the short run. Many companies recognize that they need a longer-term compensation plan in addition to the cash component.

Long-term compensation plans attempt to develop company loyalty among key employees by giving them "a piece of the action"—that is, an equity interest. These plans, generally referred to as **stock-based compensation plans**, come in many forms. Essentially, they provide the employee with the opportunity to receive stock if the performance of the company (by whatever measure) is satisfactory. Typical performance measures focus on long-term improvements that are readily measurable and that benefit the company as a whole, such as increases in earnings per share, revenues, stock price, or market share.

As indicated in our opening story, companies are changing the way they use stock-based compensation. Illustration 16-3 indicates that option expense is a much smaller element of compensation relative to **restricted stock** at companies such as Ford and Wal-Mart.

Company	Fair Value of Option Grants	Fair Value of Restricted Stock Grants
Disney	$120.6	$515.1
Ford	37.3	124.4
Urban Outfitters	1.0	35.8
Wal-Mart Stores	19.6	550.9

ILLUSTRATION 16-3
2011 Company Equity Grants ($ in millions)

The major reasons for this change are two-fold. Critics often cited the indiscriminate use of stock options as a reason why company executives manipulated accounting numbers in an attempt to achieve higher share price. As a result, many responsible companies decided to cut back on the issuance of options, both to avoid such accounting manipulations and to head off investor doubts. In addition, GAAP now results in companies recording a higher expense when stock options are granted.

The data reported in Illustration 16-4 (page 892) reinforce the point that the fair value of stock grants is significant and increasing. The study documents that compensation increased 7.7 percent for S&P 500 executives in 2011, with equity grants being the biggest source of growth.

ILLUSTRATION 16-4
Compensation Elements

($ in millions)	2011	% Change from 2010
Salary	$ 1,781.3	0.2%
Bonus	648.8	−2.8
Fair value of equity grants	8389.1	13.8
Non-equity incentive compensation	2719.2	−2.9
Pension benefits	1309.2	11.9
All other	590.6	7.8
Total executive compensation	$15,438.2	7.7%

Illustration 16-4 shows that cash compensation is less than 20 percent of total compensation. The fair value of equity grants comprised approximately 54 percent of total compensation.

The Major Reporting Issue. Suppose that as an employee for Hurdle Inc., you receive options to purchase 10,000 shares of the firm's common stock as part of your compensation. The date you receive the options is referred to as the **grant date**. The options are good for 10 years. The market price and the exercise price for the stock are both $20 at the grant date. **What is the value of the compensation you just received?**

Some believe that what you have received has no value. They reason that because the difference between the market price and the exercise price is zero, no compensation results. Others argue these options do have value. If the stock price goes above $20 any time in the next 10 years and you exercise the options, you may earn substantial compensation. For example, if at the end of the fourth year, the market price of the stock is $30 and you exercise your options, you earn $100,000 [10,000 options × ($30 − $20)], ignoring income taxes.

International Perspective

IFRS follows the same model as GAAP for recognizing share-based compensation.

The question for Hurdle is how to report the granting of these options. One approach measures compensation cost by the excess of the market price of the stock over its exercise price at the grant date. This approach is referred to as the **intrinsic-value method**. It measures what the holder would receive today if the option was immediately exercised. That intrinsic value **is the difference between the market price of the stock and the exercise price of the options at the grant date.** Using the intrinsic-value method, Hurdle would not recognize any compensation expense related to your options because at the grant date the market price equaled the exercise price. (In the preceding paragraph, those who answered that the options had no value were looking at the question from the intrinsic-value approach.)

The second way to look at the question of how to report the granting of these options bases the cost of employee stock options on the **fair value** of the stock options granted. Under this **fair value method**, companies use acceptable option-pricing models to value the options at the date of grant. These models take into account the many factors that determine an option's underlying value.[7]

GAAP requires that companies recognize compensation cost using the fair value method. [5] The FASB position is that companies should base the accounting for the cost of employee services on the fair value of compensation paid. This amount is presumed to be a measure of the value of the services received. We will discuss more about the politics of GAAP in this area later (see "Debate over Stock-Option Accounting," page 897). Let's first describe the procedures involved.

[7]These factors include the volatility of the underlying stock, the expected life of the options, the risk-free rate during the option life, and expected dividends during the option life.

ACCOUNTING FOR STOCK COMPENSATION

Stock-Option Plans

4 LEARNING OBJECTIVE
Describe the accounting for stock compensation plans.

Stock-option plans involve two main accounting issues:

1. How to determine compensation expense.
2. Over what periods to allocate compensation expense.

Determining Expense

Under the fair value method, companies compute total compensation expense based on the fair value of the options expected to vest on the date they grant the options to the employee(s) (i.e., the **grant date**).[8] Public companies estimate fair value by using an option-pricing model, with some adjustments for the unique factors of employee stock options. No adjustments occur after the grant date in response to subsequent changes in the stock price—either up or down.

Allocating Compensation Expense

In general, a company recognizes compensation expense in the periods in which its employees perform the service—the **service period**. Unless otherwise specified, the service period is the vesting period—the time between the grant date and the vesting date. Thus, the company determines total compensation cost at the grant date and allocates it to the periods benefited by its employees' services.

Stock Compensation Example

An example will help show the accounting for a stock-option plan. Assume that on November 1, 2013, the stockholders of Chen Company approve a plan that grants the company's five executives options to purchase 2,000 shares each of the company's $1 par value common stock. The company grants the options on January 1, 2014. The executives may exercise the options at any time within the next 10 years. The option price per share is $60, and the market price of the stock at the date of grant is $70 per share.

Under the fair value method, the company computes total compensation expense by applying an acceptable fair value option-pricing model (such as the Black-Scholes option-pricing model). To keep this illustration simple, we assume that the fair value option-pricing model determines Chen's total compensation expense to be $220,000.

Basic Entries. Under the fair value method, a company recognizes the value of the options as an expense in the periods in which the employee performs services. In the case of Chen Company, assume that the expected period of benefit is two years, starting with the grant date. Chen would record the transactions related to this option contract as follows.

At date of grant (January 1, 2014)		
No entry.		
To record compensation expense for 2014 (December 31, 2014)		
Compensation Expense	110,000	
Paid-in Capital—Stock Options ($220,000 ÷ 2)		110,000
To record compensation expense for 2015 (December 31, 2015)		
Compensation Expense	110,000	
Paid-in Capital—Stock Options		110,000

[8] "To vest" means "to earn the rights to." An employee's award becomes vested at the date that the employee's right to receive or retain shares of stock or cash under the award is no longer contingent on remaining in the service of the employer.

As indicated, Chen allocates compensation expense evenly over the two-year service period.

Exercise. If Chen's executives exercise 2,000 of the 10,000 options (20 percent of the options) on June 1, 2017 (three years and five months after date of grant), the company records the following journal entry.

June 1, 2017		
Cash (2,000 × $60)	120,000	
Paid-in Capital—Stock Options (20% × $220,000)	44,000	
Common Stock (2,000 × $1.00)		2,000
Paid-in Capital in Excess of Par—Common Stock		162,000

Expiration. If Chen's executives fail to exercise the remaining stock options before their expiration date, the company transfers the balance in the Paid-in Capital—Stock Options account to a more properly titled paid-in capital account, such as Paid-in Capital—Expired Stock Options. Chen records this transaction at the date of expiration as follows.

January 1, 2024 (expiration date)		
Paid-in Capital—Stock Options	176,000	
Paid-in Capital—Expired Stock Options (80% × $220,000)		176,000

Adjustment. An unexercised stock option does not nullify the need to record the costs of services received from executives and attributable to the stock option plan. Under GAAP, a company therefore does not adjust compensation expense upon expiration of the options.

However, if an employee forfeits a stock option because **the employee fails to satisfy a service requirement** (e.g., leaves employment), the company should adjust the estimate of compensation expense recorded in the current period (as a change in estimate). A company records this change in estimate by debiting Paid-in Capital—Stock Options and crediting Compensation Expense for the amount of cumulative compensation expense recorded to date (thus decreasing compensation expense in the period of forfeiture).

Restricted Stock

As indicated earlier, many companies also use restricted stock (in some cases, replacing options altogether) to compensate employees. **Restricted-stock plans** transfer shares of stock to employees, subject to an agreement that the shares cannot be sold, transferred, or pledged until vesting occurs. Similar to stock options, these shares are subject to forfeiture if the conditions for vesting are not met.[9]

Major advantages of restricted-stock plans are:

1. ***Restricted stock never becomes completely worthless.*** In contrast, if the stock price does not exceed the exercise price for a stock option, the options are worthless. The restricted stock, however, still has value.
2. ***Restricted stock generally results in less dilution to existing stockholders.*** Restricted-stock awards are usually one-half to one-third the size of stock options. For example,

[9]Most companies base vesting on future service for a period of generally three to five years. Vesting may also be conditioned on some performance target such as revenue, net income, cash flows, or some combination of these three factors. The employee also collects dividends on the restricted stock, and these dividends generally must be repaid if forfeiture occurs.

if a company issues stock options on 1,000 shares, an equivalent restricted-stock offering might be 333 to 500 shares. The reason for the difference is that at the end of the vesting period, the restricted stock will have value, whereas the stock options may not. As a result, fewer shares are involved in restricted-stock plans, and therefore less dilution results if the stock price rises.

3. ***Restricted stock better aligns the employee incentives with the companies' incentives.*** The holder of restricted stock is essentially a stockholder and should be more interested in the long-term objectives of the company. In contrast, the recipients of stock options often have a short-run focus which leads to taking risks to hype the stock price for short-term gain to the detriment of the long-term.[10]

The accounting for restricted stock follows the same general principles as accounting for stock options at the date of grant. That is, the company determines the fair value of the restricted stock at the date of grant (usually the fair value of a share of stock) and then expenses that amount over the service period. Subsequent changes in the fair value of the stock are ignored for purposes of computing compensation expense.

Restricted Stock Example

Assume that on January 1, 2014, Ogden Company issues 1,000 shares of restricted stock to its CEO, Christie DeGeorge. Ogden's stock has a fair value of $20 per share on January 1, 2014. Additional information is as follows.

1. The service period related to the restricted stock is five years.
2. Vesting occurs if DeGeorge stays with the company for a five-year period.
3. The par value of the stock is $1 per share.

Ogden makes the following entry on the grant date (January 1, 2014).

Unearned Compensation	20,000	
Common Stock (1,000 × $1)		1,000
Paid-in Capital in Excess of Par—Common Stock (1,000 × $19)		19,000

The credits to Common Stock and Paid-in Capital in Excess of Par—Common Stock indicate that Ogden has issued shares of stock. The debit to Unearned Compensation (often referred to as Deferred Compensation Expense) identifies the total compensation expense the company will recognize over the five-year period. **Unearned Compensation represents the cost of services yet to be performed, which is not an asset.** Consequently, the company reports Unearned Compensation in stockholders' equity in the balance sheet, as a contra equity account (similar to the reporting of treasury stock at cost).

At December 31, 2014, Ogden records compensation expense of $4,000 (1,000 shares × $20 × 20%) as follows.

Compensation Expense	4,000	
Unearned Compensation		4,000

Ogden records compensation expense of $4,000 for each of the next four years (2015, 2016, 2017, and 2018).

[10]One important rationale for moving away from options to restricted stock is summarized by Bill Gates of Microsoft: "When you win [with options], you win the lottery. And when you don't win, you still want it. I can imagine an employee going home at night and considering two wildly different possibilities with his compensation program. Either he can buy six summer homes or no summer homes. Either he can send his kids to college 50 times, or no times. The variation is huge; much greater than most employees have an appetite for. And so as soon as they saw that options could go both ways, we proposed an economic equivalent. So what we do now is give shares, not options." See *http://www.mystockoptions.com/pdfs/Restricted%20Stock.pdf*.

What happens if DeGeorge leaves the company before the five years has elapsed? In this situation, DeGeorge forfeits her rights to the stock, and Ogden reverses the compensation expense already recorded.

For example, assume that DeGeorge leaves on February 3, 2016 (before any expense has been recorded during 2016). The entry to record this forfeiture is as follows.

Common Stock	1,000	
Paid-in Capital in Excess of Par—Common Stock	19,000	
Compensation Expense ($4,000 × 2)		8,000
Unearned Compensation		12,000

In this situation, Ogden reverses the compensation expense of $8,000 recorded through 2015. In addition, the company debits Common Stock and Paid-in Capital in Excess of Par—Common Stock, reflecting DeGeorge's forfeiture. It credits the balance of Unearned Compensation since none remains when DeGeorge leaves Ogden.

This accounting is similar to accounting for stock options when employees do not fulfill vesting requirements. Recall that once compensation expense is recorded for stock options, it is not reversed. The only exception is if the employee does not fulfill the vesting requirement, by leaving the company before vesting occurs.

In Ogden's restricted-stock plan, vesting never occurred because DeGeorge left the company before she met the service requirement. Because DeGeorge was never vested, she had to forfeit her shares. Therefore, the company must reverse compensation expense recorded to date.[11]

Employee Stock-Purchase Plans

Employee stock-purchase plans (ESPPs) generally permit all employees to purchase stock at a discounted price for a short period of time. The company often uses such plans to secure equity capital or to induce widespread ownership of its common stock among employees. These plans are considered compensatory unless they satisfy **all three** conditions presented below.

1. Substantially all full-time employees may participate on an equitable basis.
2. The discount from market is small. That is, the discount does not exceed the per share amount of costs avoided by not having to raise cash in a public offering. If the amount of the discount is 5 percent or less, no compensation needs to be recorded.
3. The plan offers no substantive option feature.

International Perspective

IFRS requires that any discount from the market price in employee stock-purchase plans be recorded as compensation expense.

For example, Masthead Company's stock-purchase plan allowed employees who met minimal employment qualifications to purchase its stock at a 5 percent reduction from market price for a short period of time. The reduction from market price is not considered compensatory. Why? Because the per share amount of the costs avoided by not having to raise the cash in a public offering equals 5 percent.

Companies that offer their employees a compensatory ESPP should record the compensation expense over the service life of the employees. It will be difficult for some companies to claim that their ESPPs are non-compensatory (and therefore not record compensation expense) unless they change their discount policy which in the past often was 15 percent. If they change their discount policy to 5 percent, participation in these plans will undoubtedly be lower. As a result, it is likely that some companies will end up dropping these plans.

[11]There are numerous variations on restricted-stock plans, including restricted-stock units (for which the shares are issued at the end of the vesting period) and restricted-stock plans with performance targets, such as EPS or stock price growth.

Disclosure of Compensation Plans

Companies must fully disclose the status of their compensation plans at the end of the periods presented. To meet these objectives, companies must make extensive disclosures. Specifically, a company with one or more share-based payment arrangements must disclose information that enables users of the financial statements to understand:

1. The nature and terms of such arrangements that existed during the period and the potential effects of those arrangements on shareholders.
2. The effect on the income statement of compensation cost arising from share-based payment arrangements.
3. The method of estimating the fair value of the goods or services received, or the fair value of the equity instruments granted (or offered to grant), during the period.
4. The cash flow effects resulting from share-based payment arrangements.

Illustration 16-5 (on page 898) presents the type of information disclosed for compensation plans.

Debate over Stock-Option Accounting

5 LEARNING OBJECTIVE

Discuss the controversy involving stock compensation plans.

The FASB faced considerable opposition when it proposed the fair value method for accounting for stock options. This is not surprising, given that the fair value method results in greater compensation costs relative to the intrinsic-value model. One study documented that, on average, companies in the Standard & Poor's 500 stock index overstated earnings in a recent year by 10 percent through the use of the intrinsic-value method. (See the "What Do the Numbers Mean" box on page 899.) Nevertheless, some companies, such as **Coca-Cola**, **General Electric**, **Wachovia**, **Bank One**, and **The Washington Post**, decided to use the fair value method. As the CFO of Coca-Cola stated, "There is no doubt that stock options are compensation. If they weren't, none of us would want them."

Yet many in corporate America resisted the fair value method. Many small high-technology companies were especially vocal in their opposition, arguing that only through offering stock options can they attract top professional management. They contended that recognizing large amounts of compensation expense under these plans places them at a competitive disadvantage against larger companies that can withstand higher compensation charges. As one high-tech executive stated, "If your goal is to attack fat-cat executive compensation in multi-billion dollar firms, then please do so! But not at the expense of the people who are 'running lean and mean,' trying to build businesses and creating jobs in the process."

Underlying Concepts

The stock-option controversy involves economic-consequence issues. The FASB believes companies should follow the neutrality concept. Others disagree, noting that factors other than accounting theory should be considered.

The stock-option saga is a classic example of the difficulty the FASB faces in issuing new accounting guidance. Many powerful interests aligned against the Board. Even some who initially appeared to support the Board's actions later reversed themselves. These efforts undermine the authority of the FASB, which in turn damages confidence in our financial reporting system.

Transparent financial reporting—including recognition of stock-based expense—should not be criticized because companies will report lower income. We may not like what the financial statements say, but we are always better off when the statements are representationally faithful to the underlying economic substance of transactions.

ILLUSTRATION 16-5
Stock-Option Plan Disclosure

Stock-Option Plan

Description of plan

The Company has a share-based compensation plan. The compensation cost that has been charged against income for the plan was $29.4 million, and $28.7 million for 2014 and 2013, respectively.

The Company's 2014 Employee Share-Option Plan (the Plan), which is shareholder-approved, permits the grant of share options and shares to its employees for up to 8 million shares of common stock. The Company believes that such awards better align the interests of its employees with those of its shareholders. Option awards are generally granted with an exercise price equal to the market price of the Company's stock at the date of grant; those option awards generally vest based on 5 years of continuous service and have 10-year contractual terms. Share awards generally vest over five years. Certain option and share awards provide for accelerated vesting if there is a change in control (as defined by the Plan).

Valuation model assumptions

The fair value of each option award is estimated on the date of grant using an option valuation model based on the assumptions noted in the following table.

	2014	2013
Expected volatility	25%–40%	24%–38%
Weighted-average volatility	33%	30%
Expected dividends	1.5%	1.5%
Expected term (in years)	5.3–7.8	5.5–8.0
Risk-free rate	6.3%–11.2%	6.0%–10.0%

Option plan activity and balances

A summary of option activity under the Plan as of December 31, 2014, and changes during the year then ended are presented below.

Options	Shares (000)	Weighted-Average Exercise Price	Weighted-Average Remaining Contractual Term	Aggregate Intrinsic Value ($000)
Outstanding at January 1, 2014	4,660	42		
Granted	950	60		
Exercised	(800)	36		
Forfeited or expired	(80)	59		
Outstanding at December 31, 2014	4,730	47	6.5	85,140
Exercisable at December 31, 2014	3,159	41	4.0	75,816

The weighted-average grant-date fair value of options granted during the years 2014 and 2013 was $19.57 and $17.46, respectively. The total intrinsic value of options exercised during the years ended December 31, 2014 and 2013, was $25.2 million, and $20.9 million, respectively.

Option expense

As of December 31, 2014, there was $25.9 million of total unrecognized compensation cost related to nonvested share-based compensation arrangements granted under the Plan. That cost is expected to be recognized over a weighted-average period of 4.9 years. The total fair value of shares vested during the years ended December 31, 2014 and 2013, was $22.8 million and $21 million, respectively.

Restricted-Stock Awards

Restricted-stock plan details

The Company also has a restricted-stock plan. The Plan is intended to retain and motivate the Company's Chief Executive Officer over the term of the award and to bring his total compensation package closer to median levels for Chief Executive Officers of comparable companies. The fair value of grants during the year was $1,889,000, or $35.68 per share, equivalent to 92% of the market price of a share of the Company's Common Stock on the date the award was granted.

Restricted-stock activity for the year ended 2014 is as follows.

	Shares	Price
Outstanding at December 31, 2013	57,990	—
Granted	149,000	$12.68
Vested	(19,330)	—
Forfeited	—	—
Outstanding at December 31, 2014	187,660	

By leaving stock-based compensation expense out of income, reported income is biased. Biased reporting not only raises concerns about the credibility of companies' reports, but also of financial reporting in general. Even good companies get tainted by the biased reporting of a few "bad apples." If we write standards to achieve some social, economic, or public policy goal, financial reporting loses its credibility.

What do the numbers mean? A LITTLE HONESTY GOES A LONG WAY

As you have learned, GAAP requires companies to expense compensation paid in the form of stock options. However, before the change to require expensing, some companies voluntarily expensed options rather than simply disclosing the estimated costs in the notes to the financial statements. You might think investors would punish companies that decided to expense stock options. After all, most of corporate America has been battling for years to avoid having to expense them, worried that accounting for those perks would destroy earnings. And indeed, **Merrill Lynch** estimated that if all S&P 500 companies were to expense options, reported profits would fall by as much as 10 percent.

Yet, this small band of big-name companies voluntarily made the switch to expensing, and investors for the most part showered them with love. As shown in the following table, with a few exceptions, the stock prices of the "expensers," from **Cinergy** to **The Washington Post**, outpaced the market after they announced the change.

Company	Estimated EPS: Without Options	Estimated EPS: With Options Expensed	% Change Since Announcement: Company Stock Price
Cinergy	$ 2.80	$ 2.77	22.4%
The Washington Post	20.48	20.10	16.4
Computer Associates	−0.46	−0.62	11.1
Fannie Mae	6.15	6.02	6.7
Bank One	2.77	2.61	2.6
General Motors	5.84	5.45	2.6
Procter & Gamble	3.57	3.35	−2.3
Coca-Cola	1.79	1.70	−6.2
General Electric	1.65	1.61	−6.2
Amazon.com	0.04	−0.99	−11.4

Sources: Merrill Lynch; company reports.

The market's general positive reaction to the expensing of stock options provides a good case study supporting the value that investors place on transparent accounting and reporting. It is puzzling why some companies continued to fight implementation of the expensing rule.

Source: David Stires, "A Little Honesty Goes a Long Way," *Fortune* (September 2, 2002), p. 186. Reprinted by permission. See also Troy Wolverton, "Foes of Expensing Welcome FASB Delay," *TheStreet.com* (October 15, 2004).

COMPUTING EARNINGS PER SHARE

6 LEARNING OBJECTIVE
Compute earnings per share in a simple capital structure.

As indicated earlier, stockholders and potential investors widely use earnings per share in evaluating the profitability of a company. As a result, much attention is given to earnings per share by the financial press. **Earnings per share** indicates the income earned by each share of common stock. Thus, **companies report earnings per share only for common stock**. For example, if Oscar Co. has net income of $300,000 and a weighted average of 100,000 shares of common stock outstanding for the year, earnings per share is $3 ($300,000 ÷ 100,000). Because of the importance of earnings per share information, most companies must report this information on the face of the income statement.[12] **[6]** The exception, due to cost-benefit considerations, is nonpublic companies.[13] Generally, companies report earnings per share information below

[12]For an article on the usefulness of reported EPS data and the application of the qualitative characteristics of accounting information to EPS data, see Lola W. Dudley, "A Critical Look at EPS," *Journal of Accountancy* (August 1985), pp. 102–111.

[13]A nonpublic enterprise is an enterprise (1) whose debt or equity securities are not traded in a public market on a foreign or domestic stock exchange or in the over-the-counter market (including securities quoted locally or regionally), or (2) that is not required to file financial statements with the SEC. An enterprise is not considered a nonpublic enterprise when its financial statements are issued in preparation for the sale of any class of securities in a public market.

net income in the income statement. Illustration 16-6 shows Oscar Co.'s income statement presentation of earnings per share.

ILLUSTRATION 16-6
Income Statement Presentation of EPS

Net income	$300,000
Earnings per share	$3.00

When the income statement contains intermediate components of income (such as discontinued operations or extraordinary items), companies should disclose earnings per share for each component. The presentation in Illustration 16-7 is representative.

ILLUSTRATION 16-7
Income Statement Presentation of EPS Components

Earnings per share:	
Income from continuing operations	$4.00
Loss from discontinued operations, net of tax	0.60
Income before extraordinary item	3.40
Extraordinary gain, net of tax	1.00
Net income	$4.40

These disclosures enable the user of the financial statements to recognize the effects on EPS of income from continuing operations, as distinguished from income or loss from irregular items.[14]

Earnings per Share—Simple Capital Structure

A corporation's capital structure is **simple** if it consists only of common stock or includes no **potential common stock** that upon conversion or exercise could dilute earnings per common share. A capital structure is **complex** if it includes securities that could have a dilutive effect on earnings per common share.

The computation of earnings per share for a simple capital structure involves two items (other than net income)—(1) preferred stock dividends and (2) weighted-average number of shares outstanding.

Preferred Stock Dividends

As we indicated earlier, earnings per share relates to earnings per *common share*. When a company has both common and preferred stock outstanding, **it subtracts the current-year preferred stock dividend from net income to arrive at income available to common stockholders**. Illustration 16-8 shows the formula for computing earnings per share.

ILLUSTRATION 16-8
Formula for Computing Earnings per Share

$$\text{Earnings per Share} = \frac{\text{Net Income} - \text{Preferred Dividends}}{\text{Weighted-Average Number of Shares Outstanding}}$$

In reporting earnings per share information, a company must calculate income available to common stockholders. To do so, the company subtracts dividends on preferred stock from each of the intermediate components of income (income from continuing operations and income before extraordinary items) and finally from net income. If a company declares dividends on preferred stock and a net loss occurs, **the**

[14]Companies should present, either on the face of the income statement or in the notes to the financial statements, per share amounts for discontinued operations and extraordinary items.

company adds the preferred dividend to the loss for purposes of computing the loss per share.

If the preferred stock is cumulative and the company has net income but declares no dividend in the current year, it subtracts **an amount equal to the dividend that it should have declared for the current year only**. If the stock is cumulative and the company reports a net loss, but declares no dividend in the current year, it **adds** an amount equal to the dividend to the net loss. The company should have included dividends in arrears for previous years in the previous years' computations.

International Perspective

The FASB and the IASB are working together on a project to improve EPS accounting by simplifying the computational guidance and thereby increasing the comparability of EPS data on an international basis.

Weighted-Average Number of Shares Outstanding

In all computations of earnings per share, the **weighted-average number of shares outstanding** during the period constitutes the basis for the per share amounts reported. Shares issued or purchased during the period affect the amount outstanding. Companies must **weight the shares by the fraction of the period they are outstanding**. The rationale for this approach is to find the equivalent number of whole shares outstanding for the year.

To illustrate, assume that Franks Inc. has changes in its common stock shares outstanding for the period as shown in Illustration 16-9.

ILLUSTRATION 16-9
Shares Outstanding, Ending Balance—Franks Inc.

Date	Share Changes	Shares Outstanding
January 1	Beginning balance	90,000
April 1	Issued 30,000 shares for cash	30,000
		120,000
July 1	Purchased 39,000 shares	(39,000)
		81,000
November 1	Issued 60,000 shares for cash	60,000
December 31	Ending balance	141,000

Franks computes the weighted-average number of shares outstanding as follows.

ILLUSTRATION 16-10
Weighted-Average Number of Shares Outstanding

Dates Outstanding	(A) Shares Outstanding	(B) Fraction of Year	(C) Weighted Shares (A × B)
Jan. 1–Apr. 1	90,000	3/12	22,500
Apr. 1–July 1	120,000	3/12	30,000
July 1–Nov. 1	81,000	4/12	27,000
Nov. 1–Dec. 31	141,000	2/12	23,500
Weighted-average number of shares outstanding			103,000

As Illustration 16-10 shows, 90,000 shares were outstanding for three months, which is equivalent to 22,500 whole shares for the entire year. Because Franks issued additional shares on April 1, it must weight these shares for the time outstanding. When the company purchased 39,000 shares on July 1, it reduced the shares outstanding. Therefore, from July 1 to November 1, only 81,000 shares were outstanding, which is equivalent to 27,000 shares. The issuance of 60,000 shares increases shares outstanding for the last two months of the year. Franks then makes a new computation to determine the proper weighted shares outstanding.

Stock Dividends and Stock Splits. When **stock dividends** or **stock splits** occur, companies need to restate the shares outstanding before the stock dividend or split, in order to compute the weighted-average number of shares. For example, assume that Vijay Corporation had 100,000 shares outstanding on January 1 and issued a 25 percent stock dividend on June 30. For purposes of computing a weighted-average for the current year, it assumes the additional 25,000 shares outstanding as a result of the stock dividend to be **outstanding since the beginning of the year.** Thus, the weighted-average for the year for Vijay is 125,000 shares.

Companies restate the issuance of a stock dividend or stock split, but not the issuance or repurchase of stock for cash. Why? Because stock splits and stock dividends do not increase or decrease the net assets of the company. The company merely issues additional shares of stock. Because of the added shares, it must restate the weighted-average shares. Restating allows valid comparisons of earnings per share between periods before and after the stock split or stock dividend. Conversely, the issuance or purchase of stock for cash **changes the amount of net assets.** As a result, the company either earns more or less in the future as a result of this change in net assets. Stated another way, **a stock dividend or split does not change the shareholders' total investment**—it only increases (unless it is a reverse stock split) the number of common shares representing this investment.

To illustrate how a stock dividend affects the computation of the weighted-average number of shares outstanding, assume that Sabrina Company has the following changes in its common stock shares during the year.

ILLUSTRATION 16-11
Shares Outstanding, Ending Balance—Sabrina Company

Date	Share Changes	Shares Outstanding
January 1	Beginning balance	100,000
March 1	Issued 20,000 shares for cash	20,000
		120,000
June 1	60,000 additional shares (50% stock dividend)	60,000
		180,000
November 1	Issued 30,000 shares for cash	30,000
December 31	Ending balance	210,000

Sabrina computes the weighted-average number of shares outstanding as follows.

ILLUSTRATION 16-12
Weighted-Average Number of Shares Outstanding—Stock Issue and Stock Dividend

Dates Outstanding	(A) Shares Outstanding	(B) Restatement	(C) Fraction of Year	(D) Weighted Shares (A × B × C)
Jan. 1–Mar. 1	100,000	1.50	2/12	25,000
Mar. 1–June 1	120,000	1.50	3/12	45,000
June 1–Nov. 1	180,000		5/12	75,000
Nov. 1–Dec. 31	210,000		2/12	35,000
Weighted-average number of shares outstanding				180,000

Sabrina must restate the shares outstanding prior to the stock dividend. The company adjusts the shares outstanding from January 1 to June 1 for the stock dividend, so that it now states these shares on the same basis as shares issued subsequent to the stock dividend. Sabrina does not restate shares issued after the stock dividend because they are on the new basis. The stock dividend simply restates existing shares. **The same type of treatment applies to a stock split.**

If a stock dividend or stock split occurs after the end of the year but before issuing the financial statements, a company must restate the weighted-average number of shares outstanding for the year (and any other years presented in comparative form). For example, assume that Hendricks Company computes its weighted-average number of shares as 100,000 for the year ended December 31, 2014. On January 15, 2015, before issuing the financial statements, the company splits its stock 3 for 1. In this case, the weighted-average number of shares used in computing earnings per share for 2014 is now 300,000 shares. If providing earnings per share information for 2013 as comparative information, Hendricks must also adjust it for the stock split.

Comprehensive Example

Let's study a comprehensive illustration for a simple capital structure. Darin Corporation has income before extraordinary item of $580,000 and an extraordinary gain, net of tax, of $240,000. In addition, it has declared preferred dividends of $1 per share on 100,000 shares of preferred stock outstanding. Darin also has the following changes in its common stock shares outstanding during 2014.

ILLUSTRATION 16-13
Shares Outstanding, Ending Balance—Darin Corp.

Dates	Share Changes	Shares Outstanding
January 1	Beginning balance	180,000
May 1	Purchased 30,000 treasury shares	(30,000)
		150,000
July 1	300,000 additional shares (3-for-1 stock split)	300,000
		450,000
December 31	Issued 50,000 shares for cash	50,000
December 31	Ending balance	500,000

To compute the earnings per share information, Darin determines the weighted-average number of shares outstanding as follows.

ILLUSTRATION 16-14
Weighted-Average Number of Shares Outstanding

Dates Outstanding	(A) Shares Outstanding	(B) Restatement	(C) Fraction of Year	(D) Weighted Shares (A × B × C)
Jan. 1–May 1	180,000	3	4/12	180,000
May 1–July 1	150,000	3	2/12	75,000
July 1–Dec. 31	450,000		6/12	225,000
Weighted-average number of shares outstanding				480,000

In computing the weighted-average number of shares, the company ignores the shares sold on December 31, 2014, because they have not been outstanding during the year. Darin then divides the weighted-average number of shares into income before extraordinary item and net income to determine earnings per share. It subtracts its preferred dividends of $100,000 from income before extraordinary item ($580,000) to arrive at income before extraordinary item available to common stockholders of $480,000 ($580,000 − $100,000).

Deducting the preferred dividends from the income before extraordinary item also reduces net income without affecting the amount of the extraordinary item. The final amount is referred to as **income available to common stockholders**, as shown in Illustration 16-15.

ILLUSTRATION 16-15
Computation of Income Available to Common Stockholders

	(A) Income Information	(B) Weighted Shares	(C) Earnings per Share (A ÷ B)
Income before extraordinary item available to common stockholders	$480,000*	480,000	$1.00
Extraordinary gain (net of tax)	240,000	480,000	0.50
Income available to common stockholders	$720,000	480,000	$1.50

*$580,000 − $100,000

Darin must disclose the per share amount for the extraordinary item (net of tax) either on the face of the income statement or in the notes to the financial statements. Illustration 16-16 shows the income and per share information reported on the face of Darin's income statement.

ILLUSTRATION 16-16
Earnings per Share, with Extraordinary Item

Income before extraordinary item	$580,000
Extraordinary gain, net of tax	240,000
Net income	$820,000
Earnings per share:	
Income before extraordinary item	$1.00
Extraordinary item, net of tax	0.50
Net income	$1.50

Earnings per Share—Complex Capital Structure

LEARNING OBJECTIVE 7
Compute earnings per share in a complex capital structure.

The EPS discussion to this point applies to **basic EPS** for a simple capital structure. One problem with a **basic EPS** computation is that it fails to recognize the potential impact of a corporation's dilutive securities. As discussed at the beginning of the chapter, **dilutive securities** are securities that can be converted to common stock.[15] Upon conversion or exercise by the holder, the dilutive securities reduce (dilute) earnings per share. This adverse effect on EPS can be significant and, more importantly, *unexpected* unless financial statements call attention to their potential dilutive effect.

As indicated earlier, a complex capital structure exists when a corporation has convertible securities, options, warrants, or other rights that upon conversion or exercise could dilute earnings per share. When a company has a complex capital structure, **it generally reports both basic and diluted earnings per share.**

Computing **diluted EPS** is similar to computing basic EPS. The difference is that diluted EPS includes the effect of all potential dilutive common shares that were outstanding during the period. The formula in Illustration 16-17 shows the relationship between basic EPS and diluted EPS.

International Perspective

The provisions in GAAP are substantially the same as those in *International Accounting Standard No. 33*, "Earnings per Share," issued by the IASB.

Some securities are antidilutive. **Antidilutive securities** are securities that upon conversion or exercise **increase** earnings per share (or reduce the loss per share). Companies with complex capital structures will not report diluted EPS if the securities in their capital structure are antidilutive. The purpose of presenting both basic and diluted EPS is to inform financial statement users of

[15]Issuance of these types of securities is typical in mergers and compensation plans.

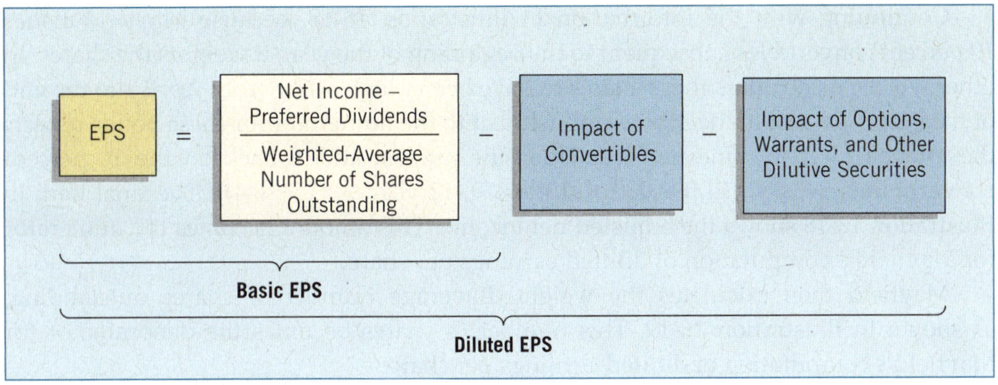

ILLUSTRATION 16-17
Relationship between Basic and Diluted EPS

situations that will likely occur (basic EPS) and also to provide "worst case" dilutive situations (dilutive EPS). If the securities are antidilutive, the likelihood of conversion or exercise is considered remote. Thus, companies that have only antidilutive securities must report only the basic EPS number. We illustrated the computation of basic EPS in the prior section. In the following sections, we address the effects of convertible and other dilutive securities on EPS calculations.

Diluted EPS—Convertible Securities

At conversion, companies exchange convertible securities for common stock. Companies measure the dilutive effects of potential conversion on EPS using the **if-converted method**. This method for a convertible bond assumes (1) the conversion of the convertible securities at the beginning of the period (or at the time of issuance of the security, if issued during the period), and (2) the elimination of related interest, net of tax. Thus, the additional shares assumed issued increase the **denominator**—the weighted-average number of shares outstanding. The amount of interest expense, net of tax associated with those potential common shares, increases the **numerator**—net income.

Comprehensive Example—If-Converted Method. As an example, Mayfield Corporation has net income of $210,000 for the year and a weighted-average number of common shares outstanding during the period of 100,000 shares. The basic earnings per share is therefore $2.10 ($210,000 ÷ 100,000). The company has two convertible debenture bond issues outstanding. One is a 6 percent issue sold at 100 (total $1,000,000) in a prior year and convertible into 20,000 common shares. The other is a 10 percent issue sold at 100 (total $1,000,000) on April 1 of the current year and convertible into 32,000 common shares. The tax rate is 40 percent.

As Illustration 16-18 shows, to determine the numerator for diluted earnings per share, Mayfield adds back the interest on the if-converted securities, less the related tax effect. Because the if-converted method assumes conversion as of the beginning of the year, Mayfield assumes that it pays no interest on the convertibles during the year. The interest on the 6 percent convertibles is $60,000 for the year ($1,000,000 × 6%). The increased tax expense is $24,000 ($60,000 × 0.40). The interest added back net of taxes is $36,000 [$60,000 − $24,000, or simply $60,000 × (1 − 0.40)].

Net income for the year	$210,000
Add: Adjustment for interest (net of tax)	
6% debentures ($60,000 × [1 − .40])	36,000
10% debentures ($100,000 × 9/12 × [1 − .40])	45,000
Adjusted net income	$291,000

ILLUSTRATION 16-18
Computation of Adjusted Net Income

Continuing with the information in Illustration 16-18, because Mayfield issues 10 percent convertibles subsequent to the beginning of the year, it weights the shares. In other words, it considers these shares to have been outstanding from April 1 to the end of the year. As a result, the interest adjustment to the numerator for these bonds reflects the interest for only nine months. Thus, the interest added back on the 10 percent convertible is $45,000 [$1,000,000 × 10% × 9/12 year × (1 − 0.4)]. The final item in Illustration 16-18 shows the adjusted net income. This amount becomes the numerator for Mayfield's computation of diluted earnings per share.

Mayfield then calculates the weighted-average number of shares outstanding, as shown in Illustration 16-19. This number of shares becomes the denominator for Mayfield's computation of diluted earnings per share.

ILLUSTRATION 16-19
Computation of Weighted-Average Number of Shares

Weighted-average number of shares outstanding	100,000
Add: Shares assumed to be issued:	
6% debentures (as of beginning of year)	20,000
10% debentures (as of date of issue, April 1; 9/12 × 32,000)	24,000
Weighted-average number of shares adjusted for dilutive securities	144,000

In its income statement, Mayfield reports basic and diluted earnings per share.[16] Illustration 16-20 shows this dual presentation.

ILLUSTRATION 16-20
Earnings per Share Disclosure

Net income for the year	$210,000
Earnings per Share (Note X)	
Basic earnings per share ($210,000 ÷ 100,000)	$2.10
Diluted earnings per share ($291,000 ÷ 144,000)	$2.02

Other Factors. The example above assumed that Mayfield sold its bonds at the face amount. If it instead sold the bonds at a premium or discount, the company must adjust the interest expense each period to account for this occurrence. Therefore, the interest expense reported on the income statement is the amount of interest expense, net of tax, added back to net income. (It is not the interest paid in cash during the period.)

In addition, the conversion rate on a dilutive security may change during the period in which the security is outstanding. For the diluted EPS computation in such a situation, the **company uses the most dilutive conversion rate available.** For example, assume that a company issued a convertible bond on January 1, 2013, with a conversion rate of 10 common shares for each bond starting January 1, 2015. Beginning January 1, 2018, the conversion rate is 12 common shares for each bond, and beginning January 1, 2022, it is 15 common shares for each bond. In computing diluted EPS in 2013, the company uses the conversion rate of 15 shares to one bond.

A final issue relates to preferred stock. For example, assume that Mayfield's 6 percent convertible debentures were instead 6 percent convertible *preferred stock.* In that case, Mayfield considers the convertible preferred as potential common shares. Thus, it includes them in its diluted EPS calculations as shares outstanding. The company does not subtract preferred dividends from net income in computing the numerator. Why

[16]Conversion of bonds is dilutive because EPS with conversion ($2.02) is less than basic EPS ($2.10). See Appendix 16B for a comprehensive evaluation of antidilution with multiple securities.

not? Because for purposes of computing EPS, it assumes conversion of the convertible preferreds to outstanding common stock. The company uses net income as the numerator—it computes **no tax effect** because preferred dividends generally are not tax-deductible.

Diluted EPS—Options and Warrants

A company includes in diluted earnings per share stock options and warrants outstanding (whether or not presently exercisable), unless they are antidilutive. Companies use the **treasury-stock method** to include options and warrants and their equivalents in EPS computations.

The treasury-stock method assumes that the options or warrants are exercised at the beginning of the year (or date of issue if later), and that the company uses those proceeds to purchase common stock for the treasury. If the exercise price is lower than the market price of the stock, then the proceeds from exercise are insufficient to buy back all the shares. The company then adds the incremental shares remaining to the weighted-average number of shares outstanding for purposes of computing diluted earnings per share.

For example, if the exercise price of a warrant is $5 and the market price of the stock is $15, the treasury-stock method increases the shares outstanding. Exercise of the warrant results in one additional share outstanding, but the $5 received for the one share issued is insufficient to purchase one share in the market at $15. The company needs to exercise three warrants (and issue three additional shares) to produce enough money ($15) to acquire one share in the market. Thus, a net increase of two shares outstanding results.

To see this computation using larger numbers, assume 1,500 options outstanding at an exercise price of $30 for a common share and a common stock market price per share of $50. Through application of the treasury-stock method, the company would have 600 incremental shares outstanding, computed as shown in Illustration 16-21.[17]

ILLUSTRATION 16-21
Computation of Incremental Shares

Proceeds from exercise of 1,500 options (1,500 × $30)	$45,000
Shares issued upon exercise of options	1,500
Treasury shares purchasable with proceeds ($45,000 ÷ $50)	(900)
Incremental shares outstanding (potential common shares)	600

Thus, if the exercise price of the option or warrant is **lower** than the market price of the stock, dilution occurs. An exercise price of the option or warrant **higher** than the market price of the stock reduces common shares. In this case, the options or warrants are **antidilutive** because their assumed exercise leads to an increase in earnings per share.

For both options and warrants, exercise is assumed only if the average market price of the stock exceeds the exercise price during the reported period.[18] As a practical

[17]The incremental number of shares may be more simply computed:

$$\frac{\text{Market price} - \text{Option price}}{\text{Market price}} \times \text{Number of options} = \text{Number of shares}$$

$$\frac{\$50 - \$30}{\$50} \times 1{,}500 \text{ options} = 600 \text{ shares}$$

[18]Options and warrants have essentially the same assumptions and computational problems, although the warrants may allow or require the tendering of some other security, such as debt, in lieu of cash upon exercise. In such situations, the accounting becomes quite complex and is beyond the scope of this textbook.

matter, a simple average of the weekly or monthly prices is adequate, so long as the prices do not fluctuate significantly.

Comprehensive Example—Treasury-Stock Method. To illustrate application of the treasury-stock method, assume that Kubitz Industries, Inc. has net income for the period of $220,000. The average number of shares outstanding for the period was 100,000 shares. Hence, basic EPS—ignoring all dilutive securities—is $2.20. The average number of shares related to options outstanding (although not exercisable at this time), at an option price of $20 per share, is 5,000 shares. The average market price of the common stock during the year was $28. Illustration 16-22 shows the computation of EPS using the treasury-stock method.

ILLUSTRATION 16-22
Computation of Earnings per Share—Treasury-Stock Method

	Basic Earnings per Share	Diluted Earnings per Share
Average number of shares related to options outstanding		5,000
Option price per share		× $20
Proceeds upon exercise of options		$100,000
Average market price of common stock		$28
Treasury shares that could be repurchased with proceeds ($100,000 ÷ $28)		3,571
Excess of shares under option over the treasury shares that could be repurchased (5,000 − 3,571)—potential common incremental shares		1,429
Average number of common shares outstanding	100,000	100,000
Total average number of common shares outstanding and potential common shares	100,000 (A)	101,429 (C)
Net income for the year	$220,000 (B)	$220,000 (D)
Earnings per share	$2.20 (B ÷ A)	$2.17 (D ÷ C)

Contingent Issue Agreement

In business combinations, the acquirer may promise to issue additional shares—referred to as **contingent shares**—under certain conditions. Sometimes the company issues these contingent shares as a result of a **passage-of-time condition** or upon the attainment of a **certain earnings or market price level**. If this passage-of-time condition occurs during the current year, or if the company meets the earnings or market price **by the end of the year**, the company considers the contingent shares as outstanding for the computation of diluted earnings per share.[19]

For example, assume that Watts Corporation purchased Cardoza Company and agreed to give Cardoza's stockholders 20,000 additional shares in 2017 if Cardoza's net income in 2016 is $90,000. In 2015, Cardoza's net income is $100,000. Because Cardoza has already attained the 2016 stipulated earnings of $90,000, in computing diluted earnings per share for 2015, Watts would include the 20,000 contingent shares in the shares-outstanding computation.

Antidilution Revisited

In computing diluted EPS, a company must consider the aggregate of all dilutive securities. But first it must determine which potentially dilutive securities are in fact individually dilutive and which are antidilutive. **A company should exclude any**

[19]In addition to contingent issuances of stock, other situations that might lead to dilution are the issuance of participating securities and two-class common shares. The reporting of these types of securities in EPS computations is beyond the scope of this textbook.

security that is antidilutive, nor can the company use such a security to offset dilutive securities.

Recall that including antidilutive securities in earnings per share computations increases earnings per share (or reduces net loss per share). With options or warrants, whenever the exercise price exceeds the market price, the security is antidilutive. Convertible debt is antidilutive if the addition to income of the interest (net of tax) causes a greater percentage increase in income (numerator) than conversion of the bonds causes a percentage increase in common and potentially dilutive shares (denominator). In other words, convertible debt is antidilutive if conversion of the security causes common stock earnings to increase by a greater amount per additional common share than earnings per share was before the conversion.

To illustrate, assume that Martin Corporation has a 6 percent, $1,000,000 debt issue that is convertible into 10,000 common shares. Net income for the year is $210,000, the weighted-average number of common shares outstanding is 100,000 shares, and the tax rate is 40 percent. In this case, assumed conversion of the debt into common stock at the beginning of the year requires the following adjustments of net income and the weighted-average number of shares outstanding.

ILLUSTRATION 16-23
Test for Antidilution

Net income for the year	$210,000	Average number of shares outstanding	100,000
Add: Adjustment for interest (net of tax) on 6% debentures $60,000 × (1 − .40)	36,000	Add: Shares issued upon assumed conversion of debt	10,000
Adjusted net income	$246,000	Average number of common and potential common shares outstanding	110,000

Basic EPS = $210,000 ÷ 100,000 = $2.10
Diluted EPS = $246,000 ÷ 110,000 = $2.24 = **Antidilutive**

As a shortcut, Martin can also identify the convertible debt as antidilutive by comparing the EPS resulting from conversion, $3.60 ($36,000 additional earnings ÷ 10,000 additional shares), with EPS before inclusion of the convertible debt, $2.10.

Companies should ignore antidilutive securities in all calculations and in computing diluted earnings per share. This approach is reasonable. The profession's intent was to inform the investor of the possible dilution that might occur in reported earnings per share and not to be concerned with securities that, if converted or exercised, would result in an increase in earnings per share. Appendix 16B to this chapter provides an extended example of how companies consider antidilution in a complex situation with multiple securities.

EPS Presentation and Disclosure

A company with a complex capital structure would present its EPS information as follows.

ILLUSTRATION 16-24
EPS Presentation—Complex Capital Structure

Earnings per common share	
Basic earnings per share	$3.30
Diluted earnings per share	$2.70

When the earnings of a period include irregular items, a company should show per share amounts (where applicable) for the following: income from continuing operations, income before extraordinary items, and net income. Companies that report a discontinued operation or an extraordinary item should present per share amounts **for those line items** either on the face of the income statement or in the notes to the financial statements. Illustration 16-25 (page 910) shows a presentation reporting extraordinary items.

ILLUSTRATION 16-25
EPS Presentation, with Extraordinary Item

Basic earnings per share	
Income before extraordinary item	$3.80
Extraordinary item	(0.80)
Net income	$3.00
Diluted earnings per share	
Income before extraordinary item	$3.35
Extraordinary item	(0.65)
Net income	$2.70

A company must show earnings per share amounts for all periods presented. Also, the company should restate all prior period earnings per share amounts presented for stock dividends and stock splits. If it reports diluted EPS data for at least one period, the company should report such data for all periods presented, even if it is the same as basic EPS. When a company restates results of operations of a prior period as a result of an error or a change in accounting principle, it should also restate the earnings per share data shown for the prior periods. Complex capital structures and dual presentation of earnings per share require the following additional disclosures in note form.

1. Description of pertinent rights and privileges of the various securities outstanding.
2. A reconciliation of the numerators and denominators of the basic and diluted per share computations, including individual income and share amount effects of all securities that affect EPS.
3. The effect given preferred dividends in determining income available to common stockholders in computing basic EPS.
4. Securities that could potentially dilute basic EPS in the future that were excluded in the computation because they would be antidilutive.
5. Effect of conversions subsequent to year-end, but before issuing statements.

Illustration 16-26 presents the reconciliation and the related disclosure to meet the requirements of this standard.[20] **[7]**

ILLUSTRATION 16-26
Reconciliation for Basic and Diluted EPS

	For the Year Ended 2014		
	Income (Numerator)	Shares (Denominator)	Per Share Amount
Income before extraordinary item	$7,500,000		
Less: Preferred stock dividends	45,000		
Basic EPS	7,455,000	3,991,666	$1.87
Warrants		30,768	
Convertible preferred stock	45,000	308,333	
4% convertible bonds (net of tax)	60,000	50,000	
Diluted EPS	$7,560,000	4,380,767	$1.73

Stock options to purchase 1,000,000 shares of common stock at $85 per share were outstanding during the second half of 2014 but were not included in the computation of diluted EPS because the options' exercise price was greater than the average market price of the common shares. The options were still outstanding at the end of year 2014 and expire on June 30, 2024.

[20]Note that GAAP has specific disclosure requirements regarding stock-based compensation plans and earnings per share disclosures as well. The earnings per share effects of noncontrolling interest (discussed in Chapter 4) should also be presented, with the amounts of income from continuing operations and discontinued operations (if present), attributable to the controlling interest disclosed. However, only the net income attributable to the controlling interest should be used in computing earnings per share.

What do the numbers mean? PRO FORMA EPS CONFUSION

Many companies are reporting pro forma EPS numbers along with GAAP-based EPS numbers in the financial information provided to investors. Pro forma earnings generally exceed GAAP earnings because the pro forma numbers exclude such items as restructuring charges, impairments of assets, R&D expenditures, and stock compensation expense. Here are some examples.

Company	GAAP EPS	Pro Forma EPS
Adaptec	$(0.62)	$ 0.05
Corning	(0.24)	0.09
General Motors	(0.41)	0.85
Honeywell International	(0.38)	0.44
International Paper	(0.57)	0.14
Qualcomm	(0.06)	0.20
Broadcom	(6.36)	(0.13)
Lucent Technologies	(2.16)	(0.27)

Source: Company press releases.

Another case of possibly misleading pro forma reporting is the case of social media darlings **Facebook**, **Zynga**, and **Groupon**. For example, social gaming company Zynga recently reported so much stock-compensation expense ($600 million) that it overwhelmed its operating profit; these expenses took operating profit negative to the tune of $406 million. The accounting? Zynga "window dressed" the expense by encouraging Wall Street analysts to use a non-GAAP pro forma accounting figure—"adjusted earnings before interest, taxes, depreciation and amortization"—that ignores the stock compensation. **LinkedIn** and Groupon also use non-GAAP metrics that exclude stock compensation. LinkedIn's $30 million stock-compensation expense roughly halved its operating profit, while Groupon's $94 million took operating profit $203 million into the red. Wall Street analysts tend to go along with the accounting hocus-pocus, as it allows them to justify higher valuations for stocks. Investors should remember, however, that employee equity awards are real costs.

As discussed in Chapter 4, SEC Regulation G requires companies to provide a clear reconciliation between pro forma and GAAP information. And this applies to EPS measures as well. This reconciliation is especially important, given the spike in pro forma reporting by companies adding back employee stock-option expense.

Sources: See M. Moran, A. J. Cohen, and K. Shaustyuk, "Stock Option Expensing: The Battle Has Been Won; Now Comes the Aftermath," *Portfolio Strategy/Accounting*, Goldman Sachs (March 17, 2005); and R. Winkler, "Stock and Awe at Facebook and Zynga," *Wall Street Journal* (February 16, 2012).

Summary of EPS Computation

As you can see, computation of earnings per share is a complex issue. It is a controversial area because many securities, although technically not common stock, have many of its basic characteristics. Indeed, some companies have issued these other securities rather than common stock in order to avoid an adverse dilutive effect on earnings per share. Illustrations 16-27 and 16-28 (page 912) display the elementary points of calculating earnings per share in a simple capital structure and in a complex capital structure.

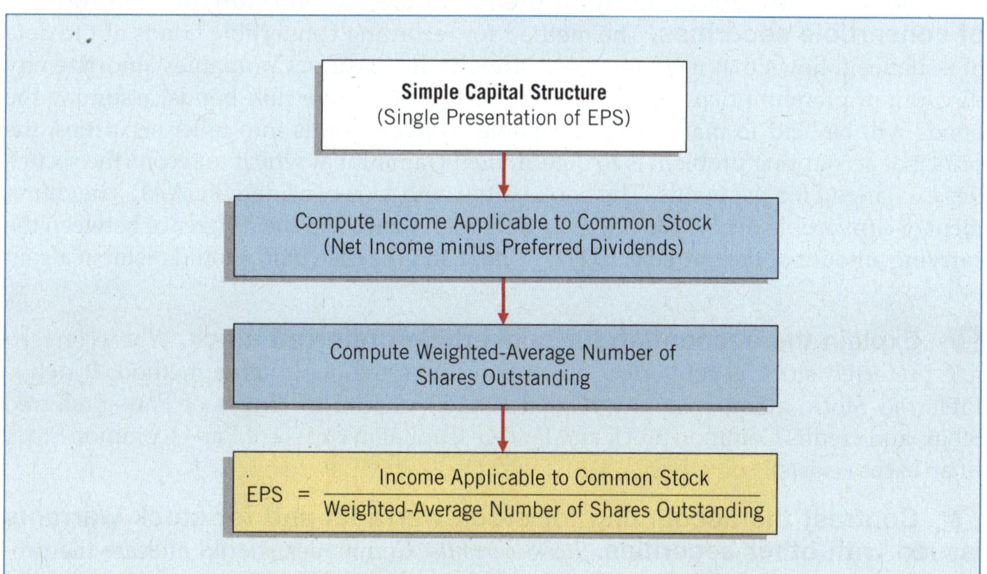

ILLUSTRATION 16-27
Calculating EPS, Simple Capital Structure

ILLUSTRATION 16-28
Calculating EPS, Complex Capital Structure

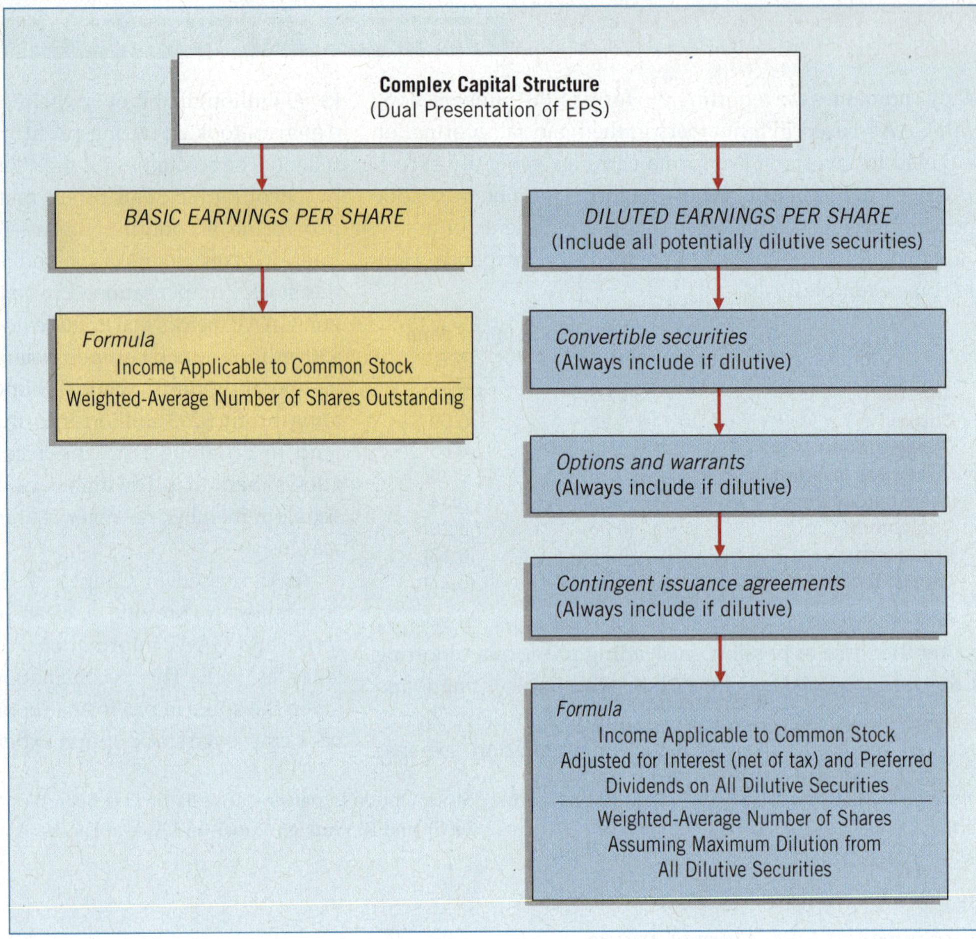

You will want to read the **IFRS INSIGHTS** on pages 941–949 for discussion of IFRS related to dilutive securities and earnings per share.

KEY TERMS

antidilutive securities, *904*
basic EPS, *904*
complex capital structure, *900*
convertible bonds, *884*
convertible preferred stock, *886*
detachable stock warrants, *888*
diluted EPS, *904*
dilutive securities, *884, 904*
earnings per share, *899*
fair value method, *892*
grant date, *892*
if-converted method, *905*
income available to common stockholders, *900*
incremental method, *889*
induced conversion, *885*

SUMMARY OF LEARNING OBJECTIVES

1 Describe the accounting for the issuance, conversion, and retirement of convertible securities. The method for recording convertible bonds at the date of issuance follows that used to record straight debt issues. Companies amortize any discount or premium that results from the issuance of convertible bonds, assuming the bonds will be held to maturity. If companies convert bonds into other securities, the principal accounting problem is to determine the amount at which to record the securities exchanged for the bonds. The book value method is considered GAAP. The retirement of convertible debt is considered a debt retirement, and the difference between the carrying amount of the retired convertible debt and the cash paid should result in a gain or loss.

2 Explain the accounting for convertible preferred stock. When convertible preferred stock is converted, a company uses the book value method. It debits Preferred Stock, along with any related Paid-in Capital in Excess of Par—Preferred Stock, and credits Common Stock and Paid-in Capital in Excess of Par—Common Stock (if an excess exists).

3 Contrast the accounting for stock warrants and for stock warrants issued with other securities. *Stock warrants*: Companies should allocate the proceeds from the sale of debt with detachable warrants between the two securities.

Warrants that are detachable can be traded separately from the debt, and therefore companies can determine their fair value. Two methods of allocation are available: the proportional method and the incremental method. Nondetachable warrants do not require an allocation of the proceeds between the bonds and the warrants; companies record the entire proceeds as debt. *Stock rights*: No entry is required when a company issues rights to existing stockholders. The company needs only to make a memorandum entry to indicate the number of rights issued to existing stockholders and to ensure that the company has additional unissued stock registered for issuance in case the stockholders exercise the rights.

4 Describe the accounting for stock compensation plans. Companies must use the fair value approach to account for stock-based compensation. Under this approach, a company computes total compensation expense based on the fair value of the options that it expects to vest on the grant date. Companies recognize compensation expense in the periods in which the employee performs the services. Restricted-stock plans follow the same general accounting principles as those for stock options. Companies estimate total compensation cost at the grant date based on the fair value of the restricted stock; they expense that cost over the service period. If vesting does not occur, companies reverse the compensation expense.

5 Discuss the controversy involving stock compensation plans. When first proposed, there was considerable opposition to the recognition provisions contained in the fair value approach. The reason: that approach could result in substantial, previously unrecognized compensation expense. Corporate America, particularly the high-technology sector, vocally opposed the proposed standard. They believed that the standard would place them at a competitive disadvantage with larger companies that can withstand higher compensation charges. Offsetting such opposition is the need for greater transparency in financial reporting, on which our capital markets depend.

6 Compute earnings per share in a simple capital structure. When a company has both common and preferred stock outstanding, it subtracts the current-year preferred stock dividend from net income to arrive at income available to common stockholders. The formula for computing earnings per share is net income less preferred stock dividends, divided by the weighted-average number of shares outstanding.

7 Compute earnings per share in a complex capital structure. A complex capital structure requires a dual presentation of earnings per share, each with equal prominence on the face of the income statement. These two presentations are referred to as basic earnings per share and diluted earnings per share. Basic earnings per share relies on the number of weighted-average common shares outstanding (i.e., equivalent to EPS for a simple capital structure). Diluted earnings per share indicates the dilution of earnings per share that will occur if all potential issuances of common stock that would reduce earnings per share takes place. Companies with complex capital structures should exclude antidilutive securities when computing earnings per share.

APPENDIX 16A ACCOUNTING FOR STOCK-APPRECIATION RIGHTS

8 LEARNING OBJECTIVE
Explain the accounting for stock-appreciation rights plans.

A major disadvantage of many stock-option plans is that an executive must pay income tax on the difference between the market price of the stock and the option price at the **date of exercise**. This feature of stock-option plans (those referred to as **nonqualified**) can be a financial hardship for an executive who wishes to keep the stock (rather than sell it immediately) because he or she would have to pay not only income tax but the option price as well. In another type of plan (an **incentive plan**), the executive pays no taxes at exercise but may need to borrow to finance the exercise price, which leads to related interest cost.

One solution to this problem was the creation of **stock-appreciation rights (SARs)**. In this type of plan, the company gives an executive the right to receive compensation equal to the share appreciation. **Share appreciation** is the excess of the market price of the stock at the date of exercise over a pre-established price. The company may pay the share appreciation in cash, shares, or a combination of both.

The major advantage of SARs is that the executive often does not have to make a cash outlay at the date of exercise, but receives a payment for the share appreciation. Unlike shares acquired under a stock-option plan, the company does not issue the shares that constitute the basis for computing the appreciation in a SARs plan. Rather, the company simply awards the executive cash or stock having a fair value equivalent to the appreciation. The accounting for stock-appreciation rights depends on whether the company classifies the rights as equity or as a liability.

SARS—SHARE-BASED EQUITY AWARDS

Companies classify SARs as **equity awards** if at the date of exercise, the holder receives shares of stock from the company upon exercise. In essence, SARs are essentially equivalent to a stock option. The major difference relates to the form of payment. With the stock option, the holder pays the exercise price and then receives the stock. In an equity SAR, the holder receives shares in an amount equal to the **share-price appreciation** (the difference between the market price and the pre-established price). The accounting for SARs when they are equity awards follows the accounting used for stock options. At the date of grant, the company determines a fair value for the SAR and then allocates this amount to compensation expense over the service period of the employees.

SARS—SHARE-BASED LIABILITY AWARDS

Companies classify SARs as liability awards if at the date of exercise, the holder receives a cash payment. In this case the holder is not receiving additional shares of stock but a cash payment equal to the amount of share-price appreciation. The company's compensation expense therefore changes as the value of the liability changes.

A company uses the following approach to record share-based liability awards:

1. Measure the fair value of the award at the grant date and accrue compensation over the service period.
2. Remeasure the fair value each reporting period, until the award is settled. Adjust the compensation cost each period for changes in fair value prorated for the portion of the service period completed.
3. Once the service period is completed, determine compensation expense each subsequent period by reporting the full change in market price as an adjustment to compensation expense.

For liability awards, the company estimates the fair value of the SARs, using an option-pricing model. The company then allocates this total estimated compensation cost over the service period, recording expense (or a decrease in expense if fair value declines) in each period. At the end of each period, total compensation expense reported to date should equal the percentage of the total service period that has elapsed, multiplied by the total estimated compensation cost.

For example, assume that the service period is 40 percent complete and total estimated compensation is $100,000. The company reports cumulative compensation expense to date of $40,000 ($100,000 × .40).

The method of allocating compensation expense is called the **percentage approach**. In this method, in the first year of, say, a four-year plan, the company charges one-fourth of the estimated cost to date. In the second year, it charges off two-fourths, or 50 percent, of the estimated cost to date, less the amount already recognized in the first year. In the third year, it charges off three-fourths of the estimated cost to date, less the amount recognized previously. In the fourth year, it charges off the remaining compensation expense.

A special problem arises when the exercise date is later than the service period. In the previous example, if the stock-appreciation rights were not exercised at the end of four years, in the fifth year the company would have to account for the difference in the market price and the pre-established price. In this case, the company adjusts compensation expense whenever a change in the market price of the stock **occurs in subsequent reporting periods, until the rights expire or are exercised, whichever comes first.**

Increases or decreases in the fair value of the SAR between the date of grant and the exercise date, therefore, result in a change in the measure of compensation. Some periods will have credits to compensation expense if the fair value decreases from one period to the next. The credit to compensation expense, however, cannot exceed previously recognized compensation expense. In other words, **cumulative compensation expense cannot be negative**.

STOCK-APPRECIATION RIGHTS EXAMPLE

Assume that American Hotels, Inc. establishes a stock-appreciation rights plan on January 1, 2014. The plan entitles executives to receive cash at the date of exercise for the difference between the market price of the stock and the pre-established price of $10 on 10,000 SARs. The fair value of the SARs on December 31, 2014, is $3, and the service period runs for two years (2014–2015). Illustration 16A-1 indicates the amount of compensation expense to be recorded each period, assuming that the executives hold the SARs for three years, at which time they exercise the rights.

STOCK-APPRECIATION RIGHTS
SCHEDULE OF COMPENSATION EXPENSE

(1) Date	(2) Fair Value	(3) Cumulative Compensation Recognizable[a]	(4) Percentage Accrued[b]	(5) Cumulative Compensation Accrued to Date	Expense 2014	Expense 2015	Expense 2016
12/31/14	$3	$30,000	50%	$ 15,000	$15,000		
				55,000		$55,000	
12/31/15	7	70,000	100%	70,000			
				(20,000)			$(20,000)
12/31/16	5	50,000	100%	$ 50,000			

[a]Cumulative compensation for unexercised SARs to be allocated to periods of service.
[b]The percentage accrued is based upon a two-year service period (2014–2015).

ILLUSTRATION 16A-1
Compensation Expense, Stock-Appreciation Rights

In 2014, American Hotels records compensation expense of $15,000 because 50 percent of the $30,000 total compensation cost estimated at December 31, 2014, is allocable to 2014. In 2015, the fair value increased to $7 per right ($70,000 total). The company recorded additional compensation expense of $55,000 ($70,000 minus $15,000).

The executives held the SARs through 2016, during which time the fair value declined to $5 (and the obligation to the executives equals $50,000). American Hotels recognizes the decrease by recording a $20,000 credit to compensation expense and a debit to Liability under Stock-Appreciation Plan. Note that after the service period ends, since the rights are still outstanding, the company adjusts the rights to market at December 31, 2016. Any such credit to compensation expense cannot exceed previous charges to expense attributable to that plan.

As the company records the compensation expense each period, the corresponding credit is to a liability account, because the company will pay the stock appreciation in cash. American Hotels records compensation expense in the first year as follows.

Compensation Expense	15,000	
Liability under Stock-Appreciation Plan		15,000

The company would credit the liability account for $55,000 again in 2015. In 2016, when it records negative compensation expense, American would debit the account for $20,000. The entry to record the negative compensation expense is as follows.

Liability under Stock-Appreciation Plan	20,000	
Compensation Expense		20,000

At December 31, 2016, the executives receive $50,000 (which equals the market price of the shares less the pre-established price). American would remove the liability with the following entry.

Liability under Stock-Appreciation Plan	50,000	
Cash		50,000

Compensation expense can increase or decrease substantially from one period to the next. The reason is that compensation expense is remeasured each year, which can lead to large swings in compensation expense.

SUMMARY OF LEARNING OBJECTIVE FOR APPENDIX 16A

KEY TERMS

percentage approach, *915*
share appreciation, *914*
stock-appreciation rights (SARs), *914*

8 Explain the accounting for stock-appreciation rights plans. The accounting for stock-appreciation rights depends on whether the rights are classified as equity- or liability-based. If equity-based, the accounting is similar to that used for stock options. If liability-based, companies remeasure compensation expense each period and allocate it over the service period using the percentage approach.

APPENDIX 16B COMPREHENSIVE EARNINGS PER SHARE EXAMPLE

LEARNING OBJECTIVE 9
Compute earnings per share in a complex situation.

This appendix illustrates the method of computing dilution when many securities are involved. We present the following section of the balance sheet of Webster Corporation for analysis. Assumptions related to the capital structure follow the balance sheet.

ILLUSTRATION 16B-1
Balance Sheet for Comprehensive Illustration

WEBSTER CORPORATION
BALANCE SHEET (PARTIAL)
AT DECEMBER 31, 2014

Long-term debt	
Notes payable, 14%	$ 1,000,000
8% convertible bonds payable	2,500,000
10% convertible bonds payable	2,500,000
Total long-term debt	$ 6,000,000
Stockholders' equity	
10% cumulative, convertible preferred stock, par value $100; 100,000 shares authorized, 25,000 shares issued and outstanding	$ 2,500,000
Common stock, par value $1, 5,000,000 shares authorized, 500,000 shares issued and outstanding	500,000
Additional paid-in capital	2,000,000
Retained earnings	9,000,000
Total stockholders' equity	$14,000,000

Notes and Assumptions
December 31, 2014

1. Options were granted in July 2012 to purchase 50,000 shares of common stock at $20 per share. The average market price of Webster's common stock during 2014 was $30 per share. All options are still outstanding at the end of 2014.
2. Both the 8 percent and 10 percent convertible bonds were issued in 2013 at face value. Each convertible bond is convertible into 40 shares of common stock. (Each bond has a face value of $1,000.)
3. The 10 percent cumulative, convertible preferred stock was issued at the beginning of 2014 at par. Each share of preferred is convertible into four shares of common stock.
4. The average income tax rate is 40 percent.
5. The 500,000 shares of common stock were outstanding during the entire year.
6. Preferred dividends were not declared in 2014.
7. Net income was $1,750,000 in 2014.
8. No bonds or preferred stock were converted during 2014.

The computation of basic earnings per share for 2014 starts with the amount based upon the weighted-average number of shares outstanding, as shown in Illustration 16B-2.

ILLUSTRATION 16B-2
Computation of Earnings per Share—Simple Capital Structure

Net income	$1,750,000
Less: 10% cumulative, convertible preferred stock dividend requirements	250,000
Income applicable to common stockholders	$1,500,000
Weighted-average number of shares outstanding	500,000
Earnings per common share ($1,500,000 ÷ 500,000)	$3.00

Note the following points concerning this calculation.

1. When preferred stock is cumulative, the company subtracts the preferred dividend to arrive at income applicable to common stock, whether the dividend is declared or not.
2. The company must compute earnings per share of $3 as a starting point, because it is the per share amount that is subject to reduction due to the existence of convertible securities and options.

DILUTED EARNINGS PER SHARE

The steps for computing diluted earnings per share are:

1. Determine, for each dilutive security, the per share effect assuming exercise/conversion.
2. Rank the results from step 1 from smallest to largest earnings effect per share. That is, rank the results from most dilutive to least dilutive.
3. Beginning with the earnings per share based upon the weighted-average number of shares outstanding ($3), recalculate earnings per share by adding the smallest per share effects from step 2. If the results from this recalculation are less than $3, proceed to the next smallest per share effect and recalculate earnings per share. Continue this process so long as each recalculated earnings per share is smaller than the previous amount. The process will end either because there are no more securities to test or a particular security maintains or increases earnings per share (is antidilutive).

We'll now apply the three steps to Webster Corporation. (Note that net income and income available to common stockholders are not the same if preferred dividends are declared or cumulative.) Webster Corporation has four securities that could reduce EPS: options, 8 percent convertible bonds, 10 percent convertible bonds, and the convertible preferred stock.

The first step in the computation of diluted earnings per share is to determine a per share effect for each potentially dilutive security. Illustrations 16B-3 through 16B-6 illustrate these computations.

ILLUSTRATION 16B-3
Per Share Effect of Options (Treasury-Stock Method), Diluted Earnings per Share

Number of shares under option	50,000
Option price per share	× $20
Proceeds upon assumed exercise of options	$1,000,000
Average 2014 market price of common	$30
Treasury shares that could be acquired with proceeds ($1,000,000 ÷ $30)	33,333
Excess of shares under option over treasury shares that could be repurchased (50,000 − 33,333)	16,667
Per share effect:	
$\frac{\text{Incremental Numerator Effect}}{\text{Incremental Denominator Effect}} = \frac{\text{None}}{\text{16,667 shares}} =$	$0

ILLUSTRATION 16B-4
Per Share Effect of 8% Bonds (If-Converted Method), Diluted Earnings per Share

Interest expense for year (8% × $2,500,000)	$200,000
Income tax reduction due to interest (40% × $200,000)	80,000
Interest expense avoided (net of tax)	$120,000
Number of common shares issued assuming conversion of bonds (2,500 bonds × 40 shares)	100,000
Per share effect:	
$\frac{\text{Incremental Numerator Effect}}{\text{Incremental Denominator Effect}} = \frac{\$120{,}000}{\text{100,000 shares}} =$	$1.20

ILLUSTRATION 16B-5
Per Share Effect of 10% Bonds (If-Converted Method), Diluted Earnings per Share

Interest expense for year (10% × $2,500,000)	$250,000
Income tax reduction due to interest (40% × $250,000)	100,000
Interest expense avoided (net of tax)	$150,000
Number of common shares issued assuming conversion of bonds (2,500 bonds × 40 shares)	100,000
Per share effect:	
$\frac{\text{Incremental Numerator Effect}}{\text{Incremental Denominator Effect}} = \frac{\$150{,}000}{\text{100,000 shares}} =$	$1.50

Dividend requirement on cumulative preferred (25,000 shares × $10)	$250,000
Income tax effect (dividends not a tax deduction)	none
Dividend requirement avoided	$250,000
Number of common shares issued assuming conversion of preferred (4 × 25,000 shares)	100,000
Per share effect:	
$\frac{\text{Incremental Numerator Effect}}{\text{Incremental Denominator Effect}} = \frac{\$250{,}000}{100{,}000 \text{ shares}} =$	$2.50

ILLUSTRATION 16B-6
Per Share Effect of 10% Convertible Preferred (If-Converted Method), Diluted Earnings per Share

Illustration 16B-7 shows the ranking of all four potentially dilutive securities.

	Effect per Share
1. Options	$ 0
2. 8% convertible bonds	1.20
3. 10% convertible bonds	1.50
4. 10% convertible preferred	2.50

ILLUSTRATION 16B-7
Ranking of per Share Effects (Smallest to Largest), Diluted Earnings per Share

The next step is to determine earnings per share giving effect to the ranking in Illustration 16B-7. Starting with the earnings per share of $3 computed previously, add the incremental effects of the options to the original calculation, as follows.

Options	
Income applicable to common stockholders	$1,500,000
Add: Incremental numerator effect of options	none
Total	$1,500,000
Weighted-average number of shares outstanding	500,000
Add: Incremental denominator effect of options (Illustration 16B-3)	16,667
Total	516,667
Recomputed earnings per share ($1,500,000 ÷ 516,667 shares)	$2.90

ILLUSTRATION 16B-8
Recomputation of EPS Using Incremental Effect of Options

Since the recomputed earnings per share is reduced (from $3 to $2.90), the effect of the options is dilutive. Again, we could have anticipated this effect because the average market price ($30) exceeded the option price ($20).

Assuming that Webster converts the 8 percent bonds, recomputed earnings per share is as shown in Illustration 16B-9.

8% Convertible Bonds	
Numerator from previous calculation	$1,500,000
Add: Interest expense avoided (net of tax)	120,000
Total	$1,620,000
Denominator from previous calculation (shares)	516,667
Add: Number of common shares assumed issued upon conversion of bonds	100,000
Total	616,667
Recomputed earnings per share ($1,620,000 ÷ 616,667 shares)	$2.63

ILLUSTRATION 16B-9
Recomputation of EPS Using Incremental Effect of 8% Convertible Bonds

Since the recomputed earnings per share is reduced (from $2.90 to $2.63), the effect of the 8 percent bonds is dilutive.

Next, assuming Webster converts the 10 percent bonds, the company recomputes earnings per share as shown in Illustration 16B-10 (page 920).

ILLUSTRATION 16B-10
Recomputation of EPS Using Incremental Effect of 10% Convertible Bonds

10% Convertible Bonds	
Numerator from previous calculation	$1,620,000
Add: Interest expense avoided (net of tax)	150,000
Total	$1,770,000
Denominator from previous calculation (shares)	616,667
Add: Number of common shares assumed issued upon conversion of bonds	100,000
Total	716,667
Recomputed earnings per share ($1,770,000 ÷ 716,667 shares)	$2.47

Since the recomputed earnings per share is reduced (from $2.63 to $2.47), the effect of the 10 percent convertible bonds is dilutive.

The final step is the recomputation that includes the 10 percent preferred stock. This is shown in Illustration 16B-11.

ILLUSTRATION 16B-11
Recomputation of EPS Using Incremental Effect of 10% Convertible Preferred

10% Convertible Preferred	
Numerator from previous calculation	$1,770,000
Add: Dividend requirement avoided	250,000
Total	$2,020,000
Denominator from previous calculation (shares)	716,667
Add: Number of common shares assumed issued upon conversion of preferred	100,000
Total	816,667
Recomputed earnings per share ($2,020,000 ÷ 816,667 shares)	$2.47

Since the recomputed earnings per share is not reduced, the effect of the 10 percent convertible preferred is not dilutive. Diluted earnings per share is $2.47. The per share effects of the preferred are not used in the computation.

Finally, Illustration 16B-12 shows Webster Corporation's disclosure of earnings per share on its income statement.

ILLUSTRATION 16B-12
Income Statement Presentation, EPS

Net income	$1,750,000
Basic earnings per common share (Note X)	$3.00
Diluted earnings per common share	$2.47

A company uses income from continuing operations (adjusted for preferred dividends) to determine whether potential common stock is dilutive or antidilutive. Some refer to this measure as the **control number**. To illustrate, assume that Barton Company provides the following information.

ILLUSTRATION 16B-13
Barton Company Data

Income from continuing operations	$2,400,000
Loss from discontinued operations	3,600,000
Net loss	$1,200,000
Weighted-average number of shares outstanding	1,000,000
Potential common stock	200,000

Barton reports basic and dilutive earnings per share as follows.

ILLUSTRATION 16B-14
Basic and Diluted EPS

Basic earnings per share	
Income from continuing operations	$2.40
Loss from discontinued operations	3.60
Net loss	$1.20
Diluted earnings per share	
Income from continuing operations	$2.00
Loss from discontinued operations	3.00
Net loss	$1.00

As Illustration 16B-14 shows, basic earnings per share from continuing operations is higher than the diluted earnings per share from continuing operations. The reason: The diluted earnings per share from continuing operations includes an additional 200,000 shares of potential common stock in its denominator.[21]

Companies use income from continuing operations as the control number because many of them show income from continuing operations (or a similar line item above net income if it appears on the income statement) but report a final net loss due to a loss on discontinued operations. If a company uses final net loss as the control number, basic and diluted earnings per share would be the same because the potential common shares are antidilutive.[22]

Gateway to the Profession

EPS Illustration with Multiple Dilutive Securities

SUMMARY OF LEARNING OBJECTIVE FOR APPENDIX 16B

KEY TERM

control number, *920*

9 **Compute earnings per share in a complex situation.** For diluted EPS, make the following computations. (1) For each potentially dilutive security, determine the per share effect assuming exercise/conversion. (2) Rank the results from most dilutive to least dilutive. (3) Recalculate EPS starting with the most dilutive, and continue adding securities until EPS does not change or becomes larger.

DEMONSTRATION PROBLEM

On January 1, 2013, Scutaro Company issued 10-year, $200,000 face value, 6% bonds at par (payable annually on January 1). Each $1,000 bond is convertible into 30 shares of Garner $2 par value common stock. The company has had 10,000 shares of common stock (and no preferred stock) outstanding throughout its life. None of the bonds have been converted as of the end of 2014.

[21] A company that does not report a discontinued operation but reports an extraordinary item should use that line item (for example, income before extraordinary items) as the control number.

[22] If a company reports a loss from continuing operations, basic and diluted earnings per share will be the same because potential common stock will be antidilutive, even if the company reports final net income. The FASB believes that comparability of EPS information will be improved by using income from continuing operations as the control number.

Scutaro also has adopted a stock-option plan that granted options to key executives to purchase 4,000 shares of the company's common stock. The options were granted on January 2, 2013, and were exercisable 2 years after the date of grant if the grantee was still an employee of the company. The options expired 6 years from the date of grant. The option price was set at $4, and the fair value option-pricing model determines the total compensation expense to be $18,000. All of the options were exercised during the year 2015: 3,000 on January 3 when the market price was $6, and 1,000 on May 1 when the market price was $7 a share. (Ignore all tax effects.)

Instructions

(a) Prepare the journal entry Scutaro would have made on January 1, 2013, to record the issuance of the bonds.

(b) Prepare the journal entry to record interest expense and compensation expense in 2014.

(c) Scutaro's net income in 2014 was $30,000 and was $27,000 in 2013. Compute basic and diluted earnings per share for Scutaro for 2014 and 2013. Scutaro's average stock price was $4.40 in 2013 and $5 in 2014.

(d) Assume that 75 percent of the holders of Scutaro's convertible bonds convert their bonds to stock on June 30, 2015, when Scutaro's stock is trading at $8 per share. Scutaro pays $2 per bond to induce bondholders to convert. Prepare the journal entry to record the conversion.

Solution

(a) Under U.S. GAAP, proceeds from the issuance of convertible debt are recorded entirely as debt.

	Debit	Credit
Cash	200,000	
Bonds Payable		200,000

(b) **December 31, 2014**

	Debit	Credit
Interest Expense	12,000	
Interest Payable		12,000
[To record interest expense for 2014 ($200,000 × 6%)]		
Compensation Expense	9,000	
Paid-in Capital—Stock Options		9,000
[To record compensation expense for 2014 (1/2 × $18,000)]		

(c)

Basic EPS	**2014**	**2013**
Net income (a)	$30,000	$27,000
Outstanding shares (b)	10,000	10,000
Basic EPS (a ÷ b)	$ 3.00	$ 2.70
Diluted EPS		
Net income	$30,000	$27,000
Add: Interest savings ($200,000 × 6%)	12,000	12,000
Adjusted net income (a)	$42,000	$39,000
Outstanding shares	10,000	10,000
Shares upon conversion (200 × 30)	6,000	6,000
Options (treasury-stock method)	800*	364*
Total shares for diluted EPS (b)	16,800	16,364
Diluted EPS (a ÷ b)	$ 2.50	$ 2.38

*Treasury-stock method:

	2014		2013	
Cash proceeds	($4 × 4,000)	$16,000		$16,000
Shares repurchased	($16,000 ÷ $5)	3,200	($16,000 ÷ $4.40)	3,636
Net shares issued	(4,000 − 3,200)	800	(4,000 − 3,636)	364

(d)			
	Bond Conversion Expense**	300	
	Bonds Payable	150,000	
	Common Stock*		9,000
	Paid-in-Capital in Excess of Par—Common Stock*		141,000
	Cash		300

*$200,000 × 75% = $150,000 of bonds converted
$150,000 ÷ $1,000 per bond = 150 bonds
150 bonds × 30 shares per bond = 4,500 new shares issued
4,500 shares × $2 par value = $9,000 increase in common stock account
$150,000 − $9,000 = $141,000 increase in paid-in capital account
**150 bonds X $2 per bond = $300 bond conversion expense

FASB CODIFICATION

FASB Codification References

[1] FASB ASC 480-10-25. [Predecessor literature: "Accounting for Certain Financial Instruments with Characteristics of Both Liabilities and Equity," *Statement of Financial Accounting Standards No. 150* (Norwalk, Conn.: FASB, 2003), par. 23.]

[2] FASB ASC 470-20-45. [Predecessor literature: "Induced Conversions of Convertible Debt," *Statement of Financial Accounting Standards No. 84* (Stamford, Conn.: FASB, 1985).]

[3] FASB ASC 470-20-25-1 to 2. [Predecessor literature: "Accounting for Convertible Debt and Debt Issued with Stock Purchase Warrants," *Opinions of the Accounting Principles Board No. 14* (New York, NY: AICPA, 1973).]

[4] FASB ASC 470-20-30. [Predecessor literature: "Accounting for Convertible Debt Instruments that May Be Settled in Cash Upon Conversion," *FASB Staff Position No. 14-1* (Norwalk, Conn: FASB, 2008).]

[5] FASB ASC 718-10-10. [Predecessor literature: "Accounting for Stock-Based Compensation," *Statement of Financial Accounting Standards No. 123* (Norwalk, Conn: FASB, 1995); and "Share-Based Payment," *Statement of Financial Accounting Standard No. 123(R)* (Norwalk, Conn: FASB, 2004).]

[6] FASB ASC 260-10-45-2. [Predecessor literature: "Earnings per Share," *Statement of Financial Accounting Standards No. 128* (Norwalk, Conn: FASB, 1997).]

[7] FASB ASC 260-10-50. [Predecessor literature: "Earnings per Share," *Statement of Financial Accounting Standards No. 128*, (Norwalk, Conn.: FASB, 1997.)]

Exercises

If your school has a subscription to the FASB Codification, go to *http://aaahq.org/ascLogin.cfm* to log in and prepare responses to the following. Provide Codification references for your responses.

CE16-1 Access the glossary ("Master Glossary") to answer the following.

(a) What is the definition of "basic earnings per share"?
(b) What is "dilution"?
(c) What is a "warrant"?
(d) What is a "grant date"?

CE16-2 For how many periods must a company present EPS data?

CE16-3 For each period that an income statement is presented, what must a company disclose about its EPS?

CE16-4 If a company's outstanding shares are increased through a stock dividend or a stock split, how would that alter the presentation of its EPS data?

An additional Codification case can be found in the Using Your Judgment section, on page 941.

Be sure to check the book's companion website for a Review and Analysis Exercise, with solution.

Note: All asterisked Questions, Exercises, and Problems relate to material in the appendices to the chapter.

QUESTIONS

1. What is meant by a dilutive security?

2. Briefly explain why corporations issue convertible securities.

3. Discuss the similarities and the differences between convertible debt and debt issued with stock warrants.

4. Bridgewater Corp. offered holders of its 1,000 convertible bonds a premium of $160 per bond to induce conversion into shares of its common stock. Upon conversion of all the bonds, Bridgewater Corp. recorded the $160,000 premium as a reduction of paid-in capital. Comment on Bridgewater's treatment of the $160,000 "sweetener."

5. Explain how the conversion feature of convertible debt has a value (a) to the issuer and (b) to the purchaser.

6. What are the arguments for giving separate accounting recognition to the conversion feature of debentures?

7. Four years after issue, debentures with a face value of $1,000,000 and book value of $960,000 are tendered for conversion into 80,000 shares of common stock immediately after an interest payment date. At that time, the market price of the debentures is 104, and the common stock is selling at $14 per share (par value $10). The company records the conversion as follows.

Bonds Payable	1,000,000	
Discount on Bonds Payable		40,000
Common Stock		800,000
Paid-in Capital in Excess of Par—Common Stock		160,000

Discuss the propriety of this accounting treatment.

8. On July 1, 2014, Roberts Corporation issued $3,000,000 of 9% bonds payable in 20 years. The bonds include detachable warrants giving the bondholder the right to purchase for $30 one share of $1 par value common stock at any time during the next 10 years. The bonds were sold for $3,000,000. The value of the warrants at the time of issuance was $100,000. Prepare the journal entry to record this transaction.

9. What are stock rights? How does the issuing company account for them?

10. Briefly explain the accounting requirements for stock compensation plans under GAAP.

11. Cordero Corporation has an employee stock-purchase plan which permits all full-time employees to purchase 10 shares of common stock on the third anniversary of their employment and an additional 15 shares on each subsequent anniversary date. The purchase price is set at the market price on the date purchased and no commission is charged. Discuss whether this plan would be considered compensatory.

12. What date or event does the profession believe should be used in determining the value of a stock option? What arguments support this position?

13. Over what period of time should compensation cost be allocated?

14. How is compensation expense computed using the fair value approach?

15. What are the advantages of using restricted stock to compensate employees?

16. At December 31, 2014, Reid Company had 600,000 shares of common stock issued and outstanding, 400,000 of which had been issued and outstanding throughout the year and 200,000 of which were issued on October 1, 2014. Net income for 2014 was $2,000,000, and dividends declared on preferred stock were $400,000. Compute Reid's earnings per common share. (Round to the nearest penny.)

17. What effect do stock dividends or stock splits have on the computation of the weighted-average number of shares outstanding?

18. Define the following terms.

(a) Basic earnings per share.

(b) Potentially dilutive security.

(c) Diluted earnings per share.

(d) Complex capital structure.

(e) Potential common stock.

19. What are the computational guidelines for determining whether a convertible security is to be reported as part of diluted earnings per share?

20. Discuss why options and warrants may be considered potentially dilutive common shares for the computation of diluted earnings per share.

21. Explain how convertible securities are determined to be potentially dilutive common shares and how those convertible securities that are not considered to be potentially dilutive common shares enter into the determination of earnings per share data.

22. Explain the treasury-stock method as it applies to options and warrants in computing dilutive earnings per share data.

23. Earnings per share can affect market prices of common stock. Can market prices affect earnings per share? Explain.

24. What is meant by the term antidilution? Give an example.

25. What type of earnings per share presentation is required in a complex capital structure?

***26.** How is antidilution determined when multiple securities are involved?

BRIEF EXERCISES

1 **BE16-1** Archer Inc. issued $4,000,000 par value, 7% convertible bonds at 99 for cash. If the bonds had not included the conversion feature, they would have sold for 95. Prepare the journal entry to record the issuance of the bonds.

1 **BE16-2** Petrenko Corporation has outstanding 2,000 $1,000 bonds, each convertible into 50 shares of $10 par value common stock. The bonds are converted on December 31, 2014, when the unamortized discount is $30,000 and the market price of the stock is $21 per share. Record the conversion using the book value approach.

2 **BE16-3** Pechstein Corporation issued 2,000 shares of $10 par value common stock upon conversion of 1,000 shares of $50 par value preferred stock. The preferred stock was originally issued at $60 per share. The common stock is trading at $26 per share at the time of conversion. Record the conversion of the preferred stock.

3 **BE16-4** Eisler Corporation issued 2,000 $1,000 bonds at 101. Each bond was issued with one detachable stock warrant. After issuance, the bonds were selling in the market at 98, and the warrants had a market price of $40. Use the proportional method to record the issuance of the bonds and warrants.

3 **BE16-5** McIntyre Corporation issued 2,000 $1,000 bonds at 101. Each bond was issued with one detachable stock warrant. After issuance, the bonds were selling separately at 98. The market price of the warrants without the bonds cannot be determined. Use the incremental method to record the issuance of the bonds and warrants.

4 **BE16-6** On January 1, 2014, Barwood Corporation granted 5,000 options to executives. Each option entitles the holder to purchase one share of Barwood's $5 par value common stock at $50 per share at any time during the next 5 years. The market price of the stock is $65 per share on the date of grant. The fair value of the options at the grant date is $150,000. The period of benefit is 2 years. Prepare Barwood's journal entries for January 1, 2014, and December 31, 2014 and 2015.

4 **BE16-7** Refer to the data for Barwood Corporation in BE16-6. Repeat the requirements assuming that instead of options, Barwood granted 2,000 shares of restricted stock.

4 **BE16-8** On January 1, 2014 (the date of grant), Lutz Corporation issues 2,000 shares of restricted stock to its executives. The fair value of these shares is $75,000, and their par value is $10,000. The stock is forfeited if the executives do not complete 3 years of employment with the company. Prepare the journal entry (if any) on January 1, 2014, and on December 31, 2014, assuming the service period is 3 years.

6 **BE16-9** Kalin Corporation had 2014 net income of $1,000,000. During 2014, Kalin paid a dividend of $2 per share on 100,000 shares of preferred stock. During 2014, Kalin had outstanding 250,000 shares of common stock. Compute Kalin's 2014 earnings per share.

6 **BE16-10** Douglas Corporation had 120,000 shares of stock outstanding on January 1, 2014. On May 1, 2014, Douglas issued 60,000 shares. On July 1, Douglas purchased 10,000 treasury shares, which were reissued on October 1. Compute Douglas's weighted-average number of shares outstanding for 2014.

6 **BE16-11** Tomba Corporation had 300,000 shares of common stock outstanding on January 1, 2014. On May 1, Tomba issued 30,000 shares. (a) Compute the weighted-average number of shares outstanding if the 30,000 shares were issued for cash. (b) Compute the weighted-average number of shares outstanding if the 30,000 shares were issued in a stock dividend.

7 **BE16-12** Rockland Corporation earned net income of $300,000 in 2014 and had 100,000 shares of common stock outstanding throughout the year. Also outstanding all year was $800,000 of 10% bonds, which are convertible into 16,000 shares of common. Rockland's tax rate is 40%. Compute Rockland's 2014 diluted earnings per share.

7 **BE16-13** DiCenta Corporation reported net income of $270,000 in 2014 and had 50,000 shares of common stock outstanding throughout the year. Also outstanding all year were 5,000 shares of cumulative preferred stock, each convertible into 2 shares of common. The preferred stock pays an annual dividend of $5 per share. DiCenta's tax rate is 40%. Compute DiCenta's 2014 diluted earnings per share.

7 **BE16-14** Bedard Corporation reported net income of $300,000 in 2014 and had 200,000 shares of common stock outstanding throughout the year. Also outstanding all year were 45,000 options to purchase common stock at $10 per share. The average market price of the stock during the year was $15. Compute diluted earnings per share.

6 **BE16-15** The 2014 income statement of Wasmeier Corporation showed net income of $480,000 and an extraordinary loss of $120,000. Wasmeier had 100,000 shares of common stock outstanding all year. Prepare Wasmeier's income statement presentation of earnings per share.

8 ***BE16-16** Ferraro, Inc. established a stock-appreciation rights (SAR) program on January 1, 2014, which entitles executives to receive cash at the date of exercise for the difference between the market price of the stock and the pre-established price of $20 on 5,000 SARs. The required service period is 2 years. The fair value of the SARs are determined to be $4 on December 31, 2014, and $9 on December 31, 2015. Compute Ferraro's compensation expense for 2014 and 2015.

EXERCISES

1 3 **E16-1 (Issuance and Conversion of Bonds)** For each of the unrelated transactions described below, present the entry(ies) required to record each transaction.

1. Grand Corp. issued $20,000,000 par value 10% convertible bonds at 99. If the bonds had not been convertible, the company's investment banker estimates they would have been sold at 95. Expenses of issuing the bonds were $70,000.
2. Hoosier Company issued $20,000,000 par value 10% bonds at 98. One detachable stock purchase warrant was issued with each $100 par value bond. At the time of issuance, the warrants were selling for $4.
3. Suppose Sepracor, Inc. called its convertible debt in 2014. Assume the following related to the transaction. The 11%, $10,000,000 par value bonds were converted into 1,000,000 shares of $1 par value common stock on July 1, 2014. On July 1, there was $55,000 of unamortized discount applicable to the bonds, and the company paid an additional $75,000 to the bondholders to induce conversion of all the bonds. The company records the conversion using the book value method.

1 **E16-2 (Conversion of Bonds)** Aubrey Inc. issued $4,000,000 of 10%, 10-year convertible bonds on June 1, 2014, at 98 plus accrued interest. The bonds were dated April 1, 2014, with interest payable April 1 and October 1. Bond discount is amortized semiannually on a straight-line basis.

On April 1, 2015, $1,500,000 of these bonds were converted into 30,000 shares of $20 par value common stock. Accrued interest was paid in cash at the time of conversion.

Instructions

(a) Prepare the entry to record the interest expense at October 1, 2014. Assume that accrued interest payable was credited when the bonds were issued. (Round to nearest dollar.)

(b) Prepare the entry(ies) to record the conversion on April 1, 2015. (Book value method is used.) Assume that the entry to record amortization of the bond discount and interest payment has been made.

1 **E16-3 (Conversion of Bonds)** Vargo Company has bonds payable outstanding in the amount of $500,000, and the Premium on Bonds Payable account has a balance of $7,500. Each $1,000 bond is convertible into 20 shares of preferred stock of par value of $50 per share. All bonds are converted into preferred stock.

Instructions

Assuming that the book value method was used, what entry would be made?

1 **E16-4 (Conversion of Bonds)** On January 1, 2013, when its $30 par value common stock was selling for $80 per share, Plato Corp. issued $10,000,000 of 8% convertible debentures due in 20 years. The conversion option allowed the holder of each $1,000 bond to convert the bond into five shares of the corporation's common stock. The debentures were issued for $10,800,000. The present value of the bond payments at the time of issuance was $8,500,000, and the corporation believes the difference between the present value and the amount paid is attributable to the conversion feature. On January 1, 2014, the corporation's $30 par value common stock was split 2 for 1, and the conversion rate for the bonds was adjusted accordingly. On January 1, 2015, when the corporation's $15 par value common stock was selling for $135 per share, holders of 30% of the convertible debentures exercised their conversion options. The corporation uses the straight-line method for amortizing any bond discounts or premiums.

Instructions

(a) Prepare in general journal form the entry to record the original issuance of the convertible debentures.

(b) Prepare in general journal form the entry to record the exercise of the conversion option, using the book value method. Show supporting computations in good form.

1 **E16-5 (Conversion of Bonds)** The December 31, 2014, balance sheet of Kepler Corp. is as follows.

10% callable, convertible bonds payable (semiannual interest dates April 30 and October 31; convertible into 6 shares of $25 par value common stock per $1,000 of bond principal; maturity date April 30, 2020)	$500,000	
Discount on bonds payable	10,240	$489,760

On March 5, 2015, Kepler Corp. called all of the bonds as of April 30 for the principal plus interest through April 30. By April 30, all bondholders had exercised their conversion to common stock as of the interest payment date. Consequently, on April 30, Kepler Corp. paid the semiannual interest and issued shares of common stock for the bonds. The discount is amortized on a straight-line basis. Kepler uses the book value method.

Instructions

Prepare the entry(ies) to record the interest expense and conversion on April 30, 2015. Reversing entries were made on January 1, 2015. (Round to the nearest dollar.)

1 **E16-6 (Conversion of Bonds)** On January 1, 2014, Gottlieb Corporation issued $4,000,000 of 10-year, 8% convertible debentures at 102. Interest is to be paid semiannually on June 30 and December 31. Each $1,000 debenture can be converted into eight shares of Gottlieb Corporation $100 par value common stock after December 31, 2015.

On January 1, 2016, $400,000 of debentures are converted into common stock, which is then selling at $110. An additional $400,000 of debentures are converted on March 31, 2016. The market price of the common stock is then $115. Accrued interest at March 31 will be paid on the next interest date.

Bond premium is amortized on a straight-line basis.

Instructions

Make the necessary journal entries for:

(a) December 31, 2015.
(b) January 1, 2016.
(c) March 31, 2016.
(d) June 30, 2016.

Record the conversions using the book value method.

3 **E16-7 (Issuance of Bonds with Warrants)** Illiad Inc. has decided to raise additional capital by issuing $170,000 face value of bonds with a coupon rate of 10%. In discussions with investment bankers, it was determined that to help the sale of the bonds, detachable stock warrants should be issued at the rate of one warrant for each $100 bond sold. The value of the bonds without the warrants is considered to be $136,000, and the value of the warrants in the market is $24,000. The bonds sold in the market at issuance for $152,000.

Instructions

(a) What entry should be made at the time of the issuance of the bonds and warrants?
(b) If the warrants were nondetachable, would the entries be different? Discuss.

3 **E16-8 (Issuance of Bonds with Detachable Warrants)** On September 1, 2014, Sands Company sold at 104 (plus accrued interest) 4,000 of its 9%, 10-year, $1,000 face value, nonconvertible bonds with detachable stock warrants. Each bond carried two detachable warrants. Each warrant was for one share of common stock at a specified option price of $15 per share. Shortly after issuance, the warrants were quoted on the market for $3 each. No fair value can be determined for the Sands Company bonds. Interest is payable on December 1 and June 1. Bond issue costs of $30,000 were incurred.

Instructions

Prepare in general journal format the entry to record the issuance of the bonds.

(AICPA adapted)

3 **E16-9 (Issuance of Bonds with Stock Warrants)** On May 1, 2014, Friendly Company issued 2,000 $1,000 bonds at 102. Each bond was issued with one detachable stock warrant. Shortly after issuance, the bonds were selling at 98, but the fair value of the warrants cannot be determined.

Instructions

(a) Prepare the entry to record the issuance of the bonds and warrants.
(b) Assume the same facts as part (a), except that the warrants had a fair value of $30. Prepare the entry to record the issuance of the bonds and warrants.

4 **E16-10 (Issuance and Exercise of Stock Options)** On November 1, 2014, Columbo Company adopted a stock-option plan that granted options to key executives to purchase 30,000 shares of the company's $10 par value common stock. The options were granted on January 2, 2015, and were exercisable 2 years after the date of grant if the grantee was still an employee of the company. The options expired 6 years from date of grant. The option price was set at $40, and the fair value option-pricing model determines the total compensation expense to be $450,000.

All of the options were exercised during the year 2017: 20,000 on January 3 when the market price was $67, and 10,000 on May 1 when the market price was $77 a share.

Instructions

Prepare journal entries relating to the stock option plan for the years 2015, 2016, and 2017. Assume that the employee performs services equally in 2015 and 2016.

4 **E16-11 (Issuance, Exercise, and Termination of Stock Options)** On January 1, 2015, Titania Inc. granted stock options to officers and key employees for the purchase of 20,000 shares of the company's $10 par common stock at $25 per share. The options were exercisable within a 5-year period beginning January 1, 2017, by grantees still in the employ of the company, and expiring December 31, 2021. The service period for this award is 2 years. Assume that the fair value option-pricing model determines total compensation expense to be $350,000.

On April 1, 2016, 2,000 options were terminated when the employees resigned from the company. The market price of the common stock was $35 per share on this date.

On March 31, 2017, 12,000 options were exercised when the market price of the common stock was $40 per share.

Instructions

Prepare journal entries to record issuance of the stock options, termination of the stock options, exercise of the stock options, and charges to compensation expense, for the years ended December 31, 2015, 2016, and 2017.

4 **E16-12 (Issuance, Exercise, and Termination of Stock Options)** On January 1, 2013, Nichols Corporation granted 10,000 options to key executives. Each option allows the executive to purchase one share of Nichols' $5 par value common stock at a price of $20 per share. The options were exercisable within a 2-year period beginning January 1, 2015, if the grantee is still employed by the company at the time of the exercise. On the grant date, Nichols' stock was trading at $25 per share, and a fair value option-pricing model determines total compensation to be $400,000.

On May 1, 2015, 8,000 options were exercised when the market price of Nichols' stock was $30 per share. The remaining options lapsed in 2017 because executives decided not to exercise their options.

Instructions

Prepare the necessary journal entries related to the stock option plan for the years 2013 through 2017.

4 **E16-13 (Accounting for Restricted Stock)** Derrick Company issues 4,000 shares of restricted stock to its CFO, Dane Yaping, on January 1, 2014. The stock has a fair value of $120,000 on this date. The service period related to this restricted stock is 4 years. Vesting occurs if Yaping stays with the company for 4 years. The par value of the stock is $5. At December 31, 2015, the fair value of the stock is $145,000.

Instructions

(a) Prepare the journal entries to record the restricted stock on January 1, 2014 (the date of grant), and December 31, 2015.

(b) On March 4, 2016, Yaping leaves the company. Prepare the journal entry (if any) to account for this forfeiture.

4 **E16-14 (Accounting for Restricted Stock)** Tweedie Company issues 10,000 shares of restricted stock to its CFO, Mary Tokar, on January 1, 2014. The stock has a fair value of $500,000 on this date. The service period related to this restricted stock is 5 years. Vesting occurs if Tokar stays with the company until December 31, 2018. The par value of the stock is $10. At December 31, 2014, the fair value of the stock is $450,000.

Instructions

(a) Prepare the journal entries to record the restricted stock on January 1, 2014 (the date of grant), and December 31, 2015.

(b) On July 25, 2018, Tokar leaves the company. Prepare the journal entry (if any) to account for this forfeiture.

6 **E16-15 (Weighted-Average Number of Shares)** Newton Inc. uses a calendar year for financial reporting. The company is authorized to issue 9,000,000 shares of $10 par common stock. At no time has Newton issued any potentially dilutive securities. Listed below is a summary of Newton's common stock activities.

1. Number of common shares issued and outstanding at December 31, 2012	2,000,000
2. Shares issued as a result of a 10% stock dividend on September 30, 2013	200,000
3. Shares issued for cash on March 31, 2014	2,000,000
Number of common shares issued and outstanding at December 31, 2014	4,200,000
4. A 2-for-1 stock split of Newton's common stock took place on March 31, 2015	

Instructions

(a) Compute the weighted-average number of common shares used in computing earnings per common share for 2013 on the 2014 comparative income statement.

(b) Compute the weighted-average number of common shares used in computing earnings per common share for 2014 on the 2014 comparative income statement.

(c) Compute the weighted-average number of common shares to be used in computing earnings per common share for 2014 on the 2015 comparative income statement.

(d) Compute the weighted-average number of common shares to be used in computing earnings per common share for 2015 on the 2015 comparative income statement.

(CMA adapted)

6 **E16-16 (EPS: Simple Capital Structure)** On January 1, 2015, Wilke Corp. had 480,000 shares of common stock outstanding. During 2015, it had the following transactions that affected the common stock account.

February 1	Issued 120,000 shares
March 1	Issued a 10% stock dividend
May 1	Acquired 100,000 shares of treasury stock
June 1	Issued a 3-for-1 stock split
October 1	Reissued 60,000 shares of treasury stock

Instructions

(a) Determine the weighted-average number of shares outstanding as of December 31, 2015.

(b) Assume that Wilke Corp. earned net income of $3,456,000 during 2015. In addition, it had 100,000 shares of 9%, $100 par nonconvertible, noncumulative preferred stock outstanding for the entire year. Because of liquidity considerations, however, the company did not declare and pay a preferred dividend in 2015. Compute earnings per share for 2015, using the weighted-average number of shares determined in part (a).

(c) Assume the same facts as in part (b), except that the preferred stock was cumulative. Compute earnings per share for 2015.

(d) Assume the same facts as in part (b), except that net income included an extraordinary gain of $864,000 and a loss from discontinued operations of $432,000. Both items are net of applicable income taxes. Compute earnings per share for 2015.

6 **E16-17 (EPS: Simple Capital Structure)** Ace Company had 200,000 shares of common stock outstanding on December 31, 2015. During the year 2016, the company issued 8,000 shares on May 1 and retired 14,000 shares on October 31. For the year 2016, Ace Company reported net income of $249,690 after a casualty loss of $40,600 (net of tax).

Instructions

What earnings per share data should be reported at the bottom of its income statement, assuming that the casualty loss is extraordinary?

6 **E16-18 (EPS: Simple Capital Structure)** Flagstad Inc. presented the following data.

Net income	$2,500,000
Preferred stock: 50,000 shares outstanding, $100 par, 8% cumulative, not convertible	5,000,000
Common stock: Shares outstanding 1/1	750,000
Issued for cash, 5/1	300,000
Acquired treasury stock for cash, 8/1	150,000
2-for-1 stock split, 10/1	

Instructions

Compute earnings per share.

6 **E16-19 (EPS: Simple Capital Structure)** A portion of the combined statement of income and retained earnings of Seminole Inc. for the current year follows.

Income before extraordinary item		$15,000,000
Extraordinary loss, net of applicable income tax (Note 1)		1,340,000
Net income		13,660,000
Retained earnings at the beginning of the year		83,250,000
		96,910,000
Dividends declared:		
On preferred stock—$6.00 per share	$ 300,000	
On common stock—$1.75 per share	14,875,000	15,175,000
Retained earnings at the end of the year		$81,735,000

Note 1. During the year, Seminole Inc. suffered a major casualty loss of $1,340,000 after applicable income tax reduction of $1,200,000.

At the end of the current year, Seminole Inc. has outstanding 8,500,000 shares of $10 par common stock and 50,000 shares of 6% preferred. On April 1 of the current year, Seminole Inc. issued 1,000,000 shares of common stock for $32 per share to help finance the casualty.

Instructions

Compute the earnings per share on common stock for the current year as it should be reported to stockholders.

6 **E16-20 (EPS: Simple Capital Structure)** On January 1, 2014, Lennon Industries had stock outstanding as follows.

6% Cumulative preferred stock, $100 par value, issued and outstanding 10,000 shares	$1,000,000
Common stock, $10 par value, issued and outstanding 200,000 shares	2,000,000

To acquire the net assets of three smaller companies, Lennon authorized the issuance of an additional 160,000 common shares. The acquisitions took place as shown below.

Date of Acquisition	Shares Issued
Company A April 1, 2014	50,000
Company B July 1, 2014	80,000
Company C October 1, 2014	30,000

On May 14, 2014, Lennon realized a $90,000 (before taxes) insurance gain on the expropriation of investments originally purchased in 2000.

On December 31, 2014, Lennon recorded net income of $300,000 before tax and exclusive of the gain.

Instructions

Assuming a 50% tax rate, compute the earnings per share data that should appear on the financial statements of Lennon Industries as of December 31, 2014. Assume that the expropriation is extraordinary.

6 **E16-21 (EPS: Simple Capital Structure)** At January 1, 2014, Langley Company's outstanding shares included the following.

280,000 shares of $50 par value, 7% cumulative preferred stock
900,000 shares of $1 par value common stock

Net income for 2014 was $2,530,000. No cash dividends were declared or paid during 2014. On February 15, 2015, however, all preferred dividends in arrears were paid, together with a 5% stock dividend on common shares. There were no dividends in arrears prior to 2014.

On April 1, 2014, 450,000 shares of common stock were sold for $10 per share, and on October 1, 2014, 110,000 shares of common stock were purchased for $20 per share and held as treasury stock.

Instructions

Compute earnings per share for 2014. Assume that financial statements for 2014 were issued in March 2015.

7 **E16-22 (EPS with Convertible Bonds, Various Situations)** In 2013, Chirac Enterprises issued, at par, 60 $1,000, 8% bonds, each convertible into 100 shares of common stock. Chirac had revenues of $17,500 and

expenses other than interest and taxes of $8,400 for 2014. (Assume that the tax rate is 40%.) Throughout 2014, 2,000 shares of common stock were outstanding; none of the bonds was converted or redeemed.

Instructions

(a) Compute diluted earnings per share for 2014.

(b) Assume the same facts as those assumed for part (a), except that the 60 bonds were issued on September 1, 2014 (rather than in 2013), and none have been converted or redeemed.

(c) Assume the same facts as assumed for part (a), except that 20 of the 60 bonds were actually converted on July 1, 2014.

7 **E16-23 (EPS with Convertible Bonds)** On June 1, 2012, Andre Company and Agassi Company merged to form Lancaster Inc. A total of 800,000 shares were issued to complete the merger. The new corporation reports on a calendar-year basis.

On April 1, 2014, the company issued an additional 400,000 shares of stock for cash. All 1,200,000 shares were outstanding on December 31, 2014.

Lancaster Inc. also issued $600,000 of 20-year, 8% convertible bonds at par on July 1, 2014. Each $1,000 bond converts to 40 shares of common at any interest date. None of the bonds have been converted to date.

Lancaster Inc. is preparing its annual report for the fiscal year ending December 31, 2014. The annual report will show earnings per share figures based upon a reported after-tax net income of $1,540,000. (The tax rate is 40%.)

Instructions

Determine the following for 2014.

(a) The number of shares to be used for calculating:
  (1) Basic earnings per share.
  (2) Diluted earnings per share.

(b) The earnings figures to be used for calculating:
  (1) Basic earnings per share.
  (2) Diluted earnings per share.

(CMA adapted)

7 **E16-24 (EPS with Convertible Bonds and Preferred Stock)** The Simon Corporation issued 10-year, $5,000,000 par, 7% callable convertible subordinated debentures on January 2, 2014. The bonds have a par value of $1,000, with interest payable annually. The current conversion ratio is 14:1, and in 2 years it will increase to 18:1. At the date of issue, the bonds were sold at 98. Bond discount is amortized on a straight-line basis. Simon's effective tax was 35%. Net income in 2014 was $9,500,000, and the company had 2,000,000 shares outstanding during the entire year.

Instructions

(a) Prepare a schedule to compute both basic and diluted earnings per share.

(b) Discuss how the schedule would differ if the security was convertible preferred stock.

7 **E16-25 (EPS with Convertible Bonds and Preferred Stock)** On January 1, 2014, Crocker Company issued 10-year, $2,000,000 face value, 6% bonds, at par. Each $1,000 bond is convertible into 15 shares of Crocker common stock. Crocker's net income in 2014 was $300,000, and its tax rate was 40%. The company had 100,000 shares of common stock outstanding throughout 2014. None of the bonds were converted in 2014.

Instructions

(a) Compute diluted earnings per share for 2014.

(b) Compute diluted earnings per share for 2014, assuming the same facts as above, except that $1,000,000 of 6% convertible preferred stock was issued instead of the bonds. Each $100 preferred share is convertible into 5 shares of Crocker common stock.

7 **E16-26 (EPS with Options, Various Situations)** Venzuela Company's net income for 2014 is $50,000. The only potentially dilutive securities outstanding were 1,000 options issued during 2013, each exercisable for one share at $6. None has been exercised, and 10,000 shares of common were outstanding during 2014. The average market price of Venzuela's stock during 2014 was $20.

Instructions

(a) Compute diluted earnings per share. (Round to nearest cent.)

(b) Assume the same facts as those assumed for part (a), except that the 1,000 options were issued on October 1, 2014 (rather than in 2013). The average market price during the last 3 months of 2014 was $20.

7 **E16-27 (EPS with Contingent Issuance Agreement)** Winsor Inc. recently purchased Holiday Corp., a large midwestern home painting corporation. One of the terms of the merger was that if Holiday's income

for 2014 was $110,000 or more, 10,000 additional shares would be issued to Holiday's stockholders in 2015. Holiday's income for 2013 was $120,000.

Instructions

(a) Would the contingent shares have to be considered in Winsor's 2013 earnings per share computations?

(b) Assume the same facts, except that the 10,000 shares are contingent on Holiday's achieving a net income of $130,000 in 2014. Would the contingent shares have to be considered in Winsor's earnings per share computations for 2013?

7 **E16-28 (EPS with Warrants)** Howat Corporation earned $360,000 during a period when it had an average of 100,000 shares of common stock outstanding. The common stock sold at an average market price of $15 per share during the period. Also outstanding were 15,000 warrants that could be exercised to purchase one share of common stock for $10 for each warrant exercised.

Instructions

(a) Are the warrants dilutive?

(b) Compute basic earnings per share.

(c) Compute diluted earnings per share.

8 ***E16-29 (Stock-Appreciation Rights)** On December 31, 2010, Beckford Company issues 150,000 stock-appreciation rights to its officers entitling them to receive cash for the difference between the market price of its stock and a pre-established price of $10. The fair value of the SARs is estimated to be $4 per SAR on December 31, 2011; $1 on December 31, 2012; $10 on December 31, 2013; and $9 on December 31, 2014. The service period is 4 years, and the exercise period is 7 years.

Instructions

(a) Prepare a schedule that shows the amount of compensation expense allocable to each year affected by the stock-appreciation rights plan.

(b) Prepare the entry at December 31, 2014, to record compensation expense, if any, in 2014.

(c) Prepare the entry on December 31, 2014, assuming that all 150,000 SARs are exercised.

8 ***E16-30 (Stock-Appreciation Rights)** Capulet Company establishes a stock-appreciation rights program that entitles its new president Ben Davis to receive cash for the difference between the market price of the stock and a pre-established price of $30 (also market price) on December 31, 2010, on 30,000 SARs. The date of grant is December 31, 2010, and the required employment (service) period is 4 years. President Davis exercises all of the SARs in 2016. The fair value of the SARs is estimated to be $6 per SAR on December 31, 2011; $9 on December 31, 2012; $15 on December 31, 2013; $6 on December 31, 2014; and $18 on December 31, 2015.

Instructions

(a) Prepare a 5-year (2011–2015) schedule of compensation expense pertaining to the 30,000 SARs granted president Davis.

(b) Prepare the journal entry for compensation expense in 2011, 2014, and 2015 relative to the 30,000 SARs.

EXERCISES SET B

See the book's companion website, at **www.wiley.com/college/kieso**, for an additional set of exercises.

PROBLEMS

1 3 4 **P16-1 (Entries for Various Dilutive Securities)** The stockholders' equity section of Martino Inc. at the beginning of the current year appears below.

Common stock, $10 par value, authorized 1,000,000 shares, 300,000 shares issued and outstanding	$3,000,000
Paid-in capital in excess of par—common stock	600,000
Retained earnings	570,000

During the current year, the following transactions occurred.

1. The company issued to the stockholders 100,000 rights. Ten rights are needed to buy one share of stock at $32. The rights were void after 30 days. The market price of the stock at this time was $34 per share.
2. The company sold to the public a $200,000, 10% bond issue at 104. The company also issued with each $100 bond one detachable stock purchase warrant, which provided for the purchase of common stock at $30 per share. Shortly after issuance, similar bonds without warrants were selling at 96 and the warrants at $8.
3. All but 5,000 of the rights issued in (1) were exercised in 30 days.
4. At the end of the year, 80% of the warrants in (2) had been exercised, and the remaining were outstanding and in good standing.
5. During the current year, the company granted stock options for 10,000 shares of common stock to company executives. The company, using a fair value option-pricing model, determines that each option is worth $10. The option price is $30. The options were to expire at year-end and were considered compensation for the current year.
6. All but 1,000 shares related to the stock-option plan were exercised by year-end. The expiration resulted because one of the executives failed to fulfill an obligation related to the employment contract.

Instructions

(a) Prepare general journal entries for the current year to record the transactions listed above.
(b) Prepare the stockholders' equity section of the balance sheet at the end of the current year. Assume that retained earnings at the end of the current year is $750,000.

1 **P16-2 (Entries for Conversion, Amortization, and Interest of Bonds)** Volker Inc. issued $2,500,000 of convertible 10-year bonds on July 1, 2014. The bonds provide for 12% interest payable semiannually on January 1 and July 1. The discount in connection with the issue was $54,000, which is being amortized monthly on a straight-line basis.

XLS

The bonds are convertible after one year into 8 shares of Volker Inc.'s $100 par value common stock for each $1,000 of bonds.

On August 1, 2015, $250,000 of bonds were turned in for conversion into common stock. Interest has been accrued monthly and paid as due. At the time of conversion, any accrued interest on bonds being converted is paid in cash.

Instructions

Prepare the journal entries to record the conversion, amortization, and interest in connection with the bonds as of the following dates. (Round to the nearest dollar.)

(a) August 1, 2015. (Assume the book value method is used.)
(b) August 31, 2015.
(c) December 31, 2015, including closing entries for end-of-year.

(AICPA adapted)

4 **P16-3 (Stock-Option Plan)** Berg Company adopted a stock-option plan on November 30, 2013, that provided that 70,000 shares of $5 par value stock be designated as available for the granting of options to officers of the corporation at a price of $9 a share. The market price was $12 a share on November 30, 2014.

XLS

On January 2, 2014, options to purchase 28,000 shares were granted to president Tom Winter—15,000 for services to be rendered in 2014 and 13,000 for services to be rendered in 2015. Also on that date, options to purchase 14,000 shares were granted to vice president Michelle Bennett—7,000 for services to be rendered in 2014 and 7,000 for services to be rendered in 2015. The market price of the stock was $14 a share on January 2, 2014. The options were exercisable for a period of one year following the year in which the services were rendered. The fair value of the options on the grant date was $4 per option.

In 2015, neither the president nor the vice president exercised their options because the market price of the stock was below the exercise price. The market price of the stock was $8 a share on December 31, 2015, when the options for 2014 services lapsed.

On December 31, 2016, both president Winter and vice president Bennett exercised their options for 13,000 and 7,000 shares, respectively, when the market price was $16 a share.

Instructions

Prepare the necessary journal entries in 2013 when the stock-option plan was adopted, in 2014 when options were granted, in 2015 when options lapsed, and in 2016 when options were exercised.

4 **P16-4 (Stock-Based Compensation)** Assume that Amazon.com has a stock-option plan for top management. Each stock option represents the right to purchase a share of Amazon $1 par value common stock in

the future at a price equal to the fair value of the stock at the date of the grant. Amazon has 5,000 stock options outstanding, which were granted at the beginning of 2014. The following data relate to the option grant.

Exercise price for options	$40
Market price at grant date (January 1, 2014)	$40
Fair value of options at grant date (January 1, 2014)	$6
Service period	5 years

Instructions

(a) Prepare the journal entry(ies) for the first year of the stock-option plan.

(b) Prepare the journal entry(ies) for the first year of the plan assuming that, rather than options, 700 shares of restricted stock were granted at the beginning of 2014.

(c) Now assume that the market price of Amazon stock on the grant date was $45 per share. Repeat the requirements for (a) and (b).

(d) Amazon would like to implement an employee stock-purchase plan for rank-and-file employees, but it would like to avoid recording expense related to this plan. Which of the following provisions must be in place for the plan to avoid recording compensation expense?

(1) Substantially all employees may participate.
(2) The discount from market is small (less than 5%).
(3) The plan offers no substantive option feature.
(4) There is no preferred stock outstanding.

7 **P16-5 (EPS with Complex Capital Structure)** Amy Dyken, controller at Fitzgerald Pharmaceutical Industries, a public company, is currently preparing the calculation for basic and diluted earnings per share and the related disclosure for Fitzgerald's financial statements. Below is selected financial information for the fiscal year ended June 30, 2014.

FITZGERALD PHARMACEUTICAL INDUSTRIES
SELECTED BALANCE SHEET INFORMATION
JUNE 30, 2014

Long-term debt	
Notes payable, 10%	$ 1,000,000
8% convertible bonds payable	5,000,000
10% bonds payable	6,000,000
Total long-term debt	$12,000,000
Shareholders' equity	
Preferred stock, 6% cumulative, $50 par value, 100,000 shares authorized, 25,000 shares issued and outstanding	$ 1,250,000
Common stock, $1 par, 10,000,000 shares authorized, 1,000,000 shares issued and outstanding	1,000,000
Additional paid-in capital	4,000,000
Retained earnings	6,000,000
Total shareholders' equity	$12,250,000

The following transactions have also occurred at Fitzgerald.

1. Options were granted on July 1, 2013, to purchase 200,000 shares at $15 per share. Although no options were exercised during fiscal year 2014, the average price per common share during fiscal year 2014 was $20 per share.
2. Each bond was issued at face value. The 8% convertible bonds will convert into common stock at 50 shares per $1,000 bond. The bonds are exercisable after 5 years and were issued in fiscal year 2013.
3. The preferred stock was issued in 2013.
4. There are no preferred dividends in arrears; however, preferred dividends were not declared in fiscal year 2014.
5. The 1,000,000 shares of common stock were outstanding for the entire 2014 fiscal year.
6. Net income for fiscal year 2014 was $1,500,000, and the average income tax rate is 40%.

Instructions

For the fiscal year ended June 30, 2014, calculate the following for Fitzgerald Pharmaceutical Industries.

(a) Basic earnings per share.
(b) Diluted earnings per share.

6 **P16-6 (Basic EPS: Two-Year Presentation)** Melton Corporation is preparing the comparative financial statements for the annual report to its shareholders for fiscal years ended May 31, 2014, and May 31, 2015. The income from operations for each year was $1,800,000 and $2,500,000, respectively. In both years, the company incurred a 10% interest expense on $2,400,000 of debt, an obligation that requires interest-only payments for 5 years. The company experienced a loss of $600,000 from a fire in its Scotland facility in February 2015, which was determined to be an extraordinary loss. The company uses a 40% effective tax rate for income taxes.

The capital structure of Melton Corporation on June 1, 2013, consisted of 1 million shares of common stock outstanding and 20,000 shares of $50 par value, 6%, cumulative preferred stock. There were no preferred dividends in arrears, and the company had not issued any convertible securities, options, or warrants.

On October 1, 2013, Melton sold an additional 500,000 shares of the common stock at $20 per share. Melton distributed a 20% stock dividend on the common shares outstanding on January 1, 2014. On December 1, 2014, Melton was able to sell an additional 800,000 shares of the common stock at $22 per share. These were the only common stock transactions that occurred during the two fiscal years.

Instructions

(a) Identify whether the capital structure at Melton Corporation is a simple or complex capital structure, and explain why.
(b) Determine the weighted-average number of shares that Melton Corporation would use in calculating earnings per share for the fiscal year ended:
(1) May 31, 2014.
(2) May 31, 2015.
(c) Prepare, in good form, a comparative income statement, beginning with income from operations, for Melton Corporation for the fiscal years ended May 31, 2014, and May 31, 2015. This statement will be included in Melton's annual report and should display the appropriate earnings per share presentations.

(CMA adapted)

7 **P16-7 (Computation of Basic and Diluted EPS)** Charles Austin of the controller's office of Thompson Corporation was given the assignment of determining the basic and diluted earnings per share values for the year ending December 31, 2015. Austin has compiled the information listed below.

1. The company is authorized to issue 8,000,000 shares of $10 par value common stock. As of December 31, 2014, 2,000,000 shares had been issued and were outstanding.
2. The per share market prices of the common stock on selected dates were as follows.

	Price per Share
July 1, 2014	$20.00
January 1, 2015	21.00
April 1, 2015	25.00
July 1, 2015	11.00
August 1, 2015	10.50
November 1, 2015	9.00
December 31, 2015	10.00

3. A total of 700,000 shares of an authorized 1,200,000 shares of convertible preferred stock had been issued on July 1, 2014. The stock was issued at its par value of $25, and it has a cumulative dividend of $3 per share. The stock is convertible into common stock at the rate of one share of convertible preferred for one share of common. The rate of conversion is to be automatically adjusted for stock splits and stock dividends. Dividends are paid quarterly on September 30, December 31, March 31, and June 30.
4. Thompson Corporation is subject to a 40% income tax rate.
5. The after-tax net income for the year ended December 31, 2015, was $11,550,000.

The following specific activities took place during 2015.

1. January 1—A 5% common stock dividend was issued. The dividend had been declared on December 1, 2014, to all stockholders of record on December 29, 2014.

2. April 1—A total of 400,000 shares of the $3 convertible preferred stock was converted into common stock. The company issued new common stock and retired the preferred stock. This was the only conversion of the preferred stock during 2015.
3. July 1—A 2-for-1 split of the common stock became effective on this date. The board of directors had authorized the split on June 1.
4. August 1—A total of 300,000 shares of common stock were issued to acquire a factory building.
5. November 1—A total of 24,000 shares of common stock were purchased on the open market at $9 per share. These shares were to be held as treasury stock and were still in the treasury as of December 31, 2015.
6. Common stock cash dividends—Cash dividends to common stockholders were declared and paid as follows.

   April 15—$0.30 per share
   October 15—$0.20 per share

7. Preferred stock cash dividends—Cash dividends to preferred stockholders were declared and paid as scheduled.

Instructions

(a) Determine the number of shares used to compute basic earnings per share for the year ended December 31, 2015.

(b) Determine the number of shares used to compute diluted earnings per share for the year ended December 31, 2015.

(c) Compute the adjusted net income to be used as the numerator in the basic earnings per share calculation for the year ended December 31, 2015.

7 **P16-8 (Computation of Basic and Diluted EPS)** The information below pertains to Barkley Company for 2015.

Net income for the year	$1,200,000
7% convertible bonds issued at par ($1,000 per bond); each bond is convertible into 30 shares of common stock	2,000,000
6% convertible, cumulative preferred stock, $100 par value; each share is convertible into 3 shares of common stock	4,000,000
Common stock, $10 par value	6,000,000
Tax rate for 2015	40%
Average market price of common stock	$25 per share

There were no changes during 2015 in the number of common shares, preferred shares, or convertible bonds outstanding. There is no treasury stock. The company also has common stock options (granted in a prior year) to purchase 75,000 shares of common stock at $20 per share.

Instructions

(a) Compute basic earnings per share for 2015.

(b) Compute diluted earnings per share for 2015.

6 **P16-9 (EPS with Stock Dividend and Extraordinary Items)** Agassi Corporation is preparing the comparative financial statements to be included in the annual report to stockholders. Agassi employs a fiscal year ending May 31.

Income from operations before income taxes for Agassi was $1,400,000 and $660,000, respectively, for fiscal years ended May 31, 2015 and 2014. Agassi experienced an extraordinary loss of $400,000 because of an earthquake on March 3, 2015. A 40% combined income tax rate pertains to any and all of Agassi Corporation's profits, gains, and losses.

Agassi's capital structure consists of preferred stock and common stock. The company has not issued any convertible securities or warrants and there are no outstanding stock options.

Agassi issued 40,000 shares of $100 par value, 6% cumulative preferred stock in 2011. All of this stock is outstanding, and no preferred dividends are in arrears.

There were 1,000,000 shares of $1 par common stock outstanding on June 1, 2013. On September 1, 2013, Agassi sold an additional 400,000 shares of the common stock at $17 per share. Agassi distributed a 20% stock dividend on the common shares outstanding on December 1, 2014. These were the only common stock transactions during the past 2 fiscal years.

Instructions

(a) Determine the weighted-average number of common shares that would be used in computing earnings per share on the current comparative income statement for:

(1) The year ended May 31, 2014.

(2) The year ended May 31, 2015.

(b) Starting with income from operations before income taxes, prepare a comparative income statement for the years ended May 31, 2015 and 2014. The statement will be part of Agassi Corporation's annual report to stockholders and should include appropriate earnings per share presentation.

(c) The capital structure of a corporation is the result of its past financing decisions. Furthermore, the earnings per share data presented on a corporation's financial statements is dependent upon the capital structure.

(1) Explain why Agassi Corporation is considered to have a simple capital structure.

(2) Describe how earnings per share data would be presented for a corporation that has a complex capital structure.

(CMA adapted)

PROBLEMS SET B

See the book's companion website, at **www.wiley.com/college/kieso**, for an additional set of problems.

CONCEPTS FOR ANALYSIS

CA16-1 (Warrants Issued with Bonds and Convertible Bonds) Incurring long-term debt with an arrangement whereby lenders receive an option to buy common stock during all or a portion of the time the debt is outstanding is a frequent corporate financing practice. In some situations, the result is achieved through the issuance of convertible bonds; in others, the debt instruments and the warrants to buy stock are separate.

Instructions

(a) (1) Describe the differences that exist in current accounting for original proceeds of the issuance of convertible bonds and of debt instruments with separate warrants to purchase common stock.

(2) Discuss the underlying rationale for the differences described in (a)(1) above.

(3) Summarize the arguments that have been presented in favor of accounting for convertible bonds in the same manner as accounting for debt with separate warrants.

(b) At the start of the year, Huish Company issued $18,000,000 of 12% bonds along with detachable warrants to buy 1,200,000 shares of its $10 par value common stock at $18 per share. The bonds mature over the next 10 years, starting one year from date of issuance, with annual maturities of $1,800,000. At the time, Huish had 9,600,000 shares of common stock outstanding. The company received $20,040,000 for the bonds and the warrants. For Huish Company, 12% was a relatively low borrowing rate. If offered alone, at this time, the bonds would have sold in the market at a 22% discount. Prepare the journal entry (or entries) for the issuance of the bonds and warrants for the cash consideration received.

(AICPA adapted)

CA16-2 (Ethical Issues—Compensation Plan) The executive officers of Rouse Corporation have a performance-based compensation plan. The performance criteria of this plan is linked to growth in earnings per share. When annual EPS growth is 12%, the Rouse executives earn 100% of the shares; if growth is 16%, they earn 125%. If EPS growth is lower than 8%, the executives receive no additional compensation.

In 2014, Joan Devers, the controller of Rouse, reviews year-end estimates of bad debt expense and warranty expense. She calculates the EPS growth at 15%. Kurt Adkins, a member of the executive group, remarks over lunch one day that the estimate of bad debt expense might be decreased, increasing EPS growth to 16.1%. Devers is not sure she should do this because she believes that the current estimate of bad debts is sound. On the other hand, she recognizes that a great deal of subjectivity is involved in the computation.

Instructions

Answer the following questions.

(a) What, if any, is the ethical dilemma for Devers?

(b) Should Devers's knowledge of the compensation plan be a factor that influences her estimate?

(c) How should Devers respond to Adkins's request?

CA16-3 (Stock Warrants—Various Types) For various reasons a corporation may issue warrants to purchase shares of its common stock at specified prices that, depending on the circumstances, may be less than, equal to, or greater than the current market price. For example, warrants may be issued:

1. To existing stockholders on a pro rata basis.
2. To certain key employees under an incentive stock-option plan.
3. To purchasers of the corporation's bonds.

Instructions

For each of the three examples of how stock warrants are used:

(a) Explain why they are used.

(b) Discuss the significance of the price (or prices) at which the warrants are issued (or granted) in relation to (1) the current market price of the company's stock, and (2) the length of time over which they can be exercised.

(c) Describe the information that should be disclosed in financial statements, or notes thereto, that are prepared when stock warrants are outstanding in the hands of the three groups listed above.

(AICPA adapted)

CA16-4 (Stock Compensation Plans) The following two items appeared on the Internet concerning the GAAP requirement to expense stock options.

> *WASHINGTON, D.C.—February 17, 2005* Congressman David Dreier (R–CA), Chairman of the House Rules Committee, and Congresswoman Anna Eshoo (D–CA) reintroduced legislation today that will preserve broad-based employee stock option plans and give investors critical information they need to understand how employee stock options impact the value of their shares.
>
> "Last year, the U.S. House of Representatives overwhelmingly voted for legislation that would have ensured the continued ability of innovative companies to offer stock options to rank-and-file employees," Dreier stated. "Both the Financial Accounting Standards Board (FASB) and the Securities and Exchange Commission (SEC) continue to ignore our calls to address legitimate concerns about the impact of FASB's new standard on workers' ability to have an ownership stake in the New Economy, and its failure to address the real need of shareholders: accurate and meaningful information about a company's use of stock options."
>
> "In December 2004, FASB issued a stock option expensing standard that will render a huge blow to the 21st century economy," Dreier said. "Their action and the SEC's apparent lack of concern for protecting shareholders, requires us to once again take a firm stand on the side of investors and economic growth. Giving investors the ability to understand how stock options impact the value of their shares is critical. And equally important is preserving the ability of companies to use this innovative tool to attract talented employees."

> *"Here We Go Again!" by Jack Ciesielski (2/21/2005, http://www.accountingobserver.com/blog/2005/02/here-we-go-again)* On February 17, Congressman David Dreier (R–CA), and Congresswoman Anna Eshoo (D–CA), officially entered Silicon Valley's bid to gum up the launch of honest reporting of stock option compensation: They co-sponsored a bill to "preserve broad-based employee stock option plans and give investors critical information they need to understand how employee stock options impact the value of their shares." You know what "critical information" they mean: stuff like the stock compensation for the top five officers in a company, with a rigged value set as close to zero as possible. Investors *crave* this kind of information. Other ways the good Congresspersons want to "help" investors: The bill "also requires the SEC to study the effectiveness of those disclosures over three years, during which time, no new accounting standard related to the treatment of stock options could be recognized. Finally, the bill requires the Secretary of Commerce to conduct a study and report to Congress on the impact of broad-based employee stock option plans on expanding employee corporate ownership, skilled worker recruitment and retention, research and innovation, economic growth, and international competitiveness."
>
> It's the old "four corners" basketball strategy: stall, stall, stall. In the meantime, hope for regime change at your opponent, the FASB.

Instructions

(a) What are the major recommendations of the stock-based compensation pronouncement?

(b) How do the provisions of GAAP in this area differ from the bill introduced by members of Congress (Dreier and Eshoo), which would require expensing for options issued to only the top five officers in a company? Which approach do you think would result in more useful information? (Focus on comparability.)

(c) The bill in Congress urges the FASB to develop a rule that preserves "the ability of companies to use this innovative tool to attract talented employees." Write a response to these Congress-people explaining the importance of neutrality in financial accounting and reporting.

CA16-5 (EPS: Preferred Dividends, Options, and Convertible Debt) "Earnings per share" (EPS) is the most featured, single financial statistic about modern corporations. Daily published quotations of stock prices have recently been expanded to include for many securities a "times earnings" figure that is based on EPS. Stock analysts often focus their discussions on the EPS of the corporations they study.

Instructions

(a) Explain how dividends or dividend requirements on any class of preferred stock that may be outstanding affect the computation of EPS.

(b) One of the technical procedures applicable in EPS computations is the "treasury-stock method." Briefly describe the circumstances under which it might be appropriate to apply the treasury-stock method.

(c) Convertible debentures are considered potentially dilutive common shares. Explain how convertible debentures are handled for purposes of EPS computations.

(AICPA adapted)

CA16-6 (EPS, Antidilution) Brad Dolan, a stockholder of Rhode Corporation, has asked you, the firm's accountant, to explain why his stock warrants were not included in diluted EPS. In order to explain this situation, you must briefly explain what dilutive securities are, why they are included in the EPS calculation, and why some securities are antidilutive and thus not included in this calculation.

Rhode Corporation earned $228,000 during the period, when it had an average of 100,000 shares of common stock outstanding. The common stock sold at an average market price of $25 per share during the period. Also outstanding were 30,000 warrants that could be exercised to purchase one share of common stock at $30 per warrant.

Instructions

Write Mr. Dolan a 1–1.5-page letter explaining why the warrants are not included in the calculation.

USING YOUR JUDGMENT

FINANCIAL REPORTING

Financial Reporting Problem

P&G

The Procter & Gamble Company (P&G)

The financial statements of P&G are presented in Appendix 5B. The company's complete annual report, including the notes to the financial statements, can be accessed at the book's companion website, **www.wiley.com/college/kieso**.

Instructions

Refer to P&G's financial statements and accompanying notes to answer the following questions.

(a) Under P&G's stock-based compensation plan, stock options are granted annually to key managers and directors.

(1) How many options were granted during 2011 under the plan?

(2) How many options were exercisable at June 30, 2011?

(3) How many options were exercised in 2011, and what was the average price of those exercised?

(4) How many years from the grant date do the options expire?

(5) To what accounts are the proceeds from these option exercises credited?

(6) What was the number of outstanding options at June 30, 2011, and at what average exercise price?

(b) What number of diluted weighted-average common shares outstanding was used by P&G in computing earnings per share for 2011, 2010, and 2009? What was P&G's diluted earnings per share in 2011, 2010, and 2009?

(c) What other stock-based compensation plans does P&G have?

Comparative Analysis Case

The Coca-Cola Company and PepsiCo, Inc.

Instructions

Go to the book's companion website and use information found there to answer the following questions related to The Coca-Cola Company and PepsiCo, Inc.

(a) What employee stock-option compensation plans are offered by Coca-Cola and PepsiCo?

(b) How many options are outstanding at year-end 2011 for both Coca-Cola and PepsiCo?

(c) How many options were granted by Coca-Cola and PepsiCo to officers and employees during 2011?

(d) How many options were exercised during 2011?

(e) What was the average exercise price for Coca-Cola and PepsiCo employees during 2011?

(f) What are the weighted-average number of shares used by Coca-Cola and PepsiCo in 2011, 2010, and 2009 to compute diluted earnings per share?

(g) What was the diluted net income per share for Coca-Cola and PepsiCo for 2011, 2010, and 2009?

Financial Statement Analysis Case

Ragatz, Inc.

Ragatz, Inc., a drug company, reported the following information. The company prepares its financial statements in accordance with GAAP.

	2014 (,000)
Current liabilities	$ 554,114
Convertible subordinated debt	648,020
Total liabilities	1,228,313
Stockholders' equity	176,413
Net income	58,333

Analysts attempting to compare Ragatz to drug companies that issue debt with detachable warrants may face a challenge due to differences in accounting for convertible debt.

Instructions

(a) Compute the following ratios for Ragatz, Inc. (Assume that year-end balances approximate annual averages.)

(1) Return on assets.

(2) Return on common stock equity.

(3) Debt to assets ratio.

(b) Briefly discuss the operating performance and financial position of Ragatz. Industry averages for these ratios in 2014 were ROA 3.5%; return on equity 16%; and debt to assets 75%. Based on this analysis, would you make an investment in the company's 5% convertible bonds? Explain.

(c) Assume you want to compare Ragatz to an IFRS company like Merck (which issues nonconvertible debt with detachable warrants). Assuming that the fair value of the equity component of Ragatz's convertible bonds is $150,000, how would you adjust the analysis above to make valid comparisons between Ragatz and Merck?

Accounting, Analysis, and Principles

On January 1, 2013, Garner issued 10-year, $200,000 face value, 6% bonds at par. Each $1,000 bond is convertible into 30 shares of Garner $2 par value common stock. The company has had 10,000 shares of common stock (and no preferred stock) outstanding throughout its life. None of the bonds have been converted as of the end of 2014. (Ignore all tax effects.)

Accounting

(a) Prepare the journal entry Garner would have made on January 1, 2013, to record the issuance of the bonds.

(b) Garner's net income in 2014 was $30,000 and was $27,000 in 2013. Compute basic and diluted earnings per share for Garner for 2014 and 2013.

(c) Assume that 75% of the holders of Garner's convertible bonds convert their bonds to stock on June 30, 2015, when Garner's stock is trading at $32 per share. Garner pays $50 per bond to induce bondholders to convert. Prepare the journal entry to record the conversion.

Analysis

Show how Garner will report income and EPS for 2014 and 2013. Briefly discuss the importance of GAAP for EPS to analysts evaluating companies based on price-earnings ratios. Consider comparisons for a company over time, as well as comparisons between companies at a point in time.

Principles

In order to converge GAAP and IFRS, the FASB is considering whether the equity element of a convertible bond should be reported as equity. Describe how the journal entry you made in part (a) above would differ under IFRS. In terms of the accounting principles discussed in Chapter 2, what does IFRS for convertible debt accomplish that GAAP potentially sacrifices? What does GAAP for convertible debt accomplish that IFRS potentially sacrifices?

BRIDGE TO THE PROFESSION

Professional Research: FASB Codification

Richardson Company is contemplating the establishment of a share-based compensation plan to provide long-run incentives for its top management. However, members of the compensation committee of the board of directors have voiced some concerns about adopting these plans, based on news accounts related to a recent accounting standard in this area. They would like you to conduct some research on this recent standard so they can be better informed about the accounting for these plans.

Instructions

If your school has a subscription to the FASB Codification, go to *http://aaahq.org/ascLogin.cfm* to log in and prepare responses to the following. Provide Codification references for your responses.

(a) Identify the authoritative literature that addresses the accounting for share-based payment compensation plans.

(b) Briefly discuss the objectives for the accounting for stock compensation. What is the role of fair value measurement?

(c) The Richardson Company board is also considering an employee share-purchase plan, but the Board does not want to record expense related to the plan. What criteria must be met to avoid recording expense on an employee stock-purchase plan?

Additional Professional Resources

See the book's companion website, at **www.wiley.com/college/kieso**, for professional simulations as well as other study resources.

IFRS INSIGHTS

10 LEARNING OBJECTIVE
Compare the accounting for dilutive securities and earnings per share under GAAP and IFRS.

The primary IFRS related to financial instruments, including dilutive securities, is *IAS 39*, "Financial Instruments: Recognition and Measurement." The accounting for various forms of stock-based compensation under IFRS is found in *IFRS 2*, "Share-Based Payment." This standard was recently amended, resulting in significant convergence between IFRS and GAAP in this area. The IFRS addressing accounting and reporting for earnings per share computations is *IAS 33*, "Earnings per Share."

RELEVANT FACTS

Following are the key similarities and differences between GAAP and IFRS related to dilutive securities and earnings per share.

Similarities

- IFRS and GAAP follow the same model for recognizing stock-based compensation: The fair value of shares and options awarded to employees is recognized over the period to which the employees' services relate.
- Although the calculation of basic and diluted earnings per share is similar between IFRS and GAAP, the Boards are working to resolve the few minor differences in EPS reporting. One proposal in the FASB project concerns contracts that can be settled in either cash or shares. IFRS requires that share settlement must be used, while GAAP gives companies a choice. The FASB project proposes adopting the IFRS approach, thus converging GAAP and IFRS in this regard.

Differences

- A significant difference between IFRS and GAAP is the accounting for securities with characteristics of debt and equity, such as convertible debt. Under GAAP, all of the proceeds of convertible debt are recorded as long-term debt. Under IFRS, convertible bonds are "bifurcated"—separated into the equity component (the value of the conversion option) of the bond issue and the debt component.
- Related to employee share-purchase plans, under IFRS, all employee share-purchase plans are deemed to be compensatory; that is, compensation expense is recorded for the amount of the discount. Under GAAP, these plans are often considered noncompensatory and therefore no compensation is recorded. Certain conditions must exist before a plan can be considered noncompensatory—the most important being that the discount generally cannot exceed 5 percent.
- Modification of a share option results in the recognition of any incremental fair value under both IFRS and GAAP. However, if the modification leads to a reduction, IFRS does not permit the reduction but GAAP does.
- Other EPS differences relate to (1) the treasury-stock method and how the proceeds from extinguishment of a liability should be accounted for, and (2) how to compute the weighted average of contingently issuable shares.

ABOUT THE NUMBERS

Accounting for Convertible Debt

Convertible debt is accounted for as a **compound instrument** because it contains both a liability and an equity component. IFRS requires that compound instruments be separated into their liability and equity components for purposes of accounting. Companies use the **"with-and-without" method** to value compound instruments. Illustration IFRS16-1 identifies the components used in the with-and-without method.

ILLUSTRATION IFRS16-1
Convertible Debt Components

Fair value of convertible debt at date of issuance (with both debt and equity components)	−	Fair value of liability component at date of issuance, based on present value of cash flows	=	Equity component at date of issuance (without the debt component)

As indicated, the equity component is the residual amount after subtracting the liability component. IFRS does not permit companies to assign a value to the equity amount first and then determine the liability component. To do so would be inconsistent with the definition of equity, which is considered a residual amount. To implement the with-and-without approach, companies do the following.

1. First, the company determines the total fair value of the convertible debt *with* both the liability and equity component. **This is straightforward, as this amount is the proceeds received upon issuance.**
2. The company then determines the liability component by computing the net present value of all contractual future cash flows discounted at the market rate of interest. This market rate is the rate the company would pay on similar nonconvertible debt.
3. In the final step, the company subtracts the liability component estimated in the second step from the fair value of the convertible debt (issue proceeds) to arrive at the equity component. That is, the equity component is the fair value of the convertible debt *without* the liability component.

Accounting at Time of Issuance

To illustrate the accounting for convertible debt, assume that **Roche Group** issues 2,000 convertible bonds at the beginning of 2013. The bonds have a four-year term with a stated rate of interest of 6 percent, and are issued at par with a face value of $1,000 per bond (the total proceeds received from issuance of the bonds are $2,000,000). Interest is payable annually at December 31. Each bond is convertible into 250 ordinary shares with a par value of $1. The market rate of interest on similar nonconvertible debt is 9 percent. The time diagram in Illustration IFRS16-2 depicts both the interest and principal cash flows.

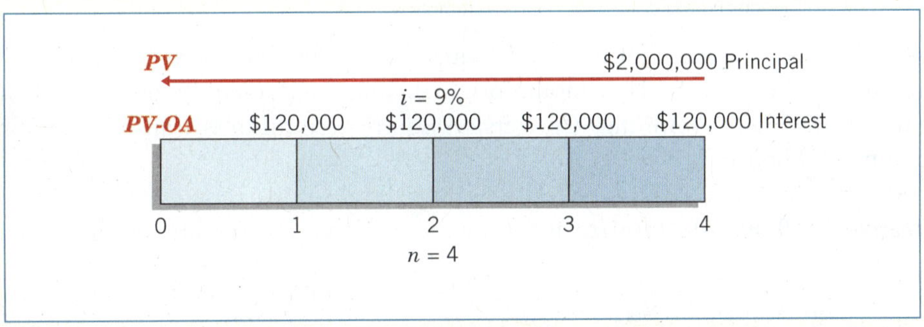

ILLUSTRATION IFRS16-2
Time Diagram for Convertible Bond

The liability component of the convertible debt is computed as shown in Illustration IFRS16-3.

Present value of principal: $2,000,000 × .70843 (Table 6-2; n = 4, i = 9%)	$1,416,860
Present value of the interest payments: $120,000 × 3.23972 (Table 6-4; n = 4, i = 9%)	388,766
Present value of the liability component	$1,805,626

ILLUSTRATION IFRS16-3
Fair Value of Liability Component of Convertible Bond

The equity component of Roche's convertible debt is then computed as shown in Illustration IFRS16-4.

Fair value of convertible debt at date of issuance	$2,000,000
Less: Fair value of liability component at date of issuance	1,805,626
Fair value of equity component at date of issuance	$ 194,374

ILLUSTRATION IFRS16-4
Equity Component of Convertible Bond

The journal entry to record this transaction is as follows.

Cash	2,000,000	
Bonds Payable		1,805,626
Share Premium—Conversion Equity		194,374

The liability component of Roche's convertible debt issue is recorded as Bonds Payable. As shown in Chapter 14, the amount of the discount relative to the face value of the bond is amortized at each reporting period so at maturity, the Bonds Payable account is reported at $2,000,000 (face value). The equity component of the convertible bond is recorded in the Share Premium—Conversion Equity account and is reported in the equity section of the statement of financial position. Because this amount is considered part of contributed capital, it does not change over the life of the convertible. **Transaction costs related to the liability and equity components are allocated in proportion to the proceeds received from the two components.** *For purposes of homework, use the Share Premium—Conversion Equity account to record the equity component.* **In practice, there may be considerable variation in the accounts used to record this component.**

Settlement of Convertible Bonds

We illustrate four settlement situations: (1) repurchase at maturity, (2) conversion at maturity, (3) conversion before maturity, and (4) repurchase before maturity.

Repurchase at Maturity. If the bonds are not converted at maturity, Roche makes the following entry to pay off the convertible debtholders.

Bonds Payable	2,000,000	
Cash		2,000,000
(To record the purchase of bonds at maturity)		

Because the carrying value of the bonds equals the face value, there is no gain or loss on repurchase at maturity. The amount originally allocated to equity of $194,374 either remains in the Share Premium—Conversion Equity account or is transferred to Share Premium—Ordinary.

Conversion of Bonds at Maturity. If the bonds are converted at maturity, Roche makes the following entry.

Share Premium—Conversion Equity	194,374	
Bonds Payable	2,000,000	
Share Capital—Ordinary		500,000
Share Premium—Ordinary		1,694,374
(To record the conversion of bonds at maturity)		

As indicated, Roche records a credit to Share Capital—Ordinary for $500,000 (2,000 bonds × 250 shares × $1 par) and the remainder to Share Premium—Ordinary for $1,694,374. There is no gain or loss on conversion at maturity. The original amount allocated to equity ($194,374) is transferred to the Share Premium—Ordinary account. As a result, Roche's equity has increased by a total of $2,194,374 through issuance and conversion of the convertible bonds. This accounting approach is often referred to as the **book value method** in that the carrying amount (book value) of the bond and related conversion equity determines the amount in the ordinary equity accounts.

Conversion of Bonds before Maturity. What happens if bonds are converted before maturity? To understand the accounting, we again use the Roche Group example. A schedule of bond amortization related to Roche's convertible bonds is shown in Illustration IFRS16-5.

ILLUSTRATION IFRS16-5
Convertible Bond Amortization Schedule

SCHEDULE OF BOND AMORTIZATION
EFFECTIVE-INTEREST METHOD
6% BOND DISCOUNTED AT 9%

Date	Cash Paid	Interest Expense	Discount Amortized	Carrying Amount of Bonds
1/1/13				$1,805,626
12/31/13	$120,000	$162,506	$42,506	1,848,132
12/31/14	120,000	166,332	46,332	1,894,464
12/31/15	120,000	170,502	50,502	1,944,966
12/31/16	120,000	175,034*	55,034	2,000,000

*$13 difference due to rounding.

Assuming that Roche converts its bonds into ordinary shares on December 31, 2014, Roche debits the Bonds Payable account for its carrying value of $1,894,464 (see Illustration IFRS16-5). In addition, Roche credits Share Capital—Ordinary for $500,000 (2,000 × 250 × $1) and credits Share Premium—Ordinary for $1,588,838. The entry to record this conversion is as follows.

Share Premium—Conversion Equity	194,374	
Bonds Payable	1,894,464	
Share Capital—Ordinary		500,000
Share Premium—Ordinary		1,588,838
(To record the conversion of bonds before maturity)		

There is no gain or loss on conversion before maturity: The original amount allocated to equity ($194,374) is transferred to the Share Premium—Ordinary account.

Repurchase before Maturity. In some cases, companies decide to repurchase the convertible debt before maturity. The approach used for allocating the amount paid upon repurchase follows the approach used when the convertible bond was originally issued. That is, Roche determines the fair value of the liability component of the convertible bonds at December 31, 2014, and then subtracts this amount from the fair value of the convertible bond issue (including the equity component) to arrive at the value for the equity. After this allocation is completed:

1. The difference between the consideration allocated to the liability component and the carrying amount of the liability is recognized as a gain or loss, and
2. The amount of consideration relating to the equity component is recognized (as a reduction) in equity.

To illustrate, instead of converting the bonds on December 31, 2014, assume that Roche repurchases the convertible bonds from the bondholders. Pertinent information related to this conversion is as follows.

- Fair value of the convertible debt (including both liability and equity components), based on market prices at December 31, 2014, is $1,965,000.
- The fair value of the liability component is $1,904,900. This amount is based on computing the present value of a nonconvertible bond with a two-year term (which corresponds to the shortened time to maturity of the repurchased bonds).

We first determine the gain or loss on the liability component, as computed in Illustration IFRS16-6.

ILLUSTRATION IFRS16-6
Gain or Loss on Debt Repurchase

Present value of liability component at December 31, 2014 (given above)	$ 1,904,900
Carrying value of liability component at December 31, 2014 (per Illustration IFRS16-5)	(1,894,464)
Loss on repurchase	$ 10,436

Roche has a loss on this repurchase because the value of the debt extinguished is greater than its carrying amount. To determine any adjustment to equity, we compute the value of the equity as shown in Illustration IFRS16-7.

ILLUSTRATION IFRS16-7
Equity Adjustment on Repurchase of Convertible Bonds

Fair value of convertible debt at December 31, 2014 (**with equity component**)	$1,965,000
Less: Fair value of liability component at December 31, 2014 (similar 2-year nonconvertible debt)	1,904,900
Fair value of equity component at December 31, 2014 (**without debt component**)	$ 60,100

Roche makes the following compound journal entry to record the entire repurchase transaction.

Bonds Payable	1,894,464	
Share Premium—Conversion Equity	60,100	
Loss on Repurchase	10,436	
Cash		1,965,000
(To record the repurchase of convertible bonds)		

In summary, the repurchase results in a loss related to the liability component and a reduction in Share Premium—Conversion Equity. The remaining balance in Share Premium—Conversion Equity of $134,274 ($194,374 − $60,100) is often transferred to Share Premium—Ordinary upon the repurchase.

Employee Share-Purchase Plans

Employee share-purchase plans (ESPPs) generally permit all employees to purchase shares at a discounted price for a short period of time. The company often uses such plans to secure equity capital or to induce widespread ownership of its ordinary shares among employees. **These plans are considered compensatory and should be recorded as expense over the service period.**

To illustrate, assume that Masthead Company offers all its 1,000 employees the opportunity to participate in an employee share-purchase plan. Under the terms of the plan, the employees are entitled to purchase 100 ordinary shares (par value $1 per share) at a 20 percent discount. The purchase price must be paid immediately upon acceptance of the offer. In total, 800 employees accept the offer, and each employee purchases on average 80 shares. That is, the employees purchase a total of 64,000 shares. The weighted-average market price of the shares at the purchase date is $30 per share, and the weighted-average purchase price is $24 per share. The entry to record this transaction is as follows.

Cash (64,000 × $24)	1,536,000	
Compensation Expense [64,000 × ($30 − $24)]	384,000	
Share Capital—Ordinary (64,000 × $1)		64,000
Share Premium—Ordinary		1,856,000
(Issue shares in an employee share-purchase plan)		

The IASB indicates that there is no reason to treat broad-based employee share plans differently from other employee share plans. Some have argued that because these plans are used to raise capital, they should not be compensatory. However, IFRS requires recording expense for these arrangements. The Board notes that because these arrangements are available only to employees, it is sufficient to conclude that the benefits provided represent employee compensation.

ON THE HORIZON

The FASB has been working on a standard that will likely converge to IFRS in the accounting for convertible debt. Similar to the FASB, the IASB is examining the classification of hybrid securities; the IASB is seeking comment on a discussion document similar to the FASB Preliminary Views document, *"Financial Instruments with Characteristics of*

Equity." It is hoped that the Boards will develop a converged standard in this area. While GAAP and IFRS are similar as to the presentation of EPS, the Boards have been working together to resolve remaining differences related to earnings per share computations.

IFRS SELF-TEST QUESTIONS

1. All of the following are key similarities between GAAP and IFRS with respect to accounting for dilutive securities and EPS **except**:
   (a) the model for recognizing stock-based compensation.
   (b) the calculation of basic and diluted EPS.
   (c) the accounting for convertible debt.
   (d) the accounting for modifications of share options, when the value increases.
2. Which of the following statements is **correct**?
   (a) IFRS separates the proceeds of a convertible bond between debt and equity by determining the fair value of the debt component before the equity component.
   (b) Both IFRS and GAAP assume that when there is choice of settlement of an option for cash or shares, share settlement is assumed.
   (c) IFRS separates the proceeds of a convertible bond between debt and equity, based on relative fair values.
   (d) Both GAAP and IFRS separate the proceeds of convertible bonds between debt and equity.
3. Under IFRS, convertible bonds:
   (a) are separated into the bond component and the expense component.
   (b) are separated into debt and equity components.
   (c) are separated into their components based on relative fair values.
   (d) All of the above.
4. Mae Jong Corp. issues $1,000,000 of 10% bonds payable which may be converted into 10,000 shares of $2 par value ordinary shares. The market rate of interest on similar bonds is 12%. Interest is payable annually on December 31, and the bonds were issued for total proceeds of $1,000,000. In accounting for these bonds, Mae Jong Corp. will:
   (a) first assign a value to the equity component, then determine the liability component.
   (b) assign no value to the equity component since the conversion privilege is not separable from the bond.
   (c) first assign a value to the liability component based on the face amount of the bond.
   (d) use the "with-and-without" method to value the compound instrument.
5. Anazazi Co. offers all its 10,000 employees the opportunity to participate in an employee share-purchase plan. Under the terms of the plan, the employees are entitled to purchase 100 ordinary shares (par value $1 per share) at a 20% discount. The purchase price must be paid immediately upon acceptance of the offer. In total, 8,500 employees accept the offer, and each employee purchases on average 80 shares at $22 share (market price $27.50). Under IFRS, Anazazi Co. will record:
   (a) no compensation since the plan is used to raise capital, not compensate employees.
   (b) compensation expense of $5,500,000.
   (c) compensation expense of $18,700,000.
   (d) compensation expense of $3,740,000.

IFRS CONCEPTS AND APPLICATION

IFRS16-1 Where can authoritative IFRS be found related to dilutive securities, stock-based compensation, and earnings per share?

IFRS16-2 Briefly describe some of the similarities and differences between GAAP and IFRS with respect to the accounting for dilutive securities, stock-based compensation, and earnings per share.

IFRS16-3 Norman Co., a fast-growing golf equipment company, uses GAAP. It is considering the issuance of convertible bonds. The bonds mature in 10 years, have a face value of $400,000, and pay interest annually at a rate of 4%. The equity component of the bond issue has a fair value of $35,000. Greg Shark is curious as to the difference in accounting for these bonds if the company were to use IFRS. (a) Prepare the entry to record issuance of the bonds at par under GAAP. (b) Repeat the requirement for part (a), assuming application of IFRS to the bond issuance. (c) Which approach provides the better accounting? Explain.

IFRS16-4 Briefly discuss the convergence efforts that are under way by the IASB and FASB in the area of dilutive securities and earnings per share.

IFRS16-5 Explain how the conversion feature of convertible debt has a value (a) to the issuer and (b) to the purchaser.

IFRS16-6 What are the arguments for giving separate accounting recognition to the conversion feature of debentures?

IFRS16-7 Four years after issue, debentures with a face value of $1,000,000 and book value of $960,000 are tendered for conversion into 80,000 ordinary shares immediately after an interest payment date. At that time, the market price of the debentures is 104, and the ordinary shares are selling at $14 per share (par value $10). At date of issue, the company recorded Share Premium—Conversion Equity of $50,000. The company records the conversion as follows.

Bonds Payable	960,000	
Share Premium—Conversion Equity	50,000	
Share Capital—Ordinary		800,000
Share Premium—Ordinary		210,000

Discuss the propriety of this accounting treatment.

IFRS16-8 Cordero Corporation has an employee share-purchase plan which permits all full-time employees to purchase 10 ordinary shares on the third anniversary of their employment and an additional 15 shares on each subsequent anniversary date. The purchase price is set at the market price on the date purchased less a 10% discount. How is this discount accounted for by Cordero?

IFRS16-9 Archer Company issued $4,000,000 par value, 7% convertible bonds at 99 for cash. The net present value of the debt without the conversion feature is $3,800,000. Prepare the journal entry to record the issuance of the convertible bonds.

IFRS16-10 Petrenko Corporation has outstanding 2,000 $1,000 bonds, each convertible into 50 shares of $10 par value ordinary shares. The bonds are converted on December 31, 2014. The bonds payable has a carrying value of $1,950,000 and conversion equity of $20,000. Record the conversion using the book value method.

IFRS16-11 Angela Corporation issues 2,000 convertible bonds at January 1, 2013. The bonds have a 3-year life, and are issued at par with a face value of $1,000 per bond, giving total proceeds of $2,000,000. Interest is payable annually at 6%. Each bond is convertible into 250 ordinary shares (par value of $1). When the bonds are issued, the market rate of interest for similar debt without the conversion option is 8%.

Instructions

(a) Compute the liability and equity component of the convertible bond on January 1, 2013.
(b) Prepare the journal entry to record the issuance of the convertible bond on January 1, 2013.
(c) Prepare the journal entry to record the repurchase of the convertible bond for cash at January 1, 2016, its maturity date.

IFRS16-12 Assume the same information in IFRS16-11, except that Angela Corporation converts its convertible bonds on January 1, 2014.

Instructions

(a) Compute the carrying value of the bond payable on January 1, 2014.
(b) Prepare the journal entry to record the conversion on January 1, 2014.
(c) Assume that the bonds were repurchased on January 1, 2014, for $1,940,000 cash instead of being converted. The net present value of the liability component of the convertible bonds on January 1, 2014, is $1,900,000. Prepare the journal entry to record the repurchase on January 1, 2014.

IFRS16-13 Assume that Sarazan Company has a share-option plan for top management. Each share option represents the right to purchase a $1 par value ordinary share in the future at a price equal to the fair value of the shares at the date of the grant. Sarazan has 5,000 share options outstanding, which were granted at the beginning of 2014. The following data relate to the option grant.

Exercise price for options	$40
Market price at grant date (January 1, 2014)	$40
Fair value of options at grant date (January 1, 2014)	$6
Service period	5 years

Instructions

(a) Prepare the journal entry(ies) for the first year of the share-option plan.

(b) Prepare the journal entry(ies) for the first year of the plan assuming that, rather than options, 700 shares of restricted shares were granted at the beginning of 2014.

(c) Now assume that the market price of Sarazan shares on the grant date was $45 per share. Repeat the requirements for (a) and (b).

(d) Sarazan would like to implement an employee share-purchase plan for rank-and-file employees, but it would like to avoid recording expense related to this plan. Explain how employee share-purchase plans are recorded.

Professional Research

IFRS16-14 Richardson Company is contemplating the establishment of a share-based compensation plan to provide long-run incentives for its top management. However, members of the compensation committee of the board of directors have voiced some concerns about adopting these plans, based on news accounts related to a recent accounting standard in this area. They would like you to conduct some research on this recent standard so they can be better informed about the accounting for these plans.

Instructions

Access the IFRS authoritative literature at the IASB website (*http://eifrs.iasb.org/*). (Click on the IFRS tab and then register for free eIFRS access if necessary.) When you have accessed the documents, you can use the search tool in your Internet browser to respond to the following questions. (Provide paragraph citations.)

(a) Identify the authoritative literature that addresses the accounting for share-based payment compensation plans.

(b) Briefly discuss the objectives for the accounting for share-based compensation. What is the role of fair value measurement?

(c) The Richardson Company board is also considering an employee share-purchase plan, but the Board does not want to record expense related to the plan. What are the IFRS requirements for the accounting for an employee share-purchase plan?

International Financial Reporting Problem
Marks and Spencer plc

IFRS16-15 The financial statements of **Marks and Spencer plc (M&S)** are available at the book's companion website or can be accessed at *http://annualreport.marksandspencer.com/_assets/downloads/Marks-and-Spencer-Annual-report-and-financial-statements-2012.pdf.*

Instructions

Refer to M&S's financial statements and the accompanying notes to answer the following questions.

(a) Under M&S's share-based compensation plan, share options are granted annually to key managers and directors.

- **(1)** How many options were granted during 2012 under the plan?
- **(2)** How many options were exercisable at 31 March 2012?
- **(3)** How many options were exercised in 2012, and what was the average price of those exercised?
- **(4)** How many years from the grant date do the options expire?
- **(5)** To what accounts are the proceeds from these option exercises credited?
- **(6)** What was the number of outstanding options at 31 March 2012, and at what average exercise price?

(b) What number of diluted weighted-average shares outstanding was used by M&S in computing earnings per share for 2012 and 2011? What was M&S's diluted earnings per share in 2012 and 2011?

(c) What other share-based compensation plans does M&S have?

ANSWERS TO IFRS SELF-TEST QUESTIONS

1. c **2.** a **3.** b **4.** d **5.** d

Remember to check the book's companion website to find additional resources for this chapter.

CHAPTER

17 Investments

LEARNING OBJECTIVES

After studying this chapter, you should be able to:

1 Identify the three categories of debt securities and describe the accounting and reporting treatment for each category.

2 Understand the procedures for discount and premium amortization on bond investments.

3 Identify the categories of equity securities and describe the accounting and reporting treatment for each category.

4 Explain the equity method of accounting and compare it to the fair value method for equity securities.

5 Describe the accounting for the fair value option and for impairments of debt and equity investments.

6 Describe the reporting of reclassification adjustments and the accounting for transfers between categories.

What to Do?

A few years ago, a bank reported an $87.3 million write-down on its mortgage-backed securities for the third quarter of 2008. However, the bank stated that it expected its actual losses to be only $44,000. The loss of $44,000 was equal to a modest loss on a condo foreclosure. The bank's regulator found "the accounting result absurd." And the bank regulator was right, as the bank, in the third quarter of 2009, raised its credit-loss estimate by **$263.1 million**, quite a difference from its original loss estimate of **$44,000**.

The discussion above highlights the challenge of valuing financial assets such as loans, derivatives, and other debt investments. The fundamental question that arose out of the example above and, more significantly, the recent financial crisis is: Should financial instruments be valued at amortized cost, fair value, or some other measure(s)? As one writer noted, the opinion that fair value accounting weakens financial and economic stability has persisted among many regulators and politicians. But some investors and others believe that fair value is the right answer because it is more transparent information. OK, so what to do?

Well, the FASB originally issued a proposal to account for just about all financial assets at fair value with gains and losses recorded in income (amortized cost would be disclosed for some financial assets). The FASB indicated this approach will provide the most relevant and transparent information about financial assets. In contrast, the IASB issued a new standard on financial assets *(IFRS 9)* that uses a mixed-attribute approach. Some of the financial assets are valued at amortized cost and others at fair value.

Interestingly, the European Union refused to consider adopting the requirements of *IFRS 9*, arguing that it contained **too much** fair value information. Nevertheless, the standard was issued and other countries that follow IFRS will have to implement the new standard in 2015. At the same time, as soon as the FASB issues its new standard, the IASB has indicated that it may revisit the valuation issue once again. Thus, the early reaction to *IFRS 9* indicates that, unfortunately, once again politics

is raising its ugly head on an accounting issue. Some European regulators have suggested that the IASB's future funding may even depend on the IASB putting more limits on the use of fair value.

Now, let's go back to the FASB. Recently, the FASB dropped its plan to value loans at fair value and permits amortized cost accounting for these loans. This decision means banks will continue to value loans as they do today. This reversal is a big victory for the banking industry, which argued that the fair value approach would hurt lending and provide unnecessary volatility in their financial results. As a consequence, the FASB is moving much closer to the IASB's position. So after much discussion about what went wrong in the accounting for financial instruments during the financial crises, it looks like we are headed back to most of the same measurement rules that occurred before the financial collapse of 2008. We deem that unfortunate.

Sources: Adapted from Jonathan Weil, "Suing Wall Street Banks Never Looked So Shady," *http://www.bloomberg.com/* (February 28, 2010); and Rachel Sanderson and Jennifer Hughes, "Carried Forward," *Financial Times Online* (April 20, 2010).

CONCEPTUAL FOCUS

> See the **Underlying Concepts** on pages 954, 955, and 957.

> Read the **Evolving Issues** on pages 968 and 975 for a discussion of the fair value controversy, and proposed classification and measurement model for financial instruments.

INTERNATIONAL FOCUS

> See the **International Perspectives** on pages 952, 953, 966, 968, 987, 989, and 995.

> Read the **IFRS Insights** on pages 1026–1039 for a discussion of:

—Accounting for financial assets
—Debt investments
—Equity investments
—Impairments

PREVIEW OF CHAPTER 17

As indicated in the opening story, the accounting for financial assets is highly controversial. How to measure, recognize, and disclose this information is now being debated and discussed extensively. In this chapter, we address the accounting for debt and equity investments. Appendices to this chapter discuss the accounting for derivative instruments, variable-interest entities, and fair value disclosures. The content and organization of this chapter are as follows.

Investments

Investments in Debt Securities	Investments in Equity Securities	Additional Measurement Issues	Reclassifications and Transfers
• Debt investment classifications • Held-to-maturity securities • Available-for-sale securities • Trading securities	• Holdings of less than 20% • Holdings between 20% and 50% • Holdings of more than 50%	• Fair value option • Impairment of value	• Reclassification adjustments • Transfers between categories • Summary

INVESTMENTS IN DEBT SECURITIES

LEARNING OBJECTIVE 1
Identify the three categories of debt securities and describe the accounting and reporting treatment for each category.

Companies have different motivations for investing in securities issued by other companies.[1] **One motivation is to earn a high rate of return.** For example, companies like Coca-Cola and PepsiCo can receive interest revenue from a debt investment or dividend revenue from an equity investment. In addition, they can realize capital gains on both types of securities. **Another motivation for investing (in equity securities) is to secure certain operating or financing arrangements with another company.** For example, Coca-Cola and PepsiCo are able to exercise some control over bottler companies based on their significant (but not controlling) equity investments.

To provide useful information, companies account for investments based on the type of security (debt or equity) and their intent with respect to the investment. As indicated in Illustration 17-1, we organize our study of investments by type of security. Within this section, we explain the accounting for investments in debt. We address equity securities later in the chapter.

ILLUSTRATION 17-1
Summary of Investment Accounting Approaches

Type of Security	Management Intent	Valuation Approach
Debt	No plans to sell	Amortized cost
	Plan to sell	Fair value
Equity	Plan to sell	Fair value
	Exercise some control	Equity method

Debt securities represent a creditor relationship with another entity. Debt securities include U.S. government securities, municipal securities, corporate bonds, convertible debt, and commercial paper. Trade accounts receivable and loans receivable are not debt securities because they do not meet the definition of a security.

Debt Investment Classifications

Companies group investments in debt securities into three separate categories for accounting and reporting purposes:

International Perspective
Under IFRS, debt investments are classified as either held-for-collection or trading.

- **Held-to-maturity**: Debt securities that the company has the positive intent and ability to hold to maturity.
- **Trading**: Debt securities bought and held primarily for sale in the near term to generate income on short-term price differences.
- **Available-for-sale**: Debt securities not classified as held-to-maturity or trading securities.

Illustration 17-2 identifies these categories, along with the accounting and reporting treatments required for each.

[1]A **security** is a share, participation, or other interest in property or in an enterprise of the issuer or an obligation of the issuer that has the following three characteristics. (1) It either is represented by an instrument issued in bearer or registered form or, if not represented by an instrument, is registered in books maintained to record transfers by or on behalf of the issuer. (2) It is commonly traded on securities exchanges or markets or, when represented by an instrument, is commonly recognized in any area in which it is issued or dealt in as a medium for investment. (3) It either is one of a class or series or by its terms is divisible into a class or series of shares, participations, interests, or obligations. [1]

See the FASB Codification section (page 1005).

Category	Valuation	Unrealized Holding Gains or Losses	Other Income Effects
Held-to-maturity	Amortized cost	Not recognized	Interest when earned; gains and losses from sale.
Trading securities	Fair value	Recognized in net income	Interest when earned; gains and losses from sale.
Available-for-sale	Fair value	Recognized as other comprehensive income and as separate component of stockholders' equity	Interest when earned; gains and losses from sale.

ILLUSTRATION 17-2
Accounting for Debt Securities by Category

International Perspective

Under IFRS, held-for-collection debt investments are valued at amortized cost; all other investments are measured at fair value.

Amortized cost is the acquisition cost adjusted for the amortization of discount or premium, if appropriate. **Fair value** is the price that would be received to sell an asset or paid to transfer a liability in an orderly transaction between market participants at the measurement date. **[2]**

Held-to-Maturity Securities

2 LEARNING OBJECTIVE
Understand the procedures for discount and premium amortization on bond investments.

Only debt securities can be classified as held-to-maturity. By definition, equity securities have no maturity date. A company like **Starbucks** should classify a debt security as **held-to-maturity** only if it has **both (1) the positive intent** and **(2) the ability to hold those securities to maturity**. It should not classify a debt security as held-to-maturity if it intends to hold the security for an indefinite period of time. Likewise, if Starbucks anticipates that a sale may be necessary due to changes in interest rates, foreign currency risk, liquidity needs, or other asset-liability management reasons, it should not classify the security as held-to-maturity.[2]

Companies account for held-to-maturity securities **at amortized cost**, not fair value. If management intends to hold certain investment securities to maturity and has no plans to sell them, fair values (selling prices) are not relevant for measuring and evaluating the cash flows associated with these securities. Finally, because companies do not adjust held-to-maturity securities to fair value, these securities do not increase the volatility of either reported earnings or reported capital as do trading securities and available-for-sale securities.

To illustrate the accounting for held-to-maturity debt securities, assume that Robinson Company purchased $100,000 of 8 percent bonds of Evermaster Corporation on January 1, 2013, at a discount, paying $92,278. The bonds mature January 1, 2018 and yield 10%. Interest is payable each July 1 and January 1. Robinson records the investment as follows.

January 1, 2013		
Debt Investments	92,278	
Cash		92,278

Calculator Solution for Bond Price

	Inputs	Answer
N	10	
I	5	
PV	?	-92,278
PMT	4,000	
FV	100,000	

[2]The FASB defines situations where, even though a company sells a security before maturity, it has constructively held the security to maturity, and thus does not violate the held-to-maturity requirement. These include selling a security close enough to maturity (such as three months) so that interest rate risk is no longer an important pricing factor.

However, companies must be extremely careful with debt securities held to maturity. If a company prematurely sells a debt security in this category, the sale may "taint" the entire held-to-maturity portfolio. That is, a management's statement regarding "intent" is no longer credible. Therefore, the company may have to reclassify the securities. This could lead to unfortunate consequences. An interesting by-product of this situation is that companies that wish to retire their debt securities early are finding it difficult to do so. The holder will not sell because the securities are classified as held-to-maturity.

Robinson uses a Debt Investments account to indicate the type of debt security purchased.[3]

As indicated in Chapter 14, companies must amortize premium or discount using the **effective-interest method** unless some other method—such as the straight-line method—yields a similar result. They apply the effective-interest method to bond investments in a way similar to that for bonds payable. To compute interest revenue, companies compute the effective-interest rate or yield at the time of investment and apply that rate to the beginning carrying amount (book value) for each interest period. The investment carrying amount is increased by the amortized discount or decreased by the amortized premium in each period.

Underlying Concepts

The use of some simpler method that yields results similar to the effective-interest method is an application of the materiality concept.

Illustration 17-3 shows the effect of the discount amortization on the interest revenue that Robinson records each period for its investment in Evermaster bonds.

ILLUSTRATION 17-3
Schedule of Interest Revenue and Bond Discount Amortization—Effective-Interest Method

8% Bonds Purchased to Yield 10%

Date	Cash Received	Interest Revenue	Bond Discount Amortization	Carrying Amount of Bonds
1/1/13				$ 92,278
7/1/13	$ 4,000[a]	$ 4,614[b]	$ 614[c]	92,892[d]
1/1/14	4,000	4,645	645	93,537
7/1/14	4,000	4,677	677	94,214
1/1/15	4,000	4,711	711	94,925
7/1/15	4,000	4,746	746	95,671
1/1/16	4,000	4,783	783	96,454
7/1/16	4,000	4,823	823	97,277
1/1/17	4,000	4,864	864	98,141
7/1/17	4,000	4,907	907	99,048
1/1/18	4,000	4,952	952	100,000
	$40,000	$47,722	$7,722	

[a]$4,000 = $100,000 × .08 × $\frac{6}{12}$
[b]$4,614 = $92,278 × .10 × $\frac{6}{12}$
[c]$614 = $4,614 − $4,000
[d]$92,892 = $92,278 + $614

Robinson records the receipt of the first semiannual interest payment on July 1, 2013 (using the data in Illustration 17-3), as follows.

July 1, 2013

Cash	4,000	
Debt Investments	614	
Interest Revenue		4,614

Because Robinson is on a calendar-year basis, it accrues interest and amortizes the discount at December 31, 2013, as follows.

December 31, 2013

Interest Receivable	4,000	
Debt Investments	645	
Interest Revenue		4,645

Again, Illustration 17-3 shows the interest and amortization amounts.

[3]Companies generally record investments acquired at par, at a discount, or at a premium in the accounts at cost, including brokerage and other fees but excluding the accrued interest. They generally do not record investments at maturity value. The use of a separate discount or premium account as a valuation account is acceptable procedure for investments, but in practice companies do not widely use it.

Robinson reports its investment in Evermaster bonds in its December 31, 2013, financial statements, as follows.

ILLUSTRATION 17-4
Reporting of Held-to-Maturity Securities

Balance Sheet	
Current assets	
Interest receivable	$ 4,000
Long-term investments	
Debt investments (held-to-maturity)	$93,537
Income Statement	
Other revenues and gains	
Interest revenue	$ 9,259

Sometimes, a company sells a held-to-maturity debt security so close to its maturity date that a change in the market interest rate would not significantly affect the security's fair value. Such a sale may be considered a sale at maturity and would not call into question the company's original intent to hold the investment to maturity. Let's assume, as an example, that Robinson Company sells its investment in Evermaster bonds on November 1, 2017, at $99^3/_4$ plus accrued interest. The discount amortization from July 1, 2017, to November 1, 2017, is $635 ($^4/_6 \times$ $952). Robinson records this discount amortization as follows.

November 1, 2017		
Debt Investments	635	
Interest Revenue		635

Illustration 17-5 shows the computation of the realized gain on the sale.

ILLUSTRATION 17-5
Computation of Gain on Sale of Bonds

Selling price of bonds (exclusive of accrued interest)		$99,750
Less: Book value of bonds on November 1, 2017:		
Amortized cost, July 1, 2017	$99,048	
Add: Discount amortized for the period July 1, 2017, to November 1, 2017	635	99,683
Gain on sale of bonds		$ 67

Robinson records the sale of the bonds as:

November 1, 2017		
Cash	102,417	
Interest Revenue (4/6 × $4,000)		2,667
Debt Investments		99,683
Gain on Sale of Investments		67

The credit to Interest Revenue represents accrued interest for four months, for which the purchaser pays cash. The debit to Cash represents the selling price of the bonds plus accrued interest ($99,750 + $2,667). The credit to Debt Investments represents the book value of the bonds on the date of sale. The credit to Gain on Sale of Investments represents the excess of the selling price over the book value of the bonds.

Available-for-Sale Securities

Underlying Concepts

Recognizing unrealized gains and losses is an application of the concept of comprehensive income.

Companies like **Amazon.com** report **available-for-sale** securities at fair value. It records the unrealized gains and losses related to changes in the fair value of available-for-sale debt securities in an unrealized holding gain or loss account. Amazon adds (subtracts) this amount to other comprehensive income for the

Calculator Solution for Bond Price

	Inputs	Answer
N	10	
I	4	
PV	?	−108,111
PMT	5,000	
FV	100,000	

period. Other comprehensive income is then added to (subtracted from) accumulated other comprehensive income, which is shown as a separate component of stockholders' equity until realized. Thus, **companies report available-for-sale securities at fair value on the balance sheet but do not report changes in fair value as part of net income until after selling the security**. This approach reduces the volatility of net income.

Example: Single Security

To illustrate the accounting for available-for-sale securities, assume that Graff Corporation purchases $100,000, 10 percent, five-year bonds on January 1, 2013, with interest payable on July 1 and January 1. The bonds sell for $108,111, which results in a bond premium of $8,111 and an effective-interest rate of 8 percent.

Graff records the purchase of the bonds as follows.

January 1, 2013

Debt Investments	108,111	
Cash		108,111

Illustration 17-6 discloses the effect of the premium amortization on the interest revenue Graff records each period using the effective-interest method.

ILLUSTRATION 17-6
Schedule of Interest Revenue and Bond Premium Amortization—Effective-Interest Method

10% Bonds Purchased to Yield 8%

Date	Cash Received	Interest Revenue	Bond Premium Amortization	Carrying Amount of Bonds
1/1/13				$108,111
7/1/13	$ 5,000[a]	$ 4,324[b]	$ 676[c]	107,435[d]
1/1/14	5,000	4,297	703	106,732
7/1/14	5,000	4,269	731	106,001
1/1/15	5,000	4,240	760	105,241
7/1/15	5,000	4,210	790	104,451
1/1/16	5,000	4,178	822	103,629
7/1/16	5,000	4,145	855	102,774
1/1/17	5,000	4,111	889	101,885
7/1/17	5,000	4,075	925	100,960
1/1/18	5,000	4,040	960	100,000
	$50,000	$41,889	$8,111	

[a]$5,000 = $100,000 × .10 × 6/12
[b]$4,324 = $108,111 × .08 × 6/12
[c]$676 = $5,000 − $4,324
[d]$107,435 = $108,111 − $676

The entry to record interest revenue on July 1, 2013, is as follows.

July 1, 2013

Cash	5,000	
Debt Investments		676
Interest Revenue		4,324

At December 31, 2013, Graff makes the following entry to recognize interest revenue.

December 31, 2013

Interest Receivable	5,000	
Debt Investments		703
Interest Revenue		4,297

As a result, Graff reports revenue for 2013 of $8,621 ($4,324 + $4,297).

To apply the fair value method to these debt investments, assume that at year-end the fair value of the bonds is $105,000 and that the carrying amount of the investments is $106,732. Comparing this fair value with the carrying amount (amortized cost) of the bonds at December 31, 2013, Graff recognizes an unrealized holding loss of $1,732 ($106,732 − $105,000). It reports this loss as other comprehensive income. Graff makes the following entry.

December 31, 2013		
Unrealized Holding Gain or Loss—Equity	1,732	
Fair Value Adjustment (available-for-sale)		1,732

Graff uses a valuation account instead of crediting the Debt Investments account. The use of the **Fair Value Adjustment** (available-for-sale) account enables the company to maintain a record of its amortized cost. Because the adjustment account has a credit balance in this case, Graff subtracts it from the balance of the Debt Investments account to determine fair value. Graff reports this fair value amount on the balance sheet. At each reporting date, Graff reports the bonds at fair value with an adjustment to the Unrealized Holding Gain or Loss—Equity account.

Underlying Concepts

Companies report some debt securities at fair value not only because the information is relevant but also because it is representationally faithful.

Example: Portfolio of Securities

To illustrate the accounting for a portfolio of securities, assume that Webb Corporation has two debt securities classified as available-for-sale. Illustration 17-7 identifies the amortized cost, fair value, and the amount of the unrealized gain or loss.

ILLUSTRATION 17-7
Computation of Fair Value Adjustment—Available-for-Sale Securities (2014)

AVAILABLE-FOR-SALE DEBT SECURITY PORTFOLIO
DECEMBER 31, 2014

Investments	Amortized Cost	Fair Value	Unrealized Gain (Loss)
Watson Corporation 8% bonds	$ 93,537	$103,600	$ 10,063
Anacomp Corporation 10% bonds	200,000	180,400	(19,600)
Total of portfolio	$293,537	$284,000	(9,537)
Previous fair value adjustment balance			-0-
Fair value adjustment—Cr.			$ (9,537)

The fair value of Webb's available-for-sale portfolio totals $284,000. The gross unrealized gains are $10,063, and the gross unrealized losses are $19,600, resulting in a net unrealized loss of $9,537. That is, the fair value of available-for-sale securities is $9,537 lower than its amortized cost. Webb makes an adjusting entry to a valuation allowance to record the decrease in value and to record the loss as follows.

December 31, 2014		
Unrealized Holding Gain or Loss—Equity	9,537	
Fair Value Adjustment (available-for-sale)		9,537

Webb reports the unrealized holding loss of $9,537 as other comprehensive income and a reduction of stockholders' equity. Recall that companies exclude from net income any unrealized holding gains and losses related to available-for-sale securities.

Sale of Available-for-Sale Securities

If a company sells bonds carried as investments in available-for-sale securities before the maturity date, it must make entries to remove from the Debt Investments account the amortized cost of bonds sold. To illustrate, assume that Webb Corporation sold the Watson bonds (from Illustration 17-7) on July 1, 2015, for $90,000, at which time it had an amortized cost of $94,214. Illustration 17-8 (on page 958) shows the computation of the realized loss.

ILLUSTRATION 17-8
Computation of Loss on Sale of Bonds

Amortized cost (Watson bonds)	$94,214
Less: Selling price of bonds	90,000
Loss on sale of bonds	$ 4,214

Webb records the sale of the Watson bonds as follows.

July 1, 2015		
Cash	90,000	
Loss on Sale of Investments	4,214	
Debt Investments		94,214

Webb reports this realized loss in the "Other expenses and losses" section of the income statement.[4] Assuming no other purchases and sales of bonds in 2015, Webb on December 31, 2015, prepares the information shown in Illustration 17-9.

ILLUSTRATION 17-9
Computation of Fair Value Adjustment—Available-for-Sale (2015)

AVAILABLE-FOR-SALE DEBT SECURITY PORTFOLIO
DECEMBER 31, 2015

Investments	Amortized Cost	Fair Value	Unrealized Gain (Loss)
Anacomp Corporation 10% bonds (total portfolio)	$200,000	$195,000	$(5,000)
Previous fair value adjustment balance—Cr.			(9,537)
Fair value adjustment—Dr.			$ 4,537

Webb has an unrealized holding loss of $5,000. However, the Fair Value Adjustment (available-for-sale) account already has a credit balance of $9,537. To reduce the adjustment account balance to $5,000, Webb debits it for $4,537, as follows.

December 31, 2015		
Fair Value Adjustment (available-for-sale)	4,537	
Unrealized Holding Gain or Loss—Equity		4,537

Financial Statement Presentation

Webb's December 31, 2015, balance sheet and the 2015 income statement include the following items and amounts (the Anacomp bonds are long-term investments but are not intended to be held to maturity).

ILLUSTRATION 17-10
Reporting of Available-for-Sale Securities

Balance Sheet	
Current assets	
Interest receivable	$ xxx
Investments	
Debt investments (available-for-sale)	$195,000
Stockholders' equity	
Accumulated other comprehensive loss	$ 5,000
Income Statement	
Other revenues and gains	
Interest revenue	$ xxx
Other expenses and losses	
Loss on sale of investments	$ 4,214

[4]On the date of sale, any unrealized gains or losses on the sold security is not adjusted in accumulated other comprehensive income. This adjustment occurs at year-end when the portfolio is evaluated for fair value adjustment.

Some favor including the unrealized holding gain or loss in net income rather than showing it as other comprehensive income.[5] However, some companies, particularly financial institutions, note that recognizing gains and losses on assets, but not liabilities, introduces substantial volatility in net income. They argue that hedges often exist between assets and liabilities so that gains in assets are offset by losses in liabilities, and vice versa. In short, to recognize gains and losses only on the asset side is unfair and not representative of the economic activities of the company.

This argument convinced the FASB. As a result, companies **do not include in net income** these unrealized gains and losses. **[3]** However, even this approach solves only some of the problems because **volatility of capital** still results. This is of concern to financial institutions because regulators restrict financial institutions' operations based on their level of capital. However, companies can still manage their net income by engaging in **gains trading** (i.e., selling the winners and holding the losers).

What do the numbers mean? *WHAT IS FAIR VALUE?*

In the fall of 2000, Wall Street brokerage firm **Morgan Stanley** told investors that rumors of big losses in its bond portfolio were "greatly exaggerated." As it turns out, Morgan Stanley also was exaggerating.

As a result, the SEC accused Morgan Stanley of violating securities laws by overstating the value of certain bonds by $75 million. The SEC said the overvaluations stemmed more from wishful thinking than reality, which violated generally accepted accounting principles. "In effect, Morgan Stanley valued its positions at the price at which it thought a willing buyer and seller should enter into an exchange, rather than at a price at which a willing buyer and a willing seller would enter into a current exchange," the SEC wrote.

Especially egregious, stated one accounting expert, were the SEC's findings that Morgan Stanley in some instances used its own more optimistic assumptions as a substitute for external pricing sources. "What that is saying is: 'Fair value is what you want the value to be. Pick a number . . .' That's especially troublesome."

As indicated in the opening story, both the FASB and the IASB are assessing what is fair and what isn't when it comes to assigning valuations. Concerns over the issue caught fire after the collapses of **Enron Corp.** and other energy traders that abused the wide discretion given them under fair value accounting. Investors have expressed similar worries about some financial companies, which use internal—and subjectively designed—mathematical models to come up with valuations when market quotes aren't available. Similar concerns have been raised when companies revalue their debt obligations when they apply the fair value option.

Sources: Adapted from Susanne Craig and Jonathan Weil, "SEC Targets Morgan Stanley Values," *Wall Street Journal* (November 8, 2004), p. C3; Floyd Norris, "Distortions in Baffling Financial Statements," *The New York Times* (November 10, 2011); and Marie Leone, "The Fair Value Deadbeat Debate Returns," *CFO.com* (June 25, 2009).

Trading Securities

Companies hold **trading securities** with the intention of selling them in a short period of time. "Trading" in this context means frequent buying and selling. Companies thus use trading securities to generate profits from short-term differences in price. Companies generally hold these securities for less than three months, some for merely days or hours.

Companies report trading securities at fair value, with unrealized holding gains and losses reported as part of net income. Similar to held-to-maturity or available-for-sale investments, companies are required to amortize any discount or premium. A **holding gain or loss** is the net change in the fair value of a security from one period to another, exclusive of dividend or interest revenue recognized but not received. In short, the FASB says to adjust the trading securities to fair value, at each reporting date. In addition, companies report the change in value as part of net income, not other comprehensive income.

[5]In Chapter 4, we discussed the concept of, and reporting for, other comprehensive income.

To illustrate, assume that on December 31, 2014, Western Publishing Corporation determined its trading securities portfolio to be as shown in Illustration 17-11. (Assume that 2014 is the first year that Western Publishing held trading securities.) At the date of acquisition, Western Publishing recorded these trading securities at cost, including brokerage commissions and taxes, in the account entitled Debt Investments. This is the first valuation of this recently purchased portfolio.

ILLUSTRATION 17-11
Computation of Fair Value Adjustment—Trading Securities Portfolio (2014)

TRADING DEBT SECURITY PORTFOLIO
DECEMBER 31, 2014

Investments	Amortized Cost	Fair Value	Unrealized Gain (Loss)
Burlington Northern 6% bonds	$ 43,860	$ 51,500	$ 7,640
GM Corporation 7% bonds	184,230	175,200	(9,030)
Time Warner 8% bonds	86,360	91,500	5,140
Total of portfolio	$314,450	$318,200	3,750
Previous fair value adjustment balance			–0–
Fair value adjustment—Dr.			$ 3,750

The total cost of Western Publishing's trading portfolio is $314,450. The gross unrealized gains are $12,780 ($7,640 + $5,140), and the gross unrealized losses are $9,030, resulting in a net unrealized gain of $3,750. The fair value of trading securities is $3,750 greater than its cost.

At December 31, Western Publishing makes an adjusting entry to a valuation allowance, referred to as Fair Value Adjustment (trading), to record the increase in value and to record the unrealized holding gain.

December 31, 2014		
Fair Value Adjustment (trading)	3,750	
Unrealized Holding Gain or Loss—Income		3,750

Because the Fair Value Adjustment account balance is a debit, Western Publishing adds it to the cost of the Debt Investments account to arrive at a fair value for the trading securities. Western Publishing reports this fair value amount on the balance sheet.

As with other debt investments, when a trading investment is sold, the Debt Investments account is reduced by the amount of the amortized cost of the bonds. Any realized gain or loss is recorded in the "Other expenses and losses" section of the income statement. The Fair Value Adjustment account is then adjusted at year-end for the unrealized gains or losses on the remaining securities in the trading investment portfolio.

When securities are actively traded, the FASB believes that the investments should be reported at fair value on the balance sheet. In addition, changes in fair value (unrealized gains and losses) should be reported in income. Such reporting on trading securities provides more relevant information to existing and prospective stockholders.

INVESTMENTS IN EQUITY SECURITIES

LEARNING OBJECTIVE 3
Identify the categories of equity securities and describe the accounting and reporting treatment for each category.

Equity securities represent ownership interests such as common, preferred, or other capital stock. They also include rights to acquire or dispose of ownership interests at an agreed-upon or determinable price, such as in warrants, rights, and call or put options. Companies do not treat convertible debt securities as equity securities. Nor do they treat as equity securities redeemable preferred stock (which must be redeemed for common stock). The cost of equity securities includes the purchase price of the security plus broker's commissions and other fees incidental to the purchase.

The degree to which one corporation (**investor**) acquires an interest in the common stock of another corporation (**investee**) generally determines the accounting treatment for the investment subsequent to acquisition. The classification of such investments depends on the percentage of the investee voting stock that is held by the investor:

1. Holdings of less than 20 percent (**fair value method**)—investor has passive interest.
2. Holdings between 20 percent and 50 percent (**equity method**)—investor has significant influence.
3. Holdings of more than 50 percent (**consolidated statements**)—investor has controlling interest.

Illustration 17-12 lists these levels of interest or influence and the corresponding valuation and reporting method that companies must apply to the investment.

ILLUSTRATION 17-12
Levels of Influence Determine Accounting Methods

Percentage of Ownership	0% ⟷ 20%	⟷ 50%	⟷ 100%
Level of Influence	Little or None	Significant	Control
Valuation Method	Fair Value Method	Equity Method	Consolidation

The accounting and reporting for equity securities therefore depend on the level of influence and the type of security involved, as shown in Illustration 17-13.

ILLUSTRATION 17-13
Accounting and Reporting for Equity Securities by Category

Category	Valuation	Unrealized Holding Gains or Losses	Other Income Effects
Holdings less than 20%			
1. Available-for-sale	Fair value	Recognized in "Other comprehensive income" and as separate component of stockholders' equity	Dividends declared; gains and losses from sale.
2. Trading	Fair value	Recognized in net income	Dividends declared; gains and losses from sale.
Holdings between 20% and 50%	Equity	Not recognized	Proportionate share of investee's net income.
Holdings more than 50%	Consolidation	Not recognized	Not applicable.

Holdings of Less Than 20%

When an investor has an interest of less than 20 percent, it is presumed that the investor has little or no influence over the investee. In such cases, if market prices are available subsequent to acquisition, the company values and reports the investment using the **fair value method**.[6] The fair value method requires that companies classify equity securities at acquisition as **available-for-sale securities** or **trading securities**. Because equity securities have no maturity date, companies cannot classify them as held-to-maturity.

[6]If an equity investment is not publicly traded, a company values the investment and reports it at cost in periods subsequent to acquisition. This approach is often referred to as the cost method. Companies recognize dividends when received. They value the portfolio and report it at acquisition cost. Companies only recognize gains or losses after selling the securities.

Available-for-Sale Securities

Upon acquisition, companies record available-for-sale securities at cost.[7] To illustrate, assume that on November 3, 2014, Republic Corporation purchased common stock of three companies, each investment representing less than a 20 percent interest.

	Cost
Northwest Industries, Inc.	$259,700
Campbell Soup Co.	317,500
St. Regis Pulp Co.	141,350
Total cost	$718,550

Republic records these investments as follows.

November 3, 2014		
Equity Investments	718,550	
Cash		718,550

On December 6, 2014, Republic receives a cash dividend of $4,200 on its investment in the common stock of Campbell Soup Co. It records the cash dividend as follows.

December 6, 2014		
Cash	4,200	
Dividend Revenue		4,200

All three of the investee companies reported net income for the year, but only Campbell Soup declared and paid a dividend to Republic. But, recall that when an investor owns less than 20 percent of the common stock of another corporation, it is presumed that the investor has relatively little influence on the investee. As a result, **net income of the investee is not a proper basis for recognizing income from the investment by the investor**. Why? Because the increased net assets resulting from profitable operations may be permanently retained for use in the investee's business. Therefore, **the investor recognizes net income only when the investee declares cash dividends**.

At December 31, 2014, Republic's available-for-sale equity security portfolio has the cost and fair value shown in Illustration 17-14.

ILLUSTRATION 17-14
Computation of Fair Value Adjustment—Available-for-Sale Equity Security Portfolio (2014)

AVAILABLE-FOR-SALE EQUITY SECURITY PORTFOLIO
DECEMBER 31, 2014

Investments	Cost	Fair Value	Unrealized Gain (Loss)
Northwest Industries, Inc.	$259,700	$275,000	$ 15,300
Campbell Soup Co.	317,500	304,000	(13,500)
St. Regis Pulp Co.	141,350	104,000	(37,350)
Total of portfolio	$718,550	$683,000	(35,550)
Previous fair value adjustment balance			-0-
Fair value adjustment—Cr.			$(35,550)

[7]Companies should record equity securities acquired in **exchange for noncash consideration** (property or services) at (1) the fair value of the consideration given, or (2) the fair value of the security received, whichever is more clearly determinable. Accounting for numerous purchases of securities requires the preservation of information regarding the cost of individual purchases, as well as the dates of purchases and sales. If specific identification is not possible, companies may use average-cost for multiple purchases of the same class of security. The **first-in, first-out method (FIFO)** of assigning costs to investments at the time of sale is also acceptable and normally employed.

For Republic's available-for-sale equity securities portfolio, the gross unrealized gains are $15,300, and the gross unrealized losses are $50,850 ($13,500 + $37,350), resulting in a net unrealized loss of $35,550. The fair value of the available-for-sale securities portfolio is below cost by $35,550.

As with available-for-sale **debt** securities, Republic records the net unrealized gains and losses related to changes in the fair value of available-for-sale **equity** securities in an Unrealized Holding Gain or Loss—Equity account. Republic reports this amount as a **part of other comprehensive income and as a component of other accumulated comprehensive income (reported in stockholders' equity) until realized**. In this case, Republic prepares an adjusting entry debiting the Unrealized Holding Gain or Loss—Equity account and crediting the Fair Value Adjustment account to record the decrease in fair value and to record the loss as follows.

December 31, 2014		
Unrealized Holding Gain or Loss—Equity	35,550	
Fair Value Adjustment (available-for-sale)		35,550

On January 23, 2015, Republic sold all of its Northwest Industries, Inc. common stock receiving net proceeds of $287,220. Illustration 17-15 shows the computation of the realized gain on the sale.

Net proceeds from sale	$287,220
Cost of **Northwest** shares	259,700
Gain on sale of stock	$ 27,520

ILLUSTRATION 17-15
Computation of Gain on Sale of Stock

Republic records the sale as follows.

January 23, 2015		
Cash	287,220	
Equity Investments		259,700
Gain on Sale of Investments		27,520

In addition, assume that on February 10, 2015, Republic purchased 20,000 shares of Continental Trucking at a market price of $12.75 per share plus brokerage commissions of $1,850 (total cost, $256,850).

Illustration 17-16 lists Republic's portfolio of available-for-sale securities, as of December 31, 2015.

AVAILABLE-FOR-SALE EQUITY SECURITY PORTFOLIO
DECEMBER 31, 2015

Investments	Cost	Fair Value	Unrealized Gain (Loss)
Continental Trucking	$256,850	$278,350	$ 21,500
Campbell Soup Co.	317,500	362,550	45,050
St. Regis Pulp Co.	141,350	139,050	(2,300)
Total of portfolio	$715,700	$779,950	64,250
Previous fair value adjustment balance—Cr.			(35,550)
Fair value adjustment—Dr.			$ 99,800

ILLUSTRATION 17-16
Computation of Fair Value Adjustment—Available-for-Sale Equity Security Portfolio (2015)

At December 31, 2015, the fair value of Republic's available-for-sale equity securities portfolio exceeds cost by $64,250 (unrealized gain). The Fair Value Adjustment account had a credit balance of $35,550 at December 31, 2015. To adjust its December 31, 2015, available-for-sale portfolio to fair value, the company debits the Fair Value Adjustment account for $99,800 ($35,550 + $64,250). Republic records this adjustment as follows.

December 31, 2015		
Fair Value Adjustment (available-for-sale)	99,800	
Unrealized Holding Gain or Loss—Equity		99,800

Trading Securities

The accounting entries to record trading equity securities are the same as for available-for-sale equity securities, except for recording the unrealized holding gain or loss. For trading equity securities, companies **report the unrealized holding gain or loss as part of net income**. Thus, the account titled Unrealized Holding Gain or Loss—Income is used.

What do the numbers mean? *MORE DISCLOSURE, PLEASE*

How to account for investment securities is a particularly sensitive area, given the large amounts of equity investments involved. And presently companies report investments in equity securities at cost, equity, fair value, and full consolidation, depending on the circumstances. As a recent SEC study noted, "there are so many different accounting treatments for investments that it raises the question of whether they are all needed."

Presented in the right-hand column is an estimate of the percentage of companies on the major exchanges that have investments in the equity of other entities.

Investments in the Equity of Other Companies

Categorized by Accounting Treatment	Percent of Companies
Presenting consolidated financial statements	91.1%
Reporting equity method investments	23.5
Reporting cost method investments*	17.4
Reporting available-for-sale investments	37.4
Reporting trading investments	6.2

*If the equity investments are not publicly traded, the company often accounts for the investment under the cost method. Changes in value are therefore not recognized unless there is impairment.

As the table indicates, many companies have equity investments of some type. These investments can be substantial. For example, the total amount of equity-method investments appearing on company balance sheets is approximately $403 billion, and the amount shown in the income statements in any one year for all companies is approximately $38 billion.

Source: "Report and Recommendations Pursuant to Section 401(c) of the Sarbanes-Oxley Act of 2002 on Arrangements with Off-Balance Sheet Implications, Special Purpose Entities, and Transparency of Filings by Issuers," United States Securities and Exchange Commission—Office of Chief Accountant, Office of Economic Analyses, Division of Corporation Finance (June 2005), pp. 36–39.

Holdings Between 20% and 50%

LEARNING OBJECTIVE 4
Explain the equity method of accounting and compare it to the fair value method for equity securities.

An investor corporation may hold an interest of less than 50 percent in an investee corporation and thus not possess legal control. However, an investment in voting stock of less than 50 percent can still give the investor the ability to exercise significant influence over the operating and financial policies of the investee company. [4] **Significant influence** may be indicated in several ways. Examples include representation on the board of directors, participation in policy-making processes, material intercompany transactions, interchange of managerial personnel, or technological dependency.

Another important consideration is the extent of ownership by an investor in relation to the concentration of other shareholdings. To achieve a reasonable degree of uniformity in application of the "significant influence" criterion, the profession concluded that an investment (direct or indirect) of 20 percent or more of the voting stock of an investee should lead to a presumption that in the absence of evidence to the contrary, an investor has the ability to exercise significant influence over an investee.[8]

[8]Cases in which an investment of 20 percent or more might not enable an investor to exercise significant influence include (1) the investee opposes the investor's acquisition of its stock, (2) the investor and investee sign an agreement under which the investor surrenders significant shareholder rights, (3) the investor's ownership share does not result in "significant influence" because majority ownership of the investee is concentrated among a small group of shareholders who operate the investee without regard to the views of the investor, and (4) the investor tries and fails to obtain representation on the investee's board of directors. [5]

In instances of "significant influence" (generally an investment of 20 percent or more), the investor must account for the investment using the **equity method**.

Equity Method

Under the **equity method**, the investor and the investee acknowledge a substantive economic relationship. The company originally records the investment at the cost of the shares acquired but subsequently adjusts the amount each period for changes in the investee's net assets. That is, **the investor's proportionate share of the earnings (losses) of the investee periodically increases (decreases) the investment's carrying amount. All cash dividends received by the investor from the investee also decrease the investment's carrying amount.** The equity method recognizes that investee's earnings increase investee's net assets, and that investee's losses and dividends decrease these net assets.

To illustrate the equity method and compare it with the fair value method, assume that Maxi Company purchases a 20 percent interest in Mini Company. To apply the fair value method in this example, assume that Maxi does not have the ability to exercise significant influence, and classifies the securities as available-for-sale. Where this example applies the equity method, assume that the 20 percent interest permits Maxi to exercise significant influence. Illustration 17-17 shows the entries.

ILLUSTRATION 17-17
Comparison of Fair Value Method and Equity Method

ENTRIES BY MAXI COMPANY

Fair Value Method			Equity Method		
On January 2, 2014, Maxi Company acquired 48,000 shares (20% of Mini Company common stock) at a cost of $10 a share.					
Equity Investments	480,000		Equity Investments	480,000	
Cash		480,000	Cash		480,000
For the year 2014, Mini Company reported net income of $200,000; Maxi Company's share is 20%, or $40,000.					
No entry			Equity Investments	40,000	
			Investment Income		40,000
At December 31, 2014, the 48,000 shares of Mini Company have a fair value (market price) of $12 a share, or $576,000.					
Fair Value Adjustment (available-for-sale)	96,000		No entry		
Unrealized Holding Gain or Loss—Equity		96,000			
On January 28, 2015, Mini Company announced and paid a cash dividend of $100,000; Maxi Company received 20%, or $20,000.					
Cash	20,000		Cash	20,000	
Dividend Revenue		20,000	Equity Investments		20,000
For the year 2015, Mini reported a net loss of $50,000; Maxi Company's share is 20%, or $10,000.					
No entry			Investment Loss	10,000	
			Equity Investments		10,000
At December 31, 2015, the Mini Company 48,000 shares have a fair value (market price) of $11 a share, or $528,000.					
Unrealized Holding Gain or Loss—Equity	48,000		No entry		
Fair Value Adjustment (available-for-sale)		48,000			

Note that under the fair value method, Maxi reports as revenue only the cash dividends received from Mini. **The earning of net income by Mini (the investee) is not**

considered a proper basis for recognition of income from the investment by Maxi (the investor). Why? Mini may permanently retain in the business any increased net assets resulting from its profitable operation. Therefore, Maxi only recognizes revenue when it receives dividends from Mini.

> **International Perspective**
>
> IFRS has similar accounting rules for significant influence equity investments.

Under the equity method, Maxi reports as revenue its share of the net income reported by Mini. Maxi records the cash dividends received from Mini as a decrease in the investment carrying value. As a result, Maxi records its share of the net income of Mini in the year when it is recognized. With significant influence, Maxi can ensure that Mini will pay dividends, if desired, on any net asset increases resulting from net income. To wait until receiving a dividend ignores the fact that Maxi is better off if the investee has earned income.

Using dividends as a basis for recognizing income poses an additional problem. For example, assume that the investee reports a net loss. However, the investor exerts influence to force a dividend payment from the investee. In this case, the investor reports income, even though the investee is experiencing a loss. **In other words, using dividends as a basis for recognizing income fails to report properly the economics of the situation.**

For some companies, equity accounting can be a real pain to the bottom line. For example, **Amazon.com**, the pioneer of Internet retailing, at one time struggled to turn a profit. Furthermore, some of Amazon's equity investments had resulted in Amazon's earnings performance going from bad to worse. At one time, Amazon disclosed equity stakes in such companies as **Altera International**, **Basis Technology**, **Drugstore.com**, and **Eziba.com**. These equity investees reported losses that made Amazon's already bad bottom line even worse, accounting for up to 22 percent of its reported loss in one year alone.

Investee Losses Exceed Carrying Amount. If an investor's share of the investee's losses exceeds the carrying amount of the investment, should the investor recognize additional losses? Ordinarily, the investor should discontinue applying the equity method and not recognize additional losses.

If the investor's potential loss is not limited to the amount of its original investment (by guarantee of the investee's obligations or other commitment to provide further financial support) or if imminent return to profitable operations by the investee appears to be assured, the investor should recognize additional losses. **[6]**

Holdings of More Than 50%

When one corporation acquires a voting interest of more than 50 percent in another corporation, it is said to have a **controlling interest**. In such a relationship, the investor corporation is referred to as the **parent** and the investee corporation as the **subsidiary**. Companies present the investment in the common stock of the subsidiary as a long-term investment on the separate financial statements of the parent.

> **International Perspective**
>
> In contrast to U.S. firms, financial statements of non-U.S. companies often include both consolidated (group) statements and parent company financial statements.

When the parent treats the investment as a subsidiary, the parent generally prepares **consolidated financial statements**. Consolidated financial statements treat the parent and subsidiary corporations as a single economic entity. (Advanced accounting courses extensively discuss the subject of when and how to prepare consolidated financial statements.) Whether or not consolidated financial statements are prepared, the parent company generally accounts for the investment in the subsidiary **using the equity method** as explained in the previous section of this chapter.

What do the numbers mean? WHO'S IN CONTROL HERE?

Molson Coors Brewing Company owns 42 percent of the MillerCoors' brewing venture operating in the United States and Puerto Rico. As part of the agreement, Molson helps the MillerCoors unit produce and sell its products in the U.S. and Puerto Rican markets. Lenovo Group owns a significant percentage (45 percent) of the shares of Beijing Lenovo Parasaga Information Technology Co. (which develops and distributes computer software). Beijing Lenovo is important to Lenovo because it develops and sells the software that is used with Lenovo computers. In return, Beijing Lenovo depends on Lenovo to provide the products that make its software and services valuable, as well as perform significant customer and market support. Indeed, it can be said that to some extent Lenovo controls Beijing Lenovo, which would likely not exist without the support of Lenovo.

As you have learned, because a company like Lenovo owns less than 50 percent of the shares, it does not consolidate Beijing Lenovo but instead accounts for its investment using the *equity method*. Under the equity method, Lenovo reports a single income item for its profits from Beijing Lenovo and only the net amount of its investment in the statement of financial position. Equity method accounting gives Lenovo a pristine statement of financial position and income statement, by separating the assets and liabilities and the profit margins of the related companies from its laptop-computer businesses.

Some are critical of equity method accounting. They argue that some investees, like Beijing Lenovo, should be consolidated. The FASB has issued rules to consider other factors, in addition to voting interests, when determining whether an entity should be consolidated. We discuss these rules in Appendix 17B. The FASB has tightened up consolidation rules, so that companies will be more likely to consolidate more of their 20–50-percent-owned investments. Consolidation of entities, such as MillerCoors and Beijing Lenovo, is warranted if Molson and Lenovo effectively control their equity method investments.

ADDITIONAL MEASUREMENT ISSUES

Fair Value Option

5 LEARNING OBJECTIVE
Describe the accounting for the fair value option and for impairments of debt and equity investments.

As indicated in earlier chapters, companies have the option to report most financial instruments at fair value, with all gains and losses related to changes in fair value reported in the income statement. This option is applied on an instrument-by-instrument basis. The fair value option is generally available only at the time a company first purchases the financial asset or incurs a financial liability. If a company chooses to use the fair value option, it must measure this instrument at fair value until the company no longer has ownership.

For example, assume that Abbott Laboratories purchased debt securities in 2014 that it classified as held-to-maturity. Abbott does not choose to report this security using the fair value option. In 2015, Abbott buys another held-to-maturity debt security. Abbott decides to report this security using the fair value option. Once it chooses the fair value option for the security bought in 2015, the decision is irrevocable (may not be changed). In addition, Abbott does not have the option to value the held-to-maturity security purchased in 2014 at fair value in 2015 or in subsequent periods.

Many support the use of the fair value option as a step closer to total fair value reporting for financial instruments. They believe this treatment leads to an improvement in financial reporting. Others argue that the fair value option is confusing. A company can choose from period to period whether to use the fair value option for any new investment in a financial instrument. By permitting an instrument-by-instrument approach, companies are able to report some financial instruments at fair value but not others. To illustrate the accounting issues related to the fair value option, we discuss two different situations.

Available-for-Sale Securities

Available-for-sale securities are presently reported at fair value, with any unrealized gains and losses recorded as part of other comprehensive income. Assume that Hardy Company purchases stock in Fielder Company during 2014 that it classifies as available-for-sale. At December 31, 2014, the cost of this security is $100,000; its fair value at December 31, 2014, is $125,000. If Hardy chooses the fair value option to account for the Fielder Company stock, it makes the following entry at December 31, 2014.

Equity Investments	25,000	
Unrealized Holding Gain or Loss—Income		25,000

In this situation, Hardy uses an account titled Equity Investments to record the change in fair value at December 31. It does not use a Fair Value Adjustment account because the accounting for a fair value option is on an investment-by-investment basis rather than on a portfolio basis. Because Hardy selected the fair value option, the unrealized gain or loss is recorded as part of net income. Hardy must continue to use the fair value method to record this investment until it no longer has ownership of the security.

Equity Method Investments

Companies may also use the fair value option for investments that otherwise follow the equity method of accounting. To illustrate, assume that Durham Company holds a 28 percent stake in Suppan Inc. Durham purchased the investment in 2014 for $930,000. At December 31, 2014, the fair value of the investment is $900,000. Durham elects to report the investment in Suppan using the fair value option. The entry to record this investment is as follows.

Unrealized Holding Gain or Loss—Income	30,000	
Equity Investments		30,000

In contrast to equity method accounting, if the fair value option is chosen, Durham does not report its pro rata share of the income or loss from Suppan. In addition, any dividend payments are credited to Dividend Revenue and therefore do not reduce the Equity Investments account.

International Perspective

IFRS does not allow the use of the fair value option for equity method investments. The FASB is considering a proposal to converge to IFRS in this area.

One major advantage of using the fair value option for this type of investment is that it addresses confusion about the equity method of accounting. In other words, what exactly does the one-line consolidation related to the equity method of accounting on the balance sheet tell investors? Many believe it does not provide information about liquidity or solvency, nor does it provide an indication of the worth of the company.

Evolving Issue FAIR VALUE CONTROVERSY

The reporting of investment securities is controversial. Some believe that all securities should be reported at fair value. Others believe they all should be stated at amortized cost. Still others favor the present approach. Here are some of the major unresolved issues:

- ***Measurement based on intent.*** Companies classify debt securities as held-to-maturity, available-for-sale, or trading. As a result, companies can report three identical debt securities in three different ways in the financial statements. Some argue such treatment is confusing. Furthermore, the held-to-maturity category relies on intent, a subjective evaluation. What is not subjective is the fair value of the debt instrument. In other words, the three classifications are subjective, resulting in arbitrary classifications.
- ***Gains trading.*** Companies can classify certain debt securities as held-to-maturity and therefore report them at amortized cost. Companies can classify other debt and equity

securities as available-for-sale and report them at fair value, with the unrealized gain or loss reported as other comprehensive income. In either case, a company can become involved in "gains trading" (also referred to as "cherry picking," "snacking," or "sell the best and keep the rest"). In **gains trading**, companies sell their "winners," reporting the gains in income, and hold on to the losers.

- ***Liabilities not fairly valued.*** Many argue that if companies report investment securities at fair value, they also should report liabilities at fair value. Why? By recognizing changes in value on only one side of the balance sheet (the asset side), a high degree of volatility can occur in the income and stockholders' equity amounts. Further, financial institutions are involved in asset and liability management (not just asset management). Viewing only one side may lead managers to make uneconomic decisions as a result of the accounting. The fair value option may address this concern to some extent. However, there is debate on the usefulness of fair value estimates for liabilities.

Impairment of Value

A company should evaluate every investment, at each reporting date, to determine if it has suffered **impairment**—a loss in value that is other than temporary. For example, if an investee experiences a bankruptcy or a significant liquidity crisis, the investor may suffer a permanent loss. **If the decline is judged to be other than temporary, a company writes down the cost basis of the individual security to a new cost basis.** The company accounts for the write-down as a realized loss. Therefore, it includes the amount in net income.

For debt securities, a company uses the impairment test to determine whether "it is probable that the investor will be unable to collect all amounts due according to the contractual terms."

For equity securities, the guideline is less precise. Any time realizable value is lower than the carrying amount of the investment, a company must consider an impairment. Factors involved include the length of time and the extent to which the fair value has been less than cost, the financial condition and near-term prospects of the issuer, and the intent and ability of the investor company to retain its investment to allow for any anticipated recovery in fair value.

To illustrate an impairment, assume that Strickler Company holds available-for-sale bond securities with a par value and amortized cost of $1 million. The fair value of these securities is $800,000. Strickler has previously reported an unrealized loss on these securities of $200,000 as part of other comprehensive income. In evaluating the securities, Strickler now determines that it probably will not collect all amounts due. In this case, it reports the unrealized loss of $200,000 as a loss on impairment of $200,000. Strickler includes this amount in income, with the bonds stated at their new cost basis. It records this impairment as follows.

Loss on Impairment	200,000	
Debt Investments		200,000

The new cost basis of the investment in debt securities is $800,000. Strickler includes subsequent increases and decreases in the fair value of impaired available-for-sale securities as other comprehensive income.[9]

Companies base impairment for debt and equity securities on a fair value test. This test differs slightly from the impairment test for loans that we discuss in Appendix 7B.

[9]In addition, any balance in the Unrealized Gain or Loss—Equity and Fair Value Adjustment accounts related to the impaired security would be eliminated. Companies may not amortize any discount related to the debt securities after recording the impairment. The new cost basis of impaired held-to-maturity securities does not change unless additional impairment occurs.

The FASB rejected the discounted cash flow alternative for securities because of the availability of market price information.[10]

An example of the criteria used by **Caterpillar** to assess impairment is provided in Illustration 17-18.

ILLUSTRATION 17-18
Disclosure of Impairment Assessment Criteria

Caterpillar, Inc.
Notes to Financial Statements

Note 1. Impairment of available-for-sale securities

Available-for-sale securities are reviewed monthly to identify market values below cost of 20% or more. If a decline for a debt security is in excess of 20% for six months, the investment is evaluated to determine if the decline is due to general declines in the marketplace or if the investment has been impaired and should be written down to market value. . . . After the six-month period, debt securities with declines from cost in excess of 20% are evaluated monthly for impairment. For equity securities, if a decline from cost of 20% or more continues for a 12-month period, an other than temporary impairment is recognized without continued analysis.

RECLASSIFICATIONS AND TRANSFERS

Reclassification Adjustments

LEARNING OBJECTIVE 6
Describe the reporting of reclassification adjustments and the accounting for transfers between categories.

As we indicated in Chapter 4, companies report changes in unrealized holding gains and losses related to available-for-sale securities as part of other comprehensive income. Companies may display the components of other comprehensive income in one of two ways: (1) in a combined statement of income and comprehensive income, or (2) in a separate statement of comprehensive income that begins with net income.

The reporting of changes in unrealized gains or losses in comprehensive income is straightforward unless a company sells securities during the year. In that case, double-counting results when the company reports realized gains or losses as part of net income but also shows the amounts as part of other comprehensive income in the current period or in previous periods.

To ensure that gains and losses are not counted twice when a sale occurs, a **reclassification adjustment** is necessary. To illustrate, assume that Open Company has the following two available-for-sale securities in its portfolio at the end of 2013 (its first year of operations).

ILLUSTRATION 17-19
Available-for-Sale Security Portfolio (2013)

Investments	Cost	Fair Value	Unrealized Holding Gain (Loss)
Lehman Inc. common stock	$ 80,000	$105,000	$25,000
Woods Co. common stock	120,000	135,000	15,000
Total of portfolio	$200,000	$240,000	40,000
Previous fair value adjustment balance			–0–
Fair value adjustment—Dr.			$40,000

The entry to record the unrealized holding gain in 2013 is as follows.

Fair Value Adjustment (available-for-sale)	40,000	
Unrealized Holding Gain or Loss—Equity		40,000

[10]The FASB is currently exploring a new impairment model for financial instruments. The model focuses on the recognition of all expected losses which are "an estimate of contractual cash flows not expected to be collected." This differs from the current model, known as the incurred loss model, which requires evidence that a loss actually has occurred before the loss can be recorded.

If Open Company reports net income in 2013 of $350,000, it presents a statement of comprehensive income as follows.

ILLUSTRATION 17-20
Statement of Comprehensive Income (2013)

OPEN COMPANY STATEMENT OF COMPREHENSIVE INCOME FOR THE YEAR ENDED DECEMBER 31, 2013	
Net income	$350,000
Other comprehensive income	
Unrealized holding gain	40,000
Comprehensive income	$390,000

At December 31, 2013, Open Company reports on its balance sheet equity investments of $240,000 (cost $200,000 plus fair value adjustment of $40,000) and accumulated other comprehensive income in stockholders' equity of $40,000. The entry to transfer the unrealized holding gain—equity to accumulated other comprehensive income is as follows.

Unrealized Holding Gain or Loss—Equity	40,000	
Accumulated Other Comprehensive Income		40,000

In 2014, Open Company sells its Lehman Inc. common stock for $105,000 and realizes a gain on the sale of $25,000 ($105,000 − $80,000). The journal entry to record this transaction is as follows.

Cash	105,000	
Equity Investments		80,000
Gain on Sale of Investments		25,000

At the end of 2014, the fair value of the Woods Co. common stock increased an additional $20,000 ($155,000 − $135,000), to $155,000. Illustration 17-21 shows the computation of the change in the Fair Value Adjustment account (based on only the Woods Co. investment).

ILLUSTRATION 17-21
Available-for-Sale Security Portfolio (2014)

Investments	Cost	Fair Value	Unrealized Holding Gain (Loss)
Woods Co. common stock	$120,000	$155,000	$35,000
Previous fair value adjustment balance—Dr.			(40,000)
Fair value adjustment—Cr.			$ (5,000)

The entry to record the unrealized holding gain in 2014 is as follows.

Unrealized Holding Gain or Loss—Equity	5,000	
Fair Value Adjustment (available-for-sale)		5,000

If we assume that Open Company reports net income of $720,000 in 2014, including the realized sale on the Lehman stock, its income statement is presented as shown in Illustration 17-22.

ILLUSTRATION 17-22
Statement of Comprehensive Income (2014)

OPEN COMPANY STATEMENT OF COMPREHENSIVE INCOME FOR THE YEAR ENDED DECEMBER 31, 2014	
Net income (includes $25,000 realized gain on Lehman shares)	$720,000
Other comprehensive income	
Unrealized holding loss	(5,000)
Comprehensive income	$715,000

At December 31, 2014, Open Company reports on its balance sheet equity investments of $155,000 (cost $120,000 plus a fair value adjustment of $35,000) and accumulated other comprehensive income in stockholders' equity of $35,000 ($40,000 – $5,000). The entry to transfer the unrealized holding loss—equity to accumulated other comprehensive income is as follows.

Accumulated Other Comprehensive Income	5,000	
Unrealized Holding Gain or Loss—Equity		5,000

In 2013, Open included the unrealized gain on the Lehman Co. common stock in comprehensive income. In 2014, Open sold the stock. It reported the realized gain ($25,000) in net income, which increased comprehensive income again. To avoid double-counting this gain, Open makes a reclassification adjustment to eliminate the realized gain from the computation of comprehensive income in 2014.

This reclassification adjustment may be made in the income statement, in accumulated other comprehensive income or in a note to the financial statements. The FASB prefers to show the reclassification amount in accumulated other comprehensive income in the notes to the financial statements.[11] For Open Company, this presentation is as shown in Illustration 17-23.

ILLUSTRATION 17-23
Note Disclosure of Reclassification Adjustments

OPEN COMPANY
NOTES TO FINANCIAL STATEMENTS
CHANGES IN ACCUMULATED OTHER COMPREHENSIVE INCOME

Beginning balance, January 1, 2014		$40,000
Current-period other comprehensive income ($155,000 – $135,000)	$ 20,000	
Amount reclassified from accumulated other comprehensive income	(25,000)	
Unrealized holding loss		(5,000)
Ending balance, December 31, 2014		$35,000

Comprehensive Example

To provide a single-period example of the reporting of investment securities and related gain or loss on available-for-sale securities, assume that on January 1, 2014, Hinges Co. had cash and common stock of $50,000.[12] At that date, the company had no other asset, liability, or equity balance. On January 2, Hinges purchased for cash $50,000 of equity securities classified as available-for-sale. On June 30, Hinges sold part of the available-for-sale security portfolio, realizing a gain as shown in Illustration 17-24.

ILLUSTRATION 17-24
Computation of Realized Gain

Fair value of securities sold	$22,000
Less: Cost of securities sold	20,000
Realized gain	$ 2,000

[11] Recently, the FASB has proposed requiring companies to provide a tabular disclosure about items reclassified out of accumulated other comprehensive income. In general, for items reclassified to net income (e.g., gains or losses on available-for-sale securities), the disclosure includes the amount reclassified and identifies the line item affected on the income statement.

[12] We adapted this example from Dennis R. Beresford, L. Todd Johnson, and Cheri L. Reither, "Is a Second Income Statement Needed?" *Journal of Accountancy* (April 1996), p. 71.

Hinges did not purchase or sell any other securities during 2014. It received $3,000 in dividends during the year. At December 31, 2014, the remaining portfolio is as shown in Illustration 17-25.

ILLUSTRATION 17-25
Computation of Unrealized Gain

Fair value of portfolio	$34,000
Less: Cost of portfolio	30,000
Unrealized gain	$ 4,000

Illustration 17-26 shows the company's income statement for 2014.

ILLUSTRATION 17-26
Income Statement

HINGES CO.
INCOME STATEMENT
FOR THE YEAR ENDED DECEMBER 31, 2014

Dividend revenue	$3,000
Realized gains on investment in securities	2,000
Net income	$5,000

The company reports its change in the unrealized holding gain in a statement of comprehensive income as follows.

ILLUSTRATION 17-27
Statement of Comprehensive Income

HINGES CO.
STATEMENT OF COMPREHENSIVE INCOME
FOR THE YEAR ENDED DECEMBER 31, 2014

Net income (includes realized gain of $2,000)	$5,000
Other comprehensive income:	
Unrealized holding gain	4,000
Comprehensive income	$9,000

Its statement of stockholders' equity appears in Illustration 17-28.

ILLUSTRATION 17-28
Statement of Stockholders' Equity

HINGES CO.
STATEMENT OF STOCKHOLDERS' EQUITY
FOR THE YEAR ENDED DECEMBER 31, 2014

	Common Stock	Retained Earnings	Accumulated Other Comprehensive Income	Total
Beginning balance	$50,000	$ -0-	$-0-	$50,000
Add: Net income		5,000		5,000
Other comprehensive income			4,000*	4,000
Ending balance	$50,000	$5,000	$4,000	$59,000

*Total holding gains of $6,000 less reclassification adjustment of $2,000.

The comparative balance sheet is shown below in Illustration 17-29.

ILLUSTRATION 17-29
Comparative Balance Sheet

HINGES CO. COMPARATIVE BALANCE SHEET	1/1/14	12/31/14
Assets		
Cash	$50,000	$25,000
Equity investments (available-for-sale)		34,000
Total assets	$50,000	$59,000
Stockholders' equity		
Common stock	$50,000	$50,000
Retained earnings		5,000
Accumulated other comprehensive income		4,000
Total stockholders' equity	$50,000	$59,000

This example indicates how an unrealized gain or loss on available-for-sale securities affects all the financial statements. Note that a company must disclose the components that comprise accumulated other comprehensive income.

Transfers Between Categories

Companies account for transfers between any of the categories at fair value. Thus, if a company transfers available-for-sale securities to held-to-maturity investments, it records the new investments (held-to-maturity) at the date of transfer at **fair value** in the new category. Similarly, if it transfers held-to-maturity investments to available-for-sale investments, it records the new investments (available-for-sale) at **fair value.** This **fair value** rule assures that a company cannot omit recognition of fair value simply by transferring securities to the held-to-maturity category. Illustration 17-30 summarizes the accounting treatment for transfers.

ILLUSTRATION 17-30
Accounting for Transfers

Gateway to the Profession

Examples of the Entries for Recording Transfers Between Categories

Type of Transfer	Measurement Basis	Impact of Transfer on Stockholders' Equity*	Impact of Transfer on Net Income*
Transfer from trading to available-for-sale	Security transferred at fair value at the date of transfer, which is the new cost basis of the security.	The unrealized gain or loss at the date of transfer increases or decreases stockholders' equity.	The unrealized gain or loss at the date of transfer is recognized in income.
Transfer from available-for-sale to trading	Security transferred at fair value at the date of transfer, which is the new cost basis of the security.	The unrealized gain or loss at the date of transfer increases or decreases stockholders' equity.	The unrealized gain or loss at the date of transfer is recognized in income.
Transfer from held-to-maturity to available-for-sale**	Security transferred at fair value at the date of transfer.	The separate component of stockholders' equity is increased or decreased by the unrealized gain or loss at the date of transfer.	None
Transfer from available-for-sale to held-to-maturity	Security transferred at fair value at the date of transfer.	The unrealized gain or loss at the date of transfer carried as a separate component of stockholders' equity is amortized over the remaining life of the security.	None

*Assumes that adjusting entries to report changes in fair value for the current period are not yet recorded.
**According to GAAP, these types of transfers should be rare.

Summary of Reporting Treatment of Securities

Illustration 17-31 summarizes the major debt and equity securities and their reporting treatment.

ILLUSTRATION 17-31
Summary of Treatment of Major Debt and Equity Securities

Category*	Balance Sheet	Income Statement
Trading (debt and equity securities)	Investments shown at fair value. Current assets.	Interest and dividends are recognized as revenue. Unrealized holding gains and losses are included in net income.
Available-for-sale (debt and equity securities)	Investments shown at fair value. Current or long-term assets. Unrealized holding gains and losses are a separate component of stockholders' equity.	Interest and dividends are recognized as revenue. Unrealized holding gains and losses are **not** included in net income but in other comprehensive income.
Held-to-maturity (debt securities)	Investments shown at amortized cost. Current or long-term assets.	Interest is recognized as revenue.
Equity method and/or consolidation (equity securities)	Investments originally are carried at cost, are periodically adjusted by the investor's share of the investee's earnings or losses, and are decreased by all dividends received from the investee. Classified as long-term.	Revenue is recognized to the extent of the investee's earnings or losses reported subsequent to the date of investment.

*Companies have the option to report financial instruments at fair value with all gains and losses related to changes in fair value reported in the income statement. If a company chooses to use the fair option for some of its financial instruments, these assets or liabilities should be reported separately from other financial instruments that use a different valuation basis. To accomplish separate reporting, a company may either (a) report separate line items for the fair value and non–fair value amounts or (b) report the total fair value and non–fair value amounts in one line and parenthetically report the fair value amount in that line also.[13]

Gateway to the Profession

Discussion of Special Issues Related to Investments

You will want to read the **IFRS INSIGHTS** on pages 1026–1039 for discussion of IFRS related to the accounting for investments.

Evolving Issue — CLASSIFICATION AND MEASUREMENT—THE LONG ROAD

As discussed in the opening story, the FASB and IASB have been on divergent approaches to financial instrument classification and measurement. These differences have narrowed recently with the decision to permit a "Fair Value through Other Comprehensive Income" category for some debt instruments. The following table summarizes the agreed-upon approach in comparison to current GAAP.

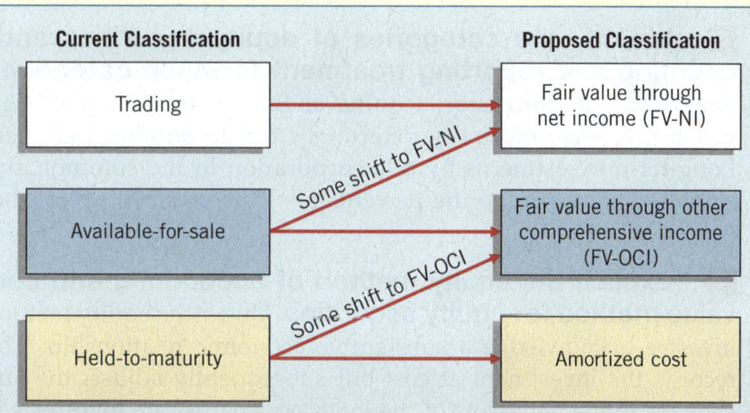

Source: J.P. Morgan.

As indicated, under the new model, there will still be three "buckets" although the proportions of financial instruments within the new classifications will change. For example, the FV-NI category will likely be larger than the current trading category because publicly traded companies will likely be required to classify all equity securities (both marketable

[13]Not surprisingly, the disclosure requirements for investments and other financial assets and liabilities are extensive. We provide an expanded discussion with examples of these disclosure requirements in Appendix 17C.

and nonmarketable) in FV-NI. Currently, companies are able to classify some equities in the available-for-sale category if particular criteria are met. To the extent a company has traditionally classified a large portion of its equity securities in the available-for-sale category, more equity instruments accounted for in the FV-NI category could create more net income volatility than under current GAAP.

The FV-OCI category may be larger or smaller than a company's current available-for-sale category. On the one hand, equities will no longer be eligible for classification in this category, which will make it smaller. On the other hand, some instruments that are currently classified as held-to-maturity will not be eligible for amortized cost classification and instead will end up being moved into the FV-OCI category.

For most companies, the amortized cost category generally will be smaller than the current held-to-maturity category because securities will no longer be eligible for classification in this category. Our expectation is that most of the instruments that will no longer meet the eligibility criteria for amortized cost accounting will likely move to the FV-OCI category.

The FASB is expected to issue a revised proposal in 2013. The IASB has specified that a revised *IFRS 9* will be effective for annual periods beginning on or after January 1, 2015.

Source: Adapted from D. Mott, "FASB and IASB Come Together on the Classification and Measurement of Debt Instruments," *Global Equity Research—Accounting Issues*, J.P. Morgan (25 May 2012).

KEY TERMS

amortized cost, *953*
available-for-sale securities, *952*
consolidated financial statements, *966*
controlling interest, *966*
debt securities, *952*
effective-interest method, *954*
equity method, *965*
equity securities, *960*
exchange for noncash consideration, *962(n)*
fair value, *953*
Fair Value Adjustment, *957*
fair value method, *961*
gains trading, *959*
held-to-maturity securities, *952*
holding gain or loss, *959*
impairment, *969*
investee, *961*
investor, *961*
parent, *966*
reclassification adjustment, *970*
security, *952(n)*
significant influence, *964*
subsidiary, *966*
trading securities, *952*

SUMMARY OF LEARNING OBJECTIVES

1 Identify the three categories of debt securities and describe the accounting and reporting treatment for each category. (1) Carry and report *held-to-maturity debt securities* at amortized cost. (2) Value *trading debt securities* for reporting purposes at fair value, with unrealized holding gains or losses included in net income. (3) Value *available-for-sale debt securities* for reporting purposes at fair value, with unrealized holding gains or losses reported as other comprehensive income and as a separate component of stockholders' equity.

2 Understand the procedures for discount and premium amortization on bond investments. Similar to bonds payable, companies should amortize discount or premium on bond investments using the effective-interest method. They apply the effective-interest rate or yield to the beginning carrying value of the investment for each interest period in order to compute interest revenue.

3 Identify the categories of equity securities and describe the accounting and reporting treatment for each category. The degree to which one corporation (investor) acquires an interest in the common stock of another corporation (investee) generally determines the accounting treatment for the investment. Long-term investments by one corporation in the common stock of another can be classified according to the percentage of the voting stock of the investee held by the investor.

4 Explain the equity method of accounting and compare it to the fair value method for equity securities. Under the equity method, the investor and the investee acknowledge a substantive economic relationship. The company originally records the investment at cost but subsequently adjusts the amount each period for changes in the net assets of the investee. That is, the investor's proportionate share of the earnings (losses) of the investee periodically increases (decreases) the investment's carrying amount. All dividends received by the investor from the investee decrease the investment's carrying amount. Under the fair value method, a company reports the equity investment at fair value each reporting period irrespective of the investee's earnings or dividends paid to it. A company applies the equity method to investment holdings between 20 percent and 50 percent of ownership. It applies the fair value method to holdings below 20 percent.

5 Describe the accounting for the fair value option and for impairments of debt and equity investments. Companies have the option to report most financial instruments at fair value, with all gains and losses related to changes in fair value reported in the income statement. This option is applied on an instrument-by-instrument basis. The fair value option is generally available only at the time a company first purchases the financial asset or incurs a financial liability. If a company chooses to use the fair value option, it must measure this instrument at fair value until the company no longer has ownership.

Impairments of debt and equity securities are losses in value that are determined to be other than temporary, are based on a fair value test, and are charged to income.

6 Describe the reporting of reclassification adjustments and the accounting for transfers between categories. A company needs a reclassification adjustment when it reports realized gains or losses as part of net income but also shows the amounts as part of other comprehensive income in the current or in previous periods. Companies should report unrealized holding gains or losses related to available-for-sale securities in other comprehensive income and the aggregate balance as accumulated comprehensive income on the balance sheet.

Transfers of securities between categories of investments should be accounted for at fair value, with unrealized holding gains or losses treated in accordance with the nature of the transfer.

APPENDIX 17A ACCOUNTING FOR DERIVATIVE INSTRUMENTS

7 LEARNING OBJECTIVE
Describe the uses of and accounting for derivatives.

Until the early 1970s, most financial managers worked in a cozy, if unthrilling, world. Since then, constant change caused by volatile markets, new technology, and deregulation has increased the risks to businesses. In response, the financial community developed products to manage these risks.

These products—called **derivative financial instruments** or simply **derivatives**—are useful for managing risk. Companies use the fair values or cash flows of these instruments to offset the changes in fair values or cash flows of the at-risk assets. The development of powerful computing and communication technology has aided the growth in derivative use. This technology provides new ways to analyze information about markets as well as the power to process high volumes of payments.

DEFINING DERIVATIVES

In order to understand derivatives, consider the following examples.

Example 1—Forward Contract. Assume that a company like Dell believes that the price of Google's stock will increase substantially in the next 3 months. Unfortunately, it does not have the cash resources to purchase the stock today. Dell therefore enters into a contract with a broker for delivery of 10,000 shares of Google stock in 3 months at the price of $110 per share.

Dell has entered into a **forward contract**, a type of derivative. As a result of the contract, Dell **has received the right** to receive 10,000 shares of Google stock in 3 months. Further, it **has an obligation** to pay $110 per share at that time. What is the benefit of this derivative contract? Dell can buy Google stock today and take delivery in 3 months. If the price goes up, as it expects, Dell profits. If the price goes down, Dell loses.

Example 2—Option Contract. Now suppose that Dell needs 2 weeks to decide whether to purchase Google stock. It therefore enters into a different type of contract, one that gives it the right to purchase Google stock at its current price any time within the next 2 weeks. As part of the contract, the broker charges $3,000 for holding the contract open for 2 weeks at a set price.

Dell has now entered into an **option contract**, another type of derivative. As a result of this contract, **it has received the right but not the obligation** to purchase this stock. If the price of the Google stock increases in the next 2 weeks, Dell exercises its option. In this case, the cost of the stock is the price of the stock stated in the contract, plus the cost of the option contract. If the price does not increase, Dell does not exercise the contract but still incurs the cost for the option.

The forward contract and the option contract both involve a future delivery of stock. The value of the contract relies on the underlying asset—the Google stock. Thus, these financial instruments are known as derivatives because they **derive their value from** values of other assets (e.g., stocks, bonds, or commodities). Or, put another way, their value relates to a market-determined indicator (e.g., stock price, interest rates, or the Standard and Poor's 500 stock composite index).

In this appendix, we discuss the accounting for three different types of derivatives:

1. Financial forwards or financial futures.
2. Options.
3. Swaps.

WHO USES DERIVATIVES, AND WHY?

Whether to protect for changes in interest rates, the weather, stock prices, oil prices, or foreign currencies, derivative contracts help to smooth the fluctuations caused by various types of risks. A company that wants to ensure against certain types of business risks often uses derivative contracts to achieve this objective.[14]

Producers and Consumers

To illustrate, assume that Heartland Ag is a large producer of potatoes for the consumer market. The present price for potatoes is excellent. Unfortunately, Heartland needs two months to harvest its potatoes and deliver them to the market. Because Heartland expects the price of potatoes to drop in the coming months, it signs a forward contract. It agrees to sell its potatoes today at the current market price for delivery in 2 months.

Who would buy this contract? Suppose on the other side of the contract is McDonald's Corporation. McDonald's wants to have potatoes (for French fries) in 2 months and believes that prices will increase. McDonald's is therefore agreeable to accepting delivery in 2 months at current prices. It knows that it will need potatoes in 2 months and that it can make an acceptable profit at this price level.

In this situation, if the price of potatoes increases before delivery, Heartland loses and McDonald's wins. Conversely, if the price decreases, Heartland wins and McDonald's loses. However, the objective is not to gamble on the outcome. Regardless of which way the price moves, both Heartland and McDonald's have received a price at

[14]Derivatives are traded on many exchanges throughout the world. In addition, many derivative contracts (primarily interest rate swaps) are privately negotiated.

which they obtain an acceptable profit. In this case, although Heartland is a **producer** and McDonald's is a **consumer**, both companies are **hedgers**. They both **hedge their positions** to ensure an acceptable financial result.

Commodity prices are volatile. They depend on weather, crop production, and general economic conditions. For the producer and the consumer to plan effectively, it makes good sense to lock in specific future revenues or costs in order to run their businesses successfully.

Speculators and Arbitrageurs

In some cases, instead of McDonald's taking a position in the forward contract, a speculator may purchase the contract from Heartland. The **speculator** bets that the price of potatoes will rise, thereby increasing the value of the forward contract. The speculator, who may be in the market for only a few hours, will then sell the forward contract to another speculator or to a company like McDonald's.

Arbitrageurs also use derivatives. These market players attempt to exploit inefficiencies in markets. They seek to lock in profits by simultaneously entering into transactions in two or more markets. For example, an arbitrageur might trade in a futures contract. At the same time, the arbitrageur will also trade in the commodity underlying the futures contract, hoping to achieve small price gains on the difference between the two. Markets rely on speculators and arbitrageurs to keep the market liquid on a daily basis.

In these illustrations, we explained why Heartland (the producer) and McDonald's (the consumer) would become involved in a derivative contract. Consider other types of situations that companies face.

1. Airlines, like **Delta**, **Southwest**, and **United**, are affected by changes in the price of jet fuel.
2. Financial institutions, such as **Citigroup**, **Bankers Trust**, and **BMO Harris**, are involved in borrowing and lending funds that are affected by changes in interest rates.
3. Multinational corporations, like **Cisco Systems**, **Coca-Cola**, and **General Electric**, are subject to changes in foreign exchange rates.

In fact, most corporations are involved in some form of derivatives transactions. Companies give these reasons (in their annual reports) as to why they use derivatives:

1. **ExxonMobil** uses derivatives to hedge its exposure to fluctuations in interest rates, foreign currency exchange rates, and hydrocarbon prices.
2. **Caterpillar** uses derivatives to manage foreign currency exchange rates, interest rates, and commodity price exposure.
3. **Johnson & Johnson** uses derivatives to manage the impact of interest rate and foreign exchange rate changes on earnings and cash flows.

Many corporations use derivatives extensively and successfully. However, derivatives can be dangerous. All parties involved must understand the risks and rewards associated with these contracts.[15]

[15]There are some well-publicized examples of companies that have suffered considerable losses using derivatives. For example, companies such as **Fannie Mae** (U.S.), **Enron** (U.S.), **Showa Shell Sekiyu** (Japan), **Metallgesellschaft** (Germany), **Procter & Gamble** (U.S.), and **Air Products & Chemicals** (U.S.) incurred significant losses from investments in derivative instruments.

BASIC PRINCIPLES IN ACCOUNTING FOR DERIVATIVES

The FASB concluded that derivatives such as forwards and options are assets and liabilities. It also concluded that companies should report them in the balance sheet **at fair value**.[16] The Board believes that fair value will provide statement users the best information about derivatives. Relying on some other basis of valuation for derivatives, such as historical cost, does not make sense. Why? Because many derivatives have a historical cost of zero. Furthermore, the markets for derivatives, and the assets upon which derivatives' values rely, are well developed. As a result, the Board believes that companies can determine reliable fair value amounts for derivatives.[17]

On the income statement, a company should recognize any unrealized gain or loss in income, if it uses the derivative for speculation purposes. If using the derivative for hedging purposes, the accounting for any gain or loss depends on the type of hedge used. We discuss the accounting for hedged transactions later in the appendix.

In summary, companies follow these guidelines in accounting for derivatives.

1. Recognize derivatives in the financial statements as assets and liabilities.
2. Report derivatives at fair value.
3. Recognize gains and losses resulting from speculation in derivatives immediately in income.
4. Report gains and losses resulting from hedge transactions differently, depending on the type of hedge.

Example of Derivative Financial Instrument—Speculation

To illustrate the measurement and reporting of a derivative for speculative purposes, we examine a derivative whose value depends on the market price of Laredo Inc. common stock. A company can realize a gain from the increase in the value of the Laredo shares with the use of a derivative, such as a call option.[18] A **call option** gives the holder the right, but not the obligation, to buy shares at a preset price. This price is often referred to as the **strike price** or the **exercise price**.

[16]GAAP covers accounting and reporting for all derivative instruments, whether financial or not. In this appendix, we focus on derivative financial instruments because of their widespread use in practice. [7]

[17]As discussed in earlier chapters, fair value is defined as "the price that would be received to sell an asset or paid to transfer a liability in an orderly transaction between market participants at the measurement date." Fair value is therefore a market-based measure. The FASB has also developed a fair value hierarchy, which indicates the priority of valuation techniques to use to determine fair value. *Level 1* fair value measures are based on observable inputs that reflect quoted prices for identical assets or liabilities in active markets. *Level 2* measures are based on inputs other than quoted prices included in Level 1 but that can be corroborated with observable data. *Level 3* fair values are based on unobservable inputs (for example, a company's own data or assumptions). Thus, Level 1 is the most reliable because it is based on quoted prices, like a closing stock price in the *Wall Street Journal*. Level 2 is the next most reliable and would rely on evaluating similar assets or liabilities in active markets. For Level 3 (the least reliable), much judgment is needed, based on the best information available, to arrive at a relevant and reliable fair value measurement. [8]

[18]Investors can use a different type of option contract—a **put option**—to realize a gain if anticipating a decline in the Laredo stock value. A put option gives the holder the option to sell shares at a preset price. Thus, a put option **increases** in value when the underlying asset **decreases** in value.

For example, assume a company enters into a call option contract with Baird Investment Co., which gives it the option to purchase Laredo stock at $100 per share.[19] If the price of Laredo stock increases above $100, the company can exercise this option and purchase the shares for $100 per share. If Laredo's stock never increases above $100 per share, the call option is worthless.

Accounting Entries. To illustrate the accounting for a call option, assume that the company purchases a call option contract on January 2, 2014, when Laredo shares are trading at $100 per share. The contract gives it the option to purchase 1,000 shares (referred to as the **notional amount**) of Laredo stock at an option price of $100 per share. The option expires on April 30, 2014. The company purchases the call option for $400 and makes the following entry.

January 2, 2014		
Call Option	400	
Cash		400

This payment is referred to as the **option premium**. It is generally much less than the cost of purchasing the shares directly. The option premium consists of two amounts: (1) intrinsic value and (2) time value. Illustration 17A-1 shows the formula to compute the option premium.

ILLUSTRATION 17A-1
Option Premium Formula

Option Premium = **Intrinsic Value** + **Time Value**

Intrinsic value is the difference between the market price and the preset strike price at any point in time. It represents the amount realized by the option holder, if exercising the option immediately. On January 2, 2014, the intrinsic value is zero because the market price equals the preset strike price.

Time value refers to the option's value over and above its intrinsic value. Time value reflects the possibility that the option has a fair value greater than zero. How? Because there is some expectation that the price of Laredo shares will increase above the strike price during the option term. As indicated, the time value for the option is $400.[20]

The following additional data are available with respect to the call option.

Date	Market Price of Laredo Shares	Time Value of Call Option
March 31, 2014	$120 per share	$100
April 16, 2014	$115 per share	$ 60

As indicated, on March 31, 2014, the price of Laredo shares increases to $120 per share. The intrinsic value of the call option contract is now $20,000. That is, the company can exercise the call option and purchase 1,000 shares from Baird Investment for $100 per share. It can then sell the shares in the market for $120 per share. This gives the

[19]Baird Investment Co. is referred to as the **counterparty**. Counterparties frequently are investment bankers or other companies that hold inventories of financial instruments.

[20]This cost is estimated using option-pricing models, such as the Black-Scholes equation. The volatility of the underlying stock, the expected life of the option, the risk-free rate of interest, and expected dividends on the underlying stock during the option term affect the Black-Scholes fair value estimate.

company a gain of $20,000 ($120,000 − $100,000) on the option contract.[21] It records the increase in the intrinsic value of the option as follows.

March 31, 2014		
Call Option	20,000	
Unrealized Holding Gain or Loss—Income		20,000

A market appraisal indicates that the time value of the option at March 31, 2014, is $100.[22] The company records this change in value of the option as follows.

March 31, 2014		
Unrealized Holding Gain or Loss—Income	300	
Call Option ($400 − $100)		300

At March 31, 2014, the company reports the call option in its balance sheet at fair value of $20,100.[23] The unrealized holding gain increases net income for the period. The loss on the time value of the option decreases net income.

On April 16, 2014, the company settles the option before it expires. To properly record the settlement, it updates the value of the option for the decrease in the intrinsic value of $5,000 ([$20 − $15]) × 1,000) as follows.

April 16, 2014		
Unrealized Holding Gain or Loss—Income	5,000	
Call Option		5,000

The decrease in the time value of the option of $40 ($100 − $60) is recorded as follows.

April 16, 2014		
Unrealized Holding Gain or Loss—Income	40	
Call Option		40

Thus, at the time of the settlement, the call option's carrying value is as follows.

Call Option

January 2, 2014	400	March 31, 2014	300
March 31, 2014	20,000	April 16, 2014	5,000
		April 16, 2014	40
Balance, April 16, 2014	15,060		

The company records the settlement of the option contract with Baird as follows.

April 16, 2014		
Cash	15,000	
Loss on Settlement of Call Option	60	
Call Option		15,060

Illustration 17A-2 summarizes the effects of the call option contract on net income.

ILLUSTRATION 17A-2
Effect on Income—Derivative Financial Instrument

Date	Transaction	Income (Loss) Effect
March 31, 2014	Net increase in value of call option ($20,000 − $300)	$19,700
April 16, 2014	Decrease in value of call option ($5,000 + $40)	(5,040)
April 16, 2014	Settle call option	(60)
	Total net income	$14,600

[21]In practice, investors generally do not have to actually buy and sell the Laredo shares to settle the option and realize the gain. This is referred to as the **net settlement** feature of option contracts.

[22]The decline in value reflects both the decreased likelihood that the Laredo shares will continue to increase in value over the option period and the shorter time to maturity of the option contract.

[23]As indicated earlier, the total value of the option at any point in time equals the intrinsic value plus the time value.

The accounting summarized in Illustration 17A-2 is in accord with GAAP. That is, because the call option meets the definition of an asset, the company records it in the balance sheet on March 31, 2014. Furthermore, it reports the call option at fair value, with any gains or losses reported in income.

Differences Between Traditional and Derivative Financial Instruments

How does a traditional financial instrument differ from a derivative one? A derivative financial instrument has the following three basic characteristics. **[9]**

1. ***The instrument has (1) one or more underlyings and (2) an identified payment provision.*** An **underlying** is a specified interest rate, security price, commodity price, index of prices or rates, or other market-related variable. The interaction of the underlying, with the face amount or the number of units specified in the derivative contract (the notional amounts), determines payment. For example, the value of the call option increased in value when the value of the Laredo stock increased. In this case, the underlying is the stock price. To arrive at the payment provision, multiply the change in the stock price by the number of shares (notional amount).
2. ***The instrument requires little or no investment at the inception of the contract.*** To illustrate, the company paid a small premium to purchase the call option—an amount much less than if purchasing the Laredo shares as a direct investment.
3. ***The instrument requires or permits net settlement.*** As indicated in the call option example, the company could realize a profit on the call option without taking possession of the shares. This **net settlement** feature reduces the transaction costs associated with derivatives.

Illustration 17A-3 summarizes the differences between traditional and derivative financial instruments. Here, we use a trading security for the traditional financial instrument and a call option as an example of a derivative one.

ILLUSTRATION 17A-3
Features of Traditional and Derivative Financial Instruments

Feature	Traditional Financial Instrument (Trading Security)	Derivative Financial Instrument (Call Option)
Payment provision	Stock price times the number of shares.	Change in stock price (underlying) times number of shares (notional amount).
Initial investment	Investor pays full cost.	Initial investment is much less than full cost.
Settlement	Deliver stock to receive cash.	Receive cash equivalent, based on changes in stock price times the number of shares.

DERIVATIVES USED FOR HEDGING

Flexibility in use and the low-cost features of derivatives relative to traditional financial instruments explain the popularity of derivatives. An additional use for derivatives is in risk management. For example, companies such as **Coca-Cola**, **ExxonMobil**, and **General Electric** borrow and lend substantial amounts in credit markets. In doing so, they are exposed to significant **interest rate risk**. That is, they face substantial risk that the fair values or cash flows of interest-sensitive assets or liabilities will change if interest rates increase or decrease. These same companies also have significant international operations. As such, they are also exposed to **exchange rate risk**—the risk that changes in foreign currency exchange rates will negatively impact the profitability of their international businesses.

Companies can use derivatives to offset the negative impacts of changes in interest rates or foreign currency exchange rates. This use of derivatives is referred to as **hedging**. GAAP established accounting and reporting standards for derivative financial instruments used in hedging activities. The FASB allows special accounting for two types of hedges—fair value and cash flow hedges.[24]

What do the numbers mean? RISKY BUSINESS

As shown in the graph below, use of derivatives has grown substantially in the past 10 years. In fact, over *$450 trillion* (in notional amounts) in derivative contracts were in play at the end of 2010. The primary players in the market for derivatives are large companies and various financial institutions, which continue to find new uses for derivatives for speculation and risk management

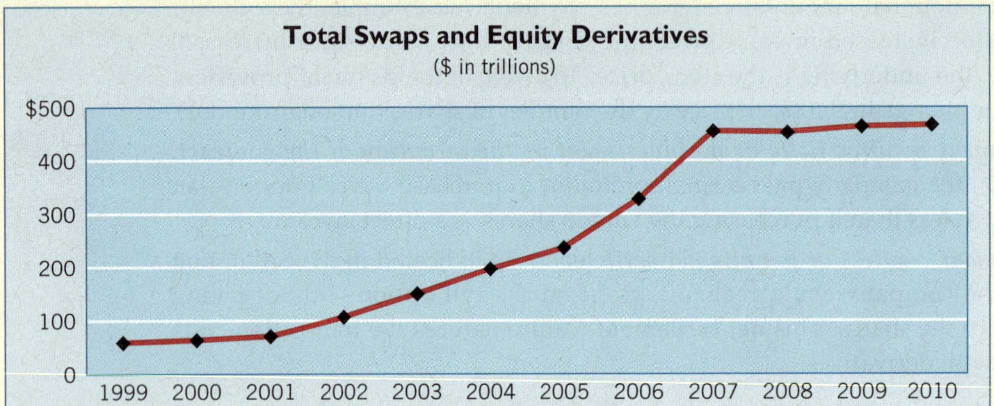

Source: Data from International Swaps and Derivatives Association Market Survey (2011).

Financial engineers continue to develop new uses for derivatives, many times through the use of increasingly complex webs of transactions, spanning a number of markets. As new uses for derivatives appear, the financial system as a whole can be dramatically affected. As a result, some market-watchers are concerned about the risk that a crisis in one company or sector could bring the entire financial system to its knees.

This was the case recently when credit default swaps were used to facilitate the sales of mortgage-backed securities (MBS). However, when the real estate market went south, the MBS defaulted, exposing large international financial institutions, like **Barclays**, **AIG**, and **Bank of America**, to massive losses. The losses were so widespread that government bailouts were required to prevent international securities markets from collapsing. In response, market regulators are proposing new rules to mitigate risks to broader markets from derivatives trading.

Source: P. Eavis, "Bill on Derivatives Overhaul Is Long Overdue," *Wall Street Journal* (April 14, 2010).

Fair Value Hedge

LEARNING OBJECTIVE 8
Explain how to account for a fair value hedge.

In a **fair value hedge**, a company uses a derivative to hedge (offset) the exposure to changes in the fair value of a recognized asset or liability or of an unrecognized commitment. In a perfectly hedged position, the gain or loss on the fair value of the derivative equals and offsets that of the hedged asset or liability.

[24]GAAP also addresses the accounting for certain foreign currency hedging transactions. In general, these transactions are special cases of the two hedges we discuss here. **[10]** Understanding of foreign currency hedging transactions requires knowledge related to consolidation of multinational entities, which is beyond the scope of this textbook.

Companies commonly use several types of fair value hedges. For example, companies use interest rate swaps to hedge the risk that changes in interest rates will impact the fair value of debt obligations. Or, they use put options to hedge the risk that an equity investment will decline in value.

To illustrate a fair value hedge, assume that on April 1, 2014, Hayward Co. purchases 100 shares of Sonoma stock at a market price of $100 per share. Hayward does not intend to actively trade this investment. It consequently classifies the Sonoma investment as available-for-sale. Hayward records this available-for-sale investment as follows.

April 1, 2014		
Equity Investments	10,000	
Cash		10,000

Hayward records available-for-sale securities at fair value on the balance sheet. It reports unrealized gains and losses in equity as part of other comprehensive income.[25] Fortunately for Hayward, the value of the Sonoma shares increases to $125 per share during 2014. Hayward records the gain on this investment as follows.

December 31, 2014		
Fair Value Adjustment (available-for-sale)	2,500	
Unrealized Holding Gain or Loss—Equity		2,500

Illustration 17A-4 indicates how Hayward reports the Sonoma investment in its balance sheet.

ILLUSTRATION 17A-4
Balance Sheet Presentation of Available-for-Sale Securities

HAYWARD CO. BALANCE SHEET (PARTIAL) DECEMBER 31, 2014	
Assets	
Equity investments (available-for-sale)	$12,500
Stockholders' Equity	
Accumulated other comprehensive income	
Unrealized holding gain	$2,500

While Hayward benefits from an increase in the price of Sonoma shares, it is exposed to the risk that the price of the Sonoma stock will decline. To hedge this risk, Hayward locks in its gain on the Sonoma investment by purchasing a put option on 100 shares of Sonoma stock.

Hayward enters into the put option contract on January 2, 2015, and designates the option as a fair value hedge of the Sonoma investment. This put option (which expires in two years) gives Hayward the option to sell Sonoma shares at a price of $125. Since the exercise price equals the current market price, no entry is necessary at inception of the put option.[26]

January 2, 2015

No entry required. A memorandum indicates the signing of the put option contract and its designation as a fair value hedge for the Sonoma investment.

At December 31, 2015, the price of the Sonoma shares has declined to $120 per share. Hayward records the following entry for the Sonoma investment.

December 31, 2015		
Unrealized Holding Gain or Loss—Income	500	
Fair Value Adjustment (available-for-sale)		500

[25]We discussed the distinction between trading and available-for-sale investments in the chapter.

[26]To simplify the example, we assume no premium is paid for the option.

Note that upon designation of the hedge, the accounting for the available-for-sale security changes from regular GAAP. That is, Hayward records the unrealized holding loss in income, not in equity. **If Hayward had not followed this accounting, a mismatch of gains and losses in the income statement would result.** Thus, special accounting for the hedged item (in this case, an available-for-sale security) is necessary in a fair value hedge.

The following journal entry records the increase in value of the put option on Sonoma shares.

December 31, 2015		
Put Option	500	
Unrealized Holding Gain or Loss—Income		500

The decline in the price of Sonoma shares results in an increase in the fair value of the put option. That is, Hayward could realize a gain on the put option by purchasing 100 shares in the open market for $120 and then exercise the put option, selling the shares for $125. This results in a gain to Hayward of $500 (100 shares × [$125 – $120]).[27]

Illustration 17A-5 indicates how Hayward reports the amounts related to the Sonoma investment and the put option.

ILLUSTRATION 17A-5
Balance Sheet Presentation of Fair Value Hedge

HAYWARD CO.
BALANCE SHEET (PARTIAL)
DECEMBER 31, 2015

Assets	
Equity investments (available-for-sale)	$12,000
Put option	500

The increase in fair value on the option offsets or hedges the decline in value on Hayward's available-for-sale security. By using fair value accounting for both financial instruments, the financial statements reflect the underlying substance of Hayward's net exposure to the risks of holding Sonoma stock. By using fair value accounting for both these financial instruments, the balance sheet reports the amount that Hayward would receive on the investment and the put option contract if Hayward sold and settled them, respectively.

Illustration 17A-6 illustrates the reporting of the effects of the hedging transaction on income for the year ended December 31, 2015.

ILLUSTRATION 17A-6
Income Statement Presentation of Fair Value Hedge

HAYWARD CO.
INCOME STATEMENT (PARTIAL)
FOR THE YEAR ENDED DECEMBER 31, 2015

Other Income	
Unrealized holding gain—put option	$ 500
Unrealized holding loss—available-for-sale securities	(500)

The income statement indicates that the gain on the put option offsets the loss on the available-for-sale securities.[28] The reporting for these financial instruments, even when

[27]In practice, Hayward generally does not have to actually buy and sell the Sonoma shares to realize this gain. Rather, unless the counterparty wants to hold Hayward shares, Hayward can "close out" the contract by having the counterparty pay it $500 in cash. This is an example of the net settlement feature of derivatives.

[28]Note that the fair value changes in the option contract will not offset *increases* in the value of the Hayward investment. Should the price of Sonoma stock increase above $125 per share, Hayward would have no incentive to exercise the put option.

they reflect a hedging relationship, illustrates why the FASB argued that fair value accounting provides the most relevant information about financial instruments, including derivatives.

Cash Flow Hedge

9 LEARNING OBJECTIVE
Explain how to account for a cash flow hedge.

Companies use **cash flow hedges** to hedge exposures to **cash flow risk**, which results from the variability in cash flows. The FASB allows special accounting for cash flow hedges. Generally, companies measure and report derivatives at fair value on the balance sheet. They report gains and losses directly in net income. However, companies account for derivatives used in cash flow hedges at fair value on the balance sheet, but they **record gains or losses in equity, as part of other comprehensive income.**

International Perspective

Under IFRS, companies record unrealized holding gains or losses on cash flow hedges as adjustments to the value of the hedged item, not as "Other comprehensive income."

To illustrate, assume that in September 2014, Allied Can Co. anticipates purchasing 1,000 metric tons of aluminum in January 2015. Concerned that prices for aluminum will increase in the next few months, Allied wants to hedge the risk that it might pay higher prices for inventory in January 2015. As a result, Allied enters into an aluminum futures contract.

A **futures contract** gives the holder the right and the obligation to purchase an asset at a preset price for a specified period of time.[29] In this case, the aluminum futures contract gives Allied the right and the obligation to purchase 1,000 metric tons of aluminum for $1,550 per ton. This contract price is good until the contract expires in January 2015. The underlying for this derivative is the price of aluminum. If the price of aluminum rises above $1,550, the value of the futures contract to Allied increases. Why? Because Allied will be able to purchase the aluminum at the lower price of $1,550 per ton.[30]

Allied enters into the futures contract on September 1, 2014. Assume that the price to be paid today for inventory to be delivered in January—the **spot price**—equals the contract price. With the two prices equal, the futures contract has no value. Therefore, no entry is necessary.

September 2014

No entry required. A memorandum indicates the signing of the futures contract.

At December 31, 2014, the price for January delivery of aluminum increases to $1,575 per metric ton. Allied makes the following entry to record the increase in the value of the futures contract.

December 31, 2014

Futures Contract	25,000	
Unrealized Holding Gain or Loss—Equity ([$1,575 − $1,550] × 1,000 tons)		25,000

Allied reports the futures contract in the balance sheet as a current asset. It reports the gain on the futures contract as part of other comprehensive income.

[29] A **futures contract** is a firm contractual agreement between a buyer and seller for a specified asset on a fixed date in the future which also trades on an exchange. The contract also has a standard specification so both parties know exactly what is being traded. A **forward** is similar but is not traded on an exchange and does not have standardized conditions.

[30] As with the earlier call option example, the actual aluminum does not have to be exchanged. Rather, the parties to the futures contract settle by paying the cash difference between the futures price and the price of aluminum on each settlement date.

Since Allied has not yet purchased and sold the inventory, this gain arises from an anticipated transaction. In this type of transaction, **a company accumulates in equity gains or losses on the futures contract as part of other comprehensive income until the period in which it sells the inventory, thereby affecting earnings.**

In January 2015, Allied purchases 1,000 metric tons of aluminum for $1,575 and makes the following entry.[31]

January 2015		
Aluminum Inventory	1,575,000	
Cash ($1,575 × 1,000 tons)		1,575,000

At the same time, Allied makes final settlement on the futures contract. It records the following entry.

January 2015		
Cash	25,000	
Futures Contract ($1,575,000 – $1,550,000)		25,000

Through use of the futures contract derivative, Allied fixes the cost of its inventory. The $25,000 futures contract settlement offsets the amount paid to purchase the inventory at the prevailing market price of $1,575,000. The result: net cash outflow of $1,550 per metric ton, as desired. As Illustration 17A-7 shows, Allied has therefore effectively hedged the cash flow for the purchase of inventory.

ILLUSTRATION 17A-7
Effect of Hedge on Cash Flows

Anticipated Cash Flows

Wish to fix cash paid for inventory at $1,550,000

=

Actual Cash Flows

Actual cash paid	$1,575,000
Less: Cash received on futures contract	(25,000)
Final cash paid	$1,550,000

There are no income effects at this point. Allied accumulates in equity the gain on the futures contract as part of other comprehensive income until the period when it sells the inventory, affecting earnings through cost of goods sold.

For example, assume that Allied processes the aluminum into finished goods (cans). The total cost of the cans (including the aluminum purchases in January 2015) is $1,700,000. Allied sells the cans in July 2015 for $2,000,000, and records this sale as follows.

July 2015		
Cash	2,000,000	
Sales Revenue		2,000,000
Cost of Goods Sold	1,700,000	
Inventory (cans)		1,700,000

Since the effect of the anticipated transaction has now affected earnings, Allied makes the following entry related to the hedging transaction.

[31] In practice, futures contracts are settled on a daily basis. For our purposes, we show only one settlement for the entire amount.

July 2015

Unrealized Holding Gain or Loss—Equity	25,000	
Cost of Goods Sold		25,000

The gain on the futures contract, which Allied reported as part of other comprehensive income, now reduces cost of goods sold. As a result, the cost of aluminum included in the overall cost of goods sold is $1,550,000. The futures contract has worked as planned. Allied has managed the cash paid for aluminum inventory and the amount of cost of goods sold.

OTHER REPORTING ISSUES

The preceding examples illustrate the basic reporting issues related to the accounting for derivatives. Next, we discuss the following additional issues:

10 LEARNING OBJECTIVE
Identify special reporting issues related to derivative financial instruments that cause unique accounting problems.

1. The accounting for embedded derivatives.
2. Qualifying hedge criteria.

Embedded Derivatives

As we indicated at the beginning of this appendix, rapid innovation in the development of complex financial instruments drove efforts toward unifying and improving the accounting standards for derivatives. In recent years, this innovation has led to the development of **hybrid securities**. These securities have characteristics of both debt and equity. They often combine traditional and derivative financial instruments.

For example, a convertible bond (discussed in Chapter 16) is a hybrid instrument. It consists of two parts: (1) a debt security, referred to as the **host security**, combined with (2) an option to convert the bond to shares of common stock, the **embedded derivative**.

To provide consistency in accounting for similar derivatives, a company must account for embedded derivatives similarly to other derivatives. Therefore, to account for an embedded derivative, a company **should separate it from the host security** and then account for it using the accounting for derivatives. This separation process is referred to as **bifurcation**.[32] Thus, a company investing in a convertible bond must separate the stock option component of the instrument. It then accounts for the derivative (the stock option) at fair value and the host instrument (the debt) according to GAAP, as if there were no embedded derivative.[33]

Qualifying Hedge Criteria

The FASB identified certain criteria that hedging transactions must meet before requiring the special accounting for hedges. The FASB designed these criteria to ensure the use of hedge accounting in a consistent manner across different hedge transactions. The general criteria relate to the following areas.

International Perspective
IFRS qualifying hedge criteria are similar to those used in GAAP.

1. ***Documentation, risk management, and designation.*** At inception of the hedge, there must be formal **documentation** of the hedging relationship, the company's **risk management** objective, and the strategy for undertaking the hedge. **Designation**

[32]A company can also designate such a derivative as a hedging instrument. The company would apply the hedge accounting provisions outlined earlier in the chapter.

[33]The issuer of the convertible bonds would not bifurcate the option component of the convertible bonds payable. GAAP explicitly precludes embedded derivative accounting for an embedded derivative that is indexed to a company's own common stock. If the conversion feature was tied to **another company's** stock, then the derivative would be bifurcated.

refers to identifying the hedging instrument, the hedged item or transaction, the nature of the risk being hedged, and how the hedging instrument will offset changes in the fair value or cash flows attributable to the hedged risk.

The FASB decided that documentation and designation are critical to the implementation of the special accounting for hedges. Without these requirements, companies might try to apply the hedge accounting provisions retroactively, only in response to negative changes in market conditions, to offset the negative impact of a transaction on the financial statements. Allowing special hedge accounting in such a setting could mask the speculative nature of the original transaction.

2. ***Effectiveness of the hedging relationship.*** At inception and on an ongoing basis, the hedging relationship should be **highly effective** in achieving offsetting changes in fair value or cash flows. Companies must assess effectiveness whenever preparing financial statements.

The general guideline for effectiveness is that the fair values or cash flows of the hedging instrument (the derivative) and the hedged item exhibit a high degree of correlation. In practice, high effectiveness is assumed when the correlation is close to one (e.g., within plus or minus .10). In our earlier hedging examples (put option and the futures contract on aluminum inventory), the fair values and cash flows are perfectly correlated. That is, when the cash payment for the inventory purchase increased, it offset, dollar for dollar, the cash received on the futures contract.

If the effectiveness criterion is not met, either at inception or because of changes following inception of the hedging relationship, the FASB no longer allows special hedge accounting. The company should then account for the derivative as a free-standing derivative.[34]

3. ***Effect on reported earnings of changes in fair values or cash flows.*** A change in the fair value of a hedged item or variation in the cash flow of a hedged forecasted transaction must have the potential to change the amount recognized in reported earnings.[35] There is no need for special hedge accounting if a company accounts for both the hedging instrument and the hedged item at fair value under existing GAAP. In this case, earnings will properly reflect the offsetting gains and losses.

For example, special accounting is not needed for a fair value hedge of a trading security, because a company accounts for both the investment and the derivative at fair value on the balance sheet with gains or losses reported in earnings. Thus, "special" hedge accounting is necessary only when there is a mismatch of the accounting effects for the hedging instrument and the hedged item under GAAP.[36]

Summary of Derivatives Accounting

Illustration 17A-8 summarizes the accounting provisions for derivatives and hedging transactions.

[34]That is, the accounting for the part of a derivative that is not effective in a hedge is at fair value, with gains and losses recorded in income.

[35]GAAP gives companies the option to measure most types of financial instruments—from equity investments to debt issued by the company—at fair value. Changes in fair value are recognized in net income each reporting period. Thus, GAAP provides companies with the opportunity to hedge their financial instruments without the complexity inherent in applying hedge accounting provisions. For example, if the fair value option is used, bifurcation of an embedded derivative is not required. **[11]**

[36]An important criterion specific to cash flow hedges is that the forecasted transaction in a cash flow hedge "is likely to occur." A company should support this probability (defined as significantly greater than the term "more likely than not") by observable facts such as frequency of similar past transactions and its financial and operational ability to carry out the transaction.

ILLUSTRATION 17A-8
Summary of Derivative Accounting under GAAP

Derivative Use	Accounting for Derivative	Accounting for Hedged Item	Common Example
Speculation	At fair value with unrealized holding gains and losses recorded in income.	Not applicable.	Call or put option on an equity security.
Hedging			
Fair value	At fair value with holding gains and losses recorded in income.	At fair value with gains and losses recorded in income.	Put option to hedge an equity investment.
Cash flow	At fair value with unrealized holding gains and losses from the hedge recorded in other comprehensive income, and reclassified in income when the hedged transaction's cash flows affect earnings.	Use other generally accepted accounting principles for the hedged item.	Use of a futures contract to hedge a forecasted purchase of inventory.

As indicated, the general accounting for derivatives relies on fair values. GAAP also establishes special accounting guidance when companies use derivatives **for hedging purposes**. For example, when a company uses a put option to hedge price changes in an available-for-sale stock investment in a fair value hedge (see the Hayward example earlier), it records unrealized gains on the investment in earnings, which is not GAAP for available-for-sale securities without such a hedge. This special accounting is justified in order to accurately report the nature of the hedging relationship in the balance sheet (recording both the put option and the investment at fair value) and in the income statement (reporting offsetting gains and losses in the same period).

Special accounting also is used for cash flow hedges. Companies account for derivatives used in qualifying cash flow hedges at fair value on the balance sheet, but record unrealized holding gains or losses in other comprehensive income until selling or settling the hedged item. In a cash flow hedge, a company continues to record the hedged item at its historical cost.

Disclosure requirements for derivatives are complex. Recent pronouncements on fair value information and financial instruments provide a helpful disclosure framework for reporting derivative instruments. Appendix 17C illustrates many of these disclosures, except for discussion of hedging issues. In general, companies that have derivatives are required to disclose the objectives for holding or issuing those instruments (speculation or hedging), the hedging context (fair value or cash flow), and the strategies for achieving risk-management objectives.

COMPREHENSIVE HEDGE ACCOUNTING EXAMPLE

To provide a comprehensive example of hedge accounting, we examine the use of an interest rate swap. First, let's consider how swaps work and why companies use them.

Options and futures trade on organized securities exchanges. Because of this, options and futures have standardized terms. Although that standardization makes the trading easier, it limits the flexibility needed to tailor contracts to specific circumstances. In addition, most types of derivatives have relatively short time horizons, thereby excluding their use for reducing long-term risk exposure.

As a result, many corporations instead turn to the swap, a very popular type of derivative. A **swap** is a transaction between two parties in which the first party promises to make a payment to the second party. Similarly, the second party promises to make a simultaneous payment to the first party.

The most common type of swap is the **interest rate swap**. In this type, one party makes payments based on a fixed or floating rate, and the second party does just the opposite. In most cases, large money-center banks bring together the two parties. These banks handle the flow of payments between the parties, as shown in Illustration 17A-9.

ILLUSTRATION 17A-9
Swap Transaction

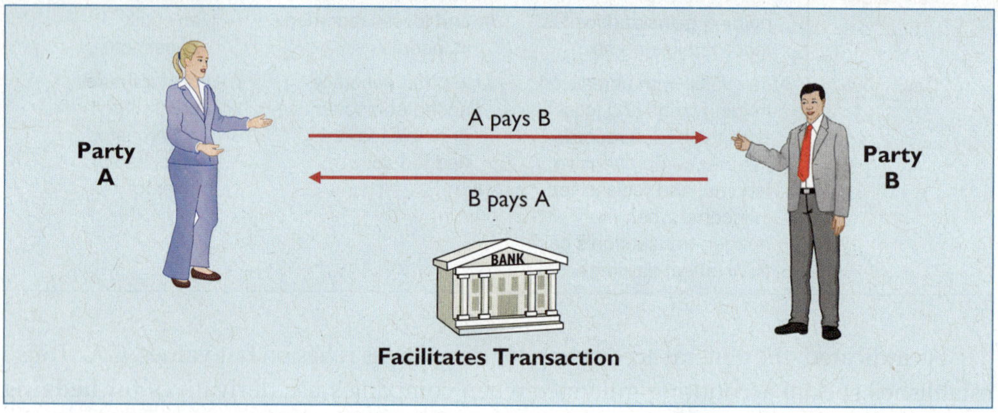

Fair Value Hedge

To illustrate the use of a swap in a fair value hedge, assume that Jones Company issues $1,000,000 of five-year, 8 percent bonds on January 2, 2014. Jones records this transaction as follows.

January 2, 2014		
Cash	1,000,000	
Bonds Payable		1,000,000

Jones offered a fixed interest rate to appeal to investors. But Jones is concerned that if market interest rates decline, the fair value of the liability will increase. The company will then suffer an economic loss.[37] To protect against the risk of loss, Jones hedges the risk of a decline in interest rates by entering into a five-year interest rate swap contract. Jones agrees to the following terms:

1. Jones will receive fixed payments at 8 percent (based on the $1,000,000 amount).
2. Jones will pay variable rates, based on the market rate in effect for the life of the swap contract. The variable rate at the inception of the contract is 6.8 percent.

As Illustration 17A-10 shows, this swap allows Jones to change the interest on the bonds payable from a fixed rate to a variable rate.

ILLUSTRATION 17A-10
Interest Rate Swap

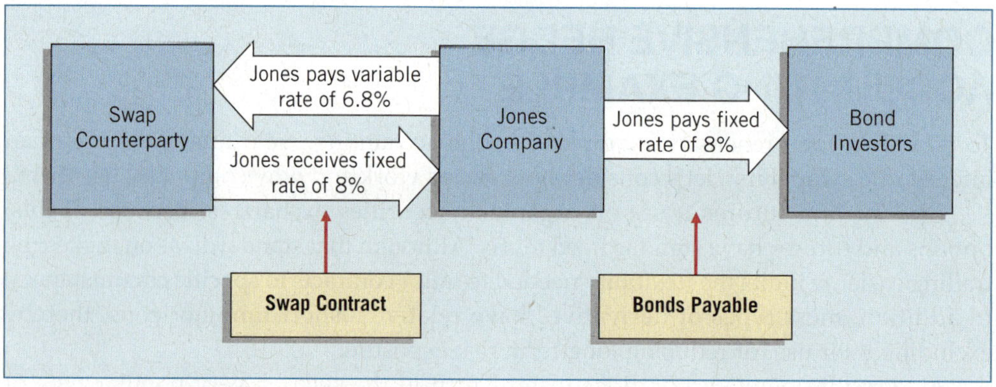

[37]This economic loss arises because Jones is locked into the 8 percent interest payments even if rates decline.

The settlement dates for the swap correspond to the interest payment dates on the debt (December 31). On each interest payment (settlement) date, Jones and the counterparty compute the difference between current market interest rates and the fixed rate of 8 percent, and determine the value of the swap.[38] If interest rates decline, the value of the swap contract to Jones increases (Jones has a gain), while at the same time Jones's fixed-rate debt obligation increases (Jones has an economic loss).

The swap is an effective risk-management tool in this setting. Its value relates to the same underlying (interest rates) that will affect the value of the fixed-rate bond payable. Thus, if the value of the swap goes up, it offsets the loss related to the debt obligation.

Assuming that Jones enters into the swap on January 2, 2014 (the same date as the issuance of the debt), the swap at this time has no value. Therefore, no entry is necessary.

January 2, 2014

No entry required. A memorandum indicates the signing of the swap contract.

At the end of 2014, Jones makes the interest payment on the bonds. It records this transaction as follows.

December 31, 2014		
Interest Expense	80,000	
Cash (8% × $1,000,000)		80,000

At the end of 2014, market interest rates have declined substantially. Therefore, the value of the swap contract increases. Recall (see Illustration 17A-9) that in the swap, Jones receives a fixed rate of 8 percent, or $80,000 ($1,000,000 × 8%), and pays a variable rate (6.8%), or $68,000. Jones therefore receives $12,000 ($80,000 − $68,000) as a settlement payment on the swap contract on the first interest payment date. Jones records this transaction as follows.

December 31, 2014		
Cash	12,000	
Interest Expense		12,000

In addition, a market appraisal indicates that the value of the interest rate swap has increased $40,000. Jones records this increase in value as follows.[39]

December 31, 2014		
Swap Contract	40,000	
Unrealized Holding Gain or Loss—Income		40,000

Jones reports this swap contract in the balance sheet. It reports the gain on the hedging transaction in the income statement. Because interest rates have declined, the company records a loss and a related increase in its liability as follows.

December 31, 2014		
Unrealized Holding Gain or Loss—Income	40,000	
Bonds Payable		40,000

Jones reports the loss on the hedging activity in net income. It adjusts bonds payable in the balance sheet to fair value (which deviates from normal accounting at amortized cost).

[38]The underlying for an interest rate swap is some index of market interest rates. The most commonly used index is the London Interbank Offer Rate, or LIBOR. In this example, we assume the LIBOR is 6.8 percent.

[39]Theoretically, this fair value change reflects the present value of expected future differences in variable and fixed interest rates.

Financial Statement Presentation of an Interest Rate Swap

Illustration 17A-11 indicates how Jones reports the asset and liability related to this hedging transaction on the balance sheet.

ILLUSTRATION 17A-11
Balance Sheet Presentation of Fair Value Hedge

JONES COMPANY
BALANCE SHEET (PARTIAL)
DECEMBER 31, 2014

Current assets	
Swap contract	$40,000
Long-term liabilities	
Bonds payable	$1,040,000

The effect on Jones's balance sheet is the addition of the swap asset and an increase in the carrying value of the bonds payable. Illustration 17A-12 indicates how Jones reports the effects of this swap transaction in the income statement.

ILLUSTRATION 17A-12
Income Statement Presentation of Fair Value Hedge

JONES COMPANY
INCOME STATEMENT (PARTIAL)
FOR THE YEAR ENDED DECEMBER 31, 2014

Interest expense ($80,000 − $12,000)		$68,000
Other income		
Unrealized holding gain—swap contract	$40,000	
Unrealized holding loss—bonds payable	(40,000)	
Net gain (loss)		$-0-

On the income statement, Jones reports interest expense of $68,000. Jones has effectively changed the debt's interest rate from fixed to variable. That is, by receiving a fixed rate and paying a variable rate on the swap, the company converts the fixed rate on the bond payable to variable. This results in an effective-interest rate of 6.8 percent in 2014.[40] Also, the gain on the swap offsets the loss related to the debt obligation. Therefore, the net gain or loss on the hedging activity is zero.

Illustration 17A-13 shows the overall impact of the swap transaction on the financial statements.

ILLUSTRATION 17A-13
Impact on Financial Statements of Fair Value Hedge

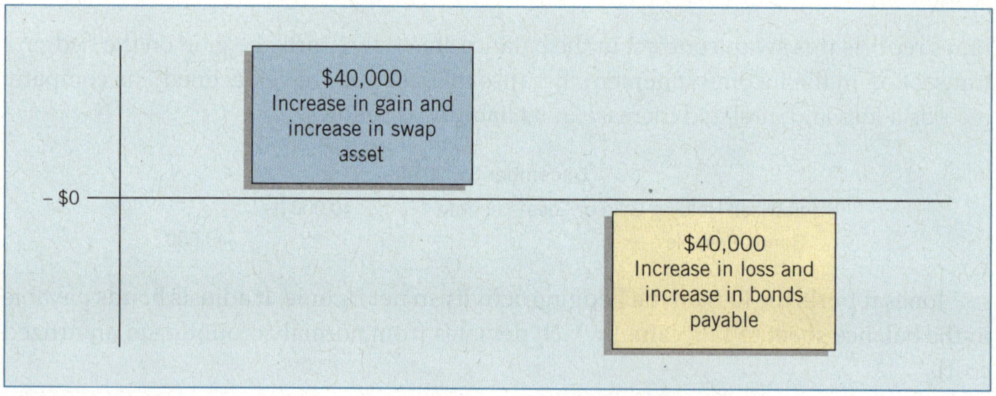

[40]Jones will apply similar accounting and measurement at future interest payment dates. Thus, if interest rates increase, Jones will continue to receive 8 percent on the swap (records a loss) but will also be locked into the fixed payments to the bondholders at an 8 percent rate (records a gain).

In summary, to account for fair value hedges (as illustrated in the Jones example) **record the derivative at its fair value in the balance sheet, and record any gains and losses in income**. Thus, the gain on the swap offsets or hedges the loss on the bond payable, due to the decline in interest rates.

By adjusting the hedged item (the bond payable in the Jones case) to fair value, with the gain or loss recorded in earnings, the accounting for the Jones bond payable deviates from amortized cost. This special accounting is justified in order to report accurately the nature of the hedging relationship between the swap and the bond payable in the balance sheet (both the swap and the debt obligation are recorded at fair value) and in the income statement (offsetting gains and losses are reported in the same period).[41]

International Perspective

International accounting for hedges (*IAS 39*) is similar to the provisions of GAAP.

CONTROVERSY AND CONCLUDING REMARKS

Companies need rules to properly measure and report derivatives in financial statements. However, some argue that reporting derivatives at fair value results in unrealized gains and losses that are difficult to interpret. Others raise concerns about the complexity and cost of implementing GAAP in this area.

However, we believe that the long-term benefits of using fair value and reporting derivatives at fair value will far outweigh any short-term implementation costs. As the volume and complexity of derivatives and hedging transactions continue to grow, so does the risk that investors and creditors will be exposed to unexpected losses arising from derivative transactions. Statement readers must have comprehensive information concerning many derivative financial instruments and the effects of hedging transactions using derivatives.

SUMMARY OF LEARNING OBJECTIVES FOR APPENDIX 17A

7 Describe the uses of and accounting for derivatives. Any company or individual that wants to ensure against different types of business risks may use derivative contracts to achieve this objective. In general, these transactions involve some type of hedge. Speculators also use derivatives, attempting to find an enhanced return. Speculators are very important to the derivatives market because they keep it liquid on a daily basis. Arbitrageurs attempt to exploit inefficiencies in various derivative contracts. A company primarily uses derivatives for purposes of hedging its exposure to fluctuations in interest rates, foreign currency exchange rates, and commodity prices.

Companies should recognize derivatives in the financial statements as assets and liabilities, and report them at fair value. Companies should recognize gains and losses resulting from speculation immediately in income. They report gains and losses resulting from hedge transactions in different ways, depending on the type of hedge.

KEY TERMS

anticipated transaction, *988*
arbitrageurs, *979*
bifurcation, *989*
call option, *980*
cash flow hedge, *987*
counterparty, *981(n)*
derivative financial instruments, derivatives, *977*
designation, *989*
documentation, *989*
embedded derivative, *989*
fair value hedge, *984*
forward contract, *977*
futures contract, *987*
hedging, *984*
highly effective, *990*
host security, *989*
hybrid security, *989*
interest rate swap, *992*
intrinsic value, *981*

[41] An interest rate swap can also be used in a cash flow hedge. A common setting is the cash flow risk inherent in having variable rate debt as part of a company's debt structure. In this situation, the variable debt issuer can hedge the cash flow risk by entering into a swap contract to receive variable rate cash flows but pay fixed rate. The cash received on the swap contract will offset the variable cash flows to be paid on the debt obligation.

net settlement, *982(n)*
notional amount, *981*
option contract, *978*
option premium, *981*
put option, *980(n)*
risk management, *989*
speculators, *979*
spot price, *987*
strike (exercise) price, *980*
swap, *991*
time value, *981*
underlying, *983*

Companies report derivative financial instruments in the balance sheet, and record them at fair value. Except for derivatives used in hedging, companies record realized and unrealized gains and losses on derivative financial instruments in income.

8 Explain how to account for a fair value hedge. A company records the derivative used in a qualifying fair value hedge at its fair value in the balance sheet, recording any gains and losses in income. In addition, the company also accounts for the item being hedged with the derivative at fair value. By adjusting the hedged item to fair value, with the gain or loss recorded in earnings, the accounting for the hedged item may deviate from GAAP in the absence of a hedge relationship. This special accounting is justified in order to report accurately the nature of the hedging relationship between the derivative hedging instruments and the hedged item. A company reports both in the balance sheet, reporting offsetting gains and losses in income in the same period.

9 Explain how to account for a cash flow hedge. Companies account for derivatives used in qualifying cash flow hedges at fair value on the balance sheet, but record gains or losses in equity as part of other comprehensive income. Companies accumulate these gains or losses, and reclassify them in income when the hedged transaction's cash flows affect earnings. Accounting is according to GAAP for the hedged item.

10 Identify special reporting issues related to derivative financial instruments that cause unique accounting problems. A company should separate a derivative that is embedded in a hybrid security from the host security, and account for it using the accounting for derivatives. This separation process is referred to as bifurcation. Special hedge accounting is allowed only for hedging relationships that meet certain criteria. The main criteria are as follows. (1) There is formal documentation of the hedging relationship, the company's risk-management objective, and the strategy for undertaking the hedge, and the company designates the derivative as either a cash flow or fair value hedge. (2) The company expects the hedging relationship to be highly effective in achieving offsetting changes in fair value or cash flows. (3) "Special" hedge accounting is necessary only when there is a mismatch of the accounting effects for the hedging instrument and the hedged item under GAAP.

APPENDIX 17B VARIABLE-INTEREST ENTITIES

LEARNING OBJECTIVE 11
Describe the accounting for variable-interest entities.

The FASB has issued rules to address the concern that some companies are not reporting the risks and rewards of certain investments and other financial arrangements in their consolidated financial statements. **[12]** As one analyst noted, **Enron** showed the world the power of the idea that "if investors can't see it, they can't ask you about it—the 'it' being assets and liabilities."

What exactly did Enron do? First, it created a number of entities whose purpose was to hide debt, avoid taxes, and enrich certain management personnel to the detriment of the company and its stockholders. In effect, these entities, called **special-purpose entities (SPEs)**, appeared to be separate entities for which Enron had a limited economic interest. However, for many of these arrangements, Enron actually had a substantial economic interest. The risks and rewards of ownership were not shifted to the entities but remained with Enron. In short, Enron was obligated to repay investors in these SPEs when they were unsuccessful. Once Enron's problems were discovered, it soon became apparent that many other companies had similar problems.

WHAT ABOUT GAAP?

A reasonable question to ask with regard to SPEs is, "Why didn't GAAP prevent companies from hiding SPE debt and other risks, by forcing companies to include these obligations in their consolidated financial statements?" To understand why, we have to look at the basic rules of consolidation.

The GAAP rules indicate that consolidated financial statements are "usually necessary for a fair presentation when one of the companies in the group directly or indirectly has a controlling financial interest in other companies." They further note that "the usual condition for a controlling financial interest is ownership of a majority voting interest."[42] In other words, if a company like **Intel** owns more than 50 percent of the voting stock of another company, Intel consolidates that company. GAAP also indicates that controlling financial interest may be achieved through arrangements that do not involve voting interests. However, applying these guidelines in practice is difficult.

Whenever GAAP uses a clear line, like "greater than 50 percent," companies sometimes exploit the criterion. For example, some companies set up joint ventures in which each party owns exactly 50 percent. In that case, neither party consolidates. Or like **Coca-Cola**, a company may own less than 50 percent of the voting stock but maintain effective control through board of director relationships, supply relationships, or through some other type of financial arrangement.

So the FASB realized that changes had to be made to GAAP for consolidations, and it issued expanded consolidation guidelines. These guidelines define when a company should use factors other than voting interest to determine controlling financial interest. In this pronouncement, the FASB created a new risk-and-reward model to be used in situations where voting interests were unclear. The risk-and-reward model answers the basic questions of who stands to gain or lose the most from ownership in an SPE when ownership is uncertain.

In other words, we now have two models for consolidation:

1. **Voting-interest model**—If a company owns more than 50 percent of another company, then consolidate in most cases.
2. **Risk-and-reward model**—If a company is involved substantially in the economics of another company, then consolidate.

Operationally, the voting-interest model is easy to apply. It sets a "bright-line" ownership standard of more than 50 percent of the voting stock. However, if companies cannot determine control based on voting interest, they must use the risk-and-reward model.

CONSOLIDATION OF VARIABLE-INTEREST ENTITIES

To answer the question of who gains or loses when voting rights do not determine consolidation, the FASB developed the risk-and-reward model. In this model, the FASB introduced the notion of a variable-interest entity. A **variable-interest entity (VIE)** is an entity that has one of the following characteristics:

1. ***Insufficient equity investment at risk.*** Stockholders are assumed to have sufficient capital investment to support the entity's operations. If thinly capitalized, the entity is considered a VIE and is subject to the risk-and-reward model.

[42]"Consolidation of Certain Special Purpose Entities," Proposed Interpretation (Norwalk, Conn.: FASB, June 28, 2002).

2. ***Stockholders lack decision-making rights.*** In some cases, stockholders do not have the influence to control the company's destiny.

3. ***Stockholders do not absorb the losses or receive the benefits of a normal stockholder.*** In some entities, stockholders are shielded from losses related to their primary risks, or their returns are capped or must be shared with other parties.

Once the company determines that an entity is a variable-interest entity, it no longer can use the voting-interest model. The question that must then be asked is, "What party is exposed to the majority of the risks and rewards associated with the VIE?" This party is called the primary beneficiary and must consolidate the VIE. Illustration 17B-1 shows the decision model for the VIE consolidation model.[43]

ILLUSTRATION 17B-1
VIE Consolidation Model

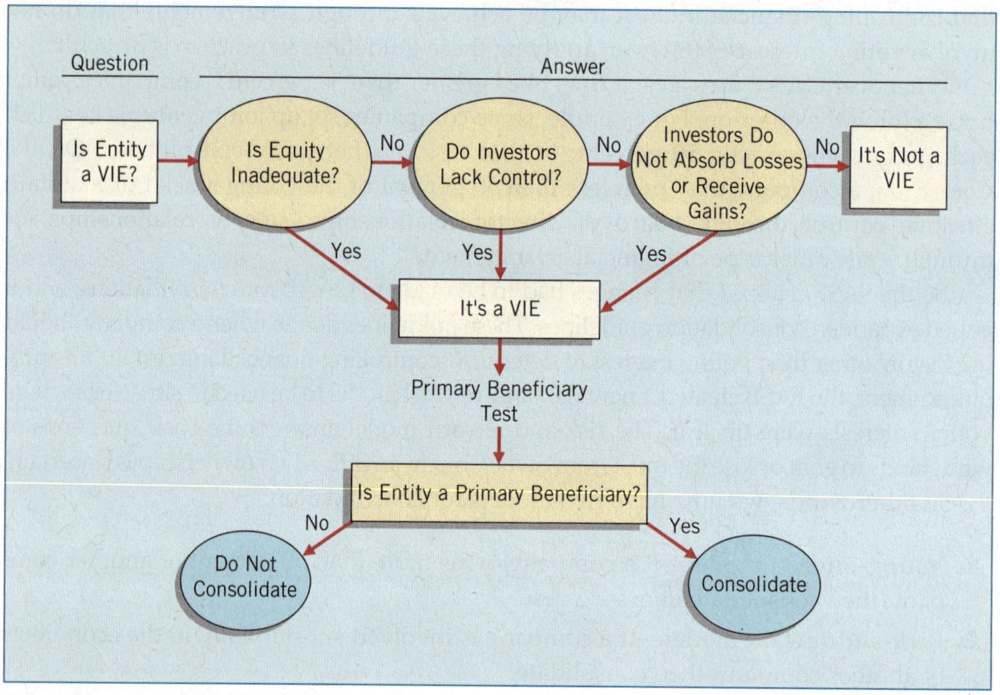

Some Examples

Let's look at a couple of examples to illustrate how this process works.

Example 1

Assume that **Citigroup** sells notes receivable to another entity called RAKO. RAKO's assets are financed in two ways: Lenders provide 90 percent, and investors provide the remaining 10 percent as an equity investment. If Citigroup does not guarantee the debt, Citigroup has low or nonexistent risk. Therefore, Citigroup would not consolidate the assets and liabilities of RAKO. On the other hand, if Citigroup guarantees RAKO's debt, then RAKO is a VIE, and Citigroup is the primary beneficiary. In that case, Citigroup must consolidate.

[43]In a recent amendment to the VIE consolidation rules, the FASB expanded the factors to be considered when deciding whether a VIE should be consolidated. The new guidelines require evaluation of qualitative factors related to the power to direct activities of the VIE and assessment of obligations to absorb losses or rights to receive benefits from the VIE. These qualitative factors must be considered in addition to the quantitative analysis of the expected losses of the entity to determine consolidation. [13] The IASB has recently issued new rules on consolidation that are similar to GAAP.

Example 2

San Diego Gas and Electric (SDGE) is required by law to buy power from small, local producers. In some cases, SDGE has contracts requiring it to purchase substantially all the power generated by these local companies over their lifetime. Because SDGE controls the outputs of the producers, they are VIEs. In this case, the risks and rewards related to ownership apply to SDGE. In other words, it is the primary beneficiary, and SDGE should include these producers in the consolidated financial statements.

Note that the primary beneficiary may have the risks and rewards of ownership through use of a variety of instruments and financial arrangements, such as equity investments, loans to the VIE, leases, derivatives, and guarantees. Potential VIEs include corporations, partnerships, limited liability companies, and majority-owned subsidiaries.

What Is Happening in Practice?

For most companies, the reporting related to VIEs will not materially affect their financial statements. As shown in Illustration 17B-2, one study of 509 companies with total market values over $500 million found that just 17 percent of the companies reviewed had a material impact when the VIE rules were first implemented.

ILLUSTRATION 17B-2
Impact of Rule Involving Risk-and-Reward Model

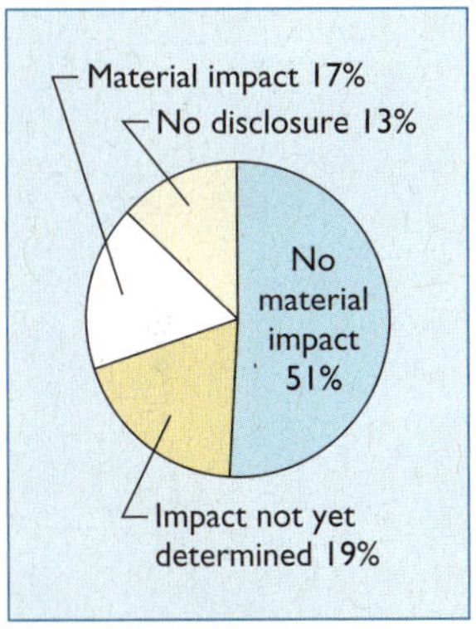

Source: Company Reports; *Glass, Lewis, & Co. Research Report* (November 6, 2003).

Of the material VIEs disclosed in the study, the most common types (42 percent) were related to joint-venture equity investments, followed by off-balance-sheet lease arrangements (22 percent). In some cases, companies restructured transactions to avoid consolidation. For example, Pep Boys, Choice Point, Inc., and Anadarko all appear to have restructured their lease transactions to avoid consolidation. On the other hand, companies like eBay, Kimberly-Clark, and Williams-Sonoma Inc. had to consolidate their VIEs. With respect to the new guidelines for VIEs, companies began reporting under these rules in 2010. Some estimates have as much as $5 trillion of assets that could be brought on-balance-sheet under the new rules. As an example, JP Morgan reported in a recent annual report that up to $160 billion of credit card receivables and other mortgage-backed loans will have to be consolidated when it adopts the new rules.

In summary, companies are required to consolidate certain investments and other financing arrangements that previously were reported off-balance-sheet. As a result, financial statements should be more complete in reporting the risks and rewards of these transactions.

SUMMARY OF LEARNING OBJECTIVE FOR APPENDIX 17B

11 Describe the accounting for variable-interest entities. Special variable-interest accounting is used in situations where control cannot be determined based on voting rights. A company is required to consolidate a variable-interest entity if it is the primary beneficiary of the variable-interest entity.

KEY TERMS

risk-and-reward model, *997*
special-purpose entity (SPE), *996*
variable-interest entity (VIE), *997*
voting-interest model, *997*

APPENDIX 17C FAIR VALUE DISCLOSURES

12 LEARNING OBJECTIVE
Describe required fair value disclosures.

As indicated in the chapter, the FASB believes that fair value information is relevant for making effective business decisions. However, others express concern about fair value measurements for two reasons: (1) the lack of reliability related to the fair value measurement in certain cases, and (2) the ability to manipulate fair value measurements to achieve financial results inconsistent with the underlying economics of the situation.

The Board recognizes these concerns and has attempted to develop a sound conceptual basis for measuring and reporting fair value information. In addition, it has placed emphasis on developing guidelines for reporting fair value information for financial instruments because many of these instruments have relatively active markets for which valuations can be reliably determined. The purpose of this appendix is to explain the disclosure requirements for financial instruments related to fair value information.

DISCLOSURE OF FAIR VALUE INFORMATION: FINANCIAL INSTRUMENTS

One requirement related to fair value disclosure is that both the cost and the fair value of all financial instruments be reported in the notes to the financial statements. **[14]** This enables readers of the financial statements to understand the fair value of the company's financial instruments and the potential gains and losses that might occur in the future as a result of these instruments.

The Board also decided that companies should disclose information that enables users to determine the extent of usage of fair value and the inputs used to implement fair value measurement. Two reasons for additional disclosure beyond the simple itemization of fair values are:

1. ***Differing levels of reliability exist in the measurement of fair value information.*** It therefore is important to understand the varying risks involved in measurement. It is difficult to incorporate these levels of uncertainty into the financial statements. Disclosure provides a framework for addressing the qualitative aspects related to risk and measurement.
2. ***Changes in the fair value of financial instruments are reported differently in the financial statements, depending on the type of financial instrument involved and whether the fair value option is employed.*** Note disclosure provides an opportunity to explain more precisely the impact that changes in the value of financial instruments have on financial results. In assessing the inputs, the Board recognizes that the reliability of the fair value measurement is of extreme importance. Many financial instruments are traded in active markets, and their valuation is not difficult. Other instruments are complex/illiquid, and their valuation is difficult.

To highlight these levels of reliability in valuation, the FASB established a fair value hierarchy. As discussed in Chapter 2 (page 57), this hierarchy identifies three broad levels—1, 2, and 3—related to the measurement of fair values. Level 1 is the most reliable measurement because fair value is based on quoted prices in active markets *for identical assets or liabilities*. Level 2 is less reliable; it is not based on quoted market prices for identical assets and liabilities but instead may be based on *similar assets or liabilities*. Level 3 is least reliable; it uses unobservable inputs that reflect the company's assumption as to the value of the financial instrument.

Illustration 17C-1 is an example of a fair value note disclosure for Sabathia Company. It includes both the fair value amounts and the reliability level. (A similar disclosure would be presented for liabilities.)

ILLUSTRATION 17C-1
Example of Fair Value Hierarchy

SABATHIA COMPANY
NOTES TO THE FINANCIAL STATEMENTS

($ in 000s)		Fair Value Measurements at Reporting Data Using		
Description	Fair Value 12/31/14	Quoted Prices in Active Markets for Identical Assets (Level 1)	Significant Other Observable Inputs (Level 2)	Significant Unobservable Inputs (Level 3)
Trading securities	$115	$105	$10	
Available-for-sale securities	75	75		
Derivatives	60	25	15	$20
Venture capital investments	10			10
Total	$260	$205	$25	$30

For assets and liabilities measured at fair value and classified as Level 3, a reconciliation of Level 3 changes for the period is required. In addition, companies should report an analysis of how Level 3 changes in fair value affect total gains and losses and their impact on net income. Illustration 17C-2 is an example of this disclosure.

ILLUSTRATION 17C-2
Reconciliation of Level 3 Inputs

SABATHIA COMPANY
NOTES TO THE FINANCIAL STATEMENTS

($ in 000s)	Fair Value Measurements Using Significant Unobservable Inputs (Level 3)		
	Derivatives	Venture Capital Investments	Total
Beginning balance	$14	$11	$25
Total gains or losses (realized/unrealized)			
Included in earnings (or changes in net assets)	11	(3)	8
Included in other comprehensive income	4		4
Purchases, issuances, and settlements	(7)	2	(5)
Transfers in and/or out of Level 3	(2)		(2)
Ending balance	$20	$10	$30
The amount of total gains or losses for the period included in earnings (or changes in net assets) attributable to the change in unrealized gains or losses relating to assets still held at the reporting date	$7	$2	$9

Gains and losses (realized and unrealized) included in earnings (or changes in net assets) for the period (above) are reported in trading revenues and in other revenues as follows.

	Trading Revenues	Other Revenues
Total gains or losses included in earnings (or changes in net assets) for the period (as shown in the table above)	$11	$(3)
Change in unrealized gains or losses relating to assets still held at reporting date	$7	$2

Sabathia Company's disclosure provides to the user of the financial statements an understanding of the following:

1. The carrying amount and the fair value of the company's financial instruments segregated by level of reliability. Thus, the reader of the financial statements has a basis for judging what credence should be given to the fair value amounts.

2. For Level 3 financial instruments, a reconciliation of the balance from the beginning to the end of the period. This reconciliation enables the reader to understand the composition of the change. It is important because these calculations are most affected by subjective estimates and could be subject to manipulation.
3. The impact of changes in fair value on the net assets of the company from one period to the next.

For companies that choose to use the fair value option for some or all of their financial instruments [15], they are permitted to incorporate the entire guidelines related to fair value measurement into one master schedule, or they can provide in a separate schedule information related solely to the fair value option.

Finally, companies must provide the following (with special emphasis on Level 3 measurements):

1. Quantitative information about significant unobservable inputs used for all Level 3 measurements.
2. A qualitative discussion about the sensitivity of recurring Level 3 measurements to changes in the unobservable inputs disclosed, including interrelationships between inputs.
3. A description of the company's valuation process.
4. Any transfers between Levels 1 and 2 of the fair value hierarchy.
5. Information about nonfinancial assets measured at fair value at amounts that differ from the assets' highest and best use.
6. The proper hierarchy classification for items that are not recognized on the balance sheet but are disclosed in the notes to the financial statements.

A typical disclosure related to Level 3 fair value measurements is presented in Illustration 17C-3.

ILLUSTRATION 17C-3
Quantitative Information about Level 3 Fair Value Measurements

($ in millions)	Fair Value at 12/31/2014	Valuation Technique(s)	Unobservable Input	Range (Weighted-Average)
Residential mortgage-backed securities	125	Discounted cash flow	Constant prepayment rate Probability of default Loss severity	3.5%–5.5% (4.5%) 5%–50% (10%) 40%–100% (60%)
Collateralized debt obligations	35	Consensus pricing	Offered quotes Comparability adjustments (%)	20–45 −10%–+15% (+5%)
Direct venture capital investments: Healthcare	53	Discounted cash flow	Weighted-average cost of capital Long-term revenue growth rate Long-term pretax operating margin Discount for lack of marketability[a] Control premium[a]	7%–16% (12.1%) 2%–5% (4.2%) 3%–20% (10.3%) 5%–20% (17%) 10%–30% (20%)
		Market-comparable companies	EBITDA multiple[b] Revenue multiple[b] Discount for lack of marketability[a] Control premium[a]	6.5–12 (9.5) 1.0–3.0 (2.0) 5%–20% (10%) 10%–20% (12%)
Credit contracts	38	Option model	Annualized volatility of credit[c] Counterparty credit risk[d] Own credit risk[d]	10%–20% 0.5–3.5% 0.3–2.0%

[a]Represents amounts used when the reporting entity has determined that market participants would take into account these premiums and discounts when pricing the investments.
[b]Represents amounts used when the reporting entity has determined that market participants would use such multiples when pricing the investments.
[c]Represents the range of the volatility curves used in the valuation analysis that the reporting entity has determined market participants would use when pricing the contracts.
[d]Represents the range of the credit default swap spread curves used in the valuation analysis that the reporting entity has determined market participants would use when pricing the contracts.

(*Note:* For liabilities, a similar table should be presented.)

DISCLOSURE OF FAIR VALUES: IMPAIRED ASSETS OR LIABILITIES

In addition to financial instruments, companies often have assets or liabilities that are remeasured on a nonrecurring basis due to impairment. In this case, the fair value hierarchy can highlight the reliability of the measurement, coupled with the related gain or loss for the period. Illustration 17C-4 highlights this disclosure for McClung Company.

ILLUSTRATION 17C-4
Disclosure of Fair Value, with Impairment

McCLUNG COMPANY
NOTES TO THE FINANCIAL STATEMENTS

($ in millions)		Fair Value Measurements Using		
Description	Year Ended 12/31/14	Quoted Prices in Active Markets for Identical Assets (Level 1)	Significant Other Observable Inputs (Level 2)	Significant Unobservable Inputs (Level 3)
Long-lived assets held and used	$75	—	$75	—
Goodwill	30	—	—	$30
Long-lived assets held for sale	26	—	26	—

Long-lived assets held and used with a carrying amount of $100 million were written down to their fair value of $75 million, resulting in an impairment charge of $25 million, which was included in earnings for the period.

Goodwill with a carrying amount of $65 million was written down to its implied fair value of $30 million, resulting in an impairment charge of $35 million, which was included in earnings for the period.

In accordance with the provisions of the Impairment or Disposal of Long-Lived Assets Subsections of FASB Codification Subtopic 360-10, long-lived assets held for sale with a carrying amount of $35 million were written down to their fair value of $26 million, less cost to sell of $6 million (or $20 million), resulting in a loss of $15 million, which was included in earnings for the period.

CONCLUSION

With recent joint FASB and IASB standard-setting efforts, we now have convergence with respect to fair value measurement, both in terms of the definition and measurement guidelines when fair value is the measurement approach in GAAP and IFRS. In addition, GAAP and IFRS have the same fair value disclosure requirements, as illustrated in this appendix. As the former chair of the IASB noted, this "marks the completion of a major convergence project and is a fundamentally important element of our joint response to the global crisis. The result is clearer and more consistent guidance on measuring fair value, where its use is already required."

SUMMARY OF LEARNING OBJECTIVE FOR APPENDIX 17C

12 Describe required fair value disclosures. The FASB has developed required fair value disclosures in response to concerns about the reliability of fair value measures. Disclosure elements include fair value amounts and reliability levels as well as impaired assets or liabilities.

DEMONSTRATION PROBLEM

Rogers Corporation carries an account in its general ledger called Investments, which contained the following debits for investment purchases and no credits.

Feb. 1, 2014	Jordy Company common stock, $100 par, 200 shares	$ 37,400
April 1	U.S. government bonds, 11%, due April 1, 2024, interest payable April 1 and October 1, 100 bonds at $1,000 each	100,000
July 1	Driver Company 12% bonds, par $50,000, dated March 1, 2010, purchased at par plus accrued interest, interest payable annually on March 1, due March 1, 2034	52,000

Instructions

(a) Prepare the entries necessary to classify the amounts into proper accounts, assuming that all the securities are classified as available-for-sale.

(b) Prepare the entry to record the accrued interest on December 31, 2014.

(c) The fair values of the securities on December 31, 2014, were:

Jordy Company common stock	$ 33,800 (1% of total shares)
U.S. government bonds	124,700
Driver Company bonds	58,600

What entry or entries, if any, would you recommend be made?

(d) The U.S. government bonds were sold on July 1, 2015, for $119,200 plus accrued interest. Give the proper entry.

(e) Now assume Rogers' investment in Jordy Company represents 30% of Jordy's shares. Prepare the 2014 entries for the investment in Jordy stock. In 2014, Jordy declared and paid dividends of $9,000 (on September 30) and reported net income of $30,000.

Solution

(a)

	Debit	Credit
Equity Investments (available-for-sale)	37,400	
Debt Investments (available-for-sale)	150,000	
Interest Revenue ($50,000 × .12 × 4/12)	2,000	
Investments		189,400

(b)

December 31, 2014

	Debit	Credit
Interest Receivable	7,750	
Interest Revenue		7,750

(c)

Available-for-Sale Portfolio
December 31, 2014

Securities	Cost	Fair Value	Unrealized Gain (Loss)
Jordy Company stock	$ 37,400	$ 33,800	$ (3,600)
U.S. government bonds	100,000	124,700	24,700
Driver Company bonds	50,000	58,600	8,600
Total	$187,400	$217,100	29,700
Previous fair value adjustment balance			0
Fair value adjustment—Dr.			$29,700

	Debit	Credit
Fair Value Adjustment (available-for-sale)	29,700	
Unrealized Holding Gain or Loss—Equity		29,700

(d)

July 1, 2015

	Debit	Credit
Cash ($119,200 + $2,750)	121,950	
Debt Investments (available-for-sale)		100,000
Interest Revenue ($100,000 × .11 × 3/12)		2,750
Gain on Sale of Investments		19,200

(e)	February 1, 2014		
	Equity Investments (Jordy Company)	37,400	
	Cash		37,400
	September 30, 2014		
	Cash	2,700	
	Equity Investments (Jordy Company) (30% × $9,000)		2,700
	December 31, 2014		
	Equity Investments (Jordy Company)	9,000	
	Investment Income (30% × $30,000)		9,000

FASB CODIFICATION

FASB Codification References

[1] FASB ASC Glossary. [Predecessor literature: "Accounting for Certain Investments in Debt and Equity Securities," *Statement of Financial Accounting Standards No. 115* (Norwalk, Conn.: FASB, 1993), par. 137.]

[2] FASB ASC 820-10-20. [Predecessor literature: "Fair Value Measurement," *Statement of Financial Accounting Standards No. 157* (Norwalk, Conn.: FASB, September 2006).]

[3] FASB ASC 220. [Predecessor literature: "Reporting Comprehensive Income," *Statement of Financial Accounting Standards No. 130* (Norwalk, Conn.: FASB, 1997).]

[4] FASB ASC 323-10-15. [Predecessor literature: "The Equity Method of Accounting for Investments in Common Stock," *Opinions of the Accounting Principles Board No. 18* (New York: AICPA, 1971), par. 17.]

[5] FASB ASC 323-10-15-10. [Predecessor literature: "Criteria for Applying the Equity Method of Accounting for Investments in Common Stock," *Interpretations of the Financial Accounting Standards Board No. 35* (Stamford, Conn.: FASB, 1981).]

[6] FASB ASC 323-10-35. [Predecessor literature: "The Equity Method of Accounting for Investments in Common Stock," *Opinions of the Accounting Principles Board No. 18* (New York: AICPA, 1971), par. 19(i).]

[7] FASB ASC 815-10-05. [Predecessor literature: "Accounting for Derivative Instruments and Hedging Activities," *Statement of Financial Accounting Standards No. 133* (Stamford, Conn.: FASB, 1998).]

[8] FASB ASC 820-10. [Predecessor literature: "Fair Value Measurement," *Statement of Financial Accounting Standards No. 157* (Norwalk, Conn.: FASB, September 2006).]

[9] FASB ASC 815-10-05-4. [Predecessor literature: "Accounting for Derivative Instruments and Hedging Activities," *Statement of Financial Accounting Standards No. 133* (Stamford, Conn.: FASB, 1998), par. 249.]

[10] FASB ASC 815-10-05-4. [Predecessor literature: "Accounting for Derivative Instruments and Hedging Activities," *Statement of Financial Accounting Standards No. 133* (Stamford, Conn.: FASB, 1998).]

[11] FASB ASC 825-10-25-1. [Predecessor literature: "The Fair Value Option for Financial Assets and Liabilities, Including an Amendment of FASB Statement No. 115," *Statement of Financial Accounting Standards No. 159* (Norwalk, Conn.: FASB, February 2007).]

[12] FASB ASC 810-10-05. [Predecessor literature: "Consolidation of Variable Interest Entities (revised)—An Interpretation of *ARB No. 51*," *Financial Accounting Standards Interpretation No. 46(R)* (Norwalk, Conn.: FASB, December 2003).]

[13] FASB ASC 810-10-15. [Predecessor literature: "Consolidation of Variable Interest Entities (revised)—An Interpretation of *ARB No. 51*," *Financial Accounting Standards Interpretation No. 46(R)* (Norwalk, Conn.: FASB, December 2003).]

[14] FASB ASC 820-10. [Predecessor literature: "Fair Value Measurement," *Statement of Financial Accounting Standards No. 157* (Norwalk, Conn.: FASB, September 2006).]

[15] FASB ASC 825-10-25-1. (Predecessor literature: "The Fair Value Option for Financial Assets and Liabilities, Including an Amendment of FASB Statement No. 115," *Statement of Financial Accounting Standards No. 159* (Norwalk, Conn.: FASB, February 2007).]

Exercises

If your school has a subscription to the FASB Codification, go to *http://aaahq.org/ascLogin.cfm* to log in and prepare responses to the following. Provide Codification references for your responses.

CE17-1 Access the glossary ("Master Glossary") to answer the following.

(a) What are trading securities?
(b) What is the definition of "holding gain or loss"?
(c) What is a cash flow hedge?
(d) What is a fair value hedge?

CE17-2 What guidance does the SEC give for disclosures regarding accounting policies used for derivatives?

CE17-3 When would an investor discontinue applying the equity method in an investment? Are there any exceptions to this rule?

CE17-4 For balance sheet purposes, can the fair value of a derivative in a loss position be netted against the fair value of a derivative in a gain position?

An additional Codification case can be found in the Using Your Judgment section, on page 1026.

Be sure to check the book's companion website for a Review and Analysis Exercise, with solution.

WileyPLUS **Brief Exercises, Exercises, Problems, and many more learning and assessment tools and resources are available for practice in WileyPLUS.**

Note: All asterisked Questions, Exercises, and Problems relate to material in the appendices to the chapter.

QUESTIONS

1. Distinguish between a debt security and an equity security.
2. What purpose does the variety in bond features (types and characteristics) serve?
3. What is the cost of a long-term investment in bonds?
4. Identify and explain the three types of classifications for investments in debt securities.
5. When should a debt security be classified as held-to-maturity?
6. Explain how trading securities are accounted for and reported.
7. At what amount should trading, available-for-sale, and held-to-maturity securities be reported on the balance sheet?
8. On July 1, 2014, Wheeler Company purchased $4,000,000 of Duggen Company's 8% bonds, due on July 1, 2021. The bonds, which pay interest semiannually on January 1 and July 1, were purchased for $3,500,000 to yield 10%. Determine the amount of interest revenue Wheeler should report on its income statement for the year ended December 31, 2014.
9. If the bonds in Question 8 are classified as available-for-sale and they have a fair value at December 31, 2014, of $3,604,000, prepare the journal entry (if any) at December 31, 2014, to record this transaction.
10. Indicate how unrealized holding gains and losses should be reported for investments securities classified as trading, available-for-sale, and held-to-maturity.
11. (a) Assuming no Fair Value Adjustment (available-for-sale) account balance at the beginning of the year, prepare the adjusting entry at the end of the year if Laura Company's available-for-sale securities have a fair value $60,000 below cost. (b) Assume the same information as part (a), except that Laura Company has a debit balance in its Fair Value Adjustment account of $10,000 at the beginning of the year. Prepare the adjusting entry at year-end.
12. Identify and explain the different types of classifications for investments in equity securities.
13. Why are held-to-maturity investments applicable only to debt securities?
14. Hayes Company sold 10,000 shares of Kenyon Co. common stock for $27.50 per share, incurring $1,770 in brokerage commissions. These securities were classified as trading and originally cost $260,000. Prepare the entry to record the sale of these securities.

15. Distinguish between the accounting treatment for available-for-sale equity securities and trading equity securities.

16. What constitutes "significant influence" when an investor's financial interest is below the 50% level?

17. Explain how the investment account is affected by investee activities under the equity method.

18. Your classmate Kate believes that the equity method is applied with a strict application of the "20%" rule. Do you agree? Explain.

19. Hiram Co. uses the equity method to account for investments in common stock. What accounting should be made for dividends received from these investments subsequent to the date of investment?

20. Raleigh Corp. has an investment with a carrying value (equity method) on its books of $170,000 representing a 30% interest in Borg Company, which suffered a $620,000 loss this year. How should Raleigh Corp. handle its proportionate share of Borg's loss?

21. Where on the asset side of the balance sheet are trading securities, available-for-sale securities, and held-to-maturity securities reported? Explain.

22. Explain why reclassification adjustments are necessary.

23. Briefly discuss how a transfer of securities from the available-for-sale category to the trading category affects stockholders' equity and income.

24. When is a debt security considered impaired? Explain how to account for the impairment of an available-for-sale debt security.

25. What is the GAAP definition of fair value?

26. What is the fair value option?

27. Franklin Corp. has an investment that it has held for several years. When it purchased the investment, Franklin classified and accounted for it as available-for-sale. Can Franklin use the fair value option for this investment? Explain.

***28.** What is meant by the term "underlying" as it relates to derivative financial instruments?

***29.** What are the main distinctions between a traditional financial instrument and a derivative financial instrument?

***30.** What is the purpose of a fair value hedge?

***31.** In what situation will the unrealized holding gain or loss on an available-for-sale security be reported in income?

***32.** Why might a company become involved in an interest rate swap contract to receive fixed interest payments and pay variable?

***33.** What is the purpose of a cash flow hedge?

***34.** Where are gains and losses related to cash flow hedges involving anticipated transactions reported?

***35.** What are hybrid securities? Give an example of a hybrid security.

***36.** Explain the difference between the voting-interest model and the risk-and-reward model used for consolidation.

***37.** What is a variable-interest entity?

BRIEF EXERCISES

2 **BE17-1** Garfield Company purchased, as a held-to-maturity investment, $80,000 of the 9%, 5-year bonds of Chester Corporation for $74,086, which provides an 11% return. Prepare Garfield's journal entries for (a) the purchase of the investment, and (b) the receipt of annual interest and discount amortization. Assume effective-interest amortization is used.

2 **BE17-2** Use the information from BE17-1 but assume the bonds are purchased as an available-for-sale security. Prepare Garfield's journal entries for (a) the purchase of the investment, (b) the receipt of annual interest and discount amortization, and (c) the year-end fair value adjustment. (Assume a zero balance in the Fair Value Adjustment account.) The bonds have a year-end fair value of $75,500.

2 **BE17-3** Carow Corporation purchased, as a held-to-maturity investment, $60,000 of the 8%, 5-year bonds of Harrison, Inc. for $65,118, which provides a 6% return. The bonds pay interest semiannually. Prepare Carow's journal entries for (a) the purchase of the investment, and (b) the receipt of semiannual interest and premium amortization. Assume effective-interest amortization is used.

2 **BE17-4** Hendricks Corporation purchased trading investment bonds for $50,000 at par. At December 31, Hendricks received annual interest of $2,000, and the fair value of the bonds was $47,400. Prepare Hendricks' journal entries for (a) the purchase of the investment, (b) the interest received, and (c) the fair value adjustment. (Assume a zero balance in the Fair Value Adjustment account.)

3 **BE17-5** Fairbanks Corporation purchased 400 shares of Sherman Inc. common stock as an available-for-sale investment for $13,200. During the year, Sherman paid a cash dividend of $3.25 per share. At year-end, Sherman stock was selling for $34.50 per share. Prepare Fairbanks' journal entries to record (a) the purchase of the investment, (b) the dividends received, and (c) the fair value adjustment. (Assume a zero balance in the Fair Value Adjustment account.)

3 **BE17-6** Use the information from BE17-5 but assume the stock was purchased as a trading security. Prepare Fairbanks' journal entries to record (a) the purchase of the investment, (b) the dividends received, and (c) the fair value adjustment.

4 **BE17-7** Zoop Corporation purchased for $300,000 a 30% interest in Murphy, Inc. This investment enables Zoop to exert significant influence over Murphy. During the year, Murphy earned net income of $180,000 and paid dividends of $60,000. Prepare Zoop's journal entries related to this investment.

3 **BE17-8** Cleveland Company has a stock portfolio valued at $4,000 (available-for-sale). Its cost was $3,300. If the Fair Value Adjustment account has a debit balance of $200, prepare the journal entry at year-end.

6 **BE17-9** The following information relates to **Starbucks** for the year ended October 2, 2011: net income 1,245.7 million; unrealized holding loss of $10.9 million related to available-for-sale securities during the year; accumulated other comprehensive income of $57.2 million on October 3, 2010. Assuming no other changes in accumulated other comprehensive income, determine (a) other comprehensive income for 2011, (b) comprehensive income for 2011, and (c) accumulated other comprehensive income at October 2, 2011.

5 **BE17-10** Hillsborough Co. has an available-for-sale investment in the bonds of Schuyler Corp. with a carrying (and fair) value of $70,000. Hillsborough determined that due to poor economic prospects for Schuyler, the bonds have decreased in value to $60,000. It is determined that this loss in value is other-than-temporary. Prepare the journal entry, if any, to record the reduction in value.

EXERCISES

1 3 **E17-1 (Investment Classifications)** For the following investments identify whether they are:

1. Trading Securities
2. Available-for-Sale Securities
3. Held-to-Maturity Securities

Each case is independent of the other.

(a) A bond that will mature in 4 years was bought 1 month ago when the price dropped. As soon as the value increases, which is expected next month, it will be sold.
(b) 10% of the outstanding stock of Farm-Co was purchased. The company is planning on eventually getting a total of 30% of its outstanding stock.
(c) 10-year bonds were purchased this year. The bonds mature at the first of next year.
(d) Bonds that will mature in 5 years are purchased. The company would like to hold them until they mature, but money has been tight recently and they may need to be sold.
(e) Preferred stock was purchased for its constant dividend. The company is planning to hold the preferred stock for a long time.
(f) A bond that matures in 10 years was purchased. The company is investing money set aside for an expansion project planned 10 years from now.

2 **E17-2 (Entries for Held-to-Maturity Securities)** On January 1, 2013, Dagwood Company purchased at par 12% bonds having a maturity value of $300,000. They are dated January 1, 2013, and mature January 1, 2018, with interest receivable December 31 of each year. The bonds are classified in the held-to-maturity category.

XLS

Instructions

(a) Prepare the journal entry at the date of the bond purchase.
(b) Prepare the journal entry to record the interest received for 2013.
(c) Prepare the journal entry to record the interest received for 2014.

2 **E17-3 (Entries for Held-to-Maturity Securities)** On January 1, 2013, Hi and Lois Company purchased 12% bonds having a maturity value of $300,000 for $322,744.44. The bonds provide the bondholders with a 10% yield. They are dated January 1, 2013, and mature January 1, 2018, with interest receivable December 31 of each year. Hi and Lois Company uses the effective-interest method to allocate unamortized discount or premium. The bonds are classified in the held-to-maturity category.

Instructions

(a) Prepare the journal entry at the date of the bond purchase.
(b) Prepare a bond amortization schedule.

(c) Prepare the journal entry to record the interest received and the amortization for 2013.
(d) Prepare the journal entry to record the interest received and the amortization for 2014.

2 **E17-4 (Entries for Available-for-Sale Securities)** Assume the same information as in E17-3 except that the securities are classified as available-for-sale. The fair value of the bonds at December 31 of each year-end is as follows.

2013	$320,500	2016	$310,000
2014	$309,000	2017	$300,000
2015	$308,000		

Instructions

(a) Prepare the journal entry at the date of the bond purchase.
(b) Prepare the journal entries to record the interest received and recognition of fair value for 2013.
(c) Prepare the journal entry to record the recognition of fair value for 2014.

2 **E17-5 (Effective-Interest versus Straight-Line Bond Amortization)** On January 1, 2013, Phantom Company acquires $200,000 of Spiderman Products, Inc., 9% bonds at a price of $185,589. The interest is payable each December 31, and the bonds mature December 31, 2015. The investment will provide Phantom Company a 12% yield. The bonds are classified as held-to-maturity.

XLS

Instructions

(a) Prepare a 3-year schedule of interest revenue and bond discount amortization, applying the straight-line method.
(b) Prepare a 3-year schedule of interest revenue and bond discount amortization, applying the effective-interest method.
(c) Prepare the journal entry for the interest receipt of December 31, 2014, and the discount amortization under the straight-line method.
(d) Prepare the journal entry for the interest receipt of December 31, 2014, and the discount amortization under the effective-interest method.

3 **E17-6 (Entries for Available-for-Sale and Trading Securities)** The following information is available for Barkley Company at December 31, 2014, regarding its investments.

Securities	Cost	Fair Value
3,000 shares of Myers Corporation Common Stock	$40,000	$48,000
1,000 shares of Cole Incorporated Preferred Stock	25,000	22,000
	$65,000	$70,000

Instructions

(a) Prepare the adjusting entry (if any) for 2014, assuming the securities are classified as trading.
(b) Prepare the adjusting entry (if any) for 2014, assuming the securities are classified as available-for-sale.
(c) Discuss how the amounts reported in the financial statements are affected by the entries in (a) and (b).

3 **E17-7 (Trading Securities Entries)** On December 21, 2013, Bucky Katt Company provided you with the following information regarding its trading securities.

December 31, 2013

Investments (Trading)	Cost	Fair Value	Unrealized Gain (Loss)
Clemson Corp. stock	$20,000	$19,000	$(1,000)
Colorado Co. stock	10,000	9,000	(1,000)
Buffaloes Co. stock	20,000	20,600	600
Total of portfolio	$50,000	$48,600	(1,400)
Previous fair value adjustment balance			–0–
Fair value adjustment—Cr.			$(1,400)

During 2014, Colorado Company stock was sold for $9,400. The fair value of the stock on December 31, 2014, was Clemson Corp. stock—$19,100; Buffaloes Co. stock—$20,500.

Instructions

(a) Prepare the adjusting journal entry needed on December 31, 2013.
(b) Prepare the journal entry to record the sale of the Colorado Company stock during 2014.
(c) Prepare the adjusting journal entry needed on December 31, 2014.

3 **E17-8 (Available-for-Sale Securities Entries and Reporting)** Satchel Corporation purchases equity securities costing $73,000 and classifies them as available-for-sale securities. At December 31, the fair value of the portfolio is $65,000.

Instructions

Prepare the adjusting entry to report the securities properly. Indicate the statement presentation of the accounts in your entry.

3 **E17-9 (Available-for-Sale Securities Entries and Financial Statement Presentation)** At December 31, 2013, the available-for-sale equity portfolio for Steffi Graf, Inc. is as follows.

Security	Cost	Fair Value	Unrealized Gain (Loss)
A	$17,500	$15,000	($2,500)
B	12,500	14,000	1,500
C	23,000	25,500	2,500
Total	$53,000	$54,500	1,500
Previous fair value adjustment balance—Dr.			400
Fair value adjustment—Dr.			$1,100

On January 20, 2014, Steffi Graf, Inc. sold security A for $15,100. The sale proceeds are net of brokerage fees.

Instructions

(a) Prepare the adjusting entry at December 31, 2013, to report the portfolio at fair value.
(b) Show the balance sheet presentation of the investment-related accounts at December 31, 2013. (Ignore notes presentation.)
(c) Prepare the journal entry for the 2014 sale of security A.

6 **E17-10 (Comprehensive Income Disclosure)** Assume the same information as E17-9 and that Steffi Graf Inc. reports net income in 2013 of $120,000 and in 2014 of $140,000. Total holding gains (including any realized holding gain or loss) total $40,000.

Instructions

(a) Prepare a statement of comprehensive income for 2013 starting with net income.
(b) Prepare a statement of comprehensive income for 2014 starting with net income.

3 **E17-11 (Equity Securities Entries)** Arantxa Corporation made the following cash purchases of securities during 2014, which is the first year in which Arantxa invested in securities.

1. On January 15, purchased 10,000 shares of Sanchez Company's common stock at $33.50 per share plus commission $1,980.
2. On April 1, purchased 5,000 shares of Vicario Co.'s common stock at $52.00 per share plus commission $3,370.
3. On September 10, purchased 7,000 shares of WTA Co.'s preferred stock at $26.50 per share plus commission $4,910.

On May 20, 2014, Arantxa sold 4,000 shares of Sanchez Company's common stock at a market price of $35 per share less brokerage commissions, taxes, and fees of $3,850. The year-end fair values per share were Sanchez $30, Vicario $55, and WTA $28. In addition, the chief accountant of Arantxa told you that Arantxa Corporation plans to hold these securities for the long term but may sell them in order to earn profits from appreciation in prices.

Instructions

(a) Prepare the journal entries to record the above three security purchases.
(b) Prepare the journal entry for the security sale on May 20.
(c) Compute the unrealized gains or losses and prepare the adjusting entries for Arantxa on December 31, 2014.

3 4 **E17-12 (Journal Entries for Fair Value and Equity Methods)** The following are two independent situations.

Situation 1: Conchita Cosmetics acquired 10% of the 200,000 shares of common stock of Martinez Fashion at a total cost of $13 per share on March 18, 2014. On June 30, Martinez declared and paid a $75,000 cash dividend. On December 31, Martinez reported net income of $122,000 for the year. At December 31, the market price of Martinez Fashion was $15 per share. The securities are classified as available-for-sale.

Situation 2: Monica, Inc. obtained significant influence over Seles Corporation by buying 30% of Seles's 30,000 outstanding shares of common stock at a total cost of $9 per share on January 1, 2014. On June 15, Seles declared and paid a cash dividend of $36,000. On December 31, Seles reported a net income of $85,000 for the year.

Instructions

Prepare all necessary journal entries in 2014 for both situations.

4 **E17-13 (Equity Method)** Parent Co. invested $1,000,000 in Sub Co. for 25% of its outstanding stock. Sub Co. pays out 40% of net income in dividends each year.

Instructions

Use the information in the following T-account for the investment in Sub to answer the following questions.

Investment in Sub Co.	
1,000,000	
110,000	
	44,000

(a) How much was Parent Co.'s share of Sub Co.'s net income for the year?
(b) How much was Parent Co.'s share of Sub Co.'s dividends for the year?
(c) What was Sub Co.'s total net income for the year?
(d) What was Sub Co.'s total dividends for the year?

3 **E17-14 (Equity Investment—Trading)** Oregon Co. had purchased 200 shares of Washington Co. for $40 each this year and classified the investment as a trading security. Oregon Co. sold 100 shares of the stock for $45 each. At year-end, the price per share of the Washington Co. stock had dropped to $35.

Instructions

Prepare the journal entries for these transactions and any year-end adjustments.

3 **E17-15 (Equity Investments—Trading)** Kenseth Company has the following securities in its trading portfolio of securities on December 31, 2013.

Investments (Trading)	Cost	Fair Value
1,500 shares of Gordon, Inc., Common	$ 73,500	$ 69,000
5,000 shares of Wallace Corp., Common	180,000	175,000
400 shares of Martin, Inc., Preferred	60,000	61,600
	$313,500	$305,600

All of the securities were purchased in 2013.

In 2014, Kenseth completed the following securities transactions.

March 1	Sold the 1,500 shares of Gordon, Inc., Common, @ $45 less fees of $1,200
April 1	Bought 700 shares of Earnhart Corp., Common, @ $75 plus fees of $1,300

Kenseth Company's portfolio of trading securities appeared as follows on December 31, 2014.

Investments (Trading)	Cost	Fair Value
5,000 shares of Wallace Corp., Common	$180,000	$175,000
700 shares of Earnhart Corp., Common	53,800	50,400
400 shares of Martin, Inc., Preferred	60,000	58,000
	$293,800	$283,400

Instructions

Prepare the general journal entries for Kenseth Company for:

(a) The 2013 adjusting entry.
(b) The sale of the Gordon stock.
(c) The purchase of the Earnhart stock.
(d) The 2014 adjusting entry for the trading portfolio.

3 4 **E17-16 (Fair Value and Equity Method Compared)** Jaycie Phelps Inc. acquired 20% of the outstanding common stock of Theresa Kulikowski Inc. on December 31, 2013. The purchase price was $1,200,000 for 50,000 shares. Kulikowski Inc. declared and paid an $0.85 per share cash dividend on June 30 and on December 31, 2014. Kulikowski reported net income of $730,000 for 2014. The fair value of Kulikowski's stock was $27 per share at December 31, 2014.

Instructions

(a) Prepare the journal entries for Jaycie Phelps Inc. for 2013 and 2014, assuming that Phelps cannot exercise significant influence over Kulikowski. The securities should be classified as available-for-sale.

(b) Prepare the journal entries for Jaycie Phelps Inc. for 2013 and 2014, assuming that Phelps can exercise significant influence over Kulikowski.

(c) At what amount is the investment in securities reported on the balance sheet under each of these methods at December 31, 2014? What is the total net income reported in 2014 under each of these methods?

4 **E17-17 (Equity Method)** On January 1, 2014, Pennington Corporation purchased 30% of the common shares of Edwards Company for $180,000. During the year, Edwards earned net income of $80,000 and paid dividends of $20,000.

Instructions

Prepare the entries for Pennington to record the purchase and any additional entries related to this investment in Edwards Company in 2014.

5 **E17-18 (Impairment of Debt Securities)** Hagar Corporation has municipal bonds classified as available-for-sale at December 31, 2013. These bonds have a par value of $800,000, an amortized cost of $800,000, and a fair value of $720,000. The unrealized loss of $80,000 previously recognized as other comprehensive income and as a separate component of stockholders' equity is now determined to be other than temporary. That is, the company believes that impairment accounting is now appropriate for these bonds.

Instructions

(a) Prepare the journal entry to recognize the impairment. No entry is needed to adjust accumulated other comprehensive income.

(b) What is the new cost basis of the municipal bonds? Given that the maturity value of the bonds is $800,000, should Hagar Corporation amortize the difference between the carrying amount and the maturity value over the life of the bonds?

(c) At December 31, 2014, the fair value of the municipal bonds is $760,000. Prepare the entry (if any) to record this information.

3 5 **E17-19 (Fair Value Measurement)** Presented below is information related to the purchases of common stock by Lilly Company during 2014.

	Cost (at purchase date)	Fair Value (at December 31)
Investment in Arroyo Company stock	$100,000	$ 80,000
Investment in Lee Corporation stock	250,000	300,000
Investment in Woods Inc. stock	180,000	190,000
Total	$530,000	$570,000

Instructions

(Assume a zero balance for any Fair Value Adjustment account.)

(a) What entry would Lilly make at December 31, 2014, to record the investment in Arroyo Company stock if it chooses to report this security using the fair value option?

(b) What entry would Lilly make at December 31, 2014, to record the investment in Lee Corporation, assuming that Lilly wants to classify this security as available-for-sale? This security is the only available-for-sale security that Lilly presently owns.

(c) What entry would Lilly make at December 31, 2014, to record the investment in Woods Inc., assuming that Lilly wants to classify this investment as a trading security?

3 5 **E17-20 (Fair Value Measurement Issues)** Assume the same information as in E17-19 for Lilly Company. In addition, assume that the investment in the Woods Inc. stock was sold during 2015 for $195,000.

At December 31, 2015, the following information relates to its two remaining investments of common stock.

	Cost (at purchase date)	Fair Value (at December 31)
Investment in Arroyo Company stock	$100,000	$140,000
Investment in Lee Corporation stock	250,000	310,000
Total	$350,000	$450,000

Net income before any security gains and losses for 2015 was $905,000.

Instructions

(a) Compute the amount of net income or net loss that Lilly should report for 2015, taking into consideration Lilly's security transactions for 2015.

(b) Prepare the journal entry to record unrealized gain or loss related to the investment in Arroyo Company stock at December 31, 2015.

2 3 5 **E17-21 (Fair Value Option)** Presented below is selected information related to the financial instruments of Dawson Company at December 31, 2014. This is Dawson Company's first year of operations.

	Carrying Amount	Fair Value (at December 31)
Investment in debt securities (intent is to hold to maturity)	$ 40,000	$ 41,000
Investment in Chen Company stock	800,000	910,000
Bonds payable	220,000	195,000

Instructions

(a) Dawson elects to use the fair value option whenever possible. Assuming that Dawson's net income is $100,000 in 2014 before reporting any securities gains or losses, determine Dawson's net income for 2014.

(b) Record the journal entry, if any, necessary at December 31, 2014, to record the fair value option for the bonds payable.

7 ***E17-22 (Derivative Transaction)** On January 2, 2014, Jones Company purchases a call option for $300 on Merchant common stock. The call option gives Jones the option to buy 1,000 shares of Merchant at a strike price of $50 per share. The market price of a Merchant share is $50 on January 2, 2014 (the intrinsic value is therefore $0). On March 31, 2014, the market price for Merchant stock is $53 per share, and the time value of the option is $200.

Instructions

(a) Prepare the journal entry to record the purchase of the call option on January 2, 2014.

(b) Prepare the journal entry(ies) to recognize the change in the fair value of the call option as of March 31, 2014.

(c) What was the effect on net income of entering into the derivative transaction for the period January 2 to March 31, 2014?

8 ***E17-23 (Fair Value Hedge)** On January 2, 2014, MacCloud Co. issued a 4-year, $100,000 note at 6% fixed interest, interest payable semiannually. MacCloud now wants to change the note to a variable-rate note.

As a result, on January 2, 2014, MacCloud Co. enters into an interest rate swap where it agrees to receive 6% fixed and pay LIBOR of 5.7% for the first 6 months on $100,000. At each 6-month period, the variable rate will be reset. The variable rate is reset to 6.7% on June 30, 2014.

Instructions

(a) Compute the net interest expense to be reported for this note and related swap transaction as of June 30, 2014.

(b) Compute the net interest expense to be reported for this note and related swap transaction as of December 31, 2014.

9 ***E17-24 (Cash Flow Hedge)** On January 2, 2014, Parton Company issues a 5-year, $10,000,000 note at LIBOR, with interest paid annually. The variable rate is reset at the end of each year. The LIBOR rate for the first year is 5.8%.

Parton Company decides it prefers fixed-rate financing and wants to lock in a rate of 6%. As a result, Parton enters into an interest rate swap to pay 6% fixed and receive LIBOR based on $10 million. The variable rate is reset to 6.6% on January 2, 2015.

Instructions

(a) Compute the net interest expense to be reported for this note and related swap transactions as of December 31, 2014.

(b) Compute the net interest expense to be reported for this note and related swap transactions as of December 31, 2015.

8 *E17-25 **(Fair Value Hedge)** Sarazan Company issues a 4-year, 7.5% fixed-rate interest only, nonprepayable $1,000,000 note payable on December 31, 2013. It decides to change the interest rate from a fixed rate to variable rate and enters into a swap agreement with M&S Corp. The swap agreement specifies that Sarazan will receive a fixed rate at 7.5% and pay variable with settlement dates that match the interest payments on the debt. Assume that interest rates have declined during 2014 and that Sarazan received $13,000 as an adjustment to interest expense for the settlement at December 31, 2014. The loss related to the debt (due to interest rate changes) was $48,000. The value of the swap contract increased $48,000.

Instructions

(a) Prepare the journal entry to record the payment of interest expense on December 31, 2014.

(b) Prepare the journal entry to record the receipt of the swap settlement on December 31, 2014.

(c) Prepare the journal entry to record the change in the fair value of the swap contract on December 31, 2014.

(d) Prepare the journal entry to record the change in the fair value of the debt on December 31, 2014.

7 *E17-26 **(Call Option)** On August 15, 2013, Outkast Co. invested idle cash by purchasing a call option on Counting Crows Inc. common shares for $360. The notional value of the call option is 400 shares, and the option price is $40. The option expires on January 31, 2014. The following data are available with respect to the call option.

Date	Market Price of Counting Crows Shares	Time Value of Call Option
September 30, 2013	$48 per share	$180
December 31, 2013	$46 per share	65
January 15, 2014	$47 per share	30

Instructions

Prepare the journal entries for Outkast for the following dates.

(a) Investment in call option on Counting Crows shares on August 15, 2013.

(b) September 30, 2013—Outkast prepares financial statements.

(c) December 31, 2013—Outkast prepares financial statements.

(d) January 15, 2014—Outkast settles the call option on the Counting Crows shares.

9 *E17-27 **(Cash Flow Hedge)** Hart Golf Co. uses titanium in the production of its specialty drivers. Hart anticipates that it will need to purchase 200 ounces of titanium in November 2014, for clubs that will be shipped in the spring and summer of 2015. However, if the price of titanium increases, this will increase the cost to produce the clubs, which will result in lower profit margins.

To hedge the risk of increased titanium prices, on May 1, 2014, Hart enters into a titanium futures contract and designates this futures contract as a cash flow hedge of the anticipated titanium purchase. The notional amount of the contract is 200 ounces, and the terms of the contract give Hart the option to purchase titanium at a price of $500 per ounce. The price will be good until the contract expires on November 30, 2014.

Assume the following data with respect to the price of the call options and the titanium inventory purchase.

Date	Spot Price for November Delivery
May 1, 2014	$500 per ounce
June 30, 2014	520 per ounce
September 30, 2014	525 per ounce

Instructions

Present the journal entries for the following dates/transactions.

(a) May 1, 2014—Inception of futures contract, no premium paid.

(b) June 30, 2014—Hart prepares financial statements.

(c) September 30, 2014—Hart prepares financial statements.

(d) October 5, 2014—Hart purchases 200 ounces of titanium at $525 per ounce and settles the futures contract.

(e) December 15, 2014—Hart sells clubs containing titanium purchased in October 2014 for $250,000. The cost of the finished goods inventory is $140,000.

(f) Indicate the amount(s) reported in the income statement related to the futures contract and the inventory transactions on December 31, 2014.

EXERCISES SET B

See the book's companion website, at **www.wiley.com/college/kieso**, for an additional set of exercises.

PROBLEMS

2 **P17-1 (Debt Securities)** Presented below is an amortization schedule related to Spangler Company's 5-year, $100,000 bond with a 7% interest rate and a 5% yield, purchased on December 31, 2012, for $108,660.

Date	Cash Received	Interest Revenue	Bond Premium Amortization	Carrying Amount of Bonds
12/31/12				$108,660
12/31/13	$7,000	$5,433	$1,567	107,093
12/31/14	7,000	5,354	1,646	105,447
12/31/15	7,000	5,272	1,728	103,719
12/31/16	7,000	5,186	1,814	101,905
12/31/17	7,000	5,095	1,905	100,000

The following schedule presents a comparison of the amortized cost and fair value of the bonds at year-end.

	12/31/13	12/31/14	12/31/15	12/31/16	12/31/17
Amortized cost	$107,093	$105,447	$103,719	$101,905	$100,000
Fair value	$106,500	$107,500	$105,650	$103,000	$100,000

Instructions

(a) Prepare the journal entry to record the purchase of these bonds on December 31, 2012, assuming the bonds are classified as held-to-maturity securities.

(b) Prepare the journal entry(ies) related to the held-to-maturity bonds for 2013.

(c) Prepare the journal entry(ies) related to the held-to-maturity bonds for 2015.

(d) Prepare the journal entry(ies) to record the purchase of these bonds, assuming they are classified as available-for-sale.

(e) Prepare the journal entry(ies) related to the available-for-sale bonds for 2013.

(f) Prepare the journal entry(ies) related to the available-for-sale bonds for 2015.

2 **P17-2 (Available-for-Sale Debt Securities)** On January 1, 2014, Novotna Company purchased $400,000, 8% bonds of Aguirre Co. for $369,114. The bonds were purchased to yield 10% interest. Interest is payable semiannually on July 1 and January 1. The bonds mature on January 1, 2019. Novotna Company uses the effective-interest method to amortize discount or premium. On January 1, 2016, Novotna Company sold the bonds for $370,726 after receiving interest to meet its liquidity needs.

Instructions

(a) Prepare the journal entry to record the purchase of bonds on January 1. Assume that the bonds are classified as available-for-sale.

(b) Prepare the amortization schedule for the bonds.

(c) Prepare the journal entries to record the semiannual interest on July 1, 2014, and December 31, 2014.

(d) If the fair value of Aguirre bonds is $372,726 on December 31, 2015, prepare the necessary adjusting entry. (Assume the fair value adjustment balance on January 1, 2015, is a debit of $3,375.)

(e) Prepare the journal entry to record the sale of the bonds on January 1, 2016.

2 3 **P17-3 (Available-for-Sale Investments)** Cardinal Paz Corp. carries an account in its general ledger called Investments, which contained debits for investment purchases, and no credits, with the following descriptions.

Feb. 1, 2014	Sharapova Company common stock, $100 par, 200 shares	$ 37,400
April 1	U.S. government bonds, 11%, due April 1, 2024, interest payable April 1 and October 1, 110 bonds of $1,000 par each	110,000
July 1	McGrath Company 12% bonds, par $50,000, dated March 1, 2014, purchased at 104 plus accrued interest, interest payable annually on March 1, due March 1, 2034	54,000

Instructions

(Round all computations to the nearest dollar.)

(a) Prepare entries necessary to classify the amounts into proper accounts, assuming that all the securities are classified as available-for-sale.

(b) Prepare the entry to record the accrued interest and the amortization of premium on December 31, 2014, using the straight-line method.

(c) The fair values of the investments on December 31, 2014, were:

Sharapova Company common stock	$ 31,800
U.S. government bonds	124,700
McGrath Company bonds	58,600

What entry or entries, if any, would you recommend be made?

(d) The U.S. government bonds were sold on July 1, 2015, for $119,200 plus accrued interest. Give the proper entry.

2 **P17-4 (Available-for-Sale Debt Investments)** Presented below is information taken from a bond investment amortization schedule with related fair values provided. These bonds are classified as available-for-sale.

	12/31/14	12/31/15	12/31/16
Amortized cost	$491,150	$519,442	$550,000
Fair value	$497,000	$509,000	$550,000

Instructions

(a) Indicate whether the bonds were purchased at a discount or at a premium.

(b) Prepare the adjusting entry to record the bonds at fair value at December 31, 2014. The Fair Value Adjustment account has a debit balance of $1,000 prior to adjustment.

(c) Prepare the adjusting entry to record the bonds at fair value at December 31, 2015.

3 **P17-5 (Equity Securities Entries and Disclosures)** Parnevik Company has the following securities in its investment portfolio on December 31, 2014 (all securities were purchased in 2014): (1) 3,000 shares of Anderson Co. common stock which cost $58,500, (2) 10,000 shares of Munter Ltd. common stock which cost $580,000, and (3) 6,000 shares of King Company preferred stock which cost $255,000. The Fair Value Adjustment account shows a credit of $10,100 at the end of 2014.

XLS

In 2015, Parnevik completed the following securities transactions.

1. On January 15, sold 3,000 shares of Anderson's common stock at $22 per share less fees of $2,150.
2. On April 17, purchased 1,000 shares of Castle's common stock at $33.50 per share plus fees of $1,980.

On December 31, 2015, the market prices per share of these securities were Munter $61, King $40, and Castle $29. In addition, the accounting supervisor of Parnevik told you that, even though all these securities have readily determinable fair values, Parnevik will not actively trade these securities because the top management intends to hold them for more than one year.

Instructions

(a) Prepare the entry for the security sale on January 15, 2015.

(b) Prepare the journal entry to record the security purchase on April 17, 2015.

(c) Compute the unrealized gains or losses and prepare the adjusting entry for Parnevik on December 31, 2015.

(d) How should the unrealized gains or losses be reported on Parnevik's balance sheet?

3 **P17-6 (Trading and Available-for-Sale Securities Entries)** McElroy Company has the following portfolio of investment securities at September 30, 2014, its last reporting date.

Trading Securities	Cost	Fair Value
Horton, Inc. common (5,000 shares)	$215,000	$200,000
Monty, Inc. preferred (3,500 shares)	133,000	140,000
Oakwood Corp. common (1,000 shares)	180,000	179,000

On October 10, 2014, the Horton shares were sold at a price of $54 per share. In addition, 3,000 shares of Patriot common stock were acquired at $54.50 per share on November 2, 2014. The December 31, 2014, fair values were Monty $106,000, Patriot $132,000, and the Oakwood common $193,000. All the securities are classified as trading.

Instructions

(a) Prepare the journal entries to record the sale, purchase, and adjusting entries related to the trading securities in the last quarter of 2014.

(b) How would the entries in part (a) change if the securities were classified as available-for-sale?

2 **P17-7 (Available-for-Sale and Held-to-Maturity Debt Securities Entries)** The following information relates to the debt securities investments of Wildcat Company.

1. On February 1, the company purchased 10% bonds of Gibbons Co. having a par value of $300,000 at 100 plus accrued interest. Interest is payable April 1 and October 1.
2. On April 1, semiannual interest is received.
3. On July 1, 9% bonds of Sampson, Inc. were purchased. These bonds with a par value of $200,000 were purchased at 100 plus accrued interest. Interest dates are June 1 and December 1.
4. On September 1, bonds with a par value of $60,000, purchased on February 1, are sold at 99 plus accrued interest.
5. On October 1, semiannual interest is received.
6. On December 1, semiannual interest is received.
7. On December 31, the fair value of the bonds purchased February 1 and July 1 are 95 and 93, respectively.

Instructions

(a) Prepare any journal entries you consider necessary, including year-end entries (December 31), assuming these are available-for-sale securities.

(b) If Wildcat classified these as held-to-maturity investments, explain how the journal entries would differ from those in part (a).

3 4 5 **P17-8 (Fair Value and Equity Methods)** Brooks Corp. is a medium-sized corporation specializing in quarrying stone for building construction. The company has long dominated the market, at one time achieving a 70% market penetration. During prosperous years, the company's profits, coupled with a conservative dividend policy, resulted in funds available for outside investment. Over the years, Brooks has had a policy of investing idle cash in equity securities. In particular, Brooks has made periodic investments in the company's principal supplier, Norton Industries. Although the firm currently owns 12% of the outstanding common stock of Norton Industries, Brooks does not have significant influence over the operations of Norton Industries.

Cheryl Thomas has recently joined Brooks as assistant controller, and her first assignment is to prepare the 2014 year-end adjusting entries for the accounts that are valued by the "fair value" rule for financial reporting purposes. Thomas has gathered the following information about Brooks' pertinent accounts.

1. Brooks has trading securities related to Delaney Motors and Patrick Electric. During this fiscal year, Brooks purchased 100,000 shares of Delaney Motors for $1,400,000; these shares currently have a fair value of $1,600,000. Brooks' investment in Patrick Electric has not been profitable; the company acquired 50,000 shares of Patrick in April 2014 at $20 per share, a purchase that currently has a value of $720,000.
2. Prior to 2014, Brooks invested $22,500,000 in Norton Industries and has not changed its holdings this year. This investment in Norton Industries was valued at $21,500,000 on December 31, 2013. Brooks' 12% ownership of Norton Industries has a current fair value of $22,225,000.

Instructions

(a) Prepare the appropriate adjusting entries for Brooks as of December 31, 2014, to reflect the application of the "fair value" rule for both classes of securities described above.

(b) For both classes of securities presented above, describe how the results of the valuation adjustments made in (a) would be reflected in the body of and notes to Brooks' 2014 financial statements.

(c) Prepare the entries for the Norton investment, assuming that Brooks owns 25% of Norton's shares. Norton reported income of $500,000 in 2014 and paid cash dividends of $100,000.

3 6 P17-9 (Financial Statement Presentation of Available-for-Sale Investments) Kennedy Company has the following portfolio of available-for-sale securities at December 31, 2014.

Security	Quantity	Percent Interest	Per Share Cost	Per Share Price
Frank, Inc.	2,000 shares	8%	$11	$16
Ellis Corp.	5,000 shares	14%	23	19
Mendota Company	4,000 shares	2%	31	24

Instructions

(a) What should be reported on Kennedy's December 31, 2014, balance sheet relative to these long-term available-for-sale securities?

On December 31, 2015, Kennedy's portfolio of available-for-sale securities consisted of the following common stocks.

Security	Quantity	Percent Interest	Per Share Cost	Per Share Price
Ellis Corp.	5,000 shares	14%	$23	$28
Mendota Company	4,000 shares	2%	31	23
Mendota Company	2,000 shares	1%	25	23

At the end of 2015, Kennedy Company changed its intent relative to its investment in Frank, Inc. and reclassified the shares to trading securities status when the shares were selling for $8 per share.

(b) What should be reported on the face of Kennedy's December 31, 2015, balance sheet relative to available-for-sale securities investments? What should be reported to reflect the transactions above in Kennedy's 2015 income statement?

3 5 P17-10 (Gain on Sale of Investments and Comprehensive Income) On January 1, 2014, Acker Inc. had the following balance sheet.

ACKER INC.
BALANCE SHEET
AS OF JANUARY 1, 2014

Assets		Equity	
Cash	$ 50,000	Common stock	$260,000
Equity investments (available-for-sale)	240,000	Accumulated other comprehensive income	30,000
Total	$290,000	Total	$290,000

The accumulated other comprehensive income related to unrealized holding gains on available-for-sale securities. The fair value of Acker Inc.'s available-for-sale securities at December 31, 2014, was $190,000; its cost was $140,000. No securities were purchased during the year. Acker Inc.'s income statement for 2014 was as follows. (Ignore income taxes.)

ACKER INC.
INCOME STATEMENT
FOR THE YEAR ENDED DECEMBER 31, 2014

Dividend revenue	$ 5,000
Gain on sale of investments	30,000
Net income	$35,000

Instructions

(Assume all transactions during the year were for cash.)

(a) Prepare the journal entry to record the sale of the available-for-sale securities in 2014.
(b) Prepare a statement of comprehensive income for 2014.
(c) Prepare a balance sheet as of December 31, 2014.

3 **P17-11 (Equity Investments—Available-for-Sale)** Castleman Holdings, Inc. had the following available-for-sale investment portfolio at January 1, 2014.

XLS

Evers Company	1,000 shares @ $15 each	$15,000
Rogers Company	900 shares @ $20 each	18,000
Chance Company	500 shares @ $9 each	4,500
Equity investments (available-for-sale) @ cost		37,500
Fair value adjustment (available-for-sale)		(7,500)
Equity investments (available-for-sale) @ fair value		$30,000

During 2014, the following transactions took place.

1. On March 1, Rogers Company paid a $2 per share dividend.
2. On April 30, Castleman Holdings, Inc. sold 300 shares of Chance Company for $11 per share.
3. On May 15, Castleman Holdings, Inc. purchased 100 more shares of Evers Co. stock at $16 per share.
4. At December 31, 2014, the stocks had the following price per share values: Evers $17, Rogers $19, and Chance $8.

During 2015, the following transactions took place.

5. On February 1, Castleman Holdings, Inc. sold the remaining Chance shares for $8 per share.
6. On March 1, Rogers Company paid a $2 per share dividend.
7. On December 21, Evers Company declared a cash dividend of $3 per share to be paid in the next month.
8. At December 31, 2015, the stocks had the following price per share values: Evers $19 and Rogers $21.

Instructions

(a) Prepare journal entries for each of the above transactions.

(b) Prepare a partial balance sheet showing the investment-related amounts to be reported at December 31, 2014 and 2015.

3 5 **P17-12 (Available-for-Sale Securities—Statement Presentation)** Fernandez Corp. invested its excess cash in available-for-sale securities during 2014. As of December 31, 2014, the portfolio of available-for-sale securities consisted of the following common stocks.

Security	Quantity		Cost	Fair Value
Lindsay Jones, Inc.	1,000 shares		$ 15,000	$ 21,000
Poley Corp.	2,000 shares		40,000	42,000
Arnold Aircraft	2,000 shares		72,000	60,000
		Totals	$127,000	$123,000

Instructions

(a) What should be reported on Fernandez's December 31, 2014, balance sheet relative to these securities? What should be reported on Fernandez's 2014 income statement?

On December 31, 2015, Fernandez's portfolio of available-for-sale securities consisted of the following common stocks.

Security	Quantity		Cost	Fair Value
Lindsay Jones, Inc.	1,000 shares		$ 15,000	$20,000
Lindsay Jones, Inc.	2,000 shares		33,000	40,000
Duff Company	1,000 shares		16,000	12,000
Arnold Aircraft	2,000 shares		72,000	22,000
		Totals	$136,000	$94,000

During the year 2015, Fernandez Corp. sold 2,000 shares of Poley Corp. for $38,200 and purchased 2,000 more shares of Lindsay Jones, Inc. and 1,000 shares of Duff Company.

(b) What should be reported on Fernandez's December 31, 2015, balance sheet? What should be reported on Fernandez's 2015 income statement?

On December 31, 2016, Fernandez's portfolio of available-for-sale securities consisted of the following common stocks.

Security	Quantity		Cost	Fair Value
Arnold Aircraft	2,000 shares		$72,000	$82,000
Duff Company	500 shares		8,000	6,000
		Totals	$80,000	$88,000

During the year 2016, Fernandez Corp. sold 3,000 shares of Lindsay Jones, Inc. for $39,900 and 500 shares of Duff Company at a loss of $2,700.

(c) What should be reported on the face of Fernandez's December 31, 2016, balance sheet? What should be reported on Fernandez's 2016 income statement?

(d) What would be reported in a statement of comprehensive income at (1) December 31, 2014, and (2) December 31, 2015?

7 ***P17-13 (Derivative Financial Instrument)** The treasurer of Miller Co. has read on the Internet that the stock price of Wade Inc. is about to take off. In order to profit from this potential development, Miller Co. purchased a call option on Wade common shares on July 7, 2014, for $240. The call option is for 200 shares (notional value), and the strike price is $70. (The market price of a share of Wade stock on that date is $70.) The option expires on January 31, 2015. The following data are available with respect to the call option.

Date	Market Price of Wade Shares	Time Value of Call Option
September 30, 2014	$77 per share	$180
December 31, 2014	75 per share	65
January 4, 2015	76 per share	30

Instructions

Prepare the journal entries for Miller Co. for the following dates.

(a) July 7, 2014—Investment in call option on Wade shares.
(b) September 30, 2014—Miller prepares financial statements.
(c) December 31, 2014—Miller prepares financial statements.
(d) January 4, 2015—Miller settles the call option on the Wade shares.

7 ***P17-14 (Derivative Financial Instrument)** Johnstone Co. purchased a put option on Ewing common shares on July 7, 2014, for $240. The put option is for 200 shares, and the strike price is $70. (The market price of a share of Ewing stock on that date is $70.) The option expires on January 31, 2015. The following data are available with respect to the put option.

Date	Market Price of Ewing Shares	Time Value of Put Option
September 30, 2014	$77 per share	$125
December 31, 2014	75 per share	50
January 31, 2015	78 per share	0

Instructions

Prepare the journal entries for Johnstone Co. for the following dates.

(a) July 7, 2014—Investment in put option on Ewing shares.
(b) September 30, 2014—Johnstone prepares financial statements.
(c) December 31, 2014—Johnstone prepares financial statements.
(d) January 31, 2015—Put option expires.

7 ***P17-15 (Free-Standing Derivative)** Warren Co. purchased a put option on Echo common shares on January 7, 2014, for $360. The put option is for 400 shares, and the strike price is $85 (which equals the price of an Echo share on the purchase date). The option expires on July 31, 2014. The following data are available with respect to the put option.

Date	Market Price of Echo Shares	Time Value of Put Option
March 31, 2014	$80 per share	$200
June 30, 2014	82 per share	90
July 6, 2014	77 per share	25

Instructions

Prepare the journal entries for Warren Co. for the following dates.

(a) January 7, 2014—Investment in put option on Echo shares.
(b) March 31, 2014—Warren prepares financial statements.
(c) June 30, 2014—Warren prepares financial statements.
(d) July 6, 2014—Warren settles the put option on the Echo shares.

8 ***P17-16 (Fair Value Hedge Interest Rate Swap)** On December 31, 2014, Mercantile Corp. had a $10,000,000, 8% fixed-rate note outstanding, payable in 2 years. It decides to enter into a 2-year swap with Chicago First Bank to convert the fixed-rate debt to variable-rate debt. The terms of the swap indicate that Mercantile will receive interest at a fixed rate of 8.0% and will pay a variable rate equal to the 6-month LIBOR rate, based on the $10,000,000 amount. The LIBOR rate on December 31, 2014, is 7%. The LIBOR rate will be reset every 6 months and will be used to determine the variable rate to be paid for the following 6-month period.

Mercantile Corp. designates the swap as a fair value hedge. Assume that the hedging relationship meets all the conditions necessary for hedge accounting. The 6-month LIBOR rate and the swap and debt fair values are as follows.

Date	6-Month LIBOR Rate	Swap Fair Value	Debt Fair Value
December 31, 2014	7.0%	—	$10,000,000
June 30, 2015	7.5%	(200,000)	9,800,000
December 31, 2015	6.0%	60,000	10,060,000

Instructions

(a) Present the journal entries to record the following transactions.

(1) The entry, if any, to record the swap on December 31, 2014.

(2) The entry to record the semiannual debt interest payment on June 30, 2015.

(3) The entry to record the settlement of the semiannual swap amount receivables at 8%, less amount payable at LIBOR, 7%.

(4) The entry to record the change in the fair value of the debt on June 30, 2015.

(5) The entry to record the change in the fair value of the swap at June 30, 2015.

(b) Indicate the amount(s) reported on the balance sheet and income statement related to the debt and swap on December 31, 2014.

(c) Indicate the amount(s) reported on the balance sheet and income statement related to the debt and swap on June 30, 2015.

(d) Indicate the amount(s) reported on the balance sheet and income statement related to the debt and swap on December 31, 2015.

9 ***P17-17 (Cash Flow Hedge)** LEW Jewelry Co. uses gold in the manufacture of its products. LEW anticipates that it will need to purchase 500 ounces of gold in October 2014, for jewelry that will be shipped for the holiday shopping season. However, if the price of gold increases, LEW's cost to produce its jewelry will increase, which would reduce its profit margins.

To hedge the risk of increased gold prices, on April 1, 2014, LEW enters into a gold futures contract and designates this futures contract as a cash flow hedge of the anticipated gold purchase. The notional amount of the contract is 500 ounces, and the terms of the contract give LEW the right and the obligation to purchase gold at a price of $300 per ounce. The price will be good until the contract expires on October 31, 2014.

Assume the following data with respect to the price of the futures contract and the gold inventory purchase.

Date	Spot Price for October Delivery
April 1, 2014	$300 per ounce
June 30, 2014	310 per ounce
September 30, 2014	315 per ounce

Instructions

Prepare the journal entries for the following transactions.

(a) April 1, 2014—Inception of the futures contract, no premium paid.

(b) June 30, 2014—LEW Co. prepares financial statements.

(c) September 30, 2014—LEW Co. prepares financial statements.

(d) October 10, 2014—LEW Co. purchases 500 ounces of gold at $315 per ounce and settles the futures contract.

(e) December 20, 2014—LEW sells jewelry containing gold purchased in October 2014 for $350,000. The cost of the finished goods inventory is $200,000.

(f) Indicate the amount(s) reported on the balance sheet and income statement related to the futures contract on June 30, 2014.

(g) Indicate the amount(s) reported in the income statement related to the futures contract and the inventory transactions on December 31, 2014.

8 ***P17-18 (Fair Value Hedge)** On November 3, 2014, Sprinkle Co. invested $200,000 in 4,000 shares of the common stock of Pratt Co. Sprinkle classified this investment as available-for-sale. Sprinkle Co. is considering making a more significant investment in Pratt Co. at some point in the future but has decided to wait and see how the stock does over the next several quarters.

To hedge against potential declines in the value of Pratt stock during this period, Sprinkle also purchased a put option on the Pratt stock. Sprinkle paid an option premium of $600 for the put option, which gives Sprinkle the option to sell 4,000 Pratt shares at a strike price of $50 per share. The option expires on July 31, 2015. The following data are available with respect to the values of the Pratt stock and the put option.

Date	Market Price of Pratt Shares	Time Value of Put Option
December 31, 2014	$50 per share	$375
March 31, 2015	45 per share	175
June 30, 2015	43 per share	40

Instructions

(a) Prepare the journal entries for Sprinkle Co. for the following dates.

(1) November 3, 2014—Investment in Pratt stock and the put option on Pratt shares.

(2) December 31, 2014—Sprinkle Co. prepares financial statements.

(3) March 31, 2015—Sprinkle prepares financial statements.

(4) June 30, 2015—Sprinkle prepares financial statements.

(5) July 1, 2015—Sprinkle settles the put option and sells the Pratt shares for $43 per share.

(b) Indicate the amount(s) reported on the balance sheet and income statement related to the Pratt investment and the put option on December 31, 2014.

(c) Indicate the amount(s) reported on the balance sheet and income statement related to the Pratt investment and the put option on June 30, 2015.

PROBLEMS SET B

See the book's companion website, at **www.wiley.com/college/kieso**, for an additional set of problems.

CONCEPTS FOR ANALYSIS

CA17-1 (Issues Raised about Investment Securities) You have just started work for Warren Co. as part of the controller's group involved in current financial reporting problems. Jane Henshaw, controller for Warren, is interested in your accounting background because the company has experienced a series of financial reporting surprises over the last few years. Recently, the controller has learned from the company's auditors that there is authoritative literature that may apply to its investment in securities. She assumes that you are familiar with this pronouncement and asks how the following situations should be reported in the financial statements.

Situation 1: Trading securities in the current assets section have a fair value that is $4,200 lower than cost.

Situation 2: A trading security whose fair value is currently less than cost is transferred to the available-for-sale category.

Situation 3: An available-for-sale security whose fair value is currently less than cost is classified as noncurrent but is to be reclassified as current.

Situation 4: A company's portfolio of available-for-sale securities consists of the common stock of one company. At the end of the prior year, the fair value of the security was 50% of original cost, and this reduction in fair value was reported as an other than temporary impairment. However, at the end of the current year, the fair value of the security had appreciated to twice the original cost.

Situation 5: The company has purchased some convertible debentures that it plans to hold for less than a year. The fair value of the convertible debentures is $7,700 below its cost.

Instructions

What is the effect upon carrying value and earnings for each of the situations above? Assume that these situations are unrelated.

CA17-2 (Equity Securities) Lexington Co. has the following available-for-sale securities outstanding on December 31, 2014 (its first year of operations).

	Cost	Fair Value
Greenspan Corp. Stock	$20,000	$19,000
Summerset Company Stock	9,500	8,800
Tinkers Company Stock	20,000	20,600
	$49,500	$48,400

During 2015, Summerset Company stock was sold for $9,200, the difference between the $9,200 and the "fair value" of $8,800 being recorded as a "Gain on Sale of Investments." The market price of the stock on December 31, 2015, was Greenspan Corp. stock $19,900; Tinkers Company stock $20,500.

Instructions

(a) What justification is there for valuing available-for-sale securities at fair value and reporting the unrealized gain or loss as part of stockholders' equity?
(b) How should Lexington Company apply this rule on December 31, 2014? Explain.
(c) Did Lexington Company properly account for the sale of the Summerset Company stock? Explain.
(d) Are there any additional entries necessary for Lexington Company at December 31, 2015, to reflect the facts on the financial statements in accordance with generally accepted accounting principles? Explain.

(AICPA adapted)

CA17-3 (Financial Statement Effect of Equity Securities) Presented below are three unrelated situations involving equity securities.

Situation 1: An equity security, whose fair value is currently less than cost, is classified as available-for-sale but is to be reclassified as trading.

Situation 2: A noncurrent portfolio with an aggregate fair value in excess of cost includes one particular security whose fair value has declined to less than one-half of the original cost. The decline in value is considered to be other than temporary.

Situation 3: The portfolio of trading securities has a cost in excess of fair value of $13,500. The available-for-sale portfolio has a fair value in excess of cost of $28,600.

Instructions

What is the effect upon carrying value and earnings for each of the situations above?

CA17-4 (Investment Accounted for under the Equity Method) On July 1, 2015, Fontaine Company purchased for cash 40% of the outstanding capital stock of Knoblett Company. Both Fontaine Company and Knoblett Company have a December 31 year-end. Knoblett Company, whose common stock is actively traded in the over-the-counter market, reported its total net income for the year to Fontaine Company and also paid cash dividends on November 15, 2015, to Fontaine Company and its other stockholders.

Instructions

How should Fontaine Company report the above facts in its December 31, 2015, balance sheet and its income statement for the year then ended? Discuss the rationale for your answer.

(AICPA adapted)

CA17-5 (Equity Investment) On July 1, 2014, Selig Company purchased for cash 40% of the outstanding capital stock of Spoor Corporation. Both Selig and Spoor have a December 31 year-end. Spoor Corporation, whose common stock is actively traded on the American Stock Exchange, paid a cash dividend on November 15, 2014, to Selig Company and its other stockholders. It also reported its total net income for the year of $920,000 to Selig Company.

Instructions

Prepare a one-page memorandum of instructions on how Selig Company should report the above facts in its December 31, 2014, balance sheet and its 2014 income statement. In your memo, identify and describe the method of valuation you recommend. Provide rationale where you can. Address your memo to the chief accountant at Selig Company.

CA17-6 (Fair Value) Addison Manufacturing holds a large portfolio of debt and equity securities as an investment. The fair value of the portfolio is greater than its original cost, even though some securities have decreased in value. Sam Beresford, the financial vice president, and Angie Nielson, the controller, are near year-end in the process of classifying for the first time this securities portfolio in accordance with GAAP. Beresford wants to classify those securities that have increased in value during the period as trading securities in order to increase net income this year. He wants to classify all the securities that have decreased in value as available-for-sale (the equity securities) and as held-to-maturity (the debt securities).

Nielson disagrees. She wants to classify those securities that have decreased in value as trading securities and those that have increased in value as available-for-sale (equity) and held-to-maturity (debt). She contends that the company is having a good earnings year and that recognizing the losses will help to smooth the income this year. As a result, the company will have built-in gains for future periods when the company may not be as profitable.

Instructions

Answer the following questions.

(a) Will classifying the portfolio as each proposes actually have the effect on earnings that each says it will?

(b) Is there anything unethical in what each of them proposes? Who are the stakeholders affected by their proposals?

(c) Assume that Beresford and Nielson properly classify the entire portfolio into trading, available-for-sale, and held-to-maturity categories. But then each proposes to sell just before year-end the securities with gains or with losses, as the case may be, to accomplish their effect on earnings. Is this unethical?

USING YOUR JUDGMENT

FINANCIAL REPORTING

Financial Reporting Problem

P&G

The Procter & Gamble Company (P&G)

The financial statements of P&G are presented in Appendix 5B. The company's complete annual report, including the notes to the financial statements, can be accessed at the book's companion website, **www.wiley.com/college/kieso**.

Instructions

Refer to P&G's financial statements and the accompanying notes to answer the following questions.

(a) What investments does P&G report in 2011, and how are these investments accounted for in its financial statements?

(b) How are P&G's investments valued? How does P&G determine fair value?

(c) How does P&G use derivative financial instruments?

Comparative Analysis Case

The Coca-Cola Company and PepsiCo, Inc.

Instructions

Go to the book's companion website and use information found there to answer the following questions related to The Coca-Cola Company and PepsiCo, Inc.

(a) Based on the information contained in these financial statements, determine each of the following for each company.

- **(1)** Cash used in (for) investing activities during 2011 (from the statement of cash flows).
- **(2)** Cash used for acquisitions and investments in unconsolidated affiliates (or principally bottling companies) during 2011.
- **(3)** Total investment in unconsolidated affiliates (or investments and other assets) at the end of 2011.

(b) (1) Briefly identify from Coca-Cola's December 31, 2011, balance sheet the investments it reported as being accounted for under the equity method. (2) What is the amount of investments that Coca-Cola reported in its 2011 balance sheet as "cost method investments," and what is the nature of these investments?

(c) In its Note 2 on Investments, what total amounts did Coca-Cola report at December 31, 2011, as: (1) trading securities, (2) available-for-sale securities, and (3) held-to-maturity securities?

Financial Statement Analysis Case

Union Planters

Union Planters is a Tennessee bank holding company (that is, a corporation that owns banks). (Union Planters is now part of Regions Bank.) Union Planters manages $32 billion in assets, the largest of which is its loan portfolio of $19 billion. In addition to its loan portfolio, however, like other banks it has significant debt investments. The nature of these investments varies from short-term in nature to long-term in nature. As a consequence, consistent with the requirements of accounting rules, Union Planters reports its investments in two different categories—trading and available-for-sale. The following facts were found in a recent Union Planters' annual report.

(all dollars in millions)	Amortized Cost	Gross Unrealized Gains	Gross Unrealized Losses	Fair Value
Trading account assets	$ 275	—	—	$ 275
Securities available for sale	8,209	$108	$15	8,302
Net income				224
Net securities gains (losses)				(9)

Instructions

(a) Why do you suppose Union Planters purchases investments, rather than simply making loans? Why does it purchase investments that vary in nature both in terms of their maturities and in type (debt versus stock)?

(b) How must Union Planters account for its investments in each of the two categories?

(c) In what ways does classifying investments into two different categories assist investors in evaluating the profitability of a company like Union Planters?

(d) Suppose that the management of Union Planters was not happy with its net income for the year. What step could it have taken with its investment portfolio that would have definitely increased reported profit? How much could it have increased reported profit? Why do you suppose it chose not to do this?

Accounting, Analysis, and Principles

Instar Company has several investments in the securities of other companies. The following information regarding these investments is available at December 31, 2014.

1. Instar holds bonds issued by Dorsel Corp. The bonds have an amortized cost of $320,000 and their fair value at December 31, 2014, is $400,000. Instar intends to hold the bonds until they mature on December 31, 2022.
2. Instar has invested idle cash in the equity securities of several publicly traded companies. Instar intends to sell these securities during the first quarter of 2015, when it will need the cash to acquire seasonal inventory. These equity securities have a cost basis of $800,000 and a fair value of $920,000 at December 31, 2014.
3. Instar has a significant ownership stake in one of the companies that supplies Instar with various components Instar uses in its products. Instar owns 6% of the common stock of the supplier, does not have any representation on the supplier's board of directors, does not exchange any personnel with the supplier, and does not consult with the supplier on any of the supplier's operating, financial, or strategic decisions. The cost basis of the investment in the supplier is $1,200,000 and the fair value of the investment at December 31, 2014, is $1,550,000. Instar does not intend to sell the investment in the foreseeable future. The supplier reported net income of $80,000 for 2014 and paid no dividends.
4. Instar owns some common stock of Forter Corp. The cost basis of the investment in Forter is $200,000 and the fair value at December 31, 2014, is $50,000. Instar believes the decline in the value of its investment in Forter is other than temporary, but Instar does not intend to sell its investment in Forter in the foreseeable future.
5. Instar purchased 25% of the stock of Slobbaer Co. for $900,000. Instar has significant influence over the operating activities of Slobbaer Co. During 2014, Slobbaer Co. reported net income of $300,000 and paid a dividend of $100,000.

Accounting

(a) Determine whether each of the investments described above should be classified as available-for-sale, held-to-maturity, trading, or equity method.

(b) Prepare any December 31, 2014, journal entries needed for Instar relating to Instar's various investments in other companies. Assume 2014 is Instar's first year of operations.

Analysis

What is the effect on Instar's 2014 net income (as reported on Instar's income statement) of Instar's investments in other companies?

Principles

Briefly explain the different rationales for the different accounting and reporting rules for different types of investments in the securities of other companies.

BRIDGE TO THE PROFESSION

Professional Research: FASB Codification

Your client, Cascade Company, is planning to invest some of its excess cash in 5-year revenue bonds issued by the county and in the stock of one of its suppliers, Teton Co. Teton's shares trade on the over-the-counter market. Cascade plans to classify these investments as available-for-sale. They would like you to conduct some research on the accounting for these investments.

Instructions

If your school has a subscription to the FASB Codification, go to *http://aaahq.org/ascLogin.cfm* to log in and prepare responses to the following. Provide Codification references for your responses.

(a) Since the Teton shares do not trade on one of the large stock markets, Cascade argues that the fair value of this investment is not readily available. According to the authoritative literature, when is the fair value of a security "readily determinable"?

(b) How is an impairment of a security accounted for?

(c) To avoid volatility in their financial statements due to fair value adjustments, Cascade debated whether the bond investment could be classified as held-to-maturity; Cascade is pretty sure it will hold the bonds for 5 years. How close to maturity could Cascade sell an investment and still classify it as held-to-maturity?

(d) What disclosures must be made for any sale or transfer from securities classified as held-to-maturity?

Additional Professional Resources

See the book's companion website, at **www.wiley.com/college/kieso**, for professional simulations as well as other study resources.

IFRS INSIGHTS

LEARNING OBJECTIVE 13

Compare the accounting for investments under GAAP and IFRS.

The accounting for investments is discussed in *IAS 27* ("Consolidated and Separate Financial Statements"), *IAS 28* ("Accounting for Investments in Associates"), *IAS 39* ("Financial Instruments: Recognition and Measurement"), and *IFRS 9* ("Financial Instruments"). Until recently, when the IASB issued *IFRS 9*, the accounting and reporting for investments under IFRS and GAAP were for the most part very similar. However, *IFRS 9* introduces new investment classifications and increases the situations when investments are accounted for at fair value, with gains and losses recorded in income.

RELEVANT FACTS

Following are the key similarities and differences between GAAP and IFRS related to investments.

Similarities

- GAAP and IFRS use similar classifications for trading investments.
- The accounting for trading investments is the same between GAAP and IFRS. Held-to-maturity (GAAP) and held-for-collection (IFRS) investments are accounted for at

amortized cost. Gains and losses on some investments are reported in other comprehensive income.

- Both GAAP and IFRS use the same test to determine whether the equity method of accounting should be used, that is, significant influence with a general guideline of over 20 percent ownership.
- GAAP and IFRS are similar in the accounting for the fair value option. That is, the option to use the fair value method must be made at initial recognition, the selection is irrevocable, and gains and losses are reported as part of income.
- The measurement of impairments is similar under GAAP and IFRS.

Differences

- While GAAP classifies investments as trading, available-for-sale (both debt and equity investments), and held-to-maturity (only for debt investments), IFRS uses held-for-collection (debt investments), trading (both debt and equity investments), and non-trading equity investment classifications.
- The basis for consolidation under IFRS is control. Under GAAP, a bipolar approach is used, which is a risk-and-reward model (often referred to as a variable-entity approach, discussed in Appendix 17B) and a voting-interest approach. However, under both systems, for consolidation to occur, the investor company must generally own 50 percent of another company.
- While the measurement of impairments is similar under GAAP and IFRS, GAAP does not permit the reversal of an impairment charge related to available-for-sale debt and equity investments. IFRS allows reversals of impairments of held-for-collection investments.
- While GAAP and IFRS are similar in the accounting for the fair value option, one difference is that GAAP permits the fair value option for equity method investments; IFRS does not.

ABOUT THE NUMBERS

Accounting for Financial Assets

A **financial asset** is cash, an equity investment of another company (e.g., ordinary or preference shares), or a contractual right to receive cash from another party (e.g., loans, receivables, and bonds). The accounting for cash is relatively straightforward and is discussed in Chapter 7. The accounting and reporting for equity and debt investments, as discussed in the opening story, is extremely contentious, particularly in light of the credit crisis in the latter part of 2008.

IFRS requires that companies determine how to measure their financial assets based on two criteria:

- The company's business model for managing its financial assets; and
- The contractual cash flow characteristics of the financial asset.

If a company has (1) a business model whose objective is to hold assets in order to collect contractual cash flows and (2) the contractual terms of the financial asset provides specified dates to cash flows that are solely payments of principal and interest on the principal amount outstanding, then the company should use amortized cost.

For example, assume that **Mitsubishi** purchases a bond investment that it intends to hold to maturity. Its business model for this type of investment is to collect interest and then principal at maturity. The payment dates for the interest rate and principal are stated on the bond. In this case, Mitsubishi accounts for the investment at amortized cost. If, on the other hand, Mitsubishi purchased the bonds as part of a trading strategy to speculate on interest rate changes (a trading investment), then the debt investment is reported at fair value. As a result, only debt investments such as receivables, loans, and bond investments that meet the two criteria above are recorded at amortized cost. All other debt investments are recorded and reported at fair value.

Equity investments are generally recorded and reported at fair value. Equity investments do not have a fixed interest or principal payment schedule and therefore cannot be accounted for at amortized cost. In summary, companies account for investments based on the type of security, as indicated in Illustration IFRS17-1.

ILLUSTRATION IFRS17-1
Summary of Investment Accounting Approaches

Type of Investment	Assessment of Accounting Criteria	Valuation Approach
Debt	Meets business model (held-for-collection) and contractual cash flow tests.	Amortized cost
	Does not meet the business model test (not held-for-collection).	Fair value
Equity	Does not meet contractual cash flow test.	Fair value
	Exercises some control.	Equity method

Debt Investments

Debt Investments—Amortized Cost

Only debt investments can be measured at amortized cost. If a company like **Carrefour** makes an investment in the bonds of **Nokia**, it will receive contractual cash flows of interest over the life of the bonds and repayment of the principal at maturity. If it is Carrefour's strategy to hold this investment in order to receive these cash flows over the life of the bond, it has a held-for-collection strategy and it will measure the investment at amortized cost.[44]

Example: Debt Investment at Amortized Cost. To illustrate the accounting for a debt investment at amortized cost, assume that Robinson Company purchased $100,000 of 8 percent bonds of Evermaster Corporation on January 1, 2014, at a discount, paying $92,278. The bonds mature January 1, 2019, and yield 10 percent; interest is payable each July 1 and January 1. Robinson records the investment as follows.

January 1, 2014		
Debt Investments	92,278	
Cash		92,278

As indicated in Chapter 14, companies must amortize premiums or discounts using the **effective-interest method**. They apply the effective-interest method to bond investments in a way similar to that for bonds payable. To compute interest revenue, companies compute the effective-interest rate or yield at the time of investment and apply that rate to the beginning carrying amount (book value) for each interest period. The investment carrying amount is increased by the amortized discount or decreased by the amortized premium in each period.

Illustration IFRS17-2 shows the effect of the discount amortization on the interest revenue that Robinson records each period for its investment in Evermaster bonds.

[44]Classification as held-for-collection does not mean the security must be held to maturity. For example, a company may sell an investment before maturity if (1) the security does not meet the company's investment strategy (e.g., the company has a policy to invest in only AAA-rated bonds but the bond investment has a decline in its credit rating), (2) a company changes its strategy to invest only in securities within a certain maturity range, or (3) the company needs to sell a security to fund certain capital expenditures. However, if a company begins trading held-for-collection investments on a regular basis, it should assess whether such trading is consistent with the held-for-collection classification.

ILLUSTRATION IFRS17-2
Schedule of Interest Revenue and Bond Discount Amortization—Effective-Interest Method

8% Bonds Purchased to Yield 10%

Date	Cash Received	Interest Revenue	Bond Discount Amortization	Carrying Amount of Bonds
1/1/14				$ 92,278
7/1/14	$ 4,000[a]	$ 4,614[b]	$ 614[c]	92,892[d]
1/1/15	4,000	4,645	645	93,537
7/1/15	4,000	4,677	677	94,214
1/1/16	4,000	4,711	711	94,925
7/1/16	4,000	4,746	746	95,671
1/1/17	4,000	4,783	783	96,454
7/1/17	4,000	4,823	823	97,277
1/1/18	4,000	4,864	864	98,141
7/1/18	4,000	4,907	907	99,048
1/1/19	4,000	4,952	952	100,000
	$40,000	$47,722	$7,722	

[a]$4,000 = $100,000 × .08 × 6/12
[b]$4,614 = $92,278 × .10 × 6/12
[c]$614 = $4,614 − $4,000
[d]$92,892 = $92,278 + $614

Robinson records the receipt of the first semiannual interest payment on July 1, 2014 (using the data in Illustration IFRS17-2), as follows.

July 1, 2014

Cash	4,000	
Debt Investments	614	
Interest Revenue		4,614

Because Robinson is on a calendar-year basis, it accrues interest and amortizes the discount at December 31, 2014, as follows.

December 31, 2014

Interest Receivable	4,000	
Debt Investments	645	
Interest Revenue		4,645

Again, Illustration IFRS17-2 shows the interest and amortization amounts. Thus, the accounting for held-for-collection investments in IFRS is the same as held-to-maturity investments under GAAP.

Debt Investments—Fair Value

In some cases, companies both manage and evaluate investment performance on a fair value basis. In these situations, these investments are managed and evaluated based on a documented risk-management or investment strategy based on fair value information. For example, some companies often hold debt investments with the intention of selling them in a short period of time. These debt investments are often referred to as **trading investments** because companies frequently buy and sell these investments to generate profits in short-term differences in price.

Companies that account for and report debt investments at fair value follow the same accounting entries as debt investments held-for-collection during the reporting period. That is, they are recorded at amortized cost. However, **at each reporting date, companies adjust the amortized cost to fair value, with any unrealized holding gain or loss reported as part of net income (fair value method)**. An **unrealized holding gain or loss** is the net change in the fair value of a debt investment from one period to another.

Example: Debt Investment at Fair Value. To illustrate the accounting for debt investments using the fair value approach, assume the same information as in our previous illustration for Robinson Company. Recall that Robinson Company purchased $100,000 of 8 percent bonds of Evermaster Corporation on January 1, 2014, at a discount, paying $92,278.[45] The bonds mature January 1, 2019, and yield 10 percent; interest is payable each July 1 and January 1.

The journal entries in 2014 are exactly the same as those for amortized cost. These entries are as follows.

January 1, 2014		
Debt Investments	92,278	
Cash		92,278
July 1, 2014		
Cash	4,000	
Debt Investments	614	
Interest Revenue		4,614
December 31, 2014		
Interest Receivable	4,000	
Debt Investments	645	
Interest Revenue		4,645

Again, Illustration IFRS17-2 shows the interest and amortization amounts. If the debt investment is held-for-collection, no further entries are necessary. To apply the fair value approach, Robinson determines that, due to a decrease in interest rates, the fair value of the debt investment increased to $95,000 at December 31, 2014. Comparing the fair value with the carrying amount of these bonds at December 31, 2014, Robinson has an unrealized holding gain of $1,463, as shown in Illustration IFRS17-3.

ILLUSTRATION IFRS17-3
Computation of Unrealized Gain on Fair Value Debt Investment (2014)

Fair value at December 31, 2014	$95,000
Amortized cost at December 31, 2014 (per Illustration IFRS17-2)	93,537
Unrealized holding gain or (loss)	$ 1,463

Robinson therefore makes the following entry to record the adjustment of the debt investment to fair value at December 31, 2014.

Fair Value Adjustment	1,463	
Unrealized Holding Gain or Loss—Income		1,463

Robinson uses a valuation account (**Fair Value Adjustment**) instead of debiting Debt Investments to record the investment at fair value. The use of the Fair Value Adjustment account enables Robinson to maintain a record at amortized cost in the accounts. Because the valuation account has a debit balance, in this case the fair value of Robinson's debt investment is higher than its amortized cost.

The Unrealized Holding Gain or Loss—Income account is reported in the other income and expense section of the income statement as part of net income. This account is closed to net income each period. The Fair Value Adjustment account is not closed each period and is simply adjusted each period to its proper valuation. The Fair Value Adjustment balance is not shown on the statement of financial position but is simply used to restate the debt investment account to fair value.

[45]Companies may incur brokerage and transaction costs in purchasing securities. For investments accounted for at fair value (both debt and equity), IFRS requires that these costs be recorded in net income as other income and expense and not as an adjustment to the carrying value of the investment.

Robinson reports its investment in Evermaster bonds in its December 31, 2014, financial statements as shown in Illustration IFRS17-4.

ILLUSTRATION IFRS17-4
Financial Statement Presentation of Debt Investments at Fair Value

Statement of Financial Position	
Current assets	
Interest receivable	$ 4,000
Debt investments (trading)	95,000
Income Statement	
Other income and expense	
Interest revenue ($4,614 + $4,645)	$ 9,259
Unrealized holding gain or (loss)	1,463

As you can see from this example, the accounting for trading debt investments under IFRS is the same as GAAP.

Equity Investments

As in GAAP, under IFRS, the degree to which one corporation (**investor**) acquires an interest in the shares of another corporation (**investee**) generally determines the accounting treatment for the investment subsequent to acquisition. To review, the classification of such investments depends on the percentage of the investee voting shares that is held by the investor:

1. Holdings of less than 20 percent (**fair value method**)—investor has passive interest.
2. Holdings between 20 percent and 50 percent (**equity method**)—investor has significant influence.
3. Holdings of more than 50 percent (**consolidated statements**)—investor has controlling interest.

The accounting and reporting for equity investments therefore depend on the level of influence and the type of security involved, as shown in Illustration IFRS17-5.

ILLUSTRATION IFRS17-5
Accounting and Reporting for Equity Investments by Category

Category	Valuation	Unrealized Holding Gains or Losses	Other Income Effects
Holdings less than 20%			
1. Trading	Fair value	Recognized in net income	Dividends declared; gains and losses from sale.
2. Non-Trading	Fair value	Recognized in "Other comprehensive income" (OCI) and as separate component of equity	Dividends declared; gains and losses from sale.
Holdings between 20% and 50%	Equity	Not recognized	Proportionate share of investee's net income.
Holdings more than 50%	Consolidation	Not recognized	Not applicable.

Equity Investments at Fair Value

When an investor has an interest of less than 20 percent, it is presumed that the investor has little or no influence over the investee. As indicated in Illustration IFRS17-5, there are two classifications for holdings less than 20 percent. Under IFRS, the presumption is that equity investments are held-for-trading. That is, companies hold these securities to profit from price changes. As with debt investments that are held-for trading, the general accounting and reporting rule for these investments is to value the securities at fair value and record unrealized gains and losses in net income (**fair value method**).[46]

However, some equity investments are held for purposes other than trading. For example, a company may be required to hold an equity investment in order to sell its products in a particular area. In this situation, the recording of unrealized gains and losses in income, as is required for trading investments, is not indicative of the company's performance with respect to this investment. As a result, IFRS allows companies to classify some equity investments as non-trading. **Non-trading equity investments** are recorded at fair value on the statement of financial position, with unrealized gains and losses reported in other comprehensive income.

Example: Equity Investment (Income). Upon acquisition, companies record equity investments at fair value. To illustrate, assume that on November 3, 2014, Republic Corporation purchased ordinary shares of three companies, each investment representing less than a 20 percent interest.

	Cost
Burberry	$259,700
Nestlé	317,500
St. Regis Pulp Co.	141,350
Total cost	$718,550

Republic records these investments as follows.

November 3, 2014		
Equity Investments	718,550	
Cash		718,550

On December 6, 2014, Republic receives a cash dividend of $4,200 on its investment in the ordinary shares of Nestlé. It records the cash dividend as follows.

December 6, 2014		
Cash	4,200	
Dividend Revenue		4,200

All three of the investee companies reported net income for the year, but only Nestlé declared and paid a dividend to Republic. But, recall that when an investor owns less than 20 percent of the shares of another corporation, it is presumed that the investor has relatively little influence on the investee. As a result, **net income of the investee is not a proper basis for recognizing income from the investment by the investor.** Why? Because the increased net assets resulting from profitable operations may be permanently retained for use in the investee's business. Therefore, **the investor recognizes net income only when the investee declares cash dividends.**

At December 31, 2014, Republic's equity investment portfolio has the carrying value and fair value shown in Illustration IFRS17-6.

[46]Fair value at initial recognition is the transaction price (exclusive of brokerage and other transaction costs). Subsequent fair value measurements should be based on market prices, if available. For non-traded investments, a valuation technique based on discounted expected cash flows can be used to develop a fair value estimate. While IFRS requires that all equity investments be measured at fair value, in certain limited cases, cost may be an appropriate estimate of fair value for an equity investment.

ILLUSTRATION IFRS17-6
Computation of Fair Value Adjustment—Equity Investment Portfolio (2014)

EQUITY INVESTMENT PORTFOLIO DECEMBER 31, 2014			
Investments	Carrying Value	Fair Value	Unrealized Gain (Loss)
Burberry	$259,700	$275,000	$ 15,300
Nestlé	317,500	304,000	(13,500)
St. Regis Pulp Co.	141,350	104,000	(37,350)
Total of portfolio	$718,550	$683,000	(35,550)
Previous fair value adjustment balance			-0-
Fair value adjustment—Cr.			$(35,550)

For Republic's equity investment portfolio, the gross unrealized gains are $15,300, and the gross unrealized losses are $50,850 ($13,500 + $37,350), resulting in a net unrealized loss of $35,550. The fair value of the equity investment portfolio is below cost by $35,550.

As with **debt** investments, Republic records the net unrealized gains and losses related to changes in the fair value of **equity** investments in an Unrealized Holding Gain or Loss—Income account. Republic reports this amount as other income and expense. In this case, Republic prepares an adjusting entry debiting the Unrealized Holding Gain or Loss—Income account and crediting the Fair Value Adjustment account to record the decrease in fair value and to record the loss as follows.

December 31, 2014		
Unrealized Holding Gain or Loss—Income	35,550	
Fair Value Adjustment		35,550

On January 23, 2015, Republic sold all of its Burberry ordinary shares, receiving $287,220. Illustration IFRS17-7 shows the computation of the realized gain on the sale.

ILLUSTRATION IFRS17-7
Computation of Gain on Sale of Burberry Shares

Net proceeds from sale	$287,220
Cost of Burberry shares	259,700
Gain on sale of shares	$ 27,520

Republic records the sale as follows.

January 23, 2015		
Cash	287,220	
Equity Investments		259,700
Gain on Sale of Equity Investment		27,520

As indicated in this example, the fair value method accounting for trading equity investments under IFRS is the same as GAAP for trading equity investments. As shown in the next section, the accounting for ***non-trading*** equity investments under IFRS is similar to the accounting for available-for-sale equity investments under GAAP.

Example: Equity Investments (OCI). The accounting entries to record non-trading equity investments are the same as for trading equity investments, except for recording the unrealized holding gain or loss. For non-trading equity investments, companies **report the unrealized holding gain or loss as other comprehensive income (OCI).** Thus, the account titled Unrealized Holding Gain or Loss—Equity is used.

To illustrate, assume that on December 10, 2014, Republic Corporation purchased $20,750 of 1,000 ordinary shares of Hawthorne Company for $20.75 per share (which represents less than a 20 percent interest). Hawthorne is a distributor for Republic products in certain locales, the laws of which require a minimum level of share ownership of a company in that region. The investment in Hawthorne meets this regulatory requirement. As a result, Republic accounts for this investment at fair value, with unrealized gains and losses recorded in OCI.[47] Republic records this investment as follows.

December 10, 2014		
Equity Investments	20,750	
Cash		20,750

On December 27, 2014, Republic receives a cash dividend of $450 on its investment in the ordinary shares of Hawthorne Company. It records the cash dividend as follows.

December 27, 2014		
Cash	450	
Dividend Revenue		450

Similar to the accounting for trading investments, when an investor owns less than 20 percent of the ordinary shares of another corporation, it is presumed that the investor has relatively little influence on the investee. Therefore, **the investor earns income when the investee declares cash dividends.**

At December 31, 2014, Republic's investment in Hawthorne has the carrying value and fair value shown in Illustration IFRS17-8.

ILLUSTRATION IFRS17-8
Computation of Fair Value Adjustment—Non-Trading Equity Investment (2014)

Non-Trading Equity Investment	Carrying Value	Fair Value	Unrealized Gain (Loss)
Hawthorne Company	$20,750	$24,000	$3,250
Previous fair value adjustment balance			0
Fair value adjustment (Dr.)			$3,250

For Republic's non-trading investment, the unrealized gain is $3,250. That is, the fair value of the Hawthorne investment exceeds cost by $3,250. Because Republic has classified this investment as non-trading, Republic records the unrealized gains and losses related to changes in the fair value of this non-trading **equity** investment in an Unrealized Holding Gain or Loss—Equity account. Republic reports this amount as **a part of other comprehensive income and as a component of other accumulated comprehensive income (reported in equity) until realized.** In this case, Republic prepares an adjusting entry crediting the Unrealized Holding Gain or Loss—Equity account and debiting the Fair Value Adjustment account to record the decrease in fair value and to record the loss as follows.

December 31, 2014		
Fair Value Adjustment	3,250	
Unrealized Holding Gain or Loss—Equity		3,250

Republic reports its equity investments in its December 31, 2014, financial statements as shown in Illustration IFRS17-9.

ILLUSTRATION IFRS17-9
Financial Statement Presentation of Equity Investments at Fair Value (2014)

Statement of Financial Position	
Investments	
Equity investments (non-trading)	$24,000
Equity	
Accumulated other comprehensive gain	$ 3,250
Statement of Comprehensive Income	
Other income and expense	
Dividend revenue	$ 450
Other comprehensive income	
Unrealized holding gain	$ 3,250

[47]The classification of an equity investment as non-trading is irrevocable. This approach is designed to provide some discipline to the application of the non-trading classification, which allows unrealized gains and losses to bypass net income.

During 2015, sales of Republic products through Hawthorne as a distributor did not meet management's goals. As a result, Republic withdrew from these markets and on December 20, 2015, Republic sold all of its Hawthorne Company ordinary shares, receiving net proceeds of $22,500. Illustration IFRS17-10 shows the computation of the realized gain on the sale.

Net proceeds from sale	$22,500
Cost of Hawthorne shares	20,750
Gain on sale of shares	$ 1,750

ILLUSTRATION IFRS17-10
Computation of Gain on Sale of Shares

Republic records the sale as follows.

December 20, 2015		
Cash	22,500	
Equity Investments		20,750
Gain on Sale of Equity Investment		1,750

Because Republic no longer holds any equity investments, it makes the following entry to eliminate the Fair Value Adjustment account.

December 31, 2015		
Unrealized Holding Gain or Loss—Equity	3,250	
Fair Value Adjustment		3,250

In summary, the accounting for non-trading equity investments deviates from the general provisions for equity investments. The IASB noted that while fair value provides the most useful information about investments in equity investments, recording unrealized gains or losses in other comprehensive income is more representative for non-trading equity investments.

Impairments

A company should evaluate every held-for-collection investment, at each reporting date, to determine if it has suffered **impairment**—a loss in value such that the fair value of the investment is below its carrying value.[48] For example, if an investee experiences a bankruptcy or a significant liquidity crisis, the investor may suffer a permanent loss. **If the company determines that an investment is impaired, it writes down the amortized cost basis of the individual security to reflect this loss in value.** The company accounts for the write-down as a realized loss, and it includes the amount in net income.

For debt investments, a company uses the impairment test to determine whether "it is probable that the investor will be unable to collect all amounts due according to the contractual terms." If an investment is impaired, the company should measure the loss due to the **impairment**. This impairment loss is calculated as the difference between the carrying amount plus accrued interest and the expected future cash flows discounted at the investment's historical effective-interest rate.

Example: Impairment Loss

At December 31, 2013, Mayhew Company has a debt investment in Bellovary Inc., purchased at par for $200,000. The investment has a term of four years, with annual interest payments at 10 percent, paid at the end of each year (the historical effective-interest rate is 10 percent). This debt investment is classified as held-for-collection. Unfortunately, Bellovary is experiencing significant financial difficulty and indicates that it will be unable

[48]Note that impairments tests are conducted only for debt investments that are held-for-collection (which are accounted for at amortized cost). Other debt and equity investments are measured at fair value each period; thus, an impairment test is not needed.

to make all payments according to the contractual terms. Mayhew uses the present value method for measuring the required impairment loss. Illustration IFRS17-11 shows the cash flow schedule prepared for this analysis.

ILLUSTRATION IFRS17-11
Investment Cash Flows

Dec. 31	Contractual Cash Flows	Expected Cash Flows	Loss of Cash Flows
2014	$ 20,000	$ 16,000	$ 4,000
2015	20,000	16,000	4,000
2016	20,000	16,000	4,000
2017	220,000	216,000	4,000
Total cash flows	$280,000	$264,000	$16,000

As indicated, the expected cash flows of $264,000 are less than the contractual cash flows of $280,000. The amount of the impairment to be recorded equals the difference between the recorded investment of $200,000 and the present value of the expected cash flows, as shown in Illustration IFRS17-12.

ILLUSTRATION IFRS17-12
Computation of Impairment Loss

Recorded investment		$200,000
Less: Present value of $200,000 due in 4 years at 10% (Table 6-2); FV($PVF_{4,10\%}$); ($200,000 × .68301)	$136,602	
Present value of $16,000 interest receivable annually for 4 years at 10% (Table 6-4); R($PVF\text{-}OA_{4,10\%}$); ($16,000 × 3.16986)	50,718	187,320
Loss on impairment		$ 12,680

The loss due to the impairment is $12,680. Why isn't it $16,000 ($280,000 − $264,000)? A loss of $12,680 is recorded because Mayhew must measure the loss at a present value amount, not at an undiscounted amount. Mayhew recognizes an impairment loss of $12,680 by debiting Loss on Impairment for the expected loss. At the same time, it reduces the overall value of the investment. The journal entry to record the loss is therefore as follows.

Loss on Impairment	12,680	
Debt Investments		12,680

Recovery of Impairment Loss

Subsequent to recording an impairment, events or economic conditions may change such that the extent of the impairment loss decreases (e.g., due to an improvement in the debtor's credit rating). In this situation, some or all of the previously recognized impairment loss shall be reversed with a debit to the Debt Investments account and a credit to Recovery of Impairment Loss. Similar to the accounting for impairments of receivables shown in Chapter 7, the reversal of impairment losses shall not result in a carrying amount of the investment that exceeds the amortized cost that would have been reported had the impairment not been recognized.

ON THE HORIZON

At one time, both the FASB and IASB have indicated that they believe that all financial instruments should be reported at fair value and that changes in fair value should be reported as part of net income. However, the recently issued IFRS indicates that the IASB believes that certain debt investments should not be reported at fair value. The IASB's decision to issue new rules on investments, prior to the FASB's completion of its deliberations on financial instrument accounting, could create obstacles for the Boards in converging the accounting in this area.

IFRS SELF-TEST QUESTIONS

1. All of the following are key similarities between GAAP and IFRS with respect to accounting for investments **except**:
   - **(a)** IFRS and GAAP have a held-to-maturity investment classification.
   - **(b)** IFRS and GAAP apply the equity method to significant influence equity investments.
   - **(c)** IFRS and GAAP have a fair value option for financial instruments.
   - **(d)** the accounting for impairment of investments is similar, although IFRS allows recovery of impairment losses.
2. Which of the following statements is **correct**?
   - **(a)** GAAP has a held-for-collection investment classification.
   - **(b)** GAAP permits recovery of impairment losses.
   - **(c)** Under IFRS, non-trading equity investments are accounted for at amortized cost.
   - **(d)** IFRS and GAAP both have a trading investment classification.
3. IFRS requires companies to measure their financial assets at fair value based on:
   - **(a)** the company's business model for managing its financial assets.
   - **(b)** whether the financial asset is a debt investment.
   - **(c)** whether the financial asset is an equity investment.
   - **(d)** All of the choices are IFRS requirements.
4. Select the investment accounting approach with the correct valuation approach:

	Not Held-for-Collection	Held-for-Collection
(a)	Amortized cost	Amortized cost
(b)	Fair value	Fair value
(c)	Fair value	Amortized cost
(d)	Amortized cost	Fair value

5. Under IFRS, a company:
   - **(a)** should evaluate only equity investments for impairment.
   - **(b)** accounts for an impairment as an unrealized loss, and includes it as a part of other comprehensive income and as a component of other accumulated comprehensive income until realized.
   - **(c)** calculates the impairment loss on debt investments as the difference between the carrying amount plus accrued interest and the expected future cash flows discounted at the investment's historical effective-interest rate.
   - **(d)** All of the above.

IFRS CONCEPTS AND APPLICATION

IFRS17-1 Where can authoritative IFRS be found related to investments?

IFRS17-2 Briefly describe some of the similarities and differences between GAAP and IFRS with respect to the accounting for investments.

IFRS17-3 Describe the two criteria for determining the valuation of financial assets.

IFRS17-4 Which types of investments are valued at amortized cost? Explain the rationale for this accounting.

IFRS17-5 Lady Gaga Co. recently made an investment in the bonds issued by Chili Peppers Inc. Lady Gaga's business model for this investment is to profit from trading in response to changes in market interest rates. How should this investment be classified by Lady Gaga? Explain.

IFRS17-6 Consider the bond investment by Lady Gaga in IFRS17-5. Discuss the accounting for this investment if Lady Gaga's business model is to hold the investment to collect interest while outstanding and to receive the principal at maturity.

IFRS17-7 Indicate how unrealized holding gains and losses should be reported for investments classified as trading and held for-collection.

IFRS17-8 Ramirez Company has a held-for-collection investment in the 6%, 20-year bonds of Soto Company. The investment was originally purchased for $1,200,000 in 2013. Early in 2014, Ramirez recorded an impairment of $300,000 on the Soto investment, due to Soto's financial distress. In 2015, Soto returned to profitability and the Soto investment was no longer impaired. What entry does Ramirez make in 2015 under (a) GAAP and (b) IFRS?

IFRS17-9 Carow Corporation purchased, as a held-for-collection investment, $60,000 of the 8%, 5-year bonds of Harrison, Inc. for $65,118, which provides a 6% return. The bonds pay interest semiannually. Prepare Carow's journal entries for (a) the purchase of the investment, and (b) the receipt of semiannual interest and premium amortization.

IFRS17-10 Fairbanks Corporation purchased 400 ordinary shares of Sherman Inc. as a trading investment for $13,200. During the year, Sherman paid a cash dividend of $3.25 per share. At year-end, Sherman shares were selling for $34.50 per share. Prepare Fairbanks' journal entries to record (a) the purchase of the investment, (b) the dividends received, and (c) the fair value adjustment.

IFRS17-11 Use the information from IFRS17-10 but assume the shares were purchased to meet a non-trading regulatory requirement. Prepare Fairbanks' journal entries to record (a) the purchase of the investment, (b) the dividends received, and (c) the fair value adjustment.

IFRS17-12 On January 1, 2014, Roosevelt Company purchased 12% bonds, having a maturity value of $500,000, for $537,907.40. The bonds provide the bondholders with a 10% yield. They are dated January 1, 2014, and mature January 1, 2019, with interest receivable December 31 of each year. Roosevelt's business model is to hold these bonds to collect contractual cash flows.

Instructions

(a) Prepare the journal entry at the date of the bond purchase.
(b) Prepare a bond amortization schedule.
(c) Prepare the journal entry to record the interest received and the amortization for 2014.
(d) Prepare the journal entry to record the interest received and the amortization for 2015.

IFRS17-13 Assume the same information as in IFRS17-12 except that Roosevelt has an active trading strategy for these bonds. The fair value of the bonds at December 31 of each year-end is as follows.

2014	$534,200	2017	$517,000
2015	$515,000	2018	$500,000
2016	$513,000		

Instructions

(a) Prepare the journal entry at the date of the bond purchase.
(b) Prepare the journal entries to record the interest received and recognition of fair value for 2014.
(c) Prepare the journal entry to record the recognition of fair value for 2015.

IFRS17-14 On December 21, 2014, Zurich Company provided you with the following information regarding its trading investments.

December 31, 2014

Investments (Trading)	Cost	Fair Value	Unrealized Gain (Loss)
Stargate Corp. shares	$20,000	$19,000	$(1,000)
Carolina Co. shares	10,000	9,000	(1,000)
Vectorman Co. shares	20,000	20,600	600
Total of portfolio	$50,000	$48,600	$(1,400)
Previous fair value adjustment balance	–0–		
Fair value adjustment—Cr.	$ (1,400)		

During 2015, Carolina Company shares were sold for $9,500. The fair value of the shares on December 31, 2015, was Stargate Corp. shares—$19,300; Vectorman Co. shares—$20,500.

Instructions

(a) Prepare the adjusting journal entry needed on December 31, 2014.
(b) Prepare the journal entry to record the sale of the Carolina Company shares during 2015.
(c) Prepare the adjusting journal entry needed on December 31, 2015.

IFRS17-15 Komissarov Company has a debt investment in the bonds issued by Keune Inc. The bonds were purchased at par for $400,000 and, at the end of 2014, have a remaining life of 3 years with annual interest payments at 10%, paid at the end of each year. This debt investment is classified as held-for-collection. Keune is facing a tough economic environment and informs all of its investors that it will be unable to make all payments according to the contractual terms. The controller of Komissarov has prepared the following revised expected cash flow forecast for this bond investment.

Dec. 31	Expected Cash Flows
2015	$ 35,000
2016	35,000
2017	385,000
Total cash flows	$455,000

Instructions

(a) Determine the impairment loss for Komissarov at December 31, 2014.

(b) Prepare the entry to record the impairment loss for Komissarov at December 31, 2014.

(c) On January 15, 2015, Keune receives a major capital infusion from a private equity investor. It informs Komissarov that the bonds now will be paid according to the contractual terms. Briefly describe how Komissarov would account for the bond investment in light of this new information.

Professional Research

IFRS17-16 Your client, Cascade Company, is planning to invest some of its excess cash in 5-year revenue bonds issued by the county and in the shares of one of its suppliers, Teton Co. Teton's shares trade on the over-the-counter market. Cascade plans to classify these investments as trading. They would like you to conduct some research on the accounting for these investments.

Instructions

Access the IFRS authoritative literature at the IASB website (*http://eifrs.iasb.org/*). (Click on the IFRS tab and then register for free eIFRS access if necessary.) When you have accessed the documents, you can use the search tool in your Internet browser to respond to the following questions. (Provide paragraph citations.)

(a) Since the Teton shares do not trade on one of the large securities exchanges, Cascade argues that the fair value of this investment is not readily available. According to the authoritative literature, when is the fair value of a security "readily determinable"?

(b) How is an impairment of a debt investment accounted for?

(c) To avoid volatility in their financial statements due to fair value adjustments, Cascade debated whether the bond investment could be classified as held-for-collection; Cascade is pretty sure it will hold the bonds for 5 years. What criteria must be met for Cascade to classify it as held-for-collection?

International Financial Reporting Problem

Marks and Spencer plc

IFRS17-17 The financial statements of **Marks and Spencer plc (M&S)** are available at the book's companion website or can be accessed at *http://annualreport.marksandspencer.com/_assets/downloads/Marks-and-Spencer-Annual-report-and-financial-statements-2012.pdf.*

Instructions

Refer to M&S's financial statements and the accompanying notes to answer the following questions.

(a) What investments does M&S report in 2012, and where are these investments reported in its financial statements?

(b) How are M&S's investments valued? How does M&S determine fair value?

(c) How does M&S use derivative financial instruments?

ANSWERS TO IFRS SELF-TEST QUESTIONS

1. a **2.** d **3.** a **4.** c **5.** c

Remember to check the book's companion website to find additional resources for this chapter.

CHAPTER

18 Revenue Recognition

LEARNING OBJECTIVES

After studying this chapter, you should be able to:

1 Understand revenue recognition issues.

2 Identify the five steps in the revenue recognition process.

3 Identify the contract with customers.

4 Identify the separate performance obligations in the contract.

5 Determine the transaction price.

6 Allocate the transaction price to the separate performance obligations.

7 Recognize revenue when the company satisfies its performance obligation.

8 Identify other revenue recognition issues.

9 Describe presentation and disclosure regarding revenue.

It's Back

Several years after passage, the accounting world continues to be preoccupied with the Sarbanes-Oxley Act of 2002 (SOX). Unfortunately, SOX did not solve one of the classic accounting issues—how to properly account for revenue. In fact, revenue recognition practices are the most prevalent reason for accounting restatements. A number of revenue recognition issues relate to possible fraudulent behavior by company executives and employees.

As a result of such revenue recognition problems, the SEC has increased its enforcement actions in this area. In some of these cases, companies made significant adjustments to previously issued financial statements. As Lynn Turner, a former chief accountant of the SEC, indicated, "When people cross over the boundaries of legitimate reporting, the Commission will take appropriate action to ensure the fairness and integrity that investors need and depend on every day."

Consider some SEC actions:

- The SEC charged the former co-chairman and CEO of **Qwest Communications International Inc.** and eight other former Qwest officers and employees with fraud and other violations of the federal securities laws. Three of these people fraudulently characterized nonrecurring revenue from one-time sales as revenue from recurring data and Internet services. The SEC release notes that internal correspondence likened Qwest's dependence on these transactions to fill the gap between actual and projected revenue to an addiction.
- The SEC filed a complaint against three former senior officers of **iGo Corp.**, alleging that the defendants collectively caused iGo to improperly recognize revenue on consignment sales and products that were not shipped or that were shipped after the end of a fiscal quarter.
- The SEC filed a complaint against the former CEO and chairman of **Homestore Inc.** and its former executive vice president of business development, alleging that they engaged in a fraudulent scheme to overstate advertising and subscription revenues. The scheme involved a complex structure of "round-trip" transactions using various third-party companies that, in essence, allowed Homestore to recognize its own cash as revenue.
- The SEC claims that **Lantronix** deliberately sent excessive product to distributors and granted them generous return rights and extended payment terms. In addition, as part of its alleged channel stuffing and to prevent product returns, Lantronix loaned funds to a third party to purchase Lantronix products from one of its distributors. The third party later returned the products. The SEC also asserted that Lantronix engaged in

CONCEPTUAL FOCUS

> See the **Underlying Concepts** on pages 1043 and 1049.

> Read the **Evolving Issue** on page 1070 for a discussion of the implementation of the recently issued revenue recognition standard.

INTERNATIONAL FOCUS

> With the issuance of the new standard ("Revenue from Contracts with Customers"), the accounting for revenue recognition is now converged under U.S. GAAP and IFRS.

> See the **International Perspective** on page 1042.

other improper revenue recognition practices, including shipping without a purchase order and recognizing revenue on a contingent sale.

Revenue numbers are attracting more attention from investors these days. For example, in a recent quarter, revenue for the S&P 500 actually decreased by a small percentage. A concern expressed recently is that revenue growth is not robust, and increases in net income (the bottom line) are caused by factors such as low financing costs and lower labor costs which in the long run may not be sustainable. So more attention is now being given to a company's top-line revenue number as many believe strong revenue growth suggests a more profitable company in the future.

Recently, the FASB and IASB issued a new standard on revenue recognition that hopefully will improve the reporting of revenue transactions. This new standard provides a set of guidelines to follow in determining when revenue should be reported and how it should be measured. The new standard is comprehensive and applies to all companies. As a result, comparability and consistency in reporting revenue should be enhanced. After studying this chapter, you should have a good understanding of the new revenue recognition concepts.

Sources: Cheryl de Mesa Graziano, "Revenue Recognition: A Perennial Problem," *Financial Executive* (July 14, 2005), *www.fei.org/mag/articles/7-2005_revenue.cfm;* and S. Taub, "SEC Accuses Ex-CFO of Channel Stuffing," *CFO.com* (September 30, 2006).

PREVIEW OF CHAPTER 18

As indicated in the opening story, the issue of when revenue should be recognized is complex. The many methods of marketing products and services make it difficult to develop guidelines that will apply to all situations. This chapter provides you with general guidelines used in most business transactions. The content and organization of the chapter are as follows.

Revenue Recognition

Overview of Revenue Recognition	The Five-Step Process	Other Revenue Recognition Issues	Presentation and Disclosure
• Background • New revenue recognition standard	• Contract with customer • Separate performance obligations • Determining the transaction price • Allocating the transaction price • Satisfying performance obligations	• Right of return • Repurchase agreements • Bill-and-hold arrangements • Principal-agent relationships • Consignments • Warranties • Nonrefundable upfront fees	• Presentation • Disclosure

OVERVIEW OF REVENUE RECOGNITION

Background

LEARNING OBJECTIVE 1
Understand revenue recognition issues.

Most revenue transactions pose few problems for revenue recognition. This is because, in many cases, the transaction is initiated and completed at the same time. However, not all transactions are that simple. For example, consider a cell phone contract between a company such as **Verizon** and a customer. The customer is often provided with a package that may include a handset, free minutes of talk time, data downloads, and text messaging service. In addition, some providers will bundle that with a fixed-line broadband service. At the same time, the customer may pay for these services in a variety of ways, possibly receiving a discount on the handset and then paying higher prices for connection fees and so forth. In some cases, depending on the package purchased, the company may provide free applications in subsequent periods. How, then, should the various pieces of this sale be reported by Verizon? The answer is not obvious.

It is therefore not surprising that a recent survey of financial executives noted that the revenue recognition process is increasingly more complex to manage, more prone to error, and more material to financial statements compared to any other area in financial reporting. The report went on to note that revenue recognition is a top fraud risk and that regardless of the accounting rules followed (GAAP or IFRS), the risk of errors and inaccuracies in revenue reporting is significant.[1]

International Perspective

The converged revenue recognition standard represents a significant milestone in the FASB/IASB convergence project.

Both the FASB and the IASB have indicated that the state of reporting for revenue was unsatisfactory. IFRS was criticized because it lacked guidance in a number of areas. For example, IFRS had one basic standard on revenue recognition—*IAS 18*—plus some limited guidance related to certain minor topics. In contrast, GAAP had numerous standards related to revenue recognition (by some counts, well over 100), but many believed the standards were often inconsistent with one another. Thus, the accounting for revenues provided a most fitting contrast of the principles-based (IFRS) and rules-based (GAAP) approaches. While both sides had their advocates, the FASB and IASB recognized a number of deficiencies in this area.[2]

See the FASB Codification section (page 1089).

Recently, the FASB and IASB issued a converged standard on revenue recognition entitled *Revenue from Contracts with Customers*. **[1]** To address the inconsistencies and weaknesses of the previous approaches, a comprehensive revenue recognition standard now applies to a wide range of transactions and industries. The Boards believe this new standard will improve GAAP and IFRS by:

(a) Providing a more robust framework for addressing revenue recognition issues.
(b) Improving comparability of revenue recognition practices across entities, industries, jurisdictions, and capital markets.

[1]See *www.softrax.com/resources/pdf/intlriskrevreporting*.

[2]See, for example, "Preliminary Views on Revenue Recognition in Contracts with Customers," *IASB/FASB Discussion Paper* (December 19, 2008). Some noted that GAAP has so many standards that at times they are inconsistent with each other in applying basic principles. In addition, even with the many standards, no comprehensive guidance was provided for service transactions. Conversely, IFRS lacked guidance in certain fundamental areas such as multiple-deliverable arrangements. In addition, there were inconsistencies in applying revenue recognition principles to long-term contracts versus other elements of revenue recognition.

(c) Simplifying the preparation of financial statements by reducing the number of requirements to which companies must refer.

(d) Requiring enhanced disclosures to help financial statement users better understand the amount, timing, and uncertainty of revenue that is recognized. **[2]**

New Revenue Recognition Standard

The new standard, *Revenue from Contracts with Customers*, adopts an **asset-liability approach** as the basis for revenue recognition. The asset-liability approach recognizes and measures revenue based on changes in assets and liabilities. The Boards decided that focusing on (a) the recognition and measurement of assets and liabilities and (b) changes in those assets or liabilities over the life of the contract brings more discipline to the measurement of revenue, compared to the "earned and realized" criteria in prior standards.

Under the asset-liability approach, companies account for revenue based on the asset or liability arising from contracts with customers. Companies analyze contracts with customers because contracts are the lifeblood of most businesses. Contracts indicate the terms of the transaction, provide the measurement of the consideration, and specify the promises that must be met by each party. Without contracts, companies cannot know whether promises will be met.

Underlying Concepts

The asset-liability approach is consistent with the conceptual framework approach to recognition.

Illustration 18-1 shows the key concepts related to this new standard on revenue recognition. The new standard first identifies the key objective of revenue recognition, followed by a five-step process that companies should use to ensure that revenue is measured and reported correctly. The culmination of the process is the **revenue recognition principle**, that is, recognition of revenue when the performance obligation is satisfied. We examine all steps in more detail in the following section.

ILLUSTRATION 18-1
Key Concepts of Revenue Recognition

KEY OBJECTIVE

Recognize revenue to depict the transfer of goods or services to customers in an amount that reflects the consideration that the company receives, or expects to receive, in exchange for these goods or services.

FIVE-STEP PROCESS FOR REVENUE RECOGNITION

1. Identify the contract with customers.
2. Identify the separate performance obligations in the contract.
3. Determine the transaction price.
4. Allocate the transaction price to the separate performance obligations.
5. Recognize revenue when each performance obligation is satisfied.

REVENUE RECOGNITION PRINCIPLE

Recognize revenue in the accounting period when the performance obligation is satisfied.

THE FIVE-STEP PROCESS

2 LEARNING OBJECTIVE
Identify the five steps in the revenue recognition process.

Assume that **Boeing Corporation** signs a contract to sell airplanes to **Delta Air Lines** for $100 million. Illustration 18-2 (page 1044) shows the five steps that Boeing follows to recognize revenue.

ILLUSTRATION 18-2
Five Steps of Revenue Recognition

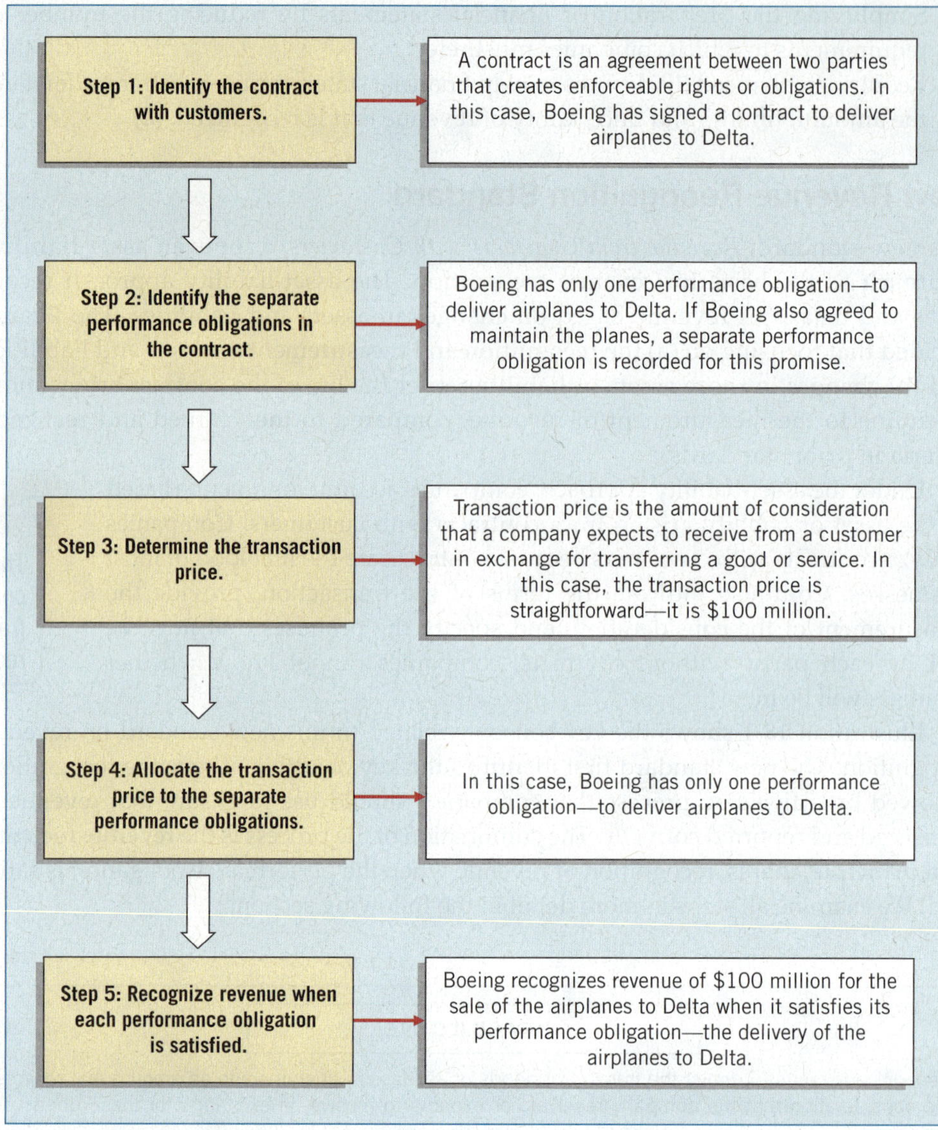

Illustration 18-2 highlights the five-step process used to recognize revenue. Step 5 is when Boeing recognizes revenue related to the sale of the airplanes to Delta. At this point, Boeing delivers the airplanes to Delta and satisfies its performance obligation. In essence, a change in control from Boeing to Delta occurs. Delta now controls the assets because it has the ability to direct the use of and obtain substantially all the remaining benefits from the airplanes. Control also includes Delta's ability to prevent other companies from directing the use of, or receiving the benefits from, the airplanes. In the following sections, we provide an expanded discussion of this five-step process.

Identifying the Contract with Customers—Step 1

LEARNING OBJECTIVE 3
Identify the contract with customers.

A **contract** is an agreement between two or more parties that creates enforceable rights or obligations. Contracts can be written, oral, or implied from customary business practice. A company applies the revenue guidance to a contract according to the following criteria in Illustration 18-3. [3]

In some cases, there are multiple contracts related to the transaction, and accounting for each contract may or may not occur, depending on the circumstances. These situations often develop when not only a product is provided but some type of service is performed as well.

ILLUSTRATION 18-3
Contract Criteria for Revenue Guidance

Apply Revenue Guidance to Contracts If:	Disregard Revenue Guidance to Contracts If:
• The contract has commercial substance; • The parties to the contract have approved the contract and are committed to perform their respective obligations; • The company can identify each party's rights regarding the goods or services to be transferred; and • The company can identify the payment terms for the goods and services to be transferred. • It is probable that the company will collect the consideration to which it will be entitled.[3]	• The contract is wholly unperformed, and • Each party can unilaterally terminate the contract without compensation.

In some cases, a company should combine contracts and account for them as one contract.

Basic Accounting

Revenue from a contract with a customer cannot be recognized until a contract exists. On entering into a contract with a customer, a company obtains rights to receive consideration from the customer and assumes obligations to transfer goods or services to the customer (performance obligations). The combination of those rights and performance obligations gives rise to an (net) asset or (net) liability. If the measure of the remaining rights exceeds the measure of the remaining performance obligations, the contract is an asset (a contract asset). Conversely, if the measure of the remaining performance obligations exceeds the measure of the remaining rights, the contract is a liability (a contract liability). However, **a company does not recognize contract assets or liabilities until one or both parties to the contract perform.** The basic accounting for a contract in which both parties perform is shown in Illustration 18-4.

ILLUSTRATION 18-4
Basic Revenue Transaction

CONTRACTS AND RECOGNITION

Facts: On March 1, 2014, Margo Company enters into a contract to transfer a product to Soon Yoon on July 31, 2014. The contract is structured such that Soon Yoon is required to pay the full contract price of $5,000 on August 31, 2014. The cost of the goods transferred is $3,000. Margo delivers the product to Soon Yoon on July 31, 2014.

***Question:* What journal entries should Margo Company make in regards to this contract in 2014?**

Solution: No entry is required on March 1, 2014, because neither party has performed on the contract. On July 31, 2014, Margo delivers the product and therefore should recognize revenue on that date as it satisfies its performance obligation by delivering the product to Soon Yoon.

The journal entry to record the sale and related cost of goods sold is as follows.

July 31, 2014

Accounts Receivable	5,000	
Sales Revenue		5,000
Cost of Goods Sold	3,000	
Inventory		3,000

After receiving the cash payment on August 31, 2014, Margo makes the following entry.

August 31, 2014

Cash	5,000	
Accounts Receivable		5,000

[3]The FASB included this criterion (which acts like a collectibility threshold) because the Board concluded that the assessment of a customer's credit risk was an important part of determining whether a contract is valid. That is, under the revenue standard (and discussed later in the chapter), collectibility is not a consideration for determining whether revenue is recognized. However, collectibility may be a consideration in assessing whether parties to the contract are committed to perform. In determining whether it is probable that a company will collect the amount of consideration to which it is entitled, the company assesses both the customer's ability and intent to pay as amounts become due. **[4]**

A key feature of the revenue arrangement is that the signing of the contract by the two parties is not recorded (does not result in a journal entry) until one or both of the parties *perform under the contract*. **Until performance occurs, no net asset or net liability occurs.**

Contract Modifications

Companies sometimes change the contract terms while it is ongoing; this is referred to as a **contract modification**. When a contract modification occurs, companies determine whether a new contract (and performance obligations) results or whether it is a modification of the existing contract.

Separate Performance Obligation A company accounts for a contract modification as a new contract if **both** of the following conditions are satisfied:

- The promised **goods or services are distinct** (i.e., the company sells them separately and they are not interdependent with other goods and services), and
- The company has the right to receive an amount of **consideration that reflects the standalone selling price** of the promised goods or services. **[5]**

For example, Crandall Co. has a contract to sell 100 products to a customer for $10,000 ($100 per product) at various points in time over a six-month period. After 60 products have been delivered, Crandall modifies the contract by promising to deliver 20 more products for an additional $1,900, or $95 per product (which is the standalone selling price of the products at the time of the contract modification). Crandall regularly sells the products separately. In this situation, the contract modification for the additional 20 products is, in effect, a **new and separate contract** because it meets both of the conditions above. That is, it does not affect the accounting for the original contract.

Given a new contract, Crandall recognizes an additional $4,000 [(100 units − 60 units) × $100] related to the original contract terms and $1,900 (20 units × $95) related to the new products. Total revenue after the modification is therefore $5,900 ($4,000 + $1,900).

Prospective Modification What if Crandall Co. determines that the additional products are not a separate performance obligation? This might arise if the new products are not priced at the proper standalone selling price or if they are not distinct. In this situation, companies generally account for the modification using a prospective approach.

Under the prospective approach, Crandall should account for the effect of the change in the period of change as well as future periods if the change affects both. Crandall should not change previously reported results. Thus, for Crandall, the amount recognized as revenue for each of the remaining products would be a blended price of $98.33, computed as shown in Illustration 18-5.

ILLUSTRATION 18-5
Revenue Under Prospective Modification

Consideration for products not yet delivered under original contract ($100 × 40)	$4,000
Consideration for products to be delivered under the contract modification ($95 × 20)	1,900
Total remaining revenue	$5,900
Revenue per remaining unit ($5,900 ÷ 60) = $98.33	

Therefore, under the prospective approach, this computation differs from that in the separate performance obligation approach in that revenue on the remaining units is recognized at the blended price. Total revenue after the modification is therefore $5,900

(60 units × $98.33). Illustration 18-6 shows the revenue reported under the two contract modification approaches for Crandall Co.

ILLUSTRATION 18-6
Comparison of Contract Modification Approaches

	Revenue Recognized Prior to Modification	Revenue Recognized After Modification	Total Revenue Recognized
Separate performance obligation	$6,000	$5,900	$11,900
No separate performance obligation—prospectively	$6,000	$5,900	$11,900

As indicated, whether a modification is treated as a separate performance obligation or prospectively, the same amount of revenue is recognized before and after the modification. However, under the prospective approach, a blended price ($98.33) is used for sales in the periods after the modification.[4]

Identifying Separate Performance Obligations—Step 2

4 LEARNING OBJECTIVE
Identify the separate performance obligations in the contract.

A **performance obligation** is a promise in a contract to provide a product or service to a customer. This promise may be explicit, implicit, or possibly based on customary business practice. To determine whether a performance obligation exists, **the company must provide a distinct product or service.** Illustration 18-7 summarizes some classic situations when revenue is recognized as a result of providing a distinct product or service, therefore satisfying a performance obligation.

ILLUSTRATION 18-7
Revenue Recognition Situations

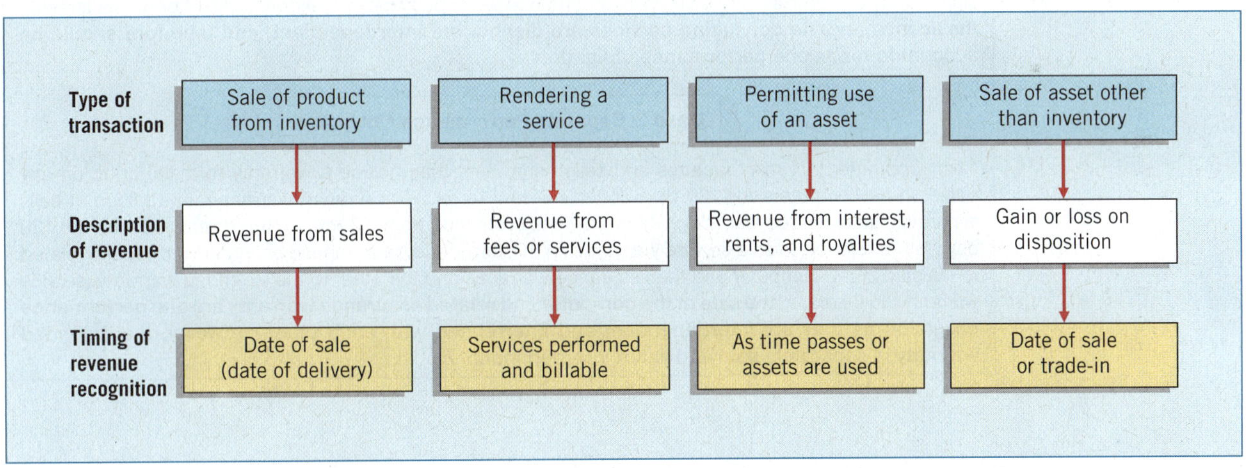

[4]Another approach to account for a contract modification is to report the information in a cumulative catch-up manner. In other words, assuming that these new products are part of the original contract, companies adjust the revenue account to reflect the cumulative effect for periods prior to when the modification occurred. An example of a catch-up situation is a long-term construction contract, which is discussed in more detail in Appendix 18A. Use of the prospective approach avoids the complexity of opening up the accounting for previously satisfied performance obligations. However, it ignores any adjustments to revenue that have already been recognized. **[6]** *For homework purposes, unless instructed otherwise, use the prospective approach for modifications that do not result in a separate performance obligation.* Expanded discussion of the prospective and cumulative catch-up (retrospective) approaches to accounting changes is provided in Chapter 22.

The accounting for the transactions in Illustration 18-7 is straightforward as only one performance obligation exists. However, many revenue arrangements may have more than one performance obligation. To determine whether a company has to account for multiple performance obligations, it evaluates a second condition. That is, **whether the product is distinct within the contract**. In other words, if the performance obligation is not highly dependent on, or interrelated with, other promises in the contract, then each performance obligation should be accounted for separately. Conversely, if each of these services is interdependent and interrelated, these services are combined and reported as one performance obligation.

To illustrate, assume that General Motors sells an automobile to Marquart Auto Dealers at a price that includes six months of telematics services such as navigation and remote diagnostics. These telematics services are regularly sold on a standalone basis by General Motors for a monthly fee. After the six-month period, the consumer can renew these services on a fee basis with General Motors. In this case, two performance obligations exist, one related to providing the automobile and the other related to the telematics services. **Both are distinct (they can be sold separately) and are not interdependent.**

Illustration 18-8 provides additional case examples of issues related to identifying performance obligations.

ILLUSTRATION 18-8
Identifying Performance Obligations

Case 1: Single Performance Obligation

SoftTech Inc. licenses customer-relationship software to Lopez Company. In addition to providing the software itself, SoftTech promises to perform consulting services by extensively customizing the software to Lopez's information technology environment, for a total consideration of $600,000. In this case, SoftTech is providing a significant service by integrating the goods and services (the license and the consulting service) into one combined item for which Lopez has contracted. In addition, the software is significantly customized by SoftTech in accordance with specifications negotiated by Lopez. As a result, **the license and the consulting services are distinct but interdependent, and therefore should be accounted for as one performance obligation.**

Case 2: Separate Performance Obligation

Chen Computer Inc. manufactures and sells computers that include a warranty to make good on any defect in its computers for 120 days (often referred to as an assurance warranty). In addition, it sells separately an extended warranty, which provides protection from defects for three years beyond the 120 days (often referred to as a service warranty). In this case, two performance obligations exist, one related to the sale of the computer and the assurance warranty, and the other to the extended warranty (service warranty). In this case, **the sale of the computer and related assurance warranty are one performance obligation as they are interdependent and interrelated with each other. However, the extended warranty is separately sold and is not interdependent.**

Determining the Transaction Price—Step 3

LEARNING OBJECTIVE 5
Determine the transaction price.

The **transaction price** is the amount of consideration that a company expects to receive from a customer in exchange for transferring goods and services. The transaction price in a contract is often easily determined because the customer agrees to pay a fixed amount to the company over a short period of time. In other contracts, companies must consider the following factors. [7]

- Variable consideration
- Time value of money
- Noncash consideration
- Consideration paid or payable to the customer

Variable Consideration

In some cases, the price of a good or service is dependent on future events. These future events might include discounts, rebates, credits, performance bonuses, or royalties. In these cases, the company estimates the amount of variable consideration it will receive from the contract to determine the amount of revenue to recognize. Companies use either the **expected value,** which is a probability-weighted amount, or the **most likely amount** in a range of possible amounts to estimate variable consideration. Companies select among these two methods based on which approach better predicts the amount of consideration to which a company is entitled. [8] Illustration 18-9 highlights the issues to be considered in selecting the appropriate method.

Underlying Concepts

The expected value approach is also illustrated in Chapter 6 to determine the liability for warranties.

ILLUSTRATION 18-9
Estimating Variable Consideration

Expected Value: Probability-weighted amount in a range of possible consideration amounts.	**Most Likely Amount:** The single most likely amount in a range of possible consideration outcomes.
• May be appropriate if a company has a large number of contracts with similar characteristics. • Can be based on a limited number of discrete outcomes and probabilities.	• May be appropriate if the contract has only two possible outcomes.

Illustration 18-10 provides an application of the two estimation methods.

ILLUSTRATION 18-10
Transaction Price—Variable Consideration

ESTIMATING VARIABLE CONSIDERATION

Facts: Peabody Construction Company enters into a contract with a customer to build a warehouse for $100,000, with a performance bonus of $50,000 that will be paid based on the timing of completion. The amount of the performance bonus decreases by 10% per week for every week beyond the agreed-upon completion date. The contract requirements are similar to contracts that Peabody has performed previously, and management believes that such experience is predictive for this contract. Management estimates that there is a 60% probability that the contract will be completed by the agreed-upon completion date, a 30% probability that it will be completed 1 week late, and only a 10% probability that it will be completed 2 weeks late.

***Question:* How should Peabody account for this revenue arrangement?**

Solution: The transaction price should include management's estimate of the amount of consideration to which Peabody will be entitled. Management has concluded that the **probability-weighted method** is the most predictive approach for estimating the variable consideration in this situation:

60% chance of $150,000 [$100,000 + ($50,000 × 1.0)] =	$ 90,000
30% chance of $145,000 [$100,000 + ($50,000 × .90)] =	43,500
10% chance of $140,000 [$100,000 + ($50,000 × .80)] =	14,000
	$147,500

Thus, the total transaction price is $147,500 based on the probability-weighted estimate. Management should update its estimate at each reporting date. Using a most likely outcome approach may be more predictive if a performance bonus is binary (Peabody either will or will not earn the performance bonus), such that Peabody earns either $50,000 for completion on the agreed-upon date or nothing for completion after the agreed-upon date. In this scenario, if management believes that Peabody will meet the deadline and estimates the consideration using the **most likely outcome**, the total transaction price would be $150,000 (the outcome with 60% probability).

A word of caution—a company only **allocates variable consideration if it is reasonably assured that it will be entitled to that amount.** Companies therefore may only recognize variable consideration if (1) they have experience with similar contracts and are able to estimate the cumulative amount of revenue, and (2) based on experience, it is highly probable that there will not be a significant reversal of revenue previously recognized.[5] If these criteria are not met, revenue recognition is constrained. **[10]** Illustration 18-11 provides an example of how the revenue constraint works.

ILLUSTRATION 18-11
Transaction Price—Revenue Constraint

REVENUE CONSTRAINT

Facts: On January 1, Shera Company enters into a contract with Hornung Inc. to perform asset-management services for 1 year. Shera receives a quarterly management fee based on a percentage of Hornung's assets under management at the end of each quarter. In addition, Shera receives a performance-based incentive fee of 20% of the fund's return in excess of the return of an observable index at the end of the year.

Shera accounts for the contract as a single performance obligation to perform investment-management services for 1 year because the services are interdependent and interrelated. To recognize revenue for satisfying the performance obligation over time, Shera selects an output method of measuring progress toward complete satisfaction of the performance obligation. Shera has had a number of these types of contracts with customers in the past.

***Question:* At what point should Shera recognize the management fee and the performance-based incentive fee related to Hornung?**

Solution: Shera should record the management fee each quarter as it is performs the management of the fund over the year. However, Shera should not record the incentive fee until the end of the year. Although Shera has experience with similar contracts, that experience is not predictive of the outcome of the current contract because the amount of consideration is highly susceptible to volatility in the market. In addition, the incentive fee has a large number and high variability of possible consideration amounts. Thus, revenue related to the incentive fee is constrained (not recognized) until the incentive fee is known at the end of the year.

Time Value of Money

Timing of payment to the company sometimes does not match the transfer of the goods or services to the customer. In most situations, companies receive consideration after the product is provided or the service performed. In essence, the company provides financing for the customer.

Companies account for the time value of money if the contract **involves a significant financing component**. When a sales transaction involves a significant financing component (i.e., interest is accrued on consideration to be paid over time), the fair value is determined either by measuring the consideration received or by discounting the payment using an imputed interest rate. The imputed interest rate is the more clearly determinable of either (1) the prevailing rate for a similar instrument of an issuer with a similar credit rating, or (2) a rate of interest that discounts the nominal amount of the instrument to the current sales price of the goods or services. The company

[5]Conditions such as one of the following would indicate that the revenue is constrained (or not recognized):

1. The amount of consideration is highly susceptible to factors outside the company's influence. Factors include volatility in a market, the judgment of third parties, weather conditions, and a high risk of obsolescence of the promised good or service.
2. The uncertainty about the amount of consideration is not expected to be resolved for a long period of time.
3. The company's experience (or other evidence) with similar types of performance obligations is limited.
4. The contract has a large number and broad range of possible consideration amounts. **[9]**

will report the effects of the financing either as interest expense or interest revenue. Illustration 18-12 provides an example of a financing transaction.

ILLUSTRATION 18-12
Transaction Price—Extended Payment Terms

EXTENDED PAYMENT TERMS

Facts: On July 1, 2014, SEK Company sold goods to Grant Company for $900,000 in exchange for a 4-year, zero-interest-bearing note with a face amount of $1,416,163. The goods have an inventory cost on SEK's books of $590,000.

***Questions:* (a) How much revenue should SEK Company record on July 1, 2014? (b) How much revenue should it report related to this transaction on December 31, 2014?**

Solution:

(a) SEK should record revenue of $900,000 on July 1, 2014, which is the fair value of the inventory in this case.

(b) SEK is also financing this purchase and records interest revenue on the note over the 4-year period. In this case, the interest rate is imputed and is determined to be 12%. SEK records interest revenue of $54,000 (12% × ½ × $900,000) at December 31, 2014.

The entry to record SEK's sale to Grant Company is as follows.

July 1, 2014		
Notes Receivable	1,416,163	
Discount on Notes Receivable		516,163
Sales Revenue		900,000

The related entry to record the cost of goods sold is as follows.

July 1, 2014		
Cost of Goods Sold	590,000	
Inventory		590,000

SEK makes the following entry to record interest revenue at the end of the year.

December 31, 2014		
Discount on Notes Receivable	54,000	
Interest Revenue (12% × ½ × $900,000)		54,000

As a practical expedient, companies are not required to reflect the time value of money to determine the transaction price if the time period for payment is less than a year. **[11]**

Noncash Consideration

Companies sometimes receive consideration in the form of goods, services, or other noncash consideration. When these situations occur, **companies generally recognize revenue on the basis of the fair value of what is received.** For example, assume that Raeylinn Company receives common stock of Monroe Company in payment for consulting services. In that case, Raeylinn Company recognizes revenue in the amount of the fair value of the common stock received. If Raeylinn cannot determine this amount, then it should estimate the selling price of the services performed and recognize this amount as revenue.

In addition, companies sometimes receive contributions (e.g., donations and gifts). A contribution is often some type of asset (e.g., securities, land, buildings, or use of facilities) but it could be the forgiveness of debt. In these cases, companies recognize revenue for the fair value of the consideration received. Similarly, customers sometimes contribute goods or services, such as equipment or labor, as consideration for goods provided or services performed. This consideration should be recognized as revenue based on the fair value of the consideration received.

Consideration Paid or Payable to Customers

Companies often make payments to their customers as part of a revenue arrangement. Consideration paid or payable may include discounts, volume rebates, coupons, free products, or services. In general, these elements reduce the consideration received and the revenue to be recognized. Illustration 18-13 provides an example of this type of transaction.

ILLUSTRATION 18-13
Transaction Price—Volume Discount

VOLUME DISCOUNT

Facts: Sansung Company offers its customers a 3% volume discount if they purchase at least $2 million of its product during the calendar year. On March 31, 2014, Sansung has made sales of $700,000 to Artic Co. In the previous 2 years, Sansung sold over $3,000,000 to Artic in the period April 1 to December 31.

***Question:* How much revenue should Sansung recognize for the first 3 months of 2014?**

Solution: In this case, Sansung should reduce its revenue by $21,000 ($700,000 × 3%) because it is probable that it will provide this rebate. Revenue is therefore $679,000 ($700,000 – $21,000). To not recognize this volume discount overstates Sansung's revenue for the first 3 months of 2014. In other words, the appropriate revenue is $679,000, not $700,000.

Given these facts, Sansung makes the following entry on March 31, 2014, to recognize revenue.

Accounts Receivable	679,000	
Sales Revenue		679,000

Assuming that Sansung's customer **meets the discount threshold**, Sansung makes the following entry.

Cash	679,000	
Accounts Receivable		679,000

If Sansung's customer **fails to meet the discount threshold**, Sansung makes the following entry upon payment.

Cash	700,000	
Accounts Receivable		679,000
Sales Discounts Forfeited		21,000

As indicated in Chapter 7 (pages 351–352), Sales Discounts Forfeited is reported in the "Other revenues and gains" section of the income statement.

In many cases, companies provide cash discounts to customers for a short period of time (often referred to as prompt settlement discounts). For example, assume that terms are payment due in 60 days, but if payment is made within five days, a two percent discount is given (referred to as 2/5, net 60). These prompt settlement discounts should reduce revenues, if material. In most cases, companies record the revenue at full price (gross) and record a sales discount if payment is made within the discount period.

Allocating the Transaction Price to Separate Performance Obligations—Step 4

LEARNING OBJECTIVE 6
Allocate the transaction price to the separate performance obligations.

Companies often have to allocate the transaction price to more than one performance obligation in a contract. If an allocation is needed, the transaction price allocated to the various performance obligations is based on their relative fair values. The best measure of fair value is what the company could sell the good or service for on a standalone basis, referred to as the **standalone selling price**. If this information is not available, companies should use their best estimate of what the good or service might sell for as a standalone unit. Illustration 18-14 summarizes the approaches that companies follow (in preferred order of use).

ILLUSTRATION 18-14
Transaction Price Allocation

Allocation Approach	Implementation
Adjusted market assessment approach	Evaluate the market in which it sells goods or services and estimate the price that customers in that market are willing to pay for those goods or services. That approach also might include referring to prices from the company's competitors for similar goods or services and adjusting those prices as necessary to reflect the company's costs and margins.
Expected cost plus a margin approach	Forecast expected costs of satisfying a performance obligation and then add an appropriate margin for that good or service.
Residual approach	If the standalone selling price of a good or service is highly variable or uncertain, then a company may estimate the standalone selling price by reference to the total transaction price less the sum of the observable standalone selling prices of other goods or services promised in the contract.[6]

Illustrations 18-15 and 18-16 (on page 1054) are examples of the measurement issues involved in allocating the transaction price.

ILLUSTRATION 18-15
Allocation—Multiple Performance Obligations

MULTIPLE PERFORMANCE OBLIGATIONS—EXAMPLE 1

Facts: Lonnie Company enters into a contract to build, run, and maintain a highly complex piece of electronic equipment for a period of 5 years, commencing upon delivery of the equipment. There is a fixed fee for each of the build, run, and maintenance deliverables, and any progress payments made are nonrefundable. All the deliverables have a standalone value. There is verifiable evidence of the selling price for the building and maintenance but not for running the equipment. It is determined that the transaction price must be allocated to the three performance obligations: building, running, and maintaining the equipment.

***Question:* What procedure should Lonnie Company use to allocate the transaction price to the three performance obligations?**

Solution: The performance obligations relate to building the equipment, running the equipment, and maintaining the equipment. As indicated, Lonnie can determine standalone values for the equipment and the maintenance agreements. The company then can make a best estimate of the selling price for running the equipment, using the adjusted market assessment approach or expected cost plus a margin approach. Lonnie next applies the relative fair value method at the inception of the transaction to determine the proper allocation to each performance obligation. Once the allocation is performed, Lonnie recognizes revenue independently for each performance obligation using regular revenue recognition criteria.

If, on the other hand, Lonnie is unable to estimate the standalone selling price for running the equipment because such an estimate is highly variable or uncertain, Lonnie may use a residual approach. In this case, Lonnie uses the fair values of the equipment and maintenance agreements and subtracts their fair value from the total transaction price to arrive at a residual value for running the equipment.

[6]A selling price is highly variable when a company sells the same good or service to different customers (at or near the same time) for a broad range of amounts. A selling price is uncertain when a company has not yet established a price for a good or service and the good or service has not previously been sold. [12]

ILLUSTRATION 18-16
Multiple Performance Obligations—Product, Installation, and Service

MULTIPLE PERFORMANCE OBLIGATIONS—EXAMPLE 2

Facts: Handler Company is an experienced manufacturer of equipment used in the construction industry. Handler's products range from small to large individual pieces of automated machinery to complex systems containing numerous components. Unit selling prices range from $600,000 to $4,000,000 and are quoted inclusive of installation and training. The installation process does not involve changes to the features of the equipment and does not require proprietary information about the equipment in order for the installed equipment to perform to specifications. Handler has the following arrangement with Chai Company.

- Chai purchases equipment from Handler for a price of $2,000,000 and chooses Handler to do the installation. Handler charges the same price for the equipment irrespective of whether it does the installation or not. (Some companies do the installation themselves because they either prefer their own employees to do the work or because of relationships with other customers.) The price of the installation service is estimated to have a fair value of $20,000.
- The fair value of the training sessions is estimated at $50,000. Other companies can also perform these training services.
- Chai is obligated to pay Handler the $2,000,000 upon the delivery and installation of the equipment.
- Handler delivers the equipment on September 1, 2014, and completes the installation of the equipment on November 1, 2014 (transfer of control is complete). Training related to the equipment starts once the installation is completed and lasts for 1 year. The equipment has a useful life of 10 years.

***Questions:* (a) What are the performance obligations for purposes of accounting for the sale of the equipment? (b) If there is more than one performance obligation, how should the payment of $2,000,000 be allocated to various components?**

Solution:

(a) The first condition for separation into a standalone unit for the equipment is met. That is, the equipment, installation, and training are distinct and not interdependent. That is, the equipment, installation, and training are three separate products or services. Each of these items has a standalone selling price and therefore is not interdependent.

(b) The total revenue of $2,000,000 should be allocated to the three components based on their relative fair values. In this case, the fair value of the equipment should be considered $2,000,000, the installation fee is $20,000, and the training is $50,000. The total fair value to consider is $2,070,000 ($2,000,000 + $20,000 + $50,000). The allocation is as follows.

Equipment	$1,932,367 [($2,000,000 ÷ $2,070,000) × $2,000,000]
Installation	$19,324 [($20,000 ÷ $2,070,000) × $2,000,000]
Training	$48,309 [($50,000 ÷ $2,070,000) × $2,000,000]

Handler makes the following entry on November 1, 2014, to record both sales revenue and service revenue on the installation, as well as unearned service revenue.

November 1, 2014

Cash	2,000,000	
Service Revenue (installation)		19,324
Unearned Service Revenue		48,309
Sales Revenue		1,932,367

Assuming the cost of the equipment is $1,500,000, the entry to record cost of goods sold is as follows.

November 1, 2014

Cost of Goods Sold	1,500,000	
Inventory		1,500,000

As indicated by these entries, Handler recognizes revenue from the sale of the equipment once the installation is completed on November 1, 2014. In addition, it recognizes revenue for the installation fee because these services have been performed.

Handler recognizes the training revenues on a straight-line basis starting on November 1, 2014, or $4,026 ($48,309 ÷ 12) per month for one year (unless a more appropriate method such as the percentage-of-completion method is warranted). The journal entry to recognize the training revenue for two months in 2014 is as follows.

December 31, 2014

Unearned Service Revenue	8,052	
Service Revenue (training) ($4,026 × 2)		8,052

Therefore, Handler recognizes revenue at December 31, 2014, in the amount of $1,959,743 ($1,932,367 + $19,324 + $8,052). Handler makes the following journal entry to recognize the training revenue in 2015, assuming adjusting entries are made at year-end.

December 31, 2015

Unearned Service Revenue	40,257	
Service Revenue (training) ($48,309 − $8,052)		40,257

When a company sells a bundle of goods or services, the selling price of the bundle is often less than the sum of the individual standalone prices. In this case, the company should allocate the discount to the product (or products) that is causing the discount and not to the entire bundle. Illustration 18-17 indicates how a discount should be allocated.

ILLUSTRATION 18-17
Allocating Transaction Price with a Discount

DISCOUNTED TRANSACTION PRICE

Facts: Colorado Joe's Golf Shop provides the following information related to three items that are often sold as a package.

Item	Standalone Selling Price	Price When Bundled
Lessons (per session)	$100	$100
Custom irons	525	500
Putter	125	25
Total	$750	$625

***Question:* How should the discount be allocated to the elements of the revenue arrangement?**

Solution: As indicated, the standalone price for the lesson, custom irons, and putter is $750, but the bundled price for all three is $625. In this case, the discount applies to the performance obligations related to the providing of the custom irons and putter. As a result, Colorado Joe's allocates the discount solely to the custom irons and putter, and not to the lessons, as follows.

	Allocated Amounts
Lessons	$100
Custom irons and putter	525
Total	$625

Recognizing Revenue When (or as) Each Performance Obligation Is Satisfied—Step 5

7 LEARNING OBJECTIVE
Recognize revenue when the company satisfies its performance obligation.

A company satisfies its performance obligation when the customer obtains control of the good or service. As indicated earlier, the concept of change in control is the deciding factor in determining when a performance obligation is satisfied. The customer controls the product or service when it has the ability to direct the use of and obtain substantially all the remaining benefits from the asset or service. Control also includes the customer's ability to prevent other companies from directing the use of, or receiving the benefits, from the asset or service. Illustration 18-18 summarizes the indicators that the customer has obtained control. **[13]**

ILLUSTRATION 18-18
Change in Control Indicators

1. The company has a right to payment for the asset.
2. The company has transferred legal title to the asset.
3. The company has transferred physical possession of the asset.
4. The customer has significant risks and rewards of ownership.
5. The customer has accepted the asset.

Companies satisfy performance obligations either at a point in time or over a period of time. Companies recognize revenue over a period of time if the customer receives and consumes the benefits as the seller performs and one of the following two criteria is met.

1. The customer controls the asset as it is created or enhanced (e.g., a builder constructs a building on a customer's property).
2. The company does not have an alternative use for the asset created or enhanced (e.g., an aircraft manufacturer builds specialty jets to a customer's specifications) and either (a) the customer receives benefits as the company performs and therefore the task would not need to be re-performed, or (b) the company has a right to payment and this right is enforceable.

Illustration 18-19 provides an example of the point in time when revenue should be recognized.

ILLUSTRATION 18-19
Satisfying a Performance Obligation

TIMING OF REVENUE RECOGNITION

Facts: Gomez Software Company enters into a contract with Hurly Company to develop and install customer relationship management (CRM) software. Progress payments are made upon completion of each stage of the contract. If the contract is terminated, then the partly completed CRM software passes to Hurly Company. Gomez Software is prohibited from redirecting the software to another customer.

***Question:* At what point should Gomez Software Company recognize revenue related to its contract with Hurly Company?**

Solution: Gomez Software does not create an asset with an alternative use because it is prohibited from redirecting the software to another customer. In addition, Gomez Software is entitled to payments for performance to date and expects to complete the project. Therefore, Gomez Software concludes that the contract meets the criteria for recognizing revenue over time.

A company recognizes revenue from a performance obligation over time by measuring the progress toward completion. The method selected for measuring progress should depict the transfer of control from the company to the customer. Companies use various methods to determine the extent of progress toward completion. The most common are the cost-to-cost and units-of-delivery methods. The objective of all these methods is to measure the extent of progress in terms of costs, units, or value added. Companies identify the various measures (costs incurred, labor hours worked, tons produced, floors completed, etc.) and classify them as input or output measures.

Input measures (e.g., costs incurred and labor hours worked) are efforts devoted to a contract. Output measures (with units of delivery measured as tons produced, floors of a building completed, miles of a highway completed, etc.) track results. Neither is universally applicable to all long-term projects. Their use requires the exercise of judgment and careful tailoring to the circumstances.

The most popular input measure used to determine the progress toward completion is the cost-to-cost basis. Under this basis, a company measures the percentage of completion by comparing costs incurred to date with the most recent estimate of the total costs required to complete the contract. The percentage-of-completion method is discussed more fully in Appendix 18A, which examines the accounting for long-term contracts.

Summary

Illustration 18-20 provides a summary of the five-step revenue recognition process.

Step in Process	Description	Implementation
1. Identify the contract with customers.	A contract is an agreement that creates enforceable rights or obligations.	A company applies the revenue guidance to contracts with customers and must determine if new performance obligations are created by a contract modification.
2. Identify the separate performance obligations in the contract.	A performance obligation is a promise in a contract to provide a product or service to a customer. A performance obligation exists if the customer can benefit from the good or service on its own or together with other readily available resources.	A contract may be comprised of multiple performance obligations. The accounting for multiple performance obligations is based on evaluation of whether the product or service is distinct within the contract. If each of the goods or services is distinct, but is interdependent and interrelated, these goods and services are combined and reported as one performance obligation.
3. Determine the transaction price.	The transaction price is the amount of consideration that a company expects to receive from a customer in exchange for transferring goods and services.	In determining the transaction price, companies must consider the following factors: (1) variable consideration, (2) time value of money, (3) noncash consideration, and (4) consideration paid or payable to customer.
4. Allocate the transaction price to the separate performance obligations.	If more than one performance obligation exists, allocate the transaction price based on relative fair values.	The best measure of fair value is what the good or service could be sold for on a standalone basis (standalone selling price). Estimates of standalone selling price can be based on (1) adjusted market assessment, (2) expected cost plus a margin approach, or (3) a residual approach.
5. Recognize revenue when each performance obligation is satisfied.	A company satisfies its performance obligation when the customer obtains control of the good or service.	Companies satisfy performance obligations either at a point in time or over a period of time. Companies recognize revenue over a period of time if (1) the customer controls the asset as it is created or (2) the company does not have an alternative use for the asset.

ILLUSTRATION 18-20
Summary of the Five-Step Revenue Recognition Process

OTHER REVENUE RECOGNITION ISSUES

8 LEARNING OBJECTIVE
Identify other revenue recognition issues.

The revenue recognition principle and the concept of control are illustrated for the following situations.

- Right of return
- Repurchase agreements
- Bill and hold
- Principal-agent relationships
- Consignments
- Warranties
- Nonrefundable upfront fees

Right of Return

Sales with rights of return have long been a challenge in the area of revenue recognition. For example, assume that Hogland Glass Works transfers control of hurricane glass to Henlo Builders. Hogland grants Henlo the **right of return** for the product for various reasons (e.g., dissatisfaction with the product) and to receive any combination of the following.

1. A full or partial refund of any consideration paid.
2. A credit that can be applied against amounts owed, or that will be owed, to the seller.
3. Another product in exchange.

To account for the transfer of this glass with a right of return (and for some services that are performed subject to a refund), Hogland should recognize all of the following.

(a) Revenue for the transferred products in the amount of consideration to which Hogland is reasonably assured to be entitled (considering the products expected to be returned).

(b) A refund liability.

(c) An asset (and corresponding adjustment to cost of sales) for its right to recover glass from Henlo on settling the refund liability.

An example of a return situation is presented in Illustration 18-21.[7]

ILLUSTRATION 18-21
Recognition—Right of Return

RIGHT OF RETURN

Facts: Venden Company sells 100 products for $100 each to Amaya Inc. for cash. Venden allows Amaya to return any unused product within 30 days and receive a full refund. The cost of each product is $60. To determine the transaction price, Venden decides that the approach that is most predictive of the amount of consideration to which it will be entitled is the most likely amount. Using the most likely amount, Venden estimates that:

1. Three products will be returned.
2. The costs of recovering the products will be immaterial.
3. The returned products are expected to be resold at a profit.

***Question:* How should Venden record this sale?**

Solution: Upon transfer of control of the products, Venden recognizes (a) revenue of $9,700 ($100 × 97 products expected not to be returned), (b) a refund liability for $300 ($100 refund × 3 products expected to be returned), and (c) an asset of $180 ($60 × 3 products) for its right to recover products from customers on settling the refund liability. Hence, the amount recognized in cost of sales for 97 products is $5,820 ($60 × 97).

Venden records the sale as follows.

Cash	10,000	
Sales Revenue		9,700
Refund Liability		300

Venden also records the related cost of goods sold with the following entry.

Cost of Goods Sold	5,820	
Estimated Inventory Returns	180	
Inventory		6,000

When a return occurs, Venden should reduce the Refund Liability and Estimated Inventory Returns accounts. In addition, Venden recognizes the returned inventory in a Returned Inventory account as shown in the following entries for the return of two products.

Refund Liability (2 × $100)	200	
Accounts Payable		200
Returned Inventory (2 × $60)	120	
Estimated Inventory Returns		120

Companies record the returned asset in a separate account from inventory to provide transparency. The carrying value of the returned asset is subject to impairment testing, separate from the inventory. If a company is unable to estimate the level of returns with any reliability, it should not report any revenue until the returns become predictive.

[7]Adapted from "Revenue from Contracts with Customers," *Proposed Accounting Standards Update (Revised)* (Norwalk, Conn.: FASB, November 14, 2011, and January 4, 2012), p. 58.

Repurchase Agreements

In some cases, companies enter into **repurchase agreements**, which allow them to transfer an asset to a customer but have an obligation or right to repurchase the asset at a later date. In these situations, the question is whether the company sold the asset.[8] Generally, companies report these transactions as a financing (borrowing). That is, if the company has an obligation or right to repurchase the asset for an amount **greater than or equal to its selling price,** then the transaction is a financing transaction by the company. Illustration 18-22 examines the issues related to a repurchase agreement.

ILLUSTRATION 18-22
Recognition—
Repurchase Agreement

REPURCHASE AGREEMENT

Facts: Morgan Inc., an equipment dealer, sells equipment on January 1, 2014, to Lane Company for $100,000. It agrees to repurchase this equipment from Lane Company on December 31, 2015, for a price of $121,000.

***Question:* Should Morgan Inc. record a sale for this transaction?**

Solution: For a sale and repurchase agreement, the terms of the agreement need to be analyzed to determine whether Morgan Inc. has transferred control to the customer, Lane Company. As indicated earlier, control of an asset refers to the ability to direct the use of and obtain substantially all the benefits from the asset. Control also includes the ability to prevent other companies from directing the use of and receiving the benefit from a good or service. In this case, Morgan Inc. continues to have control of the asset. Therefore, this agreement is a financing transaction and not a sale. Thus, the asset is not removed from the books of Morgan Inc.

Assuming that an interest rate of 10 percent is imputed from the agreement, Morgan Inc. makes the following entries to record this agreement. Morgan Inc. records the financing on January 1, 2014, as follows.

January 1, 2014

Cash	100,000	
Liability to Lane Company		100,000

Morgan Inc. records interest on December 31, 2014, as follows.

December 31, 2014

Interest Expense	10,000	
Liability to Lane Company ($100,000 × 10%)		10,000

Morgan Inc. records interest and retirement of its liability to Lane Company as follows.

December 31, 2014

Interest Expense	11,000	
Liability to Lane Company ($110,000 × 10%)		11,000
Liability to Lane Company	121,000	
Cash ($100,000 + $10,000 + $11,000)		121,000

Rather than Morgan Inc. having the obligation or right to repurchase the asset, assume that Lane Company **has the option** to require Morgan Inc. to repurchase the asset at December 31, 2015. This option is a put option; that is, Lane Company has the option to put the asset back to Morgan Inc. Recall from the discussion in Appendix 17A

[8]Beyond financing motivations, a company may transfer inventory to another party on a short-term basis to avoid inventory taxes. If the counterparty is able to use the inventory during the transfer period, the transaction may more appropriately be accounted for as a rental agreement.

that the value of a put option increases when the value of the underlying asset (in this case, the equipment) decreases. In determining how to account for this transaction, Morgan Inc. has to determine whether Lane Company will have an economic incentive to exercise this put option at the end of 2015.

Specifically, Lane Company has a significant economic incentive to exercise its put option if the value of the equipment declines. In this case, the transaction is reported as a financing transaction as shown in Illustration 18-22. That is, Lane Company will return (put) the equipment back to Morgan Inc. if the repurchase price exceeds the fair value of the equipment. For example, if the repurchase price of the equipment is $150,000 but its fair value is $125,000, Lane Company is better off returning the equipment to Morgan Inc.

Conversely, if Lane Company does not have a significant economic incentive to exercise its put option, then the transaction should be reported as a sale of a product with a right of return.

What do the numbers mean? NO TAKE-BACKS

Investors in **Lucent Technologies** were negatively affected when Lucent violated one of the fundamental criteria for revenue recognition—the "no take-back" rule. This rule holds that revenue should not be booked on inventory that is shipped if the customer can return it at some point in the future. In this particular case, Lucent agreed to take back shipped inventory from its distributors if the distributors were unable to sell the items to their customers.

In essence, Lucent was "stuffing the channel." By booking sales when goods were shipped, even though they most likely would get them back, Lucent was able to report continued sales growth. However, Lucent investors got a nasty surprise when distributors returned those goods and Lucent had to restate its financial results. The restatement erased $679 million in revenues, turning an operating profit into a loss. In response to this bad news, Lucent's share price declined $1.31 per share, or 8.5 percent. Lucent is not alone in this practice. **Sunbeam** got caught stuffing the sales channel with barbeque grills and other outdoor items, which contributed to its troubles when it was forced to restate its earnings.

Investors can be tipped off to potential channel stuffing by carefully reviewing a company's revenue recognition policy for generous return policies or use of cash incentives to encourage distributors to buy products (as was done at **Monsanto**) and by watching inventory and receivables levels. When sales increase along with receivables, that's one sign that customers are not paying for goods shipped on credit. And growing inventory levels are an indicator that customers have all the goods they need. Both scenarios suggest a higher likelihood of goods being returned and revenues and income being restated. So remember, no take-backs!

Sources: Adapted from S. Young, "Lucent Slashes First Quarter Outlook, Erases Revenue from Latest Quarter," *Wall Street Journal Online* (December 22, 2000); Tracey Byrnes, "Too Many Thin Mints: Spotting the Practice of Channel Stuffing," *Wall Street Journal Online* (February 7, 2002); and H. Weitzman, "Monsanto to Restate Results After SEC Probe," *Financial Times* (October 5, 2011).

Bill-and-Hold Arrangements

A **bill-and-hold arrangement** is a contract under which an entity bills a customer for a product but the entity retains physical possession of the product until it is transferred to the customer at a point in time in the future. Bill-and-hold sales result when the buyer is not yet ready to take delivery but does take title and accepts billing. For example, a customer may request a company to enter into such an arrangement because of (1) lack of available space for the product, (2) delays in its production schedule, or (3) more than sufficient inventory in its distribution channel.[9] Illustration 18-23 provides an example of a bill-and-hold arrangement.

[9] "Revenue from Contracts with Customers," *Proposed Accounting Standards Update* (Stamford, Conn.: FASB, June 24, 2010), p. 54.

ILLUSTRATION 18-23
Recognition—Bill and Hold

BILL AND HOLD

Facts: Butler Company sells $450,000 (cost $280,000) of fireplaces on March 1, 2014, to a local coffee shop, Baristo, which is planning to expand its locations around the city. Under the agreement, Baristo asks Butler to retain these fireplaces in its warehouses until the new coffee shops that will house the fireplaces are ready. Title passes to Baristo at the time the agreement is signed.

***Question:* When should Butler recognize the revenue from this bill-and-hold arrangement?**

Solution: When to recognize revenue in a bill-and-hold arrangement depends on the circumstances. Butler determines when it has satisfied its performance obligation to transfer a product by evaluating when Baristo obtains control of that product. For Baristo to have obtained control of a product in a bill-and-hold arrangement, all of the following criteria should be met:

(a) The reason for the bill-and-hold arrangement must be substantive.
(b) The product must be identified separately as belonging to Baristo.
(c) The product currently must be ready for physical transfer to Baristo.
(d) Butler cannot have the ability to use the product or to direct it to another customer.

In this case, it appears that the above criteria were met, and therefore revenue recognition should be permitted at the time the contract is signed. Butler has transferred control to Baristo; that is, Butler has a right to payment for the fireplaces and legal title has transferred.

Butler makes the following entry to record the bill-and-hold sale and related cost of goods sold.

March 1, 2014

Accounts Receivable	450,000	
Sales Revenue		450,000
Cost of Goods Sold	280,000	
Inventory		280,000

Principal-Agent Relationships

In a **principal-agent relationship**, the principal's performance obligation is to provide goods or perform services for a customer. The agent's performance obligation is to arrange for the principal to provide these goods or services to a customer. Examples of principal-agent relationships are as follows.

- Preferred Travel Company (agent) facilitates the booking of cruise excursions by finding customers for Regency Cruise Company (principal).
- **Priceline** (agent) facilitates the sale of various services such as car rentals at **Hertz** (principal).

In these types of situations, amounts collected on behalf of the principal are not revenue of the agent. Instead, revenue for the agent is the amount of the commission it receives (usually a percentage of total revenue). Illustration 18-24 provides an example of the issues related to principal-agent relationships.

ILLUSTRATION 18-24
Recognition—Principal-Agent Relationship

PRINCIPAL-AGENT RELATIONSHIP

Facts: Fly-Away Travel sells airplane tickets for **British Airways (BA)** to various customers.

***Question:* What are the performance obligations in this situation and how should revenue be recognized for both the principal and agent?**

Solution: The principal in this case is BA and the agent is Fly-Away Travel. Because BA has the performance obligation to provide air transportation to the customer, it is the principal. Fly-Away Travel facilitates the sale of the airline ticket to the customer in exchange for a fee or commission. Its performance obligation is to arrange for BA to provide air transportation to the customer.

Although Fly-Away collects the full airfare from the customer, it then remits this amount to BA less the commission. Fly-Away therefore should not record the full amount of the fare as revenue on its books—to do so overstates revenue. Its revenue is the commission, not the full price. Control of performing the air transportation is with BA, not Fly-Away Travel.

Some might argue that there is no harm in letting Fly-Away record revenue for the full price of the ticket and then charging the cost of the ticket against the revenue (often referred to as the **gross method** of recognizing revenue). Others note that this approach overstates the agent's revenue and is misleading. The revenue received is the commission for providing the travel services, not the full fare price (often referred to as the **net approach**). The profession believes the net approach is the correct method for recognizing revenue in a principal-agent relationship. As a result, the FASB has developed specific criteria to determine when a principal-agent relationship exists.[10] An important feature in deciding whether Fly-Away is acting as an agent is whether the amount it earns is predetermined, being either a fixed fee per transaction or a stated percentage of the amount billed to the customer.

What do the numbers mean? GROSSED OUT

As you learned in Chapter 4, many corporate executives obsess over the bottom line. However, analysts on the outside look at the big picture, which includes examination of both the top line and the important subtotals in the income statement, such as gross profit. Recently, the top line is causing some concern, with nearly all companies in the S&P 500 reporting a 2 percent decline in the bottom line while the top line saw revenue decline by 1 percent. This is troubling because it is the first decline in revenues since we crawled out of the recession following the financial crisis. **McDonald's** gave an ominous preview—it saw its first monthly sales decline in nine years. And the United States, rather than foreign markets, led the drop.

What about income subtotals like gross margin? These metrics too have been under pressure. There is concern that struggling companies may employ a number of manipulations to mask the impact of gross margin declines on the bottom line. In fact, **Rite Aid** prepares an income statement that omits the gross margin subtotal. That is not surprising when you consider that Rite Aid's gross margin has steadily declined from 28 percent in 2010 to 26 percent in 2012. Rite Aid has used a number of suspect accounting adjustments related to tax allowances and inventory gains to offset its weak gross margin.

Or, consider the classic case of **Priceline.com**, the company made famous by William Shatner's ads about "naming your own price" for airline tickets and hotel rooms. In one quarter, Priceline reported that it earned $152 million in revenues. But, that included the full amount customers paid for tickets, hotel rooms, and rental cars. Traditional travel agencies call that amount "gross bookings," not revenues. And, much like regular travel agencies, Priceline keeps only a small portion of gross bookings—namely, the spread between the customers' accepted bids and the price it paid for the merchandise. The rest, which Priceline calls "product costs," it pays to the airlines and hotels that supply the tickets and rooms.

However, Priceline's product costs came to $134 million, leaving Priceline just $18 million of what it calls "gross profit" and what most other companies would call revenues. And that's before all of Priceline's other costs—like advertising and salaries—which netted out to a loss of $102 million. The difference isn't academic. Priceline shares traded at about 23 times its reported revenues but at a mind-boggling 214 times its "gross profit." This and other aggressive recognition practices explain the stricter revenue recognition guidance, indicating that if a company performs as an agent or broker without assuming the risks and rewards of ownership of the goods, the company should report sales on a net (fee) basis.

Sources: Jeremy Kahn, "Presto Chango! Sales Are Huge," *Fortune* (March 20, 2000), p. 44; A. Catanach and E. Ketz, "RITE AID: Is Management Selling Drugs or Using Them?" *Grumpy Old Accountants* (August 22, 2011); and S. Jakab, "Weak Revenue Is New Worry for Investors," *Wall Street Journal* (November 25, 2012).

Consignments

A common principal-agent relationship involves consignments. In these cases, manufacturers (or wholesalers) deliver goods but retain title to the goods until they are sold. This specialized method of marketing certain types of products makes use of

[10] Indicators that the company's performance obligation is to arrange for the providing of goods or the performing of services by another party (i.e., the company is an agent and should recognize revenue in the net amount) include the following: (a) the other party is primarily responsible for fulfilling the contract; (b) the company does not have inventory risk before or after the customer order, during shipping, or on return; (c) the company does not have latitude in establishing prices for the other party's goods or services and, hence, the benefit that the company can receive from those goods or services is constrained; (d) the company's consideration is in the form of a commission; and (e) the company does not have customer credit risk for the amount receivable in exchange for the other party's goods or services. **[14]**

an agreement known as a **consignment**. Under this arrangement, the **consignor** (manufacturer or wholesaler) ships merchandise to the **consignee** (dealer), who is to act as an agent for the consignor in selling the merchandise. Both consignor and consignee are interested in selling—the former to make a profit or develop a market, the latter to make a commission on the sale.

The consignee accepts the merchandise and agrees to exercise due diligence in caring for and selling it. The consignee remits to the consignor cash received from customers, after deducting a sales commission and any chargeable expenses. In consignment sales, the consignor uses a modified version of the point-of-sale basis of revenue recognition. That is, the consignor recognizes revenue only after receiving notification of the sale and the cash remittance from the consignee.

The consignor carries the merchandise as inventory throughout the consignment, separately classified as Inventory (consignments). **The consignee does not record the merchandise as an asset on its books.** Upon sale of the merchandise, the consignee has **a liability for the net amount due the consignor**. The consignor periodically receives from the consignee a report called **account sales** that shows the merchandise received, merchandise sold, expenses chargeable to the consignment, and the cash remitted. Revenue is then recognized by the consignor. Analysis of a consignment arrangement is provided in Illustration 18-25.

ILLUSTRATION 18-25
Recognition—Sales on Consignment

SALES ON CONSIGNMENT

Facts: Nelba Manufacturing Co. ships merchandise costing $36,000 on consignment to Best Value Stores. Nelba pays $3,750 of freight costs, and Best Value pays $2,250 for local advertising costs that are reimbursable from Nelba. By the end of the period, Best Value has sold two-thirds of the consigned merchandise for $40,000 cash. Best Value notifies Nelba of the sales, retains a 10% commission, and remits the cash due Nelba.

***Question:* What are the journal entries that the consignor (Nelba) and the consignee (Best Value) make to record this transaction?**

Solution:

NELBA MFG. CO. (CONSIGNOR)			BEST VALUE STORES (CONSIGNEE)		
Shipment of consigned merchandise					
Inventory (consignments)	36,000		No entry (record memo of merchandise received).		
Finished Goods Inventory		36,000			
Payment of freight costs by consignor					
Inventory (consignments)	3,750		No entry.		
Cash		3,750			
Payment of advertising by consignee					
No entry until notified.			Receivable from Consignor	2,250	
			Cash		2,250
Sales of consigned merchandise					
No entry until notified.			Cash	40,000	
			Payable to Consignor		40,000
Notification of sales and expenses and remittance of amount due					
Cash	33,750		Payable to Consignor	40,000	
Advertising Expense	2,250		Receivable from Consignor		2,250
Commission Expense	4,000		Commission Revenue		4,000
Revenue from Consignment Sales		40,000	Cash		33,750
Adjustment of inventory on consignment for cost of sales					
Cost of Goods Sold	26,500		No entry.		
Inventory (consignments)		26,500			
[2/3 ($36,000 + $3,750) = $26,500]					

Under the consignment arrangement, the consignor accepts the risk that the merchandise might not sell and relieves the consignee of the need to commit part of its working capital to inventory. Consignors use a variety of systems and account titles to record consignments, but they all share the common goal of postponing the recognition of revenue until it is known that a sale to a third party has occurred. **Consignees only recognize revenue associated with commissions.**

Warranties

Companies often provide one of two types of **warranties** to customers:

1. Warranties that the product **meets agreed-upon specifications in the contract at the time the product is sold**. This type of warranty is included in the sales price of a company's product and is often referred to as an **assurance-type warranty**.
2. Warranties that provide an **additional service beyond the assurance-type warranty**. This warranty is not included in the sales price of the product and is referred to as a **service-type warranty**. As a consequence, it is recorded as a separate performance obligation.

Companies do not record a separate performance obligation for assurance-type warranties. This type of warranty is nothing more than a quality guarantee that the good or service is free from defects at the point of sale. These types of obligations should be expensed in the period the goods are provided or services performed (in other words, at the point of sale). In addition, the company should record a warranty liability. The estimated amount of the liability includes all the costs that the company will incur after sale due to the correction of defects or deficiencies required under the warranty provisions.

In addition, companies sometimes provide customers with an option to purchase a warranty separately. In most cases, these extended warranties provide the customer a service beyond fixing defects that existed at the time of sale. For example, when you purchase a TV, you are entitled to the company's warranty. You will also undoubtedly be offered an extended warranty on the product at an additional cost. These service-type warranties represent a **separate service and are an additional performance obligation**. As a result, companies should allocate a portion of the transaction price to this performance obligation. The company recognizes revenue in the period that the service-type warranty is in effect. Illustration 18-26 presents an example of both an assurance-type and a service-type warranty.

ILLUSTRATION 18-26
Recognition—Performance Obligations and Warranties

WARRANTIES

Facts: Maverick Company sold 1,000 Rollomatics during 2014 at a total price of $6,000,000, with a warranty guarantee that the product was free of any defects. The cost of Rollomatics sold is $4,000,000. The term of the assurance warranty is two years, with an estimated cost of $30,000. In addition, Maverick sold extended warranties related to 400 Rollomatics for 3 years beyond the 2-year period for $12,000.

***Question:* What are the journal entries that Maverick Company should make in 2014 related to the sale and the related warranties?**

Solution: To record the revenue and liabilities related to the warranties:

Cash ($6,000,000 + $12,000)	6,012,000	
Warranty Expense	30,000	
Warranty Liability		30,000
Unearned Warranty Revenue		12,000
Sales Revenue		6,000,000

To reduce inventory and recognize cost of goods sold:

Cost of Goods Sold	4,000,000	
Inventory		4,000,000

Similar to that illustrated in Chapter 13 (pages 720–721), Maverick Company reduces the Warranty Liability account over the first two years as the actual warranty costs are incurred. The company also recognizes revenue related to the service-type warranty over the three-year period that extends beyond the assurance warranty period (two years). In most cases, the unearned warranty revenue is recognized on a straight-line basis. The costs associated with the service-type warranty are expensed as incurred.

Nonrefundable Upfront Fees

Companies sometimes receive payments (**upfront fees**) from customers before they deliver a product or perform a service. Upfront payments generally relate to the initiation, activation, or setup of a good or service to be provided or performed in the future. In most cases, these upfront payments are nonrefundable. Examples include fees paid for membership in a health club or buying club, and activation fees for phone, Internet, or cable.

Companies must determine whether these nonrefundable advance payments are for products or services in the current period. In most situations, these payments are for future delivery of products and services and should therefore not be recorded as revenue at the time of payment. In some cases, the upfront fee is viewed similar to a renewal option for future products and services at a reduced price. An example would be a health club where once the initiation fee is paid, no additional fee is necessary upon renewal. Illustration 18-27 provides an example of an upfront fee payment.

ILLUSTRATION 18-27
Transaction Price—Upfront Fee Considerations

UPFRONT FEE CONSIDERATIONS

Facts: Erica Felise signs a 1-year contract with Bigelow Health Club. The terms of the contract are that Erica is required to pay a nonrefundable initiation fee of \$200 and an annual membership fee of \$50 per month. Bigelow determines that its customers, on average, renew their annual membership two times before terminating their membership.

Question: **What is the amount of revenue Bigelow Health Club should recognize in the first year?**

Solution: In this case, the membership fee arrangement may be viewed as a single performance obligation (similar services are provided in all periods). That is, Bigelow is providing a discounted price in the second and third years for the same services, and this should be reflected in the revenue recognized in those periods. Bigelow determines the total transaction price to be \$2,000—the upfront fee of \$200 and the three years of monthly fees of \$1,800 (\$50 × 36)—and allocates it over the three years. In this case, Bigelow would report revenue of \$55.56 (\$2,000 ÷ 36) each month for three years. *Unless otherwise instructed, use this approach for homework problems.*[11]

Summary

Illustration 18-28 (page 1066) provides a summary of the additional issues related to transfer of control and revenue recognition.

[11] The initiation fee might be viewed as a separate performance obligation (it provides a renewal option at a lower price than normally charged, perhaps with different sevices). In this situation, in the first period, Bigelow would report revenue of \$600 (\$50 × 12). The initiation fee would then be allocated to years two and three (\$100 in each year) unless forfeited earlier.

Issue	Description	Implementation
Right of return	Return of product by customer (e.g., due to dissatisfaction with the product) in exchange for refunds, a credit against amounts owed or that will be owed, and/or another product in exchange.	Seller may recognize (a) an adjustment to revenue for the products expected to be returned, (b) a refund liability, and (c) an asset for the right to recover the product.
Repurchase agreements	Seller has an obligation or right to repurchase the asset at a later date.	Generally, if the company has an obligation or right to repurchase the asset for an amount greater than its selling price, then the transaction is a financing transaction.
Bill and hold	Result when the buyer is not yet ready to take delivery but does take title and accept billing.	Revenue is recognized depending on when the customer obtains control of that product.
Principal-agent	Arrangement in which the principal's performance obligation is to provide goods or perform services for a customer. The agent's performance obligation is to arrange for the principal to provide these goods or services to a customer.	Amounts collected on behalf of the principal are not revenue of the agent. Instead, revenue for the agent is the amount of the commission it receives. The principal recognizes revenue when the goods or services are sold to a third-party customer.
Consignments	A principal-agent relationship in which the consignor (manufacturer or wholesaler) ships merchandise to the consignee (dealer), who is to act as an agent for the consignor in selling the merchandise.	The consignor recognizes revenue only after receiving notification of the sale and the cash remittance from the consignee (consignor carries the merchandise as inventory throughout the consignment). The consignee records commission revenue (usually some percentage of the selling price).
Warranties	Warranties can be assurance-type (product meets agreed-upon specifications) or service-type (provides additional service beyond the assurance-type warranty).	A separate performance obligation is not recorded for assurance-type warranties (considered part of the product). Service-type warranties are recorded as a separate performance obligation. Companies should allocate a portion of the transaction price to service type-warranties, when present.
Nonrefundable upfront fees	Upfront payments generally relate to initiation, activation, or setup activities for a good or service to be delivered in the future.	The upfront payment should be allocated over the periods benefited.

ILLUSTRATION 18-28
Summary—Other Revenue Recognition Issues

PRESENTATION AND DISCLOSURE

Presentation

LEARNING OBJECTIVE 9
Describe presentation and disclosure regarding revenue.

Companies now use an asset-liability approach to recognize revenue. For example, when **General Mills** delivers cereal to **Whole Foods Market** (satisfying its performance obligation), it has a right to consideration from Whole Foods and therefore has a contract asset. If, on the other hand, Whole Foods Market performs first, by prepaying for this cereal, General Mills has a contract liability. Companies must present these contract assets and contract liabilities on their balance sheets.

Contract Assets and Liabilities

Contract assets are of two types: (1) unconditional rights to receive consideration because the company has satisfied its performance obligation with a customer, and (2) conditional rights to receive consideration because the company has satisfied one performance obligation but must satisfy another performance obligation in the contract before it can bill the customer. Companies should report unconditional rights to receive consideration as a receivable on the balance sheet. Conditional rights on the balance sheet should be reported separately as contract assets. Illustration 18-29 provides an example of the accounting and reporting for a contract asset.

ILLUSTRATION 18-29
Contract Asset Recognition and Presentation

CONTRACT ASSET

Facts: On January 1, 2014, Finn Company enters into a contract to transfer Product A and Product B to Obermine Co. for $100,000. The contract specifies that payment of Product A will not occur until Product B is also delivered. In other words, payment will not occur until both Product A and Product B are transferred to Obermine. Finn determines that standalone prices are $30,000 for Product A and $70,000 for Product B. Finn delivers Product A to Obermine on February 1, 2014. On March 1, 2014, Finn delivers Product B to Obermine.

***Question:* What journal entries should Finn Company make in regards to this contract in 2014?**

Solution: No entry is required on January 1, 2014, because neither party has performed on the contract. On February 1, 2014, Finn records the following entry.

February 1, 2014

Contract Asset	30,000	
Sales Revenue		30,000

On February 1, Finn has satisfied its performance obligation and therefore reports revenue of $30,000. However, it does not record an accounts receivable at this point because it does not have an unconditional right to receive the $100,000 unless it also transfers Product B to Obermine. In other words, a contract asset occurs generally when a company must satisfy another performance obligation before it is entitled to bill the customer. When Finn transfers Product B on March 1, 2014, it makes the following entry.

March 1, 2014

Accounts Receivable	100,000	
Contract Asset		30,000
Sales Revenue		70,000

As indicated above, a **contract liability** is a company's obligation to transfer goods or services to a customer for which the company has received consideration from the customer. A contract liability is generally referred to as Unearned Sales Revenue, Unearned Service Revenue, or another appropriate account title. Illustration 18-30 provides an example of the recognition and presentation of a contract liability.

ILLUSTRATION 18-30
Contract Liability Recognition and Presentation

CONTRACT LIABILITY

Facts: On March 1, 2014, Henly Company enters into a contract to transfer a product to Propel Inc. on July 31, 2014. It is agreed that Propel will pay the full price of $10,000 in advance on April 15, 2014. Henly delivers the product on July 31, 2014. The cost of the product is $7,500.

***Question:* What journal entries are required in 2014?**

Solution: No entry is required on March 1, 2014, because neither party has performed on the contract. On receiving the cash on April 15, 2014, Henly records the following entry.

April 15, 2014

Cash	10,000	
Unearned Sales Revenue		10,000

On satisfying the performance obligation on July 31, 2014, Henly records the following entry to record the sale.

July 31, 2014

Unearned Sales Revenue	10,000	
Sales Revenue		10,000

In addition, Henly records cost of goods sold as follows.

Cost of Goods Sold	7,500	
Inventory		7,500

Companies are not required to use the terms "contract assets" and "contract liabilities" on the balance sheet. For example, contract liabilities are performance obligations and therefore more descriptive titles (as noted earlier) such as unearned service revenue, unearned sales revenue, repurchase liability, and return liability may be used where appropriate. For contract assets, it is important that financial statement users can differentiate between unconditional and conditional rights through appropriate account presentation.

Costs to Fulfill a Contract

Companies may also report assets associated with fulfillment costs related to a revenue arrangement. Companies divide fulfillment costs (contract acquisition costs) into two categories:

1. Those that give rise to an asset.
2. Those that are expensed as incurred.

Companies recognize an asset for the incremental costs if these costs are incurred to obtain a contract with a customer. In other words, incremental costs are those that a company would not incur if the contract had not been obtained (e.g., selling commissions). Additional examples are as follows.

(a) Direct labor, direct materials, and allocation of costs that relate directly to the contract (e.g., costs of contract management and supervision, insurance, and depreciation of tools and equipment).

(b) Costs that generate or enhance resources of the company that will be used in satisfying performance obligations in the future. Such costs include intangible design or engineering costs that will continue to give rise to benefits in the future.

Other costs that are expensed as incurred include general and administrative costs (unless those costs are explicitly chargeable to the customer under the contract) as well as costs of wasted materials, labor, or other resources to fulfill the contract that were not reflected in the price of the contract. That is, **companies only capitalize costs that are direct, incremental, and recoverable** (assuming that the contract period is more than one year). Illustration 18-31 provides an example of costs capitalized to fulfill a contract.

ILLUSTRATION 18-31
Recognition—Contract Costs

CONTRACT COSTS

Facts: Rock Integrators enters into a contract to operate Dello Company's information technology data center for 5 years. Rock Integrators incurs selling commission costs of $10,000 to obtain the contract. Before performing the services, Rock Integrators designs and builds a technology platform that interfaces with Dello's systems. That platform is not transferred to Dello. Dello promises to pay a fixed fee of $20,000 per month. Rock Integrators incurs the following costs: design services for the platform $40,000, hardware for the platform $120,000, software $90,000, and migration and testing of data center $100,000.

***Question:* What are Rock Integrators' costs for fulfilling the contract to Dello Company?**

Solution: The $10,000 selling commission costs related to obtaining the contract are recognized as an asset. The design services cost of $40,000 and the hardware for the platform of $120,000 are also capitalized. As the technology platform is independent of the contract, the pattern of amortization of this platform may not be related to the terms of the contract. The migration and testing costs are expensed as incurred; in general, these costs are not recoverable.

As a practical expedient, a company recognizes the incremental costs of obtaining a contract as an expense when incurred if the amortization period of the asset that the company otherwise would have recognized is one year or less.

Collectibility

As indicated earlier, if it is probable that the transaction price will not be collected, this is an indication that the parties are not committed to their obligations. As a result, one of the criteria for the existence of a contract is not met and therefore revenue is not recognized.

Any time a company sells a product or performs a service on account, a collectibility issue occurs. **Collectibility** refers to a customer's credit risk, that is, the risk that a customer will be unable to pay the amount of consideration in accordance with the contract. Under the revenue guidance—as long as a contract exists (it is probable that the customer will pay)—the amount recognized as revenue is not adjusted for customer credit risk.

Thus, companies report the revenue gross (without consideration of credit risk) and then present an allowance for any impairment due to bad debts (recognized initially and subsequently in accordance with the respective bad debt guidance). An impairment related to bad debts is reported as an operating expense in the income statement. Whether a company will get paid for satisfying a performance obligation is not a consideration in determining revenue recognition. **[15]**

Disclosure

The disclosure requirements for revenue recognition are designed to help financial statement users understand the nature, amount, timing, and uncertainty of revenue and cash flows arising from contracts with customers. To achieve that objective, companies disclose qualitative and quantitative information about all of the following:

- ***Contracts with customers.*** These disclosures include the disaggregation of revenue, presentation of opening and closing balances in contract assets and contract liabilities, and significant information related to their performance obligations.
- ***Significant judgments.*** These disclosures include judgments and changes in these judgments that affect the determination of the transaction price, the allocation of the transaction price, and the determination of the timing of revenue.
- ***Assets recognized from costs incurred to fulfill a contract.*** These disclosures include the closing balances of assets recognized to obtain or fulfill a contract, the amount of amortization recognized, and the method used for amortization.

To implement these requirements and meet the disclosure objectives, companies provide a range of disclosures, as summarized in Illustration 18-32.[12]

ILLUSTRATION 18-32
Revenue Disclosures

Disclosure Type	Requirements
Disaggregation of revenue	Disclose disaggregated revenue information in categories that depict how the nature, amount, timing, and uncertainty of revenue and cash flows are affected by economic factors. Reconcile disaggregated revenue to revenue for reportable segments.
Reconciliation of contract balances	Disclose opening and closing balances of contract assets (e.g., unbilled receivables) and liabilities (e.g., deferred revenue) and provide a qualitative description of significant changes in these amounts. Disclose the amount of revenue recognized in the current period relating to performance obligations satisfied in a prior period (e.g., from contracts with variable consideration). Disclose the opening and closing balances of trade receivables if not presented elsewhere.
Remaining performance obligations	Disclose the amount of the transaction price allocated to performance obligations of any remaining performance obligations not subject to significant revenue reversal. Provide a narrative discussion of potential additional revenue in constrained arrangements.
Costs to obtain or fulfill contracts	Disclose the closing balances of capitalized costs to obtain and fulfill a contract and the amount of amortization in the period. Disclose the method used to determine amortization for each reporting period.
Other qualitative disclosures	Disclose significant judgments and changes in judgments that affect the amount and timing of revenue from contracts with customers. Disclose how management determines the minimum amount of revenue not subject to the variable consideration constraint.

[12]See *PricewaterhouseCoopers Dataline 2013–2014; FASB ASC 605-10-50-1 through 19.* **[16]**

Evolving Issue — CH, CH, CH CHANGES IN REVENUE RECOGNITION

As you have learned in this chapter, the recently issued revenue recognition standard provides a comprehensive and general framework for recognizing revenue and should result in improvements in the reporting of revenue. However, these new rules reflect significant change relative to the prior revenue guidance and are expected to create implementation challenges, especially for companies that:

- Currently recognize revenue using industry-specific guidance.
- Have customer contracts with diverse terms and conditions.
- Have arrangements with goods or services delivered over long periods.
- Have systems or processes that do not easily provide new data requirements.

Among the companies that are likely to experience significant changes are those in the telecommunications, aerospace, construction, asset management, real estate, and software industries.

In the months after issuance of the new guidance, the FASB (and IASB) plans to issue documents that will address common questions posed by these industries. In addition, the Boards have created a joint transition resource group that is responsible for informing the FASB and IASB about interpretive issues that could arise when companies, institutions, and other organizations implement the revenue recognition standard. The transition group is comprised of specialists representing financial statement preparers, auditors, regulators, users, and other stakeholders, as well as members of the FASB and IASB.

The resource group solicits, analyzes, and discusses stakeholder issues that apply to common transactions that could reasonably create diversity in practice. In addition to providing a forum to discuss the application of the requirements, the transition group provides information that will help the Boards determine what, if any, action will be needed to resolve that diversity. The group itself will not issue guidance.

As noted by Russ Golden, chairman of the FASB:

> "Effective implementation of the revenue recognition standard is critical to its success in providing financial statement users with the information they need to make the right decisions about how to allocate their capital. The Boards are committed to ensuring a smooth transition to the new standard, and the transition resource group is an important tool for determining any areas that will need additional guidance before the standard becomes effective in 2017."

So change is necessary to achieve improvements in revenue recognition accounting. Hopefully, the extended transition period and expanded support by the transition group will make the change a bit less painful.

Sources: Executive Accounting Update: "Changes to Revenue Recognition," KPMG (January 22, 2014); and *Defining Issues No. 14-9*: "Implementing the Forthcoming Revenue Recognition Standard," KPMG (February 2014).

KEY TERMS

asset-liability approach, *1043*
assurance-type warranty, *1064*
bill-and-hold arrangement, *1060*
collectibility, *1069*
consignee, *1063*
consignment, *1063*
consignor, *1063*
contract, *1044*
contract assets, *1066*
contract liability, *1067*
contract modification, *1046*
performance obligation, *1047*
principal-agent relationship, *1061*
repurchase agreements, *1059*

SUMMARY OF LEARNING OBJECTIVES

1 Understand revenue recognition issues. Most revenue transactions pose few problems for revenue recognition. This is because, in many cases, the transaction is initiated and completed at the same time. Increasing complexity of business and revenue arrangements have resulted in revenue recognition practices being identified as the most prevalent reasons for accounting restatements. A number of the revenue recognition issues relate to possible fraudulent behavior by company executives and employees, but are also due to sometimes incomplete and inconsistent accounting guidelines for revenue recognition. A recent new standard provides a set of guidelines to follow in determining when revenue should be reported and how it should be measured. The standard is comprehensive and applies to all companies. As a result, comparability and consistency in reporting revenue should be enhanced.

2 Identify the five steps in the revenue recognition process. The five steps in the revenue recognition process are (1) identify the contract with customers, (2) identify the separate performance obligations in the contract, (3) determine the transaction price, (4) allocate the transaction price to the separate performance obligations, and (5) recognize revenue when each performance obligation is satisfied.

3 Identify the contract with customers. A contract is an agreement that creates enforceable rights or obligations. A company applies the revenue guidance to contracts with customers and must determine if new performance obligations are created by a contract modification.

4 **Identify the separate performance obligations in the contract.** A performance obligation is a promise in a contract to provide a product or service to a customer. A contract may be comprised of multiple performance obligations. The accounting for multiple performance obligations is based on evaluation of whether the product or service is distinct within the contract. If each of the goods or services is distinct, but is interdependent and interrelated, these goods and services are combined and reported as one performance obligation.

5 **Determine the transaction price.** The transaction price is the amount of consideration that a company expects to receive from a customer in exchange for transferring goods and services. In determining the transaction price, companies must consider the following factors: (1) variable consideration, (2) time value of money, (3) noncash consideration, and (4) consideration paid or payable to a customer.

6 **Allocate the transaction price to the separate performance obligations.** If more than one performance obligation exists in a contract, allocate the transaction price based on relative fair values. The best measure of fair value is what the good or service could be sold for on a standalone basis (standalone selling price). Estimates of standalone selling price can be based on (1) adjusted market assessment, (2) expected cost plus a margin approach, or (3) a residual approach.

7 **Recognize revenue when the company satisfies its performance obligation.** A company satisfies its performance obligation when the customer obtains control of the good or service. Companies satisfy performance obligations either at a point in time or over a period of time. Companies recognize revenue over a period of time if (1) the customer controls the asset as it is created or the company does not have an alternative use for the asset, and (2) the company has a right to payment.

8 **Identify other revenue recognition issues.** Refer to Illustration 18-28 (page 1066) for a summary of the accounting for (a) right of return, (b) repurchase agreements, (c) bill-and-hold sales, (d) principal-agent relationships, (e) consignments, (f) warranties, and (g) nonrefundable upfront fees.

9 **Describe presentation and disclosure regarding revenue.** Under the asset-liability approach, to recognize revenue, companies present contract assets and contract liabilities on their balance sheets. Contract assets are rights to receive consideration. A contract liability is a company's obligation to transfer goods or services to a customer for which the company has received consideration from the customer. Companies may also report assets associated with fulfillment costs and contract acquisition costs related to a revenue arrangement. Companies disclose qualitative and quantitative information about (a) contracts with customers with disaggregation of revenue, presentation of opening and closing balances in contract assets and contract liabilities, and significant information related to their performance obligations; (b) significant judgments that affect the determination of the transaction price, the allocation of the transaction price, and the determination of the timing of revenue; and (c) assets recognized from costs incurred to fulfill a contract.

APPENDIX 18A LONG-TERM CONSTRUCTION CONTRACTS

REVENUE RECOGNITION OVER TIME

10 LEARNING OBJECTIVE
Apply the percentage-of-completion method for long-term contracts.

For the most part, companies recognize revenue at the point of sale because that is when the performance obligation is satisfied. However, as indicated in the chapter, under certain circumstances companies recognize revenue over time. The most notable context in which revenue is recognized over time is long-term construction contract accounting.

Long-term contracts frequently provide that the seller (builder) may bill the purchaser at intervals, as it reaches various points in the project. Examples of long-term contracts are construction-type contracts, development of military and commercial aircraft, weapons-delivery systems, and space exploration hardware. When the project consists of separable units, such as a group of buildings or miles of roadway, contract provisions may provide for delivery in installments. In that case, the seller would bill the buyer and transfer title at stated stages of completion, such as the completion of each building unit or every 10 miles of road. The accounting records should record sales when installments are "delivered."

A company satisfies a performance obligation and recognizes revenue over time if at least one of the following two criteria is met: **[17]**

1. The company's performance creates or enhances an asset (for example, work in process) that the customer controls as the asset is created or enhanced; or
2. The company's performance does not create an asset with an alternative use. For example, the asset cannot be used by another customer. In addition to this alternative use element, at least *one* of the following criteria must be met:
   (a) The customer simultaneously receives and consumes the benefits of the entity's performance as the entity performs.
   (b) Another company would not need to substantially re-perform the work the company has completed to date if that other company were to fulfill the remaining obligation to the customer.
   (c) The company has a right to payment for its performance completed to date, and it expects to fulfill the contract as promised.[13]

Therefore, if criterion 1 or 2 is met, then a company recognizes revenue over time *if* **it can reasonably estimate its progress toward satisfaction of the performance obligations**. That is, it recognizes revenues and gross profits each period based upon the progress of the construction—referred to as the **percentage-of-completion method**. The company accumulates construction costs plus gross profit recognized to date in an inventory account (Construction in Process), and it accumulates progress billings in a contra inventory account (Billings on Construction in Process).

The rationale for using percentage-of-completion accounting is that under most of these contracts the buyer and seller have enforceable rights. The buyer has the legal right to require specific performance on the contract. The seller has the right to require progress payments that provide evidence of the buyer's ownership interest. As a result, a continuous sale occurs as the work progresses. Companies should recognize revenue according to that progression.

Alternatively, if the criteria for recognition over time are not met (e.g., the company cannot reasonably estimate its progress toward meeting a performance obligation), the company recognizes revenues and gross profit at a point in time, that is, when the contract is completed. This approach is referred to as the **completed-contract method**.[14]

[13] The right to payment for performance completed to date does not need to be for a fixed amount. However, the company must be entitled to an amount that would compensate the company for performance completed to date (even if the customer can terminate the contract for reasons other than the company's failure to perform as promised). Compensation for performance completed to date includes payment that approximates the selling price of the goods or services transferred to date (for example, recovery of the company's costs plus a reasonable profit margin).

[14] *Accounting Trends and Techniques—2012* reports that of the 83 of its 500 sample companies that referred to long-term construction contracts, 75 used the percentage-of-completion method and 8 used the completed-contract method. In some circumstances (e.g., in the early stages of a contract), a company may not be able to reasonably measure the outcome of a performance obligation, but it expects to recover the costs incurred in satisfying the performance obligation. In these situations, companies recognize revenue only to the extent of the costs incurred until such time that they can reasonably measure the outcome of the performance obligation. This is referred to as the cost-recovery method.

The company accumulates construction costs in an inventory account (Construction in Process), and it accumulates progress billings in a contra inventory account (Billings on Construction in Process).

Percentage-of-Completion Method

The **percentage-of-completion method** recognizes revenues, costs, and gross profit as a company makes progress toward completion on a long-term contract. To defer recognition of these items until completion of the entire contract is to misrepresent the efforts (costs) and accomplishments (revenues) of the accounting periods during the contract. In order to apply the percentage-of-completion method, a company must have some basis or standard for measuring the progress toward completion at particular interim dates.

Measuring the Progress Toward Completion

As one practicing accountant wrote, "The big problem in applying the percentage-of-completion method . . . has to do with the ability to make reasonably accurate estimates of completion and the final gross profit." Companies use various methods to determine the **extent of progress toward completion**. The most common are the *cost-to-cost* and *units-of-delivery* methods.

As indicated in the chapter, the objective of all these methods is to measure the extent of progress in terms of costs, units, or value added. Companies identify the various measures (costs incurred, labor hours worked, tons produced, floors completed, etc.) and classify them as input or output measures. **Input measures** (costs incurred, labor hours worked) are efforts devoted to a contract. **Output measures** (with units of delivery measured as tons produced, floors of a building completed, miles of a highway completed) track results. Neither measure is universally applicable to all long-term projects. Their use requires the exercise of judgment and careful tailoring to the circumstances.

Both input and output measures have certain disadvantages. The input measure is based on an established relationship between a unit of input and productivity. If inefficiencies cause the productivity relationship to change, inaccurate measurements result. Another potential problem is front-end loading, in which significant upfront costs result in higher estimates of completion. To avoid this problem, companies should disregard some early-stage construction costs—for example, costs of uninstalled materials or costs of subcontracts not yet performed—if they do not relate to contract performance.

Similarly, output measures can produce inaccurate results if the units used are not comparable in time, effort, or cost to complete. For example, using floors (stories) completed can be deceiving. Completing the first floor of an eight-story building may require more than one-eighth the total cost because of the substructure and foundation construction.

The most popular input measure used to determine the progress toward completion is the **cost-to-cost basis**. Under this basis, a company like **EDS** measures the percentage of completion by comparing costs incurred to date with the most recent estimate of the total costs required to complete the contract. Illustration 18A-1 shows the formula for the cost-to-cost basis.

$$\frac{\text{Costs incurred to date}}{\text{Most recent estimate of total costs}} = \text{Percent complete}$$

ILLUSTRATION 18A-1
Formula for Percentage-of-Completion, Cost-to-Cost Basis

Once EDS knows the percentage that costs incurred bear to total estimated costs, it applies that percentage to the total revenue or the estimated total gross profit on the contract. The resulting amount is the revenue or the gross profit to be recognized to date. Illustration 18A-2 shows this computation.

$$\text{Percent complete} \times \text{Estimated total revenue (or gross profit)} = \text{Revenue (or gross profit) to be recognized to date}$$

ILLUSTRATION 18A-2
Formula for Total Revenue (or Gross Profit) to Be Recognized to Date

To find the amounts of revenue and gross profit recognized each period, EDS subtracts total revenue or gross profit recognized in prior periods, as shown in Illustration 18A-3.

ILLUSTRATION 18A-3
Formula for Amount of Current-Period Revenue (or Gross Profit) Cost-to-Cost Basis

Revenue (or gross profit) to be recognized to date	−	Revenue (or gross profit) recognized in prior periods	=	Current-period revenue (or gross profit)

Because **the cost-to-cost method is widely used** (without excluding other bases for measuring progress toward completion), we have adopted it for use in our examples.

Example of Percentage-of-Completion Method—Cost-to-Cost Basis

To illustrate the percentage-of-completion method, assume that Hardhat Construction Company has a contract to construct a $4,500,000 bridge at an estimated cost of $4,000,000. The contract is to start in July 2014, and the bridge is to be completed in October 2016. The following data pertain to the construction period. (Note that by the end of 2015, Hardhat has revised the estimated total cost from $4,000,000 to $4,050,000.)

	2014	2015	2016
Costs to date	$1,000,000	$2,916,000	$4,050,000
Estimated costs to complete	3,000,000	1,134,000	—
Progress billings during the year	900,000	2,400,000	1,200,000
Cash collected during the year	750,000	1,750,000	2,000,000

Hardhat would compute the percent complete as shown in Illustration 18A-4.

ILLUSTRATION 18A-4
Application of Percentage-of-Completion Method, Cost-to-Cost Basis

	2014	2015	2016
Contract price	$4,500,000	$4,500,000	$4,500,000
Less estimated cost:			
Costs to date	1,000,000	2,916,000	4,050,000
Estimated costs to complete	3,000,000	1,134,000	—
Estimated total costs	4,000,000	4,050,000	4,050,000
Estimated total gross profit	$ 500,000	$ 450,000	$ 450,000
Percent complete	25%	72%	100%
	$\left(\frac{\$1,000,000}{\$4,000,000}\right)$	$\left(\frac{\$2,916,000}{\$4,050,000}\right)$	$\left(\frac{\$4,050,000}{\$4,050,000}\right)$

On the basis of the data above, Hardhat would make the following entries to record (1) the costs of construction, (2) progress billings, and (3) collections. These entries appear as summaries of the many transactions that would be entered individually as they occur during the year.

ILLUSTRATION 18A-5
Journal Entries—Percentage-of-Completion Method, Cost-to-Cost Basis

	2014		2015		2016	
To record costs of construction:						
Construction in Process	1,000,000		1,916,000		1,134,000	
Materials, Cash, Payables, etc.		1,000,000		1,916,000		1,134,000
To record progress billings:						
Accounts Receivable	900,000		2,400,000		1,200,000	
Billings on Construction in Process		900,000		2,400,000		1,200,000
To record collections:						
Cash	750,000		1,750,000		2,000,000	
Accounts Receivable		750,000		1,750,000		2,000,000

In this example, the costs incurred to date are a measure of the extent of progress toward completion. To determine this, Hardhat evaluates the costs incurred to date as a proportion of the estimated total costs to be incurred on the project. The estimated revenue and gross profit that Hardhat will recognize for each year are calculated as shown in Illustration 18A-6.

ILLUSTRATION 18A-6
Percentage-of-Completion Revenue, Costs, and Gross Profit by Year

	To Date	Recognized in Prior Years	Recognized in Current Year
2014			
Revenues ($4,500,000 × 25%)	$1,125,000		$1,125,000
Costs	1,000,000		1,000,000
Gross profit	$ 125,000		$ 125,000
2015			
Revenues ($4,500,000 × 72%)	$3,240,000	$1,125,000	$2,115,000
Costs	2,916,000	1,000,000	1,916,000
Gross profit	$ 324,000	$ 125,000	$ 199,000
2016			
Revenues ($4,500,000 × 100%)	$4,500,000	$3,240,000	$1,260,000
Costs	4,050,000	2,916,000	1,134,000
Gross profit	$ 450,000	$ 324,000	$ 126,000

Illustration 18A-7 shows Hardhat's entries to recognize revenue and gross profit each year and to record completion and final approval of the contract.

ILLUSTRATION 18A-7
Journal Entries to Recognize Revenue and Gross Profit and to Record Contract Completion—Percentage-of-Completion Method, Cost-to-Cost Basis

	2014		2015		2016	
To recognize revenue and gross profit:						
Construction in Process (gross profit)	125,000		199,000		126,000	
Construction Expenses	1,000,000		1,916,000		1,134,000	
Revenue from Long-Term Contracts		1,125,000		2,115,000		1,260,000
To record completion of the contract:						
Billings on Construction in Process					4,500,000	
Construction in Process						4,500,000

Note that **Hardhat debits gross profit (as computed in Illustration 18A-6) to Construction in Process.** Similarly, it credits Revenue from Long-Term Contracts for the amounts computed in Illustration 18A-6. Hardhat then debits the difference between the amounts recognized each year for revenue and gross profit to a nominal account, Construction Expenses (similar to Cost of Goods Sold in a manufacturing company). It reports that amount in the income statement as the actual cost of construction incurred in that period. For example, in 2014 Hardhat uses the actual costs of $1,000,000 to compute both the gross profit of $125,000 and the percent complete (25 percent).

Hardhat continues to accumulate costs in the Construction in Process account, in order to maintain a record of total costs incurred (plus recognized gross profit) to date. Although theoretically a series of "sales" takes place using the percentage-of-completion method, the selling company cannot remove the inventory cost until the construction is completed and transferred to the new owner. Hardhat's Construction in Process account for the bridge would include the following summarized entries over the term of the construction project.

ILLUSTRATION 18A-8
Content of Construction in Process Account—Percentage-of-Completion Method

Construction in Process			
2014 construction costs	$1,000,000	12/31/16	to close completed project $4,500,000
2014 recognized gross profit	125,000		
2015 construction costs	1,916,000		
2015 recognized gross profit	199,000		
2016 construction costs	1,134,000		
2016 recognized gross profit	126,000		
Total	$4,500,000	Total	$4,500,000

Recall that the Hardhat Construction Company example contained a **change in estimated costs**: In the second year, 2015, it increased the estimated total costs from $4,000,000 to $4,050,000. The change in estimate is accounted for in a **cumulative catch-up manner**, as indicated in the chapter. This is done by first adjusting the percent completed to the new estimate of total costs. Next, Hardhat deducts the amount of revenues and gross profit recognized in prior periods from revenues and gross profit computed for progress to date. That is, it accounts for the change in estimate in the period of change. That way, the balance sheet at the end of the period of change and the accounting in subsequent periods are as they would have been if the revised estimate had been the original estimate.

Financial Statement Presentation—Percentage-of-Completion

Generally, when a company records a receivable from a sale, it reduces the Inventory account. Under the percentage-of-completion method, however, the company continues to carry both the receivable and the inventory. Subtracting the balance in the **Billings account** from Construction in Process avoids double-counting the inventory. During the life of the contract, Hardhat reports in the balance sheet the difference between the Construction in Process and the Billings on Construction in Process accounts. If that amount is a debit, Hardhat reports it **as a current asset**; if it is a credit, it reports it **as a current liability**.

At times, the costs incurred plus the gross profit recognized to date (the balance in Construction in Process) exceed the billings. In that case, Hardhat reports this excess as a current asset entitled "Costs and recognized profit in excess of billings." Hardhat can at any time calculate the unbilled portion of revenue recognized to date by subtracting the billings to date from the revenue recognized to date, as illustrated for 2014 for Hardhat Construction in Illustration 18A-9.

ILLUSTRATION 18A-9
Computation of Unbilled Contract Price at 12/31/14

Contract revenue recognized to date: $\$4{,}500{,}000 \times \frac{\$1{,}000{,}000}{\$4{,}000{,}000}$	$1,125,000
Billings to date	(900,000)
Unbilled revenue	$ 225,000

At other times, the billings exceed costs incurred and gross profit to date. In that case, Hardhat reports this excess as a current liability entitled "Billings in excess of costs and recognized profit."

What happens, as is usually the case, when companies have more than one project going at a time? When a company has a number of projects, costs exceed billings on some contracts and billings exceed costs on others. In such a case, the company segregates the contracts. The asset side includes only those contracts on which costs and recognized profit exceed billings. The liability side includes only those on which billings exceed costs and recognized profit. Separate disclosures of the dollar volume of billings and costs are preferable to a summary presentation of the net difference.

Using data from the bridge example, Hardhat Construction Company would report the status and results of its long-term construction activities under the percentage-of-completion method as shown in Illustration 18A-10.

ILLUSTRATION 18A-10
Financial Statement Presentation—Percentage-of-Completion Method (2014)

HARDHAT CONSTRUCTION COMPANY		
Income Statement (from Illustration 18A-6)		2014
Revenue from long-term contracts		$1,125,000
Costs of construction		1,000,000
Gross profit		$ 125,000

Balance Sheet (12/31)		2014
Current assets		
Accounts receivable ($900,000 − $750,000)		$ 150,000
Inventory		
Construction in process	$1,125,000	
Less: Billings	900,000	
Costs and recognized profit in excess of billings		225,000

In 2015, its financial statement presentation is as follows.

ILLUSTRATION 18A-11
Financial Statement Presentation—Percentage-of-Completion Method (2015)

HARDHAT CONSTRUCTION COMPANY		
Income Statement (from Illustration 18A-6)		2015
Revenue from long-term contracts		$2,115,000
Costs of construction		1,916,000
Gross profit		$ 199,000

Balance Sheet (12/31)		
Current assets		
Accounts receivable ($150,000 + $2,400,000 − $1,750,000)		$ 800,000
Current liabilities		
Billings	$3,300,000	
Less: Construction in process	3,240,000	
Billings in excess of costs and recognized profits		60,000

In 2016, Hardhat's financial statements only include an income statement because the bridge project was completed and settled.

ILLUSTRATION 18A-12
Financial Statement Presentation—Percentage-of-Completion Method (2016)

HARDHAT CONSTRUCTION COMPANY		
Income Statement (from Illustration 18A-6)		2016
Revenue from long-term contracts		$1,260,000
Costs of construction		1,134,000
Gross profit		$ 126,000

In addition, Hardhat should disclose the following information in each year.

ILLUSTRATION 18A-13
Percentage-of-Completion Method Note Disclosure

Note 1. Summary of significant accounting policies.
Long-Term Construction Contracts. The company recognizes revenues and reports profits from long-term construction contracts, its principal business, under the percentage-of-completion method of accounting. These contracts generally extend for periods in excess of one year. The amounts of revenues and profits recognized each year are based on the ratio of costs incurred to the total estimated costs. Costs included in construction in process include direct materials, direct labor, and project-related overhead. Corporate general and administrative expenses are charged to the periods as incurred and are not allocated to construction contracts.

Completed-Contract Method

LEARNING OBJECTIVE 11
Apply the completed-contract method for long-term contracts.

Under the **completed-contract method**, companies recognize revenue and gross profit only at point of sale—that is, when the contract is completed. Under this method, companies accumulate costs of long-term contracts in process, but they make no interim charges or credits to income statement accounts for revenues, costs, or gross profit.

The principal advantage of the completed-contract method is that reported revenue reflects final results rather than *estimates* of unperformed work. Its major disadvantage is that it does not reflect current performance when the period of a contract extends into more than one accounting period. Although operations may be fairly uniform during the period of the contract, the company will not report revenue until the year of completion, creating a distortion of earnings.

Under the completed-contract method, the company would make the same **annual entries** to record costs of construction, progress billings, and collections from customers as those illustrated under the percentage-of-completion method. The significant difference is that the company **would not make entries to recognize revenue and gross profit**.

For example, under the completed-contract method for the bridge project illustrated on the preceding pages, Hardhat Construction Company would make the following entries in 2016 to recognize revenue and costs and to close out the inventory and billing accounts.

Billings on Construction in Process	4,500,000	
Revenue from Long-Term Contracts		4,500,000
Costs of Construction	4,050,000	
Construction in Process		4,050,000

Illustration 18A-14 compares the amount of gross profit that Hardhat Construction Company would recognize for the bridge project under the two revenue recognition methods.

ILLUSTRATION 18A-14
Comparison of Gross Profit Recognized under Different Methods

	Percentage-of-Completion	Completed-Contract
2014	$125,000	$ 0
2015	199,000	0
2016	126,000	450,000

Under the completed-contract method, Hardhat Construction would report its long-term construction activities as follows.

ILLUSTRATION 18A-15
Financial Statement Presentation—Completed-Contract Method

HARDHAT CONSTRUCTION COMPANY				
		2014	2015	2016
Income Statement				
Revenue from long-term contracts		—	—	$4,500,000
Costs of construction		—	—	4,050,000
Gross profit		—	—	$ 450,000
Balance Sheet (12/31)				
Current assets				
Accounts receivable		$150,000	$800,000	$ -0-
Inventory				
Construction in process	$1,000,000			
Less: Billings	900,000			
Costs in excess of billings		100,000		-0-
Current liabilities				
Billings ($3,300,000) in excess of costs ($2,916,000)			384,000	-0-

Note 1. Summary of significant accounting policies.
Long-Term Construction Contracts. The company recognizes revenues and reports profits from long-term construction contracts, its principal business, under the completed-contract method. These contracts generally extend for periods in excess of one year. Contract costs and billings are accumulated during the periods of construction, but no revenues or profits are recognized until completion of the contract. Costs included in construction in process include direct material, direct labor, and project-related overhead. Corporate general and administrative expenses are charged to the periods as incurred.

Long-Term Contract Losses

12 LEARNING OBJECTIVE
Identify the proper accounting for losses on long-term contracts.

Two types of losses can become evident under long-term contracts:

1. *Loss in the current period on a profitable contract.* This condition arises when, during construction, there is a significant increase in the estimated total contract costs but the increase does not eliminate all profit on the contract. Under the percentage-of-completion method only, the estimated cost increase requires a current-period adjustment of excess gross profit recognized on the project in prior periods. The company records this adjustment as a loss in the current period because it is a change in accounting estimate (discussed in Chapter 22).
2. *Loss on an unprofitable contract.* Cost estimates at the end of the current period may indicate that a loss will result on completion of the *entire* contract. Under both the percentage-of-completion and the completed-contract methods, the company must recognize in the current period the entire expected contract loss.

The treatment described for unprofitable contracts is consistent with the accounting custom of anticipating foreseeable losses to avoid overstatement of current and future income (conservatism). **[18]**

Loss in Current Period

To illustrate a loss in the current period on a contract expected to be profitable upon completion, we'll continue with the Hardhat Construction Company bridge project. Assume that on December 31, 2015, Hardhat estimates the costs to complete the bridge contract at $1,468,962 instead of $1,134,000 (refer to page 1074). Assuming all other data are the same as before, Hardhat would compute the percentage complete and recognize the loss as shown in Illustration 18A-16. Compare these computations with those for 2015 in Illustration 18A-4 (page 1074). The "percent complete" has dropped, from 72 percent to 66½ percent, due to the increase in estimated future costs to complete the contract.

ILLUSTRATION 18A-16
Computation of Recognizable Loss, 2015—Loss in Current Period

Cost to date (12/31/15)	$2,916,000
Estimated costs to complete (revised)	1,468,962
Estimated total costs	$4,384,962
Percent complete ($2,916,000 ÷ $4,384,962)	66½%
Revenue recognized in 2015	
($4,500,000 × 66½%) − $1,125,000	$1,867,500
Costs incurred in 2015	1,916,000
Loss recognized in 2015	$ (48,500)

The 2015 loss of $48,500 is a cumulative adjustment of the "excessive" gross profit recognized on the contract in 2014. Instead of restating the prior period, the company absorbs the prior period misstatement entirely in the current period. In this illustration, the adjustment was large enough to result in recognition of a loss.

Hardhat Construction would record the loss in 2015 as follows.

Construction Expenses	1,916,000	
Construction in Process (loss)		48,500
Revenue from Long-Term Contracts		1,867,500

Hardhat will report the loss of $48,500 on the 2015 income statement as the difference between the reported revenue of $1,867,500 and the costs of $1,916,000.[15] **Under the completed-contract method, the company does not recognize a loss in 2015.** Why not? Because the company still expects the contract **to result in a profit**, to be recognized in the year of completion.

Loss on an Unprofitable Contract

To illustrate the accounting for an **overall loss on a long-term contract**, assume that at December 31, 2015, Hardhat Construction Company estimates the costs to complete the bridge contract at $1,640,250 instead of $1,134,000. Revised estimates for the bridge contract are as follows.

	2014 Original Estimates	2015 Revised Estimates
Contract price	$4,500,000	$4,500,000
Estimated total cost	4,000,000	4,556,250*
Estimated gross profit	$ 500,000	
Estimated loss		$ (56,250)

*($2,916,000 + $1,640,250)

[15] In 2016, Hardhat Construction will recognize the remaining 33½ percent of the revenue ($1,507,500), with costs of $1,468,962 as expected, and will report a gross profit of $38,538. The total gross profit over the three years of the contract would be $115,038 [$125,000 (2014) − $48,500 (2015) + $38,538 (2016)]. This amount is the difference between the total contract revenue of $4,500,000 and the total contract costs of $4,384,962.

Under the percentage-of-completion method, Hardhat recognized $125,000 of gross profit in 2014 (see Illustration 18A-6 on page 1075). This amount must be offset in 2015 because it is no longer expected to be realized. In addition, since losses must be recognized as soon as estimable, the company must recognize the total estimated loss of $56,250 in 2015. Therefore, Hardhat must recognize a total loss of $181,250 ($125,000 + $56,250) in 2015.

Illustration 18A-17 shows Hardhat's computation of the revenue to be recognized in 2015.

ILLUSTRATION 18A-17
Computation of Revenue Recognizable, 2015—Unprofitable Contract

Revenue recognized in 2015:		
Contract price		$4,500,000
Percent complete		× 64%*
Revenue recognizable to date		2,880,000
Less: Revenue recognized prior to 2015		1,125,000
Revenue recognized in 2015		$1,755,000
*Cost to date (12/31/15)	$2,916,000	
Estimated cost to complete	1,640,250	
Estimated total costs	$4,556,250	
Percent complete: $2,916,000 ÷ $4,556,250 = 64%		

To compute the construction costs to be expensed in 2015, Hardhat adds the total loss to be recognized in 2015 ($125,000 + $56,250) to the revenue to be recognized in 2015. Illustration 18A-18 shows this computation.

ILLUSTRATION 18A-18
Computation of Construction Expense, 2015—Unprofitable Contract

Revenue recognized in 2015 (computed above)		$1,755,000
Total loss recognized in 2015:		
Reversal of 2014 gross profit	$125,000	
Total estimated loss on the contract	56,250	181,250
Construction cost expensed in 2015		$1,936,250

Hardhat Construction would record the long-term contract revenues, expenses, and loss in 2015 as follows.

Construction Expenses	1,936,250	
Construction in Process (loss)		181,250
Revenue from Long-Term Contracts		1,755,000

At the end of 2015, Construction in Process has a balance of $2,859,750 as shown below.[16]

ILLUSTRATION 18A-19
Content of Construction in Process Account at End of 2015—Unprofitable Contract

Construction in Process			
2014 Construction costs	1,000,000		
2014 Recognized gross profit	125,000		
2015 Construction costs	1,916,000	2015 Recognized loss	181,250
Balance	**2,859,750**		

[16] If the costs in 2016 are $1,640,250 as projected, at the end of 2016 the Construction in Process account will have a balance of $1,640,250 + $2,859,750, or $4,500,000, equal to the contract price. When the company matches the revenue remaining to be recognized in 2016 of $1,620,000 [$4,500,000 (total contract price) − $1,125,000 (2014) − $1,755,000 (2015)] with the construction expense to be recognized in 2016 of $1,620,000 [total costs of $4,556,250 less the total costs recognized in prior years of $2,936,250 (2014, $1,000,000; 2015, $1,936,250)], a zero profit results. Thus, the total loss has been recognized in 2015, the year in which it first became evident.

Under the completed-contract method, Hardhat also would recognize the contract loss of $56,250 through the following entry in 2015 (the year in which the loss first became evident).

Loss from Long-Term Contracts	56,250	
Construction in Process (loss)		56,250

Just as the Billings account balance cannot exceed the contract price, neither can the balance in Construction in Process exceed the contract price. In circumstances where the Construction in Process balance exceeds the billings, the company can deduct the recognized loss from such accumulated costs on the balance sheet. That is, under both the percentage-of-completion and the completed-contract methods, the provision for the loss (the credit) may be combined with Construction in Process, thereby reducing the inventory balance. In those circumstances, however (as in the 2015 example above), where the billings exceed the accumulated costs, Hardhat must report separately on the balance sheet, as a current liability, the amount of the estimated loss. That is, under both the percentage-of-completion and the completed-contract methods, Hardhat would take the $56,250 loss, as estimated in 2015, from the Construction in Process account and report it separately as a current liability titled "Estimated liability from long-term contracts."

KEY TERMS

Billings account, *1076*
completed-contract method, *1078*
cost-to-cost basis, *1073*
input measures, *1073*
output measures, *1073*
percentage-of-completion method, *1073*

SUMMARY OF LEARNING OBJECTIVES FOR APPENDIX 18A

10 Apply the percentage-of-completion method for long-term contracts. To apply the percentage-of-completion method to long-term contracts, a company must have some basis for measuring the progress toward completion at particular interim dates. One of the most popular input measures used to determine the progress toward completion is the cost-to-cost basis. Using this basis, a company measures the percentage of completion by comparing costs incurred to date with the most recent estimate of the total costs to complete the contract. The company applies that percentage to the total revenue or the estimated total gross profit on the contract, to arrive at the amount of revenue or gross profit to be recognized to date.

11 Apply the completed-contract method for long-term contracts. Under this method, companies recognize revenue and gross profit only at point of sale—that is, when the company completes the contract. The company accumulates costs of long-term contracts in process and current billings. It makes no interim charges or credits to income statement accounts for revenues, costs, and gross profit. The annual journal entries to record costs of construction, progress billings, and collections from customers would be identical to those for the percentage-of-completion method—with the significant exclusion of the recognition of revenue and gross profit.

12 Identify the proper accounting for losses on long-term contracts. Two types of losses can become evident under long-term contracts. (1) *Loss in current period on a profitable contract:* Under the percentage-of-completion method only, the estimated cost increase requires a current-period adjustment of excess gross profit recognized on the project in prior periods. The company records this adjustment as a loss in the current period because it is a change in accounting estimate. (2) *Loss on an unprofitable contract:* Under both the percentage-of-completion and the completed-contract methods, the company must recognize the entire expected contract loss in the current period.

APPENDIX 18B REVENUE RECOGNITION FOR FRANCHISES

13 LEARNING OBJECTIVE
Explain revenue recognition for franchises.

In this appendix, we cover a common yet unique type of business transaction—franchises. As indicated throughout this chapter, companies recognize revenue when performance obligations in a revenue arrangement are satisfied. **Franchises** represent a challenging area because a variety of performance obligations may exist in a given franchise agreement. As a result, companies must carefully analyze franchise agreements to identify the separate performance obligations, determine when performance obligations are met, and, therefore, when revenue should be recognized.[17]

Four types of franchising arrangements have evolved: (1) manufacturer-retailer, (2) manufacturer-wholesaler, (3) service sponsor-retailer, and (4) wholesaler-retailer. The fastest-growing category of franchising, and the one that has given rise to accounting challenges, is the third category, **service sponsor-retailer**. Included in this category are such industries and businesses as:

- Soft ice cream/frozen yogurt stores (**Tastee Freez**, **TCBY**, **Dairy Queen**)
- Food drive-ins (**McDonald's**, **KFC**, **Burger King**)
- Restaurants (**TGI Friday's**, **Pizza Hut**, **Denny's**)
- Motels (**Holiday Inn**, **Marriott**, **Best Western**)
- Auto rentals (**Avis**, **Hertz**, **National**)
- Others (**H & R Block**, **Meineke Mufflers**, **7-Eleven Stores**, **Kelly Services**)

Franchise companies derive their revenue from one or both of two sources: (1) from the sale of initial franchises and related assets or services, and (2) from continuing fees based on the operations of franchises. The **franchisor** (the party who grants business rights under the franchise) normally provides the **franchisee** (the party who operates the franchised business) with the following services.

1. Assistance in site selection: (a) analyzing location and (b) negotiating lease.
2. Evaluation of potential income.
3. Supervision of construction activity: (a) obtaining financing, (b) designing building, and (c) supervising contractor while building.
4. Assistance in the acquisition of signs, fixtures, and equipment.
5. Bookkeeping and advisory services: (a) setting up franchisee's records; (b) advising on income, real estate, and other taxes; and (c) advising on local regulations of the franchisee's business.
6. Employee and management training.
7. Quality control.
8. Advertising and promotion.

In the past, it was standard practice for franchisors to recognize the entire franchise fee at the date of sale, whether the fee was received then or was collectible over a long

[17]Franchises are an example of a license or similar rights to use intellectual property. In such arrangements, a company grants a customer the right to use, but not own, intellectual property of the company. Other examples of intellectual property include (1) software and technology; (2) motion pictures, music, and other forms of media and entertainment; and (3) patents, trademarks, and copyrights. Generally, revenue is recognized in these situations when the customer obtains control of the rights. In some cases, a license is a promise to provide a right, which transfers to the customer at a point in time. In other cases, a license is a promise to provide access to an entity's intellectual property, which transfers benefits to the customer over time. **[19]**

period of time. Frequently, franchisors recorded the entire amount as revenue in the year of sale, even though many of the services were yet to be performed and uncertainty existed regarding the collection of the entire fee. (In effect, the franchisors were counting their fried chickens before they were hatched.) However, a **franchise agreement** may provide for refunds to the franchisee if certain conditions are not met, and franchise fee profit can be reduced sharply by future costs of obligations and services to be rendered by the franchisor.

FRANCHISE ACCOUNTING

As indicated, the performance obligations in a franchise arrangement relate to the right to open a business, use of the trade name or other intellectual property of the franchisor, and continuing services, such as marketing help, training, and in some cases supplying inventory and inventory management. Franchisors commonly charge an initial franchise fee as well as continuing franchise fees. The **initial franchise fee** is payment for establishing the franchise relationship and providing some initial services. **Continuing franchise fees** are received in return for the continuing rights granted by the franchise agreement and for providing such services as management training, advertising and promotion, legal assistance, and other support. Illustration 18B-1 provides an example of a franchise arrangement.

ILLUSTRATION 18B-1
Recognition—Franchise Arrangement

FRANCHISE

Facts: Tum's Pizza Inc. enters into a franchise agreement on December 31, 2014, giving Food Fight Corp. the right to operate as a franchisee of Tum's Pizza for 5 years. Tum's charges Food Fight an initial franchise fee of $50,000 for the right to operate as a franchisee. Of this amount, $20,000 is payable when Food Fight signs the agreement, and the note balance is payable in five annual payments of $6,000 each on December 31. As part of the arrangement, Tum's helps locate the site, negotiate the lease or purchase of the site, supervise the construction activity, and provide employee training and the equipment necessary to be a distributor of its products. Similar training services and equipment are sold separately.

Food Fight also promises to pay ongoing royalty payments of 1% of its annual sales (payable each January 31 of the following year) and is obliged to purchase products from Tum's at its current standalone selling prices at the time of purchase. The credit rating of Food Fight indicates that money can be borrowed at 8%. The present value of an ordinary annuity of five annual receipts of $6,000 each discounted at 8% is $23,957. The discount of $6,043 represents the interest revenue to be accrued by Tum's over the payment period.

***Question:* What are the performance obligations in this arrangement and the point in time at which the performance obligations for Tum's are satisfied and revenue is recognized?**

Solution: To identify the performance obligations, Tum's must determine whether the promised rights, site selection and construction services, training services, and equipment are distinct.

- Rights to the trade name, market area, and proprietary know-how for 5 years are not individually distinct because each one is not sold separately and cannot be used with other goods or services that are readily available to the franchisee. Therefore, those combined rights give rise to a single performance obligation. Tum's satisfies the performance obligation to grant those rights at the point in time when Food Fight obtains control of the rights. That is, once Food Fight begins operating the store, Tum's has no further obligation with respect to these rights.
- Training services and equipment are distinct because similar services and equipment are sold separately. Tum's satisfies those performance obligations when it transfers the services and equipment to Food Fight.
- Tum's cannot recognize revenue for the royalty payments because it is not reasonably assured to be entitled to those sales-based royalty amounts. That is, these payments represent variable consideration. Therefore, Tum's recognizes revenue for the royalties when (or as) the uncertainty is resolved.

Tum's promise to stand ready to provide products to the franchisee in the future at standalone selling prices is not accounted for as a separate performance obligation in the contract because it does not provide Food Fight with a material right. Thus, revenue from those sales is recorded in the future when the sales are made.

To illustrate the accounting for this franchise, consider the following values for allocation of the transaction price at December 31, 2014.

Rights to the trade name, market area, and proprietary know-how	$20,000
Training services	9,957
Equipment (cost of $10,000)	14,000
Total transaction price	$ 43,957

Training is completed in January 2015, the equipment is installed in January 2015, and Food Fight holds a grand opening on February 2, 2015. The entries for the Tum's franchise arrangement are summarized in Illustration 18B-2.

ILLUSTRATION 18B-2
Franchise Entries—Inception and Commencement of Operations

Tum's signs the agreement and receives upfront payment and note.

December 31, 2014		
Cash	20,000	
Notes Receivable	30,000	
Discount on Notes Receivable		6,043
Unearned Franchise Revenue		20,000
Unearned Service Revenue (training)		9,957
Unearned Sales Revenue (equipment)		14,000

Franchise opens. Tum's satisfies the performance obligations related to the franchise rights, training, and equipment. That is, Tum's has no further obligations related to these elements of the franchise.

February 2, 2015		
Unearned Franchise Revenue	20,000	
Franchise Revenue		20,000
Unearned Service Revenue (training)	9,957	
Service Revenue (training)		9,957
Unearned Sales Revenue (equipment)	14,000	
Sales Revenue		14,000
Cost of Goods Sold	10,000	
Inventory		10,000

As indicated, when Food Fight begins operations, Tum's satisfies the performance obligations related to the franchise rights, training, and equipment under the franchise agreement. That is, Tum's has no further obligations related to these elements of the franchise.

During 2015, Food Fight does well, recording $525,000 of sales in its first year of operations. The entries for Tum's related to the first year of operations of the franchise are summarized in Illustration 18B-3.

ILLUSTRATION 18B-3
Franchise Entries—First Year of Franchise Operations

To record continuing franchise fees

December 31, 2015		
Accounts Receivable ($525,000 × 1%)	5,250	
Franchise Revenue		5,250

To record payment received and interest revenue on note

December 31, 2015		
Cash	6,000	
Notes Receivable		6,000
Discount on Notes Receivable ($23,957 × 8%)	1,917	
Interest Revenue		1,917

Tum's will make similar entries in subsequent years of the franchise agreement.

RECOGNITION OF FRANCHISE RIGHTS REVENUE OVER TIME

In the franchise example presented in Illustration 18B-1, Tum's transferred control of the franchise rights at a point in time—that is, when the franchisee began operations and could benefit from control of the rights—with no further involvement by Tum's. In other situations, depending on the economic substance of the rights, the franchisor may be providing **access to the right** rather than transferring control of the franchise rights. In this case, **the franchise revenue is recognized over time**, rather than at a point in time. The franchise arrangement presented in Illustration 18B-4 provides an example of a franchise agreement with revenue recognized over time.

ILLUSTRATION 18B-4
Revenue Recognition over Time—Franchise

FRANCHISE REVENUE OVER TIME

Facts: Tech Solvers Corp. is a franchisor in the emerging technology consulting service business. Tech Solvers' stores provide a range of computing services (hardware/software installation, repairs, data backup, device syncing, and network solutions) on popular Apple and PC devices. Each franchise agreement gives a franchisee the right to open a Tech Solvers store and sell Tech Solvers' products and services in the area for 5 years. Under the contract, Tech Solvers also provides the franchisee with a number of services to support and enhance the franchise brand, including (a) advising and consulting on the operations of the store; (b) communicating new hardware and software developments, and service techniques; (c) providing business and training manuals; and (d) advertising programs and training. As an almost entirely service operation (all parts and other supplies are purchased as needed by customers), Tech Solvers provides few upfront services to franchisees. Instead, the franchisee recruits service technicians, who are given Tech Solvers' training materials (online manuals and tutorials), which are updated for technology changes, on a monthly basis at a minimum.

Tech Solvers enters into a franchise agreement on December 15, 2014, giving a franchisee the rights to operate a Tech Solvers franchise in eastern Indiana for 5 years. Tech Solvers charges an initial franchise fee of $5,000 for the right to operate as a franchisee, payable upon signing the contract. Tech Solvers also receives ongoing royalty payments of 7% of the franchisee's annual sales (payable each January 15 of the following year).

***Question:* What are the performance obligations in this arrangement and the point in time at which the performance obligations will be satisfied and revenue will be recognized?**

Solution: To identify the performance obligations, Tech Solvers must determine whether the promised rights and the ongoing franchisee technology support and training services are distinct.

- Rights to the trade name, market area, and proprietary know-how for 5 years are not individually distinct because each one is not sold separately and cannot be used with other goods or services that are readily available to the franchisee. In addition, these licensed rights have a close connection with the underlying Tech Solvers' intellectual property (its ability to keep its service and training materials up-to-date). Therefore, those combined rights and the ongoing training materials are a single performance obligation. Tech Solvers satisfies the performance obligation over time. That is, once the franchisee begins operating a Tech Solvers franchise, Tech Solvers is providing access to the rights and must continue to perform updates and services.
- Tech Solvers cannot recognize revenue for the royalty payments because it is not reasonably assured to be entitled to those revenue-based royalty amounts. That is, these payments represent variable consideration. Therefore, Tech Solvers recognizes revenue for the royalties when (or as) the uncertainty is resolved.

The entries for Tech Solvers related to the franchise are summarized in Illustration 18B-5.

ILLUSTRATION 18B-5
Franchise Entries—Revenue Recognized over Time

Franchise agreement signed and receipt of upfront payment and note		
December 15, 2014		
Cash	5,000	
Unearned Franchise Revenue		5,000
Franchise begins operations in January 2015 and records $85,000 of revenue for the year ended December 31, 2015		
December 31, 2015		
Unearned Franchise Revenue	1,000	
Franchise Revenue ($5,000 ÷ 5)		1,000
Accounts Receivable	5,950	
Franchise Revenue ($85,000 × 7%)		5,950
To record payment received from franchisee		
January 31, 2016		
Cash	5,950	
Accounts Receivable		5,950

As indicated, Tech Solvers satisfies the performance obligation related to access to the franchise rights and training materials over time (in this case, on a straight-line basis). Continuing franchise fees are recognized when uncertainty related to the variable consideration is resolved.

In summary, analysis of the characteristics of the Tech Solvers' franchise indicates that it does not reflect a right that is transferred at a point in time. That is, Tech Solvers has a continuing obligation to provide updated materials and ongoing support, suggesting the control of the right has not been transferred to the franchisee. Thus, revenue from the franchise rights is recognized over time.

SUMMARY OF LEARNING OBJECTIVE FOR APPENDIX 18B

KEY TERMS

continuing franchise fees, *1084*
franchisee, *1083*
franchises, *1083*
franchisor, *1083*
initial franchise fee, *1084*

13 Explain revenue recognition for franchises. In a franchise arrangement, the franchisor satisfies its performance obligation for a franchise license when control of the franchise rights is transferred, generally when the franchisee begins operations of the franchise. In situations where the franchisor provides *access to the rights* rather than transferring control of the franchise rights, the franchise rights' revenue is recognized over time rather than at a point in time. Franchisors recognize continuing franchise fees as uncertainty related to the variable consideration is resolved, that is, over time.

DEMONSTRATION PROBLEM

Outback Industries manufactures emergency power equipment. Its most popular generator is a model called the E-Booster, which has a retail price of $1,500 and costs Outback $740 to manufacture. It sells the E-Booster on a standalone basis directly to businesses, as well as provides installation services. Outback also distributes the E-Booster through a consignment agreement with **Home Depot**. Income data for Outback's first quarter of 2014 from operations other than the E-Booster generator are as follows.

Revenues	$6,500,000
Expenses	4,350,000

Outback has the following information related to four E-Booster revenue arrangements during the first quarter of 2014.

1. Outback entered into an arrangement with the Grocers Co-op in eastern Minnesota to deliver E-Boosters for the meat lockers in the grocers' stores. Outback provides a 5% volume discount for E-Boosters purchased by Grocers if at least $450,000 of E-Boosters are purchased during 2014. By March 31, 2014, Outback has made sales of $360,000 to Grocers Co-op. Based on prior experience with this promotion in two neighboring states, Outback met the discount threshold for the year if more than one-half of the target had been met by mid-year.
2. On January 1, 2014, Outback sells 20 E-Boosters to Nick's Liquors. Nick's signs a 6-month note due in 6 months at an annual interest rate of 12%. Outback allows Nick's to return any E-Booster that it cannot use within 60 days and receive a full refund. Based on prior experience, Outback estimates that three units will be returned (using the most likely outcome approach). Outback's costs to recover the products will be immaterial, and the returned generators are expected to be resold at a profit.
3. Outback sells 30 E-Boosters to a community bank in the Florida Keys, to provide uninterrupted power for bank branches with ATMs, for a total contract price of $50,000. In addition to the E-Boosters, Outback also provides installation (at a cost of $150 per E-Booster) on a standalone basis; the fair value of this service is $200 per unit installed. The E-Boosters are delivered and installed on March 1, 2014, and full payment is made to Outback.
4. Outback ships 300 E-Boosters to Home Depot on consignment. By March 31, 2014, Home Depot has sold three-fourths of the consigned merchandise at the listed price of $1,500 per unit. Home Depot notifies Outback of the sales, retains an 8% commission, and remits the cash due to Outback.

Instructions

(a) Determine net income for Outback Industries for the first quarter of 2014. (Ignore taxes.)
(b) In reviewing the credit history of Nick's Liquors, Outback has some concerns about the collectibility of the full amount due on the note. Briefly discuss how collectibility of the note affects revenue recognition and income measurement for Outback.

Solution

(a) The amount of revenue and expense recognized on each of the arrangements is as follows.

1. Sales revenue [95% × ($1,500 × 240)]	$342,000	
Cost of goods sold ($740 × 240)	177,600	
Gross profit		$164,400
2. Sales revenue (20 × $1,500)	30,000	
Less: Estimated returns (3 × $1,500)	4,500	
Net sales	25,500	
Cost of goods sold (17 × $740)	12,580	
Gross profit	12,920	
Interest revenue ($30,000 × 12% × 3/12)	900	
Net income on this arrangement		13,820

3. The total transaction price of $50,000 is allocated between the equipment and installation. The transaction price for the equipment and installation is allocated based on relative fair values:

Equipment: $44,118 = ($45,000 ÷ $51,000) × $50,000
Installation: $5,882 = ($6,000 ÷ $51,000) × $50,000

Sales revenue	$44,118		
Cost of goods sold (30 × $740)	22,000		
Gross profit		$22,118	
Installation revenue	5,882		
Installation expense (30 × $150)	4,500		
Net profit		1,382	
Net income on this arrangement			$23,500
4. Sales revenue (225 × $1,500)		337,500	
Cost of goods sold (225 × $740)		166,500	
Gross profit		171,000	
Commission expense ($337,500 × 8%)		27,000	
Net income on this arrangement			144,000
Net income on E-Booster			$345,720

Income for the quarter: $6,500,000 − $4,350,000 + $345,720 = $2,495,720.

(b) Whether a company will get paid for satisfying a performance obligation is not a consideration in determining revenue recognition. That is, the amount recognized is not adjusted for customer credit risk. If significant doubt exists at contract inception about collectibility, Outback reports the revenue gross and then presents an allowance for any impairment due to bad debts, which will reduce net income and which is reported as an operating expense in the income statement.

FASB CODIFICATION

FASB Codification References

[1] FASB ASC 606. [Predecessor literature: None.]

[2] FASB Accounting Standards Update No. 2014-09, *Revenue from Contracts with Customers* (Topic 606) (May 2014), Summary.

[3] FASB ASC 606-10-25-1 to 4. [Predecessor literature: None.]

[4] FASB ASC 606-10-25-1 (e). [Predecessor literature: None.]

[5] FASB ASC 606-10-25-12. [Predecessor literature: None.]

[6] FASB ASC 606-10-25-13. [Predecessor literature: None.]

[7] FASB ASC 606-10-32-2 to 4. [Predecessor literature: None.]

[8] FASB ASC 606-10-32-5 to 9. [Predecessor literature: None.]

[9] FASB ASC 606-10-32-12. [Predecessor literature: None.]

[10] FASB ASC 606-10-32-11. [Predecessor literature: None.]

[11] FASB ASC 606-10-32-18. [Predecessor literature: None.]

[12] FASB ASC 606-10-32-34. [Predecessor literature: None.]

[13] FASB Accounting Standards Update No. 2014-09, *Revenue from Contracts with Customers* (Topic 606) (May 2014), pp. 5–6.

[14] FASB ASC 606-10-55-38. [Predecessor literature: None.]

[15] FASB Accounting Standards Update No. 2014-09, *Revenue from Contracts with Customers* (Topic 606) (May 2014), par. BC261.

[16] FASB ASC 606-10-50-1 to 21. [Predecessor literature: None.]

[17] FASB ASC 606-10-25-27 to 29. [Predecessor literature: None.]

[18] FASB ASC 450 *(Contingencies)*.

[19] FASB ASC 606-10-55-54 to 64. [Predecessor literature: None.]

Exercises

If your school has a subscription to the FASB Codification, go to *http://aaahq.org/asclogin.cfm* to log in and prepare responses to the following. Provide Codification references for your responses.

CE18-1 Access the glossary ("Master Glossary") to answer the following.

(a) What is the definition of a customer?
(b) What is a performance obligation?
(c) How is standalone selling price defined?
(d) What is a transaction price?

CE18-2 Briefly explain the conditions when a contract modification shall be accounted for as a separate performance obligation.

CE18-3 Describe the accounting for refund liabilities.

CE18-4 What procedures are followed in the allocation of a discount?

Be sure to check the book's companion website for a Review and Analysis Exercise, with solution.

WileyPLUS **Brief Exercises, Exercises, Problems, and many more learning and assessment tools and resources are available for practice in WileyPLUS.**

Note: All asterisked Questions, Exercises, and Problems relate to material in the appendices to the chapter.

QUESTIONS

1. Explain the current environment regarding revenue recognition.

2. What was viewed as a major criticism of GAAP as regards revenue recognition?

3. Describe the revenue recognition principle.

4. Identify the five steps in the revenue recognition process.

5. Describe the critical factor in evaluating whether a performance obligation is satisfied.

6. When is revenue recognized in the following situations? (a) Revenue from selling products, (b) revenue from services performed, (c) revenue from permitting others to use company assets, and (d) revenue from disposing of assets other than products.

7. Explain the importance of a contract in the revenue recognition process.

8. On October 10, 2014, Executor Co. entered into a contract with Belisle Inc. to transfer Executor's specialty products (sales value of $10,000, cost of $6,500) on December 15, 2014. Belisle agrees to make a payment of $5,000 upon delivery and signs a promissory note to pay the remaining balance on January 15, 2015. What entries does Executor make in 2014 on this contract? Ignore time value of money considerations.

9. Explain the accounting for contract modifications.

10. What is a performance obligation? Under what conditions does a performance obligation exist?

11. When must multiple performance obligations in a revenue arrangement be accounted for separately?

12. Engelhart Implements Inc. sells tractors to area farmers. The price for each tractor includes GPS positioning service for 9 months (which facilitates field settings for planting and harvesting equipment). The GPS service is regularly sold on a standalone basis by Engelhart for a monthly fee. After the 9-month period, the consumer can renew the service on a fee basis. Does Engelhart have one or multiple performance obligations? Explain.

13. What is the transaction price? What additional factors related to the transaction price must be considered in determining the transaction price?

14. What are some examples of variable consideration? What are the two approaches for estimating variable consideration?

15. Allee Corp. is evaluating a revenue arrangement to determine proper revenue recognition. The contract is for construction of 10 speedboats for a contract price of $400,000. The customer needs the boats in its showrooms by February 1, 2015, for the boat purchase season; the customer provides a bonus payment of $21,000 if all boats are delivered by the February 1 deadline. The bonus is reduced by $7,000 each week that the boats are delivered after the deadline until no bonus is paid if the boats are delivered after February 15, 2015. Allee frequently includes such bonus terms in it contracts and thus has good historical data for estimating the probabilities of completion at different dates. It estimates an equal probability (25%) for each full delivery outcome. What approach should Allee use to determine the transaction price for this contract? Explain.

16. Refer to the information in Question 15. Assume that Allee has limited experience with a construction project on the same scale as the 10 speedboats. How does this affect the accounting for the variable consideration?

17. In measuring the transaction price, explain the accounting for (a) time value of money, and (b) noncash consideration.

18. What is the proper accounting for volume discounts on sales of products?

19. On what basis should the transaction price be allocated to various performance obligations? Identify the approaches for allocating the transaction price.

20. Fuhremann Co. is a full-service manufacturer of surveillance equipment. Customers can purchase any combination of equipment, installation services, and training as part of Fuhremann's security services. Thus, each of these performance obligations are separate with individual standalone values. Laplante Inc. purchased cameras, installation, and training at a total price of $80,000. Estimated standalone fair values of the equipment, installation, and training are $90,000, $7,000, and $3,000, respectively. How should the transaction price be allocated to the equipment, installation, and training?

21. When does a company satisfy a performance obligation? Identify the indicators of satisfaction of a performance obligation.

22. Under what conditions does a company recognize revenue over a period of time?

23. How do companies recognize revenue from a performance obligation over time?

24. Explain the accounting for sales with right of return.

25. What are the reporting issues in a sale with a repurchase agreement?

26. Explain a bill-and-hold sale. When is revenue recognized in these situations?

27. Explain a principal-agent relationship and its significance to revenue recognition.

28. What is the nature of a sale on consignment?

29. What are the two types of warranties? Explain the accounting for each type.

30. Campus Cellular provides cell phones and 1 year of cell service to students for an upfront, nonrefundable fee of $300 and a usage fee of $5 per month. Students may renew the service for each year they are on campus (on average, students renew their service one time). What amount of revenue should Campus Cellular recognize in the first year of the contract?

31. Describe the conditions when contract assets and liabilities are recognized and presented in financial statements.

32. Explain the reporting for (a) costs to fulfill a contract and (b) collectibility.

33. What qualitative and quantitative disclosures are required related to revenue recognition?

***34.** What are the two basic methods of accounting for long-term construction contracts? Indicate the circumstances that determine when one or the other of these methods should be used.

***35.** For what reasons should the percentage-of-completion method be used over the completed-contract method whenever possible?

***36.** What methods are used in practice to determine the extent of progress toward completion? Identify some "input measures" and some "output measures" that might be used to determine the extent of progress.

***37.** What are the two types of losses that can become evident in accounting for long-term contracts? What is the nature of each type of loss? How is each type accounted for?

*38. Why in franchise arrangements may it not be proper to recognize the entire franchise fee as revenue at the date of sale?

*39. How should a franchisor account for continuing franchise fees and routine sales of equipment and supplies to franchisees?

BRIEF EXERCISES

3 **BE18-1** On May 10, 2014, Cosmo Co. enters into a contract to deliver a product to Greig Inc. on June 15, 2014. Greig agrees to pay the full contract price of $2,000 on July 15, 2014. The cost of the goods is $1,300. Cosmo delivers the product to Greig on June 15, 2014, and receives payment on July 15, 2014. Prepare the journal entries for Cosmo related to this contract.

3 **BE18-2** Stengel Co. enters into a 3-year contract to perform maintenance service to Laplante Inc. Laplante promises to pay $100,000 at the beginning of each year (the standalone selling price of the service at contract inception is $100,000 per year). At the end of the second year, the contract is modified and the fee for third year of service, which reflects a reduced menu of maintenance services to be performed at Laplante locations, is reduced to $80,000 (the standalone selling price of the services at the beginning of the third year is $80,000 per year). Briefly describe the accounting for this contract modification.

4 **BE18-3** Ismail Construction enters into a contract to design and build a hospital. Ismail is responsible for the overall management of the project and identifies various goods and services to be provided, including engineering, site clearance, foundation, procurement, construction of the structure, piping and wiring, installation of equipment, and finishing. Does Ismail have a single performance obligation to the customer in this revenue arrangement? Explain.

4 **BE18-4** Mauer Company licenses customer-relationship software to Hedges Inc. for 3 years. In addition to providing the software, Mauer promises to provide consulting services over the life of the license to maintain operability within Hedges' computer system. The total transaction price is $200,000. Based on standalone values, Mauer estimates the consulting services have a value of $75,000 and the software license has a value of $125,000. Upon installation of the software on July 1, 2014, Hedges pays $100,000; the contract balance is due on December 31, 2014. Identify the performance obligations and the revenue in 2014, assuming (a) the performance obligations are interdependent and (b) the performance obligations are not interdependent.

5 **BE18-5** Nair Corp. enters into a contract with a customer to build an apartment building for $1,000,000. The customer hopes to rent apartments at the beginning of the school year and provides a performance bonus of $150,000 to be paid if the building is ready for rental beginning August 1, 2015. The bonus is reduced by $50,000 each week that completion is delayed. Nair commonly includes these completion bonuses in its contracts and, based on prior experience, estimates the following completion outcomes:

Completed by	Probability
August 1, 2015	70%
August 8, 2015	20
August 15, 2015	5
After August 15, 2015	5

Determine the transaction price for this contract.

5 **BE18-6** Referring to the revenue arrangement in BE18-5, determine the transaction price for the contract, assuming (a) Nair is only able to estimate whether the building can be completed by August 1, 2015, or not (Nair estimates that there is a 70% chance that the building will be completed by August 1, 2015), and (b) Nair has limited information with which to develop a reliable estimate of completion by the August 1, 2015, deadline.

5 **BE18-7** On January 2, 2014, Adani Inc. sells goods to Geo Company in exchange for a zero-interest-bearing note with face value of $11,000, with payment due in 12 months. The fair value of the goods at the date of sale is $10,000 (cost $6,000). Prepare the journal entry to record this transaction on January 2, 2014. How much total revenue should be recognized in 2014?

5 **BE18-8** On March 1, 2014, Parnevik Company sold goods to Goosen Inc. for $660,000 in exchange for a 5-year, zero-interest-bearing note in the face amount of $1,062,937. The goods have an inventory cost on

Parnevik's books of $400,000. Prepare the journal entries for Parnevik on (a) March 1, 2014, and (b) December 31, 2014.

5 **BE18-9** Telephone Sellers Inc. sells prepaid telephone cards to customers. Telephone Sellers then pays the telecommunications company, TeleExpress, for the actual use of its telephone lines related to the prepaid telephone cards. Assume that Telephone Sellers sells $4,000 of prepaid cards in January 2014. It then pays TeleExpress based on usage, which turns out to be 50% in February, 30% in March, and 20% in April. The total payment by Telephone Sellers for TeleExpress lines over the 3 months is $3,000. Indicate how much income Telephone Sellers should recognize in January, February, March, and April.

5 **BE18-10** Manual Company sells goods to Nolan Company during 2014. It offers Nolan the following rebates based on total sales to Nolan. If total sales to Nolan are 10,000 units, it will grant a rebate of 2%. If it sells up to 20,000 units, it will grant a rebate of 4%. If it sells up to 30,000 units, it will grant a rebate of 6%. In the first quarter of the year, Manual sells 11,000 units to Nolan at a sales price of $110,000. Manual, based on past experience, has sold over 40,000 units to Nolan, and these sales normally take place in the third quarter of the year. Prepare the journal entry that Manual should make to record the sale of the 11,000 units in the first quarter of the year.

6 **BE18-11** Geraths Windows manufactures and sells custom storm windows for three-season porches. Geraths also provides installation service for the windows. The installation process does not involve changes in the windows, so this service can be performed by other vendors. Geraths enters into the following contract on July 1, 2014, with a local homeowner. The customer purchases windows for a price of $2,400 and chooses Geraths to do the installation. Geraths charges the same price for the windows irrespective of whether it does the installation or not. The price of the installation service is estimated to have a fair value of $600. The customer pays Geraths $2,000 (which equals the fair value of the windows, which have a cost of $1,100) upon delivery and the remaining balance upon installation of the windows. The windows are delivered on September 1, 2014, Geraths completes installation on October 15, 2014, and the customer pays the balance due. Prepare the journal entries for Geraths in 2014. (Round amounts to nearest dollar.)

6 7 **BE18-12** Refer to the revenue arrangement in BE18-11. Repeat the requirements, assuming (a) Geraths estimates the standalone value of the installation based on an estimated cost of $400 plus a margin of 20% on cost, and (b) given uncertainty of finding skilled labor, Geraths is unable to develop a reliable estimate for the fair value of the installation. (Round amounts to nearest dollar.)

8 **BE18-13** On July 10, 2014, Amodt Music sold CDs to retailers on account and recorded sales revenue of $700,000 (cost $560,000). Amodt grants the right to return CDs that do not sell in 3 months following delivery. Past experience indicates that the normal return rate is 15%. By October 11, 2014, retailers returned CDs to Amodt and were granted credit of $78,000. Prepare Amodt's journal entries to record (a) the sale on July 10, 2014, and (b) $78,000 of returns on October 11, 2014.

8 **BE18-14** Kristin Company sells 300 units of its products for $20 each to Logan Inc. for cash. Kristin allows Logan to return any unused product within 30 days and receive a full refund. The cost of each product is $12. To determine the transaction price, Kristin decides that the approach that is most predictive of the amount of consideration to which it will be entitled is the probability-weighted amount. Using the probability-weighted amount, Kristin estimates that (1) 10 products will be returned and (2) the returned products are expected to be resold at a profit. Prepare the journal entry for Kristin at the time of the sale to Logan.

8 **BE18-15** On June 1, 2014, Mills Company sells $200,000 of shelving units to a local retailer, ShopBarb, which is planning to expand its stores in the area. Under the agreement, ShopBarb asks Mills to retain the shelving units at its factory until the new stores are ready for installation. Title passes to ShopBarb at the time the agreement is signed. The shelving units are delivered to the stores on September 1, 2014, and ShopBarb pays in full. Prepare the journal entries for this bill-and-hold arrangement (assuming that conditions for recognizing the sale have been met) for Mills on June 1 and September 1, 2014. The cost of the shelving units to Mills is $110,000.

8 **BE18-16** Travel Inc. sells tickets for a Caribbean cruise on ShipAway Cruise Lines to Carmel Company employees. The total cruise package price to Carmel Company employees is $70,000. Travel Inc. receives a commission of 6% of the total price. Travel Inc. therefore remits $65,800 to ShipAway. Prepare the journal entry to record the remittance and revenue recognized by Travel Inc. on this transaction.

8 **BE18-17** Jansen Corporation shipped $20,000 of merchandise on consignment to Gooch Company. Jansen paid freight costs of $2,000. Gooch Company paid $500 for local advertising, which is reimbursable from Jansen. By year-end, 60% of the merchandise had been sold for $21,500. Gooch notified Jansen, retained a

10% commission, and remitted the cash due to Jansen. Prepare Jansen's journal entry when the cash is received.

8 **BE18-18** Talarczyk Company sold 10,000 Super-Spreaders on July 1, 2014, at a total price of $1,000,000, with a warranty guarantee that the product was free of any defects. The cost of the spreaders sold is $550,000. The assurance warranties extend for a 2-year period and are estimated to cost $40,000. Talarczyk also sold extended warranties (service-type warranties) related to 2,000 spreaders for 2 years beyond the 2-year period for $12,000. Prepare the journal entries that Talarczyk should make in 2014 related to the sale and the related warranties.

9 **BE18-19** On May 1, 2014, Mount Company enters into a contract to transfer a product to Eric Company on September 30, 2014. It is agreed that Eric will pay the full price of $25,000 in advance on June 15, 2014. Eric pays on June 15, 2014, and Mount delivers the product on September 30, 2014. Prepare the journal entries required for Mount in 2014.

8 **BE18-20** Nate Beggs signs a 1-year contract with BlueBox Video. The terms of the contract are that Nate is required to pay a nonrefundable initiation fee of $100. After the first year, membership can be renewed by paying an annual membership fee of $5 per month. BlueBox determines that its customers, on average, renew their annual membership three times after the first year before terminating their membership. What amount of revenue should BlueBox recognize in its first year?

10 ***BE18-21** Turner, Inc. began work on a $7,000,000 contract in 2014 to construct an office building. During 2014, Turner, Inc. incurred costs of $1,700,000, billed its customers for $1,200,000, and collected $960,000. At December 31, 2014, the estimated future costs to complete the project total $3,300,000. Prepare Turner's 2014 journal entries using the percentage-of-completion method.

11 ***BE18-22** Guillen, Inc. began work on a $7,000,000 contract in 2014 to construct an office building. Guillen uses the completed-contract method. At December 31, 2014, the balances in certain accounts were Construction in Process $1,715,000; Accounts Receivable $240,000; and Billings on Construction in Process $1,000,000. Indicate how these accounts would be reported in Guillen's December 31, 2014, balance sheet.

12 ***BE18-23** Archer Construction Company began work on a $420,000 construction contract in 2014. During 2014, Archer incurred costs of $278,000, billed its customer for $215,000, and collected $175,000. At December 31, 2014, the estimated future costs to complete the project total $162,000. Prepare Archer's journal entry to record profit or loss, if any, using (a) the percentage-of-completion method and (b) the completed-contract method.

13 ***BE18-24** Frozen Delight, Inc. charges an initial franchise fee of $75,000 for the right to operate as a franchisee of Frozen Delight. Of this amount, $25,000 is collected immediately. The remainder is collected in four equal annual installments of $12,500 each. These installments have a present value of $41,402. As part of the total franchise fee, Frozen Delight also provides training (with a fair value of $2,000) to help franchisees get the store ready to open. The franchise agreement is signed on April 1, 2014, training is completed, and the store opens on July 1, 2014. Prepare the journal entries required by Frozen Delight in 2014.

EXERCISES

3 5 **E18-1 (Sales with Discounts)** Jupiter Company sells goods to Danone Inc. on account on January 1, 2014. The goods have a sales price of $610,000 (cost $500,000). The terms of the sale are net 30. If Danone pays within 5 days, it receives a cash discount of $10,000. Past history indicates the cash discount will be taken.

Instructions

(a) Prepare the journal entries for Jupiter for January 1, 2014.

(b) Prepare the journal entries for Jupiter for January 31, 2014, assuming Danone does not make payment until January 31, 2014.

3 5 **E18-2 (Transaction Price)** Presented below are three revenue recognition situations.

(a) Grupo sells goods to MTN for $1,000,000, payment due at delivery.

(b) Grupo sells goods on account to Grifols for $800,000, payment due in 30 days.

(c) Grupo sells goods to Magnus for $500,000, payment due in two installments: the first installment payable in 18 months and the second payment due 6 months later. The present value of the future payments is $464,000.

Instructions

Indicate the transaction price for each of these transactions and when revenue will be recognized.

3 **E18-3 (Contract Modification)** In September 2014, Gaertner Corp. commits to selling 150 of its iPhone-compatible docking stations to Better Buy Co. for $15,000 ($100 per product). The stations are delivered to Better Buy over the next 6 months. After 90 stations are delivered, the contract is modified and Gaertner promises to deliver an additional 45 products for an additional $4,275 ($95 per station). All sales are cash on delivery.

Instructions

(a) Prepare the journal entry for Gaertner for the sale of the first 90 stations. The cost of each station is $54.

(b) Prepare the journal entry for the sale of 10 more stations after the contract modification, assuming that the price for the additional stations reflects the standalone selling price at the time of the contract modification. In addition, the additional stations are distinct from the original products as Gaertner regularly sells the products separately.

(c) Prepare the journal entry for the sale of 10 more stations (as in (b)), assuming that the pricing for the additional products *does not* reflect the standalone selling price of the additional products and the prospective method is used.

3 **E18-4 (Contract Modification)** Tyler Financial Services performs bookkeeping and tax-reporting services to startup companies in the Oconomowoc area. On January 1, 2014, Tyler entered into a 3-year service contract with Walleye Tech. Walleye promises to pay $10,000 at the beginning of each year, which at contract inception is the standalone selling price for these services. At the end of the second year, the contract is modified and the fee for the third year of services is reduced to $8,000. In addition, Walleye agrees to pay an additional $20,000 at the beginning of the third year to cover the contract for 3 additional years (i.e., 4 years remain after the modification). The extended contract services are similar to those provided in the first 2 years of the contract.

Instructions

(a) Prepare the journal entries for Tyler in 2014 and 2015 related to this service contract.

(b) Prepare the journal entries for Tyler in 2016 related to the modified service contract, assuming a prospective approach.

(c) Repeat the requirements for part (b), assuming Tyler and Walleye agree on a revised set of services (fewer bookkeeping services but more tax services) in the extended contract period and the modification results in a separate performance obligation.

5 **E18-5 (Variable Consideration)** Blair Biotech enters into a licensing agreement with Pang Pharmaceutical for a drug under development. Blair will receive a payment of $10,000,000 if the drug receives regulatory approval. Based on prior experience in the drug-approval process, Blair determines it is 90% likely that the drug will gain approval and a 10% chance of denial.

Instructions

(a) Determine the transaction price of the arrangement for Blair Biotech.

(b) Assuming that regulatory approval was granted on December 20, 2014, and that Blair received the payment from Pang on January 15, 2015, prepare the journal entries for Blair.

5 **E18-6 (Trailing Commission)** Aaron's Agency sells an insurance policy offered by Capital Insurance Company for a commission of $100. In addition, Aaron will receive an additional commission of $10 each year for as long as the policyholder does not cancel the policy. After selling the policy, Aaron does not have any remaining performance obligations. Based on Aaron's significant experience with these types of policies, it estimates that policyholders on average renew the policy for 4.5 years. It has no evidence to suggest that previous policyholder behavior will change.

Instructions

(a) Determine the transaction price of the arrangement for Aaron, assuming 100 policies are sold.

(b) Prepare the journal entries, assuming that the 100 policies are sold in January 2014 and that Aaron receives commissions from Capital.

5 **E18-7 (Sales with Discounts)** On June 3, 2014, Hunt Company sold to Ann Mount merchandise having a sales price of $8,000 (cost $5,600) with terms of 2/10, n/60, f.o.b. shipping point. Hunt estimates that merchandise with a sales value of $800 will be returned. An invoice totaling $120, terms n/30, was received by Mount on June 8 from Olympic Transport Service for the freight cost. Upon receipt of the goods, on June 5, Mount notified Hunt that $300 of merchandise contained flaws. The same day, Hunt issued a credit memo covering the defective merchandise and asked that it be returned at Hunt's expense.

Hunt estimates the returned items to have a fair value of $120. The freight on the returned merchandise was $24, paid by Hunt on June 7. On June 12, the company received a check for the balance due from Mount.

Instructions

(a) Prepare journal entries for Hunt Company to record all the events noted above assuming sales and receivables are entered at gross selling price.

(b) Prepare the journal entry assuming that Ann Mount did not remit payment until August 5.

5 **E18-8 (Sales with Discounts)** Taylor Marina has 300 available slips that rent for $800 per season. Payments must be made in full at the start of the boating season, April 1, 2015. The boating season ends October 31, and the marina has a December 31 year-end. Slips for future seasons may be reserved if paid for by December 31, 2015. Under a new policy, if payment for 2016 season slips is made by December 31, 2015, a 5% discount is allowed. If payment for 2017 season slips is made by December 31, 2015, renters get a 20% discount (this promotion hopefully will provide cash flow for major dock repairs).

On December 31, 2014, all 300 slips for the 2015 season were rented at full price. On December 31, 2015, 200 slips were reserved and paid for the 2016 boating season, and 60 slips were reserved and paid for the 2017 boating season.

Instructions

(a) Prepare the appropriate journal entries for December 31, 2014, and December 31, 2015.

(b) Assume the marina operator is unsophisticated in business. Explain the managerial significance of the above accounting to this person.

5 6 **E18-9 (Allocate Transaction Price)** Sanchez Co. enters into a contract to sell Product A and Product B on January 2, 2014, for an upfront cash payment of $150,000. Product A will be delivered in 2 years (January 2, 2016) and Product B will be delivered in 5 years (January 2, 2019). Sanchez Co. allocates the $150,000 to Products A and B on a relative standalone selling price basis as follows.

	Standalone Selling Prices	Percent Allocated	Allocated Amounts
Product A	$ 40,000	25%	$ 37,500
Product B	120,000	75%	112,500
	$160,000		$150,000

Sanchez Co. uses an interest rate of 6%, which is its incremental borrowing rate.

Instructions

(a) Prepare the journal entries necessary on January 2, 2014, and December 31, 2014.

(b) Prepare the journal entries necessary on December 31, 2015.

(c) Prepare the journal entries necessary on January 2, 2016.

6 **E18-10 (Allocate Transaction Price)** Shaw Company sells goods that cost $300,000 to Ricard Company for $410,000 on January 2, 2014. The sales price includes an installation fee, which is valued at $40,000. The fair value of the goods is $370,000. The installation is considered a separate performance obligation and is expected to take 6 months to complete.

Instructions

(a) Prepare the journal entries (if any) to record the sale on January 2, 2014.

(b) Shaw prepares an income statement for the first quarter of 2014, ending on March 31, 2014 (installation was completed on June 18, 2014). How much revenue should Shaw recognize related to its sale to Ricard?

5 **E18-11 (Allocate Transaction Price)** Crankshaft Company manufactures equipment. Crankshaft's products range from simple automated machinery to complex systems containing numerous components. Unit selling prices range from $200,000 to $1,500,000 and are quoted inclusive of installation. The installation process does not involve changes to the features of the equipment and does not require proprietary information about the equipment in order for the installed equipment to perform to specifications. Crankshaft has the following arrangement with Winkerbean Inc.

- Winkerbean purchases equipment from Crankshaft for a price of $1,000,000 and contracts with Crankshaft to install the equipment. Crankshaft charges the same price for the equipment irrespective of whether it does the installation or not. Using market data, Crankshaft determines installation service is estimated to have a fair value of $50,000. The cost of the equipment is $600,000.

- Winkerbean is obligated to pay Crankshaft the $1,000,000 upon the delivery and installation of the equipment.

Crankshaft delivers the equipment on June 1, 2014, and completes the installation of the equipment on September 30, 2014. The equipment has a useful life of 10 years. Assume that the equipment and the installation are two distinct performance obligations which should be accounted for separately.

Instructions

(a) How should the transaction price of $1,000,000 be allocated among the service obligations?

(b) Prepare the journal entries for Crankshaft for this revenue arrangement in 2014 assuming Crankshaft receives payment when installation is completed.

6 **E18-12 (Allocate Transaction Price)** Refer to the revenue arrangement in E18-11.

Instructions

Repeat requirements (a) and (b) assuming Crankshaft does not have market data with which to determine the standalone selling price of the installation services. As a result, an expected cost plus margin approach is used. The cost of installation is $36,000; Crankshaft prices these services with a 25% margin relative to cost.

6 **E18-13 (Allocate Transaction Price)** Appliance Center is an experienced home appliance dealer. Appliance Center also offers a number of services together with the home appliances that it sells. Assume that Appliance Center sells ovens on a standalone basis. Appliance Center also sells installation services and maintenance services for ovens. However, Appliance Center does not offer installation or maintenance services to customers who buy ovens from other vendors. Pricing for ovens is as follows.

Oven only	$ 800
Oven with installation service	850
Oven with maintenance services	975
Oven with installation and maintenance services	1,000

In each instance in which maintenance services are provided, the maintenance service is separately priced within the arrangement at $175. Additionally, the incremental amount charged by Appliance Center for installation approximates the amount charged by independent third parties. Ovens are sold subject to a general right of return. If a customer purchases an oven with installation and/or maintenance services, in the event Appliance Center does not complete the service satisfactorily, the customer is only entitled to a refund of the portion of the fee that exceeds $800.

Instructions

(a) Assume that a customer purchases an oven with both installation and maintenance services for $1,000. Based on its experience, Appliance Center believes that it is probable that the installation of the equipment will be performed satisfactorily to the customer. Assume that the maintenance services are priced separately. Identify the separate performance obligations related to the Appliance Center revenue arrangement.

(b) Indicate the amount of revenue that should be allocated to the oven, the installation, and to the maintenance contract.

8 **E18-14 (Sales with Returns)** Organic Growth Company is presently testing a number of new agricultural seeds that it has recently harvested. To stimulate interest, it has decided to grant to five of its largest customers the unconditional right of return to these products if not fully satisfied. The right of return extends for 4 months. Organic Growth sells these seeds on account for $1,500,000 (cost $800,000) on January 2, 2014. Customers are required to pay the full amount due by March 15, 2014.

Instructions

(a) Prepare the journal entry for Organic Growth at January 2, 2014, assuming Organic Growth estimates returns of 20% based on prior experience.

(b) Assume that one customer returns the seeds on March 1, 2014, due to unsatisfactory performance. Prepare the journal entry to record this transaction, assuming this customer purchased $100,000 of seeds from Organic Growth.

(c) Briefly describe the accounting for these sales if Organic Growth is unable to reliably estimate returns.

8 **E18-15 (Sales with Returns)** Uddin Publishing Co. publishes college textbooks that are sold to bookstores on the following terms. Each title has a fixed wholesale price, terms f.o.b. shipping point, and payment is due 60 days after shipment. The retailer may return a maximum of 30% of an order at the retailer's expense. Sales are made only to retailers who have good credit ratings. Past experience indicates that the normal return rate is 12%, and the average collection period is 72 days.

Instructions

(a) Identify the revenue recognition criteria that Uddin could employ concerning textbook sales.
(b) Briefly discuss the reasoning for your answers in (a) above.
(c) On July 1, 2014, Uddin shipped books invoiced at $15,000,000 (cost $12,000,000). Prepare the journal entry to record this transaction.
(d) On October 3, 2014, $1.5 million of the invoiced July sales were returned according to the return policy, and the remaining $13.5 was paid. Prepare the journal entries for the return and payment.

8 **E18-16 (Sales with Repurchase)** Cramer Corp. sells idle machinery to Enyart Company on July 1, 2014, for $40,000. Cramer agrees to repurchase this equipment from Enyart on June 30, 2015, for a price of $42,400 (an imputed interest rate of 6%).

Instructions

(a) Prepare the journal entry for Cramer for the transfer of the asset to Enyart on July 1, 2014.
(b) Prepare any other necessary journal entries for Cramer in 2014.
(c) Prepare the journal entry for Cramer when the machinery is repurchased on June 30, 2015.

8 **E18-17 (Repurchase Agreement)** Zagat Inc. enters into an agreement on March 1, 2014, to sell Werner Metal Company aluminum ingots in 2 months. As part of the agreement, Zagat also agrees to repurchase the ingots in 60 days at the original sales price of $200,000 plus 2%. (Because Zagat has an unconditional obligation to repurchase the ingots at an amount greater than the original sales price, the transaction is treated as a financing.)

Instructions

(a) Prepare the journal entry necessary on March 1, 2014.
(b) Prepare the journal entry for the repurchase of the ingots on May 1, 2014.

8 **E18-18 (Bill and Hold)** Wood-Mode Company is involved in the design, manufacture, and installation of various types of wood products for large construction projects. Wood-Mode recently completed a large contract for Stadium Inc., which consisted of building 35 different types of concession counters for a new soccer arena under construction. The terms of the contract are that upon completion of the counters, Stadium would pay $2,000,000. Unfortunately, due to the depressed economy, the completion of the new soccer arena is now delayed. Stadium has therefore asked Wood-Mode to hold the counters for 2 months at its manufacturing plant until the arena is completed. Stadium acknowledges in writing that it ordered the counters and that they now have ownership. The time that Wood-Mode Company must hold the counters is totally dependent on when the arena is completed. Because Wood-Mode has not received additional progress payments for the arena due to the delay, Stadium has provided a deposit of $300,000.

Instructions

(a) Explain this type of revenue recognition transaction.
(b) What factors should be considered in determining when to recognize revenue in this transaction?
(c) Prepare the journal entry(ies) that Wood-Mode should make, assuming it signed a valid sales contract to sell the counters and received at the time the $300,000 deposit.

8 **E18-19 (Consignment Sales)** On May 3, 2014, Eisler Company consigned 80 freezers, costing $500 each, to Remmers Company. The cost of shipping the freezers amounted to $840 and was paid by Eisler Company. On December 30, 2014, a report was received from the consignee, indicating that 40 freezers had been sold for $750 each. Remittance was made by the consignee for the amount due after deducting a commission of 6%, advertising of $200, and total installation costs of $320 on the freezers sold.

Instructions

(a) Compute the inventory value of the units unsold in the hands of the consignee.
(b) Compute the profit for the consignor for the units sold.
(c) Compute the amount of cash that will be remitted by the consignee.

8 **E18-20 (Warranty Arrangement)** On December 31, 2014, Grando Company sells production equipment to Fargo Inc. for $50,000. Grando includes a 1-year assurance warranty service with the sale of all its equipment. The customer receives and pays for the equipment on December 31, 2014. Grando estimates the prices to be $48,800 for the equipment and $1,200 for the cost of the warranty.

Instructions

(a) Prepare the journal entry to record this transaction on December 31, 2014.

(b) Repeat the requirements for (a), assuming that in addition to the assurance warranty, Grando sold an extended warranty (service-type warranty) for an additional 2 years (2016–2017) for $800.

8 **E18-21 (Warranties)** Celic Inc. manufactures and sells computers that include an assurance-type warranty for the first 90 days. Celic offers an optional extended coverage plan under which it will repair or replace any defective part for 3 years from the expiration of the assurance-type warranty. Because the optional extended coverage plan is sold separately, Celic determines that the 3 years of extended coverage represent a separate performance obligation. The total transaction price for the sale of a computer and the extended warranty is $3,600 on October 1, 2014, and Celic determines the standalone selling price of each is $3,200 and $400, respectively. Further, Celic estimates, based on historical experience, it will incur $200 in costs to repair defects that arise within the 90-day coverage period for the assurance-type warranty. The cost of the equipment is $1,440.

Instructions

(a) Prepare the journal entry (ies) to record the sale of the computer, cost of goods sold, and liabilities related to the warranties.

(b) Briefly describe the accounting for the service-type warranty after the 90-day assurance-type warranty period.

9 **E18-22 (Existence of a Contract)** On January 1, 2014, Gordon Co. enters into a contract to sell a customer a wiring base and shelving unit that sits on the base in exchange for $3,000. The contract requires delivery of the base first but states that payment for the base will not be made until the shelving unit is delivered. Gordon identifies two performance obligations and allocates $1,200 of the transaction price to the wiring base and the remainder to the shelving unit. The cost of the wiring base is $700; the shelves have a cost of $320.

Instructions

(a) Prepare the journal entry on January 1, 2014, for Gordon.

(b) Prepare the journal entry on February 5, 2014, for Gordon when the wiring base is delivered to the customer.

(c) Prepare the journal entry on February 25, 2014, for Gordon when the shelving unit is delivered to the customer and Gordon receives full payment.

9 **E18-23 (Existence of a Contract)** On May 1, 2014, Richardson Inc. entered into a contract to deliver one of its specialty mowers to Kickapoo Landscaping Co. The contract requires Kickapoo to pay the contract price of $900 in advance on May 15, 2014. Kickapoo pays Richardson on May 15, 2014, and Richardson delivers the mower (with cost of $575) on May 31, 2014.

Instructions

(a) Prepare the journal entry on May 1, 2014, for Richardson.

(b) Prepare the journal entry on May 15, 2014, for Richardson.

(c) Prepare the journal entry on May 31, 2014, for Richardson.

9 **E18-24 (Contract Costs)** Rex's Reclaimers entered into a contract with Dan's Demolition to manage the processing of recycled materials on Dan's various demolition projects. Services for the 3-year contract include collecting, sorting, and transporting reclaimed materials to recycling centers or contractors who will reuse them. Rex's incurs selling commission costs of $2,000 to obtain the contract. Before performing the services, Rex's also designs and builds specialty receptacles and loading equipment that interfaces with Dan's demolition equipment at a cost of $27,000. These receptacles and equipment are retained by Rex's. Dan's promises to pay a fixed fee of $12,000 per year, payable every 6 months for the services under the contract. Rex's incurs the following costs: design services for the receptacles to interface with Dan's equipment $3,000, loading equipment controllers $6,000, and special testing and OSHA inspection fees $2,000 (some of Dan's projects are on government property).

Instructions

(a) Determine the costs that should be capitalized as part of Rex's Reclaimers revenue arrangement with Dan's Demolition.

(b) Dan's also expects to incur general and administrative costs related to this contract, as well as costs of wasted materials and labor that likely cannot be factored into the contract price. Can these costs be capitalized? Explain.

9 **E18-25 (Contract Costs, Collectibility)** Refer to the information in E18-24.

Instructions

(a) Does the accounting for capitalized costs change if the contract is for 1 year rather than 3 years? Explain.

(b) Dan's Demolition is a startup company; as a result, there is more than insignificant uncertainty about Dan's ability to make the 6-month payments on time. Does this uncertainty affect the amount of revenue to be recognized under the contract? Explain.

10 ***E18-26 (Recognition of Profit on Long-Term Contracts)** During 2014, Nilsen Company started a con-
11 struction job with a contract price of $1,600,000. The job was completed in 2016. The following information is available.

	2014	2015	2016
Costs incurred to date	$400,000	$825,000	$1,070,000
Estimated costs to complete	600,000	275,000	–0–
Billings to date	300,000	900,000	1,600,000
Collections to date	270,000	810,000	1,425,000

Instructions

(a) Compute the amount of gross profit to be recognized each year, assuming the percentage-of-completion method is used.

(b) Prepare all necessary journal entries for 2015.

(c) Compute the amount of gross profit to be recognized each year, assuming the completed-contract method is used.

10 ***E18-27 (Analysis of Percentage-of-Completion Financial Statements)** In 2014, Steinrotter Construction Corp. began construction work under a 3-year contract. The contract price was $1,000,000. Steinrotter uses the percentage-of-completion method for financial accounting purposes. The income to be recognized each year is based on the proportion of cost incurred to total estimated costs for completing the contract. The financial statement presentations relating to this contract at December 31, 2014, are shown below.

Balance Sheet	
Accounts receivable	$18,000
Construction in process	65,000
Less: Billings	61,500
Costs and recognized profit in excess of billings	3,500
Income Statement	
Income (before tax) on the contract recognized in 2014	$19,500

Instructions

(a) How much cash was collected in 2014 on this contract?

(b) What was the initial estimated total income before tax on this contract?

(AICPA adapted)

10 ***E18-28 (Gross Profit on Uncompleted Contract)** On April 1, 2014, Dougherty Inc. entered into a cost plus fixed fee contract to construct an electric generator for Altom Corporation. At the contract date, Dougherty
XLS estimated that it would take 2 years to complete the project at a cost of $2,000,000. The fixed fee stipulated in the contract is $450,000. Dougherty appropriately accounts for this contract under the percentage-of-completion method. During 2014, Dougherty incurred costs of $800,000 related to the project. The estimated cost at December 31, 2014, to complete the contract is $1,200,000. Altom was billed $600,000 under the contract.

Instructions

Prepare a schedule to compute the amount of gross profit to be recognized by Dougherty under the contract for the year ended December 31, 2014. Show supporting computations in good form.

(AICPA adapted)

10 11 ***E18-29 (Recognition of Revenue on Long-Term Contract and Entries)** Hamilton Construction Company uses the percentage-of-completion method of accounting. In 2014, Hamilton began work under contract #E2-D2, which provided for a contract price of $2,200,000. Other details follow:

	2014	2015
Costs incurred during the year	$640,000	$1,425,000
Estimated costs to complete, as of December 31	960,000	–0–
Billings during the year	420,000	1,680,000
Collections during the year	350,000	1,500,000

Instructions

(a) What portion of the total contract price would be recognized as revenue in 2014? In 2015?

(b) Assuming the same facts as those above except that Hamilton uses the completed-contract method of accounting, what portion of the total contract price would be recognized as revenue in 2015?

(c) Prepare a complete set of journal entries for 2014 (using the percentage-of-completion method).

10 11 ***E18-30 (Recognition of Profit and Balance Sheet Amounts for Long-Term Contracts)** Yanmei Construction Company began operations on January 1, 2014. During the year, Yanmei Construction entered into a contract with Lundquist Corp. to construct a manufacturing facility. At that time, Yanmei estimated that it would take 5 years to complete the facility at a total cost of $4,500,000. The total contract price for construction of the facility is $6,000,000. During the year, Yanmei incurred $1,185,800 in construction costs related to the construction project. The estimated cost to complete the contract is $4,204,200. Lundquist Corp. was billed and paid 25% of the contract price.

Instructions

Prepare schedules to compute the amount of gross profit to be recognized for the year ended December 31, 2014, and the amount to be shown as "costs and recognized profit in excess of billings" or "billings in excess of costs and recognized profit" at December 31, 2014, under each of the following methods. Show supporting computations in good form.

(a) Completed-contract method.

(b) Percentage-of-completion method.

(AICPA adapted)

13 ***E18-31 (Franchise Entries)** Pacific Crossburgers Inc. charges an initial franchise fee of $70,000. Upon the signing of the agreement (which covers 3 years), a payment of $28,000 is due. Thereafter, three annual payments of $14,000 are required. The credit rating of the franchisee is such that it would have to pay interest at 10% to borrow money. The franchise agreement is signed on May 1, 2014, and the franchise commences operation on July 1, 2014.

Instructions

Prepare the journal entries in 2014 for the franchisor under the following assumptions. (Round to the nearest dollar.)

(a) No future services are required by the franchisor once the franchise starts operations.

(b) The franchisor has substantial services to perform, once the franchise begins operations, to maintain the value of the franchise.

(c) The total franchise fee includes training services (with a value of $2,400) for the period leading up to the franchise opening and for 2 months following opening.

13 ***E18-32 (Franchise Fee, Initial Down Payment)** On January 1, 2014, Lesley Benjamin signed an agreement, covering 5 years, to operate as a franchisee of Campbell Inc. for an initial franchise fee of $50,000. The amount of $10,000 was paid when the agreement was signed, and the balance is payable in five annual payments of $8,000 each, beginning January 1, 2015. The agreement provides that the down payment is nonrefundable and that no future services are required of the franchisor once the franchise commences

operations on April 1, 2014. Lesley Benjamin's credit rating indicates that she can borrow money at 11% for a loan of this type.

Instructions

(a) Prepare journal entries for Campbell for 2014-related revenue for this franchise arrangement.

(b) Prepare journal entries for Campbell for 2014-related revenue for this franchise arrangement, assuming that in addition to the franchise rights, Campbell also provides 1 year of operational consulting and training services, beginning on the signing date. These services have a value of $3,600.

(c) Repeat the requirements for part (a), assuming that Campbell must provide services to Benjamin throughout the franchise period to maintain the franchise value.

EXERCISES SET B

See the book's companion website, at **www.wiley.com/college/kieso**, for an additional set of exercises.

PROBLEMS

4 5 6 7 **P18-1 (Allocate Transaction Price, Upfront Fees)** Tablet Tailors sells tablet PCs combined with Internet service (Tablet Bundle A) that permits the tablet to connect to the Internet anywhere (set up a Wi-Fi hot spot). The price for the tablet and a 4-year Internet connection service contract is $500. The standalone selling price of the tablet is $250 (cost to Tablet Tailors $175). Tablet Tailors sells the Internet access service independently for an upfront payment of $100, plus $72 payments at the beginning of years 2–4 of the contract. With an imputed interest rate of 8%, the standalone value of the service is $286. On January 2, 2014, Tablet Tailors signed 100 contracts, receiving a total of $31,445 in cash (full payment of $500 each in cash, less the upfront fee for Internet service, less the present value of the note for the future service plan payments), delivered tablets, and started service for 100 tablet packages.

Instructions

(a) Prepare any journal entries to record this revenue arrangement on January 2, 2014.

(b) Prepare any journal entries to record this revenue arrangement on December 31, 2015.

(c) Prepare any journal entries to record this revenue arrangement on December 31, 2016.

(d) Repeat the requirements for part (a), assuming that Tablet Tailors has no reliable data with which to estimate the standalone selling price for the Internet service.

3 4 5 6 7 **P18-2 (Modification of Contract, Allocate Transaction Price)** Refer to the revenue arrangement in P18-1.

Instructions

Consider the following information and respond to the requirements indicated.

(a) In response to competitive pressures for the Internet access service for Bundle A, at the end of the second year of the 4-year contract, Tablet Tailors offers a modified contract and extension incentive. The extended contract services are similar to those provided in the first 2 years of the contract. Signing the extension and paying $120 (which equals the fair value of the revised service package) extends access for 2 more years of Internet connection. Assuming 40 Bundle A customers sign up for this offer, prepare the journal entries when the contract is signed in January 2, 2016, and at December 31, 2016, for those contracts. Assume the modification does not result in a separate performance obligation.

(b) Tablet Tailors offers a second package (Tablet Bundle B) which includes a service plan for the tablet PC covering the 4-year contract period. That product bundle sells for $600. Tablet Tailors provides the tablet service as a separate product with a standalone selling price of $160. Prepare any journal entries to record the sale of 200 of these packages on January 2, 2014.

4 5 6 7 **P18-3 (Allocate Transaction Price, Discounts, Time Value)** Grill Master Company sells total outdoor grilling solutions, providing gas and charcoal grills, accessories, and installation services for custom patio grilling stations.

Instructions

Respond to the requirements related to the following independent revenue arrangements for Grill Master products and services.

(a) Grill Master offers contract GM205, which is comprised of a free-standing gas grill for small patio use plus installation to a customer's gas line for a total price $800. On a standalone basis, the grill sells for $700 (cost $425), and Grill Master estimates that the fair value of the installation service (based on cost-plus estimation) is $150. Grill Master signed 10 GM205 contracts on April 20, 2014, and customers paid the contract price in cash. The grills were delivered and installed on May 15, 2014. Prepare journal entries for Grill Master for GM205 in April and May 2014.

(b) The State of Kentucky is planning major renovations in its parks during 2014 and enters into a contract with Grill Master to purchase 400 durable, easy maintenance, standard charcoal grills during 2014. The grills are priced at $200 each (with a cost of $160 each), and Grill Master provides a 6% volume discount if Kentucky purchases at least 300 grills during 2014. On April 17, 2014, Grill Master delivered and received payment for 280 grills. Based on prior experience with the State of Kentucky renovation projects, the delivery of this many grills makes it certain that Kentucky will meet the discount threshold. Prepare the journal entries for Grill Master for grills sold on April 17, 2014.

(c) Grill Master sells its specialty combination gas/wood-fired grills to local restaurants. Each grill is sold for $1,000 (cost $550) on credit with terms 3/30, net/90. Prepare the journal entries for the sale of 20 grills on September 1, 2014, and upon payment, assuming the customer paid on (1) September 25, 2014, and (2) October 15, 2014. Assume the company records sales net.

(d) On October 1, 2014, Grill Master sold one of its super deluxe combination gas/charcoal grills to a local builder. The builder plans to install it in one of its "Parade of Homes" houses. Grill Master accepted a 3-year, zero-interest-bearing note with face amount of $5,324. The grill has an inventory cost of $2,700. An interest rate of 10% is an appropriate market rate of interest for this customer. Prepare the journal entries on October 1, 2014, and December 31, 2014.

4 5 6 7 **P18-4 (Allocate Transaction Price, Discounts, Time Value)** Economy Appliance Co. manufactures low-price, no-frills appliances that are in great demand for rental units. Pricing and cost information on Economy's main products are as follows.

Item	Standalone Selling Price (Cost)
Refrigerator	$500 ($260)
Range	$560 ($275)
Stackable washer/dryer unit	$700 ($400)

Customers can contract to purchase either individually at the stated prices or a three-item bundle with a price of $1,800. The bundle price includes delivery and installation. Economy provides delivery and installation as a standalone service for any of its products for a price of $100.

Instructions

Respond to the requirements related to the following independent revenue arrangements for Economy Appliance Co.

(a) On June 1, 2014, Economy sold 100 washer/dryer units without installation to Laplante Rentals for $70,000. Laplante is a newer customer and is unsure how this product will work in its older rental units. Economy offers a 60-day return privilege and estimates, based on prior experience with sales on this product, 4% of the units will be returned. Prepare the journal entries for the sale and related cost of goods sold on June 1, 2014.

(b) YellowCard Property Managers operates upscale student apartment buildings. On May 1, 2014, Economy signs a contract with YellowCard for 300 appliance bundles to be delivered and installed in one of its new buildings. YellowCard pays 20% cash at contract signing and will pay the balance upon delivery and installation no later than August 1, 2014. Prepare journal entries for Economy on (1) May 1, 2014, and (2) August 1, 2014, when all appliances are delivered and installed.

(c) Refer to the arrangement in part (b). It would help YellowCard secure lease agreements with students if the delivery and installation of the appliance bundles can be completed by July 1, 2014. YellowCard offers a 10% bonus payment if Economy can complete delivery and installation by July 1, 2014. Economy estimates its chances of meeting the bonus deadline to be 60%, based on a number of prior contracts of similar scale. Repeat the requirement for part (b), given this bonus provision. Assume installation is completed by July 1, 2014.

(d) Epic Rentals would like to take advantage of the bundle price for its 400-unit project; on February 1, 2014, Economy signs a contract with Epic for delivery and installation of 400 bundles. Under the agreement, Economy will hold the appliance bundles in its warehouses until the new rental units are ready for installation. Epic pays 10% cash at contract signing. On April 1, 2014, Economy completes manufacture of the appliances in the Epic bundle order and places them in the warehouse. Economy and Epic have documented the warehouse arrangement and identified the units designated for Epic. The units are ready to ship, and Economy may not sell these units to other customers. Prepare journal entries for Economy on (1) February 1, 2014, and (2) April 1, 2014.

6 8 **P18-5 (Allocate Transaction Price, Returns, and Consignments)** Ritt Ranch & Farm is a distributor of ranch and farm equipment. Its products range from small tools, power equipment for trench-digging and fencing, grain dryers, and barn winches. Most products are sold direct via its company catalog and Internet site. However, given some of its specialty products, select farm implement stores carry Ritt's products. Pricing and cost information on three of Ritt's most popular products are as follows.

Item	Standalone Selling Price (Cost)
Mini-trencher	$ 3,600 ($2,000)
Power fence hole auger	1,200 ($800)
Grain/Hay dryer	14,000 ($11,000)

Instructions

Respond to the requirements related to the following independent revenue arrangements for Ritt Ranch & Farm.

(a) On January 1, 2014, Ritt sells augers to Mills Farm & Fleet for $48,000. Mills signs a 6-month note at an annual interest rate of 12%. Ritt allows Mills to return any auger that it cannot use within 60 days and receive a full refund. Based on prior experience, Ritt estimates that 5% of units sold to customers like Mills will be returned (using the most likely outcome approach). Ritt's costs to recover the products will be immaterial, and the returned augers are expected to be resold at a profit. Prepare the journal entry for Ritt on January 1, 2014.

(b) On August 10, 2014, Ritt sells 16 mini-trenchers to a farm co-op in western Minnesota. Ritt provides a 4% volume discount on the mini-trenchers if the co-op has a 15% increase in purchases from Ritt compared to the prior year. Given the slowdown in the farm economy, sales to the co-op have been flat, and it is highly uncertain that the benchmark will be met. Prepare the journal entry for Ritt on August 10, 2014.

(c) Ritt sells three grain/hay dryers to a local farmer at a total contract price of $45,200. In addition to the dryers, Ritt provides installation, which has a standalone sales value of $1,000 per unit installed. The contract payment also includes a $1,200 maintenance plan for the dryers for 3 years after installation. Ritt signs the contract on June 20, 2014, and receives a 20% down payment from the farmer. The dryers are delivered and installed on October 1, 2014, and full payment is made to Ritt. Prepare the journal entries for Ritt in 2014 related to this arrangement.

(d) On April 25, 2014, Ritt ships 100 augers to Farm Depot, a farm supply dealer in Nebraska, on consignment. By June 30, 2014, Farm Depot has sold 60 of the consigned augers at the listed price of $1,200 per unit. Farm Depot notifies Ritt of the sales, retains a 10% commission, and remits the cash due Ritt. Prepare the journal entries for Ritt and Farm Depot for the consignment arrangement.

8 **P18-6 (Warranty, Customer Loyalty Program)** Hale Hardware takes pride as the "shop around the corner" that can compete with the big-box home improvement stores by providing good service from knowledgeable sales associates (many of whom are retired local handymen). Hale has developed the following two revenue arrangements to enhance its relationships with customers and increase its bottom line.

1. Hale sells a specialty portable winch that is popular with many of the local customers for use at their lake homes (putting docks in and out, launching boats, etc.). The Hale winch is a standard manufacture winch that Hale modifies so the winch can be used for a variety of tasks. Hale sold 70 of these winches during 2014 at a total price of $21,000, with a warranty guarantee that the product was free of any defects. The cost of winches sold is $16,000. The assurance warranties extend for a 3-year period with an estimated cost of $2,100. In addition, Hale sold extended warranties related to 20 Hale winches for 2 years beyond the 3-year period for $400 each.
2. To bolster its already strong customer base, Hale implemented a customer loyalty program that rewards a customer with 1 loyalty point for every $10 of purchases on a select group of Hale products. Each point is redeemable for a $1 discount on any purchases of Hale merchandise in

the following 2 years. During 2014, customers purchased select group products for $100,000 (all products are sold to provide a 45% gross profit) and earned 10,000 points redeemable for future purchases. The standalone selling price of the purchased products is $100,000. Based on prior experience with incentives programs like this, Hale expects 9,500 points to be redeemed related to these sales (Hale appropriately uses this experience to estimate the value of future consideration related to bonus points).

Instructions

(a) Identify the separate performance obligations in the Hale warranty and bonus point programs, and briefly explain the point in time when the performance obligations are satisfied.
(b) Prepare the journal entries for Hale related to the sales of Hale winches with warranties.
(c) Prepare the journal entries for the bonus point sales for Hale in 2014.
(d) How much additional sales revenue is recognized by Hale in 2015, assuming 4,500 bonus points are redeemed?

8 **P18-7 (Customer Loyalty Program)** Martz Inc. has a customer loyalty program that rewards a customer with 1 customer loyalty point for every $10 of purchases. Each point is redeemable for a $3 discount on any future purchases. On July 2, 2014, customers purchase products for $300,000 (with a cost of $171,000) and earn 30,000 points redeemable for future purchases. Martz expects 25,000 points to be redeemed (based on its past experience, which is predictive of the amount of consideration to which it will be entitled). Martz estimates a standalone selling price of $2.50 per point (or $75,000 total) on the basis of the likelihood of redemption. The points provide a material right to customers that they would not receive without entering into a contract. As a result, Martz concludes that the points are a separate performance obligation.

Instructions

(a) Determine the transaction price for the product and the customer loyalty points.
(b) Prepare the journal entries to record the sale of the product and related points on July 2, 2014.
(c) At the end of the first reporting period (July 31, 2014), 10,000 loyalty points are redeemed. Martz continues to expect 25,000 loyalty points to be redeemed in total. Determine the amount of loyalty point revenue to be recognized at July 31, 2014.

4 5 6 8 **P18-8 (Comprehensive Three-Part Revenue Recognition)** Van Hatten Consolidated has three operating divisions: DeMent Publishing Division, Ankiel Securities Division, and Depp Advisory Division. Each division maintains its own accounting system.

DeMent Publishing Division
The DeMent Publishing Division sells large volumes of novels to a few book distributors, which in turn sell to several national chains of bookstores. DeMent allows distributors to return up to 30% of sales, and distributors give the same terms to bookstores. While returns from individual titles fluctuate greatly, the returns from distributors have averaged 20% in each of the past 5 years. A total of $7,000,000 of paperback novel sales were made to distributors during fiscal 2014. On November 30, 2014 (the end of the fiscal year), $1,500,000 of fiscal 2014 sales were still subject to return privileges over the next 6 months. The remaining $5,500,000 of fiscal 2014 sales had actual returns of 21%. Sales from fiscal 2013 totaling $2,000,000 were collected in fiscal 2014 less 18% returns. This division records revenue according to the revenue recognition method when the right of return exists.

Ankiel Securities Division
The Ankiel Securities Division works through manufacturers' agents in various cities. Orders for alarm systems and down payments are forwarded from agents, and the division ships the goods f.o.b. factory directly to customers (usually police departments and security guard companies). Customers are billed directly for the balance due plus actual shipping costs. The company received orders for $6,000,000 of goods during the fiscal year ended November 30, 2014. Down payments of $600,000 were received, and $5,200,000 of goods were billed and shipped. Actual freight costs of $100,000 were also billed. Commissions of 10% on product price are paid to manufacturing agents after goods are shipped to customers. Such goods are warranted for 90 days after shipment, and warranty returns have been about 1% of sales. Revenue is recognized at the point of sale by this division.

Depp Advisory Division
The Depp Advisory Division provides asset management services. This division grew out of Van Hatten's own treasury and asset management operations that several of its customers asked to have access to. On January 1, 2014, Depp entered into a contract with Scutaro Co. to perform asset management services for

1 year. Depp receives a quarterly management fee of 0.25% of Scutaro's assets under management at the end of each quarter. In addition, Depp receives a performance-based incentive fee of 20% of the fund's annual return in excess of the return of the S&P 500 index at the end of the quarter (multiplied by the assets under management at quarter-end). At the end of the first quarter of 2014, Depp was managing $2,400,000 of Scutaro assets. The annualized return on the portfolio was 6.2% (the S&P 500 index had an annualized return of 5.7%).

Instructions

(a) For each division's revenue arrangements, identify the separate performance obligations, briefly explain allocation of the transaction process to each performance obligation, and indicate when the performance obligations are satisfied.

(b) Compute the revenue to be recognized in fiscal year 2014 for each of the three operating divisions of Van Hatten in accordance with generally accepted accounting principles.

5 8 **P18-9 (Time Value, Gift Cards, Discounts)** Presented below are three independent revenue arrangements for Colbert Company.

Instructions

Respond to the requirements related to each revenue arrangement.

(a) Colbert sells 3-D printer systems. Recently, Colbert provided a special promotion of zero-interest financing for 2 years on any new 3-D printer system. Assume that Colbert sells Lyle Cartright a 3-D system receiving a $5,000 zero-interest-bearing note on January 1, 2014. The cost of the 3-D printer system is $4,000. Colbert imputes a 6% interest rate on this zero-interest note transaction. Prepare the journal entry to record the sale on January 1, 2014, and compute the total amount of revenue to be recognized in 2014.

(b) Colbert sells 20 nonrefundable $100 gift cards for 3-D printer paper on March 1, 2014. The paper has a standalone selling price of $100 (cost $80). The gift cards expiration date is June 30, 2014. Colbert estimates that customers will not redeem 10% of these gift cards. The pattern of redemption is as follows.

	Redemption Total
March 31	50%
April 30	80%
June 30	85%

Prepare the 2014 journal entries related to the gift cards at March 1, March 31, April 30, and June 30.

(c) Colbert sells 3-D printers along with a number of retail items. The package price and standalone selling prices of each item are as follows

Item	Standalone Selling Price	Price When Bundled	Bundling Discount
3-D printer (cost $4,000)	$5,000	$4,500	$500
Custom stand (cost $200)	450	450	0
Special 3-D paper (cost $135)	175	175	0
Total for bundle	$5,625	$5,125	$500

Due to the timing of delivery—the paper is delivered 6 months after the printer is delivered to the customer—Colbert chooses to account for two performance obligations: (1) the printer and stand, and (2) the paper. Prepare the journal entries for Colbert on (a) March 1, 2014, when Colbert receives $51,250 for the sale of 10 printer bundles, and (b) September 1, 2014, when the paper is delivered to customers.

10 11 ***P18-10 (Recognition of Profit on Long-Term Contract)** Shanahan Construction Company has entered into a contract beginning January 1, 2014, to build a parking complex. It has been estimated that the complex will cost $600,000 and will take 3 years to construct. The complex will be billed to the purchasing company at $900,000. The following data pertain to the construction period.

	2014	2015	2016
Costs to date	$270,000	$450,000	$610,000
Estimated costs to complete	330,000	150,000	–0–
Progress billings to date	270,000	550,000	900,000
Cash collected to date	240,000	500,000	900,000

Instructions

(a) Using the percentage-of-completion method, compute the estimated gross profit that would be recognized during each year of the construction period.

(b) Using the completed-contract method, compute the estimated gross profit that would be recognized during each year of the construction period.

10 11 12 ***P18-11 (Long-Term Contract with Interim Loss)** On March 1, 2014, Pechstein Construction Company contracted to construct a factory building for Fabrik Manufacturing Inc. for a total contract price of $8,400,000. The building was completed by October 31, 2016. The annual contract costs incurred, estimated costs to complete the contract, and accumulated billings to Fabrik for 2014, 2015, and 2016 are given below.

	2014	2015	2016
Contract costs incurred during the year	$2,880,000	$2,230,000	$2,190,000
Estimated costs to complete the contract at 12/31	3,520,000	2,190,000	–0–
Billings to Fabrik during the year	3,200,000	3,500,000	1,700,000

Instructions

(a) Using the percentage-of-completion method, prepare schedules to compute the profit or loss to be recognized as a result of this contract for the years ended December 31, 2014, 2015, and 2016. (Ignore income taxes.)

(b) Using the completed-contract method, prepare schedules to compute the profit or loss to be recognized as a result of this contract for the years ended December 31, 2014, 2015, and 2016. (Ignore incomes taxes.)

10 11 12 ***P18-12 (Long-Term Contract with an Overall Loss)** On July 1, 2014, Torvill Construction Company Inc. contracted to build an office building for Gumbel Corp. for a total contract price of $1,900,000. On July 1, Torvill estimated that it would take between 2 and 3 years to complete the building. On December 31, 2016, the building was deemed substantially completed. Following are accumulated contract costs incurred, estimated costs to complete the contract, and accumulated billings to Gumbel for 2014, 2015, and 2016.

XLS

	At 12/31/14	At 12/31/15	At 12/31/16
Contract costs incurred to date	$ 300,000	$1,200,000	$2,100,000
Estimated costs to complete the contract	1,200,000	800,000	–0–
Billings to Gumbel	300,000	1,100,000	1,850,000

Instructions

(a) Using the percentage-of-completion method, prepare schedules to compute the profit or loss to be recognized as a result of this contract for the years ended December 31, 2014, 2015, and 2016. (Ignore income taxes.)

(b) Using the completed-contract method, prepare schedules to compute the profit or loss to be recognized as a result of this contract for the years ended December 31, 2014, 2015, and 2016. (Ignore income taxes.)

13 ***P18-13 (Franchise Revenue)** Amigos Burrito Inc. sells franchises to independent operators throughout the northwestern part of the United States. The contract with the franchisee includes the following provisions.

1. The franchisee is charged an initial fee of $120,000. Of this amount, $20,000 is payable when the agreement is signed, and a $20,000 zero-interest-bearing note is payable at the end of each of the 5 subsequent years.
2. All of the initial franchise fee collected by Amigos is to be refunded and the remaining obligation canceled if, for any reason, the franchisee fails to open his or her franchise.
3. In return for the initial franchise fee, Amigos agrees to (a) assist the franchisee in selecting the location for the business, (b) negotiate the lease for the land, (c) obtain financing and assist with building design, (d) supervise construction, (e) establish accounting and tax records, and (f) provide expert advice over a 5-year period relating to such matters as employee and management training, quality control, and promotion. This continuing involvement by Amigos helps maintain the brand value of the franchise.
4. In addition to the initial franchise fee, the franchisee is required to pay to Amigos a monthly fee of 2% of sales for menu planning, recipe innovations, and the privilege of purchasing ingredients from Amigos at or below prevailing market prices.

Management of Amigos Burrito estimates that the value of the services rendered to the franchisee at the time the contract is signed amounts to at least $20,000. All franchisees to date have opened their locations at the scheduled time, and none have defaulted on any of the notes receivable. The credit ratings of all franchisees would entitle them to borrow at the current interest rate of 10%. The present value of an ordinary annuity of five annual receipts of $20,000 each discounted at 10% is $75,816.

Instructions

(a) Discuss the alternatives that Amigos Burrito Inc. might use to account for the franchise fees.

(b) Prepare the journal entries for the initial and continuing franchise fees, assuming:

- **(1)** Franchise agreement is signed on January 5, 2014.
- **(2)** Amigos completes franchise startup tasks and the franchise opens on July 1, 2014.
- **(3)** The franchisee records $260,000 in sales in the first 6 months of operations and remits the monthly franchise fee on December 31, 2014.

(c) Briefly describe the accounting for unearned franchise fees, assuming that Amigos has little or no involvement with the franchisee related to expert advice on employee and management training, quality control, and promotion, once the franchise opens.

PROBLEMS SET B

See the book's companion website, at **www.wiley.com/college/kieso**, for an additional set of problems.

CONCEPTS FOR ANALYSIS

CA18-1 (Five-Step Revenue Process) Revenue is recognized based on a five-step process that is applied to a company's revenue arrangements.

Instructions

(a) Briefly describe the five-step process.

(b) Explain the importance of contracts when analyzing revenue arrangements.

(c) How are fair value measurement concepts applied in implementation of the five-step process?

(d) How does the five-step process reflect application of the definitions of assets and liabilities?

CA18-2 (Satisfying Performance Obligations) Judy Schaeffer is getting up to speed on the new guidance on revenue recognition. She is trying to understand the revenue recognition principle as it relates to the five-step revenue recognition process.

Instructions

(a) Describe the revenue recognition principle.

(b) Briefly discuss how the revenue recognition principle relates to the definitions of assets and liabilities. What is the importance of control?

(c) Judy recalls that previous revenue recognition guidance required that revenue not be recognized unless the revenue was realized or realizable (also referred to as collectibility). Is collectibility a consideration in the recognition of revenue? Explain.

CA18-3 (Recognition of Revenue—Theory) Revenue is usually recognized at the point of sale (a point in time). Under special circumstances, however, bases other than the point of sale are used for the timing of revenue recognition.

Instructions

(a) Why is the point of sale usually used as the basis for the timing of revenue recognition?

(b) Disregarding the special circumstances when bases other than the point of sale are used, discuss the merits of each of the following objections to the point-of-sale basis of revenue recognition:

- **(1)** It is too conservative because revenue is earned throughout the entire process of production.
- **(2)** It is not conservative enough because accounts receivable do not represent disposable funds, sales returns and allowances may be made, and collection and bad debt expenses may be incurred in a later period.

(c) Revenue may also be recognized over time. Give an example of the circumstances in which revenue is recognized over time and accounting merits of its use instead of the point-of-sale basis.

(AICPA adapted)

CA18-4 (Recognition of Revenue—Theory) Revenue is recognized for accounting purposes when a performance obligation is satisfied. In some situations, revenue is recognized over time as the fair values of assets and liabilities change. In other situations, however, accountants have developed guidelines for recognizing revenue at the point of sale.

Instructions

(Ignore income taxes.)

(a) Explain and justify why revenue is often recognized at time of sale.
(b) Explain in what situations it would be appropriate to recognize revenue over time.

CA18-5 (Discounts) Fahey Company sells Stairmasters to a retailer, Physical Fitness, Inc., for $2,000,000. Fahey has a history of providing price concessions on this product if the retailer has difficulty selling the Stairmasters to customers. Fahey has experience with sales like these in the past and estimates that the maximum amount of price concessions is $300,000.

Instructions

(a) Determine the amount of revenue that Fahey should recognize at the date of the sale of Stairmasters to Physical Fitness, Inc.
(b) According to GAAP, in some situations, the amount of revenue recognized may be constrained. Explain how the accounting for the Stairmasters sales might be affected by the revenue constraint due to variable consideration or returns.
(c) Some believe that revenue recognition should be constrained by collectibility. Is such a view consistent with GAAP? Explain.

CA18-6 (Recognition of Revenue from Subscriptions) *Cutting Edge* is a monthly magazine that has been on the market for 18 months. It currently has a circulation of 1.4 million copies. Negotiations are underway to obtain a bank loan in order to update the magazine's facilities. *Cutting Edge* is producing close to capacity and expects to grow at an average of 20% per year over the next 3 years.

After reviewing the financial statements of *Cutting Edge*, Andy Rich, the bank loan officer, had indicated that a loan could be offered to *Cutting Edge* only if it could increase its current ratio and decrease its debt to equity ratio to a specified level. Jonathan Embry, the marketing manager of *Cutting Edge*, has devised a plan to meet these requirements. Embry indicates that an advertising campaign can be initiated to immediately increase circulation. The potential customers would be contacted after the purchase of another magazine's mailing list. The campaign would include:

1. An offer to subscribe to *Cutting Edge* at three-fourths the normal price.
2. A special offer to all new subscribers to receive the most current world atlas whenever requested at a guaranteed price of $2.
3. An unconditional guarantee that any subscriber will receive a full refund if dissatisfied with the magazine.

Although the offer of a full refund is risky, Embry claims that few people will ask for a refund after receiving half of their subscription issues. Embry notes that other magazine companies have tried this sales promotion technique and experienced great success. Their average cancellation rate was 25%. On average, each company increased its initial circulation threefold and in the long run increased circulation to twice that which existed before the promotion. In addition, 60% of the new subscribers are expected to take advantage of the atlas premium. Embry feels confident that the increased subscriptions from the advertising campaign will increase the current ratio and decrease the debt to equity ratio.

You are the controller of *Cutting Edge* and must give your opinion of the proposed plan.

Instructions

(a) When should revenue from the new subscriptions be recognized?
(b) How would you classify the estimated sales returns stemming from the unconditional guarantee?
(c) How should the atlas premium be recorded? Is the estimated premium claims a liability? Explain.
(d) Does the proposed plan achieve the goals of increasing the current ratio and decreasing the debt to equity ratio?

CA18-7 (Recognition of Revenue—Bonus Points) Griseta & Dubel Inc. was formed early this year to sell merchandise credits to merchants, who distribute the credits free to their customers. For example, customers can earn additional credits based on the dollars they spend with a merchant (e.g., airlines and hotels). Accounts for accumulating the credits and catalogs illustrating the merchandise for which the credits may be exchanged are maintained online. Centers with inventories of merchandise premiums have been established for redemption of the credits. Merchants may not return unused credits to Griseta & Dubel.

The following schedule expresses Griseta & Dubel's expectations as to the percentages of a normal month's activity that will be attained. For this purpose, a "normal month's activity" is defined as the level of operations expected when expansion of activities ceases or tapers off to a stable rate. The company expects that this level will be attained in the third year and that sales of credits will average $6,000,000 per month throughout the third year.

Month	Actual Credit Sales Percent	Merchandise Premium Purchases Percent	Credit Redemptions Percent
6th	30%	40%	10%
12th	60	60	45
18th	80	80	70
24th	90	90	80
30th	100	100	95

Griseta & Dubel plans to adopt an annual closing date at the end of each 12 months of operation.

Instructions

(a) Discuss the factors to be considered in determining when revenue should be recognized.
(b) Apply the revenue recognition factors to the Griseta & Dubel Inc. revenue arrangement.
(c) Provide balance sheet accounts that should be used and indicate how each should be classified.

(AICPA adapted)

CA18-8 (Revenue Recognition—Membership Fees) Midwest Health Club (MHC) offers 1-year memberships. Membership fees are due in full at the beginning of the individual membership period. As an incentive to new customers, MHC advertised that any customers not satisfied for any reason could receive a refund of the remaining portion of unused membership fees. As a result of this policy, Richard Nies, corporate controller, recognized revenue ratably over the life of the membership. MHC is in the process of preparing its year-end financial statements. Rachel Avery, MHC's treasurer, is concerned about the company's lackluster performance this year. She reviews the financial statements Nies prepared and tells Nies to recognize membership revenue when the fees are received.

Instructions

Answer the following questions.

(a) What are the ethical issues involved?
(b) What should Nies do?

***CA18-9 (Long-Term Contract—Percentage-of-Completion)** Widjaja Company is accounting for a long-term construction contract using the percentage-of-completion method. It is a 4-year contract that is currently in its second year. The latest estimates of total contract costs indicate that the contract will be completed at a profit to Widjaja Company.

Instructions

(a) What theoretical justification is there for Widjaja Company's use of the percentage-of-completion method?
(b) How would progress billings be accounted for? Include in your discussion the classification of progress billings in Widjaja Company financial statements.
(c) How would the income recognized in the second year of the 4-year contract be determined using the cost-to-cost method of determining percentage of completion?
(d) What would be the effect on earnings per share in the second year of the 4-year contract of using the percentage-of-completion method instead of the completed-contract method? Discuss.

(AICPA adapted)

USING YOUR JUDGMENT

As the new revenue recognition guidance is not yet implemented, note that the financial statements and notes for Procter & Gamble, Coca-Cola, PepsiCo, and Westinghouse reflect revenue recognition under prior standards.

FINANCIAL REPORTING

Financial Reporting Problem

P&G

The Procter & Gamble Company (P&G)

The financial statements of P&G are presented in Appendix 5B. The company's complete annual report, including the notes to the financial statements, can be accessed at the book's companion website, **www.wiley.com/college/kieso**.

Instructions

Refer to P&G's financial statements and the accompanying notes to answer the following questions.

(a) What were P&G's net sales for 2011?

(b) What was the percentage of increase or decrease in P&G's net sales from 2010 to 2011? From 2009 to 2010? From 2009 to 2011?

(c) In its notes to the financial statements, what criteria does P&G use to recognize revenue?

(d) How does P&G account for trade promotions? Does the accounting conform to accrual accounting concepts? Explain.

Comparative Analysis Case

The Coca-Cola Company and PepsiCo, Inc.

Instructions

Go to the book's companion website and use information found there to answer the following questions related to The Coca-Cola Company and PepsiCo, Inc.

(a) What were Coca-Cola's and PepsiCo's net revenues (sales) for the year 2011? Which company increased its revenue more (dollars and percentage) from 2010 to 2011?

(b) Are the revenue recognition policies of Coca-Cola and PepsiCo similar? Explain.

(c) In which foreign countries (geographic areas) did Coca-Cola and PepsiCo experience significant revenues in 2011? Compare the amounts of foreign revenues to U.S. revenues for both Coca-Cola and PepsiCo.

Financial Statement Analysis Case

Westinghouse Electric Corporation

The following note appears in the "Summary of Significant Accounting Policies" section of the Annual Report of Westinghouse Electric Corporation.

Note 1 (in part): Revenue Recognition. Sales are primarily recorded as products are shipped and services are rendered. The percentage-of-completion method of accounting is used for nuclear steam supply system orders with delivery schedules generally in excess of five years and for certain construction projects where this method of accounting is consistent with industry practice.

WFSI revenues are generally recognized on the accrual method. When accounts become delinquent for more than two payment periods, usually 60 days, income is recognized only as payments are received. Such delinquent accounts for which no payments are received in the current month, and other accounts on which income is not being recognized because the receipt of either principal or interest is questionable, are classified as nonearning receivables.

Instructions

(a) Identify the revenue recognition methods used by Westinghouse Electric as discussed in its note on significant accounting policies.

(b) Under what conditions are the revenue recognition methods identified in the first paragraph of Westinghouse's note above acceptable?

(c) From the information provided in the second paragraph of Westinghouse's note, identify the type of operation being described and defend the acceptability of the revenue recognition method.

Accounting, Analysis, and Principles

Diversified Industries manufactures sump-pumps. Its most popular product is called the Super Soaker, which has a retail price of $1,200 and costs $540 to manufacture. It sells the Super Soaker on a standalone basis directly to businesses. Diversified also provides installation services for these commercial customers, who want an emergency pumping capability (with regular and back-up generator power) at their businesses. Diversified also distributes the Super Soaker through a consignment agreement with Menards. Income data for the first quarter of 2014 from operations other than the Super Soaker are as follows.

Revenues	$9,500,000
Expenses	7,750,000

Diversified has the following information related to two Super Soaker revenue arrangements during the first quarter of 2014.

1. Diversified sells 30 Super Soakers to businesses in flood-prone areas for a total contract price of $54,600. In addition to the pumps, Diversified also provides installation (at a cost of $150 per pump). On a standalone basis, the fair value of this service is $200 per unit installed. The contract payment also includes a $10 per month service plan for the pumps for 3 years after installation (Diversified's cost to provide this service is $7 per month). The Super Soakers are delivered and installed on March 1, 2014, and full payment is made to Diversified. Any discount is applied to the pump/installation bundle.
2. Diversified ships 300 Super Soakers to Menards on consignment. By March 31, 2014, Menards has sold two-thirds of the consigned merchandise at the listed price of $1,200 per unit. Menards notifies Diversified of the sales, retains a 5% commission, and remits the cash due Diversified.

Accounting

Determine Diversified Industries' 2014 first-quarter net income. (Ignore taxes.)

Analysis

Determine free cash flow (see Chapter 5) for Diversified Industries for the first quarter of 2014. In the first quarter, Diversified had depreciation expense of $175,000 and a net increase in working capital (change in accounts receivable and accounts payable) of $250,000. In the first quarter, capital expenditures were $500,000; Diversified paid dividends of $120,000.

Principles

Explain how the five-step revenue recognition process, when applied to Diversified's two revenue arrangements, reflects the concept of control in the definition of an asset and trade-offs between relevance and faithful representation.

BRIDGE TO THE PROFESSION

Professional Research: FASB Codification

Employees at your company disagree about the accounting for sales returns. The sales manager believes that granting more generous return provisions can give the company a competitive edge and increase sales revenue. The controller cautions that, depending on the terms granted, loose return provisions might lead to non-GAAP revenue recognition. The company CFO would like you to research the issue to provide an authoritative answer.

Instructions

If your school has a subscription to the FASB Codification, go to *http://aaahq.org/ascLogin.cfm* to log in and prepare responses to the following. Provide Codification references for your responses. (Provide paragraph citations.)

(a) What is the authoritative literature addressing revenue recognition when right of return exists?

(b) What is meant by "right of return"? "Bill and hold"?

(c) Describe the accounting when there is a right of return.

(d) When goods are sold on a bill-and-hold basis, what conditions must be met to recognize revenue upon receipt of the order?

Additional Professional Resources

See the book's companion website, at **www.wiley.com/college/kieso**, for professional simulations as well as other study resources.

Remember to check the book's companion website to find additional resources for this chapter.

Notes

Notes

CHAPTER

19 Accounting for Income Taxes

LEARNING OBJECTIVES

After studying this chapter, you should be able to:

1 Identify differences between pretax financial income and taxable income.

2 Describe a temporary difference that results in future taxable amounts.

3 Describe a temporary difference that results in future deductible amounts.

4 Explain the purpose of a deferred tax asset valuation allowance.

5 Describe the presentation of income tax expense in the income statement.

6 Describe various temporary and permanent differences.

7 Explain the effect of various tax rates and tax rate changes on deferred income taxes.

8 Apply accounting procedures for a loss carryback and a loss carryforward.

9 Describe the presentation of deferred income taxes in financial statements.

10 Indicate the basic principles of the asset-liability method.

How Much Is Enough?

In the wake of the economic downturn due to the financial crisis, a number of companies and numerous banks reported operating losses. As you will learn in this chapter, the tax code allows companies that report operating losses to claim a tax credit related to these losses for taxes paid in the past (referred to as "carrybacks") and to offset taxable income in periods following the operating loss (referred to as "carryforwards"). When companies use these offsets, they reduce income tax expense, which increases net income. For tax carryforwards, companies also record a deferred tax asset, which measures the expected future net cash inflows from lower taxable income in future periods.

Citigroup is a good example of a company that has used operating loss credits to reduce its tax bill. In 2008, it had deferred tax assets (DTAs) of $28.5 billion, which represented 80 percent of stockholders' equity and nearly eclipsed the bank's market value of equity. Some analysts have raised concerns about Citi's DTAs and whether these assets will ever be realized by Citi. Why the concerns?

Well, in order to receive the tax deductions in future years, a company like Citigroup needs to be reasonably sure it will have taxable income in the future. In Citi's case, analysts predict that the struggling bank will need to earn $99 billion in taxable income over the next 20 years. Given that Citigroup recorded operating losses of $60 billion in 2008 and 2009, some are skeptical that the DTAs will be realized. As a result, market watchers are debating whether Citi should set up an allowance to reduce its deferred tax assets due to the possibility that the assets will not be realized. Not surprisingly, Citigroup has resisted setting up an allowance as it would reduce its DTAs and increase its income tax expense.

This accounting does not sit well with some market observers. As one critic noted, "Why should auditors, investors, regulators and others rely on Citigroup's projections . . . to justify the use (realizability) of their DTAs?" Former SEC chief accountant, Lynn Turner, agrees: "Citi's position defies imagination and logic. Instead of talking about making money, what Citi ought to do is to reserve for at least part of the deferred tax assets and reap the benefit of reducing the reserves once it actually makes money."

CONCEPTUAL FOCUS

> Read the **Evolving Issue** on page 1143 for a discussion of uncertain tax positions.

INTERNATIONAL FOCUS

> See the **International Perspectives** on pages 1119, 1128, 1137, 1140, and 1145.

> Read the **IFRS Insights** on pages 1175–1181 for a discussion of:
— Deferred tax asset (non-recognition)
— Statement of financial position classification

In response, Citigroup, which accumulated deferred tax assets partly because of its huge losses during the financial crisis, said it was "very comfortable with the recording of our deferred tax assets." And some market analysts sided with the bank, remarking that Citi's accounts were not out of order due to a misstatement of its DTAs. The Citigroup debate has arisen because accounting standards on DTAs are vague, stating that an allowance is not needed if management believes it is "more likely than not" the company will earn enough taxable income in the future.

This debate over Citigroup's accounting highlights the extent to which management judgment plays an important role in the accounting for taxes. After studying this chapter, you should be better able to evaluate Citigroup's accounting as well as the other judgments inherent in the accounting for income taxes.

Sources: Adapted from J. Weil, "Citigroup's Capital Was All Casing, No Meat," *www.bloomberg.net* (November 24, 2008); and F. Guerra and J. Eaglesham, "Citi Under Fire Over Deferred Tax Assets," *Financial Times* (September 6, 2010).

PREVIEW OF CHAPTER 19

As our opening story indicates, the accounting for income taxes involves significant judgment. Investors need to be knowledgeable of the accounting provisions related to taxes to be able to evaluate these judgments. Thus, companies must present financial information to the investment community that provides a clear picture of present and potential tax obligations and tax benefits. In this chapter, we discuss the basic guidelines that companies must follow in reporting income taxes. The content and organization of the chapter are as follows.

Accounting for Income Taxes

Fundamentals of Accounting for Income Taxes	Accounting for Net Operating Losses	Financial Statement Presentation	Review of the Asset-Liability Method
• Future taxable amounts and deferred taxes • Future deductible amounts and deferred taxes • Valuation allowance • Income statement presentation • Specific differences • Rate considerations	• Loss carryback • Loss carryforward • Loss carryback example • Loss carryforward example	• Balance sheet • Income statement	

FUNDAMENTALS OF ACCOUNTING FOR INCOME TAXES

LEARNING OBJECTIVE 1
Identify differences between pretax financial income and taxable income.

Up to this point, you have learned the basic guidelines that corporations use to report information to investors and creditors. Corporations also must file income tax returns following the guidelines developed by the Internal Revenue Service (IRS). Because GAAP and tax regulations differ in a number of ways, so frequently do pretax financial income and taxable income. Consequently, the amount that a company reports as tax expense will differ from the amount of taxes payable to the IRS. Illustration 19-1 highlights these differences.

ILLUSTRATION 19-1
Fundamental Differences between Financial and Tax Reporting

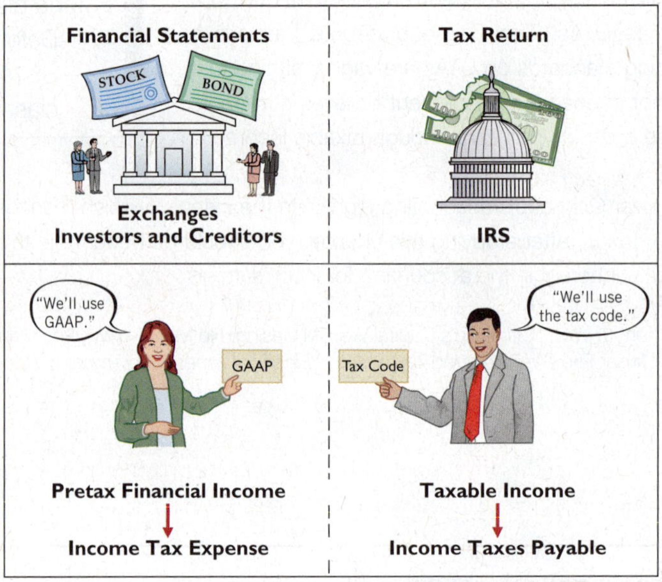

Pretax financial income is a **financial reporting** term. It also is often referred to as income before taxes, income for financial reporting purposes, or income for book purposes. Companies determine pretax financial income according to GAAP. They measure it with the objective of providing useful information to investors and creditors.

Taxable income (income for tax purposes) is a **tax accounting** term. It indicates the amount used to compute income taxes payable. Companies determine taxable income according to the Internal Revenue Code (the tax code). Income taxes provide money to support government operations.

To illustrate how differences in GAAP and IRS rules affect financial reporting and taxable income, assume that Chelsea Inc. reported revenues of $130,000 and expenses of $60,000 in each of its first three years of operations. Illustration 19-2 shows the (partial) income statement over these three years.

ILLUSTRATION 19-2
Financial Reporting Income

CHELSEA INC.
GAAP REPORTING

	2014	2015	2016	Total
Revenues	$130,000	$130,000	$130,000	
Expenses	60,000	60,000	60,000	
Pretax financial income	$ 70,000	$ 70,000	$ 70,000	$210,000
Income tax expense (40%)	$ 28,000	$ 28,000	$ 28,000	$ 84,000

For tax purposes (following the tax code), Chelsea reported the same expenses to the IRS in each of the years. But, as Illustration 19-3 shows, Chelsea reported taxable revenues of $100,000 in 2014, $150,000 in 2015, and $140,000 in 2016.

ILLUSTRATION 19-3
Tax Reporting Income

CHELSEA INC.
TAX REPORTING

	2014	2015	2016	Total
Revenues	$100,000	$150,000	$140,000	
Expenses	60,000	60,000	60,000	
Taxable income	$ 40,000	$ 90,000	$ 80,000	$210,000
Income taxes payable (40%)	$ 16,000	$ 36,000	$ 32,000	$ 84,000

Income tax expense and income taxes payable differed over the three years but were equal **in total**, as Illustration 19-4 shows.

ILLUSTRATION 19-4
Comparison of Income Tax Expense to Income Taxes Payable

CHELSEA INC.
INCOME TAX EXPENSE AND INCOME TAXES PAYABLE

	2014	2015	2016	Total
Income tax expense	$28,000	$28,000	$28,000	$84,000
Income taxes payable	16,000	36,000	32,000	84,000
Difference	$12,000	$ (8,000)	$ (4,000)	$ 0

The differences between income tax expense and income taxes payable in this example arise for a simple reason. For financial reporting, companies use the full accrual method to report revenues. For tax purposes, they use a modified cash basis. As a result, Chelsea reports pretax financial income of $70,000 and income tax expense of $28,000 for each of the three years. However, taxable income fluctuates. For example, in 2014 taxable income is only $40,000, so Chelsea owes just $16,000 to the IRS that year. Chelsea classifies the income taxes payable as a current liability on the balance sheet.

International Perspective

In some countries, taxable income equals pretax financial income. As a consequence, accounting for differences between tax and book income is insignificant.

As Illustration 19-4 indicates, for Chelsea the $12,000 ($28,000 − $16,000) difference between income tax expense and income taxes payable in 2014 reflects taxes that it will pay in future periods. This $12,000 difference is often referred to as a **deferred tax amount**. In this case, it is a **deferred tax liability**. In cases where taxes will be lower in the future, Chelsea records a **deferred tax asset**. We explain the measurement and accounting for deferred tax liabilities and assets in the following two sections.[1]

Future Taxable Amounts and Deferred Taxes

2 LEARNING OBJECTIVE
Describe a temporary difference that results in future taxable amounts.

The example summarized in Illustration 19-4 shows how income taxes payable can differ from income tax expense. This can happen when there are temporary differences between the amounts reported for tax purposes and those reported for

[1]Determining the amount of tax to pay the IRS is a costly exercise for both individuals and companies. Individuals and businesses must pay not only the taxes owed but also the costs of their own time spent filing and complying with the tax code, including (1) the tax collection costs of the IRS, and (2) the tax compliance outlays that individuals and businesses pay to help them file their taxes. One study estimated this cost to be 30 cents on every dollar sent to the government. Another study noted how big the tax compliance industry has become. According to the research, the tax compliance industry employs more people than all the workers at Wal-Mart, UPS, McDonald's, IBM, and Citigroup combined. *Source:* A. Laffer, "The 30-Cent Tax Premium," *Wall Street Journal* (April 18, 2011).

book purposes. A **temporary difference** is the difference between the tax basis of an asset or liability and its reported (carrying or book) amount in the financial statements, which will result in taxable amounts or deductible amounts in future years. **Taxable amounts** increase taxable income in future years. **Deductible amounts** decrease taxable income in future years.

In Chelsea's situation, the only difference between the book basis and tax basis of the assets and liabilities relates to accounts receivable that arose from revenue recognized for book purposes. Illustration 19-5 indicates that Chelsea reports accounts receivable at $30,000 in the December 31, 2014, GAAP-basis balance sheet. However, the receivables have a zero tax basis.

ILLUSTRATION 19-5
Temporary Difference, Sales Revenue

Per Books	12/31/14	Per Tax Return	12/31/14
Accounts receivable	$30,000	Accounts receivable	$-0-

What will happen to the $30,000 temporary difference that originated in 2014 for Chelsea? Assuming that Chelsea expects to collect $20,000 of the receivables in 2015 and $10,000 in 2016, this collection results in future taxable amounts of $20,000 in 2015 and $10,000 in 2016. These future taxable amounts will cause taxable income to exceed pretax financial income in both 2015 and 2016.

An assumption inherent in a company's GAAP balance sheet is that companies recover and settle the assets and liabilities at their reported amounts (carrying amounts). This assumption creates a requirement under accrual accounting to recognize **currently** the deferred tax consequences of temporary differences. That is, companies recognize the amount of income taxes that are payable (or refundable) when they recover and settle the reported amounts of the assets and liabilities, respectively. Illustration 19-6 shows the reversal of the temporary difference described in Illustration 19-5 and the resulting taxable amounts in future periods.

ILLUSTRATION 19-6
Reversal of Temporary Difference, Chelsea Inc.

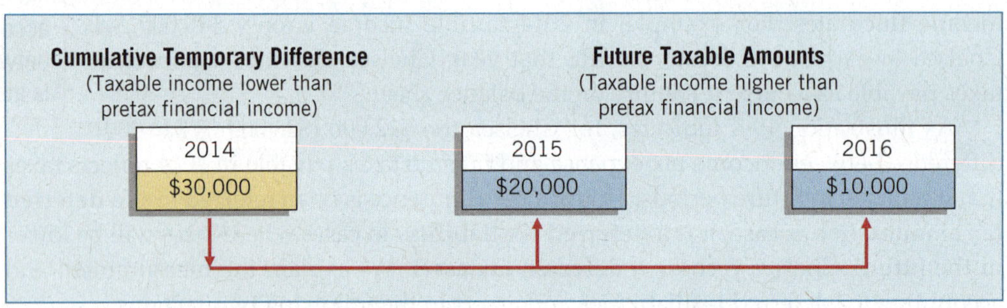

Chelsea assumes that it will collect the accounts receivable and report the $30,000 collection as taxable revenues in future tax returns. A payment of income tax in both 2015 and 2016 will occur. Chelsea should therefore record in its books in 2014 the deferred tax consequences of the revenue and related receivables reflected in the 2014 financial statements. Chelsea does this by recording a deferred tax liability.

Deferred Tax Liability

A **deferred tax liability** is the deferred tax consequences attributable to taxable temporary differences. In other words, **a deferred tax liability represents the increase in taxes payable in future years as a result of taxable temporary differences existing at the end of the current year.**

Recall from the Chelsea example that income taxes payable is $16,000 ($40,000 × 40%) in 2014 (Illustration 19-4 on page 1119). In addition, a temporary difference exists at year-end because Chelsea reports the revenue and related accounts receivable differently for book and tax purposes. The book basis of accounts receivable is $30,000, and the tax basis is zero. Thus, the total deferred tax liability at the end of 2014 is $12,000, computed as shown in Illustration 19-7.

ILLUSTRATION 19-7
Computation of Deferred Tax Liability, End of 2014

Book basis of accounts receivable	$30,000
Tax basis of accounts receivable	-0-
Cumulative temporary difference at the end of 2014	30,000
Tax rate	40%
Deferred tax liability at the end of 2014	$12,000

Companies may also compute the deferred tax liability by preparing a schedule that indicates the future taxable amounts due to existing temporary differences. Such a schedule, as shown in Illustration 19-8, is particularly useful when the computations become more complex.

ILLUSTRATION 19-8
Schedule of Future Taxable Amounts

	Future Years		
	2015	2016	Total
Future taxable amounts	$20,000	$10,000	$30,000
Tax rate	40%	40%	
Deferred tax liability at the end of 2014	$ 8,000	$ 4,000	$12,000

Because it is the first year of operations for Chelsea, there is no deferred tax liability at the beginning of the year. Chelsea computes the income tax expense for 2014 as shown in Illustration 19-9.

ILLUSTRATION 19-9
Computation of Income Tax Expense, 2014

Deferred tax liability at end of 2014	$12,000
Deferred tax liability at beginning of 2014	-0-
Deferred tax expense for 2014	12,000
Current tax expense for 2014 (income taxes payable)	16,000
Income tax expense (total) for 2014	$28,000

This computation indicates that income tax expense has two components—**current tax expense** (the amount of income taxes payable for the period) and deferred tax expense. **Deferred tax expense** is the increase in the deferred tax liability balance from the beginning to the end of the accounting period.

Companies credit taxes due and payable to Income Taxes Payable, and credit the increase in deferred taxes to Deferred Tax Liability. They then debit the sum of those two items to Income Tax Expense. For Chelsea, it makes the following entry at the end of 2014.

Income Tax Expense	28,000	
Income Taxes Payable		16,000
Deferred Tax Liability		12,000

At the end of 2015 (the second year), the difference between the book basis and the tax basis of the accounts receivable is $10,000. Chelsea multiplies this difference by the applicable tax rate to arrive at the deferred tax liability of $4,000 ($10,000 × 40%), which it reports at the end of 2015. Income taxes payable for 2015 is $36,000 (Illustration 19-3 on page 1119), and the income tax expense for 2015 is as shown in Illustration 19-10 (page 1122).

ILLUSTRATION 19-10
Computation of Income Tax Expense, 2015

Deferred tax liability at end of 2015	$ 4,000
Deferred tax liability at beginning of 2015	12,000
Deferred tax expense (benefit) for 2015	(8,000)
Current tax expense for 2015 (income taxes payable)	36,000
Income tax expense (total) for 2015	$28,000

Chelsea records income tax expense, the change in the deferred tax liability, and income taxes payable for 2015 as follows.

Income Tax Expense	28,000	
Deferred Tax Liability	8,000	
Income Taxes Payable		36,000

The entry to record income taxes at the end of 2016 reduces the Deferred Tax Liability by $4,000. The Deferred Tax Liability account appears as follows at the end of 2016.

ILLUSTRATION 19-11
Deferred Tax Liability Account after Reversals

Deferred Tax Liability			
2015	8,000	2014	12,000
2016	4,000		

The Deferred Tax Liability account has a zero balance at the end of 2016.

What do the numbers mean? "REAL LIABILITIES"

Some analysts dismiss deferred tax liabilities when assessing the financial strength of a company. But the FASB indicates that the deferred tax liability meets the definition of a liability established in *Statement of Financial Accounting Concepts No. 6*, "Elements of Financial Statements" because:

1. ***It results from a past transaction.*** In the Chelsea example, the company performed services for customers and recognized revenue in 2014 for financial reporting purposes but deferred it for tax purposes.
2. ***It is a present obligation.*** Taxable income in future periods will exceed pretax financial income as a result of this temporary difference. Thus, a present obligation exists.
3. ***It represents a future sacrifice.*** Taxable income and taxes due in future periods will result from past events. The payment of these taxes when they come due is the future sacrifice.

A study by B. Ayers indicates that the market views deferred tax assets and liabilities similarly to other assets and liabilities. Further, the study concludes that the FASB rules in this area increased the usefulness of deferred tax amounts in financial statements.

Source: B. Ayers, "Deferred Tax Accounting Under *SFAS No. 109*: An Empirical Investigation of Its Incremental Value-Relevance Relative to *APB No. 11*," *The Accounting Review* (April 1998).

Summary of Income Tax Accounting Objectives

One objective of accounting for income taxes is to recognize the amount of taxes payable or refundable for the current year. In Chelsea's case, income taxes payable is $16,000 for 2014.

A **second objective** is to recognize deferred tax liabilities and assets for the future tax consequences of events already recognized in the financial statements or tax returns. For example, Chelsea sold services to customers that resulted in accounts receivable of $30,000 in 2014. It reported that amount on the 2014 income statement, but not on the tax return as income. That amount will appear on future tax returns as income for the period **when collected**. As a result, a $30,000 temporary difference exists at the end of 2014, which will cause future taxable amounts. Chelsea reports a deferred tax liability of $12,000 on the balance sheet at the end of 2014, which represents the increase in taxes payable in future years ($8,000 in 2015 and $4,000 in 2016) as a result of a temporary difference existing at the end of the current year. The related deferred tax liability is reduced by $8,000 at the end of 2015 and by another $4,000 at the end of 2016.

In addition to affecting the balance sheet, deferred taxes impact income tax expense in each of the three years affected. In 2014, taxable income ($40,000) is less than pretax financial income ($70,000). Income taxes payable for 2014 is therefore $16,000 (based on taxable income). Deferred tax expense of $12,000 results from the increase in the Deferred Tax Liability account on the balance sheet. Income tax expense is then $28,000 for 2014.

In 2015 and 2016, however, taxable income will exceed pretax financial income, due to the reversal of the temporary difference ($20,000 in 2015 and $10,000 in 2016). Income taxes payable will therefore exceed income tax expense in 2015 and 2016. Chelsea will debit the Deferred Tax Liability account for $8,000 in 2015 and $4,000 in 2016. It records credits for these amounts in Income Tax Expense. These credits are often referred to as a **deferred tax benefit** (which we discuss again later on).

Future Deductible Amounts and Deferred Taxes

3 LEARNING OBJECTIVE

Describe a temporary difference that results in future deductible amounts.

Assume that during 2014, Cunningham Inc. estimated its warranty costs related to the sale of microwave ovens to be $500,000, paid evenly over the next two years. For book purposes, in 2014 Cunningham reported warranty expense and a related estimated liability for warranties of $500,000 in its financial statements. For tax purposes, **the warranty tax deduction is not allowed until paid**. Therefore, Cunningham recognizes no warranty liability on a tax-basis balance sheet. Illustration 19-12 shows the balance sheet difference at the end of 2014.

Per Books	12/31/14	Per Tax Return	12/31/14
Estimated liability for warranties	$500,000	Estimated liability for warranties	$-0-

ILLUSTRATION 19-12
Temporary Difference, Warranty Liability

When Cunningham pays the warranty liability, it reports an expense (deductible amount) for tax purposes. Because of this temporary difference, Cunningham should recognize in 2014 the tax benefits (positive tax consequences) for the tax deductions that will result from the future settlement of the liability. Cunningham reports this future tax benefit in the December 31, 2014, balance sheet as a **deferred tax asset**.

We can think about this situation another way. Deductible amounts occur in future tax returns. These **future deductible amounts** cause taxable income to be less than pretax financial income in the future as a result of an existing temporary difference. Cunningham's temporary difference originates (arises) in one period (2014) and reverses over two periods (2015 and 2016). Illustration 19-13 diagrams this situation.

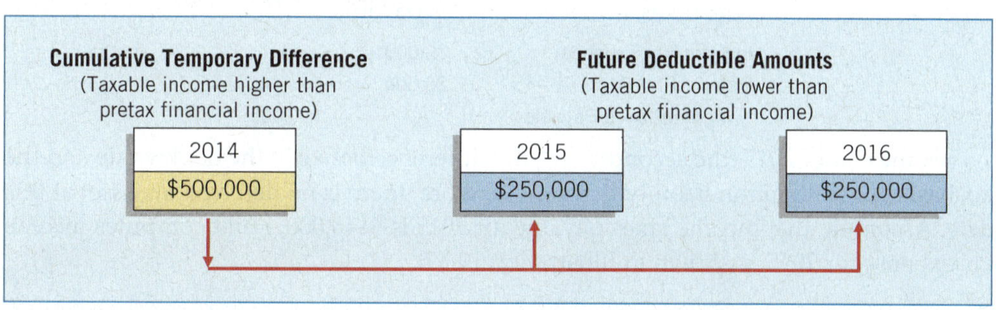

ILLUSTRATION 19-13
Reversal of Temporary Difference, Cunningham Inc.

Deferred Tax Asset

A deferred tax asset is the deferred tax consequence attributable to deductible temporary differences. In other words, a **deferred tax asset represents the increase in taxes refundable (or saved) in future years as a result of deductible temporary differences existing at the end of the current year.**

To illustrate, assume that Hunt Co. accrues a loss and a related liability of $50,000 in 2014 for financial reporting purposes because of pending litigation. Hunt cannot deduct this amount for tax purposes until the period it pays the liability, expected in 2015. As a result, a deductible amount will occur in 2015 when Hunt settles the liability (Estimated Litigation Liability), causing taxable income to be lower than pretax financial income. Illustration 19-14 shows the computation of the deferred tax asset at the end of 2014 (assuming a 40 percent tax rate).

ILLUSTRATION 19-14
Computation of Deferred Tax Asset, End of 2014

Book basis of litigation liability	$50,000
Tax basis of litigation liability	–0–
Cumulative temporary difference at the end of 2014	50,000
Tax rate	40%
Deferred tax asset at the end of 2014	$20,000

Hunt can also compute the deferred tax asset by preparing a schedule that indicates the future deductible amounts due to deductible temporary differences. Illustration 19-15 shows this schedule.

ILLUSTRATION 19-15
Schedule of Future Deductible Amounts

	Future Years
Future deductible amounts	$50,000
Tax rate	40%
Deferred tax asset at the end of 2014	$20,000

Assuming that 2014 is Hunt's first year of operations and income taxes payable is $100,000, Hunt computes its income tax expense as follows.

ILLUSTRATION 19-16
Computation of Income Tax Expense, 2014

Deferred tax asset at end of 2014	$ 20,000
Deferred tax asset at beginning of 2014	–0–
Deferred tax expense (benefit) for 2014	(20,000)
Current tax expense for 2014 (income taxes payable)	100,000
Income tax expense (total) for 2014	$ 80,000

The **deferred tax benefit** results from the increase in the deferred tax asset from the beginning to the end of the accounting period (similar to the Chelsea example earlier). The deferred tax benefit is a negative component of income tax expense. The total income tax expense of $80,000 on the income statement for 2014 thus consists of two elements—current tax expense of $100,000 and a deferred tax benefit of $20,000. For Hunt, it makes the following journal entry at the end of 2014 to record income tax expense, deferred income taxes, and income taxes payable.

Income Tax Expense	80,000	
Deferred Tax Asset	20,000	
Income Taxes Payable		100,000

At the end of 2015 (the second year), the difference between the book value and the tax basis of the litigation liability is zero. Therefore, there is no deferred tax asset at this date. Assuming that income taxes payable for 2015 is $140,000, Hunt computes income tax expense for 2015 as shown in Illustration 19-17.

ILLUSTRATION 19-17
Computation of Income Tax Expense, 2015

Deferred tax asset at the end of 2015	$ –0–
Deferred tax asset at the beginning of 2015	20,000
Deferred tax expense (benefit) for 2015	20,000
Current tax expense for 2015 (income taxes payable)	140,000
Income tax expense (total) for 2015	$160,000

The company records income taxes for 2015 as follows.

Income Tax Expense	160,000	
Deferred Tax Asset		20,000
Income Taxes Payable		140,000

The total income tax expense of $160,000 on the income statement for 2015 thus consists of two elements—current tax expense of $140,000 and deferred tax expense of $20,000. Illustration 19-18 shows the Deferred Tax Asset account at the end of 2015.

Deferred Tax Asset			
2014	20,000	2015	20,000

ILLUSTRATION 19-18
Deferred Tax Asset Account after Reversals

What do the numbers mean? "REAL ASSETS"

A key issue in accounting for income taxes is whether a company should recognize a deferred tax asset in the financial records. Based on the conceptual definition of an asset, a deferred tax asset meets the three main conditions for an item to be recognized as an asset:

1. ***It results from a past transaction.*** In the Hunt example, the accrual of the loss contingency is the past event that gives rise to a future deductible temporary difference.
2. ***It gives rise to a probable benefit in the future.*** Taxable income exceeds pretax financial income in the current year (2014). However, in the next year the exact opposite occurs. That is, taxable income is lower than pretax financial income. Because this deductible temporary difference reduces taxes payable in the future, a probable future benefit exists at the end of the current period.
3. ***The entity controls access to the benefits.*** Hunt can obtain the benefit of existing deductible temporary differences by reducing its taxes payable in the future. Hunt has the exclusive right to that benefit and can control others' access to it.

Market analysts' reactions to the **write-off** of deferred tax assets also supports their treatment as assets. When **Bethlehem Steel** reported a $1 billion charge to write off a deferred tax asset, analysts believed that Bethlehem was signaling that it would not realize the future benefits of the tax deductions. Thus, Bethlehem should write down the asset like other assets.

Source: J. Weil and S. Liesman, "Stock Gurus Disregard Most Big Write-Offs but They Often Hold Vital Clues to Outlook," *Wall Street Journal Online* (December 31, 2001).

Deferred Tax Asset—Valuation Allowance

4 LEARNING OBJECTIVE
Explain the purpose of a deferred tax asset valuation allowance.

Companies recognize a deferred tax asset for all deductible temporary differences. However, a company should reduce a deferred tax asset by a **valuation allowance** if, based on available evidence, **it is more likely than not** that it **will not realize** some portion or all of the deferred tax asset. **"More likely than not"** means a level of likelihood of at least slightly more than 50 percent.

Assume that Jensen Co. has a deductible temporary difference of $1,000,000 at the end of its first year of operations. Its tax rate is 40 percent, which means it records a deferred tax asset of $400,000 ($1,000,000 × 40%). Assuming $900,000 of income taxes payable, Jensen records income tax expense, the deferred tax asset, and income taxes payable as follows.

Income Tax Expense	500,000	
Deferred Tax Asset	400,000	
Income Taxes Payable		900,000

After careful review of all available evidence, Jensen determines that it is more likely than not that it will not realize $100,000 of this deferred tax asset. Jensen records this reduction in asset value as follows.

Income Tax Expense	100,000	
Allowance to Reduce Deferred Tax Asset to Expected Realizable Value		100,000

This journal entry increases income tax expense in the current period because Jensen does not expect to realize a favorable tax benefit for a portion of the deductible temporary difference. Jensen **simultaneously establishes a valuation allowance to recognize the reduction in the carrying amount of the deferred tax asset.** This valuation account is a contra account. Jensen reports it on the financial statements in the following manner.

ILLUSTRATION 19-19
Balance Sheet Presentation of Valuation Allowance Account

Deferred tax asset	$400,000
Less: Allowance to reduce deferred tax asset to expected realizable value	100,000
Deferred tax asset (net)	$300,000

Jensen then evaluates this allowance account at the end of each accounting period. If, at the end of the next period, the deferred tax asset is still $400,000 but now the company expects to realize $350,000 of this asset, Jensen makes the following entry to adjust the valuation account.

Allowance to Reduce Deferred Tax Asset to Expected Realizable Value	50,000	
Income Tax Expense		50,000

Jensen should consider all available evidence, both positive and negative, to determine whether, based on the weight of available evidence, it needs a valuation allowance. For example, if Jensen has been experiencing a series of loss years, it reasonably assumes that these losses will continue. Therefore, Jensen will lose the benefit of the future deductible amounts. We discuss the use of a valuation account under other conditions later in the chapter.

Income Statement Presentation

LEARNING OBJECTIVE 5
Describe the presentation of income tax expense in the income statement.

Circumstances dictate whether a company should add or subtract the change in deferred income taxes to or from income taxes payable in computing income tax expense. For example, a company adds an increase in a deferred tax liability to income taxes payable. On the other hand, it subtracts an increase in a deferred tax asset from income taxes payable. The formula in Illustration 19-20 is used to compute income tax expense (benefit).

ILLUSTRATION 19-20
Formula to Compute Income Tax Expense

Income Taxes Payable or Refundable	±	Change in Deferred Income Taxes	=	Total Income Tax Expense or Benefit

In the income statement or in the notes to the financial statements, a company should disclose the significant components of income tax expense attributable to continuing operations. Given the information related to Chelsea on page 1121, Chelsea reports its income statement as follows.

ILLUSTRATION 19-21
Income Statement Presentation of Income Tax Expense

CHELSEA INC.
INCOME STATEMENT
FOR THE YEAR ENDING DECEMBER 31, 2014

Revenues		$130,000
Expenses		60,000
Income before income taxes		70,000
Income tax expense		
Current	$16,000	
Deferred	12,000	28,000
Net income		$ 42,000

As illustrated, Chelsea reports both the current portion (amount of income taxes payable for the period) and the deferred portion of income tax expense. Another option is to simply report the total income tax expense on the income statement and then indicate in the notes to the financial statements the current and deferred portions. Income tax expense is often referred to as "Provision for income taxes." Using this terminology, the current provision is $16,000, and the provision for deferred taxes is $12,000.

Specific Differences

6 LEARNING OBJECTIVE
Describe various temporary and permanent differences.

Numerous items create differences between pretax financial income and taxable income. For purposes of accounting recognition, these differences are of two types: (1) temporary, and (2) permanent.

Temporary Differences

Taxable temporary differences are temporary differences that will result in taxable amounts in future years when the related assets are recovered. **Deductible temporary differences** are temporary differences that will result in deductible amounts in future years, when the related book liabilities are settled. As discussed earlier, taxable temporary differences give rise to recording deferred tax liabilities. Deductible temporary differences give rise to recording deferred tax assets. Illustration 19-22 provides examples of temporary differences.

ILLUSTRATION 19-22
Examples of Temporary Differences

Revenues or gains are taxable after they are recognized in financial income.

An asset (e.g., accounts receivable or investment) may be recognized for revenues or gains that will result in **taxable amounts in future years** when the asset is recovered. Examples:

1. Sales accounted for on the accrual basis for financial reporting purposes and on the installment (cash) basis for tax purposes.
2. Contracts accounted for under the percentage-of-completion method for financial reporting purposes and a portion of related gross profit deferred for tax purposes.
3. Investments accounted for under the equity method for financial reporting purposes and under the cost method for tax purposes.
4. Gain on involuntary conversion of nonmonetary asset which is recognized for financial reporting purposes but deferred for tax purposes.
5. Unrealized holding gains for financial reporting purposes (including use of the fair value option), but deferred for tax purposes.

Expenses or losses are deductible after they are recognized in financial income.

A liability (or contra asset) may be recognized for expenses or losses that will result in **deductible amounts in future years** when the liability is settled. Examples:

1. Product warranty liabilities.
2. Estimated liabilities related to discontinued operations or restructurings.
3. Litigation accruals.
4. Bad debt expense recognized using the allowance method for financial reporting purposes; direct write-off method used for tax purposes.
5. Stock-based compensation expense.
6. Unrealized holding losses for financial reporting purposes (including use of the fair value option), but deferred for tax purposes.

Revenues or gains are taxable before they are recognized in financial income.

A liability may be recognized for an advance payment for goods or services to be provided in future years. For tax purposes, the advance payment is included in taxable income upon the receipt of cash. Future sacrifices to provide goods or services (or future refunds to those who cancel their orders) that settle the liability will result in **deductible amounts in future years**. Examples:

1. Subscriptions received in advance.
2. Advance rental receipts.
3. Sales and leasebacks for financial reporting purposes (income deferral) but reported as sales for tax purposes.
4. Prepaid contracts and royalties received in advance.

Expenses or losses are deductible before they are recognized in financial income.

The cost of an asset may have been deducted for tax purposes faster than it was expensed for financial reporting purposes. Amounts received upon future recovery of the amount of the asset for financial reporting (through use or sale) will exceed the remaining tax basis of the asset and thereby result in **taxable amounts in future years**. Examples:

1. Depreciable property, depletable resources, and intangibles.
2. Deductible pension funding exceeding expense.
3. Prepaid expenses that are deducted on the tax return in the period paid.

Determining a company's temporary differences may prove difficult. A company should prepare a balance sheet for tax purposes that it can compare with its GAAP balance sheet. Many of the differences between the two balance sheets are temporary differences.

Originating and Reversing Aspects of Temporary Differences. An **originating temporary difference** is the initial difference between the book basis and the tax basis of an asset or liability, regardless of whether the tax basis of the asset or liability exceeds or is exceeded by the book basis of the asset or liability. A **reversing difference**, on the other hand, occurs when eliminating a temporary difference that originated in prior periods and then removing the related tax effect from the deferred tax account.

For example, assume that Sharp Co. has tax depreciation in excess of book depreciation of $2,000 in 2012, 2013, and 2014. Further, it has an excess of book depreciation over tax depreciation of $3,000 in 2015 and 2016 for the same asset. Assuming a tax rate of 30 percent for all years involved, the Deferred Tax Liability account reflects the following.

ILLUSTRATION 19-23
Tax Effects of Originating and Reversing Differences

	Deferred Tax Liability				
Tax Effects of Reversing Differences	2015	900	2012	600	Tax Effects of Originating Differences
	2016	900	2013	600	
			2014	600	

The originating differences for Sharp in each of the first three years are $2,000. The related tax effect of each originating difference is $600. The reversing differences in 2015 and 2016 are each $3,000. The related tax effect of each is $900.

Permanent Differences

International Perspective

If companies switch to IFRS, the impact on tax accounting methods will require consideration. For example, in cases in which GAAP and tax rules are the same, what happens if IFRS is different from GAAP? Should the tax method change to IFRS? And what might happen at the state level, due to changes in the financial reporting rules?

Some differences between taxable income and pretax financial income are permanent. **Permanent differences** result from items that (1) enter into pretax financial income but **never** into taxable income, or (2) enter into taxable income but **never** into pretax financial income.

Congress has enacted a variety of tax law provisions to attain certain political, economic, and social objectives. Some of these provisions exclude certain revenues from taxation, limit the deductibility of certain expenses, and permit the deduction of certain other expenses in excess of costs incurred. A corporation that has tax-free income, nondeductible expenses, or allowable deductions in excess of cost has an effective tax rate that differs from its statutory (regular) tax rate.

Since permanent differences affect only the period in which they occur, they do not give rise to future taxable or deductible amounts. As a result, **companies recognize no deferred tax consequences**. Illustration 19-24 shows examples of permanent differences.

ILLUSTRATION 19-24
Examples of Permanent Differences

Items are recognized for financial reporting purposes but not for tax purposes.

Examples:
1. Interest received on state and municipal obligations.
2. Expenses incurred in obtaining tax-exempt income.
3. Proceeds from life insurance carried by the company on key officers or employees.
4. Premiums paid for life insurance carried by the company on key officers or employees (company is beneficiary).
5. Fines and expenses resulting from a violation of law.

Items are recognized for tax purposes but not for financial reporting purposes.

Examples:
1. "Percentage depletion" of natural resources in excess of their cost.
2. The deduction for dividends received from U.S. corporations, generally 70% or 80%.

Examples of Temporary and Permanent Differences

To illustrate the computations used when both temporary and permanent differences exist, assume that Bio-Tech Company reports pretax financial income of $200,000 in each of the years 2012, 2013, and 2014. The company is subject to a 30 percent tax rate and has the following differences between pretax financial income and taxable income.

1. Bio-Tech reports gross profit of $18,000 from an installment sale in 2012 for tax purposes over an 18-month period at a constant amount per month beginning January 1, 2013. It recognizes the entire amount for book purposes in 2012.
2. It pays life insurance premiums for its key officers of $5,000 in 2013 and 2014. Although not tax-deductible, Bio-Tech expenses the premiums for book purposes.

The installment sale is a temporary difference, whereas the life insurance premium is a permanent difference. Illustration 19-25 shows the reconciliation of Bio-Tech's pretax financial income to taxable income and the computation of income taxes payable.

ILLUSTRATION 19-25
Reconciliation and Computation of Income Taxes Payable

	2012	2013	2014
Pretax financial income	$200,000	$200,000	$200,000
Permanent difference			
Nondeductible expense		5,000	5,000
Temporary difference			
Installment sale	(18,000)	12,000	6,000
Taxable income	182,000	217,000	211,000
Tax rate	30%	30%	30%
Income taxes payable	$ 54,600	$ 65,100	$ 63,300

Note that Bio-Tech **deducts** the installment-sales gross profit from pretax financial income to arrive at taxable income. The reason: Pretax financial income includes the installment-sales gross profit; taxable income does not. Conversely, it **adds** the $5,000 insurance premium to pretax financial income to arrive at taxable income. The reason: Pretax financial income records an expense for this premium, but for tax purposes the premium is not deductible. As a result, pretax financial income is lower than taxable income. Therefore, the life insurance premium must be added back to pretax financial income to reconcile to taxable income.

Bio-Tech records income taxes for 2012, 2013, and 2014 as follows.

December 31, 2012		
Income Tax Expense ($54,600 + $5,400)	60,000	
Deferred Tax Liability ($18,000 × 30%)		5,400
Income Taxes Payable ($182,000 × 30%)		54,600
December 31, 2013		
Income Tax Expense ($65,100 − $3,600)	61,500	
Deferred Tax Liability ($12,000 × 30%)	3,600	
Income Taxes Payable ($217,000 × 30%)		65,100
December 31, 2014		
Income Tax Expense ($63,300 − $1,800)	61,500	
Deferred Tax Liability ($6,000 × 30%)	1,800	
Income Taxes Payable ($211,000 × 30%)		63,300

Bio-Tech has one temporary difference, which originates in 2012 and reverses in 2013 and 2014. It recognizes a deferred tax liability at the end of 2012 because the temporary difference causes future taxable amounts. As the temporary difference reverses,

Bio-Tech reduces the deferred tax liability. There is no deferred tax amount associated with the difference caused by the nondeductible insurance expense because it is a permanent difference.

Although an enacted tax rate of 30 percent applies for all three years, the effective rate differs from the enacted rate in 2013 and 2014. Bio-Tech computes the **effective tax rate** by dividing total income tax expense for the period by pretax financial income. The effective rate is 30 percent for 2012 ($60,000 ÷ $200,000 = 30%) and 30.75 percent for 2013 and 2014 ($61,500 ÷ $200,000 = 30.75%).

Tax Rate Considerations

LEARNING OBJECTIVE 7
Explain the effect of various tax rates and tax rate changes on deferred income taxes.

In our previous illustrations, the enacted tax rate did not change from one year to the next. Thus, to compute the deferred income tax amount to report on the balance sheet, a company simply multiplies the cumulative temporary difference by the current tax rate. Using Bio-Tech as an example, it multiplies the cumulative temporary difference of $18,000 by the enacted tax rate, 30 percent in this case, to arrive at a deferred tax liability of $5,400 ($18,000 × 30%) at the end of 2012.

Future Tax Rates

What happens if tax rates are expected to change in the future? In this case, a company should use the **enacted tax rate** expected to apply. Therefore, a company must consider presently enacted changes in the tax rate that become effective for a particular future year(s) when determining the tax rate to apply to existing temporary differences. For example, assume that Warlen Co. at the end of 2011 has the following cumulative temporary difference of $300,000, computed as shown in Illustration 19-26.

ILLUSTRATION 19-26
Computation of Cumulative Temporary Difference

Book basis of depreciable assets	$1,000,000
Tax basis of depreciable assets	700,000
Cumulative temporary difference	$ 300,000

Furthermore, assume that the $300,000 will reverse and result in taxable amounts in the future, with the enacted tax rates shown in Illustration 19-27.

ILLUSTRATION 19-27
Deferred Tax Liability Based on Future Rates

	2012	2013	2014	2015	2016	Total
Future taxable amounts	$80,000	$70,000	$60,000	$50,000	$40,000	$300,000
Tax rate	40%	40%	35%	30%	30%	
Deferred tax liability	$32,000	$28,000	$21,000	$15,000	$12,000	$108,000

The total deferred tax liability at the end of 2011 is $108,000. Warlen may only use tax rates other than the current rate when the future tax rates have been enacted, as is the case in this example. **If new rates are not yet enacted for future years, Warlen should use the current rate.**

In determining the appropriate enacted tax rate for a given year, companies must use the **average tax rate**. The Internal Revenue Service and other taxing jurisdictions tax income on a graduated tax basis. For a U.S. corporation, the IRS taxes the first $50,000 of taxable income at 15 percent, the next $25,000 at 25 percent, with higher incremental levels of income at rates as high as 39 percent. In computing deferred income taxes, companies for which graduated tax rates are a significant factor must therefore **determine the average tax rate and use that rate.**

What do the numbers mean? GLOBAL TAX RATES

If you are concerned about your tax rate and the taxes you pay, you might want to consider moving to Switzerland, which has a personal tax rate of anywhere from zero percent to 13.2 percent. You don't want to move to Denmark though. Yes, the people of Denmark are regularly voted to be the happiest people on Earth but it's uncertain how many of these polls take place at tax time. The government in Denmark charges income tax rates ranging from 38 percent to 59 percent. So, taxes are a major item to many individuals, wherever they reside.

Taxes are also a big deal to corporations. For example, the Organisation for Economic Co-operation and Development (OECD) is an international organization of 30 countries that accepts the principles of a free-market economy. Most OECD members are high-income economies and are regarded as developed countries. However, companies in the OECD can be subject to significant tax levies, as indicated in the following list of the ten highest corporate income tax rates for the OECD countries.

United States	40.0%	Germany	29.5%
Japan	38.0	Luxembourg	28.8
Belgium	33.9	New Zealand	28.0
France	33.3	Spain	28.0
Australia	30.0	Canada	26.0

On the low end of the tax rate spectrum are Iceland and Ireland, with tax rates of 15 percent and 12.5 percent, respectively. Indeed, corporate tax rates have been dropping around the world as countries attempt to spur capital investment, which in turn spurs international tax competition. However, with stagnant global economic growth, there is concern that governments will target increases in corporate tax rates as a source of revenues to address budget shortfalls. In addition, further expansion of value-added taxes (VAT) is being considered. Indirect taxes such as VAT are charged on consumption of goods and services, which is much more stable than the corporate tax.

If these tax proposals result in changes in the tax rates applied to future deductible and taxable amounts, be prepared for significant remeasurement of deferred tax assets and liabilities.

Source: The rates reported reflect the base corporate rate in effect in 2012. Effective rates paid may vary depending on country-specific additional levies for such items as unemployment and local taxes, and, in the case of Japan, earthquake damage assessments. Effective rates may be lower due to credits for investments and capital gains. See *http://www.kpmg.com/global/en/services/tax/tax-tools-and-resources/pages/tax-rates-online.aspx*. See also P. Toscano, "The World's Highest Tax Rates," *http://www.cnbc.com/id/30727913* (May 13, 2009).

Revision of Future Tax Rates

When a change in the tax rate is enacted, companies should record its effect on the existing deferred income tax accounts immediately. **A company reports the effect as an adjustment to income tax expense in the period of the change.**

Assume that on December 10, 2011, a new income tax act is signed into law that lowers the corporate tax rate from 40 percent to 35 percent, effective January 1, 2013. If Hostel Co. has one temporary difference at the beginning of 2011 related to $3 million of excess tax depreciation, then it has a Deferred Tax Liability account with a balance of $1,200,000 ($3,000,000 × 40%) at January 1, 2011. If taxable amounts related to this difference are scheduled to occur equally in 2012, 2013, and 2014, the deferred tax liability at the end of 2011 is $1,100,000, computed as follows.

	2012	2013	2014	Total
Future taxable amounts	$1,000,000	$1,000,000	$1,000,000	$3,000,000
Tax rate	40%	35%	35%	
Deferred tax liability	$ 400,000	$ 350,000	$ 350,000	$1,100,000

ILLUSTRATION 19-28
Schedule of Future Taxable Amounts and Related Tax Rates

Hostel, therefore, recognizes the decrease of $100,000 ($1,200,000 − $1,100,000) at the end of 2011 in the deferred tax liability as follows.

Deferred Tax Liability	100,000	
Income Tax Expense		100,000

Corporate tax rates do not change often. Therefore, companies usually employ the current rate. However, state and foreign tax rates change more frequently, and they require adjustments in deferred income taxes accordingly.[2]

ACCOUNTING FOR NET OPERATING LOSSES

LEARNING OBJECTIVE 8

Apply accounting procedures for a loss carryback and a loss carryforward.

Every management hopes its company will be profitable. But hopes and profits may not materialize. For a start-up company, it is common to accumulate operating losses while expanding its customer base but before realizing economies of scale. For an established company, a major event such as a labor strike, rapidly changing regulatory and competitive forces, a disaster such as 9/11, or a general economic recession can cause expenses to exceed revenues—a net operating loss.

A **net operating loss (NOL)** occurs for tax purposes in a year when tax-deductible expenses exceed taxable revenues. An inequitable tax burden would result if companies were taxed during profitable periods without receiving any tax relief during periods of net operating losses. Under certain circumstances, therefore, the federal tax laws permit taxpayers to use the losses of one year to offset the profits of other years.

Companies accomplish this income-averaging provision through the **carryback and carryforward of net operating losses**. Under this provision, a company pays no income taxes for a year in which it incurs a net operating loss. In addition, it may select one of the two options discussed below and on the following pages.

Loss Carryback

Through use of a **loss carryback**, a company may carry the net operating loss back two years and receive refunds for income taxes paid in those years. The company must apply the loss to the earlier year first and then to the second year. It may **carry forward** any loss remaining after the two-year carryback up to 20 years to offset future taxable income. Illustration 19-29 diagrams the loss carryback procedure, assuming a loss in 2014.

ILLUSTRATION 19-29
Loss Carryback Procedure

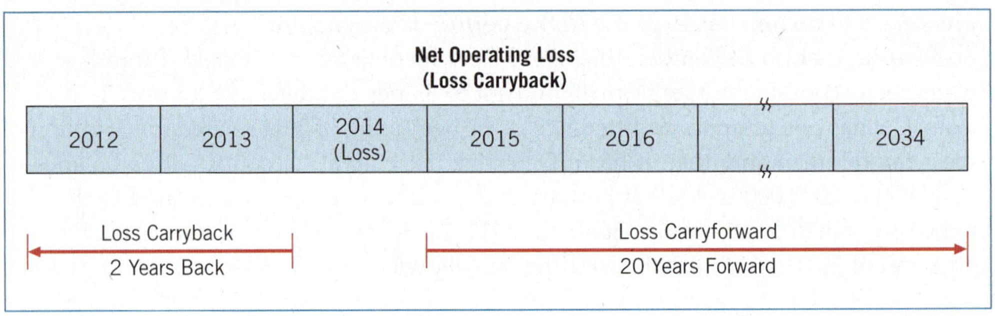

Loss Carryforward

A company may forgo the loss carryback and use only the **loss carryforward** option, offsetting future taxable income for up to 20 years. Illustration 19-30 shows this approach.

[2]Tax rate changes nearly always will substantially impact income numbers and the reporting of deferred income taxes on the balance sheet. As a result, you can expect to hear an economic consequences argument every time that Congress decides to change the tax rates. For example, when Congress raised the corporate rate from 34 percent to 35 percent in 1993, companies took an additional "hit" to earnings if they were in a deferred tax liability position. Thus, corporate America is following closely the recent budget and deficit-reduction negotiations. Some proposals will eliminate certain corporate deductions (or loopholes) in order to "broaden the tax base" and therefore allow for lower tax rates. Depending on a company's deferred tax position, a change in tax rates can have a positive or negative effect on net income.

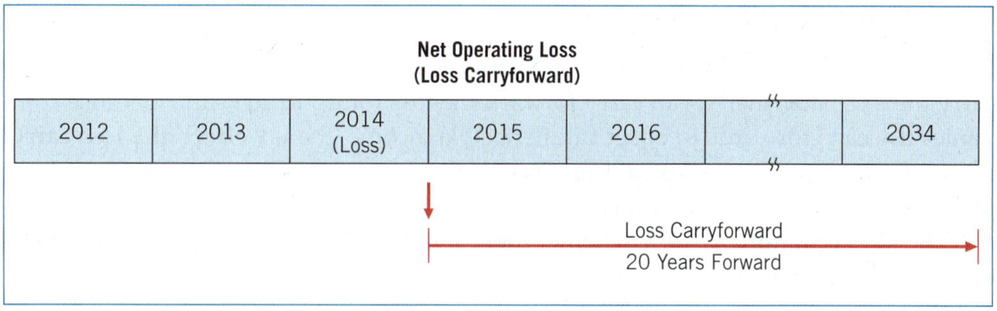

ILLUSTRATION 19-30
Loss Carryforward Procedure

Operating losses can be substantial. For example, **Yahoo!** at one time had net operating losses of approximately $5.4 billion. That amount translates into tax savings of $1.4 billion if Yahoo! is able to generate taxable income before the NOLs expire.

Loss Carryback Example

To illustrate the accounting procedures for a net operating loss carryback, assume that Groh Inc. has no temporary or permanent differences. Groh experiences the following.

Year	Taxable Income or Loss	Tax Rate	Tax Paid
2011	$ 50,000	35%	$17,500
2012	100,000	30%	30,000
2013	200,000	40%	80,000
2014	(500,000)	—	-0-

In 2014, Groh incurs a net operating loss that it decides to carry back. Under the law, Groh must apply the carryback first to the **second year preceding the loss year**. Therefore, it carries the loss back first to 2012. Then, Groh carries back any unused loss to 2013. Accordingly, Groh files amended tax returns for 2012 and 2013, receiving refunds for the $110,000 ($30,000 + $80,000) of taxes paid in those years.

For accounting as well as tax purposes, the $110,000 represents the **tax effect (tax benefit)** of the loss carryback. Groh should recognize this tax effect in 2014, the loss year. Since the tax loss gives rise to a refund that is both measurable and currently realizable, Groh should recognize the associated tax benefit in this loss period.

Groh makes the following journal entry for 2014.

Income Tax Refund Receivable	110,000	
Benefit Due to Loss Carryback (Income Tax Expense)		110,000

Groh reports the account debited, **Income Tax Refund Receivable,** on the balance sheet as a current asset at December 31, 2014. It reports the account credited on the income statement for 2014 as shown in Illustration 19-31.

GROH INC.
INCOME STATEMENT (PARTIAL) FOR 2014

Operating loss before income taxes	$(500,000)
Income tax benefit	
Benefit due to loss carryback	110,000
Net loss	$(390,000)

ILLUSTRATION 19-31
Recognition of Benefit of the Loss Carryback in the Loss Year

Since the $500,000 net operating loss for 2014 exceeds the $300,000 total taxable income from the 2 preceding years, Groh carries forward the remaining $200,000 loss.

Loss Carryforward Example

If a carryback fails to fully absorb a net operating loss, or if the company decides not to carry the loss back, then it can carry forward the loss for up to 20 years.[3] Because companies use carryforwards to offset future taxable income, the **tax effect of a loss carryforward** represents **future tax savings**. Realization of the future tax benefit depends on future earnings, an uncertain prospect.

The key accounting issue is whether there should be different requirements for recognition of a deferred tax asset for (a) deductible temporary differences, and (b) operating loss carryforwards. The FASB's position is that in substance these items are the same—both are tax-deductible amounts in future years. As a result, the Board concluded that there **should not be different requirements** for recognition of a deferred tax asset from deductible temporary differences and operating loss carryforwards.[4]

Carryforward without Valuation Allowance

To illustrate the accounting for an operating loss carryforward, return to the Groh example from the preceding section. In 2014, the company records the tax effect of the $200,000 loss carryforward as a deferred tax asset of $80,000 ($200,000 × 40%), assuming that the enacted future tax rate is 40 percent. Groh records the benefits of the carryback and the carryforward in 2014 as follows.

To recognize benefit of loss carryback		
Income Tax Refund Receivable	110,000	
Benefit Due to Loss Carryback (Income Tax Expense)		110,000

To recognize benefit of loss carryforward		
Deferred Tax Asset	80,000	
Benefit Due to Loss Carryforward (Income Tax Expense)		80,000

Groh realizes the income tax refund receivable of $110,000 immediately as a refund of taxes paid in the past. It establishes a Deferred Tax Asset account for the benefits of future tax savings. The two accounts credited are contra income tax expense items, which Groh presents on the 2014 income statement shown in Illustration 19-32.

ILLUSTRATION 19-32
Recognition of the Benefit of the Loss Carryback and Carryforward in the Loss Year

GROH INC. INCOME STATEMENT (PARTIAL) FOR 2014		
Operating loss before income taxes		$(500,000)
Income tax benefit		
Benefit due to loss carryback	$110,000	
Benefit due to loss carryforward	80,000	190,000
Net loss		$(310,000)

The **current tax benefit** of $110,000 is the income tax refundable for the year. Groh determines this amount by applying the carryback provisions of the tax law to the taxable loss for 2014. The $80,000 is the **deferred tax benefit** for the year, which results from an increase in the deferred tax asset.

[3]The length of the carryforward and carryback periods has varied. The carryforward period has increased from 7 years to 20 years over a period of time. As part of the Economic Recovery Act of 2009, Congress enacted a temporary extension of the carryback period from 2 to 5 years for operating losses incurred in 2008 and 2009. It is estimated that the companies in the S&P 500 will reap a refund of $5 billion due to this change. See D. Zion, A. Varshney, and C. Cornett, "Spinning Losses into Gold," *Equity Research—Accounting and Tax*, Credit Suisse (November 12, 2009).

[4]This requirement is controversial because many believe it is inappropriate to recognize deferred tax assets except when assured beyond a reasonable doubt. Others argue that companies should never recognize deferred tax assets for loss carryforwards until realizing the income in the future.

For 2015, assume that Groh returns to profitable operations and has taxable income of $250,000 (prior to adjustment for the NOL carryforward), subject to a 40 percent tax rate. Groh then realizes the benefits of the carryforward for tax purposes in 2015, which it recognized for accounting purposes in 2014. Groh computes the income taxes payable for 2015 as shown in Illustration 19-33.

ILLUSTRATION 19-33
Computation of Income Taxes Payable with Realized Loss Carryforward

Taxable income prior to loss carryforward	$ 250,000
Loss carryforward deduction	(200,000)
Taxable income for 2015	50,000
Tax rate	40%
Income taxes payable for 2015	$ 20,000

Groh records income taxes in 2015 as follows.

Income Tax Expense	100,000	
Deferred Tax Asset		80,000
Income Taxes Payable		20,000

The benefits of the NOL carryforward, realized in 2015, reduce the Deferred Tax Asset account to zero.

The 2015 income statement that appears in Illustration 19-34 does **not report** the tax effects of either the loss carryback or the loss carryforward because Groh had reported both previously.

ILLUSTRATION 19-34
Presentation of the Benefit of Loss Carryforward Realized in 2015, Recognized in 2014

GROH INC.
INCOME STATEMENT (PARTIAL) FOR 2015

Income before income taxes		$250,000
Income tax expense		
Current	$20,000	
Deferred	80,000	100,000
Net income		$150,000

Carryforward with Valuation Allowance

Let us return to the Groh example. Assume that it is more likely than not that Groh will *not* realize the entire NOL carryforward in future years. In this situation, Groh records the tax benefits of $110,000 associated with the $300,000 NOL carryback, as we previously described. In addition, it records Deferred Tax Asset of $80,000 ($200,000 × 40%) for the potential benefits related to the loss carryforward, and an allowance to reduce the deferred tax asset by the same amount. Groh makes the following journal entries in 2014.

To recognize benefit of loss carryback		
Income Tax Refund Receivable	110,000	
Benefit Due to Loss Carryback (Income Tax Expense)		110,000
To recognize benefit of loss carryforward		
Deferred Tax Asset	80,000	
Benefit Due to Loss Carryforward (Income Tax Expense)		80,000
To record allowance amount		
Benefit Due to Loss Carryforward (Income Tax Expense)	80,000	
Allowance to Reduce Deferred Tax Asset to Expected Realizable Value		80,000

The latter entry indicates that because positive evidence of sufficient quality and quantity is unavailable to counteract the negative evidence, Groh needs a valuation allowance.

Illustration 19-35 shows Groh's 2014 income statement presentation.

ILLUSTRATION 19-35
Recognition of Benefit of Loss Carryback Only

GROH INC. INCOME STATEMENT (PARTIAL) FOR 2014	
Operating loss before income taxes	$(500,000)
Income tax benefit	
Benefit due to loss carryback	110,000
Net loss	$(390,000)

In 2015, assuming that Groh has taxable income of $250,000 (before considering the carryforward) subject to a tax rate of 40 percent, it realizes the deferred tax asset. It thus no longer needs the allowance. Groh records the following entries.

To record current and deferred income taxes		
Income Tax Expense	100,000	
Deferred Tax Asset		80,000
Income Taxes Payable		20,000
To eliminate allowance and recognize loss carryforward		
Allowance to Reduce Deferred Tax Asset to Expected Realizable Value	80,000	
Benefit Due to Loss Carryforward (Income Tax Expense)		80,000

Groh reports the $80,000 Benefit Due to the Loss Carryforward on the 2015 income statement. The company did not recognize it in 2014 because it was more likely than not that it would not be realized. Assuming that Groh derives the income for 2015 from continuing operations, it prepares the income statement as shown in Illustration 19-36.

ILLUSTRATION 19-36
Recognition of Benefit of Loss Carryforward When Realized

GROH INC. INCOME STATEMENT (PARTIAL) FOR 2015		
Income before income taxes		$250,000
Income tax expense		
Current	$ 20,000	
Deferred	80,000	
Benefit due to loss carryforward	(80,000)	20,000
Net income		$230,000

Another method is to report only one line for total income tax expense of $20,000 on the face of the income statement and disclose the components of income tax expense in the notes to the financial statements.

Valuation Allowance Revisited

A company should consider all positive and negative information in determining whether it needs a valuation allowance. Whether the company will realize a deferred tax asset depends on whether sufficient taxable income exists or will exist within the carryforward period available under tax law. Illustration 19-37 shows possible sources of taxable income that may be available under the tax law to realize a tax benefit for deductible temporary differences and carryforwards.[5]

[5]Companies implement a tax-planning strategy to realize a tax benefit for an operating loss or tax credit carryforward before it expires. Companies consider tax-planning strategies when assessing the need for and amount of a valuation allowance for deferred tax assets.

ILLUSTRATION 19-37
Possible Sources of Taxable Income

Taxable Income Sources
a. Future reversals of existing taxable temporary differences.
b. Future taxable income exclusive of reversing temporary differences and carryforwards.
c. Taxable income in prior carryback year(s) if carryback is permitted under the tax law.
d. Tax-planning strategies that would, if necessary, be implemented to: (1) Accelerate taxable amounts to utilize expiring carryforwards. (2) Change the character of taxable or deductible amounts from ordinary income or loss to capital gain or loss. (3) Switch from tax-exempt to taxable investments. [1]

See the FASB Codification section (page 1156).

If any one of these sources is sufficient to support a conclusion that a valuation allowance is unnecessary, a company need not consider other sources.

Forming a conclusion that a valuation allowance is not needed is difficult when there is negative evidence such as cumulative losses in recent years. Companies may also cite positive evidence indicating that a valuation allowance is not needed. Illustration 19-38 presents examples (not prerequisites) of evidence to consider when determining the need for a valuation allowance.[6]

ILLUSTRATION 19-38
Evidence to Consider in Evaluating the Need for a Valuation Account

Negative Evidence
a. A history of operating loss or tax credit carryforwards expiring unused.
b. Losses expected in early future years (by a presently profitable entity).
c. Unsettled circumstances that, if unfavorably resolved, would adversely affect future operations and profit levels on a continuing basis in future years.
d. A carryback, carryforward period that is so brief that it would limit realization of tax benefits if (1) a significant deductible temporary difference is expected to reverse in a single year or (2) the enterprise operates in a traditionally cyclical business.
Positive Evidence
a. Existing contracts or firm sales backlog that will produce more than enough taxable income to realize the deferred tax asset based on existing sale prices and cost structures.
b. An excess of appreciated asset value over the tax basis of the entity's net assets in an amount sufficient to realize the deferred tax asset.
c. A strong earnings history exclusive of the loss that created the future deductible amount (tax loss carryforward or deductible temporary difference) coupled with evidence indicating that the loss is an aberration rather than a continuing condition (for example, the result of an unusual, infrequent, or extraordinary item). [2]

The use of a valuation allowance provides a company with an opportunity to manage its earnings. As one accounting expert notes, "The 'more likely than not' provision is perhaps the most judgmental clause in accounting." Some companies may set up a valuation account and then use it to increase income as needed. Others may take the income immediately to increase capital or to offset large negative charges to income.

International Perspective

Under IFRS (*IAS 12*), a company may not recognize a deferred tax asset unless realization is "probable." However, "probable" is not defined in the standard, leading to diversity in the recognition of deferred tax assets.

[6]In contrast to the valuation allowance issue for **Citigroup** in the opening story, **Sony Corp.** announced a $3.2 billion net loss, blaming a $4.4 billion write-off on a certain portion of deferred tax assets in Japan, in what would be the company's third straight year of red ink. The write-off is an admission that the March 2011 earthquake and tsunami have shattered its expectations for a robust current fiscal year. In the wake of the disaster, Sony temporarily shut 10 plants in and around the quake-hit region. Like other Japanese auto and electronics makers, Sony faced uncertainties because its recovery prospects are partially dependent on parts and materials suppliers, many of which have also been affected by the quake. Thus, the post-quake outlook put Sony in a position where it had to set aside reserves of ¥360 billion on certain deferred tax assets in its fiscal fourth quarter. See J. Osawa, "Sony Expects Hefty Loss: Electronics Giant Reverses Prediction for Full-Year Profit, Blaming Earthquake," *Wall Street Journal* (May 24, 2011).

What do the numbers mean? NOLs: GOOD NEWS OR BAD?

Here are some net operating loss numbers reported by several notable companies.

NOLs ($ in millions)

Company	Income (Loss)	Operating Loss Carryforward	Tax Benefit (Deferred Tax Asset)	Comment
Delta Air Lines, Inc.	$(5,198.00)	$7,500.00	$2,848.00	Begins to expire in 2022. Valuation allowance recorded.
Goodyear	114.80	1,306.60	457.30	Begins to expire in next year. Full valuation allowance.
Kodak	556.00	509.00	234.00	Begins to expire in next year. Valuation allowance on foreign credits only.
Yahoo!	42.82	5,400.00	1,443.50	State and federal carryforwards. Begins to expire in next year. Valuation allowance recorded.

All of these companies are using the carryforward provisions of the tax code for their NOLs. For many of them, the NOL is an amount far exceeding their reported profits. Why carry forward the loss to get the tax deduction? First, the company may have already used up the carryback provision, which allows only a two-year carryback period. (Carryforwards can be claimed up to 20 years in the future.) In some cases, management expects the tax rates in the future to be higher. This difference in expected rates provides a bigger tax benefit if the losses are carried forward and matched against future income. Is there a downside? To realize the benefits of carryforwards, a company must have future taxable income in the carryforward period in order to claim the NOL deductions. As we learned, if it is more likely than not that a company will not have taxable income, it must record a valuation allowance (and increased tax expense). As the data above indicate, recording a valuation allowance to reflect the uncertainty of realizing the tax benefits has merit. But for some, the NOL benefits begin to expire in the following year, which may be not enough time to generate sufficient taxable income in order to claim the NOL deduction.

Source: Company annual reports.

FINANCIAL STATEMENT PRESENTATION

Balance Sheet

LEARNING OBJECTIVE 9

Describe the presentation of deferred income taxes in financial statements.

Deferred tax accounts are reported on the balance sheet as assets and liabilities. Companies should classify these accounts as a net current amount and a net noncurrent amount. **An individual deferred tax liability or asset is classified as current or noncurrent based on the classification of the related asset or liability for financial reporting purposes.**

A company considers a deferred tax asset or liability to be related to an asset or liability if reduction of the asset or liability causes the temporary difference to reverse or turn around. A company should classify a deferred tax liability or asset that is unrelated to an asset or liability for financial reporting, including a deferred tax asset related to a loss carryforward, according to the expected reversal date of the temporary difference.

To illustrate, assume that Morgan Inc. records bad debt expense using the allowance method for accounting purposes and the direct write-off method for tax purposes. It currently has Accounts Receivable and Allowance for Doubtful Accounts balances of $2 million and $100,000, respectively. In addition, given a 40 percent tax rate, Morgan has a debit balance in the Deferred Tax Asset account of $40,000 (40% × $100,000). It considers the $40,000 debit balance in the Deferred Tax Asset account to be related to the Accounts Receivable and the Allowance for Doubtful Accounts balances because collection or write-off of the receivables will cause the temporary difference to reverse. Therefore,

Morgan classifies the Deferred Tax Asset account as current, the same as the Accounts Receivable and Allowance for Doubtful Accounts balances.

In practice, most companies engage in a large number of transactions that give rise to deferred taxes. Companies should classify the balances in the deferred tax accounts on the balance sheet in two categories: one for the **net current amount**, and one for the **net noncurrent amount**. We summarize this procedure as follows.

1. ***Classify the amounts as current or non-current.*** If related to a specific asset or liability, classify the amounts in the same manner as the related asset or liability. If not related, classify them on the basis of the expected reversal date of the temporary difference.
2. ***Determine the net current amount*** by summing the various deferred tax assets and liabilities classified as current. If the net result is an asset, report it on the balance sheet as a current asset; if a liability, report it as a current liability.
3. ***Determine the net non-current amount*** by summing the various deferred tax assets and liabilities classified as noncurrent. If the net result is an asset, report it on the balance sheet as a noncurrent asset; if a liability, report it as a long-term liability.

To illustrate, assume that K. Scott Company has four deferred tax items at December 31, 2014. Illustration 19-39 shows an analysis of these four temporary differences as current or noncurrent.

ILLUSTRATION 19-39
Classification of Temporary Differences as Current or Noncurrent

Temporary Difference	Resulting Deferred Tax (Asset)	Resulting Deferred Tax Liability	Related Balance Sheet Account	Classification
1. Rent collected in advance: recognized when earned for accounting purposes and when received for tax purposes.	$(42,000)		Unearned Rent	Current
2. Use of straight-line depreciation for accounting purposes and accelerated depreciation for tax purposes.		$214,000	Equipment	Noncurrent
3. Recognition of profits on installment sales during period of sale for accounting purposes and during period of collection for tax purposes.		45,000	Installment Accounts Receivable	Current
4. Warranty liabilities: recognized for accounting purposes at time of sale; for tax purpose at time paid.	(12,000)		Estimated Liability under Warranties	Current
Totals	$(54,000)	$259,000		

K. Scott classifies as current a deferred tax asset of $9,000 ($42,000 + $12,000 − $45,000). It also reports as noncurrent a deferred tax liability of $214,000. Consequently, K. Scott's December 31, 2014, balance sheet reports deferred income taxes as shown in Illustration 19-40.

ILLUSTRATION 19-40
Balance Sheet Presentation of Deferred Income Taxes

Current assets	
Deferred tax asset	$ 9,000
Long-term liabilities	
Deferred tax liability	$214,000

As we indicated earlier, a deferred tax asset or liability **may not be related** to an asset or liability for financial reporting purposes. One example is an operating loss carryforward. In this case, a company records a deferred tax asset, but there is no related, identifiable asset or liability for financial reporting purposes. In these limited situations, deferred income taxes are classified according to the **expected reversal date** of the temporary difference. That is, a company should report the tax effect of any temporary difference reversing next year as current, and the remainder as noncurrent. If a deferred tax asset is noncurrent, a company should classify it in the "Other assets" section.

The total of all deferred tax liabilities, the total of all deferred tax assets, and the total valuation allowance should be disclosed. In addition, companies should disclose the following: (1) any net change during the year in the total valuation allowance, and (2) the types of temporary differences, carryforwards, or carrybacks that give rise to significant portions of deferred tax liabilities and assets.

International Perspective

IFRS requires that deferred tax assets and liabilities be classified as noncurrent, regardless of the classification of the underlying asset or liability.

Income taxes payable is reported as a current liability on the balance sheet. Corporations make estimated tax payments to the Internal Revenue Service quarterly. They record these estimated payments by a debit to Prepaid Income Taxes. As a result, the balance of the Income Taxes Payable offsets the balance of the Prepaid Income Taxes account when reporting income taxes on the balance sheet.

What do the numbers mean? *IMAGINATION AT WORK*

Here's one thing you can say that's true about U.S. corporate taxes: The statutory rate (35 percent at the federal level, 39.2 percent when you average in state rates) is the highest on earth (see the "What Do the Numbers Mean?" box on page 1131). Here's another thing you can say that's true about U.S. corporate taxes: The average effective tax rate is more like 25 percent, and many corporations generally pay much less than that. How do they do it? Take **Apple**, for example. It uses a tax structure known as the "Double Irish with a Dutch Sandwich," which reduces taxes by routing profits through Irish subsidiaries and the Netherlands and then to the Caribbean. As a result of using this tactic, Apple paid cash taxes of $3.3 billion around the world on its reported profits of $34.2 billion in a recent year, a tax rate of just 9.8 percent. **Google** uses the same strategy to reduce its overseas tax rate to 2.4 percent, the lowest of the top five U.S. technology companies by market capitalization, according to regulatory filings in six countries.

General Electric (GE) is generally viewed as the most skilled at reducing its tax burden. GE uses a maze of shelters, tax credits, and subsidiaries to pay far less than the stated tax rate. In a recent year, it reported worldwide profits of $14.2 billion, and said $5.1 billion of the total came from its operations in the United States. Its American tax bill? Zero. In fact, GE claimed a tax benefit of $3.2 billion. GE's giant tax department is viewed by some as the world's best tax law firm. Indeed, the company's slogan, "Imagination at Work," fits this department well. The team includes former officials not just from the Treasury, but also from the IRS and virtually all the tax-writing committees in Congress. The strategies employed by Apple, Google, and GE, as well as changes in tax laws that encouraged some businesses and professionals to file as individuals, have pushed down the corporate share of the nation's tax receipts from 30 percent of all federal revenue in the mid-1950s to 6.6 percent in 2009.

One IRS provision designed to curb excessive tax avoidance is the **alternative minimum tax (AMT)**. Companies compute their potential tax liability under the AMT, adjusting for various preference items that reduce their tax bills under the regular tax code. (Examples of such preference items are accelerated depreciation methods and the installment method for revenue recognition.) Companies must pay the higher of the two tax obligations computed under the AMT and the regular tax code. But, as indicated by the cases above, some profitable companies avoid high tax bills, even in the presence of the AMT. Indeed, a recent study by the Government Accounting Office found that roughly two-thirds of U.S. and foreign corporations paid no federal income taxes from 1998–2005. Many citizens and public-interest groups cite corporate avoidance of income taxes as a reason for more tax reform.

Sources: D. Kocieniewski, "G.E.'s Strategies Let It Avoid Taxes Altogether," *The New York Times* (March 24, 2011); and J. Fox, "Why Some Multinationals Pay Such Low Taxes," *HBR Blog Network* (March 27, 2012).

Income Statement

Gateway to the Profession

Expanded Discussion of Intraperiod Tax Allocation

Companies should allocate income tax expense (or benefit) to continuing operations, discontinued operations, extraordinary items, and prior period adjustments. This approach is referred to as intraperiod tax allocation.

In addition, companies should disclose the significant components of income tax expense attributable to continuing operations:

1. Current tax expense or benefit.
2. Deferred tax expense or benefit, exclusive of other components listed below.
3. Investment tax credits.
4. Government grants (if recognized as a reduction of income tax expense).
5. The benefits of operating loss carryforwards (resulting in a reduction of income tax expense).
6. Tax expense that results from allocating tax benefits either directly to paid-in capital or to reduce goodwill or other noncurrent intangible assets of an acquired entity.
7. Adjustments of a deferred tax liability or asset for enacted changes in tax laws or rates or a change in the tax status of a company.
8. Adjustments of the beginning-of-the-year balance of a valuation allowance because of a change in circumstances that causes a change in judgment about the realizability of the related deferred tax asset in future years.

In the notes, companies must also reconcile (using percentages or dollar amounts) income tax expense attributable to continuing operations with the amount that results from applying domestic federal statutory tax rates to pretax income from continuing significant reconciling items. Illustration 19-41 (page 1142) presents an example from the 2011 annual report of **PepsiCo, Inc.**

These income tax disclosures are required for several reasons:

1. ***Assessing quality of earnings.*** Many investors seeking to assess the quality of a company's earnings are interested in the reconciliation of pretax financial income to taxable income. Analysts carefully examine earnings that are enhanced by a favorable tax effect, particularly if the tax effect is nonrecurring. For example, the tax disclosure in Illustration 19-41 indicates that PepsiCo's effective tax rate increased from 23 percent in 2010 to 26.8 percent in 2011 (due to acquisitions of PBG and PAS and "other"). This decrease in the effective tax rate increased income for 2011.
2. ***Making better predictions of future cash flows.*** Examination of the deferred portion of income tax expense provides information as to whether taxes payable are likely to be higher or lower in the future. In PepsiCo's case, analysts expect future taxable amounts and higher tax payments, primarily from lower depreciation and amortization in the future. PepsiCo expects future deductible amounts and lower tax payments due to deductions for carryforwards, employee benefits, and state taxes. These deferred tax items indicate that actual tax payments for PepsiCo will be higher than the tax expense reported on the income statement in the future.[7]

[7]An article by R. P. Weber and J. E. Wheeler, "Using Income Tax Disclosures to Explore Significant Economic Transactions," *Accounting Horizons* (September 1992), discusses how analysts use deferred tax disclosures to assess the quality of earnings and to predict future cash flows.

ILLUSTRATION 19-41
Disclosure of Income Taxes—PepsiCo, Inc.

PepsiCo, Inc.
(in millions)

Current and deferred tax expense

Tax rate reconciliation

Deferred tax liabilities and deferred tax assets

Valuation allowance adjustments

Note 5—Income Taxes (in part)	2011	2010
Income before income taxes		
U.S.	$3,964	$4,008
Foreign	4,870	4,224
	$8,834	$8,232
Provision for income taxes		
Current: U.S. Federal	611	932
Foreign	882	728
State	124	137
	1,617	1,797
Deferred: U.S. Federal	789	78
Foreign	(88)	18
State	54	1
	755	97
	$2,372	$1,894
Tax rate reconciliation		
U.S. Federal statutory tax rate	35.0%	35.0%
State income tax, net of U.S. Federal tax benefit	1.3	1.1
Lower taxes on foreign results	(8.7)	(9.4)
Acquisitions of PBG and PAS	0	(3.1)
Other, net	(0.8)	(0.6)
Annual tax rate	26.8%	23.0%
Deferred tax liabilities		
Investments in noncontrolled affiliates	$ 41	$ 74
Debt guarantee of wholly owned subsidiary	828	828
Property, plant and equipment	2,466	1,984
Intangible assets other than nondeductible goodwill	4,297	3,726
Other	184	647
Gross deferred tax liabilities	7,816	7,259
Deferred tax assets		
Net carryforwards	1,373	1,264
Stock-based compensation	429	455
Retiree medical benefits	504	579
Other employee-related benefits	695	527
Pension benefits	545	291
Deductible state tax and interest benefits	339	320
Long-term debt obligations acquired	223	291
Other	822	904
Gross deferred tax assets	4,930	4,631
Valuation allowances	(1,264)	(875)
Deferred tax assets, net	3,666	3,756
Net deferred tax liabilities (assets)	$4,150	$3,503
Deferred taxes included within:		
Assets:		
Prepaid expenses and other current assets	$ 845	$ 554
Liabilities:		
Deferred income taxes	$4,995	$4,057
Analysis of valuation allowances		
Balance, beginning of year	$ 875	$ 586
(Benefit/provision)	464	75
Other additions/(deductions)	(75)	214
Balance, end of year	$1,264	$ 875

Carryforwards and allowances

Operating loss carryforwards totaling $10.0 billion at year-end 2011 are being carried forward in a number of foreign and state jurisdictions where we are permitted to use tax operating losses from prior periods to reduce future taxable income. These operating losses will expire as follows: $0.1 billion in 2012, $8.2 billion between 2013 and 2031 and $1.7 billion may be carried forward indefinitely. We establish valuation allowances for our deferred tax assets if, based on the available evidence, it is more likely than not that some portion or all of the deferred tax assets will not be realized.

3. ***Predicting future cash flows for operating loss carryforwards.*** Companies should disclose the amounts and expiration dates of any operating loss carryforwards for tax purposes. From this disclosure, analysts determine the amount of income that the company may recognize in the future on which it will pay no income tax. For example, the PepsiCo disclosure in Illustration 19-41 indicates that PepsiCo has $10.0 billion in net operating loss carryforwards that it can use to reduce future taxes. However, the valuation allowance indicates that $1.264 million of deferred tax assets may not be realized in the future.

Loss carryforwards can be valuable to a potential acquirer. For example, as mentioned earlier, **Yahoo!** has a substantial net operating loss carryforward. A potential acquirer would find Yahoo! more valuable as a result of these carryforwards. That is, the acquirer may be able to use these carryforwards to shield future income. However the acquiring company has to be careful because the structure of the deal may lead to a situation where the deductions will be severely limited.

Much the same issue arises in companies emerging from bankruptcy. In many cases, these companies have large NOLs but the value of the losses may be limited. This is because any gains related to the cancellation of liabilities in bankruptcy must be offset against the NOLs. For example, when **Kmart Holding Corp.** emerged from bankruptcy in early 2004, it disclosed NOL carryforwards approximating $3.8 billion. At the same time, Kmart disclosed cancellation of debt gains that reduced the value of the NOL carryforward. These reductions soured the merger between Kmart and **Sears Roebuck** because the cancellation of the indebtedness gains reduced the value of the Kmart carryforwards to the merged company by $3.74 billion.[8]

Evolving Issue UNCERTAIN TAX POSITIONS

Whenever there is a contingency, companies determine if the contingency is **probable** and can be reasonably estimated. If both of these criteria are met, the company records the contingency in the financial statements. These guidelines also apply to uncertain tax positions. **Uncertain tax positions** are tax positions for which the tax authorities may disallow a deduction in whole or in part. Uncertain tax positions often arise when a company takes an aggressive approach in its tax planning. Examples are instances in which the tax law is unclear or the company may believe that the risk of audit is low. Uncertain tax positions give rise to tax benefits either by reducing income tax expense or related payables or by increasing an income tax refund receivable or deferred tax asset.

Unfortunately, companies have not applied these provisions consistently in accounting and reporting of uncertain tax positions. Some companies have not recognized a tax benefit unless it is probable that the benefit will be realized and can be reasonably estimated. Other companies have used a lower threshold, such as that found in the existing authoritative literature. As we have learned, the lower threshold—described as "**more likely than not**"—means that the company believes it has at least a 51 percent chance that the uncertain tax position will pass muster with the taxing authorities. Thus, there has been diversity in practice concerning the accounting and reporting of uncertain tax positions.

As a result, the FASB has issued rules for companies to follow to determine whether it is "more likely than not" that tax positions will be sustained upon audit. **[3]** If the probability is more than 50 percent, companies may reduce their liability or increase their assets. If the probability is less than 50 percent, companies may not record the tax benefit. In determining "more likely than not," companies must assume that they will be audited by the tax authorities. If the recognition threshold is passed, companies must then estimate the amount to record as an adjustment to their tax assets and

[8]P. McConnell, J. Pegg, C. Senyak, and D. Mott, "The ABCs of NOLs," *Accounting Issues*, Bear Stearns Equity Research (June 2005). In addition, some U.S. banks hope to cash in tax credits by acquiring weaker banks with operating losses and housing credits, arising from the credit crisis. See D. Palletta, "Goldman Looks to Buy Fannie Tax Credits," *Wall Street Journal* (November 2, 2009). The IRS frowns on acquisitions done solely to obtain operating loss carryforwards. If it determines that the merger is solely tax-motivated, the IRS disallows the deductions. But because it is very difficult to determine whether a merger is or is not tax-motivated, the "purchase of operating loss carryforwards" continues.

liabilities. (This estimation process is complex and is beyond the scope of this textbook.)

Companies will experience varying financial statement effects upon adoption of these rules. Those with a history of conservative tax strategies may have their tax liabilities decrease or their tax assets increase. For example, PepsiCo recorded a $7 million increase to retained earnings upon adoption of the guidelines. Others that followed more aggressive tax planning may have to increase their liabilities or reduce their assets, with a resulting negative effect on net income.

REVIEW OF THE ASSET-LIABILITY METHOD

LEARNING OBJECTIVE 10
Indicate the basic principles of the asset-liability method.

The FASB believes that the **asset-liability method** (sometimes referred to as the **liability approach**) is the most consistent method for accounting for income taxes. One objective of this approach is to recognize the amount of taxes payable or refundable for the current year. A second objective is to recognize **deferred tax liabilities and assets** for the **future tax consequences** of events that have been recognized in the financial statements or tax returns.

To implement the objectives, companies apply some basic principles in accounting for income taxes at the date of the financial statements, as listed in Illustration 19-42. **[4]**

ILLUSTRATION 19-42
Basic Principles of the Asset-Liability Method

Basic Principles

a. A current tax liability or asset is recognized for the estimated taxes payable or refundable on the tax return for the current year.
b. A deferred tax liability or asset is recognized for the estimated future tax effects attributable to temporary differences and carryforwards.
c. The measurement of current and deferred tax liabilities and assets is based on provisions of the enacted tax law; the effects of future changes in tax laws or rates are not anticipated.
d. The measurement of deferred tax assets is reduced, if necessary, by the amount of any tax benefits that, based on available evidence, are not expected to be realized.

Illustration 19-43 diagrams the procedures for implementing the asset-liability method.

ILLUSTRATION 19-43
Procedures for Computing and Reporting Deferred Income Taxes

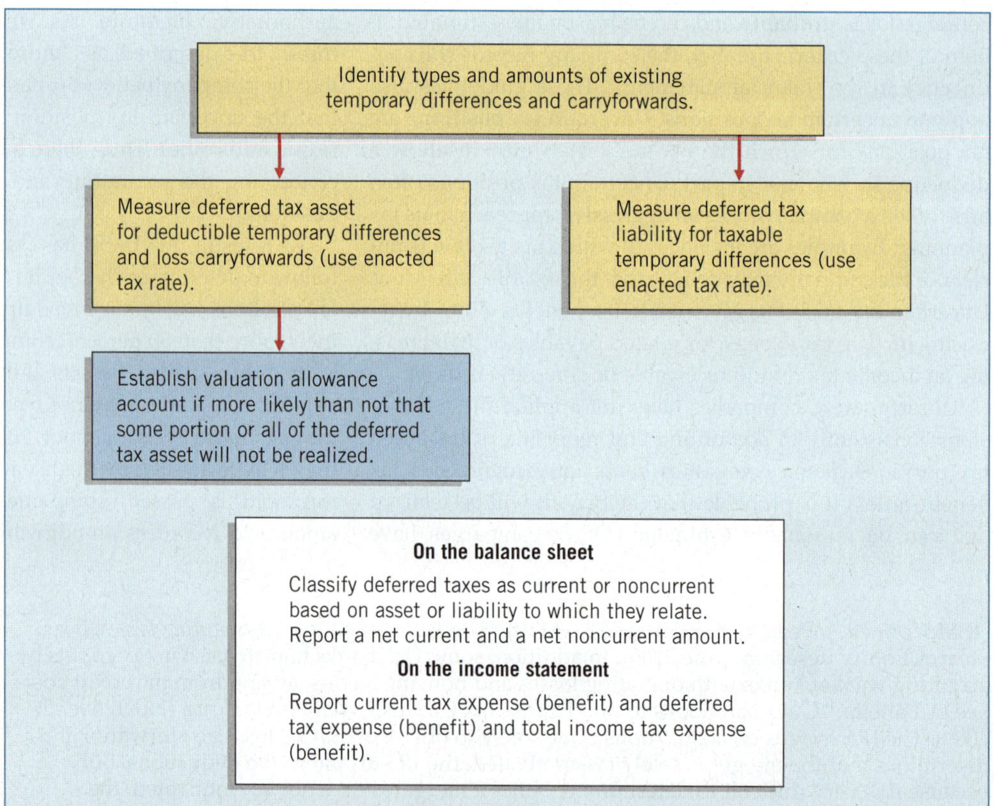

Gateway to the Profession
Discussion of Conceptual Approaches to Interperiod Tax Allocation

As an aid to understanding deferred income taxes, we provide the following glossary.

KEY DEFERRED INCOME TAX TERMS

CARRYBACKS. Deductions or credits that cannot be utilized on the tax return during a year and that may be carried back to reduce taxable income or taxes paid in a prior year. An **operating loss carryback** is an excess of tax deductions over gross income in a year. A **tax credit carryback** is the amount by which tax credits available for utilization exceed statutory limitations.

CARRYFORWARDS. Deductions or credits that cannot be utilized on the tax return during a year and that may be carried forward to reduce taxable income or taxes payable in a future year. An **operating loss carryforward** is an excess of tax deductions over gross income in a year. A **tax credit carryforward** is the amount by which tax credits available for utilization exceed statutory limitations.

CURRENT TAX EXPENSE (BENEFIT). The amount of income taxes paid or payable (or refundable) for a year as determined by applying the provisions of the enacted tax law to the taxable income or excess of deductions over revenues for that year.

DEDUCTIBLE TEMPORARY DIFFERENCE. Temporary differences that result in deductible amounts in future years when recovering or settling the related asset or liability, respectively.

DEFERRED TAX ASSET. The deferred tax consequences attributable to deductible temporary differences and carryforwards.

DEFERRED TAX CONSEQUENCES. The future effects on income taxes as measured by the enacted tax rate and provisions of the enacted tax law resulting from temporary differences and carryforwards at the end of the current year.

DEFERRED TAX EXPENSE (BENEFIT). The change during the year in a company's deferred tax liabilities and assets.

DEFERRED TAX LIABILITY. The deferred tax consequences attributable to taxable temporary differences.

INCOME TAXES. Domestic and foreign federal (national), state, and local (including franchise) taxes based on income.

INCOME TAXES CURRENTLY PAYABLE (REFUNDABLE). Refer to current tax expense (benefit).

INCOME TAX EXPENSE (BENEFIT). The sum of current tax expense (benefit) and deferred tax expense (benefit).

TAXABLE INCOME. The excess of taxable revenues over tax-deductible expenses and exemptions for the year as defined by the governmental taxing authority.

TAXABLE TEMPORARY DIFFERENCE. Temporary differences that result in taxable amounts in future years when recovering or settling the related asset or liability, respectively.

TAX-PLANNING STRATEGY. An action that meets certain criteria and that a company implements to realize a tax benefit for an operating loss or tax credit carryforward before it expires. Companies consider tax-planning strategies when assessing the need for and amount of a valuation allowance for deferred tax assets.

TEMPORARY DIFFERENCE. A difference between the tax basis of an asset or liability and its reported amount in the financial statements that will result in taxable or deductible amounts in future years when recovering or settling the reported amount of the asset or liability, respectively.

VALUATION ALLOWANCE. The portion of a deferred tax asset for which it is more likely than not that a company will not realize a tax benefit.

International Perspective

IFRS on income taxes is based on the same principles as GAAP—comprehensive recognition of deferred tax assets and liabilities.

You will want to read the **IFRS INSIGHTS** on pages 1175–1181 for discussion of IFRS related to income taxes.

KEY TERMS

alternative minimum tax (AMT), *1140*
asset-liability method, *1144*
average tax rate, *1130*
current tax expense (benefit), *1121, 1134*
deductible amounts, *1120*
deductible temporary difference, *1127*
deferred tax asset, *1123*
deferred tax expense (benefit), *1121, 1124*
deferred tax liability, *1120*
effective tax rate, *1130*
enacted tax rate, *1130*
Income Tax Refund Receivable, *1133*
loss carryback, *1132*
loss carryforward, *1132*
more likely than not, *1125*
net current amount, *1139*
net noncurrent amount, *1139*
net operating loss (NOL), *1132*
originating temporary difference, *1128*
permanent difference, *1128*
pretax financial income, *1118*
reversing difference, *1128*
taxable amounts, *1120*
taxable income, *1118*
taxable temporary difference, *1127*
tax effect (tax benefit), *1133*
temporary difference, *1120*
uncertain tax positions, *1143*
valuation allowance, *1125*

SUMMARY OF LEARNING OBJECTIVES

1 Identify differences between pretax financial income and taxable income. Companies compute pretax financial income (or income for book purposes) in accordance with generally accepted accounting principles. They compute taxable income (or income for tax purposes) in accordance with prescribed tax regulations. Because tax regulations and GAAP differ in many ways, so frequently do pretax financial income and taxable income. Differences may exist, for example, in the timing of revenue recognition and the timing of expense recognition.

2 Describe a temporary difference that results in future taxable amounts. Revenue recognized for book purposes in the period earned but deferred and reported as revenue for tax purposes when collected results in future taxable amounts. The future taxable amounts will occur in the periods the company recovers the receivable and reports the collections as revenue for tax purposes. This results in a deferred tax liability.

3 Describe a temporary difference that results in future deductible amounts. An accrued warranty expense that a company pays for and deducts for tax purposes, in a period later than the period in which it incurs and recognizes it for book purposes, results in future deductible amounts. The future deductible amounts will occur in the periods during which the company settles the related liability for book purposes. This results in a deferred tax asset.

4 Explain the purpose of a deferred tax asset valuation allowance. A deferred tax asset should be reduced by a valuation allowance if, based on all available evidence, it is more likely than not (a level of likelihood that is at least slightly more than 50 percent) that it will not realize some portion or all of the deferred tax asset. The company should carefully consider all available evidence, both positive and negative, to determine whether, based on the weight of available evidence, it needs a valuation allowance.

5 Describe the presentation of income tax expense in the income statement. Significant components of income tax expense should be disclosed in the income statement or in the notes to the financial statements. The most commonly encountered components are the current expense (or benefit) and the deferred expense (or benefit).

6 Describe various temporary and permanent differences. Examples of temporary differences are (1) revenues or gains that are taxable after recognition in financial income; (2) expenses or losses that are deductible after recognition in financial income; (3) revenues or gains that are taxable before recognition in financial income; and (4) expenses or losses that are deductible before recognition in financial income. Examples of permanent differences are (1) items recognized for financial reporting purposes but not for tax purposes, and (2) items recognized for tax purposes but not for financial reporting purposes.

7 Explain the effect of various tax rates and tax rate changes on deferred income taxes. Companies may use tax rates other than the current rate only after enactment of the future tax rates. When a change in the tax rate is enacted, a company should immediately recognize its effect on the deferred income tax accounts. The company reports the effects as an adjustment to income tax expense in the period of the change.

8 Apply accounting procedures for a loss carryback and a loss carryforward. A company may carry a net operating loss back two years and receive refunds for income taxes paid in those years. The loss is applied to the earlier year first and then to the second year. Any loss remaining after the two-year carryback may be carried forward up to 20 years to offset future taxable income. A company may forgo the loss carryback and use the loss carryforward, offsetting future taxable income for up to 20 years.

9 Describe the presentation of deferred income taxes in financial statements. Companies report deferred tax accounts on the balance sheet as assets and liabilities. These deferred tax accounts are classified as a net current and a net noncurrent amount. Companies classify an individual deferred tax liability or asset as current or noncurrent based on the classification of the related asset or liability for financial reporting. A deferred tax liability or asset that is not related to an asset or liability for financial reporting, including a deferred tax asset related to a loss carryforward, is classified according to the expected reversal date of the temporary difference.

10 Indicate the basic principles of the asset-liability method. Companies apply the following basic principles in accounting for income taxes at the date of the financial statements. (1) Recognize a current tax liability or asset for the estimated taxes payable or refundable on the tax return for the current year. (2) Recognize a deferred tax liability or asset for the estimated future tax effects attributable to temporary differences and carryforwards using the enacted tax rate. (3) Base the measurement of current and deferred tax liabilities and assets on provisions of the enacted tax law. (4) Reduce the measurement of deferred tax assets, if necessary, by the amount of any tax benefits that, based on available evidence, companies do not expect to realize.

APPENDIX 19A COMPREHENSIVE EXAMPLE OF INTERPERIOD TAX ALLOCATION

11 LEARNING OBJECTIVE
Understand and apply the concepts and procedures of interperiod tax allocation.

This appendix presents a comprehensive illustration of a deferred income tax problem with several temporary and permanent differences. The example follows one company through two complete years (2013 and 2014). **Study it carefully.** It should help you understand the concepts and procedures presented in the chapter.

FIRST YEAR—2013

Allman Company, which began operations at the beginning of 2013, produces various products on a contract basis. Each contract generates a gross profit of $80,000. Some of Allman's contracts provide for the customer to pay on an installment basis. Under these contracts, Allman collects one-fifth of the contract revenue in each of the following four years. For financial reporting purposes, the company recognizes gross profit in the year of completion (accrual basis); for tax purposes, Allman recognizes gross profit in the year cash is collected (installment basis).

Presented below is information related to Allman's operations for 2013.

1. In 2013, the company completed seven contracts that allow for the customer to pay on an installment basis. Allman recognized the related gross profit of $560,000 for financial reporting purposes. It reported only $112,000 of gross profit on installment sales on the 2013 tax return. The company expects future collections on the related installment receivables to result in taxable amounts of $112,000 in each of the next four years.
2. At the beginning of 2013, Allman Company purchased depreciable assets with a cost of $540,000. For financial reporting purposes, Allman depreciates these assets using the straight-line method over a six-year service life. For tax purposes, the assets fall in the five-year recovery class, and Allman uses the MACRS system. The depreciation schedules for both financial reporting and tax purposes are shown on page 1148.

Year	Depreciation for Financial Reporting Purposes	Depreciation for Tax Purposes	Difference
2013	$ 90,000	$108,000	$(18,000)
2014	90,000	172,800	(82,800)
2015	90,000	103,680	(13,680)
2016	90,000	62,208	27,792
2017	90,000	62,208	27,792
2018	90,000	31,104	58,896
	$540,000	$540,000	$ -0-

3. The company warrants its product for two years from the date of completion of a contract. During 2013, the product warranty liability accrued for financial reporting purposes was $200,000, and the amount paid for the satisfaction of warranty liability was $44,000. Allman expects to settle the remaining $156,000 by expenditures of $56,000 in 2014 and $100,000 in 2015.

4. In 2013, nontaxable municipal bond interest revenue was $28,000.

5. During 2013, nondeductible fines and penalties of $26,000 were paid.

6. Pretax financial income for 2013 amounts to $412,000.

7. Tax rates enacted before the end of 2013 were:

2013	50%
2014 and later years	40%

8. The accounting period is the calendar year.

9. The company is expected to have taxable income in all future years.

Taxable Income and Income Taxes Payable—2013

The first step is to determine Allman Company's income taxes payable for 2013 by calculating its taxable income. Illustration 19A-1 shows this computation.

ILLUSTRATION 19A-1
Computation of Taxable Income, 2013

Pretax financial income for 2013	$412,000
Permanent differences:	
Nontaxable revenue—municipal bond interest	(28,000)
Nondeductible expenses—fines and penalties	26,000
Temporary differences:	
Excess gross profit per books ($560,000 – $112,000)	(448,000)
Excess depreciation per tax ($108,000 – $90,000)	(18,000)
Excess warranty expense per books ($200,000 – $44,000)	156,000
Taxable income for 2013	$100,000

Allman computes income taxes payable on taxable income for $100,000 as follows.

ILLUSTRATION 19A-2
Computation of Income Taxes Payable, End of 2013

Taxable income for 2013	$100,000
Tax rate	50%
Income taxes payable (current tax expense) for 2013	$ 50,000

Computing Deferred Income Taxes—End of 2013

The schedule in Illustration 19A-3 summarizes the temporary differences and the resulting future taxable and deductible amounts.

ILLUSTRATION 19A-3
Schedule of Future Taxable and Deductible Amounts, End of 2013

	Future Years					
	2014	2015	2016	2017	2018	Total
Future taxable (deductible) amounts:						
Installment sales	$112,000	$112,000	$112,000	$112,000		$448,000
Depreciation	(82,800)	(13,680)	27,792	27,792	$58,896	18,000
Warranty costs	(56,000)	(100,000)				(156,000)

Allman computes the amounts of deferred income taxes to be reported at the end of 2013 as shown in Illustration 19A-4.

ILLUSTRATION 19A-4
Computation of Deferred Income Taxes, End of 2013

Temporary Difference	Future Taxable (Deductible) Amounts	Tax Rate	Deferred Tax (Asset)	Deferred Tax Liability
Installment sales	$448,000	40%		$179,200
Depreciation	18,000	40%		7,200
Warranty costs	(156,000)	40%	$(62,400)	
Totals	$310,000		$(62,400)	$186,400*

*Because only a single tax rate is involved in all relevant years, these totals can be reconciled: $310,000 × 40% = ($62,400) + $186,400.

A temporary difference is caused by the use of the accrual basis for financial reporting purposes and the installment method for tax purposes. This temporary difference will result in future taxable amounts and hence a deferred tax liability. Because of the installment contracts completed in 2013, a temporary difference of $448,000 originates that will reverse in equal amounts over the next four years. The company expects to have taxable income in all future years, and there is only one enacted tax rate applicable to all future years. Allman uses that rate (40 percent) to compute the entire deferred tax liability resulting from this temporary difference.

The temporary difference caused by different depreciation policies for books and for tax purposes originates over three years and then reverses over three years. This difference will cause deductible amounts in 2014 and 2015 and taxable amounts in 2016, 2017, and 2018. These amounts sum to a net future taxable amount of $18,000 (which is the cumulative temporary difference at the end of 2013). Because the company expects to have taxable income in all future years and because there is only one tax rate enacted for all of the relevant future years, Allman applies that rate to the net future taxable amount to determine the related net deferred tax liability.

The third temporary difference is caused by different methods of accounting for warranties. This difference will result in deductible amounts in each of the two future years it takes to reverse. Because the company expects to report a positive income on all future tax returns and because there is only one tax rate enacted for each of the relevant future years, Allman uses that 40 percent rate to calculate the resulting deferred tax asset.

Deferred Tax Expense (Benefit) and the Journal Entry to Record Income Taxes—2013

To determine the deferred tax expense (benefit), we need to compare the beginning and ending balances of the deferred income tax accounts. Illustration 19A-5 (on page 1150) shows that computation.

ILLUSTRATION 19A-5
Computation of Deferred Tax Expense (Benefit), 2013

Deferred tax asset at the end of 2013	$ 62,400
Deferred tax asset at the beginning of 2013	–0–
Deferred tax expense (benefit)	$ (62,400)
Deferred tax liability at the end of 2013	$186,400
Deferred tax liability at the beginning of 2013	–0–
Deferred tax expense (benefit)	$186,400

The $62,400 increase in the deferred tax asset causes a deferred tax benefit to be reported in the income statement. The $186,400 increase in the deferred tax liability during 2013 results in a deferred tax expense. These two amounts **net** to a deferred tax expense of $124,000 for 2013.

ILLUSTRATION 19A-6
Computation of Net Deferred Tax Expense, 2013

Deferred tax expense (benefit)	$ (62,400)
Deferred tax expense (benefit)	186,400
Net deferred tax expense for 2013	$124,000

Allman then computes the total income tax expense as follows.

ILLUSTRATION 19A-7
Computation of Total Income Tax Expense, 2013

Current tax expense for 2013	$ 50,000
Deferred tax expense for 2013	124,000
Income tax expense (total) for 2013	$174,000

Allman records income taxes payable, deferred income taxes, and income tax expense as follows.

Income Tax Expense	174,000	
Deferred Tax Asset	62,400	
Income Taxes Payable		50,000
Deferred Tax Liability		186,400

Financial Statement Presentation—2013

Companies should classify deferred tax assets and liabilities as current and noncurrent on the balance sheet based on the classifications of related assets and liabilities. Multiple categories of deferred taxes are classified into a net current amount and a net noncurrent amount. Illustration 19A-8 shows the classification of Allman's deferred tax accounts at the end of 2013.

ILLUSTRATION 19A-8
Classification of Deferred Tax Accounts, End of 2013

Temporary Difference	Resulting Deferred Tax (Asset)	Resulting Deferred Tax Liability	Related Balance Sheet Account	Classification
Installment sales		$179,200	Installment Receivable	Current
Depreciation		7,200	Plant Assets	Noncurrent
Warranty costs	$(62,400)		Warranty Obligation	Current
Totals	$(62,400)	$186,400		

For the first temporary difference, there is a related asset on the balance sheet, installment accounts receivable. Allman classifies that asset as current because it has a trade practice of selling to customers on an installment basis. Allman therefore classifies the resulting deferred tax liability as a current liability.

Certain assets on the balance sheet are related to the depreciation difference—the property, plant, and equipment being depreciated. Allman would classify the plant assets as noncurrent. Therefore, it also classifies the resulting deferred tax liability as noncurrent. Since the company's operating cycle is at least four years in length, Allman classifies the entire $156,000 warranty obligation as a current liability. Thus, it also classifies the related deferred tax asset of $62,400 as current.[9]

The balance sheet at the end of 2013 reports the following amounts.

ILLUSTRATION 19A-9
Balance Sheet Presentation of Deferred Taxes, 2013

Current liabilities	
Income taxes payable	$ 50,000
Deferred tax liability ($179,200 − $62,400)	116,800
Long-term liabilities	
Deferred tax liability	$ 7,200

Allman's income statement for 2013 reports the following.

ILLUSTRATION 19A-10
Income Statement Presentation of Income Tax Expense, 2013

Income before income taxes		$412,000
Income tax expense		
Current	$ 50,000	
Deferred	124,000	174,000
Net income		$238,000

SECOND YEAR—2014

1. During 2014, Allman collected $112,000 from customers for the receivables arising from contracts completed in 2013. The company expects recovery of the remaining receivables to result in taxable amounts of $112,000 in each of the following three years.
2. In 2014, the company completed four new contracts that allow for the customer to pay on an installment basis. These installment sales created new installment receivables. Future collections of these receivables will result in reporting gross profit of $64,000 for tax purposes in each of the next four years.
3. During 2014, Allman continued to depreciate the assets acquired in 2013 according to the depreciation schedules appearing on page 1148. Thus, depreciation amounted to $90,000 for financial reporting purposes and $172,800 for tax purposes.
4. An analysis at the end of 2014, of the product warranty liability account, showed the following details.

Balance of liability at beginning of 2014	$156,000
Expense for 2014 income statement purposes	180,000
Amount paid for contracts completed in 2013	(56,000)
Amount paid for contracts completed in 2014	(50,000)
Balance of liability at end of 2014	$230,000

[9]If Allman's operating cycle were less than one year in length, the company would expect to settle $56,000 of the warranty obligation within one year of the December 31, 2013, balance sheet and would use current assets to do so. Thus, $56,000 of the warranty obligation would be a current liability and the remaining $100,000 warranty obligation would be a long-term (noncurrent) liability. This would mean that Allman would classify $22,400 ($56,000 × 40%) of the related deferred tax asset as a current asset, and $40,000 ($100,000 × 40%) of the deferred tax asset as a noncurrent asset. *In doing homework problems, unless it is evident otherwise, assume a company's operating cycle is not longer than one year.*

The balance of the liability is expected to require expenditures in the future as follows.

$100,000 in 2015 due to 2013 contracts
$ 50,000 in 2015 due to 2014 contracts
$ 80,000 in 2016 due to 2014 contracts
$230,000

5. During 2014, nontaxable municipal bond interest revenue was $24,000.
6. Allman accrued a loss of $172,000 for financial reporting purposes because of pending litigation. This amount is not tax-deductible until the period the loss is realized, which the company estimates to be 2022.
7. Pretax financial income for 2014 amounts to $504,800.
8. The enacted tax rates still in effect are:

2013	50%
2014 and later years	40%

Taxable Income and Income Taxes Payable—2014

Allman computes taxable income for 2014 as follows.

ILLUSTRATION 19A-11
Computation of Taxable Income, 2014

Pretax financial income for 2014	$504,800
Permanent difference:	
Nontaxable revenue—municipal bond interest	(24,000)
Reversing temporary differences:	
Collection on 2013 installment sales	112,000
Payments on warranties from 2013 contracts	(56,000)
Originating temporary differences:	
Excess gross profit per books—2014 contracts	(256,000)
Excess depreciation per tax	(82,800)
Excess warranty expense per books—2014 contracts	130,000
Loss accrual per books	172,000
Taxable income for 2014	$500,000

Income taxes payable for 2014 are as follows.

ILLUSTRATION 19A-12
Computation of Income Taxes Payable, End of 2014

Taxable income for 2014	$500,000
Tax rate	40%
Income taxes payable (current tax expense) for 2014	$200,000

Computing Deferred Income Taxes—End of 2014

The schedule in Illustration 19A-13 summarizes the temporary differences existing at the end of 2014 and the resulting future taxable and deductible amounts.

ILLUSTRATION 19A-13
Schedule of Future Taxable and Deductible Amounts, End of 2014

	Future Years					
	2015	2016	2017	2018	2022	Total
Future taxable (deductible) amounts:						
Installment sales—2013	$112,000	$112,000	$112,000			$336,000
Installment sales—2014	64,000	64,000	64,000	$64,000		256,000
Depreciation	(13,680)	27,792	27,792	58,896		100,800
Warranty costs	(150,000)	(80,000)				(230,000)
Loss accrual					$(172,000)	(172,000)

Allman computes the amounts of deferred income taxes to be reported at the end of 2014 as follows.

ILLUSTRATION 19A-14
Computation of Deferred Income Taxes, End of 2014

Temporary Difference	Future Taxable (Deductible) Amounts	Tax Rate	Deferred Tax (Asset)	Deferred Tax Liability
Installment sales	$592,000*	40%		$236,800
Depreciation	100,800	40%		40,320
Warranty costs	(230,000)	40%	$ (92,000)	
Loss accrual	(172,000)	40%	(68,800)	
Totals	$290,800		$(160,800)	$277,120**

*Cumulative temporary difference = $336,000 + $256,000
**Because of a flat tax rate, these totals can be reconciled: $290,800 × 40% = $(160,800) + $277,120

Deferred Tax Expense (Benefit) and the Journal Entry to Record Income Taxes—2014

To determine the deferred tax expense (benefit), Allman must compare the beginning and ending balances of the deferred income tax accounts, as shown in Illustration 19A-15.

ILLUSTRATION 19A-15
Computation of Deferred Tax Expense (Benefit), 2014

Deferred tax asset at the end of 2014	$160,800
Deferred tax asset at the beginning of 2014	62,400
Deferred tax expense (benefit)	$ (98,400)
Deferred tax liability at the end of 2014	$277,120
Deferred tax liability at the beginning of 2014	186,400
Deferred tax expense (benefit)	$ 90,720

The deferred tax expense (benefit) and the total income tax expense for 2014 are, therefore, as follows.

ILLUSTRATION 19A-16
Computation of Total Income Tax Expense, 2014

Deferred tax expense (benefit)	$ (98,400)
Deferred tax expense (benefit)	90,720
Deferred tax benefit for 2014	(7,680)
Current tax expense for 2014	200,000
Income tax expense (total) for 2014	$192,320

The deferred tax expense of $90,720 and the deferred tax benefit of $98,400 net to a deferred tax benefit of $7,680 for 2014.

Allman records income taxes for 2014 with the following journal entry.

Income Tax Expense	192,320	
Deferred Tax Asset	98,400	
Income Taxes Payable		200,000
Deferred Tax Liability		90,720

Financial Statement Presentation—2014

Illustration 19A-17 (on page 1154) shows the classification of Allman's deferred tax accounts at the end of 2014.

ILLUSTRATION 19A-17
Classification of Deferred Tax Accounts, End of 2014

Temporary Difference	Resulting Deferred Tax (Asset)	Liability	Related Balance Sheet Account	Classification
Installment sales		$236,800	Installment Receivables	Current
Depreciation		40,320	Plant Assets	Noncurrent
Warranty costs	$ (92,000)		Warranty Obligation	Current
Loss accrual	(68,800)		Litigation Obligation	Noncurrent
Totals	$(160,800)	$277,120		

The new temporary difference introduced in 2014 (due to the litigation loss accrual) results in a litigation obligation that is classified as a long-term liability. Thus, the related deferred tax asset is noncurrent.

Allman's balance sheet at the end of 2014 reports the following amounts.

ILLUSTRATION 19A-18
Balance Sheet Presentation of Deferred Taxes, End of 2014

Other assets (noncurrent)	
Deferred tax asset ($68,800 – $40,320)	$ 28,480
Current liabilities	
Income taxes payable	$200,000
Deferred tax liability ($236,800 – $92,000)	144,800

The income statement for 2014 reports the following.

ILLUSTRATION 19A-19
Income Statement Presentation of Income Tax Expense, 2014

Income before income taxes		$504,800
Income tax expense		
Current	$200,000	
Deferred	(7,680)	192,320
Net income		$312,480

SUMMARY OF LEARNING OBJECTIVE FOR APPENDIX 19A

11 Understand and apply the concepts and procedures of interperiod tax allocation. Accounting for deferred taxes involves the following steps. (1) Calculate taxable income and income taxes payable for the year. (2) Compute deferred income taxes at the end of the year. (3) Determine deferred tax expense (benefit) and make the journal entry to record income taxes. (4) Classify deferred tax assets and liabilities as current or noncurrent in the financial statements.

DEMONSTRATION PROBLEM

Johnny Bravo Company began operations in 2014 and has provided the following information.

1. Pretax financial income for 2014 is $100,000.
2. The tax rate enacted for 2014 and future years is 40%.
3. Differences between the 2014 income statement and tax return are listed below.
   (a) Warranty expense accrued for financial reporting purposes amounts to $5,000. Warranty deductions per the tax return amount to $2,000.

(b) Gross profit on construction contracts using the percentage-of-completion method for books amounts to $92,000. Gross profit on construction contracts for tax purposes amounts to $62,000.
(c) Depreciation of property, plant, and equipment for financial reporting purposes amounts to $60,000. Depreciation of these assets amounts to $80,000 for the tax return.
(d) A $3,500 fine paid for violation of pollution laws was deducted in computing pretax financial income.
(e) Interest revenue earned on an investment in tax-exempt municipal bonds amounts to $1,400.
Assume (a) is short-term in nature; assume (b) and (c) are long-term in nature.

4. Taxable income is expected for the next few years.

Instructions

(a) Compute taxable income for 2014.
(b) Compute the deferred taxes at December 31, 2014, that relate to the temporary differences described above.
(c) Prepare the journal entry to record income tax expense, deferred taxes, and income taxes payable for 2014.
(d) Draft the income tax expense section of the income statement, beginning with "Income before income taxes."
(e) Assume that in 2015 Johnny Bravo reported a pretax operating loss of $100,000. There were no other temporary or permanent differences in tax and book income for 2015. Prepare the journal entry to record income tax expense for 2015. Johnny Bravo expects to return to profitability in 2016.

Solution

(a)

Pretax financial income	$100,000
Permanent differences	
Fine for pollution	3,500
Tax-exempt interest	(1,400)
Originating temporary differences	
Excess warranty expense per books ($5,000 – $2,000)	3,000
Excess construction profits per books ($92,000 – $62,000)	(30,000)
Excess depreciation per tax ($80,000 – $60,000)	(20,000)
Taxable income	$ 55,100

(b)

Temporary Difference	Future Taxable (Deductible) Amounts	Tax Rate	Deferred Tax (Asset)	Deferred Tax Liability
Warranty costs	$ (3,000)	40%	$(1,200)	
Construction contracts	30,000	40%		$12,000
Depreciation	20,000	40%		8,000
Totals	$47,000		$(1,200)	$20,000*

(c)

Income Tax Expense	40,840	
Deferred Tax Asset	1,200	
Deferred Tax Liability		20,000
Income Taxes Payable		22,040

Taxable income for 2014 [from part (a)]	$55,100
Tax rate	40%
Income taxes payable for 2014	$22,040
Deferred tax liability at the end of 2014 [from part (b)]	$20,000
Deferred tax liability at the beginning of 2014	–0–
Deferred tax expense for 2014	$20,000
Deferred tax asset at the end of 2014 [from part (b)]	$ 1,200
Deferred tax asset at the beginning of 2014	–0–
Deferred tax benefit for 2014	$ (1,200)

(d)

Income before income taxes		$100,000
Income tax expense		
Current	$22,040	
Deferred	18,800	40,840
Net income		$ 59,160

(e)

Income Tax Refund Receivable*	22,040	
Deferred Tax Asset**	17,960	
Benefit from Operating Loss Carryback		22,040
Benefit from Operating Loss Carryforward		17,960

2015 Loss	$100,000
*Carryback	(55,100) × 40% = $22,040 refund
**Carryforward	$ 44,900 × 40% = $17,960 deferred tax asset

No valuation allowance is needed since Johnny Bravo is expected to return to profitability in 2016. This is positive evidence that the deferred tax asset will be realized.

FASB CODIFICATION

FASB Codification References

[1] FASB ASC 740-10-30-18. [Predecessor literature: "Accounting for Income Taxes," *Statement of Financial Accounting Standards No. 109* (Norwalk, Conn.: FASB, 1992).]

[2] FASB ASC 740-10-30-21 & 22. [Predecessor literature: "Accounting for Income Taxes," *Statement of Financial Accounting Standards No. 109* (Norwalk, Conn.: FASB, 1992), paras. 23 and 24.]

[3] FASB ASC 740-10-25-6. [Predecessor literature: "Accounting for Uncertainty in Income Taxes," *FASB Interpretation No. 48* (Norwalk, Conn.: FASB, 2006).]

[4] FASB ASC 740-10-05. [Predecessor literature: "Accounting for Income Taxes," *Statement of Financial Accounting Standards No. 109* (Norwalk, Conn.: FASB, 1992), paras. 6 and 8.]

Exercises

If your school has a subscription to the FASB Codification, go to *http://aaahq.org/ascLogin.cfm* to log in and prepare responses to the following. Provide Codification references for your responses.

CE19-1 Access the glossary ("Master Glossary") to answer the following.

(a) What is a deferred tax asset?
(b) What is taxable income?
(c) What is the definition of valuation allowance?
(d) What is a deferred tax liability?

CE19-2 What are the two basic requirements applied to the measurement of current and deferred income taxes at the date of the financial statements?

CE19-3 A company wishes to conduct business in a foreign country that attracts businesses by granting "holidays" from income taxes for a certain period of time. Would the company have to disclose this "holiday" to the SEC? If so, what information must be disclosed?

CE19-4 When is a company allowed to initially recognize the financial statement effects of a tax position?

An additional Codification case can be found in the Using Your Judgment section, on page 1174.

Be sure to check the book's companion website for a Review and Analysis Exercise, with solution.

WileyPLUS Brief Exercises, Exercises, Problems, and many more learning and assessment tools and resources are available for practice in WileyPLUS.

QUESTIONS

1. Explain the difference between pretax financial income and taxable income.
2. What are the two objectives of accounting for income taxes?
3. Interest on municipal bonds is referred to as a permanent difference when determining the proper amount to report for deferred taxes. Explain the meaning of permanent differences, and give two other examples.
4. Explain the meaning of a temporary difference as it relates to deferred tax computations, and give three examples.
5. Differentiate between an originating temporary difference and a reversing difference.
6. The book basis of depreciable assets for Erwin Co. is $900,000, and the tax basis is $700,000 at the end of 2015. The enacted tax rate is 34% for all periods. Determine the amount of deferred taxes to be reported on the balance sheet at the end of 2015.
7. Roth Inc. has a deferred tax liability of $68,000 at the beginning of 2015. At the end of 2015, it reports accounts receivable on the books at $90,000 and the tax basis at zero (its only temporary difference). If the enacted tax rate is 34% for all periods, and income taxes payable for the period is $230,000, determine the amount of total income tax expense to report for 2015.
8. What is the difference between a future taxable amount and a future deductible amount? When is it appropriate to record a valuation account for a deferred tax asset?
9. Pretax financial income for Lake Inc. is $300,000, and its taxable income is $100,000 for 2015. Its only temporary difference at the end of the period relates to a $70,000 difference due to excess depreciation for tax purposes. If the tax rate is 40% for all periods, compute the amount of income tax expense to report in 2015. No deferred income taxes existed at the beginning of the year.
10. How are deferred tax assets and deferred tax liabilities reported on the balance sheet?
11. Describe the procedures involved in segregating various deferred tax amounts into current and noncurrent categories.
12. How is it determined whether deferred tax amounts are considered to be "related" to specific asset or liability amounts?
13. At the end of the year, Falabella Co. has pretax financial income of $550,000. Included in the $550,000 is $70,000 interest income on municipal bonds, $25,000 fine for dumping hazardous waste, and depreciation of $60,000. Depreciation for tax purposes is $45,000. Compute income taxes payable, assuming the tax rate is 30% for all periods.
14. Addison Co. has one temporary difference at the beginning of 2014 of $500,000. The deferred tax liability established for this amount is $150,000, based on a tax rate of 30%. The temporary difference will provide the following taxable amounts: $100,000 in 2015, $200,000 in 2016, and $200,000 in 2017. If a new tax rate for 2017 of 20% is enacted into law at the end of 2014, what is the journal entry necessary in 2014 (if any) to adjust deferred taxes?
15. What are some of the reasons that the components of income tax expense should be disclosed and a reconciliation between the effective tax rate and the statutory tax rate be provided?
16. Differentiate between "loss carryback" and "loss carryforward." Which can be accounted for with the greater certainty when it arises? Why?
17. What are the possible treatments for tax purposes of a net operating loss? What are the circumstances that determine the option to be applied? What is the proper treatment of a net operating loss for financial reporting purposes?
18. What controversy relates to the accounting for net operating loss carryforwards?
19. What is an uncertain tax position, and what are the general guidelines for accounting for uncertain tax positions?

BRIEF EXERCISES

1 2 **BE19-1** In 2014, Amirante Corporation had pretax financial income of $168,000 and taxable income of $120,000. The difference is due to the use of different depreciation methods for tax and accounting purposes. The effective tax rate is 40%. Compute the amount to be reported as income taxes payable at December 31, 2014.

1 2 **BE19-2** Oxford Corporation began operations in 2014 and reported pretax financial income of $225,000 for the year. Oxford's tax depreciation exceeded its book depreciation by $40,000. Oxford's tax rate for 2014 and years thereafter is 30%. In its December 31, 2014, balance sheet, what amount of deferred tax liability should be reported?

9 **BE19-3** Using the information from BE19-2, assume this is the only difference between Oxford's pretax financial income and taxable income. Prepare the journal entry to record the income tax expense, deferred income taxes, and income taxes payable, and show how the deferred tax liability will be classified on the December 31, 2014, balance sheet.

2 5 **BE19-4** At December 31, 2014, Appaloosa Corporation had a deferred tax liability of $25,000. At December 31, 2015, the deferred tax liability is $42,000. The corporation's 2015 current tax expense is $48,000. What amount should Appaloosa report as total 2015 income tax expense?

1 3 **BE19-5** At December 31, 2014, Suffolk Corporation had an estimated warranty liability of $105,000 for accounting purposes and $0 for tax purposes. (The warranty costs are not deductible until paid.) The effective tax rate is 40%. Compute the amount Suffolk should report as a deferred tax asset at December 31, 2014.

3 5 **BE19-6** At December 31, 2014, Percheron Inc. had a deferred tax asset of $30,000. At December 31, 2015, the deferred tax asset is $59,000. The corporation's 2015 current tax expense is $61,000. What amount should Percheron report as total 2015 income tax expense?

4 **BE19-7** At December 31, 2014, Hillyard Corporation has a deferred tax asset of $200,000. After a careful review of all available evidence, it is determined that it is more likely than not that $60,000 of this deferred tax asset will not be realized. Prepare the necessary journal entry.

5 **BE19-8** Mitchell Corporation had income before income taxes of $195,000 in 2014. Mitchell's current income tax expense is $48,000, and deferred income tax expense is $30,000. Prepare Mitchell's 2014 income statement, beginning with Income before income taxes.

2 3 **BE19-9** Shetland Inc. had pretax financial income of $154,000 in 2014. Included in the computation of that amount is insurance expense of $4,000 which is not deductible for tax purposes. In addition, depreciation for tax purposes exceeds accounting depreciation by $10,000. Prepare Shetland's journal entry to record 2014 taxes, assuming a tax rate of 45%.

2 **BE19-10** Clydesdale Corporation has a cumulative temporary difference related to depreciation of $580,000 at December 31, 2014. This difference will reverse as follows: 2015, $42,000; 2016, $244,000; and 2017, $294,000. Enacted tax rates are 34% for 2015 and 2016, and 40% for 2017. Compute the amount Clydesdale should report as a deferred tax liability at December 31, 2014.

7 **BE19-11** At December 31, 2014, Fell Corporation had a deferred tax liability of $680,000, resulting from future taxable amounts of $2,000,000 and an enacted tax rate of 34%. In May 2015, a new income tax act is signed into law that raises the tax rate to 40% for 2015 and future years. Prepare the journal entry for Fell to adjust the deferred tax liability.

8 **BE19-12** Conlin Corporation had the following tax information.

Year	Taxable Income	Tax Rate	Taxes Paid
2012	$300,000	35%	$105,000
2013	$325,000	30%	$ 97,500
2014	$400,000	30%	$120,000

In 2015, Conlin suffered a net operating loss of $480,000, which it elected to carry back. The 2015 enacted tax rate is 29%. Prepare Conlin's entry to record the effect of the loss carryback.

8 **BE19-13** Rode Inc. incurred a net operating loss of $500,000 in 2014. Combined income for 2012 and 2013 was $350,000. The tax rate for all years is 40%. Rode elects the carryback option. Prepare the journal entries to record the benefits of the loss carryback and the loss carryforward. Rode expects to return to profitability in 2015.

4 8 **BE19-14** Use the information for Rode Inc. given in BE19-13. Assume that it is more likely than not that the entire net operating loss carryforward will not be realized in future years. Prepare all the journal entries necessary at the end of 2014.

9 **BE19-15** Youngman Corporation has temporary differences at December 31, 2014, that result in the following deferred taxes.

Deferred tax liability—current	$38,000
Deferred tax asset—current	$62,000
Deferred tax liability—noncurrent	$96,000
Deferred tax asset—noncurrent	$27,000

Indicate how these balances would be presented in Youngman's December 31, 2014, balance sheet.

EXERCISES

2 5 **E19-1 (One Temporary Difference, Future Taxable Amounts, One Rate, No Beginning Deferred Taxes)** South Carolina Corporation has one temporary difference at the end of 2014 that will reverse and cause taxable amounts of $55,000 in 2015, $60,000 in 2016, and $65,000 in 2017. South Carolina's pretax financial income for 2014 is $300,000, and the tax rate is 30% for all years. There are no deferred taxes at the beginning of 2014.

Instructions

(a) Compute taxable income and income taxes payable for 2014.
(b) Prepare the journal entry to record income tax expense, deferred income taxes, and income taxes payable for 2014.
(c) Prepare the income tax expense section of the income statement for 2014, beginning with the line "Income before income taxes."

2 **E19-2 (Two Differences, No Beginning Deferred Taxes, Tracked through 2 Years)** The following information is available for Wenger Corporation for 2013 (its first year of operations).

1. Excess of tax depreciation over book depreciation, $40,000. This $40,000 difference will reverse equally over the years 2014–2017.
2. Deferral, for book purposes, of $20,000 of rent received in advance. The rent will be recognized in 2014.
3. Pretax financial income, $300,000.
4. Tax rate for all years, 40%.

Instructions

(a) Compute taxable income for 2013.
(b) Prepare the journal entry to record income tax expense, deferred income taxes, and income taxes payable for 2013.
(c) Prepare the journal entry to record income tax expense, deferred income taxes, and income taxes payable for 2014, assuming taxable income of $325,000.

2 5 **E19-3 (One Temporary Difference, Future Taxable Amounts, One Rate, Beginning Deferred Taxes)** Bandung Corporation began 2014 with a $92,000 balance in the Deferred Tax Liability account. At the end of 2014, the related cumulative temporary difference amounts to $350,000, and it will reverse evenly over the next 2 years. Pretax accounting income for 2014 is $525,000, the tax rate for all years is 40%, and taxable income for 2014 is $405,000.

Instructions

(a) Compute income taxes payable for 2014.
(b) Prepare the journal entry to record income tax expense, deferred income taxes, and income taxes payable for 2014.
(c) Prepare the income tax expense section of the income statement for 2014 beginning with the line "Income before income taxes."

2 3 5 6 **E19-4 (Three Differences, Compute Taxable Income, Entry for Taxes)** Zurich Company reports pretax financial income of $70,000 for 2014. The following items cause taxable income to be different than pretax financial income.

1. Depreciation on the tax return is greater than depreciation on the income statement by $16,000.
2. Rent collected on the tax return is greater than rent recognized on the income statement by $22,000.
3. Fines for pollution appear as an expense of $11,000 on the income statement.

Zurich's tax rate is 30% for all years, and the company expects to report taxable income in all future years. There are no deferred taxes at the beginning of 2014.

Instructions

(a) Compute taxable income and income taxes payable for 2014.
(b) Prepare the journal entry to record income tax expense, deferred income taxes, and income taxes payable for 2014.
(c) Prepare the income tax expense section of the income statement for 2014, beginning with the line "Income before income taxes."
(d) Compute the effective income tax rate for 2014.

2 3 5 **E19-5 (Two Temporary Differences, One Rate, Beginning Deferred Taxes)** The following facts relate to Krung Thep Corporation.

1. Deferred tax liability, January 1, 2014, $40,000.
2. Deferred tax asset, January 1, 2014, $0.
3. Taxable income for 2014, $95,000.
4. Pretax financial income for 2014, $200,000.
5. Cumulative temporary difference at December 31, 2014, giving rise to future taxable amounts, $240,000.
6. Cumulative temporary difference at December 31, 2014, giving rise to future deductible amounts, $35,000.
7. Tax rate for all years, 40%.
8. The company is expected to operate profitably in the future.

Instructions

(a) Compute income taxes payable for 2014.
(b) Prepare the journal entry to record income tax expense, deferred income taxes, and income taxes payable for 2014.
(c) Prepare the income tax expense section of the income statement for 2014, beginning with the line "Income before income taxes."

6 **E19-6 (Identify Temporary or Permanent Differences)** Listed below are items that are commonly accounted for differently for financial reporting purposes than they are for tax purposes.

Instructions

For each item below, indicate whether it involves:

(1) A temporary difference that will result in future deductible amounts and, therefore, will usually give rise to a deferred income tax asset.
(2) A temporary difference that will result in future taxable amounts and, therefore, will usually give rise to a deferred income tax liability.
(3) A permanent difference.

Use the appropriate number to indicate your answer for each.

(a) ______ The MACRS depreciation system is used for tax purposes, and the straight-line depreciation method is used for financial reporting purposes for some plant assets.
(b) ______ A landlord collects some rents in advance. Rents received are taxable in the period when they are received.
(c) ______ Expenses are incurred in obtaining tax-exempt income.
(d) ______ Costs of guarantees and warranties are estimated and accrued for financial reporting purposes.
(e) ______ Installment sales of investments are accounted for by the accrual method for financial reporting purposes and the installment method for tax purposes.
(f) ______ For some assets, straight-line depreciation is used for both financial reporting purposes and tax purposes but the assets' lives are shorter for tax purposes.
(g) ______ Interest is received on an investment in tax-exempt municipal obligations.
(h) ______ Proceeds are received from a life insurance company because of the death of a key officer. (The company carries a policy on key officers.)
(i) ______ The tax return reports a deduction for 80% of the dividends received from U.S. corporations. The cost method is used in accounting for the related investments for financial reporting purposes.
(j) ______ Estimated losses on pending lawsuits and claims are accrued for books. These losses are tax deductible in the period(s) when the related liabilities are settled.
(k) ______ Expenses on stock options are accrued for financial reporting purposes.

2 3 4 6 **E19-7 (Terminology, Relationships, Computations, Entries)**

Instructions

Complete the following statements by filling in the blanks.

(a) In a period in which a taxable temporary difference reverses, the reversal will cause taxable income to be _______ (less than, greater than) pretax financial income.
(b) If a $76,000 balance in Deferred Tax Asset was computed by use of a 40% rate, the underlying cumulative temporary difference amounts to $_______.
(c) Deferred taxes _______ (are, are not) recorded to account for permanent differences.
(d) If a taxable temporary difference originates in 2014, it will cause taxable income for 2014 to be _______ (less than, greater than) pretax financial income for 2014.
(e) If total tax expense is $50,000 and deferred tax expense is $65,000, then the current portion of the expense computation is referred to as current tax _______ (expense, benefit) of $_______.

(f) If a corporation's tax return shows taxable income of $100,000 for Year 2 and a tax rate of 40%, how much will appear on the December 31, Year 2, balance sheet for "Income taxes payable" if the company has made estimated tax payments of $36,500 for Year 2? $________.

(g) An increase in the Deferred Tax Liability account on the balance sheet is recorded by a _______ (debit, credit) to the Income Tax Expense account.

(h) An income statement that reports current tax expense of $82,000 and deferred tax benefit of $23,000 will report total income tax expense of $________.

(i) A valuation account is needed whenever it is judged to be _______ that a portion of a deferred tax asset _______ (will be, will not be) realized.

(j) If the tax return shows total taxes due for the period of $75,000 but the income statement shows total income tax expense of $55,000, the difference of $20,000 is referred to as deferred tax _______ (expense, benefit).

2 3 5 9 **E19-8 (Two Temporary Differences, One Rate, 3 Years)** Button Company has the following two temporary differences between its income tax expense and income taxes payable.

	2014	2015	2016
Pretax financial income	$840,000	$910,000	$945,000
Excess depreciation expense on tax return	(30,000)	(40,000)	(10,000)
Excess warranty expense in financial income	20,000	10,000	8,000
Taxable income	$830,000	$880,000	$943,000

The income tax rate for all years is 40%.

Instructions

(a) Assuming there were no temporary differences prior to 2014, prepare the journal entry to record income tax expense, deferred income taxes, and income taxes payable for 2014, 2015, and 2016.

(b) Indicate how deferred taxes will be reported on the 2016 balance sheet. Button's product warranty is for 12 months.

(c) Prepare the income tax expense section of the income statement for 2016, beginning with the line "Pretax financial income."

8 **E19-9 (Carryback and Carryforward of NOL, No Valuation Account, No Temporary Differences)** The pretax financial income (or loss) figures for Jenny Spangler Company are as follows.

2009	$160,000
2010	250,000
2011	80,000
2012	(160,000)
2013	(380,000)
2014	120,000
2015	100,000

Pretax financial income (or loss) and taxable income (loss) were the same for all years involved. Assume a 45% tax rate for 2009 and 2010 and a 40% tax rate for the remaining years.

Instructions

Prepare the journal entries for the years 2011 to 2015 to record income tax expense and the effects of the net operating loss carrybacks and carryforwards assuming Jenny Spangler Company uses the carryback provision. All income and losses relate to normal operations. (In recording the benefits of a loss carryforward, assume that no valuation account is deemed necessary.)

8 **E19-10 (Two NOLs, No Temporary Differences, No Valuation Account, Entries and Income Statement)** Felicia Rashad Corporation has pretax financial income (or loss) equal to taxable income (or loss) from 2006 through 2014 as follows.

	Income (Loss)	Tax Rate
2006	$ 29,000	30%
2007	40,000	30%
2008	17,000	35%
2009	48,000	50%
2010	(150,000)	40%
2011	90,000	40%
2012	30,000	40%
2013	105,000	40%
2014	(60,000)	45%

Pretax financial income (loss) and taxable income (loss) were the same for all years since Rashad has been in business. Assume the carryback provision is employed for net operating losses. In recording the benefits of a loss carryforward, assume that it is more likely than not that the related benefits will be realized.

Instructions

(a) What entry(ies) for income taxes should be recorded for 2010?
(b) Indicate what the income tax expense portion of the income statement for 2010 should look like. Assume all income (loss) relates to continuing operations.
(c) What entry for income taxes should be recorded in 2011?
(d) How should the income tax expense section of the income statement for 2011 appear?
(e) What entry for income taxes should be recorded in 2014?
(f) How should the income tax expense section of the income statement for 2014 appear?

2 3 9 **E19-11 (Three Differences, Classify Deferred Taxes)** At December 31, 2013, Belmont Company had a net deferred tax liability of $375,000. An explanation of the items that compose this balance is as follows.

Temporary Differences	Resulting Balances in Deferred Taxes
1. Excess of tax depreciation over book depreciation	$200,000
2. Accrual, for book purposes, of estimated loss contingency from pending lawsuit that is expected to be settled in 2014. The loss will be deducted on the tax return when paid.	(50,000)
3. Accrual method used for book purposes and installment method used for tax purposes for an isolated installment sale of an investment.	225,000
	$375,000

In analyzing the temporary differences, you find that $30,000 of the depreciation temporary difference will reverse in 2014, and $120,000 of the temporary difference due to the installment sale will reverse in 2014. The tax rate for all years is 40%.

Instructions

Indicate the manner in which deferred taxes should be presented on Belmont Company's December 31, 2013, balance sheet.

2 3 5 **E19-12 (Two Temporary Differences, One Rate, Beginning Deferred Taxes, Compute Pretax Financial Income)** The following facts relate to Duncan Corporation.

1. Deferred tax liability, January 1, 2014, $60,000.
2. Deferred tax asset, January 1, 2014, $20,000.
3. Taxable income for 2014, $105,000.
4. Cumulative temporary difference at December 31, 2014, giving rise to future taxable amounts, $230,000.
5. Cumulative temporary difference at December 31, 2014, giving rise to future deductible amounts, $95,000.
6. Tax rate for all years, 40%. No permanent differences exist.
7. The company is expected to operate profitably in the future.

Instructions

(a) Compute the amount of pretax financial income for 2014.
(b) Prepare the journal entry to record income tax expense, deferred income taxes, and income taxes payable for 2014.
(c) Prepare the income tax expense section of the income statement for 2014, beginning with the line "Income before income taxes."
(d) Compute the effective tax rate for 2014.

2 7 **E19-13 (One Difference, Multiple Rates, Effect of Beginning Balance versus No Beginning Deferred Taxes)** At the end of 2013, Lucretia McEvil Company has $180,000 of cumulative temporary differences that will result in reporting future taxable amounts as shown on the next page.

2014	$ 60,000
2015	50,000
2016	40,000
2017	30,000
	$180,000

Tax rates enacted as of the beginning of 2012 are:

2012 and 2013	40%
2014 and 2015	30%
2016 and later	25%

McEvil's taxable income for 2013 is $320,000. Taxable income is expected in all future years.

Instructions

(a) Prepare the journal entry for McEvil to record income taxes payable, deferred income taxes, and income tax expense for 2013, assuming that there were no deferred taxes at the end of 2012.

(b) Prepare the journal entry for McEvil to record income taxes payable, deferred income taxes, and income tax expense for 2013, assuming that there was a balance of $22,000 in a Deferred Tax Liability account at the end of 2012.

3 4 **E19-14 (Deferred Tax Asset with and without Valuation Account)** Jennifer Capriati Corp. has a deferred tax asset account with a balance of $150,000 at the end of 2013 due to a single cumulative temporary difference of $375,000. At the end of 2014, this same temporary difference has increased to a cumulative amount of $450,000. Taxable income for 2014 is $820,000. The tax rate is 40% for all years. No valuation account related to the deferred tax asset is in existence at the end of 2013.

Instructions

(a) Record income tax expense, deferred income taxes, and income taxes payable for 2014, assuming that it is more likely than not that the deferred tax asset will be realized.

(b) Assuming that it is more likely than not that $30,000 of the deferred tax asset will not be realized, prepare the journal entry at the end of 2014 to record the valuation account.

3 4 5 **E19-15 (Deferred Tax Asset with Previous Valuation Account)** Assume the same information as E19-14, except that at the end of 2013, Jennifer Capriati Corp. had a valuation account related to its deferred tax asset of $45,000.

Instructions

(a) Record income tax expense, deferred income taxes, and income taxes payable for 2014, assuming that it is more likely than not that the deferred tax asset will be realized in full.

(b) Record income tax expense, deferred income taxes, and income taxes payable for 2014, assuming that it is more likely than not that none of the deferred tax asset will be realized.

2 5 7 9 **E19-16 (Deferred Tax Liability, Change in Tax Rate, Prepare Section of Income Statement)** Novotna Inc.'s only temporary difference at the beginning and end of 2013 is caused by a $3 million deferred gain for tax purposes for an installment sale of a plant asset, and the related receivable (only one-half of which is classified as a current asset) is due in equal installments in 2014 and 2015. The related deferred tax liability at the beginning of the year is $1,200,000. In the third quarter of 2013, a new tax rate of 34% is enacted into law and is scheduled to become effective for 2015. Taxable income for 2013 is $5,000,000, and taxable income is expected in all future years.

Instructions

(a) Determine the amount reported as a deferred tax liability at the end of 2013. Indicate proper classification(s).

(b) Prepare the journal entry (if any) necessary to adjust the deferred tax liability when the new tax rate is enacted into law.

(c) Draft the income tax expense portion of the income statement for 2013. Begin with the line "Income before income taxes." Assume no permanent differences exist.

2 3 7 **E19-17 (Two Temporary Differences, Tracked through 3 Years, Multiple Rates)** Taxable income and pretax financial income would be identical for Huber Co. except for its treatments of gross profit on installment sales and estimated costs of warranties. The income computations shown on page 1164 have been prepared.

Taxable income	2013	2014	2015
Excess of revenues over expenses			
(excluding two temporary differences)	$160,000	$210,000	$90,000
Installment gross profit collected	8,000	8,000	8,000
Expenditures for warranties	(5,000)	(5,000)	(5,000)
Taxable income	$163,000	$213,000	$93,000

Pretax financial income	2013	2014	2015
Excess of revenues over expenses			
(excluding two temporary differences)	$160,000	$210,000	$90,000
Installment gross profit earned	24,000	–0–	–0–
Estimated cost of warranties	(15,000)	–0–	–0–
Income before taxes	$169,000	$210,000	$90,000

The tax rates in effect are 2013, 40%; 2014 and 2015, 45%. All tax rates were enacted into law on January 1, 2013. No deferred income taxes existed at the beginning of 2013. Taxable income is expected in all future years.

Instructions

Prepare the journal entry to record income tax expense, deferred income taxes, and income taxes payable for 2013, 2014, and 2015.

2 3 7 **E19-18 (Three Differences, Multiple Rates, Future Taxable Income)** During 2014, Kate Holmes Co.'s first year of operations, the company reports pretax financial income at $250,000. Holmes's enacted tax rate is 45% for 2014 and 40% for all later years. Holmes expects to have taxable income in each of the next 5 years. The effects on future tax returns of temporary differences existing at December 31, 2014, are summarized as follows.

	Future Years					
	2015	2016	2017	2018	2019	Total
Future taxable (deductible) amounts:						
Installment sales	$32,000	$32,000	$32,000			$ 96,000
Depreciation	6,000	6,000	6,000	$6,000	$6,000	30,000
Unearned rent	(50,000)	(50,000)				(100,000)

Instructions

(a) Complete the schedule below to compute deferred taxes at December 31, 2014.
(b) Compute taxable income for 2014.
(c) Prepare the journal entry to record income taxes payable, deferred taxes, and income tax expense for 2014.

	Future Taxable		December 31, 2014	
	(Deductible)	Tax	Deferred Tax	
Temporary Difference	Amounts	Rate	(Asset)	Liability
Installment sales	$ 96,000			
Depreciation	30,000			
Unearned rent	(100,000)			
Totals	$			

2 3 9 **E19-19 (Two Differences, One Rate, Beginning Deferred Balance, Compute Pretax Financial Income)** Andy McDowell Co. establishes a $100 million liability at the end of 2014 for the estimated site-cleanup costs at two of its manufacturing facilities. All related closing costs will be paid and deducted on the tax return in 2015. Also, at the end of 2014, the company has $50 million of temporary differences due to excess depreciation for tax purposes, $7 million of which will reverse in 2015.

The enacted tax rate for all years is 40%, and the company pays taxes of $64 million on $160 million of taxable income in 2014. McDowell expects to have taxable income in 2015.

Instructions

(a) Determine the deferred taxes to be reported at the end of 2015.
(b) Indicate how the deferred taxes computed in (a) are to be reported on the balance sheet.

(c) Assuming that the only deferred tax account at the beginning of 2014 was a deferred tax liability of $10,000,000, draft the income tax expense portion of the income statement for 2014, beginning with the line "Income before income taxes." (*Hint:* You must first compute (1) the amount of temporary difference underlying the beginning $10,000,000 deferred tax liability, then (2) the amount of temporary differences originating or reversing during the year, and then (3) the amount of pretax financial income.)

2 3 9 **E19-20 (Two Differences, No Beginning Deferred Taxes, Multiple Rates)** Teri Hatcher Inc., in its first year of operations, has the following differences between the book basis and tax basis of its assets and liabilities at the end of 2013.

	Book Basis	Tax Basis
Equipment (net)	$400,000	$340,000
Estimated warranty liability	$200,000	$ –0–

It is estimated that the warranty liability will be settled in 2014. The difference in equipment (net) will result in taxable amounts of $20,000 in 2014, $30,000 in 2015, and $10,000 in 2016. The company has taxable income of $520,000 in 2013. As of the beginning of 2013, the enacted tax rate is 34% for 2013–2015, and 30% for 2016. Hatcher expects to report taxable income through 2016.

Instructions

(a) Prepare the journal entry to record income tax expense, deferred income taxes, and income taxes payable for 2013.

(b) Indicate how deferred income taxes will be reported on the balance sheet at the end of 2013.

2 3 7 9 **E19-21 (Two Temporary Differences, Multiple Rates, Future Taxable Income)** Nadal Inc. has two temporary differences at the end of 2013. The first difference stems from installment sales, and the second one results from the accrual of a loss contingency. Nadal's accounting department has developed a schedule of future taxable and deductible amounts related to these temporary differences as follows.

	2014	2015	2016	2017
Taxable amounts	$40,000	$50,000	$60,000	$80,000
Deductible amounts		(15,000)	(19,000)	
	$40,000	$35,000	$41,000	$80,000

As of the beginning of 2013, the enacted tax rate is 34% for 2013 and 2014, and 38% for 2015–2018. At the beginning of 2013, the company had no deferred income taxes on its balance sheet. Taxable income for 2013 is $500,000. Taxable income is expected in all future years.

Instructions

(a) Prepare the journal entry to record income tax expense, deferred income taxes, and income taxes payable for 2013.

(b) Indicate how deferred income taxes would be classified on the balance sheet at the end of 2013.

2 3 9 **E19-22 (Two Differences, One Rate, First Year)** The differences between the book basis and tax basis of the assets and liabilities of Castle Corporation at the end of 2013 are presented below.

	Book Basis	Tax Basis
Accounts receivable	$50,000	$–0–
Litigation liability	30,000	–0–

It is estimated that the litigation liability will be settled in 2014. The difference in accounts receivable will result in taxable amounts of $30,000 in 2014 and $20,000 in 2015. The company has taxable income of $350,000 in 2013 and is expected to have taxable income in each of the following 2 years. Its enacted tax rate is 34% for all years. This is the company's first year of operations. The operating cycle of the business is 2 years.

Instructions

(a) Prepare the journal entry to record income tax expense, deferred income taxes, and income taxes payable for 2013.

(b) Indicate how deferred income taxes will be reported on the balance sheet at the end of 2013.

4 7 8 **E19-23 (NOL Carryback and Carryforward, Valuation Account versus No Valuation Account)** Spamela Hamderson Inc. reports the following pretax income (loss) for both financial reporting purposes and tax purposes. (Assume the carryback provision is used for a net operating loss.)

Year	Pretax Income (Loss)	Tax Rate
2012	$120,000	34%
2013	90,000	34%
2014	(280,000)	38%
2015	220,000	38%

The tax rates listed were all enacted by the beginning of 2012.

Instructions

(a) Prepare the journal entries for the years 2012–2015 to record income tax expense (benefit) and income taxes payable (refundable) and the tax effects of the loss carryback and carryforward, assuming that at the end of 2014 the benefits of the loss carryforward are judged more likely than not to be realized in the future.

(b) Using the assumption in (a), prepare the income tax section of the 2014 income statement beginning with the line "Operating loss before income taxes."

(c) Prepare the journal entries for 2014 and 2015, assuming that based on the weight of available evidence, it is more likely than not that one-fourth of the benefits of the loss carryforward will not be realized.

(d) Using the assumption in (c), prepare the income tax section of the 2014 income statement beginning with the line "Operating loss before income taxes."

4 7 8 **E19-24 (NOL Carryback and Carryforward, Valuation Account Needed)** Beilman Inc. reports the following pretax income (loss) for both book and tax purposes. (Assume the carryback provision is used where possible for a net operating loss.)

Year	Pretax Income (Loss)	Tax Rate
2012	$120,000	40%
2013	90,000	40%
2014	(280,000)	45%
2015	120,000	45%

The tax rates listed were all enacted by the beginning of 2012.

Instructions

(a) Prepare the journal entries for years 2012–2015 to record income tax expense (benefit) and income taxes payable (refundable), and the tax effects of the loss carryback and loss carryforward, assuming that based on the weight of available evidence, it is more likely than not that one-half of the benefits of the loss carryforward will not be realized.

(b) Prepare the income tax section of the 2014 income statement beginning with the line "Operating loss before income taxes."

(c) Prepare the income tax section of the 2015 income statement beginning with the line "Income before income taxes."

4 7 8 **E19-25 (NOL Carryback and Carryforward, Valuation Account Needed)** Meyer reported the following pretax financial income (loss) for the years 2012–2016.

2012	$240,000
2013	350,000
2014	120,000
2015	(570,000)
2016	180,000

Pretax financial income (loss) and taxable income (loss) were the same for all years involved. The enacted tax rate was 34% for 2012 and 2013, and 40% for 2014–2016. Assume the carryback provision is used first for net operating losses.

Instructions

(a) Prepare the journal entries for the years 2014–2016 to record income tax expense, income taxes payable (refundable), and the tax effects of the loss carryback and loss carryforward, assuming that based on the weight of available evidence, it is more likely than not that one-fifth of the benefits of the loss carryforward will not be realized.

(b) Prepare the income tax section of the 2015 income statement beginning with the line "Income (loss) before income taxes."

EXERCISES SET B

See the book's companion website, at **www.wiley.com/college/kieso**, for an additional set of exercises.

PROBLEMS

2 3 **P19-1 (Three Differences, No Beginning Deferred Taxes, Multiple Rates)** The following information is
5 available for Remmers Corporation for 2014.

1. Depreciation reported on the tax return exceeded depreciation reported on the income statement by $120,000. This difference will reverse in equal amounts of $30,000 over the years 2015–2018.
2. Interest received on municipal bonds was $10,000.
3. Rent collected in advance on January 1, 2014, totaled $60,000 for a 3-year period. Of this amount, $40,000 was reported as unearned at December 31, 2014, for book purposes.
4. The tax rates are 40% for 2014 and 35% for 2015 and subsequent years.
5. Income taxes of $320,000 are due per the tax return for 2014.
6. No deferred taxes existed at the beginning of 2014.

Instructions

(a) Compute taxable income for 2014.

(b) Compute pretax financial income for 2014.

(c) Prepare the journal entries to record income tax expense, deferred income taxes, and income taxes payable for 2014 and 2015. Assume taxable income was $980,000 in 2015.

(d) Prepare the income tax expense section of the income statement for 2014, beginning with "Income before income taxes."

3 5 **P19-2 (One Temporary Difference, Tracked for 4 Years, One Permanent Difference, Change in Rate)** The
6 pretax financial income of Truttman Company differs from its taxable income throughout each of 4 years as follows.

Year	Pretax Financial Income	Taxable Income	Tax Rate
2014	$290,000	$180,000	35%
2015	320,000	225,000	40%
2016	350,000	260,000	40%
2017	420,000	560,000	40%

Pretax financial income for each year includes a nondeductible expense of $30,000 (never deductible for tax purposes). The remainder of the difference between pretax financial income and taxable income in each period is due to one depreciation temporary difference. No deferred income taxes existed at the beginning of 2014.

Instructions

(a) Prepare journal entries to record income taxes in all 4 years. Assume that the change in the tax rate to 40% was not enacted until the beginning of 2015.

(b) Prepare the income statement for 2015, beginning with Income before income taxes.

2 5 **P19-3 (Second Year of Depreciation Difference, Two Differences, Single Rate, Extraordinary Item)** The
6 9 following information has been obtained for the Gocker Corporation.

1. Prior to 2014, taxable income and pretax financial income were identical.
2. Pretax financial income is $1,700,000 in 2014 and $1,400,000 in 2015.
3. On January 1, 2014, equipment costing $1,200,000 is purchased. It is to be depreciated on a straight-line basis over 5 years for tax purposes and over 8 years for financial reporting purposes. (*Hint:* Use the half-year convention for tax purposes, as discussed in Appendix 11A.)
4. Interest of $60,000 was earned on tax-exempt municipal obligations in 2015.
5. Included in 2015 pretax financial income is an extraordinary gain of $200,000, which is fully taxable.
6. The tax rate is 35% for all periods.
7. Taxable income is expected in all future years.

Instructions

(a) Compute taxable income and income taxes payable for 2015.
(b) Prepare the journal entry to record 2015 income tax expense, income taxes payable, and deferred taxes.
(c) Prepare the bottom portion of Gocker's 2015 income statement, beginning with "Income before income taxes and extraordinary item."
(d) Indicate how deferred income taxes should be presented on the December 31, 2015, balance sheet.

2 3 **P19-4 (Permanent and Temporary Differences, One Rate)** The accounting records of Shinault Inc. show
5 the following data for 2014 (its first year of operations).

1. Life insurance expense on officers was $9,000.
2. Equipment was acquired in early January for $300,000. Straight-line depreciation over a 5-year life is used, with no salvage value. For tax purposes, Shinault used a 30% rate to calculate depreciation.
3. Interest revenue on State of New York bonds totaled $4,000.
4. Product warranties were estimated to be $50,000 in 2014. Actual repair and labor costs related to the warranties in 2014 were $10,000. The remainder is estimated to be paid evenly in 2015 and 2016.
5. Gross profit on an accrual basis was $100,000. For tax purposes, $75,000 was recorded on the installment-sales method.
6. Fines incurred for pollution violations were $4,200.
7. Pretax financial income was $750,000. The tax rate is 30%.

Instructions

(a) Prepare a schedule starting with pretax financial income in 2014 and ending with taxable income in 2014.
(b) Prepare the journal entry for 2014 to record income taxes payable, income tax expense, and deferred income taxes.

5 7 **P19-5 (NOL without Valuation Account)** Jennings Inc. reported the following pretax income (loss) and
8 9 related tax rates during the years 2010–2016.

	Pretax Income (loss)	Tax Rate
2010	$ 40,000	30%
2011	25,000	30%
2012	50,000	30%
2013	80,000	40%
2014	(180,000)	45%
2015	70,000	40%
2016	100,000	35%

Pretax financial income (loss) and taxable income (loss) were the same for all years since Jennings began business. The tax rates from 2013–2016 were enacted in 2013.

Instructions

(a) Prepare the journal entries for the years 2014–2016 to record income taxes payable (refundable), income tax expense (benefit), and the tax effects of the loss carryback and carryforward. Assume that Jennings elects the carryback provision where possible and expects to realize the benefits of any loss carryforward in the year that immediately follows the loss year.
(b) Indicate the effect the 2014 entry(ies) has on the December 31, 2014, balance sheet.
(c) Prepare the portion of the income statement, starting with "Operating loss before income taxes," for 2014.
(d) Prepare the portion of the income statement, starting with "Income before income taxes," for 2015.

2 3 9 **P19-6 (Two Differences, Two Rates, Future Income Expected)** Presented below are two independent situations related to future taxable and deductible amounts resulting from temporary differences existing at December 31, 2014.

1. Mooney Co. has developed the following schedule of future taxable and deductible amounts.

	2015	2016	2017	2018	2019
Taxable amounts	$300	$300	$300	$ 300	$300
Deductible amount	—	—	—	(1,600)	—

2. Roesch Co. has the following schedule of future taxable and deductible amounts.

	2015	2016	2017	2018
Taxable amounts	$300	$300	$ 300	$300
Deductible amount	—	—	(2,300)	—

Both Mooney Co. and Roesch Co. have taxable income of $4,000 in 2014 and expect to have taxable income in all future years. The tax rates enacted as of the beginning of 2014 are 30% for 2014–2017 and 35% for years thereafter. All of the underlying temporary differences relate to noncurrent assets and liabilities.

Instructions

For each of these two situations, compute the net amount of deferred income taxes to be reported at the end of 2014, and indicate how it should be classified on the balance sheet.

2 5 7 **P19-7 (One Temporary Difference, Tracked 3 Years, Change in Rates, Income Statement Presentation)** Crosley Corp. sold an investment on an installment basis. The total gain of $60,000 was reported for financial reporting purposes in the period of sale. The company qualifies to use the installment-sales method for tax purposes. The installment period is 3 years; one-third of the sale price is collected in the period of sale. The tax rate was 40% in 2014, and 35% in 2015 and 2016. The 35% tax rate was not enacted in law until 2015. The accounting and tax data for the 3 years is shown below.

	Financial Accounting	Tax Return
2014 (40% tax rate)		
Income before temporary difference	$ 70,000	$70,000
Temporary difference	60,000	20,000
Income	$130,000	$90,000
2015 (35% tax rate)		
Income before temporary difference	$ 70,000	$70,000
Temporary difference	–0–	20,000
Income	$ 70,000	$90,000
2016 (35% tax rate)		
Income before temporary difference	$ 70,000	$70,000
Temporary difference	–0–	20,000
Income	$ 70,000	$90,000

Instructions

(a) Prepare the journal entries to record the income tax expense, deferred income taxes, and the income taxes payable at the end of each year. No deferred income taxes existed at the beginning of 2014.

(b) Explain how the deferred taxes will appear on the balance sheet at the end of each year. (Assume Installment Accounts Receivable is classified as a current asset.)

(c) Draft the income tax expense section of the income statement for each year, beginning with "Income before income taxes."

2 3 5 9 **P19-8 (Two Differences, 2 Years, Compute Taxable Income and Pretax Financial Income)** The information shown below and on page 1170 was disclosed during the audit of Elbert Inc.

1.

Year	Amount Due per Tax Return
2014	$130,000
2015	104,000

2. On January 1, 2014, equipment costing $600,000 is purchased. For financial reporting purposes, the company uses straight-line depreciation over a 5-year life. For tax purposes, the company uses the elective straight-line method over a 5-year life. (*Hint:* For tax purposes, the half-year convention as discussed in Appendix 11A must be used.)
3. In January 2015, $225,000 is collected in advance rental of a building for a 3-year period. The entire $225,000 is reported as taxable income in 2015, but $150,000 of the $225,000 is reported as unearned revenue in 2015 for financial reporting purposes. The remaining amount of unearned revenue is to be recognized equally in 2016 and 2017.
4. The tax rate is 40% in 2014 and all subsequent periods. (*Hint:* To find taxable income in 2014 and 2015, the related income taxes payable amounts will have to be "grossed up.")
5. No temporary differences existed at the end of 2013. Elbert expects to report taxable income in each of the next 5 years.

Instructions

(a) Determine the amount to report for deferred income taxes at the end of 2014, and indicate how it should be classified on the balance sheet.

(b) Prepare the journal entry to record income taxes for 2014.

(c) Draft the income tax section of the income statement for 2014, beginning with "Income before income taxes." (*Hint:* You must compute taxable income and then combine that with changes in cumulative temporary differences to arrive at pretax financial income.)

(d) Determine the deferred income taxes at the end of 2015, and indicate how they should be classified on the balance sheet.

(e) Prepare the journal entry to record income taxes for 2015.

(f) Draft the income tax section of the income statement for 2015, beginning with "Income before income taxes."

2 3 **P19-9 (Five Differences, Compute Taxable Income and Deferred Taxes, Draft Income Statement)**
5 6 Wise Company began operations at the beginning of 2015. The following information pertains to this
9 company.

1. Pretax financial income for 2015 is $100,000.
2. The tax rate enacted for 2015 and future years is 40%.
3. Differences between the 2015 income statement and tax return are listed below:
   (a) Warranty expense accrued for financial reporting purposes amounts to $7,000. Warranty deductions per the tax return amount to $2,000.
   (b) Gross profit on construction contracts using the percentage-of-completion method per books amounts to $92,000. Gross profit on construction contracts for tax purposes amounts to $67,000.
   (c) Depreciation of property, plant, and equipment for financial reporting purposes amounts to $60,000. Depreciation of these assets amounts to $80,000 for the tax return.
   (d) A $3,500 fine paid for violation of pollution laws was deducted in computing pretax financial income.
   (e) Interest revenue recognized on an investment in tax-exempt municipal bonds amounts to $1,500.
4. Taxable income is expected for the next few years. (Assume (a) is short-term in nature; assume (b) and (c) are long-term in nature.)

Instructions

(a) Compute taxable income for 2015.

(b) Compute the deferred taxes at December 31, 2015, that relate to the temporary differences described above. Clearly label them as deferred tax asset or liability.

(c) Prepare the journal entry to record income tax expense, deferred taxes, and income taxes payable for 2015.

(d) Draft the income tax expense section of the income statement, beginning with "Income before income taxes."

PROBLEMS SET B

See the book's companion website, at **www.wiley.com/college/kieso**, for an additional set of problems.

CONCEPTS FOR ANALYSIS

CA19-1 (Objectives and Principles for Accounting for Income Taxes) The amount of income taxes due to the government for a period of time is rarely the amount reported on the income statement for that period as income tax expense.

Instructions

(a) Explain the objectives of accounting for income taxes in general-purpose financial statements.
(b) Explain the basic principles that are applied in accounting for income taxes at the date of the financial statements to meet the objectives discussed in (a).
(c) List the steps in the annual computation of deferred tax liabilities and assets.

CA19-2 (Basic Accounting for Temporary Differences) Dexter Company appropriately uses the asset-liability method to record deferred income taxes. Dexter reports depreciation expense for certain machinery purchased this year using the modified accelerated cost recovery system (MACRS) for income tax purposes and the straight-line basis for financial reporting purposes. The tax deduction is the larger amount this year.

Dexter received rent revenues in advance this year. These revenues are included in this year's taxable income. However, for financial reporting purposes, these revenues are reported as unearned revenues, a current liability.

Instructions

(a) What are the principles of the asset-liability approach?
(b) How would Dexter account for the temporary differences?
(c) How should Dexter classify the deferred tax consequences of the temporary differences on its balance sheet?

CA19-3 (Identify Temporary Differences and Classification Criteria) The asset-liability approach for recording deferred income taxes is an integral part of generally accepted accounting principles.

Instructions

(a) Indicate whether each of the following independent situations should be treated as a temporary difference or as a permanent difference, and explain why.

- **(1)** Estimated warranty costs (covering a 3-year warranty) are expensed for financial reporting purposes at the time of sale but deducted for income tax purposes when paid.
- **(2)** Depreciation for book and income tax purposes differs because of different bases of carrying the related property, which was acquired in a trade-in. The different bases are a result of different rules used for book and tax purposes to compute the basis of property acquired in a trade-in.
- **(3)** A company properly uses the equity method to account for its 30% investment in another company. The investee pays dividends that are about 10% of its annual earnings.
- **(4)** A company reports a gain on an involuntary conversion of a nonmonetary asset to a monetary asset. The company elects to replace the property within the statutory period using the total proceeds so the gain is not reported on the current year's tax return.

(b) Discuss the nature of the deferred income tax accounts and possible classifications in a company's balance sheet. Indicate the manner in which these accounts are to be reported.

CA19-4 (Accounting and Classification of Deferred Income Taxes)

Part A: This year, Gumowski Company has each of the following items in its income statement.

1. Gross profits on installment sales.
2. Revenues on long-term construction contracts.
3. Estimated costs of product warranty contracts.
4. Premiums on officers' life insurance policies with Gumowski as beneficiary.

Instructions

(a) Under what conditions would deferred income taxes need to be reported in the financial statements?
(b) Specify when deferred income taxes would need to be recognized for each of the items above, and indicate the rationale for such recognition.

Part B: Gumowski Company's president has heard that deferred income taxes can be classified in different ways in the balance sheet.

Instructions

Identify the conditions under which deferred income taxes would be classified as a noncurrent item in the balance sheet. What justification exists for such classification?

(AICPA adapted)

CA19-5 (Explain Computation of Deferred Tax Liability for Multiple Tax Rates) At December 31, 2014, Higley Corporation has one temporary difference which will reverse and cause taxable amounts in 2015. In 2014, a new tax act set taxes equal to 45% for 2014, 40% for 2015, and 34% for 2016 and years thereafter.

Instructions

Explain what circumstances would call for Higley to compute its deferred tax liability at the end of 2014 by multiplying the cumulative temporary difference by:

(a) 45%.
(b) 40%.
(c) 34%.

CA19-6 (Explain Future Taxable and Deductible Amounts, How Carryback and Carryforward Affects Deferred Taxes) Maria Rodriquez and Lynette Kingston are discussing accounting for income taxes. They are currently studying a schedule of taxable and deductible amounts that will arise in the future as a result of existing temporary differences. The schedule is as follows.

		Future Years			
	2014	2015	2016	2017	2018
Taxable income	$850,000				
Taxable amounts		$375,000	$375,000	$375,000	$375,000
Deductible amounts				(2,400,000)	
Enacted tax rate	50%	45%	40%	35%	30%

Instructions

(a) Explain the concept of future taxable amounts and future deductible amounts as illustrated in the schedule.
(b) How do the carryback and carryforward provisions affect the reporting of deferred tax assets and deferred tax liabilities?

CA19-7 (Deferred Taxes, Income Effects) Stephanie Delaney, CPA, is the newly hired director of corporate taxation for Acme Incorporated, which is a publicly traded corporation. Ms. Delaney's first job with Acme was the review of the company's accounting practices on deferred income taxes. In doing her review, she noted differences between tax and book depreciation methods that permitted Acme to realize a sizable deferred tax liability on its balance sheet. As a result, Acme paid very little in income taxes at that time.

Delaney also discovered that Acme has an explicit policy of selling off plant assets before they reversed in the deferred tax liability account. This policy, coupled with the rapid expansion of its plant asset base, allowed Acme to "defer" all income taxes payable for several years, even though it always has reported positive earnings and an increasing EPS. Delaney checked with the legal department and found the policy to be legal, but she's uncomfortable with the ethics of it.

Instructions

Answer the following questions.

(a) Why would Acme have an explicit policy of selling plant assets before the temporary differences reversed in the deferred tax liability account?
(b) What are the ethical implications of Acme's "deferral" of income taxes?
(c) Who could be harmed by Acme's ability to "defer" income taxes payable for several years, despite positive earnings?
(d) In a situation such as this, what are Ms. Delaney's professional responsibilities as a CPA?

USING YOUR JUDGMENT

FINANCIAL REPORTING

Financial Reporting Problem

P&G **The Procter & Gamble Company (P&G)**

The financial statements of P&G are presented in Appendix 5B. The company's complete annual report, including the notes to the financial statements, can be accessed at the book's companion website, **www.wiley.com/college/kieso.**

Instructions

Refer to P&G's financial statements and the accompanying notes to answer the following questions.

(a) What amounts relative to income taxes does P&G report in its:

(1) 2011 income statement?

(2) June 30, 2011, balance sheet?

(3) 2011 statement of cash flows?

(b) P&G's income taxes in 2009, 2010, and 2011 were computed at what effective tax rates? (See the notes to the financial statements.)

(c) How much of P&G's 2011 total income taxes was current tax expense, and how much was deferred tax expense?

(d) What did P&G report as the significant components (the details) of its June 30, 2011, deferred tax assets and liabilities?

Comparative Analysis Case

The Coca-Cola Company and PepsiCo, Inc.

Instructions

Go to the book's companion website and use information found there to answer the following questions related to **The Coca-Cola Company** and **PepsiCo, Inc.**

(a) What are the amounts of Coca-Cola's and PepsiCo's provision for income taxes for the year 2011? Of each company's 2011 provision for income taxes, what portion is current expense and what portion is deferred expense?

(b) What amount of cash was paid in 2011 for income taxes by Coca-Cola and by PepsiCo?

(c) What was the U.S. federal statutory tax rate in 2011? What was the effective tax rate in 2011 for Coca-Cola and PepsiCo? Why might their effective tax rates differ?

(d) For year-end 2011, what amounts were reported by Coca-Cola and PepsiCo as (1) gross deferred tax assets and (2) gross deferred tax liabilities?

(e) Do either Coca-Cola or PepsiCo disclose any net operating loss carrybacks and/or carryforwards at year-end 2011? What are the amounts, and when do the carryforwards expire?

Financial Statement Analysis Case

Homestake Mining Company

Homestake Mining Company is a 120-year-old international gold mining company with substantial gold mining operations and exploration in the United States, Canada, and Australia. At year-end, Homestake reported the following items related to income taxes (thousands of dollars).

Total current taxes	$ 26,349
Total deferred taxes	(39,436)
Total income and mining taxes (the provision for taxes per its income statement)	(13,087)
Deferred tax liabilities	$303,050
Deferred tax assets, net of valuation allowance of $207,175	95,275
Net deferred tax liability	$207,775

Note 6: The classification of deferred tax assets and liabilities is based on the related asset or liability creating the deferred tax. Deferred taxes not related to a specific asset or liability are classified based on the estimated period of reversal.

Tax loss carryforwards (U.S., Canada, Australia, and Chile)	$71,151
Tax credit carryforwards	$12,007

Instructions

(a) What is the significance of Homestake's disclosure of "Current taxes" of $26,349 and "Deferred taxes" of $(39,436)?

(b) Explain the concept behind Homestake's disclosure of gross deferred tax liabilities (future taxable amounts) and gross deferred tax assets (future deductible amounts).

(c) Homestake reported tax loss carryforwards of $71,151 and tax credit carryforwards of $12,007. How do the carryback and carryforward provisions affect the reporting of deferred tax assets and deferred tax liabilities?

Accounting, Analysis, and Principles

DeJohn Company, which began operations at the beginning of 2012, produces various products on a contract basis. Each contract generates a gross profit of $80,000. Some of DeJohn's contracts provide for the customer to pay on an installment basis. Under these contracts, DeJohn collects one-fifth of the contract revenue in each of the following four years. For financial reporting purposes, the company recognizes gross profit in the year of completion (accrual basis). For tax purposes, DeJohn recognizes gross profit in the year cash is collected (installment basis).

Presented below is information related to DeJohn's operations for 2014:

1. In 2014, the company completed seven contracts that allow for the customer to pay on an installment basis. DeJohn recognized the related gross profit of $560,000 for financial reporting purposes. It reported only $112,000 of gross profit on installment sales on the 2014 tax return. The company expects future collections on the related installment receivables to result in taxable amounts of $112,000 in each of the next four years.
2. In 2014, nontaxable municipal bond interest revenue was $28,000.
3. During 2014, nondeductible fines and penalties of $26,000 were paid.
4. Pretax financial income for 2014 amounts to $500,000.
5. Tax rates (enacted before the end of 2014) are 50% for 2014 and 40% for 2015 and later.
6. The accounting period is the calendar year.
7. The company is expected to have taxable income in all future years.
8. The company has no deferred tax assets or liabilities at the end of 2013.

Accounting

Prepare the journal entry to record income taxes for 2014.

Analysis

Classify deferred income taxes on the balance sheet at December 31, 2014, and indicate, starting with Income before income taxes, how income taxes are reported on the income statement. What is DeJohn's effective tax rate?

Principles

Explain how the conceptual framework is used as a basis for determining the proper accounting for deferred income taxes.

BRIDGE TO THE PROFESSION

Professional Research: FASB Codification

Kleckner Company started operations in 2010. Although it has grown steadily, the company reported accumulated operating losses of $450,000 in its first four years in business. In the most recent year (2014), Kleckner appears to have turned the corner and reported modest taxable income of $30,000. In addition to a deferred tax asset related to its net operating loss, Kleckner has recorded a deferred tax asset related to product warranties and a deferred tax liability related to accelerated depreciation.

Given its past operating results, Kleckner has established a full valuation allowance for its deferred tax assets. However, given its improved performance, Kleckner management wonders whether the company can now reduce or eliminate the valuation allowance. They would like you to conduct some research on the accounting for its valuation allowance.

Instructions

If your school has a subscription to the FASB Codification, go to *http://aaahq.org/ascLogin.cfm* to log in and prepare responses to the following. Provide Codification references for your responses.

(a) Briefly explain to Kleckner management the importance of future taxable income as it relates to the valuation allowance for deferred tax assets.

(b) What are the sources of income that may be relied upon to remove the need for a valuation allowance?

(c) What are tax-planning strategies? From the information provided, does it appear that Kleckner could employ a tax-planning strategy to support reducing its valuation allowance?

Additional Professional Resources

See the book's companion website, at **www.wiley.com/college/kieso**, for professional simulations as well as other study resources.

IFRS INSIGHTS

The accounting for income taxes in IFRS is covered in *IAS 12* ("Income Taxes"), which is based on an asset-liability approach to measurement of deferred taxes.

12 LEARNING OBJECTIVE
Compare the accounting for income taxes under GAAP and IFRS.

RELEVANT FACTS

Following are the key similarities and differences between GAAP and IFRS related to accounting for taxes.

Similarities

- Similar to GAAP, IFRS uses the asset and liability approach for recording deferred taxes.

Differences

- The classification of deferred taxes under IFRS is always non-current. As indicated in the chapter, GAAP classifies deferred taxes based on the classification of the asset or liability to which it relates.
- Under IFRS, an affirmative judgment approach is used, by which a deferred tax asset is recognized up to the amount that is probable to be realized. GAAP uses an impairment approach. In this approach, the deferred tax asset is recognized in full. It is then reduced by a valuation account if it is more likely than not that all or a portion of the deferred tax asset will not be realized.
- IFRS uses the enacted tax rate or substantially enacted tax rate. ("Substantially enacted" means virtually certain.) For GAAP, the enacted tax rate must be used.
- The tax effects related to certain items are reported in equity under IFRS. That is not the case under GAAP, which charges or credits the tax effects to income.
- GAAP requires companies to assess the likelihood of uncertain tax positions being sustainable upon audit. Potential liabilities must be accrued and disclosed if the position is "more likely than not" to be disallowed. Under IFRS, all potential liabilities must be recognized. With respect to measurement, IFRS uses an expected-value approach to measure the tax liability, which differs from GAAP.

ABOUT THE NUMBERS

Deferred Tax Asset (Non-Recognition)

Under IFRS, companies recognize a deferred tax asset for all deductible temporary differences. However, based on available evidence, a company should reduce a deferred tax asset if it is probable that it **will not realize** some portion or all of the deferred tax asset. "**Probable**" means a level of likelihood of at least slightly more than 50 percent.

Assume that Jensen Co. has a deductible temporary difference of $1,000,000 at the end of its first year of operations. Its tax rate is 40 percent, which means it records a deferred tax asset of $400,000 ($1,000,000 × 40%). Assuming $900,000 of income taxes payable, Jensen records income tax expense, the deferred tax asset, and income taxes payable as follows.

Income Tax Expense	500,000	
Deferred Tax Asset	400,000	
Income Taxes Payable		900,000

After careful review of all available evidence, Jensen determines that it is probable that it will not realize $100,000 of this deferred tax asset. Jensen records this reduction in asset value as follows.

Income Tax Expense	100,000	
Deferred Tax Asset		100,000

This journal entry increases income tax expense in the current period because Jensen does not expect to realize a favorable tax benefit for a portion of the deductible temporary difference. Jensen **simultaneously recognizes a reduction in the carrying amount of the deferred tax asset**. Jensen then reports a deferred tax asset of $300,000 in its statement of financial position.

Jensen evaluates the deferred tax asset account at the end of each accounting period. If, at the end of the next period, it expects to realize $350,000 of this deferred tax asset, Jensen makes the following entry to adjust this account.

Deferred Tax Asset ($350,000 − $300,000)	50,000	
Income Tax Expense		50,000

Jensen should consider all available evidence, both positive and negative, to determine whether, based on the weight of available evidence, it needs to adjust the deferred tax asset. For example, if Jensen has been experiencing a series of loss years, it reasonably assumes that these losses will continue. Therefore, Jensen will lose the benefit of the future deductible amounts.

Generally, sufficient taxable income arises from temporary taxable differences that will reverse in the future or from a tax-planning strategy that will generate taxable income in the future. Illustration IFRS19-1 shows how Ahold describes its reporting of deferred assets.

ILLUSTRATION IFRS19-1
Deferred Tax Asset Disclosure

Ahold

Note 11. Significant judgment is required in determining whether deferred tax assets are realizable. Ahold determines this on the basis of expected taxable profits arising from recognized deferred tax liabilities and on the basis of budgets, cash flow forecasts, and impairment models. Where utilization is not considered probable, deferred taxes are not recognized.

Carryforward (Non-Recognition)

To illustrate non-recognition of a loss carryforward, assume that Groh Inc. has tax benefits of $110,000 associated with a NOL carryback and a potential deferred tax asset of $80,000 associated with an operating loss carryforward of $200,000, assuming a future tax rate of 40% ($200,000 × 40%). However, if it is probable that Groh will *not* realize the entire NOL carryforward in future years, it does not recognize this deferred tax asset. To illustrate, Groh makes the following journal entry in 2014 to record only the tax refund receivable.

To recognize benefit of loss carryback

Income Tax Refund Receivable	110,000	
Benefit Due to Loss Carryback (Income Tax Expense)		110,000

Illustration IFRS19-2 shows Groh's 2014 income statement presentation.

ILLUSTRATION IFRS19-2
Recognition of Benefit of Loss Carryback Only

GROH INC. INCOME STATEMENT (PARTIAL) FOR 2014	
Operating loss before income taxes	$(500,000)
Income tax benefit	
Benefit due to loss carryback	110,000
Net loss	$(390,000)

In 2015, assuming that Groh has taxable income of $250,000 (before considering the carryforward), subject to a tax rate of 40 percent, it realizes the deferred tax asset. Groh records the following entries.

To recognize deferred tax asset and loss carryforward		
Deferred Tax Asset	80,000	
Benefit Due to Loss Carryforward (Income Tax Expense)		80,000

To record current and deferred income taxes		
Income Tax Expense	100,000	
Deferred Tax Asset		80,000
Income Taxes Payable		20,000

Groh reports the $80,000 Benefit Due to the Loss Carryforward on the 2015 income statement. The company did not recognize it in 2014 because it was probable that it would not be realized. Assuming that Groh derives the income for 2015 from continuing operations, it prepares the income statement as shown in Illustration IFRS19-3.

ILLUSTRATION IFRS19-3
Recognition of Benefit of Loss Carryforward When Realized

GROH INC. INCOME STATEMENT (PARTIAL) FOR 2015		
Income before income taxes		$250,000
Income tax expense		
Current	$ 20,000	
Deferred	80,000	
Benefit due to loss carryforward	(80,000)	20,000
Net income		$230,000

Another method is to report only one line for total income tax expense of $20,000 on the face of the income statement and disclose the components of income tax expense in the notes to the financial statements.

Statement of Financial Position Classification

Companies classify taxes receivable or payable as current assets or current liabilities. Although current tax assets and liabilities are separately recognized and measured, they are often offset in the statement of financial position. The offset occurs because companies normally have a legally enforceable right to offset a current tax asset (Taxes Receivable) against a current tax liability (Taxes Payable) when they relate to income taxes levied by the same taxation authority. Deferred tax assets and deferred tax liabilities are also separately recognized and measured but may be offset in the statement of financial position. Companies are permitted to offset deferred tax assets and deferred tax liabilities if, and only if (1) the company has a legally enforceable right to offset current tax assets against current tax liabilities, and (2) the deferred tax assets and the deferred tax liabilities relate to income taxes levied by the same tax authority and for the same company.

The net deferred tax asset or net deferred tax liability is reported in the non-current section of the statement of financial position. Deferred tax amounts should not be discounted. The IASB apparently considers discounting to be an unnecessary complication even if the effects are material. To illustrate, assume that K. Scott Company has four deferred tax items at December 31, 2014, as shown in Illustration IFRS19-4.

ILLUSTRATION IFRS19-4
Classification of Temporary Differences

Temporary Difference	Resulting Deferred Tax (Asset)	Resulting Deferred Tax Liability
1. Rent collected in advance: recognized when earned for accounting purposes and when received for tax purposes.	$(42,000)	
2. Use of straight-line depreciation for accounting purposes and accelerated depreciation for tax purposes.		$214,000
3. Recognition of profits on installment sales during period of sale for accounting purposes and during period of collection for tax purposes.		45,000
4. Warranty liabilities: recognized for accounting purposes at time of sale; for tax purposes at time paid.	(12,000)	
Totals	$(54,000)	$259,000

As indicated, K. Scott has a total deferred tax asset of $54,000 and a total deferred tax liability of $259,000. Assuming these two items can be offset, K. Scott reports a deferred tax liability of $205,000 ($259,000 − $54,000) in the non-current liability section of its statement of financial position.

ON THE HORIZON

The IASB and the FASB have been working to address some of the differences in the accounting for income taxes. Some of the issues under discussion are the term "probable" under IFRS for recognition of a deferred tax asset, which might be interpreted to mean "more likely than not." If the term is changed, the reporting for impairments of deferred tax assets will be essentially the same between GAAP and IFRS. In addition, the IASB is considering adoption of the classification approach used in GAAP for deferred assets and liabilities. Also, GAAP will likely continue to use the enacted tax rate in computing deferred taxes, except in situations where the taxing jurisdiction is not involved. In that case, companies should use IFRS, which is based on enacted rates or substantially enacted tax rates. Finally, the issue of allocation of deferred income taxes to equity for certain transactions under IFRS must be addressed in order to converge with GAAP, which allocates the effects to income. At the time of this printing, deliberations on the income tax project have been suspended indefinitely.

IFRS SELF-TEST QUESTIONS

1. Which of the following is **false**?
   (a) Under GAAP, deferred taxes are reported based on the classification of the asset or liability to which it relates.
   (b) Under IFRS, some potential liabilities are not recognized.
   (c) Under GAAP, the enacted tax rate is used to measure deferred tax assets and liabilities.
   (d) Under IFRS, all deferred tax assets and liabilities are classified as non-current.
2. Which of the following statements is **correct** with regard to IFRS and GAAP?
   (a) Under GAAP, all potential liabilities related to uncertain tax positions must be recognized.
   (b) The tax effects related to certain items are reported in equity under GAAP; under IFRS, the tax effects are charged or credited to income.

(c) IFRS uses an affirmative judgment approach for deferred tax assets, whereas GAAP uses an impairment approach for deferred tax assets.
(d) IFRS classifies deferred taxes based on the classification of the asset or liability to which it relates.

3. Under IFRS:
(a) "probable" is defined as a level of likelihood of at least slightly more than 60%.
(b) a company should reduce a deferred tax asset when it is likely that some or all of it will not be realized by using a valuation allowance.
(c) a company considers only positive evidence when determining whether to recognize a deferred tax asset.
(d) deferred tax assets must be evaluated at the end of each accounting period.

4. Stephens Company has a deductible temporary difference of $2,000,000 at the end of its first year of operations. Its tax rate is 40 percent. Stephens has $1,800,000 of income taxes payable. After a careful review of all available evidence, Stephens determines that it is probable that it will not realize $200,000 of this deferred tax asset. On Stephens Company's statement of financial position at the end of its first year of operations, what is the amount of deferred tax asset?
(a) $2,000,000. (c) $800,000.
(b) $1,800,000. (d) $600,000.

5. Lincoln Company has the following four deferred tax items at December 31, 2014. The deferred tax assets and the deferred tax liabilities relate to income taxes levied by the same tax authority.

Temporary Difference	Deferred Tax Asset	Deferred Tax Liability
Rent collected in advance: recognized when earned for accounting purposes and when received for tax purposes.	$652,000	
Use of straight-line depreciation for accounting purposes and accelerated depreciation for tax purposes.		$330,000
Recognition of profits on installment sales during period of sale for accounting purposes and during period of collection for tax purposes.		64,000
Warranty liabilities: recognized for accounting purposes at time of sale; for tax purposes at time paid.	37,000	

On Lincoln's December 31, 2014, statement of financial position, it will report:
(a) $394,000 non-current deferred tax liability and $689,000 non-current deferred tax asset.
(b) $330,000 non-current liability and $625,000 current deferred tax asset.
(c) $295,000 non-current deferred tax asset.
(d) $295,000 current tax receivable.

IFRS CONCEPTS AND APPLICATION

IFRS19-1 Where can authoritative IFRS related to the accounting for taxes be found?

IFRS19-2 Briefly describe some of the similarities and differences between GAAP and IFRS with respect to income tax accounting.

IFRS19-3 Describe the current convergence efforts of the FASB and IASB in the area of accounting for taxes.

IFRS19-4 How are deferred tax assets and deferred tax liabilities reported on the statement of financial position under IFRS?

IFRS19-5 Describe the procedure(s) involved in classifying deferred tax amounts on the statement of financial position under IFRS.

IFRS19-6 At December 31, 2014, Hillyard Corporation has a deferred tax asset of $200,000. After a careful review of all available evidence, it is determined that it is probable that $60,000 of this deferred tax asset will not be realized. Prepare the necessary journal entry.

IFRS19-7 Rode Inc. incurred a net operating loss of $500,000 in 2014. Combined income for 2012 and 2013 was $350,000. The tax rate for all years is 40%. Rode elects the carryback option. Prepare the journal entries to record the benefits of the loss carryback and the loss carryforward.

IFRS19-8 Use the information for Rode Inc. given in IFRS19-7. Assume that it is probable that the entire net operating loss carryforward will not be realized in future years. Prepare the journal entry(ies) necessary at the end of 2014.

IFRS19-9 Youngman Corporation has temporary differences at December 31, 2014, that result in the following deferred taxes.

Deferred tax asset	$24,000
Deferred tax liability	$69,000

Indicate how these balances would be presented in Youngman's December 31, 2014, statement of financial position.

IFRS19-10 At December 31, 2014, Cascade Company had a net deferred tax liability of $450,000. An explanation of the items that compose this balance is as follows.

Temporary Differences in Deferred Taxes	Resulting Balances
1. Excess of tax depreciation over book depreciation.	$200,000
2. Accrual, for book purposes, of estimated loss contingency from pending lawsuit that is expected to be settled in 2015. The loss will be deducted on the tax return when paid.	$ (50,000)
3. Accrual method used for book purposes and installment method used for tax purposes for an isolated installment sale of an investment.	$300,000

In analyzing the temporary differences, you find that $30,000 of the depreciation temporary difference will reverse in 2015, and $120,000 of the temporary difference due to the installment sale will reverse in 2015. The tax rate for all years is 40%.

Instructions

Indicate the manner in which deferred taxes should be presented on Cascade Company's December 31, 2014, statement of financial position.

IFRS19-11 Callaway Corp. has a deferred tax asset account with a balance of $150,000 at the end of 2014 due to a single cumulative temporary difference of $375,000. At the end of 2015, this same temporary difference has increased to a cumulative amount of $500,000. Taxable income for 2015 is $850,000. The tax rate is 40% for all years.

Instructions

(a) Record income tax expense, deferred income taxes, and income taxes payable for 2015, assuming that it is probable that the deferred tax asset will be realized.

(b) Assuming that it is probable that $30,000 of the deferred tax asset will not be realized, prepare the journal entry at the end of 2015 to recognize this probability.

Professional Research

IFRS19-12 Kleckner Company started operations in 2010. Although it has grown steadily, the company reported accumulated operating losses of $450,000 in its first four years in business. In the most recent year (2014), Kleckner appears to have turned the corner and reported modest taxable income of $30,000. In addition to a deferred tax asset related to its net operating loss, Kleckner has recorded a deferred tax asset related to product warranties and a deferred tax liability related to accelerated depreciation. Given its past operating results, Kleckner has determined that it is not probable that it will realize any of the deferred tax assets. However, given its improved performance, Kleckner management wonders whether there are any accounting consequences for its deferred tax assets. They would like you to conduct some research on the accounting for recognition of its deferred tax asset.

Instructions

Access the IFRS authoritative literature at the IASB website (*http://eifrs.iasb.org/*). (Click on the IFRS tab and then register for free eIFRS access if necessary.) When you have accessed the documents, you can use the search tool in your Internet browser to respond to the following questions. (Provide paragraph citations.)

(a) Briefly explain to Kleckner management the importance of future taxable income as it relates to the recognition of deferred tax assets.

(b) What are the sources of income that may be relied upon in assessing realization of a deferred tax asset?

(c) What are tax-planning strategies? From the information provided, does it appear that Kleckner could employ a tax-planning strategy in evaluating its deferred tax asset?

International Financial Reporting Problem
Marks and Spencer plc

IFRS19-13 The financial statements of **Marks and Spencer plc (M&S)** are available at the book's companion website or can be accessed at *http://annualreport.marksandspencer.com/_assets/downloads/Marks-and-Spencer-Annual-report-and-financial-statements-2012.pdf.*

Instructions

Refer to M&S's financial statements and the accompanying notes to answer the following questions.

(a) What amounts relative to income taxes does M&S report in its:

(1) 2012 income statement?

(2) 31 March 2012 statement of financial position?

(3) 2012 statement of cash flows?

(b) M&S's provision for income taxes in 2011 and 2012 was computed at what effective tax rates? (See the notes to the financial statements.)

(c) How much of M&S's 2012 total provision for income taxes was current tax expense, and how much was deferred tax expense?

(d) What did M&S report as the significant components (the details) of its 31 March 2012 deferred tax assets and liabilities?

ANSWERS TO IFRS SELF-TEST QUESTIONS

1. b **2.** c **3.** d **4.** d **5.** c

Remember to check the book's companion website to find additional resources for this chapter.

CHAPTER

20 Accounting for Pensions and Postretirement Benefits

LEARNING OBJECTIVES

After studying this chapter, you should be able to:

1. Distinguish between accounting for the employer's pension plan and accounting for the pension fund.
2. Identify types of pension plans and their characteristics.
3. Explain alternative measures for valuing the pension obligation.
4. List the components of pension expense.
5. Use a worksheet for employer's pension plan entries.
6. Describe the amortization of prior service costs.
7. Explain the accounting for unexpected gains and losses.
8. Explain the corridor approach to amortizing gains and losses.
9. Describe the requirements for reporting pension plans in financial statements.

Where Have All the Pensions Gone?

Many companies have benefit plans that promise income and other benefits to retired employees in exchange for services during their working years. However, a shift is on from traditional defined benefit plans, in which employers bear the risk of meeting the benefit promises, to plans in which employees bear more of the risk. In some cases, employers are dropping retirement plans altogether. Here are some of the reasons for the shift.

- ***Competition.*** Newer and foreign competitors do not have the same retiree costs that older U.S. companies do. **Southwest Airlines** does not offer a traditional pension plan, but **United** has a pension deficit exceeding $100,000 per employee.
- ***Cost.*** Retirees are living longer, and the costs of retirement are higher. Combined with annual retiree healthcare costs, retirement benefits are costing the S&P 500 companies over $25 billion a year and are rising at double-digit rates.
- ***Insurance.*** Pensions are backed by premiums paid to the **Pension Benefit Guarantee Corporation (PBGC)**. When a company fails, the PBGC takes over the plan. But due to a number of significant company failures, the PBGC is running a deficit, and healthy companies are subsidizing the weak.
- ***Accounting.*** To bring U.S. standards in line with international rules, accounting rule-makers are considering rules that will require companies to "mark their pensions to market" (value them at market rates). Such a move would increase the reported volatility of the retirement plan and of company financial statements. When Great Britain made this shift, 25 percent of British companies closed their plans to new entrants.

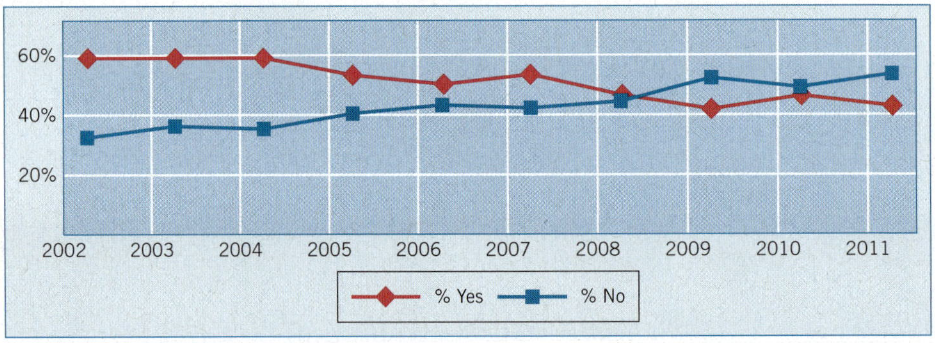

As a result of such factors, it is understandable that experts can think of no major company that has instituted a traditional pension plan in the past decade. What does this mean for you as you evaluate job offers and benefit packages? To start, you should begin building *your own* retirement nest egg, rather than relying on your employer to provide postretirement income and healthcare benefits. Recently, a sample of Americans was asked the following question: When you retire, do you think you will have enough money to live comfortably, or not?

The graph on the previous page shows a substantial change in responses from nonretired adults from 2002 to 2011.

In 2002, adults were nearly twice as likely to say they would have enough money to live comfortably (59%) as to say they would not (32%). Those views changed as time passed. By 2011, a majority said they would not have enough money to live comfortably in retirement.

General economic conditions affect how Americans look at retirement. Americans were more positive about the overall economy—and retirement—prior to the recent recession than they are now. The continuing political discussion about the fragility of the country's Social Security and Medicare programs may also reduce nonretired Americans' comfort with projections of their monetary resources in their retirement. In addition, many are beginning to realize that retirement at the age of 65 may no longer be possible given the possible extension of social benefits to later ages.

This means that retirement accounts, including individual retirement accounts and defined contribution pensions such as 401(k) plans, will need to become a bigger piece of the pie to fill the gap left by smaller government and employer-sponsored benefits. So get started now with a personal savings strategy to ensure an adequate nest egg at your retirement.

Sources: Story adapted from Nanette Byrnes with David Welch, "The Benefits Trap," *BusinessWeek* (July 19, 2004), pp. 54–72; and F. Newport, "In U.S., 53% Worry About Having Enough Money in Retirement," *http://www.gallup.com/poll/147254/%20-americans-biggest-financial-worry.aspx* (April 25, 2011).

CONCEPTUAL FOCUS

> See the **Underlying Concepts** on pages 1189, 1208, 1209, and 1213.

> Read the **Evolving Issue** on page 1202 for a discussion of the corridor approach.

INTERNATIONAL FOCUS

> See the **International Perspectives** on pages 1186 and 1207.

> Read the **IFRS Insights** on pages 1250–1266 for a discussion of:

—Accounting for pensions

—Using a pension worksheet

PREVIEW OF CHAPTER 20

As our opening story indicates, the cost of retirement benefits is steep. For example, **British Airways**' pension and healthcare costs for retirees in a recent year totaled $195 million, or approximately $6 per passenger carried. Many other companies are also facing substantial pension and other postretirement expenses and obligations. In this chapter, we discuss the accounting issues related to these benefit plans. The content and organization of the chapter are as follows.

Accounting for Pensions and Postretirement Benefits

Nature of Pension Plans
- Defined contribution plan
- Defined benefit plan
- Role of actuaries

Accounting for Pensions
- Alternative measures of liability
- Recognition of net funded status
- Components of pension expense

Using a Pension Worksheet
- 2014 entries and worksheet
- Amortization of prior service cost
- 2015 entries and worksheet
- Gain or loss
- Corridor amortization
- 2016 entries and worksheet

Reporting Pension Plans in Financial Statements
- Within the financial statements
- Within the notes to the financial statements
- Pension note disclosure
- 2017 entries and worksheet—a comprehensive example
- Special issues

NATURE OF PENSION PLANS

LEARNING OBJECTIVE 1

Distinguish between accounting for the employer's pension plan and accounting for the pension fund.

A **pension plan** is an arrangement whereby an employer provides benefits (payments) to retired employees for services they provided in their working years. Pension accounting may be divided and separately treated as **accounting for the employer** and **accounting for the pension fund**. The *company* or *employer* is the organization sponsoring the pension plan. It incurs the cost and makes contributions to the pension fund. The *fund* or *plan* is the entity that receives the contributions from the employer, administers the pension assets, and makes the benefit payments to the retired employees (pension recipients). Illustration 20-1 shows the three entities involved in a pension plan and indicates the flow of cash among them.

ILLUSTRATION 20-1
Flow of Cash among Pension Plan Participants

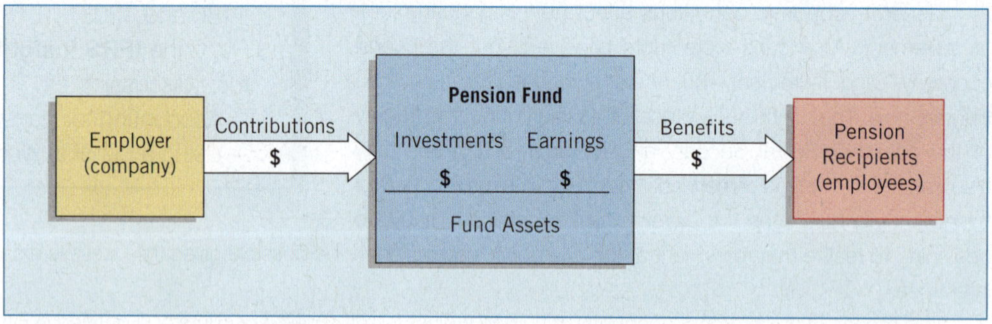

A pension plan is **funded** when the employer makes payments to a funding agency.[1] That agency accumulates the assets of the pension fund and makes payments to the recipients as the benefits come due.

Some pension plans are **contributory**. In these, the employees bear part of the cost of the stated benefits or voluntarily make payments to increase their benefits. Other plans are **noncontributory**. In these plans, the employer bears the entire cost. Companies generally design their pension plans so as to take advantage of federal income tax benefits. Plans that offer tax benefits are called **qualified pension plans**. They permit **deductibility of the employer's contributions to the pension fund and tax-free status of earnings from pension fund assets.**

The pension fund should be a separate legal and accounting entity. The pension fund, as a separate entity, maintains a set of books and prepares financial statements. Maintaining records and preparing financial statements for the fund, an activity known as "accounting for employee benefit plans," is not the subject of this chapter.[2] Instead, this chapter explains the pension accounting and reporting problems **of the employer** as the sponsor of a pension plan.

The need to properly administer and account for pension funds becomes apparent when you understand the size of these funds. Listed in Illustration 20-2 are the pension fund assets and pension expenses of six major companies.

ILLUSTRATION 20-2
Pension Funds and Pension Expense

Company ($ in millions)	Size of Pension Fund	2011 Pension Expense (Income)	Pension Expense as % of Pretax Income
General Motors	$108,980	$(490)	−8.19%
Hewlett-Packard	10,662	280	3.12%
Deere & Company	9,552	91	2.15%
Merck	12,481	543	7.40%
The Coca-Cola Company	6,171	249	2.18%
Molson Coors Brewing	3,139	19	2.45%

See the FASB Codification section (page 1229).

[1]When used as a verb, **fund** means to pay to a funding agency (as to fund future pension benefits or to fund pension cost). Used as a noun, it refers to assets accumulated in the hands of a funding agency (trustee) for the purpose of meeting pension benefits when they become due.

[2]The FASB issued a separate standard covering the accounting and reporting for employee benefit plans. **[1]**

As Illustration 20-2 indicates, pension expense is a substantial percentage of total pretax income for many companies.[3] The two most common types of pension plans are **defined contribution plans** and **defined benefit plans**, and we look at each of them in the following sections.

Defined Contribution Plan

2 LEARNING OBJECTIVE
Identify types of pension plans and their characteristics.

In a **defined contribution plan**, the employer agrees to contribute to a pension trust a certain sum each period, based on a formula. This formula may consider such factors as age, length of employee service, employer's profits, and compensation level. **The plan defines only the employer's contribution.** It makes no promise regarding the ultimate benefits paid out to the employees. A common form of this plan is a **401(k) plan**.

The size of the pension benefits that the employee finally collects under the plan depends on several factors: the amounts originally contributed to the pension trust, the income accumulated in the trust, and the treatment of forfeitures of funds caused by early terminations of other employees. A company usually turns over to an **independent third-party trustee** the amounts originally contributed. The trustee, acting on behalf of the beneficiaries (the participating employees), assumes ownership of the pension assets and is accountable for their investment and distribution. The trust is separate and distinct from the employer.

The accounting for a defined contribution plan is straightforward. The employee gets the benefit of gain (or the risk of loss) from the assets contributed to the pension plan. The employer simply contributes each year based on the formula established in the plan. As a result, the employer's annual cost (pension expense) is simply the amount that it is obligated to contribute to the pension trust. The employer reports a liability on its balance sheet only if it does not make the contribution in full. The employer reports an asset only if it contributes more than the required amount.

In addition to pension expense, the employer must disclose the following for a defined contribution plan: a plan description, including employee groups covered; the basis for determining contributions; and the nature and effect of significant matters affecting comparability from period to period. **[2]**

Defined Benefit Plan

A **defined benefit plan** outlines the benefits that employees will receive when they retire. These benefits typically are a function of an employee's years of service and of the compensation level in the years approaching retirement.

To meet the defined benefit commitments that will arise at retirement, a company must determine what the contribution should be today (a time value of money computation). Companies may use many different contribution approaches. However, the funding method should provide enough money at retirement to meet the benefits defined by the plan.

The **employees** are the beneficiaries of a defined **contribution** trust, but the **employer** is the beneficiary of a defined **benefit** trust. Under a defined benefit plan, the trust's primary purpose is to safeguard and invest assets so that there will be enough to pay the employer's obligation to the employees. **In form**, the trust is a separate entity. **In substance**, the trust assets and liabilities belong to the employer. That is, **as long as**

[3]Retirement assets in the 13 major global markets increased 4 percent to a record $27.5 trillion in 2011. The United States accounts for 59 percent of total pension assets, followed by Japan at 12 percent and the United Kingdom at 9 percent. Defined contribution assets for the seven largest markets—United States, United Kingdom, Japan, Netherlands, Canada, Australia, and Switzerland—now make up 43 percent of global retirement assets, up from 41 percent in 2005 and 38 percent in 2001. The United States, Australia, and Switzerland are the only countries with more defined contribution assets than defined benefit ones. See K. Olsen, "Global Pension Market Hits $27.5T," *http://www.pionline.com/article/20120206/PRINTSUB/302069986#* (February 6, 2012).

International Perspective

Outside the United States, private pension plans are less common because many other nations rely on government-sponsored pension plans. Consequently, accounting for defined benefit pension plans is typically a less important issue elsewhere in the world.

the plan continues, the employer is responsible for the payment of the defined benefits (without regard to what happens in the trust). The employer must make up any shortfall in the accumulated assets held by the trust. On the other hand, the employer can recapture any excess accumulated in the trust, either through reduced future funding or through a reversion of funds.

Because a defined benefit plan specifies benefits in terms of uncertain future variables, a company must establish an appropriate funding pattern to ensure the availability of funds at retirement in order to provide the benefits promised. This funding level depends on a number of factors such as turnover, mortality, length of employee service, compensation levels, and interest earnings.

Employers are at risk with defined benefit plans because they must contribute enough to meet the cost of benefits that the plan defines. The expense recognized each period is not necessarily equal to the cash contribution. Similarly, the liability is controversial because its measurement and recognition relate to unknown future variables. Thus, the accounting issues related to this type of plan are complex. **Our discussion in the following sections deals primarily with defined benefit plans.**[4]

What do the numbers mean? WHICH PLAN IS RIGHT FOR YOU?

Defined contribution plans have become much more popular with employers than defined benefit plans, as indicated in the chart below. One reason is that they are cheaper. Defined contribution plans often cost no more than 3 percent of payroll, whereas defined benefit plans can cost 5 to 6 percent of payroll.

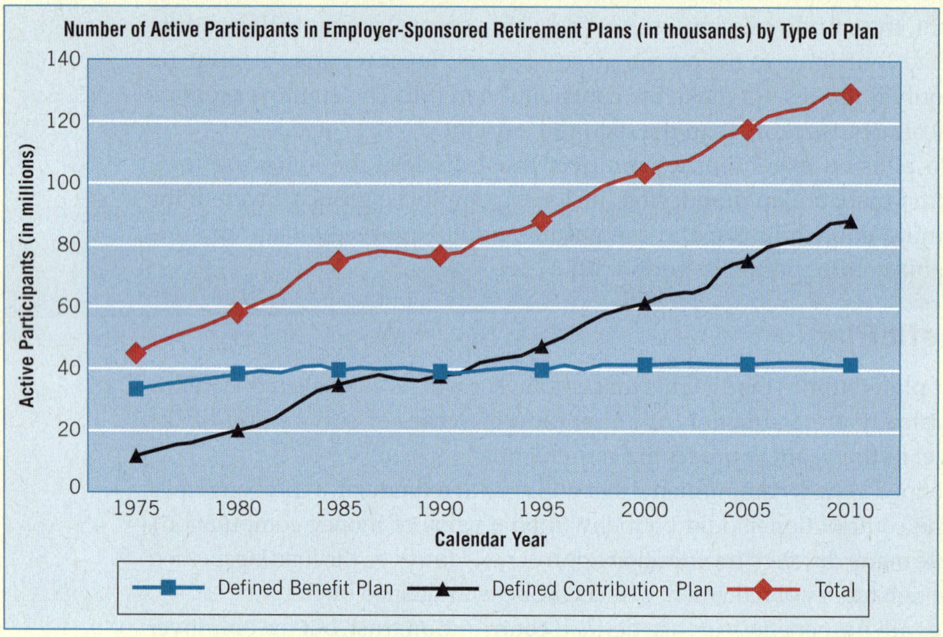

Source: Form 5500 filings with U.S. Department of Labor, November 2012, "Private Pension Plan Bulletin."

The total amount of assets held by pension plans increased 14 percent to $6.3 trillion in 2010. Defined benefit plan assets increased 12 percent to $2.4 trillion, while defined contribution plans increased 16 percent to $3.8 trillion.

[4]A recent federal law requires employees to explicitly opt out of an employer-sponsored defined contribution plan. This should help employees build their own nest eggs (as suggested in the opening story) and will contribute to further growth in defined contribution plans. However, note the following three warnings: (1) low-income workers will still not be able to stash enough away, (2) it leaves each participant alone to manage risk, and (3) companies establish a minimum contribution, which too many participants choose to use, instead of a larger contribution.

The Role of Actuaries in Pension Accounting

The problems associated with pension plans involve complicated mathematical considerations. Therefore, companies engage **actuaries** to ensure that a pension plan is appropriate for the employee group covered.[5] Actuaries are individuals trained through a long and rigorous certification program to assign probabilities to future events and their financial effects. The insurance industry employs actuaries to assess risks and to advise on the setting of premiums and other aspects of insurance policies. Employers rely heavily on actuaries for assistance in developing, implementing, and funding pension funds.

Actuaries make predictions (called *actuarial assumptions*) of mortality rates, employee turnover, interest and earnings rates, early retirement frequency, future salaries, and any other factors necessary to operate a pension plan. They also compute the various pension measures that affect the financial statements, such as the pension obligation, the annual cost of servicing the plan, and the cost of amendments to the plan. In summary, accounting for defined benefit pension plans relies heavily upon information and measurements provided by actuaries.

ACCOUNTING FOR PENSIONS

3 LEARNING OBJECTIVE
Explain alternative measures for valuing the pension obligation.

In accounting for a company's pension plan, two questions arise. (1) What is the pension obligation that a company should report in the financial statements? (2) What is the pension expense for the period? Attempting to answer the first question has produced much controversy.

Alternative Measures of the Liability

Most agree that an employer's **pension obligation** is the deferred compensation obligation it has to its employees for their service under the terms of the pension plan. Measuring that obligation is not so simple, though, because there are alternative ways of measuring it.[6]

One measure of the pension obligation is to base it only on the benefits vested to the employees. **Vested benefits** are those that the employee is entitled to receive even if he or she renders no additional services to the company. Most pension plans require a certain minimum number of years of service to the employer before an employee achieves vested benefits status. Companies compute the **vested benefit obligation** using only vested benefits, at current salary levels.

Another way to measure the obligation uses both vested and nonvested years of service. On this basis, the company computes the deferred compensation amount on all years of employees' service—**both vested and nonvested**—using current salary levels. This measurement of the pension obligation is called the **accumulated benefit obligation**.

[5]An actuary's primary purpose is to ensure that the company has established an appropriate funding pattern to meet its pension obligations. This computation involves developing a set of assumptions and continued monitoring of these assumptions to ensure their realism. That the general public has little understanding of what an actuary does is illustrated by the following excerpt from the *Wall Street Journal*: "A polling organization once asked the general public what an actuary was, and received among its more coherent responses the opinion that it was a place where you put dead actors."

[6]One measure of the pension obligation is to determine the amount that the **Pension Benefit Guaranty Corporation** would require the employer to pay if it defaulted. (This amount is limited to 30 percent of the employer's net worth.) The accounting profession rejected this approach for financial reporting because it is too hypothetical and ignores the going concern concept.

A third measure bases the deferred compensation amount on both vested and nonvested service **using future salaries**. This measurement of the pension obligation is called the **projected benefit obligation**. Because future salaries are expected to be higher than current salaries, this approach results in the largest measurement of the pension obligation.

The choice between these measures is critical. The choice affects the amount of a company's pension liability and the annual pension expense reported. The diagram in Illustration 20-3 presents the differences in these three measurements.

ILLUSTRATION 20-3
Different Measures of the Pension Obligation

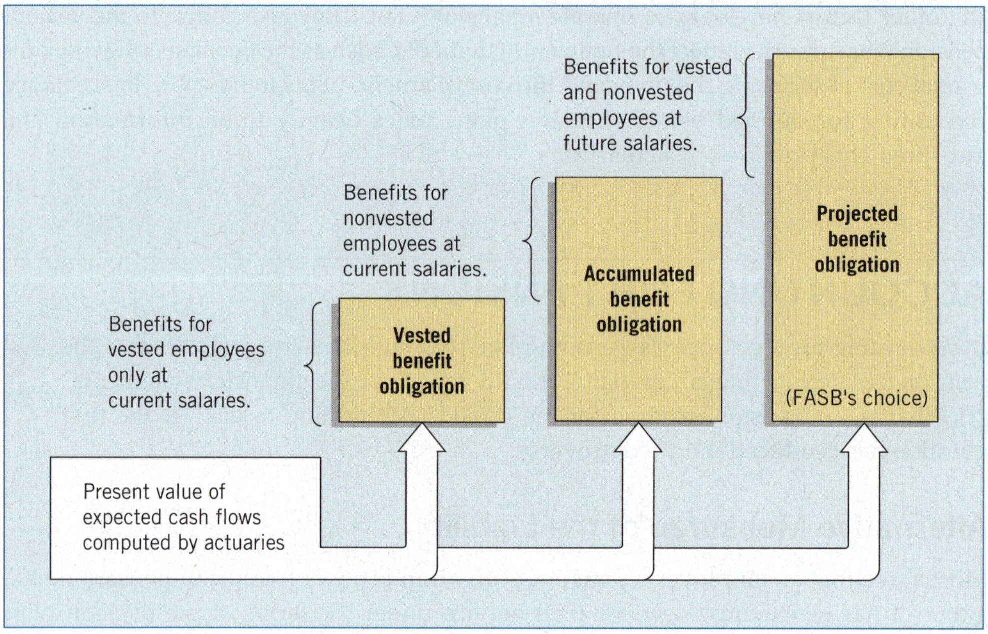

Which of these alternative measures of the pension liability does the profession favor? **The profession adopted the projected benefit obligation—the present value of vested and nonvested benefits accrued to date, based on employees' future salary levels.**[7] Those in favor of the projected benefit obligation contend that a promise by an employer to pay benefits based on a percentage of the employees' future salaries is far greater than a promise to pay a percentage of their current salary, and such a difference should be reflected in the pension liability and pension expense.

Moreover, companies discount to present value the estimated future benefits to be paid. Minor changes in the interest rate used to discount pension benefits can dramatically affect the measurement of the employer's obligation. For example, a 1 percent decrease in the discount rate can increase pension liabilities 15 percent. Accounting rules require that at each measurement date, a company must determine the appropriate discount rate used to measure the pension liability, based on current interest rates.

[7]When we use the term "present value of benefits" throughout this chapter, we really mean the *actuarial* present value of benefits. **Actuarial present value** is the amount payable adjusted to reflect the time value of money *and* the probability of payment (by means of decrements for events such as death, disability, withdrawals, or retirement) between the present date and the expected date of payment. For simplicity, though, we use the term "present value" instead of "actuarial present value" in our discussion.

Recognition of the Net Funded Status of the Pension Plan

Companies must recognize on their balance sheet the full overfunded or underfunded status of their defined benefit pension plan.[8] **[3]** The **overfunded** or **underfunded status** is measured as the difference between the fair value of the plan assets and the projected benefit obligation.

To illustrate, assume that Coker Company has a projected benefit obligation of $300,000, and the fair value of its plan assets is $210,000. In this case, Coker Company's pension plan is underfunded, and therefore it reports a pension liability of $90,000 ($300,000 − $210,000) on its balance sheet. If instead the fair value of Coker's plan assets were $430,000, it would report a pension asset of $130,000 ($430,000 − $300,000).

In 2007, by slowing the growth of pension liabilities and increasing contributions to pension funds, the S&P 500 companies reported aggregate overfunding (assets exceeded liabilities) of $47.2 billion. However, by 2011, these same pension plans were underfunded by $358.4 billion.[9]

Components of Pension Expense

4 LEARNING OBJECTIVE
List the components of pension expense.

There is broad agreement that companies should account for pension cost on the **accrual basis.**[10] The profession recognizes that **accounting for pension plans requires measurement of the cost and its identification with the appropriate time periods**. The determination of pension cost, however, is extremely complicated because it is a function of the following components.

Underlying Concepts

The expense recognition principle and the definition of a liability justify accounting for pension cost on the accrual basis. This requires recording an expense when employees earn the future benefits, and recognizing an existing obligation to pay pensions later based on current services received.

1. *Service cost.* Service cost is the expense caused by the increase in pension benefits payable (the **projected benefit obligation**) to employees because of their services rendered during the current year. Actuaries compute **service cost** as the present value of the new benefits earned by employees during the year.
2. *Interest on the liability.* Because a pension is a deferred compensation arrangement, there is a time value of money factor. As a result, companies record the pension liability on a discounted basis. **Interest expense accrues each year on the projected benefit obligation just as it does on any discounted debt.** The actuary helps to select the interest rate, referred to as the **settlement rate**.
3. *Actual return on plan assets.* The return earned by the accumulated pension fund assets in a particular year is relevant in measuring the net cost to the employer of sponsoring an employee pension plan. Therefore, **a company should adjust annual pension expense for interest and dividends that accumulate within the fund, as well as increases and decreases in the fair value of the fund assets.**
4. *Amortization of prior service cost.* Pension plan amendments (including initiation of a pension plan) often include provisions to increase benefits (or in rare situations, to decrease benefits) for employee service provided in prior years. A company grants plan amendments with the expectation that it will realize economic benefits in future periods. Thus, **it allocates the cost (prior service cost) of providing these**

[8]Recognize that GAAP applies to pensions as well as other postretirement benefit plans (OPEBs). Appendix 20A addresses the accounting for OPEBs.

[9]J. Ciesielski, "State of the Pension Promise: The S&P 500 in 2011," *The Analyst's Accounting Observer* (May 29, 2012).

[10]At one time, companies applied the **cash basis** of accounting to pension plans by recognizing the amount paid in a particular accounting period as the pension expense for the period. The problem was that the amount paid or funded in a fiscal period depended on financial management and was too often discretionary. For example, funding could depend on the availability of cash, the level of earnings, or other factors unrelated to the requirements of the plan. Application of the cash basis made it possible to manipulate the amount of pension expense appearing in the income statement simply by varying the cash paid to the pension fund.

retroactive benefits to pension expense in the future, specifically to the remaining service-years of the affected employees.

5. *Gain or loss.* Volatility in pension expense can result from sudden and large changes in the fair value of plan assets and by changes in the projected benefit obligation (which changes when actuaries modify assumptions or when actual experience differs from expected experience). Two items comprise this gain or loss: (1) the difference between the actual return and the expected return on plan assets, and (2) amortization of the net gain or loss from previous periods. We will discuss this complex computation later in the chapter.

Illustration 20-4 shows the components of pension expense and their effect on total pension expense (increase or decrease).

ILLUSTRATION 20-4
Components of Annual Pension Expense

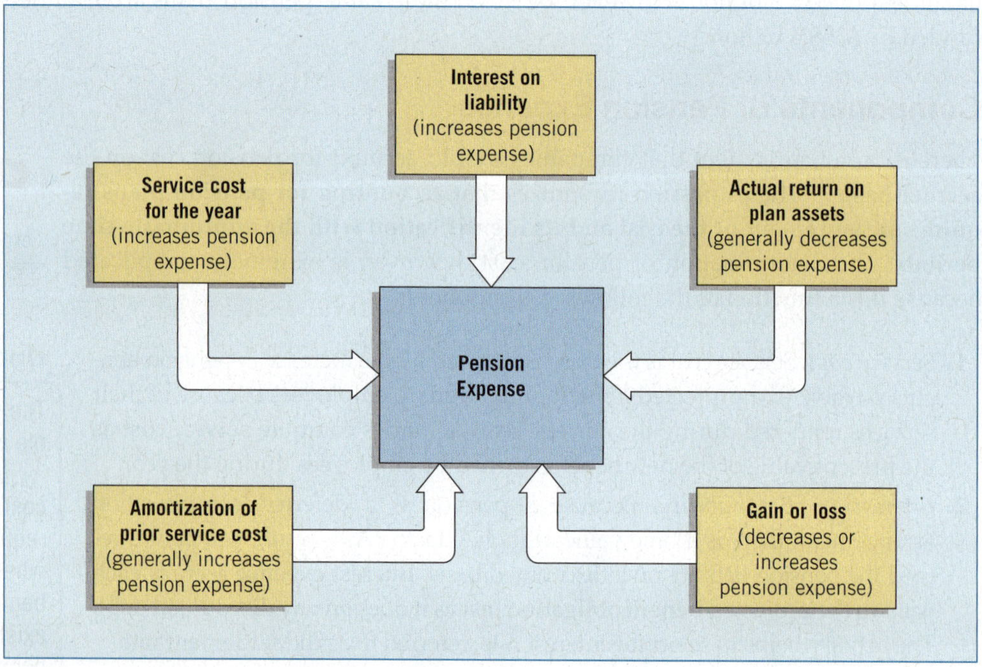

Service Cost

The service cost is the **actuarial present value of benefits attributed by the pension benefit formula to employee service during the period**. That is, the actuary predicts the additional benefits that an employer must pay under the plan's benefit formula as a result of the employees' current year's service, and then discounts the cost of those future benefits back to their present value.

The Board concluded that **companies must consider future compensation levels in measuring the present obligation and periodic pension expense if the plan benefit formula incorporates them**. In other words, the present obligation resulting from a promise to pay a benefit of 1 percent of an employee's **final pay** differs from the promise to pay 1 percent of **current pay**. To overlook this fact is to ignore an important aspect of pension expense. Thus, the FASB adopts the **benefits/years-of-service actuarial method, which determines pension expense based on future salary levels.**

Some object to this determination, arguing that a company should have more freedom to select an expense recognition pattern. Others believe that incorporating future salary increases into current pension expense is accounting for events that have not yet happened. They argue that if a company terminates the plan today, it pays only liabilities for accumulated benefits. **Nevertheless, the FASB indicates that the projected benefit obligation provides a more realistic measure of the employer's obligation under the**

plan on a going concern basis and, therefore, companies should use it as the basis for determining service cost.

Interest on the Liability

The second component of pension expense is **interest on the liability**, or **interest expense**. Because a company defers paying the liability until maturity, the company records it on a discounted basis. The liability then accrues interest over the life of the employee. **The interest component is the interest for the period on the projected benefit obligation outstanding during the period.** The FASB did not address the question of how often to compound the interest cost. To simplify our illustrations and problem materials, we use a simple interest computation, applying it to the beginning-of-the-year balance of the projected benefit liability.

How do companies determine the interest rate to apply to the pension liability? The Board states that the assumed discount rate should **reflect the rates at which companies can effectively settle pension benefits**. In determining these **settlement rates**, companies should look to rates of return on high-quality fixed-income investments currently available, whose cash flows match the timing and amount of the expected benefit payments. The objective of selecting the assumed discount rates is to measure a single amount that, if invested in a portfolio of high-quality debt instruments, would provide the necessary future cash flows to pay the pension benefits when due.

Actual Return on Plan Assets

Pension plan assets are usually investments in stocks, bonds, other securities, and real estate that a company holds to earn a reasonable return, generally at minimum risk. Employer contributions and actual returns on pension plan assets increase pension plan assets. Benefits paid to retired employees decrease them. As we indicated, the actual return earned on these assets increases the fund balance and correspondingly reduces the employer's net cost of providing employees' pension benefits. That is, the higher the actual return on the pension plan assets, the less the employer has to contribute eventually and, therefore, the less pension expense that it needs to report.

The actual return on the plan assets is the increase in pension funds from interest, dividends, and realized and unrealized changes in the fair value of the plan assets. Companies compute the actual return by adjusting the change in the plan assets for the effects of contributions during the year and benefits paid out during the year. The equation in Illustration 20-5, or a variation thereof, can be used to compute the actual return.

$$\text{Actual Return} = \left(\begin{array}{c}\text{Plan Assets} \\ \text{Ending Balance}\end{array} - \begin{array}{c}\text{Plan Assets} \\ \text{Beginning Balance}\end{array}\right) - (\text{Contributions} - \text{Benefits Paid})$$

ILLUSTRATION 20-5
Equation for Computing Actual Return

Stated another way, the actual return on plan assets is the difference between the **fair value of the plan assets** at the beginning of the period and at the end of the period, adjusted for contributions and benefit payments. Illustration 20-6 uses the equation above to compute the actual return, using some assumed amounts.

Fair value of plan assets at end of period		$5,000,000
Deduct: Fair value of plan assets at beginning of period		4,200,000
Increase in fair value of plan assets		800,000
Deduct: Contributions to plan during period	$500,000	
Less benefits paid during period	300,000	200,000
Actual return on plan assets		$ 600,000

ILLUSTRATION 20-6
Computation of Actual Return on Plan Assets

If the actual return on the plan assets is positive (a gain) during the period, a company subtracts it when computing pension expense. If the actual return is negative (a loss) during the period, the company adds it when computing pension expense.[11]

USING A PENSION WORKSHEET

LEARNING OBJECTIVE 5
Use a worksheet for employer's pension plan entries.

We will now illustrate the basic computation of pension expense using the first three components: (1) service cost, (2) interest on the liability, and (3) actual return on plan assets. We discuss the other pension expense components (amortization of prior service cost, and gains and losses) in later sections.

Companies often use a worksheet to record pension-related information. As its name suggests, the worksheet is a working tool. A worksheet is **not** a permanent accounting record. It is neither a journal nor part of the general ledger. The worksheet is merely a device to make it easier to prepare entries and the financial statements.[12] Illustration 20-7 shows the format of the **pension worksheet**.

ILLUSTRATION 20-7
Basic Format of Pension Worksheet

Pension Worksheet.xls

Home Insert Page Layout Formulas Data Review View

P18 fx

	A	B	C	D	E	F
1						
2		General Journal Entries			Memo Record	
3		Annual		Pension	Projected	
4		Pension		Asset/	Benefit	Plan
5	Items	Expense	Cash	Liability	Obligation	Assets
6						
7						
8						
9						

The "General Journal Entries" columns of the worksheet (near the left side) determine the entries to record in the formal general ledger accounts. The "Memo Record" columns (on the right side) maintain balances in the projected benefit obligation and the plan assets. The difference between the projected benefit obligation and the fair value of the plan assets is the **pension asset/liability**, which is shown in the balance sheet. If the projected benefit obligation is greater than the plan assets, a pension liability occurs. If the projected benefit obligation is less than the plan assets, a pension asset occurs.

On the first line of the worksheet, a company records the beginning balances (if any). It then records subsequent transactions and events related to the pension plan using debits and credits, using both sets of columns as if they were one. For each transaction or event, the debits must equal the credits. **The ending balance in the Pension Asset/Liability column should equal the net balance in the memo record.**

2014 Entries and Worksheet

To illustrate the use of a worksheet and how it helps in accounting for a pension plan, assume that on January 1, 2014, Zarle Company provides the following information related to its pension plan for the year 2014.

[11]At this point, we use the actual rate of return. Later, for purposes of computing pension expense, we use the expected rate of return.

[12]The use of a pension entry worksheet is recommended and illustrated by Paul B. W. Miller, "The New Pension Accounting (Part 2)," *Journal of Accountancy* (February 1987), pp. 86–94.

Plan assets, January 1, 2014, are $100,000.

Projected benefit obligation, January 1, 2014, is $100,000.

Annual service cost is $9,000.

Settlement rate is 10 percent.

Actual return on plan assets is $10,000.

Funding contributions are $8,000.

Benefits paid to retirees during the year are $7,000.

Using this data, the worksheet in Illustration 20-8 presents the beginning balances and all of the pension entries recorded by Zarle in 2014. Zarle records the beginning balances for the projected benefit obligation and the pension plan assets on the first line of the worksheet in the memo record. Because the projected benefit obligation and the plan assets are the same at January 1, 2014, the Pension Asset/Liability account has a zero balance at January 1, 2014.

ILLUSTRATION 20-8
Pension Worksheet—2014

Pension Worksheet—2014.xls

	A	B	C	D	E	F
1						
2		General Journal Entries			Memo Record	
3		Annual		Pension	Projected	
4		Pension		Asset/	Benefit	Plan
5	Items	Expense	Cash	Liability	Obligation	Assets
6	Balance, Jan. 1, 2014			—	100,000 Cr.	100,000 Dr.
7	(a) Service cost	9,000 Dr.			9,000 Cr.	
8	(b) Interest cost	10,000 Dr.			10,000 Cr.	
9	(c) Actual return	10,000 Cr.				10,000 Dr.
10	(d) Contributions		8,000 Cr.			8,000 Dr.
11	(e) Benefits				7,000 Dr.	7,000 Cr.
12						
13						
14	Journal entry for 2014	9,000 Dr.	8,000 Cr.	1,000 Cr.*		
15	Balance, Dec. 31, 2014			1,000 Cr.**	112,000 Cr.	111,000 Dr.
16						
17	*$9,000 – $8,000 = $1,000					
18	**$112,000 – $111,000 = $1,000					

Entry (a) in Illustration 20-8 records the service cost component, which increases pension expense by $9,000 and increases the liability (projected benefit obligation) by $9,000. Entry (b) accrues the interest expense component, which increases both the liability and the pension expense by $10,000 (the beginning projected benefit obligation multiplied by the settlement rate of 10 percent). Entry (c) records the actual return on the plan assets, which increases the plan assets and decreases the pension expense. Entry (d) records Zarle's contribution (funding) of assets to the pension fund, thereby decreasing cash by $8,000 and increasing plan assets by $8,000. Entry (e) records the benefit payments made to retirees, which results in equal $7,000 decreases to the plan assets and the projected benefit obligation.

Zarle makes the "formal journal entry" on December 31, which records the pension expense in 2014, as follows.

2014		
Pension Expense	9,000	
Cash		8,000
Pension Asset/Liability		1,000

The credit to Pension Asset/Liability for $1,000 represents the difference between the 2014 pension expense of $9,000 and the amount funded of $8,000. Pension Asset/Liability (credit) is a liability because Zarle underfunds the plan by $1,000. The Pension Asset/Liability account balance of $1,000 also equals the net of the balances in the memo accounts. Illustration 20-9 shows that the projected benefit obligation exceeds the plan assets by $1,000, which reconciles to the pension liability reported in the balance sheet.

ILLUSTRATION 20-9
Pension Reconciliation Schedule—December 31, 2014

Projected benefit obligation (Credit)	$(112,000)
Plan assets at fair value (Debit)	111,000
Pension asset/liability (Credit)	$ (1,000)

If the net of the memo record balances is a credit, the reconciling amount in the pension asset/liability column will be a credit equal in amount. If the net of the memo record balances is a debit, the pension asset/liability amount will be a debit equal in amount. The worksheet is designed to produce this reconciling feature, which is useful later in the preparation of the financial statements and required note disclosure related to pensions.

In this illustration (for 2014), the debit to Pension Expense exceeds the credit to Cash, resulting in a credit to Pension Asset/Liability—the recognition of a liability. If the credit to Cash exceeded the debit to Pension Expense, Zarle would debit Pension Asset/Liability—the recognition of an asset.

Amortization of Prior Service Cost (PSC)

LEARNING OBJECTIVE 6
Describe the amortization of prior service costs.

When either initiating (adopting) or amending a defined benefit plan, a company often provides benefits to employees for years of service before the date of initiation or amendment. As a result of this prior service cost, the projected benefit obligation is increased to recognize this additional liability. In many cases, the increase in the projected benefit obligation is substantial.

Should a company report an expense for these **prior service costs (PSC)** at the time it initiates or amends a plan? The FASB says no. The Board's rationale is that the employer would not provide credit for past years of service unless it expects to receive benefits in the future. As a result, a company should not recognize the **retroactive benefits** as pension expense in the year of amendment. Instead, **the employer initially records the prior service cost as an adjustment to other comprehensive income. The employer then recognizes the prior service cost as a component of pension expense over the remaining service lives of the employees who are expected to benefit from the change in the plan.**

The cost of the retroactive benefits (including any benefits provided to existing retirees) is the increase in the projected benefit obligation at the date of the amendment. An actuary computes the amount of the prior service cost. Amortization of the prior service cost is also an accounting function performed with the assistance of an actuary.

The Board prefers a **years-of-service method** that is similar to a units-of-production computation. First, the company computes the total number of service-years to be worked by all of the participating employees. Second, it divides the prior service cost by the total number of service-years, to obtain a cost per service-year (the unit cost). Third, the company multiplies the number of service-years consumed each year by the cost per service-year, to obtain the annual amortization charge.

To illustrate the amortization of the prior service cost under the years-of-service method, assume that Zarle Company's defined benefit pension plan covers 170 employees. In its negotiations with the employees, Zarle Company amends its pension plan on January 1, 2015, and grants $80,000 of prior service costs to its employees. The employees are grouped according to expected years of retirement, as shown on the next page.

Group	Number of Employees	Expected Retirement on Dec. 31
A	40	2015
B	20	2016
C	40	2017
D	50	2018
E	20	2019
	170	

Illustration 20-10 shows computation of the service-years per year and the total service-years.

ILLUSTRATION 20-10
Computation of Service-Years

	Service-Years					
Year	A	B	C	D	E	Total
2015	40	20	40	50	20	170
2016		20	40	50	20	130
2017			40	50	20	110
2018				50	20	70
2019					20	20
	40	40	120	200	100	500

Computed on the basis of a prior service cost of $80,000 and a total of 500 service-years for all years, the cost per service-year is $160 ($80,000 ÷ 500). The annual amount of amortization based on a $160 cost per service-year is computed as follows.

ILLUSTRATION 20-11
Computation of Annual Prior Service Cost Amortization

Year	Total Service-Years	×	Cost per Service-Year	=	Annual Amortization
2015	170		$160		$27,200
2016	130		160		20,800
2017	110		160		17,600
2018	70		160		11,200
2019	20		160		3,200
	500				$80,000

An alternative method of computing amortization of **prior service cost is permitted. Employers may use straight-line amortization over the average remaining service life of the employees.** In this case, with 500 service-years and 170 employees, the average would be 2.94 years (500 ÷ 170). The annual expense would be $27,211 ($80,000 ÷ 2.94). Using this method, Zarle Company would charge cost to expense in 2015, 2016, and 2017 as follows.

Year	Expense
2015	$27,211
2016	27,211
2017	25,578*
	$80,000

*.94 × $27,211

2015 Entries and Worksheet

Continuing the Zarle Company illustration into 2015, we note that the company amends the pension plan on January 1, 2015, to grant employees prior service benefits with a present value of $80,000. Zarle uses the annual amortization amounts, as computed in the previous section using the years-of-service approach ($27,200 for 2015). The following additional facts apply to the pension plan for the year 2015.

Annual service cost is $9,500.
Settlement rate is 10 percent.
Actual return on plan assets is $11,100.
Annual funding contributions are $20,000.
Benefits paid to retirees during the year are $8,000.
Amortization of prior service cost (PSC) using the years-of-service method is $27,200.
Accumulated other comprehensive income (hereafter referred to as accumulated OCI) on December 31, 2014, is zero.

Illustration 20-12 presents a worksheet of all the pension entries and information recorded by Zarle in 2015. We now add an additional column to the worksheet to record the prior service cost adjustment to other comprehensive income. In addition, as shown in rows 19, 21, and 22, the other comprehensive income amount related to prior service cost is added to accumulated other comprehensive income ("Accumulated OCI") to arrive at a debit balance of $52,800 at December 31, 2015.

Pension Worksheet—2015.xls

	A	B	C	D	E	F	G
2		General Journal Entries				Memo Record	
3–7	Items	Annual Pension Expense	Cash	Other Comprehensive Income Prior Service Cost	Pension Asset/ Liability	Projected Benefit Obligation	Plan Assets
8	Balance, Dec. 31, 2014				1,000 Cr.	112,000 Cr.	111,000 Dr.
9	(f) Prior service cost			80,000 Dr.		80,000 Cr.	0
10							
11	Balance, Jan. 1, 2015					192,000 Cr.	111,000 Dr.
12	(g) Service cost	9,500 Dr.				9,500 Cr.	
13	(h) Interest cost	19,200 Dr.				19,200 Cr.	
14	(i) Actual return	11,100 Cr.					11,100 Dr.
15	(j) Amortization of PSC	27,200 Dr.		27,200 Cr.			
16	(k) Contributions		20,000 Cr.				20,000 Dr.
17	(l) Benefits					8,000 Dr.	8,000 Cr.
18							
19	Journal entry for 2015	44,800 Dr.	20,000 Cr.	52,800 Dr.	77,600 Cr.		
20							
21	Accumulated OCI, Dec. 31, 2014			0			
22	Balance, Dec. 31, 2015			52,800 Dr.	78,600 Cr.	212,700 Cr.	134,100 Dr.
23							

ILLUSTRATION 20-12
Pension Worksheet—2015

The first line of the worksheet shows the beginning balances of the Pension Asset/ Liability account and the memo accounts. Entry (f) records Zarle's granting of prior service cost, by adding $80,000 to the projected benefit obligation and decreasing other comprehensive income—prior service cost by the same amount. Entries (g), (h), (i), (k), and (l) are similar to the corresponding entries in 2014. To compute the interest cost on the projected benefit obligation for entry (h), we use the beginning projected benefit balance of $192,000, which has been adjusted for the prior service cost amendment on January 1, 2015. Entry (j) records the 2015 amortization of prior service cost by debiting Pension Expense for $27,200 and crediting **Other Comprehensive Income (PSC)** for the same amount.

Zarle makes the following journal entry on December 31 to formally record the 2015 pension expense (the sum of the annual pension expense column), and related pension information.

2015		
Pension Expense	44,800	
Other Comprehensive Income (PSC)	52,800	
Cash		20,000
Pension Asset/Liability		77,600

Because the debits to Pension Expense and to Other Comprehensive Income (PSC) exceed the funding, Zarle credits the Pension Asset/Liability account for the $77,600 difference. That account is a liability. In 2015, as in 2014, the balance of the Pension Asset/Liability account ($78,600) is equal to the net of the balances in the memo accounts, as shown in Illustration 20-13.

Projected benefit obligation (Credit)	$(212,700)
Plan assets at fair value (Debit)	134,100
Pension asset/liability (Credit)	$ (78,600)

ILLUSTRATION 20-13
Pension Reconciliation Schedule—December 31, 2015

The reconciliation is the formula that makes the worksheet work. It relates the components of pension accounting, recorded and unrecorded, to one another.

Gain or Loss

7 LEARNING OBJECTIVE
Explain the accounting for unexpected gains and losses.

Of great concern to companies that have pension plans are the uncontrollable and unexpected swings in pension expense that can result from (1) sudden and large changes in the fair value of plan assets, and (2) changes in actuarial assumptions that affect the amount of the projected benefit obligation. If these gains or losses impact fully the financial statements in the period of realization or incurrence, substantial fluctuations in pension expense result.

Therefore, the FASB decided to reduce the volatility associated with pension expense by using **smoothing techniques** that dampen and in some cases fully eliminate the fluctuations.

Smoothing Unexpected Gains and Losses on Plan Assets

One component of pension expense, actual return on plan assets, reduces pension expense (assuming the actual return is positive). A large change in the actual return can substantially affect pension expense for a year. Assume a company has a 40 percent return in the stock market for the year. Should this substantial, and perhaps one-time, event affect current pension expense?

Actuaries ignore current fluctuations when they develop a funding pattern to pay expected benefits in the future. They develop an **expected rate of return** and multiply it by an asset value weighted over a reasonable period of time to arrive at an **expected return on plan assets**. They then use this return to determine a company's funding pattern.

The FASB adopted the actuary's approach to dampen wide swings that might occur in the actual return. That is, a company includes the **expected return** on the plan assets as a component of pension expense, not the actual return in a given year. To achieve this goal, the company multiplies the expected rate of return by the market-related value of the plan assets. The **market-related asset value** of the plan assets is either the fair value of plan assets or a calculated value that recognizes changes in fair value in a systematic and rational manner. **[4]**[13]

The difference between the expected return and the actual return is referred to as the **unexpected gain or loss**; the FASB uses the term **asset gains and losses**. **Asset gains** occur when actual return exceeds expected return; **asset losses** occur when actual return is less than expected return.

What happens to unexpected gains or losses in the accounting for pensions? Companies record asset gains and asset losses in an account, **Other Comprehensive Income (G/L)**, combining them with gains and losses accumulated in prior years. This treatment is similar to prior service cost. The Board believes this treatment is consistent with the practice of including in other comprehensive income certain changes in value that have not been recognized in net income (for example, unrealized gains and losses on available-for-sale securities). **[5]** In addition, the accounting is simple, transparent, and symmetrical.

To illustrate the computation of an unexpected gain or loss and its related accounting, assume that in 2016, Zarle Company has an actual return on plan assets of $12,000 when the expected return is $13,410 (the expected rate of return of 10% on plan assets times the beginning-of-the-year plan assets). The unexpected asset loss of $1,410 ($12,000 − $13,410) is debited to Other Comprehensive Income (G/L) and credited to Pension Expense.

What do the numbers mean? *PENSION COSTS UPS AND DOWNS*

For some companies, pension plans generated real profits in 2011. The plans not only paid for themselves but also increased earnings. This happens when the expected return on pension assets exceed the company's annual costs. At **MeadWestvaco**, pension income amounted to approximately 27 percent of operating profit. It tallied 11 percent of operating profit at **CenturyTel** and 9.5 percent at **Sun Trust Banks**. The issue is important because in these cases management is not driving the operating income—pension income is. And as a result, income can change quickly.

Unfortunately, when the stock market stops booming, pension expense substantially increases for many companies. The reason: Expected return on a smaller asset base no longer offsets pension service costs and interest on the projected benefit obligation. As a result, many companies find it difficult to meet their earnings targets, and at a time when meeting such targets is crucial to maintaining the stock price.

Smoothing Unexpected Gains and Losses on the Pension Liability

In estimating the projected benefit obligation (the liability), actuaries make assumptions about such items as mortality rate, retirement rate, turnover rate, disability rate, and salary amounts. Any change in these actuarial assumptions affects the amount of the projected benefit obligation. Seldom does actual experience coincide exactly with actuarial predictions. These unexpected gains or losses from changes in the projected benefit obligation are called **liability gains and losses**.

[13]Companies may use different ways of determining the calculated market-related value for different classes of assets. For example, an employer might use fair value for bonds and a five-year moving-average for equities. But companies should consistently apply the manner of determining market-related value from year to year for each asset class. Throughout our Zarle illustrations, we assume that market-related values based on a calculated value and the fair value of plan assets are equal. *For homework purposes, use the fair value of plan assets as the measure for the market-related value.*

Companies report liability gains (resulting from unexpected decreases in the liability balance) and liability losses (resulting from unexpected increases) in Other Comprehensive Income (G/L). Companies combine the liability gains and losses in the same Other Comprehensive Income (G/L) account used for asset gains and losses. They accumulate the asset and liability gains and losses from year to year that are not amortized in Accumulated Other Comprehensive Income. This amount is reported on the balance sheet in the stockholders' equity section.

Corridor Amortization

8 LEARNING OBJECTIVE
Explain the corridor approach to amortizing gains and losses.

The asset gains and losses and the liability gains and losses can offset each other. As a result, the Accumulated OCI account related to gains and losses may not grow very large. But, it is possible that no offsetting will occur and that the balance in the Accumulated OCI account related to gains and losses will continue to grow.

To limit the growth of the Accumulated OCI account, the FASB invented the **corridor approach** for amortizing the account's accumulated balance when it gets too large. How large is too large? The FASB set a limit of 10 percent of the larger of the beginning balances of the projected benefit obligation or the market-related value of the plan assets. **Above that size, the Accumulated OCI account related to gains and losses is considered too large and must be amortized.**

To illustrate the corridor approach, data for Callaway Co.'s projected benefit obligation and plan assets over a period of six years are shown in Illustration 20-14.

ILLUSTRATION 20-14
Computation of the Corridor

Beginning-of-the-Year Balances	Projected Benefit Obligation	Market-Related Asset Value	Corridor* +/− 10%
2013	$1,000,000	$ 900,000	$100,000
2014	1,200,000	1,100,000	120,000
2015	1,300,000	1,700,000	170,000
2016	1,500,000	2,250,000	225,000
2017	1,700,000	1,750,000	175,000
2018	1,800,000	1,700,000	180,000

*The corridor becomes 10% of the larger (in red type) of the projected benefit obligation or the market-related plan asset value.

How the corridor works becomes apparent when we portray the data graphically, as in Illustration 20-15.

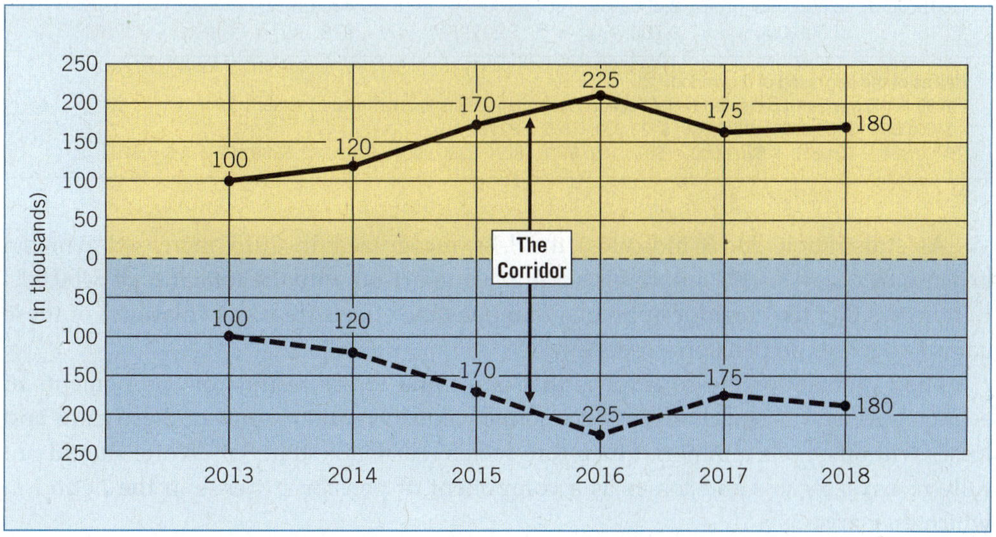

ILLUSTRATION 20-15
Graphic Illustration of the Corridor

If the balance in the Accumulated OCI account related to gains and losses stays within the upper and lower limits of the corridor, no amortization is required. In that case, Callaway carries forward unchanged the accumulated OCI related to gains and losses.

If amortization is required, the minimum amortization is the excess divided by the average remaining service period of active employees who are expected to receive benefits under the plan. Callaway may use any systematic method of amortization of gains and losses in lieu of the minimum, provided it is greater than the minimum. It must use the method consistently for both gains and losses, and must disclose the amortization method used.

Example of Gains/Losses

In applying the corridor, companies should include amortization of the net gain or loss as a component of pension expense only if, at the **beginning of the year**, the net gain or loss in Accumulated OCI exceeded the corridor. That is, if no net gain or loss exists in Accumulated OCI at the beginning of the period, the company cannot recognize pension expense gains or losses in that period.

To illustrate the amortization of net gains and losses, assume the following information for Soft-White, Inc.

	2014	2015	2016
		(beginning of the year)	
Projected benefit obligation	$2,100,000	$2,600,000	$2,900,000
Market-related asset value	2,600,000	2,800,000	2,700,000

Soft-White recorded in Other Comprehensive Income actuarial losses of $400,000 in 2014 and $300,000 in 2015.

If the average remaining service life of all active employees is 5.5 years, the schedule to amortize the net gain or loss is as shown in Illustration 20-16.

ILLUSTRATION 20-16
Corridor Test and Gain/Loss Amortization Schedule

Year	Projected Benefit Obligation[a]	Plan Assets[a]	Corridor[b]	Accumulated OCI (G/L)[a]	Minimum Amortization of Loss (For Current Year)
2014	$2,100,000	$2,600,000	$260,000	$ -0-	$ -0-
2015	2,600,000	2,800,000	280,000	400,000	21,818[c]
2016	2,900,000	2,700,000	290,000	678,182[d]	70,579[d]

[a]All as of the beginning of the period.
[b]10% of the greater of projected benefit obligation or plan assets' market-related value.
[c]$400,000 − $280,000 = $120,000; $120,000 ÷ 5.5 = $21,818.
[d]$400,000 − $21,818 + $300,000 = $678,182; $678,182 − $290,000 = $388,182; $388,182 ÷ 5.5 = $70,579.

As Illustration 20-16 indicates, the loss recognized in 2015 increased pension expense by $21,818. This amount is small in comparison with the total loss of $400,000. It indicates that the corridor approach dampens the effects (reduces volatility) of these gains and losses on pension expense.

The rationale for the corridor is that gains and losses result from refinements in estimates as well as real changes in economic value. Over time, some of these gains and losses will offset one another. It therefore seems reasonable that Soft-White should not fully recognize gains and losses as a component of pension expense in the period in which they arise.

However, Soft-White should immediately recognize in net income certain gains and losses—if they arise from a single occurrence not directly related to the operation of the pension plan and not in the ordinary course of the employer's business. For example, a gain or loss that is directly related to a plant closing, a disposal of a business component, or a similar event that greatly affects the size of the employee work force should be recognized as a part of the gain or loss associated with that event.

For example, at one time, **Bethlehem Steel** reported a quarterly loss of $477 million. A great deal of this loss was attributable to future estimated benefits payable to workers who were permanently laid off. In this situation, the loss should be treated as an adjustment to the gain or loss on the plant closing and should not affect pension cost for the current or future periods.

Summary of Calculations for Asset Gain or Loss

The difference between the actual return on plan assets and the expected return on plan assets is the **unexpected asset gain or loss** component. This component defers the difference between the actual return and expected return on plan assets in computing current-year pension expense. Thus, after considering this component, **it is really the expected return on plan assets (not the actual return) that determines current pension expense**.

Companies determine the amortized net gain or loss by amortizing the Accumulated OCI amount related to net gain or loss at the beginning of the year subject to the corridor limitation. In other words, **if the accumulated gain or loss is greater than the corridor, these net gains and losses are subject to amortization.** Soft-White computed this minimum amortization by dividing the net gains or losses subject to amortization by the average remaining service period. When the current-year unexpected gain or loss is combined with the amortized net gain or loss, we determine the current-year gain or loss. Illustration 20-17 summarizes these gain and loss computations.

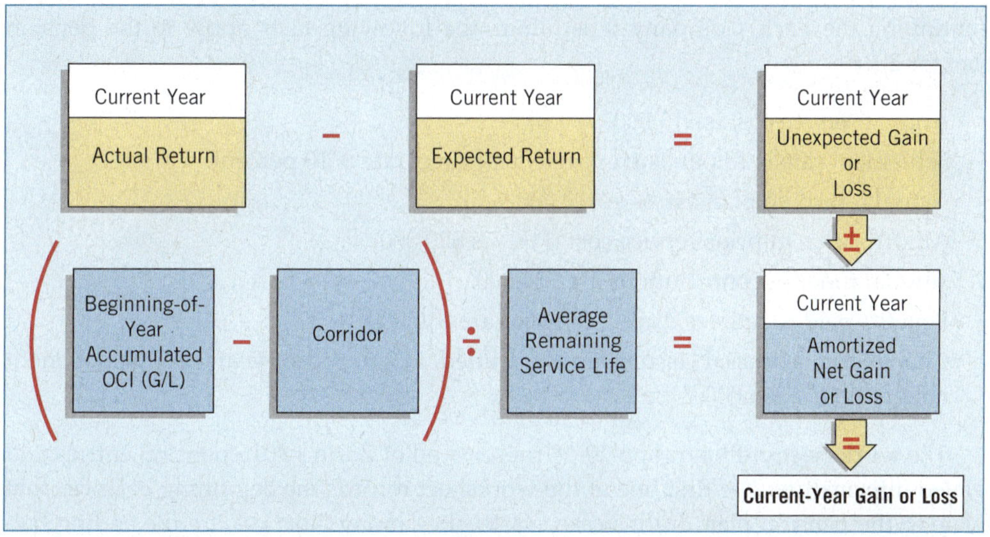

ILLUSTRATION 20-17
Graphic Summary of Gain or Loss Computation

In essence, these gains and losses are subject to *triple* smoothing. That is, companies first smooth the asset gain or loss by using the expected return. Second, they do not amortize the accumulated gain or loss at the beginning of the year unless it is greater than the corridor. Finally, they spread the excess over the remaining service life of existing employees.

Evolving Issue BYE BYE CORRIDOR

Many companies have significant actuarial losses in their pension plans, which are presently deferred through use of the corridor approach. However, companies do have a choice—they may select any method of accounting for these deferred losses as long as it is systematic, rational, and consistently applied, and meets a minimum for recognition in the income statement.

Some companies are now shifting away from the corridor approach and recognizing actuarial losses immediately. For example, **AT&T**, **Verizon Communications**, and **Honeywell International** have recently changed accounting principles from smoothing these losses to recognizing them in the year incurred.

Companies argue this approach provides more transparency for these losses that will directly affect pension expense in the current period (and this accounting is also more similar to IFRS). However, there is a silver lining for these companies—they can charge many of these deferred losses to past years. For example, the table at the top of the right-hand column indicates deferred losses as of 2009 for three major companies.

	Deferred Losses as of 2009 (in billions)	Losses as % of Pension Assets
AT&T	$23.04	49%
Verizon	$12.20	43
Honeywell	$7.57	55

When AT&T changed to immediate recognition in 2010, it restated its previous years. In 2008, for example, AT&T increased its pension cost by $24.9 billion, which led to a net loss in 2008 of $2.6 billion instead of a profit of $12.9 billion. As a result, in 2010 it recognized a much smaller pension cost of $3 billion. Skeptics suggest that AT&T made this change to charge these losses to prior periods. In other words, does anyone in 2011 care that the profit in 2008 was changed to a loss? In addition, once these losses are charged to prior periods, they no longer affect current and future earnings.

Although earnings in the future will probably be more volatile due to fluctuations in pension expense, more companies are willing to move in the direction of immediate expensing to eliminate large deferred losses which would be a drag on future income.

Source: Michael Rapoport, "Rewriting Pension History," *Wall Street Journal* (March 9, 2011).

2016 Entries and Worksheet

Continuing the Zarle Company illustration, the following facts apply to the pension plan for 2016.

Annual service cost is $13,000.

Settlement rate is 10 percent; expected earnings rate is 10 percent.

Actual return on plan assets is $12,000.

Amortization of prior service cost (PSC) is $20,800.

Annual funding contributions are $24,000.

Benefits paid to retirees during the year are $10,500.

Changes in actuarial assumptions resulted in an end-of-year projected benefit obligation of $265,000.

The worksheet in Illustration 20-18 presents all of Zarle's 2016 pension entries and related information. The first line of the worksheet records the beginning balances that relate to the pension plan. In this case, Zarle's beginning balances are the ending balances from its 2015 pension worksheet in Illustration 20-12 (page 1196).

Entries (m), (n), (o), (q), (r), and (s) are similar to the corresponding entries in 2014 or 2015.

Entries (o) and (p) are related. We explained the recording of the actual return in entry (o) in both 2014 and 2015; it is recorded similarly in 2016. In both 2014 and 2015, Zarle assumed that the actual return on plan assets was equal to the expected return on plan assets. In 2016, the expected return of $13,410 (the expected rate of return of

Pension Worksheet—2016.xls

	General Journal Entries					Memo Record	
			Other Comprehensive Income				
Items	Annual Pension Expense	Cash	Prior Service Cost	Gains/Losses	Pension Asset/ Liability	Projected Benefit Obligation	Plan Assets
Balance, Jan. 1, 2016					78,600 Cr.	212,700 Cr.	134,100 Dr.
(m) Service cost	13,000 Dr.					13,000 Cr.	
(n) Interest cost	21,270 Dr.					21,270 Cr.	
(o) Actual return	12,000 Cr.						12,000 Dr.
(p) Unexpected loss	1,410 Cr.			1,410 Dr.			
(q) Amortization of PSC	20,800 Dr.		20,800 Cr.				
(r) Contributions		24,000 Cr.					24,000 Dr.
(s) Benefits						10,500 Dr.	10,500 Cr.
(t) Liability increase				28,530 Dr.		28,530 Cr.	
Journal entry for 2016	41,660 Dr.	24,000 Cr.	20,800 Cr.	29,940 Dr.	26,800 Cr.		
Accumulated OCI, Dec. 31, 2015			52,800 Dr.	0			
Balance, Dec. 31, 2016*			32,000 Dr.	29,940 Dr.	105,400 Cr.	265,000 Cr.	159,600 Dr.
*Accumulated OCI (PSC)	$32,000 Dr.						
Accumulated OCI (G/L)	29,940 Dr.						
Accumulated OCI, Dec. 31, 2016	$61,940 Dr.						

ILLUSTRATION 20-18
Pension Worksheet—2016

10 percent times the beginning-of-the-year plan assets' balance of $134,100) is higher than the actual return of $12,000. To smooth pension expense, Zarle defers the unexpected loss of $1,410 ($13,410 − $12,000) by debiting the Other Comprehensive Income (G/L) account and crediting Pension Expense. **As a result of this adjustment, the expected return on the plan assets is the amount actually used to compute pension expense.**

Entry (t) records the change in the projected benefit obligation resulting from the change in the actuarial assumptions. As indicated, the actuary has now computed the ending balance to be $265,000. Given the PBO balance at December 31, 2015, and the related transactions during 2016, the PBO balance to date is computed as shown in Illustration 20-19.

December 31, 2015, PBO balance	$212,700
Service cost [entry (m)]	13,000
Interest cost [entry (n)]	21,270
Benefits paid [entry (s)]	(10,500)
December 31, 2016, PBO balance (before liability increases)	$236,470

ILLUSTRATION 20-19
Projected Benefit Obligation Balance (Unadjusted)

The difference between the ending balance of $265,000 and the balance of $236,470 before the liability increase is $28,530 ($265,000 − $236,470). This $28,530 increase in the employer's liability is an unexpected loss. The journal entry on December 31, 2016, to record the pension information is as follows.

Pension Expense	41,660	
Other Comprehensive Income (G/L)	29,940	
Cash		24,000
Other Comprehensive Income (PSC)		20,800
Pension Asset/Liability		26,800

As the 2016 worksheet indicates, the $105,400 balance in the Pension Asset/Liability account at December 31, 2016, is equal to the net of the balances in the memo accounts. Illustration 20-20 shows this computation.

ILLUSTRATION 20-20
Pension Reconciliation Schedule—December 31, 2016

Projected benefit obligation (Credit)	$(265,000)
Plan assets at fair value (Debit)	159,600
Pension asset/liability	$(105,400)

What do the numbers mean? ROLLER COASTER

The chart below shows what has happened to the financial health of pension plans over the last few years. It is a real roller coaster.

At the turn of the century, when the stock market was strong, pension plans were overfunded. However, the bubble burst, and by 2002 companies in the S&P 500 saw their pension plans funded at just 85 percent of reported liabilities. Then, plans bounced back, and by 2007 pension plans were overfunded again. However, due to recent downturns, plans are now underfunded again and the future is highly uncertain.

A number of factors cause a fund to change from being overfunded to underfunded. First, low interest rates decimate returns on pension plan assets. Second, using low interest rates to discount the projected benefit payments leads to a higher pension liability. Finally, more individuals are retiring, which leads to a depletion of the pension plan assets.

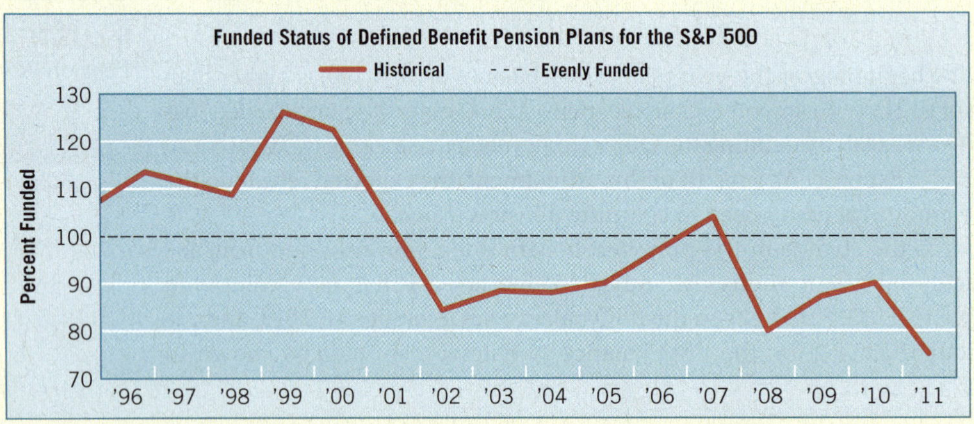

Source: D. Zion, A. Varshay, and N. Burnap, "From Bad to Worse," *Credit Suisse Equity Research* (October 10, 2011).

REPORTING PENSION PLANS IN FINANCIAL STATEMENTS

LEARNING OBJECTIVE 9
Describe the requirements for reporting pension plans in financial statements.

As you might suspect, a phenomenon as significant and complex as pensions involves extensive reporting and disclosure requirements. We will cover these requirements in two categories: (1) those within the financial statements, and (2) those within the notes to the financial statements.

Within the Financial Statements

Recognition of the Net Funded Status of the Pension Plan

Companies must recognize on their balance sheet the overfunded (pension asset) or underfunded (pension liability) status of their defined benefit pension plan. The overfunded or underfunded status is measured as the difference between the fair value of the plan assets and the projected benefit obligation.

Classification of Pension Asset or Pension Liability

No portion of a pension asset is reported as a current asset. The excess of the fair value of the plan assets over the benefit obligation is classified as a noncurrent asset. The rationale for noncurrent classification is that the pension plan assets are restricted. That is, these assets are used to fund the projected benefit obligation, and therefore noncurrent classification is appropriate.

The current portion of a net pension liability represents the amount of benefit payments to be paid in the next 12 months (or operating cycle, if longer), if that amount cannot be funded from existing plan assets. Otherwise, the pension liability is classified as a noncurrent liability.[14]

Aggregation of Pension Plans

Some companies have two or more pension plans. In such instances, a question arises as to whether these multiple plans should be combined and shown as one amount on the balance sheet. The Board takes the position that **all overfunded plans should be combined** and shown as a pension asset on the balance sheet. Similarly, if the company has two or more underfunded plans, the **underfunded plans are combined and shown as one amount** on the balance sheet.

The FASB rejected the alternative of combining *all* plans and representing the net amount as a single net asset or net liability. The rationale: A company does not have the ability to offset excess assets of one plan against underfunded obligations of another plan. Furthermore, netting all plans is inappropriate because offsetting assets and liabilities is not permitted under GAAP unless a right of offset exists.

To illustrate, assume that Cresci Company has three pension plans as shown in Illustration 20-21.

ILLUSTRATION 20-21
Multiple Pension Plans' Funded Status

	Pension Assets (at Fair Value)	Projected Benefit Obligation	Pension Asset/Liability
Plan A	$400,000	$300,000	$100,000 Asset
Plan B	600,000	720,000	120,000 Liability
Plan C	550,000	700,000	150,000 Liability

In this case, Cresci reports a pension plan asset of $100,000 and a pension plan liability of $270,000 ($120,000 + $150,000).

Actuarial Gains and Losses/Prior Service Cost

Actuarial gains and losses not recognized as part of pension expense are recognized as increases and decreases in other comprehensive income. The same type of accounting is also used for prior service cost. The Board requires that the prior service cost arising in the year of the amendment (which increases the projected benefit obligation) be recognized

[14]Recently, the FASB required more extensive disclosures related to pension plan assets. At a minimum, companies must disclose the amount of assets allocated to equities, government and corporate bonds, mortgage-backed securities, derivatives, and real estate. Also, information on concentrations of risk must be explained. Finally, fair value disclosures would be required, including classification of amounts into levels of the fair value hierarchy. **[6]**

by an offsetting debit to other comprehensive income. By recognizing both actuarial gains and losses and prior service cost as part of other comprehensive income, the Board believes that the usefulness of financial statements is enhanced.

To illustrate the presentation of other comprehensive income and related accumulated OCI, assume that Obey Company provides the following information for the year 2014. None of the Accumulated OCI on January 1, 2014, should be amortized in 2014.

Net income for 2014	$100,000
Actuarial liability loss for 2014	60,000
Prior service cost adjustment to provide additional benefits in December 2014	15,000
Accumulated OCI, January 1, 2014	40,000

Both the actuarial liability loss and the prior service adjustment decrease the funded status of the plan on the balance sheet. This results because the projected benefit obligation increases. However, neither the actuarial liability loss nor the prior service cost adjustment affects pension expense in 2014. In subsequent periods, these items will impact pension expense through amortization.

For Obey Company, the computation of "Other comprehensive loss" for 2014 is as follows.

ILLUSTRATION 20-22
Computation of Other Comprehensive Income

Actuarial liability loss	$60,000
Prior service cost benefit adjustment	15,000
Other comprehensive loss	$75,000

The computation of "Comprehensive income" for 2014 is as follows.

ILLUSTRATION 20-23
Computation of Comprehensive Income

Net income	$100,000
Other comprehensive loss	75,000
Comprehensive income	$ 25,000

The components of other comprehensive income must be reported in one of two ways: (1) in a second income statement, or (2) in a combined statement of comprehensive income. Regardless of the format used, net income must be added to other comprehensive income to arrive at comprehensive income. *For homework purposes, use the second income statement approach unless stated otherwise.* Earnings per share information related to comprehensive income is not required.

To illustrate the second income statement approach, assume that Obey Company has reported a traditional income statement. The comprehensive income statement is shown in Illustration 20-24.

ILLUSTRATION 20-24
Comprehensive Income Reporting

OBEY COMPANY
COMPREHENSIVE INCOME STATEMENT
FOR THE YEAR ENDED DECEMBER 31, 2014

Net income		$100,000
Other comprehensive loss		
Actuarial liability loss	$60,000	
Prior service cost	15,000	75,000
Comprehensive income		$ 25,000

The computation of "Accumulated other comprehensive income" as reported in stockholders' equity at December 31, 2014, is as follows.

ILLUSTRATION 20-25
Computation of Accumulated Other Comprehensive Income

Accumulated other comprehensive income, January 1, 2014	$40,000
Other comprehensive loss	75,000
Accumulated other comprehensive loss, December 31, 2014	$35,000

Regardless of the display format for the income statement, the accumulated other comprehensive loss is reported in the stockholders' equity section of the balance sheet of Obey Company as shown in Illustration 20-26. (Illustration 20-26 uses assumed data for the common stock and retained earnings information.)

ILLUSTRATION 20-26
Reporting of Accumulated OCI

OBEY COMPANY
BALANCE SHEET
AS OF DECEMBER 31, 2014
(STOCKHOLDERS' EQUITY SECTION)

Stockholders' equity	
Common stock	$100,000
Retained earnings	60,000
Accumulated other comprehensive loss	35,000
Total stockholders' equity	$125,000

By providing information on the components of comprehensive income as well as total accumulated other comprehensive income, the company communicates all changes in net assets.

In this illustration, it is assumed that the accumulated other comprehensive income at January 1, 2014, is not adjusted for the amortization of any prior service cost or actuarial gains and losses that would change pension expense. As discussed in the earlier examples, these items will be amortized into pension expense in future periods.

Within the Notes to the Financial Statements

Pension plans are frequently important to understanding a company's financial position, results of operations, and cash flows. Therefore, a company discloses the following information, either in the body of the financial statements or in the notes. [7]

1. A schedule showing all the major components of pension expense.
   Rationale: Information provided about the components of pension expense helps users better understand how a company determines pension expense. It also is useful in forecasting a company's net income.
2. A **reconciliation** showing how the projected benefit obligation and the fair value of the plan assets changed from the beginning to the end of the period.
   Rationale: Disclosing the projected benefit obligation, the fair value of the plan assets, and changes in them should help users understand the economics underlying the obligations and resources of these plans. Explaining the changes in the projected benefit obligation and fair value of plan assets in the form of a reconciliation provides a more complete disclosure and makes the financial statements more understandable.

International Perspective

The IASB and FASB are studying whether the various components of pension expense, such as interest cost and investment earnings on plan assets, should be presented separately in the income statement along with other interest expense and investment earnings.

3. A disclosure of the rates used in measuring the benefit amounts (discount rate, expected return on plan assets, rate of compensation).
Rationale: Disclosure of these rates permits users to determine the reasonableness of the assumptions applied in measuring the pension liability and pension expense.
4. A table indicating the allocation of pension plan assets by category (equity securities, debt securities, real estate, and other assets), and showing the percentage of the fair value to total plan assets. In addition, a company must include a narrative description of investment policies and strategies, including the target allocation percentages (if used by the company).
Rationale: Such information helps financial statement users evaluate the pension plan's exposure to market risk and possible cash flow demands on the company. It also will help users better assess the reasonableness of the company's expected rate of return assumption.
5. The **expected benefit payments** to be paid to current plan participants for each of the next five fiscal years and in the aggregate for the five fiscal years thereafter. Also required is disclosure of a company's best **estimate of expected contributions** to be paid to the plan during the next year.
Rationale: These disclosures provide information related to the cash outflows of the company. With this information, financial statement users can better understand the potential cash outflows related to the pension plan. They can better assess the liquidity and solvency of the company, which helps in assessing the company's overall financial flexibility.
6. The nature and amount of changes in plan assets and benefit obligations recognized in net income and in other comprehensive income of each period.
Rationale: This disclosure provides information on pension elements affecting the projected benefit obligation and plan assets and on whether those amounts have been recognized in income or deferred to future periods.
7. The accumulated amount of changes in plan assets and benefit obligations that have been recognized in other comprehensive income and that will be recycled into net income in future periods.
Rationale: This information indicates the pension-related balances recognized in stockholders' equity, which will affect future income.
8. The amount of estimated net actuarial gains and losses and prior service costs and credits that will be amortized from accumulated other comprehensive income into net income over the next fiscal year.
Rationale: This information helps users predict the impact of deferred pension expense items on next year's income.

Underlying Concepts

Does it make a difference to users of financial statements whether companies recognize pension information in the financial statements or disclose it only in the notes? The FASB was unsure, so in accord with the full disclosure principle, it decided to provide extensive pension plan disclosures.

In summary, the disclosure requirements are extensive, and purposely so. One factor that has been a challenge for useful pension reporting has been the lack of consistent terminology. Furthermore, a substantial amount of offsetting is inherent in the measurement of pension expense and the pension liability. These disclosure requirements are designed to address these concerns and take some of the mystery out of pension reporting.

Example of Pension Note Disclosure

In the following sections, we provide examples and explain the key pension disclosure elements.

Components of Pension Expense

The FASB requires disclosure of the individual pension expense components (derived from the information in the pension expense worksheet column): (1) service cost,

(2) interest cost, (3) expected return on assets, (4) other gains or losses component, and (5) prior service cost component. The purpose of such disclosure is to clarify to more sophisticated readers how companies determine pension expense. Providing information on the components should also be useful in predicting future pension expense.

Illustration 20-27 presents an example of this part of the disclosure. It uses the information from the Zarle illustration, specifically the expense component information from the worksheets in Illustrations 20-8 (page 1193), 20-12 (page 1196), and 20-18 (page 1203).

ILLUSTRATION 20-27
Summary of Expense Components—2014, 2015, 2016

ZARLE COMPANY

	2014	2015	2016
Components of Pension Expense			
Service cost	$ 9,000	$ 9,500	$13,000
Interest cost	10,000	19,200	21,270
Expected return on plan assets	(10,000)	(11,100)	(13,410)*
Amortization of prior service cost	–0–	27,200	20,800
Pension expense	$ 9,000	$44,800	$41,660

*Note that the expected return must be disclosed, not the actual return. In 2016, the expected return is $13,410, which is the actual gain ($12,000) adjusted by the unrecognized loss ($1,410).

Funded Status of Plan

Having a reconciliation of the changes in the assets and liabilities from the beginning of the year to the end of the year, statement readers can better understand the underlying economics of the plan. In essence, this disclosure contains the information in the pension worksheet for the projected benefit obligation and plan asset columns. Using the information for Zarle, the schedule in Illustration 20-28 provides an example of the reconciliation.

Underlying Concepts

This represents another compromise between relevance and faithful representation. Disclosure attempts to balance these objectives.

ILLUSTRATION 20-28
Pension Disclosure for Zarle Company—2014, 2015, 2016

ZARLE COMPANY
PENSION DISCLOSURE

	2014	2015	2016
Change in benefit obligation			
Benefit obligation at beginning of year	$100,000	$112,000	$ 212,700
Service cost	9,000	9,500	13,000
Interest cost	10,000	19,200	21,270
Amendments (Prior service cost)	–0–	80,000	–0–
Actuarial loss	–0–	–0–	28,530
Benefits paid	(7,000)	(8,000)	(10,500)
Benefit obligation at end of year	112,000	212,700	265,000
Change in plan assets			
Fair value of plan assets at beginning of year	100,000	111,000	134,100
Actual return on plan assets	10,000	11,100	12,000
Contributions	8,000	20,000	24,000
Benefits paid	(7,000)	(8,000)	(10,500)
Fair value of plan assets at end of year	111,000	134,100	159,600
Funded status (Pension asset/liability)	$ (1,000)	$ (78,600)	$(105,400)

The 2014 column reveals that Zarle underfunds the projected benefit obligation by $1,000. The 2015 column reveals that Zarle reports the underfunded liability of $78,600 in the balance sheet. Finally, the 2016 column indicates that Zarle recognizes the underfunded liability of $105,400 in the balance sheet.

2017 Entries and Worksheet—A Comprehensive Example

Incorporating the corridor computation and the required disclosures, we continue the Zarle Company pension plan accounting based on the following facts for 2017.

Service cost is $16,000.
Settlement rate is 10 percent; expected rate of return is 10 percent.
Actual return on plan assets is $22,000.
Amortization of prior service cost is $17,600.
Annual funding contributions are $27,000.
Benefits paid to retirees during the year are $18,000.
Average service life of all covered employees is 20 years.

Zarle prepares a worksheet to facilitate accumulation and recording of the components of pension expense and maintenance of amounts related to the pension plan. Illustration 20-29 shows that worksheet, which uses the basic data presented above. Beginning-of-the-year 2017 account balances are the December 31, 2016, balances from Zarle's revised 2016 pension worksheet in Illustration 20-18 (on page 1203).

Comprehensive Pension Worksheet—2017.xls

	General Journal Entries					Memo Record	
			Other Comprehensive Income				
Items	Annual Pension Expense	Cash	Prior Service Cost	Gains/Losses	Pension Asset/ Liability	Projected Benefit Obligation	Plan Assets
Balance, Dec. 31, 2016					105,400 Cr.	265,000 Cr.	159,600 Dr.
(aa) Service cost	16,000 Dr.					16,000 Cr.	
(bb) Interest cost	26,500 Dr.					26,500 Cr.	
(cc) Actual return	22,000 Cr.						22,000 Dr.
(dd) Unexpected gain	6,040 Dr.			6,040 Cr.			
(ee) Amortization of PSC	17,600 Dr.		17,600 Cr.				
(ff) Contributions		27,000 Cr.					27,000 Dr.
(gg) Benefits						18,000 Dr.	18,000 Cr.
(hh) Amortization of loss	172 Dr.			172 Cr.			
Journal entry for 2017	44,312 Dr.	27,000 Cr.	17,600 Cr.	6,212 Cr.	6,500 Dr.		
Accumulated OCI, Dec. 31, 2016			32,000 Dr.	29,940 Dr.			
Balance, Dec. 31, 2017*			14,400 Dr.	23,728 Dr.	98,900 Cr.	289,500 Cr.	190,600 Dr.
*Accumulated OCI (PSC)	$14,400 Dr.						
Accumulated OCI (G/L)	23,728 Dr.						
Accumulated OCI, Dec. 31, 2017	$38,128 Dr.						

ILLUSTRATION 20-29
Comprehensive Pension Worksheet—2017

Worksheet Explanations and Entries

Entries (aa) through (gg) are similar to the corresponding entries previously explained in the prior years' worksheets, with the exception of entry (dd). In 2016, the expected return on plan assets exceeded the actual return, producing an unexpected loss. In 2017, the actual return of $22,000 exceeds the expected return of $15,960 ($159,600 × 10%), resulting in an unexpected gain of $6,040, entry (dd). By netting the gain of $6,040 against the actual return of $22,000, pension expense is affected only by the expected return of $15,960.

A new entry (hh) in Zarle's worksheet results from application of the corridor test on the accumulated balance of net gain or loss in accumulated other comprehensive income. Zarle Company begins 2017 with a balance in the net loss account of $29,940. The company applies the corridor criterion in 2017 to determine whether the balance is excessive and should be amortized. In 2017, the corridor is 10 percent of the larger of the beginning-of-the-year projected benefit obligation of $265,000 or the plan asset's $159,600 market-related asset value (assumed to be fair value). The corridor for 2017 is $26,500 ($265,000 × 10%). Because the balance in Accumulated OCI is a net loss of $29,940, the excess (outside the corridor) is $3,440 ($29,940 − $26,500). Zarle amortizes the $3,440 excess over the average remaining service life of all employees. Given an average remaining service life of 20 years, the amortization in 2017 is $172 ($3,440 ÷ 20). In the 2017 pension worksheet, Zarle debits Pension Expense for $172 and credits that amount to Other Comprehensive Income (G/L). Illustration 20-30 shows the computation of the $172 amortization charge.

ILLUSTRATION 20-30
Computation of 2017 Amortization Charge (Corridor Test)

2017 Corridor Test	
Net (gain) or loss at beginning of year in accumulated OCI	$29,940
10% of larger of PBO or market-related asset value of plan assets	(26,500)
Amortizable amount	$ 3,440
Average service life of all employees	20 years
2017 amortization ($3,440 ÷ 20 years)	$172

Zarle formally records pension expense for 2017 as follows.

2017		
Pension Expense	44,312	
Pension Asset/Liability	6,500	
Cash		27,000
Other Comprehensive Income (G/L)		6,212
Other Comprehensive Income (PSC)		17,600

Note Disclosure

Illustration 20-31 (page 1212) shows the note disclosure of Zarle's pension plan for 2017. Note that this example assumes that the pension liability is noncurrent and that the 2018 adjustment for amortization of the net gain or loss and amortization of prior service cost are the same as 2017.

Special Issues

The Pension Reform Act of 1974

A classic example of the unfortunate consequences of an underfunded pension plan is the 1963 shutdown of the **Studebaker Automobile** operations in South Bend, Indiana, in which 4,500 workers lost 85 percent of their vested benefits. As a result of such situations, the Employee Retirement Income Security Act of 1974—**ERISA**—was passed. The legislation affects virtually every private retirement plan in the United States. It attempts

ILLUSTRATION 20-31
Minimum Note Disclosure of Pension Plan, Zarle Company, 2017

ZARLE COMPANY
NOTES TO THE FINANCIAL STATEMENTS

Note D. The company has a pension plan covering substantially all of its employees. The plan is noncontributory and provides pension benefits that are based on the employee's compensation during the three years immediately preceding retirement. The pension plan's assets consist of cash, stocks, and bonds. The company's funding policy is consistent with the relevant government (ERISA) and tax regulations.

Pension expense for 2017 is comprised of the following components of pension cost.

Components of pension expense

Service cost	$16,000	
Interest on projected benefit obligation	26,500	
Expected return on plan assets	(15,960)	
Amortization of prior service cost	17,600	
Amortization of net loss	172	
Pension expense		$44,312

Amounts recognized in other comprehensive income

Other changes in plan assets and benefit obligations recognized in other comprehensive income		
Net actuarial gain	$ 6,212	
Amortization of prior service cost	17,600	
Total recognized in other comprehensive income		(23,812)
Total recognized in pension expense and other comprehensive income		$20,500

The estimated net actuarial loss and prior service cost for the defined benefit pension plan that will be amortized from accumulated other comprehensive into pension expense over the next year are estimated to be the same as this year.

The amount recognized as a long-term liability in the balance sheet is as follows:

Amounts recognized in the balance sheet

Noncurrent liability	
Pension liability	$98,900

The amounts recognized in accumulated other comprehensive income related to pensions consist of:

Net actuarial loss	$23,728
Prior service cost	14,400
Total	$38,128

Reconciliations of pension liability and plan assets

Change in benefit obligation	
Benefit obligation at beginning of year	$265,000
Service cost	16,000
Interest cost	26,500
Amendments (Prior service cost)	–0–
Actuarial gain	–0–
Benefits paid	(18,000)
Benefit obligation at end of year	289,500
Change in plan assets	
Fair value of plan assets at beginning of year	159,600
Actual return on plan assets	22,000
Contributions	27,000
Benefits paid	(18,000)
Fair value of plan assets at end of year	190,600
Funded status (liability)	$ 98,900

Funded status of plan

Rates used to estimate plan elements

The weighted-average discount rate used in determining the 2017 projected benefit obligation was 10 percent. The rate of increase in future compensation levels used in computing the 2017 projected benefit obligation was 4.5 percent. The weighted-average expected long-term rate of return on the plan's assets was 10 percent.

to safeguard employees' pension rights by mandating many pension plan requirements, including minimum funding, participation, and vesting.

These requirements can influence the employers' cash flows significantly. Under this legislation, annual funding is no longer discretionary. An employer now must fund the plan in accordance with an actuarial funding method that over time will be sufficient to pay for all pension obligations. If companies do not fund their plans in a reasonable manner, they may be subject to fines and/or loss of tax deductions.[15]

The law requires plan administrators to publish a comprehensive description and summary of their plans, along with detailed annual reports that include many supplementary schedules and statements.

Another important provision of the act is the creation of the Pension Benefit Guaranty Corporation (PBGC). **The PBGC's purpose is to administer terminated plans** and to impose liens on an employer's assets for certain unfunded pension liabilities. If a company terminates its pension plan, the PBGC can effectively impose a lien against the employer's assets for the excess of the present value of guaranteed vested benefits over the pension fund assets. This lien generally has had the status of a tax lien; it takes priority over most other creditorship claims. This section of the act gives the PBGC the power to force an involuntary termination of a pension plan whenever the risks related to nonpayment of the pension obligation seem too great. Because ERISA restricts to 30 percent of net worth the lien that the PBGC can impose, the PBGC must monitor all plans to ensure that net worth is sufficient to meet the pension benefit obligations.

A large number of terminated plans have caused the PBGC to pay out substantial benefits. Currently the PBGC receives its funding from employers, who contribute a certain dollar amount for each employee covered under the plan.[16]

Underlying Concepts

Many plans are underfunded but still quite viable. For example, at one time Loews Corp. had a $159 million shortfall, but also had earnings of $594 million and a good net worth. Thus, the going concern assumption permits us to ignore pension underfundings in some cases because in the long run they are not significant.

What do the numbers mean? WHO GUARANTEES THE GUARANTOR?

The Pension Benefit Guaranty Corporation (PBGC) in its 2012 annual report indicates that its primary mission is to encourage the continuation and maintenance of voluntary private pension plans. It's an obligation which the PBGC takes seriously. However, the trends are ominous:

- Americans today are spending more years in retirement. They're healthier and more active, which is great news. Unfortunately, pensions haven't kept up.
- Many businesses, for competitive and other reasons, continue to reduce their support for retirement plans. Some have switched from a defined benefit plan to a defined contribution plan which costs less and comes with fewer obligations. Others offer lump-sum cash payments to employees or retirees to settle the employer's obligations.
- Left on their own, many people save less, as well as invest and plan less well. They also pay higher fees and they get lower returns.
- Many people defer retirement but still don't have enough money for retirement—and they're worried. One poll cited by the Senate Health, Education, Labor, and Pensions Committee says that 92 percent of people think there's a retirement crisis. They're right to be concerned.

Add to these concerns that obligations in pension plans today greatly exceed pension assets. Finally, the PBGC has a problem as well—a large deficit in its accounts. The chart on page 1214 indicates that downward spiral in the net worth of the PBGC over the last 10 years.

[15]In 2006, Congress passed the Pension Protection Act. This law has many provisions. One important aspect of the act is that it forced many companies to expedite their contributions to their pension plans. One group estimates that companies in the S&P 500 would have had to contribute $47 billion to their pension plans if the new rules were fully phased in for 2006. That amount is about 57 percent more than the $30 billion that companies were expecting to contribute to their plans that year. Subsequently, Congress continues to provide pension funding relief. For example, in the "Moving Ahead for Progress in the 21st Century" Act (enacted July 6, 2012), companies can use a higher discount rate based on high-grade bond yields averaged over 25 years, which helps reduce the pension liability and required contributions.

[16]Pan American Airlines is a good illustration of how difficult it is to assess when to terminate. When Pan Am filed for bankruptcy in 1991, it had a pension liability of $900 million. From 1983 to 1991, the IRS gave it six waivers so it did not have to make contributions. When Pan Am terminated the plan, there was little net worth left upon which to impose a lien. An additional accounting problem relates to the manner of disclosing the possible termination of a plan. For example, should Pan Am have disclosed a contingent liability for its struggling plan? At present this issue is unresolved, and considerable judgment is needed to analyze a company with these contingent liabilities.

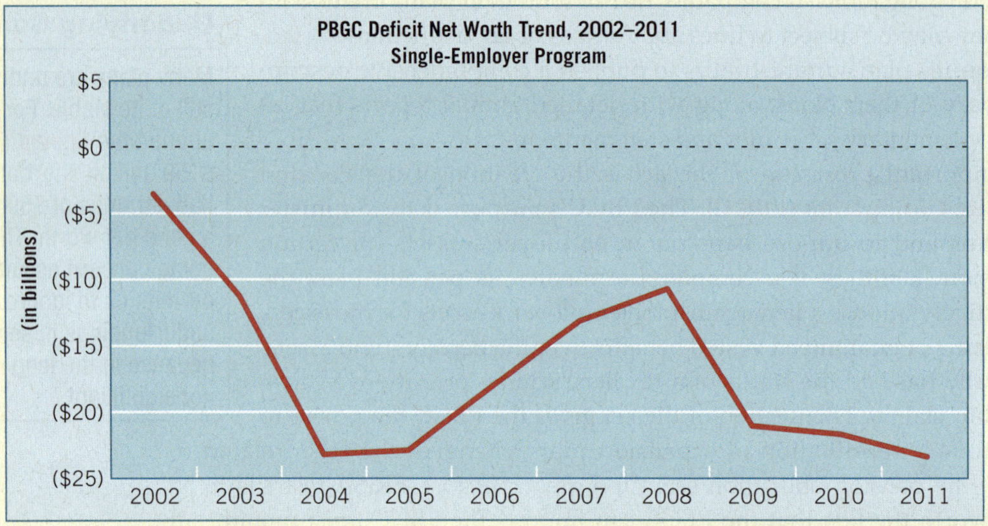

In February 2012, **American Airlines** announced that it is ending its defined benefit plans, which would result in the PBGC having to increase its deficit even more to an estimated $35 billion. The result is a growing deficit problem which is likely to continue. Who has the risk? You guessed it, the American taxpayer.

Source: Alex Pollock, "The Pension Benefit Guaranty Corporation: Who Will Guarantee This Guarantor?" *2012 Annual Report of the Pension Benefit Guarantee Corporation* (June 26, 2012).

Pension Terminations

A congressman at one time noted, "Employers are simply treating their employee pension plans like company piggy banks, to be raided at will." What this congressman was referring to is the practice of paying off the projected benefit obligation and pocketing any excess. ERISA prevents companies from recapturing excess assets unless they pay participants what is owed to them and then terminate the plan. As a result, companies were buying *annuities* to pay off the pension claimants and then used the excess funds for other corporate purposes.[17]

For example, at one time, pension plan terminations netted $363 million for **Occidental Petroleum Corp.**, $95 million for **Stroh's Brewery Co.**, $58 million for **Kellogg Co.**, and $29 million for **Western Airlines**. Recently, many large companies have terminated their pension plans and captured billions in surplus assets. The U.S. Treasury also benefits: Federal legislation requires companies to pay an excise tax of anywhere from 20 percent to 50 percent on the gains. All of this is quite legal.[18]

[17]A question exists as to whose money it is. Some argue that the excess funds belong to the employees, not the employer. In addition, given that the funds have been reverting to the employer, critics charge that cost-of-living increases and the possibility of other increased benefits are reduced because companies will be reluctant to use those remaining funds to pay for such increases.

[18]Another way that companies have reduced their pension obligations is through adoption of **cash-balance plans**. These are *hybrid* plans combining features of defined benefit and defined contribution plans. Although these plans permit employees to transfer their pension benefits when they change employers (like a defined contribution plan), they are controversial because the change to a cash-balance plan often reduces benefits to older workers.

The accounting for cash-balance plans is similar to that for defined benefit plans, because employers bear the investment risk in cash-balance plans. When an employer adopts a cash-balance plan, the measurement of the future benefit obligation to employees generally is lower, compared to a traditional defined benefit plan. See A. T. Arcady and F. Mellors, "Cash-Balance Conversions," *Journal of Accountancy* (February 2000), pp. 22–28.

The accounting issue that arises from these terminations is whether a company should recognize a gain when pension plan assets revert back to the company (often called **asset reversion** transactions). The issue is complex. In some cases, a company starts a new defined benefit plan after it eliminates the old one. Thus, some contend that there has been no change in substance but merely a change in form. However, the FASB disagrees. It requires recognition in earnings of a gain or loss when the employer settles a pension obligation either by lump-sum cash payments to participants or by purchasing nonparticipating annuity contracts. **[8]**[19]

Concluding Observations

Hardly a day goes by without the financial press analyzing in depth some issue related to pension plans in the United States. This is not surprising, since pension funds exceed over $22 trillion in assets globally. As you have seen, the accounting issues related to pension plans are complex. Recent changes to GAAP have clarified many of these issues and should help users understand the financial implications of a company's pension plans on its financial position, results of operations, and cash flows.

You will want to read the **IFRS INSIGHTS** on pages 1250–1266 for discussion of IFRS related to pension accounting.

SUMMARY OF LEARNING OBJECTIVES

1 Distinguish between accounting for the employer's pension plan and accounting for the pension fund. The company or employer is the organization sponsoring the pension plan. It incurs the cost and makes contributions to the pension fund. The fund or plan is the entity that receives the contributions from the employer, administers the pension assets, and makes the benefit payments to the pension recipients (retired employees). The fund should be a separate legal and accounting entity; it maintains a set of books and prepares financial statements.

2 Identify types of pension plans and their characteristics. The two most common types of pension arrangements are as follows. (1) *Defined contribution plans:* The employer agrees to contribute to a pension trust a certain sum each period based on a formula. This formula may consider such factors as age, length of employee service, employer's profits, and compensation level. Only the employer's contribution is defined; no promise is made regarding the ultimate benefits paid out to the employees. (2) *Defined benefit plans:* These plans define the benefits that the employee will receive at the time of retirement. The formula typically provides for the benefits to be a function of the employee's years of service and the compensation level when he or she nears retirement.

3 Explain alternative measures for valuing the pension obligation. One measure bases the pension obligation only on the benefits vested to the employees. Vested benefits are those that the employee is entitled to receive even if he or she renders no additional services under the plan. Companies compute the *vested benefit pension obligation* using current salary levels; this obligation includes only vested benefits. Another measure of the obligation, called the *accumulated benefit obligation*, computes the deferred compensation amount based on all years of service performed by employees

[19]Some companies have established *pension poison pills* as an anti-takeover measure. These plans require asset reversions from termination of a plan to benefit employees and retirees rather than the acquiring company. For a discussion of pension poison pills, see Eugene E. Comiskey and Charles W. Mulford, "Interpreting Pension Disclosures: A Guide for Lending Officers," *Commercial Lending Review* (Winter 1993–94), Vol. 9, No. 1.

KEY TERMS

accumulated benefit obligation, *1187*
actual return on plan assets, *1191*
actuarial present value, *1188(n)*
actuaries, *1187*
asset gains and losses, *1198*
cash-balance plans, *1214(n)*
components of pension expense, *1190*
contributory pension plan, *1184*
corridor approach, *1199*
defined benefit plan, *1185*
defined contribution plan, *1185*
ERISA, *1211*
expected rate of return, *1197*
expected return on plan assets, *1197*
fair value of plan assets, *1191*
funded pension plan, *1184*
funded status (overfunded or underfunded), *1189*
interest on the liability (interest expense), *1191*

under the plan—both vested and nonvested—using current salary levels. A third measure, called the *projected benefit obligation*, bases the computation of the deferred compensation amount on both vested and nonvested service using future salaries.

4 List the components of pension expense. Pension expense is a function of the following components: (1) service cost, (2) interest on the liability, (3) return on plan assets, (4) amortization of prior service cost, and (5) gain or loss.

5 Use a worksheet for employer's pension plan entries. Companies may use a worksheet unique to pension accounting. This worksheet records both the formal entries and the memo entries to keep track of all the employer's relevant pension plan items and components.

6 Describe the amortization of prior service costs. An actuary computes the amount of the prior service cost, and the company then records it as an adjustment to the projected benefit obligation and other comprehensive income. It then amortizes it, generally using a "years-of-service" amortization method, similar to a units-of-production computation. First, the company computes total estimated number of service-years to be worked by all of the participating employees. Second, it divides the accumulated prior service cost by the total number of service-years, to obtain a cost per service-year (the unit cost). Third, the company multiplies the number of service-years consumed each year times the cost per service-year, to obtain the annual amortization charge.

7 Explain the accounting for unexpected gains and losses. In estimating the projected benefit obligation (the liability), actuaries make assumptions about such items as mortality rate, retirement rate, turnover rate, disability rate, and salary amounts. Any change in these actuarial assumptions affects the amount of the projected benefit obligation. These unexpected gains or losses from changes in the projected benefit obligation are liability gains and losses. Liability gains result from unexpected decreases in the liability balance; liability losses result from unexpected increases. Companies also incur asset gains or losses. Both types of actuarial gains and losses are recorded in other comprehensive income and adjust either the projected benefit obligation or the plan assets.

8 Explain the corridor approach to amortizing gains and losses. The FASB set a limit for the size of an accumulated net gain or loss balance. That arbitrarily selected limit (called a *corridor*) is 10 percent of the larger of the beginning balances of the projected benefit obligation or the market-related value of the plan assets. Beyond that limit, an accumulated net gain or loss balance is considered too large and must be amortized. If the balance of the accumulated net gain or loss account stays within the upper and lower limits of the corridor, no amortization is required.

9 Describe the requirements for reporting pension plans in financial statements. Currently, companies must disclose the following pension plan information in their financial statements. (1) The components of pension expense for the period. (2) A schedule showing changes in the benefit obligation and plan assets during the year. (3) The amount of prior service cost and net gains and losses in accumulated OCI, including the estimated prior service cost and gains and losses that will affect net income in the next year. (4) The weighted-average assumed discount rate, the rate of compensation increase used to measure the projected benefit obligation, and the weighted-average expected long-term rate of return on plan assets. (5) A table showing the allocation of pension plan assets by category and the percentage of the fair value to total plan assets. (6) The expected benefit payments for current plan participants for each of the next five fiscal years and for the following five years in aggregate, along with an estimate of expected contributions to the plan during the next year.

APPENDIX 20A ACCOUNTING FOR POSTRETIREMENT BENEFITS

10 LEARNING OBJECTIVE
Identify the differences between pensions and postretirement healthcare benefits.

IBM's adoption of the GAAP requirements on postretirement benefits resulted in a $2.3 billion charge and a historical curiosity—IBM's first-ever quarterly loss. General Electric disclosed that its charge for adoption of the same GAAP rules would be $2.7 billion. AT&T absorbed a $2.1 billion pretax hit for postretirement benefits upon adoption. What is GAAP in this area, and how could its adoption have so grave an impact on companies' earnings?

ACCOUNTING GUIDANCE

After a decade of study, the FASB in December 1990 issued GAAP for "Employers' Accounting for Postretirement Benefits Other Than Pensions." **[9]** It alone was the cause for the large charges to income cited above. These rules cover for healthcare and other "welfare benefits" provided to retirees, their spouses, dependents, and beneficiaries.[20] These other welfare benefits include life insurance offered outside a pension plan; medical, dental, and eye care; legal and tax services; tuition assistance; day care; and housing assistance.[21] Because healthcare benefits are the largest of the other postretirement benefits, we use this item to illustrate accounting for postretirement benefits.

For many employers (about 95 percent), these GAAP rules required a change from the predominant practice of accounting for postretirement benefits on a pay-as-you-go (cash) basis to an accrual basis. Similar to pension accounting, the accrual basis necessitates measuring the employer's obligation to provide future benefits and accrual of the cost during the years that the employee provides service.

One of the reasons companies had not prefunded these benefit plans was that payments to prefund healthcare costs, unlike excess contributions to a pension trust, are not tax-deductible. Another reason was that postretirement healthcare benefits were once perceived to be a low-cost employee benefit that could be changed or eliminated at will and therefore were not a legal liability. Now, the accounting definition of a liability goes beyond the notion of a legally enforceable claim; the definition now encompasses equitable or constructive obligations as well, making it clear that the postretirement benefit promise is a liability.[22]

[20]*Accounting Trends and Techniques* recently reported that of its 500 surveyed companies, 317 reported benefit plans that provide postretirement healthcare benefits. In response to rising healthcare costs and higher premiums on healthcare insurance, companies are working to get their postretirement benefit costs under control.

[21]"OPEB" is the acronym frequently used to describe postretirement benefits other than pensions. This term came into being before the scope of guidance was narrowed from "other postemployment benefits" to "other postretirement benefits," thereby excluding postemployment benefits related to severance pay or wage continuation to disabled, terminated, or laid-off employees.

[22]"Elements of Financial Statements," *Statement of Financial Accounting Concepts No. 6* (Stamford, Conn.: 1985), p. 13, footnote 21.

DIFFERENCES BETWEEN PENSION BENEFITS AND HEALTHCARE BENEFITS

The FASB used the GAAP rules on pensions as a reference for the accounting prescribed for healthcare and other nonpension postretirement benefits.[23] Why didn't the FASB cover these other types of postretirement benefits in the earlier pension accounting statement? Because the apparent similarities between the two benefits mask some significant differences. Illustration 20A-1 shows these differences.[24]

ILLUSTRATION 20A-1
Differences between Pensions and Postretirement Healthcare Benefits

Item	Pensions	Healthcare Benefits
Funding	Generally funded.	Generally **not** funded.
Benefit	Well-defined and level dollar amount.	Generally uncapped and great variability.
Beneficiary	Retiree (maybe some benefit to surviving spouse).	Retiree, spouse, and other dependents.
Benefit payable	Monthly.	As needed and used.
Predictability	Variables are reasonably predictable.	Utilization difficult to predict. Level of cost varies geographically and fluctuates over time.

Two of the differences in Illustration 20A-1 highlight why measuring the future payments for healthcare benefit plans is so much more difficult than for pension plans.

1. Many postretirement plans do not set a limit on healthcare benefits. No matter how serious the illness or how long it lasts, the benefits continue to flow. (Even if the employer uses an insurance company plan, the premiums will escalate according to the increased benefits provided.)
2. The levels of healthcare benefit use and healthcare costs are difficult to predict. Increased longevity, unexpected illnesses (e.g., AIDS, SARS, and avian flu), along with new medical technologies and cures, cause changes in healthcare utilization.

Additionally, although the fiduciary and reporting standards for employee benefit funds under government regulations generally cover healthcare benefits, the stringent minimum vesting, participation, and funding standards that apply to pensions do not apply to healthcare benefits. Nevertheless, as you will learn, many of the basic concepts of pensions, and much of the related accounting terminology and measurement methodology, do apply to other postretirement benefits. Therefore, in the following discussion and illustrations, we point out the similarities and differences in the accounting and reporting for these two types of postretirement benefits.

[23]Other postemployment (but before retirement) benefits include, but are not limited to, salary continuation, disability-related benefits, severance benefits, and continuance of healthcare benefits and life insurance for inactive or former (e.g., terminated, disabled, or deceased) employees or their beneficiaries. These benefits are accounted for similar to accounting for compensated absences (see Chapter 13). **[10]**

[24]D. Gerald Searfoss and Naomi Erickson, "The Big Unfunded Liability: Postretirement Health-Care Benefits," *Journal of Accountancy* (November 1988), pp. 28–39.

What do the numbers mean? OPEBs—HOW BIG ARE THEY?

For many companies, *other postretirement benefit obligations* (OPEBs) are substantial. Generally, OPEBs are not well funded because companies are not permitted a tax deduction for contributions to the plan assets, as is the case with pensions. That is, the company may not claim a tax deduction until it makes a payment to the participant (pay-as-you-go).

Presented below are companies with the largest OPEB obligations, indicating their relationship with other financial items.

For year ended 12/31/2011 ($ in millions)	Obligation	% Underfunded	Obligation as a % of Stockholders' Equity
General Motors	$ 7,312	100.00%	18.75%
AT&T Inc.	34,963	71.70%	33.04%
Verizon Communications	27,369	90.40%	81.86%
General Electric	11,637	27.98%	9.85%
Boeing Company	7,997	98.72%	221.65%
Alcatel-Lucent	4,541	85.22%	76.08%

So, how big are OPEB obligations? REALLY big.

Source: Company reports.

POSTRETIREMENT BENEFITS ACCOUNTING PROVISIONS

Healthcare and other postretirement benefits for current and future retirees and their dependents are forms of deferred compensation. They are earned through employee service and are subject to accrual during the years an employee is working.

The period of time over which the postretirement benefit cost accrues is called the **attribution period**. It is the period of service during which the employee earns the benefits under the terms of the plan. The attribution period, shown in Illustration 20A-2 for a hypothetical employee, generally begins when an employee is hired and ends on the date the employee is eligible to receive the benefits and ceases to earn additional benefits by performing service, the vesting date.[25]

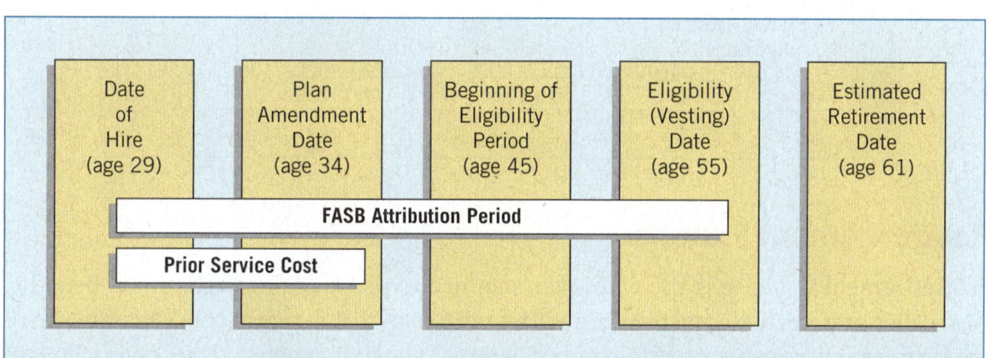

ILLUSTRATION 20A-2
Range of Possible Attribution Periods

[25]This is a benefit-years-of-service approach (the projected unit credit actuarial cost method). The FASB found no compelling reason to switch from the traditional pension accounting approach. It rejected the employee's full service period (i.e., to the estimated retirement date) because it was unable to identify any approach that would appropriately attribute benefits beyond the date when an employee attains full eligibility for those benefits. Employees attain full eligibility by meeting specified age, service, or age and service requirements of the plan.

Obligations Under Postretirement Benefits

In defining the obligation for postretirement benefits, the FASB maintained many concepts similar to pension accounting. It also designed some new and modified terms specifically for postretirement benefits. Two of the most important of these specialized terms are (a) expected postretirement benefit obligation and (b) accumulated postretirement benefit obligation.

The **expected postretirement benefit obligation (EPBO)** is the actuarial present value as of a particular date of **all benefits a company expects to pay after retirement to employees and their dependents.** Companies do not record the EPBO in the financial statements, but they do use it in measuring periodic expense.

The **accumulated postretirement benefit obligation (APBO)** is the actuarial present value of **future benefits attributed to employees' services rendered to a particular date.** The APBO is equal to the EPBO for retirees and active employees fully eligible for benefits. Before the date an employee achieves full eligibility, the APBO is only a portion of the EPBO. Or stated another way, the difference between the APBO and the EPBO is the future service costs of active employees who are not yet fully eligible.

Illustration 20A-3 contrasts the EPBO and the APBO. At the date an employee is fully eligible (the end of the attribution period), the APBO and the EPBO for that employee are equal.

ILLUSTRATION 20A-3
APBO and EPBO Contrasted

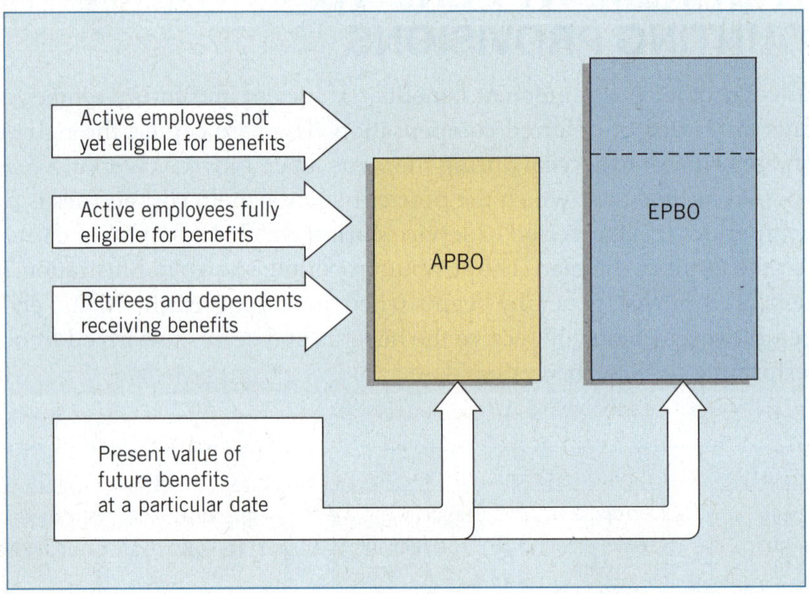

Postretirement Expense

Postretirement expense is the employer's annual expense for postretirement benefits. Also called **net periodic postretirement benefit cost**, this expense consists of many of the familiar components used to compute annual pension expense. The components of net periodic postretirement benefit cost are as follows. **[11]** [26]

1. *Service cost.* The portion of the EPBO attributed to employee service during the period.
2. *Interest cost.* The increase in the APBO attributable to the passage of time. Companies compute interest cost by applying the beginning-of-the-year discount rate to

[26] See James R. Wilbert and Kenneth E. Dakdduk, "The New FASB 106: How to Account for Postretirement Benefits," *Journal of Accountancy* (August 1991), pp. 36–41.

the beginning-of-the-year APBO, adjusted for benefit payments to be made during the period. The discount rate is based on the rates of return on high-quality, fixed-income investments that are currently available.[27]

3. ***Actual return on plan assets.*** The change in the fair value of the plan's assets adjusted for contributions and benefit payments made during the period. Because companies charge or credit the postretirement expense for the gain or loss on plan assets (the difference between the actual and the expected return), this component is actually the expected return.
4. ***Amortization of prior service cost.*** The amortization of the cost of retroactive benefits resulting from plan amendments. The typical amortization period, beginning at the date of the plan amendment, is the remaining service periods through the full eligibility date.
5. ***Gains and losses.*** In general, changes in the APBO resulting from changes in assumptions or from experience different from that assumed. For funded plans, this component also includes the difference between actual return and expected return on plan assets.

ILLUSTRATIVE ACCOUNTING ENTRIES

11 LEARNING OBJECTIVE
Contrast accounting for pensions to accounting for other postretirement benefits.

Like pension accounting, the accounting for postretirement plans must recognize in the accounts and in the financial statements effects of several significant items. These items are:

1. Expected postretirement benefit obligation (EPBO).
2. Accumulated postretirement benefit obligation (APBO).
3. Postretirement benefit plan assets.
4. Prior service cost.
5. Net gain or loss.

The EPBO is not recognized in the financial statements or disclosed in the notes. Companies recompute it each year, and the actuary uses it in measuring the annual service cost. Because of the numerous assumptions and actuarial complexity involved in measuring annual service cost, we have omitted these computations of the EPBO.

Similar to pensions, companies must recognize in the financial statements items 2 through 5 listed above. In addition, as in pension accounting, companies must know the exact amount of these items in order to compute postretirement expense. Therefore, companies use the worksheet like that for pension accounting to record both the formal general journal entries and the memo entries.

2014 Entries and Worksheet

To illustrate the use of a worksheet in accounting for a postretirement benefits plan, assume that on January 1, 2014, Quest Company adopts a healthcare benefit plan. The following facts apply to the postretirement benefits plan for the year 2014.

Plan assets at fair value on January 1, 2014, are zero.

Actual and expected returns on plan assets are zero.

Accumulated postretirement benefit obligation (APBO), January 1, 2014, is zero.

[27]The FASB concluded that the discount rate for measuring the present value of the postretirement benefit obligation and the service cost component should be the same as that applied to pension measurements. It chose not to label it the *settlement rate,* in order to clarify that the objective of the discount rate is to measure the time value of money.

Service cost is $54,000.

No prior service cost exists.

Interest cost on the APBO is zero.

Funding contributions during the year are $38,000.

Benefit payments to employees from plan are $28,000.

ILLUSTRATION 20A-4
Postretirement Worksheet—2014

Using that data, the worksheet in Illustration 20A-4 presents the postretirement entries for 2014.

Postretirement Worksheet—2014.xls

	A	B	C	D	E	F
1						
2		General Journal Entries			Memo Record	
3		Annual				
4		Postretirement		Postretirement		
5	Items	Expense	Cash	Asset/Liability	APBO	Plan Assets
6	Balance, Jan. 1, 2014					
7	(a) Service cost	54,000 Dr.			54,000 Cr.	
8	(b) Contributions		38,000 Cr.			38,000 Dr.
9	(c) Benefits				28,000 Dr.	28,000 Cr.
10						
11	Journal entry for 2014	54,000 Dr.	38,000 Cr.	16,000 Cr.*		
12	Balance, Dec. 31, 2014			16,000 Cr.**	26,000 Cr.	10,000 Dr.
13						
14	*$54,000 – $38,000 = $16,000					
15	**$26,000 – $10,000 = $16,000					
16						

Entry (a) records the service cost component, which increases postretirement expense $54,000 and increases the liability (APBO) $54,000. Entry (b) records Quest's funding of assets to the postretirement fund. The funding decreases cash $38,000 and increases plan assets $38,000. Entry (c) records the benefit payments made to retirees, which results in equal $28,000 decreases to the plan assets and the liability (APBO).

Quest's December 31 adjusting entry formally records the postretirement expense in 2014, as follows.

December 31, 2014		
Postretirement Expense	54,000	
Cash		38,000
Postretirement Asset/Liability		16,000

The credit to Postretirement Asset/Liability for $16,000 represents the difference between the APBO and the plan assets. The $16,000 credit balance is a liability because the plan is underfunded. The Postretirement Asset/Liability account balance of $16,000 also equals the net of the balances in the memo accounts.

Illustration 20A-5 shows the funded status reported in the balance sheet. (Notice its similarity to the pension schedule.)

ILLUSTRATION 20A-5
Postretirement Reconciliation Schedule—December 31, 2014

Accumulated postretirement benefit obligation (Credit)	$(26,000)
Plan assets at fair value (Debit)	10,000
Postretirement asset/liability (Credit)	$(16,000)

Recognition of Gains and Losses

Gains and losses represent changes in the APBO or the value of plan assets. These changes result either from actual experience different from that expected or from changes in actuarial assumptions. The amortization of these gains and losses follows the approach used for pensions. That is, the gains and losses are recorded in other comprehensive income.

The Corridor Approach

Consistent with pension accounting, companies amortize the gains and losses in accumulated other comprehensive income as a component of postretirement expense if, at the beginning of the period, they exceed a "corridor" limit. The corridor is measured as the greater of 10 percent of the APBO or 10 percent of the market-related value of plan assets.

The intent of the **corridor approach** is to reduce volatility of postretirement expense by providing a reasonable opportunity for gains and losses to offset over time without affecting net periodic expense.

Amortization Methods

If the company must amortize gains and losses (beyond the corridor) on postretirement benefit plans, the **minimum amortization amount** is the excess gain or loss divided by the average remaining service life to expected retirement of all active employees. Companies may use any systematic method of amortization provided that: (1) the amount amortized in any period is equal to or greater than the minimum amount, (2) the company applies the method consistently, and (3) the company applies the method similarly for gains and losses.

The company must recompute the amount of gain or loss in accumulated other comprehensive income each year and amortize the gain or loss over the average remaining service life if the net amount exceeds the "corridor."

2015 Entries and Worksheet

Continuing the Quest Company illustration into 2015, the following facts apply to the postretirement benefits plan for the year 2015.

Actual return on plan assets is $600.
Expected return on plan assets is $800.
Discount rate is 8 percent.
Increase in APBO due to change in actuarial assumptions is $60,000.
Service cost is $26,000.
Funding contributions during the year are $18,000.
Benefit payments to employees during the year are $5,000.
Average remaining service to expected retirement: 25 years.

The worksheet in Illustration 20A-6 (on page 1224) presents all of Quest's postretirement benefit entries and information for 2015. The beginning balances on the first line of the worksheet are the ending balances from Quest's 2014 postretirement benefits worksheet in Illustration 20A-4 (on page 1222).

Entries (d), (h), and (i) are similar to the corresponding entries previously explained for 2014. Entry (e) accrues the interest expense component, which increases both the liability and the postretirement expense by $2,080 (the beginning APBO multiplied by the discount rate of 8%). Entries (f) and (g) are related. The expected return of $800 is higher than the actual return of $600. To smooth postretirement expense,

Postretirement Benefits Worksheet—2015.xls

	General Journal Entries				Memo Record	
Items	Annual Postretirement Expense	Cash	Other Comprehensive Income (G/L)	Postretirement Asset/Liability	APBO	Plan Assets
Balance, Jan. 1, 2015				16,000 Cr.	26,000 Cr.	10,000 Dr.
(d) Service cost	26,000 Dr.				26,000 Cr.	
(e) Interest cost	2,080 Dr.				2,080 Cr.	
(f) Actual return	600 Cr.					600 Dr.
(g) Unexpected loss	200 Cr.		200 Dr.			
(h) Contributions		18,000 Cr.				18,000 Dr.
(i) Benefits					5,000 Dr.	5,000 Cr.
(j) Increase in APBO (Loss)			60,000 Dr.		60,000 Cr.	
Journal entry for 2015	27,280 Dr.	18,000 Cr.	60,200 Dr.	69,480 Cr.		
Accumulated OCI, Dec. 31, 2014			0			
Balance, Dec. 31, 2015			60,200 Dr.	85,480 Cr.	109,080 Cr.	23,600 Dr.

ILLUSTRATION 20A-6
Postretirement Benefits Worksheet—2015

Quest defers the unexpected loss of $200 ($800 − $600) by debiting Other Comprehensive Income (G/L) and crediting Postretirement Expense. As a result of this adjustment, the expected return on the plan assets is the amount actually used to compute postretirement expense.

Entry (j) records the change in the APBO resulting from a change in actuarial assumptions. This $60,000 increase in the employer's accumulated liability is an unexpected loss. Quest debits this loss to Other Comprehensive Income (G/L).

On December 31 Quest formally records net periodic expense for 2015 as follows.

December 31, 2015

Postretirement Expense	27,280	
Other Comprehensive Income (G/L)	60,200	
Cash		18,000
Postretirement Asset/Liability		69,480

The balance of the Postretirement Asset/Liability account at December 31, 2015, is $85,480. This balance is equal to the net of the balances in the memo accounts as shown in the reconciliation schedule in Illustration 20A-7.

ILLUSTRATION 20A-7
Postretirement Benefits Reconciliation Schedule—December 31, 2015

Accumulated postretirement benefit obligation (Credit)	$(109,080)
Plan assets at fair value (Debit)	23,600
Postretirement asset/liability (Credit)	$ (85,480)

Amortization of Net Gain or Loss in 2016

Quest has a beginning balance in Accumulated OCI related to losses of $60,200. Therefore, Quest must apply the corridor test for amortization of the balance for 2016. Illustration 20A-8 shows the computation of the amortization charge for the loss.

ILLUSTRATION 20A-8
Computation of Amortization Charge (Corridor Test)—2016

2016 Corridor Test	
Accumulated OCI at beginning of year	$60,200
10% of greater of APBO or market-related value of plan assets ($109,080 × .10)	(10,908)
Amortizable amount	$49,292
Average remaining service to expected retirement	25 years
2016 amortization of loss ($49,292 ÷ 25)	$1,972

DISCLOSURES IN NOTES TO THE FINANCIAL STATEMENTS

The disclosures required for other postretirement benefit plans are similar to and just as detailed and extensive as those required for pensions. The note disclosure for **Tootsie Roll, Inc.** in Illustration 20A-9 (page 1226) provides a good example of the extensive disclosure required for other postretirement benefit plans.

As indicated in Illustration 20A-9, Tootsie Roll shows the impact of the postretirement benefit plan on income, the balance sheet, and the cash flow statement, and it provides information on important assumptions used in the measurement of the postretirement benefit obligation. Also note that given no tax incentives for funding, Tootsie Roll (like many companies) does not have any assets set aside for its other postretirement benefit obligations.

While Tootsie Roll has only an other postretirement benefit plan, many companies sponsor both defined benefit pension and other postretirement plans. Given the similarities in accounting for these plans, companies can combine pension and other postretirement benefit disclosures.

ACTUARIAL ASSUMPTIONS AND CONCEPTUAL ISSUES

Measurement of the EPBO, the APBO, and the net periodic postretirement benefit cost is involved and complex. Due to the uncertainties in forecasting healthcare costs, rates of use, changes in government health programs, and the differences employed in nonmedical assumptions (e.g., discount rate, employee turnover, rate of pre-65 retirement, spouse-age difference), estimates of postretirement benefit costs may have a large margin of error. Is the information relevant, reliable, or verifiable? The FASB concluded that "the obligation to provide postretirement benefits meets the definition of a liability, is representationally faithful, is relevant to financial statement users, and can be measured with sufficient reliability at a justifiable cost." **[12]** Failure to accrue an obligation and an expense prior to payment of benefits would result in an unfaithful representation of what financial statements should represent.

The FASB took a momentous step by requiring recognition of a postretirement liability. Many opposed the requirement, warning that the GAAP rules would devastate earnings. Others argued that putting these numbers on the balance sheet was inappropriate. Others noted that the requirement would force companies to curtail postretirement benefits to employees.

The authors believe that the FASB deserves special praise. Because the Board addressed this issue, companies now recognize the magnitude of these costs. This recognition has

ILLUSTRATION 20A-9
Postretirement Benefit Disclosure

Tootsie Roll Industries, Inc.

Notes to Financial Statements

Note 7 Employee Benefit Plans (partial)
Postretirement health care and life insurance benefit plans:

The Company provides certain postretirement health care and life insurance benefits for corporate office and management employees based upon their age, years of service, date of hire and if they agree to contribute a portion of the cost as determined by the Company. The Company has the right to modify or terminate these benefits and does not fund postretirement health care and life insurance benefits in advance of payments for benefit claims. The Company is currently contemplating changes to its postretirement health care and life insurance benefits with the intention of reducing the Company's cost of providing such benefits. These changes are likely to include increasing retiree premium contributions, reducing and eliminating certain benefits, and taking steps to ensure that the Company does not become subject to the excise tax on high value coverage instituted by the Patient Protection and Affordability Act. The Company is not presently able to determine the effects of such changes on its financial statements.

Amounts recognized in other comprehensive income

Amounts recognized in accumulated other comprehensive loss (pre-tax) at December 31, 2011 are as follows:

Prior service credit	$ (626)
Net actuarial loss	8,255
Net amount recognized in accumulated other comprehensive loss	$7,629

The estimated actuarial loss and prior service credit to be amortized from accumulated other comprehensive income into net periodic benefit cost during 2012 are $1,146 and $(125), respectively.

Reconciliation of OPEB liability

The changes in the accumulated postretirement benefit obligation at December 31, 2011 and 2010 consist of the following:

	December 31,	
	2011	2010
Benefit obligation, beginning of year	$20,689	$16,674
Service cost	831	696
Interest cost	1,117	958
Actuarial loss	3,898	2,714
Benefits paid	(427)	(353)
Benefit obligation, end of year	$26,108	$20,689

Components of OPEB expense

Net periodic postretirement benefit cost included the following components:

	2011	2010	2009
Service cost—benefits attributed to service during the period	$ 831	$ 696	$ 704
Interest cost on the accumulated postretirement benefit obligation	1,117	958	853
Net amortization	501	128	140
Net periodic postretirement benefit cost	$2,449	$1,782	$1,697

Rates used to estimate plan elements

For measurement purposes, the 2012 annual rate of increase in the per capita cost of covered health care benefits was assumed to be 8.2% for pre-age 65 retirees, post 65 retirees and for prescription drugs; these rates were assumed to decrease gradually to 5.0% for 2019 and remain at that level thereafter. The health care cost trend rate assumption has a significant effect on the amounts reported. The weighted-average discount rate used in determining the accumulated postretirement benefit obligation was 4.31% and 5.47% at December 31, 2011 and 2010, respectively.

Increasing or decreasing the health care trend rates by one percentage point in each year would have the following effect:

	1% Increase	1% Decrease
Postretirement benefit obligation	$6,247	$(4,277)
Total of service and interest cost components	$ 484	$ (320)

The Company estimates future benefit payments will be $574, $710, $882, $993 and $1,095 in 2012 through 2016, respectively, and a total of $7,002 in 2017 through 2020. The future benefit payments are net of the annual Medicare Part D subsidy of approximately $1,094 beginning in 2012.

led to efforts to control escalating healthcare costs. As John Ruffle, a former president of the Financial Accounting Foundation noted, "The Board has done American industry a gigantic favor. Over the long term, industry will look back and say thanks."

What do the numbers mean? WANT SOME BAD NEWS?

Many companies have underfunded pension and other postretirement plans. Unfortunately, many governmental entities also have the same problem but on a much larger scale. Here are some examples.

- The actual liabilities of the federal government—including Social Security, Medicare, and federal employees' future retirement benefits—is estimated to be $86.8 trillion or 550 percent of GDP at the end of 2011. When the accrued expenses of the government's entitled programs are counted, we need to collect over $8 trillion in tax revenues annually. Even if you take all the taxable income of corporations and of individuals earning over approximately $66,000, that still falls short of the $8 trillion.
- A State Budget Crisis Task Force recently declared underfunded retirement promises as one of the six major threats to states' "fiscal sustainability."
- According to the Milliman's Public Pension Fund Study and the Pew Center for the States Report, an $859 billion gap exists between obligations for the country's 100 largest public pension plans and the funding of these plans. Nine states were 60 percent funded or less. In Illinois, just 45 percent of the state's pension liabilities were funded. California alone had $113 billion in unfunded liability.

So what does all this have to do with accounting? Similar to the FASB, there is an organization called the Governmental Accounting Standards Board (GASB), which establishes standards of financial accounting and reporting for state and local governmental agencies.

Until recently, the GASB went about its work in relative obscurity. How did the GASB get everyone's attention? It recently required that governmental units recognize postretirement benefits on their balance sheets on an accrual basis. Some states do not like this requirement and have proposed legislation that will allow them to ignore GASB standards. However, the GASB, with the support of users of government reports, has pushed for the change. They are concerned that without the new requirements, governments will continue to misrepresent the true cost of their retirement-related promises to public employees. In their view, the new accounting rules are in the best interests of municipal bondholders and the public in general. Thus, it appears that the FASB is not the only standard-setter subject to political pressure.

Sources: R. H. Attmore, "Who Do Texas Elected Officials Think They Are Fooling?" *The Bond Buyer* (June 18, 2007); Chris Cox and Bill Archer, "Why $16 Trillion Only Hints at the True U.S. Debt," *Wall Street Journal* (November 27, 2012); and "More Bad News for Public Pensions," *Wall Street Journal* (July 12, 2012). For more information on the GASB, go to *www.gasb.org/*.

SUMMARY OF LEARNING OBJECTIVES FOR APPENDIX 20A

10 Identify the differences between pensions and postretirement healthcare benefits. Pension plans are generally funded, but healthcare benefit plans are not. Pension benefits are generally well-defined and level in amount; healthcare benefits are generally uncapped and variable. Pension benefits are payable monthly; healthcare benefits are paid as needed and used. Pension plan variables are reasonably predictable, whereas healthcare plan variables are difficult to predict.

11 Contrast accounting for pensions to accounting for other postretirement benefits. Many of the basic concepts, accounting terminology, and measurement methodology that apply to pensions also apply to other postretirement benefit accounting. Because other postretirement benefit plans are unfunded, large obligations can occur. Two significant concepts peculiar to accounting for other postretirement benefits are (1) expected postretirement benefit obligation (EPBO), and (2) accumulated postretirement benefit obligation (APBO).

KEY TERMS

DEMONSTRATION PROBLEM

Jablonski Corp. sponsors a defined benefit pension plan for its employees. On January 1, 2014, the following balances related to this plan.

Plan assets (market-related value)	$170,000
Projected benefit obligation	340,000
Pension asset/liability	170,000 Cr.
Prior service cost	100,000
OCI—Loss	39,000

As a result of the operation of the plan during 2014, the actuary provided the following additional data at December 31, 2014.

Service cost for 2014	$45,000
Actual return on plan assets in 2014	27,000
Amortization of prior service cost	20,000
Contributions in 2014	85,000
Benefits paid retirees in 2014	51,000
Settlement rate	7%
Expected return on plan assets	8%
Average remaining service life of active employees	10 years

Instructions

(a) Compute pension expense for Jablonski Corp. for the year 2014 by preparing a pension worksheet that shows the journal entry for pension expense.

(b) Indicate the pension amounts reported in the financial statements.

Solution

(a)

Jablonski Corp.xls

JABLONSKI CORP.
Pension Worksheet—2014

	General Journal Entries					Memo Record	
			Other Comprehensive Income				
Items	Annual Pension Expense	Cash	Prior Service Cost	Gain/Loss	Pension Asset/ Liability	Projected Benefit Obligation	Plan Assets
Balance, Jan. 1, 2014					170,000 Cr.	340,000 Cr.	170,000 Dr.
Service cost	45,000 Dr.					45,000 Cr.	
Interest cost*	23,800 Dr.					23,800 Cr.	
Actual return	27,000 Cr.						27,000 Dr.
Unexpected gain**	13,400 Dr.			13,400 Cr.			
Amortization of PSC	20,000 Dr.		20,000 Cr.				
Amortization of loss***	500 Dr.			500 Cr.			
Contributions		85,000 Cr.					85,000 Dr.
Benefits						51,000 Dr.	51,000 Cr.
Journal entry for 2014	75,700 Dr.	85,000 Cr.	20,000 Cr.	13,900 Cr.	43,200 Dr.		
Accumulated OCI, Dec. 31, 2014			100,000 Dr.	39,000 Dr.			
Balance, Dec. 31, 2014			80,000 Dr.	25,100 Dr.	126,800 Cr.	357,800 Cr.	231,000 Dr.

*$23,800 = $340,000 × .07

**$13,400 = ($170,000 × .08) − $27,000

***

Year	1/1 Projected Benefit Obligation	Value of 1/1 Plan Assets	10% Corridor	Accumulated OCI (G/L), 1/1	Minimum Amortization of Loss for 2013
2014	$340,000	$170,000	$34,000	$39,000	$500****

**** ($39,000 − $34,000) = $5,000 ÷ 10 = $500

2014

Pension Expense	75,700	
Pension Asset/Liability	43,200	
Other Comprehensive Income (PSC)		20,000
Other Comprehensive Income (G/L)		13,400
Cash		85,000

(b) The pension amounts reported in the 2014 financial statements are as follows.

Income Statement

Pension expense		$ 75,700

Comprehensive Income Statement

Net Income		$ XXXX
Other comprehensive income		
Asset gain	$13,900	
Amortization of loss	500	
Prior service cost amortization	20,000	34,400
Comprehensive income		$ XXXX

Balance Sheet

Liabilities	
Pension liability	$126,800
Stockholders' equity	
Accumulated other comprehensive loss (PSC)	$ 80,000
Accumulated other comprehensive loss (G/L)	25,100

C FASB CODIFICATION

FASB Codification References

[1] FASB ASC 960. [Predecessor literature: "Accounting and Reporting by Defined Benefit Pension Plans," *Statement of Financial Accounting Standards No. 35* (Stamford, Conn.: FASB, 1979).]

[2] FASB ASC 715-70-50-1. [Predecessor literature: "Employers' Accounting for Pension Plans," *Statement of Financial Accounting Standards No. 87* (Stamford, Conn.: FASB, 1985), paras. 63–66.]

[3] FASB ASC 715-30-25-1. [Predecessor literature: "Employers' Accounting for Defined Benefit Pension and Other Postretirement Plans: An Amendment to SFAS Nos. 87, 88, 106, and 132(R)," *Statement of Financial Accounting Standards No. 158* (Norwalk, Conn.: FASB, 2006).]

[4] FASB ASC 715-30-35-22. [Predecessor literature: "Employers' Accounting for Pension Plans," *Statement of Financial Accounting Standards No. 87* (Stamford, Conn.: FASB, 1985), par. 30.]

[5] FASB ASC 220-10-45-13. [Predecessor literature: "Employers' Accounting for Defined Benefit Pension and Other Postretirement Plans: An Amendment of SFAS Nos. 87, 88, 106, and 132(R)," *Statement of Financial Accounting Standards No. 158* (Norwalk, Conn.: FASB, 2006), par. B41.]

[6] FASB ASC 715-20-50-1. [Predecessor literature: None.]

[7] FASB ASC 715-20-50-1. [Predecessor literature: "Employers' Disclosure about Pensions and Other Postretirement Benefits," *Statement of Financial Accounting Standards No. 132* (Stamford, Conn.: FASB, 1998; revised 2003); and "Employers' Accounting for Defined Benefit Pension and Other Postretirement Plans: An Amendment of SFAS Nos. 87, 88, 106, and 132(R)," *Statement of Financial Accounting Standards No. 158* (Norwalk, Conn.: FASB, 2006).]

[8] FASB ASC 715-30-05-9. [Predecessor literature: "Employers' Accounting for Settlements and Curtailments of Defined Benefit Pension Plans and for Termination Benefits," *Statement of Financial Accounting Standards No. 88* (Stamford, Conn.: FASB, 1985).]

[9] FASB ASC 715-60. [Predecessor literature: "Employers' Accounting for Postretirement Benefits Other Than Pensions," *Statement of Financial Accounting Standards No. 106* (Norwalk, Conn.: FASB, 1990).]

[10] FASB ASC 712-10-05. [Predecessor literature: "Employers' Accounting for Postemployment Benefits," *Statement of Financial Accounting Standards No. 112* (Norwalk, Conn.: FASB, 1992).]

[11] FASB ASC 715-60-35-9. [Predecessor literature: "Employers' Accounting for Postretirement Benefits Other Than Pensions," *Statement of Financial Accounting Standards No. 106* (Norwalk, Conn.: FASB, 1990), paras. 46–66.]

[12] FASB ASC 715-60-25. [Predecessor literature: "Employers' Accounting for Postretirement Benefits Other Than Pensions," *Statement of Financial Accounting Standards No. 106* (Norwalk, Conn.: FASB, 1990), par. 163.]

Exercises

If your school has a subscription to the FASB Codification, go to *http://aaahq.org/ascLogin.cfm* to log in and prepare responses to the following. Provide Codification references for your responses.

CE20-1 Access the glossary ("Master Glossary") to answer the following.

- **(a)** What is an accumulated benefit obligation?
- **(b)** What is a defined benefit postretirement plan?
- **(c)** What is the definition of "actuarial present value"?
- **(d)** What is a prior service cost?

CE20-2 In general, how can an employer choose an appropriate discount rate for its pension plan? What information could an employer use in choosing a discount rate?

CE20-3 If an employer has a defined benefit pension plan, what components would make up its net periodic pension cost?

CE20-4 What information about its pension plan must a publicly traded company disclose in its interim financial statements?

An additional Codification case can be found in the Using Your Judgment section, on page 1250.

Be sure to check the book's companion website for a Review and Analysis Exercise, with solution.

WileyPLUS **Brief Exercises, Exercises, Problems, and many more learning and assessment tools and resources are available for practice in WileyPLUS.**

Note: All asterisked Questions, Exercises, and Problems relate to material in the appendix to the chapter.

QUESTIONS

1. What is a private pension plan? How does a contributory pension plan differ from a noncontributory plan?

2. Differentiate between a defined contribution pension plan and a defined benefit pension plan. Explain how the employer's obligation differs between the two types of plans.

3. Differentiate between "accounting for the employer" and "accounting for the pension fund."

4. The meaning of the term "fund" depends on the context in which it is used. Explain its meaning when used as a noun. Explain its meaning when it is used as a verb.

5. What is the role of an actuary relative to pension plans? What are actuarial assumptions?

6. What factors must be considered by the actuary in measuring the amount of pension benefits under a defined benefit plan?

7. Name three approaches to measuring benefit obligations from a pension plan and explain how they differ.

8. Explain how cash-basis accounting for pension plans differs from accrual-basis accounting for pension plans. Why is cash-basis accounting generally considered unacceptable for pension plan accounting?

9. Identify the five components that comprise pension expense. Briefly explain the nature of each component.

10. What is service cost, and what is the basis of its measurement?

11. In computing the interest component of pension expense, what interest rates may be used?

12. Explain the difference between service cost and prior service cost.

13. What is meant by "prior service cost"? When is prior service cost recognized as pension expense?

14. What are "liability gains and losses," and how are they accounted for?

15. If pension expense recognized in a period exceeds the current amount funded by the employer, what kind of account arises, and how should it be reported in the financial statements? If the reverse occurs—that is, current funding by the employer exceeds the amount recognized as pension expense—what kind of account arises, and how should it be reported?

16. Given the following items and amounts, compute the actual return on plan assets: fair value of plan assets at the beginning of the period \$9,500,000; benefits paid during the period \$1,400,000; contributions made during the period \$1,000,000; and fair value of the plan assets at the end of the period \$10,150,000.

17. How does an "asset gain or loss" develop in pension accounting? How does a "liability gain or loss" develop in pension accounting?

18. What is the meaning of "corridor amortization"?

19. At the end of the current period, Agler Inc. had a projected benefit obligation of \$400,000 and pension plan assets (at fair value) of \$350,000. What are the accounts and amounts that will be reported on the company's balance sheet as pension assets or pension liabilities?

20. At the end of the current year, Pociek Co. has prior service cost of \$9,150,000. Where should the prior service cost be reported on the balance sheet?

21. Describe the accounting for actuarial gains and losses.

22. Boey Company reported net income of \$25,000 in 2015. It had the following amounts related to its pension plan in 2015: Actuarial liability gain \$10,000; Unexpected asset loss \$14,000; Accumulated other comprehensive income (G/L) (beginning balance), zero. Determine for 2015 (a) Boey's other comprehensive income, and (b) comprehensive income.

23. Describe the reporting of pension plans for a company with multiple plans, some of which are underfunded and some of which are overfunded.

24. Determine the meaning of the following terms.

(a) Contributory plan.

(b) Vested benefits.

(c) Retroactive benefits.

(d) Years-of-service method.

25. A headline in the *Wall Street Journal* stated, "Firms Increasingly Tap Their Pension Funds to Use Excess Assets." What is the accounting issue related to the use of these "excess assets" by companies?

***26.** What are postretirement benefits other than pensions?

***27.** Why didn't the FASB cover both types of postretirement benefits—pensions and healthcare—in the earlier pension accounting rules?

***28.** What are the major differences between postretirement healthcare benefits and pension benefits?

***29.** What is the difference between the APBO and the EPBO? What are the components of postretirement expense?

BRIEF EXERCISES

4 **BE20-1** AMR Corporation (parent company of American Airlines) reported the following for 2011 (in millions).

Service cost	\$366
Interest on P.B.O.	737
Return on plan assets	593
Amortization of prior service cost	13
Amortization of net loss	154

Compute AMR Corporation's 2011 pension expense.

4 **BE20-2** For Warren Corporation, year-end plan assets were \$2,000,000. At the beginning of the year, plan assets were \$1,780,000. During the year, contributions to the pension fund were \$120,000, and benefits paid were \$200,000. Compute Warren's actual return on plan assets.

5 **BE20-3** At January 1, 2014, Hennein Company had plan assets of \$280,000 and a projected benefit obligation of the same amount. During 2014, service cost was \$27,500, the settlement rate was 10%, actual and expected return on plan assets were \$25,000, contributions were \$20,000, and benefits paid were \$17,500. Prepare a pension worksheet for Hennein Company for 2014.

4 **BE20-4** For 2012, Campbell Soup Company had pension expense of \$73 million and contributed \$71 million to the pension fund. Prepare Campbell Soup Company's journal entry to record pension expense and funding.

6 **BE20-5** Mancuso Corporation amended its pension plan on January 1, 2014, and granted $160,000 of prior service costs to its employees. The employees are expected to provide 2,000 service years in the future, with 350 service years in 2014. Compute prior service cost amortization for 2014.

9 **BE20-6** At December 31, 2014, Besler Corporation had a projected benefit obligation of $560,000, plan assets of $322,000, and prior service cost of $127,000 in accumulated other comprehensive income. Determine the pension asset/liability at December 31, 2014.

8 **BE20-7** Shin Corporation had a projected benefit obligation of $3,100,000 and plan assets of $3,300,000 at January 1, 2014. Shin also had a net actuarial loss of $465,000 in accumulated OCI at January 1, 2014. The average remaining service period of Shin's employees is 7.5 years. Compute Shin's minimum amortization of the actuarial loss.

9 **BE20-8** Hawkins Corporation has the following balances at December 31, 2014.

Projected benefit obligation	$2,600,000
Plan assets at fair value	2,000,000
Accumulated OCI (PSC)	1,100,000

How should these balances be reported on Hawkins's balance sheet at December 31, 2014?

9 **BE20-9** Norton Co. had the following amounts related to its pension plan in 2014.

Actuarial liability loss for 2014	$28,000
Unexpected asset gain for 2014	18,000
Accumulated other comprehensive income (G/L) (beginning balance)	7,000 Cr.

Determine for 2014: (a) Norton's other comprehensive income (loss), and (b) comprehensive income. Net income for 2014 is $26,000; no amortization of gain or loss is necessary in 2014.

9 **BE20-10** Lahey Corp. has three defined benefit pension plans as follows.

	Pension Assets (at Fair Value)	Projected Benefit Obligation
Plan X	$600,000	$500,000
Plan Y	900,000	720,000
Plan Z	550,000	700,000

How will Lahey report these multiple plans in its financial statements?

10 11 ***BE20-11** Manno Corporation has the following information available concerning its postretirement benefit plan for 2014.

Service cost	$40,000
Interest cost	47,400
Actual and expected return on plan assets	26,900

Compute Manno's 2014 postretirement expense.

10 11 ***BE20-12** For 2014, Sampsell Inc. computed its annual postretirement expense as $240,900. Sampsell's contribution to the plan during 2014 was $180,000. Prepare Sampsell's 2014 entry to record postretirement expense.

EXERCISES

4 6 **E20-1 (Pension Expense, Journal Entries)** The following information is available for the pension plan of Radcliffe Company for the year 2014.

XLS

Actual and expected return on plan assets	$ 15,000
Benefits paid to retirees	40,000
Contributions (funding)	90,000
Interest/discount rate	10%
Prior service cost amortization	8,000
Projected benefit obligation, January 1, 2014	500,000
Service cost	60,000

Instructions

(a) Compute pension expense for the year 2014.

(b) Prepare the journal entry to record pension expense and the employer's contribution to the pension plan in 2014.

4 6 **E20-2 (Computation of Pension Expense)** Veldre Company provides the following information about its defined benefit pension plan for the year 2014.

Service cost	$ 90,000
Contribution to the plan	105,000
Prior service cost amortization	10,000
Actual and expected return on plan assets	64,000
Benefits paid	40,000
Plan assets at January 1, 2014	640,000
Projected benefit obligation at January 1, 2014	700,000
Accumulated OCI (PSC) at January 1, 2014	150,000
Interest/discount (settlement) rate	10%

Instructions

Compute the pension expense for the year 2014.

5 **E20-3 (Preparation of Pension Worksheet)** Using the information in E20-2, prepare a pension worksheet inserting January 1, 2014, balances, showing December 31, 2014, balances, and the journal entry recording pension expense.

5 **E20-4 (Basic Pension Worksheet)** The following facts apply to the pension plan of Boudreau Inc. for the year 2014.

Plan assets, January 1, 2014	$490,000
Projected benefit obligation, January 1, 2014	490,000
Settlement rate	8%
Service cost	40,000
Contributions (funding)	25,000
Actual and expected return on plan assets	49,700
Benefits paid to retirees	33,400

Instructions

Using the preceding data, compute pension expense for the year 2014. As part of your solution, prepare a pension worksheet that shows the journal entry for pension expense for 2014 and the year-end balances in the related pension accounts.

6 **E20-5 (Application of Years-of-Service Method)** Andrews Company has five employees participating in its defined benefit pension plan. Expected years of future service for these employees at the beginning of 2014 are as follows.

Employee	Future Years of Service
Jim	3
Paul	4
Nancy	5
Dave	6
Kathy	6

On January 1, 2014, the company amended its pension plan, increasing its projected benefit obligation by $72,000.

Instructions

Compute the amount of prior service cost amortization for the years 2014 through 2019 using the years-of-service method, setting up appropriate schedules.

4 **E20-6 (Computation of Actual Return)** Gingrich Importers provides the following pension plan information.

Fair value of pension plan assets, January 1, 2014	$2,400,000
Fair value of pension plan assets, December 31, 2014	2,725,000
Contributions to the plan in 2014	280,000
Benefits paid retirees in 2014	350,000

Instructions

From the data above, compute the actual return on the plan assets for 2014.

5 6 **E20-7 (Basic Pension Worksheet)** The following defined pension data of Rydell Corp. apply to the year 2014.

XLS

Projected benefit obligation, 1/1/14 (before amendment)	$560,000
Plan assets, 1/1/14	546,200
Pension liability	13,800
On January 1, 2014, Rydell Corp., through plan amendment, grants prior service benefits having a present value of	120,000
Settlement rate	9%
Service cost	58,000
Contributions (funding)	65,000
Actual (expected) return on plan assets	52,280
Benefits paid to retirees	40,000
Prior service cost amortization for 2014	17,000

Instructions

For 2014, prepare a pension worksheet for Rydell Corp. that shows the journal entry for pension expense and the year-end balances in the related pension accounts.

8 **E20-8 (Application of the Corridor Approach)** Kenseth Corp. has the following beginning-of-the-year present values for its projected benefit obligation and market-related values for its pension plan assets.

	Projected Benefit Obligation	Plan Assets Value
2013	$2,000,000	$1,900,000
2014	2,400,000	2,500,000
2015	2,950,000	2,600,000
2016	3,600,000	3,000,000

The average remaining service life per employee in 2013 and 2014 is 10 years and in 2015 and 2016 is 12 years. The net gain or loss that occurred during each year is as follows: 2013, $280,000 loss; 2014, $90,000 loss; 2015, $11,000 loss; and 2016, $25,000 gain. (In working the solution, the gains and losses must be aggregated to arrive at year-end balances.)

Instructions

Using the corridor approach, compute the amount of net gain or loss amortized and charged to pension expense in each of the four years, setting up an appropriate schedule.

9 **E20-9 (Disclosures: Pension Expense and Other Comprehensive Income)** Taveras Enterprises provides the following information relative to its defined benefit pension plan.

Balances or Values at December 31, 2014	
Projected benefit obligation	$2,737,000
Accumulated benefit obligation	1,980,000
Fair value of plan assets	2,278,329
Accumulated OCI (PSC)	210,000
Accumulated OCI—Net loss (1/1/14 balance, –0–)	45,680
Pension liability	458,671
Other pension plan data for 2014:	
Service cost	94,000
Prior service cost amortization	42,000
Actual return on plan assets	130,000
Expected return on plan assets	175,680
Interest on January 1, 2014, projected benefit obligation	253,000
Contributions to plan	93,329
Benefits paid	140,000

Instructions

(a) Prepare the note disclosing the components of pension expense for the year 2014.

(b) Determine the amounts of other comprehensive income and comprehensive income for 2014. Net income for 2014 is $35,000.

(c) Compute the amount of accumulated other comprehensive income reported at December 31, 2014.

5 **E20-10 (Pension Worksheet)** Webb Corp. sponsors a defined benefit pension plan for its employees. On January 1, 2014, the following balances relate to this plan.

Plan assets	$480,000
Projected benefit obligation	600,000
Pension asset/liability	120,000
Accumulated OCI (PSC)	100,000 Dr.

As a result of the operation of the plan during 2014, the following additional data are provided by the actuary.

Service cost	$90,000
Settlement rate, 9%	
Actual return on plan assets	55,000
Amortization of prior service cost	19,000
Expected return on plan assets	52,000
Unexpected loss from change in projected benefit obligation, due to change in actuarial predictions	76,000
Contributions	99,000
Benefits paid retirees	85,000

Instructions

(a) Using the data above, compute pension expense for Webb Corp. for the year 2014 by preparing a pension worksheet.

(b) Prepare the journal entry for pension expense for 2014.

4 9 **E20-11 (Pension Expense, Journal Entries, Statement Presentation)** Henning Company sponsors a defined benefit pension plan for its employees. The following data relate to the operation of the plan for the year 2014 in which no benefits were paid.

1. The actuarial present value of future benefits earned by employees for services rendered in 2014 amounted to $56,000.
2. The company's funding policy requires a contribution to the pension trustee amounting to $145,000 for 2014.
3. As of January 1, 2014, the company had a projected benefit obligation of $900,000, an accumulated benefit obligation of $800,000, and a debit balance of $400,000 in accumulated OCI (PSC). The fair value of pension plan assets amounted to $600,000 at the beginning of the year. The actual and expected return on plan assets was $54,000. The settlement rate was 9%. No gains or losses occurred in 2014 and no benefits were paid.
4. Amortization of prior service cost was $50,000 in 2014. Amortization of net gain or loss was not required in 2014.

Instructions

(a) Determine the amounts of the components of pension expense that should be recognized by the company in 2014.

(b) Prepare the journal entry or entries to record pension expense and the employer's contribution to the pension trustee in 2014.

(c) Indicate the amounts that would be reported on the income statement and the balance sheet for the year 2014.

4 6 7 8 9 **E20-12 (Pension Expense, Journal Entries, Statement Presentation)** Ferreri Company received the following selected information from its pension plan trustee concerning the operation of the company's defined benefit pension plan for the year ended December 31, 2014.

	January 1, 2014	December 31, 2014
Projected benefit obligation	$1,500,000	$1,527,000
Market-related and fair value of plan assets	800,000	1,130,000
Accumulated benefit obligation	1,600,000	1,720,000
Accumulated OCI (G/L)—Net gain	–0–	(200,000)

The service cost component of pension expense for employee services rendered in the current year amounted to $77,000 and the amortization of prior service cost was $120,000. The company's actual funding (contributions) of the plan in 2014 amounted to $250,000. The expected return on plan assets and the actual rate were both 10%; the interest/discount (settlement) rate was 10%. Accumulated other comprehensive income (PSC) had a balance of $1,200,000 on January 1, 2014. Assume no benefits paid in 2014.

Instructions

(a) Determine the amounts of the components of pension expense that should be recognized by the company in 2014.

(b) Prepare the journal entry to record pension expense and the employer's contribution to the pension plan in 2014.

(c) Indicate the pension-related amounts that would be reported on the income statement and the balance sheet for Ferreri Company for the year 2014.

4 6 7 8 9 **E20-13 (Computation of Actual Return, Gains and Losses, Corridor Test, and Pension Expense)** Erickson Company sponsors a defined benefit pension plan. The corporation's actuary provides the following information about the plan.

	January 1, 2014	December 31, 2014
Vested benefit obligation	$1,500	$1,900
Accumulated benefit obligation	1,900	2,730
Projected benefit obligation	2,500	3,300
Plan assets (fair value)	1,700	2,620
Settlement rate and expected rate of return		10%
Pension asset/liability	800	?
Service cost for the year 2014		400
Contributions (funding in 2014)		700
Benefits paid in 2014		200

Instructions

(a) Compute the actual return on the plan assets in 2014.
(b) Compute the amount of the other comprehensive income (G/L) as of December 31, 2014. (Assume the January 1, 2014, balance was zero.)
(c) Compute the amount of net gain or loss amortization for 2014 (corridor approach).
(d) Compute pension expense for 2014.

5 **E20-14 (Worksheet for E20-13)** Using the information in E20-13 about Erickson Company's defined benefit pension plan, prepare a 2014 pension worksheet with supplementary schedules of computations. Prepare the journal entries at December 31, 2014, to record pension expense and related pension transactions. Also, indicate the pension amounts reported in the balance sheet.

4 **E20-15 (Pension Expense, Journal Entries)** Latoya Company provides the following selected information related to its defined benefit pension plan for 2014.

Pension asset/liability (January 1)	$ 25,000 Cr.
Accumulated benefit obligation (December 31)	400,000
Actual and expected return on plan assets	10,000
Contributions (funding) in 2014	150,000
Fair value of plan assets (December 31)	800,000
Settlement rate	10%
Projected benefit obligation (January 1)	700,000
Service cost	80,000

Instructions

(a) Compute pension expense and prepare the journal entry to record pension expense and the employer's contribution to the pension plan in 2014. Preparation of a pension worksheet is not required. Benefits paid in 2014 were $35,000.
(b) Indicate the pension-related amounts that would be reported in the company's income statement and balance sheet for 2014.

8 **E20-16 (Amortization of Accumulated OCI (G/L), Corridor Approach, Pension Expense Computation)** The actuary for the pension plan of Gustafson Inc. calculated the following net gains and losses.

Incurred during the Year	(Gain) or Loss
2014	$300,000
2015	480,000
2016	(210,000)
2017	(290,000)

Other information about the company's pension obligation and plan assets is as follows.

As of January 1,	Projected Benefit Obligation	Plan Assets (market-related asset value)
2014	$4,000,000	$2,400,000
2015	4,520,000	2,200,000
2016	5,000,000	2,600,000
2017	4,240,000	3,040,000

Gustafson Inc. has a stable labor force of 400 employees who are expected to receive benefits under the plan. The total service-years for all participating employees is 5,600. The beginning balance of accumulated

OCI (G/L) is zero on January 1, 2014. The market-related value and the fair value of plan assets are the same for the 4-year period. Use the average remaining service life per employee as the basis for amortization.

Instructions

(Round to the nearest dollar.)

Prepare a schedule which reflects the minimum amount of accumulated OCI (G/L) amortized as a component of net periodic pension expense for each of the years 2014, 2015, 2016, and 2017. Apply the "corridor" approach in determining the amount to be amortized each year.

8 **E20-17 (Amortization of Accumulated OCI Balances)** Keeton Company sponsors a defined benefit pension plan for its 600 employees. The company's actuary provided the following information about the plan.

	January 1,	December 31,	
	2014	2014	2015
Projected benefit obligation	$2,800,000	$3,650,000	$4,195,000
Accumulated benefit obligation	1,900,000	2,430,000	2,900,000
Plan assets (fair value and market-related asset value)	1,700,000	2,900,000	3,790,000
Accumulated net (gain) or loss (for purposes of the corridor calculation)	–0–	198,000	(24,000)
Discount rate (current settlement rate)		9%	8%
Actual and expected asset return rate		10%	10%
Contributions		1,030,000	600,000

The average remaining service life per employee is 10.5 years. The service cost component of net periodic pension expense for employee services rendered amounted to $400,000 in 2014 and $475,000 in 2015. The accumulated OCI (PSC) on January 1, 2014, was $1,260,000. No benefits have been paid.

Instructions

(Round to the nearest dollar.)

(a) Compute the amount of accumulated OCI (PSC) to be amortized as a component of net periodic pension expense for each of the years 2014 and 2015.

(b) Prepare a schedule which reflects the amount of accumulated OCI (G/L) to be amortized as a component of pension expense for 2014 and 2015.

(c) Determine the total amount of pension expense to be recognized by Keeton Company in 2014 and 2015.

5 8 **E20-18 (Pension Worksheet—Missing Amounts)** The accounting staff of Usher Inc. has prepared the following pension worksheet. Unfortunately, several entries in the worksheet are not decipherable. The company has asked your assistance in completing the worksheet and completing the accounting tasks related to the pension plan for 2014.

Pension Worksheet—Usher Inc.xls

	A	B	C	D	E	F	G	H
1								
2				General Journal Entries			Memo Record	
3–5	Items	Annual Pension Expense	Cash	OCI—Prior Service Cost	OCI—Gain/Loss	Pension Asset/ Liability	Projected Benefit Obligation	Plan Assets
6	Balance, Jan. 1, 2014					1,100 Cr.	2,800	1,700
7	Service cost	(1)					500	
8	Interest cost	(2)					280	
9	Actual return	(3)						220
10	Unexpected gain	150			(4)			
11	Amortization of PSC	(5)		55				
12	Contributions		800					800
13	Benefits						200	200
14	Liability increase				(6)		365	
15	Journal entry	(7)	(8)	(9)	(10)	(11)		
16								
17	Accumulated OCI, Dec. 31, 2013			1,100	0			
18	Balance, Dec. 31, 2014			1,045	215	1,225	3,745	2,520
19								

Instructions

(a) Determine the missing amounts in the 2014 pension worksheet, indicating whether the amounts are debits or credits.

(b) Prepare the journal entry to record 2014 pension expense for Usher Inc.

(c) The accounting staff has heard of a pension accounting procedure called "corridor amortization." Is Usher required to record any amounts for corridor amortization in (1) 2014? In (2) 2015? Explain.

10 11 ***E20-19 (Postretirement Benefit Expense Computation)** Kreter Co. provides the following information about its postretirement benefit plan for the year 2014.

Service cost	$ 45,000
Contribution to the plan	10,000
Actual and expected return on plan assets	11,000
Benefits paid	20,000
Plan assets at January 1, 2014	110,000
Accumulated postretirement benefit obligation at January 1, 2014	330,000
Discount rate	8%

Instructions

Compute the postretirement benefit expense for 2014.

10 11 ***E20-20 (Postretirement Benefit Worksheet)** Using the information in E20-19, prepare a worksheet inserting January 1, 2014, balances, and showing December 31, 2014, balances. Prepare the journal entry recording postretirement benefit expense.

10 11 ***E20-21 (Postretirement Benefit Expense Computation)** Garner Inc. provides the following information related to its postretirement benefits for the year 2014.

Accumulated postretirement benefit obligation at January 1, 2014	$710,000
Actual and expected return on plan assets	34,000
Prior service cost amortization	21,000
Discount rate	10%
Service cost	83,000

Instructions

Compute postretirement benefit expense for 2014.

10 11 ***E20-22 (Postretirement Benefit Expense Computation)** Englehart Co. provides the following information about its postretirement benefit plan for the year 2014.

Service cost	$ 90,000
Prior service cost amortization	3,000
Contribution to the plan	56,000
Actual and expected return on plan assets	62,000
Benefits paid	40,000
Plan assets at January 1, 2014	710,000
Accumulated postretirement benefit obligation at January 1, 2014	760,000
Accumulated OCI (PSC) at January 1, 2014	100,000 Dr.
Discount rate	9%

Instructions

Compute the postretirement benefit expense for 2014.

10 11 ***E20-23 (Postretirement Benefit Worksheet)** Using the information in E20-22, prepare a worksheet inserting January 1, 2014, balances, showing December 31, 2014, balances, and the journal entry recording postretirement benefit expense.

10 11 ***E20-24 (Postretirement Benefit Worksheet—Missing Amounts)** The accounting staff of Holder Inc. has prepared the following postretirement benefit worksheet. Unfortunately, several entries in the worksheet are not decipherable. The company has asked your assistance in completing the worksheet and completing the accounting tasks related to the pension plan for 2014.

Postretirement Benefit Worksheet—Holder Inc.xls

	A	B	C	D	E	F	G
1							
2			**General Journal Entries**			**Memo Record**	
3				Other			
4		Annual		Comprehensive	Postretirement		
5	Items	Expense	Cash	Income—PSC	Asset/Liability	APBO	Plan Assets
6	Balance, Jan. 1, 2014				290,000	410,000	120,000
7	Service cost	(1)				56,000	
8	Interest cost	(2)				36,900	
9	Actual/Expected return	(3)					2,000
10	Contributions		66,000				(4)
11	Benefits					5,000	5,000
12	Amortization of PSC	3,000		(5)			
13	Journal entry for 2014	(6)	(7)	(8)	(9)		
14							
15	Accumulated OCI, Dec. 31, 2013			30,000 Dr.			
16	Balance, Dec. 31, 2014			27,000 Dr.	314,900 Cr.	497,900 Cr.	183,000 Dr.
17							

Instructions

(a) Determine the missing amounts in the 2014 postretirement worksheet, indicating whether the amounts are debits or credits.

(b) Prepare the journal entry to record 2014 postretirement expense for Holder Inc.

(c) What discount rate is Holder using in accounting for the interest on its other postretirement benefit plan? Explain.

EXERCISES SET B

See the book's companion website, at **www.wiley.com/college/kieso**, for an additional set of exercises.

PROBLEMS

5 6 7 9 **P20-1 (2-Year Worksheet)** On January 1, 2014, Harrington Company has the following defined benefit pension plan balances.

Projected benefit obligation	$4,500,000
Fair value of plan assets	4,200,000

XLS

The interest (settlement) rate applicable to the plan is 10%. On January 1, 2015, the company amends its pension agreement so that prior service costs of $500,000 are created. Other data related to the pension plan are as follows.

	2014	2015
Service cost	$150,000	$180,000
Prior service cost amortization	–0–	90,000
Contributions (funding) to the plan	240,000	285,000
Benefits paid	200,000	280,000
Actual return on plan assets	252,000	260,000
Expected rate of return on assets	6%	8%

Instructions

(a) Prepare a pension worksheet for the pension plan for 2014 and 2015.
(b) For 2015, prepare the journal entry to record pension-related amounts.

5 6 7 9 **P20-2 (3-Year Worksheet, Journal Entries, and Reporting)** Jackson Company adopts acceptable accounting for its defined benefit pension plan on January 1, 2013, with the following beginning balances: plan assets $200,000; projected benefit obligation $250,000. Other data relating to 3 years' operation of the plan are as follows.

	2013	2014	2015
Annual service cost	$16,000	$ 19,000	$ 26,000
Settlement rate and expected rate of return	10%	10%	10%
Actual return on plan assets	18,000	22,000	24,000
Annual funding (contributions)	16,000	40,000	48,000
Benefits paid	14,000	16,400	21,000
Prior service cost (plan amended, 1/1/14)		160,000	
Amortization of prior service cost		54,400	41,600
Change in actuarial assumptions establishes a December 31, 2015, projected benefit obligation of:			520,000

Instructions

(a) Prepare a pension worksheet presenting all 3 years' pension balances and activities.
(b) Prepare the journal entries (from the worksheet) to reflect all pension plan transactions and events at December 31 of each year.
(c) Indicate the pension-related amounts reported in the financial statements for 2015.

6 7 8 9 **P20-3 (Pension Expense, Journal Entries, Amortization of Loss)** Gottschalk Company sponsors a defined benefit plan for its 100 employees. On January 1, 2014, the company's actuary provided the following information.

Accumulated other comprehensive loss (PSC)	$150,000
Pension plan assets (fair value and market-related asset value)	200,000
Accumulated benefit obligation	260,000
Projected benefit obligation	380,000

The average remaining service period for the participating employees is 10 years. All employees are expected to receive benefits under the plan. On December 31, 2014, the actuary calculated that the present value of future benefits earned for employee services rendered in the current year amounted to $52,000; the projected benefit obligation was $490,000; fair value of pension assets was $276,000; the accumulated benefit obligation amounted to $365,000. The expected return on plan assets and the discount rate on the projected benefit obligation were both 10%. The actual return on plan assets is $11,000. The company's current year's contribution to the pension plan amounted to $65,000. No benefits were paid during the year.

Instructions

(a) Determine the components of pension expense that the company would recognize in 2014. (With only one year involved, you need not prepare a worksheet.)
(b) Prepare the journal entry to record the pension expense and the company's funding of the pension plan in 2014.
(c) Compute the amount of the 2014 increase/decrease in gains or losses and the amount to be amortized in 2014 and 2015.
(d) Indicate the pension amounts reported in the financial statement as of December 31, 2014.

5 6 7 8 **P20-4 (Pension Expense, Journal Entries for 2 Years)** Gordon Company sponsors a defined benefit pension plan. The following information related to the pension plan is available for 2014 and 2015.

XLS

	2014	2015
Plan assets (fair value), December 31	$699,000	$849,000
Projected benefit obligation, January 1	700,000	800,000
Pension asset/liability, January 1	140,000 Cr.	?
Prior service cost, January 1	250,000	240,000
Service cost	60,000	90,000
Actual and expected return on plan assets	24,000	30,000
Amortization of prior service cost	10,000	12,000
Contributions (funding)	115,000	120,000
Accumulated benefit obligation, December 31	500,000	550,000
Interest/settlement rate	9%	9%

Instructions

(a) Compute pension expense for 2014 and 2015.

(b) Prepare the journal entries to record the pension expense and the company's funding of the pension plan for both years.

7 8 **P20-5 (Computation of Pension Expense, Amortization of Net Gain or Loss–Corridor Approach, Journal Entries for 3 Years)** Hiatt Toothpaste Company initiates a defined benefit pension plan for its 50 employees on January 1, 2014. The insurance company which administers the pension plan provided the following selected information for the years 2014, 2015, and 2016.

	For Year Ended December 31,		
	2014	2015	2016
Plan assets (fair value)	$50,000	$ 85,000	$180,000
Accumulated benefit obligation	45,000	165,000	292,000
Projected benefit obligation	60,000	200,000	324,000
Net (gain) loss (for purposes of corridor calculation)	–0–	78,400	86,121
Employer's funding contribution (made at end of year)	50,000	60,000	105,000

There were no balances as of January 1, 2014, when the plan was initiated. The actual and expected return on plan assets was 10% over the 3-year period, but the settlement rate used to discount the company's pension obligation was 13% in 2014, 11% in 2015, and 8% in 2016. The service cost component of net periodic pension expense amounted to the following: 2014, $60,000; 2015, $85,000; and 2016, $119,000. The average remaining service life per employee is 12 years. No benefits were paid in 2014, $30,000 of benefits were paid in 2015, and $18,500 of benefits were paid in 2016 (all benefits paid at end of year).

Instructions

(Round to the nearest dollar.)

(a) Calculate the amount of net periodic pension expense that the company would recognize in 2014, 2015, and 2016.

(b) Prepare the journal entries to record net periodic pension expense, employer's funding contribution, and related pension amounts for the years 2014, 2015, and 2016.

6 7 8 **P20-6 (Computation of Prior Service Cost Amortization, Pension Expense, Journal Entries, and Net Gain or Loss)** Aykroyd Inc. has sponsored a noncontributory, defined benefit pension plan for its employees since 1991. Prior to 2014, cumulative net pension expense recognized equaled cumulative contributions to the plan. Other relevant information about the pension plan on January 1, 2014, is as follows.

1. The company has 200 employees. All these employees are expected to receive benefits under the plan. The average remaining service life per employee is 12 years.
2. The projected benefit obligation amounted to $5,000,000 and the fair value of pension plan assets was $3,000,000. The market-related asset value was also $3,000,000. Unrecognized prior service cost was $2,000,000.

On December 31, 2014, the projected benefit obligation and the accumulated benefit obligation were $4,850,000 and $4,025,000, respectively. The fair value of the pension plan assets amounted to $4,100,000 at the end of the year. A 10% settlement rate and a 10% expected asset return rate were used in the actuarial present value computations in the pension plan. The present value of benefits attributed by the pension benefit formula to employee service in 2014 amounted to $200,000. The employer's contribution to the plan assets amounted to $775,000 in 2014. This problem assumes no payment of pension benefits.

Instructions

(Round all amounts to the nearest dollar.)

(a) Prepare a schedule, based on the average remaining life per employee, showing the prior service cost that would be amortized as a component of pension expense for 2014, 2015, and 2016.

(b) Compute pension expense for the year 2014.

(c) Prepare the journal entries required to report the accounting for the company's pension plan for 2014.

(d) Compute the amount of the 2014 increase/decrease in net gains or losses and the amount to be amortized in 2014 and 2015.

5 6 7 **P20-7 (Pension Worksheet)** Hanson Corp. sponsors a defined benefit pension plan for its employees. On January 1, 2014, the following balances related to this plan.

Plan assets (market-related value)	$520,000
Projected benefit obligation	700,000
Pension asset/liability	180,000 Cr.
Prior service cost	81,000
Net gain or loss (debit)	91,000

As a result of the operation of the plan during 2014, the actuary provided the following additional data for 2014.

Service cost	$108,000
Settlement rate, 9%; expected return rate, 10%	
Actual return on plan assets	48,000
Amortization of prior service cost	25,000
Contributions	133,000
Benefits paid retirees	85,000
Average remaining service life of active employees	10 years

Instructions

Using the preceding data, compute pension expense for Hanson Corp. for the year 2014 by preparing a pension worksheet that shows the journal entry for pension expense. Use the market-related asset value to compute the expected return and for corridor amortization.

5 6 **P20-8 (Comprehensive 2-Year Worksheet)** Lemke Company sponsors a defined benefit pension plan for
7 8 its employees. The following data relate to the operation of the plan for the years 2014 and 2015.
9

	2014	2015
Projected benefit obligation, January 1	$600,000	
Plan assets (fair value and market-related value), January 1	410,000	
Pension asset/liability, January 1	190,000 Cr.	
Prior service cost, January 1	160,000	
Service cost	40,000	$ 59,000
Settlement rate	10%	10%
Expected rate of return	10%	10%
Actual return on plan assets	36,000	61,000
Amortization of prior service cost	70,000	50,000
Annual contributions	97,000	81,000
Benefits paid retirees	31,500	54,000
Increase in projected benefit obligation due to changes in actuarial assumptions	87,000	-0-
Accumulated benefit obligation at December 31	721,800	789,000
Average service life of all employees		20 years
Vested benefit obligation at December 31		464,000

Instructions

(a) Prepare a pension worksheet presenting both years 2014 and 2015 and accompanying computations and amortization of the loss (2015) using the corridor approach.

(b) Prepare the journal entries (from the worksheet) to reflect all pension plan transactions and events at December 31 of each year.

(c) For 2015, indicate the pension amounts reported in the financial statements.

5 6 **P20-9 (Comprehensive 2-Year Worksheet)** Hobbs Co. has the following defined benefit pension plan
7 balances on January 1, 2014.

Projected benefit obligation	$4,600,000
Fair value of plan assets	4,600,000

The interest (settlement) rate applicable to the plan is 10%. On January 1, 2015, the company amends its pension agreement so that prior service costs of $600,000 are created. Other data related to the pension plan are:

	2014	2015
Service cost	$150,000	$170,000
Prior service cost amortization	-0-	90,000
Contributions (funding) to the plan	200,000	184,658
Benefits paid	220,000	280,000
Actual return on plan assets	252,000	350,000
Expected rate of return on assets	6%	8%

Instructions

(a) Prepare a pension worksheet for the pension plan in 2014.

(b) Prepare any journal entries related to the pension plan that would be needed at December 31, 2014.

(c) Prepare a pension worksheet for 2015 and any journal entries related to the pension plan as of December 31, 2015.

(d) Indicate the pension-related amounts reported in the 2015 financial statements.

5 6 7 **P20-10 (Pension Worksheet—Missing Amounts)** Kramer Co. has prepared the following pension worksheet. Unfortunately, several entries in the worksheet are not decipherable. The company has asked your assistance in completing the worksheet and completing the accounting tasks related to the pension plan for 2014.

Pension Worksheet—Kramer Co.xls

	General Journal Entries					Memo Record	
Items	Annual Pension Expense	Cash	OCI—Prior Service Cost	OCI—Gain/Loss	Pension Asset/ Liability	Projected Benefit Obligation	Plan Assets
Balance, Jan. 1, 2014					120,000	325,000	205,000 Dr.
Service cost	(1)					20,000	
Interest cost	(2)					26,000	
Actual return	(3)						18,000 Dr.
Unexpected loss	2,500			(4)			
Amortization of PSC	(5)		35,000				
Contributions		41,000					41,000 Dr.
Benefits						15,000	15,000 Cr.
Increase in PBO				(6)		43,500	
Journal entry for 2014	(7)	(8)	(9)	(10)	(11)		
Accumulated OCI, Dec. 31, 2013			80,000	0			
Balance, Dec. 31, 2014			45,000	46,000	150,500 Cr.	399,500 Cr.	249,000 Dr.

Instructions

(a) Determine the missing amounts in the 2014 pension worksheet, indicating whether the amounts are debits or credits.

(b) Prepare the journal entry to record 2014 pension expense for Kramer Co.

(c) Determine the following for Kramer for 2014: (1) settlement rate used to measure the interest on the liability and (2) expected return on plan assets.

5 6 7 8 9 **P20-11 (Pension Worksheet)** The following data relate to the operation of Kramer Co.'s pension plan in 2015. The pension worksheet for 2014 is provided in P20-10.

Service cost	$59,000
Actual return on plan assets	32,000
Amortization of prior service cost	28,000
Annual contributions	51,000
Benefits paid retirees	27,000
Average service life of all employees	25 years

For 2015, Kramer will use the same assumptions as 2014 for the expected rate of returns on plan assets. The settlement rate for 2015 is 10%.

Instructions

(a) Prepare a pension worksheet for 2015 and accompanying computations and amortization of the loss, if any, in 2015 using the corridor approach.

(b) Prepare the journal entries (from the worksheet) to reflect all pension plan transactions and events at December 31.

(c) Indicate the pension amounts reported in the financial statements.

5 6 7 8 9 **P20-12 (Pension Worksheet)** Larson Corp. sponsors a defined benefit pension plan for its employees. On January 1, 2015, the following balances related to this plan.

Plan assets (market-related value)	$270,000
Projected benefit obligation	340,000
Pension asset/liability	70,000 Cr.
Prior service cost	90,000
OCI—Loss	39,000

As a result of the operation of the plan during 2015, the actuary provided the following additional data for 2015.

Service cost	$45,000
Actual return on plan assets	27,000
Amortization of prior service cost	12,000
Contributions	65,000
Benefits paid retirees	41,000
Settlement rate	7%
Expected return on plan assets	8%
Average remaining service life of active employees	10 years

Instructions

(a) Compute pension expense for Larson Corp. for the year 2015 by preparing a pension worksheet that shows the journal entry for pension expense.

(b) Indicate the pension amounts reported in the financial statements.

10 11 ***P20-13 (Postretirement Benefit Worksheet)** Hollenbeck Foods Inc. sponsors a postretirement medical and dental benefit plan for its employees. The following balances relate to this plan on January 1, 2014.

Plan assets	$200,000
Expected postretirement benefit obligation	820,000
Accumulated postretirement benefit obligation	200,000
No prior service costs exist.	

As a result of the plan's operation during 2014, the following additional data are provided by the actuary.

Service cost is $70,000
Discount rate is 10%
Contributions to plan are $65,000
Expected return on plan assets is $10,000
Actual return on plan assets is $15,000
Benefits paid to employees are $44,000
Average remaining service to full eligibility: 20 years

Instructions

(a) Using the preceding data, compute the net periodic postretirement benefit cost for 2014 by preparing a worksheet that shows the journal entry for postretirement expense and the year-end balances in the related postretirement benefit memo accounts. (Assume that contributions and benefits are paid at the end of the year.)

(b) Prepare any journal entries related to the postretirement plan for 2014 and indicate the postretirement amounts reported in the financial statements for 2014.

10 11 ***P20-14 (Postretirement Benefit Worksheet—2 Years)** Elton Co. has the following postretirement benefit plan balances on January 1, 2014.

Accumulated postretirement benefit obligation	$2,250,000
Fair value of plan assets	2,250,000

The interest (settlement) rate applicable to the plan is 10%. On January 1, 2015, the company amends the plan so that prior service costs of $175,000 are created. Other data related to the plan are:

	2014	2015
Service costs	$ 75,000	$ 85,000
Prior service costs amortization	-0-	12,000
Contributions (funding) to the plan	45,000	35,000
Benefits paid	40,000	45,000
Actual return on plan assets	140,000	120,000
Expected rate of return on assets	8%	6%

Instructions

(a) Prepare a worksheet for the postretirement plan in 2014.

(b) Prepare any journal entries related to the postretirement plan that would be needed at December 31, 2014.

(c) Prepare a worksheet for 2015 and any journal entries related to the postretirement plan as of December 31, 2015.

(d) Indicate the postretirement-benefit–related amounts reported in the 2015 financial statements.

PROBLEMS SET B

See the book's companion website, at **www.wiley.com/college/kieso**, for an additional set of problems.

CONCEPTS FOR ANALYSIS

CA20-1 (Pension Terminology and Theory) Many business organizations have been concerned with providing for the retirement of employees since the late 1800s. During recent decades, a marked increase in this concern has resulted in the establishment of private pension plans in most large companies and in many medium- and small-sized ones.

The substantial growth of these plans, both in numbers of employees covered and in amounts of retirement benefits, has increased the significance of pension costs in relation to the financial position, results of operations, and cash flows of many companies. In examining the costs of pension plans, a CPA encounters certain terms. The components of pension costs that the terms represent must be dealt with appropriately if generally accepted accounting principles are to be reflected in the financial statements of entities with pension plans.

Instructions

(a) Define a private pension plan. How does a contributory pension plan differ from a noncontributory plan?

(b) Differentiate between "accounting for the employer" and "accounting for the pension fund."

(c) Explain the terms "funded" and "pension liability" as they relate to:

- **(1)** The pension fund.
- **(2)** The employer.

(d) **(1)** Discuss the theoretical justification for accrual recognition of pension costs.

- **(2)** Discuss the relative objectivity of the measurement process of accrual versus cash (pay-as-you-go) accounting for annual pension costs.

(e) Distinguish among the following as they relate to pension plans.

- **(1)** Service cost.
- **(2)** Prior service costs.
- **(3)** Vested benefits.

CA20-2 (Pension Terminology) The following items appear on Brueggen Company's financial statements.

1. Under the caption Assets:
   Pension asset/liability.
2. Under the caption Liabilities:
   Pension asset/liability.
3. Under the caption Stockholders' Equity:
   Prior service cost as a component of Accumulated Other Comprehensive Income.
4. On the income statement:
   Pension expense.

Instructions

Explain the significance of each of the items above on corporate financial statements. (*Note:* All items set forth above are not necessarily to be found on the statements of a single company.)

CA20-3 (Basic Terminology) In examining the costs of pension plans, Helen Kaufman, CPA, encounters certain terms. The components of pension costs that the terms represent must be dealt with appropriately if generally accepted accounting principles are to be reflected in the financial statements of entities with pension plans.

Instructions

(a) **(1)** Discuss the theoretical justification for accrual recognition of pension costs.

- **(2)** Discuss the relative objectivity of the measurement process of accrual versus cash (pay-as-you-go) accounting for annual pension costs.

(b) Explain the following terms as they apply to accounting for pension plans.

- **(1)** Market-related asset value.
- **(2)** Projected benefit obligation.
- **(3)** Corridor approach.

(c) What information should be disclosed about a company's pension plans in its financial statements and its notes?

(AICPA adapted)

CA20-4 (Major Pension Concepts) Davis Corporation is a medium-sized manufacturer of paperboard containers and boxes. The corporation sponsors a noncontributory, defined benefit pension plan that covers its 250 employees. Sid Cole has recently been hired as president of Davis Corporation. While reviewing last year's financial statements with Carol Dilbeck, controller, Cole expressed confusion about several of the items in the footnote to the financial statements relating to the pension plan. In part, the footnote reads as follows.

> **Note J.** The company has a defined benefit pension plan covering substantially all of its employees. The benefits are based on years of service and the employee's compensation during the last four years of employment. The company's funding policy is to contribute annually the maximum amount allowed under the federal tax code. Contributions are intended to provide for benefits expected to be earned in the future as well as those earned to date.

The net periodic pension expense on Davis Corporation's comparative income statement was $72,000 in 2014 and $57,680 in 2013.

The following are selected figures from the plan's funded status and amounts recognized in the Davis Corporation's Statement of Financial Position at December 31, 2014 ($000 omitted).

Actuarial present value of benefit obligations:	
Accumulated benefit obligation	
(including vested benefits of $636)	$ (870)
Projected benefit obligation	$(1,200)
Plan assets at fair value	1,050
Projected benefit obligation in excess of plan assets	$ (150)

Given that Davis Corporation's work force has been stable for the last 6 years, Cole could not understand the increase in the net periodic pension expense. Dilbeck explained that the net periodic pension expense consists of several elements, some of which may increase or decrease the net expense.

Instructions

(a) The determination of the net periodic pension expense is a function of five elements. List and briefly describe each of the elements.

(b) Describe the major difference and the major similarity between the accumulated benefit obligation and the projected benefit obligation.

(c) **(1)** Explain why pension gains and losses are not recognized on the income statement in the period in which they arise.

(2) Briefly describe how pension gains and losses are recognized.

(CMA adapted)

CA20-5 (Implications of GAAP Rules on Pensions) Jill Vogel and Pete Dell have to do a class presentation on GAAP rules for reporting pension information. In developing the class presentation, they decided to provide the class with a series of questions related to pensions and then discuss the answers in class. Given that the class has all read the rules related to pension accounting and reporting, they felt this approach would provide a lively discussion. Here are the questions:

1. In an article in *BusinessWeek* prior to new rules related to pensions, it was reported that the discount rates used by the largest 200 companies for pension reporting ranged from 5% to 11%. How can such a situation exist, and does GAAP alleviate this problem?
2. An article indicated that when new GAAP rules were issued related to pensions, it caused an increase in the liability for pensions for approximately 20% of companies. Why might this situation occur?
3. A recent article noted that while "smoothing" is not necessarily an accounting virtue, pension accounting has long been recognized as an exception—an area of accounting in which at least some dampening of market swings is appropriate. This is because pension funds are managed so that their performance is insulated from the extremes of short-term market swings. A pension expense that reflects the volatility of market swings might, for that reason, convey information of little relevance. Are these statements true?

4. Understanding the impact of the changes required in pension reporting requires detailed information about its pension plan(s) and an analysis of the relationship of many factors, particularly the:
   (a) Type of plan(s) and any significant amendments.
   (b) Plan participants.
   (c) Funding status.
   (d) Actuarial funding method and assumptions currently used.
   What impact does each of these items have on financial statement presentation?
5. An article noted "You also need to decide whether to amortize gains and losses using the corridor method, or to use some other systematic method. Under the corridor approach, only gains and losses in excess of 10% of the greater of the projected benefit obligation or the plan assets would have to be amortized." What is the corridor method and what is its purpose?

Instructions

What answers do you believe Jill and Pete gave to each of these questions?

CA20-6 (Gains and Losses, Corridor Amortization) Vickie Plato, accounting clerk in the personnel office of Streisand Corp., has begun to compute pension expense for 2016 but is not sure whether or not she should include the amortization of unrecognized gains/losses. She is currently working with the following beginning-of-the-year present values for the projected benefit obligation and market-related values for the pension plan:

	Projected Benefit Obligation	Plan Assets Value
2013	$2,200,000	$1,900,000
2014	2,400,000	2,500,000
2015	2,900,000	2,600,000
2016	3,900,000	3,000,000

The average remaining service life per employee in 2013 and 2014 is 10 years and in 2015 and 2016 is 12 years. The net gain or loss that occurred during each year is as follows.

2013	$280,000 loss
2014	85,000 loss
2015	12,000 loss
2016	25,000 gain

(In working the solution, you must aggregate the unrecognized gains and losses to arrive at year-end balances.)

Instructions

You are the manager in charge of accounting. Write a memo to Vickie Plato, explaining why in some years she must amortize some of the net gains and losses and in other years she does not need to. In order to explain this situation fully, you must compute the amount of net gain or loss that is amortized and charged to pension expense in each of the 4 years listed above. Include an appropriate amortization schedule, referring to it whenever necessary.

CA20-7 (Nonvested Employees—An Ethical Dilemma) Thinken Technology recently merged with College Electronix (CE), a computer graphics manufacturing firm. In performing a comprehensive audit of CE's accounting system, Gerald Ott, internal audit manager for Thinken Technology, discovered that the new subsidiary did not record pension assets and liabilities, subject to GAAP.

The net present value of CE's pension assets was $15.5 million, the vested benefit obligation was $12.9 million, and the projected benefit obligation was $17.4 million. Ott reported this audit finding to Julie Habbe, the newly appointed controller of CE. A few days later, Habbe called Ott for his advice on what to do. Habbe started her conversation by asking, "Can't we eliminate the negative income effect of our pension dilemma simply by terminating the employment of nonvested employees before the end of our fiscal year?"

Instructions

How should Ott respond to Habbe's remark about firing nonvested employees?

USING YOUR JUDGMENT

FINANCIAL REPORTING

Financial Reporting Problem

P&G

The Procter & Gamble Company (P&G)

The financial statements of P&G are presented in Appendix 5B. The company's complete annual report, including the notes to the financial statements, can be accessed at the book's companion website, **www.wiley.com/college/kieso**.

Instructions

Refer to P&G's financial statements and the accompanying notes to answer the following questions.

(a) What kind of pension plan does P&G provide its employees in the United States?

(b) What was P&G's pension expense for 2011, 2010, and 2009 for the United States?

(c) What is the impact of P&G's pension plans for 2011 on its financial statements?

(d) What information does P&G provide on the target allocation of its pension assets? (Compare the asset allocation for "Pensions and Other Retiree Benefits.") How do the allocations relate to the expected returns on these assets?

Comparative Analysis Case

The Coca-Cola Company and PepsiCo, Inc.

Instructions

Go to the book's companion website and use information found there to answer the following questions related to The Coca-Cola Company and PepsiCo, Inc.

(a) What kind of pension plans do Coca-Cola and PepsiCo provide their employees?

(b) What net periodic pension expense (cost) did Coca-Cola and PepsiCo report in 2011?

(c) What is the year-end 2011 funded status of Coca-Cola's and PepsiCo's U.S. plans?

(d) What relevant rates were used by Coca-Cola and PepsiCo in computing their pension amounts?

(e) Compare the expected benefit payments and contributions for Coca-Cola and PepsiCo.

*Financial Statement Analysis Case

General Electric

A *Wall Street Journal* article discussed a $1.8 billion charge to income made by General Electric for postretirement benefit costs. It was attributed to previously unrecognized healthcare and life insurance cost. As financial vice president and controller for Peake, Inc., you found this article interesting because the president recently expressed interest in adopting a postemployment benefit program for Peake's employees, to complement the company's existing defined benefit plan. The president, Martha Beyerlein, wants to know how the expense on the new plan will be determined and what impact the accounting for the plan will have on Peake's financial statements.

Instructions

(a) As financial vice president and controller of Peake, Inc., explain the calculation of postemployment benefit expense under GAAP, and indicate how the accounting for the plan will affect Peake's financial statements.

(b) Discuss the similarities and differences in the accounting for the other postemployment benefit plan relative to the accounting for the defined benefit plan.

Accounting, Analysis, and Principles

PENCOMP's balance sheet at December 31, 2014, is as follows.

PENCOMP, INC.
BALANCE SHEET
AS OF DECEMBER 31, 2014

Assets		*Liabilities*	
Cash	$ 438	Notes payable	$1,000
Inventory	1,800	Pension liability	344
Total current assets	2,238	Total liabilities	1,344
Plant and equipment	2,000	*Stockholders' equity*	
Accumulated depreciation	(240)	Common stock	2,000
	1,760	Retained earnings	896
Total assets	$3,998	Accumulated other comprehensive income	(242)
		Total stockholders' equity	2,654
		Total liabilities and stockholders' equity	$3,998

Additional information concerning PENCOMP's defined benefit pension plan is as follows.

Projected benefit obligation at 12/31/14	$ 820.5
Plan assets (fair value) at 12/31/14	476.5
Unamortized past service cost at 12/31/14	150.0
Amortization of past service cost during 2015	15.0
Service cost for 2015	42.0
Discount rate	10%
Expected rate of return on plan assets in 2015	12%
Actual return on plan assets in 2015	10.4
Contributions to pension fund in 2015	70.0
Benefits paid during 2015	40.0
Unamortized net loss due to changes in actuarial assumptions and deferred net losses on plan assets at 12/31/14	92.0
Expected remaining service life of employees	15.0
Average period to vesting of prior service costs	10.0

Other information about PENCOMP is as follows.

Salary expense, all paid with cash during 2015	$ 700.0
Sales, all for cash	3,000.0
Purchases, all for cash	2,000.0
Inventory at 12/31/15	1,800.0

Property originally cost $2,000 and is depreciated on a straight-line basis over 25 years with no residual value.

Interest on the note payable is 10% annually and is paid in cash on 12/31 of each year.

Dividends declared and paid are $200 in 2015.

Accounting

Prepare an income statement for 2015 and a balance sheet as of December 31, 2015. Also, prepare the pension expense journal entry for the year ended December 31, 2015. Round to the nearest tenth (e.g., round 2.87 to 2.9).

Analysis

Compute return on equity for PENCOMP for 2015 (assume stockholders' equity is equal to year-end average stockholders' equity). Do you think an argument can be made for including some or even all of the change in accumulated other comprehensive income (due to pensions) in the numerator of return on equity? Illustrate that calculation.

Principles

Explain a rationale for why the FASB has (so far) decided to exclude from the current period income statement the effects of pension plan amendments and gains and losses due to changes in actuarial assumptions.

BRIDGE TO THE PROFESSION

Professional Research: FASB Codification

Monat Company has grown rapidly since its founding in 2004. To instill loyalty in its employees, Monat is contemplating establishment of a defined benefit plan. Monat knows that lenders and potential investors will pay close attention to the impact of the pension plan on the company's financial statements, particularly any gains or losses that develop in the plan. Monat has asked you to conduct some research on the accounting for gains and losses in a defined benefit plan.

Instructions

If your school has a subscription to the FASB Codification, go to *http://aaahq.org/ascLogin.cfm* to log in and prepare responses to the following. Provide Codification references for your responses.

(a) Briefly describe how pension gains and losses are accounted for.

(b) Explain the rationale behind the accounting method described in part (a).

(c) What is the related pension asset or liability that will show up on the balance sheet? When will each of these situations occur?

Additional Professional Resources

See the book's companion website, at **www.wiley.com/college/kieso**, for professional simulations as well as other study resources.

IFRS INSIGHTS

LEARNING OBJECTIVE 12
Compare the accounting for pensions under GAAP and IFRS.

The accounting for various forms of compensation plans under IFRS is found in *IAS 19* ("Employee Benefits") and *IFRS 2* ("Share-Based Payment"). *IAS 19* addresses the accounting for a wide range of compensation elements—wages, bonuses, postretirement benefits, and compensated absences. The underlying concepts for the accounting for postretirement benefits are similar between GAAP and IFRS—both GAAP and IFRS view pensions and other postretirement benefits as forms of deferred compensation. At present, there are significant differences in the specific accounting provisions as applied to these plans.

RELEVANT FACTS

Following are the key similarities and differences between GAAP and IFRS related to pensions.

Similarities

- IFRS and GAAP separate pension plans into defined contribution plans and defined benefit plans. The accounting for defined contribution plans is similar.
- IFRS and GAAP recognize a pension asset or liability as the funded status of the plan (i.e., defined benefit obligation minus the fair value of plan assets). (Note that defined benefit obligation is referred to as the projected benefit obligation in GAAP.)
- IFRS and GAAP compute unrecognized past service cost (PSC) (referred to as prior service cost in GAAP) in the same manner. However, IFRS recognizes past service cost as a component of pension expense in income immediately. GAAP amortizes PSC over the remaining service lives of employees.

Differences

- IFRS and GAAP include interest expense on the liability in pension expense. Regarding asset returns, IFRS reduces pension expense by the amount of interest revenue (based on the discount rate times the beginning value of pension assets). GAAP includes an asset return component based on the expected return on plan assets.
- Under IFRS, companies recognize both liability and asset gains and losses (referred to as remeasurements) in other comprehensive income. These gains and losses are not "recycled" into income in subsequent periods. GAAP recognizes liability and asset gains and losses in "Accumulated other comprehensive income" and amortizes these amounts to income over remaining service lives, using the "corridor approach."
- The accounting for pensions and other postretirement benefit plans is the same under IFRS. GAAP has separate standards for these types of benefits, and significant differences exist in the accounting.

ABOUT THE NUMBERS

Accounting for Pensions

Net Defined Benefit Obligation (Asset)

As in GAAP, under IFRS the **net defined benefit liability** (asset) is the deficit or surplus related to a defined benefit pension plan. The deficit or surplus is measured as follows.

Defined Benefit Obligation − Fair Value of Plan Assets (if any)

The deficit or surplus is often referred to as the **funded status** of the plan.

If the defined benefit obligation is greater than the plan assets, the pension plan has a deficit. Conversely, if the defined pension obligation is less than the plan assets, the pension plan has a surplus. Illustration IFRS20-1 shows these relationships.

ILLUSTRATION IFRS20-1
Presentation of Funded Status

Deficit		Surplus	
Defined benefit obligation	$1,000,000	Defined benefit obligation	$150,000
Plan assets	900,000	Plan assets	200,000
Net defined benefit obligation	$ 100,000	Net defined benefit asset	$ 50,000

The net defined benefit obligation (asset) is often referred to simply as the pension liability or the pension asset on the statement of financial position.

As indicated, companies should report either a pension asset or pension liability related to a pension plan on the statement of financial position (often referred to as the **net approach**). To illustrate, assume that at year-end Acer Company has a defined pension obligation of $4,000,000 and plan assets of $3,700,000. In this case, Acer reports $300,000 ($4,000,000 − $3,700,000) as a pension liability on its statement of financial position.

Some believe that companies should report separately both the defined benefit obligation and the plan assets on the statement of financial position. This approach (often referred to as the **gross approach**) would report Acer's defined benefit obligation of $4,000,000 and its plan assets of $3,700,000 on the statement of financial position. The IASB disagrees, indicating that offsetting these amounts is consistent with its standard on when assets and liabilities should be netted.[28]

[28]*IAS 32* states that a financial asset and a financial liability should be offset and the net amount reported in the statement of financial position when a company (a) has a legally enforceable right to set off the recognized amounts and (b) intends either to settle on a net basis, or to realize the asset and settle it simultaneously.

Reporting Changes in the Defined Benefit Obligation (Asset)

The IASB requires that all changes in the defined benefit obligation and plan assets in the current period be recognized in comprehensive income. The Board believes that immediate recognition of the effects of these changes in the statement of comprehensive income provides the most understandable and useful information to financial statement users. The IASB requires that companies report changes arising from different elements of pension liabilities and assets in different sections of the statement of comprehensive income, depending on their nature.

In the past, companies often reported only a single pension expense number in the comprehensive income statement. Providing additional segmentation of the **components of pension cost** provides additional transparency about the nature of these costs. The three components are as follows.

- *Service cost.* **Service cost** is either current service cost or past service cost. Current service cost is the increase in the present value of the defined benefit obligation from employee service in the current period. Past service cost is the change in the present value of the defined benefit obligation for employee service for prior periods—generally resulting from a plan amendment (e.g., changes to the plan). This component is reported in the statement of comprehensive income in the operating section of the statement and affects net income.
- *Net interest.* Net interest is computed by multiplying the discount rate by the funded status of the plan (defined benefit obligation minus plan assets). If the plan has a net defined benefit obligation at the end of the period, the company reports interest expense. Conversely, if it has a net defined benefit asset, it reports interest revenue. This approach is justified on the basis of its simplicity and that any financing costs should be based on the funded status of the plan. This amount is often shown below the operating section of the income statement in the financing section and affects net income.
- *Remeasurements.* Remeasurements are gains and losses related to the defined benefit obligation (changes in discount rate or other actuarial assumptions) and gains or losses on the fair value of the plan assets (actual rate of return less interest revenue included in the finance component). This component is reported in other comprehensive income, net of tax. **These remeasurement gains or losses therefore affect comprehensive income but not net income.**

Illustration IFRS20-2 shows the components of changes in the pension liability (asset) and their placement on the statement of comprehensive income.

ILLUSTRATION IFRS20-2
Reporting Changes in the Pension Obligation (Assets)

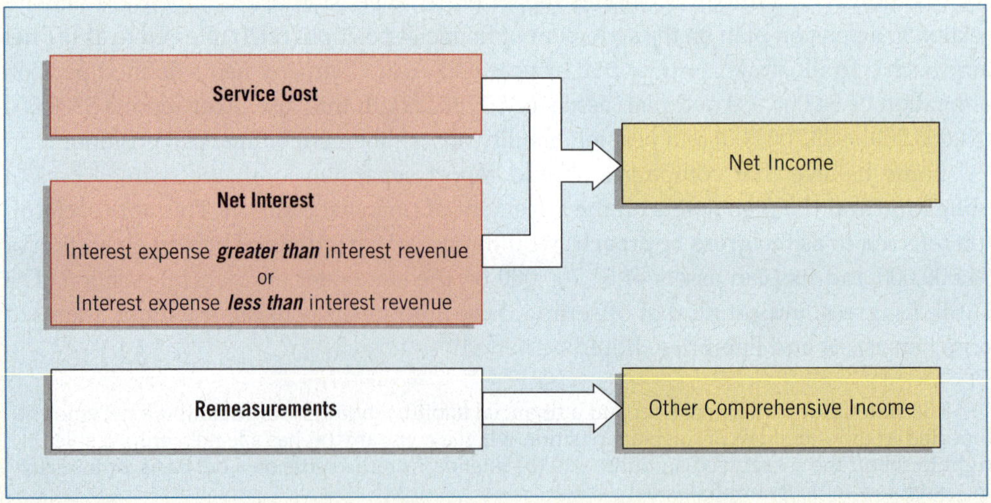

As indicated in Illustration IFRS20-2, service cost and net interest are reported in net income. We discuss determination of each of these components in the following section. Remeasurements, which are reported in other comprehensive income, are discussed in a later section.

Service Cost. To determine current service cost and the related increase in the defined benefit obligation, companies must:

1. Apply an actuarial valuation method.
2. Assign benefits to period of service.
3. Make actuarial assumptions.[29]

In applying an actuarial valuation method, the IASB concluded that **companies must consider future compensation levels in measuring the present obligation and periodic pension expense if the plan benefit formula incorporates them**. In other words, the present obligation resulting from a promise to pay a benefit of 1 percent of an employee's **final pay** differs from the promise to pay 1 percent of **current pay**. To overlook this fact is to ignore an important aspect of pension expense. Thus, the Board adopts the ***projected unit credit method*** **(often referred to as the *benefits/years-of-service method*), which determines pension expense based on future salary levels.**

Some object to this determination, arguing that a company should have more freedom to select an expense recognition pattern. Others believe that incorporating future salary increases into current pension expense is accounting for events that have not yet happened. They argue that if a company terminates the plan today, it pays only liabilities for accumulated benefits. **Nevertheless, the IASB indicates that the defined benefit obligation provides a more realistic measure of the employer's obligation under the plan on a going concern basis and, therefore, companies should use it as the basis for determining service cost.**

The assignment of benefits to periods of service is based on the actuarial valuation method. The actuary then allocates the cost of the pension benefits over the expected service life of the company's employees. In determining the proper service cost for a period, the actuary makes actuarial assumptions related to such factors as mortality; rates of employee turnover, disability, and early retirement; discount rate; benefit levels; and future salary levels. While *IAS 19* does not require use of an actuary, given the complexity of these estimates, just about all companies rely on an actuary to determine service cost and related other defined benefit measures.

Net Interest. In computing net interest, companies assume that the discount rate, the net defined benefit obligation, and the pension asset are determined at the beginning of the year.[30] The **discount rate** is based on the yields of high-quality bonds with terms consistent with the company's pension obligation. Net interest is then computed as indicated in the following equation.

Net Interest = (Defined Benefit Obligation × Discount Rate) − (Plan Assets × Discount Rate)

[29]As indicated earlier, service cost is comprised of current and past service cost. Determination of past service cost is based on the same actuarial valuation model as that used for current service cost. We discuss recognition of past service cost in a later section.

[30]The IASB indicates that if the beginning of the year amount changes materially (due to contributions to or payments out of the plan), an adjustment to the beginning balances should be made. *For homework purposes, unless information indicates that balances have changed materially, use the beginning of the year balances.*

That is, net interest is determined by multiplying the net defined pension obligation (asset) by the discount rate.

Because payment of the pension obligation is deferred, companies record the pension liability on a discounted basis. As a result, the liability accrues interest over the service life of the employee (passage of time), which is essentially interest expense (**interest on the liability**). Similarly, companies earn a return on their plan assets. That is, a company assumes that it earns interest based on multiplying the discount rate by the plan assets. While the IASB recognizes that the actual return on plan assets may differ from the assumed interest revenue computed, it believes that the change in plan assets can be divided into an amount that arises from the passage of time and amounts that arise from other changes. As we discuss in the next section, changes not related to the passage of time are reported in other comprehensive income as remeasurements. Thus, the growth in the plan assets should mirror the growth in the defined benefit obligation. In other words, the assumed interest revenue on the plan assets based on the passage of time offsets the interest expense on the defined benefit obligation.

In summary, pension expense is comprised of two components: (1) service cost and (2) net interest. Companies report each of these components in the statement of comprehensive income. In some cases, companies may choose to report these components in one section of the statement of comprehensive income and report total pension expense. Other companies may choose to report the service cost component in operating income and the net interest in a separate section related to financing.[31]

Plan Assets and Actual Return

Pension **plan assets** are usually investments in shares, bonds, other securities, and real estate that a company holds to earn a reasonable rate of return. Plan assets are reported at fair value. Companies generally hold these assets in a separate legal entity (a pension fund) that exists only to administer the employee benefit plan. These assets held by the pension fund are therefore not available to the company's own creditors (even in bankruptcy). Employer contributions and the actual return on plan assets increase pension plan assets. **Actual return on plan assets** is the increase in the pension fund assets arising from interest, dividends, and realized and unrealized changes in the fair value of the plan. Benefits paid to retired employees decrease plan assets.

To illustrate, assume that Hasbro Company has pension plan assets of $4,200,000 on January 1, 2014. During 2014, Hasbro contributed $300,000 to the plan and paid out retirement benefits of $250,000. Its actual return on plan assets was $210,000 for the year. Hasbro's plan assets at December 31, 2014, are $4,460,000, computed as shown in Illustration IFRS20-3.

ILLUSTRATION IFRS20-3
Determination of Pension Assets

Plan assets, January 1, 2014	$4,200,000
Contributions by Hasbro to plan	300,000
Actual return	210,000
Benefits paid to employees	(250,000)
Plan assets, December 31, 2014	$4,460,000

In some cases, companies compute the actual return by adjusting the change in plan assets for the effect of contributions during the year and benefits paid during the year. The equation in Illustration IFRS20-4, or a variation thereof, can be used to compute the actual return.

[31]The IASB does not provide guidance on which of these two approaches is preferred. *For homework purposes, report pension expense as a single total in income from operations in the statement of comprehensive income.*

$$\text{Actual Return} = \left(\text{Plan Assets Ending Balance} - \text{Plan Assets Beginning Balance}\right) - (\text{Contributions} - \text{Benefits Paid})$$

ILLUSTRATION IFRS20-4
Equation for Computing Actual Return

Stated another way, the actual return on plan assets is the difference between the fair value of the plan assets at the beginning of the period and at the end of the period, adjusted for contributions and benefit payments. Illustration IFRS20-5 uses the equation above to compute actual return, using the information provided in Illustration IFRS20-3.

Plan assets, December 31, 2014		$4,460,000
Plan assets, January 1, 2014		(4,200,000)
Increase in fair value of plan assets		260,000
Deduct: Contributions to plan	$300,000	
Add: Benefit payments to employees	250,000	(50,000)
Actual return		$ 210,000

ILLUSTRATION IFRS20-5
Computation of Actual Return on Plan Assets

In this case, Hasbro has a positive actual return on plan assets. Recently, some pension plans have experienced negative actual returns due to the increased volatility in global securities markets.

Using a Pension Worksheet

We will now illustrate the basic computation of pension expense using the first two components: (1) service cost and (2) net interest. We discuss remeasurements in later sections.

Companies often use a worksheet to record pension-related information. As its name suggests, the worksheet is a working tool. A worksheet is **not** a permanent accounting record: It is neither a journal nor part of the general ledger. The worksheet is merely a device to make it easier to prepare entries and the financial statements.[32] Illustration IFRS20-6 shows the format of the **pension worksheet**.

Pension Worksheet.xls

Home Insert Page Layout Formulas Data Review View

P18 fx

	A	B	C	D	E	F
1						
2		General Journal Entries			Memo Record	
3		Annual		Pension	Defined	
4		Pension		Asset/	Benefit	
5	Items	Expense	Cash	Liability	Obligation	Plan Assets
6						
7						
8						
9						
10						

ILLUSTRATION IFRS20-6
Basic Format of Pension Worksheet

The "General Journal Entries" columns of the worksheet (near the left side) determine the entries to record in the formal general ledger accounts. The "Memo Record" columns

[32]The use of a pension entry worksheet is recommended and illustrated by Paul B. W. Miller, "The New Pension Accounting (Part 2)," *Journal of Accountancy* (February 1987), pp. 86–94.

(on the right side) maintain balances in the defined benefit obligation and the plan assets. The difference between the defined benefit obligation and the fair value of the plan assets is the **pension asset/liability**, which is shown in the statement of financial position. If the defined benefit obligation is greater than the plan assets, a pension liability occurs. If the defined benefit obligation is less than the plan assets, a pension asset occurs.

On the first line of the worksheet, a company enters the beginning balances (if any). It then records subsequent transactions and events related to the pension plan using debits and credits, using both sets of columns as if they were one. For each transaction or event, the debits must equal the credits. **The ending balance in the Pension Asset/Liability column should equal the net balance in the memo record.**

2014 Entries and Worksheet

To illustrate the use of a worksheet and how it helps in accounting for a pension plan, assume that on January 1, 2014, Zarle Company provides the following information related to its pension plan for the year 2014.

Plan assets, January 1, 2014, are $100,000.

Defined benefit obligation, January 1, 2014, is $100,000.

Annual service cost is $9,000.

Discount rate is 10 percent.

Funding contributions are $8,000.

Benefits paid to retirees during the year are $7,000.

Using the data presented above, the worksheet in Illustration IFRS20-7 presents the beginning balances and all of the pension entries recorded by Zarle in 2014. Zarle records the beginning balances for the defined benefit obligation and the pension plan assets on the first line of the worksheet in the memo record. Because the defined benefit obligation and the plan assets are the same at January 1, 2014, the Pension Asset/Liability account has a zero balance at January 1, 2014.

Entry (a) in Illustration IFRS20-7 records the service cost component, which increases pension expense by $9,000 and increases the liability (defined benefit obligation)

ILLUSTRATION IFRS20-7
Pension Worksheet—2014

Pension Worksheet—2014.xls

Items	General Journal Entries			Memo Record	
	Annual Pension Expense	Cash	Pension Asset/ Liability	Defined Benefit Obligation	Plan Assets
Balance, Jan. 1, 2014			—	100,000 Cr.	100,000 Dr.
(a) Service cost	9,000 Dr.			9,000 Cr.	
(b) Interest expense	10,000 Dr.			10,000 Cr.	
(c) Interest revenue	10,000 Cr.				10,000 Dr.
(d) Contributions		8,000 Cr.			8,000 Dr.
(e) Benefits				7,000 Dr.	7,000 Cr.
Journal entry for 2014	9,000 Dr.	8,000 Cr.	1,000 Cr.*		
Balance, Dec. 31, 2014			1,000 Cr.**	112,000 Cr.	111,000 Dr.

*$9,000 – $8,000 = $1,000

**$112,000 – $111,000 = $1.000

by $9,000. Entry (b) accrues the interest expense component, which increases both the liability and the pension expense by $10,000 (the beginning defined benefit obligation multiplied by the discount rate of 10 percent). Entry (c) records the interest revenue component, which increases plan assets and decreases pension expense by $10,000. This is computed by multiplying the beginning plan assets by the discount rate of 10 percent. As a result, net interest expense (income) is zero in 2014. Entry (d) records Zarle's contribution (funding) of assets to the pension fund, thereby decreasing cash by $8,000 and increasing plan assets by $8,000. Entry (e) records the benefit payments made to retirees, which results in equal $7,000 decreases to the plan assets and the defined benefit obligation.

Zarle makes the "formal journal entry" on December 31, which records the pension expense in 2014, as follows.

2014		
Pension Expense	9,000	
Cash		8,000
Pension Asset/Liability		1,000

The credit to Pension Asset/Liability for $1,000 represents the difference between the 2014 pension expense of $9,000 and the amount funded of $8,000. Pension Asset/Liability (credit) is a liability because Zarle underfunds the plan by $1,000. The Pension Asset/Liability account balance of $1,000 also equals the net of the balances in the memo accounts. Illustration IFRS20-8 shows that the defined benefit obligation exceeds the plan assets by $1,000, which reconciles to the pension liability reported in the statement of financial position.

Defined benefit obligation (Credit)	$(112,000)
Plan assets at fair value (Debit)	111,000
Pension asset/liability (Credit)	$ (1,000)

ILLUSTRATION IFRS20-8
Pension Reconciliation Schedule—December 31, 2014

If the net of the memo record balances is a credit, the reconciling amount in the Pension Asset/Liability column will be a credit equal in amount. If the net of the memo record balances is a debit, the Pension Asset/Liability amount will be a debit equal in amount. The worksheet is designed to produce this reconciling feature, which is useful later in the preparation of the financial statements and required note disclosure related to pensions.

In this illustration (for 2014), the debit to Pension Expense exceeds the credit to Cash, resulting in a credit to Pension Asset/Liability—the recognition of a liability. If the credit to Cash exceeded the debit to Pension Expense, Zarle would debit Pension Asset/Liability—the recognition of an asset.[33]

Past Service Cost

Past service cost is the change in the present value of the defined benefit obligation resulting from a plan amendment or a curtailment.[34] For example, a plan amendment arises when a company decides to provide additional benefits to existing employees

[33]The IASB in *IAS 19* limits the amount of a pension asset that is recognized, based on a recoverability test. This test, which has been further clarified in *IFRIC 14*, limits the amount of the pension asset to the sum of unrecognized actuarial gains and losses (discussed later) and amounts that will be received by the company in the form of refunds or reduction of future contributions. *For purposes of homework, assume that a pension asset, if present, meets the criteria for full recognition.*

[34]The IASB also indicates that gains and losses on non-routine settlements are considered past service costs. A **settlement** is a payment of benefits that is not set out in the terms of the plan.

for past service. Conversely, the company may decide that it is necessary to reduce its benefit package retroactively for existing employees, thereby reducing their pension benefit. A **curtailment** occurs when the company has a significant reduction in the number of employees covered by the plan. Because a curtailment has the same effect as a reduction in benefits due to an amendment to the plan, these situations are accounted for in the same way. Illustration IFRS20-9 summarizes the nature of past service costs.

ILLUSTRATION IFRS20-9
Types of Past Service Costs

Past Service Costs (Expense in Current Period)	
Plan Amendments	Curtailments
• Introduction of a plan. • Withdrawal of a plan. • Changes to a plan.	• Significant reduction in the number of employees covered by the plan.

The accounting for past service cost is straightforward—expense past service cost in the period of the amendment or curtailment. As a result, a substantial increase (decrease) in pension expense and the defined benefit obligation often results when a plan amendment or curtailment occurs. Because current and past service costs relate directly to employment, they are reported in the operating section of the statement of comprehensive income.

Some disagree with the IASB position of expensing these costs in the year a plan is amended or curtailed. They argue that a company would not provide these additional benefits for past years of service unless it expects to receive benefits in the future. According to this reasoning, a company should not recognize the full past service cost in the year of the amendment. Instead, the past service cost should be spread out over the remaining service life of employees who are expected to benefit from the changes in the plan. Others believe that if they are truly past service costs, they should be treated retroactively as an adjustment made to prior periods.

However, the IASB decided that any changes in the defined benefit obligation or plan assets should be recognized in the current period. To do otherwise is not informative and leads to delayed recognition of costs or reduced benefits which are neither assets nor liabilities.

It is also possible to decrease past service costs by decreasing the defined benefit obligation (referred to as negative past service cost). Negative past service cost arises when an entity changes the benefits attributable to past service cost so that the present value of the defined benefit obligation decreases. In that case, pension expense is decreased. Both positive (increased pension expense) and negative (decreased pension expense) past service cost adjustments are handled in the same manner; that is, adjust pension expense immediately.

2015 Entries and Worksheet

Continuing the Zarle Company illustration into 2015, we note that the company amends the pension plan on January 1, 2015, to grant employees past service benefits with a present value of $81,600. The following additional facts apply to the pension plan for the year 2015.

Annual service cost is $9,500.
Discount rate is 10 percent.
Annual funding contributions are $20,000.
Benefits paid to retirees during the year are $8,000.

Illustration IFRS20-10 presents a worksheet of all the pension entries and information recorded by Zarle in 2015.

ILLUSTRATION IFRS20-10
Pension Worksheet—2015

Pension Worksheet—2015.xls

		General Journal Entries			Memo Record	
	Items	Annual Pension Expense	Cash	Pension Asset/ Liability	Defined Benefit Obligation	Plan Assets
6	Balance, Dec. 31, 2014			1,000 Cr.	112,000 Cr.	111,000 Dr.
7	(f) Additional PSC, 1/1/2015	81,600 Dr.			81,600 Cr.	
8	Balance, Jan. 1, 2015				193,600 Cr.	
9	(g) Service cost	9,500 Dr.			9,500 Cr.	
10	(h) Interest expense	19,360 Dr.			19,360 Cr.	
11	(i) Interest revenue	11,100 Cr.				11,100 Dr.
12	(j) Contributions		20,000 Cr.			20,000 Dr.
13	(k) Benefits				8,000 Dr.	8,000 Cr.
14	Journal entry for 2015	99,360 Dr.	20,000 Cr.	79,360 Cr.		
15	Balance, Dec. 31, 2015			80,360 Cr.	214,460 Cr.	134,100 Dr.

The first line of the worksheet shows the beginning balances of the Pension Asset/Liability account and the memo accounts. Entry (f) records Zarle's granting of past service cost, by adding $81,600 to the defined benefit obligation and to Pension Expense. Entry (g) records the current service cost; entry (h) records interest expense for the period. Because the past service cost occurred at the beginning of the year, interest is computed on the January 1, 2015, balance of the defined benefit obligation, adjusted for the past service cost. Interest expense is therefore $19,360 ($193,600 × 10%). Entry (i) records interest revenue for the period of $11,100 ($111,000 × 10%). Entries (j) and (k) are similar to the corresponding entries in 2014.

Zarle makes the following journal entry on December 31 to formally record the 2015 pension expense—the sum of the annual pension expense column.

2015		
Pension Expense	99,360	
Cash		20,000
Pension Asset/Liability		79,360

Because the expense exceeds the funding, Zarle credits the Pension Asset/Liability account for the $79,360 difference. That account is a liability. In 2015, as in 2014, the balance of the Pension Asset/Liability account ($80,360) is equal to the net of the balances in the memo accounts, as shown in Illustration IFRS20-11.

ILLUSTRATION IFRS20-11
Pension Reconciliation Schedule—December 31, 2015

Defined benefit obligation (Credit)	$(214,460)
Plan assets at fair value (Debit)	134,100
Pension asset/liability (Credit)	$ (80,360)

The **reconciliation** is the formula that makes the worksheet work. It relates the components of pension accounting, recorded and unrecorded, to one another.

Remeasurements

Of great concern to companies that have pension plans are the uncontrollable and unexpected swings that can result from (1) sudden and large changes in the fair value of plan assets and (2) changes in actuarial assumptions that affect the amount of the defined benefit obligation. How should these changes (referred to as **remeasurements**) affect the financial statements, most notably pension expense? The IASB believes that the most informative way is to recognize the remeasurement in other comprehensive income. The rationale for this reporting is that the predictive nature of remeasurements is much different than the other two components of pension benefit cost—service cost and net interest.

Remeasurements are generally of two types:

1. Gains and losses on plan assets.
2. Gains and losses on the defined benefit obligation.

Asset Gains and Losses. The gains and losses on plan assets (referred to as **asset gains and losses**) is the difference between the actual return and the interest revenue computed in determining net interest. Asset gains occur when actual returns exceed the interest revenue. Asset losses occur when the actual returns are less than interest revenue. To illustrate, assume that Shopbob Company has plan assets at January 1, 2014, of $100,000. The discount rate for the year is 6 percent, and the actual return on the plan assets for 2014 is $8,000. In 2014, Shopbob should record an asset gain of $2,000, computed as follows.

ILLUSTRATION IFRS20-12
Computation of Asset Gain

Actual return	$8,000
Less: Interest revenue ($100,000 × 6%)	6,000
Asset gain	$2,000

Shopbob therefore debits plan assets for the asset gain of $2,000 and credits Other Comprehensive Income (G/L) for the same amount. If interest revenue exceeds the actual return, Shopbob debits Other Comprehensive Income (G/L) for the asset loss and credits plan assets.

Liability Gains and Losses. In estimating the defined benefit obligation (the liability), actuaries make assumptions about such items as mortality rate, retirement rate, turnover rate, disability rate, and salary amounts. Any change in these actuarial assumptions affects the amount of the defined benefit obligation. Seldom does actual experience coincide exactly with actuarial predictions. These gains or losses from changes in the defined benefit obligation are called **liability gains and losses**.

Companies report liability gains (resulting from unexpected decreases in the liability balance) and liability losses (resulting from unexpected increases in the liability balance) in Other Comprehensive Income (G/L). Companies combine the liability gains and losses in the same Other Comprehensive Income (G/L) account used for asset gains and losses. They accumulate the asset and liability gains and losses from year to year in Accumulated Other Comprehensive Income.[35] This amount is reported on the statement of financial position in the equity section.

[35]The IASB is silent as to whether the account "Accumulated Other Comprehensive Income" should be used instead of another equity account, like Retained Earnings. *For homework purposes, use an Accumulated Other Comprehensive Income account.* The IASB also permits the transfer of the balance in the Accumulated Other Comprehensive Income account to other equity accounts at a later date.

2016 Entries and Worksheet

Continuing the Zarle Company illustration, the following facts apply to the pension plan for 2016.

Annual service cost is $13,000.

Discount rate is 10 percent.

Actual return on plan assets is $12,000.

Annual funding contributions are $24,000.

Benefits paid to retirees during the year are $10,500.

Changes in actuarial assumptions establish the end-of-year defined benefit obligation at $265,000.

The worksheet in Illustration IFRS20-13 presents all of Zarle's 2016 pension entries and related information. The first line of the worksheet records the beginning balances that relate to the pension plan. In this case, Zarle's beginning balances are the ending balances from its 2015 pension worksheet in Illustration IFRS20-10.

Pension Worksheet—2016.xls

	A	B	C	D	E	F	G
1							
2		General Journal Entries				Memo Record	
3		Annual			Pension	Defined	
4		Pension		OCI—	Asset/	Benefit	
5	Items	Expense	Cash	Gain/Loss	Liability	Obligation	Plan Assets
6	Balance, Jan. 1, 2016				80,360 Cr.	214,460 Cr.	134,100 Dr.
7	(l) Service cost	13,000 Dr.				13,000 Cr.	
8	(m) Interest expense	21,446 Dr.				21,446 Cr.	
9	(n) Interest revenue	13,410 Cr.					13,410 Dr.
10	(o) Contributions		24,000 Cr.				24,000 Dr.
11	(p) Benefits					10,500 Dr.	10,500 Cr.
12	(q) Asset loss			1,410 Dr.			1,410 Cr.
13	(r) Liability loss			26,594 Dr.		26,594 Cr.	
14	Journal entry for 2016	21,036 Dr.	24,000 Cr.	28,004 Dr.	25,040 Cr.		
15							
16	Accumulated OCI, Dec. 31, 2015			0			
17	Balance, Dec. 31, 2016			28,004 Dr.	105,400 Cr.	265,000 Cr.	159,600 Dr.
18							

ILLUSTRATION IFRS20-13
Pension Worksheet—2016

Entries (l), (m), (n), (o), and (p) are similar to the corresponding entries in 2014 or 2015. Entries (m) and (n) are related. Entry (m) records the interest expense of $21,446 ($214,460 × 10%). Entry (n) records interest revenue of $13,410 ($134,100 × 10%). Therefore, net interest expense is $8,036 ($21,446 − $13,410). Entries (o) and (p) are recorded similarly in 2016 as those in 2014 and 2015.

Entries (q) and (r) need additional explanation. As indicated, the actual return on plan assets for 2016 was $12,000. However, as indicated in entry (n), pension expense was decreased $13,410 as a result of multiplying the beginning plan assets by the discount rate to arrive at an assumed interest revenue of $13,410. As a result, Zarle has an asset loss of $1,410 ($13,410 − $12,000) because the assumed interest revenue is greater than the actual return. This asset loss is debited to Other Comprehensive Income (G/L) and credited to plan assets. Pension plan assets are then properly stated at their fair value.

Entry (r) records the change in the defined benefit obligation resulting from the changes in the actuarial assumptions related to this obligation. As indicated in the facts on page 1261, the actuary has determined that the ending balance in the defined benefit obligation should be $265,000 at December 31, 2016. However, the balance at December 31, 2016, before any adjustment for actuarial gains and losses related to the defined benefit obligation is $238,406, as shown in Illustration IFRS20-14.

ILLUSTRATION IFRS20-14
Defined Benefit Obligation Balance (Unadjusted)

December 31, 2015, DBO balance	$214,460
Service cost [entry (l)]	13,000
Interest expense [entry (m)]	21,446
Benefits paid [entry (p)]	(10,500)
December 31, 2016, DBO balance (before liability increases)	$238,406

The difference between the ending balance of $265,000 as determined by the actuary and the present balance of $238,406 is $26,594 (a liability loss on the defined benefit liability). This liability loss is debited to Other Comprehensive Income (G/L) and credited to the defined benefit obligation. After this worksheet adjustment, the defined benefit obligation is stated at its actuarial value of $265,000. The journal entry to record the information related to the pension plan at December 31, 2016, based on the pension worksheet in Illustration IFRS20-13, is as follows.

Pension Expense	21,036	
Other Comprehensive Income (G/L)	28,004	
Cash		24,000
Pension Asset/Liability		25,040

As the 2016 worksheet indicates, the $105,400 balance in the Pension Asset/Liability account at December 31, 2016, is equal to the net of the balances in the memo accounts. Illustration IFRS20-15 shows this computation.

ILLUSTRATION IFRS20-15
Pension Reconciliation Schedule—December 31, 2016

Defined benefit obligation (Credit)	$(265,000)
Plan assets at fair value (Debit)	159,600
Pension asset/liability	$(105,400)

Zarle carries the 2016 ending balances for Pension Asset/Liability and Accumulated Other Comprehensive Income forward as the beginning balances for pension plan accounting in 2017. These balances will be adjusted by changes in the defined benefit obligation and plan assets as shown in the prior examples. For example, assume that Zarle's pension plan had the following activity in 2017:

Service cost	$10,072	Contributions	$32,000
Pension expense	17,450	Benefits	11,000
Asset gain	13,150	Decrease in Pension Asset/Liability	27,700
Discount rate	7%		

The ending balances for the defined benefit obligation and plan assets are $282,622 and $204,922, respectively. These elements are summarized in the partial 2017 pension worksheet shown in Illustration IFRS20-16.

Partial Pension Worksheet—2017.xls

	A	B	C	D	E	F	G
1							
2		General Journal Entries				Memo Record	
3–5	Items	Annual Pension Expense	Cash	OCI—Gain/Loss	Pension Asset/Liability	Defined Benefit Obligation	Plan Assets
6	Balance, Jan. 1, 2017			28,004 Dr.	105,400 Cr.	265,000 Cr.	159,600 Dr.
7							
8							
9	Journal entry for 2017	17,450 Dr.	32,000 Cr.	13,150 Cr.	27,700 Dr.		
10							
11	Accumulated OCI, Jan. 1, 2017			28,004 Dr.			
12	Balance, Dec. 31, 2017			14,854 Dr.	77,700 Cr.	282,622 Cr.	204,922 Dr.
13							

ILLUSTRATION IFRS20-16
Partial Pension Worksheet—2017

Focusing on the "Journal Entry" row, in 2017 Zarle records pension expense of $17,450 and a decrease in Pension Asset/Liability of $27,700. The reduction in Pension Asset/Liability is due in part to the asset gain of $13,150 recorded in 2017. As a result, Zarle's 2017 ending balances (which become the 2018 beginning balances) are $77,700 for Pension Asset/Liability and Accumulated Other Comprehensive Income $14,854 (beginning Accumulated OCI of $28,004 − gain of $13,150).

ON THE HORIZON

The IASB and the FASB have been working collaboratively on a postretirement benefit project. The recent amendments issued by the IASB moves IFRS closer to GAAP with respect to recognition of the funded status on the statement of financial position. However, as illustrated in the *About the Numbers* section above, significant differences remain in the components of pension expense. The FASB is expected to begin work on a project that will reexamine expense measurement of postretirement benefit plans. The FASB likely will consider the recent IASB amendments in this area, which could lead to a converged standard.

IFRS SELF-TEST QUESTIONS

1. At the end of the current period, Oxford Ltd. has a defined benefit obligation of $195,000 and pension plan assets with a fair value of $110,000. The amount of the vested benefits for the plan is $105,000. What amount related to its pension plan will be reported on the company's statement of financial position?
(a) $5,000.
(b) $90,000.
(c) $85,000.
(d) $20,000.

2. At the end of the current year, Kennedy Co. has a defined benefit obligation of $335,000 and pension plan assets with a fair value of $245,000. The amount of the vested benefits for the plan is $225,000. Kennedy has an actuarial gain of $8,300. What account and amount(s) related to its pension plan will be reported on the company's statement of financial position?
(a) Pension Liability and $74,300.
(b) Pension Liability and $90,000.
(c) Pension Asset and $233,300.
(d) Pension Asset and $110,000.

3. For 2014, Carson Majors Inc. had pension expense of $77 million and contributed $55 million to the pension fund. Which of the following is the journal entry that Carson Majors would make to record pension expense and funding?

(a) Pension Expense	77,000,000	
Pension Asset/Liability		22,000,000
Cash		55,000,000
(b) Pension Expense	77,000,000	
Pension Asset/Liability	22,000,000	
Cash		99,000,000
(c) Pension Expense	55,000,000	
Pension Asset/Liability	22,000,000	
Cash		77,000,000
(d) Pension Expense	22,000,000	
Pension Asset/Liability	55,000,000	
Cash		77,000,000

4. At January 1, 2014, Wembley Company had plan assets of $250,000 and a defined benefit obligation of the same amount. During 2014, service cost was $27,500, the discount rate was 10%, actual return on plan assets was $25,000, contributions were $20,000, and benefits paid were $17,500. Based on this information, what would be the defined benefit obligation for Wembley Company at December 31, 2014?
   (a) $277,500. (c) $27,500.
   (b) $285,000. (d) $302,500.

5. Towson Company has experienced tough competition for its talented workforce, leading it to enhance the pension benefits provided to employees. As a result, Towson amended its pension plan on January 1, 2014, and granted past service costs of $250,000. Current service cost for 2014 is $52,000. Interest expense is $18,000, and interest revenue is $5,000. Actual return on assets in 2014 is $3,000. What is Towson's pension expense for 2014?
   (a) $65,000. (c) $317,000.
   (b) $302,000. (d) $315,000.

IFRS CONCEPTS AND APPLICATION

IFRS20-1 What is net interest? Identify the elements of net interest and explain how they are computed.

IFRS20-2 What is service cost, and what is the basis of its measurement?

IFRS20-3 What is meant by "past service cost"? When is past service cost recognized as pension expense?

IFRS20-4 Bill Haley is learning about pension accounting. He is convinced that in years when companies record liability gains and losses, total comprehensive income will not be affected. Is Bill correct? Explain.

IFRS20-5 At the end of the current year, Joshua Co. has a defined benefit obligation of $335,000 and pension plan assets with a fair value of $345,000. The amount of the vested benefits for the plan is $225,000. Joshua has a liability gain of $8,300 (beginning accumulated OCI is zero). What amount and account(s) related to its pension plan will be reported on the company's statement of financial position?

IFRS20-6 Villa Company has experienced tough competition, leading it to seek concessions from its employees in the company's pension plan. In exchange for promises to avoid layoffs and wage cuts, the employees agreed to receive lower pension benefits in the future. As a result, Villa amended its pension plan on January 1, 2014, and recorded negative past service cost of $125,000. Current service cost for 2014 is $26,000. Interest expense is $9,000, and interest revenue is $2,500. Actual return on assets in 2012 is $1,500. Compute Villa's pension expense in 2014.

IFRS20-7 Tevez Company experienced an actuarial loss of $750 in its defined benefit plan in 2014. For 2014, Tevez's revenues are $125,000, and expenses (excluding pension expense of $14,000, which does not include the actuarial loss) are $85,000. Prepare Tevez's statement of comprehensive income for 2014.

IFRS20-8 The following defined pension data of Doreen Corp. apply to the year 2014.

Defined benefit obligation, 1/1/14 (before amendment)	$560,000
Plan assets, 1/1/14	546,200
Pension asset/liability	13,800 Cr.
On January 1, 2014, Doreen Corp., through plan amendment, grants past service benefits having a present value of	120,000
Discount rate	9%
Service cost	58,000
Contributions (funding)	65,000
Actual return on plan assets	49,158
Benefits paid to retirees	40,000

Instructions

For 2014, prepare a pension worksheet for Doreen Corp. that shows the journal entry for pension expense and the year-end balances in the related pension accounts.

IFRS20-9 Buhl Corp. sponsors a defined benefit pension plan for its employees. On January 1, 2014, the following balances relate to this plan.

Plan assets	$480,000
Defined benefit obligation	600,000
Pension asset/liability	120,000

As a result of the operation of the plan during 2014, the following additional data are provided by the actuary.

Service cost for 2014	$90,000
Discount rate, 6%	
Actual return on plan assets in 2014	55,000
Unexpected loss from change in defined benefit obligation, due to change in actuarial predictions	76,000
Contributions in 2014	99,000
Benefits paid retirees in 2014	85,000

Instructions

(a) Using the data above, compute pension expense for Buhl Corp. for the year 2014 by preparing a pension worksheet.

(b) Prepare the journal entry for pension expense for 2014.

IFRS20-10 Linda Berstler Company sponsors a defined benefit pension plan. The corporation's actuary provides the following information about the plan.

	January 1, 2014	December 31, 2014
Defined benefit obligation	$2,500	$3,300
Plan assets (fair value)	1,700	2,620
Discount rate		10%
Pension asset/liability	800	?
Service cost for the year 2014		400
Contributions (funding in 2014)		700
Benefits paid in 2014		200

Instructions

(a) Compute the actual return on the plan assets in 2014.

(b) Compute the amount of other comprehensive income (G/L) as of December 31, 2014. (Assume the January 1, 2014, balance was zero.)

Professional Research

IFRS20-11 Jack Kelly Company has grown rapidly since its founding in 2004. To instill loyalty in its employees, Kelly is contemplating establishment of a defined benefit plan. Kelly knows that lenders and potential investors will pay close attention to the impact of the pension plan on the company's financial statements, particularly any gains or losses that develop in the plan. Kelly has asked you to conduct some research on the accounting for gains and losses in a defined benefit plan.

Instructions

Access the IFRS authoritative literature at the IASB website (*http://eifrs.iasb.org/*). (Click on the IFRS tab and then register for free eIFRS access if necessary.) When you have accessed the documents, you can use the search tool in your Internet browser to respond to the following questions. (Provide paragraph citations.)

(a) Briefly describe how pension gains and losses are accounted for.
(b) Explain the rationale behind the accounting method described in part (a).
(c) What is the related pension asset or liability that may show up on the statement of financial position? When will each of these situations occur?

International Financial Reporting Problem

Marks and Spencer plc

IFRS20-12 The financial statements of **Marks and Spencer plc (M&S)** are available at the book's companion website or can be accessed at *http://annualreport.marksandspencer.com/_assets/downloads/Marks-and-Spencer-Annual-report-and-financial-statements-2012.pdf.*

Instructions

Refer to M&S's financial statements and the accompanying notes to answer the following questions.

(a) What kind of pension plan does M&S provide its employees?
(b) What was M&S's pension expense for 2012 and 2011?
(c) What is the impact of M&S's pension plans for 2012 on its financial statements?
(d) What information does M&S provide on the target allocation of its pension assets? How do the allocations relate to the expected returns on these assets?

ANSWERS TO IFRS SELF-TEST QUESTIONS

1. c **2.** b **3.** a **4.** b **5.** d

Remember to check the book's companion website to find additional resources for this chapter.

CHAPTER

21 Accounting for Leases

LEARNING OBJECTIVES

After studying this chapter, you should be able to:

1 Explain the nature, economic substance, and advantages of lease transactions.

2 Describe the accounting criteria and procedures for capitalizing leases by the lessee.

3 Contrast the operating and capitalization methods of recording leases.

4 Explain the advantages and economics of leasing to lessors and identify the classifications of leases for the lessor.

5 Describe the lessor's accounting for direct-financing leases.

6 Identify special features of lease arrangements that cause unique accounting problems.

7 Describe the effect of residual values, guaranteed and unguaranteed, on lease accounting.

8 Describe the lessor's accounting for sales-type leases.

9 List the disclosure requirements for leases.

More Companies Ask, "Why Buy?"

Leasing has grown tremendously in popularity. Today, it is the fastest growing form of capital investment. Instead of borrowing money to buy an airplane, computer, nuclear core, or satellite, a company makes periodic payments to lease these assets. Even gambling casinos lease their slot machines. Of the 500 companies surveyed by the AICPA in 2011, more than half disclosed lease data.*

A classic example is the airline industry. Many travelers on airlines such as **United**, **Delta**, and **Southwest** believe these airlines own the planes on which they are flying. Often, this is not the case. Airlines lease many of their airplanes due to the favorable accounting treatment they receive if they lease rather than purchase. Presented below are the lease percentages for the major U.S. airlines.

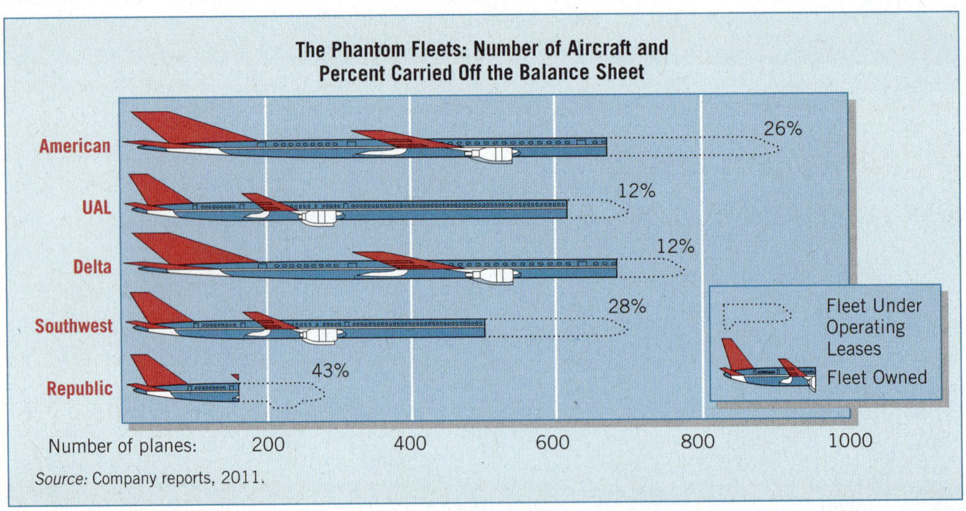

What about other companies? They are also exploiting the existing lease accounting rules to keep assets and liabilities off the books. For example, **Krispy Kreme**, a chain of 217 doughnut shops, had been showing good growth and profitability using a relatively small bit of capital. That's an impressive feat if you care about return on capital. But there's a hole in this doughnut. The company explained that it was building a $30 million new mixing plant and warehouse in Effingham, Illinois.

*AICPA, *Accounting Trends and Techniques—2011*. 277 out of 500 surveyed companies reported leased assets. Companies that lease tend to be smaller, are high growth, and are in technology-oriented industries (see *www.techlease.com*).

Yet the financial statements failed to disclose the investments and obligations associated with that $30 million. By financing through a synthetic lease, Krispy Kreme kept the investment and obligation off the books.

In a synthetic lease, a financial institution like **Bank of America** sets up a special-purpose entity (SPE) that borrows money to build the plant and then leases it to Krispy Kreme. For accounting purposes, Krispy Kreme reports only rent expense. For tax purposes, however, Krispy Kreme can be considered the owner of the asset and gets depreciation tax deductions. This is a pretty good deal for Krispy Kreme. But for investors? Not so good. This is because the Krispy Kreme financial statements failed to disclose the investments and obligations associated with that $30 million.

Another example is struggling drug store chain **Rite Aid**. Its balance sheet is in shambles. While its current assets exceed current liabilities, that's the end of any good news in the balance sheet. Total assets are $7,364 million, while total liabilities are $9,951 million, thereby yielding a shareholders' deficit of $(2,587) million. Things are even worse once you consider Rite Aid's large off-balance-sheet lease obligations. Using the data in note 10 of the financial statements, analysts estimate the company's lease liabilities to be $5,939 million. This adjustment increases total liabilities to $15,890 million, causing the stockholders' deficit to worsen to $(8,526) million.

As you will learn in this chapter, due to lease accounting rules, users of financial statements must make an educated guess on the real-but-hidden leverage of leasing only by using the information disclosed in the notes and by applying a rule-of-thumb multiple. As the chairperson for the IASB noted, "It seems odd to expect an analyst to guess the liabilities associated with leases when management already has this information at its fingertips." This concern explains why the FASB and IASB are working on a new standard on leasing, so that assets and liabilities avoid on-balance-sheet treatment simply by calling a loan a "lease."

Sources: Adapted from Seth Lubore and Elizabeth MacDonald, "Debt? Who, Me?" *Forbes* (February 18, 2002), p. 56; A. Catanach and E. Ketz, "Still Searching for the 'Rite' Stuff," *Grumpy Old Accountants* (April 30, 2012), at *http://blogs.smeal.psu.edu/grumpyoldaccountants/archives/643*; and Hans Hoogervorst, "Harmonisation and Global Economic Consequences," Public lecture at the London School of Economics (November 6, 2012).

CONCEPTUAL FOCUS

> See the **Underlying Concepts** on pages 1274 and 1307.

> Read the **Evolving Issues** on pages 1283 and 1303 for discussions of off-balance-sheet reporting of leases.

INTERNATIONAL FOCUS

> See the **International Perspectives** on pages 1272, 1276, 1285, and 1303.

> Read the **IFRS Insights** on pages 1331–1341 for a discussion of:

—Lessee accounting
—Lessor accounting

PREVIEW OF CHAPTER 21

Our opening story indicates the increased significance and prevalence of lease arrangements. As a result, the need for uniform accounting and informative reporting of these transactions has intensified. In this chapter, we look at the accounting issues related to leasing. The content and organization of this chapter are as follows.

Accounting for Leases

Leasing Environment	Accounting by Lessee	Accounting by Lessor	Special Lease Accounting Problems
• Who are players? • Advantages of leasing • Conceptual nature of a lease	• Capitalization criteria • Accounting differences • Capital lease method • Operating method • Comparison	• Economics of leasing • Classification • Direct-financing method • Operating method	• Residual values • Sales-type leases • Bargain-purchase option • Initial direct costs • Current versus noncurrent • Disclosure • Unresolved problems

THE LEASING ENVIRONMENT

LEARNING OBJECTIVE 1
Explain the nature, economic substance, and advantages of lease transactions.

Aristotle once said, "Wealth does not lie in ownership but in the use of things"! Clearly, many U.S. companies have decided that Aristotle is right, as they have become heavily involved in leasing assets rather than owning them. For example, according to the Equipment Leasing Association (ELA), the global equipment-leasing market is a $600–$700 billion business, with the United States accounting for about one-third of the global market. The ELA estimates that of the $1.3 trillion in total fixed investment expected from domestic businesses in 2012, $654 billion (50 percent) will be financed through leasing. Remember that these statistics are just for equipment leasing. Add in real estate leasing, which is probably larger, and we are talking about a very large and growing business, one that is at least in part driven by the accounting.

What types of assets are being leased? As the opening story indicated, any type of equipment can be leased, such as railcars, helicopters, bulldozers, barges, CT scanners, computers, and so on.

Illustration 21-1 summarizes, in their own words, what several major companies are leasing.

ILLUSTRATION 21-1
What Do Companies Lease?

Company (Ticker)	Description
Gap (GPS)	"We lease most of our store premises and some of our headquarters facilities and distribution centers."
ExxonMobil Corp. (XOM)	"Minimum commitments for operating leases, shown on an undiscounted basis, cover drilling equipment, tankers, service stations, and other properties."
JPMorgan Chase (JPM)	"JPMorgan Chase and its subsidiaries were obligated under a number of noncancelable operating leases for premises and equipment used primarily for banking purposes."
Maytag Corp. (MYG)	"The Company leases real estate, machinery, equipment, and automobiles under operating leases, some of which have renewal options."
McDonald's Corp. (MCD)	"The Company was the lessee at 15,235 restaurant locations through ground leases (the Company leases the land and the Company or franchisee owns the building) and through improved leases (the Company leases land and buildings)."
Starbucks Corp. (SBUX)	"Starbucks leases retail stores, roasting and distribution facilities, and office space under operating leases."
TXU Corp. (TXU)	"TXU Energy Holdings and TXU Electric Delivery have entered into operating leases covering various facilities and properties including generation plant facilities, combustion turbines, transportation equipment, mining equipment, data processing equipment, and office space."
Viacom Inc. (VIA.B)	"The Company has long-term non-cancelable operating lease commitments for office space and equipment, transponders, studio facilities, and vehicles. The Company also enters into capital leases for satellite transponders."
	Source: Company 10-K filings.

The largest group of leased equipment involves information technology equipment, followed by assets in the transportation area (trucks, aircraft, rail), and then construction and agriculture.

Who Are the Players?

A **lease** is a contractual agreement between a lessor and a lessee. This arrangement gives the **lessee** the right to use specific property, owned by the **lessor**, for a specified period of time. In return for the use of the property, the lessee makes rental payments over the lease term to the lessor.

Who are the lessors that own this property? They generally fall into one of three categories:

1. Banks.
2. Captive leasing companies.
3. Independents.

Banks

Banks are the largest players in the leasing business. They have low-cost funds, which give them the advantage of being able to purchase assets at less cost than their competitors. Banks also have been more aggressive in the leasing markets. Deciding that there is money to be made in leasing, banks have expanded their product lines in this area. Finally, leasing transactions are now more standardized, which gives banks an advantage because they do not have to be as innovative in structuring lease arrangements. Thus, banks like **Wells Fargo**, **Chase**, **Citigroup**, and **PNC** have substantial leasing subsidiaries.

Captive Leasing Companies

Captive leasing companies are subsidiaries whose primary business is to perform leasing operations for the parent company. Companies like **Caterpillar Financial Services Corp.** (for Caterpillar), **Ford Motor Credit** (for Ford), and **IBM Global Financing** (for IBM) facilitate the sale of products to consumers. For example, suppose that **Sterling Construction Co.** wants to acquire a number of earthmovers from Caterpillar. In this case, Caterpillar Financial Services Corp. will offer to structure the transaction as a lease rather than as a purchase. Thus, Caterpillar Financial provides the financing rather than an outside financial institution.

Captive leasing companies have the point-of-sale advantage in finding leasing customers. That is, as soon as Caterpillar receives a possible order, its leasing subsidiary can quickly develop a lease-financing arrangement. Furthermore, the captive lessor has product knowledge that gives it an advantage when financing the parent's product.

The current trend is for captives to focus primarily on their companies' products rather than do general lease financing. For example, **Boeing Capital** and **UPS Capital** are two captives that have left the general finance business to focus exclusively on their parent companies' products.

Independents

Independents are the final category of lessors. Independents have not done well over the last few years. Their market share has dropped fairly dramatically as banks and captive leasing companies have become more aggressive in the lease-financing area. Independents do not have point-of-sale access, nor do they have a low cost of funds advantage. What they *are* often good at is developing innovative contracts for lessees. In addition, they are starting to act as captive finance companies for some companies that do not have a leasing subsidiary. For example, **International Lease Finance Corp.** is one of the world's largest independent lessors.

According to recent data at *www.ficinc.com* on new business volume by lessor type, banks hold about 49 percent of the market, followed by captives at 32 percent. Independents had the remaining 19 percent of new business. Data on changes in market share show that both captives and independents have increased business at the expense of the banks. That is, from 2009 to 2010, captives' and independents' market shares had grown by 11.3 percent and 5.3 percent, respectively, while the banks' market share declined by 0.9 percent.

Advantages of Leasing

The growth in leasing indicates that it often has some genuine advantages over owning property, such as:

1. ***100% financing at fixed rates.*** Leases are often signed without requiring any money down from the lessee. This helps the lessee conserve scarce cash—an especially desirable feature for new and developing companies. In addition, lease payments often remain fixed, which protects the lessee against inflation and increases in the cost of money. The following comment explains why companies choose a lease instead of a conventional loan: "Our local bank finally came up to 80 percent of the purchase price but wouldn't go any higher, and they wanted a floating interest rate. We just couldn't afford the down payment, and we needed to lock in a final payment rate we knew we could live with."
2. ***Protection against obsolescence.*** Leasing equipment reduces risk of obsolescence to the lessee and in many cases passes the risk of residual value to the lessor. For example, **Merck** (a pharmaceutical maker) leases computers. Under the lease agreement, Merck may turn in an old computer for a new model at any time, canceling the old lease and writing a new one. The lessor adds the cost of the new lease to the balance due on the old lease, less the old computer's trade-in value. As one treasurer remarked, "Our instinct is to purchase." But if a new computer is likely to come along in a short time, "then leasing is just a heck of a lot more convenient than purchasing." Naturally, the lessor also protects itself by requiring the lessee to pay higher rental payments or provide additional payments if the lessee does not maintain the asset.
3. ***Flexibility.*** Lease agreements may contain less restrictive provisions than other debt agreements. Innovative lessors can tailor a lease agreement to the lessee's special needs. For instance, the duration of the lease—the **lease term**—may be anything from a short period of time to the entire expected economic life of the asset. The rental payments may be level from year to year, or they may increase or decrease in amount. The payment amount may be predetermined or may vary with sales, the prime interest rate, the Consumer Price Index, or some other factor. In most cases, the rent is set to enable the lessor to recover the cost of the asset plus a fair return over the life of the lease.
4. ***Less costly financing.*** Some companies find leasing cheaper than other forms of financing. For example, start-up companies in depressed industries or companies in low tax brackets may lease to claim tax benefits that they might otherwise lose. Depreciation deductions offer no benefit to companies that have little if any taxable income. Through leasing, the leasing companies or financial institutions use these tax benefits. They can then pass some of these tax benefits back to the user of the asset in the form of lower rental payments.

International Perspective

Some companies "double dip" on the international level too. The leasing rules of the lessor's and lessee's countries may differ, permitting both parties to own the asset. Thus, both lessor and lessee receive the tax benefits related to depreciation.

5. ***Tax advantages.*** In some cases, companies can "have their cake and eat it too" with tax advantages that leases offer. That is, for financial reporting purposes, companies do not report an asset or a liability for the lease arrangement. For tax purposes, however, companies can capitalize and depreciate the leased asset. As a result, a company takes deductions earlier rather than later and also reduces its taxes. A common vehicle for this type of transaction is a "synthetic lease" arrangement, such as that described in the opening story for **Krispy Kreme**.
6. ***Off-balance-sheet financing.*** Certain leases do not add debt on a balance sheet or affect financial ratios. In fact, they may add to borrowing capacity.[1] Such **off-balance-sheet financing** is critical to some companies.

[1]As demonstrated later in this chapter, certain types of lease arrangements are not capitalized on the balance sheet. The liabilities section is thereby relieved of large future lease commitments that, if recorded, would adversely affect the debt to equity ratio. The reluctance to record lease obligations as liabilities is one of the primary reasons some companies resist capitalized lease accounting.

What do the numbers mean? OFF-BALANCE-SHEET FINANCING

As shown in our opening story, airlines use lease arrangements extensively. This results in a great deal of off-balance-sheet financing. The following chart indicates that many airlines that lease aircraft understate debt levels by a substantial amount.

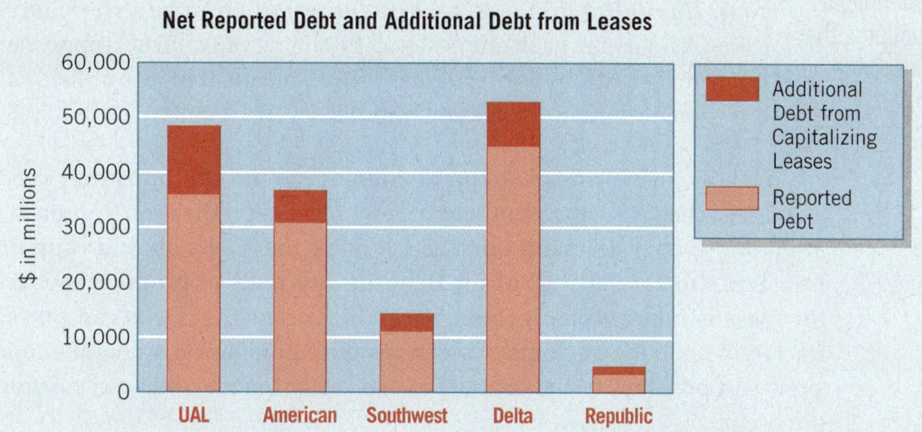

Source: Company reports, 2011.

Airlines are not the only ones playing the off-balance-sheet game. A recent study estimates that for S&P 500 companies, off-balance-sheet lease obligations total more than one-half trillion dollars, or roughly three percent of market value. Thus, analysts must adjust reported debt levels for the effects of non-capitalized leases. A methodology for making this adjustment is discussed in Eugene A. Imhoff, Jr., Robert C. Lipe, and David W. Wright, "Operating Leases: Impact of Constructive Capitalization," *Accounting Horizons* (March 1991).

Source: D. Zion and A. Varshney, "Leases Landing on Balance Sheets," *Credit Suisse Equity Research* (August 17, 2010).

Conceptual Nature of a Lease

If **Delta** borrows $47 million on a 10-year note from **Bank of America** to purchase a Boeing 737 jet plane, Delta should clearly report an asset and related liability at that amount on its balance sheet. Similarly, if Delta purchases the 737 for $47 million directly from Boeing through an installment purchase over 10 years, it should obviously report an asset and related liability (i.e., it should "capitalize" the installment transaction).

However, what if Delta **leases** the Boeing 737 for 10 years from **International Lease Finance Corp. (ILFC)**—the world's largest lessor of airplanes—through a noncancelable lease transaction with payments of the same amount as the installment purchase transaction? In that case, opinion differs over how to report this transaction. The various views on **capitalization of leases** are as follows.

1. ***Do not capitalize any leased assets.*** This view considers capitalization inappropriate because Delta does not own the property. Furthermore, a lease is an "**executory**" **contract** requiring continuing performance by both parties. Because companies do not currently capitalize other executory contracts (such as purchase commitments and employment contracts), they should not capitalize leases either.
2. ***Capitalize leases that are similar to installment purchases.*** This view holds that companies should report transactions in accordance with their economic substance. Therefore, if companies capitalize installment purchases, they should also capitalize leases that have similar characteristics. For example, Delta makes the same payments over a 10-year period for either a lease or an installment purchase. Lessees make rental payments, whereas owners make mortgage payments.

Underlying Concepts

The issue of how to report leases is the classic case of substance versus form. Although legal title does not technically pass in lease transactions, the benefits from the use of the property do transfer.

Why should the financial statements not report these transactions in the same manner?

3. ***Capitalize all long-term leases.*** This approach requires only the long-term right to use the property in order to capitalize. This property-rights approach capitalizes all long-term leases.[2]
4. ***Capitalize firm leases where the penalty for nonperformance is substantial.*** A final approach advocates capitalizing only "firm" (noncancelable) contractual rights and obligations. "Firm" means that it is unlikely to avoid performance under the lease without a severe penalty.

In short, the various viewpoints range from no capitalization to capitalization of all leases. The FASB apparently agrees with the capitalization approach when the lease is similar to an installment purchase. It notes that Delta **should capitalize a lease that transfers substantially all of the benefits and risks of property ownership, provided the lease is noncancelable**. **Noncancelable** means that Delta can cancel the lease contract only upon the outcome of some remote contingency, or that the cancellation provisions and penalties of the contract are so costly to Delta that cancellation probably will not occur.

This viewpoint leads to three basic conclusions. (1) Companies must identify the characteristics that indicate the transfer of substantially all of the benefits and risks of ownership. (2) The same characteristics should apply consistently to the lessee and the lessor. (3) Those leases that do **not** transfer substantially all the benefits and risks of ownership are operating leases. Companies should not capitalize operating leases. Instead, companies should account for them as rental payments and receipts.

ACCOUNTING BY THE LESSEE

LEARNING OBJECTIVE 2

Describe the accounting criteria and procedures for capitalizing leases by the lessee.

If Delta Airlines (the lessee) **capitalizes** a lease, it records an asset and a liability generally equal to the present value of the rental payments. ILFC (the lessor), having transferred substantially all the benefits and risks of ownership, recognizes a sale by removing the asset from the balance sheet and replacing it with a receivable. The typical journal entries for Delta and ILFC, assuming leased and capitalized equipment, appear as shown in Illustration 21-2.

ILLUSTRATION 21-2
Journal Entries for Capitalized Lease

Delta (Lessee)			ILFC (Lessor)		
Leased Equipment	XXX		Lease Receivable	XXX	
Lease Liability		XXX	Equipment		XXX

Having capitalized the asset, Delta records depreciation on the leased asset. Both ILFC and Delta treat the lease rental payments as consisting of interest and principal.

If Delta does not capitalize the lease, it does not record an asset, nor does ILFC remove one from its books. When Delta makes a lease payment, it records rental expense; ILFC recognizes rental revenue.

[2]Capitalization of most leases (based on either a right of use or on noncancelable rights and obligations) has the support of financial analysts. See Peter H. Knutson, "Financial Reporting in the 1990s and Beyond," Position Paper (Charlottesville, Va.: AIMR, 1993); and Warren McGregor, "Accounting for Leases: A New Approach," Special Report (Norwalk, Conn.: FASB, 1996). The joint FASB/IASB project on lease accounting is based on a right-of-use model, which will require expanded capitalization of lease assets and liabilities. See *http://www.fasb.org* (click on the "Projects" tab).

In order to record a lease as a **capital lease**, the lease must be noncancelable. Further, it must meet one or more of the four criteria listed in Illustration 21-3.

ILLUSTRATION 21-3
Capitalization Criteria for Lessee

Capitalization Criteria (Lessee)

- The lease transfers ownership of the property to the lessee.
- The lease contains a bargain-purchase option.[3]
- The lease term is equal to 75 percent or more of the estimated economic life of the leased property.
- The present value of the minimum lease payments (excluding executory costs) equals or exceeds 90 percent of the fair value of the leased property. **[1]**

See the FASB Codification section (page 1313).

Delta classifies and accounts for leases that **do not meet any of the four criteria** as **operating leases**. Illustration 21-4 shows that a lease meeting any one of the four criteria results in the lessee having a capital lease.

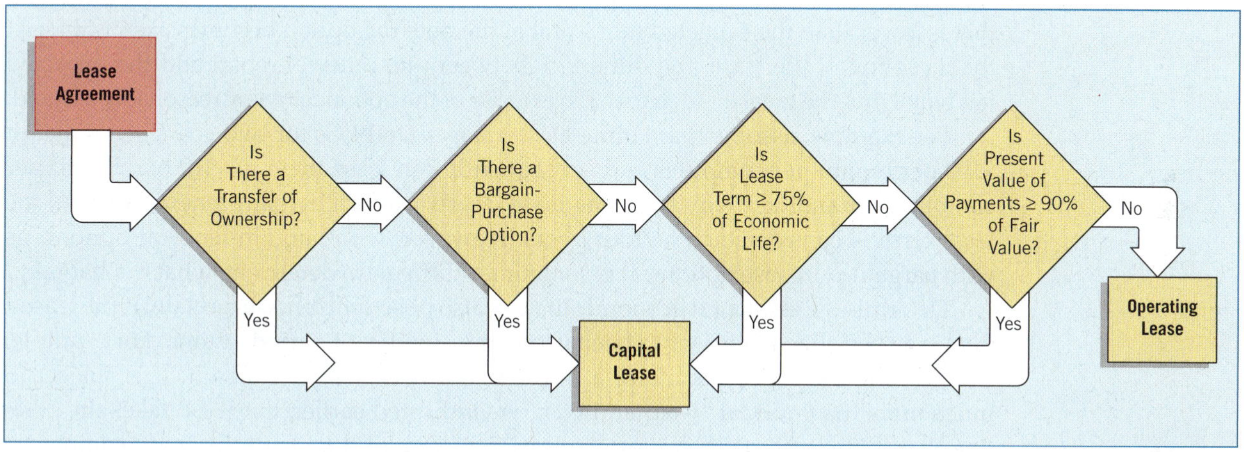

ILLUSTRATION 21-4
Diagram of Lessee's Criteria for Lease Classification

In keeping with the FASB's reasoning that a company consumes a significant portion of the value of the asset in the first 75 percent of its life, the lessee applies neither the third nor the fourth criterion when the inception of the lease occurs during the last 25 percent of the asset's life.

Capitalization Criteria

Three of the four **capitalization criteria** that apply to lessees are controversial and can be difficult to apply in practice. We discuss each of the criteria in detail on the following pages.

Transfer of Ownership Test

If the lease transfers ownership of the asset to the lessee, it is a capital lease. This criterion is not controversial and easily implemented in practice.

Bargain-Purchase Option Test

A **bargain-purchase option** allows the lessee to purchase the leased property for a price that is **significantly lower** than the property's expected fair value at the date the option becomes exercisable. At the inception of the lease, the difference between the option price and the expected fair value must be large enough to make exercise of the option reasonably assured.

[3]We define a bargain-purchase option in the next section.

For example, assume that Brett's Delivery Service was to lease a Honda Accord for \$599 per month for 40 months, with an option to purchase for \$100 at the end of the 40-month period. If the estimated fair value of the Honda Accord is \$3,000 at the end of the 40 months, the \$100 option to purchase is clearly a bargain. Therefore, Brett must capitalize the lease. In other cases, the criterion may not be as easy to apply, and determining *now* that a certain *future* price is a bargain can be difficult.

Economic Life Test (75% Test)

If the lease period equals or exceeds 75 percent of the asset's economic life, the lessor transfers most of the risks and rewards of ownership to the lessee. Capitalization is therefore appropriate. However, determining the lease term and the economic life of the asset can be troublesome.

The **lease term** is generally considered to be the fixed, noncancelable term of the lease. However, a bargain-renewal option, if provided in the lease agreement, can extend this period. A **bargain-renewal option** allows the lessee to renew the lease for a rental that is lower than the expected fair rental at the date the option becomes exercisable. At the inception of the lease, the difference between the renewal rental and the expected fair rental must be great enough to make exercise of the option to renew reasonably assured.

For example, assume that **Home Depot** leases **Dell** PCs for two years at a rental of \$100 per month per computer and subsequently can lease them for \$10 per month per computer for another two years. The lease clearly offers a bargain-renewal option; the lease term is considered to be four years. However, with bargain-renewal options, as with bargain-purchase options, it is sometimes difficult to determine what is a bargain.[4]

Determining estimated economic life can also pose problems, especially if the leased item is a specialized item or has been used for a significant period of time. For example, determining the economic life of a nuclear core is extremely difficult. It is subject to much more than normal "wear and tear." As indicated earlier, the FASB takes the position that if the lease starts during the last 25 percent of the life of the asset, companies cannot use the economic life test to classify a lease as a capital lease.

International Perspective

IFRS does not specify an exact percentage, such as 90%. Instead, it uses the term "substantially all." This difference illustrates the distinction between rules-based and principles-based standards.

Recovery of Investment Test (90% Test)

If the present value of the minimum lease payments equals or exceeds 90 percent of the fair value of the asset, then a lessee like Delta should capitalize the leased asset. Why? If the present value of the minimum lease payments is reasonably close to the fair value of the aircraft, Delta is effectively purchasing the asset.

Determining the present value of the minimum lease payments involves three important concepts: (1) minimum lease payments, (2) executory costs, and (3) discount rate.

Minimum Lease Payments. Delta is obligated to make, or expected to make, **minimum lease payments** in connection with the leased property. These payments include the following.

1. ***Minimum rental payments.*** Minimum rental payments are those that Delta must make to ILFC under the lease agreement. In some cases, the minimum rental payments may equal the minimum lease payments. However, the minimum lease payments may also include a guaranteed residual value (if any), penalty for failure to renew, or a bargain-purchase option (if any), as we note on the next page.

[4]The original lease term is also extended for leases having the following: substantial penalties for nonrenewal, periods for which the lessor has the option to renew or extend the lease, renewal periods preceding the date a bargain-purchase option becomes exercisable, and renewal periods in which any lessee guarantees of the lessor's debt are expected to be in effect or in which there will be a loan outstanding from the lessee to the lessor. The lease term, however, can never extend beyond the time a bargain-purchase option becomes exercisable. [2]

2. ***Guaranteed residual value.*** The residual value is the estimated fair (market) value of the leased property at the end of the lease term. ILFC may transfer the risk of loss to Delta or to a third party by obtaining a guarantee of the estimated residual value. The **guaranteed residual value** is either (1) the certain or determinable amount that Delta will pay ILFC at the end of the lease to purchase the aircraft at the end of the lease, or (2) the amount Delta or the third party guarantees that ILFC will realize if the aircraft is returned. (**Third-party guarantors** are, in essence, insurers who for a fee assume the risk of deficiencies in leased asset residual value.) If not guaranteed in full, the **unguaranteed residual value** is the estimated residual value exclusive of any portion guaranteed.[5]
3. ***Penalty for failure to renew or extend the lease.*** The amount Delta must pay if the agreement specifies that it must extend or renew the lease, and it fails to do so.
4. ***Bargain-purchase option.*** As we indicated earlier (in item 1), an option given to Delta to purchase the aircraft at the end of the lease term at a price that is fixed sufficiently below the expected fair value, so that, at the inception of the lease, purchase is reasonably assured.

Delta excludes executory costs (defined below) from its computation of the present value of the minimum lease payments.

Executory Costs. Like most assets, leased tangible assets incur insurance, maintenance, and tax expenses—called **executory costs**—during their economic life. If ILFC retains responsibility for the payment of these "ownership-type costs," **it should exclude**, in computing the present value of the minimum lease payments, a portion of each lease payment that represents executory costs. Executory costs do not represent payment on or reduction of the obligation.

Many lease agreements specify that the lessee directly pays executory costs to the appropriate third parties. In these cases, the lessor can use the rental payment **without adjustment** in the present value computation.

Discount Rate. A lessee like Delta generally computes the present value of the minimum lease payments using its **incremental borrowing rate**. This rate is defined as: "The rate that, at the inception of the lease, the lessee would have incurred to borrow the funds necessary to buy the leased asset on a secured loan with repayment terms similar to the payment schedule called for in the lease." **[4]**

To determine whether the present value of these payments is less than 90 percent of the fair value of the property, Delta discounts the payments using its incremental borrowing rate. Determining the incremental borrowing rate often requires judgment because the lessee bases it on a hypothetical purchase of the property.

However, there is one exception to this rule. If (1) Delta knows the **implicit interest rate computed by ILFC** and (2) it is less than Delta's incremental borrowing rate, then Delta **must use ILFC's implicit rate**. What is the **interest rate implicit in the lease**? It is the discount rate that, when applied to the minimum lease payments and any unguaranteed residual value accruing to the lessor, causes the aggregate present value to equal the fair value of the leased property to the lessor. **[5]**

The purpose of this exception is twofold. First, **the implicit rate of ILFC is generally a more realistic rate** to use in determining the amount (if any) to report as the asset and related liability for Delta. Second, the guideline ensures that Delta **does not use an artificially high incremental borrowing rate** that would cause the present value of the minimum lease payments to be less than 90 percent of the fair value of the aircraft. Use of such a rate would thus make it possible to avoid capitalization of the asset and related liability.

[5]A lease provision requiring the lessee to make up a residual value deficiency that is attributable to damage, extraordinary wear and tear, or excessive usage is not included in the minimum lease payments. Lessees recognize such costs as period costs when incurred. **[3]**

Delta may argue that it cannot determine the implicit rate of the lessor and therefore should use the higher rate. However, in most cases, Delta can approximate the implicit rate used by ILFC. The determination of whether or not a reasonable estimate could be made will require judgment, particularly where the result from using the incremental borrowing rate comes close to meeting the 90 percent test. Because Delta **may not capitalize the leased property at more than its fair value** (as we discuss later), it cannot use an excessively low discount rate.

Asset and Liability Accounted for Differently

In a capital lease transaction, Delta uses the lease as a source of financing. ILFC finances the transaction (provides the investment capital) through the leased asset. Delta makes rent payments, which actually are installment payments. Therefore, over the life of the aircraft rented, **the rental payments to ILFC constitute a payment of principal plus interest**.

Asset and Liability Recorded

Under the capital lease method, Delta treats the lease transaction as if it purchases the aircraft in a financing transaction. That is, Delta acquires the aircraft and creates an obligation. Therefore, it records a capital lease as an asset and a liability at the lower of (1) the present value of the minimum lease payments (excluding executory costs) or (2) the fair value of the leased asset at the inception of the lease. The rationale for this approach is that companies should not record a leased asset for more than its fair value.

Depreciation Period

One troublesome aspect of accounting for the depreciation of the capitalized leased asset relates to the period of depreciation. If the lease agreement transfers ownership of the asset to Delta (criterion 1) or contains a bargain-purchase option (criterion 2), Delta depreciates the aircraft consistent with its normal depreciation policy for other aircraft, **using the economic life of the asset**.

On the other hand, if the lease does not transfer ownership or does not contain a bargain-purchase option, then Delta depreciates it over the **term of the lease**. In this case, the aircraft reverts to ILFC after a certain period of time.

Effective-Interest Method

Throughout the term of the lease, Delta uses the **effective-interest method** to allocate each lease payment between principal and interest. This method produces a periodic interest expense equal to a constant percentage of the carrying value of the lease obligation. When applying the effective-interest method to capital leases, Delta must use the same discount rate that determines the present value of the minimum lease payments.

Depreciation Concept

Although Delta computes the amounts initially capitalized as an asset and recorded as an obligation at the same present value, the **depreciation of the aircraft and the discharge of the obligation are independent accounting processes** during the term of the lease. It should depreciate the leased asset by applying conventional depreciation methods: straight-line, sum-of-the-years'-digits, declining-balance, units of production, etc. The FASB uses the term "amortization" more frequently than "depreciation" to recognize intangible leased property rights. We prefer "depreciation" to describe the write-off of a tangible asset's expired services.

Capital Lease Method (Lessee)

To illustrate a capital lease, assume that **Caterpillar Financial Services Corp.** (a subsidiary of Caterpillar) and **Sterling Construction Corp.** sign a lease agreement dated January 1,

2014, that calls for Caterpillar to lease a front-end loader to Sterling beginning January 1, 2014. The terms and provisions of the lease agreement, and other pertinent data, are as follows.

- The term of the lease is five years. The lease agreement is noncancelable, requiring equal rental payments of $25,981.62 at the beginning of each year (annuity-due basis).
- The loader has a fair value at the inception of the lease of $100,000, an estimated economic life of five years, and no residual value.
- Sterling pays all of the executory costs directly to third parties except for the property taxes of $2,000 per year, which is included as part of its annual payments to Caterpillar.
- The lease contains no renewal options. The loader reverts to Caterpillar at the termination of the lease.
- Sterling's incremental borrowing rate is 11 percent per year.
- Sterling depreciates, on a straight-line basis, similar equipment that it owns.
- Caterpillar sets the annual rental to earn a rate of return on its investment of 10 percent per year; Sterling knows this fact.

The lease meets the criteria for classification as a capital lease for the following reasons.

1. The lease term of five years, being equal to the equipment's estimated economic life of five years, satisfies the 75 percent test.
2. The present value of the minimum lease payments ($100,000 as computed below) exceeds 90 percent of the fair value of the loader ($100,000).

The minimum lease payments are $119,908.10 ($23,981.62 × 5). Sterling computes the amount capitalized as leased assets as the present value of the minimum lease payments (excluding executory costs—property taxes of $2,000) as shown in Illustration 21-5.

Capitalized amount = ($25,981.62 − $2,000) × Present value of an annuity due of 1 for 5 periods at 10% (Table 6-5)
= $23,981.62 × 4.16986
= $100,000

ILLUSTRATION 21-5
Computation of Capitalized Lease Payments

Sterling uses Caterpillar's implicit interest rate of 10 percent instead of its incremental borrowing rate of 11 percent because (1) it is lower and (2) it knows about it.[6]

Sterling records the capital lease on its books on January 1, 2014, as:

Leased Equipment (under capital leases)	100,000	
Lease Liability		100,000

Note that the entry records the obligation at the net amount of $100,000 (the present value of the future rental payments) rather than at the gross amount of $119,908.10 ($23,981.62 × 5).

Sterling records the **first lease payment on January 1, 2014**, as follows.

Property Tax Expense	2,000.00	
Lease Liability	23,981.62	
Cash		25,981.62

Calculator Solution for Lease Payment

	Inputs	Answer
N	5	
I	10	
PV	?	100,000
PMT	−23,981.59*	
FV	0	

*Set payments at beginning of period.

[6]If Sterling has an incremental borrowing rate of, say, 9 percent (lower than the 10 percent rate used by Caterpillar) and it did not know the rate used by Caterpillar, the present value computation would yield a capitalized amount of $101,675.35 ($23,981.62 × 4.23972). And, because this amount exceeds the $100,000 fair value of the equipment, Sterling should capitalize the $100,000 and use 10 percent as its effective rate for amortization of the lease obligation.

Each lease payment of $25,981.62 consists of three elements: (1) a reduction in the lease liability, (2) a financing cost (interest expense), and (3) executory costs (property taxes). The total financing cost (interest expense) over the term of the lease is $19,908.10. This amount is the difference between the present value of the lease payments ($100,000) and the actual cash disbursed, net of executory costs ($119,908.10). Therefore, the annual interest expense, applying the effective-interest method, is a function of the outstanding liability, as Illustration 21-6 shows.

ILLUSTRATION 21-6
Lease Amortization Schedule for Lessee—Annuity-Due Basis

STERLING CONSTRUCTION
LEASE AMORTIZATION SCHEDULE
ANNUITY-DUE BASIS

Date	Annual Lease Payment	Executory Costs	Interest (10%) on Liability	Reduction of Lease Liability	Lease Liability
	(a)	(b)	(c)	(d)	(e)
1/1/14					$100,000.00
1/1/14	$ 25,981.62	$ 2,000	$ -0-	$ 23,981.62	76,018.38
1/1/15	25,981.62	2,000	7,601.84	16,379.78	59,638.60
1/1/16	25,981.62	2,000	5,963.86	18,017.76	41,620.84
1/1/17	25,981.62	2,000	4,162.08	19,819.54	21,801.30
1/1/18	25,981.62	2,000	2,180.32*	21,801.30	-0-
	$129,908.10	$10,000	$19,908.10	$100,000.00	

(a) Lease payment as required by lease.
(b) Executory costs included in rental payment.
(c) Ten percent of the preceding balance of (e) except for 1/1/14; since this is an annuity due, no time has elapsed at the date of the first payment and no interest has accrued.
(d) (a) minus (b) and (c).
(e) Preceding balance minus (d).

*Rounded by 19 cents.

At the end of its fiscal year, December 31, 2014, Sterling records **accrued interest** as follows.

Interest Expense	7,601.84	
Interest Payable		7,601.84

Depreciation of the leased equipment over its five-year lease term, applying Sterling's normal depreciation policy (straight-line method), results in the following entry on December 31, 2014.

Depreciation Expense (capital leases)	20,000	
Accumulated Depreciation—Capital Leases		20,000
($100,000 ÷ 5 years)		

At December 31, 2014, Sterling separately identifies the assets recorded under capital leases on its balance sheet. Similarly, it separately identifies the related obligations. Sterling classifies the portion due within one year or the operating cycle, whichever is longer, with current liabilities, and the rest with noncurrent liabilities. For example, the current portion of the December 31, 2014, total obligation of $76,018.38 in Sterling's amortization schedule is the amount of the reduction in the obligation in 2015, or $16,379.78. Illustration 21-7 shows the liabilities section as it relates to lease transactions at December 31, 2014.

ILLUSTRATION 21-7
Reporting Current and Noncurrent Lease Liabilities

Current liabilities	
Interest payable	$ 7,601.84
Lease liability	16,379.78
Noncurrent liabilities	
Lease liability	59,638.60

Sterling records the lease payment of January 1, 2015, as follows.

Property Tax Expense	2,000.00	
Interest Payable	7,601.84	
Lease Liability	16,379.78	
Cash		25,981.62

Entries through 2018 follow the pattern above. Sterling records its other executory costs (insurance and maintenance) in a manner similar to how it records any other operating costs incurred on assets it owns.

Upon expiration of the lease, Sterling has fully amortized the amount capitalized as leased equipment. It also has fully discharged its lease obligation. If Sterling does not purchase the loader, it returns the equipment to Caterpillar. Sterling then removes the leased equipment and related accumulated depreciation accounts from its books.[7]

If Sterling purchases the equipment at termination of the lease, at a price of $5,000, and the estimated life of the equipment changes from five to seven years, it makes the following entry.

Equipment ($100,000 + $5,000)	105,000	
Accumulated Depreciation—Capital Leases	100,000	
Leased Equipment (under capital leases)		100,000
Accumulated Depreciation—Equipment		100,000
Cash		5,000

Operating Method (Lessee)

Under the **operating method**, rent expense (and the associated liability) accrues day by day to the lessee as it uses the property. **The lessee assigns rent to the periods benefiting from the use of the asset and ignores, in the accounting, any commitments to make future payments.** The lessee makes appropriate accruals or deferrals if the accounting period ends between cash payment dates.

For example, assume that the capital lease illustrated in the previous section did not qualify as a capital lease. Sterling therefore accounts for it as an operating lease. The first-year charge to operations is now $25,981.62, the amount of the rental payment. Sterling records this payment on January 1, 2014, as follows.

Rent Expense	25,981.62	
Cash		25,981.62

Sterling does not report the loader, as well as any long-term liability for future rental payments, on the balance sheet. Sterling reports rent expense on the income statement. And, as discussed later in the chapter, **Sterling must disclose all operating leases that have noncancelable lease terms in excess of one year.**

What do the numbers mean? RESTATEMENTS ON THE MENU

Accounting for operating leases would appear routine, so it is unusual for a bevy of companies in a single industry—restaurants—to get caught up in the accounting rules for operating leases. Getting the accounting right is particularly important for restaurant chains because they make extensive use of leases for their restaurants and equipment.

The problem stems from the way most property (and equipment) leases cover a specific number of years (the so-called *primary lease term*) as well as renewal periods (sometimes referred to as the *option term*). In some cases, companies were calculating their lease expense for the primary term but depreciating lease-related assets over

[7]If Sterling purchases the front-end loader during the term of a "capital lease," it accounts for it like a renewal or extension of a capital lease. "Any difference between the purchase price and the carrying amount of the lease obligation shall be recorded as an adjustment of the carrying amount of the asset." **[6]**

both the primary and option terms. This practice resulted in understating the total cost of the lease and thus boosted earnings.

For example, the CFO at CKE Restaurants Inc., owner of the Hardee's and Carl's Jr. chains, noted that CKE ran into trouble because it was not consistent in calculating the lease and depreciation expense. Correcting the error at CKE reduced earnings by nine cents a share in fiscal 2002, nine cents a share in fiscal 2003, and 10 cents a share in fiscal 2004. The company now uses the shorter, primary lease terms for calculating both lease expense and depreciation. The change increases depreciation annually, which in turn decreases total assets.

CKE was not alone in improper operating lease accounting. Notable restaurateurs who ran afoul of the lease rules included Brinker International Inc., operator of Chili's; Darden Restaurants Inc., which operates Red Lobster and Olive Garden; and Jack in the Box. To correct their operating lease accounting, these restaurants reported restatements that resulted in lower earnings and assets.

Source: Steven D. Jones and Richard Gibson, *Wall Street Journal* (January 26, 2005), p. C3.

Comparison of Capital Lease with Operating Lease

LEARNING OBJECTIVE 3
Contrast the operating and capitalization methods of recording leases.

As we indicated, if accounting for the lease as an operating lease, the first-year charge to operations is $25,981.62, the amount of the rental payment. Treating the transaction as a capital lease, however, results in a first-year charge of $29,601.84: depreciation of $20,000 (assuming straight-line), interest expense of $7,601.84 (per Illustration 21-6), and executory costs of $2,000. Illustration 21-8 shows that **while the total charges to operations are the same over the lease term whether accounting for the lease as a capital lease or as an operating lease, under the capital lease treatment the charges are higher in the earlier years and lower in the later years.**[8]

ILLUSTRATION 21-8
Comparison of Charges to Operations—Capital vs. Operating Leases

STERLING CONSTRUCTION
SCHEDULE OF CHARGES TO OPERATIONS
CAPITAL LEASE VERSUS OPERATING LEASE

	Capital Lease				Operating	
Year	Depreciation	Executory Costs	Interest	Total Charge	Lease Charge	Difference
2014	$ 20,000	$ 2,000	$ 7,601.84	$ 29,601.84	$ 25,981.62	$3,620.22
2015	20,000	2,000	5,963.86	27,963.86	25,981.62	1,982.24
2016	20,000	2,000	4,162.08	26,162.08	25,981.62	180.46
2017	20,000	2,000	2,180.32	24,180.32	25,981.62	(1,801.30)
2018	20,000	2,000	—	22,000.00	25,981.62	(3,981.62)
	$100,000	$10,000	$19,908.10	$129,908.10	$129,908.10	$ -0-

If using an accelerated method of depreciation, the differences between the amounts charged to operations under the two methods would be even larger in the earlier and later years.

In addition, using the capital lease approach results in an asset and related liability of $100,000 initially reported on the balance sheet. The lessee would not report any asset

[8]The higher charges in the early years is one reason lessees are reluctant to adopt the capital lease accounting method. Lessees (especially those of real estate) claim that it is really no more costly to operate the leased asset in the early years than in the later years. Thus, they advocate an even charge similar to that provided by the operating method.

or liability under the operating method. Therefore, the following differences occur if using a capital lease instead of an operating lease.

1. An increase in the amount of reported debt (both short-term and long-term).
2. An increase in the amount of total assets (specifically long-lived assets).
3. A lower income early in the life of the lease and, therefore, lower retained earnings.

Thus, many companies believe that capital leases negatively impact their financial position: Their debt to total equity ratio increases, and their rate of return on total assets decreases. As a result, the business community resists capitalizing leases.

Whether this resistance is well founded is debatable. From a cash flow point of view, the company is in the same position whether accounting for the lease as an operating or a capital lease. Managers often argue against capitalization for several reasons. First, capitalization can more easily lead to **violation of loan covenants**. It also can affect the **amount of compensation received by owners** (for example, a stock compensation plan tied to earnings). Finally, capitalization can **lower rates of return** and **increase debt to equity relationships**, making the company less attractive to present and potential investors.[9]

Evolving Issue ARE YOU LIABLE?

Under current accounting rules, companies can keep the obligations associated with operating leases off the balance sheet. (For example, see the "What Do the Numbers Mean?" box on page 1273 for the effects of this approach for airlines.) This approach may change if the FASB and IASB are able to craft a new lease accounting rule. The current plans for a new rule in this area should result in many more operating leases on balance sheets. Analysts are beginning to estimate the expected impact of a new rule. As shown in the table below, if the FASB (and IASB) issue a new rule on operating leases, a company like **Walgreen** could see its liabilities jump a whopping 216 percent.

Retailer	Estimated Off-Balance-Sheet Lease Liabilities	Jump in Liabilities If They Were on the Balance Sheet
McDonald's	$ 7.996 billion	149%
Walgreen	23.212	216
Home Depot	5.846	27
Starbucks	3.685	146
CVS	26.913	104

And it is not just retailers who would be impacted. A PricewaterhouseCoopers survey of 3,000 international companies indicated the following impacts for several industries.

	Average Increase in Interest-Bearing Debt	Companies with over 25% Increase	Average Increase in Leverage
Retail and trade	213%	71%	64%
Other services	51	35	34
Transportation and warehousing	95	38	31
Professional services	158	52	19
Accommodation	101	41	18
All companies	58	24	13

As indicated, the expected effects are significant, with all companies expecting a 58 percent increase in their debt levels and a 13 percent increase in leverage ratios.

This is not a pretty picture, but investors need to see it if they are to fully understand a company's lease obligations.

Sources: Nanette Byrnes, "You May Be Liable for That Lease," *BusinessWeek* (June 5, 2006), p. 76; PricewaterhouseCoopers, *The Future of Leasing: Research of Impact on Companies' Financial Ratios* (2009); and J. E. Ketz, "Operating Lease Obligations to Be Capitalized," *Smartpros* (August 2010), *http://accounting.smartpros.com/x70304.xml.*

[9]One study indicates that management's behavior did change as a result of the leasing rules. For example, many companies restructure their leases to avoid capitalization. Others increase their purchases of assets instead of leasing. Still others, faced with capitalization, postpone their debt offerings or issue stock instead. However, note that the study found no significant effect on stock or bond prices as a result of capitalization of leases. See A. Rashad Abdel-khalik, "The Economic Effects on Lessees of *FASB Statement No. 13,* Accounting for Leases," Research Report (Stamford, Conn.: FASB, 1981).

ACCOUNTING BY THE LESSOR

LEARNING OBJECTIVE 4

Explain the advantages and economics of leasing to lessors and identify the classifications of leases for the lessor.

Earlier in this chapter, we discussed leasing's advantages to the lessee. Three important benefits are available to the lessor:

1. ***Interest revenue.*** Leasing is a form of financing. Banks, captives, and independent leasing companies find leasing attractive because it provides competitive interest margins.
2. ***Tax incentives.*** In many cases, companies that lease cannot use the tax benefit of the asset, but leasing allows them to transfer such tax benefits to another party (the lessor) in return for a lower rental rate on the leased asset. To illustrate, **Boeing Aircraft** might sell one of its 737 jet planes to a wealthy investor who needed only the tax benefit. The investor then leased the plane to a foreign airline, for whom the tax benefit was of no use. Everyone gained. Boeing sold its airplane, the investor received the tax benefit, and the foreign airline cheaply acquired a 737.[10]
3. ***High residual value.*** Another advantage to the lessor is the return of the property at the end of the lease term. Residual values can produce very large profits. **Citigroup** at one time estimated that the commercial aircraft it was leasing to the airline industry would have a residual value of 5 percent of their purchase price. It turned out that they were worth 150 percent of their cost—a handsome profit. At the same time, if residual values decline, lessors can suffer losses when less-valuable leased assets are returned at the conclusion of the lease. At one time, automaker **Ford** took a $2.1 billion write-down on its lease portfolio, when rising gas prices spurred dramatic declines in the resale values of leased trucks and SUVs. Such residual value losses led **Chrysler** to get out of the leasing business altogether.

Economics of Leasing

A lessor, such as Caterpillar Financial in our earlier example, determines the amount of the rental, basing it on the rate of return—the implicit rate—needed to justify leasing the front-end loader. In establishing the rate of return, Caterpillar considers the credit standing of Sterling Construction, the length of the lease, and the status of the residual value (guaranteed versus unguaranteed).

In the Caterpillar/Sterling example on pages 1278–1281, Caterpillar's implicit rate was 10 percent, the cost of the equipment to Caterpillar was $100,000 (also fair value), and the estimated residual value was zero. Caterpillar determines the amount of the lease payment as follows.

ILLUSTRATION 21-9
Computation of Lease Payments

Fair value of leased equipment	$100,000.00
Less: Present value of the residual value	–0–
Amount to be recovered by lessor through lease payments	$100,000.00
Five beginning-of-the-year lease payments to yield a 10% return ($100,000 ÷ 4.16986[a])	$ 23,981.62

[a]PV of an annuity due of 1 for 5 years at 10% (Table 6-5).

If a residual value is involved (whether guaranteed or not), Caterpillar would not have to recover as much from the lease payments. Therefore, the lease payments would be less. (Illustration 21-16, on page 1291, shows this situation.)

[10]Some would argue that there is a loser—the U.S. government. The tax benefits enable the profitable investor to reduce or eliminate taxable income.

Classification of Leases by the Lessor

For accounting purposes, the **lessor** may classify leases as one of the following:

1. Operating leases.
2. Direct-financing leases.
3. Sales-type leases.

Illustration 21-10 presents two groups of capitalization criteria for the lessor. If at the date of inception the lessor agrees to a lease that meets **one or more** of the Group I criteria (1, 2, 3, and 4) and **both** of the Group II criteria (1 and 2), the lessor shall classify and account for the arrangement as a direct-financing lease or as a sales-type lease. **[7]** Note that the Group I criteria are identical to the criteria that must be met in order for a lessee to classify a lease as a capital lease, as shown in Illustration 21-3 (on page 1275).

ILLUSTRATION 21-10
Capitalization Criteria for Lessor

Capitalization Criteria (Lessor)

Group I

1. The lease transfers ownership of the property to the lessee.
2. The lease contains a bargain-purchase option.
3. The lease term is equal to 75 percent or more of the estimated economic life of the leased property.
4. The present value of the minimum lease payments (excluding executory costs) equals or exceeds 90 percent of the fair value of the leased property.

Group II

1. Collectibility of the payments required from the lessee is reasonably predictable.
2. No important uncertainties surround the amount of unreimbursable costs yet to be incurred by the lessor under the lease (lessor's performance is substantially complete or future costs are reasonably predictable).

Why the Group II requirements? The profession wants to ensure that the lessor has really transferred the risks and benefits of ownership. If collectibility of payments is not predictable or if performance by the lessor is incomplete, then the criteria for revenue recognition have not been met. The lessor should therefore account for the lease as an operating lease.

For example, computer leasing companies at one time used to buy IBM equipment, lease the equipment, and remove the leased assets from their balance sheets. In leasing the assets, the computer lessors stated that they would substitute new IBM equipment if obsolescence occurred. However, when IBM introduced a new computer line, IBM refused to sell it to the computer leasing companies. As a result, a number of the lessors could not meet their contracts with their customers and had to take back the old equipment. The computer leasing companies therefore had to reinstate the assets they had taken off the books. Such a case demonstrates one reason for the Group II requirements.

International Perspective

GAAP is consistent with *International Accounting Standard No. 17* (Accounting for Leases). However, the international standard is a relatively simple statement of basic principles, whereas the U.S. rules on leases are more prescriptive and detailed.

The distinction for the lessor between a direct-financing lease and a sales-type lease is the presence or absence of a manufacturer's or dealer's profit (or loss). A sales-type lease involves a manufacturer's or dealer's profit, and a direct-financing lease does not. The profit (or loss) to the lessor is evidenced by the difference between the fair value of the leased property at the inception of the lease and the lessor's cost or carrying amount (book value).

Normally, sales-type leases arise when manufacturers or dealers use leasing as a means of marketing their products. For example, a computer manufacturer will lease its computer equipment (possibly through a captive) to businesses and institutions. Direct-financing leases generally result from arrangements with lessors that are primarily engaged in financing operations (e.g., banks). However, a lessor need not be a manufacturer or dealer to recognize a profit (or loss) at the inception of a lease that requires application of sales-type lease accounting.

Lessors classify and account for all leases that do not qualify as direct-financing or sales-type leases as operating leases. Illustration 21-11 shows the circumstances under which a lessor classifies a lease as operating, direct-financing, or sales-type.

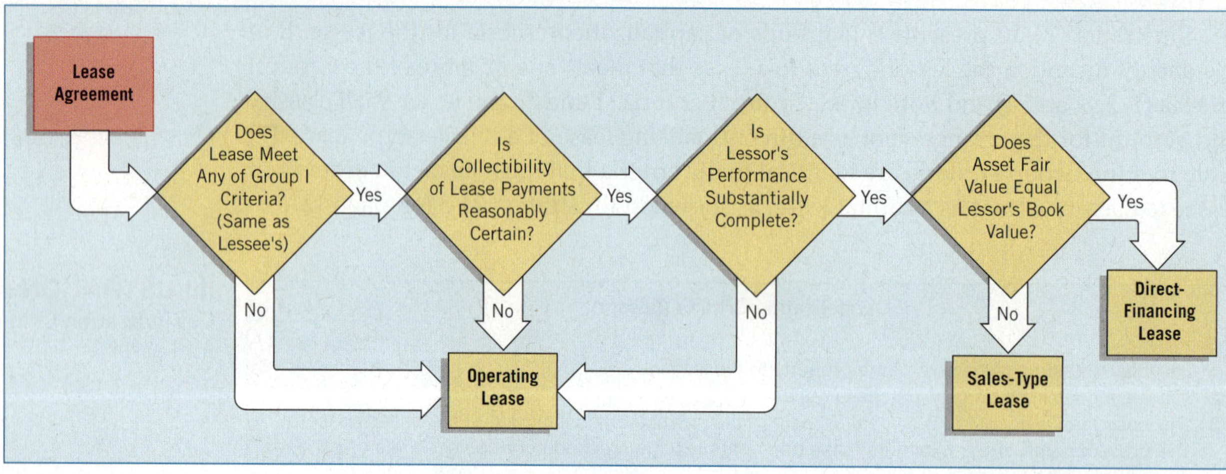

ILLUSTRATION 21-11
Diagram of Lessor's Criteria for Lease Classification

As a consequence of the additional Group II criteria for lessors, a lessor may classify a lease as an **operating** lease but the lessee may classify the same lease as a **capital** lease. In such an event, both the lessor and lessee will carry the asset on their books, and both will depreciate the capitalized asset.

For purposes of comparison with the lessee's accounting, we will illustrate only the operating and direct-financing leases in the following section. We will discuss the more complex sales-type lease later in the chapter.

Direct-Financing Method (Lessor)

LEARNING OBJECTIVE 5
Describe the lessor's accounting for direct-financing leases.

Direct-financing leases are in substance the financing of an asset purchase by the lessee. In this type of lease, the lessor records a **lease receivable** instead of a leased asset. The lease receivable is the present value of the minimum lease payments. Remember that "minimum lease payments" include:

1. Rental payments (excluding executory costs).
2. Bargain-purchase option (if any).
3. Guaranteed residual value (if any).
4. Penalty for failure to renew (if any).

Thus, the lessor records the residual value, whether guaranteed or not. Also, recall that if the lessor pays any executory costs, then it should reduce the rental payment by that amount in computing minimum lease payments.

The following presentation, using the data from the preceding Caterpillar/Sterling example on page 1279, illustrates the accounting treatment for a direct-financing lease. We repeat here the information relevant to Caterpillar in accounting for this lease transaction.

1. The term of the lease is five years beginning January 1, 2014, noncancelable, and requires equal rental payments of $25,981.62 at the beginning of each year. Payments include $2,000 of executory costs (property taxes).

2. The equipment (front-end loader) has a cost of $100,000 to Caterpillar, a fair value at the inception of the lease of $100,000, an estimated economic life of five years, and no residual value.
3. Caterpillar incurred no initial direct costs in negotiating and closing the lease transaction.
4. The lease contains no renewal options. The equipment reverts to Caterpillar at the termination of the lease.
5. Collectibility is reasonably assured and Caterpillar incurs no additional costs (with the exception of the property taxes being collected from Sterling).
6. Caterpillar sets the annual lease payments to ensure a rate of return of 10 percent (implicit rate) on its investment as shown in Illustration 21-12.

ILLUSTRATION 21-12
Computation of Lease Payments

Fair value of leased equipment	$100,000.00
Less: Present value of residual value	–0–
Amount to be recovered by lessor through lease payments	$100,000.00
Five beginning-of-the-year lease payments to yield a 10% return ($100,000 ÷ 4.16986[a])	$ 23,981.62

[a]PV of an annuity due of 1 for 5 years at 10% (Table 6-5).

The lease meets the criteria for classification as a direct-financing lease for several reasons. (1) The lease term exceeds 75 percent of the equipment's estimated economic life. (2) The present value of the minimum lease payments exceeds 90 percent of the equipment's fair value. (3) Collectibility of the payments is reasonably assured. (4) Caterpillar incurs no further costs. It is not a sales-type lease because there is no difference between the fair value ($100,000) of the loader and Caterpillar's cost ($100,000).

The Lease Receivable is the present value of the minimum lease payments (excluding executory costs which are property taxes of $2,000). Caterpillar computes it as follows.

ILLUSTRATION 21-13
Computation of Lease Receivable

Lease receivable = ($25,981.62 − $2,000) × Present value of an annuity due of 1 for 5 periods at 10% (Table 6-5)
= $23,981.62 × 4.16986
= $100,000

Caterpillar records the lease of the asset and the resulting receivable on January 1, 2014 (the inception of the lease), as follows.

Lease Receivable	100,000	
Equipment		100,000

Companies often **report** the lease receivable in the balance sheet as "Net investment in capital leases." Companies classify it either as current or noncurrent, depending on when they recover the net investment.[11]

Caterpillar replaces its investment (the leased front-end loader, a cost of $100,000), with a lease receivable. In a manner similar to Sterling's treatment of interest, Caterpillar applies the effective-interest method and recognizes interest revenue as a function of the lease receivable balance, as Illustration 21-14 (page 1288) shows.

[11]In the notes to the financial statements (see Illustration 21-32, pages 1301–1302, for lessor disclosures by **Hewlett-Packard**), the lease receivable is reported at its gross amount (minimum lease payments plus the unguaranteed residual value). In addition, the lessor also reports total unearned interest related to the lease. As a result, some lessors record lease receivable on a gross basis and record the unearned interest in a separate account. We illustrate the net approach here because it is consistent with the accounting for the lessee.

ILLUSTRATION 21-14
Lease Amortization Schedule for Lessor—Annuity-Due Basis

CATERPILLAR FINANCIAL
LEASE AMORTIZATION SCHEDULE
ANNUITY-DUE BASIS

Date	Annual Lease Payment	Executory Costs	Interest (10%) on Lease Receivable	Lease Receivable Recovery	Lease Receivable
	(a)	(b)	(c)	(d)	(e)
1/1/14					$100,000.00
1/1/14	$ 25,981.62	$ 2,000.00	$ -0-	$ 23,981.62	76,018.38
1/1/15	25,981.62	2,000.00	7,601.84	16,379.78	59,638.60
1/1/16	25,981.62	2,000.00	5,963.86	18,017.76	41,620.84
1/1/17	25,981.62	2,000.00	4,162.08	19,819.54	21,801.30
1/1/18	25,981.62	2,000.00	2,180.32*	21,801.30	-0-
	$129,908.10	$10,000.00	$19,908.10	$100,000.00	

(a) Annual rental that provides a 10% return on net investment.
(b) Executory costs included in rental payment.
(c) Ten percent of the preceding balance of (e) except for 1/1/14.
(d) (a) minus (b) and (c).
(e) Preceding balance minus (d).

*Rounded by 19 cents.

On January 1, 2014, Caterpillar records receipt of the first year's lease payment as follows.

Cash	25,981.62	
Lease Receivable		23,981.62
Property Tax Expense/Property Taxes Payable		2,000.00

On December 31, 2014, Caterpillar recognizes the interest revenue during the first year through the following entry.

Interest Receivable	7,601.84	
Interest Revenue (leases)		7,601.84

At December 31, 2014, Caterpillar reports the lease receivable in its balance sheet among current assets or noncurrent assets, or both. It classifies the portion due within one year or the operating cycle, whichever is longer, as a current asset, and the rest with noncurrent assets.

Illustration 21-15 shows the assets section as it relates to lease transactions at December 31, 2014.

ILLUSTRATION 21-15
Reporting Lease Transactions by Lessor

Current assets	
Interest receivable	$ 7,601.84
Lease receivable	16,379.78
Noncurrent assets (investments)	
Lease receivable	$59,638.60

The following entries record receipt of the second year's lease payment and recognition of the interest.

January 1, 2015

Cash	25,981.62	
Lease Receivable		16,379.78
Interest Receivable		7,601.84
Property Tax Expense/Property Taxes Payable		2,000.00

December 31, 2015		
Interest Receivable	5,963.86	
Interest Revenue (leases)		5,963.86

Journal entries through 2018 follow the same pattern except that Caterpillar records no entry in 2018 (the last year) for interest revenue. Because it fully collects the receivable by January 1, 2018, no balance (investment) is outstanding during 2018. Caterpillar **recorded no depreciation**. If Sterling buys the loader for $5,000 upon expiration of the lease, Caterpillar recognizes disposition of the equipment as follows.

Cash	5,000	
Gain on Disposal of Equipment		5,000

Operating Method (Lessor)

Under the **operating method**, the lessor records each rental receipt as rental revenue. It **depreciates the leased asset in the normal manner**, with the depreciation expense of the period matched against the rental revenue. The amount of revenue recognized in each accounting period is a level amount (straight-line basis) regardless of the lease provisions, unless another systematic and rational basis better represents the time pattern in which the lessor derives benefit from the leased asset.

In addition to the depreciation charge, the lessor expenses maintenance costs and the cost of any other services performed under the provisions of the lease that pertain to the current accounting period. The lessor **amortizes over the life of the lease** any costs paid to independent third parties, such as appraisal fees, finder's fees, and costs of credit checks, usually on a straight-line basis.

To illustrate the operating method, assume that the direct-financing lease illustrated in the previous section does not qualify as a capital lease. Therefore, Caterpillar accounts for it as an operating lease. It records the cash rental receipt, assuming the $2,000 was for property tax expense, as follows.

Cash	25,981.62	
Rent Revenue		25,981.62

Caterpillar records depreciation as follows (assuming a straight-line method, a cost basis of $100,000, and a five-year life).

Depreciation Expense (leased equipment)	20,000	
Accumulated Depreciation—Equipment		20,000

If Caterpillar pays property taxes, insurance, maintenance, and other operating costs during the year, it records them as expenses chargeable against the gross rental revenues.

If Caterpillar owns plant assets that it uses in addition to those leased to others, the company **separately classifies the leased equipment and accompanying accumulated depreciation** as Equipment Leased to Others or Investment in Leased Property. If significant in amount or in terms of activity, Caterpillar separates the rental revenues and accompanying expenses in the income statement from sales revenue and cost of goods sold.

SPECIAL LEASE ACCOUNTING PROBLEMS

6 LEARNING OBJECTIVE
Identify special features of lease arrangements that cause unique accounting problems.

The features of lease arrangements that cause unique accounting problems are:

1. Residual values.
2. Sales-type leases (lessor).
3. Bargain-purchase options.

4. Initial direct costs.
5. Current versus noncurrent classification.
6. Disclosure.

We discuss each of these features on the following pages.

Residual Values

LEARNING OBJECTIVE 7
Describe the effect of residual values, guaranteed and unguaranteed, on lease accounting.

Up to this point, in order to develop the basic accounting issues related to lessee and lessor accounting, we have generally ignored residual values. Accounting for residual values is complex and will probably provide you with the greatest challenge in understanding lease accounting.

Meaning of Residual Value

The **residual value** is the estimated fair value of the leased asset at the end of the lease term. Frequently, a significant residual value exists at the end of the lease term, especially when the economic life of the leased asset exceeds the lease term. If title does not pass automatically to the lessee (criterion 1) and if a bargain-purchase option does not exist (criterion 2), the lessee returns physical custody of the asset to the lessor at the end of the lease term.[12]

Guaranteed versus Unguaranteed

The residual value may be unguaranteed or guaranteed by the lessee. Sometimes the lessee agrees to make up any deficiency below a stated amount that the lessor realizes in residual value at the end of the lease term. In such a case, that stated amount is the **guaranteed residual value**.

The parties to a lease use guaranteed residual value in lease arrangements for two reasons. The first is a business reason: It protects the lessor against any loss in estimated residual value, thereby ensuring the lessor of the desired rate of return on investment. The second reason is an accounting benefit that you will learn from the discussion at the end of this chapter.

Lease Payments

A guaranteed residual value—by definition—has more assurance of realization than does an unguaranteed residual value. As a result, the lessor may adjust lease payments because of the increased certainty of recovery. After the lessor establishes this rate, it makes no difference from an accounting point of view whether the residual value is guaranteed or unguaranteed. The net investment that the lessor records (once the rate is set) will be the same.

Assume the same data as in the Caterpillar/Sterling illustrations except that Caterpillar estimates a residual value of $5,000 at the end of the five-year lease term. In addition, Caterpillar assumes a 10 percent return on investment (ROI),[13] whether the residual value is guaranteed or unguaranteed. Caterpillar would compute the amount of the lease payments as follows.

[12]When the lease term and the economic life are not the same, the residual value and the salvage value of the asset will probably differ. For simplicity, we will assume that residual value and salvage value are the same, even when the economic life and lease term vary.

[13]Technically, the rate of return Caterpillar demands would differ depending upon whether the residual value was guaranteed or unguaranteed. To simplify the illustrations, we are ignoring this difference in subsequent sections.

ILLUSTRATION 21-16
Lessor's Computation of Lease Payments

CATERPILLAR'S COMPUTATION OF LEASE PAYMENTS (10% ROI) GUARANTEED OR UNGUARANTEED RESIDUAL VALUE ANNUITY-DUE BASIS, INCLUDING RESIDUAL VALUE	
Fair value of leased asset to lessor	$100,000.00
Less: Present value of residual value ($5,000 × .62092, Table 6-2)	3,104.60
Amount to be recovered by lessor through lease payments	$ 96,895.40
Five periodic lease payments ($96,895.40 ÷ 4.16986, Table 6-5)	$ 23,237.09

Contrast the foregoing lease payment amount to the lease payments of $23,981.62 as computed in Illustration 21-9 (on page 1284), where no residual value existed. In the second example, the payments are less, because the present value of the residual value reduces Caterpillar's total recoverable amount from $100,000 to $96,895.40.

Lessee Accounting for Residual Value

Whether the estimated residual value is guaranteed or unguaranteed has both economic and accounting consequence to the lessee. We saw the economic consequence—lower lease payments—in the preceding example. The accounting consequence is that the **minimum lease payments**, the basis for capitalization, include the guaranteed residual value but exclude the unguaranteed residual value.

Guaranteed Residual Value (Lessee Accounting). A guaranteed residual value affects the lessee's computation of minimum lease payments. Therefore, it also affects the amounts capitalized as a leased asset and a lease obligation. In effect, the guaranteed residual value **is an additional lease payment that the lessee will pay in property or cash, or both, at the end of the lease term.**

Using the rental payments as computed by the lessor in Illustration 21-16, the minimum lease payments are $121,185.45 ([$23,237.09 × 5] + $5,000). Illustration 21-17 shows the capitalized present value of the minimum lease payments (excluding executory costs) for Sterling Construction.

ILLUSTRATION 21-17
Computation of Lessee's Capitalized Amount—Guaranteed Residual Value

STERLING'S CAPITALIZED AMOUNT (10% RATE) ANNUITY-DUE BASIS, INCLUDING **GUARANTEED** RESIDUAL VALUE	
Present value of five annual rental payments ($23,237.09 × 4.16986, Table 6-5)	$ 96,895.40
Present value of guaranteed residual value of $5,000 due five years after date of inception: ($5,000 × .62092, Table 6-2)	3,104.60
Lessee's capitalized amount	$100,000.00

Sterling prepares a schedule of interest expense and amortization of the $100,000 lease liability. That schedule, shown in Illustration 21-18 (page 1292), is based on a $5,000 final guaranteed residual value payment at the end of five years.

Sterling records the leased asset (front-end loader) and liability, depreciation, interest, property tax, and lease payments on the basis of a guaranteed residual value. (These journal entries are shown in Illustration 21-23, on page 1294.) The format of these entries is the same as illustrated earlier, although the amounts are different because of the guaranteed residual value. Sterling records the loader at $100,000 and depreciates it over five years. To compute depreciation, it subtracts the guaranteed

ILLUSTRATION 21-18
Lease Amortization Schedule for Lessee—Guaranteed Residual Value

STERLING CONSTRUCTION
LEASE AMORTIZATION SCHEDULE
ANNUITY-DUE BASIS, **GUARANTEED** RESIDUAL VALUE—GRV

Date	Lease Payment Plus GRV	Executory Costs	Interest (10%) on Liability	Reduction of Lease Liability	Lease Liability
	(a)	(b)	(c)	(d)	(e)
1/1/14					$100,000.00
1/1/14	$ 25,237.09	$ 2,000	-0-	$ 23,237.09	76,762.91
1/1/15	25,237.09	2,000	$ 7,676.29	15,560.80	61,202.11
1/1/16	25,237.09	2,000	6,120.21	17,116.88	44,085.23
1/1/17	25,237.09	2,000	4,408.52	18,828.57	25,256.66
1/1/18	25,237.09	2,000	2,525.67	20,711.42	4,545.24
12/31/18	5,000.00*		454.76**	4,545.24	-0-
	$131,185.45	$10,000	$21,185.45	$100,000.00	

(a) Annual lease payment as required by lease.
(b) Executory costs included in rental payment.
(c) Preceding balance of (e) × 10%, except 1/1/14.
(d) (a) minus (b) and (c).
(e) Preceding balance minus (d).

*Represents the guaranteed residual value.
**Rounded by 24 cents.

residual value from the cost of the loader. Assuming that Sterling uses the straight-line method, the depreciation expense each year is $19,000 ([$100,000 − $5,000] ÷ 5 years).

At the end of the lease term, before the lessee transfers the asset to Caterpillar, the lease asset and liability accounts have the following balances.

ILLUSTRATION 21-19
Account Balances on Lessee's Books at End of Lease Term—Guaranteed Residual Value

Leased equipment (under capital leases)	$100,000.00	Interest payable	$ 454.76
Less: Accumulated depreciation—capital leases	95,000.00	Lease liability	4,545.24
	$ 5,000.00		$5,000.00

If at the end of the lease the fair value of the residual value is less than $5,000, Sterling will have to record a loss. Assume that Sterling depreciated the leased asset down to its residual value of $5,000 but that the fair value of the residual value at December 31, 2018, was $3,000. In this case, Sterling would have to report a loss of $2,000. Assuming that it pays cash to make up the residual value deficiency, Sterling would make the following journal entry.

Loss on Capital Lease	2,000.00	
Interest Expense (or Interest Payable)	454.76	
Lease Liability	4,545.24	
Accumulated Depreciation—Capital Leases	95,000.00	
Leased Equipment (under capital leases)		100,000.00
Cash		2,000.00

If the fair value *exceeds* $5,000, a gain may be recognized. Caterpillar and Sterling may apportion gains on guaranteed residual values in whatever ratio the parties initially agree.

When there is a guaranteed residual value, the lessee must be careful not to depreciate the total cost of the asset. For example, if Sterling mistakenly depreciated the total cost of the loader ($100,000), a misstatement would occur. That is, the carrying amount of the asset at the end of the lease term would be zero, but Sterling would show the liability under the capital lease at $5,000. In that case, if the asset was worth $5,000, Sterling would end up reporting a gain of $5,000 when it transferred the asset back to

Caterpillar. As a result, Sterling would overstate depreciation and would understate net income in 2014–2017; in the last year (2018) net income would be overstated.

Unguaranteed Residual Value (Lessee Accounting). From the lessee's viewpoint, an **unguaranteed residual value** is the same as no residual value in terms of its effect upon the lessee's method of computing the minimum lease payments and the capitalization of the leased asset and the lease liability.

Assume the same facts as those above except that the $5,000 residual value is **unguaranteed** instead of guaranteed. The amount of the annual lease payments would be the same—$23,237.09. Whether the residual value is guaranteed or unguaranteed, Caterpillar will recover the same amount through lease rentals—that is, $96,895.40. The minimum lease payments are $116,185.45 ($23,237.09 × 5). Sterling would capitalize the amount shown in Illustration 21-20.

ILLUSTRATION 21-20
Computation of Lessee's Capitalized Amount—Unguaranteed Residual Value

STERLING'S CAPITALIZED AMOUNT (10% RATE)
ANNUITY-DUE BASIS, INCLUDING **UNGUARANTEED** RESIDUAL VALUE

Present value of 5 annual rental payments of $23,237.09 × 4.16986 (Table 6-5)	$96,895.40
Unguaranteed residual value of $5,000 (not capitalized by lessee)	–0–
Lessee's capitalized amount	$96,895.40

Illustration 21-21 shows Sterling's schedule of interest expense and amortization of the lease liability of $96,895.40, assuming an unguaranteed residual value of $5,000 at the end of five years.

ILLUSTRATION 21-21
Lease Amortization Schedule for Lessee—Unguaranteed Residual Value

STERLING CONSTRUCTION
LEASE AMORTIZATION SCHEDULE (10%)
ANNUITY-DUE BASIS, **UNGUARANTEED** RESIDUAL VALUE

Date	Annual Lease Payments	Executory Costs	Interest (10%) on Liability	Reduction of Lease Liability	Lease Liability
	(a)	(b)	(c)	(d)	(e)
1/1/14					$96,895.40
1/1/14	$ 25,237.09	$ 2,000	–0–	$23,237.09	73,658.31
1/1/15	25,237.09	2,000	$ 7,365.83	15,871.26	57,787.05
1/1/16	25,237.09	2,000	5,778.71	17,458.38	40,328.67
1/1/17	25,237.09	2,000	4,032.87	19,204.22	21,124.45
1/1/18	25,237.09	2,000	2,112.64*	21,124.45	–0–
	$126,185.45	$10,000	$19,290.05	$96,895.40	

(a) Annual lease payment as required by lease.
(b) Executory costs included in rental payment.
(c) Preceding balance of (e) × 10%.
(d) (a) minus (b) and (c).
(e) Preceding balance minus (d).

*Rounded by 19 cents.

Sterling records the leased asset and liability, depreciation, interest, property tax, and lease payments on the basis of an unguaranteed residual value. (These journal entries are shown in Illustration 21-23 on page 1294.) The format of these capital lease entries is the same as illustrated earlier. Note that Sterling records the leased asset at $96,895.40 and depreciates it over five years. Assuming that it uses the straight-line method, the depreciation expense each year is $19,379.08 ($96,895.40 ÷ 5 years). At the end of the lease term, before Sterling transfers the asset to Caterpillar, the lease asset and liability accounts have the following balances.

ILLUSTRATION 21-22
Account Balances on Lessee's Books at End of Lease Term—Unguaranteed Residual Value

Leased equipment (under capital leases)	$96,895	Lease liability	$-0-
Less: Accumulated depreciation—capital leases	96,895		
	$ -0-		

Assuming that Sterling has fully depreciated the leased asset and has fully amortized the lease liability, no entry is required at the end of the lease term, except to remove the asset from the books.

If Sterling depreciated the asset down to its unguaranteed residual value, a misstatement would occur. That is, the carrying amount of the leased asset would be $5,000 at the end of the lease, but the liability under the capital lease would be stated at zero before the transfer of the asset. Thus, Sterling would end up reporting a loss of $5,000 when it transferred the asset back to Caterpillar. Sterling would understate depreciation and would overstate net income in 2014–2017; in the last year (2018), net income would be understated because of the recorded loss.

Lessee Entries Involving Residual Values. Illustration 21-23 shows, in comparative form, Sterling's entries for both a guaranteed and an unguaranteed residual value.

ILLUSTRATION 21-23
Comparative Entries for Guaranteed and Unguaranteed Residual Values, Lessee Company

Guaranteed Residual Value			Unguaranteed Residual Value		
Capitalization of lease (January 1, 2014):					
Leased Equipment (under capital leases)	100,000.00		Leased Equipment (under capital leases)	96,895.40	
Lease Liability		100,000.00	Lease Liability		96,895.40
First payment (January 1, 2014):					
Property Tax Expense	2,000.00		Property Tax Expense	2,000.00	
Lease Liability	23,237.09		Lease Liability	23,237.09	
Cash		25,237.09	Cash		25,237.09
Adjusting entry for accrued interest (December 31, 2014):					
Interest Expense	7,676.29		Interest Expense	7,365.83	
Interest Payable		7,676.29	Interest Payable		7,365.83
Entry to record depreciation (December 31, 2014):					
Depreciation Expense (capital leases)	19,000.00		Depreciation Expense (capital leases)	19,379.08	
Accumulated Depreciation—Capital Leases ([$100,000 − $5,000] ÷ 5 years)		19,000.00	Accumulated Depreciation—Capital Leases ($96,895.40 ÷ 5 years)		19,379.08
Second payment (January 1, 2015):					
Property Tax Expense	2,000.00		Property Tax Expense	2,000.00	
Lease Liability	15,560.80		Lease Liability	15,871.26	
Interest Expense (or Interest Payable)	7,676.29		Interest Expense (or Interest Payable)	7,365.83	
Cash		25,237.09	Cash		25,237.09

Lessor Accounting for Residual Value

As we indicated earlier, the lessor will recover the same net investment whether the residual value is guaranteed or unguaranteed. That is, the lessor works on the assumption that it will realize **the residual value at the end of the lease term whether guaranteed or unguaranteed**. The lease payments required in order for the company to earn a certain return on investment are the same (e.g., $23,237.09 in our example) whether the residual value is guaranteed or unguaranteed.

To illustrate, we again use the Caterpillar/Sterling data and assume classification of the lease as a direct-financing lease. With a residual value (either guaranteed or unguaranteed) of $5,000, Caterpillar determines the payments as shown in Illustration 21-24.

ILLUSTRATION 21-24
Computation of Direct-Financing Lease Payments

Fair value of leased equipment	$100,000.00
Less: Present value of residual value ($5,000 × .62092, Table 6-2)	3,104.60
Amount to be recovered by lessor through lease payments	$ 96,895.40
Five beginning-of-the-year lease payments to yield a 10% return ($96,895.40 ÷ 4.16986, Table 6-5)	$ 23,237.09

The amortization schedule is the same for guaranteed or unguaranteed residual value, as Illustration 21-25 shows.

ILLUSTRATION 21-25
Lease Amortization Schedule, for Lessor—Guaranteed or Unguaranteed Residual Value

CATERPILLAR FINANCIAL
LEASE AMORTIZATION SCHEDULE
ANNUITY-DUE BASIS, **GUARANTEED OR UNGUARANTEED** RESIDUAL VALUE

Date	Annual Lease Payment Plus Residual Value	Executory Costs	Interest (10%) on Lease Receivable	Lease Receivable Recovery	Lease Receivable
	(a)	(b)	(c)	(d)	(e)
1/1/14					$100,000.00
1/1/14	$ 25,237.09	$ 2,000.00	$ -0-	$ 23,237.09	76,762.91
1/1/15	25,237.09	2,000.00	7,676.29	15,560.80	61,202.11
1/1/16	25,237.09	2,000.00	6,120.21	17,116.88	44,085.23
1/1/17	25,237.09	2,000.00	4,408.52	18,828.57	25,256.66
1/1/18	25,237.09	2,000.00	2,525.67	20,711.42	4,545.24
12/31/18	5,000.00	-0-	454.76*	4,545.24	-0-
	$131,185.45	$10,000.00	$21,185.45	$100,000.00	

(a) Annual lease payment as required by lease.
(b) Executory costs included in rental payment.
(c) Preceding balance of (e) × 10%, except 1/1/14.
(d) (a) minus (b) and (c).
(e) Preceding balance minus (d).
*Rounded by 24 cents.

Using the amounts computed above, Caterpillar would make the following entries for this direct-financing lease in the first year. Note the similarity to Sterling's entries in Illustration 21-23.

ILLUSTRATION 21-26
Entries for Either Guaranteed or Unguaranteed Residual Value, Lessor Company

Inception of lease (January 1, 2014):		
Lease Receivable	100,000.00	
Equipment		100,000.00
First payment received (January 1, 2014):		
Cash	25,237.09	
Lease Receivable		23,237.09
Property Tax Expense/Property Taxes Payable		2,000.00
Adjusting entry for accrued interest (December 31, 2014):		
Interest Receivable	7,676.29	
Interest Revenue		7,676.29

Sales-Type Leases (Lessor)

LEARNING OBJECTIVE 8
Describe the lessor's accounting for sale-type leases.

As already indicated, the primary difference between a direct-financing lease and a **sales-type lease** is the manufacturer's or dealer's gross profit (or loss). The diagram in Illustration 21-27 presents the distinctions between direct-financing and sales-type leases.

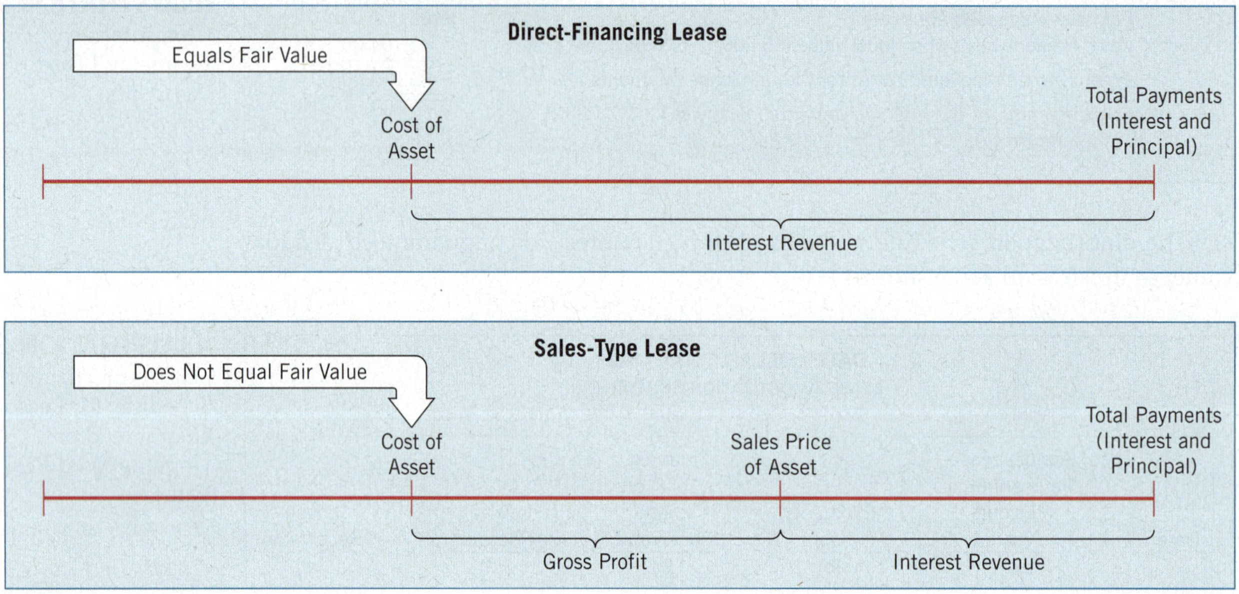

ILLUSTRATION 21-27
Direct-Financing versus Sales-Type Leases

In a sales-type lease, the lessor records the sales price of the asset, the cost of goods sold and related inventory reduction, and the lease receivable. The information necessary to record the sales-type lease is as follows.

SALES-TYPE LEASE TERMS

LEASE RECEIVABLE (also referred to as **NET INVESTMENT**). The present value of the minimum lease payments plus the present value of any unguaranteed residual value. The lease receivable therefore includes the present value of the residual value, whether guaranteed or not.

SALES PRICE OF THE ASSET. The present value of the minimum lease payments.

COST OF GOODS SOLD. The cost of the asset to the lessor, less the present value of any unguaranteed residual value.

When recording sales revenue and cost of goods sold, there is a difference in the accounting for guaranteed and unguaranteed residual values. The guaranteed residual value can be considered part of sales revenue because the lessor knows that the entire asset has been sold. But there is less certainty that the unguaranteed residual portion of the asset has been "sold" (i.e., will be realized). Therefore, the lessor recognizes sales and cost of goods sold only for the portion of the asset for which realization is assured. However, **the gross profit amount on the sale of the asset is the same whether a guaranteed or unguaranteed residual value is involved**.

To illustrate a sales-type lease with a guaranteed residual value and with an unguaranteed residual value, assume the same facts as in the preceding direct-financing lease situation (pages 1286–1287). The estimated residual value is $5,000 (the present value of which is $3,104.60), and the leased equipment has an $85,000 cost to the dealer, Caterpillar. Assume that the fair value of the residual value is $3,000 at the end of the lease term.

Illustration 21-28 shows computation of the amounts relevant to a sales-type lease.

ILLUSTRATION 21-28
Computation of Lease Amounts by Caterpillar Financial—Sales-Type Lease

	Sales-Type Lease	
	Guaranteed Residual Value	Unguaranteed Residual Value
Lease receivable	\$100,000 [\$23,237.09 × 4.16986 (Table 6-5) + \$5,000 ×.62092 (Table 6-2)]	Same
Sales price of the asset	\$100,000	\$96,895.40 (\$100,000 − \$3,104.60)
Cost of goods sold	\$85,000	\$81,895.40 (\$85,000 − \$3,104.60)
Gross profit	\$15,000 (\$100,000 − \$85,000)	\$15,000 (\$96,895.40 − \$81,895.40)

Caterpillar records the same profit (\$15,000) at the point of sale whether the residual value is guaranteed or unguaranteed. The difference between the two is that **the sales revenue and cost of goods sold amounts are different.**

In making this computation, we deduct the present value of the unguaranteed residual value from sales revenue and cost of goods sold for two reasons. (1) The criteria for revenue recognition have not been met. (2) It is improper to record an expense against revenue not yet recognized. The revenue recognition criteria have not been met **because of the uncertainty surrounding the realization of the unguaranteed residual value.**

Caterpillar makes the following entries to record this transaction on January 1, 2014, and the receipt of the residual value at the end of the lease term.

ILLUSTRATION 21-29
Entries for Guaranteed and Unguaranteed Residual Values, Lessor Company—Sales-Type Lease

Guaranteed Residual Value			Unguaranteed Residual Value		
To record sales-type lease at inception (January 1, 2014):					
Cost of Goods Sold	85,000.00		Cost of Goods Sold	81,895.40	
Lease Receivable	100,000.00		Lease Receivable	100,000.00	
Sales Revenue		100,000.00	Sales Revenue		96,895.40
Inventory		85,000.00	Inventory		85,000.00
To record receipt of the first lease payment (January 1, 2014):					
Cash	25,237.09		Cash	25,237.09	
Lease Receivable		23,237.09	Lease Receivable		23,237.09
Property Tax Exp./Pay.		2,000.00	Property Tax Exp./Pay.		2,000.00
To recognize interest revenue during the first year (December 31, 2014):					
Interest Receivable	7,676.29		Interest Receivable	7,676.29	
Interest Revenue		7,676.29	Interest Revenue		7,676.29
(See lease amortization schedule, Illustration 21-25 on page 1295)					
To record receipt of the second lease payment (January 1, 2015):					
Cash	25,237.09		Cash	25,237.09	
Interest Receivable		7,676.29	Interest Receivable		7,676.29
Lease Receivable		15,560.80	Lease Receivable		15,560.80
Property Tax Exp./Pay.		2,000.00	Property Tax Exp./Pay.		2,000.00
To recognize interest revenue during the second year (December 31, 2015):					
Interest Receivable	6,120.21		Interest Receivable	6,120.21	
Interest Revenue		6,120.21	Interest Revenue		6,120.21
To record receipt of residual value at end of lease term (December 31, 2018):					
Inventory	3,000		Inventory	3,000	
Cash	2,000		Loss on Capital Lease	2,000	
Lease Receivable		5,000	Lease Receivable		5,000

Gateway to the Profession

Expanded Discussion of Real Estate Leases and Leveraged Leases

Companies must periodically review the **estimated unguaranteed residual value in a sales-type lease**. If the estimate of the unguaranteed residual value declines, the company must revise the accounting for the transaction using the changed estimate. The decline represents a reduction in the lessor's lease receivable (net investment). The lessor recognizes the decline as a loss in the period in which it reduces the residual estimate. Companies do not recognize upward adjustments in estimated residual value.

What do the numbers mean? XEROX TAKES ON THE SEC

Xerox derives much of its income from leasing equipment. Reporting such leases as sales leases, Xerox records a lease contract as a sale, thereby recognizing income immediately. One problem is that each lease receipt consists of payments for items such as supplies, services, financing, and equipment.

The SEC *accused* Xerox of inappropriately allocating lease receipts, which affects the timing of income that it reports. If Xerox applied SEC guidelines, it would report income in different time periods. Xerox contended that its methods were correct. It also noted that when the lease term is up, the bottom line is the same using either the SEC's recommended allocation method or its current method.

Although Xerox can refuse to change its method, the SEC has the right to prevent a company from selling stock or bonds to the public if the agency rejects financial filings of the company.

Apparently, being able to access public markets is very valuable to Xerox. The company agreed to change its accounting according to SEC wishes, and Xerox will pay $670 million to settle a shareholder lawsuit related to its lease transactions. Its former auditor, KPMG LLP, will pay $80 million.

Sources: Adapted from "Xerox Takes on the SEC," *Accounting Web* (January 9, 2002), *www.account-ingweb.com*; and K. Shwiff and M. Maremont, "Xerox, KPMG Settle Shareholder Lawsuit," *Wall Street Journal Online* (March 28, 2008), p. B3.

Bargain-Purchase Option (Lessee)

As stated earlier, a bargain-purchase option allows the lessee to purchase the leased property for a future price that is substantially lower than the property's expected future fair value. The price is so favorable at the lease's inception that the future exercise of the option appears to be reasonably assured. If a bargain-purchase option exists, **the lessee must increase the present value of the minimum lease payments by the present value of the option price**.

For example, assume that Sterling Construction (see Illustration 21-18 on page 1292) had an option to buy the leased equipment for $5,000 at the end of the five-year lease term. At that point, Sterling and Caterpillar expect the fair value to be $18,000. The significant difference between the option price and the fair value creates a bargain-purchase option, and the exercise of that option is reasonably assured.

A bargain-purchase option affects the accounting for leases in essentially the same way as a guaranteed residual value. In other words, with a guaranteed residual value, the lessee must pay the residual value at the end of the lease. Similarly, a purchase option that is a bargain will almost certainly be paid by the lessee. Therefore, the computations, amortization schedule, and entries that would be prepared for this $5,000 bargain-purchase option are identical to those shown for the $5,000 guaranteed residual value (see Illustrations 21-16, 21-17, and 21-18 on pages 1291 and 1292).

The only difference between the accounting treatment for a bargain-purchase option and a guaranteed residual value of identical amounts and circumstances is in the **computation of the annual depreciation**. In the case of a guaranteed residual value, Sterling depreciates the asset over the lease term. In the case of a bargain-purchase option, it uses the **economic life** of the asset.

Initial Direct Costs (Lessor)

Initial direct costs are of two types: incremental and internal. [8] **Incremental direct costs** are paid to independent third parties for originating a lease arrangement. Examples include the cost of independent appraisal of collateral used to secure a lease, the cost of an outside credit check of the lessee, or a broker's fee for finding the lessee.

Internal direct costs are directly related to specified activities performed **by the lessor** on a given lease. Examples are evaluating the prospective lessee's financial condition; evaluating and recording guarantees, collateral, and other security arrangements; negotiating lease terms and preparing and processing lease documents; and closing the transaction. The costs directly related to an employee's time spent on a specific lease transaction are also considered initial direct costs.

However, initial direct costs should **not** include **internal indirect costs**. Such costs are related to activities the lessor performs for advertising, servicing existing leases, and establishing and monitoring credit policies. Nor should the lessor include the costs for supervision and administration or for expenses such as rent and depreciation.

The accounting for initial direct costs depends on the type of lease:

- For **operating leases**, the lessor should defer initial direct costs and **allocate them over the lease term** in proportion to the recognition of rental revenue.
- For **sales-type leases**, the lessor expenses the initial direct costs **in the period** in which it recognizes the profit on the sale.
- For a **direct-financing lease**, the lessor adds initial direct costs to the net investment in the lease and **amortizes them over the life of the lease as a yield adjustment**.

In a direct-financing lease, the lessor must disclose the unamortized deferred initial direct costs that are part of its investment in the direct-financing lease. For example, if the carrying value of the asset in the lease is $4,000,000 and the lessor incurs initial direct costs of $35,000, then the lease receivable (net investment in the lease) would be $4,035,000. The yield would be lower than the initial rate of return, and the lessor would adjust the yield to ensure proper amortization of the amount over the life of the lease.

Current versus Noncurrent

Earlier in the chapter, we presented the classification of the lease liability/receivable in an annuity-due situation. Illustration 21-7 (on page 1280) indicated that Sterling's current liability is the payment of $23,981.62 (excluding $2,000 of executory costs) to be made on January 1 of the next year. Similarly, as shown in Illustration 21-15 (on page 1288), Caterpillar's current asset is the $23,981.62 (excluding $2,000 of executory costs) it will collect on January 1 of the next year. In these annuity-due instances, the balance sheet date is December 31 and the due date of the lease payment is January 1 (less than one year), so the present value ($23,981.62) of the payment due the following January 1 is the same as the rental payment ($23,981.62).

What happens if the situation is an ordinary annuity rather than an annuity due? For example, assume that the rent is due at the **end of the year** (December 31) rather than at the beginning (January 1). GAAP does not indicate how to measure the current and noncurrent amounts. It requires that for the lessee the "obligations shall be separately identified on the balance sheet as obligations under capital leases and shall be subject to the same considerations as other obligations in classifying them with current and noncurrent liabilities in classified balance sheets." **[9] The most common method of measuring the current liability portion in ordinary annuity leases is the change-in-the-present-value method.**[14]

[14]For additional discussion on this approach and possible alternatives, see R. J. Swieringa, "When Current Is Noncurrent and Vice Versa!" *The Accounting Review* (January 1984), pp. 123–30; and A. W. Richardson, "The Measurement of the Current Portion of the Long-Term Lease Obligations—Some Evidence from Practice," *The Accounting Review* (October 1985), pp. 744–52.

To illustrate the change-in-the-present-value method, assume an ordinary-annuity situation with the same facts as the Caterpillar/Sterling case, excluding the $2,000 of executory costs. Because Sterling pays the rents at the end of the period instead of at the beginning, Caterpillar sets the five rents at $26,379.73, to have an effective-interest rate of 10 percent. Illustration 21-30 shows the ordinary-annuity amortization schedule.

ILLUSTRATION 21-30
Lease Amortization Schedule—Ordinary-Annuity Basis

STERLING/CATERPILLAR
LEASE AMORTIZATION SCHEDULE
ORDINARY-ANNUITY BASIS

Date	Annual Lease Payment	Interest 10%	Reduction of Lease Liability/Receivable	Balance of Lease Liability/Receivable
1/1/14				$100,000.00
12/31/14	$ 26,379.73	$10,000.00	$ 16,379.73	83,620.27
12/31/15	26,379.73	8,362.03	18,017.70	65,602.57
12/31/16	26,379.73	6,560.26	19,819.47	45,783.10
12/31/17	26,379.73	4,578.31	21,801.42	23,981.68
12/31/18	26,379.73	2,398.05*	23,981.68	–0–
	$131,898.65	$31,898.65	$100,000.00	

*Rounded by 12 cents.

The current portion of the lease liability/receivable under the **change-in-the-present-value method** as of December 31, 2014, would be $18,017.70 ($83,620.27 − $65,602.57). At December 31, 2014, Caterpillar classifies $65,602.57 of the receivable as noncurrent. As of December 31, 2015, the current portion would be $19,819.47 ($65,602.57 − $45,783.10).

Thus, both the annuity-due and the ordinary-annuity situations report the reduction of principal for the next period as a current liability/current asset. In the annuity-due situation, Caterpillar accrues interest during the year but is not paid until the next period. As a result, **a current asset arises for the receivable reduction and for the interest** that was recognized in the preceding period.

In the ordinary-annuity situation, the interest accrued during the period is also paid in the same period. Consequently, the lessor shows as a current asset only the principal reduction.

Disclosing Lease Data

LEARNING OBJECTIVE 9
List the disclosure requirements for leases.

The FASB requires **lessees** and **lessors** to disclose certain information about leases in their financial statements or in the notes. These requirements vary based upon the type of lease (capital or operating) and whether the issuer is the lessor or lessee. These disclosure requirements provide investors with the following information.

- General description of the nature of leasing arrangements.
- The nature, timing, and amount of cash inflows and outflows associated with leases, including payments to be paid or received for each of the five succeeding years.
- The amount of lease revenues and expenses reported in the income statement each period.
- Description and amounts of leased assets by major balance sheet classification and related liabilities.
- Amounts receivable and unearned revenues under lease agreements. **[10]**

Illustration 21-31 presents financial statement excerpts from the annual report of **Wal-Mart Stores, Inc.** dated January 31, 2012. These excerpts represent the statement and note disclosures typical of a lessee having both capital leases and operating leases.

ILLUSTRATION 21-31
Disclosure of Leases by Lessee

Wal-Mart Stores, Inc.

(dollar amounts in millions)

	Jan. 31, 2012	Jan. 31, 2011
Current Liabilities		
Obligations under capital leases due within one year	$ 326	$ 336
Noncurrent Liabilities		
Long-term obligations under capital leases	$3,009	$3,150

Description and amount of lease obligations

Note 12: Commitments

The Company and certain of its subsidiaries have long-term leases for stores and equipment. Aggregate minimum annual rentals at January 31, 2012, under non-cancelable leases are as follows (dollar amounts in millions):

General description

	Operating Leases	Capital Leases
2013	$1,644	$ 608
2014	1,590	580
2015	1,525	532
2016	1,428	497
2017	1,312	457
Thereafter	8,916	3,261
Total minimum rentals		$5,935
Less estimated executory costs		50
Net minimum lease payments		$5,885
Less imputed interest		2,550
Present value of minimum lease payments		$3,335

Description and amounts of leased assets

Rental expense was approximately $2.4 billion in 2012 and $2 billion in 2011.

Certain of the Company's leases provide for the payment of contingent rentals based on a percentage of sales. Such contingent rentals were immaterial for fiscal 2012 and 2011. Substantially all of the Company's store leases have renewal options, some of which may trigger an escalation in rentals. The Company has future lease commitments for land and buildings for approximately 425 future locations. These lease commitments have lease terms ranging from 4 to 50 years and provide for certain minimum rentals. If executed, payments under operating leases would increase by $92 million for fiscal 2013, based on current cost estimates.

Nature, timing, and amounts of cash outflows

Amount of lease rental expense

Illustration 21-32 presents the lease note disclosure from the 2011 annual report of **Hewlett-Packard Company**. The disclosure highlights required lessor disclosures.

ILLUSTRATION 21-32
Disclosure of Leases by Lessor

Hewlett-Packard Company

Notes to Financial Statements
(in millions)

Note 11: Financing Receivables and Operating Leases

Financing receivables represent sales-type and direct-financing leases resulting from the marketing of HP's and third-party products. These receivables typically have terms from two to five years and are usually collateralized by a security interest in the underlying assets. Financing receivables also include billed receivables from operating leases. The components of net financing receivables, which are included in financing receivables and long-term financing receivables and other assets, were as follows for the following fiscal years ended October 31:

General description

	2011	2010
Minimum lease payments receivable	$7,721	$7,094
Allowance for doubtful accounts	(130)	(140)
Unguaranteed residual value	233	212
Unearned income	(647)	(596)
Financing receivables, net	7,177	6,570
Less current portion	(3,162)	(2,986)
Amounts due after one year, net	$4,015	$3,584

Amount receivable and unearned revenues

ILLUSTRATION 21-32
(Continued)

Nature, timing, and amounts of cash inflows

As of October 31, 2011, scheduled maturities of HP's minimum lease payments receivable were as follows for the following fiscal years ended October 31:

	2012	2013	2014	2015	Thereafter	Total
Scheduled maturities of minimum lease payments receivable	$3,518	$2,256	$1,257	$517	$173	$7,721

Description of leased assets

Equipment leased to customers under operating leases was $4.0 billion at October 31, 2011 and $3.5 billion at October 31, 2010 and is included in machinery and equipment. Accumulated depreciation on equipment under lease was $1.3 billion at October 31, 2011 and $1.0 billion at October 31, 2010. As of October 31, 2011, minimum future rentals on non-cancelable operating leases related to leased equipment were as follows for the following fiscal years ended October 31:

Amount of future rentals

	2012	2013	2014	2015	Thereafter	Total
Minimum future rentals on non-cancelable operating leases	$1,273	$801	$414	$152	$42	$2,682

Unresolved Lease Accounting Problems

As we indicated at the beginning of this chapter, lease accounting is subject to abuse. Companies make strenuous efforts to circumvent GAAP in this area. In practice, the strong desires of lessees to resist capitalization have rendered the accounting rules for capitalizing leases partially ineffective. Leasing generally involves large dollar amounts that, when capitalized, materially increase reported liabilities and adversely affect the debt to equity ratio. Lessees also resist lease capitalization because charges to expense made in the early years of the lease term are higher under the capital lease method than under the operating method, frequently without tax benefit. As a consequence, "let's beat the lease standard" is one of the most popular games in town.[15]

To avoid leased asset capitalization, companies design, write, and interpret lease agreements to prevent satisfying any of the four capitalized lease criteria. Companies can easily devise lease agreements in such a way, by meeting the following specifications.

1. Ensure that the lease does not specify the transfer of title of the property to the lessee.
2. Do not write in a bargain-purchase option.
3. Set the lease term at something less than 75 percent of the estimated economic life of the leased property.
4. Arrange for the present value of the minimum lease payments to be less than 90 percent of the fair value of the leased property.

The real challenge lies in disqualifying the lease as a capital lease to the lessee, while having the same lease qualify as a capital (sales or financing) lease to the lessor. Unlike lessees, lessors try to avoid having lease arrangements classified as operating leases.[16]

Avoiding the first three criteria is relatively simple, but it takes a little ingenuity to avoid the "90 percent recovery test" for the lessee while satisfying it for the lessor. Two of the factors involved in this effort are (1) the use of the incremental borrowing rate by the lessee when it is higher than the implicit interest rate of the lessor, by making information about the implicit rate unavailable to the lessee, and (2) residual value guarantees.

[15]Richard Dieter, "Is Lessee Accounting Working?" *CPA Journal* (August 1979), pp. 13–19. This article provides interesting examples of abuses of GAAP in this area, discusses the circumstances that led to the current situation, and proposes a solution.

[16]The reason is that most lessors are banks, which are not permitted to hold these assets on their balance sheets except for relatively short periods of time. Furthermore, the capital lease transaction from the lessor's standpoint provides higher income flows in the earlier periods of the lease life.

The lessee's use of the higher interest rate is probably the more popular subterfuge. Lessees are knowledgeable about the fair value of the leased property and, of course, the rental payments. However, they generally are unaware of the estimated residual value used by the lessor. Therefore, the lessee who does not know exactly the lessor's implicit interest rate might use a different (higher) incremental borrowing rate.

The residual value guarantee is the other unique, yet popular, device used by lessees and lessors. In fact, a whole new industry has emerged to circumvent symmetry between the lessee and the lessor in accounting for leases. The residual value guarantee has spawned numerous companies whose principal, or even sole, function is to guarantee the residual value of leased assets.

International Perspective

The IASB and the FASB are working on a joint project to reconsider lease accounting standards.

Because the minimum lease payments include the guaranteed residual value for the lessor, this satisfies the 90 percent recovery of the fair value test. The lease is a nonoperating lease to the lessor. **But because a third-party guarantees the residual value, the minimum lease payments of the lessee exclude the guarantee.** Thus, by merely transferring some of the risk to a third party, lessees can alter substantially the accounting treatment by converting what would otherwise be capital leases to operating leases.[17]

You will want to read the **IFRS INSIGHTS** on pages 1331–1341 for discussion of IFRS related to lease accounting.

The nature of the criteria encourages much of this circumvention, stemming from weaknesses in the basic objective of the lease accounting guidelines. Accounting rule-makers continue to have poor experience with arbitrary break points or other size and percentage criteria—such as rules like "90 percent of" and "75 percent of." Some believe that a more workable solution is to require capitalization of all leases that have noncancelable payment terms in excess of one year. Under this approach, the lessee acquires an asset (a property right) and a corresponding liability, rather than on the basis that the lease transfers substantially all the risks and rewards of ownership.

Evolving Issue *LEASE ACCOUNTING—IF IT QUACKS LIKE A DUCK*

Three years after it issued a lease accounting pronouncement, a majority of the FASB expressed "the tentative view that, if the lease accounting rules were to be reconsidered, they would support a property right approach in which all leases are included as 'rights to use property' and as 'lease obligations' in the lessee's balance sheet." The FASB and IASB have issued a proposal on lease accounting to address off-balance-sheet reporting of leases. As summarized in the adjacent table, early analysis of the potential impact of the proposed leasing rules indicates significant impacts.

A quick look at the current leasing market, and some possible effects of the proposed rules:

- ***$600 billion.*** Annual volume of leased equipment.
- ***70%.*** Volume of real estate leases as a percentage of all leases held by U.S. public companies.
- ***$1.3 trillion.*** Amount of operating lease payments that U.S. public companies will bring back on balance sheets as capital leases under the proposed rule.
- ***7%.*** Potential first-year average increase in lease expense for a 3-year lease.
- ***21%.*** Potential first-year average increase in lease expense for a 10-year lease.

Source: Equipment Leasing and Finance Association, 2009; PricewaterhouseCoopers and Rotterdam School of Management, 2009.

As indicated, over $1.1 trillion of operating leases will come on-balance-sheet if the rules are adopted. In addition,

[17]As an aside, third-party guarantors have experienced some difficulty. **Lloyd's of London**, at one time, insured the fast-growing U.S. computer leasing industry in the amount of $2 billion against revenue losses, and losses in residual value, for canceled leases. Because of "overnight" technological improvements and the successive introductions of more efficient and less expensive computers, lessees in abundance canceled their leases. As the market for secondhand computers became flooded, residual values plummeted, and third-party guarantor Lloyd's of London projected a loss of $400 million. The lessees' and lessors' desire to circumvent GAAP stimulated much of the third-party guarantee business.

there will be a significant negative impact on lessee income statements in the early years of leases.

As shown below, the frontloading of lease expenses will be felt by lessees in several industry sectors.

Lease Expense Impacts by Industry Sector

Sector	Typical Lease Term (Years)	First-Year % Increase Prompted by New Rules*	Cumulative % Increase Through Peak Year*
Airline	17	26%	128%/yr. 9
Automotive fleet	3	4	N/A
Banking	10	21	64%/yr. 5
Copier/office equipment	3	7	7%/yr. 3
Equipment manufacturers	5	11	17%/yr. 2
Health-care equipment	5	11	17%/yr. 2
Information technology	3	7	7%/yr. 2
Rail	22	26	200%/yr. 12
Real estate	10	21	64%/yr. 5
Trucking	7	16	33%/yr. 4

*As compared with the straight-line method of accounting.

Source: Equipment Leasing and Finance Association, 2009.

Given these effects—increased reported debt and lower income—as a consequence of these proposed rules, it is not surprising that the FASB (and IASB) are receiving numerous comments opposing changes in lease accounting rules. At the same time, an analysis of the new rules and how they might impact the advantages of leasing presented in the following table suggests that many of the advantages of leases will remain after implementation of the new rules.

Reason for Leasing	Details	Status After Proposed New Rules Implemented
Funding source	Additional capital source, 100% financing, fixed rate, level payments, longer terms.	Still a major benefit versus a purchase—money loan financing, fixed rate, level payments—especially for smaller companies with limited sources of capital.
Low-cost capital	Low payments/rate due to tax benefits, residual and lessor's comparatively low cost of funds.	Still a benefit versus a loan.
Tax benefits	Lessee cannot use tax benefits and lease versus buy shows lease option offers lowest after tax cost.	Still a benefit.
Manage need for assets/ residual risk transfer	Lessee has flexibility to return asset.	Still a benefit.
Convenience	Quick and convenient financing process often available at point-of-sale.	Still a benefit.
Regulatory	Can help in meeting capital requirements.	Still a partial benefit if the capitalized amount is less than the cost of the asset as it is in many leases due to residuals assumed and tax benefits.
Accounting	Asset and liability off-balance-sheet.	Still a partial benefit if the capitalized amount is less than the cost of the asset as it is in many leases due to residuals assumed and tax benefits.

Source: Equipment Leasing & Finance Foundation, *2011 State of the Equipment Finance Industry Report*.

So while concerns about changes in lease accounting may be valid, accounting standard-setters are resolved to address lease accounting deficiencies. As the chairperson of the IASB remarked, ". . . a financing, in the form of a loan to purchase an asset, then it would be recorded. Call it a lease and miraculously it does not show up in your books. In my book, if it looks like a duck, swims like a duck, and quacks like a duck, then it probably is a duck. So is the case with debt— leasing or otherwise."

We hope that new accounting rules can be developed so that financial statements provide relevant and representationally faithful information about leasing arrangements.

Sources: M. Leone, "Taking the 'Ease' Out of 'Lease'?" *CFO Magazine* (December 1, 2010); and Hans Hoogervorst, "Harmonisation and Global Economic Consequences," Public lecture at the London School of Economics (November 6, 2012). For the latest on the lease project, go to *www.fasb.org* (click on Leases under the Projects tab).

SUMMARY OF LEARNING OBJECTIVES

1 Explain the nature, economic substance, and advantages of lease transactions. A lease is a contractual agreement between a lessor and a lessee that conveys to the lessee the right to use specific property (real or personal), owned by the lessor, for a specified period of time. In return, the lessee periodically pays cash (rent) to the lessor. The advantages of lease transactions are (1) 100 percent financing, (2) protection against obsolescence, (3) flexibility, (4) less costly financing, (5) possible tax advantages, and (6) off-balance-sheet financing.

2 Describe the accounting criteria and procedures for capitalizing leases by the lessee. A lease is a capital lease if it meets one or more of the following criteria. (1) The lease transfers ownership of the property to the lessee. (2) The lease contains a bargain-purchase option. (3) The lease term is equal to 75 percent or more of the estimated economic life of the leased property. (4) The present value of the minimum lease payments (excluding executory costs) equals or exceeds 90 percent of the fair value of the leased property. For a capital lease, the lessee records an asset and a liability at the lower of (1) the present value of the minimum lease payments, or (2) the fair value of the leased asset at the inception of the lease.

3 Contrast the operating and capitalization methods of recording leases. The total charges to operations are the same over the lease term whether accounting for the lease as a capital lease or as an operating lease. Under the capital lease treatment, the charges are higher in the earlier years and lower in the later years. If using an accelerated method of depreciation, the differences between the amounts charged to operations under the two methods would be even larger in the earlier and later years. If using a capital lease instead of an operating lease, the following occurs: (1) an increase in the amount of reported debt (both short-term and long-term), (2) an increase in the amount of total assets (specifically long-lived assets), and (3) lower income early in the life of the lease and, therefore, lower retained earnings.

4 Explain the advantages and economics of leasing to lessors and identify the classifications of leases for the lessor. Three important benefits available to the lessor are (1) interest revenue, (2) tax incentives, and (3) residual value profits. Lessors are essentially renting or selling assets, and in many cases are providing financing for the purchase of the asset. The lessor determines the amount of the rental, basing it on the rate of return—the implicit rate—needed to justify leasing the asset, taking into account the credit standing of the lessee, the length of the lease, and the status of the residual value (guaranteed versus unguaranteed).

A lessor may classify leases for accounting purposes as follows: (1) operating leases, (2) direct-financing leases, and (3) sales-type leases. The lessor should classify and account for an arrangement as a direct-financing lease or a sales-type lease if, at the date of the lease agreement, the lease meets one or more of the Group I criteria (as shown in Learning Objective 2 for lessees) and *both* of the following Group II criteria: (1) collectibility of the payments required from the lessee is reasonably predictable, and (2) no important uncertainties surround the amount of unreimbursable costs yet to be incurred by the lessor under the lease. The lessor classifies and accounts for all leases that fail to meet the criteria as operating leases.

5 Describe the lessor's accounting for direct-financing leases. Leases that are in substance the financing of an asset purchase by a lessee require the lessor to substitute a "lease receivable" for the leased asset. "Lease receivable" is the present value of the minimum lease payments plus the present value of the unguaranteed residual value. Therefore, lessors include the residual value, whether guaranteed or unguaranteed, as part of the lease receivable.

KEY TERMS

bargain-purchase option, *1275*
bargain-renewal option, *1276*
capitalization criteria, *1275*
capitalization of leases, *1273*
capital lease, *1275*
direct-financing lease, *1286*
effective-interest method, *1278*
executory costs, *1277*
guaranteed residual value, *1277, 1290*
implicit interest rate, *1277*
incremental borrowing rate, *1277*
initial direct costs, *1298*
lease, *1270*
lease receivable, *1286*
lease term, *1272*
lessee, *1270*
lessor, *1270*
manufacturer's or dealer's profit (or loss), *1285*
minimum lease payments, *1276*
noncancelable, *1274*
off-balance-sheet financing, *1272*
operating lease, *1275*
residual value, *1290*
sales-type lease, *1296*
third-party guarantors, *1277*
unguaranteed residual value, *1293*

6 Identify special features of lease arrangements that cause unique accounting problems. The features of lease arrangements that cause unique accounting problems are (1) residual values, (2) sales-type leases (lessor), (3) bargain-purchase options, (4) initial direct costs, (5) current versus noncurrent, and (6) disclosures.

7 Describe the effect of residual values, guaranteed and unguaranteed, on lease accounting. Whether the estimated residual value is guaranteed or unguaranteed is of both economic and accounting consequence to the lessee. The accounting consequence is that the minimum lease payments, the basis for capitalization, include the guaranteed residual value but exclude the unguaranteed residual value. A guaranteed residual value affects the lessee's computation of minimum lease payments and the amounts capitalized as a leased asset and a lease obligation. In effect, the guaranteed residual value is an additional lease payment that the lessee will pay in property or cash, or both, at the end of the lease term. An unguaranteed residual value from the lessee's viewpoint is the same as no residual value in terms of its effect upon the lessee's method of computing the minimum lease payments and the capitalization of the leased asset and the lease liability.

8 Describe the lessor's accounting for sales-type leases. A sales-type lease recognizes interest revenue like a direct-financing lease. It also recognizes a manufacturer's or dealer's profit. In a sales-type lease, the lessor records at the inception of the lease the sales price of the asset, the cost of goods sold and related inventory reduction, and the lease receivable. Sales-type leases differ from direct-financing leases in terms of the cost and fair value of the leased asset, which results in gross profit. Lease receivable and interest revenue are the same whether a guaranteed or an unguaranteed residual value is involved. The accounting for guaranteed and for unguaranteed residual values requires recording sales revenue and cost of goods sold differently. The guaranteed residual value can be considered part of sales revenue because the lessor knows that the entire asset has been sold. There is less certainty that the unguaranteed residual portion of the asset has been "sold." Therefore, lessors recognize sales and cost of goods sold only for the portion of the asset for which realization is assured. However, the gross profit amount on the sale of the asset is the same whether a guaranteed or unguaranteed residual value is involved.

9 List the disclosure requirements for leases. The disclosure requirements for the lessees and lessors vary based upon the type of lease (capital or operating) and whether the issuer is the lessor or lessee. These disclosure requirements provide investors with the following information: (1) general description of the nature of leasing arrangements; (2) the nature, timing, and amount of cash inflows and outflows associated with leases, including payments to be paid or received for each of the five succeeding years; (3) the amount of lease revenues and expenses reported in the income statement each period; (4) description and amounts of leased assets by major balance sheet classification and related liabilities; and (5) amounts receivable and unearned revenues under lease agreements.

APPENDIX 21A SALE-LEASEBACKS

LEARNING OBJECTIVE 10

Describe the lessee's accounting for sale-leaseback transactions.

The term **sale-leaseback** describes a transaction in which the owner of the property (seller-lessee) sells the property to another and simultaneously leases it back from the new owner. The use of the property is generally continued without interruption.

Sale-leasebacks are common. Financial institutions (e.g., **Bank of America** and **First Chicago**) have used this technique for their administrative offices, public utilities (**Ohio Edison** and **Pinnacle West Corporation**) for their generating plants, and airlines (**Continental** and **Alaska Airlines**) for their aircraft. The advantages of a sale-leaseback from the seller's viewpoint usually involve two primary considerations:

1. *Financing.* If the purchase of equipment has already been financed, a sale-leaseback can allow the seller to refinance at lower rates, assuming rates have dropped. In addition, a sale-leaseback can provide another source of working capital, particularly when liquidity is tight.
2. *Taxes.* At the time a company purchased equipment, it may not have known that it would be subject to an alternative minimum tax and that ownership might increase its minimum tax liability. By selling the property, the seller-lessee may deduct the entire lease payment, which is not subject to alternative minimum tax considerations.

DETERMINING ASSET USE

To the extent the **seller-lessee continues to use** the asset after the sale, the sale-leaseback is really a form of financing. Therefore, the lessor **should not recognize a gain or loss** on the transaction. In short, the seller-lessee is simply borrowing funds.

On the other hand, if the **seller-lessee gives up the right to the use** of the asset, the transaction is in substance a sale. In that case, **gain or loss recognition** is appropriate. Trying to ascertain when the lessee has given up the use of the asset is difficult, however, and the FASB has formulated complex rules to identify this situation.[18] To understand the profession's position in this area, we discuss the basic accounting for the lessee and lessor below.

Underlying Concepts

A sale-leaseback is similar in substance to the parking of inventories (discussed in Chapter 8). The ultimate economic benefits remain under the control of the "seller," thus satisfying the definition of an asset.

Lessee

If the lease meets one of the four criteria for treatment as a capital lease (see Illustration 21-3 on page 1275), the **seller-lessee accounts for the transaction as a sale and the lease as a capital lease**. The seller-lessee should defer any profit or loss it experiences from the sale of the assets that are leased back under a capital lease; it should **amortize that profit over the lease term** (or the economic life if either criterion 1 or 2 is satisfied) in proportion to the amortization of the leased assets.

For example, assume **Scott Paper** sells equipment having a book value of $580,000 and a fair value of $623,110 to **General Electric Credit** for $623,110 and leases the equipment back for $50,000 a year for 20 years. Scott should amortize the profit of $43,110 over the 20-year period at the same rate that it depreciates the $623,110. **[12]** It credits the $43,110 ($623,110 − $580,000) to **Unearned Profit on Sale-Leaseback.**

If none of the capital lease criteria are satisfied, **the seller-lessee accounts for the transaction as a sale and the lease as an operating lease**. Under an operating lease, the lessee defers such profit or loss and amortizes it in proportion to the rental payments over the period when it expects to use the assets.

[18]Sales and leasebacks of real estate are often accounted for differently. A discussion of the issues related to these transactions is beyond the scope of this textbook. **[11]**

There are exceptions to these two general rules. They are:

1. ***Losses recognized.*** When the fair value of the asset is **less than the book value** (carrying amount), the lessee must recognize a loss immediately, up to the amount of the difference between the book value and fair value. For example, if Lessee, Inc. sells equipment having a book value of $650,000 and a fair value of $623,110, it should charge the difference of $26,890 to a loss account.[19]
2. ***Minor leaseback.*** Leasebacks in which the present value of the rental payments are 10 percent or less of the fair value of the asset are **minor leasebacks**. In this case, the seller-lessee gives up most of the rights to the use of the asset sold. Therefore, the transaction is a sale, and full gain or loss recognition is appropriate. It is not a financing transaction because the risks of ownership have been transferred.[20]

Lessor

If the lease meets one of the criteria in Group I and both of the criteria in Group II (see Illustration 21-10 on page 1285), the **purchaser-lessor** records the transaction as a purchase and a direct-financing lease. If the lease does not meet the criteria, the purchaser-lessor records the transaction as a purchase and an operating lease.

SALE-LEASEBACK EXAMPLE

To illustrate the accounting treatment accorded a sale-leaseback transaction, assume that **American Airlines** on January 1, 2014, sells a used Boeing 757 having a carrying amount on its books of $75,500,000 to **CitiCapital** for $80,000,000. American immediately leases the aircraft back under the following conditions:

1. The term of the lease is 15 years, noncancelable, and requires equal rental payments of $10,487,443 at the beginning of each year.
2. The aircraft has a fair value of $80,000,000 on January 1, 2014, and an estimated economic life of 15 years.
3. American pays all executory costs.
4. American depreciates similar aircraft that it owns on a straight-line basis over 15 years.
5. The annual payments assure the lessor a 12 percent return.
6. American's incremental borrowing rate is 12 percent.

This lease is a capital lease to American because the lease term exceeds 75 percent of the estimated life of the aircraft and because the present value of the lease payments exceeds 90 percent of the fair value of the aircraft to CitiCapital. Assuming that collectibility of the lease payments is reasonably predictable and that no important uncertainties exist

[19]There can be two types of losses in sale-leaseback arrangements. One is a real economic loss that results when the carrying amount of the asset is higher than the fair value of the asset. In this case, the loss should be recognized. An artificial loss results when the sales price is below the carrying amount of the asset but the fair value is above the carrying amount. In this case, the loss is more in the form of prepaid rent, and the lessee should defer the loss and amortize it in the future.

[20]In some cases, the seller-lessee retains more than a minor part but less than substantially all. The computations to arrive at these values are complex and beyond the scope of this textbook.

in relation to unreimbursable costs yet to be incurred by CitiCapital, it should classify this lease as a direct-financing lease.

Illustration 21A-1 presents the typical journal entries to record the sale-leaseback transactions for American and CitiCapital for the first year.

ILLUSTRATION 21A-1
Comparative Entries for Sale-Leaseback for Lessee and Lessor

American Airlines (Lessee)			CitiCapital (Lessor)		
Sale of Aircraft by American to CitiCapital (January 1, 2014):					
Cash	80,000,000		Aircraft	80,000,000	
Aircraft		75,500,000	Cash		80,000,000
Unearned Profit on Sale-Leaseback		4,500,000	Lease Receivable	80,000,000	
Leased Aircraft (under capital leases)	80,000,000		Aircraft		80,000,000
Lease Liability		80,000,000			
First Lease Payment (January 1, 2014):					
Lease Liability	10,487,443		Cash	10,487,443	
Cash		10,487,443	Lease Receivable		10,487,443
Incurrence and Payment of Executory Costs by American Corp. throughout 2014:					
Insurance, Maintenance, Taxes, etc.	XXX			(No entry)	
Cash or Accounts Payable		XXX			
Depreciation Expense on the Aircraft (December 31, 2014):					
Depreciation Expense	5,333,333			(No entry)	
Accumulated Depr.—Capital Leases ($80,000,000 ÷ 15)		5,333,333			
Amortization of Profit on Sale-Leaseback by American (December 31, 2014):					
Unearned Profit on Sale-Leaseback	300,000			(No entry)	
Depreciation Expense ($4,500,000 ÷ 15)		300,000			
(*Note:* A case might be made for crediting Sales Revenue instead of Depreciation Expense.)					
Interest for 2014 (December 31, 2014):					
Interest Expense	8,341,507[a]		Interest Receivable	8,341,507	
Interest Payable		8,341,507	Interest Revenue		8,341,507[a]

[a]Partial Lease Amortization Schedule:

Date	Annual Rental Payment	Interest 12%	Reduction of Balance	Balance
1/1/14				$80,000,000
1/1/14	$10,487,443	$ -0-	$10,487,443	69,512,557
1/1/15	10,487,443	8,341,507	2,145,936	67,366,621

SUMMARY OF LEARNING OBJECTIVE FOR APPENDIX 21A

KEY TERMS

minor leaseback, *1308*
sale-leaseback, *1306*

10 Describe the lessee's accounting for sale-leaseback transactions. If the lease meets one of the four criteria for treatment as a capital lease, the seller-lessee accounts for the transaction as a sale and the lease as a capital lease. The seller-lessee defers any profit it experiences from the sale of the assets that are leased back under a capital lease. The seller-lessee amortizes any profit over the lease term (or the economic life if either criterion 1 or 2 is satisfied) in proportion to the amortization of the leased assets. If the lease satisfies none of the capital lease criteria, the seller-lessee accounts for the transaction as a sale and the lease as an operating lease. Under an operating lease, the lessee defers such profit and amortizes it in proportion to the rental payments over the period of time that it expects to use the assets.

DEMONSTRATION PROBLEM

Morgan Bakeries is involved in four different lease situations. Each of these leases is noncancelable, and in no case does Morgan receive title to the properties leased during or at the end of the lease term. All leases start on January 1, 2014, with the first rental due at the beginning of the year. Additional information is shown in the following table.

	(a) Harmon, Inc.	(b) Arden's Oven Co.	(c) Mendota Truck Co.	(d) Appleland Computer
Type of property	Cabinets	Oven	Truck	Computer
Yearly rental	$6,000	$15,000	$5,582.62	$3,557.25
Lease term	20 years	10 years	3 years	3 years
Estimated economic life	30 years	25 years	7 years	5 years
Purchase option	None	$75,000 at end of 10 years $4,000 at end of 15 years	None	$3,000 at end of 3 years, which approximates fair value
Renewal option	None	5-year renewal option at $15,000 per year	None	1 year at $1,500; no penalty for nonrenewal; standard renewal clause
Fair value at inception of lease	$60,000	$120,000	$20,000	$10,000
Cost of asset to lessor	$60,000	$120,000	$15,000	$10,000
Residual value				
Guaranteed	–0–	–0–	$7,000	–0–
Unguaranteed	$5,000	–0–	–0–	$3,000
Incremental borrowing rate of lessee	12%	12%	12%	12%
Executory costs paid by	*Lessee* $300 per year	*Lessee* $1,000 per year	*Lessee* $500 per year	*Lessor* Estimated to be $500 per year, included in lease payment
Present value of minimum lease payments				
Using incremental borrowing rate of lessee	$50,194.68	$115,153.35	$20,000	$8,224.16
Using implicit rate of lessor	Not known	Not known	Not known	Known by lessee, $8,027.48
Estimated fair value at end of lease	$5,000	$80,000 at end of 10 years $60,000 at end of 15 years	Not available	$3,000

Instructions

For each lease arrangement, determine the correct classification of the lease and prepare the journal entry at its inception.

Solution

(a) Analysis of the Harmon, Inc. lease:

1. **Transfer of title?** No.
2. **Bargain-purchase option?** No.
3. **Economic life test (75% test).** The lease term is 20 years and the estimated economic life is 30 years. Thus, it **does not** meet the 75 percent test.
4. **Recovery of investment test (90% test):**

Fair value	$60,000	Rental payments	$ 6,000
Rate	× 90%	PV of annuity due for 20 years at 12%	× 8.36578
90% of fair value	$54,000	PV of rental payments	$50,194.68

Because the present value of the minimum lease payments is less than 90 percent of the fair value, the lease does not meet the 90 percent test.

Both Morgan and Harmon should account for this lease as an operating lease, as indicated by the following January 1, 2014, entries.

Morgan Bakeries (Lessee)			Harmon, Inc. (Lessor)		
Rent Expense	6,000		Cash	6,000	
Cash		6,000	Rent Revenue		6,000

(b) Analysis of the Arden's Oven Co. lease:

1. **Transfer of title?** No.
2. **Bargain-purchase option?** The $75,000 option at the end of 10 years does not appear to be sufficiently lower than the expected fair value of $80,000 to make it reasonably assured that it will be exercised. However, the $4,000 at the end of 15 years when the fair value is $60,000 does appear to be a bargain. From the information given, criterion 2 is therefore met. Note that both the guaranteed and the unguaranteed residual values are assigned zero values because the lessor does not expect to repossess the leased asset.
3. **Economic life test (75% test):** Given that a bargain-purchase option exists, the lease term is the initial lease period of 10 years plus the five-year renewal option since it precedes a bargain-purchase option. Even though the lease term is now considered to be 15 years, this test is still not met because 75 percent of the economic life of 25 years is 18.75 years.
4. **Recovery of investment test (90% test):**

Fair value	$120,000	Rental payments	$ 15,000.00
Rate	× 90%	PV of annuity due for 15 years at 12%	× 7.62817
90% of fair value	$108,000	PV of rental payments	$114,422.55

PV of bargain-purchase option: $= \$4,000 \times (PVF_{15,12\%}) = \$4,000 \times .18270 = \$730.80$

PV of rental payments	$114,422.55
PV of bargain-purchase option	730.80
PV of minimum lease payments	$115,153.35

The present value of the minimum lease payments is greater than 90 percent of the fair value. Therefore, the lease does meet the 90 percent test.

Morgan Bakeries should account for this as a capital lease because the lease meets both criteria 2 and 4. Assuming that Arden's implicit rate is less than Morgan's incremental borrowing rate, the following entries are made on January 1, 2014.

Morgan Bakeries (Lessee)			Arden's Oven Co. (Lessor)		
Leased Equipment (oven)	115,153.35		Lease Receivable	120,000	
Lease Liability		115,153.35	Equipment (oven)		120,000

Morgan Bakeries would depreciate the leased asset over its economic life of 25 years, given the bargain-purchase option. Arden's Oven Co. does not use sales-type accounting because the fair value and the cost of the asset are the same at the inception of the lease.

(c) Analysis of the Mendota Truck Co. lease:

1. **Transfer of title?** No.
2. **Bargain-purchase option?** No.
3. **Economic life test (75% test):** The lease term is three years and the estimated economic life is seven years. Thus, it **does not** meet the 75 percent test.
4. **Recovery of investment test (90% test):**

Fair value	$20,000	Rental payments	$ 5,582.62
Rate	× 90%	PV of annuity due for 3 years at 12%	× 2.69005
90% of fair value	$18,000	PV of rental payments	$15,017.54

(*Note:* Adjusted for $0.01 due to rounding.)

PV of guaranteed residual value: $= \$7,000 \times (PVF_{3,12\%}) = \$7,000 \times .71178 = \$4,982.46$

PV of rental payments	$15,017.54
PV of guaranteed residual value	4,982.46
PV of minimum lease payments	$20,000.00

The present value of the minimum lease payments is greater than 90 percent of the fair value. Therefore, the lease meets the 90 percent test.

Assuming that Mendota's implicit rate is the same as Morgan's incremental borrowing rate, the following entries are made on January 1, 2014.

Morgan Bakeries (Lessee)			Mendota Truck Co. (Lessor)		
Leased Equipment (truck)	20,000		Lease Receivable	20,000	
Lease Liability		20,000	Cost of Goods Sold	15,000	
			Trucks		15,000
			Sales Revenue		20,000

Because the cost of the truck is less than the fair value, this is a sales-type lease for Mendota. Morgan depreciates the leased asset over three years to its guaranteed residual value.

(d) Analysis of the Appleland Computer lease:

1. **Transfer of title?** No.
2. **Bargain-purchase option?** No. The option to purchase at the end of three years at approximate fair value is clearly not a bargain.
3. **Economic life test (75% test):** The lease term is three years, and no bargain-renewal period exists. Therefore, the 75 percent test **is not** met.
4. **Recovery of investment test (90% test):**

Fair value	$10,000	Rental payments	$3,557.25
Rate	× 90%	Less executory costs	500.00
90% of fair value	$ 9,000		3,057.25
		PV of annuity-due factor for 3 years at 12%	×2.69005
		PV of minimum lease payments using incremental borrowing rate	$8,224.16

The present value of the minimum lease payments using the incremental borrowing rate is $8,224.16. Using the implicit rate, it is $8,027.48. The lessor's implicit rate is therefore higher than the incremental borrowing rate. Given this situation, the lessee uses the $8,224.16 (lower interest rate when discounting) when comparing with the 90 percent of fair value. Because the present value of the minimum lease payments is lower than 90 percent of the fair value, the lease does **not** meet the recovery of investment test.

The following entries are made on January 1, 2014, indicating an operating lease.

Morgan Bakeries (Lessee)			Appleland Computer (Lessor)		
Rent Expense	3,557.25		Cash	3,557.25	
Cash		3,557.25	Rent Revenue		3,557.25

If the lease payments had been $3,557.25 with no executory costs involved, this lease arrangement would have qualified for capital-lease accounting treatment.

FASB CODIFICATION

FASB Codification References

[1] FASB ASC 840-10-25-1. [Predecessor literature: "Accounting for Leases," *FASB Statement No. 13* as amended and interpreted through May 1980 (Stamford, Conn.: FASB, 1980), par. 7.]

[2] FASB ASC 840-10-25. [Predecessor literature: "Accounting for Leases: Sale-Leaseback Transactions Involving Real Estate; Sales-Type Leases of Real Estate; Definition of the Lease Term; Initial Direct Costs of Direct Financing Leases," *Statement of Financial Accounting Standards No. 98* (Stamford, Conn.: FASB, 1988).]

[3] FASB ASC 840-10-25-9. [Predecessor literature: "Lessee Guarantee of the Residual Value of Leased Property," *FASB Interpretation No. 19* (Stamford, Conn.: FASB, 1977), par. 3.]

[4] FASB ASC 840-10-25-22. [Predecessor literature: "Accounting for Leases," *FASB Statement No. 13* as amended and interpreted through May 1980 (Stamford, Conn.: FASB, 1980), par. 5 (l).]

[5] FASB ASC 840-10-25-31. [Predecessor literature: "Accounting for Leases," *FASB Statement No. 13* as amended and interpreted through May 1980 (Stamford, Conn.: FASB, 1980), par. 5 (k).]

[6] FASB ASC 840-30-35-14. [Predecessor literature: "Accounting for Purchase of a Leased Asset by the Lessee During the Term of the Lease," *FASB Interpretation No. 26* (Stamford, Conn.: FASB, 1978), par. 5.]

[7] FASB ASC 840-10-25-43. [Predecessor literature: "Accounting for Leases," *FASB Statement No. 13* as amended and interpreted through May 1980 (Stamford, Conn.: FASB, 1980), paras. 6, 7, and 8.]

[8] FASB ASC 840-30-30-12. [Predecessor literature: "Accounting for Nonrefundable Fees and Costs Associated with Originating or Acquiring Loans and Initial Direct Costs of Leases," *Statement of Financial Accounting Standards No. 91* (Stamford: Conn.: FASB, 1987).]

[9] FASB ASC 840-30-50-1. [Predecessor literature: "Accounting for Leases," *FASB Statement No. 13* as amended and interpreted through May 1980 (Stamford, Conn.: FASB, 1980), par. 16.]

[10] FASB ASC 840-30-50-4. [Predecessor literature: "Accounting for Leases," *FASB Statement No. 13* as amended and interpreted through May 1980 (Stamford, Conn.: FASB, 1980), paras. 16 and 23.]

[11] FASB ASC 840-40. [Predecessor literature: "Accounting for Leases: Sale-Leaseback Transactions Involving Real Estate; Sales-Type Leases of Real Estate; Definition of the Lease Term; Initial Direct Costs of Direct Financing Leases," *Statement of Financial Accounting Standards No. 98* (Stamford, Conn.: FASB, 1988).]

[12] FASB ASC 840-40. [Predecessor literature: *Statement of Financial Accounting Standards No. 28*, "Accounting for Sales with Leasebacks" (Stamford, Conn.: FASB, 1979).]

Exercises

If your school has a subscription to the FASB Codification, go to *http://aaahq.org/ascLogin.cfm* to log in and prepare responses to the following. Provide Codification references for your responses.

CE21-1 Access the glossary ("Master Glossary") to answer the following.

(a) What is a bargain-purchase option?
(b) What is the definition of "incremental borrowing rate"?
(c) What is the definition of "estimated residual value"?
(d) What is an unguaranteed residual value?

CE21-2 What comprises a lessee's minimum lease payments? What is excluded?

CE21-3 What information should a lessee disclose about its capital leases in its financial statements and footnotes?

CE21-4 How should a lessor measure its initial gross investment in either a sales-type lease or a direct-financing lease?

An additional Codification case can be found in the Using Your Judgment section, on page 1331.

Be sure to check the book's companion website for a Review and Analysis Exercise, with solution.

WileyPLUS Brief Exercises, Exercises, Problems, and many more learning and assessment tools and resources are available for practice in WileyPLUS.

Note: All asterisked Questions, Exercises, and Problems relate to material in the appendix to the chapter.
(Unless instructed otherwise, round all amounts to the nearest dollar.)

QUESTIONS

1. What are the major lessor groups in the United States? What advantage does a captive have in a leasing arrangement?

2. Bradley Co. is expanding its operations and is in the process of selecting the method of financing this program. After some investigation, the company determines that it may (1) issue bonds and with the proceeds purchase the needed assets or (2) lease the assets on a long-term basis. Without knowing the comparative costs involved, answer these questions:

(a) What might be the advantages of leasing the assets instead of owning them?

(b) What might be the disadvantages of leasing the assets instead of owning them?

(c) In what way will the balance sheet be differently affected by leasing the assets as opposed to issuing bonds and purchasing the assets?

3. Identify the two recognized lease accounting methods for lessees and distinguish between them.

4. Ballard Company rents a warehouse on a month-to-month basis for the storage of its excess inventory. The company periodically must rent space whenever its production greatly exceeds actual sales. For several years, the company officials have discussed building their own storage facility, but this enthusiasm wavers when sales increase sufficiently to absorb the excess inventory. What is the nature of this type of lease arrangement, and what accounting treatment should be accorded it?

5. Distinguish between minimum rental payments and minimum lease payments, and indicate what is included in minimum lease payments.

6. Explain the distinction between a direct-financing lease and a sales-type lease for a lessor.

7. Outline the accounting procedures involved in applying the operating method by a lessee.

8. Outline the accounting procedures involved in applying the capital lease method by a lessee.

9. Identify the lease classifications for lessors and the criteria that must be met for each classification.

10. Outline the accounting procedures involved in applying the direct-financing method.

11. Outline the accounting procedures involved in applying the operating method by a lessor.

12. Walker Company is a manufacturer and lessor of computer equipment. What should be the nature of its lease arrangements with lessees if the company wishes to account for its lease transactions as sales-type leases?

13. Metheny Corporation's lease arrangements qualify as sales-type leases at the time of entering into the transactions. How should the corporation recognize revenues and costs in these situations?

14. Alice Foyle, M.D. (lessee), has a noncancelable 20-year lease with Brownback Realty, Inc. (lessor) for the use of a medical building. Taxes, insurance, and maintenance are paid by the lessee in addition to the fixed annual payments, of which the present value is equal to the fair value of the leased property. At the end of the lease period, title becomes the lessee's at a nominal price. Considering the terms of the lease described above, comment on the nature of the lease transaction and the accounting treatment that should be accorded it by the lessee.

15. The residual value is the estimated fair value of the leased property at the end of the lease term.

(a) Of what significance is (1) an unguaranteed and (2) a guaranteed residual value in the lessee's accounting for a capitalized-lease transaction?

(b) Of what significance is (1) an unguaranteed and (2) a guaranteed residual value in the lessor's accounting for a direct-financing lease transaction?

16. How should changes in the estimated unguaranteed residual value be handled by the lessor?

17. Describe the effect of a "bargain-purchase option" on accounting for a capital lease transaction by a lessee.

18. What are "initial direct costs" and how are they accounted for?

19. What disclosures should be made by lessees and lessors related to future lease payments?

***20.** What is the nature of a "sale-leaseback" transaction?

BRIEF EXERCISES

2 **BE21-1** Callaway Golf Co. leases telecommunication equipment. Assume the following data for equipment leased from Photon Company. The lease term is 5 years and requires equal rental payments of $31,000 at the beginning of each year. The equipment has a fair value at the inception of the lease of $138,000, an estimated useful life of 8 years, and no residual value. Callaway pays all executory costs directly to third parties. Photon set the annual rental to earn a rate of return of 10%, and this fact is known to Callaway. The lease does not transfer title or contain a bargain-purchase option. How should Callaway classify this lease?

2 **BE21-2** Waterworld Company leased equipment from Costner Company. The lease term is 4 years and requires equal rental payments of $43,019 at the beginning of each year. The equipment has a fair value at the inception of the lease of $150,000, an estimated useful life of 4 years, and no salvage value. Waterworld pays all executory costs directly to third parties. The appropriate interest rate is 10%. Prepare Waterworld's January 1, 2014, journal entries at the inception of the lease.

2 **BE21-3** Rick Kleckner Corporation recorded a capital lease at $300,000 on January 1, 2014. The interest rate is 12%. Kleckner Corporation made the first lease payment of $53,920 on January 1, 2014. The lease requires eight annual payments. The equipment has a useful life of 8 years with no salvage value. Prepare Kleckner Corporation's December 31, 2014, adjusting entries.

2 **BE21-4** Use the information for Rick Kleckner Corporation from BE21-3. Assume that at December 31, 2014, Kleckner made an adjusting entry to accrue interest expense of $29,530 on the lease. Prepare Kleckner's January 1, 2015, journal entry to record the second lease payment of $53,920.

3 **BE21-5** Jana Kingston Corporation enters into a lease on January 1, 2014, that does not transfer ownership or contain a bargain-purchase option. It covers 3 years of the equipment's 8-year useful life, and the present value of the minimum lease payments is less than 90% of the fair value of the asset leased. Prepare Jana Kingston's journal entry to record its January 1, 2014, annual lease payment of $35,000.

4 5 **BE21-6** Assume that IBM leased equipment that was carried at a cost of $150,000 to Sharon Swander Company. The term of the lease is 6 years beginning January 1, 2014, with equal rental payments of $30,044 at the beginning of each year. All executory costs are paid by Swander directly to third parties. The fair value of the equipment at the inception of the lease is $150,000. The equipment has a useful life of 6 years with no salvage value. The lease has an implicit interest rate of 8%, no bargain-purchase option, and no transfer of title. Collectibility is reasonably assured with no additional cost to be incurred by IBM. Prepare IBM's January 1, 2014, journal entries at the inception of the lease.

4 5 **BE21-7** Use the information for IBM from BE21-6. Assume the direct-financing lease was recorded at a present value of $150,000. Prepare IBM's December 31, 2014, entry to record interest.

4 **BE21-8** Jennifer Brent Corporation owns equipment that cost $80,000 and has a useful life of 8 years with no salvage value. On January 1, 2014, Jennifer Brent leases the equipment to Donna Havaci Inc. for one year with one rental payment of $15,000 on January 1. Prepare Jennifer Brent Corporation's 2014 journal entries.

6 7 **BE21-9** Indiana Jones Corporation enters into a 6-year lease of equipment on January 1, 2014, which requires 6 annual payments of $40,000 each, beginning January 1, 2014. In addition, Indiana Jones guarantees the lessor a residual value of $20,000 at lease-end. The equipment has a useful life of 6 years. Prepare Indiana Jones' January 1, 2014, journal entries assuming an interest rate of 10%.

6 7 **BE21-10** Use the information for Indiana Jones Corporation from BE21-9. Assume that for Lost Ark Company, the lessor, collectibility is reasonably predictable, there are no important uncertainties concerning costs, and the carrying amount of the equipment is $202,921. Prepare Lost Ark's January 1, 2014, journal entries.

8 **BE21-11** Geiberger Corporation manufactures replicators. On January 1, 2014, it leased to Althaus Company a replicator that had cost $110,000 to manufacture. The lease agreement covers the 5-year useful life of the replicator and requires 5 equal annual rentals of $40,800 payable each January 1, beginning January 1, 2014. An interest rate of 12% is implicit in the lease agreement. Collectibility of the rentals is reasonably assured, and there are no important uncertainties concerning costs. Prepare Geiberger's January 1, 2014, journal entries.

10 ***BE21-12** On January 1, 2014, Irwin Animation sold a truck to Peete Finance for $33,000 and immediately leased it back. The truck was carried on Irwin's books at $28,000. The term of the lease is 5 years, and title transfers to Irwin at lease-end. The lease requires five equal rental payments of $8,705 at the end of each year. The appropriate rate of interest is 10%, and the truck has a useful life of 5 years with no salvage value. Prepare Irwin's 2014 journal entries.

EXERCISES

2 **E21-1 (Lessee Entries; Capital Lease with Unguaranteed Residual Value)** On January 1, 2014, Burke Corporation signed a 5-year noncancelable lease for a machine. The terms of the lease called for Burke to make annual payments of $8,668 at the beginning of each year, starting January 1, 2014. The machine has an estimated useful life of 6 years and a $5,000 unguaranteed residual value. The machine reverts back to the lessor at the end of the lease term. Burke uses the straight-line method of depreciation for all of its plant assets. Burke's incremental borrowing rate is 10%, and the Lessor's implicit rate is unknown.

Instructions

(a) What type of lease is this? Explain.
(b) Compute the present value of the minimum lease payments.
(c) Prepare all necessary journal entries for Burke for this lease through January 1, 2015.

2 **E21-2 (Lessee Computations and Entries; Capital Lease with Guaranteed Residual Value)** Pat Delaney Company leases an automobile with a fair value of $8,725 from John Simon Motors, Inc., on the following terms:

1. Noncancelable term of 50 months.
2. Rental of $200 per month (at end of each month). (The present value at 1% per month is $7,840.)
3. Estimated residual value after 50 months is $1,180. (The present value at 1% per month is $715.) Delaney Company guarantees the residual value of $1,180.
4. Estimated economic life of the automobile is 60 months.
5. Delaney Company's incremental borrowing rate is 12% a year (1% a month). Simon's implicit rate is unknown.

Instructions

(a) What is the nature of this lease to Delaney Company?
(b) What is the present value of the minimum lease payments?
(c) Record the lease on Delaney Company's books at the date of inception.
(d) Record the first month's depreciation on Delaney Company's books (assume straight-line).
(e) Record the first month's lease payment.

2 7 **E21-3 (Lessee Entries; Capital Lease with Executory Costs and Unguaranteed Residual Value)** Assume that on January 1, 2014, **Kimberly-Clark Corp.** signs a 10-year noncancelable lease agreement to lease a storage building from Sheffield Storage Company. The following information pertains to this lease agreement.

1. The agreement requires equal rental payments of $72,000 beginning on January 1, 2014.
2. The fair value of the building on January 1, 2014 is $440,000.
3. The building has an estimated economic life of 12 years, with an unguaranteed residual value of $10,000. Kimberly-Clark depreciates similar buildings on the straight-line method.
4. The lease is nonrenewable. At the termination of the lease, the building reverts to the lessor.
5. Kimberly-Clark's incremental borrowing rate is 12% per year. The lessor's implicit rate is not known by Kimberly-Clark.
6. The yearly rental payment includes $2,471 of executory costs related to taxes on the property.

Instructions

Prepare the journal entries on the lessee's books to reflect the signing of the lease agreement and to record the payments and expenses related to this lease for the years 2014 and 2015. Kimberly-Clark's corporate year-end is December 31.

5 **E21-4 (Lessor Entries; Direct-Financing Lease with Option to Purchase)** Castle Leasing Company signs a lease agreement on January 1, 2014, to lease electronic equipment to Jan Way Company. The term of the noncancelable lease is 2 years, and payments are required at the end of each year. The following information relates to this agreement:

1. Jan Way has the option to purchase the equipment for $16,000 upon termination of the lease.
2. The equipment has a cost and fair value of $160,000 to Castle Leasing Company. The useful economic life is 2 years, with a salvage value of $16,000.
3. Jan Way Company is required to pay $5,000 each year to the lessor for executory costs.
4. Castle Leasing Company desires to earn a return of 10% on its investment.
5. Collectibility of the payments is reasonably predictable, and there are no important uncertainties surrounding the costs yet to be incurred by the lessor.

Instructions

(a) Prepare the journal entries on the books of Castle Leasing to reflect the payments received under the lease and to recognize income for the years 2014 and 2015.

(b) Assuming that Jan Way Company exercises its option to purchase the equipment on December 31, 2015, prepare the journal entry to reflect the sale on Castle's books.

2 3 **E21-5 (Type of Lease; Amortization Schedule)** Mike Macinski Leasing Company leases a new machine that has a cost and fair value of $95,000 to Sharrer Corporation on a 3-year noncancelable contract. Sharrer Corporation agrees to assume all risks of normal ownership including such costs as insurance, taxes, and maintenance. The machine has a 3-year useful life and no residual value. The lease was signed on January 1, 2014. Mike Macinski Leasing Company expects to earn a 9% return on its investment. The annual rentals are payable on each December 31.

Instructions

(a) Discuss the nature of the lease arrangement and the accounting method that each party to the lease should apply.

(b) Prepare an amortization schedule that would be suitable for both the lessor and the lessee and that covers all the years involved.

8 **E21-6 (Lessor Entries; Sales-Type Lease)** Crosley Company, a machinery dealer, leased a machine to Dexter Corporation on January 1, 2014. The lease is for an 8-year period and requires equal annual payments of $35,013 at the beginning of each year. The first payment is received on January 1, 2014. Crosley had purchased the machine during 2013 for $160,000. Collectibility of lease payments is reasonably predictable, and no important uncertainties surround the amount of costs yet to be incurred by Crosley. Crosley set the annual rental to ensure an 11% rate of return. The machine has an economic life of 10 years with no residual value and reverts to Crosley at the termination of the lease.

XLS

Instructions

(a) Compute the amount of the lease receivable.

(b) Prepare all necessary journal entries for Crosley for 2014.

8 **E21-7 (Lessee-Lessor Entries; Sales-Type Lease)** On January 1, 2014, Bensen Company leased equipment to Flynn Corporation. The following information pertains to this lease.

1. The term of the noncancelable lease is 6 years, with no renewal option. The equipment reverts to the lessor at the termination of the lease.
2. Equal rental payments are due on January 1 of each year, beginning in 2014.
3. The fair value of the equipment on January 1, 2014, is $150,000, and its cost is $120,000.
4. The equipment has an economic life of 8 years, with an unguaranteed residual value of $10,000. Flynn depreciates all of its equipment on a straight-line basis.
5. Bensen set the annual rental to ensure an 11% rate of return. Flynn's incremental borrowing rate is 12%, and the implicit rate of the lessor is unknown.
6. Collectibility of lease payments is reasonably predictable, and no important uncertainties surround the amount of costs yet to be incurred by the lessor.

Instructions

(Both the lessor and the lessee's accounting period ends on December 31.)

(a) Discuss the nature of this lease to Bensen and Flynn.

(b) Calculate the amount of the annual rental payment.

(c) Prepare all the necessary journal entries for Flynn for 2014.

(d) Prepare all the necessary journal entries for Bensen for 2014.

8 **E21-8 (Lessee Entries with Bargain-Purchase Option)** The following facts pertain to a noncancelable lease agreement between Mooney Leasing Company and Rode Company, a lessee.

Inception date:	May 1, 2014
Annual lease payment due at the beginning of each year, beginning with May 1, 2014	$21,227.65
Bargain-purchase option price at end of lease term	$ 4,000.00
Lease term	5 years
Economic life of leased equipment	10 years
Lessor's cost	$65,000.00
Fair value of asset at May 1, 2014	$91,000.00
Lessor's implicit rate	10%
Lessee's incremental borrowing rate	10%

The collectibility of the lease payments is reasonably predictable, and there are no important uncertainties surrounding the costs yet to be incurred by the lessor. The lessee assumes responsibility for all executory costs.

Instructions

(Round all numbers to the nearest cent.)

(a) Discuss the nature of this lease to Rode Company.
(b) Discuss the nature of this lease to Mooney Company.
(c) Prepare a lease amortization schedule for Rode Company for the 5-year lease term.
(d) Prepare the journal entries on the lessee's books to reflect the signing of the lease agreement and to record the payments and expenses related to this lease for the years 2014 and 2015. Rode's annual accounting period ends on December 31. Reversing entries are used by Rode.

8 **E21-9 (Lessor Entries with Bargain-Purchase Option)** A lease agreement between Mooney Leasing Company and Rode Company is described in E21-8.

Instructions

(Round all numbers to the nearest cent.)
Refer to the data in E21-8 and do the following for the lessor.

(a) Compute the amount of the lease receivable at the inception of the lease.
(b) Prepare a lease amortization schedule for Mooney Leasing Company for the 5-year lease term.
(c) Prepare the journal entries to reflect the signing of the lease agreement and to record the receipts and income related to this lease for the years 2014, 2015, and 2016. The lessor's accounting period ends on December 31. Reversing entries are not used by Mooney.

5 **E21-10 (Computation of Rental; Journal Entries for Lessor)** Morgan Leasing Company signs an agreement on January 1, 2014, to lease equipment to Cole Company. The following information relates to this agreement.

1. The term of the noncancelable lease is 6 years with no renewal option. The equipment has an estimated economic life of 6 years.
2. The cost of the asset to the lessor is $245,000. The fair value of the asset at January 1, 2014, is $245,000.
3. The asset will revert to the lessor at the end of the lease term, at which time the asset is expected to have a residual value of $43,622, none of which is guaranteed.
4. Cole Company assumes direct responsibility for all executory costs.
5. The agreement requires equal annual rental payments, beginning on January 1, 2014.
6. Collectibility of the lease payments is reasonably predictable. There are no important uncertainties surrounding the amount of costs yet to be incurred by the lessor.

Instructions

(Round all numbers to the nearest cent.)

(a) Assuming the lessor desires a 10% rate of return on its investment, calculate the amount of the annual rental payment required. (Round to the nearest dollar.)
(b) Prepare an amortization schedule that would be suitable for the lessor for the lease term.
(c) Prepare all of the journal entries for the lessor for 2014 and 2015 to record the lease agreement, the receipt of lease payments, and the recognition of income. Assume the lessor's annual accounting period ends on December 31.

2 **E21-11 (Amortization Schedule and Journal Entries for Lessee)** Laura Leasing Company signs an agreement on January 1, 2014, to lease equipment to Plote Company. The following information relates to this agreement.

1. The term of the noncancelable lease is 5 years with no renewal option. The equipment has an estimated economic life of 5 years.
2. The fair value of the asset at January 1, 2014, is $80,000.
3. The asset will revert to the lessor at the end of the lease term, at which time the asset is expected to have a residual value of $7,000, none of which is guaranteed.
4. Plote Company assumes direct responsibility for all executory costs, which include the following annual amounts: (1) $900 to Rocky Mountain Insurance Company for insurance and (2) $1,600 to Laclede County for property taxes.
5. The agreement requires equal annual rental payments of $18,142.95 to the lessor, beginning on January 1, 2014.

6. The lessee's incremental borrowing rate is 12%. The lessor's implicit rate is 10% and is known to the lessee.
7. Plote Company uses the straight-line depreciation method for all equipment.
8. Plote uses reversing entries when appropriate.

Instructions

(Round all numbers to the nearest cent.)

(a) Prepare an amortization schedule that would be suitable for the lessee for the lease term.

(b) Prepare all of the journal entries for the lessee for 2014 and 2015 to record the lease agreement, the lease payments, and all expenses related to this lease. Assume the lessee's annual accounting period ends on December 31.

3 4 **E21-12 (Accounting for an Operating Lease)** On January 1, 2014, Doug Nelson Co. leased a building to Patrick Wise Inc. The relevant information related to the lease is as follows.

1. The lease arrangement is for 10 years.
2. The leased building cost $4,500,000 and was purchased for cash on January 1, 2014.
3. The building is depreciated on a straight-line basis. Its estimated economic life is 50 years with no salvage value.
4. Lease payments are $275,000 per year and are made at the end of the year.
5. Property tax expense of $85,000 and insurance expense of $10,000 on the building were incurred by Nelson in the first year. Payment on these two items was made at the end of the year.
6. Both the lessor and the lessee are on a calendar-year basis.

Instructions

(a) Prepare the journal entries that Nelson Co. should make in 2014.

(b) Prepare the journal entries that Wise Inc. should make in 2014.

(c) If Nelson paid $30,000 to a real estate broker on January 1, 2014, as a fee for finding the lessee, how much should be reported as an expense for this item in 2014 by Nelson Co.?

3 4 **E21-13 (Accounting for an Operating Lease)** On January 1, 2014, a machine was purchased for $900,000 by Young Co. The machine is expected to have an 8-year life with no salvage value. It is to be depreciated on a straight-line basis. The machine was leased to St. Leger Inc. on January 1, 2014, at an annual rental of $210,000. Other relevant information is as follows.

1. The lease term is for 3 years.
2. Young Co. incurred maintenance and other executory costs of $25,000 in 2014 related to this lease.
3. The machine could have been sold by Young Co. for $940,000 instead of leasing it.
4. St. Leger is required to pay a rent security deposit of $35,000 and to prepay the last month's rent of $17,500.

Instructions

(a) How much should Young Co. report as income before income tax on this lease for 2014?

(b) What amount should St. Leger Inc. report for rent expense for 2014 on this lease?

3 4 **E21-14 (Operating Lease for Lessee and Lessor)** On February 20, 2014, Barbara Brent Inc., purchased a machine for $1,500,000 for the purpose of leasing it. The machine is expected to have a 10-year life, no residual value, and will be depreciated on the straight-line basis. The machine was leased to Rudy Company on March 1, 2014, for a 4-year period at a monthly rental of $19,500. There is no provision for the renewal of the lease or purchase of the machine by the lessee at the expiration of the lease term. Brent paid $30,000 of commissions associated with negotiating the lease in February 2014.

Instructions

(a) What expense should Rudy Company record as a result of the facts above for the year ended December 31, 2014? Show supporting computations in good form.

(b) What income or loss before income taxes should Brent record as a result of the facts above for the year ended December 31, 2014? (*Hint:* Amortize commissions over the life of the lease.)

(AICPA adapted)

10 ***E21-15 (Sale-Leaseback)** Assume that on January 1, 2014, Elmer's Restaurants sells a computer system to Liquidity Finance Co. for $680,000 and immediately leases the computer system back. The relevant information is as follows.

1. The computer was carried on Elmer's books at a value of $600,000.
2. The term of the noncancelable lease is 10 years; title will transfer to Elmer.
3. The lease agreement requires equal rental payments of $110,666.81 at the end of each year.

4. The incremental borrowing rate for Elmer is 12%. Elmer is aware that Liquidity Finance Co. set the annual rental to insure a rate of return of 10%.
5. The computer has a fair value of $680,000 on January 1, 2014, and an estimated economic life of 10 years.
6. Elmer pays executory costs of $9,000 per year.

Instructions

Prepare the journal entries for both the lessee and the lessor for 2014 to reflect the sale and leaseback agreement. No uncertainties exist, and collectibility is reasonably certain.

10 *__E21-16 (Lessee-Lessor, Sale-Leaseback)__ Presented below are four independent situations.

(a) On December 31, 2014, Zarle Inc. sold computer equipment to Daniell Co. and immediately leased it back for 10 years. The sales price of the equipment was $520,000, its carrying amount is $400,000, and its estimated remaining economic life is 12 years. Determine the amount of deferred revenue to be reported from the sale of the computer equipment on December 31, 2014.

(b) On December 31, 2014, Wasicsko Co. sold a machine to Cross Co. and simultaneously leased it back for one year. The sale price of the machine was $480,000, the carrying amount is $420,000, and it had an estimated remaining useful life of 14 years. The present value of the rental payments for the one year is $35,000. At December 31, 2014, how much should Wasicsko report as deferred revenue from the sale of the machine?

(c) On January 1, 2014, McKane Corp. sold an airplane with an estimated useful life of 10 years. At the same time, McKane leased back the plane for 10 years. The sales price of the airplane was $500,000, the carrying amount $379,000, and the annual rental $73,975.22. McKane Corp. intends to depreciate the leased asset using the sum-of-the-years'-digits depreciation method. Discuss how the gain on the sale should be reported at the end of 2014 in the financial statements.

(d) On January 1, 2014, Sondgeroth Co. sold equipment with an estimated useful life of 5 years. At the same time, Sondgeroth leased back the equipment for 2 years under a lease classified as an operating lease. The sales price (fair value) of the equipment was $212,700, the carrying amount is $300,000, the monthly rental under the lease is $6,000, and the present value of the rental payments is $115,753. For the year ended December 31, 2014, determine which items would be reported on its income statement for the sale-leaseback transaction.

EXERCISES SET B

See the book's companion website, at **www.wiley.com/college/kieso**, for an additional set of exercises.

PROBLEMS

2 8 **P21-1 (Lessee-Lessor Entries, Sales-Type Lease)** Glaus Leasing Company agrees to lease machinery to Jensen Corporation on January 1, 2014. The following information relates to the lease agreement.

1. The term of the lease is 7 years with no renewal option, and the machinery has an estimated economic life of 9 years.
2. The cost of the machinery is $525,000, and the fair value of the asset on January 1, 2014, is $700,000.
3. At the end of the lease term, the asset reverts to the lessor and has a guaranteed residual value of $100,000. Jensen depreciates all of its equipment on a straight-line basis.
4. The lease agreement requires equal annual rental payments, beginning on January 1, 2014.
5. The collectibility of the lease payments is reasonably predictable, and there are no important uncertainties surrounding the amount of costs yet to be incurred by the lessor.
6. Glaus desires a 10% rate of return on its investments. Jensen's incremental borrowing rate is 11%, and the lessor's implicit rate is unknown.

Instructions

(Assume the accounting period ends on December 31.)

(a) Discuss the nature of this lease for both the lessee and the lessor.

(b) Calculate the amount of the annual rental payment required.

(c) Compute the present value of the minimum lease payments.
(d) Prepare the journal entries Jensen would make in 2014 and 2015 related to the lease arrangement.
(e) Prepare the journal entries Glaus would make in 2014 and 2015.

3 4 **P21-2 (Lessee-Lessor Entries, Operating Lease)** Cleveland Inc. leased a new crane to Abriendo Construction under a 5-year noncancelable contract starting January 1, 2014. Terms of the lease require payments of \$33,000 each January 1, starting January 1, 2014. Cleveland will pay insurance, taxes, and maintenance charges on the crane, which has an estimated life of 12 years, a fair value of \$240,000, and a cost to Cleveland of \$240,000. The estimated fair value of the crane is expected to be \$45,000 at the end of the lease term. No bargain-purchase or renewal options are included in the contract. Both Cleveland and Abriendo adjust and close books annually at December 31. Collectibility of the lease payments is reasonably certain, and no uncertainties exist relative to unreimbursable lessor costs. Abriendo's incremental borrowing rate is 10%, and Cleveland's implicit interest rate of 9% is known to Abriendo.

Instructions

(a) Identify the type of lease involved and give reasons for your classification. Discuss the accounting treatment that should be applied by both the lessee and the lessor.
(b) Prepare all the entries related to the lease contract and leased asset for the year 2014 for the lessee and lessor, assuming the following amounts.
  (1) Insurance \$500.
  (2) Taxes \$2,000.
  (3) Maintenance \$650.
  (4) Straight-line depreciation and salvage value \$15,000.
(c) Discuss what should be presented in the balance sheet, the income statement, and the related notes of both the lessee and the lessor at December 31, 2014.

2 8 9 **P21-3 (Lessee-Lessor Entries, Balance Sheet Presentation, Sales-Type Lease)** Winston Industries and Ewing Inc. enter into an agreement that requires Ewing Inc. to build three diesel-electric engines to Winston's specifications. Upon completion of the engines, Winston has agreed to lease them for a period of 10 years and to assume all costs and risks of ownership. The lease is noncancelable, becomes effective on January 1, 2014, and requires annual rental payments of \$413,971 each January 1, starting January 1, 2014.

Winston's incremental borrowing rate is 10%. The implicit interest rate used by Ewing Inc. and known to Winston is 8%. The total cost of building the three engines is \$2,600,000. The economic life of the engines is estimated to be 10 years, with residual value set at zero. Winston depreciates similar equipment on a straight-line basis. At the end of the lease, Winston assumes title to the engines. Collectibility of the lease payments is reasonably certain; no uncertainties exist relative to unreimbursable lessor costs.

Instructions

(a) Discuss the nature of this lease transaction from the viewpoints of both lessee and lessor.
(b) Prepare the journal entry or entries to record the transaction on January 1, 2014, on the books of Winston Industries.
(c) Prepare the journal entry or entries to record the transaction on January 1, 2014, on the books of Ewing Inc.
(d) Prepare the journal entries for both the lessee and lessor to record the first rental payment on January 1, 2014.
(e) Prepare the journal entries for both the lessee and lessor to record interest expense (revenue) at December 31, 2014. (Prepare a lease amortization schedule for 2 years.)
(f) Show the items and amounts that would be reported on the balance sheet (not notes) at December 31, 2014, for both the lessee and the lessor.

2 9 **P21-4 (Balance Sheet and Income Statement Disclosure—Lessee)** The following facts pertain to a noncancelable lease agreement between Alschuler Leasing Company and McKee Electronics, a lessee, for a computer system.

Inception date	October 1, 2014
Lease term	6 years
Economic life of leased equipment	6 years
Fair value of asset at October 1, 2014	\$300,383
Residual value at end of lease term	–0–
Lessor's implicit rate	10%
Lessee's incremental borrowing rate	10%
Annual lease payment due at the beginning of each year, beginning with October 1, 2014	\$62,700

The collectibility of the lease payments is reasonably predictable, and there are no important uncertainties surrounding the costs yet to be incurred by the lessor. The lessee assumes responsibility for all executory costs, which amount to $5,500 per year and are to be paid each October 1, beginning October 1, 2014. (This $5,500 is not included in the rental payment of $62,700.) The asset will revert to the lessor at the end of the lease term. The straight-line depreciation method is used for all equipment.

The following amortization schedule has been prepared correctly for use by both the lessor and the lessee in accounting for this lease. The lease is to be accounted for properly as a capital lease by the lessee and as a direct-financing lease by the lessor.

Date	Annual Lease Payment/ Receipt	Interest (10%) on Unpaid Liability/Receivable	Reduction of Lease Liability/Receivable	Balance of Lease Liability/Receivable
10/01/14				$300,383
10/01/14	$ 62,700		$ 62,700	237,683
10/01/15	62,700	$23,768	38,932	198,751
10/01/16	62,700	19,875	42,825	155,926
10/01/17	62,700	15,593	47,107	108,819
10/01/18	62,700	10,882	51,818	57,001
10/01/19	62,700	5,699*	57,001	–0–
	$376,200	$75,817	$300,383	

*Rounding error is $1.

Instructions

(a) Assuming the lessee's accounting period ends on September 30, answer the following questions with respect to this lease agreement.
 (1) What items and amounts will appear on the lessee's income statement for the year ending September 30, 2015?
 (2) What items and amounts will appear on the lessee's balance sheet at September 30, 2015?
 (3) What items and amounts will appear on the lessee's income statement for the year ending September 30, 2016?
 (4) What items and amounts will appear on the lessee's balance sheet at September 30, 2016?

(b) Assuming the lessee's accounting period ends on December 31, answer the following questions with respect to this lease agreement.
 (1) What items and amounts will appear on the lessee's income statement for the year ending December 31, 2014?
 (2) What items and amounts will appear on the lessee's balance sheet at December 31, 2014?
 (3) What items and amounts will appear on the lessee's income statement for the year ending December 31, 2015?
 (4) What items and amounts will appear on the lessee's balance sheet at December 31, 2015?

5 9 **P21-5 (Balance Sheet and Income Statement Disclosure—Lessor)** Assume the same information as in P21-4.

XLS

Instructions

(a) Assuming the lessor's accounting period ends on September 30, answer the following questions with respect to this lease agreement.
 (1) What items and amounts will appear on the lessor's income statement for the year ending September 30, 2015?
 (2) What items and amounts will appear on the lessor's balance sheet at September 30, 2015?
 (3) What items and amounts will appear on the lessor's income statement for the year ending September 30, 2016?
 (4) What items and amounts will appear on the lessor's balance sheet at September 30, 2016?

(b) Assuming the lessor's accounting period ends on December 31, answer the following questions with respect to this lease agreement.
 (1) What items and amounts will appear on the lessor's income statement for the year ending December 31, 2014?
 (2) What items and amounts will appear on the lessor's balance sheet at December 31, 2014?
 (3) What items and amounts will appear on the lessor's income statement for the year ending December 31, 2015?
 (4) What items and amounts will appear on the lessor's balance sheet at December 31, 2015?

2 7 **P21-6 (Lessee Entries with Residual Value)** The following facts pertain to a noncancelable lease agreement between Faldo Leasing Company and Vance Company, a lessee.

Inception date	January 1, 2014
Annual lease payment due at the beginning of each year, beginning with January 1, 2014	$124,798
Residual value of equipment at end of lease term, guaranteed by the lessee	$50,000
Lease term	6 years
Economic life of leased equipment	6 years
Fair value of asset at January 1, 2014	$600,000
Lessor's implicit rate	12%
Lessee's incremental borrowing rate	12%

The lessee assumes responsibility for all executory costs, which are expected to amount to $5,000 per year. The asset will revert to the lessor at the end of the lease term. The lessee has guaranteed the lessor a residual value of $50,000. The lessee uses the straight-line depreciation method for all equipment.

Instructions

(a) Prepare an amortization schedule that would be suitable for the lessee for the lease term.

(b) Prepare all of the journal entries for the lessee for 2014 and 2015 to record the lease agreement, the lease payments, and all expenses related to this lease. Assume the lessee's annual accounting period ends on December 31 and reversing entries are used when appropriate.

2 9 **P21-7 (Lessee Entries and Balance Sheet Presentation, Capital Lease)** Ludwick Steel Company as lessee signed a lease agreement for equipment for 5 years, beginning December 31, 2014. Annual rental payments of $40,000 are to be made at the beginning of each lease year (December 31). The taxes, insurance, and the maintenance costs are the obligation of the lessee. The interest rate used by the lessor in setting the payment schedule is 9%; Ludwick's incremental borrowing rate is 10%. Ludwick is unaware of the rate being used by the lessor. At the end of the lease, Ludwick has the option to buy the equipment for $1, considerably below its estimated fair value at that time. The equipment has an estimated useful life of 7 years, with no salvage value. Ludwick uses the straight-line method of depreciation on similar owned equipment.

Instructions

(a) Prepare the journal entry or entries, with explanations, that should be recorded on December 31, 2014, by Ludwick.

(b) Prepare the journal entry or entries, with explanations, that should be recorded on December 31, 2015, by Ludwick. (Prepare the lease amortization schedule for all five payments.)

(c) Prepare the journal entry or entries, with explanations, that should be recorded on December 31, 2016, by Ludwick.

(d) What amounts would appear on Ludwick's December 31, 2016, balance sheet relative to the lease arrangement?

2 9 **P21-8 (Lessee Entries and Balance Sheet Presentation, Capital Lease)** On January 1, 2014, Cage Company contracts to lease equipment for 5 years, agreeing to make a payment of $137,899 (including the executory costs of $6,000) at the beginning of each year, starting January 1, 2014. The taxes, the insurance, and the maintenance, estimated at $6,000 a year, are the obligations of the lessee. The leased equipment is to be capitalized at $550,000. The asset is to be depreciated on a double-declining-balance basis, and the obligation is to be reduced on an effective-interest basis. Cage's incremental borrowing rate is 12%, and the implicit rate in the lease is 10%, which is known by Cage. Title to the equipment transfers to Cage when the lease expires. The asset has an estimated useful life of 5 years and no residual value.

Instructions

(a) Explain the probable relationship of the $550,000 amount to the lease arrangement.

(b) Prepare the journal entry or entries that should be recorded on January 1, 2014, by Cage Company.

(c) Prepare the journal entry to record depreciation of the leased asset for the year 2014.

(d) Prepare the journal entry to record the interest expense for the year 2014.

(e) Prepare the journal entry to record the lease payment of January 1, 2015, assuming reversing entries are not made.

(f) What amounts will appear on the lessee's December 31, 2014, balance sheet relative to the lease contract?

2 **P21-9 (Lessee Entries, Capital Lease with Monthly Payments)** Shapiro Inc. was incorporated in 2013 to operate as a computer software service firm with an accounting fiscal year ending August 31. Shapiro's primary product is a sophisticated online inventory-control system; its customers pay a fixed fee plus a usage charge for using the system.

Shapiro has leased a large, Alpha-3 computer system from the manufacturer. The lease calls for a monthly rental of $40,000 for the 144 months (12 years) of the lease term. The estimated useful life of the computer is 15 years.

Each scheduled monthly rental payment includes $3,000 for full-service maintenance on the computer to be performed by the manufacturer. All rentals are payable on the first day of the month beginning with August 1, 2014, the date the computer was installed and the lease agreement was signed. The lease is noncancelable for its 12-year term, and it is secured only by the manufacturer's chattel lien on the Alpha-3 system.

This lease is to be accounted for as a capital lease by Shapiro, and it will be depreciated by the straight-line method with no expected salvage value. Borrowed funds for this type of transaction would cost Shapiro 12% per year (1% per month). Following is a schedule of the present value of $1 for selected periods discounted at 1% per period when payments are made at the beginning of each period.

Periods (months)	Present Value of $1 per Period Discounted at 1% per Period
1	1.000
2	1.990
3	2.970
143	76.658
144	76.899

Instructions

Prepare all entries Shapiro should have made in its accounting records during August 2014 relating to this lease. Give full explanations and show supporting computations for each entry. Remember, August 31, 2014, is the end of Shapiro's fiscal accounting period and it will be preparing financial statements on that date. Do not prepare closing entries.

(AICPA adapted)

4 7 8 **P21-10 (Lessor Computations and Entries, Sales-Type Lease with Unguaranteed Residual Value)** George Company manufactures a check-in kiosk with an estimated economic life of 12 years and leases it to National Airlines for a period of 10 years. The normal selling price of the equipment is $278,072, and its unguaranteed residual value at the end of the lease term is estimated to be $20,000. National will pay annual payments of $40,000 at the beginning of each year and all maintenance, insurance, and taxes. George incurred costs of $180,000 in manufacturing the equipment and $4,000 in negotiating and closing the lease. George has determined that the collectibility of the lease payments is reasonably predictable, that no additional costs will be incurred, and that the implicit interest rate is 10%.

Instructions

(a) Discuss the nature of this lease in relation to the lessor and compute the amount of each of the following items.

(1) Lease receivable.

(2) Sales price.

(3) Cost of sales.

(b) Prepare a 10-year lease amortization schedule.

(c) Prepare all of the lessor's journal entries for the first year.

2 6 7 **P21-11 (Lessee Computations and Entries, Capital Lease with Unguaranteed Residual Value)** Assume the same data as in P21-10 with National Airlines Co. having an incremental borrowing rate of 10%.

Instructions

(a) Discuss the nature of this lease in relation to the lessee, and compute the amount of the initial lease liability.

(b) Prepare a 10-year lease amortization schedule.

(c) Prepare all of the lessee's journal entries for the first year.

2 6 **P21-12 (Basic Lessee Accounting with Difficult PV Calculation)** In 2013, Grishell Trucking Company negotiated and closed a long-term lease contract for newly constructed truck terminals and freight storage facilities. The buildings were erected to the company's specifications on land owned by the company. On January 1, 2014, Grishell Trucking Company took possession of the lease properties. On

January 1, 2014 and 2015, the company made cash payments of $948,000 that were recorded as rental expenses.

Although the terminals have a composite useful life of 40 years, the noncancelable lease runs for 20 years from January 1, 2014, with a bargain-purchase option available upon expiration of the lease.

The 20-year lease is effective for the period January 1, 2014, through December 31, 2033. Advance rental payments of $800,000 are payable to the lessor on January 1 of each of the first 10 years of the lease term. Advance rental payments of $320,000 are due on January 1 for each of the last 10 years of the lease. The company has an option to purchase all of these leased facilities for $1 on December 31, 2033. It also must make annual payments to the lessor of $125,000 for property taxes and $23,000 for insurance. The lease was negotiated to assure the lessor a 6% rate of return.

Instructions

(a) Prepare a schedule to compute for Grishell Trucking Company the present value of the terminal facilities and related obligation at January 1, 2014.

(b) Assuming that the present value of terminal facilities and related obligation at January 1, 2014, was $7,600,000, prepare journal entries for Grishell Trucking Company to record the:

(1) Cash payment to the lessor on January 1, 2016.

(2) Amortization of the cost of the leased properties for 2016 using the straight-line method and assuming a zero salvage value.

(3) Accrual of interest expense at December 31, 2016.

Selected present value factors are as follows.

Periods	For an Ordinary Annuity of $1 at 6%	For $1 at 6%
1	.943396	.943396
2	1.833393	.889996
8	6.209794	.627412
9	6.801692	.591898
10	7.360087	.558395
19	11.158117	.330513
20	11.469921	.311805

(AICPA adapted)

4 7 8 **P21-13 (Lessor Computations and Entries, Sales-Type Lease with Guaranteed Residual Value)** Amirante Inc. manufactures an X-ray machine with an estimated life of 12 years and leases it to Chambers Medical Center for a period of 10 years. The normal selling price of the machine is $411,324, and its guaranteed residual value at the end of the noncancelable lease term is estimated to be $15,000. The hospital will pay rents of $60,000 at the beginning of each year and all maintenance, insurance, and taxes. Amirante Inc. incurred costs of $250,000 in manufacturing the machine and $14,000 in negotiating and closing the lease. Amirante Inc. has determined that the collectibility of the lease payments is reasonably predictable, that there will be no additional costs incurred, and that the implicit interest rate is 10%.

Instructions

(a) Discuss the nature of this lease in relation to the lessor and compute the amount of each of the following items.

(1) Lease receivable at inception of the lease.

(2) Sales price.

(3) Cost of sales.

(b) Prepare a 10-year lease amortization schedule.

(c) Prepare all of the lessor's journal entries for the first year.

2 7 **P21-14 (Lessee Computations and Entries, Capital Lease with Guaranteed Residual Value)** Assume the same data as in P21-13 and that Chambers Medical Center has an incremental borrowing rate of 10%.

Instructions

(a) Discuss the nature of this lease in relation to the lessee, and compute the amount of the initial lease liability.

(b) Prepare a 10-year lease amortization schedule.

(c) Prepare all of the lessee's journal entries for the first year.

2 3 7 **P21-15 (Operating Lease vs. Capital Lease)** You are auditing the December 31, 2014, financial statements of Hockney, Inc., manufacturer of novelties and party favors. During your inspection of the company garage, you discovered that a used automobile not listed in the equipment subsidiary ledger is parked there. You ask Stacy Reeder, plant manager, about the vehicle, and she tells you that the company did not list the automobile because the company was only leasing it. The lease agreement was entered into on January 1, 2014, with Crown New and Used Cars.

You decide to review the lease agreement to ensure that the lease should be afforded operating lease treatment, and you discover the following lease terms.

1. Noncancelable term of 4 years.
2. Rental of $3,240 per year (at the end of each year). (The present value at 8% per year is $10,731.)
3. Estimated residual value after 4 years is $1,100. (The present value at 8% per year is $809.) Hockney guarantees the residual value of $1,100.
4. Estimated economic life of the automobile is 5 years.
5. Hockney's incremental borrowing rate is 8% per year.

Instructions

You are a senior auditor writing a memo to your supervisor, the audit partner in charge of this audit, to discuss the above situation. Be sure to include (a) why you inspected the lease agreement, (b) what you determined about the lease, and (c) how you advised your client to account for this lease. Explain every journal entry that you believe is necessary to record this lease properly on the client's books. (It is also necessary to include the fact that you communicated this information to your client.)

2 4 7 **P21-16 (Lessee-Lessor Accounting for Residual Values)** Goring Dairy leases its milking equipment from King Finance Company under the following lease terms.

1. The lease term is 10 years, noncancelable, and requires equal rental payments of $30,300 due at the beginning of each year starting January 1, 2014.
2. The equipment has a fair value and cost at the inception of the lease (January 1, 2014) of $220,404, an estimated economic life of 10 years, and a residual value (which is guaranteed by Goring Dairy) of $20,000.
3. The lease contains no renewable options, and the equipment reverts to King Finance Company upon termination of the lease.
4. Goring Dairy's incremental borrowing rate is 9% per year. The implicit rate is also 9%.
5. Goring Dairy depreciates similar equipment that it owns on a straight-line basis.
6. Collectibility of the payments is reasonably predictable, and there are no important uncertainties surrounding the costs yet to be incurred by the lessor.

Instructions

(a) Evaluate the criteria for classification of the lease, and describe the nature of the lease. In general, discuss how the lessee and lessor should account for the lease transaction.

(b) Prepare the journal entries for the lessee and lessor at January 1, 2014, and December 31, 2014 (the lessee's and lessor's year-end). Assume no reversing entries.

(c) What would have been the amount capitalized by the lessee upon the inception of the lease if:
  (1) The residual value of $20,000 had been guaranteed by a third party, not the lessee?
  (2) The residual value of $20,000 had not been guaranteed at all?

(d) On the lessor's books, what would be the amount recorded as the Net Investment (Lease Receivable) at the inception of the lease, assuming:
  (1) The residual value of $20,000 had been guaranteed by a third party?
  (2) The residual value of $20,000 had not been guaranteed at all?

(e) Suppose the useful life of the milking equipment is 20 years. How large would the residual value have to be at the end of 10 years in order for the lessee to qualify for the operating method? (Assume that the residual value would be guaranteed by a third party.) (*Hint:* The lessee's annual payments will be appropriately reduced as the residual value increases.)

PROBLEMS SET B

See the book's companion website, at **www.wiley.com/college/kieso**, for an additional set of problems.

CONCEPTS FOR ANALYSIS

CA21-1 (Lessee Accounting and Reporting) On January 1, 2014, Evans Company entered into a noncancelable lease for a machine to be used in its manufacturing operations. The lease transfers ownership of the machine to Evans by the end of the lease term. The term of the lease is 8 years. The minimum lease payment made by Evans on January 1, 2014, was one of eight equal annual payments. At the inception of the lease, the criteria established for classification as a capital lease by the lessee were met.

Instructions

(a) What is the theoretical basis for the accounting standard that requires certain long-term leases to be capitalized by the lessee? Do not discuss the specific criteria for classifying a specific lease as a capital lease.

(b) How should Evans account for this lease at its inception and determine the amount to be recorded?

(c) What expenses related to this lease will Evans incur during the first year of the lease, and how will they be determined?

(d) How should Evans report the lease transaction on its December 31, 2014, balance sheet?

CA21-2 (Lessor and Lessee Accounting and Disclosure) Sylvan Inc. entered into a noncancelable lease arrangement with Breton Leasing Corporation for a certain machine. Breton's primary business is leasing; it is not a manufacturer or dealer. Sylvan will lease the machine for a period of 3 years, which is 50% of the machine's economic life. Breton will take possession of the machine at the end of the initial 3-year lease and lease it to another, smaller company that does not need the most current version of the machine. Sylvan does not guarantee any residual value for the machine and will not purchase the machine at the end of the lease term.

Sylvan's incremental borrowing rate is 10%, and the implicit rate in the lease is 9%. Sylvan has no way of knowing the implicit rate used by Breton. Using either rate, the present value of the minimum lease payments is between 90% and 100% of the fair value of the machine at the date of the lease agreement.

Sylvan has agreed to pay all executory costs directly, and no allowance for these costs is included in the lease payments.

Breton is reasonably certain that Sylvan will pay all lease payments. Because Sylvan has agreed to pay all executory costs, there are no important uncertainties regarding costs to be incurred by Breton. Assume that no indirect costs are involved.

Instructions

(a) With respect to Sylvan (the lessee), answer the following.

- **(1)** What type of lease has been entered into? Explain the reason for your answer.
- **(2)** How should Sylvan compute the appropriate amount to be recorded for the lease or asset acquired?
- **(3)** What accounts will be created or affected by this transaction, and how will the lease or asset and other costs related to the transaction be matched with earnings?
- **(4)** What disclosures must Sylvan make regarding this leased asset?

(b) With respect to Breton (the lessor), answer the following.

- **(1)** What type of leasing arrangement has been entered into? Explain the reason for your answer.
- **(2)** How should this lease be recorded by Breton, and how are the appropriate amounts determined?
- **(3)** How should Breton determine the appropriate amount of earnings to be recognized from each lease payment?
- **(4)** What disclosures must Breton make regarding this lease?

(AICPA adapted)

CA21-3 (Lessee Capitalization Criteria) On January 1, Santiago Company, a lessee, entered into three noncancelable leases for brand-new equipment, Lease L, Lease M, and Lease N. None of the three leases transfers ownership of the equipment to Santiago at the end of the lease term. For each of the three leases, the present value at the beginning of the lease term of the minimum lease payments, excluding that portion of the payments representing executory costs such as insurance, maintenance, and taxes to be paid by the lessor, is 75% of the fair value of the equipment.

The following information is peculiar to each lease.

1. Lease L does not contain a bargain-purchase option. The lease term is equal to 80% of the estimated economic life of the equipment.
2. Lease M contains a bargain-purchase option. The lease term is equal to 50% of the estimated economic life of the equipment.
3. Lease N does not contain a bargain-purchase option. The lease term is equal to 50% of the estimated economic life of the equipment.

Instructions

(a) How should Santiago Company classify each of the three leases above, and why? Discuss the rationale for your answer.

(b) What amount, if any, should Santiago record as a liability at the inception of the lease for each of the three leases above?

(c) Assuming that the minimum lease payments are made on a straight-line basis, how should Santiago record each minimum lease payment for each of the three leases above?

(AICPA adapted)

CA21-4 (Comparison of Different Types of Accounting by Lessee and Lessor)

Part 1: Capital leases and operating leases are the two classifications of leases described in FASB pronouncements from the standpoint of the **lessee**.

Instructions

(a) Describe how a capital lease would be accounted for by the lessee both at the inception of the lease and during the first year of the lease, assuming the lease transfers ownership of the property to the lessee by the end of the lease.

(b) Describe how an operating lease would be accounted for by the lessee both at the inception of the lease and during the first year of the lease, assuming equal monthly payments are made by the lessee at the beginning of each month of the lease. Describe the change in accounting, if any, when rental payments are not made on a straight-line basis.

Do **not** discuss the criteria for distinguishing between capital leases and operating leases.

Part 2: Sales-type leases and direct-financing leases are two of the classifications of leases described in FASB pronouncements from the standpoint of the **lessor**.

Instructions

Compare and contrast a sales-type lease with a direct-financing lease as follows.

(a) Lease receivable.

(b) Recognition of interest revenue.

(c) Manufacturer's or dealer's profit.

Do **not** discuss the criteria for distinguishing between the leases described above and operating leases.

(AICPA adapted)

CA21-5 (Lessee Capitalization of Bargain-Purchase Option) Albertsen Corporation is considering proposals for either leasing or purchasing aircraft. The proposed lease agreement involves a twin-engine turboprop Viking that has a fair value of $1,000,000. This plane would be leased for a period of 10 years beginning January 1, 2014. The lease agreement is cancelable only upon accidental destruction of the plane. An annual lease payment of $141,780 is due on January 1 of each year; the first payment is to be made on January 1, 2014. Maintenance operations are strictly scheduled by the lessor, and Albertsen Corporation will pay for these services as they are performed. Estimated annual maintenance costs are $6,900. The lessor will pay all insurance premiums and local property taxes, which amount to a combined total of $4,000 annually and are included in the annual lease payment of $141,780. Upon expiration of the 10-year lease, Albertsen Corporation can purchase the Viking for $44,440. The estimated useful life of the plane is 15 years, and its salvage value in the used plane market is estimated to be $100,000 after 10 years. The salvage value probably will never be less than $75,000 if the engines are overhauled and maintained as prescribed by the manufacturer. If the purchase option is not exercised, possession of the plane will revert to the lessor, and there is no provision for renewing the lease agreement beyond its termination on December 31, 2023.

Albertsen Corporation can borrow $1,000,000 under a 10-year term loan agreement at an annual interest rate of 12%. The lessor's implicit interest rate is not expressly stated in the lease agreement, but this rate appears to be approximately 8% based on 10 net rental payments of $137,780 per year and the initial fair value of $1,000,000 for the plane. On January 1, 2014, the present value of all net rental payments and the purchase option of $44,440 is $888,890 using the 12% interest rate. The present value of all net rental payments and the $44,440 purchase option on January 1, 2014, is $1,022,226 using the 8% interest rate implicit in the lease agreement. The financial vice president of Albertsen Corporation has established that this lease agreement is a capital lease as defined in GAAP.

Instructions

(a) What is the appropriate amount that Albertsen Corporation should recognize for the leased aircraft on its balance sheet after the lease is signed?

(b) Without prejudice to your answer in part (a), assume that the annual lease payment is $141,780 as stated in the question, that the appropriate capitalized amount for the leased aircraft is $1,000,000 on January 1, 2014, and that the interest rate is 9%. How will the lease be reported in the December 31, 2014, balance sheet and related income statement? (Ignore any income tax implications.)

(CMA adapted)

CA21-6 (Lease Capitalization, Bargain-Purchase Option) Baden Corporation entered into a lease agreement for 10 photocopy machines for its corporate headquarters. The lease agreement qualifies as an operating lease in all terms except there is a bargain-purchase option. After the 5-year lease term, the corporation can purchase each copier for $1,000, when the anticipated fair value is $2,500.

Jerry Suffolk, the financial vice president, thinks the financial statements must recognize the lease agreement as a capital lease because of the bargain-purchase option. The controller, Diane Buchanan, disagrees: "Although I don't know much about the copiers themselves, there is a way to avoid recording the lease liability." She argues that the corporation might claim that copier technology advances rapidly and that by the end of the lease term the machines will most likely not be worth the $1,000 bargain price.

Instructions

Answer the following questions.

(a) What ethical issue is at stake?

(b) Should the controller's argument be accepted if she does not really know much about copier technology? Would it make a difference if the controller were knowledgeable about the pace of change in copier technology?

(c) What should Suffolk do?

*__CA21-7 (Sale-Leaseback)__ On January 1, 2014, Perriman Company sold equipment for cash and leased it back. As seller-lessee, Perriman retained the right to substantially all of the remaining use of the equipment.

The term of the lease is 8 years. There is a gain on the sale portion of the transaction. The lease portion of the transaction is classified appropriately as a capital lease.

Instructions

(a) What is the theoretical basis for requiring lessees to capitalize certain long-term leases? **Do not discuss the specific criteria for classifying a lease as a capital lease.**

(b) (1) How should Perriman account for the sale portion of the sale-leaseback transaction at January 1, 2014?

(2) How should Perriman account for the leaseback portion of the sale-leaseback transaction at January 1, 2014?

(c) How should Perriman account for the gain on the sale portion of the sale-leaseback transaction during the first year of the lease? Why?

(AICPA adapted)

USING YOUR JUDGMENT

FINANCIAL REPORTING

Financial Reporting Problem

P&G

The Procter & Gamble Company (P&G)

The financial statements of P&G are presented in Appendix 5B. The company's complete annual report, including the notes to the financial statements, can be accessed at the book's companion website, **www.wiley.com/college/kieso**.

Instructions

Refer to P&G's financial statements, accompanying notes, and management's discussion and analysis to answer the following questions.

(a) What types of leases are used by P&G?

(b) What amount of capital leases was reported by P&G in total and for less than one year?

(c) What minimum annual rental commitments under all noncancelable leases at June 30, 2011, did P&G disclose?

Comparative Analysis Case

UAL, Inc. and Southwest Airlines

Instructions

Go to the book's companion website or the company websites and use information found there to answer the following questions related to UAL, Inc. and Southwest Airlines.

(a) What types of leases are used by Southwest and on what assets are these leases primarily used?

(b) How long-term are some of Southwest's leases? What are some of the characteristics or provisions of Southwest's (as lessee) leases?

(c) What did Southwest report in 2011 as its future minimum annual rental commitments under noncancelable leases?

(d) At year-end 2011, what was the present value of the minimum rental payments under Southwest's capital leases? How much imputed interest was deducted from the future minimum annual rental commitments to arrive at the present value?

(e) What were the amounts and details reported by Southwest for rental expense in 2011, 2010, and 2009?

(f) How does UAL's use of leases compare with Southwest's?

Financial Statement Analysis Case

Wal-Mart Stores, Inc.

Presented in Illustration 21-31 are the financial statement disclosures from the January 31, 2012, annual report of Wal-Mart Stores, Inc.

Instructions

Answer the following questions related to these disclosures.

(a) What is the total obligation under capital leases at January 31, 2012, for Wal-Mart?

(b) What is the total rental expense reported for leasing activity for the year ended January 31, 2012, for Wal-Mart?

(c) Estimate the off-balance-sheet liability due to Wal-Mart's operating leases at January 31, 2012.

Accounting, Analysis, and Principles

Salaur Company is evaluating a lease arrangement being offered by TSP Company for use of a computer system. The lease is noncancelable, and in no case does Salaur receive title to the computers during or at the end of the lease term. The lease starts on January 1, 2014, with the first rental payment due on January 1, 2014. Additional information related to the lease is as follows.

Yearly rental	$3,557.25
Lease term	3 years
Estimated economic life	5 years
Purchase option	$3,000 at end of 3 years, which approximates fair value
Renewal option	1 year at $1,500; no penalty for nonrenewal; standard renewal clause
Fair value at inception of lease	$10,000
Cost of asset to lessor	$10,000
Residual value:	
Guaranteed	–0–
Unguaranteed	$3,000
Lessor's implicit rate (known by the lessee)	12%
Executory costs paid by:	Lessor; estimated to be $500 per year (included in rental equipment)
Estimated fair value at end of lease	$3,000

Accounting

Analyze the lease capitalization criteria for this lease for Salaur Company. Prepare the journal entry for Salaur on January 1, 2014.

Analysis

Briefly discuss the impact of the accounting for this lease for two common ratios: return on assets and debt to total assets.

Principles

What element of faithful representation (completeness, neutrality, free from error) is being addressed when a company like Salaur evaluates lease capitalization criteria?

BRIDGE TO THE PROFESSION

Professional Research: FASB Codification

Daniel Hardware Co. is considering alternative financing arrangements for equipment used in its warehouses. Besides purchasing the equipment outright, Daniel is also considering a lease. Accounting for the outright purchase is fairly straightforward, but because Daniel has not used equipment leases in the past, the accounting staff is less informed about the specific accounting rules for leases.

The staff is aware of some lease rules related to a "90 percent of fair value," "75 percent of useful life," and "residual value deficiencies," but they are unsure about the meanings of these terms in lease accounting. Daniel has asked you to conduct some research on these items related to lease capitalization criteria.

Instructions

If your school has a subscription to the FASB Codification, go to *http://aaahq.org/ascLogin.cfm* to log in and prepare responses to the following. Provide Codification references for your responses.

(a) What is the objective of lease classification criteria?

(b) An important element of evaluating leases is determining whether substantially all of the risks and rewards of ownership are transferred in the lease. How is "substantially all" defined in the authoritative literature?

(c) Besides the noncancelable term of the lease, name at least three other considerations in determining the "lease term."

(d) A common issue in the accounting for leases concerns lease requirements that the lessee make up a residual value deficiency that is attributable to damage, extraordinary wear and tear, or excessive usage (e.g., excessive mileage on a leased vehicle). Do these features constitute a lessee guarantee of the residual value such that the estimated residual value of the leased property at the end of the lease term should be included in minimum lease payments? Explain.

Additional Professional Resources

See the book's companion website, at **www.wiley.com/college/kieso**, for professional simulations as well as other study resources.

IFRS INSIGHTS

11 LEARNING OBJECTIVE
Compare the accounting for leases under GAAP and IFRS.

Leasing is a global business. Lessors and lessees enter into arrangements with one another without regard to national boundaries. Although GAAP and IFRS for leasing are similar, both the FASB and the IASB have decided that the existing accounting does not provide the most useful, transparent, and complete information about leasing transactions that should be provided in the financial statements.

RELEVANT FACTS

Following are the key similarities and differences between GAAP and IFRS related to the accounting for leases.

Similarities

- Both GAAP and IFRS share the same objective of recording leases by lessees and lessors according to their economic substance—that is, according to the definitions of assets and liabilities.
- Much of the terminology for lease accounting in IFRS and GAAP is the same.
- Under IFRS, lessees and lessors use the same general lease capitalization criteria to determine if the risks and rewards of ownership have been transferred in the lease.

Differences

- One difference in lease terminology is that finance leases are referred to as capital leases in GAAP.
- GAAP for leases uses bright-line criteria to determine if a lease arrangement transfers the risks and rewards of ownership; IFRS is more general in its provisions.
- GAAP has additional lessor criteria: payments are collectible and there are no additional costs associated with a lease.
- IFRS requires that lessees use the implicit rate to record a lease unless it is impractical to determine the lessor's implicit rate. GAAP requires use of the incremental rate unless the implicit rate is known by the lessee and the implicit rate is lower than the incremental rate.
- Under GAAP, extensive disclosure of future non-cancelable lease payments is required for each of the next five years and the years thereafter. Although some international companies (e.g., Nokia) provide a year-by-year breakout of payments due in years 1 through 5, IFRS does not require it.
- The FASB standard for leases was originally issued in 1976. The standard (*SFAS No. 13*) has been the subject of more than 30 interpretations since its issuance. The IFRS leasing standard is *IAS 17*, first issued in 1982. This standard is the subject of only three interpretations. One reason for this small number of interpretations is that IFRS does not specifically address a number of leasing transactions that are covered by GAAP. Examples include lease agreements for natural resources, sale-leasebacks, real estate leases, and leveraged leases.

ABOUT THE NUMBERS

Accounting by the Lessee

If Air France (the lessee) **capitalizes** a lease, it records an asset and a liability generally equal to the present value of the rental payments. ILFC (the lessor), having transferred substantially all the benefits and risks of ownership, recognizes a sale by removing the asset from the statement of financial position and replacing it with a receivable.

Under IFRS, a lease is classified as a **finance lease** if it transfers substantially all the risks and rewards incidental to ownership. In order to record a lease as a finance lease, the lease must be non-cancelable. The IASB identifies the four criteria listed in Illustration IFRS21-1 for assessing whether the risks and rewards have been transferred in the lease arrangement.

Capitalization Criteria (Lessee)

1. The lease transfers ownership of the property to the lessee.
2. The lease contains a bargain-purchase option.
3. The lease term is for the major part of the economic life of the asset.
4. The present value of the minimum lease payments amounts to substantially all of the fair value of the leased asset.

ILLUSTRATION IFRS21-1
Capitalization Criteria for Lessee

Air France classifies and accounts for leases that **do not meet any of the four criteria** as **operating leases**. Illustration IFRS21-2 shows that a lease meeting any one of the four criteria results in the lessee having a finance lease.

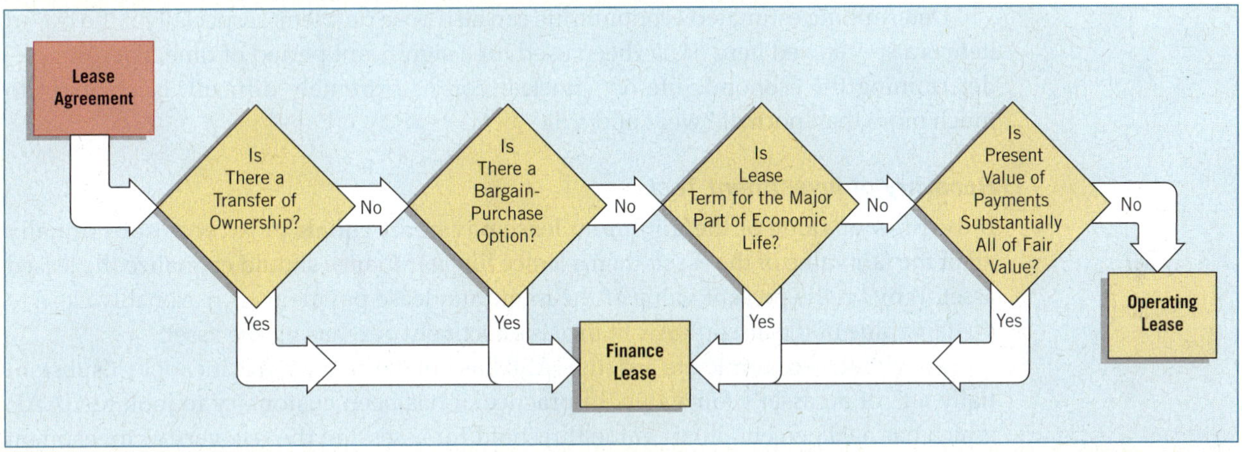

ILLUSTRATION IFRS21-2
Diagram of Lessee's Criteria for Lease Classification

Thus, the proper classification of a lease is determined based on the substance of the lease transaction rather than on its mere form. This determination often requires the use of professional judgment of whether the risks and rewards of ownership are transferred.

As indicated, the capitalization criteria for finance leases are similar to those used in GAAP for capital leases (see Illustration 21-3 on page 1275). The main differences relate to the economic life and recoverability tests, which we describe in the following sections.

Economic Life Test

If the lease period is for a major part of the asset's economic life, the lessor transfers most of the risks and rewards of ownership to the lessee. Capitalization is therefore appropriate. However, determining the lease term and what constitutes the major part of the economic life of the asset can be troublesome.

The IASB has not defined what is meant by the "major part" of an asset's economic life. In practice, following the IASB Hierarchy, it has been customary to look to GAAP, which has a 75 percent of economic life threshold for evaluating the economic life test. While the 75 percent guideline may be a useful reference point, it does not represent an automatic cutoff point. Rather, lessees and lessors should consider all relevant factors when assessing whether substantially all the risks and rewards of ownership have been transferred in the lease.[21] *For purposes of homework, assume a 75 percent threshold for the economic life test, unless otherwise stated.*

[21]See KPMG, *Insights into IFRS*, Fifth Edition (Thomson Reuters: London, 2008), p. 1011; and The International Financial Reporting Group of Ernst and Young, *International GAAP, 2009* (John Wiley and Sons: New York, 2009), p. 1356.

The **lease term** is generally considered to be the fixed, non-cancelable term of the lease. However, a bargain-renewal option, if provided in the lease agreement, can extend this period. A **bargain-renewal option** allows the lessee to renew the lease for a rental that is lower than the expected fair rental at the date the option becomes exercisable. At the inception of the lease, the difference between the renewal rental and the expected fair rental must be great enough to make exercise of the option to renew reasonably assured.

For example, assume that **Carrefour** leases **Lenovo** PCs for two years at a rental of $100 per month per computer and subsequently can lease them for $10 per month per computer for another two years. The lease clearly offers a bargain-renewal option; the lease term is considered to be four years. However, with bargain-renewal options, as with bargain-purchase options, it is sometimes difficult to determine what is a bargain.

Determining estimated economic life can also pose problems, especially if the leased item is a specialized item or has been used for a significant period of time. For example, determining the economic life of a nuclear core is extremely difficult. It is subject to much more than normal "wear and tear."

Recovery of Investment Test

If the present value of the minimum lease payments equals or exceeds substantially all of the fair value of the asset, then a lessee like **Air France** should capitalize the leased asset. Why? If the present value of the minimum lease payments is reasonably close to the fair value of the aircraft, Air France is effectively purchasing the asset.

As with the economic life test, the IASB has not defined what is meant by "substantially all" of an asset's fair value. In practice, it has been customary to look to GAAP, which has a 90 percent of fair value threshold for assessing the recovery of investment test. Again, rather than focusing on any single element of the lease classification indicators, lessees and lessors should consider all relevant factors when evaluating lease classification criteria.[22] *For purposes of homework, assume a 90 percent threshold for the recovery of investment test.*

Determining the present value of the minimum lease payments involves three important concepts: (1) minimum lease payments, (2) executory costs, and (3) discount rate. The IFRS guidelines for minimum lease payments and executory costs are the same as that of GAAP.

Discount Rate. A lessee, like Air France, computes the present value of the minimum lease payments using the **implicit interest rate**. This rate is defined as the discount rate that, at the inception of the lease, causes the aggregate present value of the minimum lease payments and the unguaranteed residual value to be equal to the fair value of the leased asset.

While Air France may argue that it cannot determine the implicit rate of the lessor, in most cases Air France can approximate the implicit rate used by ILFC. In the event that it is impracticable to determine the implicit rate, Air France should use its incremental borrowing rate. The incremental borrowing rate is the rate of interest the lessee would have to pay on a similar lease or the rate that, at the inception of the lease, the lessee would incur to borrow over a similar term the funds necessary to purchase the asset.

[22] *Ibid.* The 75 percent of useful life and 90 percent of fair value "bright-line" cutoffs in GAAP have been criticized. Many believe that lessees structure leases so as to just miss the 75 and 90 percent cutoffs, thereby avoiding classifying leases as finance leases and keeping leased assets and the related liabilities off the statement of financial position. See Warren McGregor, "Accounting for Leases: A New Approach," Special Report (Norwalk, Conn.: FASB, 1996).

If known or practicable to estimate, use of the implicit rate is preferred. This is because **the implicit rate of ILFC is generally a more realistic rate** to use in determining the amount (if any) to report as the asset and related liability for Air France. In addition, use of the implicit rate avoids use of **an artificially high incremental borrowing rate** that would cause the present value of the minimum lease payments to be lower, supporting an argument that the lease does not meet the recovery of investment test. Use of such a rate would thus make it more likely that the lessee avoids capitalization of the leased asset and related liability.

The determination of whether or not a reasonable estimate could be made will require judgment, particularly where the result from using the incremental borrowing rate comes close to meeting the fair value test. Because Air France **may not capitalize the leased property at more than its fair value** (as we discuss later), it cannot use an excessively low discount rate.

Finance Lease Method (Lessee)

To illustrate a finance lease, assume that **CNH Capital** (a subsidiary of CNH Global) and **Ivanhoe Mines Ltd.** sign a lease agreement dated January 1, 2014, that calls for CNH to lease a front-end loader to Ivanhoe beginning January 1, 2014. The terms and provisions of the lease agreement, and other pertinent data, are as follows.

- The term of the lease is five years. The lease agreement is non-cancelable, requiring equal rental payments of $25,981.62 at the beginning of each year (annuity-due basis).
- The loader has a fair value at the inception of the lease of $100,000, an estimated economic life of five years, and no residual value.
- Ivanhoe pays all of the executory costs directly to third parties except for the property taxes of $2,000 per year, which is included as part of its annual payments to CNH.
- The lease contains no renewal options. The loader reverts to CNH at the termination of the lease.
- Ivanhoe's incremental borrowing rate is 11 percent per year.
- Ivanhoe depreciates similar equipment that it owns on a straight-line basis.
- CNH sets the annual rental to earn a rate of return on its investment of 10 percent per year; Ivanhoe knows this fact.

The lease meets the criteria for classification as a finance lease for the following reasons:

1. The lease term of five years, being equal to the equipment's estimated economic life of five years, satisfies the economic life test.
2. The present value of the minimum lease payments ($100,000 as computed below) equals the fair value of the loader ($100,000).

The minimum lease payments are $119,908.10 ($23,981.62 × 5). Ivanhoe computes the amount capitalized as leased assets as the present value of the minimum lease payments (excluding executory costs—property taxes of $2,000) as shown in Illustration IFRS21-3.

Capitalized amount	=	($25,981.62 − $2,000) × Present value of an annuity due of 1 for 5 periods at 10% (Table 6-5)
	=	$23,981.62 × 4.16986
	=	$100,000

ILLUSTRATION IFRS21-3
Computation of Capitalized Lease Payments

Calculator Solution for Lease Payment

	Inputs	Answer
N	5	
I	10	
PV	?	100,000
PMT	–23,981.59*	
FV	0	

*Set payments to beginning of period.

Ivanhoe uses CNH's implicit interest rate of 10 percent instead of its incremental borrowing rate of 11 percent because it knows about it.[23] Ivanhoe records the finance lease on its books on January 1, 2014, as:

Leased Equipment (under finance leases)	100,000	
Lease Liability		100,000

Note that the entry records the obligation at the net amount of $100,000 (the present value of the future rental payments) rather than at the gross amount of $119,908.10 ($23,981.62 × 5).

Ivanhoe records the **first lease payment on January 1, 2014**, as follows.

Property Tax Expense	2,000.00	
Lease Liability	23,981.62	
Cash		25,981.62

Each lease payment of $25,981.62 consists of three elements: (1) a reduction in the lease liability, (2) a financing cost (interest expense), and (3) executory costs (property taxes). The total financing cost (interest expense) over the term of the lease is $19,908.10. This amount is the difference between the present value of the lease payments ($100,000) and the actual cash disbursed, net of executory costs ($119,908.10). The annual interest expense, applying the effective-interest method, is a function of the outstanding liability, as Illustration IFRS21-4 shows.

ILLUSTRATION IFRS21-4
Lease Amortization Schedule for Lessee—Annuity-Due Basis

IVANHOE MINES
LEASE AMORTIZATION SCHEDULE
ANNUITY-DUE BASIS

Date	Annual Lease Payment (a)	Executory Costs (b)	Interest (10%) on Liability (c)	Reduction of Lease Liability (d)	Lease Liability (e)
1/1/14					$100,000.00
1/1/14	$ 25,981.62	$ 2,000	$ –0–	$ 23,981.62	76,018.38
1/1/15	25,981.62	2,000	7,601.84	16,379.78	59,638.60
1/1/16	25,981.62	2,000	5,963.86	18,017.76	41,620.84
1/1/17	25,981.62	2,000	4,162.08	19,819.54	21,801.30
1/1/18	25,981.62	2,000	2,180.32*	21,801.30	–0–
	$129,908.10	$10,000	$19,908.10	$100,000.00	

(a) Lease payment as required by lease.
(b) Executory costs included in rental payment.
(c) Ten percent of the preceding balance of (e) except for 1/1/14; since this is an annuity due, no time has elapsed at the date of the first payment and no interest has accrued.
(d) (a) minus (b) and (c).
(e) Preceding balance minus (d).
*Rounded by 19 cents.

At the end of its fiscal year, December 31, 2014, Ivanhoe records **accrued interest** as follows.

Interest Expense	7,601.84	
Interest Payable		7,601.84

Depreciation of the leased equipment over its five-year lease term, applying Ivanhoe's normal depreciation policy (straight-line method), results in the following entry on December 31, 2014.

[23]If it is impracticable for Ivanhoe to determine the implicit rate and it has an incremental borrowing rate of, say, 9 percent (lower than the 10 percent rate used by CNH), the present value computation would yield a capitalized amount of $101,675.35 ($23,981.62 × 4.23972). Thus, use of an unrealistically low discount rate could lead to a lessee recording a leased asset at an amount exceeding the fair value of the equipment, which is generally prohibited in IFRS. This explains why the implicit rate should be used to capitalize the minimum lease payments.

Depreciation Expense (finance leases)	20,000	
Accumulated Depreciation—Finance Leases ($100,000 ÷ 5 years)		20,000

At December 31, 2014, Ivanhoe separately identifies the assets recorded under finance leases on its statement of financial position. Similarly, it separately identifies the related obligations. Thus, once a lessee capitalizes a finance lease, the accounting under IFRS is the same as that applied for capital leases under GAAP.

Accounting by the Lessor

For accounting purposes, under IFRS the **lessor** also classifies leases as operating or finance leases. Finance leases may be further subdivided into direct-financing and sales-type leases.

As with lessee accounting, if the lease transfers substantially all the risks and rewards incidental to ownership, the lessor shall classify and account for the arrangement as a finance lease. Lessors evaluate the same criteria shown in Illustration IFRS21-1 to make this determination.

The distinction for the lessor between a direct-financing lease and a sales-type lease is the presence or absence of a manufacturer's or dealer's profit (or loss). A sales-type lease involves a manufacturer's or dealer's profit, and a direct-financing lease does not. The profit (or loss) to the lessor is evidenced by the difference between the fair value of the leased property at the inception of the lease and the lessor's cost or carrying amount (book value).

Normally, sales-type leases arise when manufacturers or dealers use leasing as a means of marketing their products. For example, a computer manufacturer will lease its computer equipment (possibly through a captive) to businesses and institutions. Direct-financing leases generally result from arrangements with lessors that are primarily engaged in financing operations (e.g., banks).

Lessors classify and account for all leases that do not qualify as direct-financing or sales-type leases as operating leases. Illustration IFRS21-5 shows the circumstances under which a lessor classifies a lease as operating, direct-financing, or sales-type.

ILLUSTRATION IFRS21-5
Diagram of Lessor's Criteria for Lease Classification

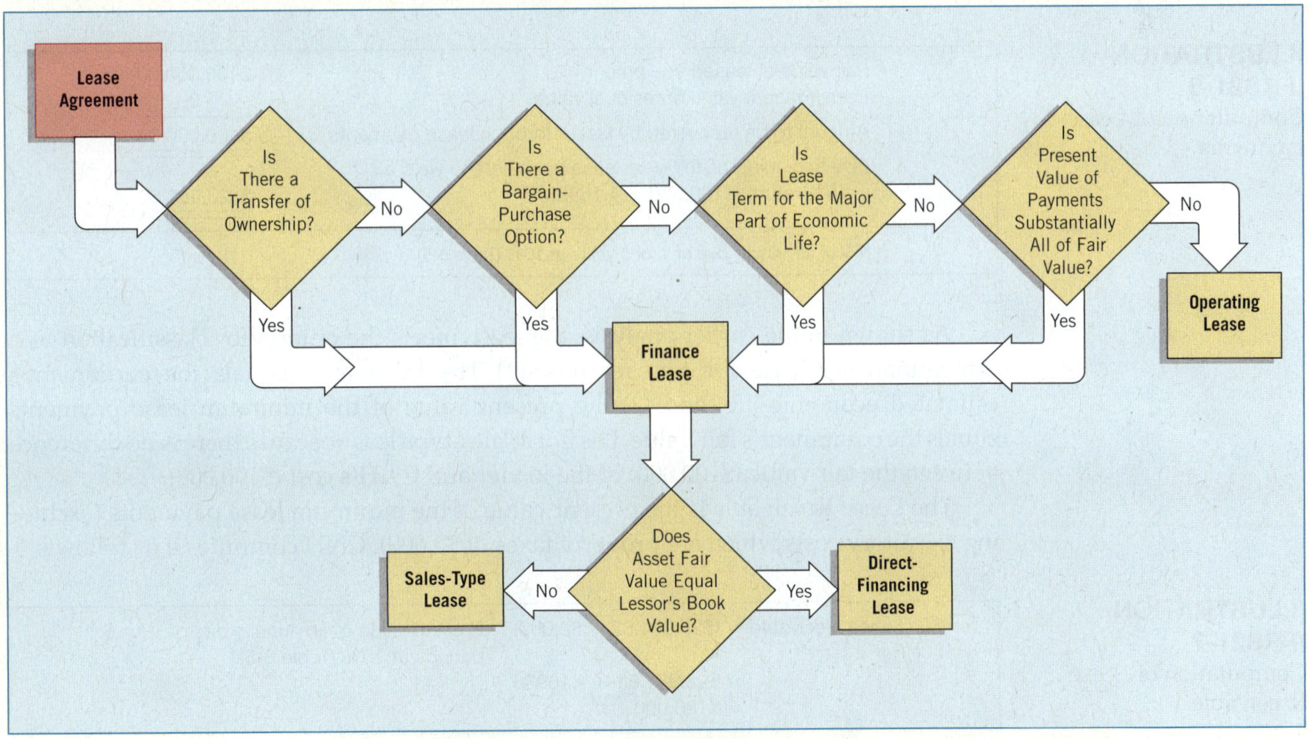

For purposes of comparison with the lessee's accounting, we will illustrate only the operating and direct-financing leases in the following section.

Direct-Financing Method (Lessor)

Direct-financing leases are in substance the financing of an asset purchase by the lessee. In this type of lease, the lessor records a **lease receivable** instead of a leased asset. The lease receivable is the present value of the minimum lease payments plus the present value of the unguaranteed residual value. Remember that "minimum lease payments" include (1) rental payments (excluding executory costs), (2) bargain-purchase option (if any), (3) guaranteed residual value (if any), and (4) penalty for failure to renew (if any).

Thus, the lessor records the residual value, whether guaranteed or not. Also, recall that if the lessor pays any executory costs, then it should reduce the rental payment by that amount in computing minimum lease payments.

The following presentation, using the data from the preceding CNH/Ivanhoe example on pages 1335–1337, illustrates the accounting treatment for a direct-financing lease. We repeat here the information relevant to CNH in accounting for this lease transaction.

1. The term of the lease is five years beginning January 1, 2014, non-cancelable, and requires equal rental payments of $25,981.62 at the beginning of each year. Payments include $2,000 of executory costs (property taxes).
2. The equipment (front-end loader) has a cost of $100,000 to CNH, a fair value at the inception of the lease of $100,000, an estimated economic life of five years, and no residual value.
3. CNH incurred no initial direct costs in negotiating and closing the lease transaction.
4. The lease contains no renewal options. The equipment reverts to CNH at the termination of the lease.
5. CNH sets the annual lease payments to ensure a rate of return of 10 percent (implicit rate) on its investment, as shown in Illustration IFRS21-6.

ILLUSTRATION IFRS21-6
Computation of Lease Payments

Fair value of leased equipment	$100,000.00
Less: Present value of residual value	–0–
Amount to be recovered by lessor through lease payments	$100,000.00
Five beginning-of-the-year lease payments to yield a 10% return ($100,000 ÷ 4.16986[a])	$ 23,981.62

[a]PV of an annuity due of 1 for 5 years at 10% (Table 6-5).

As shown in the earlier analysis, the lease meets the criteria for classification as a direct-financing lease for two reasons. (1) The lease term equals the equipment's estimated economic life, and (2) the present value of the minimum lease payments equals the equipment's fair value. It is not a sales-type lease because there is no difference between the fair value ($100,000) of the loader and CNH's cost ($100,000).

The Lease Receivable is the present value of the minimum lease payments (excluding executory costs which are property taxes of $2,000). CNH computes it as follows.

ILLUSTRATION IFRS21-7
Computation of Lease Receivable

Lease receivable = ($25,981.62 − $2,000) × Present value of an annuity due of 1 for 5 periods at 10% (Table 6-5)
= $23,981.62 × 4.16986
= $100,000

CNH records the lease of the asset and the resulting receivable on January 1, 2014 (the inception of the lease), as follows.

Lease Receivable	100,000	
Equipment		100,000

Companies often **report** the lease receivable in the statement of financial position as "Net investment in finance leases." Companies classify it either as current or non-current, depending on when they recover the net investment.

Under IFRS, once a lessor determines classification of a lease as either direct-financing or sales-type, the accounting for the lease arrangement is the same as GAAP (as shown on pages 1286–1289 and 1296–1298).

ON THE HORIZON

Lease accounting is one of the areas identified in the IASB/FASB Memorandum of Understanding. The Boards have issued proposed rules based on "right of use," which requires that all leases, regardless of their terms, be accounted for in a manner similar to how finance leases are treated today. That is, the notion of an operating lease will be eliminated, which will address the concerns under current rules in which no asset or liability is recorded for many operating leases. A final standard is expected in 2013. You can follow the lease project at either the FASB (*http://www.fasb.org*) or IASB (*http://www.iasb.org*) websites.

IFRS SELF-TEST QUESTIONS

1. Which of the following is **not** a criterion for a lease to be recorded as a finance lease?
   (a) There is transfer of ownership.
   (b) The lease is cancelable.
   (c) The lease term is for the major part of the economic life of the asset.
   (d) There is a bargain-purchase option.
2. Under IFRS, in computing the present value of the minimum lease payments, the lessee should:
   (a) use its incremental borrowing rate in all cases.
   (b) use either its incremental borrowing rate or the implicit rate of the lessor, whichever is higher, assuming that the implicit rate is known to the lessee.
   (c) use either its incremental borrowing rate or the implicit rate of the lessor, whichever is lower, assuming that the implicit rate is known to the lessee.
   (d) use the implicit rate of the lessor, unless it is impracticable to determine the implicit rate.
3. A lease that involves a manufacturer's or dealer's profit is a(an):
   (a) direct financing lease.
   (b) finance lease.
   (c) operating lease.
   (d) sales-type lease.
4. Which of the following statements is **true** when comparing the accounting for leasing transactions under GAAP with IFRS?
   (a) IFRS for leases is more "rules-based" than GAAP and includes many bright-line criteria to determine ownership.
   (b) IFRS requires that companies provide a year-by-year breakout of future non-cancelable lease payments due in years 1 through 5.
   (c) The IFRS leasing standard is the subject of over 30 interpretations since its issuance in 1982.
   (d) IFRS does not provide detailed guidance for leases of natural resources, sale-leasebacks, and leveraged leases.
5. All of the following statements about lease accounting under IFRS and GAAP are true **except**:
   (a) IFRS requires a year-by-year breakout of payments related to leasing arrangements.
   (b) IFRS is more general in its lease accounting provisions than is GAAP.
   (c) The IFRS leasing standard, *IAS 17*, is the subject of only three interpretations.
   (d) Finance leases under IFRS are referred to as capital leases under GAAP.

IFRS CONCEPTS AND APPLICATION

IFRS21-1 Where can authoritative IFRS related to the accounting for leases be found?

IFRS21-2 Briefly describe some of the similarities and differences between GAAP and IFRS with respect to the accounting for leases.

IFRS21-3 Briefly discuss the IASB and FASB efforts to converge their accounting guidelines for leases.

IFRS21-4 Outline the accounting procedures involved in applying the operating lease method by a lessee.

IFRS21-5 Outline the accounting procedures involved in applying the finance lease method by a lessee.

IFRS21-6 Identify the lease classifications for lessors and the criteria that must be met for each classification.

IFRS21-7 Rick Kleckner Corporation recorded a finance lease at $300,000 on January 1, 2014. The interest rate is 12%. Kleckner Corporation made the first lease payment of $53,920 on January 1, 2014. The lease requires eight annual payments. The equipment has a useful life of 8 years with no residual value. Prepare Kleckner Corporation's December 31, 2014, adjusting entries.

IFRS21-8 Use the information for Rick Kleckner Corporation from IFRS21-7. Assume that at December 31, 2014, Kleckner made an adjusting entry to accrue interest expense of $29,530 on the lease. Prepare Kleckner's January 1, 2015, journal entry to record the second lease payment of $53,920.

IFRS21-9 Brecker Company leases an automobile with a fair value of $10,906 from Emporia Motors, Inc., on the following terms:

1. Non-cancelable term of 50 months.
2. Rental of $250 per month (at end of each month). (The present value at 1% per month is $9,800.)
3. Estimated residual value after 50 months is $1,180. (The present value at 1% per month is $715.) Brecker Company guarantees the residual value of $1,180.
4. Estimated economic life of the automobile is 60 months.
5. Brecker Company's incremental borrowing rate is 12% a year (1% a month). It is impracticable to determine Emporia's implicit rate.

Instructions

(a) What is the nature of this lease to Brecker Company?
(b) What is the present value of the minimum lease payments?
(c) Record the lease on Brecker Company's books at the date of inception.
(d) Record the first month's depreciation on Brecker Company's books (assume straight-line).
(e) Record the first month's lease payment.

IFRS21-10 The following facts pertain to a non-cancelable lease agreement between Lennox Leasing Company and Gill Company, a lessee. (Round all numbers to the nearest cent.)

Inception date: May 1, 2014

Annual lease payment due at the beginning of each year, beginning with May 1, 2014: $18,829.49

Bargain-purchase option price at end of lease term: $4,000.00

Lease term: 5 years

Economic life of leased equipment: 10 years

Lessor's cost: $65,000.00; fair value of asset at May 1, 2014, $81,000.00

Lessor's implicit rate: 10%; lessee's incremental borrowing rate 10%

The lessee assumes responsibility for all executory costs.

Instructions

(a) Discuss the nature of this lease to Gill Company.
(b) Discuss the nature of this lease to Lennox Company.
(c) Prepare a lease amortization schedule for Gill Company for the 5-year lease term.
(d) Prepare the journal entries on the lessee's books to reflect the signing of the lease agreement and to record the payments and expenses related to this lease for the years 2014 and 2015. Gill's annual accounting period ends on December 31. Reversing entries are used by Gill.

IFRS21-11 A lease agreement between Lennox Leasing Company and Gill Company is described in IFRS21-10. Refer to the data in IFRS21-10 and do the following for the lessor. (Round all numbers to the nearest cent.)

Instructions

(a) Compute the amount of the lease receivable at the inception of the lease.

(b) Prepare a lease amortization schedule for Lennox Leasing Company for the 5-year lease term.

(c) Prepare the journal entries to reflect the signing of the lease agreement and to record the receipts and income related to this lease for the years 2014, 2015, and 2016. The lessor's accounting period ends on December 31. Reversing entries are not used by Lennox.

Professional Research

IFRS21-12 Daniel Hardware Co. is considering alternative financing arrangements for equipment used in its warehouses. Besides purchasing the equipment outright, Daniel is also considering a lease. Accounting for the outright purchase is fairly straightforward, but because Daniel has not used equipment leases in the past, the accounting staff is less informed about the specific accounting rules for leases. The staff is aware of some general lease rules related to "risks and rewards," but they are unsure about the meanings of these terms in lease accounting. Daniel has asked you to conduct some research on these items related to lease capitalization criteria.

Instructions

Access the IFRS authoritative literature at the IASB website (*http://eifrs.iasb.org/*). (Click on the IFRS tab and then register for free eIFRS access if necessary.) When you have accessed the documents, you can use the search tool in your Internet browser to respond to the following questions. (Provide paragraph citations.)

(a) What is the objective of lease classification criteria?

(b) An important element of evaluating leases is determining whether substantially all of the risks and rewards of ownership are transferred in the lease. How is "substantially all" defined in the authoritative literature?

(c) Besides the non-cancelable term of the lease, name at least three other considerations in determining the "lease term."

International Financial Reporting Problem

Marks and Spencer plc

IFRS21-13 The financial statements of **Marks and Spencer plc (M&S)** are available at the book's companion website or can be accessed at *http://annualreport.marksandspencer.com/_assets/downloads/Marks-and-Spencer-Annual-report-and-financial-statements-2012.pdf.*

Instructions

Refer to M&S's financial statements and the accompanying notes to answer the following questions.

(a) What types of leases are used by M&S?

(b) What amount of finance leases was reported by M&S in total and for less than one year?

(c) What minimum annual rental commitments under all non-cancelable leases at 31 March 2012 did M&S disclose?

ANSWERS TO IFRS SELF-TEST QUESTIONS

1. b **2.** d **3.** d **4.** d **5.** a

Remember to check the book's companion website to find additional resources for this chapter.

CHAPTER

22 Accounting Changes and Error Analysis

LEARNING OBJECTIVES

After studying this chapter, you should be able to:

1. Identify the types of accounting changes.
2. Describe the accounting for changes in accounting principles.
3. Understand how to account for retrospective accounting changes.
4. Understand how to account for impracticable changes.
5. Describe the accounting for changes in estimates.
6. Identify changes in a reporting entity.
7. Describe the accounting for correction of errors.
8. Identify economic motives for changing accounting methods.
9. Analyze the effect of errors.

In the Dark

The FASB's conceptual framework describes comparability (including consistency) as one of the qualitative characteristics that contribute to the usefulness of accounting information. Unfortunately, companies are finding it difficult to maintain comparability and consistency due to the numerous changes in accounting principles mandated by the FASB. In addition, a number of companies have faced restatements due to errors in their financial statements. For example, the table below shows types and numbers of recent accounting changes.

Business combinations	49	Debt–equity financial instruments	18
Noncontrolling interests	38	Transfers of financial instruments	12
Fair value measurements	32	Earnings per share	6
Defined benefit pension and postretirement plans	21	Other, including depreciation, stock-based compensation, derivatives, inventory, and revenue	75

Although the percentage of companies reporting material changes or errors is small, readers of financial statements still must be careful. The reason: The amounts in the financial statements may have changed due to changing accounting principles and/or restatements. The chart below indicates the recent trends in restatements.

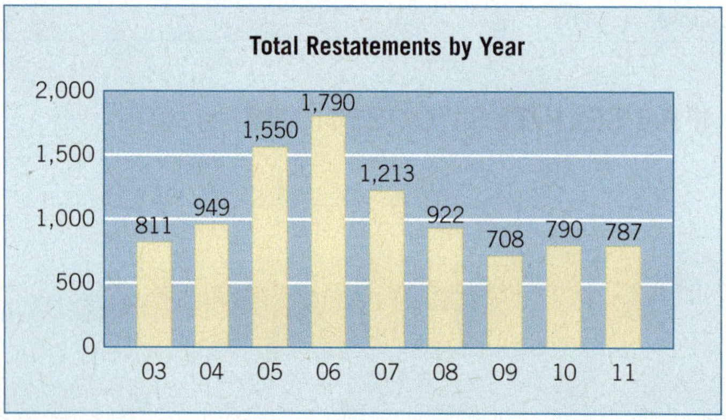

There is much good news in the chart. In 2007, restatements declined by 32.2 percent (from 1,790 to 1,213). In 2008, restatements declined another 24 percent (from 1,213 to 922). The declining trend continued in 2009, with restatements stabilized at pre-crisis levels in 2010 and 2011. However, investors can be in the dark when a company has an error that requires restatement. It may take some time for companies to sort out the source of an error, prepare corrected statements, and get auditor

sign-off. Recent data indicate it takes on average about 3 months to resolve a restatement. The following table reports the range of periods when investors are in the dark due to a restatement.

Time to File Restated Financial Statements	% of All Restatements
Up to 3 Months	77
3–9 Months	11
Greater than 9 Months	12

While most companies (77%) resolve their errors within 3 months, 12 percent (or over 200 companies) take more than 9 months to file corrected statements.

These lengthy "dark periods" have caught the attention of policy-setters and were a topic of discussion of the Committee for Improvements in Financial Reporting (CIFR). As one member of CIFR noted, "The dark period is bad for users." As a result, the committee is proposing that for some errors, companies might not need to go through the pain of restatement, but enhanced disclosures about errors are needed.

Sources: Accounting change data from *Accounting Trends and Techniques—2011–2012* (New York: AICPA, 2011–2012). Restatement data from *2011 Financial Restatements: A Nine Year Comparison*, Audit Analytics (April 2012), p. 3; M. Leone, "Materiality Debate Emerges from the Dark," *CFO.com* (July 14, 2008); and B. Badertscher and J. Burks, "Accounting Restatements and the Timeliness of Disclosures," *Accounting Horizons* (December 2011), pp. 609–629.

CONCEPTUAL FOCUS

> See the **Underlying Concepts** on pages 1344, 1346, and 1366.

INTERNATIONAL FOCUS

> See the **International Perspectives** on pages 1345 and 1355.

> Read the **IFRS Insights** on pages 1404–1408 for a discussion of:

—Direct and indirect effects of changes

—Impracticability

PREVIEW OF CHAPTER 22

As our opening story indicates, changes in accounting principles and errors in financial information have increased substantially in recent years. When these changes occur, companies must follow specific accounting and reporting requirements. In addition, to ensure comparability among companies, the FASB has standardized reporting of accounting changes, accounting estimates, error corrections, and related earnings per share information. In this chapter, we discuss these reporting standards, which help investors better understand a company's financial condition. The content and organization of the chapter are as follows.

Accounting Changes and Error Analysis

- **Accounting Changes**
- **Changes in Principle**
  - Retrospective
  - Direct and indirect effects
  - Impracticability
- **Changes in Estimates**
  - Prospective
  - Disclosures
- **Changes in Entity**
- **Accounting Errors**
  - Example
  - Summary
  - Motivations
- **Error Analysis**
  - Balance sheet errors
  - Income statement errors
  - Balance sheet and income statement errors
  - Comprehensive example
  - Preparation of statements with error corrections

ACCOUNTING CHANGES

LEARNING OBJECTIVE 1
Identify the types of accounting changes.

Accounting alternatives diminish the comparability of financial information between periods and between companies; they also obscure useful historical trend data. For example, if **Ford** revises its estimates for equipment useful lives, depreciation expense for the current year will not be comparable to depreciation expense reported by Ford in prior years. Similarly, if **OfficeMax** changes to FIFO inventory pricing while **Staples** uses LIFO, it will be difficult to compare these companies' reported results. A reporting framework helps preserve comparability when there is an accounting change.

See the FASB Codification section (page 1381).

The FASB has established a reporting framework, which involves three types of accounting changes. **[1]** The three types of accounting changes are:

Underlying Concepts

While changes in accounting may enhance the qualitative characteristic of *usefulness*, these changes may adversely affect the enhancing characteristics of *comparability* and *consistency*.

1. *Change in accounting principle.* A change from one generally accepted accounting principle to another one. For example, a company may change its inventory valuation method from LIFO to average-cost.
2. *Change in accounting estimate.* A change that occurs as the result of new information or additional experience. For example, a company may change its estimate of the useful lives of depreciable assets.
3. *Change in reporting entity.* A change from reporting as one type of entity to another type of entity. As an example, a company might change the subsidiaries for which it prepares consolidated financial statements.

A fourth category necessitates changes in accounting, though it is not classified as an accounting change.

4. *Errors in financial statements.* Errors result from mathematical mistakes, mistakes in applying accounting principles, or oversight or misuse of facts that existed when preparing the financial statements. For example, a company may incorrectly apply the retail inventory method for determining its final inventory value.

The FASB classifies changes in these categories because each category involves different methods of recognizing changes in the financial statements. In this chapter, we discuss these classifications. We also explain how to report each item in the accounts and how to disclose the information in comparative statements.

CHANGES IN ACCOUNTING PRINCIPLE

LEARNING OBJECTIVE 2
Describe the accounting for changes in accounting principles.

By definition, a **change in accounting principle involves a change from one generally accepted accounting principle to another**. For example, a company might change the basis of inventory pricing from average-cost to LIFO. Or, it might change its method of revenue recognition for long-term construction contracts from the completed-contract to the percentage-of-completion method.

Companies must carefully examine each circumstance to ensure that a change in principle has actually occurred. **Adoption of a new principle** in recognition of events that have occurred for the first time or that were previously immaterial is not an accounting change. For example, a change in accounting principle has not occurred when a company adopts an inventory method (e.g., FIFO) for **newly** acquired items of inventory, even if FIFO differs from that used for **previously recorded** inventory. Another example is certain marketing expenditures that were previously immaterial and expensed in the period incurred. It would not be considered a change in accounting principle if they become material and so may be acceptably deferred and amortized.

Finally, what if a company previously followed an accounting principle that was not acceptable? Or what if the company applied a principle incorrectly? In such cases, the profession considers a change to a generally accepted accounting principle **a correction of an error**. For example, a switch from the cash (income tax) basis of accounting to the accrual basis is a correction of an error. Or, if a company deducted salvage value when computing double-declining depreciation on plant assets and later recomputed depreciation without deducting estimated salvage value, it has corrected an error.

There are three possible approaches for reporting changes in accounting principles:

1. ***Report changes currently.*** In this approach, companies report the cumulative effect of the change in the current year's income statement as an irregular item. The **cumulative effect** is the difference in prior years' income between the newly adopted and prior accounting method. Under this approach, the effect of the change on prior years' income appears only in the current-year income statement. The company does not change **prior year financial statements**.

   Advocates of this position argue that changing prior years' financial statements results in a loss of confidence in financial reports. How do investors react when told that the earnings computed three years ago are now entirely different? Changing prior periods, if permitted, also might upset contractual arrangements based on the old figures. For example, profit-sharing arrangements computed on the old basis might have to be recomputed and completely new distributions made, creating numerous legal problems. Many practical difficulties also exist. The cost of changing prior period financial statements may be excessive, or determining the amount of the prior period effect may be impossible on the basis of available data.

2. ***Report changes retrospectively.*** **Retrospective application** refers to the application of a different accounting principle to recast previously issued financial statements—**as if the new principle had always been used**. In other words, the company "goes back" and adjusts **prior years' statements** on a basis consistent with the newly adopted principle. The company shows any cumulative effect of the change as an adjustment to beginning retained earnings of the earliest year presented.

   Advocates of this position argue that retrospective application ensures comparability. Think for a moment what happens if this approach is not used. The year *previous* to the change will be on the old method, the year *of the change* will report the entire cumulative adjustment, and the *following* year will present financial statements on the new basis without the cumulative effect of the change. Such lack of consistency fails to provide meaningful earnings-trend data and other financial relationships necessary to evaluate the business.

3. ***Report changes prospectively (in the future).*** In this approach, previously reported results remain. As a result, companies do not adjust opening balances to reflect the change in principle. Advocates of this position argue that once management presents financial statements based on acceptable accounting principles, they are final. Management cannot change prior periods by adopting a new principle. According to this line of reasoning, the current-period cumulative adjustment is not appropriate because that approach includes amounts that have little or no relationship to the current year's income or economic events.

International Perspective

IFRS (*IAS 8*) generally requires retrospective application to prior years for accounting changes. However, *IAS 8* permits the prospective method if a company cannot reasonably determine the amounts to which to restate prior periods.

Given these three possible approaches, which does the accounting profession prefer? The FASB **requires that companies use the retrospective approach.** Why? Because it provides financial statement users with more useful information than the cumulative-effect or prospective approaches. [2] The rationale is that changing the prior statements to be on the same basis as the newly adopted principle results in greater consistency across accounting periods. Users can then better compare results from one period to the next.[1]

What do the numbers mean? QUITE A CHANGE

The cumulative-effect approach results in a loss of comparability. Also, reporting the cumulative adjustment in the period of the change can significantly affect net income, resulting in a misleading income figure. For example, at one time Chrysler Corporation changed its inventory accounting from LIFO to FIFO. If Chrysler had used the cumulative-effect approach, it would have reported a $53,500,000 adjustment to net income. That adjustment would have resulted in net income of $45,900,000, instead of a net loss of $7,600,000.

A second case: In the early 1980s, the railroad industry switched from the retirement-replacement method of depreciating railroad equipment to more generally used methods such as straight-line depreciation. Using cumulative treatment, railroad companies would have made substantial adjustments to income in the period of change. Many in the industry argued that including such large cumulative-effect adjustments in the current year would distort the information and make it less useful.

Such situations lend support to retrospective application so that comparability is maintained.

Retrospective Accounting Change Approach

LEARNING OBJECTIVE 3
Understand how to account for retrospective accounting changes.

Underlying Concepts
Retrospective application contributes to comparability.

A presumption exists that once a company adopts an accounting principle, it should not change. That presumption is understandable, given the idea that consistent use of an accounting principle enhances the usefulness of financial statements. However, the environment continually changes, and companies change in response. Recent standards on such subjects as stock options, exchanges of nonmonetary assets, and derivatives indicate that changes in accounting principle will continue to occur.

When a company changes an accounting principle, it should report the change using retrospective application. In general terms, here is what it must do:

1. *It adjusts its financial statements for each prior period presented.* Thus, financial statement information about prior periods is on the same basis as the new accounting principle.
2. *It adjusts the carrying amounts of assets and liabilities as of the beginning of the first year presented.* By doing so, these accounts reflect the cumulative effect on periods prior to those presented of the change to the new accounting principle. The company also makes an offsetting adjustment to the opening balance of retained earnings or other appropriate component of stockholders' equity or net assets as of the beginning of the first year presented.

For example, assume that Target decides to change its inventory valuation method in 2014 from the retail inventory method (FIFO) to the retail inventory method (average-cost). It provides comparative information for 2012 and 2013 based on the new method. Target would adjust its assets, liabilities, and retained earnings for periods prior to 2012 and report these amounts in the 2012 financial statements, when it prepares comparative financial statements.

[1]Adoption of the retrospective approach contributes to international accounting convergence. As discussed throughout the textbook, the FASB and the IASB are collaborating on a project in which they have agreed to converge around high-quality solutions to resolve differences between GAAP and IFRS. By adopting the retrospective approach, which is the method used in IFRS, the FASB agreed that this approach is superior to the current approach.

Retrospective Accounting Change: Long-Term Contracts

To illustrate the retrospective approach, assume that Denson Company has accounted for its income from long-term construction contracts using the completed-contract method. In 2014, the company changed to the percentage-of-completion method. Management believes this approach provides a more appropriate measure of the income earned. For tax purposes, the company uses the completed-contract method and plans to continue doing so in the future. (We assume a 40% enacted tax rate.)

Illustration 22-1 shows portions of three income statements for 2012–2014—for both the completed-contract and percentage-of-completion methods (2012 was Denson's first year of operations in the construction business).

ILLUSTRATION 22-1
Comparative Income Statements for Completed-Contract versus Percentage-of-Completion Methods

COMPLETED-CONTRACT METHOD
DENSON COMPANY
INCOME STATEMENT (PARTIAL)
FOR THE YEARS ENDED DECEMBER 31

	2012	2013	2014
Income before income tax	$400,000	$160,000	$190,000
Income tax (40%)	160,000	64,000	76,000
Net income	$240,000	$ 96,000	$114,000

PERCENTAGE-OF-COMPLETION METHOD
DENSON COMPANY
INCOME STATEMENT (PARTIAL)
FOR THE YEARS ENDED DECEMBER 31

	2012	2013	2014
Income before income tax	$600,000	$180,000	$200,000
Income tax (40%)	240,000	72,000	80,000
Net income	$360,000	$108,000	$120,000

To record a change from the completed-contract to the percentage-of-completion method, we analyze the various effects, as Illustration 22-2 shows.

ILLUSTRATION 22-2
Data for Retrospective Change Example

	Pretax Income from		Difference in Income		
Year	Percentage-of-Completion	Completed-Contract	Difference	Tax Effect 40%	Income Effect (net of tax)
Prior to 2013	$600,000	$400,000	$200,000	$80,000	$120,000
In 2013	180,000	160,000	20,000	8,000	12,000
Total at beginning of 2014	$780,000	$560,000	$220,000	$88,000	$132,000
Total in 2014	$200,000	$190,000	$ 10,000	$ 4,000	$ 6,000

The entry to record the change at the beginning of 2014 would be:

Construction in Process	220,000	
Deferred Tax Liability		88,000
Retained Earnings		132,000

The Construction in Process account increases by $220,000 (as indicated in the first column under "Difference in Income" in Illustration 22-2). The credit to Retained Earnings of $132,000 reflects the cumulative income effects prior to 2014 (third column under "Difference in Income" in Illustration 22-2). The company credits Retained Earnings because prior years' income is closed to this account each year. The credit to Deferred Tax Liability represents the adjustment to prior years' tax expense. The company now recognizes that amount, $88,000, as a tax liability for future taxable amounts. That is, in future periods, taxable income will be higher than book income as a result of current temporary differences. Therefore, Denson must report a deferred tax liability in the current year.

What do the numbers mean? CHANGE MANAGEMENT

Halliburton offers a case study in the importance of good reporting of an accounting change. Note that Halliburton uses percentage-of-completion accounting for its long-term construction-services contracts. The SEC questioned the company about its change in accounting for disputed claims.

Prior to the year of the change, Halliburton took a very conservative approach to its accounting for disputed claims. That is, the company waited until all disputes were resolved before recognizing associated revenues. In contrast, in the year of the change, the company recognized revenue for disputed claims *before* their resolution, using estimates of amounts expected to be recovered. Such revenue and its related profit are more tentative and subject to possible later adjustment. The accounting method adopted is more aggressive than the company's former policy but is within the boundaries of GAAP.

It appears that the problem with Halliburton's accounting stems more from how the company handled its accounting change than from the new method itself. That is, Halliburton did not provide in its annual report in the year of the change an explicit reference to its change in accounting method. In fact, rather than stating its new policy, the company simply deleted the sentence that described how it accounted for disputed claims. Then later, in its next year's annual report, the company stated its new accounting policy.

When companies make such changes in accounting, investors need to be informed about the change and about its effects on the financial results. With such information, investors and analysts can compare current results with those of prior periods and can make a more informed assessment about the company's future prospects.

Source: Adapted from "Accounting Ace Charles Mulford Answers Accounting Questions," *Wall Street Journal Online* (June 7, 2002).

Reporting a Change in Principle. The disclosure of accounting changes is particularly important. Financial statement readers want consistent information from one period to the next. Such consistency ensures the usefulness of financial statements. The major disclosure requirements are as follows.

1. The nature of and reason for the change in accounting principle. This must include an explanation of why the newly adopted accounting principle is preferable.
2. The method of applying the change, and:
   (a) A description of the prior period information that has been retrospectively adjusted, if any.
   (b) The effect of the change on income from continuing operations, net income (or other appropriate captions of changes in net assets or performance indicators), any other affected line item, and any affected per share amounts for the current period and for any prior periods retrospectively adjusted.
   (c) The cumulative effect of the change on retained earnings or other components of equity or net assets in the statement of financial position as of the beginning of the earliest period presented.[2]

To illustrate, Denson will prepare comparative financial statements for 2013 and 2014 using the percentage-of-completion method (the new construction accounting method). Illustration 22-3 indicates how Denson presents this information.

[2]Presentation of the effect on financial statement subtotals and totals other than income from continuing operations and net income (or other appropriate captions of changes in the applicable net assets or performance indicator) is not required. [3]

ILLUSTRATION 22-3
Comparative Information Related to Accounting Change (Percentage-of-Completion)

DENSON COMPANY
INCOME STATEMENT (PARTIAL)
FOR THE YEAR ENDED

	2014	2013 As Adjusted (Note A)
Income before income tax	$200,000	$180,000
Income tax (40%)	80,000	72,000
Net income	$120,000	$108,000

Note A: Change in Method of Accounting for Long-Term Contracts. The company has accounted for revenue and costs for long-term construction contracts by the percentage-of-completion method in 2014, whereas in all prior years, revenue and costs were determined by the completed-contract method. The new method of accounting for long-term contracts was adopted to recognize . . . [state justification for change in accounting principle] . . . and financial statements of prior years have been restated to apply the new method retrospectively. For income tax purposes, the completed-contract method has been continued. The effect of the accounting change on income of 2014 was an increase of $6,000 net of related taxes and on income of 2013 as previously reported was an increase of $12,000 net of related taxes. The balances of retained earnings for 2013 and 2014 have been adjusted for the effect of applying retroactively the new method of accounting. As a result of the accounting change, retained earnings as of January 1, 2013, increased by $120,000 compared to that reported using the completed-contract method.

As Illustration 22-3 shows, Denson Company reports net income under the newly adopted percentage-of-completion method for both 2013 and 2014. The company retrospectively adjusted the 2013 income statement to report the information on a percentage-of-completion basis. Also, the note to the financial statements indicates the nature of the change, why the company made the change, and the years affected.

In addition, companies are required to provide data on important differences between the amounts reported under percentage-of-completion versus completed-contract. When identifying the significant differences, some companies show the *entire* financial statements and line-by-line differences between percentage-of-completion and completed-contract. However, most companies will show only line-by-line differences. For example, Denson would show the differences in construction in process, retained earnings, gross profit, and net income for 2013 and 2014 under the completed-contract and percentage-of-completion methods.

Retained Earnings Adjustment. As indicated earlier, one of the disclosure requirements is to show the cumulative effect of the change on retained earnings as of the beginning of the earliest period presented. For Denson Company, that date is January 1, 2013. Denson disclosed that information by means of a narrative description (see Note A in Illustration 22-3). Denson also would disclose this information in its retained earnings statement. Assuming a retained earnings balance of $1,360,000 at the beginning of 2012, Illustration 22-4 shows Denson's retained earnings statement under the completed-contract method—that is, before giving effect to the change in accounting principle. (The income information comes from Illustration 22-1 on page 1347.)

ILLUSTRATION 22-4
Retained Earnings Statement before Retrospective Change

DENSON COMPANY
RETAINED EARNINGS STATEMENT
FOR THE YEAR ENDED

	2014	2013	2012
Retained earnings, January 1	$1,696,000	$1,600,000	$1,360,000
Net income	114,000	96,000	240,000
Retained earnings, December 31	$1,810,000	$1,696,000	$1,600,000

If Denson presents comparative statements for 2013 and 2014 under percentage-of-completion, then it must change the beginning balance of retained earnings at

January 1, 2013. The difference between the retained earnings balances under completed-contract and percentage-of-completion is computed as follows.

Retained earnings, January 1, 2013 (percentage-of-completion)	$1,720,000
Retained earnings, January 1, 2013 (completed-contract)	(1,600,000)
Cumulative-effect difference	$ 120,000

The $120,000 difference is the cumulative effect. Illustration 22-5 shows a comparative retained earnings statement for 2013 and 2014, giving effect to the change in accounting principle to percentage-of-completion.

ILLUSTRATION 22-5
Retained Earnings Statement after Retrospective Application

DENSON COMPANY
RETAINED EARNINGS STATEMENT
FOR THE YEAR ENDED

	2014	2013
Retained earnings, January 1, as reported	–	$1,600,000
Add: Adjustment for the cumulative effect on prior years of applying retrospectively the new method of accounting for construction contracts		120,000
Retained earnings, January 1, as adjusted	$1,828,000	1,720,000
Net income	120,000	108,000
Retained earnings, December 31	$1,948,000	$1,828,000

Denson adjusted the beginning balance of retained earnings on January 1, 2013, for the excess of percentage-of-completion net income over completed-contract net income in 2012. This comparative presentation indicates the type of adjustment that a company needs to make. It follows that this adjustment would be much larger if a number of prior periods were involved.

Retrospective Accounting Change: Inventory Methods

As a second illustration of the retrospective approach, assume that Lancer Company has accounted for its inventory using the LIFO method. In 2014, the company changes to the FIFO method because management believes this approach provides a more appropriate reporting of its inventory costs. Illustration 22-6 provides additional information related to Lancer Company.

ILLUSTRATION 22-6
Lancer Company Information

1. Lancer Company started its operations on January 1, 2012. At that time, stockholders invested $100,000 in the business in exchange for common stock.
2. All sales, purchases, and operating expenses for the period 2012–2014 are cash transactions. Lancer's cash flows over this period are as follows.

	2012	2013	2014
Sales	$300,000	$300,000	$300,000
Purchases	90,000	110,000	125,000
Operating expenses	100,000	100,000	100,000
Cash flow from operations	$110,000	$ 90,000	$ 75,000

3. Lancer has used the LIFO method for financial reporting since its inception.
4. Inventory determined under LIFO and FIFO for the period 2012–2014 is as follows.

	LIFO Method	FIFO Method	Difference
January 1, 2012	$ 0	$ 0	$ 0
December 31, 2012	10,000	12,000	2,000
December 31, 2013	20,000	25,000	5,000
December 31, 2014	32,000	39,000	7,000

ILLUSTRATION 22-6
(Continued)

5. Cost of goods sold under LIFO and FIFO for the period 2012–2014 are as follows.

	Cost of Goods Sold LIFO	Cost of Goods Sold FIFO	Difference
2012	$ 80,000	$ 78,000	$2,000
2013	100,000	97,000	3,000
2014	113,000	111,000	2,000

6. Earnings per share information is not required on the income statement.
7. All tax effects for this illustration should be ignored.

Given the information about Lancer Company, Illustration 22-7 shows its income statement, retained earnings statement, balance sheet, and statement of cash flows for 2012–2014 under LIFO.

ILLUSTRATION 22-7
Lancer Financial Statements (LIFO)

LANCER COMPANY
INCOME STATEMENT
FOR THE YEAR ENDED DECEMBER 31

	2012	2013	2014
Sales	$300,000	$300,000	$300,000
Cost of goods sold (LIFO)	80,000	100,000	113,000
Operating expenses	100,000	100,000	100,000
Net income	$120,000	$100,000	$ 87,000

LANCER COMPANY
RETAINED EARNINGS STATEMENT
FOR THE YEAR ENDED DECEMBER 31

	2012	2013	2014
Retained earnings (beginning)	$ 0	$120,000	$220,000
Add: Net income	120,000	100,000	87,000
Retained earnings (ending)	$120,000	$220,000	$307,000

LANCER COMPANY
BALANCE SHEET
AT DECEMBER 31

	2012	2013	2014
Cash	$210,000	$300,000	$375,000
Inventory (LIFO)	10,000	20,000	32,000
Total assets	$220,000	$320,000	$407,000
Common stock	$100,000	$100,000	$100,000
Retained earnings	120,000	220,000	307,000
Total liabilities and stockholders' equity	$220,000	$320,000	$407,000

LANCER COMPANY
STATEMENT OF CASH FLOWS
FOR THE YEAR ENDED DECEMBER 31

	2012	2013	2014
Cash flows from operating activities			
Sales	$300,000	$300,000	$300,000
Purchases	90,000	110,000	125,000
Operating expenses	100,000	100,000	100,000
Net cash provided by operating activities	110,000	90,000	75,000
Cash flows from financing activities			
Issuance of common stock	100,000	—	—
Net increase in cash	210,000	90,000	75,000
Cash at beginning of year	0	210,000	300,000
Cash at end of year	$210,000	$300,000	$375,000

As Illustration 22-7 indicates, under LIFO Lancer Company reports $120,000 net income in 2012, $100,000 net income in 2013, and $87,000 net income in 2014. The amount of inventory reported on Lancer's balance sheet reflects LIFO costing.

Illustration 22-8 shows Lancer's income statement, retained earnings statement, balance sheet, and statement of cash flows for 2012–2014 under **FIFO**. You can see that **the cash flow statement under FIFO is the same as under LIFO**. Although the net incomes are different in each period, there is no cash flow effect from these differences in net income. (If we considered income taxes, a cash flow effect would result.)

ILLUSTRATION 22-8
Lancer Financial Statements (FIFO)

LANCER COMPANY
INCOME STATEMENT
FOR THE YEAR ENDED DECEMBER 31

	2012	2013	2014
Sales	$300,000	$300,000	$300,000
Cost of goods sold (FIFO)	78,000	97,000	111,000
Operating expenses	100,000	100,000	100,000
Net income	$122,000	$103,000	$ 89,000

LANCER COMPANY
RETAINED EARNINGS STATEMENT
FOR THE YEAR ENDED DECEMBER 31

	2012	2013	2014
Retained earnings (beginning)	$ 0	$122,000	$225,000
Add: Net income	122,000	103,000	89,000
Retained earnings (ending)	$122,000	$225,000	$314,000

LANCER COMPANY
BALANCE SHEET
AT DECEMBER 31

	2012	2013	2014
Cash	$210,000	$300,000	$375,000
Inventory (FIFO)	12,000	25,000	39,000
Total assets	$222,000	$325,000	$414,000
Common stock	$100,000	$100,000	$100,000
Retained earnings	122,000	225,000	314,000
Total liabilities and stockholders' equity	$222,000	$325,000	$414,000

LANCER COMPANY
STATEMENT OF CASH FLOWS
FOR THE YEAR ENDED DECEMBER 31

	2012	2013	2014
Cash flows from operating activities			
Sales	$300,000	$300,000	$300,000
Purchases	90,000	110,000	125,000
Operating expenses	100,000	100,000	100,000
Net cash provided by operating activities	110,000	90,000	75,000
Cash flows from financing activities			
Issuance of common stock	100,000	—	—
Net increase in cash	210,000	90,000	75,000
Cast at beginning of year	0	210,000	300,000
Cash at end of year	$210,000	$300,000	$375,000

Compare the financial statements reported in Illustration 22-7 and Illustration 22-8. You can see that under retrospective application, the change to FIFO inventory valuation affects reported inventories, cost of goods sold, net income, and retained earnings. In the following sections, we discuss the accounting and reporting of Lancer's accounting change from LIFO to FIFO.

Given the information provided in Illustrations 22-6, 22-7, and 22-8, we now are ready to account for and report on the accounting change.

Our first step is to adjust the financial records for the change from LIFO to FIFO. To do so, we perform the analysis in Illustration 22-9.

ILLUSTRATION 22-9
Data for Recording Change in Accounting Principle

	Net Income		Difference in Income
Year	LIFO	FIFO	
2012	$120,000	$122,000	$2,000
2013	100,000	103,000	3,000
Total at beginning of 2014	$220,000	$225,000	$5,000
Total in 2014	$ 87,000	$ 89,000	$2,000

The entry to record the change to the FIFO method at the beginning of 2014 is as follows.

Inventory	5,000	
Retained Earnings		5,000

The change increases the Inventory account by $5,000. This amount represents the difference between the ending inventory at December 31, 2013, under LIFO ($20,000) and the ending inventory under FIFO ($25,000). The credit to Retained Earnings indicates the amount needed to change the prior year's income, assuming that Lancer had used FIFO in previous periods.

Reporting a Change in Principle. Lancer Company will prepare comparative financial statements for 2013 and 2014 using FIFO (the new inventory method). Illustration 22-10 indicates how Lancer might present this information.

ILLUSTRATION 22-10
Comparative Information Related to Accounting Change (FIFO)

LANCER COMPANY
INCOME STATEMENT
FOR THE YEAR ENDED DECEMBER 31

	2014	2013 As adjusted (Note A)
Sales	$300,000	$300,000
Cost of goods sold	111,000	97,000
Operating expenses	100,000	100,000
Net income	$ 89,000	$103,000

Note A

Change in Method of Accounting for Inventory Valuation On January 1, 2014, Lancer Company elected to change its method of valuing its inventory to the FIFO method; in all prior years, inventory was valued using the LIFO method. The Company adopted the new method of accounting for inventory to better report cost of goods sold in the year incurred. Comparative financial statements of prior years have been adjusted to apply the new method retrospectively. The following financial statement line items for years 2014 and 2013 were affected by the change in accounting principle.

Nature and reason for change; description of prior period information adjusted

	2014			2013		
Balance Sheet	LIFO	FIFO	Difference	LIFO	FIFO	Difference
Inventory	$ 32,000	$ 39,000	$7,000	$ 20,000	$ 25,000	$5,000
Retained earnings	307,000	314,000	7,000	220,000	225,000	5,000
Income Statement						
Cost of goods sold	$113,000	$111,000	$2,000	$100,000	$ 97,000	$3,000
Net income	87,000	89,000	2,000	100,000	103,000	3,000

Effect of change on key performance indicators

Statement of Cash Flows

(no effect)

As a result of the accounting change, retained earnings as of January 1, 2013, increased from $120,000, as originally reported using the LIFO method, to $122,000 using the FIFO method.

Cumulative effect on retained earnings

As Illustration 22-10 shows, Lancer Company reports net income under the newly adopted FIFO method for both 2013 and 2014. The company retrospectively adjusted the 2013 income statement to report the information on a FIFO basis. In addition, the note to the financial statements indicates the nature of the change, why the company made the change, and the years affected. The note also provides data on important differences between the amounts reported under LIFO versus FIFO. (When identifying the significant differences, some companies show the *entire* financial statements and line-by-line differences between LIFO and FIFO.)

Retained Earnings Adjustment. As indicated earlier, one of the disclosure requirements is to show the cumulative effect of the change on retained earnings as of the beginning of the earliest period presented. For Lancer Company, that date is January 1, 2013. Lancer disclosed that information by means of a narrative description (see Note A in Illustration 22-10). Lancer also would disclose this information in its retained earnings statement. Illustration 22-11 shows Lancer's retained earnings statement under LIFO—that is, before giving effect to the change in accounting principle. (This information comes from Illustration 22-7 on page 1351.)

ILLUSTRATION 22-11
Retained Earnings Statements (LIFO)

	2014	2013	2012
Retained earnings, January 1	$220,000	$120,000	$ 0
Net income	87,000	100,000	120,000
Retained earnings, December 31	$307,000	$220,000	$120,000

If Lancer presents comparative statements for 2013 and 2014 under FIFO, then it must change the beginning balance of retained earnings at January 1, 2013. The difference between the retained earnings balances under LIFO and FIFO is computed as follows.

Retained earnings, January 1, 2013 (FIFO)	$122,000
Retained earnings, January 1, 2013 (LIFO)	(120,000)
Cumulative effect difference	$ 2,000

The $2,000 difference is the cumulative effect. Illustration 22-12 shows a comparative retained earnings statement for 2013 and 2014, giving effect to the change in accounting principle to FIFO.

ILLUSTRATION 22-12
Retained Earnings Statements after Retrospective Application

	2014	2013
Retained earnings, January 1, as reported		$120,000
Add: Adjustment for the cumulative effect on prior years of applying retrospectively the new method of accounting for inventory		2,000
Retained earnings, January 1, as adjusted	$225,000	122,000
Net income	89,000	103,000
Retained earnings, December 31	$314,000	$225,000

Lancer adjusted the beginning balance of retained earnings on January 1, 2013, for the excess of FIFO net income over LIFO net income in 2012. This comparative presentation indicates the type of adjustment that a company needs to make. It follows that the amount of this adjustment would be much larger if a number of prior periods were involved.

Direct and Indirect Effects of Changes

Are there other effects that a company should report when it makes a change in accounting principle? For example, what happens when a company like Lancer has a bonus plan based on net income and the prior year's net income changes when FIFO is retrospectively applied? Should Lancer also change the reported amount of bonus expense? Or what happens if we had not ignored income taxes in the Lancer example? Should Lancer adjust net income, given that taxes will be different under LIFO and FIFO in prior periods? The answers depend on whether the effects are direct or indirect.

Direct Effects

The FASB takes the position that companies should retrospectively apply the **direct effects of a change in accounting principle**. An example of a **direct effect** is an adjustment to an inventory balance as a result of a change in the inventory valuation method. For example, Lancer Company should change the inventory amounts in prior periods to indicate the change to the FIFO method of inventory valuation. Another inventory-related example would be an impairment adjustment resulting from applying the lower-of-cost-or-market test to the adjusted inventory balance. Related changes, such as deferred income tax effects of the impairment adjustment, are also considered direct effects. This entry was illustrated in the Denson example, in which the change to percentage-of-completion accounting resulted in recording a deferred tax liability.

Indirect Effects

In addition to direct effects, companies can have **indirect effects related to a change in accounting principle**. An **indirect effect** is any change to current or future cash flows of a company that result from making a change in accounting principle that is applied retrospectively. An example of an indirect effect is a change in profit-sharing or royalty payment that is based on a reported amount such as revenue or net income. **Indirect effects do not change prior period amounts.**

For example, let's assume that Lancer has an employee profit-sharing plan based on net income. As Illustration 22-9 showed (on page 1353), Lancer would report higher income in 2012 and 2013 if it used the FIFO method. In addition, let's assume that the profit-sharing plan requires that Lancer pay the incremental amount due based on the FIFO income amounts. In this situation, Lancer reports this additional expense **in the current period**; it would not change prior periods for this expense. If the company prepares comparative financial statements, it follows that it does not recast the prior periods for this additional expense.[3]

> **International Perspective**
>
> IFRS does not explicitly address the accounting and disclosure of indirect effects.

If the terms of the profit-sharing plan indicate that *no payment is necessary* in the current period due to this change, then the company need not recognize additional profit-sharing expense in the current period. Neither does it change amounts reported for prior periods.

When a company recognizes the indirect effects of a change in accounting principle, it includes in the financial statements a description of the indirect effects. In doing so, it discloses the amounts recognized in the current period and related per share information.

[3]The rationale for this approach is that companies should recognize, in the period the adoption occurs (not the prior period), the effect on the cash flows that is caused by the adoption of the new accounting principle. That is, the accounting change is a necessary "past event" in the definition of an asset or liability that gives rise to the accounting recognition of the indirect effect in the current period. **[4]**

Impracticability

LEARNING OBJECTIVE 4
Understand how to account for impracticable changes.

It is not always possible for companies to determine how they would have reported prior periods' financial information under retrospective application of an accounting principle change. Retrospective application is considered **impracticable** if a company cannot determine the prior period effects using every reasonable effort to do so.

Companies should not use retrospective application if one of the following conditions exists:

1. The company cannot determine the effects of the retrospective application.
2. Retrospective application requires assumptions about management's intent in a prior period.
3. Retrospective application requires significant estimates for a prior period, and the company cannot objectively verify the necessary information to develop these estimates.

If any of the above conditions exists, it is deemed impracticable to apply the retrospective approach. In this case, the company **prospectively applies** the new accounting principle as of the earliest date it is practicable to do so. [5]

For example, assume that Williams Company changed its inventory method from FIFO to LIFO, effective January 1, 2015. Williams prepares statements on a calendar-year basis and has used the FIFO method since its inception. Williams judges it impracticable to retrospectively apply the new method. Determining prior period effects would require subjective assumptions about the LIFO layers established in prior periods. These assumptions would ordinarily result in the computation of a number of different earnings figures.

As a result, the only adjustment necessary may be to restate the beginning inventory to a cost basis from a lower-of-cost-or-market approach (which establishes the beginning LIFO layer). Williams must disclose only the effect of the change on the results of operations in the period of change. Also, the company should explain the reasons for omitting the computations of the cumulative effect for prior years. Finally, it should disclose the justification for the change to LIFO. [6][4] Illustration 22-13, from the annual report of The Quaker Oats Company, shows the type of disclosure needed.

ILLUSTRATION 22-13
Disclosure of Change to LIFO

The Quaker Oats Company

Note 1 (In Part): Summary of Significant Accounting Policies

Inventories. Inventories are valued at the lower of cost or market, using various cost methods, and include the cost of raw materials, labor and overhead. The percentage of year-end inventories valued using each of the methods is as follows:

June 30	Current Year	Prior Year
Average quarterly cost	21%	54%
Last-in, first-out (LIFO)	65%	29%
First-in, first-out (FIFO)	14%	17%

Effective July 1, the Company adopted the LIFO cost flow assumption for valuing the majority of remaining U.S. Grocery Products inventories. The Company believes that the use of the LIFO method better matches current costs with current revenues. The cumulative effect of this change on retained earnings at the beginning of the year is not determinable, nor are the pro-forma effects of retroactive application of LIFO to prior years. The effect of this change on current-year fiscal results was to decrease net income by $16.0 million, or $.20 per share.

If the LIFO method of valuing certain inventories were not used, total inventories would have been $60.1 million higher in the current year, and $24.0 million higher in the prior year.

[4] In practice, many companies defer the formal adoption of LIFO until year-end. Management thus has an opportunity to assess the impact that a change to LIFO will have on the financial statements and to evaluate the desirability of a change for tax purposes. As indicated in Chapter 8, many companies use LIFO because of the advantages of this inventory valuation method in a period of inflation.

CHANGES IN ACCOUNTING ESTIMATES

5 LEARNING OBJECTIVE
Describe the accounting for changes in estimates.

To prepare financial statements, companies must estimate the effects of future conditions and events. For example, the following items require estimates.

1. Uncollectible receivables.
2. Inventory obsolescence.
3. Useful lives and salvage values of assets.
4. Periods benefited by deferred costs.
5. Liabilities for warranty costs and income taxes.
6. Recoverable mineral reserves.
7. Change in depreciation methods.

A company cannot perceive future conditions and events and their effects with certainty. Therefore, estimation requires the exercise of judgment. Accounting estimates will change as new events occur, as a company acquires more experience, or as it obtains additional information.

Prospective Reporting

Companies report prospectively changes in accounting estimates. That is, companies should not adjust previously reported results for changes in estimates. Instead, they account for the effects of all changes in estimates in (1) the period of change if the change affects that period only, or (2) the period of change and future periods if the change affects both. The FASB views changes in estimates as **normal recurring corrections and adjustments**, the natural result of the accounting process. It prohibits retrospective treatment.

The circumstances related to a change in estimate differ from those for a change in accounting principle. If companies reported changes in estimates retrospectively, continual adjustments of prior years' income would occur. It seems proper to accept the view that, because new conditions or circumstances exist, the revision fits the new situation (not the old one). Companies should therefore handle such a revision in the current and future periods.

To illustrate, Underwriters Labs Inc. purchased for $300,000 a building that it originally estimated to have a useful life of 15 years and no salvage value. It recorded depreciation for 5 years on a straight-line basis. On January 1, 2014, Underwriters Labs revises the estimate of the useful life. It now considers the asset to have a total life of 25 years. (Assume that the useful life for financial reporting and tax purposes and depreciation method are the same.) Illustration 22-14 shows the accounts at the beginning of the sixth year.

Buildings	$300,000
Less: Accumulated depreciation—buildings (5 × $20,000)	100,000
Book value of building	$200,000

ILLUSTRATION 22-14
Book Value after Five Years' Depreciation

Underwriters Labs records depreciation for the year 2014 as follows.

Depreciation Expense	10,000	
Accumulated Depreciation—Buildings		10,000

The company computes the $10,000 depreciation charge as shown in Illustration 22-15.

$$\text{Depreciation Charge} = \frac{\textbf{Book Value of Asset}}{\textbf{Remaining Service Life}} = \frac{\$200{,}000}{25 \text{ years} - 5 \text{ years}} = \$10{,}000$$

ILLUSTRATION 22-15
Depreciation after Change in Estimate

Companies sometime find it difficult to differentiate between a change in estimate and a change in accounting principle. Is it a change in principle or a change in estimate when a company changes from deferring and amortizing marketing costs to expensing them as incurred because future benefits of these costs have become doubtful? If it is impossible to determine whether a change in principle or a change in estimate has occurred, the rule is this: **Consider the change as a change in estimate.** This is often referred to as a **change in estimate effected by a change in accounting principle**.

Another example of a change in estimate effected by a change in principle is a change in depreciation (as well as amortization or depletion) methods. Because companies change depreciation methods based on changes in estimates about future benefits from long-lived assets, it is not possible to separate the effect of the accounting principle change from that of the estimates. **As a result, companies account for a change in depreciation methods as a change in estimate effected by a change in accounting principle. [7]**

A similar problem occurs in differentiating between a change in estimate and a correction of an error, although here the answer is more clear-cut. How does a company determine whether it overlooked the information in earlier periods (an error), or whether it obtained new information (a change in estimate)? Proper classification is important because the accounting treatment differs for corrections of errors versus changes in estimates. The general rule is this: **Companies should consider careful estimates that later prove to be incorrect as changes in estimate.** Only when a company obviously computed the estimate incorrectly because of lack of expertise or in bad faith should it consider the adjustment an error. There is no clear demarcation line here. Companies must use good judgment in light of all the circumstances.[5]

Disclosures

Illustration 22-16 shows disclosure of a change in estimated useful lives, which appeared in the annual report of Ampco–Pittsburgh Corporation.

ILLUSTRATION 22-16
Disclosure of Change in Estimated Useful Lives

Ampco–Pittsburgh Corporation

Note 11: Change in Accounting Estimate. The Corporation revised its estimate of the useful lives of certain machinery and equipment. Previously, all machinery and equipment, whether new when placed in use or not, were in one class and depreciated over 15 years. The change principally applies to assets purchased new when placed in use. Those lives are now extended to 20 years. These changes were made to better reflect the estimated periods during which such assets will remain in service. The change had the effect of reducing depreciation expense and increasing net income by approximately $991,000 ($.10 per share).

For the most part, companies need not disclose changes in accounting estimates made as part of normal operations, such as bad debt allowances or inventory obsolescence, unless such changes are material. However, for a change in estimate that affects several periods (such as a change in the service lives of depreciable assets), companies should disclose the effect on income from continuing operations and related per share

[5]In evaluating reasonableness, the auditor should use one or a combination of the following approaches.

(a) Review and test the process used by management to develop the estimate.
(b) Develop an independent expectation of the estimate to corroborate the reasonableness of management's estimate.
(c) Review subsequent events or transactions occurring prior to completion of fieldwork.

"Auditing Accounting Estimates," *Statement on Auditing Standards No. 57* (New York: AICPA, 1988).

amounts of the current period. When a company has a change in estimate effected by a change in accounting principle, it must indicate why the new method is preferable. In addition, companies are subject to all other disclosure guidelines established for changes in accounting principle.

CHANGES IN REPORTING ENTITY

6 LEARNING OBJECTIVE
Identify changes in a reporting entity.

Occasionally, companies make changes that result in different reporting entities. In such cases, companies report the change by **changing the financial statements of all prior periods presented**. The revised statements show the financial information for the **new reporting entity** for all periods.

Examples of a change in reporting entity are:

1. Presenting consolidated statements in place of statements of individual companies.
2. Changing specific subsidiaries that constitute the group of companies for which the entity presents consolidated financial statements.
3. Changing the companies included in combined financial statements.
4. Changing the cost, equity, or consolidation method of accounting for subsidiaries and investments.[6] In this case, a change in the reporting entity does not result from creation, cessation, purchase, or disposition of a subsidiary or other business unit.

In the year in which a company changes a reporting entity, it should disclose in the financial statements the nature of the change and the reason for it. It also should report, for all periods presented, the effect of the change on income before extraordinary items, net income, and earnings per share. These disclosures need not be repeated in subsequent periods' financial statements.

Illustration 22-17 shows a note disclosing a change in reporting entity, from the annual report of **Hewlett-Packard Company**.

ILLUSTRATION 22-17
Disclosure of Change in Reporting Entity

Hewlett-Packard Company

Note: Accounting and Reporting Changes (In Part)

Consolidation of Hewlett-Packard Finance Company. The company implemented a new accounting pronouncement on consolidations. With the adoption of this new pronouncement, the company consolidated the accounts of Hewlett-Packard Finance Company (HPFC), a wholly owned subsidiary previously accounted for under the equity method, with those of the company. The change resulted in an increase in consolidated assets and liabilities but did not have a material effect on the company's financial position. Since HPFC was previously accounted for under the equity method, the change did not affect net earnings. Prior years' consolidated financial information has been restated to reflect this change for comparative purposes.

ACCOUNTING ERRORS

7 LEARNING OBJECTIVE
Describe the accounting for correction of errors.

No business, large or small, is immune from errors. As the opening story discusses, the number of accounting errors that lead to restatement are beginning to decline. However, without accounting and disclosure guidelines for the reporting of errors, investors can be left in the dark about the effects of errors.

Certain errors, such as misclassifications of balances within a financial statement, are not as significant to investors as other errors. Significant errors would be those resulting in overstating assets or income, for example. However, investors should know

[6]An exception to retrospective application occurs when changing from the equity method. We provide an expanded illustration of the accounting for a change from or to the equity method in Appendix 22A.

the potential impact of all errors. Even "harmless" misclassifications can affect important ratios. Also, some errors could signal important weaknesses in internal controls that could lead to more significant errors.

In general, accounting errors include the following types:

1. A change from an accounting principle that is **not** generally accepted to an accounting principle that is acceptable. The rationale is that the company incorrectly presented prior periods because of the application of an improper accounting principle. For example, a company may change from the cash (income tax) basis of accounting to the accrual basis.
2. Mathematical mistakes, such as incorrectly totaling the inventory count sheets when computing the inventory value.
3. Changes in estimates that occur because a company did not prepare the estimates in good faith. For example, a company may have adopted a clearly unrealistic depreciation rate.
4. An oversight, such as the failure to accrue or defer certain expenses and revenues at the end of the period.
5. A misuse of facts, such as the failure to use salvage value in computing the depreciation base for the straight-line approach.
6. The incorrect classification of a cost as an expense instead of an asset, and vice versa.

Accounting errors occur for a variety of reasons. Illustration 22-18 indicates 11 major categories of accounting errors that drive restatements.

ILLUSTRATION 22-18
Accounting-Error Types

Accounting Category	Type of Restatement
Expense recognition	Recording expenses in the incorrect period or for an incorrect amount.
Revenue recognition	Improper revenue accounting. This category includes instances in which revenue was improperly recognized, questionable revenues were recognized, or any other number of related errors that led to misreported revenue.
Misclassification	Misclassifying significant accounting items on the balance sheet, income statement, or statement of cash flows. These include restatements due to misclassification of short- or long-term accounts or those that impact cash flows from operations.
Equity—other	Improper accounting for EPS, restricted stock, warrants, and other equity instruments.
Reserves/Contingencies	Errors involving bad debts related to accounts receivable, inventory reserves, income tax allowances, and loss contingencies.
Long-lived assets	Asset impairments of property, plant, and equipment; goodwill; or other related items.
Taxes	Errors involving correction of tax provision, improper treatment of tax liabilities, and other tax-related items.
Equity—other comprehensive income	Improper accounting for comprehensive income equity transactions including foreign currency items, unrealized gains and losses on certain investments in debt, equity securities, and derivatives.
Inventory	Inventory costing valuations, quantity issues, and cost of sales adjustments.
Equity—stock options	Improper accounting for employee stock options.
Other	Any restatement not covered by the listed categories including those related to improper accounting for acquisitions or mergers.

Source: T. Baldwin and D. Yoo, "Restatements—Traversing Shaky Ground," *Trend Alert*, Glass Lewis & Co. (June 2, 2005), p. 8.

As soon as a company discovers an error, it must correct the error. Companies record **corrections of errors** from prior periods as an adjustment to the beginning balance of retained earnings in the current period. Such corrections are called **prior period adjustments**.[7] **[8]**

[7]See Mark L. Defond and James Jiambalvo, "Incidence and Circumstances of Accounting Errors," *The Accounting Review* (July 1991) for examples of different types of errors and why these errors might have occurred.

If it presents comparative statements, a company should restate the prior statements affected, to correct for the error.[8] The company need not repeat the disclosures in the financial statements of subsequent periods.

Example of Error Correction

To illustrate, in 2015 the bookkeeper for Selectro Company discovered an error. In 2014, the company failed to record $20,000 of depreciation expense on a newly constructed building. This building is the only depreciable asset Selectro owns. The company correctly included the depreciation expense in its tax return and correctly reported its income taxes payable. Illustration 22-19 presents Selectro's income statement for 2014 (starting with income before depreciation expense) with and without the error.

ILLUSTRATION 22-19
Error Correction Comparison

SELECTRO COMPANY
INCOME STATEMENT
FOR THE YEAR ENDED, DECEMBER 31, 2014

		Without Error		With Error
Income before depreciation expense		$100,000		$100,000
Depreciation expense		20,000		0
Income before income tax		80,000		100,000
Current income tax expense	$32,000		$32,000	
Deferred income tax expense	-0-	32,000	8,000	40,000
Net income		$ 48,000		$ 60,000

Illustration 22-20 shows the entries that Selectro should have made and did make for recording depreciation expense and income taxes.

ILLUSTRATION 22-20
Error Entries

Entries Company Should Have Made (Without Error)			Entries Company Did Make (With Error)		
Depreciation Expense	20,000		No entry made for depreciation		
Accumulated Depreciation —Buildings		20,000			
Income Tax Expense	32,000		Income Tax Expense	40,000	
Income Taxes Payable		32,000	Deferred Tax Liability		8,000
			Income Taxes Payable		32,000

As Illustration 22-20 indicates, the $20,000 omission error in 2014 results in the following effects.

Income Statement Effects

Depreciation expense (2014) is understated $20,000.
Income tax expense (2014) is overstated $8,000 ($20,000 × 40%).
Net income (2014) is overstated $12,000 ($20,000 − $8,000).

Balance Sheet Effects

Accumulated depreciation—buildings is understated $20,000.
Deferred tax liability is overstated $8,000 ($20,000 × 40%).

To make the proper correcting entry in 2015, Selectro should recognize that net income in 2014 is overstated by $12,000, the Deferred Tax Liability is overstated by $8,000,

[8]The term **restatement** is used for the process of revising previously issued financial statements to reflect the correction of an error. This distinguishes an error correction from a change in accounting principle. **[9]**

and Accumulated Depreciation—Buildings is understated by $20,000. The entry to correct this error in 2015 is as follows.

Retained Earnings	12,000	
Deferred Tax Liability	8,000	
Accumulated Depreciation—Buildings		20,000

The debit to Retained Earnings results because net income for 2014 is overstated. The debit to Deferred Tax Liability is made to remove this account, which was caused by the error. The credit to Accumulated Depreciation—Buildings reduces the book value of the building to its proper amount. Selectro will make the same journal entry to record the correction of the error in 2015 whether it prepares single-period (noncomparative) or comparative financial statements.

Single-Period Statements

To demonstrate how to show this information in a single-period statement, assume that Selectro Company has a beginning retained earnings balance at January 1, 2015, of $350,000. The company reports net income of $400,000 in 2015. Illustration 22-21 shows Selectro's retained earnings statement for 2015.

ILLUSTRATION 22-21
Reporting an Error—Single-Period Financial Statement

SELECTRO COMPANY
RETAINED EARNINGS STATEMENT
FOR THE YEAR ENDED DECEMBER 31, 2015

Retained earnings, January 1, as reported		$350,000
Correction of an error (depreciation)	$20,000	
Less: Applicable income tax reduction	8,000	(12,000)
Retained earnings, January 1, as adjusted		338,000
Add: Net income		400,000
Retained earnings, December 31		$738,000

The balance sheet in 2015 would not have any deferred tax liability related to the building, and Accumulated Depreciation—Buildings is now restated at a higher amount. The income statement would not be affected.

Comparative Statements

If preparing comparative financial statements, a company should make adjustments to correct the amounts for all affected accounts reported in the statements for **all periods** reported. The company should restate the data to the correct basis for each year presented. It should **show any catch-up adjustment as a prior period adjustment to retained earnings for the earliest period it reported**. These requirements are essentially the same as those for reporting a change in accounting principle.

For example, in the case of Selectro, the error of omitting the depreciation of $20,000 in 2014, discovered in 2015, results in the restatement of the 2014 financial statements. Illustration 22-22 shows the accounts that Selectro restates in the 2014 financial statements.

ILLUSTRATION 22-22
Reporting an Error—Comparative Financial Statements

In the balance sheet:	
Accumulated depreciation—buildings	$20,000 increase
Deferred tax liability	$ 8,000 decrease
Retained earnings, ending balance	$12,000 decrease
In the income statement:	
Depreciation expense—buildings	$20,000 increase
Income tax expense	$ 8,000 decrease
Net income	$12,000 decrease
In the retained earnings statement:	
Retained earnings, ending balance (due to lower net income for the period)	$12,000 decrease

Selectro prepares the 2015 financial statements in comparative form with those of 2014 **as if the error had not occurred.** In addition, Selectro must disclose that it has restated its previously issued financial statements, and it describes the nature of the error. Selectro also must disclose the following.

1. The effect of the correction on each financial statement line item and any per share amounts affected for each prior period presented.
2. The cumulative effect of the change on retained earnings or other appropriate components of equity or net assets in the statement of financial position, as of the beginning of the earliest period presented. **[10]**

Summary of Accounting Changes and Correction of Errors

Having guidelines for reporting accounting changes and corrections has helped resolve several significant and long-standing accounting problems. Yet, because of diversity in situations and characteristics of the items encountered in practice, use of professional judgment is of paramount importance. In applying these guidelines, the primary objective is to serve the users of the financial statements. Achieving this objective requires accuracy, full disclosure, and an absence of misleading inferences.

Illustration 22-23 summarizes the main distinctions and treatments presented in the discussion in this chapter.

ILLUSTRATION 22-23
Summary of Guidelines for Accounting Changes and Errors

Changes in accounting principle

Employ the retrospective approach by:

a. Changing the financial statements of all prior periods presented.
b. Disclosing in the year of the change the effect on net income and earnings per share for all prior periods presented.
c. Reporting an adjustment to the beginning retained earnings balance in the retained earnings statement in the earliest year presented.

If impracticable to determine the prior period effect (e.g., change to LIFO):

a. Do not change prior years' income.
b. Use opening inventory in the year the method is adopted as the base-year inventory for all subsequent LIFO computations.
c. Disclose the effect of the change on the current year, and the reasons for omitting the computation of the cumulative effect and pro forma amounts for prior years.

Changes in accounting estimate

Employ the current and prospective approach by:

a. Reporting current and future financial statements on the new basis.
b. Presenting prior period financial statements as previously reported.
c. Making no adjustments to current-period opening balances for the effects in prior periods.

Changes in reporting entity

Employ the retrospective approach by:

a. Restating the financial statements of all prior periods presented.
b. Disclosing in the year of change the effect on net income and earnings per share data for all prior periods presented.

Changes due to error

Employ the restatement approach by:

a. Correcting all prior period statements presented.
b. Restating the beginning balance of retained earnings for the first period presented when the error effects occur in a period prior to the first period presented.

Changes in accounting principle are appropriate **only** when a company demonstrates that the newly adopted generally accepted accounting principle is **preferable** to the existing one. Companies and accountants determine preferability on the basis of whether the new principle constitutes an **improvement in financial reporting**, not on the basis of the income tax effect alone.[9]

But it is not always easy to determine an improvement in financial reporting. **How does one measure preferability or improvement?** Such measurement varies from company to company. Quaker Oats Company, for example, argued that a change in accounting principle to LIFO inventory valuation "better matches current costs with current revenues" (see Illustration 22-13, page 1356). Conversely, another company might change from LIFO to FIFO because it wishes to report a more realistic ending inventory. How do you determine which is the better of these two arguments? Determining the preferable method requires some "standard" or "objective." Because no universal standard or objective is generally accepted, the problem of determining preferability continues to be difficult.

Initially, the SEC took the position that the auditor should indicate whether a change in accounting principle was preferable. The SEC has since modified this approach, noting that greater reliance may be placed on management's judgment in assessing preferability. Even though the preferability criterion is difficult to apply, the general guidelines have acted as a deterrent to capricious changes in accounting principles.[10] **If a FASB rule creates a new principle, expresses preference for, or rejects a specific accounting principle, a change is considered clearly acceptable.**

What do the numbers mean? CAN I GET MY MONEY BACK?

When companies report restatements, investors usually lose money. What should investors do if a company misleads them by misstating its financial results? Join other investors in a class-action suit against the company and in some cases, the auditor.

Class-action activity has picked up in recent years, and settlements can be large. To find out about class actions, investors can go online to see if they are eligible to join any class actions. Below are some recent examples.

Company	Settlement Amount	Contact for Claim
Samsung	$1 billion	*www.lawyersandsettlements.com*
Merck	$950 million	*www.lawyersandsettlements.com*
Wal-Mart	$13.5 million	*www.lawyersandsettlements.com*

The amounts reported are *before* attorney's fees, which can range from 15 to 30 percent of the total. Also, investors may owe taxes if the settlement results in a capital gain on the investment. Thus, investors can get back some of the money they lost due to restatements, but they should be prepared to pay an attorney and the government first.

Sources: Adapted from C. Coolidge, "Lost and Found," *Forbes* (October 1, 2001), pp. 124–125; data from *www.lawyersandsettlements.com* as of 11/13/12.

[9]A change in accounting principle, a change in the reporting entity (special type of change in accounting principle), and a correction of an error require an explanatory paragraph in the auditor's report discussing lack of consistency from one period to the next. A change in accounting estimate does not affect the auditor's opinion relative to consistency. However, if the change in estimate has a material effect on the financial statements, disclosure may still be required. Error correction not involving a change in accounting principle does not require disclosure relative to consistency.

[10]If management has not provided reasonable justification for the change in accounting principle, the auditor should express a qualified opinion. Or, if the effect of the change is sufficiently material, the auditor should express an adverse opinion on the financial statements. "Reports on Audited Financial Statements," *Statement on Auditing Standards No. 58* (New York: AICPA, 1988).

Motivations for Change of Accounting Method

8 LEARNING OBJECTIVE
Identify economic motives for changing accounting methods.

Difficult as it is to determine which accounting standards have the strongest conceptual support, other complications make the process even more complex. These complications stem from the fact that managers have self-interest in how the financial statements make the company look. They naturally wish to show their financial performance in the best light. A **favorable profit picture** can influence investors, and a strong liquidity position can influence creditors. **Too favorable a profit picture**, however, can provide union negotiators and government regulators with ammunition during bargaining talks. Hence, managers might have varying motives for reporting income numbers.

Research has provided additional insight into why companies may prefer certain accounting methods.[11] Some of these reasons are as follows.

1. ***Political costs.*** As companies become larger and more politically visible, politicians and regulators devote more attention to them. The larger the firm, the more likely it is to become subject to regulation such as antitrust, and the more likely it is to be required to pay higher taxes. Therefore, companies that are politically visible may seek to report low income numbers, to avoid the scrutiny of regulators. In addition, other constituents, such as labor unions, may be less willing to ask for wage increases if reported income is low. Researchers have found that the larger the company, the more likely it is to adopt income-decreasing approaches in selecting accounting methods.
2. ***Capital structure.*** A number of studies have indicated that the capital structure of the company can affect the selection of accounting methods. For example, a company with a high debt to equity ratio is more likely to be constrained by debt covenants. The debt covenant may indicate that the company cannot pay dividends if retained earnings fall below a certain level. As a result, such a company is more likely to select accounting methods that will increase net income.
3. ***Bonus payments.*** Studies have found that if compensation plans tie managers' bonus payments to income, management will select accounting methods that maximize their bonus payments.
4. ***Smooth earnings.*** Substantial earnings increases attract the attention of politicians, regulators, and competitors. In addition, large increases in income are difficult to achieve in following years. Further, executive compensation plans would use these higher numbers as a baseline and make it difficult for managers to earn bonuses in subsequent years. Conversely, investors and competitors might view large decreases in earnings as a signal that the company is in financial trouble. Also, substantial decreases in income raise concerns on the part of stockholders, lenders, and other interested parties about the competency of management. For all these reasons, companies have an incentive to "manage" or "smooth" earnings. In general, management tends to believe that a steady 10 percent growth a year is much better than a 30 percent growth one year and a 10 percent decline the next.[12] In other words, managers usually prefer a gradually increasing income report and sometimes change accounting methods to ensure such a result.

[11]See Ross L. Watts and Jerold L. Zimmerman, "Positive Accounting Theory: A Ten-Year Perspective," *The Accounting Review* (January 1990) for an excellent review of research findings related to management incentives in selecting accounting methods.

[12]O. Douglas Moses, "Income Smoothing and Incentives: Empirical Tests Using Accounting Changes," *The Accounting Review* (April 1987). The findings provide evidence that earnings smoothing is associated with firm size, the existence of bonus plans, and the divergence of actual earnings from expectations.

Management pays careful attention to the accounting it follows and often changes accounting methods, not for conceptual reasons, but for economic reasons. As indicated throughout this textbook, such arguments have come to be known as **economic consequences** arguments. These arguments focus on the supposed impact of the accounting method on the behavior of investors, creditors, competitors, governments, or managers of the reporting companies themselves.[13]

Underlying Concepts

Neutrality is an important element of faithful representation.

To counter these pressures, standard-setters such as the FASB have declared, as part of their conceptual framework, that they will assess the merits of proposed standards from a position of **neutrality**. That is, they evaluate the soundness of standards on the basis of conceptual soundness, not on the grounds of possible impact on behavior. It is not the FASB's place to choose standards according to the kinds of behavior it wishes to promote and the kinds it wishes to discourage. At the same time, it must be admitted that some standards often **will have** the effect of influencing behavior. Yet their justification should be conceptual, and not viewed in terms of their economic impact.

ERROR ANALYSIS

LEARNING OBJECTIVE 9

Analyze the effect of errors.

In this section, we show some additional types of accounting errors. Companies generally do not correct for errors that do not have a significant effect on the presentation of the financial statements. For example, should a company with a total annual payroll of $1,750,000 and net income of $940,000 correct its financial statements if it finds it failed to record accrued wages of $5,000? No—it would not consider this error significant or material.

Obviously, defining materiality is difficult, and managers and auditors must use experience and judgment to determine whether adjustment is necessary for a given error. We assume **all errors discussed in this section to be material and to require adjustment**. (Also, we ignore all tax effects in this section.)

Companies must answer three questions in error analysis:

1. What type of error is involved?
2. What entries are needed to correct for the error?
3. After discovery of the error, how are financial statements to be restated?

As indicated earlier, companies treat errors **as prior period adjustments and report them in the current year as adjustments to the beginning balance of Retained Earnings**. If a company presents comparative statements, it restates the prior affected statements to correct for the error.

Balance Sheet Errors

Balance sheet errors affect only the presentation of an asset, liability, or stockholders' equity account. Examples are the classification of a short-term receivable as part of the investment section, the classification of a note payable as an account payable, and the classification of plant assets as inventory.

When the error is discovered, the company reclassifies the item to its proper position. If the company prepares comparative statements that include the error year, it should correctly restate the balance sheet for the error year.

[13]Lobbyists use economic consequences arguments—and there are many of them—to put pressure on standard-setters. We have seen examples of these arguments in the oil and gas industry about successful-efforts versus full-cost in the technology area, with the issue of mandatory expensing of research and developmental costs and stock options.

Income Statement Errors

Income statement errors involve the improper classification of revenues or expenses. Examples include recording interest revenue as part of sales, purchases as bad debt expense, and depreciation expense as interest expense. An income statement classification error has no effect on the balance sheet and **no effect on net income**.

A company must make a reclassification entry when it discovers the error, if it makes the discovery in the same year in which the error occurs. If the error occurred in prior periods, the company does not need to make a reclassification entry at the date of discovery because the accounts for the current year are correctly stated. (Remember that the company has closed the income statement accounts from the prior period to retained earnings.) If the company prepares comparative statements that include the error year, it restates the income statement for the error year.

Balance Sheet and Income Statement Errors

The third type of error involves both the balance sheet and income statement. For example, assume that the bookkeeper overlooked accrued wages payable at the end of the accounting period. The effect of this error is to understate expenses, understate liabilities, and overstate net income for that period of time. This type of error affects both the balance sheet and the income statement. We classify this type of error in one of two ways—counterbalancing or noncounterbalancing.

Counterbalancing errors are those that will be offset or corrected over two periods. For example, the failure to record accrued wages is a counterbalancing error because over a two-year period the error will no longer be present. In other words, the failure to record accrued wages in the previous period means: (1) net income for the first period is overstated, (2) accrued wages payable (a liability) is understated, and (3) wages expense is understated. In the next period, net income is understated, accrued wages payable (a liability) is correctly stated, and wages expense is overstated. For the two **years combined**: (1) net income is correct, (2) wages expense is correct, and (3) accrued wages payable at the end of the second year is correct. Most errors in accounting that affect both the balance sheet and income statement are counterbalancing errors.

Noncounterbalancing errors are those that are not offset in the next accounting period. An example would be the failure to capitalize equipment that has a useful life of five years. If we expense this asset immediately, expenses will be overstated in the first period but understated in the next four periods. At the end of the second period, the effect of the error is not fully offset. Net income is correct in the aggregate only at the end of five years because the asset is fully depreciated at this point. Thus, **noncounterbalancing errors are those that take longer than two periods to correct themselves**.

Only in rare instances is an error never reversed. An example would be if a company initially expenses land. Because land is not depreciable, theoretically the error is never offset, unless the land is sold.

Counterbalancing Errors

We illustrate the usual types of counterbalancing errors on the following pages. In studying these illustrations, keep in mind a couple of points.

First, determine whether the company has closed the books for the period in which the error is found:

1. **If the company has closed the books in the current year:**
   - **(a)** If the error is already counterbalanced, no entry is necessary.
   - **(b)** If the error is not yet counterbalanced, make an entry to adjust the present balance of retained earnings.

2. If the company has not closed the books in the current year:

(a) If the error is already counterbalanced, make an entry to correct the error in the current period and to adjust the beginning balance of Retained Earnings.

(b) If the error is not yet counterbalanced, make an entry to adjust the beginning balance of Retained Earnings.

Second, if the company presents comparative statements, it must restate the amounts for comparative purposes. **Restatement is necessary even if a correcting journal entry is not required.**

To illustrate, assume that Sanford's Cement Co. failed to accrue revenue in 2012 when it fulfilled its performance obligation, but recorded the revenue in 2013 when it received payment. The company discovered the error in 2015. It does not need to make an entry to correct for this error because the effects have been counterbalanced by the time Sanford discovered the error in 2015. However, if Sanford presents comparative financial statements for 2012 through 2015, it must **restate the accounts and related amounts for the years 2012 and 2013 for financial reporting purposes.**

The sections that follow demonstrate the accounting for the usual types of counterbalancing errors.

Failure to Record Accrued Wages. On December 31, 2014, Hurley Enterprises did not accrue wages in the amount of $1,500. The entry in 2015 to correct this error, assuming Hurley has not closed the books for 2015, is:

Retained Earnings	1,500	
Salaries and Wages Expense		1,500

The rationale for this entry is as follows. (1) When Hurley pays the 2014 accrued wages in 2015, it makes an additional debit of $1,500 to 2015 Salaries and Wages Expense. (2) Salaries and Wages Expense—2015 is overstated by $1,500. (3) Because the company did not record 2014 accrued wages as Salaries and Wages Expense in 2014, the net income for 2014 was overstated by $1,500. (4) Because 2014 net income is overstated by $1,500, the Retained Earnings account is overstated by $1,500 (because net income is closed to Retained Earnings).

If Hurley has closed the books for 2015, it makes no entry because the error is counterbalanced.

Failure to Record Prepaid Expenses. In January 2014, Hurley Enterprises purchased a two-year insurance policy costing $1,000. It debited Insurance Expense, and credited Cash. The company made no adjusting entries at the end of 2014.

The entry on December 31, 2015, to correct this error, assuming Hurley has not closed the books for 2015, is:

Insurance Expense	500	
Retained Earnings		500

If Hurley has closed the books for 2015, it makes no entry because the error is counterbalanced.

Understatement of Unearned Revenue. On December 31, 2014, Hurley Enterprises received $50,000 as a prepayment for renting certain office space for the following year. At the time of receipt of the rent payment, the company recorded a debit to Cash and a credit to Rent Revenue. It made no adjusting entry as of December 31, 2014. The entry on December 31, 2015, to correct for this error, assuming that Hurley has not closed the books for 2015, is:

Retained Earnings	50,000	
Rent Revenue		50,000

If Hurley has closed the books for 2015, it makes no entry because the error is counterbalanced.

Overstatement of Accrued Revenue. On December 31, 2014, Hurley Enterprises accrued as interest revenue $8,000 that applied to 2015. On that date, the company recorded a debit to Interest Receivable and a credit to Interest Revenue. The entry on December 31, 2015, to correct for this error, assuming that Hurley has not closed the books for 2015, is:

Retained Earnings	8,000	
Interest Revenue		8,000

If Hurley has closed the books for 2015, it makes no entry because the error is counterbalanced.

Overstatement of Purchases. Hurley's accountant recorded a purchase of merchandise for $9,000 in 2014 that applied to 2015. The physical inventory for 2014 was correctly stated. The company uses the periodic inventory method. The entry on December 31, 2015, to correct for this error, assuming that Harley has not closed the books for 2015, is:

Purchases	9,000	
Retained Earnings		9,000

If Hurley has closed the books for 2015, it makes no entry because the error is counterbalanced.

Noncounterbalancing Errors

The entries for noncounterbalancing errors are more complex. Companies must make correcting entries, even if they have closed the books.

Failure to Record Depreciation. Assume that on January 1, 2014, Hurley Enterprises purchased a machine for $10,000 that had an estimated useful life of five years. The accountant incorrectly expensed this machine in 2014, but discovered the error in 2015. If we assume that Hurley uses straight-line depreciation on this asset, the entry on December 31, 2015, to correct for this error, given that Hurley has not closed the books, is:

Equipment	10,000	
Depreciation Expense	2,000	
Retained Earnings		8,000*
Accumulated Depreciation—Equipment (20% × $10,000 × 2)		4,000

*Computations:

Retained Earnings	
Overstatement of expense in 2014	$10,000
Proper depreciation for 2014 (20% × $10,000)	(2,000)
Retained earnings understated as of Dec. 31, 2014	$ 8,000

If Hurley has closed the books for 2015, the entry is:

Equipment	10,000	
Retained Earnings		6,000*
Accumulated Depreciation—Equipment		4,000

*Computations:

Retained Earnings	
Retained earnings understated as of Dec. 31, 2014	$ 8,000
Proper depreciation for 2015 (20% × $10,000)	(2,000)
Retained earnings understated as of Dec. 31, 2015	$ 6,000

Failure to Adjust for Bad Debts. Companies sometimes use a specific charge-off method in accounting for bad debt expense when a percentage of sales is more appropriate. They then make adjustments to change from the specific write-off to some type of allowance method. For example, assume that Hurley Enterprises has recognized bad debt expense when it has the following uncollectible debts.

	2014	2015
From 2014 sales	$550	$690
From 2015 sales		700

Hurley estimates that it will charge off an additional $1,400 in 2016, of which $300 is applicable to 2014 sales and $1,100 to 2015 sales. The entry on December 31, 2015, assuming that Hurley **has not closed the books for 2015**, is:

Bad Debt Expense	410	
Retained Earnings	990	
Allowance for Doubtful Accounts		1,400

Allowance for doubtful accounts: Additional $300 for 2014 sales and $1,100 for 2015 sales.

Bad debts and retained earnings balance:

	2014	2015
Bad debts charged for	$1,240*	$ 700
Additional bad debts anticipated in 2016	300	1,100
Proper bad debt expense	1,540	1,800
Charges currently made to each period	(550)	(1,390)
Bad debt adjustment	$ 990	$ 410

*$550 + $690 = $1,240

If Hurley **has closed the books for 2015**, the entry is:

Retained Earnings	1,400	
Allowance for Doubtful Accounts		1,400

Comprehensive Example: Numerous Errors

In some circumstances a combination of errors occurs. The company therefore prepares a worksheet to facilitate the analysis. The following problem demonstrates use of the worksheet. The mechanics of its preparation should be obvious from the solution format. The income statements of Hudson Company for the years ended December 31, 2013, 2014, and 2015, indicate the following net incomes.

2013	$17,400
2014	20,200
2015	11,300

An examination of the accounting records for these years indicates that Hudson Company made several errors in arriving at the net income amounts reported:

1. The company consistently omitted from the records wages earned by workers but not paid at December 31. The amounts omitted were:

December 31, 2013	$1,000
December 31, 2014	$1,400
December 31, 2015	$1,600

   When paid in the year following that in which they were earned, Hudson recorded these amounts as expenses.

2. The company overstated merchandise inventory on December 31, 2013, by $1,900 as the result of errors made in the footings and extensions on the inventory sheets.
3. On December 31, 2014, Hudson expensed prepaid insurance of $1,200, applicable to 2015.
4. The company did not record on December 31, 2014, interest receivable in the amount of $240.
5. On January 2, 2014, Hudson sold for $1,800 a piece of equipment costing $3,900. At the date of sale, the equipment had accumulated depreciation of $2,400. The

company recorded the cash received as Miscellaneous Income in 2014. In addition, the company continued to record depreciation for this equipment in both 2014 and 2015 at the rate of 10 percent of cost.

The first step in preparing the worksheet is to prepare a schedule showing the corrected net income amounts for the years ended December 31, 2013, 2014, and 2015. Each correction of the amount originally reported is clearly labeled. The next step is to indicate the balance sheet accounts affected as of December 31, 2015. Illustration 22-24 shows the completed worksheet for Hudson Company.

ILLUSTRATION 22-24
Worksheet to Correct Income and Balance Sheet Errors

HUDSON COMPANY.xls

HUDSON COMPANY
Worksheet to Correct Income and Balance Sheet Errors

	A	B	C	D	E	F	G	H
4		Worksheet Analysis of Changes in Net Income				Balance Sheet Correction at December 31, 2015		
5		2013	2014	2015	Totals	Debit	Credit	Account
6	Net income as reported	$17,400	$20,200	$11,300	$48,900			
7	Wages unpaid, 12/31/13	(1,000)	1,000		-0-			
8	Wages unpaid, 12/31/14		(1,400)	1,400	-0-			
9	Wages unpaid, 12/31/15			(1,600)	(1,600)		$1,600	Salaries and Wages Payable
10	Inventory overstatement, 12/31/13	(1,900)	1,900		-0-			
11	Prepaid insurance, 12/31/14		1,200	(1,200)	-0-			
12	Interest receivable, 12/31/14		240	(240)	-0-			
13	Correction for entry made upon sale of equipment, 1/2/14[a]		(1,500)		(1,500)	$2,400		Accumulated Depreciation—Equipment
							3,900	Equipment
14	Overcharge of depreciation, 2014		390		390	390		Accumulated Depreciation—Equipment
15	Overcharge of depreciation, 2015			390	390	390		Accumulated Depreciation—Equipment
16	Corrected net income	$14,500	$22,030	$10,050	$46,580			
17	[a]Cost	$ 3,900						
18	Less: Accumulated depreciation	2,400						
19	Book value	1,500						
20	Less: Proceeds from sale	1,800						
21	Gain on sale	300						
22	Income reported	(1,800)						
23	Adjustment	$(1,500)						

Assuming that Hudson Company **has not closed the books**, correcting entries on December 31, 2015, are:

Retained Earnings	1,400	
Salaries and Wages Expense		1,400
(To correct improper charge to Salaries and Wages Expense for 2015)		
Salaries and Wages Expense	1,600	
Salaries and Wages Payable		1,600
(To record proper wages expense for 2015)		

Insurance Expense	1,200	
Retained Earnings		1,200
(To record proper insurance expense for 2015)		
Interest Revenue	240	
Retained Earnings		240
(To correct improper credit to Interest Revenue in 2015)		
Retained Earnings	1,500	
Accumulated Depreciation—Equipment	2,400	
Equipment		3,900
(To record write-off of equipment in 2014 and adjustment of Retained Earnings)		
Accumulated Depreciation—Equipment	780	
Depreciation Expense		390
Retained Earnings		390
(To correct improper charge for depreciation expense in 2014 and 2015)		

If Hudson Company has closed the books for 2015, the correcting entries are:

Retained Earnings	1,600	
Salaries and Wages Payable		1,600
(To record proper wage expense for 2015)		
Retained Earnings	1,500	
Accumulated Depreciation—Equipment	2,400	
Equipment		3,900
(To record write-off of equipment in 2014 and adjustment of Retained Earnings)		
Accumulated Depreciation—Equipment	780	
Retained Earnings		780
(To correct improper charge for depreciation expense in 2014 and 2015)		

What do the numbers mean? GUARD THE FINANCIAL STATEMENTS!

Restatements sometimes occur because of financial fraud. Financial frauds involve the intentional misstatement or omission of material information in the organization's financial reports. Common methods of financial fraud manipulation include recording fictitious revenues, concealing liabilities or expenses, and artificially inflating reported assets. Financial frauds made up around 8 percent of the frauds in a recent study on occupational fraud but caused a median loss of more than $1 million in 2012 ($4 million in 2010)—by far the most costly category of fraud. The following chart compares loss amounts for 2012 versus 2010 for financial statement fraud, corruption, and asset misappropriation.

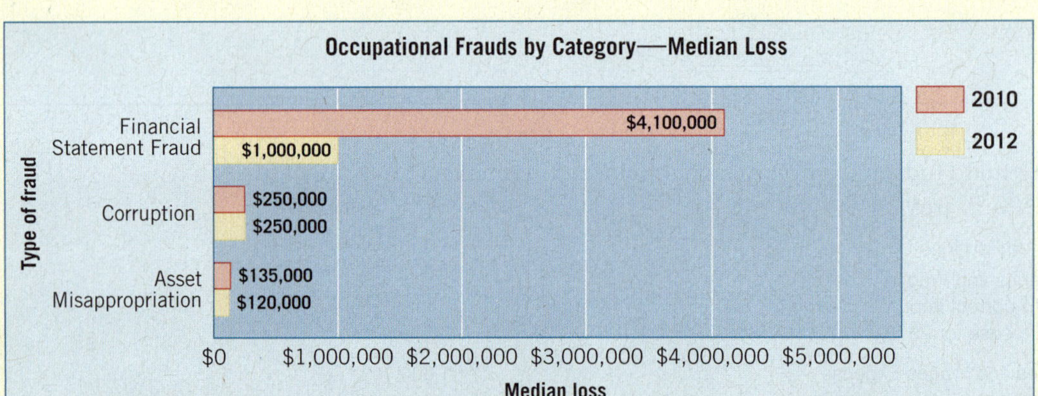

While the trend in the dollar amount of losses is going in the right direction, another study indicates that the number of fraud reports at 1,400 companies in the "Quarterly Corporate Fraud Index" is on the climb—with 2,348 reported frauds in the 2nd quarter of 2005 to over 7,800 in the 2nd quarter of 2012. While there is some debate about whether the reporting of fraud has increased with regulation that provides whistle-blower protections (i.e., the incidence of fraud is not increasing as much as the reporting of fraud), companies must increase their efforts to protect their statements from the negative effects of fraud.

Sources: Report to the Nations on Occupational Fraud and Abuse, 2012 Global Fraud Study, Association of Certified Fraud Examiners (2012), p. 11; and C. McDonald, "Fraud Reports Climb Still Higher," *CFO.com* (September 26, 2012).

Preparation of Financial Statements with Error Corrections

Up to now, our discussion of error analysis has focused on identifying the type of error involved and accounting for its correction in the records. We have noted that companies must present the correction of the error on comparative financial statements.

The following example illustrates how a company would restate a typical year's financial statements, given many different errors.

Dick & Wally's Outlet is a small retail outlet in the town of Holiday. Lacking expertise in accounting, the company does not keep adequate records, and numerous errors occurred in recording accounting information.

1. The bookkeeper inadvertently failed to record a cash receipt of $1,000 on the sale of merchandise in 2015.
2. Accrued wages expense at the end of 2014 was $2,500; at the end of 2015, $3,200. The company does not accrue for wages; all wages are charged to Administrative Expenses.
3. The company had not set up an allowance for estimated uncollectible receivables. Dick and Wally decided to set up such an allowance for the estimated probable losses, as of December 31, 2015, for 2014 accounts of $700, and for 2015 accounts of $1,500. They also decided to correct the charge against each year so that it shows the losses (actual and estimated) relating to that year's sales. The company has written off accounts to bad debt expense (selling expense) as follows.

	In 2014	In 2015
2014 accounts	$400	$2,000
2015 accounts		1,600

4. Prepaid insurance not recorded at the end of 2014 was $600, and at the end of 2015, $400. All insurance is charged to Administrative Expenses.
5. An account payable of $6,000 should have been a note payable.
6. During 2014, the company sold for $7,000 an asset that cost $10,000 and had a book value of $4,000. At the time of sale, Cash was debited and Miscellaneous Income was credited for $7,000.
7. As a result of the last transaction, the company overstated depreciation expense (an administrative expense) in 2014 by $800 and in 2015 by $1,200.

Illustration 22-25 (page 1374) presents a worksheet that begins with the unadjusted trial balance of Dick & Wally's Outlet. You can determine the correcting entries and their effect on the financial statements by examining the worksheet.

DICK & WALLY'S OUTLET.xls

Home | Insert | Page Layout | Formulas | Data | Review | View

P18 fx

DICK & WALLY'S OUTLET
Worksheet Analysis to Adjust Financial Statements for the Year 2015

		Trial Balance Unadjusted		Adjustments		Income Statement Adjusted		Balance Sheet Adjusted	
		Dr.	Cr.	Dr.	Cr.	Dr.	Cr.	Dr.	Cr.
8	Cash	3,100		(1) 1,000				4,100	
9	Accounts Receivable	17,600						17,600	
10	Notes Receivable	8,500						8,500	
11	Inventory	34,000						34,000	
12	Property, Plant, and Equipment	112,000			(6) 10,000[a]			102,000	
13	Accumulated Depreciation—		83,500	(6) 6,000[a]					75,500
	Equipment			(7) 2,000					
14									
15	Investments	24,300						24,300	
16	Accounts Payable		14,500	(5) 6,000					8,500
17	Notes Payable		10,000		(5) 6,000				16,000
18	Capital Stock		43,500						43,500
19	Retained Earnings		20,000	(3) 2,700[b]					
20				(6) 4,000[a]	(4) 600				
21				(2) 2,500	(7) 800				12,200
22	Sales Revenue		94,000		(1) 1,000		95,000		
23	Cost of Goods Sold	21,000				21,000			
24	Selling Expenses	22,000			(3) 500[b]	21,500			
25	Administrative Expenses	23,000		(2) 700	(4) 400	22,700			
26				(4) 600	(7) 1,200				
27	Totals	265,500	265,500						
28									
29	Salaries and Wages Payable				(2) 3,200				3,200
30	Allowance for Doubtful				(3) 2,200[b]				2,200
31	Accounts								
32	Prepaid Insurance			(4) 400				400	
33	Net Income					29,800			29,800
34	Totals			25,900	25,900	95,000	95,000	190,900	190,900
35									

Computations:

[a]Machinery	
Proceeds from sale	$ 7,000
Book value of machinery	(4,000)
Gain on sale	3,000
Less: Income credited	7,000
Retained earnings adjustment	$(4,000)

[b]Bad Debts	2014	2015
Bad debts charged for	$2,400	$1,600
Additional bad debts anticipated	700	1,500
	3,100	3,100
Charges currently made to each year	(400)	(3,600)
Bad debt adjustment	$2,700	$ (500)

ILLUSTRATION 22-25
Worksheet to Analyze Effect of Errors in Financial Statements

You will want to read **IFRS INSIGHTS** on pages 1404–1408 for discussion of IFRS related to accounting changes and errors.

SUMMARY OF LEARNING OBJECTIVES

1 Identify the types of accounting changes. The three different types of accounting changes are as follows. (1) *Change in accounting principle:* a change from one generally accepted accounting principle to another generally accepted accounting principle. (2) *Change in accounting estimate:* a change that occurs as the result of new information or as additional experience is acquired. (3) *Change in reporting entity:* a change from reporting as one type of entity to another type of entity.

2 Describe the accounting for changes in accounting principles. A change in accounting principle involves a change from one generally accepted accounting principle to another. A change in accounting principle is not considered to result from the adoption of a new principle in recognition of events that have occurred for the first time or that were previously immaterial. If the accounting principle previously followed was not acceptable or if the principle was applied incorrectly, a change to a generally accepted accounting principle is considered a correction of an error.

3 Understand how to account for retrospective accounting changes. The general requirement for changes in accounting principle is retrospective application. Under retrospective application, companies change prior years' financial statements on a basis consistent with the newly adopted principle. They treat any part of the effect attributable to years prior to those presented as an adjustment of the earliest retained earnings presented.

4 Understand how to account for impracticable changes. Retrospective application is impracticable if the prior period effect cannot be determined using every reasonable effort to do so. For example, in changing to LIFO, the base-year inventory for all subsequent LIFO calculations is generally the opening inventory in the year the company adopts the method. There is no restatement of prior years' income because it is often too impractical to do so.

5 Describe the accounting for changes in estimates. Companies report changes in estimates prospectively. That is, companies should make no changes in previously reported results. They do not adjust opening balances nor change financial statements of prior periods.

6 Identify changes in a reporting entity. An accounting change that results in financial statements that are actually the statements of a different entity should be reported by restating the financial statements of all prior periods presented, to show the financial information for the new reporting entity for all periods.

7 Describe the accounting for correction of errors. Companies must correct errors as soon as they discover them, by proper entries in the accounts, and report them in the financial statements. The profession requires that a company treat corrections of errors as prior period adjustments, record them in the year in which it discovered the errors, and report them in the financial statements in the proper periods. If presenting comparative statements, a company should restate the prior statements affected to correct for the errors. The company need not repeat the disclosures in the financial statements of subsequent periods.

8 Identify economic motives for changing accounting methods. Managers might have varying motives for income reporting, depending on economic times and whom they seek to impress. Some of the reasons for changing accounting methods are (1) political costs, (2) capital structure, (3) bonus payments, and (4) smoothing of earnings.

KEY TERMS

9 **Analyze the effect of errors.** Three types of errors can occur. (1) *Balance sheet errors,* which affect only the presentation of an asset, liability, or stockholders' equity account. (2) *Income statement errors,* which affect only the presentation of revenue, expense, gain, or loss accounts in the income statement. (3) *Balance sheet and income statement errors,* which involve both the balance sheet and income statement. Errors are classified into two types. (1) *Counterbalancing errors* are offset or corrected over two periods. (2) *Noncounterbalancing errors* are not offset in the next accounting period and take longer than two periods to correct themselves.

As an aid to understanding accounting changes, we provide the following glossary.

KEY TERMS RELATED TO ACCOUNTING CHANGES

ACCOUNTING CHANGE. A change in (1) an accounting principle, (2) an accounting estimate, or (3) the reporting entity. The correction of an error in previously issued financial statements is not an accounting change.

CHANGE IN ACCOUNTING PRINCIPLE. A change from one generally accepted accounting principle to another generally accepted accounting principle when two or more generally accepted accounting principles apply or when the accounting principle formerly used is no longer generally accepted.

CHANGE IN ACCOUNTING ESTIMATE. A change that has the effect of adjusting the carrying amount of an existing asset or liability or altering the subsequent accounting for existing or future assets or liabilities. Changes in accounting estimates result from new information.

CHANGE IN ACCOUNTING ESTIMATE EFFECTED BY A CHANGE IN ACCOUNTING PRINCIPLE. A change in accounting estimate that is inseparable from the effect of a related change in accounting principle.

CHANGE IN THE REPORTING ENTITY. A change that results in financial statements that, in effect, are those of a different reporting entity (see page 1359).

DIRECT EFFECTS OF A CHANGE IN ACCOUNTING PRINCIPLE. Those recognized changes in assets or liabilities necessary to effect a change in accounting principle.

ERROR IN PREVIOUSLY ISSUED FINANCIAL STATEMENTS. An error in recognition, measurement, presentation, or disclosure in financial statements resulting from mathematical mistakes, mistakes in the application of GAAP, or oversight or misuse of facts that existed at the time the financial statements were prepared. A change from an accounting principle that is not generally accepted to one that is generally accepted is a correction of an error.

INDIRECT EFFECTS OF A CHANGE IN ACCOUNTING PRINCIPLE. Any changes to current or future cash flows of an entity that result from making a change in accounting principle that is applied retrospectively.

RESTATEMENT. The process of revising previously issued financial statements to reflect the correction of an error in those financial statements.

RETROSPECTIVE APPLICATION. The application of a different accounting principle to one or more previously issued financial statements, or to the statement of financial position at the beginning of the current period, as if that principle had always been used, or a change to financial statements of prior accounting periods to present the financial statements of a new reporting entity as if it had existed in those prior years. **[11]**

APPENDIX 22A CHANGING FROM OR TO THE EQUITY METHOD

10 LEARNING OBJECTIVE
Make the computations and prepare the entries necessary to record a change from or to the equity method of accounting.

As noted in the chapter, companies generally should report an accounting change that results in financial statements for a different entity by **changing the financial statements of all prior periods presented**.

An example of a change in reporting entity is when a company's level of ownership or influence changes, such as when it changes from or to the equity method. When changing **to** the equity method, companies use retrospective application. Companies treat a change **from** the equity method prospectively. We present examples of these changes in entity in the following two sections.

CHANGE FROM THE EQUITY METHOD

If the investor level of influence or ownership falls below that necessary for continued use of the equity method, a company must change from the equity method to the fair value method. The earnings or losses that the investor previously recognized under the equity method should **remain as part of the carrying amount** of the investment, with no retrospective application to the new method.

When a company changes **from the equity method to the fair value method, the cost basis for accounting purposes is the carrying amount of the investment at the date of the change**. The investor applies the new method in its entirety once the equity method is no longer appropriate. At the next reporting date, the investor should record the unrealized holding gain or loss to recognize the difference between the carrying amount and fair value.[14]

Dividends in Excess of Earnings

In subsequent periods, dividends received by the investor company may exceed its share of the investee's earnings for such periods (all periods following the change in method). To the extent that they do so, the investor company should account for such dividends as a **reduction of the investment carrying amount**, rather than as revenue. The reason: Dividends in excess of earnings are viewed as a liquidating dividend, with this excess then accounted for as a reduction of the equity investment.

To illustrate, assume that on January 1, 2013, Investor Company purchased 250,000 shares of Investee Company's 1,000,000 shares of outstanding stock for $8,500,000. Investor correctly accounted for this investment using the equity method. After accounting for dividends received and investee net income, in 2013 Investor reported its investment in Investee Company at $8,780,000 at December 31, 2013. On January 2, 2014, Investee Company sold 1,500,000 additional shares of its own common stock to the public, thereby reducing Investor Company's ownership from 25 percent to 10 percent. Illustration 22A-1 (page 1378) shows the net income (or loss) and dividends of Investee Company for the years 2014 through 2016.

[14]A retrospective application for this type of change is impracticable in many cases. Determining fair values on a portfolio basis for securities in previous periods may be quite difficult. As a result, prospective application is used.

ILLUSTRATION 22A-1
Income Earned and Dividends Received

Year	Investor's Share of Investee Income (Loss)	Investee Dividends Received by Investor
2014	$600,000	$ 400,000
2015	350,000	400,000
2016	–0–	210,000
Totals	$950,000	$1,010,000

Assuming a change from the equity method to the fair value method as of January 2, 2014, Investor Company's reported investment in Investee Company and its reported income would be as shown in Illustration 22A-2.

ILLUSTRATION 22A-2
Impact on Investment Carrying Amount

Year	Dividend Revenue Recognized	Cumulative Excess of Share of Earnings over Dividends Received	Investment at December 31
2014	$400,000	$200,000[a]	$8,780,000
2015	400,000	150,000[b]	8,780,000
2016	150,000	(60,000)[c]	$8,780,000 – $60,000 = $8,720,000

[a]$600,000 – $400,000 = $200,000
[b]($350,000 – $400,000) + $200,000 = $150,000
[c]$150,000 – $210,000 = $(60,000)

Investor Company would record the dividends and earnings data for the three years subsequent to the change in methods as shown by the following entries.

2014 and 2015

Cash	400,000	
Dividend Revenue		400,000
(To record dividend received from Investee Company)		

2016

Cash	210,000	
Equity Investments (available-for-sale)		60,000
Dividend Revenue		150,000
(To record dividend revenue from Investee Company in 2016 and to recognize cumulative excess of dividends received over share of Investee earnings in periods subsequent to change from equity method)		

CHANGE TO THE EQUITY METHOD

When converting to the equity method, companies use retrospective application. Such a change involves adjusting the carrying amount of the investment, results of current and prior operations, and retained earnings of the investor **as if the equity method has been in effect during all of the previous periods in which this investment was held. [12]** When changing from the fair value method to the equity method, companies also must eliminate any balances in the Unrealized Holding Gain or Loss—Equity account and the Fair Value Adjustment account. In addition, they eliminate the available-for-sale classification for this investment, and they record the investment under the equity method.

For example, on January 2, 2014, Amsted Corp. purchased, for $500,000 cash, 10 percent of the outstanding shares of Cable Company common stock. On that date, the net identifiable assets of Cable Company had a fair value of $3,000,000. The excess of cost over the underlying equity in the net identifiable assets of Cable Company is goodwill.

On January 2, 2016, Amsted Corp. purchased an additional 20 percent of Cable Company's stock for $1,200,000 cash when the fair value of Cable's net identifiable assets was $4,000,000. The excess of cost over fair value related to this additional investment is goodwill. Now having a 30 percent interest, Amsted Corp. must use the equity method.

From January 2, 2014, to January 2, 2016, Amsted Corp. used the fair value method and categorized these securities as available-for-sale. At January 2, 2016, Amsted has a credit balance of $92,000 in its Unrealized Holding Gain or Loss—Equity account and a debit balance in its Fair Value Adjustment account of the same amount. This change in fair value occurred in 2014. (Income tax effects are ignored.) Illustration 22A-3 shows the net income reported by Cable Company and the Cable Company dividends received by Amsted during the period 2014 through 2016.

ILLUSTRATION 22A-3
Income Earned and Dividends Received

Year	Cable Company Net Income	Cable Co. Dividends Paid to Amsted
2014	$ 500,000	$ 20,000
2015	1,000,000	30,000
2016	1,200,000	120,000

Amsted makes the following journal entries from January 2, 2014, through December 31, 2016, relative to Amsted Corp.'s investment in Cable Company, reflecting the data above and a change from the fair value method to the equity method.[15]

	Debit	Credit
January 2, 2014		
Equity Investments (available-for-sale)	500,000	
Cash		500,000
(To record the purchase of a 10% interest in Cable Company)		
December 31, 2014		
Cash	20,000	
Dividend Revenue		20,000
(To record the receipt of cash dividends from Cable Company)		
Fair Value Adjustment (available-for-sale)	92,000	
Unrealized Holding Gain or Loss—Equity		92,000
(To record increase in fair value of securities)		
December 31, 2015		
Cash	30,000	
Dividend Revenue		30,000
(To record the receipt of cash dividends from Cable Company)		
January 2, 2016		
Equity Investments (Cable Company)	1,300,000	
Cash		1,200,000
Retained Earnings		100,000
(To record the purchase of an additional interest in Cable Company and to reflect retrospectively a change from the fair value method to the equity method of accounting for the investment. The $100,000 adjustment is computed as follows:)		

	2014	2015	Total
Amsted Corp. equity in earnings of Cable Company (10%)	$50,000	$100,000	$150,000
Dividend received	(20,000)	(30,000)	(50,000)
Retrospective application	$30,000	$ 70,000	$100,000

[15]Adapted from Paul A. Pacter, "Applying APB Opinion No. 18—Equity Method," *Journal of Accountancy* (September 1971), pp. 59–60.

	Debit	Credit
January 2, 2016		
Equity Investments (Cable Company)	500,000	
Equity Investments (available-for-sale)		500,000
(To reclassify initial 10% interest to equity method)		
January 2, 2016		
Unrealized Holding Gain or Loss—Equity	92,000	
Fair Value Adjustment (available-for-sale)		92,000
(To eliminate fair value accounts for change to equity method)		
December 31, 2016		
Equity Investments (Cable Company)	360,000	
Investment Revenue		360,000
[To record equity in earnings of Cable Company (30% of $1,200,000)]		
Cash	120,000	
Equity Investments (Cable Company)		120,000
(To record the receipt of cash dividends from Cable Company)		

Companies change to the equity method by placing the accounts related to and affected by the investment on the same basis **as if the equity method had always been the basis of accounting for that investment**. Thus, they report the effects of this accounting change using the retrospective approach.[16]

SUMMARY OF LEARNING OBJECTIVE FOR APPENDIX 22A

10 Make the computations and prepare the entries necessary to record a change from or to the equity method of accounting. When changing *from* the equity method to the fair value method, the cost basis for accounting purposes is the carrying amount used for the investment at the date of change. The investor company applies the new method in its entirety once the equity method is no longer appropriate. When changing *to* the equity method, the company adjusts the accounts to be on the same basis as if the equity method had always been used for that investment.

DEMONSTRATION PROBLEM

Wangerin Company is in the process of adjusting and correcting its books at the end of 2014. In reviewing its records, the following information is compiled.

1. At December 31, 2014, Wangerin decided to change the depreciation method on its office equipment from double-declining-balance to straight-line. The equipment had an original cost of $200,000 when purchased on January 1, 2012. It has a 10-year useful life and no salvage value. Depreciation expense recorded prior to 2014 under the double-declining-balance method was $72,000. Wangerin has already recorded 2014 depreciation expense of $25,600 using the double-declining-balance method.

[16]The change to the equity method illustration assumes that the fair value and the book value of the net identifiable assets of the investee are the same. However, the fair value of the net identifiable assets of the investee may be greater than their book value. In this case, this excess (if depreciable or amortizable) reduces the net income reported by the investor from the investee. For example, assume that the fair value of an investee's building is $1,000,000 and its book value is $800,000 at the time of change to the equity method. In that case, this difference of $200,000 is depreciated over the useful life of the building, thereby reducing the amount of investee's net income reported on the investor's books.

2. Before 2014, Wangerin accounted for its income from long-term construction contracts on the completed-contract basis. Early in 2014, Wangerin changed to the percentage-of-completion basis for accounting purposes. It continues to use the completed-contract method for tax purposes. Income for 2014 has been recorded using the percentage-of-completion method. The following information is available.

	Pretax Income	
	Percentage-of-Completion	Completed-Contract
Prior to 2014	$450,000	$315,000
2014	180,000	60,000

3. Insurance for a 12-month period purchased on November 1 of this year was charged to insurance expense in the amount of $3,300 because "the amount of the check is about the same every year."
4. Reported sales revenue for the year is $1,908,000. This includes all sales taxes collected for the year. The sales tax rate is 6%. Because the sales tax is forwarded to the state's Department of Revenue, the Sales Tax Expense account is debited. The bookkeeper thought that "the sales tax is a selling expense." At the end of the current year, the balance in the Sales Tax Expense account is $103,400.

Instructions

Prepare the journal entries necessary at December 31, 2014, to record the above corrections and changes. The books are still open for 2014. The income tax rate is 40%. Wangerin has not yet recorded its 2014 income tax expense and payable amounts so current-year tax effects may be ignored. Prior-year tax effects must be considered in item 2.

Solution

1.	Accumulated Depreciation—Equipment	9,600	
	Depreciation Expense		9,600*
	*Equipment cost	$200,000	
	Depreciation before 2012	(72,000)	
	Book value	$128,000	
	Depreciation recorded	$ 25,600	
	Depreciation to be taken ($128,000/8)	(16,000)	
	Difference	$ 9,600	
2.	Construction in Process	135,000	
	Deferred Tax Liability		54,000*
	Retained Earnings		81,000
	*($450,000 − $315,000) × 40%		
3.	Prepaid Insurance ($3,300 × 10/12)	2,750	
	Insurance Expense		2,750
4.	Sales Revenue [$1,908,000 ÷ (1.00 + .06) × 6%]	108,000	
	Sales Taxes Payable		108,000
	Sales Taxes Payable	103,400	
	Sales Tax Expense		103,400

FASB CODIFICATION

FASB Codification References

[1] FASB ASC 250-10-05-1. [Predecessor literature: "Accounting Changes and Error Corrections," *Statement of Financial Accounting Standards No. 154* (Stamford, Conn.: FASB, 2005).]

[2] FASB ASC 250-10-05-2. [Predecessor literature: "Accounting Changes and Error Corrections," *Statement of Financial Accounting Standards No. 154* (Stamford, Conn.: FASB, 2005).]

[3] FASB ASC 250-10-50-1. [Predecessor literature: "Accounting Changes and Error Corrections," *Statement of Financial Accounting Standards No. 154* (Stamford, Conn.: FASB, 2005), par. 17.]

[4] FASB ASC 250-10-50-1. [Predecessor literature: "Accounting Changes and Error Corrections," *Statement of Financial Accounting Standards No. 154* (Stamford, Conn.: FASB, 2005), par. B19.]

[5] FASB ASC 250-10-45-6. [Predecessor literature: "Accounting Changes and Error Corrections," *Statement of Financial Accounting Standards No. 154* (Stamford, Conn.: FASB, 2005), paras. 8–11.]

[6] FASB ASC 250-10-50-1. [Predecessor literature: "Accounting Changes and Error Corrections," *Statement of Financial Accounting Standards No. 154* (Stamford, Conn.: FASB, 2005), par. 17.]

[7] FASB ASC 250-10-45-18. [Predecessor literature: "Accounting Changes and Error Corrections," *Statement of Financial Accounting Standards No. 154* (Stamford, Conn.: FASB, 2005), par. 20.]

[8] FASB ASC 250-10-45-24. [Predecessor literature: "Prior Period Adjustments," *Statement of Financial Accounting Standards No. 16* (Stamford, Conn.: FASB, 1977), p. 5.]

[9] FASB ASC 250-10-50-4. [Predecessor literature: "Accounting Changes and Error Corrections," *Statement of Financial Accounting Standards No. 154* (Stamford, Conn.: FASB, 2005), par. 2.]

[10] FASB ASC 250-10-50-7. [Predecessor literature: "Accounting Changes and Error Corrections," *Statement of Financial Accounting Standards No. 154* (Stamford, Conn.: FASB, 2005), par. 26.]

[11] FASB ASC 250-10-50-1. [Predecessor literature: "Accounting Changes and Error Corrections," *Statement of Financial Accounting Standards No. 154* (Stamford, Conn.: FASB, 2005), par. 2.]

[12] FASB ASC 323-10-35-33. [Predecessor literature: "The Equity Method of Accounting for Investments in Common Stock," *Opinions of the Accounting Principles Board No. 18* (New York: AICPA, 1971), par. 17.]

Exercises

If your school has a subscription to the FASB Codification, go to *http://aaahq.org/ascLogin.cfm* to log in and prepare responses to the following. Provide Codification references for your responses.

CE22-1 Access the glossary ("Master Glossary") to answer the following.

(a) What is a change in accounting estimate?

(b) What is a change in accounting principle?

(c) What is a restatement?

(d) What is the definition of "retrospective application"?

CE22-2 When a company has to restate its financial statements to correct an error, what information must the company disclose?

CE22-3 What reporting requirements does retrospective application require?

CE22-4 If a company registered with the SEC justifies a change in accounting method as preferable under the circumstances, and the circumstances change, can that company switch back to its prior method of accounting before the change? Why or why not?

An additional Codification case can be found in the Using Your Judgment section, on page 1404.

Be sure to check the book's companion website for a Review and Analysis Exercise, with solution.

WileyPLUS **Brief Exercises, Exercises, Problems, and many more learning and assessment tools and resources are available for practice in WileyPLUS.**

Note: All asterisked Questions, Exercises, and Problems relate to material in the appendix to the chapter.

QUESTIONS

1. In recent years, the *Wall Street Journal* has indicated that many companies have changed their accounting principles. What are the major reasons why companies change accounting methods?

2. State how each of the following items is reflected in the financial statements.

(a) Change from FIFO to LIFO method for inventory valuation purposes.

(b) Charge for failure to record depreciation in a previous period.

(c) Litigation won in current year, related to prior period.

(d) Change in the realizability of certain receivables.

(e) Write-off of receivables.

(f) Change from the percentage-of-completion to the completed-contract method for reporting net income.

3. Discuss briefly the three approaches that have been suggested for reporting changes in accounting principles.

4. Identify and describe the approach the FASB requires for reporting changes in accounting principles.

5. What is the indirect effect of a change in accounting principle? Briefly describe the reporting of the indirect effects of a change in accounting principle.

6. Define a change in estimate and provide an illustration. When is a change in accounting estimate effected by a change in accounting principle?

7. Lenexa State Bank has followed the practice of capitalizing certain marketing costs and amortizing these costs over their expected life. In the current year, the bank determined that the future benefits from these costs were doubtful. Consequently, the bank adopted the policy of expensing these costs as incurred. How should the bank report this accounting change in the comparative financial statements?

8. Indicate how the following items are recorded in the accounting records in the current year of Coronet Co.

(a) Impairment of goodwill.

(b) A change in depreciating plant assets from accelerated to the straight-line method.

(c) Large write-off of inventories because of obsolescence.

(d) Change from the cash basis to accrual basis of accounting.

(e) Change from LIFO to FIFO method for inventory valuation purposes.

(f) Change in the estimate of service lives for plant assets.

9. Whittier Construction Co. had followed the practice of expensing all materials assigned to a construction job without recognizing any salvage inventory. On December 31, 2014, it was determined that salvage inventory should be valued at $52,000. Of this amount, $29,000 arose during the current year. How does this information affect the financial statements to be prepared at the end of 2014?

10. Parsons Inc. has proposed a change from the completed-contract to the percentage-of-completion method for financial reporting purposes. The auditor indicates that a change would be permitted only if it is to a preferable method. What difficulties develop in assessing preferability?

11. Discuss how a change to the LIFO method of inventory valuation is handled when it is impracticable to determine previous LIFO inventory amounts.

12. How should consolidated financial statements be reported this year when statements of individual companies were presented last year?

13. Simms Corp. controlled four domestic subsidiaries and one foreign subsidiary. Prior to the current year, Simms Corp. had excluded the foreign subsidiary from consolidation. During the current year, the foreign subsidiary was included in the financial statements. How should this change in accounting entity be reflected in the financial statements?

14. Distinguish between counterbalancing and noncounterbalancing errors. Give an example of each.

15. Discuss and illustrate how a correction of an error in previously issued financial statements should be handled.

16. Prior to 2014, Heberling Inc. excluded manufacturing overhead costs from work in process and finished goods inventory. These costs have been expensed as incurred. In 2014, the company decided to change its accounting methods for manufacturing inventories to full costing by including these costs as product costs. Assuming that these costs are material, how should this change be reflected in the financial statements for 2013 and 2014?

17. Elliott Corp. failed to record accrued salaries for 2013, $2,000; 2014, $2,100; and 2015, $3,900. What is the amount of the overstatement or understatement of Retained Earnings at December 31, 2016?

18. In January 2014, installation costs of $6,000 on new machinery were charged to Maintenance and Repairs Expense. Other costs of this machinery of $30,000 were correctly recorded and have been depreciated using the straight-line method with an estimated life of 10 years and no salvage value. At December 31, 2015, it is decided that the machinery has a remaining useful life of 20 years, starting with January 1, 2015. What entry(ies) should be made in 2015 to correctly record transactions related to machinery, assuming the machinery has no salvage value? The books have not been closed for 2015 and depreciation expense has not yet been recorded for 2015.

19. On January 2, 2014, $100,000 of 11%, 10-year bonds were issued for $97,000. The $3,000 discount was charged to Interest Expense. The bookkeeper, Mark Landis, records interest only on the interest payment dates of January 1 and July 1. What is the effect on reported net income for 2014 of this error, assuming straight-line amortization of the discount? What entry is necessary to correct for this error, assuming that the books are not closed for 2014?

20. An entry to record Purchases and related Accounts Payable of $13,000 for merchandise purchased on December 23, 2015, was recorded in January 2016. This merchandise was not included in inventory at December 31, 2015. What effect does this error have on reported net income for 2015? What entry should be made to correct for this error, assuming that the books are not closed for 2015?

21. Equipment was purchased on January 2, 2014, for $24,000, but no portion of the cost has been charged to depreciation. The corporation wishes to use the straight-line method for these assets, which have been estimated to have a life of 10 years and no salvage value. What effect does this error have on net income in 2014? What entry is necessary to correct for this error, assuming that the books are not closed for 2014?

BRIEF EXERCISES

3 **BE22-1** Wertz Construction Company decided at the beginning of 2014 to change from the completed-contract method to the percentage-of-completion method for financial reporting purposes. The company will continue to use the completed-contract method for tax purposes. For years prior to 2014, pretax income under the two methods was as follows: percentage-of-completion $120,000, and completed-contract $80,000. The tax rate is 35%. Prepare Wertz's 2014 journal entry to record the change in accounting principle.

3 **BE22-2** Refer to the accounting change by Wertz Construction Company in BE22-1. Wertz has a profit-sharing plan, which pays all employees a bonus at year-end based on 1% of pretax income. Compute the indirect effect of Wertz's change in accounting principle that will be reported in the 2014 income statement, assuming that the profit-sharing contract explicitly requires adjustment for changes in income numbers.

3 **BE22-3** Shannon, Inc., changed from the LIFO cost flow assumption to the FIFO cost flow assumption in 2014. The increase in the prior year's income before taxes is $1,200,000. The tax rate is 40%. Prepare Shannon's 2014 journal entry to record the change in accounting principle.

5 **BE22-4** Tedesco Company changed depreciation methods in 2014 from double-declining-balance to straight-line. Depreciation prior to 2014 under double-declining-balance was $90,000, whereas straight-line depreciation prior to 2014 would have been $50,000. Tedesco's depreciable assets had a cost of $250,000 with a $40,000 salvage value, and an 8-year remaining useful life at the beginning of 2014. Prepare the 2014 journal entries, if any, related to Tedesco's depreciable assets.

5 **BE22-5** Sesame Company purchased a computer system for $74,000 on January 1, 2013. It was depreciated based on a 7-year life and an $18,000 salvage value. On January 1, 2015, Sesame revised these estimates to a total useful life of 4 years and a salvage value of $10,000. Prepare Sesame's entry to record 2015 depreciation expense.

7 **BE22-6** In 2014, Bailey Corporation discovered that equipment purchased on January 1, 2012, for $50,000 was expensed at that time. The equipment should have been depreciated over 5 years, with no salvage value. The effective tax rate is 30%. Prepare Bailey's 2014 journal entry to correct the error.

7 **BE22-7** At January 1, 2014, Beidler Company reported retained earnings of $2,000,000. In 2014, Beidler discovered that 2013 depreciation expense was understated by $400,000. In 2014, net income was $900,000 and dividends declared were $250,000. The tax rate is 40%. Prepare a 2014 retained earnings statement for Beidler Company.

7 **BE22-8** Indicate the effect—Understate, Overstate, No Effect—that each of the following errors has on 2014 net income and 2015 net income.

	2014	2015
(a) Equipment purchased in 2012 was expensed.	____	____
(b) Wages payable were not recorded at 12/31/14.	____	____
(c) Equipment purchased in 2014 was expensed.	____	____
(d) 2014 ending inventory was overstated.	____	____
(e) Patent amortization was not recorded in 2015.	____	____

3 5 **BE22-9** Roundtree Manufacturing Co. is preparing its year-end financial statements and is considering the accounting for the following items.

1. The vice president of sales had indicated that one product line has lost its customer appeal and will be phased out over the next 3 years. Therefore, a decision has been made to lower the estimated lives on related production equipment from the remaining 5 years to 3 years.
2. The Hightone Building was converted from a sales office to offices for the Accounting Department at the beginning of this year. Therefore, the expense related to this building will now appear as an administrative expense rather than a selling expense on the current year's income statement.
3. Estimating the lives of new products in the Leisure Products Division has become very difficult because of the highly competitive conditions in this market. Therefore, the practice of deferring and amortizing preproduction costs has been abandoned in favor of expensing such costs as they are incurred.

Identify and explain whether each of the above items is a change in principle, a change in estimate, or an error.

3 7 **BE22-10** Palmer Co. is evaluating the appropriate accounting for the following items.

1. Management has decided to switch from the FIFO inventory valuation method to the LIFO inventory valuation method for all inventories.
2. When the year-end physical inventory adjustment was made for the current year, the controller discovered that the prior year's physical inventory sheets for an entire warehouse were mislaid and excluded from last year's count.
3. Palmer's Custom Division manufactures large-scale, custom-designed machinery on a contract basis. Management decided to switch from the completed-contract method to the percentage-of-completion method of accounting for long-term contracts.

Identify and explain whether each of the above items is a change in accounting principle, a change in estimate, or an error.

10 ***BE22-11** Simmons Corporation owns stock of Armstrong, Inc. Prior to 2014, the investment was accounted for using the equity method. In early 2014, Simmons sold part of its investment in Armstrong, and began using the fair value method. In 2014, Armstrong earned net income of $80,000 and paid dividends of $95,000. Prepare Simmons's entries related to Armstrong's net income and dividends, assuming Simmons now owns 10% of Armstrong's stock.

10 ***BE22-12** Oliver Corporation has owned stock of Conrad Corporation since 2011. At December 31, 2014, its balances related to this investment were:

Equity Investments	$185,000
Fair Value Adjustment (AFS)	34,000 Dr.
Unrealized Holding Gain or Loss—Equity	34,000 Cr.

On January 1, 2015, Oliver purchased additional stock of Conrad Company for $475,000 and now has significant influence over Conrad. If the equity method had been used in 2011–2014, Oliver's share of income would have been $33,000 greater than dividends received. Prepare Oliver's journal entries to record the purchase of the investment and the change to the equity method.

EXERCISES

3 **E22-1 (Change in Principle—Long-Term Contracts)** Pam Erickson Construction Company changed from the completed-contract to the percentage-of-completion method of accounting for long-term construction contracts during 2015. For tax purposes, the company employs the completed-contract method and will continue this approach in the future. (*Hint:* Adjust all tax consequences through the Deferred Tax Liability account.) The appropriate information related to this change is as follows.

	Pretax Income from:		
	Percentage-of-Completion	Completed-Contract	Difference
2014	$780,000	$590,000	$190,000
2015	700,000	480,000	220,000

Instructions

(a) Assuming that the tax rate is 35%, what is the amount of net income that would be reported in 2015?
(b) What entry(ies) are necessary to adjust the accounting records for the change in accounting principle?

3 **E22-2 (Change in Principle—Inventory Methods)** Holder-Webb Company began operations on January 1, 2012, and uses the average-cost method of pricing inventory. Management is contemplating a change in inventory methods for 2015. The following information is available for the years 2012–2014.

	Net Income Computed Using		
	Average-Cost Method	FIFO Method	LIFO Method
2012	$15,000	$19,000	$12,000
2013	18,000	23,000	14,000
2014	20,000	25,000	17,000

Instructions

(Ignore all tax effects.)

(a) Prepare the journal entry necessary to record a change from the average-cost method to the FIFO method in 2015.

(b) Determine net income to be reported for 2012, 2013, and 2014, after giving effect to the change in accounting principle.

(c) Assume Holder-Webb Company used the LIFO method instead of the average-cost method during the years 2012–2014. In 2015, Holder-Webb changed to the FIFO method. Prepare the journal entry necessary to record the change in principle.

3 **E22-3 (Accounting Change)** Taveras Co. decides at the beginning of 2014 to adopt the FIFO method of inventory valuation. Taveras had used the LIFO method for financial reporting since its inception on January 1, 2012, and had maintained records adequate to apply the FIFO method retrospectively. Taveras concluded that FIFO is the preferable inventory method because it reflects the current cost of inventory on the balance sheet. The following table presents the effects of the change in accounting principles on inventory and cost of goods sold.

	Inventory Determined by		Cost of Goods Sold Determined by	
Date	LIFO Method	FIFO Method	LIFO Method	FIFO Method
January 1, 2012	$ 0	$ 0	$ 0	$ 0
December 31, 2012	100	80	800	820
December 31, 2013	200	240	1,000	940
December 31, 2014	320	390	1,130	1,100

Other information:

1. For each year presented, sales are $3,000 and operating expenses are $1,000.
2. Taveras provides two years of financial statements. Earnings per share information is not required.

Instructions

(a) Prepare income statements under LIFO and FIFO for 2012, 2013, and 2014.

(b) Prepare income statements reflecting the retrospective application of the accounting change from the LIFO method to the FIFO method for 2014 and 2013.

(c) Prepare the note to the financial statements describing the change in method of inventory valuation. In the note, indicate the income statement line items for 2014 and 2013 that were affected by the change in accounting principle.

(d) Prepare comparative retained earnings statements for 2013 and 2014 under FIFO. Retained earnings reported under LIFO are as follows:

	Retained Earnings Balance
December 31, 2012	$1,200
December 31, 2013	2,200
December 31, 2014	3,070

3 **E22-4 (Accounting Change)** Gordon Company started operations on January 1, 2009, and has used the FIFO method of inventory valuation since its inception. In 2015, it decides to switch to the average-cost method. You are provided with the following information.

	Net Income		Retained Earnings (Ending Balance)
	Under FIFO	Under Average-Cost	Under FIFO
2009	$100,000	$ 90,000	$100,000
2010	70,000	65,000	160,000
2011	90,000	80,000	235,000
2012	120,000	130,000	340,000
2013	300,000	290,000	590,000
2014	305,000	310,000	780,000

Instructions

(a) What is the beginning retained earnings balance at January 1, 2011, if Gordon prepares comparative financial statements starting in 2011?

(b) What is the beginning retained earnings balance at January 1, 2014, if Gordon prepares comparative financial statements starting in 2014?

(c) What is the beginning retained earnings balance at January 1, 2015, if Gordon prepares single-period financial statements for 2015?

(d) What is the net income reported by Gordon in the 2014 income statement if it prepares comparative financial statements starting with 2012?

3 **E22-5 (Accounting Change)** Presented below are income statements prepared on a LIFO and FIFO basis for Kenseth Company, which started operations on January 1, 2013. The company presently uses the LIFO method of pricing its inventory and has decided to switch to the FIFO method in 2014. The FIFO income statement is computed in accordance with the requirements of GAAP. Kenseth's profit-sharing agreement with its employees indicates that the company will pay employees 10% of income before profit-sharing. Income taxes are ignored.

	LIFO Basis		FIFO Basis	
	2014	2013	2014	2013
Sales	$3,000	$3,000	$3,000	$3,000
Cost of goods sold	1,130	1,000	1,100	940
Operating expenses	1,000	1,000	1,000	1,000
Income before profit-sharing	870	1,000	900	1,060
Profit-sharing expense	87	100	96	100
Net income	$ 783	$ 900	$ 804	$ 960

Instructions

Answer the following questions.

(a) If comparative income statements are prepared, what net income should Kenseth report in 2013 and 2014?

(b) Explain why, under the FIFO basis, Kenseth reports $100 in 2013 and $96 in 2014 for its profit-sharing expense.

(c) Assume that Kenseth has a beginning balance of retained earnings at January 1, 2014, of $8,000 using the LIFO method. The company declared and paid dividends of $500 in 2014. Prepare the retained earnings statement for 2014, assuming that Kenseth has switched to the FIFO method.

5 **E22-6 (Accounting Changes—Depreciation)** Kathleen Cole Inc. acquired the following assets in January of 2012.

Equipment, estimated service life, 5 years; salvage value, $15,000	$525,000
Building, estimated service life, 30 years; no salvage value	$693,000

The equipment has been depreciated using the sum-of-the-years'-digits method for the first 3 years for financial reporting purposes. In 2015, the company decided to change the method of computing depreciation to the straight-line method for the equipment, but no change was made in the estimated service life or salvage value. It was also decided to change the total estimated service life of the building from 30 years to 40 years, with no change in the estimated salvage value. The building is depreciated on the straight-line method.

Instructions

(a) Prepare the general journal entry to record depreciation expense for the equipment in 2015.

(b) Prepare the journal entry to record depreciation expense for the building in 2015. (Round all computations to two decimal places.)

5 **7** **E22-7 (Change in Estimate and Error; Financial Statements)** Presented below are the comparative income and retained earnings statements for Denise Habbe Inc. for the years 2014 and 2015.

	2015	2014
Sales	$340,000	$270,000
Cost of sales	200,000	142,000
Gross profit	140,000	128,000
Expenses	88,000	50,000
Net income	$ 52,000	$ 78,000
Retained earnings (Jan. 1)	$125,000	$ 72,000
Net income	52,000	78,000
Dividends	(30,000)	(25,000)
Retained earnings (Dec. 31)	$147,000	$125,000

The following additional information is provided:

1. In 2015, Denise Habbe Inc. decided to switch its depreciation method from sum-of-the-years'-digits to the straight-line method. The assets were purchased at the beginning of 2014 for $100,000 with an estimated useful life of 4 years and no salvage value. (The 2015 income statement contains depreciation expense of $30,000 on the assets purchased at the beginning of 2014.)
2. In 2015, the company discovered that the ending inventory for 2014 was overstated by $24,000; ending inventory for 2015 is correctly stated.

Instructions

Prepare the revised retained earnings statement for 2014 and 2015, assuming comparative statements. (Ignore income taxes.)

3 5 **E22-8 (Accounting for Accounting Changes and Errors)** Listed below are various types of accounting
7 changes and errors.

______ **1.** Change in a plant asset's salvage value.
______ **2.** Change due to overstatement of inventory.
______ **3.** Change from sum-of-the-years'-digits to straight-line method of depreciation.
______ **4.** Change from presenting unconsolidated to consolidated financial statements.
______ **5.** Change from LIFO to FIFO inventory method.
______ **6.** Change in the rate used to compute warranty costs.
______ **7.** Change from an unacceptable accounting principle to an acceptable accounting principle.
______ **8.** Change in a patent's amortization period.
______ **9.** Change from completed-contract to percentage-of-completion method on construction contracts.
______ **10.** Change from FIFO to average-cost inventory method.

Instructions

For each change or error, indicate how it would be accounted for using the following code letters:

(a) Accounted for prospectively.
(b) Accounted for retrospectively.
(c) Neither of the above.

5 7 **E22-9 (Error and Change in Estimate—Depreciation)** Joy Cunningham Co. purchased a machine on January 1, 2012, for $550,000. At that time, it was estimated that the machine would have a 10-year life and no salvage value. On December 31, 2015, the firm's accountant found that the entry for depreciation expense had been omitted in 2013. In addition, management has informed the accountant that the company plans to switch to straight-line depreciation, starting with the year 2015. At present, the company uses the sum-of-the-years'-digits method for depreciating equipment.

Instructions

Prepare the general journal entries that should be made at December 31, 2015, to record these events. (Ignore tax effects.)

5 **E22-10 (Depreciation Changes)** On January 1, 2011, Jackson Company purchased a building and equipment that have the following useful lives, salvage values, and costs.

Building, 40-year estimated useful life, $50,000 salvage value, $800,000 cost
Equipment, 12-year estimated useful life, $10,000 salvage value, $100,000 cost

The building has been depreciated under the double-declining-balance method through 2014. In 2015, the company decided to switch to the straight-line method of depreciation. Jackson also decided to change the total useful life of the equipment to 9 years, with a salvage value of $5,000 at the end of that time. The equipment is depreciated using the straight-line method.

Instructions

(a) Prepare the journal entry(ies) necessary to record the depreciation expense on the building in 2015.
(b) Compute depreciation expense on the equipment for 2015.

5 **E22-11 (Change in Estimate—Depreciation)** Peter M. Dell Co. purchased equipment for $510,000 which was estimated to have a useful life of 10 years with a salvage value of $10,000 at the end of that time. Depreciation has been entered for 7 years on a straight-line basis. In 2015, it is determined that the total estimated life should be 15 years with a salvage value of $5,000 at the end of that time.

Instructions

(a) Prepare the entry (if any) to correct the prior years' depreciation.
(b) Prepare the entry to record depreciation for 2015.

5 **E22-12 (Change in Estimate—Depreciation)** Gerald Englehart Industries changed from the double-declining-balance to the straight-line method in 2015 on all its plant assets. There was no change in the assets' salvage values or useful lives. Plant assets, acquired on January 2, 2012, had an original cost of $1,600,000, with a $100,000 salvage value and an 8-year estimated useful life. Income before depreciation expense was $270,000 in 2014 and $300,000 in 2015.

Instructions

(a) Prepare the journal entry(ies) to record depreciation expense in 2015.

(b) Starting with income before depreciation expense, prepare the remaining portion of the income statement for 2014 and 2015.

3 **E22-13 (Change in Principle—Long-Term Contracts)** Cullen Construction Company, which began operations in 2014, changed from the completed-contract to the percentage-of-completion method of accounting for long-term construction contracts during 2015. For tax purposes, the company employs the completed-contract method and will continue this approach in the future. The appropriate information related to this change is as follows.

	Pretax Income		
	Percentage-of-Completion	Completed-Contract	Difference
2014	$880,000	$590,000	$290,000
2015	900,000	480,000	420,000

Instructions

(a) Assuming that the tax rate is 40%, what is the amount of net income that would be reported in 2015?
(b) What entry(ies) are necessary to adjust the accounting records for the change in accounting principle?

3 **E22-14 (Various Changes in Principle—Inventory Methods)** Below is the net income of Anita Ferreri Instrument Co., a private corporation, computed under the three inventory methods using a periodic system.

	FIFO	Average-Cost	LIFO
2012	$26,000	$24,000	$20,000
2013	30,000	25,000	21,000
2014	28,000	27,000	24,000
2015	34,000	30,000	26,000

Instructions

(Ignore tax considerations.)

(a) Assume that in 2015 Ferreri decided to change from the FIFO method to the average-cost method of pricing inventories. Prepare the journal entry necessary for the change that took place during 2015, and show net income reported for 2012, 2013, 2014, and 2015.
(b) Assume that in 2015 Ferreri, which had been using the LIFO method since incorporation in 2012, changed to the FIFO method of pricing inventories. Prepare the journal entry necessary to record the change in 2015 and show net income reported for 2012, 2013, 2014, and 2015.

7 **E22-15 (Error Correction Entries)** The first audit of the books of Bruce Gingrich Company was made for the year ended December 31, 2015. In examining the books, the auditor found that certain items had been overlooked or incorrectly handled in the last 3 years. These items are:

1. At the beginning of 2013, the company purchased a machine for $510,000 (salvage value of $51,000) that had a useful life of 6 years. The bookkeeper used straight-line depreciation, but failed to deduct the salvage value in computing the depreciation base for the 3 years.
2. At the end of 2014, the company failed to accrue sales salaries of $45,000.
3. A tax lawsuit that involved the year 2013 was settled late in 2015. It was determined that the company owed an additional $85,000 in taxes related to 2013. The company did not record a liability in 2013 or 2014 because the possibility of loss was considered remote, and charged the $85,000 to a loss account in 2015.
4. Gingrich Company purchased a copyright from another company early in 2013 for $45,000. Gingrich had not amortized the copyright because its value had not diminished. The copyright has a useful life at purchase of 20 years.
5. In 2015, the company wrote off $87,000 of inventory considered to be obsolete; this loss was charged directly to Retained Earnings.

Instructions

Prepare the journal entries necessary in 2015 to correct the books, assuming that the books have not been closed. Disregard effects of corrections on income tax.

7 **E22-16 (Error Analysis and Correcting Entry)** You have been engaged to review the financial statements of Gottschalk Corporation. In the course of your examination, you conclude that the bookkeeper hired during the current year is not doing a good job. You notice a number of irregularities as follows.

1. Year-end wages payable of $3,400 were not recorded because the bookkeeper thought that "they were immaterial."
2. Accrued vacation pay for the year of $31,100 was not recorded because the bookkeeper "never heard that you had to do it."

3. Insurance for a 12-month period purchased on November 1 of this year was charged to insurance expense in the amount of $2,640 because "the amount of the check is about the same every year."
4. Reported sales revenue for the year is $2,120,000. This includes all sales taxes collected for the year. The sales tax rate is 6%. Because the sales tax is forwarded to the state's Department of Revenue, the Sales Tax Expense account is debited. The bookkeeper thought that "the sales tax is a selling expense." At the end of the current year, the balance in the Sales Tax Expense account is $103,400.

Instructions

Prepare the necessary correcting entries, assuming that Gottschalk uses a calendar-year basis.

7 **E22-17 (Error Analysis and Correcting Entry)** The reported net incomes for the first 2 years of Sandra Gustafson Products, Inc., were as follows: 2014, $147,000; 2015, $185,000. Early in 2016, the following errors were discovered.

1. Depreciation of equipment for 2014 was overstated $17,000.
2. Depreciation of equipment for 2015 was understated $38,500.
3. December 31, 2014, inventory was understated $50,000.
4. December 31, 2015, inventory was overstated $16,200.

Instructions

Prepare the correcting entry necessary when these errors are discovered. Assume that the books are closed. (Ignore income tax considerations.)

7 9 **E22-18 (Error Analysis)** Peter Henning Tool Company's December 31 year-end financial statements contained the following errors.

	December 31, 2014	December 31, 2015
Ending inventory	$9,600 understated	$8,100 overstated
Depreciation expense	$2,300 understated	—

An insurance premium of $66,000 was prepaid in 2014 covering the years 2014, 2015, and 2016. The entire amount was charged to expense in 2014. In addition, on December 31, 2015, fully depreciated machinery was sold for $15,000 cash, but the entry was not recorded until 2016. There were no other errors during 2014 or 2015, and no corrections have been made for any of the errors. (Ignore income tax considerations.)

Instructions

(a) Compute the total effect of the errors on 2015 net income.
(b) Compute the total effect of the errors on the amount of Henning's working capital at December 31, 2015.
(c) Compute the total effect of the errors on the balance of Henning's retained earnings at December 31, 2015.

7 9 **E22-19 (Error Analysis; Correcting Entries)** A partial trial balance of Julie Hartsack Corporation is as follows on December 31, 2015.

	Dr.	Cr.
Supplies	$ 2,700	
Salaries and wages payable		$ 1,500
Interest receivable	5,100	
Prepaid insurance	90,000	
Unearned rent		–0–
Interest payable		15,000

Additional adjusting data:

1. A physical count of supplies on hand on December 31, 2015, totaled $1,100.
2. Through oversight, the Salaries and Wages Payable account was not changed during 2015. Accrued salaries and wages on December 31, 2015, amounted to $4,400.
3. The Interest Receivable account was also left unchanged during 2015. Accrued interest on investments amounts to $4,350 on December 31, 2015.
4. The unexpired portions of the insurance policies totaled $65,000 as of December 31, 2015.
5. $28,000 was received on January 1, 2015, for the rent of a building for both 2015 and 2016. The entire amount was credited to rent revenue.
6. Depreciation on equipment for the year was erroneously recorded as $5,000 rather than the correct figure of $50,000.
7. A further review of depreciation calculations of prior years revealed that equipment depreciation of $7,200 was not recorded. It was decided that this oversight should be corrected by a prior period adjustment.

Instructions

(a) Assuming that the books have not been closed, what are the adjusting entries necessary at December 31, 2015? (Ignore income tax considerations.)

(b) Assuming that the books have been closed, what are the adjusting entries necessary at December 31, 2015? (Ignore income tax considerations.)

(c) Repeat the requirements for items 6 and 7, taking into account income tax effects (40% tax rate) and assuming that the books have been closed.

7 9 **E22-20 (Error Analysis)** The before-tax income for Lonnie Holdiman Co. for 2014 was $101,000 and $77,400 for 2015. However, the accountant noted that the following errors had been made:

1. Sales for 2014 included amounts of $38,200 which had been received in cash during 2014, but for which the related products were delivered in 2015. Title did not pass to the purchaser until 2015.
2. The inventory on December 31, 2014, was understated by $8,640.
3. The bookkeeper in recording interest expense for both 2014 and 2015 on bonds payable made the following entry on an annual basis.

Interest Expense	15,000	
Cash		15,000

The bonds have a face value of $250,000 and pay a stated interest rate of 6%. They were issued at a discount of $15,000 on January 1, 2014, to yield an effective-interest rate of 7%. (Assume that the effective-yield method should be used.)

4. Ordinary repairs to equipment had been erroneously charged to the Equipment account during 2014 and 2015. Repairs in the amount of $8,500 in 2014 and $9,400 in 2015 were so charged. The company applies a rate of 10% to the balance in the Equipment account at the end of the year in its determination of depreciation charges.

Instructions

Prepare a schedule showing the determination of corrected income before taxes for 2014 and 2015.

7 9 **E22-21 (Error Analysis)** When the records of Debra Hanson Corporation were reviewed at the close of 2015, the errors listed below were discovered. For each item, indicate by a check mark in the appropriate column whether the error resulted in an overstatement, an understatement, or had no effect on net income for the years 2014 and 2015.

	2014			2015		
Item	Over-statement	Under-statement	No Effect	Over-statement	Under-statement	No Effect
1. Failure to record amortization of patent in 2015.						
2. Failure to record the correct amount of ending 2014 inventory. The amount was understated because of an error in calculation.						
3. Failure to record merchandise purchased in 2014. Merchandise was also omitted from ending inventory in 2014 but was not yet sold.						
4. Failure to record accrued interest on notes payable in 2014; that amount was recorded when paid in 2015.						
5. Failure to reflect supplies on hand on balance sheet at end of 2014.						

10 ***E22-22 (Change from Fair Value to Equity)** On January 1, 2014, Beyonce Co. purchased 25,000 shares (a 10% interest) in Elton John Corp. for $1,400,000. At the time, the book value and the fair value of John's net assets were $13,000,000.

On July 1, 2015, Beyonce paid $3,040,000 for 50,000 additional shares of John common stock, which represented a 20% investment in John. The fair value of John's identifiable assets net of liabilities was equal to their carrying amount of $14,200,000. As a result of this transaction, Beyonce owns 30% of John and can exercise significant influence over John's operating and financial policies.

John reported the following net income and declared and paid the following dividends.

	Net Income	Dividend per Share
Year ended 12/31/14	$700,000	None
Six months ended 6/30/15	500,000	None
Six months ended 12/31/15	815,000	$1.55

Instructions

(Any excess fair value is attributed to goodwill.)

Determine the ending balance that Beyonce Co. should report as its investment in John Corp. at the end of 2015.

10 ***E22-23 (Change from Equity to Fair Value)** Dan Aykroyd Corp. was a 30% owner of Steve Martin Company, holding 210,000 shares of Martin's common stock on December 31, 2013. The investment account had the following entries.

Investment in Martin

1/1/12 Cost	$3,180,000	12/6/12 Dividend received	$150,000
12/31/12 Share of income	390,000	12/5/13 Dividend received	240,000
12/31/13 Share of income	510,000		

On January 2, 2014, Aykroyd sold 126,000 shares of Martin for $3,440,000, thereby losing its significant influence. During the year 2014, Martin experienced the following results of operations and paid the following dividends to Aykroyd.

	Martin Income (Loss)	Dividends Paid to Aykroyd
2014	$300,000	$50,400

At December 31, 2014, the fair value of Martin shares held by Aykroyd is $1,570,000. This is the first reporting date since the January 2 sale.

Instructions

(a) What effect does the January 2, 2014, transaction have upon Aykroyd's accounting treatment for its investment in Martin?

(b) Compute the carrying amount of the investment in Martin as of December 31, 2014 (prior to any fair value adjustment).

(c) Prepare the adjusting entry on December 31, 2014, applying the fair value method to Aykroyd's long-term investment in Martin Company securities.

EXERCISES SET B

See the book's companion website, at **www.wiley.com/college/kieso**, for an additional set of exercises.

PROBLEMS

2 5 7 **P22-1 (Change in Estimate and Error Correction)** Holtzman Company is in the process of preparing its financial statements for 2014. Assume that no entries for depreciation have been recorded in 2014. The following information related to depreciation of fixed assets is provided to you.

1. Holtzman purchased equipment on January 2, 2011, for $85,000. At that time, the equipment had an estimated useful life of 10 years with a $5,000 salvage value. The equipment is depreciated on a

straight-line basis. On January 2, 2014, as a result of additional information, the company determined that the equipment has a remaining useful life of 4 years with a $3,000 salvage value.

2. During 2014, Holtzman changed from the double-declining-balance method for its building to the straight-line method. The building originally cost $300,000. It had a useful life of 10 years and a salvage value of $30,000. The following computations present depreciation on both bases for 2012 and 2013.

	2013	2012
Straight-line	$27,000	$27,000
Declining-balance	48,000	60,000

3. Holtzman purchased a machine on July 1, 2012, at a cost of $120,000. The machine has a salvage value of $16,000 and a useful life of 8 years. Holtzman's bookkeeper recorded straight-line depreciation in 2012 and 2013 but failed to consider the salvage value.

Instructions

(a) Prepare the journal entries to record depreciation expense for 2014 and correct any errors made to date related to the information provided. (Ignore taxes.)

(b) Show comparative net income for 2013 and 2014. Income before depreciation expense was $300,000 in 2014, and was $310,000 in 2013. (Ignore taxes.)

3 5 7 **P22-2 (Comprehensive Accounting Change and Error Analysis Problem)** Botticelli Inc. was organized in late 2012 to manufacture and sell hosiery. At the end of its fourth year of operation, the company has been fairly successful, as indicated by the following reported net incomes.

2012	$140,000[a]	2014	$205,000
2013	160,000[b]	2015	276,000

[a]Includes a $10,000 increase because of change in bad debt experience rate.
[b]Includes extraordinary gain of $30,000.

The company has decided to expand operations and has applied for a sizable bank loan. The bank officer has indicated that the records should be audited and presented in comparative statements to facilitate analysis by the bank. Botticelli Inc. therefore hired the auditing firm of Check & Doublecheck Co. and has provided the following additional information.

1. In early 2013, Botticelli Inc. changed its estimate from 2% of sales to 1% on the amount of bad debt expense to be charged to operations. Bad debt expense for 2012, if a 1% rate had been used, would have been $10,000. The company therefore restated its net income for 2012.
2. In 2015, the auditor discovered that the company had changed its method of inventory pricing from LIFO to FIFO. The effect on the income statements for the previous years is as follows.

	2012	2013	2014	2015
Net income unadjusted—LIFO basis	$140,000	$160,000	$205,000	$276,000
Net income unadjusted—FIFO basis	155,000	165,000	215,000	260,000
	$ 15,000	$ 5,000	$ 10,000	$ (16,000)

3. In 2015, the auditor discovered that:
   (a) The company incorrectly overstated the ending inventory (under both LIFO and FIFO) by $14,000 in 2014.
   (b) A dispute developed in 2013 with the Internal Revenue Service over the deductibility of entertainment expenses. In 2012, the company was not permitted these deductions, but a tax settlement was reached in 2015 that allowed these expenses. As a result of the court's finding, tax expenses in 2015 were reduced by $60,000.

Instructions

(a) Indicate how each of these changes or corrections should be handled in the accounting records. (Ignore income tax considerations.)

(b) Present comparative income statements for the years 2012 to 2015, starting with income before extraordinary items. (Ignore income tax considerations.)

3 5 7 **P22-3 (Error Corrections and Accounting Changes)** Penn Company is in the process of adjusting and correcting its books at the end of 2014. In reviewing its records, the following information is compiled.

1. Penn has failed to accrue sales commissions payable at the end of each of the last 2 years, as follows.

December 31, 2013	$3,500
December 31, 2014	$2,500

2. In reviewing the December 31, 2014, inventory, Penn discovered errors in its inventory-taking procedures that have caused inventories for the last 3 years to be incorrect, as follows.

December 31, 2012	Understated	$16,000
December 31, 2013	Understated	$19,000
December 31, 2014	Overstated	$ 6,700

Penn has already made an entry that established the incorrect December 31, 2014, inventory amount.

3. At December 31, 2014, Penn decided to change the depreciation method on its office equipment from double-declining-balance to straight-line. The equipment had an original cost of $100,000 when purchased on January 1, 2012. It has a 10-year useful life and no salvage value. Depreciation expense recorded prior to 2014 under the double-declining-balance method was $36,000. Penn has already recorded 2014 depreciation expense of $12,800 using the double-declining-balance method.
4. Before 2014, Penn accounted for its income from long-term construction contracts on the completed-contract basis. Early in 2014, Penn changed to the percentage-of-completion basis for accounting purposes. It continues to use the completed-contract method for tax purposes. Income for 2014 has been recorded using the percentage-of-completion method. The following information is available.

	Pretax Income	
	Percentage-of-Completion	Completed-Contract
Prior to 2014	$150,000	$105,000
2014	60,000	20,000

Instructions

Prepare the journal entries necessary at December 31, 2014, to record the above corrections and changes. The books are still open for 2014. The income tax rate is 40%. Penn has not yet recorded its 2014 income tax expense and payable amounts so current-year tax effects may be ignored. Prior-year tax effects must be considered in item 4.

5 **P22-4 (Accounting Changes)** Aston Corporation performs year-end planning in November of each year before its calendar year ends in December. The preliminary estimated net income is $3 million. The CFO, Rita Warren, meets with the company president, J. B. Aston, to review the projected numbers. She presents the following projected information.

ASTON CORPORATION
PROJECTED INCOME STATEMENT
FOR THE YEAR ENDED DECEMBER 31, 2014

Sales		$29,000,000
Cost of goods sold	$14,000,000	
Depreciation	2,600,000	
Operating expenses	6,400,000	23,000,000
Income before income tax		6,000,000
Income tax		3,000,000
Net income		$ 3,000,000

ASTON CORPORATION
SELECTED BALANCE SHEET INFORMATION
AT DECEMBER 31, 2014

Estimated cash balance	$ 5,000,000
Available-for-sale securities (at cost)	10,000,000
Fair value adjustment (1/1/14)	–0–

Estimated fair value at December 31, 2014:

Security	Cost	Estimated Fair Value
A	$ 2,000,000	$ 2,200,000
B	4,000,000	3,900,000
C	3,000,000	3,100,000
D	1,000,000	1,800,000
Total	$10,000,000	$11,000,000

Other information at December 31, 2014:

Equipment	$3,000,000
Accumulated depreciation (5-year SL)	1,200,000
New robotic equipment (purchased 1/1/14)	5,000,000
Accumulated depreciation (5-year DDB)	2,000,000

The corporation has never used robotic equipment before, and Warren assumed an accelerated method because of the rapidly changing technology in robotic equipment. The company normally uses straight-line depreciation for production equipment.

Aston explains to Warren that it is important for the corporation to show a $7,000,000 income before taxes because Aston receives a $1,000,000 bonus if the income before taxes and bonus reaches $7,000,000. Aston also does not want the company to pay more than $3,000,000 in income taxes to the government.

Instructions

(a) What can Warren do within GAAP to accommodate the president's wishes to achieve $7,000,000 in income before taxes and bonus? Present the revised income statement based on your decision.

(b) Are the actions ethical? Who are the stakeholders in this decision, and what effect do Warren's actions have on their interests?

3 **P22-5 (Change in Principle—Inventory—Periodic)** The management of Utrillo Instrument Company had concluded, with the concurrence of its independent auditors, that results of operations would be more fairly presented if Utrillo changed its method of pricing inventory from last-in, first-out (LIFO) to average-cost in 2014. Given below is the 5-year summary of income under LIFO and a schedule of what the inventories would be if stated on the average-cost method.

UTRILLO INSTRUMENT COMPANY
STATEMENT OF INCOME AND RETAINED EARNINGS
FOR THE YEARS ENDED MAY 31

	2010	2011	2012	2013	2014
Sales—net	$13,964	$15,506	$16,673	$18,221	$18,898
Cost of goods sold					
Beginning inventory	1,000	1,100	1,000	1,115	1,237
Purchases	13,000	13,900	15,000	15,900	17,100
Ending inventory	(1,100)	(1,000)	(1,115)	(1,237)	(1,369)
Total	12,900	14,000	14,885	15,778	16,968
Gross profit	1,064	1,506	1,788	2,443	1,930
Administrative expenses	700	763	832	907	989
Income before taxes	364	743	956	1,536	941
Income taxes (50%)	182	372	478	768	471
Net income	182	371	478	768	470
Retained earnings—beginning	1,206	1,388	1,759	2,237	3,005
Retained earnings—ending	$ 1,388	$ 1,759	$ 2,237	$ 3,005	$ 3,475
Earnings per share	$1.82	$3.71	$4.78	$7.68	$4.70

SCHEDULE OF INVENTORY BALANCES USING AVERAGE-COST METHOD
FOR THE YEARS ENDED MAY 31

2009	2010	2011	2012	2013	2014
$1,010	$1,124	$1,101	$1,270	$1,500	$1,720

Instructions

Prepare comparative statements for the 5 years, assuming that Utrillo changed its method of inventory pricing to average-cost. Indicate the effects on net income and earnings per share for the years involved. Utrillo Instruments started business in 2009. (All amounts except EPS are rounded up to the nearest dollar.)

5 7 9 **P22-6 (Accounting Change and Error Analysis)** On December 31, 2014, before the books were closed, the management and accountants of Madrasa Inc. made the following determinations about three pieces of equipment.

XLS

1. Equipment A was purchased January 2, 2011. It originally cost $540,000 and, for depreciation purposes, the straight-line method was originally chosen. The asset was originally expected to be

useful for 10 years and have a zero salvage value. In 2014, the decision was made to change the depreciation method from straight-line to sum-of-the-years'-digits, and the estimates relating to useful life and salvage value remained unchanged.

2. Equipment B was purchased January 3, 2010. It originally cost $180,000 and, for depreciation purposes, the straight-line method was chosen. The asset was originally expected to be useful for 15 years and have a zero residual value. In 2014, the decision was made to shorten the total life of this asset to 9 years and to estimate the residual value at $3,000.
3. Equipment C was purchased January 5, 2010. The asset's original cost was $160,000, and this amount was entirely expensed in 2010. This particular asset has a 10-year useful life and no residual value. The straight-line method was chosen for depreciation purposes.

Additional data:

1. Income in 2014 before depreciation expense amounted to $400,000.
2. Depreciation expense on assets other than A, B, and C totaled $55,000 in 2014.
3. Income in 2013 was reported at $370,000.
4. Ignore all income tax effects.
5. 100,000 shares of common stock were outstanding in 2013 and 2014.

Instructions

(a) Prepare all necessary entries in 2014 to record these determinations.

(b) Prepare comparative retained earnings statements for Madrasa Inc. for 2013 and 2014. The company had retained earnings of $200,000 at December 31, 2012.

7 9 **P22-7 (Error Corrections)** You have been assigned to examine the financial statements of Zarle Company for the year ended December 31, 2014. You discover the following situations.

1. Depreciation of $3,200 for 2014 on delivery vehicles was not recorded.
2. The physical inventory count on December 31, 2013, improperly excluded merchandise costing $19,000 that had been temporarily stored in a public warehouse. Zarle uses a periodic inventory system.
3. A collection of $5,600 on account from a customer received on December 31, 2014, was not recorded until January 2, 2015.
4. In 2014, the company sold for $3,700 fully depreciated equipment that originally cost $25,000. The company credited the proceeds from the sale to the Equipment account.
5. During November 2014, a competitor company filed a patent-infringement suit against Zarle claiming damages of $220,000. The company's legal counsel has indicated that an unfavorable verdict is probable and a reasonable estimate of the court's award to the competitor is $125,000. The company has not reflected or disclosed this situation in the financial statements.
6. Zarle has a portfolio of trading securities. No entry has been made to adjust to market. Information on cost and fair value is as follows.

	Cost	Fair Value
December 31, 2013	$95,000	$95,000
December 31, 2014	$84,000	$82,000

7. At December 31, 2014, an analysis of payroll information shows accrued salaries of $12,200. The Salaries and Wages Payable account had a balance of $16,000 at December 31, 2014, which was unchanged from its balance at December 31, 2013.
8. A large piece of equipment was purchased on January 3, 2014, for $40,000 and was charged to Maintenance and Repairs Expense. The equipment is estimated to have a service life of 8 years and no residual value. Zarle normally uses the straight-line depreciation method for this type of equipment.
9. A $12,000 insurance premium paid on July 1, 2013, for a policy that expires on June 30, 2016, was charged to insurance expense.
10. A trademark was acquired at the beginning of 2013 for $50,000. No amortization has been recorded since its acquisition. The maximum allowable amortization period is 10 years.

Instructions

Assume the trial balance has been prepared but the books have not been closed for 2014. Assuming all amounts are material, prepare journal entries showing the adjustments that are required. (Ignore income tax considerations.)

7 9 **P22-8 (Comprehensive Error Analysis)** On March 5, 2015, you were hired by Hemingway Inc., a closely held company, as a staff member of its newly created internal auditing department. While reviewing the company's records for 2013 and 2014, you discover that no adjustments have yet been made for the items listed on the next page.

Items

1. Interest income of $14,100 was not accrued at the end of 2013. It was recorded when received in February 2014.
2. A computer costing $4,000 was expensed when purchased on July 1, 2013. It is expected to have a 4-year life with no salvage value. The company typically uses straight-line depreciation for all fixed assets.
3. Research and development costs of $33,000 were incurred early in 2013. They were capitalized and were to be amortized over a 3-year period. Amortization of $11,000 was recorded for 2013 and $11,000 for 2014.
4. On January 2, 2013, Hemingway leased a building for 5 years at a monthly rental of $8,000. On that date, the company paid the following amounts, which were expensed when paid.

Security deposit	$20,000
First month's rent	8,000
Last month's rent	8,000
	$36,000

5. The company received $36,000 from a customer at the beginning of 2013 for services that it is to perform evenly over a 3-year period beginning in 2013. None of the amount received was reported as unearned revenue at the end of 2013.
6. Merchandise inventory costing $18,200 was in the warehouse at December 31, 2013, but was incorrectly omitted from the physical count at that date. The company uses the periodic inventory method.

Instructions

Indicate the effect of any errors on the net income figure reported on the income statement for the year ending December 31, 2013, and the retained earnings figure reported on the balance sheet at December 31, 2014. Assume all amounts are material, and ignore income tax effects. Using the following format, enter the appropriate dollar amounts in the appropriate columns. Consider each item independent of the other items. It is not necessary to total the columns on the grid.

	Net Income for 2013		Retained Earnings at 12/31/14	
Item	Understated	Overstated	Understated	Overstated

(CIA adapted)

7 9 **P22-9 (Error Analysis)** Lowell Corporation has used the accrual basis of accounting for several years. A review of the records, however, indicates that some expenses and revenues have been handled on a cash basis because of errors made by an inexperienced bookkeeper. Income statements prepared by the bookkeeper reported $29,000 net income for 2013 and $37,000 net income for 2014. Further examination of the records reveals that the following items were handled improperly.

1. Rent was received from a tenant in December 2013. The amount, $1,000, was recorded as revenue at that time even though the rental pertained to 2014.
2. Salaries and wages payable on December 31 have been consistently omitted from the records of that date and have been entered as expenses when paid in the following year. The amounts of the accruals recorded in this manner were:

December 31, 2012	$1,100
December 31, 2013	1,200
December 31, 2014	940

3. Invoices for supplies purchased have been charged to expense accounts when received. Inventories of supplies on hand at the end of each year have been ignored, and no entry has been made for them.

December 31, 2012	$1,300
December 31, 2013	940
December 31, 2014	1,420

Instructions

Prepare a schedule that will show the corrected net income for the years 2013 and 2014. All items listed should be labeled clearly. (Ignore income tax considerations.)

7 9 **P22-10 (Error Analysis and Correcting Entries)** You have been asked by a client to review the records of Roberts Company, a small manufacturer of precision tools and machines. Your client is interested in buying the business, and arrangements have been made for you to review the accounting records. Your examination reveals the following information.

1. Roberts Company commenced business on April 1, 2012, and has been reporting on a fiscal year ending March 31. The company has never been audited, but the annual statements prepared by the bookkeeper reflect the following income before closing and before deducting income taxes.

Year Ended March 31	Income Before Taxes
2013	$ 71,600
2014	111,400
2015	103,580

2. A relatively small number of machines have been shipped on consignment. These transactions have been recorded as ordinary sales and billed as such. On March 31 of each year, machines billed and in the hands of consignees amounted to:

2013	$6,500
2014	none
2015	5,590

Sales price was determined by adding 25% to cost. Assume that the consigned machines are sold the following year.

3. On March 30, 2014, two machines were shipped to a customer on a C.O.D. basis. The sale was not entered until April 5, 2014, when cash was received for $6,100. The machines were not included in the inventory at March 31, 2014. (Title passed on March 30, 2014.)
4. All machines are sold subject to a 5-year warranty. It is estimated that the expense ultimately to be incurred in connection with the warranty will amount to ½ of 1% of sales. The company has charged an expense account for warranty costs incurred.

   Sales per books and warranty costs were as follows.

Year Ended March 31	Sales	Warranty Expense for Sales Made in 2013	2014	2015	Total
2013	$ 940,000	$760			$ 760
2014	1,010,000	360	$1,310		1,670
2015	1,795,000	320	1,620	$1,910	3,850

5. Bad debts have been recorded on a direct write-off basis. Experience of similar enterprises indicates that losses will approximate ¼ of 1% of sales. Bad debts written off were:

	Bad Debts Incurred on Sales Made in 2013	2014	2015	Total
2013	$750			$ 750
2014	800	$ 520		1,320
2015	350	1,800	$1,700	3,850

6. The bank deducts 6% on all contracts financed. Of this amount, ½% is placed in a reserve to the credit of Roberts Company that is refunded to Roberts as finance contracts are paid in full. (Thus, Roberts should have a receivable for these payments and should record revenue when the net balance is remitted each year.) The reserve established by the bank has not been reflected in the books of Roberts. The excess of credits over debits (net increase) to the reserve account with Roberts on the books of the bank for each fiscal year were as follows.

2013	$ 3,000
2014	3,900
2015	5,100
	$12,000

7. Commissions on sales have been entered when paid. Commissions payable on March 31 of each year were as follows.

2013	$1,400
2014	900
2015	1,120

8. A review of the corporate minutes reveals the manager is entitled to a bonus of 1% of the income before deducting income taxes and the bonus. The bonuses have never been recorded or paid.

Instructions

(a) Present a schedule showing the revised income before income taxes for each of the years ended March 31, 2013, 2014, and 2015. (Make computations to the nearest whole dollar.)

(b) Prepare the journal entry or entries you would give the bookkeeper to correct the books. Assume the books have not yet been closed for the fiscal year ended March 31, 2015. Disregard correction of income taxes.

(AICPA adapted)

10 *__P22-11 (Fair Value to Equity Method with Goodwill)__ On January 1, 2014, Millay Inc. paid $700,000 for 10,000 shares of Genso Company's voting common stock, which was a 10% interest in Genso. At that date, the net assets of Genso totaled $6,000,000. The fair values of all of Genso's identifiable assets and liabilities were equal to their book values. Millay does not have the ability to exercise significant influence over the operating and financial policies of Genso. Millay received dividends of $1.50 per share from Genso on October 1, 2014. Genso reported net income of $550,000 for the year ended December 31, 2014.

On July 1, 2015, Millay paid $2,325,000 for 30,000 additional shares of Genso Company's voting common stock which represents a 30% investment in Genso. The fair values of all of Genso's identifiable assets net of liabilities were equal to their book values of $6,550,000. As a result of this transaction, Millay has the ability to exercise significant influence over the operating and financial policies of Genso. Millay received dividends of $2.00 per share from Genso on April 1, 2015, and $2.50 per share on October 1, 2015. Genso reported net income of $650,000 for the year ended December 31, 2015, and $350,000 for the 6 months ended December 31, 2015.

Instructions

(For both purchases, assume any excess of cost over book value is due to goodwill.)

(a) Prepare a schedule showing the income or loss before income taxes for the year ended December 31, 2014, that Millay should report from its investment in Genso in its income statement issued in March 2015.

(b) During March 2016, Millay issues comparative financial statements for 2014 and 2015. Prepare schedules showing the income or loss before income taxes for the years ended December 31, 2014 and 2015, that Millay should report from its investment in Genso.

(AICPA adapted)

10 *__P22-12 (Change from Fair Value to Equity Method)__ On January 3, 2013, Martin Company purchased for $500,000 cash a 10% interest in Renner Corp. On that date, the net assets of Renner had a book value of $3,700,000. The excess of cost over the underlying equity in net assets is attributable to undervalued depreciable assets having a remaining life of 10 years from the date of Martin's purchase.

The fair value of Martin's investment in Renner securities is as follows: December 31, 2013, $560,000, and December 31, 2014, $515,000.

On January 2, 2015, Martin purchased an additional 30% of Renner's stock for $1,545,000 cash when the book value of Renner's net assets was $4,150,000. The excess was attributable to depreciable assets having a remaining life of 8 years.

During 2013, 2014, and 2015, the following occurred.

	Renner Net Income	Dividends Paid by Renner to Martin
2013	$350,000	$15,000
2014	450,000	20,000
2015	550,000	70,000

Instructions

On the books of Martin Company, prepare all journal entries in 2013, 2014, and 2015 that relate to its investment in Renner Corp., reflecting the data above and a change from the fair value method to the equity method.

PROBLEMS SET B

See the book's companion website, at **www.wiley.com/college/kieso**, for an additional set of problems.

CONCEPTS FOR ANALYSIS

CA22-1 (Analysis of Various Accounting Changes and Errors) Mathys Inc. has recently hired a new independent auditor, Karen Ogleby, who says she wants "to get everything straightened out." Consequently, she has proposed the following accounting changes in connection with Mathys Inc.'s 2014 financial statements.

1. At December 31, 2013, the client had a receivable of $820,000 from Hendricks Inc. on its balance sheet. Hendricks Inc. has gone bankrupt, and no recovery is expected. The client proposes to write off the receivable as a prior period item.
2. The client proposes the following changes in depreciation policies.
   (a) For office furniture and fixtures, it proposes to change from a 10-year useful life to an 8-year life. If this change had been made in prior years, retained earnings at December 31, 2013, would have been $250,000 less. The effect of the change on 2014 income alone is a reduction of $60,000.
   (b) For its new equipment in the leasing division, the client proposes to adopt the sum-of-the-years'-digits depreciation method. The client had never used SYD before. The first year the client operated a leasing division was 2014. If straight-line depreciation were used, 2014 income would be $110,000 greater.
3. In preparing its 2013 statements, one of the client's bookkeepers overstated ending inventory by $235,000 because of a mathematical error. The client proposes to treat this item as a prior period adjustment.
4. In the past, the client has spread preproduction costs in its furniture division over 5 years. Because its latest furniture is of the "fad" type, it appears that the largest volume of sales will occur during the first 2 years after introduction. Consequently, the client proposes to amortize preproduction costs on a per-unit basis, which will result in expensing most of such costs during the first 2 years after the furniture's introduction. If the new accounting method had been used prior to 2014, retained earnings at December 31, 2013, would have been $375,000 less.
5. For the nursery division, the client proposes to switch from FIFO to LIFO inventories because it believes that LIFO will provide a better matching of current costs with revenues. The effect of making this change on 2014 earnings will be an increase of $320,000. The client says that the effect of the change on December 31, 2013, retained earnings cannot be determined.
6. To achieve an appropriate recognition of revenues and expenses in its building construction division, the client proposes to switch from the completed-contract method of accounting to the percentage-of-completion method. Had the percentage-of-completion method been employed in all prior years, retained earnings at December 31, 2013, would have been $1,075,000 greater.

Instructions

(a) For each of the changes described above, decide whether:
   (1) The change involves an accounting principle, accounting estimate, or correction of an error.
   (2) Restatement of opening retained earnings is required.

(b) What would be the proper adjustment to the December 31, 2013, retained earnings?

CA22-2 (Analysis of Various Accounting Changes and Errors) Various types of accounting changes can affect the financial statements of a business enterprise differently. Assume that the following list describes changes that have a material effect on the financial statements for the current year of your business enterprise.

1. A change from the completed-contract method to the percentage-of-completion method of accounting for long-term construction-type contracts.
2. A change in the estimated useful life of previously recorded fixed assets as a result of newly acquired information.
3. A change from deferring and amortizing preproduction costs to recording such costs as an expense when incurred because future benefits of the costs have become doubtful. The new accounting method was adopted in recognition of the change in estimated future benefits.
4. A change from including the employer share of FICA taxes with payroll tax expenses to including it with "Retirement benefits" on the income statement.
5. Correction of a mathematical error in inventory pricing made in a prior period.
6. A change from presentation of statements of individual companies to presentation of consolidated statements.
7. A change in the method of accounting for leases for tax purposes to conform with the financial accounting method. As a result, both deferred and current taxes payable changed substantially.
8. A change from the FIFO method of inventory pricing to the LIFO method of inventory pricing.

Instructions

Identify the type of change that is described in each item above and indicate whether the prior year's financial statements should be recast when presented in comparative form with the current year's financial statements.

CA22-3 (Analysis of Three Accounting Changes and Errors) The following are three independent, unrelated sets of facts relating to accounting changes.

Situation 1: Sanford Company is in the process of having its first audit. The company has used the cash basis of accounting for revenue recognition. Sanford president, B. J. Jimenez, is willing to change to the accrual method of revenue recognition.

Situation 2: Hopkins Co. decides in January 2015 to change from FIFO to weighted-average pricing for its inventories.

Situation 3: Marshall Co. determined that the depreciable lives of its fixed assets are too long at present to fairly match the cost of the fixed assets with the revenue produced. The company decided at the beginning of the current year to reduce the depreciable lives of all of its existing fixed assets by 5 years.

Instructions

For each of the situations described, provide the information indicated below.

(a) Type of accounting change.
(b) Manner of reporting the change under current generally accepted accounting principles, including a discussion where applicable of how amounts are computed.
(c) Effect of the change on the balance sheet and income statement.

CA22-4 (Analysis of Various Accounting Changes and Errors) Katherine Irving, controller of Lotan Corp., is aware of a pronouncement on accounting changes. After reading the pronouncement, she is confused about what action should be taken on the following items related to Lotan Corp. for the year 2014.

1. In 2014, Lotan decided to change its policy on accounting for certain marketing costs. Previously, the company had chosen to defer and amortize all marketing costs over at least 5 years because Lotan believed that a return on these expenditures did not occur immediately. Recently, however, the time differential has considerably shortened, and Lotan is now expensing the marketing costs as incurred.
2. In 2014, the company examined its entire policy relating to the depreciation of plant equipment. Plant equipment had normally been depreciated over a 15-year period, but recent experience has indicated that the company was incorrect in its estimates and that the assets should be depreciated over a 20-year period.
3. One division of Lotan Corp., Hawthorne Co., has consistently shown an increasing net income from period to period. On closer examination of its operating statement, it is noted that bad debt expense and inventory obsolescence charges are much lower than in other divisions. In discussing this with the controller of this division, it has been learned that the controller has increased his net income each period by knowingly making low estimates related to the write-off of receivables and inventory.
4. In 2014, the company purchased new machinery that should increase production dramatically. The company has decided to depreciate this machinery on an accelerated basis, even though other machinery is depreciated on a straight-line basis.
5. All equipment sold by Lotan is subject to a 3-year warranty. It has been estimated that the expense ultimately to be incurred on these machines is 1% of sales. In 2014, because of a production breakthrough, it is now estimated that $\frac{1}{2}$ of 1% of sales is sufficient. In 2012 and 2013, warranty expense was computed as $64,000 and $70,000, respectively. The company now believes that these warranty costs should be reduced by 50%.
6. In 2014, the company decided to change its method of inventory pricing from average-cost to the FIFO method. The effect of this change on prior years is to increase 2012 income by $65,000 and increase 2013 income by $20,000.

Instructions

Katherine Irving has come to you, as her CPA, for advice about the situations above. Prepare a report, indicating the appropriate accounting treatment that should be given for each of these situations.

CA22-5 (Change in Principle, Estimate) As a certified public accountant, you have been contacted by Joe Davison, CEO of Sports-Pro Athletics, Inc., a manufacturer of a variety of athletic equipment. He has asked you how to account for the following changes.

1. Sports-Pro appropriately changed its depreciation method for its machinery from the double-declining-balance method to the units-of-production method effective January 1, 2014.
2. Effective January 1, 2014, Sports-Pro appropriately changed the salvage values used in computing depreciation for its office equipment.
3. On December 31, 2014, Sports-Pro appropriately changed the specific subsidiaries constituting the group of companies for which consolidated financial statements are presented.

Instructions

Write a 1–1.5 page letter to Joe Davison explaining how each of the above changes should be presented in the December 31, 2014, financial statements.

CA22-6 (Change in Estimate) Mike Crane is an audit senior of a large public accounting firm who has just been assigned to the Frost Corporation's annual audit engagement. Frost has been a client of Crane's firm for many years. Frost is a fast-growing business in the commercial construction industry. In reviewing the fixed asset ledger, Crane discovered a series of unusual accounting changes, in which the useful lives of assets, depreciated using the straight-line method, were substantially lowered near the midpoint of the original estimate. For example, the useful life of one dump truck was changed from 10 to 6 years during its fifth year of service. Upon further investigation, Mike was told by Kevin James, Frost's accounting manager, "I don't really see your problem. After all, it's perfectly legal to change an accounting estimate. Besides, our CEO likes to see big earnings!"

Instructions

Answer the following questions.

(a) What are the ethical issues concerning Frost's practice of changing the useful lives of fixed assets?
(b) Who could be harmed by Frost's unusual accounting changes?
(c) What should Crane do in this situation?

USING YOUR JUDGMENT

FINANCIAL REPORTING

Financial Reporting Problem

The Procter & Gamble Company (P&G)

The financial statements of P&G are presented in Appendix 5B. The company's complete annual report, including the notes to the financial statements, can be accessed at the book's companion website, **www.wiley.com/college/kieso**.

Instructions

Refer to P&G's financial statements and the accompanying notes to answer the following questions.

(a) Were there changes in accounting principles reported by P&G during the three years covered by its income statements (2009–2011)? If so, describe the nature of the change and the year of change.
(b) What types of estimates did P&G discuss in 2011?

Comparative Analysis Case

The Coca-Cola Company and PepsiCo, Inc.

Instructions

Go to the book's companion website and use information found there to answer the following questions related to The Coca-Cola Company and PepsiCo, Inc.

(a) Identify the changes in accounting principles reported by Coca-Cola during the 3 years covered by its income statements (2009–2011). Describe the nature of the change and the year of change.
(b) Identify the changes in accounting principles reported by PepsiCo during the 3 years covered by its income statements (2009–2011). Describe the nature of the change and the year of change.
(c) For each change in accounting principle by Coca-Cola and PepsiCo, identify, if possible, the cumulative effect of each change on prior years and the effect on operating results in the year of change.

Accounting, Analysis, and Principles

In preparation for significant expansion of its international operations, ABC Co. has adopted a plan to gradually shift to the same accounting methods as used by its international competitors. Part of this plan includes a switch from LIFO inventory accounting to FIFO (recall that IFRS does not allow LIFO). ABC decides to make the switch to FIFO at January 1, 2014. The following data pertains to ABC's 2014 financial statements (in millions of dollars).

Sales	$550
Inventory purchases	350
12/31/14 inventory (using FIFO)	580
Compensation expense	17

All sales and purchases were with cash. All of 2014's compensation expense was paid with cash. (Ignore taxes.) ABC's property, plant, and equipment cost $400 million and has an estimated useful life of 10 years with no salvage value.

ABC Co. reported the following for fiscal 2013 (in millions of dollars):

ABC CO.
BALANCE SHEET AT DECEMBER 31, 2013

	2013	2012		2013	2012
Cash	$ 365	$ 200	Common stock	$ 500	$ 500
Inventory	500	480	Retained earnings	685	540
Property, plant, and equipment	400	400			
Accumulated depreciation	(80)	(40)			
Total assets	*$1,185*	*$1,040*	*Total equity*	*$1,185*	*$1,040*

ABC CO.
INCOME STATEMENT
FOR THE YEAR ENDED DECEMBER 31, 2013

	2013
Sales	$ 500
Cost of goods sold	(300)
Depreciation expense	(40)
Compensation expense	(15)
Net income	*$ 145*

Summary of Significant Accounting Policies
Inventory: The company accounts for inventory by the LIFO method. The current cost of the company's inventory, which approximates FIFO, was $60 and $50 higher at the end of fiscal 2013 and 2012, respectively, than those reported in the balance sheet.

Accounting

Prepare ABC's December 31, 2014, balance sheet and an income statement for the year ended December 31, 2014. In columns beside 2014's numbers, include 2013's numbers *as they would appear in the 2014 financial statements* for comparative purposes.

Analysis

Compute ABC's inventory turnover for 2013 and 2014 under both LIFO and FIFO. Assume averages are equal to year-end balances where necessary. What causes the differences in this ratio between LIFO and FIFO?

Principles

Briefly explain, in terms of the principles discussed in Chapter 2, why GAAP requires that companies that change accounting methods recast prior year's financial statement data.

BRIDGE TO THE PROFESSION

Professional Research: FASB Codification

As part of the year-end accounting process and review of operating policies, Cullen Co. is considering a change in the accounting for its equipment from the straight-line method to an accelerated method. Your supervisor wonders how the company will report this change in principle. He read in a newspaper article that the FASB has issued a standard in this area and has changed GAAP for a "change in estimate that is effected by a change in accounting principle." (Thus, the accounting may be different from what he learned in intermediate accounting.) Your supervisor wants you to research the authoritative guidance on a change in accounting principle related to depreciation methods.

Instructions

If your school has a subscription to the FASB Codification, go to *http://aaahq.org/ascLogin.cfm* to log in and prepare responses to the following. Provide Codification references for your responses.

(a) What are the accounting and reporting guidelines for a change in accounting principle related to depreciation methods?

(b) What are the conditions that justify a change in depreciation method, as contemplated by Cullen Co.?

(c) What guidance does the SEC provide concerning the impact that recently issued accounting standards will have on the financial statements in a future period?

Additional Professional Resources

See the book's companion website, at **www.wiley.com/college/kieso**, for professional simulations as well as other study resources.

IFRS INSIGHTS

ACCOUNTING CHANGES AND ERRORS

LEARNING OBJECTIVE 11
Compare the procedures for accounting changes and error analysis under GAAP and IFRS.

The IFRS addressing accounting and reporting for changes in accounting principles, changes in estimates, and errors is *IAS 8* ("Accounting Policies, Changes in Accounting Estimates and Errors"). Various presentation issues related to restatements are addressed in *IAS 1* ("Presentation of Financial Statements"). As indicated in the chapter, the FASB has issued guidance on changes in accounting principles, changes in estimates, and corrections of errors, which essentially converges GAAP to *IAS 8*.

RELEVANT FACTS

Following are the key similarities and differences between GAAP and IFRS related to the procedures for accounting changes.

Similarities

- The accounting for changes in estimates is similar between GAAP and IFRS.
- Under GAAP and IFRS, if determining the effect of a change in accounting policy is considered impracticable, then a company should report the effect of the change in the period in which it believes it practicable to do so, which may be the current period.

Differences

- One area in which GAAP and IFRS differ is the reporting of error corrections in previously issued financial statements. While both sets of standards require restatement, GAAP is an absolute standard—that is, there is no exception to this rule.

- Under IFRS, the impracticality exception applies both to changes in accounting principles and to the correction of errors. Under GAAP, this exception applies only to changes in accounting principle.
- IFRS (*IAS 8*) does not specifically address the accounting and reporting for indirect effects of changes in accounting principles. As indicated in the chapter, GAAP has detailed guidance on the accounting and reporting of indirect effects.

ABOUT THE NUMBERS

Direct and Indirect Effects of Changes

Are there other effects that a company should report when it makes a change in accounting policy? For example, what happens when a company like Lancer (see pages 1350–1354) has a bonus plan based on net income and the prior year's net income changes when FIFO is retrospectively applied? Should Lancer also change the reported amount of bonus expense? Or, what happens if we had not ignored income taxes in the Lancer example? Should Lancer adjust net income, given that taxes will be different under average-cost and FIFO in prior periods? The answers depend on whether the effects are direct or indirect.

Direct Effects

Similar to GAAP, IFRS indicates that companies should retrospectively apply the **direct effects of a change in accounting policy**. An example of a **direct effect** is an adjustment to an inventory balance as a result of a change in the inventory valuation method. For example, referring to Lancer Company on pages 1350–1354, Lancer should change the inventory amounts in prior periods to indicate the change to the FIFO method of inventory valuation. Another inventory-related example would be an impairment adjustment resulting from applying the lower-of-cost-or-net realizable value test to the adjusted inventory balance. Related changes, such as deferred income tax effects of the impairment adjustment, are also considered direct effects. This entry was illustrated in the Denson example on page 1349, in which the change to percentage-of-completion accounting resulted in recording a deferred tax liability.

Indirect Effects

In addition to direct effects, companies can have **indirect effects related to a change in accounting policy**. An **indirect effect** is any change to current or future cash flows of a company that results from making a change in accounting policy that is applied retrospectively. An example of an indirect effect is a change in profit-sharing or royalty payment that is based on a reported amount such as revenue or net income. The IASB is silent on what to do in this situation. GAAP (likely because its standard in this area was issued after *IAS 8*) requires that indirect effects do not change prior period amounts.

For example, let's assume that Lancer Company has an employee profit-sharing plan based on net income and it changed from the weighted-average inventory method to FIFO in 2014. Lancer reports higher income in 2013 and 2014 if it used the FIFO method. In addition, let's assume that the profit-sharing plan requires that Lancer pay the incremental amount due based on the FIFO income amounts. In this situation, Lancer reports this additional expense **in the current period**; it would not change prior periods for this expense. If the company prepares comparative financial statements, it follows that it does not recast the prior periods for this additional expense. If the terms of the profit-sharing plan indicate that *no payment is necessary* in the current period due to this change, then the company need not recognize additional profit-sharing expense in the current period. Neither does it change amounts reported for prior periods.

When a company recognizes the indirect effects of a change in accounting policy, it includes in the financial statements a description of the indirect effects. In doing so, it discloses the amounts recognized in the current period and related per share information.

Impracticability

It is not always possible for companies to determine how they would have reported prior periods' financial information under retrospective application of an accounting policy change. Retrospective application is considered **impracticable** if a company cannot determine the prior period effects using every reasonable effort to do so.

Companies should not use retrospective application if one of the following conditions exists:

1. The company cannot determine the effects of the retrospective application.
2. Retrospective application requires assumptions about management's intent in a prior period.
3. Retrospective application requires significant estimates for a prior period, and the company cannot objectively verify the necessary information to develop these estimates.

If any of the above conditions exists, it is deemed impracticable to apply the retrospective approach. In this case, the company **prospectively applies** the new accounting policy as of the earliest date it is practicable to do so.

For example, assume that Williams Company changed its accounting policy for depreciable assets so as to more fully apply component depreciation under revaluation accounting. Unfortunately, the company does not have detailed accounting records to establish a basis for the components of these assets. As a result, Williams determines it is not practicable to account for the change to full component depreciation using the retrospective application approach. It therefore applies the policy prospectively, starting at the beginning of the current year.

Williams must disclose only the effect of the change on the results of operations in the period of change. Also, the company should explain the reasons for omitting the computations of the cumulative effect for prior years. Finally, it should disclose the justification for the change to component depreciation.

ON THE HORIZON

For the most part, IFRS and GAAP are similar in the area of accounting changes and reporting the effects of errors. Thus, there is no active project in this area. A related development involves the presentation of comparative data. Under IFRS, when a company prepares financial statements on a new basis, two years of comparative data are reported. GAAP requires comparative information for a three-year period. Use of the shorter comparative data period must be addressed before U.S. companies can adopt IFRS.

IFRS SELF-TEST QUESTIONS

1. Which of the following is **false**?
   (a) GAAP and IFRS have the same absolute standard regarding the reporting of error corrections in previously issued financial statements.
   (b) The accounting for changes in estimates is similar between GAAP and IFRS.
   (c) Under IFRS, the impracticability exception applies both to changes in accounting principles and to the correction of errors.
   (d) GAAP has detailed guidance on the accounting and reporting of indirect effects; IFRS does not.

2. Which of the following is **not** classified as an accounting change by IFRS?
   (a) Change in accounting policy.
   (b) Change in accounting estimate.
   (c) Errors in financial statements.
   (d) None of the above.
3. IFRS requires companies to use which method for reporting changes in accounting policies?
   (a) Cumulative effect approach.
   (b) Retrospective approach.
   (c) Prospective approach.
   (d) Averaging approach.
4. Under IFRS, the retrospective approach should **not** be used if:
   (a) retrospective application requires assumptions about management's intent in a prior period.
   (b) the company does not have trained staff to perform the analysis.
   (c) the effects of the change have counterbalanced.
   (d) the effects of the change have not counterbalanced.
5. Which of the following is **true** regarding whether IFRS specifically addresses the accounting and reporting for effects of changes in accounting policies?

	Direct effects	Indirect effects
(a)	Yes	Yes
(b)	No	No
(c)	No	Yes
(d)	Yes	No

IFRS CONCEPTS AND APPLICATION

IFRS22-1 Where can authoritative IFRS related to accounting changes be found?

IFRS22-2 Briefly describe some of the similarities and differences between GAAP and IFRS with respect to reporting accounting changes.

IFRS22-3 How might differences in presentation of comparative data under GAAP and IFRS affect adoption of IFRS by U.S. companies?

IFRS22-4 What is the indirect effect of a change in accounting policy? Briefly describe the approach to reporting the indirect effects of a change in accounting policy under IFRS.

IFRS22-5 Discuss how a change in accounting policy is handled when it is impracticable to determine previous amounts.

IFRS22-6 Joblonsky Inc. has recently hired a new independent auditor, Karen Ogleby, who says she wants "to get everything straightened out." Consequently, she has proposed the following accounting changes in connection with Joblonsky Inc.'s 2014 financial statements.

1. At December 31, 2013, the client had a receivable of $820,000 from Hendricks Inc. on its statement of financial position. Hendricks Inc. has gone bankrupt, and no recovery is expected. The client proposes to write off the receivable as a prior period item.
2. The client proposes the following changes in depreciation policies.
   (a) For office furniture and fixtures, it proposes to change from a 10-year useful life to an 8-year life. If this change had been made in prior years, retained earnings at December 31, 2013, would have been $250,000 less. The effect of the change on 2014 income alone is a reduction of $60,000.
   (b) For its new equipment in the leasing division, the client proposes to adopt the sum-of-the-years'-digits depreciation method. The client had never used SYD before. The first year the client operated a leasing division was 2014. If straight-line depreciation were used, 2014 income would be $110,000 greater.
3. In preparing its 2013 statements, one of the client's bookkeepers overstated ending inventory by $235,000 because of a mathematical error. The client proposes to treat this item as a prior period adjustment.
4. In the past, the client has spread preproduction costs in its furniture division over 5 years. Because its latest furniture is of the "fad" type, it appears that the largest volume of sales will occur during the first 2 years after introduction. Consequently, the client proposes to amortize preproduction costs on a per-unit basis, which will result in expensing most of such costs during the first 2 years after the furniture's introduction. If the new accounting method had been used prior to 2014, retained earnings at December 31, 2013, would have been $375,000 less.

5. For the nursery division, the client proposes to switch from FIFO to average-cost inventories because it believes that average-cost will provide a better income measure. The effect of making this change on 2014 earnings will be an increase of $320,000. The client says that the effect of the change on December 31, 2013, retained earnings cannot be determined.
6. To achieve an appropriate recognition of revenues and expenses in its building construction division, the client proposes to switch from the cost-recovery method of accounting to the percentage-of-completion method. Had the percentage-of-completion method been employed in all prior years, retained earnings at December 31, 2013, would have been $1,075,000 greater.

Instructions

(a) For each of the changes described above, decide whether:
  (1) The change involves an accounting policy, accounting estimate, or correction of an error.
  (2) Restatement of opening retained earnings is required.
(b) What would be the proper adjustment to the December 31, 2013, retained earnings?

Professional Research

IFRS22-7 As part of the year-end accounting process and review of operating policies, Cullen Co. is considering a change in the accounting for its equipment from the straight-line method to an accelerated method. Your supervisor wonders how the company will report this change in accounting. It has been a few years since he took intermediate accounting, and he cannot remember whether this change would be treated in a retrospective or prospective manner. Your supervisor wants you to research the authoritative guidance on a change in accounting policy related to depreciation methods.

Instructions

Access the IFRS authoritative literature at the IASB website (*http://eifrs.iasb.org/*). (Click on the IFRS tab and then register for free eIFRS access if necessary.) When you have accessed the documents, you can use the search tool in your Internet browser to respond to the following questions. (Provide paragraph citations.)

(a) What are the accounting and reporting guidelines for a change in accounting policy related to depreciation methods?
(b) What are the conditions that justify a change in depreciation method, as contemplated by Cullen Co.?

International Financial Reporting Problem
Marks and Spencer plc

IFRS22-8 The financial statements of Marks and Spencer plc (M&S) are available at the book's companion website or can be accessed at *http://annualreport.marksandspencer.com/assets/downloads/Marks-and-Spencer-Annual-report-and-financial-statements-2012 pdf.*

Instructions

Refer to M&S's financial statements and the accompanying notes to answer the following questions.

(a) Were there changes in accounting policies reported by M&S during the two years covered by its income statements (2011–2012)? If so, describe the nature of the change and the year of change.
(b) What types of estimates did M&S discuss in 2012?

ANSWERS TO IFRS SELF-TEST QUESTIONS

1. a **2.** c **3.** b **4.** a **5.** d

Remember to check the book's companion website to find additional resources for this chapter.

CHAPTER 23 Statement of Cash Flows

LEARNING OBJECTIVES

After studying this chapter, you should be able to:

1 Describe the purpose of the statement of cash flows.

2 Identify the major classifications of cash flows.

3 Prepare a statement of cash flows.

4 Differentiate between net income and net cash flow from operating activities.

5 Determine net cash flows from investing and financing activities.

6 Identify sources of information for a statement of cash flows.

7 Contrast the direct and indirect methods of calculating net cash flow from operating activities.

8 Discuss special problems in preparing a statement of cash flows.

9 Explain the use of a worksheet in preparing a statement of cash flows.

Show Me the Money!

Investors usually look to net income as a key indicator of a company's financial health and future prospects. The following graph shows the net income of one company over a seven-year period.

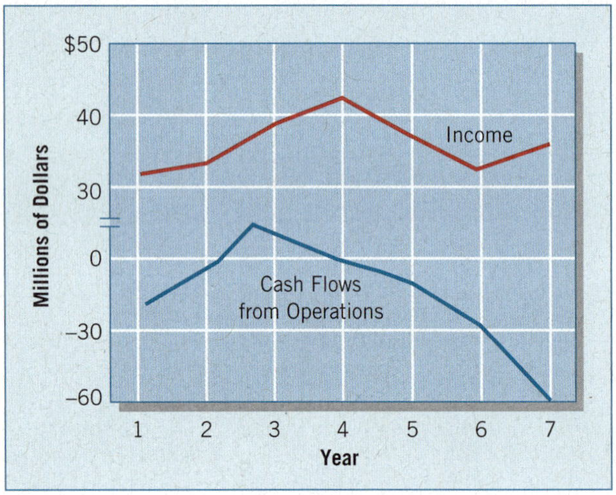

The company showed a pattern of consistent profitability and even some periods of income growth. Between years 1 and 4, net income for this company grew by 32 percent, from $31 million to $41 million. Would you expect its profitability to continue? The company had consistently paid dividends and interest. Would you expect it to continue to do so? Investors answered these questions by buying the company's stock. Eighteen months later, this company—**W. T. Grant**—filed for bankruptcy, in what was then the largest bankruptcy filing in the United States.

How could this happen? As indicated by the second line in the graph, the company had experienced several years of negative cash flow from its operations, even though it reported profits. How can a company have negative cash flows while reporting profits? The answer lays partly in the fact that W. T. Grant was having trouble collecting the receivables from its credit sales, causing cash flow to be less than

net income. Investors who analyzed the cash flows would have been likely to find an early warning signal of W. T. Grant's operating problems.

Investors can also look to cash flow information to sniff out companies that can be good buys. As one analyst stated when it comes to valuing stocks: "Show me the money!" Here's the thinking behind that statement. Start with the "cash flows from operations" reported in the statement of cash flows, which (as you will learn in this chapter) consists of net income with non-cash charges (like depreciation and deferred taxes) added back and cash-draining events (like an inventory pile-up) taken out. Now subtract capital expenditures and dividends. What you're left with is free cash flow (as discussed in Chapter 5).

CONCEPTUAL FOCUS

- See the **Underlying Concepts** on pages 1412 and 1437.
- Read the **Evolving Issue** on page 1433 for a discussion of the direct versus indirect method.

INTERNATIONAL FOCUS

- See the **International Perspectives** on pages 1413, 1415, and 1434.
- Read the **IFRS Insights** on pages 1480–1485 for a discussion of:
  —Significant non-cash transactions
  —Special disclosures

Many analysts like companies trading at low multiples of their free cash flow—low, that is, in relation to rivals today or the same company in past years. Why? They know that reported earnings can be misleading. Case in point: Computer-game firm **Activision Blizzard** reported net income of $113 million in a recent year. But it did better than that. It took in an additional $300 million, mostly for subscriptions to online multiplayer games. It gets the cash now but records the revenue only over time, as the subscriptions run out. A couple of investment houses put this stock on their buy list on the strength of its cash flows. So watch cash flow—to get an indicator of companies headed for trouble, as well as companies that may be undervalued.

Sources: Adapted from James A. Largay III and Clyde P. Stickney, "Cash Flows, Ratio Analysis, and the W. T. Grant Company Bankruptcy," *Financial Analysts Journal* (July–August 1980), p. 51; and D. Fisher, "Cash Doesn't Lie," *Forbes* (April 12, 2010), pp. 52–55.

PREVIEW OF CHAPTER 23

As the opening story indicates, examination of **W. T. Grant**'s cash flows from operations would have shown the financial inflexibility that eventually caused the company's bankruptcy. This chapter explains the main components of a statement of cash flows and the types of information it provides. The content and organization of the chapter are as follows.

Statement of Cash Flows

Preparation of the Statement	Illustrations—Tax Consultants	Special Problems in Statement Preparation	Use of a Worksheet
• Usefulness of statement • Classification of cash flows • Format of statement • Steps in preparation	• Change in cash • Operating cash flows • Cash flows from investing and financing • Statement of cash flows—2013 • Illustrations—2014 and 2015 • Sources of information • Indirect vs. direct method	• Adjustments to net income • Accounts receivable (net) • Other working capital changes • Net losses • Significant non-cash transactions	• Preparation of worksheet • Analysis of transactions • Preparation of final statement

PREPARATION OF THE STATEMENT OF CASH FLOWS

LEARNING OBJECTIVE 1
Describe the purpose of the statement of cash flows.

The primary purpose of the **statement of cash flows** is to provide information about a company's cash receipts and cash payments during a period. A secondary objective is to provide cash-basis information about the company's operating, investing, and financing activities. The statement of cash flows therefore reports cash receipts, cash payments, and net change in cash resulting from a company's operating, investing, and financing activities during a period. Its format reconciles the beginning and ending cash balances for the period.

Usefulness of the Statement of Cash Flows

See the FASB Codification section (page 1454).

The statement of cash flows provides information to help investors, creditors, and others assess the following **[1]**:

Underlying Concepts

Reporting information in the statement of cash flows contributes to meeting the objective of financial reporting.

1. ***The entity's ability to generate future cash flows.*** A primary objective of financial reporting is to provide information with which to predict the amounts, timing, and uncertainty of future cash flows. By examining relationships between items such as sales and net cash flow from operating activities, or net cash flow from operating activities and increases or decreases in cash, it is possible to better predict the future cash flows than is possible using accrual-basis data alone.
2. ***The entity's ability to pay dividends and meet obligations.*** Simply put, cash is essential. Without adequate cash, a company cannot pay employees, settle debts, pay out dividends, or acquire equipment. A statement of cash flows indicates where the company's cash comes from and how the company uses its cash. Employees, creditors, stockholders, and customers should be particularly interested in this statement, because it alone shows the flows of cash in a business.
3. ***The reasons for the difference between net income and net cash flow from operating activities.*** The net income number is important: It provides information on the performance of a company from one period to another. But some people are critical of accrual-basis net income because companies must make estimates to arrive at it. Such is not the case with cash. Thus, as the opening story showed, financial statement readers can benefit from knowing why a company's net income and net cash flow from operating activities differ, and can assess for themselves the reliability of the income number.
4. ***The cash and noncash investing and financing transactions during the period.*** Besides operating activities, companies undertake investing and financing transactions. *Investing* activities include the purchase and sale of assets other than a company's products or services. *Financing* activities include borrowings and repayments of borrowings, investments by owners, and distributions to owners. By examining a company's investing and financing activities, a financial statement reader can better understand why assets and liabilities increased or decreased during the period. For example, by reading the statement of cash flows, the reader might find answers to the following questions:
   - Why did cash decrease for **Home Depot** when it reported net income for the period?
   - How much did **Southwest Airlines** spend on property, plant, and equipment last year?
   - Did dividends paid by **Campbell's Soup** increase?
   - How much money did **Coca-Cola** borrow last year?
   - How much cash did **Hewlett-Packard** use to repurchase its common stock?

Classification of Cash Flows

2 LEARNING OBJECTIVE
Identify the major classifications of cash flows.

The statement of cash flows classifies cash receipts and cash payments by operating, investing, and financing activities.[1] Transactions and other events characteristic of each kind of activity are as follows.

1. **Operating activities** involve the cash effects of transactions that enter into the determination of net income, such as cash receipts from sales of goods and services, and cash payments to suppliers and employees for acquisitions of inventory and expenses.
2. **Investing activities** generally involve long-term assets and include (a) making and collecting loans, and (b) acquiring and disposing of investments and productive long-lived assets.
3. **Financing activities** involve liability and stockholders' equity items and include (a) obtaining cash from creditors and repaying the amounts borrowed, and (b) obtaining capital from owners and providing them with a return on, and a return of, their investment.

Illustration 23-1 classifies the typical cash receipts and payments of a company according to operating, investing, and financing activities. The operating activities category is the most important. It shows the cash provided by company operations. This source of cash is generally considered to be the best measure of a company's ability to generate enough cash to continue as a going concern.

ILLUSTRATION 23-1
Classification of Typical Cash Inflows and Outflows

Activities	
Operating	
Cash inflows	
From sales of goods or services.	
From returns on loans (interest) and on equity securities (dividends).	
Cash outflows	**Income Statement Items**
To suppliers for inventory.	
To employees for services.	
To government for taxes.	
To lenders for interest.	
To others for expenses.	
Investing	
Cash inflows	
From sale of property, plant, and equipment.	
From sale of debt or equity securities of other entities.	
From collection of principal on loans to other entities.	**Generally Long-Term Asset Items**
Cash outflows	
To purchase property, plant, and equipment.	
To purchase debt or equity securities of other entities.	
To make loans to other entities.	
Financing	
Cash inflows	
From sale of equity securities.	
From issuance of debt (bonds and notes).	**Generally Long-Term Liability and Equity Items**
Cash outflows	
To stockholders as dividends.	
To redeem long-term debt or reacquire capital stock.	

International Perspective

According to IFRS, companies can define "cash and cash equivalents" as "net monetary assets"—that is, as "cash and demand deposits and highly liquid investments less short-term borrowings."

[1]The basis recommended by the FASB for the statement of cash flows is actually "cash and cash equivalents." **Cash equivalents** are short-term, highly liquid investments that are both (a) readily convertible to known amounts of cash, and (b) so near their maturity that they present insignificant risk of changes in interest rates. Generally, only investments with original maturities of three months or less qualify under this definition. Examples of cash equivalents are Treasury bills, commercial paper, and money market funds purchased with cash that is in excess of immediate needs.

Although we use the term "cash" throughout our discussion and illustrations, we mean cash and cash equivalents when reporting the cash flows and the net increase or decrease in cash.

Note the following general guidelines about the classification of cash flows.

1. Operating activities involve income statement items.
2. Investing activities involve cash flows resulting from changes in investments and long-term asset items.
3. Financing activities involve cash flows resulting from changes in long-term liability and stockholders' equity items.

Companies classify some cash flows relating to investing or financing activities as operating activities.[2] For example, companies classify receipts of investment income (interest and dividends) and payments of interest to lenders as operating activities. Why are these considered operating activities? Companies report these items in the income statement, where the results of operations are shown.

Conversely, companies classify some cash flows relating to operating activities as investing or financing activities. For example, a company classifies the cash received from the sale of property, plant, and equipment at a gain, although reported in the income statement, as an investing activity. It excludes the effects of the related gain in net cash flow from operating activities. Likewise, a gain or loss on the payment (extinguishment) of debt is generally part of the cash outflow related to the repayment of the amount borrowed. It therefore is a financing activity.

What do the numbers mean? HOW'S MY CASH FLOW?

To evaluate overall cash flow, it is useful to understand where in the product life cycle a company is. Generally, companies move through several stages of development, which have implications for cash flow. As the following graph shows, the pattern of cash flows from operating, financing, and investing activities will vary depending on the stage of the product life cycle.

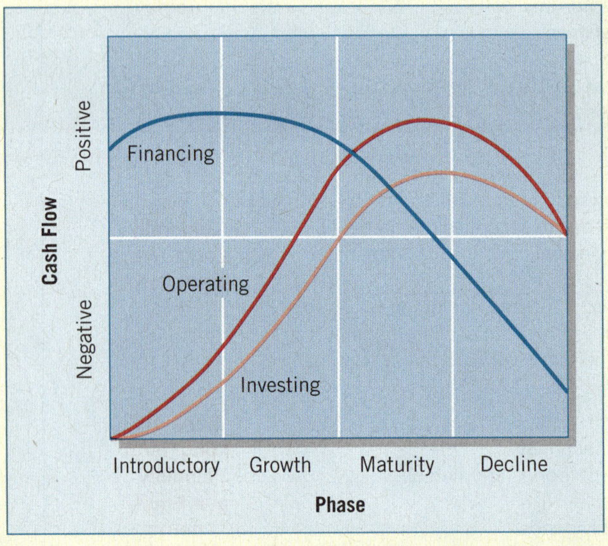

In the introductory phase, the product is likely not generating much revenue (operating cash flow is negative). Because the company is making heavy investments to get a product off the ground, cash flow from investment is negative, and financing cash flows are positive.

[2]Banks and brokers must classify cash flows from purchases and sales of loans and securities specifically for resale and carried at fair value **as operating activities**. This requirement recognizes that for these firms these assets are similar to inventory in other businesses. [2]

As the product moves to the growth and maturity phases, these cash flow relationships reverse. The product generates more cash flow from operations, which can be used to cover investments needed to support the product, and less cash is needed from financing. So is a negative operating cash flow bad? Not always. It depends on the product life cycle.

Source: Adapted from Paul D. Kimmel, Jerry J. Weygandt, and Donald E. Kieso, *Financial Accounting: Tools for Business Decision Making*, 6th ed. (New York: John Wiley & Sons, 2011), p. 628.

Format of the Statement of Cash Flows

The three activities we discussed above constitute the general format of the statement of cash flows. The operating activities section always appears first. It is followed by the investing activities section and then the financing activities section.

A company reports the individual inflows and outflows from investing and financing activities separately. That is, a company reports them gross, not netted against one another. Thus, a cash outflow from the purchase of property is reported separately from the cash inflow from the sale of property. Similarly, a cash inflow from the issuance of debt is reported separately from the cash outflow from its retirement.

The net increase or decrease in cash reported during the period should reconcile the beginning and ending cash balances as reported in the comparative balance sheets. The general format of the statement of cash flows presents the results of the three activities discussed previously–operating, investing, and financing. Illustration 23-2 shows a widely used form of the statement of cash flows.

ILLUSTRATION 23-2
Format of the Statement of Cash Flows

COMPANY NAME
STATEMENT OF CASH FLOWS
PERIOD COVERED

Cash flows from operating activities		
Net income		XXX
Adjustments to reconcile net income to net cash provided (used) by operating activities:		
(List of individual items)	XX	XX
Net cash provided (used) by operating activities		XXX
Cash flows from investing activities		
(List of individual inflows and outflows)	XX	
Net cash provided (used) by investing activities		XXX
Cash flows from financing activities		
(List of individual inflows and outflows)	XX	
Net cash provided (used) by financing activities		XXX
Net increase (decrease) in cash		XXX
Cash at beginning of period		XXX
Cash at end of period		XXX

International Perspective

Both IFRS and GAAP specify that companies must classify cash flows as operating, investing, or financing.

Steps in Preparation

Companies prepare the statement of cash flows differently from the three other basic financial statements. For one thing, it is not prepared from an adjusted trial balance. The cash flow statement requires detailed information concerning the changes in account balances that occurred between two points in time. An adjusted trial balance will not provide the necessary data. Second, the statement of cash flows deals with cash receipts and payments. As a result, the company must adjust the effects of the use of accrual accounting to determine cash flows. The information to prepare this statement usually comes from three sources:

1. **Comparative balance sheets** provide the amount of the changes in assets, liabilities, and equities from the beginning to the end of the period.
2. **Current income statement data** help determine the amount of cash provided by or used by operations during the period.
3. **Selected transaction data** from the general ledger provide additional detailed information needed to determine how the company provided or used cash during the period.

Preparing the statement of cash flows from the data sources above involves three major steps:

Step 1. ***Determine the change in cash.*** This procedure is straightforward. A company can easily compute the difference between the beginning and the ending cash balance from examining its comparative balance sheets.

Step 2. ***Determine the net cash flow from operating activities.*** This procedure is complex. It involves analyzing not only the current year's income statement but also comparative balance sheets as well as selected transaction data.

Step 3. ***Determine net cash flows from investing and financing activities.*** A company must analyze all other changes in the balance sheet accounts to determine their effects on cash.

On the following pages, we work through these three steps in the process of preparing the statement of cash flows for Tax Consultants Inc. over several years.

ILLUSTRATIONS—TAX CONSULTANTS INC.

LEARNING OBJECTIVE 3
Prepare a statement of cash flows.

We show the steps in preparing the statement of cash flows using data for Tax Consultants Inc. To begin, we use the **first year of operations** for Tax Consultants Inc. The company started on January 1, 2013, when it issued 60,000 shares of $1 par value common stock for $60,000 cash. The company rented its office space, furniture, and equipment, and performed tax consulting services throughout the first year. The comparative balance sheets at the beginning and end of the year 2013 appear in Illustration 23-3.

ILLUSTRATION 23-3
Comparative Balance Sheets, Tax Consultants Inc., Year 1

TAX CONSULTANTS INC.
COMPARATIVE BALANCE SHEETS

Assets	Dec. 31, 2013	Jan. 1, 2013	Change Increase/Decrease
Cash	$49,000	$-0-	$49,000 Increase
Accounts receivable	36,000	-0-	36,000 Increase
Total	$85,000	$-0-	
Liabilities and Stockholders' Equity			
Accounts payable	$ 5,000	$-0-	$ 5,000 Increase
Common stock ($1 par)	60,000	-0-	60,000 Increase
Retained earnings	20,000	-0-	20,000 Increase
Total	$85,000	$-0-	

Illustration 23-4 shows the income statement and additional information for Tax Consultants.

ILLUSTRATION 23-4
Income Statement, Tax Consultants Inc., Year 1

TAX CONSULTANTS INC. INCOME STATEMENT FOR THE YEAR ENDED DECEMBER 31, 2013	
Revenues	$125,000
Operating expenses	85,000
Income before income taxes	40,000
Income tax expense	6,000
Net income	$ 34,000

Additional Information
Examination of selected data indicates that a dividend of $14,000 was declared and paid during the year.

Step 1: Determine the Change in Cash

To prepare a statement of cash flows, the first step is to **determine the change in cash.** This is a simple computation. Tax Consultants had no cash on hand at the beginning of the year 2013. It had $49,000 on hand at the end of 2013. Thus, cash changed (increased) in 2013 by $49,000.

Step 2: Determine Net Cash Flow from Operating Activities

4 LEARNING OBJECTIVE
Differentiate between net income and net cash flow from operating activities.

To determine net cash flow from operating activities,[3] companies adjust net income in numerous ways. A useful starting point is to understand why net income must be converted to net cash provided by operating activities.

Under generally accepted accounting principles, most companies use the accrual basis of accounting. As you have learned, this basis requires that companies record revenue when a performance obligation is met and record expenses when incurred. Revenues may include credit sales for which the company has not yet collected cash. Expenses incurred may include some items that the company has not yet paid in cash. Thus, under the accrual basis of accounting, net income is not the same as net cash flow from operating activities.

To arrive at net cash flow from operating activities, a company must determine revenues and expenses on a **cash basis. It does this by eliminating the effects of income statement transactions that do not result in an increase or decrease in cash.** Illustration 23-5 shows the relationship between net income and net cash flow from operating activities.

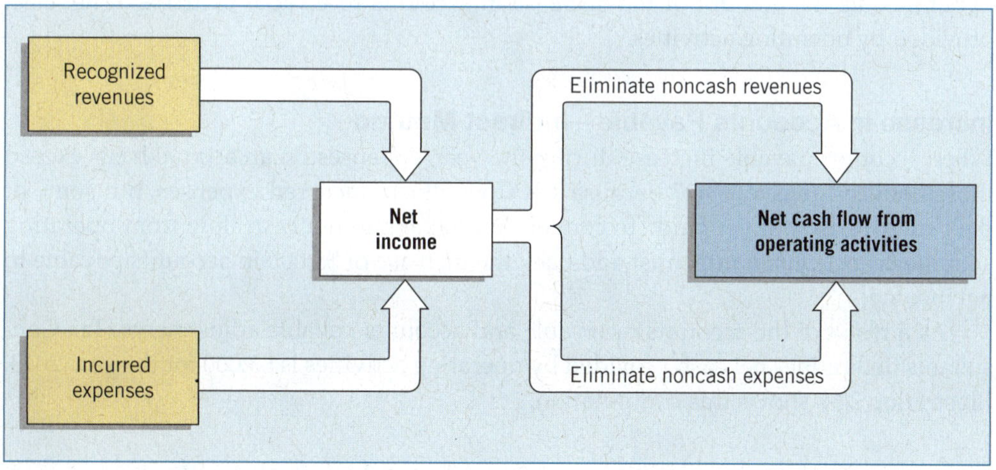

ILLUSTRATION 23-5
Net Income versus Net Cash Flow from Operating Activities

[3]"Net cash flow from operating activities" is a generic phrase, replaced in the statement of cash flows with either "Net cash **provided by** operating activities" if operations increase cash, or "Net cash **used by** operating activities" if operations decrease cash.

In this chapter, we use the term net income to refer to accrual-based net income. A company may convert net income to net cash flow from operating activities through either a direct method or an indirect method. Due to its widespread use in practice, in the following sections we illustrate use of the indirect method. Later in the chapter, we describe the direct method and discuss the advantages and disadvantages of the two methods.[4]

The **indirect method** (or **reconciliation method**) starts with net income and converts it to net cash flow from operating activities. In other words, **the indirect method adjusts net income for items that affected reported net income but did not affect cash.** To compute net cash flow from operating activities, a company adds back noncash charges in the income statement to net income and deducts noncash credits. We explain the two adjustments to net income for Tax Consultants, namely, the increases in accounts receivable and accounts payable, as follows.

Increase in Accounts Receivable—Indirect Method

Tax Consultants' accounts receivable increased by $36,000 (from $0 to $36,000) during the year. For Tax Consultants, this means that cash receipts were $36,000 lower than revenues. The Accounts Receivable account in Illustration 23-6 shows that Tax Consultants had $125,000 in revenues (as reported on the income statement), but it collected only $89,000 in cash.

ILLUSTRATION 23-6
Analysis of Accounts Receivable

Accounts Receivable				
1/1/13	Balance	–0–	Receipts from customer	89,000
	Revenues	125,000		
12/31/13	Balance	36,000		

As shown in Illustration 23-7, to adjust net income to net cash provided by operating activities, Tax Consultants must deduct the increase of $36,000 in accounts receivable from net income. When the Accounts Receivable balance *decreases*, cash receipts are higher than revenue recognized under the accrual basis. Therefore, the company adds to net income the amount of the decrease in accounts receivable to arrive at net cash provided by operating activities.

Increase in Accounts Payable—Indirect Method

When accounts payable increase during the year, expenses on an accrual basis exceed those on a cash basis. Why? Because Tax Consultants incurred expenses, but some of the expenses are not yet paid. To convert net income to net cash flow from operating activities, Tax Consultants must add back the increase of $5,000 in accounts payable to net income.

As a result of the accounts receivable and accounts payable adjustments, Tax Consultants determines net cash provided by operating activities is $3,000 for the year 2013. Illustration 23-7 shows this computation.

[4]*Accounting Trends and Techniques—2012* reports that out of its 500 surveyed companies, 495 (99 percent) used the indirect method, and only 5 used the direct method. *In doing homework assignments, you should follow instructions for use of either the direct or indirect method.*

Net income		$ 34,000
Adjustments to reconcile net income to net cash provided by operating activities:		
Increase in accounts receivable	$(36,000)	
Increase in accounts payable	5,000	(31,000)
Net cash provided by operating activities		$ 3,000

ILLUSTRATION 23-7
Computation of Net Cash Flow from Operating Activities, Year 1—Indirect Method

What do the numbers mean? *EARNINGS AND CASH FLOW MANAGEMENT?*

Investors must be vigilant in their monitoring of management incentives to manipulate both earnings and cash flows. That is, financial success is dependent not only on a company's ability to generate revenues and earnings, but also cash flow. A company that shows profits but is unable to generate cash will also experience waning investor enthusiasm.

Thus, management has an incentive to make operating cash flow look good because Wall Street has paid a premium for companies that generate a lot of cash from operations, rather than through borrowings. However, similar to earnings, companies have ways to pump up cash flow from operations.

One way that companies can boost their operating cash flow is by "securitizing" receivables. That is, companies can speed up cash collections by selling their receivables. For example, **Federated Department Stores** reported a $2.2 billion increase in cash flow from operations. This seems impressive until you read the fine print, which indicates that a big part of the increase was due to the sale of receivables. As discussed in this section, decreases in accounts receivable increase cash flow from operations. So while it appeared that Federated's core operations had improved, the company really did little more than accelerate collections of its receivables. In fact, the cash flow from the securitizations represented more than half of Federated's operating cash flow.

Similarly, companies may time the recognition of noncash gains to mask cash flow problems. Take the example of **Chesapeake Energy Corp.** In a recent quarter, Chesapeake, the second-largest U.S. gas producer, reported a $929 million net profit, nearly double from a year earlier. These results seem pretty good until you take a closer look. Falling commodity prices for natural gas resulted in a 45 percent decrease in Chesapeake's operating cash flow. To plug the hole in its bottom line, the company sold pipeline assets. As a result, all but $3 million of its net income came from these sales and other noncash gains. Thus, in evaluating the quality of accounting, investors must keep an eye on the quality of earnings and cash flows.

Source: Adapted from Ann Tergesen, "Cash Flow Hocus Pocus," *BusinessWeek* (July 16, 2002), pp. 130–131. See also C. Mulford and A. Lopez de Mesa, *Cash Flow Trends and Their Fundamental Drivers: Comprehensive Industry Review*, Georgia Tech Financial Analysis Lab (October 2, 2012); and D. Gilbert, "Chesapeake Plans Increase in Asset Sales as Net Rises," *Wall Street Journal* (August 6, 2012).

Step 3: Determine Net Cash Flows from Investing and Financing Activities

5 LEARNING OBJECTIVE
Determine net cash flows from investing and financing activities.

After Tax Consultants has computed the net cash provided by operating activities, the next step is to determine whether any other changes in balance sheet accounts caused an increase or decrease in cash.

For example, an examination of the remaining balance sheet accounts for Tax Consultants shows increases in both common stock and retained earnings. The common stock increase of $60,000 resulted from the issuance of common stock for cash. The issuance of common stock is reported in the statement of cash flows as a receipt of cash from a financing activity.

Two items caused the retained earnings increase of $20,000:

1. Net income of $34,000 increased retained earnings.
2. Declaration of $14,000 of dividends decreased retained earnings.

Tax Consultants has converted net income into net cash flow from operating activities, as explained earlier. The additional data indicate that it paid the dividend. Thus, the company reports the dividend payment as a cash outflow, classified as a financing activity.

Statement of Cash Flows—2013

We are now ready to prepare the statement of cash flows. The statement starts with the operating activities section. Tax Consultants uses the indirect method to report net cash flow from operating activities.

Illustration 23-8 shows the statement of cash flows for Tax Consultants Inc., for year 1 (2013).

ILLUSTRATION 23-8
Statement of Cash Flows, Tax Consultants Inc., Year 1

TAX CONSULTANTS INC.
STATEMENT OF CASH FLOWS
FOR THE YEAR ENDED DECEMBER 31, 2013

Cash flows from operating activities		
Net income		$ 34,000
Adjustments to reconcile net income to net cash provided by operating activities:		
Increase in accounts receivable	$(36,000)	
Increase in accounts payable	5,000	(31,000)
Net cash provided by operating activities		3,000
Cash flows from financing activities		
Issuance of common stock	60,000	
Payment of cash dividends	(14,000)	
Net cash provided by financing activities		46,000
Net increase in cash		49,000
Cash, January 1, 2013		-0-
Cash, December 31, 2013		$ 49,000

As indicated, the $60,000 increase in common stock results in a financing activity cash inflow. The payment of $14,000 in cash dividends is a financing activity outflow of cash. The $49,000 increase in cash reported in the statement of cash flows agrees with the increase of $49,000 shown in the comparative balance sheets as the change in the Cash account.

Illustration—2014

Tax Consultants Inc. continued to grow and prosper in its second year of operations. The company purchased land, building, and equipment, and revenues and net income increased substantially over the first year. Illustrations 23-9 and 23-10 present information related to the second year of operations for Tax Consultants Inc.

Step 1: Determine the Change in Cash

To prepare a statement of cash flows from the available information, the first step is to determine the change in cash. As indicated from the information presented, cash decreased $12,000 ($49,000 − $37,000).

ILLUSTRATION 23-9
Comparative Balance Sheets, Tax Consultants Inc., Year 2

TAX CONSULTANTS INC.
COMPARATIVE BALANCE SHEETS
AS OF DECEMBER 31

Assets	2014	2013	Change Increase/Decrease
Cash	$ 37,000	$ 49,000	$ 12,000 Decrease
Accounts receivable	26,000	36,000	10,000 Decrease
Prepaid expenses	6,000	-0-	6,000 Increase
Land	70,000	-0-	70,000 Increase
Buildings	200,000	-0-	200,000 Increase
Accumulated depreciation—buildings	(11,000)	-0-	11,000 Increase
Equipment	68,000	-0-	68,000 Increase
Accumulated depreciation—equipment	(10,000)	-0-	10,000 Increase
Total	$386,000	$ 85,000	
Liabilities and Stockholders' Equity			
Accounts payable	$ 40,000	$ 5,000	$ 35,000 Increase
Bonds payable	150,000	-0-	150,000 Increase
Common stock ($1 par)	60,000	60,000	-0-
Retained earnings	136,000	20,000	116,000 Increase
Total	$386,000	$ 85,000	

ILLUSTRATION 23-10
Income Statement, Tax Consultants Inc., Year 2

TAX CONSULTANTS INC.
INCOME STATEMENT
FOR THE YEAR ENDED DECEMBER 31, 2014

Revenues		$492,000
Operating expenses (excluding depreciation)	$269,000	
Depreciation expense	21,000	290,000
Income from operations		202,000
Income tax expense		68,000
Net income		$134,000

Additional Information

(a) The company declared and paid an $18,000 cash dividend.
(b) The company obtained $150,000 cash through the issuance of long-term bonds.
(c) Land, building, and equipment were acquired for cash.

Step 2: Determine Net Cash Flow from Operating Activities—Indirect Method

Using the indirect method, we adjust net income of $134,000 on an accrual basis to arrive at net cash flow from operating activities. Explanations for the adjustments to net income follow.

Decrease in Accounts Receivable. Accounts receivable decreased during the period because cash receipts (cash-basis revenues) are higher than revenues reported on an accrual basis. To convert net income to net cash flow from operating activities, the decrease of $10,000 in accounts receivable must be added to net income.

Increase in Prepaid Expenses. When prepaid expenses (assets) increase during a period, expenses on an accrual-basis income statement are lower than they are on a cash-basis income statement. The reason: Tax Consultants has made cash payments in the current period, but expenses (as charges to the income statement) have been deferred to future periods. To convert net income to net cash flow from operating activities, the company must deduct from net income the increase of $6,000 in prepaid expenses. An increase in prepaid expenses results in a decrease in cash during the period.

Increase in Accounts Payable. Like the increase in 2013, Tax Consultants must add the 2014 increase of $35,000 in accounts payable to net income, to convert to net cash flow from operating activities. The company incurred a greater amount of expense than the amount of cash it disbursed.

Depreciation Expense (Increase in Accumulated Depreciation). The purchase of depreciable assets is a use of cash, shown in the investing section in the year of acquisition. Tax Consultants' depreciation expense of $21,000 (also represented by the increase in accumulated depreciation) is a noncash charge; the company adds it back to net income, to arrive at net cash flow from operating activities. The $21,000 is the sum of the $11,000 depreciation on the building plus the $10,000 depreciation on the equipment.

Certain other periodic charges to expense do not require the use of cash. Examples are the amortization of intangible assets and depletion expense. Such charges are treated in the same manner as depreciation. Companies frequently list depreciation and similar noncash charges as the first adjustments to net income in the statement of cash flows.

As a result of the foregoing items, net cash provided by operating activities is $194,000 as shown in Illustration 23-11.

ILLUSTRATION 23-11
Computation of Net Cash Flow from Operating Activities, Year 2—Indirect Method

Net income		$134,000
Adjustments to reconcile net income to		
net cash provided by operating activities:		
Depreciation expense	$21,000	
Decrease in accounts receivable	10,000	
Increase in prepaid expenses	(6,000)	
Increase in accounts payable	35,000	60,000
Net cash provided by operating activities		$194,000

Step 3: Determine Net Cash Flows from Investing and Financing Activities

After you have determined the items affecting net cash provided by operating activities, the next step involves analyzing the remaining changes in balance sheet accounts. Tax Consultants Inc. analyzed the following accounts.

Increase in Land. As indicated from the change in the Land account, the company purchased land of $70,000 during the period. This transaction is an investing activity, reported as a use of cash.

Increase in Buildings and Related Accumulated Depreciation. As indicated in the additional data and from the change in the Buildings account, Tax Consultants acquired an office building using $200,000 cash. This transaction is a cash outflow, reported in the investing section. The $11,000 increase in accumulated depreciation results from recording depreciation expense on the building. As indicated earlier, the reported depreciation expense has no effect on the amount of cash.

Increase in Equipment and Related Accumulated Depreciation. An increase in equipment of $68,000 resulted because the company used cash to purchase equipment. This transaction is an outflow of cash from an investing activity. The depreciation expense entry for the period explains the increase in Accumulated Depreciation—Equipment.

Increase in Bonds Payable. The Bonds Payable account increased $150,000. Cash received from the issuance of these bonds represents an inflow of cash from a financing activity.

Increase in Retained Earnings. Retained earnings increased $116,000 during the year. Two factors explain this increase. (1) Net income of $134,000 increased retained earnings, and (2) dividends of $18,000 decreased retained earnings. As indicated earlier, the company adjusts net income to net cash provided by operating activities in the operating activities section. Payment of the dividends is a financing activity that involves a cash outflow.

Statement of Cash Flows—2014

Combining the foregoing items, we get a statement of cash flows for 2014 for Tax Consultants Inc., using the indirect method to compute net cash flow from operating activities.

ILLUSTRATION 23-12
Statement of Cash Flows, Tax Consultants Inc., Year 2

TAX CONSULTANTS INC. STATEMENT OF CASH FLOWS FOR THE YEAR ENDED DECEMBER 31, 2014		
Cash flows from operating activities		
Net income		$ 134,000
Adjustments to reconcile net income to net cash provided by operating activities:		
Depreciation expense	$ 21,000	
Decrease in accounts receivable	10,000	
Increase in prepaid expenses	(6,000)	
Increase in accounts payable	35,000	60,000
Net cash provided by operating activities		194,000
Cash flows from investing activities		
Purchase of land	(70,000)	
Purchase of building	(200,000)	
Purchase of equipment	(68,000)	
Net cash used by investing activities		(338,000)
Cash flows from financing activities		
Issuance of bonds	150,000	
Payment of cash dividends	(18,000)	
Net cash provided by financing activities		132,000
Net decrease in cash		(12,000)
Cash, January 1, 2014		49,000
Cash, December 31, 2014		$ 37,000

Illustration—2015

Our third example, covering the 2015 operations of Tax Consultants Inc., is more complex. It again uses the indirect method to compute and present net cash flow from operating activities.

Tax Consultants Inc. experienced continued success in 2015 and expanded its operations to include the sale of computer software used in tax-return preparation and tax planning. Thus, inventory is a new asset appearing in the company's December 31, 2015, balance sheet. Illustrations 23-13 and 23-14 (on page 1424) show the comparative balance sheets, income statements, and selected data for 2015.

Step 1: Determine the Change in Cash

The first step in the preparation of the statement of cash flows is to determine the change in cash. As the comparative balance sheets show, cash increased $17,000 in 2015.

ILLUSTRATION 23-13
Comparative Balance Sheets, Tax Consultants Inc., Year 3

TAX CONSULTANTS INC.
COMPARATIVE BALANCE SHEETS
AS OF DECEMBER 31

Assets	2015	2014	Change Increase/Decrease
Cash	$ 54,000	$ 37,000	$ 17,000 Increase
Accounts receivable	68,000	26,000	42,000 Increase
Inventory	54,000	–0–	54,000 Increase
Prepaid expenses	4,000	6,000	2,000 Decrease
Land	45,000	70,000	25,000 Decrease
Buildings	200,000	200,000	–0–
Accumulated depreciation—buildings	(21,000)	(11,000)	10,000 Increase
Equipment	193,000	68,000	125,000 Increase
Accumulated depreciation—equipment	(28,000)	(10,000)	18,000 Increase
Totals	$569,000	$386,000	
Liabilities and Stockholders' Equity			
Accounts payable	$ 33,000	$ 40,000	$ 7,000 Decrease
Bonds payable	110,000	150,000	40,000 Decrease
Common stock ($1 par)	220,000	60,000	160,000 Increase
Retained earnings	206,000	136,000	70,000 Increase
Totals	$569,000	$386,000	

ILLUSTRATION 23-14
Income Statement, Tax Consultants Inc., Year 3

TAX CONSULTANTS INC.
INCOME STATEMENT
FOR THE YEAR ENDED DECEMBER 31, 2015

Revenues		$890,000
Cost of goods sold	$465,000	
Operating expenses	221,000	
Interest expense	12,000	
Loss on sale of equipment	2,000	700,000
Income from operations		190,000
Income tax expense		65,000
Net income		$125,000

Additional Information

(a) Operating expenses include depreciation expense of $33,000 and expiration of prepaid expenses of $2,000.
(b) Land was sold at its book value for cash.
(c) Cash dividends of $55,000 were declared and paid.
(d) Interest expense of $12,000 was paid in cash.
(e) Equipment with a cost of $166,000 was purchased for cash. Equipment with a cost of $41,000 and a book value of $36,000 was sold for $34,000 cash.
(f) Bonds were redeemed at their book value for cash.
(g) Common stock ($1 par) was issued for cash.

Step 2: Determine Net Cash Flow from Operating Activities—Indirect Method

We explain the adjustments to net income of $125,000 as follows.

Increase in Accounts Receivable. The increase in accounts receivable of $42,000 represents recorded accrual-basis revenues in excess of cash collections in 2015. The company deducts this increase from net income to convert from the accrual basis to the cash basis.

Increase in Inventory. The $54,000 increase in inventory represents an operating use of cash, not an expense. Tax Consultants therefore deducts this amount from net income, to arrive at net cash flow from operations. In other words, when inventory purchased exceeds inventory sold during a period, cost of goods sold on an accrual basis is lower than on a cash basis.

Decrease in Prepaid Expenses. The $2,000 decrease in prepaid expenses represents a charge to the income statement for which Tax Consultants made no cash payment in the current period. The company adds back the decrease to net income, to arrive at net cash flow from operating activities.

Decrease in Accounts Payable. When accounts payable decrease during the year, cost of goods sold and expenses on a cash basis are higher than they are on an accrual basis. To convert net income to net cash flow from operating activities, the company must deduct the $7,000 in accounts payable from net income.

Depreciation Expense (Increase in Accumulated Depreciation). Accumulated Depreciation—Buildings increased $10,000 ($21,000 − $11,000). The Buildings account did not change during the period, which means that Tax Consultants recorded depreciation expense of $10,000 in 2015.

Accumulated Depreciation—Equipment increased by $18,000 ($28,000 − $10,000) during the year. But Accumulated Depreciation—Equipment decreased by $5,000 as a result of the sale during the year. Thus, depreciation for the year was $23,000. The company reconciled Accumulated Depreciation—Equipment as follows.

Beginning balance	$10,000
Add: Depreciation for 2015	23,000
	33,000
Deduct: Sale of equipment	5,000
Ending balance	$28,000

The company must add back to net income the total depreciation of $33,000 ($10,000 + $23,000) charged to the income statement, to determine net cash flow from operating activities.

Loss on Sale of Equipment. Tax Consultants Inc. sold for $34,000 equipment that cost $41,000 and had a book value of $36,000. As a result, the company reported a loss of $2,000 on its sale. To arrive at net cash flow from operating activities, it must add back to net income the loss on the sale of the equipment. The reason is that the loss is a noncash charge to the income statement. The loss did not reduce cash, but it did reduce net income.[5]

From the foregoing items, the company prepares the operating activities section of the statement of cash flows, as shown in Illustration 23-15.

ILLUSTRATION 23-15
Operating Activities Section of Cash Flow Statement

Cash flows from operating activities		
Net income		$125,000
Adjustments to reconcile net income to net cash provided by operating activities:		
Depreciation expense	$ 33,000	
Loss on sale of equipment	2,000	
Increase in accounts receivable	(42,000)	
Increase in inventory	(54,000)	
Decrease in prepaid expenses	2,000	
Decrease in accounts payable	(7,000)	(66,000)
Net cash provided by operating activities		59,000

[5]A similar adjustment is required for unrealized gains or losses recorded on trading security investments or other financial assets and liabilities accounted for under the fair value option. Marking these assets and liabilities to fair value results in an increase or decrease in income, but there is no effect on cash flows.

Step 3: Determine Net Cash Flows from Investing and Financing Activities

By analyzing the remaining changes in the balance sheet accounts, Tax Consultants identifies cash flows from investing and financing activities.

Land. Land decreased $25,000 during the period. As indicated from the information presented, the company sold land for cash at its book value. This transaction is an investing activity, reported as a $25,000 source of cash.

Equipment. An analysis of the Equipment account indicates the following.

Beginning balance	$ 68,000
Purchase of equipment	166,000
	234,000
Deduct: Sale of equipment	41,000
Ending balance	$193,000

The company used cash to purchase equipment with a fair value of $166,000—an investing transaction reported as a cash outflow. The sale of the equipment for $34,000 is also an investing activity, but one that generates a cash inflow.

Bonds Payable. Bonds payable decreased $40,000 during the year. As indicated from the additional information, the company redeemed the bonds at their book value. This financing transaction used $40,000 of cash.

Common Stock. The Common Stock account increased $160,000 during the year. As indicated from the additional information, Tax Consultants issued common stock of $160,000 at par. This financing transaction provided cash of $160,000.

Retained Earnings. Retained earnings changed $70,000 ($206,000 − $136,000) during the year. The $70,000 change in retained earnings results from net income of $125,000 from operations and the financing activity of paying cash dividends of $55,000.

Statement of Cash Flows—2015

Tax Consultants Inc. combines the foregoing items to prepare the statement of cash flows shown in Illustration 23-16.

Sources of Information for the Statement of Cash Flows

LEARNING OBJECTIVE 6
Identify sources of information for a statement of cash flows.

Important points to remember in the preparation of the statement of cash flows are these:

1. Comparative balance sheets provide the basic information from which to prepare the report. Additional information obtained from analyses of specific accounts is also included.
2. An analysis of the Retained Earnings account is necessary. The net increase or decrease in Retained Earnings without any explanation is a meaningless amount in the statement. Without explanation, it might represent the effect of net income, dividends declared, or prior period adjustments.
3. The statement includes all changes that have passed through cash or have resulted in an increase or decrease in cash.
4. Write-downs, amortization charges, and similar "book" entries, such as depreciation of plant assets, represent neither inflows nor outflows of cash because they have no effect on cash. To the extent that they have entered into the determination of net income, however, the company must add them back to or subtract them from net income, to arrive at net cash provided (used) by operating activities.

ILLUSTRATION 23-16
Statement of Cash Flows, Tax Consultants Inc., Year 3

TAX CONSULTANTS INC.
STATEMENT OF CASH FLOWS
FOR THE YEAR ENDED DECEMBER 31, 2015

Cash flows from operating activities		
Net income		$ 125,000
Adjustments to reconcile net income to net cash provided by operating activities:		
Depreciation expense	$ 33,000	
Loss on sale of equipment	2,000	
Increase in accounts receivable	(42,000)	
Increase in inventory	(54,000)	
Decrease in prepaid expenses	2,000	
Decrease in accounts payable	(7,000)	(66,000)
Net cash provided by operating activities		59,000
Cash flows from investing activities		
Sale of land	25,000	
Sale of equipment	34,000	
Purchase of equipment	(166,000)	
Net cash used by investing activities		(107,000)
Cash flows from financing activities		
Redemption of bonds	(40,000)	
Sale of common stock	160,000	
Payment of dividends	(55,000)	
Net cash provided by financing activities		65,000
Net increase in cash		17,000
Cash, January 1, 2015		37,000
Cash, December 31, 2015		$ 54,000

Indirect Method—Additional Adjustments

For consistency and comparability and because it is the most widely used method in practice, we used the indirect method in the Tax Consultants' illustrations. We determined net cash flow from operating activities by adding back to or deducting from net income those items that had no effect on cash. Illustration 23-17 presents a more complete set of common adjustments that companies make to net income to arrive at net cash flow from operating activities.

ILLUSTRATION 23-17
Adjustments Needed to Determine Net Cash Flow from Operating Activities—Indirect Method

Net Income

Additions	Deductions
Depreciation expense	Amortization of bond premium
Amortization of intangibles and deferred charges	Decrease in deferred income tax liability
Amortization of bond discount	Income on investment in common stock using equity method
Increase in deferred income tax liability	Gain on sale of plant assets
Loss on investment in common stock using equity method	Increase in receivables
Loss on sale of plant assets	Increase in inventory
Loss on impairment of assets	Increase in prepaid expense
Decrease in receivables	Decrease in accounts payable
Decrease in inventory	Decrease in accrued liabilities
Decrease in prepaid expense	
Increase in accounts payable	
Increase in accrued liabilities	

= **Net Cash Flow from Operating Activities**

The additions and deductions in Illustration 23-17 reconcile net income to net cash flow from operating activities, illustrating why the indirect method is also called the reconciliation method.

Net Cash Flow from Operating Activities—Direct Method

7 LEARNING OBJECTIVE
Contrast the direct and indirect methods of calculating net cash flow from operating activities.

Two different methods are available to adjust income from operations on an accrual basis to net cash flow from operating activities. We showed the indirect method in the Tax Consultants' illustrations in the prior sections.

The **direct method** reports cash receipts and cash disbursements from operating activities. The difference between these two amounts is the net cash flow from operating activities. In other words, the direct method deducts operating cash disbursements from operating cash receipts. The direct method results in the presentation of a condensed cash receipts and cash disbursements statement.

As indicated from the accrual-based income statement (see Illustration 23-4 on page 1417), Tax Consultants reported revenues of $125,000. However, because the company's accounts receivable increased during 2013 by $36,000, the company collected only $89,000 ($125,000 − $36,000) in cash from these revenues. Similarly, Tax Consultants reported operating expenses of $85,000. However, accounts payable increased during the period by $5,000. Assuming that these payables relate to operating expenses, cash operating expenses were $80,000 ($85,000 − $5,000). Because no taxes payable exist at the end of the year, the company must have paid $6,000 income tax expense for 2013 in cash during the year. Tax Consultants computes net cash flow from operating activities as shown in Illustration 23-18.

ILLUSTRATION 23-18
Computation of Net Cash Flow from Operating Activities, Year 1—Direct Method

Cash collected from revenues	$89,000
Cash payments for expenses	80,000
Income before income taxes	9,000
Cash payments for income taxes	6,000
Net cash provided by operating activities	$ 3,000

"Net cash provided by operating activities" is the equivalent of cash basis net income. ("Net cash used by operating activities" is equivalent to cash basis net loss.)

The FASB encourages use of the direct method and permits use of the indirect method. Yet, if the direct method is used, the Board requires that companies provide in a separate schedule a reconciliation of net income to net cash flow from operating activities. Therefore, under either method, companies must prepare and report information from the indirect (reconciliation) method.

Direct Method—Expanded Example

Under the direct method, the statement of cash flows reports net cash flow from operating activities as major classes of *operating cash receipts* (e.g., cash collected from customers and cash received from interest and dividends) and *cash disbursements* (e.g., cash paid to suppliers for goods, to employees for services, to creditors for interest, and to government authorities for taxes).

We illustrate the direct method here in more detail to help you understand the difference between accrual-based income and net cash flow from operating activities. This example also illustrates the data needed to apply the direct method. Emig Company, which began business on January 1, 2014, has the following selected balance sheet information.

ILLUSTRATION 23-19
Balance Sheet Accounts, Emig Co.

	December 31, 2014	January 1, 2014
Cash	$159,000	-0-
Accounts receivable	15,000	-0-
Inventory	160,000	-0-
Prepaid expenses	8,000	-0-
Property, plant, and equipment (net)	90,000	-0-
Accounts payable	60,000	-0-
Accrued expenses payable	20,000	-0-

Emig Company's December 31, 2014, income statement and additional information are as follows.

ILLUSTRATION 23-20
Income Statement, Emig Co.

Sales revenue		$780,000
Cost of goods sold		450,000
Gross profit		330,000
Operating expenses	$160,000	
Depreciation	10,000	170,000
Income before income taxes		160,000
Income tax expense		48,000
Net income		$112,000

Additional Information

(a) Dividends of $70,000 were declared and paid in cash.
(b) The accounts payable increase resulted from the purchase of merchandise.
(c) Prepaid expenses and accrued expenses payable relate to operating expenses.

Under the **direct method**, companies compute net cash provided by operating activities by **adjusting each item in the income statement** from the accrual basis to the cash basis. To simplify and condense the operating activities section, only major classes of operating cash receipts and cash payments are reported. As Illustration 23-21 shows, the difference between these major classes of cash receipts and cash payments is the net cash provided by operating activities.

ILLUSTRATION 23-21
Major Classes of Cash Receipts and Payments

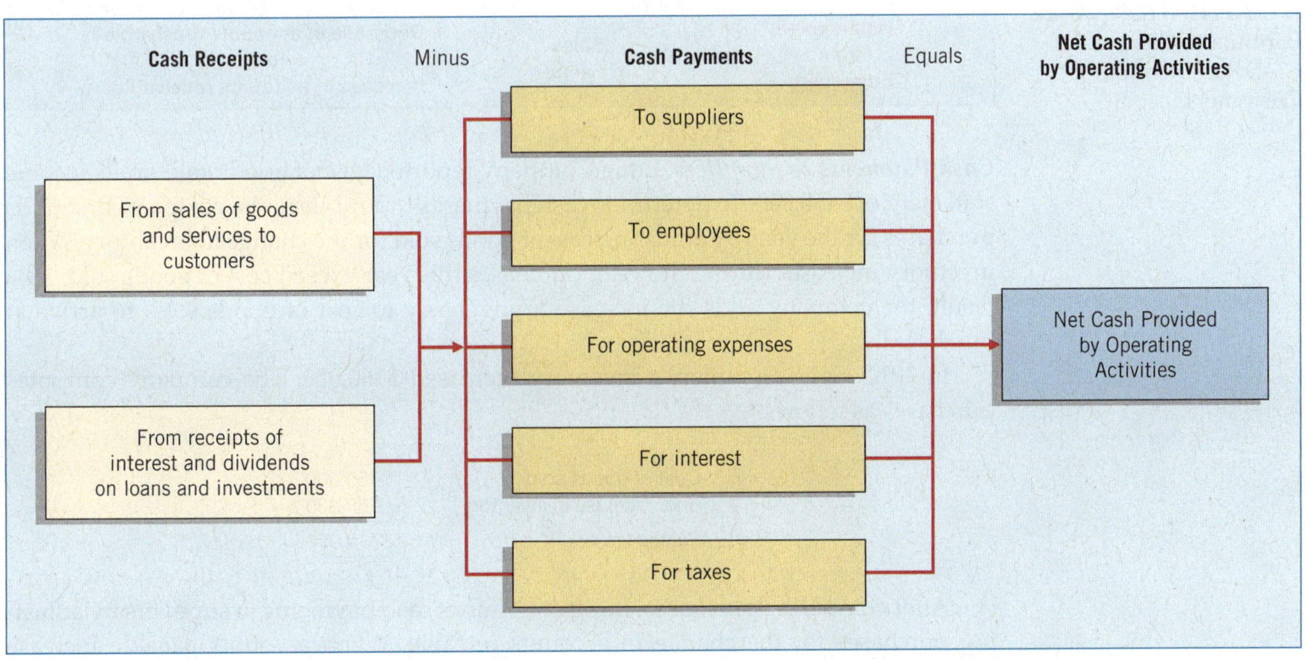

An efficient way to apply the direct method is to analyze the revenues and expenses reported in the income statement in the order in which they are listed. The company then determines cash receipts and cash payments related to these revenues and expenses. In the following sections, we present the direct method adjustments for Emig Company in 2014, to determine net cash provided by operating activities.

Cash Receipts from Customers. The income statement for Emig Company reported revenues from customers of $780,000. To determine cash receipts from customers, the company considers the change in accounts receivable during the year.

When accounts receivable increase during the year, revenues on an accrual basis are higher than cash receipts from customers. In other words, operations led to increased revenues, but not all of these revenues resulted in cash receipts. To determine the amount of increase in cash receipts, deduct the amount of the increase in accounts receivable from the total sales revenue. Conversely, a decrease in accounts receivable is added to sales revenue because cash receipts from customers then exceed sales revenue.

For Emig Company, accounts receivable increased $15,000. Thus, cash receipts from customers were $765,000, computed as follows.

Sales revenue	$780,000
Deduct: Increase in accounts receivable	15,000
Cash receipts from customers	$765,000

Emig could also determine cash receipts from customers by analyzing the Accounts Receivable account as shown below.

Accounts Receivable				
1/1/14	Balance	–0–	Receipts from customers	765,000
	Sales revenue	780,000		
12/31/14	Balance	15,000		

Illustration 23-22 shows the relationships between cash receipts from customers, sales revenue, and changes in accounts receivable.

ILLUSTRATION 23-22
Formula to Compute Cash Receipts from Customers

Cash receipts from customers	=	**Sales revenue**	**+ Decrease in accounts receivable** **or** **– Increase in accounts receivable**

Cash Payments to Suppliers. Emig Company reported cost of goods sold on its income statement of $450,000. To determine cash payments to suppliers, the company first finds purchases for the year, by adjusting cost of goods sold for the change in inventory. When inventory increases during the year, purchases this year exceed cost of goods sold. As a result, the company adds the increase in inventory to cost of goods sold, to arrive at purchases.

In 2014, Emig Company's inventory increased $160,000. The company computes purchases as follows.

Cost of goods sold	$450,000
Add: Increase in inventory	160,000
Purchases	$610,000

After computing purchases, Emig determines cash payments to suppliers by adjusting purchases for the change in accounts payable. When accounts payable increase during the year, purchases on an accrual basis are higher than they are on a cash basis. As a result, the company deducts from purchases the increase in accounts payable to arrive at cash payments to suppliers. Conversely, if cash payments to suppliers exceed purchases, Emig adds to purchases the decrease in accounts payable. Cash payments to suppliers were $550,000, computed as follows.

Purchases	$610,000
Deduct: Increase in accounts payable	60,000
Cash payments to suppliers	$550,000

Emig also can determine cash payments to suppliers by analyzing Accounts Payable, as shown below.

Accounts Payable				
Payments to suppliers	550,000	1/1/14	Balance	–0–
			Purchases	610,000
		12/31/14	Balance	60,000

Illustration 23-23 shows the relationships between cash payments to suppliers, cost of goods sold, changes in inventory, and changes in accounts payable.

Cash payments to suppliers	=	Cost of goods sold	+ Increase in inventory or – Decrease in inventory	+ Decrease in accounts payable or – Increase in accounts payable

ILLUSTRATION 23-23
Formula to Compute Cash Payments to Suppliers

Cash Payments for Operating Expenses. Emig reported operating expenses of $160,000 on its income statement. To determine the cash paid for operating expenses, it must adjust this amount for any changes in prepaid expenses and accrued expenses payable.

For example, when prepaid expenses increased $8,000 during the year, cash paid for operating expenses was $8,000 higher than operating expenses reported on the income statement. To convert operating expenses to cash payments for operating expenses, the company adds to operating expenses the increase of $8,000. Conversely, if prepaid expenses decrease during the year, it deducts from operating expenses the amount of the decrease.

Emig also must adjust operating expenses for changes in accrued expenses payable. When accrued expenses payable increase during the year, operating expenses on an accrual basis are higher than they are on a cash basis. As a result, the company deducts from operating expenses an increase in accrued expenses payable, to arrive at cash payments for operating expenses. Conversely, it adds to operating expenses a decrease in accrued expenses payable, because cash payments exceed operating expenses.

Emig's cash payments for operating expenses were $148,000, computed as follows.

Operating expenses	$160,000
Add: Increase in prepaid expenses	8,000
Deduct: Increase in accrued expenses payable	20,000
Cash payments for operating expenses	$148,000

The relationships among cash payments for operating expenses, changes in prepaid expenses, and changes in accrued expenses payable are shown in Illustration 23-24 (page 1432).

ILLUSTRATION 23-24
Formula to Compute Cash Payments for Operating Expenses

Cash payments for operating expenses	=	Operating expenses	+ Increase in prepaid expense or − Decrease in prepaid expense	+ Decrease in accrued expenses payable or − Increase in accrued expenses payable

Note that the company did not consider depreciation expense because it is a noncash charge.

Cash Payments for Income Taxes. The income statement for Emig shows income tax expense of $48,000. This amount equals the cash paid. How do we know that? Because the comparative balance sheet indicated no income taxes payable at either the beginning or end of the year.

Summary of Net Cash Flow from Operating Activities—Direct Method

The following schedule summarizes the computations illustrated above.

ILLUSTRATION 23-25
Accrual Basis to Cash Basis

Accrual Basis			Adjustment	Add (Subtract)	Cash Basis
Sales revenue	$780,000	−	Increase in accounts receivable	$ (15,000)	$765,000
Cost of goods sold	450,000	+	Increase in inventory	160,000	
		−	Increase in accounts payable	(60,000)	550,000
Operating expenses	160,000	+	Increase in prepaid expenses	8,000	
		−	Increase in accrued expenses payable	(20,000)	148,000
Depreciation expense	10,000	−	Depreciation expense	(10,000)	-0-
Income tax expense	48,000				48,000
Total expense	668,000				746,000
Net income	$112,000		Net cash provided by operating activities		$ 19,000

Illustration 23-26 shows the presentation of the direct method for reporting net cash flow from operating activities for the Emig Company illustration.

ILLUSTRATION 23-26
Operating Activities Section—Direct Method, 2014

EMIG COMPANY
STATEMENT OF CASH FLOWS (PARTIAL)

Cash flows from operating activities		
Cash received from customers		$765,000
Cash payments:		
To suppliers	$550,000	
For operating expenses	148,000	
For income taxes	48,000	746,000
Net cash provided by operating activities		$ 19,000

If Emig Company uses the direct method to present the net cash flow from operating activities, it must provide in a separate schedule the reconciliation of net income to net cash provided by operating activities. The reconciliation assumes the identical form and content of the indirect method of presentation, as the following shows.

EMIG COMPANY RECONCILIATION		
Net income		$112,000
Adjustments to reconcile net income to net cash provided by operating activities:		
Depreciation expense	$ 10,000	
Increase in accounts receivable	(15,000)	
Increase in inventory	(160,000)	
Increase in prepaid expenses	(8,000)	
Increase in accounts payable	60,000	
Increase in accrued expense payable	20,000	(93,000)
Net cash provided by operating activities		$ 19,000

ILLUSTRATION 23-27
Reconciliation of Net Income to Net Cash Provided by Operating Activities

When the direct method is used, the company may present this reconciliation at the bottom of the statement of cash flows or in a separate schedule.

Evolving Issue DIRECT VERSUS INDIRECT

The most contentious decision that the FASB faced related to cash flow reporting was choosing between the direct method and the indirect method of determining net cash flow from operating activities. Companies lobbied *against* the direct method, urging adoption of the indirect method. Commercial lending officers expressed to the FASB a strong preference in favor of the direct method. What are the arguments in favor of each of the methods?

In Favor of the Direct Method

The principal advantage of the direct method is that **it shows operating cash receipts and payments**. Thus, it is more consistent with the objective of a statement of cash flows—to provide information about cash receipts and cash payments—than the indirect method, which does not report operating cash receipts and payments.

Supporters of the direct method contend that knowledge of the specific sources of operating cash receipts and the purposes for which operating cash payments were made in past periods is useful in estimating future operating cash flows. Furthermore, information about amounts of major classes of operating cash receipts and payments is more useful than information only about their arithmetic sum (the net cash flow from operating activities). Such information is more revealing of a company's ability (1) to generate sufficient cash from operating activities to pay its debts, (2) to reinvest in its operations, and (3) to make distributions to its owners. [3]

Many companies indicate that they do not currently collect information in a manner that allows them to determine amounts such as cash received from customers or cash paid to suppliers directly from their accounting systems. But supporters of the direct method contend that the incremental cost of determining operating cash receipts and payments is not significant.

In Favor of the Indirect Method

The principal advantage of the indirect method is that **it focuses on the differences between net income and net cash flow from operating activities**. That is, it provides a useful link between the statement of cash flows and the income statement and balance sheet.

Many companies contend that it is less costly to adjust net income to net cash flow from operating activities (indirect) than it is to report gross operating cash receipts and payments (direct). Supporters of the indirect method also state that the direct method, which effectively reports income statement information on a cash rather than an accrual basis, may erroneously suggest that net cash flow from operating activities is as good as, or better than, net income as a measure of performance.

In their joint financial statement presentation project, the FASB and the IASB have proposed to allow only the direct method. However, there has been significant pushback on this proposal, which suggests that the choice of either the direct or indirect method will continue to be available.

Source: See *http://www.fasb.org*; click on Projects and then on Inactive Joint FASB/IASB Projects.

Special Reporting Rules Applying to Direct and Indirect Methods

Companies that use the direct method are required, at a minimum, to report separately the following classes of operating cash receipts and payments:

International Perspective

Consolidated statements of cash flows may be of limited use to analysts evaluating multinational companies. Without disaggregation, users of such statements are not able to determine "where in the world" the funds are sourced and used.

Receipts

1. Cash collected from customers (including lessees, licensees, etc.).
2. Interest and dividends received.
3. Other operating cash receipts, if any.

Payments

1. Cash paid to employees and suppliers of goods or services (including suppliers of insurance, advertising, etc.).
2. Interest paid.
3. Income taxes paid.
4. Other operating cash payments, if any.

The FASB encourages companies to provide further breakdowns of operating cash receipts and payments that they consider meaningful.

Companies using the indirect method must disclose separately changes in inventory, receivables, and payables in order to reconcile net income to net cash flow from operating activities. In addition, they must disclose, elsewhere in the financial statements or in accompanying notes, interest paid (net of amount capitalized) and income taxes paid.[6] The FASB requires these separate and additional disclosures so that users may approximate the direct method. Also, an acceptable alternative presentation of the indirect method is to report net cash flow from operating activities as a single line item in the statement of cash flows and to present the reconciliation details elsewhere in the financial statements.

Finally, the FASB **encourages** the use of the direct method over the indirect method. If a company uses the direct method of reporting net cash flow from operating activities, the FASB **requires** that the company provide in a separate schedule a reconciliation of net income to net cash flow from operating activities. If a company uses the indirect method, it can either report the reconciliation within the statement of cash flows or can provide it in a separate schedule, with the statement of cash flows reporting only the **net** cash flow from operating activities. [4]

SPECIAL PROBLEMS IN STATEMENT PREPARATION

LEARNING OBJECTIVE 8

Discuss special problems in preparing a statement of cash flows.

We discussed some of the special problems related to preparing the statement of cash flows in connection with the preceding illustrations. Other problems that arise with some frequency in the preparation of this statement include the following.

1. Adjustments to net income.
2. Accounts receivable (net).
3. Other working capital changes.
4. Net losses.
5. Significant noncash transactions.

[6] *Accounting Trends and Techniques—2012* reports that of the 500 companies surveyed, 207 disclosed interest paid in notes to the financial statements, 257 disclosed interest paid at the bottom of the statement of cash flows, 7 disclosed interest paid within the statement of cash flows, and 29 reported no separate amount. Income taxes paid during the year were disclosed in a manner similar to interest payments.

Adjustments to Net Income

Depreciation and Amortization

Depreciation expense is the most common adjustment to net income that companies make to arrive at net cash flow from operating activities. But there are numerous other noncash expense or revenue items. Examples of expense items that companies must add back to net income are the **amortization of limited-life intangible assets** such as patents, and the **amortization of deferred costs** such as bond issue costs. These charges to expense involve expenditures made in prior periods that a company amortizes currently. These charges reduce net income without affecting cash in the current period.

Also, **amortization of bond discount or premium** on long-term bonds payable affects the amount of interest expense. However, neither affects cash. As a result, a company should add back discount amortization and subtract premium amortization from net income to arrive at net cash flow from operating activities.

Postretirement Benefit Costs

If a company has postretirement costs such as an employee pension plan, chances are that the pension expense recorded during a period will either be higher or lower than the cash funded. It will be higher when there is an unfunded liability and will be lower when there is a pension asset. When the expense is higher or lower than the cash paid, **the company must adjust net income by the difference between cash paid and the expense reported** in computing net cash flow from operating activities.

Changes in Deferred Income Taxes

Changes in deferred income taxes affect net income but have no effect on cash. For example, Delta Airlines reported an increase in its liability for deferred taxes of approximately $1.2 billion. This change in the liability increased tax expense and decreased net income, but did not affect cash. Therefore, Delta added back $1.2 billion to net income on its statement of cash flows.

Equity Method of Accounting

Another common adjustment to net income is **a change related to an investment in common stock** when recording income or loss under the equity method. Recall that under the equity method, the investor (1) debits the investment account and credits revenue for its share of the investee's net income, and (2) credits dividends received to the investment account. Therefore, the net increase in the investment account does not affect cash flow. A company must deduct the net increase from net income to arrive at net cash flow from operating activities.

Assume that Victor Co. owns 40 percent of Milo Inc. During the year, Milo reports net income of $100,000 and pays a cash dividend of $30,000. Victor reports this in its statement of cash flows as a deduction from net income in the following manner—Equity in earnings of Milo, net of dividends, $28,000 [($100,000 − $30,000) × 40%].

Losses and Gains

Realized Losses and Gains. In the illustration for Tax Consultants, the company experienced a loss of $2,000 from the sale of equipment. The company added this loss to net income to compute net cash flow from operating activities because **the loss is a noncash charge in the income statement**.

If Tax Consultants experiences a **gain** from a sale of equipment, it too requires an adjustment to net income. Because a company reports the gain in the statement of cash flows as part of the cash proceeds from the sale of equipment under investing activities, **it deducts the gain from net income to avoid double-counting**—once as part of net income and again as part of the cash proceeds from the sale.

To illustrate, assume that Tax Consultants had land with a carrying value of $200,000, which was condemned by the state government for a highway project. The condemnation proceeds received were $205,000, resulting in a gain of $5,000. In the statement of cash flows (indirect method), the company would deduct the $5,000 gain from net income in the operating activities section. It would report the $205,000 cash inflow from the condemnation as an investing activity, as follows.

Cash flows from investing activities	
Condemnation of land	$205,000

Unrealized Losses and Gains. Unrealized losses and gains generally occur for debt investments and for equity investments. For example, assume that Target purchases the following two investments on January 10, 2014.

1. Debt investment for $1 million that is classified as trading. During 2014, the debt investment has an unrealized holding gain of $110,000 (recorded in net income).
2. Equity investment for $600,000 that is classified as available-for-sale. During 2014, the available-for-sale equity investment has an unrealized holding loss of $50,000 (recorded in other comprehensive income).

For Target, the unrealized holding gain of $110,000 on the debt investment increases net income but does not increase net cash flow from operating activities. As a result, the unrealized holding gain of $110,000 is deducted from net income to compute net cash flow from operating activities.

On the other hand, the unrealized holding loss of $50,000 that Target incurs on the available-for-sale equity investment does not affect net income or cash flows—this loss is reported in the other comprehensive income section. As a result, no adjustment to net income is necessary in computing net cash flow from operating activities.

Thus, the general rule is that unrealized holding gains or losses that affect net income must be adjusted to determine net cash flow from operating activities. Conversely, unrealized holding gains or losses that do not affect net income are not adjusted to determine net cash flow from operating activities.

Stock Options

Recall for share-based compensation plans that companies are required to use the fair value method to determine total compensation cost. The compensation cost is then recognized as an expense in the periods in which the employee provides services. When Compensation Expense is debited, Paid-in Capital—Stock Options is often credited. Cash is not affected by recording the expense. **Therefore, the company must increase net income by the amount of compensation expense from stock options in computing net cash flow from operating activities.**

To illustrate how this information should be reported on a statement of cash flows, assume that First Wave Inc. grants 5,000 options to its CEO, Ann Johnson. Each option entitles Johnson to purchase one share of First Wave's $1 par value common stock at $50 per share at any time in the next two years (the service period). The fair value of the options is $200,000. First Wave records compensation expense in the first year as follows.

Compensation Expense ($200,000 ÷ 2)	100,000	
Paid-in Capital—Stock Options		100,000

In addition, if we assume that First Wave has a 35 percent tax rate, it would recognize a deferred tax asset of $35,000 ($100,000 × 35%) in the first year as follows.

Deferred Tax Asset	35,000	
Income Tax Expense		35,000

Therefore, on the statement of cash flows for the first year, First Wave reports the following (assuming a net income of $600,000).

Net income	$600,000
Adjustments to reconcile net income to net cash provided by operating activities:	
Share-based compensation expense	100,000
Increase in deferred tax asset	(35,000)

As shown in First Wave's statement of cash flows, it adds the share-based compensation expense to net income because it is a noncash expense. The increase in the deferred tax asset and the related reduction in income tax expense increase net income. Although the negative income tax expense increases net income, it does not increase cash. Therefore, it should be deducted.

Subsequently, if Ann Johnson exercises her options, First Wave reports "Cash provided by exercise of stock options" in the financing section of the statement of cash flows.[7]

Extraordinary Items

Companies should report **either as investing activities or as financing activities** cash flows from extraordinary transactions and other events whose effects are included in net income, but which are not related to operations.

For example, assume that Tax Consultants had land with a carrying value of $200,000, which was condemned by the state of Maine for a highway project. The condemnation proceeds received were $205,000, resulting in an extraordinary gain of $5,000 less $2,000 of taxes. In the statement of cash flows (indirect method), the company would deduct the $5,000 gain from net income in the operating activities section. It would report the $205,000 cash inflow from the condemnation as an investing activity, as follows.

Cash flows from investing activities	
Condemnation of land	$205,000

Note that Tax Consultants handles the gain at its **gross** amount ($5,000), not net of tax. The company reports the cash received in the condemnation as an investing activity at $205,000, also exclusive of the tax effect.

The FASB requires companies to classify **all income taxes paid as operating cash outflows**. Some suggested that income taxes paid be allocated to investing and financing transactions. But the Board decided that allocation of income taxes paid to operating, investing, and financing activities would be so complex and arbitrary that the benefits, if any, would not justify the costs involved. Under both the direct method and the indirect method, companies must disclose the total amount of income taxes paid.[8]

Underlying Concepts

By rejecting the requirement to allocate taxes to the various activities, the FASB invoked the cost constraint. The information would be beneficial, but the cost of providing such information would exceed the benefits of providing it.

[7]Companies receive a tax deduction related to share-based compensation plans at the time employees exercise their options. The amount of the deduction is equal to the difference between the market price of the stock and the exercise price at the date the employee purchases the stock, which in most cases is much larger than the total compensation expense recorded. When the tax deduction exceeds the total compensation recorded, this provides an additional cash inflow to the company. For example, in a recent year **Cisco Systems** reported an additional cash inflow related to its stock-option plans equal to $537 million. Under GAAP, this tax-related cash inflow is reported in the financing section of the statement of cash flows. **[5]**

[8]For an insightful article on some weaknesses and limitations in the statement of cash flows, see Hugo Nurnberg, "Inconsistencies and Ambiguities in Cash Flow Statements Under *FASB Statement No. 95*," *Accounting Horizons* (June 1993), pp. 60–73. Nurnberg identifies the inconsistencies caused by the three-way classification of all cash receipts and cash payments, gross versus net of tax, the ambiguous disclosure requirements for noncash investing and financing transactions, and the ambiguous presentation of third-party financing transactions. See also Paul B. W. Miller and Bruce P. Budge, "Nonarticulation in Cash Flow Statements and Implications for Education, Research, and Practice," *Accounting Horizons* (December 1996), pp. 1–15; and Charles Mulford and Michael Ely, "Calculating Sustainable Cash Flow: A Study of the S&P 100," *Georgia Tech Financial Analysis Lab* (October 2004).

Accounts Receivable (Net)

Up to this point, we assumed no allowance for doubtful accounts—a contra account—to offset accounts receivable. However, if a company needs an allowance for doubtful accounts, how does that allowance affect the company's determination of net cash flow from operating activities? For example, assume that Redmark Co. reports net income of $40,000. It has the accounts receivable balances as shown in Illustration 23-28.

ILLUSTRATION 23-28
Accounts Receivable Balances, Redmark Co.

	2014	2013	Change Increase/Decrease
Accounts receivable	$105,000	$90,000	$15,000 Increase
Allowance for doubtful accounts	(10,000)	(4,000)	6,000 Increase
Accounts receivable (net)	$ 95,000	$86,000	9,000 Increase

Indirect Method

Because an increase in Allowance for Doubtful Accounts results from a charge to bad debt expense, a company should add back an increase in Allowance for Doubtful Accounts to net income to arrive at net cash flow from operating activities. Illustration 23-29 shows one method for presenting this information in a statement of cash flows.

ILLUSTRATION 23-29
Presentation of Allowance for Doubtful Accounts—Indirect Method

REDMARK CO.
STATEMENT OF CASH FLOWS (PARTIAL)
FOR THE YEAR 2014

Cash flows from operating activities		
Net income		$40,000
Adjustments to reconcile net income to net cash provided by operating activities:		
Increase in accounts receivable	$(15,000)	
Increase in allowance for doubtful accounts	6,000	(9,000)
		$31,000

As we indicated, the increase in the Allowance for Doubtful Accounts balance results from a charge to bad debt expense for the year. Because bad debt expense is a noncash charge, a company must add it back to net income in arriving at net cash flow from operating activities.

Instead of separately analyzing the allowance account, a short-cut approach is to net the allowance balance against the receivable balance and compare the change in accounts receivable on a net basis. Illustration 23-30 shows this presentation.

ILLUSTRATION 23-30
Net Approach to Allowance for Doubtful Accounts—Indirect Method

REDMARK CO.
STATEMENT OF CASH FLOWS (PARTIAL)
FOR THE YEAR 2014

Cash flows from operating activities	
Net income	$40,000
Adjustments to reconcile net income to net cash provided by operating activities:	
Increase in accounts receivable (net)	(9,000)
	$31,000

This short-cut procedure works also if the change in the allowance account results from a write-off of accounts receivable. This reduces both Accounts Receivable and Allowance for Doubtful Accounts. No effect on cash flows occurs. *Because of its simplicity, use the net approach for your homework assignments.*

Direct Method

If using the direct method, a company **should not net** Allowance for Doubtful Accounts against Accounts Receivable. To illustrate, assume that Redmark Co.'s net income of $40,000 consisted of the items shown in Illustration 23-31.

ILLUSTRATION 23-31
Income Statement, Redmark Co.

REDMARK CO.
INCOME STATEMENT
FOR THE YEAR 2014

Sales revenue		$100,000
Expenses		
Salaries	$46,000	
Utilities	8,000	
Bad debts	6,000	60,000
Net income		$ 40,000

If Redmark deducts the $9,000 increase in accounts receivable (net) from sales for the year, it would report cash sales at $91,000 ($100,000 − $9,000) and cash payments for operating expenses at $60,000. Both items would be misstated: Cash sales should be reported at $85,000 ($100,000 − $15,000), and total cash payments for operating expenses should be reported at $54,000 ($60,000 − $6,000). Illustration 23-32 shows the proper presentation.

ILLUSTRATION 23-32
Bad Debts—Direct Method

REDMARK CO.
STATEMENT OF CASH FLOWS (PARTIAL)
FOR THE YEAR 2014

Cash flows from operating activities		
Cash received from customers		$85,000
Salaries paid	$46,000	
Utilities paid	8,000	54,000
Net cash provided by operating activities		$31,000

An added complication develops when a company writes off accounts receivable. Simply adjusting sales for the change in accounts receivable will not provide the proper amount of cash sales. The reason is that the write-off of the accounts receivable is not a cash collection. Thus, an additional adjustment is necessary.

What do the numbers mean? NOT WHAT IT SEEMS

The controversy over direct and indirect methods highlights the importance that the market attributes to operating cash flow. By showing an improving cash flow, a company can give a favorable impression of its ongoing operations. For example, WorldCom concealed declines in its operations by capitalizing certain operating expenses—to the tune of $3.8 billion! This practice not only "juiced up" income but also made it possible to report the cash payments in the investing section of the cash flow statement rather than as a deduction from operating cash flow.

The SEC recently addressed a similar cash flow classification issue with automakers like Ford, GM, and Chrysler. For years, automakers classified lease receivables and other dealer-financing arrangements as investment cash flows. Thus, they reported an increase in lease or loan receivables from cars sold as a use of cash in the investing section of the statement of cash flows. The SEC objected and now requires automakers to report these receivables as operating cash flows, since the leases and loans are used to facilitate car sales. At GM, these reclassifications reduced its operating cash flows from $7.6 billion to $3 billion in the year before the change.

In the banking industry, how banks classify their investments, deposits, and cash flow from acquisitions results in huge swings in operating cash flows, both downward (**Bank of America**) and upward (**KeyCorp**). According to one analyst, "As it stands now, banks can't be reliably compared to each other by their recorded cash flow from operations . . . operating cash flow for a bank is basically meaningless." Another questionable cash flow classification for banks is the characterization of increases and decreases in deposits as financing cash flow. Many analysts believe customer-driven deposits should be accounted for under operating cash flow (rather than as a financing cash flow) since "the very health of a bank's operations depends on its deposit base and its ability to attract a growing stream of deposits." So while the overall cash flow—from operations, investing, and financing—remained the same, operating cash flow at these companies looked better than it really was.

Sources: Peter Elstrom, "How to Hide $3.8 Billion in Expenses," *BusinessWeek Online* (July 8, 2002); Judith Burns, "SEC Tells US Automakers to Retool Cash-Flow Accounting," *Wall Street Journal Online* (February 28, 2005); and Sarah Johnson, "Cash Flow: A Better Way to Know Your Bank?" *CFO.com* (July 9, 2009).

Other Working Capital Changes

Up to this point, we showed how companies handled all of the changes in working capital items (current asset and current liability items) as adjustments to net income in determining net cash flow from operating activities. You must be careful, however, because **some changes in working capital, although they affect cash, do not affect net income**. Generally, these are investing or financing activities of a current nature.

One activity is the purchase of **short-term available-for-sale securities**. For example, the purchase of short-term available-for-sale securities for $50,000 cash has no effect on net income but it does cause a $50,000 decrease in cash. A company reports this transaction as a cash flow from investing activities as follows. **[6]**

Cash flows from investing activities	
Purchase of short-term available-for-sale securities	$(50,000)

What about **trading securities?** Because companies hold these investments principally for the purpose of selling them in the near term, companies should classify the cash flows from purchases and sales of trading securities as cash flows from **operating activities**. **[7]**[9]

Another example is the issuance of a **short-term nontrade note payable** for cash. This change in a working capital item has no effect on income from operations but it increases cash by the amount of the note payable. For example, a company reports the issuance of a $10,000 short-term note payable for cash in the statement of cash flows as follows.

Cash flows from financing activities	
Issuance of short-term note	$10,000

Another change in a working capital item that has no effect on income from operations or on cash is a **cash dividend payable**. Although a company will report the cash dividends when paid as a financing activity, it does not report the declared but unpaid dividend on the statement of cash flows.

Net Losses

If a company reports a net loss instead of a net income, it must adjust the net loss for those items that do not result in a cash inflow or outflow. The net loss, after adjusting for

[9]If the basis of the statement of cash flows is **cash and cash equivalents** and the short-term investment is considered a cash equivalent, then a company reports nothing in the statement because the transaction does not affect the balance of cash and cash equivalents. The Board notes that cash purchases of short-term investments generally are part of the company's cash management activities rather than part of its operating, investing, or financing activities.

the charges or credits not affecting cash, may result in a negative or a positive cash flow from operating activities.

For example, if the net loss is $50,000 and the total amount of charges to add back is $60,000, then net cash provided by operating activities is $10,000. Illustration 23-33 shows this computation.

ILLUSTRATION 23-33
Computation of Net Cash Flow from Operating Activities—Cash Inflow

Net loss		$(50,000)
Adjustments to reconcile net income to net cash provided by operating activities:		
Depreciation of plant assets	$55,000	
Amortization of patents	5,000	60,000
Net cash provided by operating activities		$ 10,000

If the company experiences a net loss of $80,000 and the total amount of the charges to add back is $25,000, the presentation appears as follows.

ILLUSTRATION 23-34
Computation of Net Cash Flow from Operating Activities—Cash Outflow

Net loss	$(80,000)
Adjustments to reconcile net income to net cash used by operating activities:	
Depreciation of plant assets	25,000
Net cash used by operating activities	$(55,000)

Although not illustrated in this chapter, a negative cash flow may result even if the company reports a net income.

Significant Noncash Transactions

Because the statement of cash flows reports only the effects of operating, investing, and financing activities in terms of cash flows, it omits some **significant noncash transactions** and other events that are investing or financing activities. Among the more common of these noncash transactions that a company should report or disclose in some manner are the following.

1. Acquisition of assets by assuming liabilities (including capital lease obligations) or by issuing equity securities.
2. Exchanges of nonmonetary assets.
3. Refinancing of long-term debt.
4. Conversion of debt or preferred stock to common stock.
5. Issuance of equity securities to retire debt.

A company does not incorporate these noncash items in the statement of cash flows. If material in amount, these disclosures may be either narrative or summarized in a separate schedule at the bottom of the statement, or they may appear in a separate note or supplementary schedule to the financial statements.[10] Illustration 23-35 (page 1442) shows the presentation of these significant noncash transactions or other events in a separate schedule at the bottom of the statement of cash flows.

[10]Some noncash investing and financing activities are part cash and part noncash. Companies should report only the cash portion on the statement of cash flows. The noncash component should be reported at the bottom of the statement or in a separate note.

ILLUSTRATION 23-35
Schedule Presentation of Noncash Investing and Financing Activities

Net increase in cash	$3,717,000
Cash at beginning of year	5,208,000
Cash at end of year	$8,925,000
Noncash investing and financing activities	
Purchase of land and building through issuance of 250,000 shares of common stock	$1,750,000
Exchange of Steadfast, NY, land for Bedford, PA, land	$2,000,000
Conversion of 12% bonds to 50,000 shares of common stock	$500,000

Or, companies may present these noncash transactions in a separate note, as shown in Illustration 23-36.

ILLUSTRATION 23-36
Note Presentation of Noncash Investing and Financing Activities

Note G: Significant noncash transactions. During the year, the company engaged in the following significant noncash investing and financing transactions:

Issued 250,000 shares of common stock to purchase land and building	$1,750,000
Exchanged land in Steadfast, NY, for land in Bedford, PA	$2,000,000
Converted 12% bonds to 50,000 shares of common stock	$500,000

Companies do not generally report certain other significant noncash transactions or other events in conjunction with the statement of cash flows. Examples of these types of transactions are **stock dividends, stock splits, and restrictions on retained earnings.** Companies generally report these items, neither financing nor investing activities, in conjunction with the statement of stockholders' equity or schedules and notes pertaining to changes in capital accounts.

What do the numbers mean? *CASH FLOW TOOL*

By understanding the relationship between cash flow and income measures, analysts can gain better insights into company performance. Because earnings altered through creative accounting practices generally do not change operating cash flows, analysts can use the relationship between earnings and operating cash flow to detect suspicious accounting practices. Also, by monitoring the ratio between cash flow from operations and operating income, they can get a clearer picture of developing problems in a company.

For example, the following chart plots the ratio of operating cash flows to earnings for Xerox Corp. in the years leading up to the SEC singling it out in 2000 for aggressive revenue recognition practices on its leases.

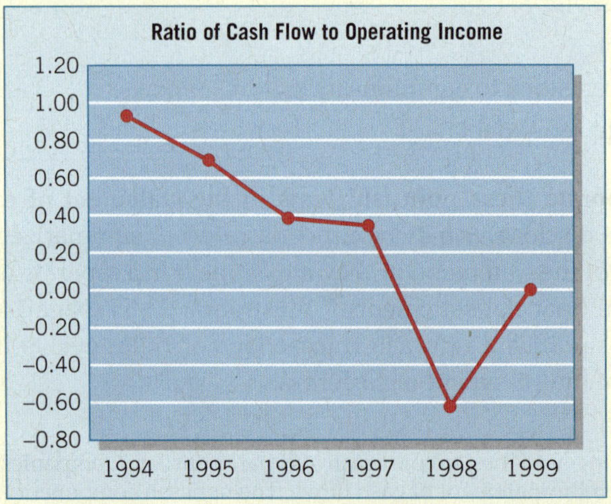

Similar to W. T. Grant in the opening story, Xerox was reporting earnings growth in the years leading up to its financial breakdown in 2000 but teetering near bankruptcy in 2001. However, Xerox's ratio of cash flow to earnings showed a declining trend and became negative well before its revenue recognition practices were revealed. The trend revealed in the graph should have given any analyst reason to investigate Xerox further. As one analyst noted, "Earnings growth that exceeds the growth in operating cash flow cannot continue for extended periods and should be investigated."

Source: Adapted from Charles Mulford and Eugene Comiskey, *The Financial Numbers Game: Detecting Creative Accounting Practices* (New York: John Wiley & Sons, 2002), Chapter 11, by permission.

USE OF A WORKSHEET

9 LEARNING OBJECTIVE
Explain the use of a worksheet in preparing a statement of cash flows.

When numerous adjustments are necessary or other complicating factors are present, companies often use **a worksheet to assemble and classify the data that will appear on the statement of cash flows**. The worksheet is merely a device that aids in the preparation of the statement. Its use is optional. Illustration 23-37 shows the skeleton format of the worksheet for preparation of the statement of cash flows using the indirect method.

ILLUSTRATION 23-37
Format of Worksheet for Preparation of Statement of Cash Flows

XYZ COMPANY.xls

Home Insert Page Layout Formulas Data Review View

P18 *fx*

	A	B	C	D	E
1					
2	**XYZ COMPANY**				
3	**Statement of Cash Flows for the Year Ended...**				
4	Balance Sheet Accounts	End of Prior Year Balances	Reconciling Items Debits	Reconciling Items Credits	End of Current Year Balances
5	Debit balance accounts	XX	XX	XX	XX
6		XX	XX	XX	XX
7	Totals	XXX			XXX
8	Credit balance accounts	XX	XX	XX	XX
9		XX	XX	XX	XX
10	Totals	XXX			XXX
11	Statement of Cash Flows Effects				
12	Operating activities				
13	Net income		XX		
14	Adjustments		XX	XX	
15	Investing activities				
16	Receipts and payments		XX	XX	
17	Financing activities				
18	Receipts and payments		XX	XX	
19	Totals		XXX	XXX	
20	Increase (decrease) in cash		(XX)	XX	
21	Totals		XXX	XXX	
22					

The following guidelines are important in using a worksheet.

1. In the balance sheet accounts section, **list accounts with debit balances separately from those with credit balances**. This means, for example, that Accumulated Depreciation is listed under credit balances and not as a contra account under debit balances. Enter the beginning and ending balances of each account in the appropriate columns. Then, enter the transactions that caused the change in the account balance during the year as reconciling items in the two middle columns.

After all reconciling items have been entered, each line pertaining to a balance sheet account should foot across. That is, the beginning balance plus or minus the reconciling item(s) must equal the ending balance. When this agreement exists for all balance sheet accounts, all changes in account balances have been reconciled.

2. The bottom portion of the worksheet consists of the operating, investing, and financing activities sections. Accordingly, it provides the information necessary to prepare the formal statement of cash flows. **Enter inflows of cash as debits in the reconciling columns, and outflows of cash as credits in the reconciling columns.** Thus, in this section, a company would enter the sale of equipment for cash at book value as a debit under inflows of cash from investing activities. Similarly, it would enter the purchase of land for cash as a credit under outflows of cash from investing activities.
3. **Do not enter in any journal or post to any account the reconciling items shown in the worksheet.** These items do not represent either adjustments or corrections of the balance sheet accounts. They are used only to facilitate the preparation of the statement of cash flows.

Preparation of the Worksheet

The preparation of a worksheet involves the following steps.

Step 1. Enter the balance sheet accounts and their beginning and ending balances in the balance sheet accounts section.

Step 2. Enter the data that explain the changes in the balance sheet accounts (other than cash) and their effects on the statement of cash flows in the reconciling columns of the worksheet.

Step 3. Enter the increase or decrease in cash on the cash line and at the bottom of the worksheet. This entry should enable the totals of the reconciling columns to be in agreement.

To illustrate the preparation and use of a worksheet and to illustrate the reporting of some of the special problems discussed in the prior section, we present a comprehensive example for Satellite Corporation. Again, the indirect method serves as the basis for the computation of net cash provided by operating activities. Illustrations 23-38 and 23-39 (page 1446) present the balance sheet, combined statement of income and retained earnings, and additional information for Satellite Corporation.

The discussion that follows provides additional explanations related to the preparation of the worksheet.

Analysis of Transactions

The following discussion explains the individual adjustments that appear on the worksheet in Illustration 23-40 (page 1450). Because cash is the basis for the analysis, Satellite reconciles the Cash account last. Because income is the first item that appears on the statement of cash flows, it is handled first.

Change in Retained Earnings

Net income for the period is $117,000. The entry for it on the worksheet is as follows.

(1)		
Operating—Net Income	117,000	
Retained Earnings		117,000

ILLUSTRATION 23-38
Comparative Balance Sheet, Satellite Corporation

SATELLITE CORPORATION.xls

SATELLITE CORPORATION
Comparative Balance Sheet–December 31, 2014 and 2013

Assets	2014	2013	Increase or (Decrease)
Cash	$ 59,000	$ 66,000	$ (7,000)
Accounts receivable (net)	104,000	51,000	53,000
Inventory	493,000	341,000	152,000
Prepaid expenses	16,500	17,000	(500)
Investment in Porter Co. (equity method)	18,500	15,000	3,500
Land	131,500	82,000	49,500
Equipment	187,000	142,000	45,000
Accumulated depreciation—equipment	(29,000)	(31,000)	(2,000)
Buildings	262,000	262,000	–
Accumulated depreciation—buildings	(74,100)	(71,000)	3,100
Trademarks	7,600	10,000	(2,400)
Total assets	$1,176,000	$884,000	
Liabilities			
Accounts payable	$ 132,000	$ 131,000	$ 1,000
Accrued liabilities	43,000	39,000	4,000
Income taxes payable	3,000	16,000	(13,000)
Notes payable (long-term)	60,000	–	60,000
Bonds payable	100,000	100,000	–
Premium on bonds payable	7,000	8,000	(1,000)
Deferred tax liability (long-term)	9,000	6,000	3,000
Total liabilities	354,000	300,000	
Stockholders' Equity			
Common stock ($1 par)	60,000	50,000	10,000
Paid-in capital in excess of par—common stock	187,000	38,000	149,000
Retained earnings	592,000	496,000	96,000
Treasury stock	(17,000)	–	17,000
Total stockholders' equity	822,000	584,000	
Total liabilities and stockholders' equity	$1,176,000	$884,000	

Satellite reports net income on the bottom section of the worksheet. This **is the starting point for preparation of the statement of cash flows (under the indirect method).**

A stock dividend and a cash dividend also affected retained earnings. The retained earnings statement reports a stock dividend of $15,000. The worksheet entry for this transaction is as follows.

(2)

Retained Earnings	15,000	
Common Stock		1,000
Paid-in Capital in Excess of Par—Common Stock		14,000

The issuance of stock dividends is not a cash operating, investing, or financing item. Therefore, **although the company enters this transaction on the worksheet for reconciling purposes, it does not report it in the statement of cash flows.**

ILLUSTRATION 23-39
Income and Retained Earnings Statements, Satellite Corporation

SATELLITE CORPORATION
COMBINED STATEMENT OF INCOME AND RETAINED EARNINGS
FOR THE YEAR ENDED DECEMBER 31, 2014

Net sales		$526,500
Other revenue		3,500
Total revenues		530,000
Expense		
Cost of goods sold		310,000
Selling and administrative expenses		47,000
Other expenses and losses		12,000
Total expenses		369,000
Income before income tax and extraordinary item		161,000
Income tax		
Current	$47,000	
Deferred	3,000	50,000
Income before extraordinary item		111,000
Gain on condemnation of land (net of $2,000 tax)		6,000
Net income		117,000
Retained earnings, January 1		496,000
Less:		
Cash dividends	6,000	
Stock dividend	15,000	21,000
Retained earnings, December 31		$592,000
Per share:		
Income before extraordinary item		$2.02
Extraordinary item		.11
Net income		$2.13

Additional Information

(a) Other revenue of $3,500 represents Satellite's equity share in the net income of Porter Co., an equity investee. Satellite owns 22% of Porter Co.

(b) An analysis of the equipment account and related accumulated depreciation indicates the following:

	Equipment Dr./(Cr.)	Accum. Dep. Dr./(Cr.)	Gain or (Loss)
Balance at end of 2013	$142,000	$(31,000)	
Purchases of equipment	53,000		
Sale of equipment	(8,000)	2,500	$(1,500)
Depreciation for the period		(11,500)	
Major repair charged to accumulated depreciation		11,000	
Balance at end of 2014	$187,000	$(29,000)	

(c) Land in the amount of $60,000 was purchased through the issuance of a long-term note; in addition, certain parcels of land costing $10,500 were condemned. The state government paid Satellite $18,500, resulting in an $8,000 gain which has a $2,000 tax effect.

(d) The change in the Accumulated Depreciation—Buildings, Trademarks, and Premium on Bonds Payable accounts resulted from depreciation and amortization entries.

(e) An analysis of the paid-in capital accounts in stockholders' equity discloses the following.

	Common Stock	Paid-In Capital in Excess of Par—Common Stock
Balance at end of 2013	$50,000	$ 38,000
Issuance of 2% stock dividend	1,000	14,000
Sale of stock for cash	9,000	135,000
Balance at end of 2014	$60,000	$187,000

(f) Interest paid (net of amount capitalized) is $9,000; income taxes paid is $62,000.

The $6,000 cash dividend paid represents a financing activity cash outflow. Satellite makes the following worksheet entry:

(3)

Retained Earnings	6,000	
Financing—Cash Dividends		6,000

The company reconciles the beginning and ending balances of retained earnings by entry of the three items above.

Accounts Receivable (Net)

The increase in accounts receivable (net) of $53,000 represents adjustments that did not result in cash inflows during 2014. As a result, the company would deduct from net income the increase of $53,000. Satellite makes the following worksheet entry.

(4)

Accounts Receivable (net)	53,000	
Operating—Increase in Accounts Receivable (net)		53,000

Inventory

The increase in inventory of $152,000 represents an operating use of cash. The incremental investment in inventory during the year reduces cash without increasing the cost of goods sold. Satellite makes the following worksheet entry.

(5)

Inventory	152,000	
Operating—Increase in Inventory		152,000

Prepaid Expense

The decrease in prepaid expenses of $500 represents a charge in the income statement for which there was no cash outflow in the current period. Satellite should add that amount back to net income through the following entry.

(6)

Operating—Decrease in Prepaid Expenses	500	
Prepaid Expenses		500

Investment in Stock

Satellite's investment in the stock of Porter Co. increased $3,500. This amount reflects Satellite's share of net income earned by Porter (its equity investee) during the current year. Although Satellite's revenue and therefore its net income increased $3,500 by recording Satellite's share of Porter Co.'s net income, no cash (dividend) was provided. Satellite makes the following worksheet entry.

(7)

Equity Investments (Porter Co.)	3,500	
Operating—Equity in Earnings of Porter Co.		3,500

Land

Satellite purchased land in the amount of $60,000 through the issuance of a long-term note payable. This transaction did not affect cash. It is a significant noncash investing/financing transaction that the company would disclose either in a separate schedule below the statement of cash flows or in the accompanying notes. Satellite makes the following entry to reconcile the worksheet.

(8)

Land	60,000	
Notes Payable		60,000

In addition to the noncash transaction involving the issuance of a note to purchase land, the Land account was decreased by the condemnation proceedings. The following worksheet entry records the receipt of $18,500 for land having a book value of $10,500.

(9)

Investing—Proceeds from Condemnation of Land	18,500	
Land		10,500
Operating—Gain on Condemnation of Land		8,000

In reconciling net income to net cash flow from operating activities, Satellite deducts from net income the extraordinary gain of $8,000. The reason is that the transaction that gave rise to the gain is an item whose cash effect is already classified as an investing cash inflow. The Land account is now reconciled.

Equipment and Accumulated Depreciation

An analysis of Equipment and Accumulated Depreciation—Equipment shows that a number of transactions have affected these accounts. The company purchased equipment in the amount of $53,000 during the year. Satellite records this transaction on the worksheet as follows.

(10)

Equipment	53,000	
Investing—Purchase of Equipment		53,000

In addition, Satellite sold at a loss of $1,500 equipment with a book value of $5,500. It records this transaction as follows.

(11)

Investing—Sale of Equipment	4,000	
Operating—Loss on Sale of Equipment	1,500	
Accumulated Depreciation—Equipment	2,500	
Equipment		8,000

The proceeds from the sale of the equipment provided cash of $4,000. In addition, the loss on the sale of the equipment has reduced net income but did not affect cash. Therefore, the company adds back to net income the amount of the loss, in order to accurately report cash provided by operating activities.

Satellite reported depreciation on the equipment at $11,500 and recorded it on the worksheet as follows.

(12)

Operating—Depreciation Expense—Equipment	11,500	
Accumulated Depreciation—Equipment		11,500

The company adds depreciation expense back to net income because that expense reduced income but did not affect cash.

Finally, the company made a major repair to the equipment. It charged this expenditure, in the amount of $11,000, to Accumulated Depreciation—Equipment. This expenditure required cash, and so Satellite makes the following worksheet entry.

(13)

Accumulated Depreciation—Equipment	11,000	
Investing—Major Repairs of Equipment		11,000

After adjusting for the foregoing items, Satellite has reconciled the balances in the Equipment and related Accumulated Depreciation—Equipment accounts.

Building Depreciation and Amortization of Trademarks

Depreciation expense on the buildings of $3,100 and amortization of trademarks of $2,400 are both expenses in the income statement that reduced net income but did not require cash outflows in the current period. Satellite makes the following worksheet entry.

(14)

Operating—Depreciation Expense—Buildings	3,100	
Operating—Amortization of Trademarks	2,400	
Accumulated Depreciation—Buildings		3,100
Trademarks		2,400

Other Noncash Charges or Credits

Analysis of the remaining accounts indicates that changes in the Accounts Payable, Accrued Liabilities, Income Taxes Payable, Premium on Bonds Payable, and Deferred Tax Liability balances resulted from charges or credits to net income that did not affect cash. The company should individually analyze each of these items and enter them in the worksheet. The following compound entry summarizes these noncash, income-related items.

(15)

Income Taxes Payable	13,000	
Premium on Bonds Payable	1,000	
Operating—Increase in Accounts Payable	1,000	
Operating—Increase in Accrued Liabilities	4,000	
Operating—Increase in Deferred Tax Liability	3,000	
Operating—Decrease in Income Taxes Payable		13,000
Operating—Amortization of Bond Premium		1,000
Accounts Payable		1,000
Accrued Liabilities		4,000
Deferred Tax Liability		3,000

Common Stock and Related Accounts

Comparison of the Common Stock balances and the Paid-in Capital in Excess of Par—Common Stock balances shows that transactions during the year affected these accounts. First, Satellite issues a stock dividend of 2 percent to stockholders. As the discussion of worksheet entry (2) indicated, no cash was provided or used by the stock dividend transaction. In addition to the shares issued via the stock dividend, Satellite sold shares of common stock at $16 per share. The company records this transaction as follows.

(16)

Financing—Sale of Common Stock	144,000	
Common Stock		9,000
Paid-in Capital in Excess of Par—Common Stock		135,000

Also, the company purchased shares of its common stock in the amount of $17,000. It records this transaction on the worksheet as follows.

(17)

Treasury Stock	17,000	
Financing—Purchase of Treasury Stock		17,000

Final Reconciling Entry

The final entry to reconcile the change in cash and to balance the worksheet is shown below. The $7,000 amount is the difference between the beginning and ending cash balance.

(18)

Decrease in Cash	7,000	
Cash		7,000

Once the company has determined that the differences between the beginning and ending balances per the worksheet columns have been accounted for, it can total the reconciling transactions columns, and they should balance. Satellite can prepare the statement of cash flows entirely from the items and amounts that appear at the bottom of the worksheet under "Statement of Cash Flows Effects," as shown in Illustration 23-40.

ILLUSTRATION 23-40
Completed Worksheet for Preparation of Statement of Cash Flows, Satellite Corporation

SATELLITE CORPORATION.xls

	A	B	C	D	E	F	G
1							
2				SATELLITE CORPORATION			
3				Worksheet for Preparation of Statement of Cash Flows			
4				for the Year Ended December 31, 2014			
5		Balance 12/31/13		Reconciling Items–2014 Dr.		Cr.	Balance 12/31/14
6	Debits						
7	Cash	$ 66,000			(18)	$ 7,000	$ 59,000
8	Accounts receivable (net)	51,000	(4)	$ 53,000			104,000
9	Inventory	341,000	(5)	152,000			493,000
10	Prepaid expenses	17,000			(6)	500	16,500
11	Investment in Porter Co. (equity method)	15,000	(7)	3,500			18,500
12	Land	82,000	(8)	60,000	(9)	10,500	131,500
13	Equipment	142,000	(10)	53,000	(11)	8,000	187,000
14	Buildings	262,000					262,000
15	Trademarks	10,000			(14)	2,400	7,600
16	Treasury stock		(17)	17,000			17,000
17	Total debits	$986,000					$1,296,100
18	Credits						
19	Accum. depr.–equipment	$ 31,000	(11)	2,500	(12)	11,500	
20			(13)	11,000			$ 29,000
21	Accum. depr.–buildings	71,000			(14)	3,100	74,100
22	Accounts payable	131,000			(15)	1,000	132,000
23	Accrued liabilities	39,000			(15)	4,000	43,000
24	Income taxes payable	16,000	(15)	13,000			3,000
25	Notes payable	-0-			(8)	60,000	60,000
26	Bonds payable	100,000					100,000
27	Premium on bonds payable	8,000	(15)	1,000			7,000
28	Deferred tax liability	6,000			(15)	3,000	9,000
29	Common stock	50,000			(2)	1,000	
30					(16)	9,000	60,000
31	Paid-in capital in excess of	38,000			(2)	14,000	
32	par—common stock				(16)	135,000	187,000
33	Retained earnings	496,000	(2)	15,000	(1)	117,000	
34			(3)	6,000			592,000
35	Total credits	$986,000					$1,296,100
36	Statement of Cash Flows Effects						
37	Operating activities						
38	Net income		(1)	117,000			
39	Increase in accounts receivable (net)				(4)	53,000	
40	Increase in inventory				(5)	152,000	
41	Decrease in prepaid expenses		(6)	500			
42	Equity in earnings of Porter Co.				(7)	3,500	
43	Gain on condemnation of land				(9)	8,000	
44	Loss on sale of equipment		(11)	1,500			
45	Depr. expense–equipment		(12)	11,500			
46	Depr. expense–buildings		(14)	3,100			
47	Amortization of trademarks		(14)	2,400			
48	Increase in accounts payable		(15)	1,000			
49	Increase in accrued liabilities		(15)	4,000			
50	Increase in deferred tax liability		(15)	3,000			
51	Decrease in income taxes payable				(15)	13,000	
52	Amortization of bond premium				(15)	1,000	
53	Investing activities						
54	Proceeds from condemnation of land		(9)	18,500			
55	Purchase of equipment				(10)	53,000	
56	Sale of equipment		(11)	4,000			
57	Major repairs of equipment				(13)	11,000	
58	Financing activities						
59	Payment of cash dividend				(3)	6,000	
60	Issuance of common stock		(16)	144,000			
61	Purchase of treasury stock				(17)	17,000	
62	Totals			697,500		704,500	
63	Decrease in cash		(18)	7,000			
64	Totals			$704,500		$704,500	
65							

Preparation of Final Statement

Illustration 23-41 presents a formal statement of cash flows prepared from the data compiled in the lower portion of the worksheet.

ILLUSTRATION 23-41
Statement of Cash Flows, Satellite Corporation

SATELLITE CORPORATION
STATEMENT OF CASH FLOWS
FOR THE YEAR ENDED DECEMBER 31, 2014

Cash flows from operating activities		
Net income		$117,000
Adjustments to reconcile net income to net cash used by operating activities:		
Depreciation expense	$ 14,600	
Amortization of trademarks	2,400	
Amortization of bond premium	(1,000)	
Equity in earnings of Porter Co.	(3,500)	
Gain on condemnation of land	(8,000)	
Loss on sale of equipment	1,500	
Increase in deferred tax liability	3,000	
Increase in accounts receivable (net)	(53,000)	
Increase in inventory	(152,000)	
Decrease in prepaid expenses	500	
Increase in accounts payable	1,000	
Increase in accrued liabilities	4,000	
Decrease in income taxes payable	(13,000)	(203,500)
Net cash used by operating activities		(86,500)
Cash flows from investing activities		
Proceeds from condemnation of land	18,500	
Purchase of equipment	(53,000)	
Sale of equipment	4,000	
Major repairs of equipment	(11,000)	
Net cash used by investing activities		(41,500)
Cash flows from financing activities		
Payment of cash dividend	(6,000)	
Issuance of common stock	144,000	
Purchase of treasury stock	(17,000)	
Net cash provided by financing activities		121,000
Net decrease in cash		(7,000)
Cash, January 1, 2014		66,000
Cash, December 31, 2014		$ 59,000

Supplemental Disclosures of Cash Flow Information:
Cash paid during the year for:

Interest (net of amount capitalized)	$ 9,000
Income taxes	$ 62,000

Supplemental Schedule of Noncash Investing and Financing Activities:
Purchase of land for $60,000 in exchange for a $60,000 long-term note.

Gateway to the Profession

Discussion of the T-Account Approach to Preparation of the Statement of Cash Flows

You will want to read **IFRS INSIGHTS** on pages 1480–1485 for discussion of IFRS related to the statement of cash flows.

SUMMARY OF LEARNING OBJECTIVES

1 Describe the purpose of the statement of cash flows. The primary purpose of the statement of cash flows is to provide information about cash receipts and cash payments of an entity during a period. A secondary objective is to report the entity's operating, investing, and financing activities during the period.

KEY TERMS

cash equivalents, *1413(n)*
direct method, *1428*
financing activities, *1413*
indirect method, *1418*
investing activities, *1413*
operating activities, *1413*

significant noncash transactions, *1441*
statement of cash flows, *1412*

2 Identify the major classifications of cash flows. Companies classify cash flows as follows. (1) *Operating activities*—transactions that result in the revenues, expenses, gains, and losses that determine net income. (2) *Investing activities*—lending money and collecting on those loans, and acquiring and disposing of investments, plant assets, and intangible assets. (3) *Financing activities*—obtaining cash from creditors and repaying loans, issuing and reacquiring capital stock, and paying cash dividends.

3 Prepare a statement of cash flows. Preparing the statement involves three major steps. (1) *Determine the change in cash.* This is the difference between the beginning and the ending cash balance shown on the comparative balance sheets. (2) *Determine the net cash flow from operating activities.* This procedure is complex; it involves analyzing not only the current year's income statement but also the comparative balance sheets and the selected transaction data. (3) *Determine cash flows from investing and financing activities.* Analyze all other changes in the balance sheet accounts to determine the effects on cash.

4 Differentiate between net income and net cash flow from operating activities. Companies must adjust net income on an accrual basis to determine net cash flow from operating activities because some expenses and losses do not cause cash outflows, and some revenues and gains do not provide cash inflows.

5 Determine net cash flows from investing and financing activities. Once a company has computed the net cash flow from operating activities, the next step is to determine whether any other changes in balance sheet accounts caused an increase or decrease in cash. Net cash flows from investing and financing activities can be determined by examining the changes in noncurrent balance sheet accounts.

6 Identify sources of information for a statement of cash flows. The information to prepare the statement usually comes from three sources. (1) *Comparative balance sheets*: Information in these statements indicates the amount of the changes in assets, liabilities, and equities during the period. (2) *Current income statement*: Information in this statement is used in determining the cash provided by operations during the period. (3) *Selected transaction data*: These data from the general ledger provide additional detailed information needed to determine how cash was provided or used during the period.

7 Contrast the direct and indirect methods of calculating net cash flow from operating activities. Under the direct approach, companies calculate the major classes of operating cash receipts and cash disbursements. Companies summarize the computations in a schedule of changes from the accrual- to the cash-basis income statement. Presentation of the direct approach of reporting net cash flow from operating activities takes the form of a condensed cash-basis income statement. The indirect method adds back to net income the noncash expenses and losses and subtracts the noncash revenues and gains.

8 Discuss special problems in preparing a statement of cash flows. These special problems are (1) adjustments to income (depreciation and amortization, postretirement benefit costs, change in deferred income taxes, equity method of accounting, losses and gains, stock options, extraordinary items); (2) accounts receivable (net); (3) other working capital changes; (4) net losses; and (5) significant noncash transactions.

9 Explain the use of a worksheet in preparing a statement of cash flows. When numerous adjustments are necessary or other complicating factors are present, companies often use a worksheet to assemble and classify the data that will appear on the statement of cash flows. The worksheet is merely a device that aids in the preparation of the statement. Its use is optional.

DEMONSTRATION PROBLEM

Data presented below are from the records of Antonio Brasileiro Company.

	December 31, 2014	December 31, 2013
Cash	$ 15,000	$ 8,000
Current assets other than cash	85,000	60,000
Long-term investments	10,000	53,000
Plant assets	335,000	215,000
	$445,000	$336,000
Accumulated depreciation	$ 20,000	$ 40,000
Current liabilities	40,000	22,000
Bonds payable	75,000	-0-
Common stock	254,000	254,000
Retained earnings	56,000	20,000
	$445,000	$336,000

Additional information:

1. In 2014, the company sold for $34,000 available-for-sale investments carried at a cost of $43,000 on December 31, 2014. The loss (not extraordinary) was incorrectly charged directly to Retained Earnings.
2. In 2014, the company sold for $8,000 plant assets that cost $50,000 and were 80% depreciated. The loss (not extraordinary) was incorrectly charged directly to Retained Earnings.
3. Net income as reported on the income statement for the year was $57,000.
4. The company paid dividends totaling $10,000.
5. Depreciation charged for the year was $20,000.

Instructions

Prepare a statement of cash flows for the year 2014 using the indirect method.

Solution

ANTONIO BRASILEIRO COMPANY
STATEMENT OF CASH FLOWS
FOR THE YEAR ENDED DECEMBER 31, 2014
INDIRECT METHOD

Cash flows from operating activities		
Net income ($57,000 – $9,000 – $2,000)		$ 46,000
Adjustments to reconcile net income to net cash provided by operating activities:		
Depreciation expense	$ 20,000	
Loss on sale of investments	9,000	
Loss on sale of plant assets	2,000	
Increase in current assets other than cash	(25,000)	
Increase in current liabilities	18,000	24,000
Net cash provided by operating activities		70,000
Cash flows from investing activities		
Sale of plant assets	8,000	
Sale of held-to-maturity investments	34,000	
Purchase of plant assets*	(170,000)	
Net cash used by investing activities		(128,000)
Cash flows from financing activities		
Issuance of bonds payable	75,000	
Payment of dividends	(10,000)	
Net cash provided by financing activities		65,000
Net increase in cash		7,000
Cash balance, January 1, 2014		8,000
Cash balance, December 31, 2014		$ 15,000

*Supporting computation (purchase of plant assets):

Plant assets, December 31, 2014	$335,000
Less: Plant assets, December 31, 2013	215,000
Net change	120,000
Plant assets sold	50,000
Plant assets purchased	$170,000

FASB CODIFICATION

FASB Codification References

[1] FASB ASC 230-10-10-2. [Predecessor literature: "The Statement of Cash Flows," *Statement of Financial Accounting Standards No. 95* (Stamford, Conn.: FASB, 1987), paras. 4 and 5.]

[2] FASB ASC 230-10-45-18 through 21. [Predecessor literature: "Statement of Cash Flows—Exemption of Certain Enterprises and Classification of Cash Flows from Certain Securities Acquired for Resale (amended)," *Statement of Financial Accounting Standards No. 102* (February 1989).]

[3] FASB ASC 230-10-45-25. [Predecessor literature: "Statement of Cash Flows," *Statement of Financial Accounting Standards No. 95* (Stamford, Conn.: FASB, 1987), paras. 107 and 111.]

[4] FASB ASC 230-10-45-31. [Predecessor literature: "The Statement of Cash Flows," *Statement of Financial Accounting Standards No. 95* (Stamford, Conn.: FASB, 1987), paras. 27 and 30.]

[5] FASB ASC 230-10-45-14. [Predecessor literature: "Share-Based Payment," *Statement of Financial Accounting Standard No. 123(R)* (Norwalk, Conn.: FASB, 2004), par. 68.]

[6] FASB ASC 320-10-45-11. [Predecessor literature: "Accounting for Certain Investments in Debt and Equity Securities," *Statement of Financial Accounting Standards No. 115* (Norwalk, Conn.: 1993), par. 118.]

[7] FASB ASC 320-10-45-11. [Predecessor literature: "Accounting for Certain Investments in Debt and Equity Securities," *Statement of Financial Accounting Standards No. 115* (Norwalk, Conn.: 1993), par. 118.]

Exercises

If your school has a subscription to the FASB Codification, go to *http://aaahq.org/ascLogin.cfm* to log in and prepare responses to the following. Provide Codification references for your responses.

CE23-1 Access the glossary ("Master Glossary") to answer the following.

(a) What are cash equivalents?
(b) What are financing activities?
(c) What are investing activities?
(d) What are operating activities?

CE23-2 Name five cash inflows that would qualify as a "financing activity."

CE23-3 How should cash flows from purchases, sales, and maturities of available-for-sale securities be classified and reported in the statement of cash flows?

CE23-4 Do companies need to disclose information about investing and financing activities that do not affect cash receipts or cash payments? If so, how should such information be disclosed?

An additional codification case can be found in the Using Your Judgment section, on page 1479.

Be sure to check the book's companion website for a Review and Analysis Exercise, with solution.

WileyPLUS **Brief Exercises, Exercises, Problems, and many more learning and assessment tools and resources are available for practice in WileyPLUS.**

QUESTIONS

1. What is the purpose of the statement of cash flows? What information does it provide?

2. Of what use is the statement of cash flows?

3. Differentiate between investing activities, financing activities, and operating activities.

4. What are the major sources of cash (inflows) in a statement of cash flows? What are the major uses (outflows) of cash?

5. Identify and explain the major steps involved in preparing the statement of cash flows.

6. Identify the following items as (1) operating, (2) investing, or (3) financing activities: purchase of land, payment of dividends, cash sales, and purchase of treasury stock.

7. Unlike the other major financial statements, the statement of cash flows is not prepared from the adjusted trial balance. From what sources does the information to prepare this statement come, and what information does each source provide?

8. Why is it necessary to convert accrual-based net income to a cash basis when preparing a statement of cash flows?

9. Differentiate between the direct method and the indirect method by discussing each method.

10. Broussard Company reported net income of $3.5 million in 2014. Depreciation for the year was $520,000; accounts receivable increased $500,000; and accounts payable increased $300,000. Compute net cash flow from operating activities using the indirect method.

11. Collinsworth Co. reported sales on an accrual basis of $100,000. If accounts receivable increased $30,000 and the allowance for doubtful accounts increased $9,000 after a write-off of $2,000, compute cash sales.

12. Your roommate is puzzled. During the last year, the company in which she is a stockholder reported a net loss of $675,000, yet its cash increased $321,000 during the same period of time. Explain to your roommate how this situation could occur.

13. The board of directors of Gifford Corp. declared cash dividends of $260,000 during the current year. If dividends payable was $85,000 at the beginning of the year and $90,000 at the end of the year, how much cash was paid in dividends during the year?

14. Explain how the amount of cash payments to suppliers is computed under the direct method.

15. The net income for Letterman Company for 2014 was $320,000. During 2014, depreciation on plant assets was $124,000, amortization of patent was $40,000, and the company incurred a loss on sale of plant assets of $21,000. Compute net cash flow from operating activities.

16. Each of the following items must be considered in preparing a statement of cash flows for Blackwell Inc. for the year ended December 31, 2014. State where each item is to be shown in the statement, if at all.

(a) Plant assets that had cost $18,000 6½ years before and were being depreciated on a straight-line basis over 10 years with no estimated scrap value were sold for $4,000.

(b) During the year, 10,000 shares of common stock with a stated value of $20 a share were issued for $41 a share.

(c) Uncollectible accounts receivable in the amount of $22,000 were written off against Allowance for Doubtful Accounts.

(d) The company sustained a net loss for the year of $50,000. Depreciation amounted to $22,000, and a gain of $9,000 was realized on the sale of available-for-sale securities for $38,000 cash.

17. Classify the following items as (1) operating, (2) investing, (3) financing, or (4) significant non-cash investing and financing activities, using the direct method.

(a) Cash payments to employees.

(b) Redemption of bonds payable.

(c) Sale of building at book value.

(d) Cash payments to suppliers.

(e) Exchange of equipment for furniture.

(f) Issuance of preferred stock.

(g) Cash received from customers.

(h) Purchase of treasury stock.

(i) Issuance of bonds for land.

(j) Payment of dividends.

(k) Purchase of equipment.

(l) Cash payments for operating expenses.

18. Stan Conner and Mark Stein were discussing the presentation format of the statement of cash flows of Bombeck Co. At the bottom of Bombeck's statement of cash flows was a separate section entitled "Noncash investing and financing activities." Give three examples of significant non-cash transactions that would be reported in this section.

19. During 2014, Simms Company redeemed $2,000,000 of bonds payable for $1,880,000 cash. Indicate how this transaction would be reported on a statement of cash flows, if at all.

20. What are some of the arguments in favor of using the indirect (reconciliation) method as opposed to the direct method for reporting a statement of cash flows?

21. Why is it desirable to use a worksheet when preparing a statement of cash flows? Is a worksheet required to prepare a statement of cash flows?

BRIEF EXERCISES

5 **BE23-1** Wainwright Corporation had the following activities in 2014.

1. Sale of land $180,000.
2. Purchase of inventory $845,000.
3. Purchase of treasury stock $72,000.
4. Purchase of equipment $415,000.
5. Issuance of common stock $320,000.
6. Purchase of available-for-sale securities $59,000.

Compute the amount Wainwright should report as net cash provided (used) by investing activities in its 2014 statement of cash flows.

5 **BE23-2** Stansfield Corporation had the following activities in 2014.

1. Payment of accounts payable $770,000.
2. Issuance of common stock $250,000.
3. Payment of dividends $350,000.
4. Collection of note receivable $100,000.
5. Issuance of bonds payable $510,000.
6. Purchase of treasury stock $46,000.

Compute the amount Stansfield should report as net cash provided (used) by financing activities in its 2014 statement of cash flows.

2 **BE23-3** Novak Corporation is preparing its 2014 statement of cash flows, using the indirect method. Presented below is a list of items that may affect the statement. Using the code below, indicate how each item will affect Novak's 2014 statement of cash flows.

Code Letter	Effect
A	Added to net income in the operating section
D	Deducted from net income in the operating section
R-I	Cash receipt in investing section
P-I	Cash payment in investing section
R-F	Cash receipt in financing section
P-F	Cash payment in financing section
N	Noncash investing and financing activity

Items

____ **(a)** Purchase of land and building.
____ **(b)** Decrease in accounts receivable.
____ **(c)** Issuance of stock.
____ **(d)** Depreciation expense.
____ **(e)** Sale of land at book value.
____ **(f)** Sale of land at a gain.
____ **(g)** Payment of dividends.
____ **(h)** Increase in accounts receivable.
____ **(i)** Purchase of available-for-sale investment.
____ **(j)** Increase in accounts payable.
____ **(k)** Decrease in accounts payable.
____ **(l)** Loan from bank by signing note.
____ **(m)** Purchase of equipment using a note.
____ **(n)** Increase in inventory.
____ **(o)** Issuance of bonds.
____ **(p)** Redemption of bonds payable.
____ **(q)** Sale of equipment at a loss.
____ **(r)** Purchase of treasury stock.

4 7 **BE23-4** Bloom Corporation had the following 2014 income statement.

Sales revenue	$200,000
Cost of goods sold	120,000
Gross profit	80,000
Operating expenses (includes depreciation of $21,000)	50,000
Net income	$ 30,000

The following accounts increased during 2014: Accounts Receivable $12,000; Inventory $11,000; Accounts Payable $13,000. Prepare the cash flows from operating activities section of Bloom's 2014 statement of cash flows using the direct method.

4 7 **BE23-5** Use the information from BE23-4 for Bloom Corporation. Prepare the cash flows from operating activities section of Bloom's 2014 statement of cash flows using the indirect method.

7 **BE23-6** At January 1, 2014, Eikenberry Inc. had accounts receivable of $72,000. At December 31, 2014, accounts receivable is $54,000. Sales revenue for 2014 total $420,000. Compute Eikenberry's 2014 cash receipts from customers.

7 **BE23-7** Moxley Corporation had January 1 and December 31 balances as follows.

	1/1/14	12/31/14
Inventory	$95,000	$113,000
Accounts payable	61,000	69,000

For 2014, cost of goods sold was $500,000. Compute Moxley's 2014 cash payments to suppliers.

3 **BE23-8** In 2014, Elbert Corporation had net cash provided by operating activities of $531,000; net cash used by investing activities of $963,000; and net cash provided by financing activities of $585,000. At January 1, 2014, the cash balance was $333,000. Compute December 31, 2014, cash.

4 7 **BE23-9** Loveless Corporation had the following 2014 income statement.

Revenues	$100,000
Expenses	60,000
	$ 40,000

In 2014, Loveless had the following activity in selected accounts.

Accounts Receivable

1/1/14	20,000		
Revenues	100,000	1,000	Write-offs
		90,000	Collections
12/31/14	29,000		

Allowance for Doubtful Accounts

		1,200	1/1/14
Write-offs	1,000	1,840	Bad debt expense
		2,040	12/31/14

Prepare Loveless's cash flows from operating activities section of the statement of cash flows using (a) the direct method and (b) the indirect method.

4 **BE23-10** Hendrickson Corporation reported net income of $50,000 in 2014. Depreciation expense was $17,000. The following working capital accounts changed.

Accounts receivable	$11,000 increase
Available-for-sale securities	16,000 increase
Inventory	7,400 increase
Nontrade note payable	15,000 decrease
Accounts payable	12,300 increase

Compute net cash provided by operating activities.

4 **BE23-11** In 2014, Wild Corporation reported a net loss of $70,000. Wild's only net income adjustments were depreciation expense $81,000, and increase in accounts receivable $8,100. Compute Wild's net cash provided (used) by operating activities.

8 **BE23-12** In 2014, Leppard Inc. issued 1,000 shares of $10 par value common stock for land worth $40,000.

(a) Prepare Leppard's journal entry to record the transaction.
(b) Indicate the effect the transaction has on cash.
(c) Indicate how the transaction is reported on the statement of cash flows.

9 **BE23-13** Indicate in general journal form how the items below would be entered in a worksheet for the preparation of the statement of cash flows.

(a) Net income is $317,000.
(b) Cash dividends declared and paid totaled $120,000.
(c) Equipment was purchased for $114,000.
(d) Equipment that originally cost $40,000 and had accumulated depreciation of $32,000 was sold for $10,000.

EXERCISES

2 **E23-1 (Classification of Transactions)** Red Hot Chili Peppers Co. had the following activity in its most recent year of operations.

(a) Purchase of equipment.
(b) Redemption of bonds payable.
(c) Sale of building.
(d) Depreciation.
(e) Exchange of equipment for furniture.
(f) Issuance of capital stock.
(g) Amortization of intangible assets.
(h) Purchase of treasury stock.
(i) Issuance of bonds for land.
(j) Payment of dividends.
(k) Increase in interest receivable on notes receivable.
(l) Pension expense exceeds amount funded.

Instructions

Classify the items as (1) operating—add to net income; (2) operating—deduct from net income; (3) investing; (4) financing; or (5) significant non-cash investing and financing activities. Use the indirect method.

2 4 **E23-2 (Statement Presentation of Transactions—Indirect Method)** Each of the following items must be considered in preparing a statement of cash flows (indirect method) for Turbulent Indigo Inc. for the year ended December 31, 2014.

(a) Plant assets that had cost $20,000 6 years before and were being depreciated on a straight-line basis over 10 years with no estimated scrap value were sold for $5,300.
(b) During the year, 10,000 shares of common stock with a stated value of $10 a share were issued for $43 a share.
(c) Uncollectible accounts receivable in the amount of $27,000 were written off against Allowance for Doubtful Accounts.
(d) The company sustained a net loss for the year of $50,000. Depreciation amounted to $22,000, and a gain of $9,000 was realized on the sale of land for $39,000 cash.
(e) A 3-month U.S. Treasury bill was purchased for $100,000. The company uses a cash and cash equivalent basis for its cash flow statement.
(f) Patent amortization for the year was $20,000.
(g) The company exchanged common stock for a 70% interest in Tabasco Co. for $900,000.
(h) During the year, treasury stock costing $47,000 was purchased.

Instructions

State where each item is to be shown in the statement of cash flows, if at all.

4 7 **E23-3 (Preparation of Operating Activities Section—Indirect Method, Periodic Inventory)** The income statement of Vince Gill Company is shown below.

XLS

VINCE GILL COMPANY
INCOME STATEMENT
FOR THE YEAR ENDED DECEMBER 31, 2014

Sales revenue		$6,900,000
Cost of goods sold		
Beginning inventory	$1,900,000	
Purchases	4,400,000	
Goods available for sale	6,300,000	
Ending inventory	1,600,000	
Cost of goods sold		4,700,000
Gross profit		2,200,000
Operating expenses		
Selling expenses	450,000	
Administrative expenses	700,000	1,150,000
Net income		$1,050,000

Additional information:

1. Accounts receivable decreased $360,000 during the year.
2. Prepaid expenses increased $170,000 during the year.
3. Accounts payable to suppliers of merchandise decreased $275,000 during the year.
4. Accrued expenses payable decreased $100,000 during the year.
5. Administrative expenses include depreciation expense of $60,000.

Instructions

Prepare the operating activities section of the statement of cash flows for the year ended December 31, 2014, for Vince Gill Company, using the indirect method.

4 7 **E23-4 (Preparation of Operating Activities Section—Direct Method)** Data for the Vince Gill Company are presented in E23-3.

XLS

Instructions

Prepare the operating activities section of the statement of cash flows using the direct method.

4 7 **E23-5 (Preparation of Operating Activities Section—Direct Method)** Krauss Company's income statement for the year ended December 31, 2014, contained the following condensed information.

Service revenue		$840,000
Operating expenses (excluding depreciation)	$624,000	
Depreciation expense	60,000	
Loss on sale of equipment	26,000	710,000
Income before income taxes		130,000
Income tax expense		40,000
Net income		$ 90,000

Krauss's balance sheet contained the following comparative data at December 31.

	2014	2013
Accounts receivable	$37,000	$54,000
Accounts payable	41,000	31,000
Income taxes payable	4,000	8,500

(Accounts payable pertains to operating expenses.)

Instructions

Prepare the operating activities section of the statement of cash flows using the direct method.

4 7 **E23-6 (Preparation of Operating Activities Section—Indirect Method)** Data for Krauss Company are presented in E23-5.

Instructions

Prepare the operating activities section of the statement of cash flows using the indirect method.

4 7 **E23-7 (Computation of Operating Activities—Direct Method)** Presented below are two independent situations.

Situation A: Annie Lennox Co. reports revenues of $200,000 and operating expenses of $110,000 in its first year of operations, 2014. Accounts receivable and accounts payable at year-end were $71,000 and $29,000, respectively. Assume that the accounts payable related to operating expenses. (Ignore income taxes.)

Instructions

Using the direct method, compute net cash provided by operating activities.

Situation B: The income statement for Blues Traveler Company shows cost of goods sold $310,000 and operating expenses (exclusive of depreciation) $230,000. The comparative balance sheet for the year shows that inventory increased $26,000, prepaid expenses decreased $8,000, accounts payable (related to merchandise) decreased $17,000, and accrued expenses payable increased $11,000.

Instructions

Compute (a) cash payments to suppliers and (b) cash payments for operating expenses.

4 7 **E23-8 (Schedule of Net Cash Flow from Operating Activities—Indirect Method)** Ballard Co. reported $145,000 of net income for 2014. The accountant, in preparing the statement of cash flows, noted the following items occurring during 2014 that might affect cash flows from operating activities.

1. Ballard purchased 100 shares of treasury stock at a cost of $20 per share. These shares were then resold at $25 per share.
2. Ballard sold 100 shares of IBM common at $200 per share. The acquisition cost of these shares was $145 per share. This investment was shown on Ballard's December 31, 2013, balance sheet as an available-for-sale security.
3. Ballard revised its estimate for bad debts. Before 2014, Ballard's bad debt expense was 1% of its net sales. In 2014, this percentage was increased to 2%. Net sales for 2014 were $500,000, and net accounts receivable decreased by $12,000 during 2014.
4. Ballard issued 500 shares of its $10 par common stock for a patent. The market price of the shares on the date of the transaction was $23 per share.
5. Depreciation expense is $39,000.
6. Ballard Co. holds 40% of the Nirvana Company's common stock as a long-term investment. Nirvana Company reported $27,000 of net income for 2014.
7. Nirvana Company paid a total of $2,000 of cash dividends to all investees in 2014.
8. Ballard declared a 10% stock dividend. One thousand shares of $10 par common stock were distributed. The market price at date of issuance was $20 per share.

Instructions

Prepare a schedule that shows the net cash flow from operating activities using the indirect method. Assume no items other than those listed above affected the computation of 2014 net cash flow from operating activities.

7 **E23-9 (SCF—Direct Method)** Los Lobos Corp. uses the direct method to prepare its statement of cash flows. Los Lobos's trial balances at December 31, 2014 and 2013, are as follows.

	December 31	
	2014	2013
Debits		
Cash	$ 35,000	$ 32,000
Accounts receivable	33,000	30,000
Inventory	31,000	47,000
Property, plant, and equipment	100,000	95,000
Unamortized bond discount	4,500	5,000
Cost of goods sold	250,000	380,000
Selling expenses	141,500	172,000
General and administrative expenses	137,000	151,300
Interest expense	4,300	2,600
Income tax expense	20,400	61,200
	$756,700	$976,100
Credits		
Allowance for doubtful accounts	$ 1,300	$ 1,100
Accumulated depreciation—plant assets	16,500	15,000
Accounts payable	25,000	15,500
Income taxes payable	21,000	29,100
Deferred tax liability	5,300	4,600
8% callable bonds payable	45,000	20,000
Common stock	50,000	40,000
Paid-in capital in excess of par	9,100	7,500
Retained earnings	44,700	64,600
Sales revenue	538,800	778,700
	$756,700	$976,100

Additional information:

1. Los Lobos purchased $5,000 in equipment during 2014.
2. Los Lobos allocated one-third of its depreciation expense to selling expenses and the remainder to general and administrative expenses.
3. Bad debt expense for 2014 was $5,000, and write-offs of uncollectible accounts totaled $4,800.

Instructions

Determine what amounts Los Lobos should report in its statement of cash flows for the year ended December 31, 2014, for the following items.

(a) Cash collected from customers.
(b) Cash paid to suppliers.
(c) Cash paid for interest.
(d) Cash paid for income taxes.
(e) Cash paid for selling expenses.

2 8 **E23-10 (Classification of Transactions)** Following are selected balance sheet accounts of Allman Bros. Corp. at December 31, 2014 and 2013, and the increases or decreases in each account from 2013 to 2014. Also presented is selected income statement information for the year ended December 31, 2014, and additional information.

Selected balance sheet accounts	2014	2013	Increase (Decrease)
Assets			
Accounts receivable	$ 34,000	$ 24,000	$ 10,000
Property, plant, and equipment	277,000	247,000	30,000
Accumulated depreciation—plant assets	(178,000)	(167,000)	(11,000)
Liabilities and stockholders' equity			
Bonds payable	$ 49,000	$ 46,000	$ 3,000
Dividends payable	8,000	5,000	3,000
Common stock, $1 par	22,000	19,000	3,000
Additional paid-in capital	9,000	3,000	6,000
Retained earnings	104,000	91,000	13,000

Selected income statement information for the year ended December 31, 2014	
Sales revenue	$ 155,000
Depreciation	33,000
Gain on sale of equipment	14,500
Net income	31,000

Additional information:

1. During 2014, equipment costing $45,000 was sold for cash.
2. Accounts receivable relate to sales of merchandise.
3. During 2014, $20,000 of bonds payable were issued in exchange for property, plant, and equipment. There was no amortization of bond discount or premium.

Instructions

Determine the category (operating, investing, or financing) and the amount that should be reported in the statement of cash flows for the following items.

(a) Payments for purchase of property, plant, and equipment.
(b) Proceeds from the sale of equipment.
(c) Cash dividends paid.
(d) Redemption of bonds payable.

3 **E23-11 (SCF—Indirect Method)** Condensed financial data of Pat Metheny Company for 2014 and 2013 are presented below.

PAT METHENY COMPANY
COMPARATIVE BALANCE SHEET
AS OF DECEMBER 31, 2014 AND 2013

	2014	2013
Cash	$1,800	$1,150
Receivables	1,750	1,300
Inventory	1,600	1,900
Plant assets	1,900	1,700
Accumulated depreciation	(1,200)	(1,170)
Long-term investments (held-to-maturity)	1,300	1,420
	$7,150	$6,300
Accounts payable	$1,200	$ 900
Accrued liabilities	200	250
Bonds payable	1,400	1,550
Capital stock	1,900	1,700
Retained earnings	2,450	1,900
	$7,150	$6,300

PAT METHENY COMPANY
INCOME STATEMENT
FOR THE YEAR ENDED DECEMBER 31, 2014

Sales revenue	$6,900
Cost of goods sold	4,700
Gross margin	2,200
Selling and administrative expense	930
Income from operations	1,270
Other revenues and gains	
Gain on sale of investments	80
Income before tax	1,350
Income tax expense	540
Net income	810
Cash dividends	260
Income retained in business	$ 550

Additional information:

During the year, $70 of common stock was issued in exchange for plant assets. No plant assets were sold in 2014.

Instructions

Prepare a statement of cash flows using the indirect method.

3 **E23-12 (SCF—Direct Method)** Data for Pat Metheny Company are presented in E23-11.

Instructions

Prepare a statement of cash flows using the direct method. (Do not prepare a reconciliation schedule.)

3 **E23-13 (SCF—Direct Method)** Brecker Inc., a greeting card company, had the following statements prepared as of December 31, 2014.

BRECKER INC.
COMPARATIVE BALANCE SHEET
AS OF DECEMBER 31, 2014 AND 2013

	12/31/14	12/31/13
Cash	$ 6,000	$ 7,000
Accounts receivable	62,000	51,000
Short-term investments (available-for-sale)	35,000	18,000
Inventory	40,000	60,000
Prepaid rent	5,000	4,000
Equipment	154,000	130,000
Accumulated depreciation—equipment	(35,000)	(25,000)
Copyrights	46,000	50,000
Total assets	$313,000	$295,000
Accounts payable	$ 46,000	$ 40,000
Income taxes payable	4,000	6,000
Salaries and wages payable	8,000	4,000
Short-term loans payable	8,000	10,000
Long-term loans payable	60,000	69,000
Common stock, $10 par	100,000	100,000
Contributed capital, common stock	30,000	30,000
Retained earnings	57,000	36,000
Total liabilities and stockholders' equity	$313,000	$295,000

BRECKER INC.
INCOME STATEMENT
FOR THE YEAR ENDING DECEMBER 31, 2014

Sales revenue		$338,150
Cost of goods sold		175,000
Gross profit		163,150
Operating expenses		120,000
Operating income		43,150
Interest expense	$11,400	
Gain on sale of equipment	2,000	9,400
Income before tax		33,750
Income tax expense		6,750
Net income		$ 27,000

Additional information:

1. Dividends in the amount of $6,000 were declared and paid during 2014.
2. Depreciation expense and amortization expense are included in operating expenses.
3. No unrealized gains or losses have occurred on the investments during the year.
4. Equipment that had a cost of $20,000 and was 70% depreciated was sold during 2014.

Instructions

Prepare a statement of cash flows using the direct method. (Do not prepare a reconciliation schedule.)

3 **E23-14 (SCF—Indirect Method)** Data for Brecker Inc. are presented in E23-13.

Instructions

Prepare a statement of cash flows using the indirect method.

3 **E23-15 (SCF—Indirect Method)** Presented below are data taken from the records of Alee Company.

	December 31, 2014	December 31, 2013
Cash	$ 15,000	$ 8,000
Current assets other than cash	85,000	60,000
Long-term investments	10,000	53,000
Plant assets	335,000	215,000
	$445,000	$336,000
Accumulated depreciation	$ 20,000	$ 40,000
Current liabilities	40,000	22,000
Bonds payable	75,000	–0–
Capital stock	254,000	254,000
Retained earnings	56,000	20,000
	$445,000	$336,000

Additional information:

1. Held-to-maturity securities carried at a cost of $43,000 on December 31, 2013, were sold in 2014 for $34,000. The loss (not extraordinary) was incorrectly charged directly to Retained Earnings.
2. Plant assets that cost $50,000 and were 80% depreciated were sold during 2014 for $8,000. The loss (not extraordinary) was incorrectly charged directly to Retained Earnings.
3. Net income as reported on the income statement for the year was $57,000.
4. Dividends paid amounted to $10,000.
5. Depreciation charged for the year was $20,000.

Instructions

Prepare a statement of cash flows for the year 2014 using the indirect method.

2 4 5 **E23-16 (Cash Provided by Operating, Investing, and Financing Activities)** The balance sheet data of Brown Company at the end of 2014 and 2013 follow.

	2014	2013
Cash	$ 30,000	$ 35,000
Accounts receivable (net)	55,000	45,000
Inventory	65,000	45,000
Prepaid expenses	15,000	25,000
Equipment	90,000	75,000
Accumulated depreciation—equipment	(18,000)	(8,000)
Land	70,000	40,000
	$307,000	$257,000
Accounts payable	$ 65,000	$ 52,000
Accrued expenses	15,000	18,000
Notes payable—bank, long-term	–0–	23,000
Bonds payable	30,000	–0–
Common stock, $10 par	189,000	159,000
Retained earnings	8,000	5,000
	$307,000	$257,000

Land was acquired for $30,000 in exchange for common stock, par $30,000, during the year; all equipment purchased was for cash. Equipment costing $10,000 was sold for $3,000; book value of the equipment was $6,000. Cash dividends of $10,000 were declared and paid during the year.

Instructions

Compute net cash provided (used) by:

(a) Operating activities.
(b) Investing activities.
(c) Financing activities.

3 **E23-17 (SCF—Indirect Method and Balance Sheet)** Jobim Inc. had the following condensed balance sheet at the end of operations for 2013.

JOBIM INC.
BALANCE SHEET
DECEMBER 31, 2013

Cash	$ 8,500	Current liabilities	$ 15,000
Current assets other than cash	29,000	Long-term notes payable	25,500
Investments	20,000	Bonds payable	25,000
Plant assets (net)	67,500	Capital stock	75,000
Land	40,000	Retained earnings	24,500
	$165,000		$165,000

During 2014, the following occurred.

1. A tract of land was purchased for $9,000.
2. Bonds payable in the amount of $15,000 were redeemed at par.
3. An additional $10,000 in capital stock was issued at par.
4. Dividends totaling $9,375 were paid to stockholders.
5. Net income was $35,250 after allowing depreciation of $13,500.
6. Land was purchased through the issuance of $22,500 in bonds.
7. Jobim Inc. sold part of its investment portfolio for $12,875. This transaction resulted in a gain of $2,000 for the company. The company classifies the investments as available-for-sale.
8. Both current assets (other than cash) and current liabilities remained at the same amount.

Instructions

(a) Prepare a statement of cash flows for 2014 using the indirect method.
(b) Prepare the condensed balance sheet for Jobim Inc. as it would appear at December 31, 2014.

3 8 **E23-18 (Partial SCF—Indirect Method)** The accounts below appear in the ledger of Anita Baker Company.

	Retained Earnings	Dr.	Cr.	Bal.
Jan. 1, 2014	Credit Balance			$ 42,000
Aug. 15	Dividends (cash)	$15,000		27,000
Dec. 31	Net Income for 2014		$40,000	67,000

	Equipment	Dr.	Cr.	Bal.
Jan. 1, 2014	Debit Balance			$140,000
Aug. 3	Purchase of Equipment	$62,000		202,000
Sept. 10	Cost of Equipment Constructed	48,000		250,000
Nov. 15	Equipment Sold		$56,000	194,000

	Accumulated Depreciation—Equipment	Dr.	Cr.	Bal.
Jan. 1, 2014	Credit Balance			$ 84,000
Apr. 8	Extraordinary Repairs	$21,000		63,000
Nov. 15	Accum. Depreciation on Equipment Sold	25,200		37,800
Dec. 31	Depreciation for 2014		$16,800	54,600

Instructions

From the postings in the accounts above, indicate how the information is reported on a statement of cash flows by preparing a partial statement of cash flows using the indirect method. The loss on sale of equipment (November 15) was $5,800.

9 **E23-19 (Worksheet Analysis of Selected Accounts)** Data for Anita Baker Company are presented in E23-18.

Instructions

Prepare entries in journal form for all adjustments that should be made on a worksheet for a statement of cash flows.

9 **E23-20 (Worksheet Analysis of Selected Transactions)** The transactions below took place during the year 2014.

1. Convertible bonds payable with a par value of $300,000 were exchanged for unissued common stock with a par value of $300,000. The market price of both types of securities was par.
2. The net income for the year was $410,000.
3. Depreciation expense for the building was $90,000.
4. Some old office equipment was traded in on the purchase of some dissimilar office equipment, and the following entry was made.

Equipment	50,000	
Accum. Depreciation—Equipment	30,000	
Equipment		40,000
Cash		34,000
Gain on Disposal of Plant Assets		6,000

The Gain on Disposal of Plant Assets was credited to current operations as ordinary income.

5. Dividends in the amount of $123,000 were declared. They are payable in January of next year.

Instructions

Show by journal entries the adjustments that would be made on a worksheet for a statement of cash flows.

9 **E23-21 (Worksheet Preparation)** Below is the comparative balance sheet for Stevie Wonder Corporation.

	Dec. 31, 2014	Dec. 31, 2013
Cash	$ 16,500	$ 21,000
Short-term investments	25,000	19,000
Accounts receivable	43,000	45,000
Allowance for doubtful accounts	(1,800)	(2,000)
Prepaid expenses	4,200	2,500
Inventory	81,500	65,000
Land	50,000	50,000
Buildings	125,000	73,500
Accumulated depreciation—buildings	(30,000)	(23,000)
Equipment	53,000	46,000
Accumulated depreciation—equipment	(19,000)	(15,500)
Delivery equipment	39,000	39,000
Accumulated depreciation—delivery equipment	(22,000)	(20,500)
Patents	15,000	–0–
	$379,400	$300,000

	Dec. 31, 2014	Dec. 31, 2013
Accounts payable	$ 26,000	$ 16,000
Short-term notes payable (trade)	4,000	6,000
Accrued payables	3,000	4,600
Mortgage payable	73,000	53,400
Bonds payable	50,000	62,500
Capital stock	140,000	102,000
Paid-in capital in excess of par	10,000	4,000
Retained earnings	73,400	51,500
	$379,400	$300,000

Dividends in the amount of $15,000 were declared and paid in 2014.

Instructions

From this information, prepare a worksheet for a statement of cash flows. Make reasonable assumptions as appropriate. The short-term investments are considered available-for-sale and no unrealized gains or losses have occurred on these securities.

EXERCISES SET B

See the book's companion website, at **www.wiley.com/college/kieso**, for an additional set of exercises.

PROBLEMS

3 4 8 **P23-1 (SCF—Indirect Method)** The following are Sullivan Corp.'s comparative balance sheet accounts at December 31, 2014 and 2013, with a column showing the increase (decrease) from 2013 to 2014.

Comparative Balance Sheets

	2014	2013	Increase (Decrease)
Cash	$ 815,000	$ 700,000	$115,000
Accounts receivable	1,128,000	1,168,000	(40,000)
Inventory	1,850,000	1,715,000	135,000
Property, plant, and equipment	3,307,000	2,967,000	340,000
Accumulated depreciation	(1,165,000)	(1,040,000)	(125,000)
Investment in Myers Co.	310,000	275,000	35,000
Loan receivable	250,000	—	250,000
Total assets	$6,495,000	$5,785,000	$710,000
Accounts payable	$1,015,000	$ 955,000	$ 60,000
Income taxes payable	30,000	50,000	(20,000)
Dividends payable	80,000	100,000	(20,000)
Lease liability	400,000	—	400,000
Common stock, $1 par	500,000	500,000	—
Paid-in capital in excess of par—common stock	1,500,000	1,500,000	—
Retained earnings	2,970,000	2,680,000	290,000
Total liabilities and stockholders' equity	$6,495,000	$5,785,000	$710,000

Additional information:

1. On December 31, 2013, Sullivan acquired 25% of Myers Co.'s common stock for $275,000. On that date, the carrying value of Myers's assets and liabilities, which approximated their fair values, was $1,100,000. Myers reported income of $140,000 for the year ended December 31, 2014. No dividend was paid on Myers's common stock during the year.
2. During 2014, Sullivan loaned $300,000 to TLC Co., an unrelated company. TLC made the first semi-annual principal repayment of $50,000, plus interest at 10%, on December 31, 2014.
3. On January 2, 2014, Sullivan sold equipment costing $60,000, with a carrying amount of $38,000, for $40,000 cash.
4. On December 31, 2014, Sullivan entered into a capital lease for an office building. The present value of the annual rental payments is $400,000, which equals the fair value of the building. Sullivan made the first rental payment of $60,000 when due on January 2, 2015.
5. Net income for 2014 was $370,000.
6. Sullivan declared and paid the following cash dividends for 2014 and 2013.

	2014	2013
Declared	December 15, 2014	December 15, 2013
Paid	February 28, 2015	February 28, 2014
Amount	$80,000	$100,000

Instructions

Prepare a statement of cash flows for Sullivan Corp. for the year ended December 31, 2014, using the indirect method.

(AICPA adapted)

3 6 8 **P23-2 (SCF—Indirect Method)** The comparative balance sheets for Hinckley Corporation show the following information.

	December 31	
	2014	2013
Cash	$ 33,500	$13,000
Accounts receivable	12,250	10,000
Inventory	12,000	9,000
Investments	–0–	3,000
Buildings	–0–	29,750
Equipment	45,000	20,000
Patents	5,000	6,250
	$107,750	$91,000
Allowance for doubtful accounts	$ 3,000	$ 4,500
Accumulated depreciation—equipment	2,000	4,500
Accumulated depreciation—building	–0–	6,000
Accounts payable	5,000	3,000
Dividends payable	–0–	5,000
Notes payable, short-term (nontrade)	3,000	4,000
Long-term notes payable	31,000	25,000
Common stock	43,000	33,000
Retained earnings	20,750	6,000
	$107,750	$91,000

Additional data related to 2014 are as follows.

1. Equipment that had cost $11,000 and was 40% depreciated at time of disposal was sold for $2,500.
2. $10,000 of the long-term note payable was paid by issuing common stock.
3. Cash dividends paid were $5,000.
4. On January 1, 2014, the building was completely destroyed by a flood. Insurance proceeds on the building were $30,000 (net of $2,000 taxes).
5. Investments (available-for-sale) were sold at $1,700 above their cost. The company has made similar sales and investments in the past.
6. Cash was paid for the acquisition of equipment.
7. A long-term note for $16,000 was issued for the acquisition of equipment.
8. Interest of $2,000 and income taxes of $6,500 were paid in cash.

Instructions

Prepare a statement of cash flows using the indirect method. Flood damage is unusual and infrequent in that part of the country.

3 **P23-3 (SCF—Direct Method)** Mortonson Company has not yet prepared a formal statement of cash flows for the 2014 fiscal year. Comparative balance sheets as of December 31, 2013 and 2014, and a statement of income and retained earnings for the year ended December 31, 2014, are presented as follows.

MORTONSON COMPANY
STATEMENT OF INCOME AND RETAINED EARNINGS
FOR THE YEAR ENDED DECEMBER 31, 2014
($000 OMITTED)

Sales revenue		$3,800
Expenses		
Cost of goods sold	$1,200	
Salaries and benefits	725	
Heat, light, and power	75	
Depreciation	80	
Property taxes	19	
Patent amortization	25	
Miscellaneous expenses	10	
Interest	30	2,164

MORTONSON COMPANY
STATEMENT OF INCOME AND RETAINED EARNINGS
FOR THE YEAR ENDED DECEMBER 31, 2014
(CONTINUED)

Income before income taxes	1,636
Income taxes	818
Net income	818
Retained earnings—Jan. 1, 2014	310
	1,128
Stock dividend declared and issued	600
Retained earnings—Dec. 31, 2014	$ 528

MORTONSON COMPANY
COMPARATIVE BALANCE SHEETS
AS OF DECEMBER 31
($000 OMITTED)

Assets	2014	2013
Current assets		
Cash	$ 333	$ 100
U.S. Treasury notes (available-for-sale)	10	50
Accounts receivable	780	500
Inventory	720	560
Total current assets	1,843	1,210
Long-term assets		
Land	150	70
Buildings and equipment	910	600
Accumulated depreciation—buildings and equipment	(200)	(120)
Patents (less amortization)	105	130
Total long-term assets	965	680
Total assets	$2,808	$1,890
Liabilities and Stockholders' Equity		
Current liabilities		
Accounts payable	$ 420	$ 330
Income taxes payable	40	30
Notes payable	320	320
Total current liabilities	780	680
Long-term notes payable—due 2016	200	200
Total liabilities	980	880
Stockholders' equity		
Common stock	1,300	700
Retained earnings	528	310
Total stockholders' equity	1,828	1,010
Total liabilities and stockholders' equity	$2,808	$1,890

Instructions

Prepare a statement of cash flows using the direct method. Changes in accounts receivable and accounts payable relate to sales and cost of goods sold. Do not prepare a reconciliation schedule.

(CMA adapted)

3 6 8 **P23-4 (SCF—Direct Method)** Michaels Company had available at the end of 2014 the information shown on the next page.

MICHAELS COMPANY
COMPARATIVE BALANCE SHEETS
AS OF DECEMBER 31, 2014 AND 2013

	2014	2013
Cash	$ 10,000	$ 4,000
Accounts receivable	20,500	12,950
Short-term investments	22,000	30,000
Inventory	42,000	35,000
Prepaid rent	3,000	12,000
Prepaid insurance	2,100	900
Supplies	1,000	750
Land	125,000	175,000
Buildings	350,000	350,000
Accumulated depreciation—buildings	(105,000)	(87,500)
Equipment	525,000	400,000
Accumulated depreciation—equipment	(130,000)	(112,000)
Patents	45,000	50,000
Total assets	$910,600	$871,100
Accounts payable	$ 22,000	$ 32,000
Income taxes payable	5,000	4,000
Salaries and wages payable	5,000	3,000
Short-term notes payable	10,000	10,000
Long-term notes payable	60,000	70,000
Bonds payable	400,000	400,000
Premium on bonds payable	20,303	25,853
Common stock	240,000	220,000
Paid-in capital in excess of par—common stock	25,000	17,500
Retained earnings	123,297	88,747
Total liabilities and stockholders' equity	$910,600	$871,100

MICHAELS COMPANY
INCOME STATEMENT AND DIVIDEND INFORMATION
FOR THE YEAR ENDED DECEMBER 31, 2014

Sales revenue		$1,160,000
Cost of goods sold		748,000
Gross margin		412,000
Operating expenses		
Selling expenses	$ 79,200	
Administrative expenses	156,700	
Depreciation/Amortization expense	40,500	
Total operating expenses		276,400
Income from operations		135,600
Other revenues/expenses		
Gain on sale of land	8,000	
Gain on sale of short-term investment	4,000	
Dividend revenue	2,400	
Interest expense	(51,750)	(37,350)
Income before taxes		98,250
Income tax expense		39,400
Net income		58,850
Dividends to common stockholders		(24,300)
To retained earnings		$ 34,550

Instructions

Prepare a statement of cash flows for Michaels Company using the direct method accompanied by a reconciliation schedule. Assume the short-term investments are classified as available-for-sale.

3 6 8 **P23-5 (SCF—Indirect Method)** You have completed the field work in connection with your audit of Alexander Corporation for the year ended December 31, 2014. The balance sheet accounts at the beginning and end of the year are shown below.

	Dec. 31, 2014	Dec. 31, 2013	Increase or (Decrease)
Cash	$ 277,900	$ 298,000	($20,100)
Accounts receivable	469,424	353,000	116,424
Inventory	741,700	610,000	131,700
Prepaid expenses	12,000	8,000	4,000
Investment in subsidiary	110,500	–0–	110,500
Cash surrender value of life insurance	2,304	1,800	504
Machinery	207,000	190,000	17,000
Buildings	535,200	407,900	127,300
Land	52,500	52,500	–0–
Patents	69,000	64,000	5,000
Copyrights	40,000	50,000	(10,000)
Bond discount and issue costs	4,502	–0–	4,502
	$2,522,030	$2,035,200	$486,830
Income taxes payable	$ 90,250	$ 79,600	$ 10,650
Accounts payable	299,280	280,000	19,280
Dividends payable	70,000	–0–	70,000
Bonds payable—8%	125,000	–0–	125,000
Bonds payable—12%	–0–	100,000	(100,000)
Allowance for doubtful accounts	35,300	40,000	(4,700)
Accumulated depreciation—buildings	424,000	400,000	24,000
Accumulated depreciation—machinery	173,000	130,000	43,000
Premium on bonds payable	–0–	2,400	(2,400)
Common stock—no par	1,176,200	1,453,200	(277,000)
Paid-in capital in excess of par—common stock	109,000	–0–	109,000
Retained earnings—unappropriated	20,000	(450,000)	470,000
	$2,522,030	$2,035,200	$486,830

STATEMENT OF RETAINED EARNINGS
FOR THE YEAR ENDED DECEMBER 31, 2014

January 1, 2014	Balance (deficit)	$(450,000)
March 31, 2014	Net income for first quarter of 2014	25,000
April 1, 2014	Transfer from paid-in capital	425,000
	Balance	–0–
December 31, 2014	Net income for last three quarters of 2014	90,000
	Dividend declared—payable January 21, 2015	(70,000)
	Balance	$ 20,000

Your working papers from the audit contain the following information:

1. On April 1, 2014, the existing deficit was written off against paid-in capital created by reducing the stated value of the no-par stock.
2. On November 1, 2014, 29,600 shares of no-par stock were sold for $257,000. The board of directors voted to regard $5 per share as stated capital.
3. A patent was purchased for $15,000.
4. During the year, machinery that had a cost basis of $16,400 and on which there was accumulated depreciation of $5,200 was sold for $9,000. No other plant assets were sold during the year.
5. The 12%, 20-year bonds were dated and issued on January 2, 2002. Interest was payable on June 30 and December 31. They were sold originally at 106. These bonds were redeemed at 100.9 plus accrued interest on March 31, 2014.
6. The 8%, 40-year bonds were dated January 1, 2014, and were sold on March 31 at 97 plus accrued interest. Interest is payable semiannually on June 30 and December 31. Expense of issuance was $839.
7. Alexander Corporation acquired 70% control in Crimson Company on January 2, 2014, for $100,000. The income statement of Crimson Company for 2014 shows a net income of $15,000.
8. Extraordinary repairs to buildings of $7,200 were charged to Accumulated Depreciation—Buildings.
9. Interest paid in 2014 was $10,500 and income taxes paid were $34,000.

Instructions

From the information given, prepare a statement of cash flows using the indirect method. A worksheet is not necessary, but the principal computations should be supported by schedules or general ledger accounts. The company uses straight-line amortization for bond interest.

3 4 7 8 **P23-6 (SCF—Indirect Method, and Net Cash Flow from Operating Activities, Direct Method)** Comparative balance sheet accounts of Marcus Inc. are presented below.

MARCUS INC.
COMPARATIVE BALANCE SHEET ACCOUNTS
AS OF DECEMBER 31, 2014 AND 2013

	December 31	
Debit Accounts	2014	2013
Cash	$ 42,000	$ 33,750
Accounts Receivable	70,500	60,000
Inventory	30,000	24,000
Investments (available-for-sale)	22,250	38,500
Machinery	30,000	18,750
Buildings	67,500	56,250
Land	7,500	7,500
	$269,750	$238,750
Credit Accounts		
Allowance for Doubtful Accounts	$ 2,250	$ 1,500
Accumulated Depreciation—Machinery	5,625	2,250
Accumulated Depreciation—Buildings	13,500	9,000
Accounts Payable	35,000	24,750
Accrued Payables	3,375	2,625
Long-Term Notes Payable	21,000	31,000
Common Stock, no-par	150,000	125,000
Retained Earnings	39,000	42,625
	$269,750	$238,750

Additional data (ignoring taxes):

1. Net income for the year was $42,500.
2. Cash dividends declared and paid during the year were $21,125.
3. A 20% stock dividend was declared during the year. $25,000 of retained earnings was capitalized.
4. Investments that cost $25,000 were sold during the year for $28,750.
5. Machinery that cost $3,750, on which $750 of depreciation had accumulated, was sold for $2,200.

Marcus's 2014 income statement follows (ignoring taxes).

Sales revenue		$540,000
Less: Cost of goods sold		380,000
Gross margin		160,000
Less: Operating expenses (includes $8,625 depreciation and $5,400 bad debts)		120,450
Income from operations		39,550
Other: Gain on sale of investments	$3,750	
Loss on sale of machinery	(800)	2,950
Net income		$ 42,500

Instructions

(a) Compute net cash flow from operating activities using the direct method.
(b) Prepare a statement of cash flows using the indirect method.

3 6 7 8 **P23-7 (SCF—Direct and Indirect Methods from Comparative Financial Statements)** Chapman Company, a major retailer of bicycles and accessories, operates several stores and is a publicly traded company. The comparative balance sheet and income statement for Chapman as of May 31, 2014, are as follows. The company is preparing its statement of cash flows.

CHAPMAN COMPANY
COMPARATIVE BALANCE SHEET
AS OF MAY 31

	2014	2013
Current assets		
Cash	$ 28,250	$ 20,000
Accounts receivable	75,000	58,000
Inventory	220,000	250,000
Prepaid expenses	9,000	7,000
Total current assets	332,250	335,000
Plant assets		
Plant assets	600,000	502,000
Less: Accumulated depreciation—plant assets	150,000	125,000
Net plant assets	450,000	377,000
Total assets	$782,250	$712,000
Current liabilities		
Accounts payable	$123,000	$115,000
Salaries and wages payable	47,250	72,000
Interest payable	27,000	25,000
Total current liabilities	197,250	212,000
Long-term debt		
Bonds payable	70,000	100,000
Total liabilities	267,250	312,000
Stockholders' equity		
Common stock, $10 par	370,000	280,000
Retained earnings	145,000	120,000
Total stockholders' equity	515,000	400,000
Total liabilities and stockholders' equity	$782,250	$712,000

CHAPMAN COMPANY
INCOME STATEMENT
FOR THE YEAR ENDED MAY 31, 2014

Sales revenue	$1,255,250
Cost of goods sold	722,000
Gross profit	533,250
Expenses	
Salaries and wages expense	252,100
Interest expense	75,000
Depreciation expense	25,000
Other expenses	8,150
Total expenses	360,250
Operating income	173,000
Income tax expense	43,000
Net income	$ 130,000

The following is additional information concerning Chapman's transactions during the year ended May 31, 2014.

1. All sales during the year were made on account.
2. All merchandise was purchased on account, comprising the total accounts payable account.
3. Plant assets costing $98,000 were purchased by paying $28,000 in cash and issuing 7,000 shares of stock.
4. The "other expenses" are related to prepaid items.
5. All income taxes incurred during the year were paid during the year.
6. In order to supplement its cash, Chapman issued 2,000 shares of common stock at par value.
7. Cash dividends of $105,000 were declared and paid at the end of the fiscal year.

Instructions

(a) Compare and contrast the direct method and the indirect method for reporting cash flows from operating activities.

(b) Prepare a statement of cash flows for Chapman Company for the year ended May 31, 2014, using the direct method. Be sure to support the statement with appropriate calculations. (A reconciliation of net income to net cash provided is not required.)

(c) Using the indirect method, calculate only the net cash flow from operating activities for Chapman Company for the year ended May 31, 2014.

3 6 8 **P23-8 (SCF—Direct and Indirect Methods)** Comparative balance sheet accounts of Sharpe Company are presented below.

SHARPE COMPANY
COMPARATIVE BALANCE SHEET ACCOUNTS
AS OF DECEMBER 31

Debit Balances	2014	2013
Cash	$ 70,000	$ 51,000
Accounts Receivable	155,000	130,000
Inventory	75,000	61,000
Investments (available-for-sale)	55,000	85,000
Equipment	70,000	48,000
Buildings	145,000	145,000
Land	40,000	25,000
Totals	$610,000	$545,000
Credit Balances		
Allowance for Doubtful Accounts	$ 10,000	$ 8,000
Accumulated Depreciation—Equipment	21,000	14,000
Accumulated Depreciation—Buildings	37,000	28,000
Accounts Payable	66,000	60,000
Income Taxes Payable	12,000	10,000
Long-Term Notes Payable	62,000	70,000
Common Stock	310,000	260,000
Retained Earnings	92,000	95,000
Totals	$610,000	$545,000

Additional data:

1. Equipment that cost $10,000 and was 60% depreciated was sold in 2014.
2. Cash dividends were declared and paid during the year.
3. Common stock was issued in exchange for land.
4. Investments that cost $35,000 were sold during the year.
5. There were no write-offs of uncollectible accounts during the year.

Sharpe's 2014 income statement is as follows.

Sales revenue		$950,000
Less: Cost of goods sold		600,000
Gross profit		350,000
Less: Operating expenses (includes depreciation expense and bad debt expense)		250,000
Income from operations		100,000
Other revenues and expenses		
Gain on sale of investments	$15,000	
Loss on sale of equipment	(3,000)	12,000
Income before taxes		112,000
Income taxes		45,000
Net income		$ 67,000

Instructions

(a) Compute net cash provided by operating activities under the direct method.

(b) Prepare a statement of cash flows using the indirect method.

3 6 8 **P23-9 (Indirect SCF)** Dingel Corporation has contracted with you to prepare a statement of cash flows. The controller has provided the following information.

	December 31	
	2014	2013
Cash	$ 38,500	$13,000
Accounts receivable	12,250	10,000
Inventory	12,000	10,000
Investments	–0–	3,000
Buildings	–0–	29,750
Equipment	40,000	20,000
Copyrights	5,000	5,250
Totals	$107,750	$91,000
Allowance for doubtful accounts	$ 3,000	$ 4,500
Accumulated depreciation—equipment	2,000	4,500
Accumulated depreciation—buildings	–0–	6,000
Accounts payable	5,000	4,000
Dividends payable	–0–	5,000
Notes payable, short-term (nontrade)	3,000	4,000
Long-term notes payable	36,000	25,000
Common stock	38,000	33,000
Retained earnings	20,750	5,000
	$107,750	$91,000

Additional data related to 2014 are as follows.

1. Equipment that had cost $11,000 and was 30% depreciated at time of disposal was sold for $2,500.
2. $5,000 of the long-term note payable was paid by issuing common stock.
3. Cash dividends paid were $5,000.
4. On January 1, 2014, the building was completely destroyed by a flood. Insurance proceeds on the building were $33,000 (net of $4,000 taxes).
5. Investments (available-for-sale) were sold at $1,500 above their cost. The company has made similar sales and investments in the past.
6. Cash and long-term note for $16,000 were given for the acquisition of equipment.
7. Interest of $2,000 and income taxes of $5,000 were paid in cash.

Instructions

(a) Use the indirect method to analyze the above information and prepare a statement of cash flows for Dingel. Flood damage is unusual and infrequent in that part of the country.

(b) What would you expect to observe in the operating, investing, and financing sections of a statement of cash flows of:

(1) A severely financially troubled firm?

(2) A recently formed firm that is experiencing rapid growth?

PROBLEMS SET B

See the book's companion website, at **www.wiley.com/college/kieso**, for an additional set of problems.

CONCEPTS FOR ANALYSIS

CA23-1 (Analysis of Improper SCF) The following statement was prepared by Maloney Corporation's accountant.

MALONEY CORPORATION
STATEMENT OF SOURCES AND APPLICATION OF CASH
FOR THE YEAR ENDED SEPTEMBER 30, 2014

Sources of cash	
Net income	$111,000
Depreciation and depletion	70,000
Increase in long-term debt	179,000
Changes in current receivables and inventories, less current liabilities (excluding current maturities of long-term debt)	14,000
	$374,000
Application of cash	
Cash dividends	$ 60,000
Expenditure for property, plant, and equipment	214,000
Investments and other uses	20,000
Change in cash	80,000
	$374,000

The following additional information relating to Maloney Corporation is available for the year ended September 30, 2014.

1. Salaries and wages expense attributable to stock option plans was $25,000 for the year.
2. | | |
   |---|---|
   | Expenditures for property, plant, and equipment | $250,000 |
   | Proceeds from retirements of property, plant, and equipment | 36,000 |
   | Net expenditures | $214,000 |
3. A stock dividend of 10,000 shares of Maloney Corporation common stock was distributed to common stockholders on April 1, 2014, when the per share market price was $7 and par value was $1.
4. On July 1, 2014, when its market price was $6 per share, 16,000 shares of Maloney Corporation common stock were issued in exchange for 4,000 shares of preferred stock.
5. | | |
   |---|---|
   | Depreciation expense | $ 65,000 |
   | Depletion expense | 5,000 |
   | | $ 70,000 |
6. | | |
   |---|---|
   | Increase in long-term debt | $620,000 |
   | Less: Redemption of debt | 441,000 |
   | Net increase | $179,000 |

Instructions

(a) In general, what are the objectives of a statement of the type shown above for Maloney Corporation? Explain.

(b) Identify the weaknesses in the form and format of Maloney Corporation's statement of cash flows without reference to the additional information. (Assume adoption of the indirect method.)

(c) For each of the six items of additional information for the statement of cash flows, indicate the preferable treatment and explain why the suggested treatment is preferable.

(AICPA adapted)

CA23-2 (SCF Theory and Analysis of Improper SCF) Teresa Ramirez and Lenny Traylor are examining the following statement of cash flows for Pacific Clothing Store's first year of operations.

PACIFIC CLOTHING STORE
STATEMENT OF CASH FLOWS
FOR THE YEAR ENDED JANUARY 31, 2014

Sources of cash	
From sales of merchandise	$ 382,000
From sale of capital stock	380,000
From sale of investment	120,000
From depreciation	80,000
From issuance of note for truck	30,000
From interest on investments	8,000
Total sources of cash	1,000,000

PACIFIC CLOTHING STORE
STATEMENT OF CASH FLOWS
FOR THE YEAR ENDED JANUARY 31, 2014
(CONTINUED)

Uses of cash	
For purchase of fixtures and equipment	330,000
For merchandise purchased for resale	253,000
For operating expenses (including depreciation)	170,000
For purchase of investment	95,000
For purchase of truck by issuance of note	30,000
For purchase of treasury stock	10,000
For interest on note	3,000
Total uses of cash	891,000
Net increase in cash	$ 109,000

Teresa claims that Pacific's statement of cash flows is an excellent portrayal of a superb first year, with cash increasing $109,000. Lenny replies that it was not a superb first year—that the year was an operating failure, the statement was incorrectly presented, and $109,000 is not the actual increase in cash.

Instructions

(a) With whom do you agree, Teresa or Lenny? Explain your position.

(b) Using the data provided, prepare a statement of cash flows in proper indirect method form. The only noncash items in income are depreciation and the gain from the sale of the investment (purchase and sale are related).

CA23-3 (SCF Theory and Analysis of Transactions) Ashley Company is a young and growing producer of electronic measuring instruments and technical equipment. You have been retained by Ashley to advise it in the preparation of a statement of cash flows using the indirect method. For the fiscal year ended October 31, 2014, you have obtained the following information concerning certain events and transactions of Ashley.

1. The amount of reported earnings for the fiscal year was $700,000, which included a deduction for an extraordinary loss of $110,000 (see item 5 below).
2. Depreciation expense of $315,000 was included in the income statement.
3. Uncollectible accounts receivable of $40,000 were written off against the allowance for doubtful accounts. Also, $51,000 of bad debt expense was included in determining income for the fiscal year, and the same amount was added to the allowance for doubtful accounts.
4. A gain of $6,000 was realized on the sale of a machine. It originally cost $75,000, of which $30,000 was undepreciated on the date of sale.
5. On April 1, 2014, lightning caused an uninsured building loss of $110,000 ($180,000 loss, less reduction in income taxes of $70,000). This extraordinary loss was included in determining income as indicated in item 1 above.
6. On July 3, 2014, building and land were purchased for $700,000. Ashley gave in payment $75,000 cash, $200,000 market price of its unissued common stock, and signed a $425,000 mortgage note payable.
7. On August 3, 2014, $800,000 face value of Ashley's 10% convertible debentures was converted into $150,000 par value of its common stock. The bonds were originally issued at face value.

Instructions

Explain whether each of the seven numbered items above is a cash inflow or outflow, and explain how it should be disclosed in Ashley's statement of cash flows for the fiscal year ended October 31, 2014. If any item is neither an inflow nor an outflow of cash, explain why it is not, and indicate the disclosure, if any, that should be made of the item in Ashley's statement of cash flows for the fiscal year ended October 31, 2014.

CA23-4 (Analysis of Transactions' Effect on SCF) Each of the following items must be considered in preparing a statement of cash flows for Cruz Fashions Inc. for the year ended December 31, 2014.

1. Fixed assets that had cost $20,000 6½ years before and were being depreciated on a 10-year basis, with no estimated scrap value, were sold for $4,750.
2. During the year, goodwill of $15,000 was considered impaired and was completely written off to expense.
3. During the year, 500 shares of common stock with a stated value of $25 a share were issued for $32 a share.
4. The company sustained a net loss for the year of $2,100. Depreciation amounted to $2,000 and patent amortization was $400.
5. Uncollectible accounts receivable in the amount of $2,000 were written off against Allowance for Doubtful Accounts.

6. Investments (available-for-sale) that cost $12,000 when purchased 4 years earlier were sold for $10,600. The loss was considered ordinary.
7. Bonds payable with a par value of $24,000 on which there was an unamortized bond premium of $2,000 were redeemed at 101. The gain was credited to ordinary income.

Instructions

For each item, state where it is to be shown in the statement and then how you would present the necessary information, including the amount. Consider each item to be independent of the others. Assume that correct entries were made for all transactions as they took place.

CA23-5 (Purpose and Elements of SCF) GAAP requires the statement of cash flows be presented when financial statements are prepared.

Instructions

(a) Explain the purposes of the statement of cash flows.

(b) List and describe the three categories of activities that must be reported in the statement of cash flows.

(c) Identify and describe the two methods that are allowed for reporting cash flows from operations.

(d) Describe the financial statement presentation of noncash investing and financing transactions. Include in your description an example of a noncash investing and financing transaction.

CA23-6 (Cash Flow Reporting) Brockman Guitar Company is in the business of manufacturing top-quality, steel-string folk guitars. In recent years, the company has experienced working capital problems resulting from the procurement of factory equipment, the unanticipated buildup of receivables and inventories, and the payoff of a balloon mortgage on a new manufacturing facility. The founder and president of the company, Barbara Brockman, has attempted to raise cash from various financial institutions, but to no avail because of the company's poor performance in recent years. In particular, the company's lead bank, First Financial, is especially concerned about Brockman's inability to maintain a positive cash position. The commercial loan officer from First Financial told Barbara, "I can't even consider your request for capital financing unless I see that your company is able to generate positive cash flows from operations."

Thinking about the banker's comment, Barbara came up with what she believes is a good plan: With a more attractive statement of cash flows, the bank might be willing to provide long-term financing. To "window dress" cash flows, the company can sell its accounts receivables to factors and liquidate its raw materials inventories. These rather costly transactions would generate lots of cash. As the chief accountant for Brockman Guitar, it is your job to tell Barbara what you think of her plan.

Instructions

Answer the following questions.

(a) What are the ethical issues related to Barbara Brockman's idea?

(b) What would you tell Barbara Brockman?

USING YOUR JUDGMENT

FINANCIAL REPORTING

Financial Reporting Problem

P&G

The Procter & Gamble Company (P&G)

The financial statements of P&G are presented in Appendix 5B. The company's complete annual report, including the notes to the financial statements, can be accessed at the book's companion website, **www.wiley.com/college/kieso**.

Instructions

Refer to P&G's financial statements and the accompanying notes to answer the following questions.

(a) Which method of computing net cash provided by operating activities does P&G use? What were the amounts of net cash provided by operating activities for the years 2009, 2010, and 2011? Which two items were most responsible for the decrease in net cash provided by operating activities in 2011?

(b) What was the most significant item in the cash flows used for investing activities section in 2011? What was the most significant item in the cash flows used for financing activities section in 2011?

(c) Where is "deferred income taxes" reported in P&G's statement of cash flows? Why does it appear in that section of the statement of cash flows?

(d) Where is depreciation reported in P&G's statement of cash flows? Why is depreciation added to net income in the statement of cash flows?

Comparative Analysis Case

The Coca-Cola Company and PepsiCo, Inc.

Instructions

Go to the book's companion website and use information found there to answer the following questions related to The Coca-Cola Company and PepsiCo, Inc.

(a) What method of computing net cash provided by operating activities does Coca-Cola use? What method does PepsiCo use? What were the amounts of cash provided by operating activities reported by Coca-Cola and PepsiCo in 2011?

(b) What was the most significant item reported by Coca-Cola and PepsiCo in 2011 in their investing activities sections? What is the most significant item reported by Coca-Cola and PepsiCo in 2011 in their financing activities sections?

(c) What were these two companies' trends in net cash provided by operating activities over the period 2009 to 2011?

(d) Where is "depreciation and amortization" reported by Coca-Cola and PepsiCo in their statements of cash flows? What is the amount and why does it appear in that section of the statement of cash flows?

(e) Based on the information contained in Coca-Cola's and PepsiCo's financial statements, compute the following 2011 ratios for each company. These ratios require the use of statement of cash flows data. (These ratios were covered in Chapter 5.)

(1) Current cash debt coverage.

(2) Cash debt coverage.

(f) What conclusions concerning the management of cash can be drawn from the ratios computed in (e)?

Financial Statement Analysis Case

Vermont Teddy Bear Co.

Founded in the early 1980s, the Vermont Teddy Bear Co. designs and manufactures American-made teddy bears and markets them primarily as gifts called Bear-Grams or Teddy Bear-Grams. Bear-Grams are personalized teddy bears delivered directly to the recipient for special occasions such as birthdays and anniversaries. The Shelburne, Vermont, company's primary markets are New York, Boston, and Chicago. Sales have jumped dramatically in recent years. Such dramatic growth has significant implications for cash flows. Provided below are the cash flow statements for two recent years for the company.

	Current Year	Prior Year
Cash flows from operating activities:		
Net income	$ 17,523	$ 838,955
Adjustments to reconcile net income to net cash provided by operating activities		
Deferred income taxes	(69,524)	(146,590)
Depreciation and amortization	316,416	181,348
Changes in assets and liabilities:		
Accounts receivable, trade	(38,267)	(25,947)
Inventories	(1,599,014)	(1,289,293)
Prepaid and other current assets	(444,794)	(113,205)
Deposits and other assets	(24,240)	(83,044)
Accounts payable	2,017,059	(284,567)
Accrued expenses	61,321	170,755
Accrued interest payable, debentures	—	(58,219)
Other	—	(8,960)
Income taxes payable	—	117,810
Net cash provided by (used for) operating activities	236,480	(700,957)
Net cash used for investing activities	(2,102,892)	(4,422,953)
Net cash (used for) provided by financing activities	(315,353)	9,685,435
Net change in cash and cash equivalents	(2,181,765)	4,561,525

Other information:

	Current Year	Prior Year
Current liabilities	$ 4,055,465	$ 1,995,600
Total liabilities	4,620,085	2,184,386
Net sales	20,560,566	17,025,856

Instructions

(a) Note that net income in the current year was only $17,523 compared to prior-year income of $838,955, but net cash flow from operating activities was $236,480 in the current year and a negative $700,957 in the prior year. Explain the causes of this apparent paradox.

(b) Evaluate Vermont Teddy Bear's liquidity, solvency, and profitability for the current year using cash flow-based ratios.

Accounting, Analysis, and Principles

The income statement for the year ended December 31, 2014, for Laskowski Manufacturing Company contains the following condensed information.

LASKOWSKI CO.
INCOME STATEMENT

Revenues		$6,583,000
Operating expenses (excluding depreciation)	$4,920,000	
Depreciation expense	880,000	5,800,000
Income before income tax		783,000
Income tax expense		353,000
Net income		$ 430,000

Included in operating expenses is a $24,000 loss resulting from the sale of machinery for $270,000 cash. The company purchased machinery at a cost of $750,000.

Laskowski reports the following balances on its comparative balance sheets at December 31.

LASKOWSKI CO.
COMPARATIVE BALANCE SHEETS (PARTIAL)

	2014	2013
Cash	$672,000	$130,000
Accounts receivable	775,000	610,000
Inventory	834,000	867,000
Accounts payable	521,000	501,000

Income tax expense of $353,000 represents the amount paid in 2014. Dividends declared and paid in 2014 totaled $200,000.

Accounting

Prepare the statement of cash flows using the indirect method.

Analysis

Laskowski has an aggressive growth plan, which will require significant investments in plant and equipment over the next several years. Preliminary plans call for an investment of over $500,000 in the next year. Compute Laskowski's free cash flow (from Chapter 5) and use it to evaluate the investment plans with the use of only internally generated funds.

Principles

How does the statement of cash flows contribute to achieving the objective of financial reporting?

BRIDGE TO THE PROFESSION

Professional Research: FASB Codification

As part of the year-end accounting process for your company, you are preparing the statement of cash flows according to GAAP. One of your team, a finance major, believes the statement should be prepared to report the change in working capital, because analysts many times use working capital in ratio analysis. Your supervisor would like research conducted to verify the basis for preparing the statement of cash flows.

Instructions

If your school has a subscription to the FASB Codification, go to *http://aaahq.org/ascLogin.cfm* to log in and prepare responses to the following. Provide Codification references for your responses.

(a) What is the primary objective for the statement of cash flows? Is working capital the basis for meeting this objective?

(b) What information is provided in a statement of cash flows?

(c) List some of the typical cash inflows and outflows from operations.

Additional Professional Resources

See the book's companion website, at **www.wiley.com/college/kieso**, for professional simulations as well as other study resources.

IFRS INSIGHTS

LEARNING OBJECTIVE 10

Compare the statement of cash flows under GAAP and IFRS.

As in GAAP, the statement of cash flows is a required statement for IFRS. In addition, the content and presentation of a U.S. statement of cash flows is similar to one used for IFRS. However, the disclosure requirements related to the statement of cash flows are more extensive under GAAP. *IAS 7* ("Cash Flow Statements") provides the overall IFRS requirements for cash flow information.

RELEVANT FACTS

Following are the key similarities and differences between GAAP and IFRS related to the statement of cash flows.

Similarities

- Both GAAP and IFRS require that companies prepare a statement of cash flows.
- Both IFRS and GAAP require that the statement of cash flows should have three major sections—operating, investing, and financing—along with changes in cash and cash equivalents.
- Similar to GAAP, the cash flow statement can be prepared using either the indirect or direct method under IFRS. For both IFRS and GAAP, most companies use the indirect method for reporting net cash flow from operating activities.
- The definition of cash equivalents used in IFRS is similar to that used in GAAP.

Differences

- A major difference in the definition of cash and cash equivalents is that in certain situations, bank overdrafts are considered part of cash and cash equivalents under IFRS (which is not the case in GAAP). Under GAAP, bank overdrafts are classified as financing activities.
- IFRS requires that non-cash investing and financing activities be excluded from the statement of cash flows. Instead, these non-cash activities should be reported elsewhere. This requirement is interpreted to mean that non-cash investing and financing activities should be disclosed in the notes to the financial statements instead of in the financial statements. Under GAAP, companies may present this information in the cash flow statement.

- One area where there can be substantive differences between IFRS and GAAP relates to the classification of interest, dividends, and taxes. IFRS provides more alternatives for disclosing these items, while GAAP requires that except for dividends paid (which are classified as a financing activity), these items are all reported as operating activities.

ABOUT THE NUMBERS

Significant Non-Cash Transactions

Because the statement of cash flows reports only the effects of operating, investing, and financing activities in terms of cash flows, it omits some **significant non-cash transactions** and other events that are investing or financing activities. Among the more common of these non-cash transactions that a company should report or disclose in some manner are the following.

1. Acquisition of assets by assuming liabilities (including finance lease obligations) or by issuing equity securities.
2. Exchanges of non-monetary assets.
3. Refinancing of long-term debt.
4. Conversion of debt or preference shares to ordinary shares.
5. Issuance of equity securities to retire debt.

Investing and financing transactions that do not require the use of cash are excluded from the statement of cash flows. If material in amount, these disclosures may be either narrative or summarized in a separate schedule. This schedule may appear in a separate note or supplementary schedule to the financial statements.

Illustration IFRS23-1 shows the presentation of these significant non-cash transactions or other events in a separate schedule in the notes to the financial statements.

Note G: Significant non-cash transactions. During the year, the company engaged in the following significant non-cash investing and financing transactions:

Issued 250,000 ordinary shares to purchase land and building	$1,750,000
Exchanged land in Steadfast, New York, for land in Bedford, Pennsylvania	$2,000,000
Converted 12% bonds to 50,000 ordinary shares	$ 500,000

ILLUSTRATION IFRS23-1
Note Presentation of Non-Cash Investing and Financing Activities

Companies do not generally report certain other significant non-cash transactions or other events in conjunction with the statement of cash flows. Examples of these types of transactions are **share dividends, share splits, and restrictions on retained earnings**. Companies generally report these items, neither financing nor investing activities, in conjunction with the statement of changes in equity or schedules and notes pertaining to changes in equity accounts.

Special Disclosures

IAS 7 indicates that cash flows related to interest received and paid, and dividends received and paid, should be separately disclosed in the statement of cash flows. IFRS allows flexibility in how these items are classified in the statement of cash flows. However, each item should be classified in a consistent manner from period to period as operating, investing, or financing cash flows. *For homework purposes, classify interest received and paid and dividends received as part of cash flows from operating activities and dividends paid as cash flows from financing activities.* The justification for reporting the first three items in cash flows from operating activities is that each item affects net income. Dividends paid, however, do not affect net income and are often considered a cost of financing.

Companies should also disclose income taxes paid separately in the cash flows from operating activities unless they can be separately identified as part of investing or financing activities. While tax expense may be readily identifiable with investing or financing activities, the related tax cash flows are often impracticable to identify and may arise in a different period from the cash flows of the underlying transaction. Therefore, taxes paid are usually classified as cash flows from operating activities. IFRS requires that the cash paid for taxes, as well as cash flows from interest and dividends received and paid, be disclosed. The category (operating, investing, or financing) that each item was included in must be disclosed as well.

An example of such a disclosure from the notes to Daimler's financial statements is provided in Illustration IFRS23-2.

ILLUSTRATION IFRS23-2
Note Disclosure of Interest, Taxes, and Dividends

Daimler

Cash provided by operating activities includes the following cash flows:

(in millions of €)	2012	2011	2010
Interest paid	(894)	(651)	(1,541)
Interest received	471	765	977
Income taxes paid, net	(358)	(898)	(1,020)
Dividends received	109	67	69

Other companies choose to report these items directly in the statement of cash flows. In many cases, companies start with income before income taxes and then show income taxes paid as a separate item. In addition, they often add back interest expense on an accrual basis and then subtract interest paid. Reporting these items in the operating activities section is shown for Mermel Company in Illustration IFRS23-3.

ILLUSTRATION IFRS23-3
Reporting of Interest, Taxes, and Dividends in the Operating Section

MERMEL COMPANY
STATEMENT OF CASH FLOWS ($000,000)
(OPERATING ACTIVITIES SECTION ONLY)

Income before income tax		$ 4,000
Adjustments to reconcile income before income tax to net cash provided by operating activities:		
Depreciation expense	$1,000	
Interest expense	500	
Investment revenue (dividends)	(650)	
Decrease in inventories	1,050	
Increase in trade receivables	(310)	1,590
Cash generated from operations		5,590
Interest paid	(300)	
Income taxes paid	(760)	(1,060)
Net cash provided by operating activities		$ 4,530

Companies often provide a separate section to identify interest and income taxes paid.

ON THE HORIZON

Presently, the IASB and the FASB are involved in a joint project on the presentation and organization of information in the financial statements. With respect to the cash flow statement specifically, the notion of *cash equivalents* will probably not be retained. The definition of cash in the existing literature would be retained, and the statement of cash flows would present information on changes in cash only. In addition, the IASB and FASB favor presentation of operating cash flows using the direct method only. This approach is generally opposed by the preparer community.

IFRS SELF-TEST QUESTIONS

1. Which of the following is **true** regarding the statement of cash flows under IFRS?
   - **(a)** The statement of cash flows has two major sections—operating and non-operating.
   - **(b)** The statement of cash flows has two major sections—financing and investing.
   - **(c)** The statement of cash flows has three major sections—operating, investing, and financing.
   - **(d)** The statement of cash flows has three major sections—operating, non-operating, and financing.
2. In the case of a bank overdraft:
   - **(a)** GAAP typically includes the amount in cash and cash equivalents.
   - **(b)** IFRS typically includes the amount in cash equivalents but not in cash.
   - **(c)** GAAP typically treats the overdraft as a liability, and reports the amount in the financing section of the statement of cash flows.
   - **(d)** IFRS typically treats the overdraft as a liability, and reports the amount in the investing section of the statement of cash flows.
3. Under IFRS, significant non-cash transactions:
   - **(a)** are classified as operating, if they are related to income items.
   - **(b)** are excluded from the statement of cash flows and disclosed in a narrative form or summarized in a separate schedule.
   - **(c)** are classified as an investing or financing activity.
   - **(d)** are classified as an operating activity, unless they can be specifically identified with financing or investing activities.
4. For purposes of the statement of cash flows, under IFRS interest paid is treated as:
   - **(a)** an operating activity in all cases.
   - **(b)** an investing or operating activity, depending on use of the borrowed funds.
   - **(c)** either a financing or investing activity.
   - **(d)** either an operating or financing activity, but treated consistently from period to period.
5. For purposes of the statement of cash flows, under IFRS income taxes paid are treated as:
   - **(a)** cash flows from operating activities unless they can be separately identified as part of investing or financing activities.
   - **(b)** an operating activity in all cases.
   - **(c)** an investing or operating activity, depending on whether a refund is received.
   - **(d)** either operating, financing, or investing activity, but treated consistently to other companies in the same industry.

IFRS CONCEPTS AND APPLICATION

IFRS23-1 Where can authoritative IFRS related to the statement of cash flows be found?

IFRS23-2 Briefly describe some of the similarities and differences between GAAP and IFRS with respect to cash flow reporting.

IFRS23-3 What are some of the key obstacles for the FASB and IASB within their accounting guidance in the area of cash flow reporting? Explain.

IFRS23-4 Stan Conner and Mark Stein were discussing the statement of cash flows of Bombeck Co. In the notes to the statement of cash flows was a schedule entitled "Non-cash investing and financing activities." Give three examples of significant non-cash transactions that would be reported in this schedule.

IFRS23-5 Springsteen Co. had the following activity in its most recent year of operations.

- **(a)** Pension expense exceeds amount funded.
- **(b)** Redemption of bonds payable.
- **(c)** Sale of building at book value.
- **(d)** Depreciation.
- **(e)** Exchange of equipment for furniture.
- **(f)** Issuance of ordinary shares.
- **(g)** Amortization of intangible assets.
- **(h)** Purchase of treasury shares.
- **(i)** Issuance of bonds for land.
- **(j)** Payment of dividends.
- **(k)** Increase in interest receivable on notes receivable.
- **(l)** Purchase of equipment.

Instructions

Classify the items as (1) operating—add to net income, (2) operating—deduct from net income, (3) investing, (4) financing, or (5) significant non-cash investing and financing activities. Use the indirect method.

IFRS23-6 Following are selected statement of financial position accounts of Sander Bros. Corp. at December 31, 2014 and 2013, and the increases or decreases in each account from 2013 to 2014. Also presented is selected income statement information for the year ended December 31, 2014, and additional information.

Selected statement of financial position accounts	2014	2013	Increase (Decrease)
Assets			
Property, plant, and equipment	$277,000	$247,000	$30,000
Accumulated depreciation	(178,000)	(167,000)	(11,000)
Accounts receivable	34,000	24,000	10,000
Equity and liabilities			
Share capital—ordinary, $1 par	$ 22,000	$ 19,000	$ 3,000
Share premium—ordinary	9,000	3,000	6,000
Retained earnings	104,000	91,000	13,000
Bonds payable	49,000	46,000	3,000
Dividends payable	8,000	5,000	3,000

Selected income statement information for the year ended December 31, 2014	
Sales revenue	$155,000
Depreciation	38,000
Gain on sale of equipment	14,500
Net income	31,000

Additional information:

1. During 2014, equipment costing $45,000 was sold for cash.
2. Accounts receivable relate to sales of merchandise.
3. During 2014, $25,000 of bonds payable were issued in exchange for property, plant, and equipment.

There was no amortization of bond discount or premium.

Instructions

Determine the category (operating, investing, or financing) and the amount that should be reported in the statement of cash flows for the following items.

(a) Payments for purchase of property, plant, and equipment.
(b) Proceeds from the sale of equipment.
(c) Cash dividends paid.
(d) Redemption of bonds payable.

IFRS23-7 Dingel Corporation has contracted with you to prepare a statement of cash flows. The controller has provided the following information.

	December 31	
	2014	2013
Buildings	$ -0-	$29,750
Equipment	45,000	20,000
Patents	5,000	6,250
Investments	-0-	3,000
Inventory	12,000	9,000
Accounts receivable	12,250	10,000
Cash	33,500	13,000
	$107,750	$91,000
Share capital—ordinary	$ 43,000	$33,000
Retained earnings	20,750	6,000
Allowance for doubtful accounts	3,000	4,500
Accumulated depreciation on equipment	2,000	4,500
Accumulated depreciation on buildings	-0-	6,000
Accounts payable	5,000	3,000
Dividends payable	-0-	5,000
Long-term notes payable	31,000	25,000
Notes payable, short-term (non-trade)	3,000	4,000
	$107,750	$91,000

Additional data related to 2014 are as follows.

1. Equipment that had cost $11,000 and was 40% depreciated at time of disposal was sold for $2,500.
2. $10,000 of the long-term notes payable was paid by issuing ordinary shares.
3. Cash dividends paid were $5,000.
4. On January 1, 2014, the building was completely destroyed by a flood. Insurance proceeds on the building were $32,000.
5. Equity investments (non-trading) were sold at $1,700 above their cost.
6. Cash was paid for the acquisition of equipment.
7. A long-term note for $16,000 was issued for the acquisition of equipment.
8. Interest of $2,000 and income taxes of $6,500 were paid in cash.

Instructions

Prepare a statement of cash flows using the indirect method.

Professional Research

IFRS23-8 As part of the year-end accounting process for your company, you are preparing the statement of cash flows according to IFRS. One of your team, a finance major, believes the statement should be prepared to report the change in working capital because analysts many times use working capital in ratio analysis. Your supervisor would like research conducted to verify the basis for preparing the statement of cash flows.

Instructions

Access the IFRS authoritative literature at the IASB website (*http://eifrs.iasb.org/*). (Click on the IFRS tab and then register for free eIFRS access if necessary.) When you have accessed the documents, you can use the search tool in your Internet browser to respond to the following questions. (Provide paragraph citations.)

(a) What is the primary objective for the statement of cash flows? Is working capital the basis for meeting this objective?

(b) What information is provided in a statement of cash flows?

(c) List some of the typical cash inflows and outflows from operations.

International Financial Reporting Problem

Marks and Spencer plc

IFRS23-9 The financial statements of **Marks and Spencer plc (M&S)** are available at the book's companion website or can be accessed at *http://annualreport.marksandspencer.com/_assets/downloads/Marks-and-Spencer-Annual-report-and-financial-statements-2012.pdf.*

Instructions

Refer to M&S's financial statements and the accompanying notes to answer the following questions.

(a) Which method of computing net cash provided by operating activities does M&S use? What were the amounts of net cash provided by operating activities for the years 2011 and 2012? Which two items were most responsible for the increase in net cash provided by operating activities in 2012?

(b) What was the most significant item in the cash flows used for investing activities section in 2012? What was the most significant item in the cash flows used for financing activities section in 2012?

(c) Where is "deferred income taxes" reported in M&S's statement of cash flows? Why does it appear in that section of the statement of cash flows?

(d) Where is depreciation reported in M&S's statement of cash flows? Why is depreciation added to net income in the statement of cash flows?

ANSWERS TO IFRS SELF-TEST QUESTIONS

1. c **2.** c **3.** b **4.** d **5.** a

Remember to check the book's companion website to find additional resources for this chapter.

CHAPTER 24 Full Disclosure in Financial Reporting

LEARNING OBJECTIVES

After studying this chapter, you should be able to:

1. Review the full disclosure principle and describe implementation problems.
2. Explain the use of notes in financial statement preparation.
3. Discuss the disclosure requirements for related-party transactions, post-balance-sheet events, and major business segments.
4. Describe the accounting problems associated with interim reporting.
5. Identify the major disclosures in the auditor's report.
6. Understand management's responsibilities for financials.
7. Identify issues related to financial forecasts and projections.
8. Describe the profession's response to fraudulent financial reporting.

High-Quality Financial Reporting—Always in Fashion

Here are excerpts from leading experts regarding the importance of high-quality financial reporting:

Warren E. Buffett, Chairman and Chief Executive Officer, **Berkshire Hathaway Inc.**:

> Financial reporting for Berkshire Hathaway, and for me personally, is the beginning of every decision that we make around here in terms of capital. I'm punching out 10-Ks and 10-Qs every single day. We look at the numbers and try to evaluate the quality of the financial reporting, and then we try to figure out what that means for the bonds and stocks that we're looking at, and thinking of either buying or selling.

Judy Lewent, Executive Vice President and Chief Financial Officer, **Merck & Co., Inc.**:

> Higher standards, when properly implemented, drive excellence. I can make a parallel to the pharmaceutical industry. If you look around the world at where innovations come from, economists have studied and seen that where regulatory standards are the highest is where innovation is also the highest.

Floyd Norris, Chief Financial Correspondent, **New York Times**:

> We are in a situation now in our society where the temptations to provide "bad" financial reporting are probably greater than they used to be. The need to get the stock price up, or to keep it up, is intense. So, the temptation to play games, the temptation to manage earnings—some of which can be legitimate and some of which cannot be—is probably greater than it used to be.

Abby Joseph Cohen, Chair, Investment Policy Committee, **Goldman, Sachs & Co.**:

> High-quality financial reporting is perhaps the most important thing we can expect from companies. For investors to make good decisions—whether those investors are buying stocks or bonds or making private investments—they need to know the truth. And we think that when information is as clear as possible and is reported as frequently as makes sense, investors can do their jobs as best they can.

We can also get insight into the importance of high-quality reporting based on the market assessment of companies perceived to have poor-quality reporting. In a recent quarter, **Coach, Inc.** stopped reporting as separate items sales from regular stores (full price) and factory outlets. As a result, readers of its financial statements have a hard time determining the source of Coach's sales growth. Analysts are especially concerned that the less-transparent reporting may obscure slowing sales at its regular stores, as consumers cut down on luxury goods in the sluggish economy. Did Coach's stock price suffer as a result of this lower-quality reporting? You bet, as shown in the price graph on the next page.

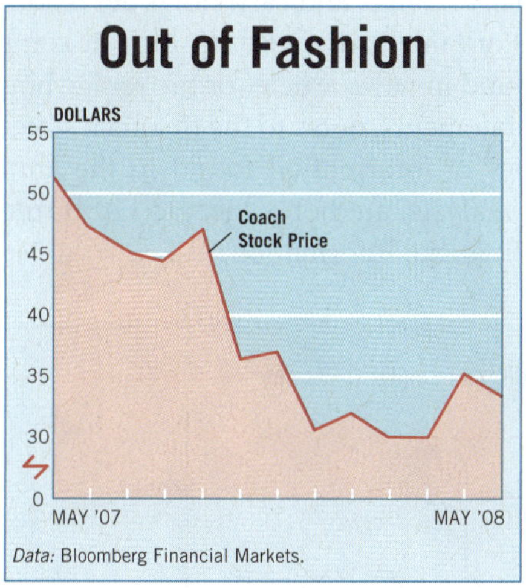

CONCEPTUAL FOCUS

> See the **Underlying Concepts** on pages 1488, 1490, 1496, 1503, 1514, 1520, 1522, and 1525.

> Read the **Evolving Issues** on pages 1490 and 1507 for discussions on financial disclosure and interim reporting.

INTERNATIONAL FOCUS

> See the **International Perspectives** on pages 1489, 1507, and 1523.

> Read the **IFRS Insights** on pages 1548–1557 for a discussion of:

—Differential disclosure
—Subsequent events
—Interim reports

In the year following the change in reporting, Coach's stock price was down 34 percent. As one analyst noted, "It's never a good sign when you reduce transparency . . . It's a sign of weakness."

In short, the analyst's comments above illustrate why high-quality reporting is always in fashion—for companies, investors, and the capital markets. And, as the Coach example illustrates, full disclosure is at the heart of high-quality reporting.

Sources: Excerpts taken from video entitled "Financially Correct with Ben Stein," Financial Accounting Standards Board (Norwalk, Conn.: FASB, 2002). By permission. See also J. Porter, "As Belts Tighten, Coach Feels the Pinch," *BusinessWeek* (May 29, 2008), p. 66.

PREVIEW OF CHAPTER 24

As the opening story indicates, our markets will not function properly without transparent, complete, and truthful reporting of financial performance. Investors and other interested parties need to read and understand all aspects of financial reporting—the financial statements, the notes, the president's letter, and management's discussion and analysis. In this chapter, we cover the full disclosure principle in more detail and examine disclosures that must accompany financial statements so that they are not misleading. The content and organization of this chapter are as follows.

Full Disclosure in Financial Reporting

Full Disclosure Principle	Notes to Financial Statements	Disclosure Issues	Auditor's and Management's Reports	Current Reporting Issues
• Increase in reporting requirements • Differential disclosure	• Accounting policies • Common notes	• Special transactions or events • Post-balance-sheet events • Diversified companies • Interim reports	• Auditor's report • Management's reports	• Reporting on forecasts and projections • Internet financial reporting • Fraudulent financial reporting • Criteria for accounting and reporting choices

FULL DISCLOSURE PRINCIPLE

LEARNING OBJECTIVE 1
Review the full disclosure principle and describe implementation problems.

According to the FASB Conceptual Framework, some useful information is best provided in the financial statements, and some is best provided by means other than in financial statements. For example, earnings and cash flows are readily available in financial statements—but investors might do better to look at comparisons to other companies in the same industry, found in news articles or brokerage house reports.

FASB rules directly affect financial statements, notes to the financial statements, and supplementary information. Other types of information found in the annual report, such as management's discussion and analysis, are not subject to FASB rules. Illustration 24-1 indicates the various types of financial information.

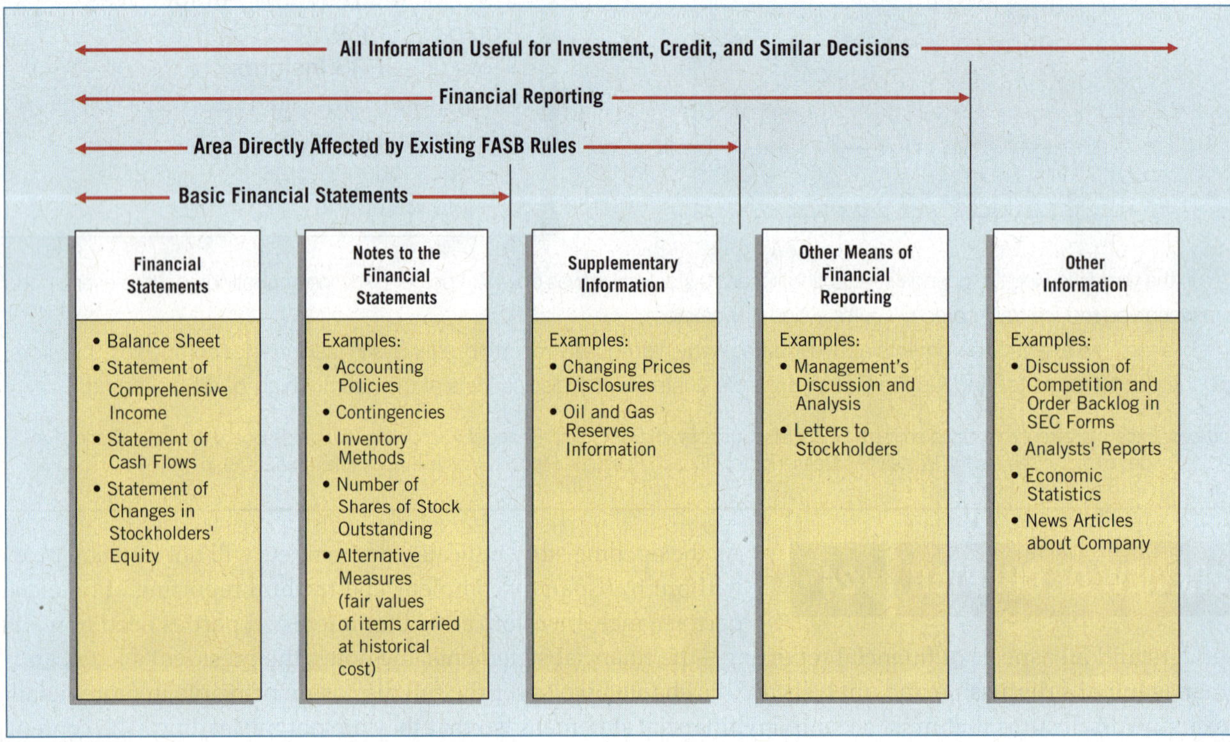

ILLUSTRATION 24-1
Types of Financial Information

As Chapter 2 indicated, the profession has adopted a **full disclosure principle**. The full disclosure principle calls for financial reporting of **any financial facts significant enough to influence the judgment of an informed reader**. In some situations, the benefits of disclosure may be apparent but the costs uncertain. In other instances, the costs may be certain but the benefits of disclosure not as apparent.

Underlying Concepts
Here is a good example of the trade-off between cost considerations and the benefits of full disclosure.

For example, the SEC required companies to provide expanded disclosures about their contractual obligations. In light of the off-balance-sheet accounting frauds at companies like **Enron**, the benefits of these expanded disclosures seem fairly obvious to the investing public. While no one has documented the exact costs of disclosure in these situations, they would appear to be relatively small.

On the other hand, the cost of disclosure can be substantial in some cases and the benefits difficult to assess. For example, at one time the *Wall Street Journal* reported that if segment reporting were adopted, a company like **Fruehauf** would have had to increase its accounting staff 50 percent, from 300 to 450 individuals. In this case, the cost of disclosure can be measured, but the benefits are less well defined.

Some even argue that the reporting requirements are so detailed and substantial that users have a difficult time absorbing the information. These critics charge the profession with engaging in **information overload**.

Financial disasters at **Microstrategy**, **PharMor**, **WorldCom**, and **Lehman** highlight the difficulty of implementing the full disclosure principle. They raise the issue of why investors were not aware of potential problems. Was the information these companies presented not comprehensible? Was it buried? Was it too technical? Was it properly presented and fully disclosed as of the financial statement date, but the situation later deteriorated? Or was it simply not there? In the following sections, we describe the elements of high-quality disclosure that will enable companies to avoid these disclosure pitfalls.

Increase in Reporting Requirements

Disclosure requirements have increased substantially. One survey showed that the size of many companies' annual reports is growing in response to demands for increased transparency. For example, annual report page counts ranged from 70 pages for **Gateway** up to a whopping 244 pages in **Eastman Kodak**'s annual report. And annual report lengths continue to grow in the post-Sarbanes-Oxley environment, with the number of companies producing reports over 100 pages increasing from 19 percent to 37 percent—almost double.[1] This result is not surprising. As illustrated throughout this textbook, the FASB has issued many pronouncements in recent years that have substantial disclosure provisions.

The reasons for this increase in disclosure requirements are varied. Some of them are:

- ***Complexity of the business environment.*** The increasing complexity of business operations magnifies the difficulty of distilling economic events into summarized reports. Such areas as derivatives, leasing, business combinations, pensions, financing arrangements, revenue recognition, and deferred taxes are complex. As a result, companies extensively use **notes to the financial statements** to explain these transactions and their future effects.
- ***Necessity for timely information.*** Today, more than ever before, users are demanding information that is current and predictive. For example, users want more complete **interim data**. Also, the SEC recommends published financial forecasts, long avoided and even feared by management.
- ***Accounting as a control and monitoring device.*** The government has recently sought public disclosure of such phenomena as management compensation, off-balance-sheet financing arrangements, and related-party transactions. An "Enronitis" concern is expressed in many of these newer disclosure requirements, and the SEC has selected accountants and auditors as the agents to assist in controlling and monitoring these concerns.

Differential Disclosure

A trend toward **differential disclosure** is also occurring. For example, the SEC requires that companies report to it certain substantive information that is not found in annual reports to stockholders. Likewise, the FASB, recognizing that certain disclosure requirements are costly and unnecessary for certain companies, has eliminated reporting requirements for nonpublic enterprises in such areas as fair value of financial instruments and segment reporting.

International Perspective

IFRS allows different accounting rules for small- and medium-sized entities.

[1]MWW Group, *MWW White Paper: Annual Report* (Winter 2012). See also *Final Report of the Advisory Committee on Improvements to Financial Reporting to the United States Securities and Exchange Commission* (August 1, 2008) for discussion of the need to address the growing volume and complexity of the financial reports and disclosures.

Underlying Concepts

Surveys indicate that users differ in their needs for information and that not all companies should report all elements of information. Thus, some contend that companies should report only information that users and preparers agree is needed in the particular circumstances.

Some still complain that the FASB has not gone far enough. They note that certain types of companies (small or nonpublic) should not have to follow complex GAAP requirements such as those for deferred income taxes, leases, or pensions. This issue, often referred to as "**big GAAP versus little GAAP**," continues to be controversial.[2]

The FASB has traditionally taken the position that there should be one set of GAAP. However, due to the growing concern about differential costs and benefits of a "one size fits all" reporting package, the FASB is working with an advisory committee to explore ways that its standards can be more cost-effective for all companies, regardless of size. The Board is studying such areas as fair value measurement disclosures, and the accounting for consolidations, financial instruments, presentation of comprehensive income, and leases. In addition, the FASB has initiated a project to develop a framework, including a set of decision criteria, for determining whether and when to adjust the requirements for recognition, measurement, presentation, disclosure, effective dates, and transition methods for financial accounting standards that apply to private companies.[3]

Evolving Issue DISCLOSURE—QUANTITY AND QUALITY

There is no better illustration of the adage that both quality and quantity are important than the issue of financial disclosure. While the full disclosure principle holds that more is better, how much more and of what form? An evaluation of this issue requires careful analysis of costs and benefits. Furthermore, as noted by one FASB member, the usefulness of expanded required disclosure also depends on users' ability to distinguish between the form of reporting (i.e., disclosed versus recognized items in financial statements). Research to date is inconclusive on this matter. So it is not just the amount but the quality.

Indeed, the SEC Committee on Improvement in Financial Reporting recommended the development of a disclosure framework that integrates existing SEC and FASB disclosure requirements into a cohesive whole to ensure meaningful communication and logical presentation of disclosures, based on consistent objectives and principles. This would eliminate redundancies and provide a single source of disclosure guidance across all financial reporting standards. Adopting such a framework should lead to disclosure of the principal assumptions, estimates, and sensitivity analyses that may impact a company's business, as well as a qualitative discussion of the key risks and uncertainties that could significantly change these amounts over time. This would encompass transactions recognized and measured in the financial statements, as well as events and uncertainties that are not recorded.

The FASB (and IASB) have responded to this recommendation by initiating a project with the objective and primary focus of improving the effectiveness of disclosures in notes to financial statements by clearly communicating the information that is most important to users of each company's financial statements. Achieving the objective of improving effectiveness will require development of a framework that promotes consistent decisions about disclosure requirements by standard-setters and the appropriate exercise of discretion by reporting companies. The FASB has issued an invitation to comment, seeking input on whether and, if so, how to provide guidance to improve the organization, formatting, and style of notes to financial statements. The FASB notes that while reducing the volume of the notes to financial statements is not the primary focus, the Board hopes that a sharper focus on important information will result in reduced volume in most cases. That is, get the quantity as well as the quality of disclosure right.

Sources: K. Schipper, "Required Disclosures in Financial Reports," Presidential Address to the American Accounting Association Annual Meeting (San Francisco, Calif., August 2005); *Final Report of the Advisory Committee on Improvements to Financial Reporting to the United States Securities and Exchange Commission* (August 1, 2008); and FASB, *Invitation to Comment: Disclosure Framework* (July 12, 2012).

[2] In response to cost-benefit concerns, the SEC has exempted some small public companies from certain rules implemented in response to the Sarbanes-Oxley Act. For example, smaller companies have more time to comply with the internal control rules required by the Sarbanes-Oxley law and have more time to file annual and interim reports.

[3] See "Private Company Decision-Making Framework: A Framework for Evaluating Financial Accounting and Reporting Guidance for Private Companies," *FASB Invitation to Comment* (July 31, 2012).

NOTES TO THE FINANCIAL STATEMENTS

2 LEARNING OBJECTIVE
Explain the use of notes in financial statement preparation.

As you know from your study of this textbook, notes are an integral part of the financial statements of a business enterprise. However, readers of financial statements often overlook them because they are highly technical and often appear in small print. **Notes are the means of amplifying or explaining the items presented in the main body of the statements.** They can explain in qualitative terms information pertinent to specific financial statement items. In addition, they can provide supplementary data of a quantitative nature to expand the information in the financial statements. Notes also can explain restrictions imposed by financial arrangements or basic contractual agreements. Although notes may be technical and difficult to understand, they provide meaningful information for the user of the financial statements.

Accounting Policies

Accounting policies are the specific accounting principles and methods a company currently uses and considers most appropriate to present fairly its financial statements. GAAP states that information about the accounting policies adopted by a reporting entity is essential for financial statement users in making economic decisions. It recommends that companies should present **as an integral part of the financial statements a statement identifying the accounting policies adopted and followed by the reporting entity**. Companies should present the disclosure as the first note or in a separate Summary of Significant Accounting Policies section preceding the notes to the financial statements.

The Summary of Significant Accounting Policies answers such questions as: What method of depreciation is used on plant assets? What valuation method is employed on inventories? What amortization policy is followed in regard to intangible assets? How are marketing costs handled for financial reporting purposes?

Refer to the financial statements and notes to the financial statements for **The Procter & Gamble Company** (available at the book's companion website, **www.wiley.com/college/kieso**) for an illustration of note disclosure of accounting policies (Note 1) and other notes accompanying the audited financial statements.

Analysts examine carefully the summary of accounting policies to determine whether a company is using conservative or liberal accounting practices. For example, depreciating plant assets over an unusually long period of time is considered liberal. Using LIFO inventory valuation in a period of inflation is generally viewed as conservative.

Companies that fail to adopt high-quality reporting policies may be heavily penalized by the market. For example, when **Microstrategy** disclosed that it would restate prior-year results due to use of aggressive revenue recognition policies, its share price dropped over 60 percent in one day. Investors viewed Microstrategy's quality of earnings as low.

Common Notes

We have discussed many of the **notes to the financial statements** throughout this textbook, and will discuss others more fully in this chapter. The more common are as follows.

MAJOR DISCLOSURES

INVENTORY. Companies should report the basis upon which inventory amounts are stated (lower-of-cost-or-market) and the method used in determining cost (LIFO, FIFO, average-cost, etc.). Manufacturers should report, either in the balance sheet or in a separate schedule in the notes, the inventory composition (finished goods, work in process, raw materials). Unusual or significant financing arrangements relating to inventories that may require disclosure include transactions with related parties, product financing arrangements, firm purchase commitments, involuntary liquidation of LIFO inventories, and pledging of inventories as collateral. Chapter 9 (pages 494–495) illustrates these disclosures.

PROPERTY, PLANT, AND EQUIPMENT. Companies should state the basis of valuation for property, plant, and equipment. It is usually historical cost. Companies also should disclose pledges, liens, and other commitments related to these assets. In the presentation of depreciation, companies should disclose the following in the financial statements or in the notes: (1) depreciation expense for the period; (2) balances of major classes of depreciable assets, by nature and function, at the balance sheet date; (3) accumulated depreciation, either by major classes of depreciable assets or in total, at the balance sheet date; and (4) a general description of the method or methods used in computing depreciation with respect to major classes of depreciable assets. Finally, companies should explain any major impairments. Chapter 11 (pages 609–611) illustrates property, plant, and equipment.

CREDITOR CLAIMS. Investors normally find it extremely useful to understand the nature and cost of creditor claims. However, the liabilities section in the balance sheet can provide the major types of liabilities only in the aggregate. Note schedules regarding such obligations provide additional information about how a company is financing its operations, the costs that it will bear in future periods, and the timing of future cash outflows. Financial statements must disclose for each of the five years following the date of the statements the aggregate amount of maturities and sinking fund requirements for all long-term borrowings. Chapter 14 (pages 785–787) illustrates these disclosures.

EQUITYHOLDERS' CLAIMS. Many companies present in the body of the balance sheet information about equity securities: the number of shares authorized, issued, and outstanding and the par value for each type of security. Or, companies may present such data in a note. Beyond that, a common equity note disclosure relates to contracts and senior securities outstanding that might affect the various claims of the residual equityholders. An example would be the existence of outstanding stock options, outstanding convertible debt, redeemable preferred stock, and convertible preferred stock. In addition, it is necessary to disclose certain types of restrictions currently in force. Generally, these types of restrictions involve the amount of earnings available for dividend distribution. Examples of these types of disclosures are illustrated in Chapter 15 (pages 847–848) and Chapter 16 (pages 909–910).

CONTINGENCIES AND COMMITMENTS. A company may have gain or loss contingencies that are not disclosed in the body of the financial statements. These contingencies include litigation, debt and other guarantees, possible tax assessments, renegotiation of government contracts, and sales of receivables with recourse. In addition, companies should disclose in the notes commitments that relate to dividend restrictions, purchase agreements (through-put and take-or-pay), hedge contracts, and employment contracts. Disclosures of such items are illustrated in Chapter 7 (page 372), Chapter 9 (page 483), and Chapter 13 (pages 728–729).

FAIR VALUES. Companies that have assets or liabilities measured at fair value must disclose both the cost and the fair value of all financial instruments in the notes to the financial statements. Fair value measurements may be used for many financial assets and liabilities, investments, impairments of long-lived assets, and some contingencies. Companies also provide disclosure of information that enables users to determine the extent of usage of fair value and the inputs used to implement fair value measurement. This fair value hierarchy identifies three broad levels related to the measurement of fair values (Levels 1, 2, and 3). The levels indicate the reliability of the measurement of fair value information. Appendix 17C (pages 999–1003) discusses in detail fair value disclosures.

DEFERRED TAXES, PENSIONS, AND LEASES. The FASB also requires extensive disclosure in the areas of deferred taxes, pensions, and leases. Chapter 19 (pages 1138–1144), Chapter 20 (pages 1204–1215), and Chapter 21 (pages 1300–1302) discuss in detail each of these disclosures. Users of financial statements should carefully read notes to the financial statements for information about off-balance-sheet commitments, future financing needs, and the quality of a company's earnings.

CHANGES IN ACCOUNTING PRINCIPLES. The profession defines various types of accounting changes and establishes guides for reporting each type. Companies discuss, either in the summary of significant accounting policies or in the other notes, changes in accounting principles (as well as material changes in estimates and corrections of errors). See Chapter 22 (pages 1363–1364).

In earlier chapters, we discussed the disclosures listed above. The following sections of this chapter illustrate four additional disclosures of significance—special transactions or events, subsequent events, segment reporting, and interim reporting.

What do the numbers mean? *FOOTNOTE SECRETS*

Often, note disclosures are needed to give a complete picture of a company's financial position. A good example of such disclosures is the required disclosure of debt triggers that may be buried in financing arrangements. These triggers can require a company to pay off a loan immediately if the debt rating collapses; they are one of the reasons **Enron** crumbled so quickly. But few Enron stockholders knew about the debt triggers until the gun had gone off. Companies are also disclosing more about their bank credit lines, liquidity, and any special-purpose entities. (The latter were major villains in the Enron drama.)

How can you get better informed about note disclosures that may contain important information related to your investments? Beyond your study in this class, a good Web resource for understanding the contents of note disclosures is *http://www.footnoted.org/*. This site highlights "the things companies bury in their SEC filings." It notes that company reports are more complete of late, but only the largest companies are preparing documents that are readable. As the editor of the site noted, "[some companies] are being dragged kicking and screaming into plain English."

Sources: Gretchen Morgenson, "Annual Reports: More Pages, but Better?" *The New York Times* (March 17, 2002); and D. Stead, "The Secrets in SEC Filings," *BusinessWeek* (August 25, 2008), p. 12.

DISCLOSURE ISSUES

Disclosure of Special Transactions or Events

3 LEARNING OBJECTIVE
Discuss the disclosure requirements for related-party transactions, post-balance-sheet events, and major business segments.

Related-party transactions, errors and fraud, and illegal acts pose especially sensitive and difficult problems. The accountant/auditor who has responsibility for reporting on these types of transactions must take care to properly balance the rights of the reporting company and the needs of users of the financial statements.

Related-party transactions arise when a company engages in transactions in which one of the parties has the ability to significantly influence the policies of the other. They may also occur when a nontransacting party has the ability to influence the policies of the two transacting parties.[4] Competitive, free-market dealings may not exist

[4]Examples of related-party transactions include transactions between (a) a parent company and its subsidiaries; (b) subsidiaries of a common parent; (c) a company and trusts for the benefit of employees (controlled or managed by the enterprise); and (d) a company and its principal owners, management, or members of immediate families, and affiliates. Two classic cases of related-party transactions were **Enron**, with its misuse of special-purpose entities, and **Tyco International**, which forgave loans to its management team.

in related-party transactions, and so an "arm's-length" basis cannot be assumed. Transactions such as borrowing or lending money at abnormally low or high interest rates, real estate sales at amounts that differ significantly from appraised value, exchanges of nonmonetary assets, and transactions involving enterprises that have no economic substance ("shell corporations") suggest that related parties may be involved.

See the FASB Codification section (page 1530).

In order to make adequate disclosure, companies should report the economic substance, rather than the legal form, of these transactions. GAAP requires the following disclosures of material related-party transactions. [1]

1. The nature of the relationship(s) involved.
2. A description of the transactions (including transactions to which no amounts or nominal amounts were ascribed) for each of the periods for which income statements are presented.
3. The dollar amounts of transactions for each of the periods for which income statements are presented.
4. Amounts due from or to related parties as of the date of each balance sheet presented.

Illustration 24-2, from the annual report of **Harley-Davidson, Inc.**, shows disclosure of related-party transactions.

ILLUSTRATION 24-2
Disclosure of Related-Party Transactions

Harley-Davidson, Inc.

22. Related Party Transactions

The Company has the following material related party transactions. A director of the Company is Chairman and Chief Executive Officer and an equity owner of Fred Deeley Imports Ltd. (Deeley Imports), the exclusive distributor of the Company's motorcycles in Canada. The Company recorded motorcycles and related products revenue and financial services revenue from Deeley Imports during 2011, 2010 and 2009 of $155.2 million, $158.7 million and $177.2 million, respectively, and had finance receivables balances due from Deeley Imports of $14.5 million, $21.0 million and $13.9 million at December 31, 2011, 2010 and 2009, respectively. All such products were provided in the ordinary course of business at prices and on terms and conditions that the Company believes are the same as those that would result from arm's-length negotiations between unrelated parties.

Many companies are involved in related-party transactions. Errors, fraud (sometimes referred to as irregularities), and illegal acts, however, are the exception rather than the rule. Accounting **errors** are **unintentional** mistakes, whereas **fraud** (misappropriation of assets and fraudulent financial reporting) involves **intentional** distortions of financial statements.[5] As indicated earlier, companies should correct the financial statements when they discover errors. The same treatment should be given fraud. The discovery of fraud, however, gives rise to a different set of procedures and responsibilities for the accountant/auditor.[6]

Illegal acts encompass such items as illegal political contributions, bribes, kickbacks, and other violations of laws and regulations.[7] In these situations, the accountant/auditor

[5] "Consideration of Fraud in a Financial Statement Audit," *Statement on Auditing Standards No. 99* (New York: AICPA, 2002). We have an expanded discussion of fraudulent financial reporting later in this chapter. Since passage of the Sarbanes-Oxley Act, auditors of public companies are regulated by the Public Company Accounting Oversight Board (PCAOB). The PCAOB is now the audit standard-setter for auditors of public companies. It has adopted much of the prior auditing standards issued by the Auditing Standards Board of the AICPA.

[6] The profession became so concerned with certain management frauds that affect financial statements that it established a National Commission on Fraudulent Financial Reporting. The major purpose of this organization was to determine how fraudulent reporting practices could be constrained. Fraudulent financial reporting is discussed later in this chapter.

[7] "Illegal Acts by Clients," *Statement on Auditing Standards No. 54* (New York: AICPA, 1988).

must evaluate the adequacy of disclosure in the financial statements. For example, if a company derives revenue from an illegal act that is considered material in relation to the financial statements, this information should be disclosed. The Sarbanes-Oxley Act is intended to deter these illegal acts. This law adds significant fines and longer jail time for those who improperly sign off on the correctness of financial statements that include willing and knowing misstatements.

Disclosure plays a very important role in these types of transactions because the events are more qualitative than quantitative and involve more subjective than objective evaluation. Users of the financial statements need some indication of the existence and nature of these transactions, through disclosures, modifications in the auditor's report, or reports of changes in auditors.

Post-Balance-Sheet Events (Subsequent Events)

Notes to the financial statements should explain any significant financial events that took place after the formal balance sheet date, but before the statement is issued. These events are referred to as **post-balance-sheet events**, or just plain **subsequent events**. Illustration 24-3 shows a time diagram of the subsequent events period.

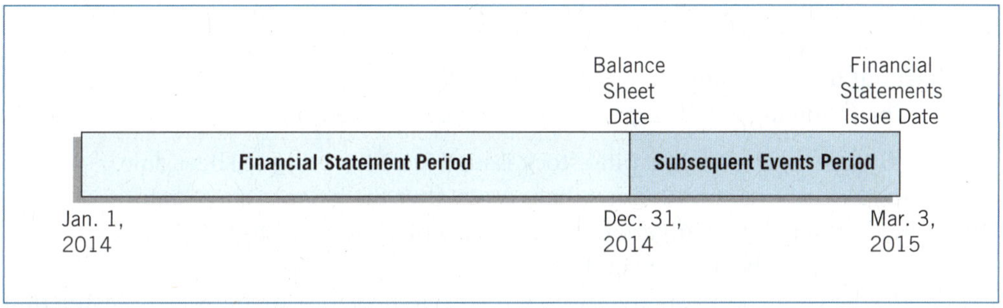

ILLUSTRATION 24-3
Time Periods for Subsequent Events

A period of several weeks, and sometimes months, may elapse after the end of the fiscal year but before the company issues financial statements. Various activities involved in closing the books for the period and issuing the statements all take time: taking and pricing the inventory, reconciling subsidiary ledgers with controlling accounts, preparing necessary adjusting entries, ensuring that all transactions for the period have been entered, obtaining an audit of the financial statements by independent certified public accountants, and printing the annual report. During the period between the balance sheet date and its distribution to stockholders and creditors, important transactions or other events may occur that materially affect the company's financial position or operating situation.

Many who read a balance sheet believe the balance sheet condition is constant, and they project it into the future. However, readers must be told if the company has experienced a significant change—e.g., sold one of its plants, acquired a subsidiary, suffered extraordinary losses, settled significant litigation, or experienced any other important event in the post-balance-sheet period. Without an explanation in a note, the reader might be misled and draw inappropriate conclusions.

Two types of events or transactions occurring after the balance sheet date may have a material effect on the financial statements or may need disclosure so that readers interpret these statements accurately:

1. Events that provide additional evidence about conditions **that existed** at the balance sheet date, including the estimates inherent in the process of preparing financial statements. These events are referred to as **recognized subsequent events** and

require adjustments to the financial statements. All information available prior to the issuance of the financial statements helps investors and creditors evaluate estimates previously made. To ignore these subsequent events is to pass up an opportunity to improve the accuracy of the financial statements. This first type of event encompasses information that an accountant would have recorded in the accounts had the information been known at the balance sheet date.

For example, if a loss on an account receivable results from a customer's bankruptcy subsequent to the balance sheet date, the company adjusts the financial statements before their issuance. The bankruptcy stems from the customer's poor financial health existing at the balance sheet date.

The same criterion applies to settlements of litigation. The company must adjust the financial statements if the events that gave rise to the litigation, such as personal injury or patent infringement, took place prior to the balance sheet date.

2. Events that provide evidence about conditions that **did not exist** at the balance sheet date but arise subsequent to that date. These events are referred as **nonrecognized subsequent events** and do not require adjustment of the financial statements. To illustrate, a loss resulting from a customer's fire or flood *after* the balance sheet date does not reflect conditions existing at that date. Thus, adjustment of the financial statements is not necessary. A company should not recognize subsequent events that provide evidence about conditions that did not exist at the date of the balance sheet but that arose after the balance sheet date.

The following are examples of nonrecognized subsequent events:

Underlying Concepts

A company also should consider supplementing the historical financial statements with pro forma financial data. Occasionally, a nonrecognized subsequent event may be so significant that disclosure can best be made by means of pro forma financial data.

(a) Sale of a bond or capital stock issued after the balance sheet date.
(b) A business combination that occurs after the balance sheet date.
(c) Settlement of litigation when the event giving rise to the claim took place after the balance sheet date.
(d) Loss of plant or inventories as a result of fire or natural disaster that occurred after the balance sheet date.
(e) Losses on receivables resulting from conditions (such as a customer's major casualty) arising after the balance sheet date.
(f) Changes in the quoted market prices of securities or foreign exchange rates after the balance sheet date.
(g) Entering into significant commitments or contingent liabilities, for example, by issuing significant guarantees after the balance sheet date. **[2]**[8]

Some nonrecognized subsequent events may have to be disclosed to keep the financial statements from being misleading. For such events, a company discloses the nature of the event and an estimate of its financial effect.

Illustration 24-4 presents an example of subsequent events disclosure, excerpted from the annual report of **Commercial Metals Company**.

Many subsequent events or developments do not require adjustment of or disclosure in the financial statements. Typically, these are nonaccounting events or conditions

[8]The effects from natural disasters, like hurricanes Katrina, Rita, and Sandy, which occurred after the year-end for companies with August fiscal years, require disclosure in order to keep the statements from being misleading. Some companies may have to consider whether these disasters affect their ability to continue as going concerns. *Accounting Trends and Techniques—2012* listed the following types of subsequent events and their frequency of occurrence among the 500 companies surveyed: acquisitions, 32; debt incurred, reduced, or refinanced, 31; business combinations pending or effected, 29; capital stock issued or purchased, 18; discontinued operations or asset disposals, 15; litigation, 14; and restructuring/bankruptcy, 13.

ILLUSTRATION 24-4
Disclosure of Subsequent Events

Commercial Metals Company

NOTE 22. SUBSEQUENT EVENTS (August 31 Fiscal Year End)
On October 7, 2011, The Company announced its decision to exit the business in CMCS by way of sale and/or closure. During 2011, the Company made operational improvements in the business but not to a level which would restore profitability for the long run. Additionally, delayed entry in the European Union, cyclical demand for tubular products, unsustainable losses and increased demand for capital resources resulted in the decision to exit the business. The operation will service any existing customer commitments and the Company expects to wind down operations and liquidate inventory over the next several months. In connection with this decision, the Company expects to incur severance and other closure costs between $25 million and $40 million in fiscal 2012.

that management normally communicates by other means. These events include legislation, product changes, management changes, strikes, unionization, marketing agreements, and loss of important customers.

Reporting for Diversified (Conglomerate) Companies

In certain business climates, companies have a tendency to diversify their operations. Take the case of conglomerate General Electric (GE), whose products include locomotives and jet engines, credit card services, and water purification systems. Or, consider cable giant Comcast; its NBC Universal subsidiary owns NBC TV, Telemundo, Universal Pictures, and Universal Parks and Resorts. When businesses are so diversified, investors and investment analysts want more information about the details behind conglomerate financial statements. Particularly, they want income statement, balance sheet, and cash flow information on the **individual segments** that compose the total income figure.

Illustration 24-5 shows **segmented** (disaggregated) financial information of an office equipment and auto parts company.

ILLUSTRATION 24-5
Segmented Income Statement

OFFICE EQUIPMENT AND AUTO PARTS COMPANY
INCOME STATEMENT DATA
(IN MILLIONS)

	Consolidated	Office Equipment	Auto Parts
Net sales	$78.8	$18.0	$60.8
Manufacturing costs			
Inventories, beginning	12.3	4.0	8.3
Materials and services	38.9	10.8	28.1
Wages	12.9	3.8	9.1
Inventories, ending	(13.3)	(3.9)	(9.4)
	50.8	14.7	36.1
Selling and administrative expenses	12.1	1.6	10.5
Total operating expenses	62.9	16.3	46.6
Income before taxes	15.9	1.7	14.2
Income taxes	(9.3)	(1.0)	(8.3)
Net income	$ 6.6	$ 0.7	$ 5.9

Much information is hidden in the aggregated totals. If the analyst has only the consolidated figures, he/she cannot tell the extent to which the differing product lines **contribute to the company's profitability, risk, and growth potential**. For example, in Illustration 24-5, the office equipment segment looks like a risky venture. Segmented reporting would provide useful information about the two business segments and would be useful for making an informed investment decision regarding the whole company.

In addition to the example of **Coach, Inc.** in the opening story, a classic situation that demonstrates the need for segmented data involved **Caterpillar, Inc.** The SEC cited Caterpillar because it failed to tell investors that nearly a quarter of its income in one year came from a Brazilian unit and was nonrecurring in nature. The company knew that different economic policies in the next year would probably greatly affect earnings of the Brazilian unit. But Caterpillar presented its financial results on a consolidated basis, not disclosing the Brazilian operations. The SEC found that Caterpillar's failure to include information about Brazil left investors with an incomplete picture of the company's financial results and denied investors the opportunity to see the company "through the eyes of management."

Companies have always been somewhat hesitant to disclose segmented data for various reasons:

1. Without a thorough knowledge of the business and an understanding of such important factors as the competitive environment and capital investment requirements, the investor may find the segmented information meaningless or may even draw improper conclusions about the reported earnings of the segments.
2. Additional disclosure may be helpful to competitors, labor unions, suppliers, and certain government regulatory agencies, and thus harm the reporting company.
3. Additional disclosure may discourage management from taking intelligent business risks because segments reporting losses or unsatisfactory earnings may cause stockholder dissatisfaction with management.
4. The wide variation among companies in the choice of segments, cost allocation, and other accounting problems limits the usefulness of segmented information.
5. The investor is investing in the company as a whole and not in the particular segments, and it should not matter how any single segment is performing if the overall performance is satisfactory.
6. Certain technical problems, such as classification of segments and allocation of segment revenues and costs (especially "common costs"), are formidable.

On the other hand, the advocates of segmented disclosures offer these reasons in support of the practice:

1. Investors need segmented information to make an intelligent investment decision regarding a diversified company.
   (a) Sales and earnings of individual segments enable investors to evaluate the differences between segments in growth rate, risk, and profitability, and to forecast consolidated profits.
   (b) Segmented reports help investors evaluate the company's investment worth by disclosing the nature of a company's businesses and the relative size of the components.
2. The absence of segmented reporting by a diversified company may put its unsegmented, single product-line competitors at a competitive disadvantage because the conglomerate may obscure information that its competitors must disclose.

The advocates of segmented disclosures appear to have a much stronger case. Many users indicate that segmented data are the most useful financial information provided, aside from the basic financial statements. As a result, the FASB has issued extensive reporting guidelines in this area.

Objective of Reporting Segmented Information

The objective of reporting segmented financial data is to provide information about the **different types of business activities** in which an enterprise engages and the **different economic environments** in which it operates. Meeting this objective will help users of financial statements do the following.

(a) Better understand the enterprise's performance.

(b) Better assess its prospects for future net cash flows.

(c) Make more informed judgments about the enterprise as a whole.

Basic Principles

Financial statements can be disaggregated in several ways. For example, they can be disaggregated by products or services, by geography, by legal entity, or by type of customer. However, it is not feasible to provide all of that information in every set of financial statements. GAAP requires that general-purpose financial statements include selected information on a single basis of segmentation. Thus, a company can meet the segmented reporting objective by providing financial statements segmented based on how the company's operations are managed. The method chosen is referred to as the **management approach**. [3] **The management approach reflects how management segments the company for making operating decisions.** The segments are evident from the components of the company's organization structure. These components are called **operating segments**.

Identifying Operating Segments

An **operating segment** is a component of an enterprise:

(a) That engages in business activities from which it earns revenues and incurs expenses.

(b) Whose operating results are regularly reviewed by the company's chief operating decision-maker to assess segment performance and allocate resources to the segment.

(c) For which discrete financial information is available that is generated by or based on the internal financial reporting system.

Companies may aggregate information about two or more operating segments only if the segments have the same basic characteristics in each of the following areas.

(a) The nature of the products and services provided.

(b) The nature of the production process.

(c) The type or class of customer.

(d) The methods of product or service distribution.

(e) If applicable, the nature of the regulatory environment.

After the company decides on the possible segments for disclosure, it makes a quantitative materiality test. This test determines whether the segment is significant enough to warrant actual disclosure. An operating segment is deemed significant, and therefore a reportable segment, if it satisfies **one or more** of the following quantitative thresholds.

1. Its **revenue** (including both sales to external customers and intersegment sales or transfers) is 10 percent or more of the combined revenue of all the company's operating segments.
2. The absolute amount of its **profit or loss** is 10 percent or more of the greater, in absolute amount, of (a) the combined operating profit of all operating segments that

did not incur a loss, or (b) the combined loss of all operating segments that did report a loss.

3. Its **identifiable assets** are 10 percent or more of the combined assets of all operating segments.

In applying these tests, the company must consider two additional factors. First, segment data must explain a significant portion of the company's business. Specifically, the segmented results must equal or exceed 75 percent of the combined sales to unaffiliated customers for the entire company. This test prevents a company from providing limited information on only a few segments and lumping all the rest into one category.

Second, the profession recognizes that reporting too many segments may overwhelm users with detailed information. The FASB decided that 10 is a reasonable upper limit for the number of segments that a company must disclose.

To illustrate these requirements, assume a company has identified six possible reporting segments, as shown in Illustration 24-6 (000s omitted).

ILLUSTRATION 24-6
Data for Different Possible Reporting Segments

Segments	Total Revenue (Unaffiliated)	Operating Profit (Loss)	Identifiable Assets
A	$ 100	$10	$ 60
B	50	2	30
C	700	40	390
D	300	20	160
E	900	18	280
F	100	(5)	50
	$2,150	$85	$970

The company would apply the respective tests as follows.

Revenue test: 10% × $2,150 = $215; C, D, and E meet this test.

Operating profit (loss) test: 10% × $90 = $9 (note that the $5 loss is ignored because the test is based on non-loss segments); A, C, D, and E meet this test.

Identifiable assets tests: 10% × $970 = $97; C, D, and E meet this test.

The reporting segments are therefore A, C, D, and E, assuming that these four segments have enough sales to meet the 75 percent of combined sales test. The 75 percent test is computed as follows.

75% of combined sales test: 75% × $2,150 = $1,612.50. The sales of A, C, D, and E total $2,000 ($100 + $700 + $300 + $900); therefore, the 75 percent test is met.

Measurement Principles

The accounting principles that companies use for segment disclosure need not be the same as the principles they use to prepare the consolidated statements. This flexibility may at first appear inconsistent. But, preparing segment information in accordance with generally accepted accounting principles would be difficult because some principles are not expected to apply at a segment level. Examples are accounting for the cost of company-wide employee benefit plans, accounting for income taxes in a company that files a consolidated tax return, and accounting for inventory on a LIFO basis if the pool includes items in more than one segment.

The FASB does not require allocations of joint, common, or company-wide costs solely for external reporting purposes. **Common costs** are those incurred for the benefit of more than one segment and whose interrelated nature prevents a completely objective division of costs among segments. For example, the company president's salary is difficult to allocate to various segments. Allocations of common costs are inherently arbitrary and may not be meaningful. There is a presumption that if companies allocate common costs to segments, these allocations are either directly attributable or reasonably allocable.

Segmented Information Reported

The FASB requires that an enterprise report the following.

1. ***General information about its operating segments.*** This includes factors that management considers most significant in determining the company's operating segments, and the types of products and services from which each operating segment derives its revenues.
2. ***Segment profit and loss and related information.*** Specifically, companies must report the following information about each operating segment if the amounts are included in determining segment profit or loss.
   (a) Revenues from transactions with external customers.
   (b) Revenues from transactions with other operating segments of the same enterprise.
   (c) Interest revenue.
   (d) Interest expense.
   (e) Depreciation, depletion, and amortization expense.
   (f) Unusual items.
   (g) Equity in the net income of investees accounted for by the equity method.
   (h) Income tax expense or benefit.
   (i) Extraordinary items.
   (j) Significant noncash items other than depreciation, depletion, and amortization expense.
3. ***Segment assets.*** A company must report each operating segment's total assets.
4. ***Reconciliations.*** A company must provide a reconciliation of the total of the segments' revenues to total revenues, a reconciliation of the total of the operating segments' profits and losses to its income before income taxes, and a reconciliation of the total of the operating segments' assets to total assets.
5. ***Information about products and services and geographic areas.*** For each operating segment not based on geography, the company must report (unless it is impracticable): (1) revenues from external customers, (2) long-lived assets, and (3) expenditures during the period for long-lived assets. This information, if material, must be reported (a) in the enterprise's country of domicile and (b) in each other country.
6. ***Major customers.*** If 10 percent or more of company revenue is derived from a single customer, the company must disclose the total amount of revenue from each such customer by segment.

Illustration of Disaggregated Information

Illustration 24-7 (page 1502) shows the segment disclosure for **Johnson & Johnson**.

Interim Reports

4 LEARNING OBJECTIVE
Describe the accounting problems associated with interim reporting.

Another source of information for the investor is interim reports. As noted earlier, **interim reports** cover periods of less than one year. The stock exchanges, the SEC, and the accounting profession have an active interest in the presentation of interim information.

The SEC mandates that certain companies file a **Form 10-Q**, in which a company discloses quarterly data similar to that disclosed in the annual report. It also requires

Johnson & Johnson
(notes excluded)

Segments of Business and Geographic Areas

(Dollars in Millions)	Sales to Customers 2011	2010	2009
Consumer—United States	$ 5,151	$ 5,519	$ 6,837
International	9,732	9,071	8,966
Total	14,883	14,590	15,803
Pharmaceutical—United States	12,386	12,519	13,041
International	11,982	9,877	9,479
Total	24,368	22,396	22,520
Medical Devices and Diagnostics—United States	11,371	11,412	11,011
International	14,408	13,189	12,563
Total	25,779	24,601	23,574
Worldwide total	$65,030	$61,587	$ 61,897

(Dollars in Millions)	Operating Profit 2011	2010	2009	Identifiable Assets 2011	2010	2009
Consumer	$ 2,096	$ 2,342	$ 2,475	$ 24,210	$ 23,753	$24,671
Pharmaceutical	6,406	7,086	6,413	23,747	19,961	21,460
Medical Devices and Diagnostics	5,263	8,272	7,694	23,609	23,277	22,853
Total	13,765	17,700	16,582	71,566	66,991	68,984
Less: Expense not allocated to segments	1,404	753	827			
General corporate				42,078	35,917	25,698
Worldwide total	$12,361	$16,947	$15,755	$113,644	$102,908	$94,682

(Dollars in Millions)	Additions to Property, Plant & Equipment 2011	2010	2009	Depreciation and Amortization 2011	2010	2009
Consumer	$ 670	$ 526	$ 439	$ 631	$ 532	$ 513
Pharmaceutical	729	508	535	958	912	922
Medical Devices and Diagnostics	1,095	1,113	1,114	1,331	1,270	1,124
Segments total	2,494	2,147	2,088	2,920	2,714	2,559
General corporate	399	237	277	238	225	215
Worldwide total	$2,893	$2,384	$2,365	$3,158	$2,939	$2,774

(Dollars in Millions)	Sales to Customers 2011	2010	2009	Long-Lived Assets 2011	2010	2009
United States	$28,908	$29,450	$30,889	$ 23,529	$ 23,315	$22,399
Europe	17,129	15,510	15,934	19,056	16,791	17,347
Western Hemisphere excluding U.S.	6,418	5,550	5,156	3,517	3,653	3,540
Asia-Pacific, Africa	12,575	11,077	9,918	2,163	2,089	1,868
Segments total	65,030	61,587	61,897	48,265	45,848	45,154
General corporate				750	715	790
Other non long-lived assets				64,629	56,345	48,738
Worldwide total	$65,030	$61,587	$61,897	$113,644	$102,908	$94,682

ILLUSTRATION 24-7
Segment Disclosure

those companies to disclose selected quarterly information in notes to the annual financial statements. Illustration 24-8 presents the selected quarterly disclosure of **Tootsie Roll Industries, Inc.** In addition to Form 10-Q, GAAP narrows the reporting alternatives related to interim reports. **[4]**

Because of the short-term nature of the information in these reports, there is considerable controversy as to the general approach companies should employ. One group,

ILLUSTRATION 24-8
Disclosure of Selected Quarterly Data

Tootsie Roll Industries, Inc.

For the Year Ended December 31, 2011

(Thousands of dollars except per share data)

	First	Second	Third	Fourth	Total
Net product sales	$108,323	$104,884	$186,784	$128,378	$528,369
Product gross margin	34,799	33,898	54,554	39,893	163,144
Net earnings	8,330	6,486	18,855	10,267	43,938
Net earnings per share	0.14	0.11	0.33	0.18	0.76

	Stock Prices 2011		Dividends 2011
	High	Low	
1st Qtr	$29.45	$27.06	$0.08
2nd Qtr	$29.68	$27.78	$0.08
3rd Qtr	$29.80	$23.52	$0.08
4th Qtr	$25.95	$22.85	$0.08

which favors the **discrete approach**, believes that companies should treat each interim period as a separate accounting period. Using that treatment, companies would follow the principles for deferrals and accruals used for annual reports. In this view, companies should report accounting transactions as they occur, and expense recognition should not change with the period of time covered.

Underlying Concepts

For information to be relevant, it must be available to decision-makers before it loses its capacity to influence their decisions (timeliness). Interim reporting is an excellent example of this concept.

Another group, which favors the **integral approach**, believes that the interim report is an integral part of the annual report and that deferrals and accruals should take into consideration what will happen for the entire year. In this approach, companies should assign estimated expenses to parts of a year on the basis of sales volume or some other activity base.

At present, many companies follow the discrete approach for certain types of expenses and the integral approach for others, because the standards currently employed in practice are vague and lead to differing interpretations.

Interim Reporting Requirements

Generally, companies should use the same accounting principles for interim reports and for annual reports. They should recognize revenues in interim periods on the same basis as they are for annual periods. For example, if Cedars Corp. uses the installment-sales method as the basis for recognizing revenue on an annual basis, then it should use the installment basis for interim reports as well. Also, Cedars should treat costs directly associated with revenues (product costs, such as materials, labor and related fringe benefits, and manufacturing overhead) in the same manner for interim reports as for annual reports.

Companies should use the same inventory pricing methods (FIFO, LIFO, etc.) for interim reports and for annual reports. However, the following exceptions are appropriate at interim reporting periods.

1. Companies may use the gross profit method for interim inventory pricing. But they must disclose the method and adjustments to reconcile with annual inventory.
2. When a company liquidates LIFO inventories at an interim date and expects to replace them by year-end, cost of goods sold should include the expected cost of replacing the liquidated LIFO base, rather than give effect to the interim liquidation.

3. Companies should not defer inventory market declines beyond the interim period unless they are temporary and no loss is expected for the fiscal year.
4. Companies ordinarily should defer planned variances under a standard cost system; such variances are expected to be absorbed by year-end.

Companies often charge to the interim period, as incurred, costs and expenses other than product costs (often referred to as **period costs**). But companies may allocate these costs among interim periods on the basis of an estimate of time expired, benefit received, or activity associated with the periods. Companies display considerable latitude in accounting for these costs in interim periods, and many believe more definitive guidelines are needed.

Regarding disclosure, companies should report the following interim data at a minimum.

1. Sales or gross revenues, provision for income taxes, extraordinary items, and net income.
2. Basic and diluted earnings per share where appropriate.
3. Seasonal revenue, cost, or expenses.
4. Significant changes in estimates or provisions for income taxes.
5. Disposal of a component of a business and extraordinary, unusual, or infrequently occurring items.
6. Contingent items.
7. Changes in accounting principles or estimates.
8. Significant changes in financial position.

The FASB encourages, but does not require, companies to publish an interim balance sheet and statement of cash flows. If a company does not present this information, it should disclose significant changes in such items as liquid assets, net working capital, long-term liabilities, and stockholders' equity.

Unique Problems of Interim Reporting

GAAP reflects a preference for the integral approach. However, within this broad guideline, a number of unique reporting problems develop related to the following items.

Advertising and Similar Costs. The general guidelines are that companies should defer in an interim period costs such as advertising if the benefits extend beyond that period; otherwise, the company should expense those costs as incurred. But such a determination is difficult, and even if the company defers the costs, how should it allocate them between quarters?

Because of the vague guidelines in this area, accounting for advertising varies widely. At one time, some companies in the food industry, such as **RJR Nabisco** and **Pillsbury**, charged advertising costs as a percentage of sales and adjusted to actual at year-end, whereas **General Foods** and **Kellogg** expensed these costs as incurred.

The same type of problem relates to such items as Social Security taxes, research and development costs, and major repairs. For example, should the company expense Social Security costs (payroll taxes) on highly paid personnel early in the year, or allocate and spread them to subsequent quarters? Should a major repair that occurs later in the year be anticipated and allocated proportionately to earlier periods?

Expenses Subject to Year-End Adjustment. Companies often do not know with a great deal of certainty amounts of bad debts, executive bonuses, pension costs, and inventory shrinkage until year-end. **They should estimate these costs and allocate them to interim periods as best they can.** Companies use a variety of allocation techniques to accomplish this objective.

Income Taxes. Not every dollar of corporate taxable income is taxed at the same rate; the tax rate is progressive. This aspect of business income taxes poses a problem in preparing interim financial statements. Should the company use the **annualized approach**, which is to annualize income to date and accrue the proportionate income tax for the period to date? Or should it follow the **marginal principle approach**, which is to apply the lower rate of tax to the first amount of income earned? At one time, companies generally followed the latter approach and accrued the tax applicable to each additional dollar of income.

The profession now, however, uses the annualized approach. This requires that "at the end of each interim period the company should make its best estimate of the effective tax rate expected to be applicable for the full fiscal year. The rate so determined should be used in providing for income taxes on income for the quarter." **[5]**[9]

Because businesses did not uniformly apply this guideline in accounting for similar situations, the FASB issued authoritative guidance. GAAP now requires companies, when computing the year-to-date tax, to apply the **estimated annual effective tax rate** to the year-to-date "ordinary" income at the end of each interim period. Further, the **interim period tax** related to "ordinary" income shall be the difference between the amount so computed and the amounts reported for previous interim periods of the fiscal period. **[6]**[10]

Extraordinary Items. Extraordinary items consist of unusual and nonrecurring material gains and losses. In the past, companies handled them in interim reports in one of three ways: (1) absorbed them entirely in the quarter in which they occurred, (2) prorated them over four quarters, or (3) disclosed them only by note. **The required approach now is to charge or credit the loss or gain in the quarter in which it occurs**, instead of attempting some arbitrary multiple-period allocation. This approach is consistent with the way in which companies must handle extraordinary items on an annual basis. No attempt is made to prorate the extraordinary items over several years.

Some favor the omission of extraordinary items from the quarterly net income. They believe that inclusion of extraordinary items that may be large in proportion to interim results distorts the predictive value of interim reports. Many, however, consider such an omission inappropriate because it deviates from actual results.

Earnings per Share. Interim reporting of earnings per share has all the problems inherent in computing and presenting annual earnings per share, and then some. If a company issues shares in the third period, EPS for the first two periods will not reflect year-end EPS. If an extraordinary item is present in one period and the company sells new equity shares in another period, the EPS figure for the extraordinary item will change for the year. On an annual basis, only one EPS figure can be associated with an extraordinary item and that figure does not change; the interim figure is subject to change.

For purposes of computing earnings per share and making the required disclosure determinations, each interim period should stand alone. That is, all applicable tests should be made for that single period.

[9]The estimated annual effective tax rate should reflect anticipated tax credits, foreign tax rates, percentage depletion, capital gains rates, and other available tax-planning alternatives.

[10]"Ordinary" income (or loss) refers to "income (or loss) from continuing operations before income taxes (or benefits)" excluding extraordinary items and discontinued operations.

Seasonality. **Seasonality** occurs when most of a company's sales occur in one short period of the year while certain costs are fairly evenly spread throughout the year. For example, the natural gas industry has its heavy sales in the winter months. In contrast, the beverage industry has its heavy sales in the summer months.

The problem of seasonality is related to the expense recognition principle in accounting. Generally, expenses are associated with the revenues they create. In a seasonal business, wide fluctuations in profits occur because off-season sales do not absorb the company's fixed costs (for example, manufacturing, selling, and administrative costs that tend to remain fairly constant regardless of sales or production).

To illustrate why seasonality is a problem, assume the following information.

ILLUSTRATION 24-9
Data for Seasonality Example

Selling price per unit	$1
Annual sales for the period (projected and actual)	
100,000 units @ $1	$100,000
Manufacturing costs	
Variable	10¢ per unit
Fixed	20¢ per unit or $20,000 for the year
Nonmanufacturing costs	
Variable	10¢ per unit
Fixed	30¢ per unit or $30,000 for the year

Sales for four quarters and the year (projected and actual) were:

ILLUSTRATION 24-10
Sales Data for Seasonality Example

		Percent of Sales
1st Quarter	$ 20,000	20%
2nd Quarter	5,000	5
3rd Quarter	10,000	10
4th Quarter	65,000	65
Total for the year	$100,000	100%

Under the present accounting framework, the income statements for the quarters might be as shown in Illustration 24-11.

ILLUSTRATION 24-11
Interim Net Income for Seasonal Business—Discrete Approach

	1st Qtr	2nd Qtr	3rd Qtr	4th Qtr	Year
Sales	$20,000	$ 5,000	$10,000	$65,000	$100,000
Manufacturing costs					
Variable	(2,000)	(500)	(1,000)	(6,500)	(10,000)
Fixed[a]	(4,000)	(1,000)	(2,000)	(13,000)	(20,000)
	14,000	3,500	7,000	45,500	70,000
Nonmanufacturing costs					
Variable	(2,000)	(500)	(1,000)	(6,500)	(10,000)
Fixed[b]	(7,500)	(7,500)	(7,500)	(7,500)	(30,000)
Net income	$ 4,500	$(4,500)	$ (1,500)	$31,500	$ 30,000

[a]The fixed manufacturing costs are inventoried, so that equal amounts of fixed costs do not appear during each quarter.
[b]The fixed nonmanufacturing costs are not inventoried, so equal amounts of fixed costs appear during each quarter.

An investor who uses the first quarter's results might be misled. If the first quarter's earnings are $4,500, should this figure be multiplied by four to predict annual earnings of $18,000? Or, if first-quarter sales of $20,000 are 20 percent of the predicted sales for the year, would the net income for the year be $22,500 ($4,500 × 5)? Both figures are obviously wrong, and after the second quarter's results occur, the investor may become even more confused.

The problem with the conventional approach is that the fixed nonmanufacturing costs are not charged in proportion to sales. Some enterprises have adopted a way of avoiding this problem by making all fixed nonmanufacturing costs follow the sales pattern, as shown in Illustration 24-12.

ILLUSTRATION 24-12
Interim Net Income for Seasonal Business—Integral Approach

	1st Qtr	2nd Qtr	3rd Qtr	4th Qtr	Year
Sales	$20,000	$ 5,000	$10,000	$65,000	$100,000
Manufacturing costs					
Variable	(2,000)	(500)	(1,000)	(6,500)	(10,000)
Fixed	(4,000)	(1,000)	(2,000)	(13,000)	(20,000)
	14,000	3,500	7,000	45,500	70,000
Nonmanufacturing costs					
Variable	(2,000)	(500)	(1,000)	(6,500)	(10,000)
Fixed	(6,000)	(1,500)	(3,000)	(19,500)	(30,000)
Net income	$ 6,000	$ 1,500	$ 3,000	$19,500	$ 30,000

This approach solves some of the seasonality problems of interim reporting. Sales in the first quarter are 20 percent of total sales for the year, and net income in the first quarter is 20 percent of total income. In this case, as in the previous example, the investor cannot rely on multiplying any given quarter by four but can use comparative data or rely on some estimate of sales in relation to income for a given period.

The greater the degree of seasonality experienced by a company, the greater the possibility of distortion. Because there are no definitive guidelines for handling such items as the fixed nonmanufacturing costs, variability in income can be substantial. To alleviate this problem, the profession recommends that companies subject to material seasonal variations disclose the seasonal nature of their business and consider supplementing their interim reports with information for 12-month periods ended at the interim date for the current and preceding years.

The two illustrations highlight the difference between the **discrete** and **integral** approaches. Illustration 24-11 represents the discrete approach, in which the fixed nonmanufacturing expenses are expensed as incurred. Illustration 24-12 shows the integral approach, in which expenses are charged to expense on the basis of some measure of activity.

International Perspective

IFRS requires that interim financial statements use the discrete method, except for tax expenses.

Evolving Issue *IT'S FASTER BUT IS IT BETTER?*

The profession has developed some rules for interim reporting, but much still has to be done. As yet, it is unclear whether the discrete or the integral method, or some combination of the two, will be settled on.

Discussion also persists about the independent auditor's involvement in interim reports. Many auditors are reluctant to express an opinion on interim financial information, arguing that the data are too tentative and subjective. On the other hand, more people are advocating some examination of interim reports. As a compromise, the SEC currently requires that auditors perform a review of interim financial information. Such a review, which is much more limited in its procedures than the annual audit, provides some assurance that the interim information appears to be in accord with GAAP. (See "Interim Financial Information," *Statement on Auditing Standards No. 101* (New York: AICPA, 2002).)

Analysts and investors want financial information as soon as possible, before it's old news. We may not be far from a continuous database system in which corporate financial records can be accessed via the Internet. Investors might be able to access a company's financial records whenever they wish and put the information in the format they need. Thus, they could learn about sales slippage, cost increases, or earnings changes as they happen, rather than waiting until after the quarter has ended.

A step in this direction is the SEC's mandate for companies to file their financial statements electronically with the SEC. The system, called EDGAR (electronic data gathering and retrieval), provides interested parties with computer access to financial information such as periodic filings, corporate prospectuses, and proxy materials.

The SEC also believes that timeliness of information is of extreme importance. First, the SEC has said that large public companies will have only 60 days to complete their annual reports, down from 90 days. Quarterly reports must be done within 40 days of the close of the quarter, instead of 45. In addition, corporate executives and shareholders with more than 10 percent of a company's outstanding stock now have two days to disclose their sale or purchase of stock.

Finally, in a bid to increase Internet disclosure, the SEC encourages companies to post current, quarterly, and annual reports on their websites—or explain why they don't. The Internet postings would have to be made by the day the company submits the information to the SEC, rather than within 24 hours as current rules allow.

A steady stream of information from the company to the investor could be very positive because it might alleviate management's continual concern with short-run interim numbers. Today, many contend that U.S. management is too oriented to the short-term. The truth of this statement is echoed by the words of the president of a large company who decided to retire early: "I wanted to look forward to a year made up of four seasons rather than four quarters."

AUDITOR'S AND MANAGEMENT'S REPORTS

Auditor's Report

LEARNING OBJECTIVE 5
Identify the major disclosures in the auditor's report.

Another important source of information, which is often overlooked, is the **auditor's report**. An **auditor** is an accounting professional who conducts an independent examination of a company's accounting data.

If satisfied that the financial statements present the financial position, results of operations, and cash flows fairly in accordance with generally accepted accounting principles, the auditor expresses an **unqualified opinion**. An example is shown in Illustration 24-13.[11]

In preparing the report, the auditor follows these reporting standards.

1. The report states whether the financial statements are in accordance with generally accepted accounting principles.
2. The report identifies those circumstances in which the company has not consistently observed such principles in the current period in relation to the preceding period.
3. Users are to regard the informative disclosures in the financial statements as reasonably adequate unless the report states otherwise.
4. The report contains either an expression of opinion regarding the financial statements taken as a whole or an assertion to the effect that an opinion cannot be expressed. When the auditor cannot express an overall opinion, the report should state the reasons. In all cases where an auditor's name is associated with financial statements, the report should contain a clear-cut indication of the character of the auditor's examination, if any, and the degree of responsibility being taken.

In most cases, the auditor issues a standard **unqualified** or **clean opinion**. That is, the auditor expresses the opinion that the financial statements present fairly, in all material respects, the financial position, results of operations, and cash flows of the entity in conformity with generally accepted accounting principles.

[11]This auditor's report is in exact conformance with the specifications contained in "Reports on Audited Financial Statements," *Statement on Auditing Standards No. 58* (New York: AICPA, 1988). The last paragraph refers to the assessment of the company's internal controls, as required by the PCAOB.

ILLUSTRATION 24-13
Auditor's Report

Best Buy Co., Inc.

Report of Independent Registered Public Accounting Firm

To the Board of Directors and Shareholders of Best Buy Co., Inc.:

We have audited the accompanying consolidated balance sheets of Best Buy Co., Inc. and subsidiaries (the "Company") as of March 3, 2012 and February 26, 2011 and the related consolidated statements of earnings, cash flows, and changes in shareholders' equity for each of the three fiscal years in the period ended March 3, 2012. Our audits also included the financial statement schedule listed in the Index at Item 15(a). These financial statements and financial statement schedule are the responsibility of the Company's management. Our responsibility is to express an opinion on these financial statements and financial statement schedule based on our audits.

We conducted our audits in accordance with the standards of the Public Company Accounting Oversight Board (United States). Those standards require that we plan and perform the audit to obtain reasonable assurance about whether the financial statements are free of material misstatement. An audit includes examining, on a test basis, evidence supporting the amounts and disclosures in the financial statements. An audit also includes assessing the accounting principles used and significant estimates made by management, as well as evaluating the overall financial statement presentation. We believe that our audits provide a reasonable basis for our opinion.

In our opinion, such consolidated financial statements present fairly, in all material respects, the financial position of Best Buy Co., Inc. and subsidiaries as of March 3, 2012 and February 26, 2011, and the results of their operations and their cash flows for each of the three fiscal years in the period ended March 3, 2012, in conformity with accounting principles generally accepted in the United States of America. Also, in our opinion, such financial statement schedule, when considered in relation to the basic consolidated financial statements taken as a whole, presents fairly, in all material respects, the information set forth therein. We have also audited, in accordance with the standards of the Public Company Accounting Oversight Board (United States), the Company's internal control over financial reporting as of March 3, 2012, based on the criteria established in *Internal Control-Integrated Framework* issued by the Committee of Sponsoring Organizations of the Treadway Commission and our report dated May 1, 2012, expressed an unqualified opinion on the Company's internal control over financial reporting.

Deloitte & Touche LLP

Minneapolis, Minnesota
May 1, 2012

Certain circumstances, although they do not affect the auditor's unqualified opinion, may require the auditor to add an explanatory paragraph to the audit report. Some of the more important circumstances are as follows.

1. *Going concern.* The auditor must evaluate whether there is substantial doubt about the entity's **ability to continue as a going concern** for a reasonable period of time, taking into consideration all available information about the future. (The future is at least, but not limited to, 12 months from the end of the reporting period.) If substantial doubt exists about the company continuing as a going concern, the auditor adds to the report an explanatory note describing the potential problem. **[7]**[12]

[12]The FASB has a project requiring certain disclosures when management concludes it is *more likely than not* that the company will not be able to meet its obligations in the ordinary course of business for a reasonable period of time. When management concludes it is *probable* that the entity will not be able to meet its obligations in the ordinary course of business for a reasonable period of time, a statement that there is substantial doubt about the entity's ability to continue as a going concern would also be required. Similar to auditing standards, the Board defines a *reasonable period of time* as 12 months from the balance sheet date. However, management would also consider events that are probable of resulting in an entity's potential inability to meet its obligations beyond 12 months. The combined assessment period would not exceed 24 months. See *http://www.fasb.org/*; click on the Projects tab and scroll down to the Going Concern link. See also the project on liquidation accounting.

2. *Lack of consistency.* If a company has changed accounting principles or the method of their application in a way that has a material effect on the comparability of its financial statements, the auditor should refer to the change in an explanatory paragraph of the report. Such an explanatory paragraph should identify the nature of the change and refer readers to the note in the financial statements that discusses the change in detail. The auditor's concurrence with a change is implicit unless the auditor takes exception to the change in expressing an opinion as to fair presentation in conformity with generally accepted accounting principles.
3. *Emphasis of a matter.* The auditor may wish to emphasize a matter regarding the financial statements but nevertheless intends to express an unqualified opinion. For example, the auditor may wish to emphasize that the entity is a component of a larger business enterprise or that it has had significant transactions with related parties. The auditor presents such explanatory information in a separate paragraph of the report.

In some situations, however, the auditor is required to express (1) a **qualified** opinion or (2) an **adverse** opinion, or (3) to **disclaim** an opinion.

A **qualified opinion** contains an exception to the standard opinion. Ordinarily, the exception is not of sufficient magnitude to invalidate the statements as a whole; if it were, an adverse opinion would be rendered. The usual circumstances in which the auditor may deviate from the standard unqualified short-form report on financial statements are as follows.

1. The scope of the examination is limited or affected by conditions or restrictions.
2. The statements do not fairly present financial position or results of operations because of:
   (a) Lack of conformity with generally accepted accounting principles and standards.
   (b) Inadequate disclosure.

If confronted with one of the situations noted above, the auditor must offer a qualified opinion. A qualified opinion states that, except for the effects of the matter to which the qualification relates, the financial statements present fairly, in all material respects, the financial position, results of operations, and cash flows in conformity with generally accepted accounting principles.

Illustration 24-14 shows an example of an auditor's report with a qualified opinion. The auditor qualified the opinion because the company used an accounting principle at variance with generally accepted accounting principles.

ILLUSTRATION 24-14
Qualified Auditor's Report

Helio Company

Independent Auditor's Report

(Same first and second paragraphs as the standard report)

Helio Company has excluded, from property and debt in the accompanying balance sheets, certain lease obligations that, in our opinion, should be capitalized in order to conform with generally accepted accounting principles. If these lease obligations were capitalized, property would be increased by $1,500,000 and $1,300,000, long-term debt by $1,400,000 and $1,200,000, and retained earnings by $100,000 and $50,000 as of December 31, in the current and prior year, respectively. Additionally, net income would be decreased by $40,000 and $30,000 and earnings per share would be decreased by $.06 and $.04, respectively, for the years then ended.

In our opinion, except for the effects of not capitalizing certain lease obligations as discussed in the preceding paragraph, the financial statements referred to above present fairly, in all material respects, the financial position of Helio Company, and the results of its operations and its cash flows for the years then ended in conformity with generally accepted accounting principles.

An **adverse opinion** is required in any report in which the exceptions to fair presentation are so material that in the independent auditor's judgment, a qualified opinion is not justified. In such a case, the financial statements taken as a whole are not presented in accordance with generally accepted accounting principles. Adverse opinions are rare, because most companies change their accounting to conform with GAAP. The SEC will not permit a company listed on an exchange to have an adverse opinion.

A **disclaimer of an opinion** is appropriate when the auditor has gathered so little information on the financial statements that no opinion can be expressed.

The audit report should provide useful information to the investor. One investment banker noted, "Probably the first item to check is the auditor's opinion to see whether or not it is a clean one—'in conformity with generally accepted accounting principles'—or is qualified in regard to differences between the auditor and company management in the accounting treatment of some major item, or in the outcome of some major litigation."

What do the numbers mean? *HEART OF THE MATTER*

As we discussed in the opening story, financial disclosure is one of a number of institutional features that contribute to vibrant security markets. In fact, a recent study of disclosure and other mechanisms (such as civil lawsuits and criminal sanctions) found that good disclosure is the most important contributor to a vibrant market. The study, which compared disclosure and other legal and regulatory elements across 49 countries, found that countries with the best disclosure laws have the biggest stock markets.

Countries with more successful market environments also tend to have regulations that make it relatively easy for private investors to sue corporations that provide bad information. That is, while criminal sanctions can be effective in some circumstances, disclosure and other legal and regulatory elements encouraging good disclosure are the most important determinants of highly liquid and deep securities markets.

These findings hold for nations in all stages of economic development, with particular importance for nations that are in the early stages of securities regulation. In addition, countries with fewer market protections likely will benefit the most from adoption of international standards for market regulation and disclosure. The lesson: Disclosure is good for your market.

Sources: Rebecca Christie, "Study: Disclosure at Heart of Effective Securities Laws," *Wall Street Journal Online* (August 11, 2003); and L. Hail, C. Leuz, and P. Wysocki, "Global Accounting Convergence and the Potential Adoption of IFRS by the U.S. (Part I): Conceptual Underpinnings and Economic Analysis," *Accounting Horizons* (September 2010).

Management's Reports

Management's Discussion and Analysis

6 LEARNING OBJECTIVE
Understand management's responsibilities for financials.

The SEC mandates inclusion of **management's discussion and analysis (MD&A)**. This section covers three financial aspects of an enterprise's business—liquidity, capital resources, and results of operations. In it, management highlights favorable or unfavorable trends and identifies significant events and uncertainties that affect these three factors. This approach obviously involves subjective estimates, opinions, and soft data. However, the SEC believes that the relevance of this information exceeds the potential lack of faithful representation.

Illustration 24-15 (page 1512) presents an excerpt from the MD&A section (2009 "Business Risks" only) of **PepsiCo**'s annual report.

The MD&A section also must provide information about the effects of inflation and changing prices, if they are material to financial statement trends. The SEC has not required specific numerical computations, and companies have provided little analysis on changing prices.

An additional disclosure provided in the MD&A of many companies is discussion of the company's critical accounting policies. This disclosure identifies accounting

ILLUSTRATION 24-15
Management's Discussion and Analysis

PepsiCo, Inc.

MD&A Our business risks (in part)

Risk Management Framework

The achievement of our strategic and operating objectives will necessarily involve taking risks. Our risk management process is intended to ensure that risks are taken knowingly and purposefully. As such, we leverage an integrated risk management framework to identify, assess, prioritize, manage, monitor and communicate risks across the Company. This framework includes:

- The PepsiCo Risk Committee (PRC), comprised of a cross-functional, geographically diverse, senior management group which meets regularly to identify, assess, prioritize and address strategic and reputational risks;
- Division Risk Committees (DRCs), comprised of cross-functional senior management teams which meet regularly to identify, assess, prioritize and address division-specific operating risks;
- PepsiCo's Risk Management Office, which manages the overall risk management process, provides ongoing guidance, tools and analytical support to the PRC and the DRCs, identifies and assesses potential risks, and facilitates ongoing communication between the parties, as well as to PepsiCo's Audit Committee and Board of Directors;
- PepsiCo Corporate Audit, which evaluates the ongoing effectiveness of our key internal controls through periodic audit and review procedures; and
- PepsiCo's Compliance Department, which leads and coordinates our compliance policies and practices.

Market Risks

We are exposed to market risks arising from adverse changes in:

- commodity prices, affecting the cost of our raw materials and energy,
- foreign exchange rates, and
- interest rates.

In the normal course of business, we manage these risks through a variety of strategies, including productivity initiatives, global purchasing programs and hedging strategies. Ongoing productivity initiatives involve the identification and effective implementation of meaningful cost saving opportunities or efficiencies. Our global purchasing programs include fixed-price purchase orders and pricing agreements.

policies that require management to make subjective judgments regarding uncertainties, resulting in potentially significant effects on the financial results.[13] For example, in its critical accounting policy disclosure, PepsiCo showed the impact on stock-based compensation expense in response to changes in estimated interest rates and stock return volatility. Through this voluntary disclosure, companies can expand on the information contained in the notes to the financial statements to indicate the sensitivity of the financial results to accounting policy judgments.

Gateway to the Profession

Expanded Discussion of Accounting for Changing Prices

Management's Responsibilities for Financial Statements

The Sarbanes-Oxley Act requires the SEC to develop guidelines for *all* publicly traded companies to report on management's responsibilities for, and assessment of, the internal control system. An example of the type of disclosure that public companies are now making is shown in Illustration 24-16.[14]

[13] See *Cautionary Advice Regarding Disclosure about Critical Accounting Policies,* Release Nos. 33-8040; 34-45149; FR-60 (Washington, D.C.: SEC); and *Proposed Rule: Disclosure in Management's Discussion and Analysis about the Application of Critical Accounting Policies,* Release Nos. 33-8098; 34-45907; International Series Release No. 1258; File No. S7-16-02 (Washington, D.C.: SEC).

[14] As indicated in this disclosure, management is responsible for preparing the financial statements and establishing and maintaining an effective system of internal controls. The auditor provides an independent assessment of whether the financial statements are prepared in accordance with GAAP, and for public companies, whether the internal controls are effective (see the audit opinion in Illustration 24-13 on page 1509).

ILLUSTRATION 24-16
Report on Management's Responsibilities

Home Depot

Management's Responsibility for Financial Statements

The financial statements presented in this Annual Report have been prepared with integrity and objectivity and are the responsibility of the management of The Home Depot, Inc. These financial statements have been prepared in conformity with U.S. generally accepted accounting principles and properly reflect certain estimates and judgments based upon the best available information.

The financial statements of the Company have been audited by KPMG LLP, an independent registered public accounting firm. Their accompanying report is based upon an audit conducted in accordance with the standards of the Public Company Accounting Oversight Board (United States).

The Audit Committee of the Board of Directors, consisting solely of independent directors, meets five times a year with the independent registered public accounting firm, the internal auditors and representatives of management to discuss auditing and financial reporting matters. In addition, a telephonic meeting is held prior to each quarterly earnings release. The Audit Committee retains the independent registered public accounting firm and regularly reviews the internal accounting controls, the activities of the independent registered public accounting firm and internal auditors and the financial condition of the Company. Both the Company's independent registered public accounting firm and the internal auditors have free access to the Audit Committee.

Management's Report on Internal Control over Financial Reporting

Our management is responsible for establishing and maintaining adequate internal control over financial reporting, as such term is defined in Rule 13a-15(f) promulgated under the Securities Exchange Act of 1934, as amended (the "Exchange Act"). Under the supervision and with the participation of our management, including our Chief Executive Officer and Chief Financial Officer, we conducted an evaluation of the effectiveness of our internal control over financial reporting as of January 29, 2012 based on the framework in *Internal Control—Integrated Framework* issued by the Committee of Sponsoring Organizations of the Treadway Commission (COSO). Based on our evaluation, our management concluded that our internal control over financial reporting was effective as of January 29, 2012 in providing reasonable assurance regarding the reliability of financial reporting and the preparation of financial statements for external purposes in accordance with U.S. generally accepted accounting principles. The effectiveness of our internal control over financial reporting as of January 29, 2012 has been audited by KPMG LLP, an independent registered public accounting firm, as stated in their report which is included on page 28 in this Form 10-K.

Francis S. Blake Chairman & Chief Executive Officer	Carol B. Tomé Chief Financial Officer & Executive Vice President—Corporate Services

CURRENT REPORTING ISSUES

Reporting on Financial Forecasts and Projections

7 LEARNING OBJECTIVE
Identify issues related to financial forecasts and projections.

In recent years, the investing public's demand for more and better information has focused on disclosure of corporate expectations for the future.[15] These disclosures take one of two forms:[16]

- ***Financial forecasts.*** A **financial forecast** is a set of prospective financial statements that present, to the best of the responsible party's knowledge and belief, a company's expected financial position, results of operations, and cash flows. The

[15]Some areas in which companies are using financial information about the future are equipment lease-versus-buy analysis, analysis of a company's ability to successfully enter new markets, and examination of merger and acquisition opportunities. In addition, companies also prepare forecasts and projections for use by third parties in public offering documents (requiring financial forecasts), tax-oriented investments, and financial feasibility studies. Use of forward-looking data has been enhanced by the increased capability of microcomputers to analyze, compare, and manipulate large quantities of data.

[16]"Financial Forecasts and Projections" and "Guide for Prospective Financial Information," *Codification of Statements on Standards for Attestation Engagements* (New York: AICPA 2006), paras. 3.04 and 3.05.

responsible party bases a financial forecast on conditions it expects to exist and the course of action it expects to take.

- ***Financial projections.*** Financial projections are prospective financial statements that present, to the best of the responsible party's knowledge and belief, given one or more *hypothetical assumptions*, an entity's expected financial position, results of operations, and cash flows. The responsible party bases a financial projection on conditions it expects *would* exist and the course of action it expects *would* be taken, given one or more hypothetical assumptions.

The difference between a financial forecast and a financial projection is clear-cut. A forecast provides information on what is **expected** to happen, whereas a projection provides information on what **might** take place but is not necessarily expected to happen.

Whether companies should be required to provide financial forecasts is the subject of intensive discussion with journalists, corporate executives, the SEC, financial analysts, accountants, and others. Predictably, there are strong arguments on either side. Listed below are some of the arguments.

Arguments for requiring published forecasts:

1. Investment decisions are based on future expectations. Therefore, information about the future facilitates better decisions.
2. Companies already circulate forecasts informally. This situation should be regulated to ensure that the forecasts are available to all investors.
3. Circumstances now change so rapidly that historical information is no longer adequate for prediction.

Arguments against requiring published forecasts:

1. No one can foretell the future. Therefore, forecasts will inevitably be wrong. Worse, they may mislead, if they convey an impression of precision about the future.
2. Companies may strive only to meet their published forecasts, thereby failing to produce results that are in the stockholders' best interest.
3. If forecasts prove inaccurate, there will be recriminations and probably legal actions.[17]
4. Disclosure of forecasts will be detrimental to organizations, because forecasts will inform competitors (foreign and domestic) as well as investors.

Underlying Concepts

The profession indicates that the legal environment discourages companies from disclosing forward-looking information. Companies should not have to expand reporting of forward-looking information unless there are more effective deterrents to unwarranted litigation.

The AICPA has issued a statement on standards for accountants' services on prospective financial information. This statement establishes guidelines for the preparation and presentation of financial forecasts and projections.[18] It requires accountants to provide (1) a summary of significant assumptions used in the forecast or projection and (2) guidelines for minimum presentation.

To encourage management to disclose prospective financial information, the SEC has a safe harbor rule. It provides protection to a company that presents an erroneous forecast, as long as the company prepared the forecast on a reasonable basis

[17]The issue is serious. Over a recent three-year period, 8 percent of the companies on the NYSE were sued because of an alleged lack of financial disclosure. Companies complain that they are subject to lawsuits whenever the stock price drops. And as one executive noted, "You can even be sued if the stock price goes up—because you did not disclose the good news fast enough."

[18]*Op. cit.*, par. 1.02.

and disclosed it in good faith.[19] However, many companies note that the safe harbor rule does not work in practice, since it does not cover oral statements, nor has it kept them from investor lawsuits.

What do the numbers mean? GLOBAL FORECASTS

Great Britain permits financial forecasts, and the results have been fairly successful. Some significant differences do exist between the English and the U.S. business and legal environments. The British system, for example, does not permit litigation on forecasted information, and the solicitor (lawyer) is not permitted to work on a contingent-fee basis.

But such differences probably could be overcome if influential interests in this country cooperated to produce an atmosphere conducive to quality forecasting. A typical British forecast adapted from a construction company's report to support a public offering of stock is as follows.

> Profits have grown substantially over the past 10 years and directors are confident of being able to continue this expansion. . . . While the rate of expansion will be dependent on the level of economic activity in Ireland and England, the group is well structured to avail itself of opportunities as they arise, particularly in the field of property development, which is expected to play an increasingly important role in the group's future expansion.
>
> Profits before taxation for the half year ended 30th June were 402,000 pounds. On the basis of trading experiences since that date and the present level of sales and completions, the directors expect that in the absence of unforeseen circumstances, the group's profits before taxation for the year to 31st December will be not less than 960,000 pounds.
>
> No dividends will be paid in respect of the current year. In a full financial year, on the basis of above forecasts (not including full year profits) it would be the intention of the board, assuming current rates of tax, to recommend dividends totaling 40% (of after-tax profits), which will be payable in the next two years.

A general narrative-type forecast issued by a U.S. corporation might appear as follows.

> On the basis of promotions planned by the company for the second half of the fiscal year, net earnings for that period are expected to be approximately the same as those for the first half of the fiscal year, with net earnings for the third quarter expected to make the predominant contribution to net earnings for the second half of the year.

As indicated, the U.S. version is much less specific in its forecasted information.

Source: See "A Case for Forecasting—The British Have Tried It and Find That It Works," *World* (New York: Peat, Marwick, Mitchell & Co., Autumn 1978), pp. 10–13. In a recent survey, U.K. companies remain stubbornly backward-looking. Just 5 percent of FTSE 100 companies address the future of the business in their discussion and analysis. See PricewaterhouseCoopers, "Guide to Forward-looking Information: Don't Fear the Future" (2006).

Questions of Liability

What happens if a company does not meet its forecasts? Can the company and the auditor be sued? If a company, for example, projects an earnings increase of 15 percent and achieves only 5 percent, should stockholders be permitted to have some judicial recourse against the company?

One court case involving **Monsanto Chemical Corporation** set a precedent. In this case, Monsanto predicted that sales would increase 8 to 9 percent and that earnings would rise 4 to 5 percent. In the last part of the year, the demand for Monsanto's products dropped as a result of a business turndown. Instead of increasing, the company's earnings declined. Investors sued the company because the projected earnings figure was erroneous, but a judge dismissed the suit because the forecasts were the best estimates of qualified people whose intents were honest.

As indicated earlier, the SEC's safe harbor rules are intended to protect companies that provide good-faith projections. However, much concern exists as to how the SEC

[19] "Safe-Harbor Rule for Projections," *Release No. 5993* (Washington, D.C.: SEC, 1979). The Private Securities Litigation Reform Act of 1995 recognizes that some information that is useful to investors is inherently subject to less certainty or reliability than other information. By providing safe harbor for forward-looking statements, Congress has sought to facilitate access to this information by investors.

and the courts will interpret such terms as "good faith" and "reasonable assumptions" when erroneous forecasts mislead users of this information.

Internet Financial Reporting

Most companies now use the power and reach of the Internet to provide more useful information to financial statement readers. All large companies have Internet sites, and a large proportion of companies' websites contain links to their financial statements and other disclosures. The popularity of such reporting is not surprising since it reduces the companies' costs of printing and disseminating paper reports.

Does Internet financial reporting improve the usefulness of a company's financial reports? Yes, in several ways. First, dissemination of reports via the Web allows firms **to communicate more easily and quickly with users** than do traditional paper reports. In addition, **Internet reporting allows users to take advantage of tools** such as search engines and hyperlinks to quickly find information about the firm and to download the information for analysis. Finally, **Internet reporting can help make financial reports more relevant** by allowing companies to report expanded disaggregated data and more timely data than is possible through paper-based reporting. For example, some companies voluntarily report weekly sales data and segment operating data on their websites.

Given the widespread use of the Internet by investors and creditors, it is not surprising that organizations are developing new technologies and standards to further enable and enhance Internet financial reporting. An example is the increasing use of eXtensible Business Reporting Language (XBRL). **XBRL** is a computer language adapted from the code of the Internet. It "tags" accounting data to correspond to financial reporting items that are reported in the balance sheet, income statement, and the cash flow statement. Once tagged, any company's XBRL data can be easily processed using spreadsheets and other computer programs. In fact, the SEC is phasing in requirements for all companies and mutual funds to prepare their financial reports using XBRL, thereby allowing users to more easily search a company's reports, extract and analyze data, and perform financial comparisons within industries.[20]

To complement the implementation of XBRL use, the SEC has also announced a major upgrade to its EDGAR database. The new system is called IDEA (short for Interactive Data Electronic Applications). This replacement of EDGAR marks the SEC's transition from collecting forms and documents to making the information itself freely available to investors in a timely form they can readily use. With IDEA, investors will be able to quickly collate information from thousands of companies and forms and create reports and analyses on the fly, in any way they choose. It is hoped that IDEA will open the door for both the SEC and investors to the new world of financial disclosure in interactive data (XBRL) format.[21]

[20]See *SEC Interactive Data Rules for Operating Companies* (*http://www.sec.gov/rules/final/2009/33-9002.pdf*); and C. Twarowski, "Financial Data 'on Steroids'," *Washington Post* (August 19, 2008), p. D01. See also *www.xbrl.org/us/us/BusinessCaseForXBRL.pdf* for additional information on XBRL. The IASB and the FASB are collaborating to implement XBRL with their standards. See *http://www.ifrs.org/XBRL/XBRL/htm*.

[21]See *http://www.sec.gov/edgar/aboutedgar.htm*. The SEC has implemented other regulations to ensure that investors get high-quality disclosures. For example, as discussed in Chapter 4, the SEC was concerned that companies may use pro forma reporting to deflect investor attention from bad news. In response, the SEC issued Regulation G, which requires companies to reconcile non-GAAP financial measures to GAAP. This regulation provides investors with a roadmap to analyze adjustments companies make to their GAAP numbers to arrive at pro forma results. [See SEC Regulation G, "Conditions for Use of Non-GAAP Financial Measures," Release No. 33-8176 (March 28, 2003).] Regulation FD (Release Nos. 33-7881) was issued in 2000 to address the concern that some analysts were receiving information sooner than the general public (e.g., during conference calls with analysts when earnings releases were discussed). Regulation FD requires that when relevant information is released, all have equal access to it.

What do the numbers mean? NEW FORMATS, NEW DISCLOSURE

As indicated in earlier chapters in the *IFRS Insights* discussions, the FASB and the IASB are exploring better ways to present information in the financial statements. Recently, these two standard-setters have issued a discussion paper that requests input on a proposed reformatting of the financial statements. The table below provides a "snapshot" of the proposed changes (go to *http://www.fasb.org* to learn more about this joint international project).

Statement of Financial Position	Statement of Comprehensive Income	Statement of Cash Flows
Business	Business	Business
• Operating assets and liabilities	• Operating income and expenses	• Operating cash flows
• Investing assets and liabilities	• Investing income and expenses	• Investing cash flows
Financing	Financing	Financing
• Financing assets	• Financing asset income	• Financing asset cash flows
• Financing liabilities	• Financing liability expenses	• Financing liability cash flows
Income Taxes	Income Taxes	Income Taxes

As indicated, each statement will use the same format. While the proposed changes will not affect the measurement of individual financial statement elements, the use of a consistent format (e.g., Business, Financing, Income Taxes) will help users understand the interrelationships in the financial statements. In addition, a new schedule reconciling cash flows to comprehensive income will be provided. As part of this schedule, changes in fair value will be included. It is a good thing the timeline for the project is lengthy, as these changes in presentation are significant.

Fraudulent Financial Reporting

8 LEARNING OBJECTIVE
Describe the profession's response to fraudulent financial reporting.

Economic crime is on the rise around the world. A recent global survey of over 3,000 executives from 54 countries documented the types of economic crimes, as shown in Illustration 24-17 and Illustration 24-18 (page 1518).

ILLUSTRATION 24-17
Types of Economic Crime

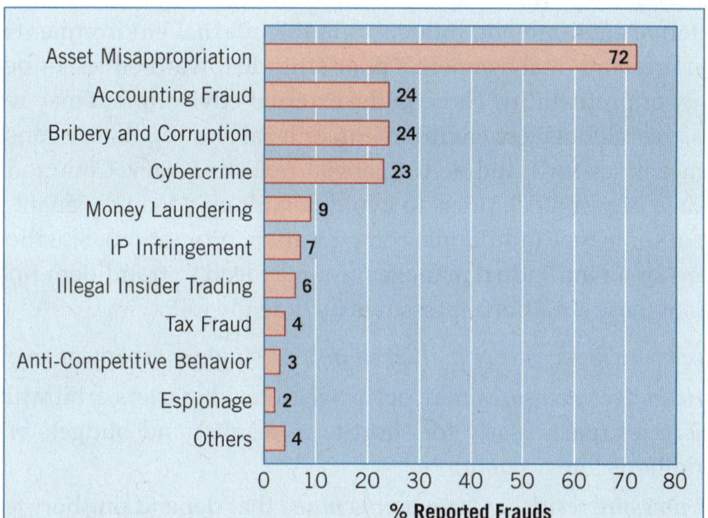

% Respondents who experienced economic crimes in the last 12 months.

As indicated, a wide range of economic crimes are reported. As shown in Illustration 24-18, while the trend for the top three areas is improving, accounting fraud consistently is in the top three.

Fraudulent financial reporting is defined as "intentional or reckless conduct, whether act or omission, that results in materially misleading financial statements."[22] Fraudulent

[22]"Report of the National Commission on Fraudulent Financial Reporting" (Washington, D.C., 1987), page 2. Unintentional errors as well as corporate improprieties (such as tax fraud, employee embezzlements, and so on) which do not cause the financial statements to be misleading are excluded from the definition of fraudulent financial reporting.

ILLUSTRATION 24-18
Trends in Reported Fraud

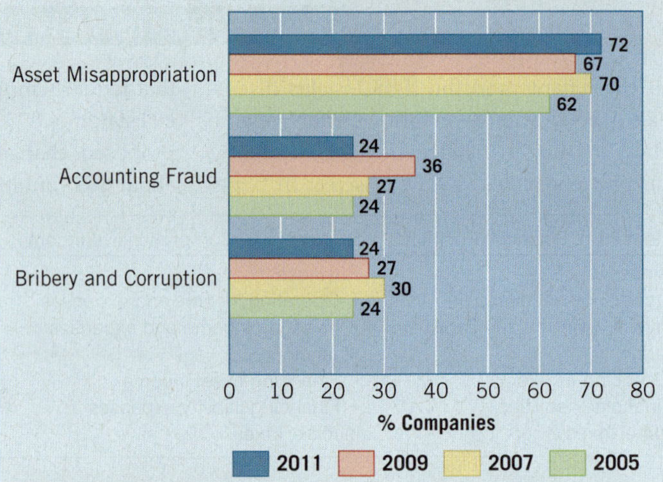

Source: PricewaterhouseCoopers, *The Global Economic Crime Survey: Economic Crime in a Downturn* (November 2011).

reporting can involve gross and deliberate distortion of corporate records (such as inventory count tags), or misapplication of accounting principles (failure to disclose material transactions). Although frauds are unusual, recent events involving such well-known companies as **Enron**, **WorldCom**, **Adelphia**, and **Tyco** indicate that more must be done to address this issue.

Causes of Fraudulent Financial Reporting

Fraudulent financial reporting usually occurs because of conditions in a company's internal or external environment. Influences in the **internal environment** relate to poor internal control systems, management's poor attitude toward ethics, or perhaps a company's liquidity or profitability. Those in the **external environment** may relate to industry conditions, overall business environment, or legal and regulatory considerations.

General incentives for fraudulent financial reporting vary. Common ones are the desire to obtain a higher stock price, to avoid default on a loan covenant, or to make a personal gain of some type (additional compensation, promotion). Situational pressures on the company or an individual manager also may lead to fraudulent financial reporting. Examples of these situational pressures include the following.

- ***Sudden decreases in revenue or market share*** for a single company or an entire industry.
- ***Unrealistic budget pressures*** may occur when headquarters arbitrarily determines profit objectives (particularly for short-term results) and budgets without taking actual conditions into account.
- ***Financial pressure resulting from bonus plans*** that depend on short-term economic performance. This pressure is particularly acute when the bonus is a significant component of the individual's total compensation.

Opportunities for fraudulent financial reporting are present in circumstances when the fraud is easy to commit and when detection is difficult. Frequently, these opportunities arise from:

1. ***The absence of a board of directors or audit committee*** that vigilantly oversees the financial reporting process.
2. ***Weak or nonexistent internal accounting controls.*** This situation can occur, for example, when a company's revenue system is overloaded as a result of a rapid

expansion of sales, an acquisition of a new division, or the entry into a new, unfamiliar line of business.

3. ***Unusual or complex transactions*** such as the consolidation of two companies, the divestiture or closing of a specific operation, and the purchase and sale of derivative instruments.
4. ***Accounting estimates requiring significant subjective judgment*** by company management, such as the allowance for loan losses and the estimated liability for warranty expense.
5. ***Ineffective internal audit staffs*** resulting from inadequate staff size and severely limited audit scope.

A weak corporate ethical climate contributes to these situations. Opportunities for fraudulent financial reporting also increase dramatically when the accounting principles followed in reporting transactions are nonexistent, evolving, or subject to varying interpretations.[23]

The AICPA has issued numerous auditing standards in response to concerns of the accounting profession, the media, and the public.[24] For example, the standard on fraudulent financial reporting "raises the bar" on the performance of financial statement audits by explicitly requiring auditors to assess the risk of material financial misstatement due to fraud.[25] As indicated earlier, the Sarbanes-Oxley Act now raises the penalty substantially for executives who are involved in fraudulent financial reporting.

What do the numbers mean? DISCLOSURE OVERLOAD

As we discussed in Chapter 1 and throughout the textbook, IFRS is gaining popularity around the world. The U.S. Securities and Exchange Commission is still studying whether and how to incorporate IFRS in the accounting rules used by publicly traded companies in the United States. There is some debate on U.S. readiness to make the switch. For example, there are several areas in which the FASB and the IASB must iron out a number of technical accounting issues before they reach a substantially converged set of accounting standards. Here is a list of six important areas yet to be converged.

1. ***Error correction.*** According to *IAS 8*, it's not always necessary to retrospectively restate financial results when a company corrects errors, especially if the adjustment is impractical or too costly. GAAP, on the other hand, requires restatements in many error-correction cases.
2. ***Death of LIFO.*** Last-in, first-out (LIFO) inventory accounting is prohibited under *IAS 2*, so any U.S. company using the method will have to abandon it (and the tax benefits) and move to another methodology. Although LIFO is permitted under GAAP, the repeal of LIFO for tax purposes is an ongoing debate.
3. ***Reversal of impairments.*** *IAS 36* permits companies to reverse impairment losses up to the amount of the original impairment when the reason for the charge decreases or no longer exists. However, GAAP bans reversal.
4. ***PP&E revaluation.*** *IAS 16* allows for the revaluation of property, plant, and equipment, but the entire asset class must be revalued. That means a company can choose to use the revaluation model if the asset class's fair value can be measured reliably. But, it must choose to use one

[23]The discussion in this section is based on the Report of the National Commission on Fraudulent Financial Reporting, pp. 23–24 (2004). See also "2012 Report to the Nation on Occupational Fraud and Abuse, Association of Certified Fraud Examiners" (*http://www.acfe.com/uploadedFiles/ACFE_Website/Content/rttn/2012-report-to-nations.pdf*), for fraudulent financial reporting causes and consequences.

[24]Because the profession believes that the role of the auditor is not well understood outside the profession, much attention has been focused on the expectation gap. The **expectation gap** is the gap between (1) the expectation of financial statement users concerning the level of assurance they believe the independent auditor provides, and (2) the assurance that the independent auditor actually does provide under generally accepted auditing standards.

[25]"Consideration of Fraud in a Financial Statement Audit," *Statement on Auditing Standards No. 99* (New York: AICPA, 2002).

model or the other; both cannot be used at the same time. GAAP does not allow revaluation.

5. *Component depreciation.* Also under *IAS 16*, companies must recognize and depreciate equipment components separately if the components can be physically separated from the asset and have different useful life spans. In practical terms, that means controllers will have to rely on the operations side of the business to help assess equipment components. GAAP allows component depreciation, but it is not required.
6. *Development costs.* Based on *IAS 38*, companies are permitted to capitalize development costs as long as they meet six criteria. However, research costs are still expensed. GAAP requires that all R&D costs be charged to expense when incurred.

Some are already debating what will happen if and when U.S. companies adopt these new standards. It is almost certain that expanded disclosure will be needed to help users navigate accounting reports upon adoption of IFRS. As one accounting analyst remarked, "Get ready for an avalanche of footnotes." Since using IFRS requires more judgment than using GAAP, two to three times as many footnotes will be needed to explain the rationales for accounting approaches. So while principles-based standards should promote more comparability, they require investors to dig into the disclosures in the footnotes.

Source: Marie Leone, "GAAP and IFRS: Six Degrees of Separation," *CFO.com* (June 30, 2010).

Criteria for Making Accounting and Reporting Choices

Underlying Concepts

The FASB concept statements on the objective of financial reporting, elements of financial statements, qualitative characteristics of accounting information, and recognition and measurement are important steps in the right direction.

Throughout this textbook, we have stressed the need to provide information that is useful to predict the amounts, timing, and uncertainty of future cash flows. To achieve this objective, companies must make judicious choices between alternative accounting concepts, methods, and means of disclosure. You are probably surprised by the large number of choices that exist among acceptable alternatives.

You should recognize, however, as indicated in Chapter 1, that accounting is greatly influenced by its environment. It does not exist in a vacuum. Therefore, it is unrealistic to assume that the profession can entirely eliminate alternative presentations of certain transactions and events. Nevertheless, we are hopeful that the profession, by adhering to the conceptual framework, will be able to focus on the needs of financial statement users and eliminate diversity where appropriate. The SEC's and FASB's projects on principles-based standards are directed at these very issues. They seek to develop guidance that will result in accounting and financial reporting that reflects the economic substance of the transactions, not the desired financial result of management. The profession must continue its efforts to develop a sound foundation upon which to build financial standards and practice. As Aristotle said, "The correct beginning is more than half the whole."

You will want to read **IFRS INSIGHTS** on pages 1548–1557 for discussion of IFRS related to disclosure.

KEY TERMS

accounting policies, 1491
adverse opinion, 1511
auditor, 1508
auditor's report, 1508
common costs, 1500
differential disclosure, 1489
disclaimer of an opinion, 1511
discrete approach, 1503
errors, 1494
financial forecast, 1513

SUMMARY OF LEARNING OBJECTIVES

1 Review the full disclosure principle and describe implementation problems. The full disclosure principle calls for financial reporting of any financial facts significant enough to influence the judgment of an informed reader. Implementing the full disclosure principle is difficult because the cost of disclosure can be substantial and the benefits difficult to assess. Disclosure requirements have increased because of (1) the growing complexity of the business environment, (2) the necessity for timely information, and (3) the use of accounting as a control and monitoring device.

2 Explain the use of notes in financial statement preparation. Notes are the accountant's means of amplifying or explaining the items presented in the main body of the statements. Notes can explain in qualitative terms information pertinent to specific financial statement items, and can provide supplementary data of a quantitative nature. Common note disclosures relate to such items as accounting policies; inventories; property, plant, and equipment; creditor claims; contingencies and commitments; and subsequent events.

3 Discuss the disclosure requirements for related-party transactions, post-balance-sheet events, and major business segments. In related-party transactions, one party has the ability to significantly influence the policies of the other. As a result, GAAP requires disclosure of the relationship(s) involved, a description and dollar amounts of the transactions, and amounts due from or to related parties. For post-balance-sheet events, companies should disclose recognized subsequent events as well as nonrecognized subsequent events. Finally, aggregated figures hide much information about the composition of these consolidated figures. There is no way to tell from the consolidated data the extent to which the differing product lines contribute to the company's profitability, risk, and growth potential. As a result, the profession requires segment information in certain situations.

4 Describe the accounting problems associated with interim reporting. Interim reports cover periods of less than one year. Two viewpoints exist regarding interim reports. The discrete approach holds that each interim period should be treated as a separate accounting period. The integral approach is that the interim report is an integral part of the annual report and that deferrals and accruals should take into consideration what will happen for the entire year.

Companies should use the same accounting principles for interim reports that they use for annual reports. A number of unique reporting problems develop related to the following items: (1) advertising and similar costs, (2) expenses subject to year-end adjustment, (3) income taxes, (4) extraordinary items, (5) earnings per share, and (6) seasonality.

5 Identify the major disclosures in the auditor's report. The auditor expresses an unqualified opinion if satisfied that the financial statements present the financial position, results of operations, and cash flows fairly in accordance with generally accepted accounting principles. A qualified opinion contains an exception to the standard opinion; ordinarily the exception is not of sufficient magnitude to invalidate the statements as a whole.

An adverse opinion is required when the exceptions to fair presentation are so material that a qualified opinion is not justified. A disclaimer of an opinion is appropriate when the auditor has so little information on the financial statements that no opinion can be expressed.

6 Understand management's responsibilities for financials. Management's discussion and analysis (MD&A) section covers three financial aspects of an enterprise's business: liquidity, capital resources, and results of operations. Management's responsibility for the financial statements is often indicated in a letter to stockholders in the annual report.

7 Identify issues related to financial forecasts and projections. The SEC has indicated that companies are permitted (not required) to include profit forecasts in their reports. To encourage management to disclose such information, the SEC issued a safe harbor rule. The rule provides protection to a company that presents an erroneous forecast, as long as it prepared the projection on a reasonable basis and disclosed it in good faith. However, the safe harbor rule has not worked well in practice.

8 Describe the profession's response to fraudulent financial reporting. Fraudulent financial reporting is intentional or reckless conduct, whether through act or omission, that results in materially misleading financial statements. Fraudulent financial reporting usually occurs because of poor internal control, management's poor attitude toward ethics, poor performance, and so on. The Sarbanes-Oxley Act has numerous provisions intended to help prevent fraudulent financial reporting.

APPENDIX 24A BASIC FINANCIAL STATEMENT ANALYSIS

LEARNING OBJECTIVE 9
Understand the approach to financial statement analysis.

What would be important to you in studying a company's financial statements? The answer depends on your particular interest—whether you are a creditor, stockholder, potential investor, manager, government agency, or labor leader. For example, **short-term creditors** such as banks are primarily interested in the ability of the firm to pay its currently maturing obligations. In that case, you would examine the current assets and their relation to short-term liabilities to evaluate the short-run solvency of the firm.

Bondholders, on the other hand, look more to long-term indicators, such as the enterprise's capital structure, past and projected earnings, and changes in financial position. **Stockholders**, present or prospective, also are interested in many of the features considered by a long-term creditor. As a stockholder, you would focus on the earnings picture, because changes in it greatly affect the market price of your investment. You also would be concerned with the financial position of the company, because it affects indirectly the stability of earnings.

The **managers** of a company are concerned about the composition of its capital structure and about the changes and trends in earnings. This financial information has a direct influence on the type, amount, and cost of external financing that the company can obtain. In addition, the company managers find financial information useful on a day-to-day operating basis in such areas as capital budgeting, break-even analysis, variance analysis, gross margin analysis, and for internal control purposes.

PERSPECTIVE ON FINANCIAL STATEMENT ANALYSIS

Readers of financial statements can gather information by examining relationships between items on the statements and identifying trends in these relationships. The relationships are expressed numerically in ratios and percentages, and trends are identified through comparative analysis.

Underlying Concepts

Because financial statements report on the past, they emphasize the *qualitative characteristic of feedback value.* This feedback value is useful because it can be used to better achieve the *qualitative characteristic of predictive value.*

A problem with learning how to analyze statements is that the means may become an end in itself. Analysts could identify and calculate thousands of possible relationships and trends. If one knows only how to calculate ratios and trends without understanding how such information can be used, little is accomplished. Therefore, a logical approach to financial statement analysis is necessary, consisting of the following steps.

1. *Know the questions for which you want to find answers.* As indicated earlier, various groups have different types of interest in a company.
2. *Know the questions that particular ratios and comparisons are able to help answer.* These will be discussed in this appendix.
3. *Match 1 and 2 above.* By such a matching, the statement analysis will have a logical direction and purpose.

Several caveats must be mentioned. **Financial statements report on the past.** Thus, analysis of these data is an examination of the past. When using such information in a decision-making (future-oriented) process, analysts assume that the past is a reasonable basis for predicting the future. This is usually a reasonable approach, but its limitations should be recognized.

Also, ratio and trend analyses will help identify a company's present strengths and weaknesses. They may serve as "red flags" indicating problem areas. In many cases, however, such analyses will not reveal **why** things are as they are. Finding answers about "why" usually requires an in-depth analysis and an awareness of many factors about a company that are not reported in the financial statements.

Another caveat is that a **single ratio by itself is not likely to be very useful**. For example, analysts may generally view a current ratio of 2 to 1 (current assets are twice current liabilities) as satisfactory. However, if the industry average is 3 to 1, such a conclusion may be invalid. Even given this industry average, one may conclude that the particular company is doing well if one knows the previous year's ratio was 1.5 to 1. Consequently, to derive meaning from ratios, analysts need some standard against which to compare them. Such a standard may come from industry averages, past years' amounts, a particular competitor, or planned levels.

Finally, **awareness of the limitations of accounting numbers used in an analysis** is important. We will discuss some of these limitations and their consequences later in this appendix.

International Perspective

Some companies outside the United States provide "convenience" financial statements for U.S. readers. These financial statements have been translated into English, and they may also translate the currency units into U.S. dollars. However, the statements are *not restated* using U.S. accounting principles; financial statement analysis needs to take this fact into account.

RATIO ANALYSIS

In analyzing financial statement data, analysts use various devices to bring out the comparative and relative significance of the financial information presented. These devices include ratio analysis, comparative analysis, percentage analysis, and examination of related data. No one device is more useful than another. Every situation is different, and analysts often obtain the needed answers only upon close examination of the interrelationships among all the data provided. Ratio analysis is the starting point. Ratios can be classified as follows.

10 LEARNING OBJECTIVE

Identify major analytic ratios and describe their calculation.

MAJOR TYPES OF RATIOS

LIQUIDITY RATIOS. Measures of the company's short-run ability to pay its maturing obligations.

ACTIVITY RATIOS. Measures of how effectively the company is using the assets employed.

PROFITABILITY RATIOS. Measures of the degree of success or failure of a given company or division for a given period of time.

COVERAGE RATIOS. Measures of the degree of protection for long-term creditors and investors.[26]

We have integrated discussions and illustrations about the computation and use of these financial ratios throughout this book. Illustration 24A-1 (page 1524) summarizes all of the ratios presented in the book and identifies the specific chapters that presented that material.

[26]Some analysts use other terms to categorize these ratios. For example, liquidity ratios are sometimes referred to as *solvency* ratios; activity ratios as *turnover* or *efficiency* ratios; and coverage ratios as *leverage* or *capital structure* ratios.

ILLUSTRATION 24A-1
Summary of Financial Ratios

SUMMARY OF RATIOS PRESENTED IN EARLIER CHAPTERS

Ratio	Formula for Computation	Reference
I. Liquidity		
1. Current ratio	$\frac{\text{Current assets}}{\text{Current liabilities}}$	Chapter 13, p. 729
2. Quick or acid-test ratio	$\frac{\text{Cash, short-term investments, and net receivables}}{\text{Current liabilities}}$	Chapter 13, p. 730
3. Current cash debt coverage	$\frac{\text{Net cash provided by operating activities}}{\text{Average current liabilities}}$	Chapter 5, p. 234
II. Activity		
4. Accounts receivable turnover	$\frac{\text{Net sales}}{\text{Average trade receivables (net)}}$	Chapter 7, p. 373
5. Inventory turnover	$\frac{\text{Cost of goods sold}}{\text{Average inventory}}$	Chapter 9, p. 496
6. Asset turnover	$\frac{\text{Net sales}}{\text{Average total assets}}$	Chapter 11, p. 611
III. Profitability		
7. Profit margin on sales	$\frac{\text{Net income}}{\text{Net sales}}$	Chapter 11, p. 612
8. Return on assets	$\frac{\text{Net income}}{\text{Average total assets}}$	Chapter 11, p. 612
9. Return on common stock equity	$\frac{\text{Net income minus preferred dividends}}{\text{Average common stockholders' equity}}$	Chapter 15, p. 849
10. Earnings per share	$\frac{\text{Net income minus preferred dividends}}{\text{Weighted-average number of shares outstanding}}$	Chapter 16, p. 900
11. Payout ratio	$\frac{\text{Cash dividends}}{\text{Net income}}$	Chapter 15, p. 850
IV. Coverage		
12. Debt to assets ratio	$\frac{\text{Total liabilities}}{\text{Total assets}}$	Chapter 14, p. 787
13. Times interest earned	$\frac{\text{Income before income taxes and interest expense}}{\text{Interest expense}}$	Chapter 14, p. 787
14. Cash debt coverage	$\frac{\text{Net cash provided by operating activities}}{\text{Average total liabilities}}$	Chapter 5, p. 234
15. Book value per share	$\frac{\text{Common stockholders' equity}}{\text{Outstanding shares}}$	Chapter 15, p. 850

Gateway to the Profession
Financial Analysis Primer

You can find additional coverage of these ratios, accompanied by assignment material, at the book's companion website, at **www.wiley.com/college/kieso**. This supplemental coverage takes the form of a comprehensive case adapted from the annual report of a large international chemical company that we have disguised under the name of Anetek Chemical Corporation.

Limitations of Ratio Analysis

LEARNING OBJECTIVE 11
Explain the limitations of ratio analysis.

The reader of financial statements must understand the basic limitations associated with ratio analysis. As analytical tools, ratios are attractive because they are simple and convenient. But too frequently, decision-makers base their decisions on only these simple computations. The ratios are only as good as the data upon which they are based and the information with which they are compared.

One important limitation of ratios is that they generally are **based on historical cost, which can lead to distortions in measuring performance**. Inaccurate assessments of the enterprise's financial condition and performance can result from failing to incorporate fair value information.

Also, investors must remember that **where estimated items (such as depreciation and amortization) are significant, income ratios lose some of their credibility**. For example, income recognized before the termination of a company's life is an approximation. In analyzing the income statement, users should be aware of the uncertainty surrounding the computation of net income. As one writer aptly noted, "The physicist has long since conceded that the location of an electron is best expressed by a probability curve. Surely an abstraction like earnings per share is even more subject to the rules of probability and risk."[27]

Probably the greatest limitation of ratio analysis is the **difficult problem of achieving comparability among firms in a given industry**. Achieving comparability requires that the analyst (1) identify basic differences in companies' accounting principles and procedures, and (2) adjust the balances to achieve comparability. Basic differences in accounting usually involve one of the following areas.

Underlying Concepts

Consistency and comparability are important concepts for financial statement analysis. If the principles and assumptions used to prepare the financial statements are continually changing, accurate assessments of a company's progress become difficult.

1. Inventory valuation (FIFO, LIFO, average-cost).
2. Depreciation methods, particularly the use of straight-line versus accelerated depreciation.
3. Capitalization versus expensing of certain costs.
4. Capitalization of leases versus noncapitalization.
5. Investments in common stock carried at equity versus fair value.
6. Differing treatments of postretirement benefit costs.
7. Questionable practices of defining discontinued operations, impairments, and extraordinary items.

The use of these different alternatives can make a significant difference in the ratios computed. For example, at one time **Anheuser-Busch InBev** noted that if it had used average-cost for inventory valuation instead of LIFO, inventories would have increased approximately $33,000,000. Such an increase would have a substantive impact on the current ratio. Several studies have analyzed the impact of different accounting methods on financial statement analysis. The differences in income that can develop are staggering in some cases. Investors must be aware of the potential pitfalls if they are to be able to make the proper adjustments.[28]

Finally, analysts should recognize that a **substantial amount of important information** is not included in a company's financial statements. Events involving such things as industry changes, management changes, competitors' actions, technological developments, government actions, and union activities are often critical to a company's successful operation. These events occur continuously, and information about them must come from careful analysis of financial reports in the media and other sources. Indeed many argue, in what is known as the **efficient-market hypothesis**, that financial statements contain "no surprises" to those engaged in market activities. They contend that the effect of these events is known in the marketplace—and the price of the company's stock adjusts accordingly—well before the issuance of such reports.

[27]Richard E. Cheney, "How Dependable Is the Bottom Line?" *The Financial Executive* (January 1971), p. 12.

[28]See, for example, Eugene A. Imhoff, Jr., Robert C. Lipe, and David W. Wright, "Operating Leases: Impact of Constructive Capitalization," *Accounting Horizons* (March 1991).

COMPARATIVE ANALYSIS

LEARNING OBJECTIVE 12
Describe techniques of comparative analysis.

Comparative analysis presents the same information for two or more different dates or periods, so that like items may be compared. Ratio analysis provides only a single snapshot, for one given point or period in time. In a comparative analysis, an investment analyst can concentrate on a given item and determine whether it appears to be growing or diminishing year by year and the proportion of such change to related items. Generally, companies present comparative financial statements. They typically include two years of balance sheet information and three years of income statement information.

In addition, many companies include in their annual reports five- or ten-year summaries of pertinent data that permit readers to examine and analyze trends. As indicated in GAAP, "the presentation of comparative financial statements in annual and other reports enhances the usefulness of such reports and brings out more clearly the nature and trends of current changes affecting the enterprise." Illustration 24A-2 presents a five-year condensed statement, with additional supporting data, of Anetek Chemical Corporation.

ILLUSTRATION 24A-2
Condensed Comparative Financial Information

ANETEK CHEMICAL CORPORATION
CONDENSED COMPARATIVE STATEMENTS
(000,000 OMITTED)

	2014	2013	2012	2011	2010	10 Years Ago 2004	20 Years Ago 1994
Sales and other revenue:							
Net sales	$1,600.0	$1,350.0	$1,309.7	$1,176.2	$1,077.5	$636.2	$170.7
Other revenue	75.0	50.0	39.4	34.1	24.6	9.0	3.7
Total	1,675.0	1,400.0	1,349.1	1,210.3	1,102.1	645.2	174.4
Costs and other charges:							
Cost of sales	1,000.0	850.0	827.4	737.6	684.2	386.8	111.0
Depreciation and amortization	150.0	150.0	122.6	115.6	98.7	82.4	14.2
Selling and administrative expenses	225.0	150.0	144.2	133.7	126.7	66.7	10.7
Interest expense	50.0	25.0	28.5	20.7	9.4	8.9	1.8
Income taxes	100.0	75.0	79.5	73.5	68.3	42.4	12.4
Total	1,525.0	1,250.0	1,202.2	1,081.1	987.3	587.2	150.1
Net income for the year	$ 150.0	$ 150.0	$ 146.9	$ 129.2	$ 114.8	$ 58.0	$ 24.3
Other Statistics							
Earnings per share on common stock (in dollars)[a]	$ 5.00	$ 5.00	$ 4.90	$ 3.58	$ 3.11	$ 1.66	$ 1.06
Cash dividends per share on common stock (in dollars)[a]	2.25	2.15	1.95	1.79	1.71	1.11	0.25
Cash dividends declared on common stock	67.5	64.5	58.5	64.6	63.1	38.8	5.7
Stock dividend at approximate market value				46.8		27.3	
Taxes (major)	144.5	125.9	116.5	105.6	97.8	59.8	17.0
Wages paid	389.3	325.6	302.1	279.6	263.2	183.2	48.6
Cost of employee benefits	50.8	36.2	32.9	28.7	27.2	18.4	4.4
Number of employees at year end (thousands)	47.4	36.4	35.0	33.8	33.2	26.6	14.6
Additions to property	306.3	192.3	241.5	248.3	166.1	185.0	49.0

[a]Adjusted for stock splits and stock dividends.

PERCENTAGE (COMMON-SIZE) ANALYSIS

13 LEARNING OBJECTIVE
Describe techniques of percentage analysis.

Analysts also use percentage analysis to help them evaluate and compare companies. **Percentage analysis** consists of reducing a series of related amounts to a series of percentages of a given base. For example, analysts frequently express all items in an income statement as a percentage of sales or sometimes as a percentage of cost of goods sold. They may analyze a balance sheet on the basis of total assets. Percentage analysis facilitates comparison and is helpful in evaluating the relative size of items or the relative change in items. A conversion of absolute dollar amounts to percentages may also facilitate comparison between companies of different size.

Illustration 24A-3 shows a comparative analysis of the expense section of Anetek for the last two years.

ILLUSTRATION 24A-3
Horizontal Percentage Analysis

ANETEK CHEMICAL CORPORATION
HORIZONTAL COMPARATIVE ANALYSIS
(000,000 OMITTED)

	2014	2013	Difference	% Change Inc. (Dec.)
Cost of sales	$1,000.0	$850.0	$150.0	17.6%
Depreciation and amortization	150.0	150.0	0	0
Selling and administrative expenses	225.0	150.0	75.0	50.0
Interest expense	50.0	25.0	25.0	100.0
Income taxes	100.0	75.0	25.0	33.3

This approach, normally called **horizontal analysis**, indicates the proportionate change over a period of time. It is especially useful in evaluating trends, because absolute changes are often deceiving.

Another comparative approach, called **vertical analysis**, is the proportional expression of each financial statement item in a given period to a base figure. For example, Anetek Chemical's income statement using this approach appears in Illustration 24A-4.

ILLUSTRATION 24A-4
Vertical Percentage Analysis

ANETEK CHEMICAL CORPORATION
INCOME STATEMENT
(000,000 OMITTED)

	Amount	Percentage of Total Revenue
Net sales	$1,600.0	96%
Other revenue	75.0	4
Total revenue	1,675.0	100
Less:		
Cost of sales	1,000.0	60
Depreciation and amortization	150.0	9
Selling and administrative expenses	225.0	13
Interest expense	50.0	3
Income taxes	100.0	6
Total expenses	1,525.0	91
Net income	$ 150.0	9%

Vertical analysis is frequently called **common-size analysis** because it reduces all of the statement items to a "common size." That is, all of the elements within each statement are expressed in percentages of some common number and always add up to 100 percent. Common-size (percentage) analysis reveals the composition of each of the financial statements.

In the analysis of the balance sheet, common-size analysis answers such questions as: What percentage of the capital structure is stockholders' equity, current liabilities, and long-term debt? What is the mix of assets (percentage-wise) with which the company has chosen to conduct business? What percentage of current assets is in inventory, receivables, and so forth?

Common-size analysis of the income statement typically relates each item to sales. It is instructive to know what proportion of each sales dollar is absorbed by various costs and expenses incurred by the enterprise.

Analysts may use common-size statements to compare one company's statements from different years, to detect trends not evident from comparing absolute amounts. Also, common-size statements provide intercompany comparisons regardless of size because they recast financial statements into a comparable common-size format.

KEY TERMS

accounts receivable turnover, *1524*
acid-test ratio, *1524*
activity ratios, *1523*
asset turnover, *1524*
book value per share, *1524*
cash debt coverage, *1524*
common-size analysis, *1527*
comparative analysis, *1526*
coverage ratios, *1523*
current cash debt coverage, *1524*
current ratio, *1524*
debt to assets ratio, *1524*
earnings per share, *1524*
horizontal analysis, *1527*
inventory turnover, *1524*
liquidity ratios, *1523*
payout ratio, *1524*
percentage analysis, *1527*
profit margin on sales, *1524*
profitability ratios, *1523*
quick ratio, *1524*
return on assets, *1524*
return on common stock equity, *1524*
times interest earned, *1524*
vertical analysis, *1527*

SUMMARY OF LEARNING OBJECTIVES FOR APPENDIX 24A

9 Understand the approach to financial statement analysis. Basic financial statement analysis involves examining relationships between items on the statements (ratio and percentage analysis) and identifying trends in these relationships (comparative analysis). Analysis is used to predict the future, but ratio analysis is limited because the data are from the past. Also, ratio analysis identifies present strengths and weaknesses of a company, but it may not reveal *why* they are as they are. Although single ratios are helpful, they are not conclusive. For maximum usefulness, analysts must compare them with industry averages, past years, planned amounts, and the like.

10 Identify major analytic ratios and describe their calculation. Ratios are classified as liquidity ratios, activity ratios, profitability ratios, and coverage ratios. (1) *Liquidity ratio analysis* measures the short-run ability of a company to pay its currently maturing obligations. (2) *Activity ratio analysis* measures how effectively a company is using its assets. (3) *Profitability ratio analysis* measures the degree of success or failure of a company to generate revenues adequate to cover its costs of operation and provide a return to the owners. (4) *Coverage ratio analysis* measures the degree of protection afforded long-term creditors and investors.

11 Explain the limitations of ratio analysis. Ratios are based on historical cost, which can lead to distortions in measuring performance. Also, where estimated items are significant, income ratios lose some of their credibility. In addition, comparability problems exist because companies use different accounting principles and procedures. Finally, analysts must recognize that a substantial amount of important information is not included in a company's financial statements.

12 Describe techniques of comparative analysis. Companies present comparative data, which generally includes two years of balance sheet information and three years of income statement information. In addition, many companies include in their annual reports five- to ten-year summaries of pertinent data that permit the reader to analyze trends.

13 Describe techniques of percentage analysis. Percentage analysis consists of reducing a series of related amounts to a series of percentages of a given base. Analysts use two approaches. *Horizontal analysis* indicates the proportionate change in financial statement items over a period of time; such analysis is most helpful in evaluating trends. *Vertical analysis* (common-size analysis) is a proportional expression of each item on the financial statements in a given period to a base amount. It analyzes the composition of each of the financial statements from different years (a) to detect trends not evident from the comparison of absolute amounts and (b) to make intercompany comparisons of different-sized enterprises.

DEMONSTRATION PROBLEM

Konetzke Corporation, a publicly traded company, is preparing the interim financial data which it will issue to its stockholders and the Securities and Exchange Commission (SEC) for the fiscal year ending December 31, 2014. Your job as a member of the accounting team is to help determine the appropriate disclosures and any other potential year-end adjustments. You have collected the following information.

1. Konetzke is involved in four separate industries. The following information is available for each of the four industries. Konetzke wonders which segments are reportable.

Operating Segment	Total Revenue	Operating Profit (Loss)	Identifiable Assets
Badger	$ 60,000	$15,000	$167,000
Spartan	10,000	1,500	83,000
Cornhusker	23,000	(2,000)	21,000
Hawkeye	9,000	1,000	19,000
	$102,000	$15,500	$290,000

2. On February 3, 2015, one of Konetzke's customers declared bankruptcy. At December 31, 2014, this company owed Konetzke $15,000, of which $3,000 was paid in January 2015.
3. On January 18, 2015, one of the three major plants of the client burned down.
4. On January 23, 2015, a strike was called at one of Konetzke's largest plants, which halted 30% of its production. As of today (February 13), the strike has not been settled.
5. On February 1, 2013, the board of directors adopted a resolution accepting the offer of an investment banker to guarantee the marketing of $1,200,000 of preferred stock.

Instructions

(a) State in each case how the 2014 financial statements would be affected, if at all.

(b) Moving ahead to the first quarter of 2015, your team has compiled the following summarized revenue and expense data for the first quarter of the year.

Sales revenue	$30,000
Cost of goods sold	18,000
Variable selling expenses	500
Fixed selling expenses	1,500

Included in the fixed selling expenses was the single lump-sum payment of $800 for Internet advertisements for the entire year. Address the following with respect to the first quarter report. (1) Explain whether Konetzke should report its operating results for the quarter as if the quarter were a separate reporting period in and of itself, or as if the quarter were an integral part of the annual reporting period. (2) State how the sales revenue, cost of goods sold, and fixed selling expenses would be reflected in Konetzke's quarterly report prepared for the first quarter of 2015.

Solution

(a) 1. Konetzke first conducts the following three tests:

Revenue test: 10% × $102,000 = $10,200. The Badger ($23,000) and Cornhusker ($60,000) segments both meet this test.

Operating profit (loss) test: 10% × ($15,000 + $1,500 + $1,000) = $1,750. The Badger ($15,000) and Cornhusker ($2,000 absolute amount) segments both meet this test.

Identifiable assets test: 10% × $290,000 = $29,000. The Badger ($167,000) and Spartan ($83,000) segments both meet this test.

Thus, Konetzke has three reportable segments for which segment information should be disclosed.

Regarding the post-balance-sheet events:

2. The financial statements should be adjusted for the expected loss pertaining to the remaining receivable of $12,000. Such adjustment should reduce accounts receivable to their realizable value as of December 31, 2015.
3. Report the fire loss in a footnote to the balance sheet and refer to it in connection with the income statement, since earnings power is presumably affected.
4. Strikes are considered general knowledge and therefore disclosure is not required. Many auditors, however, would encourage disclosure in all cases.
5. Report the action of the new stock issue in a footnote to the balance sheet.

(b) 1. The company should report its quarterly results as if each interim period is an integral part of the annual period.

2. The company's revenue and expenses would be reported as follows on its quarterly report prepared for the first quarter of 2015:

Sales revenue	$30,000
Cost of goods sold	18,000
Variable selling expenses	500
Fixed selling expenses	
Advertising ($800 ÷ 4)	200
Other ($1,500 – $800)	700

Sales revenue and cost of goods sold receive the same treatment as if this were an annual report. Costs and expenses other than product costs should be charged to expense in interim periods as incurred or allocated among interim periods. Consequently, the variable selling expenses and the portion of fixed selling expenses not related to Internet advertising should be reported in full. One-fourth of the Internet advertising is reported as an expense in the first quarter, assuming the advertising is constant throughout the year. These costs can be deferred within the fiscal period if the benefits of the expenditure clearly extend beyond the interim period in which the expenditure is made.

FASB CODIFICATION

FASB Codification References

[1] FASB ASC 850-10-05 [Predecessor literature: "Related Party Disclosures," *Statement of Financial Accounting Standards No. 57* (Stamford, Conn.: FASB, 1982).]

[2] FASB ASC 855-10-05 [Predecessor literature: "Subsequent Events," *Statement on Auditing Standards No. 1* (New York: AICPA, 1973), pp. 123–124.]

[3] FASB ASC 280-10-05-3. [Predecessor literature: "Disclosures about Segments of an Enterprise and Related Information," *Statement of Financial Accounting Standards No. 131* (Norwalk, Conn.: FASB, 1997).]

[4] FASB ASC 270-10. [Predecessor literature: "Interim Financial Reporting," *Opinions of the Accounting Principles Board No. 28* (New York: AICPA, 1973).]

[5] FASB ASC 740-270-30-2 through 3. [Predecessor literature: "Interim Financial Reporting," *Opinions of the Accounting Principles Board No. 28* (New York: AICPA, 1973), par. 19.]

[6] FASB ASC 740-270-35-4. [Predecessor literature: "Accounting for Income Taxes in Interim Periods," *FASB Interpretation No. 18* (Stamford, Conn.: FASB, March 1977), par. 9.]

[7] FASB ASC 205-30 [Predecessor literature: "The Auditor's Consideration of an Entity's Ability to Continue as a Going Concern," *Statement on Auditing Standards No. 59* (New York: AICPA, 1988).]

Exercises

If your school has a subscription to the FASB Codification, go to *http://aaahq.org/ascLogin.cfm* to log in and prepare responses to the following. Provide Codification references for your responses.

CE24-1 Access the glossary ("Master Glossary") to answer the following.

(a) What is the definition of "ordinary income" (loss)?
(b) What is an error in previously issued financial statements?

(c) What is the definition of "earnings per share"?
(d) What is a publicly traded company?

CE24-2 What are some examples of related parties?

CE24-3 What are the quantitative thresholds that would require a public company to report separately information about an operating segment?

CE24-4 If an SEC-registered company uses the gross profit method to determine cost of goods sold for interim periods, would it be acceptable for the company to state that it's not practicable to determine components of inventory at interim periods? Why or why not?

An additional Codification case can be found in the Using Your Judgment section, on page 1548.

Be sure to check the book's companion website for a Review and Analysis Exercise, with solution.

WileyPLUS **Brief Exercises, Exercises, Problems, and many more learning and assessment tools and resources are available for practice in WileyPLUS.**

Note: All asterisked Questions, Exercises, and Problems relate to material in the appendix to the chapter.

QUESTIONS

1. What are the major advantages of notes to the financial statements? What types of items are usually reported in notes?

2. What is the full disclosure principle in accounting? Why has disclosure increased substantially in the last 10 years?

3. The FASB requires a reconciliation between the effective tax rate and the federal government's statutory rate. Of what benefit is such a disclosure requirement?

4. What type of disclosure or accounting do you believe is necessary for the following items?

(a) Because of a general increase in the number of labor disputes and strikes, both within and outside the industry, there is an increased likelihood that a company will suffer a costly strike in the near future.

(b) A company reports an extraordinary item (net of tax) correctly on the income statement. No other mention is made of this item in the annual report.

(c) A company expects to recover a substantial amount in connection with a pending refund claim for a prior year's taxes. Although the claim is being contested, counsel for the company has confirmed the client's expectation of recovery.

5. The following information was described in a note of Canon Packing Co.

"During August, Holland Products Corporation purchased 311,003 shares of the Company's common stock which constitutes approximately 35% of the stock outstanding. Holland has since obtained representation on the Board of Directors."

"An affiliate of Holland Products Corporation acts as a food broker for Canon Packing in the greater New York City marketing area. The commissions for such services after August amounted to approximately $20,000."

Why is this information disclosed?

6. What are the major types of subsequent events? Indicate how each of the following "subsequent events" would be reported.

(a) Collection of a note written off in a prior period.

(b) Issuance of a large preferred stock offering.

(c) Acquisition of a company in a different industry.

(d) Destruction of a major plant in a flood.

(e) Death of the company's chief executive officer (CEO).

(f) Additional wage costs associated with settlement of a four-week strike.

(g) Settlement of a federal income tax case at considerably more tax than anticipated at year-end.

(h) Change in the product mix from consumer goods to industrial goods.

7. What are diversified companies? What accounting problems are related to diversified companies?

8. What quantitative materiality test is applied to determine whether a segment is significant enough to warrant separate disclosure?

9. Identify the segment information that is required to be disclosed by GAAP.

10. What is an operating segment, and when can information about two operating segments be aggregated?

11. The controller for Lafayette Inc. recently commented, "If I have to disclose our segments individually, the only people who will gain are our competitors and the only people that will lose are our present stockholders." Evaluate this comment.

12. An article in the financial press entitled "Important Information in Annual Reports This Year" noted that annual reports include a management's discussion and analysis section. What would this section contain?

13. "The financial statements of a company are management's, not the accountant's." Discuss the implications of this statement.

14. Olga Conrad, a financial writer, noted recently, "There are substantial arguments for including earnings projections in annual reports and the like. The most compelling is that it would give anyone interested something now available to only a relatively select few—like large stockholders, creditors, and attentive bartenders." Identify some arguments against providing earnings projections.

15. The following comment appeared in the financial press: "Inadequate financial disclosure, particularly with respect to how management views the future and its role in the marketplace, has always been a stone in the shoe. After all, if you don't know how a company views the future, how can you judge the worth of its corporate strategy?" What are some arguments for reporting earnings forecasts?

16. What are interim reports? Why are balance sheets often not provided with interim data?

17. What are the accounting problems related to the presentation of interim data?

18. Dierdorf Inc., a closely held corporation, has decided to go public. The controller, Ed Floyd, is concerned with presenting interim data when a LIFO inventory valuation is used. What problems are encountered with LIFO inventories when quarterly data are presented?

19. What approaches have been suggested to overcome the seasonality problem related to interim reporting?

20. What is the difference between a CPA's unqualified opinion or "clean" opinion and a qualified one?

21. Jane Ellerby and Sam Callison are discussing the recent fraud that occurred at LowRental Leasing, Inc. The fraud involved the improper reporting of revenue to ensure that the company would have income in excess of $1 million. What is fraudulent financial reporting, and how does it differ from an embezzlement of company funds?

*22. "The significance of financial statement data is not in the amount alone." Discuss the meaning of this statement.

*23. A close friend of yours, who is a history major and who has not had any college courses or any experience in business, is receiving the financial statements from companies in which he has minor investments (acquired for him by his now-deceased father). He asks you what he needs to know to interpret and to evaluate the financial statement data that he is receiving. What would you tell him?

*24. Distinguish between ratio analysis and percentage analysis relative to the interpretation of financial statements. What is the value of these two types of analyses?

*25. In calculating inventory turnover, why is cost of goods sold used as the numerator? As the inventory turnover increases, what increasing risk does the business assume?

*26. What is the relationship of the asset turnover to the return on assets?

*27. Explain the meaning of the following terms: (a) common-size analysis, (b) vertical analysis, (c) horizontal analysis, and (d) percentage analysis.

*28. Presently, the profession requires that earnings per share be disclosed on the face of the income statement. What are some disadvantages of reporting ratios on the financial statements?

BRIEF EXERCISES

2 **BE24-1** An annual report of Crestwood Industries states, "The company and its subsidiaries have long-term leases expiring on various dates after December 31, 2014. Amounts payable under such commitments, without reduction for related rental income, are expected to average approximately $5,711,000 annually for the next 3 years. Related rental income from certain subleases to others is estimated to average $3,094,000 annually for the next 3 years." What information is provided by this note?

2 **BE24-2** An annual report of Ford Motor Corporation states, "Net income a share is computed based upon the average number of shares of capital stock of all classes outstanding. Additional shares of common stock may be issued or delivered in the future on conversion of outstanding convertible debentures, exercise of outstanding employee stock options, and for payment of defined supplemental compensation. Had such additional shares been outstanding, net income a share would have been reduced by 10¢ in the current year and 3¢ in the previous year. . . . As a result of capital stock transactions by the company during the current year (primarily the purchase of Class A Stock from Ford Foundation), net income a share was increased by 6¢." What information is provided by this note?

3 **BE24-3** Morlan Corporation is preparing its December 31, 2014, financial statements. Two events that occurred between December 31, 2014, and March 10, 2015, when the statements were issued, are described below.

1. A liability, estimated at $160,000 at December 31, 2014, was settled on February 26, 2015, at $170,000.
2. A flood loss of $80,000 occurred on March 1, 2015.

What effect do these subsequent events have on 2014 net income?

3 **BE24-4** Tina Bailey, a student of intermediate accounting, was heard to remark after a class discussion on segment reporting, "All this is very confusing to me. First we are told that there is merit in presenting the consolidated results, and now we are told that it is better to show segmental results. I wish they would make up their minds." Evaluate this comment.

3 **BE24-5** Foley Corporation has seven industry segments with total revenues as follows.

Penley	$600	Cheng	$225
Konami	650	Takuhi	200
KSC	250	Molina	700
Red Moon	275		

Based only on the revenues test, which industry segments are reportable?

3 **BE24-6** Operating profits and losses for the seven industry segments of Foley Corporation are:

Penley	$ 90	Cheng	$ (20)
Konami	(40)	Takuhi	34
KSC	25	Molina	150
Red Moon	50		

Based only on the operating profit (loss) test, which industry segments are reportable?

3 **BE24-7** Identifiable assets for the seven industry segments of Foley Corporation are:

Penley	$500	Cheng	$200
Konami	550	Takuhi	150
KSC	250	Molina	475
Red Moon	400		

Based only on the identifiable assets test, which industry segments are reportable?

10 ***BE24-8** Answer each of the questions in the following unrelated situations.

(a) The current ratio of a company is 5:1 and its acid-test ratio is 1:1. If the inventories and prepaid items amount to $500,000, what is the amount of current liabilities?

(b) A company had an average inventory last year of $200,000 and its inventory turnover was 5. If sales volume and unit cost remain the same this year as last and inventory turnover is 8 this year, what will average inventory have to be during the current year?

(c) A company has current assets of $90,000 (of which $40,000 is inventory and prepaid items) and current liabilities of $40,000. What is the current ratio? What is the acid-test ratio? If the company borrows $15,000 cash from a bank on a 120-day loan, what will its current ratio be? What will the acid-test ratio be?

(d) A company has current assets of $600,000 and current liabilities of $240,000. The board of directors declares a cash dividend of $180,000. What is the current ratio after the declaration but before payment? What is the current ratio after the payment of the dividend?

10 ***BE24-9** Heartland Company's budgeted sales and budgeted cost of goods sold for the coming year are $144,000,000 and $99,000,000, respectively. Short-term interest rates are expected to average 10%. If Heartland can increase inventory turnover from its present level of 9 times a year to a level of 12 times per year, compute its expected cost savings for the coming year.

EXERCISES

3 **E24-1 (Post-Balance-Sheet Events)** Madrasah Corporation issued its financial statements for the year ended December 31, 2014, on March 10, 2015. The following events took place early in 2015.

(a) On January 10, 10,000 shares of $5 par value common stock were issued at $66 per share.

(b) On March 1, Madrasah determined after negotiations with the Internal Revenue Service that income taxes payable for 2014 should be $1,270,000. At December 31, 2014, income taxes payable were recorded at $1,100,000.

Instructions

Discuss how the preceding post-balance-sheet events should be reflected in the 2014 financial statements.

3 **E24-2 (Post-Balance-Sheet Events)** For each of the following subsequent (post-balance-sheet) events, indicate whether a company should (a) adjust the financial statements, (b) disclose in notes to the financial statements, or (c) neither adjust nor disclose.

_______ 1. Settlement of federal tax case at a cost considerably in excess of the amount expected at year-end.
_______ 2. Introduction of a new product line.
_______ 3. Loss of assembly plant due to fire.
_______ 4. Sale of a significant portion of the company's assets.
_______ 5. Retirement of the company president.
_______ 6. Prolonged employee strike.
_______ 7. Loss of a significant customer.
_______ 8. Issuance of a significant number of shares of common stock.
_______ 9. Material loss on a year-end receivable because of a customer's bankruptcy.
_______ 10. Hiring of a new president.
_______ 11. Settlement of prior year's litigation against the company (no loss was accrued).
_______ 12. Merger with another company of comparable size.

3 **E24-3 (Segmented Reporting)** Carlton Company is involved in four separate industries. The following information is available for each of the four industries.

Operating Segment	Total Revenue	Operating Profit (Loss)	Identifiable Assets
W	$ 60,000	$15,000	$167,000
X	10,000	3,000	83,000
Y	23,000	(2,000)	21,000
Z	9,000	1,000	19,000
	$102,000	$17,000	$290,000

Instructions

Determine which of the operating segments are reportable based on the:

(a) Revenue test.
(b) Operating profit (loss) test.
(c) Identifiable assets test.

10 ***E24-4 (Ratio Computation and Analysis; Liquidity)** As loan analyst for Utrillo Bank, you have been presented the following information.

	Toulouse Co.	Lautrec Co.
Assets		
Cash	$ 120,000	$ 320,000
Receivables	220,000	302,000
Inventories	570,000	518,000
Total current assets	910,000	1,140,000
Other assets	500,000	612,000
Total assets	$1,410,000	$1,752,000
Liabilities and Stockholders' Equity		
Current liabilities	$ 305,000	$ 350,000
Long-term liabilities	400,000	500,000
Capital stock and retained earnings	705,000	902,000
Total liabilities and stockholders' equity	$1,410,000	$1,752,000
Annual sales	$ 930,000	$1,500,000
Rate of gross profit on sales	30%	40%

Each of these companies has requested a loan of $50,000 for 6 months with no collateral offered. Because your bank has reached its quota for loans of this type, only one of these requests is to be granted.

Instructions

Which of the two companies, as judged by the information given above, would you recommend as the better risk and why? Assume that the ending account balances are representative of the entire year.

10 ***E24-5 (Analysis of Given Ratios)** Picasso Company is a wholesale distributor of professional equipment and supplies. The company's sales have averaged about $900,000 annually for the 3-year period 2012–2014. The firm's total assets at the end of 2014 amounted to $850,000.

The president of Picasso Company has asked the controller to prepare a report that summarizes the financial aspects of the company's operations for the past 3 years. This report will be presented to the board of directors at their next meeting.

In addition to comparative financial statements, the controller has decided to present a number of relevant financial ratios which can assist in the identification and interpretation of trends. At the request of the controller, the accounting staff has calculated the following ratios for the 3-year period 2012–2014.

	2012	2013	2014
Current ratio	1.80	1.89	1.96
Acid-test (quick) ratio	1.04	0.99	0.87
Accounts receivable turnover	8.75	7.71	6.42
Inventory turnover	4.91	4.32	3.42
Debt to assets	51.0%	46.0%	41.0%
Long-term debt to assets	31.0%	27.0%	24.0%
Sales to fixed assets (fixed asset turnover)	1.58	1.69	1.79
Sales as a percent of 2012 sales	1.00	1.03	1.07
Gross margin percentage	36.0%	35.1%	34.6%
Net income to sales	6.9%	7.0%	7.2%
Return on assets	7.7%	7.7%	7.8%
Return on common stock equity	13.6%	13.1%	12.7%

In preparation of the report, the controller has decided first to examine the financial ratios independent of any other data to determine if the ratios themselves reveal any significant trends over the 3-year period.

Instructions

(a) The current ratio is increasing while the acid-test (quick) ratio is decreasing. Using the ratios provided, identify and explain the contributing factor(s) for this apparently divergent trend.

(b) In terms of the ratios provided, what conclusion(s) can be drawn regarding the company's use of financial leverage during the 2012–2014 period?

(c) Using the ratios provided, what conclusion(s) can be drawn regarding the company's net investment in plant and equipment?

10 ***E24-6 (Ratio Analysis)** Edna Millay Inc. is a manufacturer of electronic components and accessories with total assets of $20,000,000. Selected financial ratios for Millay and the industry averages for firms of similar size are presented below.

	Edna Millay			2014 Industry Average
	2012	2013	2014	
Current ratio	2.09	2.27	2.51	2.24
Quick ratio	1.15	1.12	1.19	1.22
Inventory turnover	2.40	2.18	2.02	3.50
Net sales to stockholders' equity	2.71	2.80	2.99	2.85
Return on common stock equity	0.14	0.15	0.17	0.11
Total liabilities to stockholders' equity	1.41	1.37	1.44	0.95

Millay is being reviewed by several entities whose interests vary, and the company's financial ratios are a part of the data being considered. Each of the parties listed below must recommend an action based on its evaluation of Millay's financial position.

Archibald MacLeish Bank. The bank is processing Millay's application for a new 5-year term note. Archibald MacLeish has been Millay's banker for several years but must reevaluate the company's financial position for each major transaction.

Robert Lowell Company. Lowell is a new supplier to Millay and must decide on the appropriate credit terms to extend to the company.

Robert Penn Warren. A brokerage firm specializing in the stock of electronics firms that are sold over-the-counter, Robert Penn Warren must decide if it will include Millay in a new fund being established for sale to Robert Penn Warren's clients.

Working Capital Management Committee. This is a committee of Millay's management personnel chaired by the chief operating officer. The committee is charged with the responsibility of periodically reviewing the company's working capital position, comparing actual data against budgets, and recommending changes in strategy as needed.

Instructions

(a) Describe the analytical use of each of the six ratios presented on page 1535.

(b) For each of the four entities described above, identify two financial ratios, from the ratios presented on page 1535, that would be most valuable as a basis for its decision regarding Millay.

(c) Discuss what the financial ratios presented in the question reveal about Millay. Support your answer by citing specific ratio levels and trends as well as the interrelationships between these ratios.

(CMA adapted)

EXERCISES SET B

See the book's companion website, at **www.wiley.com/college/kieso**, for an additional set of exercises.

PROBLEMS

3 **P24-1 (Subsequent Events)** Your firm has been engaged to examine the financial statements of Almaden Corporation for the year 2014. The bookkeeper who maintains the financial records has prepared all the unaudited financial statements for the corporation since its organization on January 2, 2009. The client provides you with the following information.

ALMADEN CORPORATION
BALANCE SHEET
DECEMBER 31, 2014

Assets		Liabilities	
Current assets	$1,881,100	Current liabilities	$ 962,400
Other assets	5,171,400	Long-term liabilities	1,439,500
		Capital	4,650,600
	$7,052,500		$7,052,500

An analysis of current assets discloses the following.

Cash (restricted in the amount of $300,000 for plant expansion)	$ 571,000
Investments in land	185,000
Accounts receivable less allowance of $30,000	480,000
Inventories (LIFO flow assumption)	645,100
	$1,881,100

Other assets include:

Prepaid expenses	$ 62,400
Plant and equipment less accumulated depreciation of $1,430,000	4,130,000
Cash surrender value of life insurance policy	84,000
Unamortized bond discount	34,500
Notes receivable (short-term)	162,300
Goodwill	252,000
Land	446,200
	$5,171,400

Current liabilities include:

Accounts payable	$ 510,000
Notes payable (due 2017)	157,400
Estimated income taxes payable	145,000
Premium on common stock	150,000
	$ 962,400

Long-term liabilities include:

Unearned revenue	$ 489,500
Dividends payable (cash)	200,000
8% bonds payable (due May 1, 2019)	750,000
	$1,439,500

Capital includes:

Retained earnings	$2,810,600
Common stock, par value $10; authorized 200,000 shares, 184,000 shares issued	1,840,000
	$4,650,600

The supplementary information below is also provided.

1. On May 1, 2014, the corporation issued at 95.4, $750,000 of bonds to finance plant expansion. The long-term bond agreement provided for the annual payment of interest every May 1. The existing plant was pledged as security for the loan. Use the straight-line method for discount amortization.
2. The bookkeeper made the following mistakes.
   (a) In 2012, the ending inventory was overstated by $183,000. The ending inventories for 2013 and 2014 were correctly computed.
   (b) In 2014, accrued wages in the amount of $225,000 were omitted from the balance sheet, and these expenses were not charged on the income statement.
   (c) In 2014, a gain of $175,000 (net of tax) on the sale of certain plant assets was credited directly to retained earnings.
3. A major competitor has introduced a line of products that will compete directly with Almaden's primary line, now being produced in a specially designed new plant. Because of manufacturing innovations, the competitor's line will be of comparable quality but priced 50% below Almaden's line. The competitor announced its new line on January 14, 2015. Almaden indicates that the company will meet the lower prices that are high enough to cover variable manufacturing and selling expenses, but permit recovery of only a portion of fixed costs.
4. You learned on January 28, 2015, prior to completion of the audit, of heavy damage because of a recent fire to one of Almaden's two plants; the loss will not be reimbursed by insurance. The newspapers described the event in detail.

Instructions

Analyze the above information to prepare a corrected balance sheet for Almaden in accordance with proper accounting and reporting principles. Prepare a description of any notes that might need to be prepared. The books are closed and adjustments to income are to be made through retained earnings.

3 **P24-2 (Segmented Reporting)** Cineplex Corporation is a diversified company that operates in five different industries: A, B, C, D, and E. The following information relating to each segment is available for 2015.

	A	B	C	D	E
Sales revenue	$40,000	$ 75,000	$580,000	$35,000	$55,000
Cost of goods sold	19,000	50,000	270,000	19,000	30,000
Operating expenses	10,000	40,000	235,000	12,000	18,000
Total expenses	29,000	90,000	505,000	31,000	48,000
Operating profit (loss)	$11,000	$ (15,000)	$ 75,000	$ 4,000	$ 7,000
Identifiable assets	$35,000	$ 80,000	$500,000	$65,000	$50,000

Sales of segments B and C included intersegment sales of $20,000 and $100,000, respectively.

Instructions

(a) Determine which of the segments are reportable based on the:
   (1) Revenue test.
   (2) Operating profit (loss) test.
   (3) Identifiable assets test.
(b) Prepare the necessary disclosures required by GAAP.

10 12 ***P24-3 (Ratio Computations and Additional Analysis)** Bradburn Corporation was formed 5 years ago through a public subscription of common stock. Daniel Brown, who owns 15% of the common stock, was one of the organizers of Bradburn and is its current president. The company has been successful, but it currently is experiencing a shortage of funds. On June 10, 2014, Daniel Brown approached the Topeka National Bank, asking for a 24-month extension on two $35,000 notes, which are due on June 30, 2015, and September 30, 2015. Another note of $6,000 is due on March 31, 2016, but he expects no difficulty in paying this note on its

due date. Brown explained that Bradburn's cash flow problems are due primarily to the company's desire to finance a $300,000 plant expansion over the next 2 fiscal years through internally generated funds.

The commercial loan officer of Topeka National Bank requested the following financial reports for the last 2 fiscal years.

BRADBURN CORPORATION
BALANCE SHEET
MARCH 31

Assets	2015	2014
Cash	$ 18,200	$ 12,500
Notes receivable	148,000	132,000
Accounts receivable (net)	131,800	125,500
Inventories (at cost)	105,000	50,000
Plant & equipment (net of depreciation)	1,449,000	1,420,500
Total assets	$1,852,000	$1,740,500
Liabilities and Stockholders' Equity		
Accounts payable	$ 79,000	$ 91,000
Notes payable	76,000	61,500
Accrued liabilities	9,000	6,000
Common stock (130,000 shares, $10 par)	1,300,000	1,300,000
Retained earnings[a]	388,000	282,000
Total liabilities and stockholders' equity	$1,852,000	$1,740,500

[a]Cash dividends were paid at the rate of $1 per share in fiscal year 2014 and $2 per share in fiscal year 2015.

BRADBURN CORPORATION
INCOME STATEMENT
FOR THE FISCAL YEARS ENDED MARCH 31

	2015	2014
Sales revenue	$3,000,000	$2,700,000
Cost of goods sold[a]	1,530,000	1,425,000
Gross margin	1,470,000	1,275,000
Operating expenses	860,000	780,000
Income before income taxes	610,000	495,000
Income taxes (40%)	244,000	198,000
Net income	$ 366,000	$ 297,000

[a]Depreciation charges on the plant and equipment of $100,000 and $102,500 for fiscal years ended March 31, 2014 and 2015, respectively, are included in cost of goods sold.

Instructions

(a) Compute the following items for Bradburn Corporation.

(1) Current ratio for fiscal years 2014 and 2015.

(2) Acid-test (quick) ratio for fiscal years 2014 and 2015.

(3) Inventory turnover for fiscal year 2015.

(4) Return on assets for fiscal years 2014 and 2015. (Assume total assets were $1,688,500 at 3/31/13.)

(5) Percentage change in sales, cost of goods sold, gross margin, and net income after taxes from fiscal year 2014 to 2015.

(b) Identify and explain what other financial reports and/or financial analyses might be helpful to the commercial loan officer of Topeka National Bank in evaluating Daniel Brown's request for a time extension on Bradburn's notes.

(c) Assume that the percentage changes experienced in fiscal year 2015 as compared with fiscal year 2014 for sales and cost of goods sold will be repeated in each of the next 2 years. Is Bradburn's desire to finance the plant expansion from internally generated funds realistic? Discuss.

(d) Should Topeka National Bank grant the extension on Bradburn's notes considering Daniel Brown's statement about financing the plant expansion through internally generated funds? Discuss.

13 ***P24-4 (Horizontal and Vertical Analysis)** Presented below is the comparative balance sheet for Gilmour Company.

XLS

GILMOUR COMPANY
COMPARATIVE BALANCE SHEET
AS OF DECEMBER 31, 2015 AND 2014

	December 31	
	2015	2014
Assets		
Cash	$ 180,000	$ 275,000
Accounts receivable (net)	220,000	155,000
Short-term investments	270,000	150,000
Inventories	1,060,000	980,000
Prepaid expenses	25,000	25,000
Plant & equipment	2,585,000	1,950,000
Accumulated depreciation	(1,000,000)	(750,000)
	$3,340,000	$2,785,000
Liabilities and Stockholders' Equity		
Accounts payable	$ 50,000	$ 75,000
Accrued expenses	170,000	200,000
Bonds payable	450,000	190,000
Capital stock	2,100,000	1,770,000
Retained earnings	570,000	550,000
	$3,340,000	$2,785,000

Instructions

(Round to two decimal places.)

(a) Prepare a comparative balance sheet of Gilmour Company showing the percent each item is of the total assets or total liabilities and stockholders' equity.
(b) Prepare a comparative balance sheet of Gilmour Company showing the dollar change and the percent change for each item.
(c) Of what value is the additional information provided in part (a)?
(d) Of what value is the additional information provided in part (b)?

10 ***P24-5 (Dividend Policy Analysis)** Matheny Inc. went public 3 years ago. The board of directors will be meeting shortly after the end of the year to decide on a dividend policy. In the past, growth has been financed primarily through the retention of earnings. A stock or a cash dividend has never been declared. Presented below is a brief financial summary of Matheny Inc. operations.

	($000 omitted)				
	2015	2014	2013	2012	2011
Sales revenue	$20,000	$16,000	$14,000	$6,000	$4,000
Net income	2,400	1,400	800	700	250
Average total assets	22,000	19,000	11,500	4,200	3,000
Current assets	8,000	6,000	3,000	1,200	1,000
Working capital	3,600	3,200	1,200	500	400
Common shares:					
Number of shares outstanding (000)	2,000	2,000	2,000	20	20
Average market price	$9	$6	$4	–	–

Instructions

Gateway to the Profession

Additional Financial Statement Analysis Problems

(a) Suggest factors to be considered by the board of directors in establishing a dividend policy.
(b) Compute the return on assets, profit margin on sales, earnings per share, price-earnings ratio, and current ratio for each of the 5 years for Matheny Inc.
(c) Comment on the appropriateness of declaring a cash dividend at this time, using the ratios computed in part (b) as a major factor in your analysis.

PROBLEMS SET B

See the book's companion website, at **www.wiley.com/college/kieso**, for an additional set of problems.

CONCEPTS FOR ANALYSIS

CA24-1 (General Disclosures; Inventories; Property, Plant, and Equipment) Koch Corporation is in the process of preparing its annual financial statements for the fiscal year ended April 30, 2015. Because all of Koch's shares are traded intrastate, the company does not have to file any reports with the Securities and Exchange Commission. The company manufactures plastic, glass, and paper containers for sale to food and drink manufacturers and distributors.

Koch Corporation maintains separate control accounts for its raw materials, work in process, and finished goods inventories for each of the three types of containers. The inventories are valued at the lower-of-cost-or-market.

The company's property, plant, and equipment are classified in the following major categories: land, office buildings, furniture and fixtures, manufacturing facilities, manufacturing equipment, and leasehold improvements. All fixed assets are carried at cost. The depreciation methods employed depend on the type of asset (its classification) and when it was acquired.

Koch Corporation plans to present the inventory and fixed asset amounts in its April 30, 2015, balance sheet as shown below.

Inventories	$4,814,200
Property, plant, and equipment (net of depreciation)	6,310,000

Instructions

What information regarding inventories and property, plant, and equipment must be disclosed by Koch Corporation in the audited financial statements issued to stockholders, either in the body or the notes, for the 2014–2015 fiscal year?

(CMA adapted)

CA24-2 (Disclosures Required in Various Situations) Ace Inc. produces electronic components for sale to manufacturers of radios, television sets, and digital sound systems. In connection with her examination of Ace's financial statements for the year ended December 31, 2015, Gloria Rodd, CPA, completed field work 2 weeks ago. Ms. Rodd now is evaluating the significance of the following items prior to preparing her auditor's report. Except as noted, none of these items have been disclosed in the financial statements or notes.

Item 1: A 10-year loan agreement, which the company entered into 3 years ago, provides that dividend payments may not exceed net income earned after taxes subsequent to the date of the agreement. The balance of retained earnings at the date of the loan agreement was $420,000. From that date through December 31, 2015, net income after taxes has totaled $570,000 and cash dividends have totaled $320,000. On the basis of these data, the staff auditor assigned to this review concluded that there was no retained earnings restriction at December 31, 2015.

Item 2: Recently Ace interrupted its policy of paying cash dividends quarterly to its stockholders. Dividends were paid regularly through 2014, discontinued for all of 2015 to finance purchase of equipment for the company's new plant, and resumed in the first quarter of 2016. In the annual report, dividend policy is to be discussed in the president's letter to stockholders.

Item 3: A major electronics firm has introduced a line of products that will compete directly with Ace's primary line, now being produced in the specially designed new plant. Because of manufacturing innovations, the competitor's line will be of comparable quality but priced 50% below Ace's line. The competitor announced its new line during the week following completion of field work. Ms. Rodd read the announcement in the newspaper and discussed the situation by telephone with Ace executives. Ace will meet the lower prices that are high enough to cover variable manufacturing and selling expenses but will permit recovery of only a portion of fixed costs.

Item 4: The company's new manufacturing plant building, which cost $2,400,000 and has an estimated life of 25 years, is leased from Wichita National Bank at an annual rental of $600,000. The company is obligated to pay property taxes, insurance, and maintenance. At the conclusion of its 10-year noncancelable lease, the company has the option of purchasing the property for $1. In Ace's income statement, the rental payment is reported on a separate line.

Instructions

For each of the above items, discuss any additional disclosures in the financial statements and notes that the auditor should recommend to her client. (The cumulative effect of the four items should not be considered.)

CA24-3 (Disclosures, Conditional and Contingent Liabilities) Presented below are three independent situations.

Situation 1: A company offers a one-year warranty for the product that it manufactures. A history of warranty claims has been compiled, and the probable amounts of claims related to sales for a given period can be determined.

Situation 2: Subsequent to the date of a set of financial statements but prior to the issuance of the financial statements, a company enters into a contract that will probably result in a significant loss to the company. The amount of the loss can be reasonably estimated.

Situation 3: A company has adopted a policy of recording self-insurance for any possible losses resulting from injury to others by the company's vehicles. The premium for an insurance policy for the same risk from an independent insurance company would have an annual cost of $4,000. During the period covered by the financial statements, there were no accidents involving the company's vehicles that resulted in injury to others.

Instructions

Discuss the accrual or type of disclosure necessary (if any) and the reason(s) why such disclosure is appropriate for each of the three independent sets of facts above.

(AICPA adapted)

CA24-4 (Post-Balance-Sheet Events) At December 31, 2014, Coburn Corp. has assets of $10,000,000, liabilities of $6,000,000, common stock of $2,000,000 (representing 2,000,000 shares of $1 par common stock), and retained earnings of $2,000,000. Net sales for the year 2014 were $18,000,000, and net income was $800,000. As auditors of this company, you are making a review of subsequent events on February 13, 2015, and you find the following.

1. On February 3, 2015, one of Coburn's customers declared bankruptcy. At December 31, 2014, this company owed Coburn $300,000, of which $60,000 was paid in January 2015.
2. On January 18, 2015, one of the three major plants of the client burned.
3. On January 23, 2015, a strike was called at one of Coburn's largest plants, which halted 30% of its production. As of today (February 13), the strike has not been settled.
4. A major electronics enterprise has introduced a line of products that would compete directly with Coburn's primary line, now being produced in a specially designed new plant. Because of manufacturing innovations, the competitor has been able to achieve quality similar to that of Coburn's products but at a price 50% lower. Coburn officials say they will meet the lower prices, which are high enough to cover variable manufacturing and selling costs but which permit recovery of only a portion of fixed costs.
5. Merchandise traded in the open market is recorded in the company's records at $1.40 per unit on December 31, 2014. This price had prevailed for 2 weeks, after release of an official market report that predicted vastly enlarged supplies; however, no purchases were made at $1.40. The price throughout the preceding year had been about $2, which was the level experienced over several years. On January 18, 2015, the price returned to $2, after public disclosure of an error in the official calculations of the prior December, correction of which destroyed the expectations of excessive supplies. Inventory at December 31, 2015, was on a lower-of-cost-or-market basis.
6. On February 1, 2015, the board of directors adopted a resolution accepting the offer of an investment banker to guarantee the marketing of $1,200,000 of preferred stock.

Instructions

State in each case how the 2014 financial statements would be affected, if at all.

CA24-5 (Segment Reporting) You are compiling the consolidated financial statements for Winsor Corporation International. The corporation's accountant, Anthony Reese, has provided you with the segment information shown on the next page.

Note 7: Major Segments of Business
WCI conducts funeral service and cemetery operations in the United States and Canada. Substantially all revenues of WCI's major segments of business are from unaffiliated customers. Segment information for fiscal 2015, 2014, and 2013 follows.

	Funeral	Floral	Cemetery	(thousands) Real Estate	Dried Whey	Limousine	Consolidated
Revenues							
2015	$302,000	$10,000	$ 73,000	$ 2,000	$7,000	$12,000	$406,000
2014	245,000	6,000	61,000	4,000	4,000	4,000	324,000
2013	208,000	3,000	42,000	3,000	1,000	3,000	260,000
Operating Income							
2015	74,000	1,500	18,000	(36,000)	500	2,000	60,000
2014	64,000	200	12,000	(28,000)	200	400	48,800
2013	54,000	150	6,000	(21,000)	100	350	39,600
Capital Expenditures							
2015	26,000	1,000	9,000	400	300	1,000	37,700
2014	28,000	2,000	60,000	1,500	100	700	92,300
2013	14,000	25	8,000	600	25	50	22,700
Depreciation and Amortization							
2015	13,000	100	2,400	1,400	100	200	17,200
2014	10,000	50	1,400	700	50	100	12,300
2013	8,000	25	1,000	600	25	50	9,700
Identifiable Assets							
2015	334,000	1,500	162,000	114,000	500	8,000	620,000
2014	322,000	1,000	144,000	52,000	1,000	6,000	526,000
2013	223,000	500	78,000	34,000	500	3,500	339,500

Instructions

Determine which of the above segments must be reported separately and which can be combined under the category "Other." Then, write a one-page memo to the company's accountant, Anthony Reese, explaining the following.

(a) What segments must be reported separately and what segments can be combined.
(b) What criteria you used to determine reportable segments.
(c) What major items for each must be disclosed.

CA24-6 (Segment Reporting—Theory) Presented below is an excerpt from the financial statements of **H. J. Heinz Company**.

Segment and Geographic Data

The company is engaged principally in one line of business—processed food products—which represents over 90% of consolidated sales. Information about the business of the company by geographic area is presented in the table below.

There were no material amounts of sales or transfers between geographic areas or between affiliates, and no material amounts of United States export sales.

		Foreign					
(in thousands of U.S. dollars)	Domestic	United Kingdom	Canada	Western Europe	Other	Total	Worldwide
Sales	$2,381,054	$547,527	$216,726	$383,784	$209,354	$1,357,391	$3,738,445
Operating income	246,780	61,282	34,146	29,146	25,111	149,685	396,465
Identifiable assets	1,362,152	265,218	112,620	294,732	143,971	816,541	2,178,693
Capital expenditures	72,712	12,262	13,790	8,253	4,368	38,673	111,385
Depreciation expense	42,279	8,364	3,592	6,355	3,606	21,917	64,196

Instructions

(a) Why does H. J. Heinz not prepare segment information on its products or services?
(b) What are export sales, and when should they be disclosed?
(c) Why are sales by geographical area important to disclose?

CA24-7 (Segment Reporting—Theory) The following article appeared in the *Wall Street Journal*.

WASHINGTON—The Securities and Exchange Commission staff issued guidelines for companies grappling with the problem of dividing up their business into industry segments for their annual reports.

An industry segment is defined by the Financial Accounting Standards Board as a part of an enterprise engaged in providing a product or service or a group of related products or services primarily to unaffiliated customers for a profit.

Although conceding that the process is a "subjective task" that "to a considerable extent, depends on the judgment of management," the SEC staff said companies should consider . . . various factors . . . to determine whether products and services should be grouped together or reported as segments.

Instructions

(a) What does financial reporting for segments of a business enterprise involve?
(b) Identify the reasons for requiring financial data to be reported by segments.
(c) Identify the possible disadvantages of requiring financial data to be reported by segments.
(d) Identify the accounting difficulties inherent in segment reporting.

CA24-8 (Interim Reporting) Snider Corporation, a publicly traded company, is preparing the interim financial data which it will issue to its stockholders and the Securities and Exchange Commission (SEC) at the end of the first quarter of the 2014–2015 fiscal year. Snider's financial accounting department has compiled the following summarized revenue and expense data for the first quarter of the year.

Sales revenue	$60,000,000
Cost of goods sold	36,000,000
Variable selling expenses	1,000,000
Fixed selling expenses	3,000,000

Included in the fixed selling expenses was the single lump-sum payment of $2,000,000 for television advertisements for the entire year.

Instructions

(a) Snider Corporation must issue its quarterly financial statements in accordance with generally accepted accounting principles regarding interim financial reporting.
   (1) Explain whether Snider should report its operating results for the quarter as if the quarter were a separate reporting period in and of itself, or as if the quarter were an integral part of the annual reporting period.
   (2) State how the sales revenue, cost of goods sold, and fixed selling expenses would be reflected in Snider Corporation's quarterly report prepared for the first quarter of the 2014–2015 fiscal year. Briefly justify your presentation.

(b) What financial information, as a minimum, must Snider Corporation disclose to its stockholders in its quarterly reports?

(CMA adapted)

CA24-9 (Treatment of Various Interim Reporting Situations) The following statement is an excerpt from the FASB pronouncement related to interim reporting.

> Interim financial information is essential to provide investors and others with timely information as to the progress of the enterprise. The usefulness of such information rests on the relationship that it has to the annual results of operations. Accordingly, the Board has concluded that each interim period should be viewed primarily as an integral part of an annual period.
>
> In general, the results for each interim period should be based on the accounting principles and practices used by an enterprise in the preparation of its latest annual financial statements unless a change in an accounting practice or policy has been adopted in the current year. The Board has concluded, however, that certain accounting principles and practices followed for annual reporting purposes may require modification at interim reporting dates so that the reported results for the interim period may better relate to the results of operations for the annual period.

Instructions

Listed on the next page are six independent cases on how accounting facts might be reported on an individual company's interim financial reports. For each of these cases, state whether the method proposed to be used for interim reporting would be acceptable under generally accepted accounting principles applicable to interim financial data. Support each answer with a brief explanation.

(a) J. D. Long Company takes a physical inventory at year-end for annual financial statement purposes. Inventory and cost of sales reported in the interim quarterly statements are based on estimated gross profit rates, because a physical inventory would result in a cessation of operations. Long Company does have reliable perpetual inventory records.

(b) Rockford Company is planning to report one-fourth of its pension expense each quarter.

(c) Republic Company wrote inventory down to reflect lower-of-cost-or-market in the first quarter. At year-end, the market exceeds the original acquisition cost of this inventory. Consequently, management plans to write the inventory back up to its original cost as a year-end adjustment.

(d) Gansner Company realized a large gain on the sale of investments at the beginning of the second quarter. The company wants to report one-third of the gain in each of the remaining quarters.

(e) Fredonia Company has estimated its annual audit fee. It plans to pro rate this expense equally over all four quarters.

(f) LaBrava Company was reasonably certain it would have an employee strike in the third quarter. As a result, it shipped heavily during the second quarter but plans to defer the recognition of the sales in excess of the normal sales volume. The deferred sales will be recognized as sales in the third quarter when the strike is in progress. LaBrava Company management thinks this is more representative of normal second- and third-quarter operations.

CA24-10 (Financial Forecasts) An article in *Barron's* noted the following.

Okay. Last fall, someone with a long memory and an even longer arm reached into that bureau drawer and came out with a moldy cheese sandwich and the equally moldy notion of corporate forecasts. We tried to find out what happened to the cheese sandwich—but, rats!, even recourse to the Freedom of Information Act didn't help. However, the forecast proposal was dusted off, polished up and found quite serviceable. The SEC, indeed, lost no time in running it up the old flagpole—but no one was very eager to salute. Even after some of the more objectionable features—compulsory corrections and detailed explanations of why the estimates went awry—were peeled off the original proposal.

Seemingly, despite the Commission's smiles and sweet talk, those craven corporations were still afraid that an honest mistake would lead them down the primrose path to consent decrees and class action suits. To lay to rest such qualms, the Commission last week approved a "Safe Harbor" rule that, providing the forecasts were made on a reasonable basis and in good faith, protected corporations from litigation should the projections prove wide of the mark (as only about 99% are apt to do).

Instructions

(a) What are the arguments for preparing profit forecasts?

(b) What is the purpose of the "safe harbor" rule?

(c) Why are corporations concerned about presenting profit forecasts?

CA24-11 (Disclosure of Estimates) Nancy Tercek, the financial vice president, and Margaret Lilly, the controller, of Romine Manufacturing Company are reviewing the financial ratios of the company for the years 2014 and 2015. The financial vice president notes that the profit margin on sales ratio has increased from 6% to 12%, a hefty gain for the 2-year period. Tercek is in the process of issuing a media release that emphasizes the efficiency of Romine Manufacturing in controlling cost. Margaret Lilly knows that the difference in ratios is due primarily to an earlier company decision to reduce the estimates of warranty and bad debt expense for 2015. The controller, not sure of her supervisor's motives, hesitates to suggest to Tercek that the company's improvement is unrelated to efficiency in controlling cost. To complicate matters, the media release is scheduled in a few days.

Instructions

(a) What, if any, is the ethical dilemma in this situation?

(b) Should Lilly, the controller, remain silent? Give reasons.

(c) What stakeholders might be affected by Tercek's media release?

(d) Give your opinion on the following statement and cite reasons: "Because Tercek, the vice president, is most directly responsible for the media release, Lilly has no real responsibility in this matter."

CA24-12 (Reporting of Subsequent Events) In June 2014, the board of directors for McElroy Enterprises Inc. authorized the sale of $10,000,000 of corporate bonds. Jennifer Grayson, treasurer for McElroy Enterprises Inc., is concerned about the date when the bonds are issued. The company really needs the cash, but she is worried that if the bonds are issued before the company's year-end (December 31, 2014) the additional liability will have an adverse effect on a number of important ratios. In July, she explains to company president William McElroy that if they delay issuing the bonds until after December 31 the bonds will not affect the ratios until December 31, 2015. They will have to report the issuance as a subsequent event which requires only footnote disclosure. Grayson expects that with expected improved financial performance in 2015, ratios should be better.

Instructions

(a) What are the ethical issues involved?
(b) Should McElroy agree to the delay?

*__CA24-13 (Effect of Transactions on Financial Statements and Ratios)__ The transactions listed below relate to Wainwright Inc. You are to assume that on the date on which each of the transactions occurred, the corporation's accounts showed only common stock ($100 par) outstanding, a current ratio of 2.7:1, and a substantial net income for the year to date (before giving effect to the transaction concerned). On that date, the book value per share of stock was $151.53.

Each numbered transaction is to be considered completely independent of the others, and its related answer should be based on the effect(s) of that transaction alone. Assume that all numbered transactions occurred during 2015 and that the amount involved in each case is sufficiently material to distort reported net income if improperly included in the determination of net income. Assume further that each transaction was recorded in accordance with generally accepted accounting principles and, where applicable, in conformity with the all-inclusive concept of the income statement.

For each of the numbered transactions you are to decide whether it:

(a) Increased the corporation's 2015 net income.
(b) Decreased the corporation's 2015 net income.
(c) Increased the corporation's total retained earnings directly (i.e., not via net income).
(d) Decreased the corporation's total retained earnings directly.
(e) Increased the corporation's current ratio.
(f) Decreased the corporation's current ratio.
(g) Increased each stockholder's proportionate share of total stockholders' equity.
(h) Decreased each stockholder's proportionate share of total stockholders' equity.
(i) Increased each stockholder's equity per share of stock (book value).
(j) Decreased each stockholder's equity per share of stock (book value).
(k) Had none of the foregoing effects.

Instructions

List the numbers 1 through 9. Select as many letters as you deem appropriate to reflect the effect(s) of each transaction as of the date of the transaction by printing beside the transaction number the letter(s) that identifies that transaction's effect(s).

Transactions

_____ **1.** In January, the board directed the write-off of certain patent rights that had suddenly and unexpectedly become worthless.

_____ **2.** The corporation sold at a profit land and a building that had been idle for some time. Under the terms of the sale, the corporation received a portion of the sales price in cash immediately, the balance maturing at 6-month intervals.

_____ **3.** Treasury stock originally repurchased and carried at $127 per share was sold for cash at $153 per share.

_____ **4.** The corporation wrote off all of the unamortized discount and issue expense applicable to bonds that it refinanced in 2015.

_____ **5.** The corporation called in all its outstanding shares of stock and exchanged them for new shares on a 2-for-1 basis, reducing the par value at the same time to $50 per share.

_____ **6.** The corporation paid a cash dividend that had been recorded in the accounts at time of declaration.

_____ **7.** Litigation involving Wainwright Inc. as defendant was settled in the corporation's favor, with the plaintiff paying all court costs and legal fees. In 2012, the corporation had appropriately established a special contingency for this court action. (Indicate the effect of reversing the contingency only.)

_____ **8.** The corporation received a check for the proceeds of an insurance policy from the company with which it is insured against theft of trucks. No entries concerning the theft had been made previously, and the proceeds reduce but do not cover completely the loss.

_____ **9.** Treasury stock, which had been repurchased at and carried at $127 per share, was issued as a stock dividend. In connection with this distribution, the board of directors of Wainwright Inc. had authorized a transfer from retained earnings to permanent capital of an amount equal to the aggregate market value ($153 per share) of the shares issued. No entries relating to this dividend had been made previously.

(AICPA adapted)

USING YOUR JUDGMENT

FINANCIAL REPORTING

Financial Reporting Problem

P&G

The Procter & Gamble Company (P&G)

As stated in the chapter, notes to the financial statements are the means of explaining the items presented in the main body of the statements. Common note disclosures relate to such items as accounting policies, segmented information, and interim reporting. The financial statements of P&G are presented in Appendix 5B. The company's complete annual report, including the notes to the financial statements, can be accessed at the book's companion website, **www.wiley.com/college/kieso**.

Instructions

Refer to P&G's financial statements and the accompanying notes to answer the following questions.

(a) What specific items does P&G discuss in its Note 1—Summary of Significant Accounting Policies? (List the headings only.)

(b) For what segments did P&G report segmented information? Which segment is the largest? Who is P&G's largest customer?

(c) What interim information was reported by P&G?

Comparative Analysis Case

The Coca-Cola Company and PepsiCo, Inc.

Instructions

Go to the book's companion website and use information found there to answer the following questions related to The Coca-Cola Company and PepsiCo, Inc.

(a) (1) What specific items does Coca-Cola discuss in its Note 1—Accounting Policies? (Prepare a list of the headings only.)

(2) What specific items does PepsiCo discuss in its Note 2—Our Summary of Significant Accounting Policies? (Prepare a list of the headings only.)

(b) For what lines of business or segments do Coca-Cola and PepsiCo present segmented information?

(c) Note and comment on the similarities and differences between the auditors' reports submitted by the independent auditors of Coca-Cola and PepsiCo for the year 2011.

*Financial Statement Analysis Case

RNA Inc. manufactures a variety of consumer products. The company's founders have run the company for 30 years and are now interested in retiring. Consequently, they are seeking a purchaser who will continue its operations, and a group of investors, Morgan Inc., is looking into the acquisition of RNA. To evaluate its financial stability and operating efficiency, RNA was requested to provide the latest financial statements and selected financial ratios. Summary information provided by RNA is as follows.

RNA INC.
INCOME STATEMENT
FOR THE YEAR ENDED NOVEMBER 30, 2015
(IN THOUSANDS)

Sales (net)	$30,500
Interest income	500
Total revenue	31,000
Costs and expenses	
Cost of goods sold	17,600
Selling and administrative expenses	3,550
Depreciation and amortization expense	1,890
Interest expense	900
Total costs and expenses	23,940
Income before taxes	7,060
Income taxes	2,800
Net income	$ 4,260

RNA INC.
BALANCE SHEET
AS OF NOVEMBER 30
(IN THOUSANDS)

	2015	2014
Cash	$ 400	$ 500
Short-term investments (at cost)	300	200
Accounts receivable (net)	3,200	2,900
Inventory	6,000	5,400
Total current assets	9,900	9,000
Property, plant, & equipment (net)	7,100	7,000
Total assets	$17,000	$16,000
Accounts payable	$ 3,700	$ 3,400
Income taxes payable	900	800
Accrued expenses	1,700	1,400
Total current liabilities	6,300	5,600
Long-term debt	2,000	1,800
Total liabilities	8,300	7,400
Common stock ($1 par value)	2,700	2,700
Paid-in capital in excess of par	1,000	1,000
Retained earnings	5,000	4,900
Total stockholders' equity	8,700	8,600
Total liabilities and stockholders' equity	$17,000	$16,000

SELECTED FINANCIAL RATIOS

	RNA INC.		Current Industry
	2014	2013	Average
Current ratio	1.61	1.62	1.63
Acid-test ratio	.64	.63	.68
Times interest earned	8.55	8.50	8.45
Profit margin on sales	13.2%	12.1%	13.0%
Asset turnover	1.84	1.83	1.84
Inventory turnover	3.17	3.21	3.18

Instructions

(a) Calculate a new set of ratios for the fiscal year 2015 for RNA based on the financial statements presented.

(b) Explain the analytical use of each of the six ratios presented, describing what the investors can learn about RNA's financial stability and operating efficiency.

(c) Identify two limitations of ratio analysis.

(CMA adapted)

Accounting, Analysis, and Principles

Savannah, Inc. is a company that manufactures and sells a single product. Unit sales for each of the four quarters of 2014 are projected as follows.

Quarter	Units
First	80,000
Second	150,000
Third	550,000
Fourth	120,000
Annual Total	900,000

Savannah incurs variable manufacturing costs of $0.40 per unit and variable nonmanufacturing costs of $0.35 per unit. Savannah will incur fixed manufacturing costs of $720,000 and fixed nonmanufacturing costs of $1,080,000. Savannah will sell its product for $4.00 per unit.

Accounting

Determine the amount of net income Savannah will report in each of the four quarters of 2014, assuming actual sales are as projected and employing the integral approach to interim financial reporting. (Ignore income taxes.)

Analysis

Compute Savannah's profit margin on sales for each of the four quarters of 2014 under both the integral and discrete approaches. What effect does employing the integral approach instead of the discrete approach have on the degree to which Savannah's profit margin on sales varies from quarter to quarter?

Principles

Explain the conceptual rationale behind the integral approach to interim financial reporting.

BRIDGE TO THE PROFESSION

Professional Research: FASB Codification

As part of the year-end audit, you are discussing the disclosure checklist with your client. The checklist identifies the items that must be disclosed in a set of GAAP financial statements. The client is surprised by the disclosure item related to accounting policies. Specifically, since the audit report will attest to the statements being prepared in accordance with GAAP, the client questions the accounting policy checklist item. The client has asked you to conduct some research to verify the accounting policy disclosures.

Instructions

If your school has a subscription to the FASB Codification, go to *http://aaahq.org/ascLogin.cfm* to log in and prepare responses to the following. Provide Codification references for your responses.

(a) In general, what should disclosures of accounting policies encompass?

(b) List some examples of the most commonly required disclosures.

Additional Professional Resources

See the book's companion website, at **www.wiley.com/college/kieso**, for professional simulations as well as other study resources.

IFRS INSIGHTS

LEARNING OBJECTIVE 14
Compare the disclosure requirements under GAAP and IFRS.

IFRS and GAAP disclosure requirements are similar in many regards. The IFRS addressing various disclosure issues are *IAS 24* ("Related Party Disclosures"), disclosure and recognition of post-statement of financial position events in *IAS 10* ("Events after the Balance Sheet Date"), segment reporting IFRS provisions in *IFRS 8* ("Operating Segments"), and interim reporting requirements in *IAS 34* ("Interim Financial Reporting").

RELEVANT FACTS

Following are the key similarities and differences between GAAP and IFRS related to disclosures.

Similarities

- GAAP and IFRS have similar standards on post-statement of financial position (subsequent) events. That is, under both sets of standards, events that occurred after the statement of financial position date, and which provide additional evidence of conditions that existed at the statement of financial position date, are recognized in the financial statements.
- Like GAAP, IFRS requires that for transactions with related parties, companies disclose the amounts involved in a transaction; the amount, terms, and nature of the outstanding balances; and any doubtful amounts related to those outstanding balances for each major category of related parties.
- Following the recent issuance of *IFRS 8*, "Operating Segments," the requirements under IFRS and GAAP are very similar. That is, both standards use the management approach to identify reportable segments, and similar segment disclosures are required.
- Neither GAAP nor IFRS require interim reports. Rather, the SEC and securities exchanges outside the United States establish the rules. In the United States, interim reports generally are provided on a quarterly basis; outside the United States, six-month interim reports are common.

Differences

- Due to the broader range of judgments allowed in more principles-based IFRS, note disclosures generally are more expansive under IFRS compared to GAAP.
- Subsequent (or post-statement of financial position) events under IFRS are evaluated through the date that financial instruments are "authorized for issue." GAAP uses the date when financial statements are "issued." Also, for share dividends and splits in the subsequent period, IFRS does not adjust but GAAP does.
- Under IFRS, there is no specific requirement to disclose the name of the related party, which is this case under GAAP.
- Under IFRS, interim reports are prepared on a discrete basis; GAAP generally follows the integral approach.

ABOUT THE NUMBERS

Differential Disclosure

A trend toward **differential disclosure** is occurring. The IASB has developed IFRS for small- and medium-sized entities (SMEs). SMEs are entities that publish general-purpose financial statements for external users but do not issue shares or other securities in a public market. Many believe a simplified set of standards makes sense for these companies because they do not have the resources to implement full IFRS. Simplified IFRS for SMEs is a single standard of fewer than 230 pages. It is designed to meet the needs and capabilities of SMEs, which are estimated to account for over 95 percent of all companies around the world. Compared with full IFRS (and many national accounting standards), simplified IFRS for SMEs is less complex in a number of ways:

- Topics not relevant for SMEs are omitted. Examples are earnings per share, interim financial reporting, and segment reporting.
- Simplified IFRS for SMEs allows fewer accounting policy choices. Examples are no option to revalue property, equipment, or intangibles, and no corridor approach for actuarial gains and losses.
- Many principles for recognizing and measuring assets, liabilities, revenue, and expenses are simplified. For example, goodwill is amortized (as a result, there is no annual impairment test), and all borrowing and R&D costs are expensed.

- Significantly fewer disclosures are required (roughly 300 versus 3,000).
- To further reduce standard overload, revisions to the IFRS for SMEs will be limited to once every three years.

Thus, the option of using simplified IFRS helps SMEs meet the needs of their financial statement users while balancing the costs and benefits from a preparer perspective.[29]

Events after the Reporting Period (Subsequent Events)

Notes to the financial statements should explain any significant financial events that took place after the formal statement of financial position date, but before the statements are authorized for issuance (hereafter referred to as the authorization date). These events are referred to as **events after the reporting date**, or **subsequent events**. Illustration IFRS24-1 shows a time diagram of the subsequent events period.

ILLUSTRATION IFRS24-1
Time Periods for Subsequent Events

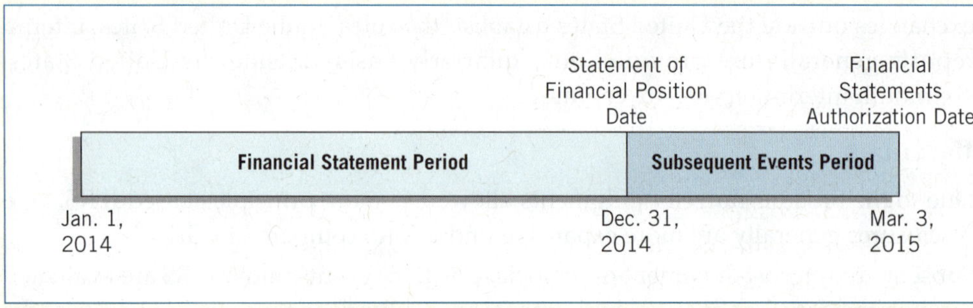

A period of several weeks, and sometimes months, may elapse after the end of the fiscal year but before the management or the board of directors authorizes issuance of the financial statements. Various activities involved in closing the books for the period and issuing the statements all take time: taking and pricing the inventory, reconciling subsidiary ledgers with controlling accounts, preparing necessary adjusting entries, ensuring that all transactions for the period have been entered, obtaining an audit of the financial statements by independent certified public accountants, and printing the annual report. During the period between the statement of financial position date and its authorization date, important transactions or other events may occur that materially affect the company's financial position or operating situation.

Many who read a statement of financial position believe the financial condition is constant, and they project it into the future. However, readers must be told if the company has experienced a significant change—e.g., sold one of its plants, acquired a subsidiary, suffered unusual losses, settled significant litigation, or experienced any other important event in the post-statement of financial position period. Without an explanation in a note, the reader might be misled and draw inappropriate conclusions.

Two types of events or transactions occurring after the statement of financial position date may have a material effect on the financial statements or may need disclosure so that readers interpret these statements accurately:

[29]In the United States, there has been a preference for one set of GAAP except in unusual situations. With the advent of simplified IFRS for SMEs, this position is under review. Both the FASB and the AICPA are studying the big GAAP/little GAAP issue to ensure that any kind of differential reporting is conceptually sound and meets the needs of users. As discussed in the chapter, the FASB has formed a Private Company Financial Reporting Committee, whose primary objectives are to provide recommendations on FASB standard-setting for privately held enterprises (see *http://www.pcfr.org/*).

1. Events that provide additional evidence about conditions **that existed** at the statement of financial position date, including the estimates inherent in the process of preparing financial statements. These events are referred to as **adjusted subsequent events** and require adjustments to the financial statements. All information available prior to the authorization date of the financial statements helps investors and creditors evaluate estimates previously made. To ignore these subsequent events is to pass up an opportunity to improve the accuracy of the financial statements. This first type of event encompasses information that an accountant would have recorded in the accounts had the information been known at the statement of financial position date.

   For example, if a loss on an account receivable results from a customer's bankruptcy subsequent to the statement of financial position date, the company adjusts the financial statements before their issuance. The bankruptcy stems from the customer's poor financial health existing at the statement of financial position date.

   The same criterion applies to settlements of litigation. The company must adjust the financial statements if the events that gave rise to the litigation, such as personal injury or patent infringement, took place prior to the statement of financial position date.

2. Events that provide evidence about conditions that **did not exist** at the statement of financial position date but arise subsequent to that date. These events are referred to as **non-adjusted subsequent events** and do not require adjustment of the financial statements. To illustrate, a loss resulting from a customer's fire or flood *after* the statement of financial position date does not reflect conditions existing at that date.

   Thus, adjustment of the financial statements is not necessary. A company should not recognize subsequent events that provide evidence about conditions that did not exist at the date of the statement of financial position but that arose after the statement of financial position date.

   The following are examples of non-adjusted subsequent events:

   - A major business combination after the reporting period or disposing of a major subsidiary.
   - Announcing a plan to discontinue an operation or commencing the implementation of a major restructuring.
   - Major purchases of assets, other disposals of assets, or expropriation of major assets by government.
   - The destruction of a major production plant or inventories by a fire or natural disaster after the reporting period.
   - Major ordinary share transactions and potential ordinary share transactions after the reporting period.
   - Abnormally large changes after the reporting period in asset prices, foreign exchange rates, or taxes.
   - Entering into significant commitments or contingent liabilities, for example, by issuing significant guarantees after the statement date.[30]

[30]The effects from natural disasters, like the recent eruption of the Icelandic volcano, which occurred after the year-end for companies with March fiscal years, require disclosure in order to keep the statements from being misleading. Some companies may have to consider whether these disasters affect their ability to continue as going concerns.

Some non-adjusted subsequent events may have to be disclosed to keep the financial statements from being misleading. For such events, a company discloses the nature of the event and an estimate of its financial effect. Illustration IFRS24-2 presents an example of subsequent events disclosure, excerpted from the annual report of Magyar Telecom plc.

ILLUSTRATION IFRS24-2
Disclosure of Subsequent Events

Magyar Telecom plc

Note 37. Events After the Reporting Period (in part)

On March 1, 2011 the Hungarian Government announced that as part of its long-term effort to reduce the Hungarian budget deficit it intends to amend existing law that provides for a reduction in corporate tax rates from the current 19% to 10% starting in 2013. When the law reducing future corporate tax rates was enacted in 2010, the Group recalculated its deferred tax balances, resulting in the reversal of net deferred tax liabilities of HUF 14.5 billion (see Note 9.3) in the 2010 income statement of comprehensive income. The recent announcement of the intended cancellation of the scheduled reduction of the tax rate from 2013 is expected to cause the recognition of a substantially higher amount of net deferred tax liabilities in 2011 and result in a negative impact on deferred tax expense in 2011 equivalent in magnitude to the positive impact on net deferred tax expense in 2010.

Many subsequent events or developments do not require adjustment of or disclosure in the financial statements. Typically, these are non-accounting events or conditions that management normally communicates by other means. These events include legislation, product changes, management changes, strikes, unionization, marketing agreements, and loss of important customers.

Interim Reports

Another source of information for the investor is interim reports. As noted earlier, **interim reports** cover periods of less than one year. The securities exchanges, market regulators, and the accounting profession have an active interest in the presentation of interim information.

Because of the short-term nature of the information in these reports, there is considerable controversy as to the general approach companies should employ. One group, which favors the **discrete approach**, believes that companies should treat each interim period as a separate accounting period. Using that treatment, companies would follow the principles for deferrals and accruals used for annual reports. In this view, companies should report accounting transactions as they occur, and expense recognition should not change with the period of time covered.

Another group, which favors the **integral approach**, believes that the interim report is an integral part of the annual report and that deferrals and accruals should take into consideration what will happen for the entire year. In this approach, companies should assign estimated expenses to parts of a year on the basis of sales volume or some other activity base. In general, IFRS requires companies to follow the discrete approach.

Interim Reporting Requirements

Under IFRS, companies should use the same accounting policies for interim reports and for annual reports. They should recognize revenues in interim periods on the same basis as they are for annual periods. For example, if Cedars Corp. uses the percentage-of-completion method as the basis for recognizing revenue on an annual basis, it should use the percentage-of-completion method for interim reports as well. Also, Cedars should treat costs directly associated with revenues (product costs, such as materials, labor and related fringe benefits, and manufacturing overhead) in the same manner for interim reports as for annual reports.

Companies should use the same inventory pricing methods (FIFO, average-cost, etc.) for interim reports and for annual reports. However, companies may use the gross profit method for interim inventory pricing. But, they must disclose the method and adjustments to reconcile with annual inventory.

Discrete Approach. Following the discrete approach, companies record in interim reports revenues and expenses according to the revenue and expense recognition principles. This includes costs and expenses other than product costs (often referred to as period costs). No accruals or deferrals in anticipation of future events during the year should be reported. For example, the cost of a planned major periodic maintenance or overhaul for a company like **Airbus** or other seasonal expenditure that is expected to occur late in the year is not anticipated for interim reporting purposes. The mere intention or necessity to incur expenditure related to the future is not sufficient to give rise to an obligation.

Or, a company like **Carrefour** may budget certain costs expected to be incurred irregularly during the financial year, such as advertising and employee training costs. Those costs generally are discretionary even though they are planned and tend to recur from year to year. However, recognizing an obligation at the end of an interim financial reporting period for such costs that have not yet been incurred generally is not consistent with the definition of a liability.

While year-to-date measurements may involve changes in estimates of amounts reported in prior interim periods of the current financial year, the principles for recognizing assets, liabilities, income, and expenses for interim periods are the same as in annual financial statements. For example, **Wm Morrison Supermarkets plc** records losses from inventory write-downs, restructurings, or impairments in an interim period similar to how it would treat these items in the annual financial statements (when incurred). However, if an estimate from a prior interim period changes in a subsequent interim period of that year, the original estimate is adjusted in the subsequent interim period.

Interim Disclosures. IFRS does not require a complete set of financial statements at the interim reporting date. Rather, companies may comply with the requirements by providing condensed financial statements and selected explanatory notes. Because users of interim financial reports also have access to the most recent annual financial report, companies only need provide explanation of significant events and transactions since the end of the last annual reporting period. Companies should report the following interim data at a minimum.

1. Statement that the same accounting policies and methods of computation are followed in the interim financial statements as compared with the most recent annual financial statements or, if those policies or methods have been changed, a description of the nature and effect of the change.
2. Explanatory comments about the seasonality or cyclicality of interim operations.
3. The nature and amount of items affecting assets, liabilities, equity, net income, or cash flows that are unusual because of their nature, size, or incidence.
4. The nature and amount of changes in accounting policies and estimates of amounts previously reported.
5. Issuances, repurchases, and repayments of debt and equity securities.
6. Dividends paid (aggregate or per share) separately for ordinary shares and other shares.

7. Segment information, as required by *IFRS 8*, "Operating Segments."
8. Changes in contingent liabilities or contingent assets since the end of the last annual reporting period.
9. Effect of changes in the composition of the company during the interim period, such as business combinations, obtaining or losing control of subsidiaries and long-term investments, restructurings, and discontinued operations.
10. Other material events subsequent to the end of the interim period that have not been reflected in the financial statements for the interim period.

If a complete set of financial statements is provided in the interim report, companies comply with the provisions of *IAS 1*, "Presentation of Financial Statements."

ON THE HORIZON

Hans Hoogervorst, chairperson of the IASB, recently noted: "High quality financial information is the lifeblood of market-based economies. If the blood is of poor quality, then the body shuts down and the patient dies. It is the same with financial reporting. If investors cannot trust the numbers, then financial markets stop working. For market-based economies, that is really bad news. It is an essential public good for market-based economies. . . . And in the past 10 years, most of the world's economies—developed and emerging—have embraced IFRSs." While the United States has yet to adopt IFRS, there is no question that IFRS and GAAP are converging quickly. We have provided expanded discussion in the *International Perspectives* and *IFRS Insights* to help you understand the issues surrounding convergence as they relate to intermediate accounting. After reading these discussions, you should realize that IFRS and GAAP are very similar in many areas, with differences in those areas revolving around some minor technical points. In other situations, the differences are major; for example, IFRS does not permit LIFO inventory accounting. Our hope is that the FASB and IASB can quickly complete their convergence efforts, resulting in a single set of high-quality accounting standards for use by companies around the world.

IFRS SELF-TEST QUESTIONS

1. Which of the following is **false**?
   (a) In general, IFRS note disclosures are more expansive compared to GAAP.
   (b) GAAP and IFRS have similar standards on subsequent events.
   (c) Both IFRS and GAAP require interim reports although the reporting frequency varies.
   (d) Segment reporting requirements are very similar under IFRS and GAAP.
2. Differential reporting for small- and medium-sized entities:
   (a) is required for all companies less than a certain size.
   (b) omits accounting topics not relevant for SMEs, such as earnings per share, and interim and segment reporting.
   (c) has different rules for topics such as earnings per share, and interim and segment reporting.
   (d) requires significantly more disclosures, since more items are not recognized in the financial statements.
3. Subsequent events are reviewed through which date under IFRS?
   (a) Statement of financial position date.
   (b) Sixty days after the year-end date.
   (c) Date of independent auditor's opinion.
   (d) Authorization date of the financial statements.

4. Under IFRS, share dividends declared after the statement of financial position date but before the end of the subsequent events period are:
   (a) accounted for similar to errors as a prior period adjustment.
   (b) adjusted subsequent events, because they are paid from prior year earnings.
   (c) not adjusted in the current year's financial statements.
   (d) recognized on a prospective basis from the date of declaration.
5. Interim reporting under IFRS:
   (a) is prepared using the discrete approach.
   (b) is prepared using a combination of the discrete and integral approach.
   (c) requires a complete set of financial statements for each interim period.
   (d) permits companies to omit disclosure of material events subsequent to the interim reporting date.

IFRS CONCEPTS AND APPLICATION

IFRS24-1 Where can authoritative IFRS be found related to the various disclosure issues discussed in the chapter?

IFRS24-2 What are the major types of subsequent events? Indicate how each of the following "subsequent events" would be reported.

(a) Collection of a note written off in a prior period.
(b) Issuance of a large preference share offering.
(c) Acquisition of a company in a different industry.
(d) Destruction of a major plant in a flood.
(e) Death of the company's chief executive officer (CEO).
(f) Additional wage costs associated with settlement of a four-week strike.
(g) Settlement of an income tax case at considerably more tax than anticipated at year-end.
(h) Change in the product mix from consumer goods to industrial goods.

IFRS24-3 Morlan Corporation is preparing its December 31, 2014, financial statements. Two events that occurred between December 31, 2014, and March 10, 2015, when the statements were authorized for issue, are described below.

1. A liability, estimated at $160,000 at December 31, 2014, was settled on February 26, 2015, at $170,000.
2. A flood loss of $80,000 occurred on March 1, 2015.

Instructions

What effect do these subsequent events have on 2014 net income?

IFRS24-4 Keystone Corporation's financial statements for the year ended December 31, 2014, were authorized for issue on March 10, 2015. The following events took place early in 2015.

(a) On January 10, 10,000 ordinary shares of $5 par value were issued at $66 per share.
(b) On March 1, Keystone determined after negotiations with the taxing authorities that income taxes payable for 2014 should be $1,320,000. At December 31, 2014, income taxes payable were recorded at $1,100,000.

Instructions

Discuss how the preceding subsequent events should be reflected in the 2014 financial statements.

IFRS24-5 For each of the following subsequent events, indicate whether a company should (a) adjust the financial statements, (b) disclose in notes to the financial statements, or (c) neither adjust nor disclose.

_______ 1. Settlement of a tax case at a cost considerably in excess of the amount expected at year-end.
_______ 2. Introduction of a new product line.
_______ 3. Loss of assembly plant due to fire.
_______ 4. Sale of a significant portion of the company's assets.
_______ 5. Retirement of the company president.

_________ 6. Issuance of a significant number of ordinary shares.
_________ 7. Loss of a significant customer.
_________ 8. Prolonged employee strike.
_________ 9. Material loss on a year-end receivable because of a customer's bankruptcy.
_________ 10. Hiring of a new president.
_________ 11. Settlement of prior year's litigation against the company (no loss was accrued).
_________ 12. Merger with another company of comparable size.

IFRS24-6 What are interim reports? Why is a complete set of financial statements often not provided with interim data? What are the accounting problems related to the presentation of interim data?

IFRS24-7 Dierdorf Inc., a closely held corporation, has decided to go public. The controller, Ed Floyd, is concerned with presenting interim data when an inventory write-down is recorded. What problems are encountered with inventories when quarterly data are presented?

IFRS24-8 Bill Novak is working on an audit of an IFRS client. In his review of the client's interim reports, he notes that the reports are prepared on a discrete basis. That is, each interim report is viewed as a distinct period. Is this acceptable under IFRS? If so, explain how that treatment could affect comparisons to a GAAP company.

IFRS24-9 Snider Corporation, a publicly traded company, is preparing the interim financial data which it will issue to its shareholders at the end of the first quarter of the 2014–2015 fiscal year. Snider's financial accounting department has compiled the following summarized revenue and expense data for the first quarter of the year.

Sales revenue	$60,000,000
Cost of goods sold	36,000,000
Variable selling expenses	1,000,000
Fixed selling expenses	3,000,000

Included in the fixed selling expenses was the single lump-sum payment of $2,000,000 for television advertisements for the entire year.

Instructions

(a) Snider Corporation must issue its quarterly financial statements in accordance with IFRS regarding interim financial reporting.

(1) Explain whether Snider should report its operating results for the quarter as if the quarter were a separate reporting period in and of itself, or as if the quarter were an integral part of the annual reporting period.

(2) State how the sales revenue, cost of goods sold, and fixed selling expenses would be reflected in Snider Corporation's quarterly report prepared for the first quarter of the 2014–2015 fiscal year. Briefly justify your presentation.

(b) What financial information, as a minimum, must Snider Corporation disclose to its shareholders in its quarterly reports?

Professional Research

IFRS24-10 As part of the year-end audit, you are discussing the disclosure checklist with your client. The checklist identifies the items that must be disclosed in a set of IFRS financial statements. The client is surprised by the disclosure item related to accounting policies. Specifically, since the audit report will attest to the statements being prepared in accordance with IFRS, the client questions the accounting policy checklist item. The client has asked you to conduct some research to verify the accounting policy disclosures.

Instructions

Access the IFRS authoritative literature at the IASB website (*http://eifrs.iasb.org/*). (Click on the IFRS tab and then register for free eIFRS access if necessary.) When you have accessed the documents, you can use the search tool in your Internet browser to respond to the following questions. (Provide paragraph citations.)

(a) In general, what should disclosures of accounting policies encompass?

(b) List some examples of the most commonly required disclosures.

International Financial Reporting Problem
Marks and Spencer plc

IFRS24-11 The financial statements of **Marks and Spencer plc (M&S)** are available at the book's companion website or can be accessed at *http://annualreport.marksandspencer.com/_assets/downloads/Marks-and-Spencer-Annual-report-and-financial-statements-2012.pdf.*

Instructions

Refer to M&S's financial statements and the accompanying notes to answer the following questions.

(a) What specific items does M&S discuss in its Note 1—Summary of Significant Accounting Policies? (List the headings only.)

(b) For what segments did M&S report segmented information? Which segment is the largest? Who is M&S's largest customer?

(c) What interim information was reported by M&S?

ANSWERS TO IFRS SELF-TEST QUESTIONS

1. c **2.** b **3.** d **4.** c **5.** a

Remember to check the book's companion website to find additional resources for this chapter.

INDEX